Total Language Accessibility

For over 150 years, Oxford's hallmarks of integrity and authority have been adapted to meet the changing needs of dictionary users. Today, with a dramatically more open style, Oxford dictionaries and thesauruses offer total language accessibility and many new benefits.

Rapid-Access Design

Oxford's new quick-access page designs offer clear margins, with special typefaces and symbols to ensure exceptional clarity. Paper and binding styles are carefully selected for their durability. All Oxford thesauruses are in clear A–Z form, and entries are written in jargon-free English, without confusing abbreviations, or long impenetrable paragraphs.

True To The Facts

Thesaurus entries are compiled after wide scrutiny of real evidence, drawn from millions of unique citations, in order to provide the most accurate picture of the language.

Most Useful Words Listed First

In many of the larger thesauruses, the commonest synonyms in today's English are listed first. In smaller thesauruses, an A–Z listing provides easy access to the information you need.

Reliable Guidance On Usage

In order to show the context in which words can be used—whether they are, for example, colloquial, slang, dialect, formal, or literary—reliable guidance is provided by usage markers and extensive example phrases or sentences.

Additional Language Benefits

All Oxford thesauruses offer extra help to the user in the form of special language features. These benefits may include dual-access entry, with an index as well as an A–Z listing; cross-referencing to related or opposite words; vocabulary tables of people, places, and things; or appendices which list complex or unusual alternatives for a variety of common words, phrases, and proper nouns as a vocabulary builder and for success in word games.

The Most Trusted Range In The World

In addition to its comprehensive range of thesauruses, Oxford publishes a wide variety of dictionaries for children, native speakers, and learners; on paper or CD-ROM; in English, French, Spanish, German, Italian, Russian, Japanese, Latin, Ancient and Modern Greek, Arabic, Turkish, Portuguese, Hungarian, Hindi, Gujarati, and Chinese.

The Greatest Exploration of English Ever Undertaken

Oxford—the world leader in authenticating new words and describing language—has developed the most rigorous research programme in operation anywhere in the world today.

The Oxford World Reading Programme

Tracking the growth of English worldwide lies at the heart of this, the world's greatest language research programme and the most comprehensive one in operation in the world today. On average 18,000 examples of new words, idioms, meanings, and turns of phrase are collected every month by a 60-strong international network of readers.

The Oxford Special Subject Advisers

Once sufficient evidence for a new word has been collected, a new entry is prepared. Specialist lexicographers research the meaning and origin of the word, and consult the panel of Oxford Special Subject Advisers, a 150-strong international consultative body working in some of the world's greatest institutions, universities, and companies.

The Oxford Bank of New Words

Finalized new entries are deposited with The Oxford Bank of New Words, the database that feeds new editions of all Oxford dictionaries and which, typically, holds over 3,000 properly authenticated entries at any one time.

The British National Corpus

How are the words of our language actually used? What are the most frequently used meanings of common words? To answer such questions accurately Oxford uses The British National Corpus, an unrivalled balanced collection of 100 million words of text representing every kind of writing and speech in English. Using rapid computer search-and-analysis techniques, Oxford lexicographers can answer the most complex language queries.

OWLS The Oxford Word & Language Service

This is a unique word-help centre set up to answer special language-related questions raised by teachers, writers, specialist institutes, and everyday native speakers of English worldwide.

The Oxford College Thesaurus

Compiled by

Betty Kirkpatrick

OXFORD UNIVERSITY PRESS
1998

Oxford University Press, Great Clarendon Street, Oxford OX2 6DP

Oxford New York

Athens Auckland Bangkok Bogota Bombay
Buenos Aires Calcutta Cape Town Dar es Salaam
Delhi Florence Hong Kong Istanbul Karachi
Kuala Lumpur Madras Madrid Melbourne
Mexico City Nairobi Paris Singapore
Taipei Tokyo Toronto Warsaw
and associated companies in
Berlin Ibadan

Oxford is a trade mark of Oxford University Press

Published in the United States by
Oxford University Press Inc., New York

© Oxford University Press 1994, 1998
First published as the Oxford Paperback Thesaurus 1994
This edition first published 1998

British Library Cataloguing in Publication Data
Data available

Library of Congress Cataloging in Publication Data
Data available
ISBN 0-19-860157-3

10 9 8 7 6 5 4 3 2 1

Printed in Great Britain by
Mackays PLC
Chatham, Kent

Preface

There are nowadays two quite distinct forms of thesaurus. One is the Roget-type where the material is arranged according to themes: the other is the synonym-type where the headwords are arranged in alphabetical order and are followed by lists of words that approximate to them in meaning to a greater or lesser extent.

In synonym-type thesauruses the word synonym is used rather loosely. It refers not only to a word which is exactly the same in meaning as another word but to a word which is nearly the same or has the same connotations.

The synonym-type thesaurus, into which category the present volume falls, is particularly useful for people who already know roughly the word they want to use but cannot quite call it to mind. They may, for example, be in search of an alternative for a word which they have already used several times in a piece of writing, for example, an essay, dissertation, or application.

The promotional department of Oxford University Press have opted to describe this book as "helpful". Compared with many publishing claims this may seem rather low-key; usually something more in the way of exaggeration is chosen.

"Helpful", however, is exactly what this book is. Much care and attention has been devoted to presenting the material in a way that a wide range of users will find useful and easy and quick to follow. Too often people are put off reference books because they feel that they are too complex or that they are only for the educational élite.

This book has several features which are particularly helpful. These include the addition of example sentences and phrases, and the style of ordering synonyms.

Where a headword has more than one set of meanings each set is not only differentiated by a number but also by a short example phrase or sentence. These have been kept simple and to the point. People seeking the right word for the right place are frequently in a hurry and this feature will certainly help to speed up the search process.

Many synonym-type thesauruses have their synonyms as well as their headwords arranged alphabetically. I personally find this system time-consuming and the order of synonyms in this book is based on frequency of usage, with the more common synonyms coming first.

I used to wonder why most thesauruses have their synonyms arranged alphabetically. I now know why. It is an extremely difficult task to arrange them in order of frequency of usage, certainly not the kind of task that can be accomplished by the flick of a computer switch.

Indeed so many times did I change my mind about the ideal order that I forsook my word processor in favour of old-fashioned pen and paper, finding it easier to make the relevant changes by this means. So much for the new technology!

Opinions may vary about what is the ideal order based on usage and some synonyms are just about as common as each other. However, the usage system makes it much easier to identify the looked-for synonym and at the very least makes sure that the user in pursuit of a synonym or near equivalent does not encounter the most difficult or least likely one first, as may well happen when the synonyms are arranged in alphabetical order.

In the compilation of reference books it is exceptionally true that several heads are better than one. My thanks are due to the editorial staff of the reference department of Oxford University Press and to the editorial staff of Market House Books for their contributions to this project.

Betty Kirkpatrick

Guide to the Thesaurus

The Headwords

The text of the *Thesaurus* is organized under headwords, which are printed in bold type. The headwords are listed in strict alphabetical order. Many English words have two or more different acceptable spellings; in this book, the one used is the one regarded as being the most common. If two or more different forms are common, alternatives are given, for example:

cagey, cagy adj guarded, secretive, non-committal, cautious, chary, wary, careful, shrewd, wily.

However, alternatives are not listed in all such cases. For instance, in British English many words ending in -ize can also be spelled with an -ise ending. Variants of this type have not been included.

Parts of Speech

Headwords are always followed by a label indicating the part of speech of the entry. The part-of-speech labels used in the *Thesaurus* are listed later.

When a word has two or more different parts of speech, it is listed more than once with separate entries for each, for example:

captive n *take captives*...prisoner, prisoner-of-war, hostage,....

captive adj *captive animals* imprisoned, incarcerated, locked up,....

The order of parts of speech is based on usage, with the most common form placed first. Not all possible parts of speech of a word are necessarily included as headwords. For example, many words that function as adjectives can also function as adverbs. These are included only when they have useful sets of synonyms.

Homonyms

Certain words have the same spelling but different meanings and different origins (etymologies). Such words, known as homonyms, are treated as separate headwords, even when they have the same part of speech. They are distinguished by homonym numbers. For example:

cape[1] n *wearing a black cape* cloak, mantle, shawl, wrap, poncho, pelisse, pelerine, domino, cope.

cape[2] n *drowned off the cape* headland, head, point, promontory, neck, tongue, peninsula.

When headwords have different homonym numbers and different parts of speech, the entries with the same homonym numbers are etymologically related. For instance:

bank[1] n *a grassy bank* slope, rise, incline,.....

bank[1] v *bank an aircraft* tilt, slope, slant,.....

bank[2] n *borrow from the bank*...high-street bank, clearing bank,.....

bank[2] v *bank the money* deposit, save, save up,.....

In this case, the noun **bank**[1] (a grassy bank) and the verb **bank**[1] (to bank an aircraft) are etymologically related. Similarly, the noun **bank**[2] and the verb **bank**[2] are also etymologically related.

Homonym numbers are given in order to distinguish identical headwords with the same part of speech for the purposes of cross-referencing. If the headwords are identical and the parts of speech differ, there can be no ambiguity in cross references and homonym numbers are not used. This does not necessarily imply that the different part-of-speech entries have the same etymology.

The Entries

Each entry contains a list of words that are synonyms of the headword; i.e. the words can be used in place of the headword in most (although not all) contexts. When a word has more than one meaning, the different senses of the word are numbered.

Example sentences (in italic type) indicate the particular sense and illustrate the use of the word. In some cases, two or more examples are given; these are separated by a vertical bar. For example:

assimilate v **1.** *assimilate food/facts | assimilate people into a group* absorb, take in, incorporate, digest, ingest. **2.** *assimilate your way of life to theirs* adapt, adjust, accustom, acclimatize, become like/similar, blend in, fit, homogenize.

Note that a solidus (/) is used to separate alternative words in order to save space. The solidus applies only to the two words it separates; thus 'assimilate food/facts' can be read as 'assimilate food' and 'assimilate facts'.

Groups Within Senses

In general, the synonyms in an entry are separated by commas. However, there are cases in which the words fall naturally into two or more distinct groups, which are separated by a semicolon. There are various reasons for subdividing a sense in this way:
• **grammatical differences** Some of the words may function in a different way than others, for example:

briefing...*recruits being given their briefing* brief, information, guidance, preparation; instructions, directions....

In this case the words *instructions* and *directions* have been grouped separately because they are plural nouns. There are other grammatical reasons why synonyms may be split into groups. For example, the headword may function as both a transitive and intransitive verb, whereas some of the synonyms may be intransitive only.
• **non-synonyms** In certain entries, lists of words have been included that are not strict synonyms of the headword. For example:

car n...motor car, motor, vehicle,...; limousine, hatchback, estate....

Here, words such as *limousine* and *hatchback* have been grouped separately because they are types of car, rather than synonyms for the word **car**.

• *informal words* Words that are not used in standard formal English have been grouped at the end of lists and given the label *inf*. No distinction is made between colloquial, informal, and slang levels of usage. For example:

babble v...jabber, gibber, gabble, burble, chatter, mutter, mumble, prate, drivel, bleat, cackle; *inf* rabbit, waffle, run on.

The label *inf* applies to all the words following in the group.

• *restricted usage* Synonyms have been separated into labelled groups when they are used in different regions or in particular fields. For example:

baby n *holding a tiny baby* infant, newborn, child, babe, tiny tot; *inf* sprog; *Scots* bairn; *Med* neonate.

A full list of labels used in the *Thesaurus* is given later.

Sub-entries

Verb phrases are included as sub-entries under their main entry. For example:

call *call out in pain* cry, cry out, shout, exclaim...**call for** *this calls for a celebration* need, require, be grounds for,...**call off** *call off the dogs* order off, order away....

Cross References

Cross-reference to main entries is indicated by small capitals. Where necessary, the part of speech and sense number are also given. For example:

barbaric adj....see BARBARIAN *adj* 1.

Abbreviations

The following labels have been used:

Parts of Speech

adj	adjective
adv	adverb
conj	conjunction
interj	interjection
n	noun
npl	plural noun
pfx	prefix
prep	preposition
pron	pronoun
v	verb

Other Abbreviations

Amer	American
Aust	Australian
dial	dialect
fml	formal
inf	informal
lit	literary
Med	Medicine
Tech	Technical fields
vulg	vulgar

abandon v **1** *abandon one's wife* desert, leave, forsake, depart from, leave behind, cast aside, jilt; *inf* run out on. **2** *abandon ship* leave, depart from, go away from, vacate, withdraw from, quit. **3** *abandon hope* give up, renounce, relinquish, dispense with, forgo, desist from, forswear. **4** *abandon a country to the enemy* yield, surrender, give up, cede, relinquish, abdicate, deliver up, resign. **5** *abandon smoking* stop, give up, cease, drop, forgo, desist from, dispense with, abjure; *inf* kick in, jack in, pack in. **6** *abandon oneself to despair* give way to, give oneself up to, yield to, indulge in, lose oneself to/in.

abandon n *behave with gay abandon* recklessness, lack of restraint/inhibition, unrestraint, carelessness, wildness, impulse, impetuosity, immoderation, wantonness.

abandoned adj **1** *an abandoned wife* deserted, forsaken, cast aside. *see* ABANDON V 1. **2** *an abandoned ship* vacated, evacuated, deserted, unoccupied, empty, unused. *see* ABANDON V 2. **3** *abandoned behaviour* reckless, unrestrained, uninhibited, impetuous, wild, careless, wanton. **4** *an abandoned young man* dissipated, debauched, profligate, dissolute, immoral, corrupt, depraved, reprobate, wild, unrestrained, reckless, wanton.

abase v *abase oneself before the emperor* | *abase one's servants* humiliate, humble, belittle, lower, degrade, disparage, debase, demean, discredit, mortify, bring low, demote, reduce.

abasement n humiliation, belittlement, lowering, degradation, disparagement, debasement, mortification, demotion, reduction. *see* ABASE.

abashed adj embarrassed, ashamed, shamefaced, mortified, humiliated, taken aback, disconcerted, nonplussed, discomfited, discomposed, perturbed, confounded, dismayed, dumbfounded, confused, put out of countenance, discountenanced.

abate v **1** *the storm/pain abated* die down, lessen, ease, subside, let up, decrease, diminish, moderate, decline, fade, slacken, wane, ebb, alleviate, attenuate. **2** *trying to abate the pain* ease, lessen, decrease, diminish, moderate, soothe, relieve, dull, blunt,

alleviate, mitigate, allay, assuage, palliate, appease, attenuate. **3** *attempts to abate the noise levels* decrease, reduce, lessen, lower, diminish.

abatement n **1** *the abatement of the wind* lessening, moderation, decrease, decline, ebb, alleviation, attenuation. *see* ABATE 1. **2** *the abatement of the pain* easing, decrease, moderation, relief, mitigation, assuagement, palliation, appeasement, attenuation. *see* ABATE 2. **3** *the abatement of noise levels* decrease, reduction, lowering. *see* ABATE 3.

abbey n religious house; monastery, priory, cloister, friary, convent, nunnery, coenoby.

abbreviate v shorten, reduce, cut, cut short/down, contract, condense, compress, abridge, truncate, clip, crop, shrink, constrict, summarize, abstract, précis, synopsize, digest.

abbreviation n **1** *the abbreviation of his name* shortening, reduction, cutting, contraction, condensation, compression, abridgement. *see* ABBREVIATE. **2** *the abbreviation for the United Kingdom is UK* shortened form, contraction, abridgement.

abdicate v **1** *the King abdicated in 1936* resign, stand down, retire, quit. **2** *abdicate the throne* give up, renounce, resign from, relinquish, abjure, cede; *Law* disclaim. **3** *abdicate all responsibility* give up, renounce, relinquish, abjure, repudiate, reject, disown, waive, yield, forgo, refuse, abandon, surrender, cast aside, drop, turn one's back on, wash one's hands of.

abdication n **1** *abdication from the throne* giving up of, renunciation of, resignation from, relinquishment of, abjuration of, ceding of. **2** *abdication of responsibility* renunciation, relinquishment, abjuration, repudiation, rejection, waiving, refusal, abandonment, surrender. *see* ABDICATE 2.

abdomen n stomach, belly, intestines; *inf* tummy, tum, insides, guts, pot, paunch, corporation, maw, bread basket.

abdominal adj gastric, intestinal, stomachic, visceral, coeliac, ventral.

abduct v kidnap, carry off, run away/off with, make off with, seize, hold as hostage, hold to ransom; *inf* snatch.

aberrant adj deviant, deviating, divergent, anomalous, abnormal, irregular, atypical, freakish.

aberration n **1** *a statistical aberration* deviation, divergence, anomaly, abnormality, irregularity, variation, freak. **2** *in a moment of aberration* abnormality, irregularity, eccentricity, deviation, straying, abberancy. **3** *suffering from a mental aberration* disorder, disease, irregularity, instability, derangement, vagary.

abet v assist, aid, help, support, back, second, encourage, promote, cooperate with, connive at, endorse, sanction, succour.

abeyance n *the decision was in abeyance* a state of suspension/dormancy/latency, suspension, suspense, remission; *inf* cold storage.

abhor v detest, loathe, hate, abominate, feel aversion to, shrink/recoil from, dislike, execrate.

abhorrent adj detestable, loathsome, hateful, hated, abominable, repellent, repugnant, repulsive, revolting, disgusting, distasteful, horrible, horrid, heinous, obnoxious, odious, offensive, execrable; *inf* yucky.

abide v **1** *abide by the rules* keep to, comply with, observe, follow, obey, agree to, hold to, conform to, adhere to, stick to, stand by. **2** *I cannot abide them or their habits* stand, tolerate, bear, put up with, endure, stomach, suffer, accept, brook.

abiding adj lasting, everlasting, eternal, unending, continuing, durable, constant, permanent, stable, enduring, persisting, unchanging, steadfast, immutable.

ability n **1** *a person of outstanding ability* talent, competence, competency, proficiency, skill, expertise, expertness, adeptness, aptitude, dexterity, adroitness, qualification, cleverness, flair, gift, knack, *savoir faire*; *inf* know-how. **2** *the ability to cope* capacity, capability, potential, potentiality, power, aptness, facility, faculty, propensity.

abject adj **1** *abject poverty* wretched, miserable, hopeless, pathetic, pitiable, piteous, stark, forlorn. **2** *an abject coward* base, low, vile, worthless, contemptible, debased, degraded, despicable, ignominious, mean. **3** *an abject apology* obsequious, grovelling, servile, cringing, snivelling, ingratiating, toadying, sycophantic, submissive.

abjure v **1** *abjure a claim* give up, renounce, relinquish, retract, abandon, deny, abdicate, disclaim, disavow, forswear, renege on. **2** *abjure worldly pleasures* give up, renounce, relinquish, abandon, forswear,

forgo, forsake, abstain from, refrain from, reject, repudiate, eschew, abnegate; *inf* kick, jack in, pack in.

ablaze adj **1** *the house was ablaze* on fire, burning, blazing, alight, flaming; *lit* afire, aflame. **2** *the house was ablaze with lights* lit up, alight, gleaming, glowing, aglow, illuminated, brilliant, radiant, shimmering, sparkling, flashing, incandescent. **3** *ablaze with excitement/anger* passionate, aroused, excited, stimulated, animated, impassioned, ardent, fervent, frenzied.

able adj *an able pupil* competent, capable, talented, skilful, skilled, clever, intelligent, accomplished, gifted, proficient, apt, fit, expert, adept, efficient, effective, qualified, adroit.

able-bodied adj healthy, in good health, fit, robust, strong, sound, sturdy, vigorous, hardy, hale and hearty, muscular, strapping, tough, powerful, mighty, rugged, burly, stalwart, staunch; in good shape, in tip-top condition.

ablution n *perform one's ablutions* washing, cleansing, bathing, showering, scrubbing, purification; wash, bath, shower; *fml* lavage, lavation.

abnegation n **1** *monks leading a life of abnegation/self-abnegation* renunciation, self-denial, self-sacrifice, resignation, abstinence, temperance. **2** *the abnegation of a doctrine* giving up, renunciation, denial, rejection, relinquishment, abdication.

abnormal adj unusual, strange, odd, peculiar, uncommon, curious, queer, weird, eccentric, extraordinary, unexpected, exceptional, irregular, unnatural, erratic, singular, atypical, non-typical, anomalous, deviant, deviating, divergent, aberrant; *inf* oddball; *Amer inf* off the wall, wacko.

abnormality n **1** *the abnormality of their behaviour* unusualness, strangeness, oddness, eccentricity, unexpectedness, irregularity, singularity, atypicality, anomalousness, deviation, divergence, aberrance, aberration. **2** *X-rays showing a physical abnormality* irregularity, malformation, deformity, anomaly, flaw, deviation, aberration.

abode n *welcome to my humble abode* home, house, place of residence/habitation, dwelling-place, domicile, dwelling, habitat; accommodation, habitation; quarters, lodgings; *inf* pad.

abolish v do away with, put an end to, end, stop, terminate, axe, eliminate, eradicate, exterminate, destroy, annihilate, stamp out, obliterate, wipe out, extinguish, quash, expunge, extirpate, annul, cancel, invalidate, nullify, void, rescind, repeal, revoke, vitiate, abrogate.

abolition n ending, termination, elimination, extermination, destruction, annihilation, obliteration, extirpation, annulment, cancellation, nullification, invalidation, rescindment, repeal, revocation, vitiation, abrogation.

abominable adj hateful, loathsome, detestable, odious, obnoxious, base, despicable, contemptible, damnable, cursed, disgusting, revolting, repellent, repulsive, offensive, repugnant, abhorrent, reprehensible, foul, vile, wretched, horrible, nasty, disagreeable, unpleasant, execrable; *inf* yucky, god-awful.

abominate v detest, loathe, hate, abhor, dislike, feel aversion/revulsion to, shudder at, recoil from.

abomination n **1** *regard with abomination* detestation, loathing, hatred, aversion, antipathy, repulsion, abhorrence, repugnance, disgust, distaste, dislike; *fml* odium, execration. **2** *the child/building is an abomination* atrocity, disgrace, horror, obscenity, curse, torment, anathema, bugbear, *bête noir.*

aboriginal adj indigenous, native, original, earliest, first, ancient, primitive, primeval, primordial, autochthonous, autochthonal, autochthonic.

abort v **1** *abort a pregnancy/foetus* terminate. **2** *the expectant mother aborted* miscarry, have a miscarriage. **3** *abort a space mission* call off, halt, stop, end, terminate, axe, arrest, nullify. **4** *the space mission aborted* come to a halt, end, terminate, fail.

abortion n **1** *she had an abortion* termination, miscarriage, foeticide. **2** *the mission was an abortion* failure, non-success, fiasco, misadventure, disappointment, defeat.

abortive adj *an abortive attempt/plan* failed, unsuccessful, non-successful, vain, futile, useless, worthless, ineffective, ineffectual, fruitless, unproductive, unavailing.

abound v **1** *weeds abound around here* be plentiful, proliferate, superabound, thrive, flourish. **2** *a river abounding with/in fish* be full of, overflow with, teem with, be packed/crowded/thronged/jammed with, be alive, swarm with; *inf* be crawling/lousy with.

about prep **1** *talk about it* with reference to, referring to, with regard to, regarding, concerning, with respect to, respecting, relating to, on, touching on, dealing with, with relevance to, connected with; *inf* re.

2 *somewhere about here* near, nearby, close to, adjacent to, beside, around. **3** *about ten o'clock* approximately, roughly, nearly, in the neighbourhood of. **4** *dancing about the maypole* round, around, encircling, surrounding. **5** *travelling about the world* round, throughout, over, all over, in all parts, through. **6** *when you're about it* occupied with, concerned with, busy with. **about to** *they're about to die* on the point of, on the verge/brink of, going to, ready to, preparing to, soon to, intending to.

about adv **1** *running and jumping about* around, here and there, to and fro, from place to place, hither and thither. **2** *it costs about £10* approximately, roughly, nearly, in the neighbourhood/region of. **3** *she's somewhere about* around, near, nearby, about the place, in the vicinity, hereabouts. **4** *turn the ship about* in the reverse/opposite direction, into reverse, backwards. **5** *a lot of 'flu about* around, in circulation, going on, in existence, current, prevailing, prevalent, happening, in the air. **6** *just about enough* nearly, almost, not quite, scarcely, barely.

above prep **1** *above the horizon* over, higher than, on top of; atop. **2** *the rank above captain* over, higher than, superior to. **3** *a temperature above the average* over, higher than, greater than, more than, exceeding, in excess of, over and above, surpassing. **4** *above suspicion* beyond, not subject/liable/open to, superior to. **5** *prize honour above life* in preference to, more than, rather than, before, in favour of. **6** *above the bridge* upstream from, northwards of, north from. **above oneself** conceited, proud, arrogant, self-important; *inf* cocky, stuck-up, big-headed.

above adv **1** *on the shelf above* overhead, on/at the top, on/at a higher place, high up; *fml* on high. **2** *as stated above* earlier, previously, before, formerly.

above adj *the above reference* aforementioned, aforesaid, preceding, earlier, foregoing, previous, prior.

above-board adv/adj *the deal was made above-board/an above-board discussion* honest, fair, open, frank, straight, overt, candid, forthright, unconcealed, unequivocal.

abrasion n **1** *skin abrasions* graze, scrape, scratch, sore, ulcer, chafe. **2** *the abrasion of the rock* erosion, wearing down/away, corrosion, chafing, rubbing, scraping, excoriation.

abrasive adj **1** *an abrasive substance* erosive, eroding, corrosive, chafing, rubbing, coarse, harsh. **2** *an abrasive manner* caustic, cutting, grating, biting, rough, harsh, irritating, sharp, nasty.

abreast adv **1** *running abreast* side by side, alongside, level, beside each other, shoulder to shoulder. **2** *keeping abreast of the news/changes* up to date with, up with, in touch with, familiar/acquainted with, informed/knowledgeable about, conversant with, *au courant* with, *au fait* with.

abridge v shorten, cut down, condense, contract, compress, abbreviate, reduce, decrease, diminish, curtail, truncate, lessen, trim, summarize, abstract, epitomize, synopsize, digest.

abridgement, abridgment, n **1** *prepare an abridgement of the report* summary, synopsis, précis, abstract, outline, résumé, shortening, digest. **2** *the abridgement of a novel* shortening, cutting, condensation, contraction, reduction, summarization. *see* ABRIDGE.

abroad adv **1** *go abroad on holiday* overseas, out of the country, to/in foreign parts, to/in a foreign country/land, beyond the seas. **2** *spreading the rumour abroad* about, widely, far and wide, everywhere, publicly, extensively, at large, forth, in circulation, circulating.

abrogation n repeal, annulment, cancellation, countermanding, reversal, withdrawal, revocation, retraction, abolition, ending, quashing, scrapping, invalidation, nullification, voiding, repudiation, rescission.

abrupt adj **1** *an abrupt ending* sudden, quick, hurried, hasty, swift, rapid, precipitate, headlong, instantaneous, surprising, unexpected, unanticipated, unforeseen. **2** *an abrupt manner* curt, blunt, brusque, short, terse, brisk, crisp, gruff, snappish, unceremonious, rough, rude. **3** *an abrupt slope* steep, sheer, precipitous, sudden, sharp; *fml* declivitous. **4** *an abrupt style of writing* jerky, uneven, irregular, disconnected, discontinuous, broken, rough, inelegant.

abscess n ulcer, ulceration, boil, pustule, carbuncle, pimple, papule.

abscond v run away, bolt, clear out, flee, make off, escape, take flight, fly, decamp, disappear, slip/steal/sneak away, take to one's heels, make a quick getaway, beat a hasty retreat, show a clean pair of heels, run for it; *inf* do a bunk, do a moonlight flit, cut and run, skedaddle, skip, do a runner.

absence n **1** *the teacher noted their absence* non-attendance, non-appearance, truancy, absenteeism. **2** *in the absence of proof* lack, want, non-existence, unavailability, deficiency, omission, default, need, privation.

absent adj **1** *absent overseas | absent from school* away, off, out, gone, missing, truant, lacking, unavailable, non-existent, non-attendant. **2** *an absent expression* absent-minded, distracted, preoccupied, daydreaming, dreaming, far-away, blank, empty, vacant, inattentive, vague, absorbed, abstracted, musing, unheeding, wool-gathering, *distrait*.

absent-minded adj *an absent-minded professor* distracted, preoccupied, absorbed, abstracted, vague, inattentive, forgetful, oblivious, in a brown study, *distrait*. *see* ABSENT 2.

absolute adj **1** *absolute trust* complete, total, utter, out and out, outright, perfect, entire, undivided, unqualified, unadulterated, unalloyed, downright, undiluted, solid, consummate, unmitigated. **2** *the absolute truth* certain, positive, definite, unquestionable, undoubted, unequivocal, decisive, unconditional, categorical, conclusive, confirmed, infallible. **3** *an absolute standard* fixed, independent, non-relative, non-variable, rigid, established, set, definite. **4** *absolute power* unlimited, unrestricted, unrestrained, unbounded, boundless, infinite, ultimate, total, supreme, unconditional, full, utter, sovereign, omnipotent. **5** *absolute monarch* despotic, dictatorial, autocratic, tyrannical, authoritarian, arbitrary, autonomous, sovereign.

absolutely adv **1** *absolutely correct* completely, totally, utterly, perfectly, entirely, wholly, fully, thoroughly. **2** *absolutely the worst driver* certainly, positively, definitely, unquestionably, undoubtedly, without a doubt, unequivocally, unconditionally, conclusively, unreservedly. **3** *absolutely pouring down* positively, actually, in actual fact, really, in truth. **4** *ruling absolutely* despotically, dictatorially, autocratically, tyrannically, arbitrarily, unrestrictedly, totally, supremely, unconditionally, utterly, omnipotently. *see* ABSOLUTE 4, 5.

absolutely interj *are you going? absolutely!* certainly, yes, indeed, of course, positively, naturally, without doubt, unquestionably.

absolution n forgiveness, pardoning, exoneration, freedom, liberation, deliverance, remission, dispensation, condoning, vindication, exculpation; pardon, acquittal, reprieve, discharge, amnesty, release, delivery.

absolve v **1** *absolve them from blame* acquit, exonerate, discharge, release, free, deliver, liberate, let off, clear, exempt, exculpate.

2 *absolve repentant sinners* forgive, pardon, excuse, reprieve, give amnesty to, give dispensation/indulgence to, clear, set free, vindicate.

absorb v **1** *absorb liquid* soak up, suck up, draw up/in, take up/in, blot up, mop, sponge up, sop up. **2** *absorb food* consume, devour, eat up, swallow, assimilate, digest, ingest. **3** *absorb smaller companies* take in, incorporate, assimilate, appropriate, co-opt; *derog* swallow up. **4** *absorb them | absorb their attention* occupy, engage, preoccupy, captivate, engross, monopolize, rivet.

absorbed adj *absorbed in a book* occupied with, taken up with/by, engaged in, preoccupied with, engrossed in, immersed in, captivated by, riveted by.

absorbent adj absorptive, porous, spongy, spongelike, permeable, pervious, penetrable, assimilative, receptive, soaking, blotting, sorbefacient.

absorbing adj *an absorbing book* fascinating, gripping, interesting, captivating, engrossing, riveting, spellbinding, intriguing.

absorption n **1** *absorption of liquid* soaking up, sucking up. *see* ABSORB 1. **2** *absorption of food* consumption, devouring, assimilation, ingestion. *see* ABSORB 2. **3** *absorption of small companies* incorporation, assimilation, appropriation, co-opting. *see* ABSORB 3. **4** *absorption of their attention* occupying, engagement, engaging, preoccupation, engrossment, monopolization, riveting, intentness, raptness, involvement. *see* ABSORB 4.

abstain v **1** *abstain from voting* refrain, decline, forbear, desist, hold back, keep from, refuse, renounce, avoid, shun, eschew. **2** *most voted but I abstained* decline/refuse to vote. **3** *the young people drink but the parents abstain* be teetotal, take the pledge; *inf* be on the wagon.

abstemious adj moderate, temperate, abstinent, self-denying, austere, sober, self-restrained, ascetic, puritanical, non-indulgent, self-abnegating.

abstention n *abstention from voting* abstaining, refraining, forbearing, desistance, refusal, renunciation, self-control, self-denial.

abstinence n **1** *practise total abstinence* teetotalism, temperance, sobriety, nephalism. *see* ABSTAIN 3. **2** *abstinence from pleasure* refraining, forbearing, desistance, renunciation. *see* ABSTAIN 1.

abstract adj **1** *beauty is abstract* theoretical, conceptual, notional, intellectual, metaphysical, philosophical. **2** *abstract art* non-representational, non-realistic, unrealistic. **3** *abstract theories of cosmology* complex, abstruse, recondite, obscure, deep.

abstract n *an abstract of/from a scientific paper* summary, synopsis, précis, résumé, outline, abridgement, condensation, digest.

abstract v **1** *abstract metal from ore* extract, remove, take out/away, separate, detach, draw away, isolate. **2** *abstract goods from the shop* steal, rob, thieve, appropriate, make off with, filch, purloin; *inf* pinch, nick. **3** *abstract a book* abridge, summarize, précis, condense, compress, shorten, cut down, abbreviate, contract, synopsize.

abstracted adj **1** *an abstracted expression* absent-minded, distracted, preoccupied, far-away, inattentive, thoughtful, pensive, musing, absorbed, wool-gathering, absent, *distrait*. **2** *an abstracted book* abridged, summarized, condensed, compressed, abbreviated. *see* ABSTRACT V 3.

abstraction n **1** *the abstraction of metal from ore* extraction, removal, separation, detachment. *see* ABSTRACT V 1. **2** *lost in abstraction* absent-mindedness, distraction, preoccupation, daydreaming, inattentiveness, thoughtfulness, absorption. *see* ABSTRACTED 1. **3** *facts rather than an abstraction* concept, generality, generalization, idea, theory, hypothesis, supposition, notion, presumption.

abstruse adj obscure, deep, profound, complex, hidden, esoteric, mysterious, incomprehensible, unfathomable, inscrutable, enigmatic, perplexing, puzzling, recondite, arcane, nebulous.

absurd adj ridiculous, foolish, silly, idiotic, stupid, nonsensical, senseless, inane, crazy, ludicrous, funny, laughable, comical, preposterous, farcical, hare-brained, asinine; *inf* daft.

absurdity n **1** *the absurdity of the situation* ridiculousness, foolishness, silliness, idiocy, stupidity, inanity, folly, incongruity, irrationality, ludicrousness, funniness, comedy, humour, joke, farce. *see* ABSURD. **2** *talking absurdities* nonsense, foolishness, rubbish, twaddle, gibberish, drivel, balderdash; *inf* claptrap, bunk.

abundance n plenty, plentifulness, profusion, copiousness, amplitude, affluence, lavishness, bountifulness; *inf* heaps, bags, stacks, loads, tons, oodles.

abundant adj plentiful, large, great, huge, ample, well-supplied, well-provided, profuse, copious, lavish, bountiful, teeming, overflowing; *inf* galore.

abuse v **1** *abuse power/alcohol* misuse, misapply, misemploy, mishandle, exploit. **2** *abuse children* mistreat, maltreat, ill-use, ill-treat, manhandle, injure, hurt, harm, beat, damage, wrong, oppress, torture. **3** *abusing trespassers* insult, swear at, curse, scold, rebuke, upbraid, reprove, castigate, inveigh against, revile, vilify, vituperate against, slander.

abuse n **1** *the abuse of power* | *alcohol abuse* misuse, misapplication, misemployment, mishandling, exploitation. **2** *child abuse* mistreatment, maltreatment, ill-use, ill-treatment, manhandling, injury, hurt, harm, beating, damage, wronging, oppression, torture. **3** *guilty of political abuse* corruption, wrongdoing, wrong, misconduct, misdeeds, offence, crime, fault, sin. **4** *torrents of abuse* swearing, cursing, scolding, rebuke, upbraiding, reproval, invective, castigation, revilement, vilification, vituperation, defamation, slander; insults, curses, expletives, swear-words.

abusive adj *abusive remarks* | *becoming abusive* insulting, rude, blasphemous, offensive, vulgar, vituperative, reproachful, reproving, derisive, scornful, castigating, slanderous, defamatory, opprobrious, calumniating.

abut v adjoin, border, verge on, join, touch, meet, impinge on.

abutting adj adjacent, next to, neighbouring, adjoining, contiguous, bordering, verging, joining, touching, meeting.

abysmal adj *abysmal ignorance/poverty* extreme, utter, complete, thorough, profound, deep, endless, immeasurable, boundless, incalculable, unfathomable, bottomless.

abyss n **1** *a yawning abyss* chasm, gorge, cavity, void, pit, bottomless pit, hole, gulf, depth, ravine, canyon, crevasse. **2** *the abyss of despair* chasm, void, bottomless pit, hell, hell-hole; depths.

academic adj **1** *academic considerations* educational, scholastic, instructional, pedagogical. **2** *of an academic turn of mind* scholarly, studious, literary, well-read, intellectual, erudite, learned, cultured, bookish, highbrow, pedantic, donnish, cerebral; *inf* brainy. **3** *an academic rather than a practical solution* theoretical, hypothetical, abstract, conjectural, notional, impractical, unrealistic, speculative, ivory-towerish.

academic n scholar, lecturer, don, teacher, tutor, professor, fellow, bluestocking, bookworm, egghead, pedant, pedagogue.

accede v **1** *accede to the request* agree to, consent to, accept, assent, acquiesce, endorse, comply with, go along with, concur, grant, yield to. **2** *accede to the throne* succeed to, assume, attain, come to, inherit.

accelerate v **1** *the car accelerated* speed up, go faster, pick up speed; *inf* open up. **2** *the process accelerated* speed up, go faster, hasten, hurry, quicken, advance rapidly. **3** *accelerate the process* speed up, hasten, quicken, expedite, step up, advance, forward, further, spur on, facilitate, precipitate, stimulate.

acceleration n **1** *the acceleration of the car* increased speed; speeding up; *inf* opening up. **2** *the acceleration of the process* speeding up, hastening, quickening, expedition, stepping up, advancement, forwarding, facilitation, precipitation, stimulation. *see* ACCELERATE 3.

accent n **1** *a Scottish accent* pronunciation, intonation, enunciation, articulation, inflection, tone, modulation, utterance. **2** *the accent on the first syllable* stress, emphasis, accentuation, force, beat, prominence; primary stress, secondary stress. **3** *the accent on comfort* emphasis, stress, prominence, importance, accentuation, priority, underlining, underscoring. **4** *an acute accent* | *an accent on the e* accent mark, mark, diacritic, diacritical mark, sign; circumflex, acute accent, grave accent, cedilla, umlaut, tilde.

accent v **1** *accent the first syllable* stress, put/lay the stress on, emphasize, put/lay the emphasis on, put the force on, accentuate. **2** *accent the advantages* accentuate, emphasize, highlight, underline, draw attention. *see* ACCENTUATE 1.

accentuate v **1** *the black dress accentuated her paleness* emphasize, stress, highlight, underline, draw attention to, give prominence to, heighten, point up, underscore, accent. **2** *accentuate the pulse of the music* stress, put the stress/emphasis on, emphasize, accent. *see* ACCENT V 1.

accept v **1** *accept the award* receive, take, take receipt of, get, gain, obtain, acquire, come by. **2** *accept the decision* accede to, agree to, consent to, acquiesce in, concur with, endorse, comply with, go along with, defer to, put up with, recognize, acknowledge, cooperate with, adopt, admit. **3** *accept the responsibility/project* take on, undertake, assume, bear, tackle, be responsible for. **4** *accept their story* | *accept what they say* believe, trust, credit, be convinced of, have faith in, count/rely on. **5** *never accepted as* *one of the family* welcome, receive, receive favourably, embrace, offer friendship to, integrate. **6** *accept the invitation* say yes to, reply in the affirmative, comply with.

acceptable adj **1** *an acceptable present* welcome, agreeable, delightful, pleasing, desirable, satisfying, gratifying. **2** *a standard of work not acceptable* satisfactory, good enough, adequate, passable, admissible, tolerable. **3** *an acceptable risk* allowable, tolerable, admissible, bearable, supportable.

acceptance n **1** *the acceptance of an award* receipt, receiving, taking, obtaining, acquiring. *see* ACCEPT 1. **2** *the acceptance of a decision* accedence, accession, acquiescence, endorsement, recognition, acknowledgement, adoption, admission. *see* ACCEPT 2. **3** *the acceptance of responsibility* undertaking, assumption, tackling, adoption. *see* ACCEPT 3. **4** *the acceptance of their story | acceptance of what they said* belief in, trust in, faith in, credibility, reliance on. *see* ACCEPT 4. **5** *acceptance as one of the family* welcome, welcoming, favourable reception, embracing, integration, approval, adoption. *see* ACCEPT 5. **6** *acceptances to an invitation* yes, affirmative reply, affirmation, confirmation, ratification.

accepted adj **1** *an accepted opinion* approved, recognized, sanctioned, authorized, received, allowable, acceptable. **2** *the accepted manner of behaving* usual, customary, normal, expected, standard, conventional, recognized, acknowledged, established, traditional, confirmed.

access n **1** *a building with a rear access | access to the building* entry, entrance, way in, means of entry/entrance; admittance, admission; approachability, accessibility; approach, means of approach; gateway, driveway, road, path, avenue, passage. **2** *access to the prison/prisoner | access to secret information* admission, admittance, entrée, right of entry, permission/opportunity to enter/reach/use; accessibility, attainability. **3** *an access of anger* fit, outburst, attack, paroxysm, onset.

access v *access the data/information* gain access to, retrieve, gain, acquire.

accessibility n **1** *the accessibility of sources of entertainment* attainability, reachability, availability, approachability, achievability. *see* ACCESSIBLE 1. **2** *accessibility of the manager to the staff* approachability, availability, informality, friendliness, agreeableness, congeniality, affability, cordiality. *see* ACCESSIBLE 2. **3** *accessibility of information* comprehensibility, intelligibility, penetrability. *see* ACCESSIBLE 3.

accessible n **1** *an accessible source of entertainment* attainable, reachable, available, approachable, obtainable, achievable; *inf* get-at-able. **2** *accessible to the staff* approachable by, available, easygoing, informal, friendly, pleasant, agreeable, obliging, congenial, affable, cordial. **3** *accessible information* understandable, comprehensible, intelligible, penetrable, fathomable, graspable.

accession n **1** *accession to the throne/title* succession, inheritance. *see* ACCEDE 2. **2** *accession to the request/treaty* agreement, consent, acceptance, acquiescence. *see* ACCEDE 1. **3** *a recent accession to the museum collection* addition, increase, augmentation, increment, gain, enlargement, expansion, extension.

accessory n **1** *his accessories in the raid* accomplice, associate, confederate, abettor, helper, assistant, partner. **2** *bicycle accessories* attachment, fitment, extra, addition, adjunct, appendage, supplement. **3** *accessories matching her outfit* adornment, finery, trimming, ornament, ornamentation, embellishment, trappings, fashion detail, frill; handbag, shoes, gloves, hat, belt, ribbon.

accessory adj *an accessory part/factor* additional, extra, supplementary, contributory, subsidiary, ancilliary, auxiliary, secondary, assisting.

accident n **1** *an accident at work | an industrial accident* mishap, casualty, misfortune, misadventure, injury, disaster, tragedy, blow, catastrophe, calamity. **2** *the police were called to an accident* crash, collision; *inf* smash, smash-up, pile-up. **3** *met by accident* chance, mere chance, fate, twist of fate, fortune, good fortune, luck, good luck, fortuity, hazard; *inf* fluke.

accidental adj **1** *accidental death | an accidental meeting* chance, occurring by chance/ accident, unintentional, unintended, inadvertent, unexpected, unforeseen, unlooked-for, fortuitous, unanticipated, unplanned, uncalculated, unpremeditated, unwitting, adventitious. **2** *an accidental consideration* non-essential, inessential, incidental, extraneous, extrinsic, supplementary, subsidiary, subordinate, secondary, accessory, irrelevant.

accidentally adv *killed/met accidentally* by accident, by chance, unintentionally, inadvertently, without design, unexpectedly, adventitiously, unwittingly; *inf* by a fluke. *see* ACCIDENTAL 1.

acclaim v *acclaim his victory* applaud, cheer, celebrate, salute, welcome, approve, honour, praise, commend, hail, extol, laud, eulogize, exalt. **2** *acclaim her queen* declare, announce, proclaim, hail.

acclaim n *returning to the acclaim of the crowd* applause, ovation, praise, commendation, approval, approbation, homage, tribute, extolment, laudation; cheers, congratulations, plaudits, bouquets, salutes, eulogies.

acclamation n **1** *acknowledge the acclamations of the crowd* applause, ovation, praise, salutation, welcome, homage, tribute, approval; cheers, congratulations, plaudits. *see* ACCLAIM n. **2** *the acclamation of her as queen* declaration, announcement, proclamation, hailing. **3** *elected by acclamation* shouting, calling out, oral vote, non-ballot; shouts.

acclimatization n *acclimatization to the heat | acclimatization to new conditions* adjustment, adaptation, habituation, accommodation, familiarization, inurement, naturalization, acclimation, acculturation.

acclimatize v *acclimatize to tropical conditions* adjust, adapt, accustom, get used, accommodate, accustom/habituate oneself, become seasoned, familiarize oneself, become innured, become naturalized.

accommodate v **1** *we can accommodate four people* put up, house, cater for, board, lodge, provide shelter for, shelter, provide with a roof, harbour, billet. **2** *accommodate oneself to new circumstances | accommodate our plans to suit yours* adapt, adjust, modify, reconcile, fit, harmonize, conform. **3** *accommodate you with a loan* provide, supply, furnish, serve, grant. **4** *accommodate them whenever possible* help, assist, aid, lend a hand to, oblige, meet the needs/wants of, do a favour to, favour, indulge.

accommodating adj *an accommodating person/attitude* obliging, cooperative, helpful, adaptable, pliable, compliant, complaisant, considerate, unselfish, willing, polite, kindly, hospitable, kind, friendly, agreeable.

accommodation n **1** *provide accommodation for four | do you have accommodation?* housing, lodging, board, shelter; place of residence, house, billet; lodgings, quarters; *inf* digs. **2** *the accommodation to new circumstances | accommodation of our plans to suit yours* adaptation, adjustment, modification, reconciliation, fitting, harmonization. *see* ACCOMMODATE 2. **3** *the accommodation of the firm with a loan* provision, supply, supplying, furnishing, serving. *see* ACCOMMODATE 3. **4** *the accommodation of the younger members* help, assistance, aid, obliging, favouring, indulgence. *see* ACCOMMODATE 4.

accompaniment n **1** *the accompaniment of speech with/by gestures* coexistence, coinci-

dence, concurrence, supplement. **2** *a musical accompaniment* backup, support, background, obbligato. **3** *salad as an accompaniment* supplement, addition, adjunct, appendage, complement.

accompany v **1** *accompany her to the dance* escort, go with, go along with, keep company, squire, attend on, usher, conduct, convoy, chaperon. **2** *meat accompanied by vegetables | speech accompanied with gestures* go with, go along with, go together with, coexist/occur/coincide with, supplement. **3** *accompany them on the piano* play a musical accompaniment, play with/for, back up, support.

accomplice n confederate, accessory, collaborator, abettor, associate, partner, ally, assistant, helper, aider, henchman, right hand, right-hand man, fellow-conspirator, mate, friend; *inf* sidekick.

accomplish v **1** *accomplish an aim* achieve, carry out, fulfil, perform, attain, realize, succeed in, bring off, bring about, effect, execute, effectuate. **2** *accomplish a task* finish, complete, carry through, do, perform, conclude, effect, execute, consummate.

accomplished adj **1** *an accomplished player* skilled, skilful, expert, gifted, talented, proficient, adept, masterly, polished, practised, capable, able, competent, experienced, professional, deft, consummate. **2** *an accomplished aim* achieved, fulfilled, realized. *see* ACCOMPLISH 1. **3** *an accomplished task* finished, completed, executed. *see* ACCOMPLISH 2.

accomplishment n **1** *a woman of accomplishment | proud of her social accomplishments* talent, ability, skill, gift, attainment, achievement, capability, proficiency. **2** *the army's proud accomplishments* achievement, act, deed, exploit, performance, attainment, feat, coup, triumph. **3** *the accomplishment of aims* achievement, fulfilment, attainment, realization, success, effecting, execution. *see* ACCOMPLISH 1. **4** *the accomplishment of tasks* finishing, completion, performance, conclusion, execution, consummation. *see* ACCOMPLISH 2.

accord v **1** *his statement does not accord with hers* agree, concur, fit, correspond, tally, match, conform, harmonize, suit, be in tune. **2** *accord them permission | accord a welcome* give, grant, confer, bestow, tender, offer, present, award, vouchsafe, concede.

accord n *accord between former enemies | in accord with our plans* agreement, harmony, rapport, unison, concord, amity, sympathy, unanimity, accordance. **of one's own accord** *leaving of their own accord* of one's own free will, voluntarily, willingly, freely, unforced. **with one accord** unanimously, in complete agreement, with one mind, of one voice, unitedly, concertedly.

accordance n **1** *the accordance of permission | the accordance of a welcome* granting, conferring, bestowal, tendering. *see* ACCORD V 2. **2** *accordance between opponents* accord, agreement, harmony, concord, rapport. *see* ACCORD n. **3** *acting in accordance with their wishes* agreement conformity, compliance.

according adj **according to 1** *according to the manager* as stated/maintained by, as claimed by, on the authority of, on the report of. **2** *acting according to their principles* in accordance with, in agreement with, in line with, in keeping with, in compliance with, in harmony with, in conformity with, in obedience to, following, after. **3** *salary according to experience* in proportion to, commensurate with, in relation to.

accordingly adv **1** *you know the truth and must act accordingly* appropriately, correspondingly, suitably, properly, fitly, consistently. **2** *they could not pay the rent and accordingly left* as a result, consequently, therefore, so, thus, as a consequence, in consequence, hence, *ergo.*

accost v **1** *the police accosted him in the street* address, speak to, confront, approach, greet, hail, salute; *inf* buttonhole. **2** *accosted by a prostitute* solicit, importune.

account n **1** *a full account of the accident* statement, report, description, record, narration, narrative, story, recital, explanation, tale, chronicle, history, relation, version. **2** *pay their accounts on time* bill, invoice, reckoning, tally; charges, debts. **3** *accounts with several banks* bank account; current account, deposit account, savings account. **4** *the firm's accounts are in good order* ledger, balance sheet, financial statement; books. **5** *a person/matter of no account* importance, consequence, significance. **on account of** because of, owing to, on grounds of. **on no account** not under any circumstances, under no circumstances, certainly not, absolutely not, in any event.

account v *they are accounted guilty | account her to be guilty* consider, regard, reckon, believe, think, look upon, view as, judge, count, deem. **account for 1** *they must account for the delay* explain, explain away, give reasons for, show grounds for, justify, elucidate. **2** *oil accounts for most of their exports* be responsible for, make up, supply, provide, give. **3** *the army accounted for hundreds of terrorists* kill, destroy, put out of action, incapacitate.

accountability n **1** *the accountability of the police for their actions* responsibility, answerability, liability. *see* ACCOUNTABLE 1. **2** *their accountability to the manager* responsibility, answerability, reporting, obedience. *see* ACCOUNTABLE 2. **3** *the accountability of his actions* explicability, comprehensibility, intelligibility.

accountable adj **1** *accountable for one's actions* responsible, answerable, liable, chargeable. **2** *accountable to the manager* responsible, answerable, reporting to, under the charge of, obeying. **3** *his actions are not accountable* explicable, explainable, understandable, comprehensible, intelligible.

accoutrements npl equipment, gear, tackle, paraphernalia, apparatus, adornment, ornamentation; trappings, appurtenances, furnishings, appointments, fittings; *inf* things, bits and pieces.

accredit v **1** *accredited with the invention* credit with, have ascribed/attributed to, receive the credit for. **2** *accredited to Shakespeare* ascribe, attribute.

accredited adj **1** *our accredited representative* official, authorized, legal, appointed, approved, recognized, certified, sanctioned. **2** *accredited theories* accepted, recognized, believed, endorsed, orthodox. **3** *an accredited herd* certified, attested, licensed.

accrue v **1** *bank interest accrued* accumulate, build/mount up, amass, collect, gather, grow, increase, augment. **2** *medical advances accrued from the new technology* arise, follow, ensue, result/emanate from.

accumulate v **1** *dust accumulated over the weeks* gather, pile/build up, collect, amass, increase, augment, cumulate, accrue. **2** *accumulate money/books* amass, gather, collect, stockpile, pile/heap up, store, hoard, cumulate.

accumulation n **1** *an accumulation of rubbish/money* stockpile, pile, heap, mass, collection, build-up, gathering, stock, store, hoard, stack, cumulation, accrual, aggregation. **2** *the accumulation of piles of dust | the accumulation of his collection of coins* gathering, collection, amassing, building up, stockpiling, cumulation, accrual. *see* ACCUMULATE.

accuracy n **1** *the accuracy of the statistics* correctness, precision, exactness, rightness, validity. *see* ACCURATE 1. **2** *the accuracy of the description | say with any accuracy* correctness, exactness, closeness, faithfulness, truth, authenticity, veracity. *see* ACCURATE 2. **3** *the accuracy of the aim* precision, carefulness, meticulousness. *see* ACCURATE 3.

accurate adj **1** *accurate statistics* correct, precise, exact, right, errorless, without error, valid; *inf* spot on, bang on. **2** *an accurate description* correct, exact, close, faithful, true, truthful, authentic, factual, literal, veracious, strict. **3** *take accurate aim* precise, careful, meticulous, painstaking.

accursed adj **1** *that accursed noise | those accursed money-lenders* hateful, detestable, despicable, horrible, foul, abominable, odious, obnoxious, execrable; *inf* yucky. **2** *the witch and her accursed victims* under a curse, cursed, curse-laden, bewitched, bedevilled, damned, doomed, ill-fated, wretched, blighted.

accusation n *deny the accusation* charge, allegation, attribution, incrimination, imputation, denouncement, indictment, arraignment, impeachment, citation, inculpation, incrimation, blame.

accuse v **1** *in court accused of murder* charge, indict, arraign, impeach, summon, cite, inculpate. **2** *accuse her of tearing the curtain* blame for, lay the blame on, hold responsible/accountable/answerable, impute blame to; *inf* lay at the door of, stick on.

accustom v *accustom herself to the new situation* adapt, adjust, acclimatize, get used to, make familiar/aquainted with, habituate.

accustomed adj **1** *his accustomed style* usual, normal, customary, habitual, regular, routine, ordinary, fixed, set, typical, established, common, general. **2** *accustomed to public speaking | accustomed to the situation* used to, familiar/acquainted with, adapted, adjusted, habituated, inured.

ace n *a tennis ace* expert, champion, master, star, winner, genius, virtuoso, adept; *inf* wizard, dab hand, hotshot, whiz.

ace adj *an ace player* expert, champion, brilliant, great, superb, outstanding, excellent, first-rate, fine, skilful, adept; *inf* crack, A1, tiptop, hotshot.

acerbic adj **1** *an acerbic wit/tone* harsh, sarcastic, sharp, biting, stinging, caustic, trenchant, bitter, astringent, vitriolic, virulent, mordant. **2** *an acerbic taste* sour, tart, bitter, acid, sharp, acrid, acidulous, pungent.

ache n **1** *an ache in my back* pain, dull pain, soreness; pang, throb, twinge, smarting, gnawing, stabbing, spasm; suffering. **2** *an ache in my heart* suffering, sorrow, misery, distress, grief, anguish, affliction, woe, mourning. **3** *feel an ache for old times* longing, yearning, craving, desire, hunger, hungering, pining, hankering.

ache v **1** *my head aches* hurt, be sore, be painful, be in pain, pain; throb, pound, twinge, smart, gnaw. **2** *my heart aches* grieve, be sorrowful, be distressed, be in distress, be miserable, mourn, agonize, suffer. **3** *she aches for sunshine* long for, yearn for, crave, desire, hunger for, pine for, hanker for/after, covet.

achieve v **1** *achieve success* attain, reach, arrive at, gain, earn, realize, win, acquire, obtain, procure, get, wrest. **2** *achieve all the tasks begun* complete, finish, accomplish, carry through, fulfil, execute, conclude, perform, effect, consummate.

achievement n **1** *the achievement of success/objectives* attainment, gaining, realization, acquiral, procurement. *see* ACHIEVE 1. **2** *the achievement of tasks begun* completion, finishing, accomplishment, fulfilment, execution, conclusion, consummation. *see* ACHIEVE 2. **3** *proud of their child's achievement* accomplishment, feat, performance, act, action, deed, effort, exploit.

acid adj **1** *an acid taste/fruit* sour, tart, bitter, sharp, biting, acrid, pungent, acerbic, vinegary, vinegarish, acetic, acetous, acidulous. *see* ACERBIC 2. **2** *an acid wit/reply* acerbic, sarcastic, sharp, caustic, trenchant, vitriolic, mordant. *see* ACERBIC 1.

acknowledge v **1** *acknowledge the need for reform* admit, grant, allow, recognize, accept, subscribe to, approve, agree to, acquiesce in, concede. **2** *acknowledge him with a wave* greet, salute, address, hail, recognize, notice. **3** *acknowledge a letter* answer, reply to, respond to, react to. **4** *acknowledge help* show appreciation for/of, express gratitude for, give thanks for, thank.

acknowledged adj *the acknowledged leader* admitted, recognized, accepted, approved, accredited, declared, avowed.

acknowledgement n **1** *the acknowledgement of the need for reform* admission, granting, recognition, acceptance, approval, agreement, acquiescence. *see* ACKNOWLEDGE 1. **2** *the acknowledgement of his presence with a wave* greeting, saluting, recognition, notice. *see* ACKNOWLEDGE 2. **3** *the acknowledgement of a letter | an acknowledgement* answering, answer, reply, response, reaction. *see* ACKNOWLEDGE 3. **4** *the/an acknowledgement of help* expression of appreciation/gratitude, thanks. *see* ACKNOWLEDGE 4.

acme n peak, pinnacle, zenith, climax, culmination, height, high point, crown, summit, optimum, apex.

acolyte n assistant, helper, attendant, follower.

acquaint v *acquaint oneself/you with the facts* familiarize, make familiar/conversant, make known to, make aware of, advise of, inform, apprise of, enlighten, let know.

acquaintance n **1** *an acquaintance, not a close friend* associate, colleague, contact; *fml* confrère. **2** *our acquaintance with them* association, relationship, contact, social contact, fellowship, companionship. **3** *have some acquaintance with his poetry* familiarity, knowledge, awareness, understanding, cognizance.

acquainted adj **1** *acquainted with his poems* familiar with, conversant with, well versed in, knowledgeable in, cognizant in, apprised of, instructed in. **2** *acquainted with the mayor* known to, on friendly terms with, friendly with, on a sociable footing with.

acquiesce v consent, agree, accept, concur, approve, assent, allow, comply, conform, concede, go along with, bow to, yield.

acquiescence n consent, agreement, acceptance, concurrence, approval, assent, compliance, conforming, conceding, concession, yielding. *see* ACQUIESCE.

acquiescent adj **1** *their response was acquiescent rather than disapproving* consenting, concurrent, compliant, concessionary. *see* ACQUIESCE. **2** *an acquiescent personality/attitude* submissive, servile, subservient, obsequious, ingratiating, toadying, Uriah Heepish, self-effacing; *inf* bootlicking.

acquire v obtain, come by, get, receive, gain, procure, earn, win, secure, take possession of, gather, collect, pick up, achieve, attain, appropriate, amass.

acquirement n **1** *acquirements are as important as natural talent* attainment, achievement, accomplishment, skill, qualification. **2** *the acquirement of money* acquisition, obtaining, procurement, collecting, collection, achievement, attainment, appropriation. *see* ACQUIRE.

acquisition n **1** *the library's/museum's recent acquisitions* gain, purchase, buy, possession, accession, addition; accretion, property. **2** *the acquisition of money* obtaining, procurement, collecting, attainment, appropriation. *see* ACQUIREMENT 2.

acquisitive adj greedy, grasping, covetous, avaricious, predatory, avid, rapacious, mercenary.

acquisitiveness n greed, covetousness, avarice, avidity, rapaciousness, rapacity. *see* ACQUISITIVE.

acquit v **1** *acquit the accused of the offence* clear, absolve, exonerate, discharge, release, vindicate, liberate, free, deliver; *fml* exculpate. **2** *they acquitted themselves well/badly* perform, act, behave, conduct oneself, comport oneself, bear oneself. **3** *acquit oneself of the task/duty* perform, discharge, execute, accomplish, carry out, effect.

acquittal n **1** *the acquittal of the accused* clearing, absolution, exoneration, discharge, release, vindication, liberation, deliverance; *fml* exculpation. **2** *the acquittal of the task/duty* performance, discharge, execution, accomplishment. *see* ACQUIT 3.

acrid adj **1** *an acrid taste/smell* pungent, sharp, sour, bitter, tart, harsh, acid, stinging, burning, irritating, vinegary, acerbic, acetic, acetous. **2** *an acrid wit/remark* acerbic, sarcastic, sharp, stinging, caustic, astringent, trenchant, vitriolic, virulent. *see* ACERBIC 1.

acrimonious adj *an acrimonious attitude/remark* bitter, caustic, cutting, sarcastic, harsh, sharp, acid, acerbic, virulent, trenchant, stringent, spiteful, crabbed, vitriolic, venomous, irascible.

acrimony n bitterness, causticity, sarcasm, harshness, sharpness, acidity, acerbicity, virulence, trenchancy, stringency, spitefulness, crabbedness, irascibility. *see* ACRIMONIOUS.

acrobatics npl **1** *acrobatics in the circus ring* gymnastics, gymnastic feats/skills; agility, skill. **2** *mental acrobatics* agility, skill, quick thinking.

act n **1** *a daring/shameful act | acts of bravery/cowardice* deed, action, feat, performance, undertaking, operation, execution, exploit, enterprise, achievement, accomplishment. **2** *acts of parliament* bill, law, decree, statute, edict, dictum, enactment, resolution, ruling, judgement, ordinance, measure. **3** *an act of a play* division, part, section, segment. **4** *a music hall act* performance, turn, routine, show, sketch, skit. **5** *putting on an act | it's just an act* pretence, sham, fake, make-believe, show, feigning, affectation, counterfeit, front, posture, pose, dissimulation, dissemblance.

act v **1** *you must act now | act wisely* take action, do, move, be active, perform, function, react, behave, be employed, be busy. **2** *the painkiller will act soon* work, take effect, operate, function, be efficacious. **3** *she's acting in a Shakespeare play* perform, play, play a part, be an actor/actress, be one of the cast; *inf* tread the boards. **4** *he's acting the part of Lear* perform, play, portray, enact, represent, characterize, personify, stage. **5** *he's not ill but just acting* pretend, sham, fake, feign, put it on, dissemble, pose, dissimulate. **act for** *act for his sick father* represent, stand/fill in for, deputize/ cover/substitute for, replace, take the place of, act in place of. **act on/upon 1** *alcohol acts on the brain* affect, have an effect on, influence, alter, change, modify, transform. **2** *act on official instructions* act in accordance with, follow, obey, comply with, take heed/notice of, heed, conform to. **act up** *my car/child is acting up* misbehave, give/cause trouble, malfunction; *inf* play up.

acting n **1** *she wants to go in for acting* the theatre, drama, the performing arts, dramatics, stagecraft, theatricals, performing, portraying. **2** *acting now will save trouble* taking action, moving, functioning, reacting. *see* ACT v 1. **3** *the quick acting of the pills* action, working, taking effect. *see* ACT v 2. **4** *the acting of the part of Lear* performance, playing, portrayal, enacting. *see* ACT v 4. **5** *his acting is sometimes taken as real illness* pretending, pretence, play-acting, shamming, posturing, dissimulation. *see* ACT v 5.

acting adj *an acting head of department* deputy, substitute, temporary, interim, provisional, pro tem, *pro tempore; inf* fill-in.

action n **1** *their prompt action saved lives* act, deed, move, effort, operation, performance, undertaking, manoeuvre, endeavour, exertion, exploit. **2** *time for action | put ideas into action* acting, activity, doing, movement, motion, operating, operation, work, working, functioning, performance, effort, exertion. **3** *men of action* activity, energy, vitality, vigour, forcefulness, spirit, liveliness, vim; *inf* get-up-and-go. **4** *the action of acid on metal* effect, influence, power, result, consequence. **5** *the action of the play is set in Spain* activity; events, happenings, incidents, episodes. **6** *a piece of the action | miss the action* activity, excitement, bustle; happenings, incidents; *inf* goingson. **7** *soldiers seeing action overseas* conflict, combat, warfare, fighting, battle. **8** *the military action at Ypres* battle, fighting, engagement, clash, encounter, skirmish, affray. **9** *raise an action* lawsuit, case, prosecution, litigation; legal proceedings.

actions npl *a man is judged by his actions, not his beliefs* behaviour, conduct, activity, comportment, deportment; ways.

activate v **1** *activate the alarm system* switch on, turn on, start off, set going, trigger off, set in motion, actuate, energize. **2** *activated by envy* actuate, motivate, stimulate, move, drive, rouse, prompt. *see* ACTUATE 1.

active adj **1** *an active member of the team | an active volcano* working, functioning, operat-ing, operative, in action, in operation, in force, effective. **2** *active people | old people leading active lives* mobile, energetic, vigorous, vital, sprightly, lively, spry, busy, bustling, occupied, involved; *inf* on the go/ move; *Amer inf* go-go. **3** *the active ingredients* effective, effectual, operational, powerful, potent, non-passive, non-inert.

activity n **1** *markets are places of great activity* business, bustle, hustle and bustle, liveliness, movement, life, stir, animation, commotion, flurry, tumult; *inf* toing and froing, comings and goings. **2** *schoolwork and outside activities* interest, hobby, pastime, pursuit, occupation, venture, undertaking, enterprise, project, scheme. **3** *return to activity after being ill* functioning, mobility, effectiveness, vigour, strength, potency.

actor, actress n performer, player, dramatic artist, Thespian; stage performer/ player, play actor, film actor, film star, starlet, leading man/woman, trouper, tragedian.

actual adj *her actual words/the actual cost* real, true, factual, genuine, authentic, verified, confirmed, veritable, existing.

actually adv **1** *he's actually brilliant rather than stupid | Actually, he's very clever* really, in fact, in point of fact, as a matter of fact, in reality, indeed, truly, in truth. **2** *she was actually expected to lie* literally, even, in reality.

actuate v **1** *people actuated by greed* motivate, stimulate, move, drive, rouse, arouse, prompt, influence, impel, incite, spur on, urge, goad, animate, excite, kindle, awaken, activate. **2** *actuate an electrical device* activate, start off, trigger off. *see* ACTIVATE 2.

acumen n *showing business acumen* astuteness, shrewdness, sharpness, cleverness, smartness, judgement, discernment, wisdom, perspicacity, ingenuity, insight, perspicuity, sagacity, penetration.

acute adj **1** *an acute sense of hearing* sharp, keen, penetrating, discerning, sensitive, incisive. **2** *an acute mind/analysis* astute, shrewd, sharp, clever, smart, discerning, perceptive, perspicacious, penetrating, incisive, piercing, discriminating, sagacious, judicious. **3** *an acute shortage of food* severe, critical, crucial, grave, serious, urgent, pressing, vital, dangerous, precarious. **4** *an acute pain* sharp, shooting, piercing, keen, penetrating, stabbing, intense, excruciating, fierce, racking; *fml* exquisite. **5** *an acute illness* intense, severe, short and sharp, short-lasting.

acutely adv *acutely conscious of his poverty* very, markedly, extremely, intensely, deeply, profoundly, keenly, sharply, painfully.

adage n *as the old adage has it* saying, maxim, axiom, proverb, aphorism, saw, dictum, precept, truism, platitude; *fml* apophthegm, gnome.

adamant adj resolute, determined, firm, immovable, unshakable, uncompromising, unrelenting, unyielding, unbending, inflexible, obdurate, inexorable, intransigent.

adapt v **1** *adapt a dress/novel | adapt one's way of life* adjust, tailor, convert, change, alter, modify, transform, remodel, reshape. **2** *you must adapt to the new environment* adjust, conform, acclimatize, accommodate, familiarize oneself with, habituate oneself.

adaptable adj **1** *an adaptable dress | an adaptable way of life* adjustable, convertible, alterable, modifiable, variable, versatile. **2** *you must try to be adaptable* adjustable, flexible, pliant, compliant, malleable, versatile, resilient, easygoing, conformable.

adaptation n **1** *the adaptation of a dress/novel* adjustment, tailoring, converting, alteration, changing, modification, remodelling. *see* ADAPT 1. **2** *the adaptation to a new environment* adjustment, conformity, acclimatization, accommodation, familiarization, habituation.

add v **1** *he added an extra sentence* include, put on/in, attach, append, affix; *fml* adjoin. **2** *add all the numbers* add up, add together, total, count, count up, compute; *inf* tot up. **3** *"That's fine," he added* go on to say, state further; *inf* tack on, tag on; *fml* superimpose. **add to** *this added to their pain* increase, magnify, amplify, augment, intensify, aggravate, exacerbate. **add up 1** *add up the column of figures* add, add together, total, count, count up, compute; *inf* tot up. **2** *it adds up to £100* amount to, come to. **3** *it all adds up to a disaster* amount to, constitute, comprise, signify; *inf* spell, spell out. **4** *it doesn't add up* make sense, be/seem reasonable, be/seem plausible; *inf* ring true, hold water, stand to reason.

addendum n addition, appendix, codicil, postscript, appendage, supplement, adjunct.

addict n **1** *a drugs/heroin addict* abuser, user; *inf* junkie, freak, head, fiend, tripper. **2** *a film addict* fan, enthusiast, devotee, follower, adherent; *inf* buff, freak, nut.

addicted adj **1** *addicted to drugs* dependent, dependent on; *inf* hooked. **2** *addicted to the cinema* devoted, obsessed, dedicated; *inf* hooked.

addiction n *an addiction to drugs | addiction to the cinema* dependency, craving, devotion, obsession, dedication, enslavement, habit.

addition n **1** *the addition of an extra sentence* inclusion, adding on, attachment, appendage. *see* ADD 1. **2** *the addition of a row of figures | check my addition* adding up, counting, totalling, computation, calculation; *inf* totting up. *see* ADD 2. **3** *an addition to the family/library* increase, increment, extension, augmentation, gain, supplement, appendage. **in addition** *in addition, you may take three books | in addition to Jane* additionally, besides, as well, as well as.

additional adj *additional help* extra, supplementary, further, more, other, over and above, fresh, supplemental.

additionally adv *additionally he gave money* in addition, also, as well, besides, moreover, further, into the bargain, to boot.

additive n *additives to food | chemical additives* supplement, addition, add-on; preservative, E number.

address n **1** *the address on the envelope* inscription, label, superscription; directions. **2** *moved to a new address* house, home, location, place, residence, abode, domicile, dwelling, situation; whereabouts. **3** *an address to the crowd* speech, lecture, talk, dissertation, discourse, oration, sermon, harangue, diatribe, disquisition, phillipic.

address v **1** *address an envelope* direct, label, inscribe, superscribe. **2** *address the audience* talk to, speak to, give a talk to, make a speech to, lecture, give a discourse/dissertation/oration to, preach to, declaim to, harangue; *inf* spout to. **3** *address someone across the street* greet, speak to, hail, salute. **4** *how to address the mayor* name, call, speak to, write, describe, designate; *fml* denominate. **5** *address any remarks to the manager* direct, send, communicate, convey, forward, remit. **6** *address a ball* take aim at, aim at, face. **address onself to** apply oneself to, attend to, direct one's attention to, turn to, get down to, devote oneself to, take up, engage in, undertake, concentrate on.

adduce v cite, put forward, mention, point out, quote, name, instance, present, offer, advance, propose, proffer.

adept adj *adept at games | adept at growing roses* expert, clever, proficient, skilful, accomplished, brilliant, talented, first-rate, masterly; *inf* top-notch, A1, wizard, ace.

adept n *an adept at chess/tennis* expert, past master, genius, ace, virtuoso; *inf* wizard, dab hand, hotshot.

adequacy n **1** *dispute the adequacy of their salary* sufficiency, ampleness, reasonableness. *see* ADEQUATE 1. **2** *work noted for its adequacy rather than its excellence* passableness, tolerableness, acceptability, mediocrity, indifference. *see* ADEQUATE 2. **3** *not disputing his adequacy* capability, competence, suitability, ability, qualifications, fitness. *see* ADEQUATE 3.

adequate adj **1** *adequate grounds for divorce | an adequate salary* sufficient, enough, ample, reasonable, satisfactory, requisite. **2** *your work is adequate but not good* passable, tolerable, acceptable, fair, middle-of-the-road, mediocre, unexceptional, indifferent, average, so-so, minimal; *inf* nothing to write home about, no great shakes. **3** *he did not feel adequate to the task* up to, equal to, capable, competent, suited, suitable, able, qualified, fit.

adhere v **1** *sticky tape adhering to the wall* stick, stick fast, cling, hold fast, cohere, be fixed, be pasted/glued. **2** *adhering to their principles* stick to, hold to, abide by, comply with, stand by, be faithful to, follow, obey, fulfil. **3** *adhere to the democratic party* be attached to, support, give support to, be connected with, be affiliated to, be a member of, follow.

adherent n **1** *an adherent of communism* supporter, follower, upholder, advocate, disciple, votary, partisan, sectary, member; *inf* hanger-on. **2** *an adherent of the cinema* fan, admirer, follower, enthusiast, devotee, lover, addict, aficionado; *inf* buff, freak, fiend.

adherent adj *an adherent surface* sticky, sticking, adhering, clinging, viscous, adhesive. *see* ADHESIVE adj.

adhesive adj *an adhesive substance* sticky, sticking, adhering, adherent, clinging, tacky, gluey, gummy, cohesive, viscous, viscid, glutinous; *fml* mucilaginous.

adhesive n glue, fixative, gum, paste, cement; *fml* mucilage.

adieu interj/n goodbye, farewell. *see* GOODBYE.

adjacent adj adjoining, neighbouring, next door, abutting, close, near, bordering, alongside, contiguous, proximate, attached, touching, conjoining.

adjoining adj *an adjoining house* neighbouring, next door, adjacent, abutting, bordering, connected, connecting, contiguous, interconnecting, attached. *see* ADJACENT.

adjourn v **1** *adjourn our meeting* break off, discontinue, interrupt, suspend, dissolve, postpone, put off, defer, delay, shelve, prorogue. **2** *the court adjourns for lunch* break off, discontinue, pause; *Amer* take a recess. **3** *the women adjourned to the drawing room* withdraw, retire, retreat; *fml* repair.

adjournment n **1** *the adjournment of our meeting* breaking-off, discontinuation, interruption, suspension, postponement, deferment, deferral, delay, shelving, prorogation. *see* ADJOURN 1. **2** *the court's adjournment* breaking-off, break, discontinuation, pause. **3** *the adjournment of the women to the drawing-room* withdrawing, retirement, retreat; *fml* repairing.

adjudicate v **1** *adjudicate at a musical competition* judge, arbitrate, referee, umpire. **2** *adjudicate a tribunal claim* judge, decide on, settle, determine, pronounce on, give a ruling on.

adjudication n **1** *the adjudication at a competition* judging, arbitration, refereeing, umpiring. **2** *a tribunal adjudication* judgement, decision, pronouncement, ruling, settlement, determination, finding, verdict.

adjunct n *a mere adjunct to the rest of the equipment* extra, addition, attachment, accessory, appendage, addendum, appurtenance, supplement.

adjust v **1** *I cannot adjust to the new situation* adapt, become accustomed to, get used to, accommodate, acclimatize, reconcile oneself, habituate oneself, assimilate. **2** *adjust the dress* adapt, rearrange, alter, modify, change, remodel. **3** *adjust the brakes* regulate, modify, fix, repair, rectify, put in working order, set to rights, tune.

adjustable adj **1** *adjustable seat-belts* alterable, adaptable, modifiable, movable. **2** *adjustable people* adaptable, accommodating, amenable, obliging, flexible, malleable, pliable, pliant, tractable.

adjustment n **1** *the adjustment to a new situation* adaptation, accustoming, accommodation, acclimatization, reconciliation, habituation, assimilation. **2** *the adjustment of the dress* adaptation, alteration, modification. *see* ADJUST 2. **3** *the adjustment of the brakes* regulating, modifying, modification, fixing, repair. *see* ADJUST 3. **4** *make a small adjustment* adaptation, alteration, change, modification, rearrangement.

ad lib v *the speaker cannot ad lib* extemporize, improvise, speak off the cuff, make an impromptu speech, speak impromptu.

ad lib adj *an ad lib speech* off the cuff, impromptu, on the spot, extempore, improvised, unrehearsed, extemporaneous.

ad lib adv *speak ad lib* off the cuff, impromptu, extempore, without preparation, without rehearsal, extemporaneously; *inf* off the top of one's head.

administer v **1** *administer the firm's financial affairs* manage, direct, control, conduct, run, govern, operate, superintend, supervise, oversee, preside over. **2** *administer justice/comfort* dispense, hand out, discharge, allot, deal, distribute, mete out, disburse, bestow, provide. **3** *administer a remedy/medicine* apply, give, dispense, provide, treat with.

administration n **1** *he's in business/hospital administration* management, direction, control, conduct, execution, government, operation, supervision. **2** *the Tory administration* government, ministry, regime, executive; term of office. **3** *the administration of justice* dispensation, discharge, allotment, dealing, distribution, disbursement, bestowal. *see* ADMINISTER 2. **4** *the administration of a remedy* application, dispensation, provision. *see* ADMINISTER 3.

administrative adj *in an administrative role* managerial, management, directorial, executive, organizational, controlling, governmental, supervisory, regulatory.

administrator n manager, director, executive, controller, head, chief, superintendent, supervisor.

admirable adj **1** *admirable conduct in the circumstances* worthy, commendable, praiseworthy, laudable, good, estimable, honourable. **2** *an admirable musical performance* excellent, superb, brilliant, first-rate, first-class, supreme, great, fine, masterly, marvellous.

admiration n **1** *filled with admiration for his courage* approval, regard, high regard, respect, approbation, appreciation, praise, esteem, veneration. **2** *she was the admiration of the whole village* object of admiration, pride, pride and joy, wonder, delight, marvel, sensation.

admire v **1** *admire his courage* approve of, respect, think highly of, appreciate, applaud, praise, hold in high regard/esteem, venerate. **2** *she admired her hat* approve of, like, express admiration for, compliment, sing the praises of, be taken with. **3** *he admired her from afar* adore, love, be enamoured of, idolize; *inf* carry a torch for.

admirer n **1** *an admirer of modern art* enthusiast, fan, devotee, aficionado, supporter, adherent, follower, disciple, votary; *inf* buff, freak. **2** *they teased her about her admirer* suitor, wooer, beau, sweetheart, lover, boyfriend, girlfriend.

admissible adj *admissible evidence/behaviour* allowable, allowed, permissible, permitted, acceptable, passable, justifiable, tolerable.

admission n **1** *admission to university | admission to the palace* admittance, entry, right of entry, entrance, access, entrée; *fml* ingress. **2** *admission is £3* entrance fee, entry charge, ticket. **3** *an admission of guilt/failure* acknowledgement, confession, revelation, disclosure, divulgence, expression, declaration, utterance, avowal.

admit v **1** *one ticket admits two people | the window admits little light* let in, allow/permit entry, give access to. **2** *the scheme does not admit non-shareholders* give admission to, allow, permit, accept, receive, let in. **3** *the room admits only 30 people* accommodate, cater for, hold. **4** *they admitted their guilt | admitting that they were wrong* acknowledge, confess, reveal, make known, disclose, divulge, declare, avow. **5** *admit that you may be right* concede, accept, grant, acknowledge, agree, allow, concur.

admittance n *no admittance to the palace* entry, right of entry, entrance, access. *see* ADMISSION 1.

admonish v **1** *admonish the boys for smoking* reprimand, rebuke, scold, reprove, upbraid, chide, censure, berate; *inf* tell off. **2** *she admonished us to seek help* advise, urge, caution, warn, counsel, exhort.

admonition n **1** *deliver an admonition to the culprits* reprimand, rebuke, scolding; *inf* telling-off. *see* ADMONISH 1. **2** *gave them an admonition to seek help* piece of advice, warning, exhortation; advice. *see* ADMONISH 2.

admonitory adj **1** *admonitory remarks to the culprits* admonishing, reprimanding, rebuking, reproving, reproachful. *see* ADMONISH 1. **2** *admonitory suggestions to seek help* admonishing, advisory, cautioning, cautionary, counselling, exhortative. *see* ADMONISH 2.

ado n *we set off without further ado* fuss, trouble, bother, commotion, upset, agitation, hubbub, confusion, disturbance, hurly-burly, flurry, to-do; *dial* pother; *Amer* fuss and feathers.

adolescence n *have acne during adolescence* teenage years, teens, youth, pubescence.

adolescent adj **1** *adolescent problems* teenage, youthful, pubescent. **2** *despite her* *age she has a silly adolescent sense of humour* immature, juvenile, childish, puerile.

adolescent n *adolescents are sometimes moody* teenager, youngster, young person, youth.

adopt v **1** *adopt a child* take as one's own child, be adoptive parents to, take in, take care of. **2** *adopt eastern customs* assume, take on, take over, affect, embrace, espouse, appropriate, arrogate. **3** *adopt a candidate* select, choose, vote for. **4** *adopt the new measures* approve, endorse, accept, ratify, sanction, support, back.

adoption n **1** *the adoption of a child* adopting, taking as one's own, taking in. *see* ADOPT 1. **2** *the adoption of eastern customs* assumption, taking on, affecting, affectation, espousal, appropriation, arrogation. *see* ADOPT 2. **3** *the adoption of the political candidate* selection, choosing, choice, voting for. *see* ADOPT 3. **4** *the adoption of the new measures by parliament* approval, endorsement, acceptance, ratification, sanctioning, support, backing. *see* ADOPT 4.

adorable adj lovable, appealing, charming, sweet, enchanting, captivating, dear, darling, delightful, attractive, winsome, winning, fetching.

adoration n **1** *the adoration of their children* love, loving, doting, devotion, idolization, worship. *see* ADORE 1. **2** *the adoration of God* worship, glorification, praising, praise, homage, exaltation, magnification, extolment, veneration. *see* ADORE 2. **3** *their adoration of travel* love, liking, enjoyment, great liking/enjoyment, relishing. *see* ADORE 3.

adore v **1** *adore their children* love, be devoted to, dote on, cherish, hold dear, idolize, worship. **2** *let us adore God* worship, glorify, praise, revere, reverence, exalt, magnify, laud, extol, esteem, venerate. **3** *they adore ice cream* like, love, be fond of, enjoy, delight in, take pleasure in, relish.

adorn v *flowers adorn the room* decorate, embellish, add ornament to, ornament, trim, enhance, beautify, enrich, bedeck, deck, array, grace, emblazon.

adornment n **1** *the adornment of the Christmas tree* decorating, decoration, embellishment, ornamentation, trimming, arraying, enhancement, beautification, enrichment. *see* ADORN. **2** *simply dressed with no adornment* ornamentation, ornament, embellishment, frippery, decoration; frills, accessories, trimmings.

adrift adj **1** *a boat adrift on the sea* drifting, unmoored, unanchored. **2** *young people adrift in city streets* aimless, purposeless,

without purpose/goal, directionless, unsettled, rootless. **3** *the tarpaulin on the load came adrift* unfastened, loose, untied, detached, unsecured. **4** *our plans have gone badly adrift* wrong, awry, amiss, astray, off course.

adroit adj **1** *his adroit handling of the boat* | *adroit at tennis* skilful, skilled, expert, adept, dextrous, deft, clever, able, capable, competent, masterly, proficient. **2** *an adroit politician* skilful, expert, adept, clever, quick-thinking, quick-witted, cunning, artful, resourceful, astute, shrewd.

adroitness n **1** *her adroitness at sailing* skill, skilfulness, expertise, adeptness, dexterity, deftness, cleverness, ability, capability, competence, proficiency. *see* ADROIT 1. **2** *his political adroitness* skill, skilfulness, expertise, adeptness, cleverness, quick-wittedness, cunning, artfulness, resourcefulness. *see* ADROIT 2.

adulation n *adulation of pop stars* worship, hero-worship, idolization, adoration, glorification, praising, praise, flattery; blandishments.

adult adj **1** *an adult women/tree* mature, grown-up, fully grown, full-grown, fully developed; *fml* of age. **2** *adult magazines/ videos* sexually explicit, obscene, pornographic; *inf* full-frontal.

adulterate v *adulterate the water/brandy* make impure, debase, degrade, spoil, contaminate, taint, doctor, water down, weaken, bastardize; *fml* vitiate.

advance v **1** *the army advanced* go/come/ move forward, proceed, go ahead, move along, press on, push forward, make progress, make headway, forge ahead, gain ground **2** *advance the date of publication* | *advance our lunch appointment* bring/put forward, make earlier. **3** *advance his promotion* | *advance the building schedule* speed up, accelerate, step up, hasten, expedite, hurry, quicken, forward. **4** *advance his chances of promotion* further, forward, help, assist, facilitate, promote, boost, improve, benefit, foster. **5** *her career advanced rapidly* go forward, go ahead, progress, develop, improve, thrive, flourish. **6** *advance a suggestion/theory* put forward, suggest, propose, submit, recommend, present, introduce, offer, proffer, adduce. **7** *the company advanced him £200* pay in advance lend, supply on credit. **8** *prices are advancing rapidly* rise, increase, go up, mount **9** *war advanced prices* raise, increase, put up, inflate; *inf* jack up, hike up.

advance n **1** *the advance of the army* going/ coming/moving forward, movement forward, progress, headway. *see* ADVANCE V 1.

2 *the advance of civilization* progress, development, advancement, movement forward, headway, improvement, betterment, furtherance. **3** *recent medical advances* development, discovery, breakthrough, finding, invention. **4** *an advance in the price of oil* rise, increase, mark-up. **5** *they paid me an advance of £20* down payment, deposit, retainer. **in advance** beforehand, ahead of time, earlier, previously.

advance adj **1** *the advance party sent ahead*, leading, first. **2** *given advance warning* early, previous, prior, beforehand.

advanced adj **1** *advanced technology* progressive, forward, highly developed, modern, ultra modern, avant-garde, ahead of the times. **2** *advanced studies* higher-level.

advancement n **1** *furthering the advancement of knowledge* progress, development, improvement, furtherance. *see* ADVANCE n 2, 3. **2** *a job offering advancement* promotion, improvement, progress, betterment, growth, rise, preferment.

advances npl *make friendly advances* approaches, overtures, moves, proposals, propositions.

advantage n **1** *the main advantage is the size of the garden* benefit, asset, good point, boon, blessing. **2** *he had an advantage over her | the advantage of age* benefit, superiority, dominance, ascendancy, supremacy, power, mastery, upper hand, whiphand, trump card. **3** *little advantage in going | not to one's advantage* benefit, profit, gain, good.

advantageous adj **1** *in an advantageous position* favourable, superior, dominant, powerful. **2** *advantageous to your career* beneficial, of benefit, helpful, of assistance, useful, valuable, of service, profitable.

advent n *the advent of war | advent of modern techniques* arrival, coming, appearance, approach, occurrence.

adventitious adj **1** *an adventitious encounter* accidental, unexpected, unplanned, chance, fortuitous, casual. **2** *adventitious influences* outside, external, extraneous, foreign, alien, extrinsic.

adventure n **1** *a spirit of adventure | a life full of adventure* risk, hazard, danger, peril, gamble, gambling, uncertainty, precariousness. **2** *tales of the sailor's adventures* exploit, deed, feat, experience, incident.

adventurous adj **1** *adventurous young men* daring, daredevil, bold, intrepid, audacious; *fml* adventuresome, venturesome. **2** *an adventurous life* risky, dangerous, perilous, hazardous, precarious.

adversary n opponent, opposer, antagonist, rival, enemy, foe, fellow contestant/competitor.

adverse adj **1** *adverse circumstances | adverse weather conditions* unfavourable, unlucky, disadvantageous, inauspicious, unpropitious, unfortunate, untoward. **2** *adverse criticism* hostile, unfriendly, unfavourable, antagonistic, negative, opposing, inimical, antipathetic. **3** *adverse to health* harmful, dangerous, injurious, detrimental, disadvantageous, hurtful.

adversity n **1** *face adversity with courage* misfortune, ill luck, bad luck, trouble, hardship, distress, disaster, suffering, affliction, sorrow, misery, tribulation, woe; hard times. **2** *many adversities in their lives* misfortune, mishap, accident, shock, reverse, setback, disaster, catastrophe, tragedy, calamity, trial.

advertise v **1** *advertise details of a meeting* make known/public, publicize, give publicity to, announce, broadcast, proclaim, call attention to. **2** *advertise a product* promote, publicize, give publicity to, call attention to, display, puff, give a puff to, tout, promulgate; *inf* push, plug.

advertisement n **1** *put an advertisement in the paper* notice, announcement, display; *inf* advert, ad. **2** *a television advertisement | an advertisement for soap* promotion, display, commercial, puff, blurb; *inf* advert, ad, push, plug. **3** *the advertisement of products* advertising, promotion, publicizing, touting; *inf* plugging, pushing.

advice n **1** *give advice to young people* guidance, counselling, counsel, help; recommendations, suggestions, hints, tips, ideas, opinions, views. **2** *an advice sent from the bank* notification, communication, information; data.

advisability n desirability, wisdom, soundness, prudence, appropriateness, fitness, suitability, aptness, judiciousness, expediency.

advisable adj desirable, best, wisest, sensible, sound, prudent, proper, appropriate, suitable, fitting, apt, judicious, recommended, suggested, expedient, politic.

advise v **1** *cannot advise you on your affairs* give guidance, guide, counsel, give counsel, give recommendations, offer suggestions/opinions, give hints/tips, instruct. **2** *advise you of the facts* inform, notify, give notice, apprise, acquaint with, report on, warn. **3** *advise caution* suggest, commend, recommend, admonish, urge.

adviser, advisor n counsellor, mentor, guide, consultant, confidant, confidante, coach, teacher, tutor, therapist.

advisory adj advising, consultative, counselling, recommendatory, assisting.

advocacy adj *advocacy of political freedom* advising, recommending, support for, backing, arguing/argument for, promotion. *see* ADVOCATE V.

advocate v *advocate reducing expenditure* recommend, advise, favour, support, uphold, back, subscribe to, champion, speak for, campaign on behalf of, argue/plead/press for, urge, promote.

advocate n **1** *an advocate of political freedom* supporter, upholder, backer, champion, spokesman, spokeswoman, spokesperson, speaker, campaigner, pleader, promoter, proponent, exponent, apostle, apologist. **2** barrister, counsel, *Amer* attorney.

aegis n protection, guardianship, support, patronage, sponsorship, safeguarding, defence, championship, aid, guaranty; auspices.

aeon n age, long period, eternity; ages.

affability n friendliness, amiability, geniality, congeniality, cordiality, pleasantness, agreeableness, good-humouredness, kindliness, courtesy, civility, approachability, sociability.

affable adj friendly, amiable, genial, congenial, cordial, pleasant, agreeable, easygoing, good-humoured, good-natured, kindly, courteous, civil, approachable, sociable.

affair n **1** *that's my own affair* concern, business, matter, responsibility. **2** *forget the sad affair* event, happening, occurrence, incident, episode, circumstance, adventure, case. **3** *an informal affair* party, function, reception, gathering, *inf* get-together, do. **4** *an affair with a married man* love affair, relationship, romance, liaison, affair of the heart, intrigue, amour, *affaire*.

affairs npl *commercial/foreign affairs* concerns, matters, activities, transactions, undertakings, ventures, business.

affect[1] v **1** *it affected his health* | *affected our attitude* have an effect on, influence, act on, work on, have an impact on, change, alter, transform. **2** *the disease affected his lungs* attack, strike at, infect, take hold of. **3** *the experience deeply affected us* move, touch, upset, disturb, trouble, perturb, agitate, stir, tug at the heartstrings.

affect[2] v **1** *affect long words* | *affect bright clothes* assume, put on, adopt, like, have a liking for, espouse. **2** *affect a foreign accent* |

affect ignorance pretend, feign, fake, counterfeit, sham, simulate.

affectation n **1** *tired of her affectation* | *without affectation* pretence, pretension, pretentiousness, affectedness, artificiality, insincerity, posturing. **2** *her affectations annoy me* airs, airs and graces, pretensions; posing, posturing. **3** *an affectation of interest* façade, show, appearance, false display, pretence, feigning, shamming, simulation.

affected[1] adj influenced, altered, changed. *see* AFFECT[1].

affected[2] adj **1** *an affected style of writing* pretentious, artificial, unnatural, assumed, high-flown, ostentatious, contrived, studied, pompous, mannered. **2** *an affected politeness* put on, pretended, feigned, fake, counterfeit, sham, simulated.

affecting adj *an affecting scene* moving, touching, poignant, upsetting, pathetic, heart-rending. *see* AFFECT[1] 3.

affection n *affection for her sister* love, liking, fondness, warmth, devotion, caring, attachment, friendship, amity; warm feelings.

affectionate adj *an affectionate wife/hug* loving, fond, devoted, caring, tender, doting, friendly. *see* AFFECTION.

affianced adj engaged, betrothed, contracted, pledged.

affiliate v *they are affiliated to the union* | *the college is affiliated with the university* associate with, unite with, combine with, join with, ally with, amalgamate with, coalesce, form a federation/confederation, annex to, merge with, incorporate into.

affiliation n **1** *the affiliation of the college to the university* uniting, combining, allying, amalgamation. *see* AFFILIATE. **2** *affiliations between clubs* connection, link, bond, tie, relationship; communication.

affinity n **1** *the human's affinity with the ape* likeness, similarity, resemblance, correspondence, analogy, similitude. **2** *have an affinity for each other* liking, fondness, attraction, inclination, rapport, sympathy, partiality, penchant, predilection. **3** *the witness's affinity with the accused* relationship, kinship, connection, propinquity.

affirm v state, assert, declare, aver, proclaim, pronounce, swear, attest; *fml* asseverate.

affirmation n statement, assertion, declaration, averment, proclamation, pronouncement, swearing, attestation; *fml* asseveration.

affirmative adj assenting, consenting, agreeing, concurring, corroborative, favourable, approving, positive.

affix v **1** *affix a stamp to the envelope* attach, stick, fasten, fix, tack, glue, paste. **2** *affix a signature to a document* append, add, add on, attach.

afflict v trouble, burden, distress, beset, harass, oppress, torment, plague, rack, smite.

affliction n **1** *bearing affliction bravely* trouble, distress, pain, misery, suffering, wretchedness, hardship, misfortune, sorrow, torment, tribulation, woe. **2** *the afflictions of the old* trouble, disorder, disease, pain, suffering, trial, hardship, ordeal, scourge, plague, woe.

affluence n wealth, prosperity, opulence, fortune, richness; riches, resources. *see* AFFLUENT.

affluent adj rich, wealthy, prosperous, opulent, well off, moneyed, well-to-do, comfortable; *inf* well-heeled, in the money, loaded.

afford v **1** *cannot afford a new dress* pay for, meet the expense of, spare the price of. **2** *cannot afford the loss of staff* bear, sustain, stand. **3** *the tree affords shade* provide, supply, offer, give, impart, bestow, furnish, yield. **4** *the orchard affords a large crop* yield, produce, bear, supply, give.

affray n fight, brawl, battle, quarrel, row, set-to, wrangle, fracas, altercation, disturbance, commotion, breach of the peace, mêlée, scrap, clash, scuffle, tussle; *inf* free-for-all.

affront n *sexist remarks are an affront to women* insult, offence, indignity, slight, snub, aspersion, provocation, injury, outrage; *inf* slap in the face.

affront v *he was affronted by her behaviour* insult, offend, outrage, provoke, slight, hurt, pique.

afoot adj/adv *trouble afoot | evil plans afoot* around, going on, abroad, circulating, current, stirring; *inf* on the go; *lit* astir.

aforesaid adj aforementioned, aforenamed, previously described, foregoing, preceding, earlier, previous.

afraid adj **1** *afraid of death | afraid to die* frightened, scared, terrified, apprehensive, fearful, nervous, alarmed at, intimidated by, terror-stricken. **2** *I'm afraid I can't help* sorry, regretful, apologetic, unhappy.

afresh adv anew, again, over again, once again, once more.

after prep **1** *leave after lunch* following, subsequent to, at the close/end of, later than. **2** *shut the door after you* behind, following, in the rear of. **3** *B comes after A* following, next to, nearest to, below. **4** *run after the thief | be after a job* in pursuit of, in search of, in quest of. **5** *after the way he acted she hates him* following, because of, as a result of, in view of, owing to, on account of. **6** *after all that she still loves him* despite, in spite of, regardless of, notwithstanding. **7** *enquire after her health* about, concerning, regarding, with reference to, apropos. **8** *they called their son after his grandfather* with the name of, the same as, in honour of, as a tribute to; *Amer* for. **9** *a painting after Rubens* in the style of, in the manner of, in imitation of, on the model of, following the pattern of.

after adv **1** *the week after* later, following, afterwards, subsequently, thereafter. **2** *following on after* behind, in the rear, at the back.

after adj *in after years* later, succeeding, subsequent, following.

afterlife n *Christians believe in an afterlife* life after death, the hereafter, afterworld.

aftermath n after-effects, effects, consequences, results; end result, outcome, upshot, issue, end.

afterwards adv *afterwords they left* later, subsequently, then, thereupon, after, next.

again adv **1** *start again* once more, afresh, anew, a second time, another time. **2** *again there is the question of money* moreover, besides, also, furthermore, further. **3** *he might come and again he might not* on the other hand, on the contrary, conversely. **4** *half as much again* in addition, over and above, also, too. **again and again** often, frequently, repeatedly, over and over, time and time again, continually, persistently.

against prep **1** *people against the movement* opposed to, in opposition to, hostile to, at odds with, in disagreement with, versus, at cross-purposes with. **2** *rowing against the tide* in opposition to, counter to, resisting. **3** *leaning against the fence* touching, in contact with, close up to, up against, abutting. **4** *silhouetted against a black background* in contrast to, as a foil to. **5** *saving against a rainy day* in preparation for, in anticipation of, in expectation of, as provision for. **6** *his age is against him* disadvantageous to, unfavourable to, damaging to, detrimental to, prejudicial to. **7** *the exchange rate against the dollar* in exchange for, in return for, in compensation for.

age n **1** *what age is the tree?* number of years, lifetime, duration, stage of life, generation; years. **2** *wisdom comes with age* | *age can bring infirmity* maturity, seniority, elderliness, oldness, old age; advancing years, declining years; *fml* senescence. **3** *the Elizabethan/nuclear age* era, epoch, period, time. **4** *we waited for an age* | *it took ages* a long time, an eternity; hours, days, months, years, aeons, hours/days/months on end.

age v *she has aged well* mature, ripen, grow up, come of age; grow old, decline, wither, fade, become obsolete.

aged adj *a white-haired aged man* old, elderly, superannuated; *fml* senescent; as old as the hills.

agency n **1** *advertising agency* business, organization, company, firm, office, bureau, concern. **2** *through the agency of heat* activity, action, effect, influence, force, power, work. **3** *a young couple brought together through the agency of friends* good offices, mediation, intervention, intercession, instrumentality.

agenda n programme, schedule, timetable, plan, list, scheme.

agent n **1** *an insurance agent* representative, negotiator, emissary, envoy, factor, go-between; *inf* rep. **2** *an enemy agent* spy; *inf* mole; *Amer inf* spook. **3** *our agents will be in touch* solicitor, lawyer; *Amer* attorney. **4** *the agent of his ruin* executor, author, performer, perpetrator, doer, operator, operative, mover. **5** *a cleansing agent* moving force, agency, cause, instrument, vehicle, means, power, force.

agglomeration n collection, accumulation, mass, cluster, lump, clump, pile, heap, aggregate, miscellany, jumble, hotchpotch.

aggravate v **1** *aggravate the situation/pain* worsen, make worse, exacerbate, inflame, intensify, increase, heighten, magnify. **2** *aggravate the teacher* annoy, irritate, anger, exasperate, provoke, irk, vex, get on one's nerves, rub up the wrong way; *inf* needle.

aggravation n **1** *the aggravation of the situation/pain* worsening, exacerbation, intensification, increase, magnification. *see* AGGRAVATE 1. **2** *the aggravation of the teacher* annoyance, irritation, angering, exasperation, provocation, vexation; *inf* needling. *see* AGGRAVATE 2. **3** *just one more aggravation* irritant, nuisance, pest, grievance, thorn in the flesh; *inf* headache.

aggregate n **1** *the aggregate of goals* total, sum total, whole amount, totality, entirety, summation, gross. **2** *an aggregate of minerals* collection, accumulation, mass, cluster, clump, lump, pile, heap, concentration, assemblage, mixture, combination, agglomeration.

aggregate adj **1** *the aggregate score* total, combined, whole, added. **2** *aggregate rock* composite, compound, combined, massed, clustered.

aggression n **1** *an act of aggression* attack, assault, injury, encroachment, offence, invasion, infringement. **2** *a bloody aggression* attack, assault, onslaught, foray, raid, sortie, offensive, invasion.

aggressive adj **1** *an aggressive person* quarrelsome, argumentative, belligerent, pugnacious, militant, warring. **2** *an aggressive act* hostile, belligerent, warring, combative, bellicose, invasive, intrusive. **3** *an aggressive salesman* | *aggressive sales promotion* assertive, forceful, insistent, vigorous, energetic, dynamic, bold, enterprising, go-ahead, zealous, pushing; *inf* pushy.

aggressor n attacker, assaulter, invader, assailant, provoker, instigator, initiator.

aggrieved adj **1** *aggrieved at her treatment* resentful, angry, distressed, disturbed, piqued; *inf* peeved. **2** *the aggrieved party* wronged, injured, abused, harmed, mistreated, ill-used.

aghast adj horrified, appalled, astounded, amazed, thunderstruck, stunned, shocked, flabbergasted, awestruck; *inf* floored.

agile adj **1** *an agile body* active, nimble, spry, lithe, fit, supple, sprightly, in good condition, lively, quick-moving, limber. **2** *an agile mind* active, nimble, alert, sharp, acute, clever, quick-witted.

agility n **1** *the agility of their bodies* activeness, nimbleness, litheness, fitness, suppleness. *see* AGILE 1. **2** *the agility of her mind* activeness, nimbleness, alertness. *see* AGILE 2.

agitate v **1** *she was agitated by the delay* upset, work up, perturb, fluster, ruffle, disconcert, disquiet, flurry, trouble, worry. **2** *agitate the mixture* stir, whisk, beat, churn, shake, toss. **3** *agitate for tax reductions* campaign, argue, debate, dispute, wrangle.

agitation n **1** *the agitation caused by delays* upset, perturbation, fluster, disconcertment, flurry, trouble, worry. *see* AGITATE 1. **2** *the agitation of the mixture* stirring, whisking, churning. *see* AGITATE 2. **3** *agitation for/against tax changes* campaigning, arguing, argument, wrangling. *see* AGITATE 3.

agitator n troublemaker, instigator, *agent provocateur*, inciter, rabble-rouser, provoker, fomenter, firebrand, revolutionary, demagogue.

agnostic n sceptic, unbeliever, disbeliever, doubter, questioner, doubting Thomas.

ago adv in the past, in time gone by, since, formerly.

agog adv eager, excited, impatient, in suspense, keen, curious, expectant, enthralled, enthusiastic, avid.

agonizing adj excruciating, harrowing, racking, painful, acute, searing, insufferable, piercing, unendurable, torturous, tormenting; *lit* exquisite.

agony n suffering, pain, hurt, distress, torture, torment, anguish, misery, woe; pangs, throes.

agree v 1 *agree with you | agree with your proposals* concur, be of the same mind/opinion, comply, see eye to eye, accord. 2 *agree to your proposals* consent to, accept, approve, acquiesce in, assent to, concede to, allow, admit, grant. 3 *the statements do not agree with each other* match, accord, correspond, conform, coincide, fit, tally, harmonize; *inf* square. 4 *we agreed a time* settle on, arrange, arrive at, decide on. 5 *the warm climate agrees with me* suit, be good for.

agreeable adj 1 *agreeable occasion* pleasant, pleasing, delightful, enjoyable, pleasurable, to one's liking. 2 *an agreeable youngster/manner* pleasant, likeable, charming, amiable, nice, friendly, good-natured. 3 *if you want us to go we are agreeable* willing, amenable, compliant, consenting, assenting, accommodating, tractable.

agreement n 1 *we are in total agreement* accord, assent, concurrence, harmony, accordance, unity, concord. 2 *sign a business/international agreement* contract, compact, treaty, covenant, pact, bargain, settlement, proposal; *inf* deal; *fml* concordat. 3 *the agreement of the statements* matching, similarity, accordance, correspondence, conformity, coincidence, harmony. *see* AGREE 3.

agriculture n farming, husbandry; animal husbandry, cultivation, tillage, horticulture, viticulture; agribusiness, agronomics, agronomy.

aground adv/adj beached, grounded, foundered, ashore, stuck, shipwrecked, on the ground/bottom.

ahead adv 1 *they went ahead* in the front, at the head, in the lead, in the vanguard. 2 *the way ahead* forward, onwards, on.

ahead of 1 *straight ahead of us* in front of, towards the front of, before. 2 *ahead of time* in advance of, before, earlier than. 3 *he's ahead of us in maths* further on, more advanced, superior to, outdistancing, outstripping.

aid v 1 *aid us in our effort | aid our effort* help, assist, support, lend a hand, succour, sustain, second. 2 *aid recovery/sleep* help, speed up, hasten, facilitate, expedite, encourage, promote.

aid n 1 *give aid to a motorist* help, assistance, support, a helping hand, succour, encouragement. 2 *foreign aid* contribution, subsidy, gift, donation. 3 *a hospital aid* helper, assistant, girl/man Friday.

ailing adj ill, unwell, sick, sickly, poorly, weak, indisposed, under the weather.

ailment n illness, disease, disorder, sickness, complaint, infection.

aim v 1 *aim a gun* point, direct, take aim, train, sight, focus, position. 2 *aim at a scholarship* set one's sights on, try for, strive for, work towards, be after, seek, aspire to. 3 *aim to increase profits* plan, intend, resolve, propose, purpose, design.

aim n 1 *the aim of a gun* pointing, directing, training; line of sight. *see* AIM v 1. 2 *our aim is to win* goal, ambition, objective, object, end, target, intention, plan, purpose, aspiration, resolve, proposal, design, desire, wish.

aimless adj 1 *an aimless life* purposeless, pointless, goalless, futile, undirected, objectless. 2 *aimless young people* goalless, unambitious, purposeless, undirected, drifting, wandering.

air n 1 *the birds of the air | propelled through the air* atmosphere, sky, heavens, aerospace. 2 *let's get some air* breeze, breath of air, puff of wind, whiff of wind, zephyr, draught. 3 *an air of peace* impression, appearance, look, atmosphere, mood, quality, ambience, aura, manner, bearing, character, feeling, flavour, effect, tone. 4 *playing an old air* tune, melody, song, theme, strain.

air v 1 *air the room/clothes* ventilate, aerate, freshen. 2 *air one's views/objections* make public, publicize, express, voice, publish, vent, disseminate, circulate, communicate, broadcast, reveal, proclaim, divulge.

airily adv *"goodbye," he said airily* lightly, light-heartedly, breezily, flippantly, gaily, blithely, jauntily, nonchalantly, cheerfully.

airing n 1 *the airing of the room/clothes* ventilating, ventilation, aerating, freshening. 2 *take for an airing* outing, walk, stroll, excursion, jaunt; *fml* promenade. 3 *the air-*

ing of one's views publicizing, expression, voicing, publishing, venting, dissemination, circulation, communication, revelation, proclamation, divulgence. *see* AIR v 2.

airless adj stuffy, close, stifling, suffocating, unventilated, sultry, muggy, oppressive.

airs npl affectedness, posing, posturing; affectations, pretensions; *inf* swank.

airtight adj **1** *an airtight tin* closed, sealed, shut tight, impermeable. **2** *an airtight alibi* indisputable, incontrovertible, incontestable, irrefutable, unassailable.

airy adj **1** *an airy day* breezy, windy, blowy, gusty. **2** *a light and airy office* well-ventilated, spacious, open. **3** *an airy being* delicate, insubstantial, ethereal, flimsy, wispy, incorporeal, vaporous. **4** *an airy promise/reply* light-hearted, breezy, flippant, blithe, gay, jaunty, nonchalant, insubstantial, cheerful.

aisle n gangway, passageway, passage, corridor, path, lane, alley.

ajar adj/adv half open, slightly, open, unfastened, unsecured, unlatched.

akin adj *akin to sailing/murder* related to, allied with, connected with, similar to, corresponding to.

alacrity n readiness, promptness, willingness, eagerness, enthusiasm, haste, swiftness.

alarm n **1** *have/hear a burglar/fire alarm* warning sound/device, alarm signal, alarm bell, danger/distress signal, siren, alert, tocsin. **2** *rumours causing alarm* fear, fright, terror, apprehension, panic, trepidation, nervousness, anxiety, unease, distress, consternation, disquiet, perturbation.

alarm v **1** *crowds alarm her* frighten, scare, terrify, panic, startle, unnerve, distress, intimidate; put the wind up. **2** *fire! you must alarm the neighbourhood* warn, alert, arouse, signal.

alarming adj frightening, disturbing, terrifying, startling, shocking, distressing, dismaying, perturbing.

alarmist n scaremonger, voice of doom, doomster, doom merchant.

alcohol n strong drink, liquor, intoxicating liquor; spirits; *inf* booze, tipple, the demon drink; *dial* bevvy.

alcoholic adj *alcoholic not soft drinks* intoxicating, inebriating, strong, hard, spirituous, vinous.

alcoholic n *a confirmed alcoholic* alcohol addict, dipsomaniac, hard/heavy drinker, drunk, drunkard, tippler, sot, toper, inebriate, imbiber; *inf* boozer, lush, alchy, dipso, soak, tosspot, wino, sponge.

alcove n niche, recess, nook, opening, bay, hollow, cavity, corner.

alert adj **1** *an alert mind/youngster* wideawake, sharp, bright, quick, keen, perceptive; *inf* on the ball, on one's toes, quick off the mark. **2** *you must always be alert to danger* wideawake, on the look-out, aware, heedful, watchful, attentive, vigilant, observant, circumspect, wary, on one's guard; *fml* on the qui vive.

alias adv also known as, also called, otherwise known as, otherwise; *inf* a.k.a.

alias n assumed name, false name, pseudonym, stage name, *nom de plume*, sobriquet; *fml nom de guerre*.

alibi n defence, plea, justification, explanation, reason, vindication, excuse, pretext.

alien adj **1** *an alien culture* foreign, overseas, non-native, unnaturalized. **2** *an alien environment* strange, unfamiliar, unknown, outlandish, remote, exotic. **3** *behaviour alien to his principles* opposed, conflicting, contrary, adverse, incompatible, unacceptable, repugnant, hostile, antagonistic, inimical.

alien n **1** *aliens deported in war-time* foreigner, outsider, stranger. **2** *aliens from Mars* extraterrestrial; *inf* little green man.

alienate v **1** *alienate his daughter from her mother* estrange, set against, turn away, make hostile, sever, divorce, separate, cut off, divide. **2** *alienate property* transfer, convey.

alienation v **1** *alienation of his daughter* estrangement, severance, divorce, separation, cutting off. *see* ALIENATE 1. **2** *alienation of property* transfer, conveyance.

alight adj **1** *set alight* on fire, ablaze, burning, lighted, lit, blazing, flaming, ignited. **2** *faces alight with joy* lit up, shining, bright, brilliant, illuminated.

alight v **1** *alight from the bus* get off, dismount, disembark, descend. **2** *birds alighting on branches* land, come down, come to rest, touch down, settle, perch.

align v **1** *align the books on the shelves* line up, range, arrange in line, rank, put in order, straighten. **2** *align with a political party* affiliate, ally, associate, join, cooperate, side, sympathize, agree.

alignment n **1** *the alignment of the books* lining up, ranging, arrangement in line, straightening. *see* ALIGN 1. **2** *the alignment with a political party* affiliation, alliance, association, siding, sympathy. *see* ALIGN 2.

alike adj *the sisters are so alike* like, similar, the same, indistinguishable, resembling, identical, interchangeable, corresponding.

alike adv *think alike* similarly, the same, just the same, in the same way, identically, in like manner.

alimony n maintenance, support, keep, sustenance, livelihood; *Scots* aliment.

alive adj **1** *at least the captives are alive* living, live, breathing; *inf* in the land of the living, alive and kicking; *fml* animate. **2** *interest/ debate is still very much alive* active, continuing, going on, existing, extant, prevalent, functioning, in the air/wind, in existence, in operation; *fml* existent. **3** *seeming very much alive today* full of life, lively, active, energetic, alert, animated, vivacious, vigorous, spry, sprightly, vital, zestful, spirited. **4** *alive to the possibilities* alert to, awake to, aware/cognizant of. **5** *alive with vermin/ crowds* overflowing, teeming, crowded, packed, bristling, swarming, thronged, bustling; *inf* crawling, hopping, lousy; *Scots* hotching.

all adj **1** *all animals are equal* each, each one of, every, every one of, every single. **2** *he worked all summer / buy all the wood* the whole of, every bit of, the complete, the entire, the totality of. **3** *in all earnestness* complete, entire, total, full, utter, greatest, perfect.

all n **1** *all died* everyone, everybody, every/ each person; *inf* the whole lot. **2** *all were thrown away* everything, each thing; *inf* the whole lot, lock, stock and barrel. **3** *take all of it* everything, the whole/total amount, the entirety, the sum total, the aggregate.

all adv *dressed all in black* completely, entirely, totally, wholly, altogether, fully, utterly.

allay v *allay suffering/fears* lessen, diminish, reduce, relieve, calm, lull, alleviate, assuage, appease, quell, check, mitigate.

allegation n claim, charge, accusation, professing, declaration, statement, assertion, averment, avowal, deposition, plea, affirmation; *fml* asseveration.

allege v claim, profess, declare, state, assert, aver, avow, affirm; *fml* asseverate.

alleged adj supposed, so-called, claimed, professed, declared, stated, designated. *see* ALLEGE.

allegiance n loyalty, obedience, fidelity, faithfulness, duty, devotion, constancy, adherence, homage; *fml* fealty.

allegorical adj symbolic, metaphorical, figurative, emblematic, parabolic.

allegory n **1** *Spenser's 'Faerie Queen' is an allegory* parable, fable, apologue. **2** *illustrate by allegory* symbolism, symbol, metaphor, analogy.

allergic adj **1** *allergic to cow's milk* hypersensitive, sensitive, susceptible. **2** *allergic to work* averse, opposed, loath, hostile, antagonistic, disinclined.

allergy n **1** *an allergy to cow's milk* hypersensitivity, sensitivity, susceptibility. **2** *an allergy to work* aversion, antipathy, opposition, hostility, antagonism, dislike.

alleviate v *alleviate pain/poverty* reduce, lessen, diminish, relieve, ease, allay, abate, mitigate, assuage, palliate.

alley n alleyway, lane, passage, passageway, path, pathway, corridor, backstreet.

alliance n **1** *form an alliance / working in alliance with the French* union, association, coalition, league, confederation, federation, partnership, affiliation. **2** *the alliance between physics and maths* affinity, association, relationship.

allied adj *a union of allied trades* associated, related, connected, linked, kindred.

allocate v allot, assign, distribute, give out, share/mete/parcel out, dispense, apportion.

allocation n **1** *spend our allocation for the year* allowance, quota, share, ration, portion, lot. **2** *the allocation of resources* allotment, assignment, distribution, giving out, apportionment. *see* ALLOCATE.

allot v **1** *we allotted money for expenses* set aside, designate, earmark, assign, appropriate. **2** *allot portions to everyone* allocate, distribute, give out, dispense, apportion. *see* ALLOCATE.

allotment n **1** *the allotment of money for expenses* setting aside, appropriation. *see* ALLOT 1. **2** *the allotment of portions* allocation, distribution, dispensing, apportionment. *see* ALLOT 2. **3** *your allotment for the year* allocation, allowance, quota. *see* ALLOCATION. **4** *digging his allotment* rented land, plot.

all-out adj thorough, thorough-going, complete, total, exhaustive, vigorous, determined.

allow v **1** *allow them to enter* permit, give permission to, let, authorize, sanction; *inf* give the go-ahead to, give the green light to. **2** *allow £5 for expenses* allocate, allot, grant, give, assign, remit, spare. **3** *allow for wastage* plan for, take into consideration/ account, make provision for, provide for. **4** *I allow that you won* admit, acknowledge, concede, grant, own, confess, agree.

allowable adj *allowable expenses* permissible, admissible, authorized, sanctioned, justifiable, legitimate, lawful, legal; *inf* legit.

allowance n **1** *father gives her an allowance* remittance, payment, subsidy, grant, contribution. **2** *our book allowance* allocation, quota, share, ration, portion. **3** *tax/business allowances* rebate, discount, deduction, reduction, concession. **make allowances 1** *make allowances for his youth* take into consideration/account, bear in mind, have regard to. **2** *make allowances for him* make excuses, excuse, forgive, pardon.

alloy n compound, mixture, amalgam, blend, combination, admixture, composite.

all right adj **1** *the children are all right* safe, safe and sound, secure, unharmed, uninjured, well, fine; *inf* OK. **2** *the coffee's all right?* satisfactory, acceptable, adequate, fine, passable; *inf* OK.

all right adv **1** *reached home all right* safely; *inf* OK. **2** *worked out all right* satisfactorily, acceptably, fine; *inf* OK.

all right interj *all right! I'll go* right, yes, very well; *inf* OK.

allude v refer to, mention, touch upon, mention in passing, *en passant*, make an allusion to, cite.

allure v attract, fascinate, entice, seduce, charm, enchant, bewitch, beguile, captivate, tempt, lure.

alluring adj attractive, fascinating, charming, enchanting, captivating.

allusion n reference, citation, mention, hint, intimation, suggestion.

ally n confederate, partner, associate, accomplice, colleague, friend, helper, accessory, abettor.

ally v *allied with France* unite, join, join forces, band together, go into partnership, combine, go into league, affiliate, form an alliance.

almanac n yearbook, calendar, register, annual, annals.

almighty adj **1** *Almighty God* all-powerful, omnipotent, supreme, most high. **2** *an almighty row* terrible, awful, dreadful, great.

almost adv nearly, close to, just about, not quite, all but, not far from, approximately, practically, as good as, virtually, approaching, verging on, bordering on, well-nigh.

alone adj/adv **1** *be alone in the house* by oneself, solitary, unaccompanied, unattended, unescorted, companionless. **2** *succeed alone* by oneself, single-handed, unassisted, unaided. **3** *left all alone* solitary, lonely, deserted, abandoned, forsaken, forlorn, desolate, isolated. **4** *house standing alone* by itself, sep-

arate, detached, apart, unconnected. **5** *in his area the professor stands alone* unique, unparalleled, unequalled, unsurpassed, matchless, peerless. **6** *you alone can help* only, solely, just, exclusively, no one else, nothing but.

along prep **1** *walk along the corridor/road* throughout the length of, from one end of to the other, through. **2** *grew along the verge* beside, by the side of, alongside, close by, on the edge of. **3** *somewhere along the way* in the course of, during, in the middle of.

along adv **1** *move along* on, onwards, ahead, forwards. **2** *bring a friend along* in accompaniment, in company, as a partner. **along with** *poverty along with illness* together, in addition to, plus, coupled with, accompanying, accompanied by.

aloof adv *stand aloof* at a distance, apart, separately, distanced, at arm's length.

aloof adj *she's rather aloof* distant, detached, unresponsive, remote, unapproachable, standoffish, indifferent, unsympathetic, unsociable, unfriendly, cold, chilly.

aloud adv out loud, audibly, clearly, distinctly, plainly, intelligibly.

already adv **1** *known already* by this time, by now, before, before now, previously. **2** *young children reading already* as early as this, as soon as this, so soon, so early.

also adv **1** *come along also* too, as well, besides, in addition, additionally, into the bargain, on top of that, to boot. **2** *also, he's ill* besides, furthermore, moreover, in addition, too, plus.

alter v **1** *alter one's life style | alter a skirt* change, make different, adjust, adapt, modify, convert, reshape, remodel, vary, transform, transfigure, diversify, metamorphose. **2** *he's altered a lot* change, make different, metamorphose, suffer a sea change.

alteration n *make an alteration* change, adjustment, adaptation, modification, conversion, variation, revision, amendment, transformation, transfiguration, metamorphosis.

altercation n quarrel, row, argument, fight, wrangle, squabble, fracas; *inf* set-to.

alternate adj **1** *alternate weeks* every other, every second. **2** *alternate joy and sadness* in rotation, rotating, occurring in turns, interchanging, following in sequence, sequential. **3** *take an alternate route* alternative, different. see ALTERNATIVE adj **1**.

alternate v *rain and sun alternated | rain alternated with sunshine* take turns, rotate, interchange, oscillate.

alternative adj **1** *an alternative route* another, other, second, different. **2** *alternative medicine* non-standard.

alternative n **1** *no alternative but to go* choice, option. **2** *have the alternative of going* choice, option, preference, election, substitute.

alternatively adv *alternatively, you can stay on the other hand*, otherwise, instead, if not, or, as an alternative.

although conj though, even though, even if, even supposing, despite the fact that, while, whilst, albeit, notwithstanding the fact that.

altitude n height, elevation; tallness, loftiness.

altogether adv **1** *not altogether happy* completely, thoroughly, totally, entirely, absolutely, fully, utterly, perfectly, quite. **2** *altogether the day was fine* on the whole, all things considered, all in all, by and large, in general, in the main. **3** *nine of us altogether* in all, all told, *in toto*, taken together, in sum.

altruistic adj unselfish, self-sacrificing, non-egotistical, public-spirited, philanthropic, humanitarian, charitable, open-handed.

always adv **1** *he always comes early* every time, on every occasion, consistently, invariably, without exception, regularly, repeatedly, unfailingly. **2** *she's always complaining* continually, constantly, forever, repeatedly, perpetually, incessantly, eternally. **3** *you can always go by bus* whatever the circumstances, no matter what, in any event, in any case, come what may. **4** *he will love her always* forever, forever and ever, evermore, eternally, ever, everlastingly, endlessly.

amalgamate v combine, merge, unite, integrate, fuse, blend, mingle, intermingle, mix, intermix, incorporate; *lit* commingle.

amass v collect, gather, accumulate, pile/heap up, hoard, store up, assemble, garner; *inf* stash away.

amateur n non-professional, dilettante, layman, dabbler.

amateurish adj unprofessional, unskilful, inexpert, incompetent, clumsy, crude, bungling.

amaze v astonish, astound, surprise, dumbfound, flabbergast, daze, shock, stagger, stun, startle, bewilder, stupefy; *inf* bowl over, strike dumb.

amazement n astonishment, surprise, shock, bewilderment, stupefaction, wonder. *see* AMAZE.

ambassador n diplomat, consul, envoy, emissary, legate, attaché, plenipotentiary, representative, deputy.

ambiguity n **1** *the ambiguity of his remark* equivocacy, ambivalence, two-edgedness. **2** *the ambiguity of his meaning* doubtfulness, dubiety, obscurity, unclearness, vagueness, uncertainty, abstruseness. *see* AMBIGUOUS 2. **3** *full of ambiguities* equivocation, double-talk, obscurity, doubt, dubiety, uncertainty, puzzle, enigma, paradox.

ambiguous adj **1** *we misunderstood because his remark was ambiguous* equivocal, ambivalent, two-edged. **2** *his meaning was ambiguous* cryptic, obscure, doubtful, dubious, unclear, vague, uncertain, indefinite, abstruse, puzzling, perplexing, enigmatic, paradoxical.

ambition n **1** *full of ambition to succeed* desire, aspiration, drive, striving, force, enterprise, eagerness, zeal, longing, yearning, hankering; *inf* get up and go, oomph. **2** *her ambition is to be boss* goal, aim, objective, purpose, intent, desire, wish, design, end, dream, hope.

ambitious adj **1** *an ambitious man* aspiring, forceful, enterprising, go-ahead, zealous, purposeful, assertive, designing; *inf* pushy, on the make. **2** *ambitious to be promoted* eager, enthusiastic, desirous of, striving, longing, avid, hankering after. **3** *an ambitious task* challenging, demanding, exacting, formidable, arduous, difficult, bold.

ambivalent adj *an ambivalent attitude* equivocal, uncertain, doubtful, indecisive, inconclusive, irresolute, unresolved, hesitating, fluctuating, vacillating, mixed, opposing, conflicting, clashing.

amble v stroll, saunter, dawdle, wander, ramble; *inf* mosey along.

ambush n **1** *wait in ambush* hiding, concealment, cover, shelter, retreat, ambuscade. **2** *lay an ambush* trap, snare, pitfall, lure, ambuscade.

ambush v *ambush the soldiers* waylay, lay a trap for, lie in wait for, trap, entrap, ensnare, decoy, ambuscade.

amenable adj **1** *find her amenable to suggestion* tractable, agreeable, responsive, pliant, flexible, persuadable, adaptable, acquiescent, manageable, susceptible. **2** *amenable to the law* accountable, answerable, subject, liable, responsible.

amend v **1** *amend a text* revise, alter, correct, modify, change, adjust. **2** *amend the* *situation* improve, remedy, ameliorate, better, fix, set right, repair, enhance.

amendment n **1** *the amendment of the text* revision, alteration, modification, adjustment. *see* AMEND 1. **2** *the amendment of the situation* improvement, remedying, amelioration, betterment, fixing. *see* AMEND 2. **3** *amendments to the government bill* alteration, addendum, addition, adjunct, attachment, appendage.

amends npl *make amends for the mistake* compensation, recompense, reparation.

amenity n **1** *amenities provided by the hotel* facility, service, convenience, resource, advantage. **2** *the amenity of his surroundings* pleasantness, agreeableness, pleasurableness, enjoyableness, niceness.

amiable adj friendly, pleasant, agreeable, pleasing, charming, delightful, good-natured, sociable, genial, congenial.

amicable adj *an amicable settlement* friendly, good-natured, civil, harmonious, cordial, non-hostile, peaceful.

amid prep in the midst of, amidst, in the middle/course of, among, amongst, in the thick of.

amiss adj *something was amiss|flowers wouldn't seem amiss* wrong, awry, faulty, out of order, defective, unsatisfactory, incorrect, inappropriate.

ammunition n **1** *running out of ammunition for the guns* projectiles; bullets, cartridges, shells, shot, slugs, grenades, gunpowder, powder, bombs, missiles. **2** *run out of ammunition in an argument* information, data, input; pointers, points, advantages.

amnesty n general pardon, pardon, pardoning, reprieve; absolution, forgiveness, dispensation, indulgence.

amok adv frenziedly, in a frenzy, berserk, wildly, uncontrollably, maniacally, crazedly, insanely, violently, destructively.

among, amongst prep **1** *live among trees/ friends* in the midst of, amid, amidst, in the middle of, surrounded by, in the thick of. **2** *divide it among you* between, to each of. **3** *among us was a doctor* included in, out of, in the group of, in the number of, in the company of. **4** *decide among yourselves* by the joint action of, by all of, by the whole of, with one another, together, mutually, reciprocally.

amorous adj loving, passionate, sexual, lustful, erotic, amatory.

amorphous adj formless, unformed, shapeless, unshaped, structureless, unstructured, indeterminate, ill-organized, vague, nebulous; *fml* inchoate.

amount n **1** *a large amount of money/cloud/ experience* quantity, measure, mass, volume, bulk, expanse, extent. **2** *the full amount* total, grand/sum total, aggregate; *inf* whole caboodle, whole shebang.

amount v amount to **1** *the bill amounted to £50* add up to, total, come to, run to. **2** *their silence amounts to a confession* equal, add up to, be equivalent to, correspond to, approximate to. **3** *he never amounted to anything* become, grow/develop into, mature into, progress/advance to.

ample adj **1** *ample food to live on* enough, sufficient, adequate, plenty, more than enough, enough and to spare. **2** *an ample supply of wine* plentiful, abundant, copious, lavish, generous, liberal, profuse, bountiful, plenteous. **3** *of ample proportions|an ample bosom* large, big, substantial, extensive, wide, spacious, roomy, capacious, commodious.

amplify v **1** *amplify the sound/signal* increase, boost, magnify, intensify, heighten, augment, supplement. **2** *amplify your statement* expand, enlarge on, elaborate on, add to, develop, flesh out, go into detail about, expound on, expatiate on, explicate.

amputate v cut off, sever, remove, excise, lop, lop off, dismember.

amuse v **1** *the clowns amused them* entertain, gladden, cheer, please, charm, delight, divert, beguile, enliven, regale with. **2** *amuse yourselves when I'm out* occupy, interest, entertain, divert, absorb, engross.

amusement n **1** *smiling with amusement* mirth, laughter, fun, merriment, gaiety, hilarity, enjoyment, pleasure, delight. **2** *provide a range of amusements* entertainment, diversion, interest, recreation, sport, pastime, hobby. **3** *the amusement of the children* entertaining, entertainment, diverting. *see* AMUSE 1.

amusing adj *an amusing tale/story-teller* humorous, funny, comical, witty, entertaining, hilarious, facetious, droll, jocular.

anaemic adj **1** *anaemic and frail* weak, pale, wan, colourless, pallid, ashen; *inf* bloodless. **2** *an anaemic effort/group* weak, feeble, powerless, impotent, vigourless, ineffective, ineffectual, enervated.

anaesthetic n *give an anaesthetic to the patient* narcotic, opiate, soporific, stupefacient, painkiller, sedative, analgesic, anodyne; general anaesthetic, local anaesthetic.

anaesthetic adj *an anaesthetic substance/ effect* numbing, deadening, dulling, narcotic, opiate, soporific, stupefacient, painkilling, sedative, analgesic, anodyne.

analogous adj similar, parallel, comparable, like, corresponding, related, kindred, matching, equivalent, homologous.

analogy n similarity, parallel, correspondence, likeness, resemblance, correlation, relation, equivalence, similitude, homology.

analyse v **1** *analyse the sample/structure* break down, dissect, separate out, fractionate, assay, decompose, examine; *fml* anatomize. **2** *analyse the results of the match* study, examine, investigate, enquire into, dissect, review, evaluate, interpret.

analysis n **1** *carry out analysis of the sample/ structure* breakdown, dissection, fractionation, decomposition, assay, examination; *fml* anatomization. **2** *the analysis of the match results* study, examination, investigation, enquiry, dissection, review, evaluation, interpretation.

analytical, analytic adj *an analytical mind/ approach* investigative, enquiring, dissecting, inquisitive, searching, critical, interpretative, diagnostic.

anarchic adj lawless, ungoverned.

anarchist n revolutionist, revolutionary, nihilist, rebel, insurgent, terrorist.

anarchy n **1** *state of anarchy in the country* absence of government, nihilism, lawlessness, mobocracy, misgovernment, misrule, revolution. **2** *anarchy in the classroom* riot, disorder, chaos, rebellion, mutiny, tumult, mayhem, insurrection, disorganization.

anathema n **1** *racism is anathema to them* abomination, abhorrence, aversion, bane, bugbear, *bête noir*. **2** *following an anathema of the Church* excommunication, damnation, proscription, denunciation, curse, ban, malediction.

anatomy n **1** *the anatomy of dogs* structure, make-up, composition, framework. **2** *undertake the anatomy of the animal/plant* dissection, cutting up, division, dismemberment, vivisection, zootomy. **3** *the anatomy of crime* analysis, examination, study, investigation, scrutiny, research, enquiry.

ancestor n forbear, progenitor, forerunner, precursor, prototype.

ancestral adj *ancestral home* inherited, hereditary, lineal.

ancestry n **1** *of noble ancestry* lineage, descent, extraction, parentage, origin, derivation, genealogy, pedigree, blood,

stock. **2** *research into one's ancestry* ancestors, antecedents, forefathers, forbears, progenitors; family tree.

anchor n **1** *a ship's anchor* mooring, kedge, grapnel, killick, drogue. **2** *mother was the family's anchor* mainstay, support, protection; stability, security.

anchor v **1** *anchor the boat* secure by anchor, secure, fasten. **2** *anchor the bush to a trellis* fasten, attach, connect, bind, affix.

ancient adj **1** *in ancient times* earliest, early, of long ago, primeval, prehistoric, primordial. **2** *an ancient custom* age-old, time-worn, antique, long-lived, very old. **3** *positively ancient ideas* antiquated, old-fashioned, out of date, outmoded, archaic, bygone, obsolete, *passé*, superannuated, atavistic.

ancillary adj auxiliary, secondary, subsidiary, subordinate, accessory, contributory, supplementary, additional, extra, attendant.

and conj along with, with, together with, as well as, also, in addition to, including, plus.

anecdote n story, tale, narrative, yarn, sketch, reminiscence.

anew adv again, afresh, once more, once again, over again.

angel n **1** *heavenly angels* messenger of god, heavenly messenger; archangel, seraph, cherub. **2** *thanks! you're an angel* darling, dear, gem, saint, paragon. **3** *a play staged with an angel's help* backer, supporter, benefactor, promoter.

angelic adj **1** *angelic beings* seraphic, cherubic, celestial, heavenly, ethereal; *fml* empyrean. **2** *an angelic child* virtuous, innocent, pure, good, saintly, beautiful, adorable.

anger n *shout in anger* annoyance, rage, fury, indignation, temper, wrath, exasperation, irritation, vexation, ire, ill humour, irritability, outrage, pique, spleen; *lit* choler.

anger v *it angered him* annoy, infuriate, enrage, exasperate, irritate, incense, madden, vex, outrage, provoke, nettle, rile, pique, gall, fret.

angle[1] n **1** *a right angle | the angle of the walls* intersection, inclination; projection, corner, bend, fork, nook, niche, recess, elbow. **2** *take an angle on a news story* slant, approach, viewpoint, standpoint, point of view, position, opinion.

angle[1] v **1** *angle the cam* slant, tilt, slope, turn. **2** *angle a news item* slant, skew, distort.

angle² v **1** *angle by the riverside* fish, cast, go fishing. **2** *angle for a compliment* seek, solicit, scheme, aim, try, fish; *inf* be after.

angry adj annoyed, furious, infuriated, indignant, enraged, irate, wrathful, exasperated, irritated, irascible, heated, incensed, maddened, ill-humoured, hot-tempered, outraged, vexed, provoked; *inf* mad, hot under the collar; *fml* choleric. *see* ANGER V.

angst n anxiety, fear, apprehension, foreboding, disquiet.

anguish n agony, suffering, torture, torment, pain, distress, misery, sorrow, grief, woe; pangs, throes.

angular adj **1** *an angular shape* sharp-cornered, pointed, V-shaped, Y-shaped, forked, bifurcate. **2** *an angular woman* bony, gaunt, raw-boned, rangy, scrawny, spare, skinny, lean.

animal n **1** *plants and animals* beast, creature, brute. **2** *the man was an animal* beast, brute, monster, barbarian, savage, fiend; *inf* swine.

animal adj **1** *animal as opposed to plant characteristics* animalistic, zooid, zooidal. **2** *animal passions* carnal, sensual, fleshly, bodily, physical, brutish, bestial.

animate v **1** *a smile animated her face | music animated the group* give life to, enliven, liven up, cheer up, gladden, vitalize; *inf* buck up, pep up. **2** *fresh hope animated them* encourage, hearten, inspire, excite, fire, rouse, stir, stimulate, incite, energize.

animate adj *something animate* living, alive, live, breathing.

animated adj **1** *an animated discussion* lively, energetic, active, vigorous, excited, enthusiastic, spirited, fiery, passionate, dynamic, forceful, vital, fervent, vivacious, buoyant. **2** *an animated cartoon* moving.

animation n *the animation of the discussion* liveliness, energy, vigour, excitement, enthusiasm, fieriness dynamism, passion, forcefulness, vitality, fervour, vivacity, buoyancy, verve, zest, sparkle; *inf* zing.

annals npl archives, chronicles, records, accounts; register, history.

annex v **1** *annex a garage to the house* add, attach, join, connect, append, adjoin, affix. **2** *annex a smaller country* take over, occupy, seize, conquer, appropriate, expropriate, arrogate.

annexe, annex n *a school annexe* supplementary/additional building, extension, wing, ell.

annihilate v destroy, wipe out, exterminate, decimate, eliminate, liquidate, abolish, obliterate, eradicate, extinguish, erase, root out, extirpate.

annotate v *annotate a text* gloss, comment on, add notes/footnotes to, explain, interpret, elucidate, explicate.

annotation n **1** *annotations in the margin* note, comment, gloss, commentary, footnote, explanation, interpretation, observation, elucidation, explication. **2** *the annotation of the text* glossing, commenting on, explaining, explanation. *see* ANNOTATE.

announce v **1** *announce the results* make known/public, give out, declare, intimate, proclaim, report, disclose, reveal, divulge, publicize, broadcast, publish, advertise, promulgate. **2** *announce a guest* give the name of, name, herald, usher in. **3** *cigar smoke announcing his approach* signal, indicate, signify, give notice of, warn, foretell, herald, betoken, augur, portend, harbinger.

announcement n **1** *the announcement of the results* declaration, intimation, proclamation, report, disclosure. *see* ANNOUNCE 1. **2** *make an announcement | give out an announcement* statement, report, intimation, bulletin, communiqué, message; information.

announcer n commentator, presenter, newsreader, newscaster, broadcaster, reporter, anchorman, master of ceremonies, MC, herald.

annoy v **1** *their behaviour annoyed her* irritate, exasperate, vex, ruffle, rile, irk, provoke, displease, anger, madden, rub one up the wrong way, get on one's nerves; *inf* get to, bug. **2** *don't annoy her when she's reading* bother, disturb, pester, worry, harass, trouble, plague, harry.

annoyance n **1** *to our annoyance* irritation, exasperation, displeasure, anger, vexation, ire. **2** *an annoyance to work late* nuisance, pest, bother, trial, irritant; *inf* bind, bore, pain, pain in the neck, hassle.

annual adj **1** *annual report* yearly, once a year. **2** *annual subscription* year-long.

annually adv **1** *payable annually* yearly, by the year, once a year, per annum. **2** *visit annually* once a year, every year, each year.

annul v nullify, declare null and void, quash, cancel, invalidate, rescind, revoke, repeal, abrogate, void, negate.

anodyne n *an anodyne for the patient* analgesic, painkiller, pain-reliever, palliative.

anoint v **1** *anoint the body* oil, apply ointment; spread over, smear, rub, embrocate.

29

2 *anoint the new king* consecrate, sanctify, bless, ordain, hallow.

anomalous adj abnormal, atypical, irregular, deviant, deviating, aberrant, exceptional, rare, unusual, eccentric, odd, bizarre, peculiar, inconsistent.

anomaly n abnormality, irregularity, deviation, aberration, departure, rarity, eccentricity, oddity, peculiarity, inconsistency.

anon adv soon, shortly, presently, in a short time, in a little while, by and by, before long, ere long.

anonymous adj *an anonymous donor* unnamed, nameless, unidentified, unknown, unspecified, undesignated, unacknowledged, uncredited, unsigned, incognito; *fml* innominate.

another adj **1** *another chance* second, further, additional. **2** *it was another girl, not Jane* different, some other, not the same.

answer n **1** *receive an answer* reply, response, acknowledgement, rejoinder, retort, riposte; *inf* comeback. **2** *the answer to the clue* solution, explanation, resolution. **3** *his answer to the charge* defence, plea, refutation, rebuttal, vindication. **4** *his answer was to leave the room* reaction, response.

answer v **1** *answer a question/letter* reply to, respond to, acknowledge, come back to, make a rejoinder, retort, riposte. **2** *answer the bell/phone* respond to, react to. **3** *answer to the description* fit, match, correspond to, be similar to, conform to, correlate to. **4** *answer our requirements* meet, satisfy, fulfil, fill, measure up to, serve. **answer back** talk back, be cheeky, be impertinent, contradict, argue with, disagree with. **answer for 1** *answer for her crimes* pay for, suffer for, be punished for, make amends for, make reparation for, atone for. **2** *cannot answer for my sister* vouch for, be responsible for, be accountable for, be liable for, take the blame for; *inf* take the rap for.

answerable adj *answerable to the manager | answerable for your safety* responsible, accountable, liable.

antagonism n hostility, opposition, animosity, antipathy, enmity, rivalry, competition, dissension, friction, conflict.

antagonist n adversary, enemy, foe, opponent, rival, competitor, contender.

antagonistic adj hostile, ill-disposed, opposed, dissenting, adverse, antipathetic, inimical, at odds with.

antagonize v arouse hostility/enmity in, alienate, put against, estrange; *fml* disaffect.

antecedents npl **1** *inherited from his antecedents* ancestors, forefathers, forebears, predecessors. **2** *check his antecedents* record, history, past, background.

antedate v **1** *antedate a cheque* backdate, assign to an earlier date. **2** *antedate the civil war* precede, come/go before, anticipate.

antediluvian adj **1** *in antediluvian times* prehistoric, primeval, primordial; *inf* before the flood; *fml* autochthonal. **2** *antediluvian attitudes* antiquated, old-fashioned, outmoded, out of date, archaic, obsolete; *inf* out of the ark.

anteroom n outer room, waiting-room, reception area, vestibule, lobby, foyer; *fml* antechamber.

anthem n **1** *church anthems* hymn, psalm, song of praise, plainsong, chorale, chant, canticle. **2** *a national anthem* song of praise, paean, state song.

anthology n collection, compendium, treasury, compilation, miscellany, selection; *lit* garland; *fml* collectanea, ana, analects.

anticipate v **1** *anticipate trouble | anticipate that trouble will occur* expect, foresee, predict, forecast; count on, look for, prepare for, await, contemplate. **2** *anticipating her birthday with pleasure* look forward to, await, look towards; *inf* lick one's lips over. **3** *anticipate his chess move* forestall, intercept, prevent, nullify; *inf* beat one to it, beat to the draw. **4** *anticipate the invention of radio* antedate, come/go before, be earlier than.

anticipation n **1** *in anticipation of success/war* expectation, prediction, preparation, awaiting, contemplation. **2** *full of anticipation before the party* expectancy, hope, hopefulness.

anticlimax n let-down, disappointment, comedown; disillusionment; *lit* bathos.

antics npl pranks, capers, larks, tricks, romps, frolics; horseplay.

antidote n **1** *an antidote to poison* antitoxin, countermeasure. **2** *an antidote to sadness* cure, remedy, corrective, countermeasure, counteragent.

antipathy n aversion, hostility, dislike, enmity, opposition, antagonism, animosity, hatred, abhorrence, loathing, repugnance, animus.

antiquated adj *antiquated attitudes* out of date, old-fashioned, outmoded, passé, outworn, archaic, obsolete, antediluvian; *inf* superannuated.

antique adj **1** *antique furniture* antiquarian, old, vintage. **2** *antique customs* age-old, time-

worn, early, earliest, prehistoric, primeval, primordial. **3** *antique attitudes* old-fashioned. *see* ANTIQUATED.

antique n *the chair's an antique* heirloom, object of virtu, relic, curio.

antiseptic adj **1** *an antiseptic substance* disinfectant, germicidal, bactericidal. **2** *an antiseptic surface* sterile, germ-free, uncontaminated, unpolluted, aseptic, sanitary, hygienic. **3** *antiseptic surroundings* clinical, characterless, undistinguished, unexciting.

antiseptic n *swab with antiseptic* disinfectant, germicide, bactericide.

antisocial adj **1** *dropping litter is antisocial* disruptive, disorderly, lawless, rebellious, asocial. **2** *feeling antisocial* unsociable, uncommunicative, reserved, unfriendly, withdrawn, retiring.

antithesis n **1** *white is the antithesis of black* opposite, converse, reverse, inverse, other extreme. **2** *an attitude the antithesis of mine* opposite, contrast, contrariety, inverse, reversal.

anxiety n **1** *anxiety about the future* worry, concern, uneasiness, apprehension, disquiet, nervousness, tenseness, misgiving, angst. **2** *full of anxiety to win* eagerness, desire, longing, yearning, avidity.

anxious adj **1** *anxious about the future* | *anxious about her health* worried, concerned, uneasy, apprehensive, fearful, nervous, disturbed, tense. **2** *anxious to please* eager, keen, longing, yearning, avid.

any adj **1** *did you get any books/meat?* a, an, one, some, a single one, a single part. **2** *any book will do* any one, every, whatever, whichever; *inf* any old.

any pron **1** *there are the thieves but do you recognize any?* anyone, anybody, somebody, someone. **2** *don't give him any* even one, even the smallest amount.

any adv *is your father any better?* at all, in the least, to any extent, to some extent, somewhat, in any degree.

anyhow adv **1** *go anyhow you like* in any way, anyway, in any manner, by any means. **2** *anyhow, you must go* in any case, in any event, at all events, no matter what. **3** *lying around anyhow* haphazardly, carelessly, heedlessly, negligently.

apart adv **1** *with feet apart* separate, separately, separated, at a distance. **2** *a person/house standing apart* to one side, aside, to the side, separately, alone, by oneself/itself, distant, isolated. **3** *a couple living apart* separate, separately, separated, divorced, not together. **4** *blow/break apart* to pieces, in

pieces, to bits, asunder. **apart from** no-one apart from him except, but, other than, aside from, excluding, not counting, save.

apartment n **1** *the royal/furnished apartments* accommodation, lodging, suite; living quarters, quarters, rooms. **2** *an appartment in New York* flat.

apathetic adj uninterested, unmoved, unconcerned, unfeeling, unemotional, emotionless, unresponsive, indifferent, impassive, passive, listless, lethargic, languid, phlegmatic, torpid.

apathy n lack of interest/concern/feeling/ emotion, unconcern, unresponsiveness, indifference, impassivity, passivity, dispassion, dispassionateness, listlessness, lethargy, languor, torpor.

ape v imitate, mimic, copy, echo, mock, parody, parrot.

aperture n opening, gap, hole, orifice, window, crack, slit, space, chink, fissure, perforation, breach, eye, interstice.

apex n top, summit, peak, pinnacle, tip, crest, vertex, acme, zenith, apogee.

aphrodisiac n love potion, philtre, stimulant, stimulative.

apiece adv each, for/from/to each, respectively, individually, separately.

aplomb n poise, assurance, self-confidence, self-assurance, calmness, composure, collectedness, equanimity, equilibrity, level-headedness, sang-froid.

apocryphal adj **1** *apocryphal evidence* unverified, unauthenticated, unsubstantiated, spurious, debatable, questionable, dubious, doubtful. **2** *apocryphal tales of his sexual prowess* mythical, fictitious, legendary, false, untrue, phony.

apologetic adj sorry, regretful, contrite, remorseful, penitent, repentant, rueful.

apologize v say one is sorry, say sorry, make an apology, express regret, ask forgiveness, ask for pardon, beg pardon; *inf* eat humble pie.

apology n **1** *deliver an apology* expression of regret; regrets. **2** *present my apologies for my absence* excuses. **3** *an/the apology for their beliefs* defence, vindication, justification, argument, apologia; plea, excuse. **4** *an apology for a man/meal* travesty, poor excuse, excuse, mockery, caricature, imitation, substitute, makeshift, stopgap.

apostle n **1** *Christian apostles* missionary, evangelical, evangelic, preacher, teacher, reformer, spreader of the faith/word; *fml* proselytizer. **2** *an apostle of acupuncture* advocate, supporter, crusader, campaigner, proponent, propagandist, pioneer.

appal v shock, dismay, horrify, outrage, astound, alarm.

appalling adj shocking, horrifying, frightful, outrageous, terrible, awful, dreadful, ghastly, hideous, harrowing, dire.

apparatus n 1 *laboratory/gymnastic apparatus* equipment, gear, tackle, mechanism, outfit, plant; appliance, machine, device, contraption; instruments, tools. 2 *the apparatus of government* structure, system, organization, network, set-up, hierarchy.

apparel n clothing, dress, attire, outfit, wear, costume, garb, habit; clothes, garments, robes, vestments, habiliments; *inf* gear.

apparent adj 1 *problems apparent from the start* clear, plain, obvious, evident, discernible, perceivable, perceptible, manifest, patent. 2 *apparent calmness* seeming, ostensible, outward, superficial, specious, quasi.

apparently adv *apparently he's ill* seemingly, it seems that, it appears that, on the face of it.

apparition n 1 *frightened of the apparition* ghost, spectre, phantom, spirit, wraith; *inf* spook; *fml/lit* shade, revenant, visitant. 2 *the sudden apparition of the black figure* appearance, manifestation, materialization, emergence, visitation.

appeal n 1 *an appeal for help* request, call, plea, entreaty, petition, supplication, solicitation, imploration. 2 *barrister asking for an appeal* reconsideration, re-examination, review, another opinion. 3 *hold little appeal* attraction, attractiveness, allure, charm, interest, fascination, temptation, enticement.

appeal v 1 *appeal for money* ask for, request, put in a plea for, entreat, beg/beseech/plead for, implore, solicit, petition for. 2 *appeal to a higher court* apply for an appeal. *see* APPEAL n 2. 3 *appeals to her* attract, charm, interest, engage, fascinate, tempt, entice, allure, invite.

appear v 1 *a messenger/solution appeared* come into view/sight, emerge, come forth, arrive, turn/show/crop up, materialize, surface, loom. 2 *he may appear at the meeting* attend, be present at, turn up at; *inf* show up, show. 3 *she appeared sad* seem, look, have the appearance/air of being, give the impression of being. 4 *the new furniture range finally appeared | has his new book appeared?* come into being/existence, come out, become available, come on the market, be published/produced. 5 *she appears*

nightly perform, play, act, take part, be on stage, come on.

appearance n 1 *the appearance of the messenger/solution* coming into view, emergence, arrival, advent, materialization, surfacing, looming. *see* APPEAR 1. 2 *his weekly appearance at meetings* attendance, presence, turning up. *see* APPEAR 2. 3 *having an appearance of sadness* look, air, expression, impression, manner, demeanour, bearing, aspect; *lit* mien. 4 *poor but giving the appearance of being rich* semblance, guise, show, pretence, image, outward appearance, front, impression.

appease v 1 *appease the enemy with gifts* placate, pacify, make peace with, conciliate, calm, tranquillize, soothe, quieten down, mollify, soften, propitiate. 2 *appease one's appetite/curiosity* satisfy, assuage, take the edge off, blunt, relieve, quench, diminish.

appeasement n 1 *policy of appeasement* conciliation, placation, concession, acquiescence, acceding, peace-offering, accommodation, propitiation. 2 *the appeasement of the enemy* placating, pacification, conciliation, calming. *see* APPEASE 1. 3 *the appeasement of one's appetite* satisfying, assuagement. *see* APPEASE 2.

append v *append one's signature | append a clause* add, attach, affix, adjoin.

appendage n 1 *an appendage to a will/family* addition, attachment, adjunct, addendum, appurtenance, accessory, affix. 2 *an animal's appendage* extremity, protuberance, projection, member, limb, tail.

appendix n *appendix to a book* supplement, addendum, postscript, addition, extension, adjunct, codicil.

appertain v **appertain to** belong to, relate to, be connected with, be part of, be relevant to, have relevance to, have to do with, be pertinent to, have reference to, have a bearing upon.

appetite n 1 *an appetite for food* hunger, taste, palate, desire, relish. 2 *an appetite for adventure* hunger, thirst, need, liking, inclination, passion, longing, craving, yearning, hankering, zest, gusto, propensity, proclivity; *fml* appetency.

appetizer n starter, hors d'oeuvre, antipasto, canapé.

appetizing adj 1 *an appetizing dish* mouthwatering, tasty, succulent, delicious, palatable. 2 *an appetizing prospect* tempting, inviting, enticing, appealing, alluring.

applaud v 1 *the audience applauded* clap, cheer, whistle, give a standing ovation to, ask for an encore, put one's hands

together; *inf* give someone a big hand.
2 *applaud their courage* praise, express admiration/approval for, admire, compliment on, commend, acclaim, extol, laud.

applause n **1** *the applause of the audience* clapping, handclapping, cheering, whistling, standing ovation; cheers, whistles, encores, bravos, curtain calls. **2** *won the applause of the neighbourhood* praise, admiration, approval, approbation, commendation, acclaim, acclamation, eulogy, extolment, laudation; compliments, accolades, plaudits.

appliance n **1** *an electrical appliance* device, gadget, apparatus, implement, machine, instrument, tool, mechanism. **2** *the appliance of force* application, use. *see* APPLICATION 1.

applicable adj **1** *rules applicable to everyone* relevant, appropriate, pertinent, apposite, apropos. **2** *an applicable remedy* fitting, suitable, useful.

applicant n candidate, interviewee, competitor, enquirer, claimant, suppliant, supplicant, petitioner, suitor, postulant.

application n **1** *the application of force* use, exercise, administration, employment, putting into operation/practice, practice. **2** *a remark having no application to the case* relevance, bearing, significance, pertinence, aptness, appositeness, germaneness. **3** *the application of ointment* putting on, rubbing in. *see* APPLY 3. **4** *students with application* industry, diligence, attentiveness, effort, hard work, assiduity, commitment, dedication, perseverance, persistence, sedulousness. **5** *an application for a job | application for a tax rebate* enquiry, request, claim, appeal, petition, entreaty, suit, solicitation, requisition, demand. **6** *a healing application* ointment, lotion, cream, rub, emollient, balm, poultice, unguent.

apply v **1** *apply force/tact | apply the brakes* use, put to use, employ, utilize, administer, exercise, put into practice, bring into effect/play, bring to bear. **2** *the remark did not apply to the situation* be relevant/significant/pertinent, be apt/apposite/germane, have a bearing on. **3** *apply ointment* put on, rub in, cover with, spread, smear. **4** *apply for a job | apply for tax relief* make/put in an application, put in for, try for, enquire after, request, claim, seek, appeal, petition, make an entreaty, solicit, sue. **apply one-self** be industrious/diligent/assiduous, study, work hard, make an effort, pay attention, be attentive, commit/devote oneself, persevere, persist, put one's shoulder to the wheel; *inf* buckle to.

appoint v **1** *appoint him manager* name, designate, nominate, select, choose, elect, install as. **2** *appoint a time* set, fix, arrange, choose, establish, settle, determine, assign, designate, allot.

appointment n **1** *cancel an appointment* meeting, engagement, date, interview, arrangement, rendezvous, assignation; *lit* tryst. **2** *his new appointment as manager* job, post, position, situation, place, office, station. **3** *the appointment of him as boss* naming, nomination, selection. *see* APPOINT 1. **4** *the appointment of a time* setting, arrangement, establishment. *see* APPOINT 2.

apportion v allocate, distribute, share out, divide out, hand/deal out, ration/mete/dole out, allot, dispense, assign.

apposite adj appropriate, suitable, fitting, apt, relevant, to the point, pertinent, applicable, germane.

appraisal n **1** *make an appraisal of the house* valuation, pricing, survey. **2** *an appraisal of their ability* assessment, evaluation, summing-up, estimation, estimate, judgement, sizing-up.

appraise v **1** *appraise the property* value, survey, price, set a price on. **2** *appraise his ability* assess, evaluate, sum up, estimate, gauge, judge, review; *inf* size up.

appreciable adj *an appreciable amount* considerable, substantial, significant, sizeable, visible, goodly.

appreciate v **1** *appreciate your help* be appreciative of, be thankful/grateful for, give thanks for, be indebted/beholden for. **2** *appreciate good staff/wine* value, hold in high regard, hold in esteem, prize, cherish, treasure, rate highly, respect, think highly of, think much of. **3** *appreciate the importance of* recognize, acknowledge, realize, know, be aware of, be conscious/cognizant of, be alive to, understand, comprehend, perceive, discern. **4** *the house appreciated in value* increase, gain, grow, rise, mount, inflate, escalate.

appreciation n **1** *express his appreciation for their help* gratitude, gratefulness, thankfulness, indebtedness, obligation; thanks. **2** *the appreciation of good staff/wine* valuing, esteem, regard, prizing, respect. *see* APPRECIATE 2. **3** *the appreciation of its importance* recognition, acknowledgement, realization, awareness, consciousness, cognizance, comprehension, perception, discernment. *see* APPRECIATE 3. **4** *the appreciation of house values* increase, rise, growth, gain, improvement, inflation, escalation. **5** *an appreciation of the poetry* review, critique, criticism, critical analysis, notice, commentary; praise, acclamation.

appreciative adj **1** *most appreciative of your help* grateful, thankful, indebted, obliged, beholden; grateful for, thankful for. **2** *an appreciative audience* enthusiastic, responsive, supportive, encouraging, sympathetic, sensitive.

apprehend v **1** *apprehend the criminal* arrest, catch, seize, capture, take prisoner, take into custody, haul in, detain; *inf* collar, nab, nail, run in, nick, pinch, bust. **2** *apprehend the significance* understand, grasp, realize, recognize, appreciate, comprehend, discern, perceive; *inf* twig, get the picture.

apprehension n **1** *full of apprehension about the interview/future* anxiety, dread, alarm, worry, uneasiness, unease, nervousness, fear, misgiving, disquiet, concern, trepidation, perturbation, foreboding, presentiment, angst; nerves; *inf* butterflies in the stomach, the willies, the heebie-jeebies. **2** *the apprehension of criminals* arrest, seizure, capture, detention; *inf* collaring, nabbing, nailing. *see* APPREHEND 1. **3** *the apprehension of problems* understanding, realization, recognition, appreciation, comprehension, discernment, perception. *see* APPREHEND 2.

apprehensive adj anxious, alarmed, worried, uneasy, nervous, frightened, fearful, mistrustful, concerned. *see* APPREHENSION 1.

apprentice n trainee, learner, beginner, probationer, pupil, student, cub, greenhorn, tiro, novice, neophyte; *Amer inf* rookie.

apprise v inform, notify, tell, let know; *inf* clue in, fill in.

approach v **1** *someone's approaching the house* come/go/draw near/nearer, come/go/draw close/closer, move/edge near/nearer, draw nigh, catch up, gain on, near, advance, push forward, reach, arrive. **2** *don't approach strangers in the street* talk/speak to, make conversation with, engage in conversation, greet, address, salute, hail. **3** *approach them for a contribution* apply/appeal to, broach the matter to, make advances/overtures to, make a proposal to, sound out, proposition, solicit. **4** *approach the problem with care* set about, tackle, begin, start, commence, embark on, make a start on, undertake. **5** *a price approaching £600* come near/close to, approximate, be comparable/similar to, compare with.

approach n **1** *the approach of footsteps* coming near/nearer, nearing, advance, advent, arrival. *see* APPROACH v 1. **2** *the approach to the manor* driveway, drive, access road, road,

avenue, street, passageway. **3** *make an approach to | make approaches* application, appeal, proposal, proposition; advances, overtures. **4** *the merest approach to a smile* approximation, likeness, semblance. **5** *a new approach to teaching* method, procedure, technique, style, way, manner, mode, *modus operandi*; means.

appropriate adj *an appropriate time/remark* suitable, fitting, befitting, proper, seemly, right, apt, relevant, pertinent, apposite, applicable, congruous, opportune, felicitous, germane; *fml* appurtenant.

appropriate v **1** *appropriate a country/house* take possession of, take over, seize, commandeer, expropriate, annex, arrogate. **2** *appropriate money for education* set apart/aside, assign, allot, allocate, earmark, devote, apportion. **3** *appropriate company money* embezzle, misappropriate, steal, pilfer, filch, pocket, purloin; *inf* pinch, nick, swipe; *fml* peculate.

approval n **1** *look on with approval* favour, liking, approbation, acceptance, admiration, appreciation, regard, esteem, respect, commendation, applause, acclaim, acclamation, praise. **2** *give approval to the minutes/application* acceptance, agreement, consent, assent, sanction, endorsement, blessing, permission, leave, confirmation, ratification, authorization, mandate, licence, validation, acquiescence, concurrence, imprimatur; *inf* the go-ahead, the green light, the OK. **on approval** on trial, under probation; *inf* on appro.

approve v **1** *approve of their behaviour* think well of, like, look on with favour, give one's blessing to, be pleased with, admire, hold in regard/esteem, commend, favour, applaud, acclaim, praise. **2** *approve the minutes/application* accept, pass, agree to, sanction, consent/assent to, ratify, authorize, validate, accede to, acquiesce in, concur in, warrant; *inf* give the go-ahead to, give the OK to, give the green light to, give the word to, buy.

approximate adj **1** *the approximate price* rough, estimated, near, close, inexact; *inf* guesstimate. **2** *your approximate neighbour* adjacent, next door, next, neighbouring, near, nearby, close by, adjoining, contiguous.

approximate v *approximating to the truth* be close/near to, come close/near to, approach, border on, verge on, resemble, be similar to.

approximately adv *approximately 40 miles* roughly, about, just about, around, *circa*, or so, more or less, in the neighbourhood of, in the region of, nearly, not far off, close to, near to, almost.

approximation n **1** *200 is an approximation* guess, estimate, estimation, conjecture, rough calculation, rough idea; guesswork; *inf* guesstimate. **2** *an approximation to the truth* semblance, similarity, likeness, correspondence. *see* APPROXIMATE V.

appurtenances npl appendages, accoutrements, accessories, belongings, trappings; equipment, paraphernalia, impedimenta.

apron n pinafore, overall; *inf* pinny.

apropos adj **1** *the remark was extremely apropos* appropriate, pertinent, relevant, apposite, apt, applicable, germane. **2** *apropos the meeting* | *apropos of that remark* with reference to, with regard/respect to, regarding, respecting, on the subject of, re.

apropos adv **1** *talked apropos* appropriately, pertinently. **2** *apropos, we're not going* by the way, incidentally.

apt adj **1** *an apt remark* suitable, fitting, appropriate, applicable, apposite, felicitous, apropos. **2** *apt to get angry* inclined, given, likely, liable, disposed, prone, ready, subject. **3** *an apt pupil* quick to learn, quick, bright, sharp, clever, smart, intelligent, able, gifted, talented, adept, competent, astute.

aptitude n *an aptitude for drawing* talent, gift, flair, bent, skill, knack; ability, proficiency, quickness, competence, capability, potential, capacity, faculty.

aptness n **1** *the aptness of the remark* suitability, appropriateness, applicability. *see* APT 1. **2** *the aptness of the pupil* quickness, brightness, sharpness, cleverness, intelligence. *see* APT 3.

aquatic adj *aquatic plants/sports* water, sea, river, marine, maritime, fluvial.

aqueduct n channel, conduit, race, watercourse, waterway, bridge.

aquiline adj eagle-like, hooked, curved.

arable adj ploughable, tillable, cultivable, cultivatable, farmable; fertile, productive, fruitful, fecund.

arbiter n **1** *an arbiter of fashion* authority, judge, determiner, controller, director, governor, master, expert, pundit. **2** *the arbiter in the case* adjudicator. *see* ARBITRATOR.

arbitrary adj **1** *a completely arbitrary decision* discretionary, discretional, personal, subjective, random, chance, whimsical, capricious, erratic, inconsistent, unreasoned, unreasonable, unsupported, irrational. **2** *an arbitrary ruler* despotic, tyrannical,

tyrannous, absolute, autocratic, dictatorial, imperious, domineering, high-handed.

arbitrate v adjudicate, judge, referee, umpire, adjudge, sit in judgement, pass judgement, settle, decide, determine.

arbitration n adjudication, judgement, settlement, decision, determination; *fml* arbitrament.

arbitrator n adjudicator, judge, referee, umpire, arbiter.

arbour n bower, alcove, grotto, recess, pergola, gazebo.

arc n curve, bow, arch, bend, crescent, halfmoon, semicircle, circular section/line; curvature.

arcade n gallery, colonnade, cloister, loggia, piazza, portico, shopping mall/precinct.

arcane adj secret, mysterious, hidden, concealed, recondite, covert, enigmatic, inscrutable, abstruse, esoteric, cryptic, occult.

arch n **1** *a bridge with three arches* archway, vault, span. **2** *the arch of the rainbow* arc, bow, curve, semicircle; curvature, convexity.

arch v *the cat arched its back* curve, bow, bend, arc; *fml* embow.

arch adj *an arch smile* playful, mischievous, roguish, saucy, artful, sly, knowing, frolicsome.

arch- pfx *archbishop* | *arch-enemy* chief, foremost, principal, leading, main, top, highest, greatest, pre-eminent.

archaic adj old, obsolete, out of date, oldfashioned, outmoded, bygone, *passé*, antiquated, antique; *inf* old hat.

arched adj curved, vaulted, domed; *fml* embowed.

archer n bowman, toxophilite.

archetype n prototype, original, pattern, model, standard, exemplar, mould, paradigm, ideal.

architect n **1** *the architect of the house* designer, planner, building consultant, draughtsman. **2** *the architect of the scheme* author, engineer, creator, originator, planner, deviser, instigator, founder, inventor, contriver, prime mover.

architecture n **1** *studying architecture* design, planning, building, construction; *fml* architectonics. **2** *eighteenth-century architecture* construction, style, design, structure, framework.

archives npl **1** *study the firm's archives* records, annals, chronicles, papers, documents, registers, rolls; history, documentation; *fml* muniments. **2** *the archives are situated in the basement* records office, registry, museum, repository, chancery.

arctic adj **1** *arctic regions* polar, far northern, northern; *fml* boreal, hyperborean. **2** *arctic conditions* freezing, frigid, frozen, icy, glacial, frosty, chilly, cold; *fml* gelid.

ardent adj passionate, avid, impassioned, fervent, fervid, zealous, eager, earnest, enthusiastic, emotional, vehement, intense, fierce, fiery, profound, consuming.

ardour n passion, avidity, fervour, zeal, eagerness, enthusiasm, earnestness, emotion, emotionalism, vehemence, intensity, fierceness, fire, fieriness, profundity.

arduous adj taxing, difficult, hard, onerous, heavy, laborious, burdensome, exhausting, wearying, fatiguing, tiring, strenuous, gruelling, punishing, vigorous, tough, formidable, Herculean.

area n **1** *the area around the city* region, district, zone, sector, territory, tract, stretch, quarter, locality, neighbourhood, domain, realm, sphere. **2** *the area of the room | the area of my knowledge* extent, size, expanse, scope, compass, range; measurements. **3** *specializing in the area of finance* field, sphere, discipline, realm, department, sector, province, domain, territory. **4** *the changing area* section, space, sector, part, portion. **5** *the area of a basement flat* yard, enclosure.

arena n **1** *circus/boxing arena* ground, field, stadium, ring, stage, platform, amphitheatre, colosseum; *inf* park; *Amer* bowl. **2** *the political arena* area/field of conflict, sphere of action/activity, battleground, battlefield, area, scene, sphere, realm, province, territory, domain, sector, theatre, lists.

argue v **1** *the children are always arguing* disagree, quarrel, squabble, bicker, fight, wrangle, dispute, feud; *inf* fall out, argy-bargy. **2** *argue that they are right* assert, declare, maintain, insist, hold, claim, contend, expostulate. **3** *argue the point/case* debate, dispute, discuss, controvert. **4** *argue him out of going | argue him into going* talk round, persuade, convince, prevail upon. **5** *the essay argued much research* point to, indicate, demonstrate, show, suggest, imply, exhibit, denote, be evidence of, display, evince.

argument n **1** *the children had an argument* disagreement, quarrel, squabble, fight, row, difference of opinion, dispute, wrangle, clash, altercation, controversy, feud; *inf* tiff, barney, falling out, set-to, dust-up. **2** *stick to the argument that they are right*

assertion, declaration, claim, plea, contention, expostulation. **3** *the argument against capital punishment* line of reasoning, reasoning, logic, case, defence, evidence, argumentation, polemic; reasons, grounds. **4** *the argument of the biography* theme, topic, subject-matter, gist, outline, plot, storyline, summary, synopsis, abstract, précis.

argumentative adj quarrelsome, belligerent, disputatious, contentious, combative, litigous, dissentient.

arid adj **1** *arid areas* dry, dried up, desert, waterless, moistureless, parched, baked, scorched, dehydrated, desiccated, barren. **2** *arid surroundings/discussion* uninspiring, unstimulating, dull, dreary, drab, dry, colourless, flat, boring, uninteresting, monotonous, lifeless, tedious, vapid, jejune.

aright adv *hear aright* correctly, rightly, accurately, properly, exactly; *inf* OK.

arise v **1** *a difficulty arose* appear, come to light, make an appearance, crop/turn up, spring up, emerge, occur, ensue, set in, come into being/existence, begin. **2** *accidents arising from carelessness* result, be caused by, proceed, follow, stem, originate, emanate, ensue. **3** *arise and go* rise, stand up, get to one's feet, get up. **4** *birds arising* rise, ascend, go up, mount, climb, fly, soar.

aristocracy n nobility, peerage, gentry, upper class, privileged/ruling class, élite, high society, patriciate; *inf* upper crust; *lit* haut monde.

aristocrat n noble, nobleman, noblewoman, lord, lady, peer, peeress, patrician, grandee.

aristocratic adj **1** *an aristocratic family* noble, titled, blue-blooded, high-born, upper-class, patrician, élite. **2** *aristocratic bearing/manners* well-bred, dignified, courtly, refined, elegant, stylish, gracious, fine, polite, haughty, proud.

arm n **1** *arms and legs* limb, upper limb, forelimb, member, appendage. **2** *arm of the sea* inlet, estuary, channel, branch, strait, sound, firth. **3** *an arm of the civil service* branch, offshoot, section, department, division, sector, detachment, extension. **4** *the arm of the law* power, force, authority, strength, might, potency.

arm v **1** *arm with guns/information* provide, supply, equip, furnish, issue with. **2** *arm oneself against criticism* prepare, forearm, make ready, brace, steel, fortify, gird one's loins.

armada n fleet, flotilla, navy, squadron.

armaments npl arms, weapons, firearms, munitions; weaponry, ordnance, *matériel*.

armistice n truce, ceasefire, peace, suspension of hostilities.

armour n armour-plate, protective covering, covering, protection, sheathing, chain-armour, chain-mail; coat armour.

armoury n arms depot, ordnance depot, arsenal, magazine, ammunition dump.

arms npl **1** *carrying arms* weapons, firearms, guns, armaments; weaponry. **2** *the family arms* heraldic device, coat of arms, emblem, crest, insignia, escutcheon, shield, blazonry.

army n **1** *the invading army* armed/military force, land force, soldiery, infantry; troops, soldiers, land forces; *Amer* military. **2** *an army of tourists* horde, pack, host, multitude, mob, crowd, swarm, throng, array.

aroma n smell, scent, odour, bouquet, fragrance, perfume, redolence.

aromatic adj fragrant, sweet-smelling, scented, perfumed, balmy, piquant, spicy, savoury, pungent, odoriferous.

around prep **1** *around the tree* about, on all sides of, on every side of, circling, encircling, surrounding, encompassing. **2** *thrown around the room* about, here and there, all over, everywhere, in all parts of. **3** *around 9 o'clock | around three miles* about, approximately, roughly, close to, near to, nearly, circa. **4** *turn around* in the opposite direction, in reverse, backwards, to the rear.

around adv **1** *litter scattered around* about, here and there, all over, everywhere, in all directions, throughout. **2** *can't see anyone around* nearby, near, close by, close, at hand, at close range.

arouse v **1** *arouse them at dawn* rouse, awaken, waken, wake, wake up. **2** *arouse panic* cause, induce, stir up, inspire, call forth, kindle, provoke, foster, whip up, sow the seeds of. **3** *arouse the crowd* rouse, incite, excite, provoke, goad, prompt, spur on, urge, encourage, egg on, animate, inflame, build a fire under. **4** *arouse sexually* excite, stimulate; *inf* turn on.

arraign v **1** *arraign for murder* accuse, charge, lay charges against, indict, impeach. **2** *arraign the assembled crowd* criticize, censure, find fault with, upbraid, reproach, rebuke, reprove, take to task.

arrange v **1** *arrange the books/flowers* put in order, order, set out, group, sort, organize, tidy, position, dispose, marshal, range, align, line up, rank, file, classify, categorize, array, systematize. **2** *arrange to meet | arrange an appointment* settle on, decide,

determine, agree, come to an agreement, settle on, come to terms about, plan, schedule, devise, contrive; *inf* fix up. **3** *arrange for her to be met* make preparations, prepare, plan, organize. **4** *music arranged for the piano* score, adapt, orchestrate, instrument, harmonize.

arrangement n **1** *the arrangement of books/flowers* order, ordering, grouping, organization, positioning, system, disposition, marshalling, ranging, alignment, filing, classification, categorization, array. **2** *make an arrangement | make arrangements* preparations, plans, provisions; agreement, contract, compact. **3** *a musical arrangement* score, adaptation, orchestration, instrumentation, harmonization.

arrant adj utter, downright, outright, absolute, out and out, rank, thorough, thoroughgoing, through and through, total, unmitigated, blatant, barefaced.

array n **1** *an array of bottles/facts* collection, arrangement, assembling, assemblage, line-up, formation, ordering, disposition, marshalling, muster, amassing, show, display, agglomeration, aggregation. **2** *in silken array* attire, apparel, clothing, dress, garb, finery; garments.

array v **1** *the books/troops are arrayed* assemble, arrange, draw up, group, order, range, rank, line up, place, position, dispose, marshall, muster, amass, agglomerate, aggregate. **2** *they were arrayed in silk* attire, clothe, dress, fit out, garb, deck, robe, apparel, accoutre.

arrears npl **1** *pay the arrears* outstanding payment, debt, balance, deficit. **2** *arrears of work* backlog, accumulation, pile-up. **in arrears** behind, behindhand, late, overdue, in the red, in default, in debt.

arrest v **1** *arrest the thief* apprehend, take into custody, take prisoner, detain, seize, capture, catch, lay hold of, haul in; *inf* nick, run in, nab, pinch, collar, bust, nail, pick up. **2** *arrest the spread of disease* stop, halt, end, bring to a standstill, check, block, hinder, delay, interrupt, prevent, obstruct, inhibit, slow down, retard, nip in the bud, stay. **3** *arrest their attention* attract, capture, catch, catch hold of, grip, engage, absorb, occupy, rivet, engross.

arrest n **1** *the arrest of the thieves* apprehension, taking into custody, detention, seizure, capture; *inf* nicking, running in. *see* ARREST V 1. **2** *the arrest of the disease* stopping, stoppage, halt, ending, end, check, blocking, hindrance, delay, interruption, prevention, obstruction, retardation. *see* ARREST V 2.

arresting adj *an arresting face* striking, impressive, remarkable, extraordinary, unusual, noticeable, outstanding, conspicuous, stunning.

arrival n **1** *the arrival of the guest/winter* coming, advent, appearance, entrance, entry, occurrence, approach. **2** *several recent arrivals* incomer, newcomer, visitor, visitant, guest, immigrant.

arrive v **1** *the guests/winter arrived* come, appear, put in an appearance, come on the scene, enter, get here/there, happen, occur, present itself, turn/show up; *inf* blow in. **2** *the actor's really arrived* succeed, make good, reach the top, prosper, flourish, get ahead, become famous, achieve recognition; *inf* make it, make the grade, get somewhere.

arrogance n haughtiness, pride, self-importance, conceit, egotism, snobbishness, snobbery, pomposity, superciliousness, high-handedness, condescencion, disdain, imperiousness, lordliness, presumption, pretentiousness, swagger, bluster, bumptiousness, insolence; *inf* stuck-upness, uppitiness. *see* ARROGANT.

arrogant adj haughty, proud, self-important, conceited, egotistic, snobbish, pompous, supercilious, overbearing, overweening, high-handed, condescending, disdainful, imperious, lordly, presumptuous, pretentious, swaggering, blustering, bumptious, insolent; *inf* stuck-up, uppity, high and mighty.

arrogate v appropriate, assume, expropriate, seize, avail oneself of, commandeer.

arrow n **1** *bow and arrow* shaft, bolt, dart, quarrel. **2** *follow the arrows* pointer, indicator, marker.

arsenal n **1** *weapons in the arsenal* arms depot, magazine, armoury, ammunition dump, ordnance depot, repository. **2** *an arsenal of sharp remarks* store, supply, stock, stockpile, storehouse.

arson n incendiarism, pyromania.

art n **1** *studying art* painting, drawing, design; visual arts. **2** *the art of writing/conversation* skill, craft, aptitude, talent, flair, gift, knack, facility; artistry, mastery, dexterity, expertness, skilfulness, adroitness, cleverness, ingenuity, virtuosity. **3** *use art to win* artfulness, cunning, deceit, deception, wiliness, slyness, craft, craftiness, guile, trickery, duplicity, artifice; wiles.

artery n **1** *a blocked artery* blood vessel, aorta. **2** *crowded arteries* main road, high road, motorway, *autoroute, autobahn; Amer* throughway, highway.

artful adj cunning, deceitful, wily, sly, crafty, duplicitous, scheming, designing, shrewd, politic, ingenious.

article n **1** *three black articles* object, thing, item, commodity; *inf* thingummy, thingumajig, thingumabob, what-d'ye-call-it. **2** *an article in the newspaper* item, piece, story, feature, report, account, write-up. **3** *an article in a legal document | articles of faith* clause, section, point, paragraph, division, part, passage.

articulate adj **1** *an articulate speaker* eloquent, fluent, well-spoken, communicative, coherent, lucid, expressive, silver-tongued, vocal. **2** *an articulate speech* eloquent, clear, fluent, intelligible, comprehensible, understandable, lucid, coherent. **3** *articulate limbs* articulated, jointed, segmented.

articulate v **1** *articulate words/ideas* enunciate, pronounce, voice, say, utter, express, vocalize. **2** *articulated parts* joint, hinge, connect, link, couple.

artifice n **1** *an artifice to mislead* trick, stratagem, ruse, dodge, subterfuge, machination, manoeuvre, tactic, device, contrivance. **2** *win by using artifice* trickery, strategy, cunning, deceit, deception, craftiness, artfulness, wiliness, slyness, duplicity, guile, chicanery.

artificial adj **1** *artificial silk/flowers* manmade, manufactured, synthetic, imitation, simulated, pseudo, ersatz, plastic, mock, sham, fake, bogus, counterfeit; *inf* phoney. **2** *an artificial smile* feigned, false, affected, unnatural, assumed, pretended, insincere, contrived, forced, laboured, strained, hollow, spurious, meretricious; *inf* phoney.

artisan n craftsman, craftswoman, skilled worker, journeyman, artificer, technician.

artist n **1** *the artist's exhibition* painter, drawer, sculptor, old master. **2** *furniture carved by an artist* craftsman, craftswoman, expert, adept, genius, past-master, maestro.

artistic adj **1** *an artistic person* creative, talented, gifted, accomplished, imaginative, sensitive, cultivated. **2** *an artistic flower arrangement* decorative, beautiful, attractive, lovely, tasteful, graceful, stylish, elegant, exquisite, aesthetic, ornamental. **3** *the artistic temperament* temperamental, unconventional, bohemian, nonconformist.

artistry n art, skill, ability, talent, genius, brilliance, expertness, flair, gift, creativity, proficiency, virtuosity, craftsmanship, workmanship.

artless adj *an artless smile/remark* natural, simple, innocent, childlike, naive, ingenuous, guileless, sincere, frank, unpretentious.

as conj **1** *she came as we were leaving* just as, at the same time that, during the time that, at the time that, while, when. **2** *I must go home as it's late* since, because, seeing that, considering that, on account of. **3** *old as he is, he's healthy* although, though, even if. **4** *do as I say* in the manner that, in the way that. **5** *they live as their ancestors did* in the same manner that, in the same way that, like. **6** *the well-paid, as doctors, lawyers and accountants* such as, like, for instance, for example, namely, viz. **7** *as you know, he's dead* a fact which, that which. **as for/to** on the subject of, as regards, with reference to, with regard to, with respect to. **as it were** so to speak, in a manner of speaking, in a way. **as yet** until now, up to now, up to the present time.

as prep **1** *dressed as a policeman* in the guise of, with the appearance of, in the character of, so as to appear to be. **2** *as their employer I must sack them* in the role of, being, acting as, functioning as.

ascend v climb, go/move up, mount, scale, rise, levitate, fly up, soar, slope upwards.

ascendancy, ascendency n dominance, domination, control, power, authority, mastery, rule, command, supremacy, sway, sovereignty, the upper hand.

ascendant, ascendent adj ascending, rising, going up, climbing, mounting, on the way up, on the rise, growing, increasing, flourishing, on the up and up, up-and-coming.

ascertain v find out, get to know, ferret out, establish, discover, learn, determine, settle, identify, decide, verify, make certain, confirm; *inf* pin down.

ascetic n *an ascetic living alone in the forest* recluse, hermit, solitary, anchorite, self-denier, abstainer, celibate, nun, monk, stylite, fakir, dervish, yogi.

ascetic adj *an ascetic way of life* self-denying, abstinent, abstemious, self-disciplined, austere, frugal, rigorous, strict, moderate, temperate, celibate, Spartan, puritanical.

ascribe v attribute, assign, accredit, credit, give credit to, put/set down to, chalk up to, impute, charge with, lay on, blame.

ashamed adj **1** *ashamed of his conduct* humiliated, conscience-stricken, sorry, mortified, abashed, crestfallen, shamefaced, remorseful, discomfited, embarrassed, distressed, sheepish, red-faced, blushing, with one's tail between one's legs. **2** *ashamed to say* reluctant, unwilling, hesitant, restrained.

ashen adj pale, pale-faced, pallid, wan, grey, grey-faced, white, colourless, anaemic, washed out, bleached, ghostly, deathlike, livid, leaden.

ashes npl **1** *ashes in the grate* cinders, embers; residue. **2** *the city was left in ashes* rubble, ruin; ruins. **3** *bury her ashes* remains.

ashore adv to/on the shore, on land, on dry land, on the beach, shorewards, landwards.

aside adv **1** *stand aside* to/on one side, to the side, alongside, apart, away, separately, detached, in isolation. **2** *joking aside* apart, notwithstanding.

aside n *make an aside* whispered/confidential remark casual remark, soliloquy, monologue.

asinine adj stupid, silly, idiotic, foolish, brainless, nonsensical, senseless, half-witted, fatuous, inane, imbecilic, moronic; *inf* daft, dopey, balmy, batty, nutty, dumb, gormless.

ask v **1** *ask her why|ask her about it* inquire, question, put a question to, query, interrogate, quiz, cross-examine, catechize; *inf* grill, pump, give the third degree to. **2** *asked a favour|ask the boss for a rise* request, demand, appeal to, apply to, petition, call upon, entreat, beg, implore, beseech, plead, sue, supplicate. **3** *ask them to dine* invite, bid, summon.

askance adv **1** *look askance at her neighbour* sideways, indirectly, obliquely, out of the corner of one's eye. **2** *look askance at their antics* disapprovingly, mistrustfully, suspiciously, with distrust/doubt.

askew adv/adj to one side, sideways, at an oblique angle, awry, out of line.

asleep adj/adv **1** *asleep in bed* sleeping, fast asleep, sound asleep, in a deep sleep, slumbering, napping, catnapping, dozing, resting, reposing, dormant, comatose; *inf* snoozing, dead to the world, out like a light, kipping; *lit* in the arms of Morpheus. **2** *my leg's asleep* numb, without feeling, deadened, benumbed.

aspect n **1** *look at every aspect of the problem* feature, facet, side, angle, slant, viewpoint, standpoint, light. **2** *a man with a fierce aspect* appearance, look, expression, air, countenance, demeanour, bearing; features; *fml* mien. **3** *the southern aspect of the house* direction, situation, position, location, exposure, outlook. **4** *affording a pleasant aspect* outlook, view, scene, prospect.

asperity n harshness, sharpness, roughness, severity, acerbity, bitterness, acrimony, sourness, astringency, virulence, sarcasm, irritability, irascibility, churlishness, crabbedness, peevishness, crossness.

aspersions npl *resent your aspersions* | *cast aspersions* disparaging/denigrating/malicious remark, defamatory/slanderous remark; disparagement, deprecation, denigration, defamation, slander.

asphyxiate v choke, suffocate, smother, stifle, throttle, strangle, strangulate.

aspiration n *aspirations to succeed* desire, longing, yearning, hankering, wish, ambition, hope, aim, objective, goal, object, dream, eagerness, enthusiasm, endeavour.

aspire v desire, long to/for, yearn to/for, hanker after, be ambitious, hope to/for, wish to/for, dream of, hunger for, aim to/for, seek, pursue.

aspiring adj *an aspiring leader* would-be, expectant, hopeful, ambitious, enterprising, optimistic, eager, striving, wishful.

ass n **1** *riding on an ass* donkey, burro; *inf* moke. **2** *a silly ass* fool, idiot, dolt, ninny, imbecile, nincompoop, blockhead, numskull, halfwit, dunce, simpleton, jackass; *inf* twit, twerp, chump, nerd, nitwit, dimwit, dickhead, fathead.

assail v **1** *assail the enemy with blows* | *a mind assailed by doubts* attack, assault, set about, lay into, beset, fall/set upon, accost, mug, charge; *inf* jump. **2** *assailed with angry words/insults* bombard, berate, belabour, lash, abuse, criticize, harangue, revile, lambast, fulminate against; *inf* sail into, tear into.

assailant n attacker, mugger, aggressor, assaulter, accoster, assailer.

assassin n murderer, killer, slayer, executioner, liquidator; *inf* hit man, contract man.

assassinate v murder, kill, slay, execute, liquidate, eliminate; *inf* hit.

assault n **1** *lead an army assault* attack, onslaught, onset, charge, offensive, act of aggression, storming. **2** *found guilty of assault* violent act, physical/verbal attack; sexual assault, sexual misconduct, molesting, sexual interference, rape.

assault v **1** *assault the enemy forces* attack, make an onslaught/onset on, charge, undertake an offensive, storm. **2** *assault a policeman* attack, strike, hit, aim blows at. **3** *assault and murder a woman* sexually assault, molest, rape, interfere with.

assay v **1** *assay metals* test, check, analyse, assess, evaluate, appraise, examine, inspect, investigate, scrutinize, probe. **2** *assay a reply* attempt, venture, try.

assay n *metal assays* test, trial, check, analysis, assessment, evaluation, appraisal, examination, investigation, inspection, probe.

assemblage n *an assemblage of old vases* collection, accumulation, conglomeration, cluster, medley, jumble.

assemble v **1** *assemble the children/books/evidence* get together, bring/put together, gather, collect, round up, marshal, muster, summon, congregate, accumulate, amass, rally, convoke. **2** *the crowd assembled* gather, collect, come together, foregather, meet, congregate, convene, flock together. **3** *assemble the parts of the wardrobe* put together, piece/fit together, build, fabricate, construct, erect, manufacture, set up, connect, join.

assembly n **1** *talking to a crowded assembly* gathering, meeting, group, body of people, crowd, throng, congregation, convention. **2** *the assembly of furniture/cars* putting/fitting together, building, fabrication, construction, erection, manufacture. *see* ASSEMBLE 3.

assent n *give one's assent* agreement, concurrence, acceptance, approval, consent, acquiescence, compliance, approbation, permission, sanction, accord, accordance, accession.

assert v **1** *assert that she is innocent* declare, state, announce, maintain, pronounce, proclaim, contend, aver, swear, avow, attest, affirm, allege, claim, postulate, asseverate. **2** *assert one's rights* uphold, press/push for, insist upon, stand up for, defend, vindicate. **assert oneself** behave confidently, make one's presence felt, exert one's influence.

assertive adj *an assertive personality* positive, confident, self-assured, dogmatic, aggressive, self-assertive, strong-willed, forceful, dominant, domineering; *inf* pushy.

assess v **1** *assess the quality/value* evaluate, judge, gauge, rate, estimate, appraise, determine, weigh up, compute. **2** *assess taxation contributions* fix, evaluate, levy, impose, demand, rate.

assessment n **1** *continuous assessment* | *the assessment of quality* evaluation, judgement, gauging, rating, estimation, appraisal. *see* ASSESS 1. **2** *tax assessment* evaluation, levy, charge, rate, toll, tariff, demand, fee.

asset n *make the most of one's assets* | *an asset to the school* advantage, benefit, blessing, strong point, strength, boon, aid, help.

assets npl property, estate, capital, wealth, money; resources, reserves, securities, holdings, possessions, effects, goods, valuables, belongings, chattels.

assiduous adj diligent, industrious, hardworking, studious, persevering, persistent, laborious, unflagging, indefatigible, zealous, sedulous.

assign v **1** *assign duties to all* allocate, allot, distribute, give out, dispense, apportion, consign. **2** *assign him to the post* appoint, select, install, designate, nominate, name, delegate, commission. **3** *assign Thursdays for trips* fix, appoint, decide on, determine, set aside/apart, stipulate, appropriate. **4** *assign her behaviour to jealousy* ascribe, put down to, attribute, accredit, chalk up to. **5** *assign her property* transfer, make over, convey, consign.

assignation n *lovers making an assignation* rendezvous, tryst, date, appointment, meeting.

assignment n **1** *carry out an assignment* task, job, duty, commission, charge, mission, responsibility, obligation. **2** *the assignment of duties* allocation, allotment, dispensation, apportionment, consignment. **3** *his assignment to the post* appointment, selection, installation, nomination. *see* ASSIGN 2. **4** *its assignment to jealousy* ascribing. *see* ASSIGN 4. **5** *the assignment of property* transfer, conveyance.

assimilate v **1** *assimilate food/facts | assimilate people into a group* absorb, take in, incorporate, digest, ingest. **2** *assimilate your way of life to theirs* adapt, adjust, accustom, acclimatize, accommodate, become like/similar, blend in, fit, homogenize.

assist v **1** *assist the old lady | assist the police* help, aid, lend a hand, succour, support, cooperate/collaborate with, abet, work with, play a part. **2** *he was only assisting his senior* be the assistant/subordinate to, help out, support, back, second. **3** *assist the factory's smooth operation* make easier, facilitate, expedite.

assistance n help, aid, succour, support, reinforcement, cooperation, collaboration; a helping hand.

assistant n **1** *her assistant's in charge* subordinate, deputy, auxiliary, second in command, right hand man/woman, man/girl Friday, henchman. **2** *an assistant in the project* helper, colleague, associate, partner, confederate, accomplice, collaborator, accessory, abettor. **3** *an assistant in a department store* shop/sales assistant, salesperson, saleswoman, salesman, server, checkout girl/person/operator; *Amer* clerk.

associate v **1** *associate wine with France* link, connect, relate, think of together, couple. **2** *they associate with criminals* mix, keep company, mingle, socialize, hobnob, fraternize; *inf* run around, hang out, pal up. **3** *their clubs are associated* combine, join, connect, attach, affiliate, band together, ally, syndicate, incorporate, conjoin.

assorted adj mixed, varied, variegated, miscellaneous, diverse, diversified, motley, sundry, heterogeneous.

assortment n mixture, variety, miscellany, selection, medley, *mélange*, diversity, jumble, mishmash, hotchpotch, pot-pourri, farrago, salmagundi.

assuage v **1** *assuage the pain* relieve, ease, alleviate, soothe, mitigate, lessen, allay, moderate, diminish, calm, palliate, abate, lull, temper, mollify. **2** *assuage their hunger/thirst* appease, satisfy, relieve, slake, quench, dull, blunt, allay, pacify, take the edge off.

assume v **1** *assume he's coming* suppose, take for granted, presuppose, presume, imagine, think, believe, fancy, expect, accept, suspect, surmise, understand, gather; *Amer* guess. **2** *assume a thorough knowledge* feign, pretend, simulate, put on, counterfeit, sham. **3** *assume an air of authority | assume massive proportions* adopt, take on, acquire, come to have. **4** *assume a position of responsibility* undertake, enter upon, begin, set about, take on/up, embark on, take upon oneself, accept, shoulder. **5** *the invaders assumed power* seize, take, take over, appropriate, usurp, pre-empt, commandeer.

assumed adj *an assumed name* false, fictitious, fake, feigned, pretended, made-up, bogus, sham, spurious, make-believe, counterfeit, pseudo; *inf* phoney; *fml* pseudonymous.

assumption n **1** *on the assumption that you're right* supposition, presupposition, presumption, premise, belief, expectation, conjecture, surmise, guess, theory, hypothesis, suspicion, postulation. **2** *the assumption of a thorough knowledge* feigning, pretending, simulation. *see* ASSUME 2. **3** *the assumption of an air of authority* adoption, taking on. *see* ASSUME 3. **4** *the assumption of a position of responsibility* undertaking, entering upon, setting about, embarkation on. *see* ASSUME 4. **5** *the invaders' assumption of power* seizure, appropriation, usurping. *see* ASSUME 5. **6** *amazed at his assumption* arrogance, presumption, conceit, impertinence.

assurance n **1** *shows remarkable assurance for her age* self-assurance, self-confidence, confidence, self-reliance, nerve, poise, positiveness. **2** *you have my assurance that I'll be there* word of honour, word, guarantee, promise, pledge, vow, oath, affirmation. **3** *no assurance of her success* certainty, guarantee. *see* ASSURE 3. **4** *life assurance* insurance.

assure v **1** *I assure you that he's wrong* declare, affirm, give one's word, guarantee, promise, swear, certify, pledge, vow, attest. **2** *they assured him of their ability* convince, persuade, reassure, prove to. **3** *success is assured* ensure, make certain, make sure, secure, guarantee, seal, clinch, confirm. **4** *assure his life* insure.

assured adj **1** *an assured manner* self-assured, self-confident, confident, self-reliant, poised, positive. **2** *an assured market* certain, sure, guaranteed, secure, reliable, dependable.

astonish v amaze, astound, dumbfound, stagger, surprise, stun, take aback, confound, take one's breath away; *inf* flabbergast, floor.

astonishing adj amazing, astounding, staggering, surprising, breathtaking, striking, impressive, bewildering, stunning.

astonishment n *he failed to conceal his astonishment* surprise, amazement, wonder, disbelief, shock, numbness, bewilderment, confusion.

astound v amaze, astonish, dumbfound, stagger, surprise. *see* ASTONISH.

astounding adj amazing, astonishing, staggering, surprising. *see* ASTONISHING.

astray adv/adj **1** *go astray in the fog* off course, off the right track, adrift; lost. **2** *led astray by wicked men* into wrongdoing, into error/sin, to the bad.

astringent adj **1** *an astringent lotion* contracting, constricting, constrictive, constringent, styptic. **2** *astringent criticism/ conditions* severe, stern, harsh, rough, stringent, acerbic, austere, caustic, mordant, trenchant.

astronaut n spaceman, spacewoman, cosmonaut, space traveller.

astute adj shrewd, sharp, acute, quick, quick-witted, clever, cunning, artful, ingenious, perceptive, discerning, crafty, wily, calculating, perspicacious, sagacious.

asunder adv into pieces, to pieces, to bits, apart.

asylum n **1** *seek an asylum in the church | political asylum* refuge, sanctuary, shelter, safety, safe keeping, protection; haven, retreat, harbour, port in a storm. **2** *shut away in an asylum* mental hospital, psychi-

atric hospital, institution; *derog* madhouse, nuthouse, loony bin, funny farm.

asymmetrical adj disproportionate, misproportioned, irregular, uneven, distorted, malformed, formless.

atavism n reversion, throwback; recurrence, reappearance, resurgence.

atheism n disbelief, nonbelief, unbelief, heresy, godlessness, scepticism, irreligion, heathenism, freethinking, apostasy, nihilism.

atheist n non-believer, disbeliever, unbeliever, heretic, sceptic, heathen, freethinker, nihilist, infidel.

athlete n sportsman, sportswoman, runner, player; gymnast, competitor, contestant; *inf* keep-fit buff/freak.

athletic adj **1** *an athletic person | of an athletic build* muscular, powerful, robust, able-bodied, sturdy, strong, strapping, vigorous, hardy, stalwart, well-built, brawny, thickset, Herculean; *inf* husky. **2** *an athletic event* sports, sporting, games, gymnastics.

athletics npl sporting events, track and field events, sports, games, matches, contests, gymnastics.

atmosphere n **1** *the world's polluted atmosphere* air, aerosphere, aerospace, sky, heavens. **2** *a friendly/unfriendly atmosphere* environment, milieu, medium, background, setting, air, ambience, aura, climate, mood, feeling, character, tone, tenor, spirit, quality, flavour; surroundings.

atom n iota, jot, bit, whit, particle, scrap, shred, trace, speck, spot, dot, crumb, fragment, grain, morsel, mite.

atone v make amends/reparation, compensate, pay the penalty, pay for, recompense, expiate, do penance.

atonement n reparation, compensation, recompense, redress, indemnity, restitution, expiation, penance, redemption.

atrocious adj **1** *atrocious crimes* brutal, barbaric, barbarous, savage, vicious, wicked, cruel, ruthless, merciless, villainous, murderous, heinous, nefarious, monstrous, inhuman, infernal, fiendish, diabolical, flagrant, outrageous. **2** *atrocious weather* very bad, unpleasant, appalling, dreadful, terrible, shocking.

atrocity n **1** *atrocities committed in wartime* act of brutality/barbarity/savagery, crime, offence, injury; brutality, cruelty, barbarity. **2** *the atrocity of war* abomination, enormity, outrage, horror, evil, monstrosity, violation.

atrophy v waste, waste away, wither, shrivel up, shrink, dry up, decay, wilt, decline, deteriorate, degenerate.

attach v **1** *attach a label to the briefcase* fasten, fix, affix, join, connect, couple, link, secure, tie, stick, adhere, pin, hitch, bond, add, append, annex, subjoin. **2** *attach oneself to a group* affiliate with, join, join forces with, associate/combine with, ally/unite with, latch on to. **3** *attach no significance to it* ascribe, assign, attribute, accredit, apply, put, place, lay, impute, invest with. **4** *the state attaching criminals' property* seize, confiscate, appropriate; Law distrain. **5** *he is attached to the military unit* assign, second, allot, allocate, detail, appoint.

attached adj **1** *is she attached?* married, engaged, having a partner, spoken for; inf going steady. **2** *she is attached to her father* be fond of, full of regard for, devoted to.

attachment n **1** *a strong attachment to one's aunt* fondness, love, liking, affection, devotion, loyalty, tenderness, bond, affinity. **2** *an electric drill and attachments* supplementary part, accessory, extension, fitting, extra, adjunct, addition, appurtenance, appendage, accoutrement. **3** *the cable attachment is loose* junction, connector, coupling, fastening, link, clamp. **4** *on attachment to the unit* assignment, secondment, detail, appointment. **5** *the attachment of a label* fastening, fixing, affixing. see ATTACH 1. **6** *my/the attachment of others to the group* affiliation, joining, association. see ATTACH 2. **7** *the attachment of criminals' property* seizure, confiscation, appropriation; Law distrainment.

attack v **1** *attack the enemy | let us attack* assault, set/fall upon, strike at, rush, storm, charge, pounce upon, beset, besiege, beleaguer; strike, begin hostilities; inf lay into, let one have it. **2** *an article attacking the writer* criticize, censure, berate, reprove, rebuke, impugn, harangue, find fault with, blame, revile, fulminate against, vilify; inf slate, have a go at, knock, slam. **3** *attack a pile of work* set about, get/go to work on, get started on, undertake, embark on. **4** *a disease attacking the nervous system* affect, have an effect on, infect.

attack n **1** *an attack on the enemy* assault, onslaught, offensive, onset, strike, storming, charge, foray, rush, incursion, inroad. see ATTACK v 1. **2** *launch an attack on his writing* criticism, censure, berating, rebuke, reproval, impugnment, blame, revilement, vilification; inf slating, knocking. see ATTACK v 2. **3** *mount an attack on a pile of work* start, beginning, commencement, undertaking, onslaught. **4** *an asthmatic attack* fit, bout,

seizure, spasm, convulsion, paroxysm, stroke; fml access.

attacker n assailant, aggressor, assaulter, striker, mugger.

attain v achieve, accomplish, obtain, gain, procure, secure, get, grasp, win, earn, acquire, reach, arrive at, realize, fulfil, succeed in, bring off, be successful.

attainable adj achievable, obtainable, accessible, within reach, at hand, reachable, winnable, realizable, practicable, feasible, possible, potential, conceivable, imaginable.

attainment n **1** *the attainment of his goal* achievement, accomplishment, gaining, procurement, acquiral, acquirement, acquisition, realization, fulfilment, completion, consummation, success. see ATTAIN. **2** *musical attainment* accomplishment, ability, art, skill, proficiency, mastery, talent, gift, capability, competence.

attempt v **1** *attempt to explain* try, strive, aim, venture, endeavour, seek, undertake, set out, do one's best, take it upon oneself, essay; inf give it a whirl. **2** *attempt an escape* try, venture, undertake, tackle, have a go/shot at, essay; inf have a crack at.

attempt n effort, try, endeavour, venture, trial, experiment, essay; crack, go, shot.

attend v **1** *attend a meeting | can you attend?* be present, be at, be here/there, appear, put in an appearance, turn up, visit, frequent, haunt; inf show up, show. **2** *attend the sick* look after, take care of, care for, tend, nurse, mind, minister to. **3** *she was told but was not attending* pay attention, concentrate, listen, pay heed, heed, follow, take note, observe, notice, mark, watch. **4** *attend to this matter/customer* deal/cope with, see to, handle, take care of, give one's attention to, take charge of. **5** *the queen attended by her bodyguard* accompany, escort, guard, chaperon, squire, convoy. **6** *a plan attended with problems* accompanied by, be associated/connected with, go hand in hand with, occur/coexist with, result/arise from, follow upon, be a consequence of.

attendance n **1** *attendance at church is not compulsory* presence, attending, appearance, being there; inf showing up, showing. **2** *attendances vary* number present, turnout, crowd, audience, house, gate. **in attendance** present, giving assistance, supervising, monitoring, on guard.

attendant n **1** *cloakroom attendant* assistant, helper, auxiliary, steward, waiter, servant, menial. **2** *the queen and her attendants* companion, escort, aide, guard, custodian, guide, usher, equerry, squire, lackey, flunkey.

attendant adj *attendant circumstances* accompanying, concomitant, related, accessory, resultant, consequent.

attention n **1** *wandering attention | give more attention to the problem* concentration, attentiveness, intentness, notice, observation, heed, heedfulness, regard, contemplation, deliberation, scrutiny; thought, thinking, studying. **2** *attract their attention* notice, awareness, observation, consciousness, heed, recognition, regard. **3** *for the personal attention of the manager* consideration, action, notice, investigation. **4** *medical attention* care, treatment, ministration, therapy. **5** *appreciate his attentions* civility, politeness, courtesy, respect, gallantry, urbanity, deference; compliments.

attentive adj **1** *keen and attentive* alert, aware, awake, watchful, wideawake, observant, noticing, concentrating, heeding, heedful, mindful, vigilant, on guard; *inf* all ears; *fml* on the qui vive. **2** *an attentive host* considerate, thoughtful, kind, polite, courteous, gracious, conscientious, civil, obliging, accommodating, gallant, chivalrous.

attenuated adj **1** *attenuated limbs | attenuated lengths of silk* thin, slender, threadlike, thinned down, stretched out, drawn out. **2** *attenuated force* weakened, reduced, lessened, decreased, diminished, impaired, enervated.

attest v **1** *witnesses attest his account* affirm, aver, asseverate, confirm, testify to, vouch for, bear witness to, bear out, endorse, back up, support, corroborate, verify, authenticate. **2** *footsteps attested to his presence* prove, give proof of, provide evidence of, evidence, demonstrate, evince, display, exhibit, show, manifest, substantiate, confirm, verify, vouch for.

attic n loft, garret, mansard.

attire n *evening attire* clothing, dress, wear, outfit, apparel, garb, ensemble, costume, array, habit, wardrobe; clothes, garments, accoutrements; *inf* gear, togs, glad rags, rig-out.

attire v *attired in silk* dress, clothe, dress up, fit out, garb, robe, array, deck out, turn out, costume, accoutre; *inf* doll up, rig out; *fml* apparel.

attitude n **1** *one's attitude to marriage* point of view, viewpoint, opinion, frame of mind, outlook, perspective, reaction, stance, position, approach; thoughts, ideas. **2** *bodies adopting different attitudes* position, stance, pose, stand; bearing, deportment, carriage.

attract v **1** *magnets attract iron filings* draw, pull, magnetize. **2** *men attracted by small women | moths attracted to light* allure, entice, tempt, interest, fascinate, charm, engage, enchant, captivate, bewitch, seduce, inveigle.

attraction n **1** *magnetic attraction* pull, draw, magnetism. **2** *the attraction of foreign travel* appeal, attractiveness, allure, pull, draw, enticement, temptation, inducement, interest, charm, fascination, glamour, enchantment, captivation, seduction; *inf* come-on. **3** *one of the city attractions* interest, feature, entertainment, activity, diversion.

attractive adj **1** *an attractive proposal* appealing, agreeable, pleasing, inviting, tempting, interesting. **2** *an attractive woman/man* good-looking, striking, beautiful, handsome, pretty, stunning, gorgeous, prepossessing, fetching, comely, captivating, charming, fascinating, interesting, appealing, enchanting, alluring.

attribute n **1** *kindness is one their attributes* quality, feature, characteristic, property, mark, trait, distinction, idiosyncrasy. **2** *the throne is an attribute of a king* symbol, indicator, mark, sign, trademark, status symbol.

attribute v *success attributed to hard work* ascribe, assign, accredit, put down to, lay at the door of, chalk up to.

attrition n **1** *the smoothing of rock by attrition* abrasion, friction, rubbing, chafing, corroding, corrosion, erosion, eating away, grinding, scraping, wearing away, excoriation, detrition. **2** *defeat the enemy by a war of attrition* wearing down, weakening, debilitation, enfeebling, enervation, sapping, attenuation, harassment, harrying.

attune v **1** *not yet attuned to the situation | attuned to their ideas* accustom, adjust, adapt, familiarize, acclimatize, assimilate, tailor, be fitted, be in tune/harmony/accord, homologize. **2** *attune an instrument* tune, regulate, modulate, harmonize.

auburn adj reddish-brown, Titian, chestnut-coloured, chestnut, copper-coloured, copper, rust-coloured, russet, hennaed.

audacious adj **1** *an audacious scheme/traveller* bold, daring, fearless, intrepid, brave, courageous, valiant, adventurous, plucky, daredevil, reckless; *inf* gutsy, spunky. **2** *an audacious youth/remark* impudent, impertinent, insolent, presumptuous, cheeky, forward, rude, brazen, shameless, pert, saucy, defiant.

audacity n **1** *the audacity of the scheme/man* boldness, daring, fearlessness, intrepidity, bravery, courage, valour, pluck, reckless-ness; *inf* guts, spunk. **2** *the child had the audacity to swear* impudence, impertinence, insolence, presumption, cheek, forward-ness, rudeness, brazenness, shamelessness, pertness, sauce, defiance.

audible adj heard, hearable, clear, distinct, perceptible, discernible.

audience n **1** *a concert/TV audience* listeners, spectators, viewers, onlookers; assembly, gathering, crowd, assemblage, house, turnout, congregation, gallery. **2** *publica-tions aimed at a wide audience* public, mar-ket, following; fans, devotees, aficionados; *inf* buffs, freaks. **3** *an audience with the Pope* interview, meeting, hearing, consultation, discussion, reception.

audit n *an audit of the firm's accounts* inspec-tion, examination, scrutiny, investigation, review, check.

audit v *audit the books* inspect, examine, go over/through, scrutinize, investigate, review, check.

augment v **1** *augment one's income | augment the audience* increase, make larger/bigger/greater, boost, build up, enlarge, add to, expand, extend, amplify, raise, enhance, heighten, multiply, magnify, elevate, swell, inflate, escalate, intensify. **2** *his fortune aug-mented* increase, grow, build up, enlarge, expand, extend, rise, multiply, swell, inflate, escalate.

augur v *it augurs well that they're talking* be a sign of, foretell, forecast, predict, prophesy, bode, foreshadow, promise, presage, por-tend, herald, betoken, harbinger.

augur n *augurs foretelling disasters* seer, soothsayer, prophet, oracle.

august adj dignified, solemn, majestic, stately, magnificent, noble, regal, impos-ing, impressive, exalted, lofty, grand, high-ranking, illustrious, distinguished, awe-inspiring.

aura n ambience, atmosphere, air, quality, mood, character, spirit, feeling, tone, sug-gestion, emanation; vibrations; *inf* vibes.

auspices npl *under the auspices of* patronage, guidance, influence, responsibility, control, protection.

auspicious adj propitious, favourable, promising, bright, optimistic, hopeful, encouraging, opportune, timely, lucky, for-tunate, providential, felicitous, rosy.

austere adj **1** *an austere manner* harsh, stern, severe, strict, unfeeling, hard, rigorous, stringent, grim, cold, distant, formal, stiff, aloof, forbidding, grave, solemn, serious, unsmiling, unyielding, unbending, unre-

lenting, inflexible. **2** *monks leading an aus-tere life* strict, self-denying, self-abnegating, ascetic, Spartan, abstemious, abstinent, moral, upright, celibate, chaste, puritani-cal. **3** *decorated in an austere style* plain, sim-ple, severe, unadorned, unornamented, unembellished, stark, subdued, sombre.

authentic adj **1** *an authentic painting* gen-uine, true, bona fide, rightful, legitimate, lawful, legal, valid; *inf* the real McCoy, kosher. **2** *an authentic statement* reliable, dependable, trustworthy, true, truthful, honest, faithful, credible; *inf* straight from the horse's mouth.

authenticate v **1** *authenticate an agreement* validate, ratify, confirm, certify, seal, endorse, guarantee, warrant, underwrite. **2** *authenticate the work as being Shakespeare's* verify, substantiate, support, prove, evi-dence.

authenticity n **1** *the authenticity of the paint-ing* genuineness, rightfulness, legitimacy, legality, validity. **2** *the authenticity of the statement* reliability, dependability, trust-worthiness, truth, honesty, faithfulness, credibility.

author n **1** *the author of the book/article* writer, composer; novelist, dramatist, play-wright, screenwriter, poet, essayist, biogra-pher, librettist, lyricist, songwriter, journalist, columnist, reporter. **2** *the author of their misfortune* cause, creator, originator, initiator, founder, planner, prime mover, designer.

authoritarian n *the new headmaster is an authoritarian* disciplinarian, autocrat, despot, dictator, tyrant, absolutist.

authoritarian adj *an authoritarian approach* disciplinarian, harsh, strict, autocratic, despotic, dictatorial, tyrannical, domineer-ing, dogmatic, imperious, absolute, Dra-conian.

authoritative adj **1** *an authoritative biogra-phy* official, approved, authorized, sanc-tioned, validated, authentic, genuine; *inf* kosher. **2** *authoritative information* sound, dependable, reliable, trustworthy, authen-tic, valid, certified, attested, definitive, fac-tual, accurate, scholarly. **3** *an authoritative manner* self-assured, confident, assertive, imposing, masterful, dogmatic, peremp-tory, arrogant, commanding, dominating, domineering, imperious, overbearing, authoritarian.

authorities npl administration, the estab-lishment, government, officialdom, man-agement, legislation, the police, bureaucracy, red tape; the powers that be.

authority n **1** *have the authority to decide | a person of/in authority* authorization, right, power, might, sanction, influence, force, control, charge, prerogative, jurisdiction, rule, command, dominion, sovereignty, ascendancy, supremacy; *inf* say-so. **2** *he is an authority on ecology* expert, specialist, professional, master, scholar, adept, pundit; *inf* walking encyclopedia, bible. **3** *quoting authorities used* source, reference, documentation, bibliography, citation, quotation, quote, excerpt, passage. **4** *have his authority to act* permission, authorization, sanction, licence, warrant; *inf* say-so. **5** *have on their authority that they were there* testimony, evidence, witness, attestation, sworn statement, declaration, word, avowal, deposition, profession.

authorize v **1** *authorize them to represent us* give authority to, commission, empower, entitle, enable, accredit, license, certify, validate. **2** *authorize the sale* give authority/permission for, permit, allow, approve, give one's assent to, agree to, sanction, ratify, warrant, give leave for, countenance, accede to; *inf* give the green light to, give the go-ahead for.

autobiography n memoirs; life-story, diary, journal.

autocratic adj despotic, dictatorial, tyrannical, domineering, imperious, omnipotent, all-powerful, absolute, Draconian, oppressive, high-handed; *inf* bossy.

autograph n *get an actor's autograph* signature, inscription, mark, cross, X.

autograph v *autograph a programme* sign, attach one's signature, initial, countersign, mark, put one's cross/X.

automatic adj **1** *an automatic washing machine* automated, mechanized, mechanical, push-button, robotic, self-activating, self-regulating, self-directing, self-propelling. **2** *an automatic reaction* instinctive, spontaneous, involuntary, unconscious, reflex, natural, mechanical. **3** *promotion is automatic* inevitable, routine, certain, assured, unavoidable, necessary.

autonomy n *the people fought for autonomy | the region gained autonomy* independence, self-determination, autarchy; self-sufficiency, individualism.

available adj *tickets are still available* unoccupied, free, untaken, vacant, usable, employable, ready; accessible, obtainable, at hand, convenient.

avarice n *she turned to crime because of avarice* greed, acquisitiveness, covetousness, materialism; selfishness, self-interest, meanness, miserliness.

average n *she calculated the average* mean, median, midpoint, centre; norm, standard, yardstick, rule.

average adj **1** *the team played an average game | the house was an average size* ordinary, normal, typical, everyday; common, widespread, prevalent. **2** *she wrote average essays | his ability was no better than average* mediocre, moderate, unexceptional; second-rate, banal; pedestrian.

aversion n *she had an aversion to spiders | his aversion to work became a problem* dislike, distaste, hatred, repugnance; avoidance, evasion, shunning, reluctance, unwillingness.

avid adj *she was an avid reader | he was an avid fan* keen, eager, enthusiastic, partial to, fond of, fervent, zealous, passionate about; *inf* crazy about, mad about.

avoid v *he tried to avoid paying taxes | he avoided her in the street* shun, keep away from, eschew, steer clear of; evade, hide from, elude, shirk, dodge; abstain from, refrain from, hold back from.

aware adj **1** *he was aware of the problem | she was aware of hostility* conscious of, informed of, familiar with, sensitive to; *inf* clued up on, in the know. **2** *he was aware of every movement | the watchmen were always aware* awake, watchful, vigilant, alert, cautious, paying attention.

awe n *she gazed in awe | they were filled with awe* amazement, wonder, astonishment, stupefaction; reverence, honour, veneration; dread, fear.

awful adj **1** *she had an awful cough | his new coat looked awful* nasty, unpleasant, distressing, troublesome, horrible; serious, severe; ugly, unattractive, foul, disgusting. **2** *the awful power of the gods | the awful presence of the high priestess* awe-inspiring, awesome, venerable, demanding respect, admirable, impressive, authoritative, daunting.

awkward adj **1** *the appointment was at an awkward time* inconvenient, difficult, problematic; unhelpful, annoying, obstructive, vexatious, perverse. **2** *the gymnast had been an awkward child* clumsy, ungainly, inelegant, inept, gauche; lumbering, out of proportion, unwieldy.

awry adj *the storm left the fence awry* lopsided, uneven, unequal, asymmetrical, askew, crooked.

Bb

babble v **1** *babbling away unintelligibly* jabber, gibber, gabble, burble, chatter, mutter, mumble, prate, drivel, bleat, cackle; *inf* rabbit, waffle, run on. **2** *he babbled the secret* blab, blurt out, reveal, divulge, let slip. **3** *the stream babbled quietly* murmur, whisper, gurgle.

babble n *the babble of voices* jabbering, gabble, gabbling, gibberish, chatter, muttering, mumbling, clamour.

babe n **1** *a new-born babe* baby, infant, child. **2** *just a babe in the world of business* innocent, ingénue, babe in arms, greenhorn, novice, tiro, beginner.

babel n commotion, clamour, babble, hubbub, tumult, uproar, din.

baby n **1** *holding a tiny baby* infant, newborn, child, babe, tiny tot; *inf* sprog; *Scots* bairn; *Med* neonate. **2** *the baby of the team* junior, youngest, subordinate.

baby v *baby the children | baby his wife* pamper, spoil, cosset, indulge, pet, humour, coddle, mollycoddle, overindulge, spoonfeed, feather-bed.

baby adj *baby carrots* miniature, mini, diminutive, dwarf, tiny, minute, small, little, wee, midget.

babyish adj childish, immature, infantile, juvenile, puerile, adolescent, jejune, pathetic, inane, namby-pamby.

back n **1** *hurt one's back* spine, backbone, spinal column; human posterior; *Med* dorsum. **2** *the back of the building* rear, rear end, far end, end, reverse, reverse side, other side; hind part, posterior, tail end, backside, hindquarters, stern. **behind one's back** secretly, deceitfully, slyly, sneakily, surreptitiously, covertly.

back adj **1** *back garden/shed/teeth* rear, hind, end, hindmost, posterior. **2** *back copies* past, previous, earlier, former, bygone, expired, elapsed, obsolete.

back adv **1** *without looking back* backwards, behind, to the rear, rearwards. **2** *a few days back* earlier, previously, before, since, ago, heretofore. **3** *standing back from the road* to the rear, at a distance, remote from.

back v **1** *back the proposal/candidate* support, endorse, approve, favour, advocate, help, assist, aid, promote, uphold, champion, encourage, second, abet. **2** *back the theatrical venture* sponsor, finance, subsidize, underwrite, subscribe to. **3** *back her statement* support, confirm, corroborate, substantiate, endorse, second, bolster, reinforce, stand by, side with, vouch for, attest to, sanction. **4** *back a horse/runner* bet on, place a bet on, gamble on. **5** *the car backed out* go/move backwards, reverse. **back away** withdraw, retire, retreat, fall back, recede, turn tail. **back down** yield, submit, surrender, give in, climb down, concede, concede defeat, backtrack, backpedal, retract. **back out** go back on, withdraw from, cancel, renege on, abandon, retreat from, get cold feet, recant; *inf* chicken out of. **back up** support, confirm. *see* BACK v 3.

backbiting n slander, libel, defamation, abuse, scandalmongering, disparagement, denigration, detraction, malice, spite, spitefulness, cattiness, vilification, vituperation, calumny; slurs, aspersions; *inf* bitching, knocking, slagging off, mud-slinging; *Amer inf* bad-mouthing.

backbone n **1** *an injured backbone* spine, spinal/vertebral column. **2** *the backbone of the organization* framework, mainstay, support, basis, foundation, structure. **3** *lacking backbone* strength of character, firmness, determination, resolve, resolution, steadfastness, character, courage, grit, nerve, mettle, pluck, fortitude, tenacity, stamina, will-power; *inf* bottle.

backer n **1** *the theatre's backers* sponsor, patron, financer, benefactor, subsidizer, underwriter, well-wisher, Maecenas; *inf* angel. **2** *backers of the plan/candidate* supporter, advocate, promoter, upholder, champion, seconder, second, abettor.

backfire v **1** *the engine backfired* explode, detonate, discharge. **2** *the plan backfired* miscarry, rebound, recoil, boomerang, fail, disappoint; *inf* flop.

background n **1** *in the background of the painting* distance, rear, horizon. **2** *models posing against a white background* setting, backcloth, backdrop, scene, stage. **3** *check the employee's background* upbringing, rearing, education, history, environment, class, culture, experience; family circumstances, circumstances, qualifications, credentials.

4 *the political background* conditions, circumstances, environment, milieu, framework; factors, influences.

backhanded adj indirect, oblique, ambiguous, equivocal, double-edged, two-edged, sarcastic, ironic, sardonic.

backing n 1 *have the school's backing* support, approval, commendation, help, assistance, aid, helping hand, encouragement, cooperation, championship, promotion, advocacy, endorsement. 2 *set up with the backing of the directors* sponsorship, financing; finance, grant, subsidy; funds. 3 *the backing of the bank* security, surety, collateral, assurance, insurance, guarantee, warranty. 4 *musical backing* accompaniment, backup, harmony, obbligato.

backlash n reaction, counteraction, repercussion, recoil, kickback, rebound, boomerang, retroaction, retaliation.

backlog n accumulation, stockpile, heap, excess, hoard, stock, supply; arrears, reserves; *inf* mountain.

back-pedal v retract, take back, withdraw, retreat, reverse, backtrack, back down, renege, do an about-face, shift ground, tergiversate.

backslide v relapse, lapse, regress, retrogress, revert, fall back, slip/fall from grace, stray, go astray, leave the straight and narrow, degenerate, deteriorate, turn one's back, tergiversate, apostatize.

backslider n recidivist, turncoat, relapser, renegade, deserter, regressor, apostate, fallen angel, tergiversator.

backward adj 1 *a backward look/somersault* rearward, towards the back/rear, reverse. 2 *a backward area* slow, behind, behindhand, underdeveloped, undeveloped, retarded, unprogressive, dull, sluggish, subnormal, unsophisticated. 3 *rather backward in a crowd* bashful, shy, retiring, diffident, hesitant, shrinking, timid, demure, chary, reluctant.

backwards adv 1 *look backwards* rearwards, towards the back/rear, behind. 2 *running backwards* in reverse. 3 *a country going backwards* in reverse, worse, retrogressively, retrogradely.

backwash n 1 *backwash of a ship* wash, backflow, wake, path, churning, disturbance. 2 *the backwash of the war* aftermath, result, effect; repercussions, reverberations, consequences, after-effects.

backwoods npl wildnerness, no man's land; *Aust* bush, outback; *inf* back of beyond, middle of nowhere, the wilds, the sticks.

bacteria npl germs, microorganisms, microbes, parasites, bacilli; *inf* bugs.

bad adj 1 *bad workmanship | a bad driver* poor, unsatisfactory, inadequate, deficient, imperfect, defective, inferior, substandard, faulty, unacceptable, useless, worthless, inept, ineffectual; *inf* duff, ropy. 2 *smoking is a bad habit | it's bad for you* harmful, hurtful, damaging, dangerous, injurious, detrimental, destructive, ruinous, deleterious, unhealthy, unwholesome, poisonous. 3 *a bad man | leading a bad life* immoral, wicked, wrong, evil, sinful, corrupt, base, reprobate, depraved, dishonest, dishonourable, crooked. 4 *a bad child* naughty, mischievous, disobedient, unruly, wayward, refractory. 5 *bad weather | having a bad time* disagreeable, unpleasant, unwelcome, uncomfortable, nasty, terrible, dreadful, adverse, grim, gloomy, unfortunate, unfavourable, unlucky, distressing. 6 *a bad time for house-buying* adverse, difficult, unfavourable, unfortunate, unsuitable, inappropriate, inapt. 7 *a bad mistake/accident* serious, severe, grave, disastrous, terrible, critical, acute. 8 *bad eggs | meat going bad* rotten, off, decayed, mouldy, putrid, tainted, contaminated, putrescent, putrefacient. 9 *an invalid feeling bad* ill, unwell, sick, poorly, indisposed, ailing, weak, feeble, diseased; *inf* under the weather, below par. 10 *feeling bad about their actions* sorry, apologetic, regretful, conscience-stricken, contrite, remorseful, guilty, penitent, rueful, sad, upset. 11 *a bad cheque* worthless, invalid, counterfeit, false, spurious, fraudulent, fake; *inf* bogus, phoney. **not bad** all right, quite good, passable, tolerable, fair, average, moderate; *inf* OK, so-so.

badge n 1 *a badge on a cap/blazer* crest, emblem, insignia, device, shield, escutcheon, brand. 2 *showing the badge of servility* mark, sign, symbol, indication, indicator, signal, characteristic, trademark.

badger v pester, harass, plague, torment, bother, provoke, hound, nag, chivvy, goad, bully, importune, harry; *inf* bug, hassle.

badinage n banter, repartee, wordplay, raillery, chaff, drollery, waggery; pleasantries; *inf* joshing, kidding, ribbing, ragging.

badly adv 1 *do the job badly* poorly, wrongly, incorrectly, unsatisfactorily, inadequately, imperfectly, defectively, faultily, ineptly, inefficiently, shoddily, carelessly, ineffectually. 2 *work out badly* unsuccessfully, unfortunately, unhappily, unluckily, unfavourably. 3 *badly hurt/defeated* greatly, deeply, severely, seriously, extremely, intensely, exceedingly, gravely, acutely. **4** *behave badly* naughtily, wrongly, immorally, wickedly, improperly, evilly, criminally. **5** *want something badly* very much, greatly, exceedingly, extremely, enormously, tremendously, considerably.

baffle v **1** *baffled by the problem* puzzle, perplex, mystify, nonplus, stump, flummox, confound, dumbfound, bamboozle, bewilder, confuse, amaze, stagger, stun. **2** *baffle their plans* thwart, frustrate, foil, balk, check, block, hinder, obstruct, bar, prevent, deflect, divert.

bag n receptacle; handbag, shoulder bag, case, suitcase, briefcase, attaché case, grip, flight bag, backpack, rucksack, haversack, satchel, duffel bag.

bag v **1** *bag three pheasants* catch, capture, shoot, kill, trap, snare, land. **2** *bag good seats* acquire, obtain, get, keep, come by, secure. **3** *the trousers bagged* sag, hang loosely, bulge, swell, balloon, fill out, inflate.

baggage n luggage, gear, equipment, pack; belongings, things, suitcases, bags, effects, paraphernalia, trappings, impedimenta, accoutrements.

baggy adj loose, slack, roomy, oversize, shapeless, ill-fitting, sagging, seated, bulging, ballooning, floppy.

bail n *pay the prisoner's bail* surety, security, bond, guarantee, warranty, pledge, collateral.

bail v **bail out, bale out 1** *bail them out of their financial difficulties* help, assist, aid, rescue, relieve, give/lend a helping hand to. **2** *they bailed out before the crash* escape, get out, withdraw, retreat, beat a retreat, quit.

bait n **1** *used as bait for the fish/mice* lure, decoy, troll, plug. **2** *low prices as bait for the consumer* attraction, lure, incentive, snare, temptation; allurement, enticement, incitement, inducement.

bait v *bait the prisoner* torment, persecute, badger, plague, harry, harass, hound, provoke, tease, annoy, irritate; *inf* hassle, needle, give a hard time to, wind up, nark.

bake v **1** *bake the bread/meat* cook. **2** *earth baked by the sun* scorch, burn, sear, parch, dry, desiccate, fire.

balance n **1** *weigh it on the balance* scales, weighing machine. **2** *maintain the balance of international power* equilibrium, evenness, symmetry, parity, equity, equipoise, correspondence, uniformity, equivalence. **3** *I tripped and lost my balance* steadiness, stability. **4** *people of ability and balance* compo-

sure, poise, equanimity, aplomb, stability, assurance, confidence, self-possession, coolness, level-headedness, sang-froid. **5** *her practicality acts as a balance to his genius* counterbalance, countercheck, counterweight, stabilizer, compensation, recompense, ballast, make-weight. **6** *pay the balance of the account | collect the balance of the order* remainder, rest, residue, difference, surplus, excess. **in the balance** uncertain, at a turning-point, critical, at a crisis. **on balance** taking everything into consideration, considering everything, all in all.

balance v **1** *balancing the book on her head* steady, stabilize, poise. **2** *the weights must balance each other | advantages balancing disadvantages* counterbalance, counterweigh, counteract, offset, equalize, neutralize, compensate for, make up for, counterpoise. **3** *the profit and loss columns must balance | leisure and work time must balance* correspond, match, be level/parallel. **4** *balance the advantages and disadvantages* weigh, compare, evaluate, consider, deliberate, assess, appraise, estimate, review.

balcony n **1** *the balcony of a villa* veranda, terrace, portico, loggia. **2** *the balcony of a theatre* gallery, upper circle; *inf* the gods.

bald adj **1** *a shining bald head* hairless, baldheaded, depilated, glabrous. **2** *a bald landscape* barren, treeless, bare, uncovered, stark, exposed, bleak, unsheltered. **3** *a concise bald statement* blunt, direct, forthright, straight, straightforward, downright, outright, plain, simple, unadorned, unvarnished, unembellished, stark, severe, austere.

balderdash n nonsense, rubbish, twaddle, drivel, foolishness, gibberish, bunkum, claptrap, stuff and nonsense; *inf* bunk, piffle, hot air, bilge, bosh, cobblers, poppycock, rot, tommy-rot, bullshit, crap, guff, balls.

bale n bundle, truss, pack, parcel, load.

bale v **bale out** *see* BAIL v bail out.

baleful adj threatening, menacing, evil, wicked, malevolent, malignant, sinister, venomous, harmful, injurious, dangerous, deadly, noxious, pernicious.

balk v **1** *balk at the high fence* refuse, demur, hesitate over, draw back from, flinch/shrink/shy from, jib, recoil, evade, shirk, dodge, resist, eschew. **2** *balk their advance* hinder, prevent, impede, obstruct, thwart, foil, check, stop, halt, bar, block, forestall, frustrate, baffle.

ball[1] n **1** *a rubber ball | a ball of wool* sphere, globe, orb, globule, spheroid. **2** *cannon ball* projectile; shot, grapeshot, bullet, pellet, slug.

ball[2] n **1** *a fancy-dress ball* dance, social gathering; *inf* hop. **2** *they had a ball* great time; fun.

ballad n folk-song, song, broadside, ditty.

ballast n stabilizer, weight, counterweight; packing, filling.

balloon n *travel in a balloon* hot-air balloon, airship, dirigible, Zeppelin, blimp, montgolfier.

balloon v *skirts ballooning* swell out, puff out, fill out, billow, blow up, inflate, belly.

ballot n vote, poll, election, referendum, plebiscite; voting, polling.

ballyhoo n **1** *disturbed by the ballyhoo from the party* fuss, commotion. to-do, hullabaloo, racket. **2** *a lot of ballyhoo about the new film* publicity, propaganda, promotion, build-up; *inf* hype.

balm n **1** *apply balm to the burns* ointment, lotion, cream, salve, emollient, embrocation, liniment, unguent, balsam. **2** *balm for a troubled mind* remedy, curative, cure, restorative, palliative, anodyne, solace, consolation, comfort.

balmy adj **1** *balmy breezes* mild, gentle, temperate, calm, tranquil, soothing, soft, fragrant, scented, perfumed. **2** *a balmy idea* foolish, stupid. *see* BARMY.

bamboozle v **1** *bamboozled by their actions* puzzle, perplex, mystify, baffle, stump, bewilder, confuse, confound. **2** *bamboozle them into agreeing* trick, cheat, deceive, delude, hoodwink, mislead, hoax, fool, dupe, defraud, swindle; *inf* gull, con.

ban v *ban smoking* prohibit, forbid, veto, disallow, bar, debar, outlaw, proscribe, suppress, interdict, reject, restrict, banish.

ban n *impose a ban on smoking* prohibition, veto, bar, embargo, boycott, proscription, interdict, interdiction, suppression, stoppage, restriction, taboo; censorship, banishment.

banal adj hackneyed, trite, clichéd, cliché-ridden, commonplace, platitudinous, humdrum, stock, stereotyped, pedestrian, unoriginal, unimaginative, stale, uninspired, prosaic, dull, everyday, ordinary, tired, inane, fatuous, jejune; *inf* old hat.

banality n **1** *the banality of his remarks* triteness, platitudinousness, pedestrianism, lack of originality, unimaginativeness, staleness, prosaicness, dullness, ordinariness, fatuity. *see* BANAL. **2** *talking in banalities* cliché, trite phrase, platitude, truism, bromide, triviality.

band[1] n **1** *iron/rubber band* bond, binding, cord, strap, tie, connection, link, chain, thong, fetter, manacle, shackle, ligature, ring, hoop. **2** *a band round the waist/hair* belt, cord, braid, sash, girdle, ribbon, fillet, cincture; waistband, headband, hatband, wristband, sweatband. **3** *a band of white on the black* strip, stripe, streak, line, bar, striation.

band[2] n **1** *a band of robbers* group, troop, company, gang, mob, pack, bunch, body, gathering, crowd, horde, throng, assembly, assemblage, association, society, club, clique, set, coterie. **2** *a singer with the band* | *a brass/jazz band* musical group, group, pop group, combo, ensemble, orchestra.

band[2] v *band together* join, group, unite, merge, combine, team up, gather, ally, affiliate, associate, federate, consolidate.

bandage n dressing, gauze, compress, plaster, ligature; *Trademark* Elastoplast.

bandage v bind, bind up, dress, cover, plaster.

bandit n robber, brigand, outlaw, desperado, hijacker, plunderer, marauder, gangster, criminal, crook, thief, gunman, highwayman, footpad, pirate, racketeer.

bandy adj *having bandy legs* bandy-legged, bowed, bow-legged, curved, crooked, bent, misshapen.

bandy v **1** *bandy words* exchange, swap, trade, interchange, barter, reciprocate. **2** *bandy rumours about* circulate, spread, pass, toss about, disseminate.

bane n ruin, death, ruination, destruction, scourge, torment, plague, affliction, calamity, despair, misery, woe, trouble, nuisance, trial, burden, blight, curse, nightmare, *bête noir*.

bang **1** *a loud bang* explosive noise, report, burst, boom, clash, clang, peal, clap, pop, slam, thud, thump. **2** *a bang on the head* blow, bump, hit, slap, punch, knock, stroke, smack, whack, rap, cuff, box, buffet; *inf* wallop, bash, sock.

bang v **1** *bang the table* | *banged her nose* hit, strike, beat, thump, hammer, knock, rap, pound, thud, pummel, whack; *inf* bash. **2** *bang the door* slam, crash, clatter. **3** *the fireworks banged* explode, burst, blow up, detonate, pop, resound, echo.

bang adv **1** *fell bang on the floor* | *bang went her hopes* noisily, violently, suddenly, abruptly. **2** *bang in the middle* precisely, right, exactly, absolutely, directly; *inf* slap-bang, smack. **3** *bang up to date* completely, totally, right, absolutely.

bangle n bracelet, wristlet, anklet, armlet.

banish v **1** *banish from the country* exile, deport, expel, eject, drive away, expatriate, cast out, outlaw, transport, oust, evict, throw out, exclude, proscribe, excommunicate. **2** *banished from her presence* | *banish fear* dismiss, drive/send away, dispel, oust, cast/shut out, get rid of, ban, bar, exclude, eliminate, dislodge.

banishment n exile, deportation, expulsion, expatriation, transportation, proscription. *see* BANISH 1.

banisters npl handrail, railing, rail, balustrade; balusters.

bank¹ n *a grassy bank* slope, rise, incline, gradient, mound, hillock, knoll. **2** *a river/canal bank* edge, side, shore, brink, margin, embankment.

bank¹ v *bank an aircraft* tilt, slope, slant, incline, pitch. **bank up 1** *bank up the leaves* | *snow banked up* pile/heap up, stack up, gather, accumulate. **2** *bank up the fire/flames* damp down, stifle.

bank² n **1** *borrow from the bank* financial institution; commercial bank, high-street bank, clearing bank, merchant bank, savings bank, building society. **2** *empty the child's bank* piggy bank, cash-box, safe, strongbox, coffer. **3** *the card-game bank* kitty, pool, pot. **4** *a bank of information* | *blood bank* store, reserve, accumulation, stock, stockpile, reservoir, supply, fund, hoard, storehouse, repository, depository.

bank² v **1** *bank the money* deposit, save, save up, keep, lay by, put aside, put by for a rainy day; *inf* salt away, stash away. **2** *bank with the national bank* deal with, do business with, invest with. **bank on/upon** rely on, count on, depend on, lean on, trust, believe in, have/place confidence in, pin one's hopes on.

bank³ n *a bank of switches* row, line, tier, array, group, series, chain, course, progression, rank, succession.

bankrupt adj **1** *bankrupt businessmen/businesses* insolvent, failed, ruined, penurious, impecunious, financially embarrassed, distressed, in the red; *inf* on the rocks, broke, hard up, on one's uppers. **2** *bankrupt of funds/ideas* lacking, in need of, deficient in, wanting, without, deprived of, bereft of, exhausted of, depleted of.

bankrupt v ruin, beggar, cripple, impoverish; *inf* bust.

bankruptcy n insolvency, liquidation, indebtedness, failure, ruin, ruination, disaster, penury; straitened circumstances.

banner n **1** *the king's banner* flag, standard, pennant, pennon, gonfalon. **2** *the banners in the procession* placard, sign.

banquet n dinner, dinner party, feast, meal, party, repast, treat, revel.

banter n *indulge in light-hearted banter* repartee, *badinage*, chaff, teasing, joking, jesting, jocularity, raillery, wordplay, mockery, ridicule, persiflage; pleasantries; *inf* kidding, ribbing, joshing.

banter v *bantering not insulting* chaff, tease, joke, jest, mock, ridicule, make fun of, twit; *inf* kid, rib, rag, josh.

baptism n **1** *the baptism of the child* christening, naming, immersion, sprinkling; *fml* aspersing. **2** *survive his baptism as a teacher* debut, initiation, introduction, inauguration, launch, beginning, commencement, rite of passage.

baptize v **1** *baptize a baby* christen, name, immerse, sprinkle. **2** *baptize as a teacher* initiate, introduce, inaugurate, launch.

bar n **1** *an iron bar* | *a window bar* rod, pole, stake, stick, batten, shaft, rail, pale, paling, spar, crosspiece. **2** *a bar of soap/gold* block, cake, wedge, lump. **3** *no bar to promotion* | *colour bar* obstacle, barrier, obstruction, hindrance, impediment, check, stop, deterrent, drawback, stumbling block, fly in the ointment. **4** *prisoner at the bar* | *the bar of the House of Commons* barrier, rail, railing, barricade. **5** *members of the Bar* barristers, advocates; counsel. **6** *bar of light* band, strip, line, belt, streak, stripe. **7** *a ship stuck on a bar* shoal, shallow, reef, sandbank, ridge, ledge, shelf. **8** *drinking in a bar* pub, public house, inn, tavern; saloon, snug, lounge. **9** *sandwich/breakfast bar* counter, table, buffet.

bar v **1** *bar the door* bolt, lock, fasten, padlock, secure, latch. **2** *barred from entering* | *barred from the competition* debar, prohibit, preclude, forbid, ban, exclude, keep out, block, impede; obstruct, hinder, restrain, check, stop, defer.

bar prep *bar a few* except, excepting, except for, with the exception of, apart from, besides, other than, excluding, barring, omitting, leaving out.

barb n **1** *a barb in one's finger* thorn, needle, spike, prickle, bristle, prong, point, spicule. **2** *the barbs of his rival* insult, sneer, gibe, affront; scoffing, scorn, sarcasm, contumely; *inf* dig.

barbarian n **1** *knights defeating the barbarians* savage, brute, wild man/woman, troglodyte, monster. **2** *a classroom full of bar-*

barians ruffian, lout, vandal, hooligan, boor, ignoramus, philistine, yahoo.

barbarian adj **1** *barbarian tribes* savage, uncivilized, primitive, brutish, wild, heathen. **2** *barbarian football supporters* loutish, hooligan, boorish, uncivilized, wild, rough, coarse, gross, uncouth, vulgar, philistine.

barbaric adj **1** *barbaric tribes* savage, uncivilized, primitive. *see* BARBARIAN adj 1. **2** *barbaric customs* brutal, savage, cruel, vicious, fierce, ferocious, bestial, barbarous, murderous, inhuman, ruthless, remorseless.

barbarism n **1** *the barbarism of ancient tribes* savagery, uncivilizedness, primitiveness, brutishness, heathenism. **2** *the barbarism of the punishment* brutality, savagery, cruelty, barbarity. *see* BARBARITY 1. **3** *a speech full of barbarisms* misuse, misusage, misapplication, corruption, catachresis; error, slip, solecism.

barbarity n **1** *the barbarity of the punishment* brutality, savagery, cruelty, viciousness, bestiality, inhumanity, ruthlessness. **2** *barbarities committed* atrocity, brutality, outrage, enormity.

barbarous adj **1** *barbarous tribes* savage, uncivilized, barbarian. *see* BARBARIAN adj 1. **2** *barbarous punishment* brutal, savage, cruel, barbaric. *see* BARBARIC adj 2. **3** *barbarous tastes* unrefined, unsophisticated, uncultivated, uncultured, ignorant, vulgar, crude, uncouth, coarse.

barbecue n *hold a barbecue* picnic, alfresco lunch/dinner, outdoor meal.

barbecue v *barbecue the steaks* grill, charcoal, broil.

bare adj **1** *sunbathing bare | a bare chest* naked, stark naked, nude, uncovered, exposed, unclothed, undressed, unclad, stripped, denuded. **2** *a bare room* empty, vacant, unfurnished, unadorned, uncovered, stark, austere, unembellished. **3** *a bare landscape* bleak, unsheltered, unprotected, unshielded, desolate, barren, treeless, without vegetation. **4** *the bare facts* simple, plain, bald, basic, essential, straightforward, stark, unvarnished, unembellished, cold, hard, sheer, literal. **5** *the bare minimum* mere, basic, meagre, scanty, inadequate. **6** *a cupboard bare of food* without, lacking, devoid of, wanting, destitute of.

barefaced adj blatant, flagrant, glaring, arrant, shameless, brazen, bold, impudent, insolent, audacious, brash, open, undisguised, unconcealed, transparent, patent, manifest, palpable.

barely adv hardly, scarcely, only just, just, by the skin of one's teeth.

bargain n **1** *make a bargain* agreement, contract, pact, transaction, deal, treaty, negotiation, arrangement, compact, covenant, concordant, understanding, pledge, promise, engagement. **2** *get a bargain* discount, reduction, good buy, sales article; *inf* snip, steal, giveaway. **into the bargain** *into the bargain it rained* moreover, besides, also, over and above that, additionally, as well.

bargain v *buyer and seller were bargaining* haggle, barter, deal, trade, traffic. **bargain for** *more than we bargained for* expect, anticipate, be prepared for, allow for, take into account/consideration, forsee, look for, contemplate, imagine. **bargain on** *bargaining on victory* rely on, depend on, count on, bank on, hope for, plan on, expect, anticipate.

barge n *a barge holiday* canal boat, flatboat, narrow boat, lighter, houseboat.

barge v **1** *barge in during prayers* burst in, break in, intrude, interrupt; *inf* butt in, horn in. **2** *people barging into each other* bump, crash, collide, cannon, plough, smash. **3** *she was barging around* lurch, rush about.

bark[1] n *the bark of a tree/shrub* covering, cortex, husk, coating, casing, crust, skin; hide, rind, shell, hull, sheath, integument.

bark[1] v *bark one's shin* scrape, skin, abrade, rub, excoriate, strip, flay, shave.

bark[2] v **1** *the dog barked* howl, woof, yelp, yap, bay, growl, snarl. **2** *the teacher barked at the pupils* shout, yell, bawl, thunder, scream, screech, shriek, snap, snarl, bluster.

barmy adj *a barmy idea | a barmy old man* mad, foolish, stupid, idiotic, insane, silly, odd, queer, eccentric, peculiar, weird; *inf* crazy, daft, batty, nutty, loony, loopy, crackpot, goofy, off one's head, round the bend/twist, out to lunch.

barn n outbuilding, shed, outhouse, shelter, byre; stables, mews.

baron n **1** *the king and the barons* noble, nobleman, aristocrat, peer, lord. **2** *oil barons* tycoon, magnate, executive, industrialist, financier, captain of industry.

baroque adj ornate, elaborate, decorated, embellished, flamboyant, ostentatious, extravagant, showy, fussy, florid, convoluted; rococo, grotesque.

barracks npl billet, garrison, camp, encampment, fort, cantonment, casern; quarters.

barrage n **1** *soldiers killed by the enemy's barrage* gunfire, bombardment, shelling, battery, cannonade, volley, broadside, salvo, fusillade, wall/curtain/barrier of fire. **2** *a barrage of criticism* deluge, stream, storm, torrent, onslaught, flood, avalanche, hail, burst, mass, abundance, superabundance, plethora, profusion.

barrel n cask, keg, butt, vat, tun, tub, tank, firkin, hogshead.

barren adj **1** *a barren woman* infertile, sterile, childless; *fml* infecund. **2** *barren land* infertile, unproductive, uncultivable, unfruitful, arid, desert, waste, desolate. **3** *barren discussion | barren way of life* uninteresting, boring, dull, uninspiring, stale, prosaic, futile, worthless, useless, valueless, unrewarding, purposeless, vapid, lacklustre.

barricade n *barricades keeping back the crowd* barrier, obstacle, blockade, bar, fence, obstruction, roadblock, bulwark, stockade, rampart, palisade.

barricade v *barricade the door/house* blockade, obstruct, close up, bar, shut off/in, fence in, defend, fortify.

barrier n **1** *the barrier in the car park* barricade, bar, fence, railing, obstacle, blockade, roadblock. **2** *a barrier to success | the language barrier* obstacle, hindrance, impediment, drawback, check, hurdle, restriction, stumbling-block, handicap, difficulty, restraint.

barrister n professional pleader, counsel; *Scots* advocate; *Amer* attorney.

barter n *an economy based on barter* trading, trade-off, exchange, swapping, bargaining, haggling, trafficking.

barter v *barter his horse for food* trade, trade off, exchange, swap, bargain, traffic, haggle.

base n **1** *the base of a column* foundation, support, prop, stay, stand, pedestal, rest, bottom, bed, foot, substructure, plinth. **2** *paints with an oil base* basis, core, essence, component, essential, fundamental, root, heart, principal, source, origin. **3** *mountaineers setting up a base* headquarters, centre, camp, site, station, settlement, post, starting-point.

base v **1** *based on historical facts* found, build, construct, form, establish, ground, rest, root, fasten, hinge, derive. **2** *based in London* locate, station, situate, post, place, install.

base adj **1** *base motives* low, mean, sordid, bad, wrong, immoral, dishonourable, evil, wicked, debased, sinful, unprincipled, dissolute, disreputable, reprobate, corrupt, depraved, vile, shameful, scandalous, infa-

mous, ignoble, vulgar, foul, despicable, contemptible. **2** *base servitude* menial, subservient, servile, lowly, mean, low, slavish, grovelling, snivelling, cowering, wretched, downtrodden, obsequious, sycophantic. **3** *base coin* debased, alloyed, impure, adulterated, spurious, counterfeit, pinchbeck. **4** *base metal* low-value, inferior, nonprecious.

baseless adj groundless, unfounded, foundationless, unsupported, unsubstantiated, uncorroborated, unconfirmed, unjustifiable, unjustified.

basement n cellar, crypt, vault, garden flat; *inf* below stairs.

bashful adj shy, reserved, diffident, retiring, modest, self-conscious, coy, demure, reticent, self-effacing, hesitant, shrinking, backward, timid, timorous, abashed, blushing, embarrassed, shamefaced, sheepish.

bashfulness n shyness, reserve, modesty, self-consciousness, coyness, demureness, reticence, self-effacement, hesitancy, timidity, timorousness, embrrassment. *see* BASHFUL.

basic adj **1** *basic principles* fundamental, elementary, rudimentary, primary, radical, key, central, essential, vital, necessary, indispensable, intrinsic, underlying. **2** *basic salary* bottom, lowest-level, lowest, starting, ground, undermost, without commission. **3** *pretty basic accommodation* plain, simple, spartan, sparse, stark, unadorned, without frills.

basically adv fundamentally, at bottom, at heart, intrinsically, essentially, inherently, primarily, firstly, radically, mostly, for the most part, in the main, in substance.

basics npl fundamentals, essentials, facts, hard facts, rudiments, principles, practicalities, realities, the ABC; *inf* nitty-gritty, brass tacks, nuts and bolts.

basin n **1** *carry water in a basin* container, receptacle, vessel; bowl, dish, pan. **2** *the river basin* bed, channel.

basis n **1** *no scientific basis for the statement* support, foundation, base, footing, reasoning, back-up; grounds. **2** *the statement will form the basis of the discussion* starting-point, premise, fundamental point/principle, principal constituent, main ingredient; groundwork, core, essence. **3** *on a part-time basis* footing, procedure, condition, status, position.

bask v **1** *bask in the sunshine* lie, laze, lounge, relax, loll, sunbathe, sun/warm oneself. **2** *bask in their admiration* luxuriate, revel, wallow, enjoy, delight, take pleasure in, rejoice in, relish, savour, indulge oneself in.

basket n container, receptacle; hamper, creel, pannier, punnet.

bass adj deep, deep-pitched, deep-toned, low, low-pitched, low-toned, resonant, sonorous.

bastard n **1** *the King's bastard* illegitimate child, love child, natural son/daughter. **2** *a rotten bastard* scoundrel, cad, blackguard, villain, rascal.

bastard adj **1** *bastard child* illegitimate, natural. **2** *a bastard language* adulterated, impure, hybrid, alloyed, inferior, imperfect, spurious, counterfeit, artificial, sham, false, fake.

bastardize v *bastardize the language/coinage* debase, degrade, devalue, depreciate, corrupt, adulterate, defile, contaminate.

bastion n **1** *the bastion of a fort* projection, bulwark, rampart, parapet. **2** *storm the enemy bastion* fort, fortress, citadel, keep, stronghold, garrison. **3** *the last bastion of privilege* protection, protector, defence, defender, support, supporter, prop, mainstay, stronghold.

batch n group, quantity, lot, bunch, accumulation, mass, cluster, set, collection, assemblage, pack, crowd, aggregate, conglomeration.

bath n **1** *install a bath* bath-tub, tub, hip-bath, sitz-bath, whirlpool bath, sauna, steam bath. **2** *have a bath* wash, soak, dip, shower, douche, soaping.

bath v *bath every day* have/take a bath, bathe, wash, soak, shower, douche, soap oneself.

bathe v **1** *bathe the wound* clean, cleanse, wash, soak, steep, immerse, wet, moisten, rinse, suffuse. **2** *bathe in the sea* swim, take a dip. **3** *bathed in sunlight* envelope, suffuse.

bathe n *a quick bathe in the sea* swim, dip.

bathing-costume n bathing-suit, swim-suit, swimming-costume, swimming-trunks, trunks, bikini, monokini, one-piece swimsuit; *Aust inf* cossie, bathers.

bathos n anticlimax, let-down; sentimentality, mawkishness.

baton n stick, bar, wand, rod, staff, club, truncheon, mace.

battalion n **1** *military battalions* unit; troops, forces; garrison, division, regiment, brigade, squadron, company, platoon, section, detachment, contingent, legion. **2** *battalions of protesters* crowd, mob, throng, horde, multitude, herd, host.

batten¹ n *a wooden batten* board, strip, bar, bolt, clamp.

batten¹ v *batten down the hatches* fasten, fix, secure.

batten² v *batten on the poor* thrive/flourish/prosper/fatten/increase/wax at the expense of, be a parasite on.

batter v **1** *battering their children* hit, strike, beat, bash, assault, wallop, thump, thrash, lash, pound, deliver/rain blows on, pummel, buffet, belabour, abuse; *inf* whack. **2** *countries battered by war* damage, injure, hurt, harm, bruise, wound, crush, shatter, smash, destroy, demolish, ruin, squash, impair, mar, spoil.

battered adj *battered children* beaten, assaulted, thrashed, abused. *see* BATTER 1.

battery n **1** *a battery of tests/units* series, sequence, set, cycle, chain, string, progression, succession. **2** *convicted of assault and battery* attack, mugging, grievous bodily harm, GBH, beating, striking, thumping, thrashing, bashing; aggression. **3** *the military battery* artillery, cannonry; guns, cannons.

battle n **1** *battle between enemy forces* war, armed conflict, conflict, fight, clash, contest, struggle, skirmish, engagement, affray, encounter, confrontation, collision, meeting, campaign, crusade, tussle, scuffle, scrap, mêlée; fighting, warfare, combat, action; hostilities. **2** *a battle of wills* clash, conflict, contest, competition, tournament, struggle, disagreement, argument, dispute, controversy, debate; dissension, altercation, strife.

battle v **1** *battling against the elements | battle for a pay-rise* fight, struggle, strive, combat, contend, war, feud. **2** *battle one's way through the wind* fight, struggle, labour, push. **3** *neighbours constantly battling* fight, war, feud, argue, quarrel, disagree, bicker, wrangle, cross swords, lock horns.

battleaxe n *a battleaxe of a headmistress* dragon, harridan, tartar, martinet, termagant, virago, shrew, fury, stramullion.

battle-cry n **1** *the battle-cry of the invaders* war cry, war whoop, rallying call. **2** *the battle-cry of the women's movement* slogan, motto, watchword, catchword, catchphrase, shibboleth.

battlefield n battleground, front, battlefront, battle lines, field of operations, field of battle, combat zone, theatre/arena of war, battle stations.

battlement n parapet, rampart, balustrade, wall, bulwark, barbican, bartizan; fortification, breastwork, crenellation, circumvallation, outwork.

battleship n warship, man-of-war, ship of the line, gunboat, cruiser, battle cruiser, capital ship.

batty adj mad, foolish, stupid, idiotic, insane, silly, odd, queer, eccentric; *inf* crazy, daft, bats, barmy, bonkers, nutty, nuts, crackers, dotty, potty, loony, off one's head, round the bend, out to lunch.

bauble n trinket, knick-knack, trifle, ornament, toy, plaything, gewgaw, gimcrack, bagatelle, kickshaw, bibelot.

bawd n prostitute, whore, street-walker, woman of the streets; *inf* hooker.

bawdy adj pornographic, obscene, vulgar, indecent, blue, racy, titillating, crude, coarse, rude, gross, ribald, lewd, dirty, filthy, smutty, off-colour, naughty, suggestive, indelicate, unseemly, indecorous, salacious, erotic, prurient, lascivious, licentious, risqué, scatalogical, Rabelaisian, near the bone, near the knuckle; *inf* raunchy, nudge-nudge.

bawl v **1** *he bawled a reply | bawl to his brother* shout, call/cry out, yell, roar, bellow, screech, scream, howl, whoop, vociferate; *Amer inf* holler. **2** *a child bawling* cry, sob, weep, wail, blubber, snivel, squall.

bay¹ n *ships moored in the bay* cove, inlet, indentation, natural harbour, gulf, basin, sound, arm, bight, firth.

bay² n *a table in the bay* alcove, recess, niche, opening, nook.

bay³ n *the bay of the hounds* baying, howl, howling, bark, cry, ululation. *see* BAY³ v.

bay³ v *hounds baying* howl, bark, yelp, cry, growl, bellow, roar, clamour, ululate.

bayonet n blade, knife, dagger, poniard.

bazaar n **1** *an eastern bazaar* market, market-place, mart, exchange, souk. **2** *the church bazaar* fête, fair, sale, bring-and-buy.

be v **1** *will there be many such people at the party?* exist, live, be alive, have life/being, breathe. **2** *the lamp is on the table | Mary is at the farm* be situated, be located, dwell, reside. **3** *the concert is tomorrow* take place, occur, come about, come to pass, arise, crop up, transpire, befall. **4** *she has been there all her life* remain, stay, last, continue, survive, endure, persist, prevail, obtain. **5** *he was at church* attend, be present, be at.

beach n *sunbathing at/on the beach* seaside, coast; seashore, shore, water's edge, coastline, sands, sand, shingle, strand, plage, lido, margin; *fml* littoral.

beachcomber n **1** *beachcombers collecting wood* scavenger, forager, gatherer, collector, accumulator. **2** *beachcombers and other homeless* tramp, vagrant, hobo, wanderer, scrounger; *inf* bum.

beached adj aground, ashore, grounded, high and dry, stuck fast, marooned, stranded, wrecked, abandoned.

beacon n warning fire/light, signal fire/light, bonfire, smoke signal, flare, beam, rocket, signal, danger signal; lighthouse, pharos, watchtower.

bead n **1** *glass beads* ball, pellet, pill, globule, spheroid, oval. **2** *beads of sweat* drop, droplet, bubble, blob, dot, glob, dewdrop, teardrop.

beads npl **1** *wearing beads and earrings* string of beads, necklace, necklet, pendant, choker. **2** *telling one's beads* rosary, chaplet.

beak n **1** *a bird's beak* bill, nib, mandible; *dial* neb. **2** *the fellow's large beak* nose, snout, proboscis. **3** *a ship's beak* prow, bow, bowsprit, stem, rostrum, ram.

beam n **1** *the roof beams* board, timber, plank, joist, rafter, girder, spar, support, lath, scantling. **2** *a beam of light* ray, shaft, stream, streak, flash, gleam, glow, glimmer, glint, flare, bar; radiation, emission. **3** *a beam of happiness* smile, grin, bright look.

beam v **1** *light beamed from the window* emit, radiate, shine. **2** *beam radio/television programmes* broadcast, transmit, direct, aim. **3** *beaming from ear to ear* smile, grin.

bear v **1** *bear gifts* carry, bring, transport, move, convey, take, fetch, haul; *inf* tote. **2** *bear tales* spread, transmit, carry. **3** *bear a signature/inscription* carry, display, show, be marked with. **4** *bear a crop* yield, produce, give forth, give, provide, supply, generate. **5** *bear a son* give birth to, breed, bring forth, beget, engender. **6** *bear the cost* carry, sustain, support, shoulder, uphold. **7** *cannot bear his attitude | can't bear the thought* stand, endorse, tolerate, put up with, abide, stomach, permit, allow, admit, brook; *Scots* thole. **8** *much pain to bear* suffer, endure, undergo, tolerate, put up with, experience, go through, support, weather. **9** *bear a grudge | bear evil thoughts* have, hold, harbour, possess, entertain, cherish. **10** *bear left* veer, curve, go, move, turn, fork, diverge, deviate, bend. **bear out** *bear out the facts* confirm, corroborate, substantiate, endorse, vindicate, give credence to, support, ratify, warrant, uphold, justify, prove, authenticate, verify. **bear up** *bearing up against disaster* cope, persevere, carry on, manage, endure, withstand, grin and bear.

bear with *bear with the delay* tolerate, put up with, endure, make allowances for, be patient with, show forbearance towards, suffer.

bearable adj endurable, tolerable, supportable, sufferable, sustainable, admissible, passable, manageable.

beard n *a man with a beard* facial hair, whiskers, bristle, stubble, designer stubble, five o'clock shadow; full beard, goatee, beaver, imperial, Vandyke, Abe Lincoln, side-whiskers, sideboards, sideburns, mutton-chops.

beard v *beard the management* brave, confront, face, challenge, come face-to-face with, oppose, defy, stand up against, dare, throw down the gauntlet at.

bearded adj unshaven, whiskered, bewhiskered, stubbly, bristly, hairy, hirsute, bushy, shaggy.

bearer n **1** *a coffin/luggage bearer* carrier, porter, conveyor, transporter. **2** *a bearer of good news* messenger, agent, runner, courier. **3** *pay the bearer of the cheque* payee, consignee, beneficiary.

bearing n **1** *having a distinguished bearing* deportment, posture, carriage, gait. **2** *her bearing throughout the trial* attitude, behaviour, manner, demeanour, air, aspect, mien. **3** *the bearing of a ship* course, direction. **4** *have a bearing on the case* relevance, pertinence, connection. **5** *lose one's bearings* orientation, location, position, situation, whereabouts, track, way.

beast n **1** *a beast of the jungle* animal, creature, brute; mammal, quadruped. **2** *a cruel beast to his wife and children* brute, monster, savage, swine, pig, ogre, fiend, sadist, barbarian.

beastly adj **1** *a beastly apparition* beastlike, bestial, animal, animal-like, brutal, theroid. **2** *a beastly cold* awful, terrible, horrible, rotten, nasty, foul, unpleasant, disagreeable, vile; *inf* shitty.

beat v **1** *beat the drum* bang, hit, strike, pound. **2** *he beats the dog/child* hit, strike, batter, thump, wallop, hammer, punch, knock, thrash, pound, pummel, slap, smack, flay, whip, lash, chastise, thwack, cuff, bruise, buffet, box, cudgel, club, birch, maul, pelt, drub; *inf* belt, bash, whack, clout, slug, tan, biff, bop, lay into, do over, knock about, rough up, fill in. **3** *their hearts beating* throb, pound, thump, pulsate, pulse, palpitate, vibrate, tremble. **4** *the bird's wings beat* flap, flutter, quiver, tremble, vibrate. **5** *beat the eggs* mix, blend, whip, whisk, stir. **6** *waves beating against/on*

the shore strike, dash, break against, lap, wash. **7** *beating metal into rods* hammer, forge, form, shape, work, stamp, fashion, model. **8** *beat a path* tread, tramp, trample, wear, track, groove. **9** *beat the opposition* defeat, conquer, vanquish, trounce, rout, overpower, overcome, overwhelm, overthrow, subdue, quash; *inf* lick. **10** *beat the record* outdo, surpass, exceed, eclipse, transcend, top, outstrip. **beat up** assault, attack, mug, batter, thrash; *inf* knock about/around, do over, work over, clobber, rough up, duff up, fill in.

beat n **1** *the beat of the drum* | *three beats of the carpet* bang, banging, stroke, striking, blow, hit, punch, pound, pummel, slap, smack, thwack. **2** *the beat of his heart* throb, throbbing, pounding, pulsating, pulsing, beating, thumping, palpitating, vibrating, vibration. **3** *musical/metrical beat* rhythm, stress, metre, time, measure, accent, cadence. **4** *policeman's beat* round, circuit, course, route, way, path, orbit.

beat adj *dead beat after the walk* exhausted, tired, worn out, fatigued, wearied, spent.

beaten adj **1** *the beaten contestant/army* defeated, vanquished, trounced, routed, overcome, overwhelmed, overpowered, bested, quashed; *inf* licked. **2** *beaten metal* hammered, forged, formed, shaped, worked. *see* BEAT v 7. **3** *beaten paths* trodden, well-trodden, much-trodden, well-used, much-travelled, trampled, worn, well-worn. **4** *the beaten eggs/cake mixture* mixed, blended, whipped, whisked, stirred, frothy, foamy.

beatific adj **1** *a beatific existence* blessed, blissful, heavenly, celestial, paradisical. **2** *children with beatific smiles* rapturous, joyful, ecstatic, blissful, happy, glad.

beating n **1** *the savage beating of the children* hitting, striking, battering, thrashing; corporal punishment, chastisement; *inf* belting, bashing, pasting. *see* BEAT v 2. **2** *recovering from their beating by the opposition* defeat, conquest, vanquishing, trouncing, overthrow, downfall. *see* BEAT v 9. **3** *the beating of their hearts* throb, pulsating, pulse, pulsing, palpitating. *see* BEAT n 2. **4** *the beating of the waves* striking, dashing, breaking. *see* BEAT v 6.

beatitude n blessedness, bliss, ecstasy, exaltation, supreme happiness, divine rapture, sainthood.

beau n **1** *his sister's beau* boyfriend, sweetheart, lover, fiancé, partner, significant other, escort, admirer, suitor, follower; *lit* swain. **2** *beaux of the eighteenth century* dandy, fop, coxcomb, gallant, cavalier, popinjay; *inf* swell, toff.

beautiful adj ravishing, gorgeous, stunning, alluring, lovely, attractive, pretty, handsome, good-looking, pleasing, comely, charming, delightful, glamorous, appealing, fair, fine, becoming, seemly, winsome, graceful, elegant, exquisite; *fml* beauteous, pulchritudinous; *Scots* bonny.

beautify v **1** *beautify the surroundings* adorn, embellish, enhance, decorate, ornament, garnish, gild, smarten, prettify, glamorize. **2** *beautify oneself* apply make-up/cosmetics, prettify, glamorize, prink, primp, preen; *inf* do/doll oneself up.

beauty n **1** *the beauty of the women/surroundings* loveliness, attractiveness, prettiness, handsomeness, allure, allurement, charm, glamour, grace, artistry, symmetry; *fml* beauteousness, pulchritude. *see* BEAUTIFUL. **2** *the sisters were all great beauties* belle, charmer, enchantress, seductress, *femme fatale*, Venus, goddess; *inf* good-looker, lovely, stunner, knockout, dish, cracker. **3** *the beauty of the scheme* attraction, good thing, advantage, benefit, asset, strong point, boon, blessing. **beaver away** work hard/assiduously/conscientiously, exert oneself, persevere, persist, hammer away; *inf* slog, peg away, plug away, graft, get one's head down.

becalmed adj motionless, at a halt, still, at a standstill, stranded, stuck, marooned.

because conj *he left because he was ill* since, as, in view of the fact that, owing to the fact that, seeing that. **because of** *leaving because of ill health* on account of, as a result of, owing to, by reason of, as a consequence of, thanks to, by virtue of.

beckon v **1** *beckon to the waiter* signal, gesture, make a gesture, gesticulate, motion, wave, nod, call summon, bid. **2** *the sea beckons him* draw, pull, call, invite, attract, tempt, entice, allure, coax, persuade, induce.

become v **1** *she became rich | become a scientist* come to be, turn out to be, grow, grow into, mature into, evolve into, pass into, change into, turn into, alter into, transform into, be transformed into, be converted into, metamorphose into. **2** *the dress becomes her* suit, flatter, look good on, set off, enhance, embellish, ornament, grace. **3** *it ill becomes you to behave like that* befit, behove, suit, be suitable/fitting to. **4** *what became of him?* happen to, befell, be the fate/lot of.

becoming adj **1** *a becoming hat* flattering, comely, attractive, lovely, pretty, handsome, stylish, elegant, chic, tasteful. **2** *hardly becoming behaviour* suitable, fitting, appropriate, apt, proper, right, decent, seemly, worthy, decorous, graceful, *comme il faut*. **3** *behaviour becoming to a teacher* befitting, suitable for, appropriate to, in keeping with, compatible with, consistent with, congruous with.

bed n **1** *she liked to sleep in her own bed* divan, bunk, cot, berth, couch, pallet, palliasse, hammock, litter, stretcher, double bed, single bed, four-poster, bunk-bed, camp-bed, water-bed, crib, cradle, bassinet; *inf* kip, sack. **2** *the importance of bed in relationships* sexual intercourse, sex, lovemaking, physical relationship, intimacy, conjugality. **3** *a flower bed* plot, area, lot, patch, space, border, strip, row. **4** *a bed of concrete* base, basis, foundation, bottom, support, substructure, substratum; groundwork.

bed v **1** *bricks bedded in concrete* embed, set, fix into, insert, inlay, implant, bury, base, establish, found. **2** *anxious to bed a woman* go to bed with, have sex with, sleep with, seduce, spend the night with. **3** *bed out the pansies* plant, plant out, set in beds/soil.

bed down 1 *bed down in the shed* go to bed/sleep, retire, settle down, have a nap; *inf* turn in, hit the sack/hay. **2** *bed the children down* put to bed, tuck in, settle down, say goodnight to.

bedclothes npl bedding, bedcovers, covers; blankets, duvets, quilts, eiderdowns, counterpanes, sheets, bed linen, linen.

bedeck v deck, decorate, adorn, ornament, trim, festoon, array, embellish, garnish.

bedevil v afflict, torment, beset, plague, harass, distress, trouble, worry, frustrate, annoy, vex, irritate, irk, pester, torture.

bedlam n uproar, pandemonium, commotion, confusion, furore, hubbub, clamour, disorder, chaos, turmoil, tumult, noise, disarray; *inf* madhouse.

bedraggled adj muddy, muddied, wet, dirty, messy, sodden, soaking, soaking wet, soaked, drenched, saturated, dripping, soggy, splashed, soiled, stained, dishevelled, disordered, untidy, unkempt.

bedridden adj confined to bed, housebound; *inf* laid up, flat on one's back.

bedrock n **1** *the bedrock beneath the soil* substratum, solid, foundation, rock bed. **2** *the finance is at bedrock* lowest point/level, rock bottom, nadir. **3** *the bedrock of their beliefs | get down to bedrock* basis, core, nitty-gritty; basics, fundamentals, essentials.

beef n **1** *more noted for his beef than his brain* brawn, muscle, muscularity, heftiness, burliness, bulk, physique, strength, powerfulness, robustness. *see* BEEFY 1. **2** *tired of the beef about the traffic* complaint, grumbling, grumble, criticism, objection, protestation, grievance; *inf* griping, gripe, grousing, grouse, nit-picking.

beefy adj **1** *beefy wrestler* brawny, muscular, hefty, burly, hulking, strapping, thickset, solid, strong, powerful, heavy, robust, sturdy, stocky. **2** *a beefy young woman* heavy, solid, fat, chubby, plump, overweight, stout, buxom, obese, fleshy, podgy, rotund, portly, corpulent, paunchy, dumpy.

beer n mild, bitter, ale, real ale, stout, lager.

beetling adj *beetling brows/cliffs* overhanging, projecting, protruding, sticking/jutting out.

befall v happen, occur, take place, chance, crop up, arise, come about, come to pass, transpire, materialize, ensue, follow, result, fall, supervene.

befitting adj fitting, fit, suitable, appropriate, apt, proper, right, seemly, decorous.

before adv **1** *we've met before* previously, earlier, formerly, hitherto, in the past. **2** *they went on before* ahead, in front, in advance, in the lead.

before prep **1** *before lunch | before the war | before going out* prior to, previous to, earlier than. **2** *B comes before C* in front of, ahead of, in advance of. **3** *said before witnesses* in the presence of, in the sight of, before the very eyes of, under the nose of. **4** *death before dishonour* in preference to, rather/sooner than.

beforehand adv before, before now, earlier, previously, in advance, in readiness, ahead of time, already, sooner.

befriend v make friends with, make a friend of, look after, protect, keep an eye on, help, assist, aid, support, back, stand by, side with, encourage, sustain, uphold, succour, advise.

befuddled adj **1** *befuddled old people* confused, dazed, groggy, muddled, bewildered, fuddled, stunned, numbed; *inf* woozy. **2** *befuddled drunks* drunk, drunken, intoxicated, inebriated, stupefied, muddled, dazed, bewildered; *inf* blotto, bombed, out of it, blitzed, legless, paralytic, smashed, wasted, wrecked, zonked.

beg v **1** *beg in order to live* ask for money, solicit money, seek charity/alms, cadge, scrounge; *inf* sponge, bum; *Amer inf* mooch. **2** *beg for money/mercy* ask for, request, seek, look for, desire, crave, solicit, plead for, beseech, entreat, importune, plead with.

beget v **1** *fathers begetting able sons* father, sire, procreate, generate, engender, spawn. **2** *differing opinion begetting strife* cause, give rise to, bring, bring about, create, produce, result in, occasion, effect, bring to pass, engender.

beggar n **1** *accosted by a beggar* tramp, vagrant, mendicant, cadger, vagabond, pauper, down-and-out, derelict; *inf* scrounger, sponger, bum; *Amer inf* moocher, bag lady, hobo. **2** *what a lucky beggar!* fellow, person, bloke, individual, creature.

beggar v *a nation beggared by war* impoverish, make poor, reduce to poverty, bankrupt, pauperize.

beggarly adj **1** *a beggarly wage* inadequate, meagre, paltry, slight, miserly, pitiful, pathetic, stingy, niggardly, ungenerous, contemptible, despicable. **2** *beggarly accommodation* miserable, wretched, mean, base, vile, foul, sordid, shabby, shoddy, despicable. **3** *beggarly creatures* poor, poverty-stricken, impoverished, needy, penniless, destitute, indigent, impecunious.

beggary n poverty, penury, destitution, indigence, impecuniousness, bankruptcy, insolvency, need, neediness, pauperism, pauperdom, mendicancy, vagrancy.

begin v **1** *begin work* start, commence, set about, embark on, initiate, set in motion, institute, inaugurate, get ahead with. **2** *begin now!* start, commence, go ahead, get going; *inf* fire away, kick off, get the show on the road, get to it, start the ball rolling, take the plunge. **3** *trouble began immediately* start, commence, arise, come into existence/being, happen, occur, spring up, crop up, emerge, dawn, appear, originate. **4** *rain began to fall* start, commence.

beginner n novice, trainee, learner, apprentice, student, pupil, recruit, raw recruit, tiro, fledgling, neophyte, initiate, novitiate, tenderfoot, fresher; *inf* greenhorn, rookie.

beginning n **1** *from the beginning of time | beginning of the match* start, starting-point, commencement, onset, outset, dawn, birth, inception, conception, emergence, rise; *inf* kick-off. **2** *the beginning of the book* start, commencement, first part, opening, prelude, preface, introduction. **3** *philosophy having its beginnings in religion* origin, source, starting-point, fountainhead, spring, mainspring, embryo, germ; roots, seeds.

begrudge v **1** *begrudge him his success* grudge, envy, resent, be jealous of. **2** *begrudge the time spent* grudge, resent, give unwillingly, be dissatisfied with.

beguile v 1 *beguiled by her beauty* charm, attract, delight, please, enchant, bewitch, seduce. 2 *the comedian beguiling the audience* entertain, amuse, occupy, absorb, engage, distract, divert, engross. 3 *beguile the hours* pass, while away, spend.

beguiling adj *a beguiling smile* charming, attractive, delightful, pleasing, enchanting, bewitching, seductive.

behalf n 1 *acting on behalf of his client | on his client's behalf* for, representing, as a representative of, in the interests of, in the name of, in place of. 2 *collecting on behalf of the blind* in the interests of, for, for the benefit/good/sake of, to the advantage/profit of, on account of, in support of.

behave v 1 *the children must behave themselves* act correctly/properly, conduct oneself well, act in a polite way, show good manners, mind one's manners. 2 *they behaved well/badly* act, perform, conduct oneself, acquit oneself, comport oneself. 3 *she behaves like a dictator | the engine behaved badly/well* act, perform, function, operate.

behaviour n 1 *criticize his children's/opponent's behaviour* conduct, way of acting, response, comportment, deportment, bearing; actions, manners, ways. 2 *the erratic behaviour of the machine | study the behaviour of bees* action, performance, functioning, operation, reaction, response; actions, reactions, responses.

behead v decapitate, guillotine.

behest n order, command, decree, edict, rule, ruling, directive, direction, instruction, request, requirement, charge, bidding, wish, dictate, injunction, mandate, precept.

behind prep 1 *behind the woodshed* at the back of, at the rear of, beyond, on the further side of, on the other side of; *Amer* in back of. 2 *running behind us* after, at the back of, to the rear of, following, in the wake of, close upon, hard on the heels of. 3 *trouble is behind us* now in the past of. 4 *behind the others in English* less advanced than, slower than, weaker than, inferior to. 5 *behind schedule* late in relation to, later than, after. 6 *he's behind the trouble* at the back of, at the bottom of, responsible for, causing, the cause/source of, giving rise to, instigating, initiating, urging. 7 *we're behind you all the way* backing, supporting, for, on the side of, in agreement with, financing.

behind adv 1 *with the dog running behind* after, at the back, in the rear, in the wake. 2 *look behind* to/towards the back/rear, over one's shoulder. 3 *stay/leave behind* after-

wards, remaining after departure. 4 *we're behind so don't stop* behindhand, behind schedule, late, slow. 5 *behind in payments* behindhand, in arrears, overdue, in debt.

behindhand adv 1 *behindhand in paying* late, slow, dilatory, tardy, remiss. 2 *too behindhand for modern times* out of date, old-fashioned, behind the times/time, backward.

behold v look at, see, observe, view, watch, survey, gaze at, stare at, scan, witness, regard, contemplate, inspect, take note of, mark, consider, pay heed to.

behold interj look!, see!, lo!, *ecce!*

beholden adj indebted, under obligation, obligated, bound, owing, thankful, grateful.

behove v 1 *it behoves him to take over his father's business* be incumbent on, be obligatory for, be necessary for, be essential for, be expected of, be advisable for, be sensible for, be wise for. 2 *it ill behoves him to have an affair with his brother's fiancé* be fitting, befit, be suitable, be seemly, be proper, be decorous.

beige adj fawn, mushroom, neutral, buff, sand, oatmeal, ecru, biscuit, coffee, *café au lait.*

being n 1 *the purpose of our being* existence, living, life, animation, animateness, actuality, life blood, vital force, entity; *fml* esse. 2 *shocked to the depths of her being* spirit, soul, nature, essence, substance, entity, quiddity. 3 *a sentient being* creature, person, human being, human, individual, mortal, living thing, man, animal.

belabour v 1 *belabour the boy with blows* beat, hit, strike, batter, attack, flog, thrash, whip, lambaste, bombard, pelt. 2 *belabour the actor* criticize, attack, berate, censure, castigate, lay into, flay. 3 *belabour the point* overelaborate, discuss at length, go through with a fine-tooth comb; *inf* flog to death.

belated adj late, overdue, behindhand, behind time, delayed, tardy, unpunctual.

belch v 1 eruct, eructate, hiccup, break wind, bring up wind, burp. 2 *factory chimneys belching smoke* give out, give off, pour out, discharge, emit, issue, vent, gush, eject, disgorge, spew out, vomit, cough up; *fml* disembogue.

beleaguered adj 1 *a beleaguered city* besieged, under siege, surrounded, blockaded, encircled, hemmed in, under attack. 2 *a film star beleaguered by fans* besieged, badgered, harassed, bothered, beset, pestered, plagued, tormented, vexed, set upon, persecuted.

belie v **1** *her smile belied her anger* contradict, deny, give the lie to, disprove, refute, gainsay, confute. **2** *the official report belies the enormity of the disaster* misrepresent, falsify, distort, conceal, disguise. **3** *her performance belied our faith in her* fail to justify, be at odds with, not to live up to.

belief n **1** *it is my belief that she is dead* opinion, feeling, impression, view, viewpoint, conviction, judgement, thinking, way of thinking, theory, notion. **2** *no belief in his powers* faith, credence, freedom from doubt, trust, reliance, confidence. **3** *Christian/political beliefs* doctrine, teaching, creed, dogma, ideology, principles, tenet, canon, credence, credo.

believable adj credible, plausible, likely, creditable, probable, possible, acceptable, within the bounds of possibility, conceivable, imaginable.

believe v **1** *I don't believe you* consider honest/true, be convinced by, trust. **2** *don't believe his story* regard/accept as true, accept, credit, be convinced by, trust; *inf* swallow, fall for, buy. **3** *I believe he's retired | believed the earth to be flat* think, be of the opinion that, understand, suppose, assume, presume, conjecture, surmise, reckon, guess, postulate/theorize that. **believe in 1** *believe in God/fairies* be convinced/sure/persuaded of the existence of. **2** *believe in alternative medicine* have faith in, trust, be convinced/persuaded by, set store by, value, swear by; *inf* rate.

believer n follower, adherent, supporter, disciple, upholder.

belittle v disparage, decry, deprecate, undervalue, underrate, underestimate, minimize, make light of, slight, detract from, downgrade, play down, depreciate, derogate, scoff at, sneer at.

belligerent adj **1** *in a belligerent mood | a belligerent young woman quarrelling with everyone* aggressive, antagonistic, militant, pugnacious, quarrelsome, argumentative, disputatious, combative, quick-tempered, hot-tempered, irascible, captious. **2** *belligerent nations* at war, warring, battling, contending, militant, martial, warlike, warmongering.

bellow v roar, shout, bawl, yell, shriek, howl, scream, screech, call, cry out, whoop, ululate; *Amer inf* holler.

belly n **1** *a stabbing pain in the belly* stomach, abdomen, paunch; intestines, innards; *inf* tummy, tum, insides, guts, corporation, pot, bread basket, pot belly, beer belly. **2** *the belly of the planes* underside, underpart, underbelly.

belly v *the sail bellied out* swell, billow, bulge, fill out, balloon out, bag.

belong v **1** *where does this book belong?* have a place/home, be classified, be categorized. **2** *they do not belong here* fit in, be suited to, have a rightful place, be part of; *inf* go, click. **belong to 1** *the house belongs to them* be owned by, be the property of, be under the ownership of, be held by, be at the disposal of. **2** *she belongs to the sailing club/it belongs to the cat family* be a member of, be affiliated to, be allied to, be associated with, be connected to, be included in, be an adherent of. **3** *this lid belongs to that box* be part of, be an adjunct of, attach to, go with, relate to, be relevant to.

belongings npl possessions, personal possessions/effects, effects, goods, accoutrements, appurtenances; property, paraphernalia; *inf* gear, things, stuff, junk.

beloved adj **1** *my beloved children* dear, dearest, darling, adored, much loved, precious, cherished, sweet, treasured, prized, worshipped, idolized. **2** *beloved of everyone* loved, liked, adored, admired, respected, valued, esteemed, revered.

beloved n *married her beloved* sweetheart, fiancé, fiancée, boyfriend, girlfriend, love, lover, betrothed; *fml* paramour, inamorato, inamorata.

below adv **1** *we could see it down below* further/lower down, in/to a lower position, underneath, beneath, downstairs. **2** *for further details see below* further on, at a later point/place.

below prep **1** *skirts below the knee | the valley below the village* further down than, lower than, under, underneath. **2** *prices/temperatures below average* less/lower than. **3** *ranking below him | work below standard* lower than, inferior to, subordinate to. **4** *that remark was below you* unworthy of, undignified for, degrading to, not befitting, unsuitable for, inappropriate for.

belt n **1** *wearing a leather belt* girdle, sash, cummerbund, waistband, band, girth; *fml* cincture, baldric, cestus. **2** *mechanics mending the machine's belt* band, conveyor belt, fan belt. **3** *America's corn belt* zone, region, area, district, tract, stretch, extent. **4** *a belt of white in the black* strip, band, stripe, bar, line, stria. **5** *a belt across the ears* blow, punch, smack, bang, thump; *inf* clout, bash, wallop.

belt v **1** *with her waist belted* encircle, gird, encompass, bind, tie, fasten. **2** *teachers can no longer belt children with a strap* strap, flog, whip, lash, cane, thrash, scourge, flail, birch, flagellate. **3** *belt the child with his fists* strike, hit, beat, punch, smack, thrash, thump, bang, batter, pound, pummel; *inf* bash, sock, slog.

bemoan v lament, mourn, deplore, regret, grieve for/over, express sorrow for, sorrow for, bewail, sigh over, weep over, repent, rue.

bemused adj *a bemused look | bemused by the events* confused, bewildered, puzzled, perplexed, dazed, stunned, muddled, overwhelmed, disconcerted, discomfited, astonished, astounded, stupefied, preoccupied, absent-minded, engrossed.

bench n 1 *pupils sitting on a bench* form, long seat, seat, pew, stall, settle. 2 *carpenters at the bench* workbench, worktable, table, counter, trestle table, board. 3 *appear before the bench* court, bar, courtroom, tribunal. 4 *a member of the bench* judges, magistrates; judiciary, judicature.

benchmark n standard, point of reference, gauge, criterion, norm, guideline, specification, model, pattern, touchstone, yardstick.

bend v 1 *bend the iron bar | bend the little finger* make crooked/curved, curve, crook, flex, twist, bow, arch, contort. 2 *the road bends to the right* curve, turn, twist, swerve, veer, incline, diverge, curl, deviate, deflect, coil, spiral, loop, divagate, incurvate. 3 *bend down over the sink* stoop, crouch, lean down/over, bow, hunch. 4 *bend them to our will* mould, shape, direct, force, influence, compel, persuade, subdue, sway, subjugate. 5 *bend our steps homeward | bend our minds to the task* direct, point, aim, turn, train, steer, set.

bend n curve, turn, corner, twist, angle, arc, swerve, veer, incline, divergence, crook, curling, deviation, deflection, coiling, spiral, loop, hook, incurvation; dogleg, hairpin bend, zigzag.

beneath adv *upon the earth beneath* below, underneath, in/to a lower place.

beneath prep 1 *sank beneath the waves* below, under, underneath, lower than. 2 *people beneath her socially* below, lower than, inferior to, secondary to, subservient to. 3 *beneath him to behave like that* below, unworthy of, undignified for, unbefitting, unbecoming.

benediction n 1 *say a benediction* blessing, prayer, invocation; grace, thanksgiving; *lit* orison. 2 *a state of benediction* blessedness, grace, beatitude, bliss, favour.

benefactor n helper, patron, backer, sponsor, supporter, promoter, contributor, subscriber, subsidizer, donor, philanthropist, sympathizer, well-wisher; *inf* angel, friend.

beneficial adj advantageous, favourable, propitious, promising, helpful, accommodating, obliging, useful, serviceable, valuable, profitable, rewarding, gainful.

beneficiary n heir, inheritor, recipient, receiver, legatee, payee, assignee.

benefit n 1 *for the benefit of all* advantage, good, gain, profit, help, aid, assistance, interest, welfare, well-being, betterment, asset, avail, use, service. 2 *enjoy the benefits of modern medicine* advantage, blessing, boon; good, usefulness; perquisites, perks, fringe benefits. 3 *living on government benefit* social security payment, insurance money, allowance, sick pay, unemployment benefit.

benefit v 1 *discoveries benefiting society* do good to, be of service to, profit, serve, be of advantage to, advantage, help, aid, assist, contribute to, better, improve, advance, further. 2 *criminals benefiting from their deeds* profit, gain, reap benefits, make money; *inf* cash in, make a killing.

benevolence n kindness, kind-heartedness, goodness, generosity, charity, altruism, goodwill, humanity, compassion, humanitarianism, philanthropism.

benevolent adj 1 *a benevolent attitude to others* kind, kindly, kind-hearted, friendly, amiable, benign, generous, magnanimous, warm-hearted, considerate, thoughtful, well-meaning, altruistic, humane, compassionate, caring, sympathetic, obliging, helpful, humanitarian, philanthropic, bountiful, liberal, bounteous, beneficent. 2 *a benevolent institution* charitable, non-profit making, alms-giving, eleemosynary.

benighted adj ignorant, unenlightened, backward, uncivilized, uncultured, uneducated, illiterate, crude.

benign adj 1 *with a benign smile/attitude* kind, kindly, friendly, amiable, genial, gracious, cordial, generous, benevolent, gentle, sympathetic, obliging, accommodating, liberal. 2 *a benign climate* healthy, health-giving, wholesome, salubrious, temperate, pleasant, mild, balmy, agreeable, refreshing. 3 *in benign circumstances* favourable, advantageous, beneficial, propitious, auspicious, lucky, opportune, providential, encouraging, conducive, helpful, benevolent. 4 *a benign tumour* non-malignant, non-dangerous, harmless, innocent, curable, remediable, treatable.

bent adj 1 *a bent iron rod* curved, crooked, twisted, bowed, angled, warped, contorted. 2 *bent backs* bowed, arched, curved, stooped, hunched. 3 *a bent policeman* corrupt, dishonest, crooked, fraudulent, unprincipled, bribable. **4** *her husband turned out to be bent* homosexual, gay; *inf* homo, queer. **bent on** *bent on winning* determined to, set on, insistent on, resolved to, fixed on, inclined to, disposed to, predisposed to.

bent n *an artistic bent | a bent for design* inclination, predisposition, disposition, leaning, tendency, penchant, bias, predilection, proclivity, propensity, talent, gift, flair, ability, knack, aptitude, facility, skill, capability, capacity, forte, genius.

bequeath v **1** *bequeath her estate to her son* leave, will, make over, cede, endow on, bestow on, consign, commit, entrust, grant, transfer. **2** *ideas bequeathed by previous inventors* hand down/on, pass down/on, impart, transmit.

bequest n **1** *receive a bequest of £10,000* legacy, inheritance, endowment, estate, heritage, bestowal, bequeathal, gift, settlement. **2** *the bequest of her collection to the museum* bequeathing, leaving, willing, making over. *see* BEQUEATH 1.

berate v scold, rebuke, reprimand, chide, reprove, upbraid, castigate, censure, criticize, rail at, harangue, lambaste, fulminate against, vituperate, read the riot act to; *inf* tell off, give a dressing-down to, tear a strip off, bawl out.

bereave v *an accident bereaved him of his wife* deprive, dispossess, rob, divest, strip.

bereavement n **1** *sympathize with her in her bereavement* loss, deprivation, dispossession. *see* BEREAVE. **2** *a series of family bereavements* death, loss, passing, demise, decease, quietus.

bereft adj **bereft of** deprived of, robbed of, cut off from, parted from, devoid of, wanting, lacking, destitute of, minus.

berserk adj frenzied, mad, insane, crazed, crazy, out of one's mind, hysterical, maniacal, manic, raving, wild, enraged, raging, uncontrollable, amok, unrestrainable; *inf* off one's head, hyper, ape.

berth n **1** *book a berth in the train/ship* bed, bunk, sleeping accommodation, billet, hammock, cot. **2** *ships at their berths* anchorage, mooring, docking site. **3** *a cosy well-paid berth* job, post, position, situation, place, employment, appointment, living.

berth v **1** *berth the ship* moor, dock, anchor, land, tie up. **2** *the ship berthed at dawn* moor, dock, drop anchor, land. **3** *the yacht berths four* provide beds for, sleep, accommodate, put up, house, shelter, lodge.

beseech v beg, implore, entreat, ask, plead with, pray, petition, call upon, appeal to, supplicate, invoke, adjure, crave.

beset v **1** *beset with fears | beset by anxieties* attack, harass, assail, worry, plague, bother, trouble, perplex, torment, pester, hound, nag, bedevil, harry. **2** *beset by enemy forces* surround, besiege, encircle, ring round, enclose, encompass, hem in, shut/fence in.

besetting adj *his besetting sins* habitual, persistent, inveterate, prevalent, troublesome, harassing, assailing.

beside prep **1** *walking beside him* alongside, by/at the side of, abreast of, next to, with, by, adjacent to, cheek by jowl with, close to, near, nearby, neighbouring, next door to. **2** *beside her work, his is poor* compared with, in comparison with, next to, against, contrasted with, in contrast to/with.

beside oneself berserk, frenzied, in a frenzy, mad, frantic, demented, insane, crazed, crazy, deranged, unbalanced, distraught, hysterical, uncontrolled, unrestrained, unhinged, out of one's mind.

beside the point irrelevant, not applicable, immaterial.

besides adv *besides, it's too late* also, in addition, additionally, moreover, furthermore, further, as well, too, what's more.

besides prep *three besides him* apart from, in addition to, aside from, over and above, other than, not counting, excluding, not including, without.

besiege v **1** *the castle besieged by the enemy* lay siege to, beleaguer, blockade, surround, encircle, encompass. **2** *film stars besieged by reporters* surround, enclose, encircle, beleaguer, beset, shut in, hem in, fence in, hedge in. **3** *besieged with doubts* harass, assail, worry, plague, beset. *see* BESET 1.

besmirch v *besmirch the firm's reputation* sully, slander, defame, tarnish, smear, stain, taint, damage.

besotted adj **1** *besotted with his secretary* infatuated with, doting on, smitten, bewitched by, spellbound by, hypnotized by. **2** *besotted with drink* befuddled, drunk, intoxicated, stupefied, confused, muddled, dazed, bewildered; *inf* blotto, bombed, out of it, smashed, zonked. *see* BEFUDDLED.

bespatter v spatter, splatter, splash, bedaub, muddy, dirty, smear, besmirch, besprinkle, sully, begrime, befoul.

bespeak v **1** *actions bespeaking a kind heart* give evidence of, indicate, demonstrate, exhibit, show, display, evince, manifest, reveal, betray, testify to, bear witness to. **2** *bespeak goods* order in advance, order pre-arranged, reserve, requisition.

best adj **1** *the best player* foremost, finest, leading, top, chief, principal, highest, worthiest, supreme, superlative, unsurpassed, unexcelled, excellent, first-class, first-rate, outstanding, pre-eminent; *inf* crack, ace. **2** *the best way to get there* | *the best solution* right, correct, most fitting, most suitable, most desirable, apt, advantageous.

best adv **1** *he played best* in the best way, superlatively, unsurpassedly, excellently, outstandingly. **2** *he likes tennis best* to the highest/greatest degree, greatly, extremely. **3** *her behaviour is best ignored* most sensibly, most wisely, most suitably, most fittingly, most advantageously.

best n **1** *only the best may enter* finest, first class, top, cream, pick, flower, choice, élite. **2** *do your best* utmost, hardest, best endeavour; *inf* damnedest. **3** *at his best in the morning* peak, prime, top form, height, apex. **4** *the best of having a car* most favourable/advantageous/pleasant aspect, advantage, asset, blessing, boon. **5** *dressed in her best* best clothes, finery, finest clothes; *inf* Sunday best, best bib and tucker. **6** *give him my best* best wishes, regards, kindest regards, greetings, love.

best v *best the opposition* defeat, beat, conquer, get the better of, trounce, thrash, triumph over, get the upper hand of, prevail over, outdo, outclass, surpass, outwit, outsmart, worst; *inf* lick, make mincemeat of.

bestial adj **1** *bestial treatment of prisoners* brutish, savage, brutal, inhuman, beastly, barbarous, barbaric, abominable, atrocious, cruel, primitive, wild, heathen. **2** *bestial sexual practices* depraved, vile, sordid, degenerate, degraded, gross, carnal, lustful, lecherous, prurient, lascivious, lewd, crude. **3** *bestial shapes* beastlike, animal, theroid, theriomorphic.

bestow n give, present, confer on, grant, donate, endow with, hand over, allot, assign, consign, apportion, distribute, bequeath, impart, accord, award, honour with, entrust with, commit.

bestride v **1** *bestriding the horse* straddle, bestraddle, sit/stand astride. **2** *a bridge bestriding the river* straddle, span, extend across, pass over, cross.

bet v **1** *bet £100 that he wins* wager, gamble, stake, pledge, risk, venture, hazard, chance. **2** *he never bets* gamble, wager, speculate; *inf* punt. **3** *you can bet they've gone* be certain/sure, state confidently, predict.

bet n **1** *enter into a bet* wager, gamble, speculation, venture, game of chance, lottery, sweepstake, long shot. **2** *place a bet of £100* wager, stake, ante, pledge. **3** *my bet is that*

they'll go prediction, forecast, opinion, belief, feeling, view, theory. **4** *they're/that's our best bet* choice, option, alternative, selection, possibility, course of action.

bête noire n anathema, pet aversion, aversion, pet hate, bugbear, abomination.

betide v happen, occur, take place, befall, supervene, transpire, come to pass, ensue, chance.

betoken v **1** *white betokening chastity* indicate, denote, signify, suggest, evidence, typify, represent, show, demonstrate, manifest, bespeak. **2** *activities betokening war* augur, forebode, bode, portend, presage, foreshadow, prophesy, prognosticate, promise.

betray v **1** *betray one's friends* inform on/against, be disloyal/unfaithful to, treat treacherously, break faith with, break one's promise to; *inf* tell on, double-cross, stab in the back, sell down the river, sell out, blow the whistle on, squeal on. **2** *betray a secret* | *a smile betraying his feelings* reveal, disclose, divulge, give away, let slip, blurt out, blab, lay bare, bring to light, uncover, expose, exhibit, manifest, unmask. **3** *betrayed him into a wrong course of action* mislead, lead astray, delude, deceive, beguile, dupe, fool, hoodwink, cheat, trap, ensnare, gull, cozen. **4** *betrayed his mistress for another woman* abandon, desert, forsake, walk out on, jilt; *inf* leave flat.

betrayal n **1** *the betrayal of his friends* informing on/against, being disloyal to, breaking faith with; *inf* double-crossing. see BETRAY 1. **2** *the betrayal of a secret* | *betrayal of his feelings* revelation, disclosure, divulgence, giving away. see BETRAY 2. **3** *the betrayal into a wrong course of action* misleading, delusion, deception, duping, hoodwinking. see BETRAY 3. **4** *the betrayal of his mistress* abandonment, desertion, forsaking. see BETRAY 4. **5** *appalled by their betrayal* act of betrayal, breach of faith, bad faith, disloyalty, treachery, perfidy, duplicity, double-dealing, sedition, treason, subversion; *inf* double-crossing, back-stabbing, sell out, whistle-blowing.

betroth v engage, affiance, plight, contract, covenant; *lit* espouse.

betrothal n engagement, betrothment, marriage contract, plighting of one's truth, compact, covenant; *lit* espousal.

better adj **1** *the better players* finer, of higher quality, greater, superior, worthier, fitter. **2** *a better course of action* more fitting, more suitable, more appropriate, more desirable, more advantageous, more useful, more valuable. **3** *feeling better* healthier, fitter, less ill, stronger, well, cured, recovered, recovering, progressing, improving; *inf* mending, on the mend.

better adv **1** *he plays better now* in a better way, in a superior/finer way, to a higher standard. **2** *I understand him better* more, to a greater degree. **3** *her advice is better ignored* more sensibly, more wisely, more suitably, more fittingly, more advantageously.

better v **1** *better the lot of the poor* make better, raise, improve, ameliorate, advance, promote, forward, further, amend, rectify, relieve, reform, enhance, enrich. **2** *better the previous record* improve on, beat, surpass, exceed, top, cap, outstrip, outdo, excel, go one better than.

betterment n improvement, amelioration, furtherance, reform, enhancement, enrichment.

between prep **1** *standing between them | sharing things between them* in the middle of, amidst, in the midst of, among. **2** *somewhere between the two cities* on the way along, on the course connecting, in the space separating. **3** *the bond between mother and baby* connecting, linking, joining, uniting, allying. **4** *the difference between them* separating, distinguishing, differentiating, discriminating.

bevel n slope, slant, oblique, tilt, angle, cant, bezel, chamfer.

beverage n drink, potation, potable; refreshment, liquid, liquor; *inf* libation, bevvy.

bevy n **1** *a bevy of quails/birds* flock, flight. **2** *a bevy of beautiful girls* collection, gathering, assembly, array, galaxy, group, band, troupe, cluster; *inf* bunch, gaggle.

bewail v mourn, lament, grieve over, sorrow for/over, express woe/sorrow for, cry/weep over, wail/keen over, bemoan, regret, deplore, repent, rue, pine for.

beware v *you must beware | beware of thieves* be careful/wary, be cautious, be on one's guard, take heed, watch out, look out, watch/look/mind out for, be on the lookout/alert for.

bewilder v confuse, mix up, muddle, puzzle, perplex, baffle, mystify, nonplus, disconcert, confound, bemuse, daze, stupefy, befuddle, obfuscate; *inf* stump, bamboozle.

bewildered adj confused, muddled, puzzled, perplexed, nonplussed, uncertain, speechless, startled, taken aback, all at sea, thrown off balance. *see* BEWILDER.

bewitch v **1** *the wizard bewitched the prince* put a spell on, cast a spell over, enchant, entrance, curse; *Amer inf* hex. **2** *he was* bewitched by her beauty charm, enchant, beguile, captivate, entrance, fascinate, delight, allure, enrapture, spellbind, hypnotize, mesmerize, transfix.

bewitched adj charmed, enchanted, beguiled, captivated, entranced, fascinated, enraptured, spellbound, hypnotized, mesmerized.

beyond prep **1** *beyond the mountains* on the farther/far side of, on the other side of, further on than, past, after, over, behind. **2** *beyond midnight | beyond retirement age* after, past, later than, on the other side of. **3** *beyond our understanding/repair* outside the reach/range of, outside the limitations of, beyond the power/capacity of, surpassing. **4** *inflation beyond 10%* above, more than, greater than, exceeding, in excess of, over and above. **5** *notice nothing beyond his beard* other than, apart from, except.

beyond adv *what lies beyond | the mountains beyond* yonder, further on, far off, far away, at a distance, afar.

bias n **1** *cut on the bias* slant, cross, diagonal, skew, angle, oblique, slope. **2** *have a bias in favour of/against socialism | have a musical bias* tendency, inclination, leaning, bent, partiality, penchant, predisposition, propensity, proclivity, proneness, predilection, prejudice, bigotry, intolerance, narrowmindedness, one-sidedness.

bias v **1** *bias the judges* prejudice, influence, sway, predispose. **2** *bias their decision* prejudice, influence, sway, distort, bend, twist, warp, weight, predispose.

biased adj *a biased attitude* prejudiced, partial, one-sided, influenced, slanted, weighted, swayed, distorted, predisposed.

Bible n **1** *Christians studying the Bible* Holy Writ, the Holy Scriptures, the Good Book; New English Bible, Gideon Bible. **2** *the gardener's bible* authority, handbook, manual, guide, textbook, primer, vade-mecum.

bibliography n book list, list, catalogue, compilation, record.

bicker v wrangle, quarrel, argue, squabble, have a row, fight, fall out, have a disagreement, disagree, dispute, spar; *inf* row, scrap.

bicycle n bike, cycle; tandem, unicycle, tricycle, racer, mountain bike; *inf* push-bike, bone-shaker.

bid v **1** *bid £100 for the vase* offer, tender, proffer, propose, submit, put forward, advance. **2** *they bade him go* command, order, instruct, ask, tell, call for, direct, demand, enjoin, charge, summon, require, invite. **3** *bid them farewell* wish, greet, tell, call, say.

bid n **1** *put in a bid of £3000* offer, proposition, proffer, proposal, submission, tender, advance, ante, price, sum, amount. **2** *a bid for power* attempt, effort.

biddable adj obedient, amenable, tractable, complaisant, cooperative, teachable, docile, meek.

bidding n **1** *he left at his father's bidding* command, order, instruction, injunction, direction, demand, mandate, charge, summons, request, call, behest, invitation. **2** *present at the bidding* auction; making of bids, tendering; offers, tenders, proposals.

big adj **1** *a big garden/car* large, sizeable, great, huge, enormous, immense, vast, massive, extensive, substantial, spacious, colossal, gigantic, mammoth, prodigious. **2** *a big man* large, tall, bulky, burly, hulking, huge, enormous, muscular, beefy, brawny, strapping, thickset, heavy, solid, corpulent, fat, obese, stout, gargantuan, elephantine, Brobdingnagian. **3** *a big boy now* | *a big sister* grown-up, adult, grown, mature, elder. **4** *a big decision/moment* important, significant, serious, momentous, salient, weighty, paramount. **5** *a big figure in the movement* important, influential, powerful, prominent, outstanding, leading, well-known, principal, foremost, noteworthy, notable, eminent, distinguished. **6** *big ideas/talk* arrogant, pretentious, ambitious, inflated, pompous, proud, haughty, conceited, boastful, bragging, bombastic. **7** *a big heart* generous, kindly, kind-hearted, benevolent, magnanimous, unselfish, altruistic, philanthropic, beneficient, humane.

bigot n fanatic, zealot, sectarian, dogmatist, chauvinist, jingoist, racist, sexist.

bigoted adj prejudiced, intolerant, fanatical, narrow-minded, illiberal, biased, partial, one-sided, dogmatic, warped, twisted, jaundiced, chauvinistic, jingoistic, racist, sexist.

bigotry n prejudice, intolerance, fanaticism, narrow-mindedness, bias, partiality, dogmatism, discrimination, unfairness, injustice, chauvinism, jingoism, racism, sexism, provincialism. *see* BIGOTED.

bigwig n VIP, dignitary, notable, notability, personage, celebrity, panjandrum; *inf* somebody, heavyweight, big shot, big noise, big gun, big cheese, nob.

bilge n *don't talk bilge* rubbish, nonsense, drivel, gibberish, balderdash, bunkum,

hogwash, twaddle; *inf* rot, codswallop, poppycock, claptrap, piffle, guff, tosh.

bilious adj **1** *feeling bilious* liverish, out of sorts, queasy, nauseated, sick. **2** *of a bilious temperament* bad-tempered, ill-tempered, short-tempered, ill-humoured, cross, irritable, crotchety, grumpy, peevish, edgy, touchy, tetchy, crabby, cantankerous, testy, nasty; *inf* grouchy, ratty. **3** *bilious colours* violent, garish, distasteful, nauseating.

bilk v swindle, cheat, defraud, exploit, fleece, deceive, trick, bamboozle, rook, gull; *inf* con, do, diddle.

bill¹ n **1** *a bill for damages* | *a restaurant bill* account, invoice, statement, note/list of charges, reckoning, tally, score; *Amer* check; *Amer inf* tab. **2** *post no bills* | *distribute bills* poster, advertisement, flier, notice, announcement, leaflet, circular, handout, handbill, brochure, placard, bulletin, broadsheet, broadside; *inf* advert, ad. **3** *top of the bill* programme, playbill, list, listing, agenda, card, schedule, timetable, syllabus, roster, calendar, catalogue, inventory. **4** *a parliamentary bill* proposal, measure, projected/proposed law, piece of legislation.

bill¹ v **1** *bill them for the goods* invoice, send an invoice to, charge for, debit, send a statement to, tabulate/list costs/expenditure. **2** *bill it all over the building* advertise, announce, post, give notice of, put up in lights. **3** *bill it for tomorrow* programme, schedule, enter on the timetable, timetable, put on the agenda.

bill² n *a bird's bill* beak; *dial* neb.

billet n **1** *billets for soldiers* quarters, living quarters, barracks, rooms; accommodation, lodging, housing, cantonment. **2** *an easy well-paid billet* job, post, situation, position, office, appointment, commission, assignment; employment.

billet v *billet the soldiers in the town* accommodate, put up, lodge, house, quarter, station, shelter.

billow n wave, surge, swell, tide, rush, deluge, flood, breaker, roller.

billow v puff up, swell, fill out, balloon, belly, surge, roll.

billowy adj wavelike, swelling, surging, undulating, rolling, tossing, rising, rising and falling, ebbing and flowing.

bin n container, receptacle, box, can, crate.

bind v **1** *bind the sheaves together* | *with their legs bound* tie, tie up, fasten, secure, attach, rope, strap, truss, lash, tether, fetter, chain, hitch, wrap. **2** *bind the wound* bandage, dress, tape, wrap, cover, swathe, encase. **3** *bind the surfaces together* stick, glue, cement, paste. **4** *bind the seams with gold* edge, trim, hem, border, finish. **5** *bound to answer/secrecy* compel, obligate, oblige, constrain, force, impel, engage, require, prescribe. **6** *bound by family ties* constrain, restrain, restrict, hamper, hinder, inhibit, yoke.

bind n **1** *waiting for them is a bind* nuisance, bore, irritation, inconvenience, vexation; *inf* drag. **2** *we're in a bind over what to do* quandary, dilemma, predicament, difficulty, spot, tight spot.

binding adj *the agreement is binding* irrevocable, unalterable, compulsory, obligatory, indissoluble, imperative, mandatory, necessary, conclusive.

binge n spree, orgy, drinking/eating bout, fling; *inf* bender, jag, blinder.

biography n life history, life, life story, memoir, profile, account; *inf* bio.

bird n songbird, songster, warbler, fowl, fledgling, feathered friend; bird of prey.

birth n **1** *present at the child's birth* childbirth, delivery, parturition, confinement, nativity. **2** *the birth of jazz* origin, beginnings, start, source, emergence, commencement, fountainhead, genesis. **3** *of noble birth* origin, descent, ancestry, lineage, line, extraction, derivation, family, parentage, house, blood, breeding, genealogy, pedigree, heritage, patrimony, stock, race, strain, background.

birthmark n blemish, discoloration, naevus, patch, mole.

birthright n right, due, privilege, heritage, patrimony, legacy.

bisect v cut in half, halve, cut/divide/split in two, split down the middle, cleave, separate into two, bifurcate, dichotomize.

bisexual adj hermaphrodite, androgynous, epicene; *tech* monoclinous; *inf* AC/DC, swinging both ways, kicking with both feet, ambidextrous, bi.

bit¹ n **1** *bits of bread/cheese/sawdust* small piece, piece, section, part, segment, chunk, lump, hunk, portion, butt, stump, particle, fragment, atom, flake, sliver, chip, crumb, grain, speck, scrap, shred, trace, morsel, mouthful, iota, jot, tittle, whit, modicum, shard, hint, tinge, suggestion **2** *see you in a bit* little, little while, short time, moment, minute, second, instant, short spell, short period, flash, blink of an eye; *inf* jiffy, tick, before you know it, two shakes of a lamb's tail.

bit² n *a horse's bit/a tool's bit* restraint, restrainer, check, curb, brake, snaffle.

bitch n **1** *his wife's a real bitch* shrew, vixen, cat, virago, harpy, she-devil. **2** *this job's a real bitch* problem, difficulty, predicament, dilemma.

bitch v **1** *stop bitching about your work* complain, grumble, moan, find fault, find fault with, carp, grouse, whine; *inf* gripe, beef, bellyache. **2** *she's always bitching about her friends and relations* be spiteful about, blacken the name of, slander, decry, disparage, malign; *fml* calumniate. **3** *that workman bitches up everything* botch, bungle, spoil, ruin, wreck, make a mess of; *inf* mess up, screw up.

bitchy adj nasty, mean, spiteful, malicious, catty, vindictive, rancorous, venomous, snide, shrewish, vixenish, cruel, backbiting.

bite v **1** *bite into the food | bite one's nails* chew, munch, crunch, champ, masticate, eat; nibble at, gnaw at. **2** *dogs biting people* sink one's teeth into, nip, snap at, tear at, wound. **3** *insects biting them* sting, prick, pierce, puncture, wound. **4** *biting on his pipe* clamp, grip, hold on to. **5** *acids biting into the metal* eat into, corrode, burn, eat away at, erode, dissolve, wear away. **6** *measures beginning to bite* take effect, work, have results. **7** *fish biting | new clients not biting* take the bait, be lured, be enticed, be tempted, be allured. **8** *what's biting you?* annoy, irritate, bother, displease, peeve, provoke, vex; *inf* bug, get at, needle.

bite n **1** *the dog gave her a playful bite* nip, snap. **2** *suffering from insect bites* sting, prick, puncture, wound, lesion, itch, smarting. **3** *a bite of the apple/food* mouthful, piece, morsel, bit. **4** *have a bite to eat* snack, light meal, refreshment. **5** *the sauce had a bite to it* sharpness, spiciness, piquancy, pungency, edge; *inf* kick, punch.

biting adj **1** *biting winds* sharp, freezing, cold, bitterly cold, harsh, nipping, stinging, piercing, penetrating. **2** *biting words* sharp, bitter, cutting, caustic, sarcastic, scathing, trenchant, mordant, stinging, withering, incisive, acid.

bitter adj **1** *a bitter substance* acid, pungent, acrid, tart, sour, biting, harsh, unsweetened, vinegary, acetous, acerbic. **2** *a bitter old woman | feeling bitter* resentful, embittered, rancorous, acrimonious, piqued, ill-disposed, indignant, sullen, crabbed, sour, morose, begrudging, petulant, peevish, with a chip on one's shoulder. **3** *from bitter experience | bitter memories* painful, distressing, distressful, harrowing, heartbreaking, heart-rending, agonizing, unhappy, sad, poignant, grievous, tragic, galling, vexa-

tious. **4** *bitter north winds* biting, sharp,
intensely cold, freezing, harsh, stinging,
piercing, penetrating, fierce. **5** *bitter quar-
rels/controversy* virulent, acrimonious, hostile, antagonistic, spiteful, vicious,
rancorous, vindictive, malicious, malevolent, venomous.

bitterness n **1** *the bitterness of the medicine*
acidity, pungency, acridity, tartness, sourness, vinegariness, acerbity. *see* BITTER 1.
2 *the bitterness of the old woman* resentment,
resentfulness, embitteredness, rancour,
animosity, acrimony, grudge, sullenness,
crabbedness, sourness. *see* BITTER 2. **3** *the bitterness of the experience/memories* pain,
painfulness, distress, agony, unhappiness,
sadness, poignancy, tragedy. *see* BITTER 3.
4 *the bitterness of the wind* sharpness, harshness, coldness, intensity, penetration.
see BITTER 4. **5** *the bitterness of the quarrel/
controversy* acrimony, hostility, antagonism,
spitefulness, rancour, malice, malevolence,
venom. *see* BITTER 5.

bizarre adj strange, weird, peculiar, odd,
unusual, uncommon, curious, abnormal,
extraordinary, queer, freakish, offbeat, outlandish, unconventional, fantastic, *outré*,
eccentric, grotesque, ludicrous, comical,
ridiculous, droll, deviant, aberrant; *inf* oddball, rum, wacky, way-out, off-the-wall.

blab v **1** *blab a secret* blurt out, let slip,
reveal, disclose, divulge, tell. **2** *they won't
know unless he's blabbed* tell, inform, report,
let the cat out of the bag, tattle; *inf* squeal,
sing. **3** *blabbing away at the bus-stop* gossip,
chat, chatter, tittle-tattle, blabber.

black adj **1** *black horses* dark, pitch-black,
pitch-dark, pitch, jet-black, jet, ebony,
raven, sable, inky, coal-black, dusky,
swarthy, blackish, nigrescent, stygian. **2** *the
Black races* Negro, Negroid, coloured, dark-
skinned. **3** *black nights/skies* dark, starless,
moonless, unlit, unlighted, unilluminated,
gloomy, dusky, dim, overcast, crepuscular,
tenebrous, Stygian, Cimmerian. **4** *children
with black hands | black corners* dirty, grubby,
filthy, grimy, unclean, muddy, sooty,
soiled, stained, dingy. **5** *black news | a black
day* sad, melancholy, depressing, dismal,
distressing, gloomy, hopeless, sombre,
doleful, mournful, lugubrious, funereal,
pessimistic, ominous, foreboding. **6** *the
crowd in a black mood* angry, threatening,
menacing, hostile, furious, aggressive, bel-
ligerent, resentful, sullen. **7** *a black deed |
black hearts* evil, wicked, sinful, bad, vile,
villainous, criminal, iniquitous, nefarious,
heinous, foul, ignoble, base, corrupt,
depraved, devilish, diabolic. **8** *black humour*
cynical, sick, macabre.

black v **1** *black the cargo | black the delivery
firm* boycott, embargo, put an embargo on,
blacklist, ban, bar. **2** *black his eye* blacken,
make black, bruise, injure. **3** *black shoes*
blacken, make black/blacker, polish.

black n **in the black** solvent, in credit, in
funds, without debt. **in black and white**
1 *wish to see the proposals in black and white*
in print, written down, clearly/plainly/
explicitly defined. **2** *see everything in black
and white* in absolute terms, unequivocally,
categorically, uncomprisingly, without
shades of grey.

blackball v vote against, blacklist, debar,
bar, ban, exclude, shut out, expel, drum
out, oust, cashier, ostracize, reject, repudiate, boycott, snub, shun, give the cold
shoulder to.

blacken v **1** *smoke blackening the walls* make
black, darken, make dirty/sooty/smoky,
begrime, besmudge, befoul. **2** *the sky blackened* grow/become black, darken, grow dim.
3 *they blackened his character* defame, speak
ill/evil of, slander, libel, denigrate, disparage, slur, sully, decry, run down, vilify,
malign, defile, impugn, smear, besmirch,
tarnish, taint, stain, dishonour, drag
through the mud, calumniate, traduce.

blackguard n scoundrel, rogue, villain,
wretch, cad, rascal, devil, miscreant; *inf*
jerk, rat, creep, louse, rotter, bounder,
blighter, swine; *derog* bastard; *inf* scumbag.

blacklist v debar, bar, ban, exclude, shut
out, preclude, reject, repudiate, boycott,
proscribe, blackball. *see* BLACKBALL.

blackmail n *get the money by blackmail* extortion, exaction, extraction, intimidation,
bribery, wresting, wringing, milking,
bleeding, bloodsucking.

blackmail v **1** *blackmail large sums of money
from them* extort, exact, extract, bribe,
wrest, force. *see* BLACKMAIL n. **2** *blackmail people into paying* hold to ransom, threaten,
coerce, force, compel.

blackout n **1** *suffer a blackout* loss of consciousness, faint, coma, passing-out, period
of oblivion, swoon; *inf* flaking-out; *Med* syncope. **2** *using candles during a sudden blackout*
power cut, electricity failure. **3** *information
blackout* cut-off, suppression, withholding,
non-communication, censorship.

blame v **1** *blame him for the accident* hold
responsible/accountable, accuse, condemn,
find guilty, assign/attribute fault/liability/
guilt. **2** *blame the accident on him* ascribe,
attribute, impute to, lay at the door of; *inf*
pin on, stick on. **3** *they're always blaming the
child* find fault with, criticize, censure, rep-

rimand, reproach, reprove, upbraid, scold, chide, berate, take to task.

blame n **1** *put the blame for the accident on him* responsibility, guilt, accountability, liability, onus, culpability, fault; *inf* rap. **2** *incur much blame for his behaviour* censure, criticism, incrimination, accusation, condemnation, reprimanding, reproach, recrimination, reproof, castigation, complaint, indictment, berating. *see* BLAME v 3.

blameless adj innocent, not to blame, guiltless, above reproach/suspicion, in the clear, without fault, virtuous, moral, upright, irreproachable, unimpeachable, unoffending, sinless.

blameworthy adj to blame, guilty, at fault, culpable, offending, wrong, erring, condemnable.

blanch v **1** *blanch in fear* go/become pale, pale, whiten, go white, become pallid. **2** *staying indoors had blanched her skin | sun blanching the carpet* made pale, whiten, made pallid, bleach, grey, wash out. **3** *blanch the almonds/peppers* scald, boil.

bland adj **1** *bland food* tasteless, flavourless, mild, insipid. **2** *a bland speech* dull, middle-of-the-road, mediocre, nondescript, humdrum, boring, uninteresting, monotonous, unexciting, tedious, non-stimulating, uninspiring, weak, vapid. **3** *a bland manner* suave, urbane, smooth, affable, amiable, agreeable, gentle, gracious, courteous, congenial, unemotional, undemonstrative. **4** *bland breezes* mild, soft, calm, temperate, balmy, soothing, benign, mollifying, nonirritating, non-irritant.

blandishments npl flattery, cajolery, coaxing, wheedling, praise, fawning, toadying, ingratiating, inveiglement; compliments, soft words; *inf* sweet talk, soft soap.

blank adj **1** *a blank sheet of paper* void, empty, unfilled, unmarked, unwritten, clear, bare, clean, plain, spotless, white, vacant. **2** *a blank expression* expressionless, empty, vacant, deadpan, impassive, poker-faced, vacuous, lifeless, uninterested, emotionless, indifferent, uncomprehending. **3** *he looked blank | my mind went blank* uncomprehending, without ideas, at a loss, confused, puzzled, perplexed, bewildered, disconcerted, nonplussed, muddled, dumbfounded; *inf* floored. **4** *a blank refusal* outright, absolute, unqualified, utter, complete, thorough, unalloyed.

blank n empty space, space, gap, emptiness, void, vacuum, vacancy, vacuity, nothingness.

blanket n **1** *cover with a warm blanket* cover, covering, coverlet, bedcover, spread, rug, afghan; *Amer* throw. **2** *a blanket of snow/mist* covering, mass, layer, coat, coating, film, sheet, carpet, veneer, overlay, cloak, mantle, envelope, wrapping.

blanket adj *a blanket agreement* across the board, overall, inclusive, all-inclusive, comprehensive, general, wide-ranging, sweeping.

blanket v **1** *snow blanketing the earth | mist blanketing the hills* cover, overlay, coat, carpet, conceal, hide, mask, cloud, cloak, veil, shroud, envelop, surround. **2** *blanket out the television picture | shouting blanketing out his speech* obscure, suppress, extinguish.

blankness n **1** *blankness of the paper/walls* voidness, emptiness, bareness, whiteness. *see* BLANK adj 1. **2** *the blankness of her expression* expressionlessness, vacancy, lifelessness, emotionlessness, indifference, abstraction. *see* BLANK adj 2. **3** *the blankness of her mind* lack of ideas, obliviousness, no recollection, lack of comprehension, confusion, perplexity, bewilderment. *see* BLANK adj 3. **4** *the blankness of the refusal* outrightness, absoluteness, lack of qualification. *see* BLANK adj 4.

blare v **1** *car horns blaring* sound loudly, trumpet, blast, clamour, boom, roar, bellow, resound, honk, toot, peal, clang, screech. **2** *radios blaring out loud music* utter/give out loudly, blast out, boom out, screech out.

blarney n smooth talk, flattery, cajolery, coaxing, wheedling; blandishments, soft/honeyed words, compliments; *inf* sweet talk, soft soap.

blasé adj indifferent, apathetic, uninterested, unexcited, nonchalant, uncaring, unmoved, emotionless, phlegmatic, lukewarm, unconcerned, offhand, bored, weary, world-weary, jaded, surfeited, glutted, cloyed, satiated.

blaspheme v **1** *drunks blaspheming* swear, curse, utter oaths/profanities, damn, execrate, anathematize; *inf* cuss. **2** *blaspheming Christ* profane, desecrate, revile, abuse.

blasphemous adj profane, sacrilegious, irreligious, irreverent, impious, ungodly, godless, unholy.

blasphemy n **1** *guilty of blasphemy* profaneness, profanity, sacrilege, irreligiousness, irreverence, impiety, impiousness, ungodliness, unholiness, desecration, execration. **2** *utter blasphemies* cursing, swearing, execration; curses, oaths, profanities.

blast n **1** *a sudden blast of cold air* gust, rush, draught, blow, gale, squall, storm. **2** *a sudden blast of noise* blare, blaring, trumpeting, clamour, bellow, bellowing, boom, roar, clang, screech, wail, toot, honk, peal. **3** *people killed by the blast* explosion, detonation, discharge, blow-up, blowing-up, eruption, bang, burst. **4** *receive a blast from the teacher* outburst, attack, reprimand, rebuke, criticism, castigation, reproof.

blast v **1** *car horns blasting away | blast the car horn* sound loudly, trumpet, blare, boom, roar. *see* BLARE 1. **2** *radios blasting out pop* utter/give out loudly, blare out, boom out, screech out. **3** *blast the building to bits* blow, demolish, blow to pieces, shatter, explode, break up, destroy, ruin, raze to the ground. **4** *frost blasted the plants* blight, kill, destroy, wither, shrivel. **5** *poverty blasting their hopes* kill, destroy, crush, dash, blight, wreck, ruin, spoil, mar, annihilate, disappoint, frustrate. **6** *blasting the pupils for being late* attack, reprimand, rebuke, criticize, upbraid, berate, castigate, reprove, rail at, flay. **7** *guns blasting* shoot, fire, blaze away, discharge, let fly. **blast off** *the rocket blasted off successfully* be launched, take off, lift off.

blasted adj *blasted plants/hopes* blighted, destroyed, withered, shrivelled, ruined, devastated, spoiled, wasted.

blatant adj flagrant, glaring, obtrusive, obvious, overt, manifest, conspicuous, prominent, pronounced, bare-faced, naked, sheer, outright, out and out, unmitigated, brazen, shameless, flaunting.

blaze n **1** *the house was destroyed in the blaze* fire, conflagration, holocaust; flames. **2** *a sudden blaze of light* beam, flash, flare, glare, streak, glitter; brightness, radiance, brilliance. **3** *left in a blaze of anger* outburst, burst, eruption, flare-up, explosion, outbreak, storm, torrent, blast, rush.

blaze v **1** *the logs blazed up* burn, be ablaze, flame, burst into flames, catch fire. **2** *lights blazed in the street* shine, beam, flash, flare, glare, glitter. **3** *she blazed with fury* flare up, blow up, explode, seethe, fume, boil, smoulder; *inf* see red, work oneself up, get steamed up. **4** *blaze away at the birds* shoot, fire, blast, discharge, let fly.

blazon v *blazoned all over the newspapers* publicize, proclaim, broadcast, advertise, publish, make known, trumpet.

bleach v **1** *the sun bleaching her hair/carpet* make white/whiter, make pale/paler, lighten, blanch, fade, wash out, decolour, decolorize, peroxide, etiolate. **2** *bones bleaching in the desert* grow white/whiter, grow pale/paler, lighten, blanch, fade.

bleached adj lightened, blanched, faded, washed-out, decolorized, peroxided, stone-washed, etiolated.

bleak adj **1** *a bleak landscape* bare, barren, desolate, exposed, unsheltered, open, windswept, windy, chilly, cold, waste, arid, desert, uncultivable, uncultivatable, unproductive. **2** *bleak surroundings/prospects* dreary, dismal, dark, gloomy, drab, sombre, wretched, depressing, grim, miserable, cheerless, joyless, uninviting, discouraging, disheartening, unpromising, hopeless.

bleary adj **1** *bleary eyes* blurred, blurry, tired, watery, rheumy. **2** *bleary view* indistinct, dim, unclear, hazy, foggy, fogged, fuzzy, clouded, misty, murky.

bleed v **1** *the wounded/wounds were bleeding badly* shed/lose blood, emit blood. **2** *doctors formerly bled patients* draw blood from, remove/take blood from; *fml* phlebotomize. **3** *sap bleeding from a cut in the trunk* flow, run, ooze, seep, exude, trickle, weep, gush, spurt. **4** *bleeding money from the old man* extort, extract, squeeze, fleece, milk. **5** *bleeding their resources* drain, exhaust, sap, deplete, reduce. **6** *hearts are bleeding for them* ache, grieve, mourn, sorrow, suffer, agonize, anguish, sympathize, feel.

blemish n **1** *a blemish on the fruit skin* mark, blotch, spot, patch, bruise, scar, speck, speckle, imperfection, discoloration, disfigurement, birthmark, naevus. **2** *a character blemish* defect, flaw, blot, taint, stain, smirch, dishonour, disgrace.

blemish v **1** *frost blemishing the fruit | her blemished skin* damage, mar, spoil, flaw, mark, spot, speckle, blotch, disfigure, discolour, deface. **2** *blemishing his reputation* sully, tarnish, blot, taint, stain, besmirch, injure, damage, impair, flaw.

blench v flinch, start, shy, recoil, wince, quiver, shudder, tremble, quake, shrink, quail, cower.

blend v **1** *blend the ingredients* mix, combine, intermix, admix, commix, mingle, commingle, amalgamate, coalesce, unite, merge, compound, alloy, fuse, synthesize, homogenize. **2** *colours blending with each other* harmonize, go with, go well with, complement, fit, suit.

blend n *a blend of teas* mixture, mix, combination, admixture, mingling, commingling, amalgamation, amalgam, uniting, union, merging, compound, alloy, fusion, composite, concoction, synthesis, homogenization.

bless v **1** *bless the altar* consecrate, sanctify, hallow, dedicate. **2** *bless God's name* glorify, praise, laud, exalt, magnify, extol. **3** *the priest blessed the children* ask God's favour/ protection for, give a benediction for, invoke happiness on. **4** *I bless the day I met her*|*bless you for helping* give thanks for/to, thank. **5** *they were blessed with good looks*| *blessed with three children* endow, bestow, favour, provide, grace. **6** *the committee blessed the enterprise* sanction, approve, give approval for, be in favour of, endorse, support, give consent, smile upon.

blessed adj **1** *a blessed place* consecrated, sanctified, hallowed, sacred, holy, divine, venerated, revered, beatified. **2** *the blessed Virgin* glorified, exalted, magnified, extolled. **3** *the blessed section of society* fortunate, lucky, favoured, endowed. **4** *blessed days of peace* happy, joyful, joyous, blissful, glad, cheerful, blithe, contented.

blessing n **1** *utter a blessing* benediction, dedication, thanksgiving, consecration, invocation, commendation; grace. **2** *give the plan his blessing* approval, approbation, sanction, endorsement, support, backing, permission, leave, consent, assent, concurrence; good wishes. **3** *have the blessing of a quiet mind*|*what a blessing you're here* advantage, benefit, help, boon, godsend, favour, gift; luck, good fortune, gain, profit, bounty.

blight n **1** *plants killed by blight* disease, canker, infestation, pestilence, fungus, mildew. **2** *the blight which destroyed the city* affliction, plague, scourge, bane, woe, curse, misfortune, calamity, trouble, tribulation, evil, corruption, pollution, contamination.

blight v **1** *trees blighted by frost* kill, destroy, wither, shrivel, blast, mildew. **2** *hopes blighted by war* kill, destroy, crush, dash, blast, wreck, ruin. *see* BLAST v 5.

blind adj **1** *guide dogs for blind people* unsighted, sightless, visually impaired, visionless, unseeing, stone-blind, partially sighted, half-blind, purblind, eyeless; *inf* visually challenged. **2** *he must be blind not to know she loves him* imperceptive, slow, slowwitted, dim-witted, obtuse, dense, thick. **3** *blind to danger* unmindful of, careless of, heedless of, oblivious to, inattentive to, indifferent to, neglectful of, unaware of, unconscious of, unobservant of, ignorant of, insensitive to. **4** *blind loyalty* unreasoned, uncritical, unthinking, mindless, injudicious, undiscerning, indiscriminate, prejudiced, biased. **5** *in a blind rage* rash, impetuous, hasty, reckless, uncontrolled, uncontrollable, unrestrained, wild, frantic, violent, furious, irrational. **6** *a blind*

entrance concealed, hidden, obscured, out of sight. **7** *a blind alley* dead-end, without exit, exitless, blocked, closed, barred, impassable. **8** *blind after the party* drunk, blind drunk, intoxicated; *inf* smashed, paralytic, sloshed, plastered. *see* DRUNK adj.

blind v **1** *blinded in the accident* make blind, deprive of sight/vision, render unsighted/ sightless, put one's eyes out, gouge out the eyes of. **2** *blinding the driver* obscure/block one's vision, get in one's line of vision, dazzle. **3** *blinded by love* deprive of judgement/ reason/sense, deceive, delude, beguile, hoodwink. **4** *blind with science/facts* bewilder, confuse, overwhelm, overawe, swamp.

blind n **1** *a window blind* screen, shade, curtain, shutter; Venetian blind, roller blind. **2** *his job's a blind for his spying activities* camouflage, screen, smokescreen, front, façade, cover, disguise, cloak, pretext, masquerade, mask, feint.

blindly adv **1** *feeling his way blindly* without sight, sightlessly, unseeingly. **2** *rushing on blindly* unmindfully, carelessly, heedlessly, rashly, impetuously, recklessly, uncontrolledly, wildly, frantically, irrationally. *see* BLIND adj 3, 5. **3** *loving him blindly* uncritically, injudiciously, undiscerningly, indiscriminately. *see* BLIND adj 4.

blink v **1** *eyes blinking in the light* flutter, flicker, wink, bat, nictitate, nictate. **2** *people blinking in the sunlight* wink, peer, squint, screw up the eyes. **3** *city lights blinking* flicker, twinkle, waver, wink, glimmer, glitter, sparkle, shimmer, scintillate, flash, gleam, shine. **4** *teachers blinking at truancy* turn a blind eye to, take no notice of, disregard, overlook, ignore, condone, connive at.

bliss n **1** *it's bliss to be on holiday* ecstasy, joy, elation, rapture, euphoria, happiness, delight, gladness, pleasure, heaven, paradise, seventh heaven, Eden, Utopia, Arcadia; halcyon days. **2** *in a state of bliss* blessedness, heavenly joy, divine happiness, beatitude.

blister n **1** *blisters on the skin caused by burns* bleb, pustule, pimple, boil, cyst, abscess, carbuncle, ulcer, blain, papule, vesication, wen, furuncle. **2** *blisters on the paintwork* bubble, swelling, bulge, protuberance.

blistering adj **1** *at blistering speed*|*in blistering heat* extreme, very great, greatest, intense, maximum, utmost. **2** *blistering criticism* scathing, fierce, severe, savage, sharp, biting, harsh, sarcastic, caustic, searing, mordant, trenchant.

blithe n **1** *in a blithe mood* happy, cheerful, cheery, light-hearted, jolly, merry, gay, joyful, carefree, buoyant, jaunty, animated, sprightly, vivacious, spirited, frisky, gladsome, mirthful. **2** *with a blithe disregard for others* casual, indifferent, careless, thoughtless, nonchalant, uncaring, unconcerned, heedless, untroubled, cool, blasé.

blitz n **1** *the blitz on London* bombardment, attack, assault, raid, offensive, onslaught, strike, blitzkrieg. **2** *a blitz on cleaning* attack, onslaught, all-out effort, onset, setto, endeavour.

blizzard n snowstorm, snow blast/squall.

bloat v swell, puff up/out, blow up, distend, inflate, balloon, enlarge, expand, dilate.

blob n **1** *a blob of cream* globule, glob, drop, droplet, bead, ball, bubble, pellet, pill. **2** *a blob of paint* spot, dab, splash, daub, blotch, blot, smudge, smear, mark.

bloc n alliance, coalition, union, federation, league, ring, group, syndicate, combine, entente, party, wing, faction, cabal, clique, coterie.

block n **1** *block of chocolate/soap* bar, cake, brick, chunk, hunk, lump, cube, ingot, wedge, mass, piece, wad. **2** *building a new science block* building, complex. **3** *block of seats/shares* group, batch, band, cluster, set, section, quantity. **4** *a block in the pipe* blockage, obstruction, stoppage. **5** *a block to progress* obstacle, bar, barrier, impediment, hindrance, deterrent, check, hurdle, stumbling-block, drawback, hitch.

block v **1** *block the pipe* clog, stop up, choke, plug, close, obstruct; *inf* bung up. **2** *block progress* hinder, obstruct, impede, halt, stop, bar, check, arrest, deter, thwart, frustrate, stand in the way of. **3** *block hats* shape, mould, form, fashion, frame, tailor.

blockade n **1** *blockade of the city* siege, beleaguerment, investment, encirclement. **2** *a blockade at the border | a blockade to progress* barrier, barricade, obstacle, obstruction, block, hindrance, impediment, check, deterrent, hurdle, stoppage.

blockage n **1** *a blockage in the pipes* obstruction, stoppage, block, occlusion, impediment. **2** *the blockage of the pipes* obstructing, blocking, stopping up, occluding.

blockhead n dunce, numskull, dolt, fool, dullard, idiot, ignoramus, bonehead, nincompoop; *inf* thickhead, dickhead, chump, pillock, wally, dork, geek; *Aust/Amer inf* dingbat.

bloke n man, boy, male, individual, body; *inf* chap, fellow, guy, bod, punter, character, customer.

blond, blonde adj fair, fair-haired, goldenhaired, flaxen, tow-coloured, tow-headed; fair-skinned, fair-complexioned, light, light-coloured, light-toned whitish.

blood n **1** *a blood disease | blood was flowing* lifeblood, vital fluid, gore, whole blood; *lit* ichor. **2** *of noble blood* ancestry, lineage, line, family, birth, extraction, descent, origin, genealogy, heritage, stock, race, pedigree, kinship, consanguinity. **3** *own flesh and blood* relations, kin, kindred; relationship, kinship. **4** *of hot blood* temperament, disposition, nature, humour, temper, spirit, feeling.

blood-curdling adj spine-chilling, chilling, terrifying, hair-raising, horrifying, horrific, horrendous, frightening, fearful, appalling, scaring.

bloodless adj **1** *an invalid looking bloodless* anaemic, pale, wan, colourless, pallid, ashen, chalky, pasty, sallow, sickly, peaked, ghostlike, white as a sheet; *inf* peaky. **2** *a bloodless young man* listless, languid, feeble, sluggish, languorous, apathetic, spiritless, passionless, phlegmatic, torpid, lackadaisical.

bloodshed n killing, slaughter, slaying, carnage, butchery, massacre, murder, bloodletting, blood bath, gore, pogrom, decimation.

bloodthirsty adj murderous, homicidal, savage, vicious, ruthless, barbarous, barbaric, brutal, bloody, sadistic, slaughterous, warlike, bellicose; *fml* sanguinary.

bloody adj **1** *a bloody nose* bleeding, unstaunched. **2** *a bloody cloth* bloodstained, blood-soaked, blood-marked, blood-spattered; *fml* sanguinary. **3** *bloody actions/thoughts* bloodthirsty, murderous, homicidal, savage, vicious, slaughterous; *fml* sanguinary. *see* BLOODTHIRSTY.

bloom n **1** *perfect blooms* flower, blossom, floweret; flowering, blossoming, efflorescence. **2** *beauty losing its bloom* freshness, glow, lustre, sheen, radiance, flush, perfection, blush. **3** *genius no longer in full bloom* prime, perfection, heyday, vigour, flourishing, strength.

bloom v **1** *plants blooming* flower, blossom, be in flower/blossom, come into flower/blossom, open, open out, bud, burgeon. **2** *they've bloomed since moving to the country* flourish, thrive, be in good health, get on well, prosper, succeed, progress.

blossom n *apple blossom* blooms, flowers, flowerets; blossoming, efflorescence.

blossom v **1** *trees blossoming* be in flower, flower, bloom, burgeon. **2** *she blossomed in her new environment | the friendship blossomed* bloom, flourish, thrive, get on well, prosper, succeed, progress, develop, grow, mature.

blot n **1** *blots of ink/grease* spot, blotch, splodge, smudge, patch, dot, mark, speck, smear. **2** *a blot on his character* stain, blemish, taint, flaw, fault, defect, tarnishing, imperfection, disgrace.

blot v **1** *paper blotted with ink-spots* spot, blotch, smudge, dot, mark, speckle, smear, bespatter. **2** *the event blotting his reputation* stain, sully, tarnish, taint, besmirch, blacken. **3** *blot up the grease* soak up, absorb, dry up, dry out, take up. **blot out 1** *typing fluid to blot out the print* erase, obliterate, delete, rub out. **2** *a tree blotting out the view* hide, conceal, obscure, obliterate, darken, dim, shadow. **3** *time blotting out memories* wipe out, erase, efface, obliterate, expunge, destroy, exterminate.

blotch n **1** *a blotch of ink* splodge, patch, smudge, dot, spot, speck, blot, stain, smear. **2** *a blotch on the skin* patch, blemish, mark, spot, eruption, birthmark, naevus.

blow¹ v **1** *the wind was blowing* be in motion, puff, flurry, bluster, blast. **2** *hair blowing in the breeze* move, wave, flap, flutter, waft, stream, drift, whirl, undulate. **3** *wind blowing the leaves/boats* move, waft, toss, sweep, whisk, drive, buffet, whirl, transport, convey. **4** *blow cigarette smoke* breathe out, puff out, exhale, emit, expel. **5** *he was blowing a bit* breathe hard, puff, pant, wheeze, gasp, huff and puff. **6** *blow the trumpet* sound, play, toot, blare, blast. **7** *blow £100 on a meal* squander, fritter away, spend freely, lavish, dissipate. **8** *blow one's chances* spoil, ruin, bungle, make a mess of, muff; *inf* botch, make a hash of, screw up. **9** *blow about his big house* boast, brag, crow; *inf* talk big. **blow out 1** *blow out the candle* put out, extinguish, snuff, douse, stifle. **2** *the walls suddenly blew out* break open, burst, explode, blow up, shatter, rupture, crack. **blow over** pass away, pass, die down, be forgotten, sink into oblivion, come to an end, disappear, vanish, cease, subside, settle down, terminate. **blow up 1** *the bombed building blew up* explode, burst open, break open, shatter, rupture. **2** *the bomb blew up* explode, go off, detonate, erupt. **3** *blow up the building* bomb, detonate, explode, blast. **4** *blow up the tyre/stomach* inflate, pump up, fill up, swell, enlarge, distend, expand, puff up, balloon. **5** *blow up the story* exaggerate, overstate, embroider, colour, magnify, heighten, expand on. **6** *he blew up at the news* lose one's temper, become angry/enraged/furious, go into a rage/fury, erupt, go wild, rage; *inf* hit the roof, go off the deep end, fly off the handle.

blow¹ n **1** *a bit of a blow today* wind, breeze, gust, puff of wind, flurry, blast, gale, storm, tempest; turbulence. **2** *a blow on the trumpet* blast, blare, toot, sound.

blow² n **1** *a blow on the head* hit, knock, bang, punch, thump, smack, whack, thwack, buffet, stroke, rap; *inf* bash, belt, clout, sock, wallop, battering, lick, slosh, bat. **2** *her death was a blow* shock, upset, calamity, catastrophe, disaster, misfortune, setback, disappointment, jolt, reversal.

blow-out n **1** *a blow-out at the minefield* explosion, blast, detonation. **2** *crash owing to a blow-out* puncture, flat tyre, burst tyre, leak; *inf* flat. **3** *a birthday blow-out* party, feast, celebration, binge, spree; *inf* bash, knees-up, beanfeast, shindig, beano, rave, rave-up.

blowzy adj **1** *a dirty blowzy young woman* dishevelled, slovenly, sluttish, slatternly, tousled, unkempt, untidy, sloppy, slipshod, messy, bedraggled. **2** *a blowzy drunk* coarse-looking, florid, ruddy-complexioned, red-faced.

bludgeon n *beaten with a bludgeon* club, cudgel, stick, truncheon, heavy weapon.

bludgeon v **1** *bludgeoned to death* club, cudgel, strike, hit, beat, beat up; *inf* clobber. **2** *bludgeoned into agreeing* coerce, force, compel, browbeat, dragoon, bulldoze, bully, railroad, steamroller, pressurize, hector; *inf* strong-arm.

blue adj **1** *a blue dress | blue walls* azure, sky-blue, powder-blue, deep blue, royal blue, sapphire, ultramarine, navy blue, navy, indigo, cyan, cobalt, cerulean. **2** *feeling blue* depressed, gloomy, dejected, despondent, low, downcast, downhearted, unhappy, sad, melancholy, glum, morose, dismal; *inf* down in the dumps. **3** *blue jokes* obscene, indecent, dirty, coarse, vulgar, bawdy, lewd, risqué, improper, smutty, offensive; *inf* naughty, near the knuckle/bone, nudge-nudge.

blueprint n plan, design, prototype, draft, outline, sketch, pattern, layout, representation.

blues npl *a fit of the blues* depression, gloominess, gloom, dejection, despondency, downheartedness, unhappiness, sadness, melancholy, glumness, moroseness, dismalness; low spirits, doldrums; *inf* dumps, the hump.

bluff¹ v **1** *he's only bluffing* pretend, sham, fake, feign, put it on, lie. **2** *he's bluffing you* deceive, delude, mislead, trick, hoodwink, hoax, take in, humbug, bamboozle, cozen; *inf* put one over on.

bluff¹ n *it's just a bluff* deception, deceit, pretence, sham, subterfuge, fake, show, false show, idle boast, feint, delusion, hoax, fraud; humbug, bluster.

bluff² adj **1** *a bluff manner | a bluff old man* frank, open, candid, outspoken, blunt, direct, plain-spoken, straightforward, downright, hearty, rough. **2** *a bluff slope* steep, sheer, vertical, precipitous, abrupt, sudden, acclivitous, perpendicular.

bluff² n cliff, headland, ridge, promontory, peak, crag, bank, slope, height, escarpment, scarp.

blunder n mistake, error, inaccuracy, fault, slip, oversight, *faux pas*, gaffe; *inf* slip-up, clanger, boob, boo-boo, howler, bloomer.

blunder v **1** *management blundered badly* make a mistake, err; *inf* slip up, screw up, blow it. **2** *blundering about in the dark* stumble, flounder, lurch, stagger, falter. **3** *blunder the situation* mismanage, botch, bungle, make a mess of.

blunt adj **1** *a blunt knife/blade* not sharp, unsharpened, dull, dulled, edgeless. **2** *a blunt remark/manner/person* frank, candid, outspoken, plain-spoken, straightforward, direct, bluff, to the point, brusque, abrupt, curt, short; *inf* upfront.

blunt v **1** *blunt the blade* make less sharp, make blunt/dull. **2** *blunt the appetite/enthusiasm* dull, take the edge off, deaden, dampen, numb, weaken, impair, appease.

blur v **1** *blurring the view* make indistinct, make vague, obscure, dim, bedim, make hazy, befog, fog, cloud, becloud, mask, veil. **2** *blur the windscreen* smear, besmear, smudge, spot, blotch, blot, stain, besmirch. **3** *blur one's judgement/memory* dull, numb, make dim, make less sharp, deaden.

blur n **1** *just a blur on the landscape | a blur in my memory* something hazy/indistinct/ vague, haze; haziness, indistinctness, obcureness, obcurity, dimness, fogginess, cloudiness. **2** *a blur on the windscreen* smear, smudge, spot, blotch, blot, stain.

blurred adj hazy, indistinct, faint, fuzzy, blurry, misty, foggy, unclear, vague, lacking definition, out of focus, nebulous.

blurt v *blurt out* call out, cry out, utter suddenly, exclaim, ejaculate, blab, disclose, divulge, reveal, let slip, babble, let the cat out of the bag, give the game away; *inf* spill the beans, spout.

blush v *blushing in embarrassment* redden, go pink/red, turn red/crimson/scarlet, flush, colour, crimson, burn up.

blush n *hiding her blushes* flush; reddening, high colour, colour, rosiness, pinkness, ruddiness.

bluster v **1** *wind blustering* blow fiercely, blast, gust, storm, roar. **2** *bullies blustering* rant, bully, domineer, hector, harangue, threaten, boast, brag, swagger, throw one's weight about, be overbearing, lord it, vaunt.

bluster n **1** *the bluster of the wind* noise, roar, tumult, blasting, gusting, storming. **2** *the bullies' bluster* ranting, bravado, domineering, hectoring, bombast, boasting, bragging, swaggering, braggadocio; empty threats.

blustery adj stormy, gusty, gusting, squally, wild, tempestuous; *inf* blowy.

board n **1** *a wooden board* plank, beam, panel, slat, length of timber, piece of wood. **2** *pay for one's board* food, sustenance; meals, daily meals, provisions, victuals; *inf* grub, nosh. **3** *on the board of the firm* committee, council, panel, directorate, advisory group, advisorate, panel of trustees.

board v **1** *board up the windows* cover up/ over, close up, shut up, seal. **2** *they board with her* lodge, live, have rooms, room, be quartered, be housed. **3** *she boards three people* take in, put up, lodge, accommodate, house, feed. **4** *board the plane/train/bus* get on, enter, go on board, go aboard, step aboard, embark, mount; *fml* emplane, entrain, embus.

boast v **1** *always boasting about his achievements* brag, crow, exaggerate, overstate, swagger, blow one's own trumpet, sing one's own praises, congratulate oneself, pat oneself on the back; *inf* swank, talk big, blow hard. **2** *the town boasts two museums* possess, have, own, enjoy, pride oneself/ itself on.

boast n **1** *his boast is that he's best* brag, overstatement, self-praise, bluster, vaunt; bragging, crowing, blustering; *inf* swank, swanking; *lit* fanfaronade. *see* BOAST v 1. **2** *the building is the boast of the town* pride, pride and joy, treasure, gem, pearl, valued object, source of satisfaction.

boastful adj bragging, braggart, crowing, swaggering, cocky, conceited, arrogant, vain, egotistical, overbearing, blustering, overweening, vaunting; *fml* vainglorious; *inf* swanking, swanky, big-headed, swollen-headed.

boat n vessel, craft; yacht, dinghy, sloop, coracle, sailing-boat, motorboat, speedboat, rowing-boat, punt, canoe, kayak.

bob v **1** *bobbing in the water* move up and down, float, bounce, quiver, wobble. **2** *bobbed her head* nod, jerk, twitch, duck, waggle. **3** *bobbing on the dance floor* dance, bounce, skip, leap, jerk, weave.

bode v augur, presage, portend, betoken, foretell, prophesy, predict, forebode, foreshadow, indicate, signify, purport.

bodily adj *bodily functions/injuries* physical, corporeal, corporal, carnal, fleshly.

bodily adv **1** *the audience rising bodily* as a body/group/mass, in a mass, as a whole, together, as one, collectively, en masse. **2** *threw him bodily into the river* wholly, completely, entirely, totally.

body n **1** *well-formed bodies* frame, form, figure, shape, build, physique, framework, skeleton, trunk, torso. **2** *a body in the morgue* dead body, corpse, cadaver, carcass; remains, relics; *inf* stiff. **3** *a lift accommodating six bodies* person, individual, being, human being, human, creature, mortal. **4** *the body of the plane* main part, principal part, hub, core. **5** *a body of water* mass, expanse, extent, aggregate. **6** *the body of political opinion* majority, preponderance, bulk, mass. **7** *the ruling body* group, party, band, association, company, confederation, bloc, congress, corporation, society. **8** *material with little body* substance, firmness, solidity, density, shape, structure.

bog n marsh, marshland, swamp, mire, quagmire, morass, slough, fen; *dial* sump.

bogged v **bogged down** stuck, impeded, obstructed, halted, stopped, delayed, stalled, slowed down; trapped, entangled, ensnared.

bogey n **1** *children imagining a bogey* bogeyman, evil spirit, bogle, ghost, apparition, spectre, phantom, hobgoblin, witch; *inf* spook. **2** *always a bogey of mine* bugbear, pet hate, bane, anathema, *bête noire*, dread, bugaboo.

boggle v **1** *boggled at paying so much* hesitate to, jib at, demur at, shrink/flinch from, hang back from, waver/falter at. **2** *they boggled at the sight* be surprised, take fright, start, be startled, be astounded/staggered, shy. **3** *the sight boggled my mind* startle, astound, astonish, amaze, overwhelm, shock, bowl over; *inf* flabbergast.

bogus adj fraudulent, counterfeit, fake, spurious, false, forged, sham, artificial, mock, make-believe, quasi, pseudo; *inf* phoney, pseud.

bohemian adj *a bohemian lifestyle* unconventional, unorthodox, nonconformist, offbeat, avant-garde, original, eccentric, alternative, artistic; *inf* arty, arty-farty, way-out, off-the-wall, oddball.

bohemian n *bohemians of the 1960s* unconventional person, nonconformist, hippy, beatnik, drop-out, artistic person.

boil v **1** *the soup is boiling* bubble, simmer, cook, seethe, heat, stew. **2** *boil the soup* bring to the boil, simmer, cook, heat. **3** *the sea was boiling* seethe, bubble, churn, froth, foam, fizz, effervesce, be agitated. **4** *the teacher was boiling* be/made angry/furious/indignant, rage, fume, seethe, rant, rave, storm, fulminate, bluster, explode, flare up; *inf* blow one's top, fly off the handle, go off the deep end, hit the roof, go up the wall, blow a fuse.

boiling adj **1** *boiling hot | boiling weather* very hot, scorching, roasting, baking, blistering, sweltering, searing, torrid. **2** *she was boiling at his insults* furious, incensed, fuming, enraged, infuriated, seething, indignant, irate, angry; *inf* mad.

boisterous adj **1** *boisterous children/ parties* lively, active, bouncy, frisky, exuberant, spirited, noisy, loud, rowdy, unruly, wild, unrestrained, romping, rollicking, disorderly, rumbustious. **2** *boisterous winds* blustery, gusting, gusty, breezy, stormy, squally, rough, turbulent, raging, wild.

bold adj **1** *a bold explorer | bold deeds* daring, intrepid, audacious, courageous, brave, valiant, fearless, gallant, heroic, adventurous, enterprising, confident, undaunted, valorous. **2** *a bold young woman* brazen, shameless, forward, brash, impudent, audacious, cheeky, saucy, pert, immodest, unabashed, barefaced, bold as brass; *inf* brassy. **3** *bold colours* striking, vivid, bright, eye-catching, conspicuous, distinct, pronounced, prominent, well- marked, showy, flashy.

bolshie adj uncooperative, awkward, perverse, difficult, disobliging, stubborn, unhelpful, annoying; *inf* bloody-minded.

bolster n *laid his head on the bolster* pillow, cushion, pad, support.

bolster v *bolster morale/bolster up the economy* strengthen, reinforce, support, boost, give a boost to, prop up, buoy up, shore up, hold up, maintain, buttress, aid, assist, help, revitalize, invigorate.

bolt n **1** *window bolts* bar, catch, latch, lock, fastener, hasp. **2** *nuts and bolts* rivet, pin, peg. **3** *bolt of lightning* flash, shaft, streak, burst, discharge, flare. **4** *escape in one bolt | make a bolt for it* dash, dart, run, sprint, rush, bound, spring, leap, jump. **5** *firing bolts* arrow, dart, shaft, missile, projectile, thunderbolt, quarrel. **6** *a bolt of cloth* roll, quantity.

bolt v **1** *bolt the door* bar, lock, fasten, latch. **2** *bolt the pieces together* rivet, pin, clamp, fasten, batten. **3** *they bolted from the room* dash, dart, run, sprint, hurtle, rush, bound, hurry, flee, fly, spring, leap, abscond, escape, make a break/run for it; *inf* tear from. **4** *bolting his food* gulp, gobble, devour, wolf, guzzle, cram, stuff.

bolt adv **bolt upright** straight up, very straight, rigid, stiff, completely upright.

bomb n explosive, incendiary device, incendiary, blockbuster; grenade, shell, missile, torpedo, projectile, trajectile; letter-bomb, petrol-bomb, nuclear bomb.

bomb v bombard, blow up; shell, torpedo, blitz, strafe, cannonade.

bombard v **1** *bombard military establishments* bomb, shell, torpedo, pound, blitz, strafe, pepper, cannonade, fusillade, fire at, attack, assault, raid. **2** *bombard with questions* assail, attack, besiege, beset, bother, subject to, hound, belabour.

bombardment n **1** *the bombardment of London* bombing, shelling, strafing, torpedoing, blitz, blitzkrieg, air-raid, strafe, cannonade, fusillade, attack, assault. **2** *the bombardment of the film star with press questions* assailing, attack, besieging, barraging. *see* BOMBARD 2.

bombast n pomposity, ranting, rant, bluster, turgidity, verbosity, pretentiousness, affectedness, ostentation, grandiloquence, magniloquence, periphrasis, euphuism, fustian, braggadocio, rodomontade.

bona fide adj genuine, authentic, real, true, actual, sterling, sound, legal, legitimate.

bonanza n windfall, godsend, stroke/run of luck, boon, bonus.

bond n **1** *the bond/bonds of friendship* tie, link, binding, connection, attachment, union, ligature, nexus. **2** *freed from his bonds* chains, fetters, shackles, manacles; rope, cord. **3** *enter into a bond* | *sign a bond* agreement, contract, pact, transaction, bargain, deal, covenant, compact, pledge, promise, treaty, concordat.

bond v *bond the pieces of metal together* join, connect, fasten, stick, unite, attach, bind; glue, gum, fuse, weld.

bondage n slavery, enslavement, captivity, servitude, thraldom, serfdom, oppression.

bonus n **1** *the pleasant environment was a bonus* extra, plus, gain, benefit, boon, perquisite, dividend, premium. **2** *a Christ-mas bonus* gratuity, tip, gift, perk, honorarium, reward, bounty, commission.

bony adj *a bony frame* angular, rawboned, gaunt, scraggy, scrawny, skinny, thin, emaciated, skeletal, cadaverous.

book n **1** *read/publish a book* volume, tome, work, publication, title, opus, treatise, manual. **2** *the exercise/rent book* booklet, pad, looseleaf notebook, notebook, jotter, ledger, log.

book v **1** *book a room* | *book the seats/speaker* reserve, make reservations for, arrange in advance, engage, charter. **2** *book the meeting* arrange, programme, schedule, line up. **book in** *book in at the hotel* | *book in for the competition* register, enrol, enter, record/log one's arrival.

bookish adj studious, scholarly, academic, literary, intellectual, brainy, highbrow, erudite, learned, pedantic, pedagoguish, bluestocking, impractical, ivory-towerish.

books npl *checking the books* accounts, records.

boom v **1** *guns booming in the distance* resound, sound loudly, explode, bang, blast, blare, roar, bellow, rumble, reverberate, thunder. **2** *the teacher boomed* roar, bellow, shout, thunder. **3** *property market booming* burgeon, flourish, thrive, prosper, progress, do well, succeed, grow, develop, expand, increase, swell, intensify, mushroom, put on a spurt.

boom n **1** *the boom of the guns* resounding, loud noise, explosion, banging, bang, blasting, blast, blare, roaring, roar, bellow, rumble, reverberation, thundering, thunder. **2** *the boom in private housing* increase, upturn, upsurge, upswing, advance, growth, spurt, progress, development, expansion, improvement, boost, success.

boomerang v rebound, come back, spring back, return, recoil, reverse, ricochet, backfire.

boon n benefit, advantage, gain, plus, bonus, good thing, blessing, godsend, windfall, perk, perquisite.

boon adj *a boon companion* close, intimate, favourite, special, best, inseparable.

boor n lout, oaf, rough, churl, philistine, vulgarian, yahoo, barbarian; *inf* clodhopper, clod, peasant, yobbo, yob, plonker, casual.

boorish adj rough, rude, coarse, ill-bred, ill-mannered, uncouth, churlish, gruff, uncivilized, unsophisticated, unrefined, crude, vulgar, gross, brutish, bearish, barbaric; *inf* yobbish, clodhopping.

boost v **1** *boost him up the tree* lift, raise, hoist, push, thrust, shove, heave, elevate, help, assist; *inf* hoick. **2** *boost morale* raise, increase, improve, encourage, heighten, help, promote, foster, inspire, uplift. **3** *boost sales* increase, expand, raise, add to, improve, enlarge, inflate, promote, advance, develop, further, foster, facilitate, help, assist; *inf* jack up, hike, hike up. **4** *boost their products* promote, advertise, publicize, praise, write up; *inf* plug, give a plug to.

boost n **1** *give him a boost into the tree* lift up, hoist up, push, thrust, shove, heave; *inf* hoick up. **2** *give a boost to morale* uplift, shot in the arm; encouragement, help, inspiration, stimulus. **3** *a boost in sales* increase, expansion, rise, improvement, advance; *inf* jacking up, hike. *see* BOOST v **3**. **4** *a boost for their products* promotion, advertisement, write-up; publicity, publicization; *inf* plug, puff.

boot n footwear; wellington, gumboot, combat boot, climbing boot, football boot, ski boot, *Trademark* Doc Marten; *inf* welly, bovver boot.

boot v **1** *boot the ball* kick, knock, punt. **2** *boot him out* throw out, kick out, dismiss, sack, expel, eject, oust. **3** *boot a computer* load, prepare, make ready.

booth n **1** *market booth* stall, stand, counter. **2** *telephone booth* cubicle, compartment, enclosure, cupboard, carrel.

bootless adj *bootless attempts* futile, vain, unsuccessful, useless, ineffective, ineffectual, abortive, unproductive, fruitless, unavailing; *lit* Sisyphean.

booty n spoil, loot, plunder, pillage, prize, haul; spoils, profits, pickings, takings, winnings; *inf* swag, boodle, the goods.

bordello n brothel, house of ill repute, house of prostitution, bawdy house, whorehouse, bagnio.

border n **1** *the border of the lake/lawn* edge, verge, perimeter, boundary, margin, brink, skirt; fringes, bounds, limits, confines. **2** *passport checks at the border* frontier, boundary, march.

border v **1** *woods bordering the fields* edge, skirt, bound. *see* BORDER n **1**. **2** *Portugal borders Spain | his garden borders on mine* adjoin, abut on, be adjacent to, be next to, neighbour, touch, join, connect, border on. **3** *border the skirt with lace* edge, fringe, hem, trim, bind, decorate, rim. **4** *border his territory* be/come close to, border on. **border on** *his reply is bordering on rudeness | bordering on the obscene* verge on, approximate to,

approach, come close to, be near/similar to, resemble.

bore¹ v *bore into the wood | bore a hole* pierce, perforate, puncture, penetrate, drill, tap, tunnel, burrow, mine, dig out, gouge out, sink.

bore¹ n **1** *sink a bore to find oil* borehole, hole, shaft, tunnel. **2** *the bore of a rifle* calibre, diameter, gauge.

bore² v *the talk/speaker bored her* weary, pall on, be tedious to, tire, fatigue, send to sleep, exhaust, wear out; bore to tears, bore to death, bore out of one's mind.

bore² n tiresome person/thing, tedious person/thing, nuisance, bother, pest; *inf* drag, pain, pain in the neck.

boredom n tedium, tediousness, dullness, monotony, flatness, sameness, humdrum, dreariness, weariness, apathy, languor, ennui, world-weariness, malaise.

boring adj tedious, dull, monotonous, humdrum, repetitious, unvaried, uninteresting, unexciting, flat, dry-as-dust, weary, wearisome, tiring, tiresome; *inf* samey.

borrow v **1** *borrow some money* ask for the loan of, receive/take as a loan, use/have temporarily; *inf* cadge, mooch, scrounge, sponge, beg, bum. **2** *borrow another writer's plots* appropriate, commandeer, use as one's own, copy, plagiarize, pirate, take, adopt, purloin, steal, grab, filch, pinch, help oneself to, abstract, imitate, simulate. **3** *English borrowing words from French* adopt, appropriate, take in, take over, acquire, embrace.

bosom n **1** *woman with a large bosom* breasts, bust, chest; *inf* boobs, tits, knockers, bristols. **2** *bosom of the family/Church* heart, centre, core, midst, circle, protection, shelter, aegis. **3** *nurturing warm feelings in their bosoms* heart, soul, being; emotions, affections.

bosom adj *bosom friends/companions* close, intimate, boon, confidential, dear, inseparable, faithful, thick as thieves.

boss n *the boss of the factory* head, chief, manager, director, executive, administrator, leader, superintendent, supervisor, foreman, overseer, controller, employer, master, owner; *inf* gaffer, governor; *Amer inf* Mister Big, honcho, numero uno.

boss v **1** *he's always bossing his brothers about* order about/around, give orders/commands to, bully, push around, domineer, dominate, ride roughshod over, control; throw one's weight about. **2** *he bosses the whole business* be in charge of, head, manage, run, administrate, direct, control, command, preside over, superintend, supervise, own.

bossy adj domineering, dominating, over-bearing, dictatorial, authoritarian, despotic, imperious, high-handed, auto-cratic.

botch v *botch the situation/repair* bungle, do badly/clumsily, make a mess of, spoil, mar, muff, mismanage, mangle, fumble, throw a spanner in the works; *inf* mess up, make a hash of, hash, foul up, screw up, blow, louse up, cock up, balls up.

both adj/pron *both boys|both are here* the two, the two together.

bother v 1 *don't bother your father* disturb, trouble, worry, pester, harass, annoy, upset, irritate, vex, inconvenience, pro-voke, plague, torment, nag, molest; *inf* has-sle, give someone a hard time, get in one's hair. 2 *don't bother yourself with that|don't bother* concern oneself, occupy/busy one-self, take the time, make the effort, trouble oneself, go to trouble, inconvenience one-self, worry oneself. 3 *it bothers me that I lost it* upset, trouble, worry, concern, distress, perturb, disconcert, fret.

bother n 1 *don't go to any bother* trouble, effort, inconvenience, fuss, flurry, bustle, hustle and bustle, exertion, strain; pains; *inf* hassle. 2 *what a bother we've missed it* nui-sance, pest, annoyance, irritation, incon-venience, difficulty, problem, vexation. 3 *a bit of bother in the pub* trouble, disturbance, commotion, uproar, disorder, fighting, furore, brouhaha.

bottle n 1 *a bottle of milk/wine* container; flask, carafe, decanter, pitcher, flagon, car-boy, demijohn, magnum, jeroboam, methuselah, balthazar. 2 *fond of the bottle* alcoholic drink, alcohol, drink, liquor; *inf* booze. 3 *the bottle to fight* courage, bravery, nerve, boldness, confidence, daring, pluck; *inf* guts, spunk.

bottle v **bottle up** *bottle up feelings* keep back, suppress, restrain, keep in check, curb, contain, shut in, conceal.

bottleneck n constriction, narrowing, obstruction, congestion, block, blockage, jam, hold-up.

bottom n 1 *the bottom of the hill/pile* foot, lowest part/point, base. 2 *the bottom of the pillar* base, foundation, basis, support, pedestal, substructure, substratum, groundwork, underpinning. 3 *the bottom of the car* underside, lower side, underneath, undersurface, belly. 4 *the bottom of the sea* floor, bed, depths. 5 *the bottom of the garden* the furthest part, the farthest point, the

far end. 6 *the bottom of the class* lowest level/position, least important/successful part, least honourable/valuable part. 7 *sitting on his bottom* hindquarters, buttocks; rear end, rear, seat, tail, posterior, rump; *inf* back-side, behind, bum, fundament, *derrière*, jacksy, arse; *Amer inf* butt, ass. 8 *drinking too much was at the bottom of it* origin, cause, root, source, starting-point, core, centre, heart, base. 9 *get to the bottom of it* basis, foundation, reality, essence, nitty-gritty, substance; essentials.

bottom adj *on the bottom shelf* lowest, last, undermost, ground.

bottomless adj 1 *bottomless pit* deep, immeasurable, fathomless, unfathomable, unfathomed. 2 *bottomless reserves of energy* boundless, inexhaustible, infinite, unlim-ited, immeasurable.

bough n branch, limb, twig.

boulder n rock, stone.

boulevard n avenue, drive, broad road, roadway, thoroughfare, promenade.

bounce v 1 *the ball bounced* rebound, spring back, bob, recoil, ricochet, jounce. 2 *chil-dren bouncing about* leap, bound, jump, spring, bob, skip, prance, romp, caper, hur-tle. 3 *bounce the troublemakers* throw out, eject, remove, expel, oust, get rid of, evict; *inf* kick out, boot out.

bounce n 1 *ball/material not having much bounce* spring, springiness, rebound, recoil, resilience, elasticity, give. 2 *losing bounce over the years* vitality, vigour, energy, vivac-ity, liveliness, life, animation, spiritedness, spirit, dynamism; *inf* go, get-up-and-go, pep, oomph, pizazz, zing, zip. 3 *with a run and a bounce* leap, bound, jump, spring, bob, skip.

bouncing adj *a bouncing young woman/baby| in bouncing health* robust, strong, vigorous, healthy, thriving, flourishing, blooming.

bound[1] adj 1 *the bound prisoners* tied, tied up, secured, roped, tethered, fettered. *see* BIND v 1. 2 *the bound sheets* fastened, secured, fixed, cased. 3 *she's bound to win* certain, sure, very likely, destined, predestined, fated. 4 *doctors bound by their professional code* obligated, obliged, duty-bound, con-strained, pledged to, committed to, beholden to, compelled, required. 5 *a future bound up with hers* connected with, tied up with, allied to, attached to, dependent on. 6 *bound up in their own affairs* occupied with, busy with, preoccupied with, engrossed in, obsessed with.

bound[2] v *bound over the fence|bound into the room* leap, jump, spring, bounce, hop, vault, hurdle, skip, bob, dance, prance, romp, caper, frisk, frolic, gambol, curvet.

bound² n *reach the finishing-post in one bound | the bounds of the lambs* leap, jump, spring, bounce, hop, vault, hurdle; skip, bob, dance, prance, romp, caper, frisk, frolic, gambol, curvet.

bound³ v **1** *views bounded by prejudice* limit, confine, restrict, cramp, straiten, restrain, demarcate, delimit, circumscribe, define. **2** *estates bounded by walls* enclose, surround, wall in, encircle, hem in, circumscribe. **3** *Germany is bounded on the west by France | Germany bounds on France* border, adjoin, abut, be next/adjacent to, be contiguous with.

boundary n **1** *the boundary between the countries* border, frontier, partition, dividing/ bounding line. **2** *the boundary of the forest* bounds, border, periphery, perimeter; confines, limits, extremities, margins, edges. *see* BOUNDS 2. **3** *the boundary between sentiment and sentimentality* dividing line, borderline, demarcation line. **4** *pushing back the boundaries of knowledge* bounds, limits, outer limits, confines, extremities, barriers.

boundless adj limitless, without limit, unlimited, illimitable, unbounded, endless, unending, never-ending, without end, inexhaustible, infinite, interminable, unceasing, everlasting, untold, immeasurable, measureless, incalculable, immense, vast, great.

bounds npl **1** *within the bounds of possibility* limits, boundaries, confines, restrictions, limitations, demarcations. **2** *within the bounds of the estate* boundaries, borders, confines, limits, extremeties, margins, edges, fringes, marches; periphery, perimeter, precinct, pale.

bountiful adj **1** *a bountiful hostess* generous, magnanimous, liberal, kind, giving, openhanded, unstinting, unsparing, munificent, benevolent, beneficent, philanthropic; *fml* eleemosynary. **2** *a bountiful supply of food* ample, abundant, bumper, superabundant, plentiful, copious, lavish, prolific, profuse, bounteous, princely, luxuriant, exuberant, plenteous.

bounty n *a bounty for finding the treasure* reward, recompense, remuneration, gratuity, tip, premium, bonus.

bouquet n **1** *the bride carrying a bouquet* bunch/spray of flowers, spray, posy, wreath, garland, nosegay, boutonnière, chaplet, corsage, buttonhole. **2** *the wine's bouquet* aroma, smell, fragrance, perfume, scent, redolence, savour, odour; odiferousness. **3** *bouquets from the management* compliment, commendation, tribute, eulogy; praise; congratulations.

bourgeois adj **1** *the bourgeois classes, not the nobility* middle-class, property-owning, propertied. **2** *bourgeois values* materialistic, capitalistic, non-Communist, moneyoriented. **3** *bourgeois way of life* conventional, ordinary, uncultured, philistine, uncreative, unimaginative.

bout n **1** *bouts of inactivity* spell, period, time, stretch, stint, turn, fit, run, session, round, season. **2** *a bout of flu* attack, fit, spell, paroxysm. **3** *defeated in the last bout* match, contest, round, competition, encounter, fight, struggle, set-to.

bovine adj **1** *bovine creatures* cowlike, cattlelike. **2** *bovine people hating activity* lifeless, sluggish, stolid, inanimate, phlegmatic, torpid. **3** *too bovine to grasp the facts* stupid, thick, dense, slow, dim-witted, dull-witted, doltish.

bow¹ v **1** *bow to the queen* incline the head/ body, make obeisance, nod, curtsey, bob, genuflect, bend the knee, salaam, prostrate oneself. **2** *age had bowed his back* bend, stoop, curve, arch, crook. **3** *bow to the inevitable* give in, give way to, yield, submit, surrender, succumb, capitulate, accept, defer, acquiesce in, comply with, kowtow. **4** *enemy activities bowing down the tribes* subjugate, subdue, conquer, vanquish, overcome, crush, overpower, bring to one's knees, humble, humiliate. **5** *bowing them into the restaurant* usher, conduct, show, guide, direct, escort. **bow out** leave, resign, retire, withdraw, step down, give up, get out, quit, pull out, back out.

bow¹ n *make a bow to the queen* inclination of the head/body, obeisance, nod, curtsey, bob, salaam; genuflection, prostration.

bow² n *the bow of a ship* prow, front, forepart, fore-end, stem, head, beak.

bowdlerize v expurgate, censor, bluepencil; *inf* clean up.

bowel n intestine, small intestine, large intestine, colon.

bowels npl **1** *an infection affecting the bowels* intestines, entrails, guts; *inf* insides, innards; *fml* viscera. **2** *the bowels of the earth/ machine* interior, inside, core, belly, cavity; depths; *inf* innards.

bower n **1** *a bower in the garden* arbour, shady place, leafy shelter, alcove, pergola, grotto. **2** *taking tea in the bower* summerhouse, gazebo, conservatory. **3** *ladies' bowers* boudoir, chamber, bedroom.

bowl n **1** *a bowl of fruit* dish, basin, vessel, container. **2** *the bowl of a tobacco pipe* hollow part, hollow, depression, dip. **3** *dust-bowl hollow*, crater, hole, depression, dip, valley. **4** *American football bowl* stadium, arena, amphitheatre, coliseum.

bowl v **1** *bowl a fast ball* throw, pitch, hurl, fling, spin, send, deliver. **2** *bowl the balls in the skittles alley* roll, pitch. **3** *bowling along in their cars* trundle, move, travel, drive, go, proceed. **4** *bowl a wicket* strike, hit, knock. **bowl over 1** *bowled over by her beauty/news* overwhelm, astound, amaze, astonish, dumbfound, stagger, flabbergast, stun, surprise. **2** *bowl over an old woman* knock down, bring down, fell, floor.

box¹ n **1** *a box of cigars/tea* container, receptacle, crate, case, carton, pack, package, chest, trunk, bin, coffer, casket. **2** *a theatre/telephone box* compartment, cubicle, enclosure, kiosk, cabin, hut.

box¹ v *box the goods* package, pack, wrap, bundle up. **box in/up** enclose, shut in, hem in, fence in, confine, restrain, constrain, cage in, coop up.

box² n *give him a box on the ears* thump, cuff, slap, punch. *see* BOX² v 2.

box² v **1** *he boxes professionally* fight, spar, grapple, take to fisticuffs. **2** *box him on the ears* strike, hit, thump, cuff, slap, punch, knock, wallop, batter, pummel, thwack, buffet; *inf* belt, sock, clout, whack, slug, slam, whop.

boxer n fighter, pugilist, prizefighter, sparring partner.

boy n **1** *men and boys* youth, lad, youngster, young person, kid, schoolboy, junior, stripling, whippersnapper. **2** *send for the boy* page, servant, waiter, *garçon*, boots.

boycott v **1** *boycott their company|the party* stay away from, ostracize, spurn, avoid, eschew, shun, reject, send to Coventry, blackball, blacklist. **2** *boycott their goods* ban, bar, black, blacklist, embargo, place an embargo on, prohibit, debar, outlaw, proscribe.

boyfriend n sweetheart, young man, lover, man, suitor, admirer; *inf* steady, date; *Amer* beau.

boyish adj youthful, young, childlike, immature, adolescent, juvenile, childish, callow, green, puerile.

brace n **1** *holding the pieces of metal in a brace* clamp, vice, fastener, coupling. **2** *the wall's brace* support, prop, beam, strut, stay, truss, reinforcement, buttress, shoring-up, stanchion. **3** *a brace of pheasants* two, couple, pair, duo. **4** *printing braces* bracket, parenthesis.

brace v **1** *beams firmly braced* support, strengthen, reinforce, fortify, shore up, prop up, hold up, buttress. **2** *braced his foot against the wall* steady, secure, stabilize, make fast. **3** *brace oneself for the results* prepare, steady, strengthen, fortify, tense.

bracelet n bangle, band, wristlet, circlet, armlet, anklet.

bracing adj invigorating, refreshing, stimulating, energizing, exhilarating, reviving, fortifying, strengthening, restorative, tonic, vitalizing, rousing, healthful, health-giving, fresh, brisk, crisp, cool.

bracket n **1** *a wall bracket* support, prop, buttress. **2** *put the words in brackets* parenthesis, round bracket, square bracket, angle bracket, brace. **3** *in a different social/financial bracket* group, grouping, category, categorization, grade, grading, classification, class, set, section, division, order.

brackish adj slightly salty/briny, saline, bitter, impure, undrinkable, unsavoury.

brag v boast, crow, show off, bluster, blow one's own trumpet, sing one's own praises, pat oneself on the back; *inf* talk big, blow hard, lay it on thick; *Amer inf* shoot the bull, speak for Buncombe; *lit* vaunt, roister, hyperbolize.

braggart n boaster, brag, show-off, blusterer, trumpeter, braggadocio, fanfaronade, gasconader; *inf* blow-hard, big-mouth, bag of wind, windbag, loud-mouth, gasbag, bullshitter, bull-shooter.

braid v **1** *braid the thread/hair* weave, interweave, plait, entwine, twine, intertwine, interlace, twist, wind, interthread. **2** *braid the jacket* trim, decorate, edge, fringe, befrill.

braid n **1** *trim it with braid* cord, thread, tape, twine, yarn. **2** *hair in braids* plait, pigtail.

brain n **1** *studying the brain* cerebral matter; *fml* encephalon. **2** *have a good brain* mind, intellect, brainpower, intelligence, wit, head; powers of reasoning; *inf* grey matter. **3** *one of the brains of our year* genius, intellectual, intellect, thinker, mind, scholar, mastermind, sage, pundit, polymath; *inf* highbrow, egghead, Einstein.

brains npl *not to have the brains to do it* mind, intellect, intelligence, wit, head, sense, cleverness, brightness, understanding, shrewdness, sagacity, acumen, capacity, capability; *inf* nous, savvy.

brainwashing n indoctrination, inculcation, persuasion, conditioning, infixation.

brainy adj clever, intelligent, bright, brilliant, smart, gifted.

brake n *a brake on spending/enthusiasm* curb, check, damper, restraint, constraint, rein, control.

brake v *brake approaching the junction* reduce speed, slow, slow down, decelerate, put on the brakes, hit the brake.

branch n **1** *the branch of a tree* bough, limb, stem, twig, shoot, sprig, arm. **2** *the branch of the deer's antlers* offshoot, prong. **3** *the local branch of the bank* division, subdivision, section, subsection, department, part, wing, office. **4** *branches of the railway/stream* subdivision, subsidiary, tributary, feeder.

branch v **1** *the road branches before the village | the road branched off* fork, divide, subdivide, furcate, bifurcate, divaricate; separate, diverge. **2** *they branched off from the motorway/topic* diverge from, deviate from, depart from, turn aside from, shoot off from, go off at a tangent to. **branch out** *the firm must branch out into new areas* extend, spread out, widen, broaden, diversify, open up, expand, enlarge, increase, proliferate, multiply.

brand n **1** *a brand of canned soup* make, kind, type, sort, variety, line, label, trade name, trade mark, registered trade mark. **2** *her particular brand of humour* kind, type, sort, variety, style, stamp, cast. **3** *recognize the cow by its brand* identifying mark, identification, tag, marker, earmark. **4** *a brand on him for life* stigma, stain, blot, taint, slur.

brand v **1** *identifying marks branded on cattle* burn, burn in, scorch, sear, stamp, mark. **2** *unhappy experiences branded on his mind* stamp, imprint, print, engrave, impress, fix. **3** *branded as a thief* stigmatize, mark, disgrace, discredit, denounce, besmirch, taint.

brandish v wave, flourish, wield, raise, swing, shake, wag, display, flaunt, show off.

brash adj **1** *a loud brash young man* bold, self-confident, self-assertive, audacious, aggressive, brazen, forward, cocky, impudent, insolent, impertinent, rude, cheeky. **2** *brash actions* hasty, rash, impetuous, impulsive, reckless, precipitate, careless, heedless, incautious. **3** *brash colours* loud, showy, garish, gaudy, ostentatious, vulgar, tasteless, tawdry.

brassy adj **1** *a brassy blonde* loud, brazen, shameless, forward, bold, self-assertive, brash, pert, impudent, insolent, cheeky, flashy, vulgar, showy, garish; *inf* pushy. **2** *brassy ornaments* brass, brazen, metallic. **3** *brassy music* blaring, loud, noisy, thundering, deafening, harsh, raucous, dissonant,

cacophonous, jangling, grating, jarring, strident, piercing, shrill.

brat n imp, rascal, urchin, minx, whippersnapper, spoiled brat.

bravado n show of courage/confidence, swagger, swaggering, boldness, audacity, blustering, boasting, boastfulness, bragging, bombast, swashbuckling; *lit* vaunting, braggadocio, fanfaronade.

brave adj **1** *brave soldiers* courageous, valiant, intrepid, fearless, plucky, game, gallant, heroic, bold, daring, audacious, resolute, undaunted, dauntless, lionhearted, valorous, doughty, mettlesome; *inf* gutsy, spunky. **2** *a brave show* splendid, spectacular, fine, ostentatious, showy.

brave n *Indian braves* warrior, soldier, fighter, fighting man.

brave v *brave the weather* face, stand up to, endure, put up with, bear, suffer, withstand, defy, challenge, confront; bell the cat, beard the lion in his den, bite the bullet.

bravery n courage, courageousness, valour, intrepidity, fearlessness, pluck, pluckiness, gameness, gallantry, heroism, boldness, daring, audacity, resolution, fortitude, grit, mettle, spirit, dauntlessness, doughtiness, hardihood; *inf* guts, spunk.

bravo interj well done!, take a bow!, encore!

brawl n *a brawl in a public house* fight, affray, fracas, wrangle, mêlée, rumpus, scuffle, altercation, squabble, clash, quarrel, argument, disagreement, free-for-all, tussle, brouhaha, commotion, uproar, donnybrook; fisticuffs; *inf* row, punch-up, scrap, ruckus.

brawl v *brawling in the street* fight, wrangle, wrestle, scuffle, tussle, clash, battle, quarrel, argue, altercate; *inf* row, scrap.

brawn n brawniness, muscle, muscular strength, muscularity, burliness, heftiness, huskiness, physical strength, physique, robustness, might; *inf* beefiness, beef.

brawny adj muscular, burly, hefty, powerfully built, strong, robust, sturdy, powerful, strapping, husky, bulky, stalwart, mighty, sinewy, well-knit.

bray v whinny, neigh, hee haw.

brazen adj **1** *a brazen hussy* bold, audacious, defiant, forward, brash, presumptuous, pushing, impudent, insolent, impertinent, brassy, cheeky, pert, saucy, shameless, immodest, unashamed, unabashed; *inf* pushy. **2** *brazen objects* brass, brassy, metallic.

brazen v **brazen it out** be defiant, be unrepentant, be impenitent, be unashamed, be unabashed, stand one's ground, show a bold front, put a bold face on it.

breach n **1** *a breach in the sea wall* break, rupture, split, crack, fissure, fracture, rent, rift, cleft, opening, gap, hole, aperture, chasm, gulf. **2** *a breach of the agreement* | *a breach of confidence* breaking, contravention, violation, infringement, non-observance, transgression, neglect, infraction; breach of promise, breach of the peace. **3** *a breach in diplomatic relations* | *a breach between the two families* breaking-off, estrangement, separation, severance, parting, parting of the ways, division, rift, schism, disunion, alienation, disaffection, variance, difference, dissension, falling-out, quarrel, discord.

breach v **1** *breach the enemy defences* break/burst through, rupture, split, make a gap in, open up. **2** *breach the contract/law* break, contravene, violate, infringe, defy, disobey, flaunt, transgress against, infract.

bread n **1** *serve bread with the soup* | *loaves of bread* white bread, brown bread, rye bread, whole-wheat bread, whole-grain bread, granary bread, unleavened bread, soda bread, sourdough bread, French bread, French stick, baguette, pitta bread, paratha, nan, chapatti, breakfast roll, scone, bap, bun, croissant, brioche, bagel. **2** *earn the children's bread* | *our daily bread* food, nourishment, sustenance, subsistence, fare, nutriment, diet; provisions, victuals, viands; *fml* aliment. **3** *spend the bread* money, cash, finance; funds; *inf* dough, brass, dosh, the needful, the necessary, shekels, tin, dibs, spondulicks.

breadth n **1** *the breadth of the room* width, broadness, wideness, thickness, span, spread. **2** *the breadth of her knowledge* | *the breadth of support* extent, extensiveness, scope, range, scale, degree, compass, spread, sweep, comprehensiveness, vastness, expanse, magnitude, measure, volume, immensity; dimensions. **3** *breadth of spirit* liberality, liberalness, broad-mindedness, open-mindedness, freedom, latitude, magnanimity.

break v **1** *break the cup/bag* | *broke his arm* smash, shatter, crack, fracture, split, burst, fragment, splinter, shiver, crash, snap, rend, tear, divide, sever, separate, part, demolish, disintegrate. **2** *the cup/bag/arm broke* smash, shatter, crack, fracture, split, burst, fragment, splinter, crash, snap, tear, sever, separate. **3** *the machine broke* become damaged, cease to operate/work/function,

be unusable; *inf* go kaput. **4** *the skin is not broken* pierce, puncture, perforate, penetrate, open up. **5** *break the law* contravene, violate, infringe, breach, commit a breach of, defy, disobey, flaunt, transgress against; *fml* infract. **6** *break for tea* take a break, stop, pause, discontinue, rest, give up; *inf* knock off, take five. **7** *break one's concentration/journey/sleep* interrupt, suspend, discontinue, cut, disturb, interfere with. **8** *break his resolve* | *it broke her morale* overcome, crush, overpower, overwhelm, subdue, defeat, cow, suppress, extinguish, weaken, impair, undermine, dispirit, demoralize, incapacitate, cripple, enfeeble. **9** *he broke under questioning* be overcome, crack, collapse, give in, yield, cave in, crumple, go to pieces. **10** *the recession/scandal broke him* ruin, crush, bring to one's knees, humble, degrade, reduce to nothing, bankrupt, make bankrupt, pauperize. **11** *break the news gently* tell, announce, impart, reveal, divulge, disclose, let out, make public, proclaim. **12** *break the record* beat, surpass, outdo, better, exceed, outstrip, top; *inf* cap. **13** *break the code* decipher, decode, unravel, solve, figure out. **14** *the day/storm/scandal broke* begin, come into being, come forth, emerge, erupt, burst out, appear, occur. **15** *the weather broke* change, alter, vary, shift, metamorphose. **16** *break one's fall* cushion, soften, lessen, diminish, moderate. **17** *waves breaking against the sea wall* crash, hurl, dash, hit, collide with. **break away 1** *the prisoner broke away* run away, make a break for it, flee, make off, escape, decamp; *inf* make a run for it, run for it, hook it, leg it. **2** *break away from the main political party* break with, detach oneself from, secede from, separate from, part company with, leave, form a splinter group. **break down 1** *the car broke down* stop working, cease to function, seize up, fail; *inf* conk out, go kaput. **2** *the talks broke down* | *law and order broke down* fail, collapse, come to nothing, founder, fall through, come to grief, disintegrate; *inf* fizzle out. **3** *he broke down and cried* lose control, collapse, cave in, crumble, be overcome, go to pieces, disintegrate, come apart at the seams; *inf* lose one's cool, crack up. **4** *break down the resistance* overcome, crush, overpower, overwhelm, subdue, defeat, cow, suppress. *see* BREAK v 8. **5** *break down and analyse the figures* separate/divide out, segregate, analyse, dissect, categorize, classify, itemize. **break in 1** *break in hurriedly* burst in, barge in, push/thrust one's way in. **2** *he broke in with his own comments* interrupt, butt in, intervene, cut in, intrude, interfere, put one's oar in. **3** *he broke in last night* break and enter, commit burglary, burgle, rob. **4** *break in the horse | break in the new recruits* train, tame, condition, prepare, initiate, show the ropes to. **5** *break in new shoes* begin to wear/use, become/get used to, accustom, habituate. **break into 1** *break into the conversation* interrupt, butt into, intervene in. **2** *break into a gallop/song* begin suddenly, commence, launch into, burst into, give way to. **3** *break into his savings* begin to use, use part of, open and use. **4** *break into the room hurriedly* burst/barge into, push/thrust one's way into. **5** *break into the house* burgle, rob. **break off 1** *break off a branch* pull off, snap off, detach, separate, sever. **2** *the handle broke off* come off, snap off, become detached, separate off, become separated/severed. **3** *break off diplomatic relations | broke off their engagement* end, bring to an end, terminate, stop, cease, finish, discontinue, call a halt to, suspend, desist from. **break out 1** *break out of prison* escape, make one's escape, break loose, burst out, get free, free oneself, flee, abscond, bolt. **2** *war/fighting broke out* start/commence/occur suddenly, erupt, burst out, set in, arise. **3** *it's time she broke out and made her own decisions* become free/liberated, become emancipated, unshackle/unfetter oneself. **4** *break out in a rash* erupt, burst out. **5** *"Wait!" he broke out* exclaim, call out, cry, shout, utter, yell. **break up 1** *the meeting broke up at midnight | school breaks up tomorrow* adjourn, end, come to an end, stop, discontinue, terminate. **2** *the crowd broke up* disperse, scatter, disband, part, separate, go their separate ways, part company. **3** *the police broke up the crowd* disperse, scatter, disband, separate, put to rout, send off. **4** *the couple have broken up* separate, part, divorce, split up, dissolve a marriage/relationship, come to the parting of the ways. **5** *jealousy broke up their marriage* bring to an end, end, terminate, bring to a stop/halt, kill, destroy. **6** *breaking up at his jokes* laugh, burst out laughing, giggle, chuckle, chortle, guffaw, double up, split one's sides, hold one's sides; *inf* fall about, be in stitches.

break n **1** *a break in the sea wall* crack, hole, gap, opening, gash, chink, fracture, split, fissure, tear, rent, rupture, rift, chasm, cleft. **2** *a break for tea* interval, stop, pause, halt, rest, respite, breathing-space, lull, interlude, intermission, recess; tea break, coffee break, supper break; *inf* breather, breathing-spell, let-up, time out, down time. **3** *a weekend break* holiday, vacation, time off, recess. **4** *a break in their education* interruption, discontinuation, suspension,

hiatus, lacuna. **5** *a break in the weather* change, alteration, variation. **6** *a break in diplomatic relations* rift, breach, split, rupture, discontinuation, schism, chasm, alienation, disaffection. **7** *although losing, we got a lucky break* stroke of luck, advantage, gain, opportunity, chance, opening.

breakable adj fragile, frangible, frail, delicate, flimsy, insubstantial, brittle, crumbly, friable, not shatter-proof, destructible, gimcrack, jerry-built.

breakdown n **1** *the car's/machine's breakdown* stopping, stoppage, seizing up, failure, malfunctioning; *inf* conking-out. *see* BREAK v break down 1. **2** *the breakdown of the talks* failure, collapse, foundering, falling-through; *inf* fizzling-out. *see* BREAK v break down 2. **3** *suffer a breakdown* collapse, nervous breakdown, loss of control, going to pieces, disintegration, caving-in; *inf* crack-up. *see* BREAK v break down 3. **4** *a breakdown of the figures* separation, division, segregation, itemization, analysis, dissection, categorization, classification.

breaker n *children jumping over the breakers* wave, roller, comber, billow; white horses.

break-in n *break-ins in the neighbourhood* breaking and entering, house-breaking, burglary, forced/unlawful entry; robbery, theft. *see* BREAK v break in3.

breakneck adj fast, rapid, speedy, swift, reckless, dangerous.

breakthrough n *a breakthrough in cancer research* advance, step forward, leap, quantum leap, discovery, find, development, improvement; progress.

breakup n *the breakup of their marriage/partnership* end, termination, cessation, dissolution, disintegration, splitting up, breakdown, failure, collapse, foundering. *see* BREAK v break up 4, 5.

breakwater n sea wall, jetty, embankment, barrier, mole, groyne.

breast n **1** *her plump breasts* bust, bosom, chest, front, thorax; *inf* boob, tit, knocker; *tech* mamma. **2** *warm feelings in their breasts* heart, soul, being, core, seat of the emotions/affections; feelings.

breath n **1** *take a deep breath* gulp of air, inhalation, inspiration, exhalation, expiration, pant, gasp, wheeze; breathing, respiration. **2** *no breath left in him* breath of life, life, life force, animation, vital force. **3** *hardly a breath of air* breeze, puff, gust, waft, zephyr. **4** *a breath of spring* hint, suggestion, whiff, undertone, trace, touch, whisper, suspicion. **5** *stop for breath* break, interval, pause, lull, rest, respite, breathing-space; *inf* breather. **6** *all over in a breath* moment, instant, minute, second.

breathe v **1** *she breathed deeply* respire, inhale, inspire, exhale, expire, puff, pant, gasp, wheeze, gulp. **2** *as long as he breathes* be alive, live, have life. **3** *breathe new life/ courage into them* infuse, instil, inject, impart, imbue with, transfuse. **4** *breathe a message of love* whisper, murmur, sigh, say, utter, voice, articulate, express. **5** *her whole appearance breathed defiance* express, suggest, indicate, manifest, intimate, betoken, augur. **6** *the wind breathing through the trees* blow, whisper, murmur, sigh.

breather n **1** *let's take a breather from work* break, interval, stop, pause, halt, rest, respite, lull, breathing-space, recess. *see* BREAK n 2. **2** *I'm going out for a breather* breath of air, fresh air.

breathless adj **1** *getting breathless climbing stairs* out of breath, wheezing, panting, puffing, gasping, choking, gulping, winded. **2** *breathless with excitement* agog, all agog, with bated breath, avid, eager, excited, on edge, on tenterhooks, in suspense, open-mouthed, anxious.

breathtaking adj spectacular, impressive, magnificent, awesome, awe-inspiring, astounding, astonishing, amazing, thrilling, stunning, exciting.

breed v **1** *lions breeding in captivity* reproduce, procreate, multiply, give birth, bring forth young, beget, propagate. **2** *breed horses* raise, rear, nurture. **3** *born and bred in the town* bring up, rear, raise, develop, educate, train, nurture. **4** *breed disease/discontent* cause, bring about, give rise to, create, produce, generate, arouse, stir up, induce, originate, occasion, make for.

breed n **1** *a breed of cows* family, variety, type, kind, class, strain, stock, line. **2** *of European breed* stock, race, lineage, extraction, pedigree. **3** *a new breed of doctor* kind, type, variety, class, brand, strain.

breeding n **1** *the season for breeding* reproducing, reproduction, generation, multiplying, propagation. *see* BREED v 1. **2** *the breeding of horses/plants* raising, rearing, nurturing. **3** *a lady by breeding* upbringing, rearing, education, training, nurture. **4** *people of breeding* refinement, cultivation, culture, polish, civility, gentility, courtesy; manners.

breeze n gentle wind, breath of wind, puff of air, zephyr, gust, flurry, waft, current of air, draught; sea breeze, land breeze, onshore breeze.

breeze v *the family breezed along/in* stroll, sally, sail, sweep, glide, drift, flit.

breezy adj **1** *a breezy day* windy, blowy, blustery, gusty, squally, airy, fresh. **2** *a breezy manner/individual* jaunty, cheerful, cheery, light-hearted, carefree, blithe, free and easy, easygoing, casual, airy, sprightly, lively, spirited, buoyant, sparkling, animated, vivacious, frisky, sunny; *inf* bright-eyed and bushy-tailed.

brevity n **1** *the brevity of the speech/report* shortness, briefness, conciseness, succinctness, compactness, terseness, economy of language, pithiness, crispness, concision, condensation, pointedness, curtness, compendiousness, brachylogy. **2** *the brevity of summer/the brevity of his life* shortness, briefness, transitoriness, transience, impermanence, ephemerality.

brew v **1** *brew beer* make, ferment. **2** *brew tea* infuse, prepare. **3** *the tea is brewing* infuse, be in preparation; *dial* mash. **4** *trouble is brewing* gather, gather force, form, loom, be in the offing, be imminent, be threatening, be impending, impend. **5** *brewing something evil* plot, scheme, hatch, plan, devise, invent, concoct, stir up, foment; *inf* cook up.

brew n **1** *favourite brew/home brew* drink, beverage, liquor, ale, beer, tea; infusion, preparation; witches' brew. **2** *a brew of sex, violence and horror* mixture, blend, concoction, potpourri, *mélange*, conglomeration.

bribe n *give the minister a bribe to get the contract* inducement, enticement, lure, subornation, carrot, sop to Cerberus; *inf* backhander, sweetener, graft, hush money, protection money, boodle, kickback; *Amer inf* payola.

bribe v *bribe the local mayor* buy off, corrupt, give an inducement to, suborn; *inf* grease/ oil the palm of, get at, pay off, give a backhander/sweetener to, fix, square.

bric-à-brac n knick-knacks, trinkets, gewgaws, baubles, curios, ornaments, bibelots.

bridal adj nuptial, marital, matrimonial, connubial, conjugal; *lit* hymeneal, epithalamic.

bride n newlywed, honeymooner, blushing bride; war bride, GI bride.

bridge n **1** *a bridge over the river* arch, span, overpass, flyover, viaduct. **2** *a bridge between the two families* bond, link, tie, connection, cord, binding.

bridge v **1** *bridge the river* span, cross, cross over, go over, pass over, traverse, extend across, reach across, arch over. **2** *bridge our* *differences* join, unite, link, connect, tie, attach, bind, bridge the gap between.

bridle n **1** *a horse's bridle* halter; *Amer* hackamore, headstall. **2** *put a bridle on her tongue* curb, check, restraint, control.

bridle v **1** *bridle your tongue/anger* curb, restrain, hold back, keep control of, keep in check, put a check on, check, govern, master, subdue. **2** *she bridled at his insults* bristle, get angry, become indignant, rear up, draw oneself up, feel one's hackles rise.

brief adj **1** *a brief speech/report* short, concise, succinct, to the point, compact, terse, economic, pithy, crisp, condensed, compressed, pointed, curt, thumbnail, epigrammatic, sparing, compendious. **2** *brief summer days | a brief life* short, short-lived, fleeting, momentary, passing, fading, transitory, transient, temporary, impermanent, ephemeral, evanescent, fugacious. **3** *a brief skirt* short, scanty, skimpy. **4** *the boss was rather brief with him* short, abrupt, curt, sharp, brusque, blunt.

brief n **1** *a brief of the proceedings* outline, summary, abstract, résumé, synopsis, précis, sketch, digest, epitome. **2** *the barrister's brief* argument, case, proof, data, defence, evidence, contention, demonstration. **3** *getting his brief for his new job* briefing, information, guidance, preparation, priming, data, intelligence; instructions, directions; *inf* gen, run-down, low-down.

brief v *brief the barrister/ambassador* instruct, inform, give instructions/information/directions, direct, guide, advise, prepare, prime; *inf* give someone the gen/run-down/low-down, fill in, gen up, put someone in the picture.

briefing n **1** *at a briefing to discuss the situation* conference, meeting, discussion, forum, seminar, symposium. **2** *recruits being given their briefing* brief, information, guidance, preparation; instructions, directions. *see* BRIEF n 3.

briefly adv **1** *he spoke briefly* concisely, succinctly, to the point, tersely, economically, sparingly. **2** *briefly, I want to say goodbye* in brief, concisely, succinctly, in a few words, in a nutshell. **3** *living briefly* fleetingly, momentarily, transitorily, transiently, temporarily, ephemerally.

brigade n *fire brigade | the brigade of workers* group, band, team, squad, party, association, body, contingent, crew, force, outfit, section, organization.

brigand n robber, bandit, outlaw, ruffian, desperado, plunderer, marauder, gangster, criminal, highwayman, pirate, freebooter.

bright adj **1** *a bright light* shining, brilliant, vivid, intense, blazing, dazzling, beaming, sparkling, flashing, glittering, scintillating, gleaming, glowing, twinkling, glistening, shimmering; illuminated, luminous, lustrous, radiant, effulgent, incandescent, phosphorescent. **2** *a bright day* clear, cloudless, unclouded, fair, sunny, pleasant, clement. **3** *bright colours* vivid, brilliant, intense, glowing, bold, rich. **4** *bright children/minds* clever, intelligent, sharp, quick-witted, quick, smart, brainy, brilliant, astute, acute, ingenious, inventive, resourceful, proficient, accomplished. **5** *a bright smile/personality* happy, genial, cheerful, jolly, joyful, gay, merry, light-hearted, vivacious, lively, buoyant. **6** *a bright future* promising, optimistic, hopeful, favourable, propitious, auspicious, providential, encouraging, lucky, fortunate, good, excellent, golden.

brighten v **1** *lights brightening the room* make bright/brighter, light up, lighten, illuminate, illumine, irradiate. **2** *her mood brightening* cheer up, perk up. **3** *brightening her day/mood* cheer up, gladden, enliven, buoy up, animate; *inf* buck up, pep up.

brilliance n **1** *the brilliance of the lights* brightness, vividness, intensity, blaze, beam, dazzle, sparkle, flash, glitter, luminosity, lustre, radiance, effulgence, refulgence, resplendence. **2** *the brilliance of the spectacle* magnificence, splendour, splendidness, grandeur, glamour, pomp, lustre, resplendence, illustriousness, éclat.

brilliant adj **1** *a brilliant light* bright, shining, vivid, intense, ablaze, radiant, beaming, gleaming, dazzling, luminous, lustrous, scintillating, resplendent, effulgent, refulgent, coruscating. **2** *brilliant children* bright, clever, intelligent, smart, brainy, intellectual, gifted, talented, accomplished, educated, scholarly, learned, erudite, cerebral, precocious. **3** *a brilliant course of action* clever, intelligent, smart, astute, cute, acute, masterly, resourceful, inventive, discerning. **4** *a brilliant display* magnificent, splendid, superb, impressive, remarkable, exceptional, glorious, illustrious. **5** *having a brilliant time | a brilliant film* excellent, superb, very good, outstanding, exceptional; *inf* brill.

brim n **1** *the brim of the cup | full to the brim* rim, lip, brink, edge. **2** *the brim of the hat/cap* projecting edge, visor, shield, shade.

brim v *the cup was brimming | eyes brimming with tears* be full, be filled up, be filled to the top, be full to capacity, overflow, run/well over.

brimful adj brimming, full, filled, overfull, running over, flush.

bring v 1 *bring books/water* come conveying/ carrying, carry, bear, take, fetch, convey, transport, send, deliver, lead, guide, conduct, usher, escort. 2 *war brought hardship* cause, create, produce, result in, wreak, effect, contribute to, engender, occasion. 3 *bring a legal action* put forward, prefer, propose, initiate, institute. 4 *his job brings him a huge wage* make, fetch, yield, net, gross, return, produce, command. **bring about 1** *bring about reforms* cause to happen/occur, cause, create, produce, give rise to, achieve, result in, effect, occasion, bring to pass, effectuate. 2 *bring a ship about* turn, turn round, reverse, reverse the direction of. **bring down 1** *bring down prices* cause to fall, lower, reduce, cut. 2 *bring down the government* cause to fall, overthrow, pull down, lay low. 3 *the bad news brought her down* depress, sadden, cast down, make desolate, weigh down. **bring forward** *bring forward points for discussion* raise, put forward, propose, suggest, table, adduce. **bring in 1** *his son/job brings in £3000* earn, yield, gross, net, return, fetch in, realize. 2 *bring in a new bill* introduce, launch, inaugurate, initiate, institute, usher in. **bring off** *bring off the attempt* pull off, carry off, achieve, succeed in, accomplish, bring about, carry out, execute, perform, discharge, complete. **bring up 1** *bring up the children* rear, raise, train, educate, care for, nurture, foster, develop. 2 *bring up the subject* raise, broach, introduce, mention, allude to, touch upon, propose, submit.

brink n 1 *the brink of the cliff/lake* edge, verge, margin, rim, extremity, limit, border, boundary, fringe, skirt. 2 *on the brink of disaster* verge, edge, threshold, point.

brisk adj 1 *at a brisk pace* quick, rapid, fast, swift, speedy, energetic, lively, vigorous, agile, nimble, spry, sprightly, spirited, alacritous. 2 *brisk weather* bracing, fresh, crisp, keen, biting, invigorating, refreshing, exhilarating, energizing; *inf* nippy. 3 *a brisk manner/brisk speech* no-nonsense, brusque, abrupt, sharp, curt, crisp, snappy. 4 *business was brisk* rapid, busy, bustling, active, hectic.

bristle n 1 *shave off his bristles* hair, stubble, designer stubble; whiskers. 2 *a hedgehog's bristles* prickle, spine, quill, thorn, barb.

bristle v 1 *the dog's hair bristled* rise, stand up, stand on end, horripilate. 2 *she bristled at the insults* bridle, get angry/infuriated, become indignant, be irritated/defensive, rear up, draw oneself up. 3 *a place bristling with tourists* swarm, teem, crawl; *inf* be thick, be alive.

bristly adj hairy, stubbly, unshaven, whiskered, whiskery, bewhiskered, bearded, rough, prickly.

brittle adj 1 *a brittle substance* breakable, splintery, shatterable, hard, crisp, fragile, frail, delicate, frangible. 2 *a brittle laugh* harsh, hard, sharp, strident, grating, rasping. 3 *a brittle young woman* edgy, on edge, nervous, nervy, tense, stiff; *inf* uptight.

broach v 1 *broach the subject* introduce, bring up, raise, mention, open, put forward, propound, propose, suggest, submit. 2 *broach a bottle* open, uncork, start; *inf* crack. 3 *broach a barrel* pierce, puncture, tap, draw off.

broad adj 1 *a broad street* wide, large. 2 *broad plains* extensive, vast, spacious, expansive, sweeping, boundless. 3 *offers a broad range of subjects* wide, wide-ranging, broad-ranging, general, comprehensive, inclusive, encyclopedic, all-embracing, universal, unlimited. 4 *the broad outline of the plan* general, undetailed, non-detailed, nonspecific, unspecific, vague, loose. 5 *a broad hint* clear, obvious, direct, plain, explicit, straightforward, clear-cut, unmistakable, undisguised, unconcealed. 6 *broad daylight* full, complete, total, clear, open. 7 *a woman of broad views* broad-minded, liberal, openminded, tolerant, unprejudiced, unbiased, fair, just, free-thinking, progressive. 8 *somewhat broad humour* coarse, vulgar, gross, unrefined, indelicate, indecent, improper, blue; *inf* near the bone/knuckle.

broadcast v 1 *broadcast programmes* transmit, relay, beam, send out, put on the air, radio, televise, telecast. 2 *broadcast the news of his downfall* make public, announce, report, publicize, publish, advertise, proclaim, air, spread, circulate, pass round, disseminate, promulgate, blazon. 3 *broadcast seed* scatter, sow, disperse, strew.

broadcast n *appear on a radio/television broadcast* programme, radio/television show, show, transmission, telecast.

broaden v 1 *broaden the road* make broader, widen, make wider. 2 *his shoulders broadened* become broader, widen, become wider, fill out. 3 *broaden his knowledge/experience/ horizons* widen, expand, enlarge, extend, increase, augment, supplement, add to, amplify, fill out, develop, open up, swell.

broad-minded adj open-minded, liberal, tolerant, forbearing, indulgent, impartial, unprejudiced, unbiased, unbigoted, undogmatic, catholic, flexible, dispassionate, just, fair, progressive, free-thinking.

broadside n **1** *fire a broadside in war* volley, salvo, cannonade, barrage. **2** *receive broadsides from the press* attack, criticism, censure, assault, onslaught, abuse, battering, harangue, diatribe, philippic; *inf* slating, flak, brickbats.

brochure n booklet, leaflet, pamphlet, folder, handbill, hand-out, circular, notice, advertisement; *Amer* flyer.

broil v **1** *broil meat* grill, barbecue, fry, toast. **2** *he was broiling in the sun* be hot, be roasting, be burning, be boiling.

broiling adj *a broiling day* hot, scorching, roasting, boiling/burning hot, blistering, blistering/searing hot.

broke adj penniless, moneyless, bankrupt, insolvent, poverty-stricken, impoverished, impecunious, penurious, indigent, destitute, ruined, without a penny to one's name, stony-broke, flat broke; *inf* on one's uppers, cleaned out, strapped for cash, on one's beam ends, bust, skint.

broken adj **1** *a broken cup/bag/arm* smashed, shattered, cracked, fractured, split, burst, fragmented, splintered, shivered, crushed, snapped, rent, torn, separated, severed, destroyed, demolished, disintegrated. **2** *the machine is broken* damaged, faulty, defective, out of order/commission, non-functioning, inoperative, imperfect; kaput, bust. **3** *broken skin* pierced, punctured, perforated. **4** *broken laws* contravened, violated, infringed, disobeyed, disregarded, ignored, flaunted, transgressed, infracted. **5** *a broken sleep/journey | a broken chain of thought* interrupted, disturbed, disconnected, disrupted, discontinuous, fragmentary, incomplete, intermittent, spasmodic, erratic. **6** *a broken man/army* beaten, defeated, vanquished, overpowered, overwhelmed, subdued, crushed, humbled, dishonoured, ruined, crippled, demoralized, dispirited, discouraged. **7** *broken firms* ruined, crushed, bankrupt, bankrupted, pauperized, brought low, humbled. **8** *broken English* halting, hesitating, disjointed, faltering, stumbling, stammering, imperfect.

broken-down adj **1** *a broken-down machine* broken, damaged, faulty, defective, out of order/commission, non-functioning, inoperative; *inf* on the blink, kaput, bust, clapped out. **2** *a broken-down old cottage* dilapidated, in disrepair, ramshackle.

broken-hearted adj heartbroken, grief-stricken, desolate, despairing, devastated, inconsolable, prostrated, miserable, overwhelmed, wretched, sorrowing, mourning, forlorn, woeful, bowed down, crestfallen.

broker n agent, negotiator, middleman, intermediary, factor, dealer, broker-dealer, stockbroker, insurance broker.

bronze adj bronze-coloured, copper-coloured, copper, reddish-brown, chestnut, metallic brown, rust-coloured, rust, henna.

brooch n pin, clip, breast-pin, tie-pin, tie-clip.

brood n **1** *the hen and her brood* young, offspring, progeny, family, hatch, clutch, nest, litter. **2** *Mrs Smith and her brood* children, offspring, family; youngsters; *inf* kids.

brood v **1** *brood over/about the problem* worry, fret, agonize, think, ponder, meditate, muse, mull, dwell upon, ruminate. **2** *hens brooding* sit on/hatch/incubate eggs, cover young.

brook n *a mountain brook* stream, streamlet, burn, rivulet, rill, brooklet, runnel; *dial* beck, gill.

brook v *brook no delay* tolerate, stand, bear, allow.

brothel n bordello, house of ill repute, house of prostitution, bawdy house, whorehouse, bagnio; *inf* knocking-shop.

brother n **1** *she has two brothers* sibling, sib, blood-brother; kinsman. **2** *brothers in crime* associate, colleague, companion, partner, comrade; *inf* mate, pal, chum; *fml* confrère compeer. **3** *brothers praying* cleric, monk, friar, religious.

brotherhood n **1** *ties of brotherhood* brotherliness, fraternalism, kinship. **2** *feelings of brotherhood* comradeship, fellowship, companionship, camaraderie, friendship, *esprit de corps*. **3** *a brotherhood of merchants* association, alliance, society, union, league, guild, coalition, affiliation, consortium, fraternity, club, lodge, sodality, clique, coterie.

brotherly adj **1** *siblings ignoring brotherly ties* fraternal. **2** *the Bible tells us to practise brotherly love* friendly, affectionate, amicable, kind, kindly, cordial, sympathetic, benevolent, neighbourly, philanthropic, charitable, altruistic.

brow n **1** *furrowing her brow* forehead, temple. **2** *plucking her brows* eyebrows. **3** *the brow of the hill* top, summit, peak, crown, apex, brink.

browbeat v bully, force, coerce, compel, badger, dragoon, intimidate, tyrannize, hector, terrorize; *inf* bulldoze.

brown adj **1** *of a brown colour | brown hair/ horses* dark brown, blackish-brown, chocolate, cocoa, umber, fuscous, reddish-brown, auburn, copper, copper-coloured, coppery, bronze, henna, mahogany, walnut, maroon, rust, brick, terracotta, puce, yellowish-brown, tan, tawny, ginger, cinnamon, hazel, gold, light brown, fawn, dun, donkey brown, beige, ecru; brunette; bay, chestnut, sorrel, roan. **2** *brown bodies in the sun* tanned, sunburnt, browned, bronze, bronzed.

brown v *brown the meat* sear, seal, fry, grill, sauté

browned off adj fed up, discontented, disgruntled, discouraged, disheartened, bored, weary; inf hacked off.

browse v **1** *not reading in detail, just browsing* scan, skim, glance/look through, thumb/leaf/flip through, dip in. **2** *not buying anything, just browsing* look round, have a look, window-shop, peruse. **3** *cows browsing* graze, feed, eat, nibble, crop, pasture.

bruise v **1** *bruise the skin* make black and blue, discolour, blacken, mark, blemish, contuse, injure, hurt. **2** *bruise the fruit* damage, mark, discolour, spoil, blemish. **3** *her feelings are easily bruised* hurt, upset, offend, insult, wound, displease, peeve, vex, distress.

bruise n *a bruise on her face* black-and-blue mark, skin discoloration, blackening, mark, blemish, contusion, injury, swelling, oedema.

brunette adj dark, dark-haired, brown-haired, black-haired, darkish.

brunt n *bear the brunt of it* full force, force, impact, shock, burden, thrust, violence, pressure, strain, stress; repercussions, consequences.

brush n **1** *sweep/clean/paint with a brush* broom, besom, whisk, sweeper, sweeping brush, hairbrush, clothes brush, scrubbing brush, toothbrush, paintbrush. **2** *with a brush of his arm* touch, stroke, hit; inf swipe. **3** *a brush with the law/enemy* encounter, clash, conflict, confrontation, skirmish, tussle, fight, battle, engagement; inf scrap, set-to. **4** *lost in the brush* brushwood, undergrowth, underwood, scrub, wood, thicket, copse; bushes.

brush v **1** *brush the floor | brush one's clothes/teeth* sweep, groom, clean, buff. **2** *lips brushing her cheek* touch, flick, caress, kiss, glance, contact, stroke, sweep, scrape. **brush aside** *brush aside his objections* put aside, sweep aside, dismiss, shrug off, disregard, ignore, think no more of, forget about, have no time for. **brush off** *brush him off* cold-shoulder, rebuff, snub, cut, dismiss, ignore, spurn, slight, disregard, reject, repudiate, refuse, disown, deny,

scorn, disdain. **brush up 1** *brush up his French* revise, read up, polish up, go over, study, refresh one's memory of, relearn, cram; inf rub up, bone up. **2** *brush yourself up* smarten, clean up.

brusque adj abrupt, curt, blunt, short, sharp, terse, caustic, gruff, bluff, hasty, outspoken, plain-spoken, discourteous, impolite, rude, churlish.

brutal adj **1** *a brutal attack/murderer* savage, cruel, bloodthirsty, vicious, ruthless, callous, heartless, merciless, pitiless, remorseless, uncivilized, inhuman, barbarous. **2** *brutal instincts* bestial, brutish, beastly, animal, coarse, carnal, sensual.

brute n **1** *jungle brutes* beast, wild beast, wild animal, animal, creature. **2** *a murderous brute | a brute to his wife and children* beast, monster, animal, swine, savage, sadist, barbarian, devil, fiend, ogre. **3** *that brute of a neighbour was rude* lout, oaf, boor, dolt.

bubble n **1** *blowing soap bubbles | bubbles in champagne* globule, glob, bead, blister, drop, droplet, vesicle, air cavity. **2** *the property bubble* illusion, delusion, fantasy, dream, chimera.

bubble v **1** *champagne bubbling* fizz, effervesce, sparkle, foam, froth, spume. **2** *stew bubbling on the stove* boil, simmer, seethe, percolate. **3** *bubble with happiness* overflow, brim over, be filled.

bubbly adj **1** *bubbly mineral water | bubbly detergent* fizzy, effervescent, carbonated, sparkling, foamy, frothy, sudsy. **2** *a bubbly personality* bubbling, vivacious, effervescent, sparkling, animated, ebullient, scintillating, bouncy, buoyant, excited, elated, lively, merry, happy.

buccaneer n pirate, corsair, sea rover, freebooter, Viking.

buck v **buck up 1** *buck up or you'll be late* hurry, hurry/speed up, make haste, hasten, rush; inf get a move on, step on it, shake a leg. **2** *buck up, don't be sad* cheer up, perk up, take heart, rally. **3** *a holiday will buck you up* cheer up, perk/brighten/buoy up, enliven, gladden, make happier.

bucket n pail, scuttle, can, pitcher.

buckle n **1** *the belt buckle* clasp, clip, catch, fastener, fastening, hasp. **2** *a buckle in the railway track* kink, warp, curve, distortion, wrinkle, bulge.

buckle v **1** *buckling his trousers* fasten, hook, strap, tie, secure, clasp, catch, clip. **2** *the railway track buckled* become warped, become twisted, become curved, become distorted, become contorted, develop a kink/wrinkle/fold, bulge, crumple, cave in.

bucolic adj rural, rustic, pastoral, country, agricultural.

bud n *buds on the flowers/trees* shoot, sprout, burgeon, flowerlet, floret.

bud v *flowers/trees were budding* sprout, send out shoots, form/develop buds, germinate, burgeon, pullulate.

budding adj promising, potential, developing, beginning, fledgling, growing, burgeoning, incipient, embryonic, nascent.

budge v **1** *the car won't budge* move, shift, stir, go, proceed. **2** *I can't budge the car* move, shift, remove, dislodge, get/set going. **3** *he's obstinate so he won't budge* change one's mind, give way, give in, yield, acquiesce. **4** *you won't budge him as he's determined* influence, sway, convince, persuade, bend.

budget n **1** *draw up a budget for the year* financial plan/estimate/statement/blueprint. **2** *be over budget for the term* allowance, allocation, allotment, quota, ration.

budget v **1** *budget her money/time* plan, schedule, allocate, ration, apportion. **2** *budget for a new car | we can budget £5000* plan, allow, save, set aside money, set aside.

buff adj *buff envelopes* beige, straw-coloured, sandy, yellowish, yellowish-brown.

buff v *buff one's nails | buff metal* polish, burnish, rub up, rub, smooth, polish, shine.

buff n *a theatre buff* fan, enthusiast, devotee, aficionado, addict, admirer, expert; *inf* freak.

buffer n cushion, bulwark, guard, safeguard, shield, screen, intermediary.

buffet¹ n **1** *the station buffet* café, cafeteria, snack bar, salad bar, refreshment stall/counter. **2** *a wedding buffet* cold table, cold meal, smorgasbord, self-service. **3** *buying a buffet for the dining room* sideboard, cabinet, china cabinet/cupboard.

buffet² n **1** *a buffet on the head* blow, slap, smack, bang, box, cuff, thump, wallop, clout, whack, thwack, battering, knock, rap, poke, jab. **2** *the buffets of life* shock, jolt, jar.

buffet² v **1** *winds buffeting the trees* batter, beat/knock against, strike, hit, bang, push against. **2** *robbers buffeted the old man* slap, smack, thump, wallop, clout, whack, thwack, cuff.

buffoon n **1** *the buffoons in Shakespeare's plays* fool, clown, jester, comic, comedian, wit, wag, merry andrew, droll. **2** *he's just a buffoon* fool, dolt, idiot, nincompoop; *inf*

chump, numskull, dope, twit, nitwit, halfwit.

bug n **1** *bitten by bugs* insect, flea, mite; *inf* creepy-crawly. **2** *an illness caused by a bug | he's caught a bug* bacterium, germ, virus, micro-organism; infection. **3** *he's caught the dancing bug* craze, fad, mania, obsession, passion, fixation. **4** *get rid of all the bugs in the machine* fault, flaw, defect, imperfection, failing, error, obstruction, gremlin; *inf* snarl-up. **5** *place a bug in the phone* listening device, wire-tap, phone-tap, tap.

bug v **1** *they've bugged his phone* tap, wire-tap, phone-tap. **2** *bugging his conversation* tap, listen in, eavesdrop on. **3** *he really bugs me* annoy, irritate, exasperate, anger, irk, vex, infuriate, inflame, provoke, try one's patience, get one's hackles up; *inf* get one's back up, get on one's nerves, get in one's hair, be a thorn in one's flesh.

bugbear n bane, anathema, abomination, pet hate, hate, bogey, nightmare, horror, dread, *bête noire*.

build v **1** *build a house/road/car* construct, erect, put up, assemble, set up, raise, make, manufacture, fabricate, form. **2** *hopes built on false premises* found, base, establish. **3** *build a business from nothing | build a new career* establish, found, set up, originate, institute, start, begin, inaugurate, initiate, develop. **build up 1** *build up a business* establish, develop, expand. *see* BUILD v 3. **2** *build up her morale* boost, strengthen, increase. **3** *build up the product* advertise, promote, publicize, puff; *inf* plug, hype. **4** *important to build up his strength* develop, increase, improve, strengthen, augment, intensify, escalate. **5** *the wind is building up* strengthen, get stronger, increase, intensify, escalate.

build n *of a heavy build* body, frame, physique, figure, form, structure, shape.

building n **1** *putting up new buildings* structure, construction, edifice, erection, pile. **2** *the building of new houses* construction, erection, putting up, raising.

build-up n **1** *the build-up of resources* expansion, increase, growth, enlargement, escalation, development, accumulation. **2** *the build-up of paperwork/traffic* accumulation, stockpile, accretion, mass, heap, store, stack, pile. **3** *tired of the play's/product's build-up* promotion, publicity, advertising, puff; *inf* hype, plugging, plug, ballyhoo.

built-in adj **1** *built-in wardrobes* integral, integrated, incorporated. **2** *built-in disadvantages* in-built, inherent, intrinsic, incorporated, inseparable, included, essential, implicit.

bulge n **1** *a bulge in her pocket* | *body bulges* swelling, bump, lump, protuberance, protrusion, prominence, projection. **2** *a population bulge* boost, increase, rise, surge, intensification, augmentation.

bulge v *with pockets/stomach bulging* swell, swell out, puff up/out, stick out, bag, belly, balloon, balloon up/out, project, protrude, jut out, distend, expand, dilate, enlarge, bloat.

bulk n **1** *the sheer bulk of the rubbish/work* size, volume, bulkiness, quantity, weight, extent, mass, substance, magnitude, massiveness, hugeness, largeness, bigness, ampleness, amplitude; dimensions. **2** *the bulk of the applicants are women* majority, greater part/number, most, preponderance, major/main/better part, mass, body, generality, lion's share.

bulk v *bulk the book out with pictures* make thicker, make bigger, make larger, expand, pad out, fill out, stretch out, augment.
bulk large be important, be prominent, carry weight, dominate, preponderate, loom large.

bulky adj **1** *bulky bags of rubbish* large, big, substantial, huge, enormous, massive, vast, immense, voluminous, colossal, hulking, heavy, weighty, ponderous. **2** *Mr. Smith's bulky body* stout, thickset, plump, fat, chubby, portly, tubby, obese. **3** *bulky items of furniture* awkward-shaped, awkward, unwieldy, cumbersome, unmanageable.

bulldoze v **1** *bulldoze the area/buildings* demolish, flatten, level, raze. **2** *bulldoze his way through* | *bulldoze a path through the crowds* force, push, drive, shove, propel. **3** *they bulldozed him into going* bully, browbeat, coerce, intimidate, cow, bludgeon, dragoon, steamroller, railroad; *inf* strongarm.

bullet n pellet, ball, slug, shot, missile, projectile.

bulletin n **1** *a television bulletin* news report, report, statement, announcement, newsflash, flash, account, message, communication, communiqué, dispatch, notification. **2** *an in-house bulletin* newspaper, newsletter, pamphlet, leaflet, broadsheet; listings.

bullish adj **1** *bullish stock market* rising, improving, confident. **2** *feeling very bullish about the future* optimistic, hopeful, confident, positive, assured, cheerful, sanguine.

bully n *the school bully* browbeater, intimidator, coercer, oppressor, persecutor, tyrant, tormentor, tough, bully-boy, ruffian, thug.

bully v *bully the younger children* browbeat, intimidate, coerce, oppress, domineer, persecute, cow, tyrannize, pressurize, pressure, bulldoze; *inf* push around, strongarm, play the heavy with.

bully adj *a bully performance* excellent, firstrate, very good, fine, admirable; *inf* A1, wicked.

bulwark n **1** *the castle's bulwarks* rampart, fortification, buttress, bastion, embankment, outwork, mole, breastwork, redoubt. **2** *a bulwark of classical education* support, mainstay, defence, guard, safeguard; defendant, protector.

bum[1] n bottom, rear, rear end; buttocks; *inf* sit-upon, BTM, arse; *Amer inf* ass. *see* BOTTOM n 7.

bum[2] n **1** *a bum begging for money* tramp, vagrant, beggar, derelict, mendicant; *Amer* bag lady, hobo. **2** *just a lazy bum* loafer, idler, wastrel, good-for-nothing, ne'er-do-well, scrounger, cadger.

bum[2] v **1** *bum money from him* borrow, cadge, scrounge, sponge; *Amer inf* mooch. **2** *bum around* loaf, lounge, idle, laze, wander.

bum[2] adj *bum personal stereos* useless, worthless, inferior, unsatisfactory, low-grade, poor, bad.

bumble v **1** *the speaker was bumbling away* ramble, babble, mumble, mutter, stumble. **2** *drunks bumbling through the woods* stumble, lurch, blunder, muddle about, flounder about.

bumbling adj *a bumbling idiot* clumsy, blundering, awkward, bungling, incompetent, inept, inefficient, muddled, stumbling, lumbering, botching, foolish.

bump v **1** *the bus bumped the car* hit, bang, strike, knock, crash into, collide with; *inf* slam. **2** *bump his head on the bar* hit, bang, strike, knock, hurt, injure, damage. **3** *the cart bumping along the road* bounce, jolt, jerk, rattle, shake, jounce. **4** *bump the car out of the mud* move, shift, budge, dislodge.
bump into 1 *the cars bumped into each other* collide with, crash/smash into, run into. **2** *we bumped into old schoolfriends* run into, come/run across, meet by chance, meet, meet up with, encounter, chance/happen upon, light upon. **bump off** *bump off his enemy* kill, murder, do away with, assassinate, eliminate, liquidate, dispatch.

bump n **1** *hear a bump* thud, thump, bang, crash. **2** *land with a bump* collision, jolt, crash, smash, bang, thud, thump, knock, rap, impact. **3** *he has a bump on his head* lump, swelling, injury, contusion, nodule, node, tumescence, intumescence, protuberance. **4** *a bump on the road surface* bulge, hump, knob, knot, protuberance.

bumper adj *a bumper crop* large, big, abundant, huge, massive, bountiful, exceptional, unusual, excellent; *inf* whopping.

bumpkin n country bumpkin, yokel, clodhopper, oaf, boor, lout, peasant, rustic; *Amer inf* hill-billy, hick, hayseed, rube.

bumptious adj self-important, conceited, arrogant, self-assertive, full of oneself, overbearing, puffed up, self-opinionated, cocky, presumptuous, pompous, forward; *inf* pushy.

bumpy adj **1** *a bumpy road* uneven, rough, potholed, rutted, pitted, lumpy, knobby. **2** *a bumpy flight* choppy, jolting, jolty, jerky, jarring, bouncy, rough.

bunch n **1** *a bunch of flowers* bouquet, spray, posy, sheaf, nosegay, corsage. **2** *a bunch of keys/bananas* cluster, assemblage, collection. **3** *a bunch of papers* batch, pile, stack, heap, bundle, mass, quantity, accumulation, agglomeration. **4** *a bunch of people* group, collection, gathering, band, gang, knot, cluster, party, crowd, flock, swarm, troop, mob, multitude.

bunch v **1** *the crowd bunched together* cluster, huddle, gather, group, bundle, pack, herd, crowd, flock, mass, cram. **2** *cloth bunching up* gather, fold, pleat.

bundle n **1** *a bundle of papers* collection, batch, pile, stack, heap, bunch, mass, quantity, accumulation, agglomeration. **2** *send off bundles of mail/clothes* package, pack, bale, parcel, packet. **3** *a bundle of sticks* bunch, bale, truss, faggot, fascicle.

bundle v **1** *bundle the clothes into a bag | bundle them up* tie, tie up, tie together, package, parcel, wrap, bind, fasten together, bale, truss. **2** *bundle people inside/outside | bundled them off the road* hurry, hustle, rush, push, shove, thrust, throw. **3** *bundle children up in warm clothes* clothe, wrap, cover, muffle, swathe.

bungle v botch, muff, spoil, make a mess of, mess up, mishandle, mismanage, fudge, mar, ruin; *inf* louse up, screw up, foul up, cock up, bodge.

bungling adj clumsy, incompetent, inept, unskilful, inexpert, botching, blundering, maladroit; *inf* ham-fisted, ham-handed, cack-handed.

bunk[1] n bed, berth, bunk-bed.

bunk[2] n **do a bunk** run away, flee, bolt, fly, take flight, take off, clear out, take to one's heels, show a clean pair of heels, escape, make a run for it, abscond, decamp; *inf* cut

and run, do a runner, scarper, beat it, skedaddle, scram.

bunk[3] n nonsense, bunkum.

bunkum n nonsense, rubbish, balderdash, stuff and nonsense, twaddle, claptrap, humbug, tomfoolery; *inf* rot, poppycock, baloney, piffle, bilge, bosh, hooey; *vulg* bullshit; *Amer* hogwash.

buoy n **1** *a harbour buoy* anchored float, marker; mooring, navigation mark, guide, beacon, signal. **2** *the buoy kept him afloat* lifebuoy, life-belt, life-jacket, life-preserver, Mae West.

buoy v **buoy up** **1** *buoying up the bereaved woman* cheer, cheer up, hearten, encourage, support, sustain; *inf* keep afloat. **2** *buoying up her spirits* cheer up, raise, boost, uplift, lift, give a lift to.

buoyancy n **1** *the buoyancy of the boat/water* floatability, lightness, levity, lifting effect, lift. **2** *the buoyancy of her mood/personality* cheerfulness, cheeriness, light-heartedness, carefreeness, joy, vivacity, animation, liveliness, high spirits, verve, sparkle, sprightliness, spiritedness, blitheness, jauntiness, breeziness, pep, happiness, merriment; *inf* zing, zip.

buoyant adj **1** *a buoyant substance* floatable, floating, afloat, light. **2** *a buoyant mood/personality* cheerful, cheery, light-hearted, bouncy, carefree, joyful, vivacious, animated, lively, high-spirited, sparkling, sprightly, blithe, jaunty, breezy, happy, merry; *inf* peppy, zingy, zippy.

burden n **1** *the donkey's burden* load, cargo, weight, freight. **2** *the burden of parenthood* responsibility, onus, charge, duty, obligation, tax, trouble, care, worry, anxiety, tribulation, difficulty, strain, stress, weight, encumbrance, millstone, albatross; trials, tribulations.

burden v **1** *donkeys burdened with heavy loads* load, be laden, weight, charge, weigh down, encumber, hamper. **2** *burdened with great sorrow* oppress, trouble, worry, distress, bother, afflict, torment, strain, stress, tax, overwhelm.

bureau n **1** *a travel bureau* agency, office, service. **2** *a government bureau* department, division, branch. **3** *polish the bureau* writing-desk, desk, writing-table.

bureaucracy n **1** *rule by bureaucracy* civil service, central administration, directorate; government officials, government ministries. **2** *cut through the bureaucracy to get a passport* red tape, officialdom, bumbledom; rules and regulations.

bureaucrat n administrator, official, office-holder, civil servant, public servant, government servant, minister, functionary, mandarin, *apparatchik*, jack-in-office.

bureaucratic adj official, administrative, governmental, ministerial, red-tape, by the book, rigid, inflexible.

burgeon v **1** *flowers burgeoning* bud, sprout, put forth shoots, shoot, germinate, pullulate. **2** *a population burgeoning* grow, develop, flourish, thrive, mushroom, proliferate, snowball, increase, multiply, expand, escalate.

burglar n housebreaker, cat burglar, thief, sneak-thief, robber, pilferer, filcher, picklock; *Amer inf* second-story man/worker/thief.

burglary n **1** *done for burglary* housebreaking, breaking and entry, breaking in, forced entry, theft, robbery, larceny, pilfering, filching. **2** *suffered a burglary* break-in, theft, robbery.

burial n **1** *the burial of the body* burying, interment, entombment, inhumation, sepulture. **2** *present at the burial* funeral, sepulture; obsequies, exequies.

burial-ground n burial-place, cemetery, graveyard, churchyard, necropolis; *Amer* memorial park, potter's field; *lit* golgotha, God's acre.

burlesque n parody, caricature, travesty, farce, mockery, imitation, satire, lampoon; *inf* send-up, take-off, spoof.

burly adj thickset, brawny, powerfully built, well-built, muscular, strapping, big, hulking, hefty, beefy, bulky, sturdy, stocky, stout, strong-man.

burn v **1** *the house is burning* be on fire, be afire, be ablaze, blaze, go up, smoke, flame, be aflame, flare, flash, flicker, glow. **2** *he burned the papers* set on fire, set alight, ignite, put a match to, light, kindle, incinerate, reduce to ashes. **3** *burn the shirt with the iron* | *burn the bread* scorch, singe, sear, char. **4** *her forehead's burning* be hot, be warm, feel hot, be feverish, be fevered; *inf* be on fire. **5** *his throat's burning* smart, sting, tingle, be sore, hurt, throb. **6** *liquid burning his throat* sting, bite, prickle, irritate, pain, hurt. **7** *burn with excitement/passion* be aroused, be emotional, simmer, smoulder, seethe. **8** *he was burning to get the prize* long, yearn, desire, be consumed with the desire, hunger after, lust, itch, pant, wish, want. **9** *burn energy* use, use up, consume, expend, eat up, exhaust.

burning adj **1** *a burning house* blazing, aflaming, flaring, raging, ignited, glowing,

flickering, smouldering, scorching. **2** *the burning meat* scorching, singeing, searing, charring. **3** *a burning forehead/day* hot, warm; *inf* scorching, roasting, boiling, baking. **4** *a burning sensation* smarting, stinging, biting, prickling, irritating, caustic, searing, corroding, corrosive, painful. **5** *a burning desire* intense, fervent, fervid, ardent, passionate, eager. **6** *the burning issues of the day* important, crucial, significant, urgent, pressing, compelling, critical, vital, essential, acute, pivotal, climacteric.

burnish v polish, shine, brighten, rub, buff, buff up, smooth.

burp v belch, bring up wind, eruct, eructate; *dial* rift.

burrow n *rabbit burrows* tunnel, hole, hollow, excavation, lair, den, retreat.

burrow v **1** *burrowing holes* dig, tunnel, excavate, hollow out, gouge out, scoop out. **2** *burrow one's way out* dig, tunnel. **3** *burrowing under the bedclothes* go under, hide, shelter, conceal oneself. **4** *burrow for matches/information* search for, look for, delve for, hunt for, ferret out.

burst v **1** *the pipe has burst* split, split open, break open, rupture, crack, fracture, fragment, shatter, shiver, fly open. **2** *the cold weather burst the pipes* split, break open, tear apart, rupture, crack, fracture, fragment, shatter, shiver, rend asunder. **3** *the grenade burst* blow up, explode, detonate, fulminate. **4** *the water burst through the dam* break out, burst forth, pour forth, gush out, surge out, rush out. **5** *he burst into/from the room* barge, push/thrust/shove one's way. **6** *burst into tears/laughter* begin/start/commence suddenly, break out, erupt. **burst out 1** *"toward," she burst out* exclaim, cry out, call out, shout, yell. **2** *burst out crying* begin/start/commence suddenly. **3** *burst out of jail* break out, break loose, make one's escape, escape, get free. *see* BREAK v **break out 1**.

bury v **1** *bury the corpse* inter, lay to rest, consign to the grave, entomb, inhume, sepulchre; *lit* inearth. **2** *bury her head in her hands* conceal, hide, cover with, put out of sight, submerge, sink, secrete, enshroud. **3** *bury the nail in the wood* drive in, embed, implant, sink, submerge. **4** *bury yourself in your work* | *be buried in a book* absorb oneself, immerse oneself, occupy oneself with, engross oneself, engage oneself, interest oneself.

bush n **1** *planting bushes in the garden* | *throw in the bushes* shrub, woody plant; thicket, undergrowth, shrubbery. **2** *lost in the Aus-*

tralian bush brush, scrub land, scrub, the wild; backwoods.

bushy adj thick, shaggy, fuzzy, fluffy, luxuriant, unruly, rough.

business n **1** *what business is he in* occupation, line, profession, career, trade, work, employment, job, pursuit, vocation, *métier*. **2** *do business with the French* trade, trading, commerce, trafficking, buying and selling, merchandizing, bargaining; dealings, transactions, proceedings. **3** *owning her own business* firm, company, concern, enterprise, organization, corporation, establishment, house, shop, venture, industry. **4** *that's none of your business* concern, affair, responsibility, duty, function, task, assignment, obligation, problem. **5** *the main business of the meeting* matter, subject, topic, point of discussion, theme, issue, question, problem, thesis. **6** *it was a peculiar business* affair, matter, thing, case, set of circumstances, issue.

businesslike adj **1** *businesslike behaviour* professional, efficient, methodical, systematic, orderly, organized, well-ordered, practical, pragmatic, thorough, painstaking, meticulous, correct. **2** *a businesslike performance of the play* workaday, routine, prosaic, down-to-earth, conventional, unimaginative.

bust n **1** *a woman with a large bust* chest, breasts, bosom, torso; *inf* boobs, tits, knockers. **2** *a bust of Julius Caesar* sculptured/carved head and shoulders, head and shoulders.

bust v **1** *they bust the machine* break, fracture, burst, rupture, crack. **2** *the crash will bust him* bankrupt, ruin, impoverish, pauperize, break. **3** *the police busted him* arrest, capture, catch, seize, raid; *inf* collar, cop, nab.

bust adj **go bust** become bankrupt, fail, be ruined, become insolvent, break.

bustle v **1** *bustle about | bustle to and fro* hurry, rush, dash, scuttle, scurry, hasten, scamper, scramble, flutter, fuss; *inf* tear. **2** *bustle the children out* hurry, rush, hasten, speed up, push.

bustle n *the bustle of the market-place* activity, flurry, hurly-burly, stir, busyness, briskness, commotion, tumult, excitement, agitation, fuss; *inf* to-do; *lit* pother.

busy adj **1** *the doctor's busy* occupied, engaged, working, at work, on duty, in a meeting, otherwise engaged. **2** *busy wrapping up goods* occupied in, engaged in, employed in, involved in, absorbed in, engrossed in, preoccupied with, working at, labouring at, toiling at, slaving at. **3** *a*

busy day active, energetic, strenuous, full, hectic, exacting, bustling. **4** *busy as bees* active, energetic, industrious, lively, tireless, restless; *inf* on the go. **5** *busy patterns* ornate, overelaborate, overdetailed, overdecorated, cluttered, fussy. **6** *a busy old woman* interfering, meddlesome, meddling, prying, inquisitive, snooping; *inf* nosy, snoopy.

busy v *busy himself in the garden* occupy, engage, employ, absorb, immerse, engross, involve, interest.

busybody n meddler, interferer, snooper, pry, mischief-maker, troublemaker, gossip, scandalmonger, muckraker; *inf* nosy parker.

but conj **1** *she's ill but she's going* nevertheless, yet, still, however. **2** *he went but she did not* on the other hand, on the contrary. **3** *cannot choose but to do it* other than, otherwise than, except.

but prep **1** *everyone but him* except, with the exception of, excepting, other than, excluding, bar, barring, save. **2** *but for the rain he would have gone* without, except for, barring, notwithstanding.

but adv *we can but try* only, just, simply, merely.

butch adj mannish, masculine, lesbian.

butcher n **1** *buy steak from the butcher* meat merchant, meat seller, meat retailer. **2** *the general was a butcher* slaughterer, murderer, mass murderer, slayer, killer, serial killer, homicide, homicidal maniac, bloodshedder.

butcher v **1** *butchering cattle* slaughter, cut up, carve up, joint, slice up, prepare, dress. **2** *butchering the enemy* slaughter, slay, massacre, murder, kill, put to death, exterminate, liquidate, assassinate, put to the sword, cut down, destroy. **3** *butcher the piano concerto | butcher the piece of joinery* botch, make a botch/mess of, wreck, ruin, spoil, bungle; *inf* make a hash of, louse up, screw up, foul up.

butchery n **1** *he's taken up butchery* meat selling, meat retailing, butchering. **2** *tribes noted for their butchery | the butchery of the enemy* slaughter, massacre, slaying, murdering, murder, mass murdering, homicide, blood shedding.

butt[1] n **1** *the butt of a gun* handle, shaft, hilt, haft. **2** *the butt of a cigarette* stub, end, tail-end, remnant; *inf* fag-end. **3** *sitting on his butt* bottom, buttocks.

butt[2] n *the butt of his jokes* scapegoat, dupe, target, victim, laughing-stock, object, subject.

butt[3] n *a butt of ale* barrel, cask, pipe.

butt[4] v **1** *the ram butted her with his horns* push, thrust, shove, ram, bump, buffet, prod, poke, jab, knock, bunt. **2** *his land butts mine* abut, join, meet, conjoin. **3** *butt into a conversation | butt into a private matter* interrupt, intrude/interfere in, put one's oar into; *inf* stick one's nose into.

buttocks n bottom, posterior, rump; hindquarters; *inf* behind, bum, backside, sit-upon, BTM, arse; *Amer inf* butt, ass.

button n **1** *buttons on the sweater* fastener, stud, link. **2** *the button on the radio* disc, knob, switch.

buttonhole v *buttonhole the MP* accost, waylay, take aside, importune, detain, grab, catch, talk at.

buttress n **1** *a stone buttress* prop, support, abutment, strut, reinforcement, stanchion, pier. **2** *a buttress to the family* mainstay, upholder, sustainer, cornerstone, pillar.

buttress v *buttress the economy | buttress your argument* strengthen, reinforce, prop up, support, shore up, underpin, brace, uphold, defend, back up.

buxom adj plump, large-bosomed, big-bosomed, full-bosomed, shapely; *inf* busty.

buy v **1** *buy a house* purchase, make a purchase of, pay for, invest in, procure. **2** *he bought his way in* bribe, suborn, corrupt; *inf* grease someone's palm, square, fix, rig. **3** *buy off the customers* pay off, drop charges.

buy n *a good buy* purchase, acquisition, deal, bargain.

buzz n **1** *the buzz of the bees* buzzing, hum, humming, murmur, drone, whirr, whirring, hiss, sibilation, whisper; *lit* bombination, bombilation, susurration, susurrus. **2** *the buzz of the telephone/machines* ring, ringing, purr, purring. **3** *the buzz is he's gone* rumour, gossip, news, chitchat, report, whisper, scandal, hearsay.

buzz v **1** *bees buzzing* hum, murmur, drone, whirr, hiss, whisper, sibilate; *lit* bombinate, bombilate, susurrate. **2** *telephone/machines buzzing* ring, reverberate, purr. **3** *tongues buzzing* gossip, chatter, natter, tattle, spread rumours. **4** *people buzzing about* bustle, rush, dash, hurry. **5** *the place was buzzing* be active, be busy, be bustling.

by prep **1** *the house by the school* next to, beside, alongside, near, close to. **2** *enter by the side door | come by the quiet roads* through, along, over, by way of, via. **3** *go by the building* past, in front of. **4** *be there by midday* no later than, at, before. **5** *arrested by the police | contact him by telephone* through the agency/means/instrumentality of, under the aegis of, through. **6** *meet by chance* through, because of, as a result of.

bygone adj past, departed, dead, former, one-time, previous, forgotten, lost, of old, olden, ancient, antiquated, of yore, obsolete, extinct, out of date, outmoded, *passé*.

by-law, bye-law n local regulation, rule, regulation, statute.

bypass n *a bypass round the city* ring road, detour, circuitous route, roundabout way, alternative route.

bypass v **1** *bypass the city* make a detour round, go round, pass round. **2** *bypass the difficulties* get round, circumvent, find a way round, avoid, evade. **3** *bypass the salesman and go the manager* ignore, pass over, miss out, circumvent, avoid, go over the head of; *inf* short-circuit.

bystander n onlooker, looker-on, observer, eyewitness, witness, spectator, watcher, viewer, beholder, gaper, passer-by; *inf* gawper, rubberneck.

byword n **1** *a byword for reliability* slogan, catchword, motto, example of, personification of, embodiment of. **2** *old bywords dying out* proverb, maxim, adage, aphorism, apophthegm.

cab n **1** *order a cab* taxi, taxicab, minicab, hackney carriage, hackney. **2** *the driver's cab* cabin, compartment, quarters, cubicle, cubby-hole.

cabal n **1** *a political plot laid by a cabal* clique, faction, coterie, league, confederacy, band, gang, party, set, ring, junta, junto. **2** *the cabal was discovered in time* intrigue, conspiracy, plot, scheme, plan, design.

cabaret n **1** *watching the hotel's cabaret* entertainment, show, floorshow. **2** *employed as a singer in a cabaret* nightclub, club, nightspot, disco, discothèque.

cabbage n **1** green cabbage, white cabbage, red cabbage, winter cabbage, savoy, Chinese cabbage. **2** *she's become a cabbage since her marriage* inert/inactive/apathetic/sluggish/vegetating/stagnating person, couch potato.

cabin n **1** *a cabin by the lake* log cabin, hut, chalet, shack, shanty, shed; *Scots* bothy. **2** *a first-class cabin in the ship* stateroom, sleeping-quarters, berth, compartment, deck-house. **3** *an aircraft's cabin* compartment, passenger space, passenger accommodation. **4** *a driver's cabin* cab, compartment. see CAB 2.

cabinet n **1** *a china cabinet | a filing cabinet* cupboard, chest, locker, dresser, closet, chiffonier, case, container. **2** *the Prime Minister and the Cabinet* ministry, ministers, administration, council, counsellors, senate.

cable n **1** *tied with cable* rope, cord, wire, line, cordage. **2** *send a cable* cablegram, telegram, telegraph, telemessage, wire.

cable v *cable the news* telegraph, wire, radio.

cache n **1** *secrete the treasure in a cache* hiding-place, hide-out, secret place, hole; *inf* hidy-hole. **2** *find the cache of jewels* hoard, store, collection, fund, supply, hidden treasure, treasure, loot; *inf* stash.

cachet n prestige, distinction, stature, eminence, respect, admiration, approbation, approval, seal of approval, stamp of approval.

cackle v **1** *hens cackling* cluck, clack, squawk. **2** *the audience cackling at his jokes* chuckle, chortle, laugh, giggle, titter, snig-

ger, tee-hee. **3** *people cackling at the bus-stop* chatter, jabber, prattle, babble, gabble, clack, gibber, blather, clatter, blab; *inf* spout away.

cacophony n discord, dissonance, discordance, jarring, stridency, grating, rasping, caterwauling.

cad n scoundrel, rat, rogue, rascal, double-crosser, knave; *inf* bounder, rotter, heel.

cadaver n corpse, dead body, remains, carcass; *inf* stiff.

cadaverous adj corpse-like, death-like, gaunt, haggard, drawn, emaciated, skeletal, thin, hollow-eyed, ashen, pale, wan, ghostly.

cadence n **1** *musical/metrical cadence* rhythm, beat, pulse, rhythmical flow/pattern, measure, metre, tempo, swing, lilt, cadency. **2** *the cadence of her speech* intonation, inflection, accent, modulation.

café n coffee bar, coffee shop, snack bar, tearoom, teashop, restaurant, cafeteria, wine bar, bistro.

cafeteria n self-service restaurant, self-service canteen.

cage n *cages in the zoo* enclosure, pen, pound, lock-up, coop; *Amer* corral; birdcage, aviary, mew, hen coop.

cage v **1** *cage the animals* confine, shut in, impound, pen, lock up, immure, incarcerate, imprison, coop, coop up, mew; *Amer* corral. **2** *don't cage him in — he likes freedom* confine, hem in, restrict, restrain.

cagey, cagy adj guarded, secretive, noncommittal, cautious, chary, wary, careful, shrewd, wily.

cajole v wheedle, coax, beguile, flatter, seduce, lure, entice, tempt, inveigle, manoeuvre, humour, jolly; *inf* sweet-talk, soft-soap, butter up.

cake n **1** *cakes from the baker* gateau, cupcake, fairy cake, sponge cake, angel cake, chocolate cake, Battenberg, Madeira cake, layer cake, fruit cake, seed-cake, Genoa cake, Christmas cake, cheesecake, gingerbread, shortcake, teacake, bun, pastry. **2** *a cake of chocolate/soap* block, bar, slab, lump, mass, cube, loaf, chunk.

cake v **1** *blood caking on the bodies* solidify, harden, thicken, dry, bake, coagulate, consolidate, ossify; *lit* inspissate. **2** *boots caked with mud* cover, coat, encrust, plaster.

calamitous adj disastrous, catastrophic, cataclysmic, devastating, ruinous, dire, tragic, fatal, wretched, woeful.

calamity n disaster, catastrophe, tragedy, misfortune, cataclysm, devastation, scourge, misadventure, mischance, mishap, ruin, tribulation, woe.

calculate v **1** *calculate the sum* work out, compute, estimate, count up, figure out, reckon up, evaluate, enumerate, determine, gauge. **2** *she calculated her chances* estimate, gauge, judge, measure, weigh up, reckon, rate. **3** *the car was calculated to appeal to children* design, plan, aim, intend. **4** *we calculated on their early arrival* rely, depend, count, bank.

calculated adj *a calculated crime/risk* considered, planned, premeditated, deliberate, intentional, intended, purposeful.

calculating adj *a calculating young woman/killer* scheming, designing, contriving, devious, shrewd, manipulative, sharp, sly, crafty, Machiavellian.

calculation n **1** *by their calculations it will cost £3000* computation, estimation, estimate, reckoning, figuring, forecast, gauging, judgement. *see* CALCULATE 1, 2. **2** *the calculation is wrong* result, answer. **3** *she got the job by sheer calculation* scheming, designing, contriving, deviousness, shrewdness, manipulation, slyness, craft, expedience, circumspection, deliberation.

calibre n **1** *the calibre of a gun* bore, diameter. **2** *statesmen of his calibre* quality, worth, distinction, stature, excellence, merit, ability, talent, capability, competence, capacity, endowments, gifts, strengths, scope.

call v **1** *call out in pain* cry, cry out, shout, exclaim, yell, scream, shriek, roar. **2** *call him in the morning* awaken, waken, arouse, rouse. **3** *call her tomorrow* call up, ring, phone, phone up, telephone, give one a ring; *inf* buzz, give one a buzz, give one a tinkle. **4** *call at the house* pay a call, pay a visit, pay a brief visit, stop by; *inf* drop in, pop in. **5** *call a meeting* call together, convene, summon, order, convoke, assemble, announce, declare, proclaim, decree. **6** *call a doctor/taxi* send for, ask for, summon, contact, order, bid, fetch. **7** *they called the baby Jane | the flowers are called primulas* name, christen, style, designate, dub, entitle, denominate, describe as, label, term. **8** *I call it disgraceful* consider, think, regard, judge, estimate. **9** *called to the Bar | he was called to the Church* appoint, elect, ordain.

call for 1 *this calls for a celebration | rudeness is not called for* need, require, be grounds for, justify, necessitate, demand, entail. **2** *call for the goods* collect, pick up, fetch, go for; *dial* uplift. **call off 1** *call off the dogs* order off, order away, stop, hold back, check, rein in. **2** *call off the date* cancel, postpone, countermand, rescind, revoke. **call on 1** *call on his aunt* visit, pay a visit to, go and see; *inf* look up, look in on, drop in on. **2** *call on/upon them to help* appeal to, ask, request, entreat, urge, supplicate, invoke.

call up 1 *call her up tomorrow* call, ring, telephone, phone. *see* CALL v 3. **2** *it calls up painful memories* recall, bring/call to mind, summon up, evoke. **3** *call up all the young men* enlist, recruit, sign up; *Amer* draft.

call n **1** *a call of pain* cry, shout, exclamation, yell, scream, shriek, roar. **2** *the calls of the bird* cry, song, chirp, chirping, tweet. **3** *have a prearranged call* signal, hail, whoop, coee. **4** *give her a call tomorrow* telephone call, ring; *inf* buzz, tinkle. **5** *make a call on her* visit, brief visit. **6** *first call for the plane | a call for unity* summons, invitation, request, plea, bidding, order, command, appeal, notice. **7** *there's no call to be rude* need, occasion, reason, cause, justification, grounds, excuse. **8** *there's no call for expensive wine here* demand, request, requirement, need, want, requisition. **9** *the call of the wild* attraction, lure, allurement, fascination, appeal, bewitchment.

call girl n prostitute, whore, harlot, street walker, courtesan, woman of ill repute, fallen woman, loose woman, scarlet woman, woman of the night, woman of the town, *fille de joie*; *inf* hooker, hustler.

calling n vocation, occupation, career, profession, business, work, employment, job, trade, craft, line, line of work, pursuit, *métier*, walk of life, province, field.

callous adj **1** *a callous jail warden* hard, hardened, tough, harsh, cold, insensitive, unfeeling, cold-hearted, hard-hearted, heartless, stony-hearted, hard-bitten, cruel, obdurate, case-hardened, indurate, indurated, inured, uncaring, unsympathetic, unresponsive, unsusceptible, indifferent, soulless. **2** *callous skin* hard, hardened, thickened, leathery.

callow adj immature, inexperienced, uninitiated, naïve, unsophisticated, innocent, undeveloped, adolescent.

calm adj **1** *a calm day* still, windless, mild, tranquil, balmy, halcyon, quiet, peaceful, pacific, undisturbed, restful. **2** *a calm sea* still, smooth, motionless, placid, waveless, unagitated, storm free. **3** *be/remain calm during the trouble* composed, collected, cool, cool-headed, controlled, self-controlled, self-possessed, quiet, tranquil, unruffled, relaxed, serene, unexcited, unexcitable, unflappable, undisturbed, unagitated, imperturbable, unemotional, unmoved, equable, stoical; *inf* together.

calm n **1** *the calm before the storm | disturbing the day's calm* stillness, tranquillity, serenity, quietness, quietude, peace, peacefulness, harmony, restfulness, repose. **2** *nothing disturbs her calm* composure, coolness, self-control, tranquillity, serenity, equanimity, unflappability, imperturbability, equability, poise, sang-froid; *inf* cool.

calm v **1** *try to calm the child | calm her fears* soothe, quieten, pacify, hush, lull, tranquillize, mollify, appease, allay, alleviate, assuage. **2** *the wind eventually calmed* quieten, still, settle, settle down, die down. **calm down** quieten; relax, settle.

calumny n slander, calumniation, defamation, libel, misrepresentation, false accusation, denigration, vilification, aspersions, mud-slinging, backbiting, detraction, disparagement, deprecation, evil-speaking, insult, abuse, vituperation, obloquy, revilement, smear campaign.

camaraderie n comradeship, companionship, brotherliness, fellowship, friendship, closeness, affinity, sociability.

camouflage n *the soldiers' khaki uniforms were a camouflage | the polar bear's coat is a camouflage* disguise, protective colouring, mask, screen, cloak, cover, cover-up, false front, front, façade, masquerade, blind, concealment, subterfuge.

camouflage v *camouflaged in white against the snow* disguise, hide, conceal, mask, screen, veil, cloak, cover, cover up, obscure.

camp¹ n **1** *soldier's/Scout camp* encampment, camping ground, camp-site, tents, bivouac, cantonment. **2** *the right-wing camp* faction, party, group, clique, coterie, set, sect, cabal.

camp² v *we camped in a field* pitch tents, pitch camp, set up camp, encamp, tent. **camp out 1** *we camped out in that field* sleep out, camp. **2** *we're camping out here till the house is decorated* live rough, live simply; *inf* rough it, slum it, pig it.

camp³ v **camp it up** overdo it, overact, behave theatrically, posture, behave affectedly, ham it, lay it on, spread it on thick.

camp³ adj **1** *camp mannerisms* effeminate, affected, artificial, posturing, mannered, studied, homosexual, gay; *inf* campy; *inf* derog poncy, limp-wristed. **2** *camp humour*

exaggerated, theatrical, flamboyant, overdone, extravagant, overdrawn, artificial; *inf* over the top, camped up.

campaign n **1** *Napoleon's Russian Campaign* war, battle, expedition, offensive, attack, crusade. **2** *an advertising campaign | a campaign against litter* course of action, operation, promotion, strategy, set of tactics, drive, push, crusade, movement, manoeuvre, battle plan.

campaign v *campaigning for civil rights* fight, battle, work, push, crusade, strive, struggle, agitate.

can n *a can of beans | a can of hot water* tin, container, receptacle.

can v *can fruit* tin, preserve, bottle.

canal n **1** *barges on the canal* channel, race, watercourse, waterway. **2** *the alimentary canal* tube, duct, conduit, pipe.

cancel v **1** *cancel a holiday/date* call off, stop, discontinue, give up, withdraw from, countermand, revoke, rescind. **2** *cancel an order* annul, declare void, declare null and void, nullify, quash, invalidate, set aside, retract, negate, revoke, rescind, repudiate, abrogate, repeal, abolish. **3** *cancel that last paragraph* delete, cross out, erase, strike out, rub out, blot out, expunge, eliminate, obliterate, eradicate, efface. **4** *his friendliness cancels out her hostility* counterbalance, balance, offset, compensate, make up for, counteract, neutralize, redeem, countervail.

cancer n **1** *cancer of the breast* tumour, malignant tumour, malignancy, growth, malignant growth; *Med* carcinoma, sarcoma, melanoma, metastasis. **2** *a cancer in our society* canker, blight, evil, corruption, rot, sickness, disease, pestilence, scourge, plague.

candid adj **1** *she's always candid | candid remarks* frank, open, honest, truthful, sincere, forthright, direct, plain-spoken, outspoken, blunt, unequivocal, bluff, brusque; *inf* straight from the shoulder. **2** *candid camera shots* unposed, spontaneous, impromptu, extemporary, uncontrived, informal, unstudied.

candidate n **1** *two candidates for the post | parliamentary candidates* applicant, job applicant, office seeker, contender, nominee, contestant, aspirant, possibility; *inf* runner. **2** *candidates for the final exams* entrant, examination-taker.

candle n taper; tallow candle, wax candle, rush candle, Christmas candle, votary candle.

candour n frankness, openness, honesty, truthfulness, sincerity, forthrightness, directness, plainspokenness, outspokenness, unequivocalness, bluntness, bluffness, brusqueness.

candy n **1** *boil sugar to make candy* sugarcandy, toffee. **2** *American children asking for candy* sweets, sweetmeats, confectionery, bonbons.

cane n **1** *a walking cane|canes supporting plants* stick, staff, rod, stave; walking stick, alpenstock, shepherd's crook. **2** *sugar-cane* stem, stalk, shoot, reed.

cane v **1** *cane the children* beat, strike, hit, flog, thrash, lash, strap, scourge; *inf* tan one's hide. **2** *we really caned the opposition* trounce, thrash, vanquish, defeat, rout, put to rout.

canker n **1** *a canker in the dog's ear* ulcer, ulceration, sore, running sore, lesion, blister, abscess. **2** *tree canker* fungus disease, blight, plant rot. **3** *a canker in society* cancer, blight, evil, corruption, rot, sickness, scourge. *see* CANCER 2.

cannibal n anthropophagite, man-eater, people-eater; savage, barbarian, wild man.

cannon n gun, field gun, mounted gun; *inf* big gun.

cannonade n barrage, bombardment, shelling, battery, pounding, attack, salvo, volley, broadside.

canny adj **1** *canny savers* careful, cautious, prudent, thrifty. **2** *a canny businesswoman* shrewd, sharp, astute, discerning, penetrating, perspicacious, clever, sensible, wise, judicious, sagacious, circumspect.

canon[1] n **1** *the canons of good taste* rule, ruling, principle, standard, criterion, test, measure, yardstick, benchmark, pattern, model, exemplar, precept, norm, formula, convention. **2** *a Church canon* law, rule, regulation, statute, decree, edict, dictate. **3** *a canon of saints|the canon of Shakespeare's plays* official list, list, catalogue, enumeration, litany, roll.

canon[2] n prebendary. *see* ECCLESIASTIC n.

canopy n awning, shade, sunshade, cover, covering, tarpaulin, tester, baldachin; *lit* cope.

cant[1] n **1** *thieve's cant* slang, jargon, patter, lingo, terminology, argot. **2** *religious cant* hypocrisy, insincerity, sanctimony, sanctimoniousness, humbug, pseudo-piety, sham holiness, lip service, pretence.

cant[2] n *the table is on a cant* slant, slope, tilt, angle, inclination.

cant[2] v *the boat began to cant* tilt, tip, slope, slant, lean, incline, angle, overturn.

cantakerous adj bad-tempered, shorttempered, ill-natured, crabbed, crabby, surly, irascible, irritable, grumpy, brusque, curt, abrupt, difficult, disagreeable, quarrelsome, touchy, perverse, testy, peevish, crusty, peppery, choleric, captious; *inf* grouchy, crotchety, cranky.

canter n amble, saunter, trot, jog, dogtrot, lope, gallop.

canvass v **1** *canvassing during the general election* solicit votes, seek votes, campaign, electioneer, drum up support, persuade, convince. **2** *canvassing people's views|canvass buying habits* investigate, find out, enquire into, look into, examine, scrutinize, explore, study, analyse, sift, evaluate, survey, scan, poll. **3** *canvass an idea/suggestion/theory* discuss, debate, air, ventilate, argue, dispute.

canyon n ravine, gully, valley, gorge, chasm, gulf, abyss.

cap n **1** *doffing his cap* hat, bonnet, headgear; *inf* lid; peaked cap, flat cap, school cap, baseball cap, jockey cap, bathing cap, skullcap, nightcap, mobcap, stocking cap. *see* HAT. **2** *replace the cap on the bottle* top, lid, stopper, cork, bung, plug. **3** *the cap of a wave|mountain caps* top, crest, peak, summit, apex, pinnacle.

cap v **1** *mountains capped with snow* cover, top, crown, overlie, overspread, coat, blanket. **2** *cap his story|cap the ground record* beat, better, surpass, excel, outshine, transcend, eclipse, overshadow, outdo, outstrip, exceed. **3** *he's been capped for Wales* choose, select, pick, include. **4** *cap the price* limit, set a limit to, restrict, keep within bounds, curb. **cap it all** provide as a finishing touch, suffer as a final straw, suffer/find on top of everything else.

capability n **1** *have the capability to do well| the capability of winning* ability, capacity, potential, aptitude, faculty, facility, power, competence, efficiency, effectiveness, proficiency, accomplishment, talent, adeptness, skill, skilfulness, experience, cleverness, intelligence, smartness. *see* CAPABLE. **2** *offer capabilities* talent, gifts, skill, aptitude, flair, knack, forte, strong point.

capable adj *a very capable young woman* able, competent, adequate, efficient, effective, proficient, accomplished, talented, gifted, adept, skilful, masterly, experienced, practised, qualified, clever, intelligent, smart. **capable of 1** *capable of murder/lying* having the inclination/temperament to do, having a tendency/propensity to do, tending to, inclined to, predisposed to, prone to, liable to, likely to do. **2** *capable of improvement* needing, in need of, requiring, wanting, susceptible to, admitting of, receptive of.

capacious adj roomy, commodious, spacious, ample, large, voluminous, sizeable, substantial, vast, immense.

capacity n **1** *the capacity to seat twenty* space, room, size, largeness, ampleness, amplitude, scope, magnitude, dimensions, proportions, extent. **2** *have the capacity to do the job* ability, capability, aptitude, potential, faculty, facility, power, competence, competency, proficiency, accomplishment, cleverness, intelligence, brains, head. *see* CAPABILITY. **3** *in his capacity as a teacher* position, post, job, office, function, role, appointment, province.

cape[1] n *wearing a black cape* cloak, mantle, shawl, wrap, poncho, pelisse, pelerine, domino, cope.

cape[2] n *drowned off the cape* headland, head, point, promontory, neck, tongue, peninsula.

caper v *goats/children capering about* frolic, frisk, romp, skip, gambol, cavort, prance, dance, leap, hop, jump, bound, spring, bounce.

caper n **1** *the energetic capers of the children/goats* frolics, frisking, romping, skipping, gambols, gambolling, cavorting, prancing, dancing, leap. *see* CAPER V. **2** *tired of their mischievous capers* prank, trick, practical joke, antics, lark, jest, jesting, jape, high jinks, mischief, escapade, stunt, game, sport, fun; *inf* shenanigan; *Amer inf*, dido.

capital adj **1** *our capital concern* | *take capital decisions* principal, chief, main, major, prime, paramount, foremost, predominant, overruling, leading, cardinal, central, key. **2** *make a capital error* grave, vital, important, serious, crucial, fatal. **3** *a capital show* | *a capital piece of work* splendid, excellent, first-rate, first-class, superb, fine, outstanding; *inf* super, tip-top, A1, crack, top-notch.

capital n **1** *Edinburgh is the capital of Scotland* first city, seat of government, centre of administration. **2** *write in capitals* capital letter, upper-case letter, majuscule, uncial, uncial letter; *inf* cap. **3** *enough capital to buy the firm* money, finance, finances, funds, cash, hard cash, wherewithal, means, assets, liquid assets, wealth, resources, reserves, stock, principal; working capital, investment capital.

capitalism n free enterprise, private enterprise, private ownership, privatized industries, *laissez-faire*.

capitalist n financier, investor, banker, tycoon, moneyman; wealthy/rich person, plutocrat, nabob, bloated capitalist; *inf* yuppie, loadsamoney.

capitalize v *capitalize the firm* finance, back, provide backing for, fund, sponsor. **capitalize on** *capitalize on her rival's mistakes* take advantage of, put to advantage, profit from, turn to account, cash in on, make the most of, exploit.

capitulate v surrender, yield, submit, give in, give up, come to terms, succumb, accede, back down, cave in, relent, acquiesce; *inf* throw in the towel/sponge.

caprice n whim, whimsy, vagary, fancy, notion, fad, freak, humour, impulse, quirk, crotchet; changeableness, fickleness, volatility, inconstancy, fitfulness.

capricious adj changeable, unpredictable, fickle, variable, inconstant, unstable, mercurial, volatile, impulsive, erratic, fanciful, faddish, freakish, irregular, fitful, whimsical, wayward, quirky.

capsize v overturn, turn over, upset, upend, knock over, tip over, invert, keel over, turn turtle.

capsule n **1** *pain-relieving capsules* pill, tablet, lozenge, bolus, troche. **2** *plant capsules* seed case, pod, pericarp. **3** *remove the capsule from the wine bottle* seal, cap, cover. **4** *space capsule* craft, probe; detachable compartment, section.

captain n **1** *the captain of the ship* commander, master, skipper; *inf* old man. **2** *team captain* leader, head, skipper. **3** *captains of industry* chief, head, leader, boss, principal *inf* number one; *Amer inf* honcho.

caption n heading, title, wording, head, legend, inscription.

captious adj carping, criticizing, critical, fault-finding, quibbling, cavilling; *inf* nit-picking.

captivate v charm, delight, enchant, bewitch, fascinate, beguile, enthral, entrance, enrapture, attract, allure, lure, win, infatuate, seduce, ravish, ensnare, dazzle, hypnotize, mesmerize.

captive n *take captives* | *captives clamouring for freedom* prisoner, prisoner-of-war, hostage, slave, bondsman, convict, jailbird, detainee; *inf* con.

captive adj *captive animals* imprisoned, incarcerated, locked up, caged, interned, confined, penned up, detained, restrained; in captivity, in bondage.

captivity n imprisonment, custody, detention, confinement, internment, incarceration, restraint, constraint, committal, bondage, slavery, servitude, enslavement, subjection, thraldom.

capture v catch, arrest, apprehend, take prisoner, take captive, take into custody, seize, take, lay hold of, trap; *inf* nab, collar, pinch, lift, nail, bag.

capture n 1 *involved in the criminal's capture* arrest, apprehension, taking prisoner, taking captive, imprisonment, seizure, trapping; *inf* nabbing, collaring, pinching. *see* CAPTURE v. 2 *the captures of war* prize, trophy, gain; booty, pickings, pillage.

car n 1 *hiring a car* motor car, motor, vehicle, motor vehicle, automobile, motorized vehicle, machine; *Amer* sedan; *inf* wheels, heap, crate, jalopy, limo; *Amer inf* auto; limousine, executive, open top, four-wheel drive, hatchback, estate, coupé, cabriolet, off-roader, hard top, soft top, saloon car, sports car, racing car, company car, hired car, stock car, police car, patrol car, Panda car. 2 *railway car* carriage, coach, van; buffet car, dining car, sleeping car, Pullman, cable car.

carafe n flask, decanter, jug, pitcher, flagon.

caravan n 1 *holiday in a caravan* mobile home, camper, Dormobile; *Amer* trailer; *inf* van. 2 *a gypsy caravan* wagon, covered cart, cart, van. 3 *merchant caravans in the desert* convoy, troop, band, company, group, cavalcade, procession.

carcass n 1 *sheep carcasses* corpse, dead body, body; remains; *Med* cadaver; *inf* stiff. 2 *shift your carcass* body, person, self, oneself. 3 *the carcass of the building* frame, framework, skeleton, shell, hulk.

card n 1 *use card to make the model* cardboard, pasteboard. 2 *send a card to her* postcard, greetings card, Christmas card, birthday card, good luck card, get well card, sympathy card. 3 *here's my card* identification; business card, calling card, ID card, identification card. 4 *deal the cards* playing cards, picture cards, face cards, tarot cards; pack of cards; card-game. **on the cards** *an election's on the cards* likely, possible, probable, liable, in the wind, in the air.

cardinal adj 1 *cardinal sins/errors* main, chief, capital, principal, important, greatest, highest, vital, key, central, major, essential, foremost, leading, prime, paramount, pre-eminent, fundamental, basic, primary. 2 *painted cardinal* red, scarlet, crimson, vermillion.

cardinal n *cardinals in Rome* cardinal bishop, cardinal priest, high priest, archpriest. *see* ECCLESIASTIC n.

care n 1 *bowed down with care* worry, anxiety, trouble, disquiet, unease, distress, sorrow, anguish, grief, sadness, affliction, woe, hardship, tribulation, responsibility, stress, pressure, strain; burdens. 2 *no care for others* concern, regard, attention, interest, solicitude, looking after, sympathy. 3 *arrange the flowers with care* carefulness, attention, thought, regard, heed, forethought, mindfulness, conscientiousness, painstakingness, pains, accuracy, precision, meticulousness, punctiliousness, fastidiousness. 4 *cross the road with care* attention, caution, heedfulness, alertness, watchfulness, vigilance, wariness, awareness, circumspection, prudence. 5 *in the care of her uncle | in the care of the local authority* charge, protection, custody, keeping, safe keeping, control, management, ministration, supervision; guardianship, wardship.

care v 1 *she doesn't care about her work | he didn't care what happened* be concerned, be interested, interest oneself, have regard, worry, trouble, bother, mind; *inf* give a damn, give a hoot, give a rap, give a hang. **care for** 1 *he cares for his wife deeply* love, be fond of, be in love with, cherish, hold dear, treasure. 2 *I don't care for her* like, be fond of, find congenial. 3 *would you care for some tea?* wish, want, desire, fancy, hanker after, long for; *inf* have a yen for. 4 *care for the children* take care of, look after, mind, watch, tend, attend to, minister to, foster, nurse, provide for.

career n 1 *choose a career* occupation, profession, vocation, calling, employment, job, métier. 2 *watch the career of the political party* course, progress, progression, procedure, passage, path. 3 *stop the horse in mid-career* rush, onrush, run, race, bolt, dash, gallop, impetus.

carefree adj light-heated, happy-go-lucky, cheerful, cheery, happy, merry, jolly, buoyant, breezy, easygoing, jaunty, frisky, blithe, airy, nonchalant, unworried, untroubled, insouciant; *inf* upbeat.

careful adj 1 *be careful crossing the road* cautious, heedful, alert, aware, attentive, watchful, vigilant, wary, on guard, chary, circumspect, prudent, mindful. 2 *be careful of your reputation* mindful, heedful, protective; *be careful about what you say* solicitous, thoughtful, attentive, concerned, having regard. 3 *a careful worker* attentive, conscientious, painstaking, meticulous, accurate, precise, scrupulous, punctilious, fastidious. **4** *a careful housekeeper | careful with her money* canny, cautious, thrifty, economical, economic.

careless adj **1** *a careless driver* inattentive, thoughtless, unthinking, forgetful, absent-minded, negligent, remiss, irresponsible, slapdash, slipshod, lax, slack; *inf* sloppy. **2** *a careless piece of work* hasty, cursory, perfunctory, inaccurate, disorganized, slapdash, slipshod; *inf* sloppy. **3** *a careless remark* unthinking, thoughtless, insensitive, indiscreet, unguarded. **4** *careless of her appearance* negligent, remiss, slapdash, slipshod, untidy, slovenly, slatternly; *inf* sloppy, messy. **5** *careless rapture* carefree, light-hearted, happy-go-lucky, cheerful, merry, buoyant, blithe, nonchalant. *see* CAREFREE. **6** *careless elegance* unstudied, artless, casual, nonchalant, informal.

caress n *a loving caress* touch, stroke, fondle, fondling, pat, embrace, cuddle, hug, nuzzle, kiss.

caress v *caress her* cuddle, fondle, pet, pat, embrace, hug, nuzzle, kiss; *caress her throat* kiss, touch/stroke lovingly.

caretaker n superintendent, janitor, warden, porter, custodian, keeper, watchman, steward, curator, concierge.

cargo n freight, freightage, load, lading, haul, consignment, contents, goods, merchandise, baggage; shipment, shipload, boatload, lorryload, truckload.

caricature n cartoon, parody, burlesque, mimicry, travesty, distortion, satire, farce, lampoon, pasquinade; *inf* send-up, take-off, spoof.

caricature v parody, mimic, mock, ridicule, distort, satirize, lampoon, burlesque; *inf* send up, take off.

carnage n slaughter, wholesale slaughter, butchery, massacre, mass murder, mass destruction, indiscriminate bloodshed; blood bath, holocaust, pogrom; *inf* shambles.

carnal adj sexual, sensual, fleshly, erotic, lustful, lascivious, libidinous, lecherous, lewd, prurient, salacious, coarse, gross, lubricious.

carnival n **1** *we are looking forward to the carnival* fiesta, festival, fête, gala, jamboree, holiday; revelry, revels, merrymaking, festivity, celebration; Mardi gras. **2** *the carnival has moved to another town* fair, amusement show, sideshows, circus.

carol n Christmas song, nativity song, hymn, canticle; *inf* noel.

carol v *children carolling loudly* sing carols, go carolling, sing, chorus, warble, trill, chant.

carouse v go on a spree, go on a drinking bout, go on a binge, binge, make merry, party, paint the town red, over-indulge, drink freely, roister, wassail, live it up, go on a bender, go on a pub-crawl.

carp v complain, fault-find, find fault, criticize, cavil, pick on, quibble, censure, reproach, nag; *inf* nit-pick.

carpenter n joiner, cabinet-maker, woodworker.

carpet n **1** *the lounge carpet* floor-covering, runner, matting, mat, rug; Persian carpet, Turkish carpet, Axminster, fitted carpet, magic carpet. **2** *a carpet of leaves* covering, layer, expanse.

carriage n **1** *carriages of former times* coach, cab; coach-and-four, trap, stage coach, hackney, hansom, landau, barouche, gig, chaise, calash, tilbury, phaeton, surrey. **2** *a railway carriage* compartment, car. *see* CAR 2. **3** *an elegant carriage* posture, bearing, stance, deportment, comportment, attitude, manner, presence, air, guise, demeanour, mien, behaviour, conduct. **4** *free carriage* transport, transportation, freight, freightage, conveyance, delivery, carrying.

carry v **1** *carry a parcel* transport, convey, transfer, move, take, bring, bear, lug, haul, shift, fetch; conduct, pass on, transmit, relay. **2** *carry the weight of the column | carry responsibilities* support, sustain, bear, shoulder. **3** *carry the day/victory/motion* win, capture, gain, secure, effect, accomplish. **4** *a store carrying a brand* sell, stock, offer, have for sale, retail. **5** *carrying the latest news* communicate, give, release, publish, broadcast. **6** *carry the audience/crowd* influence, affect, have an effect on, motivate, stimulate, urge, spur on, impel, drive. **7** *women carrying themselves well* bear oneself, hold oneself, comport oneself, deport oneself, conduct oneself. **carry on 1** *carry on talking* go on, continue, keep, keep on, persist in, maintain, persevere in. **2** *carry on a business* run, operate, conduct, manage, administer, transact. **3** *he's carrying on with his secretary* have an affair, commit adultery; *inf* have it off. **4** *children carrying on* misbehave, make mischief, be mischievous, cause a fuss/commotion; *inf* create. **carry out 1** *carry out a promise/threat* fulfil, carry through, achieve, implement, realize, execute, effect, discharge. **2** *carry out an experiment/enquiry* conduct, perform, implement, execute.

cart n **1** *collect garden rubbish in a cart* handcart, barrow, wheelbarrow, pushcart. **2** *tractor-drawn carts* wagon, hay-cart, four-wheeled cart, dray, tumbrel.

cart v **1** *cart away the rubbish* transport, convey, haul, transfer, move, shift. **2** *carting the luggage on holiday* lug, tote, carry; *dial* humph.

carton n box, package, cardboard box, container, case, pack, packet.

cartoon n **1** *children's cartoons* comic strip; animated film, animated cartoon; animation. **2** *a political cartoon | newspaper cartoons* caricature, parody, lampoon, satire, burlesque, pasquinade; *inf* take-off, send-up, spoof.

cartridge n case, container, cylinder, capsule, cassette, magazine.

carve v **1** *carve a figure out of stone* sculpt, sculpture, cut, chisel, hew, whittle, chip, form, shape, fashion, mould. **2** *carve initials on a tree* engrave, etch, notch, cut in, incise. **3** *carve meat* slice, cut up. **carve up** *carve up the territory* divide, partition, parcel out, apportion, dole out, subdivide, split up, separate out.

cascade n waterfall, falls, fountain, water chute, shower, cataract, torrent, flood, deluge, outpouring, avalanche.

cascade v tumble, descend, pour, gush, surge, spill, overflow.

case[1] n **1** *a cigarette case* container, box, receptacle, holder, canister. **2** *a case of wine* crate, box, carton, pack, bin, coffer, casket. **3** *bullet case | tape case* casing, covering, sheath, sheathing, wrapper, wrapping, cover, envelope, housing, jacket, capsule, folder, integument. **4** *checking in cases at the airport* suitcase, trunk, piece of luggage, item of baggage, briefcase; luggage, baggage. **5** *display case* cabinet, cupboard, chiffonier, bureau.

case[2] n **1** *as has been the case previously* stated position, situation, circumstances, instance, occurrence, happening, occasion, conditions, plight, predicament, event, contingency, phenomenon. **2** *a case of cheating* instance, occurrence, occasion, example, illustration, specimen. **3** *the case comes up next week* lawsuit, suit, action, trial, proceedings, legal proceedings, legal process, legal cause, legal dispute. **4** *his case was that he was elsewhere* statement, plea, claim, alibi, postulation, explanation, exposition, thesis, testing, presentation. **5** *terminal cases* patient, sick person, invalid, sufferer, victim.

cash n **1** *no cash with me* money, ready money, coinage, notes, bank notes, currency; *fml* specie, legal tender. **2** *he has no cash of any kind* money, finance, wherewithal, resources, funds, capital, investment capital; *inf* dough, bread, the ready.

cash v *cash the cheque/bills* encash, realize, exchange, change, turn into cash/money.

cashier n bank clerk, bank teller, teller, banker, treasurer, bursar, purser, accountant, controller, money man.

cashier v dismiss, discharge, expel, drum out, throw out, cast out, discard, get rid of; *inf* sack, give the boot to, boot out.

casino n gambling club, gaming club, gambling house, gambling den.

cask n barrel, keg, tun, vat, vessel, hogshead, firkin, pipe.

casket n **1** *a jewel casket* box, case, container, receptacle, chest, coffer. **2** *funeral casket* coffin, pall, sarcophagus; *inf* box; *sl* wooden overcoat.

cast v **1** *cast a stone in the lake* throw, toss, fling, pitch, hurl, sling, heave, shy, lob, launch, let fly. **2** *cast their skins/coats* shed, discard, slough off, peel off, throw off, get rid of, let fall, let drop. **3** *cast a glance* shoot, direct, turn, throw, send out. **4** *cast a soft light* emit, give off, send out, shed, radiate, diffuse, spread out; *cast a shadow* form, create. **5** *cast doubt* throw, bestow, impart, confer, give, grant. **6** *cast one's vote* register, record, enter, vote. **7** *cast bronze | cast figures in bronze* shape, fashion, form, mould, model, sculpt. **8** *cast actors for the play* choose, select, pick, name, assign, appoint, allot. **9** *cast up the figures* add, total, reckon, sum. **10** *cast a fortune* predict, forecast, foretell, foresee, prophesy. **cast about** *cast about for his sock | cast about for an excuse* search, seek, look, grope about. **cast down** *the weather cast him down a bit* depress, deject, dispirit, discourage, dishearten, desolate.

cast n **1** *the cast of a dice* throw, toss, fling, pitch, hurl, shy, lob. *see* CAST v 1. **2** *cast of features/mind* sort, kind, style, type, stamp, nature. **3** *plaster cast* figure, shape, mould, form. **4** *a cast in her eye* squint, twist, defect.

caste n *a member of the upper caste* class, social class, order, social order, grade, grading, station, place, standing, position, status.

castigate v punish, discipline, chastise, rebuke, reproach, scold, reprimand, censure, reprove, upbraid, berate, chide, admonish, criticize, chasten, take to task, dress down, give a dressing-down to, haul over the coals.

castle n stronghold, fortress, keep, hold, citadel, fastness, peel, palace, chateau.

casual adj **1** *a casual meeting* chance, accidental, unintentional, unexpected, unforeseen, unanticipated, fortuitous, serendipitous. **2** *a casual remark* offhand, random, impromptu, spontaneous, unpremeditated, unthinking. **3** *casual work* part-time, temporary, irregular. **4** *a casual read* cursory, perfunctory, superficial, desultory, hasty, hurried. **5** *a casual attitude to work* indifferent, apathetic, uncaring, uninterested, unconcerned, lackadaisical, blasé, nonchalant, luke-warm, insouciant, pococurante. **6** *casual clothes* informal, not formal, unceremonious, relaxed, leisure; *inf* sporty. **7** *a casual acquaintance* slight, superficial, shallow.

casualties npl *the casualties of the last war* dead, fatalities, losses, dead and wounded, wounded, injured, missing in action, missing.

casualty n **1** *a war causality* fatality, dead/wounded/injured person, victim. **2** *the firm was a casualty of the recession* victim, sufferer, loser, loss.

cat n **1** *a cat by the fire* feline, domestic cat; *inf* pussy, pussy cat, puss, moggy; *lit* grimalkin; tabby, tomcat, tom, ginger tom, tortoiseshell, marmalade cat, Siamese, Burmese, kitten, mouser, wild cat, alley cat; **2** *the cats of Africa* big cat; lion, tiger, leopard, lynx. **3** *spiteful cat* shrew, vixen, virago; *inf* bitch.

catacombs npl underground tunnels/labyrinth/maze, tomb, underground cemetery, underground burial ground.

catalogue n *a catalogue of library books* list, record, register, inventory, directory, index, roll, table, calendar, classification, guide, brochure.

catalogue v list, classify, categorize, index, make an inventory of, inventory, record, register, file, alphabetize.

catapult n *kill the creature with a catapult* sling, trebuchet, ballista, mortar, arbalest.

catapult v *he was catapulted to freedom/success* launch/propel rapidly, hurtle, shoot, be flung.

cataract n **1** *cataracts falling from the rocks* cascade, waterfall, falls, rapids, torrent, downpour. **2** *eye surgeons operate on cataracts* opacity, opaqueness.

catastrophe n disaster, calamity, tragedy, blow, adversity, trouble, trials, mishap,

misfortune, mischance, misadventure, failure, reverses, affliction, distress.

catcall n whistle, boo, hiss, jeer; *inf* the bird, a raspberry.

catch v **1** *catch the ball* grasp, snatch, grab, seize, grip, clutch, clench, pluck, receive, acquire, come into the possession of, intercept. **2** *catch the prisoner* capture, seize, take captive, apprehend, take, arrest, lay hold of, trap, snare; *inf* nab, collar. **3** *catch what he said* understand, follow, grasp, comprehend, make out, take in, fathom, discern, perceive, apprehend; *inf* get the drift of, get the hang of, twig. **4** *catch him unawares* surprise, discover, come across, startle, detect. **5** *catch pneumonia* contract, get, become infected with, develop, succumb to, suffer from; *inf* go/come down with. **6** *catch his attention/fancy* capture, attract, draw, captivate, bewitch. **7** *catch a likeness* capture, reproduce, represent, photograph, draw, paint. **catch on 1** *sports catching on* become popular, become fashionable, come into fashion/vogue; *inf* become trendy, become all the rage. **2** *eventually catch on to his intentions* see through, find out, fathom, grasp, understand, comprehend, see the light about; *inf* twig, latch on, figure out, get the picture about.

catch n **1** *the catch of the door/suitcase* bolt, lock, fastener, fastening, clasp, hasp, hook, clip, latch, snib; *Scots* sneck. **2** *what's the catch?* snag, disadvantage, drawback, stumbling block, hitch, fly in the appointment, trap, trick, snare; catch-22. **3** *sell the catch at the market* bag, hawl, net, take, yield. **4** *he/she is quite a catch* eligible man/woman/person, marriage prospect, suitable husband/wife/spouse.

catching adj **1** *a catching disease | is it catching?* contagious, infectious, communicable, transmittable, transmissible. **2** *a catching manner* attractive, appealing, winning, captivating, charming, fetching, taking, fascinating, enchanting, bewitching, alluring.

catchword n slogan, motto, password, watchword, byword, shibboleth, formula, refrain, saying.

catchy adj memorable, popular, appealing, captivating, haunting, melodious, singable.

catechize v interrogate, cross-examine, question, quiz, examine, grill, pump, give the third degree to, put through the third degree.

categorical adj unqualified, unconditional, unequivocal, explicit, unambiguous, unreserved, absolute, direct, downright, emphatic, positive, express, conclusive.

categorize v classify, class, group, grade, order, arrange, sort, rank, break down, catalogue, list, tabulate.

category n class, classification, group, grouping, head, heading, list, listing, designation, type, sort, kind, variety, grade, grading, order, rank, status, division, section, department.

cater v 1 *cater for all needs* provide, furnish, supply, purvey. 2 *cater for large parties* provide food, feed, provision, victual.

caterwauling n howl, howling, screech, screeching, shriek, shrieking, scream, screaming.

catharsis n purging, purgation, purification, cleansing, depuration, lustration, release, emotional release; *Tech* abreaction.

cathartic adj purgative, purifying, cleansing, lustral, release-bringing.

catholic adj 1 *of catholic interest* general, universal, widespread, global, world-wide, comprehensive, all-encompassing, all-embracing, all-inclusive. 2 *catholic tastes/views* wide, broad, broad-based, eclectic, liberal, open-minded, tolerant, unbigoted, unsectarian, ecumenical.

cattle n cows, bovines, beasts; stock, livestock.

catty adj *catty female/remark* spiteful, malicious, venomous, malevolent, nasty, ill-natured, mean.

caucus n 1 *attend a Senate caucus* assembly, meeting, gathering, session, conference, convention, conclave. 2 *a local parliamentary caucus* group, party, bloc, faction, cabal, clique, coterie.

cause n 1 *the cause of the fire | the cause of her misfortune* origin, root, source, beginning, genesis, occasion, mainspring, originator, author, creator, producer, agent, prime mover, maker. 2 *no cause for alarm* reason, grounds, justification, call, basis, motive, motivation. 3 *devoted to the cause of human rights* principle, ideal, belief, conviction, tenet, object, aim, objective, purpose, *raison d'être*. 4 *plead his cause* case, point of view, contention.

cause v *cause trouble | cause the explosion* be the cause of, make happen, bring about, give rise to, begin, create, produce, originate, occasion, generate, effect, engender, lead to, result in, precipitate, provoke.

caustic adj 1 *caustic chemical substances* corrosive, corroding, mordant, burning, acrid, destructive. 2 *a caustic wit* sarcastic, cutting, biting, mordant, stinging, sharp, scathing, trenchant, virulent, acrimonious, astringent.

cauterize v burn, sear, singe, disinfect, sterilize.

caution n 1 *proceed with caution* alertness, care, carefulness, attention, wariness, attentiveness, heed, heedfulness, watchfulness, vigilance, guardedness, circumspection, discretion, forethought, prudence, mindfulness. 2 *receive a caution from the police/headmaster* warning, admonition, injunction, monition; counsel. 3 *her uncle's a caution* comic, comedian, wit, humorist, wag, clown, joker, jester.

caution v 1 *caution against driving fast | caution not to go* warn, advise, counsel, urge, admonish. 2 *cautioned by the judge* give/deliver a caution to, admonish, warn, give an injunction to.

cautious adj careful, wary, watchful, shrewd, prudent, circumspect, discreet, guarded, chary, alert, heedful, attentive, vigilant, mindful; *inf* cagey.

cavalcade n procession, parade, march, column, troop, file, train, caravan, cortège, retinue.

cavalier n 1 *cavaliers dying for King Charles* royalist, king's man. 2 *footsoldiers and cavaliers* horseman, horse soldier, equestrian, knight, chevalier. 3 *the lady and her latest cavalier | cavaliers at the ball* escort, beau, gallant, gentleman, courtier.

cavalier adj *a cavalier attitude towards his colleagues* offhand, condescending, haughty, arrogant, lofty, lordly, disdainful, supercilious, patronizing, scornful, contemptuous, discourteous, insolent.

cavalry n 1 *infantry and cavalry* mounted troops, horse soldiers, horsemen, horse, troopers; light cavalry, heavy cavalry, dragoons, lancers, hussars. 2 *the cavalry arrived just as we were going bankrupt* timely/fortuitous help, help, aid, white knight, saviour.

cave n cavern, grotto, hollow, cavity, pothole, underground chamber, tunnel, cellar, dugout, den.

caveat n warning, caution, admonition, monition; *inf* red flag, alarm bells.

caveman n *cavemen and their stone tools* primitive man, prehistoric man, primordial man, Stone Age man, palaeolithic man, Neanderthal man.

caveman adj *women resenting caveman tactics* primitive, uncivilized, crude, brutal, savage; masterful, domineering, autocratic.

cavern n large cave, cave, grotto, hollow, pothole. *see* CAVE.

cavernous adj *cavernous depths/eyes* large, huge, deep, hollow, sunken, yawning, unfathomable, dark.

cavil v carp, find fault, quibble, complain, criticize, censure, object, make objections; *inf* nit-pick.

cavity n hole, hollow, crater, pit, orifice, aperture, gap, dent.

cease v 1 *cease working* stop, discontinue, desist, desist from, end, finish, leave off, quit, conclude, terminate, suspend, bring to a halt, bring to an end, break off. 2 *the rain ceased* stop, halt, finish, come to a stop, come to an end, let up, die away, abate, terminate.

cease adv **without cease** continuously, incessantly, unendingly, unremittingly, without cessation/stopping/let-up, without a pause/break, on and on, time without end. *see* CESSATION.

ceaseless adj incessant, unceasing, unending, endless, never-ending, interminable, non-stop, constant, continuous, continual, uninterrupted, eternal, perpetual, unremitting, persistent.

cede v yield, surrender, concede; abdicate, resign, hand over; relinquish, renounce, forsake, abandon, make over, turn over, transfer, deliver up, grant, give, bequeath.

ceiling n 1 *the ceiling of the building* overhead, upper side, roof. 2 *a ceiling on prices* limit, upper limit, maximum, summit, pinnacle.

celebrate v 1 *celebrate the poet's anniversary* commemorate, observe, honour, mark, keep, drink to, toast. 2 *celebrate after the exams* make merry, rejoice, enjoy oneself, party, paint the town; *inf* go on a spree, go out on the town, whoop it up. 3 *celebrate his achievement* proclaim, make known, herald, announce, publicize, broadcast, advertise, promulgate. 4 *a poem celebrating the joys of love* praise, laud, extol, glorify, exalt, eulogize, reverence. 5 *celebrate a religious ceremony* perform, solemnize, ceremonialize.

celebrated adj famous, famed, notable, noted, renowned, well-known, popular, prominent, distinguished, great, eminent, pre-eminent, outstanding, illustrious, acclaimed, revered, glorious, legendary, lionized.

celebration n 1 *the celebration of his birthday | anniversary celebrations* commemoration, observance, honouring, keeping, remembrance. 2 *having a celebration* party, carousal, festival, fête, carnival, gala; festivity, merry-making, revelry, jollification,

junketing; *inf* spree, binge, beanfeast, bash. 3 *celebration of a religious ceremony* performance, solemnization.

celebrity n 1 *celebrities at a charity ball* VIP, famous person, dignitary, big name, name, personality, star, superstar, lion, notable, luminary, personage; *inf* bigwig, big shot, bit noise; *Amer inf* big wheel. 2 *his celebrity spread far* fame, renown, notability, popularity, reputation, honour, prominence, prestige, distinction, eminence, pre-eminence, glory, illustriousness, stardom.

celestial adj 1 *celestial beings* heavenly, divine, godly, godlike, ethereal, sublime, paradisical, elysian, spiritual, empyrean, immortal, angelic, seraphic, cherubic. 2 *celestial bodies/navigation* heavenly, astronomical, extraterrestrial, stellar, of the sky/heavens.

celibacy n chastity, singleness, abstinence, self-denial, self-restraint, continence, abnegation, asceticism, virginity, bachelorhood, spinsterhood, monkhood, nunhood, monasticism; *inf* single blessedness.

cell n 1 *a prison/monastic cell* cubicle, room, apartment, compartment, chamber, stall, enclosure, dungeon, lock-up. 2 *honeycomb cells* compartment, cavity, hole. 3 *a political cell* faction, caucus, nucleus, clique, coterie, group, party, unit.

cement n adhesive, bonding, binder, glue, superglue, gum, paste.

cement v bind, bond, stick, join, unite, attach, cohere, combine, affix, glue, gum, paste, solder, weld.

cemetery n graveyard, burial ground, burial place, necropolis, churchyard, charnel house, golgotha.

censor v *censor letters | censor the play* cut, delete, delete from, make cuts/changes to, blue-pencil, expurgate, bowdlerize.

censor n *the film censor* examiner, inspector, expurgator, bowdlerizer.

censorious adj fault-finding, critical, disapproving, condemnatory, reproachful, censuring, captious, carping, cavilling.

censure v *censure him for his behaviour* criticize, condemn, blame, castigate, denounce, disapprove of, berate, upbraid, reprove, reproach, rebuke, reprimand, scold, chide, reprehend.

censure n *open to public censure | a vote of censure* criticism, condemnation, blame, castigation, denunciation, disapproval, berating, upbraiding, reproval, reproof, reproach, rebuke, reprimand, scolding, chiding, reprehension, obloquy.

central adj **1** *a central position* middle, mid, median, medial, mesial, mean. **2** *central London/America* middle, mid, inner, interior. **3** *a central issue* main, chief, principal, foremost, fundamental, basic, key, essential, primary, pivotal, focal, core, cardinal.

centralize v *centralize the administration* concentrate, centre, concentre, consolidate, amalgamate, condense, compact, unify, incorporate, streamline, focus, rationalize.

centre n *the centre of the town* middle, middle point, midpoint, nucleus, heart, core, hub, kernel, focus, focal point, pivot.

centre v *her interests centre on sport* concentrate, focus, pivot, converge, concentre, close in.

ceramics npl pottery, earthenware, clay pots, crocks.

cereal n **1** *farmers growing cereals* grain, corn; wheat, rye, oats, barley, maize. **2** *she ate her cereal* breakfast food, cornflakes, porridge, muesli.

ceremonial adj *ceremonial occasion/dress* formal, ritual, ritualistic, stately, solemn, dignified, celebratory, sacramental, liturgical.

ceremonial n *the ceremonial of coronations* ceremony, rite, ritual, formality, custom, solemnity, sacrament, liturgy.

ceremonious adj **1** *a ceremonious occasion* ceremonial, formal, ritual. *see* CEREMONIAL adj. **2** *behave in a ceremonious manner* formal, punctilious, precise, scrupulous, stately, courtly, courteous, civil, deferential, stiff, rigid, affected; *inf* starchy, just-so.

ceremony n **1** *a wedding ceremony* rite, service, formality, observance, function, custom, sacrament, show. *see* CEREMONIAL n. **2** *conducted with ceremony* formalities, niceties, pomp, protocol, decorum, etiquette, propriety, conventionality, punctilio, attention to detail; *inf* fuss.

certain adj **1** *I'm certain he's guilty* sure, positive, confident, convinced, assured, unwavering, unshaken, secure, satisfied, persuaded. **2** *her success/failure is certain* sure, assured, destined, fated, inevitable, reliable, inescapable, bound to happen, inexorable, ineluctable; *inf* in the bag. **3** *it is certain that he will go* sure, definite, unquestionable, beyond question, indubitable, undeniable, irrefutable, incontrovertible, incontestable, obvious, evident, plain, clear, conclusive. **4** *no certain cure* | *a certain sign* sure, definite, assured, unfailing, unquestionable, undisputed, dependable, reliable, trustworthy, sound, foolproof; *inf* sure-fire. **5** *there is no certain date yet* definite, decided, settled, fixed,

established, determined. **6** *a certain lady/ place that will remain anonymous* particular, specific, individual, special, especial, precise. **7** *to a certain extent* indeterminate, moderate, minimum.

certainly adv **1** *he will certainly die* surely, definitely, assuredly, undoubtedly, undeniably, obviously, plainly, clearly. *see* CERTAIN 3. **2** *certainly, he'll be there* yes, of course, by all means.

certainty n **1** *I cannot say with certainty* sureness, assuredness, positiveness, confidence, conviction, reliability, validity, conclusiveness, authoritativeness, truth, fact, factualness. **2** *it's a certainty that Britain will lose* inevitability, indubitability, inescapability, fact; *inf* sure thing, cinch. **3** *that horse's a certainty* certain winner, certain happening; *inf* sure-fire winner, cert, dead cert, cinch.

certificate n certification, document, authorization, credentials, testimonial, warrant, licence, voucher, diploma.

certify v **1** *a document certifying their marriage* testify to, attest, corroborate, substantiate, verify, confirm, endorse, validate, vouch for, guarantee, authenticate, document, bear witness to, ratify, warrant; *certified dead* verified as, confirmed as, officially declared, vouched. **2** *she has been certified as a teacher* give a certificate/diploma to, recognize, accredit, license, authorize, qualify.

cessation n end, termination, finish, conclusion, pause, break, respite, let-up; ceasing, stopping, halting, ending, finishing.

chafe v **1** *chafe the child's feet* rub, warm, warm up. **2** *his neck chafed by his shirt* rub, abrade, graze, excoriate, scrape, scratch, rasp. **3** *material chafed by the rock* wear, wear away/down, wear out, wear to shreds, fray, tatter, erode. **4** *the passengers were chafed by the delay* annoy, anger, irritate, exasperate, infuriate, enrage, incense, inflame, provoke, vex, worry, peeve, irk, ruffle. **5** *passengers chafing at the delay* be impatient, be angry/annoyed/irritated/exasperated, fret, fume; *inf* blow one's top, blow a fuse.

chaff n **1** *chaff from the grain* husks, hulls, pods, shells, cases, casing. **2** *chaff for the cattle* straw, hay, fodder, silage. **3** *throw away the chaff* | *separate the chaff from the wheat* rubbish, refuse, waste, garbage, trash, dregs, remains, debris, junk, dross, detritus. **4** *the chaff of her classmates* | *the chaff of the comedian* banter, bantering, joking, jesting, badinage, raillery, teasing, joshing, waggishness, humour, wit, repartee, persiflage; *inf* kidding, ragging, wisecracking, ribbing.

chaff v *chaffing his sister* banter, tease, josh; *inf* kid, rag, rib.

chagrin n *feeling chagrin at their treatment* annoyance, anger, irritation, vexation, displeasure, worry, dissatisfaction, resentment, rankling, smarting, discomposure, discomfiture, disquiet, fretfulness, spleen, embarrassment, mortification, humiliation, shame.

chagrin v *chagrined by their treatment* annoy, anger, enrage, irritate, vex, displease, worry, peeve, irk, chafe, fret, dissatisfy, discompose, discomfit, disquiet, embarrass, mortify, humiliate, shame. *see* CHAGRIN n.

chain n 1 *a gold chain* series of links. 2 *a chain of events* series, succession, string, sequence, train, progression, course, set, cycle, line, row, concatenation. 3 *a chain of shops* group; firm, company. 4 *see* CHAINS.

chain v *chain the dog to the wall* fasten, secure, tie, bind, tether, shackle, fetter, manacle, hitch, moor, handcuff, confine, restrain, trammel, gird, imprison.

chains npl *prisoners in chains* bonds, fetters, shackles, manacles, trammels.

chair n 1 *tables and chairs* seat; armchair, easy chair, rocking chair, wing chair, swivel chair, wheelchair, stool, bench, pew, stall, throne. 2 *a university chair* professorship, professorate, headship. 3 *elected chair of the society* chairperson, chairman, chairwoman, president, spokesperson, spokesman, spokeswoman, MC, master/mistress of ceremonies. 4 *sent to the chair* electric chair; electrocution, execution; *inf* hot seat.

chair v *chair the meeting* preside over, lead, direct, manage, control, oversee, supervise.

chalk v **chalk up 1** *chalk it up to experience* put down, ascribe, attribute, accredit, impute, charge. 2 *chalk up the score* record, register, enter, mark, log, score.

chalky adj white, pale, wan, pallid, ashen, pasty, waxen, blanched, bleached, colourless.

challenge n 1 *accept a sporting challenge* summons, call, invitation, bidding. 2 *a challenge to tradition | a challenge to the government* questioning, interrogation, opposition, stand, countercharge, defiance, confrontation, test, ultimatum. 3 *a new challenge in his life* difficult task/venture, hazard, risk, obstacle. **challenge to** questioning of, interrogation of, stand against, countercharge, ultimatum; opposition to, defiance, confrontation with.

challenge v 1 *challenge someone to a competition* dare, summon, invite, bid, throw down the gauntlet to; defy to. 2 *challenge their authority* question, call into question, dispute, protest against, take exception to,

object to, disagree with, demur against, be a dissenter of. 3 *the job really challenges him* test, tax, stimulate, arouse, inspire, excite, spur on.

chamber n 1 *the judge's chambers* room, apartment, compartment, cubicle, hall. 2 *the princess retiring to her chamber* room, bedroom, bedchamber, boudoir. 3 *the chambers in the caves/heart* compartment, cavity, hollow, cell. 4 *the upper chamber of the government* legislative body, legislature, assembly, council, house.

champion n 1 *the champion of the competition* winner, title-holder, victor, conqueror, hero. 2 *the champion of the cause* defender, protector, upholder, supporter, advocate, backer, patron; *inf* angel. 3 *ladies' champions taking part in a tournament* knight, man-at-arms, paladin, hero, warrior.

champion v *champion the cause* defend, protect, uphold, support, stand up for, fight for, speak for, advocate, back, promote, espouse.

chance n 1 *meet by chance* accident, coincidence, fortuity, serendipity, fate, destiny, fortune, luck, providence. 2 *a good chance that he'll win* prospect, possibility, probability, likelihood, likeliness, conceivability, odds. 3 *to get a second chance* opportunity, opening, occasion, turn, time; *inf* shot. 4 *take a chance and run* risk, gamble, hazard, venture, speculation, long shot.

chance v 1 *it chanced that they arrived last* happen, occur, take place, come about, come to pass, befall, turn up, crop up. 2 *have to chance it* take a chance that, risk, hazard, gamble, venture, speculate, try one's luck, take a leap in the dark. **chance on/upon** *chance upon an old friend | chanced on the answer* come across, stumble on, come upon, meet, encounter; *inf* bump into, run into.

chance adj *a chance meeting/discovery* accidental, unexpected, unanticipated, unforeseen, unforeseeable, unlooked-for, unintended, unintentional, unpremeditated, unplanned, fortuitous, serendipitous.

chancy adj risky, uncertain, hazardous, speculative, perilous, dangerous; *inf* dicey, dodgy.

change v 1 *change one's attitude/plans* alter, modify, transform, convert, vary, remodel, recast, restyle, reconstruct, reorder, reorganize, metamorphose, transmute, permutate, permute. 2 *she's changed | the world's changed* alter, be transformed, move on, evolve, metamorphose, fluctuate, diversify; *inf* do an about-face, do a U-turn. 3 *change* *jobs/sides | change a pair of trousers* exchange, interchange, substitute, switch, replace, trade, barter; *inf* swap.

change n **1** *a change in attitude/plan* difference, alteration, modification, transformation, conversion, variation, remodelling, reconstruction, reorganization, transition, innovation, metamorphosis, transfiguration, vicissitude, transmutation, mutation, permutation; *inf* about-turn, U-turn. *see* CHANGE v **1**. **2** *a change of jobs* exchange, interchange, substitution, switch, trade, bartering; *inf* swap. **3** *he's tired and needs a change* holiday, diversion, variation, variety; *inf* break. **4** *have no change* coins, coinage, cash, silver, petty cash.

changeable adj **1** *of changeable moods | changeable weather* changing, variable, varying, changeful, chameleon-like, chameleonic, protean, shifting, vacillating, volatile, mercurial, capricious, fluctuating, fluctuant, fluid, kaleidoscopic, fitful, wavering, unstable, unsteady, unsettled, irregular, erratic, unreliable, inconstant, fickle, mutable, unpredictable, many-faceted, chequered, vicissitudinous. **2** *changeable structures/laws* alterable, modifiable, convertible, mutable, permutable.

channel n **1** *the channel connecting the seas* passage, sea-passage, strait, neck, narrows, waterway, watercourse, fiord. **2** *the channel of the canal* bed, floor, bottom, depths. **3** *rainwater running through the channels* gutter, groove, furrow, conduit, duct, culvert, ditch. **4** *new channels for their energy* course, way, direction, path, route, approach. **5** *channels of communication* means, medium, agency, vehicle, route.

channel v **1** *grooves channelling the rock* furrow, groove, flute, hollow out, cut. **2** *channelling water/energies* transmit, convey, transport, conduct, direct, guide.

chant n *a religious chant | a victory chant* song, singing, chorus, melody, ditty, carol, psalm.

chant v **1** *chant the liturgy* sing, recite, intone, cantillate. **2** *football fans chanting* shout, sing, chorus, carol.

chaos n disorder, confusion, pandemonium, bedlam, tumult, upset, upheaval, disorganization, uproar, disruption, disarray, anarchy, lawlessness, riot.

chaotic adj in chaos, disordered, confused, tumultuous, upset, disorganized, jumbled, topsy-turvy, askew, awry, disrupted, in disarray, anarchic, lawless, orderless.

chap v *wind having chapped her hands* roughen, make raw, crack, make sore, redden, chafe.

chap n man, fellow, male, boy; *inf* bloke, guy, sort, cove, customer.

chaperon n *the young lady's chaperon* companion, duenna, protectress, escort.

chaperon v *chaperoning the girls to the ball* accompany, escort, attend, shepherd, watch over, take care of, keep an eye on, protect, guard, safeguard.

chapter n **1** *the next chapter in the book* division, section, part, portion, episode. **2** *a tragic chapter in the club's history* period, time, phase, stage, episode. **3** *a chapter of accidents* series, sequence, succession, chain, progression, set. **4** *chapter of the cathedral* council, assembly, convocation, convention, synod, consistory. **5** *a chapter of the society* branch, section, division, wing, offshoot, lodge.

char v *char the paper* scorch, singe, sear, toast, carbonize, cauterize.

character n **1** *her character's changed | the character of the town has altered* personality, nature, disposition, temperament, temper; essential quality, ethos, individuality, complexion, constitution, make-up, cast, attributes, bent, genius. **2** *a person of character* moral strength/fibre, strength, honour, integrity, rectitude, uprightness, fortitude, backbone. **3** *damage his character* reputation, name, standing, position, status. **4** *he's one of the village's characters* eccentric, oddity, odd fellow, original, individual; *inf* oddball, queer fish, odd fish, card. **5** *they're all friendly characters* person, individual, human being, fellow; *inf* chap, bloke, guy, sort, type, customer. **6** *characters in Austen's novels* persona, person, portrayal, representation, role, part. **7** *in bold characters | Chinese characters* letter, sign, mark, symbol, type, cipher, hieroglyph, figure, device, rune, logo, emblem.

characteristic n *one of her appealing/annoying characteristics* quality, essential quality, attribute, feature, trait, property, mannerism, mark, trademark, idiosyncrasy, peculiarity, quirk.

characteristic adj *their characteristic modesty* typical, distinguishing, distinctive, particular, special, individual, specific, peculiar, idiosyncratic, singular, representative, symbolic, symptomatic, diagnostic.

characterize v **1** *the landscape is characterized by hills and rivers* typify, distinguish, identify, specify, signalize, indicate, denote, designate, mark, stamp, brand, label. **2** *the playwright characterizing the heroine as hysterical* portray, depict, present, represent, describe.

charade n pretence, travesty, fake, farce, parody, pantomime.

charge v **1** *what do you charge for a room?* ask in payment, ask, fix a charge/price, expect, impose, levy. **2** *charge it to my account* debit, put down to, bill. **3** *charge him with murder* accuse of, indict, arraign, impeach, impute, blame, incriminate. **4** *charge the enemy* attack, storm, assault, rush, open fire on, fall on; *inf* lay into, tear into. **5** *charged with the guardianship of the child* entrust, tax, weigh, weigh down, load, burden, encumber, hamper, saddle. **6** *charge a vessel/gun* fill, fill up, load, load up, pack, plug. **7** *charged with emotion* fill, load, imbue, suffuse, pervade, permeate, infuse, instil. **8** *I charge you to confess* order, command, bid, direct, exhort, instruct, enjoin, adjure, demand, require.

charge n **1** *what is the charge for a room?* cost, price, fee, amount, rate, payment, expense, expenditure, outlay, dues, levy, toll. **2** *charges of murder* accusation, allegation, indictment, arraignment, impeachment, citation, imputation, blame, incrimination. **3** *the charge of the cavalry* attack, storming, assault, onrush, onslaught, onset, sortie, incursion. **4** *have charge of the children* responsibility, care, custody, guardianship, trust, protection, safekeeping, surveillance. **5** *your charge is to drive the car* duty, task, job, responsibility, office, obligation, assignment, business, burden. **6** *pay for his charge's education* ward, protégé, dependant, minor. **7** *the judge's charge to the jury* instruction, direction, order, command, dictate, injunction, exhortation, mandate.

charitable adj **1** *be charitable towards the poor* philanthropic, giving, benevolent, generous, liberal, open-handed, kind, magnanimous, beneficent, bountiful, bounteous, munificent, big-hearted, humane, almsgiving, eleemosynary. **2** *a charitable interpretation of the situation* generous, liberal, tolerant, broad-minded, understanding, sympathetic, compassionate, lenient, indulgent, forgiving, kindly, favourable, gracious.

charity n **1** *relying on charity for survival* financial assistance, donations, contributions, hand-outs, gifts, funding, endowments, financial relief, alms-giving, philanthropy, benefaction. **2** *behave with charity towards fellow men* goodwill, compassion, humanity, humanitarianism, kindliness, love, sympathy, tolerance, indulgence, altruism, thoughtfulness, generosity, liberality, benevolence, benignity.

charlatan n quack, mountebank, sham, fraud, fake, impostor, confidence trickster, confidence man, pretender, cheat, deceiver, swindler; *inf* con man, phoney.

charm n **1** *the charm of the resort/hostess* attractiveness, attraction, appeal, allure, allurement, fascination, captivation, pleasingness, desirability, engagingness, delightfulness. **2** *captivated by her charms* attractiveness, appeal, allure, beauty, wiles, blandishments. **3** *the sorcerer's charm* spell, magic formula, magic word, abracadabra; sorcery, magic. **4** *the charms on her bracelet* trinket, ornament, bauble, souvenir, *bijou*. **5** *wear/carry a lucky charm* good-luck charm, amulet, talisman, fetish, periapt, phylactery.

charm v *charmed by the little girl | charmed by the music* delight, please, attract, win, win over, captivate, allure, lure, draw, fascinate, bewitch, beguile, enchant, enrapture, enamour, seduce, cajole, hypnotize, mesmerize.

charming adj delightful, pleasing, pleasant, appealing, attractive, winning, fetching, taking, captivating, winsome, engaging, lovely, agreeable, alluring, fascinating, bewitching, beguiling, enchanting, delectable, irresistible, seductive.

chart n *plot it out on a chart* graph, table, map, diagram, plan, blueprint, guide, scheme, tabulation.

chart v **1** *chart the results* tabulate, map, map out, plot, graph, delineate, diagram, sketch, chart a course of, draft. **2** *chart their progress* follow, record, register, note.

charter n **1** *privileges granted by royal charter* authority, authorization, sanction, warrant, document, covenant, deed, bond, permit, prerogative, privilege, right. **2** *the charter of the United Nations* constitution, code, canon, body of laws; principles, rules, laws. **3** *the charter of a boat* hiring, leasing, renting, engaging. **4** *have a charter to run a ferry* permit, licence, warrant, concession, franchise, indenture.

charts npl *pop charts* list, listing, league, catalogue, index.

chary adj cautious, wary, leery, careful, circumspect, watchful, distrustful, apprehensive.

chase v **1** *dogs chasing rabbits | police chasing after burglars* give chase to, pursue, run after, follow, hunt, hound, track, trail, tail. **2** *chase away the intruder* put to flight, drive, send, send packing. **3** *chase round doing the work* rush, hurry, make haste. **chase up** pester, harass.

chase n *take part in the chase* pursuit, hunt, trail; hunting, coursing.

chasm n **1** *a landscape full of chasms* gorge, abyss, canyon, ravine, pit, crater, crevasse, hole, hollow, opening, gap, fissure, crevice, cleft, rift, rent. **2** *a chasm between their points of view* schism, breach, gulf, rift; separation, alienation.

chassis n framework, frame, skeleton, substructure, fuselage, bodywork, anatomy.

chaste adj **1** *a chaste young woman* | *nuns leading a chaste life* virgin, virginal, vestal, celibate, abstinent, self-restrained, unmarried. **2** *chaste conduct/speech* virtuous, good, innocent, pure, decent, moral, decorous, modest, wholesome, righteous, upright, uncorrupted, incorrupt, uncontaminated, undefiled, unsullied. **3** *a chaste style* simple, plain, unadorned, unembellished, unaffected, unpretentious, austere, restrained.

chasten v **1** *chastened by the experience* subdue, restrain, tame, curb, check, humble, cow, tone down. **2** *chasten the pupils* discipline, punish, penalize, castigate, scold, upbraid, reprimand, reprove, chide, take to task, haul over the coals.

chastity n **1** *nuns taking vows of chastity* chasteness, virginity, celibacy, abstinence, self-restraint, self-denial, continence, singleness, unmarried state; virtue, immaculateness. **2** *chastity of conduct/speech* virtue, goodness, innocence, purity, decency, morality, decorum, modesty, wholesomeness, righteousness. *see* CHASTE 2. **3** *chastity of style* simplicity, plainness, unpretentiousness, austerity. *see* CHASTE 3.

chastize v **1** *schoolmasters chastising children* punish, discipline, castigate, beat, thrash, smack, flog, whip, strap, cane, lash, birch, scourge; *inf* wallop, thump, tan one's hide. **2** *the staff were chastized for arriving late* scold, upbraid, reprimand, reprove, chide, take to task, haul over the coals, chasten, castigate.

chat v *chat with her colleagues* talk, gossip, chatter, have a conversation with, converse, tittle-tattle, prattle, clack, jabber, prate; *inf* natter, gas, have, a confab with, have a chin-wag with, chin-wag, jaw, chew the rag/fat with. **chat up** flirt/trifle with.

chat n *have a chat with* talk, gossip, conversation, chatter, heart-to-heart, tête à tête; *inf* natter, confab, chin-wag.

chatter v *children chattering in groups* chat, gossip, jabber, prattle, babble, tittle-tattle,

tattle, blather; *inf* natter, chin-wag. *see* CHAT V.

chatter n *tired of the children's/village chatter* talk, gossip, chit-chat, chitter-chatter, jabber, prattling, babbling, tittle-tattle, tattle, blathering, nattering, confab, chin-wag. *see* CHAT n.

chatterbox n gossiper, jabberer, babbler, tittle-tattler, blatherer; *inf* natterer, windbag.

chatty adj **1** *a chatty person* talkative, gossipy, gossiping, garrulous, loquacious, voluble, glib, effusive, gushing. **2** *a chatty style* informal, conversational, colloquial, gossipy, familiar, friendly, lively; *inf* newsy.

chauvinism n jingoism, partisanship, excessive loyalty, prejudice, bias, machismo.

cheap adj **1** *cheap prices/housing* inexpensive, low-priced, low-cost, economical, reasonable, moderately priced, keenly priced, keen, bargain, cut-price, economy, sale, reduced, marked-down, slashed, discounted; *inf* bargain-basement. **2** *cheap and gaudy jewellery* poor-quality, inferior, shoddy, common, trashy, tawdry, tatty, paltry, worthless, second-rate, cheapjack, gimcrack; *inf* tacky. **3** *a cheap joke* despicable, contemptible, low, base, unpleasant, mean, sordid, vulgar. **4** *she felt so cheap at her behaviour* ashamed, shameful, embarrassed, humiliated, mortified, debased, degraded, abashed, discomfited, disconcerted. **5** *he's a cheap operator* mean, stingy, parsimonious, tight-fisted, niggardly, money-grubbing, cheese-paring, pennypinching, frugal, sparing, cheapskate.

cheapen v **1** *cheapen the cost of travel* lower, reduce, cut, mark down, slash, discount, depreciate. **2** *cheapening herself by working in that club* degrade, debase, demean, devalue, lower, belittle, denigrate, discredit, depreciate, derogate.

cheat v **1** *cheat his partner* | *cheat into giving him money* deceive, trick, swindle, defraud, dupe, hoodwink, double-cross, gull; exploit, take advantage of, victimize; *inf* do, con, diddle, bamboozle, finagle, bilk; rip off, fleece, take for a ride. **2** *cheat out of his inheritance* deprive of, deny, thwart, prevent from, preclude from, foil, frustrate, baulk, defeat. **3** *cheat the bad weather* | *cheat death* avoid, elude, evade, dodge, escape, steer clear of, shun, eschew. **4** *husbands and wives cheating on each other* be unfaithful to, commit adultery *inf* two-time.

cheat n **1** *a cheat at sport* | *a cheat for a business partner* cheater, swindler, fraud, confidence trickster, confidence man/woman, trickster, deceiver, double-crosser, crook, rogue, shark, charlatan; *inf* con man. **2** *win by a cheat* swindle, fraud, deception, deceit, trick, trickery, imposture, artifice; *inf* con.

check v **1** *luggage checked at the airport* examine, inspect, look at, look over, scrutinize, test, monitor, investigate, probe, enquire into, study; *inf* give the once-over to. **2** *check the door's locked* confirm, make sure, verify, corroborate, validate, substantiate. **3** *check the vehicle's progress* stop, arrest, halt, bring to a standstill, slow down, brake, bar, obstruct, impede, block, retard, curb, delay. **4** *check one's laughter/ tears* restrain, suppress, repress, contain, control, bridle, inhibit; *inf* nip in the bud. **5** *check the children* scold, rebuke, reprimand, chide, reprove, berate, discipline, punish; *inf* give a row to, tell off, read the riot act to. **6** *their stories don't check* correspond, agree, tally, dovetail, harmonize.
check up 1 *check up that he's telling the truth* check, investigate, confirm, ascertain, make sure, verify, corroborate, validate, substantiate. **2** *check up on his background* investigate, examine, inspect, research, scrutinize, probe, enquire into.

check n **1** *a luggage check* examination, inspection, scrutiny, scrutinization, test, monitoring, investigation, probe, enquiry, study; *inf* once-over. **2** *make a check that you have everything* confirmation, verification, corroboration. see CHECK v 2. **3** *a check in the production rate* stop, stopping, stoppage, arrest, halt, slowing-down, braking, obstruction, retardation, delay. see CHECK v 3. **4** *act as a check to the riot/ celebration* restraint, constraint, control, deterrent, hindrance, impediment, obstruction, inhibition, limitation, curb. **5** *the American asked for his check* bill, account, invoice, reckoning, tally; *Amer* tab.

checkmate n **1** *the checkmate of the chess player's king* check, block, blockage, stop, stoppage, halt, arrest. **2** *the checkmate of the other army* defeat, beating, overthrow, rout, conquest, vanquishment, trouncing, drubbing.

checkmate v **1** *checkmate his king* check, block, stop, halt, arrest. **2** *checkmate the opposing army* defeat, beat, overthrow, rout, vanquish, trounce, give a drubbing to.

check-up n *a check-up from the doctor | giving the car a check-up* examination, inspection, appraisal, assessment, analysis, scrutinization, scrutiny, exploration, probe.

cheek n **1** jowl, chop, gill. **2** *have the cheek to appear* impudence, audacity, temerity, brazenness, effrontery, nerve, imperti-

nence, insolence; *inf* gall, brass neck, sauce, lip. **3** *give the teacher cheek* impudence, impertinence, insolence, disrespect; *inf* sauce, lip. **4** *the baby's inflamed cheeks* buttocks, bottom, rump; *inf* behind, rear-end, arse. see BOTTOM n 7.

cheeky adj impudent, audacious, impertinent, insolent, forward, pert, disrespectful, insulting; *inf* saucy; *Amer inf* sassy.

cheep v chirp, chirrup, twitter, tweet, warble, trill, chatter.

cheer v **1** *crowds cheering the popstar/queen* hail, acclaim, hurrah, hurray, applaud, shout at, clap. **2** *his arrival cheered her* raise the spirits of, brighten, buoy up, perk up, enliven, animate, elate, exhilarate, hearten, uplift, give a lift to, gladden, encourage, incite, stimulate, arouse, comfort, solace, console, inspirit; *inf* buck up.
cheer up 1 *his arrival cheered her up* raise the spirits of. see CHEER v 2. **2** *she cheered up on his arrival* brighten, perk up, liven up, rally; *inf* buck up.

cheer n **1** *the cheers of the crowd* acclaim, acclamation, hurrah, hurray, applause, ovation, plaudit, hailing, shout, shouting, clapping. **2** *Christmas is a time of cheer* cheerfulness, gladness, happiness, merriment, mirth, gaiety, joy, pleasure, blitheness, jubilation, high spirits, animation, buoyancy, light-heartedness, glee, optimism, hopefulness, merry-making, rejoicing, revelry, festivity. **3** *larders laden with Christmas cheer* fare, food, provisions, foodstuffs, drink; *inf* eats.

cheerful adj **1** *a cheerful mood/disposition* happy, bright, merry, glad, gladsome, gay, sunny, joyful, jolly, blithe, animated, buoyant, light-hearted, sparkling, gleeful, carefree, happy-go-lucky, breezy, cheery, sprightly, jaunty, smiling, laughing, bright-eyed and bushy-tailed, optimistic, hopeful, positive; in good spirits; *Amer inf* peppy, chipper. **2** *a cheerful room/colour* bright, sunny, cheering, pleasant, agreeable, friendly, happy. **3** *his cheerful acceptance of the situation* willing, obliging, cooperative, compliant, complying, acquiescent, agreeing, assenting.

cheerio interj goodbye, cheers, so long, farewell, adieu, *au revoir*, ciao, *auf Wiedersehen*, adios; *inf* bye, bye bye, see you later, ta-ta, toodle-oo.

cheerless adj gloomy, dreary, miserable, dull, depressing, dismal, bleak, drab, grim, austere, desolate, dark, dingy, sombre, uninviting, comfortless, forlorn.

cheers interj **1** here's to you, good luck, here's health, *skol, slainte, prosit*; *inf* here's

mud in your eye, bottoms up, down the
hatch. **2** goodbye, cheerio. *see* CHEERIO.

cheery adj cheerful, happy, merry, glad; in
good spirits. *see* CHEERFUL 1.

chef n cook, cordon bleu cook, food pre-
parer, baker, pastrycook, sous chef, com-
mis chef, *chef de cuisine*; *Amer inf* short-order
cook.

chef-d'-oeuvre n masterpiece, magnum
opus, masterwork, *pièce de résistance*, *tour de
force*, jewel in the crown.

chequered adj *a chequered career* mixed, varied, diverse, diversified, eventful; full of
ups and downs.

cherish v **1** *cherish his loved one* care for, cosset, treasure, prize, hold dear, love, dote
on, adore, idolize, revere, indulge. **2** *cherish
the plants/orphans* care for, look after, tend,
protect, preserve, shelter, support, nurture,
foster. **3** *cherish hopes* have, entertain, harbour, cling to, foster, nurture.

cherub n **1** *heavenly cherub* angel, seraph.
2 *cherubs in the baby contest* baby, babe,
infant, innocent child, pretty child, lovable
child, well-behaved child.

chest n **1** *injured her chest* thorax, breast,
sternum. **2** *pack his goods in chests* box,
crate, case, trunk, container, coffer, casket.

chew v *chew one's food* masticate, munch,
champ, crunch, bite, gnaw, grind. **chew
over** meditate on, ruminate on, mull over,
consider, weigh up, ponder on, deliberate
upon, reflect upon, muse upon, cogitate
about.

chic adj stylish, fashionable, smart, elegant,
modish, voguish; *inf* trendy, dressy, snazzy.

chicanery n misleading talk, fraud, fraudulence, deception, deceitfulness, duplicity,
guile, cheating, duping, hoodwinking, dishonesty, subterfuge, craftiness, wiles,
sophistry.

chide v scold, upbraid, rebuke, reprimand,
reproach, admonish, lecture, call to
account, take to task, berate, castigate; *inf*
give a dressing-down to.

chief n **1** *the chief of the tribe/village* head,
headman, leader, chieftain, ruler, overlord,
lord and master, commander, suzerain;
Amer sachem. **2** *the chief of the firm* head,
principal, leader, director, chairman, chairperson, chief executive, manager, superintendent, master, foreman; *inf* boss,
bossman, gaffer, kingpin, top dog, big
cheese, Mr Big.

chief adj **1** *chief priest* supreme, head, foremost, principal, highest, leading, grand,
superior, premier, directing, governing.

2 *the chief point* main, principal, most
important, uppermost, primary, prime,
cardinal, central, key, vital, essential, predominant, pre-eminent.

chiefly adv mainly, in the main, principally, primarily, predominantly, especially,
particularly, essentially, mostly, for the
most part, on the whole, above all.

child n **1** *two adults and a child* youngster,
young person, young one, little one, boy,
girl, baby, babe, infant, toddler, tot, tiny
tot, adolescent, youth, juvenile, minor;
derog brat, chit; *inf* kid, nipper, shaver,
sprog; *Scots* bairn, wean. **2** *parents and their
children* offspring, progeny, issue; descendant, scion; son, daughter, son and heir.

childbirth n labour, confinement, parturition, delivery, *accouchement*, travail.

childhood n youth, infancy, babyhood, pre-
teens, minority, nonage, juniority, immaturity; boyhood, girlhood.

childish adj **1** *the childish behaviour of the
adults* immature, infantile, juvenile,
puerile, silly, foolish, irresponsible, jejune.
2 *childish laughter* children's, childlike,
youthful; boyish, girlish.

childlike adj **1** *childlike activities* children's,
youthful. **2** *childlike reactions/innocence*
ingenuous, innocent, artless, guileless,
simple, naive, trusting, trustful, credulous,
gullible.

chill n **1** *a chill in the air* chilliness, coldness,
coolness, iciness, crispness, rawness, sharpness, nip, bite, frigidity, gelidity. **2** *catch a
chill* cold, flu, influenza, respiratory infection, virus. **3** *a chill in her manner* chilliness,
coldness, coolness, aloofness, distance,
unresponsiveness, lack of sympathy, frigidity, lack of welcome, hostility, unfriendliness. **4** *cast a chill over the proceedings* dread,
fear, gloom, cloud, depression, damper,
check to happiness, check to joy.

chill adj **1** *a chill wind* chilly, cold, cool, icy,
raw, biting. *see* CHILLY 1. **2** *a chill manner*
chilly, cold, cool, aloof, distant, frigid,
unresponsive, hostile. *see* CHILLY 3.

chill v **1** *chilled by the wind* made cold, made
colder, cool down. **2** *chill food* make colder,
cool down, freeze, cook-chill, congeal.
3 *chill the enthusiasm/party spirit* lessen,
reduce, dampen, depress, dispirit, discourage, dishearten.

chilly adj **1** *a chilly breeze* cold, cool, icy,
crisp, brisk, fresh, raw, sharp, biting, penetrating, freezing, frigid, chill; *inf* nippy.
2 *feeling chilly* cold, cool, freezing, frozen to
the marrow, shivery. **3** *a chilly manner* cold,
cool, aloof, distant, unresponsive, unsym-

pathetic, frigid, unwelcoming, hostile, unfriendly.

chime v **1** *bells chiming* ring, peal, toll, sound, ding, dong, clang, boom, tinkle, resound, reverberate. **2** *chime the bells* ring, peal, toll, strike, sound, tintinnabulate. **3** *bells/clock chiming 6 o'clock* indicate, mark, show. **chime in 1** *their ideas chime in with ours* harmonize, blend, correspond, be complementary, agree, be in agreement, accord, be in accordance. **2** *he's always chiming in when we're talking* interrupt, cut in, interpose; *inf* chip in, butt in.

chimes npl bells, carillon, angelus, tocsin.

china n **1** *ornaments made of china* porcelain, eggshell porcelain, eggshell china, faience, ceramics, pottery; Wedgewood, delftware. **2** *set out the best china* dishes, tableware, dinner/tea service.

chink n crack, fissure, crevice, cleft, cut, rift, split, slit, gap, opening, aperture, cavity, cranny.

chip n **1** *chips on the sawmill's floor* shaving, paring, shard, flake, shred, sliver, splinter, fragment, snippet, scrap. **2** *the cup with a chip in it* nick, crack, notch, snick, fault, flaw, dent. **3** *gambling chips* counter, token, disc, man. **4** *steak and chips* potato straw, fried potato, game chip; *Amer* French fry.

chip v **1** *chip a glass* nick, crack, snick, gash, damage. **2** *the paint chips easily* break off, crack, fragment, crumble. **3** *chipping away at a chunk of wood* whittle, chisel, hew. **chip in 1** *he's always chipping in with his suggestions* interrupt, cut in, interpose; *inf* chime in, butt in. **2** *chip in to buy a present* contribute, make a contribution, subscribe, donate, make a donation, pay.

chirp v chirrup, cheep, twitter, tweet, warble, trill, chatter.

chirpy adj cheerful, cheery, happy, lighthearted, carefree, merry; in good spirits; *inf* upbeat.

chit-chat n chat, chatting, small talk, idle gossip, gossip, chatter, tittle-tattle.

chivalrous adj **1** *behaving in a chivalrous way towards women* gallant, gentlemanly, courteous, gracious, mannerly, well-mannered, polite, thoughtful, protective, courtly. **2** *chivalrous followers of King Arthur* knightly, courtly, bold, courageous, brave, valiant, heroic, daring, intrepid, honourable, highminded, just, fair, loyal, constant, true, gallant, magnanimous, protective.

chivalry n **1** *his chivalry towards women* gallantry, gentlemanliness, courtesy, courteousness, graciousness, mannerliness, politeness, thoughtfulness, protectiveness,

courtliness. **2** *chivalry at medieval courts* knightly code, knighthood, knight errantry; courtly manners. **3** *the chivalry of Arthur's followers* knightliness, courtliness, boldness, courage, bravery, valour, heroism, daring, intrepidity, honour, highmindedness, integrity, justice, justness, fairness, loyalty, constancy, trueness, truthfulness, magnanimity, protectiveness.

chivvy v prod, urge, goad, nag, pester, badger, hound, pressure, pressurize, harass, annoy; *inf* hassle.

choice n **1** *the questions are open to choice not compulsory | the choice of candidate* choosing, selection, picking, option, preference, election, adoption. **2** *no choice but to resign* alternative, option, possibility, solution, answer, way out. **3** *a wide choice of confectionery* selection, range, variety, supply, store, array, display. **4** *he was considered the right choice* selection, appointment, appointee, nominee, candidate.

choice adj **1** *choice fruit* best, select, superior, first-class, first-rate, excellent, prime, prize, special, rare, exclusive, hand-picked. **2** *a few choice phrases* well-chosen, select, hand-picked, appropriate, apposite, apt.

choke v **1** *choke her to death with his hands* strangle, strangulate, throttle. **2** *smoke choking him* asphyxiate, suffocate, smother, stifle, overpower. **3** *he choked on a fishbone* gag, gasp, retch, struggle for air, asphyxiate, suffocate. **4** *the drains are choked* clog, block, obstruct, occlude, plug, dam up, congest. **choke back** *choke back her tears* check, restrain contain, suppress, control, repress, curb, bridle.

choose v **1** *choose a book/career* select, pick, pick out, hand-pick, take, opt for, settle on, decide on, fix on, single out, adopt, designate, elect, espouse. **2** *do as you choose* prefer, like, wish, want, desire, fancy, favour.

choosy adj fussy, finicky, pernickety, faddy, fastidious, particular, exacting, discriminating.

chop v **1** *chop the trees* cut down, fell, hew, bring down, hack down, saw down. **2** *chop branches* cut off, lop, sever, hack off, saw off, cleave, sunder. **3** *chop services | the plans have been chopped* cut, reduce, decrease, decimate, axe, stop, halt. **4** *chop meat/vegetables* cut up, cube, dice, fragment, crumble. **chop down** cut, hew, fell, hack. *see* CHOP 1. **chop off** sever, cleave, sunder. *see* CHOP 2. **chop up** cut up, fragment. *see* CHOP 4.

choppy adj rough, bumpy, turbulent, blustery, stormy, tempestuous, squally.

chore n task, job, duty, errand, burden, routine; work, domestic work.

chortle v chuckle, cackle, guffaw, laugh uproariously, roar/shake with laughter, split one's sides, be convulsed.

chorus n 1 *singing in the festival chorus* choir, ensemble, choral group; choristers, singers, vocalists. 2 *girls of the chorus* dance troupe, corps de ballet; dancing girls. 3 *the chorus of the song* refrain, burden, strain, response. **in chorus** *give a reply in chorus* unison, concert, harmony.

christen v 1 *christen a child in church* baptize, give a name to, name, sprinkle, immerse. 2 *she was christened Sara* name, call, dub, style, term, designate, denominate. 3 *christen the glasses* begin using, break in.

chronic adj 1 *a chronic illness* persistent, long-lasting, long-standing, constant, continual, continuous, incessant, lingering, unabating, deep-rooted, deep-seated, ingrained. 2 *a chronic liar* inveterate, confirmed, habitual, hardened. 3 *a chronic case of plagiarism* very bad, appalling, atrocious, dreadful, awful.

chronicle n *a chronicle of historical events* register, record, annals, calendar, diary, journal, log, account, archive, history, story.

chronicle v *chronicle events* record, put on record, set down, document, register, report, enter, note, relate, tell about.

chronological adj sequential, consecutive, progressive, serial, ordered, historical; in order of time, in sequence.

chubby adj plump, tubby, rotund, stout, portly, round, dumpy, fat, fleshy, flabby, paunchy.

chuck v 1 *chuck it in the bucket* toss, fling, throw, cast, pitch, hurl, shy, heave, sling, let fly. 2 *chuck his job/girlfriend* abandon, give up, relinquish, quit, forsake; *inf* drop, pack in.

chuckle v laugh quietly, laugh to oneself, chortle, giggle, titter, cackle.

chum n friend, bosom friend, companion, comrade, crony, *alter ego*; *inf* pal, mate, buddy; *dial* marrow.

chunk n lump, hunk, block, slab, mass, square, wedge, dollop, piece, portion, part; *inf* wodge.

church n place of worship, the house of God, the Lord's house; cathedral, minster, chapel, temple, tabernacle, mosque, synagogue.

churlish adj boorish, oafish, loutish, ill-mannered, unmannerly, rude, impolite, discourteous, uncivil, surly, sullen, crabbed, ill-tempered, curt, brusque, rough.

churn v 1 *churn milk into butter* beat, whip up, agitate. 2 *churning the peaceful waters* agitate, disturb, stir up, shake up. 3 *water churning under the rocks* seethe, foam, froth, boil, swirl, toss, convulse.

cigarette n filter-tip, king-size, menthol cigarette, cigar; *inf* cig, ciggie, smoke, fag, gasper, cancer stick, coffin nail.

cinder n ash, ember, clinker, charcoal.

cinema n films, pictures, movies, motion pictures; *inf* big screen, silver screen.

cipher n 1 *written in cipher* code, secret writing; coded message, cryptograph. 2 *a row of ciphers* zero, nil, naught. 3 *Arabic ciphers* number, numeral, figure, digit, integer, character, symbol, sign. 4 *he's just a cipher in the firm* nobody, nonentity, nothing, nonperson.

circle n 1 *draw a circle* round, ring, disc, loop, circumference, ball, globe, sphere, orb. 2 *move in different circles* area of activity, field of interest, scene, sphere, domain, province, realm, range, region, circuit, orbit, compass. 3 *her circle of friends* group, set, company, crowd, ring, coterie, clique, assembly, fellowship, class.

circle v 1 *vultures circling above* move round, rotate, revolve, circulate, wheel, whirl, gyrate, pivot, swivel. 2 *circle the estate* surround, encircle, ring, ring round, enclose, envelop, hedge in, hem in, gird, belt, circumscribe; *circle the world* go round, orbit, circumnavigate.

circuit n 1 *run a circuit of the track* round, lap, turn, beat, ambit, cycle, loop, compass, circumference. 2 *the circuit of the estate/field* border, boundary, bounding line, bounds, compass, limits, circumference. 3 *the judge's circuit* tour, journey, trip, excursion, travels, wanderings, peregrination, perambulation.

circuitous adj roundabout, winding, meandering, tortuous, twisting, rambling, indirect, maze-like, labyrinthine.

circular adj round, discoid, ring-shaped, annular, spherical, spheroid, globular.

circulate v 1 *circulate the news* spread, spread around, disseminate, propagate, distribute, transmit, give out, issue, make known, make public, broadcast, publicize, advertise, publish, promulgate, pronounce. 2 *blood/air circulating* flow, move round, go round, rotate, revolve, whirl, gyrate.

circumference n perimeter, periphery, border, boundary, bounds, limits, confines,

113

circumlocution · claim

outline, circuit, compass, extremity, edge, rim, verge, fringe, skirt.

circumlocution n periphrasis, pleonasm, tautology, redundancy, convolution, discursiveness, circuitousness, verbosity, wordiness, prolixity, long-windedness, gobbledegook.

circumscribe v 1 *circumscribe a circle* enclose, encircle, bound, encompass, gird, circumvent; define, delineate, outline, demarcate, delimit, mark off. 2 *activities circumscribed by poverty* restrict, limit, curb, confine, restrain, trammel, hamper.

circumspect adj wary, cautious, careful, chary, watchful, alert, attentive, guarded, canny, vigilant, observant, suspicious, apprehensive, leery, prudent, judicious, politic, discerning, sagacious.

circumstances npl 1 *I know nothing of the circumstances | in the circumstances* situation, state of affairs, conditions, set of conditions, position, event, occurence, background. 2 *living in poor circumstances* state, situation, conditions, times, financial position, plight, predicament, lot, fortune, means, resources, life style, station.

circumstantial adj 1 *circumstantial evidence* based on circumstances, indirect, incidental, evidential, deduced, presumed, inferential, conjectural. 2 *a circumstantial account* detailed, precise, particular, exact, accurate, minute, explicit, pointed, to the point.

citadel n fortress, fort, fortification, stronghold, keep, castle, tower, bastion, fastness, donjon.

citation n 1 *citations from the Romantic poets* quotation, quote, extract, excerpt, reference, illustration, allusion, passage, source. 2 *a citation for gallantry* commendation, award, honour, mention. 3 *a citation from the courts* summons, subpoena, arraignment.

cite v 1 *cite the statistics as evidence | cite extracts from the poem* quote, mention, name, enumerate, evidence, refer to, allude to, exemplify, excerpt, extract. 2 *cite him for his gallantry* commend, recommend, pay tribute to, mention. 3 *cited by the courts* summon, subpoena, arraign, serve with a writ.

citizen n resident, inhabitant, dweller, denizen, townsman, townswoman, burgher, burgess, taxpayer, voter, freeman, subject.

city n conurbation, metropolitan area, inner city, metropolis, municipality, town, burgh, megapolis, urban sprawl, concrete jungle.

civic adj municipal, public, community, local, communal, urban, metropolitan.

civil adj 1 *civil war* interior, internal, domestic, home. 2 *civil responsibilities* civic, municipal, public, community, local. see CIVIC. 3 *civil government/rulers* civilian, lay, non-military, non-religious, secular. 4 *a civil young man | in a civil manner* polite, courteous, well-mannered, mannerly, well-bred, gentlemanly, ladylike, refined, urbane, polished, cultured, cultivated, civilized, cordial, genial, pleasant, affable, amiable.

civilian n *civilians called up* ordinary citizen, private citizen, non-military person, layperson.

civilian adj *a civilian guard* civil, lay, non-military. see CIVILIAN n.

civility n 1 *treat even his opponents with civility* courtesy, courteousness, politeness, good manners, mannerliness, graciousness, cordiality, geniality, pleasantness, affability, amiability, urbanity, gallantry. 2 *observe the civilities* polite act, courtesy; etiquette, protocol, propriety, decorum.

civilization n 1 *a threat to modern civilization* development, advancement, progress, enlightenment, culture, cultivation, edification, refinement, sophistication. 2 *ancient civilizations* society, community, nation, country, people, way of life. 3 *the civilization of the tribes* civilizing, enlightenment, socialization, humanizing, edification, education, improvement. see CIVILIZE.

civilize v enlighten, socialize, humanize, edify, cultivate, educate, instruct, improve, culture, refine, polish, sophisticate.

civilized adj 1 *civilized tribes* enlightened, socialized, educated. see CIVILIZE. 2 *she's very civilized but he's a boor* cultured, cultivated, sophisticated, educated, enlightened, urbane.

clad adj *clad in wool | warmly clad* clothed, dressed, attired, covered, apparelled.

claim v 1 *claim the prize* lay claim to, ask as one's right, establish rights to, ask for, demand, request, requisition, require. 2 *claim that he's innocent* profess, maintain, assert, declare, protest, avow, aver, allege, postulate, affirm, hold. 3 *the fire claimed lives* take, cause, result in, involve.

claim n 1 *a claim for damages* demand, request, application, petition, call. 2 *put forward his claim to the crown* right, rights, title, prerogative, privilege, heritage, inheritance, legacy. 3 *dispute his claims of innocence* profession, assertion, declaration, protestation, avowal, averment, allegation, postulation, affirmation.

claimant n applicant, candidate, petitioner, supplicant, suppliant, suitor, postulant, pretender, plaintiff.

clairvoyance n second sight, psychic powers, ESP, extrasensory perception, telepathy, sixth sense.

clamber v scramble, climb, scale, ascend, mount, shin, shinny, scrabble, claw one's way.

clammy adj moist, damp, humid, sweaty, sticky.

clamour n **1** *the clamour of children's voices* uproar, noise, din, racket, shout, shouting, yelling, babel, blaring, commotion, bróuhaha, hubbub, hullabaloo, outcry, vociferation. **2** *answer their clamours for more money* demand, call, petition, request, urging, protest, complaint, insistence, exigency.

clamp n **1** *held tightly in a clamp* vice, press, brace, clasp, fastener, hasp. **2** *a clamp on the car* immobilizer, stop, check, block, obstruction, impediment, obstacle.

clamp v **1** *a pipe clamped between his teeth* grip, hold, fix, clench, press, squeeze, secure, make fast, brace. **2** *clamp a curfew on the city* impose, inflict, lay on, set, charge, burden. **3** *clamp a car* put a clamp on, immobilize, impede, obstruct. *see* CLAMP n 2. **clamp down on** *clamp down on spending/crime* limit, restrain, restrict, confine, hold in check, crack down on, be severe with, suppress, prevent.

clamp-down n *a clamp-down on spending/crime* limitation, restraint, restriction, holding in check, crack-down, severe treatment, suppression, prevention.

clan n **1** *the Scottish clans* family, house, sept, tribe, gens, line. **2** *tired of the business clan* set, circle, crowd, in-crowd, gang, band, group, faction, clique, coterie, fraternity, brotherhood, community, society, sodality.

clandestine adj secret, undercover, surreptitious, cloak-and-dagger, back-alley, furtive, concealed, hidden, hugger-mugger, underhand.

clang n *the clang of the bell | the clang of two gates closing* ringing, ring, resounding, reverberation, clank, clash, clangour, bong, chime, toll, clink, clunk, jangle.

clang v *bells clanging | gates clanging shut* ring, resound, reverberate, clank, clash, bong, clink, chime, toll, peal.

clanger n mistake, blunder, gaffe, bungle, muff, slip-up; *inf* bloomer, howler, goof.

clank n *the clank of chains* metallic sound, clang, clangour, clink, clunk, jangle.

clank v *chains clanking* clang, clink, clunk, jangle.

clannish adj cliquish, insular, exclusive, narrow, parochial, provincial.

clap v **1** *clap on the back* strike, slap, smite, smack, bang, whack, wallop, clatter; *clap one's hands* strike/slap together. **2** *the audience clapping the cast/performance* applaud, cheer, acclaim; show one's appreciation, put one's hands together. **3** *clap him in jail/chains* cast, thrust, push, pitch, hurl, toss.

claptrap n nonsense, drivel, rubbish, humbug, insincerity; *inf* bunk, guff, flannel.

clarify v **1** *clarify the situation* make clear, clear up, resolve, make plain, explain, elucidate, illuminate, throw light on, make simple, simplify. **2** *clarify butter* purify, refine.

clarity n **1** *the clarity of his prose* clearness, lucidity, lucidness, plainness, simplicity, intelligibility, comprehensibility, obviousness, explicitness, unambiguity, precision. **2** *the clarity of the water* clearness, transparency, limpidity, translucence, pellucidity, glassiness.

clash v **1** *clash the cymbals* strike, bang, clang, crash, clatter, clank, clink, rattle, jangle. **2** *the two sides clashed* be in conflict, war, fight, contend, do battle, come to blows, feud, grapple, wrangle, quarrel, cross swords, lock horns. **3** *the appointments clash* coincide, occur simultaneously, synchronize, conflict. **4** *the colours clash* be discordant, not match, lack harmony, jar, be incompatible; *inf* scream.

clash n **1** *the clash of cymbals* striking, bang, clang, crash, clatter, clank. *see* CLASH v 1. **2** *the clash of the opposing sides* conflict, collision, confrontation, brush, warring, fighting, contending, feud, grappling, wrangling, quarrelling. **3** *the clash of the dates* coincidence, co-occurrence, concurrence, synchronization, conflict. **4** *the clash of the colours* discordance, discord, lack of harmony, incompatibility, jarring.

clasp n **1** *the clasp of the necklace* catch, fastener, fastening, clip; hook, hook and eye, snap fastener, buckle, hasp. **2** *wearing a diamond clasp* pin, brooch. **3** *engage in a loving clasp* embrace, hug, cuddle, hold, grip, grasp.

class n **1** *middle classes | professional class* social order, social division, stratum, rank, level, status, sphere, grade, group, grouping, set, classification, caste. **2** *in the highest class | degrees divided into three classes* category, classification, division, section, group, set, grade. **3** *a class of objects* category, group, set, kind, sort, type, collection, denomination, order, species, genre, genus. **4** *what class is the student/pupil in* study group, school group, seminar, tutorial. **5** *a player of class | a woman of class* quality, excellence, distinction, stylishness, elegance, chic.

class v *books classed as textbooks* classify, categorize, group, grade, arrange, order, sort, codify, file, index, pigeonhole.

classic adj **1** *a classic performance* first-rate, first-class, excellent, brilliant, finest, outstanding, exemplary, masterly, consummate. **2** *a classic case/example* typical, standard, model, guiding, archetypal, stock, true-to-form, paradigmatic, prototypical. **3** *classic styles* simple, traditional, timeless, ageless, long-lasting, enduring, abiding, time-honoured, long-standing, long-established.

classic n **1** *reading the classics* great work, established work, standard work, masterpiece. **2** *the match was a classic* masterpiece, excellent example. *see* CLASSIC adj 1.

classical adj **1** *a classical scholar | classical architecture* Greek, Grecian, Hellenic, Attic, Roman, Latin. **2** *classical music* serious, symphonic, concert, traditional, long-lasting. **3** *a classical style of design* simple, plain, restrained, pure, understated, harmonious, well-proportioned, balanced, symmetrical, elegant, aesthetic.

classification n *the classification of books/ blood* classifying, categorizing, categorization, grouping, grading, arrangement, codifying, codification, taxonomy. *see* CLASSIFY.

classify v *classify books/blood* categorize, class, group, grade, arrange, order, sort, type, rank, rate, designate, codify, catalogue, tabulate, file, index, assign, pigeonhole, brand.

clatter v rattle, clang, clank, clunk, bang.

clause n *clause 9 of the document* section, paragraph, article, note, item, point, passage, part, heading, condition, provision, proviso, stipulation.

claw n *a cat's/bird's/lobster's claws* nail, talon, unguis, pincer, nipper, chela.

claw v *claw his face* scratch, tear, lacerate, scrape, graze, rip, dig into, maul.

clay n **1** *clay used for pottery* argil, slip, kaolin, adobe, loam. **2** *buried beneath the clay* earth, ground, soil, sod.

clean adj *clean hands/clothes* unsoiled, spotless, unstained, unspotted, unsullied, unblemished, immaculate, speckless,

hygienic, sanitary, washed, cleansed, laundered, scrubbed. **2** *clean air* pure, clear, natural, unpolluted, unadulterated, uncontaminated, untainted, unmixed. **3** *living clean lives* good, upright, honourable, respectable, virtuous, righteous, moral, reputable, upstanding, exemplary, innocent, guiltless, pure, decent, chaste, undefiled. **4** *a clean piece of paper* unused, unmarked, blank, vacant, void. **5** *the clean lines of the aeroplane* stream-lined, smooth, well-defined, definite, clean-cut, regular, symmetrical, simple, elegant, graceful, uncluttered, trim, shapely. **6** *a clean break to the marriage* complete, thorough, total, entire, conclusive, decisive, final. **7** *found to be clean after investigation* innocent, guiltless, guilt-free, crime-free.

clean adv *a bullet clean through his shoulder | go clean out of my mind* completely, entirely, totally, fully, wholly, thoroughly, altogether, quite, utterly, absolutely.

clean v **1** *clean one's hands/walls* wash, cleanse, wipe, sponge, scrub, scour, swab. **2** *clean one's clothes* dry-clean, launder. **3** *clean the room* tidy, set to rights; vacuum, hoover, dust, mop, sweep; *inf* do.

cleanse v **1** *cleanse the wound* clean, make clean, clean up, wash, bathe, rinse, disinfect. **2** *cleanse of his sins* purify, purge, absolve, lustrate.

clear adj **1** *a clear day | clear weather* bright, cloudless, unclouded, fair, fine, light, undimmed, sunny, sunshiny. **2** *clear water/ glass* transparent, limpid, pellucid, translucent, crystalline, diaphanous, see-through. **3** *it was clear that he was guilty* obvious, evident, plain, apparent, sure, definite, unmistakable, manifest, indisputable, patent, incontrovertible, irrefutable, palpable, beyond doubt, beyond question. **4** *a clear account of the incident* understandable, comprehensible, intelligible, plain, explicit, lucid, coherent, distinct. **5** *a clear thinker* astute, keen, sharp, quick, perceptive, discerning, perspicacious, penetrating. **6** *a clear road/view* open, empty, free, unobstructed, unimpeded, unhindered, unlimited. **7** *a clear conscience* untroubled, undisturbed, peaceful, at peace, tranquil, serene, calm, innocent, guiltless, guilt-free, clean, sinless, stainless. **8** *four clear days* whole, full, entire, complete, total.

clear adv **1** *hear him loud and clear* clearly, distinctly, plainly, audibly. **2** *stand clear of the door* away from, at a distance from, apart from, out of contact with. **3** *got clear away* completely, entirely, thoroughly, fully, wholly, clear. *see* CLEAR adj 8.

clear v **1** *the weather cleared* clear up, brighten, lighten, break. **2** *clear the plates* remove, take away, tidy up/away. **3** *clear the drains* unblock, unclog, unstop. **4** *clear the room of objects* empty, vacate, evacuate, void, free, rid. **5** *clear the accused of charges* absolve, acquit, discharge, let go, exonerate, vindicate, excuse, pardon. **6** *clear the fence* jump, vault, leap, hop, pass over. **7** *clear £500 net*, make a profit of, realize a profit of, gain, earn, make, acquire, secure, bring, reap. **8** *clear goods | the ship was cleared* authorize, sanction, pass, approve, give consent to, permit/allow to pass, give one's seal of approval to; *inf* give the go-ahead to, give the green light to. **clear out 1** *clear out the cupboard* empty, evacuate, tidy, tidy up. **2** *clear out the rubbish* get rid of, throw out, throw away, eject, eliminate. **3** *boys told to clear out* go away, get out, leave, depart, take oneself off, make oneself scarce, withdraw, retire, decamp. **clear up 1** *clear up the mystery/problem* solve, resolve, straighten out, find an answer to, unravel, untangle, explain, elucidate; *inf* crack. **2** *clear up the room/mess* tidy, tidy up, put in order, straighten up, clean up. **3** *the weather cleared up* improve, brighten. *see* CLEAR v 1.

clearance n **1** *slum clearance* clearing, removal, evacuation, eviction, emptying, depopulation, unpeopling, withdrawal, decanting. **2** *the clearance under the bridge* clearing, space, gap, allowance, margin, headroom, leeway, room to spare. **3** *get clearance for their plans* authorization, consent, permission, sanction, go-ahead, leave, endorsement; *inf* green light.

clear-cut adj *clear-cut proposals* definite, specific, precise, explicit, unambiguous, unequivocal.

clearly adv *clearly he's ill | clearly a mistake* obviously, undoubtedly, without doubt, indubitably, plainly, undeniably, decidedly, surely, certainly, incontrovertibly, irrefutably, incontestably, patently.

cleave¹ v **1** *cleave the logs* split, split open, open, crack, lay open, divide, hew, hack, chop/slice up, sunder, sever, rend, rive. **2** *cleave a path* make, cut, plough, drive, bulldoze.

cleave² v **cleave to** cling to, stick to, hold to, stand by, abide by, adhere to, be loyal/faithful to.

cleaver n knife, chopper, hatchet, axe; butcher's knife, kitchen knife.

cleft n split, crack, gap, fissure, crevice, rift, break, fracture.

clemency n **1** *treat the prisoners with clemency* mercy, leniency, compassion, humanity, pity, sympathy, kindness, magnanimity, fairness, temperance, moderation, indulgence. **2** *the clemency of the weather* mildness, balminess, warmness.

clench v **1** *clench the teeth* close, shut, seal, fasten. **2** *clench the table edge* grip, grasp, clutch, hold, seize.

clergy n clergymen, churchmen, clerics, ecclesiastics; ministry, priesthood, holy orders, the cloth, first estate. *see* ECCLESIASTIC n.

clergyman n churchman, man of the cloth, man of God, cleric, ecclesiastic, divine; vicar, parson, pastor, priest, father, padre, reverend, rector, rabbi, imam, curate, chaplain. *see* ECCLESIASTIC n.

clerical adj **1** *a clerical post in the office | clerical duties* secretarial, office, writing, typing, filing, bookkeeping; *inf* pen-pushing. **2** *clerical clothes* ecclesiastical, churchly, priestly, pastoral, sacerdotal, prelatic, apostolic, canonical.

clever adj **1** *both stupid and clever people* intelligent, bright, sharp-witted, quick-witted, talented, gifted, smart, capable, able, competent, apt, knowledgeable, educated, sagacious; *inf* brainy. **2** *a clever move* shrewd, astute, adroit, canny, cunning, ingenious, artful, wily, inventive. **3** *clever with their hands* dextrous, skilful, adroit, nimble, deft, handy.

cliché n hackneyed phrase, platitude, commonplace, banality, truism, saw, maxim, bromide; *inf* old chestnut.

click n *the click of the key in the lock* clink, clack, chink, snap, tick.

click v **1** *the key clicked in the lock* clink, clack, chink, snap, tick. **2** *I see it's suddenly clicked* become clear, fall into place, come home to one, make sense. **3** *the two girls clicked immediately* get on, take to each other, hit it off, be compatible, be on the same wavelength, feel a rapport. **4** *the new toys clicked with the children* make a hit, prove popular, be successful, be a success, succeed, go down well.

client n customer, patron, regular, habitué, buyer, purchaser, shopper, consumer, user, patient.

clientele n clients, customers, patrons, regulars; patronage, following, trade, business, market. *see* CLIENT.

cliff n precipice, rock-face, face, crag, bluff, escarpment, scar, scarp, overhang, promontory, tor.

climate n **1** *temperate climate* weather pattern, weather conditions, weather, temperature. **2** *visit various climates* clime, country, place, region, area, zone. **3** *the political climate* atmosphere, mood, temper, spirit, feeling, feel, ambience, aura, ethos.

climax n **1** *the climax of her campaign/career* culmination, height, peak, pinnacle, high point, summit, top, highlight, acme, zenith, apex, apogee, crowning point, *ne plus ultra*. **2** *reach climax* sexual climax, orgasm.

climax v **1** *the campaign climaxed in victory* culminate, peak, come to a head, result, end. **2** *climax together* have an orgasm, orgasm; *inf* come.

climb v **1** *climb up the ladder | climb to the top* go up, ascend, mount, scale, clamber up, shin up. **2** *prices/temperatures are climbing* go up, rise, increase, shoot up, soar. **3** *the road climbs steeply* slope upward, incline, bank. **4** *climb up the ranks* make progress, get ahead, advance, work one's way up, make strides. **climb down 1** *climb down the ladder/tree* go down, descend, shin down. **2** *the government forced to climb down* back down, retract, retreat, eat one's words, eat humble pie.

clinch v **1** *clinch the deal* settle, secure, seal, set the seal on, complete, confirm, conclude, assure, cap, close, wind up; *inf* sew up. **2** *clinch a nail* fasten, make fast, secure, fix, clamp, bolt, rivet, pinion. **3** *boxers/lovers clinching* hug, embrace, cuddle, squeeze, clutch, grasp, grapple.

cling v *the surfaces clung together* stick, adhere, hold, grip, clasp, clutch. **cling to 1** *cling to the rope | clung to his friend* hold on to, hang on to, clutch, grip, grasp, clasp, cleave to, attach to, embrace. **2** *cling to one's beliefs* stick to, hold to, stand by, abide by, adhere to, be loyal/faithful to, remain true to, remain attached to; *inf* stick with.

clinic n medical centre, outpatients' clinic, polyclinic.

clinical adj **1** *a clinical attitude to others' problems* objective, dispassionate, detached, uninvolved, cold, unsympathetic, unfeeling **2** *clinical designs* plain, simple, unadorned, unornamented, stark, austere, severe, Spartan.

clip[1] v **1** *clip hair/fleece/hedges* cut, cut short, crop, snip, trim, shear, prune, pollard. **2** *clip him round the ear* hit, strike, box, cuff, smack, wallop, thump, punch, knock; *inf* clout, whack; *Scots* skelp. **3** *the train was clipping along* speed, go fast, race, gallop, rush, dash, zoom, whip along, spank along, go like lightning.

clip[1] n **1** *need a hair clip* cut, trim, shorten, shear, shearing, pruning. **2** *a clip round the*

ear box, cuff, smack, wallop; *inf* clout. *see* CLIP[1] v 2. **3** *going at a clip* speed, fast rate, swift pace, velocity; *inf* fair old rate. **4** *a clip from a film/newspaper* clipping, cutting, extract, excerpt, snippet, fragment.

clip[2] v *clip the papers together* pin, staple, fasten, fix, attach, hold.

clip[2] n *a paper-clip | bicycle clips* fastener, coupler, clasp.

clique n coterie, circle, crowd, in-crowd, set, gang, group, clan, faction, pack, band, ring, fraternity, society, mob.

cloak n **1** *wearing a black cloak* cape, mantle, wrap, shawl, pelisse, pelerine, dolman, domino, capote, cope, coat. **2** *a cloak of darkness/secrecy* cover, screen, blind, mask, mantle, veil, shroud, shield, front, camouflage, pretext.

cloak v *meetings cloaked in secrecy* hide, conceal, cover, cover up, screen, mask, veil, shroud, shield, cloud, camouflage, obscure, disguise.

clock n timekeeper, timepiece, timer; chronometer, chronograph, digital clock, analogue clock, quartz clock, grandfather clock, carriage clock, alarm clock, travelling clock, cuckoo clock, pendulum clock, water clock.

clock v **1** *clock the race* time, record the time; *inf* stopwatch. **2** *she clocked a record time* register, record, achieve, attain; *inf* do. **clock up** *we've clocked up 500 miles* register, record, attain, achieve; *inf* do.

clog n sabot, wooden shoe, wooden-soled shoe.

clog v **1** *leaves clogging up the drains* block, obstruct, dam, congest, jam, occlude; stop up, dam up. **2** *clogging the system* obstruct, hinder, impede, hamper, shackle, burden.

cloister n **1** *ecclesiastics in a cloister* convent, nunnery, monastery, abbey, priory, friary. **2** *walking in the cloisters* covered walk, walkway, corridor, aisle, arcade, gallery, piazza, ambulatory.

cloistered adj *leading cloistered lives* secluded, sheltered, sequestered, shielded, shut-off, withdrawn, confined, restricted, insulated, reclusive, hermitic, cloistral.

close[1] v **1** *close the door* shut, slam, fasten, secure, lock, bolt, bar, latch, padlock. **2** *close the bottle/opening* stop up, plug, seal, clog, choke, obstruct, occlude. **3** *close the meeting* bring to an end, end, conclude, finish, terminate, wind up, adjourn, discontinue. **4** *he closed by praying* come to an end, end, conclude, finish, cease, wind up, adjourn. **5** *close the bargain* complete, conclude, settle, clinch, seal, establish, fix, agree. **6** *the gap closed* narrow, lessen, grow smaller, dwindle, reduce. **7** *his arms closed around her | the boxers closed* come together, join, connect, come into contact, unite, clutch one another, grip, clench, grapple, couple.

close¹ n *at close of day/play* end, finish, conclusion, termination, cessation, completion, culmination, finale, wind-up.

close² n *city closes* courtyard, quadrangle, enclosure, piazza, cul-de-sac; *Scots* entry.

close² adj **1** *houses close to each other* near, adjacent, in close proximity, adjoining, neighbouring, hard by, abutting; *birthdays close together* near, occurring/falling near. **2** *a close resemblance | close in appearance* near, similar, like, alike, comparable, parallel, corresponding, akin. **3** *a close friend* intimate, dear, bosom, close-knit, inseparable, loving, devoted, attached, confidential; *inf* matey, chummy, pally; *Amer inf* buddy-buddy, palsy-walsy. **4** *close print | close formation* dense, condensed, compact, crowded, packed, solid, tight, cramped, congested, crushed, squeezed. **5** *a close game* evenly matched, well-matched, hard-fought, sharply contested, neck-and-neck, nose-to-nose; *inf* fifty-fifty. **6** *a close description* accurate, true, faithful, literal, exact, precise, conscientious. **7** *pay close attention | on close examination* careful, concentrated, attentive, assiduous, alert, vigilant, intent, dogged, painstaking, detailed, minute, intense, keen, thorough, rigorous, searching. **8** *under close arrest* strict, stringent, rigorous, thorough, tight. **9** *close weather* humid, muggy, airless, stuffy, fuggy, heavy, oppressive, stifling, suffocating, musty, unventilated. **10** *he's very close about his affairs* quiet, reticent, uncommunicative, reserved, private, unforthcoming, secretive, evasive. **11** *close with his money* mean, miserly, stingy, niggardly, parsimonious, penny-pinching, tight-fisted, tight, near; *inf* mingy.

closet n *a clothes closet* cupboard, wardrobe, cabinet, locker, storage room.

closet adj *a closet homosexual/socialist* secret, unrevealed, undisclosed, hidden, concealed, furtive.

closet v *closeted with the manager* shut away, sequester, seclude, cloister, confine, isolate.

closure n closing down, shutting down, winding up, cessation of operations, cessation, termination, finish, conclusion.

clot n **1** *a clot of blood* glob, lump, gob, clump, mass, obstruction, thrombus. **2** *a*

silly clot fool, idiot, dolt, nitwit, half-wit; *inf* dope, chump.

clot v *blood clotting* coagulate, set, congeal, jell, thicken, cake, curdle.

cloth n *silk cloth* fabric, material, stuff; textiles, dry goods, soft goods.

clothe v **1** *clothed in pure wool* dress, attire, rig, rig out, turn out, apparel, fit out, outfit, robe, garb, array, deck out, drape, accoutre, trap out, habit, invest; *inf* doll up. **2** *hills clothed in cloud* cover, wrap, cloak, envelop, swathe, swaddle.

clothes npl *put away one's clothes | wearing expensive clothes* garments, articles of clothing/dress; clothing, attire, outfits. see CLOTHING.

clothing n clothes, garments; dress, attire, apparel, outfit, costume, garb, ensemble, vestments, raiment; *inf* clobber, gear, rigout, togs, get-up.

cloud n **1** *clouds in the sky* rain cloud, storm cloud, thundercloud, fleecy cloud, billowy cloud, billow; cirrus, cumulus, altostratus, altocumulus, cumulonimbus; haze, cloudbank, mackerel sky. **2** *a cloud of smoke* pall, shroud, mantle, cloak, screen, cover. **3** *a cloud on their happiness* shadow, threat; gloom, darkness. **4** *a cloud of insects* swarm, flock, mass, multitude, host, horde, throng.

cloudy adj **1** *a cloudy sky* overcast, hazy, dark, grey, sombre, leaden, heavy, gloomy, dim, lowering, sunless, starless. **2** *cloudy recollections* blurred, vague, indistinct, hazy, indefinite, nebulous, obscure, confused, muddled. **3** *cloudy liquids* opaque, nontransparent, murky, muddy, milky, emulsified, opalescent, turbid.

clout v *clout the child* hit, strike, smack, slap, cuff, box, thump, wallop; *inf* whack, clobber, sock.

clout n **1** *give him a clout* smack, slap, thump. see CLOUT v. **2** *carry clout in the firm* influence, power, pull, weight, authority, prestige, standing.

clown n **1** *circus clowns* jester, fool, buffoon, zany, harlequin, pierrot, merry andrew. **2** *he's sedate but his brother's a real clown* joker, comedian, comic, humorist, funnyman, wag, wit, prankster. **3** *the clown crashed my car* fool, idiot, dolt, nitwit, half-wit; *inf* clot, dope.

clown v *clown around* fool, act foolishly, jest, joke; *inf* mess, muck, muck about.

cloy v satiate, pall, surfeit, dull, sicken, nauseate.

cloying adj sickly-sweet, sugary, saccharine, sickening, nauseating.

club n **1** *hit him with a club* cudgel, bludgeon, cosh, stick, staff, truncheon, bat, baton; *Amer* blackjack. **2** *a swimming/bridge club* society, group, association, organization, circle, set, clique, coterie, affiliation, league, union, federation, company, fraternity, brotherhood, sorority.

club v hit, strike, beat, batter, bash, cudgel, bludgeon, cosh, truncheon, baste; *inf* clout, clobber. **club together** join forces, pool resources, make a kitty, make a joint contribution, divide costs; *inf* have a whip-round.

clue n hint, indication, sign, evidence, information, intimation, pointer, guide, lead, tip, tip-off, inkling.

clump n **1** *a clump of trees* group, cluster, bunch, collection, assembly, assemblage. **2** *clump of earth | clump of blood cells* mass, lump, clod, glob, agglutination.

clump v **1** *houses clumped together* group, cluster, bunch, collect, assemble, congregate, mass, lump, bundle, pack. **2** *clump around in heavy boots* clomp, stamp, stump, stomp, thump, thud, bang, tramp, lumber, plod, trudge, stumble.

clumsy adj **1** *clumsy and always breaking things* awkward, uncoordinated, ungainly, blundering, bungling, bumbling, inept, maladroit, inexpert, unhandy, unskilful, like a bull in a china shop; *inf* cack-handed, ham-fisted, ham-handed, butter-fingered. **2** *a clumsy piece of furniture* awkward, unwieldy, hulking, heavy, solid, unmanoeuvrable. **3** *a clumsy apology* awkward, gauche, graceless, tactless, unpolished, crude, uncouth, crass.

cluster n **1** *a cluster of berries/flowers* bunch, clump, collection, knot, group; *Tech* raceme, panicle. **2** *cluster of people* gathering, group, collection, bunch, band, company, knot, body, assemblage, congregation.

cluster v *people clustering round the church* gather, collect, assemble, congregate, group, come together, flock together, forgather.

clutch v **1** *clutching her purse* grip, grasp, clasp, cling to, hang on to, clench. **2** *clutch at the branch* reach for, snatch at, grab, make a grab for, seize, catch at, claw at.

clutch n *a clutch of eggs* set, setting, hatch, hatching, nest, incubation.

clutches npl *fall into the clutches of moneylenders* hands, power, control, hold, grip, grasp, claws, tyranny, possession, keeping, custody.

clutter n **1** *a clutter of papers* mess, jumble, litter, heap, hotchpotch. **2** *his room in a clutter* mess, muddle, disorder, chaos, disarray, state of confusion/untidiness.

clutter v *papers cluttering up the room* litter, make untidy, make a mess of, mess up, be strewn about, be scattered about.

coach[1] n **1** *travel by express coach* bus, motorcoach, omnibus, charabanc. **2** *railway coaches* carriage, wagon; *Amer* car. **3** *horses pulling a coach* stage coach, carriage, hackney, brougham, landau, gig, phaeton, barouche; *Amer* surrey.

coach[2] n *tennis/maths coach* instructor, trainer, teacher, tutor, mentor.

coach[2] v *coach in tennis/mathematics* instruct, train, teach, tutor, drill, prime, cram, put one through one's paces.

coagulate v congeal, clot, gel, thicken, curdle.

coalesce v unite, join together, combine, merge, amalgamate, integrate, affiliate, blend, fuse; *lit* commingle.

coalition n union, alliance, affiliation, league, association, federation, confederacy, bloc, compact, amalgamation, merger, conjunction, combination, fusion.

coarse adj **1** *coarse material* rough, bristly, scratchy, prickly, hairy, shaggy. **2** *coarse features* heavy, rough, rugged, craggy, unrefined. **3** *coarse flour* crude, unrefined, unprocessed, unpurified. **4** *coarse behaviour/ manners* rude, ill-mannered, uncivil, rough, boorish, loutish, churlish, uncouth, crass. **5** *coarse humour* bawdy, earthy, blue, ribald, vulgar, smutty, obscene, indelicate, indecent, offensive, lewd, pornographic, prurient; *inf* raunchy.

coarsen v roughen, thicken, toughen, harden, harshen.

coast n *a rugged coast* coastline, shore, seashore, shoreline, seacoast, beach, foreshore, strand, seaboard, water's edge, littoral.

coast v *bicycles coasting downhill | coasting through life* freewheel, cruise, taxi, drift, glide, sail.

coat n **1** *a winter coat* overcoat, jacket; greatcoat, trench coat, waterproof, mackintosh, raincoat, Burberry, fur coat, fur. **2** *animals' coats* fur, hair, wool; fleece, hide, pelt, skin. **3** *a coat of paint* layer, covering, overlay, coating. **4** *a coat of dust* coating, layer, film. *see* COATING.

coating n covering, layer, film, coat, dusting, blanket, sheet, glaze, skin, veneer, finish, lamination, patina, membrane.

coax v wheedle, cajole, talk into, beguile, flatter, inveigle, entice, induce, persuade, prevail upon, win over; *inf* sweet-talk, soft-soap.

cock n *hens and cock* cockerel, chanticleer; *Amer* rooster.

cock v **1** *a dog cocking its leg* raise, lift, lift up. **2** *cocked his hat* tilt, tip, slant, incline.

cocky adj arrogant, conceited, egotistical, swollen-headed, vain, cocksure, swaggering, brash.

coddle v pamper, cosset, mollycoddle, indulge, spoil, baby, humour, pet, feather-bed.

code n **1** *a message in code* cipher, secret writing; coded message, cryptograph. **2** *code of honour* ethics, morals, principles, maxims; morality, convention, etiquette, custom. **3** *highway code | legal code* laws, rules, regulations, system, canon.

coerce v compel, force, pressure, pressurize, drive, impel, constrain, oblige; *inf* twist one's arm, lean on, put the screws on, strong-arm.

coffer n strongbox, moneybox, money chest, safe, chest, casket, box.

coffin n casket, box, sarcophagus; *inf* wooden overcoat.

cogent adj convincing, forceful, forcible, effective, conclusive, persuasive, compelling, powerful, strong, potent, weighty, influential, authoritative, telling.

cogitate v think, ponder, contemplate, consider, give consideration to, deliberate, meditate, reflect, mull over, muse, ruminate.

cognate adj **1** *cognate words* related, kindred, akin, allied, congeneric, consanguine. **2** *cognate sciences* allied, affiliated, associated, similar, alike, connected, corresponding, correlated, analogous.

cognition n perception, discernment, understanding, awareness, comprehension, apprehension, enlightenment, insight, intelligence, reason.

cognizant adj aware, conscious, knowing, alive to, sensible of, familiar with, acquainted with, conversant with; *inf* wise to.

cohabit v live together, sleep with; *inf* shack up with.

coherent adj *a coherent argument* logical, rational, reasoned, lucid, articulate, systematic, orderly, organized, consistent, comprehensible, intelligible.

cohort n troop, brigade, legion, squad, squadron, column, group, company, body, band.

coil v wind, spiral, loop, curl, twist, twine, entwine, snake, wreathe, convolute.

coin n **1** *gold coins* piece. **2** *pay in coin* coins, coinage, change, specie, silver, copper, gold.

coin v **1** *coin a word* invent, create, make up, devise, conceive, originate, think up, dream up, formulate, fabricate. **2** *coin money* mint, mould, stamp out, die, monetize.

coincide v **1** *dates coinciding* be concurrent, occur simultaneously, happen together, coexist, concur, synchronize. **2** *stories coinciding* accord, agree, correspond, concur, match, square, tally, harmonize.

coincidence n **1** *arrive together by coincidence* accident, chance, fluke, luck, fortuity, serendipity. **2** *the coincidence of events/stories* coinciding. *see* COINCIDE.

coincidental adj **1** *a coincidental meeting* accidental, chance, unplanned, unintentional, casual, lucky, fortuitous, serendipitous; *inf* flukey. **2** *coincidental concerts* simultaneous, concurrent, synchronous, co-existent.

cold adj **1** *a cold day* chilly, chill, cool, freezing, bitter, raw, icy, frigid, wintry, frosty, arctic, inclement, sunless, windy, glacial, polar, gelid, brumal; *inf* nippy. **2** *feeling cold* chilly, chilled, cool, freezing, frozen, frozen stiff, frozen/chilled to the bone/marrow, shivery, numbed, benumbed. **3** *a cold woman/attitude* frigid, unresponsive, unfeeling, unemotional, phlegmatic, unexcitable, passionless, spiritless, unmoved, indifferent, lukewarm, apathetic, dispassionate, aloof, distant, reserved, remote, standoffish, insensitive, unsympathetic, uncaring, heartless, callous, cold-hearted, stony-hearted, unfriendly, inhospitable, glacial. **4** *the story is cold* dead, gone, extinguished, finished, defunct.

cold-blooded adj savage, inhuman, barbarous, heartless, ruthless, pitiless, merciless, stony-hearted.

collaborate v **1** *collaborate on a book* cooperate, work together/jointly, join forces, join, unite, combine. **2** *collaborate with the enemy* conspire, fraternize, collude.

collaborator n **1** *his collaborator on the book* co-worker, associate, colleague, partner, confederate. **2** *collaborators executed* conspirator, fraternizer, traitor, quisling, turncoat, colluder.

collapse v 1 *the roof collapsed* fall in, cave in, give way, come apart, fall to pieces, crumple, subside. 2 *the onlooker collapsed* faint, pass out, lose consciousness, fall unconscious, keel over, fall prostrate, swoon. 3 *the business/talks collapsed* break down, fall through, fail, disintegrate, fold, founder, fall flat, miscarry, come to nothing; *inf* flop. 4 *collapse in tears* break down, go to pieces; *inf* crack up.

collapse n 1 *the collapse of the roof* fall-in, cave-in, giving way, subsidence. *see* COLLAPSE v 1. 2 *the collapse of the onlooker* fainting, faint, passing out, loss of consciousness, swooning, swoon. *see* COLLAPSE v 2. 3 *the collapse of the talks/firm* breakdown, failure, disintegration, unsuccessfulness, foundering; *inf* flop. *see* COLLAPSE v 3. 4 *suffer a collapse* breakdown, nervous breakdown, attack, seizure, prostration; *inf* crack-up.

collar n *the shirt collar* neckband; ruff, ruche, wimple, bertha, rabato.

collar v *collar the thief* catch, seize, grab, capture, arrest, apprehend.

collate v 1 *collate a new edition with an older one* compare, contrast, set side by side, juxtapose, weigh against, differentiate, discriminate. 2 *collate pages/information*, arrange, put in order, order, sort, categorize.

collateral n *collateral for a bank loan* security, surety, guarantee, pledge.

colleague n associate, partner, team-mate, workmate, fellow-worker, co-worker, collaborator, confederate, comrade, confrère.

collect v 1 *collect jumble* gather, accumulate, assemble, amass, pile up, stockpile, save, store, hoard, heap up, aggregate. 2 *a crowd collected* gather, assemble, congregate, forgather, converge, cluster, flock together, mass, convene, rally. 3 *collect money for a present* gather, solicit, raise, secure, obtain, acquire. 4 *collect the dry-cleaning* call for, fetch, go and get. 5 *collect one's wits/strength* get together, muster, summon, assemble, rally.

collected adj *calm and collected* cool, calm, serene, poised, controlled, composed, unperturbed, unruffled, unshaken.

collection n 1 *a collection of jumble* accumulation, pile, stockpile, store, supply, stock, hoard, heap, mass, aggregation. 2 *a collection of people* gathering, assembly, assemblage, crowd, body, group, cluster, company, number, throng, congregation, flock, convocation. 3 *a collection of stamps* set, series, array, assortment. 4 *a collection of essays* anthology, corpus, compilation,

ana, collectanea, miscellanea, garland; collected works, analects, analecta. 5 *the amount of the collection for the present* subscription, donation, contribution, gift, alms. 6 *the church collection* offering, offertory, tithe.

collective adj *collective action* joint, united, combined, shared, common, concerted, cooperative, corporate, collaborative, cumulative, aggregate.

college n 1 *she went to college* educational establishment/institution; college of further education, FE, polytechnic, poly, technical college, college of education, music college, PE college, university. 2 *the College of Heralds* association, fellowship, society, academy, union.

collide v 1 *cars colliding* crash, crash head on, come into collision, smash, bump, bang. 2 *views collide* conflict, be in conflict, clash, differ, disagree, be at variance.

collision n 1 *a motorway collision* crash, accident, smash, pile-up, bump, impact; *inf* prang. 2 *a collision of views* conflict, clash, difference, disagreement, variance, opposition. 3 *take part in a military collision* confrontation, encounter, skirmish.

colloquial adj conversational, informal, everyday, casual, familiar, chatty, idiomatic, vernacular, demotic.

collusion n connivance, complicity, secret understanding, collaboration, intrigue, plotting; *inf* cahoots.

colonize v settle, people, populate, pioneer, open up, found.

colonnade n peristyle, portico, arcade, covered walk, cloisters.

colony n 1 settlement, territory, province, dominion, protectorate, dependency, possession, satellite state. 2 *the Chinese colony in London* community, section, ghetto, district, quarter. 3 *a nudist colony* community, group, association, commune, settlement.

colossal adj 1 *a colossal building* huge, gigantic, immense, enormous, massive, vast, gargantuan, mammoth, prodigious, mountainous, elephantine, Brobdingnagian. 2 *a colossal task* huge, enormous, immense, prodigious, herculean, monumental, titanic.

colour n 1 *a red colour* hue, shade, tint, tone, tinge. 2 *paint in water-colours* paint, pigment, tint, colorant, coloration, dye. 3 *add colour to her cheeks* pinkness, rosiness, redness, ruddiness, blush, flush, glow, bloom. 4 *nations of different colours* skin-colour, skin-colouring, skin-tone, complexion, colouring, pigmentation. 5 *add colour* *to the description* vividness, life, animation, richness. **6** *under colour of friendship* outward appearance, false show, guise, show, front, facade, cloak, mask, semblance, pretence, pretext.

colour v **1** *colour the walls/fabric yellow* tint, paint, dye, stain, colourwash, tinge. **2** *she coloured* blush, flush, redden, go red, crimson, go crimson, burn. **3** *attitude coloured by childhood experiences* influence, affect, prejudice, distort, slant, taint, pervert, warp. **4** *colour the account* exaggerate, overstate, overdraw, embroider, varnish, misrepresent, falsify, disguise, garble.

colourful adj **1** bright-coloured, deep-coloured, bright, brilliant, intense, vivid, rich, vibrant, multicoloured, many-coloured, motley, variegated, psychedelic; *inf* jazzy. **2** *a colourful description* vivid, graphic, interesting, lively, animated, rich.

colourless adj **1** *colourless fabric* uncoloured, achromatic, achromic, white, bleached, faded. **2** *colourless city girls* pale, wan, anaemic, washed-out, ashen, sickly. **3** *colourless accounts* uninteresting, dull, boring, tame, lifeless, dreary, lack-lustre, characterless, insipid, vapid, vacuous. **colours** npl **1** *the King's colours* flag, standard, banner, ensign. **2** *a club's colours* badge, uniform, insignia, ribbon, rosette. **3** *see things in their true colours* nature, character, identity, aspect.

column n **1** *marble columns* pillar, support, upright, post, shaft; pilaster, caryatid, obelisk, telamon. **2** *a column of people* line, file, row, queue, rank, string, procession, train, progression, cavalcade. **3** *a newspaper column* article, piece, item; editorial, leader, gossip column, agony column.

coma n unconsciousness, insensibility, stupor, oblivion, black-out, torpor, trance, sopor.

comatose adj **1** *comatose after the accident* in a coma, unconscious, insensible, out cold, blacked-out, torpid, insentient, soporose. **2** *feeling comatose after night shift* drowsy, sleepy, sluggish, lethargic, somnolent, torpid.

comb n **1** *a brush and comb* hair comb, fine-tooth comb, curry-comb. **2** *a fowl's comb* coxcomb, crest, tuft, plume, caruncle.

comb v **1** *comb one's hair* groom, untangle, curry, arrange, dress. **2** *comb wool* dress, card, tease, hackle, heckle, hatchel. **3** *comb the area for clues* search, scour, ransack, go over with a fine-tooth comb, rake, hunt, sift, rummage.

combat n *engage in mortal combat* battle, fight, conflict, clash, skirmish, encounter, engagement, single combat, hand-to-hand combat; fighting, hostilities.

combat v **1** *combat with the enemy* fight, do battle, wage war, clash with, enter into conflict, take up arms, grapple; *combat the enemy* fight with/against. **2** *combat disease* fight, battle against, oppose, strive against, make a stand against, resist, withstand, defy.

combatant n **1** *several combatants injured* fighter, fighting man/woman, soldier, serviceman, servicewoman, warrior, battler, contender. **2** *the combatants in the dispute* adversary, antagonist, contender, opponent, enemy, foe, rival.

combatant adj *combatant forces/parties* combating, fighting, warring, battling, opposing, conflicting, clashing, contending, belligerent.

combative adj pugnacious, belligerent, aggressive, militant, bellicose, warlike, quarrelsome, argumentative, contentious, antagonistic, truculent.

combination n **1** *in combination with the other forces* cooperation, association, union, alliance, partnership, coalition, league, consortium, syndication, federation. **2** *a combination of guilt and grief* mixture, mix, blend, amalgam, amalgamation, compound, alloy, composite.

combine v **1** *combine to finish their work* join forces, get together, unite, team up, cooperate, associate, ally, pool resources, club together, amalgamate, merge, integrate. **2** *combine their efforts* join, put together, unite, pool, merge, integrate, fuse, marry, unify, synthesize. **3** *combine the ingredients* mix, blend, admix, amalgamate, bind, bond, compound, alloy, homogenize.

combustible adj inflammable, flammable, incendiary, explosive, conflagratory.

combustion n burning, firing, fire, kindling, igniting, ignition.

come v **1** *come to us* approach, advance, near, draw near, reach; move/travel towards, bear down on, close in on. **2** *they came last night* arrive, appear, put in an appearance, turn up, enter, materialize; *inf* show up, fetch up, blow in. **3** *Easter came in March* occur, fall, take place, happen, transpire, come about, come to pass. **4** *the dress comes to her ankles* reach, extend, stretch. **5** *the car does not come in red* be available, be made, be produced, be on offer. **6** *come the fool* act, play, play the part of, behave like, imitate. **7** *come* climax, achieve orgasm,

orgasm. **come about** happen, occur, take place, arise, come to pass, transpire, result, befall. **come across 1** *come across an old friend | come across an interesting fact* meet, encounter, run into, run across, chance upon, stumble upon, happen upon, light upon, hit upon, find, discover, unearth; *inf* bump into. **2** *his message/sadness came across* be communicated, be understood, be clear, be perceived. **3** *come across with the money/information* give, hand over, deliver, produce, pay up; *inf* come up with, fork out, cough up. **come along 1** *pupils/patients coming along well* progress, make progress, develop, improve, show improvement, make headway, get better, pick up, rally, recover, mend. **2** *come along there!* hurry, hurry up, make haste, speed up; *inf* get a move on, move it, step on it, make it snappy. **come apart** break up, fall to pieces, disintegrate, come unstuck, crumble, separate, split, tear. **come by** get, obtain, acquire, procure, get possession of, get/lay hold of, get one's hands on, secure, win. **come clean** make a clean breast of it, own up, confess, admit to one's actions/crimes/sins. **come down** *the report came down against punishment | they came down in favour of an increase* decide, reach a decision, recommend, choose, opt. **come down on** rebuke, reprimand, reproach, criticize, berate; *inf* jump on. **come down to** amount to, boil down to, end up as, result in. **come down with** fall ill with, become sick with, catch, contract, take, fall victim to, be stricken with. **come forward** *helpers coming forward* step forward, volunteer, offer/offer one's services. **come into** *come into money* inherit, be left, be willed, succeed to, come in for, acquire, obtain. **come in for 1** *come in for some money* come into, inherit, acquire, obtain. *see* COME, COME INTO. **2** *come in for criticism* get, receive, suffer, endure, bear the brunt of. **come off** *the attempt did not come off* succeed, be successful, be accomplished, work out, transpire, occur, happen, take place. **come on** *vegetables coming on nicely* progress, develop. *see* COME, COME ALONG 1. **come out 1** *the newspaper comes out daily* be published, appear, be in print. **2** *the full story came out* become known, become common knowledge, be revealed, be divulged, be disclosed, be publicized, be released. **3** *flowers coming out* come into bloom, flower, appear. **4** *come out all right* end, finish, conclude, terminate. **5** *debutantes coming out* enter society, be presented, debut. **6** *come out* declare oneself a homosexual, come out of the closet. **come out with** *come out with an oath* utter, say, speak, let out, blurt out. **come round**

1 *coming round annually* occur, take place, happen. **2** *come round after fainting* come to, regain consciousness, revive, wake up, recover. **3** *come round to one's way of thinking* be converted to, be persuaded by, give way to, yield to. **4** *come round in the evening* visit, call; *inf* drop in, drop by, stop by, pop in. **come through 1** *come through the war* get through, survive, outlast, outlive. **2** *we have come through* get through, survive, remain alive, live on, endure. **come to 1** *the bill comes to £5* total, add up to, amount to. **2** *come to after fainting* come round, regain consciousness, awaken. *see* COME, COME ROUND 2. **come up** *something came up* arise, occur, happen, crop up, turn up, spring up. **come up to 1** *she came up to his shoulder* come to, reach, extend to. **2** *come up to their standards* reach, measure up to, match up to, compare with, admit of comparison, bear comparison with, hold a candle to. **come up with** *come up with a plan* suggest, propose, submit, put forward, present, advance, put up, offer.

comeback n **1** *the actor making a comeback* return, rally, resurgence, recovery, revival, rebound. **2** *children making cheeky comebacks* retort, reply, rejoinder, response, answer, retaliation, riposte.

comedian n **1** *television comedian* comic, stand-up comic, funny man, funny woman, humorist. **2** *her uncle's a real comedian* comic, joker, wit, wag, jester, clown; *inf* card, laugh.

comedown n loss of status, loss of face, demotion, downgrading, degradation, humiliation, deflation, decline, reversal, anticlimax.

comedy n **1** *theatres staging both comedy and tragedy* light entertainment, humorous play, farce, musical comedy, situation comedy, comedy of errors, burlesque, pantomime, slapstick, satire, vaudeville, comic opera; *inf* sitcom. **2** *the comedy of the situation* humour, fun, funniness, wit, wittiness, joking, hilarity, levity, facetiousness, farce, drollery.

comely adj **1** *a comely young woman* attractive, good-looking, pretty, beautiful, beauteous, handsome, lovely, bonny, fair, fetching, appealing, charming, winsome, pleasing, engaging. **2** *not comely behaviour* fit, fitting, suitable, proper, seemly, decent, decorous.

come-on n inducement, lure, enticement, allurement, temptation, tantalization.

comeuppance n deserved fate, just deserts, deserts, due reward, retribution, punishment, recompense, requital.

comfort n **1** *live in comfort* ease, easefulness, freedom from hardship, serenity, repose, tranquillity, contentment, content, well-being, cosiness, plenty, sufficiency, luxury, opulence. **2** *bring comfort to the bereaved* consolation, solace, condolence, sympathy, commiseration, help, support, succour, relief, easement, alleviation, cheer, gladdening. **3** *a comfort to her parents* solace, consolation, help, aid, support.

comfort v **1** *comfort the bereaved* bring comfort to, console, solace, give condolences to, give sympathy to, help, support, succour, reassure, soothe, assuage, cheer, gladden. **2** *comforted by the fire* ease, soothe, refresh, revive, hearten, cheer, invigorate, strengthen.

comfortable adj **1** *a comfortable room* homelike, homely, cosy, snug. **2** *comfortable clothes/shoes* well-fitting, loose-fitting, roomy. **3** *a comfortable lifestyle* pleasant, adequate, free from hardship, well-off, well-to-do, affluent, luxurious, opulent. **4** *feeling comfortable* at ease, at one's ease, relaxed, serene, tranquil, contented, cosy.

comforting adj consoling, consolatory, soothing, easing, cheering, reassuring, encouraging, assuaging.

comic adj funny, humorous, amusing, entertaining, diverting, droll, jocular, joking, facetious, comical, witty, farcical, hilarious, zany, side-splitting, priceless, waggish, whimsical.

comic n **1** *a television comic* stand-up comic, comedian, funny man, funny woman, humorist. **2** *he's a real comic* comedian, joker, wag. see COMEDIAN 2. **3** *reading a comic* comic paper, funny magazine; *inf* funny.

comical adj **1** *a comical performance* comic, funny, humorous, amusing. see COMIC adj. **2** *a comical hat* absurd, ridiculous, silly, laughable, ludicrous, risible.

coming n *the coming of Christ/summer* advent, approach, nearing, arrival, appearance, accession.

coming adj **1** *the coming appearance | the coming storm* approaching, advancing, forthcoming, nearing, imminent, impending, close at hand, in store, in the wind. **2** *the coming actor* promising, aspiring.

command v **1** *command you to go* order, give orders to, direct, charge, instruct, bid, enjoin, adjure, summon, prescribe, require. **2** *he commands the unit* be in command of, have charge of, control, have control of, rule, govern, direct, preside over, head, lead, manage, supervise, superintend.

command n **1** *follow the commands* order, decree, dictate, edict, instruction, directive, direction, bidding, injunction, behest, mandate, fiat, precept, commandment, enjoining. see COMMAND v 1. **2** *under the command of the French* charge, control, authority, power, mastery, ascendancy, government, direction, management, administration, supervision, dominion, sway, domination.

commandeer v seize, take possession of, requisition, expropriate, appropriate, sequestrate, sequester, hijack, arrogate.

commander n **1** *the commander of the expedition* leader, head, director, chief, boss; *inf* number one, top dog, kingpin, big cheese, big white chief. **2** *naval commander* officer, captain. **3** *army commander* commander-in-chief, C in C, commanding officer, CO.

commanding adj **1** *a commanding position/lead* controlling, directing, dominating, dominant, superior, advantageous. **2** *a commanding manner/personality* authoritative, autocratic, masterful, assertive, peremptory, imposing, impressive, august.

commemorate v celebrate, pay tribute to, pay homage to, remember, honour, salute, mark, memorialize.

commemorative adj memorial, celebratory, celebrative, remembering, honouring, saluting, in honour of, in memory of, in remembrance of, in tribute to.

commence v **1** *ready to commence* begin, start, make a beginning/start, go ahead, be off, embark, set sail, set the ball rolling, get something off the ground; *inf* get the show on the road. **2** *commence the proceedings* begin, start, open, enter/embark upon, inaugurate, initiate, originate.

commend v **1** *commend his work* praise, applaud, speak highly of, approve, acclaim, extol, laud, eulogize. **2** *commend action* recommend, approve, endorse, advocate. **3** *commend her to your care* entrust, trust, deliver, commit, hand over, give, consign, assign.

commendable adj praiseworthy, admirable, laudable, estimable, meritorious, creditable, reputable, worthy, deserving.

commendation n **1** *receive the judge's commendation* praise, applause, high opinion, acclaim, acclamation, approval, approbation, good opinion, credit, eulogies, extolment, laudation, encomium, panegyric. **2** *the commendation of his soul to God* entrust, trusting, committal. see COMMEND 3.

125

commensurate adj **1** *a commensurate amount of water to wine* equivalent, equal, corresponding, comparable, proportionate, proportion, commensurable. **2** *a salary commensurate with experience* in accordance with, according to, proportionate to, appropriate to, consistent with, corresponding to.

comment v **1** *he commented unfavourably on her actions* remark, speak, make remarks, make a comment on, express an opinion on, say something about. **2** *"Good," he commented* say, remark, state, observe, interpose. **3** *comment on the text* write notes, annotate, explain, interpret, elucidate, clarify, shed light on.

comment n **1** *pass comments on her appearance | arouse comment* remark, opinion, observation, view, statement, criticism. **2** *textual comment* annotation, note, footnote, gloss, marginalia, explanation, interpretation, elucidation, exposition.

commentary n **1** *a television commentary* narration, description, account, review, analysis. **2** *textual commentary* annotation, notes, interpretation, analysis, exegesis, critique. *see* COMMENT n 2.

commentator n **1** *television commentator* reporter, commenter, broadcaster, narrator, correspondent; newscaster, sportscaster. **2** *text commentator* annotator, interpreter, expositor, critic, glossist, scholiast. **3** *commentator on society* commenter. *see* COMMENT V 1, WRITER, AUTHOR, SPEAKER, LECTURER.

commerce n **1** *work in commerce* business, trade, buying and selling, merchandizing, dealing, financial transaction, marketing, traffic. **2** *everday social commerce* social relations, socializing, communication, dealings, traffic, intercourse.

commercial adj **1** *commercial training* business, trade, marketing, merchandizing, sales, mercantile. **2** *not a commercial proposition* profitable, profit-making, business. **3** *town becoming too commercial* profit-orientated, money-orientated, mercantile, materialistic, mercenary.

commission n **1** *get commission on the sale* percentage, brokerage, share, fee, compensation; *inf* cut, rake-off. **2** *given the commission of designing the building* task, employment, piece of work, work, duty, charge, mission, responsibility. **3** *receive the commission to be official representative* authority, sanction, warrant, licence. **4** *set up a commission of enquiry* committee, board, board of commissioners, council, advisory body, delegation. **5** *the commission of a*

commensurate · commonplace

crime | sin of commission committing, committal, execution, perpetration, performance.

commission v **1** *commission an artist to paint a portrait* employ, engage, contract, appoint, book, authorize. **2** *commission a portrait* order, put in an order for, place an order for, contract for, pay for, authorize. **3** *commission the representatives* authorize, empower, accredit, sanction, invest.

commit v **1** *commit a crime | commit suicide* perform, carry out, execute, enact, perpetrate, effect, do. **2** *commit to one's care* entrust, trust, deliver, hand over, give, consign, assign. **3** *commit oneself to take part* pledge, promise, engage, bind oneself, covenant, obligate oneself, dedicate oneself. **4** *commit the thief to prison* imprison, jail, confine, lock up, custody, put away. **5** *commit the suicidal woman* hospitalize, institutionalize, confine.

commitment n **1** *have too many commitments* undertaking, obligation, responsibility, duty, liability, tie, task, engagement. **2** *have no commitment to the job* dedication, devotion, involvement in, loyalty, allegiance, adherence. **3** *make a commitment to go* pledge, promise, vow, assurance, covenant.

commodious adj roomy, spacious, capacious, large, extensive, ample.

commodity n thing, item, article, product, article of merchandise.

common adj **1** *the common people* ordinary, average, normal, typical, unexceptional, run-of-the-mill, plain, simple. **2** *a common style of writing* ordinary, unexceptional, undistinguished, run-of-the-mill, workaday, commonplace, common-or-garden, mediocre, pedestrian, hackneyed, trite, humdrum. **3** *a common occurrence* usual, ordinary, everyday, daily, regular, frequent, customary, habitual, routine, standard, repeated, recurrent, commonplace, run-of-the-mill. **4** *a common response* usual, ordinary, familiar, routine, stock, standard, conventional, traditional. **5** *a common belief* widespread, general, universal, popular, accepted, prevalent, prevailing. **6** *for the common good* communal, collective, community, public, popular. **7** *a common young woman* low, vulgar, coarse, uncouth, inferior, plebeian.

commonplace adj **1** *a commonplace novel/youngster* ordinary, unexceptional, undistinguished, mediocre, pedestrian, dull, uninteresting, humdrum, hackneyed, trite. **2** *foreign holidays are commonplace | commonplace events* common, usual, ordinary, routine. *see* COMMON 2.

common sense n good sense, sense, practicality, judgement, native wit/intelligence, level-headedness, prudence, discernment, astuteness, shrewdness, judiciousness, wisdom; *inf* horse sense, gumption, nous.

commotion n disturbance, racket, uproar, rumpus, tumult, clamour, riot, hubbub, hullabaloo, brouhaha, furore, hurly-burly, disorder, confusion, upheaval, disruption, agitation, excitement, fuss, disquiet, ferment, to-do, bustle, hustle and bustle.

communal adj common, collective, shared, joint, general, public, community, cooperative, communalist.

commune v 1 *commune with close friends* converse, talk, communicate, speak, have a tête-à-tête, confer, confide. 2 *commune with nature* feel in close touch, feel at one, empathize, identify.

commune n collective, cooperative, co-op, community, kibbutz.

communicable adj infectious, contagious, catching, transmittable, transmissible, transferable; *inf* taking.

communicate v 1 *communicate information* transmit, pass on, transfer, impart, convey, relay, spread, disseminate, make known, publish, broadcast, announce, report, divulge, disclose, unfold, proclaim. 2 *not to communicate with him* be in touch, be in contact, have dealings, interface. 3 *you must be able to communicate* get one's ideas/message across, interface, be articulate, be fluent, be eloquent. 4 *communicate a disease* transmit, pass on, transfer, spread. 5 *her room communicates with his* connect, be connected to, adjoin, abut on.

communication n 1 *communication is difficult* information transmission/transfer, transmission, dissemination, contact, getting in touch, radio/telephone link, connection, interface, social intercourse. 2 *received the communication* message, letter, report, statement, dispatch, news, information, data, intelligence, word.

communications n 1 *all communications under enemy control* links, channels, routes, passages. 2 *studying communications* electronic communication, telecommunications, data communications, information technology, IT; *inf* comms.

communicative adj *not a very communicative person* expansive, forthcoming, talkative, loquacious, voluble, chatty, conversational, informative, frank, open, candid.

communion n 1 *a strange communion between each other* | *communion with nature* rapport, empathy, sympathy, accord, affinity, fellowship, togetherness, harmony, closeness, agreement, sharing, concord, unity, fusion, communication. 2 *Holy Communion* Eucharist.

communiqué n official communication, bulletin, dispatch, report, news flash, announcement.

communism n state ownership, collectivism, Sovietism, Bolshevism, Marxism, Leninism.

community n 1 *move to a new community* locality, district, neighbourhood. 2 *the community condemned her* residents, inhabitants; population, populace. 3 *work for the community* society, public, general public, body politic, nation, state. 4 *the Jewish community in Paris* group, section, body, company, set, ghetto. 5 *religious community* brotherhood, sisterhood, association. 6 *community of interests* similarity, likeness, agreement, affinity. 7 *community of property* shared possession, joint liability, common ownership, joint participation.

commute v 1 *commute from Richmond to London* travel to and from, travel back and forth, shuttle. 2 *commute a sentence/penalty* lessen, reduce, shorten, curtail, mitigate, modify. 3 *commute an annuity to a lump sum* exchange, change, interchange, substitute, trade, barter, switch.

commuter n daily traveller; *inf* straphanger.

compact adj 1 *a compact parcel* dense, packed close, pressed together, close, firm, solid, compressed, condensed. 2 *a compact car/flat/machine* small, economic of space, neat. 3 *a compact style* concise, succinct, terse, brief, condensed, pithy, to the point, epigrammatic, compendious.

compact v *compact the sand* pack down, press down, compress, press together, condense, tamp.

compact n *the two sides signed the compact* contract, agreement, covenant, pact, indenture, bond, treaty, alliance, bargain, deal, transaction, settlement, entente.

companion n 1 *with an unknown companion* | *the girl and her companions* partner, escort, consort, friend, crony, comrade, colleague, associate, ally, confederate; *inf* buddy, mate. 2 *the princess and her companion* attendant, aide, chaperon, duenna, squire. 3 *the companion of this book-end/volume* fellow, mate, twin, match, counterpart, complement. 4 *the Angler's Companion* guide, handbook, manual, reference book, *vade-mecum*.

companionship n friendship, fellowship, company, society, togetherness, social intercourse, comradeship, camaraderie, association, brotherhood, sisterhood, intimacy, rapport.

company n **1** *enjoy their company* companionship, friendship, fellowship. *see* COMPANIONSHIP. **2** *address the company* assembly, assemblage, gathering, meeting, audience, group, crowd, throng, congregation, convention. **3** *a company of actors/archers* group, band, party, body, association, society, fellowship, troupe, collection, circle, league, crew, guild. **4** *a retail company* business, firm, concern, corporation, house, establishment, conglomerate; *inf* outfit. **5** *a company of soldiers* subdivision, unit, detachment. **6** *expecting company* guest(s), visitor(s), caller(s).

comparable adj **1** *his acting is not comparable with his father's* as good as, equal, on a par, in the same class/league, on a level. **2** *comparable pay for comparable work* equivalent, commensurable, corresponding, proportional, proportionate, similar, like, parallel, analogous, related.

comparative adj *living in comparative affluence* relative, in/by comparison, qualified, modified.

compare v **1** *compare the two styles* contrast, juxtapose, weigh/balance/measure the differences between, collate, differentiate. **2** *the island has been compared to heaven* liken, equate, analogize. **3** *his work does not compare with Hardy's* bear comparison, be comparable, be the equal, be on a par, be in the same class, compete, match, approach, come up to, hold a candle. *see* COMPARABLE 1.

comparison n **1** *make a comparison* contrast, juxtaposition, collation, differentiation. *see* COMPARE 1. **2** *no comparison between their works* comparability, analogy, resemblance, likeness, similarity, correlation.

compartment n **1** *luggage/bomb compartment* section, part, partition, bay, chamber, niche. **2** *compartments of one's life* part, section, division, department, area. **3** *train compartment* carriage, coach; *Amer* car.

compass n *within the compass of his power* scope, range, area, extent, reach, span, stretch, limits, bounds, field, sphere, zone, circumference.

compassion n pity, tender-heartedness, soft-heartedness, tenderness, gentleness, mercy, leniency, fellow-feeling, understanding, sympathy, concern, consideration, humanity, kindness, kind-heartedness, charity, benevolence.

compassionate adj soft-hearted, tender, gentle, merciful, lenient, understanding,

sympathetic, pitying, humanitarian, humane, kindly, kind-hearted, charitable, benevolent.

compatible adj **1** *couples not compatible* well-suited, suited, like-minded, of the same mind, in agreement, in tune, in harmony, reconcilable, having affinity/rapport, accordant. **2** *views not compatible with actions* consistent, in keeping, reconcilable, consonant, congruous, congruent.

compatriot n fellow-countryman, fellow-countrywoman, countryman, countrywoman, fellow-citizen.

compel v **1** *compel them to leave* force, make, coerce, drive, pressure, pressurize, dragoon, constrain, impel, oblige, necessitate, urge; *inf* bulldoze, railroad, twist one's arm, strong-arm, put the screws on. **2** *compel obedience* force, enforce, exact, insist upon, necessitate, extort.

compelling adj **1** *a compelling story* fascinating, gripping, enthralling, irresistible, hypnotic, mesmeric. **2** *compelling reasons* cogent, convincing, forceful, powerful, weighty, telling, conclusive, irrefutable.

compensate v **1** *compensate for his evil deed* make amends, make restitution, make reparation, make up for, atone, expiate. **2** *compensate her for her loss* recompense, repay, reimburse, requite, indemnify. **3** *the cargo compensating for the light boat* counterbalance, counterpoise, counteract, balance, cancel out, neutralize, nullify.

compensation n **1** *receive compensation for her loss* recompense, repayment, reimbursement, requital, indemnification, indemnity, damages. **2** *make compensation for his deed* amends, restitution, redress, atonement, expiation.

compete v **1** *compete in the race* take part, enter, go in for, participate, be a contestant; *inf* throw one's hat in the ring, be in the running. **2** *compete against/with his brother* contend, vie, strive, struggle, fight, pit oneself against.

competence n **1** *the competence of the player* capability, ability, capacity, proficiency, adeptness, expertise, skill. **2** *the competence of the answer* adequacy, appropriateness, suitability, pertinence, appositeness. **3** *competence to plead* fitness, qualification. **4** *a small competence* income, unearned income.

competent adj **1** *a very competent player* capable, able, proficient, qualified, efficient, adept, accomplished, skilful. **2** *a competent answer* adequate, appropriate, suitable, pertinent, apposite. **3** *not competent to plead* fit, fitted, qualified.

competition n **1** *a chess competition* contest, match, game, tournament, event, meet, quiz. **2** *in competition with them* rivalry, vying, contest, opposition, struggle, contention, strife. **3** *the competition is poor* field, opposition; challengers, opponents, rivals.

competitive adj **1** *a very competitive young man* competition-orientated, ambitious, vying, combative, aggressive. **2** *a competitive industry* aggressive, dog-eat-dog, cutthroat.

competitor n **1** *competitors in the race* contestant, contender, challenger, participant, candidate, entrant. **2** *his business competitors* rival, opponent, adversary, antagonist; opposition.

compilation n *a compilation of short stories* collection, anthology, album, corpus, garland, ana, collectanea.

compile v gather, collect, accumulate, amass, assemble, put together, collate, marshal, organize, systematize, anthologize.

complacent adj smug, self-satisfied, pleased with oneself, satisfied, contented, self-contented, pleased, gratified, placid, serene, bovine, self-righteous.

complain v **1** *complain about the service* lodge a complaint, criticize, find fault, carp, make a fuss; *inf* kick up a fuss. **2** *always complaining* grumble, grouse, gripe, moan, grouch, whine, lament, bewail; *inf* bellyache, beef, bitch.

complaint n **1** *manager attending to complaints* criticism, grievance, charge, accusation, protest, remonstrance, statement of dissatisfaction; fault-finding; *Law* plaint. **2** *always full of complaint* grumbling, grumble, grousing, grouse. *see* COMPLAIN 2. **3** *a painful complaint* illness, disease, ailment, disorder, sickness, affliction, malady.

complement n **1** *the perfect complement to the food* companion, addition, supplement, accessory, final/finishing touch. **2** *the school's full complement* amount, allowance, total, aggregate, load, capacity, quota.

complement v *wine complementing the food* complete, round/set off, add to, go well with, be the perfect companion/addition to, add the final/finishing touch to, supplement.

complementary adj complemental, completing, finishing, perfecting, culminative, consummative.

complete adj **1** *the complete collection* entire, whole, full, total, intact, unbroken, undivided, uncut, unshortened, unabridged, plenary. **2** *the task is complete* completed, finished, ended, concluded, accomplished,

finalized. **3** *a complete fool* absolute, out-and-out, thoroughgoing, thorough, utter, total, perfect, consummate, unqualified, dyed-in-the-wool.

complete v **1** *complete the task* finish, end, conclude, finalize, realize, accomplish, achieve, fulfil, execute, effect, discharge, settle, clinch, do; *inf* wrap up, polish off. **2** *complete the outfit* finish off, round off, make perfect, perfect, crown, cap, add the final/finishing touch.

completely adv *completely exhausted* totally, utterly, absolutely, thoroughly, quite, wholly, altogether.

completion n finish, ending, conclusion, close, finalization, realization, accomplishment, achievement, fulfilment, execution, consummation.

complex adj **1** *a complex subject* complicated, difficult, involved, intricate, convoluted, knotty, perplexing, puzzling, cryptic, enigmatic. **2** *a complex structure* composite, compound, compounded, multiple, manifold, multiplex, heterogenous.

complex n **1** *building complex* | *complex of regulations* structure, scheme, composite, conglomerate, aggregation, network, system, organization, synthesis. **2** *a complex about her nose* obsession, phobia, fixation, preoccupation, *idée fixe*.

complexion n **1** *a beautiful/sallow complexion* skin, skin colour, skin colouring, skin tone, colouring, pigmentation. **2** *put a new complexion on it* aspect, appearance, guise, look, light countenance, angle. **3** *his brother is of a different complexion* character, nature, disposition, cast, stamp.

complexity n *the complexities of the situation* complication, difficulty, intricacy, convolution, problem, puzzle, enigma, ramification, entanglement.

compliance n **1** *compliance with the law* obedience, observance, abiding by, conforming, acquiescence, assent, agreement, accordance. **2** *noted for his compliance* yielding, submissiveness, submission, deference, passivity, subservience, servility.

complicate v make difficult, make involved/intricate, confuse, muddle, jumble, snarl up, entangle.

complicated adj difficult, involved, intricate, complex, convoluted, perplexing, puzzling, enigmatic, cryptic, entangled, Byzantine.

complication n **1** *meet complications* difficulty, problem, drawback, snag, obstacle, aggravation. **2** *a great deal of complication* difficulty, intricacy, complexity, confusion, muddle.

complicity n collusion, conspiracy, collaboration, connivance, abetment.

compliment n *receive compliments* flattering remark/comment, bouquet; praise, tribute, homage, admiration, flattery, commendation, laudation, eulogy.

compliment v congratulate, felicitate, speak highly of, praise, sing the praises of, pay tribute/homage to, salute, admire, flatter, commend, honour, acclaim, laud, eulogize.

complimentary adj **1** *complimentary remarks* congratulatory, admiring, appreciative, approving, flattering, commendatory, laudatory, eulogizing, panegyrical. **2** *complimentary tickets* free of charge, given free.

compliments npl *the compliments of the season* greetings, good wishes, regards, respects, salutations.

comply v *comply with the ruling* obey, observe, abide by, adhere to, conform to, acquiesce with, assent to, consent to, accord with, agree with, follow, respect, yield, submit.

component n part, piece, section, constituent, element, unit, module, item.

component adj constituent, composing, integral, integrant, sectional, fractional.

compose v **1** *compose a poem* write, make up, create, think up, devise, concoct, invent, compile, contrive, formulate, fashion, produce. **2** *compose one's dress/plans* put together, arrange, put in order, align, organize, assemble, collate, systematize. **3** *peoples composing a nation* make up, form, constitute, comprise. **4** *compose oneself* calm, calm down, quiet, collect, control, soothe, still, tranquillize, quell, pacify, assuage. **5** *compose a dispute* settle, resolve, reconcile, find a solution to.

composed adj *feeling composed | a composed manner* calm, cool, collected, cool and collected, serene, tranquil, relaxed, poised, at ease, unruffled, self-controlled, untroubled, undisturbed, unperturbed, unworried, confident, self-possessed, level-headed; *inf* together.

composite adj *a composite structure* compound, complex, conglomerate, combined, blended, mixed, synthesized.

composite n *a composite of various elements* compound, amalgam, blend, mixture, complex, combination, fusion, conglomerate, synthesis.

composition n **1** *the composition of the soil* structure, constitution, make-up, conformation, configuration, organization, arrangement, lay-out, character. **2** *an adhesive composition* compound, amalgam, blend, mixture, mix, admixture. see COMPOUND n. **3** *the composition of a poem* writing, making-up, creation, concoction, invention, compilation. see COMPOSE 1. **4** *a brilliant composition* work of art, creation, literary/musical/artistic work, poem, novel, opus, arrangement, symphony, picture. **5** *pupils writing a composition* essay, theme, piece of writing. **6** *admire the painting's composition* arrangement, proportions, harmony, balance, symmetry.

compost n fertilizer, manure, humus, mulch.

composure n aplomb, poise, self-possession, presence of mind, sang-froid, equanimity, equilibrium, self-control, self-command, calm, calmness, coolness, collectedness, serenity, tranquillity, imperturbability, inexcitability, placidity.

compound n *a chemical/verbal compound* amalgam, blend, mixture, admixture, complex, combination, fusion, alloy, conglomerate, synthesis, medley, hybrid.

compound adj *a compound substance* composite, complex, conglomerate, blended, not simple, fused. see COMPOUND n.

compound v **1** *compound the two ideas/substances* mix, blend, combine, put together, amalgamate, unite, coalesce, alloy, fuse, mingle, intermingle, synthesize. **2** *compound the sin/fear compounded with poverty* worsen, make worse, add to, augment, exacerbate, magnify, aggravate, intensify, heighten.

comprehend v **1** *comprehend the facts* understand, grasp, take in, assimilate, fathom, perceive, discern, apprehend. **2** *cannot comprehend how he won* understand, conceive, imagine. see FATHOM 2. **3** *comprehend the whole school* include, take in, encompass, involve, embrace, contain, comprise.

comprehensible adj intelligible, understandable, graspable, fathomable, discernible, conceivable, plain, clear, explicit, coherent, lucid.

comprehension n *beyond one's comprehension* understanding, grasp, perception, ken, discernment, conception.

comprehensive adj inclusive, all-inclusive, all-embracing, complete, full, encyclopedic, exhaustive, thorough, extensive, broad, widespread, far-reaching, blanket, umbrella, universal, catholic.

compress v **1** *compress the pile of sand* pack down, press down, press together, squeeze together, squash, crush, condense, compact, cram, tamp, constrict. **2** *compress the text* abbreviate, shorten, abridge, contract, reduce.

comprise v **1** *a board comprising only men* consist of, contain, include, be composed of, take in, embrace, encompass, comprehend. **2** *children comprising the audience* make up, form, constitute, compose.

compromise v **1** *compromise on the wording* come to terms, come to an understanding, make a deal, make concessions, find a happy medium, find the middle grounds, strike a balance, meet halfway, give and take, take part in a trade-off. **2** *compromise him | compromise his reputation* discredit, dishonour, bring shame to, bring into disrepute, shame, embarrass, endanger, jeopardize, imperil. **3** *compromise his chances* prejudice, damage, injure, endanger, weaken.

compromise n *reach a compromise* understanding, deal, happy medium, middle course, balance, trade-off, settlement by concession; terms; middle ground, give and take, adjustment.

compulsion n **1** *under no compulsion to go* obligation, force, duress, constraint, coercion, pressure, oppression, enforcement. **2** *feel a compulsion to travel* urge, need, desire, motivation, necessity, preoccupation, obsession.

compulsive adj **1** *compulsive viewing* fascinating, gripping, irresistible, compelling. *see* COMPELLING 1. **2** *a compulsive desire to wash* obsessive, uncontrollable, irresistible, compelling, driving, overwhelming, urgent, besetting. **3** *compulsive eating* addictive, obsessional, obsessive, uncontrollable, out of control, ungovernable. **4** *a compulsive gambler/drinker* addicted, addictive, obsessive, obsessional, dependent; *inf* hooked.

compulsory adj obligatory, mandatory, required, binding, forced, necessary, essential, *de rigueur.*

compunction n remorse, regret, pangs of conscience, guilt, contrition, contriteness, penitence, repentance; scruples.

compute v calculate, reckon, count, add up, total, figure out, work out, enumerate, sum, tally, cast up, measure, rate.

comrade n companion, friend, colleague, partner, associate, co-worker, fellow-worker, mate, team-mate, ally, confederate, compatriot, compeer; *inf* pal, buddy.

con v *con the old lady* swindle, deceive, cheat, hoodwink, mislead, delude, bamboozle.

con n con trick, confidence trick, swindle, deception, cheating; con man, confidence trickster, swindler, deceiver, cheater.

concave adj curved in, incurved, incurvate, hollow, hollowed out, depressed, sunken, indented, scooped-out.

conceal v **1** *conceal her face | conceal the letter* hide, cover, keep out of sight, keep hidden, screen, obscure, disguise, camouflage, mask, secrete, shelter, bury, tuck away. **2** *conceal his identity* hide, keep secret, keep dark, hush up, cover up, dissemble; *inf* keep the lid on.

concealed adj *a concealed entrance* hidden, obscured, unseen, invisible, screened, secreted, tucked away.

concealment n *a place of concealment* hiding, hide-away, hide-out, retreat; secrecy, privacy, sheltering, secretion, camouflage.

concede v **1** *concede defeat* acknowledge, admit, accept, own, allow, grant, accede, confess, recognize. **2** *concede some territory/ goals* give up, yield, surrender, relinquish, cede, hand over.

conceit n **1** *the winner full of conceit* pride, arrogance, vanity, self-admiration, self-love, self-importance, self-adulation, narcissism, *amour propre*, egotism, complacency, self-satisfaction, boasting, swagger, vainglory. **2** *conceits in the metaphysical poets* comparison, metaphor, simile, image; imagery, ornament, decoration. **3** *exchanging clever conceits* witticism, quip, *bon mot*, pleasantry, epigram. **4** *a mind occupied with conceits* fancy idea, notion, whim; fantasy, imagination, whimsy, vagary.

conceited adj proud, arrogant, vain, self-important, cocky, haughty, supercilious, overweening, narcissistic, immodest, egotistical, puffed up, self-satisfied, complacent, boastful, swaggering, vainglorious; *inf* big-headed, swollen-headed, swell-headed, stuck-up.

conceivable adj *not conceivable that he would lose* credible, believable, imaginable, thinkable, possible, understandable, comprehensible.

conceive v **1** *women unable to conceive* become pregnant, become impregnated, become fertilized. **2** *conceive the idea | conceive a plan* think up, draw up, form, formulate, produce, develop, project, devise, contrive, conjure up, envisage. **3** *cannot conceive that/ how he lost* imagine, think, believe, realize, appreciate, suppose, understand, comprehend, perceive, grasp, apprehend, envisage, visualize, fancy.

concentrate v **1** *concentrate one's attention/ efforts on* focus, centre, converge, centralize, consolidate, bring to bear, congregate, cluster. **2** *concentrate on one's studies* be absorbed in, focus attention on, be engrossed in, give one's attention/mind to, put one's mind to, think about closely, consider closely, rack one's brains about/ over. **3** *troops concentrating on the border* | *concentrate troops* collect, gather, congregate, accumulate, amass, cluster, rally, huddle. **4** *concentrate the liquid* condense, boil down, reduce, compress, distil.

concentrated adj *a concentrated effort* intensive, intense, consolidated, rigorous, vigorous; *inf* all-out.

concentration n **1** *lose one's concentration* close attention, absorption, application, engrossment, single-mindedness, heed. **2** *the concentration of one's attention/efforts* focusing, centralization, consolidation. *see* CONCENTRATE 1. **3** *the concentration of troops* collection, gathering, congregation. *see* CONCENTRATE 3.

concept n idea, notion, abstraction, conceptualization, conception, hypothesis, theory, image, view.

conception n **1** *when conception took place* conceiving, fertilization, impregnation, fecundation, inception of pregnancy. **2** *in at the conception of the project* inception, beginning, origination, origin, birth, initiation, formation, launching, invention, outset. **3** *a brilliant conception* plan, design, invention, creation, project, scheme, proposal. **4** *the conception of maths* idea, abstraction, concept. *see* CONCEPT. **5** *no conception of how to behave* idea, notion, perception, appreciation, understanding, clue, inkling, impression, picture.

concern v **1** *affairs not concerning you* be the business of, affect, be relevant to, involve, apply to, pertain to, have a bearing on, bear on, be of interest to, touch. **2** *a report concerning cancer* be about, deal with, be connected with, relate to, have to do with, appertain to. **3** *concern herself in their affairs* interest/involve oneself in, be interested/ involved in, take/have a hand in, busy oneself with, devote one's time to, be busy with. **4** *children's behaviour concerned teachers* worry, disturb, trouble, bother, perturb, make anxious, cause disquiet to, distress.

concern n **1** *none of your concern* business, affair, interest, matter of interest, involvement, responsibility, charge, duty, job, task, occupation, mission, department,

field, subject, discipline. **2** *news of concern to all of us* interest, importance, relevance, bearing, applicability. **3** *parents full of concern* worry, disturbance, anxiety, disquiet, perturbation, distress, apprehension. **4** *parents demonstrating their concern* care, caringness, solicitude, attentiveness, attention, consideration, regard. **5** *start a publishing concern* business, firm, company, enterprise, organization, corporation, establishment, house.

concerned adj **1** *concerned parties* interested, involved, implicated, in on, party to. **2** *concerned parents going to the police* worried, disturbed, anxious, upset, uneasy, troubled, perturbed, distressed, bothered, exercised, apprehensive. **3** *both concerned and uncaring parents* caring, attentive, solicitous, responsible, considerate.

concerning prep about, on the subject of, relating to, relevant to, regarding, as regards, with regard to, with reference to, referring to, with respect to, respecting, as to, touching on, in the matter of, re, apropos of.

concert n **1** *a hall designed for concerts* musical entertainment, performance; symphony concert, variety concert, music hall, pop concert, rock concert. **2** *no concert in their actions* agreement, accordance, accord, unanimity, harmony, concord, concordance, unity, unison, consensus. **In concert** *act in concert* together, jointly, in combination, cooperatively, in cooperation, in collaboration, in league, in unison, shoulder to shoulder, side by side, concertedly.

concerted adj *a concerted effort* jointly planned, combined, cooperative, joint, coordinated, united, collaborative, synchronized, interactive, synergetic.

concession n **1** *the concession of defeat* acknowledgement, admission, acceptance, allowance, recognition. *see* CONCEDE 1. **2** *the concession of territory* yielding, surrender, relinquishment, ceding. *see* CONCEDE 2. **3** *make concessions* | *as a concession to their youth* allowance, adjustment, modification, compromise, indulgence, exception. **4** *price concessions* reduction, cut, discount, decrease. **5** *grant the concession* franchise, licence, permit, warrant, authorization.

conciliate v placate, appease, pacify, propitiate, mollify, assuage, calm down, soothe, humour, reconcile, disarm, win over, restore harmony to.

conciliatory adj placatory, appeasing, pacifying, pacificatory, propitiative, mollifying, assuaging, disarming, reconciliatory, peacemaking; *fml* irenic.

concise adj succinct, compact, terse, brief, short, condensed, compressed, crisp, pithy, to the point, epigrammatic, compendious, summary, synoptic.

conclave n private meeting, secret meeting, conference, council, parley, session, assembly, congress, gathering, forgathering, congregation.

conclude v **1** *the meeting concluded at 9 o'clock* end, finish, close, come/draw to an end, halt, cease, terminate, discontinue; *inf* wind up. **2** *we concluded the meeting* end, finish, close, bring to an end. **3** *conclude an agreement* negotiate, come terms on, reach terms on, bring about, pull off, clinch, work out, accomplish, fix, effect, establish, engineer, settle, decide, determine, resolve. **4** *conclude that he had won* come to the conclusion, deduce, infer, decide, gather, reckon, judge, assume, presume, suppose, conjecture, surmise.

conclusion n **1** *the conclusion of the meeting* end, finish, close, halting, cessation, termination, discontinuance; *inf* wind-up. **2** *the conclusion of the agreement* negotiation, clinching, accomplishment, establishment, settling, resolution. *see* CONCLUDE 3. **3** *a predictable conclusion* outcome, result, upshot, issue, culmination, consequence. **4** *reach the conclusion that he was guilty* deduction, inference, decision, opinion, judgement, verdict, conviction, assumption, presumption. *see* CONCLUDE 4. **in conclusion** in closing, to sum up, finally, lastly, in winding up.

conclusive adj decisive, clinching, definitive, definite, final, ultimate, categorical, incontestable, irrefutable, convincing, cogent.

concoct v **1** *concoct a meal/stew* prepare, put together, make, cook, muster, mix, blend, brew; *inf* rustle up. **2** *concoct an excuse* devise, invent, make up, think up, dream up, fabricate, form, formulate, hatch, plot, forge, scheme, design, fashion, brew; *inf* cook up.

concoction n **1** *a tasty concoction* preparation, mixture, blend, combination, brew, creation. **2** *don't believe that concoction* invention, fabrication, plot, scheme, designing.

concomitant adj attendant, accompanying, associated, belonging, linked, affiliated, accessory, auxiliary.

concord n agreement, harmony, accord, unity, oneness, consensus.

concrete adj **1** *concrete evidence* actual, real, factual, definite, genuine, substantial, material, tangible, unimaginary, specific. **2** *a concrete substance* solid, solidified, firm, consolidated, compact, dense, condensed, compressed, coalesced, petrified, calcified.

concubine n mistress, paramour, kept woman, courtesan, odalisque.

concupiscence n sexual desire, desire, passion, sexual appetite, libido, lust, lustfulness, lechery, lasciviousness, libidinousness; *inf* randiness, horniness.

concur v **1** *they concur on/over the verdict* agree, be in accord, accord, be in harmony, acquiesce, assent, be in assent, be of the same mind, be in concord. **2** *the two events concurred* coincide, happen/occur together, be simultaneous, coexist, synchronize. **3** *they concurred in the attempt* cooperate, combine, unite, collaborate, join forces, act together, work together, pool resources.

concurrent adj **1** *concurrent sentences* simultaneous, parallel, coexisting, coexistent, coincident, contemporaneous, synchronous, side-by-side. **2** *concurrent lines* converging, convergent, meeting, joining, uniting, intersecting. **3** *concurrent attitudes* agreeing, in agreement, in accord, in harmony, harmonious, assenting, in assent, of the same mind, like-minded, as one, at one, in rapport, compatible, consentient. **4** *concurrent action* cooperative, combined, united, joint, collaborative.

concussion n **1** *suffer concussion in the accident* brain injury, brain incapacity, unconsciousness, loss of consciousness. **2** *damage caused by concussion* jarring, jar, jolting, jolt, shaking, shock, blow, bump, impact, clash, collision.

condemn v **1** *condemn all violence | condemn him for his action* censure, denounce, deprecate, disapprove of, criticize, berate, upbraid, reprove, reproach, blame, reprehend, reprobate. **2** *condemn him to death* sentence, pass sentence on, convict. **3** *condemn the building* declare unfit, forbid the use of, proscribe, ban, bar. **4** *his action condemned him* declare guilty, prove one's guilt, accuse, incriminate, indict, inculpate, implicate. **5** *condemned to misery/poverty* doom, damn, force, compel, coerce, impel.

condemnatory adj condemning, censuring, censorious, denunciatory, deprecatory, disapproving, critical, reproving, vituperative, reproachful.

condensation n **1** *the condensation of the soup* concentration, concentrating, boiling down, reduction. *see* CONDENSE 1. **2** *the condensation of steam* liquefaction, liquidization, deliquescence, precipitation, distillation. **3** *the condensation of the report* shortening, abridgement, abbreviation, cutting, summarization. *see* CONDENSE 3. **4** *read the condensation* abridgement, summary, précis, digest, abstract, synopsis.

condense v **1** *condense the soup by boiling* concentrate, thicken, boil down, reduce, solidify, coagulate. **2** *steam condensing on the mirror* liquefy, liquidize, deliquesce, precipitate. **3** *condense the report* shorten, abridge, abbreviate, cut, compress, contract, compact, curtail, summarize, précis, epitomize, encapsulate.

condescend v **1** *condescend to speak to him* lower oneself, deign, stoop, descend, unbend, humble/demean oneself, vouchsafe; *inf* come down from one's high horse. **2** *condescend to younger people* treat condescendingly, patronize, talk down to, look down one's nose at.

condescending adj patronizing, disdainful, supercilious, superior, snobbish, lofty, lordly; *inf* snooty, snotty, toffee-nosed.

condition n **1** *the human condition | the condition of slavery* state, state of existence, circumstance, situation, predicament. **2** *in a miserable condition* state, state of affairs, circumstance, situation, position, plight, predicament, quandary. **3** *athletes in good/poor condition* shape, form, order, fitness, physical fitness, health, state of health, fettle, kilter, trim, working order. **4** *a condition of the job* qualification, requirement, necessity, essential, demand, prerequisite, stipulation; terms. **5** *the conditions of the agreement | make certain conditions* restriction, rule, provision, proviso, contingency, stipulation, prerequisite, limitation, modification; terms, limits. **6** *a heart condition* disease, disorder, illness, complaint, problem, ailment, weakness, infirmity, malady. **7** *people of various conditions* social position, class, rank, status, station, stratum, grade, order, footing, caste, estate.

condition v **1** *lotions conditioning the skin/leather* make healthy, improve, tone, tone up, prepare, make ready. **2** *cats conditioned to live in flats* train, teach, educate, coach, tutor, accustom, adapt, habituate, inure. **3** *childhood experiences conditioning later responses* influence, affect, govern, determine.

conditional adj **1** *an offer conditional on references* dependent on, contingent on, subject to, based upon. **2** *given a conditional offer* qualified, having conditions, with reservations, restrictive, provisional, provisory, stipulatory.

conditioned adj *a conditioned response* learned, trained, taught, habituated.

conditions npl *live in pleasant conditions* circumstances, surroundings, environment, situation, milieu, way of life.

condolence n commiseration, sympathy, fellow feeling, compassion, feeling, pity, solace, comfort.

condom n contraceptive, barrier contraceptive, sheath, French letter; *inf* rubber.

condone v overlook, disregard, let pass, turn a blind eye to, wink at, excuse, pardon, forgive, make allowances for, forget.

conducive adj *hardly conducive to study* contributing, contributory, helpful, instrumental, useful, favourable, advantageous.

conduct n **1** *guilty of evil conduct* behaviour, way of behaving, comportment, bearing, deportment; actions, ways, habits, practices, manners. **2** *the conduct of the war* direction, running, management, administration, organization, control, guidance, supervision, leadership.

conduct v **1** *conduct oneself well/badly* behave, act, comport, deport, acquit. **2** *conduct the proceedings* direct, run, be in charge of, manage, administer, organize, handle, be in control of, control, govern, regulate, supervise, lead, preside over. **3** *conduct us to our seats* show, guide, lead, escort, accompany, take.

conduit n duct, pipe, tube, channel, canal, trough, passageway.

confectionery n sweets, sweetmeats, chocolates, bonbons; *Amer* candy.

confederate n *the villain had his confederates* accomplice, abettor, accessory, ally, associate, collaborator, colleague, partner.

confederate adj *the confederate states* federal, federated, allied, in alliance, associated, united, combined, amalgamated.

confer v **1** *confer a title/favour* bestow, present, grant, award, give, give out, hand out, accord. **2** *confer with her colleagues* have discussions, discuss, talk, consult, converse, exchange views, discourse, parley.

conference n **1** *attend a conference* meeting, congress, convention, seminar, symposium, colloquium, forum, convocation. **2** *be in conference* discussion, consultation, conversation, deliberation, debate, communication, dialogue.

confess v **1** *confess her guilt* admit, acknowledge, make a clean breast of, own up to, declare, make known, disclose, reveal, divulge, blurt out, expose. **2** *criminals forced to confess* own up, admit guilt, plead guilty, accept blame/responsibility, make a clean breast of it, unbosom oneself; *inf* tell all, spill the beans, get something off one's chest. **3** *I must confess I don't know* admit, acknowledge, concede, grant, allow, own, say, declare, affirm, profess, assert.

confession n *listening to their confession* admission, owning-up, disclosure, revelation, divulgence, exposure, acknowledgement, avowal, unbosoming.

confidant, confidante n close friend, bosom friend, friend, crony, intimate, familiar, *alter ego*, second self; *inf* chum, pal, mate, buddy.

confide v **1** *confide a secret to | confide that he was ill* disclose, reveal, divulge, impart, tell, intimate, confess, admit. **2** *confide in a friend* open one's heart to, unburden oneself to, unbosom oneself to, tell one's all to. **3** *confide a task* entrust, consign, hand over, make over, turn over, give over, commit, commend, assign.

confidence n **1** *candidates full of confidence* self-confidence, self-assurance, assurance, self-reliance, self-possession, aplomb, poise, nerve, firmness, courage, boldness, mettle, fortitude. **2** *have no confidence in them* trust, reliance, faith, dependence, belief, credence. **3** *exchange confidences* secret, private affair, confidentiality, intimacy.

confidential adj **1** *confidential information* secret, private, classified, non-public, off-the-record, restricted, personal, intimate, privy; *inf* hush-hush. **2** *a confidential friend* close, bosom, dear, intimate, familiar, trusted, trustworthy, trusty, faithful, reliable, dependable.

confidentially adv *told confidentially* in confidence, in secret, in private, privately, between ourselves, behind closed doors, in camera, *sub rosa*.

confine v **1** *birds confined in a cage* enclose, shut up, shut, cage, keep, coop up, pen, box up, lock up, imprison, intern, hold captive, incarcerate, impound, immure. **2** *remarks confined to the discussion | confined to bed* restrict, limit, keep within the limits of.

confinement n **1** *keep in confinement* custody, imprisonment, detention, captivity, internment, incarceration. **2** *a difficult confinement* childbirth, labour, delivery, lying-in, travail, *accouchement*; *Med* parturition.

confirm v **1** *evidence confirming her statement | a letter confirming a booking* bear out, verify, corroborate, prove, endorse, validate, authenticate, substantiate, give credence to, evidence. **2** *confirm that he would appear* reassert, assert, give assurance, assure, affirm, pledge, promise, guarantee. **3** *confirm his appointment* ratify, endorse, approve, sanction, underwrite, authorize, warrant, accredit. **4** *confirm my doubts* strengthen, make firmer, reinforce, fortify.

confirmation n **1** *confirmation of her statement/booking* verification, corroboration, proof, evidence, endorsement, validation, authentication, substantiation. **2** *confirmation of the appointment* ratification, endorsement, approval, sanction, authorization, accreditation.

confirmed adj *a confirmed bachelor* long-established, established, dyed-in-the-wool, habitual, inveterate, through-and-through, seasoned, inured, settled, set, fixed, rooted.

confiscate v seize, impound, take possession of, appropriate, commandeer, expropriate, sequestrate, sequester, arrogate.

conflagration n blaze, raging fire, wall/sheet of flames, holocaust.

conflict n **1** *the military conflict* battle, fight, war, warfare, clash, engagement, encounter, hostilities, contest, combat, collision, struggle, strife, tussle, scuffle, fracas, scrap; *inf* set-to. **2** *bitter conflict between the families* disagreement, dissension, hostility, feud, discord, friction, strife, antagonism, antipathy, ill will, bad blood, contention. **3** *the conflict between love and duty* clash, variance, divided loyalties, opposition, friction, schism.

conflict v **1** *their opinions conflict* clash, differ, disagree, be at variance, be in opposition, be at odds, be incompatible, collide. **2** *conflict for victory* contend, contest, fight, combat, struggle, strive.

conflicting adj *conflicting opinions/statements* clashing, differing, disagreeing, contradictory, contrary, opposing, incompatible, inconsistent, discordant, paradoxical, at odds, at variance.

conform v **1** *refuse to conform* follow convention, be conventional, comply, obey the rules, adapt, adjust, follow the crowd, run with the pack, swim with the stream. **2** *conform to accepted standards* comply with, fall in with, follow, obey, adapt to, accommodate to, adjust, observe, yield. **3** *conform with my idea of an actor* fit, match, agree with, correspond to, tally with, square with, accord with, harmonize.

conformation n **1** *a rocky conformation* structure, form, shape, formation, framework, build, configuration. **2** *conformation* *to accepted standards* compliance, adjustment, adaptation, accommodation.

conformist n conventionalist, traditionalist, yes-man, stick-in-the-mud.

conformity n 1*noted for their conformity* conventionality, traditionalism, orthodoxy. *see* CONFORM 1. 2 *their conformity to accepted standards* compliance, obedience, observance, adaptation, adjustment, accommodation. *see* CONFORM 2. 3 *having a certain conformity* likeness, similarity, resemblance, correspondence, agreement, harmony, accord, affinity, compatibility, congruity, consonance.

confound v 1 *confounded at the news* dumbfound, astound, amaze, astonish, stun, flabbergast, surprise, startle, disconcert, perplex, puzzle, mystify, baffle, nonplus, confuse, bewilder, dismay. 2 *confound the enemy* defeat, beat, overwhelm, overthrow, trounce. 3 *confound the argument* refute, contradict, demolish, annihilate, explode.

confront v 1 *confronting the enemy* face, face up to, stand up to, resist, defy, oppose, challenge, attack, assault, accost, waylay. 2 *confront one's problems* face, tackle, come to grips with, meet head on. 3 *confront them with the proof* bring face to face, show, present. 4 *the problems confronting us* face, be in one's way, threat, trouble, harass, annoy, molest.

confrontation n *a confrontation with the government* conflict, clash, contest, collision, encounter; *inf* set-to, showdown.

confuse v 1 *confused by all the questions* bewilder, bemuse, perplex, baffle, puzzle, mystify, nonplus, befog. 2 *confuse the issue* muddle, mix up, jumble, throw into disorder, disorder, disarrange, tangle up; *inf* snarl up. 3 *his talk confused with irrelevancies* obscure, make unclear, make indistinct. 4 *confuse the twins with each other* mistake, mix up. 5 *old age confused her mind* muddle, addle, befuddle, disorient, disorientate.

confused adj 1 *a confused recollection* unclear, blurred, indistinct, hazy, foggy, obscure. 2 *a confused mess* muddled, jumbled, untidy, higgledy-piggledy, disordered, disorderly, disarranged, out of order, chaotic, disorganized, upset, topsy-turvy, at sixes and sevens. 3 *a confused old woman* muddled, addled, befuddled, bewildered, dazed, disoriented, disorientated, at sea, unbalanced, unhinged, demented; *inf* discombobulated.

confusing adj *confusing instructions* unclear, puzzling, baffling, complicated, difficult, ambiguous, misleading, inconsistent.

confusion n 1 *people in a state of confusion* bewilderment, perplexity, bafflement, puzzlement, mystification, muddle, disorientation, befuddlement. 2 *the room in a state of confusion* muddle, jumble, jumbledness, untidiness, disorder, chaos, shambles, disorderliness, disarrangement, disorganization. 3 *frightened by the confusion at the airport* muddle, disorganization, bustle, commotion, upheaval, turmoil.

congeal v solidify, harden, coagulate, thicken, set, concentrate, cake.

congenial adj 1 *a congenial companion* genial, agreeable, friendly, pleasant, kindly, pleasing, amiable, nice, companionable, good-natured, sympathetic, compatible, like-minded, kindred. 2 *congenial work/places* agreeable, pleasant, pleasing, nice, suitable, well-suited, fit, favourable.

congenital adj 1 *a congenital disease* inborn, inbred, innate, inherent, constitutional, inherited, hereditary, connate. 2 *a congenital liar|congenital dishonesty* inveterate, dyed-in-the-wool, thorough-going, thorough, utter, complete, established, rooted, ingrained, fixed, settled, set.

congested adj 1 *congested roads* crowded, overcrowded, packed, jammed, blocked, obstructed, overflowing, teeming. 2 *congested lungs/noses* blocked, clogged, choked, plugged, stopped up, gorged.

congestion n 1 *congestion on the roads* overcrowding, crowding, obstruction, jam, bottleneck; *inf* snarl up. 2 *congestion of the lungs* blocking, clogging, choking, plugging.

conglomerate n 1 *an international conglomerate* corporation, multinational, merger, joint concern, firm, company, trust, cartel. 2 *a rocky conglomerate* aggregate, agglomerate.

conglomerate adj *a conglomerate mass* aggregate, agglomerate, amassed, gathered, clustered, combined.

congratulate v wish joy to, felicitate, compliment, offer good wishes to.

congratulations npl felicitations, compliments, good wishes, best wishes, greetings.

congregate v gather, assemble, group, flock together, convene, forgather, meet, amass, crowd, cluster, throng, rendezvous.

congregation n 1 *a congregation of people* gathering, assembly, group, flock, convention, meeting, crowd, conference, congress, mass, throng, conclave, convocation, conventicle. 2 *the minister's congregation* flock, parishioners, parish.

congress n 1 *attend an international congress* assembly, meeting, gathering, conference, convention, convocation, council, synod, conventicle. **2** *join a professional congress* society, association, league, guild. **3** *vote for congress* legislative assembly, legislature, parliament, chamber of deputies, diet; representatives.

conic, conical adj cone-shaped, conoid, pyramid-shaped, pyramidal, tapered, tapering, pointed, funnel-shaped, infundibular.

conjecture v *conjecture that he would win* guess, surmise, speculate, infer, imagine, fancy, suspect, assume, suppose, believe, think, presume, presuppose, theorize, hypothesize.

conjecture n *just a conjecture | open to conjecture* guess, guesstimate, inference, fancy, notion, suspicion, presumption, presupposition, theory, hypothesis; guessing, surmise, surmising, imagination, speculation, theorizing.

conjugal adj connubial, matrimonial, nuptial, marital, married, wedded, spousal, bridal, hymeneal, epithalamic.

conjunction n **1** *the conjunction of workers* association, union, uniting, affiliation, cooperation, combination, collaboration, coaction, alliance, federation. **2** *the conjunction of events* coincidence, co-occurence, simultaneousness, coexistence, contemporaneousness, concomitance.

conjure v **1** *conjuring at the party* juggle, do tricks, do magic. **2** *conjure rabbits from a hat* summon, call up, invoke, rouse, raise up. **conjure up** *conjure up memories* recall, bring/call to mind, call up, evoke, recreate.

connect v **1** *connect the hose to the tap* join, attach, fasten, affix, couple, clamp, secure, rivet, fuse, solder, weld. **2** *a road connecting the villages* join, link, unite, bridge. **3** *houses connecting with each other* adjoin, abut, touch, neighbour, lie next to, border, be adjacent to, impinge upon. **4** *she connects him with sadness* associate, link, relate to, identify, equate, bracket, draw a parallel with.

connection n **1** *the connection has come loose* attachment, fastening, coupling, clamp, clasp, joint. **2** *the connection between the events* link, relationship, relation, relatedness, association, bond, tie-in, correspondence, parallel, analogy. **3** *in connection with this | in that connection* context, reference, frame of reference, relation. **4** *get a job through a connection* contact, friend, acquaintance, ally, associate, sponsor. **5** *dislike her husband's connection* relative, relation, kinsman, kinswoman; kin, kindred.

connive v **1** *connive with others in the plot* conspire, collaborate, collude, be in collusion with, intrigue, plot, scheme, be a party to, abet, be an accessory to. **2** *connive at their behaviour* disregard, overlook, condone, turn a blind eye to, close/shut one's eyes to, let pass, ignore, look the other way, wink at, blink at, gloss over, pass over.

conniving adj *a conniving rogue* scheming, colluding, nasty, unprincipled.

connoisseur n gourmet, epicure, aesthete, arbiter of taste, expert, authority, specialist, pundit, cognoscente, one of the cognoscenti, devotee, aficionado, appreciator, fan, savant; *inf* buff.

connotation n undertone, undermeaning, nuance, hint, intimation, suggestion, implication, allusion, insinuation, reference.

conquer v **1** *conquer the enemy* defeat, beat, overpower, overthrow, vanquish, subdue, rout, trounce, subjugate, triumph over, crush, quell. **2** *conquer the territory* seize, take possession of, occupy, invade, annex, appropriate, overrun, win. **3** *conquer one's fears* overcome, get the better of, vanquish, master, surmount, rise above, prevail over.

conqueror n victor, winner, vanquisher, defeater, subjugator, champion, hero, lord, master, conquistador.

conquest n **1** *the conquest of/over the enemy* conquering, victory, defeat, beating, overpowering, overthrow, vanquishment, rout, trouncing, subjugation, triumph, mastery, crushing, discomfiture. **2** *the conquest of the territory* seizing, possession, occupation, invasion, annexation, appropriation, overrunning, subjection. **3** *the conquest of the young ladies* captivation, enchantment, bewitching, seduction, enticement, enthralment. **4** *yet another of her conquests* captive, catch, acquisition, prize, admirer, fan, adherent, follower, supporter, worshipper; *inf* push-over, walk-over.

conscience n sense of right and wrong, moral sense, still small voice; morals, scruples, principles, ethics.

conscience-stricken adj contrite, penitent, repentant, remorseful, sorry, regretful, guilty, guilt-ridden, troubled, ashamed.

conscientious adj **1** *a conscientious person* diligent, careful, attentive, thorough, meticulous, punctilious, painstaking, hardworking, dedicated. **2** *a conscientious piece of work* careful, thorough, meticulous, precise, accurate, detailed.

conscious adj **1** *a conscious attempt at humour* deliberate, calculated, premeditated, on purpose, reasoned, knowing, studied, willed, volitional. **2** *in a conscious state* awake, aware, sentient, responsive, alert. **3** *conscious of the problem* aware, awake to, alert to, alive to, cognizant, sensible of, percipient; wise to.

consciousness n **1** *regain consciousness* wakefulness, awakeness, awareness, sentience, responsiveness, alertness. **2** *lack of consciousness of the situation* awareness, realization, cognizance, perception, apprehension, recognition.

conscript v *conscript recruits* enlist, recruit, call up, mobilize, levy.

consecrate v **1** *consecrate the building* sanctify, bless, make holy, hallow, dedicate to God. **2** *a life consecrated to religion* dedicate, devote, pledge, commit, vow, set apart.

consecutive adj successive, succeeding, following, in sequence, sequential, serial, in turn, progressive, step-by-step, continuous, uninterrupted, unbroken, chronological, seriate.

consensus n agreement, consent, common consent, unanimity, harmony, concord, unity, concurrence.

consent v *consent to their proposals* agree to, accept, approve, go along with, acquiesce in, accede to, concede to, yield to, give in to, submit to, comply with, abide by, concur with, conform to.

consent n *give their assent* agreement, assent, acceptance, approval, permission, sanction, acquiescence, compliance, concurrence; *inf* go-ahead, OK, green light.

consequence n **1** *the consequence of the decision* result, effect, upshot, outcome, issue, event, end, aftermath, repercussion, reverberation. **2** *a matter of consequence* importance, note, significance, import, moment, weight, substance, portent. **3** *a person of consequence* importance, note, distinction, standing, status, prominence, prestige, eminence, repute, mark, esteem, rank.

consequent adj resulting, resultant, ensuing, following, subsequent, successive, sequential.

consequently adv as a result, therefore, thus, hence, subsequently, accordingly, *ergo*.

conservation n preservation, protection, safeguarding, safekeeping, guarding, saving, care, charge, custody, husbandry, supervision, upkeep, maintenance.

conservative adj **1** *politically conservative* right-wing, reactionary, traditionalist,

Tory. **2** *the young are more conservative than the old* conventional, traditional, reactionary, orthodox, cautious, prudent, careful, moderate, middle-of-the-road, temperate, stable, unchanging, old-fashioned, unprogressive, hide-bound, sober. **3** *a conservative attitude to the environment* conserving, preservative, protective, saving.

conservatory n **1** *plants in the conservatory* greenhouse, glasshouse, hot house. **2** *studying at the conservatory* conservatoire, music school, drama school, academy/institute of music/drama.

conserve v preserve, save, keep, protect, take care of, hoard, store up, husband, use sparingly, reserve, nurse.

consider v **1** *consider your application* think about, weigh up, give thought to, examine, study, mull over, ponder, contemplate, deliberate over, cogitate about, chew over, meditate over, ruminate over, turn over in one's mind. **2** *consider the feelings of others* take into consideration, take into account, make allowances for, respect, bear in mind, have regard to, reckon with, remember. **3** *consider you suitable* think, believe, regard as, deem, hold to be, judge, rate. **4** *consider the horizon* contemplate, look at, observe, regard, survey, view, scrutinize, scan, examine, inspect.

considerable adj **1** *a considerable amount* sizeable, substantial, appreciable, goodly, tolerable, fair, reasonable, tidy, ample, plentiful, abundant, marked, noticeable, comfortable, decent, great, large, lavish. **2** *in considerable pain* much, a lot of, a great deal of, great, a fair amount of. **3** *a considerable artist* distinguished, noteworthy, noted, important, significant, influential, illustrious, renowned.

considerably adv *considerably older* much, very much, a great deal, significantly, substantially, markedly, appreciably.

considerate adj thoughtful, attentive, concerned, solicitous, mindful, heedful, kind, kindly, unselfish, compassionate, sympathetic, patient, charitable, generous, obliging, accommodating.

consideration n **1** *give consideration to the proposal* thought, attention, heed, notice, regard, deliberation, discussion, reflection, contemplation, cogitation, rumination, examination, inspection, scrutiny, analysis, review. **2** *show consideration to their parents* considerateness, thoughtfulness, attentiveness, concern, solicitousness, solicitude, mindfulness, kindness, kindliness, unselfishness, compassion, sympathy, patience, charity, generosity, benevolence, friendliness. **3** *money a major consideration* issue, factor, point, concern, item, detail, aspect. **4** *for a small consideration* payment, fee, remuneration, compensation, recompense, emolument, perquisite. **5** *take age into consideration* account, reckoning, allowance.

considering prep **1** *considering her age* taking into consideration, giving consideration to, bearing in mind, keeping in mind, in view of, in the light of. **2** *she's very well, considering* all things considered, considering everything, all in all.

consign v **1** *consign her to his care* hand over, give over, deliver, assign, entrust, commend, remit, bequeath. **2** *consign to the dustbin | consign to misery* put away, deposit, commit. **3** *consign the package by air* send, dispatch, transmit, convey, post, mail.

consignment n **1** *consignment to his care* handing over, assignment, entrusting, commendation. *see* CONSIGN 1. **2** *the consignment of parcels by air* sending, dispatch, conveyance. *see* CONSIGN 3. **3** *a consignment of coal* delivery, batch, shipment, containerload.

consist v **1** *consist of flour and water* be composed of, be made up of, be formed of, comprise, contain, include, incorporate, embody, involve. **2** *her beauty consisting in her colouring* lie, reside, inhere, have its existence/being, be contained.

consistency n **1** *mix to the right consistency* degree of thickness, degree of density, thickness, density, firmness, solidity, viscosity, cohesion. **2** *attitudes lacking consistency* steadiness, dependability, constancy, uniformity, lack of change, lack of deviation. **3** *the injuries showing consistency with stabbing* compatibility, conformity, congruity, agreement, accordance, consonance.

consistent adj **1** *consistent attitudes* steady, dependable, constant, uniform, unchanging, undeviating, true to type. **2** *injuries consistent with stabbing | behaviour consistent with politeness* compatible, conforming to, congruous, agreeing, accordant, consonant.

consolation n **1** *words of consolation* comfort, solace, sympathy, compassion, pity, commiseration, relief, help, support, cheer, encouragement, soothing, easement, succour, assuagement, alleviation. **2** *the baby is a consolation to her* comfort, solace, help, support.

console v *console the loser* comfort, solace, sympathize with, express sympathy to, pity, commiserate with, help, cheer,

encourage, ease, succour, alleviate, assuage.

consolidate v **1** *consolidate his position* make stronger, strengthen, make secure, secure, make stable, stabilize, reinforce, fortify, cement. **2** *consolidate the territories | firms consolidating* combine, unite, merge, amalgamate, join, affiliate, fuse, federate. **3** *time for the business to consolidate* become stronger, become more secure, stabilize, strengthen one's position.

consonant adj *behaviour consonant with status | consonant to wealth* compatible, consistent, in accordance, in harmony, suitable for, suited to, appropriate to.

consort n *the queen and her consort* spouse, partner, companion, escort; husband, wife.

consort v **consort with 1** *consort with criminals* associate with, keep company with, hang around with, go around with, mix with, spend time with, fraternize with, have dealings with. **2** *conduct consorting ill with his rank* go with, be in harmony with, be consistent with, accord with, be consonant with.

conspicuous adj **1** *conspicuous changes* easily seen, clear, visible, obvious, evident, apparent, noticeable, observable, recognizable, discernible, perceptible, distinguishable, manifest, vivid. **2** *conspicuous colours | conspicuous modern buildings* striking, glaring, obtrusive, blatant, flagrant, showy, garish, bold, ostentatious. **3** *conspicuous members of the community* distinguished, outstanding, prominent, eminent, wellknown, notable, famous, renowned, celebrated, illustrious.

conspiracy n **1** *a conspiracy to overthrow the government* plot, scheme, stratagem, plan, machination, cabal; *inf* frame-up. **2** *guilty of conspiracy* plotting, collusion, intrigue, connivance, collaboration, machination, treason.

conspirator n conspirer, plotter, schemer, intriguer, colluder, collaborator, confederate, cabalist, traitor.

conspire v **1** *conspire against the leader* form a conspiracy, plot, hatch a plot, scheme, intrigue, collude, collaborate, cabal, machinate; *inf* be in cahoots with. **2** *events conspire against us* act together, work together, combine, join, unite, join forces, cooperate, coact, gang up on.

constancy n **1** *her lover's constancy* faithfulness, fidelity, devotion, loyalty, staunchness, dependability, adherence, fealty. **2** *constancy of purpose* firmness, steadfastness, steadiness, resolution, resoluteness, fixedness, determination, perseverance, tenacity, application, doggedness. **3** *constancy of temperature* uniformity, evenness, regularity, stability, steadiness, invariableness, unchangingness, immutability.

constant adj **1** *at a constant speed/temperature* uniform, even, regular, stable, steady, fixed, invariable, unvarying, unchanging, immutable. **2** *a constant stream of people* continuous, unbroken, uninterrupted. **3** *constant chattering* continual, never-ending, endless, unending, non-stop, incessant, unceasing, ceaseless, perpetual, persistent, interminable, unremitting, sustained, relentless, unrelenting. **4** *a constant lover* faithful, devoted, loyal, staunch, dependable, true, trustworthy, trusty. **5** *constant in his purpose* firm, steadfast, steady, resolute, determined, persevering, tenacious, dogged, unwavering, unflagging, unshaken.

constantly adv always, all the time, continually, continuously, endlessly, non-stop, incessantly, ceaselessly, perpetually, persistently, interminably, relentlessly.

consternation n surprise, amazement, astonishment, dismay, bewilderment, perturbation, mystification, confusion, anxiety, distress, alarm, panic, fear, fright, dread, horror, trepidation, shock, terror, awe.

constituent adj *constituent parts* component, integral, elemental, basic, essential.

constituent n **1** *analyse the constituents* component, component part, part, ingredient, element, integral part, unit, piece, fragment. **2** *talking to his constituents* voter, elector.

constitute v **1** *the countries that constitute the European Union* form, make up, compose, comprise. **2** *a suggestion constituting a warning* be tantamount to, be the equivalent of, be, be regarded as, act as. **3** *constitute a committee* appoint, inaugurate, formally establish, authorize, commission, charter, induct, invest, empower, ordain. **4** *constitute a new school* establish, found, set up, institute, create.

constitution n **1** *the British constitution | the society's constitution* body of law, system of laws/rules, code, charter, canon; laws, rules, fundamental principles. **2** *the constitution of the committees varies* composition, make-up, structure, organization. **3** *the constitution of a new school* establishment, founding, foundation, setting up, institution, creation. **4** *people having a strong constitution* state of health, health, physique, physical condition, physical strength. **5** *peo-*

ple of a nervous constitution mental make-up, disposition, temperament, temper, nature, character, mood.

constitutional adj **1** *a constitutional body* constituted, legal, lawful, legitimate, authorized, statutory, chartered, vested. **2** *a constitutional weakness* inherent, inbred, intrinsic, congenital, organic, inborn, innate.

constitutional n *go for a constitutional* walk, stroll, saunter, turn, airing.

constrain v **1** *feel constrained to cooperate* force, compel, coerce, drive, impel, oblige, press, pressure, pressurize, urge, railroad, hustle. **2** *research constrained by lack of resources* hold back, restrict, hinder, impede, hamper, limit, curb, check, restrain. **3** *constrain political opponents* restrain, restrict, curb, confine, chain, shut in, lock up, imprison, incarcerate.

constrained adj *a constrained manner* forced, uneasy, unnatural, inhibited, reserved, reticent, guarded.

constraint n **1** *act under constraint* force, compulsion, coercion, obligation, pressure, impulsion. **2** *no constraints on their activities* restriction, hindrance, impediment, hampering, limitation, curb, check, restraint, damper. **3** *subject political opponents to constraint* restraint, restriction, confinement, imprisonment, incarceration. see CONSTRAIN 3. **4** *constraint of manner* forcedness, uneasiness, unnaturalness, inhibition, reservedness, reticence, guardedness, repression.

constrict v **1** *constricted blood vessels* narrow, make smaller, tighten, compress, contract, squeeze, strangle, strangulate. **2** *constrict the flow of traffic* impede, obstruct, hinder, hamper, limit, restrict, check, curb, inhibit.

construct v **1** *construct a housing estate | construct a bridge* build, erect, put up, set up, raise, elevate, establish, assemble, manufacture, fabricate, make. **2** *construct a plan/theory* form, formulate, put together, create, devise, design, invent, compose, fashion, mould, model, shape, frame, forge, engineer, fabricate, manufacture.

construction n **1** *a bridge under construction* building, erection, elevation, establishment, assembly, manufacture, fabrication. see CONSTRUCT 1. **2** *an impressive construction* structure, building, edifice, assembly, framework. **3** *the construction of a sentence* composition, formation, structure. **4** *put a different construction on her words* interpretation, reading, meaning, explanation, inference, explication.

constructive adj *constructive suggestions* useful, helpful, productive, practical, positive, valuable.

consul n attaché, consul general; consulate, consulship.

consult v **1** *consult an expert* ask, seek advice/information from, call in, turn to, take counsel from. **2** *consult a reference book* look up, refer to, turn to. **3** *consult with his colleagues* confer, discuss, talk, talk over, exchange views, deliberate, parley, powwow, palaver; *inf* talk turkey. **4** *consult her feelings before acting* consider, take into consideration/account, have regard to, respect, have an eye to.

consultant n **1** *a business consultant* adviser, expert, authority. **2** *a hospital consultant* senior doctor, specialist.

consultation n **1** *have a consultation with one's adviser* meeting, talk, discussion, interview, session, audience, tête-à-tête, parley, powwow, colloquy. **2** *international consultations* conference, convention, symposium, forum, session, seminar.

consume v **1** *consume cakes/lemonade* eat, eat up, drink, drink up, devour, ingest, swallow, gobble, gobble up, guzzle, snack on; *inf* tuck into, scoff, down, put away, polish off, graze on. **2** *consumed by a desire* absorb, preoccupy, engross, eat up, devour, obsess, grip, monopolize, enthral. **3** *buildings consumed by fire* destroy, demolish, lay waste, wipe out, annihilate, devastate, raze, gut, ravage. **4** *cars consuming too much petrol* use, use up, utilize, expend, deplete, exhaust, waste, squander, drain, dissipate, fritter away.

consumer n user, buyer, purchaser, customer, shopper, client, patron.

consuming adj *a consuming passion* absorbing, compelling, pre-occupying, engrossing, devouring, obsessive, gripping, overwhelming.

consummate adj complete, total, utter, absolute, perfect, superb, supreme, superior, ultimate, accomplished, expert, proficient, skilful, skilled, masterly, talented, gifted, polished, practised.

consummate v *consummate his life's work* put the finishing touch to, perfect, complete, finish, accomplish, achieve, execute, carry out, perform, end, conclude, effectuate, crown, cap, set the seal on.

consumption n **1** *unfit for human consumption* eating, drinking, devouring, ingestion. *see* CONSUME 1. **2** *consumption by fire* destruction, demolition, annihilation, devastation, razing, gutting. *see* CONSUME 3. **3** *the con-*

sumption of petrol using, using up, utilization, expending, expenditure, depletion, exhaustion, waste, draining, dissipation. *see* CONSUME 4.

contact n **1** *following contact with chemicals | on contact with an infected person* touch, touching, proximity, exposure, contiguity, junction, union, tangency. **2** *be in contact with* touch, communication, connection, correspondence, association. **3** *get a job through contacts* connection, acquaintance.

contact v *contact head office* get/be in touch with, get hold of, communicate with, be in communication with; write to, write, notify, phone, call, ring up, speak to, reach.

contagious adj catching, communicable, transmittable, transmissible, transferable, spreadable, infectious, epidemic, pandemic, pestilential, pestiferous, epizootic.

contain v **1** *the boat contained four people* hold, have capacity for, carry, accommodate, seat. **2** *the committee contains six members* include, comprise, embrace, take in, incorporate, involve. **3** *could not contain themselves | contain your mirth* keep back, hold in, restrain, control, keep under control, keep in check, suppress, repress, curb, stifle.

container n receptacle, vessel, holder, repository.

contaminate v make impure, pollute, adulterate, defile, debase, corrupt, taint, infect, foul, spoil, soil, sully, tarnish, stain, befoul, vitiate, radioactivate.

contemplate v **1** *contemplate the portrait* look at, view, regard, examine, inspect, observe, survey, scrutinize, scan, stare at, gaze at, eye. **2** *contemplate the future* think about, meditate over, consider, ponder, reflect over, mull over, muse on, dwell on, deliberate over, cogitate over, ruminate over, turn over in one's mind. **3** *he is contemplating going* think about, give thought to, consider, have in mind/view, envisage, intend, plan, propose, aim at, foresee, expect to.

contemplation n **1** *his contemplation of the painting* viewing, examination, inspection, observation, survey, scrutiny, scanning, gazing at, eyeing. *see* CONTEMPLATE 1. **2** *contemplation of the future* meditation, consideration, pondering, reflection, rumination, deliberation, cogitation. *see* CONTEMPLATE 2. **3** *lost in contemplation* thought, meditation, reflection; *inf* brown study.

contemplative adj *a contemplative mood/look* thoughtful, pensive, reflective, meditative, musing, ruminative, introspective, intent, rapt, deep/lost in thought; *inf* in a brown study.

contemporary adj **1** *Shakespeare and his contemporary writers* contemporaneous, coexisting, coexistent, concurrent, coeval, synchronous; *fml* coetaneous. **2** *contemporary fashion* modern, present-day, present, current, present-time, up-to-date, up-to-the-minute, fashionable, latest, recent, ultramodern, newfangled, à la mode; *inf* with it.

contemporary n *Yeats and his contemporaries* peer, compeer, fellow.

contempt n **1** *feel/show contempt for the bully* scorn, disdain, disrespect, condescension, derision, mockery, disgust, loathing, abhorrence, contumely. **2** *fined for contempt of court* disregard, disrespect, slighting, neglect, contumely.

contemptible adj *contemptible behaviour* despicable, detestable, ignominious, lamentable, pitiful, low, mean, shameful, abject, unworthy, worthless, base, vile, shabby, cheap, sordid, degenerate.

contemptuous adj *with a contemptuous shrug* scornful, disdainful, disrespectful, insulting, insolent, derisory, derisive, mocking, sneering, jeering, condescending, supercilious, arrogant, high and mighty; *fml* contumelious.

contend v **1** *armies contending with each other | the contending teams* compete, oppose, challenge, vie, contest, clash, strive, struggle, tussle, grapple, wrestle, scuffle, skirmish, battle, combat, fight, war, wage war, join battle, cross swords. **2** *contending with problems* cope with, face, grapple with, take on, pit oneself against. **3** *contend that he's mad* state, declare, assert, maintain, hold, claim, profess, allege, affirm, aver, pronounce.

content[1] n **1** *the content of the mixture* component parts/elements. *see* CONTENTS 1. **2** *the essay content is good, the style poor* subject matter, subject, material, substance, matter, theme, ideas, burden, gist. **3** *foods with a low sodium content* amount, proportion, quantity. **4** *the boiler's content* volume, capacity, size.

content[2] adj *content with life* contented, satisfied, pleased, happy, cheerful, glad, gratified, fulfilled, at ease, at peace, comfortable, serene, tranquil, unworried, untroubled, complacent.

content[2] n *filled with content* contentment, contentedness, satisfaction, pleasure, happiness. *see* CONTENTMENT.

content[2] v **1** *content oneself with a little* make content, satisfy, be pleased/happy/glad, be fulfilled, be gratified. **2** *sweets will content the child* pacify, placate, soothe, appease, mollify.

contented adj content, satisfied, pleased. *see* CONTENT[2] adj.

contention n **1** *two groups in contention for the title* competition, contest, rivalry, vying, opposition, striving, struggle, tussle, grappling, combat, battle, fighting, war. *see* CONTEND 1. **2** *much contention between the families* argument, disagreement, quarreling, dispute, discord, feuding, hostility, enmity, strife, dissension. **3** *it was her contention that she won* argument, assertion, declaration, affirmation, allegation, claim, stand, position, opinion, view, belief, thesis.

contentious adj **1** *contentious people* argumentative, quarrelsome, bickering, wrangling, disputatious, captious, factious, cavilling, litigious, competitive, combative, pugnacious, cross, perverse, querulous. **2** *a contentious subject* controversial, disputable, debatable, controvertible.

contentment n content, contentedness, satisfaction, pleasure, happiness, cheerfulness, gladness, gratification, fulfilment, ease, comfort, peace, equanimity, serenity, tranquillity, repletion, complacency.

contents npl **1** *the contents of the mixture/box* constituents, components, ingredients, elements, items; content, load; *inf* guts. **2** *the contents of the book* text, subject matter, theme; sections, divisions, chapters.

contest n **1** *take part in a sports/dancing contest* competition, match, game, event, tournament, meet, trial. **2** *a leadership contest* struggle, vying, conflict, battle, fight, combat, tussle, skirmish.

contest v **1** *contest the seat* compete for, contend for, vie for, fight for, fight over, battle for, struggle for, tussle for. **2** *contest the decision* challenge, question, call into question, oppose, doubt, dispute, object to, litigate. **3** *contest the point* argue, debate, dispute, quarrel over, be in contention about.

contestant n competitor, entrant, candidate, participant, player, contender, rival, opponent, adversary, antagonist, aspirant.

context n **1** *in the present financial context* circumstances, conditions; situation, state of affairs, background, environment. **2** *take a statement out of its context* text, frame of reference, contextual relationship, subject, theme, topic.

contiguous adj touching, in contact, meeting, joining, connecting, abutting, bordering, neighbouring, adjacent, near, nearby, close, vicinal.

continent adj 1 *continent in one's drinking habits* self-restrained, abstemious, abstinent, sober, austere, ascetic, self-denying. 2 *sexually continent* chaste, celibate, pure, virtuous, self-restrained, virgin, virginal.

contingency n chance event, event, eventuality, incident, happening, occurrence, juncture, accident, chance, possibility, fortuity, emergency, uncertainty.

contingent adj 1 *help contingent upon resources* conditional on, dependent on, subject to, hinging on, controlled by. 2 *contingent effects* chance, incidental, accidental, possible, fortuitous, uncertain, random, haphazard.

contingent n *an advance contingent* detachment, group, party, body, division, section, company, complement, deputation, mission; *inf* bunch.

continual adj 1 *continual complaints* frequent, repeated, constant, regular, persistent, habitual, recurrent, repetitive, oft-repeated. 2 *continual noise* continuous, perpetual, endless, constant, interminable. *see* CONTINUOUS.

continually adv *continually interrupted* frequently, repeatedly, constantly, regularly, habitually, recurrently.

continuance n continuation, persistence, staying power, endurance, survival, protraction.

continuation n 1 *support the continuation of the search* continuance, carrying on, extension, furtherance, prolongation, perpetuation, continuity, progression. 2 *favour the continuation of the search in the morning* resumption, renewal, recommencement. 3 *appreciate the continuation of the story | the continuation of Godber's TV play* sequel, postscript, addition, supplement, appendix. 4 *the road is a continuation of the High Street* extension, prolongation.

continue v 1 *the desert continues for miles* go on, extend, keep on, carry on, maintain course, drag on. 2 *the firm may continue* go on, carry on, last, remain, stay, endure, survive, live on, persist, subsist, abide. 3 *continue the session as long as possible* maintain, sustain, retain, prolong, protract, perpetuate, preserve. 4 *continue trying* go on, carry on, keep on, keep at, not stop, persist in, persevere in, prolong, pursue; *inf* stick with/at. 5 *continue the search after a break* resume, renew, recommence, start again,

carry on with, return to, take up. 6 *continue after lunch* go on, carry on, resume, recommence, proceed, pick up where one has left off.

continuity n 1 *ensure continuity of supplies* continuousness, uninterruptedness, flow, regular flow, progression. 2 *lack of continuity in the prose* cohesion, coherence, connection, interrelatedness, linkage, sequence.

continuous adj *a continuous supply | continuous noise* uninterrupted, unbroken, consecutive, constant, without stopping, non-stop, perpetual, ceaseless, incessant, unceasing, unremitting, endless, everlasting, interminable, undivided.

contort v twist, wrench/bend out of shape, wrap, deform, misshape.

contour n outline, silhouette, profile, figure, shape, form; lines, curves.

contraband n *accused of contraband* smuggling, illegal traffic, trafficking, black marketing, black marketeering, bootlegging, drug trafficking.

contraband adj *contraband goods* illegal, illicit, unlawful, prohibited, banned, proscribed, taboo, interdicted, smuggled, black-market, bootleg, bootlegged.

contraceptive n oral contraceptive, birth-control pill, the pill, the mini-pill, the morning-after pill, barrier contraceptive, diaphragm, IUD, intrauterine device, coil, loop, condom, sheath; *Amer* prophylactic; *inf* rubber, French letter.

contract n agreement, compact, covenant, pact, settlement, arrangement, understanding, transaction, bargain, deal, treaty, concordant, convention, bond, commitment, entente, *entente cordiale*.

contract v 1 *metals contracting* get smaller, become smaller, become shorter, shrink, reduce, shrivel. 2 *contracting metals* make smaller, make shorter, shrink. *see* CONTRACTION. 3 *blood vessels contracting | muscles contracting* become narrower, narrow, tighten, become tighter, tense, draw in. 4 *contract your muscles* make narrower, narrow, constrict, tighten, make tighter, tense, draw in. 5 *contract a word/text* shorten, abbreviate, abridge, lessen, compress, condense, curtail, concentrate, précis, summarize, synopsize. 6 *contract with them to do the work* arrange, agree, reach an arrangement, establish, come to terms, negotiate, bargain, strike a bargain, close/clinch a deal, close, engage, settle, covenant. 7 *contract a disease* catch, get, come/go down with, develop, become infected with, be afflicted with. **8** *contract a debt* incur, acquire, fall into.

contraction n **1** *the contraction of metals* getting smaller, shrinking. *see* CONTRACT v 1, 2. **2** *the contraction of blood vessels|muscle contraction* narrowing, tightening, constricting, tensing. *see* CONTRACT v 3, 4. **3** *pregnant women experiencing contractions* muscletightening/-tensing, womb-tightening, cramps. **4** *isn't is a contraction* shortened form, short form, shortening, elision, abridgement, abbreviation.

contradict v **1** *contradict his father* say the opposite of, oppose, challenge, counter, be at variance with. **2** *contradict his father's statement* say the opposite of, oppose, deny, challenge, dispute, counter, refute, rebut, be at variance with, controvert, impugn, confute. **3** *the two set of facts contradict each other* be at variance with, disagree with, be in conflict with, clash, contravene, run counter to, be inconsistent with, dissent from, negate.

contradiction n **1** *the contradiction of his statement* denial, disputing, countering, refuting, rebuttal, controverting, impugning, confutation. **2** *the contradiction between the two statements* variance, variation, disagreement, conflict, clash, inconsistency, dissension, contravention, negation.

contradictory adj **1** *hold a contradictory view* opposing, opposite, dissentient, dissenting, contrary, dissident; at variance, at odds. **2** *contradictory statements* contradicting, disagreeing, conflicting, clashing, contrasting, incompatible, irreconcilable, inconsistent, incongruous, contravening, negating, antithetical.

contraption n device, machine, mechanism, gadget, contrivance, apparatus, invention, appliance; *inf* thingumajig, thingumabob, whatsit, doodah, gismo.

contrary adj **1** *holding contrary views* opposite, opposing, contradictory, clashing, conflicting, contrasting, incompatible, irreconcilable, inconsistent, incongruous, antithetical. **2** *a contrary young woman* perverse, awkward, wilful, wayward, obstinate, stubborn, headstrong, pigheaded, unaccommodating, intractable, recalcitrant, intransigent, refractory, cantankerous; *inf* stroppy, cussed; *Scot inf* thrawn.

contrary n *the contrary is true* opposite, antithesis, reverse, contrariety. **on the contrary** quite the opposite, just the reverse, not at all, conversely, in contrast.

contrary adv **contrary to** against, in opposition to, not in accord with.

contrast n **1** *a marked contrast between them* difference, dissimilarity, distinction, disparity, dissimilitude, differentiation, distinguishment. **2** *he is a complete contrast to his brother* opposite, foil, antithesis. **3** *fair by contrast with his sister* comparison, differentiation, distinguishment.

contrast v **1** *contrast the two writers* compare, juxtapose, set side by side, distinguish, differentiate, discriminate. **2** *theories and actions contrast sharply* form a contrast, contradict, be at variance, be contrary, diverge, differ.

contravene v **1** *contravene a law* disobey, break, infringe, violate, transgress. **2** *evidence contravening the theory* contradict, be in conflict with, be in opposition to, clash with, be at variance with, run counter to, refute, rebut.

contretemps n mishap, misadventure, unfortunate occurrence, accident, awkward moment.

contribute v **1** *contribute money/help to the charity* give, donate, subscribe, give a donation/subscription, hand out, present, grant, endow, bestow, accord, confer, provide, supply, furnish; *inf* chip in, pitch in. **2** *contributing articles to magazines* supply, provide. **3** *sensible eating contributing to good health* be conducive to, lead to, be instrumental in, have a hand in, bear a part in, add to, conduce to, help, promote, advance.

contribution n **1** *contributions to the fund* donation, gift, subscription, offering, present, grant, bestowal, allowance, subsidy, endowment. **2** *accept contributions to the paper* article, piece, story, item. **3** *contribution to the discussion* input, participation; *inf* one's pennyworth.

contributor n **1** *the charity's contributors* giver, donor, subscriber, patron, supporter, backer, benefactor, subsidizer. **2** *newspaper contributors* correspondent, journalist, reporter, columnist, writer, critic, reviewer, freelance writer, freelance.

contrite adj penitent, repentant, remorseful, regretful, sorry, chastened, consciencestricken, guilt-ridden, in sackcloth and ashes.

contrivance n **1** *a contrivance for ploughing* device, invention, gadget, contraption, appliance, apparatus, implement, tool, machine, mechanism, equipment, gear, tackle. **2** *fooled by a clever contrivance* stratagem, scheme, ruse, trick, plot, plan, dodge, intrigue, machination, expedient, fabrication, artifice. **3** *have to admire the contrivance* *of the plotter* inventiveness, ingenuity, creativity, originality.

contrive v **1** *contrive a brilliant scheme* devise, concoct, engineer, invent, originate, create, construct, design, plan, work out, think/dream up, plot, fabricate. **2** *contrive to win* manage, find a way, engineer, manoeuvre, plot, plan, intrigue, scheme.

contrived adj unnatural, artificial, forced, strained, laboured, overdone, elaborate, planned, invented, non-spontaneous.

control v **1** *control the organization* be in control of, be in charge of, head, manage, direct, preside over, conduct, be in authority over, command, rule, govern, lead, supervise, superintend, oversee, dominate, master, reign over, be in the driver's seat of, be in the saddle of; *inf* be the boss of. **2** *control prices | control the fire* keep in check, restrain, curb, contain, hold back, restrict, limit, regulate, constrain, subdue, bridle. **3** *control the traffic/machine* regulate, guide, monitor, steer, pilot.

control n **1** *have control over the organization* charge, management, authority, power, command, direction, rule, government, jurisdiction, supervision, superintendence, guidance, dominance, mastery, reign, supremacy. **2** *get control of oneself* self-control, self-restraint, restraint, hold, check, curb, constraint. **3** *arms control | import controls* limitation, restriction, regulation, restraint, check, curb, brake. **4** *used as an experimental control* standard of comparison, standard, check. **5** *mission control* headquarters, base, centre of operations, command post.

controls npl **1** *import controls* means of limitation/restriction. *see* CONTROL n 3. **2** *the machine's controls* instruments, levers, switches, dials, knobs; control panel, console, dashboard.

controversial adj open to discussion/question, disputed, disputable, debatable, under discussion, at issue, contentious, contended, controvertible.

controversy n dispute, argument, debate, disagreement, dissension, contention, altercation, wrangle, wrangling, quarrelling, squabbling, bickering, polemic.

contumely n insult, scorn, derision, abuse, insolence, rudeness, churlishness, discourtesy.

contusion n bruise, discoloration, blemish, injury, bump, lump.

conundrum n **1** *children solving conundrums* riddle, puzzle, wordgame; *inf* brain-teaser. **2** *a conundrum for the politicians* puzzle,

problem, difficult question, enigma, mystery.

convalescence n recovery, recuperation, improvement, getting better, rehabilitation, return to health, mending, restoration.

convene v **1** *convene a meeting* call, call together, summon, convoke, round up, rally. **2** *the meeting convened* assemble, gather, collect, congregate, meet, forgather, muster.

convenience n **1** *books arranged alphabetically for convenience* accessibility, handiness, availability. **2** *the convenience of the time* suitability, appropriateness, fitness, fittingness, favourableness, advantageousness, opportuneness, propitiousness, timeliness, expedience, usefulness, utility, serviceability. **3** *do it at your convenience* suitable opportunity, leisure, freedom, spare moment, spare time, free time. **4** *for the convenience of all* service, use, benefit, advantage, accommodation, enjoyment, satisfaction, comfort, ease. **5** *few conveniences in the kitchen* gadget, labour-saving device, appliance, device, appurtenance, amenity, facility.

convenient adj **1** *shops convenient for the houses* accessible, handy, at hand, close at hand, within reach, nearby, just round the corner, at one's fingertips, available, propinquant. **2** *choose a convenient time/setting* suitable, suited, appropriate, fit, fitting, favourable, advantageous, opportune, timely, well-timed, seasonable, expedient, useful, serviceable.

convent n nunnery, religious community, priory, motherhouse; convent school.

convention n **1** *a medical convention* conference, congress, gathering, meeting, assembly, convocation, council of delegates/representatives, synod, conclave. **2** *follow convention | obey the conventions* conventionality, etiquette, formality, protocol, propriety, code, punctilio, custom, tradition, usage, practice. **3** *draw up a convention between countries* agreement, contract, pact, treaty, bargain, deal, compact, concordat.

conventional adj **1** *conventional behaviour/attitudes* accepted, expected, customary, usual, standard, regular, normal, ordinary, correct, decorous, proper, orthodox, traditional, prevailing, prevalent, conformist, conservative, formal, ritual; *inf* square, strait-laced. **2** *conventional works of art* run-of-the-mill, commonplace, common, ordinary, everyday, common-or-garden, prosaic, routine, stereotyped, pedestrian, hackneyed, unoriginal, clichéd, trite, platitudinous, bourgeois.

converge v **1** *lines/opinions converging* meet, intersect, join, merge, unite, come together, become one, coincide, concur. **2** *crowds converging on the palace* approach, move towards, come closer to, close in on, centre on, focus on.

conversant adj acquainted with, familiar with, knowledgeable about, well-versed in, informed about, well-informed about, apprised of, *au fait* with, experienced in, proficient in, practised in, skilled in; *inf* well up on.

conversation n **1** *deep in conversation* talk, discussion, chat, dialogue, discourse, communication, conference, gossip, colloquy, intercourse. **2** *having a conversation* talk, discussion, chat, dialogue, exchange, gossip, powwow, tête-à-tête; *inf* chinwag, confab.

conversational adj **1** *conversational English* informal, colloquial, chatty. **2** *a conversational person/talent* communicative, expansive, talkative, chatty, loquacious, garrulous, voluble.

converse[1] v *converse with others* talk, speak, discuss, chat, have a talk/discussion with, communicate with.

converse[1] n *deep in converse* conversation, talk, discussion. *see* CONVERSATION.

converse[2] n *the converse is true* opposite, contrary, reverse, antithesis, obverse, other side of the coin; *inf* flip side.

converse[2] adj *converse views* opposite, opposing, contrary, reverse, counter, antithetical, obverse.

conversion n **1** *the conversion of coal/liquid to gas* change, transformation, metamorphosis, transfiguration, transmutation, sea change; *inf* transmogrification. **2** *the conversion of the building* alteration, adaptation, modification, reshaping, refashioning, remodelling, remaking, reconstruction, rebuilding. **3** *religious conversion* reformation, regeneration, proselytization. **4** *the conversion of yards to metres | conversion of pounds to dollars* change, turning, exchange, substitution, switch.

convert v **1** *convert coal/liquid to gas* change, transform, metamorphose, transfigure, transmute; *inf* transmogrify. **2** *the sofa converts to a bed* change into, make into, adapt to, transform into. **3** *convert the building* alter, adapt, modify, reshape, refashion, remodel, restyle, remake, reconstruct, rebuild, reorganize. **4** *convert the heathens* reform, regenerate, convince, cause to change beliefs, bring to God, baptize, proselytize, cause to be reborn. **5** *convert yards to metres | convert pounds to dollars* change,

turn into; exchange for, substitute by, switch from.

convey v **1** *convey the goods* transport, carry, bring, fetch, bear, move, shift, transfer, cart, lug. **2** *pipes conveying water* conduct, transmit, channel, guide. **3** *convey information | convey the idea* transmit, pass on, hand on, send, dispatch, communicate, make known, impart, relate, announce, tell, reveal, disclose. **4** *convey property* give the rights to, transfer, transmit, grant, cede, devolve, lease, bequeath, will; *Law* demise.

conveyance n **1** *by public conveyance* transport, transportation, carriage, transfer, transference, transmission, movement, haulage, portage, cartage, shipment, freightage. **2** *the conveyance broke down* transport, vehicle; car, bus, coach, van, lorry. **3** *the conveyance of information* transmission, passing on, communication, imparting. *see* CONVEY 3. **4** *conveyance of property* transfer, granting, ceding, cession. *see* CONVEY 4.

convict v *convict him of the crime* declare/find/pronounce/judge guilty, sentence, condemn.

convict n *ex-convicts getting jobs* prisoner, jailbird, criminal, offender, law-breaker, felon; *inf* crook, con, old lag.

conviction n **1** *she has previous convictions* declaration/pronouncement of guilt, sentence, judgement, condemnation. **2** *she spoke with conviction* confidence, assurance, belief, certainty, certitude, persuasion, firmness, trust, earnestness. **3** *my conviction is that he is dead* belief, opinion, view, thought, idea, persuasion. **4** *a person of conviction* principle, belief, faith, creed.

convince v **1** *she convinced me that I was wrong* make one certain, prove to, satisfy, assure, reassure. **2** *convince him to vote for them* persuade, prevail upon, sway, talk round, bring around, win over.

convincing adj **1** *a convincing argument* cogent, powerful, persuasive, plausible, incontrovertible, conclusive. **2** *a convincing person* persuasive, plausible, credible. **3** *a convincing victory* impressive, decisive, conclusive.

convivial adj genial, cordial, sociable, friendly, affable, amiable, congenial, agreeable, jolly, cheerful.

convocation n assembly, gathering, meeting, congregation, conference, convention, congress, conclave, synod.

convolution n **1** *carvings with curves and convolutions* twist, turn, coil, spiral, curl, twirl, kink, curlicue, whorl, sinuosity. **2** *the convo-*

lutions of the plot complication, complexity, involvement, entanglement.

convoy n **1** *the convoy set off* group, company, assemblage, line, fleet, cortège, caravan. **2** *a fleet/company under convoy* escort, protection, guard, bodyguard, defence, shield, guidance.

convoy v **1** *convoy a company of ships* escort, accompany, attend, protect, guard, defend, guide, shepherd, flank. **2** *convoy the children home* escort, accompany, go along with, attend, chaperon.

convulse v **1** *audiences convulsed with laughter* shake, churn up, discompose, unsettle. **2** *a city convulsed with rioting* shake, agitate, disturb, upset, disorder, unsettle, wrack. **3** *the comedian convulsed the audience* greatly amuse/entertain, divert; *inf* slay, knock, knock them dead, crack up.

convulsion n **1** *the child went into convulsions* fit, seizure, paroxysm, spasm, contractions, attack. **2** *political convulsions in the city* turmoil, tumult, commotion, upheaval, agitation, disturbance, disruption, unrest, upset, disorder, chaos. **3** *have the audience in convulsions* uncontrollable laughter, fit of laughter, paroxysm.

cook v **1** *cook a dish/meal* prepare, put together, improvise; bake, roast, grill, stew, steam, braise, sauté, fry, deep-fry. **2** *cook the books* falsify, forge, alter. **3** *what's cooking?* happen, occur, take place. **cook up** concoct, make up, put together, devise, invent, create, contrive, fabricate, prepare, improvise, plot, plan, scheme.

cool adj **1** *a cool drink | cool weather* fresh, refreshing, coldish, chilly, chilled, chilling, nippy, unheated, sunless, windy, breezy, draughty. **2** *keep cool in an emergency* calm, composed, collected, self-possessed, self-controlled, level-headed, unexcited, unperturbed, unmoved, unruffled, unemotional, relaxed, placid, quiet, serene; *inf* together. **3** *a cool young woman* aloof, distant, reserved, stand-offish, unfriendly, offhand, unwelcoming, uncommunicative, frigid, chilly, impassive, undemonstrative, unresponsive, apathetic, unenthusiastic, lukewarm, indifferent, unconcerned, uninterested, incurious. **4** *the cool way she stole* bold, audacious, brazen, presumptuous, overconfident, impudent, insolent, impertinent, forward, cheeky, shameless. **5** *a cool attempt at murder* calculated, premeditated, planned, deliberate, intentional, purposeful. **6** *thinks she's really cool* sophisticated, urbane, cosmopolitan, elegant; *inf* streetwise. **7** *what a cool idea* marvellous, excellent, very good, splendid; *inf* Al.

cool v **1** *cool the milk* cool down, make cold/colder, chill, refrigerate, freeze. **2** *the metal/milk cooled* cool down, become cold/colder, lose heat. **3** *cool his ardour* lessen, abate, moderate, temper, diminish, reduce, dampen, quiet, soothe, assuage, allay, mollify, settle. **4** *his ardour cooled* cool off, lessen, abate, moderate, diminish.

cool n **1** *lose one's cool* self-control, control, calmness, composure, poise, self-possession, self-discipline. **2** *the cool of the evening* coolness, freshness, crispness, coldness, chill.

coop n *chicken's coop* cage, pen, enclosure, hutch, pound, lock-up.

coop v **coop up** *chickens/children cooped up* cage, cage/pen in, confine, enclose, hem in, shut/lock up, imprison, immure.

cooperate v **1** *cooperate in the venture* work together, act/pull together, join forces, unite, act jointly, combine, collaborate, pool resources, conspire, connive, concur, coordinate, coact. **2** *he'll be released if he cooperates* be of assistance, assist, help, lend a hand, contribute, aid, abet, participate, go along; *inf* pitch in, play ball.

cooperation n **1** *the cooperation between the departments* combined effort, working together, joint action, unity, collaboration, connivance, concurrence, coordination, teamwork, give and take, synergy. **2** *thank you for your cooperation* assistance, help, aid, contribution, helping hand, participation, support, backing, good offices.

cooperative adj **1** *a cooperative venture* joint, united, shared, unified, combined, concerted, collected, coordinated, collaborative, coactive. **2** *the public being cooperative* of assistance, assisting, helpful, helping, obliging, accommodating, aiding, contributing, participating, responsive.

coordinate v **1** *coordinate the effort* arrange, organize, order, integrate, synchronize, correlate, harmonize, systematize. **2** *coordinating for the common good* cooperate, unite, combine, collaborate, coact, interrelate.

cope v *single parents unable to cope* manage, succeed, survive, carry on, get through, get on, get along, get by, subsist, make the grade, come through, hold one's own; *inf* make out. **cope with** *cope with the situation* handle, deal with, treat, weather, contend with, take care of, dispose of, grapple with, wrestle with, struggle with, tussle with.

copious adj abundant, superabundant, plentiful, plenteous, ample, profuse, full, extensive, generous, lavish, rich, liberal, bounteous, bountiful, exuberant, luxuriant, overflowing, abounding.

copse n thicket, grove, wood, coppice, boscage; *Amer* brush.

copy n **1** *a copy of the document* facsimile, duplicate, duplication, carbon, carbon copy, photocopy, Xerox, Photostat, transcript. **2** *a clever copy of the vase* imitation, reproduction, replica, replication, likeness, counterfeit, forgery, fake, sham. **3** *three copies of the paper* specimen, example, sample.

copy v **1** *copy the document* duplicate, photocopy, Xerox, Photostat, transcribe. **2** *copy the vase/painting* reproduce, replicate, forge, counterfeit. **3** *copy his style* imitate, mimic, emulate, follow, echo, mirror, simulate, ape, parrot.

cord n **1** string, rope, twine, cable, line, ligature. **2** *cords of friendship* bond, link, tie, connection.

cordial adj **1** *a cordial welcome* friendly, warm, genial, affable, amiable, pleasant, gracious, warm-hearted, good-natured, welcoming, sincere, affectionate, hearty, whole-hearted, heart-felt. **2** *cordial dislike* intense, acute, strong, fierce, keen, whole-hearted, heart-felt.

cordon n **1** *a police/military cordon* barrier, line, chain, ring; picket line. **2** *wearing a cordon indicating rank* braid, cord, ribbon, riband, sash, decoration.

cordon v **cordon off** *cordon off the area* close off, fence off, shut off, separate off, isolate, enclose, encircle, surround, picket.

core n centre, heart, nucleus, nub, kernel, crux, heart of the matter, essence, quintessence, substance, gist, pith; *inf* nitty-gritty.

cork n stopper, stop, plug, bung.

corn n **1** *corn used to make bread* cereal, cereal crop; wheat, oats, rye, maize, Indian corn. **2** *corn served as a first course* sweet corn, corn on the cob.

corner n **1** *the corner of the road* angle, bend, curve, crook, turn. **2** *the corner where the roads meet* angle, projecting angle, intersection, junction, fork, convergence, juncture. **3** *hidden in odd corners* nook, cranny, niche, recess, crevice, cavity, hole, secret place, hideaway; *inf* hidey-hole. **4** *in a remote corner of England* part, region, area, district, section, quarter; *inf* neck of the woods. **5** *in a difficult corner* predicament, plight, tight spot; *inf* pickle, hole. **6** *establish a corner of the property market* control, position of control, dominance, monopoly.

corner v **1** *corner the enemy* drive into a corner, run to earth, block off, trap, bring to bay. **2** *corner the market* gain control/dominance of, control, dominate, monopolize; *inf* hog.

corny adj banal, trite, hackneyed, stale, commonplace, stereotyped, platitudinous, inane, fatuous, jejune, sentimental, mawkish, weak, feeble; *inf* old hat.

corollary n consequence, result, upshot, conclusion.

coronation n crowning, enthronement, enthroning, accession to the throne, investiture, anointing, inauguration.

coronet n crown, circlet, garland, wreath, chaplet.

corporal adj bodily, fleshly, physical, corporeal, material, carnal, somatic.

corporate adj combined, joint, united, communal, collective, shared, pooled, merged, allied, collaborative.

corporation n **1** *a business corporation* company, firm, trust, partnership, combine, conglomerate. **2** *municipal corporation* council, town council, municipal authorities, civic authorities. **3** *a man with a huge corporation* paunch, pot-belly, pot, beer belly.

corps n **1** *an army corps* unit, division, detachment, company, troop, contingent, squad, squadron. **2** *diplomatic/dancing corps* group, body, band, team, party, contingent, troupe, gang, pack, crew.

corpse n dead body, body, cadaver, carcass, skeleton; remains; *inf* stiff.

corpulent adj fat, obese, plump, portly, stout, tubby, chubby, podgy, overweight, beefy, thickset, heavy, heavy-set, burly, bulky, well-padded, fleshy, rotund, roly-poly.

correct adj **1** *the correct answer* right, accurate, true, actual, exact, precise, unerring, close, faithful, strict, faultless, flawless; *inf* OK, on the mark, on the beam, spot on. **2** *correct behaviour* proper, suitable, fit, fitting, befitting, appropriate, apt, seemly, conventional, approved, accepted, standard, usual, customary, *comme il faut*; *inf* OK.

correct v **1** *correct the spelling errors* make/set right, rectify, right, amend, emend, remedy, redress, cure, improve, better, ameliorate, repair. **2** *correct an exam paper* indicate errors in, show mistakes in, point out faults in. **3** *correct a defect* rectify, counteract, offset, counterbalance, compensate for, make up for, neutralize. **4** *correct an instrument* adjust, regulate, fix, set, standardize, normalize, make conform. **5** *cor-*

rect the children scold, rebuke, chide, reprimand, reprove, admonish, lecture, berate, discipline, punish, chastise.

correction n 1 *the correction of the text* amendment, emendation, rectifying, rectification, improvement, modification, alteration, amelioration, repair. 2 *a house of correction* punishment, discipline, chastisement, castigation, admonition, reproof, reformation.

corrective adj 1 *corrective surgery* remedial, therapeutic, restorative, curative, reparatory, reparative, rehabilitative. 2 *corrective training* punitive, disciplinarian, penal, castigatory, castigative, reformatory.

correctly adv 1 *answer correctly* right, rightly, accurately, unerringly, precisely, faultlessly. 2 *dressed correctly* properly, suitably, fittingly, appropriately, aptly.

correlate v 1 *subjects correlating with each other* correspond, tie in, equate, interact, relate, agree, coordinate. 2 *correlate the facts* bring together, compare, show a connection/relationship/association/correspondence, connect.

correlation n correspondence, equivalence, reciprocity, mutual relationship, interrelationship, interdependence, interaction, mutuality, connection, relationship.

correspond v 1 *accounts not corresponding* agree, be in agreement, accord, concur, coincide, conform, match, fit together, square, tally, dovetail, correlate. 2 *Congress corresponds to Parliament* be analogous, be similar, be comparable, be equivalent, be akin, compare with. 3 *correspond with a friend* exchange letters, write to, communicate, keep in touch/contact.

correspondence n 1 *lack of correspondence between the accounts* agreement, accordance, accord, concurrence, coincidence, conformity, harmony, matching. 2 *the correspondence between Congress and Parliament* analogy, similarity, resemblance, comparability, correlation, relation. 3 *a backlog of correspondence* post, mail, communication; letters. 4 *enter into correspondence* letterwriting, writing, written communication.

correspondent n 1 *her family are regular correspondents* letter-writer, pen-friend, pen-pal, communicator. 2 *newspaper correspondent* reporter, journalist, contributor, newspaperman, newspaperwoman; special correspondent, foreign correspondent; *inf* stringer.

correspondent adj *correspondent forms of legislature* analogous, similar, like, comparable, parallel, equivalent, akin, kindred.

corridor n passage, passageway, aisle; hallway.

corroborate v confirm, verify, bear out, authenticate, validate, certify, endorse, ratify, substantiate, back up, uphold, support, attest to, sustain, evidence.

corrode v 1 *pipes corroded by rust* eat away, wear away, erode, gnaw, abrade, destroy, consume, rust, oxidize, oxidate. 2 *the metal has corroded* wear away, waste away, rust, disintegrate, crumble, fragment, be destroyed.

corrosive adj *acid is corrosive* corroding, eroding, erosive, abrasive, biting, caustic, acrid, mordant, consumptive, destructive.

corrugated adj furrowed, grooved, ridged, fluted, channelled, folded, crinkled, puckered, creased, wrinkled, crumpled, striate.

corrupt adj 1 *corrupt officials* dishonest, bribable, crooked, fraudulent, dishonourable, unscrupulous, untrustworthy, venal; *inf* bent, shady. 2 *a corrupt young man | corrupt acts* immoral, depraved, wicked, evil, sinful, degenerate, reprobate, perverted, dissolute, debauched, decadent, abandoned, lascivious, lewd, lecherous. 3 *a corrupt society/atmosphere* rotten, polluted, putrid, decayed, putrescent, tainted, infected, contaminated. 4 *a corrupt substance* adulterated, impure, alloyed, contaminated, tainted.

corrupt v 1 *corrupt the new official* bribe, suborn, buy, buy off, induce, lure, entice; *inf* pay off, grease the palm of. 2 *corrupt the young boy* deprave, pervert, warp, make degenerate, debauch. 3 *corrupt the atmosphere* make rotten, pollute, putrefy, taint, infect, contaminate, blight, mar. 4 *corrupt the substance* adulterate, alloy, contaminate, taint, defile, debase. 5 *corrupt the text* alter, tamper with, falsify, doctor.

corruption n 1 *officials involved in corruption* bribery, bribing, subornation, extortion, jobbery, dishonesty, crookedness, fraud, fraudulence, unscrupulousness, shadiness, profiteering, criminality, villainy, venality; *inf* graft. 2 *found guilty of moral corruption* immorality, depravity, vice, wickedness, evil, sin, iniquity, turpitude, degeneracy, perversion, dissolution, debauchery, decadence, lasciviousness, lewdness, lechery, impurity. 3 *corruption of the atmosphere* pollution, contamination. *see* CORRUPT v 3. 4 *corruption of the substance* adulteration, debasement. *see* CORRUPT v 4. 5 *text corruptions* alteration, falsification.

corsair n pirate, buccaneer, marauder, raider, plunderer, freebooter.

corset n girdle, panty girdle, belt, foundation garment, foundation, support garment, corselet, stays.

cortège n 1 *a funeral cortège* procession, column, file, line, parade, cavalcade. 2 *the prince and his cortège* retinue, entourage, train; attendants.

cosmetic n *apply cosmetics* beauty product, beauty aid, bit of make-up. *see* MAKE-UP 1.

cosmetic adj 1 *a cosmetic product* make-up, beauty, beautifying. 2 *a purely cosmetic improvement* superficial, surface, touching-up. 3 *cosmetic surgery* beautifying, improving, non-essential, non-medical.

cosmic adj 1 *cosmic laws* universal, worldwide. 2 *cosmic rays/dust* in/from space, occurring in space. 3 *disasters of cosmic proportion* vast, huge, immense, enormous, immeasurable, measureless, infinite, limitless.

cosmonaut n astronaut, spaceman, spacewoman.

cosmopolitan adj 1 *a cosmopolitan city/ cosmopolitan influences* international, multiracial, universal, global, worldwide. 2 *a cosmopolitan attitude* liberal, broad-minded, unprejudiced, sophisticated, urbane, worldly, wordly-wise, well-travelled, jet-setting, globe-trotting, unprovincial, cultivated, cultured.

cost v 1 *the book costs £30* be priced at, sell for, be valued at, fetch, come to, amount to; *inf* set one back. 2 *valuers costing the goods* price, value, put a price on, estimate the cost/price of, evaluate. 3 *tragedy costing lives | work costing effort* involve, result in, lead to, involve the loss/expense/sacrifice of, necessitate. 4 *it cost them dear* do a disservice to, harm, hurt, injure, damage.

cost n 1 *the cost of the house/holiday* price, asking price, selling price, charge, amount, value, valuation, quotation, rate, worth, payment, expenditure, expense, outlay; *inf* damage. 2 *the cost in lives | work done at great cost* sacrifice, expense, loss, penalty, suffering, harm, hurt, injury, damage, deprivation, detriment.

costly adj 1 *a costly house* expensive, dear, high-cost, high-priced, valuable, exorbitant, extortionate, extravagant; *inf* steep. 2 *a costly victory* ruinous, catastrophic, disastrous, sacrificial, damaging, harmful, loss-making, deleterious, pyrrhic, Cadmean.

costs npl expenses, outgoings; expenditure, money spent.

costume n 1 *dressed in national costume* style of dress, dress, fashion, clothing, attire, apparel, garb, ensemble, outfit, uniform, livery, habit; clothes, garments, robes; *inf* get-up, gear, togs. 2 *a woman in a green costume* suit, outfit, ensemble.

cosy adj snug, comfortable, warm, homelike, homely, sheltered, secure, safe, at ease; *inf* comfy, snug as a bug.

coterie n clique, set, crowd, circle, gang, club, community, league, alliance, faction, cabal.

cottage n *a country cottage | a holiday cottage* small house, cabin, chalet, shack; *Scots* but and ben.

couch n *a couch and matching chairs* sofa, settee; ottoman, *chaise longue*, chesterfield, divan, day bed, love-seat.

couch v *couched in loving terms* express, phrase, word, say, state, utter, set forth, frame, style.

cough v *cough noisily* hack, hawk, clear one's throat, hem, bark.

cough n *coughs and sneezes* hack, hawking, hem, bark; *inf* frog/tickle in one's throat.

council n 1 *the town council* local authority, governing body, parliament, cabinet, chamber, ministry. 2 *the design council* advisory body, board, board of directors, committee, assembly, panel, trustees, synod, diet, convocation. 3 *the committee is in council* conference, conclave, assembly, convocation; meeting, gathering.

counsel n 1 *seek expert counsel* advice, guidance, direction, recommendation, information; opinion, suggestion, warning, admonition, caution. 2 *hold counsel with a friend* consultation, discussion, conference, deliberation, dialogue. 3 *counsel handling his case* barrister, advocate, attorney.

counsel v *counsel him against going* advise, give guidance/direction, guide, direct, recommend, give one's opinion/suggestions, warn, admonish, caution.

counsellor n adviser, guidance counsellor, director, mentor, confidant, guide.

count v 1 *count the numbers* add up, total, sum up, calculate, tot up, compute, reckon up, enumerate, tally, cast up. 2 *count the people* keep a count of, count off, enumerate, tell, keep a tally of. 3 *counting everyone* include, take into account/consideration, number among, embrace, embody. 4 *count himself lucky* consider, think, regard, look upon, hold, judge, rate, deem, esteem. 5 *his presence does not count* matter, enter into consideration, be of account, signify, carry weight, weigh, mean anything, amount to anything, rate, tell; *inf* cut any ice, have any clout. **count on/upon** rely on, depend on, lean on, bank on, trust, believe in, put/

pin one's faith in, swear by, take for granted, take on trust. **count out** exclude, disregard, leave out, ignore, except, pass over, neglect.

count n **1** *after the election count* counting, enumeration, calculation, computation, telling, tally, tallying, totting up, poll. **2** *the pollen count* total number, total, sum/grand total, amount, full amount, aggregate, whole, tally, reckoning.

countenance n **1** *angry countenance* face, features, facial expression, expression, look, appearance, aspect, air, complexion, visage, physiognomy; *lit* mien. **2** *not give countenance to the plan* support, backing, encouragement, endorsement, assistance, aid, approval, sanction, approbation, favour, acceptance, adoption, advocacy. **3** *lose countenance* composure, calmness, coolness, poise, self-possession, self-control, level-headedness, cool-headedness, equanimity, equilibrium; *inf* one's cool.

countenance v **1** *cannot countenance such behaviour* tolerate, approve, put up with, permit, allow, endure, brook; *inf* stand for. **2** *countenance him in his project* encourage, support, back, help, aid, assist, champion, abet, take the side of, sanction, condone, endorse, warrant.

counter n **1** *drinks on the counter* top, horizontal surface; worktop, working top, work surface, table, checkout, stand. **2** *game counters* token, disc, piece, man, marker, wafer.

counter adv *run counter to expectation* against, in opposition to, contrary to, at variance with, in defiance of, in the reverse/wrong direction, against the tide, contrarily, contrariwise, conversely.

counter adj *a counter-attack* opposing, opposed, opposite, contrary, adverse, conflicting, contradictory, contrasting, obverse.

counter v *counter the attack* oppose, resist, rebut, combat, dispute, argue against, parry, hit back at, contradict, retaliate, ward off.

counteract v **1** *counteract the attack* act against, act counter to, hinder, oppose, thwart, frustrate, foil, impede, check, restrain, resist, withstand, defeat. **2** *counteract the effects* counterbalance, offset, neutralize, annul, negate, invalidate, countervail, counterpoise.

counterbalance v balance, equalize, compensate for, make up for, neutralize, offset, set off, undo, countervail, counterpoise.

counterfeit adj *counterfeit money* fake, faked, copied, forged, imitation, feigned, simulated, fraudulent, sham, spurious, bogus, ersatz; *inf* phoney, pseud, pseudo.

counterfeit n *not the original, a counterfeit* fake, copy, forgery, reproduction, imitation, fraud, sham; *inf* phoney.

counterfeit v *counterfeit money* fake, copy, reproduce, imitate, simulate, feign, falsify, sham.

countermand v cancel, annul, revoke, rescind, reverse, repeal, retract, abrogate, quash, override, invalidate.

counterpart n equivalent, equal, opposite number, parallel, complement, match, twin, mate, fellow, analogue, correlative, copy, duplicate.

countless adj innumerable, incalculable, immeasurable, endless, limitless, without end/limit, boundless, infinite, inexhaustible, untold, legion, myriad, no end of/to.

country n **1** *countries at war* nation, state, sovereign state, kingdom, realm, people, community, commonwealth. **2** *his country right or wrong* native land, homeland, fatherland, motherland, mother country, land of one's birth; one's roots. **3** *driving through rough country* terrain, land, territory; region, area, district, part, neighbourhood; parts; *inf* neck of the woods. **4** *voted in by the country* people, nation, public, population, populace, community, citizenry; inhabitants, residents, citizens, electors, voters, grass roots. **5** *live in the country, not the city* countryside, rural area/district, farmland, greenbelt, great outdoors; *Aust* outback, bush; *derog* provinces, backwoods, sticks, wilds, back of beyond, wilderness, middle of nowhere; *Amer inf* boondocks.

country adj rural, agrarian, agricultural, rustic, provincial, pastoral, Arcadian, bucolic; *lit* georgic, sylvan.

countryman, countrywoman n **1** *meet a fellow countryman abroad* compatriot, fellow citizen. **2** *countrymen and countrywomen at market* country dweller, farmer, farmhand, rustic, peasant, provincial; *derog* yokel, bumpkin, bogtrotter; *dial* hind; *Amer inf* hayseed, hick.

countryside n **1** *surrounded by beautiful countryside* landscape, scenery; scene, panorama, view, prospect, vista. **2** *living in the countryside* country, rural area/district, farmland. *see* COUNTRY n 5.

county n *the southern counties* shire, province, region, territory, administrative unit.

county adj *county types* aristocratic, land-owning, gentry, upper-class, tweedy; *inf* upper crust, up-market, top-drawer, huntin', shootin', fishin'.

coup n **1** *pull off the coup of getting the pop star to attend* successful action/act, feat, master-stroke, deed, accomplishment, stroke, stroke of genius, manoeuvre, stratagem, stunt, *tour de force.* **2** *a coup in a South American country* overthrow, seizure of power, *coup d'etat*, violent change, revolt, revolution, rebellion, mutiny, insurgence.

couple n *an established couple* pair, duo, two-some, dyad, brace, span; partners, lovers, husband and wife, cohabitees. **a couple of** **1** *a couple of drinks* two, two or three, a few, a small number of. **2** *a couple of men* two, a pair.

couple v **1** *couple the joints* join, fasten, attach, connect, unite, hitch together, fuse, weld, bind, buckle, clasp, conjoin, marry. **2** *their names coupled together* join, link, associate, connect, ally. **3** *lovers coupling* copulate, have sex/intercourse, have sexual relations, make love, fornicate.

coupon n **1** *petrol coupon* voucher, token, ticket, slip, certificate, stub, detachable portion. **2** *fill in the coupon* form, entry/application form.

courage n bravery, valour, gallantry, hero-ism, fearlessness, intrepidity, lion-hearted-ness, stout-heartedness, pluck, nerve, grit, boldness, daring, audacity, dauntlessness, hardihood, mettle, fortitude, firmness, resolution, tenacity, determination; *inf* bottle, spunk, guts.

courageous adj brave, valiant, valorous, gallant, heroic, fearless, intrepid, lion-hearted, plucky, bold, daring, audacious, dauntless, mettlesome, firm, resolute, tenacious, determined, indomitable.

courier n **1** *send the parcel/information by courier* messenger, special messenger, dispatch rider, letter-carrier, mail-carrier, bearer, conveyor, envoy, emissary, harbinger, herald. **2** *the courier took them round the palace* guide, tour guide/director, drago-man.

course n **1** *the course of history* progression, progress, advance, advancement, rise, march, furtherance, proceeding, development, unfolding, flow, movement, continuity, sequence, order, succession. **2** *go a bit off course* route, way, track, direction, tack, path, line, lane, road, passage, channel, trail, trajectory, orbit, circuit, ambit. **3** *pursue a different course of action* method, way, line of action, process, procedure, manner, mode of behaviour/conduct, plan, system,

policy, programme, regimen. **4** *in the course of an hour* duration, passing, passage, lapse, period, term, span, spell, sweep. **5** *taking an English course* course of study, set of lectures, curriculum, programme, schedule; classes, lectures, studies. **6** *a course of treatment* sequence, series, system, regimen. **7** *a waterlogged course* racecourse, track, circuit, ground. **in due course** in time, at the appropriate time, in the course of time, when the time is ripe, sooner or later, in the end, eventually. **of course** naturally, obviously, certainly, definitely, undoubt-edly, without a doubt, indubitably.

course v **1** *blood coursing* flow, move, run, rush, surge, gush, race, hurry, speed, charge, dash. **2** *coursing hares* hunt, pursue, chase, follow, run after, track.

court n **1** *appear in court* court of law, law-court, bench, bar, court of justice, justiciary, tribunal, forum, chancery, assizes. **2** *the queen's court* royal household, retinue, entourage, train, suite, cortège; attendants. **3** *situated near the queen's court* royal residence, palace, castle, manor, hall, chateau. **4** *monarch holding court* assembly, reception. **5** *paying court to the young lady* attention, homage, deference, suit, wooing, courtship; respects, addresses, blandish-ments. **6** *walking in the castle court* court-yard, quadrangle, square, cloister, esplanade, patio, piazza, plaza; *inf* quad. **7** *tennis/squash court* playing area/enclosure, game area/enclosure, arena.

court v **1** *he's courting her sister* pay court to, woo, pursue, chase, run after, set one's cap at, pay addresses to, pay suit to. **2** *the couple are courting* go out, go out together, go with each other, go steady, date, keep company. **3** *court the manager* curry favour with, cultivate, try to win over, pander to, fawn upon, toady to, wheedle; *inf* soft-soap, butter up, bootlick. **4** *court fame* seek, solicit, ask for, crave. **5** *court disaster* invite, risk, provoke, lead to, cause, bring on, elicit.

courteous adj polite, well-mannered, man-nerly, civil, chivalrous, gallant, gracious, kind, considerate, pleasant, tactful, diplo-matic, politic, cordial, genial, affable, respectful, deferential, well-bred, polished, refined, civilized, urbane.

courtesan n prostitute, harlot, whore, woman of ill repute, street-walker, call-girl, strumpet, lady of the night, *fille de joie.*

courtesy n **1** *have the courtesy to wait* polite-ness, civility, courteousness, chivalry, gal-lantry, gallantness, good breeding, gentility, graciousness, kindness, consider-ation, tact, cordiality, respect, respectfulness, deference, decorousness, refinement, urbanity, courtliness, elegance; good manners, manners. **2** *the outing by courtesy of the firm* kindness, generosity, benevolence, indulgence, favour, consideration, consent, permission.

courtier n attendant, henchman, follower; lady-in-waiting, page, squire, cup-bearer, train-bearer, liegeman.

courtly adj polite, well-mannered, civil, courteous, chivalrous, gallant, gentlemanly, ladylike, aristocratic, well-bred, dignified, decorous, formal, ceremonious, stately, proper, polished, refined, cultivated, urbane, elegant, suave, debonair.

courtship n **1** *his courtship of her* courting, wooing, pursuit, suit. *see* COURT v 1. **2** *married after a long courtship* romance, affair, love affair, going steady, dating, keeping company.

courtyard n quadrangle, square, cloister, esplanade, court. *see* COURT n 6.

cove[1] n *a sandy cove* bay, inlet, bight, creek, sound, anchorage; *Scots* firth, frith.

cove[2] n *a funny cove* man, fellow; *inf* chap, bloke, guy.

covenant n *sign a covenant* contract, guarantee, agreement, bond, deed, warrant, pledge, promise, indenture, trust, commitment, compact, bargain, pact, arrangement, deal, treaty, concordat, convention.

covenant v *covenant £100 to the school* pledge, promise, settle, contract, guarantee, engage, agree on, undertake.

cover v **1** *a pile of earth covering potatoes* place over, place under cover, protect, shield, shelter, conceal, hide, house, secrete, bury. **2** *snow covering the fields* overlay, overspread, blanket, carpet, overlie, extend over, coat, layer, film, mantle, pave, submerge. **3** *girls covered in silk* clothe, attire, outfit, garb, robe, wrap, accoutre, swaddle, encase, sheathe. **4** *cover all the entrances* protect, defend, guard, shield, safeguard. **5** *cover several fields* include, deal with, contain, take in, comprise, involve, provide for, embrace, embody, incorporate, subsume, refer to, consider, examine, review, survey, take stock of. **6** *journalists covering the trial* report, write up, describe, tell of, give an account of, give details of, investigate. **7** *doctors covering for each other* relieve, act/double/substitute for, take over from, replace, stand/fill in for, take someone's place. **8** *the thief's sister covering for him* give an alibi to, provide with an alibi, alibi, shield, protect. **9** *money to cover expenses* be enough for, offset, balance, counterbal-

ance, compensate for, make up for. **10** *cover against fire* insure, provide for, indemnify, protect. **11** *cover 30 miles | cover the ground rapidly* travel, travel/pass over, traverse, cross, range/tramp over. **cover up 1** *trying to cover up the mistake/scandal* conceal, hide, keep secret, hush up, keep dark, suppress, stonewall; *inf* whitewash. **2** *cover up the potatoes* cover, place under cover, protect, shield, shelter. *see* COVER v 1. **3** *cover yourself up* put on more clothes, dress, wrap up, swathe.

cover n **1** *take cover from the storm* covering, protection, shield, shelter, concealment, housing, refuge, sanctuary, haven, hiding-place. **2** *the jam-pot cover* lid, top, cap, covering. **3** *a cover of dust/snow* layer, coat, coating, film, blanket, overlay, carpet, mantle, canopy, crust. **4** *the business is a cover for spying* cover-up, disguise, front, camouflage, pretence, facade, pretext, false front, screen, smokescreen, mask, cloak, veil, window-dressing. **5** *the artillery providing cover for the infantry* protection, defence, guard, shield. **6** *provide cover for the doctor* relief, replacement, stand-in, substitute, locum. **7** *a policy giving cover against fire* insurance, protection, compensation, indemnification, indemnity. **8** *the covers of the book* jacket, dust jacket, wrapper, binding. **9** *under plain cover* envelope, wrapper, package; wrapping, packaging. **10** *game-birds in cover* undergrowth, woods, shrubbery, thicket, copse. **11** *pull up the covers* bedclothes, sheets, blankets; bedcover, duvet, bedspread.

coverage n *news coverage* reporting, reportage; reports, accounts, articles, pieces, stories.

covering n **1** *provide covering for the children* cover, protection, shelter, housing. *see* COVER n 1. **2** *a covering of dust/snow* layer, coat, coating, film, blanket, carpet. *see* COVER n 3. **3** *the boiler covering* casing, case, wrapping, sheathe, sheathing, jacket, housing.

covering adj *a covering letter* accompanying, explanatory, introductory.

coverlet n bedspread, bedcover, counterpaine, eiderdown, quilt.

covert adj secret, concealed, hidden, surreptitious, furtive, stealthy, private, underground.

covet v desire, want, wish for, long/yearn for, crave, hanker/lust after, thirst for, hunger after, set one's heart on, aspire to, aim after, envy, begrudge.

covetous adj *covetous of her sister's house* desirous of, wanting, craving, yearning/

longing for, greedy for, envious of. *see* COVET.

cow n **1** *cows and pigs* bovine, heifer. **2** *what a cow!* bitch, minx, vixen, slut.

cow v *teachers cowing the pupils* intimidate, overawe, awe, daunt, dismay, subdue, scare, frighten, petrify, terrorize, unnerve, browbeat, bully, domineer, bulldoze.

coward n poltroon, craven, dastard, recreant, renegade; *inf* chicken, scaredy-cat, funk, yellow-belly, sissy, big baby.

cowardly adj lily-livered, faint-hearted, chicken-hearted, craven, base, spineless, timorous, timid, fearful, shrinking, pusillanimous, dastardly, afraid of one's shadow; *inf* chicken, yellow, weak-kneed, gutless, yellow-bellied.

cowboy n **1** *cowboys herding cattle* cowhand, cowman, cattleman, cowherd, herd, herdsman, drover, stockman, rancher, ranchero; *Amer inf* cowpuncher, cowpoke, broncobuster; gaucho. **2** *the builders were cowboys* scoundrel, rogue, rascal, unscrupulous/irresponsible operator.

cower v cringe, shrink, flinch, draw back, recoil, crouch, slink, wince, blench, quail, quake, tremble, quiver, grovel.

coy adj arch, coquettish, flirtatious, kittenish, skittish, shy, modest, bashful, reticent, diffident, retiring, backward, self-effacing, shrinking, withdrawn, timid, demure, prudish, unconfident, lacking confidence, unsure.

cozen v cheat, deceive, beguile, trick, double-cross, swindle, take advantage of, play one false.

crabbed adj **1** *a crabbed old man* crabby, bad-tempered, ill-tempered, ill-natured, ill-humoured, cross, cantankerous, crotchety, irritable, touchy, testy, grouchy, snappy, prickly, crusty, peevish, churlish, surly, sour, morose, acrimonious, captious, waspish, perverse, difficult, trying. **2** *crabbed handwriting* cramped, squeezed, scribbled, laboured, illegible, unreadable, undecipherable, hieroglyphical.

crabby adj cross, bad-tempered, surly, grouchy, discontented. *see* CRABBED 1.

crack v **1** *crack the cup* chip, fracture, fragment, break, chop, split, splinter, snap, cleave, craze. **2** *the rifle cracked* ring out, go bang, pop, snap, crackle, boom, explode, detonate. **3** *crack his head on a beam* hit, bang, bump, strike, knock, smack, whack, thump; *inf* wallop, clout, clip. **4** *crack under questioning* give way, break down, collapse, go to pieces, lose control, yield, succumb, founder; *inf* fall/come apart at the seams.

5 *crack the problem* solve, work out, get the answer to, find the solution to, fathom, decipher. **6** *crack a bottle* open, uncork, broach, drink. **crack up** break down, have a breakdown, collapse, go to pieces, lose control, go out of one's mind, go mad; *inf* fall/come apart at the seams, go crazy, freak out.

crack n **1** *a crack in the cup/wall* chip, fracture, break, split, crevice, fissure, chink, gap, cavity, breach, rift, rupture, cleft, slit, cranny, interstice. **2** *the crack of the gun* bang, report, pop, snap, crackle, boom, explosion, detonation. **3** *get a crack on the head* blow, hit, bang, bump, strike, knock, smack, whack, thump; *inf* wallop, clout, clip. **4** *another crack at the competition* attempt, try, shot, opportunity; *inf* go, stab. **5** *laugh at his cracks* joke, funny remark, quip, witticism, wisecrack, gag, jibe, satirical remark, insult; *inf* dig.

crack adj *a crack tennis-player | crack shot* expert, first-rate, first-class, excellent, brilliant, elite, choice, superior; *inf* ace, A1.

cracked adj **1** *cracked cups/walls* chipped, fractured, broken, split, splintered, damaged, defective, flawed, imperfect, crazed. **2** *he seems a bit cracked* mad, insane, out of one's mind, touched, crazed, crack-brained; *inf* crazy, nuts, nutty, bats, batty, crackpot, off one's head/nut, round the bend/twist, loony, not the full shilling/pound.

crackle v crack, crepitate, decrepitate, snap.

cradle n **1** *babies sleeping in cradles* crib, bassinet, Moses' basket, cot, carry-cot. **2** *the cradle of democracy* birthplace, fount, fountainhead, source, place of origin, wellspring, beginning, breeding-place, nursery; origins, beginnings.

cradle v *cradle the baby | cradle his head in her arms* hold, rock, nestle, shelter, support.

craft n **1** *admire the artist's craft* skill, skilfulness, expertise, expertness, ability, mastery, artistry, art, technique, workmanship, aptitude, dexterity, talent, flair, knack, cleverness, genius; *inf* know-how. **2** *use craft to get his way* craftiness, cunning, artfulness, artifice, scheming, guile, subterfuge, stratagem, slyness, wiliness, shrewdness, trickery, duplicity, deceit; wiles, ruses. **3** *take up a new craft* occupation, trade, vocation, calling, pursuit, business, line, work, employment. **4** *pilot a craft* vessel, ship, boat, aircraft, plane, spacecraft.

craftsman, craftswoman n master, expert, skilled worker, dedicated/meticulous worker, artist, artificer, artisan, technician, maker, smith, wright.

craftsmanship n workmanship, technique, artistry, expertise, skill, mastery.

crafty adj cunning, artful, scheming, designing, calculating, wily, sly, devious, guileful, tricky, foxy, shrewd, astute, canny, sharp, duplicitous, deceitful, subtle, insidious, treacherous, crooked, fraudulent, underhand, underhanded.

crag n cliff, bluff, escarpment, scarp, ridge, peak, pinnacle, tor.

cram v 1 *cram clothes into the suitcase* stuff, push/shove/force into, pack in, ram down, press into, squeeze/jam/crush into, compress, compact, condense. 2 *cram the baskets | a bus crammed with people* stuff, overfill, fill, fill up, fill to overflowing, stuff to the gills, fill to the brim, overcrowd. 3 *cram for exams* study, revise, grind, grind away; *inf* swot, swot/mug up.

cramp v *cramp one's progress/style* restrict, limit, hamper, hinder, impede, hamstring, constrain, check, arrest, bridle, handicap, inhibit, thwart, stymie, obstruct, restrain, confine, shackle, encumber, clog.

cramp n *suffer from cramp* muscular contraction, muscle spasm, pang, twinge, pain, shooting pain, ache, crick, stiffness, convulsion.

cramped adj 1 *cramped accommodation* narrow, small, restricted, limited, confined, uncomfortable, closed in, hemmed in, tight, crowded, overfull, packed, squeezed, jammed in, congested. 2 *cramped handwriting* close, tightly packed, small, squeezed, crabbed, illegible, unreadable, indecipherable.

crane n derrick, winch, hoist, davit, windlass, tackle.

cranium n skull, head, crown; *inf* brain-pan, noddle, nut.

crank[1] n *pedals attached to a crank* lever, arm, bar, shaft, spindle, crankshaft.

crank[1] v 1 *crank an engine* start, turn over, get going, rev, rev up. 2 *crank up production* speed up, accelerate, hasten, hurry up, increase, improve.

crank[2] n *a fitness crank* eccentric, oddity, character, fanatic, zealot, maniac, enthusiast, devotee, fan, buff; *inf* nut.

cranky adj 1 *a cranky old man | a cranky diet* eccentric, unconventional, odd, peculiar, queer, strange, bizarre, idiosyncratic, quirky, freakish, freaky, obsessive, fanatical; *inf* funny, wacky. 2 *a cranky teacher* bad-tempered, cross, crabby.

cranny n chink, crack, crevice, slit, split, fissure, rift, cleft, opening, gap, cavity, hole, nook, interstice.

crash v 1 *the sea crashed against the rocks | the glass crashed on the floor* smash, batter, dash, shatter, break, disintegrate, shiver, splinter, fracture, fragment. 2 *the cymbals crashed* clash, clang, clank, clatter, bang, smash, boom, thunder, explode. 3 *the trees crashed to the ground* fall, topple, tumble, overbalance, pitch, plunge, hurtle, lurch. 4 *the car crashed into the van* bump/run/drive/bang into, collide with, hit, hurtle/smash/plough into, jolt, jar. 5 *crash the car* smash, wreck, bump; *inf* write off. 6 *the business crashed* collapse, fail, fold, fold up, go under, smash, founder, be ruined, cave in; *inf* go broke/bust, come a cropper, go to the wall. 7 *crash the party* gatecrash, come uninvited to, intrude, sneak/slip into, invade; *inf* horn in on.

crash n 1 *the crash of crockery/cymbals* clash, clank, clang, clatter, bang, smash, clangour, racket, din, boom, thunder, explosion. 2 *involved in a crash* accident, smash, smash-up, collision, pile-up, bump, bang, thud; *inf* prang. 3 *lost money in the crash* collapse, failure, bankruptcy, fold, smash, fall, ruin, ruination, downfall, depression, débâcle.

crash adj *a crash course/diet* intensive, concentrated, telescoped, rapid, urgent.

crass adj 1 *don't be so crass* stupid, insensitive, blundering, dense, thick, doltish, oafish, boorish, asinine, coarse, gross, vulgar, crude, rude, uncouth, unsophisticated, unrefined. 2 *crass ignorance* gross, utter, downright, out-and-out, very great, complete, blatant, glaring, undisguised, naked.

crate n box, case, packing case, tea chest, basket, hamper, container, receptacle.

crater n hole, hollow, depression, dip, cavity, chasm.

crave v 1 *crave a chocolate* long/yearn for, desire, want, wish for, hanker after, need, require, hunger/thirst for, be dying for, cry out for, lust after, pant for, be panting for, pine/sigh for; *inf* fancy, have a yen for. 2 *crave pardon* ask for, plead/beg for, seek, entreat, beseech, implore, petition, pray for, solicit/sue for, supplicate.

craven adj cowardly, chicken-hearted, lily-livered, faint-hearted, timorous, fearful, timid, base, pusillanimous, dastardly, recreant, poltroon; *inf* chicken, yellow.

craving n longing, yearning, desire, hankering, need, urge, hunger, thirst, lust, appetite, addiction, *cacoethes*; *inf* yen.

crawl v creep, go on all fours, move on hands and knees, inch, drag/pull oneself along, drag, trail, slither, squirm, wriggle, writhe, worm one's way, advance slowly/stealthily, sneak.

craze n fad, vogue, trend, fashion, enthusiasm, passion, infatuation, obsession, mania, fixation, fancy, novelty, whim, fascination, preoccupation, rage; *inf* thing, the latest.

crazed adj insane, mad, wild, unbalanced, crazy. *see* CRAZY 1.

crazy adj **1** *a crazy person* crazed, of unsound mind, insane, mad, mad as a hatter, mad as March hare, lunatic, idiotic, wild, unbalanced, demented, deranged, berserk, unhinged, touched, maniacal, delirious, out of one's mind/head; *inf* cracked, daft, bats, batty, loony, barmy, nuts, nutty, nutty as a fruit cake, cuckoo, bonkers, potty, mental, not all there, a bit lacking, round the bend/twist. **2** *a crazy idea* absurd, idiotic, stupid, silly, ridiculous, foolish, peculiar, odd, strange, queer, weird, eccentric, bizarre, fantastic, outrageous, wild, fatuous, inane, puerile, impracticable, senseless, unworkable, foolhardy, unrealistic, unwise, imprudent, ill-conceived, preposterous; *inf* potty, cockeyed, half-baked. **3** *crazy about opera* enthusiastic, mad, avid, keen, infatuated, passionate, smitten, fanatical, devoted to, fond/enamoured of, zealous, fervent, fervid, excited; *inf* nuts on, gone on.

creak v squeak, screech, squeal, groan, grate, grind, jar, rasp, scrape, scratch.

cream n **1** *beauty/shoe/antiseptic cream* lotion, emulsion, emolient, paste; cosmetic, ointment, salve, unguent, liniment. **2** *the cream of the college* best/choice part, flower, elite, pick, prime, quintessence, *crème de la crème*.

cream adj *a cream dress* cream-coloured, off-white, whitish, yellowish-white, buff.

crease n **1** *a trouser crease* ridge, furrow, groove, corrugation, fold, line, ruck, pleat, tuck. **2** *facial creases* wrinkle, line, crinkle, pucker; crow's feet.

crease v **1** *the dress was creased in the journey* crumple, wrinkle, crinkle, rumple, pucker, ruck up. **2** *crease the trousers/paper* put a crease/fold in, ridge, furrow, groove, corrugate, pleat, tuck. **3** *jokes creasing them up* amuse greatly, amuse, entertain, make laugh; *inf* make one fall about, have rolling in the aisles.

create v **1** *create a new generation* bring into being/existence, give birth/life to, procreate, father, sire, beget, spawn. **2** *create a*

new environment generate, originate, invent, initiate, engender, produce, design, devise, make, frame, fabricate, build, construct, erect, develop, shape, form, mould, forge, concoct, hatch. **3** *create a good impression* produce, make, result in, cause, be the cause of, bring about, give rise to, lead to. **4** *create new life* peers | *create a new system of government* invest, appoint, install, make, establish, found, institute, constitute, inaugurate, set up.

creation n **1** *the creation of a new generation* birth, procreation, fathering, begetting, genesis, spawning. *see* CREATE 1. **2** *the creation of a new environment* generation, origination, invention, initiation, inception, design, devising, formation, production, fabrication, building, shaping, hatching. *see* CREATE 2. **3** *everything in creation* the world, the living/natural world, the universe, the cosmos, nature, life; all living things. **4** *the creation of new life* peers investing, investiture, appointment, installation, establishment, foundation, institution, inauguration. **5** *the poet's creation* work, work of art, achievement, production, opus, invention, handiwork, masterpiece, *pièce de résistance*, *magnum opus*, *chef-d'oeuvre*. **6** *Paris creations* fashion, design, dress; clothes, hats.

creative adj inventive, imaginative, original, artistic, inspired, visionary, talented, gifted, resourceful, ingenious, clever, productive, fertile.

creator n **1** *praise their Creator* God, the Almighty. *see* GOD. **2** *the creator of the series* author, inventor, originator, initiator, maker, designer, producer, architect, prime mover, begetter, generator.

creature n **1** *all God's creatures* living thing/entity, being. **2** *the creatures of the forest* animal, beast; *Amer inf* critter. **3** *beautiful/poor creatures* person, human being, human, individual, character, fellow, soul, mortal; *inf* body. **4** *the King's creature* minion, lackey, puppet, tool, hanger-on, parasite, dependant, toady, sycophant, hireling, retainer, vassal.

credence n *place no credence in his statement* belief, faith, trust, confidence, reliance.

credentials npl testimonial, proof of identity/qualifications, certificate, diploma, document, warrant, licence, permit, card, voucher, passport, letter of introduction/recommendation, missive, deed, title; references; attestation, documentation.

credibility n **1** *the credibility of the story* plausibility, tenability. *see* CREDIBLE 1. **2** *the government lacking credibility* acceptability, faith, trust, trustworthiness, reliability, dependability, integrity.

credible adj **1** *a scarcely credible story* believable, conceivable, imaginable, plausible, tenable. **2** *the more credible party* acceptable, trustworthy, reliable, dependable.

credit v **1** *he couldn't credit it* believe, accept, put confidence in, trust, have faith in, rely on, depend on; *inf* fall for, swallow, buy. **2** *credit him with the discovery* ascribe to, attribute to, assign to, accredit, give credit to, chalk up to, put down to, impute to.

credit n **1** *receive credit for his performance* praise, acclaim, approval, commendation, acknowledgement, tribute, kudos, glory, recognition, regard, esteem, respect, merit, veneration, laudation; thanks. **2** *he gained credit in the city* name, reputation, repute, character, prestige, influence, standing, status, regard, esteem, estimation, acceptability, credibility; *inf* clout. **3** *a credit to the town* source of honour/pride, feather in the cap, asset, proud, boast, glory, flower, gem. **4** *the story gaining credit* belief, believability, credence, faith, reliability, reliance, confidence. **5** *his credit is good* financial standing/status, solvency. **on credit** *buy on credit* on hire purchase, on the HP, by instalments, by deferred payment, on account; *inf* on tick, on the slate, on the never-never.

creditable adj praiseworthy, commendable, laudable, meritorious, admirable, exemplary, worthy, up to the mark, respectable, reputable, estimable, honourable, deserving.

credulity n credulousness, gullibility, gullibleness, naïvety, naïveness, blind faith, greenness. *see* CREDULOUS.

credulous adj over-trusting, over-trustful, gullible, naïve, green, dupable, deceivable, unsuspicious, unsceptical, uncritical; *inf* wet behind the ears.

creed n set of principles, system/statement of beliefs, profession of faith, teaching, doctrine, canon, dogma, tenet, catechism; beliefs, principles, rules, articles of faith, maxims.

creek n *boats sailing in the creek* inlet, bay, cove, bight; *Scots* firth, frith.

creep v **1** *creeping along the ground* crawl, go on all fours, move on hands and knees, inch, slither, squirm, wriggle, writhe, worm one's way, insinuate. *see* CRAWL. **2** *creep up on them* move stealthily, steal, sneak, tiptoe, approach unnoticed, slink, skulk. **3** *employees creeping to the boss* grovel, toady, kowtow, bow and scrape, fawn,

cower, cringe, truckle; *inf* suck up to, bootlick.

creep n *hate the little creep* sycophant, toady, fawner, sneak; *inf* bootlicker.

creeper n trailing plant, trailer, climbing plant, climber, rambler.

creeps npl *gave me the creeps* feeling of horror/fear/terror/disgust/repulsion/revulsion.

creepy adj *a creepy film* horrifying, horrific, horrible, frightening, scaring, terrifying, hair-raising, awful, disturbing, eerie, sinister, weird, nightmarish, macabre, menacing, ominous, threatening, disgusting, repellent, repulsive, revolting; *inf* scary.

crescent n *shaped like a crescent* half-moon, new moon, old moon, demilune, lunula, meniscus, sickle-shape.

crest n **1** *a cock's crest | the helmet crest* cockscomb, comb, tuft, plume, topknot, tassel, mane, panache, aigrette; *Tech* caruncle. **2** *the crest of the hill* summit, top, pinnacle, peak, crown, apex, ridge; heights. **3** *the club crest* regalia, insignia, badge, emblem, device, coat of arms; *Herald* bearing, charge.

crestfallen adj downcast, dejected, depressed, glum, downhearted, disheartened, discouraged, dispirited, despondent, disappointed, disconsolate, in the doldrums, down in the dumps.

crevice n fissure, cleft, chink, crack, cranny, split, rift, slit, gash, rent, fracture, opening, gap, hole, interstice.

crew n **1** *the ship's crew* hands, sailors, seamen, mariners, ship's company, ship's complement. **2** *the camera crew* team, company, party, working party, gang, squad, force, corps, posse. **3** *that peculiar crew over there* crowd, lot, gang, mob, pack, horde, multitude, troop, swarm, herd, band, group, bunch, set.

crib n **1** *a baby's crib* cradle, bassinet, cot, carry-cot. **2** *a crib of animal fodder* stall, manger, bin, box, rack, bunker, container. **3** *a text crib* key, translation, guide. **4** *his answer is a crib of hers* copy, plagiarism, plagiarization, reproduction, replica, duplication, piracy. **5** *a country crib* cottage, shack, hut, hovel, shanty; *Scots* bothy.

crib v **1** *crib someone's essay* copy, plagiarize, reproduce, duplicate, pirate. **2** *crib the animals* enclose, shut in/up, confine, pen, coop, coop up, box in/up, hem in, fence in, rail in, corral, cage, imprison.

crick n pain, cramp, twinge, spasm, pang; stiffness.

crier n town crier, announcer, proclaimer, herald.

crime n 1 *convicted of the crime* offence, unlawful/illegal act, misdemeanour, misdeed, wrong, felony, violation, transgression, trespass, fault, injury; *Law* malfeasance, tort. 2 *a crime against humanity* sin, immoral act, evil, evil action, wrong, wrongdoing, vice, iniquity. 3 *crime is on the increase* lawbreaking, delinquency, wrongdoing, villainy, malefaction, illegality, misconduct, felony, corruption, wickedness, evil; *Law* malfeasance.

criminal adj 1 *a criminal act* unlawful, illegal, lawbreaking, illicit, lawless, felonious, indictable, delinquent, culpable, wrong, villainous, corrupt, evil, wicked, iniquitous, nefarious; *Law* malfeasant; *inf* crooked, bent. 2 *a criminal waste of resources* deplorable, scandalous, preposterous, shameful, reprehensible, senseless, foolish, ridiculous, sinful, immoral.

criminal n lawbreaker, offender, wrongdoer, felon, delinquent, miscreant, malefactor, culprit, villain, gangster, bandit, transgressor, sinner, trespasser; *Law* malfeasant; *inf* crook, con, crim.

crimp v 1 *crimp cloth/paper* flute, ruffle, pleat, corrugate, furrow, groove, ridge, crease, wrinkle, crinkle, crumple, pucker, gather, smock. 2 *crimp hair* wave, curl, frizz, frizzle.

cringe v 1 *cringe in fear* cower, shrink, draw back, quail, flinch, recoil, start, shy, blench, dodge, duck, crouch, wince, tremble, quiver, shake. 2 *cringe to the boss* kowtow, grovel, toady/fawn to; *inf* crawl, creep, bootlick.

crinkly adj wrinkled, wrinkly, crinkled, creased, crimped, corrugated, fluted, furrowed, ridged, gathered, puckered, smocked. *see* CRIMP 1.

cripple v 1 *the accident crippled him* make lame, disable, incapacitate, debilitate, impair, damage, hamstring, maim, weaken, enfeeble, paralyse. 2 *businesses crippled by the recession* damage, injure, ruin, destroy, weaken, impair, hamstring, hamper, impede, cramp, spoil, bring to a standstill, paralyse, enfeeble, vitiate.

crippled adj lame, disabled, incapacitated, physically impaired/handicapped, deformed, housebound, bedridden; *inf* laid up.

crisis n 1 *the crisis of the fever | reaching a crisis* turning-point, critical/decisive point, crux, climax, climacteric, culmination, height, moment of truth, zero hour, Rubicon; *inf*

crunch. 2 *a financial crisis* emergency, disaster, catastrophe, calamity, extremity, predicament, plight, mess, trouble, difficulty, dilemma, quandary, exigency; dire straits; *inf* fix, pickle, scrape.

crisp adj 1 *crisp toast* brittle, crispy, crumbly, crunchy, breakable, friable. 2 *crisp lettuce* firm, fresh, unwilted, unwithered. 3 *crisp weather* brisk, bracing, fresh, refreshing, invigorating, dry, cool, chilly. 4 *a crisp account* brief, terse, succinct, concise, short, incisive, clear, pithy. 5 *a crisp manner* brisk, vigorous, decisive, brusque, curt, abrupt. 6 *a crisp appearance* clean-cut, neat, smart, spruce, trim, well-groomed; *inf* snappy; *dial* trig.

criterion n measure, gauge, scale, yardstick, standard, norm, benchmark, touchstone, barometer, model, exemplar, classic example, rule, law, principle, canon.

critic n 1 *theatre critics* reviewer, commentator, pundit, arbiter, evaluator, analyst, judge, expounder. 2 *answer his critics* faultfinder, attacker, censurer, detractor, carper, backbiter, caviller, reviler, villifier; *inf* knocker, nit-picker.

critical adj 1 *a critical point in history* crucial, deciding, decisive, climacteric, pivotal, important, momentous, high-priority, serious, vital, urgent, pressing, compelling, essential, exigent. 2 *in a critical condition* dangerous, grave, serious, risky, perilous, hazardous, touch-and-go, uncertain, precarious; *inf* chancy. 3 *a critical attitude* faultfinding, captious, censorious, carping, cavilling, quibbling, niggling, disapproving, disparaging, judgemental, hypercritical, overcritical; *inf* nit-picking. 4 *a critical essay* evaluative, analytic, interpretative, expository, commentative, explanatory, explicative, elucidative, annotative.

criticism n 1 *actions receiving criticism* faultfinding, censure, reproof, condemnation, disapproval, disparagement, captiousness, carping, cavilling, animadversion; *inf* nitpicking, brickbats, flak, bad press, bad notices, knocking, panning, slating, slamming. 2 *studying literary criticism* evaluation, comment, commentary, assessment, appreciation, appraisal, analysis, interpretation, explanation, explication, elucidation, annotation. 3 *read the criticism* review, notice, commentary, evaluation, critique, analysis, appraisal; *inf* write-up.

criticize v *criticize his behaviour* find fault with, censure, denounce, blame, condemn, pick holes in, disapprove of, disparage, carp at, cavil at, excoriate, animadvert on/upon; *inf* nit-pick, hand out brickbats, give flak to, give a knocking/panning/slating/ slamming to, knock, pan, slate, slam.

critique n evaluation, analysis, assessment, appraisal; textual examination, commentary, critical essay, review.

croak v **1** *"who's there?" he croaked* speak/utter hoarsely/huskily/throatily/harshly, rasp, speak thickly, squawk, caw, grunt, wheeze. **2** *always croaking about something* grumble, complain, moan, grouse, whine, mutter, murmur. **3** *when the crook croaked* die, pass away, perish, expire; *inf* kick the bucket. **4** *he croaked the cat* kill, butcher, murder.

crock n **1** *a crock of salt* earthenware pot, pot, jar, vessel, container, pitcher, jug, ewer. **2** *a bit of a crock now* invalid, infirm person, broken-down person/thing, decrepit person/thing.

crockery n dishes, earthenware, pottery, china, stoneware, porcelain.

crony n friend, companion, chum, mate, comrade, associate, confederate; *inf* pal, buddy.

crook n **1** *crooks imprisoned* criminal, villain, rogue, lawbreaker, thief, robber, swindler, cheat, racketeer; *inf* crim, shark, con-man. **2** *the crook of one's arm | crook of the river* bend, curve, curvature, angle, bow, flexure.

crook v *crook one's finger* bend, curve, angle, flex, hook, bow.

crooked adj **1** *a crooked branch/road* bent, curved, twisted, contorted, warped, irregular, angled, bowed, hooked, flexed, winding, twisting, zigzag, meandering, deviating, sinuous, tortuous, serpentine, anfractuous. **2** *a crooked back* deformed, misshapen, out of shape, disfigured, crippled. **3** *the picture's crooked* not straight, tilted, at an angle, angled, slanted, aslant, slanting, sloping, askew, awry, to one side, off-centre, lopsided, uneven, unsymmetrical, asymmetric. **4** *a crooked fellow/deal* criminal, dishonest, corrupt, dishonourable, unscrupulous, unprincipled, fraudulent, illegal, unlawful, nefarious, crafty, deceitful, shifty, underhand, questionable, dubious; *inf* shady, bent.

croon v hum, sing softly, warble.

crop n **1** *the apple crop* year's growth, harvest, yield, produce, vintage, gathering, reaping, gleaning, garnering, garner; fruits. **2** *the year's crop of students* batch, lot, collection, assortment, selection, supply. **3** *a bird's crop* craw, gullet, maw, throat.

crop v **1** *crop the dog's tail/hair | crop the grass* cut, cut short, clip, trim, snip, shear, lop, curtail, reduce, mow, prune. **2** *sheep cropping* graze, nibble, browse. **3** *crop the fruits*

harvest, pick, gather, collect, reap, garner, gather in, bring home. **crop up** *something cropped up* happen, occur, arise, turn up, spring up, emerge, appear, come to pass.

cross n **1** *the sign of the cross* crucifix, rood. **2** *a cross to bear* trouble, worry, burden, trial, disaster; tribulation, affliction, misfortune, adversity, misery, woe, pain, suffering, calamity, catastrophe. **3** *a cross between two breeds/types* cross-breed, hybrid, hybridization, mixture, amalgam, blend, combination, mongrel, cur.

cross v **1** *the bridge crossing the river* go across, span, extend/stretch across, pass over, bridge, ford. **2** *cross the road* go/travel across, cut across, traverse. **3** *the roads/lines crossed there* intersect, meet, join, converge, crisscross, interweave, intertwine, zigzag. **4** *hates being crossed* oppose, resist, thwart, frustrate, foil, obstruct, impede, hinder, hamper, block, check, deny, contradict. **5** *cross two species* cross-breed, interbreed, cross-fertilize, cross-pollinate, intercross, hybridize, mix, intermix, blend. **cross out** *cross out his name* delete, strike out, bluepencil, cancel, eliminate, obliterate.

cross adj **1** *she was cross at the children* angry, annoyed, irritated, in a bad mood, peeved, vexed, upset, piqued, out of humour, put out. **2** *a cross old woman* irritable, shorttempered, bad-tempered, ill-humoured, surly, churlish, disagreeable, irascible, touchy, snappy, snappish, impatient, peevish, petulant, fractious, crotchety, grouchy, grumpy, querulous, cantakerous, testy, captious, splenetic, waspish. **3** *cross ideas* contrary, opposing, opposite, adverse, unfavourable.

cross-examine v cross-question, question, interrogate, quiz, pump, catechize; *inf* grill.

crossing n **1** *a crash at the crossing* junction, crossroads, intersection. **2** *cross the street at the crossing* pedestrian crossing, street crossing, pelican crossing, underpass; *inf* the green man.

crotch n crutch, groin.

crotchet n whim, whimsy, fancy, fad, vagary, notion, caprice, quirk, eccentricity.

crotchety adj cross, bad-tempered, illnatured, ill-humoured, crabbed, crabby, awkward, difficult, grumpy, grouchy, disagreeable, irritable, irascible, churlish, surly, touchy, testy, fractious, crusty, cantakerous, curmudgeonly.

crouch v squat, bend, bend down, hunker, stoop, hunch over, cower, cringe.

crow v *the winners were crowing over/about their victory* boast, brag, trumpet, gloat, show off, glory/exult in, vaunt, parade, swagger, bluster, strut; *inf* blow one's own trumpet.

crowd n **1** *crowds of people* throng, horde, mob, rabble, large number, mass, multitude, host, army, herd, flock, drove, swarm, troupe, pack, press, crush, flood, collection, company, gathering, assembly, assemblage, array, congregation, convention, concourse. **2** *he always follows the crowd and doesn't think for himself* majority, multitude, common people, populace, general public, mob, rank and file, hoi polloi, proletariat, riff-raff; *masses*. **3** *the wine-bar crowd* group, set, lot, gang, bunch, circle, fraternity, clique, coterie. **4** *the pop group played to a capacity crowd* gate, house, turnout, audience, attendance; spectators, listeners, viewers.

crowd v **1** *crowd round the teacher* gather, cluster, forgather, congregate, flock, swarm, throng, huddle, concentrate. **2** *people crowding into the hall* push, push one's way, shove, thrust forward, jostle, elbow, squeeze, pile in, pack. **3** *tourists crowding the streets | streets crowded with tourists* throng, pack, fill, overfill, congest. **4** *crowd people into the trains* pack, squeeze, cram, jam, bundle, stuff, pile. **5** *give him time! Don't crowd him* pressure, pressurize, harass, badger, pester, hound, nag, torment, plague; *inf* hassle.

crowded adj *crowded streets/buses* full, overfull, busy, overflowing, packed, jam-packed, crushed, cramped, congested, teeming, swarming, thronged, populous; *Amer* mobbed; *inf* full to bursting.

crown n **1** *the king's crown* diadem, coronet, coronal, tiara, chaplet, circlet, wreath. **2** *the champion winning the crown* laurel wreath, victor's garland, prize, trophy; honour, distinction, glory, kudos; laurels, bays. **3** *the power of the Crown* monarchy, monarch, sovereignty, sovereign, ruler, king, queen, emperor, empress, royalty; *inf* royals. **4** *the crown of the hill* top, crest, summit, apex, head, tip, pinnacle. **5** *the crown of his achievements* climax, height, culmination, pinnacle, zenith, acme, ultimate, flower.

crown v **1** *crown the queen* invest, inaugurate, induct, install. **2** *crown his career* cap, round off, be the culmination/climax of, put the finishing touch/touches to, consummate, top off, complete, perfect, conclude. **3** *the steeple crowning the church* top, surmount, overtop. **4** *he crowned his attacker* hit over the head, strike, box, bang, cuff, punch, buffet; *inf* biff, wallop, bash.

crucial adj **1** *a crucial moment in the talks* decisive, critical, determining, pivotal, cen-

tral, testing, trying, searching. **2** *the matter is of crucial importance* very important, high-priority, essential, momentous, vital, urgent, pressing, compelling.

crucify v **1** *crucify the wrongdoers* nail to a cross, execute/put to death on a cross. **2** *bullies crucifying the new pupils* persecute, torment, distress, harrow, torture. **3** *his play was crucified by the critics* tear apart, tear to pieces, criticize, attack, lampoon; *inf* pan, slate.

crude adj **1** *crude oil/flour* raw, unrefined, natural, coarse, unprocessed, unmilled, unpolished. **2** *a crude sculpture/dwelling* rudimentary, primitive, rough, rough-and-ready, rough-hewn, makeshift, unfinished, unpolished, unformed, undeveloped, rude. **3** *a crude sense of humour* coarse, vulgar, rude, uncouth, indelicate, earthy, indecent, dirty, bawdy, smutty, obscene, offensive, lewd, ribald, boorish, crass, tasteless; *inf* blue, raunchy.

cruel adj **1** *a cruel dictator/action* savage, brutal, inhuman, barbaric, barbarous, bloodthirsty, vicious, ferocious, fierce, evil, fiendish, callous, cold-blooded, sadistic, ruthless, merciless, pitiless, unrelenting, remorseless, unfeeling, heartless, inhumane, severe, harsh, stern, stony-hearted, hard-hearted, inclement, flinty. **2** *a cruel stroke of fate* unkind, painful, distressing, harrowing, harsh, grim, heartless.

cruelty n **1** *the cruelty of the dictator | cruelty of his actions* savageness, savagery, brutality, inhumanity, barbarism, barbarousness, viciousness, ferocity, fierceness, evil, fiendishness, callousness, sadism, ruthlessness, pitilessness, relentlessness, severity, harshness, inclemency. *see* CRUEL 1. **2** *the cruelty of the blow* unkindness, painfulness, harshness, grimness, heartlessness; pain, resulting distress.

cruise v **1** *ships cruising* sail, voyage, journey. **2** *cars cruising along* coast, travel steadily, drift.

cruise n *go on a cruise* sea/boat trip, voyage, sail.

crumb n bit, fragment, morsel, particle, grain, atom, speck, scrap, shred, sliver, snippet, mite.

crumble v **1** *crumble the biscuits* break up, crush, pulverize, pound, grind, powder, granulate, fragment, shiver, triturate, comminute. **2** *the empire was crumbling* disintegrate, fall to pieces, fall apart, collapse, break down/up, tumble down, decay, deteriorate, degenerate, fall into decay, go to rack and ruin, decompose, rot, rot away, moulder, perish, vanish, fade away, come to dust.

crumple v **1** *crumple the dress* crush, crease, rumple, wrinkle, crinkle. **2** *the child's face crumpled* pucker, screw up. **3** *resistance crumpling* collapse, fail, cave in, fall apart, give way, go to pieces, topple, shrivel.

crunch v **1** *crunch biscuits* chew noisily, bite, munch, champ, chomp, gnaw, masticate; *inf* scrunch. **2** *crunch the snow* crush, grind, pulverize, pound, smash. **3** *crunch through the snow* move noisily, sound noisy/harsh, scrunch.

crunch n crux, crisis, critical point, test, moment of truth/decision.

crusade n **1** *knights/soldiers on a crusade* military campaign, holy war, jihad. **2** *a crusade against smoking* campaign, drive, push, struggle, cause, movement.

crusade v *crusading for more resources* campaign, fight, work, do battle, take up arms, take up a cause.

crusader n campaigner, fighter, battler, champion, advocate, reformer.

crush v **1** *crush the grapes* squash, squeeze, mash, press, press down, compress, bruise. **2** *crush the material* crease, crumple, rumple, wrinkle, crinkle. **3** *crush the stones* break up, smash, shatter, pound, pulverize, grind, crumble, crunch, shiver, splinter, comminute. **4** *crush the rebellion* | *crush their opponents* put down, quell, quash, suppress, subdue, overcome, overwhelm, overpower, stamp out, defeat, conquer, vanish, extinguish. **5** *crushed by his criticism* mortify, humiliate, abash, quash, shame, chagrin; *inf* put down. **6** *crush her in his arms* embrace, enfold, hug, squeeze, hold/press tight, clutch.

crush n **1** *a crush at the cinema* crowd, jam, congestion, huddle. **2** *a crush on the teacher* infatuation, fancy, liking, love, passion; *inf* pash. **3** *fruit crush* squash, fruit juice.

crust n **1** *the crust of the bread/pie* outside, casing, shell, husk. **2** *a crust of hard snow/ skin* covering, cover, coating, caking, topping, layer, film, skin, blanket, mantle, incrustation, concretion, scab.

crusty adj **1** *crusty pastry* crisp, crispy, brittle, hard, well-baked, well-done, friable. **2** *a crusty old fellow* | *a crusty manner* brusque, surly, curt, gruff, cross, crabbed, crabby, grouchy, bad-tempered, short-tempered, irritable, irascible, ill-humoured, ill-natured, snappish, prickly, fretful, touchy, testy, snarling, cantankerous, choleric, splenetic, captious.

cry v **1** *babies/women crying* shed tears, weep, sob, wail, snivel, blubber, whimper, whine, bawl, howl. **2** *he cried out her name* | *cried in terror* call out, exclaim, yell, scream, screech, bawl, shout, bellow, howl. **cry down** *cry down his achievement* decry, run down, disparage, belittle, denigrate. **cry off** *cry off the appointment* cancel, withdraw, withdraw from, back out, back out of, beg off, excuse oneself.

cry n **1** *the baby's cries* weeping, sobbing, snivelling, blubbering, wailing, lamenting, lamentation, keening; sobs, wails, howls. **2** *cry of terror/pain* call, exclamation, scream, screech, yell, shout, bellow, howl.

crypt n tomb, vault, undercroft, burial chamber, sepulchre.

cub n **1** *lion and her cubs* young, offspring, whelp. **2** *newspaper cubs* trainee, learner, recruit, tenderfoot, youngster; *inf* greenhorn.

cubbyhole n **1** *put the document in his cubbyhole* pigeonhole, compartment, slot, recess, niche. **2** *the janitor in his cubbyhole* small room, den, snug.

cube n six-sided body/shape, hexahedron, parallelepiped.

cuddle v **1** *cuddling his wife* hug, embrace, enfold, clasp. **2** *couples cuddling in cars* embrace, make love, pet, fondle; *inf* canoodle, neck, smooch. **3** *cuddle up in bed* snuggle, nestle, curl up.

cuddly adj cuddlesome, huggable, warm, soft, buxom, plump, curvaceous.

cudgel n *hit with a cudgel* club, bludgeon, stick, baton, truncheon, cosh, bat, bastinado; *Amer* blackjack; *dial* shillelagh.

cudgel v *the attacker cudgelled his victim* bludgeon, cosh, club, beat/strike with a stick, truncheon.

cue n **1** *"away" is your cue* catchword, keyword, prompt, prompt-word, prompting, reminder. **2** *your cue to begin* signal, sign, indication, hint, suggestion, intimation.

cuff v *cuff the child* slap, strike, hit, buffet. **off the cuff** impromptu, ad lib, extempore, extemporaneously, off the top of one's head, unrehearsed, improvised, offhand, on the spur of the moment, spontaneous, spontaneously.

cuisine n cookery, cooking, *cordon bleu*.

cul-de-sac n blind alley, dead end.

culminate v come to a climax, peak, reach a pinnacle, come to a crescendo, come to an end, end, close, finish, conclude, terminate, come to a head; *inf* wind up.

culmination n high point, height, top, summit, climax, peak, pinnacle, crest, crown, crowning touch, zenith, acme, apex, high noon, consummation, completion, close, finish, conclusion, termination.

culpable adj at fault, in the wrong, guilty, answerable, blameworthy, blamable, to blame, censurable, reproachable, reprovable, reprehensible, sinful; *fml* peccant.

culprit n person responsible, guilty party, wrongdoer, evildoer, lawbreaker, criminal, miscreant, delinquent, reprobate, transgressor, felon, sinner, malefactor; *inf* baddie, bad guy.

cult n **1** *belong to a strange religious cult* sect, religion, church, denomination, body, affiliation, faith, belief, persuasion, following, party, school, faction, clique. **2** *the modern pop-music cult* craze, fashion, fad; admiration, devotion, obsession, homage, worship, reverence, veneration, idolization.

cultivate v **1** *cultivate the fields* till, farm, work, plough, dig, prepare, fertilize. **2** *cultivate a crop* plant, raise, tend, bring on, produce. **3** *cultivate the mind* culture, educate, train, civilize, enlighten, enrich, improve, better, develop, refine, polish, ameliorate, elevate. *see* CULTIVATED. **4** *cultivate people* seek the friendship/company of, run after, make advances to, ingratiate oneself with, curry favour with, woo, court, dance attendance on, associate/consort with; *inf* butter up, suck up to. **5** *cultivate a friendship* pursue, devote oneself to, foster, promote, advance, further, forward, encourage, support, back, aid, help, assist, abet.

cultivated adj *a cultivated young woman* cultured, educated, civilized, enlightened, refined, polished, sophisticated, discerning, discriminating, urbane.

cultural adj **1** *cultural interests* artistic, educational, educative, enlightening, enriching, broadening, developmental, edifying, civilizing, elevating. **2** *cultural differences* life-style, ethnic, folk, racial.

culture n **1** *a woman of culture* cultivation, education, enlightenment, accomplishment, edification, erudition, refinement, polish, sophistication, urbanity, discernment, discrimination, good taste, taste, breeding, politeness, gentility, *savoir faire*. **2** *seek culture* the arts, works of art, intellectual achievements; intellectual achievement, intellectual activity. **3** *belong to a different culture* civilization, way of life, lifestyle; customs, habits, ways, mores. **4** *cereal culture* cultivation, farming, agriculture, husbandry, agronomy.

cultured adj cultivated, artistic, educated, enlightened, learned, knowledgeable, intellectual, highbrow, scholarly, well-informed, well-read, erudite, accomplished, well-versed, refined, genteel, polished, sophisticated, urbane.

culvert n channel, conduit, drain, gutter, watercourse.

cumbersome adj **1** *cumbersome packages* awkward, unwieldy, bulky, weighty, heavy, hefty, clumsy, unmanageable, burdensome, cumbrous, inconvenient, incommodious. **2** *cumbersome procedures* slow, slow-moving, inefficient, unwieldy, cumbrous.

cumulative adj accumulative, increasing, growing, enlarging, swelling, accruing, snowballing, collective, aggregate, amassed.

cunning adj **1** *a cunning thief* crafty, devious, deceitful, wily, sly, shifty, artful, foxy, tricky, guileful, shrewd, astute, sharp, knowing, subtle, Machiavellian. **2** *a cunning device/artist* clever, ingenious, resourceful, inventive, imaginative, skilful, deft, adroit, subtle, dexterous.

cunning n **1** *the cunning of the thief* craftiness, deviousness, deceitfulness, deceit, wiliness, slyness, artfulness, foxiness, trickery, trickiness, guile, shrewdness, astuteness, sharpness, subtlety. **2** *admire the cunning of the process/artist* cleverness, ingenuity, resourcefulness, inventiveness, imaginativeness, skill, skilfulness, deftness, adroitness, subtlety, finesse, dexterity, ability, capability.

cup n **1** *cups, saucers and plates* teacup, coffee cup, mug, beaker, demitasse. **2** *win the cup* trophy, chalice. **3** *two cups of sugar* cupful, teacupful, measuring cup. **4** *a fruit/wine cup* punch, drink, squash, draught, potion.

cupboard n cabinet, locker, press, closet, storeroom, pantry.

Cupid n **1** *a statue of Cupid* god of love, Eros, amoretto. **2** *acting Cupid* matchmaker, marriage broker.

cupidity n greed, avarice, avariciousness, acquisitiveness, covetousness, rapacity, rapaciousness, voracity, voraciousness, desire, avidity.

cur n **1** *bitten by a cur* mongrel, lurcher; *inf* mutt. **2** *married to a nasty cur* scoundrel, cad, blackguard, wastrel, ne'er do well, villain; *inf* rat, creep, louse, rotter, bounder, blighter.

curate n assistant priest. *see* ECCLESIASTIC n.

curative adj curing, healing, therapeutic, medicinal, remedial, restorative, sanative.

curator n keeper, custodian, conservator, guardian, caretaker, steward.

curb v *curb one's anger* restrain, check, keep in check, control, constrain, contain, hold back, bite back, repress, suppress, moderate, dampen, put a brake on, impede, retard, subdue, bridle, nozzle.

curb n *curbs on expenditure* restraint, check, control, constraint, deterrent, curtailment, limitation, limit, damper, brake, rein, suppressant, hindrance, retardant.

curdle v turn, turn sour, congeal, coagulate, clot, solidify, thicken, condense.

cure n *a cure for cancer* remedy, curative, medicine, cure-all, panacea, restorative, corrective, antidote, nostrum; treatment, therapy, healing, alleviation.

cure v **1** *cure the patient* heal, restore, restore to health, make well/better, rehabilitate, treat. **2** *cure the disease* heal, remedy, doctor, put/set right, fix, repair. **3** *cure meat* preserve, smoke, salt, dry, kipper, pickle.

curio n trinket, knick-knack, bibelot, *objet d'art*.

curiosity n **1** *curiosity about what is happening* inquisitiveness, spirit of inquiry, interest, investigativeness, researching, querying, asking questions, questioning, prying, snooping; *inf* nosiness. **2** *the object having curiosity value* strangeness, oddness, peculiarity, eccentricity, idiosyncrasy, deviation, aberration. **3** *he is a curiosity* eccentric, individual, oddity, character, card, freak, original; *inf* weirdo, oddball. **4** *looking at the curiosities of the East* novelty, oddity, phenomenon, rarity, wonder, marvel, sight, spectacle.

curious adj **1** *curious to know the facts* inquisitive, inquiring, interested, investigating, searching, researching, querying, questioning, interrogative, puzzled, burning with curiosity. **2** *curious about other's affairs* inquisitive, prying, snooping, meddling, meddlesome, interfering, intrusive; *inf* nosy, snoopy. **3** *a curious site* strange, unusual, rare, odd, peculiar, out of the ordinary, unexpected, extraordinary, remarkable, singular, novel, queer, bizarre, unconventional, unorthodox, phenomenal, weird, freakish, marvellous, wonderful, prodigious, exotic, mysterious, puzzling, quaint, unique; *inf* rum, far out.

curl v **1** *the smoke/road curled upwards* spiral, coil, twist, twist and turn, wind, curve, bend, loop, twirl, wreathe, meander, snake, corkscrew. **2** *the heat curled the leaves up* bend, twist, curve, coil, crisp. **3** *curl the hair* crimp, crinkle, kink, frizz, coil, wave, corkscrew.

curl n **1** *put curls in one's hair* kink, ringlet, coil, wave, curlicue, corkscrew. **2** *curls of smoke* spiral, coil, twist, whorl, helix.

curly adj **1** *curly hair* curling, curled, crimped, crinkly, kinked, wavy, waved, frizzy, permed, fuzzy, corkscrew. **2** *a curly pattern* spiralled, spiralling, coiling, coiled, curving, winding, corkscrew. *see* CURL v 1.

currency n **1** *foreign currency* money, medium of exchange, legal tender, cash, coinage, coin, specie, paper money; coins, bank notes, notes, bills. *see* MONEY. **2** *story gaining currency* prevalence, acceptance, popularity, vogue, circulation, communication, transmission, dissemination, publicity, exposure.

current adj **1** *current fashions* present, present-day, contemporary, ongoing, extant, existing, popular, modern, fashionable, in fashion/vogue, up to date, up to the minute; *inf* trendy, now, in. **2** *ideas no longer current* prevalent, prevailing, accepted, in circulation, circulating, going around, making the rounds, talked of, common, general, popular, widespread, rife, on everyone's lips.

current n **1** *current of air* steady flow, draught, up/down draught, wind, thermal. **2** *swimmers swept away by the current | a strong current* steady flow, stream, tide, channel. **3** *disturb the even current of village life* course, flow, progress, progression, tide. **4** *currents of opinion* trend, drift, tendency, tenor.

curse n **1** *the witches'/priest's curse* malediction, evil eye, execration, imprecation, anathema, damnation, excommunication; *inf* jinx. **2** *angrily uttering curses* oath, swearword, expletive, profanity, obscenity; swearing, blasphemy, bad/foul language. **3** *the curse of poverty* evil, affliction, burden, cross, bane, misfortune, misery, trouble, blight, harm, disaster, calamity, ordeal, tribulation, scourge, plague, torment.

curse v **1** *the witch/priest cursed them* put a curse on, accurse, put the evil eye on, execrate, imprecate, anathematize, damn, excommunicate; *inf* put a jinx on, jinx. **2** *curse at the policeman* utter oaths, swear, use bad/foul language, blaspheme, take God's/the Lord's name in vain, be foul-mouthed; *Amer inf* cuss. **3** *poverty cursed his childhood* blight, afflict, trouble, beset, harm, burden, plague, torment, destroy, ruin, scourge.

cursed adj **1** *that cursed table/ neighbour* accursed, annoying, confounded, unpleasant, hateful, detestable, odious, loathsome, foul, damnable, abominable, vile pestilential, infernal, devilish, fiendish, infamous, nefarious, pernicious. **2** *the cursed people died* accursed, under a curse, curse-laden, doomed, ill-fated, damned, execrated, anathematized; *inf* jinxed. *see* CURSE v 1.

cursory adj hasty, rapid, hurried, quick, superficial, perfunctory, desultory, ephemeral, fleeting, passing, transient.

curt adj terse, abrupt, brusque, blunt, short-spoken, short, snappy, snappish, sharp, crisp, tart, gruff, offhand, summary, rude, impolite, unceremonious, ungracious, uncivil, brief, concise, succinct, compact, pithy.

curtail v reduce, cut short, cut, cut down/back, decrease, lessen, diminish, retrench, slim down, tighten up, pare down, trim, dock, lop, truncate, shorten, abridge, abbreviate, contract, compress, shrink.

curtain n **1** *hang curtains* window hanging, screen, blind; *Amer* drape. **2** *a curtain of secrecy* screen, cover, shield, cloak, veil. **curtain off** shut off, separate off, screen off, isolate, hide, conceal, shield.

curtsy, curtsey v drop a curtsy, bob, bow, genuflect, salaam.

curve n arc, bend, arch, turn, bow, loop, hook, half-moon, crescent; winding, camber, curvature.

curve v bend, arc, arch, bow, turn, inflect, incurve, swerve, twist, wind, hook, loop, spiral, coil.

curved adj bent, arched, rounded, bowed, twisted, crooked, humped, sinuous. *see* CURVE v.

cushion n *resting on a cushion* pillow, bolster, pad, hassock, mat, squab, pillion, scatter cushion, floor cushion, beanbag.

cushion v **1** *cushioning her head* pillow, bolster, cradle, support, prop up. **2** *cushion the blow* soften, lessen, diminish, mitigate, allay, deaden, muffle, stifle. **3** *cushion the child from reality* protect, shield, buttress.

custody n **1** *in the custody of his mother* | *having custody of the children* guardianship, wardship, trusteeship, charge, care, keeping, keep, safe-keeping, protection, guidance, supervision, superintendence, surveillance, control, tutelage, aegis; auspices. **2** *suspects in custody* imprisonment, detention, confinement, incarceration, restraint, constraint, duress.

custom n **1** *it was their custom to leave early* habit, practice, routine, way, wont, policy, rule. **2** *local customs* practice, convention, ritual, procedure, ceremony, form, formality, usage, observance, way, fashion, mode,

style, praxis. **3** *thank than for their custom* trade, business, patronage, purchasing.

customarily adv as a rule, usually, generally, in the ordinary way, ordinarily, normally, commonly, habitually, routinely, traditionally.

customary adj *customary to tip* | *her customary practice* accustomed, usual, regular, common, habitual, traditional, routine, fixed, set, established, everyday, familiar, wonted, confirmed, normal, ordinary, favourite, popular, stock, well-worn.

customer n patron, client, buyer, purchaser, shopper, consumer; clientele; *inf* regular.

customs npl import taxes; duty, toll, levy, tariff.

cut v **1** *cut his finger/throat* gash, slash, lacerate, slit, nick, notch, pierce, penetrate, wound, lance, incise, score. **2** *cut the logs/meat* cut up, chop, sever, divide, cleave, carve, slice. **3** *cut a key/gem* shape, fashion, form, mould, chisel, carve, sculpt, sculpture, chip away, whittle. **4** *cut a design* carve, engrave, incise, score. **5** *cut their hair* | *cut the hedge/the grass* trim, clip, snip, crop, prune, dock, shear, shave, pare, mow. **6** *cut some flowers* detach, gather, harvest, reap. **7** *cut expenditure* reduce, curtail, curb, retrench, cut back down/on, decrease, lessen, lower, diminish, contract, ease up on, prune, slash, slim down, rationalize, slenderize, economize on. **8** *cut the text* shorten, abridge, condense, abbreviate, contract, compact, précis, summarize, epitomize. **9** *cut the unsuitable parts* delete, edit out, blue-pencil, excise. **10** *his behaviour cut me* hurt, offend, wound, distress, grieve, pain, sting, trouble, discomfort. **11** *his old friend cut him* shun, ignore, snub, spurn, give the cold shoulder to, cold-shoulder, look right through, turn one's back on, slight, scorn, send to Coventry, insult; *inf* freeze out. **12** *the lines cut here* intersect, bisect, cross, decussate. **13** *cut the engine* | *the engine suddenly cut* stop, come to a stop, halt, turn off, switch off, stop working, malfunction. **14** *cut a record/tape* record, make a recording on, put on disc/tape, make a tape of, tape-record. **cut across** *cut across national prejudices* transcend, go beyond, rise above. **cut back** *cut back on expenditure* economize, reduce. *see* CUT v 7. **cut down 1** *cut down a tree* fell, saw down, hew, chop/hack down. **2** *cut down on expenditure* economize, reduce. *see* CUT v 7. **3** *cut down in his prime* kill, slay, slaughter, massacre, mow down, dispatch. **cut in** *"wait", he cut in* | *cut in on a conversation* interrupt, interpose, break in, intervene, intrude; *inf* butt in. **cut off 1** *cut off supplies/communication* break off, disconnect, interrupt, suspend, bring to an end, discontinue, halt, stop, intercept, obstruct, hinder, thwart. **2** *cut off from the town by snow* isolate, separate, sever. **3** *cut off without a penny* disinherit, disown, renounce. **4** *cut off in his prime* kill. *see* CUT DOWN 3. **cut out 1** *cut out the bad part* remove, delete, excise, extract. **2** *cut out eating chocolate* give up, refrain from, stop, cease. **3** *cut out the middleman* leave out, omit, eliminate, exclude, do away with. **4** *cut out the competition* oust, supplant, displace, supersede. **5** *the engine cut out* stop, stop working. *see* CUT v 13. **6** *not cut out for teaching* suit, equip/design for. **cut short** *cut short a holiday* interrupt, break off, leave unfinished, truncate, abort, bring to an untimely end. **cut up** v **1** *cut up the meat* slice, carve, chop, dice, mince, grind, divide up. **2** *the mugger cut up the old man* slash, knife, stab, lacerate, wound, injure. **3** *the teacher really cut up his essay/friend* criticize, ridicule, find fault with, tear to pieces/shreds, take apart, give a hard time to; *inf* pan, slate, knock.

cut n **1** *a cut on his finger* gash, slash, laceration, incision, slit. **2** *a cut of meat* section, piece. **3** *go for a cut at the hairdresser* trim, clip, crop. **4** *a cut in expenditure/salary* cutback, decrease, reduction, lessening, curtailment, retrenchment, contraction. **5** *cut of her jacket* fashion, style. **6** *power cut* loss, temporary interruption. **7** *I want my cut* share, portion, proportion.

cut-price adj reduced, cheap, bargain.

cutthroat n *set upon by cutthroats* thug, killer, murderer, assassin, homicide,

butcher, liquidator, slayer, executioner; *inf* hit man.

cutthroat adj **1** *a cutthroat attack* murderous, death-dealing, homicidal, savage, violent, bloody, bloodthirsty, fierce, ferocious, barbarous, cruel. **2** *a cutthroat business* ruthless, merciless, pitiless, unfeeling, relentless, dog-eat-dog, fiercely competitive.

cutting adj **1** *a cutting wind* biting, bitter, piercing, raw, keen, penetrating, stinging, sharp, chill, chilling, icy. **2** *a cutting remark* hurtful, wounding, caustic, acid, barbed, acrimonious, trenchant, mordant, scathing, acerbic, sarcastic, sardonic, spiteful, vicious, malicious.

cutting n **1** *collect cuttings about his famous mother* clipping, newspaper clip, clip. **2** *plant cuttings* slip, scion. **3** *a cutting from the length of material* piece, part, bit.

cycle n **1** *occur in cycles* recurrent period, rotation, round, revolution. **2** *compare the completed cycles* series, sequence, succession, run. **3** *travel by cycle* bicycle, bike, tandem, tricycle, monocycle.

cyclone n windstorm, storm, gale, squall, hurricane, whirlwind, tornado, typhoon.

cynic n pessimist, doom merchant, doomster, doom and gloom merchant, sceptic, scoffer, doubter, misanthrope.

cynical adj pessimistic, sceptical, scoffing, doubting, unbelieving, disbelieving, distrustful, suspicious, misanthropic, critical, sardonic.

cynicism n pessimism, scepticism, scoffing, doubt, unbelief, disbelief, distrust, suspicion, misanthropy, criticism, sardonicism.

Dd

dab v *dab one's eyes | dab paint on* pat, press, touch, blot, smudge, besmear, bedaub.

dab n **1** *give one's eyes a quick dab* pat, press, touch, blot, smudge. **2** *add a dab of paint/butter* touch, bit, speck, spot, trace, drop, dash, soupçon, tinge, suggestion, hint, modicum.

dabble v **1** *dabble in politics* toy with, dip into, scratch the surface of, flirt with, tinker with, potter about with, trifle with, play with, fiddle with, dally with, have a smattering of. **2** *dabble one's fingers/feet in water* dip, splash, paddle, wet, moisten, dampen, sprinkle, spray, spatter, slosh.

dabbler n *a dabbler in art* dilettante, amateur, non-professional, layman, laywoman, tinkerer, potterer, trifler, dallier.

daft adj **1** *a daft idea* silly, absurd, stupid, foolish, idiotic, insane, crazy, mad, lunatic, nonsensical, senseless, fatuous, ridiculous, ludicrous, asinine, witless; *inf* dopey, cracked. **2** *the daft boy in the village* simple, simple-minded, feeble-minded, slow-witted, dim-witted, dull-witted, touched, deranged, unhinged, demented, out of one's mind, insane, mad; *inf* not all there, not quite right, crazy, mental, nuts, nutty, dopey, crackers, cracked, potty, barmy, batty, cuckoo, bonkers, dotty, dippy. **3** *she's daft about him* besotted by, infatuated with, obsessed by, doting on, enthusiastic about; *inf* crazy/nuts/nutty about, potty/dotty about, sweet/gone on.

dagger n stiletto, dirk, poniard, skean, bayonet, knife, blade, sheath knife, bowie knife.

daily adj **1** *a daily newspaper* of/occurring each day, everyday, diurnal, quotidian, circadian. **2** *a daily occurrence* everyday, day-to-day, routine, ordinary, common, commonplace, usual, regular, habitual, customary, wonted.

daily adv *visit her daily* every day, once a day, day after day, day by day, per diem.

dainty adj **1** *dainty china figures | dainty little girls* petite, neat, delicate, exquisite, refined, tasteful, fine, elegant, graceful, trim, pretty. **2** *a dainty morsel* tasty, delicious, appetizing, choice, delectable, palatable, flavoursome, savoury, toothsome, luscious, juicy, succulent. **3** *a dainty eater* particular, discriminating, fastidious, fussy, choosy, finicky, finical, refined, nice, scrupulous, meticulous, squeamish.

dainty n *dainties with afternoon tea* titbit, delicacy, sweetmeat, confection, fancy, *bonne bouche*.

dais n platform, stage, stand, podium, pulpit.

dale n valley, vale, glen, dell, coomb; *Scots* strath.

dally v **1** *dallying on the way home* dawdle, delay, loiter, linger, tarry, waste/kill time, take one's time, while away time; *inf* dilly-dally. **2** *dally with his affections | dally with an idea* trifle, toy, flirt, tinker; *inf* fool.

dam n *a river dam* barricade, barrier, barrage, wall, embankment, obstruction, hindrance.

damage v *damage one's property/reputation* do damage to, harm, injure, hurt, impair, abuse, spoil, mar, deface, defile, vandalize, wreck, destroy, ruin, play havoc with, devastate, do mischief to, tamper with, mutilate.

damage n **1** *damage to one's property/reputation* harm, injury, hurt, impairment, abuse, defilement, defacement, detriment, vandalism, destruction, ruin, havoc, devastation, mischief, outrage, accident, loss, suffering. **2** *what's the damage?* cost, expense, charge, bill, account, total.

damages npl *receive damages from the court* compensation, indemnity, reparation, reimbursement, restitution, satisfaction.

dame n peeress, baroness, noblewoman, lady, dowager, aristocrat, *grande dame*.

damn v **1** *damned by the priest* curse, doom, execrate, imprecate, excommunicate, anathematize, proscribe, interdict. **2** *habitually damning* curse, swear, blaspheme, maledict, use bad language. **3** *damned by his neighbours* condemn, censure, criticize, castigate, denounce, berate, reprimand, reprove, abuse, inveigh against, excoriate. **4** *a play damned by the critics* criticize, attack, flay; *inf* pan, slam, slate, knock, blast, take to pieces, take apart.

damn n *not be worth a damn | not care a damn* jot, whit, iota, hoot, two hoots; *inf* tinker's damn, brass farthing.

damnable adj **1** *damnable cruelty* accursed, cursed, diabolical, fiendish, infernal, abominable, atrocious, execrable, base, wicked, heinous, vile, despicable, detestable, hateful, horrible, hideous, obnoxious, revolting, repulsive, foul, repugnant. **2** *damnable weather* nasty, unpleasant, disagreeable, foul, objectionable.

damnation n **1** *suffer damnation* sending to hell, eternal punishment, perdition, doom. **2** *the damnation of/by the priest* curse, execration, imprecation, excommunication, anathema, anathematization, proscription, interdict. **3** *the damnation of his neighbours* condemnation, censure, criticism, castigation, denunciation. *see* DAMN v 3. **4** *the damnation of the play* criticism, attacking. *see* DAMN v 4.

damned adj **1** *damned souls* cursed, accursed, doomed, lost, condemned, execrated, excommunicated, anathematized. *see* DAMN v 1. **2** *this damned machine/weather* annoying, confounded, uncooperative, nasty, hateful, detestable, odious.

damning adj *damning evidence* incriminating, condemnatory, condemning, damnatory, implicating, implicatory, accusatorial.

damp adj **1** *damp clothes/grass* wettish, moist, dank, soggy, dewy. **2** *a damp day | damp weather* wettish, rainy, drizzly, humid, clammy, muggy, misty, foggy, vaporous.

damp n **1** *the damp in the house* dampness, wetness, moisture, dankness. **2** *the damp of the day* dampness, wetness, raininess, humidity, clamminess, mugginess; rain, drizzle. *see* DAMPNESS 2. **3** *act as a damp on our enjoyment* damper, discouragement, check, curb, obstacle. *see* DAMPER.

damp v **1** *damp the clothes* dampen, wet, moisten, humidify. **2** *damp their enthusiasm | damp down his enjoyment* dampen, discourage, dull, dispirit, depress, dash, cool, chill, check, curb, restrain, stifle, inhibit, deter, lessen, limit, diminish, allay, put a damper on, throw cold water on. **3** *damp the noise | damp down the vibrations* reduce, lessen, diminish, decrease, moderate. **4** *damp the fire | damp down the furnace* bank, smother, stifle, extinguish.

dampen v **1** *dampen the clothes/atmosphere* wet, moisten, damp, humidify, vaporize. **2** *dampen their enthusiasm* damp, damp down, discourage, dull, dash, check, stifle, inhibit, put a damper on. *see* DAMP v 2.

damper n *act as a damper on our enthusiasm* discouragement, depression, chill, pall, gloom, cloud, check, curb, obstacle, hin-

drance, impediment, restraint, deterrent; *inf* wet blanket.

dampness n **1** *dampness in the house* damp, wetness, moisture, dankness. **2** *the dampness of the weather* damp, wetness, raininess, drizzliness, dankness, humidity, clamminess, mugginess; wet, mist, fog, vapour, rain, drizzle.

damsel n young woman, girl, young lady, maid, maiden, lass.

dance v **1** *dance in the dancehall | dance with her* move/sway to music, execute dance steps, twirl, pirouette; *inf* shake a leg, hoof it; *Amer inf* cut a rug. **2** *children dancing about* caper, skip, prance, hop, frolic, gambol, jump, jig, romp, bounce, whirl, spin. **3** *dance a child on one's knee* bounce, jiggle, dandle, ride.

dance n **1** *go to a dance* ball, dancing party; *inf* hop. **2** *learn/perform a dance | study dance* ballroom dance, folk dance, modern dance; ballet, eurhythmics.

dandle v *dandle a child on one's knee* dance, bounce, jiggle, ride.

dandy n fop, coxcomb, popinjay, beau, blade, man about town, boulevardier, sharp dresser.

danger n **1** *an element of danger* risk, peril, hazard, jeopardy, endangerment, imperilment, precariousness, insecurity, instability. **2** *a danger to society* menace, threat, peril, risk, minacity, imminence.

dangerous adj **1** *involved in a dangerous venture* risky, perilous, hazardous, chancy, precarious, uncertain, insecure, unsound, unsafe, exposed, defenceless; *inf* hairy. **2** *a dangerous crook/omen* menacing, threatening, alarming, ominous, nasty, ugly, treacherous, minacious.

dangle v **1** *keys dangling from her waist* hang, hang down, swing, sway, trail, droop, depend. **2** *dangle the keys* swing, sway, wave, brandish, flourish, flaunt. **3** *he is always dangling after her* follow, follow on the heels of, hang around, attach oneself to. **4** *he dangled the temptation of a holiday* hold out, entice someone with, lure someone with, tempt someone with.

dangling adj hanging, drooping, swinging, swaying, trailing, unconnected, disconnected, loose.

dank adj damp, wet, moist, humid, clammy, chilly.

dapper adj **1** *a dapper man dressed in black* smartly dressed, smart, well-groomed, well turned out, neat, trim, spruce, out of a bandbox, stylish, chic; *inf* natty. **2** *dapper* *for his age* active, agile, spry, sprightly, nimble, lively, brisk.

dapple v *dapple with paint | sunlight dappling the leaves* dot, spot, fleck, bespeckle, mottle, stipple, bedaub.

dappled adj *dappled leaves | a dappled horse* spotted, marked, mottled, flecked, blotched, blotchy, variegated, particoloured, pied, piebald, brindled, pinto.

dare v **1** *dare not go* have the courage to, pluck up courage to, take the risk to, be brave enough to, have the nerve to, risk, hazard, venture, make bold to. **2** *dare him to go* challenge, throw down the gauntlet, provoke, goad, taunt. **3** *dare his father's anger | dared the rapids* defy, brave, face, meet, meet head on, confront, stand up to.

dare n *accept his dare* challenge, provocation, goad, taunt, ultimatum.

daredevil adj *a daredevil attitude | daredevil actions* daring, adventurous, bold, audacious, courageous, intrepid, fearless, undaunted, dauntless, rash, heedless, madcap, hare-brained, foolhardy, impetuous, imprudent, incautious, desperate.

daredevil n *daredevils on the racing circuit* adventurer, desperado, stunt man, madcap, exhibitionist; *inf* show-off.

daring adj *a daring person/plan* bold, adventurous, brave, courageous, valiant, audacious, intrepid, fearless, undaunted, dauntless, unshrinking, rash, reckless, madcap, foolhardy, wild, daredevil, desperate.

daring n *the daring of the explorers* boldness, adventurousness, bravery, courage, courageousness, valour, audacity, nerve, pluck, grit, intrepidity, fearlessness, rashness, recklessness, temerity, foolhardiness, wildness, desperation; *inf* guts, spunk.

dark adj **1** *a dark night* black, pitch-black, pitch-dark, inky, jet-black, unlit, unlighted, ill-lighted, poorly lit, dim, dingy, indistinct, shadowy, shady, murky, foggy, misty, cloudy, overcast, sunless. **2** *dark of hair* dark-haired, brunette, dark brown, jet-black, sable, ebony. **3** *dark of skin* dark-skinned, swarthy, sallow, olive-skinned, dusky, black, ebony. **4** *dark thoughts* dismal, gloomy, sombre, cheerless, bleak, joyless, drab, dreary, depressed, dejected, melancholy, grim, grave, funereal, morose, mournful, doleful. **5** *in a dark mood* angry, moody, brooding, sullen, dour, glum, morose, sulky, frowning, scowling, glowering, forbidding, threatening, ominous. **6** *dark deeds* evil, wicked, sinful, villainous, iniquitous, vile, base, foul, horrible, atrocious, abominable, nefarious, barbaric, barbarous, sinister, damnable, fiendish, infernal, satanic, hellish, flagitious. **7** *the dark ages* unenlightened, ignorant, uneducated, unschooled, uncultivated, uncultured, unlettered, benighted. **8** *a dark meaning* abstruse, recondite, arcane, profound, deep, incomprehensible, obscure, unfathomable, puzzling, enigmatic, cryptic, complicated, complex, difficult, intricate. **9** *a dark secret | keep it dark* concealed, hidden, veiled, secret, mysterious, mystic, esoteric, occult.

dark n **1** *sitting in the dark* darkness, blackness, absence of light, gloom, gloominess, dimness, murk, murkiness, shadowiness, shade; *lit* tenebrosity. **2** *when dark comes/falls* night, night-time, nightfall, dead of night, evening, twilight. **3** *in the dark about his motives* a state of ignorance/unenlightenment.

darken v **1** *the sky darkened* grow dark/darker, blacken, cloud over, dim, grow dim. **2** *darken the room* make dark/darker, make dim, shade. **3** *darken one's skin* make dark/darker, tan, blacken, black, make opaque, begrime. **4** *his mood/face darkened* blacken, grow angry/annoyed, grow/become gloomy, become depressed/dispirited, grow troubled, sadden.

darkness n **1** *the darkness of the room | darkness fell* dark, blackness, gloom, dimness, murk, shadowiness; twilight, nightfall. *see* DARK n 1, 2. **2** *the darkness of the middle ages* ignorance, lack of knowledge, unenlightenment. **3** *the darkness of her secret* mystery, concealment, secrecy, obscurity, veiledness.

darling n **1** *goodbye, darling* dear, dearest, dear one, love, sweetheart, beloved, sweet, honey. **2** *the child's a little darling* charmer, pet, sweetheart, honey; *inf* poppet, sweetie. **3** *the darling of the press* favourite, pet, apple of one's eye, toast; *inf* blue-eyed boy; *Amer inf* fair-haired boy.

darling adj **1** *his darling wife* dear, dearest, loved, beloved, adored, cherished, treasured, precious, prized, valued. **2** *a darling little girl* adorable, sweet, lovely, attractive, charming, winsome, enchanting, engaging, captivating, bewitching, alluring; *inf* cute.

darn v *darn socks* mend, repair, sew up, stitch, patch.

darn n *the darn is obvious* repair, mend, patch, reinforcement.

dart n **1** *throwing a poisoned dart* arrow, barb, quarrel. **2** *make a sudden dart* dash, rush, run, bolt, bound, spring, leap, start.

dart v **1** *dart into the bushes* dash, rush, bolt, fly, flash, sprint, tear, run, bound, shoot, spring, leap, start, scuttle; *inf* scoot. **2** *dart an angry look* throw, cast, shoot, send, fling, toss, flash, hurl, sling, propel, project.

dash n **1** *make a dash for freedom* rush, bolt, run, race, flight, dart, sprint, sortie, spurt; *inf* scoot. **2** *a dash of water on his face* splash, sprinkle, spattering, plash. **3** *a dash of salt* little, bit, drop, pinch, sprinkling, grain, touch, trace, tinge, smack, suspicion, suggestion, soupçon. **4** *carry it off with dash* élan, style, verve, vigour, spirit, vivacity, liveliness, flair, panache, flourish, brio; *inf* pizzazz.

dash v **1** *dash into the road* rush, hurry, hasten, bolt, run, race, fly, dart, sprint, tear, speed; *inf* scoot. **2** *waves dashing against the shore* strike, beat, break, crash, smash, batter, splinter, shatter. **3** *dash the plate to the floor* smash, crash, throw, hurl, fling, slam, sling, cast, pitch, catapult. **4** *dash her hopes* shatter, destroy, ruin, blight, spoil, frustrate, thwart, baulk, check. **5** *spirits dashed by the misfortune* depress, dispirit, deject, cast down, lower, sadden, dishearten, discourage, daunt, abash, dampen.

dashing adj **1** *a dashing young officer* debonair, stylish, spirited, lively, buoyant, energetic, animated, dynamic, gallant, bold, daring, plucky, dazzling, swashbuckling; *inf* peppy. **2** *dashing uniforms* smart, jaunty, sporty, stylish, elegant, fashionable, chic, dazzling, showy, flamboyant.

dastardly adj cowardly, craven, fearful, faint-hearted, cowering, chicken-livered; *inf* yellow.

data npl basic facts, facts, figures, statistics, details; information, material, input.

date n **1** *on a certain date* day, point in time. **2** *artefacts from a previous date* time, age, period, era, century, decade, year, stage. **3** *we have a lunch date* appointment, engagement, meeting, rendezvous, assignation, tryst. **4** *who is her date?* partner, escort, girlfriend, boyfriend, beau; *inf* steady. **to date** so far, as of now, up to now, up to the present, up to this point. **out of date** *out-of-date ideas/clothes* outdated, dated, old-fashioned, unfashionable, outmoded, obsolete, antiquated, archaic, *passé*; *inf* old-hat. **up to date** *up-to-date ideas/clothes* modern, up to the minute, current, contemporary, fashionable, à la mode; *inf* trendy.

date v **1** *the vase dates from the seventeenth century* originate in, come from, belong to, exist from, bear the date of. **2** *can you date this table?* assign a date to, put a date to, determine the date of, fix the period of. **3** *clothes beginning to date* become dated, become old-fashioned/outmoded/obsolete, show one's age, pass out of use, obsolesce. **4** *he's dating the girl next door* go out/around with, go with, take out; *inf* go steady with.

dated adj *dated fashions* out of date, outdated, old-fashioned, outmoded, antiquated, *passé*; *inf* old-hat.

daub v **1** *daub paint on* smear, plaster, smudge, spatter, splatter, slap, slop. **2** *daub the walls with paint* smear, besmear, bedaub, plaster, spatter, splatter, cover, coat, deface.

daub n *a daub of paint* smear, smudge, blot, spot, patch, blotch, splotch, splodge.

daunt v intimidate, frighten, scare, alarm, overawe, dismay, disconcert, unnerve, take aback, abash, cow, unman, discourage, dishearten, dispirit, deter, put off.

dawdle v go/walk slowly, move at a snail's pace, loiter, take one's time, dally, linger, delay, lag/trail behind, kill/waste time, fritter time away, idle, potter about; *inf* dilly-dally.

dawn n **1** *get up at dawn* daybreak, break of day, sunrise, first light, early morning, crack of dawn, cock crow; *Amer* sun-up; *lit* aurora, dayspring. **2** *the dawn of civilization* dawning, beginning, birth, start, rise, emergence, commencement, origin, inception, genesis, outset, onset, advent, appearance, arrival, unfolding, development.

dawn v **1** *day dawned* begin, break, grow light, lighten, brighten, gleam. **2** *civilization dawning* begin, be born, come into being/existence, start, rise, emerge, commence, originate, appear, arrive, unfold, develop. **3** *the truth suddenly dawned on them* occur to one, strike, hit, register, cross/enter one's mind, come into one's head, come to mind, pass through one's mind, flash across one's mind.

day n **1** *when day dawns* daytime, daylight, daylight hours, broad daylight. **2** *work all day* twenty-four hours, full day, working day, solar day. **3** *in this modern day | in the days of Henry VIII* period, time, age, era, epoch, generation. **4** *the steam train has had its day* prime, heyday, full flowering, useful/productive lifetime, peak, zenith, ascendancy. **5** *set a day* date, set time, time, particular day, appointed day. **day after day** *raining day after day* continuously, relentlessly, persistently, without respite, continually, ceaselessly, regularly. **day by day** *grow bigger day by day* daily, gradually, steadily, progressively.

daybreak n dawn, break of day, sunrise, first light. see DAWN n 1.

daydream n 1 *lost in a daydream* reverie, wool-gathering, musing, imagining, fantasy, vision, fancy, hallucination. 2 *their daydream never materialized* dream, pipedream, figment of the imagination; wishful thinking; fond hopes, wishes, castles in the air, castles in Spain.

daydream v dream, muse, be lost in thought, stare into space, indulge in wool-gathering, fantasize, indulge in fancy, hallucinate.

daylight n 1 *look at the colours in daylight* light of day, natural light, sunlight. 2 *children coming home in daylight* daytime, daylight hours; broad daylight. 3 *wake at daylight* dawn, daybreak, break of day, sunrise. see DAWN n 1. **see daylight** 1 *after being confused she finally saw daylight* understand, comprehend, see the light, fathom, penetrate, discern; *inf* get the idea, catch on, get the hang of it, twig, get the picture. 2 *his project never saw daylight* be completed/accomplished, see light of day, come to public attention.

daze v 1 *dazed by the blow* stun, stupefy, shock, confuse, bewilder, befuddle, muddle, addle, numb, benumb, paralyse. 2 *dazed by the news* stun, shock, amaze, astonish, astound, dumbfound, stagger, startle, surprise, dismay, disconcert, take aback, bewilder, perplex, nonplus; *inf* flabbergast, floor, take one's breath away.

daze n *in a daze* stupor, state of shock, trancelike state, confused state; confusion, bewilderment, distraction, numbness.

dazzle v 1 *dazzled by the car's headlights* blind, temporarily, deprive of sight, bedazzle, daze, overpower. 2 *dazzled by her beauty/wit* overpower, overwhelm, overawe, awe, stagger, fascinate, hypnotize, strike dumb, dumbfound, strike, impress, amaze, astonish; *inf* bowl over, take one's breath away.

dazzle n 1 *overcome by the dazzle of the lights* brightness, brilliance, gleam, flash. 2 *fascinated by the dazzle of the circus* brilliance, splendour, magnificence, glitter, sparkle, glory; *inf* razzle-dazzle, razzmatazz, pizzazz.

dead adj 1 *the dead man/flower* deceased, late, defunct, departed, lifeless, extinct, perished, gone, no more, passed on/away. 2 *dead matter* inanimate, lifeless, without life, exanimate. 3 *a dead issue/language* obsolete, outmoded, outdated, extinct, lapsed, passed, *passé*, discontinued, disused, fallen into disuse, stagnant, inactive, invalid, ineffective, inoperative, not work-

ing, barren, sterile. 4 *dead to my pleas* unresponsive, insensitive, indifferent, apathetic, dispassionate, unsympathetic, emotionless, unemotional, unfeeling, lukewarm, cold, frigid, wooden, inert. 5 *dead fingers* numb, numbed, benumbed, unfeeling, paralysed. 6 *dead eyes* emotionless, glazed, glassy, spiritless, impassive. 7 *dead desire* extinguished, finished, terminated, quenched, quashed, quelled, suppressed, smothered, stifled. 8 *a dead place to live*|*a dead time of day* dull, boring, uninteresting, tedious, tiresome, wearisome, uneventful, humdrum, flat, stale, insipid, vapid; *inf* dead-and-alive. 9 *a dead loss/cert* complete, absolute, total, entire, outright, utter, downright, out-and-out, thorough, unqualified, unmitigated. 10 *come to a dead halt* abrupt, sudden, quick, rapid, swift, hurried, instantaneous, unexpected, unforeseen. 11 *a dead shot* accurate, exact, precise, unerring, unfailing, sure, correct, direct. 12 *feeling dead* tired, tired out, exhausted, worn out, fatigued, spent; *inf* dead beat, played out, pooped.

dead adv *dead right/serious/tired* completely, absolutely, totally, entirely, exactly, utterly, thoroughly, categorically, without qualification.

deaden v 1 *deaden the pain*|*deaden the effects of the blow* blunt, dull, muffle, weaken, diminish, reduce, subdue, suppress, moderate, soothe, assuage, abate, mitigate, alleviate, smother, stifle, damp, damp down, numb. 2 *deaden the sound* dull, muffle, reduce, moderate, stifle, damp down, mute. 3 *emotions deadened by grief* render/make insensitive, desensitize, numb, benumb, anaesthetize, impair, incapacitate, paralyse.

deadlock n 1 *the talks ended in deadlock* stalemate, checkmate, impasse, standstill, halt, stop, stoppage, cessation, standoff. 2 *the game ended in deadlock* tie, draw, dead heat.

deadly adj 1 *deadly poisons* fatal, lethal, mortal, death-dealing, dangerous, destructive, harmful, pernicious, noxious, malignant, venomous, toxic, poisonous, virulent. 2 *deadly enemies* mortal, hated, hostile, murderous, fierce, implacable, remorseless, unrelenting, grim, savage; *inf* at each other's throats. 3 *deadly seriousness* intense, great, marked, extreme, excessive, immoderate, inordinate. 4 *deadly paleness* death-like, deathly, ashen, ghostly, white, pallid, wan, pale, ghastly. 5 *a deadly aim* precise, accurate, unerring, unfailing, sure, true, on target, on the mark. 6 *a deadly speaker/speech* boring, dull, tedious, uninteresting, dry, monotonous, wearisome, humdrum, lack-lustre.

deadly adv completely, absolutely. *see* DEAD adv.

deaf adj **1** *born deaf* with impaired hearing, unhearing, hard of hearing, stone deaf, deaf as a post. **2** *deaf to their pleas* unmoved by, indifferent to, oblivious to, heedless of, unconcerned with, unmindful of.

deafen v *the noise deafened us* make temporarily deaf, deprive of hearing, impair one's hearing, burst one's eardrums.

deafening adj very loud, ear-splitting, ear-piercing, overpowering, overwhelming, booming, thunderous, resounding, reverberating, ringing, dinning.

deal v **1** *deal with a problem* attend to, see to, take care of, cope with, handle, manage, sort out, tackle, take measures. **2** *the book deals with skin problems* be about, have to do with, concern, concern itself with, discuss, consider, treat of. **3** *deal honourably with the prisoners* act, behave, conduct oneself. **4** *deal in stocks and shares* trade, traffic, do business, buy and sell, be concerned/engaged in, negotiate, bargain. **5** *deal cards* distribute, give out, share out, divide out, hand out, dole out, mete out, allocate, dispense, allot, assign, apportion, bestow. **6** *deal a blow* deliver, administer, give, direct, aim.

deal n **1** *a deal of trouble | a great deal of money | feel a good deal better* amount, quantity, degree. **2** *finalize the deal* arrangement, transaction, agreement, negotiation, bargain, contract, pact, understanding, compact, concordat. **3** *be given a fair deal* treatment, handling, usage, procedure.

dealer n **1** *a dealer in used cars* trader, salesman, saleswoman, salesperson, tradesman, merchant, marketer, retailer, wholesaler, vendor, chandler, trafficker, pedlar. **2** *a dealer in the stock market* jobber, broker.

dealing n *a business noted for fair dealing* business methods/practices, actions; treatment, policy, behaviour, conduct.

dealings npl *have dealings with the firm* business, trade, commerce, trafficking, truck; transactions, relations, negotiations.

dean n **1** *dean of the arts faculty* faculty head, head of department, university official, provost. **2** *the cathedral dean* chapter head, supervisor; rural dean. *see* ECCLESIASTIC n.

dear adj **1** *his dear wife | dear friends* beloved, loved, darling, adored, cherished, close, intimate, esteemed, respected. **2** *her dearest possessions/possessions dear to him* precious, treasured, valued, prized, cherished,

favourite, favoured. **3** *what a dear child* sweet, darling, endearing, lovable, attractive, winning, enchanting, winsome, angelic. **4** *a dear brand of car* expensive, costly, highly priced, high-priced, overpriced, exorbitant, valuable, at a premium, up-market; *inf* pricey, steep.

dear n **1** *goodbye, my dear* love, beloved, darling, loved one, sweetheart, sweet, honey, pet, precious, treasure. **2** *his mother's a dear* lovable person, darling, sweetheart, pet, angel.

dear adv *a victory costing dear | sell dear* at a high price, at great cost, at a heavy cost, much, with great loss/damage.

dearly adv **1** *loving her dearly* very much, greatly, deeply, extremely, profoundly. **2** *pay dearly for mistakes* dear, at great cost, much, with great loss/damage. *see* DEAR adv.

dearth n lack, scarcity, scarceness, want, deficiency, shortage, shortness, insufficiency, paucity, sparseness, meagreness, scantiness, rareness, exiguity.

death n **1** *death by drowning* dying, decease, demise, end, passing, passing away, passing on, loss of life, expiration, quietus, departure from life, final exit, eternal rest; *inf* curtains. *see* DIE 1. **2** *the death of his hopes* end, finish, termination, cessation, ruin, ruination, extinction, destruction, extermination, eradication, annihilation, obliteration, extirpation. **3** *death came in the night* angel of death, grim reaper. **4** *their deaths were on his conscience* killing, slaying, murder, slaughter, fatality; bloodshed, massacre, carnage.

deathless adj immortal, undying, eternal, everlasting, unfading, perpetual, imperishable, timeless, memorable.

debacle n fiasco, failure, downfall, collapse, disintegration, disaster, catastrophe, tumult, turmoil, havoc, ruin, ruination, devastation, defeat, rout, overthrow.

debar v **1** *debarred from the club* shut out, exclude, bar, keep out, preclude. **2** *debarred from voting* exclude, bar, prevent, prohibit, forbid, proscribe, disallow, veto.

debase v **1** *debase the sport | debase oneself* degrade, devalue, demean, drag down, disgrace, dishonour, shame, bring shame to, discredit, lower/reduce the status of, cheapen, humble, humiliate. **2** *debase coins | debase the mixture* alloy, adulterate, depreciate, dilute, contaminate, pollute, taint, corrupt, bastardize, vitiate.

debatable adj arguable, disputable, questionable, open to question, controversial, contentious, doubtful, open to doubt, dubious, uncertain, unsure, unsettled, unde-cided, borderline, moot.

debate n **1** *a formal debate* | *open to debate* dis-cussion, argument, dispute, disputation, difference of opinion, wrangle, altercation, controversy, contention, war of words, polemic. **2** *after some debate with himself* con-sideration, deliberation, reflection, contem-plation, musing, meditation, cogitation.

debate v **1** *debate the issue* discuss, argue, argue the pros and cons of, dispute, wran-gle, bandy words, contend, contest, alter-cate, controvert, moot; *inf* kick around. **2** *he debated with himself* consider, think over, deliberate, reflect, contemplate, muse, meditate, cogitate.

debauched adj dissipated, dissolute, degenerate, corrupt, immoral, abandoned, profligate, intemperate, licentious, promis-cuous, wanton.

debauchery n dissipation, dissoluteness, degeneracy, corruption, immorality, profli-gacy, intemperance, licentiousness, promiscuity, wantonness, rakishness, liber-tinism, perversion.

debilitate v *debilitated by his illness* weaken, make feeble, enfeeble, enervate, incapaci-tate, cripple, impair, sap, undermine, exhaust, wear out, prostrate, devitalize.

debility n weakness, feebleness, frailty, infirmity, enfeeblement, enervation, inca-pacity, impairment, lack of energy, exhaus-tion, fatigue, lack of vitality, sickliness, decrepitude, malaise.

debonair adj **1** *a debonair young man* suave, urbane, self-assured, elegant, refined, well-bred, genteel, smart, dashing, dapper, charming, courteous, mannerly, gallant, chivalrous; *inf* smooth. **2** *debonair young peo-ple* carefree, jaunty, light-hearted, cheerful, cheery, merry, vivacious, buoyant, breezy, sprightly.

debris n rubble, wreckage, detritus, rub-bish, litter; remains, ruins, fragments.

debt n **1** *pay my debts* money owing, bill, account, score, tally; dues, arrears, debits. **2** *acknowledge his debt to his family* indebted-ness, obligation, liability. **3** *customers in debt* | *got himself into debt* a state of owing money, indebtedness, arrears; *inf* the red.

debunk v cut down to size, deflate, punc-ture, expose, show up, show in one's/its true light, mock, ridicule.

debut n first appearance, first performance, first time, *première*, beginning, introduc-tion, launching, coming-out, entrance.

decadence n **1** *the decadence of the empire* decay, degeneration, deterioration, decline,

wane, ebb, debasement, degradation, retro-gression. **2** *the decadence of the wealthy set* dissipation, dissoluteness, moral decay, debauchery, degeneracy, immorality, self-indulgence, licentiousness, hedonism, epi-cureanism, corruption, depravity.

decadent adj **1** *a decadent empire* decaying, degenerating, deteriorating, declining, waning, ebbing, debased, degraded, falling off, on the wane. **2** *decadent behaviour/people* dissipated, dissolute, debauched, degener-ate, immoral, self-indulgent, licentious, hedonistic, epicurean, corrupt, depraved.

decamp v **1** *the manager decamped with the firm's takings* make off, run off/away, flee, take off, abscond, escape, cut and run; *inf* skedaddle, hightail it, hotfoot it, vamoose, skip, do a moonlight flit. **2** *the soldiers decamped* break camp, strike tents, move on.

decant v pour out, draw off, drain, tap.

decapitate v behead, execute, guillotine, put on the block.

decay v **1** *food/material decaying* rot, go bad, decompose, putrefy, spoil, perish, corrode. **2** *an empire decaying* degenerate, deterio-rate, decline, fail, wane, ebb, dwindle, crumble, disintegrate, fall to pieces, sink, collapse, moulder, shrivel, wither, die, waste/wear away, atrophy.

decay n **1** *the decay of the food/material* rot-ting, going bad, decomposition, putrefac-tion, putrescence, putridity, spoilage, perishing, corrosion. **2** *spot the decay in the food/teeth/flesh* rot, decomposition; caries, gangrene. **3** *the decay of the empire* degenera-tion, deterioration, decline, failure, wan-ing, ebb, crumbling, disintegration, collapse, withering, death, atrophy. *see* DECAY v 2.

decease n *the decease of his wife* death, dying, demise, passing, passing away/on, expiration, quietus. *see* DEATH 1.

decease v *he deceased before his wife* die, pass away/on, expire, perish, meet one's death.

deceased adj *his deceased wife* late, dead, departed, defunct, lost, expired. *see* DEAD adj 1.

deceit n **1** *practise deceit* deceitfulness, deception, duplicity, double-dealing, fraud, fraudulence, cheating, trickery, duping, chicanery, underhandedness, cunning, craftiness, craft, wiliness, guile, dissimula-tion, dissembling, pretence, artifice, treachery; *inf* hanky-panky. **2** *win by a deceit* deception, trick, stratagem, ruse, dodge, subterfuge, fraud, cheat, swindle, sham, imposture, hoax, pretence, fake, misrepresentation, blind, wile, artifice, shift, Trojan horse; *inf* leg-pull.

deceitful adj **1** *don't believe that deceitful child* lying, untruthful, dishonest, mendacious, insincere, false, disingenuous, untrustworthy, two-faced, underhand, crafty, cunning, sly, guileful, hypocritical, perfidious.
2 *deceitful practices* deceptive, duplicitous, misleading, double-dealing, fraudulent, cheating, underhand, crooked, counterfeit, sham, bogus, dissembling, treacherous, perfidious, illusory, spurious, specious; *inf* sneaky, tricky.

deceive v **1** *his friendliness deceived us* take in, mislead, delude, fool, pull the wool over one's eyes, throw dust in the eyes of, misguide, lead on, trick, hoodwink, hoax, dupe, swindle, outwit, bamboozle, seduce, ensnare, entrap, beguile, double cross, cozen, gull; *inf* con, pull a fast one on, pull one's leg, take one for a ride. **2** *he's deceiving his wife* be unfaithful to, betray; *inf* two-time; *Amer inf* cheat on.

decelerate v slow down, reduce speed, brake, put the brakes on, ease up.

decency n propriety, decorum, seemliness, modesty, good taste, respectability, purity, correctness, good form, etiquette, delicacy, dignity, appropriateness, fitness, suitability.

decent adj **1** *a scarcely decent exhibition* decorous, seemly, modest, proper, nice, tasteful, polite, respectable, pure, correct, dignified, delicate, appropriate, fitting, fit, suitable, becoming, *comme il faut*. **2** *decent kind of fellow* obliging, helpful, accommodating, generous, kind, thoughtful, courteous, civil, honest, honourable, trustworthy, dependable, worthy, respectable, upright. **3** *earning quite a decent salary* acceptable, adequate, sufficient, ample, average, competent.

deception n **1** *practise deception* deceit, deceitfulness, double-dealing, duplicity, fraud, fraudulence, cheating, chicanery, trickery, underhandedness, cunning, dissimulation, pretence, artifice. *see* DECEIT 1. **2** *win by a deception* trick, stratagem, ruse, dodge, subterfuge, fraud, cheat, swindle, sham, pretence, blind. *see* DECEIT 2.

deceptive adj **1** *appearances can be deceptive* deceiving, misleading, false, illusory, delusive, fallacious, ambiguous, specious, spurious, mock, pseudo. **2** *deceptive practices* deceitful, duplicitous, fraudulent, cheating, underhand, cunning, crafty, crooked, counterfeit, sham, bogus, dissembling; *inf* sneaky, tricky.

decide v **1** *to decide to go | I cannot decide* come to a decision, reach/make a decision, make up one's mind, resolve, come to a conclusion, commit oneself, choose. **2** *that decided the matter* settle, resolve, bring to a conclusion, determine, work out, clinch; *inf* sew up. **3** *the judge will decide the case | the judge decided for/against the defence* judge, adjudge, adjudicate, arbitrate, umpire, referee; make a judgement on, pass/pronounce judgement, give a verdict, make a ruling.

decided adj **1** *a decided difference between them* distinct, clear, clear-cut, definite, certain, marked, pronounced, obvious, express, unmistakable, absolute, emphatic, categorical, unambiguous, undeniable, unequivocal, indisputable, undisputed, unquestionable. **2** *he's quite decided | a decided effort* determined, resolute, firm, strong-minded, dogged, purposeful, unhesitating, unwavering, unswerving, unfaltering, incisive, forceful, emphatic. **3** *the matter was decided* settled, resolved, concluded, determined, clinched; *inf* sewn up. *see* DECIDE 2.

decidedly adv *decidedly unwell* distinctly, clearly, definitely, certainly, positively, markedly, unmistakably, absolutely, downright, undeniably, unquestionably. *see* DECIDED 1.

deciding adj **1** *the deciding factor* crucial, critical, decisive, determining, conclusive, most influential, significant, chief, principal, prime. **2** *the deciding vote* casting, determining, conclusive.

decipher v **1** *decipher the coded message* decode, translate, interpret, construe, solve, work out, figure out, unravel, unfold, reveal; *inf* crack. **2** *cannot decipher her handwriting* make out, read, understand, comprehend, deduce.

decision n **1** *come to a decision* resolution, conclusion, determination, settling, settlement. **2** *the judge announced his decision* judgement, ruling, pronouncement, verdict, adjudgement, adjudication, arbitration; findings. **3** *a man of decision* decisiveness, determination, resolution, resoluteness, resolve, firmness, strong-mindedness, doggedness, strength of mind/will, firmness of purpose, purpose, purposefulness.

decisive adj **1** *a decisive person* determined, resolute, firm, dogged, purposeful, unhesitating, unwavering, unswerving, unfaltering, incisive, forceful, emphatic. **2** *a decisive factor* deciding, determining, determinate, definitive, conclusive, final, settling, critical, crucial, momentous, emphatic, absolute, categorical, significant, influential, important, definite, positive.

deck v **1** *deck the rooms for Christmas* bedeck, decorate, adorn, ornament, trim, embellish, garnish, festoon, garland, trick out, beautify, prettify, enhance, grace, enrich. **2** *people all decked out in their Sunday best* dress up, clothe, attire, array, apparel, rig out, tog up, outfit; *inf* be got up.

declaim v **1** *ministers declaiming from the pulpit* make a speech, speak, hold forth, lecture, harangue, rant, rail, pronounce, sermonize, speechify, spout, make an oration, orate, perorate; *inf* sound off, spiel. **2** *the preacher declaiming against adultery* speak out, protest, rail, inveigh.

declamation n *a passionate declamation* speech, address, oration, lecture, delivery, sermon, discourse, recitation, harangue, tirade; *Amer inf* stump speech.

declamatory adj *declamatory style* rhetorical, oratorical, theatrical, high-flown, bombastic, pompous, pretentious, orotund, fustian.

declaration n **1** *the declaration of his interests | declaration of war* announcement, statement, proclamation, notification, pronouncement, publishing, broadcasting, promulgation, edict, manifesto, pronunciamento. **2** *his declaration that he was innocent* statement, assertion, maintaining, insistence, protestation, averment, affirmation, contention, profession, claim, allegation, avowal, swearing. **3** *his behaviour is a declaration of his innocence* acknowledgement, revelation, disclosure, manifestation, confirmation, proof, testimony, validation, certification, attestation.

declare v **1** *declare one's interests | declare war* announce, make known, proclaim, pronounce, publish, broadcast, promulgate, trumpet, blazon. **2** *he declared that he was innocent* state, assert, maintain, aver, affirm, contend, profess, claim, allege, avow, swear. **3** *his behaviour declared his innocence* show, make known, reveal, disclose, manifest, confirm, prove, testify to, validate, certify, attest.

decline v **1** *decline an invitation | we must decline | decline to comment* turn down, give the thumbs down to, rebuff, repudiate, forgo; refuse, say no, send one's regrets. **2** *his influence declined* get less, lessen, decrease, diminish, wane, dwindle, fade, ebb, fall/taper off, abate, flag. **3** *the empire is declining | his strength is declining* deteriorate, degenerate, decay, fail, fall, wither, weaken, fade away, wane, ebb, sink. **4** *the*

terrain declines here descend, slope/slant down, dip, sink.

decline n **1** *the decline of his influence/strength* lessening, decrease, downturn, downswing, diminishing, diminution, waning, dwindling, fading, ebb, falling-off, abatement, slump, plunge, nosedive. *see* DECLINE v 2. **2** *the decline of the empire* deterioration, degeneration, decay, failure, fall, withering, enfeeblement, wane, ebb, atrophy. *see* DECLINE v 3. **3** *hikers sighting a decline* slope, declivity, dip.

decompose v **1** *corpses decomposing* decay, rot, go bad, putrefy, fester. **2** *the structure gradually decomposing* break up, fall apart, disintegrate, crumble. **3** *decompose the chemical substance* separate, break up/down, divide, disintegrate, dissect, analyse, atomize, dissolve, resolve.

decomposition n **1** *the decomposition of the corpses* decay, rot, rotting, putrefaction, putrescence, putridity, cariosity, cariousness. **2** *the decomposition of the structure* disintegration, crumbling. *see* DECOMPOSE 2. **3** *the decomposition of the substance* separation, breakup, breakdown, division, disintegration, dissection, analysis, atomization, dissolution, resolution.

decor n decoration, furnishing, furbishing, colour scheme, ornamentation.

decorate v **1** *decorate the Christmas tree* adorn, ornament, trim, embellish, garnish, festoon, garland, trick out, beautify, prettify, enhance, grace, enrich. **2** *decorate the house* paint, wallpaper, paper, renovate, refurbish, furbish; *inf* do up, spruce up. **3** *decorated for bravery* cite, honour, confer an award, give a medal to, pin a medal on.

decoration n **1** *the decoration of the tree* adornment, ornamentation, trimming, embellishment, garnishing, beautification, prettification, enhancement. *see* DECORATE 1. **2** *admire the decoration* furnishing, colour scheme. *see* DECOR. **3** *buy tree decorations* ornament, trinket, bauble, spangle, knickknack, gimcrack, doodah, gewgaw, fandangle; trimming, tinsel. **4** *a dress with many decorations* trimming, frill, flounce, furbelow, falderal, frippery, flourish, scroll, arabesque, curlicue. **5** *a decoration for bravery* award, medal, badge, star, ribbon, laurel, wreath; colours, insignia.

decorative adj *decorative features* ornamental, fancy, adorning, embellishing, garnishing, beautifying, prettifying, enhancing, nonfunctional.

decorous adj **1** *decorous behaviour* proper, seemly, decent, becoming, befitting, tasteful, in good taste, correct, *comme il faut*, appropriate, suitable, fitting, apt, apposite, polite, well-mannered, mannerly, well-behaved, genteel, refined, well-bred, dignified, respectable. **2** *decorous young ladies* modest, demure, reserved, sedate, staid.

decorum n **1** *behave with decorum* decorousness, propriety, properness, seemliness, decency, good taste, correctness, appropriateness, politeness, courtesy, refinement, breeding, deportment, dignity, respectability. **2** *observe decorum* etiquette, protocol, punctilio, customary behaviour, good form, politeness, *politesse*, conformity; *inf* the thing to do.

decoy n *a dead animal as a decoy | chocolates used as a decoy* lure, bait, enticement, inducement, temptation, attraction, allurement, ensnarement, entrapment, snare, trap, pitfall.

decoy v *decoy the deer/child* lure, entice, induce, tempt, seduce, inveigle, ensnare, entrap, snare, trap.

decrease v **1** *numbers/volume decreasing* lessen, grow less, diminish, reduce, drop, fall off, decline, dwindle, contract, shrink. **2** *decrease the numbers/amount* lessen, make fewer/less, lower, reduce, cut down/back, cut down/back on, curtail, contract, diminish. **3** *the wind/storm decreased* die down, abate, subside, let up, slacken, ebb, wane, taper off, peter out.

decrease n **1** *the decrease in numbers/amount* lessening, lowering, reduction, drop, decline, falling-off, downturn, cut-back, curtailment, diminution, contraction, shrinkage. **2** *the decrease in the wind/storm* dying down, abatement, subsidence, letting-up, slackening, ebb, wane.

decree n **1** *the emperor's decree* edict, order, law, statute, act, ordinance, regulation, rule, injunction, enactment, command, mandate, proclamation, dictum, precept, manifesto, pronunciamento. **2** *the judge's decree* ruling, verdict, judgement, decision; findings.

decree v *the emperor decreed it | fate decreed it* ordain, rule, order, command, dictate, lay down, prescribe, pronounce, proclaim, enact, adjudge, enjoin, direct, decide, determine.

decrepit adj **1** *decrepit old men* feeble, enfeebled, infirm, weak, weakened, weakly, frail, wasted, debilitated, disabled, incapacitated, crippled, doddering, tottering, aged, old, elderly, senile, superannuated, effete, emasculated, senescent. **2** *decrepit old furniture/houses* dilapidated, rickety, broken-down, tumbledown, ramshackle, run-down, worn-out, battered, decayed,

deteriorated, antiquated, superannuated, the worse for wear, on its last legs.

decry v disparage, deprecate, belittle, cry down, discredit, depreciate, devalue, play down, derogate, detract, diminish, minimize, underestimate, underrate, undervalue, criticize, carp at, cavil at, censure, blame, condemn, denounce, run down, rail against, rap, traduce; *inf* knock, do a hatchet job on.

dedicate v **1** *dedicate her life to the Church* devote, give, give over, commit, pledge, surrender. **2** *dedicate the book to him* inscribe, address, name, assign, offer. **3** *dedicate a church* devote to God, bless, make holy, consecrate, sanctify, hallow.

dedicated adj *a dedicated teacher* devoted, committed, wholehearted, single-minded, enthusiastic, zealous, sworn, pledged.

dedication n **1** *work with dedication* devotion, devotedness, commitment, wholeheartedness, single-mindedness, enthusiasm, zeal. **2** *her dedication to the Church* devotion, commitment, allegiance, loyalty, faithfulness, adherence. **3** *the dedication in the book* inscription, address, message. **4** *the dedication of the church* blessing, consecration, sanctification, hallowing.

deduce v conclude, come to the conclusion that, infer, reason, gather, glean, come to understand, understand, assume, presume; *inf* suss out.

deduct v subtract, take away, take off, withdraw, abstract, remove, discount; *inf* knock off.

deduction n **1** *the detectives' sound deduction* conclusion, inference, reasoning, assumption, presumption, corollary; results, findings. **2** *the deduction of tax* subtraction, taking-off, withdrawal, abstraction, removal. *see* DEDUCT.

deed n **1** *brave deeds* act, action, feat, exploit, performance, achievement, accomplishment, undertaking, enterprise. **2** *in deed but not in name* fact, reality, truth. **3** *legal deeds* signed document, contract, legal agreement, indenture, instrument; title deed, deed of covenant.

deem v think, believe, consider, judge, feel, imagine, conceive, regard, see, hold, estimate, calculate, suppose, reckon, account.

deep adj **1** *a deep hole/wound* extending far down/in, cavernous, yawning, profound, bottomless, immeasurable, fathomless, unfathomable. **2** *a deep voice* low, low-pitched, full-toned, bass, rich, powerful, resonant, sonorous, rumbling, booming, resounding. **3** *a deep red colour* dark, intense, vivid, rich, strong. **4** *deep distrust* profound, extreme, intense, very great, great, grave, deep-seated, deep-rooted. **5** *a deep thinker/person* clever, intellectual, learned, wise, sagacious, sage, discerning, penetrating, perspicacious. **6** *deep affection* intense, heart-felt, deep-felt, fervent, ardent, impassioned, deep-seated, deep-rooted. **7** *a deep plot* cunning, crafty, artful, shrewd, astute, devious, scheming, designing, insidious, wily, ingenious. **8** *a deep mystery/secret* obscure, unclear, abstruse, mysterious, hidden, secret, unfathomable, recondite, esoteric, enigmatic, arcane. **9** *deep in thought* absorbed, engrossed, preoccupied, rapt, immersed, lost, intent, engaged.

deep adv **1** *dig deep* far down, far in. **2** *deep into the wood/night* far, long, late.

deep n **the deep 1** *ships wrecked on the deep* sea, ocean, main; high seas; *inf* the briny. **2** *in the deep of the night* deepness, middle, midst, mid-point, central point.

deepen v **1** *his distress/love deepened* grow, increase, intensify. **2** *deepen the hole* dig out, excavate, scoop out, hollow out. **3** *deepen his distress/love* increase, add to, intensify, magnify, strengthen, heighten, reinforce.

deeply adv **1** *deeply impressed/hurt* very, greatly, extremely, profoundly, intensely, keenly, acutely. **2** *feel his death deeply* acutely, keenly, intensely, sharply, with feeling, feelingly, passionately, with distress.

deface v *deface the book/wall with writing* spoil, disfigure, mar, blemish, deform, ruin, sully, tarnish, damage, vandalize, injure, uglify.

de facto adj *a de facto ruler* actual, existing, existent, real.

de facto adv *ruling de facto* in fact, in reality, really, actually, in actuality, in effect.

defamation n slander, libel, character assassination, aspersion, calumny, smear campaign, backbiting, vilification, traducement, defilement, obloquy, contumely, malicious gossip, scandal, abuse, malediction, disparagement, denigration, detraction, derogation; smear, slur, insult; *inf* mud-slinging.

defamatory adj slanderous, libellous, calumnious, calumniatory, slurring, backbiting, vilifying, traducing, defiling, contumelious, malicious, abusive, injurious, maledictory, maledictive, disparaging, denigratory, detracting, derogatory, insulting; *inf* mud-slinging.

defame v slander, libel, cast aspersions on, asperse, blacken the name/character of, malign, smear, run down, speak evil of, backbite, vilify, traduce, besmirch, defile, stigmatize, disparage, denigrate, discredit, decry, insult; *inf* do a hatchet job on, sling/fling/throw mud at, drag through the mud; *Amer inf* bad-mouth.

default n **1** *debtors guilty of default* non-payment, failure to pay, non-remittance; *inf* welshing, bilking. **2** *lose the game by default* | *in default of evidence* absence, failure to appear, non-appearance, omission, lack, want, deficiency, neglect, negligence, delinquency, dereliction.

defaulter n **1** *defaulters ordered to pay* non-payer, debt-dodger, levanter; *inf* welsher, bilker. **2** *several defaulters in the competition* non-appearer, absentee.

defeat v **1** *defeat their team/army* beat, conquer, win a victory over, get the better of, vanquish, rout, trounce, thrash, overcome, overpower, overthrow, overwhelm, crush, quash, quell, subjugate, subdue, repulse; *inf* wipe the floor with, clobber, zap. **2** *your attitude defeats me* | *the problem defeats me* baffle, puzzle, perplex, confound, frustrate. **3** *defeat your own purpose* hinder, prevent, ruin, thwart, frustrate, foil, balk, hamper, obstruct, impede, discomfit; *inf* put the kibosh on, nip in the bud. **4** *the motion was defeated* reject, overthrow, throw out, outvote.

defeat n **1** *suffer defeat by the enemy* conquest, vanquishment, rout, beating, trouncing, thrashing, debacle, reverse, overpowering, overthrow, subjugation. *see* DEFEAT V 1. **2** *the defeat of their plans* downfall, breakdown, collapse, failure, ruin, abortion, miscarriage; undoing, reverse, disappointment, setback, discomfiture, rejection, overthrow.

defeatist n quitter, yielder, pessimist, prophet of doom, doomwatcher, reneger; *inf* doomster.

defecate v pass/discharge/excrete faeces, have a bowel movement, void excrement, have diarrhoea; *inf* do number two, have a BM, do a pooh, do a woopsie.

defect n **1** *a defect in the machine/writing* fault, flaw, imperfection, deficiency, weakness, weak spot/point, shortcoming, failing, snag, kink, deformity, blemish, crack, break, tear, scratch, spot, mistake, error; *inf* bug. **2** *defects in the educational system* deficiency, shortage, shortfall, inadequacy, insufficiency, shortcoming, lack, want, omission, weakness, failing, fault, flaw, absence.

defect v **1** *soldiers defected | party members defecting* go over to the enemy, desert, turn traitor, change sides/allegiances, *desert one's side/cause*, shift ground, break faith, tergiversate, be apostate, apostatize. **2** *defect from one's country/party* desert, abandon, forsake, renounce, repudiate, secede from, rebel against, revolt against; *inf* rat on.

defection n *soldiers guilty of defection* desertion, treason, betrayal, changing sides/allegiances, disloyalty, rebellion, mutiny, perfidy, tergiversation, apostasy, secession, dereliction, recreancy.

defective adj **1** *a defective machine* faulty, flawed, imperfect, weak, deficient, deformed, incomplete, malfunctioning, in disrepair, cracked, torn, scratched. **2** *defective in character* lacking, wanting, deficient, inadequate, insufficient, short, low, scant. **3** *mentally defective* having learning difficulties, impaired, retarded, abnormal, subnormal.

defector n deserter, turncoat, traitor, renegade, tergiversator, apostate, recreant; *inf* rat.

defence n **1** *built as a defence against the enemy* protection, shield, safeguard, guard, security, cover, shelter, screen, fortification, resistance, deterrent. **2** *build defences against the enemy* barricade, fortification, rampart, bulwark, buttress, fortress, fastness, keep, bastion. **3** *money spent on defence* military measures/resources, armaments, weapons. **4** *published a defence of his ideas* vindication, justification, apologia, apology, argument, plea, explanation, explication, excuse, extenuation, exoneration, palliation. **5** *the accused gave his defence* denial, rebuttal, plea, pleading, testimony, declaration, case, excuse, alibi.

defenceless adj **1** *defenceless old people* helpless, vulnerable, weak, powerless, impotent. **2** *defenceless cities* undefended, unprotected, unguarded, unfortified, unarmed, vulnerable, open to attack, wide open, exposed, endangered.

defend v **1** *defend the city* protect, guard, safeguard, watch over, keep from harm, preserve, secure, shield, shelter, screen, fortify, garrison, fight for. **2** *defend one's ideas* vindicate, justify, argue/speak for, speak on behalf of, give an apologia for, make a case for, plead for, explain, give reasons for, give the rationale behind, exonerate, palliate. **3** *the newspaper defended its journalist* support, back, stand by, stand/stick up for, argue for, champion, endorse, uphold, sustain, bolster.

defendant n accused, prisoner at the bar, appellant, litigant, respondent.

defender n **1** *defenders of the city* protector, guard, bodyguard, guardian, preserver, keeper. **2** *defenders of the faith* supporter, backer, champion, upholder, endorser, sustainer, bolsterer.

defensible adj **1** *a defensible position/attitude* defendable, justifiable, arguable, tenable, valid, maintainable, sustainable, plausible, permissible, excusable, pardonable, vindicable. **2** *defensible terrain* invulnerable, impregnable, impenetrable, secure, safe, unattackable, unassailable, fortified.

defensive adj **1** *defensive enemy tactics* defending, protecting, protective, safeguarding, shielding, watchful, averting, withstanding, opposing. *see* DEFEND 1. **2** *the child's defensive attitude* self-defensive, oversensitive, thin-skinned, prickly; *inf* uptight.

defer[1] v *defer the meeting* postpone, put off, adjourn, delay, hold over, shelve, put on ice, pigeon-hole, suspend, table, stay, hold in abeyance, prorogue.

defer[2] v *defer to the expert | defer to your superior knowledge* yield, submit, bow, give way, give in, surrender, accede, capitulate, acquiesce, comply with, respect.

deference n **1** *showing deference for the old* respect, regard, consideration, attentiveness, attention, thoughtfulness, esteem, courteousness, courtesy, politeness, civility, dutifulness, reverence, veneration, homage. **2** *his deference to the expert* yielding, submission, surrender, capitulation, accession, acquiescence, complaisance, obeisance.

deferential adj **1** *a deferential regard for the old* respectful, considerate, thoughtful, attentive, courteous, polite, civil, reverent, reverential, dutiful, regardful. **2** *a deferential attitude to the experts* respectful, reverential, yielding, submissive, acquiescent, compliant, complaisant, tractable, obsequious, obeisant.

deferment n **1** *the deferment of the meeting* postponement, deferral, putting off, adjournment, delay, shelving, suspension, tabling. **2** *be granted a deferment* postponement, respite, stay, moratorium, reprieve.

defiance n **1** *treat the enemy with defiance* resistance, opposition, confrontation, noncompliance, disobedience, recalcitrance, rebelliousness, insubordination, contempt, disregard, scorn, insolence, contumacy. **2** *a spirit of defiance* challenge, provocation, daring, boldness, audacity, bravado, aggression, truculence; *lit* derring-do.

defiant adj **1** *defiant opposition* resistant, non-compliant, disobedient, recalcitrant, rebellious, insubordinate, mutinous, refractory, contemptuous, scornful, indifferent, insolent. **2** *with a defiant air* challenging, provocative, bold, audacious, aggressive, truculent.

deficiency n **1** *vitamin deficiency* lack, want, shortage, dearth, insufficiency, inadequacy, scarcity, deficit, scantiness, paucity, absence. **2** *a deficiency in the system* defect, fault, flaw, imperfection, weakness, weak point/spot, failing, shortcoming, snag.

deficient adj **1** *deficient in vitamins* lacking, wanting, short of, low on, defective. **2** *deficient quantities* insufficient, inadequate, scanty, meagre, skimpy, sketchy, exiguous. **3** *a deficient system* defective, faulty, flawed, imperfect, incomplete.

deficit n **1** *the deficit is £100* shortfall, deficiency, shortage, slippage. **2** *we made a deficit* loss, minus amount; indebtedness, debt.

defile v **1** *streets defiled by filth* pollute, foul, befoul, dirty, soil. **2** *defile young minds* corrupt, contaminate, taint, infect, tarnish, sully, pervert, vitiate. **3** *defile reputations* defame, sully, blacken, cast asperions on, cast a slur on, denigrate, besmirch, stigmatize. **4** *defile the altar* desecrate, profane, treat sacrilegiously, make impure, contaminate, vitiate. **5** *defile young girls* ravish, rape, deflower, violate.

definable adj determinable, ascertainable, fixable, fixed, definite, clear-cut, precise, exact, specific.

define v **1** *define one's terms* give the meaning of, state precisely, spell out, describe, explain, expound, interpret, elucidate, clarify. **2** *define one's position* describe, determine, set out, outline, detail, specify, designate. **3** *define the boundary* mark out, fix, establish, settle, demarcate, bound, delimit, delineate, circumscribe. **4** *a tree defined against the light* outline, delineate, silhouette.

definite adj **1** *definite plans* specific, particular, precise, exact, defined, well-defined, clear, clear-cut, explicit, express, determined, fixed, established, confirmed. **2** *it's definite that he's going* certain, sure, positive, guaranteed, settled, decided, assured, conclusive, final. **3** *definite boundaries* fixed, marked, demarcated, delimited, circumscribed.

definitely adv *definitely the best applicant* certainly, surely, for sure, without doubt/question, beyond any doubt, undoubtedly, indubitably, positively, absolutely, undeniably, unmistakably, plainly, clearly, obviously, categorically, decidedly, unequivocally, easily, far and away, without fail.

definition n **1** *the definition of one's terms* meaning, statement of meaning, description, explanation, exposition, expounding, interpretation, elucidation, clarification. **2** *the definition of the boundaries* marking out, fixing, settling, establishment, determination, demarcation, bounding, delimiting, delimitation, delineation, circumscribing. **3** *the definition of the image* precision, sharpness, distinctness, clearness, clarity, contrast, visibility, focus.

definitive adj **1** *the definitive answer* conclusive, final, ultimate, decisive, unconditional, unqualified, absolute, categorical. **2** *the definitive edition* authoritative, most reliable, most complete, exhaustive, most perfect.

deflate v **1** *deflate the air-bed* let down, collapse, flatten, void, puncture. **2** *the air-bed deflated* collapse, empty of air, shrink, contract, flatten. **3** *deflate the pompous man* squash, humble, humiliate, mortify, chasten, subdue, dispirit; *inf* put down, debunk. **4** *deflate a currency* | *deflate the economy* devalue, depreciate, depress, diminish, reduce.

deflect v **1** *cause the bullet to deflect* turn aside/away, turn, alter course, change course/direction, diverge, deviate, veer, swerve, slew, drift, bend, twist, curve, shy, ricochet, glance off, divaricate, divagate. **2** *deflect the projectile* | *deflect him from his purpose* turn aside/away, turn, divert, switch, avert, sidetrack.

deflection n deviation, divergence, diversion, declination, aberration, divarication, divagation; turn, veer, swerve, drift, bend, curve.

deform v **1** *faces and bodies deformed by the fire* disfigure, deface, misshape, mar, ruin, spoil, uglify, damage, maim, injure, cripple, mutilate, mangle. **2** *deform the pieces of metal* misshape, distort, contort, buckle, twist, warp, malform, gnarl.

deformed adj **1** *deformed bodies* misshapen, malformed, distorted, contorted, twisted, crooked, curved, gnarled, crippled, maimed, humpbacked, hunchbacked, disfigured, ugly, unsightly, damaged, marred, mutilated, mangled. **2** *deformed minds* twisted, warped, perverted, corrupted, depraved, vile, gross.

deformity n **1** *deformity of the body* malformation, misshapenness, misproportion, disfigurement, imperfection, abnormality, irregularity, defacement, distortion, crookedness, ugliness, unsightliness; defect, flaw. **2** *deformity of minds* warpedness, perversion, corruption, depravity, vileness, grossness.

defraud v cheat, swindle, rob, fleece, rook, bilk, trick, fool, take in, hoodwink, mislead, delude, deceive, beguile, outwit; *lit* cozen; *inf* gyp, con, do, diddle, rip off, take for a ride, pull a fast one on, put one over on.

deft adj dexterous, adroit, nimble, nimble-fingered, handy, agile, skilful, skilled, proficient, adept, able, clever, expert, experienced.

defunct adj **1** *defunct ancestors* dead, deceased, departed, extinct, gone. **2** *defunct practices/organizations* obsolete, expired, non-existent, inoperative, invalid, non-functioning, bygone, outmoded, old-fashioned, *passé*.

defy v **1** *defied their parents* disobey, disregard, ignore, slight, flout, fly in the face of, thumb one's nose at, snap one's fingers at, spurn, scoff at, deride, scorn. **2** *defy the enemy forces* resist, withstand, brave, stand up to, confront, face, meet head-on, square up to, beard, defeat, repulse, repel, thwart, frustrate, foil, baffle. **3** *I defy you to stay* challenge, dare, throw down the gauntlet.

degeneracy n corruption, decadence, immorality, depravity, dissoluteness, debauchery, profligacy, wickedness, vileness, sinfulness, baseness, turpitude.

degenerate adj *degenerate function/person* degenerated, deteriorated, debased, declined, degraded, corrupt, decandent, immoral, depraved, dissolute, debauched, abandoned, profligate, wicked, vile, sinful, vice-ridden, disreputable, despicable, base, sordid, low, mean, ignoble.

degenerate v deteriorate, decline, worsen, decay, rot, fail, fall off, sink, slip, slide, go downhill, regress, retrogress, lapse; *inf* go to pot, go to the dogs, hit the skids.

degenerate n pervert, deviant, deviate, fiend, wretch.

degeneration n deterioration, debasement, degradation, regression, retrogression; decay, decline, descent, drop, sinking, slide, lapse. *see* DEGENERATE V.

degradation n **1** *the degradation of his family* debasement, discrediting, demeaning, deprecation, shaming, disgracing, dishonouring, humiliation, mortification. *see* DEGRADE 1. **2** *the degradation of the officers* downgrading, demotion, reduction to the ranks, deposition. *see* DEGRADE 2. **3** *witnessing a scene of degradation* degeneracy, corruption, decadence, immorality, depravity, dissolution, debauchery, vice, wickedness, sordidity, squalor.

degrade v **1** *his family degraded by his behaviour* debase, discredit, cheapen, belittle, demean, deprecate, deflate, devalue, lower, reduce, shame, disgrace, dishonour, humble, humiliate, mortify, abase, vitiate. **2** *officers degraded* downgrade, demote, reduce/lower in rank, reduce to the ranks, disrate, strip of rank, cashier, depose, remove from office, unseat, dethrone; *inf* kick upstairs, drum out. **3** *degraded by her immoral associates* debase, corrupt, pervert, defile, sully, debauch.

degraded adj *an immoral degraded crowd* degenerate, debased, corrupt, decadent, immoral, depraved, dissolute, debauched, abandoned, profligate, despicable, sordid. *see* DEGENERATE adj.

degrading adj *a degrading experience* debasing, discrediting, cheapening, belittling, demeaning, lowering, shaming, shameful, humiliating, mortifying, disgraceful, dishonourable, undignified; *inf* infra dig.

degree n **1** *reach a high degree of competence | third-degree burns* stage, level, grade, step, gradation, rung, point, mark, measure, notch, limit. **2** *to a marked degree* extent, measure, magnitude, level, amount, quality, intensity, strength, proportion, ratio. **3** *people of higher degree* rank, class, standing, status, station, position, grade, level, order, condition, estate. **by degrees** gradually, slowly, by stages, step by step, little by little, bit by bit, inch by inch.

dehydrate v **1** *they dehydrated the vegetables | heat was dehydrating the walkers* dry, dry up/out, sun-dry, desiccate, exsiccate, parch, sear. **2** *plants/bodies dehydrating* dry up, lose water, become thirsty.

deify v idolize, exalt, aggrandize, worship, adore, venerate, revere, pay homage to.

deign v condescend, stoop, lower oneself, think/see fit, deem worthy, consent.

deity n God, god, goddess, divine being, celestial being, supreme being, divinity, demiurge; godhead. *see* GOD.

dejected adj depressed, dispirited, discouraged, disheartened, downhearted, crestfallen, cast down, downcast, down, disappointed, unhappy, sad, miserable, blue, wretched, despondent, woebegone, forlorn, sorrowful, disconsolate, doleful, glum, gloomy, melancholy, morose, low in spirits, low-spirited, long-faced; *inf* down in the mouth/dumps.

dejection n depression, downheartedness, dispiritedness, discouragement, disappointment, unhappiness, sadness, misery, wretchedness, despondency, sorrowfulness, sorrow, disconsolateness, disconsolation, dolefulness, glumness, gloom, melancholy, despair; low spirits, blues; *inf* the dumps.

delay v 1 *delay our meeting* postpone, put off, adjourn, defer, hold over, shelve, suspend, table, stay, hold in abeyance, put on ice, put on the back burner. *see* DEFER 1. 2 *visitors delayed by the traffic* hold up/back, detain, slow up, set back, hinder, obstruct, hamper, impede, bog down, check, hold in check, restrain, halt, stop, arrest. 3 *Hurry up! Don't delay!* linger, loiter, hold back, dawdle, dally, dilly-dally, lag/fall behind, not keep pace, procrastinate, stall, tarry.

delay n 1 *the delay to the meeting* postponement, adjournment, deferment, suspension, tabling, stay. *see* DELAY v 1. 2 *holiday traffic delays* hold-up, wait, set-back, detainment, detention, hindrance, obstruction, impediment, check, stoppage, halt, interruption. 3 *the delay between trains* wait, waiting period, interval, lull, interlude, intermission. 4 *her delay made us late* lingering, loitering, dawdling, dallying, dilly-dallying, procrastination, stalling, tarrying. *see* DELAY v 3.

delectable adj 1 *delectable food* delicious, appetizing, inviting, tasty, savoury, enjoyable, luscious, palatable, flavoursome, toothsome; *inf* scrumptious, yummy, ambrosial. 2 *delectable girls/entertainment* delightful, charming, enchanting, adorable, captivating, winning, engaging, winsome, dainty, attractive, pleasing, agreeable, ravishing, exciting, titillating.

delectation n *for your delectation* delight, pleasure, enjoyment, entertainment, amusement, diversion, happiness, gratification, satisfaction, excitement, relish, titillation.

delegate n *our country's/conference delegate* representative, deputy, agent, spokesman, spokeswoman, spokesperson, ambassador, envoy, legate, messenger, go-between, proxy, emissary, commissary.

delegate v 1 *delegate tasks* pass on, hand over, transfer, give, commit, entrust, assign, relegate, consign, devolve. 2 *delegate him leader* appoint, designate, nominate, name, authorize, depute, commission,

mandate, empower, choose, select, elect, ordain.

delegation n 1 *our country's delegation* deputation, legation, contingent, mission, commission, embassy; delegates, envoys. 2 *the delegation of tasks* transference, committal, entrustment, assignment, relegation, consignment, devolution. *see* DELEGATE v 1. 3 *his delegation as leader* appointment, designation, nomination, authorization, commissioning, selection, election. *see* DELEGATE v 2.

delete v cross/strike out, rub out, cut out, erase, cancel, blue-pencil, edit out, remove, take out, expunge, eradicate, obliterate, efface, wipe/blot out.

deleterious adj harmful, injurious, hurtful, damaging, destructive, ruinous, bad, disadvantageous, noxious.

deliberate adj 1 *a deliberate act* intentional, planned, considered, calculated, designed, studied, studious, painstaking, conscious, purposeful, wilful, premeditated, pre-planned, prearranged, preconceived, predetermined, aforethought. 2 *slow deliberate speech/steps* careful, unhurried, cautious, thoughtful, steady, regular, measured, unwavering, unhesitating, unfaltering, determined, resolute, ponderous, laborious.

deliberate v 1 *looking out of the window deliberating* think, ponder, muse, meditate, reflect, cogitate, ruminate, brood, excogitate, be in a brown study. 2 *deliberate the advantages* think over, consider, ponder, reflect on, mull over, review, weigh up, evaluate. 3 *deliberate with colleagues* discuss, debate, confer, consult.

deliberately adv 1 *deliberately hurt her* intentionally, on purpose, purposefully, by design, knowingly, wittingly, consciously, premeditatedly, calculatedly, in cold blood. *see* DELIBERATE adj 1. 2 *speak/walk very deliberately* carefully, unhurriedly, cautiously, steadily, measuredly, unwaveringly, unhesitatingly, determinedly, ponderously. *see* DELIBERATE adj 2.

deliberation n 1 *after his deliberation* thinking, thought, consideration, pondering, musing, mulling, meditation, reflection, cogitation, rumination, brooding, weighing up, excogitation. *see* DELIBERATE v 1, 2. 2 *after deliberation with colleagues* discussion, debate, consultation, conferring, conference. 3 *speak with deliberation* care, carefulness, no hurry, caution, thoughtfulness, steadiness, determination, resoluteness, laboriousness. *see* DELIBERATE adj 2.

delicacy n 1 *the delicacy of the china/material* fineness, exquisiteness, fragility, slenderness, slightness, elegance, gracefulness, grace, daintiness, flimsiness, silkiness. *see* DELICATE 1. **2** *the delicacy of his health/wife* frailty, fragility, weakness, debilitation; sickliness, infirmity, poor/ill health. **3** *delicacy of the colours* paleness, mutedness, subtlety, softness, understatement. **4** *delicacy of the situation* difficulty, trickiness, sensitivity, ticklishness, precariousness. **5** *handle the matter with delicacy* care, consideration, sensitivity, sensibility, tact, discretion, finesse, diplomacy, politeness. **6** *the delicacy of her palate* discrimination, discernment, refinement, perceptiveness, criticalness, fastidiousness. *see* DELICATE 6. **7** *the delicacy of the mechanism* sensitivity, precision, accuracy, exactness. **8** *delicacy of touch* deftness, skill, expertise. **9** *buying some delicacies* gourmet food, titbit, dainty, treat, luxury, savoury, appetizer, *bonne bouche*.

delicate adj **1** *delicate china/material* fine, exquisite, fragile, slender, slight, elegant, graceful, dainty, flimsy, silky, gauzy, gossamer, wispy. **2** *his wife is delicate* frail, sickly, weak, debilitated, infirm, ailing, in poor health, unwell. **3** *delicate colours* pastel, pale, muted, subtle, soft, subdued, understated, faint. **4** *a delicate matter/situation* difficult, tricky, sensitive, ticklish, critical, precarious, touchy; *inf* sticky, dicey. **5** *require delicate handling* careful, considerate, sensitive, tactful, discreet, diplomatic, politic, kid-glove. **6** *a delicate palate* discriminating, discerning, refined, perceptive, critical, fastidious, finicky, pernickety, squeamish. **7** *a delicate mechanism* sensitive, precise, accurate, exact. **8** *a delicate touch* deft, skilled, skilful, expert. **9** *delicate food* dainty, choice, delicious. *see* DELICACY 9.

delicious adj **1** *delicious food* tasty, appetizing, mouth-watering, delectable, choice, dainty, savoury, flavoursome, flavourful, luscious, palatable, toothsome, ambrosial, ambrosian, nectareous, nectarean; *inf* scrumptious, yummy. **2** *a delicious evening* delightful, enchanting, exquisite, enjoyable, pleasurable, entertaining, amusing, diverting, pleasant, agreeable, charming, nice.

delight n *filled with delight* pleasure, joy, happiness, gladness, gratification, bliss, rapture, ecstasy, elation, jubilation, excitement, entertainment, amusement; *trans-*ports.

delight v **1** *delighted by the news* please, gladden, cheer, gratify, thrill, excite, transport, enchant, captivate, entrance, charm, entertain, amuse, divert; *inf* send. **2** *delight in reading* take/find pleasure, indulge, glory.

delighted adj pleased, joyful, happy, glad, gratified, overjoyed, blissful, enraptured, ecstatic, jubilant, thrilled, transported, excited, enchanted, captivated, entranced, charmed, entertained, amused, diverted; *inf* sent.

delightful adj *a delightful occasion/woman* pleasant, pleasing, agreeable, enjoyable, amusing, entertaining, diverting, pleasurable, pleasure-giving, gratifying, delectable, joyful, exciting, thrilling, rapturous, enchanting; captivating, fascinating, entrancing, ravishing, charming, attractive, beautiful, pretty, engaging, winning.

delineate v **1** *delineate her features* trace, draw the lines of, outline, draw, sketch, draft, block in, contour. **2** *delineate the statistics* make a diagram of, make a chart of, chart, map, map out, diagram. **3** *delineate his achievements* describe, define, set forth, outline, depict, portray.

delinquency n **1** *juvenile delinquency* wrongdoing, misdemeanour, misconduct, misbehaviour, mischievousness, transgression; offence, misdeed, crime. **2** *the soldier's delinquency* negligence, remissness, dereliction, omission, failure.

delinquent n *damage done by delinquents* offender, wrongdoer, culprit, lawbreaker, criminal, hooligan, vandal, ruffian, hoodlum, miscreant, malefactor, transgressor; juvenile delinquent, young offender.

delinquent adj **1** *delinquent young people* mischievous, culpable, transgressing, offending, criminal. **2** *delinquent policemen* negligent, neglectful, remiss, careless, slack, derelict.

delirious adj **1** *delirious patients* raving, incoherent, babbling, light-headed, irrational, deranged, demented, unhinged, mad, insane, crazy, out of one's mind; *inf* off one's head. **2** *delirious at the good news* ecstatic, euphoric, beside oneself, carried away, transported, hysterical, frenzied, wild with excitement, distracted, frantic, out of one's wits, feverish, Corybantic.

delirium n **1** *affected by delirium* temporary madness/insanity, irrationality, light-headedness, raving, incoherence, babbling. **2** *happy delirium* ecstasy, euphoria, hysteria, frenzy, wild emotion, wildness, excitement, distraction, feverishness, fever, passion.

deliver v **1** *deliver the mail/groceries* distribute, carry, bring, take, transport, convey, send, dispatch, remit. **2** *deliver the prisoners to the enemy* hand over, turn over, transfer, commit, grant, make over, give up, yield, surrender, relinquish, cede, resign. **3** *deliver* *them from enemies* set free, free, liberate, release, save, rescue, set loose, loose, extricate, discharge, ransom, emancipate, redeem, manumit. **4** *deliver a speech/sigh* utter, give voice to, voice, speak, give, give forth, express, pronounce, enunciate, proclaim, announce, declare, read, recite, broadcast, promulgate. **5** *deliver a blow | deliver a shot at* direct, aim, give, deal, administer, launch, inflict, throw, strike, hurl, pitch, discharge. **6** *deliver better sales figures* come up with, achieve, attain, provide, supply.

deliverance n **1** *deliverance from prison/evil* liberation, release, rescue, escape, discharge, ransom, emancipation, salvation, redemption, manumission. **2** *deliverances from the pulpit* pronouncement, declaration, announcement, proclamation, report, lecture, sermon, speech.

delivery n **1** *delivery is extra* distribution, carriage, transporting, transport, conveyance, dispatch. **2** *receive a delivery* consignment, load, batch. **3** *admire his clear delivery* manner of speaking, enunciation, articulation, intonation, elocution, utterance, presentation. **4** *a mother having a difficult delivery* confinement, labour, childbirth, parturition. **5** *delivery from the enemy* deliverance, liberation, release, rescue, escape. *see* DELIVERANCE 1. **6** *the delivery of a blow/ball* directing, aiming, launching, throwing, pitching. *see* DELIVER 5.

delude v mislead, deceive, fool, take in, trick, dupe, cheat, hoodwink, beguile, outwit, misguide, lead on, bamboozle, defraud, swindle, double-cross; *lit* cozen; *inf* con, pull a fast one on, lead up the garden path, take for a ride, put one over on, two-time.

deluge n **1** *houses swept away by the deluge* flood, spate, inundation, overflowing, flash flood, cataclysm. **2** *caught in the deluge without an umbrella* downpour, torrent, torrential rain, cloudburst. **3** *a deluge of correspondence* flood, rush, spate, torrent, avalanche, barrage, outpouring.

deluge v **1** *towns deluged with polluted water* flood, inundate, swamp, engulf, submerge, drown, soak, drench, douse. **2** *deluged by correspondence* inundate, flood, overrun, overwhelm, engulf, swamp, overload.

delusion n **1** *delusions of grandeur* false impression, false belief, misconception, misapprehension, misunderstanding, misbelief, mistake, self-deception, deception, error, fallacy, illusion, fancy, phantasm, fool's paradise. **2** *the delusion of the old lady*

deluding, misleading, deception, fooling, tricking, duping. *see* DELUDE.

de luxe adj luxurious, sumptuous, palatial, opulent, lavish, grand, rich, superior, exclusive, choice, select, elegant, splendid, costly, expensive; *inf* plush, up-market.

delve v **1** *delve into one's pockets/cupboards* search, rummage, ransack, dig into, ferret around, hunt through. **2** *delve into local history* research, investigate, look into, examine, probe, dig into, hunt through. **3** *animals delving* burrow, dig, excavate.

demagogue n political agitator, agitator, soapbox orator, rabble-rouser, firebrand, haranguer, troublemaker.

demand v **1** *workers demanding a rise* ask/call for, request, press for, insist on, urge, clamour for, make a claim for, lay claim to, claim. **2** *"What's that?" he demanded* ask, inquire, question, interrogate, challenge. **3** *work demanding care* require, need, necessitate, call for, take, involve, want, cry out for. **4** *parents demanding obedience | demand payment* expect, insist on, exact, impose, order, requisition.

demand n **1** *give in to their demands* request, entreaty, claim, requisition; insistence, pressure, clamour. **2** *answer his demand* inquiry, question, interrogation, challenge. **3** *the demands of the job* requirement, need, necessity, want, claim, imposition, exigency. **in demand** requested, required, sought after, popular, in vogue, fashionable; *inf* trendy.

demanding adj **1** *demanding children/wives* nagging, harassing, clamorous, importunate, insistent, imperious. **2** *demanding jobs* challenging, taxing, exacting, exigent, tough, hard, difficult, tiring, wearing, exhausting.

demarcation n **1** *the demarcation of the areas* boundary, border, limit, bound, margin, frontier. **2** *the demarcation of the factory jobs* separation, division, distinction, differentiation, delimitation, marking off, definition.

demean v lower, degrade, debase, devalue, demote, humble, abase, belittle, deprecate.

demeanour n behaviour, conduct, bearing, air, appearance, mien, deportment, carriage, comportment.

demented adj insane, mad, crazy, crazed, deranged, of unsound mind, out of one's mind, unhinged, unbalanced, touched, *non compos mentis*, maniacal, manic, frenzied, distraught, foolish, idiotic, crack-brained, lunatic; *inf* daft, barmy, dotty, loopy, batty, potty, crackpot, dippy, wacky.

dementia n madness; senile dementia, Alzheimer's disease, Alzheimer's.

demise n death, decease, passing, expiration, end, termination, cessation, quietus.

democracy n representative government, constitutional government, popular government, self-government; republic, commonwealth.

democratic adj of the people, representative, popular, popularist, egalitarian, republican, self-governing, autonomous.

demolish v **1** *demolish the building* knock down, pull/tear down, bring down, flatten, raze, level, bulldoze, dismantle, break up, pulverize. **2** *demolish the argument | demolish his self-confidence* destroy, put an end to, ruin, wreck, undo. **3** *demolish the opposition* defeat, conquer, vanquish, overthrow, overturn, quell, quash, suppress, destroy, annihilate, wipe out, finish off. **4** *demolish a plate of cakes* eat up, consume, devour, gobble up, put away.

demolition n **1** *the demolition of the buildings* knocking down, pulling down, flattening, razing, levelling, bulldozing. *see* DEMOLISH 1. **2** *the demolition of the argument* destruction, ruin, ruination, wrecking, undoing. **3** *demolition of the opposition* defeat, conquest, vanquishing, overthrow, destruction, annihilation. *see* DEMOLISH 3.

demon n **1** *the demons from hell* devil, evil/malignant spirit, fiend, cacodemon. **2** *the dictator's a demon* devil, fiend, brute, monster, savage, beast, barbarian, villain. **3** *the demon of creativity* daimon, eudemon, genius, guardian/ministering angel, familiar spirit, numen. **4** *he's a real demon for work* man/woman of action, hard worker, powerhouse, human dynamo, workaholic; *inf* whizz kid, eager beaver, busy bee. **5** *a demon at sailing | a demon tennis player* master, wizard, addict, fanatic; *inf* ace, freak.

demonic, demoniac, demoniacal adj **1** *demonic spirits* diabolic, diabolical, devilish, fiendish, satanic, hellish, infernal, evil, wicked, Mephistophelian, cacodemonic. **2** *demonic eyes/laughter* like one possessed, maniacal, manic, mad, crazed, frenzied, frantic, feverish, frenetic, hectic, furious, hysterical.

demonstrable adj provable, verifiable, attestable, confirmable, evincible.

demonstrate v **1** *demonstrate the proof of the proposition* show, indicate, determine, prove, validate, confirm, verify, establish. **2** *blushes demonstrating embarrassment* show, indicate, display, exhibit, express, manifest, evince, evidence. **3** *demonstrate putting*

on a bandage show, illustrate, give an idea of, teach, describe, explain, make clear, explicate, expound. **4** *demonstrate against nuclear weapons* protest, march, parade, rally, sit in, picket.

demonstration n **1** *demonstration of the proof of the proposition* indication, substantiation, confirmation, affirmation, verification, validation. *see* DEMONSTRATE 1. **2** *a demonstration of his embarrassment* indication, expression, manifestation, evincement; evidence. **3** *a demonstration of putting on a bandage* illustration, description, explanation, exposition, teach-in. **4** *a demonstration of the new product* exposition, presentation, exhibition; *inf* expo. **5** *take part in a student demonstration* protest, protest march, march, parade, rally, mass rally/lobby, sit-in, picket; *inf* demo.

demonstrative adj **1** *a demonstrative person/reaction* emotional, unreserved, unrestrained, expressive, open, effusive, expansive, gushing, non-reticent, affectionate, loving, warm. **2** *demonstrative of their skill* indicative, illustrative, evincive, expository. **3** *demonstrative evidence* conclusive, convincing, telling, material, incontrovertible, irrefutable.

demoralize v **1** *workers demoralized by the setbacks* discourage, dishearten, cast down, dispirit, deject, depress, daunt, unman, crush, sap, shake, undermine, devitalize, cripple, paralyse, weaken, enervate. **2** *brutes demoralizing the young* corrupt, deprave, debauch, pervert, debase, contaminate, defile, vitiate.

demote v downgrade, lower/reduce in rank, relegate, degrade, declass, strip of rank, reduce to the ranks, humble, disrate; *inf* kick upstairs.

demur v raise objections, object, take exception, express reluctance/reservations/doubts, be unwilling, protest, lodge a protest, dispute, refuse, dissent, balk at, hesitate, cavil.

demur n *go without demur* objection, protest, dispute, dissent, reluctance, reservation, unwillingness; doubts, qualms, misgivings.

demure adj **1** *demure young girls* modest, unassuming, decorous, meek, reserved, quiet, shy, bashful, retiring, diffident, reticent, timid, timorous, shrinking, serious, grave, sedate, staid. **2** *demure young ladies* over-modest, coy, affected, mincing, prim, priggish, prissy, prudish, goody-goody, strait-laced, puritanical.

den n **1** *the fox's den* lair, hole, hollow, shelter, hide-out; *inf* hidey-hole. **2** *the bar's a real den | den of iniquity* place of crime/vice, site, haunt; *inf* dive, joint. **3** *writing in his den* study, retreat, sanctum, *sanctum sanctorum*, sanctuary, hideaway, snuggery, cubbyhole.

denial n **1** *a denial of the statement* contradiction, repudiation, disclaimer, retraction, abjuration, disaffirmation; negation, dissent. **2** *the denial of the request* refusal, rejection, dismissal, rebuff, repulse, declination, veto, turndown; *inf* thumbs down. **3** *the denial of Christ* renunciation, renouncement, disowning, repudiation, disavowal.

denigrate v disparage, belittle, diminish, deprecate, detract from, decry, blacken one's character, defame, slander, libel, cast aspersions on, malign, vilify, calumniate, besmirch, run down, abuse, revile; *Amer* bad-mouth.

denizen n inhabitant, habitant, dweller, resident, occupier, occupant.

denomination n **1** *of various religious denominations* creed, faith, religious belief, Church, sect, religious group, persuasion, communion, order, fraternity, brotherhood, sisterhood, school. **2** *coins/weights of various denominations* value, unit, grade, size. **3** *creatures under various denominations* classification, class, category, grouping, group, type. **4** *things going under various denominations* name, title, term, designation, appellation, epithet, style, label, tag; *inf* handle, moniker.

denote v **1** *a smile denoting delight | the colour yellow denoting happiness* indicate, be a sign/mark of, signify, betoken, symbolize, represent, stand for, typify. **2** *the word bankruptcy denotes financial ruin* mean, convey, designate, suggest, bring to mind, intimate, refer to, allude to, imply, connote.

denouement n **1** *miss the denouement of the plan* resolution, solution, clarification, unravelling, final/last act, finale. **2** *the denouement of the argument* outcome, upshot, result, culmination, climax.

denounce v **1** *denounce the council's policies* condemn, criticize, attack, censure, castigate, decry, rail/inveigh/fulminate against, declaim against, arraign, denunciate, revile. **2** *denounce his partner* accuse, inform against, incriminate, implicate, inculpate, charge, file charges, indict, impeach, take to court.

dense adj **1** *a dense forest/crowd* close-packed, tightly packed, crowded, thickset, closely set, jammed together, crammed, compressed, compacted. **2** *a dense liquid/substance* of high density, heavy, concentrated, condensed. **3** *dense fog/smoke* thick, concentrated, opaque, impenetrable. **4** *too dense to understand* stupid, thick, slow-witted, slow,

dull-witted, blockish, obtuse, bovine, lumpish, stolid; *inf* dim.

deny v **1** *deny the charge/statement* declare untrue, contradict, negate, nullify, dissent from, disagree with, repudiate, refute, controvert, disclaim, retract, take back, backpedal, abjure, disaffirm, gainsay. **2** *deny the request* refuse, reject, turn down, dismiss, repulse, decline, veto; *inf* give the thumbs down to, give the red light to. **3** *to deny Christ* renounce, disown, turn one's back on, repudiate, discard, disavow.

deodorant n **1** *body deodorant* antiperspirant. **2** *room deodorants* air-freshener, deodorizer, fumigant; *inf* odour-eater.

depart v **1** *they departed at midday* leave, go, go away/off, take one's leave/departure, take oneself off, withdraw, absent oneself, set off/out, start out, get going, get under way, quit, make an exit, exit, break camp, decamp, retreat, retire; *inf* make tracks, shove off, split, cut out, vamoose, hightail it. **2** *depart from the norm* deviate, diverge, differ, vary, digress, veer, branch off, fork, swerve, turn aside.

departed adj *departed loved ones* dead, deceased, late, gone, passed away/on, expired.

department n **1** *the housing/books department* section, division, subdivision, unit, branch, segment, compartment, office, bureau, agency. **2** *that's the cook's department* area, area of responsibility, responsibility, area of interest, speciality, line, province, sphere, sphere of activity, domain, realm, jurisdiction, authority, function. **3** *the departments of France* administrative district, district, region, province, sector, division; territory, state, county, shire.

departure n **1** *the hour of their departure* leaving, leave-taking, going, going away/off, withdrawal, setting off/out, starting out, exit, exodus, decamping, retreat, retiral. *see* DEPART 1. **2** *a departure from the norm* deviation, divergence, variation, digression, veering, branching off, swerving. *see* DEPART 2. **3** *the export market is a new departure for the firm* change of direction, change, difference of emphasis, shift, innovation, branching out, novelty.

depend v **1** *success depends on hard work | it depends on how he proceeds* be dependent on, turn/hinge on, hang on, rest on, be contingent upon, be subject to, be controlled/determined by, be based on, revolve around, be influenced by, be resultant from, be subordinate to. **2** *depend on him for help* rely on, place reliance on, count/bank on, lean on, cling to, reckon/calculate on, trust in, put one's faith in, have confidence in, swear by, be sure of, be supported/sustained by.

dependable adj reliable, trustworthy, trusty, faithful, responsible, steady, stable, sure unfailing, true, steadfast.

dependant n minor, child, charge, protégé; minion, parasite, hanger-on, henchman.

dependence n 1 *the venture's dependence on hard work* reliance, turning on, hingeing on, determination, bearing, relevancy, relationship, connection, interconnection, interdependence. *see* DEPEND 1. 2 *their dependence on their mother* reliance, trust, faith, confidence. *see* DEPEND 2. 3 *pity the children's dependence* helplessness, weakness, defencelessness, vulnerability, exposure. 4 *alcohol dependence* addiction, over-reliance, reliance, dependency; abuse.

dependency n 1 *his dependency on his mother* dependence, reliance. *see* DEPEND 2. 2 *the children's utter dependency* dependence, helplessness, defencelessness. *see* DEPENDENCE 3. 3 *alcohol dependency* dependence, addiction, over-reliance, reliance. 4 *formerly a dependency of the US* colony, protectorate, province, fief. 5 *a dependency of the parent firm* subsidiary, adjunct, appendage, auxiliary, subject, attachment.

dependent adj 1 *dependent on circumstances* depending on, conditional on, contingent on, determined by, subject to. 2 *dependent on their mother* relying on, reliant on, counting on, leaning on, supported by, sustained by. *see* DEPEND 2. 3 *dependent children* reliant, helpless, weak, defenceless, vulnerable, immature. 4 *dependent countries* subsidiary, subject, subservient.

depict v 1 *a painting depicting him sitting* portray, represent, draw, paint, sketch, illustrate, delineate, outline, reproduce, render, limn, chart, map out. 2 *an account depicting his faults* describe, set forth/out, outline, sketch, detail, relate, narrate, recount, record, chronicle.

deplete v exhaust, use up, consume, expend, spend, drain, empty, milk, evacuate, bankrupt, impoverish, reduce, decrease, diminish, lessen, lower, attenuate.

depletion n exhaustion, using up, consumption, expenditure, draining, emptying, reduction, decrease, dwindling, diminution, lessening, lowering, attenuation.

deplorable adj 1 *deplorable behaviour* disgraceful, shameful, dishonourable, blameworthy, disreputable, scandalous,

reprehensible, despicable, abominable, base, sordid, vile, contemptible, execrable, opprobrious. 2 *in deplorable circumstances* lamentable, regrettable, unfortunate, wretched, dire, miserable, pitiable, pathetic, unhappy, sad, tragic, disastrous, distressing, grievous, calamitous.

deplore v 1 *deplore his dreadful behaviour* be scandalized/shocked by, be offended by, disapprove of, condemn, censure, deprecate, denounce, decry, abhor. 2 *deplore the passing of the trams* regret, lament, mourn, rue, bemoan, grieve/sorrow over, bewail, pine for, shed tears for, weep over.

deploy v 1 *deploy troops* arrange, position, dispose, spread out, extend, redistribute, station. 2 *deploy new arguments* use, utilize, set out/up, bring into play, have recourse to.

deport v 1 *deport the refugees* banish, expel, exile, evict, transport, oust, expatriate, extradite. 2 *deport oneself badly* behave, conduct oneself, act, acquit oneself, comport oneself, bear/carry/hold oneself.

deportation n *the deportation of refugees* banishment, expulsion, exile, eviction, ousting, transportation, extradition, expatriation.

deportment n 1 *have lessons in deportment* carriage, bearing, posture, comportment, stance, attitude, demeanour, mien, air, appearance, aspect, style, manner. 2 *complain about the child's deportment* behaviour, conduct, etiquette; manners, actions.

depose v 1 *depose the leader/king* remove from office, remove, unseat, dethrone, oust, displace, dismiss, discharge, cashier, strip of rank, demote; *inf* sack, fire, give the push/boot to. 2 *depose that one saw the accused* make a deposition, swear, testify, attest to. *see* DEPOSITION 2.

deposit v 1 *deposit the parcel on the floor* put, lay, set, set/put/lay down, drop, let fall. 2 *rivers depositing mud* let settle, set down, precipitate, dump. 3 *deposit money/jewels in the bank* bank, lodge, entrust, consign, save, store, hoard, stow, put away, lay in, squirrel away.

deposit n 1 *leaving a chemical deposit* precipitation, sediment, sublimate, accumulation, deposition; dregs, lees; silt, alluvium. 2 *coal/iron deposits* bed, vein, lode, layer. 3 *put a deposit on the goods* down/part payment, instalment, security, retainer, pledge, stake. 4 *put the jewels in a deposit* depository, storehouse, warehouse. *see* DEPOSITORY.

deposition n **1** *the deposition of the leader* removal, unseating, dethronement, ousting, displacement, dismissal, discharge, demotion. *see* DEPOSE 1. **2** *the witnesses' depositions* testimony, evidence, sworn statement/declaration, affidavit, attestation, affirmation.

depository n repository, store, storehouse, warehouse, depot, reservoir, safe deposit, deposit, bank.

depot n **1** *buses/trains returning to the depot* terminal, terminus; bus/railway station, garage. **2** *stored in the depot* storehouse, warehouse, repository, depository, magazine, cache, arsenal.

deprave v corrupt, debauch, lead astray, pervert, seduce, debase, degrade, make degenerate, defile, pollute, contaminate, vitiate, brutalize, abuse.

depraved adj corrupt, corrupted, immoral, unprincipled, reprobate, debauched, dissolute, abandoned, perverted, degenerate, profligate, debased, degraded, wicked, sinful, vile, base, iniquitous, criminal, vicious, brutal, lewd, licentious, lascivious, lecherous, prurient, obscene, indecent, libertine.

depravity n corruption, corruptness, corruptedness, immorality, debauchery, dissoluteness, abandonment, perversion, degradation, degeneracy, profligacy, contamination, vitiation, wickedness, sinfulness, vileness, baseness, iniquity, criminality, viciousness, brutality, brutishness, lewdness, licentiousness, lasciviousness, lechery, prurience, obscenity, indecency, libertinism.

deprecate v **1** *deprecate the committee's actions* disapprove of, criticize, deplore, frown upon, censure, condemn, protest against, inveigh/rail against, denounce; *inf* slate, knock. **2** *deprecate his achievement* belittle, disparage, denigrate, decry, discredit, deflate, diminish, depreciate. *see* DEPRECIATE 3.

deprecatory adj **1** *make deprecatory remarks about the opposition* disapproving, critical, protesting, condemnatory, reproachful, upbraiding, castigatory, admonishing, denunciatory; *inf* slating, knocking. *see* DEPRECATE 1. **2** *give a deprecatory smile at his mistake* apologetic, regretful, sorry, remorseful, contrite, penitent, repentant, rueful, compunctious, propitiatory. **3** *a deprecatory account of their achievement* belittling, disparaging, denigratory, derogatory, discrediting, deflating, diminishing, disdainful, derisive, snide, sneering, mocking, jibing.

depreciate v **1** *the furniture has depreciated* decrease in value, lose value, decline in price. **2** *depreciate the value | depreciate the furniture* devalue, reduce, lower in value/price, mark down, cheapen, cut, slash. **3** *depreciate efforts to help* belittle, disparage, denigrate, decry, deprecate, make light of, discredit, underrate, undervalue, underestimate, deflate, detract from, derogate, diminish, minimize, run down, disdain, ridicule, deride, sneer at, mock, defame, traduce.

depreciation n **1** *the depreciation of the furniture* devaluation, decrease/lowering/reduction in value, cheapening, mark-down. *see* DEPRECIATE 1, 2. **2** *the depreciation of their efforts* belittlement, disparagement, denigration, decrial, deprecation, discrediting, underrating, undervaluing. *see* DEPRECIATE 3.

depredation n *the depredation of the town by the army/storm* plundering, pillaging, ravaging, despoliation, devastation, laying waste.

depress v **1** *news that depressed her* make sad/unhappy, sadden, deject, cast down, make gloomy/despondent, dispirit, dishearten, discourage, dampen the spirits of, daunt, desolate, make desolate, weigh down, oppress. **2** *depress economic activity* slow down/up, weaken, lower, reduce, sap, enervate, debilitate, devitalize, impair, enfeeble, exhaust, drain. **3** *depress prices* reduce, lower, cut, cheapen, put/keep down, slash, depreciate, devalue, diminish, downgrade. **4** *depress the lever/grass* push down, press down, lower, level, flatten.

depressant n sedative, tranquillizer, sleeping pill, soporific, opiate, hypnotic; *inf* downer.

depressed adj **1** *depressed at the news* sad, saddened, unhappy, gloomy, blue, glum, dejected, downhearted, cast down, downcast, down, crestfallen, despondent, dispirited, low, low in spirits, low-spirited, melancholy, disheartened, discouraged, fed up, daunted, desolate, moody, morose, pessimistic, weighed down, oppressed; *inf* down in the dumps. **2** *a depressed section of land* sunken, hollow, concave, indented, dented, pushed in, recessed, set back. **3** *a depressed economy* weak, weakened, enervated, debilitated, devitalized, impaired. *see* DEPRESS 2. **4** *depressed prices* reduced, lowered, cut, cheapened, slashed, devalued, marked-down, discounted. **5** *a depressed area* poverty-stricken, poor, destitute, disadvantaged, deprived, needy, distressed, run-down, down-at-heel.

depressing adj *depressing news* saddening, sad, unhappy, gloomy, dismal, bleak, black, sombre, grave, dreary, melancholy, dispiriting, disheartening, dejecting, discouraging, daunting, distressing, painful, heart-breaking.

depression n **1** *patients suffering from depression* clinical depression, endogenous depression, reactive depression, melancholia. **2** *bad news caused her depression* sadness, unhappiness, despair, gloom, glumness, dejection, downheartedness, despondency, dispiritedness, melancholy, discouragement, desolation, dolefulness, moodiness, moroseness, pessimism, hopelessness; low spirits, blues; *inf* the dumps. **3** *a depression in the landscape* hollow, indentation, dent, cavity, concavity, dip, valley, pit, hole, bowl, sink, sink-hole, excavation. **4** *an economic depression* slump, recession, decline, slowdown, standstill; paralysis, inactivity, stagnation; hard/bad times.

deprivation v **1** *the deprivation of their rights* withholding, denial, withdrawal, removal, dispossession, taking away, stripping, expropriation, seizure, confiscation, robbing, appropriation, divestment, divestiture, wresting. **2** *areas of social deprivation* poverty, hardship, privation, destitution, disadvantage, need, neediness, want, distress, detriment.

deprive v *deprive them of their rights* dispossess, strip, expropriate, divest, wrest, rob.

deprived adj *the deprived section of the community* poor, destitute, disadvantaged, needy, in need, in want, lacking, distressed, forlorn.

depth n **1** *measure the depth of the hole* deepness, distance downwards/inwards, drop, vertical extent, profundity. **2** *a person/thinker of depth* deepness, profoundness, profundity, wisdom, understanding, sagacity, discernment, insight, awareness, intuition, penetration, astuteness, acumen, shrewdness, acuity. **3** *an essay/issue of great depth* deepness, gravity, seriousness, weight, importance, moment, solemnity, complexity, intricacy, obtuseness, abstruseness, obscurity, reconditeness. **4** *the depth of the colour* deepness, intensity, richness, darkness, vividness, strength, brilliance. **5** *investigating the depths of the cave/sea* deepest part, remotest area, bottom, floor, bed, abyss, back, pit; bowels. **in depth** *investigate in depth* thoroughly, extensively, comprehensively, intensively.

deputation n **1** *a deputation representing the homeless* delegation, legation, commission, embassy, committee; delegates, envoys, deputies. **2** *the deputation of the delegation* appointment, designation, nomination, commission, assignment, installation, investiture, induction, ordination.

depute v **1** *depute a representative* appoint, designate, nominate, commission, assign, install, invest, ordain. **2** *depute authority* delegate, transfer, assign, pass on, consign.

deputize v *deputize for the chairman* take the place of, act for, stand in for, understudy, do a locum for.

deputy n *act as the chairman's deputy* substitute, stand-in, representative, second in command, assistant, surrogate, proxy, delegate, agent, spokesperson, ambassador, lieutenant, legate, commissioner, envoy, go-between, mediator, nuncio, vice-regent, vice-president, vice-chancellor; *inf* vice.

deputy adj *a deputy manager* assistant, substitute, stand-in, representative, surrogate, proxy, subordinate.

deranged adj *mentally deranged*, disturbed, unbalanced, unhinged, touched, insane, mad, crazy, crazed, demented, irrational, of unsound mind, *non compos mentis*, berserk, frenzied; *inf* cracked, bonkers, potty, dotty, nuts, balmy, barmy, bats, batty, dippy, cuckoo, screwy, off one's trolley/rocker/chump, out to lunch.

derelict adj **1** *derelict factories/ships* abandoned, forsaken, deserted, discarded, rejected, cast off, relinquished, ownerless. **2** *living in derelict properties* dilapidated, ramshackle, tumbledown, run-down, broken-down, in disrepair, crumbling, falling to pieces, rickety, neglected. **3** *derelict officers* negligent, neglectful, remiss, lax, careless, sloppy, slipshod, slack, irresponsible, delinquent.

derelict n *derelicts begging in the street* down and out, vagrant, tramp, beggar, outcast, pariah, ne'er do well, good-for-nothing, wastrel; *inf* dosser; *Amer inf* hobo.

dereliction n **1** *the dereliction of the factories/ships* abandonment, forsaking, desertion, rejection, relinquishment, renunciation. *see* DERELICT adj 1. **2** *accused of dereliction* negligence, neglect, neglectfulness, remissness, laxity, carelessness, sloppiness, slackness, irresponsibility, non-performance, delinquency, *laissez-faire*.

deride v mock, ridicule, jeer at, scoff at, sneer at, make fun of, poke fun at, laugh at, scorn, pooh-pooh, flout at, lampoon, satirize, taunt, insult, torment, rag, tease, chaff, disdain, disparage, denigrate, slight, detract from, vilify; *fml* contemn.

derision n mockery, ridicule, jeering, scoffing, sneering, scorn, contempt, taunting, ragging, teasing, raillery, disdain, disrespect, disparagement, denigration, vilification, contumely; jeers, sneers, taunts, insults; satire, lampoon. *see* DERIDE.

derisive adj *derisive shouts* mocking, ridiculing, jeering, scoffing, scornful, contemptuous, taunting, insulting, satirical, sarcastic, disdainful, disparaging, denigratory, derisory.

derisory adj **1** *a derisory wage increase* laughable, ludicrous, ridiculous, insulting, contemptible, preposterous, outrageous, inadequate, tiny, minimal. **2** *derisory shouts* derisive, mocking, ridiculing, jeering, scoffing, scornful, contemptuous, taunting. *see* DERISIVE.

derivation n **1** *the derivation of the word/ custom* origin, source, root, etymology, fountainhead, wellspring, origination, beginning, foundation, basis, cause; ancestry, descent, genealogy, development, evolution. *see* DERIVE 1. **2** *undertake the derivation of the custom* tracing, following back. *see* DERIVE 2. **3** *the derivation of satisfaction from work* deriving, acquisition, extraction. *see* DERIVE 4. **4** *the derivation of facts* deriving, collecting, collection, gathering, gleaning, drawing out, eliciting, eduction, deduction, inference. *see* DERIVE 5.

derivative adj **1** *derivative conclusions* derived, collected, elicited, educed, deduced, inferred. *see* DERIVE 5. **2** *derivative research* imitative, unoriginal, uninventive, non-innovative, copied, plagiaristic, plagiarized, second-hand, secondary, rehashed, warmed-up, thinly disguised.

derivative n **1** *a derivative of coal* by-product, spin-off, offshoot, outgrowth. **2** *a word and its derivatives* derived word, descendant.

derive v **1** *derive from a Latin word* originate in, have one's/its origins in, have as a source, stem from, descend from, spring from, arise in. **2** *derive a word* trace back, follow back, etymologize. **3** *happiness deriving from marriage* originate in, stem from, proceed, flow, emanate, issue. **4** *derive satisfaction* acquire, obtain, get, gain, procure, extract. **5** *derive sufficient facts* collect, gather, glean, winnow, draw out, elicit, educe, deduce, infer.

derogate v **1** *derogate their achievement/character* disparage, denigrate, belittle, diminish, deprecate, depreciate, downplay, detract from, deflate, decry, discredit, downgrade, defame, vilify. **2** *derogate from old standards* deviate, degenerate, deteriorate, decline, worsen, retrogress, retrograde.

derogatory adj *a derogatory remark* disparaging, denigratory, belittling, diminishing, slighting, deprecatory, depreciatory, depreciative, detracting, deflating, discrediting, dishonouring, unfavourable, disapproving, uncomplimentary, unflattering, insulting, offensive, damaging, injurious, defamatory, vilifying.

descend v **1** *descend the hill/stairs* go down, come down, move down, climb down, pass down. **2** *the balloon descended* go down, come down, drop, fall, sink, subside, plummet, plunge, tumble, slump. **3** *descend from the train* get down, get off, alight, dismount, disembark; detrain, deplane. **4** *the hill descended to the valley* go down, slope, incline, dip, slant. **5** *will not descend to talk to servants* condescend, stoop, lower/abase oneself. **6** *descend in quality/values* degenerate, deteriorate, decline, sink, go downhill; *inf* go to pot, go to the dogs. **7** *enemies/visitors descending on us* attack, assault, assail, pounce, raid, swoop, charge, come in force, arrive in hordes. **8** *a family descended from William the Conqueror* be a descendant of, derive/originate from, issue/spring from. **9** *houses descending from father to son* be handed/passed down, pass by heredity, be transferred by inheritance.

descendants npl offspring, progeny, issue, family; scions.

descent n **1** *the descent of the hill* going down, coming down. *see* DESCEND 1. **2** *the descent of the balloon* going down, drop, fall, sinking, subsiding, plummeting, plunge. *see* DESCEND 2. **3** *the descent from the train* getting down/off, alighting. *see* DESCEND 3. **4** *walk down the descent* slope, incline, dip, drop, gradient, declivity, declination, slant. **5** *descent in quality/values* degeneracy, deterioration, decline, debasement, degradation, sinking, decadence. *see* DESCEND 6. **6** *the descent of enemies/visitors* attack, assault, assailing, raid, charge, onslaught, incursion, foray, sortie. **7** *of noble descent* ancestry, parentage, lineage, extraction, genealogy, heredity, succession, stock, line, pedigree, blood, strain; origins.

describe v **1** *describe the incident* give a description/account of, give details of, detail, tell, narrate, put into words, express, recount, relate, report, set out, chronicle, define, explain, elucidate, illustrate. **2** *he was described as brilliant* call, designate, pronounce, style, label, characterize, portray, depict. **3** *describe a circle* draw, delineate, mark out, outline, trace, sketch.

description n **1** *give a description of the incident* account, detailed statement, report, setting out, chronicle, narration, recounting, relation, commentary, explanation, elucidation, illustration; details. **2** *the description of him as dishonest* calling, designation, pronouncement, styling, labelling, characterization, portrayal, depiction. **3** *the description of a circle* drawing, delineation, outline, tracing. see DESCRIBE 3. **4** *vegetables of some description* kind, sort, variety, type, brand, breed, category, class, designation, genre, ilk, kidney, grain, stamp, mould.

descriptive adj detailed, explanatory, elucidatory, graphic, vivid, striking, expressive, illustrative, pictorial, depictive, picturesque, circumstantial.

descry v catch sight of, see, make out, notice, discern, perceive, observe, detect, distinguish.

desecrate v violate, defile, profane, treat sacrilegiously, blaspheme, pollute, contaminate, infect, befoul, debase, degrade, dishonour, vitiate.

desert v **1** *desert one's wife/post* abandon, forsake, give up, cast off, leave, turn one's back on, leave high and dry, leave in the lurch, throw over, betray, jilt, strand, leave stranded, maroon, neglect, shun, relinquish, renounce; *inf* walk/run out on, rat on. **2** *the soldier has deserted* abscond, defect, run away, make off, decamp, flee, fly, bolt, turn tail, go AWOL, take French leave, depart, quit, escape. **3** *desert a cause* abandon, forsake, turn one's back on, relinquish, renounce, betray, renege, apostatize.

desert n **1** *lost in the African desert* wasteland, waste, wilderness, barrenness, solitude; wilds. **2** *living in a cultural desert* uninteresting place/period, unproductive place/period, wasteland.

desert adj **1** *African desert regions* arid, dry, moistureless, parched, scorched, dried up, burnt, hot, burning, torrid. **2** *Arctic desert region* desolate, barren, bare, wild, empty, uninhabited, solitary, lonely, uncultivable, uncultivatable, infertile, unproductive, sterile, uncultivated, untilled.

deserted adj **1** *a deserted wife* abandoned, forsaken, cast off, betrayed, jilted, stranded, marooned, neglected, shunned, relinquished, renounced, forlorn, bereft. **2** *deserted buildings* abandoned, forsaken, neglected, empty, vacant, uninhabited, unoccupied, untenanted, tenantless, unfrequented, secluded, isolated, desolate, lonely, solitary, godforsaken.

deserter n **1** *army deserters* absconder, defector, runaway, fugitive, truant, escapee, derelict. **2** *deserters from the cause* defector, renegade, turncoat, traitor, betrayer, apostate, derelict; *inf* rat.

desertion n **1** *the desertion of his wife | sued for desertion* abandonment, forsaking, betrayal, relinquishment, renunciation. **2** *desertion from the army | disciplined for desertion* absconding, defection, decamping, flight, truancy, going AWOL, French leave, departure, escape, dereliction. **3** *desertion from/of the cause* defection, betrayal, apostasy.

deserve v merit, be worthy of, warrant, rate, justify, earn, be entitled to, have a right to, have a claim on, be qualified for.

deserved adj well-earned, merited, warranted, justified, justifiable, earned, rightful, due, right, just, fair, fitting, appropriate, suitable, proper, reasonable, condign.

deserving adj worthy, meritorious, commendable, praiseworthy, laudable, admirable, estimable, creditable, virtuous, righteous, upright, good.

design v **1** *draughtsmen designing the structure* plan, draw, draw plans of, sketch, outline, map out, plot, block out, delineate, draft, depict. **2** *designing clothes | designing schemes in his head* create, invent, originate, think up, conceive, fashion, fabricate, hatch, innovate; *inf* dream up. **3** *words designed to hurt | a course designed for beginners* intend, aim, devise, contrive, purpose, plan, tailor, mean, destine.

design n **1** *the design was left in the office* plan, blueprint, drawing, sketch, outline, map, plot, diagram, delineation, draft, depiction, scheme, model. **2** *admire the fabric designs* pattern, motif, style, arrangement, composition, make-up, constitution, configuration, organization, construction, shape, figure. **3** *a clever design to defeat the enemy* plan, enterprise, undertaking, scheme, plot, intrigue, expedient, stratagem, device, artifice. **4** *with the design of entering* intention, aim, purpose, plan, objective, goal, end, target, point, hope, desire, wish, dream, aspiration, ambition.

designate v **1** *a new category designated helpers* call, name, entitle, term, christen, dub, style, label, denominate, nickname. **2** *designated ambassador* appoint, nominate, depute, delegate, select, choose, elect, assign, allot, ordain, induct. **3** *designate the place | at designated times* state, appoint, specify, define, stipulate, particularize, earmark, set aside, pinpoint. **4** *arrows* *designating direction* show, indicate, point out, mark, denote.

designation n **1** *going under the designation of financial consultant* title, name, label, appellation, epithet, tag, style, denomination, nickname, sobriquet, cognomen; *inf* moniker. **2** *opposing his designation as ambassador* appointment, nomination, selection, election, induction. *see* DESIGNATE 2. **3** *the designation of place and time* specification, defining, stipulation, earmarking. *see* DESIGNATE 3. **4** *the designation of direction by arrows* indication, marking, denotement, denoting. *see* DESIGNATE 4.

designer n **1** *designer of bridges/buildings/fabrics* creator, inventor, deviser, fashioner, originator, author, producer, architect, artificer. **2** *dress designer* couturier, fashion designer, creator, fashioner. **3** *a troublemaking designer* plotter, schemer, intriguer, conniver, conspirator, machinator.

designing adj scheming, plotting, intriguing, conspiring, convincing, calculating, Machiavellian, cunning, crafty, artful, wily, devious, shrewd, astute, sharp, insidious, treacherous, sly, underhand, deceitful, tricky; *inf* crooked.

desirability n **1** *the desirability of the property* attractiveness, allure, appeal, popularity, eligibility, agreeableness, excellence, worth. *see* DESIRABLE 1. **2** *the desirability of no one knowing* preferableness, advisability, advantageousness, advantage, benefit, merit, value, profit, expedience. **3** *the desirability of the young woman* sexual attraction/attractiveness, attractiveness, seductiveness, allurement, eroticism, fascination; *inf* sexiness.

desirable adj **1** *a desirable job* attractive, sought-after, in demand, popular, covetable, enviable, eligible, agreeable, appealing, pleasant, admirable, worthwhile, profitable, good, excellent. **2** *it is desirable that no one knows* preferable, advisable, recommendable, advantageous, beneficial, expedient, in everyone's interests. **3** *a desirable young woman* sexually attractive, attractive, seductive, alluring, erotic, fetching, fascinating, beguiling; *inf* sexy.

desire v **1** *desire happiness* wish for, want, long/yearn for, crave, set one's heart on, hanker after, have a fancy for, fancy, be bent on, covet, aspire to; *inf* have a yen for. **2** *desire to go wish*, want, feel like, long, crave, have a fancy to. **3** *desire his/her body* lust after, burn for; *inf* letch after, have the hots for. **4** *desire a cup of tea* request, ask for, want.

desire n **1** *express a desire to go | her desire for success* wish, want, fancy, inclination, preference; wanting, longing, yearning, craving, eagerness, enthusiasm, hankering, predilection, aspiration, proclivity, predisposition. **2** *overcome by desire* sexual attraction, lust, lustfulness, sexual appetite, passion, carnal passion, concupiscence, libido, sensuality, sexuality, lasciviousness, lechery, salaciousness, libidinousness, prurience; *inf* the hots.

desired adj **1** *fitted to the desired length* required, necessary, proper, right, correct, exact, accurate, precise, specific, particular, appropriate, fitting, suitable, preferred, expected, express. **2** *the desired prize* wished for, longed for, yearned for, craved, coveted. *see* DESIRE v 1.

desirous adj **1** *desirous of success* desiring, wishing, wishful of, hopeful of, avid/eager/anxious for, craving, ambitious for. **2** *desirous to win* desiring, keen, avid, eager, ambitious, hoping, aspiring, anxious, willing, wishing, ready.

desist v *they've been asked to desist | desist from laughing* stop, cease, discontinue, abstain, give up, forbear/refrain from, break/leave off.

desolate adj **1** *desolate moors* bare, barren, bleak, dismal, desert, waste, wild. **2** *desolate farms* deserted, uninhabited, unoccupied, depopulated, forsaken, abandoned, unpeopled, untenanted, unfrequented, unvisited, solitary, lonely, isolated. **3** *desolate at the sad news* sad, unhappy, miserable, brokenhearted, wretched, downcast, cast down, dejected, downhearted, melancholy, gloomy, despondent, depressed, disconsolate, forlorn, cheerless, distressed, grieving, bereft.

desolation n **1** *the desolation of the remote landscape by war* destruction, laying waste, ruin, ruination, devastation, despoliation, havoc, ravaging. **2** *the desolation of the landscape* bareness, barrenness, bleakness, dismalness, wildness, isolation, solitude, solitariness, loneliness, remoteness; wasteland, wilderness, desert. **3** *her desolation at the news* sadness, unhappiness, misery, broken-heartedness, wretchedness, dejection, downheartedness, depression, melancholy, gloom, despondency, distress, grief.

despair n **1** *unemployed and full of despair* hopelessness, dejection, depression, desperation, disheartenment, discouragement, despondency, disconsolateness, defeatism, pessimism, resignedness, melancholy, gloom, melancholia, misery, wretchedness, distress, anguish. **2** *the boy is the despair of the teacher* hopeless case, bane, burden, bother, scourge.

despair v lose hope, give up hope, give up, lose heart, be discouraged, be despondent, be pessimistic, resign oneself, throw in the towel/sponge.

despairing adj hopeless, dejected, depressed, desperate, suicidal, disheartened, discouraged, despondent, disconsolate, inconsolable, defeatist, pessimistic, resigned, melancholy, gloomy, downcast, forlorn, miserable, wretched, distressed, broken-hearted, heartbroken, grief-stricken, sorrowing, anguished.

despatch v, n see DISPATCH v, n.

desperado n criminal, lawbreaker, gangster, terrorist, outlaw, bandit, gunman, thug, ruffian, hooligan, villain, hoodlum, mugger.

desperate adj **1** *a desperate criminal* reckless, rash, hasty, impetuous, foolhardy, audacious, daring, bold, madcap, wild, violent, frantic, mad, frenzied, lawless. **2** *a desperate act* reckless, rash, foolhardy, risky, hazardous, daring, precipitate, harebrained, wild, imprudent, incautious, injudicious, indiscreet, ill-conceived. **3** *in desperate need* urgent, pressing, compelling, acute, critical, crucial, drastic, serious, grave, dire, extreme, great. **4** *desperate for money* in great need of, urgently requiring, in want of, lacking. **5** *the desperate state of the country* grave, very bad, appalling, outrageous, intolerable, deplorable, lamentable. **6** *trying to help desperate people* despairing, hopeless, wretched. see DESPAIRING. **7** *desperate measures* last-ditch, last-resort, do-or-die, futile.

desperately adv *desperately ill/poor* seriously, gravely, severely, extremely, critically, acutely, dangerously, perilously.

desperation n **1** *the desperation of the act* recklessness, rashness, impetuosity, foolhardiness, riskiness, audacity, boldness, wildness, imprudence, injudiciousness, violence, frenziedness, lawlessness. see DESPERATE 1, 2. **2** *the desperation of their state* urgency, criticalness, crucialness, seriousness, gravity, direness, extremity. **3** *the desperation of the homeless* hopelessness, despair, dejection, depression, despondency, disconsolateness, forlornness, melancholy, gloom, misery, wretchedness, distress, anguish, sorrow, pain. see DESPAIR n 1.

despicable adj contemptible, beyond contempt, reprehensible, vile, base, low, mean, scurvy, abominable, loathsome, hateful, detestable, odious, disreputable, infamous, villainous, ignoble, disgusting, sordid, distasteful, shameful, degrading, ignominious, cheap, shabby, miserable, wretched, sorry.

despise v scorn, look down on, spurn, shun, disdain, slight, undervalue, deride, scoff/jeer at, sneer at, mock, revile, hate, detest, loathe, abhor, abominate, execrate; *fml* contemn.

despite prep in spite of, notwithstanding, regardless of, in defiance of, in the face of.

despoil v **1** *despoil the country* plunder, pillage, rob, ravage, harry, maraud, ravish, rape, depredate, raid, forage, ransack, loot, sack, rifle, devastate, lay waste, wreak havoc on, vandalize, destroy, ruin, wreck. **2** *despoil the city of its treasures* rob, dispossess, strip, deprive, denude, divest.

despondency n hopelessness, disheartenment, discouragement, disconsolateness, dispiritedness, downheartedness, despair, defeatism, melancholy, gloom, melancholia, misery, wretchedness, distress, sorrow, sadness; low spirits, doldrums, blues.

despondent adj hopeless, downcast, cast down, down, low, disheartened, discouraged, disconsolate, low-spirited, dispirited, downhearted, in despair, despairing, defeatist, blue, melancholy, gloomy, glum, morose, doleful, woebegone, miserable, wretched, distressed, sorrowful, sad.

despot n absolute ruler, autocrat, dictator, tyrant, oppressor, monocrat.

despotic adj absolute, autocratic, dictatorial, tyrannical, oppressive, totalitarian, domineering, imperious, arrogant, highhanded, authoritarian, arbitrary, unconstitutional.

despotism n absolutism, autocracy, dictatorship, tyranny, oppression, totalitarianism, monocracy, autarchy.

destination n *London was our destination* journey's end, landing place, point of disembarkation, terminus, end of the line, end, station, stop, stopping-place, port of call.

destined adj **1** *a plane destined for London* bound for, en route for, heading for/towards, directed/routed to, scheduled for. **2** *destined for the state* designed, intended, meant, set, set apart, designated, appointed, alloted. **3** *destined to die young* fated, ordained, preordained, foreordained, predestined, predetermined, doomed, foredoomed, certain, sure, bound, written in the cards.

destiny n **1** *couldn't escape his destiny* fate, fortune, lot, portion, cup, due, future, doom. **2** *destiny drew them together* fate, divine decree, predestination, luck, fortune, chance, karma, kismet; the stars.

destitute adj **1** *destitute refugees* poverty-stricken, indigent, impoverished, penurious, impecunious, penniless, insolvent, beggarly, beggared, down and out, poor, needy, hard up, badly off, on the breadline, hard-pressed, distressed, pauperized; *inf* on one's uppers, up against it. **2** *destitute of ideas* devoid of, without, bereft of, deficient in, lacking, wanting, deprived of, empty, drained.

destitution n **1** *the destitution of the refugees* dire poverty, poverty, indigence, penury, insolvency, privation, financial distress, pauperdom; impoverishment, impecuniousness, neediness. **2** *destitution of ideas* deficiency, dearth, lack, want, need, scarcity, meagreness, deprivation.

destroy v **1** *destroy the bridge* demolish, knock down, pull down, tear down, level, raze, fell, dismantle, wreck, smash, shatter, crash, blow up, blow to bits, explode, annihilate, wipe out, bomb, torpedo. **2** *destroy the countryside* ruin, spoil, devastate, lay waste, ravage, wreak havoc on, ransack. **3** *destroy their confidence* terminate, quash, quell, crush, stifle, subdue, squash, extinguish, extirpate. **4** *destroy the herd/tribe* kill, kill off, slaughter, put to sleep, exterminate; slay, murder, assassinate, wipe out, massacre, liquidate, decimate. **5** *destroy the enemy/opponents* defeat, beat, conquer, vanquish, trounce, rout, drub; *inf* lick, thrash.

destruction n **1** *the destruction of the building* demolition, knocking down, pulling down, tearing down, levelling, razing, dismantling, wrecking, smashing, blowing up, wiping out, annihilation. *see* DESTROY 1. **2** *the destruction of the countryside* ruination, spoiling, devastation, laying waste, desolation, ravaging; ruin, havoc. *see* DESTROY 2. **3** *the destruction of their confidence* termination, quashing, quelling, crushing, stifling, subduing, extinguishing, extinction. *see* DESTROY 3. **4** *the destruction of the herd/tribe* killing, slaughter, slaying, murder, assassination, massacre. *see* DESTROY 4. **5** *the destruction of the enemy/opponents* defeat, beating, conquest, vanquishing, trouncing, rout. *see* DESTROY 5.

destructive adj **1** *destructive winds/wars* ruinous, devastating, disastrous, catastrophic, calamitous, cataclysmic, ravaging, fatal, deadly, dangerous, lethal, damaging, pernicious, noxious, injurious, harmful, detrimental, deleterious, disadvantageous. **2** *destructive children* damaging, injurious, harmful, hurtful, mischievous,

pernicious. **3** *destructive comments/criticism* non-constructive, negative, unfavourable, adverse, antagonistic, hostile, unfriendly, contrary, discrediting, invalidating, derogatory, denigrating, disparaging, disapproving, discouraging, undermining.

desultory adj half-hearted, haphazard, random, aimless, rambling, erratic, irregular, unmethodical, unsystematic, chaotic, inconsistent, inconstant, fitful, capricious.

detach v **1** *detach the collar* unfasten, disconnect, unhitch, remove, separate, uncouple, loosen, free, sever, tear off, disengage, disjoin, disunite. **2** *detach oneself from the group* separate, move off, dissociate, segregate, isolate, cut off, disconnect, divide.

detached adj **1** *a detached house* standing alone, separate, unconnected, not attached. **2** *a detached collar* unfastened, disconnected, unhitched, separate, loosened, free, severed. *see* DETACH 1. **3** *observing in a detached way* dispassionate, aloof, indifferent, unconcerned, reserved, unemotional, impersonal, cool, remote. **4** *detached commentators* objective, disinterested, unbiased, unprejudiced, impartial, non-partisan, neutral, fair.

detachment n **1** *the detachment of the collar* unfastening, disconnection, unhitching, separation, uncoupling, loosening, severing, disengagement, disuniting. *see* DETACH 1. **2** *look on with detachment* dispassionateness, dispassion, aloofness, indifference, unconcern, lack of concern/emotion, reserve, coolness, remoteness. **3** *the detachment of the panel* objectivity, disinterest, lack of bias/prejudice, impartiality, non-partisanship, neutrality, fairness. **4** *a detachment of soldiers* separate/specialized unit, task force, detail, patrol.

detail n **1** *to the smallest detail* item, particular, fact, point, factor, element, circumstance, aspect, feature, respect, attribute, part, unit, component, member, accessory. **2** *don't bother with such a detail* unimportant point, insignificant item, trivial fact. **3** *fill in the details* particulars, fine points, niceties, minutiae, trivia. **4** *the detail of soldiers for fatigue duty* assignment, allotment, delegating, deputing. **5** *pass a detail of soldiers* detachment, task force, patrol. *see* DETACHMENT 4. **in detail** point by point, item by item, comprehensively, fully, thoroughly, exhaustively, blow by blow.

detail v **1** *detail the arrangements* specify, set forth, set out, list, enumerate, tabulate, catalogue, spell out, delineate, relate, recount, narrate, recite, rehearse, describe, cite, point out, indicate, portray, depict,

detailed · determined

itemize, particularize, individualize.
2 *detail personnel for duty* appoint, assign,
allocate, delegate, select, choose, name,
nominate, elect, charge, commission, send.

detailed adj **1** *a detailed bill/description* itemized, particularized, full, comprehensive,
thorough, exhaustive, all-inclusive, circumstantial, precise, exact, specific, particular,
meticulous. **2** *a detailed picture/story* complex, involved, elaborate, complicated,
intricate, convoluted, entangled.

detain v **1** *detained by business* hold/keep
back, hold up, delay, keep, slow up/down,
hinder, impede, check, retard, inhibit, stay.
2 *detain the accused* put/keep in custody,
confine, imprison, lock up, incarcerate,
impound, intern, restrain, hold, arrest; *inf*
collar.

detect v **1** *detect hostility/smoke* notice, note,
discern, perceive, make out, observe, spot,
become aware of, recognize, distinguish,
identify, catch, decry, sense, see, smell.
2 *accountants detected the theft* discover, find
out, turn up, uncover, bring to light,
expose, unearth, reveal, unmask, unveil.
3 *police detecting the crime* investigate, probe,
track down, ferret out, sleuth.

detection n **1** *the detection of hostility/smoke*
noticing, discernment, perception, observation, awareness, recognition, distinguishing, identification. *see* DETECT 1. **2** *the early
detection of the crime* discovery, uncovering,
exposure, exposé, revelation, unmasking.
see DETECT 2. **3** *the police detection* investigating, probe, tracking down, sleuthing.

detective n investigator; private investigator, CID man/woman, police officer; *inf*
sleuth, tec, dick, private eye, private dick,
tail, shadow; *Amer inf* gumshoe. *see* POLICE-
MAN.

detention n **1** *unavoidable detention at work*
holding up, delay, slowing up, hindrance,
impediment, check, retardation. *see* DETAIN
1. **2** *kept in detention/boys with a detention
after school* custody, confinement, imprisonment, incarceration, internment, restraint,
detainment, duress, quarantine, arrest;
keeping in, punishment. *see* DETAIN 2.

deter v put off, prevent, stop, discourage,
dissuade, talk out of, check, restrain, caution, frighten, intimidate, daunt, scare off,
warn against, hold back, prohibit, hinder,
impede, obstruct, block, inhibit.

detergent n cleaner, cleanser; soap pow-
der/flakes, washing-up liquid.

detergent adj cleaning, cleansing, abster-
gent.

deteriorate v **1** *moral values deteriorating* get
worse, worsen, decline, degenerate, sink,
slip, go downhill, slide, lapse, fail, fall,
drop, ebb, wane, retrograde, retrogress,
slump, depreciate; *inf* go to pot, go to the
dogs. **2** *deteriorate their moral values* corrupt,
debase, defile, impair. **3** *buildings/food deteriorating* disintegrate, become dilapidated,
decline, degenerate, crumble, fall apart,
fall to pieces, fall down, break up, decay,
decompose, go bad.

deterioration n **1** *the deterioration of morals*
worsening, decline, degeneration, lapse,
failure, downturn, ebb, waning, retrogression, slump, depreciation; corruption,
debasement, defilement, contamination,
pollution, vitiation, tainting, corrosion,
impairment. *see* DETERIORATE 1, 2. **2** *the deterioration of buildings/food* disintegration, dilapidation, decline, degeneration, crumbling,
falling apart, erosion, decay, decomposition. *see* DETERIORATE 3.

determination n **1** *behave with determination*
firmness, firmness of purpose, resoluteness, steadfastness, tenacity, single-mindedness, resolve, drive, push, thrust,
fortitude, dedication, backbone, stamina,
mettle, strong will, persistence, pertinacity, perseverance, conviction, doggedness,
stubbornness, obduracy, intransigence.
2 *the committee's determination/the legal determination* decision, conclusion, judgement,
verdict, opinion, decree, solution, result,
arbitration, settlement, diagnosis, prognosis.

determine v **1** *determine the place of meeting/
determine who should go* settle, fix, decide,
agree on, establish, judge, arbitrate,
decree, ordain. **2** *determine the argument* settle, decide, resolve, conclude, end, terminate, finish. **3** *determine the room dimensions*
find out, discover, learn, establish, calculate, work out, ascertain, check, verify, certify. **4** *determine to go alone* make up one's
mind, decide, resolve, choose, elect, fix on,
purpose. **5** *what determined him to go?* made,
prompt, impel, induce, influence, sway,
lead. **6** *conditions determining the nature of the
soil* affect, influence, act/work on, condition, regulate, decide, control, direct, rule,
dictate, govern, form, shape, modify.

determined adj **1** *a determined person/atti-
tude* firm, resolute, steadfast, tenacious,
purposeful, single-minded, dedicated,
strong-willed, mettlesome, plucky, persistent, pertinacious, persevering, dogged,
unflinching, unwavering, stubborn, obdurate, intransigent, indomitable, inflexible.
2 *determined to go/determined on going* bent
on, intent on, set on.

determining adj *determining factors* deciding, conclusive, settling, decisive, definitive, crucial, critical, pivotal, important, essential.

deterrent n curb, disincentive, discouragement, check, restraint, obstacle, hindrance, impediment, obstruction, block, barrier, inhibition.

detest v loathe, abhor, hate, despise, abominate, execrate, feel aversion/hostility/animosity towards, feel disgust/distaste for, recoil/shrink from, feel repugnance towards.

detestable adj loathsome, abhorrent, hateful, odious, despicable, contemptible, abominable, reprehensible, execrable, distasteful, disgusting, repugnant; *inf* beastly.

detonate v **1** *the bomb detonated* explode, go off, blow up, burst apart; bang, blast, boom. **2** *detonate the bomb* explode, set off, discharge, ignite, kindle, light, spark.

detour n indirect course, roundabout/circuitous route, scenic/tourist route, diversion, digression, deviation, bypass, byway, bypath.

detract v **1** *their conduct detracts from their achievement* take away from, diminish, reduce, lessen, lower, devalue, devaluate, depreciate. **2** *detract his attention* distract, divert, turn away, deflect, avert, shift.

detractor n *criticism from her detractors | detractors from his achievement/reputation* belittler, disparager, denigrator, deprecator, deflater, defamer, vilifier, backbiter, carper, caviller, scandalmonger, muckraker.

detriment n injury, harm, damage, impairment, hurt, loss, disadvantage, disservice, ill, wrong, mischief.

detrimental adj injurious, harmful, damaging, hurtful, deleterious, destructive, pernicious, disadvantageous, adverse, unfavourable, inimical, prejudicial.

detritus n debris, rubble, rubbish; remains, fragments, shards, ruins; flotsam and jetsam, grit, gravel, sand, powder, dust.

devastate v **1** *devastate the cities* lay waste, leave desolate, destroy, ruin, demolish, wreck, raze, level, annihilate, ravage, ransack, sack, harry, despoil, spoil. **2** *devasted by the news* overcome, overwhelm, shock, traumatize, take aback, confound, bewilder, nonplus, disconcert, discompose, discomfit, perturb, chagrin; *inf* floor.

devastating adj **1** *devastating storms/criticism* destructive, ruinous, wrecking, deleterious, harmful, savage, annihilative. **2** *devastating news* overwhelming, shocking,

traumatic, confounding, bewildering, disconcerting. *see* DEVASTATE 2. **3** *looking devastating in evening dress* stunning, glamorous, dazzling, ravishing, gorgeous, beautiful, lovely; *inf* out of this world. **4** *devastating wit* effective, incisive, cutting, keen, mordant, biting, trenchant, satirical, sardonic, sarcastic, withering, savage.

devastation n **1** *a scene of devastation* desolation, destruction, waste, ruin, wreckage; ruins, ravages. **2** *the devastation of the cities* laying waste, destruction, demolition, razing, annihilation, sacking, harrying. *see* DEVASTATE 1. **3** *her complete devastation* shock, traumatization, bewilderment, discomposure, discomfiture, perturbation. *see* DEVASTATE 2.

develop v **1** *cities developing rapidly* grow, evolve, mature, expand, enlarge, spread, advance, progress, prosper, flourish, make headway. **2** *children developing into adults* grow, mature, turn. **3** *develop a plan* begin, commence, start, set in motion, originate, invent, form, establish, institute, fashion, generate. **4** *develop a new breed of pig/rose* generate, breed, propagate, rear, cultivate. **5** *develop a cough* begin to have, acquire, contract, pick up. **6** *develop a theme* elaborate, unfold, work out, enlarge on, expand, broaden, dilate on, amplify, add to, augment, magnify, supplement, reinforce. **7** *a row developed* begin, start, come about, follow, happen, result, ensue, break out.

development n **1** *the development of cities* growth, evolution, maturing, expansion, spread, progress, headway. *see* DEVELOP 1. **2** *the development of a plan* originating, invention, forming, establishment, institution, generation. **3** *the development of a new breed* generation, breeding, propagation, rearing, cultivation. **4** *the development of themes* elaboration, unfolding, unravelling, enlarging, expansion, augmentation. *see* DEVELOP 6. **5** *new developments in the affair* event, turn of events, occurrence, happening, circumstance, incident, situation, issue, outcome, upshot. **6** *a housing development* complex, estate, structure, conglomeration.

deviant adj *deviant behaviour* deviating, aberrant, divergent, digressive, abnormal, irregular, non-standard, anomalous, odd, freakish, peculiar, curious, queer, bizarre, eccentric, idiosyncratic, unorthodox, offbeat, wayward, perverse, devious, warped, twisted, perverted; *inf* bent, kinky, quirky.

deviant n nonconformist, misfit, freak, rare bird, queer fellow, odd sort, pervert; *inf* oddball, weirdo, dingbat.

deviate v diverge, turn aside, step aside, depart from, digress, deflect, differ, vary, change, veer, swerve, bend, drift, stray, tack, slew.

deviation n *deviation from the norm* divergence, turning aside, departure, digression, deflection, difference, variation, alteration, veering, straying, fluctuation, aberration, abnormality, irregularity, anomaly, inconsistency, discrepancy, variableness, oddness, freakishness; change, shift, veer, swerve, bend, drift.

device n 1 *a handy device* appliance, gadget, implement, utensil, tool, piece of equipment/apparatus, apparatus, instrument, machine, contrivance, contraption, invention; *inf* gizmo. 2 *win by a cunning device* design, plan, plot, scheme, ploy, project, stratagem, trick, artifice, ruse, dodge, stunt, gambit, shift, subterfuge, blind, manoeuvre, expedient, machination, strategy, improvisation, intrigue, conspiracy, fraud, wile, deception, imposture, sleight, humbug. 3 *the club device* emblem, symbol, insignia, crest, coat-of-arms, seal, badge, token, motif, design, mark, figure, motto, slogan, legend, logo, colophon, trademark.

devil n 1 *the Devil defeated by God* Satan, Lucifer, Prince of Darkness, the Evil One, the Arch-fiend, Beelzebub, Belial, Apollyon, the Tempter, Lord of the Flies; *inf* Old Nick, Old Harry; *Scots inf* Auld Nick, Auld Clootie, the Auld One. 2 *tempted by devils* demon, fiend, evil spirit, cacodemon. 3 *the master was a devil* brute, savage, beast, monster, ogre, demon, fiend, terror, barbarian, blackguard, rogue, thug, scoundrel, villain, bully, knave. 4 *the child's a little devil* imp, scamp, rascal, rogue, mischief-maker, troublemaker. 5 *feel pity for the poor devils* wretch, unfortunate, beggar, creature, thing, sad case.

devilish adj 1 *devilish practices* diabolic, diabolical, demonic, demoniacal, fiendish, satanic, infernal, hellish. 2 *a devilish creature* wicked, evil, abominable, atrocious, detestable, execrable, villainous, sinister, accursed, damnable.

devilish adv *devilish expensive* extremely, very, exceedingly, intensely, excessively, inordinately, fiendishly, hellishly.

devil-may-care adj careless, reckless, heedless, rash, audacious, wanton, impetuous, impulsive, jaunty, swaggering, nonchalant, happy-go-lucky, easygoing, casual, flippant, indifferent, unconcerned, cavalier, insouciant.

devilry, deviltry n 1 *enemy leaders full of devilry* evil, wickedness, vice, iniquity, sin, malevolence, maliciousness, malice, viciousness, nefariousness, cruelty, savagery, villainy. 2 *the devilry of the children* devilment, mischief-making, troublemaking, roguery, rascality, impishness; mischief; *inf* monkey business. 3 *dealing in devilry* black magic, sorcery, witchcraft, black art, diablerie, diabolism.

devious adj 1 *a devious merchant* underhand, cunning, crafty, sly, wily, artful, guileful, scheming, designing, calculating, dishonest, deceitful, double-dealing, treacherous, misleading, subtle, insidious, surreptitious, furtive, secretive; *inf* crooked. 2 *go by a devious route* indirect, roundabout, deviating, circuitous, tortuous, rambling, wandering, erratic, digressive, excursive.

devise v concoct, contrive, work out, plan, form, formulate, plot, scheme, project, invent, originate, create, compose, construct, frame, think/dream up, conceive, imagine, fabricate, hatch, put together, arrange, prepare, order.

devoid adj *devoid of water/people/interest* lacking, wanting, without, deficient in, empty/vacant of, void/bare/barren of, bereft/denuded of, free from.

devolve v 1 *power devolved to the regions* pass, hand over, transfer, delegate, consign, entrust. 2 *property devolving to a cousin* hand down, pass to, transfer, convey; *Law* alienate. 3 *the argument devolves on a belief in God* depend, be dependent, rely, turn, hinge.

devote v assign, allot, allocate, set aside, set apart, reserve, commit, apply, consign, pledge, give, offer, dedicate, surrender.

devoted adj 1 *a devoted follower* loyal, faithful, true, true blue, staunch, steadfast, constant, committed, dedicated, devout, fond, loving, admiring, affectionate, caring, attentive, warm, ardent. 2 *time devoted to the children* assigned, allotted, set aside, dedicated. *see* DEVOTE. 3 *buildings devoted to God* dedicated, consecrated, blessed, sanctified, hallowed.

devotee n enthusiast, fan, admirer, addict, follower, adherent, disciple, supporter, champion, advocate, votary, fanatic, zealot; *inf* buff, freak.

devotion n 1 *the devotion of his followers* loyalty, faithfulness, fidelity, trueness, staunchness, steadfastness, constancy, commitment, adherence, allegiance, dedication, devoutness, fondness, love, admiration, affection, attentiveness, care, caring, warmness, closeness. 2 *churchmen full of devotion* devoutness, piety, religiousness, spirituality, godliness, holiness, sanctity, saintliness. 3 *look at her husband with devo-*

tion ardour, idolization, love, fondness, affection, infatuation, passion, fervour, admiration, eagerness, yearning. **4** *morning devotions* religious worship, worship, religious observance; prayers, vespers, matins; prayer meeting, church service.

devour v **1** *devour the feast* eat greedily/hungrily, eat up, consume, swallow up, gulp down, gobble up, bolt, wolf down, guzzle, stuff down, cram in, gorge oneself on; feast on; *inf* tuck into, pack away, dispatch, polish off, stuff one's face with, pig oneself on. **2** *flames devouring the house* consume, engulf, envelop, destroy, devastate, lay waste, demolish, wipe out, ruin, wreck, annihilate. **3** *hobbies devouring time/money* consume, use up, cost, spend, waste. **4** *children devouring books* be absorbed in, be engrossed in, take in, drink in/up, feast on, revel in, delight in, enjoy, relish, appreciate. **5** *devoured by anxiety/jealousy* consume, swallow up, engulf, swamp, overcome, overwhelm.

devout adj **1** *a devout Christian* pious, religious, reverent, church-going, godly, saintly, holy, prayerful, orthodox, pure, righteous. **2** *devout hope* sincere, genuine, deep, profound, heartfelt, earnest, fervent, fervid, intense, ardent, vehement, passionate, zealous.

dexterity n **1** *craftsmen showing dexterity* manual dexterity, deftness, adroitness, nimbleness of fingers, nimbleness, agility, skilfulness, skill, knack, adeptness, handiness, facility, proficiency, expertise, talent, artistry, craft, mastery, finesse, effortlessness, felicity. **2** *the firm's board showing dexterity* mental dexterity/agility, cleverness, shrewdness, smartness, astuteness, cunning, craft, sagacity, sharp-wittedness, acuteness, ingenuity, resourcefulness, inventiveness.

dexterous adj **1** *dexterous craftsmen* deft, adroit, nimble, agile, skilful, skilled, adept, handy, proficient, expert, talented, accomplished, artistic. *see* DEXTERITY 1. **2** *a dexterous businessman* clever, shrewd, smart, astute, cunning, crafty, wily, artful, sagacious, sharp-witted, acute, ingenious, resourceful, inventive. *see* DEXTERITY 2.

diabolic adj **1** *diabolic forces* devilish, fiendish, demonic, demoniacal, satanic, infernal, hellish, cacodemonic. **2** *a diabolic slave master* fiendish, wicked, evil, sinful, savage, brutish, monstrous, barbaric, cruel, malevolent, malicious, black-hearted, nasty, abominable, hateful, execrable, damnable. **3** *a diabolic task* difficult, compli-

cated, complex, tricky, nasty, unpleasant, dreadful, vile.

diabolical adj **1** *see* DIABOLIC. **2** *diabolical taste/food* very bad, horrible, excruciating, appalling, shocking, outrageous, atrocious, vile. **3** *a diabolical liberty* very great, extreme, excessive, intolerable, unreasonable, undue, inordinate, uncalled-for.

diadem n crown, coronet, tiara, circlet, headband, wreath, chaplet, fillet.

diagnose v *diagnose measles* identify, determine, distinguish, recognize, detect, pinpoint, pronounce.

diagnosis n **1** *a diagnosis of measles* identification, recognition, detection, pinpointing. *see* DIAGNOSE. **2** *consultants confirming the GP's diagnosis* opinion, pronouncement, judgement, conclusion, interpretation.

diagonal adj crossing, crossways, crosswise, slanting, slanted, sloping, oblique, angled, cornerways, cornerwise.

diagonally adv crossways, crosswise, on the cross, on the slant, aslant, obliquely, at an angle, on the bias, cornerways, cornerwise.

diagram n line drawing, drawing, sketch, draft, illustration, picture, representation, outline, delineation.

dial v *dial the number* telephone, phone, ring, call.

dialect n regional language, variety of language, vernacular, patois, non-standard language; regionalism, localism, provincialism; *inf* local lingo.

dialectic n discussion, debate, dialogue, disputation, argument, argumentation, contention, polemic, war of words, reasoning, ratiocination.

dialectic adj dialectical, logical, analytical, disputatious, argumentative, contentious, polemic, rational, rationalistic.

dialogue n **1** *the dialogue between friends* | *dialogue between the two sides* conversation, talk, tête-à-tête, chat, chit-chat, gossip, communication, debate, argument, exchange of views, discourse, discussion, conference, converse, colloquy, interlocution, duologue, confabulation, parley, palaver; *inf* pow-wow, rap session. **2** *the dialogue of the novel/play* conversation, spoken part, script; lines.

diameter n breadth, width, thickness, calibre.

diametrical adj *diametrical differences/opposition* direct, absolute, complete, exact, extreme, diametrically opposite, opposite, contrasting, conflicting, contrary, counter, antithetical, antipodal.

diaphanous adj sheer, fine, delicate, light, thin, silken, chiffony, gossamer, gauzy, cobwebby, translucent, transparent, see-through.

diarrhoea n loose motions, looseness of the bowels; *inf* the skitters, the runs, the trots, gippy tummy, holiday tummy, Delhi belly, Montezuma's revenge.

diary n **1** *noted the meeting in her diary* appointment/engagement book, personal organizer; *Trademark* Filofax. **2** *keep a diary of her holiday* day-by-day account, daily record, journal, chronicle, log, logbook, history, annal.

diatribe n tirade, harangue, verbal onslaught, stream of abuse, denunciation, philippic, reproof, reprimand, rebuke, upbraiding; invective, vituperation, abuse, castigation, criticism, stricture; *inf* tongue-lashing, slating, knocking.

dicey adj uncertain, risky, chancy, difficult, tricky, dodgy, dangerous, ticklish; *inf* hairy.

dicky adj unsound, unsteady, unstable, unreliable, shaky, fluttery, weak, infirm, queer.

dictate v **1** *dictate the letter* read out, read aloud, speak, say, utter, recite. **2** *dictate terms* prescribe, lay down, impose, set down, order, command, decree, ordain, direct, pronounce, enjoin, promulgate. **3** *always dictating to others* give orders, order about, lay down the law, impose one's will, boss about, domineer, act the tin god; *inf* call the shots, throw one's weight around.

dictate n **1** *at the commander's dictate* order, command, decree, edict, ordinance, dictum, direction, bidding, charge, behest, pronouncement, mandate, requirement, enjoining, injuction, ultimatum, promulgation. **2** *the dictates of conscience* code, guiding principle, law, rule, precept, dictum, axiom, maxim.

dictator n absolute ruler, despot, autocrat, tyrant, oppressor.

dictatorial adj **1** *dictatorial government* absolute, unlimited, unrestricted, arbitrary, omnipotent, all-powerful, autocratic, totalitarian, authoritarian, despotic, tyrannical, autarchic. **2** *dictatorial bosses* tyrannical, despotic, oppressive, iron-handed, imperious, overbearing, domineering, peremptory, high-handed, authoritarian, dogmatic, high and mighty; *inf* bossy.

dictatorship n **1** *living in dictatorships* autarchy, totalitarian state, absolute monarchy, reign of terror. **2** *revolting*

against dictatorship absolute rule, despotism, autocracy, tyranny, authoritarianism, totalitarianism, absolutism.

diction n **1** *learn diction at elocution lessons* enunciation, articulation, elocution, pronunciation, speech, intonation, inflection, delivery, fluency, rhetoric. **2** *impressed by the writer's diction* style, language, phraseology, phrasing, wording, usage, vocabulary, terminology, expression, idiom.

dictionary n wordbook, vocabulary list, glossary, lexicon, concordance.

dictum n **1** *the chairman's dictum* utterance, pronouncement, direction, injunction, assertion, statement, dictate, command, order, decree, edict. **2** *as the dictum has it* saying, maxim, axiom, proverb, adage, aphorism, saw, truism, platitude, cliché.

didactic adj *didactic prose* instructive, instructional, educational, educative, informative, informational, edifying, preceptive, pedagogic, propaedeutic, pedantic, moralistic, homiletic.

die v **1** *she died last night* pass away, pass on, lose one's life, depart this life, expire, decease, breathe one's last, meet one's end, lay down one's life, be no more, perish, go to one's last resting-place, cross the Styx; *inf* give up the ghost, kick the bucket, push up the daisies, bite the dust, snuff it, croak, turn up one's toes, cash in one's chips, hop the twig. **2** *hope died* come to an end, end, vanish, disappear, pass, fade, fall away, dwindle, melt away, dissolve, subside, decline, sink, lapse, ebb, wane, wilt, wither, evanesce. **3** *the engine died* stop, halt, fail, break down, peter out, fizzle out, run down, fade away, lose power. **4** *die of boredom/laughter* collapse with, be overcome with, be overwhelmed/overpowered by, succumb to. **5** *she's dying for water | dying to see you* be eager, be desperate, long.

die-hard adj ultraconservative, conservative, reactionary, dyed in the wool, intransigent, inflexible, immovable, unchanging, uncompromising, unyielding, indomitable, adamant, rigid.

diet[1] n **1** *eat a healthy diet* selection of food, food and drink, food, fare; foodstuffs, provisions, victuals, comestibles, edibles, viands, rations, commons; nourishment, nutriment, sustenance, aliment. **2** *go on a diet* dietary regimen/regime, abstinence, period of fasting, fast; restricted diet, crash diet.

diet[1] v *dieting to lose several pounds* follow a diet, be on a diet, eat sparingly/selectively, abstain, fast, slim, reduce, lose weight.

diet² n **1** *elected to the diet* legislative assembly, congress, parliament, council, senate, synod. **2** *attend an international diet* conference, convention, assembly, convocation, conventicle, conclave, session.

differ v **1** *tastes differ* be different, be unlike, be dissimilar, be distinguishable, vary, diverge. **2** *results differing from the norm* vary, diverge, deviate from, depart from, run counter to, contravene, contradict, contrast with. **3** *parties agreeing to differ* disagree, fail to agree, dissent, be at variance, be in dispute/opposition, oppose, take issue, conflict, clash, quarrel, argue, wrangle, quibble, squabble, altercate.

difference n **1** *the difference between/in their lifestyles* dissimilarity, unlikeness, dissimilitude, contrast, distinction, distinctness, differentiation, variance, variation, divergence, deviation, contrariety, antithesis, contradiction, contradistinction, nonconformity, disparity, imbalance, incongruity. **2** *spot the difference* distinction, peculiarity, oddity, idiosyncrasy, singularity, eccentricity, individuality. **3** *the two had a difference* difference of opinion, disagreement, dispute, disputation, argument, debate, misunderstanding, quarrel, row, wrangle, set-to, tiff, altercation, contretemps, clash, controversy, feud, vendetta. **4** *pay the difference* balance, remainder, rest, residue, residuum, excess.

different adj **1** *our lifestyles are different | tastes different from ours* unlike, dissimilar, non-identical, contrastive, contrasting, diverse, divergent, deviating, disparate, incompatible, inconsistent, opposed, at variance, at odds, clashing, conflicting, discrepant. **2** *looking completely different from last year* changed, altered, modified, transformed, metamorphosed, other. **3** *a different dress every day* separate, other, not the same, non-identical, distinct, individual, discrete. **4** *different people have commented | available in different colours* various, several, many, numerous, some, sundry, certain, assorted, varied, miscellaneous, diverse, manifold, multifarious, motley, variegated. **5** *looking for something different* unusual, out of the ordinary, uncommon, distinctive, rare, unique, novel, special, singular, remarkable, extraordinary, noteworthy, unconventional, atypical, odd, strange, bizarre; *inf* something else.

differential adj *differential treatment/rates* distinctive, distinguishing, discriminating, discriminatory, different.

differential n *maintain salary differentials* distinction, discrimination, difference;

amount of difference, disparity, discrepancy.

differentiate v **1** *differentiate between grades | can you differentiate the twins?* distinguish, discriminate, make a distinction, contrast, see/discern a difference; tell apart, set apart, separate, mark off. **2** *the yellow beak differentiates the male bird* make different, distinguish, set apart, contrast, identify. **3** *in time the species differentiated* modify, alter, change, become different, transform, adapt.

difficult adj **1** *digging in this soil is difficult* hard, strenuous, arduous, laborious, demanding, formidable, tough, onerous, burdensome, exhausting, tiring, wearisome, back-breaking, painful, oppressive; *inf* no picnic. **2** *a difficult problem* hard, complicated, complex, involved, intricate, puzzling, problematic, baffling, perplexing, knotty, thorny, ticklish, delicate, obscure, abstract, abstruse, recondite, enigmatic, profound, deep. **3** *a difficult child* troublesome, tiresome, demanding, unmanageable, intractable, perverse, recalcitrant, obstreperous, refractory, fractious, unaccommodating, uncooperative, uncompliant, unamenable. **4** *difficult people to choose presents for* hard to please/satisfy, fussy, particular, fastidious, perfectionist, critical, hypercritical, finicky, finical. **5** *arrive at a difficult time* inconvenient, ill-timed, disadvantageous, unfavourable. **6** *go through difficult times* hard, straitened, hard-pressed, bad, tough, grim, dark.

difficulty n **1** *dig with difficulty* difficultness, hardness, strenuousness, arduousness, laboriousness, toughness, struggling, awkwardness; labour, strain, struggle. **2** *the difficulty of the problem* difficultness, hardness, complicatedness, complexity, intricacy, perplexity, knottiness, delicacy, obscurity, abstruseness. *see* DIFFICULT 2. **3** *encounter a difficulty* complication, problem, snag, hitch, hindrance, obstacle, pitfall, hurdle, impediment, obstruction, barrier. **4** *raise difficulties* protest, objection, complaint, gripe, demur, cavil. **5** *in difficulty | in financial difficulties* predicament, quandary, dilemma, plight, distress, embarrassment, trouble, hot/deep water; straits; *inf* fix, jam, spot, scrape. **6** *the difficulty of the times* hardship, trial, tribulation, ordeal, exigency.

diffidence n shyness, bashfulness, modesty, sheepishness, timidity, timidness, timorousness, apprehension, reserve, hesitancy, reluctance, constraint, doubt, insecurity, distrust, suspicion, unobtrusiveness, self-effacement, humility, meekness.

diffident adj shy, bashful, modest, sheepish, unconfident, unassertive, timid, timorous, apprehensive, fearful, shrinking, reserved, withdrawn, hesitant, reluctant, doubtful, unsure, insecure, distrustful, suspicious, unobtrusive, self-effacing, unassuming, humble, meek.

diffuse adj **1** *diffuse light* diffused, spread out, scattered, dispersed, not concentrated. **2** *a diffuse style* verbose, wordy, prolix, long-winded, copious, profuse, discursive, rambling, wandering, meandering, maundering, digressive, circuitous, roundabout, circumlocutory, periphrastic, waffling, loose, vague.

diffuse v spread around, send out, scatter, disperse, disseminate, dissipate, dispel, distribute, dispense, circulate, propagate, broadcast, promulgate, effuse.

diffusion n **1** *the diffusion of light/knowledge* scattering, spreading, dispersal, dissemination, dispelling, distribution, dispensation, circulation, propagation, broadcasting, promulgation, effusion. **2** *writers given to diffusion* diffuseness, verbosity, verbiage, wordiness, prolixity, long-windedness, loquaciousness, loquacity, profuseness, discursiveness, rambling, wandering, digressiveness, circuitousness, circumlocution, periphrasis, waffling. *see* DIFFUSE adj 2.

dig v **1** *enjoy digging | dig the earth* break up soil/ground; work, break up, loosen up, turn over, spade, delve, till, cultivate, harrow, plough. **2** *dig a tunnel/hole* dig out, excavate, quarry, hollow out, scoop out, gouge, tunnel, burrow, mine, channel. **3** *dig someone in the ribs* poke, prod, jab, thrust, drive, push, punch. **4** *dig into the history* delve, search, probe, investigate, research. **5** *dig potatoes* unearth, dig up. **6** *dig the music* like, love, enjoy, appreciate. **7** *dig the statement* understand, comprehend, follow, grasp, make out; *inf* get. **dig up 1** *dig up the corpse* exhume, bring to the surface, unearth. **2** *dig up new information* unearth, uncover, root out, extricate, bring to light, come up with, expose, discover, find, come across.

dig n **1** *a dig in the ribs* poke, prod, jab, thrust, push, punch. **2** *tired of digs at his baldness* cutting remark, gibe, jeer, taunt, sneer, insult, slur, quip, insinuation; *inf* wisecrack, crack.

digest v **1** *digest food* assimilate, absorb, break down, dissolve, macerate. **2** *digest the facts* assimilate, absorb, take in, understand, comprehend, grasp, master, consider, think about, contemplate, mull over, weigh up, reflect on, ponder, meditate on,

study. **3** *digest the leaflets* classify, catalogue, tabulate, codify, arrange, order, dispose, systematize, methodize. **4** *digest the information* shorten, reduce, condense, abridge, compress, compact, summarize, précis.

digest n *a digest of the week's news* summary, synopsis, abstract, précis, résumé, outline, abridgement, epitome, review, compendium.

digestion n **1** *digestion of food* assimilation, absorption, breaking down, dissolution, maceration. **2** *digestion of facts* assimilation, absorption, understanding, comprehension, mastery, consideration, contemplation. *see* DIGEST V 2.

dignified adj stately, noble, solemn, grave, formal, decorous, reserved, ceremonious, courtly, majestic, august, lofty, exalted, regal, lordly, imposing, impressive, grand.

dignify v add dignity/distinction to, distinguish, honour, grace, adorn, exalt, enhance, ennoble, glorify, elevate, make lofty, aggrandize, upgrade.

dignitary n public figure, notable, notability, worthy, personage, luminary, VIP, pillar of society, leading light, celebrity, big name, somebody, star, lion; *inf* bigwig, top brass, big gun, big shot/noise, big wheel, celeb, lord/lady muck.

dignity n **1** *the dignity of the occasion* stateliness, nobleness, nobility, solemnity, gravity, formality, decorum, propriety, reserve, ceremoniousness, courtliness, majesty, augustness, loftiness, exaltedness, regalness, regality, lordliness, impressiveness, grandeur. **2** *the dignity of work* worthiness, honourability, nobility, excellence, respectability; worth, merit, virtue. **3** *achieve dignity in the state/Church* high rank, high standing, high station, status, elevation, eminence, honour, glory, greatness, importance. **4** *conscious of their dignity* pride, self-esteem, self-conceit, self-regard, self-importance, self-respect, *amour propre*.

digress v get off the subject, stray from the point, deviate/deflect from the topic, go off at a tangent, diverge, turn aside, depart, drift, ramble, wander, meander, maunder.

digression n **1** *his usual digression from the subject* straying, deviation, divergence, diversion, departure, drifting, rambling. *see* DIGRESS. **2** *an essay full of digressions* aside, deviation, deflection, detour, excursion, excursus, apostrophe, incidental remark, *obiter dictum*.

dilapidated adj run-down, broken-down, tumbledown, ramshackle, in ruins, ruined, falling to pieces, falling apart, in disrepair, shabby, battered, rickety, shaky, crumbling, decayed, decaying, decrepit, worn-out, neglected, uncared-for.

dilate v **1** *her pupils dilated* enlarge, widen, expand. **2** *dilate on the subject* expand, enlarge, expound, expatiate, elaborate.

dilatory adj slow, tardy, sluggish, snail-like, lazy, slack, indolent, delaying, dallying, dilly-dallying, loitering, lingering, dawdling, tarrying, procrastinating, postponing, deferring, putting off, tabling, shelving, temporizing, stalling, time-wasting, Fabian.

dilemma n difficult choice, Scylla and Charybdis, devil and the deep blue sea, Catch-22, vicious circle, quandary, predicament, plight, difficulty, tight corner/spot, problem, puzzle, mess, muddle; trouble, perplexity, confusion, embarrassment.

dilettante n **1** *dilettantes not seriously interested* dabbler, potterer, trifler, dallier, amateur, non-professional. **2** *dilettantes always at the art gallery* art lover, lover of the arts, connoisseur, aesthete, member of the *cognoscenti*, arbiter elegantiae/elegantiarum.

diligence n assiduity, assiduousness, application, concentration, industriousness, conscientiousness, attentiveness, heedfulness, constancy, intentness, earnestness, perseverance, sedulousness, persistence, tenacity, pertinacity, doggedness, laboriousness; care, attention, industry. *see* DILIGENT.

diligent adj assiduous, industrious, conscientious, hard-working, painstaking, meticulous, thorough, careful, attentive, heedful, intent, earnest, studious, constant, persevering, sedulous, persistent, tenacious, pertinacious, zealous, active, busy, untiring, tireless, indefatigable, dogged, plodding, slogging, laborious.

dilly-dally v dally, dawdle, loiter, linger, take one's time, delay, waste time, tarry, hover, kill time, potter, trifle, procrastinate, dither, hesitate, falter, vacillate, waver, shilly-shally, hem and haw, fluctuate.

dilute v **1** *dilute the solution* make weaker, weaken, make thinner, thin out, water down, cut, adulterate, mix. **2** *dilute the colourful details* | *dilute standards* make weaker, weaken, attenuate, reduce, diminish, decrease, lessen, mitigate, temper.

dim adj **1** *a dim light* faint, weak, feeble, pale, dull, dingy, lustreless, muted. **2** *dim skies* dark, darkish, grey, overcast, leaden, gloomy, sombre, dusky, lowering, cloudy, hazy, misty, foggy, crepuscular, tenebrous. **3** *dim corridors* dark, darkened, gloomy, badly lit, poorly lit, dingy, dismal. **4** *a dim shape* vague, ill-defined, indistinct, unclear, shadowy, blurred, blurry, fuzzy, imperceptible, nebulous, obscured, bleared, bleary, obfuscated. **5** *a dim recollection* vague, indistinct, hazy, confused, blurred, shadowy, imperfect, obscure, remote. **6** *rather dim people* stupid, thick, dense, slow-witted, slow, dull, doltish, limited, obtuse; *inf* dumb, slow on the uptake. **7** *prospects are rather dim* gloomy, sombre, unpromising, unfavourable, discouraging, disheartening, depressing, dispiriting.

dim v **1** *dim the stage lights* turn down, lower, dip. **2** *the light dimmed* grow dim, fade, grow faint/feeble, dull, pale, blur. **3** *the skies dimmed* grow dark, darken, cloud over, grow leaden. *see* DIM adj 2. **4** *memories/ recollections dimming* grow dim, fade, blur, become blurred/confused.

dimension n **1** *of huge dimension* | *the dimensions of the tank* measured extent, extent; length, width, breadth, depth, area, size, volume, capacity, bulk; proportions. **2** *underestimate the dimensions of the problem* size, extent, scope, measure, scale, range, magnitude, greatness, importance. **3** *add another dimension to entertainment* aspect, side, feature, facet, element.

diminish v **1** *their power/strength diminished* lessen, grow less, decrease, reduce, shrink, contract, abate, grow weak/weaker. **2** *time diminished their power/strength* lessen, lower, decrease, reduce, curtail, cut, contract, narrow, constrict, truncate, retrench. **3** *the storm/empire diminished* subside, ebb, recede, wane, dwindle, slacken, die/fall away, fade, decline, die/peter out. **4** *try to diminish him* | *diminish his reputation* belittle, disparage, denigrate, depreciate, deprecate, derogate, devalue, demean, detract from, cheapen, defame, vilify.

diminution n **1** lessening, lowering, decrease, reduction, contraction, abatement, weakening, curtailment, cut, cutback, constriction, truncating, retrenchment. *see* DIMINISH 1, 2. **2** *the diminution of the storm/empire* subsidence, ebb, receding, wane, slackening, dying away, failing, decline. *see* DIMINISH 3.

diminutive adj small, little, tiny, petite, slight, elfin, minute, miniature, mini, small-scale, compact, microscopic, midget, undersized, dwarfish, pygmy, homuncular, Lilliputian; *inf* wee, baby, half-pint.

din n loud noise, uproar, row, racket, commotion, hullabaloo, hubbub, tumult, clangour, outcry, brouhaha, crash, clatter, clash, shouting, yelling; clamour, noise, pandemonium, bedlam, babel.

din v **1** *music dinning* | *loud voices dinning* blare, blast, clang, clatter, crash, clamour, shout, roar, yell, bellow, bawl. **2** *din the facts into pupils* drum, instil, hammer, inculcate, teach.

dine v **1** *we dine at eight* have dinner/supper, eat, sup, feed, feast, banquet. *see* DINNER. **2** *dine on game* eat, consume, feed on.

dingy adj dark, dull, dim, gloomy, drab, dismal, dreary, cheerless, dusky, sombre, murky, hazy, smoggy, smoky, sooty, dirty, discoloured, grimy, soiled, faded, shabby, worn, seedy, run-down, tacky.

dinky adj *a dinky little girl/car* small, petite, dainty, neat, trim, cute, diminutive, mini, miniature.

dinner n *come to dinner* | *the firm's annual dinner* evening meal, supper, main meal, lunch, repast, refection; feast, banquet, collation; *inf* spread, blow-out.

dint n *a dint on the car's roof* dent, indentation, depression. **by dint of** by means of, by use of, by virtue of.

dip v **1** *dip the garment in dye* immerse, submerge, plunge, duck, dunk, lower, sink, souse, douse, soak, drench, steep, bathe, rinse. **2** *the sun dipping behind the horizon* sink, set, go/drop down, descend, fade, disappear, subside. **3** *profits dipping* fall, go down, drop, drop/fall off, decrease, decline, slump. **4** *the road dips* slope down, slope, descend, go down, fall, sink, decline, slant down, droop, sag. **5** *dip water* scoop up, scoop, spoon, ladle. **dip into 1** *dip into a book* skim, browse, look through, glance at, run through. **2** *dip into art* dabble in, scratch the surface of, play at, sample. **3** *dip into one's purse* | *dip into the barrel* reach into, put one's hand into, go into. **4** *dip into one's savings* draw on, use/spend part of.

dip n **1** *give the garment/sheep a dip* immersion, plunge, ducking, dunking, sousing, dousing, soaking, drenching. *see* DIP v 1. **2** *take a dip* swim, bathe, dive, plunge, paddle. **3** *a sheep dip* liquid preparation/mixture, solution; disinfectant, preservative. **4** *a cheese dip* creamy preparation/mixture, concoction, sauce. **5** *a dip in profits* fall, falling-off, drop, dropping-off, decrease, decline, lowering, slump. **6** *a dip in the terrain* slope, incline, decline, slant, descent, hollow, concavity, depression, basin.

diplomacy n **1** *ministers skilled in diplomacy* statesmanship, statecraft, international relations/politics; negotiations. **2** *treating her parents' objections with diplomacy* tactfulness, subtlety, discretion, judiciousness, prudence, delicacy, sensitivity, finesse, *savoir faire*, politeness, cleverness, artfulness, cunning. tact, care, skill.

diplomat n **1** *an international meeting of diplomats* ambassador, envoy, emissary, legate, consul, attaché. **2** *the diplomat of the firm* tactful person, conciliator, reconciler, peace-maker, mediator, negotiator, tactitian, arbitrator, intermediary, moderator, go-between, middleman, public relations officer.

diplomatic adj **1** *a diplomatic post* ambassadorial, consular, foreign office. **2** *diplomatic handling* | *a diplomatic young woman* tactful, subtle, discreet, judicious, prudent, careful, delicate, sensitive, polite, politic, clever, skilful, artful.

dire adj **1** *in dire straits* | *dire poverty* terrible, dreadful, appalling, frightful, awful, horrible, atrocious, grim, cruel, grievous, disastrous, ruinous, miserable, wretched, woeful, calamitous, catastrophic, cataclysmic, distressing, harrowing, alarming, unspeakable, shocking, outrageous. **2** *dire warnings* ominous, sinister, portentous, gloomy, gloom-and-doom, grim, dreadful, dismal, unpropitious, inauspicious, unfavourable, pessimistic. **3** *in dire need of money* urgent, desperate, drastic, pressing, crying, vital, grave, critical, crucial, extreme, compelling, exigent.

direct v **1** *direct the operation* administer, manage, be in charge/control/command of, lead, run, command, control, govern, conduct, handle, preside over, rule, supervise, superintend, oversee, guide, mastermind, regulate, orchestrate, engineer, dispose, dominate, domineer; *inf* be the boss of, run the show, call the shots. **2** *directed to work late* command, order, give orders to, instruct, charge, bid, dictate, adjure, enjoin. **3** *direct them to the station* give directions to, show/point/indicate the way, guide, steer, lead, conduct, accompany, usher, escort, navigate, pilot. **4** *remarks directed at parents* aim at, address to, intend/mean for, destine for, focus on, point/level at, train, turn on, fix on. **5** *direct the correspondence* address, label, superscribe, post, send, mail.

direct adj **1** *a direct road* straight, undeviating, unswerving, uncircuitous, shortest. **2** *a direct train/journey* straight through, through, non-stop, unbroken, uninterrupted. **3** *a direct approach* immediate, firsthand, personal, face to face, head-on, non-interventional. **4** *a direct statement/manner* frank, blunt, straightforward, straight,

straight to the point, explicit, clear, plain, unequivocal, unambiguous, honest, candid, open, sincere, plain-spoken, outspoken, forthright, downright, point blank, matter-of-fact, categorical. **5** *the direct opposite* exact, absolute, complete, downright, thorough, diametrical. **6** *a direct quotation* exact, precise, word for word, verbatim, accurate, correct.

direction n **1** *the/his direction of the project* administration, management, government, supervision, superintendence, regulation, orchestration; control, command, conduct, handling, running, overseeing, masterminding, disposal; leadership, guidance. *see* DIRECT V 1. **2** *ignore the teacher's direction* command, order, instruction, bidding, charge, dictate, enjoinment, prescription. *see* DIRECTIVE. **3** *which direction did they take?* way, route, course, path, track, road, line, run, bearing, orientation. **4** *the direction of their policy/statement* drift, aim, tack, scope, bent, bias, tendency, current, trend, tenor, inclination, leaning, proclivity, orientation. **5** *make out the direction on the parcel* address, label, mark, superscription.

directions npl instructions, guidelines, rules, regulations, recommendations, indications; guidance, briefing; plan.

directive n direction, command, order, instruction, charge, bidding, injunction, ruling, regulation, dictate, decree, edict, notice, ordinance, enjoinment, prescription, mandate, fiat.

directly adv **1** *travel directly* straight, in a straight line, as the crow flies, by the shortest route, without deviation. **2** *leave directly* immediately, at once, instantly, right/straight away, now, instantaneously, without delay/hesitation, quickly, speedily, promptly, soon, as soon as possible, shortly, in a little while; *inf* pronto. **3** *speak directly* frankly, bluntly, straightforwardly, explicitly, clearly, plainly, unequivocally, unambiguously, sincerely, truthfully, outspokenly, forthrightly, point-blank, matter-of-factly, categorically, without prevarication. **4** *talk directly to the manager* at first hand, personally, face to face, head on. **5** *it's directly opposite* exactly, immediately, diametrically.

director n administrator, controller, manager, executive, chairman, chairwoman, chairperson, chair, head, chief, principal, leader, governor, president, superintendent, supervisor, overseer, organizer, producer; *inf* boss, kingpin, top dog, gaffer; *Amer inf* honcho.

dirge n elegy, lament, funeral song/chant, burial hymn, dead march, requiem, keen, threnody.

dirt n **1** *clean the dirt from the room* grime, dust, soot, smut, muck, mud, filth, mire, sludge, slime, ooze, waste, dross, pollution; smudge, stain, tarnish; *inf* crud, yuk, grot, gunge. **2** *piles of dirt by the roadside* earth, soil, loam, clay, silt. **3** *disapprove of the dirt in modern novels* obscenity, indecency, smut, sordidness, coarseness, bawdiness, ribaldry, salaciousness, lewdness, pornography; *inf* sleaze, sleaziness. *see* DIRTY adj 2. **4** *spreading dirt about the neighbours* scandal, gossip, talk, rumour, slander, libel; revelations.

dirty adj **1** *dirty rooms/clothes* unclean, soiled, grimy, begrimed, grubby, messy, dusty, sooty, mucky, muddy, filthy, bedraggled, slimy, polluted, sullied, foul, stained, spotted, smudged, tarnished, defiled, nasty; *inf* cruddy, yukky, grotty, gungy. **2** *dirty jokes* blue, obscene, indecent, vulgar, smutty, coarse, bawdy, suggestive, ribald, salacious, risqué, prurient, lewd, lascivious, licentious, pornographic; *Amer* off colour; *inf* sleazy. **3** *a dirty cheat* nasty, unpleasant, mean, base, low, vile, contemptible, despicable, cowardly, ignominious, sordid, beggarly, squalid. **4** *a dirty trick | dirty play* unsporting, unfair, dishonourable, unscrupulous, dishonest, crooked, illegal, deceitful, fraudulent, double-dealing, corrupt, treacherous. **5** *give a dirty look* full of dislike/hate, malevolent, smouldering, resentful, bitter, angry, indignant, annoyed, peeved, offended. **6** *dirty weather* unpleasant, nasty, foul, stormy, squally, gusty, rainy, misty, gloomy, murky, overcast, louring. **7** *a dirty shade of white* dingy, dull, muddy, dark, cloudy, not clear/pure. **8** *a dirty rumour* nasty, unkind, scandalous, defamatory, slanderous, libellous.

dirty v *dirty clothes* soil, stain, muddy, begrime, blacken, mess up, spatter, smudge, smear, spot, splash, spoil, sully, pollute, foul, defile, besmirch.

dirty adv *a dirty great jewel* very, extremely, exceedingly.

disability n **1** *suffering from a physical disability* impairment, disablement, infirmity, defect, handicap, disorder, affliction, ailment, complaint, illness, malady. **2** *physical disability prevented him going* incapacity, infirmity, unfitness, weakness, powerlessness, impotence, incapability, inability, incompetence, ineptitude, disqualification.

disable v **1** *the accident disabled him* incapacitate, impair, damage, put out of action, debilitate, indispose, weaken, enfeeble, make unfit, render infirm, cripple, lame, handicap, immobilize, hamstring, paralyse, prostrate. **2** *disable the machinery* render inoperative, make ineffective, paralyse, make harmless. **3** *disabled from voting* disqualify, invalidate, declare incapable, disenable.

disabled adj physically challenged, incapacitated, impaired, handicapped, debilitated, unfit, out of action, infirm, weak, weakened, enfeebled, crippled, lame, immobilized, bedridden, paralysed.

disabuse v undeceive, set right/straight, open the eyes of, wake someone up, disenchant.

disadvantage n **1** *the advantages and disadvantages of the situation* drawback, snag, downside, weak spot/point, weakness, flaw, defect, fault, handicap, trouble, liability, nuisance, hindrance, obstacle, impediment; *inf* minus, fly in the ointment. **2** *people suffering from financial disadvantage* deprivation, privation, hardship, lack, burden. **3** *to their disadvantage* disservice, detriment, prejudice, harm, damage; loss, injury, hurt, mischief.

disadvantaged adj deprived, in need, in want, in distress, poor, poverty-stricken, discriminated against.

disadvantageous adj unfavourable, adverse, unfortunate, unlucky, hapless, detrimental, prejudicial, deleterious, harmful, damaging, injurious, hurtful, destructive, inconvenient, inopportune, ill-timed, inexpedient, inadvisable.

disaffected adj alienated, estranged, unfriendly, disunited; dissatisfied, disgruntled, discontented, disloyal, rebellious, mutinous, seditious, up in arms, hostile, antagonistic.

disagree v **1** *the two sides disagreed* differ, fail to agree, dissent, stand opposed, be in dispute/contention, be at variance/odds, diverge, disaccord. **2** *the stories disagreed | stories disagreeing with each other* differ, be dissimilar, be unlike, be different, vary, conflict, clash, contrast, diverge, not correspond, not accord, be discordant. **3** *children constantly disagreeing* quarrel, argue, bicker, wrangle, squabble, spar, dispute, debate, take issue with, altercate; *inf* fall out, have words. **4** *food disagreeing with him* be incompatible with, make ill/unwell, cause discomfort/distress, be injurious to.

disagreeable adj **1** *a disagreeable experience* unpleasant, displeasing, nasty, horrible, dreadful, hateful, detestable, abominable, odious, objectionable, offensive, obnoxious, repugnant, repulsive, repellent, revolting, disgusting, distasteful, nauseating, unsavoury, unpalatable. **2** *a disagreeable old man* bad-tempered, ill-natured, unfriendly, unpleasant, difficult, nasty, cross, irritable, rude, surly, discourteous, impolite, churlish, peevish, brusque, abrupt, disobliging, contrary.

disagreement n **1** *the disagreement of the two sides* lack of agreement, difference of opinion, dissent, dispute, variance, contention, disaccord, discord. **2** *the disagreement of/between the accounts* difference, dissimilarity, unlikeness, variation, variance, discrepancy, disparity, dissimilitude, incompatibility, incongruity, contradiction, conflict, clash, contrast, divergence, deviation, contravention, non-conformity, diversity. **3** *the disagreement between the children* quarrel, argument, wrangle, squabble, altercation, dispute, debate, disputation, discord, strife, conflict, war of words; bickering, sparring, contention, dissension, disharmony; *inf* falling out.

disallow v reject, say no to, refuse, dismiss, rebuff, repel, repulse, repudiate, ban, bar, debar, forbid, prohibit, veto, embargo, proscribe, negative, cancel, disclaim, disown, abjure, disavow.

disappear v **1** *the sun disappearing behind the horizon* pass from sight, cease to be visible, vanish from sight, vanish, be lost to view/sight, recede, recede from view, fade, fade/melt away, withdraw, depart, retire, go, pass, flee, retreat, ebb, wane, dematerialize, evanesce, evaporate; *inf* vamoose. **2** *customs/railways which have disappeared* die out, die, cease to be/exist, be no more, come to an end, end, vanish, pass away, expire, perish, become extinct, fade, melt away, leave no trace, pass into oblivion.

disappearance n **1** *the disappearance of the sun* passing from sight, vanishing, receding from view, fading, melting away, withdrawal, departure, exit, retiral, passing, retreat, ebb, wane, eclipse, dematerialization, evanescence, evaporation. *see* DISAPPEAR 1. **2** *the disappearance of the customs/trams* dying out, death, vanishing, passing away, expiry, perishing, eclipse, extinction.

disappoint v **1** *sorry to disappoint you | the news disappointed him* let down, fail, dishearten, depress, dispirit, upset, sadden, dash the hopes of, chagrin, dismay, disgruntle, disenchant, disillusion, dissatisfy, vex. **2** *disappoint their plans* thwart, frustrate, baulk, foil, defeat, baffle, hinder, obstruct, hamper, impede, interfere with.

disappointed adj **1** *disappointed children* upset, saddened, let down, disheartened, downhearted, cast down, downcast, depressed, dispirited, despondent, distressed, chagrined, disgruntled, disenchanted, disillusioned, discontented, dissatisfied, vexed. **2** *disappointed plans* thwarted, frustrated, baulked, foiled, defeated, failed, baffled. *see* DISAPPOINT 2.

disappointing adj **1** *disappointing news* upsetting, saddening, disagreeable, disheartening, discouraging, depressing, dispiriting, distressing, disenchanting, dissatisfying, disconcerting, vexing. *see* DISAPPOINT 1. **2** *a disappointing effort* unsatisfactory, inadequate, insufficient, unworthy, inferior, second-rate, pathetic, lame.

disappointment n **1** *hide one's disappointment* sadness, regret, depression, dispiritedness, despondency, distress, chagrin, disgruntlement, displeasure, disenchantment, disillusionment, discontent, dissatisfaction, vexation. **2** *the disappointment of their plans* thwarting, frustration, baulking, foiling; defeat, failure, non-success, ill-success, unfulfilment. **3** *the event was a disappointment* let-down, failure, fiasco, setback, blow, misfortune, disaster; *inf* wash-out.

disapproval n disapprobation, disfavour, displeasure, dislike, dissatisfaction, criticism, censure, blame, condemnation, denunciation, objection, exception, reproach, rebuke, reproof, remonstration, disparagement, deprecation, animadversion.

disapprove v **1** *disapprove of their behaviour* have/express a poor opinion of, dislike, find unacceptable, be against, be dissatisfied/displeased with, deplore, criticize, frown on, take a dim view of, look askance at, censure, blame, condemn, denounce, object to, take exception to, reproach, rebuke, reprove, remonstrate against, disparage, deprecate, animadvert; *inf* look down one's nose at. **2** *disapprove the plans* turn down, reject, veto, disallow, set aside; *inf* give the thumbs down to.

disarm v **1** *disarm the terrorists/nation* unarm, deprive of arms, demilitarize, demobilize, render defenceless, make powerless. **2** *the country is disarming* lay down arms, demilitarize; *lit* sheathe the sword, turn swords into ploughshares. **3** *disarmed by his smile* charm, win over, persuade, convert, mollify, appease, placate, conciliate, propitiate.

disarmament n demilitarization, demobilization, arms reduction, weapons control, arms limitation; nuclear disarmament.

disarming adj *a disarming smile* charming, winning, persuasive, irresistible, conciliatory. *see* DISARM 3.

disarrange v bring/throw into disorder, order, make disorderly, disorder, untidy, make untidy, mess up, displace, disorganize, disturb, confuse, jumble, mix up, muddle, turn upside-down, upset, unsettle, throw into disarray, derange, discompose, scatter, shake up, dishevel, tousle, rumple; *inf* turn topsy-turvy; *Amer inf* muss up.

disarray n **1** *troops in disarray* disorder, confusion, upset; disorderliness, disorganization, discomposure, unsettledness, disunity, indiscipline, unruliness. **2** *rooms/clothes in disarray* disorder, untidiness, confusion, chaos, dishevelment; mess, muddle, clutter, jumble, mix-up, tangle; shambles; *Scots* guddle.

disaster n **1** *natural disasters* catastrophe, calamity, cataclysm, tragedy, act of God, accident, mishap, misadventure, mischance, stroke of ill-luck, setback, reverse of fortune, reversal, heavy blow, shock, buffet; adversity, trouble, misfortune, ruin, ruination. **2** *the play was a disaster* failure, fiasco; *inf* flop, dud, wash-out.

disastrous adj *disastrous events* catastrophic, calamitous, cataclysmic, tragic, adverse, devastating, ravaging, dire, terrible, shocking, appalling, dreadful, black, harmful, injurious, detrimental, ruinous, unfortunate, unlucky, hapless, ill-fated, ill-starred.

disavowal n denial, contradiction, disclaimer, repudiation, renunciation, disowning, rejection.

disband v **1** *the group disbanded* break up, disperse, dissolve, separate, go separate ways. **2** *disband the group* break up, dissolve, disperse, dismiss, demobilize.

disbelief n unbelief, lack of belief, scepticism, incredulity, non-conviction, doubt, dubiety, discredit, distrust, mistrust, questioning, agnosticism, atheism, nihilism.

disbelieve v not believe, not credit, give no credence to, be incredulous, be unconvinced, discredit, discount, not accept, reject, repudiate, distrust, mistrust, question, challenge, scoff at.

disbeliever n unbeliever, sceptic, doubter, doubting Thomas, questioner, challenger, scoffer, agnostic, atheist, nihilist.

disburse v pay out, lay out, spend, expend; *inf* fork out, shell out, dish out.

discard v throw away/out, get rid of, dispose of, toss out, jettison, scrap, dispense with, cast aside, reject, repudiate, abandon, relinquish, forsake, drop, have done with, shed; *inf* dump, ditch.

discern v see, notice, observe, perceive, make out, distinguish, detect, descry, recognize, determine, differentiate.

discernible adj visible, noticeable, observable, perceptible, perceivable, distinguishable, detectable, recognizable, apparent, obvious, clear, manifest, conspicuous, patent.

discerning adj discriminating, astute, shrewd, ingenious, clever, intelligent, perceptive, sharp, quick, perspicacious, penetrating, critical, percipient, judicious, sensitive, subtle, prudent, sound, wise, aware, knowing, sagacious, sapient.

discharge v 1 *discharge the prisoner* set free, free, let go, release, liberate, acquit, clear, absolve, pardon, exonerate, reprieve, exculpate, emancipate, manumit. 2 *discharge from employment* dismiss, remove, get rid of, discard, eject, oust, expel, cashier, deprive of office; *inf* sack, fire, axe, send packing, give the boot to, boot out. 3 *discharge a weapon* fire, shoot, let/set off, explode, detonate. 4 *discharge pus/fumes* exude, ooze, excrete, give off, leak, dispense, emit, send out, send/pour forth, eject, release, gush, void, disembogue. 5 *discharge a duty* carry out, perform, do, accomplish, achieve, fulfil, execute, observe, abide by. 6 *discharge a load* unload, disburden, remove, unburden, off-load, relieve. 7 *discharge a debt/obligation* pay, settle, clear, honour, meet, liquidate, satisfy; *inf* square.

discharge n 1 *prisoners receiving a discharge* release, liberation, acquittal, clearance, absolution, pardon, exoneration, reprieve, exculpation, manumission. 2 *hear about his discharge from the firm* dismissal, removal, ejection, ousting, expulsion, cashiering, *congé; inf* the sack, firing, axeing, the boot. *see* DISCHARGE V 2. 3 *the/a discharge from a weapon* discharging, firing, shooting, explosion, detonation, blast, burst, pop, report, volley, salvo, fusillade. 4 *the discharge of pus/ fumes* exuding, oozing, excretion, emission, ejection, release, emptying, voiding, voidance, disemboguement. 5 *exuding a watery discharge* excretion, exudate, emission, flow, secretion, ooze, suppuration, pus, seepage. 6 *discharge of one's duty* carrying out, performing, doing, accomplishment, achievement, fulfilment, execution, observance; performance. 7 *the discharge of a debt* payment, settlement, clearance, honouring, meeting. *see* DISCHARGE V 7.

disciple n apostle, follower, pupil, student, believer, adherent, devotee, votary,

upholder, supporter, advocate, proponent, satellite, partisan.

disciplinarian n martinet, authoritarian, hard taskmaster, stickler for order/punishment, formalist, tyrant, despot.

discipline n 1 *school discipline|yoga is a useful discipline* training, drilling, exercise, regimen, routine, method; instruction, coaching, teaching, indoctrination, inculcation, systematization. 2 *discipline required for the exercise* control, self-control, self-restraint, strictness, orderliness, regulation, direction, government, restriction, limitation; restraint, check, curb. 3 *pupils in need of discipline* punishment, chastisement, castigation, correction; penalty, reprimand, rebuke, reproof. 4 *literature and other disciplines* field of study, field, branch of knowledge, course of study, course, area, subject, specialist subject, speciality, specialty.

discipline v 1 *discipline the troops* train, drill, break in, exercise, instruct, coach, teach, educate, tutor, prepare, ground, indoctrinate, inculcate, inure, toughen. 2 *discipline oneself* control, restrain, regulate, govern, restrict, limit, check, curb. 3 *discipline the children* punish, chastise, castigate, correct, penalize, reprimand, rebuke, reprove.

disclaim v deny, renounce, repudiate, reject, refuse, decline, disown, cast off, discard, abandon, wash one's hands of, turn one's back on, abjure, forswear, disavow, disaffirm.

disclaimer n denial, renunciation, repudiation, rejection, abjuration, disavowal, disaffirmation.

disclose v 1 *disclose confidential details* make known, reveal, divulge, tell, impart, communicate, make public, broadcast, publish, release, unveil, leak, let slip, blurt out, blab, admit, confess, avow; *inf* spill the beans about, let the cat out of the bag about, blow the gaff, blow the lid off, squeal about. 2 *disclose the contents of the box* reveal, show, exhibit, expose, uncover, lay bare, unveil, bring to light.

disclosure n 1 *make disclosures of secret ceremonies* revelation, divulgence, exposé, communication, leak, admission, confession, avowal. 2 *the disclosure of vice by the newspaper* revealing, revelation, bringing to light, divulging, divulgence, broadcasting, publishing, uncovering, laying bare, unveiling; release, announcement, declaration, exposure.

discoloration n stain, soiling, mark, streak, spot, blotch, tarnishing; blemish, flaw.

discolour v stain, soil, mark, streak, spot, tarnish, fade, bleach, wash out.

discomfit v **1** *discomfited by personal questions* embarrass, disconcert, make uncomfortable, take aback, nonplus, abash, confuse, ruffle, fluster, upset, disturb, perturb, discompose, discomfort; *inf* faze, rattle, discombobulate. **2** *discomfit the enemy's plans* thwart, frustrate, foil, obstruct, hinder, hamper, check, upset.

discomfiture n *the discomfiture of the interviewee* embarrassment, disconcertment, uneasiness, unease, confusion, discomposure. *see* DISCOMFIT 1.

discomfort n **1** *experience some discomfort in the injured leg* ache, pain, soreness, twinge, hurt, irritation, pang, throb, smart, malaise. **2** *lead the life of discomfort* lack of comfort/ease, trouble, unpleasantness, hardship, distress. **3** *blushing with discomfort* embarrassment, anxiety, disconcertment, unease, uneasiness, discomfiture, discomposure, disquietude. **4** *the discomforts of travel* inconvenience, difficulty, trouble, bother, nuisance, vexation, drawback, disadvantage, problem, trial, tribulation.

discomfort v *discomforted by the hostile audience* make uncomfortable/uneasy, embarrass, disconcert, upset, ruffle, discompose, discomfit.

discomposure n agitation, fluster, flurry, restlessness, nervousness, perturbation, disturbance, anxiety, uneasiness, unease, disquiet, disquietude, embarrassment, disconcertment, confusion, discomfiture, discomfort.

disconcert v **1** *disconcerted by the silence in the room* unsettle, shake, disturb, perturb, daunt, take aback, abash, nonplus, confuse, bewilder, fluster, ruffle, upset, agitate, worry, embarrass, discomfit, discompose, perplex, confound, distract, throw off balance, put off one's stroke; *inf* throw, faze, rattle. **2** *disconcerting their plans* thwart, frustrate, foil, obstruct, hinder, hamper, upset, undo.

disconcerting adj *a disconcerting habit of grinning* unsettling, disturbing, perturbing, daunting, confusing, bewildering, upsetting, worrying, alarming, embarrassing, discomfiting, perplexing, bothering, bothersome, distracting, dismaying, awkward; *inf* off-putting.

disconnect v **1** *disconnect the electrical supply* undo, cut off, sever, uncouple, disengage, detach, unhook, unhitch, unlink, disjoin, disunite. **2** *cannot disconnect the two philosophies* separate, sever, divide, part, split up, dissociate, disentangle. **3** *our telephone con-*

versation got disconnected discontinue, interrupt, suspend, halt, stop.

disconnected adj **1** *disconnected ideas* unconnected, separate, separated, unattached, dissociated. **2** *disconnected speech* disjointed, garbled, confused, jumbled, mixed-up, incoherent, unintelligible, rambling, wandering, disordered, illogical, irrational, uncoordinated.

disconsolate adj sad, unhappy, miserable, despondent, wretched, heartbroken, forlorn, grief-stricken, inconsolable, woebegone, dejected, low, low-spirited, dispirited, down, depressed, downcast, gloomy, melancholy, blue; *inf* down in the mouth/dumps.

discontent n discontentment, dissatisfaction, restlessness, impatience, fretfulness, displeasure, unhappiness, misery, wretchedness, envy, regret, umbrage, disaffection, disquiet, vexation, exasperation, irritation, chagrin, pique.

discontented adj dissatisfied, fed up, restless, impatient, fretful, complaining, displeased, disgruntled, querulous, unhappy, miserable, wretched, envious, regretful, disaffected, exasperated, irritated, chagrined, annoyed, peeved, piqued; *inf* browned off, cheesed off, hacked off, brassed off, pissed off.

discontinue v **1** *discontinue the service* stop, end, put an end/stop to, finish, bring to a halt, terminate, cease, abandon, give up, break off, cancel, drop, refrain from, quit, suspend, interrupt; *inf* cut out. **2** *the road/conversation discontinued* stop, come to a stop/halt, terminate, leave off, pause.

discontinued adj *a discontinued line/product* no longer available/produced, abandoned, given up, ended, finished, terminated, halted.

discord n **1** *bitter discord between the deputy heads* disagreement, difference of opinion, dissension, dispute, argument, conflict, friction, contention, strife, opposition, hostility, wrangling, clashing, quarrelling, falling-out, war, division, incompatibility, variance, disunity, rupture. **2** *the discord of the instruments* lack of harmony, disharmony, dissonance, cacophony, harshness, jarring, jangling, din, racket.

discordant adj **1** *discordant attitudes* disagreeing, differing, contradictory, contrary, dissenting, disputatious, conflicting, at variance, at odds, contentious, opposing, hostile, clashing, divergent, incompatible, incongruous. **2** *discordant sounds* inharmonious, harsh, strident, shrill, grating, jarring, jangling, dissonant, cacophonous.

discount v **1** *discount what he says* disregard, ignore, pass over, overlook, pay no attention to, take no notice of, brush off, gloss over. **2** *discount £5 from the price* deduct, take off, rebate; *inf* knock off. **3** *discount the regular price* reduce, lower, lessen; *inf* knock down. **4** *discount the products* mark down, reduce, put on sale.

discount n **1** *a good discount on the goods* mark down, deduction, price cut, cut, rebate, concession. **2** *goods at a discount* lower price, cut price, concessionary price, reduction.

discourage v **1** *he was discouraged by lack of success* dishearten, dispirit, deject, cast down, depress, demoralize, disappoint, daunt, put off, intimidate, cow, unnerve, unman. **2** *discourage them from applying* put off, dissuade, deter, talk out of, advise against, urge against, caution against, restrain, inhibit, divert from, sidetrack from. **3** *discourage the idea* oppose, disapprove of, repress, deprecate, put a damper on, throw cold water on. **4** *a preparation discouraging damp* prevent, check, curb, hinder, obstruct, suppress, inhibit.

discouraged adj *discouraged job hunters* disheartened, dispirited, dejected, cast down, downcast, depressed, demoralized, disappointed, daunted, put off, crestfallen, glum; *inf* down in the mouth/dumps. *see* DISCOURAGE 1.

discouragement n **1** *experience discouragement* dispiritedness, downheartedness, dejection, depression, demoralization, disappointment, despondency, hopelessness, lack of confidence, pessimism, despair, gloom, melancholy; low spirits. **2** *ideas meeting with discouragement* opposition, disapproval, repression, deprecation. **3** *tired of discouragements to progress* deterrent, hindrance, obstacle, impediment, barrier, curb, check, damper, restraint, constraint, restriction, disincentive, setback, rebuff; *inf* put-down.

discouraging adj *discouraging news* disheartening, dispiriting, depressing, demoralizing, disappointing, off-putting, gloomy, unfavourable, unpropitious, inauspicious.

discourse n **1** *engage in discourse* conversation, talk, dialogue, communication, discussion, conference, colloquy, converse, verbal exchange, chat, chit-chat, palaver, confabulation; *inf* confab, rap. **2** *a discourse on art* address, speech, lecture, oration, sermon, homily, essay, treatise, dissertation, paper, study, disquisition.

discourse v **1** *discourse with colleagues* converse, talk, discuss, debate, confer, speak, chat; *inf* have a confab/chin-wag, chew the fat, rap. **2** *discourse on morals* give an address/talk, deliver a speech/lecture, lecture, sermonize, preach, hold forth, write learnedly, write at length, expatiate; *inf* spout.

discourteous adj rude, impolite, ill-mannered, bad-mannered, unmannerly, uncivil, curt, abrupt, brusque, short, gruff, boorish, churlish, ungracious, ungentlemanly, unladylike, ill-bred, uncouth, disrespectful, ungallant, insolent, impertinent, impudent.

discourtesy n rudeness, impoliteness, lack of civility, incivility, ill-manneredness, unmannerliness, curtness, abruptness, brusqueness, ungraciousness, ill-breeding, uncouthness, disrespect, disrespectfulness, insolence. *see* DISCOURTEOUS.

discover v **1** *discover a new holiday place | discover new talent* find, come across/upon, stumble upon, chance upon, light upon, locate, bring to light, uncover, unearth, turn up; *inf* dig up. **2** *discover that he was lying* find out, come to know, learn, realize, detect, determine, ascertain, recognize, see, spot, notice, perceive, reveal, disclose; *inf* twig, get wise to the fact. **3** *discover a new drug* invent, originate, devise, pioneer, design, contrive, conceive of. **4** *discover America* found, explore, pioneer.

discoverer n **1** *the discoverer of America* founder, explorer, pioneer. **2** *the discoverer of penicillin* inventor, originator, pioneer, deviser, designer, initiator.

discovery n **1** *the discovery of a quiet village | new talent* finding, locating, location, uncovering. *see* DISCOVER 1. **2** *the discovery that they lied* finding out, learning, realization, detection, determination, recognition, revelation, disclosure; *inf* twigging. *see* DISCOVER 2. **3** *discovery of new drugs* invention, origination, devising, pioneering, introduction. **4** *recent discoveries* find, invention, breakthrough, innovation, lucky strike, bonanza; findings. **5** *a voyage of discovery* exploration, pioneering, research.

discredit v **1** *discredit their rivals* detract from, bring into disrepute, defame, slur, slander, cast aspersions on, vilify, disparage, deprecate, denigrate, devalue, devaluate, degrade, belittle, decry, dishonour, disgrace, censure. **2** *evidence to discredit the research* disprove, invalidate, refute, dispute, challenge, destroy the credibility of, shake one's faith in, reject, deny. **3** *the jury discredited the witness* disbelieve, give no credence to, discount, doubt, distrust, mistrust.

discredit n **1** *bring discredit on the neighbourhood* disrepute, ill-repute, infamy, disgrace, dishonour, shame, humiliation, ignominy, stigma, harm, damage, censure, blame, reproach, scandal, odium, opprobrium. **2** *regard the story with discredit* disbelief, lack of credence, incredulity, question, doubt, distrust, mistrust, scepticism, suspicion.

discredited adj brought into disrepute, disproved, invalidated, refuted, rejected, discarded, denied, exploded, debunked.

discreet adj careful, cautious, prudent, judicious, circumspect, wary, guarded, chary, tactful, reserved, diplomatic, considerate, politic, strategic, wise, sensible, sagacious.

discrepancy n inconsistency, variance, variation, disparity, deviation, divergence, incongruity, difference, disagreement, dissimilarity, contrariety, conflict, discordance, gap, lacuna.

discrete adj separate, distinct, individual, detached, unattached, disconnected, discontinuous, disjunct.

discretion n **1** *act with discretion* care, carefulness, caution, prudence, judiciousness, judgement, circumspection, wariness, guardedness, chariness, tactfulness, tact, reserve, diplomacy, consideration, strategy, discrimination, wisdom, sense, good sense, discernment, sagacity, acumen, forethought, maturity. **2** *at the discretion of the manager* choice, option, volition, will, preference, inclination, pleasure, liking, wish, desire, predilection, election, disposition, mind.

discretionary adj optional, elective, open, open to choice, non-mandatory, unrestricted, voluntary, volitional.

discriminate v **1** *discriminate between right and wrong* distinguish, make/draw a distinction, differentiate, tell the difference, make a difference, discern; separate, separate the sheep from the goats, separate the wheat from the chaff, segregate. **2** *discriminate against women | discriminate in favour of Europeans* show prejudice against/towards, be biased against/towards, treat differently, treat as inferior/superior, disfavour/favour, be intolerant/overtolerant towards.

discriminating adj **1** *a discriminating concert-goer* discerning, perceptive, astute, shrewd, selective, particular, fastidious, critical, keen, tasteful, refined, sensitive, cultivated, cultured, artistic, aesthetic. **2** *discriminating rules* distinguishing, differentiating, prejudiced. *see* DISCRIMINATORY 1.

discrimination n **1** *wine lovers of discrimination* discernment, perception, penetration, perspicacity, acumen, astuteness, shrewdness, selectivity, fastidiousness, judgement, keenness, taste, refinement, sensitivity, insight, subtlety, cultivation, culture, artistry, aestheticism. **2** *guilty of discrimination* prejudice, bias, unfairness, inequity, intolerance, bigotry, narrow-mindedness, favouritism, segregation; positive discrimination.

discriminatory adj **1** *discriminatory employment rules* prejudiced, prejudicial, biased, preferential, unfair, unjust, inequitable, weighted, one-sided, partisan. **2** *a discriminatory drinker* discerning, critical. *see* DISCRIMINATING 1.

discursive adj digressive, rambling, wandering, meandering, diffuse, episodic, circuitous, verbose, long-winded, wordy, prolix, circumlocutory.

discuss v *discuss the problem with colleagues* talk over, talk/chat about, converse about, confer about, debate, exchange views on/about, deliberate, consider, go into, thrash out, examine, review, study, scrutinize, analyse, weigh up, sift, ventilate, argue, dispute; *inf* kick around.

discussion n talk, conversation, dialogue, chat, conference, debate, discourse, exchange of views, symposium, seminar, consultation, deliberation, parley, examination, review, study, scrutiny, analysis, ventilation, argument, dispute; *inf* confab.

disdain n *look with disdain on pantomimes* scorn, scornfulness, contempt, contemptuousness, derision, sneering, deprecation, disparagement, denigration, contumely, opprobrium, arrogance, superciliousness, haughtiness, hauteur, snobbishness, aloofness, indifference, dislike, abhorrence.

disdain v *disdain offers of help* scorn, show contempt for, spurn, reject, refuse, rebuff, disregard, sneer at, pooh-pooh, deride, belittle, undervalue, slight, despise, look down on, misprize; *inf* look down one's nose at.

disdainful adj scornful, contemptuous, sneering, derisive, slighting, disparaging, arrogant, proud, supercilious, haughty, superior, lordly, pompous, snobbish, insolent, aloof, indifferent; *inf* high and mighty, hoity-toity.

disease n illness, sickness; disorder, complaint, malady, ailment, affliction, condition, indisposition, upset, infirmity, disability, abnormality; infectious disease, infection, contagious disease, contagion, viral disease, pestilence, plague, cancer, canker, blight; *inf* bug, virus.

diseased adj unhealthy, ill, ailing, sick, sickly, unwell, unsound, unwholesome, infirm, infected, abnormal, blighted, rotten, cankerous.

disembark v land, arrive, get off, step off, alight, go ashore, dismount, deplane, detrain; *inf* pile out.

disembodied adj bodiless, incorporeal, discarnate, immaterial, intangible, insubstantial, impalpable, spiritual, ghostly, spectral, phantom, wraith-like.

disembowel v eviscerate, exenterate, gut, draw.

disenchanted adj disillusioned, disabused, undeceived, set straight, disappointed, let down, blasé, cynical, soured, jaundiced, sick, out of love, indifferent.

disenchantment n disillusion, cynicism; disillusionment, disappointment, rude awakening.

disengage v *disengage the clutch | disengage oneself from an embrace* release, loosen, loose, unfasten, detach, separate, disjoin, disunite, uncouple, undo, unhook, unloose, unhitch, unclasp, untie, free, set free, liberate, disentangle, disentwine, extricate.

disentangle v 1 *disentangle the knotted wool* unravel, straighten, unwind, untwist, undo, unknot, untie, unsnarl, unkink, smooth out, comb, card. 2 *disentangle oneself* extricate, disentwine, release, loosen, detach, unfasten, unclasp, free, set free, liberate, disconnect.

disfavour n 1 *look upon with disfavour* lack of favour, disapproval, disapprobation, dislike, displeasure, dissatisfaction, disregard, low opinion, low esteem. 2 *fall into disfavour* disapproval, unpopularity, discredit, disrepute, ill repute, ignominy, disgrace, shame, opprobrium. 3 *do someone a disfavour* disservice, bad turn, ill deed, discourtesy.

disfigure v deface, deform, mutilate, blemish, flaw, scar, make ugly, uglify, spoil, mar, damage, injure, maim, vandalize, ruin, disfeature.

disfigurement n 1 *the disfigurement of the landscape* defacement, mutilation, scarring, spoiling, uglification, damaging, vandalizing, ruin. *see* DISFIGURE. 2 *an obvious disfigurement* blemish, flaw, blotch, imperfection, defect, scar, deformity, malformation, injury.

disgorge v 1 *volcanoes disgorging lava | disgorging phlegm* spit out, spew out, belch, discharge, spout, vomit, regurgitate, throw up, eject, emit, expel, empty. 2 *disgorging their hold on the territory* give up, surrender, yield, cede, relinquish, hand over, renounce, resign, abandon.

disgrace n 1 *the disgrace of being in prison* shame, humiliation, dishonour, scandal, degradation, ignominy, infamy, discredit, debasement, vitiation. 2 *be in disgrace | brought him disgrace* disfavour, discredit, disrepute, loss of face, disrespect, disapproval, disapprobation, disesteem, contempt, opprobrium, obloquy. 3 *his behaviour was a disgrace* blot, stain, blemish, black mark, scandal, smear, smirch, stigma, slur, dishonour, aspersion, defamation.

disgrace v 1 *disgrace the family* bring disgrace to, bring shame upon, shame, humiliate, bring dishonour to, dishonour, discredit, degrade, debase, sully, besmirch, taint, stain, slur, stigmatize, brand, drag through the mud. 2 *the soldier was publicly disgraced* discredit, reproach, censure, blame, dishonour, disfavour, humiliate, mortify, disparage, demean, denigrate, belittle.

disgraceful adj 1 *disgraceful behaviour by the minister* scandalous, shocking, outrageous, shameful, shameless, dishonourable, disreputable, degrading, ignominious, blameworthy, culpable, contemptible, despicable, reprehensible, improper, unseemly, unworthy. 2 *your work is disgraceful* very bad, appalling, dreadful, terrible, shocking, intolerable, unworthy.

disgruntled adj discontented, dissatisfied, displeased, unhappy, disappointed, annoyed, exasperated, vexed, irritated, peeved, put out, resentful, sulky, sullen, petulant, grumpy, churlish, testy; *inf* fed up, cheesed off, hacked off.

disguise v 1 *disguised as a policeman* camouflage, dress up, be under cover, be incognito, cover up, conceal, hide, mask, screen, shroud, veil, cloak. 2 *disguise the truth* cover up, misrepresent, falsify, give a false picture of, fake, fudge, feign, dissemble, dissimulate, gloss over, varnish.

disgust v 1 *the slimy food disgusted me* sicken, nauseate, turn one's stomach, put off, revolt, repel, cause aversion; *inf* turn off. 2 *her behaviour disgusted me* offend, outrage, shock, appal, scandalize, displease, dissatisfy, annoy, anger.

disgust n 1 *look with disgust at the food* revulsion, repugnance, repulsion, aversion, nausea, distaste, disrelish, abhorrence, loathing, detestation. 2 *disgust at her behaviour* offence, outrage, shock, disapproval, displeasure, dissatisfaction, annoyance, anger.

disgusting adj **1** *disgusting food* sickening, nauseating, nauseous, revolting, repellent, off-putting, unpalatable, foul, nasty, unappetizing, distasteful, abhorrent, loathsome, detestable, obnoxious, odious; *inf* grotty. **2** *disgusting behaviour* offensive, objectionable, outrageous, shocking, shameless, shameful, appalling, scandalous, vulgar, gross, vile, displeasing, annoying.

dish n **1** *food in dishes* container, receptacle, bowl, plate, platter, salver. **2** *prepare a new dish* food, fare, recipe, dish of the day, *plat du jour*.

dish v *dish one's plans* ruin, destroy, put an end to, spoil, wreck, torpedo. **dish out** distribute, hand out, deal out, allocate, dole out, mete out. **dish up 1** *dish up the potatoes* serve, serve up, spoon, ladle, scoop. **2** *dish up the old material in new form* present, offer, produce, prepare.

dishearten v discourage, cast down, dispirit, make dispirited/dejected, depress, crush, make crestfallen/downhearted, dash, dampen, put a damper on, daunt, disappoint, deter, sadden, weigh down.

dishevelled adj untidy, tousled, rumpled, bedraggled, disordered, disarranged, messy, in a mess, unkempt, uncombed, slovenly, slatternly, blowsy, frowzy; *Amer inf* mussed.

dishonest adj fraudulent, cheating, untrustworthy, false, untruthful, dishonourable, unscrupulous, unprincipled, corrupt, swindling, deceitful, deceiving, deceptive, lying, crafty, cunning, designing, mendacious, double-dealing, underhand, treacherous, perfidious, unfair, unjust, disreputable, rascally, roguish, knavish; *inf* crooked, shady, bent.

dishonesty n fraud, fraudulence, cheating, chicanery, untrustworthiness, falseness, falsity, falsehood, untruthfulness, dishonour, unscrupulousness, corruption, criminality, sharp practice, deceit, deception, duplicity, lying, craft, cunning, trickery, wiliness, guile, double-dealing, underhandedness, treachery, perfidy, graft, unfairness, unjustness, improbity, rascality, knavishness; *inf* crookedness, shadiness.

dishonour n **1** *bring dishonour to the regiment* disgrace, shame, humiliation, scandal, discredit, degradation, ignominy, infamy, disrepute, ill-repute, loss of face, disfavour, debasement, abasement, odium, opprobrium, obloquy, vitiation. **2** *do him a dishonour* indignity, insult, affront, offence, abuse, outrage, slight, discourtesy. **3** *a dis-*

honour to his profession disgrace, blot, blemish, stigma. *see* DISGRACE n **3**.

dishonour v **1** *dishonour the flag* disgrace, bring dishonour/shame to, shame, humiliate, discredit, degrade, debase, sully, stain, stigmatize. *see* DISGRACE v **1**. **2** *dishonour their hosts* insult, affront, abuse, slight, offend. **3** *dishonour the captives* rape, violate, ravish, defile, seduce, deflower.

dishonourable adj **1** *a dishonourable act* disgraceful, shameful, shameless, shaming, disreputable, degrading, debasing, ignominious, ignoble, blameworthy, contemptible, despicable, reprehensible, base. **2** *a dishonourable man* unprincipled, blackguardly, unscrupulous, corrupt, untrustworthy, treacherous, perfidious, traitorous, disreputable, discreditable; *inf* shady.

disillusion v disabuse, disenchant, open the eyes of, shatter the illusions of, undeceive, set straight, enlighten, disappoint, make sadder and wiser.

disincentive n discouragement, deterrent, damper, dissuasion, impediment, hindrance.

disinclination n reluctance, lack of enthusiasm, hesitancy, hesitance, unwillingness, loathness, aversion, dislike, distaste, objection, demur, resistance, opposition, recalcitrance.

disinclined adj reluctant, unenthusiastic, not in the mood, hesitant, unwilling, loath, averse, antipathetic, resistant, opposed, recalcitrant.

disinfect v sterilize, sanitize, clean, cleanse, purify, fumigate, decontaminate.

disinfectant n antiseptic, bactericide, germicide, sterilizer, sanitizer, cleansing agent, cleanser, fumigant, decontaminant.

disingenuous adj insincere, feigned, deceitful, underhand, underhanded, duplicitous, double-dealing, two-faced, false, lying, untruthful, artful, cunning, crafty, wily, sly, shifty, scheming, calculating, designing, insidious.

disinherit v cut off, cut off without a penny, dispossess, oust, disown, repudiate, renounce.

disintegrate v fall apart, fall to pieces, break up, break apart, shatter, splinter, crumble, decompose, decay, rot, moulder, erode, dissolve, go to wrack and ruin.

disinterested adj **1** *disinterested judges* unbiased, unprejudiced, impartial, detached, objective, uninvolved, dispassionate, impersonal, open-minded, neutral, outside, fair, just, equitable, even-handed, unselfish. **2** *disinterested in the lecture* unin-

terested, unconcerned, uninvolved, unresponsive, indifferent, bored, apathetic,
blasé.

disjointed n **1** *a disjointed talk* incoherent,
unconnected, disconnected, without unity,
ununified, discontinous, rambling, wandering, disorganized, confused, disordered, fitful, spasmodic, aimless, directionless.
2 *disjointed limbs* dislocated, displaced, dis-
membered, disconnected, severed, separated, disarticulated, torn apart, disunited.

dislike v have no liking for, have an aversion to, regard with distaste/animosity, feel
hostility towards, be unable to tolerate/
stomach, hold in disfavour, disfavour, have
no taste for, object to, hate, detest, loathe,
abominate, abhor, despise, scorn, shun,
have a grudge against, execrate, disrelish,
antipathize.

dislike n aversion, disapproval, disapprobation, distaste, animosity, hostility, antipathy, antagonism, disinclination, disfavour,
disesteem, hate, detestation, loathing, disgust, repugnance, enmity, abhorrence, disrelish, animus.

dislocate v **1** *dislocate a bone* put out of
joint, put out of place, displace, disjoint,
disconnect, disengage; *Med* luxate. **2** *dislo-
cate plans | dislocate air services* disrupt, dis-
turb, throw into disorder/disarray/
confusion, confuse, disorganize, mess up,
disorder, disarrange, turn topsy turvy.

dislodge v remove, displace, force out,
oust, eject, evict, unseat; *inf* sack.

disloyal adj unfaithful, faithless, false,
false-hearted, untrue, inconstant, untrustworthy, treacherous, perfidious, traitorous,
disaffected, subversive, seditious, unpatri-
otic, renegade, apostate, dissident, two-
faced, double-dealing, deceitful.

disloyalty n unfaithfulness, infidelity,
faithlessness, breach of trust, breaking of
faith, falseness, false-heartedness, falsity,
inconstancy, untrustworthiness, treachery,
perfidy, treason, disaffection, subversion,
sedition, apostasy, dissidence, double dealing, Punic faith.

dismal adj **1** *children looking dismal* gloomy,
sad, unhappy, miserable, wretched,
despondent, disconsolate, sorrowful,
solemn, blue, melancholy, morose, woebegone, forlorn, lugubrious. **2** *dismal surroundings* gloomy, dreary, bleak, drab, dull,
dark, dingy, cheerless, desolate, depressing, grim, funereal, comfortless, inhospitable, uninviting. **3** *a dismal piece of work*
bad, poor, inept, bungling, disgraceful.

dismantle v take apart, take to pieces, dis-
assemble, pull apart, tear down, demolish,
fell, destroy.

dismay v **1** *dismayed by the appearance of the
police* disconcert, take aback, startle, surprise, shock, disturb, perturb, upset, jolt,
unsettle, unnerve, unman, alarm, frighten,
scare. **2** *dismayed by their failure* discourage,
put off, dishearten, dispirit, cast down,
depress, disappoint, daunt, abash.

dismiss v **1** *dismissed from the firm for theft*
give notice to, discharge, expel, cashier,
remove, oust, eject, lay off, make/declare
redundant, deselect; *inf* sack, give the sack
to, fire, give one one's cards/books, give
one one's marching orders, send packing,
give the push/boot/heave-ho to, boot out.
2 *dismiss an assembly/army* disband, disperse, dissolve, discharge, send away, let
go, release, free. **3** *dismiss foolish thoughts*
put away, banish, think no more of, put
out of one's mind, set/lay aside, abandon,
have done with, reject, drop, disregard,
repudiate, spurn, pooh-pooh.

dismissal n **1** *his dismissal from the firm*
notice, discharge, expulsion, removal, ejection; *inf* the sack, sacking, firing, the push,
the boot, the heave-ho. *see* DISMISS 1. **2** *the
dismissal of the assembly* disbandment, dispersal, dissolution, discharge, permission
to go/depart/leave, release, congé.

disobedience n insubordination, unruliness, waywardness, indiscipline, rebellion,
defiance, mutiny, revolt, recalcitrance,
delinquency, non-compliance, infraction,
perversity, naughtiness, mischievousness,
mischief, contumacy. *see* DISOBEDIENT.

disobedient adj insubordinate, unruly,
wayward, undisciplined, rebellious, defiant, mutinous, recalcitrant, intractable,
wilful, refractory, obstreperous, disorderly,
delinquent, non-compliant, perverse,
naughty, mischievous, contrary, contumacious.

disobey v defy, not comply with, disregard,
flout, contravene, infringe, overstep, resist,
rebel against, fly in the face of, transgress,
violate, set at naught.

disobliging adj unhelpful, uncooperative,
unaccommodating, unfriendly, unsympathetic, discourteous, uncivil.

disorder n **1** *tidy up the disorder* untidiness,
mess, chaos, muddle, clutter, jumble, confusion, disorderliness, disarray, disorganization; *inf* shambles. **2** *police quelling the
disorder* disturbance, disruption, tumult,
riot, breach of the peace, fracas, rumpus,
brouhaha, mêlée, unrest. **3** *a disorder of the*

211

kidneys disease, ailment, complaint, affliction, malady, sickness, illness.

disorderly adj **1** *disorderly rooms* untidy, messy, chaotic, cluttered, jumbled, muddled, out of order, out of place, in disarray, disorganized, confused, deranged, upside-down, at sixes and sevens, unsystematic, irregular; *inf* shambolic. **2** *disorderly crowds* unruly, boisterous, rough, rowdy, disobedient, undisciplined, lawless, wild, unmanageable, uncontrollable, ungovernable, obstreperous, refractory, rebellious, mutinous, turbulent, tumultuous, rioting.

disorganized adj **1** *disorganized piles of books* disorderly, chaotic, jumbled, muddled, out of order, in disarray, confused, haphazard, random, unsystematic, irregular; *inf* shambolic. **2** *a disorganized person* unorganized, unmethodical, unsystematic, haphazard, muddled, careless; *inf* hit-or-miss.

disown v repudiate, renounce, reject, cast off, abandon, forsake, turn one's back on, disclaim, deny, disallow, abnegate, disavow, disinherit.

disparage v **1** *disparage their efforts* belittle, slight, decry, depreciate, devalue, devaluate, downgrade, demean, detract from, discredit, deprecate, denigrate, derogate, deflate, minimize, undervalue, underestimate, underrate, make light of, play down, disdain, dismiss, ridicule, deride, mock, scorn, lampoon. **2** *disparage their competitors* defame, run down, slander, libel, malign, speak ill/evil of, cast aspersions on, impugn, calumniate, vilify, traduce; *inf* do a hatchet job on, rubbish; *Amer inf* bad-mouth.

disparity n discrepancy, inequality, unevenness, inconsistency, imbalance, incongruity, difference, dissimilarity, contrast, gap.

dispassionate adj **1** *a dispassionate attitude to suffering* unemotional, emotionless, unmoved, unexcited, unexcitable, unflappable, unperturbed, nonchalant, unruffled, cool, collected, cool and collected, calm, composed, self-possessed, level-headed, self-controlled, temperate, sober, placid, equable, tranquil, serene; *inf* laid-back, together. **2** *dispassionate judges* detached, impartial, objective, disinterested, indifferent, uninvolved, impersonal, unbiased, unprejudiced, neutral, fair, just, equitable, even-handed, square dealing, open-minded.

dispatch, despatch v **1** *dispatch a parcel* send, send off, post, mail, forward, transmit, consign, remit, convey. **2** *dispatch the meeting in an hour* | *dispatch the task* finish, dispose of, conclude, settle, discharge, ex-

ecute, perform, expedite, push through, accelerate, hasten, speed up, hurry on; *inf* make short work of. **3** *enemy bullets dispatched the terrorists* kill, put to death, slay, do to death, put an end to, finish off, take the life of, slaughter, murder, assassinate, execute; *inf* bump off, do in, knock off, eliminate, erase.

dispatch, despatch n **1** *carried out with dispatch* promptness, promptitude, speed, alacrity, quickness, haste, hurry, swiftness, rapidity, expedition, expeditiousness. **2** *mentioned in military dispatches* | *a journalist's dispatch* communication, communiqué, bulletin, report, account, document, missive, letter, epistle, message, item, piece, article, news, instruction. **3** *guilty of the dispatch of the enemy* killing, death, slaying, slaughter, murder, assassination, execution. see DISPATCH v 3.

dispel v drive away, drive off, chase away, banish, rout, expel, disperse, scatter, dissipate, disseminate, dismiss, eliminate, allay.

dispensable adj expendable, disposable, unnecessary, unessential, non-essential, needless, superflous, uncalled-for.

dispensation n **1** *dispensation of supplies* distribution, handing out, dealing out, dividing out, division, allocation, allotment, apportionment, assignment, bestowal, conferment, supplying, disbursement. see DISPENSE 1. **2** *receive a dispensation of food* quota, portion, share, part, award. **3** *the dispensation of justice* administration, discharge, execution, implementation, application, enforcement, effectuation, operation, direction. **4** *the political/religious dispensation* system, order, scheme, plan, arrangement, organization, management, disposal, regulation, stewardship. **5** *given dispensation from a duty* | *given a dispensation from attending* exemption, immunity, exception, indulgence; release, relief, reprieve, remission, relaxation, absolution; *inf* letting off, let-off.

dispense v **1** *dispense supplies* distribute, hand out, deal out, dole out, share out, divide out, parcel out, allocate, allot, apportion, assign, bestow, confer, supply, disburse. **2** *dispense justice* administer, discharge, carry out, execute, implement, apply, enforce, effectuate, operate, direct. **3** *dispense medicines* make up, prepare, mix, supply. **4** *dispense him from eating fish on Fridays* grant a dispensation to, exempt, excuse, except, release, relieve, reprieve, absolve; *inf* let off. **dispense with 1** *dispense with formalities* waive, do without, omit, forgo, give up, relinquish, renounce,

ignore, disregard, pass over, brush aside.
2 *dispense with their services* do away with,
get rid of, dispose of, abolish, revoke,
rescind, cancel, shake off, manage without.

disperse v **1** *the crowd dispersed* break up,
disband, separate, go separate ways, scatter, dissolve, leave, vanish, melt away. **2** *the
wind dispersed the clouds* break up, scatter,
dissipate, dispel, drive away, banish, dissolve. **3** *disperse seeds* scatter, scatter to the
winds, disseminate, distribute, sow, sprinkle, spread, diffuse, strew, bestrew. **4** *disperse information* put into circulation,
circulate, broadcast, publish, publicize,
spread, diffuse.

dispirit v dishearten, discourage, cast
down, make dejected, depress, crush, dash,
dampen the spirits of, daunt, disappoint,
deter, sadden; *inf* throw cold water on.

displace v **1** *displace the furniture* put out of
place/order, disarrange, move, shift, relocate, transpose, derange, disorder, throw
into disorder, dislocate. **2** *displace from office*
remove, dismiss, discharge, depose, dislodge, eject, expel, force out, discard,
cashier; *inf* sack, fire, turf out. **3** *displaced
the old headmaster* replace, take the place of,
take over from, supplant, oust, supersede,
succeed; *inf* crowd out.

display v **1** *display the goods* put on show,
show, exhibit, put on view, expose to view,
present, unveil, set forth, arrange, dispose,
array, demonstrate, advertise, publicize.
2 *display their military power* show off,
flaunt, parade, flourish, boast, vaunt; *inf*
flash. **3** *display emotion* show, evince, manifest, betray, show evidence of, reveal, disclose.

display n **1** *put on a display of sculpture* show,
exhibition, exhibit, presentation, demonstration, spectacle, array. **2** *military display*
show, spectacle, parade, pageant; pomp,
flourish, ostentation. **3** *the display of emotion*
showing, evincement, manifestation,
betrayal, evidence, revelation, disclosure.

displease v dissatisfy, put out, annoy, irritate, anger, irk, vex, provoke, offend,
pique, peeve, gall, nettle, incense, exasperate, upset, perturb, disturb, discompose,
disgust; *inf* aggravate.

displeasure n dissatisfaction, discontentment, disgruntlement, disfavour, disapproval, disapprobation, distaste,
annoyance, irritation, anger, ire, wrath,
pique, chagrin, offence, rancour, indignation, exasperation, perturbation, disturbance, disgust.

disposable adj **1** *disposable plates* throw-
away, non-returnable, paper, plastic,

biodegradable. **2** *disposable assets* available,
usable, accessible, obtainable.

disposal n **1** *the disposal of rubbish* throwing
away, clearance, discarding, jettisoning,
ejection, scrapping, destruction; *inf* dump-
ing. **2** *the disposal of the business matters*
settlement, determination, deciding, conclusion. *see* DISPOSE, DISPOSE OF 2. **3** *the disposal of his estate* distribution, allotment,
allocation, transfer, transference, making
over, conveyance, bestowal, gift, bequest,
sale. *see* DISPOSE, DISPOSE OF 3. **4** *the disposal of
the troops* arrangement, ordering, positioning, placement, lining-up, setting-up, organization, marshalling, grouping. *see*
DISPOSE 1. **5** *at one's disposal* power, authority, control, direction, discretion, responsibility, management, government,
determination, regulation.

dispose v **1** *troops disposed in rows* arrange,
order, place, put, position, array, range,
line up, set up, organize, marshal, group,
rank, categorize, systematize, adjust, fix,
regulate. **2** *behaviour not disposing me to
believe him* incline, make willing, predispose, make, move, prompt, lead, induce,
tempt, actuate, motivate, bias, influence,
condition, direct. **dispose of 1** *dispose of the
rubbish* get rid of, throw away/out, clear
out, discard, jettison, eject, unload, scrap,
destroy; *inf* dump. **2** *dispose of the business*
deal with, settle, determine, decide, finish,
conclude, end. **3** *dispose of his estate* distribute, give out, allot, allocate, assign, part
with, transfer, make over, give away,
bestow, sell, auction. **4** *dispose of his enemy*
kill, do away with, put to death, slay, murder, slaughter; *inf* bump off, knock off.
5 *rapidly disposed of the food* consume, eat
up, devour, finish off, put away; *inf* polish
off.

disposed adj **1** *well-disposed to them* inclined,
predisposed, minded. **2** *disposed to help them*
inclined, willing, of a mind to, in the mood
to, ready, prepared. **3** *disposed to black moods*
inclined, given, prone, liable, apt.

disposition n **1** *people of a calm disposition*
nature, character, temperament, humour,
make-up, constitution, spirit, temper,
mood. **2** *a disposition to moodiness* inclination, tendency, proneness, propensity,
leaning, proclivity, bias, bent, predilection,
weakness, habit, readiness. **3** *the disposition
of the troops* disposal, arrangement, ordering, positioning, placement, lining-up,
setting-up, organization, marshalling,
grouping. **4** *disposition of property* disposal,
distribution, allocation, transfer, transference, bestowal. *see* DISPOSAL 3. **5** *have in one's*

disposition disposal, power, authority, control, direction, management. *see* DISPOSAL 5.

dispossess v **1** *dispossess them of their property* deprive, divest, strip, bereave. **2** *dispossess the tenants* dislodge, oust, eject, drive out, evict, turn out, dismiss.

disproportionate adj *heads disproportionate to bodies | a reaction disproportionate to the danger* out of proportion, not in proportion, not commensurate, unbalanced, uneven, unequal, irregular, relatively too large/long/much, relatively too small/short/little, excessive, unreasonable.

disprove v prove false, invalidate, refute, give the lie to, negate, rebut, confute, deny, contradict, controvert, discredit, expose.

disputable adj debatable, open to discussion, arguable, contestable, controvertible, moot, open to question, questionable, doubtful.

disputation n *a disputation ensued | open to disputation* debate, dispute; argumentation, altercation, dissension; polemics.

disputatious adj disputative, argumentative, contentious, captious, quarrelsome, litigious, polemical.

dispute v **1** *dispute with colleagues | dispute over what to do* debate, discuss, argue, disagree, have an altercation, altercate, clash, quarrel, wrangle, bicker, squabble. **2** *dispute his right to go* question, call into question, challenge, contest, deny, doubt, contradict, object to, oppose, controvert, impugn, gainsay.

dispute n **1** *open to dispute* debate, discussion, argument, controversy, contention, disagreement, altercation, dissension, conflict, friction, strife, discord, litigation. **2** *have a dispute over boundaries* argument, row, altercation, clash, quarrel, wrangle, squabble, feud, disturbance, fracas, brawl.

disqualify v *disqualify the runner* declare ineligible, rule out, preclude, debar, prohibit, disentitle.

disquiet n disquietude, inquietude, uneasiness, unease, unrest, anxiety, anxiousness, angst, nervousness, agitation, perturbation, upset, worry, concern, distress, trouble, alarm, fear, fretfulness, restlessness, dread, foreboding.

disquiet v make uneasy/anxious/nervous, agitate, perturb, upset, disturb, unsettle, discompose, ruffle, worry, concern, distress, trouble, bother, alarm, frighten, make fretful/restless, vex.

disregard v **1** *disregard the consequences* ignore, take no notice/account of, pay no attention/heed to, discount, set aside, neglect, forget, never mind, overlook, turn a blind eye to, pass over, gloss over, brush aside, laugh off, make light of; *inf* play down. **2** *disregard the neighbours | disregard their achievement* slight, disparage, denigrate, disdain, despise, shun, cold shoulder, insult, affront; *inf* turn one's nose up at.

disregard n **1** *treat danger with disregard* lack of notice/attention/heed, inattention, heedlessness, carelessness, neglect, negligence, indifference. **2** *treat staff/achievements with disregard* scorn, contempt, disparagement, denigration, disdain, disrespect, disesteem.

disrepair n dilapidation, deterioration, decay, collapse, shabbiness, ruin, ruination, decrepitude.

disreputable adj **1** *disreputable dealer* of bad reputation, infamous, dishonourable, dishonest, unprincipled, villainous, notorious, ignominious, corrupt, unworthy, base, low, mean, questionable, unsavoury, unscrupulous, rascally, contemptible, reprehensible, despicable, discreditable, disgraceful, shameful, shocking, outrageous, scandalous; *inf* crooked, shady. **2** *of disreputable appearance* shabby, slovenly, down-at-heel, seedy, dilapidated, threadbare, untidy, dishevelled, bedraggled; *inf* scruffy.

disrepute n *fall into disrepute* bad reputation, lack of respectability, notoriety, discredit, ill repute, unpopularity, disfavour, ill favour, disesteem, disgrace, shame, dishonour, infamy, ignominy, degradation, odium, opprobrium, obloquy.

disrespect n lack of respect, discourtesy, lack of civility, incivility, impoliteness, unmannerliness, rudeness, ungraciousness, irreverence, lack of consideration, disregard, insolence, impudence, cheek, churlishness, scorn, contempt; ill manners.

disrespectful adj discourteous, uncivil, impolite, unmannerly, ill-mannered, rude, irreverent, inconsiderate, insolent, impudent, impertinent, cheeky, churlish, scornful, contemptuous, insulting.

disrupt v **1** *disrupt the meeting/traffic* throw into disorder/disarray, disorder, disorganize, cause confusion/turmoil in, disarrange, disturb, upset, interrupt, suspend, discontinue, interfere with, obstruct, impede, hamper; *inf* throw a spanner in the works. **2** *disrupt the capsule* break open/apart, shatter, split, sever, separate, cleave, split asunder, sunder, rive, rend.

disruption n *the disruption of meetings/services* disorderliness, disorder, disorganization, confusion, turmoil, disarrangement, disarray, disturbance, upset, interruption, suspension, discontinuation, stoppage, interference, obstruction, impeding, hampering.

disruptive adj *disruptive children* troublemaking, troublesome, divisive, unruly, disorderly, undisciplined, obstreperous, upsetting, disturbing, distracting, noisy.

dissatisfaction n discontent, discontentment, disapproval, disapprobation, disappointment, frustration, unhappiness, regret, chagrin, dismay, vexation, annoyance, irritation, anger, exasperation, resentment, disquiet, restlessness, malaise, *Weltschmerz*.

dissatisfied adj discontented, displeased, disgruntled, disapproving, unsatisfied, disappointed, unfulfilled, frustrated, unhappy, regretful, vexed, angry, resentful, restless. *see* DISSATISFACTION.

dissect v 1 *dissect the corpse* cut up, cut/lay open, dismember, anatomize, vivisect. 2 *dissect the information* analyse, break down, examine, study, inspect, scrutinize, probe, explore, investigate.

dissection n 1 *dissection of the corpse* cutting up, cutting open, dismemberment; anatomy, vivisection, autopsy, post-mortem, zootomy. 2 *the dissection of the information* analysis, breakdown, examination, study, inspection, scrutinization, probing, exploration, investigation.

disseminate v *disseminate ideas/seeds* spread, circulate, broadcast, publish, publicize, proclaim, promulgate, propagate, dissipate, scatter, distribute, disperse, diffuse, bruit abroad.

dissension n disagreement, difference of opinion, dispute, argument, dissent, non-conformity, variance, conflict, friction, strife, discord, contention, quarrelling, wrangling, bickering.

dissent v 1 *dissent from official policy* express disagreement with, disagree with, differ from, be at variance with, decline/refuse, to support, not ratify, protest against, object to, dispute. 2 *dissent from the established Church practices* reject, repudiate, renounce, abjure, secede from, apostatize.

dissenter n dissident, objector, protester, protestant, disputant, rebel, revolutionary, non-conformist, recusant, apostate, sectarian, heretic.

dissentient adj dissenting, dissident, disagreeing, differing, protesting, objecting, opposing, non-conformist, non-compliant,

recusant, apostate, schismatic, unorthodox, heterodox.

dissertation n treatise, thesis, discourse, essay, critique, exposition, disquisition.

disservice n bad/ill turn, dirty trick, disfavour, unkindness, injury, harm, hurt, damage, wrong, injustice; *inf* kick in the teeth.

dissident adj *dissident opinions in the organizations* dissentient, dissenting, disagreeing, differing, non-conformist, recusant, apostate, schismatic, heterodox. *see* DISSENTIENT.

dissident n *expelling dissidents from the party* dissenter, rebel, objector, protester, non-conformist, recusant, apostate, heretic. *see* DISSENTER.

dissimilar adj unlike, unalike, different, varying, variant, disparate, unrelated, divergent, deviating, diverse, various, contrasting, mismatched, distinct.

dissimilarity n difference, unlikeness, dissimilitude, variance, disparity, unrelatedness, discrepancy, divergence, deviation, diversity, variation, non-uniformity, contrast, distinction, incomparability.

dissipate v 1 *dissipate one's fears* disperse, scatter, drive away, dispel, dissolve. 2 *the crowd dissipated* break up, disperse, scatter, dissolve, disappear, vanish, melt away, melt into thin air, evaporate. 3 *dissipate their resources* squander, fritter, misspend, lavish, waste, exhaust, drain, deplete, spend, expend, burn up, use up, consume, run through.

dissipated adj 1 *a dissipated young man* dissolute, debauched, intemperate, profligate, abandoned, rakish, licentious, promiscuous, drunken, self-indulgent, wild, unrestrained, wanton, depraved, degenerate, corrupt. 2 *dissipated resources* squandered, frittered away, wasted, exhausted, depleted, consumed. *see* DISSIPATE 3.

dissociate v 1 *dissociate his actions from his theories* separate, set apart, segregate, isolate, detach, disconnect, sever, divorce. 2 *dissociate the teams* disband, break up, dissolve, disperse, scatter, dismiss. **dissociate oneself from** sever connections with, break off relations with, withdraw from, part company with, quit, take one's leave of.

dissolute adj debauched, dissipated, intemperate, profligate, abandoned, rakish, licentious, promiscuous, drunken, self-indulgent, wild, unrestrained, depraved, degenerate, corrupt. *see* DISSIPATED.

dissolution n 1 *the dissolution of salt in water* dissolving, liquefaction, melting, deliques-

cence. **2** *the dissolution of the compound*
breaking up, separation, resolution,
decomposition, disintegration. **3** *the dissolution of the Roman empire* breaking up, disintegration, decay, collapse, death, demise,
extinction, destruction, ruin, overthrow.
4 *the dissolution of hopes* disappearance, vanishing, evaporation, dwindling, dispersal,
dissipation, evanescence. *see* DISSOLVE 3.
5 *the dissolution of the partnership/marriage*
end, ending, finish, termination, conclusion, breakup, discontinuation, winding-up, disbanding, suspension. **6** *the dissolution of the societies/crowds* disbandment, separation, dispersal, scattering. *see* DISSOLVE 5.
7 *the dissolution of the rich young people*
debauchery, dissipation, intemperance,
profligacy, abandonment, licentiousness,
promiscuity, drunkenness, self-indulgence,
wildness, lack of restraint, depravity,
degeneracy, corruption.

dissolve v **1** *salt dissolves in water* go into
solution, liquefy, melt, deliquesce. **2** *dissolve the salt in water* liquefy, melt, form into
a solution, solvate. **3** *his hopes dissolved* disappear, vanish, melt away, evaporate,
dwindle, disperse, dissipate, disintegrate,
crumble, decompose, perish, die, evanesce.
4 *dissolve a partnership/society* bring to an
end, end, terminate, break up, discontinue,
wind up, disband, dismiss, suspend, ruin.
5 *the societies/crowds dissolved* break up, split
up, disband, separate, sever, disunite, disjoin, disperse, scatter, go their separate
ways. **6** *dissolve in tears/mirth* break into, collapse into, be overcome with.

dissonance n **1** *the dissonance of the music*
discordance, inharmoniousness, unmelodiousness, cacophony, harshness, stridency,
grating, jarring, jangle. **2** *the dissonance
between their actions and theories* disagreement, difference, dissimilarity, variance,
inconsistency, disparity, discrepancy,
incongruity. **3** *the dissonance between the
families* discord, disagreement, difference
of opinion, dissension, quarrelling, wrangling, feuding.

dissuade v persuade/advise against, persuade/advise/urge not to, put off, stop; talk
out of, discourage/deter from, divert, turn
aside from, disincline from.

distance n **1** *the distance between the fields*
space, interval, span, gap, separation,
stretch, extent; length, width, depth. **2** *the
distance of the farm from the town* remoteness, farness. **3** *upset by her colleague's distance* aloofness, reserve, remoteness,
reticence, coolness, coldness, frigidity, stiffness, formality, restraint, unresponsiveness. *see* DISTANT 6. **in the distance** far

away, far off, on the horizon, just in view,
afar, yonder.

distance v **1** *distance oneself from the organization* place far-off, set apart, separate, dissociate, remove. **2** *distance the rest of the
runners* outdistance, outstrip, outrun, leave
behind, pass, outdo, surpass.

distant adj **1** *a distant place* far, far-away,
far-off, remote, out of the way, outlying,
abroad, far-flung. **2** *a distant time* far-off,
long ago. **3** *three miles distant from each other*
away, off, apart, separated, dispersed, scattered. **4** *a distant relative/likeness* not close,
remote, indirect, slight. **5** *a distant memory*
vague, faint, indistinct, obscure, uncertain.
6 *a distant smile* aloof, reserved, remote,
uncommunicative, unapproachable, standoffish, withdrawn, reticent, restrained,
cool, cold, frigid, stiff, formal, ceremonious, unresponsive, unfriendly, haughty,
condescending.

distaste n dislike, displeasure, disfavour,
disinclination, dissatisfaction, disrelish,
aversion, disgust, revulsion, repugnance,
antipathy, loathing, detestation, horror.

distasteful adj **1** *distasteful behaviour*
unpleasant, disagreeable, displeasing,
undesirable, off-putting, uninviting, objectionable, offensive, obnoxious, unsavoury,
disgusting, revolting, repugnant, abhorrent, loathsome, detestable. **2** *distasteful
food* unpalatable, unsavoury, unappetizing,
disgusting, sickening, nauseating, nauseous.

distended adj enlarged, swollen, puffed-up,
puffy, inflated, ballooning, bloated, dilated,
stretched, expanded, extended, tumescent.

distil v **1** *distil fresh water from sea water*
vaporize/evaporate and condense, sublime,
sublimate, fractionate. **2** *distil the essence
from a plant* extract, press out, squeeze out,
express, draw out. **3** *distil the chemical* separate, concentrate, purify, refine, rectify.
4 *distilling beads of liquid* exude, give out,
drip, leak, dribble.

distillation n essence, extract, spirit, quintessence, elixir.

distinct adj **1** *a distinct resemblance* clear,
clear-cut, well-defined, sharp, marked,
decided, definite, unmistakable, recognizable, obvious, plain, plain as day, evident,
apparent, manifest, patent, palpable,
unambiguous, unequivocal. **2** *two distinct
jobs* separate, individual, different, unconnected, unassociated, detached, discrete,
dissimilar, unalike, disparate.

distinction n **1** *make the distinction between
right and wrong* differentiation, contradis-

tinction, discrimination, division, separation, dividing line, contrast. **2** *fail to notice the identifying distinctions* difference, dissimilarity, dissimilitude, contrast, differential, subtlety, nicety, nuance. **3** *the distinctions of wealth and rank* feature, characteristic, mark, individuality, peculiarity. **4** *pass the exam with distinction* honour, credit, excellence, merit. **5** *people of distinction* note, consequence, importance, account, significance, greatness, prestige, prominence, eminence, repute, reputation, renown, fame, mark, celebrity, honour, merit, worth, excellence, glory, name, rank, quality, superiority.

distinctive adj distinguishing, characteristic, typical, individual, particular, peculiar, special, different, uncommon, unusual, remarkable, singular, extraordinary, noteworthy, original, idiosyncratic.

distinctly adv **1** *distinctly annoyed* clearly, markedly, decidedly, definitely, unmistakably, obviously, plainly, evidently, apparently, manifestly, patently, palpably. **2** *speak distinctly* clearly, plainly, intelligibly, precisely.

distinguish v **1** *distinguish one colour from another* tell apart, differentiate, discriminate, determine; tell the difference between, decide between. **2** *his hair distinguishes him from the others* make distinctive, set apart, separate, single out, mark off, characterize, individualize, designate, categorize, classify. **3** *distinguish a black shape* make out, see, discern, perceive, observe, notice, detect, recognize, identify, pick out, descry, apprehend, espy. **4** *distinguish himself in battle* make famous, bring fame/honour to, bestow honour on, ennoble, dignify, glorify, win acclaim for, lionize, immortalize.

distinguishable adj *no distinguishable difference* clear, plainly seen, obvious, evident, marked, well-defined, conspicuous, noticeable, discernible, perceptible, recognizable, manifest.

distinguished adj *a distinguished scientist* famous, famed, eminent, renowned, prominent, well-known, noted, notable, esteemed, acclaimed, illustrious, celebrated, respected, legendary.

distinguishing adj *a distinguishing mark* distinctive, differentiating, discriminating, determining, individualistic, peculiar, singular, characteristic, typical.

distort v **1** *distort the metal | distort their features* twist, warp, contort, bend, buckle, deform, misshape, disfigure, mangle, wrench, wring, wrest. **2** *distort the facts* mis-

represent, pervert, twist, falsify, garble, slant, bias, colour, tamper with, alter, change, torture.

distortion n **1** *a distortion in the metal* twist, warp, contortion, bend, buckle, curvature, deformation, deformity, malformation, gnarl, knot; crookedness. **2** *a distortion of the truth* misrepresentation, perversion, twisting, falsification, garbling, colouring, alteration; slant, bias, change.

distract v **1** *distract them from work* deflect, divert, sidetrack, turn aside, draw away. **2** *distract the children* amuse, entertain, divert, beguile, absorb, engage, occupy. **3** *bright lights distracting her* confuse, bewilder, perplex, puzzle, disturb, fluster, agitate, disconcert, discompose, confound, annoy, trouble, harass, worry, torment; *inf* hassle. **4** *grief distracting her* make frantic, drive/make mad, madden, drive insane, make crazy, derange, throw into a frenzy.

distracted adj **1** *rushing around in a distracted way* confused, bewildered, bemused, perplexed, agitated, flustered, troubled, harassed, worried; *inf* hassled, in a flap. *see* DISTRACT 3. **2** *distracted women mourning their sons* grief-stricken, distraught, frantic, frenzied, raving, wild, hysterical, overwrought, mad, maddened, insane, crazed, deranged, out of one's mind.

distraction n **1** *distraction from their work* diversion, interruption, disturbance, interference, obstruction. **2** *distractions laid on for the children* amusement, entertainment, diversion, pastime, recreation, hobby, game, occupation, divertissement. **3** *the distraction of the child at the crowds* confusion, bewilderment, befuddlement, perplexity, disturbance, agitation, perturbation, harassment. *see* DISTRACT 3. **4** *pity the distraction of the widow* frenzy, hysteria, mental distress, madness, insanity, crazedness, mania, derangement, delirium, alienation.

distress n **1** *the lost child's distress* anguish, suffering, pain, agony, ache, affliction, torment, torture, misery, wretchedness, discomfort, heartache, heartbreak, sorrow, grief, woe, sadness, desolation, trouble, worry, anxiety, perturbation, uneasiness, angst; tribulations, cries, wails. **2** *old people in distress* hardship, adversity, misfortune, trouble, calamity, need, want, poverty, lack, privation, destitution, indigence, impoverishment, penury, beggary; difficulties, dire straits.

distress v **1** *the news distressed her* cause anguish/suffering, pain, upset, make miserable/wretched, grieve, sadden, trouble, worry, bother, arouse anxiety in, perturb, disturb, vex, harrow, torment. **2** *distress the furniture* damage, spoil, dent, scratch, simulate age/wear in.

distressing adj *distressing news/sights* disturbing, worrying, upsetting, affecting, painful, sad, heartbreaking.

distribute v **1** *distribute rations to the crowd* give out, hand out, allocate, allot, issue, dispense, administer, apportion, assign, deal out, share out, divide out, dole out, measure out, mete out, parcel out, dispose. **2** *distribute advertising leaflets* circulate, pass round, hand out, deliver, convey, transmit. **3** *distribute seeds evenly* disseminate, disperse, diffuse, scatter, spread, strew, sow. **4** *luggage distributed in categories* place, position, arrange, organize, dispose, group, class, classify, categorize, file, assort, compart, locate.

distribution n **1** *distribution of rations* giving out, allocation, allotment, dispensation, administering, assignment, dealing out, division. see DISTRIBUTE 1. **2** *distribution of seeds* dissemination, dispersal, diffusion, scattering. see DISTRIBUTE 3. **3** *the distribution of luggage in categories* placement, position, arrangement, organization, disposition, grouping, classification, assortment, location. see DISTRIBUTE 4. **4** *in charge of sales and distribution* handling, delivery, transport, transportation, conveyance, mailing. **5** *an abnormal statistical distribution* frequency/probability of occurrence, prevalence, incidence.

district n **1** *live in a pleasant district* area, region, place, locality, neighbourhood, quarter, sector, vicinity, territory, domain. **2** *an administrative district* administrative division, ward, parish, community, constituency, department, canton.

distrust v mistrust, be suspicious of, be wary/chary of, be sceptical of, have doubts about, doubt, have misgivings about, wonder about, question, suspect, disbelieve, discredit; *inf* be leery of.

distrust n mistrust, lack of trust, no confidence, lack of faith, suspicion, wariness, chariness, scepticism, doubt, doubtfulness, dubiety, misgiving, questioning, qualms, disbelief, unbelief, incredulity, incredulousness, discredit; *inf* leeriness.

disturb v **1** *disturb them while they are working* interrupt, butt in on, distract, bother, trouble, pester, intrude on, interfere with, hinder, plague, harass, molest; *inf* hassle. **2** *disturb papers on a desk* disarrange, muddle, disorganize, disorder, confuse, throw into disorder/confusion, derange, unsettle. **3** *the news disturbed them* concern, perturb,

trouble, worry, upset, agitate, fluster, discomfit, disconcert, alarm, frighten, startle, dismay, distress, discompose, unsettle, ruffle, shake, confuse, bewilder, perplex, confound, excite. **4** *disturb the water* agitate, churn up, convulse, roil. **5** *don't disturb yourself* inconvenience, put out, put to trouble.

disturbance n **1** *resent the disturbance to their work* interruption, distraction, intrusion, interference, hindrance, harassment. see DISTURB 1. **2** *the disturbance of papers* disarrangement, muddling, disorganization, confusing; muddle, disorder, confusion. **3** *causing emotional disturbance* concern, perturbation, trouble, worry, upset, agitation, discomfiture, alarm, distress, bewilderment. see DISTURB 3. **4** *the disturbance of the water* agitation, churning. see DISTURB 4. **5** *police called to a disturbance* uproar, commotion, row, rumpus, hullabaloo, tumult, turmoil, fracas, affray, brawl, riot; *inf* ruction; *Amer inf* ruckus.

disturbed adj *emotionally disturbed* upset, troubled, unbalanced, disordered, maladjusted, neurotic, psychotic; *inf* screwed up.

disturbing adj *disturbing news* perturbing, troubling, worrying, upsetting, agitating, disconcerting, alarming, disquieting, startling, dismaying, frightening, distressing, unsettling, bewildering. see DISTURB 3.

disuse n non-use, non-employment, lack of use, desuetude, neglect, abandonment, cessation, discontinuance, obsolescence.

disused adj unused, neglected, abandoned, discontinued, obsolete.

ditch n trench, channel, watercourse, dyke, canal, drain, gutter, gully, moat, furrow, rut.

ditch v **1** *be engaged in digging and ditching* dig, trench, excavate, gouge, hollow out, drain. **2** *ditch the plan* abandon, throw out, discard, drop, scrap, jettison, get rid of, dispose of; *inf* dump. **3** *ditch the police* evade, escape, elude, shake off, defeat, frustrate, baulk.

diurnal adj **1** *a diurnal occurrence* daily, occurring every day, daytime, quotidian, circadian. **2** *a diurnal flower/animal* of the day, daytime, non-nocturnal.

divan n sofa, couch, settee, *chaise longue*, davenport, ottoman, chesterfield, day bed.

dive v **1** *dive from the springboard* plunge/descend into water, go/jump into water, plummet, jump, leap, bound, spring, nosedive, fall, descend, submerge, drop, swoop, dip, pitch, bellyflop. **2** *dive out of sight* move quickly, leap, jump, lunge, rush, dart, dash, duck, dodge.

dive n **1** *a dive from the springboard* plunge, plummet, jump, leap, spring, nosedive, fall, drop, swoop, bellyflop. **2** *a quick dive under the bed* leap, jump, lunge, rush, dart, dash, duck, dodge. **3** *drinking in dives* sleazy bar/nightclub; *inf* drinking-joint, drinking-den, low joint, dump.

diverge v **1** *the roads diverged* separate, divide, subdivide, split, part, disunite, fork, branch off, radiate, spread out, bifurcate, divaricate, ramify. **2** *opinions diverge* differ, disagree, be at variance/odds, conflict, clash. **3** *diverge from the norm* deviate, digress, depart, veer, stray, drift, turn aside, wander, divagate.

divergence n **1** *the divergence of the roads* separation, dividing, parting, forking, branching, bifurcation; fork, division. *see* DIVERGE 1. **2** *divergence of opinions* difference, disagreement, variance, varying, conflict. *see* DIVERGE 2. **3** *divergence from the norm* deviation, digression, departure, straying, deflection, divagation.

divergent adj **1** *divergent opinions* differing, different, diverse, disagreeing, in disagreement, varying, conflicting, clashing, dissenting. **2** *divergent statistical results* deviating, digressing, abnormal, aberrant, divagating.

divers adj several, numerous, many, some; sundry, various, different, manifold.

diverse adj various, miscellaneous, assorted, mixed, diversified, variegated, varied, varying, heterogeneous, different, differing, distinct, unlike, dissimilar, distinctive, contrasting, conflicting.

diversify v **1** *diversify the range* vary, bring variety to, variegate, modify, assort, mix, alter, change, transform. **2** *firms must diversify* extend operations/products, expand, spread.

diversion n **1** *the diversion of the stream* redirection, turning aside, deflection, digression, deviation, divergence. **2** *take the diversion* alternative route, detour. **3** *diversions provided for the children* amusement, entertainment, pastime, distraction, recreation, fun, relaxation, game, play, sport, hobby, pleasure, delight, enjoyment, beguilement, enchantment, divertissement.

diversity n *diversity of opinion* diverseness, variety, miscellany, assortment, mixture, range, medley, multiplicity, variegation, heterogeneity, diversification, difference,

unlikeness, dissimilarity, distinctiveness, dissimilitude, contrast, conflict.

divert v **1** *divert the stream* turn aside, deflect, draw away, avert, switch/change the course of, redirect. **2** *divert him from his work* distract, detract, sidetrack, lead away, turn aside, deflect. **3** *clowns diverting the children* amuse, entertain, distract, delight, give pleasure to, beguile, enchant, interest, occupy, absorb, engross, recreate.

diverting adj amusing, entertaining, humorous, fun, enjoyable, pleasurable, recreational, beguiling, interesting, absorbing.

divest v **1** *divest them of their clothes | divested himself of his coat* unclothe, undress, disrobe, strip, denude; take off, remove, doff. **2** *divest them of power/property* deprive, strip, dispossess, relieve, bereave, despoil.

divide v **1** *divide the rope in two | divide one group from another* cut up, sever, split, shear, bisect, halve, quarter, cleave, rend, sunder, rive; separate, part, segregate, partition, detach, disconnect, disjoin. **2** *the road divides here* diverge, branch, fork, split in two, divaricate. **3** *divide the food* share out, allocate, allot, apportion, portion out, distribute, dispense, deal out, hand out, dole out, measure out, parcel out. **4** *politics divided them* estrange, alienate, break up, separate, spilt up, disunite, disaffect, set/pit against one another, cause disagreement between, sow dissension between, set at variance/odds, come between. **5** *divide into types* classify, sort, arrange, order, group, grade, rank, categorize, dispose, separate, segregate.

dividend n **1** *dividends paid to shareholders* share, portion, gain, surplus; *inf* cut, divvy. **2** *dividends brought by hard work* bonus, extra, plus, benefit, fringe benefit, perquisite; *inf* perk.

divine adj **1** *a divine being* godly, godlike, heavenly, celestial, holy, angelic, seraphic, spiritual, saintly. **2** *divine worship* religious, holy, sacred, sanctified, consecrated, spiritual. **3** *divine music* supernatural, superhuman, mystical, exalted, beatific, blissful, ethereal, transcendental, transcendent, transmundane. **4** *looking divine | a divine evening* lovely, beautiful, charming, perfect, excellent, superlative, wonderful, glorious, marvellous, admirable; *inf* super, stunning.

divine n theologian, clergyman, churchman, churchwoman, cleric, ecclesiastic, minister, priest, pastor, parson, reverend.

divine v **1** *divine their plans | divine that they are going* guess, surmise, conjecture, speculate, suspect, suppose, assume, presume,

deduce, infer, theorize, hypothesize.
2 *divine their need* intuit, discern, perceive,
understand, grasp, apprehend, compre-
hend. **3** *divine the future* foretell, predict,
foresee, forecast, presage, augur, portend,
prognosticate, forebode. **4** *divine for water*
dowse.

divinity n **1** *the divinity of the being* divine
nature, divineness, deity, godhead, godliness, holiness, sanctity. **2** *worship the divinity* deity, god, goddess, genius, spirit,
guardian, angel, daemon. **3** *study divinity*
theology, religious studies, religion, scripture.

division n **1** *the division of the rope/groups*
dividing, cutting up, severance, splitting,
bisection, cleaving; parting, separation,
segregation, partitioning, disconnection,
detachment. *see* DIVIDE 1. **2** *the division of
rations* sharing out, allocation, allotment,
apportionment, distribution. *see* DIVIDE 3.
3 *cross the division* dividing line, divide,
boundary, boundary line, border, partition,
line of demarcation. **4** *divisions of equal size*
section, part, portion, piece, bit, segment,
slice, fragment, chunk, component, share;
compartment, category, class, group,
grade, family. **5** *divisions of the firm* branch,
department, section, sector, arm. **6** *a bitter
division between the families* disagreement,
difference of opinion, feud, breach, rupture, split; dissension, conflict, discord,
variance, disunion, estrangement, alienation.

divisive adj alienating, estranging, disruptive, troublemaking, troublesome, detrimental, damaging, injurious, pernicious,
discordant, inharmonious.

divorce n **1** *marriage ended in divorce* dissolution, disunion, breakup, split-up, annul-
ment, official separation, separation,
severance, breach, rupture. **2** *the divorce
between their theories and their actions* separation, severance, division, split, partition.

divorce v **1** *the couple divorced* annul/dissolve
a marriage, split up, break up, separate,
part. **2** *she divorced him* end a marriage
with/to, have a marriage annulled/dis-
solved. **3** *their views are divorced from reality*
separate, disconnect, divide, dissociate,
detach, disunite, sever, disjoin, split, sunder.

divulge v disclose, reveal, make known,
tell, impart, communicate, publish, broadcast, proclaim, promulgate, declare, utter,
expose, uncover, bring into the open, let
slip, leak, let the cat out of the bag about,
confess, betray; *inf* spill the beans about.

dizzy adj **1** *get dizzy on top of the ladder* giddy,
light-headed, faint, vertiginous, weak at
the knees, shaky, wobbly, off-balance, reeling, staggering; *inf* woozy. **2** *feeling dizzy at
the amount of information* dazed, bewildered,
confused, muddled, bemused, befuddled,
puzzled, perplexed; *inf* woozy. **3** *dizzy
heights/speeds* giddy-making, vertiginous,
bewildering. **4** *dizzy young girls* giddy, scatterbrained, feather-brained, flighty, foolish,
silly, light-headed, fickle, capricious, inconstant.

do v **1** *do as you would be done by* act, behave,
conduct oneself, comport oneself. **2** *do the
job* perform, carry out, undertake, discharge, execute, accomplish, implement,
achieve, complete, finish, conclude, bring
about, effect, effectuate, realize, produce,
engineer. **3** *this amount will do* be enough,
be sufficient, be adequate, suffice, be satisfactory, be of use, fill/fit the bill, answer/
serve the purpose, meet the needs, pass
muster, measure up. **4** *do the meals* make,
prepare, get ready, fix, produce, see to,
arrange, organize, be responsible for, be in
charge of, look after, take on. **5** *do a large
picture* create, make, produce, originate,
form, fashion, design, fabricate, manufacture. **6** *they're doing three plays* put on, perform, act, present, produce, give. **7** *do me a
favour* render, afford, give, bestow, grant,
pay. **8** *can't do this maths problem* solve,
resolve, work out, puzzle out, figure out,
decipher. **9** *what does he do?* work at, be
employed at, have as a job/profession/occu-
pation, earn a living at. **10** *how are you
doing?* get on/along, progress, fare, make
out, manage, continue. **11** *the play was done
in Russian* translate, put, render, adapt,
transform. **12** *the car was doing 90 mph*
travel at, go/proceed at, be driven at. **13** *we
did 50 miles* travel, journey, cover, traverse.
14 *they're doing Edinburgh today* sightsee,
look at, visit, tour; *inf* rubberneck. **15** *the
crooked shopkeeper did us* cheat, defraud,
swindle, fleece, bilk, trick, deceive, dupe,
take advantage of, hoax, take one for a
ride; *lit* cozen. **16** *the journey did me in* tire
out, exhaust, wear out, fatigue; *inf* do in,
fag out, shatter. **17** *the thieves did the pub
last night* burgle, rob, break into. **do away
with 1** *do away with the penalty* abolish, get
rid of, discard, remove, discontinue, eliminate, repeal, revoke, rescind, cancel, annul,
nullify. **2** *do away with his enemy* kill, put to
death, slay, murder, slaughter, liquidate,
assassinate, execute, dispatch; *inf* do in,
bump off, knock off, eliminate. **do in 1** *do
in his enemy* kill, put to death, slay, murder,
assassinate; *inf* do away with, bump off.

2 *do in his business* ruin, reduce to nothing, wreck, destroy, smash, crush, wreak havoc on. **3** *the walk did me in* tire out, exhaust, wear out, fatigue, weary; *inf* fag out, shatter, do. **do out of** prevent from having, deprive of, swindle/cheat/trick out of; *inf* con/diddle out of. **do without** forgo, dispense with, abstain from, give up, refrain from, eschew.

do n party, function, affair, event, occasion, fête, soirée; *inf* beanfeast, bash, blow-out, rave-up, thrash, knees-up.

docile adj manageable, controllable, tractable, malleable, manipulable, amenable, accommodating, compliant, pliant, obedient, biddable, dutiful, submissive, yielding, ductile.

dock n *tie up at the dock* pier, quay, wharf, jetty, marina, waterfront.

dock v **1** *dock the dogs' tails* cut, cut short, shorten, crop, lop, truncate. **2** *dock money from wages* deduct, subtract, remove, take off. **3** *dock their wages* reduce, decrease, lessen, diminish.

docket n *the docket with the package* document, documentation, paperwork, chit, chitty, certificate, counterfoil, label, tag, ticket, tab, bill, receipt.

docket v *docket the package* document, label, tag, tab, mark, ticket.

doctor n medical practitioner, physician, medical man/person; general practitioner, GP, hospital doctor, consultant, house doctor, registrar, senior registrar; *inf* doc, quack.

doctor v **1** *doctor the patients* treat, prescribe for, attend to, minister to, care for, cure, heal. **2** *doctor the machinery* patch up, repair, fix, mend, botch, cobble. **3** *doctor the drinks* adulterate, contaminate, dilute, water down, weaken, mix, cut, lace; *inf* spike. **4** *doctor the evidence* tamper with, interfere with, alter, change, falsify, disguise, fudge, pervert, misrepresent.

doctrinaire adj **1** *doctrinaire teachers* dogmatic, authoritarian, rigid, inflexible, insistent, domineering, opinionated, intolerant, biased, prejudiced, fanatical. **2** *doctrinaire schemes* impractical, unpragmatic, unrealistic, theoretical, hypothetical, ideological, speculative, visionary.

doctrine n creed, credo, dogma, belief, conviction, teaching; tenet, principle, precept, maxim; articles of faith, canons.

document n *business documents* official paper, legal paper, paper, form, certificate, record, report, deed, voucher, instrument, charter; paperwork, documentation.

document v **1** *document their statement* prove, back up, support, give weight to, corroborate, substantiate, authenticate, verify, validate, certify. **2** *the war was well documented in the press | his marriage is not documented* report, record, detail, tabulate, chart, register, cite, instance.

documentary adj **1** *documentary evidence* documented, recorded, registered, tabulated, charted, written. **2** *a documentary film* factual, non-fictional, real-life, true to life, realistic.

dodder v totter, teeter, stagger, shuffle, shamble, falter, shake, tremble, quiver.

doddering adj doddery, tottering, tottery, staggering, shuffling, shambling, faltering, shaky, unsteady, trembling, trembly, quivering, infirm, decrepit, aged, in one's dotage, senile.

dodge v **1** *dodge behind the door* dart, duck, dive, swerve, sidestep, veer, jump away, move aside. **2** *dodge the police* evade, elude, escape, fend off, avoid, stay/steer clear of, deceive, trick; *inf* give the slip to. **3** *dodge awkward questions* evade, get out of, parry, fend off, fudge. **4** *dodge hard work* avoid, evade, shirk, shun, stay/steer clear of.

dodge n **1** *a dodge to the right* dart, duck, dive, swerve, jump. **2** *a dodge to avoid work | a tax dodge* ruse, ploy, scheme, stratagem, subterfuge, trick, wile, deception, manoeuvre, device, machination, contrivance, artifice, expedient; sharp practice; *inf* wheeze.

doer n **1** *the doer of the deed* performer, executor, accomplisher, effectuator. **2** *doers rather than thinkers* worker, organizer, achiever, high achiever, activist, hustler, entrepreneur; *inf* busy bee, live wire, go-getter, whizz kid, powerhouse, wheeler-dealer.

doff v **1** *doff their hats* raise, lift, remove, take off, touch, tip. **2** *doff their clothes* take off, remove, shed, strip off, throw off, cast off.

dog n **1** *cats and dogs* canine, hound, mongrel, cur, tyke; bitch, male dog, pup, puppy, whelp, wild dog; *inf* doggy, pooch, mutt. **2** *he's a dirty dog* scoundrel, blackguard, beast, cad, rogue, villain, cur, knave, heel, bastard. **3** *a lucky dog* person, fellow; *inf* chap, guy. **4** *dogs related to the domesticated breeds* dingo, wolf, coyote, fox, jackal, hyena.

dog v *dogged by ill luck* pursue, follow, track, trail, shadow, hound, plague, trouble, haunt; *inf* tail.

dogged adj determined, resolute, obstinate, stubborn, tenacious, relentless, intent, single-minded, unshakable, unflagging, indefatigable, tireless, unfaltering, unwavering, persistent, persevering, pertinacious, unyielding, obdurate, firm, steadfast, steady, staunch.

doggedness n determination, resolution, obstinacy, stubborness, tenacity, relentlessness, single-mindedness, tirelessness, persistence, perseverance, pertinacity, obdurance, endurance, steadfastness, steadiness. *see* DOGGED.

dogma n **1** *Christian dogma* creed, credo, code of belief, conviction, teaching; belief, tenet, principle, precept, maxim; articles of faith, canons. **2** *tired of political dogma* unquestioned belief, unchallengeable conviction, arrogant conviction.

dogmatic adj **1** *dogmatic papal statements* doctrinal, doctrinaire, canonical, authoritative, *ex cathedra*, oracular. **2** *dogmatic denial/attitude/youth* assertive, insistent, emphatic, categorical, downright, authoritarian, opinionated, peremptory, domineering, imperious, arrogant, overbearing, dictatorial, intolerant, biased, prejudiced; *inf* pushy.

dogsbody n skivvy, drudge, slave, menial, general factotum, man/maid of all work.

doing n **1** *the doing of the deed* performance, carrying out, discharging, execution, accomplishment, implementation, achievement, effectuation, realization. **2** *famous for brave doings* deed, act, action, feat, exploit, work, enterprise, achievement; handiwork. **3** *take a lot of doing* effort, activity, exertion, work, application, struggle. **4** *get a doing from his father* beating, thrashing, thumping, battering, castigation, scolding.

doings npl *have you got the doings for the repair?* necessary thing/part, relevant equipment, needful, doodah, thingumajig, thingummy, thingumabob, what's its name, what d'you call it; *inf* doofer.

doldrums npl **1** *a fit of the doldrums* downheartedness, dejection, depression, melancholy, gloom, inertia, apathy, listlessness, malaise, boredom, tedium, ennui; blues, low spirits. **2** *a business in the doldrums* inactivity, inertia, flatness, stagnation, dullness, sluggishness, torpor.

dole n **1** *redundant workers receiving the dole* unemployment benefit, benefit, social security, welfare; *Scots* buroo. **2** *dole given grudgingly to the poor* alms; charity, benefit; gift, donation, allowance, grant, portion, pittance, mite.

dole v **dole out** deal out, allocate, allot, apportion, share out, mete out, distribute, divide up, dispense, hand out, give out, issue, assign, administer.

doleful adj mournful, sorrowful, sad, dejected, disconsolate, depressed, gloomy, melancholy, blue, miserable, wretched; *inf* down in the mouth/dumps.

doll n figure, figurine, model, puppet, marionette, toy, plaything; *inf* dolly.

dolour n sorrow, grief, sadness, heartache, anguish, misery, distress, suffering.

dolt n blockhead, dunderhead, thickhead, numskull, nitwit, dunce, fool, idiot, ass, simpleton, nincompoop, ignoramus, dullard, booby; *inf* dope, chump, clot, dimwit, nerd; *Amer inf* airhead, meatball.

domain n **1** *the king's domain* realm, kingdom, empire, dominion, estate. *see* DOMINION 2. **2** *working in the scientific domain* area, field, region, province, sphere, section, discipline.

dome n cupola, rotunda; hemisphere.

domestic adj **1** *an unhappy domestic life | domestic water supply* home, family, household, domiciliary, private. **2** *preferring domestic people* domesticated, housewifely, stay-at-home, home-loving, homely. **3** *a domestic animal* domesticated, tame, pet, house-trained, trained, not wild. **4** *domestic markets* home, internal, not foreign, not export. **5** *domestic plants* native, indigenous, home-grown, home-bred, aboriginal, autochthonous.

domestic n *employ a domestic* domestic help, help, maid, domestic servant, servant, charwoman, daily help, daily, au pair, home help, menial, skivvy; *Amer* hired help.

domesticate v **1** *domesticate an animal* tame, house-train, train, break in, gentle. **2** *domesticate a foreign tree* naturalize, acclimatize, habituate, accustom, familiarize, assimilate.

domesticated adj **1** *domesticated animals* tame, tamed, pet, house-trained, broken-in. **2** *domesticated plants* naturalized, acclimatized, habituated. **3** *domesticated people* domestic, housewifely; *inf* house-trained. *see* DOMESTIC adj 2.

domicile n home, house, residence, residency, dwelling, dwelling-place, abode, habitation, lodging, accommodation.

domicile v *they are domiciled in Switzerland* establish, settle, make one's home, take up one's abode, ensconce oneself.

dominant adj **1** *the dominant member of the committee* ruling, governing, controlling, commanding, ascendant, presiding, supreme, authoritative, most influential, superior, most assertive, domineering. **2** *the dominant issue* predominant, most important, chief, main, principal, leading, primary, paramount, pre-eminent, outstanding, prominent, prevailing.

dominate v **1** *dominate the council* rule, govern, control, exercise control over, command, direct, preside over, have ascendancy/mastery over, master, domineer, tyrannize, intimidate, have the upper/whip hand over, ride roughshod over; have under one's thumb, be in the driver's seat, be in the saddle, wear the trousers; *inf* boss, call the shouts. **2** *hostility/silence dominated* predominate, be paramount, be pre-eminent, prevail, be conspicuous, be most obvious, be most important. **3** *the hill dominates the town* overlook, tower above, stand over, project/jut over, hang/loom over, bestride.

domination n *under foreign domination* rule, government, control, command, direction, authority, power, mastery, supremacy, sway, tyranny, intimidation, oppression, dictatorship.

domineer v browbeat, bully, intimidate, hector, lord it over, tyrannize, be overbearing, ride roughshod over, trample on, have under one's thumb, rule with an iron hand, rule with a rod of iron, bend to one's will, subjugate; *inf* boss around/about.

domineering adj overbearing, imperious, authoritarian, high-handed, autocratic, peremptory, arrogant, haughty, dictatorial, masterful, forceful, coercive, tyrannical, despotic, oppressive, subjugating, iron-fisted, iron-handed; *inf* bossy, pushy.

dominion n **1** *have dominion over smaller states* supremacy, ascendancy, sway, mastery, rule, government, sovereignty, jurisdiction, control, command, direction, authority, power, domination, the upper/whip hand, overlordship, suzerainty. **2** *the king's dominions* realm, kingdom, empire, domain, country, province, territory, region, estate.

don v put on, slip on, slip into, get into, pull on, dress/clothe/accoutre oneself in, rig oneself out in.

don n university teacher/lecturer, college tutor, academic, scholar, pedagogue; *inf* egghead.

donate v give, contribute, make a contribution of, subscribe, make a gift of, gift, present, pledge, put oneself down for, bestow; *inf* chip in; *Amer inf* kick in.

donation n contribution, subscription, gift, present, grant, offering, gratuity; alms; charity, benefaction, largesse.

done adj **1** *the job is done* accomplished, complete, completed, executed, perfected, finished, ended, concluded, terminated, realized, consummated. **2** *the meat is done* cooked, ready. **3** *our store of logs is done* finished, used up, exhausted, depleted, spent. **4** *feeling done after the walk* worn out, exhausted, tired out, weary; *inf* done in. see DONE adj done in. **5** *such behaviour is not done* acceptable, proper, seemly, decorous, conventional, *de rigueur*. **6** *we were done by the shopkeeper* swindled, cheated, tricked, deceived, duped, hoodwinked; *inf* conned, taken for a ride. **be done with** see DONE adj have done with. **done for** finished, ruined, destroyed, broken, wrecked, undone, dashed, dead, doomed, lost, defeated, beaten, foiled, frustrated, thwarted; *inf* washed-up. **done in** worn out, exhausted, tired out, weary, fatigued, played out, on one's last legs, fit to drop; *inf* done, dog-tired, all in, dead beat, shattered, knackered, fagged out, bushed, pooped, worn to a frazzle. **have done with** be finished/through with, have no further dealings with, be no longer involved with/in, end relations with, give up, wash one's hands of.

done interj *you're offering £10? Done!* agreed, settled, that's a bargain, accepted, right; *inf* OK, you're on.

donkey n **1** *an overloaded donkey* ass, mule, jackass, jack, jenny, hinny; *Amer* burro; *inf* moke. **2** *a silly donkey* fool, ass, idiot, nincompoop, nitwit, blockhead, dolt; *inf* dope, chump, nerd.

donnish adj scholarly, scholastic, pedagogic, erudite, bookish, pedantic.

donor n giver, contributor, donator, grantor, benefactor, benefactress, supporter, backer, philanthropist; *inf* angel.

doom n **1** *what doom has in store* grim/terrible fate, destiny, fortune, lot, portion. **2** *companies/people facing doom* ruin, ruination, rack and ruin, downfall, destruction, catastrophe, disaster, extinction, annihilation, death, termination, quietus. **3** *the prisoner hearing his doom* condemnation, guilty verdict, sentence, judgement, pronouncement, decree, damnation. **4** *predicting doom* the Last Judgement, Judgement Day, doomsday, Armageddon, end of the world.

doom v **1** *children doomed to be poor* fate, destine, predestine, ordain, preordain, foreordain, consign, condemn. **2** *prisoners doomed* *to die* condemn, sentence, judge, pronounce, decree, damn.

doomed adj *doomed plans/lovers* ill-fated, star-crossed, foredoomed, unlucky, damned, bedevilled, ruined, crushed.

door n **1** *wooden doors* doorway, portal, entrance, entry, exit, barrier; front door, back door, side door, cupboard door, sliding door, revolving door, trapdoor. **2** *doors to academic success* entrance, entry, access, opening, entrée, gateway, way, path, road, ingress. **out of doors** outside, outdoors, out, in/into the open air, alfresco.

dope n **1** *smuggling dope* drugs, narcotics. *see* DRUG n **2**. **2** *a stupid dope* dolt, blockhead, dunderhead, thickhead, dunce, fool, idiot, nincompoop, nitwit; *inf* chump, dimwit, nerd. **3** *give the dope on the situation* information, inside information, story, news; facts, data, details; *inf* info, gen, low-down.

dope v **1** *dope the hostage/horse* drug, administer drugs/narcotics/opiates to, knock out, anaesthetize, stupefy, sedate, narcotize. **2** *dope his drink* add drugs/narcotics/opiates to, doctor; *inf* spike.

dormant adj sleeping, asleep, slumbering, inactive, inert, latent, fallow, quiescent, inoperative, hibernating, comatose, stagnant, sluggish, lethargic, torpid, passive, motionless, immobile.

dose n **1** *a dose of cough mixture* amount, quantity, measure, portion, draught. **2** *a dose of flu* bout, attack, spell.

dot n spot, speck, fleck, point, mark, dab, particle, atom, iota, jot, mote, mite; full stop, decimal point. **on the dot** **3** *o'clock on the dot* | *arrive on the dot* exactly, precisely, to the minute, on time, punctually, promptly; *inf* on the button.

dot v **1** *dotted with stains/ships* spot, fleck, bespeckle, mark, dab, stud, bestud, stipple, pock, freckle, sprinkle, scatter, pepper. **2** *dot the letters* mark with a dot, add a dot to, punctuate.

dotage n senility, old age, caducity, second childhood, decrepitude, infirmity, feebleness; declining years.

dote v *she dotes on/upon her grandchildren* idolize, adore, hold dear, love dearly, treasure, prize, make much of, lavish affection on, indulge, spoil, pamper.

doting adj adoring, devoted, loving, fond, indulgent, pampering.

double adj **1** *double yellow lines* | *a double eggcup* duplicate, twin, paired, in pairs, coupled, dual, twofold, binal, binate. **2** *a double portion* doubled, twice as much/many as usual, twofold, large. **3** *a double thickness* doubled, twofold, folded, folded in two, two-ply. **4** *a double meaning* dual, ambiguous, double-edged, two-edged, ambivalent, equivocal. **5** *a double life* dual, deceitful, false, dishonest, hypocritical, insincere, double-dealing, two-faced, treacherous, perfidious, Janus-faced.

double adv **1** *seeing double* two together, two at a time, in twos, by twos, two by two. **2** *pay double* twice, twice over, twice the amount.

double v **1** *double the amount* multiply by two, increase twofold, enlarge, magnify. **2** *double as a bed and sofa* have/serve a dual purpose, have a dual role. **3** *he doubled for the main part* | *she doubles in the musical* be an understudy/subsitute, understudy; act two roles/parts. **4** *double paper* fold, bend over.

double n the *double of his cousin* | *the double of the other picture* look-alike, twin, clone, doppleganger, duplicate, replica, copy, facsimile, counterpart, match, mate, fellow; *inf* spitting image, dead spit/ringer, ringer. **at/on the double** at full speed, as fast as possible, very quickly, rapidly, briskly, with haste, in double-quick time, post-haste, right away, immediately, without delay, straight away; *inf* p.d.q. (= pretty damn quick).

double-cross v betray, cheat, defraud, trick, hoodwink, mislead, deceive, swindle; *inf* two-time, take for a ride.

double-dealing n duplicity, treachery, betrayal, double-crossing, bad faith, perfidy, breach of trust, fraud, fraudulence, underhandedness, cheating, dishonesty, untrustworthiness, mendacity, deception, two-facedness, trickery, deceit, hypocrisy; *inf* crookedness.

double entendre n ambiguity, double meaning, suggested meaning, innuendo, play on words, wordplay, pun.

doubt v **1** *doubt his motives* have/entertain doubts about, be suspicious of, harbour suspicions about, suspect, distrust, mistrust, lack confidence in, have misgivings about, feel uneasy/apprehensive about, call in question, query, question. **2** *doubt that it is genuine* have doubts, be dubious, hesitate to believe, feel uncertain, be undecided, lack conviction, have scruples, query, question, challenge. **3** *still doubting last week* have doubts, be undecided, hesitate, waver, vacillate, demur.

doubt n **1** *have doubts about his motives* distrust, mistrust, lack of confidence/faith, scepticism, uneasiness, apprehension; reservations, misgivings, suspicions, qualms. **2** *express doubt that it is genuine* dubiety, dubiousness, lack of certainty, uncertainty, indecision, lack of conviction, incredulity; queries, questions. **3** *full of doubts/doubt about his faith* uncertainty, indecision, hesitation; hesitancy, wavering, vacillation, irresolution, lack of conviction, demurral. **in doubt** *the issue is still in doubt | he is in doubt about it* doubtful, uncertain, undecided, unsettled, unresolved, confused, open to question, ambiguous, problematic; in a quandary/dilemma. **no doubt** *no doubt he will win* doubtless, certainly, of course, surely, assuredly, admittedly, probably, it is likely that.

doubter n sceptic, questioner, disbeliever, doubting Thomas, unbeliever, agnostic, scoffer, dissenter, pessimist, doomster.

doubtful adj **1** *it is doubtful that he will come* in doubt, uncertain, unsure, unconfirmed, unsettled, improbable, unlikely. **2** *doubtful of/about his motives* suspicious, distrustful, mistrustful, sceptical, having reservations/misgivings, apprehensive, uneasy, questioning, unsure, incredulous. **3** *its genuineness is doubtful* uncertain, dubious, open to question, questionable, debatable, disputable, not definite, inconclusive, unresolved, unconfirmed, unsettled. **4** *the meaning of the word is doubtful* dubious, unclear, ambiguous, equivocal, obscure, vague, nebulous. **5** *doubtful about his religious convictions* uncertain, indecisive, hesitating, irresolute, wavering, vacillating. **6** *mixing with doubtful people* dubious, questionable, suspicious, suspect, under suspicion, unreliable, potentially disreputable.

doubtless adv undoubtedly, without doubt, no doubt, of course, certainly, truly, assuredly, surely, positively, beyond a doubt, unquestionably, indisputably, clearly, obviously, very probably, very/most likely, presumably.

dour adj unsmiling, sullen, morose, sour, gruff, churlish, uncommunicative, unfriendly, forbidding, grim, stern, severe, austere, harsh, dismal, dreary, gloomy.

douse, dowse v **1** *douse the walls with soapy water* drench, saturate, soak, souse, flood, deluge, wet, splash, hose down. **2** *douse the clothes in the tub* plunge, immerse, submerge, dip, dunk. **3** *douse the light* extinguish, put out, blow out, quench, snuff.

dovetail v **1** *dovetail the pieces of wood* join, unite, fit, fit together, link, interlock, splice, mortise, tenon. **2** *our plans dovetailed with theirs* fit in, go together, coincide, go hand in glove, fall in, correspond, concur, agree, tally, accord, harmonize.

dowdy adj *dowdy clothes/people* frumpish, frumpy, drab, dull, old-fashioned, unfashionable, not smart, inelegant, shabby, untidy, dingy, frowzy; *inf* tacky.

down¹ adv **1** *the lift going down* to a lower point/part, to a low point, in a lower place/position. **2** *fall down* to the ground, to the floor, below, beneath.

down¹ prep **1** *walk down the street* to a lower part of, along, through. **2** *down the centuries* through, throughout.

down¹ adj **1** *feeling down* downcast, downhearted, dejected, depressed, sad, unhappy, miserable, wretched, low, blue, gloomy, melancholy; *inf* down in the mouth/dumps. **2** *the computer is down* not working, non-functioning, inoperative.

down¹ v **1** *down three of the enemy* knock/throw/bring down, floor, fell, prostrate, tackle, trip up, overthrow, defeat, conquer, subdue. **2** *down three pints* drink, gulp down, swallow, drain, toss off, put away; *inf* swill.

down¹ n *having a down | ups and downs* fit/period of depression, unpleasant time, reversal, setback, comedown. **have a down on** be against, be prejudiced against, be set against, bear a grudge towards, show antagonism to, be hostile to, show/feel ill-will towards.

down² n fluff, fuzz, bloom, soft feathers, fine hair.

down-at-heel adj shabby, shabbily-dressed, poorly-dresed, out-at-elbows, seedy, run-down, slovenly, slipshod.

downbeat adj **1** *bored and downbeat* down, downcast, low, depressed, dejected, miserable, gloomy, pessimistic. **2** *talk in a downbeat manner* relaxed, nonchalant, casual, non-emphatic, insouciant, blasé; *inf* laid-back.

downcast adj *downcast at the news* disheartened, dispirited, downhearted, dejected, depressed, discouraged, daunted, dismayed, disappointed, disconsolate, crestfallen, despondent, sad, unhappy, miserable, wretched, down, low, blue, gloomy, glum, melancholy, sorrowful, doleful, mournful.

downfall n **1** *the downfall of the leader* loss of power/prestige/wealth, fall, collapse, undoing, ruin, ruination, crash, destruction, debasement, degradation, disgrace, overthrow, defeat. **2** *soaked in a downfall* downpour, rainstorm, snowstorm, heavy rain/snow, deluge, cloudburst. *see* DOWNPOUR.

downgrade v **1** *downgrade the office-bearers* demote, reduce in rank, remove from office, degrade, humble, debase; *inf* take down a peg or two. **2** *downgrade their achievement* disparage, denigrate, detract from, run down, decry, belittle, make light of, minimize, defame; *Amer inf* bad-mouth.

downhearted adj disheartened, dispirited, downcast, dejected, depressed, discouraged, daunted, dismayed, disappointed, disconsolate, crestfallen, despondent. *see* DOWNCAST.

downpour n rainstorm, snowstorm, deluge, torrential/pouring rain, cloudburst, downfall; torrents of rain.

downright adj **1** *a downright lie* complete, total, absolute, out and out, outright, utter, sheer, thorough, thoroughgoing, categorical, unmitigated, unqualified, unconditional, positive, simple, wholesale, all out, arrant, rank. **2** *a very downright person* frank, forthright, straightforward, open, candid, plain-spoken, matter-of-fact, outspoken, blunt, bluff, brusque.

downright adv *downright rude* completely, totally, absolutely, utterly, thoroughly, profoundly, categorically, positively.

down-to-earth adj practical, sensible, realistic, matter-of-fact, no-nonsense, hard-headed, sane, mundane, unromantic, unidealistic.

downtrodden adj oppressed, burdened, weighed down, overwhelmed, tyrannized, ground down, under the heel, helpless, powerless, prostrate, poor, miserable, wretched, distressed.

downward adj going down, moving down, descending, sliding down, earthbound.

dowry n marriage portion/settlement, *dot*; *Scots* tocher.

doze v sleep lightly, nap, take a nap, catnap, slumber, take a siesta; *inf* nod off, drift off, snooze, have a snooze, snatch forty winks, kip, get some kip/shut-eye, zizz, have a zizz.

drab adj **1** *drab clothes/surroundings* dull, dull-coloured, colourless, mousy, dun-coloured, grey, greyish, dingy, dreary, dismal, cheerless, gloomy, sombre, depressing. **2** *a drab talk* uninteresting, boring, tedious, dry, dreary, lifeless, lacklustre, uninspired; *Scots inf* dreich.

draft n **1** *a draft of the speech* preliminary version, rough sketch, outline, plan, skeleton, abstract. **2** *a draft of the new building* plan, sketch, drawing, line drawing, diagram, blueprint, delineation. **3** *a bank draft* money order, cheque, bill of exchange, postal order.

drag v **1** *drag the body from the sea* haul, pull, draw, tug, yank, trail, tow, lug. **2** *time dragged* go/move slowly, creep/limp along, crawl, go at a snail's pace. **3** *the film dragged* | *his lecture dragged on* go on too long, go on and on, become tedious. **drag out** *drag out the lecture* protract, prolong, draw out, spin out, stretch out, lengthen, extend.

drag n *the child/job is a drag* nuisance, source of annoyance, pest, trouble, bother, bore; *inf* pain in the neck.

dragoon n cavalryman, mounted soldier.

dragoon v *dragoon them into helping* force, coerce, compel, drive, impel, constrain, browbeat, bully, tyrannize; *inf* strong-arm, put the screws on.

drain v **1** *drain the water from the tank* draw off, extract, withdraw, remove, pump off, milk, bleed, tap, filter. **2** *drain the tank* empty, void, evacuate. **3** *the liquid drained away* flow out, ooze, trickle, seep out, well out, leak, discharge, exude, effuse. **4** *legal costs draining resources* use up, exhaust, deplete, consume, expend, empty, sap, strain, tax, bleed. **5** *drain a drink* drink up, finish, gulp down, swallow, quaff; *inf* down.

drain n **1** *a sewage drain* channel, conduit, culvert, duct, gutter, sewer, trench, ditch, dyke, pipe, outlet. **2** *a drain on resources* exhaustion, depletion, consumption, expenditure, outflow, sapping, strain, tax.

drama n **1** *studying drama* dramatic art, stagecraft, theatre, acting, dramaturgy, dramatics. **2** *a Restoration drama* play, show; stage play, screenplay, radio play, television play, stage show, theatrical work, theatrical piece. **3** *the drama at the police station* exciting/emotional scene, thrilling/tense/ sensational spectacle, excitement, crisis; dramatics, theatrics, histrionics.

dramatic adj **1** *dramatic art* theatrical, stage, dramaturgic, Thespian. **2** *dramatic scenes in court* exciting, sensational, spectacular, startling, unexpected, thrilling, tense, suspenseful, electrifying, stirring, affecting. **3** *a dramatic view/description* striking, impressive, vivid, spectacular, breathtaking, moving, affecting, emotive, graphic, effective, powerful. **4** *a dramatic gesture* theatrical, artificial, exaggerated, overdone, stagy, histrionic.

dramatist n playwright, scriptwriter, screenwriter, tragedy writer, comedy writer, dramaturgist, dramaturge.

dramatize v **1** *dramatize the novel* turn/adapt into a play, make a stage/screen play of, put into dramatic form. **2** *dramatize the incident* exaggerate, make a drama/performance of, overdo, overstate; *inf* lay it on thick, ham up.

drape v **1** *drape the walls in tapestry* cover, envelope, swathe, blanket, overlay, cloak, veil, shroud, decorate, adorn, array, deck, festoon. **2** *drape a shawl round her* hang, arrange, let fall in folds. **3** *drape an arm on the chair* hang, let fall, place loosely, lean, dangle, droop.

drastic adj extreme, severe, desperate, dire, radical, harsh, sharp, forceful, rigorous, Draconian.

draw v **1** *draw a chair up | draw the table away* pull, haul, tow, trail, tug, yank, lug. **2** *draw alongside/level | drew to a close* move, go, come, proceed, approach. **3** *draw a sword/gun* pull out, take out, bring out, extract, withdraw, produce, unsheathe. **4** *draw curtains* shut, close, pull together. **5** *draw attention | draw large crowds* attract, allure, lure, entice, invite, engage, interest, win, catch the eye of, capture, captivate, fascinate, tempt, seduce. **6** *draw a breath* breathe in, inhale, suck in, inspire, respire. **7** *draw a salary* take, take in, receive, be in receipt of, get, procure, obtain, earn. **8** *draw a conclusion* deduce, infer, conclude, derive, gather, glean. **9** *draw liquid* drain, siphon off, pump off, tap, milk, bleed, filtrate. **10** *draw lots/straws* choose, pick, select, opt for, make a choice of, decide on, single out. **11** *draw a house | she loved to draw in the garden* make a drawing of, sketch, make a picture/diagram of, portray, depict, delineate, represent, trace, map out, mark out, chart, paint, design; make drawings/pictures. **12** *draw a document* compose, formulate, write out. *see* DRAW v draw up 2. **draw on** *draw on experience* make use of, use, have recourse to, exploit, employ, rely on, back on. **draw out 1** *draw out a gun* pull out. *see* DRAW v 3. **2** *draw out the talk* prolong, protract, extend, lengthen, stretch out, drag out, spin out, make go on and on. **3** *draw the child out* induce to talk, persuade to speak, put at ease. **draw up 1** *draw up at the kerb* pull up, come to a halt/stop, halt, stop, rein in. **2** *draw up a document | draw up a set of rules* compose, formulate, frame, write out, put in writing, put down on paper, draft, prepare. **3** *troops drawn up for battle* arrange, put into position, order, marshal, range, rank.

draw n **1** *the draw of the circus* attraction, lure, allure, pull, enticement, magnetism. **2** *there will be a draw at the dance* lottery, raffle, sweepstake. **3** *the match ended in a draw* tie, dead heat, stalemate.

drawback n disadvantage, snag, catch, problem, difficulty, trouble, flaw, hitch, stumbling-block, handicap, hindrance, obstacle, impediment, hurdle, obstruction, barrier, curb, check, discouragement, deterrent, damper, inconvenience, nuisance, detriment, fault, weak spot, weakness, imperfection, defect; *inf* fly in the ointment.

drawing n sketch, picture, illustration, representation, portrayal, delineation, depiction, composition, study, diagram, outline.

drawl v speak slowly, draw out one's vowels/speech, twang, drone.

drawn adj *pale and drawn* pinched, haggard, hollow-cheeked, strained, tense, taut, stressed, fraught, fatigued, tired, worn, drained, wan, sapped.

dread v *dread the bully's arrival* fear, be afraid of, be terrified by, worry about, be anxious about, have forebodings about, tremble/shudder about, cringe/shrink from, quail/cower/flinch from; *inf* have cold feet about, be in a blue funk about.

dread n fear, fearfulness, fright, alarm, terror, apprehension, trepidation, horror, anxiety, concern, foreboding, dismay, perturbation, trembling, shuddering, flinching; *inf* blue funk, heebie-jeebies. *see* DREAD v.

dread adj *the dread monster/exams* dreaded, feared, frightening, alarming, terrifying, frightful, terrible, horrible, dreadful, awful, dire, awesome.

dreadful adj **1** *a dreadful sight/accident* terrible, frightful, horrible, grim, awful, dire, frightening, terrifying, alarming, distressing, shocking, appalling, harrowing, ghastly, fearful, hideous, horrendous, gruesome, tragic, calamitous, grievous. **2** *a dreadful man to deal with | dreadful weather spoiled the picnic* nasty, unpleasant, disagreeable, frightful, shocking, very bad, distasteful, repugnant, odious. **3** *a dreadful waste of time* shocking, outrageous, inordinate, great, tremendous.

dream n **1** *saw his mother in a dream* dream sequence, nightmare; vision, fantasy, hallucination. *see* DREAM v 1, 2. **2** *his dream to become rich* ambition, aspiration, goal, design, plan, aim, hope, yearning, desire, wish, notion, daydream, fantasy; castles in the air, castles in Spain. **3** *the bride was a dream* beauty, vision of loveliness, vision, delight, pleasure to behold, joy, marvel. **4** *go around in a dream* daydream, reverie, state of unreality, trance, daze, stupor; *Scots* dwam.

dream v **1** *dream at night* have dreams/ nightmares. **2** *he thought he saw a ghost but he was dreaming* hallucinate, have a vision, imagine things, fantasize. **3** *she was dreaming instead of working* daydream, be in a trance/reverie, be lost in thought, muse, be preoccupied, be abstracted. **4** *not dream of upsetting them | never dream that they would go* think, consider, visualize, conceive, suppose. **dream up** *dream up new schemes* conjure up, think up, invent, concoct, devise, create, hatch, fabricate; *inf* cook up.

dreamer n daydreamer, visionary, fantasist, fantasizer, fantast, romantic, romancer, idealist, impractical/unrealistic person, theorizer, Utopian, Don Quixote.

dreamland n **1** *existing only in dreamland* land of make-believe, never-never land, fairyland, world of fantasy, cloudland, cloud-cuckoo-land. **2** *children in dreamland* sleep, slumber, land of Nod.

dreamy adj **1** *a dreamy person* visionary, fanciful, fantasizing, romantic, idealistic, impractical, unrealistic, theorizing, daydreaming, quixotic. **2** *in a dreamy mood* daydreaming, thoughtful, lost in thought, pensive, speculative, preoccupied, abstracted, absent-minded, in a brown study, with one's head in the clouds. **3** *a dreamy recollection of the events* dreamlike, vague, dim, hazy, shadowy, misty, faint, indistinct, unclear. **4** *dreamy music* romantic, relaxing, soothing, calming, lulling, gentle, tranquil, peaceful. **5** *a dreamy young man | a dreamy dress* wonderful, marvellous, terrific, fabulous, heavenly; *inf* fab, wicked.

dreary adj **1** *a dreary day* gloomy, dismal, bleak, sombre, dull, dark, overcast, depressing. **2** *lead a dreary life* dull, drab, uninteresting, flat, dry, colourless, lifeless, tedious, wearisome, boring, humdrum, routine, monotonous, uneventful, run-of-the-mill, prosaic, commonplace, unvaried, repetitive. **3** *in a dreary frame of mind* gloomy, glum, sad, miserable, wretched, downcast, dejected, depressed, despondent, doleful, mournful, melancholic.

dregs npl **1** *the dregs of the wine* sediment, deposit, residue, residuum, precipitate, sublimate, scum, debris, dross, detritus, refuse, draff; lees, grounds, scourings. **2** *the dregs of society* scum, riff-raff, rabble, refuse; down-and-outs, good-for-nothings, outcasts, dead-beats, tramps, vagrants.

drench v soak, saturate, permeate, drown, inundate, flood, steep, douse, souse, wet, slosh.

dress n **1** *wearing a black dress* frock, gown, garment, robe. **2** *with her dress in disarray* clothes, garments; clothing, attire, apparel, costume, outfit, ensemble, garb; *inf* gear, rig-out, get-up, togs, duds; *fml* habiliment. **3** *birds/trees in their winter dress* covering, outer covering, plumage, feathers, pelt.

dress v **1** *she was dressed in black* clothe, attire, garb, fit out, turn out, array, apparel, robe, accoutre. **2** *she dressed quickly* put on clothes, don clothes, slip into clothes. **3** *dress for dinner* change, wear formal clothes, put on evening dress. **4** *dress the Christmas tree* decorate, adorn, ornament, trim, furbish, deck, bedeck, embellish, array, rig, drape; *inf* trick out. **5** *dress poultry* prepare, get ready, clean. **6** *dress one's hair* comb, arrange, do, groom, put in order, straighten, adjust, preen; *inf* fix. **7** *dress a wound* cover, bandage, bind up, put a plaster on. **8** *dress troops* line up, put in line, align, straighten, arrange, put into order, dispose, set out. **9** *dress land/soil* till, cultivate, work, dig, plough, fertilize, manure. **dress down** reprimand, scold, upbraid, rebuke, reprove, berate, castigate, haul over the coals; *inf* tell off, carpet.

dress up 1 *dress up for the occasion* dress formally/smartly, wear evening dress; *inf* doll oneself up, dress to the nines, put on one's glad rags. **2** *dress the child up* dress smartly; *inf* doll up. **3** *dress up the plain garment | dress the room up* decorate, adorn, ornament, trim, embellish, titivate, beautify, prettify. **4** *dress up as Santa Claus | dress up for the fancy dress party* put on fancy dress, put on a disguise, disguise oneself, wear disguise.

dressing n **1** *a dressing for the salad/fish* relish, sauce, condiment; oil and vinegar, French dressing. **2** *put a dressing on the wound* covering, bandage, plaster, gauze; *Trademark* Elastoplast. **3** *a top dressing on the soil* fertilizer, manure; dung.

dressmaker n couturier, tailor, tailoress, modiste, seamstress, needlewoman.

dribble v **1** *water dribbling from the tap* drip, trickle, fall in drops, drop, leak, ooze, exude, seep. **2** *the baby's dribbling* drool, slaver, slobber; *Scots* slabber.

dribble n *a dribble of water* trickle, drip, small stream.

drift v **1** *boats/leaves drifting along* be carried along/away, be borne, be wafted, float, go with the current, coast. **2** *people drifting about* wander aimlessly, wander, roam, rove, meander, coast, stray. **3** *snow drifting* pile up, bank up, accumulate, gather, form heaps, amass.

drift n **1** *a drift to the right* movement, deviation, digression, variation. **2** *the drift of his* *argument* gist, essence, meaning, substance, core, significance, import, purport, tenor, vein, implication, direction, course, tendency, trend. **3** *a snow drift* pile, heap, bank, mound, mass, accumulation.

drill v **1** *drill the new recruits* train, instruct, coach, teach, ground, inculcate, discipline, exercise, rehearse, put one through one's paces. **2** *drill the wood* bore/make a hole in, bore, pierce, puncture, penetrate, perforate.

drill n **1** *military drill* training, instruction, coaching, teaching, grounding, indoctrination. *see* DRILL v 1. **2** *children doing drill* exercises, physical exercises; strict training, workout. **3** *not to know the drill* procedure, routine, practice. **4** *an electric drill* boring/drilling tool, revolving/rotary tool.

drink v **1** *drink the water* swallow, gulp down, drain, quaff, imbibe, partake of, swill, toss off, guzzle, sup, sip; *inf* swig. **2** *her husband drinks* take alcohol, be a serious/hard drinker, tipple, indulge, be an alcoholic; *inf* take a drop, hit the bottle, booze, knock a few back. **3** *drink one's health* drink to, toast, propose a toast to. **drink in** be absorbed/rapt/lost in, be fascinated by, pay close attention to. **drink to** toast, propose a toast to, wish success/luck/health to, salute.

drink n **1** *food and drink | water is the commonest drink* beverage, drinkable/potable liquid, liquid refreshment; alcoholic drink, soft drink, non-alcoholic drink, cold drink, hot drink, thirst-quencher. **2** *no drink at the dance* alcoholic/strong drink, alcohol, liquor, intoxicating liquor; spirits; *inf* booze, hard stuff, hooch. **3** *take a drink from the cup* swallow, gulp, sip, draught, swill; *inf* swig, slug. **4** *a drink of water* cup, glass, mug, container. **5** *the kids drowned in the drink* sea, ocean; *inf* briny.

drinkable adj fit to drink, potable.

drinker n social drinker, heavy/hard drinker, serious drinker, alcoholic, chronic alcoholic, problem drinker, alcohol-abuser, drunk, drunkard, dipsomaniac, tippler, toper, sot, inebriate, imbiber; *inf* boozer, soak, lush, wino, alky, sponge, elbow-bender.

drip v *water/blood/coffee is dripping* drop, dribble, trickle, splash, sprinkle, plop, leak, ooze, exude, filter, percolate.

drip n **1** *paint drips* drop, dribble, trickle, splash, plop, leak. **2** *a boring drip* ineffective person, weakling, ninny, milksop; *inf* weed, wet, wally.

drive v **1** *drive a car* operate, steer, handle, guide, direct, manage. **2** *we drove here* come/go/travel by car, motor; *inf* travel on wheels. **3** *he drove us here* chauffeur, run, give one a lift. **4** *drive cattle to the barn* move, get going, urge, press, push, impel, propel, herd, round-up. **5** *driven to steal/despair* force, compel, constrain, impel, oblige, coerce, make, pressure, goad, spur, prod. **6** *drove himself too hard* work, overwork, tax, overtax, overburden. **7** *drive the stake into the ground* hammer, ram, bang, sink, plunge, thrust, stab. **drive at 1** *what are you driving at?* mean, suggest, imply, infer, hint at, refer to, allude to, intimate, indicate, have in mind; *inf* get at. **2** *she drove at the task* work hard, hasten, rush.

drive n **1** *go for a drive* run, trip, jaunt, outing, journey, excursion, tour, turn; *Scots* hurl; *inf* spin, joyride. **2** *the tree-lined drive* driveway, road, roadway, avenue. **3** *a sales drive* effort, push, sales push, campaign, publicity campaign, crusade, surge. **4** *a young man with drive* energy, vigour, verve, ambition, push, enterprise, motivation, initiative, action, aggressiveness; *inf* get-up-and-go, zip, pizazz, punch.

drivel n **1** *speaking drivel* nonsense, twaddle, gibberish, balderdash, rubbish, stuff and nonsense, bunkum, mumbo-jumbo; *inf* rot, tommy rot, poppycock, garbage, tripe, waffle, bosh, bunk, blah, hogwash, crap. **2** *wipe away the drivel* saliva, drool, drooling, dribble, slaver, slobber.

drivel v **1** *drivel about the rules* talk nonsense/rubbish, babble, ramble, gibber, blather, blether, prate, maunder; *inf* waffle, witter on, gab, gabble, talk through one's hat. **2** *babies drivelling* drool, slaver, slobber, dribble; *Scots* slabber.

driver v **1** *passengers paying the driver | drivers of heavy vehicles* chauffeur, taxi-driver, cab-driver; operator; engine-driver, train-driver, bus-driver, lorry-driver, truck-driver. **2** *drivers charged with drink driving* car-driver, motorist.

drizzle n *a drizzle falling* fine rain, Scotch mist, sprinkle of rain, light shower; *dial* mizzle.

droll adj **1** funny, humorous, amusing, comic, comical, clownish, farcical, zany, laughable, ridiculous, ludicrous, risible, jocular, facetious, waggish, witty, whimsical, entertaining, diverting. **2** *a droll little girl* quaint, odd, strange, queer, eccentric, outlandish, bizarre, whimsical.

drone[1] v **1** *aircraft droning overhead* make a humming noise, hum, buzz, whirr, vibrate, murmur, purr, whisper, sigh. **2** *drone on* *about cutting costs* go on and on, speak monotonously/boringly, talk interminably, intone.

drone[1] n *the drone of aircraft* hum, buzz, whirr, whirring, vibration, purr, whispering, sigh.

drone[2] n *the workers and the drones in the firm* idler, loafer, layabout, lounger, do-nothing, sluggard, laggard, parasite, leech, hanger-on; *inf* lazybones, scroungers, sponger.

droop v **1** *flowers drooping* hang, hang down, bend, bow, stoop, sag, sink, slump, fall down, drop. **2** *drooping after the news | spirits drooping* be despondent, lose heart, give up hope, become dispirited/dejected, flag, fade, languish, falter, weaken, wilt, shrivel, wither, decline, diminish, deteriorate.

drop n **1** *a drop of water* droplet, globule, bead, bubble, blob, spheroid, oval. **2** *add just a drop* little, bit, dash, spot, dribble, driblet, splash, sprinkle, trickle, taste, trace, pinch, dab, speck, particle, modicum; *inf* smidgen; *Amer inf* tad. **3** *a drop in prices* decline, decrease, reduction, cut, cutback, lowering, falling-off, fall-off, downturn, depreciation, devaluation, mark, slump. **4** *the path ended in a sudden drop* descent, incline, declivity, slope, plunge; abyss, chasm, precipice, cliff.

drop v **1** *water dropping from the trees* fall in drops, fall, drip, dribble, trickle, plop, leak. **2** *the plane dropped out of the sky* drop down, fall, descend, plunge, plummet, dive, tumble. **3** *she dropped the parcel/ball* let fall/go, fail to hold. **4** *the girl dropped from exhaustion* fall/sink down, collapse, faint, swoon, drop/fall dead. **5** *prices dropped* fall, decrease, lessen, diminish, depreciate, go into decline, dwindle, sink, slacken off, plunge, plummet. **6** *drop singing lessons* give up, discontinue, end, stop, cease, terminate, finish with, withdraw/retire from, abandon, forgo, relinquish, dispense with, throw up. **7** *drop his girlfriend* desert, abandon, forsake, leave, throw over, jilt, discard, reject, repudiate, renounce, disown; *inf* ditch, chuck, run out on, leave flat. **8** *drop half the workforce* dismiss, discharge, let go, declare/make redundant; *inf* sack, fire, boot out. **9** *drop his aitches* omit, leave out, eliminate, elide, contract, slur. **drop off 1** *sales have dropped off* drop, fall, decrease, decline, plummet. *see* DROP v 5. **2** *drop the goods/passengers off* deliver, deposit, set down, unload, leave, put off, allow to alight. **3** *people dropping off* fall asleep, doze, doze off, have a nap, catnap, drowse; *inf* nod off, snooze, take forty winks, get some shut-eye. **drop out** *students*

dropping out of college give up, abandon, renounce, leave, quit, forsake, back out, withdraw from, renege on, turn one's back on.

drought n dry spell/period, lack of rain; *Scots* drouth.

drove n **1** *a drove of cattle/sheep/livestock* herd, flock, pack. **2** *droves of people going shopping* crowd, horde, swarm, multitude, mob, throng, host, collection, gathering, assembly, company, herd, crush, press, rabble.

drown v **1** *engineers drowning the valley* flood, submerge, immerse, inundate, deluge, swamp, engulf, drench. **2** *outside noise drowning her speech* drown out, make inaudible, muffle, be louder than, deaden, stifle, overpower, overwhelm, overcome, engulf, swallow up. **3** *drowning his grief in work* suppress, deaden, stifle, quash, quench, extinguish, obliterate, wipe out, get rid of.

drowsy adj **1** *feeling drowsy* sleepy, half-asleep, tired, weary, dozy, dozing, heavy, heavy-eyed, yawning, lethargic, sluggish, somnolent, slumberous, comatose, dazed, drugged; *inf* dopey. **2** *drowsy weather* sleepy, sleep-inducing, soporific, lulling, soothing, dreamy, somniferous.

drubbing n beating, thrashing, walloping, thumping, battering, trouncing, whipping, flogging, pounding, pummelling, bludgeoning; *inf* hammering, licking, clobbering, work-over, working-over.

drudge n *drudges working in the kitchen* menial, servant, slave, labourer, char, charwoman, hack, worker, toiler, maid/man of all work, general factotum; *inf* skivvy, dogsbody.

drudge v toil, labour, slave, plod on, grind/slog away, keep one's nose to the grindstone.

drudgery n menial/hard work, donkeywork, toiling, toil, labour, hard/sweated labour, slavery, hack work, plodding; chores; *inf* skivvying, grind, slog.

drug n **1** *a new cancer drug* medical drug, medicine, medication, medicament, remedy, cure, cure-all, panacea, physic, magic bullet. **2** *addicted to drugs* addictive drug, narcotic; opiate, barbiturate, amphetamine; hashish, marijuana, heroin, cocaine, ecstasy, LSD; *inf* dope, downer, upper, speed, grass, hash, pot, horse, the big H, smack, coke, crack, E, acid.

drug v **1** *drug the patient before the operation | drug the kidnapped child* anaesthetize, give an anaesthetic to, knock out, make/render unconscious, make/render insensible, stu-

drugged · duck

pefy, befuddle, narcotize; *inf* dope. **2** *drug the patient rather than give counselling* give/ administer drugs to, give medication/ medicament to, medicate, dose, treat.

drugged adj anaesthetized, knocked out, comatose, stupefied, insensible, befuddled, narcotized; *inf* doped, stoned, dopey, on a trip, spaced out, zonked, high, high as a kite, turned on, flying, charged up.

drum n tambour, tabor, kettledrum, bass drum, snare drum, war drum, tom-tom.

drum v **1** *drum on the table | drum one's fingers* tap, beat, rap, knock, strike, tattoo, thrum. **2** *drum information into pupils* drive home, din, instil, hammer, inculcate. **drum out** *drum out of the club/regiment* expel from, dismiss/discharge from, throw out, oust from. **drum up** *drum up business/support* gather, collect, round up, summon, obtain, get, attract, canvass, solicit, petition, bid for.

drunk adj *drunk after hours in the pub* drunken, drunk as a lord, blind drunk, dead drunk, intoxicated, inebriated, inebriate, the worse for drink, under the influence, tipsy, soused, befuddled, gin-soaked, maudlin, sottish, tippling, toping, bibulous, crapulent, crapulous; *inf* tight, tiddly, squiffy, merry, happy, woozy, pie-eyed, half-seas-over, one over the eight, three sheets to the wind, under the table, out of it, legless, plastered, smashed, paralytic, sloshed, pissed, stoned, well-oiled, sozzled, blotto, blitzed, lit up, canned, bevvied, stewed, pickled, tanked-up, soaked, bombed, liquored up, tired and emotional, steaming; *Scots inf* fou.

drunk n drunkard, inebriate, heavy/hard drinker, sot, toper, tippler, alcoholic, dipsomaniac, serious/problem drinker; *inf* soak, boozer, lush, alky, wino, elbow-bender.

drunken adj **1** *drunken party-goers* drunk, intoxicated, inebriated. *see* DRUNK adj. **2** *a drunken party* debauched, dissipated, riotous, carousing, revelling, intemperate, roistering, orgiastic, bacchanalian, bacchic, wassailing, dionysian, saturnalian.

drunkenness n intoxication, inebriation, inebriety, insobriety, tipsiness, intemperance, over-indulging, debauchery, hard drinking, serious drinking, alcoholism, alcohol abuse, dipsomania, sottishness, bibulousness, crapulence.

dry adj **1** *dry ground/regions* arid, dried up/ out, parched, scorched, dehydrated, desiccated, waterless, unwatered, moistureless, rainless, torrid, thirsty, droughty, barren, unproductive, sterile. **2** *dry leaves* withered, shrivelled, wilted, dehydrated, desiccated, wizened, sapless, juiceless. **3** *dry cheese* dried out, hard, hardened, stale. **4** *a dry talk* dull, uninteresting, boring, tedious, tiresome, wearisome, dreary, monotonous, flat, unimaginative, commonplace, prosaic, run-of-the-mill, humdrum, vapid; *Scots inf* dreich. **5** *a dry wit* subtle, low-key, deadpan, laconic, sly, sharp, ironic, sarcastic, satirical, cynical, droll, waggish. **6** *a dry response/ greeting* unemotional, indifferent, cool, cold, aloof, remote, impersonal. **7** *a dry state* prohibitionist, teetotal, alcohol-free.

dry v **1** *the sun drying the earth* make dry, dry out/up, parch, scorch, dehydrate, desiccate, dehumidify, sear. **2** *the sun drying the leaves* dry up, wither, shrivel, wilt, dehydrate, desiccate, wizen, mummify. **3** *dry meat* dehydrate, desiccate, preserve, cure. **4** *dry the wet patch* dry off, mop up, blot up, towel, drain. **dry up 1** *dry up the ground* parch, scorch, dehydrate. *see* DRY v 1. **2** *dry up leaves/skin* wither, shrivel, wizen, mummify. *see* DRY v 2. **3** *inspiration dried up* fail, become unproductive, grow barren/sterile, cease to yield. **4** *actors drying up | she dried up at the sight* stop speaking/talking, forget one's lines/words, shut up.

dual adj double, twofold, duplicate, duplex, binary, twin, matched, paired, coupled.

dub v **1** *dubbed the greatest jazz singer* call, name, christen, designate, term, entitle, style, label, denominate, nominate, tag, nickname. **2** *queen dubbing a courtier* knight, confer/bestow a knighthood on, invest with a knighthood.

dubiety n doubtfulness, uncertainty, lack of certainty, unsureness, hesitancy, dubiosity, incertitude; doubt.

dubious adj **1** *dubious about going* doubtful, uncertain, unsure, hesitant, undecided, wavering, vacillating, irresolute, on the horns of a dilemma, sceptical, suspicious; *inf* iffy. **2** *the outcome is dubious* doubtful, undecided, unsure, unsettled, undetermined, indefinite, unresolved, up in the air, open, equivocal, debatable, questionable. **3** *give a dubious reply* equivocal, ambiguous, indeterminate, indefinite, unclear, vague, imprecise, hazy, puzzling, enigmatic, cryptic. **4** *a dubious character* questionable, suspicious, suspect, under suspicion, untrustworthy, unreliable, undependable; *inf* shady, fishy.

duck v **1** *duck behind the wall* bend, bow down, bob down, stoop, crouch, squat, hunch down, hunker down. **2** *duck one's head* bow, lower, drop. **3** *duck him in the pond* immerse, submerge, plunge, dip, souse, douse, dunk. **4** *duck the police/work* dodge, evade, sidestep, avoid, steer clear of, elude, escape, shirk, shun.

duct n pipe, tube, conduit, channel, passage, canal, culvert.

ductile adj **1** *a ductile substance* pliable, pliant, flexible, plastic, malleable, tensile. **2** *ductile people* pliable, malleable, compliant, tractable, manipulable, docile, accommodating, cooperative, gullible.

dud n *the lightbulb/teacher is a dud* failure, flop; *inf* wash-out, lemon, loser.

dud adj *a dud lightbulb/teacher* defective, broken, not working, not functioning, inoperative, ineffectual, failed, worthless; *inf* bust, kaput, duff.

dudgeon n **in high dudgeon** angry, annoyed, furious, in a temper, indignant, enraged, fuming, vexed, offended, resentful; *inf* peeved.

due adj **1** *money/thanks due to them* owing, owed, payable, payable now, receivable immediately, outstanding. **2** *recognition due to a hero* deserved by, merited by, earned by, justified by, appropriate to, fit for, fitting to, suitable for, right for. **3** *treat with due respect* proper, right and proper, correct, rightful, fitting, appropriate, apt, adequate, sufficient, enough, ample, satisfactory, requisite, apposite. **4** *the essay is due tomorrow* scheduled, expected, required, awaited, anticipated. **due to** *due to uncertainty* attributable to, ascribed to, ascribable to, caused by, assignable to, because of.

due adv *due north* directly, straight, without deviating, undeviatingly, dead, exactly.

due n *receive only his due* rightful treatment; rights, just deserts, deserts; *inf* comeuppance.

duel n **1** *challenge his rival to a duel* affair of honour; single combat. **2** *engage in a duel of wits* contest, competition, struggle, clash, battle, fight, encounter, engagement.

dues npl *pay one's dues to the club* fee, membership fee, subscription, charge, levy; charges.

duffer n bungler, blunderer, oaf, fool, dunce, numskull, dunderhead, booby; *inf* galoot, wally.

dulcet adj sweet, melodious, musical, lyrical, silver-toned, euphonious, pleasant, agreeable, soothing, mellow.

dull adj **1** *dull of wit* dull-witted, slow, slow-witted, unintelligent, stupid, dense, doltish, stolid, vacuous; *inf* dim, dim-witted, thick, dumb, bird-brained. **2** *a dull reaction to others' pain* insensitive, unfeeling,

unemotional, indifferent, unsympathetic, unresponsive, apathetic, blank, uncaring, passionless, callous. **3** *feeling dull in the winter* inactive, inert, slow, slow-moving, sleepy, drowsy, idle, sluggish, stagnant, lethargic, listless, languid, heavy, apathetic, torpid, phlegmatic, vegetative. **4** *trade is dull* slow, slack, sluggish, stagnant, depressed. **5** *a dull speech* dull as dishwater, uninteresting, boring, tedious, tiresome, wearisome, dry, monotonous, flat, bland, unimaginative, commonplace, prosaic, run-of-the-mill, humdrum, uneventful, vapid; *Scots inf* dreich. **6** *dull weather* overcast, cloudy, gloomy, dark, dim, dismal, dreary, bleak, sombre, leaden, murky, sunless, lowering. **7** *dull colours* drab, dreary, sombre, dark, subdued, muted, toned-down, lacklustre, lustreless, colourless, faded, washed-out; *fml* subfusc. **8** *a dull sound* muffled, muted, indistinct, feeble. **9** *a dull edge* blunt, blunted, not sharp, unkeen, unsharpened, dulled, edgeless.

dull v **1** *dull the appetite | dulled their grief* take the edge off, blunt, lessen, decrease, diminish, reduce, deaden, mute, tone down, allay, ease, soothe, assuage, alleviate, palliate. **2** *drugs dulling the senses* numb, benumb, stupefy, drug, sedate, tranquillize, narcotize. **3** *time dulling the colours* fade, bleach, wash out, decolourize, decolour. **4** *the sky dulled by clouds* darken, dim, bedim, obscure. **5** *spirits dulled by the bad news* dispirit, dishearten, depress, deject, sadden, discourage, cast down, dampen, put a damper on, cast a pall over.

duly adv **1** *suggestions duly noted* in due manner, properly, correctly, rightly, fittingly, appropriately. **2** *he duly arrived* in due time, at the proper/right time, on time, punctually.

dumb adj **1** *dumb from birth* without speech, mute. **2** *struck dumb at the sight* speechless, wordless, silent, mute, at a loss for words, voiceless, soundless, inarticulate, taciturn, uncommunicative, tongue-tied; *inf* mum. **3** *dumb people and clever people* stupid, dull, dull-witted, slow, slow-witted, unintelligent, dense, foolish, doltish; *inf* dim, dim-witted, thick.

dumbfound v astound, astonish, amaze, startle, surprise, stun, take aback, stagger, overwhelm, confound, shock, confuse, bewilder, baffle, nonplus, perplex, disconcert; *inf* flabbergast, throw, shake, knock for six, knock sideways.

dummy n **1** *a tailor's/ventriloquist's dummy* lifelike model, mannequin, manikin, figure, lay figure. **2** *not a real book/shoe, just a dummy* representation, reproduction, sample, copy, imitation, counterfeit, sham, substitute. **3** *that dummy can't do anything* idiot, fool, dolt, dunce, blockhead, numskull, oaf, nincompoop, ninny, ass, donkey, dullard; *inf* clot, nitwit, dim-wit, dope, chump, bonehead, jerk; *Amer inf* airhead, schmuck.

dump v **1** *dump the goods on the floor* place, put, put down, lay down, deposit, drop, let fall, throw down, fling down. **2** *dump the unwanted goods* dispose of, get rid of, throw away/out, scrap, jettison. **3** *the tanker dumped its load* discharge, empty out, pour out, tip out, unload, jettison. **4** *dump his wife* abandon, desert, leave, leave in the lurch, forsake, walk out on.

dump n **1** *take the debris to the dump* refuse/ rubbish dump, tip, rubbish tip, rubbish heap, junkyard, scrapyard; *Scots* midden. **2** *what a dump!* hovel, shack, slum, shanty, pigsty; *Scots* bothy; *inf* hole, joint.

dumps npl **in the dumps** depressed, dejected, gloomy, despondent, downcast, disconsolate, melancholic; *inf* blue.

dun v *dun people for payment* press, importune, pressurize, solicit, plague, pester, nag, beset.

dun adj *dun-coloured horses* greyish-brown, mud-coloured, muddy, khaki, umber.

dunce n dolt, blockhead, dunderhead, thickhead, numskull, nincompoop, ninny, simpleton, halfwit, idiot, moron, ass, donkey, ignoramus, dullard; *inf* dim-wit, dummy, bonehead, deadhead.

dungeon n underground cell, cell, lock-up, black hole, oubliette; donjon, keep.

duplicate adj *a duplicate set of keys* identical, twin, matching, matched, paired, corresponding, twofold.

duplicate n **1** *a duplicate of the chair* copy, replica, facsimile, reproduction, exact/close likeness, twin, double, clone, match, mate, fellow, counterpart; *inf* lookalike, spitting image, ringer, dead ringer. **2** *make a duplicate of the document* copy, carbon copy, carbon, photocopy, facsimile, fax; *Trademark* Photostat, Xerox.

duplicate v **1** *duplicate the documents* copy, make a carbon/facsimile of, photocopy, fax, reproduce, make a replica of, replicate, clone; *Trademark* Photostat, Xerox. **2** *duplicate the task* repeat, do over again, perform again, replicate.

duplicity n deceitfulness, double-dealing, trickery, guile, chicanery, artifice, dishonesty, knavery, two-facedness.

durable adj **1** *durable affection* lasting, long-lasting, enduring, persisting, persistent, abiding, continuing, constant, stable, fast, firm, fixed, permanent, unfading, changeless, unchanging, invariable, dependable, reliable. **2** *durable clothing/goods* long-lasting, hard-wearing, strong, sturdy, sound, tough, resistant, substantial, imperishable.

duress n **1** *sent away under duress* force, compulsion, coercion, pressure, pressurization, constraint, arm-twisting, enforcement, exaction. **2** *prisoners of war kept in duress* imprisonment, confinement, incarceration, detention, custody, captivity, restraint, constraint, bondage.

during conj throughout, through, throughout the time of, for the time of, in, within.

dusk n twilight, evening, sunset, sundown, nightfall; dark, gloom, murk; *dial* gloaming, eventide.

dusky adj **1** *dusky maidens* dark, dark-skinned, dark-complexioned, dark-coloured, olive-skinned, swarthy. **2** *dusky light* shadowy, dim, dark, darkish, gloomy, murky, cloudy, misty, hazy, foggy, crepuscular, tenebrous.

dust n **1** *dust on the furniture* fine powder, dirt, grime, smut, soot. **2** *kneel in the dust* ground, earth, soil, dirt, clay. **3** *kick up a dust* fuss, row, commotion, disturbance, uproar, fracas, rumpus, racket.

dust v **1** *dust the furniture* wipe, brush, flick clean, clean, mop. **2** *dust with icing sugar* sprinkle, dredge, sift, scatter, powder, spray, cover, spread, strew.

dusty adj **1** *a dusty room* dust-covered, dust-filled, undusted, dirty, grubby, grimy, unclean, sooty. **2** *a dusty substance* powdery, chalky, crumbly, friable. **3** *a dusty pink* greyish, muted, dull, pale. **4** *a dusty answer* curt, abrupt, terse, bad-tempered, unhelpful, rejecting.

dutiful adj respectful, filial, deferential, reverent, reverential, conscientious, devoted, considerate, thoughtful, obedient, compliant, pliant, docile, submissive.

duty n **1** *a sense of duty to one's country/parents* responsibility, obligation, obedience, allegiance, loyalty, faithfulness, fidelity, respect, deference, reverence, homage. **2** *share out the duties* task, job, chore, assignment, commission, mission, function, office, charge, part, role, requirement, responsibility, obligation; work, burden, onus. **3** *pay duty* tax, levy, tariff, excise, toll, fee, impost; customs, dues. **off duty** not working, at leisure, on holiday, off, off work, free. **on duty** at work, working, busy, occupied, engaged, tied up; *inf* on the job.

dwarf v **1** *dwarfed by the effects of a drug* stunt, arrest/check growth, atrophy, bedwarf. **2** *a novelist dwarfing his contemporaries* tower above/over, overshadow, stand head and shoulders over, dominate, overtop. **3** *their efforts dwarfing his* overshadow, diminish, minimize.

dwell v *dwell in Kensington* reside, live, be domiciled, lodge, stay, abide; *inf* hang out. **dwell on/upon** *dwell on details/complaints* spend time on, linger over, harp on, discuss at length, expatiate on, elaborate on, expound on, keep talking/writing about, be preoccupied by, be obsessed by.

dwelling n dwelling-place, residence, home, house, abode, domicile, establishment.

dwindle v **1** *savings/hope dwindling* become/grow less, become/grow smaller, decrease, lessen, diminish, shrink, contract, fade, wane. **2** *the Roman empire dwindling* decline, fail, sink, ebb, wane, degenerate, deteriorate, decay, wither, rot, disappear, vanish, die out; *inf* peter out.

dye n **1** *dip the dress in a dye* colourant, colouring agent, colouring, pigment, tint,

stain, wash. **2** *of a green dye* colour, shade, hue, tint.

dye v *dye a dress* colour, tint, pigment, shade, stain.

dyed-in-the-wool adj entrenched, inveterate, established, deep-rooted, confirmed, complete, absolute, through and through, utter, thorough-going.

dying adj **1** *a dying woman* terminally ill, at death's door, breathing one's last, on one's deathbed, in the jaws of death, having one foot in the grave, passing away, sinking fast, expiring, moribund, *in extremis*; *inf* on one's/it's last legs. **2** *dying customs* passing, fading, vanishing, failing, ebbing, waning. **3** *dying words* final, last.

dynamic adj energetic, active, lively, alive, spirited, vital, vigorous, strong, forceful, powerful, potent, effective, effectual, high-powered, magnetic, aggressive, go-ahead, driving, electric; *inf* go-getting, zippy, peppy.

dynasty n line, succession, house, regime, rule, reign, dominion, empire; sovereignty, ascendancy, government, authority, administration, jurisdiction.

each adj *each pupil received a book* every, every single.

each pron *each was nastier than the other* each one, every one, each and every one, one and all.

each adv *give a pound each* apiece, per person, per capita, to each, for each, from each, individually.

eager adj **1** *eager pupils* keen, enthusiastic, impatient, avid, fervent, earnest, diligent, zealous, passionate, wholehearted, ambitious, enterprising; *inf*bright-eyed and bushy-tailed. **2** *eager to learn* | *eager for news* agog, anxious, intent, longing, yearning, itching, wishing, desirous, hopeful, thirsty, hungry, greedy; *inf* hot.

eagerness n keenness, enthusiasm, impatience, avidity, fervour, earnestness, diligence, zeal, passion, wholeheartedness, desire, longing, yearning, wishing, itch, hope, thirst, hunger, greed, ambition, enterprise. see EAGER.

ear n **1** *an infection of the ear* inner ear, middle ear, external ear, outer ear. **2** *have the ear of the king* attention, attentiveness, notice, heed, regard, consideration. **3** *an ear for a good song/musical* appreciation, discrimination, perception, musical taste.

early adv **1** *get up and set off early* early in the day, in the early morning, at dawn, at daybreak, at cock-crow, with the lark. **2** *guests should not arrive early* ahead of time, too soon, beforehand, before the usual/appointed time, prematurely. **3** *you should arrive early for the interview* in good time, before the appointed time, ahead of schedule.

early adj **1** *an early crop/birth* advanced, forward, premature, precocious, untimely. **2** *an early reply* prompt, without delay, quick, speedy, rapid, fast, expeditious, timely. **3** *early man/settlements* primitive, primeval, primordial, prehistoric, autochthonous.

earmark v *earmark the money for a holiday* set/lay aside, keep back, allocate, reserve, designate, label, tag.

earn v **1** *earn a good salary* make, get, receive, obtain, draw, clear, collect, bring in, take home, pull in, pocket, gross, net. **2** *earn their admiration* gain, win, rate, merit, attain, achieve, secure, obtain, deserve, be entitled to, be worthy of, have a right to, warrant.

earnest[1] adj **1** *an earnest young man* serious, solemn, grave, intense, staid, studious, thoughtful, committed, dedicated, assiduous, keen, diligent, zealous, steady, hardworking. **2** *her earnest request/hope* sincere, fervent, fervid, ardent, passionate, warm, intense, heartfelt, wholehearted, profound, enthusiastic, zealous, urgent.

earnest[1] n **in earnest 1** *he was in earnest about the punishment* serious, not joking, unsmiling, sincere. **2** *they set to work in earnest* zealously, ardently, fervently, fervidly, passionately, wholeheartedly, with dedication/commitment, determinedly, resolutely.

earnest[2] n *as earnest of my intent* guarantee, pledge, promise, security, token, deposit, down payment.

earnings npl income, salary, wage, pay, take-home pay, gross/net pay, remuneration, emolument, fee, stipend, honorarium, revenue, yield, profit, gain, return; wages, fringe benefits ; *inf* perks.

earth n **1** *earth, moon and stars* globe, world, planet, sphere, orb. **2** *dig up the earth* soil, loam, clay, dirt, sod, clod, turf, ground. **3** *between the earth and the sky* ground, dry ground, land.

earthenware n pottery, crockery, stoneware; pots, crocks, ceramics.

earthly adj **1** *earthly beings* terrestrial, telluric, tellurian. **2** *earthly joys* worldly, temporal, secular, mortal, human, mundane, material, non-spiritual, materialistic, carnal, fleshly, physical, corporeal, gross, sensual, base, sordid, vile, profane. **3** *no earthly chance* feasible, possible, conceivable, imaginable, likely.

earthy adj **1** *earthy smell* soil-like, dirtlike. **2** *earthy peasants/pleasures* down-to-earth, unsophisticated, unrefined, homely, simple, plain, unpretentious, natural, uninhibited, rough, robust. **3** *an earthy sense of humour* bawdy, crude, coarse, rough, ribald, blue, indecent, indecorous, obscene.

ease n **1** *succeed with ease* no difficulty, no trouble/bother, facility, facileness, simplicity, effortlessness, deftness, adroitness, dexterity, proficiency, mastery. **2** *his ease of manner* naturalness, casualness, informality, unceremoniousness, lack of reserve/constraint, relaxedness, amiability, affability, unconcern, composure, aplomb, nonchalance, insouciance, urbanity, suaveness. **3** *ease of mind* peace, peacefulness, calmness, tranquillity, composure, serenity, repose, restfulness, quiet, contentment, security, comfort. **4** *a life of ease* comfort, contentment, content, enjoyment, affluence, wealth, prosperity, prosperousness, luxury, opulence; bed of roses.

ease *v* **1** *ease the pain* mitigate, lessen, reduce, lighten, diminish, moderate, abate, ameliorate, relieve, assuage, allay, soothe, soften, palliate, mollify, appease. **2** *the storm/pain eased* lessen, grow less, moderate, abate, diminish, quieten, slacken off. **3** *ease her mind* comfort, give solace to, solace, console, soothe, calm, quieten, pacify. **4** *ease his promotion* make easy/easier, facilitate, expedite, speed up, assist, help, aid, advance, further, forward, smooth/clear the way for, simplify. **5** *ease it into position* guide, manoeuvre, inch, edge, steer, slide, slip, squeeze.

easy *adj* **1** *an easy task* not difficult, simple, effortless, uncomplicated, straightforward, undemanding, painless, trouble-free, facile, idiot-proof. **2** *an easy prey* compliant, exploitable, susceptible, accommodating, obliging, amenable, biddable, docile, gullible, manageable, manoeuvrable, tractable, pliant, yielding, trusting, acquiescent. **3** *an easy manner* natural, casual, informal, unceremonious, unreserved, unconstrained, unforced, easygoing, amiable, affable, unconcerned, composed, carefree, nonchalant, insouciant, urbane, suave; *inf* laid-back. **4** *an easy mind* at ease, trouble-free, untroubled, unworried, at peace, calm, tranquil, composed, serene, quiet, contented, secure, relaxed, comfortable. **5** *go at an easy pace* even, steady, regular, comfortable, moderate, unexacting, undemanding, leisured, unhurried.

easygoing *adj* even-tempered, placid, happy-go-lucky, serene, relaxed, carefree, nonchalant, insouciant, tolerant, undemanding, amiable, patient, understanding, imperturbable; *inf* laid-back, together.

eat *v* **1** *eat chocolate* consume, devour, swallow, chew, munch, gulp down, bolt, wolf, ingest, tuck into; *inf* put away, scoff. **2** *eat out | eat in the evening* have a meal, take food, feed, partake of food; breakfast, lunch, dine, banquet; *inf* snack, graze. **3** *eat away material/rock* erode, corrode, wear,

gnaw away, crumble, dissolve, waste away, rot, decay, destroy.

eavesdrop *v* listen in, snoop, spy; monitor, tap, wire-tap, overhear; *inf* bug.

ebb *v* **1** *the tide ebbed* go out, flow back, retreat, draw back, fall back, fall away, recede, abate, subside, retrocede. **2** *its popularity ebbed* decline, die/fade away, die out, lessen, wane, decrease, diminish, flag, dwindle, peter out, sink, weaken, deteriorate, decay, degenerate.

ebb *n* **1** *the ebb of the tide* going out, flowing back, retreat, retreating, drawing back, receding, abating, subsiding, retrocession. *see* EBB *v* 1. **2** *the ebb of popularity* decline, dying/fading away, lessening, waning, decrease, flagging, diminution, dwindling, petering out, sinking, deterioration, decay, degeneration. *see* EBB *v* 2.

ebony *adj* black, jet black, pitch black, coal black, black as night/pitch/hell, sable, inky, sooty.

ebullience *n* exuberance, effervescence, buoyancy, exhilaration, elation, euphoria, high-spiritedness, jubilation, animation, sparkle, vivacity, enthusiasm, zest, irrepressibility; high spirits.

ebullient *adj* exuberant, effervescent, buoyant, exhilarated, elated, euphoric, high-spirited, in high spirits, jubilant, animated, sparkling, vivacious, enthusiastic, irrepressible.

eccentric *adj* odd, queer, strange, peculiar, weird, bizarre, outlandish, freakish, uncommon, irregular, abnormal, aberrant, anomalous, non-conformist, unconventional, singular, idiosyncratic, capricious, whimsical, quirky; *inf* way-out, off-beat, dotty, nutty, screwy.

eccentric *n* oddity, queer fish, freak, character, case, crank; *inf* oddball, weirdo, nut, nutter, screwball.

eccentricity *n* oddness, queerness, strangeness, weirdness, bizarreness, freakishness, unconventionality; peculiarity, irregularity, abnormality, anomaly, foible, idiosyncracy, caprice, whimsy, quirk; *inf* way-outness, off-beatness. *see* ECCENTRIC *adj*.

ecclesiastic *n* clergyman, minister, parson, priest, vicar, chaplain, padre, churchman, churchwoman, man/woman of the cloth, preacher, reverend, cleric, holy man/woman, prelate, abbé, divine, theologian.

ecclesiastic *adj* church, churchly, religious, spiritual, non-secular, non-temporal, pastoral, priestly, ministerial, holy, divine, clerical, sacerdotal; *inf* churchy.

echelon n level, grade, rank, step, rung, tier, degree.

echo n **1** *the cave's echo | the echo of her call* reverberation, reverberating, resounding, ringing, repeating. **2** *the son an echo of his father* copy, imitation, reproduction, clone, duplicate, repeat, reflection, mirror image, parallel, parody. **3** *echoes of Picasso* suggestion, hint, trace, allusion, memory, reminder, remembrance, evocation, intimation; overtones, reminiscences.

echo v **1** *echo round the room* reverberate, resound, reflect, ring, repeat. **2** *echo a statement | echo the main theme* copy, imitate, reproduce, repeat, reiterate, parrot, reflect, mirror, parallel, parody.

eclectic adj **1** *eclectic interests* wide-ranging, broad, broad-based, comprehensive, general, varied, diverse, diversified, catholic, liberal, all-embracing, non-exclusive, many-sided, multifaceted, multifarious. **2** *eclectic philosophy* selective, selecting, choosing, picking and choosing.

eclipse v **1** *eclipse the sun* blot out, block, cover, obscure, conceal, cast a shadow over, darken, shade, veil, shroud. **2** *eclipse his rival/success* outshine, overshadow, dwarf, put in the shade, surpass, excel, exceed, outstrip, transcend, outrival.

eclipse n **1** *the eclipse of the sun* blotting out, blocking, covering, obscuring, concealing, veiling, shrouding, occultation, adumbration. *see* ECLIPSE v 1. **2** *the eclipse of the empire* decline, fall, failure, deterioration, degeneration, weakening, ebb, waning. **3** *the eclipse of his rival/success* outshining, overshadowing, dwarfing, surpassing, excelling, outstripping, transcending. *see* ECLIPSE v 2.

economic adj **1** *the government's economic policy* financial, monetary, budgetary, fiscal, commercial, trade, mercantile. **2** *an economic venture* profitable, profit-making, money-making, remunerative, viable, cost-effective, productive, solvent. **3** *an economic holiday* economical, cheap. *see* ECONOMICAL 2.

economical adj **1** *economical with resources | economical with the salt* economizing, thrifty, sparing, careful, prudent, frugal, scrimping, mean, niggardly, stingy, penny-pinching, parsimonious, conservationist. **2** *an economical holiday* cheap, inexpensive, reasonable, low-cost, low-price, low-budget, budget.

economize v *we must economize because we are short of money* cut back, retrench, budget, cut expenditure, be economical, be sparing/frugal, reduce/decrease wastage,

scrimp, save, scrimp and save, cut corners, tighten one's belt, draw in one's horns.

economy n **1** *the national economy* wealth, resources; financial state, financial management. **2** *practise economy | use with economy* thriftiness, sparingness, carefulness, prudence, frugalness, scrimping, meanness, niggardliness, stinginess, penny-pinching, parsimony, parsimoniousness; thrift, care, restraint, frugality, husbandry, conservation.

ecstasy n bliss, rapture, elation, euphoria, joy, joyousness, jubilation, exultation, cloud nine, seventh heaven; transports, rhapsodies. *see* ECSTATIC.

ecstatic adj blissful, enraptured, rapturous, joyful, joyous, overjoyed, jumping for joy, jubilant, exultant, elated, in transports, rhapsodic, delirious with happiness/delight, in a frenzy of delight, orgasmic, on cloud nine, in seventh heaven.

eddy n whirlpool, vortex, maelstrom, swirling, swirl, counter-current, counter-flow.

eddy v swirl, swirl round, whirl.

edge n **1** *the edge of the lake/plate* border, side, boundary, rim, margin, fringe, outer limit, extremity, verge, brink, lip, contour, perimeter, periphery, parameter, ambit. **2** *a voice with an edge* sting, bite; sharpness, severity, pointedness, acerbity, causticity, acidity, acrimony, virulence, trenchancy, pungency. **3** *have the edge on her* advantage, upper hand, whip hand, lead, head start, dominance, superiority, ascendancy. **on edge** edgy, nervous, tense, uneasy. *see* EDGY.

edge v **1** *edge the shears* put an edge on, sharpen, hone, whet, strop, file. **2** *edge with lace* trim, bind, hem, border, fringe, rim, verge. **3** *edge one's way through the crowd* inch, ease, elbow, worm, work, sidle, sidestep, gravitate, steal. **4** *edge forward* inch, sidle, creep, steal.

edgy adj on edge, nervous, tense, ill at ease, anxious, on tenterhooks, keyed up, restive, apprehensive, uneasy, irritable, irascible, touchy, tetchy; *inf* nervy, twitchy, uptight, wired.

edible adj fit/good to eat, consumable, digestible, palatable, comestible.

edict n decree, order, command, law, rule, ruling, regulation, act, enactment, statute, injunction, mandate, manifesto, proclamation, pronouncement, ordinance, dictate, dictum, fiat, pronunciamento, ukase.

edification n instruction, education, tuition, teaching, schooling, tutoring, coaching, guidance, enlightenment, improvement, uplifting, elevation.

edifice n building, structure, construction, erection; *inf* pile.

edify v instruct, educate, teach, school, tutor, coach, guide, inform, enlighten, improve, uplift, elevate.

edit v **1** *edit her book* copy-edit, revise, correct, emend, polish, check, modify, rewrite, rephrase, prepare/adapt/assemble for publication, redact; *inf* clean up. **2** *he edits the paper* be the editor of, run, direct, be in charge of, be chief of, head, head up.

edition n **1** *morning editions of the paper/programme* issue, number, printing, version. **2** *a first edition of the book* printing, impression, publication, issue.

educate v instruct, teach, school, tutor, coach, train, drill, prime, inform, indoctrinate, inculcate, enlighten, edify, cultivate, develop, improve, prepare, rear, nurture, foster.

educated adj *educated people* literate, schooled, well-read, informed, knowledgeable, enlightened, lettered, erudite, cultivated, cultured, refined; *inf* highbrow.

education n **1** *the education of the children* schooling, teaching, instruction, tuition, coaching, training, tutelage, drilling, disciplining, priming, informing, indoctrination, inculcation, enlightenment, edification, cultivation, development, improvement, preparation, rearing, nurturing, fostering. **2** *people of education* literacy, schooling, scholarship, knowledge, enlightenment, cultivation, culture, refinement; letters.

educational adj **1** *an educational establishment* academic, learning, teaching, pedagogic. **2** *the film is educational* educative, instructive, informative, enlightening, edifying, improving, didactic, heuristic.

educator n educationalist, teacher, schoolteacher, schoolmaster, schoolmistress, lecturer, tutor, coach, academic, pedagogue.

eerie adj uncanny, unearthly, ghostly, spectral, mysterious, strange, unnatural, frightening, fearful, scaring, chilling, spine-chilling, blood-curdling; *Scots* eldritch; *inf* spooky, scary, creepy.

efface v **1** *efface the sketch/memory* remove, rub out, blot out, wipe out, blank out, obliterate, erase, delete, eradicate, expunge, eliminate, excise, annihilate, extirpate. **2** *efface oneself | be self-effacing* make inconspicuous, withdraw, keep out of the limelight, regard/treat as unimportant, be modest/diffident/retiring.

effect n **1** *the effect of the changes* result, net result, outcome, upshot, consequence, conclusion, aftermath, issue; results, fruits. **2** *with effect from tomorrow* force, enforcement, operation, implementation, execution, action. **3** *speak to great effect | act with great effect* effectiveness, success, influence, efficacy, effectuality, weight, power, cogency. see EFFECTIVENESS. **4** *or words to that effect* sense, meaning, drift, tenor, significance, import, purport, essence. **in effect** effectively, actually, really, in actual fact, in reality, in truth, to all intents and purposes, for all practical purposes, essentially, in essence, virtually. **take effect** **1** *rules taking effect from tomorrow* come into being/force/operation, begin, become operative, become valid, become law. **2** *medicine taking effect* be effective, work, produce results, have the desired effect.

effect v *effect a plan* effectuate, bring about, carry out, cause, make, produce, create, give rise to, perform, achieve, accomplish, complete, fulfil, implement, execute, actuate, initiate.

effective adj **1** *effective administration* successful, productive, competent, capable, able, efficient, efficacious, effectual, useful, adequate, active, energetic. **2** *effective lighting* striking, impressive, exciting, attractive. **3** *effective arguments* powerful, forceful, forcible, cogent, compelling, potent, telling, persuasive, convincing, moving. **4** *rules effective from tomorrow* valid, in force, in operation, operative, active, effectual.

effectiveness n **1** *the effectiveness of the administration* success, productiveness, competence, competency, capability, ability, efficiency, efficacy, effectuality, effectualness, usefulness, adequacy. see EFFECTIVE 1. **2** *the effectiveness of the argument* power, force, forcefulness, cogency, potency, persuasion, persuasiveness. see EFFECTIVE 3.

effects npl belongings, possessions, goods, goods and chattels, trappings, accoutrements, paraphernalia; property, luggage, baggage, bag and baggage, gear, equipment, tackle; *inf* things, bits and pieces.

effectual adj **1** *effectual actions/measures* effective, successful, efficacious, productive, efficient, powerful, potent, capable, competent, useful, functional, forcible. **2** *effectual documents* valid, legal, binding, lawful, in force, sound, licit.

effectuate v effect, bring about, cause, make, produce, achieve, accomplish, implement, execute, actuate. see EFFECT v.

effeminate adj womanish, unmanly, effete, milksoppish; *inf* wimpish, pansy-like, sissy.

effervesce v 1 *wine effervescing* sparkle, bubble, fizz, froth, foam, ferment. 2 *the engaged couple effervescing* sparkle, be animated, be lively, be jubilant, be exuberant. *see* EFFERVESCENT 2.

effervescence n 1 *the effervescence of the wine/water* bubbliness, sparkle, carbonation, fizziness, frothiness, foam, fermentation. 2 *the effervescence of the happy young people* vivacity, animation, liveliness, buoyancy, exuberance, exhilaration, ebullience, jubilation, sparkle, bubbliness, merriment, irrepressibility.

effervescent adj 1 *effervescent wine* sparkling, carbonated, bubbly, bubbling, fizzy, fizzing, frothy, foamy, fermenting. 2 *effervescent holiday-makers* vivacious, animated, lively, buoyant, exuberant, exhilarated, ebullient, jubilant, sparkling, bubbly, merry, irrepressible.

effete adj 1 *effete civilization* weakened, worn out, exhausted, finished, burnt out, played out, drained, spent, enfeebled, enervated, powerless. 2 *effete young men* effeminate, womanish, unmanly, milksoppish; *inf* pansy-like, sissy, wimpish.

efficacious adj effective, successful, efficient, effectual, productive, useful, competent, adequate, capable, able, potent, powerful.

efficacy n effectiveness, success, successfulness, efficiency, effectuality, productiveness, usefulness, potency. *see* EFFICACIOUS.

efficiency n 1 *admire her efficiency* capability, ability, competence, competency, effectiveness, productivity, skill, expertise, proficiency, adeptness, deftness, mastery, organization. *see* EFFICIENT 1. 2 *the efficiency of the office* organization, well-orderedness, streamlinedness. *see* EFFICIENT 2.

efficient adj 1 *an efficient person* capable, able, competent, effective, productive, skilful, expert, proficient, adept, deft, organized, workmanlike, businesslike. 2 *an efficient office* organized, well-organized, well-run, well-ordered, streamlined, labour-saving.

effigy n likeness, image, model, dummy, representation, guy, carving, statue, bust.

effluent n 1 *factory effluent* waste, sewage, pollutant, pollution, effluvium. 2 *the effluent of the dirty water* discharge, outflow, emission, emanation, exhalation.

effort n 1 *put effort into it* exertion, force, power, energy, work, muscle, application, labour, striving, endeavour, toil, struggle, strain, stress; *lit* travail; *inf* elbow grease. 2 *win at the third effort* attempt, try, endeavour; *inf* shot, go, crack, stab. 3 *admire his artistic efforts* achievement, accomplishment, attainment, result, creation, production, opus, feat, deed.

effortless adj easy, simple, uncomplicated, undemanding, unexacting, painless, trouble-free, facile.

effrontery n impertinence, insolence, impudence, cheek, audacity, temerity, presumption, gall, rashness, bumptiousness; *inf* nerve, face, neck, brass neck.

effulgent adj shining, bright, brilliant, dazzling, blazing, glowing, radiant, luminous, lustrous, incandescent, fluorescent, vivid, splendid; *lit* refulgent, lucent.

effusion n 1 *effusion of blood* gush, stream, outpouring, outflow, discharge, issue, efflux, spilling, shedding, voidance, extravasation. 2 *amazed at her passionate effusion* outburst, outpouring, stream of words, flow of speech, utterance, wordiness, speech, address, talk; words, writings.

effusive adj gushing, unrestrained, unreserved, extravagant, fulsome, demonstrative, lavish, enthusiastic, rhapsodic, lyrical, exuberant, ebullient, expansive, wordy, verbose, long-winded, profuse; *inf* over the top, OTT, smarmy.

egg v **egg on** encourage, urge, push, drive, goad, spur on, prod, prompt, excite, exhort.

egghead n intellectual, academic, scholar, brain, genius, blue-stocking, bookworm, pedagogue, pedant; *inf* highbrow, Einstein, know-it-all, walking encyclopedia.

ego n self, the self, oneself, identity; self-importance, self-esteem, self-conceit, self-image, *amour propre*, self-confidence.

egoism n self-interest, self-centredness, selfishness, egocentricity, egomania, egotism, looking out for number one, self-seeking, self-absorption, self-love, narcissism, vanity, conceit, pride, self-esteem, self-importance.

egoist n self-seeker, egocentric, egomaniac, egotist, narcissist.

egoistic adj self-centred, selfish, egocentric, egotistic, self-seeking, self-absorbed, self-obsessed, self-loving, narcissistic, vain, conceited, proud, self-important.

egotism n self-admiration, self-love, egomania, egocentricity, egoism, narcissism, self-conceit, conceit, vanity, pride, arrogance, self-esteem, self-importance, self-glorification, superiority, self-praise, boastfulness, bragging, braggadocio, fanfaronade; *inf* blowing one's own trumpet.

egotist n self-admirer, egomaniac, egocentric, egoist, boaster, bragger; *inf* blowhard, bighead.

egotistic adj self-admiring, egocentric, egoistic, narcissistic, conceited, vain, proud, arrogant, self-important, superior, boastful, bragging.

egregious adj glaring, flagrant, blatant, gross, outrageous, monstrous, rank, enormous, shocking, scandalous, appalling, heinous, intolerable, infamous, notorious, grievous, arrant.

egress n **1** *seek a means of egress* exit, way out, door/gate out, out-passage, out-lane, escape route, outlet, vent. **2** *the egress of the crowd* leaving, departure, exit, withdrawal, exodus, issue, emergence, flowing out, escape, emanation, debouchment.

ejaculate v **1** *ejaculate fluid/semen/vomit* emit, eject, discharge, release, expel, spurt. **2** *men unable to ejaculate* emit/discharge semen, climax, have an orgasm, orgasm; *inf* come. **3** *ejaculate a cry* utter, call out, voice, vocalize. **4** *"Watch out!" he ejaculated* cry out, call out, exclaim, shout out, blurt out, yell.

ejaculation n **1** *the ejaculation of fluid/semen/vomit* emission, ejection, discharge, release. *see* EJACULATE 1. **2** *his premature ejaculation* emission/discharge of semen, climax, orgasm; *inf* coming. **3** *they heard an ejaculation* cry, call, exclamation, shout, yell, utterance.

eject v **1** *eject sewage/smoke/semen* emit, discharge, exude, excrete, expel, cast out, release, spew out, disgorge, spout, vomit, ejaculate. **2** *he was ejected from the plane/vehicle* propel, thrust out, throw out, expel. **3** *eject the intruder from the building | eject him from his house | ejected from the country* throw out, turn out, put out, cast out, remove, evict, expel, oust, put out in the street, dispossess, banish, deport, exile; *inf* chuck out, kick out, turf out, boot out, heave out, bounce. **4** *eject her from a senior job* sack, dismiss, discharge, oust, dislodge, get rid of, send packing; *inf* fire, axe, hand someone his/her cards, chuck out, kick out, boot out, give the boot to.

ejection n **1** *ejection of sewage/smoke/semen* emission, discharge, exudation, excretion, expulsion, ejaculation, release. *see* EJECT 1. **2** *his ejection from the plane* propulsion, expulsion. *see* EJECT 2. **3** *ejection from the building/house/country* throwing out, removal, eviction, expulsion, ousting, dispossessing, banishment, deportation, exile;

inf chucking out, turfing out, bouncing. *see* EJECT 3. **4** *her ejection from the senior job* sacking, dismissal, discharge, ousting, dislodgement; *inf* firing, axing, chucking out, turfing out, the boot, heave-ho. *see* EJECT 4.

eke v **eke out** **1** *eke out a living* scrape, scratch, scrimp. **2** *you must eke out the butter ration* be economical with, economize on, be frugal/sparing with, husband; *inf* go easy with. **3** *eke out the meat with vegetables* stretch out, add to, increase, supplement, augment, enlarge.

elaborate adj **1** *elaborate plans* complicated, detailed, complex, involved, intricate, studied, painstaking, careful. **2** *elaborate patterns* detailed, complex, ornate, fancy, showy, fussy, ostentatious, extravagant, baroque, rococo, precious; *inf* flash.

elaborate v **1** *elaborate on a plan* expand on, enlarge on, amplify, flesh out, add flesh to, add detail to, expatiate on. **2** *elaborate the plan* develop, work out, improve, refine, polish, perfect, embellish, enhance, ornament, embroider.

élan n style, flair, flourish, dash, verve, panache, spirit, vivacity, vitality, zest, brio, *esprit*; *inf* oomph, pizazz.

elapse v pass, go by, go on, slip away, slip by, roll by, slide by, steal by.

elastic adj **1** *elastic material* stretchy, stretchable, springy, flexible, pliant, pliable, supple, yielding, rubbery, plastic, rebounding, recoiling, resilient. **2** *elastic plans/attitudes* flexible, adaptable, fluid, adjustable, accommodating, variable, yielding; *inf* easy.

elasticity n **1** *elasticity of the fibre* stretchiness, springiness, flexibility, pliancy, suppleness, rubberiness, plasticity, resilience; *inf* give. **2** *elasticity of plans/attitude* flexibility, adaptability, adjustability, fluidity, variability.

elated adj *elated at the news | an elated smile* overjoyed, ecstatic, blissful, joyful, jubilant, euphoric, exultant, rhapsodic, transported, exhilarated, ebullient, delighted, cheered, excited, animated, roused, gleeful, over the moon, in seventh heaven. *see* ECSTATIC.

elation n ecstasy, bliss, euphoria, rapture, joy, jubilation, exhilaration, rhapsody, transport, ebullience, delight, glee, excitement, animation.

elbow n **1** *leaning on one's elbow* arm-joint, bend of the arm. **2** *elbow of the pipe* bend, joint, turning, corner, right angle, crook, flexure.

elbow v *elbow out of the way* | *elbow one's way through the crowd* push, jostle, nudge, shoulder, knock, bump, crowd, bulldoze.

elbow-room n space, room, breathing-space, scope, freedom, latitude, leeway, *Lebensraum*.

elder adj older, senior, first-born.

elderly adj oldish, advanced in years, ageing, aged, old, grey-haired, ancient, superannuated, past one's prime, senescent; *inf* over the hill, long in the tooth.

elderly npl **the elderly** elderly people, older people, senior citizens, pensioners, old-age pensioners, OAPs, retired people; *inf* golden oldies, wrinklies, woopies (= well-off older people).

elect v *elect an MP* | *elect a team captain* vote for, cast one's vote for, choose by ballot, choose, pick, select, appoint, opt for, decide on, plump for, designate, determine.

elect npl **the elect** the chosen, the selected, the preferred, the appointed, the designated, the élite.

election n **1** *vote in an election* ballot, poll; hustings; general election, local election. **2** *the election of the MP* | *the election for team captain* voting, choosing, picking, selection, choice, appointment; vote, ballot. *see* ELECT v.

elector n voter, member of the electorate, constituent, selector, chooser.

electric adj **1** *electric power* generated by electricity, galvanic, voltaic. **2** *electric kettles* electric-powered, electrically operated/powered, mains-operated, battery-operated, electrically charged. **3** *an electric moment* | *the effect was electric* tense, charged, exciting, dynamic, thrilling, startling, stimulating, rousing, stirring, moving, jolting, shocking, galvanizing.

electrify v excite, thrill, startle, shock, arouse, rouse, move, stimulate, stir, animate, fire, charge, invigorate, jolt, galvanize.

elegance n style, gracefulness, grace, taste, tastefulness, fashion, culture, beauty, charm, polish, refinement, exquisiteness, finesse, discernment, dignity, distinction, propriety, luxury, sumptuousness, opulence, *haute couture*.

elegant adj stylish, graceful, tasteful, artistic, fashionable, cultured, beautiful, lovely, charming, exquisite, polished, cultivated, refined, aesthetic, suave, debonair, modish, dignified, luxurious, sumptuous, opulent.

elegiac adj funereal, lamenting, doleful, mournful, dirgelike, melancholic, plaintive, keening, sad, nostalgic, valedictory; *fml* threnodic.

elegy n funeral poem/song, lament, dirge, plaint, requiem, keening; *fml* threnody, threnode.

element n **1** *an element of truth* | *a stable element of the group* basis, ingredient, factor, feature, detail, trace, component, constituent, part, section, portion, piece, segment, member, unit, module, subdivision, integrand. **2** *in his natural element* environment, habitat, medium, milieu, sphere, field, domain, realm, circle, resort, haunt.

elemental adj **1** *elemental truth* basic, fundamental, rudimentary, embryonic, primitive, radical, essential, elementary. **2** *elemental influences* natural, atmospheric, meteorological, environmental.

elementary adj **1** *elementary puzzle* easy, simple, straightforward, uncomplicated, rudimentary, facile, simplistic. **2** *elementary maths* basic, fundamental, rudimentary, primary, preparatory, introductory.

elements npl **1** *exposed to the elements* weather, climate, atmospheric conditions/forces, environment; *lit* clime. **2** *the elements of good manners* basics, essentials, principles, foundations, fundamentals, rudiments.

elephantine adj huge, massive, enormous, immense, hulking, bulky, mammoth, gargantuan, heavy, weighty, ponderous, lumbering, clumsy, laborious.

elevate v **1** *elevate the load* raise, lift, hoist, hike up, raise up/aloft. **2** *elevate to management* promote, give promotion, upgrade, improve the position/status of, advance, give advancement, exalt, prefer, aggrandize; *inf* kick upstairs. **3** *elevate her spirits* | *she felt elevated* cheer, gladden, brighten, perk up, give a lift/boost to, lighten; cheer up, animate, exhilarate, elate, boost, buoy up, uplift.

elevated adj **1** *elevated banners* raised, lifted up, hoisted, high up, aloft, upraised, uplifted. **2** *an elevated position* high, higher, high/higher up, great, grand, lofty, dignified, noble, exalted, magnificent, sublime, inflated, pompous, bombastic, orotund, fustian. **3** *elevated spirits/state* cheerful, cheered up, glad, joyful, happy, overjoyed, gleeful, excited, animated, elated, exhilarated, in high spirits, blithe. **4** *elevated literary style* lofty, exalted, inflated, pompous, bombastic, orotund, fustian.

elevation n **1** *elevation of the building* height, altitude, tallness. **2** *the elevation behind the town* height, rise, raised/rising ground, hill, ·mountain, hillock, mound, mount, eminence; *fml* acclivity. **3** *elevation to the board* promotion, upgrading, advancement, preferment, aggrandizement, step up the ladder; *inf* kick upstairs. **4** *elevation of thought* grandeur, greatness, nobility, magnificence, loftiness, majesty, grandioseness, sublimity.

elf n fairy, pixie, sprite, dwarf, gnome, goblin, hobgoblin, imp, brownie, leprechaun, puck, troll, banshee, kobold, nix, nixie.

elfin adj **1** *elfin features/child* elflike, elfish, elvish, pixie-like, puckish, small, little, tiny, dainty, diminutive, wee, pint-sized, Lilliputian. **2** *elfin mischief* mischievous, impish, puckish, playful, arch.

elicit v obtain, bring out, draw out, extract, extort, exact, wrest, evoke, derive, call forth, educe.

élite n **1** *the élite among the students* the best, the pick, the cream, *crème de la crème*, the elect, meritocracy. **2** *the élite of society* aristocracy, nobility, gentry, establishment, high society, jet set, beautiful people, beau monde, *haut monde*.

elixir n **1** *an elixir for all ills* panacea, cure-all, universal/sovereign remedy, wonder drug, magic bullet, nostrum. **2** *elixir of eucalyptus* extract, essence, concentrate, quintessence, pith, mixture, solution, potion, tincture.

elliptical adj **1** *an elliptical shape* oval, egg-shaped, ovate, ovoid. **2** *an elliptical style of writing* terse, concise, succinct, compact, economic. **3** *elliptical prose/speech* abstruse, cryptic, ambiguous, obscure, recondite.

elocution n diction, speech, enunciation, articulation, voice production, pronunciation, phrasing, delivery, utterance, speech-making, public speaking, oratory, declamation.

elongate v lengthen, stretch out, make longer, extend, draw out, prolong, protract.

elope v **1** *elope to Gretna Green* run off/away together, run off/away with a lover, run away to marry, slip away, sneak off, steal away. **2** *elope from the camp* escape, make one's escape, flee, abscond, bolt, decamp.

eloquence n **1** *the eloquence of the speaker/argument/speech* expressiveness, articulacy, articulateness, fluency, facility, diction, enunciation, command of language, power of speech, oratory, rhetoric, persuasiveness, forcefulness; *inf* gift of the gab. **2** *the*

eloquence of the glance expressiveness, significance, meaningfulness, suggestiveness, revelation, pregnancy.

eloquent adj **1** *an eloquent speaker/argument/speech* expressive, well-spoken, articulate, fluent, graceful, silver-tongued, smooth-tongued, well-expressed, vivid, effective, graphic, pithy, persuasive, glib, forceful. **2** *an eloquent look* expressive, significant, meaningful, suggestive, revealing, telling, pregnant.

elsewhere adv somewhere else, in/to another place, in/to a different place, not here, not present, absent, away, abroad, hence.

elucidate v *please elucidate!* | *elucidate the meaning* explain; make clear/plain, interpret, illuminate, throw light on, comment on, annotate, gloss, spell out; *fml* explicate.

elucidation n explanation, clarification, interpretation, illumination, comment, commentary, annotation, gloss, explication, exposition.

elude v *the fox eluded the hunter* avoid, get away from, dodge, evade, escape, lose, duck, shake off, give the slip to, throw off the scent, flee, circumvent, bilk; *inf* ditch.

elusive adj **1** *an elusive person* difficult to catch/find, evasive, slippery, shifty, cagey. **2** *an elusive perfume* indefinable, subtle, unanalysable, intangible, impalpable, fleeting, transient, transitory, fugitive. **3** *an elusive answer* ambiguous, baffling, puzzling, misleading, evasive, equivocal, deceitful, deceptive, fallacious, fraudulent, elusory.

Elysium n heaven, paradise, eternity, kingdom come.

emaciated adj thin as a rake, wasted, gaunt, skeletal, anorexic, scrawny, cadaverous, shrivelled, shrunken, withered, haggard, drawn, pinched, wizened, attenuated, atrophied.

emaciation n gauntness, scrawniness, cadaverousness, haggardness. *see* EMACIATED.

emanate v **1** *desire emanating from jealousy* arise, originate, stem, derive, emerge, proceed, come forth, issue. **2** *emanating fumes* give off, give out, send out, send forth, discharge, emit, exhale, radiate.

emanation n **1** *emanation of hostility from rivalry* arising, origination, derivation, emergence. **2** *a foul smelling emanation* discharge, emission, effluent, exhalation, radiation, effusion, efflux.

emancipate v **1** *emancipate slaves* free, set free, liberate, release, let loose, deliver, discharge, unchain, unfetter, unshackle, untie, unyoke, manumit. **2** *emancipate* *women* allow to vote, give voting rights to, enfranchise, affranchise; free from restriction/restraint.

emancipation n **1** *emancipation of slaves* setting free, liberation, release, deliverance, discharge, unfettering, unshackling, manumission; freedom, liberty. *see* EMANCIPATE 1. **2** *the emancipation of women* enfranchisement, affranchisement; right to vote.

emasculate v **1** *emasculate a bull* castrate, neuter, geld, spay, desex, unman. **2** *emasculate the power of the state* weaken, make feeble/feebler, enfeeble, debilitate, enervate, impoverish, remove the sting from, pull the teeth of.

embalm v **1** *embalm a corpse* preserve, anoint, mummify, lay out. **2** *embalm memories* remember, keep in mind, look back on, reminisce about, cherish, treasure, conserve, store, consecrate, immortalize, enshrine. **3** *flowers embalming the air* perfume, make fragrant, scent, aromatize.

embargo n ban, bar, prohibition, stoppage, interdict, proscription; restriction, restraint, blockage, check, barrier, impediment, obstruction, hindrance.

embargo v ban, bar, prohibit, stop, interdict, debar, proscribe; restrict, restrain, block, check, impede, obstruct, hinder.

embark v **1** *passengers embarking* board ship, enplane, go on board, go aboard, take ship; set sail, put to sea, weigh anchor, take off. **2** *embark on an adventure* begin, start, commence, undertake, set about, enter on, go into, take up, venture into, launch into, turn one's hand to, engage in, broach, institute, initiate; *inf* have a go at.

embarrass v make uncomfortable/awkward, make self-conscious, upset, disconcert, discomfit, discompose, confuse, fluster, agitate, nonplus, discountenance, distress, chagrin, shame, humiliate, abash, mortify.

embarrassed adj uncomfortable, awkward, self-conscious, disconcerted, upset, discomfited, discomposed, confused, flustered, agitated, nonplussed, discountenanced, distressed, chagrined, shamed, humiliated, abashed, mortified; *inf* with egg on one's face.

embarrassing adj **1** *embarrassing remark* disconcerting, discomfiting, discomposing, upsetting, confusing, flustering, agitating, discountenancing, distressing, shaming, humiliating, mortifying. **2** *embarrassing moment* awkward, compromising, tricky.

embarrassment n **1** *overcome with embarrassment* discomfort, awkwardness, self-consciousness, bashfulness, discomfiture, discomposure, confusion, agitation, distress, chagrin, shame, humiliation, mortification. **2** *financial embarrassment* difficulty, predicament, plight, mess, dilemma, entanglement, imbroglio; *inf* bind, pickle, fix, scrape, quandary. **3** *embarrassment of riches* excess, surplus, abundance, overabundance, profusion, glut, surfeit, superfluity, avalanche, deluge, *embarras de choix*.

embassy n **1** *the British embassy* consulate, legation, ministry. **2** *the archbishop's embassy* envoy, representative, legate; delegation, deputation.

embed, imbed v insert, implant, plant, set/fix in, root, drive in, hammer in, ram in, sink.

embellish v *embellish a ceiling | embellish the truth* decorate, adorn, ornament, dress, dress up, beautify, enhance, trim, garnish, gild, varnish, embroider, enrich, deck, bedeck, festoon, emblazon, bespangle, elaborate, exaggerate.

embellishment n *the embellishment of a ceiling/story* decoration, ornamentation, adornment, beautification, enhancement, trimming, garnishing, gilding, varnishing, embroidery, enrichment, bedecking, festooning, emblazoning, elaboration, exaggeration.

embezzle v steal, rob, thieve, pilfer, appropriate, misappropriate, purloin, filch, abstract, put one's hand in the till, dip into the public purse, peculate, defalcate; *inf* nick, rip off.

embezzlement n thieving, stealing, robbing, fraud, larceny, pilfering, appropriation, misappropriation, purloining, filching, abstraction, peculation, defalcation; theft, robbery, misuse of funds; *inf* nicking, ripping off.

embitter v **1** *embittered by her divorce* make bitter, make resentful, sour, anger, disillusion, poison, disaffect, envenom. **2** *embitter the situation* aggravate, worsen, exacerbate, exaggerate.

emblazon v **1** *emblazoning a shield* decorate, adorn, ornament, embellish, illuminate, colour, paint. **2** *emblazoned on the screen* proclaim, publicize, publish, trumpet, glorify, extol, praise, laud.

emblem n crest, badge, symbol, device, representation, token, image, figure, mark, sign; insignia.

embodiment n **1** *the embodiment of new design features in the car* incorporation, combination, bringing together, collecting, inclusion, consolidation, assimilation, integration, organization, systemization. *see* EMBODY 1. **2** *he is the embodiment of good manners | the embodiment of renaissance man* personification, representation, incarnation, incorporation, symbol, symbolization, type, exemplification, example, exemplar, realization, manifestation, expression, reification. *see* EMBODY 2.

embody v **1** *a vehicle embodying technological advances* incorporate, combine, bring together, comprise, collect, include, contain, constitute, take in, consolidate, encompass, assimilate, integrate, concentrate, organize, systematize. **2** *he embodies good manners | embodying renaissance man* personify, represent, symbolize, stand for, typify, exemplify, incorporate, realize, manifest, express, incarnate, concretize, reify.

embolden v give courage to, make brave/ braver, encourage, hearten, strengthen, rouse, stir, stimulate, cheer, fire, inflame, animate, invigorate, vitalize, inspirit.

embrace v **1** *embrace his wife* take/hold in one's arms, hold, hug, cuddle, clasp, squeeze, clutch, seize, grab, nuzzle, enfold, enclasp, encircle; *inf* canoodle with, neck with. **2** *embrace the new philosophy* welcome, accept, receive enthusiastically/wholeheartedly, take up, adopt; *fml* espouse. **3** *embrace the whole area* cover, include, take in, deal with, involve, take into account, contain, comprise, incorporate, encompass, embody, subsume, comprehend, enfold.

embrace n hug, bear hug, cuddle, squeeze, clasp, hold, clutch, clinch, nuzzle; *inf* necking session.

embroider v **1** *embroider a design/tablecloth* sew, decorate with needlework. **2** *embroider the story/truth* touch up, dress up, embellish, elaborate, colour, enlarge on, exaggerate, paint, gild, invent, fabricate.

embroidery n **1** *thread for embroidery* needlework, needlepoint, sewing, tatting; tapestry, sampler. **2** *embroidery of the story/truth* touching up, dressing up, embellishment, adornment, ornamentation, elaboration, colouring, exaggeration, gilding; invention, fabrication, tall story, fisherman's tale, angler's tale.

embryonic adj just beginning, early, undeveloped, unformed, rudimentary, immature, incipient, primary, elementary, seminal, germinal, inchoate.

emend v edit, correct, revise, alter, rewrite, rectify, improve, polish, refine, expurgate, censor, bowdlerize, redact.

emendation n editing, correction, revision, alteration, rewriting, rectification, improving, improvement, polishing, refinement, expurgation, censoring, bowdlerization, redaction.

emerge v **1** *emerge from a building | emerge from a state of depression* come out, come into view, appear, come up, become visible, surface, spring up, crop up, materialize, arise, proceed, issue, come forth, emanate. **2** *facts emerging* become known, become common knowledge, come out, come to light, get around, become apparent, transpire, come to the fore.

emergence n **1** *his emergence from the building* coming out, appearance, arrival, arising, surfacing, springing up, materializing, materialization, issue, emanation. **2** *emergence of the facts* becoming known, coming to light, disclosure, exposure, unfolding, publication, publicizing, publishing, broadcasting.

emergency n *supplies for an emergency* urgent situation, crisis, danger, accident, difficulty, plight, predicament, quandary, dilemma, crunch, scrape, extremity, exigency, necessity; unforeseen circumstances, dire/desperate straits; *inf* pickle.

emergency adj *emergency exit/supplies* urgent, accident, danger; reserve, back-up, substitute, alternative, spare, extra.

emergent adj emerging, developing, beginning, coming out, budding, arising, dawning, embryonic.

emigrate v move abroad, leave one's country, migrate, relocate, resettle, defect, trek.

emigration n moving abroad, migration, departure, relocation, resettling, expatriation, exodus, defection, trekking.

eminence n **1** *eminence of the statesman* importance, greatness, prestige, reputation, fame, distinction, renown, pre-eminence, celebrity, illustriousness, notability, rank, standing, station, note, dignity. **2** *church built on an eminence* elevation, rise, rising/ raised ground, height.

eminent adj important, great, distinguished, well-known, celebrated, famous, renowned, noted, prominent, esteemed, noteworthy, pre-eminent, superior, outstanding, high-ranking, exalted, revered, elevated, august, paramount.

eminently adv *eminently suitable* very, well, greatly, highly, exceedingly, extremely, exceptionally, remarkably, outstandingly, strikingly, notably, prominently, surpassingly, signally.

emissary n ambassador, envoy, agent, delegate, representative, deputy, go-between, attaché, legate, courier, herald, scout, spy.

emission n **1** *the emission of fumes/light* discharge, outpouring, issue, oozing, leaking, excretion, secretion, ejection, emanation, radiation, exhalation, exudation, effusion, ejaculation, disgorgement, issuance. **2** *a deafening emission* utterance, declaration, expression, pronouncement, vocalization.

emit v **1** *emit fumes/light* discharge, pour out, give out/off, issue, send forth, throw out, ooze, leak, excrete, secrete, eject, emanate, radiate, exhale, ejaculate, exude. **2** *emit a terrified scream* utter, express, voice, pronounce, declare, articulate, vocalize.

emolument n payment, pay, salary, income, fee, stipend, revenue, return, profit, gain, reward, compensation, recompense, honorarium; wages, earnings, fees, profits, proceeds.

emotion n feeling, sentiment, passion, reaction, response, sensation; warmth, ardour, fervour, vehemence, joy, sorrow, pity, fear, horror.

emotional adj **1** *emotional person* feeling, passionate, hot-blooded, warm, responsive, demonstrative, tender, loving, sentimental, ardent, fervent, sensitive, excitable, temperamental, melodramatic. **2** *an emotional farewell* moving, touching, affecting, poignant, emotive, pathetic, tear-jerking, heart-rending, soul-stirring, impassioned.

emotionless adj *emotionless person/response/stave* unemotional, unfeeling, undemonstrative, cold, cold-blooded, impassive, indifferent, detached, remote, imperturbable, frigid, phlegmatic, glacial, blank, toneless.

emotive adj *an emotive issue* sensitive, delicate, controversial, touchy, awkward.

empathize v identify with, be in tune with, be on the same wavelength as, talk the same language as; sympathize, understand.

emperor n ruler, sovereign, king; tsar, kaiser, imperator, khan, mikado.

emphasis n **1** *putting the emphasis on the first syllable* stress, accent, accentuation, weight. **2** *putting the emphasis on talent* importance, stress, attention, priority, weight, urgency, force, accent, accentuation, insistence, significance, prominence, underlining, intensity, import, mark, power, moment, pre-eminence, underscoring.

emphasize v **1** *emphasize the first word* put the stress/accent/force on, stress, accentuate. **2** *emphasize the problems* put/lay stress on, give an emphasis to, stress, accent, accentuate, underline, call attention to, highlight, give prominence to, point up, spotlight, play up, feature, intensify, strengthen, heighten, deepen, italicize, underscore, insist on.

emphatic adj **1** *emphatic improvement* marked, pronounced, decided, positive, definite, distinctive, unmistakable, important, significant, strong, striking, powerful, resounding, telling, momentous. **2** *he was emphatic| an emphatic denial* definite, decided, certain, determined, absolute, direct, forceful, forcible, earnest, energetic, vigorous, categorical, unequivocal.

empire n **1** *Napoleon guarding his empire* kingdom, realm, domain, territory, jurisdiction, province, commonwealth. **2** *hold empire over* command, rule, control, authority, power, supremacy, government, sovereignty, sway, dominion.

empirical, empiric adj practical, observed, pragmatic, seen, experimental, experiental, heuristic.

employ v **1** *employ three people* hire, have in employment, engage, take on, take into employment, sign up, put on the payroll, enrol, commission, enlist, retain, indenture, apprentice. **2** *employed in polishing the floor* occupy, engage, keep busy. **3** *employ all his waking hours* occupy, take up, use up, put to use, make use of, fill, spend. **4** *employ cunning* use, apply, make use of, exercise, exert, utilize, ply, bring to bear.

employed adj **1** *no longer employed* in work, working, in employment, in a job. **2** *employed in gazing out of the window* occupied, busy, engaged, preoccupied.

employee n worker, blue-collar worker, white-collar worker, workman, member of staff, wage-earner, hand, hired hand, assistant, labourer, hireling.

employer n boss, manager, owner, proprietor, patron, contractor, director, head man/woman, top man/woman; firm of employment, organization; *inf* skipper, gaffer, governor; *Amer inf* honcho.

employment n **1** *the employment of new staff* hiring, hire, engagement, taking on, signing up, enrolment, commissioning, enlisting, apprenticing. **2** *employment as a teacher* job, work, business, line, occupation, profession, trade, calling, vocation, craft, métier, employ, service, pursuit. **3** *employment of resources/cunning* use, application, exercise, utilization, exertion.

emporium n **1** *traders in the emporium* bazaar, market place, market, fair, mart, shopping quarter. **2** *an old-fashioned emporium replaced by a supermarket* shop, store, department store, establishment.

empower v **1** *empowered to arrest you* authorize, license, certify, accredit, qualify, sanction, warrant, commission, delegate. **2** *resources empowering him to act* allow, enable, give power/means/strength to, equip.

emptiness n **1** *an emptiness in her life* vacuum, void, hiatus. **2** *the emptiness of the place/house/page* vacantness, hollowness, voidness, desolation, bareness, barrenness, lack of contents/adornment, blankness, clearness. **3** *the emptiness of the threats/ gestures* meaninglessness, futility, ineffectiveness, ineffectuality, uselessness, worthlessness, fruitlessness, insubstantiality, idleness. **4** *the emptiness of her existence* aimlessness, purposelessness, meaninglessness, worthlessness, hollowness, barrenness, senselessness, silliness, banality, frivolity, inanity, triviality. **5** *the emptiness of the expression/stare* blankness, expressionlessness, vacantness, vacuousness, unintelligence.

empty adj **1** *empty bowl/house/page* containing nothing, without contents, unfilled, vacant, hollow, void, unoccupied, uninhabited, desolate, bare, unadorned, barren, blank, clear. **2** *empty threats/gestures* meaningless, futile, ineffective, ineffectual, useless, worthless, idle, insubstantial, fruitless. **3** *empty existence* aimless, purposeless, meaningless, hollow, barren, senseless, unsatisfactory, silly, banal, inane, frivolous, trivial, worthless, valueless, profitless. **4** *empty expression/stare* blank, expressionless, vacant, unintelligent, deadpan, vacuous, absent. **5** *thirsty and empty* hungry, starving, famished, ravenous, unfed.

empty v **1** *empty the room/lorry* make vacant, vacate, clear, evacuate, void, unload, unburden. **2** *empty the liquid* drain, pour out, exhaust, use up, deplete, sap. **3** *the room emptied* clear, become vacant/empty. **4** *the liquid emptied* flow out, pour out, drain, discharge, issue, emit, exude, ooze.

empty-headed adj stupid, silly, brainless, hare-brained, scatterbrained, featherbrained, scatty, giddy, skittish, flighty, frivolous, dizzy, vacuous; *inf* dopey, batty, dotty.

enable v **1** *enable you to vote* allow, permit, authorize, entitle, qualify, fit, license, sanction, warrant, accredit, validate, commission, delegate, legalize, empower. **2** *enable you to cross the river* allow, permit, give the

means/resources to, equip, prepare, facilitate, capacitate.

enact v **1** *enact Hamlet | enact the role of Hamlet* act, act out, play, perform, stage, appear as, portray, depict, represent, impersonate, personify; *fml* personate. **2** *a bill enacted by Parliament* command, order, decree, ordain, legislate, rule, make law, pass, pronounce, approve, ratify, sanction.

enactment n **1** *the enactment of scene 3 | enactments of King Lear* acting, playing, performing, staging, performance, appearance, portrayal, depiction, representation, personification; *fml* personation. **2** *the enactment of the new law* passing, decreeing, ordaining, legislating, approval, ratification, sanction. **3** *enactments of Parliament* law, bill, act, order, decree, regulation, statute, edict, measure, motion, proclamation, command, commandment, pronouncement, ordinance, dictate, ratification; legislation.

enamoured adj in love, loving, infatuated, captivated, charmed, enchanted, fascinated, bewitched, enthralled, entranced, enraptured; *inf* smitten, mad, crazy, nuts, wild.

encampment n camp, military camp, bivouac, camp-site, camping ground.

encapsulate v **1** *encapsulate the views of the committee* sum up, summarize, condense, abridge, précis, compress, digest, epitomize. **2** *encapsulate all the main points* include, contain, embrace, capture.

enchant v bewitch, make spellbound, fascinate, charm, captivate, entrance, enthrall, beguile, hypnotize, mesmerize, enrapture, delight, enamour.

enchanter n wizard, witch, sorcerer, warlock, necromancer, magician, spell-binder, magus, conjuror, hypnotist, mesmerist, witch doctor, medicine man, soothsayer, seer.

enchanting adj bewitching, charming, delightful, attractive, appealing, captivating, irresistible, fascinating, engaging, endearing, entrancing, alluring, winsome, ravishing.

enchantment n **1** *witches with powers of enchantment* magic, witchcraft, sorcery, wizardry, necromancy, conjuration, hypnotism, mesmerism, charm, incantation. **2** *a time of enchantment* bliss, ecstasy, heaven, rapture, joy; transports. **3** *the enchantment of the view/dancing* charm, delight, attractiveness, appeal, captivation, irresistibility, fascination, entrancement, allure, allurement, glamour.

enchantress n witch, sorceress, fairy, fairy godmother, siren, Circe, hex. *see also* ENCHANTER.

encircle v **1** *enemy troops encircling the town* | *encircle the error* surround, enclose, circle, ring, encompass, circumscribe. **2** *trees encircling the lake* close in, shut in, fence in, wall in, hem in, confine.

enclose v **1** *enclosing the garden* surround, circle, ring, close in, shut in, fence/wall/hedge in, hem in, confine, encompass, encircle, circumscribe, encase; *fml* gird. **2** *enclose a cheque* include, send with, put in, insert, enfold.

enclosure n **1** *spectators/cattle in the enclosure* special/assigned area, arena; compound, ring, yard, pen, pound, fold, paddock, stockade, sty, corrall, krall, court, cloister, close; precincts; *fml* pale, enceinte, circumvallation. **2** *the enclosure of a cheque* inclusion, insertion, enfolding. **3** *an enclosure with the letter* insertion, thing enclosed.

encompass v **1** *encompass the castle* surround, enclose, ring, encircle, close in, shut in, fence/wall/hedge in, hem in, confine. **2** *encompassing all disciplines* include, cover, embrace, take in, contain, envelop, deal with, comprise, incorporate, embody.

encore n *play/take an encore* repeat, repeat/extra performance, replay; curtain call.

encounter v **1** *encounter an old friend* meet, meet by chance, run into, run across, come upon, stumble across, chance/happen upon; *inf* bump into. **2** *encounter problems* be faced with, confront, content with, tussle with. **3** *encounter the enemy* accost, confront; fight, do battle with, clash with, come into conflict with, engage with, struggle with, contend with, combat, skirmish with, tussle with.

encounter n **1** *an encounter with an old friend* meeting, chance meeting. *see* ENCOUNTER V 1. **2** *an encounter with the enemy* fight, battle, clash, conflict, contest, dispute, combat, collision, confrontation, engagement, skirmish, scuffle, tussle, brawl; *inf* run-in, set-to, brush.

encourage v **1** *encourage the losers* cheer, rally, stimulate, motivate, inspire, stir, incite, animate, hearten, invigorate, embolden, inspirit; *inf* buck up. **2** *encourage him to try again* urge, persuade, egg on, prompt, influence, exhort, sway, spur, goad. **3** *encourage exports* help, assist, aid, support, back, advocate, abet, boost, favour, promote, further, advance, forward, foster, strengthen.

encouragement n **1** *the encouragement of the losers* rallying, stimulation, motivation, inspiration, incitement, animation, heartening, invigorating, emboldening, inspiriting. **2** *encouragement to go ahead* urging, persuasion, egging on, prompting, exhortation; spur, goad. **3** *encouragement of exports* help, assistance, support, promotion, furtherance, advocacy, backing, boosting, favouring, furthering, advancing, forwarding, fostering, strengthening.

encroach v trespass, intrude, invade, infringe, impinge, infiltrate, overrun, usurp, appropriate, tread on someone's toes; *inf* muscle in on, invade someone's space.

encroachment n trespassing, intrusion, invasion, infringement, impingeing, infiltration, incursion, overrunning, usurping, appropriation.

encumber v **1** *injury encumbered his efforts* | *encumbered with two small children* hinder, hamper, obstruct, impede, inconvenience, handicap, retard, check, cramp, constrain, restrain. **2** *a room encumbered with old furniture* block up, fill up, stuff, clog, congest. **3** *encumbered with taxes* burden, load, weigh down, tax, overtax, saddle, trammel, stress, strain.

encumbrance n **1** *the encumbrance of heavy luggage* hindrance, hampering, obstruction, impediment, inconvenience, handicap, restraint, constraint. **2** *the encumbrance of a room with old furniture* blocking up, filling, stuffing, clogging, congestion. **3** *debts are an encumbrance* burden, weight, load, responsibility, obligation, stress, strain, tax, onus, trammel.

encyclopedic adj comprehensive, complete, wide-ranging, all-inclusive, thorough, exhaustive, all-embracing, universal, all-encompassing, vast, compendious.

end n **1** *the end of the table* | *the north end* edge, border, boundary, extremity, limit, margin, furthermost part, point, tip, extent. **2** *the end of the affair/novel* ending, finish, close, conclusion, termination, completion, resolution, climax, finale, culmination, denouement, epilogue; *inf* wind-up. **3** *a cigarette end* | *the end of a pencil* remnant, remainder, fragment, vestige; leftovers. **4** *her end in life* aim, goal, purpose, intention, intent, objective, object, design, motive, aspiration, raison d'être. **5** *the commercial end of the business* side, section, area, field, part, share, portion, segment, province; responsibility, burden, load. **6** *a peaceful/sad end* death, dying, demise, doom, extinction, annihilation, extermination; ruin, ruination, destruction, dissolution; death-blow, *coup de grâce*, finishing stroke; curtains. **7** *the end was that he shot himself* result, consequence, outcome, upshot, issue.

end v **1** *the show/book ended* come to an end, finish, close, stop, cease, conclude, terminate, discontinue, break off, fade away, peter out; *inf* wind up. **2** *to end a relationship/book* bring to an end, finish, close, stop, cease, conclude, terminate, break off, discontinue, complete, dissolve, resolve; *inf* wind up. **3** *end his life/hopes* put an end to, destroy, annihilate, extinguish.

endanger v *endangering the species* threaten, put in danger, expose to danger, put at risk, expose, risk, jeopardize, imperil, hazard, compromise.

endearing adj charming, attractive, adorable, lovable, sweet, engaging, winning, captivating, enchanting, winsome.

endearment n **1** *affectionate endearments* sweet talk, sweet nothings, soft words, blandishments. **2** *words of endearment* love, affection, fondness, liking, attachment.

endeavour v *endeavour to win* try, attempt, strive, work at, try one's hand at, do one's best, venture, aspire, undertake, struggle, labour, essay; *inf* have a go/shot/stab at.

endeavour n *make an endeavour to win* | *his best endeavour* try, attempt, trial, effort, striving, venture, undertaking, aspiration, enterprise, struggle, labouring, essay; *inf* go, crack, shot, stab.

ending n end, finish, close, conclusion, stopping, cessation, termination, expiration, resolution, completion.

endless adj **1** *endless patience* unending, without end, unlimited, infinite, limitless, boundless, continual, everlasting, unceasing, interminable, incessant, measureless, untold, incalculable. **2** *an endless chain* continuous, uninterrupted, unbroken, whole, entire, never-ending. **3** *endless love* unending, without end, constant, everlasting, unfading, perpetual, immortal, deathless. **4** *endless talk/travelling* non-stop, interminable, monotonous, over-long, unremitting, boring.

endorse v **1** *endorse a cheque* countersign, sign, autograph, underwrite, superscribe, validate. **2** *endorse the course of action* approve, support, back, favour, recommend, advocate, champion, subscribe to, uphold, authorize, ratify, sanction, warrant, affirm, confirm, vouch for, corroborate.

endorsement n **1** *the endorsement on the document/cheque* | *endorsement of the signature*

countersignature, autograph, underwriting, validation. **2** *the endorsement of their actions* approval, support, backing, recommendation, advocacy, championship, authorization, ratification, warrant, affirmation, corroboration. *see* ENDORSE 2.

endow v **1** *endow with talent* provide, give, present, gift, confer, bestow, enrich, supply, furnish, award, invest; *fml* endue. **2** *endow a foundation* | *endow a hospital bed* bequeath money for, bestow, will, donate money for, leave money for, make over to, settle on; pay for, finance, fund.

endowment n **1** *an endowment of money* | *endowment of a scholarship* gift, present, bestowal, grant, donation, award, proffering, bequeathing, settlement, legacy, provision; largesse, finance, funding, revenue, income. **2** *natural endowments* ability, gift, talent, flair, aptitude, genius, attribute, power, strength, capability, capacity, facility, faculty, qualification, characteristic, quality, feature.

endurance n **1** *endurance of his love/Christianity* lasting power, durability, stability, permanence, continuance, continuity, changelessness, immutability, longevity, everlastingness, immortality. **2** *beyond endurance* toleration, sufferance, fortitude, forbearance, perseverance, acceptance, patience, resignation. **3** *sports which are tests of endurance* stamina, staying power, fortitude, perseverance, tenacity; *inf* guts.

endure v **1** *love endures* last, live on, continue, persist, remain, stay, hold on, survive, wear well; *lit* abide, bide, tarry. **2** *endure the difficult situation* | *can't endure the new manager* put up with, stand, bear, tolerate, suffer, abide, submit to, countenance, brook; *inf* stick, stomach, swallow. **3** *endure poverty/pain* experience, undergo, go through, meet, encounter; bear, tolerate, cope with, suffer, brave, withstand, sustain, weather; *Scots* thole.

enduring adj lasting, long-lasting, durable, permanent, stable, steady, steadfast, imperishable, continuing, remaining, persisting, prevailing, abiding, eternal, immortal, perennial, unwavering, unfaltering.

enemy n foe, opponent, rival, adversary, antagonist, hostile party; opposition, competition.

energetic adj **1** *energetic exercises/person* active, lively, vigorous, strenuous, brisk, dynamic, spirited, animated, vital, vibrant, sprightly, tireless, indefatigable, peppy, zippy; bright-eyed and bushy-tailed. **2** *energetic approach* forceful, forcible, determined, emphatic, aggressive, high-powered, driving, effective, effectual, powerful, potent.

energize v **1** *energize him to get up* activate, stimulate, arouse, rouse, motivate, stir, goad, spur on, prompt. **2** *music might energize the party* enliven, liven up, animate, invigorate, pep up, electrify, vitalize. **3** *energize the device* activate, start up, switch on, turn on, get going.

energy n vigour, strength, stamina, forcefulness, power, might, potency, effectiveness, efficiency, efficacy, cogency, drive, push, exertion, enterprise, enthusiasm, animation, life, liveliness, pep, vivacity, vitality, spirit, spiritedness, fire, zest, verve, dash, *élan*, sparkle, buoyancy, effervescence, exuberance, *brio*, ardour, zeal, passion; *inf* vim, zip, zing.

enervate v weaken, make feeble, exhaust, tire, fatigue, wear out, strain, wash out, debilitate, enfeeble, sap, incapacitate, devitalize, prostrate.

enfold v **1** *mist enfolded the valley* enclose, fold, envelop, encircle, swathe, shroud, swaddle. **2** *enfolded in his arms* clasp, embrace, hug, hold, wrap.

enforce v **1** *enforce the law* apply, carry out, administer, implement, bring to bear, impose, discharge, fulfil, execute, prosecute, put through. **2** *enforce silence* force, compel, insist on, require, necessitate, oblige, urge, exact, coerce, pressure, pressurize, dragoon, bulldoze, constrain, extort.

enforced adj *enforced silence* forced, compelled, required, prescribed, imposed, necessitated, obliged, urged, exacted, coerced, pressured, pressurized, dragooned, bulldozed, constrained, extorted; unwilling, involuntary, unwarranted.

enforcement n **1** *enforcement of the law* application, carrying out, administering, implementation, imposition, discharge, fulfilment, execution, prosecution. **2** *enforcement of silence* coercement, exactment, coercing, exacting, requiring, pressurizing, dragooning, bulldozing.

enfranchise v *enfranchise women* gives the vote to, give voting rights to, give/grant suffrage to, give/grant franchise to, naturalize, give citizenship to.

engage v **1** *engage a housekeeper* employ, hire, take on, appoint, put on the payroll, enlist, enrol, commission. **2** *engage a boat/room* rent, hire, book, reserve, charter, lease, prearrange, bespeak. **3** *engage one's interest | engaged in a book* occupy, fill, employ, hold, grip, secure; preoccupy,

absorb, engross. **4** *engage one's attention/affection* catch, attract, draw, gain, win, capture, captivate, arrest. **5** *engage in a project | engage in many sports* enter into, become involved in, undertake, occupy oneself with, embark on, set about, take part in, join in, participate, partake in/of, launch into, throw oneself into, tackle **6** *engage in a contract | engage to marry* contract, promise, agree, guarantee, undertake, pledge, oblige, obligate, vouch, vow, commit oneself, bind oneself, covenant. **7** *engaging at dawn | engage in battle* join battle, do battle with, fight with, wage war with, attack, enter into combat, clash with, encounter, take on, set to, skirmish with, grapple with, wrest with, take the field. **8** *engage gear* fit together, join together, join, interconnect, mesh, intermesh.

engaged adj **1** *the manager is engaged* busy, occupied, in conference, unavailable; *inf* tied up. **2** *the toilet/room is engaged* occupied, in use, unavailable, reserved, booked. **3** *engaged couples* betrothed, affianced, plighted, espoused; *inf* spoken for.

engagement n **1** *her engagement as housekeeper* employment, appointment, work, job, post, situation, hire, business, stint. **2** *the engagement of a boat/room* rent, hire, booking, reservation, charter, lease, prearrangement. **3** *enter into a contractual engagement* contract, agreement, bond, pact, compact, promise, obligation, stipulation. **4** *they broke off their engagement* betrothal, marriage pledge. **5** *total engagement in the subject* absorption, preoccupation. **6** *a previous engagement* appointment, date, commitment, arrangement, meeting, interview, assignation, rendezvous, tryst. **7** *an engagement at sea* fight, battle, clash, conflict, struggle, attack, assault, confrontation, encounter, offensive; warfare, action, combat, strife; hostilities.

engaging adj attractive, charming, appealing, pleasing, pleasant, agreeable, delightful, likeable, lovable, sweet, winning, taking, captivating, fetching, enchanting, winsome, fascinating.

engender v **1** *engender feelings of hostility | engender hostility* cause, produce, create, give rise to, bring about, lead to, arouse, rouse, excite, provoke, incite, induce, instigate, generate, hatch, effect, occasion, effectuate, foment. **2** *engender sons* give birth to, father, breed, create, conceive, procreate, reproduce, bring forth, propagate, spawn, sire, beget.

engine n **1** *the engine of the car* motor, mechanism, machine, power source, turbine, dynamo, generator; internal combustion engine. **2** *engines of war* instrument, implement, device, appliance; machinery, apparatus, means.

engineer n **1** *the engineer who designed the bridge* civil engineer, electrical engineer, mechanical engineer, aeronautical engineer, chemical engineer; planner, designer, builder, architect, inventor, originator, deviser, contriver. **2** *ship's engineer* operator, controller, handler, director, driver.

engineer v bring about, cause, plan, plot, scheme, contrive, devise, manoeuvre, manipulate, orchestrate, mastermind, originate, manage, control, superintend, direct, conduct, handle, concoct; *inf* wangle.

engrave v **1** *engrave the silver cup | engrave her initials* carve, etch, inscribe, cut, chisel, imprint, impress, print, mark, chase. **2** *word's engraved on my heart* fix, set, imprint, stamp, brand, impress, embed, ingrain, lodge.

engraving n **1** *the engraving of the stone* carving, etching, sculpting, inscribing, inscription, cutting, chiselling, chasing, lithography, photoengraving, dry-point. **2** *we bought three engravings* carving, etching, print, lithograph, impression, block, plate, dry-point, cut, woodcut.

engross v **1** *engross my attention* occupy, preoccupy, absorb, engage, rivet, grip, hold, interest, catch, captivate, arrest, immerse, involve, envelop, engulf, fixate. **2** *engross the market* corner, monopolize, capture, sew up. **3** *engross a legal document* reproduce, copy, type; rewrite/reproduce in larger form.

engrossed adj *looking completely engrossed* preoccupied, absorbed, engaged, riveted, gripped, caught up, captivated, immersed, intent, rapt, involved, enveloped, engulfed.

engrossing adj *an engrossing article* absorbing, riveting, gripping, captivating, arresting, interesting, fascinating, intriguing, compelling, enthralling.

engulf v consume, overwhelm, flood, deluge, swamp, swallow up, submerge, bury, immerse, inundate, envelop, encompass.

enhance v **1** *enhance her beauty/reputation* add to, increase, heighten, stress, emphasize, strengthen, improve, augment, boost, intensify, reinforce, magnify, amplify, enrich, complement. **2** *enhance property prices* raise, lift, increase, escalate, elevate, augment, swell, exalt, aggrandize; *inf* jack up, hike.

enhancement n **1** *enhancement of beauty* heightening, emphasis, stress, strengthening, augmenting, intensification, reinforcement, magnification, amplification, enrichment. **2** *enhancement of property prices* rise, increase, increment, escalation, elevation, augmentation, swelling, exaltation, aggrandizement; *inf* jacking-up, hike.

enigma n mystery, puzzle, riddle, conundrum, paradox, problem, quandary, dilemma, labyrinth, maze, a closed book; *inf* poser, teaser, brain-teaser.

enigmatic adj mysterious, puzzling, baffling, obscure, perplexing, mystifying, cryptic, unfathomable, incomprehensible, inexplicable, inscrutable, Sphinx-like, recondite, esoteric, arcane, secret; ambiguous, equivocal, paradoxical, doubtful.

enjoin v **1** *enjoin people to stay indoors* direct, order, command, urge, bid, demand, instruct, decree, ordain, warn, require, call upon, charge, advise, counsel. **2** *enjoin late-night opening* ban, bar, prohibit, forbid, disallow, embargo, interdict, place an injunction on, proscribe, preclude, obstruct, restrain.

enjoy v **1** *enjoy music* like, love, be entertained/amused by, find/take pleasure in, delight in, appreciate, rejoice in, relish, revel in, savour, luxuriate in; *inf* fancy. **2** *enjoy good health/facilities | enjoy a good standard of living* have, possess, own, benefit from, have the benefit/advantage/use of, avail oneself of, be blessed/favoured with. **enjoy oneself** have fun, have a good time, have the time of one's life, party, make merry; *inf* have a ball, let one's hair down.

enjoyable adj entertaining, amusing, delightful, nice, pleasant, lovely, fine, good, great, agreeable, pleasurable, delicious, delectable, diverting, satisfying, gratifying.

enjoyment n **1** *find enjoyment in reading | eat with enjoyment* amusement, entertainment, diversion, recreation, pleasure, delight, happiness, gladness, joy, fun, gaiety, jollity, satisfaction, gratification, delectation, zeal, relish, gusto. **2** *the enjoyment of good health/facilities* possession, use, ownership, benefit, advantage, blessing, favour, exercise.

enlarge v **1** *enlarge the living area* make larger/bigger, expand, extend, add to, stretch, amplify, augment, supplement, magnify, multiply; widen, broaden, lengthen, elongate, deepen, thicken; *inf* jumboize. **2** *his spleen is enlarged* distend, dilate, swell, blow up, inflate, bloat, bulge, tumefy, protuberate. **3** *enlarge a photograph* make larger/bigger, blow up. **4** *enlarge on the topic* elaborate, expatiate.

enlargement n **1** *enlargement of the living area* increase, expansion, extension, magnification, amplification, augmentation, supplementation, supplement, multiplication, broadening, lengthening, elongation, deepening, thickening. **2** *enlargement of the spleen* distension, dilation, swelling, bloating, intumescence, tumefaction, protuberation; bulge, protuberance. **3** *photographic enlargement* magnification, blow-up, large print.

enlighten v inform, make aware, instruct, teach, educate, tutor, indoctrinate, illuminate, apprise, edify, civilize, cultivate, counsel, advise.

enlightened adj informed, aware, educated, knowledgeable, learned, wise, literate, intellectual, tutored, indoctrinated, illuminated, apprised; civilised, refined, cultured, cultivated, sophisticated, liberal, open-minded, broad-minded.

enlightenment n awareness, understanding, insight, education, learning, knowledge, erudition, wisdom, instruction, teaching, indoctrination, illumination, edification, awakening; culture, refinement, cultivation, civilization, sophistication, liberalism, open-mindedness, broad-mindedness.

enlist v **1** *enlist soldiers/staff* | *enlist her help* enrol, sign up, recruit, hire, employ, register, take on, engage, obtain, procure, secure, gather, muster. **2** *enlist in the army/venture* join, join up, enrol/register in, sign on/up for, enter into, volunteer for.

enliven v brighten up, cheer up, wake up, give a lift/boost to, ginger up, buoy up, hearten, gladden, excite, stimulate, rouse, refresh, exhilarate, invigorate, revitalize, vitalize, light a fire under; *inf* perk up, jazz up.

enmity n hostility, ill-will, hate, hatred, antagonism, antipathy, aversion, animosity, bitterness, spite, malice, venom, rancour, malevolence, animus.

en masse adv as a group, in a body, as one, as a whole, in a mass.

ennoble v *ennobled by grief* | *ennobling the author* make noble/great, dignify, exalt, elevate, raise, enhance, magnify, aggrandize, nobilitate, honour, glorify, lionize.

ennui n boredom, tedium, listlessness, lethargy, lassitude, languor, sluggishness, dissatisfaction, melancholy.

enormity n **1** *the enormity of the crime/act/suggestion* outrageousness, wickedness, evilness, vileness, monstrousness, hideousness, dreadfulness, heinousness, atrocity, cruelty, brutality, depravity,

nefariousness. **2** *commit enormities in wartime* outrage, horror, evil, crime, atrocity, abomination, violation, villainy, transgression, disgrace.

enormous adj huge, immense, massive, vast, gigantic, colossal, astronomic, mammoth, mountainous, gargantuan, prodigious, tremendous, stupendous, excessive, titanic, Herculean, Brobdingnagian; *inf* jumbo.

enormously adv *enormously wealthy* to a very large/great extent, tremendously, markedly, hugely, massively.

enormousness n *enormousness of the head* hugeness, massiveness, vastness, immenseness, magnitude, greatness, largeness.

enough adj *enough food/time* sufficient, adequate, ample, abundant.

enough n *we've had enough* sufficient/adequate amount, sufficiency, adequacy, ample supply, abundance, amplitude; plenty, full measure; *inf* plenitude.

enough adv *not warm enough* | *paints well enough* sufficiently, adequately, amply, satisfactorily, passably, tolerably, reasonably, fairly.

en passant adv in passing, by the way, talking of, while on the subject, that reminds me, apropos.

enquire v *see* INQUIRE.

enquiry n *see* INQUIRY.

enrage v annoy, anger, infuriate, irritate, madden, exasperate, provoke, incense, irk, agitate, inflame, incite, make one's hackles rise, make one's blood boil; *inf* wind up, get one's back/dander up.

enraged adj angry, angered, furious, annoyed, irate, livid, raging, fuming, irritated, maddened, exasperated, incensed, provoked, irked, agitated, inflamed; *inf* mad, wild, wound-up.

enrapture v delight, thrill, charm, captivate, fascinate, enchant, bewitch, entrance, enthrall, beguile, transport, ravish; *inf* blow one's mind, turn on.

enrich v **1** *a nation enriched by oil* make rich/richer, feather the nest of. **2** *enrich the soil* | *enrich one's quality of life* make richer, improve, enhance, add to, augment, supplement, upgrade, refine, polish, ameliorate, aggrandize. **3** *enrich the fabric* decorate, adorn, ornament, embellish, beautify, garnish, gild, grace.

enrol v **1** *enrol three new pupils* register, sign on/up, take on, enlist, recruit, enter, engage, admit, accept. **2** *he enrolled for military service* | *enrolling for a new course* sign on, volunteer, register, matriculate. **3** *enrol the statistics* record, enter, put down, note.

enrolment n **1** *the enrolment of pupils/soldiers* registration, signing on/up, joining up, enlisting, recruitment, engagement, admission, acceptance. **2** *the enrolment of statistics* record, register, list, note, catalogue.

en route adv on the way, in transit, along/on the road.

ensconce v settle, install, establish, nestle, curl up, snuggle up.

ensemble n **1** *the parts forming a pleasing ensemble* whole, whole thing, collection, set, combination, accumulation, sum, total, totality, entirety, assemblage, aggregate, composite; *inf* whole caboodle. **2** *a green ensemble* outfit, costume, suit, coordinates, matching; *inf* get-up, gear, rigout. **3** *a jazz ensemble* group, band, company, troupe, cast, chorus, circle, association; trio, quartet, quintet.

enshrine v **1** *enshrine the saint's relic* sanctify, dedicate, consecrate, hallow, deify, exalt. **2** *enshrine it in his heart* preserve, cherish, revere, hold sacred, treasure, venerate, immortalize.

enshroud v shroud, cloak, cloud, veil, enfold, enwrap, cover, obscure, bury, conceal, hide, pall, mask.

ensign n **1** *ensign of the ship* flag, banner, standard, pennant, streamer. **2** *ensign of the family* badge, shield, crest, escutcheon; coat of arms, armorial bearings.

ensnare v catch, capture, trap, net, snare, entangle, embroil, enmesh, entrap.

ensue v follow, come next/after, result, occur, happen, turn up, arise, come to pass, transpire, befall, proceed, succeed, issue, derive, stem, supervene.

ensure v **1** *ensure success | ensure that he will win* make certain, make sure, guarantee, secure, effect, warrant, certify, confirm. **2** *ensure his inheritance* make safe, protect, guard, safeguard, secure.

entail v *entails hard work* involve, require, call for, necessitate, demand, impose; cause, bring about, produce, result in, lead to, give rise to, occasion.

entangle v **1** *entangle wool* tangle, twist, ravel, knot, intertwine, jumble, snarl up, mat. **2** *entangle in a net* catch, trap, snare, ensnare, entrap, enmesh. **3** *entangled business affairs* complicate, confuse, muddle, jumble, mix up. **4** *entangle them in his affairs* involve, implicate, embroil, incriminate, inculpate.

entanglement n **1** *the entanglement of his business affairs* complication, involvement, confusion, muddle, jumble, tangle, mix-up, mess. **2** *his entanglement with his secretary* affair, liaison, amour, intrigue.

enter v **1** *enter a room | a river entering the sea | a bullet entering the chest* come in/into, go in/into, pass into, move into, flow into, penetrate, pierce, puncture. **2** *enter the army | enter the teaching profession* become a member of, join, enrol in, enlist in, sign up for, take up, become connected/associated with, commit oneself to. **3** *enter a competition | entered for the marathon/school* take part in, become a competitor in, participate in, put one's name down for, go in for, obtain/gain entrance to. **4** *enter the date of birth* record, register, put down, set/take down, note, mark down, catalogue, document, list, log, file, index. **5** *enter a protest* put forward, offer, present, proffer, submit, register, tender. **6** *enter another term of office | enter into negotiations* begin, start, commence, embark on, engage in, undertake, venture on. **7** *enter into details/conversation* become involved with/in, concern oneself with, participate in, engage in, join in.

enterprise n **1** *the festival is a challenging enterprise* venture, undertaking, project, operation, endeavour, effort, task, plan, scheme, campaign. **2** *a young person with enterprise* resourcefulness, resource, initiative, drive, gumption, imagination, imaginativeness, spirit, spiritedness, enthusiasm, zest, dash, ambition, energy, vigour, vitality, boldness, daring, spirit of adventure, audacity, courage, intrepidity; *inf* get-up-and-go, go, push, oomph, zip, vim. **3** *a thriving enterprise | private enterprise* business, industry, firm, commercial concern/operation, corporation, establishment, house.

enterprising adj resourceful, go-ahead, entrepreneurial, imaginative, spirited, enthusiastic, eager, keen, zealous, ambitious, energetic, active, vigorous, vital, bold, daring, adventurous, audacious, courageous, intrepid; *inf* peppy, pushy, up-and-coming.

entertain v **1** *entertain the guests with music* amuse, divert, delight, please, charm, cheer, beguile, interest, engage, occupy. **2** *entertain at home* play host/hostess, have/receive guests, provide hospitality, have people round, have company, hold/throw a party, keep open house, have a dinner/lunch party. **3** *entertain colleagues at home* play host/hostess to, show hospitality to, invite to a meal/party, wine and dine, treat, welcome, fête. **4** *entertain evil intentions* harbour, nurture, foster, cherish, hold, have, possess, hide, conceal. **5** *entertain the idea/proposal* consider, give consideration to, take into consideration, give some thought to, think about/over, contemplate, weigh up, ponder, muse over, cogitate, bear in mind, heed, pay attention to.

entertainer n performer, artiste, actor, actress, comedian, comedienne, singer, dancer, comic, impressionist, mime artist, acrobat, conjuror, magician.

entertaining adj *an entertaining recital/comic* amusing, diverting, recreational, delightful, pleasurable, pleasing, charming, enchanting, cheering, beguiling, engaging, interesting, funny, humorous, witty, comical, hilarious.

entertainment n **1** *play the piano for entertainment* amusement, fun, enjoyment, diversion, recreation, distraction; pastime, hobby, leisure activity/pursuit, sport. **2** *a one-woman entertainment* show, performance, concert, play, cabaret, presentation, spectacle, pageant.

enthrall v **1** *enthralled by the performance* hold spellbound, captivate, enchant, beguile, entrance, fascinate, bewitch, grip, rivet, charm, delight, enrapture, transport, carry away, intrigue, mesmerize, hypnotize. **2** *conquerors enthralling the villagers* enslave, subjugate, subdue, vanquish, conquer.

enthralling adj spellbinding, captivating, enchanting, fascinating, bewitching, gripping, riveting, charming, delightful, intriguing, mesmerizing, hypnotic.

enthuse v **1** *enthuse about astronomy* be enthusiastic, rave, praise to the skies, gush, wax lyrical, bubble over, effervesce; *inf* get all worked up, go over the top. **2** *her excitement enthused the others* make enthusiastic. *see* ENTHUSIASTIC.

enthusiasm n **1** *greet with enthusiasm* eagerness, keenness, ardour, fervour, warmth, passion, zeal, zest, vehemence, fire, excitement, exuberance, ebullience, avidity, wholeheartedness, commitment, devotion, devotedness, fanaticism, earnestness. **2** *stamp-collecting, is one of the child's enthusiasms* hobby, pastime, interest, recreation, passion, fad, craze, mania.

enthusiast n fan, supporter, follower, devotee, lover, admirer, fanatic, zealot, aficionado; *inf* buff, freak.

enthusiastic adj eager, keen, ardent, fervent, warm, passionate, zealous, vehement, excited, exuberant, ebullient, spirited, avid, hearty, wholehearted, committed, devoted, fanatical, earnest.

entice v lure, tempt, seduce, inveigle, lead astray/on, beguile, coax, cajole, wheedle, decoy, bait.

enticement n **1** *enticements such as high salaries* lure, temptation, allure, attraction, bait, decoy; *inf* come-on. **2** *the enticement of the child* luring, tempting, seduction, inveiglement, beguilement, coaxing, cajoling, decoying.

entire adj **1** *one's entire life* whole, complete, total, full, continuous, unbroken. **2** *not an entire success* absolute, total, outright, unqualified, thorough, unreserved, unmitigated, unmodified, unrestricted. **3** *emerge entire from the accident | an entire unblemished peach* sound, intact, undamaged, unmarked, unharmed, perfect, unbroken, unimpaired, unblemished, unflawed, unspoiled, unmutilated.

entirely adv **1** *not entirely correct* absolutely, completely, totally, fully, wholly, altogether, utterly, in every respect, unreservedly, without reservation, without exception, thoroughly, perfectly. **2** *entirely yours* only, solely, exclusively.

entirety n **1** *the population in its entirety* totality, wholeness, completeness, fullness, unity, undividedness. **2** *the entirety of the firm's outgoings* sum, total, aggregate.

entitle v **1** *entitle you to claim the estate* give the right to, qualify, make eligible, authorize, sanction, allow, permit, enable, empower, warrant, accredit, enfranchise, capacitate. **2** *they entitled the book 'Doom'* call, name, give the title of.

entity n **1** *a living entity* body, being, person, creature, individual, organism, object, article, thing, real thing, substance, quantity, existence, ens. **2** *the organization's very entity* being, inner being, existence, life, substance, essence, essential nature, quintessence, quiddity.

entourage n **1** retinue, escort, attendant, company, cortege, train, suite, bodyguard; attendants, companions, members of court, followers, camp followers, associates; *inf* groupies. **2** *a pleasant entourage* surroundings, environs, circumstances; environment, milieu, element, ambience.

entrails npl intestines, internal organs, bowels, vital organs, viscera; *inf* guts, insides, innards.

entrance v **1** *they entranced us with their dancing/beauty* hold spellbound, captivate, enchant, bewitch, beguile, enthrall, enrapture, ravish, send into transports/raptures, charm, delight. **2** *children entranced by a wizard* put under a spell, put in a trance, bewitch, hypnotize, mesmerize.

entrance n **1** *the entrance to the building* way in, entry, means of entry/access, access, approach, door, doorway, gate, gateway, drive, driveway, passageway, gangway, entrance hall, foyer, lobby, porch, portal, threshold. **2** *the entrance of the gladiators | the hero making an entrance* coming/going in, entry, appearance, arrival, introduction, ingress. **3** *refused entrance to the club* entry, admission, admittance, permission to enter, right of entry, access, ingress, *entrée*.

entrant n **1** *entrants to the college* new member, beginner, newcomer, fresher, freshman, new arrival, probationer, trainee, novice, tiro, initiate, neophyte, proselyte, cub, greenhorn; *inf* rookie. **2** *the entrants for javelin throwing* competitor, contestant, participant, player, candidate, applicant, rival, opponent.

entrap v **1** *entrap his prey* trap, snare, catch, net, enmesh, bag. **2** *entrap him into marriage* lure, trick, inveigle, seduce, lead on, entice, bait, decoy.

entreat v beg, implore, beseech, plead with, appeal to, petition, solicit, pray, crave, exhort, enjoin, importune, supplicate.

entreaty n appeal, plea, beseeching, pleading, petition, solicitation, prayer, importuning, supplication, suit. *see* ENTREAT.

entrée n *entrée to high society* entry, entrance, means of entry, access, admission, admittance, right of entry, permission to enter.

entrench, intrench v **1** *the army entrenched across the river | the party entrenched on the opposition benches* install, settle, establish, ensconce, lodge, set, root, plant, embed, anchor, seat; *inf* dig in. **2** *entrench on their neighbour's territory* encroach on, trespass on, infringe on, impinge on, intrude on, infiltrate, invade, interlope.

entrenched, intrenched adj *entrenched political bias* deep-seated, deep-rooted, rooted, well-established, fixed, set firm, firm, ingrained, unshakable, irremovable, indelible, dyed in the wool.

entrepreneur n businessman, businesswoman, business person, business executive; commercial intermediary, intermediary, enterpriser, middleman, promotor; *inf* whiz-kid.

entrust v **1** *entrust his children to her* give custody of, hand over, make over, commit, assign, consign, deliver. **2** *entrusted with the task | entrust the responsibility to him* give into the charge/care/custody of, charge, invest, commit; turn over, hand over, consign, delegate, depute, commend; put into the hands of.

entry n **1** *the main entry to the building* way in, entrance, means of access, access, approach, door, doorway, gate, gateway, driveway, passageway, entrance hall, foyer, lobby, porch, portal, threshold. *see* ENTRANCE n 1. **2** *the entry of the soldiers/actors* coming/going in, entrance, appearance, arrival, introduction, ingress. **3** *refuse entry to the gatecrashers* entrance, admission, admittance, permission to enter, access. *see* ENTRANCE n 3. **4** *an entry in a profit and loss account | an entry in his diary* item, statement, listing, record, note, jotting, memo, account, description. **5** *fifty entries in the competition* entrant, competitor, contestant, participant, player, candidate. *see* ENTRANT 2. **6** *you can submit four entries* attempt, try, effort, turn, submission; entry form; *inf* go.

entwine v wind round, twist round, intertwine, interlink, interlace, interweave, twine, link, lace, braid, plait, knit, crisscross, entangle.

enumerate v **1** *enumerate the qualities required* list, itemize, specify, spell out, name, give, cite, detail, recite, quote, relate, recount. **2** *enumerate the sums of money involved* count, calculate, add up, total, compute, tally, sum up, reckon, number.

enunciate v **1** *enunciate her words with clarity* pronounce, articulate, sound, speak, say, utter, voice, vocalize, enounce. **2** *enunciate his controversial opinions* give voice to, express, utter, state, declare, pronounce, assert, affirm, put forward, propound, proclaim, promulgate, publish, broadcast.

envelop v *the coat/fog enveloped him* enfold, cover, wrap, enwrap, swathe, swaddle, cloak, blanket, surround, engulf, encircle, encompass, conceal, hide, obscure.

envelope n *put the letter in an envelope* wrapper, wrapping, wrap, cover, covering, casing, case, jacket, shell, sheath, skin, coating, capsule, holder, container.

enviable adj *exciting envy*, desirable, worth having, covetable, tempting, excellent, fortunate, lucky, favoured.

envious adj jealous, covetous, desirous, green with envy, green, green-eyed, grudging, begrudging, resentful, jaundiced.

environment n surroundings, conditions, circumstances; habitat, territory, domain, milieu, medium, element, situation, location, locale, background, setting, scene, context, ambience, atmosphere, mood.

environmentalist n conservationist, preservationist, ecologist, green, eco-activist; *inf* econut, ecofreak.

environs npl *London and its environs* surrounding area, neighbourhood, vicinity, locality; precincts, outskirts, suburbs, purlieus.

envisage v 1 *envisage the future/consequences* foresee, predict, imagine, visualize, picture, anticipate, envision. 2 *cannot envisage failure* imagine, contemplate, conceive of, think of, visualize, accept.

envoy n 1 *envoys living in the embassy* legate, consul, attaché, chargé d'affaires, plenipotentiary. 2 *the Archbishop of Canterbury's envoy* emissary, accredited messenger, courier, representative, intermediary, delegate, deputy, agent, mediator, go-between.

envy n 1 *envy of her beautiful hair | envy of his rich neighbour* enviousness, covetousness, jealousy, desire; resentment, resentfulness, discontent, spite. 2 *it was the envy of the town* object/source of envy.

envy v *envy him his large house* be envious of, be jealous of, be covetous of, covet, begrudge, grudge.

ephemeral adj fleeting, short-lived, transitory, momentary, transient, brief, short, temporary, passing, impermanent, evanescent, fugitive, fugacious.

epic n *epics by Homer | direct an epic* long poem, long film, long story, heroic poem, saga, history, legend. see EPIC adj.

epic adj 1 *an epic poem* heroic, grand, long. 2 *of epic proportions | an epic journey* very great, very large, huge, very long, grand, extraordinary, ambitious.

epicene adj 1 *epicene individuals* bisexual, hermaphrodite, androgynous. 2 *epicene creatures* neuter, sexless, asexual. 3 *epicene men* effeminate, womanish, unmanly, effete, weak.

epicure n 1 *a restaurant guide for epicures* gourmet, *bon viveur, bon vivant*, gastronome, connoisseur; *inf* foodie. 2 *epicures interested only in sensual pleasures* hedonist, sensualist, sybarite, voluptuary, libertine, glutton, gourmand.

epicurean adj 1 pleasure-seeking, hedonistic, sensualist, self-indulgent, sybaritic, libertine, gluttonous, gourmandizing. 2 *epicurean attitude to food* gourmet, gastronomic.

epidemic n 1 *many people died in the epidemic* widespread illness/disease, outbreak,

plague, scourge. 2 *an epidemic of burglaries* outbreak, wave, upsurge, upswing, upturn, increase, growth, rise, mushrooming.

epidemic adj *reaching epidemic proportions* rife, rampant, wide-ranging, extensive, widespread, sweeping, prevalent, predominant.

epigram n 1 *puns and epigrams* witticism, quip, *bon mot*, pun, *double entendre, jeu d'esprit*, Atticism. 2 *proverbs and epigrams* saying, proverb, maxim, adage, axiom, aphorism, saw; words of wisdom.

epigrammatic adj succinct, concise, terse, compact, crisp, short, brief, tight, pointed, to the point, witty, pithy, sharp, pungent, well-tuned.

epilogue n conclusion; concluding speech, concluding programme, swan song, postscript, PS, afterword, coda, codicil, appendix, tailpiece, postlude.

episode n 1 *the second episode of the story* instalment, part, section, chapter, passage, scene. 2 *an episode in his life* incident, occurrence, event, happening, experience, adventure, occasion, matter, affair, business, interlude, circumstance.

episodic adj intermittent, irregular, sporadic, occasional, rambling, disconnected, digressive, discursive, wandering, anecdotal, picaresque.

epistle n letter, missive, communication, correspondence, message, bulletin, note, line.

epitaph n inscription, commemoration, elegy.

epithet n 1 *'blessed' was an epithet often applied to her | his epithet was 'the Iron Duke'* description, descriptive word/expression/ phrase, appellation, designation, label, tag; nickname, name, pet name, title. 2 *shouting epithets at the policeman* term of abuse, oath, curse, swear-word, obscenity, expletive, four-letter word.

epitome n 1 *the epitome of politeness* personification, embodiment, essence, quintessence, archetype, representation, model, typification, type, example, exemplar, prototype. 2 *an epitome of his written works* summary, précis, résumé, outline, synopsis, abstract, digest, abridgement, abbreviation, condensation, conspectus, compendium.

epitomize v 1 *epitomize the spirit of the age* personify, embody, exemplify, typify, represent, be representative of, symbolize, illustrate, incarnate. 2 *epitomize his works* summarize, précis, make a résumé/outline of, abridge, condense, shorten, reduce.

epoch n era, age, period, time, date.

equable adj **1** *an equable disposition* even-tempered, easygoing, calm, composed, collected, cool, calm and collected, serene, tranquil, placid, level-headed, imperturbable, unexcitable, unflappable, unruffled; *inf* unfazed. **2** *equable temperatures* uniform, even, constant, steady, stable, regular, unvarying, consistent, unchanging. **3** *an equable climate* uniform, moderate, non-extreme.

equal adj **1** *of equal height* the same, one and the same, identical, alike, like, comparable, commensurate. **2** *a sum equal to the previous sum* the same as, identical to, equivalent to, commensurate with, proportionate to, tantamount to, on a par with. **3** *an equal contest* even, evenly matched, evenly balanced, balanced, level, evenly proportioned; *inf* fifty-fifty, level pegging, neck and neck. **4** *equal to the task* capable of, fit for, up to, strong/good enough for, adequate for, sufficient for, suitable for, suited, ready for. **5** *receive equal treatment* the same, identical, like, uniform, unbiased, impartial, non-partisan, fair, just, even-handed, egalitarian. **6** *keep it at an equal temperature* even, constant, uniform, steady, stable, level, unchanging, unvarying, unfluctuating.

equal n *treat their staff as equals | they are equals in strength* equivalent, peer, compeer, coequal, mate, twin, alter ego, counterpart, match, parallel.

equal v **1** *four plus five equals nine* be equal to, be equivalent to, come to, amount to, add up to, make, total, correspond to. **2** *she equals him in strength* be equal/even/level with, be equivalent to, match, parallel, correspond to, come up to, measure up to, 'equate with, be tantamount to, vie with, rival, emulate. **3** *equal the previous record* match, be level with, reach, parallel, come up to, measure up to, achieve.

equality n sameness, identicalness, identity, equitability, parity, likeness, similarity, uniformity, evenness, levelness, balance, correspondence, parallelism, comparability, fairness, justness, impartiality, egalitarianism, equal opportunity.

equalize v **1** *equalize the score* make equal, make even, even up, make level, level up, balance, square, match. **2** *equalize the irregularities* level, level off, smooth, even off, balance, make uniform, regularize.

equanimity n composure, presence of mind, self-possession, self-control, level-headedness, even-temperedness, equilibrium, poise, aplomb, sang-froid, calmness, calm, coolness, cool-headedness, serenity, placidity, tranquillity, phlegm, imperturbability, unexcitability; *inf* cool, unflappability.

equate v **1** *equate disagreement with disloyalty* regard as the same, regard as identical, liken, compare, bracket together, associate, think of together, connect, link, ally. **2** *the two sides of the accounts do not equate* be equal, be alike, balance, correspond, agree, be commensurate, square, tally, compare, match, be equivalent, be parallel.

equation n equality, equalization, likeness, identity, balance, balancing, correspondence, equivalence, agreement, comparison, matching, equating, paralleling.

equatorial adj tropical, torrid, sultry, humid, steamy, sweltering, jungle-like.

equestrian adj *an equestrian event/statue* on horseback, mounted, in the saddle.

equestrian n horseman, horsewoman, rider; mounted soldier, mounted policeman, cavalryman, Horse Guard, trooper, hussar, cossack, cowboy.

equilibrium n **1** *a state of equilibrium between the physical forces* balance, stability, steadiness, evenness, symmetry, equipoise, counterpoise, equipollence. **2** *losing her equilibrium and shouting* equanimity, composure, calmness, coolness, sang-froid, tranquillity, collectedness, serenity, poise, self-possession, imperturbability, steadiness, stability; *inf* cool, unflappability.

equip v *equipped for the sea crossing | not equipped for academic life* fit out, kit out, rig out, prepare, provide, supply, stock, arm, array, attire, dress, outfit, accoutre; suit, endow.

equipment n gear, tools, tackle, stuff, apparatus, baggage, luggage, outfit, furniture, *matériel*; things, supplies, paraphernalia, accoutrements, furnishings; *inf* box of tricks.

equipoise n **1** *physical forces in equipoise* equilibrium, balance, stability, steadiness. *see* EQUILIBRIUM 1. **2** *scales using an equipoise* counterweight, counterbalance, counterpoise, ballast, stabilizer, makeweight; compensation.

equitable adj fair, fair-minded, just, even-handed, right, rightful, proper, reasonable, honest, impartial, unbiased, unprejudiced, non-discriminatory, disinterested, dispassionate, open-minded.

equity n equitableness, fairness, fair-mindedness, fair play, justness, justice, even-handedness, rightness, rightfulness, rectitude, righteousness, properness, rea-

sonableness, honesty, integrity, uprightness, impartiality, lack of discrimination/
bias/prejudice, disinterest, disinterestedness, open-mindedness.

equivalence n equalness, equality, sameness, identicalness, identity, similarity,
likeness, comparability, interchangeability,
correspondence, commensurateness. *see*
EQUIVALENT n.

equivalent adj *a job with equivalent status*
equal, the same, much the same, identical,
similar, like, alike, interchangeable, comparable, corresponding, correspondent,
commensurate, matching, on a par, tantamount, synonymous, homologous.

equivalent n *an ambassador or his equivalent*
equal, counterpart, parallel, alternative,
match, double, twin, peer, opposite number.

equivocal adj **1** *an equivocal reply* ambiguous, ambivalent, two-edged, indefinite,
vague, obscure, unclear, uncertain, hazy,
indeterminate, roundabout, oblique, circuitous, misleading, evasive, duplicitous,
paradoxical. **2** *equivocal character* doubtful,
dubious, questionable, suspicious, suspect.

equivocate v prevaricate, evade/dodge the
issue, beat about the bush, sit on the
fence, hedge, hedge one's bets, quibble,
fence, parry questions, fudge the issue,
vacillate, shilly-shally, hesitate, hum and
haw, shuffle about, tergiversate; *inf* pussyfoot around, waffle, flannel.

equivocation n prevarication, evasion,
dodging, hedging, quibbling, quibble, fencing, parrying, fudging, vacillation, shilly-
shallying, hesitation, humming and
hawing, shuffling, qualification, tergiversation; *inf* pussyfooting, waffle, flannel,
weasel words. *see* EQUIVOCATE.

era n age, epoch, aeon, period, time, generation, stage, cycle, season; times, days.

eradicate v get rid of, root out, uproot,
remove, extirpate, wipe out, weed out,
eliminate, do away with, abolish, stamp
out, annihilate, extinguish, excise, erase,
obliterate, efface, expunge, destroy, kill,
deracinate.

eradication n removal, extirpation, elimination, abolition, annihilation, extinguishing, excision, erasure, obliteration,
effacement, expunging, expunction,
destruction, killing, deracination.

erase v remove, rub out, wipe out, wipe
off, blot out, scrape off, obliterate, efface,
expunge, excise, cross out, strike out,
delete, cancel, blue-pencil.

erect v **1** *erect a building* build, construct,
put up, assemble, put together. **2** *erect a*
flagpole put up, raise, elevate, mount.
3 *erect a tent* put up, set up, set upright,
assemble. **4** *erect a theory/institution* establish, form, set up, found, institute, initiate,
create, organize.

erect adj **1** *stand erect | erect rows of soldiers*
upright, straight, vertical. **2** *erect flagpoles*
raised, elevated. **3** *an erect penis* hard, rigid,
stiff, firm.

erection n **1** *the erection of the building* building, construction, putting up, assembly. *see*
ERECT v 1. **2** *the erection of a flagpole* raising,
elevation. *see* ERECT v 2. **3** *the erection of a*
theory/institution establishment, formation,
setting up, foundation, institution, initiation, creation, organization. **4** *an ugly brick*
erection building, structure, edifice, construction; *inf* pile. **5** *unable to achieve an erec-*
tion tumescence, tumidity, turgescence.

erode v *wind eroded the rocks | envy eroded the*
friendship wear, wear away/down, eat, eat
away at, corrode, abrade, gnaw, gnaw away
at, grind down, excoriate, consume,
devour, spoil, disintegrate, deteriorate,
destroy.

erosion n wearing away, corrosion, abrasion, excoriation, consumption, disintegration, deterioration, attrition, destruction.

erotic adj titillating, sexually stimulating,
sexually exciting/arousing, erogenous,
aphrodisiac, seductive, sensual, carnal,
amatory, salacious, suggestive, pornographic; *inf* sexy, steamy.

err v **1** *err in thinking them guilty* be in error,
be wrong, be incorrect, be inaccurate,
make a mistake, be mistaken, mistake,
make a blunder, blunder, misjudge, miscalculate, misunderstand, misapprehend, misconstrue, get things/it wrong, bark up the
wrong tree, get the wrong end of the stick,
be wide of the mark; *inf* slip up, boob,
make a bloomer/booboo. **2** *to err is human*
do wrong, go wrong, go astray, sin, behave
badly, misbehave, transgress, trespass, fall
from grace, lapse, degenerate.

errand n message, task, job, commission,
chore, assignment, undertaking, charge,
mission.

errant adj **1** *errant knights of old* itinerant,
peripatetic, roaming, roving, wandering,
journeying, travelling, nomadic. **2** *errant*
schoolboys erring, mischievous, badly
behaved, misbehaving, lawless, criminal,
delinquent, sinning, offending, transgressing, aberrant, deviant.

erratic adj **1** *erratic conduct* inconsistent, variable, varying, irregular, unstable, unreliable, unpredictable, capricious, whimsical, fitful, wayward, abnormal, eccentric, aberrant, deviant. **2** *steer an erratic course* wandering, meandering, wavering, directionless.

erring adj errant, mischievous, badly behaved, misbehaving, lawless, criminal, delinquent, sinning. *see* ERRANT 2.

erroneous adj wrong, incorrect, inaccurate, inexact, untrue, false, mistaken, fallacious, unfounded, without foundation, spurious, invalid, faulty, flawed, unsound, specious.

error n **1** *detect an error in the arithmetic* | *errors in his report* mistake, inaccuracy, miscalculation, misreckoning, blunder, fault, flaw, oversight, misprint, literal, erratum, misinterpretation, misreading, fallacy, misconception, delusion; *inf* slip-up, bloomer, boob, booboo, howler, boner. **2** *done in error* mistake, erroneousness, oversight, misjudgement, miscalculation, misconception. **3** *see the error of his ways* wrongdoing, mischief, mischievousness, misbehaviour, misconduct, lawlessness, criminality, delinquency, sin, sinfulness, evil, evildoing.

ersatz adj artificial, imitation, fake, simulated, synthetic, substitute, man-made, plastic, sham, counterfeit, pretended, pretend, bogus, spurious; *inf* phoney, pseudo, pseud.

erudite adj learned, educated, well-read, well-educated, scholarly, intellectual, knowledgeable, literate, lettered, cultivated, cultured; *inf* brainy, highbrow.

erudition n learning, scholarship, education, intellect, knowledge, literacy, cultivation, culture; letters.

erupt v **1** *lava erupted from the volcano* | *the volcano erupted* belch/pour forth, gush, vent, spew, boil over; become active, flare up, eject/vent material, eruct, eructate. **2** *violence erupted* break out, flare up, blow up, burst forth, explode, go off. **3** *spots erupted on her face* break out, flare up, appear suddenly, burst forth, make an appearance, pop up, emerge, become visible.

eruption n **1** *an eruption of violence* | *volcanic eruptions* outbreak, outburst, flare-up, explosion, flaring, venting. **2** *a skin eruption* outbreak, rash, inflammation.

escalate v **1** *the war effort escalated* | *the war escalated* grow/develop rapidly, mushroom, increase, be increased, be stepped up, heighten, intensify, accelerate, be extended, be enlarged, be magnified, be amplified. **2** *prices will escalate* go up,

mount, soar, climb, spiral; *inf* be jacked/hiked up, go through the roof/cceiling.

escapade n adventure, act of recklessness, stunt, prank, trick, caper, romp, frolic, fling, spree; antics; *inf* lark, skylarking, scrape, fooling around, shennanigans.

escape v **1** *the prisoners escaped* make one's escape, get away, run away, run off, break out, break free, make a break for it, flee, make one's getaway, bolt, abscond, decamp, fly, slip away, steal away; *inf* do a bunk, vamoose, skedaddle, hightail it, do a runner, fly the coop; *Amer inf* take a powder. **2** *escape punishment* avoid, evade, dodge, elude, sidestep, circumvent, shake off, give the slip to, keep out of the way of, shun, steer clear of, shirk; *inf* duck, bilk; *Scots inf* body-swerve. **3** *gas escaping* leak, seep, pour out/forth, gush, spurt, issue, flow, discharge, emanate, drain.

escape n **1** *the escape from jail* | *an escape route* running away, breakout, flight, getaway, bolting, absconding, decamping, fleeing. *see* ESCAPE v 1. **2** *an escape from punishment/death* avoidance, evasion, dodging, eluding, elusion, circumvention; *inf* ducking, bilking, body-swerve. *see* ESCAPE v 2. **3** *a gas/water escape* leak, leakage, seepage, gush, spirt, issue, flow, discharge, outflow, outpouring, emanation, efflux. **4** *write as a means of escape* escapism, fantasy, fantasizing, wool-gathering, non-realism, getting away from it all. *see* ESCAPISM.

escapism n fantasy, fantasizing, dreaming, daydreaming, wool-gathering, wishful thinking.

eschew v avoid, abstain from, give up, refrain from, forgo, shun, renounce, forswear, swear off, abjure, steer clear of, have nothing to do with, give a wide berth to, fight shy of; *inf* kick, pack in, jack in.

escort n **1** *the royal party and its escort* | *the ship's escort* entourage, retinue, train, cortège, attendant company, protection, bodyguard, defence, convoy, contingent; attendant, guide, chaperon, guard, protector, safeguard, defender. **2** *her escort for the evening* | *an escort agency* partner, companion, beau, attendant, gigolo, call-girl, prostitute, rent-boy; *inf* date.

escort v **1** *escort the royal party* | *escort the ship/ambulance* accompany, guide, conduct, lead, usher, shepherd, guard, protect, safeguard, defend, convoy. *see* ESCORT n 1. **2** *escort her to the dance* partner, accompany, take out, go out with, attend on.

esoteric adj abstruse, obscure, cryptic, recondite, arcane, abstract, inscrutable, mysterious, hidden, secret, private, mystic, magical, occult, cabbalistic.

especial adj **1** *people of especial talent* special, exceptional, extraordinary, out of the ordinary, uncommon, unusual, outstanding, striking, remarkable, marked, notable, noteworthy, signal, superior, eminent, distinguished. **2** *her own especial brand of charm* special, individual, particular, distinctive, peculiar, personal, own, unique, singular, exclusive, specific, private.

especially adv **1** *especially talented* exceptionally, extraordinarily, uncommonly, unusually, outstandingly, strikingly, remarkably, markedly, notably, signally, eminently. **2** *especially in the summer* particularly, above all, mainly, chiefly, principally. **3** *bought especially for you* specially, specifically, with someone in mind, exclusively, expressly, particularly, uniquely.

espionage n spying, intelligence, undercover work, surveillance, infiltration, reconnaissance, counter-espionage, counter-intelligence; *inf* bugging, wiretapping.

espousal n *the espousal of Christianity/socialism* embracing, adoption, taking up, support, backing, championship, promotion, advocacy, defence. *see* ESPOUSE.

espouse v *espouse Christian/socialist principles* embrace, adopt, take up, take to one's heart, side with, be on the side of, support, back, champion, promote, advocate, defend, stand up for.

espy v catch sight of, glimpse, spot, see, notice, observe, make out, spy, sight, discern, behold, perceive, descry.

essay n **1** *write an essay* composition, dissertation, paper, article, thesis, discourse, treatise, tract, disquisition; *inf* piece. **2** *make a final essay* attempt, try, effort, endeavour, venture, undertaking; *inf* shot, go, crack, stab, bash.

essay v *essay the higher ascent* attempt, make an attempt at, try, try one's hand at, venture, undertake, take on; *inf* have a shot/go/crack/stab at.

essence n **1** *the essence of truth* essential part/constituent, fundamental nature/quality, innermost being/entity, quintessence, substance, sum and substance, nature, crux, heart, soul, life, lifeblood, kernel, marrow, pith, quiddity, *esse*, reality, actuality. **2** *essence of peppermint* extract, concentrate, concentration, distillate, tincture, elixir, abstraction; scent, perfume. **in essence** basically, fundamentally, to all intents and purposes, essentially, in effect,

substantially, in the main, materially, at heart, virtually. **of the essence** essential, necessary, indispensable, vital, crucial, of the greatest/utmost importance.

essential adj **1** *cost-cutting is essential* necessary, indispensable, vital, crucial, requisite, important, needed. **2** *the essential theme of the play* basic, fundamental, inherent, intrinsic, innate, elemental, characteristic, indigenous, principal, cardinal. **3** *the essential gentleman* absolute, complete, perfect, ideal, quintessential.

essential n *experience is an essential* necessity, prerequisite, requisite, basic, fundamental, *sine qua non*, rudiment; *inf* must.

establish v **1** *establish a new firm/colony* set up, form, found, institute, start, begin, bring into being, create, inaugurate, organize, build, construct, install, plant. **2** *establish his guilt* | *establish that he is guilty* prove, show to be true, show, demonstrate, attest to, certify, confirm, verify, evidence, substantiate, corroborate, validate, authenticate, ratify.

established adj accepted, official, conventional, traditional, proven, settled, fixed, entrenched, dyed in the wool, inveterate.

establishment n **1** *the establishment of the firm/colony* setting up, formation, founding, foundation, inception, creation, inauguration, organization, building, construction, installation. *see* ESTABLISH 1. **2** *a gentleman's establishment* residence, house, household, home, dwelling, abode, domicile, estate. **3** *clients patronizing his establishment* firm, business, place of business, company, shop, store, office, factory, emporium, commercial concern, concern, organization, enterprise, corporation, conglomerate. **the Establishment** the authorities, the powers that be, the system, bureaucracy, officialdom; *inf* Big Brother.

estate n **1** *a large country estate* property, piece of land, landholding, manor, domain; lands. **2** *an industrial/housing estate* area, piece of land, land, region, tract; development. **3** *his estate on death amounted to £300,000* assets, resources, effects, possessions, belongings; wealth, fortune, property. **4** *the three estates* social/political group, level, order, stratum, grade, class, rank, standing, status, caste. **5** *the estate of matrimony* state, condition, situation, circumstance, lot, position.

estate agent n property agent, property dealer; *Amer* realtor, real-estate agent.

esteem n *hold in high esteem* estimation, good opinion, regard, respect, admiration, honour, reverence, deference, veneration, appreciation, approval, approbation, favour, credit.

esteem v **1** *esteem it a favour* consider, regard as, think, deem, hold, view as, judge, adjudge, rate, reckon, account, believe; *lit* opine. **2** *highly esteemed by the community* regard, respect, value, admire, honour, look up to, think highly of, revere, venerate, appreciate, approve of, favour, like, love, cherish, prize, treasure.

estimate v **1** *estimate the cost* make an estimate, calculate roughly/approximately, work out, assess, compute, gauge, reckon, evaluate, judge, appraise, guess; *inf* guesstimate. **2** *I estimate him to be honest* consider, believe, think, regard as, judge, rate, view as, reckon, guess, conjecture, surmise; *lit* opine.

estimate n **1** *the joiner's estimate* estimated price/cost/value, price, costing, valuation, evaluation, assessment, appraisal. **2** *make an estimate of the cost* estimation, approximate/rough calculation, educated/informed guess, rough guess; *inf* guesstimate. **3** *in my estimate he is dishonest* estimation, opinion, judgement, consideration, mind, thinking, way of thinking, view, point of view, viewpoint, feeling, conviction, deduction, conclusion, guess, conjecture, surmise.

estimation n **1** *in my estimation he is the better candidate* estimate, opinion, judgement, consideration, mind, way of thinking, view, feeling, deduction, conclusion, surmise. *see* ESTIMATE n 3. **2** *go down in one's estimation* esteem, good opinion, favourable opinion, regard, respect, admiration, deference, veneration, appreciation, approval, approbation, favour. *see* ESTEEM n.

estrange v *circumstances estranged him from his wife* alienate, drive apart, set apart, part, separate, divorce, sever, disunite, make hostile/unfriendly towards, antagonize, cause antagonism between, set against, set at odds, destroy the affections of, disaffect.

estrangement n alienation, parting, separation, divorce, breakup, split, breach, severance, disunity, division, hostility, antagonism, antipathy, embitteredness, disaffection.

estuary n inlet, river mouth, cove, bay, creek, arm of the sea; *Scots* firth.

et cetera, etcetera adv and so on, and so forth, and the rest, and/or the like, and/or more of the same, et al., etc.; *inf* and what have you.

etch v engrave, carve, cut, furrow, burn into, eat into, imprint, impress, stamp, inscribe, ingrain, infix.

etching n engraving, carving, cut, print, imprint, impression, stamp, inscription.

eternal adj **1** *life eternal* everlasting, without end, endless, never-ending, immortal, infinite, enduring, deathless, permanent, immutable, indestructible, imperishable. **2** *stop that eternal row | those eternal questions* endless, never-ending, without end, ceaseless, incessant, non-stop, constant, continuous, continual, unbroken, without respite, interminable, unremitting, relentless, persistent, perpetual.

eternally adv **1** *eternally in hell | eternally yours* everlastingly, forever, for always, evermore, for all time, till the end of time, world without end. **2** *eternally on the phone* constantly, continuously, morning noon and night, day and night, perpetually, incessantly, unceasingly, interminably, persistently.

eternity n **1** *believe in eternity* immortality, everlasting life, afterlife, the hereafter, world without end, world hereafter, next world, heaven, paradise, nirvana. **2** *on the phone for an eternity* long time, age, seemingly forever, the duration; ages, ages and ages.

ethereal adj **1** *ethereal beauty/fabric* delicate, fairy-like, fragile, exquisite, dainty, fine, gossamer-like, gossamery, wispy, diaphanous, insubstantial, airy, shadowy, subtle, tenuous. **2** *ethereal regions/music* heavenly, celestial, unearthly, otherworldly, paradisical, Elysian, sublime, divine.

ethical adj moral, honourable, upright, righteous, good, virtuous, high-minded, decent, principled, honest, just, fair, right, correct, proper, fitting, seemly, decorous.

ethics npl moral code, morality; morals, moral principles, moral values, principles, rules of conduct, standards, virtues, dictates of conscience.

ethnic adj racial, cultural, national, tribal, native, indigenous, aboriginal, autochthonous, traditional, folk.

ethos n spirit, character, tenor, flavour, disposition, rationale, code, morality, moral code; attitudes, beliefs, principles, standards, ethics.

etiolated adj blenched, bleached, whitened, white, colourless, pale, chalky, chalk-white, faded, washed-out, wan, ghostly.

etiquette n rules of conduct/behaviour, good manners, manners; code of behaviour/conduct, code of practice, proper/good conduct, accepted behaviour, protocol, good form, form, courtesy, politeness, civility, propriety, decorum, convention, custom, usage, politesse.

eugenics npl racial improvement, controlled/selective breeding, planned evolution.

eulogize v praise highly, praise to the skies, sing the praises of, wax lyrical about, extol, laud, acclaim, pay tribute to, applaud, magnify, exalt, glorify, panegyrize, commend, compliment, pay compliments to, offer bouquets to; *inf* rave about.

eulogy n praise, accolade, extolment, lauding, acclamation, acclaim, paean, panegyric, tribute, applause, magnification, exaltation, glorification, encomium, commendation; praises, plaudits, compliments, bouquets; *inf* raving. *see* EULOGIZE.

euphemism n understatement, softening, substitute, polite term, politeness, genteelism, hypocorism.

euphemistic adj understated, softened, indirect, vague, inoffensive, polite, genteel.

euphonious adj harmonious, melodious, melodic, musical, pleasant-sounding, sweet-sounding, mellow, mellifluous, tuneful, dulcet, lyrical, rhythmical, symphonious, canorous.

euphoria n elation, joy, joyousness, jubilation, ecstasy, rapture, bliss, exhilaration, exaltation, glee, excitement, buoyancy, intoxication, merriment; high spirits.

euphoric adj elated, joyful, jubilant, ecstatic, enraptured, rapturous, blissful, exhilarated, exalted, high-spirited, gleeful, excited, buoyant, intoxicated, merry, on cloud nine, in seventh heaven, over the moon; *inf* on a high.

euphuism n high-flown language, purple pose, grandiloquence, floweriness, ornateness, floridity, bombast, periphrasis, circumlocution.

euthanasia n mercy-killing, merciful release, quietus.

evacuate v **1** *people evacuated the bombed town* leave, vacate, abandon, move out of, quit, withdraw from, retreat from, flee, depart from, go away from, retire from, decamp from, desert, forsake; *inf* pull out of. **2** *firemen evacuated the room* empty, make empty, clear. **3** *evacuate waste matter* | *evacuate the bowels* excrete, expel, eject, discharge, eliminate, void, purge, empty out, drain, defecate.

evacuation n **1** *the people's evacuation of the town* leaving, vacating, abandonment, withdrawal, retreat, exodus, departure, flight, desertion, forsaking. *see* EVACUATE 1. **2** *evacuation of waste products* | *bodily evacuations* excretion, expulsion, ejection, discharge, elimination, voiding, voidance, purging, emptying, draining, defecation; bowel movement/motion, stool, excrement, urination, urine; faeces, egesta.

evade v **1** *evade the enemy* | *evade one's share of the work* avoid, dodge, escape from, elude, sidestep, circumvent, shake off, give the slip to, keep out of the way of, keep one's distance from, steer clear of, shun, shirk; *inf* duck, bilk; *Scots inf* body-swerve. **2** *evade the question/issue* avoid, quibble about, be equivocal/evasive about, dodge, hedge, fence, fend off, parry, skirt round, fudge, not give a straight answer to; *inf* duck, cop out of.

evaluate v assess, put a value/price on, appraise, size up, weigh up, gauge, judge, rate, rank, estimate, calculate, reckon, measure, determine.

evaluation n assessment, appraisal, assay, weighing up, gauging, ranking, estimation, reckoning. *see* EVALUATE.

evanesce v vanish, vanish into thin air, fade, disappear, evaporate, melt away, peter out, disperse, dissolve.

evanescent adj **1** *evanescent summer days* vanishing, fading, evaporating. *see* EVANESCE. **2** *evanescent youth* ephemeral, fleeting, short-lived, transitory, transient, fugitive, fugacious, momentary, temporary, brief.

evangelical adj **1** *evangelical beliefs* according to the Gospel, scriptural, biblical, canonical, textual, orthodox. **2** *evangelical spirit* evangelistic, missionary, converting. *see* EVANGELISTIC.

evangelist n missionary, preacher, revivalist, reformer, converter, crusader, propagandist, campaigner, gospeller, proselytizer.

evangelistic adj missionary, preaching, revivalist, reforming, converting, crusading, propagandist, campaigning, evangelical, proselytizing.

evangelize v spread the faith/word, act as a missionary, preach, reform, convert, crusade, campaign, spread propaganda, proselytize.

evaporate v **1** *water evaporates in heat* become vapour, vaporize, volatilize. **2** *the hot sun evaporated the puddles* vaporize, dry, dry up, dry out, remove moisture from, dehydrate, desiccate, sear, parch. **3** *the vision evaporated* vanish, fade, disappear, melt away, dissolve, disperse, dissipate, dematerialize, evanesce.

evaporation n **1** *the evaporation of water* vaporizing, volatilization. **2** *the evaporation of the vision* vanishing, fading, disappearance, dispersal, evanescence. *see* EVAPORATE 3.

evasion n **1** *the evasion of the enemy* | *evasion of one's share of the work* avoidance, dodging, escape, eluding, elusion, sidestepping, circumvention, shunning, shirking; *inf* ducking, the go-by. *see* EVADE 1. **2** *skilled at evasion* subterfuge, deception, trickery, cunning, prevarication, quibbling, equivocation, dodging, hedging, fencing, fending, parrying, skirting round, fudging; *inf* ducking, flannel, waffle.

evasive adj **1** *evasive tactics* avoiding, dodging, escaping, eluding, sidestepping, shunning, shirking. *see* EVADE 1. **2** *evasive replies* prevaricating, quibbling, equivocating, equivocal, parrying, fudging, indirect, roundabout, circuitous, oblique, cunning, artful, casuistic; *inf* flannelling, waffling, cagey.

eve n **1** *on the eve of the election* evening before, night before, day before, period before. **2** *a summer eve* evening, night.

even adj **1** *an even surface* level, flat, plane, smooth, uniform, flush, true. **2** *an even temperature/colour/breathing* uniform, constant, steady, stable, consistent, unvarying, unchanging, unwavering, unfluctuating, regular. **3** *even amounts* | *even chances of success* equal, the same, much the same, identical, like, alike, similar, to the same degree, comparable, commensurate, corresponding, parallel, on a par, on an equal footing, evenly matched; *inf* even steven. **4** *the players/scores are even* all square, drawn, tied, level, level pegging, neck and neck, nip and tuck, neck and crop; *inf* even steven. **5** *of an even disposition* even-tempered, equable, placid, serene, well-balanced, composed, calm, tranquil, cool, unperturbable, unexcitable, unruffled, unflappable, peaceful. **get even** have/take one's revenge, be revenged, revenge oneself, even the score, settle accounts, get one's own back, give as good as one gets, return tit for tat, pay someone back, reciprocate. **get even with** have/take one's revenge on, be revenged on, revenge oneself on, get one's own back on one, repay.

even adv **1** *even colder yet*, still, more so, all the more, all the greater, to a greater extent. **2** *even a kid can do it* | *even the teacher laughed* unexpectedly, paradoxically, surprisingly. **3** *she was attractive, beautiful even* indeed, to be sure, you could say, possibly, more precisely, veritably. **4** *I could not even get up at all*, not quite, so much as, hardly, barely, scarcely, no more than. **even as** *even as we speak* at the very time/moment that, just as, as, exactly when, while, whilst, during the time that. **even so** *even so I shall attend* nevertheless, nonetheless, all the same, despite that, in spite of the fact, be that as it may, still, yet, notwithstanding.

even v **1** *even out the bumps/imperfections* smooth, level, flatten, make flush, plane. **2** *even up the differences in wages* make equal, make the same, make uniform, make comparable, balance up, standardize, regularize, equalize.

even-handed adj fair, just, impartial, unbiased, unprejudiced, non-partisan, non-discriminatory, disinterested, dispassionate, equitable.

evening n **1** *go out in the evening* late afternoon, night, close of day, twilight, dusk, nightfall, sunset, sundown; *lit* eve, even, eventide. **2** *the evening of her life* | *the evening of the Renaissance* close, end, declining years, last/latter part, epilogue.

event n **1** *sudden death is a sad event* | *the garden party was a successful event* occasion, affair, business, matter, happening, occurrence, episode, experience, circumstance, fact, eventuality, phenomenon. **2** *track events* | *the javelin event* competition, contest, game, tournament, round, bout, race. **3** *in the event he won* end, conclusion, outcome, result, upshot, consequence, issue, termination, effect, aftermath. **at all events** in any event, at any rate, in any case, anyhow, anyway, whatever happens, come what may, regardless, regardless of what happens, willy-nilly.

eventful adj busy, event-filled, action-packed, full, lively, active, important, noteworthy, memorable, notable, remarkable, outstanding, fateful, momentous, significant, crucial, critical, historic, consequential, decisive.

eventual adj final, end, closing, concluding, last, ultimate, later, resulting, ensuing, consequent, subsequent.

eventuality n event, occurrence, happening, case, contigency, chance, likelihood, possibility, probability.

eventually adv in the end, at the end of the day, ultimately, in the long run, finally, when all is said and done, one day, some day, sooner or later, sometime.

eventuate v **1** *the election eventuated in a change of government* end in, result in, have as a result/consequence. **2** *after the war famine eventuated* be the result, be a consequence, follow, ensue, come about, happen, occur, take place.

ever adv **1** *'twas ever thus* always, at all times, forever, eternally, everlastingly, until the end of time; *inf* until the twelfth of never, until the cows come home. **2** *will he ever go?* at any point, at any time, on any occasion, in any circumstances. **3** *grew ever larger | ever present | ever changing* always, at all times, constantly, continually, endlessly, unendingly, everlastingly, incessantly, unceasingly, perpetually, repeatedly, habitually, recurrently, unremittingly. **4** *ever so easy* very, to the greatest extent/degree, very much so. **5** *when will she ever learn?* at all, in any way, on earth. **6** *as beautiful as ever* up till now, until now, before.

everlasting adj **1** *everlasting life* never-ending, endless, without end, eternal, perpetual, undying, immortal, deathless, indestructible, abiding, enduring, infinite, boundless, timeless. **2** *their everlasting complaints* endless, interminable, never-ending, non-stop, incessant, ceaseless, constant, continual, continuous, unremitting, relentless, uninterrupted, recurrent, monotonous, tedious, wearisome, tiresome, boring.

evermore adv forever, always, for always, for all time, until the end of time, until death, until death do us part, endlessly, without end, ceaselessly, unceasingly, constantly.

every adj **1** *every house/child* each, every single. **2** *there is every chance of recovery* as much/great/likely as possible, all possible, all probable.

everyday adj **1** *an everyday occurrence* daily, diurnal, circadian, quotidian. **2** *everyday wear* ordinary, common, usual, regular, customary, habitual, accustomed, familiar, frequent, routine, run-of-the-mill, stock, conventional, plain, workaday, mundane, unimaginative, prosaic, dull.

everyone pron everybody, each one, every person, each person, each and every one, all, one and all, all and sundry, the whole world, every mother's son, every Tom, Dick and Harry, every man jack.

everything pron each thing, each item/article, every single thing, all, the lot, the whole lot, the entirety, the total, the aggregate; *inf* the whole caboodle, the whole

shooting match, the whole shebang, everything but the kitchen sink.

everywhere adv all around, all over, in all places, in every place/spot/part, in each place, far and wide, near and far, high and low, throughout the land, the world over, ubiquitously.

evict v turn out, put out, throw out, throw out on the streets, throw out on one's ear, eject, expel, oust, remove, dispossess, dislodge, drum out, show the door to; *inf* chuck out, kick out, turf out, boot out, heave out, give the heave-ho to, bounce, give the bum's rush to.

eviction n ejection, expulsion, removal, dispossession, dislodgement, clearance. *see* EVICT.

evidence n **1** *produce evidence of guilt* proof, confirmation, verification, substantiation, corroboration, affirmation, authentication, support; grounds. **2** *give evidence in court* testimony, sworn statement, attestation, deposition, declaration, allegation, affidavit. **3** *evidence of a struggle* sign, indication, mark, manifestation, token; signs. **In evidence** *with police very much in evidence* obvious, noticeable, conspicuous, visible, on view, on display.

evidence v *blushes evidencing guilt* indicate, show, be evidence of, reveal, display, exhibit, manifest, denote, evince, signify, testify to.

evident adj obvious, clear, apparent, plain, plain as daylight, plain as the nose on your face, unmistakable, noticeable, conspicuous, perceptible, visible, discernible, transparent, manifest, patent, palpable, tangible, indisputable, undoubted, incontrovertible, incontestable.

evidently adj **1** *evidently he disagrees* it seems, it would seem, it appears, apparently, seemingly, so it seems, as far as one can tell/judge, from all appearances, outwardly, ostensibly. **2** *quite evidently furious* obviously, clearly, plainly, unmistakably, perceptibly, indisputably, undoubtedly, without question. *see* EVIDENT.

evil adj **1** *evil deeds* wicked, bad, wrong, morally wrong, immoral, sinful, vile, base, corrupt, iniquitous, depraved, heinous, villainous, nefarious, reprobate, sinister, atrocious, vicious, malicious, malevolent, demonic, devilish, diabolic. **2** *evil influence* bad, harmful, hurtful, injurious, destructive, detrimental, deleterious, mischievous, pernicious, malignant, venomous, noxious. **3** *evil weather/temper* unpleasant, nasty, disagreeable, horrible, foul, vile. **4** *fall on evil times* unlucky, unfortunate, unfavourable, adverse, unhappy, disastrous, catastrophic, ruinous, calamitous, unpropitious, inauspicious, dire, woeful.

evil n **1** *more evil in the world than good* wickedness, bad, badness, wrong, wrongdoing, sin, sinfulness, immorality, vice, iniquity, vileness, baseness, corruption, depravity, villainy, atrocity, malevolence, devilishness. *see* EVIL adj 1. **2** *the evils of war* harm, pain, hurt, misery, sorrow, suffering, disaster, misfortune, catastrophe, ruin, calamity, affliction, woe; ills.

evince v indicate, show, reveal, display, exhibit, make clear/plain, manifest, demonstrate, signify, evidence.

evocative adj reminiscent, suggestive, reawakening, rekindling.

evoke v **1** *evoke a response* cause, bring about, bring forth, induce, arouse, excite, awaken, give rise to, stir up, kindle, stimulate, elicit, educe. **2** *evoke memories/spirits* summon, summon up, call forth, conjure up, invoke, raise, recall.

evolution n evolvement, development, unfolding, unrolling, growth, progress, progression, working out, expansion; natural selection, Darwinism. *see* EVOLVE1.

evolve v **1** *the subject evolved* develop, unfold, unroll, grow, progress, open out, work out, mature, expand, elaborate, disclose. **2** *gases were evolved* emit, yield, give off.

exacerbate v aggravate, make worse, worsen, intensify, exasperate, add fuel to the fire, put salt on the wound.

exact adj **1** *an exact description* precise, accurate, correct, unerring, faithful, close, true, just, veracious, literal, strict, errorless; *inf* on the nail, spot on. **2** *an exact person* precise, careful, meticulous, painstaking, methodical, punctilious, conscientious, rigorous, scrupulous, exacting.

exact v **1** *exact obedience* demand, require, insist on, compel, command, call for, impose, request. **2** *exact a ransom* demand, extort, extract, force, wring, wrest, squeeze; *inf* bleed.

exacting adj **1** *an exacting task* demanding, difficult, hard, arduous, tough, laborious, tiring, taxing, troublesome, stringent, onerous. **2** *an exacting person* demanding, strict, stern, firm, rigorous, harsh, rigid, unyielding, unsparing, imperious.

exactly adv **1** *exactly right | exactly as I expected* precisely, absolutely, just, quite, in every respect; *inf* on the nail, bang on, spot on. **2** *work the prices out exactly* precisely, accurately, correctly, without error. **3** *repeat my words exactly* word for word, lit-

erally, to the letter, closely, faithfully. **not exactly** *not exactly pleased to see us* not at all, by no means, not by any means, in no way, certainly not; not really.

exactly interj precisely, just so, quite so, quite, indeed, absolutely, truly, certainly, definitely, assuredly, undoubtedly.

exactness n **1** *the exactness of the description* precision, accuracy, accurateness, correctness, veracity. *see* EXACT adj 1. **2** *the exactness of our teacher* precision, care, meticulousness, punctiliousness, conscientiousness, rigour. *see* EXACT adj 2.

exaggerate v **1** *exaggerate the difficulties | exaggerate how difficult it was* overstate, overemphasize, overstress, overestimate, overvalue, magnify, amplify, aggrandize. **2** *he's not that tall — you're exaggerating* overstate, embellish, amplify, embroider, colour, add colour, overelaborate, overdraw, make a mountain out of a molehill, hyperbolize; *inf* lay it on thick, lay it on with a trowel.

exaggerated adj **1** *an exaggerated account* overstated, overemphasized, extravagant, inflated, highly coloured, excessive, hyperbolic; *inf* tall. **2** *an exaggerated frown | exaggerated make-up* overdone, extravagant, theatrical.

exaggeration n **1** *say without exaggeration* overstatement, overemphasis, magnification, amplification, embroidery, embellishment, extravagance, excessiveness, excess, pretentiousness, hyperbole; *inf* purple prose, puffery. **2** *the exaggeration of their ability* overstatement, overestimation, overvaluation, aggrandizement.

exalt v **1** *exalt to the highest rank* elevate, promote, raise, advance, upgrade, ennoble, aggrandize. **2** *exalt the composer* praise, extol, glorify, acclaim, pay homage/tribute to, laud, reverence, worship, revere, lionize, magnify. **3** *exalt one's spirits* excite, stimulate, animate, enliven, exhilarate, uplift, elevate, inspire.

exaltation n **1** *exaltation to high rank* promotion, advancement, raising, ennoblement, aggrandizement; rise, elevation. **2** *the exaltation of royalty* high rank, eminence, grandeur, dignity, honour, loftiness, prestige, fame. **3** *greet with exaltation* praise, extolment, glorification, acclamation, applause, homage, tribute, reverence, worship; plaudits. **4** *exaltation of the spirits* stimulation, animation, exhilaration, elevation, inspiration. **5** *full of exaltation* elation, exultation, joy, rapture, rhapsody, ecstasy, bliss, transport, happiness, delight.

exalted · exception

exalted adj **1** *from his exalted position in the firm* high, high-ranking, lofty, grand, eminent, prestigious, elevated, august. **2** *exalted aims* high-minded, lofty, elevated, noble, intellectual, ideal, sublime, inflated, pretentious. **3** *in an exalted mood* elated, exultant, jubilant, joyful, triumphant, rapturous, rhapsodic, ecstatic, blissful, transported.

exam n *an English exam* examination, test, set of questions/exercises; paper, question paper, oral, viva.

examination n **1** *the examination of the facts* study, inspection, scrutiny, investigation, analysis, review, research, observation, exploration, consideration, appraisal. *see* EXAMINE 1. **2** *the physical examination of a patient* check-up, inspection, assessment, observation, scrutiny. **3** *examination of witnesses* questioning, interrogation, cross-examination, cross-questioning, third degree. *see* EXAMINE 3. **4** *sit the examination* exam, test. *see* EXAM.

examine v **1** *examine the facts* look at, look into, study, inspect, survey, scrutinize, investigate, analyse, review, scan, observe, research, sift, explore, probe, check out, consider, appraise, weigh, weigh up, vet. **2** *examine a patient* look at, inspect, check over, give a check-up to, assess, observe, scrutinize. **3** *examine the candidates/witnesses* put/address questions to, question, test, quiz, interrogate, cross-examine, cross-question, catechize, give the third degree to; *inf* grill, pump.

example n **1** *an example of cave painting* sample, specimen, instance, representative case, case in point, illustration. **2** *follow someone else's example* model, pattern, precedent, paradigm, standard, parallel case, criterion. **3** *the hero is an example to everyone* model, ideal, pattern, standard, paradigm, paragon. **4** *someone as an example to other prisoners* warning, caution, lesson, admonition. **for example** for instance, e.g., to give an example/instance, by way of illustration, as an illustration, to illustrate.

exasperate v **1** *exasperate the teacher* anger, annoy, infuriate, irritate, incense, madden, enrage, provoke, irk, vex, gall, pique, try the patience of, get on the nerves of, make one's blood boil; *inf* bug, needle, get to, rile. **2** *exasperate a difficult situation* aggravate, make worse, worsen, exacerbate. *see* EXACERBATE.

exasperation n **1** *show exasperation at their behaviour* anger, annoyance, fury, irritation, rage, vexation, pique. *see* EXASPERATE 1. **2** *the*

exasperation of the difficulties aggravation, exacerbation. *see* EXASPERATE 2.

excavate v **1** *excavate a trench* dig, dig out, hollow out, scoop out, gouge, cut out, quarry, mine. **2** *excavate an ancient city/vase* unearth, dig up, uncover, bring to the surface, reveal, disinter, exhume.

excavation n **1** *the excavation of the site* digging, hollowing, quarrying. *see* EXCAVATE 1. **2** *mining/archaeological excavations* hole, hollow, cavity, pit, crater, cutting, trench, trough; burrow, quarry, mine, colliery.

exceed v **1** *if the price exceeds £10* be greater/more than, go beyond, pass, top. **2** *her abilities far exceed his* be greater than, surpass, be superior to, better, pass, beat, outdo, outstrip, outshine, transcend, top, cap, overshadow, eclipse. **3** *exceed the speed limit | exceed one's responsibility* go beyond, go over, do more than, overstep, go for the burn, out-Herod Herod, go over the top.

exceedingly adv extremely, exceptionally, extraordinarily, tremendously, enormously, vastly, greatly, highly, hugely, supremely, inordinately, surpassingly, superlatively, especially, unusually, very.

excel v **1** *excel at tennis* be pre-eminent/outstanding, be skilful/talented, be proficient, shine, be master, wear the crown. **2** *her cousin excels her at games* be better than, be superior to, surpass, outshine, eclipse, overshadow, outdo, outrival, outclass, outstrip, beat hollow, top, pass, transcend.

excellence n merit, eminence, pre-eminence, distinction, greatness, fineness, quality, superiority, supremacy, transcendence, value, worth, skill.

excellent adj very good, of high quality, of a high standard, first-rate, first-class, great, fine, distinguished, superior, superb, outstanding, marvellous, brilliant, noted, notable, eminent, pre-eminent, supreme, superlative, admirable, worthy, sterling, prime, select; *inf* A1, ace, brill, capital, top-notch, tip-top, champion; *Aust inf* beaut.

except prep *except you | except for me* with the exception of, excepting, excluding, leaving out, but, besides, barring, bar, other than, omitting, with the omission/exclusion of, exclusive of, saving, save.

except v *I except present company* exclude, leave out, omit, rule out, pass over, bar.

exception n **1** *with the exception of you* exclusion, omission, non-inclusion. *see* EXCEPT V. **2** *the case being an exception* special case, departure, deviation, anomaly, irregularity, inconsistency, quirk, peculiarity, oddity, freak. **take exception** object, be offended, take offence, raise an objection, resent, take umbrage, demur, disagree, cavil.

exceptionable adj *rude and exceptionable behaviour* objectionable, offensive, disagreeable, obnoxious, repugnant. *see* OBJECTIONABLE.

exceptional adj **1** *this noise is exceptional* unusual, uncommon, abnormal, out of the ordinary, atypical, rare, odd, anomalous, singular, peculiar, inconsistent, deviant, divergent, aberrant. **2** *a person of exceptional ability* unusually good, excellent, extraordinary, remarkable, outstanding, special, especial, phenomenal, prodigious.

excerpt n extract, citation, quotation, quote, passage, selection, part, section, fragment, piece, portion, pericope.

excess n **1** *an excess of fat/enthusiasm* surplus, surfeit, overabundance, superabundance, superfluity, plethora, glut, overkill, oversufficiency; too much, more than enough, enough and to spare. **2** *throw out the excess* remainder, residue, overload, overflow; leftovers. **3** *a life of excess* immoderation, lack of restraint, overindulgence, prodigality, intemperance, debauchery, dissipation, dissoluteness.

excess adj *excess baggage/food* extra, additional, too much, surplus, superfluous, spare, redundant.

excessive adj too much, to too great a degree, superfluous, immoderate, extravagant, lavish, superabundant, unreasonable, undue, uncalled-for, extreme, inordinate, unwarranted, unnecessary, needless, disproportionate, exorbitant, enormous, outrageous, intemperate, unconscionable; *inf* over the top, OTT.

excessively adv to too great a degree, unduly, immoderately, unreasonably. *see* EXCESSIVE.

exchange v *exchange compliments* trade, swap, barter, interchange, reciprocate, bandy.

exchange n **1** *the exchange of information* interchange, trade, trade-off, swapping, barter, giving and taking, bandying, traffic, reciprocity, tit for tat; dealings. **2** *the floor of the exchange* stock exchange, money market, bourse.

excise v **1** *surgeons excised the spleen* cut out, cut off, remove, eradicate, extirpate; *Tech* resect. **2** *excise the offending passage* remove, delete, cut out, cut, cross/strike out, erase, blue-pencil, expunge, eliminate, expurgate, bowdlerize.

excise n duty, tariff, toll, levy; customs.

excitable adj temperamental, emotional, highly strung, nervous, edgy, mercurial, volatile, tempestuous, hot-tempered, quick-tempered, hot-headed, passionate, fiery, irascible, testy, moody, choleric.

excite v **1** *excite the children too much* stimulate, rouse, arouse, animate, move, thrill, discompose, inflame, titillate; *inf* turn on, wind up. **2** *excite feelings of love* cause, bring about, rouse, arouse, awaken, incite, provoke, stimulate, kindle, evoke, stir up, elicit. **3** *excite a rebellion* cause, incite, bring about, stir up, instigate, foment.

excited adj *excited children* stimulated, aroused, animated, thrilled, agitated, overwrought, feverish, wild; *inf* high, wound up, turned on. *see* EXCITE 1.

excitement n **1** *jumping up and down with excitement* agitation, animation, emotion, anticipation, exhileration, elation, enthusiasm, feverishness, discomposure, perturbation, ferment, tumult. **2** *one of the excitements of travel* adventure, thrill, pleasure, stimulation; *inf* kick. **3** *the excitement of feelings* arousal, awakening, stimulation, evocation, kindling. *see* EXCITE 2.

exciting adj *an exciting event* thrilling, stirring, stimulating, exhilarating, intoxicating, rousing, electrifying, invigorating, moving, inspiring, titillating, provocative, sensational; *inf* sexy.

exclaim v call, cry, call/cry out, shout, yell, roar, bellow, shriek, ejaculate, utter, proclaim; *fml* vociferate.

exclamation n call, cry, shout, yell, roar, bellow, shriek, ejaculation, interjection, utterance, expletive.

exclude v **1** *exclude women from membership* debar, bar, keep out, shut out, prohibit, forbid, prevent, disallow, refuse, ban, blackball, veto, stand in the way of, proscribe, interdict. **2** *exclude the possibility* eliminate, rule out, preclude, count out, reject, set aside, except, repudiate, omit, pass over, leave out, ignore. **3** *the price excludes drinks* be exclusive of, not include, not be inclusive of, omit, leave out. **4** *exclude from a building* throw out, turn out, eject, remove, evict, expel, oust, ban; *inf* bounce, chuck out, kick/boot out.

exclusion n **1** *the exclusion of women* debarment, barring, keeping out, prevention, refusal, proscription. *see* EXCLUDE 1. **2** *the exclusion of robbery as a motive* elimination, ruling out, precluding, rejection, omission. *see* EXCLUDE 2. **3** *the exclusion of meals from the price* non-inclusion, omission, leaving out. *see* EXCLUDE 3. **4** *the exclusion of drunks* throwing out, ejection, removal, eviction, expulsion. see EXCLUDE 4.

exclusive adj **1** *an exclusive club* select, selective, choice, restrictive, restricted, closed, private, limited, discriminating, cliquish, clannish, snobbish, fashionable, chic, elegant, luxurious, high-class, aristocratic, top-people's; *inf* posh, ritzy, classy, swish, up-market. **2** *my exclusive attention* complete, undivided, full, absolute, entire, whole, total, all of, unshared. **3** *the exclusive means of travel* sole, only, unique, individual, single, one-off. **4** *exclusive of drinks* not including, excluding, leaving out, omitting, excepting, with the exception of, except for, not counting, barring. **5** *mutually exclusive* incompatible, inimical, antithetical.

excommunicate v exclude, expel, cast out, banish, eject, remove, bar, debar, proscribe, interdict, repudiate; *fml* anathematize, unchurch.

excoriate v **1** *excoriate skin* abrade, scrape, scratch, flay, strip, peel, skin, decorticate. **2** *excoriate the wrongdoers* denounce, censure, condemn, criticize, blame, accuse, berate, upbraid, rebuke, reprimand, reprove, scold, chide, read someone the riot act, chastise, castigate, inveigh/rail against, let fly at, abuse, attack, revile, vilify; *inf* carpet, lambaste, bawl out, give someone a rocket, tear someone off a strip, tear into, give someone what for.

excrement n waste matter, ordure, dung, manure; excreta, faeces, stools, droppings.

excrescence n **1** *excrescence on the body/tree* growth, lump, swelling, protuberance, outgrowth, eruption; cancer, boil, carbuncle, pustule. **2** *excrescence on the landscape* something ugly, eyesore, monstrosity, disfigurement; *inf* sight.

excrete v *excrete faeces/urine* pass, void, discharge, eject, evacuate, expel, eliminate, exude, emit, egest; defecate, urinate.

excruciating adj *an excruciating pain* agonizing, racking, torturous, insufferable, unbearable, severe, intense, extreme, harrowing, searing, piercing, acute; *fml* exquisite.

excursion n **1** *an excursion to the seaside* | *a shopping excursion* trip, day trip, expedition, jaunt, outing, journey, tour. **2** *an excursion from the main topic* digression, deviation, detour, wandering, rambling.

excusable adj forgivable, pardonable, defensible, justifiable, understandable, condonable, venial.

excuse v **1** *excuse the wrongdoer* forgive, pardon, exonerate, absolve, acquit, make

allowances for, bear with, tolerate, indulge; *fml* exculpate. **2** *excuse their behaviour* forgive, pardon, condone, justify, defend, vindicate, mitigate, explain. **3** *excuse them from heavy work* let off, exempt, spare, absolve, release, relieve, free, liberate.

excuse n **1** *their excuse for being late* defence, justification, reason, explanation, apology, vindication, mitigation; grounds, mitigating circumstances. **2** *his illness was just an excuse for his absence* pretext, ostensible reason, pretence, front, cover-up, subterfuge, fabrication, evasion, escape; *inf* cop-out. **3** *an excuse for a man/car* apology, travesty, poor specimen, pitiful example, mockery, poor substitute.

execrable adj abominable, abhorrent, loathsome, odious, heinous, hateful, detestable, despicable, foul, vile, deplorable, invidious, atrocious, offensive, disgusting, repulsive, obnoxious, nauseous, damnable.

execrate v **1** *execrate violence* abhor, abominate, loathe, hate, detest, despise, deplore, be repelled by, have an aversion to, feel hostility to, not be able to stand. **2** *execrate and blaspheme* curse, swear at, revile, imprecate, inveigh, fulminate, vituperate, condemn, damn, censure, denounce, excoriate.

execute v **1** *execute a murderer* put to death, carry out a sentence of death, kill; hang, send to the gibbet, behead, guillotine, decapitate, electrocute, send to the electric chair, send to the chair, shoot, put before a firing squad, send to the gas chamber, crucify, stone to death; *inf* string up. **2** *execute a plan of action* carry out, accomplish, perform, implement, effect, bring off, achieve, complete, fulfil, enact, enforce, put into effect, do, discharge, prosecute, engineer, administer, attain, realize, render. **3** *execute a dance* | *execute a piece of music* perform, present, stage, render.

execution n **1** *the execution of a murderer* putting to death, capital punishment; death sentence. see EXECUTE 1. **2** *the execution of a plan* carrying out, accomplishment, performance, implementation, effecting, bringing off, achievement, completion, fulfilment, enactment, enforcement, discharge, prosecution, engineering, administering, attainment, realization, rendering. **3** *execution of a piece of music* | *her superb execution of the dance* performance, presentation, staging, rendition, delivery, technique, style, mode.

executioner n **1** *public executioner* hangman, headsman, firing squad, Jack Ketch.

267

2 *the executioner of a member of a rival gang* assassin, killer, murderer; *inf* hit man, slayer.

executive n **1** *a bank executive* administrator, official, director, manager, VIP; *inf* boss, bigwig, big wheel, big Daddy/Chief; *Amer inf* honcho. **2** *the executive has increased in number* administration, leadership, management, hierachy; *inf* top brass.

executive adj *executive powers* administrative, decision-making, directing, controlling, managerial; law-making.

exegesis n *exegis of a Scriptural text* explanation, explication, interpretation, exposition, elucidation, clarification, annotation.

exemplar n **1** *an exemplar of morality* model, ideal, standard of perfection/excellence, epitome, paradigm, paragon, pattern, criterion, benchmark. **2** *an exemplar of birds of prey* example, specimen, exemplification, type, illustration, prototype, instance.

exemplary adj **1** *exhibiting exemplary behaviour* ideal, model, perfect, excellent, admirable, commendable, faultless, laudable, praiseworthy, meritorious, honourable. **2** *exemplary jail sentences* warning, cautionary, admonitory, monitory, example-setting, lesson-teaching. **3** *exemplary member of the species* typical, representative, illustrative, characteristic, epitomic.

exemplify v **1** *exemplify Impressionist painting* typify, epitomize, represent, personify, embody, illustrate. **2** *exemplify the talk with slides* illustrate, give an example/instance of, demonstrate, instance, depict.

exempt v *exempt from taxation* free from, release from, make an exception of/for, exclude from, excuse from, let off, give/grant immunity from, absolve/except from, liberate from, spare, exonerate from, relieve of, discharge from, dismiss from; *inf* let off.

exempt adj *declared exempt from taxation* free from, excused from, immune to, not subject/liable to, absolved/excepted from, spared, released from, discharged from, dismissed from. *see* EXEMPT V.

exemption n *be granted exemption from military service* immunity, indemnity, dispensation, freedom, exclusion, release, absolution, exception, exoneration, relief, discharge, special treatment, privilege, favouritism.

exercise n **1** *physical exercise* activity, exertion, effort, action, work, movement, training, physical training, drill, drilling, discipline; work-out, warm-up, limbering-up; gymnastics, sports, aerobics, callisthen-

ics, keep fit. **2** *the exercise of patience* employment, use, application, utilization, implementation, practice, operation, exertion, discharge, accomplishment. **3** *an English exercise* problem, task, piece of work; practice, schooling, drilling.

exercise v **1** *exercise in order to lose weight* do exercises, work out, train, exert oneself, drill. *see* EXERCISE n **1**. **2** *exercise patience* employ, use, make use of, utilize, apply, implement, practise, exert. **3** *a problem exercising the mind* worry, disturb, trouble, perplex, distress, preoccupy, annoy, make uneasy, perturb, vex, gall, peeve, stir up, afflict, pain, burden.

exert v **1** *exert pressure* exercise, employ, use, make use of, utilize, apply, wield, bring into play, bring to bear, set in motion, expend, spend. **2** *exert yourself and you will be able to do it* apply oneself, put oneself out, make an effort, spare no effort, try hard, do one's best, give one's all, strive, endeavour, struggle, labour, toil, strain, work, push, drive, go all out; *inf* put one's back into it.

exertion n **1** *physical exertion* effort, exercise, work, struggle, strain, stress, endeavour, toil, labour, action, industry, assiduity; pains. **2** *the exertion of pressure* exercise, employment, use, utilization, expenditure, application.

exhaust v **1** *the climb exhausted them* tire, tire out, wear out, fatigue, drain, weary, sap, enervate, tax, overtax, debilitate, prostrate, enfeeble, disable; *inf* take it out of, knacker, poop, fag out, knock out, burn out. **2** *exhaust the supply of fuel* use up, consume, finish, deplete, expend, spend, run through, dissipate, waste, squander, fritter away; *inf* blow. **3** *exhaust a well of its water* empty, drain, void, evacuate, deplete. **4** *exhaust the subject* say all there is to say about, treat in detail, treat thoroughly, develop completely, expound in detail about, study in great detail, research completely, go over with a fine-toothed comb.

exhausted adj **1** *cold and exhausted* tired out, worn out, fatigued, weary, sapped, enervated, weak, faint, debilitated, prostrate, enfeebled, spent; *inf* all in, done in, dead beat, dead tired, dog-tired, knackered, ready to drop, dead on one's feet, burnt out, played out. **2** *exhausted supplies* used up, at an end, consumed, finished, depleted. *see* EXHAUST **2**. **3** *an exhausted well* empty, drained, depleted, dry, void. *see* EXHAUST **3**.

exhausting adj tiring, wearing, fatiguing, gruelling, punishing, strenuous, arduous, back-breaking, taxing, laborious, enervating, sapping, debilitating. *see* EXHAUST 1.

exhaustion n **1** *fail to go on because of exhaustion* fatigue, great tiredness, weakness, debility, collapse, weariness, faintness, prostration, enervation, lassitude; *Med* asthenia. **2** *the exhaustion of resources* using up, consumption, depletion, dissipation. *see* EXHAUST 2.

exhaustive adj all-inclusive, comprehensive, intensive, all-out, in-depth, total, all-embracing, encyclopedic, thorough, complete, full, thoroughgoing, extensive, profound, far-reaching, sweeping.

exhibit v **1** *exhibit products* put on display/show/view, display, show, demonstrate, set out/forth, present, model, expose, air, unveil, array, flaunt, parade. **2** *exhibit signs of sadness* show, express, indicate, reveal, display, demonstrate, make clear/plain, betray, give away, disclose, manifest, evince, evidence.

exhibit n *a furniture exhibit* display, show, showing, demonstration, presentation, exhibition, viewing.

exhibition n **1** *a book exhibition* display, show, fair, demonstration, presentation, exhibit, exposition, mounting, spectacle. *see* EXHIBIT v 1. **2** *an exhibition of bad temper* display, show, expression, indication, revelation, demonstration, betrayal, disclosure, manifestation.

exhilarate v make happy/cheerful, cheer up, enliven, elate, gladden, delight, brighten, excite, thrill, animate, invigorate, lift, stimulate, raise the spirits of, revitalize, exalt, inspirit; *inf* perk/pep up.

exhilaration n elation, joy, happiness, gladness, delight, excitement, gaiety, merriment, mirth, hilarity, glee, animation, vivacity, invigoration, stimulation, revitalization, exaltation; high spirits.

exhort v urge, persuade, press, encourage, sway, prompt, advise, counsel, incite, goad, stimulate, push, beseech, entreat, bid, enjoin, admonish, warn.

exhortation n urging, persuasion, pressing, insistence, encouragement, prompting, advice, recommendation, counselling, incitement, pushing, beseeching; entreaty, enjoinder, admonition, warning, instruction, injunction, lecture, harangue. *see* EXHORT.

exhume v *exhume a corpse | exhume old memories* dig up, unearth, disinter, disentomb, unbury, resurrect, reincarnate.

exigency n **1** *a situation of exigency* urgency, emergency, crisis, criticalness, necessity,

imperativeness, stress, extremity, difficulty, trouble, pressure. **2** *the exigencies of war* need, demand, requirement, necessity, want, essential, requisite.

exiguous adj scant, scanty, meagre, sparse, bare, slim, slight, slender, paltry, skimpy, negligible, mere, trifling, diminutive.

exile v *be exiled from one's native country* banish, expatriate, deport, expel, drive out, eject, oust, proscribe, outlaw, bar, ban, ostracize, uproot, separate, excommunicate.

exile n **1** *sent into exile* banishment, expatriation, deportation, expulsion; uprooting, separation. *see* EXILE v. **2** *exiles from their homeland* expatriate, deportee, displaced person, refugee, outlaw, outcast, pariah; *inf* DP, expat.

exist v **1** *querying that ghosts exist* be, have being, have existence, live, have life, be living, subsist, breathe, draw breath, be extant, be viable. **2** *cannot exist in a cold climate* live, survive, subsist, occur, remain, continue, last, endure, prevail. **3** *enough money barely to exist on* survive, live, stay alive, eke out a living, subsist.

existence n **1** *come into existence | the existence of ghosts* being, existing, actuality, reality, fact, living, subsistence, survival, *esse*. **2** *a poverty-stricken existence* way of life, life style, manner of living/survival, mode of being. **3** *alien existences* being, entity, creation.

existent adj existing, in existence, living, extant, surviving, remaining, abiding, enduring, prevailing, present, current.

exit n **1** *theatre/motorway exit* way out, door, gate, door/gate out, passage out, out-lane, outlet, vent, egress. **2** *his exit from politics* departure, leaving, withdrawal, retirement, going, retreat, leave-taking, flight, exodus, farewell, adieu.

exodus n mass departure, flight, withdrawal, exit, leaving, escape, fleeing, evacuation, migration, emigration, retreat, retirement, hegira.

exonerate v **1** *exonerate from any responsibility* absolve, acquit, clear, discharge, vindicate, exculpate, declare innocent, dismiss, let off, excuse, pardon, justify. **2** *exonerate from duty* excuse, exempt, except, release, relieve, free, let off, liberate, discharge.

exoneration n **1** *exoneration from responsibility* aquittal, absolution, discharge, vindication, exculpation, dismissal, excusing, pardon, amnesty, justification. **2** *exoneration from duty* excusing, exemption, release, liberation, freedom, discharge, indemnity, immunity, dispensation.

exorbitant adj excessive, extortionate, extreme, unreasonable, immoderate, inordinate, outrageous, preposterous, monstrous, unwarranted, undue, unconscionable.

exorcise v 1 *exorcise the evil spirit* drive out, cast out, expel. 2 *exorcise a place of evil spirits* deliver, free, purify, rid, disenchant.

exorcism n 1 *exorcism of evil spirits* driving out, casting out, expulsion. 2 *exorcism of a place of evil spirits* deliverance, freeing, purification, ridding, disenchantment.

exordium n introduction, opening, beginning, preface, prelude, foreword, preamble, prologue, proem, prolegomenon.

exotic adj 1 *exotic fruits* foreign, non-native, tropical, imported, introduced, novel, alien, external, extraneous, extrinsic. 2 *exotic clothing* striking, outrageous, colourful, extraordinary, extravagant, sensational, unusual, remarkable, astonishing, strange, outlandish, bizarre, peculiar, impressive, glamorous, fascinating, mysterious, curious, different, unfamiliar. 3 *exotic dancing* erotic, go-go, striptease, titillating, risqué, sexy.

expand v 1 *metals expand when heated | the company is expanding* become/grow larger, enlarge, increase, increase in size/scope, swell, inflate, magnify, amplify, distend, lengthen, stretch, extend, multiply. 2 *expand the territory/business* make larger/greater/bigger, increase, magnify, amplify, add to, extend, multiply. 3 *petals expanding in the sunshine | faces expanding in smiles* open out, spread out, unfold, unfurl, unroll, unravel. 4 *expand one's account of the accident* elaborate on, add detail to, amplify, embellish, enlarge on, flesh out, expatiate on, develop, expound, pad out. 5 *guests losing their reserve and expanding* become relaxed, relax, grow friendlier, become less shy/reserved, become sociable; *inf* loosen up.

expanse n *an expanse of green/water* area, stretch, region, tract, breadth, extent, sweep, space, plain, field, extension, vastness.

expansion n 1 *expansion of metals/business* enlargement, increase, magnification, amplification, stretching, distension, protraction, extension, multiplication. 2 *flowers expanding in the sun* opening out, unfolding, unfurling, unrolling, unravelling. 3 *an expansion of one's account* elaboration, amplification, embellishment,

fleshing out, expatiation, development, expounding, padding out.

expansive adj 1 *the expansive qualities of metal when heated* expandable, expanding, extendable, extending; extensive, wide. 2 *on an expansive scale* extensive, wide-ranging, broad, wide, widespread, all-embracing, comprehensive, thorough, universal. 3 *guests growing expansive* sociable, friendly, outgoing, affable, unreserved, talkative, communicative, uninhibited, frank, open, genial, garrulous, loquacious, extrovert.

expatiate v *expatiate on the plans* expand on, enlarge on, elaborate on, amplify, embellish, expound, go into detail about, discourse on, dwell on, dissertate on.

expatriate v *expatriate criminals* deport, exile, banish, expel, cast out, proscribe, outlaw.

expatriate n *expatriates working abroad* emigrant, émigré, exile, displaced person, refugee, outcast, *Gastarbeiter; inf* expat, DP.

expatriate adj emigrant, living abroad, exiled, banished, cast out, deported.

expect v 1 *don't expect that he will come* think, believe, assume, suppose, imagine, presume, conjecture, calculate, surmise, reckon. 2 *expect a letter | expect a large crowd* anticipate, await, envisage, look for, look forward to, watch for, hope for, contemplate, bargain for, have in prospect, predict, forecast. 3 *teachers expect complete obedience* insist on, require, demand, exact, count on, call for, rely on, look for, wish, want, hope for.

expectancy n 1 *in a state of excited expectancy* anticipation, expectation, eagerness, hope, waiting, suspense, conjecture, anxiety. 2 *life expectancy* prospect, outlook, likelihood, probability.

expectant adj 1 *children's expectant faces* anticipating, anticipatory, expecting, awaiting, eager, hopeful, in suspense, ready, watchful, anxious, on tenterhooks. 2 *expectant mothers* pregnant, expecting, expecting a child, in the family way; *Tech* gravid.

expectation n 1 *in expectation of the arrival of Father Christmas* anticipation, expectancy, readiness, hope. see EXPECTANCY 1. 2 *an expectation that she will win* assumption, belief, supposition, presumption, assurance, conjecture, surmise, reckoning, calculation; confidence. 3 *future expectations* prospects, hopes; outlook, speculation, good fortune.

expecting adj pregnant, expectant. *see* EXPECTANT 2.

expediency, expedience n *interested only in the expediency of the plan, not in moral principles* convenience, advantageousness, advantage, usefulness, benefit, profitability, profit, gain, gainfulness, practicality, utilitarianism, utility, pragmatism, desirability, suitability, advisability, appropriateness, aptness, fitness, effectiveness, helpfulness, judiciousness, timeliness, opportunism, propitiousness.

expedient adj *expedient to tell a white lie | an expedient rather than moral course of action* convenient, advantageous, useful, beneficial, profitable, gainful, practical, pragmatic, desirable, suitable, advisable, appropriate, apt, fit, effective, helpful, politic, judicious, timely, opportune, propitious.

expedient n *an expedient to achieve an end* means, measure, method, resource, scheme, plan, plot, stratagem, manoeuvre, machination, agency, trick, ruse, artifice, device, tool, contrivance, invention, shift, stopgap.

expedite v **1** *expedite the procedure of obtaining planning permission* accelerate, speed up, hurry, hasten, step up, precipitate, quicken, urge on, forward, advance, facilitate, further, promote, press. **2** *expedite the task* finish/accomplish/achieve quickly, dispatch; *inf* dash off, make short work of.

expedition n **1** *an expedition to find a lost tribe* organized journey/voyage, undertaking, enterprise, mission, project, quest, exploration, safari, trek. **2** *a shopping expedition* trip, excursion, outing, journey, jaunt. **3** *three members of the expedition died* group, team, party, company, crew, band, troop, crowd. **4** *carry out orders with maximum expedition* speed, haste, promptness, swiftness, alacrity, quickness, rapidity, velocity, celerity, readiness, dispatch.

expeditious adj *an expeditious response* speedy, immediate, instant, prompt, swift, quick, rapid, fast, punctual, ready, brisk, nimble, hasty, summary.

expel v **1** *expel them from the country* banish, exile, evict, oust, drive out, throw out, cast out, expatriate, deport, proscribe, outlaw; *inf* chuck out, kick/boot out, turf out, heave out, give the bum's rush to, send packing. **2** *expel someone from a club* bar, ban, debar, blackball, throw out, drum out, oust, reject, dismiss, ostracize. **3** *expel cooking smells* discharge, eject, eliminate, excrete, evacuate, belch, void, spew out.

expend v **1** *expend time and money on acquiring luxuries* spend, lay out, pay out, disburse, lavish, squander, waste, fritter,

dissipate; *inf* fork out, shell out, dish out. **2** *expend all one's ammunition/energy* use up, consume, exhaust, deplete, drain, sap, empty, finish off.

expendable adj *workers considered expendable* dispensable, able/likely to be sacrificed, replaceable, non-essential, inessential, unimportant.

expenditure n **1** *limit expenditure and save money* spending, outlay; outgoings, costs, expenses, payments. **2** *the expenditure of money on defence* spending, outlay, disbursement, lavishing, squandering. *see* EXPEND 1. **3** *the expenditure of one's ammunition* using up, consumption, exhaustion, depletion, draining, sapping.

expense n **1** *the expense of private schooling* cost, price, charge, outlay, fee, amount, rate, figure, quotation. **2** *the expense of time, energy and money* spending, outlay, laying out, paying out, disbursement, lavishing, squandering. *see* EXPEND 1. **3** *victory at the expense of lives* cost, sacrifice.

expensive adj *expensive clothes/tastes* dear, costly, high-priced, exorbitant, extortionate, overpriced, lavish, extravagant; *inf* steep.

experience n **1** *experience of teaching | experience of prison life* involvement in, practice, participation in, contact with, familiarity with, acquaintance with, exposure to, observation of, understanding of, impression of. **2** *a frightening/wonderful experience* event, incident, occurrence, happening, affair, episode, adventure, encounter, circumstance, case, test, trial, ordeal. **3** *experience more valuable than a university degree* skill, practical knowledge, practice, training, learning, understanding, wisdom, *savoir faire*, maturity; *inf* know-how.

experience v *experience hardship | experience great happiness* have experience of, undergo, encounter, meet, feel, know, become familiar with, come into contact with, face, participate in, live/go through, sustain, suffer.

experienced adj **1** *experienced workers* having experience, practised, accomplished, skilful, proficient, seasoned, trained, expert, adept, competent, capable, knowledgeable, qualified, well-versed, professional, mature, master, veteran. **2** *experienced woman, not an innocent girl* worldly wise, sophisticated, knowing, mature, worldly, initiated; *inf* having been around.

experiment n **1** *medical experiments with rats* test, investigation, trial, trial run, try-out, examination, observation, enquiry, questioning, pilot study, demonstration, venture. **2** *results obtained by experiment* research, experimentation, observation, trial and error, try-out, analysis, testing.

experiment v *experiment on animals | experiment with new methods* conduct experiments, carry out trials/tests, conduct research; test, investigate, examine, explore, observe.

experimental adj *experimental basis/stage* trial, test, trial and error, exploratory, empirical, investigational, observational, pilot, tentative, speculative, preliminary, probationary, at the trial stage, under review, under the microscope, on the drawing-board.

expert n *an expert on ancient Rome | experts at playing golf* authority, past master, specialist, professional, adept, pundit, maestro, virtuoso, wizard, connoisseur; *cognoscenti*; *inf* old hand, dab hand, ace, buff, pro.

expert adj *an expert tennis player* skilful, experienced, practised, qualified, knowledgeable, specialist, professional, proficient, adept, master, masterly, brilliant, accomplished, able, deft, dexterous, adroit, apt, capable, competent, clever, well-versed, *au fait*; *inf* wizard, ace, crack, top-notch.

expertise n skill, skilfulness, mastery, masterliness, proficiency, knowledge, command, professionalism, deftness, dexterity, facility, ability, knack, capability, competence, cleverness; *inf* know-how.

expiate v *expiate his wrongdoing* atone for, make amends for, make up for, do penance for, pay for, redress, make redress/reparation for, make recompense for.

expiation n atonement, redemption, penance, redress, reparation, recompense, purgation; amends.

expire v **1** *your bus ticket has expired | your period of contract expires in May* be no longer valid, run out, finish, end, come to an end, terminate, conclude, discontinue, stop, cease, lapse. **2** *the old lady expired at midnight* die, pass away/on, decease, depart this life, perish, breathe one's last, meet one's Maker, give up the ghost, go to the great beyond, cross the great divide; *inf* kick the bucket. **3** *expire slowly while the X-ray is being taken* breathe out, exhale.

expiry n **1** *the expiry of the contract period | expiry of the lease* finish, end, termination, conclusion, discontinuation, cessation, lapse, expiration, invalidity. **2** *the expiry of the patient* death, passing away/on, decease, demise. *see* EXPIRE 2.

explain v **1** *explain the procedure* give an explanation of, describe, define, make clear/plain/intelligible, spell out, interpret, unfold, clarify, throw light on, clear up, decipher, decode, elucidate, expound, explicate, delineate, demonstrate, teach, illustrate, expose, resolve, solve. **2** *explain their actions* give an explanation for, account for, give a reason/justification for, justify, give an excuse/alibi/apologia for, defend, vindicate, mitigate.

explanation n **1** *the explanation of the procedure* description, definition, interpretation, clarification, deciphering, decoding, elucidation, expounding, explication, demonstration, illustration, exposure, resolution, solution. **2** *an explanation of their motives* account, justification, reason, excuse, defence, vindication, mitigation, apologia.

explanatory adj by way of explanation, descriptive, illustrative, interpretive, demonstrative, illuminative, elucidative, elucidatory, explicative, expository, justificatory, exegetic.

expletive n swear-word, oath, curse, obscenity, epithet, exclamation; *inf* dirty word, four-letter word; *Amer inf* cuss-word.

explicable adj explainable, accountable, definable, understandable, interpretable, intelligible, ascertainable, resolvable, soluble, justificatory.

explicate v **1** *explicate a literary text* explain, explain in detail, make explicit, clarify, make plain/clear, spell out, interpret, elucidate, illuminate, expound, unfold, untangle, put into plain English. **2** *explicate an idea* develop, evolve, work out, construct, formulate, devise, build, concoct, assemble.

explicit adj **1** *explicit instructions* clearly expressed, easily understandable, detailed, clear, crystal clear, direct, plain, obvious, precise, exact, straightforward, definite, distinct, categorical, specific, positive, unequivocal, unambiguous. **2** *explicit criticism | explicit sexual description* outspoken, unrestrained, unreserved, uninhibited, open, candid, frank, forthright, direct, plain-spoken, point-blank, full-frontal, no holds barred.

explode v **1** *the firework/boiler exploded* blow up, detonate, burst, fly apart, fly into pieces, go off, erupt; *inf* go bang. **2** *explode the firework* detonate, set off, let off, fire off, let fly. **3** *explode in anger* give vent to, blow up, rage, rant and rave, storm, bluster; *inf* fly off the handle, hit the roof, blow one's cool/top, blow a fuse, flip one's lid, freak out. **4** *explode a myth* disprove, invalidate, refute, repudiate, discredit, debunk, belie, give the lie to, ridicule, blow up, blow sky-high, knock the bottom from. **5** *world population exploding* increase suddenly/rapidly/dramatically, mushroom, escalate, burgeon, rocket, accelerate, heighten.

exploit n feat, deed, adventure, stunt, achievement, accomplishment, attainment.

exploit v **1** *exploit natural resources* make use of, put to use, utilize, use, use to good advantage, turn/put to good use, turn to account, profit from/by, make capital out of, capitalize on; *inf* cash in on, milk. **2** *exploit the workers | exploit his good nature* make use of, take advantage of, abuse, impose upon, play upon, misuse; *inf* walk all over, walk over, take for a ride, put one over on.

exploration n **1** *the exploration of space | a voyage of exploration* investigation, study, survey, research, inspection, probe, examination, scrutiny, observation, search, inquiry, analysis. **2** *conduct an exploration into the interior of the continent* expedition, trip, tour, survey, reconnaissance; travels.

exploratory adj investigative, probing, fact-finding, analytic, experimental, trial, searching.

explore v **1** *explore the Antarctic* travel, traverse, tour, range over, survey, take a look at, inspect, scout, reconnoitre, prospect. **2** *explore several possible solutions* investigate, look into, enquire into, consider, examine, research, survey, scrutinize, study, review, take stock of.

explorer n traveller, discover, tourer, surveyor, scout, reconnoitrer, prospector.

explosion n **1** *a loud explosion* bang, blast, boom, rumble, crash, crack, report, thunder, roll, clap, detonation, discharge, eruption. **2** *an angry explosion* outburst, flare-up, fit, outbreak, paroxysm, eruption. **3** *an explosion of population* sudden/rapid/dramatic increase, mushrooming, escalation, burgeoning, rocketing, acceleration, speeding-up, heightening.

explosive adj **1** *explosive substance* inflammable, volatile, eruptive, unstable. **2** *explosive temperament* fiery, angry, touchy, stormy, violent, vehement, volatile, volcanic. **3** *an explosive situation* tense, charged, critical, serious, inflammable, volcanic, dangerous, perilous, hazardous, ugly, overwrought.

exponent n **1** *an exponent of traditional teaching methods* advocate, supporter, upholder, backer, defender, champion, spokesperson, promoter, propagandist, proponent. **2** *an exponent lecturing on modern art* interpreter,

commentator, expounder, explainer, expositor, elucidator, illustrator, demonstrator. **3** *a famous exponent of mime* practioner, performer, player, interpreter, executant, presenter. **4** *the finest extant exponent of cave painting* example, illustration, specimen, sample, type, exemplar, instance, model, representation.

export v **1** *export goods* sell overseas/abroad, market overseas/abroad, send overseas/abroad. **2** *export ideas* transmit, spread.

expose v **1** *expose the skin to sunlight* uncover, lay bare, bare, leave unprotected, strip, reveal, denude. **2** *expose to danger/abuse* lay open to, leave unprotected from, put at risk of, put in jeopardy of, make vulnerable to, make subject to, subject to; endanger, risk, hazard. **3** *expose one's ignorance* reveal, uncover, show, display, make obvious, exhibit, disclose, manifest, unveil. **4** *expose a crime/criminal* bring to light, disclose, uncover, reveal, make known, let out, divulge, denounce, unearth, unmask, detect, betray, smoke out; *inf* spill the beans on, blow the whistle on, pull the plug on. **5** *expose to new ideas* bring into contact with, introduce to, present with, make familiar/conversant/acquainted with, familiarize/acquaint with, make aware of.

expose oneself display/reveal/show the genitalia; *inf* flash.

exposé n exposure, disclosure, uncovering, revelation, divulgence.

exposed adj *an exposed hillside* open, unprotected, without shelter/protection, unsheltered, open to the elements/weather.

exposition n **1** *the exposition of modern educational theories* explanation, interpretation, description, elucidation, explication, illustration; *fml* exegesis. **2** *give an exposition of the advantages of nuclear power* explanation, account, description, commentary, study, treatise, discourse, dissertation, critique. **3** *a trade exposition* exhibition, fair, display, show, presentation, demonstration; *inf* expo, demo.

expository adj *an expository statement of the theory* explanatory, interpretative, descriptive, elucidatory, explicatory, explicative, illustrative; *fml* exegetic, hermeneutic.

expostulate v *expostulate with an opponent* remonstrate with, argue with, reason with, make a protest to, raise an objection with.

exposure n **1** *the exposure of the skin to sunlight* uncovering, baring, stripping, revelation, denudation. **2** *exposure to danger/abuse* subjection/submission to, laying open to. *see* EXPOSE 2. **3** *exposure of one's ignorance* revelation, uncovering, showing, display, exhi-

273

bition, disclosure, manifestation, unveiling. **4** *exposure of a crime/criminal* disclosure, uncovering, revelation, divulgence, denunciation, unmasking, detection, betrayal. *see* EXPOSE 4. **5** *exposure to new ideas* contact with, introduction/presentation to. *see* EXPOSE 5. **6** *resent the exposure given to the affair* publicity, publicizing, advertising, broadcasting, airing. **7** *a sunny exposure* position, setting, location, aspect, view, outlook, frontage.

expound v **1** *expound one's views on education* explain, detail, spell out, set forth, describe, discuss. **2** *expound the Scriptures* interpret, explain, give a commentary on, annotate, illustrate, explicate.

express v **1** *express one's feelings in a speech* put into words, state, voice, give voice to, enunciate, communicate, utter, pronounce, articulate, verbalize, give vent to, word, couch, proclaim, assert, point out, speak, say. **2** *express appreciation with a gift* show, indicate, demonstrate, convey, communicate, intimate, denote, exhibit, illustrate, manifest, make manifest, reveal, evince, evidence, symbolize, embody. **3** *express juice from fruit* press out, squeeze, extract, force out. **express onself** communicate one's thoughts/opinions/views, put thoughts into words, speak one's mind, say one's piece.

express adj **1** *express service* rapid, swift, fast, quick, speedy, prompt, high-speed, brisk, expeditious, direct, non-stop. **2** *express instructions* explicit, clear, plain, distinct, unambiguous, precise, specific, well-defined, unmistakable, unequivocal, pointed, exact, outright. **3** *done with the express purpose of embarrassing them* particular, sole, purposeful, special, especial, specific, singular.

expression n **1** *public expression of grievances* statement, voicing, uttering, utterance, pronouncement, articulation, verbalization, venting, wording, proclamation, assertion. **2** *send flowers as an expression of appreciation* indication, demonstration, show, conveyance, communication, intimation, exhibition, illustration, manifestation, revelation, embodiment. **3** *a particularly apt expression* word, phrase, term, choice of words, turn of phrase, wording, language, phrasing, phraseology, speech, diction, idiom, style, delivery, intonation, execution; *fml* locution. **4** *a sad expression on her face* look, appearance, air, countenance, aspect; *fml* mien. **5** *playing the piano with expression* feeling, emotion, passion, intensity, poignancy, artistry, depth,

spirit, vividness, ardour, power, force, imagination.

expressionless adj **1** *expressionless reading of poetry* dull, dry, boring, wooden, undemonstrative, apathetic, unimpassioned, weak, devoid of feeling/emotion. *see* EXPRESSION 5. **2** *a totally expressionless face* blank, deadpan; *inf* poker-faced, inscrutable, emotionless, vacuous.

expressive adj **1** *an expressive face/gesture* full of emotion/feeling, indicating emotion/feeling, emotional, eloquent, telling, demonstrative, suggestive, vivid. **2** *an expressive piece of music* emotional, eloquent, passionate, intense, poignant, moving, striking, evocative, sympathetic, artistic, vivid, graphic, ardent, powerful, imaginative. **3** *expressive of their contempt* showing, indicative, demonstrating, demonstrative, suggesting, revealing, underlining.

expressly adv **1** *expressly forbidden* absolutely, explicitly, clearly, plainly, distinctly, precisely, specifically, unequivocally. **2** *laws expressly made to stop vandalism* purposefully, particularly, solely, specially, especially, specifically, singularly.

expropriate v seize, take away, take over, take, appropriate, take possession of, misappropriate, requisition, commandeer, impound, confiscate, usurp, assume, arrogate.

expulsion n **1** *expulsion from school* removal, eviction, ejection, banishment, debarment, dismissal, discharge; *inf* sacking, drumming out. **2** *the expulsion of waste materials* ejection, discharge, elimination, excretion, voiding, voidance, evacuation.

expunge v erase, remove, rub out, wipe out, cross out, strike out, delete, eradicate, cancel, blot out, efface, destroy, obliterate, annul, extinguish, abolish, annihilate.

expurgate v bowdlerize, censor, bluepencil, clean up, purge, purify, sanitize, emasculate.

exquisite adj **1** *exquisite skin/grace* beautiful, lovely, delicate, fragile, elegant, fine, subtle, ethereal. **2** *exquisite taste* discriminating, discerning, sensitive, selective, refined, cultivated, cultured, appreciative, educated, fastidious, impeccable, polished, consummate. **3** *exquisite pain* intense, acute, keen, piercing, sharp, excruciating, poignant.

extant adj still existing, in existence, living, alive, surviving, remaining, undestroyed, subsisting, present, existent.

extemporaneous, extempory adj *an extemporaneous vote of thanks* extempore, impromptu, spontaneous, ad lib, improvised, unrehearsed, unplanned, unprepared, unpremeditated; *inf* off the cuff; *fml* improvisatory.

extempore adj *an extempore speech* impromptu, spontaneous, ad lib, improvised, unrehearsed, unplanned, unprepared, extemporaneous. *inf* off the cuff, off the top of one's head.

extempore adv *he spoke extempore* ad lib, spontaneously, extemporaneously; *inf* off the cuff.

extemporize v improvise, ad lib, play it by ear, think on one's feet. *see* EXTEMPORE adj.

extend v **1** *extend the territory/spring* expand, increase, enlarge; lengthen, widen, broaden, stretch, stretch out, draw out, elongate. **2** *extend the scope of the law* widen, increase, add to, expand, broaden, enlarge, augment, amplify, supplement, enhance, develop. **3** *extend the period of credit* prolong, increase, lengthen, stretch out, protract, spin out, drag out. **4** *extend one's arms* stretch out, reach out, spread out, straighten out, unroll, unfurl. **5** *extend a welcome* offer, give, grant, proffer, present, confer, hold out, advance, impart, put forth, reach out. **6** *the road extends for many miles* continue, stretch, stretch out, carry on, run on, last, unroll, unfurl, range.

extended adj **1** *extended credit facilities | extended hours* longer lasting, prolonged, increased, lengthened, elongated, protracted. **2** *extended family* widened, enlarged, expanded, far-reaching, comprehensive, broad.

extension n **1** *the extension of the territory/spring* expansion, increase, enlargement; elongation. *see* EXTEND 1. **2** *the extension of a period of credit* prolongation, increase, lengthening, protraction. *see* EXTEND 3. **3** *an extension to the house/collection* annexe, wing; addition, add-on, adjunct, addendum, augmentation, supplement, appendage. **4** *ask for an extension to complete an essay* more/extra time, increased time, additional time, a longer period.

extensive adj **1** *extensive grounds around the house* large, large-scale, sizeable, substantial, spacious, considerable, capacious, commodious, vast, immense. **2** *an extensive knowledge of the subject* comprehensive, thorough, complete, broad, wide, wide-ranging, all-inclusive, all-embracing, wholesale, universal, boundless, catholic.

extent n **1** *the full extent of the track/parklands* length, area, expanse, stretch, range, scope. **2** *the extent of her knowledge* coverage, breadth, range, scope, degree, comprehen-

siveness, thoroughness, completeness, all-inclusiveness.

extenuating adj *extenuating circumstances* mitigating, palliating, palliative, justifying, moderating, qualifying.

exterior n *the exterior of the building* outside, outside surface, outer/external surface, outward appearance/aspect, façade, covering, shell.

exterior adj *the exterior layer* outer, outside, outermost, outward, external, surface, superficial.

exterminate v kill, destroy, eradicate, annihilate, eliminate, abolish, extirpate; *inf* bump off.

external adj **1** *an external wall* outer, outside, outward, exterior, surface, superficial, extraneous, extrinsic. **2** *an external student* extramural; outside, visiting, non-resident.

extinct adj **1** *an extinct species* died out, defunct, no longer existing, vanished, wiped out, gone, lost. **2** *an extinct volcano/fire* inactive, no longer active; extinguished, burnt out, quenched, put out, doused. **3** *extinct beliefs/passions* dead, defunct, ended, terminated, obsolete, outmoded, out of date, antiquated, *passea*.

extinction n dying out, death, vanishing, extinguishing, quenching, ending, termination. *see* EXTINCT.

extinguish v **1** *extinguish the light/fire* put out, blow out, quench, smother, douse, snuff out, stifle, dampen down, choke. **2** *extinguish passion* destroy, kill, end, remove, annihilate, wipe out, eliminate, abolish, eradicate, erase, expunge, exterminate, extirpate, obscure, suppress.

extol v praise, praise highly, praise to the skies, sing the praises of, applaud, acclaim, pay tribute to, laud, eulogize about, exalt, commend, congratulate, celebrate, compliment, glorify, panegyrize, magnify; *inf* cry up.

extort v *extort money | extort a confession* extract, force, exact, coerce, wring, wrest, squeeze, milk, obtain by blackmail; *inf* put the screws on to obtain; *Aust inf* put the bite on to obtain.

extortion n *obtain money by extortion* force, coercion, compulsion, exaction, oppression, blackmail. *see* EXTORT.

extortionate adj **1** *extortionate prices* exorbitant, excessive, outrageous, preposterous, immoderate, unreasonable, inordinate, inflated, sky-high. **2** *extortionate methods* exacting, grasping, blood-sucking, avaricious, rapacious, usurious, harsh, severe, rigorous, hard, oppressive.

extortionist, extortioner n blackmailer, blood-sucker, exacter, rack-renter.

extra adj **1** *extra money required* more, additional, further, supplementary, supplemental, added, auxiliary, ancillary, subsidiary, other, accessory. **2** *we always have extra food left after lunch* spare, surplus, left over, excess, superfluous, redundant, reserve, unused.

extra adv **1** *try extra hard* especially, exceptionally, extremely, unusually, particularly, extraordinarily, uncommonly, remarkably; *inf* with all the stops out. **2** *charge postage and package extra* in addition, as well, besides, over and above, on top, into the bargain, to boot.

extra n **1** *an optional extra* addition, supplement, adjunct, addendum. **2** *film extras* extra person/actor, supernumerary, walking on part, walk-on, spear-carrier.

extract v **1** *extract a tooth* draw out, pull out, remove, take out, pluck out, prize out, wrench out, tear out, uproot, withdraw, extirpate; *fml* deracinate. **2** *extract money* extort, force, exact, elicit, coerce, wrest, wring, squeeze. **3** *extract juice* squeeze, press, express, distil, separate, take out. **4** *extract a section from a chapter* abstract, select, choose, reproduce, copy, quote, cite, cull. **5** *extract a principle* deduce, educe, derive, elicit, develop, evolve.

extract n **1** *extract of malt* concentrate, essence, distillate, juice, solution, decoction. **2** *extracts from newspapers* excerpt, passage, abstract, citation, selection, quotation, cutting, clipping, fragment; analects.

extraction n **1** *the extraction of a tooth* removal, drawing out, pulling out, uprooting, extirpation; *fml* deracination. *see* EXTRACT v 1. **2** *extraction of money* extortion, exacting, wresting. *see* EXTRACT v 2. **3** *extraction of juice* squeezing, expressing, distillation, separation. *see* EXTRACT v 3. **4** *Irish by extraction* descent, ancestry, parentage, lineage, blood, derivation, origin, race.

extradite v *extradite a criminal* deport, expel, banish, exile, outlaw.

extradition n deportation, expulsion, banishment, exile, outlawing.

extraneous adj **1** *extraneous forces* external, outside, exterior, extrinsic, alien, foreign. **2** *extraneous material* irrelevant, immaterial, inapplicable, inapt, inappropriate, inapposite, unrelated, unconnected, off the subject, peripheral, beside the point, wide of the mark, not pertinent, not germane.

extraordinary adj **1** *extraordinary talent* exceptional, unusual, uncommon, rare, unique, singular, signal, peculiar, unprecedented, outstanding, striking, remarkable, phenomenal, marvellous, wonderful; *inf* fabulous. **2** *how extraordinary that we met* amazing, surprising, strange, unusual, remarkable, astounding, curious. **3** *an extraordinary colour combination* odd, weird, strange, curious, bizarre, unconventional.

extravagance n **1** *extravagance leading to debt* spendthrift behaviour/ways, squandering, overspending, profligacy, prodigality, wastefulness, lavishness, recklessness, excess. **2** *the extravagance of his compliments* excessiveness, exaggeration, exaggeratedness, unreservedness, outrageousness, immoderation, preposterousness, absurdity; irrationality, recklessness, wildness; excess, overkill, lack of restraint/reserve. **3** *extravagance of the prices/clothes* exorbitance, excessiveness, expensiveness, unreasonableness, immoderation; costliness; *inf* steepness.

extravagant adj **1** *extravagant way of life* spendthrift, squandering, thriftless, profligate, prodigal, improvident, wasteful, lavish, reckless, imprudent, excessive. **2** *extravagant compliments* excessive, exaggerated, unrestrained, unreserved, outrageous, immoderate, preposterous, absurd, irrational, reckless, wild; *inf* over-the-top, OTT. **3** *extravagant prices/clothes* exorbitant, excessive, extortionate, unreasonable, immoderate, inordinate; expensive, dear, costly, overpriced; *inf* steep.

extravaganza n spectacle, pageant, spectacular/impressive show/display.

extreme adj **1** *in extreme danger* | *extreme cold* utmost, uttermost, maximum, supreme, greatest, great, acute, intense, severe, highest, high, ultimate, exceptional, extraordinary. **2** *extreme punitive measures* harsh, severe, Draconian, stringent, stern, strict, drastic, unrelenting, relentless, unbending, unyielding, uncompromising, unmitigated, radical, overzealous. **3** *a person of extreme views* | *an extreme radical* immoderate, intemperate, fanatical, exaggerated, excessive, overzealous, outrageous, inordinate, unreasonable; *inf* over-the-top, OTT. **4** *on the extreme edge* | *in the extreme south* outermost, farthest, most remote, remotest, most distant, outlying, far-off, far-away, ultimate, last, endmost, final, terminal, apogean.

extreme n **1** *the extremes of heat/wrath* highest/greatest degree, maximum, height, ultimate, zenith, pinnacle, climax, acme, apex, ne plus ultra. **2** *the extremes of bliss and despair* opposite, pole, contrary, counter, contradiction, antonym. **in the extreme** *generous in the extreme* extremely, exceedingly, exceptionally, excessively, extravagantly, inordinately.

extremely adv very, exceedingly, exceptionally, intensely, greatly, acutely, utterly, excessively, inordinately, extraordinarily, markedly, uncommonly, severely; *inf* awfully, terribly.

extremist n radical, fanatic, zealot, diehard, ultra.

extremity n **1** *the extremities of the territory* limit, outer limit, farthest point, end, boundary, bound, border, frontier, edge, margin, termination, periphery, verge, brink, horizon; *fml* ambit. **2** *frostbite of the extremities* limb, appendage, digit; arm, leg, hand, foot, finger, toe. **3** *the extremity of the heat* the greatest/highest degree, extreme, maximum degree, intensity, acuteness, excess, zenith, pinnacle, top, acme, apex; *fml* apogee. **4** *help the poor in their extremity* hardship, adversity, trouble, misfortune, plight, destitution, indigence, exigency; crisis, emergency, setback; dire straits, hard times.

extricate v *extricate oneself/someone from a difficult situation* extract, free, release, disentangle, get out, remove, withdraw, let loose, detach, disengage, liberate, rescue, save, disencumber, deliver; *inf* get off the hook.

extrinsic adj **1** *extrinsic influence* extraneous, external, exterior, outside, outward, alien, foreign, not intrinsic. **2** *extrinsic information* extraneous, irrelevant, immaterial, inapplicable, inapt, inappropriate, inapposite, unrelated, unconnected, off the subject, peripheral, beside the point, wide of the mark, not pertinent, not germane.

extrovert, extroverted adj outgoing, outwardly directed, sociable, socializing, social, friendly, people-oriented, lively, cheerful, effervescent, exuberant.

extrovert n outgoing person, socializer, mixer, mingler, life and soul of the party.

extrude v **1** *extrude glue from a tube* force out, thrust out, press out, squeeze out, eject, expel. **2** *a branch extruding from the tree* protrude, project, jut out, stick out, poke out, extend, hang out, beetle.

exuberant adj **1** *exuberant with joy at winning* elated, animated, exhilarated, lively, high-spirited, spirited, buoyant, cheerful, sparkling, full of life, effervescent, vivacious, excited, ebullient, exultant, enthusi-

astic, irrepressible, energetic, vigorous, zestful; *inf* bouncy, upbeat. **2** *exuberant expressions of thanks* effusive, lavish, fulsome, exaggerated, unreserved, unrestrained, unlimited, wholehearted, generous, excessive, superfluous, prodigal. **3** *exuberant foliage* profuse, luxuriant, lush, thriving, abundant, superabundant, prolific, teeming, lavish, copious, rich, plentiful, abounding, overflowing, rank.

exude v **1** *sweat exuding through the pores* ooze, seep, filter, filtrate, leak, discharge, trickle, drip, issue. **2** *exuding beads of sweat* ooze, secrete, excrete, discharge, emit, issue, emanate, give out, pour out, gush, jet. **3** *exuding confidence* ooze, give out, give forth, send out, issue, emit, emanate, display.

exult v **1** *exult at/in his sister's success* rejoice, be overjoyed, be joyful, be jubilant, be elated, be delighted, be ecstatic, jump for joy, revel, be in ecstasy, be over the moon, be on cloud nine, be in seventh heaven. **2** *exulting over their opponents* triumph, gloat, crow, glory.

exultant adj exulting, rejoicing, overjoyed, joyful, jubilant, elated, triumphant, delighted, ecstatic, cock-a-hoop, gleeful, enraptured, transported.

exultation n rejoicing, joy, jubilation, elation, exhilaration, delight, ecstasy, glee, rapture, triumph, glory; transports.

eye n **1** *injury to the eye* organ of sight, eyeball; *inf* peeper; *lit* orb. **2** *have sharp eyes* eyesight, vision, sight, observation; powers of observation. **3** *an eye for art* appreciation, perception, discernment, discrimination, taste, judgement, recognition, awareness, sensitivity. **4** *keep an eye on | under her mother's eagle eye* watch, observance, lookout; observation, surveillance, vigilance, view, notice. **5** *to my eye/in my eyes they are guilty* estimation, opinion, view, point of view, judgement, belief, viewpoint, mind. **6** *eye of the needle* hole, aperture, perforation, eyelet. **7** *the eye of a daisy* centre, middle, heart, kernel, hub. **see eye to eye** agree, be in agreement/accord, concur, be on the same wavelength, get on, get along. **up to one's eyes** fully occupied, very busy, engrossed, engaged, overwhelmed, inundated, caught up, wrapped up; *inf* up to here.

eye v **1** *eye with longing* look at, gaze at, stare at, contemplate, study, survey, view, inspect, scrutinize, scan, glance at, regard, behold; *inf* clock; *Amer inf* eyeball. **2** *eye the girls* ogle, leer at, make eyes at; *inf* give the glad eye to.

eye-catching adj striking, arresting, spectacular, captivating, attractive, showy.

eyeful n **1** *get an eyeful of that* look, good look, stare, gaze, view; *inf* shufti, gander, butcher's, load. **2** *the model is quite an eyeful* vision, dream, beauty, dazzler; *inf* stunner, good-looker, knockout, sight for sore eyes, bobby-dazzler.

eyesight n sight, vision, range of vision, observation, perception.

eyesore n blemish, blot, scar, blight, disfigurement, defacement, defect, monstrosity, carbuncle, atrocity, disgrace, ugliness; *inf* sight.

eyewitness n witness, observer, onlooker, looker-on, bystander, spectator, watcher, viewer, beholder, passer-by; *inf* rubberneck.

fable n **1** *a fable about a fox* moral tale, parable, apologue; bestiary. **2** *heroes in Norse fables* story, legend, myth, traditional story, saga, epic, lay. **3** *children telling fables* lie, untruth, falsehood, white lite, fib, piece of fiction, fabrication, invention, story, fairy story, cock and bull story, figment of the imagination, fantasy; *inf* tall story, yarn, terminological inexactitude.

fabric n **1** *made of a silky fabric* cloth, material, textile, stuff, web. **2** *the fabric of the building | the fabric of society* framework, frame, structure, make-up, constitution, essence.

fabricate v **1** *fabricate the furniture from components* assemble, construct, build, erect, put together, make, form, frame, fashion, shape, manufacture, produce. **2** *fabricate a reason for lateness* make up, invent, think up, concoct, hatch, trump up, devise, formulate, coin. **3** *fabricate a document* forge, falsify, fake, counterfeit.

fabulous adj **1** *of fabulous wealth* incredible, unbelievable, inconceivable, unimaginable, astounding, amazing, astonishing, breathtaking, prodigious, phenomenal, remarkable, extraordinary, tremendous; *inf* legendary. **2** *a fabulous time at the party* marvellous, wonderful, great, superb, spectacular; *inf* fab, fantastic, super, super-duper, out of this world. **3** *fabulous creatures* mythical, imaginary, legendary, fantastical, fictitious, fictional, made-up, invented, unreal, hypothetical, apocryphal.

façade n **1** *the façade of the building* front, frontage, face, exterior, outside. **2** *a façade of friendliness* show, appearance, guise, semblance, mask, veneer, masquerade, camouflage, pretence, illusion.

face n **1** *a beautiful face* countenance, visage, physiognomy; features, lineaments; *inf* mug, dial, phizog, phiz, kisser, clock. **2** *a furious face* expression, look, air, demeanour, aspect. **3** *what a face! | make a face* scowl, grimace, frown, pout, moue. **4** *the face of the building* front, frontage, façade. *see* FAÇADE 1. **5** *the face of the country-side* outward appearance, appearance, aspect, air. **6** *put a brave/bold face on it* appearance, façade, display, show, exterior, guise, mask, veneer, camouflage, pretence. **7** *lose face* prestige, standing, status, dignity, honour, respect, image. **8** *have the face to turn up* audacity, effrontery, impudence, impertinence, cheek, boldness, presumption, temerity, bumptiousness; *inf* nerve, gall, brass neck, neck, sauce. **face to face** facing, confronting, opposing, conflicting; *inf* eyeball to eyeball. **on the face of it** from appearances, to all appearances, so it appears/seems, so it would appear/seem, apparently, seemingly.

face v **1** *buildings facing the sea* front onto, look towards, look onto, overlook, give onto, be opposite to. **2** *the problems facing us* confront, present itself, meet, be in the way, stand in the way. **3** *face rejection* encounter, meet, come across, be confronted by, come up against, experience. **4** *face facts* face up to, come to terms with, accept, confront, meet head-on, cope with, deal with, get to grips with, brazen out. **5** *face criticism/danger* encounter, meet, face out, meet head-on, confront, dare, brave, defy, oppose, resist, withstand. **6** *face the collar of the coat* put a facing on, cover, line. **7** *face stone* dress, finish, polish, smooth, level, coat, cover, surface, clad, veneer. **face up to** face, come to terms with, accept, confront, cope with. *see* FACE v 4.

facet n **1** *one facet of the problem* aspect, angle, side, slant, feature, characteristic, factor, element, point, part, phase. **2** *facet of a gem* side, plane, surface, face.

facetious adj jocular, flippant, playful, frivolous, light-hearted, non-serious, funny, amusing, humorous, comical, comic, joking, jesting, witty, droll, whimsical, tongue-in-cheek, waggish, jocose.

facile adj **1** *facile speeches/charm* superficial, shallow, glib, slick, urbane, suave, bland. **2** *facile tasks* easy, simple, uncomplicated, unchallenging, like falling off a log; *inf* easy-peasy.

facilitate v make easy/easier, ease, make smooth/smoother, smooth, smooth the path of, assist, help, aid, expedite, speed up, accelerate, forward, advance, promote, further, encourage.

facility n **1** *perform the task with facility* ease, effortlessness, smoothness, absence/lack of difficulty. **2** *facility of expression* ease, smoothness, fluency, eloquence, articulateness, slickness, glibness. **3** *a facility for wood-carving* skill, skilfulness, dexterity, adroitness, adeptness, deftness, aptitude, ability, gift, talent, expertise, expertness, knack, proficiency, bent, readiness. **4** *leisure facilities* amenity, resource, appliance, aid, opportunity, advantage, convenience, benefit; means, equipment.

facing n **1** *the facing of a jacket lapel* covering, lining, interfacing, reinforcement. **2** *the facing of the building* façade, front, surface, fronting, false front, coating, covering, cladding, veneer, protective/decorative layer, overlay, stucco, revetment.

facsimile n copy, replica, reproduction, duplicate, carbon, carbon copy, photocopy, Xerox, Photostat, Mimeograph, transcript, reprint, clone, image, fax.

fact n **1** *a fact not a rumour* actuality, reality, certainty, factuality, certitude; truth, naked truth, gospel. **2** *do not omit a single fact* detail, particular, point, item, piece of information/data, factor, feature, element, component, circumstance, specific. *see* FACTS. **3** *charged with being an accessory after the fact* happening, occurrence, incident, event, act, deed. **in fact** *in fact he's gone already* actually, in point of fact, indeed, in truth, in reality.

faction n **1** *the younger faction | a more radical faction* sector, section, group, side, party, band, set, ring, division, contingent, lobby, camp, bloc, clique, coalition, confederacy, coterie, caucus, cabal, junta, ginger group, splinter group, pressure group, minority group; *inf* gang, crew. **2** *a club full of faction* infighting, dissension, discord, strife, contention, conflict, friction, argument, difference of opinion, disagreement, controversy, quarrelling, division, divisiveness, clashing, disharmony, disunity, variance, rupture, tumult, turbulence, upheaval, dissidence, rebellion, insurrection, sedition, mutiny, schism.

factious adj dissenting, contentious, discordant, conflicting, argumentative, disagreeing, disputatious, quarrelling, quarrelsome, divisive, clashing, warring, at variance, at loggerheads, at odds, disharmonious, tumultuous, turbulent, dissident, rebellious, insurrectionary, seditious, mutinous, schismatic, sectarian, partisan.

factor n **1** *the financial factor* element, part, component, ingredient, constituent, point, detail, item, facet, aspect, feature, characteristic, consideration, influence, circumstance, thing, determinant. **2** *a business factor* agent, representative, deputy, middleman, intermediary, go-between; *Scots*

land-agent, estate manager, land steward, reeve.

factory n manufacturing building/complex, plant; works; workshop, mill, foundry.

factotum n general employee, odd-job man, general handyman, man/maid of all work, Jack of all trades, man Friday, girl Friday; *inf* Mr Fix-it.

facts npl *the police just want the facts* information, itemized information, whole story; details, data; *inf* info, gen, low-down, score, dope.

factual adj *a factual account* fact-based, realistic, real, true to life, circumstantial, true, truthful, accurate, authentic, genuine, sure, veritable, exact, precise, strict, honest, faithful, literal, matter-of-fact, verbatim, word for word, unbiased, objective, unprejudiced, unvarnished, unadorned, unadulterated, unexaggerated.

faculties npl *old people in possession of all their faculties* powers, capabilities, senses, wits; reason, intelligence.

faculty n **1** *the faculty of speech* power, capability, capacity, attribute, property. **2** *a faculty for learning languages* aptitude, ability, facility, flair, gift, talent, bent, knack, disposition, proficiency, readiness, skill, dexterity, adroitness. **3** *the arts faculty* department, university/college department, division, section. **4** *the whole faculty approved of the decision* members of a profession, profession, discipline. **5** *the Church conferring the faculty to conduct marriage services* authorization, licence, power, right, prerogative, privilege, permission, sanction.

fad n craze, mania, rage, enthusiasm, fancy, passing fancy, whim, vogue, fashion, trend, mode.

faddy adj faddish, fussy, finicky, hard to please, fastidious, particular, over-particular; *inf* choosy, picky, pernickety.

fade v **1** *the curtains/colour faded* lose colour, become pale/paler, grow pale, pale, become bleached, become washed out, dull, dim, grow dull/dim, lose lustre. **2** *time had faded the colours* pale, bleach, whiten, wash out, dull, discolour, decolorize, dim, etiolate. **3** *flowers fading* wither, wilt, die, droop, shrivel, decay, etiolate. **4** *light/hope fading* grow less, dim, die away, dwindle, grow faint, fail, wane, disappear, vanish, die, decline, dissolve, peter out, melt away, evanesce. **5** *the Roman empire was fading* die out, diminish, decline, fail, deteriorate, degenerate. *see* FAIL v 9.

faeces npl excrement, bodily waste, waste matter, ordure, dung, manure; excreta, stools, droppings.

fail v **1** *their attempt failed* not succeed, be unsuccessful, lack success, fall through, fall flat, break down, abort, miscarry, be defeated, suffer defeat, be in vain, be frustrated, collapse, founder, misfire, not come up to scratch, meet with disaster, come to grief, come to nothing/naught, fizzle out, miss the mark, run aground, go astray; *inf* flop, come a cropper, bite the dust. **2** *fail the exam | failed twice* not pass, be unsuccessful, be found wanting/deficient/defective, not make the grade, not pass muster, not come up to scratch, be rejected; *inf* flunk. **3** *fail to understand/attend* be unable; omit, neglect, forget. **4** *fail them in their hour of need* let down, neglect, desert, forsake, abandon, disappoint. **5** *the crops failed* be insufficient, be inadequate, be deficient, be wanting, be lacking, fall short. **6** *the light/ hope failing* fade, grow less, dim, die away, dwindle, wane, disappear, vanish, peter out, dissolve. *see* FADE 4. **7** *the engine failed* break down, stop working, cease to function, cut out; *inf* conk out, become kaput. **8** *the old man is failing* grow weak/weaker, become feeble, lose strength, flag, become ill, sink. **9** *her health failed | the empire failed* decline, go into decline, fade, diminish, dwindle, wane, ebb, deteriorate, sink, collapse, pass, decay, crumble, degenerate. **10** *his business failed* collapse, crash, smash, go under, go to the wall, go bankrupt, become insolvent, go into receivership, cease trading, be closed, close down; *inf* fold, flop, go bust/broke.

fail n failure, non-success. *see* FAILURE 1. **without fail** for certain, certainly, with certainty, definitely, whatever happens.

failing n *unpunctuality is his failing* fault, shortcoming, weakness, weak spot, imperfection, defect, flaw, blemish, frailty, foible, drawback.

failing prep *failing some disaster we shall come* in the absence of, in default of, lacking, notwithstanding.

failure n **1** *the failure of their attempt* nonsuccess, lack of success, non-fulfilment, abortion, miscarriage, defeat, frustration, collapse, foundering, misfiring, coming to nothing, fizzling out. *see* FAIL v 1. **2** *their plan was a failure* vain attempt, abortion, defeat, fiasco, debacle, botch, blunder; *inf* flop, wash-out. **3** *he feels a failure since losing his job* incompetent, loser, non-achiever, ne'er-do-well, disappointment; *inf* flop, dud, no-hoper, non-starter, wash-out. **4** *failure to*

attend | failure in the line of duty omission, neglect; negligence, remissness, non-observance, non-performance, dereliction, delinquency. **5** *the failure of the crops* insufficiency, inadequacy, deficiency, lack, dearth, scarcity, shortfall. **6** *the failure of the light* fading, lessening, dimming, waning, vanishing. *see* FAIL v 6. **7** *the failure of the engine* breaking down, non-function, cutting out; *inf* conking out. **8** *the failure of his health | failure of the empire* failing, decline, fading, dwindling, waning, sinking, deterioration, collapse, breakdown, loss, decay, crumbling, degeneration. **9** *the failure of his business* collapse, crashing, going under, bankruptcy, close-down, ruin; *inf* folding, flop.

faint adj **1** *a faint mark | faint traces* indistinct, unclear, dim, obscure, pale, faded, bleached. **2** *a faint noise* indistinct, scarcely audible/perceptible, vague, low, soft, muted, muffled, stifled, subdued, weak, feeble, whispered. **3** *a faint chance of success* slight, small, remote, vague, minimal. **4** *a faint response | faint praise* weak, feeble, unenthusiastic, half-hearted, low-key. **5** *feeling faint* giddy, dizzy, light-headed, weak-headed, muzzy, weak, vertiginous; *inf* woozy.

faint v *faint from loss of blood* lose consciousness, black out, pass out, collapse; *inf* flake out, keel over, conk out; *lit* swoon.

faint n *fall over in a faint* loss of consciousness, blackout, collapse, fainting fit; *lit* swoon; *Med* syncope.

faint-hearted adj timid, timorous, fearful, spiritless, weak, cowardly, unmanly, lily-livered; *inf* chicken-hearted, yellow.

faintly adv **1** *not faintly amusing* slightly, remotely, vaguely, somewhat, a little, in the least. **2** *call faintly* indistinctly, softly, weakly, feebly, in a whisper, in subdued tones.

fair adj **1** *a fair trial* just, impartial, unbiased, unprejudiced, objective, even-handed, dispassionate, disinterested, detached, equitable, above-board, lawful, legal, legitimate, proper, square; *inf* on the level. **2** *a fair person* fair-minded, just, impartial, unbiased, unprejudiced, open-minded, honest, upright, honourable, trustworthy, above-board. **3** *fair weather* fine, dry, bright, clear, sunny, cloudless, unclouded. **4** *fair winds* favourable, advantageous, helpful, beneficial. **5** *fair hair | fair and dark children* blond/blonde, yellow, flaxen, light brown, strawberry blonde, fair-haired, light-haired, flaxen-haired, tow-headed. **6** *fair skin* pale, light-coloured, white, cream-coloured, creamy, peaches and cream, chalky. **7** *fair maidens* beautiful, pretty, lovely, attractive, good-looking, bonny, comely, well-favoured; *lit* beauteous. **8** *a fair number of people* | *a fair chance of winning* reasonable, passable, tolerable, satisfactory, respectable, decent, all right, goodish, pretty good, not bad, moderate, so-so, average, middling, ample, adequate, sufficient. **9** *a fair copy of the essay* clean, clear, unblemished.

fair n **1** *a trade fair* exhibition, display, show, exhibit, exposition; *inf* expo. **2** *the county fair* fête, gala, festival, carnival. **3** *an agricultural fair* market, open-air market, mart, exchange.

fairly adv **1** *treated fairly* justly, equitably, impartially, without prejudice, objectively, even-handedly, properly, lawfully, legally, legitimately. **2** *fairly good* quite, reasonably, passably, tolerably, satisfactorily, moderately, rather, somewhat, adequately; *inf* pretty. **3** *children fairly shrieking with laughter* positively, really, absolutely, decidedly, veritably.

fair-minded adj fair, just, impartial, unprejudiced, open-minded, honest, honourable. *see* FAIR adj 2.

fairness n **1** *treat everyone with fairness* justness, impartiality, even-handedness, objectivity, disinterest, equitability, equity, legality, properness. *see* FAIR adj 1. **2** *the fairness of the judge* fair-mindedness, justness, impartiality, open-mindedness, honesty, integrity, probity, rectitude, trustworthiness. *see* FAIR adj 2. **3** *the fairness of the maidens* beauty, prettiness, loveliness, attractiveness, comeliness.

fairy n pixie, elf, sprite, imp, brownie, leprechaun, kelpie, dwarf, gnome, goblin, hobgoblin, nix, peri, puck.

fairy tale n **1** *read the child a fairy tale* fairy story, folk tale, legend, romance. **2** *the child's telling fairy tales* lie, white lie, untruth, tall story, fairy story, fabrication, invention, piece of fiction; *inf* cock-and-bull story, terminological inexactitude.

faith n **1** *have faith in the cure/doctor* trust, belief, confidence, conviction, credence, credit, reliance, dependence, optimism, hopefulness. **2** *of what faith are they?* religion, church, persuasion, belief, creed, teaching, dogma, doctrine, sect, denomination. **3** *keep/break faith* loyalty, allegiance, faithfulness, fidelity, fealty, constancy, devotion, obedience, commitment.

faithful adj **1** *faithful followers* loyal, constant, devoted, dependable, reliable, true, true-blue, trusty, trustworthy, staunch,

unswerving, unwavering, steadfast, obedient, dutiful, dedicated, committed. **2** *a faithful copy* accurate, true, exact, precise, close, strict, without error, unerring, just so; *inf* spot on, on the button.

faithful n **the faithful** believers, loyal members, adherents, followers, communicants; congregation, brethren.

faithfulness n **1** *the faithfulness of the followers* fidelity, loyalty, constancy, devotion, dependability, reliability, trustworthiness, staunchness, steadfastness, obedience, duty, dedication, commitment, allegiance, adherence, fealty. **2** *the faithfulness of the description* accuracy, truth, exactness, precision, closeness, strictness, justness.

faithless adj **1** *faithless followers* unfaithful, disloyal, false, false-hearted, untrue, untrustworthy, traitorous, treacherous, perfidious, inconstant, fickle, unreliable, undependable, deceitful, two-faced. **2** *faithless heathens* unbelieving, disbelieving, doubting, sceptical, agnostic, atheistic, irreligious.

faithlessness n unfaithfulness, infidelity, disloyalty, falseness, false-heartedness, betrayal, untrustworthiness, traitorousness, treachery, perfidy, inconstancy, fickleness, unreliability, undependability, deceit, deceitfulness, two-facedness.

fake adj **1** *a fake five pound note* counterfeit, forged, sham, imitation, fraudulent, false, bogus, spurious, pseudo; *inf* phoney. **2** *fake furs/pearls* sham, imitation, artificial, synthetic, mock, simulated, reproduction, ersatz. **3** *a fake accent* affected, put-on, assumed, feigned, pseudo, insincere; *inf* phoney, pseud.

fake n **1** *the note is a fake* counterfeit, forgery, copy, sham, imitation, fraud, reproduction, hoax; *inf* phoney. **2** *the doctor is a fake* charlatan, impostor, mountebank, quack; *inf* phoney.

fall v **1** *leaves/rain falling* come/go down, descend, drop, drop down, sink, gravitate, cascade, plop, plummet. **2** *the child fell* fall down, fall over, trip, trip over, stumble, slip, slide, tumble, topple over, keel over, go head over heels, collapse, fall in a heap, take a spill. **3** *ground falling* fall away, slope, slope down, incline/slant downwards. **4** *water levels falling* sink, sink lower, subside, recede, abate, settle. **5** *demand/prices fell* fall off, drop off, go down, decline, decrease, grow less, diminish, dwindle, depreciate, plummet, slump, deteriorate. **6** *empires falling* die, fade, fail, decline, deteriorate, flag, wane, ebb, degenerate, go downhill; *inf* go to the dogs. **7** *soldiers* *falling in war* die, be killed/slain, be a casualty/fatality, be lost, drop dead, perish, meet one's end. **8** *towns falling to the enemy* | *fall to temptation* surrender, yield, submit, give in, give up, give way, capitulate, succumb, resign oneself; be overthrown by, be taken by, be defeated by, be conquered by, lose one's position to, pass into the hands of. **9** *Christmas falls on a Saturday* | *darkness fell* take place, occur, happen, come about, come to pass. **10** *it so fell that she died* occur, happen, come about, come to pass, befall, chance, arise, result, fall out. **11** *the horse fell lame* | *she fell asleep* | *falling in love* become, grow, pass into. **12** *God punishing angels for falling* sin, do wrong, transgress, err, go astray, yield to temptation, commit an offence, lapse, fall from grace, backslide, trespass. **fall apart** *the wardrobe/system fell apart* fall/come to pieces, fall/come to bits, disintegrate, break up, crumble, dissolve. **fall back** retreat, withdraw, draw back, retire. **fall back on** resort to, call upon, call into play/action, call/press into service, have recourse to, make use of, use, employ, rely on, depend on. **fall behind 1** *fall behind in the race* be/get left behind, fall/drop back, lose one's place, lag, trail, not keep up. **2** *fall behind with the rent* get into arrears/debt, not keep up with. **fall down 1** *the child fell down* fall, fall over, trip. *see* FALL v 2. **2** *fall down on the task* fail, be unsuccessful, not succeed, not make the grade, not come up to expectations, fall short, disappoint. **fall for 1** *fall for his friend's sister* fall in love with, become infatuated with, desire, be attracted/smitten by, lose one's heart to; *inf* fancy. **2** *fall for an old trick* be taken in by, be fooled/deceived/duped by, accept; *inf* swallow. **fall in** *the roof fell in* cave in, collapse, sink inwards, come down about one's ears, crash in, crumble. **fall in with 1** *fall in with bad company* meet, encounter, get involved with, take up with. **2** *fall in with their plans* agree to/with, accept, assent to, concur with, go along with, support, back, give one's backing to, cooperate with. **fall off** *demand fell off* drop off, go down, decrease, decline, slump, deteriorate. *see* FALL v 5. **fall out 1** *husband and wife falling out* quarrel, argue, squabble, fight, bicker, have a difference of opinion, differ, have a disagreement, disagree, clash, wrangle, get into conflict, get into a dispute. **2** *it fell out that we lost* happen, occur, come about, take place, turn out, chance, arise, befall, result. **fall short** *the charity appeal fell short* | *fall short of perfection* be deficient, be/prove inadequate, disappoint; fail to meet/reach, fail to live up to, miss. **fall through** come to nothing,

fail, fail to happen, miscarry, abort, go awry; *inf* fizzle out. **fall to** *fall to and eat/work* set to, begin, start, commence, set/go about, get to work, set the ball rolling, put one's shoulder to the wheel, get moving, get the show on the road.

fall n **1** *the child had a fall* trip, tumble, spill, stumble, slipping, slip, slide, topple, keeling over, nosedive, collapse. **2** *a fall in demand/prices* fall-off, drop, dropping off, decline, decrease, cut, lessening, lowering, dip, diminishing, dwindling, reduction, depreciation, plummeting, slump, deterioration. **3** *the fall of the Roman empire* death, demise, downfall, ruin, collapse, failure, decline, deterioration, wane, ebb, degeneration, destruction, overthrow. **4** *the fall of the city to the enemy* surrender, yielding, submission, giving in, capitulation, succumbing, resignation, defeat. **5** *the fall of the land* slope, downward slope/slant/incline, declivity, descent, downgrade. **6** *the fall of Lucifer* sin, wrongdoing, transgression, error, yielding to temptation, offence, lapse, fall from grace, backsliding; original sin, the Fall.

fallacious adj false, erroneous, untrue, wrong, incorrect, faulty, flawed, inaccurate, inexact, imprecise, mistaken, misleading, fictitious, spurious, counterfeit, deceptive, fraudulent, delusive, delusory, illusory, sophistic; *inf* bogus, phoney.

fallacy n mistaken belief, misbelief, misconception, false notion, misapprehension, misjudgement, miscalculation, error, mistake, untruth, inconsistency, illusion, delusion, deceit, deception, sophism; sophistry, casuistry.

fallen adj **1** *fallen women* immoral, loose, shamed, disgraced, dishonoured, ruined, sinful, unchaste. **2** *fallen soldiers* dead, killed, slain, lost, perished, slaughtered.

fallible adj liable/prone/open to error, error-prone, erring, errant, imperfect, flawed, frail, weak, mortal.

fallow adj *fallow land* | *fields/ideas lying fallow* uncultivated, unploughed, untilled, unplanted, unsown, unseeded, unused, undeveloped, dormant, resting, inactive, idle, inert, empty, neglected, barren, unproductive.

false adj **1** *a false interpretation/account* untrue, incorrect, wrong, erroneous, faulty, invalid, unfounded; untruthful, fictitious, concocted, fabricated, invented, inaccurate, inexact, imprecise, flawed, unreal, counterfeit, forged, fraudulent, spurious, misleading. **2** *a false friend* false-hearted, unfaithful, faithless, treacherous, disloyal, traitorous, perfidious, two-faced, double-dealing, untrustworthy, untrue, deceitful, deceiving, deceptive, dishonourable, dishonest, duplicitous, hypocritical, unreliable, unsound, untruthful, lying, mendacious. **3** *false furs/pearls* fake, artificial, imitation, synthetic, simulated, sham, mock, bogus, ersatz, spurious, counterfeit, feigned, forged, make-believe, pseudo; *inf* phoney.

falsehood n **1** *telling falsehoods* lie, fib, untruth, false statement, falsification, perjury, fabrication, invention, piece of fiction, fiction, story, fairy story/tale, exaggeration; *inf* terminological inexactitude. **2** *guilty of falsehood* deceit, deception, deceitfulness, two-facedness, double-dealing, dissimulation, prevarication, equivocation, mendacity, untruthfulness, perjury, perfidy, treachery, treason, casuistry.

falsetto n high voice, high-pitched tone, squeak, squeal.

falsify v **1** *falsify a document* alter, counterfeit, forge, fake, doctor, tamper with, distort, adulterate, pervert. **2** *falsify their statement* disprove, show to be false, prove unsound, refute, confute, rebut, contradict, oppose; misrepresent, garble, misstate, misquote.

falter v **1** *falter before proceeding* hesitate, waver, oscillate, fluctuate, delay, vacillate, be undecided, blow hot and cold, shilly-shally, hum and haw, drag one's feet, sit on the fence. **2** *falter over her words* stammer, stutter, stumble, speak haltingly.

fame n renown, celebrity, eminence, notability, note, distinction, mark, prominence, esteem, importance, greatness, account, pre-eminence, glory, honour, illustriousness, stardom, reputation, repute; notoriety, infamy.

familiar adj **1** *familiar face/task/excuse* well-known, known, recognized, customary, accustomed, common, everyday, ordinary, commonplace, frequent, habitual, usual, repeated, routine, stock, mundane, run-of-the-mill, conventional, household, domestic; *inf* common or garden. **2** *a familiar atmosphere* informal, casual, relaxed, comfortable, easy, free, free-and-easy, at ease, at home, friendly, unceremonious, unrestrained, unconstrained, unreserved, open, natural, simple. **3** *familiar acquaintances* close, intimate, dear, near, confidential, bosom, friendly, neighbourly, sociable, amicable, hail fellow well met; *inf* pally, chummy, buddy-buddy, thick, thick as thieves. **4** *object to him being familiar with the staff* over-familiar, over-free, presumptuous, disrespectful, forward, bold, impudent, impertinent, intrusive; *inf* pushy.

familiar with *familiar with the system* acquainted with, conversant with, versed in, well up in, with knowledge of, knowledgeable about, instructed in, *au fait* with, at home with, no stranger to, *au courant* with.

familiarity n **1** *his familiarity with the technique* acquaintance with, acquaintanceship with, knowledge of, grasp of, mastery of, understanding of, comprehension of, experience of, skill with. **2** *the familiarity of the atmosphere* informality, casualness, ease, comfortableness, friendliness, lack of ceremony/restraint/reserve, naturalness, simplicity. *see* FAMILIAR 2. **3** *the familiarity of their relationship* closeness, intimacy, nearness, friendliness; *inf* chumminess. *see* FAMILIAR 3. **4** *object to his familiarity* overfamiliarity, presumption, presumptuousness, disrespect, forwardness, boldness, impudence, impertinence, intrusiveness; liberties.

familiarize v **1** *familiarize the pupils with the system* make familiar with, make conversant with, acquaint with, accustom to, habituate to, instruct in, coach in, train in, teach in, school in, prime in, indoctrinate in, initiate into. **2** *naturalists/broadcasters familiarizing exotic plants* make known, bring to notice, bring to public attention, make familiar.

family n **1** *two families living together* parent/parents and child/children, household, *ménage*, clan, tribe; nuclear family, extended family. **2** *she wants a family* children, offspring, little ones, progeny, descendants, issue, scions; brood; *inf* kids. **3** *the old man had no family* relatives, relations, people, kin, next of kin, kinsfolk, kinsmen, one's own flesh and blood, folk. **4** *of a noble family* ancestry, extraction, parentage, birth, pedigree, genealogy, background, family tree, descent, lineage, line, bloodline, blood, race, strain, stock, breed, stirps; dynasty, house; forebears, forefathers, antecedents, roots. **5** *a family of plants* class genus, species, kind, type, class, group, taxonomic group.

famine n **1** *famine striking the village* scarcity of food, food shortage. **2** *water famine* scarcity, lack, dearth, want, deficiency, shortage, insufficiency, paucity, exiguity, drought. **3** *dying of famine* starvation, hunger, food-deprivation, lack of food, anorexia, inanition.

famished adj starving, starving to death, starved, ravenous, hungry, undernourished.

famous adj well-known, renowned, celebrated, famed, prominent, noted, notable, great, eminent, pre-eminent, distinguished, esteemed, respected, venerable, illustrious, acclaimed, honoured, exalted, glorious, remarkable, signal, popular, legendary, lionized, much-publicized.

fan[1] n *install a fan* air-conditioner, aircooler, ventilator, blower, aerator, flabellum, punkah.

fan[1] v **1** *fan the atmosphere|fanning her face* cool, ventilate, air, aerate, blow, freshen, refresh. **2** *fan the flames/passion* intensify, increase, arouse, excite, agitate, ignite, kindle, stimulate, stir up, work up, whip up, incite, instigate, provoke. **3** *people/flags fanning out* spread, spread out, open out, open up, unfurl, unfold, outspread, stretch out.

fan[2] n *a fan of the local pop group* admirer, lover, enthusiast, devotee, addict, aficionado, zealot, follower, disciple, adherent, supporter, backer, champion, votary; *inf* buff, fiend, freak, nut, groupie.

fanatic n *a religious fanatic* zealot, extremist, radical, activist, militant, sectarian, bigot, partisan, devotee, addict, enthusiast, visionary.

fanatical adj **1** *a fanatical religious sect* extremist, extreme, zealous, radical, activist, militant, sectarian, bigoted, dogmatic, prejudiced, intolerant, narrow-minded, partisan, rabid. **2** *a fanatical film-goer* enthusiastic, eager, keen, fervent, passionate, over-enthusiastic, obsessive, immoderate, frenzied, frenetic; *inf* wild, gung-ho.

fanciful adj **1** *fanciful notions/beings* imaginary, fancied, fantastic, romantic, mythical, fabulous, legendary, unreal, illusory, visionary, made-up, make-believe, fairytale, extravagant. **2** *a fanciful child* imaginative, inventive, impractical, whimsical, capricious, visionary, chimerical. **3** *fanciful decoration* imaginative, creative, curious, extravagant, fantastic, bizarre, strange, eccentric.

fancy n **1** *a child subject to fancy* caprice, whimsy, sudden impulse, vagary, eccentricity, peculiarity; whim, quirk, notion, kink. **2** *have a fancy for an icecream* desire, urge, wish, want, yearning, longing, inclination, bent, hankering, impulse; fondness, liking, love, partiality, preference, predilection, taste, relish, humour, penchant; *inf* yen, itch. **3** *the poet's fancy* imagination, imaginative power, creativity, conception; images, mental images, visualizations. **4** *the spaceship was only a fancy* figment of the imagination, hallucination, illusion, delusion,

fantasy, vision, dream, reverie, daydream. **5** *I have a fancy it will rain* idea, vague idea, guess, thought, notion, supposition, opinion.

fancy v **1** *we fancy it will rain* have an idea, guess, think, think it likely/conceivable, believe, suppose, surmise, suspect, conjecture, reckon. **2** *he fancies a drink* would like, wish for, want, desire, long for, yearn for, crave, have a yearning/craving for, hanker after, covet; *inf* have a yen for. **3** *he fancies the new girl* find attractive, be attracted/captivated/infatuated by, take to, desire, lust after, burn for; *inf* have taken a shine to, have a crush on, be wild/mad about, go for, lech after.

fancy adj **1** *fancy decorations* ornate, elaborate, ornamented, ornamental, decorated, decorative, adorned, embellished, intricate, lavish, ostentatious, showy, luxurious, sumptuous, baroque, rococo; *inf* jazzy, ritzy, snazzy, posh, classy. **2** *fancy notions* fanciful, imaginary, fantastic, romantic, make-believe, far-fetched, illusory, delusive, extravagant, flighty, whimsical, capricious, chimerical; *inf* far-out.

fanfare n **1** *the queen greeted by a fanfare* flourish, trumpet call, blast of trumpets, fanfaronade. **2** *the new store opened with much fanfare* show, showiness, display, ostentation, commotion, fuss, publicity, sensationalism, ballyhoo; *inf* to-do, hype, pizazz.

fantastic adj **1** *fantastic notions* fanciful, imaginary, romantic, unreal, illusory, make-believe, irrational, extravagant, wild, mad, absurd, incredible, strange, eccentric, whimsical, capricious. **2** *fantastic shapes* strange, weird, queer, peculiar, outlandish, eccentric, bizarre, grotesque, freakish, whimsical, fanciful, quaint, imaginative, exotic, unreal, extravagant, elaborate, ornate, intricate, rococo, baroque, phantasmagoric, Kafkaesque. **3** *a fantastic amount of work* tremendous, enormous, huge, very great, terrific, impressive, overwhelming. **4** *the film was fantastic* marvellous, wonderful, sensational, superb, excellent, brilliant, first-class, top-notch; *inf* ace, brill, magic.

fantasy, phantasy n **1** *novels full of fantasy* fancy, imagination, creativity, invention, originality, vision, myth, romance. **2** *indulge in fantasy* fancy, speculation, daydreaming, reverie; flight of fancy, fanciful notion, dream, daydream, pipe-dream. **3** *seeing fantasies* apparition, phantom, spectre, ghost, figment of the imagination, hallucination, vision, illusion, mirage.

far adv **1** *it's not far to the house* | *far away* | *far into the night* a long way, a great distance, any great distance, a good way, afar. **2** *far the best* | *far too soon* to a great extent/degree, very much, much, by much, by a great amount, considerably, by a long way, markedly, immeasurably, decidedly, by far. **by far, by far and away** to a great extent/ degree, very much, much, by a great amount/deal, by a long way/chalk/shot, considerably, immeasurably, decidedly, markedly, positively, easily, beyond the shadow of a doubt. **far and wide** *search far and wide* everywhere, in all places, extensively, here, there and everywhere, widely, broadly, worldwide. **far out** *her clothes/ideas are far out* weird, bizarre, outlandish, unorthodox, unconventional, radical, extreme, esoteric; *inf* way out, kinky. **go far** *the young man will go far* get on, get on in the world, be successful, succeed, make one's way in the world, make headway/ progress, gain advancement, make a name for oneself, climb the ladder of success, rise in the world, set the Thames/world/ heather on fire, cut a swath; *inf* go places. **so far** *the play's OK so far* up till/to now, until now, up to this point, to date.

far adj *visit far places* far-away, far-off, distant, remote, out of the way, far-flung, far-removed, outlying, inaccessible, back of beyond, God-forsaken.

farce n **1** *starring in a bedroom farce* slapstick, slapstick comedy, burlesque, satire, parody, travesty, buffoonery, absurdity, ridiculousness. **2** *the interviews were just a farce* mockery, absurdity, sham, pretence, piece of futility, joke.

farcical adj **1** *a farcical situation* ridiculous, ludicrous, absurd, laughable, risible, preposterous, facetious, silly, foolish, nonsensical, asinine. **2** *a farcical play* comic, slapstick, custard-pie, humorous, amusing.

fare n **1** *how much is the bus fare?* ticket price, transport cost, price, cost, charge, fee. **2** *pick up three fares* passenger, traveller, fare payer, ticket payer; *inf* pick-up. **3** *the canteen serving plain fare* food, menu, diet, table, nourishment, nutriment; meals, eatables, rations, provisions, commons, victuals, viands; *inf* eats, nosh.

fare v **1** *how did you fare?* get on, proceed, get along, progress, make out, do, manage, succeed, prosper. **2** *it fared badly with him* turn out, go, happen, proceed, progress.

farewell interj goodbye, so long, cheerio, adieu, ciao, *adios, auf Wiedersehen*; *inf* see you, see you later.

farewell n *farewells are sad* goodbye, adieu, leave-taking, parting, send-off, departure, departing, going away.

far-fetched adj improbable, unlikely, remote, implausible, incredible, scarcely credible, unbelievable, difficult to believe, dubious, doubtful, unconvincing, strained, laboured, strange, fantastic, fanciful, unrealistic; *inf* hard to swallow/take.

farm n farmland, land; smallholding, holding, farmstead, steading, homestead, grange, plantation; *Scots* croft; *Amer* ranch; *Aust* station.

farm v **1** *farm the land* cultivate, bring under cultivation, till, work, plough, plant. **2** *her husband farms* be a farmer, practise farming, cultivate/till/work the land, rear livestock, do agricultural work. **3** *farm her former neighbour's children* foster, care for, have in care, mind, babysit. **farm out 1** *farm out his work* contract out, subcontract, delegate, assign to others. **2** *farm out a franchise* rent, rent out, lease, let. **3** *farm out the child* have fostered, have cared for, send to a childminder, put in care.

farmer n agriculturalist, agronomist, smallholder, yeoman; *Scots* crofter; *Amer* rancher.

farming n agriculture, agronomy, husbandry, tilling, tillage, cultivation, agribusiness, geoponics.

far-sighted adj **1** *not near-sighted, but far-sighted* long-sighted, hyperopic, hypermetropic. **2** *far-sighted in his choice* having foresight, prudent, prescient, discerning, judicious, shrewd, provident, politic, canny, cautious, careful, watchful, wise, sagacious.

farther adj *the farther boat is almost out of sight* more distant/advanced. *see* FURTHER adj 2.

farther adv *she stopped and would come no farther* to a more advanced point. *see* FURTHER adv 2.

farthest adj most distant. *see* FURTHEST.

fascinate v captivate, enchant, beguile, bewitch, enthral, infatuate, enrapture, entrance, hold spellbound, transfix, rivet, mesmerize, hypnotize, allure, lure, tempt, entice, draw, tantalize, charm, attract, intrigue, delight, absorb, engross.

fascinating adj captivating, enchanting, beguiling, bewitching, enthralling, ravishing, entrancing, compelling, spellbinding, riveting, gripping, alluring, tempting, enticing, irresistible, seductive, charming, attractive, intriguing, delightful, absorbing.

fascination n captivation, enchantment, allure, lure, allurement, attraction, attractiveness, appeal, charm, magnetism, pull, draw, spell, sorcery, magic, glamour.

fashion n **1** *the fashion in clothes/behaviour* current/latest style, style, vogue, trend, latest thing, latest taste, mode, craze, rage, fad, general tendency, convention, custom, practice. **2** *she works in fashion* clothes, clothes industry, clothes design, couture; *inf* rag trade. **3** *people of fashion* fashionable society, high society, society, social elite, the beautiful people, beau monde; *inf* jet set. **4** *working in an untidy fashion* manner, way, style, method, mode, system, approach. **5** *they built a boat of some fashion* kind, type, sort, make, design, description. **after a fashion** *he put the tent up after a fashion* somehow or other, somehow, in a way, in a rough way, in an approximate manner, to a certain extent, in a manner of speaking.

fashion v *fashion a boat out of logs* make, construct, build, manufacture, create, devise, shape, form, mould, forge, hew, carve.

fashionable adj **1** *fashionable clothes* in fashion, stylish, up to date, up to the minute, modern, voguish, in vogue, modish, popular, all the rage, trendsetting, latest, smart, chic, elegant, natty; *inf* trendy, with it, ritzy. **2** *fashionable areas/restaurants* high-class, high-toned; *inf* classy, swank.

fast adj **1** *at a fast pace* quick, rapid, swift, speedy, brisk, fleet-footed, hasty, hurried, accelerated, express, flying. **2** *remain fast friends* loyal, devoted, faithful, firm, steadfast, staunch, constant, lasting, unchanging, unwavering, enduring. **3** *the door is fast* fastened, closed, shut, secured, secure, firmly fixed. **4** *fast women* promiscuous, licentious, dissolute, loose, wanton. **5** *lead fast lives* wild, dissipated, dissolute, debauched, promiscuous, intemperate, immoderate, rakish, unrestrained, reckless, profligate, self-indulgent, extravagant.

fast adv **1** *run fast* quickly, rapidly, swiftly, speedily, briskly, hastily, with all haste, in haste, hurriedly, in a hurry, post-haste, expeditiously, with dispatch, like the wind, like a shot/flash, hell for leather, like a bat out of hell; *inf* lickety-split. **2** *stuck fast* firmly, tightly, securely, immovably, fixedly. **3** *fast asleep* sound, deeply, completely. **4** *live fast* wildly, dissipatedly, intemperately, rakishly, recklessly. *see* FAST adj 5.

fast v *fasting during Lent* abstain from food, refrain from eating, deny oneself food, go without food, go hungry, eat nothing, starve oneself, go on hunger strike.

fasten v **1** *fasten a brooch to the dress* attach, fix, affix, clip, pin, tack. **2** *fasten the door* bolt, lock, secure, make secure/fast, chain, seal. **3** *fasten the links of the chain* join, connect, couple, unite, link. **4** *fasten the goat to the tree* attach, tie, bind, tether, hitch, anchor. **5** *fasten his gaze on her* direct, aim, point, focus, fix, rivet, concentrate, zero in. **6** *the dress fastens at the back* become closed, close; button, zip. **7** *the gang fastening on the younger boys* take hold of, seize, catch/grab hold of, grab, snatch.

fastidious adj hard to please, critical, overcritical, hypercritical, fussy, finicky, overparticular; *inf* choosy, picky, pernickety.

fat adj **1** *fat old men* plump, stout, overweight, obese, heavy, large, solid, corpulent, chubby, tubby, portly, rotund, podgy, flabby, gross, pot-bellied, paunchy; *inf* beefy, roly-poly, elephantine. **2** *fat substances* fatty, greasy, oily, oleaginous, adipose, unctuous, sebaceous. **3** *fat land* fertile, productive, fruitful, rich, lush, flourishing, thriving. **4** *a fat part in a play* substantial, large, sizeable, major, important, significant, considerable. **5** *a fat income* large, substantial, profitable, remunerative, lucrative. **6** *a fat book* thick, big, substantial, broad, extended. **7** *fat chance* very little, not much, minimal, hardly any.

fat n **1** *too much fat in the meat* fatty tissue, fat cells, adipose tissue. **2** *he'll have to get rid of his fat* excessive weight, fatness, plumpness, stoutness, obesity, chubbiness, tubbiness, flabbiness, corpulence, bulk; *inf* flab, blubber, beef. *see* FAT adj 1. **3** *add fat to the cake* animal/vegetable fat; lard, suet, butter, margarine.

fatal adj **1** *a fatal blow/illness* causing death, mortal, deadly, lethal, death dealing, killing, terminal, final, incurable. **2** *fatal to our plans* ruinous, destructive, disastrous, catastrophic, calamitous, cataclysmic. **3** *the fatal moment* fateful, critical, crucial, decisive, determining, pivotal, momentous, important.

fatalism n stoicism, resignation, passive acceptance, acceptance; predeterminism, predestinarianism, necessitarianism.

fatality n **1** *three fatalities in the accident* dead person, death, casualty, mortality, loss; dead. **2** *the fatality of the blow* deadliness, lethalness. **3** *a road noted for its fatalities* fatal accident, disaster, catastrophe.

fate n **1** *fate meant them to meet* destiny, providence, God's will, nemesis, kismet, predestination, predetermination, chance, astral influence, one's lot in life; the stars. **2** *courts deciding our fate* future, outcome, issue, upshot, end. **3** *met his fate in battle* death, end, destruction, ruin, doom, catastrophe, downfall, disaster, collapse, defeat.

fated adj *a fated meeting* | *fated to meet* predestined, preordained, foreordained, destined, inevitable, inescapable, sure, ineluctable, doomed.

fateful adj **1** *a fateful meeting* critical, crucial, decisive, determining, pivotal, momentous, important, fated. **2** *a fateful course of action* disastrous, ruinous, destructive, fatal, lethal, deadly.

father n **1** male parent, begetter, paterfamilias, patriarch; adoptive father, stepfather; *inf* dad, daddy, pop, poppa, pa, old boy, old man, governor, gaffer, pater. **2** *investigate the history of his fathers* forefather, ancestor, forebear, progenitor, primogenitor, predecessor, forerunner, precursor. **3** *the father of modern history* founder, originator, initiator, prime mover, architect, inventor, creator, maker, author. **4** *the city fathers* leader, elder, patriarch, senator. **5** *God bless you, Father* priest, pastor, padre, parson, clergyman, father confessor, abbé, curé. **6** *Father in heaven* God, our Lord, the Lord God, the Deity.

father v **1** *he fathered three sons* sire, beget, procreate, engender, bring into being, give life to. **2** *father the project* found, establish, institute, originate, initiate, invent, create, generate, conceive.

fatherland n native land/country, native soil/heath, homeland, home, one's mother country, motherland, land of one's birth/ fathers, the old country.

fatherly adj paternal, kindly, kind, affectionate, tender, caring, benevolent, sympathetic, understanding, indulgent, protective, supportive, patriarchal.

fathom v **1** *fathom the depth of the water* sound, plumb, measure, estimate, gauge, probe. **2** *fathom their motives* understand, comprehend, grasp, perceive, penetrate, divine, search out, get to the bottom of, ferret out.

fatigue v *it fatigues him to walk* tire, tire out, overtire, make weary, weary, exhaust, wear out, drain, prostrate, enervate; *inf* take it out of, do in, fag out, whack, poop.

fatigue n *suffering from fatigue* tiredness, overtiredness, weariness, exhaustion, prostration, lassitude, debility, enervation, lethargy, listlessness.

fatness n plumpness, stoutness, obesity, heaviness, largeness, corpulence, portliness, chubbiness, tubbiness, rotundity, podginess, flabbiness, grossness; *inf* beefiness.

fatten v **1** *fatten the cattle for market* make fat/fatter, feed up, feed, build up, overfeed, bloat. **2** *children fattening up on good food* grow fat/fatter, get fat, put on weight, gain weight, get heavier, thicken, widen, broaden, expand, spread out. **3** *fatten the land* feed, fertilize, nourish, nurture, enrich.

fatty adj fat, greasy, oily, oleaginous, adipose, unctuous, sebaceous.

fatuous adj silly, foolish, stupid, inane, pointless, senseless, nonsensical, childish, puerile, idiotic, brainless, mindless, vacuous, asinine, moronic, witless, ridiculous, ludicrous, laughable, risible.

fault n **1** *a fault in the material* defect, flaw, imperfection, blemish, snag. **2** *a fault in her character* defect, flaw, failing, shortcoming, weakness, weak point, infirmity, lack, deficiency. **3** *a fault in the calculation* error, mistake, inaccuracy, blunder, oversight; *inf* slip-up, boob. **4** *blame one child for another's faults* misdeed, wrongdoing, offence, misdemeanour, misconduct, sin, vice, lapse, indiscretion, peccadillo, transgression, trespass. **5** *whose fault was the accident?* culpability, blameworthiness, responsibility, accountability, answerability. **at fault** *which driver was at fault?* to blame, blameworthy, blamable, in the wrong, culpable, responsible, accountable, answerable. **to a fault** *generous to a fault* excessively, unduly, in the extreme, immoderately, out of all proportion, overmuch, needlessly; *Scots* overly; *inf* over the top, OTT.

fault v **1** *cannot fault his behaviour* find fault with, criticize, complain about, quibble about, find lacking, censure, impugn, pick holes in. **2** *the judge failed to fault him* hold responsible/accountable/blameworthy/culpable, hold to blame, call to account.

fault-finding n criticism, carping, complaining, captiousness, cavilling, quibbling, niggling, hair-splitting; *inf* nit-picking.

fault-finding adj critical, overcritical, hypercritical, censorious, carping, captious, cavilling, quibbling, niggling, hair-splitting, pettifogging; *inf* nit-picking.

faultless adj **1** *a faultless piece of work* without fault, perfect, flawless, without blemish, unblemished, impeccable, accurate, correct, exemplary, model. **2** *the wife of the prisoner was faultless* innocent, without guilt, guiltless, blameless, above reproach, irreproachable, sinless, pure, unsullied.

faulty adj **1** *a faulty lock* broken, not working, malfunctioning, out of order, damaged, defective, unsound; *inf* on the blink, kaput. **2** *faulty reasoning* defective, flawed, unsound, wrong, inaccurate, incorrect, erroneous, imprecise, fallacious, impaired, weak, invalid.

faux pas n blunder, gaffe, mistake, slip-up, indiscretion, impropriety, lapse of etiquette, solecism, peccadillo; *inf* boob, boo-boo.

favour n **1** *do me a favour* good turn, service, kind act, good deed, kindness, courtesy, benefit, boon. **2** *look on him with favour* approval, approbation, esteem, goodwill, kindness, benevolence, friendliness. **3** *owe his job to favour rather than merit* favouritism, bias, partiality, prejudice, partisanship. **4** *enjoy the favour of the King* patronage, backing, support, aid, assistance, championship, aegis; auspices. **5** *wear political favours* ribbons, rosette, badge, token. **in favour of** *in favour of hanging* on the side of, for, pro, giving support/backing to, right behind; all for.

favour v **1** *he favours returning* advocate, approve of, recommend, support, back, endorse, sanction. **2** *the young man favoured blondes* prefer, go in for, go for, choose, opt for, select, pick, plump for, single out, fancy, like, incline towards. **3** *the father favours his son* show favouritism towards, have a bias towards, treat with partiality, indulge, pamper, spoil. **4** *the wind favoured the other team* be to the advantage of, be advantageous to, benefit, help, assist, aid, advance, abet, succour. **5** *favour us with a smile* do a favour/service to, do a good turn to, oblige, serve, accommodate.

favourable adj **1** *a favourable report* good, approving, commendatory, praising, well-disposed, enthusiastic. **2** *the circumstances are favourable* in one's favour, advantageous, beneficial, on one's side, helpful, good, hopeful, promising, fair, auspicious, propitious, opportune, timely, encouraging, conducive, convenient, suitable, fit, appropriate. **3** *a favourable reply* affirmative, in the affirmative, positive, encouraging. **4** *make a favourable impression* good, pleasing, agreeable, successful, positive.

favourite adj *my favourite book* best-loved, most-liked, pet, favoured, dearest, preferred, chosen, choice, treasured, ideal.

favourite n **1** *the daughter is the father's favourite* preference, first choice, choice, pick, pet, beloved, darling, idol, god, goddess, jewel, jewel in the crown; *inf* blue-eyed boy, teacher's pet. **2** *the favourite won* expected/probable winner, front-runner.

favouritism n *guilty of favouritism* bias, partiality, prejudice, unfair preference, partisanship, one-sidedness, nepotism, inequality, unfairness, inequity.

fawn adj *fawn trousers* yellowish-brown, greyish-brown, buff, beige, greige, neutral.

fawn v *fawning on the manager* kowtow to, toady to, truckle to, bow and scrape to, grovel before, be obsequious/servile to, curry favour with, pay court to, ingratiate oneself with, dance attendance on, lick the boots of; *inf* butter up.

fawning adj obsequious, servile, sycophantic, toadyish, slavish, bowing and scraping, grovelling, abject, crawling, creeping, cringing, prostrate, flattering, ingratiating, over-deferential; *inf* bootlicking.

fear n **1** *filled with fear at the danger* fright, fearfulness, terror, alarm, panic, trepidation, apprehensiveness, dread, nervousness, fear and trembling, timidity, disquiet, trembling, quaking, quivering, consternation, dismay; shivers, butterflies, tremors; *inf* funk, blue funk. **2** *all her fears were removed* phobia, aversion, dread, bête noire, bugbear, bogey, nightmare, horror, terror; *inf* the creeps. **3** *express fear that he would die* anxiety, worry, unease, uneasiness, apprehension, nervousness, agitation, concern, disquiet, disquietude, foreboding, misgiving, doubt, suspicion, angst. **4** *filled with fear at the sight of the angel* awe, wonder, amazement, reverence, veneration. **5** *there is little fear of her leaving* likelihood, probability, possibility, chance, prospect.

fear v **1** *they fear their father* be afraid/fearful/apprehensive of, be scared of, dread, live in fear/dread of, go in terror of. **2** *she fears spiders* be afraid of, dread, have a horror/dread of, have a phobia about, shudder at, take fright at; *inf* have brown trousers at. **3** *fear to go out* be too afraid/scared/apprehensive to, dare not, hesitate to; *inf* have cold feet about. **4** *I fear for her health* worry about, feel anxious/concerned about, have anxieties/qualms about, feel disquiet for, be solicitous for. **5** *they fear God* stand in awe of, revere, reverence, venerate. **6** *I fear that you may be right* be afraid, suspect, have a suspicion, expect, anticipate, foresee, have a foreboding, apprehend.

fearful adj **1** *fearful of making a noise* afraid, frightened, scared, terrified, alarmed, apprehensive, uneasy, nervous, tense, nervy, panicky, timid, timorous, faint-hearted, diffident, intimidated, hesitant, disquieted, trembling, quaking, quivering,

289

 289

shrinking, cowering, cowardly, pusillanimous; *inf* jittery, jumpy. **2** *a fearful accident* terrible, dreadful, appalling, frightful, ghastly, horrific, horrible, horrendous, shocking, awful, atrocious, hideous, monstrous, dire, grim, unspeakable, gruesome, distressing, harrowing, alarming. **3** *a fearful cold/mess* terrible, appalling, very bad, extremely bad, very great. **4** *the angels were a fearful sight* awesome, awe-inspiring, imposing, impressive, venerable.

fearfully adv **1** *crawl forward fearfully* apprehensively, in fear and trembling, uneasily, nervously, timidly, timorously, diffidently, hesitantly, with one's heart in one's mouth. **2** *she's fearfully polite* extremely, exceedingly, remarkably; *inf* tremendously, awfully, terribly, frightfully.

fearless adj unafraid, brave, courageous, valiant, intrepid, valorous, gallant, plucky, lion-hearted, stout-hearted, heroic, bold, daring, confident, audacious, indomitable, doughty, undaunted, unflinching, unshrinking, unblenching, unabashed; *inf* game, gutsy, spunky.

fearsome adj *a fearsome sight* frightening, alarming, unnerving, daunting, horrifying, horrendous, dismaying, awe-inspiring, awesome.

feasibility n practicability, possibility, workability, viability, suitability, expedience. *see* FEASIBLE.

feasible adj practicable, possible, likely, workable, doable, achievable, attainable, accomplishable, realizable, reasonable, viable, realistic, within reason, useful, suitable, expedient.

feast n **1** banquet, celebration meal, lavish dinner, repast, treat, entertainment, jollification, junket, orgy; revels, festivities; *inf* beanfeast, blow-out, spread, beano, bash, thrash. **2** *the feast of St Stephen* celebration, festival, religious festival, feast day, saint's day, holy day, holiday, fête, gala day, festivity. **3** *a feast for the eyes* pleasure, gratification, delight, treat, joy.

feast v **1** *feast on venison and claret* wine and dine, banquet, gorge oneself on, eat one's fill of, partake of, indulge in, overindulge in, gormandize, stuff one's face with, stuff oneself with. **2** *feast the visiting King* throw a feast for, hold a banquet for, wine and dine, regale, entertain, treat. **3** *feast our eyes on the beauty* delight, please, give pleasure to, gratify, gladden, treat, thrill.

feat n deed, act, action, exploit, performance, accomplishment, achievement, attainment, manoevure, move, stunt.

feather n **1** *a bird's feather* plume, quill, pinion, plumule, pinna. **2** *the bird's feathers* plumage, down, hackles; crest, tuft.

feathery adj **1** *feathery chicks* feathered, downy, fluffy, fleecy, plumed, plumy, plumose, plumate. **2** *feathery material* light, feather-like, light as a feather, gossamer-like, wispy, unsubstantial, ethereal.

feature n **1** *one feature of life in the country* aspect, characteristic, facet, side, point, attribute, quality, property, trait, mark, hallmark, trademark, peculiarity, idiosyncracy. **2** *make a feature of the tombola at the fair* special attraction, attraction, highlight, focal point, focus, draw; *inf* crowd-puller. **3** *read the features in the magazine section* main item/article, article, piece, item, report, story, column.

feature v **1** *the festival features a new opera* present, give prominence to, promote, star, spotlight, highlight, emphasize, play up, accentuate. **2** *do women feature in his life?* have prominence, play a part, have a place.

features npl face, countenance, visage, physiognomy; lineaments; *inf* mug, kisser.

fecund adj fruitful, productive, fertile, potent, prolific, proliferating, propagative.

federal adj federated, federative, confederate, allied, in alliance, in league, united, linked, banded together.

federation n confederation, confederacy, federacy, league, alliance, coalition, union, syndicate, association, amalgamation, combination, combine, entente, society, fraternity, Bund.

fee n charge, price, cost, payment, remuneration, emolument.

feeble adj **1** *old people grown feeble* weak, weakly, weakened, frail, infirm, delicate, slight, sickly, puny, failing, ailing, helpless, powerless, debilitated, decrepit, doddering, tottering, enervated, enfeebled, effete, etiolated; *Scots* shilpit. **2** *a feeble attempt at humour* ineffective, ineffectual, unsuccessful, inadequate, unconvincing, futile, poor, weak, tame, paltry, slight. **3** *he's too feeble to stand up to his boss* weak, ineffective, ineffectual, inefficient, incompetent, inadequate, indecisive, wishy-washy. **4** *a feeble light* dim, indistinct, faint, unclear, vague.

feeble-minded adj **1** *the child was declared feeble-minded* mentally defective, retarded, simple, slow-witted. **2** *he must be feeble-minded to believe that* stupid, idiotic, foolish, half-witted, vacant, slow on the uptake; *inf* bone-headed, dumb, soft in the head, not the full shilling, off one's trolley, out to lunch.

feed v **1** *feed the baby* give food/nourishment to, nurture; suckle, breast-feed, bottle-feed. **2** *feed the family/guests* give food to, nourish, sustain, cater for, provide for, wine and dine. **3** *the baby is feeding* eat, take nourishment, partake of food, consume, devour food. **4** *cattle feeding* graze, browse, crop. **5** *feed on grass* live on, exist on, subsist on. **6** *feed his self-esteem* gratify, bolster up, strengthen, augment, add to, encourage, minister to, add fuel to. **7** *feed information to the troops* supply, provide, give, furnish.

feed n **1** *cattle feed* food, fodder, provender, forage, pasturage, silage. **2** *have a good feed* feast, meal, dinner, repast, banquet; *inf* nosh, nosh-up, spread, tuck-in.

feel v **1** *feel her face* touch, stroke, caress, fondle, finger, thumb, handle, manipulate, paw, maul. **2** *feel the ship's motion* be aware/conscious of, notice, observe, perceive, be sensible of, have a sensation of. **3** *feel pain* experience, know, have, undergo, go through, bear, endure, suffer. **4** *feel one's way* grope, fumble, poke, explore. **5** *feel the temperature of the water* sense, try, try out, test, sound out. **6** *he feels that he should go* think, believe, consider it right, consider, be of the opinion, hold, judge, deem. **7** *I feel that he's hiding something* have a feeling, sense, get the impression, feel in one's bones, have a hunch, have a funny feeling, just know, intuit. **8** *the air feels damp* seem, appear, strike one as. **feel for** *feel for the poor* sympathize with, be sorry for, pity, feel sympathy/compassion for, be moved by, weep for, grieve for, one's heart bleeds for, commiserate with, condole with, empathize with. **feel like** *feel like a holiday* would like, want, wish, desire, fancy, feel in need of; *inf* have a yen for.

feel n **1** *you can tell by feel* touch, sense of touch, tactile sense. **2** *the material has a nice feel* texture, surface, finish. **3** *I don't like the feel of the place* atmosphere, ambience, aura, mood, air, impression; *inf* vibrations, vibes. **4** *have a feel for that kind of work* knack, aptitude, flair, talent, gift, art, trick, faculty.

feeler n **1** *the creature's feeler* antenna, tentacle, whisker. **2** *put out feelers to get people's opinions* probe, trial balloon, tentative proposal/suggestion, advance, leak; overtures.

feeling n **1** *tell what it is by feeling* feel, touch, sense of touch, tactile sense. **2** *a feeling of pain* awareness, consciousness, sensation, sense, perception. **3** *I had a feeling that you would be there* idea, vague idea, funny feeling, impression, suspicion, sneaking suspicion, notion, inkling, hunch, apprehension, presentiment, premonition, fore-

boding. **4** *look at him with feeling* emotion, affection, fondness, warmth, love, sentiment, passion, ardour, fervour, intensity, heat, fire, vehemence. **5** *show feeling for others* sympathy, pity, compassion, understanding, concern, sensitivity, tender-heartedness, grief, commiseration, condolence, empathy, fellow-feeling. **6** *my feeling is that he will go* instinct, opinion, intuition, impression, point of view, thought, way of thinking, theory, hunch. **7** *a feeling of neglect about the place* feel, atmosphere, ambience, aura, mood, air, impression; *inf* vibrations, vibes.

feeling adj **1** *a feeling person* sensitive, warm, tender, caring, soft-hearted, sympathetic, compassionate, responsive, sentient, sensible, emotional, demonstrative. **2** *a feeling letter* emotional, passionate, impassioned, ardent, intense, fervent, fervid.

feelings npl *hurt their feelings | strong feelings* sensibilities, sensitivities, self-esteem, ego; emotions, passions, sentiments.

feign v **1** *feign sleep* fake, simulate, sham, affect, give the appearance of. **2** *he's only feigning* pretend, fake, make believe, sham, put it on, act, play-act, malinger.

felicitations npl congratulations, good wishes, best wishes, blessings, greetings, salutations, compliments.

felicitous adj **1** *a felicitous expression* apt, well-chosen, well-expressed, well-put, fitting, suitable, appropriate, apposite, pertinent, germane, to the point. **2** *a felicitous event* happy, joyful, harmonious, fortunate, lucky, successful, prosperous.

feline adj catlike, leonine, graceful, sinuous, slinky, sensual, stealthy, insidious.

fell v **1** *fell a tree/building* cut down, hew, level, raze, raze to the ground, demolish, knock down. **2** *fell him with one blow* knock down/over, strike down, flatten, ground, floor, prostrate, overthrow, kill.

fellow n **1** *that fellow over there* man, male, boy, person, individual; *inf* chap, bloke, guy, codger, character, customer. **2** *the drunk and his fellows were thrown out* friend, companion, crony, mate, associate, colleague, comrade, partner, co-worker; *inf* chum, pal, buddy. **3** *wish to impress his fellows* peer, compeer, equal, contemporary, confrère. **4** *the fellow of the shoe* counterpart, mate, partner, match, twin, brother, double.

fellowship n **1** *join the club for fellowship* companionship, companionability, sociability, comradeship, fraternization, camaraderie, friendship, amiability, amity, affability, geniality, kindliness, cordiality, intimacy, social intercourse; *inf* chumminess, palliness, clubbiness. **2** *the church fellowship* association, society, club, league, union, guild, affiliation, order, fraternity, brotherhood, sorority, sodality, amalgamation, consortium, corporation.

female n **1** *two males and a female* woman, lady, girl, lass; *inf* bird, chick, dame. **2** *animals which are female* cow, duck, bitch, ewe, mare, sow, nanny goat, hen, doe, vixen.

female adj feminine, womanly, womanlike, ladylike.

feminine adj **1** *a very feminine young woman* soft, delicate, gentle, tender, graceful, womanly, ladylike, girlish, refined, modest. **2** *a feminine man* effeminate, womanish, effete, unmanly, unmasculine, weak; *inf* sissy, sissyish, limp-wristed.

fence n **1** *a fence round the field/town* enclosure, barrier, paling, railing, rail, wall, hedge; barricade, rampart, stockade, palisade, circumvallation. **2** *stolen goods from the fence* receiver, dealer. **on the fence** uncommitted, uncertain, undecided, vacillating, irresolute, neutral, impartial.

fence v **1** *fence the garden | fence off the field* enclose, surround, circumscribe, encircle, encompass. **2** *fence in the cows* shut in, confine, pen, separate off, secure, imprison. **3** *he fences as a hobby* go fencing, engage in swordplay/swordsmanship. **4** *fence when asked questions* hedge, be evasive, beat about the bush, dodge the issue, parry questions, prevaricate, equivocate, fudge the issue, shilly-shally, vacillate, tergiversate.

fend v *fend off their blows | fend off questions* ward off, keep off, turn aside, stave off, divert, deflect, avert, defend oneself against, guard against, parry, forestall. **fend for oneself** provide/shift for oneself, take care of oneself, get by.

ferment n **1** *use a ferment in the beer* fermenting substance, fermentation agent, yeast, mould, bacteria, leaven, leavening. **2** *children in a ferment of excitement* stir, fever, furore, frenzy, brouhaha, confusion, fuss, stew, hubbub, hurly-burly, racket, imbroglio; tumult, commotion, uproar, turmoil, agitation, disruption, turbulence.

ferment v **1** *beer/yeast mixtures fermenting* undergo fermentation, foam, froth, bubble, effervesce, seethe, boil, rise, work. **2** *ferment the beer/yeast mixture* subject to fermentation, cause to effervesce. **3** *his words fermenting the crowd* excite, agitate, inflame, incite. **4** *ferment trouble* cause, incite, excite, provoke, arouse, stir up, foment. **5** *the*

crowd fermenting with excitement seethe, smoulder, boil, be agitated.

ferocious adj **1** *a ferocious animal* fierce, savage, wild, feral, untamed, predatory, rapacious. **2** *ferocious troops* fierce, savage, ruthless, brutal, brutish, cruel, pitiless, merciless, vicious, violent, inexorable, barbarous, barbaric, inhuman, bloodthirsty, murderous, tigerish, wolfish. **3** *ferocious heat* fierce, very great, intense, extreme, acute.

ferret v **1** *ferreting in her handbag* rummage, search about, scrabble around, rifle through, forage around, sift through. **2** *ferret out the facts* search out, unearth, discover, disclose, elicit, bring to light, get at, run to earth, track down, dig up, root out, hunt out, drive out, fish out, nose out, sniff out, smell out.

ferry n *the ferry runs hourly* ferryboat, shuttle, packet boat, packet.

ferry v **1** *the boat ferries across everyday* go back and forth, come and go, run, shuttle. **2** *ferry the passengers across the water* carry, transport, convey, run, ship, shuttle, chauffeur.

fertile adj **1** *fertile soil* fruitful, productive, fecund, rich. **2** *fertile young people* potent, virile, child-producing, fecund, generative, reproductive, propagative. **3** *fertile imaginations* inventive, creative, original, ingenious, resourceful, visionary, constructive, productive.

fertilize v **1** *fertilize the soil* add fertilizer to, feed, enrich, mulch, compost, dress, top-dress. **2** *fertilize the egg/cow* impregnate, inseminate, fecundate, make pregnant. **3** *fertilize the plant* pollinate, make fruitful, fructify.

fertilizer n plant food, manure, dung, compost, dressing, top-dressing; bone-meal, guano, marl.

fervent adj passionate, ardent, impassioned, intense, vehement, heartfelt, fervid, emotional, emotive, warm, devout, sincere, eager, earnest, zealous, enthusiastic, excited, animated, spirited; *lit* perfervid.

fervid adj fervent, passionate, ardent, impassioned, intense. *see* FERVOUR.

fervour n fervency, passion, ardour, impassionedness, intensity, vehemency, fervidness, emotion, warmth, devoutness, sincerity, eagerness, earnestness, zeal, enthusiasm, excitement, animation, spirit; *inf* perfervidness.

fester v **1** *a wound festering* suppurate, matter, come to a head, gather, maturate, run, discharge. **2** *animal corpses festering* rot, decay, go bad, go off, decompose, disintegrate. **3** *resentment festering in their minds* rankle, chafe, gnaw, cause bitterness/resentment/vexation.

festival n **1** *a church festival* saint's day, holy day, feast day, holiday, anniversary, commemoration, rite, ritual, day of observance. **2** *the Edinburgh festival* festival of music and drama, musical festival, festival of music, arts festival, science festival. **3** *take part in the town's annual festival* fête, gala day, carnival; celebrations, festivities; *Welsh* eisteddfod.

festive adj *festive occasions* joyous, joyful, happy, jolly, merry, gay, jovial, light-hearted, cheerful, cheery, jubilant, convivial, good-time, gleeful, mirthful, uproarious, rollicking, back-slapping, celebratory, gala, holiday, carnival, sportive, festal.

festivity n **1** *the festivity of the occasion* joyfulness, jollity, merriment, pleasure, amusement, gaiety, cheerfulness, jubilance, convivialness, cheeriness, gleefulness, glee, mirthfulness, mirth, revelry, sportiveness. **2** *enjoy the festivities* festive event, celebration, festival, entertainment, party, jollification, revelry, carousal, sport; fun and games, celebrations, festive proceedings.

festoon n *a festoon of flowers* garland, wreath, chaplet, lei, swathe, swag.

festoon v *be festooned with flowers* garland, wreathe, hang, drape, decorate, adorn, ornament, array, deck, bedeck, swathe, beribbon.

fetch v **1** *fetch the milk/doctor* go and get, get, go for, bring, carry, deliver, convey, transport, escort, conduct, lead, usher in. **2** *the vase fetched £40* sell for, go for, bring in, realize, yield, earn, cost, afford.

fetching adj attractive, charming, enchanting, sweet, winsome, taking, captivating, fascinating, alluring.

fête n gala, fair, garden party, sale of work.

fetish n **1** *a foot/leather fetish* fixation, sexual fixation, compulsion, obsession, mania, *idée fixe*; *inf* thing. **2** *carry a fetish* talisman, charm, amulet.

fetter v **1** *fetter the prisoners* chain, chain up, shackles, bind, tie, tie up, hobble. **2** *fettered by petty restrictions* restrict, hinder, impede, obstruct, constrain, confine, restrain.

fetters npl chains, shackles, bond, irons, manacles, trammels; restraint, check.

fettle n condition, shape, form, state, order, way; *inf* kilter.

feud n **1** *a state of feud between the families* vendetta, rivalry, hostility, enmity, conflict, strife, discord, bad blood, animosity, antagonism, unfriendliness, grudge, estrangement, schism. **2** *start a feud* vendetta, quarrel, conflict, argument, bickering, falling-out, broil.

fever n **1** *the child's fever subsided* feverishness, febricity; *Med* pyrexia; *inf* temperature, temp. **2** *in a fever of excitement* ferment, frenzy, furore; turmoil, agitation, excitement, restlessness, unrest, passion, intensity.

feverish adj **1** *the child is feverish* fevered, febrile, burning, hot. **2** *look feverish* flushed, red-faced, red. **3** *feverish excitement* frenzied, frenetic, agitated, excited, restless, nervous, worked up, overwrought, frantic, distracted, flustered, impatient; *inf* in a tizzy.

few adj **1** *few people were there* not many, hardly any, scarcely any, one or two, a handful of, a sprinkling of; *inf* a couple of. **2** *very few buses* few and far between, infrequent, sporadic, irregular. **3** *opportunities are few* scarce, rare, negligible, scant, thin on the ground.

few n *a few were there* a small number, one or two, a handful, a sprinkling.

fiancé, fiancée n husband-to-be, wife-to-be, bride-to-be, future husband/wife, prospective husband/wife, prospective spouse, betrothed; *inf* intended.

fiasco n failure, disaster, catastrophe, mess, ruination, débâcle, abortion; *inf* flop, wash-out.

fib n *tell a fib* lie, white lie, untruth, falsehood, fabrication, piece of fiction, fiction, fairy story, tall tale; *inf* terminological inexactitude, whopper.

fibre n **1** *the fibres of the carpet* thread, strand, tendril, filament, fibril. **2** *made of a coarse fibre* material, substance, cloth, stuff. **3** *a person of a different fibre* character, nature, make-up, spirit, disposition, temperament. see MORAL FIBRE.

fickle adj capricious, changeable, variable, unpredictable, volatile, mercurial, inconstant, unstable, vacillating, unsteady, unfaithful, faithless, irresolute, flighty, giddy, erratic, fitful, irregular, mutable.

fickleness n capriciousness, unpredictableness, volatility, inconstancy, instability, vacillation, unfaithfulness, fitfulness, mutability. see FICKLE.

fiction n **1** *a work of fiction* story telling, story narration, romance, fable, fantasy, legend. **2** *guilty of a polite fiction* piece of fiction, fabrication, invention, concoction, lie, fib, untruth, falsehood, fairy tale/story, tall story, improvisation, prevarication; *inf* cock and bull story, whopper, angler's tale.

fictional adj *a fictional character* fictitious, made up, invented, imaginary, unreal, non-existent.

fictitious adj **1** *a fictitious character* made up, imaginary. *see* FICTIONAL. **2** *a fictitious address* false, untrue, bogus, sham, counterfeit, fake, fabricated. **3** *a fictitious name* false, assumed, invented, made up, concocted, spurious, improvised. **4** *his account is fictitious* made up, untrue, false, imagined, imaginary, apocryphal.

fiddle n **1** *play the fiddle* violin, viola, cello, double bass. **2** *the new appointment was a fiddle* fraud, fix, swindle, wangle, racket, bit of sharp practice.

fiddle v **1** *stop fiddling with your pencil* | *he's fiddling about* fidget with, play with, fuss with, toy with, finger, mess about with, fool around with; waste time, act aimlessly. **2** *he's fiddling with the engine* tinker with, play about with, tamper with, interfere with; *inf* monkey around with. **3** *fiddle one's tax return* falsify; *inf* cook. **4** *someone in the accounts department has been fiddling* cheat, swindle; *inf* diddle, finagle, cook the books.

fiddling adj *a fiddling amount* trifling, insignificant, trivial, petty, small; *inf* piddling.

fidelity n **1** *his fidelity to his wife/king* faithfulness, loyalty, devotedness, devotion, allegiance, commitment, constancy, true-heartedness, trustworthiness, dependability, reliability, staunchness, obedience. **2** *the fidelity of the copy* accuracy, exactness, exactitude, precision, preciseness, strictness, closeness, faithfulness, correspondence, conformity, authenticity.

fidget v **1** *children fidgeting* move restlessly, wriggle, squirm, twitch, jiggle; *inf* have ants in one's pants. **2** *fidget with one's pencil* fiddle with, play with, fuss with. *see* FIDDLE V 1. **3** *his silence fidgeted her* worry, make uneasy, agitate, bother, upset, ruffle.

fidgety adj restless, restive, on edge, jumpy, uneasy, nervous, nervy, twitchy; *inf* jittery, like a cat on hot bricks.

field n **1** *cows in the field* pasture, meadow; grassland; *lit* glebe, lea, mead, sward, greensward. **2** *specializing in the field of electronics* area, area of activity, sphere, regime, discipline, province, department, line, speciality, métier. **3** *in his field of vision* range, scope, purview; limits, confines. **4** *the field for the race/job is high quality* applicants, candidates, entrants, competitors, runners, possibles, possibilities; competition.

field v **1** *field the ball* catch, stop, retrieve, return, throw back. **2** *field questions deftly* deal with, handle, cope with, deflect, turn aside.

fiend n **1** *fiends of hell* devil, demon, evil spirit, cacodemon. **2** *the slavemaster was a fiend* brute, savage, beast, barbarian, monster, ogre, sadist, blackguard. **3** *a drugs fiend* addict, abuser, user. **4** *a cinema fiend* addict, fanatic, maniac, enthusiast, devotee, fan, aficionado; *inf* buff, freak, nut.

fiendish adj **1** *a fiendish stepfather* wicked, cruel, brutal, brutish, savage, barbaric, barbarous, inhuman, murderous, vicious, bloodthirsty, ferocious, ruthless, heartless, pitiless, merciless, black-hearted, unfeeling, malevolent, malicious, villainous, odious, base, malignant, devilish, diabolical, hellish, demonic, satanic, ungodly. **2** *a fiendish plan to leave early* cunning, clever, ingenious. **3** *a fiendish problem* difficult, complex, complicated, intricate.

fierce adj **1** *a fierce animal/enemy* ferocious, savage, wild, vicious, feral, untamed, bloodthirsty, dangerous, cruel, brutal, murderous, slaughterous, menacing, threatening, terrible, grim, tigerish, wolfish. **2** *a fierce love* intense, ardent, passionate, impassioned, fervent, fervid, fiery, uncontrolled. **3** *a fierce wind* violent, strong, stormy, blustery, gusty, boisterous, tempestuous, raging, furious, turbulent, tumultuous, cyclonic, typhonic. **4** *suffer from fierce headaches* very bad, severe, intense, grave, awful, dreadful. **5** *fierce competition* competitive, keen, intense, strong, relentless, cut-throat.

fight v **1** *the armies fought* battle, do battle, give battle, war, wage war, go to war, make war, attack, mount an attack, take up arms, combat, engage, meet, come to blows, exchange blows, close, clash, skirmish, struggle, contend, grapple, wrestle, scuffle, tussle, collide, spar, joust, tilt. **2** *the two men fought* come to blows, exchange blows, attack/assault each other, hit/punch each other, box, brawl; *inf* scrap. **3** *the two families have been fighting for years* feud, quarrel, argue, bicker, squabble, wrangle, dispute, be at odds, disagree, battle, altercate; *inf* fall out. **4** *we fought the council's decision* contest, take a stand against, oppose, dispute, object to, withstand, resist, defy, strive/struggle against, take issue with. **5** *fight a battle* wage, carry on, conduct, engage in, wage, prosecute. **fight**

back 1 *children told to fight back* defend oneself, put up a fight, retaliate, counterattack, give tit for tat, reply. **2** *fight back the tears* suppress, repress, check, curb, restrain, contain, bottle up. **fight off** ward off, beat off, stave off, repel, repulse, hold at bay, resist.

fight n **1** *the army lost the last fight* battle, engagement, action, clash, conflict, combat, contest, encounter, skirmish, scuffle, tussle, brush, exchange. **2** *a fight outside the pub* brawl, row, affray, fracas, mêlée, sparring match, exchange, free-for-all, struggle, disturbance; fisticuffs; *inf* set-to, scrap, punch-up. **3** *the two families have had a fight* quarrel, disagreement, difference of opinion, dispute, argument, altercation, feud. **4** *lose all the fight in him* spirit, will to win, gameness, pluck, aggression, belligerence, militancy, resistance, power to resist.

fighter n **1** *the military fighters* fighting man/woman, soldier, man-at-arms, warrior; armed aircraft. **2** *place bets on the younger fighter* boxer, pugilist, wrestler; prizefighter, champion wrestler; *inf* champ, bruiser. **3** *fighters for the title* contestant, contender, competitor, rival.

figurative adj non-literal, metaphorical, allegorical, representative, emblematic, symbolic, imagistic.

figure n **1** *illegible figures | add up the figures* number, whole number, numeral, digit, integer, cipher, numerical symbol. **2** *be unable to put a figure on the work involved* cost, price, amount, value, total, sum, aggregate. **3** *figures unrecognizable in the mist* shape, form, outline, silhouette. **4** *have a well-developed figure* body, physique, build, frame, torso; proportions; *inf* vital statistics, chassis. **5** *see figure 20* diagram, illustration, picture, drawing, sketch, chart, plan, map. **6** *artists good at drawing figures* human representation, likeness, image of a person. **7** *the lily is a figure of purity* symbol, emblem, sign, representative. **8** *the figures on the wood* pattern, design, motif, device, depiction. **9** *one of the figures of the town council* dignitary, notable, notability, personage, somebody, worthy, celebrity, leader, force, personality, presence, character; *inf* big shot, big noise, bigwig, big Daddy, Mr Big.

figure v **1** *figure up the row of numbers* count, calculate, add up, tot up, work out, total, sum, tally, reckon, compute. **2** *she figures in his autobiography* appear, feature, be featured/mentioned, be referred to, play a part/role, be conspicuous. **3** *we figure that they'll go* think, consider, conclude. **4** *that*

figures be likely/probable, be understandable, make sense. **figure out 1** *figure out the cost* work out, calculate, compute, reckon, assess. **2** *figure out why they came* understand, comprehend, work out, make out, fathom, see, reason, imagine, decipher, resolve; *inf* make head or tail of, twig.

figurehead n **1** *the king is just a figurehead* titular head, nominal leader, cipher, token, mouthpiece, puppet, man of straw. **2** *figurehead on the ship's prow* carving, bust, sculpture, image, statue.

figures npl *good at figures* arithmetic, counting; calculations, statistics.

filament n fibre, fibril, thread, strand, string, tendril, wire, cable, cord.

filch v steal, thieve, pilfer, rob, take, purloin, abstract, misappropriate, embezzle, shoplift; *inf* walk off with, nick, swipe, snaffle, lift, snitch, knock off.

file¹ n **1** *put documents/data in a file* folder, box, portfolio, document case, filing cabinet; card file, computer file, data file. **2** *get out your file* dossier, information; documents, records, data, particulars, case notes. **3** *a file of people* line, column, row, string, chain, queue.

file¹ v **1** *file the information* categorize, classify, organize, put in place, put in order, pigeonhole, put on record, record, enter, store. **2** *file for divorce* apply for, put in for, register for, sign up for. **3** *people filing in* walk/march in a line, march, parade, troop, pass in formation.

file² v *file one's nails* smooth, shape, buff, rub, rub down, polish, burnish, furbish, refine, scrape, abrade, rasp, sandpaper, pumice.

filigree n wirework, fretwork, fret, latticework, lattice, grillwork, scrollwork.

fill v **1** *fill the cup | the pond slowly filled* make/become full, fill up, fill to the brim, fill to overflowing. **2** *people filled the room* occupy all of, crowd, overcrowd, congest, cram, pervade. **3** *fill the shelves* stock, pack, load, supply, furnish, provide, replenish, restock, refill. **4** *fill the children* feed fully, satisfy, stuff, cram, satiate, sate, surfeit, glut. **5** *perfume/hostility filled the air* pervade, spread throughout, permeate, suffuse, imbue, charge, saturate. **6** *fill the hole* stop, stop up, block up, bung up, plug, seal, close, clog. **7** *he filled the post of manager* occupy, hold, take up. **8** *fill the order/commission* carry out, execute, perform, complete, fulfil. **fill in 1** *fill in the form* complete, answer, fill up; *Amer* fill out. **2** *fill in for the manager* deputize, substitute, stand in, take over. **3** *fill me in on the events* inform, advise, tell, notify, acquaint, apprise, up date; *inf* put wise, put in the picture. **fill out 1** *the children have filled out* grow fatter, become plumper/rounder. **2** *fill out the story* round out, expand.

fill n *one's fill* eat one's fill | have had one's fill *of her* all one wants, as much as one can take, enough, more than enough, plenty, ample, sufficient.

fillip n stimulus, incentive, encouragement, inducement, motivation, spur, goad, prod, push.

film n **1** *a film of dust* layer, coat, coating, covering, cover, dusting, sheet, blanket, skin, tissue, membrane, pellicle. **2** *see the mountain through a film* haze, mist, cloud, blur, veil; murkiness. **3** *see a recent film* movie, picture; *Amer* motion picture; *inf* flick.

film v **1** *film the wedding* photograph, record on film, take pictures of, shoot, make a film of, televise, video. **2** *her eyes filmed over* become blurred, blur, cloud over, mist over, dull, blear.

filmy adj diaphanous, transparent, see-through, translucent, sheer, gauzelike, gauzy, gossamer, gossamery, cobwebby, delicate, fine, light, thin, airy, floaty, fragile, flimsy, unsubstantial.

filter n *strain the coffee through a filter* strainer, sieve, sifter, riddle, colander, gauze, netting, cheesecloth.

filter v **1** *filter the coffee* strain, sieve, sift, riddle, filtrate; clarify, purify, clear, refine. **2** *liquid filtering through* trickle, ooze, seep, leak, dribble, percolate, flow out, drain, well, exude, escape, leach.

filth n **1** *the floors covered in filth | the filth of the house* dirt, muck, grime, mud, mire, sludge, slime, squalor, foul matter, excrement, dung, manure, ordure, sewage, rubbish, refuse, garbage, trash, pollution, contamination, defilement, rotting material, decay, putrefaction, putrescence; filthiness, uncleanness, foulness, nastiness; *inf* crud. **2** *objecting to filth in magazines* pornography, obscenity, indecency, smut, corruption, vulgarity, vileness; *inf* porn, hard porn, raunchiness.

filthy adj **1** *filthy canals* dirty, mucky, muddy, murky, slimy, squalid, unclean, foul, nasty, feculent, polluted, contaminated, rotten, decaying, smelly, fetid, putrid, faecal. **2** *filthy faces/clothes* unwashed, unclean, dirty, dirt-encrusted, grubby, muddy, mucky, black, blackened, begrimed. **3** *a filthy liar* low, despicable,

contemptible, base, mean, vile, nasty, sordid. **4** *filthy magazines* pornographic, obscene, indecent, smutty, corrupt, coarse, bawdy, vulgar, lewd, licentious, vile, depraved, foul, dirty, impure; *inf* blue, raunchy.

final adj **1** *the final act* last, closing, concluding, finishing, end, ending, terminating, terminal, ultimate, eventual, endmost. **2** *their decision is final* absolute, conclusive, irrevocable, unalterable, irrefutable, incontrovertible, indisputable, unappealable, decisive, definitive, definite, settled, determinate.

finale n end, finish, close, conclusion, climax, culmination, denouement, last act, final scene, final curtain, epilogue; *inf* wind-up.

finality n conclusiveness, decisiveness, definiteness, definitiveness, completeness, absoluteness, irrevocableness, irrefutability, inevitability, unavoidableness.

finalize v complete, conclude, settle, decide, agree on, work out, tie up, wrap up, put the finishing touches to; *inf* sew up, clinch.

finally adv **1** *we finally won* in the end, at last, at long last, ultimately, eventually, at the last minute, at the very last minute, at length, in the long run, when all was said and done. **2** *"finally, I declare the meeting over"* to conclude, in conclusion, lastly. **3** *they have separated finally* absolutely, conclusively, irrevocably, decisively, definitively, definitely, for ever, for good, for all time, once and for all, permanently, inexorably.

finance n **1** *she lectures/works in finance* financial affairs, money matters, pecuniary/fiscal matters, economics; money management, commerce, business, investment, banking, accounting. **2** *finances are low* funds, assets, resources; money, capital, cash, wealth, wherewithal, revenue, stock; financial condition/state.

finance v pay for, fund, back, subsidize, underwrite, capitalize, guarantee, provide capital/security for, furnish credit for.

financial adj money, monetary, pecuniary, fiscal, economic, budgetary.

find v **1** *find a gold watch* come across, chance upon, light upon, happen upon, stumble on. **2** *find a cure/answer/hotel* discover, come up with, hit upon, turn up, bring to light, uncover, unearth, ferret out, locate, lay one's hands on, encounter. **3** *we found the missing glove* get back, recover, retrieve, regain, repossess, recoup. **4** *find the money | find happiness* get, obtain, acquire, procure, gain, earn, achieve, attain, win. **5** *find it pays to be honest* | *found that everyone had gone* discover, become aware, realize, learn, conclude, detect, observe, notice, note, perceive. **6** *find the cheese too strong* consider, regard as, think, judge, deem, gauge, rate. **7** *the arrow found its mark* reach, attain, arrive at, gain, achieve. **find out** *we found out they were lying* discover, become aware that, realize, learn. *see* FIND v 5. **2** *find out the truth* discover, detect, bring to light, reveal, expose, unearth, disclose, unmask, ferret out, lay bare.

find n *the vase is quite a find* asset, acquisition, lucky discovery, catch, bargain, good buy, godsend, boon, windfall.

finding n *the finding of the committee* | *the findings of the court* decision, verdict, conclusion, pronouncement, judgement, decree, order, recommendation.

fine adj **1** *that's fine with me* all right, satisfactory, acceptable, agreeable, convenient, suitable, good; *inf* OK, tickety-boo. **2** *I'm fine, thanks* all right, in good health, quite well; *inf* OK. **3** *a fine painting/performance/wine* excellent, first-class, first-rate, great, exceptional, outstanding, admirable, quality, superior, splendid, magnificent, beautiful, exquisite, choice, select, prime, supreme, rare; *inf* A1, splendiferous, top-notch, top-hole. **4** *a fine day* fair, dry, bright, clear, cloudless, sunny, balmy, clement. **5** *fine china/bones* fragile, delicate, frail, dainty, slight. **6** *fine material* sheer, light, lightweight, chiffony, diaphanous, filmy, gossamer, gossamery, gauzelike, gauzy, cobwebby, transparent, translucent, airy, ethereal, thin, flimsy. **7** *a fine sand/powder* fine-grained, powdery, powdered, ground, crushed, pulverized, comminuted, triturated. **8** *fine clothes* expensive, elegant, stylish, smart, chic, fashionable, modish, high-fashion, lavish. **9** *fine gold* refined, pure, sterling, solid, unadulterated, unalloyed, unpolluted, one hundred per cent. **10** *a fine distinction* subtle, fine-drawn, tenuous, hair-splitting, precise, minute, elusive, abstruse, nice, over-nice. **11** *a fine taste in art* discriminating, discerning, tasteful, fastidious, critical, sensitive, refined, intelligent. **12** *a fine mind* keen, acute, sharp, quick, perspicacious, clever, intelligent, brilliant, finely honed/tuned. **13** *a fine young man/woman* good-looking, attractive, handsome, lovely, pretty, striking, well-favoured, bonny, smart-looking, comely, fair, seemly.

fine n *get a fine for illegal parking* penalty, financial penalty, punishment, forfeit, forfeiture, mulct; damages.

fine v *fine for stealing* impose a fine on, exact a penalty, penalize, punish by fining, mulct.

finery n Sunday best, frippery, adornment, splendour, showiness, gaudiness, trumpery; elaborate/best clothes, trappings, decorations, gewgaws; *inf* glad rags, best gear, best bib and tucker.

finesse n **1** *handle the problem with finesse* tact, discretion, diplomacy, delicacy, refinement, grace, elegance, sophistication, subtlety, polish, *savoir faire*, skill, expertise, wisdom, worldly wisdom, craft; tactfulness, adroitness, adeptness, skilfulness, cleverness, artfulness. **2** *win by a clever finesse* trick, stratagem, ruse, manoeuvre, scheme, artifice, machination, bluff, wile; *inf* dodge.

finger v *finger the fruit/material* touch, feel, handle, toy with, play about with, fiddle with, stroke, caress, maul, meddle with; *inf* paw.

finicky adj fussy, over-particular, fastidious, pernickety, hard to please, overcritical, difficult; *inf* picky, choosy.

finish v **1** *finish the task* complete, accomplish, execute, discharge, carry out, deal with, do, get done, fulfil, achieve, attain, end, conclude, close, bring to a conclusion/end/close, finalize, stop, cease, terminate, round off, put the finishing touches to; *inf* wind up, wrap up, sew up, polish off, knock off. **2** *finish working* stop, cease, discontinue, give up, have done with, suspend. **3** *finish the milk* | *finish up/off the food* use, use up, consume, eat, devour, drink, exhaust, empty, deplete, drain, expend, dispatch, dispose of. **4** *the job finished her* | *finish off the enemy* overcome, defeat, overpower, conquer, overwhelm, get the better of, best, worst, rout, bring down, put an end to, do away with, dispose of, get rid of, destroy, annihilate, kill, exterminate, liquidate, drive to the wall; *inf* wipe out, do in. **5** *finish her education* perfect, polish, refine, put the final/finishing touches to, crown. **6** *finish the surface of the table/vase* put a finish on, varnish, lacquer, stain, coat, veneer, wax, gild, glaze, give a shine to, polish, burnish, smooth off.

finish n **1** *at the finish of the task/race* completion, accomplishment, execution, fulfilment, achievement, consummation, end, conclusion, close, closing, cessation, final act, finale, denouement; last stages; *inf* winding-up. **2** *the finish of the enemy* defeat, overpowering, destruction, rout, bringing down, end, annihilation, death, extermination, liquidation, ruination; *inf* ruin, curtains. **3** *people of finish* cultivation, culture, refinement, polish, style, sophistication, suaveness, urbanity, education. **4** *a table/ material with a beautiful finish* surface, texture, grain, veneer, coating, lacquer, glaze, lustre, gloss, polish, shine, patina, smoothness.

finished adj **1** *finished tasks* completed, accomplished, executed, over and done with, over, in the past; *inf* wrapped up, sewn up. *see* FINISH v 1. **2** *the finished milk bottle* empty, drained, used up, exhausted, spent. **3** *a finished performance* accomplished, expert, proficient, masterly, polished, impeccable, classic, consummate, flawless, skilful, skilled, dexterous, adroit, professional, talented, gifted, elegant, graceful. **4** *finished hopes/firms which are finished* at an end, gone, gone to the wall, over with, doomed, lost, ruined, bankrupt, wrecked; *inf* washed up.

finite adj not infinite, bounded, limited, subject to limitations, restricted, delimited, demarcated, terminable.

fire n **1** *killed in a fire* blaze, conflagration, inferno, holocaust; flames. **2** *hit by enemy fire* gunfire, sniping, flak, bombardment, shelling; volley, barrage, fusillade, salvo. **3** *people of fire* energy, spirit, life, liveliness, animation, vigour, verve, vivacity, sparkle, scintillation, dash, vim, gusto, *élan*, enthusiasm, fervour, fervency, eagerness, impetuosity, force, potency, driving power, vehemence, ardour, passion, intensity, zeal; *inf* pep. **4** *writings with fire* passion, ardour, intensity, inspiration, imagination, creativity, inventiveness, flair. **on fire** **1** *houses on fire* burning, ablaze, blazing, aflame, in flames, flaming, alight, fiery. **2** *on fire with passion* passionate, ardent, fervent, intense, excited, eager, enthusiastic.

fire v **1** *fire the haystacks* set fire to, set on fire, set alight, set ablaze, put a match to, light, ignite, kindle, enkindle. **2** *fire the guns* shoot, let off, discharge, trigger, set off. **3** *fire a missile* launch, hurl, discharge, eject. **4** *fire the explosives* explode, detonate, touch off. **5** *they fired him with enthusiasm* arouse, rouse, stir up, excite, enliven, inflame, put/ breathe life into, animate, inspire, motivate, stimulate, incite, galvanize, electrify, impassion. **6** *fire the assistant* dismiss, discharge, declare redundant, give someone his/her marching orders, get rid of, show someone the door, oust, depose, cashier; *inf* sack, give the sack to, axe.

firebrand n troublemaker, agitator, rabble-rouser, demagogue, tub-thumper, soapbox orator.

fire-proof adj non-inflammable, non-flammable, incombustible, unburnable, fire-resistant, flame-resistant, flame-retardant.

fireworks npl **1** *a fireworks display on Guy Fawkes night* pyrotechnics, *feu d'artifice*. **2** *there were fireworks when she heard the news* tantrums, hysterics, paroxysms, pyrotechnics; outburst, fit, frenzy, uproar, row.

firm adj **1** *a firm surface* hard, hardened, stiff, rigid, inflexible, inelastic, unyielding, resistant, solid, solidified, compacted, compressed, condensed, dense, close-grained, congealed, frozen, set, jelled, stony, steely, adamantine. **2** *the poles were firm in the ground* fixed, fast, secure, secured, stable, set, established, tight, immovable, irremovable, unshakable, stationary, motionless, taut, anchored, rooted, embedded; riveted, braced, cemented, nailed, tied. **3** *firm plans* fixed, settled, decided, definite, established, unalterable, unchangeable. **4** *a firm handshake* strong, vigorous, sturdy. **5** *a firm friendship* constant, unchanging, enduring, abiding, durable, deep-rooted, long-standing, long-lasting, steady, stable, staunch. **6** *firm about not going* resolute, determined, decided, resolved, unfaltering, unwavering, unflinching, unswerving, unyielding, unbending, inflexible, obdurate, obstinate, stubborn, hard line, strict, intransigent, unmalleable.

firm n *a manufacturing firm* company, business, concern, house, establishment, organization, corporation, conglomerate, partnership, cooperative; *inf* outfit.

firmament n sky, heaven, blue sky, the blue, vault of heaven, vault, celestial sphere; heavens, skies; *lit* empyrean, welkin.

firmness n **1** *the firmness of the surface* hardness, stiffness, rigidity, inflexibility, inelasticity, resistance, solidity. *see* FIRM adj 1. **2** *the firmness of the handshake* strength, vigour, sturdiness. **3** *the firmness of the friendship* constancy, endurance, durability, steadiness, stability, staunchness. *see* FIRM adj 5. **4** *the firmness of the refusal/teacher* resolution, determination, resolve, strength/fixity of purpose, obduracy, inflexibility, stubbornness, strictness, intransigence. *see* FIRM adj 6.

first adj **1** *the first stages of man* earliest, initial, opening, introductory, original, premier, primitive, primeval, primordial, pristine. **2** *first principles* primary, beginning, basic, fundamental, key, rudimentary, cardinal. **3** *the first people in the land* leading, foremost, principal, highest, ruling, chief, head, main, major, greatest, pre-eminent, supreme.

first adv **1** *first he said he was a doctor* at first, to begin with, at the beginning/start, at the outset, initially. **2** *first we must wash our hands* before anything/all else, first and foremost. **3** *first, I don't want it, second...* in the first place, firstly. **4** *I'd die first* sooner, rather, in preference, more willingly.

first n *from the first* beginning, very beginning, start, outset, commencement; *inf* the word go.

firsthand adv/adj *learn firsthand* direct, directly, from the original source, straight from the horse's mouth.

first-rate adj first-class, second to none, top, premier, superlative, prime, excellent, superb, outstanding, exceptional, tip-top, admiral; *inf* top-notch, ace, A1, crack.

fiscal adj financial, economic, monetary, money, pecuniary, capital.

fish v **1** *boys fishing in the stream* go fishing, angle, cast. **2** *fish for keys* look for, search for, hunt for, grope for, delve for, cast about for. **fish out** pull out, haul out, extricate, extract, retrieve, produce.

fisher n fisherman, angler, piscator, piscatorian.

fishy adj **1** *a fishy smell* fishlike, piscatorial, piscine. **2** *fishy eyes* expressionless, inexpressive, vacant, deadpan, wooden, dull, lacklustre, glassy, glass-eyed. **3** *something fishy about it* questionable, dubious, doubtful, suspect, suspicious, odd, queer, peculiar, strange, not quite right; *inf* funny, shady, not kosher.

fission n splitting, parting, division, cleaving, rupture, breaking, severance, disjuncture, scission.

fissure n opening, crack, crevice, cleft, chink, cranny, groove, slit, gash, gap, hole, breach, break, fracture, fault, rift, rupture, split, rent, interstice, scission.

fit adj **1** *feeling fit* well, healthy, in good health, in shape, in good shape, in good trim, in trim, in good condition, strong, robust, hale and hearty, sturdy, hardy, stalwart, vigorous. **2** *fit to drive* able, capable, competent, adequate, good enough, satisfactory, ready, prepared, qualified, trained, equipped, eligible, worthy; *inf* up to scratch. **3** *a fit occasion* | *fit behaviour* fitting, proper, due, seemly, decorous, decent, right, correct, apt, appropriate, *comme il faut*, suitable, convenient, apposite, relevant, pertinent.

fit v **1** *the shoes don't fit* be the right/correct size, be big/small enough, be the right shape. **2** *facts fitting our theory* agree with, be in agreement with, accord with, concur with, correspond with, match, dovetail with, tally with, suit, go with, be congruent with, conform to, be consonant with. **3** *fit the parts together* join, connect, put together. **4** *fit the carpet* put in place/position, position, lay, fix, insert, arrange, adjust, shape. **5** *fit your expenditure to your income* adjust, adapt, modify, alter, regulate, accommodate. **6** *the training will fit him for many jobs* make suitable, qualify, prepare, make ready, prime, condition, train. **7** *fit the kitchen with units* fit out, equip, provide, supply, furnish. **fit in** belong to, match, square with; accord, agree, concur, conform. **fit out/up** *fit out the caravan/army* equip, provide, supply, furnish, kit/rig out, outfit, accoutre.

fit n **1** *an epileptic fit* convulsion, spasm, paroxysm, seizure, attack; *Med* ictus. **2** *a fit of coughing* attack, bout, spell. **3** *a fit of the giggles* bout, burst, outburst, outbreak. **4** *she'll have a fit* fit of temper, tantrum, outburst of anger/rage. **5** *when the fit was on him* mood, whim, fancy, impulse, caprice. **by fits and starts** on and off, off and on, spasmodically, intermittently, sporadically, erratically, irregularly, interruptedly, fitfully.

fitful adj *fitful sleep* broken, disturbed, irregular, uneven, intermittent, sporadic, spasmodic, disconnected, unsteady, variable.

fitness n **1** *improve your fitness* physical fitness, health, good health, condition, shape, good condition/shape, strength, robustness, sturdiness, vigour. **2** *his fitness to drive* ability, capability, competency, preparedness, qualification, eligibility, worthiness. *see* FIT adj 2. **3** *the fitness of the occasion* properness, propriety, seemliness, correctness, aptness, suitability, convenience, relevance, pertinence. *see* FIT adj 3.

fitted adj **1** *not fitted to the life* suited, suitable, right, equipped, cut out for. **2** *fitted wardrobes* built-in, fixed, permanent. **3** *fitted sheets* fitting tightly/well, shaped.

fitting adj *a fitting occasion* | *not fitting to go early* fit, proper, due, right, suitable, appropriate, *comme il faut. see* FIT adj 3.

fitting n **1** *an electrical fitting* part, piece, component, attachment, accessory. **2** *kitchen fittings* furnishings, units, fixtures, appointments, accoutrements, appurtenances; furniture, equipment.

fix v **1** *fix the shelf to the wall* fasten, secure, make fast, attach, connect, join, couple;

stick, glue, cement, pin, nail, screw, bolt, clamp, bind, tie, pinion. **2** *fix the post in the ground* plant, implant, install, anchor, embed, establish, position, station, situate. **3** *fix a date/price* decide on, settle, set, agree on, arrive at, arrange, determine, establish, define, name, specify. **4** *fix the car* repair, mend, sort, see to, patch up, put right, put to rights, restore, remedy, rectify, adjust. **5** *fix her gaze on them* direct, focus, level at, rivet. **6** *fix the colour/dye* make fast, set, make permanent. **7** *has the glue fixed?* set, solidify, congeal, harden, stiffen. **8** *fix one's hair* arrange, put in order, adjust, dress. **9** *fix something to eat* prepare, make, make ready, put together, cook. **10** *I'll fix him for that* get even with, revenge oneself on, get one's revenge on, wreak vengeance on, take retribution on, give someone his/her just deserts, punish, deal with; *inf* get one's own back, pay someone back, sort someone out, settle someone's hash, cook someone's goose. **11** *fix the outcome of the race* rig, manipulate, manoeuvre, arrange fraudulently; *inf* fiddle. **12** *fix the judges* bribe, influence, influence unduly. **fix up 1** *fix up a meeting* fix, arrange, organize, plan, agree on, settle on, decide on. **2** *fix you up a room|fix you up with a bed* provide with, supply with, furnish with, accommodate with, lay on.

fix n *in a bit of a fix* predicament, plight, quandary, dilemma, difficulty, spot of trouble, bit of bother, muddle, mess, corner, ticklish/tricky situation, tight spot; *inf* pickle, jam, hole, spot, scrape, bind.

fixation n obsession, preoccupation, complex, compulsion, mania, monomania, *idée fixe*, phobia; *inf* hang-up, thing.

fixture n **1** *kitchen fixtures* fixed appliance, attachment, fixity. **2** *a Sunday fixture* sporting event, match, game, competition, contest, meet, race.

fizz v **1** *wine fizzing* bubble, effervesce, sparkle, froth, foam. **2** *the solution fizzing* hiss, sputter, fizzle, sibilate.

fizzle v **fizzle out** peter out, come to nothing, fall through, come to grief, end in failure, fail, miscarry, abort, collapse; *inf* flop, fold.

fizzy adj bubbly, bubbling, sparkling, effervescent, carbonated, gassy.

flabbergast v astound, amaze, dumbfound, strike dumb, render speechless, stun, stagger, confound, daze, overcome, overwhelm, nonplus, disconcert; *inf* bowl over.

flabby adj flaccid, unfirm, out of tone, drooping, pendulous, limp; *inf* out of shape.

flaccid adj flabby, unfirm, drooping, limp. *see* FLABBY.

flag¹ n standard, ensign, banner, banderole, pennant, pennon, gonfalon, streamer; bunting; colours.

flag¹ v **1** *flag the places on the map* indicate, mark, mark out, label, tab, docket. **2** *the police flagged him down* wave down, signal to stop, signal, hail, gesture/motion to stop.

flag² v **1** *I'm flagging* tire, become fatigued, grow tired/weary, weaken, grow weak, lose one's strength. **2** *his strength/interest is flagging* fade, fail, decline, wane, ebb, diminish, decrease, taper off. **3** *flowers flagging* droop, sag, hang down, wilt.

flagon n bottle, decanter, carafe, flask, jug, ewer, pitcher, crock.

flagrant adj glaring, obvious, blatant, outrageous, scandalous, shocking, disgraceful, shameless, dreadful, terrible, gross, enormous, heinous, atrocious, monstrous, wicked, iniquitous, villainous.

flagstone n paving stone, stone block/slab, slab, flag.

flail v **1** *with arms flailing* swing wildly, wave helplessly, thrash about, move erratically. **2** *flail the corn/enemy* thresh, thrash, beat, strike, batter, drub.

flair n **1** *have a flair for languages* natural ability, ability, aptitude, capability, facility, skill, talent, gift, knack, bent, feel, genius. **2** *all the women of the family had flair* style, panache, elegance, dash, *élan*, taste, good taste, discernment, discrimination.

flake n *a flake of paint/snow* chip, shaving, peeling, scale, sliver, wafer, fragment, bit, particle.

flake v *paint/skin flaking* chip, peel, peel off, scale off, blister; *Tech* desquamate, exfoliate. **flake out** faint, pass out, collapse, drop, keel over; *lit* swoon.

flamboyant adj **1** *flamboyant gestures* extravagant, theatrical, showy, ostentatious, dashing, swashbuckling. **2** *flamboyant clothes/colours* colourful, brilliantly coloured, bright, exciting, dazzling, glamorous, splendid, resplendent, gaudy, flashy. **3** *flamboyant architecture* elaborate, ornate, fancy, baroque, rococo, arabesque.

flame n **1** *see the flames in the distance* fire, blaze, conflagration. **2** *burn with a flame* brilliant light, brightness, glow, gleam. **3** *flame is a bright colour* red, reddish-orange. **4** *the flame of love* passion, passionateness, warmth, ardour, fervour, fervency, fire, excitement, intensity, keenness, eagerness, enthusiasm. **5** *an old flame* boyfriend, girlfriend, sweetheart, lover, partner, beloved, beau, inamorato, inamorata.

flame v **1** *the wood flamed* burn, blaze, burst into flame, catch fire. **2** *the light flamed* glow, shine, flash, beam, glare, sparkle.

flame-proof adj non-flammable, non-inflammable, flame-resistant, fire-resistant, incombustible.

flaming adj **1** *a flaming bonfire* blazing, ablaze, burning, on fire, afire, in flames, aflame, ignited, fiery, red-hot, raging, glowing. **2** *a flaming mood* furious, enraged, fuming, incensed, infuriated, mad, angry, raging, wrathful; *inf* livid. **3** *a flaming row* angry, furious, violent, vehement, frenzied, incensed, passionate, raging. **4** *flaming colours* bright, brilliant, vivid, flamboyant, red, reddish-orange, scarlet. **5** *a flaming idiot* utter, absolute, damned, damnable.

flank n **1** *the animal's flank* side, haunch, loin, quarter, thigh. **2** *the flank of the enemy/ mountain* side, wing.

flank v *lawns flank the house* be situated along, border, edge, bound, fringe, skirt.

flannel n *talk a lot of flannel* nonsense, rubbish, prevarication, hedging, equivocation, evasion, flattery, blarney; *inf* baloney, rot, waffle, soft soap, sweet talk.

flannel v prevaricate, hedge, equivocate, be evasive, talk blarney, use flattery; flatter; *inf* waffle, soft-soap, sweet-talk, butter up.

flap v **1** *flap one's wings/arms* move up and down, flutter, beat, thresh, thrash, wave, agitate, vibrate, wag, waggle, shake, swing, oscillate. **2** *with wings/arms flapping* move up and down, beat, flail. **3** *curtains flapping at the window* flutter, swing, sway. **4** *the hostess is flapping* panic, go into a panic, become flustered, be agitated, fuss; *inf* press the panic button, be in a state, be in a tizzy/dither/twitter.

flap n **1** *the flap of wings* flutter, beat, fluttering, beating, waving, shaking, flailing. *see* FLAP v 1, 2. **2** *a flap of material* fold, overlap, overhang, covering, tab, apron, lappet. **3** *the hostess is in a flap* panic, fluster, state of panic/agitation; *inf* state, dither, twitter, tizzy, blue funk, stew.

flare v **1** *the fire flared* flare up, blaze, flame, burn unsteadily. **2** *lights flared on the shore* flash, gleam, glow, sparkle, glitter, flicker. **3** *his nostrils flared* spread outwards, broaden, widen, widen at the bottom, splay. **flare up 1** *the fire flared up* blaze, burn violently. *see* FLARE v 1. **2** *trouble/disease flared up* broke out, burst out, recur. **3** *the two women flared up* lose one's temper, lose control, become blazing mad, explode, fly

into a temper/passion, boil over, boil over with rage, fire up, go berserk, throw a tantrum; *inf* blow one's top, fly off the handle, lose one's cool.

flare n **1** *burn with a flare* unsteady flame, blaze, burst, flash, flicker, glimmer, shimmer, dazzle, glare, gleam. **2** *flares for ships* signal, distress-signal, rocket, beacon, light, flashlight. **3** *a skirt with a flare* gradual widening, outward spread.

flash v **1** *lights flashed* light up, shine out, flare, blaze, glare, beam, gleam, glint, sparkle, flicker, shimmer, twinkle, glimmer, glisten, scintillate, coruscate, fulgurate. **2** *the runners/cars/time flashed past* dart, dash, tear, shoot, zoom, streak, fly, whistle, rush, bolt, race, bound, speed, career; *inf* scoot, skedaddle. **3** *flash her new ring* show off, flaunt, flourish, display, exhibit. **4** *the peculiar man flashed at the girls* expose oneself, show one's genitals.

flash n **1** *a flash of light* blaze, burst, glare, flare, shaft, ray, streak, gleam, glint, sparkle, flicker, shimmer, twinkle, glimmer. *see* FLASH v 1. **2** *he came in a flash* instant, moment, second, split second, minute, trice, twinkling, twinkling of an eye, twinkle, wink of an eye, two shakes, two shakes of a lamb's tail; *inf* jiffy, bat of an eye. **3** *a flash of enthusiasm/wit* sudden show, outburst, burst, outbreak, brief display/exhibition. **4** *flashes on animals/uniforms* patch, bright patch, streak, stripe; emblem, insignia.

flash adj *flash clothes* ostentatious, showy, vulgar, tasteless, cheap, tawdry; *inf* tacky. *see* FLASHY.

flashy adj *flashy clothes/cars* ostentatious, showy, in bad/poor taste, tasteless, pretentious, cheap, cheap and nasty, tawdry, garish, loud, flamboyant, gawdy, meretricious; *inf* tacky, snazzy, jazzy, glitzy, ritzy.

flask n bottle, flagon, decanter, carafe, pitcher, jug, ewer.

flat adj **1** *a flat surface* level, horizontal, levelled, even, smooth, unbroken, plane. **2** *lying flat on the ground* stretched out, spread-eagled, prone, supine, prostrate, recumbent. **3** *a flat dish* shallow, not deep. **4** *a flat tyre* deflated, collapsed, blown out, burst, punctured, ruptured. **5** *a flat denial* outright, direct, out and out, downright, straight, plain, explicit, absolute, definite, positive, firm, final, conclusive, complete, utter, categorical, unqualified, unconditional, unquestionable, unequivocal. **6** *in a flat voice|flat jokes* monotonous, boring, dull, tedious, uninteresting, lifeless, lacklustre, dead, vapid, bland, insipid, prosaic.

7 *feeling rather flat* depressed, dejected, dispirited, low, down, without energy, enervated. **8** *the market is flat* slow, inactive, sluggish, slack, not busy.

flat *adv she told him flat that she was going* outright, directly, straight, plainly, explicitly, absolutely, definitely, conclusively, categorically. *see* FLAT *adj* 5. **flat out** at full speed, all out, as fast as possible, posthaste, at full tilt, full steam ahead; *inf* hell for leather.

flat *n* apartment, set of rooms; rooms; *inf* pad.

flatten *v* **1** *flatten the surface* make flat, level, level out/off, make even, even out, smooth, smooth out/off, plane. **2** *children flattening the grass* compress, trample, press down, crush, squash, compact. **3** *flatten the old buildings* demolish, tear down, knock down, raze, raze to the ground. **4** *flatten his opponent* knock down, knock to the ground, floor, knock off one's feet, fell, prostrate. **5** *even sarcasm fails to flatten him* crush, quash, squash, deflate, snub, humiliate; *inf* put down.

flatter *v* **1** *courtiers flattering the queen* compliment, praise, sing the praises of, praise to excess, praise to the skies, eulogize, puff up, pay court to, pay blandishments to, blandish, fawn upon, cajole, humour, flannel, wheedle; *inf* sweet-talk, soft-soap, butter up, lay it on thick, lay it on with a trowel, play up to. **2** *that dress flatters her colouring* suit, become, set off, show to advantage, enhance; *inf* do something for.

flattering *adj* **1** *flattering words* complimentary, fulsome, adulatory, praising, blandishing, laudatory, honeyed, sugary, ingratiating, cajoling; *inf* sweet-talking, soft-soaping. *see* FLATTER 1. **2** *a flattering dress* becoming, enhancing.

flattery *n* praise, adulation, overpraise, false praise, eulogy, puffery, laudation, blarney, fulsomeness, fawning, cajolery, wheedling; compliments, blandishments, honeyed words; *inf* sweet talk, soft soap, buttering-up, flannel.

flatulence *n* wind, intestinal gas; belching; *inf* farting.

flaunt *v* show off, parade, display ostentatiously, exhibit, draw attention to, make a show of, wave, dangle, brandish.

flavour *n* **1** *dislike the flavour of the herb* taste, savour, tang, relish. **2** *add some flavour to the sauce* flavouring, seasoning, tastiness, tang, relish, piquancy, spiciness, zest; *inf* zing. **3** *capture the flavour of the poem/place* spirit, essence, soul, nature, character, quality,

feel, feeling, ambience, tone, style, stamp, property.

flavour *v* **1** *flavour the stew* add flavour/flavouring to, season, add seasoning/herbs/spices to, spice, add piquancy to, ginger up. **2** *flavour the punch with cinnamon* season, lace, imbue, infuse.

flavouring *n* **1** *add flavouring to the stew* flavour, seasoning. *see* FLAVOUR *n* 2. **2** *vanilla flavouring* essence, extract, tincture.

flaw *n* **1** *a flaw in his character* fault, defect, imperfection, blemish, failing, foible, shortcoming, weakness, weak spot. **2** *a flaw in the china/material* fault, defect, crack, chip, fracture, break, crevice, fissure, rent, split, tear.

flawless *adj* **1** *a flawless performance* faultless, perfect, impeccable. **2** *a flawless complexion* perfect, blemish-free, unflawed, unimpaired, unmarred. **3** *a flawless piece of china* perfect, whole, intact, sound, unbroken, undamaged.

fleck *n* *a fleck of white in the black cloth* spot, mark, speck, speckle, freckle.

fleck *v* *black material flecked with white* spot, mark, speckle, dot, sprinkle, spatter, stipple, mottle, streak, freckle.

flee *v* **1** *she fled from the blaze | the burglar fled when disturbed* run, run away, run off, bolt, rush, speed, take flight, take to flight, make off, fly, abscond, retreat, beat a retreat, beat a hasty retreat, depart hastily/abruptly, make a quick exit, run for it, make a run for it, take off, take to one's heels, decamp, escape, make one's escape/getaway, show a clean pair of heels, do a disappearing act, vanish; *inf* cut and run, make oneself scarce, scarper, beat it, do a bunk, skedaddle, split, scram, light out. **2** *they fled the country* run away from, leave hastily/abruptly, fly, escape from; *inf* skip.

fleece *n* *a sheep's fleece* wool, coat.

fleece *v* **1** *fleece the sheep* shear, clip. **2** *fleece the old lady of her savings* swindle, defraud, cheat, rob, strip, mulct, bilk, overcharge; *inf* con, take for a ride, diddle, rip off, sting, bleed, take to the cleaners, soak.

fleecy *adj* woolly, downy, fluffy, shaggy, soft, smooth; fleecelike, lanate, lanose.

fleet *n* *the fleet set sail* flotilla, naval force, squadron, armada; *lit* navy, argosy.

fleet *adj* swift, fast, rapid, quick, speedy, expeditious, nimble, fleet of foot, nimble-footed, swift-footed, like the wind.

fleeting *adj* rapid, swift, brief, short-lived, short, momentary, transient, transitory, ephemeral, fugitive, evanescent, fugacious, vanishing, flying, passing, flitting, here today and gone tomorrow, temporary, impermanent.

fleetness n swiftness, fastness, rapidity, quickness, speed, speediness, velocity, celerity, nimbleness, nimble-footedness, swift-footedness.

flesh n 1 *flesh and bones* muscle, tissue, muscle tissue, brawn. 2 *carry too much flesh* fat; fatness, obesity, corpulence. 3 *not much flesh in the essay* substance, pith, matter, body. 4 *the spirit is willing but the flesh is weak | the pleasure of the flesh* body, human body, human nature, physical nature, physicality, corporeality, carnality, animality, sensuality, sensualism. 5 *all flesh would perish in such conditions* mankind, man, humankind, people, human race/species, humanity, *Homo sapiens*; animate life, the living; human beings, living creatures. **flesh and blood** *ignored their own flesh and blood* family, kin, kinsfolk; relatives, relations, blood relations; *inf* folk. **in the flesh** *saw the actor in the flesh* in person, before one's eyes, in front of one, in one's presence.

flesh v **flesh out** 1 *the children have fleshed out a bit* put on weight, grow fatter, fatten up. 2 *flesh out the material* fill out, expand, make more substantial, add substance/detail to.

flex n *electric flex* cable, wire; *Amer* cord.

flex v 1 *flex one's muscles* contract, tighten, make taught. 2 *flex one's arm* bend, curve, crook, angle.

flexible adj 1 *flexible materials* bendable, pliant, pliable, elastic, springy, plastic, mouldable. 2 *flexible young bodies* supple, agile, limber, lithe, lissom, double-jointed. 3 *my arrangements are flexible* adaptable, adjustable, open-ended, open, open to change, changeable, variable. 4 *the young man is too flexible* tractable, malleable, compliant, manageable, amenable, biddable, docile, submissive, yielding.

flick v 1 *flick the horse with a whip* strike, hit, rap, tap, touch. 2 *flick on the switch* click, snap, flip, tap. 3 *cows' tails flicking* swish, wag, waggle. **flick through** skim, flip over, glance over/through, browse through, thumb through, skip over.

flicker v 1 *lights flickering* twinkle, sparkle, blink, flash, shimmer, glitter, glimmer, glint, flare. 2 *with eyelids flickering* flutter, quiver, vibrate, bat, open and shut.

flight[1] n 1 *watching the flight of the eagle* flying, soaring, mounting. 2 *a flight of geese/birds* flying group, flock; skein, bevy, covey;

migration. 3 *a flight of bees* swarm, cloud. 4 *a history of flight* aviation, flying, air transport, aerial navigation; aeronautics. 5 *have a good flight* airline trip, journey, shuttle; *inf* plane trip. 6 *climb two flights* flight of stairs, staircase, set of steps/stairs.

flight[2] n *the flight of the beaten army* fleeing, running away, absconding, retreat, departure, hasty departure, exit, exodus, decamping, escape, get away, disappearance, vanishing. *see* FLEE. **put to flight** chase, chase off, drive off, scare off, rout, scatter, scatter to the four winds, disperse, stampede. **take flight** flee, run away, bolt, make off, fly, abscond, beat a hasty retreat, take off, decamp.

flighty adj frivolous, giddy, scatterbrained, hare-brained, fickle, changeable, inconstant, unsteady, whimsical, capricious, skittish.

flimsy adj 1 *a flimsy box* insubstantial, unsubstantial, slight, makeshift, jerry-built, gimcrack, rickety, ramshackle, shaky, fragile, frail. 2 *made of a flimsy material* thin, light, lightweight, delicate, sheer, filmy, diaphanous, transparent, translucent, see-through, chiffony, gossamer, gauzy, cobwebby. 3 *a flimsy excuse* feeble, weak, poor, inadequate, thin, transparent, unconvincing, implausible, unsatisfactory, paltry, trifling, trivial, shallow.

flinch v 1 *did not flinch when being caned* draw back, pull back, start back, recoil, withdraw, shrink back, shy away, cringe, cower, crouch, quail, wince, blench. 2 *flinch from his duty* shrink from, shy away from, shirk, turn away from, swerve from, dodge, avoid, duck, baulk at.

fling v *fling the clothes in the river* throw, toss, hurl, cast, pitch, sling, heave, fire, shy, launch, propel, catapult, send flying, let fly; *inf* lob, chuck.

fling n 1 *with one fling of the javelin* throw, toss, hurl, cast, pitch, shot, heave; *inf* lob, chuck. *see* FLING V. 2 *have a last fling before marriage* binge, spree, good time, bit of fun, night on the town. 3 *have a fling at winning the match* try, attempt, go, shot, stab, venture; *inf* crack, bash, whirl.

flip v 1 *flip a coin* flick, toss, throw, pitch, cast, spin, twist. 2 *flip a switch* flick, click, snap, tap. **flip through** skim, glance through. *see* FLICK, FLICK THROUGH.

flippant adj *a flippant remark* frivolous, superficial, shallow, glib, thoughtless, carefree, irresponsible, insouciant, offhand, disrespectful, impertinent, impudent, irreverent, cheeky, pert, saucy; *inf* flip.

flirt v **1** *she's always flirting with the boys* toy with, trifle with, make eyes at, ogle, lead on; philander with, dally with; *inf* chat up. **2** *flirt with the idea of going | flirt with antiques* toy with, trifle with, play with, entertain the idea/possibility of, consider, give thought to, dabble in.

flirt n *the new girl's a flirt* coquette, tease, vamp, heartbreaker, trifler, philanderer, wanton; *inf* cockteaser.

flirtatious adj coquettish, provocative, teasing, amorous, philandering, dallying, come-hither.

float v **1** *things light enough to float on water* stay afloat, be buoyant, be buoyed up. **2** *craft floating along* bob, glide, sail, slip, slide, drift. **3** *not working, just floating about* move aimlessly, drift, wander, meander; *inf* bum around. **4** *float a company* launch, get going, get off the ground, establish, set up, instigate, initiate, promote.

floating adj **1** *floating substances* buoyant, buoyed up, non-submerged, afloat; suspended, drifting. **2** *floating craft* gliding, sailing. see FLOAT 2. **3** *floating voters* uncommitted, unattached, fluctuating, variable. **4** *a floating population* not fixed, moving, unsettled, wandering, migratory. **5** *floating currencies* fluctuating, variable, not fixed.

flock v collect, gather, foregather, come together, assemble, group, bunch, congregate, converge, crowd, herd, troop, throng, swarm, mill, huddle.

flock n **1** *a flock of sheep* fold, drove, herd. **2** *a flock of birds/geese* flight, bevy, skein, gaggle. **3** *a flock of people* crowd, gathering, assembly, company, collection, congregation, group, throng, mass, host, multitude, troop, herd, convoy.

flog v **1** *slave-drivers flogging slaves* whip, horsewhip, lash, flay, flagellate, birch, scourge, belt, cane, strap, thrash, beat, whack, wallop, chastise, trounce; *inf* lambaste, tan the hide of. **2** *flog oneself to finish in time* drive, push, strain, punish, tax, overtax, make every effort, overexert, overwork; *inf* kill oneself, pull out all the stops. **3** *flog the goods cheaply* sell, put on sale, offer for sale.

flogging n whipping, horsewhipping, lashing, flaying, flagellation, birching, belting, caning, beating; *inf* lambasting, hiding. see FLOG 1.

flood n **1** *houses damaged in the flood* deluge, inundation, torrent, spate, overflow, flash flood, freshet. **2** *a flood of rain* downpour, torrent, cloudburst. **3** *a flood of mail* profusion, overabundance, superabundance, plethora, superfluity, glut; *inf* tons, heaps. **4** *a flood of tears* outpouring, rush, stream, flow.

flood v **1** *rivers flooding* overflow, break the banks, brim over, swell, surge, pour forth, disembogue. **2** *flood the town* inundate, deluge, pour over, immerse, submerge, swamp, drown, engulf. **3** *mail flooding in | relief flooded through her* pour, flow, surge. **4** *flood the market with fruit* overfill, oversupply, saturate, glut, overwhelm.

floor n *on the second floor* storey, level, tier, deck.

floor v **1** *floor him with one blow* knock down, ground, fell, prostrate. **2** *this problem/attitude floors me* defeat, beat, baffle, stump, perplex, puzzle, nonplus, confound, dumbfound, confuse, discomfit, disconcert; *inf* throw.

flop v **1** *flop into a chair* collapse, slump, drop, fall, tumble. **2** *the old man's head flopped to the side* dangle, droop, sag, hang limply. **3** *the play flopped* fail, fall flat, founder, close, be unsuccessful, be a disaster, miss the mark, go down like a lead balloon; *inf* bomb.

flop n *the play was a flop* failure, fiasco, loser, disaster, debacle; *inf* no-hoper, no-go, washout, dud, lemon.

floral adj *a floral dress* flower-patterned, flowery.

florid adj **1** *a florid complexion* ruddy, redfaced, red, reddish, high-coloured, flushed, blushing, blowsy, rubicund, rubescent, erubescent. **2** *florid decorations* ornate, flamboyant, overelaborate, embellished, busy, fussy, baroque. **3** *florid prose* high-flown, flowery, verbose, overelaborate, grandiloquent, purple, euphuistic. see FLOWERY 2.

flotsam n **1** *flotsam floating from the ship* wreckage, floating remains. **2** *clear up the flotsam and jetsam in the yard* rubbish, junk, odds and ends, debris, detritus.

flounder v **1** *floundering about in the mud/dark* thrash, struggle, stumble, blunder, fumble, grope. **2** *he's floundering when it comes to maths* struggle, find difficulties, be confused, be in the dark, be out of one's depth. **3** *flounder his way through the speech* stumble, falter, blunder, muddle, bungle.

flourish v **1** *flourish the sword/prize* brandish, wave, twirl, wield, swing, swish, shake, wag, hold aloft, display, exhibit, flaunt, parade, vaunt; *inf* show off. **2** *the plants are flourishing* thrive, grow, grow/do well, develop, burgeon, bloom, blossom, bear fruit, burst forth. **3** *we are all flourishing* be well, be in good health, be strong, be vigorous, bloom, thrive, get on/ahead, get on well, prosper, be successful, succeed, make progress/headway; *inf* be in the pink, be fine and dandy, go great guns.

flout v *flout convention | flout the rules* defy, scorn, disdain, show contempt for, spurn, scoff at, mock, laugh at, deride, ridicule, sneer at, jeer at, gibe at, insult, poke fun at, make a fool of; *inf* cock a snook at.

flow v **1** *blood/rivers flowing* move, go along, course, run, circulate, proceed, glide, stream, ripple, swirl, surge, sweep, roll, rush, whirl, drift, slide, trickle, gurgle, babble. **2** *blood flowing from the wound* gush, stream, well, spurt, spout, squirt, spew, jet, spill, leak, seep, ooze, drip. **3** *springs flowing from the mountains | ideas flowing from her pen* arise, issue, spring, originate, derive, emanate, emerge, pour, proceed. **4** *the lands flowed with milk and honey* overflow with, be abundant in, abound in, teem with, be rich in, be full of.

flow n **1** *the flow of the water* course, current, drift, stream, spate, tide. **2** *stem the flow of blood* gush, stream, welling, spurting, spouting, outpouring, outflow. *see* FLOW v 2. **3** *a flow of words/complaints* flood, deluge, outpouring, outflow, abundance, superabundance, plethora, excess, effusion, succession, train.

flower n **1** *pick/plant several flowers* bloom, blossom, floweret, floret; annual, perennial. **2** *in the flower of their youth* prime, peak, zenith, acme, height, heyday, springtime; salad days. **3** *the flower of the nation died in battle* finest, best, pick, choice, choicest, most select, élite, cream, *crème de la crème*.

flowery adj **1** *flowery patterns* floral, flower-covered, flower-patterned. **2** *flowery language* high-flown, ornate, fancy, elaborate, overelaborate, highly figurative, verbose, grandiloquent, purple, rhetorical, euphuistic, bombastic, baroque, pleonastic.

flowing adj **1** *flowing streams* coursing, gliding, rippling, swirling, drifting, trickling. *see* FLOW v 1. **2** *lands flowing with milk and honey* overflowing with, abounding in, teeming with, rich in, full of. **3** *flowing prose* fluent, free-flowing, effortless, smooth, unbroken, uninterrupted, continuous, graceful, elegant. **4** *flowing hair* loose, hanging loose/free, unconfined.

fluctuate v **1** *prices fluctuating* rise and fall, go up and down, see-saw, yo-yo, be unstable, be unsteady, vary, shift, change, alter, swing, oscillate, undulate, ebb and flow. **2** *she fluctuates between going and not going* waver, vacillate, hesitate, change one's

mind, alternate, veer, shilly-shally, hem and haw, teeter, totter, see-saw, yo-yo, blow hot and cold.

fluctuation n **1** *fluctuation in prices/results* rise and fall, rising and falling, see-sawing, yo-yoing, instability, unsteadiness, variation, shift, change, alteration, swing, oscillation, undulation, ebb and flow. **2** *the fluctuation of her opinion* wavering, vacillation, hesitation, alternation, shilly-shallying, inconstancy, fickleness. *see* FLUCTUATE 2.

flue n duct, passage, channel, shaft, air passage, airway, vent.

fluency n **1** *fluency as a speaker* articulacy, articulateness, eloquence, volubility. **2** *the fluency of the prose* smoothness, flowingness, fluidity, gracefulness, effortlessness, naturalness. *see* FLUENT 2. **3** *her fluency in German* command, facility, articulacy.

fluent adj **1** *a fluent after-dinner speaker* articulate, eloquent, smooth-spoken, silver-tongued, voluble. **2** *fluent prose* smooth, flowing, fluid, graceful, effortless, natural, easy, elegant, smooth-sounding, mellifluous, euphonious. **3** *fluent in French* having a command of, articulate in.

fluff n **1** *fluff off the blankets* down, fuzz, lint, nap, pile, dust, dustball, fuzzball; *Scots* oose. **2** *the fluff of the chicks* down, downiness, fuzz, soft fur. **3** *not notice the actor's fluff* mistake, error, bungle, forgetfulness; *inf* foul-up, screw-up, cock-up.

fluff v **1** *actors fluffing their lines* forget, deliver badly, bungle, muddle up, make a mess of; *inf* mess up, foul up, screw up, cock up. **2** *the cricketer fluffing a catch* miss, bungle.

fluid n flowing substance; liquid, gas, solution.

fluid adj **1** *a fluid substance moving along the pipe* gaseous, gassy, liquid, liquefied, melted, molten, uncongealed, running, flowing, fluxional. **2** *a fluid prose style | a fluid movement* fluent, smooth, smooth-flowing, flowing, graceful, elegant, effortless, easy, natural. **3** *our plans are fluid* flexible, open to change, adaptable, adjustable, not fixed, not settled, variable, mutable. **4** *the situation is fluid* subject/likely to change, unstable, unsteady, ever-shifting, fluctuating, mobile, mercurial, protean.

fluke n *win by a fluke* lucky stroke, stroke of luck, stroke of good fortune, piece of good luck, lucky chance/shot/break.

flunkey n **1** *Queen Elizabeth I and her flunkeys* manservant, footman, valet, liveried servant, lackey, page. **2** *the politician and his* *flunkeys* lackey, toady, minion, yes-man, sycophant, hanger-on, camp-follower, tool, puppet, cat's paw; *inf* bootlicker.

flurry n **1** *a flurry of snow/rain* squall, gust, shower. **2** *a sudden flurry of activity* burst, spurt, outbreak, spell, bout. **3** *the hostess in a flurry of excitement* fluster, fuss, bustle, whirl, stir, ferment, hubbub, commotion, hustle, flap, tumult, hurry, pother, agitation, disturbance, furore, excitement, perturbation; *inf* to-do.

flurry v *the unexpected guests flurried her* fluster, upset, disconcert, ruffle, unsettle, put off one's stroke, put on edge, unnerve, bother, agitate, disturb, confuse, bewilder, muddle, hustle; *inf* rattle, hassle.

flush v **1** *she flushed in embarrassment* blush, turn red, go red/rosy, redden, crimson, colour, colour up, burn up, flame up, glow, suffuse with colour, mantle. **2** *flush the toilet* wash out, rinse out, cleanse, hose down, swab. **3** *flush away the waste* eject, expel. **4** *rivers flushing the meadows* flood, overflow, overrun, swamp. *see* FLOOD v 1, 2.

flush n **1** *embarrassed flushes* blush, high colour, colouring up. *see* FLUSH v 1. **2** *the first flush of youth* bloom, glow, freshness, radiance, vigour.

flushed adj **1** *flushed faces* blushing, red, reddened, crimson, ruddy, rosy, rubicund, burning, fiery, flaming, glowing, feverish. **2** *flushed with success* elated, delighted, thrilled, exhilarated, excited, worked up, animated, aroused, inflamed, impassioned, intoxicated; *inf* high.

fluster v *unexpected guests fluster her* make nervous, agitate, ruffle, flurry, unsettle, upset, bother, put on edge, discompose, panic, perturb, disconcert, confuse, throw off balance, confound, nonplus; *inf* hassle, rattle, faze, put into a flap, throw into a tizz.

fluster n *unexpected guests putting her into a fluster | causing fluster* nervous state, state of agitation, flurry, bustle, flutter, panic, upset; discomposure, agitation, perturbation, confusion, turmoil, commotion; *inf* dither, flap, state, tizz.

flutter v **1** *a bird fluttering its wings* flap, beat, quiver, agitate, vibrate, ruffle. **2** *flutter one's eyelashes* flicker, bat. **3** *butterflies fluttering in the air* flit, hover, flitter. **4** *flags fluttering in the breeze* flap, wave, flop, ripple, quiver, shiver, tremble. **5** *with hearts fluttering* beat rapidly, pulsate, palpitate.

flutter n **1** *the flutter of the birds' wings* flapping, beating, quivering. *see* FLUTTER v 1. **2** *the flutter of her eyelashes* flickering, batting. **3** *the flutter of the flags* flapping, waving, flopping, rippling. *see* FLUTTER v 4. **4** *in a flutter at the unexpected news* fluster, flurry, bustle, panic; *inf* dither, state, flap, tizz. *see* FLUSTER n. **5** *have a flutter on a horse* bet, gamble, wager.

fly v **1** *birds flying overhead* flutter, flit, hover, soar, wing, wing its way, take wing, take to the air, mount. **2** *flying to Paris* go by aeroplane, travel/go by air; *inf* plane it. **3** *fly the plane* pilot, operate, control, manoeuvre. **4** *ships flying the British flag* display, show, wave. **5** *flags flying* flap, wave, flutter, toss. **6** *time flew past* go quickly, pass swiftly, slip past, race, rush/tear past. **7** *the runners flew by* race, dash, shoot, rush, tear, bolt, zoom, scoot, dart, speed, hasten, hurry, scamper, career, go like the wind; *inf* be off like a shot, hare off. **8** *the beaten army plan to fly* flee, run, run away, bolt, take flight, make off, abscond, beat a retreat, run for it, take to one's heels, decamp, make one's escape; *inf* cut and run, scarper, do a bunk, skedaddle. *see* FLEE. **fly at** attack, assault, strike, strike out at, hit, lay into, pitch into, light into, rush at, charge, fall upon, pounce upon; *inf* have a go at, get stuck into. **2** *she just let fly at him* lose one's temper, explode, erupt with anger, let someone have it, give free reign to one's emotions, keep nothing back, give vent to one's emotions, lash out at.

flying adj **1** *flying creatures* airborne, fluttering, flitting, hovering, soaring, winging. *see* FLY 1. **2** *a flying visit* brief, short, short-lived, hurried, hasty, rushed, fleeting, transitory, transient, fugacious. **3** *her flying footsteps* fast, rapid, swift, quick, speedy, fleet; *lit* winged.

foal n young horse, colt, filly, pony.

foam n *the foam on the beer | washing-up foam* froth, bubbles, fizz, effervescence, head, spume, lather, suds.

foam v froth, froth up, cream, bubble, fizz, effervesce, spume, lather.

focus n **1** *the focus of attention/activity* focal point, centre, central point, centre of attention, core, hub, pivot, magnet, cynosure. **2** *the focus of the light* focal point, point of convergence.

focus v **1** *focus the camera on her* turn, converge, bring into focus, bring to a focus. **2** *focus our attention on budgets* concentrate, fix, bring to bear, centre, pinpoint, rivet; *inf* zero/zoom in on.

foe n enemy, opponent, adversary, rival, antagonist, combatant, fellow-contestant.

foetus n embryo, fertilized egg, unborn baby.

fog n **1** *fog decreasing visibility* mist, mistiness, smog, murk, murkiness, haze, brume, gloom; *inf* pea-souper. **2** *go around in a mental fog* haze, daze, stupor, trance; bewilderment, confusion, perplexity, bafflement, vagueness, stupefaction, disorientation.

fog v **1** *windscreens fogging over/up* mist over, become misty, cloud over, steam up. **2** *alcohol fogging their minds/judgement* befuddle, becloud, bedim, bewilder, confuse, muddle, perplex, baffle, blind, darken, obscure, daze, stupefy, obfuscate.

foggy adj **1** *a foggy day* misty, smoggy, dark, dim, grey, overcast, murky, hazy, gloomy; *inf* soupy. **2** *have only a foggy recollection of the event* vague, indistinct, dim, hazy, shadowy, cloudy, clouded, dark, obscure, unclear, befuddled, confused, bewildered, muddled, dazed, stupefied.

foible n weakness, weak point, failing, shortcoming, flaw, blemish, defect, frailty, infirmity, quirk, idiosyncrasy; *inf* hang-up.

foil n *the perfect foil for her blonde beauty* contrast, striking difference, antithesis, complement.

foil v *foil the attempt* thwart, frustrate, put a stop to, stop, baffle, defeat, check, checkmate, circumvent, counter, baulk, disappoint, impede, obstruct, hamper, hinder, cripple, nip in the bud; *inf* mess up, screw up.

foist v **1** *foist his ideas on everyone* | *foist the vase off as antique* force upon, impose upon, thrust upon, unload upon; palm off, pass off, fob off, get rid of. **2** *foist an illegal clause into the document* sneak, insinuate, interpolate, insert, introduce, stick, squeeze, edge.

fold¹ n **1** *a sheep fold* enclosure, pen. **2** *welcome them into the fold of the church* congregation, assembly, body, church membership, brethren; parishioners, churchgoers; *inf* flock.

fold² n **1** *a fold in the cloth* folded portion, double thickness, overlap, layer, pleat, turn, gather, crease, knife-edge. **2** *a fold in the skin* wrinkle, pucker, furrow, crinkle; crow's foot.

fold² v **1** *fold the paper* double, double over, double up, crease, turn under, turn up, bend, overlap, tuck, gather, pleat, crimp, crumple, dog-ear. **2** *fold her in his arms* enfold, wrap, wrap up, enclose, envelop, clasp, embrace, hug, squeeze. **3** *the firm folded* fail, collapse, go out of business, close, shut down, go bankrupt, crash, go to the wall; *inf* go bust, go under, flop.

folder n file, binder, portfolio, envelope.

foliage n leaves; leafage, frondescence, vegetation.

folk n **1** *country folk* people, citizenry, populace, population, general public, public, race, clan, tribe, ethnic group. **2** *has she no folk of her own?* relatives, relations, family, kinsfolk, kinsmen, kin, kindred, flesh and blood.

folklore n legend, myth, mythology, lore, oral history, tradition, folk tradition; legends, fables, myths, old wives' tales.

follow v **1** *children following after each other* go behind/after, come behind/after, walk behind, tread on the heels of. **2** *he followed his father as mayor* come after, succeed, replace, take the place of, step into the shoes of, supersede, supplant. **3** *he objects to his sister following him around* come/go after, go with, escort, accompany, attend, trail; *inf* tag. **4** *dogs following rabbits* | *detectives following criminals* chase, pursue, run after, trail, shadow, hunt, stalk, track, dog, hound, course; *inf* tail. **5** *follow the rules* | *follow etiquette* obey, observe, comply with, conform to, heed, pay attention to, note, have regard to, mind, be guided by, accept, yield to. **6** *his conclusion follows from your theory* | *the conclusion follows logically* result from, be consequent on, arise from, develop from, ensue from, emanate from, issue from, proceed from, spring from, flow from; result, arise, ensue, supervene. **7** *cannot follow your argument* understand, comprehend, take in, grasp, fathom, get, catch on to, appreciate, keep up with, see; *inf* latch on to. **8** *he followed the poetic style of Shelley* | *he follows Shelley* copy, imitate, emulate, take as a pattern/example; pattern oneself on, adopt the style of, style oneself on. **9** *he follows fantasy fiction* be a follower of, be a fan/admirer/devotee of, be devoted to, be interested in, cultivate an interest in, be a supporter of, support, keep abreast of, keep up to date with. **follow through** *follow through a project* continue to the end, complete, bring to completion, bring to a finish, see something through. **follow up** *follow up the findings* research, investigate, find out about, look into, check out, make enquiries into, pursue.

follower n **1** *the new prime minister and his followers* companion, escort, attendant, henchman, retainer, minion, lackey, toady, servant, page, squire; *inf* hanger-on, sidekick. **2** *Picasso and his followers* imitator, emulator, copier; *inf* copycat. **3** *followers of Christ* apostle, disciple, adherent, supporter, believer, worshipper, votary, pupil. **4** *followers of the Beatles* supporter, enthusiast, fan, admirer, devotee; *inf* groupie, camp-follower, rooter.

following adj **1** *the following day* next, ensuing, succeeding, subsequent, successive. **2** *will the following people leave* about to be mentioned/specified. **3** *there was a quarrel and a following fight* resulting, ensuing, consequent, consequential.

following n *the new ideas/leaders have quite a following* body of support, backing, clientele, public, audience, circle, coterie, retinue, train; supporters, backers, admirers, fans, adherents, devotees, advocates, patrons.

folly n foolishness, absurdity, absurdness, stupidity, silliness, nonsense, nonsensicalness, senselessness, illogicality, inanity, madness, craziness, idiocy, imbecility, lunacy, ridiculousness, ludicrousness, fatuousness, fatuity, rashness, recklessness, imprudence, indiscretion, irrationality; *inf* daftness.

foment v instigate, incite, provoke, agitate, excite, stir up, arouse, encourage, urge, actuate, initiate.

fond adj **1** *fond of music* having a liking/love for, having a taste/fancy for, partial to, keen on, attached to, in love with, enamoured of, having a soft spot for, addicted to; *inf* hooked on. **2** *his fond wife* adoring, devoted, loving, affectionate, caring, warm, tender, amorous, doting, indulgent, overindulgent, overfond; uxorious. **3** *fond hopes of success* foolish, naive, overoptimistic, deluded, delusory, credulous, absurd, empty, vain, Panglossian.

fondle v caress, stroke, pat, pet, cuddle, hug, nuzzle, dandle.

fondness n **1** *look upon his brother with fondness* affection, love, warmth, tenderness, kindness, devotion, care, attachment, excessive devotion, dotingness; uxoriousness. **2** *have a fondness for chocolate* liking, love, taste, partiality, preference, weakness, soft spot, penchant, predilection, fancy, susceptibility.

food n **1** *give food to the children* nourishment, sustenance, nutriment, subsistence, aliment, fare, diet, menu, table, bread, daily bread, board, provender, cooking, cuisine; foodstuffs, refreshments, edibles, meals, provisions, rations, stores, viands, victuals, commons, comestibles; solids; *inf* eats, eatables, nosh, grub, chow, scoff. **2** *food for the cattle* fodder, feed, provender, forage. **3** *food for thought* stimulus, mental nourishment, something to think about, pabulum.

fool n **1** *don't try to explain—he's a fool* idiot, ass, nitwit, halfwit, numskull, nincompoop, ninny, blockhead, dunce, dunderhead, dolt, ignoramus, dullard, illiterate, moron, simpleton, silly, donkey, jackass, loon, mooncalf; *inf* dope, clot, chump, bonehead, fathead, birdbrain, twit, zombie, twerp, nerd; *Amer inf* airhead. **2** *she always makes him look like a fool* | *make a fool of him* dupe, butt, laughing-stock, gull, pushover, easy mark, tool, cat's-paw; *inf* stooge, sucker, sap, mug, fall guy. **3** *the fools of Shakespeare's day* jester, clown, buffoon, comic, jokester, zany, Merry Andrew, Harlequin, motley, Pierrot, Punchinello.

fool v **1** *they certainly fooled the teacher* deceive, trick, play a trick on, hoax, make a fool of, dupe, take in, mislead, hoodwink, bluff, delude, beguile, bamboozle, cozen, gull; *inf* con, kid, put one over on, have on. **2** *we thought he was dead but he was only fooling* pretend, make believe, feign, put on an act, act, sham, fake, counterfeit; *inf* kid. **3** *the boys are always fooling* play the fool, jest, joke, play tricks, clown around, caper, cavort; *inf* mess about. **4** *fool around with their cutlery* fiddle, play, fiddle/play around, toy, trifle, meddle, tamper, mess, interfere, monkey, monkey around. **5** *fool with someone else's wife* have an affair, philander, flirt, commit adultery.

foolery n fooling, clowning, tomfoolery, hoaxing, horseplay, mischief, buffoonery, silliness, larking about; antics, capers, practical jokes, pranks, shenanigans, monkey tricks, larks.

foolhardy adj reckless, rash, daredevil, devil-may-care, impulsive, hot-headed, impetuous, madcap, heedless, precipitate, daring, bold, adventurous, venturous, venturesome, incautious, imprudent, irresponsible, injudicious, desperate; *lit* temerarious.

foolish adj **1** *a foolish plan/idea* silly, absurd, senseless, nonsensical, unintelligent, inane, pointless, fatuous, ridiculous, laughable, derisible, risible, imprudent, incautious, irresponsible, injudicious, indiscreet, unwise, unreasonable, ill-considered, ill-advised, impolitic; *inf* damfool, dotty, crack-brained, nutty, for the birds. **2** *a foolish fellow* stupid, silly, idiotic, simple, unintelligent, halfwitted, brainless, doltish, dull, dull-witted, dense, ignorant, illiterate, moronic, witless, weak-minded, mad, crazy; *inf* dumb, dopey, daft, potty, dotty, barmy, batty, dippy, cuckoo, screwy, wacky.

foolishness n **1** *the foolishness of their actions* folly, stupidity, silliness, imprudence, lack of caution/foresight, indiscretion, irresponsibility, foolhardiness, senselessness, absurdity, inanity, madness, craziness, lunacy. **2** *talking foolishness* nonsense, rubbish, bunkum, gobbledegook, humbug, balderdash, claptrap, hogwash, rigmarole; *inf* rot, tommy rot, bunk, tosh, poppycock, piffle, hooey, garbage, crap.

foolproof adj infallible, never-failing, unfailing, certain, sure, guaranteed, safe, dependable, trustworthy.

foot n **1** *an animal's foot* paw, hoof, trotter, pad. **2** *the foot of the structure* base, bottom, foundation, substructure, understructure. **3** *the foot of the road* bottom, end, edge, boundary, extremity, limit, border.

footing n **1** *lose one's footing* foothold, secure position, grip, toehold, support. **2** *his business was on a secure footing* basis, foundation, groundwork, establishment. **3** *on a friendly footing* relationship, standing, state, condition, position, basis, foundation; relations, terms.

footling adj trivial, trifling, petty, insignificant, unimportant, minor, silly, pointless, immaterial, irrelevant, time-wasting, fiddling; *inf* piddling, piffling.

footstep n **1** *hear her footsteps* footfall, step, tread. **2** *see footsteps in the snow* footprint, footmark, trace, track.

fop n dandy, coxcomb, popinjay, beau, poseur; *inf* peacock, swell, toff.

forage n **1** *forage for cattle* fodder, feed, food, foodstuff, provender, herbage, pasturage. **2** *an enemy forage into the castle* raid, foray, assault, invasion, incursion, plundering, ravaging, looting.

forage v **1** *forage about for food | forage for her keys* search for, seek; look around for, hunt for, cast about for, rummage around for, scratch around for, scour for; *inf* go on the scrounge for, scrounge for. **2** *the enemy forces foraged the village* raid, assault, invade, plunder, ravage, loot.

forbear v refrain from, abstain from, desist from, keep from, restrain oneself from, hold back from, resist the temptation to, stop oneself from, withhold from, eschew, avoid, shun, decline, cease, give up, leave off, break off.

forbearance n **1** *teachers showing great forbearance* tolerance, toleration, patience, resignation, endurance, long-sufferingness, self-control, restraint, leniency, lenity, clemency, moderation, temperance, indulgence. **2** *his forbearance from speaking* refraining, abstinence, desisting, resistance, withholding, avoidance. *see* FORBEAR.

forbid v *dog fighting is forbidden* prohibit, ban, bar, debar, outlaw, veto, proscribe, disallow, interdict, preclude, exclude, rule out, stop, declare taboo.

forbidden adj *forbidden territory* prohibited, out of bounds, banned, debarred, outlawed, vetoed, proscribed, interdicted, taboo, *verboten*.

forbidding adj **1** *a forbidding manner* stern, harsh, grim, hard, tough, hostile, unfriendly, disagreeable, nasty, mean, abhorrent, repellent; *inf* off-putting. **2** *a forbidding landscape* frightening, threatening, ominous, menacing, sinister, daunting, foreboding.

force n **1** *requiring a lot of force* strength, power, potency, vigour, energy, might, muscle, stamina, effort, exertion, impact, pressure, life, vitality, stimulus, dynamism; *inf* punch. **2** *use force to persuade them* compulsion, coercion, duress, pressure, pressurization, constraint, enforcement, violence; *inf* arm twisting. **3** *arguments with force* persuasiveness, cogency, validity, weight, effectiveness, efficacy, efficaciousness, influence, power, strength, vehemence, significance; *inf* bite, punch. **4** *from force of habit* agency, effect, influence. **5** *speaking with great force* vehemence, intensity, vigour, drive, fierceness, feeling, passion, vividness. **6** *a task force / a military force* body of people, corps, detachment, unit, squad, squadron, battalion, division, patrol, regiment, army. **in force 1** *rules no longer in force* in operation, operative, valid, on the statute book, current, effective, binding. **2** *the fans were out in force* in full strength, in great numbers, in great quantities, in hordes.

force v **1** *force them to go* exert/use use force on, compel, coerce, make, use duress on, bring pressure to bear on, pressurize, pressure, press-gang, constrain, impel, drive, oblige, necessitate, urge by force; *inf* put the squeeze/bite on, use strong-arm tactics on. **2** *force the door/safe* force open, break open, burst open, blast, prise open, crack. **3** *the wind forced them back* drive, propel, push, thrust, shove, press. **4** *force a confession from them* wrest, extract, wring, extort, drag.

forced adj **1** *a forced confession* enforced, compulsory, compelled, obligatory, mandatory, involuntary, unwilling. **2** *a forced laugh* strained, unnatural, artificial, false, feigned, overdone, affected, contrived, stilted, laboured, wooden, self-conscious.

forceful n *forceful speakers/arguments* vigorous, powerful, potent, strong, weighty, dynamic, energetic, assertive, effective, cogent, telling, persuasive, convincing, compelling, moving, impressive, valid.

forcible adj **1** *forcible entry* by force, using force, forced, violent. **2** *forcible conscription* compulsory, obligatory, imposed, required, binding. **3** *forcible arguments* forceful, vigorous, powerful, potent. *see* FORCEFUL.

forcibly adv **1** *thrown out forcibly* compulsorily, under compulsion, by force, under coercion, against one's will, under protest, of necessity, willy-nilly. **2** *speak forcibly* forcefully, vigorously, powerfully, potently, dynamically, energetically, assertively, effectively, cogently, tellingly, persuasively, convincingly, movingly, impressively.

forebear n forefather, ancestor, forerunner, progenitor, primogenitor, predecessor, father.

forebode v augur, presage, portend, foreshadow, foreshow, foretoken, betoken, prefigure, presignify, signify, mean, indicate, point to, foretell, forecast, predict, prophesy, forewarn, warn of, prognosticate.

foreboding n **1** *a foreboding that the car would crash* presentiment, premonition, intuition, sixth sense, feeling, vague feeling, misgiving, suspicion, anxiety, apprehension, apprehensiveness, fear, dread. **2** *listening to the forebodings of the soothsayer* augury, prophecy, prediction, presage, prognostication, forecast, warning, omen, portent, sign, foretoken, token.

forecast v *he forecast that they would be late* predict, foretell, foresee, prophesy, forewarn, prognosticate, augur, divine, guess, hazard a guess, conjecture, speculate, estimate, calculate.

forecast n *his forecast proved wrong* prediction, prophecy, forewarning, prognostication, augury, guess, conjecture, speculation, prognosis, projection; *inf* guesstimate.

forefather n forebear, ancestor, forerunner. *see* FOREBEAR.

forefront n **1** *in the forefront of my mind* front, forward/foremost position, fore, foreground. **2** *in the forefront of the party* lead, leading position, head, position of prominence, van, vanguard, spearhead.

forego *see* FORGO.

foregoing adj preceding, precedent, prior, previous, former, above, aforesaid, aforementioned, antecedent, anterior.

foregone adj **1** *in foregone days* past, former, earlier, previous, prior. **2** *foregone conclu-*

sions predetermined, predecided, preordained, predestined, fixed, cut-and-dried, inevitable.

foreground n **1** *in the foreground of the picture* front, fore, forefront. **2** *in the foreground* forefront, lead, position of prominence, vanguard. *see* FOREFRONT 2.

foreign adj **1** *from foreign parts* overseas, alien, distant, remote. **2** *foreign objects* strange, unfamiliar, unknown, exotic, outlandish, odd, peculiar, curious. **3** *matters foreign to the discussion* irrelevant, not pertinent, unrelated, unconnected, inappropriate, inapposite, extraneous, extrinsic, outside.

foreigner n non-native, alien, immigrant, incomer, newcomer, stranger, outsider.

foreman n chargehand, overseer, supervisor, manager, superintendent; *inf* boss, gaffer; *Amer inf* honcho.

foremost adj leading, principal, premier, prime, top, first, primary, front, advanced, paramount, chief, main, most important, supreme, highest, pre-eminent.

forerunner n predecessor, precursor, ancestor, antecedent, forefather, herald, harbinger, usher, advance guard.

foresee v foreknow, anticipate, envisage, predict, foretell, forecast, prophesy, divine, prognosticate, forebode, augur.

foreshadow v forebode, bode, presage, augur, portend, omen, foretoken, betoken, foreshow, indicate, signify, mean, point to, suggest, signal, prefigure, promise.

foresight n forethought, discernment, farsightedness, circumspection, prudence, presence of mind, judiciousness, discrimination, perspicacity, care, caution, precaution, readiness, preparedness, anticipation, provision, prescience.

forest n wood, woodland, tree plantation, plantation; woods, trees.

forestall v pre-empt, intercept, anticipate, be beforehand, get ahead of, steal a march on, thwart, frustrate, stave off, ward off, fend off, avert, prevent, hinder, impede, obstruct, sidetrack.

forestry n forest management, forest planting, tree growing, arboriculture, silviculture, dendrology.

foretell v **1** *she foretold his death* predict, forecast, foresee, prophesy, forewarn, prognosticate, augur, divine. **2** *the first match foretold the final result* forebode, augur, presage, portend, foreshadow, foreshow, foretoken, betoken, prefigure, point to, indicate.

forethought n foresight, far-sightedness, circumspection, prudence, judiciousness, care, precaution, anticipation, provision. *see* FORESIGHT.

forever adv **1** *loving each other forever* always, ever, evermore, for all time, till the end of time, till the cows come home, till hell freezes over, till Doomsday, eternally, undyingly, world without end, perpetually, in perpetuity; *inf* for keeps, for good and all. **2** *he's forever playing loud music* all the time, incessantly, continually, constantly, perpetually, endlessly, unremittingly, interminably, everlastingly.

forewarn v prewarn, warn, give advance/ fair warning to, put on one's guard, tip off, put on the qui vive, alert, caution, advise, apprise, precaution, premonish.

foreword n introduction, preface, preamble, preliminary/front matter, prologue, prolegomenon.

forfeit n *pay/suffer a forfeit as a punishment* forfeiture, fine, penalty, mulct; damages; confiscation, loss, relinquishment, amercement; *Law* sequestration.

forfeit v *children having to forfeit their sweets/ treats* relinquish, hand over, give up, surrender, renounce, be stripped/deprived of; *Law* escheat.

forge¹ v **1** *blacksmiths forging horseshoes* hammer out, beat into shape, shape, form, fashion, mould, found, cast, make, manufacture, frame, construct, create. **2** *forge an excuse* invent, make up, devise, coin, fabricate, put together. **3** *forge handwriting/banknotes* copy, copy fraudulently, imitate, fake, falsify, counterfeit.

forge² v *soldiers forging on* advance steadily/ gradually, press on, push on, plod along. **forge ahead** advance rapidly, progress quickly, make swift progress, increase speed, put a spurt on.

forger n counterfeiter, falsifier, faker, copyist, coiner.

forgery n **1** *accused of forgery of signatures/ coins* fraudulent copying/imitation, falsification, faking, counterfeiting, coining. **2** *the vase is a forgery* fake, counterfeit, sham, fraud, imitation, reproduction; *inf* phoney.

forget v **1** *forget her phone number* fail to remember/recall, fail to think of, let slip. **2** *it's best to forget unhappy times* cease to remember, put out of one's mind, disregard, ignore, let bygones be bygones. **3** *I forgot my gloves* leave behind, omit to take, overlook. **forget oneself** misbehave, behave improperly.

forgetful adj **1** *old people growing forgetful* apt to forget, absent-minded, amnesic, amnesiac, abstracted, vague. **2** *forgetful of one's duties* neglectful, negligent, heedless, careless, unmindful, inattentive, oblivious, lax, remiss, disregardful.

forgetfulness n **1** *suffering from forgetfulness* absent-mindedness, amnesia, poor memory, lapse of memory, abstraction, vagueness, wool-gathering. **2** *guilty of forgetfulness of their duty* negligence, heedlessness, carelessness, inattention, obliviousness, laxness, remissness, disregard.

forgive v pardon, excuse, exonerate, absolve, acquit, let off, let bygones be bygones, bear no malice, harbour no grudge, bury the hatchet; *inf* let someone off the hook.

forgiveness n pardon, amnesty, exoneration, absolution, acquittal, remission, absence of malice/grudges, mercy.

forgiving adj *a forgiving nature* lenient, merciful, compassionate, magnanimous, humane, clement, mild, soft-hearted, forbearing, tolerant, placable.

forgo, forego v do/go without, waive, renounce, relinquish, sacrifice, forswear, surrender, abjure, abandon, cede, yield, abstain from, refrain from, eschew.

forgotten adj unremembered, out of mind, past recollection, beyond/past recall, consigned to oblivion, obliterated, blotted out, buried, left behind, bygone, past, gone, lost, irrecoverable.

fork v *our road forks left | the road forks* branch, branch off, diverge, bifurcate, divaricate, divide, split, separate, go in different directions, go separate ways.

forked adj branching, branched, diverging, bifurcate, divaricate, Y-shaped, V-shaped, pronged, divided, split, separated.

forlorn adj **1** *children looking forlorn* unhappy, sad, miserable, wretched, pathetic, woebegone, lonely, disconsolate, desolate, cheerless, pitiable, pitiful, uncared-for. **2** *a forlorn farmhouse* abandoned, forsaken, deserted, forgotten, neglected. **3** *a forlorn attempt* hopeless, desperate, despairing, in despair.

form v **1** *form shapes* make, fashion, shape, model, mould, forge, found, construct, build, assemble, put together, set up, erect, create, produce, concoct, devise. **2** *form plans* formulate, devise, think up, plan, draw up, frame, forge, hatch, develop, organize; *inf* dream up. **3** *form an alliance* set up, bring about, devise, establish, found, organize, institute, inaugurate.

311

4 *shapes began to form* take shape, materialize, appear, show up, become visible, come into being/existence. **5** *form bad habits* acquire, develop, get, pick up, contract, grow into; *inf* get into. **6** *form the children into lines* arrange, draw up, line up, assemble, organize, order, range, dispose, rank, grade. **7** *these books form the complete series* make, make up, comprise, constitute, compose. **8** *this plank will form the bridge* constitute, serve as, be a component/element/part of. **9** *forming young children's minds* develop, train, teach, instruct, educate, school, drill, discipline.

form n **1** *observe the form of the crystals* shape, configuration, formation, conformation, structure, construction, arrangement, disposition, outward form/appearance, exterior. **2** *of a well-built form* body, physique, figure, shape, build, frame, anatomy, silhouette, contour. **3** *help in the form of the postman* shape, appearance, manifestation, semblance, guise, character, description. **4** *a form of punishment* type, kind, sort, variety, species, genus, genre, stamp, kidney. **5** *admire the form of the painting | his literary work lacks form* structure, framework, format, organization, planning, order, orderliness, symmetry, proportion. **6** *put the mixture into a form* mould, cast, shape, matrix, pattern. **7** *the form of the athletes matters most* fitness, condition, good condition, health, shape, trim, fettle. **8** *not good form to yawn* manners; polite behaviour, acceptable conduct, etiquette, convention, protocol; *inf* done thing. **9** *know the form for organizing the garden party* manner, method, mode, style, system, formula, set formula, procedure, correct/usual way, convention, custom, ritual, protocol, etiquette; rules. **10** *fill in the forms* document, application form, application, sheet of paper, paper. **11** *what form is your daughter in?* class, year; *Amer* grade.

formal adj **1** *formal documents/procedures* official, set, fixed, conventional, standard, regular, customary, approved, prescribed, pro forma, legal, lawful, ceremonial, ritual. **2** *a formal dinner* ceremonial, ceremonious, ritualistic, elaborate. **3** *a very formal person | have a formal manner* reserved, aloof, remote, correct, proper, conventional, precise, exact, punctilious, stiff, unbending, inflexible, standoffish, prim, stuffy, straitlaced. **4** *a formal garden* symmetrical, regular, orderly, arranged, methodical.

formality n **1** *dislike the formality of the occasion* conventionality, ceremoniousness, ritual, red tape, decorum, etiquette, protocol. **2** *obey the formalities* rule, convention,

custom, matter of form, official procedure, formal gesture; form, punctilio.

formation n **1** *planes flying in formation* configuration, format, structure, organization, order, arrangement, pattern, design, disposition, grouping, layout. **2** *the formation of the new buildings is nearly complete* manufacture, making, construction, building, erecting, fashioning, shaping. see FORM v 1. **3** *the formation of a new government* setting up, establishment, founding, institution, creation, inauguration. **4** *dislike the formation of the committee* composition, make-up, constitution, organization. **5** *the formation of the national character* genesis, development, evolution, emergence.

formative adj **1** *in a child's formative years* developing, developmental, growing, mouldable, malleable, impressionable, susceptible, educable, teachable. **2** *a formative influence on the child* forming, shaping, moulding, determinative, influential.

former adj **1** *the former ruler* ex-, previous, prior, preceding, precedent, foregoing, earlier, one-time, quondam, erstwhile, antecedent, anterior, ci-devant, late, sometime. **2** *in former times* earlier, past, long past, bygone, long ago, long departed, long gone, old, ancient, of yore. **3** *the former person* first-mentioned, first.

formerly adv previously, at an earlier time, in earlier times, at one time, once, once upon a time, in times past, heretofore.

formidable adj **1** *of a formidable appearance* intimidating, redoubtable, daunting, alarming, frightening, terrifying, petrifying, horrifying, dreadful, awesome, fearsome, menacing, threatening, dangerous; *inf* scary. **2** *a formidable task* arduous, onerous, difficult, tough, colossal, mammoth, challenging, overwhelming, staggering, huge, tremendous; *inf* mind-boggling, mind-blowing. **3** *a formidable opponent* strong, powerful, mighty, impressive, terrific, tremendous, great, redoubtable, indomitable, invincible.

formula n **1** *a legal/mathematical formula* formulary, established form of words, set of words/symbols, set expression, code. **2** *the formula for writing a successful novel* recipe, prescription, rubric, blueprint, method, procedure, convention, ritual, *modus operandi*; principles, rules, precepts.

formulate v **1** *formulate one's thoughts in plain English* express/state clearly, define, articulate, set down, frame, give form to, specify, particularize, itemize, detail, designate, systematize, indicate. **2** *formulate our plans* draw up, work out, map out, plan, prepare, compose, devise, think up, conceive, create, invent, originate, coin, design.

fornication n sexual intercourse, sex, coitus, copulation.

forsake v **1** *forsake his wife and children* desert, abandon, leave, leave in the lurch, quit, throw over, jilt, cast off, discard, repudiate, reject, disown; *inf* leave flat; *Amer inf* give someone the air. **2** *forsake her life of luxury* give up, renounce, relinquish, forgo, turn one's back on, repudiate, have done with, discard, set aside.

forsaken adj **1** *forsaken wives* deserted, abandoned, cast off, discarded, jilted, rejected. **2** *what a forsaken place* godforsaken, remote, isolated, marooned, lonely, solitary, deserted, derelict, desolate, dreary, forlorn.

forswear v *forswear drinking* give up, renounce, abjure, reject, relinquish, forgo, quit, do without; *inf* cut out.

fort n fortress, stronghold, citadel, fastness, garrison, castle, tower, donjon, keep, turret, fortification, redoubt, battlement.

forte n strong point, strength, *métier*, speciality, talent, skill, gift, bent; *inf* bag, thing.

forth adv **1** *from that day forth* onward, onwards, forward, forwards. **2** *go forth from the tent* out, outside, away, off, away from home, abroad.

forthcoming adj **1** *forthcoming events* future, coming, approaching, expected, prospective, imminent, impending. **2** *no reply was forthcoming* made available, available, ready, at hand, accessible, obtainable, at one's disposal; *inf* on tap. **3** *the children are not very forthcoming* communicative, informative, talkative, expansive, voluble, chatty, conversational, loquacious, open, unreserved.

forthright adj *a forthright person* direct, frank, candid, blunt, outspoken, plain-speaking, plain-spoken, downright, straightforward, open, honest.

forthwith adv right away, immediately, at once, instantly, this instant, directly, straightaway, without delay, quickly.

fortification n **1** *the fortification of the walls* strengthening, reinforcement, bracing. **2** *soldiers manning the fortifications* battlement, rampart, bastion, bulwark, parapet, blockhouse, barricade, buttress, stronghold, palisade, stockade, outwork.

fortify v **1** *fortify the town* build defences round, garrison, embattle, guard, cover, protect, secure. **2** *fortify the walls* strengthen, reinforce, shore up, brace, buttress. **3** *fortify himself with a drink* strengthen, invigorate, energize, revive, embolden, give courage to, encourage, cheer, hearten, buoy up, reassure, make confident, brace, sustain. **4** *fortify wine* add spirits/alcohol to. **5** *fortify food* add vitamins/minerals to.

fortitude n strength, strength of mind, moral strength, firmness of purpose, backbone, grit, mettle, courage, nerve, pluck, bravery, fearlessness, valour, intrepidity, stout-heartedness, endurance, patience, long-sufferingness, forbearance, tenacity, pertinacity, perseverance, resolution, resoluteness, determination.

fortress n fort, stronghold, citadel, fastness. *see* FORT.

fortuitous adj chance, unexpected, unanticipated, unforeseen, unlooked-for, serendipitous, casual, haphazard, random, accidental, unintentional, unplanned, unpremeditated, incidental; lucky, fortunate, felicitous; *inf* fluky.

fortunate adj **1** *a fortunate person* lucky, in luck, favoured, blessed, born with a silver spoon in one's mouth, born under a lucky star, having a charmed life, happy, felicitous, prosperous, well-off, successful, flourishing; *inf* sitting pretty, jammy. **2** *in a fortunate position* advantageous, favourable, helpful, providential, auspicious, propitious, promising, encouraging, opportune, felicitous, profitable, fortuitous, timely, well-timed, convenient.

fortune n **1** *a merchant of great fortune* wealth, treasure, affluence, opulence, opulency, prosperity, substance, property; riches, assets, means, possessions, estates. **2** *the ring cost a fortune* huge amount, mint, king's ransom; *inf* packet, bundle, bomb, pile. **3** *by good fortune he won* chance, mere chance, accident, coincidence, contingency, happy chance, fortuity, serendipity, luck, providence. **4** *tell one's fortune* destiny, fate, lot, cup, portion, kismet; stars. **5** *fortune smiled on him* Lady Luck, Dame Fortune, fate. **6** *the fortunes of the club* state of affairs, condition, position; circumstances.

fortune-teller n seer, soothsayer, prophet, prophetess, augur, diviner, sibyl, oracle, astrologer, clairvoyant.

forum n **1** *a forum for discussion about the new road* meeting, assembly, symposium, round table conference, debate, discussion place, discussion medium. **2** *awarded damages by the forum* court, tribunal. **3** *Caesar and Brutus meeting in the forum* public meeting place, public square, market place.

forward adj **1** *a forward movement* moving forwards/ahead, onward, advancing, progressing, progressive. **2** *the plants are forward this year* advanced, well-advanced, early, premature, precocious. **3** *the forward force* front, at the front/fore, fore, frontal, foremost, head, leading, advance. **4** *a forward young woman* bold, brash, brazen, brazen-faced, barefaced, audacious, presumptuous, presuming, assuming, familiar, overfamiliar, overassertive, overconfident, overweening, aggressive, thrusting, pert, impudent, impertinent, cheeky, insolent, unabashed; *inf* pushy, cocky, brass-necked, fresh. **5** *forward planning* future, for the future, prospective.

forward adv **1** *move forward* towards the front, frontwards, onward, onwards, on, ahead, forth. **2** *step forward for the prize* out, forth, into view, into the open, into public notice, into prominence. **3** *from today forward* on, onward, hence.

forward v **1** *forward the letter/parcel* send on, send, pass on, dispatch, transmit, post, mail, ship, freight, deliver. **2** *his help forwarded our plans* advance, further, speed up, hasten, hurry along, expedite, accelerate, step up, aid, assist, help, foster, encourage, promote, favour, support, back, give backing to.

forward-looking adj progressive, go-ahead, modern, enterprising, reforming, radical, liberal; *inf* go-getting.

forwardness n *the forwardness of the young woman* boldness, brashness, brazenness, audacity, presumption, overfamiliarity, overconfidence, aggressiveness, pertness, impudence, impertinence, cheek, cheekiness, insolence; *inf* pushiness, cockiness.

forwards adv towards the front, frontwards. see FORWARD adv 1.

fossil n remains, reliquae, petrified remains; surviving trace/impression, remnant, relic.

foster v **1** *foster freedom of thought* encourage, promote, further, stimulate, boost, advance, forward, cultivate, foment, help, aid, assist, support, uphold, back, give backing to, facilitate. **2** *foster a child* bring up, rear, raise, care for, take care of, mother, parent. **3** *foster hopes of being rich* cherish, harbour, entertain, nurse, nourish, nurture, hold, sustain.

foul adj **1** *that foods looks foul* disgusting, revolting, repulsive, nauseating, sickening, loathsome, abominable, odious, offensive, nasty. **2** *that cheese smells foul* foul-smelling, evil-smelling, ill-smelling, stinking, high, fetid, rank, mephitic; *lit* noisome. **3** *foul water* contaminated, polluted, adulterated, infected, tainted, defiled, impure, filthy, dirty, unclean. **4** *foul carcasses* rotten, rotting, decayed, decomposed, putrid, putrescent, putrefactive, carious. **5** *use foul language* foul-mouthed, blasphemous, profane, obscene, vulgar, gross, coarse, filthy, dirty, indecent, indelicate, suggestive, smutty, blue, off-colour, low, lewd, ribald, salacious, scatological, offensive, abusive. **6** *he's a foul creature* horrible, detestable, abhorrent, loathsome, hateful, despicable, contemptible, abominable, offensive, odious, disgusting, revolting, dishonourable, disgraceful, base, low, mean, sordid, vile, wicked, vicious, heinous, execrable, iniquitous, nefarious, notorious, infamous, scandalous, egregious, flagitious. **7** *foul play by their competitors* unfair, unjust, dishonourable, dishonest, underhand, unsportsmanlike, unsporting, unscrupulous, unprincipled, immoral, crooked, fraudulent, dirty; *inf* shady. **8** *foul clothes* dirty, filthy, unwashed, soiled, grimy, grubby, stained, dirt-encrusted, muddied, begrimed, feculent. **9** *foul weather* dirty, nasty, disagreeable, bad, rough, wild, stormy, rainy, wet, blustery, squally, misty, foggy, murky, gloomy.

foul v **1** *foul the pavement/water* dirty, soil, stain, blacken, muddy, begrime, splash, spatter, smear, besmear, besmirch, defile, pollute, contaminate, taint, sully. **2** *foul up the fishing line* snarl, entangle, twist, tangle, muddle. **3** *foul the traffic/drains* clog, choke, block, jam.

found v **1** *found a new company* establish, set up, institute, originate, initiate, bring into being, create, start, inaugurate, constitute, endow, organize, develop. **2** *found the building* lay the foundations of, build, construct, erect, put up, elevate. **3** *found his story in South America* base, set, locate, ground, root.

foundation n **1** *the foundation of the building* base, bottom, bedrock, substructure, substratum, understructure, underpinning. **2** *lay the foundations of maths* basis, groundwork; principles, fundamentals, rudiments. **3** *the foundation of the company* founding, establishing, setting up, institution, initiation, inauguration, constitution, endowment. see FOUND 1. **4** *set up an educational foundation* endowed institution, institution.

founder n builder, constructor, maker, establisher, institutor, initiator, beginner, inventor, discoverer, framer, designer, architect, creator, author, originator, organizer, developer, generator, prime mover, father, patriarch.

founder v **1** *ships foundered* sink, submerge, go to the bottom, go down, be lost at sea, capsize, run aground, be swamped; *inf* go to Davy Jones's locker. **2** *plans foundered* fail, not succeed, fall through, break down, go wrong/awry, misfire, come to grief/ nothing, miscarry, abort, flounder, collapse; *inf* come a cropper. **3** *the horse foundered* stumble, trip, stagger, lurch, fall, topple, sprawl, go lame, collapse.

foundling n abandoned infant, orphan, waif, stray, outcast.

fountain n **1** *fountains built in the square* water fountain, jet, spray, spout, spurt, well, fount. **2** *fountains welling up from the mountain* spring, stream, source, well, fountainhead. **3** *the fountain of knowledge* fount, fountainhead, source, rise, well-head, wellspring, well, beginning, commencement, origin, cause, birth, genesis, root, mainspring, derivation, inception, inspiration, *fons et origo*.

fowl n domestic fowl; chicken, hen, cock, bantam, duck, turkey, goose; poultry.

foyer n entrance hall, reception area, hall, vestibule, lobby, anteroom, antechamber.

fracas n disturbance, quarrel, altercation, fight, brawl, affray, row, rumpus, scuffle, tussle, skirmish, free-for-all, brouhaha, mêlée, donnybrook, riot, uproar, commotion; trouble, tumult, turmoil, pandemonium; *Scots* stushie.

fraction n **1** *a fraction of the population* part, subdivision. **2** *cost a fraction of what you paid*|*move a fraction closer* small part, tiny piece, minute amount, bit, mite, scrap, trifle.

fractious adj **1** *fractious children* cross, irritable, fretful, bad-tempered, crabbed, peevish, petulant, ill-humoured, ill-natured, querulous, testy, snappish, touchy, irascible, sulky, sullen, morose. **2** *the fractious element on the committee* unruly, rebellious, insubordinate, stubborn, obstinate, contrary, refractory, recalcitrant, unmanageable, intractable.

fracture n **1** *the fracture of a bone* breaking, breakage, splitting, cleavage, rupture. **2** *a fracture in the bone* break, breakage, crack, split. **3** *a fracture in the rock* split, crack, fissure, cleft, rift, slit, rent, chink, crevice, gap, opening, aperture.

fracture v *the bone/material fractured* break, crack, split, splinter, rupture.

fragile adj **1** *fragile pottery* easily broken, breakable, brittle, frangible, smashable, splintery, flimsy, frail, insubstantial, delicate, dainty, fine. **2** *feeling fragile after the party* ill, unwell, ailing, sickly, delicate, weak, infirm, unsound.

fragment n **1** *fragments of glass from the bowl* piece, part, particle, chip, chink, shard, sliver, splinter, smithereen. **2** *a fragment of cloth* scrap, bit, snip, snippet, wisp, tatter. **3** *find the fragments of a book* remnant, remainder, fraction; remains, shreds.

fragmentary, fragmental adj *fragmentary evidence* incomplete, disconnected, disjointed, broken, discontinuous, uneven, piecemeal, incoherent, scrappy, bitty, sketchy, unsystematic.

fragrance n **1** *the fragrance of the roses* fragrancy, scent, perfume, bouquet, aroma, smell, sweet smell, redolence, balm, balminess. **2** *a bottle of fragrance* scent, perfume, toilet water; cologne, eau-de-Cologne.

fragrant adj *fragrant flowers* scented, perfumed, aromatic, sweet smelling, redolent, balmy, odorous, odiferous.

frail adj **1** *frail china* fragile, easily broken, breakable, frangible, delicate. *see* FRAGILE 1. **2** *frail old ladies* infirm, weak, delicate, slight, slender, puny, unsound, ill, ailing, unwell, sickly. **3** *frail creatures* weak, easily led/tempted, susceptible, impressionable, malleable, vulnerable, fallible.

frailty n **1** *the frailty of the china* fragility, brittleness, frangibility, flimsiness, insubstantiality, delicacy, daintiness, fineness. **2** *the frailty of the old* infirmness, infirmity, weakness, delicacy, slightness, puniness, illness. *see* FRAIL 2. **3** *the frailty of human nature* weakness, susceptibility, impressionability, vulnerability, fallibility. *see* FRAIL 3. **4** *excuse their frailties* foible, weakness, weak point, flaw, blemish, defect, failing, fault, shortcoming, deficiency, peccadillo.

frame n **1** *built on a frame of steel* framework, substructure, structure, shell, casing, support, skeleton, scaffolding, foundation, body, chassis. **2** *the man had a huge frame* body, physique, build, figure, shape, size, skeleton, carcass. **3** *a photograph frame* mount, mounting, setting. **4** *alter the frame of society* order, organization, scheme, system, plan, fabric, form, constitution. **5** *a sad frame of mind* state, condition; mood, humour, temper, spirit, attitude.

frame v **1** *frame the structure* assemble, put together, put/set up, build, construct, erect, elevate, make, fabricate, manufacture, fashion, mould, shape, forge. **2** *frame a policy* put together, formulate, draw up, plan, draft, map/plot/sketch out, shape, compose, form, devise, create, establish, conceive, think up, hatch; *inf* dream up, cook up. **3** *frame a picture*|*hair framing his* *face* enclose, encase, surround. **4** *to frame a colleague* incriminate, fabricate charges/evidence against; *inf* fit up.

frame-up n false charge, trumped-up charge, plot, conspiracy, collusion; *inf* put-up job, fit-up.

framework n **1** *the framework of the building* frame, substructure, shell, skeleton. *see* FRAME n 1. **2** *the framework of society* frame, order, organization, scheme, fabric. *see* FRAME n 4.

franchise n **1** *women given the franchise* right to vote, the vote, suffrage, enfranchisement. **2** *grant him a fast-food franchise | the corporation was given a franchise* warrant, warranty, charter, licence; permission, leave, consent, privilege, prerogative.

frank adj **1** *a frank person/reply* candid, direct, forthright, plain, plain-spoken, straight, straight from the shoulder, downright, explicit, outspoken, blunt, bluff, open, sincere, honest, truthful, undissembling, guileless, artless. **2** *show frank admiration* open, obvious, transparent, patent, manifest, undisguised, unconcealed, unmistakable, evident, noticeable, visible.

frank v *frank a letter* stamp, postmark, mark, imprint.

frankly adv **1** *frankly, I think he is lying* to be frank/honest, candidly, honestly, truthfully. *see* FRANK adj 1. **2** *he spoke frankly* candidly, directly, plainly, explicitly, bluntly, openly, honestly, truthfully, without dissembling.

frantic adj panic-stricken, panic-struck, panicky, beside oneself, at one's wits' end, frenzied, wild, hysterical, frenetic, berserk, distraught, overwrought, worked up, distracted, agitated, distressed, out of control, uncontrolled, unhinged, mad, crazed, out of one's mind, maniacal; *inf* fraught.

fraternity n **1** *a strong bond of fraternity in the family* brotherhood, kinship. **2** *the teaching fraternity* profession, band of workers. **3** *join a university fraternity* club, society, association, guild, set, circle.

fraternize v associate, mix, go around with, keep company with, hobnob with, socialize, mingle, consort; *inf* hang around/out with.

fraud n **1** *found guilty of fraud* fraudulence, sharp practice, cheating, swindling, trickery, deceit, double-dealing, duplicity, treachery, chicanery, skulduggery, imposture, embezzlement, crookedness; *inf* monkey business. **2** *perpetrate a fraud* ruse, trick, hoax, deception, subterfuge, stratagem, wile, artifice, swindle; *inf* con, rip-off. **3** *the*

man is a fraud impostor, fake, sham, cheat, cheater, swindler, double-dealer, trickster, confidence trickster, pretender, charlatan, quack, mountebank; *inf* phoney, con man. **4** *the vase/banknote is a fraud* fake, sham, counterfeit, forgery; *inf* phoney.

fraudulent adj dishonest, cheating, swindling, criminal, deceitful, double-dealing, duplicitous, dishonourable, unscrupulous; *inf* crooked, sharp, shady.

fraught adj **1** *fraught with danger* full of, filled with, teeming with, attended by, accompanied by. **2** *the fraught young mother* anxious, overwrought, distraught, worked up, distracted, agitated, distressed.

fray v **1** *the cloth is fraying* unravel, wear, wear thin, wear out/away, become threadbare, become tattered/ragged. **2** *tempers/nerves were frayed by the experience* strain, tax, overtax, irritate, put on edge, make edgy/tense.

freak n **1** *that animal is a freak* freak of nature, aberration, abnormality, irregularity, oddity, monster, monstrosity, malformation, mutant, *rara avis*. **2** *the neighbours think he's a bit of a freak* oddity, peculiar person; *inf* queer fish, odd bod, oddball, weirdo, weirdie, way-out person, nutcase, nut. **3** *they are film freaks* enthusiast, fan, fanatic, addict, aficionado, devotee; *inf* buff, fiend, nut. **4** *she is full of freaks* whim, caprice, vagary, fad, fancy, quirk, crotchet. **5** *by a freak he discovered the answer* anomaly, unusual occurrence, peculiar turn of events, quirk, quirk/twist of fate; chance; *inf* fluke.

freak adj *a freak storm* abnormal, unusual, atypical, aberrant, exceptional, unaccountable, unpredictable, unforeseeable, bizarre, queer, odd, unparalleled; *inf* fluky.

free adj **1** *a free booklet* free of charge, for nothing, complimentary, gratis, without charge, at no cost; *inf* for free, on the house. **2** *free of responsibilities* without, devoid of, lacking in, exempt from, not liable to, safe from, immune to, unaffected by, clear of, unencumbered by, relieved of, released from, rid of; *inf* sans. **3** *he is not free today* unoccupied, available, not at work, not busy, not tied up, idle, at leisure, with time on one's hands, with time to spare. **4** *is this place free?* empty, vacant, available, spare, unoccupied, untaken, uninhabited, tenantless. **5** *a free nation* independent, self-governing, self-governed, self-ruling, self-directing, sovereign, autonomous, democratic, emancipated, enfranchised, manumitted. **6** *the animals are free* at liberty, at large, loose, on the loose, unconfined, unbound, untied, unchained, unshackled, unfettered, unrestrained, wild. **7** *free to choose* able, allowed, permitted, unrestricted. **8** *a free flow of water* | *is the way forward free?* unobstructed, unimpeded, unhampered, clear, unblocked. **9** *the free end of the rope* not fixed, unattached, unfastened, loose. **10** *free with their money* generous, lavish, liberal, openhanded, unstinting, giving, munificent, bountiful, bounteous, charitable, extravagant, prodigal. **11** *a free natural manner* free and easy, easygoing, natural, open, frank, relaxed, casual, informal, unceremonious, unforced, spontaneous, uninhibited, artless, ingenuous; *inf* laid-back. **12** *he's a bit too free in his manner for my liking* familiar, overfamiliar, presumptuous, forward, bold, assertive, aggressive, impudent; *inf* cheeky, cocky. **free and easy** easygoing, natural, relaxed, casual, informal, tolerant. *see* FREE adj 11.

free v **1** *free the prisoners/animals* set free, release, let go, set at liberty, liberate, set/ let/turn loose, untie, unchain, unfetter, unshackle, unmanacle, uncage, unleash, deliver. **2** *free the accident victims from the car* get free, rescue, release, get loose, extricate, disentangle, disengage, disencumber. **3** *freed from paying tax* exempt, make exempt, except, excuse, relieve.

freedom n **1** *colonies seeking their freedom* independence, self-government, sovereignty, autonomy, democracy, emancipation, manumission, enfranchisement, home rule. **2** *prisoners/animals enjoying their freedom* liberty, release, deliverance, non-confinement. **3** *freedom from tax* exemption, immunity, impunity. **4** *freedom of speech* right, privilege, prerogative. **5** *freedom to move around* | *freedom to operate* scope, latitude, elbow room, wide margin, flexibility, facility, free rein, licence. **6** *admire her freedom of manner* naturalness, openness, lack of reserve/inhibition, casualness, informality, lack of ceremony, spontaneity, artlessness, ingenuousness. **7** *he treats her with too much freedom* familiarity, overfamiliarity, presumption, forwardness, impudence; *inf* cheek. *see* FREE adj 12.

freely adv **1** *speaking freely, I do not like them* frankly, openly, candidly, plainly, bluntly, unreservedly, without constraint. **2** *prisoners not allowed to speak freely* of one's own volition/accord, voluntarily, of one's own free will.

freeze v **1** *the lake has frozen* ice over/up, glaciate, solidify, harden. **2** *freeze to death* | *I'm freezing* get chilled, get chilled to the bone/marrow, go numb with cold, turn blue with cold, shiver, shiver with cold, feel Jack Frost's fingers. **3** *freeze the vegetables* deep-freeze. **4** *he froze as he saw the gun* stop dead, stop in one's tracks, stop, stand still, stand stock still, go rigid, become motionless. **5** *freeze prices* fix, hold, peg, suspend.

freezing adj **1** *freezing winds* bitterly cold, chill, chilling, frosty, glacial, arctic, wintry, raw, biting, piercing, penetrating, cutting, stinging, numbing, Siberian. **2** *freezing children/toes* chilled through, chilled to the bone/marrow, numb with cold, frostbitten.

freight n **1** *a separate charge for the freight* transportation, conveyance, freightage, carriage, portage, haulage. **2** *unload the freight* cargo, load, lading, consignment, merchandise; goods.

frenzied adj frantic, frenetic, panic-stricken, panic-struck, beside oneself, at one's wits' end, wild, hysterical, distraught, distracted, overwrought, agitated, mad, crazed, out of one's mind, maniacal; *inf* fraught. *see* FRANTIC.

frenzy n **1** *go into a frenzy at the news* mental derangement, madness, mania, insanity, wild excitement, wildness, hysteria, distraction, agitation; fit, seizure, paroxysm. **2** *a frenzy of activity* bout, outburst, fit, spasm.

frequency n **1** *the frequency of accidents on that road* frequentness, recurrence, repetition, persistence. **2** *infant mortality has decreased in frequency* rate of occurrence, rate of repetition, commonness.

frequent adj **1** *frequent accidents* occurring often, recurrent, repeated, persistent, continuing, many, numerous, quite a few/lot, several. **2** *a frequent caller* regular, habitual, customary, common, usual, familiar, everyday, continual, constant, incessant.

frequent v visit, visit often, go to regularly/repeatedly, attend, attend frequently, haunt, patronize; *inf* hang out at.

frequenter n regular visitor, regular customer, regular, habitué, haunter.

frequently adv often, very often, many times, many a time, again and again, over and over again, on several occasions, repeatedly, recurrently, habitually, continually, constantly.

fresh adj **1** *is the fruit fresh?* garden-fresh, newly harvested, crisp, unwilted, unfaded, not stale. **2** *fresh, not tinned fruit* raw, natural, unprocessed, unpreserved, undried, uncured, crude. **3** *fresh ideas* new, brand-new, recent, latest, up to date, modern, modernistic, ultra-modern, new fangled, different, innovative, original, novel, unusual, unconventional, unorthodox. **4** *feeling very fresh on holiday* energetic, vigorous, invigorated, vital, lively, vibrant, spry, sprightly, bright, alert, bouncing, refreshed, rested, restored, revived, like a new person, fresh as a daisy; *inf* full of vim/beans, rarin' to go, bright-eyed and bushy-tailed; *Amer inf* chipper. **5** *a fresh complexion* healthy-looking, healthy, clear, bright, youthful-looking, wholesome, blooming, glowing, fair, rosy, pink, reddish, ruddy. **6** *curtains looking fresh* bright, clean, spick and span, unfaded. **7** *fresh supplies* more, other, additional, further, extra, supplementary, auxiliary. **8** *a fresh morning*|*fresh air* bright, clear, cool, crispy, crisp, sparkling; pure, unpolluted, clean, refreshing. **9** *fresh winds* cool, chilly, brisk, bracing, invigorating. **10** *fresh recruits* young, youthful, new, newly arrived, untrained, unqualified, inexperienced, untried, raw, callow, green, immature, artless, ingenuous, naïve; *inf* wet behind the ears. **11** *a fresh young man* familiar, overfamiliar, presumptuous, forward, bold, audacious, brazen, impudent, impertinent, insolent, disrespectful, pert, saucy; *inf* cheeky, cocky, brass-necked.

freshen v **1** *a walk will freshen you*|*the swim freshened her up* refresh, rouse, stimulate, revitalize, restore, revive, liven up. **2** *freshen the room* air, ventilate, deodorize, purify. **3** *freshen a drink* top up, refill. **4** *I must freshen up* wash oneself, tidy oneself, tidy/spruce oneself up, titivate oneself.

fret v **1** *fretting about her mother's absence* be distressed, be upset, feel unhappy, be anxious, worry, agonize, anguish, pine, brood, mope, fuss, make a fuss, complain, grumble, whine; *inf* feel peeved. **2** *the loud noise frets him* irritate, annoy, infuriate, exasperate, anger, rile, provoke, vex, irk, gall, pique, rankle with, nettle, ruffle, harass, torment, bother, trouble, disturb; *inf* peeve.

fretful adj distressed, upset, miserable, cross, crabbed, fractious, peevish, petulant, tetchy, out of sorts, bad-tempered, irritable, ill-natured, edgy, irascible, grumpy, crotchety, touchy, captious, testy, querulous, complaining, grumbling, whining; *Amer* cranky.

friction n **1** *ropes worn by friction* rubbing, abrading, abrasion, attrition, chafing, fretting, gnawing, grating, rasping, scraping, excoriation. **2** *cause friction in the family* dissension, dissent, disagreement, discord, strife, conflict, clashing, contention, dispute, disputation, arguing, argument, quarrelling, bickering, squabbling, wrangling, fighting, hostility, rivalry, animosity, antagonism, resentment, bad feeling, ill feeling, bad blood, disharmony.

friend n **1** *on holiday with friends* companion, boon companion, crony, mate, bosom friend, comrade, playmate, soul mate, intimate, confidante, confidant, familiar, *alter ego*, shadow, ally, associate; *inf* pal, chum, china; *Amer inf* buddy. **2** *friends of the local theatre* patron, backer, supporter, benefactor, well-wisher; *inf* angel. **3** *their brother/sister and his/her friend* girl friend, boy friend, partner, lover; *inf* live-in; *Scots inf* bidie-in.

friendless adj companionless, alone, all alone, by oneself, lone, lonely, lonesome, with no one to turn to, solitary, with no ties, unattached, single, forlorn, unpopular, unbefriended.

friendliness n affability, amiability, warmth, geniality, affection, companionability, cordiality, conviviality, sociability, comradeship, neighbourliness, approachability, communicativeness, amenability, good-naturedness, benevolence. *see* FRIENDLY 1.

friendly adj **1** *a friendly person* affable, amiable, warm, genial, agreeable, affectionate, companionable, cordial, convivial, sociable, hospitable, comradely, neighbourly, outgoing, approachable, accessible, communicative, open, unreserved, easygoing, good-natured, kindly, benign, amenable, well-disposed, sympathetic, benevolent; *inf* matey, chummy; *Amer inf* clubby, buddy-buddy. **2** *on friendly terms* amicable, congenial, cordial, close, intimate, familiar, peaceable, peaceful, conciliatory, non-hostile, unwarlike; *inf* thick with. **3** *a friendly wind swept the boat to the shore* helpful, favourable, advantageous, benevolent, well-disposed.

friendship n **1** *their friendship lasted years* companionship, friendly/close relationship, intimacy, amity, mutual affection, affinity, rapport, mutual understanding, harmony, comradeship, fellowship, attachment, alliance; cordial relations. **2** *she always shows friendship to new people* friendliness, affability, amiability, warmth, geniality, cordiality, good-naturedness, neighbourliness, kindliness. *see* FRIENDLINESS.

fright n **1** *start back in fright* fear, fear and trembling, terror, alarm, horror, dread, fearfulness, apprehension, trepidation, consternation, dismay, perturbation, disquiet, panic, nervousness, jitteriness; *inf* blue funk, jitters, heebie-jeebies, willies. **2** *give them a fright* scare, shock; shivers; *inf* jitters, a fit of the heebie-jeebies. **3** *woke up* *looking a fright* ugly/horrible/grotesque sight, eyesore; *inf* mess, sight.

frighten v scare, alarm, startle, terrify, terrorize, petrify, give a shock to, shock, appal, panic, throw into panic, unnerve, unman, intimidate, cow, daunt, dismay, make one's blood run cold, freeze one's blood; *inf* scare the living daylights out of, scare stiff, scare out of one's wits, scare witless, make one's hair stand on end, make one's hair curl, put the wind up, throw into a blue funk, make someone jump out of his/her skin, spook.

frightful adj **1** *the corpse was a frightful sight* dreadful, terrible, horrible, horrid, hideous, ghastly, grisly, gruesome, macabre, grim, dire, abhorrent, revolting, repulsive, loathsome, odious, fearful, fearsome, terrifying, alarming, shocking, harrowing, appalling, daunting, unnerving. **2** *a frightful woman* unpleasant, disagreeable, dreadful, horrible, terrible, awful, appalling, ghastly, insufferable, unbearable, annoying, irritating. **3** *have a frightful cold* very bad, terrible, dreadful, awful, ghastly, nasty.

frigid adj **1** *frigid conditions* very cold, bitterly cold, bitter, freezing, frozen, icy, frosty, chilly, wintry, arctic, glacial, Siberian, polar, gelid, Hyperborean. **2** *a frigid look/welcome* cold, icy, austere, distant, aloof, remote, unapproachable, forbidding, stiff, formal, unbending, cool, unfeeling, unemotional, unfriendly, hostile, unenthusiastic. **3** *a frigid woman* sexually unresponsive, cold, passionless, passive, inorgasmic.

frill n flounce, ruffle, ruff, furbelow, ruche, ruching, gather, tuck, fringe, purfle.

frills npl *a plain meal with no frills* ornamentation, decoration, embellishment, fanciness, ostentation, fuss; trimmings, falderals, affectations, extras, additions, superfluities, bits and pieces; *inf* jazz, flash, fandangle.

fringe n **1** *a skirt with a fringe* border, trimming, frill, edging; tassels. **2** *on the fringe of the wood* | *the fringe of society* outer edge, edge, borderline, perimeter, periphery, margin, rim; limits, borders, outskirts, verges, marches.

fringe adj *fringe theatre* experimental, unconventional, unorthodox.

fringe v **1** *fringe a skirt* trim, edge, befringe. **2** *trees fringe the lake* edge, border, skirt, surround, enclose.

frisk v **1** *lambs frisking* frolic, gambol, cavort, caper, cut capers, skip, dance, leap, romp, trip, prance, hop, jump, bounce, rollick,

sport, curvet. **2** *frisked at the airport* search, check, inspect; *Amer inf* shake down.

frisky adj lively, bouncy, active, frolicsome, coltish, playful, romping, rollicking, sportive, spirited, in high spirits, high-spirited, exuberant, joyful; *inf* high, full of beans.

fritter v **1** *fritter away money* squander, waste, overspend, misspend, spend like water, dissipate, run through, get through. **2** *fritter away time* waste, squander, misuse, idle away, while away, dally away.

frivolity n **1** *the serious student needs a little frivolity* light-heartedness, levity, gaiety, fun, silliness, foolishness. **2** *the frivolity of the girls* frivolousness, giddiness, flightiness, dizziness, flippancy, silliness, zaniness, empty-headedness. *see* FRIVOLOUS 1. **3** *the frivolity of the remark* frivolousness, flippancy, superficiality, shallowness. *see* FRIVOLOUS 2.

frivolous adj **1** *frivolous young girls* lacking seriousness, non-serious, lacking in sense, senseless, flippant, giddy, flighty, dizzy, silly, foolish, facetious, zany, light-hearted, merry, superficial, shallow, empty-headed, feather-brained; *inf* flip. **2** *a frivolous remark* non-serious, flippant, ill-considered, superficial, shallow, inane, facetious; *inf* flip. **3** *frivolous clothes* impractical, flimsy, frothy. **4** *frivolous details* trivial, trifling, minor, petty, insignificant, unimportant, paltry, niggling, peripheral.

frolic v frisk, gambol, cavort, caper, skip. *see* FRISK 1.

frolic n **1** *enjoy a frolic in the garden* game, romp, lark, antic, caper, escapade, prank, revel, spree. **2** *the children's frolic* fun, fun and games, gaiety, merriment, mirth, amusement, laughter, jollity; *inf* skylarking, high jinks.

front n **1** *towards the front of the building* fore, forepart, foremost part, forefront, foreground, anterior. **2** *paint the front of the building* frontage, face, facing, façade. **3** *at the front in the battle* front line, vanguard, van, first line, firing line. **4** *at the front of the queue* beginning, head, top, lead. **5** *put a brave front on it* look, appearance, face, exterior, air, manner, expression, show, countenance, demeanour, bearing, mien, aspect. **6** *his shop is a front for his drug dealing* cover, cover-up, blind, façade, disguise, pretext, mask. **in front 1** *the runners in front* in the lead, to the fore, ahead, in the van, in advance. **2** *in front of her in the queue* ahead of, before, preceding.

front adj *the front runners* first, foremost, leading, lead.

front v *the house fronts on the lake* face towards, look out on, overlook, lie opposite to.

frontier n border, boundary, bound, limit, edge, rim; confines, marches.

frost n **1** *there was a frost last night* freeze, freeze-up; *inf* Jack Frost. **2** *frost on the trees* white frost, hoar-frost, rime. **3** *frost in her greeting* coldness, coolness, iciness, glaciality, frigidity, hostility, unfriendliness.

frosty adj **1** *a frosty morning* freezing, frozen, rimy, frigid, glacial, arctic, icy, wintry, bitterly cold, bitter, cold; *inf* nippy. **2** *a frosty welcome* cold, cool, icy, glacial, frigid, unfriendly, unwelcoming, unenthusiastic.

froth n *a froth on the liquid* foam, spume, fizz, effervescence, scum, lather; head; bubbles, suds.

froth v *beer frothing in the glass|soap suds frothing* foam, spume, cream, bubble, fizz, effervesce, lather.

frothy adj **1** *frothy lemonade* foaming, foamy, foam-like, spumy, spumous, spumescent, bubbling, bubbly, fizzy, effervescent, sparkling. **2** *a frothy dress* frilly, flouncy, insubstantial. **3** *a frothy novel* light, lightweight, insubstantial, lacking substance, trivial, trifling, petty, paltry, insignificant, worthless, trite, hackneyed.

frown v **1** *the teacher frowning at the pupils* scowl, glower, glare, lower, look daggers at, give black looks to; *inf* give a dirty look to. **2** *frowning in thought* knit one's brows. **3** *the club frowned at/on scruffy clothes* disapprove of, show/indicate disapproval of, view with dislike/disfavour, dislike, discourage, look askance at, not take kindly to, not think much of, take a dim view of.

frozen adj **1** *frozen ground* ice-covered, icy, icebound, frosted, hard, hard as iron. **2** *frozen conditions* frosty, icy, bitterly cold, glacial, frigid, arctic, Siberian, polar. **3** *children are frozen* freezing, very cold, chilled, chilled to the bone/marrow, numb with cold, shivering; *inf* frozen to death.

frugal adj **1** *a frugal old man* thrifty, sparing, economical, saving, careful, prudent, provident, unwasteful, abstemious, scrimping, niggardly, cheese-paring, penny-pinching, miserly, parsimonious, stingy. **2** *a frugal amount of food* meagre, scanty, paltry, insufficient.

fruitful adj **1** *fruitful trees* fruit-bearing, fructiferous, fruiting. **2** *a fruitful family* fertile, fecund, potent, fructuous, generative, progenitive. **3** *fruitful discussions* useful, worthwhile, productive, well-spent, prof-

itable, advantageous, beneficial, rewarding, gainful, successful, effective.

fruition n fulfilment, realization, materialization, actualization, achievement, attainment, success, completion, consummation, perfection, maturity, maturation, ripening.

fruitless adj futile, vain, in vain, useless, abortive, to no avail, worthless, pointless, to no effect, idle, ineffectual, ineffective, inefficacious, unproductive, unrewarding, profitless, unsuccessful, unavailing.

fruits npl *the fruits of our labours* results, consequences, effects, advantages; outcome, upshot, benefit, profit, reward.

fruity adj **1** *a fruity chuckle* rich, deep, resonant, full. **2** *a fruity story* bawdy, blue, smutty, racy, risqué, juicy, indecent, indelicate, vulgar, coarse, off-colour, suggestive, titillating, salacious, sexy; *inf* near the knuckle, spicy.

frustrate v **1** *frustrate their attempts* defeat, thwart, check, block, counter, foil, baulk, disappoint, forestall, baffle, stymie, stop, spoil, cripple, nullify, obstruct, impede, hamper, hinder, circumvent. **2** *lack of success frustrated him* discourage, dishearten, dispirit, depress, dissatisfy, make discontented, anger, annoy, vex, irk, irritate, embitter.

frustration n **1** *the frustration of their plans* defeat, lack of success, non-success, non fulfilment, thwarting, foiling, baulking, forestalling, hampering, circumvention. *see* FRUSTRATE 1. **2** *full of frustration at their failure* dissatisfaction, disappointment, discontentment, anger, annoyance, irritation, vexation, resentment, bitterness.

fuddled adj **1** *a fuddled mind* confused, muddled, bewildered, muzzy, stupefied, addled; *inf* woozy, woolly-minded. **2** *fuddled people from the pub* drunk, inebriated, intoxicated, tipsy, tight; *inf* legless, loaded, bevied. *see* DRUNK.

fuddy-duddy n old fogy, museum piece, conservative; *inf* stick-in-the-mud, square, stuffed shirt.

fudge v **1** *fudge the issue* evade, dodge, skirt, shift ground about, avoid. **2** *fudge the accounts* falsify, fake; *inf* cook. **3** *fudge his way through the speech* waffle, equivocate, hedge, hem and haw, shuffle.

fuel n **1** *fuel for the heating/car* heat/power source; coal, wood, oil, petrol, diesel oil, paraffin, kerosene. **2** *need fuel on cold mornings* nourishment, food, sustenance, fodder. **3** *his answer was fuel to her anger* incitement, provocation, goading, stimulus, incentive, encouragement, ammunition.

fuel v **1** *fuel the steam engine* supply with fuel, fire, stoke up, charge, power. **2** *fuel her anger* fan, inflame, incite, provoke, goad, stimulate, encourage.

fugitive n escapee, runaway, deserter, refugee.

fugitive adj **1** *a fugitive prisoner* escaping, runaway, fleeing, deserting; *inf* AWOL, on the run. **2** *fugitive happiness* transient, transitory, fleeting, ephemeral, evanescent, fugacious, flitting, momentary, short-lived, short, brief, passing, impermanent.

fulfil v **1** *fulfil his task* carry out, accomplish, achieve, execute, perform, discharge, implement, complete, bring to completion, finish, conclude, effect, effectuate, perfect. **2** *fulfil his desire* satisfy, realize, attain, consummate. **3** *fulfil the job requirements* fill, answer, meet, obey, comply with, satisfy, conform to, observe.

fulfilled adj *she doesn't feel fulfilled* satisfied, content, happy.

full adj **1** *the cup is full* filled, filled up, filled to the brim, brimful, brimming, filled to capacity. **2** *the shop was full* crowded, packed, crammed, solid with people, chock-a-block, chock-full; *inf* jam-packed, wall-to-wall. **3** *the seats/rooms are full* occupied, taken, in use. **4** *full supermarket shelves* filled, loaded, well-stocked. **5** *children feeling full* replete, satisfied, sated, gorged, glutted, cloyed. **6** *a full list of names* complete, entire, whole, comprehensive, thorough, exhaustive, detailed, all-inclusive, all-encompassing, extensive, unabridged. **7** *a full programme of events | give full details* abundant, plentiful, copious, ample, sufficient, broad-ranging, satisfying, complete. **8** *full of energy/smiles/mistakes* filled with, abounding in, brimful of. **9** *a full figure* well-rounded, rounded, plump, buxom, shapely, curvaceous, voluptuous; *inf* busty. **10** *a full skirt* loose-fitting, baggy, voluminous, capacious. **11** *a full voice* rich, deep, resonant, loud, strong; *inf* fruity.

full n **in full** *give me the account in full* in its entirety, in total, *in toto*, without omission/abridgement. **to the full** *live life to the full* fully, thoroughly, completely, to the utmost, to capacity.

full adv *hit him full in the face* directly, right, straight, squarely; *inf* smack, smack bang.

full-grown adj fully grown, mature, adult, grown-up, of age, fully developed, fully fledged, in full bloom, ripe, in one's prime.

fullness n **1** *the fullness of the list* completeness, comprehensiveness, thoroughness, exhaustiveness, extensiveness. *see* FULL adj

6. **2** *the fullness of her figure* roundedness, plumpness, buxomness, shapeliness, curvaceousness. *see* FULL adj **9**. **3** *the fullness of his voice* richness, resonance, loudness, strength; *inf* fruitiness. **4** *the doctors detected a fullness in her stomach* swelling, enlargement, distension, dilation, tumescence. **in the fullness of time** in due course, when the time is ripe, eventually.

full-scale adj **1** *a full-scale search/reorganization* thorough, comprehensive, extensive, exhaustive, all-out, all-encompassing, all-inclusive, thoroughgoing, wide-ranging, sweeping, major, in-depth. **2** *a full-scale drawing* full-size, unreduced.

fully adv **1** *fully covered by the insurance* completely, entirely, wholly, totally, thoroughly, in all respects, utterly. **2** *fully staffed* completely, amply, sufficiently, satisfactorily, enough. **3** *he's fully 80 years old* quite, at least, without exaggeration.

fully-fledged adj mature, fully developed, trained, qualified, proficient, experienced, time-served.

fulminate v **1** *fulminate against the government* protest against, rail against, declaim against, inveigh against, denounce, decry, disparage, condemn, criticize, censure, arraign. **2** *chemicals fulminating* explode, detonate, blow up.

fulmination n *his fulmination against the government* denunciation, violent protest, railing, decrying, condemnation, invective, tirade, diatribe, philippic, obloquy.

fulsome adj *fulsome compliments* excessive, extravagant, overdone, immoderate, inordinate, overappreciative, insincere, ingratiating, fawning, sycophantic, adulatory, cloying, nauseating, sickening, saccharine, unctuous; *inf* over-the-top, OTT, smarmy.

fumble v **1** *fumble for his keys* grope, feel about, search blindly, scrabble around. **2** *fumble around in the dark* feel/grope one's way, stumble, blunder, flounder. **3** *fumble her speech* bungle, botch, mismanage, mishandle, muff, spoil; *inf* make a mess/hash of, fluff, screw up, foul up; *Amer inf* flub. **4** *fumble a ball* fail to catch, miss, drop, mishandle, misfield.

fume v *the teacher is fuming* be enraged, seethe, boil, be livid, rage, rant and rave, be furious, be incensed, flare up; *inf* be up in arms, get hot under the collar, fly off the handle, be at boiling point, foam at the mouth, get all steamed up, raise the roof, flip one's lid, blow one's top.

fumes npl **1** *fumes from the exhaust* vapour, gas, smoke, exhalation, exhaust, pollution.

2 *the petrol fumes sickened her* smell, stink, reek, stench.

fumigate v disinfect, purify, sterilize, sanitize, sanitate, cleanse, clean out.

fun n **1** *what do you do for fun?* amusement, entertainment, relaxation, recreation, enjoyment, pleasure, diversion, distraction, play, good time, jollification, junketing, merrymaking; *inf* living it up. **2** *she's full of fun* merriment, gaiety, mirth, laughter, hilarity, glee, gladness, cheerfulness, joy, jollity, zest; high spirits. **3** *a figure of fun* joking, jest, teasing, banter, badinage. **fun and games** play, playfulness, horseplay, clowning/fooling around, tomfoolery, buffoonery; *inf* skylarking. **in fun** jokingly, as a joke, in jest, to tease, teasingly, for a laugh. **make fun of** ridicule, rag, deride, mock, scoff at, sneer at, taunt, jeer at, parody, lampoon; *inf* rib, send up, take off.

fun adj **1** *a fun time* amusing, entertaining, enjoyable, diverting, pleasurable. **2** *a fun person* amusing, witty, entertaining, lively, convivial.

function n **1** *his function in the firm* role, capacity, responsibility, duty, task, chore, job, post, situation, office, occupation, employment, business, charge, concern, province, part, activity, operation, line, mission, *raison d'être*; *inf* thing, bag, line of country. **2** *what is that machine's function?* use, purpose, task. **3** *invited to a function* social event/occasion, affair, gathering, reception, party; *inf* do, beanfeast.

function v **1** *is the machine functioning?* work, go, run, be in working/running order, operate. **2** *he functions as her butler* | *the sofa functions as a bed* serve, act, perform, operate, officiate, do duty, have/do the job of, play the role of, act the part of.

functional adj **1** *functional clothes* practical, useful, serviceable, utilitarian, utility, working, work-a-day, hard-wearing. **2** *is the machine functional?* working, in working order, going, running, operative, in operation, in commission.

functionary n official, office-bearer, officeholder, public servant, civil servant, bureaucrat, red tapist.

fund n **1** *the church preservation fund* reserve, pool, collection, kitty, endowment, foundation, grant, investment, capital; savings. **2** *a fund of knowledge* stock, store, accumulation, mass, mine, reservoir, supply, storehouse, treasury, treasure-house, hoard, repository.

fund v *fund the project* finance, back, pay for, capitalize, provide finance/capital for, subsidize, stake, endow, support, float.

fundamental adj *fundamental principles* basic, basal, foundational, rudimentary, elemental, underlying, primary, cardinal, initial, original, prime, first, principal, chief, key, central, structural, organic, constitutional, inherent, intrinsic, vital, essential, important, indispensable, necessary.

fundamentally adj *fundamentally he is an honest man* basically, at heart, at bottom, deep down, essentially, intrinsically.

fundamentals npl *get down to fundamentals* basics, first/basic principles, essentials, rudiments; crux, crux of the matter, *sine qua non*; *inf* nuts and bolts, nitty-gritty.

funds npl *totally out of funds* money, ready money, cash, hard cash, capital, the wherewithal; means, assets, resources, savings; *inf* dough, bread, the ready, folding money.

funeral n burial, burying, interment, inhumation, entombment, cremation; funeral rites, obsequies, exequies.

funereal adj **1** *funereal colours* black, dark, drab. **2** *a funereal atmosphere* | *wearing a funereal expression* gloomy, dismal, dreary, depressing, sombre, grave, solemn, sad, melancholy, lugubrious.

fungus n parasite, saprophyte; mushroom, toadstool, mould, mildew, rust.

funny adj **1** *a funny story/situation* amusing, comic, comical, humorous, hilarious, entertaining, diverting, laughable, hysterical, riotous, side-splitting, droll, absurd, rich, ridiculous, ludicrous, risible, farcical, silly, slapstick; *inf* killing. **2** *he can be very funny* amusing, humorous, entertaining, droll, witty, waggish, facetious, jolly, jocular. **3** *what a funny hat* strange, peculiar, odd, queer, weird, bizarre, curious. **4** *he's a funny character* strange, peculiar, odd, mysterious, suspicious, dubious; *inf* shady.

furious adj **1** *furious parents* enraged, raging, infuriated, fuming, boiling, incensed, inflamed, frenzied, very angry, indignant, mad, raving mad, maddened, wrathful, beside oneself, in high dudgeon; *inf* livid, hot under the collar, up in arms, foaming at the mouth. **2** *a furious storm/struggle* violent, fierce, wild, intense, vehement, unrestrained, tumultuous, turbulent, tempestuous, stormy, boisterous.

furnish v **1** *furnish a room* provide with furniture, fit out, rig out, appoint, outfit. **2** *furnish you with what you require* supply, equip, provide, provision, give, grant, present, offer, bestow, endow.

furniture n furnishings, house fittings, appointments, effects, movables, chattels; *inf* stuff, things.

furore n **1** *a furore when they found out* commotion, uproar, disturbance, hullabaloo, turmoil, tempest, tumult, brouhaha, stir, excitement, to-do, outburst, outcry. **2** *in a furore* rage, madness, frenzy, fit. **3** *a furore for old films* craze, enthusiasm, mania, fad, obsession.

furrow n **1** groove, trench, channel, rut, trough, hollow, ditch, seam. **2** *furrows on her brow/skin* crease, line, wrinkle, corrugation, crinkle, crow's foot.

further adj **1** *further supplies* additional, more, extra, supplementary, other, new, fresh. **2** *the further boat is almost out of sight* more distant/advanced/remote, remoter, further away/off, farther.

further adv **1** *further, you will go now* furthermore, moreover, what's more, also, besides, additionally, as well, to boot, on top of that, over and above that, by the same token. **2** *she stopped and would come no further* to a more advanced point, more forward/onward, farther.

further v *further our plans* advance, forward, facilitate, aid, assist, help, lend a hand to, abet, expedite, hasten, speed up, push, give a push to, promote, back, contribute to, encourage, foster, champion.

furtherance n **1** *furtherance in the firm* advancement, promotion, elevation, preferment; *inf* step-up. **2** *the furtherance of our plans* furthering, advancement, forwarding, facilitating, aiding, assisting, pushing, promotion, backing. *see* FURTHER v.

furthermore adv moreover, what's more, also, besides, additionally, as well, further. *see* FURTHER adv 1.

furthest adj furthest away, farthest, furthermost, most distant, most remote, outermost, outmost, extreme, uttermost, ultimate.

furtive adj secret, secretive, stealthy, surreptitious, sneaky, sneaking, skulking, slinking, clandestine, hidden, covert, cloaked, conspiratorial, sly, underhand, under the table, wily.

fury n **1** *the fury of the parents* great anger, rage, ire, wrath, madness, passion, frenzy, furore. **2** *the fury of the storm* fierceness, ferocity, violence, turbulence, tempestuousness, severity, intensity, vehemence, force, great force, power, potency. **3** *she is a real fury* virago, hell-cat, termagant, spitfire, vixen, shrew, hag.

fuse v **1** *fuse the ingredients* combine, amalgamate, put together, unite, blend, intermix, intermingle, merge, meld, coalesce, compound, agglutinate, join, integrate,

weld, solder. **2** *fuse the solid* melt, melt down, smelt, dissolve, liquefy.

fuss n **1** *the fuss over the preparations* fluster, flurry, bustle, to-do, ado, agitation, excitement, bother, stir, commotion, confusion, tumult, uproar, upset, worry, over-anxiety, pother, palaver, storm in a teacup, much ado about nothing; *inf* flap, tizzy, stew. **2** *a fuss in the pub last night* row, altercation, squabble, argument, quarrel, dispute, upset; trouble, bother, unrest; *inf* dust-up, barney, hassle. **3** *make a fuss about the service* complaint, objection; *inf* grouse, gripe.

fuss v **1** *organizers fussing around the place | fuss over details* bustle, bustle about, dash about, rush about, tear around, buzz around; worry, be agitated/worried, make a big thing out of nothing, make a mountain out of a molehill; *inf* get worked up over nothing, be in a flap, flap, be in a tizzy, be in a stew. **2** *fuss about the service* kick up a fuss, make a fuss, complain, raise an objection; *inf* grouse, gripe. **3** *the baby is fussing* be upset, fret, cry, be cross, be crabbed; *inf* take on. **4** *fuss their mother* irritate, annoy, vex, bother, pester, disturb, nag.

fussy adj **1** *a fussy eater* particular, over-particular, finicky, pernickety, faddish, faddy, fastidious, hard to please, difficult, exacting, demanding, discriminating, selective, dainty; *inf* choosy, picky, nit-picking. **2** *fussy rooms/paintings* busy, cluttered, overdecorated, over-embellished, over-elaborate, over-ornate, rococo.

futile adj **1** *a futile search* vain, in vain, to no avail, unavailing, useless, ineffectual, ineffective, inefficacious, unsuccessful, fruitless, abortive, unproductive, impotent, barren, unprofitable, hollow. **2** *a futile statement* trivial, unimportant, petty, trifling, valueless, worthless, inconsequential, idle.

futility n **1** *the futility of the search* uselessness, ineffectiveness, fruitlessness, abortiveness. *see* FUTILE 1. **2** *the futility of the statement* triviality, unimportance, pettiness, worthlessness. *see* FUTILE 2.

future n **1** *things might improve in the future* time to come, time ahead, hereafter; coming times. **2** *no future in the firm* prospects, expectations; anticipation, outlook, likely success/advancement/improvement.

fuzzy adj **1** *masses of fuzzy hair | a fuzzy-skinned peach* frizzy, downy, down-covered, woolly, linty, napped. **2** *everything's gone all fuzzy* out of focus, unfocused, blurred, blurry, bleary, misty, indistinct, unclear, distorted, ill-defined, indefinite. **3** *fuzzy recollection* confused, muddled, fuddled, befuddled, foggy, misty, shadowy, blurred.

Gg

gabble v *old women gabbling away* jabber, babble, chatter, chitter-chatter, prattle, rattle, blabber, gaggle, gibber, cackle, drivel, blab, gossip, splutter; *inf* blah, blah-blah.

gabble n *tired of their gabble* jabbering, babbling, chattering, gibbering, babble, chatter, gibberish, drivel, gossip, twaddle; *inf* flannel, waffle, blah. *see* GABBLE v.

gad v *he's always gadding about* gallivant, roam, wander, travel around, rove, ramble, run around, range, flit about, meander, stray; *inf* traipse; *Scots* stravaig.

gadabout n gallivanter, rambler, rover, wanderer, traveller, nomad, globe-trotter.

gadget n appliance, apparatus, instrument, implement, tool, contrivance, device, mechanism, invention, thing; *inf* contraption, widget, gismo.

gaffe n mistake, blunder, slip, indiscretion, solecism, *faux pas*, gaucherie; *inf* clanger, bloomer, howler, boob, boo-boo.

gaffer n **1** *old gaffers sitting in the square* old man, old fellow; *inf* old bloke, old boy, old guy, grandad, old geezer; *Amer* old-timer. **2** *he's the gaffer of the factory* foreman, ganger, overseer, supervisor, manager, superintendent; *inf* boss; *Amer* honcho.

gag n *his gags amused her* joke, jest, witticism, quip, funny remark, hoax, prank; *inf* wisecrack, crack.

gag v **1** *gag her mouth* put a gag on, stop up, block, plug, clog, stifle, smother, muffle. **2** *the press have been gagged* silence, muzzle, curb, check, restrain, suppress, repress. **3** *he gagged when he saw the corpse* choke, retch, gasp, struggle for breath, convulse, almost vomit, keck, heave.

gaiety n **1** *appreciating the gaiety of the children* gayness, light-heartedness, cheerfulness, merriment, glee, blitheness, gladness, happiness, high spirits, good spirits, delight, pleasure, joy, joyfulness, joyousness, exuberance, elation, jollity, hilarity, mirth, joviality, liveliness, vivacity, animation, effervescence, buoyancy, sprightliness, exultation, *joie de vivre*. **2** *join in the gaiety of the fair* fun, festivity, merrymaking, revelry, revels, jollification, celebration, gala, frolics. **3** *the gaiety of the dresses* colourfulness, brightness, brilliance, sparkle, glitter, gaudiness, showiness, show, garishness.

gain v **1** *gain an advantage* obtain, get, acquire, procure, secure, attain, build up, achieve, arrive at, come to have, win, capture, net, pick up, reap, gather. **2** *gain experience/weight* get more of, increase in, add on. **3** *gain a wage* earn, bring in, make, get, clear, gross, net, realize, produce. **4** *the police were gaining on the escaped prisoner* catch up with, catch up on, narrow the gap between, get nearer to, close in on, overtake, come up to, approach. **5** *the escaped prisoner was gaining on the police* widen the gap between, get further ahead of, leave behind, draw away from, outdistance, do better than. **6** *the ship gained the shore* reach, arrive at, get to, come to, attain. **gain time** stall, procrastinate, delay, use delaying tactics, temporize, use Fabian tactics, dally, use dilatory tactics; *inf* put on the back burner.

gain n **1** *his gain from the deal was negligible* profit, earnings, income, advantage, benefit, reward, emolument, yield, return, winnings, proceeds, dividend, interest; *inf* pickings. **2** *a gain in experience/weight* more of, increase, augmentation, addition, rise, increment, accretion, accumulation. **3** *their gain against the enemy* advance, advancement, progress, forward movement, headway, improvement, step forward. **4** *show off his latest gains* acquisition, acquirement, achievement.

gainful adj profitable, remunerative, paying, financially rewarding, rewarding, lucrative, money-making, productive, beneficial, advantageous, worthwhile, useful.

gainsay v *there's no gainsaying his honesty* deny, dispute, disagree with, disbelieve, contradict, contravene, challenge, oppose, controvert, disaffirm.

gait n walk, step, stride, pace, tread, manner of walking, bearing, carriage.

gala n *children having a gala* festival, fête, festivities, carnival, pageant, jamboree, party, celebration.

gala adj *a gala occasion* festive, holiday, carnival, celebratory, merry, gay, joyous, joyful, jovial, diverting, entertaining.

spectacular, showy, ceremonial, ceremonious.

galaxy n **1** *look at a galaxy through a telescope* constellation, stars, the heavens, Milky Way. **2** *a galaxy of stars* dazzling assemblage, host, brilliant gathering, illustrious group.

gale n **1** *lost at sea in a gale* storm, tempest, squall, hurricane, tornado, cyclone, typhoon, mistral, sirocco. **2** *gales of laughter* outburst, peal, ring, shriek, shout, roar, scream, howl, fit, eruption.

gall¹ n **1** *have the gall to answer back* impudence, insolence, impertinence, cheek, nerve, face, audacity, brashness, effrontery, temerity, sauciness; *inf* brass, brass neck, sauce, chutzpah. **2** *words full of gall* bitterness, resentment, rancour, acrimony, malice, spite, malignity, venom, malevolence, virulence, sourness, acerbity, asperity, animosity, antipathy, hostility, enmity, bad blood, ill feeling, animus, bile, spleen.

gall² n **1** *a gall on the horse's skin* sore, abrasion, scrape, scratch, graze, canker, ulceration. **2** *the children are a gall to him* source of vexation/irritation/annoyance, vexation, irritation, irritant, annoyance, pest, nuisance, provocation, bother, torment, plague; *inf* botheration, aggravation.

gall² v **1** *gall the skin* abrade, chafe, rub, rub raw, scrape, graze, skin, scratch, excoriate, fret, rasp, bark. **2** *her attitude galls him* vex, irritate, infuriate, irk, annoy, rub up the wrong way, provoke, exasperate, pique, rile, nettle, bother, ruffle, fret, pester, torment, harass, rankle, embitter; *inf* aggravate, peeve.

gallant adj **1** *gallant soldiers* brave, courageous, valiant, valorous, bold, plucky, daring, fearless, intrepid, manly, manful, dashing, heroic, heroical, lion-hearted, stout-hearted, doughty, mettlesome, great-spirited, honourable, noble. **2** *a gallant courtier|gallant to the ladies* chivalrous, gentlemanly, courtly, courteous, mannerly, polite, attentive, gracious, considerate, thoughtful, obliging, deferential. **3** *a gallant ship* fine, great, dignified, stately, noble, splendid, elegant, magnificent, majestic, imposing, glorious, regal, august.

gallant n **1** *the gallants of the court of King Arthur* knight, champion, hero, paladin, valiant, adventurer, cavalier, chevalier, *preux chevalier*. **2** *young gallants at a ball* man about town, man of fashion, man of the world, ladies' man, lady-killer, dandy, fop, beau. **3** *a young lady and her gallant* beau, escort, partner, suitor, wooer, admirer, lover, boyfriend, paramour.

gallantry n **1** *the gallantry of the troops* bravery, braveness, courage, courageousness, valour, boldness, pluck, daring, fearlessness, intrepidity, manliness, heroism, doughtiness. *see* GALLANT adj **1**. **2** *the gallantry of the courtiers* chivalry, chivalrousness, gentlemanliness, courtliness, courteousness, politeness, mannerliness, attentiveness, graciousness, consideration, thoughtfulness. *see* GALLANT adj **2**.

galling adj *a galling experience* vexing, vexatious, irritating, infuriating, irksome, annoying, provoking, exasperating, troublesome, bothering, harassing, rankling, embittering, bitter. *see* GALL² v **2**.

gallivant v gad about, roam, wander, travel around, rove, ramble. *see* GAD.

gallop v **1** *the horse galloped* go at full speed, canter, lope, prance, frisk. **2** *the children galloped home* race, rush, dash, tear, sprint, bolt, fly, run, shoot, dart, hurry, hasten, speed, career, scamper, scurry, scud, zoom.

gallows n gibbet, scaffold.

galore adv *have books/food/friends galore* in abundance, in profusion, in great quantity, in plenty, aplenty, in huge numbers, to spare, everywhere, all over the place.

galvanize v *galvanize them into action* electrify, shock, startle, jolt, stir, excite, rouse, arouse, awaken, spur, prod, urge, stimulate, give a stimulus to, invigorate, fire, animate, vitalize, energize, exhilarate, thrill, dynamize, inspire.

gambit n stratagem, manoeuvre, machination, move, play, ruse, trick, ploy, artifice.

gamble v **1** *he loves to gamble* bet, wager, place a bet, lay a wager/bet, back the horses, game, stake, try one's luck on the horses; *inf* punt, play the ponies, have a flutter. **2** *he gambled when he invested in that firm* take a chance, take a risk, take a leap in the dark, leave things to chance, speculate, venture, buy a pig in a poke; *inf* stick one's neck out, go out on a limb; *Amer* take a flier. **3** *gamble on his parents being absent* act in the hope that, trust that, chance that, take a chance that, bank on.

gamble n **1** *have a gamble on the horses* bet, wager, punt; *inf* flutter. **2** *it was a gamble but they decided to go* risk, hazard, chance, lottery, speculation, venture, random shot, leap in the dark, pig in a poke, pot luck, blind bargain.

gambol v frolic, frisk, cavort, caper, cut capers, skip, dance, leap, romp, trip, prance, hop, jump, spring, bounce, rollick, curvet.

game n **1** *children playing a game* pastime, diversion, entertainment, amusement, recreation, play, sport, distraction, frolic, romp, fun, merriment. **2** *we were only playing a game on him* joke, practical joke, prank, jest, trick, hoax; *inf* lark. **3** *there's a game tomorrow* match, contest, tournament, meeting, sports meeting, event, athletic event, round, bout. **4** *he's in the oil game* business, line, occupation, trade, profession, industry, enterprise, activity, calling; *inf* line of country. **5** *what's his game?* scheme, trick, plot, ploy, stratagem, strategy, cunning plan, crafty designs, tactics, artifice, device, manoeuvre. **6** *they went shooting game* wild animals, wild fowl, quarry, prey, big game. **make game of** make fun of, make a fool of, poke fun at, ridicule, deride, make a laughing-stock of, mock, scoff at, jeer at, make sport of, make the butt of one's jokes, taunt; *inf* rib, rag, send up. **play the game** play by the rules, play fair, be a good sport.

game v gamble, bet, wager. *see* GAMBLE V 1.

game adj **1** *who's game enough to knock at her door?* plucky, brave, courageous, valiant, unafraid, fearless, gallant, bold, intrepid, stout-hearted, lion-hearted, dauntless, undaunted, daring, dashing, spirited, unblenching, unflinching. **2** *I'm game to go abroad if you are* willing, favourably inclined, desirous, eager, interested, enthusiastic, ready, prepared, disposed.

gamut n entire range, whole spectrum, complete scale, complete sequence, whole series, full sweep, full compass, entire scope, entire area, full catalogue.

gang n **1** *a gang of people gathered* group, band, crowd, company, gathering, pack, horde, mob, herd. **2** *the young man and his gang* clique, circle, social set, coterie, lot, ring, club; fraternity, sorority; *inf* crew. **3** *gang of labourers/roadmen* squad, team, troop, shift, detachment, posse, troupe.

gangling, gangly adj *gangling lad of sixteen* lanky, rangy, spindly, spindling, loosely built, loosely jointed, stringy, skinny, angular, awkward, awkwardly tall.

gangster n gang-member, racketeer, bandit, brigand, robber, ruffian, thug, hoodlum, tough, desperado, Mafioso, terrorist; *inf* crook; *Amer inf* mobster, hood.

gap n **1** *a gap in the wall* opening, cavity, hole, aperture, space, breach, orifice, break, fracture, rift, rent, fissure, cleft, chink, crack, crevice, cranny, divide, discontinuity, interstice. **2** *gaps in the musical programme for refreshment* pause, intermission, interval, interlude, break; *Amer* recess. **3** *gaps in his account* omission, blank, lacuna, hiatus, void, vacuity. **4** *the gap between the old and the young* breach, difference, divergence, disparity.

gape v **1** *gaping at the procession* stare, stare in wonder, goggle, gaze, ogle; *inf* gawk, rubberneck. **2** *the chasm gaped before them* open wide, become open wide, open up, yawn, part, crack, split.

garb n **1** *admire the fine garb* clothes, clothing, garments, dress, attire, apparel, costume, outfit, wear, habit, uniform, array, habiliment, vestments, livery, trappings; *inf* gear, get-up, togs, rig-out, duds. **2** *dressed in the garb of a soldier* clothes, attire, uniform, kit, style, fashion, look. **3** *wearing the garb of sanity* outward appearance, appearance, guise, outward form, exterior, aspect, semblance, look.

garb v *garbed in black* clothe, dress, attire, apparel, array, robe, cover, outfit, fit, rig out, kit out.

garbage n **1** *put the garbage out* waste material, waste, domestic rubbish, rubbish, refuse, debris, litter, junk, filth, discarded matter; swill, detritus, scraps, scourings, leftovers, remains, slops; *inf* muck; *Amer* trash. **2** *talking a lot of garbage* nonsense, rubbish, twaddle, drivel, foolishness, balderdash; *inf* hogwash, poppycock, rot, tommy-rot, tosh, bosh, piffle.

garble v **1** *the child accidentally garbled the message* mix up, get mixed up, jumble, confuse. **2** *the enemy deliberately garbled the message* change around, distort, twist, twist around, warp, slant, mutilate, tamper with, doctor, falsify, pervert, corrupt, adulterate, misstate, misquote, misreport, misrender, misrepresent, mistranslate, misinterpret, misunderstand.

gargantuan adj extremely big/large, gigantic, giant, enormous, monstrous, huge, colossal, vast, immense, tremendous, massive, hulking, towering, mammoth, prodigious, elephantine, mountainous, monumental, titanic, Brobdingnagian; *inf* whopping.

garish adj *garish colours* | *wearing a garish shirt* flashy, loud, showy, gaudy, glaring, flaunting, bold-coloured, glittering, tinselly, brassy, tawdry, raffish, tasteless, in bad taste, vulgar, meretricious, cheap, Brummagem; *inf* flash.

garland n *wear a garland of flowers* wreath, festoon, lei, loop of flowers, laurel, laurels, bays, coronet, crown, coronal, chaplet, fillet, headband.

garland v *garland in flowers* wreathe, festoon, adorn, decorate, deck, crown.

garment n **1** *wearing a white garment* piece of clothing, article of clothing, item of dress, cover, covering. **2** *wearing strange garments* clothes, clothing, dress, attire, apparel, costume, outfit, garb. *see* GARB n 1.

garner v *squirrels garnering nuts* gather, collect, accumulate, heap, pile up, amass, assemble, stack up, store, lay up/by, put/stow away, hoard, stockpile, deposit, husband, reserve, save, preserve, save for a rainy day.

garner n granary, store, storehouse, depository, vault, treasure-house.

garnish v *garnish the dish with parsley* decorate, adorn, trim, ornament, embellish, deck, deck out, bedeck, festoon, enhance, grace, beautify, prettify, set off, add the finishing touch to.

garnish n *a parsley garnish for the meat* decoration, adornment, trim, trimming, garniture, ornament, ornamentation, embellishment, enhancement, beautification, finishing touch.

garret n attic, loft, cock-loft, roof-space.

garrison n **1** *the garrison arrived at the fort* armed force, military detachment/unit, platoon, brigade, squadron; troops, militia, soldiers. **2** *the garrison was under siege* fort, fortress, fortification, stronghold, blockhouse, citadel, camp, encampment, command post, base, station; barracks.

garrison v **1** *the town was garrisoned by the allied forces* defend, guard, protect, preserve, fortify, man, occupy, supply with troops. **2** *troops garrisoned in the town* station, post, put on duty, assign, position, billet; send in.

garrulity n **1** *the garrulity of the old man* garrulousness, talkativeness, chattiness, loquacity, gift of the gab, long-windedness, volubility, verbosity, prating, prattling; *inf* mouthiness, gabbiness. *see* GARRULOUS 1. **2** *the garrulity of the account* wordiness, long-windedness, verbosity, prolixity, diffuseness, prosiness. *see* GARRULOUS 2.

garrulous adj **1** *a garrulous old man* talkative, chatty, chattering, gossiping, loquacious, voluble, verbose, long-winded, babbling, prattling, prating, blathering, jabbering, gushing, effusive; *inf* mouthy, gabby. **2** *a garrulous account* long-winded, wordy, verbose, rambling, prolix, diffuse, prosy, gossipy, chatty; *inf* windy, gassy.

gash n *a gash in his hand* cut, slash, wound, tear, laceration, gouge, incision, slit, split, rent, nick, cleft.

gash v *gash his hand* cut, slash, wound, tear, lacerate, gouge, incise, slit, split, rend, nick, cleave.

gasp v *gasping as he climbed the hill* pant, puff, pant and puff, puff and blow, blow, catch one's breath, draw in one's breath, gulp, choke, fight for breath, wheeze.

gasp n **1** *she gave a gasp of surprise* exclamation, ejaculation, gulp, drawing-in of breath. **2** *his final gasps* breath, pant, puff, blowing, gulp, choke.

gastric adj stomach, stomachical, abdominal, intestinal, coeliac.

gate n **1** *build a gate* barrier, door, portal; wicket, postern, lich-/lych-gate, five-barred gate. **2** *crowds blocking the gates to the match* gateway, doorway, access, entrance, exit, egress, opening, passage.

gather v **1** *people gathered in the square* come together, collect, assemble, congregate, meet, group, cluster together, crowd, mass, flock together, forgather, convene, muster, converge, accumulate. **2** *gather the school together* call together, summon, get together, assemble, collect, congregate, convene, round up, muster, marshal. **3** *gather stocks of food | gather the facts* get/put together, collect, accumulate, amass, assemble, garner, store, stockpile, heap up, pile up, stack up, hoard; *inf* stash away. **4** *the event gathered a huge audience* attract, draw, draw together/in, pull, pull in, collect, pick up. **5** *we gather that he is dead* understand, be given to understand, believe, be led to believe, hear, learn, infer, draw the inference, deduce, conclude, come to the conclusion, assume, surmise. **6** *gather to one's bosom* embrace, clasp, enfold, hold, hug, cuddle. **7** *gather in the harvest* harvest, collect, pick, pluck, cull, garner, crop, reap, glean. **8** *gather in strength/force* increase, grow, rise, build, expand, enlarge, swell, extend, wax, intensify, deepen, heighten, thicken. **9** *gather the waist of the dress* ruffle, shirr, pleat, pucker, tuck, fold. **10** *the boil has gathered* come to a head, swell up, suppurate, fester.

gathering n **1** *a gathering of people* assembly, assemblage, collection, company, congregation, group, party, band, knot, crowd, flock, throng, mass, mob, horde, meeting, meet, convention, conclave, rally, turn-out, congress, convocation, concourse, muster; *inf* get-together. **2** *his gathering of coins* collection, accumulation, assemblage, aggregation, aggregate, mass, store, stock, stockpile, heap, pile, cluster, agglomeration, conglomeration, concentration. **3** *the gathering of stores/facts* collecting, accumula-

tion, assembly, assembling, garnering. see
GATHER 3. **4** *a gathering on the back of his neck*
boil, abscess, carbuncle, pustule, pimple,
spot, sore, ulcer, tumour; *inf* zit.

gauche adj *a gauche manner/person/remark*
awkward, clumsy, gawky, ungainly, bumbling, lumbering, maladroit, socially inept,
lacking in social graces, inelegant, graceless, unpolished, unsophisticated, uncultured, uncultivated.

gaudy adj *wearing a very gaudy shirt* bold-
coloured, over-bright, garish, loud, glaring,
bright, brilliant, flashy, showy, ostentatious, tawdry, raffish, tasteless, in bad
taste, vulgar, meretricious, cheap, Brummagem; *inf* flash.

gauge v **1** *gauge the thickness of the metal*
measure, calculate, compute, determine,
count, weigh, check, ascertain. **2** *you must
gauge his aptitude* evaluate, appraise, assess,
place a value on, estimate, guess, judge,
adjudge, rate, reckon, determine; *inf*
guesstimate.

gauge n **1** *find a gauge of his abilities* measure, basis, standard, guide, guideline,
touchstone, yardstick, benchmark, criterion, rule, norm, example, model, pattern,
exemplar, sample, test, indicator. **2** *the
gauge of a barrel/gun/wire/railway* extent,
degree, scope, area, size, measure, capacity, magnitude, depth, height, width, thickness, span, bore.

gaunt adj **1** *a gaunt old woman* haggard,
drawn, cadaverous, skeletal, emaciated,
skin-and-bones, skinny, spindly, stalky,
over-thin, spare, bony, angular, lank, lean,
raw-boned, pinched, hollow-cheeked,
starved-looking, scrawny, scraggy, shrivelled, wasted, withered; *inf* looking like
death warmed up. **2** *gaunt landscape* bleak,
barren, bare, desolate, dreary, dismal, forlorn, grim, stern, harsh, forbidding.

gawk v stare, gape, goggle, gaze, ogle; *inf*
rubberneck.

gawky adj *a shy gawky teenager* ungainly,
lanky, clumsy, lumbering, blundering,
gauche, maladroit, oafish, loutish, doltish,
clodhopping, lumpish.

gay adj **1** *feeling gay* merry, jolly, light-
hearted, cheerful, mirthful, jovial, glad,
happy, bright, in good spirits, in high spirits, joyful, elated, exuberant, cock-a-hoop,
animated, lively, sprightly, vivacious, buoyant, effervescent, playful, frolicsome.
2 *have a gay time* merry, festive, amusing,
enjoyable, entertaining, convivial, hilari-
ous. **3** *gay colours | wearing a very gay shirt*
bright, brightly coloured, vivid, brilliant,
richly coloured, many-coloured, multi-

coloured, flamboyant, gaudy. **4** *gay men/
women* homosexual, lesbian, homoerotic;
derog inf bent, queer, camp, poofy, limp-
wristed, butch.

gay n homosexual, lesbian; *derog inf* queer,
poof, homo, dyke.

gaze v *gaze at the scene* stare, look fixedly,
gape, goggle, stand agog, watch in wonder,
ogle, eye, take a good look, contemplate;
inf gawk, rubberneck, give the once-over.

gaze n *fix his gaze on her* stare, fixed look,
intent look, gape.

gazette n newspaper, journal, periodical,
paper, news-sheet, newsletter, organ; *derog*
rag.

gear n **1** *the car's gear* gearwheel, tooth-
wheel, cog, cogwheel. **2** *the steering gear of a
boat* gears, mechanism, machinery, works.
3 *the workman's gear* equipment, apparatus,
tools, kit, implements, tackle, appliances,
contrivances, utensils, supplies, accoutrements, trappings, accessories, paraphernalia; *inf* stuff. **4** *teenagers like modern gear*
clothes, clothing, garments, dress, attire,
apparel, garb, outfit, wear, costume, array,
habit, vestments; *inf* get-up, togs, rig-out,
duds. **5** *their daughter and all her gear*
belongings, things, luggage, baggage, kit,
effects, goods and chattels, chattels, paraphernalia, accoutrements, personal possessions; trappings, impedimenta; *inf* stuff.

gelatinous adj jelly-like, glutinous, viscid,
viscous, gummy, sticky, gluey, mucilaginous, slimy; *inf* gooey.

geld v castrate, neuter, emasculate, asexu-
alize.

gelid adj freezing, frozen, icy, ice-cold, arctic, glacial, polar, frosty, wintry, snowy, bitterly cold, chilly, Siberian, hyperborean,
hyperboreal; *Med* algid.

gem n **1** *a ring set with gems* jewel, precious
stone, semiprecious stone, stone, solitaire,
brilliant, *bijou*. **2** *the gem of his collection of
books* jewel, jewel in the crown, pick,
flower, cream, *crème de la crème*, wonder,
prize, treasure, pearl, masterpiece, *chef-
d'oeuvre*.

genealogy n pedigree, family tree, ancestry, line, lineage, descent, parentage, birth,
derivation, extraction, family, dynasty,
house, race, strain, stock, breed, blood-line,
stemma, stirps, heritage, history, roots.

general adj **1** *the general practice is to apply in
writing* usual, customary, common, ordi-
nary, normal, standard, regular, typical,
conventional, everyday, habitual, run-of-
the-mill. **2** *in general use | the general feeling*
common, extensive, widespread, broad,

wide, accepted, prevalent, prevailing, universal, popular, public, generic. **3** *a general pay-rise/rule* across-the-board, blanket, universal, sweeping, broad, broad-ranging, comprehensive, all-inclusive, encyclopedic, indiscriminate, catholic. **4** *a general store| his general knowledge* mixed, assorted, miscellaneous, variegated, diversified, composite, heterogeneous. **5** *a general account* non-detailed, undetailed, broad, loose, approximate, non-specific, unspecific, vague, ill-defined, indefinite, inexact, imprecise, rough. **6** *a general view* panoramic, sweeping, extended, bird's-eye.

generality n **1** *talking in generalities* generalization, general statement, general principle, non-specific statement, loose/vague statement, indefinite statement, sweeping statement. **2** *a situation not conforming to the generality* general principle/rule/law. **3** *the generality of people are kind* majority, greater part, bulk, mass, body. **4** *the generality of its use* commonness, widespread nature, broadness, prevalence, universality, popularity. *see* GENERAL 2. **5** *the generality of the board* universality, broadness, comprehensiveness, all-inclusiveness, catholicity. *see* GENERAL 3. **6** *the generality of the statement* lack of detail, broadness, looseness, approximation, lack of specification, vagueness, indefiniteness, inexactitude, imprecision, roughness. *see* GENERAL 5.

generally adv **1** *it generally rains there in the spring* in general, usually, as a rule, normally, ordinarily, almost always, customarily, habitually, typically, regularly, for the most part, mainly, by and large, on average, on the whole, in most cases. **2** *not generally known* commonly, widely, extensively, comprehensively, universally. *see* GENERAL 2. **3** *speaking generally* in a general sense, without detail, loosely, approximately, broadly, in non-specific terms. *see* GENERAL 5. **4** *they are generally liked* mostly, for the most part, mainly, in the main, largely, chiefly, predominantly, on the whole.

generate v **1** *generate electricity* bring into being, cause to exist, produce. **2** *generating children* beget, procreate, engender, sire, father, breed, spawn, produce, propagate. **3** *generate argument* cause, give rise to, create, produce, initiate, originate, occasion, sow the seeds of, arouse, whip up, propagate.

generation n **1** *the generation of the human race* begetting, procreation, engendering, genesis, reproduction, siring, propagation. **2** *the generation of ideas* causing, creation, production, initiation, origination, inception, occasioning, propagation. **3** *people of*

the same generation age, age group, peer group. **4** *a generation ago* life span, lifetime. **5** *generations ago* age, era, epoch, times, days.

generic adj **1** *alcoholic drink, a generic name for beer, wines and spirits* non-specific, general, common, collective, inclusive, all-inclusive, all-encompassing, comprehensive, blanket, sweeping, universal. **2** *goods having a trademark rather than generic goods* non-exclusive, non-trademarked, non-registered.

generosity n **1** *the generosity of our host* liberalness, liberality, kindness, magnanimity, benevolence, beneficence, bounteousness, bounty, munificence, hospitality, charitableness, charity, open-handedness, lavishness. *see* GENEROUS 1. **2** *the generosity of his spirit* nobility, nobleness, magnanimity, loftiness, high-mindedness, honourableness, honour, goodness, unselfishness, altruism, lack of prejudice, disinterest.

generous adj **1** *generous with money | a generous host* liberal, kind, magnanimous, benevolent, beneficent, bountiful, bounteous, munificent, hospitable, charitable, open-handed, lavish, ungrudging, unstinting, free-handed, princely. **2** *a generous spirit* noble, magnanimous, lofty, high-minded, honourable, good, unselfish, altruistic, unprejudiced, disinterested. **3** *a generous supply of cakes* liberal, abundant, plentiful, lavish, ample, copious, rich, superabundant, overflowing.

genesis n beginning, commencement, start, outset, birth, origin, source, root, creation, engendering, inception, generation, propagation.

genial adj *genial person/manner/smile* amiable, affable, good-humoured, good-natured, warm, warm-natured, pleasant, agreeable, cordial, well-disposed, amenable, cheerful, cheery, friendly, congenial, amicable, sociable, convivial, kind, kindly, benign, happy, sunny, jovial, easygoing, sympathetic.

geniality n amiability, affability, good humour, warmth, pleasantness, agreeableness, cordiality, cheerfulness, cheeriness, friendliness, congeniality, amicableness, sociability, conviviality, kindness, happiness, joviality.

genius n **1** *the boy is a genius* brilliant person, virtuoso, prodigy, master, mastermind, master-hand, maestro, mental giant, gifted child, intellectual, intellect, expert, adept; *inf* brains, Einstein. **2** *a person of genius* brilliance, great intelligence/intellect, remarkable cleverness, brains, fine mind, creative power. **3** *a genius for carpentry/cooking* gift, talent, flair, bent, turn, knack, aptitude, forte, faculty, ability, capability, capacity, endowment, propensity, inclination.

genre n genus, species, kind, sort, type, variety, style.

genteel adj **1** *living in genteel poverty* well-born, aristocratic, noble, blue-blooded, patrician, well-bred, respectable, refined, ladylike, gentlemanly. **2** *genteel behaviour* polite, well-mannered, mannerly, courteous, civil, decorous, gracious, courtly, polished, cultivated, stylish, elegant. **3** *the old lady is very genteel* over-polite, mannered, with affected manners, affected, exaggeratedly well-mannered, affectedly refined, ultra-refined.

gentility n **1** *proud of her gentility* nobility, noble birth, blue blood, good breeding, respectability, refinement, ladylikeness, gentlemanliness. **2** *the gentility of their behaviour* politeness, good manners, mannerliness, courteousness, civility, decorum, propriety, graciousness, courtliness, polish, cultivation, stylishness, elegance. **3** *the gentility of the old lady* over-politeness, affectation, ultra-refinement.

gentle adj **1** *a gentle person* kind, kindly, tender, benign, humane, lenient, merciful, clement, compassionate, tender-hearted, sweet-tempered, placid, serene, mild, soft, quiet, still, tranquil, peaceful, pacific, reposeful, meek, dove-like. **2** *a gentle wind* mild, moderate, light, temperate, balmy, soft, zephyr-like. **3** *her gentle touches* soft, light, smooth, soothing. **4** *a gentle animal* tame, placid, docile, biddable, manageable, tractable, meek, easily handled, trained, schooled, broken. **5** *a gentle slope* gradual, slight, easy, imperceptible. **6** *of gentle birth* genteel, aristocratic, noble, well-born, well-bred, blue-blooded, patrician, upper-class, high-born, respectable, refined, cultured, elegant, polished, polite, ladylike, gentlemanly.

gentlemanly adj gentlemanlike, mannerly, well-mannered, well-bred, well-behaved, civil, courteous, polite, chivalrous, considerate, obliging, accommodating, honourable, gallant, noble, cultivated, cultured, civilized, polished, refined, suave, urbane.

genuine adj **1** *a genuine diamond* real, authentic, true, pure, actual, bona fide, veritable, sound, sterling, pukka, legitimate, lawful, legal, valid, non-counterfeit, non-fake, original, unadulterated, unal-

loyed; *inf* the real McCoy, kosher, honest-to-goodness. **2** *she's a very genuine person* sincere, truthful, honest, frank, candid, open, undeceitful, natural, unaffected, artless, ingenuous; *inf* up-front.

genus n **1** *a botanical genus* subdivision, subfamily. **2** *a genus of table* kind, sort, type, variety, class, species, category, genre.

germ n **1** *illness caused by a germ* microbe, micro-organism, bacillus, bacterium, virus; *inf* bug. **2** *the germ of an idea* beginning, start, commencement, inception, seed, embryo, bud, root, rudiment, origin, source, fountain, fountain head. **3** *a fertilized germ* egg, ovum, ovule, embryo, nucleus, seed, bud.

germane adj relevant, pertinent, material, applicable, related, connected, akin, allied, analogous, a propos, apposite, appropriate, apt, fitting, suited, felicitous, proper, to the point, to the purpose.

germinate v **1** *plants germinating* sprout, burgeon, bud, develop, grow, shoot, shoot up, spring up, swell, vegetate, pullulate. **2** *an idea germinating in his mind* originate, grow, begin, start, commence, take root, develop.

gestation n development, incubation, maturation, ripening, pregnancy, gravidity, parturiency.

gesticulate v gesture, make a sign, sign, signal, motion, wave, indicate.

gesture n **1** *make a gesture for them to sit down* sign, signal, motion, motioning, wave, indication, gesticulation. **2** *a political/ friendly gesture* action, deed, act.

gesture v gesticulate, make a sign, signal, motion, wave, indicate.

get v **1** *get a new book | where did you get that hat from?* acquire, obtain, come by, come into possession of, procure, secure, buy, purchase. **2** *get a letter from her father* receive, be sent, be given. **3** *go and get that book | she got her hat from the hall* go for, fetch, bring, collect, carry, transport, convey. **4** *get what you want* gain, acquire, achieve, attain, reach, win, find; *inf* bag. **5** *get £200 per week* earn, be paid, bring in, make, clear, gross, net, pocket; *inf* pull in, take home. **6** *the police got the thief* capture, seize, grab, lay hold of, grasp, collar, take captive, arrest, apprehend, take, trap, entrap; *inf* nab, bag. **7** *get flu/measles* catch, become infected by, contract, be smitten by, come/go down with, be afflicted by, take. **8** *try to get him on the phone/radio* telephone, call, phone, ring, radio, reach, communicate with, contact, get in touch with.

9 *I didn't get what he said* hear, catch, take in, perceive. **10** *don't you get what he means?* understand, grasp, comprehend, see, fathom, follow, work out, apprehend, make head or tail of; *inf* catch on, get the hang of. **11** *we got home/there early* arrive, reach, come; *inf* make it. **12** *we got her to go* persuade, induce, coax, wheedle into, talk into, prevail upon, influence, sway, convince, win over. **13** *get to see the new film* manage, succeed, fix, arrange, organize, contrive. **14** *get fat/wet/old* become, grow, come to be, turn, turn into, wax. **15** *get a meal* prepare, make preparations for, get ready, cook; *Amer inf* fix. **16** *that music gets me* affect, have an effect on, move, touch, touch to the quick, stir, arouse, stimulate, excite, grip, impress, leave an impression on; *inf* send, turn on. **17** *I'll get him for that* avenge oneself on, take vengeance on, get even with, pay someone back, return like for like, give tit for tat, settle the score with, demand an eye for an eye and a tooth for a tooth; *inf* get back at, get one's own back on. **18** *you've got me there, I don't know* baffle, puzzle, stump, mystify, confound, nonplus. **19** *she really gets me | her nagging is beginning to get to me* irritate, get on someone's nerves, annoy, vex, provoke, anger, exasperate, infuriate, rile, get someone's back up, rub someone up the wrong way, upset, bother, nettle, pique; *inf* bug, get someone's goat. **get about** *can he get about yet?* move about, move around, travel.

get across *get across the message* communicate, get over, put over, make understood/clear, impart, convey, transmit. **get ahead** *young man getting ahead* make good, do well, succeed, be successful, progress, advance, prosper, flourish, rise in the world; *inf* go places, get somewhere. **get along 1** *I don't get along with his mother* get on, be on friendly terms, be friendly, be in harmony, be compatible, agree, see eye to eye; *inf* hit it off. **2** *how are you getting along?* get on, fare, manage, progress, advance, cope; *inf* get by, make out. **get around 1** *get around his objections* circumvent, bypass, outmanoeuvre, outwit; *inf* outsmart. **2** *get around his father* persuade, induce, prevail upon, talk round, wheedle, coax, win over, convert, sway. **3** *she certainly gets around* travel, visit, circulate, socialize. **get at 1** *always getting at the pupil* pick on, find fault with, carp, criticize, nag, taunt. **2** *what are you getting at?* suggest, hint, imply, intend, lead up to, mean. **3** *the jockey was got at* bribe, buy off, influence, corrupt, suborn. **get away** *the prisoners got away* escape, make good one's escape, flee, break free, break out, decamp, depart. **get**

back 1 *get back at dawn* return, come home, come back, arrive home, arrive back. **2** *get back her lost gloves* recover, retrieve, regain, repossess, recoup. **3** *get back at his torturer* take vengeance on, avenge oneself on, get even with, get. *see* GET 17. **get by** *get by on little money* cope, manage, subsist, survive, exist, fare, get along, contrive to get along, make both ends meet, keep the wolf from the door; *inf* keep one's head above water, make out. **get off** *get off the bus* alight from, climb off, dismount from, leave; descend from, disembark, exit. **get on 1** *get on the bus* board, climb on; mount, ascend, embark. **2** *how are you getting on?* get along, fare, manage, cope; *inf* make out. *see* GET, GET ALONG 2. **3** *husband and wife do not get on* get along, be on friendly terms, be in harmony. *see* GET, GET ALONG 1. **get out 1** *let's get out now* leave, depart, go away, be off, withdraw; *inf* vamoose, clear out. **2** *prisoners getting out* escape, break free, break out, free oneself, extricate oneself, abscond, decamp. **3** *the news has got out* be made public, become known, be revealed, be publicized, be disclosed, leak, be leaked, spread, circulate, be noised abroad. **get out of** *get out of digging the garden* avoid, dodge, evade, escape, shirk. **get over 1** *get over flu* recover from, recuperate from, get better after, pull through, survive. **2** *get over a lover | she hasn't got over her love affair* forget, think no more of, write off, come round from. **3** *get the message over* communicate, get across, make understood, impart. *see* GET, GET ACROSS. **4** *get over one's fear of dogs* overcome, master, get the better of, shake off, defeat, win a battle over. **get round**. *see* GET, GET AROUND. **get together 1** *get together the evidence* collect, gather, assemble, accumulate, compile, amass. **2** *we must get together soon* meet, meet up, have a meeting, see each other, socialize, forgather, congregate; *inf* party.

getaway n escape, flight, break-out, break, abscondment, decampment.

get-together n meeting, party, social gathering, gathering; *inf* do, beanfeast, bash, thrash.

get-up n outfit, clothes, clothing, dress, garb, apparel, garments; *inf* rig-out.

get-up-and-go n go, energy, vigour, vitality, dynamism, vim, enthusiasm, eagerness, drive, push, initiative, ambition; *inf* bounce.

ghastly adj **1** *a ghastly murder/accident* terrible, horrible, frightful, dreadful, awful, horrid, horrendous, hideous, shocking, grim, grisly, gruesome, gory, terrifying, frightening. **2** *feel ghastly* ill, unwell, sick; *inf* awful, terrible, dreadful. **3** *feels ghastly about losing her temper* bad, ashamed, shameful; *inf* awful, terrible, dreadful. **4** *a ghastly mistake* very bad, serious, grave, critical, unforgivable; *inf* awful, terrible, dreadful. **5** *what a ghastly man* odious, loathsome, nasty, foul, contemptible, low, mean, base; *inf* horrible, dreadful, abominable, appalling. **6** *her ghastly appearance* death-like, deathly pale, pale, pallid, wan, ashen, colourless, white, white as a sheet, haggard, drawn, ghostlike, spectral, cadaverous.

ghost n **1** *haunted by a ghost* spectre, apparition, phantom, spirit, wraith, revenant, phantasm, soul, manes, lemures; *lit* shade; *inf* spook. **2** *the ghost of a smile* suggestion, hint, trace, glimmer, semblance, shadow, impression, faint appearance.

ghostly adj *a ghostly figure* ghostlike, spectral, phantom-like, phantom, wraithlike, phantasmal, phantasmic, unearthly, supernatural, other-worldly, insubstantial, illusory, shadowy, eerie, weird, uncanny; *inf* spooky.

giant n *giants in legend* colossus, titan, man mountain, behemoth.

giant adj *a giant insect* gigantic, enormous, colossal, huge, immense, vast, mammoth, monumental, monstrous, gargantuan, titanic, elephantine, prodigious, stupendous, very large, Brobdingnagian; *inf* jumbo, industrial-size.

gibberish n meaningless talk, babble, gabble, jabbering, nonsense, rubbish, twaddle, drivel, balderdash, mumbo-jumbo, blather, double-talk, prattle; *inf* poppycock, gobbledegook, rot, tommy-rot, bosh, piffle.

gibe, jibe v *the students gibed at the politician* jeer, mock, sneer at, scoff at, taunt, scorn, deride, ridicule, hold up to ridicule, laugh at, poke fun at, make fun of, tease, twit; *inf* rib, rag.

gibe, jibe n *the gibes of the crowd* taunt, sneer, jeer; mocking, sneering, scoffing, taunts, scorn, derision, ridicule, teasing, sarcasm; *inf* dig.

giddy adj **1** *get giddy climbing ladders* dizzy, light-headed, faint, reeling, unsteady, vertiginous; *inf* woozy. **2** *a giddy girl* flighty, silly, frivolous, skittish, irresponsible, flippant, whimsical, capricious, light-minded, featherbrained, scatterbrained, fickle, erratic, changeable, inconstant, irresolute, mercurial, volatile, unsteady, unstable, unbalanced, impulsive, reckless, wild, care-

less, thoughtless, heedless, carefree, insouciant.

gift n **1** *receive a birthday/leaving gift | gift shop/token* present, offering, bounty, largesse, donation, contribution, boon, grant, bonus, gratuity, benefaction, bequest, legacy, inheritance, endowment. **2** *the gift of a car* giving, presentation, bestowal, conferment, donation, contribution, grant, endowment. **3** *a gift for foreign languages* talent, flair, aptitude, facility, knack, bent, turn, aptness, ability, faculty, capacity, capability, attribute, skill, expertise, genius; mind for.

gift v *gift a cup to the school* present, give, bestow, confer, proffer, donate, contribute, endow, bequeath, leave, will.

gifted adj *gifted child | gifted at singing/dancing* talented, brilliant, intelligent, clever, bright, smart, sharp, ingenious, able, accomplished, capable, masterly, skilled, adroit, proficient, expert.

gigantic adj giant, enormous, colossal, huge, immense, vast, mammoth, gargantuan, Brobdingnagian; *inf* jumbo. *see* GIANT adj.

giggle v titter, snigger, snicker, chuckle, chortle, laugh, cackle; *inf* tee-hee, ha-ha.

gigolo n **1** *hire a gigolo for the evening* male escort, male companion, dancing partner. **2** *a gigolo who hangs round rich women* male prostitute, ladies' man, lady-killer; *inf* toy boy.

gild v **1** *gild the table top* make golden/gilt/aureate, aurify, inlay with gold, cover with gold, paint/lacquer gold. **2** *gild the lily* adorn, decorate, embellish, ornament, bedeck, deck, garnish, array, enrich, enhance, brighten up, dress up, prettify, beautify, grace. **3** *gild the truth* dress up, embroider, sugar-coat, window-dress, camouflage, disguise.

gimcrack adj shoddy, cheap, tawdry, kitsch, flimsy, badly made, jerry-built; *inf* tacky, tatty.

gimmick n publicity, device, contrivance, eye-catching novelty, stunt, scheme, trick, dodge, ploy, stratagem.

gingerly adv cautiously, with caution, warily, charily, cannily, carefully, attentively, heedfully, vigilantly, watchfully, guardedly, prudently, circumspectly, judiciously, suspiciously, hesitantly, reluctantly, timidly, timorously.

gird v **1** *gird on his sword* belt, bind, fasten. **2** *trees girded the lake* surround, circle, encircle, ring, enclose, encompass, compass, confine, hem in, pen, enfold, engird, girdle.

3 *gird oneself for battle* prepare, make ready, get ready, ready, brace, fortify, steel, buttress.

girdle n **1** *wearing a red girdle round the dress* sash, belt, cummerbund, band, braid, obi, fillet; *lit* cincture. **2** *a light-support girdle* corset, corselet, foundation garment, pantie-girdle; *Med* truss.

girdle v *trees girdling the lake* surround, circle, encircle, ring, enclose, encompass, gird. *see* GIRD 2.

girl n **1** *a teenage girl | he has a boy and a girl* female child, daughter, miss, lass, young woman, young lady, young unmarried woman; *Scots* lassie; *inf* bird; *derog inf* tart, piece; *Amer inf* babe, chick. **2** *he and his girl* girlfriend, sweetheart, fiancée, lover, ladylove, mistress, inamorata.

girth n circumference, size, bulk, measure, perimeter.

gist n substance, essence, quintessence, drift, sense, general sense, significance, idea, import, core, nucleus, nub, kernel, pith, marrow, burden, crux, important point.

give v **1** *gave him the book | give a donation to the hospital* hand, present, donate, bestow, contribute, confer, hand over, turn over, award, grant, accord, leave, will, bequeath, make over, entrust, consign, vouchsafe. **2** *give out the prizes* distribute, allocate, allot, mete out, hand out, disperse, apportion, dole out, assign; *inf* dish out. **3** *give the impression* show, display, demonstrate, set forth, indicate, manifest, evidence. **4** *give them time* allow, permit, grant, accord, offer. **5** *give a reprimand* administer, deliver, deal. **6** *give advice* provide, supply, furnish, proffer, offer. **7** *give no trouble* cause, be a source of, make, create. **8** *give news of the battle* impart, communicate, announce, transmit, convey, transfer, send, purvey. **9** *land giving a good crop | giving good results* produce, yield, afford, result in. **10** *the car gave a jolt* perform, execute, make, do. **11** *give a shout/yell* let out, utter, issue, emit. **12** *give his life for his country* give up, sacrifice, relinquish, devote. **13** *give place to others* surrender, concede, yield, give up, cede. **14** *she gave me to believe* lead, made, cause, force. **15** *the chair gave* give way, collapse, break, break down, fall apart, come apart; bend, buckle. **give away 1** *give away secrets* reveal, disclose, divulge, let slip, leak, let out, expose, uncover. **2** *give his friend away* betray, inform on; *inf* grass on, rat on, blow the whistle on. **give in** give up, surrender, admit defeat, concede defeat, concede, yield, capitulate, submit,

comply, succumb, quit, retreat; *inf* throw in the sponge/towel. **give off** emit, send out, pour out, throw out, discharge, exude, exhale, release, vent, produce. **give out 1** *give out fumes* give off, emit, send out, discharge, exude. *see* GIVE, GIVE OFF. **2** *give out that he is leaving* announce, declare, make known, communicate, impart, broadcast, publish, disseminate. **3** *supplies were giving out* run out, be used up, be consumed, be exhausted, be depleted, come to an end, fail. **give up 1** *give up smoking* stop, cease, quit, desist from, leave off, swear off, renounce, forswear, abandon, discontinue; *inf* chuck, cut out. **2** *give up in the face of the enemy* give in, surrender, concede defeat, yield, capitulate. *see* GIVE, GIVE IN. **3** *she's just given up* despair, lose heart, abandon hope, give up hope.

giver n donor, donator, contributor, granter, grantor, benefactor, backer, fairy godmother; *inf* angel.

glacial adj *glacial conditions* freezing, frozen, icy, icy-cold, frigid, bitterly cold, wintry, arctic, polar, gelid, Siberian; *Med* algid.

glad adj **1** *glad you're here* happy, pleased, pleased as Punch, well-pleased, delighted, gratified, thrilled, overjoyed, elated, over the moon, satisfied, contented, grateful; *inf* chuffed, tickled pink. **2** *glad to help* willing, more than willing, eager, ready, prepared, happy, pleased, delighted. **3** *hear the glad news* happy, joyful, delightful, welcome, cheering, cheerful, pleasing, gratifying. **4** *the children's glad laughter* merry, gay, jolly, cheerful, cheery, joyful, joyous, gleeful, mirthful, happy, animated.

gladden v make happy, delight, cheer, cheer up, hearten, brighten up, raise the spirits of, please, elate, buoy up, give a lift to; *inf* buck up.

gladly adv *I'll gladly help* with pleasure, happily, willingly, cheerfully, eagerly, ungrudgingly.

glamorous adj **1** *a glamorous woman* alluring, dazzling, glittering, well-dressed, smart, elegant, beautiful, lovely, attractive, charming, fascinating, exciting, beguiling, bewitching, enchanting, entrancing, irresistible, tantalizing; *inf* glitzy, ritzy. **2** *a glamorous career* exciting, fascinating, stimulating, thrilling, high-profile, dazzling, glossy, glittering; *inf* ritzy, glitzy.

glamour n **1** *women with glamour* beauty, loveliness, attractiveness, allure, attraction, elegance, charm, fascination; *inf* glitz, pizzazz. *see* GLAMOROUS 1. **2** *the glamour of foreign travel* allure, attraction, charm, fascination, excitement, enchantment, captivation, magic, spell.

glance v **1** *glance at the stranger* look quickly/briefly at, take a quick look at, cast a brief look at, look hurriedly at, glimpse, catch a glimpse of, peek at, peep at; *inf* sneak a look at. **2** *glance through the paper* | *glance over his work* skim through, leaf through, flick through, flip through, thumb through, scan, dip into. **3** *lights glancing on water* flash, gleam, glitter, glisten, glint, glimmer, shimmer, flicker, sparkle, twinkle, reflect, coruscate. **4** *the arrow glanced off the tree* ricochet, rebound, be deflected; bounce/fly off. **5** *the car glanced the wall* graze, skim, touch, brush. **6** *glance at/over the subject of money* touch upon, mention in passing, give a mention to, mention, refer to, allude to, make an allusion to, skim over.

glance n **1** *take a glance at* brief look, quick look, rapid look, glimpse, peek, peep; *inf* gander, once-over. **2** *the glance of the sun on the water* flash, gleam, glitter, glittering, glint, glimmer, shimmer, flicker, sparkle, twinkle. *see* GLANCE v 3.

glare v **1** *teachers glaring at pupils* stare angrily, glower, scowl, frown, lour, give someone black looks, look threateningly/menacingly at, give someone dirty looks, look daggers. **2** *lights glaring* blaze, flare, flame, beam, dazzle.

glare n **1** *give a glare at his enemy* angry stare, glower, scowl, frown, lour, black look, threatening/menacing look, dirty look. **2** *the glare of lights* blaze, flare, flame, harsh beam, dazzle.

glaring adj **1** *glaring lights* blazing, dazzling. *see* GLARE v 2. **2** *a glaring error* conspicuous, obvious, overt, manifest, patent, visible, unconcealed, flagrant, blatant, egregious, outrageous, gross.

glass n *a glass of water* tumbler, flute, schooner, balloon, beaker, goblet, chalice; wineglass, sherry-glass, brandy-glass.

glasses npl *put on his glasses* spectacles, eye-glasses, bifocals, sun-glasses, lorgnette, monocle, pince-nez, field-glasses, binoculars, opera-glasses.

glassy adj **1** *a glassy surface on the table* glasslike, shiny, glossy, highly-polished, smooth. **2** *the sea is glassy* glasslike, mirror-like, smooth, clear, crystal-clear, transparent, translucent, limpid, pellucid. **3** *the pavements are glassy* slippery, icy, ice-covered. **4** *a glassy stare* expressionless, glazed, blank, empty, vacant, vacuous, deadpan, fixed, unmoving, motionless, lifeless.

glaze v **1** *glaze china* enamel, lacquer, varnish, coat, polish, burnish, gloss. **2** *glaze the cake/pie/apples* coat, cover, ice, frost. **3** *his eyes glazed over* become glassy, grow expressionless, go blank, be motionless. *see* GLASSY 4.

glaze n **1** *add a glaze to the china* enamel, lacquer, gloss, lustre, finish. *see* GLAZE v 1. **2** *put a glaze on the cake/pie* coating, icing, frosting.

gleam n **1** *a gleam of light* beam, flash, glow, shaft, ray, flare, glint. *see* GLEAM v. **2** *the gleam of the polished brass* glow, lustre, gloss, shine, sheen, brightness, brilliance, flash, coruscation. **3** *a gleam of hope* glimmer, flicker, ray, trace, suggestion, hint, inkling, grain.

gleam v *lights gleaming* shine, radiate, flash, glow, flare, glint, glisten, glitter, beam, shimmer, glimmer, glance, sparkle, twinkle, scintillate.

glee n merriment, gaiety, mirth, mirthfulness, delight, joy, joyfulness, joyousness, gladness, happiness, pleasure, jollity, hilarity, jocularity, joviality, exhilaration, high spirits, blitheness, cheerfulness, exaltation, elation, exuberance, verve, liveliness, triumph.

gleeful adj merry, gay, delighted, mirthful, joyful, overjoyed, joyous, glad, happy, pleased, jolly, jovial, exhilarated, high-spirited, blithe, cheerful, elated, exuberant, cock-a-hoop, triumphant.

glib adj slick, smooth, smooth-talking, smooth-spoken, fast-talking, plausible, quick/ready of tongue, fluent, suave, talkative, voluble, loquacious, having kissed the Blarney Stone, unctuous; *inf* sweet-talking, having the gift of the gab.

glide v **1** *skaters/ships gliding along* slide, move smoothly, slip, skim, sail, skate, float, drift, flow, coast. **2** *time glided by* pass, slip, elapse, steal away, roll on.

glimmer n **1** *a glimmer of light* gleam, flash, flicker, glint, shimmer, blink, twinkle, sparkle, glow, ray. **2** *a glimmer of hope* gleam, flicker, ray, trace. *see* GLEAM n 3.

glimmer v *lights glimmering* gleam, flash, flicker, shimmer, blink, twinkle, sparkle, glow.

glimpse n glance, brief look, quick look, peek, peep. *see* GLANCE n 1.

glimpse v catch a glimpse of, catch sight of, catch a quick sight of, spot, spy, espy, descry.

glint v *diamonds glinting* shine, sparkle, flash, twinkle, glitter, glimmer, blink, wink, shimmer, glisten, dazzle, gleam, scintillate.

glint n *the glint of diamonds* sparkle, flash, twinkle, glitter, glimmer, blink, gleam. *see* GLINT V.

glisten v *face glistened with tears/sweat* shine, shimmer, sparkle, twinkle, flicker, blink, wink, glint, glance, gleam, flash, scintillate, coruscate.

glitter v *stars glittering* sparkle, twinkle, flicker, blink, wink, shimmer, glimmer, glint, gleam, flash, scintillate, coruscate.

glitter n **1** *the glitter of stars* sparkle, twinkle, flicker, blink, winking. *see* GLITTER V. **2** *the glitter of show business* showiness, flashiness, ostentation, glamour, pageantry, fanfare, splendour; *inf* razzle-dazzle, glitz, ritziness, pizzazz.

gloat v relish, take pleasure in, delight in, revel in, rejoice in, glory in, exult in, triumph over, crow about; *inf* rub it in.

global adj **1** *global recession* worldwide, world, universal, international, planetary. **2** *a global rule* general, comprehensive, all-inclusive, all-encompassing, all-out, encyclopedic, exhaustive, thorough, total, across-the-board, with no exceptions.

globe n **1** *everywhere in the globe* world, universe, earth, planet. **2** *in the shape of a globe* sphere, orb, ball, round.

globule n bead, ball, drop, droplet, pearl, particle.

gloom n **1** *the gloom of the night/room* gloominess, dimness, darkness, dark, blackness, murkiness, murk, shadowiness, shadow, shade, shadiness, cloud, cloudiness, dullness, obscurity, dusk, twilight. **2** *a state of gloom* low spirits, melancholy, sadness, unhappiness, sorrow, grief, woe, despondency, misery, dejection, downheartedness, dispiritedness, glumness, desolation, depression, the blues, despair, pessimism, hopelessness.

gloomy adj **1** *a gloomy day* dark, cloudy, overcast, sunless, dull, dim, shadowy, dismal, dreary. **2** *a gloomy room* dark, black, unlit, murky, shadowy, sombre, dingy, dismal, dreary, crepuscular; *lit* tenebrous, Stygian. **3** *gloomy news* bad, black, sad, saddening, distressing, sombre, melancholy, depressing, dispiriting, disheartening, disappointing, cheerless, comfortless, pessimistic, hopeless. **4** *feeling gloomy* in low spirits, melancholy, sad, unhappy, sorrowful, woebegone, despondent, disconsolate, miserable, dejected, downcast, downhearted, dispirited, glum, desolate,

depressed, blue, despairing, pessimistic, morose; *inf* down in the mouth.

glorify v **1** *glorify God* worship, adore, exalt, extol, pay homage to, pay tribute to, honour, revere, reverence, venerate. **2** *wars glorified the position of the king* add lustre to, aggrandize, ennoble, exalt, elevate, raise, lift up, magnify, add dignity to, dignify, augment, increase, advance, boost, promote. **3** *glorify the conqueror* praise, sing/sound the praises of, extol, laud, eulogize, magnify, panegyrize, acclaim, applaud, cheer, hail, celebrate, lionize, cry up.

glorious adj **1** *our glorious monarch* illustrious, noble, celebrated, famous, famed, renowned, distinguished, honoured, eminent, excellent, magnificent, majestic, splendid, supreme, sublime, triumphant, victorious. **2** *a glorious day* beautiful, bright, brilliant, sunny, perfect. **3** *have a glorious time* splendid, marvellous, wonderful, delightful, enjoyable, pleasurable, excellent, fine; *inf* terrific, great, fab.

glory n **1** *to the glory of God* worship, adoration, exaltation, extolment, honour, reverence, veneration, thanksgiving. **2** *win glory in battle* renown, fame, prestige, honour, distinction, illustriousness, acclaim, credit, accolade, recognition, laudation, extolment; *inf* kudos. **3** *the glory of Versailles* splendour, resplendence, magnificence, grandeur, majesty, pomp, pageantry, beauty.

glory v *glory in their success* exult in, rejoice in, take pleasure in, take pride in, preen oneself on, be proud of, delight in, revel in, triumph over, boast about, crow about, gloat about.

gloss[1] n **1** *the gloss of the furniture* shine, sheen, lustre, gleam, brightness, brilliance, sparkle, shimmer, polish, burnish. **2** *a gloss of respectability* façade, front, camouflage, disguise, mask, false appearance, semblance, show, deceptive show, veneer, surface.

gloss[1] v **1** *gloss the furniture* make glossy, shine, give a shine to, polish, burnish. **2** *gloss the china* glaze, varnish, lacquer, enamel, japan. **3** *gloss over the truth* deal rapidly with, evade, avoid, smooth over, conceal, hide, cover up, camouflage, disguise, mask, veil, draw/pull a veil over, whitewash.

gloss[2] n *add glosses to the text* explanation, explication, interpretation, elucidation, annotation, commentary, comment, note, footnote, scholium, translation.

gloss[2] v *gloss the text* give an explanation/explication of, explain, interpret, elucidate, annotate, add a commentary to, comment on, add notes/footnotes to, translate, construe.

glossy adj **1** *glossy furniture* shining, shiny, glassy, gleaming, bright, brilliant, sparkling, shimmering, polished, burnished, glazed. **2** *glossy hair* shining, gleaming, sleek, smooth, silky, silken.

glow n **1** *the glow from the light* subdued light, gleam, glimmer, incandescence, luminosity, phosphorescence, lambency. **2** *the glow of the garden flowers* brightness, vividness, brilliance, colourfulness, richness, radiance, splendour. **3** *the glow of her complexion* blush, flush, rosiness, pinkness, redness, crimson, scarlet, reddening, bloom. **4** *induce a warm glow* warmth, happiness, contentment, satisfaction. **5** *the glow of his love* passion, ardour, fervour, vehemence, intensity, earnestness, impetuosity.

glow v **1** *the light glowed* shed a glow, gleam, glimmer, shine. **2** *the fire glowed* burn without flames, smoulder. **3** *she glowed with pleasure* blush, flush, redden, grow pink, crimson, go scarlet, colour, be suffused with colour. **4** *glow with pride* radiate, thrill, tingle.

glower v *glower at his enemy* scowl, stare angrily, glare, frown, lour, give someone black/dirty looks, look daggers.

glower n *give a glower* scowl, angry stare, glare, frown, lour, black look, dirty look.

glowing adj **1** *glowing coals* aglow, smouldering, incandescent, candescent, luminous, phosphorescent, lambent. **2** *a glowing complexion* rosy, pink, reddish, red, ruddy, florid. **3** *glowing colours* bright, vivid, brilliant, colourful, rich, radiant. **4** *a glowing report* complimentary, highly favourable, enthusiastic, ecstatic, rhapsodic, eulogistic, laudatory, acclamatory, panegyrical, adulatory; *inf* rave.

glue n *stick pictures on with glue* adhesive, fixative, gum, paste, cement, mucilage, epoxy resin.

glue v *glue the pages together* stick, gum, paste, affix, fix, cement, agglutinate, conglutinate.

glum adj in low spirits, gloomy, melancholy, sad, despondent, miserable, dejected, downcast, downhearted, dispirited, depressed; *inf* down in the mouth. *see* GLOOMY 4.

glut n *a glut of apples* surplus, excess, surfeit, superfluity, overabundance, superabundance, oversupply, overprofusion, saturation.

glut v **1** *glut the market* saturate, supersaturate, overload, oversupply, flood, inundate, deluge. **2** *glut the children* cram full, stuff, gorge, satiate, overfeed, fill up. **3** *glut the passage* clog, choke up, obstruct, stop up, dam up.

glutinous adj glue-like, sticky, gummy, adhesive, viscid, mucilaginous, viscous, pasty, tacky, mucous.

glutton n gourmand, gormandizer, gorger, gobbler, guzzler; *inf* pig, greedy pig, gannet, greedy guts.

gluttonous adj greedy, gormandizing, gourmand, insatiable, voracious, edacious; *inf* piggish, hoggish, gutsy.

gluttony n greed, greediness, gourmandism, gormandizing, insatiability, voraciousness, voracity, edaciousness, edacity; *inf* piggishness, hoggishness, gutsiness.

gnarled adj **1** *a gnarled tree* knotty, knotted, lumpy, bumpy, nodular, knurled, rough, twisted, crooked, distorted, contorted. **2** *gnarled hands* knotty, lumpy, knurled, rough, twisted, arthritic, leathery, wrinkled, rugged, weather-beaten. **3** *a gnarled disposition* cantankerous, crabbed, crabby, crotchety, grumpy, snappish, peevish, disagreeable; *inf* grouchy; *Amer* cranky.

gnash v grind, strike together, grit, rasp, grate.

gnaw v **1** *dogs gnawing the bone* chew, munch, crunch, masticate, bite, nibble, worry. **2** *rust gnawing away the metal* erode, corrode, wear away, wear down, eat away, fret, consume, devour. **3** *worry gnawing at her prey* on someone's mind, nag, torment, plague, harry, harass, fret, distress, trouble, worry.

go v **1** *go forward/backward/up* move, proceed, progress, pass, walk, travel, journey, repair. **2** *time to go* go away, leave, depart, withdraw, set off, set out, decamp; *inf* beat it, scram. **3** *does the machine go?* work, be in working order, function, operate, be operative, run, perform. **4** *go grey/peculiar/bad* become, grow, get, come to be, wax. **5** *go bang/"moo"* | *the bell went* make/emit a sound, sound, sound out, resound. **6** *this road goes all the way to the sea* extend to, stretch to, reach, spread to, give access to, lead to. **7** *as time went by* pass, pass by, elapse, lapse, slip away, tick away, fly. **8** *where does this book go?* belong, have a place, fit in, be located, be situated, be found, lie, stand. **9** *her headache has gone* stop, cease, disappear, vanish, be no more, fade away, melt away. **10** *all my money has gone* be finished, be spent, be used up, be exhausted, be consumed. **11** *the old lady has gone* die, be dead, pass away, decease, expire, perish; *inf* give up the ghost, kick the bucket. **12** *these clothes will have to go* be discarded, be thrown away, be disposed of. **13** *some of the staff will have to go* be dismissed, be made redundant; *inf* be sacked, be axed, get the axe/chop. **14** *the money will go to charity* be assigned to, be allotted to, be applied to, be devoted to, be awarded to, be granted/given to, be ceded to. **15** *how did your interview go?* turn out, work out, fare, progress, develop, result, end, end up, eventuate. **16** *the carpet and curtains don't go* go together, go with each other, match, harmonize, blend, suit each other, be suited, complement each other, be in accord, accord, be compatible. **17** *his behaviour does not go with his theories* fit, fit in with, conform to, comply with, be in line with. **18** *this goes to prove his theory* serve, contribute, help, incline, tend. **19** *the bridge went* break, give way, collapse, fall down, cave in, crumble, disintegrate, fall to pieces. **go about 1** *a rumour going about* circulate, pass around; be passed around, be spread, be broadcast. **2** *how do you go about buying a house?* set about, begin, approach, tackle, undertake. **go ahead** *work is going ahead* go, progress, make progress, proceed, advance. **go along with 1** *we went along with our neighbours* go with, accompany, escort. **2** *I'll go along with your plans* comply with, cooperate with, acquiesce in, follow, agree with, assent to, concur with. **go around**. *see* GO *v* go about 1. **go back on** *go back on one's word* renege on, repudiate, retract. **go by 1** *as time goes by* pass, elapse, move on, proceed, flow. **2** *go by the rules* follow, obey, observe, be guided by, take as a guide, heed. **go down 1** *the ship went down in a storm* sink, be submerged, founder, go under. **2** *prices are going down* decrease, drop, fall, become lower, be reduced, decline, plummet. **3** *the champion is going down in the first round* be beaten, be defeated, suffer defeat, lose, fail, collapse. **4** *his name will go down in history* be commemorated, be remembered, be recalled, be immortalized. **go far** *a young man bound to go far* do well, do well for oneself, be successful, succeed, make progress, get on, get on in the world, get ahead, make a name for oneself, advance oneself, set the world/Thames/heather on fire. **go for 1** *go for the newspapers* go and get, fetch. **2** *the dog went for him* attack, assault, assail, launch oneself at, set upon, spring at/upon, rush at. **3** *he doesn't go for clever women* be attracted to, be fond of, admire, favour, like, prefer, choose, hold with. **go in for** *go in for sport* engage in, take part in, participate in,

practise, pursue, take up, espouse, adopt, embrace. **go into 1** *go into everything wholeheartedly* participate in, take part in, undertake, enter. **2** *the police are going into the evidence thoroughly* investigate, research, inquire into, look into, examine, study, review, check, scrutinize, analyse, delve into, dig into, pursue, probe. **go off 1** *the bomb went off* explode, detonate, blow up, burst, erupt; *inf* go bang. **2** *we went off at dawn* leave, go away, depart, set out, set off, decamp, move out. **3** *the cheese has gone off* go bad, go stale, go sour, be rotten, be past the sell-by date. **go on 1** *how long did the talk go on?* last, continue, proceed, endure, persist, stay, remain, happen, occur. **2** *she does go on a bit* ramble on, talk on and on, carry on talking, chatter, prattle, blether; *inf* waffle, witter on. **go out 1** *he has gone out of the office* leave, exit, depart from. **2** *the lights/passion went out* be extinguished, be turned off, be doused, be quenched, fade, die out. **3** *a boy and girl going out together* go with each other, court; *inf* go steady, date. *see* GO *v* go together 2. **go over** *go over the accounts* read over, look over, inspect, examine, study, scan, run over; *inf* give the once-over. **go through 1** *go through torture* undergo, be subjected to, suffer, experience, bear, stand, tolerate, endure, weather, brook, brave. **2** *go through money* spend, use up, run through, consume, exhaust. **3** *go through someone's pockets* look through, search, hunt through, check, inspect, examine; *inf* frisk. **go together 1** *the carpets and curtains do not go together* go, match, harmonize, blend, suit each other. *see* GO *v* 16. **2** *they have been going together for months* go out, go out together, go with each other, see each other, court, keep company, woo; *inf* go steady, date. **go under 1** *the ship went under in a storm* go down, sink, be submerged. *see* GO *v* go down 1. **2** *the firm has gone under* fail, founder, go bankrupt, go into receivership, go to the wall; *inf* go bust, fold, flop. **go with 1** *we'll go with you* go along with, accompany, escort. **2** *the carpets do not go with the curtains* match, complement, harmonize/blend/accord with. **3** *his sister is going with her brother* go out with, see; *inf* go steady with, date. *see* GO *v* go together 2 . **go without 1** *go without chocolate* do without, abstain from, deny oneself, be denied, lack, want. **2** *she went without to feed her children* go short, be in need, be in want.

go *n* **1** *have a go at hang-gliding* try, attempt, effort, bid, essay, endeavour; *inf* shot, stab, crack, whirl, whack. **2** *people with a lot of go* energy, vigour, dynamism, force, verve, vim, vitality, spirit, animation, vivacity, drive, push, determination, enterprise; *inf* get-up-and-go, pep, oomph.

goad n **1** *a goad to spur cattle* spiked stick, stick, spike, prod, staff, crook, pole, rod. **2** *a goad to action* stimulus, incentive, incitement, instigation, inducement, stimulation, impetus, motivation, pressure, spur, prick, jolt, poke.

go-ahead n *get the go-ahead for the scheme* permission, assent, consent, authorization, sanction, leave, warranty, confirmation, imprimatur; *inf* green light, OK, okay, thumbs up.

go-ahead adj *a go-ahead firm | a very go-ahead young man* enterprising, ambitious, progressive, pioneering; *inf* up-and-coming, go-getting.

goal n *the goals of the organization* aim, objective, object, end, purpose, target, ambition, design, intention, intent, aspiration, ideal.

goat n **1** *farmers keeping goats* billy-goat, billy, nanny-goat, nanny, kid. **2** *he's a silly goat* fool, idiot, nincompoop, ninny, dolt, ass; *inf* nitwit, halfwit, twit, chump, nerd; *Amer inf* dingbat. **3** *an old goat chasing young girls* lecher, lascivious man; *inf* dirty old man, DOM.

gobble v gulp, swallow hurriedly, wolf, bolt, guzzle, devour, stuff down, gluttonize, gormandize; *inf* scoff, shovel.

gobbledegook n jargon, obscure language, unintelligible language, pretentious language, verbosity, prolixity, verbiage, circumlocution, periphrasis; *inf* gibberish.

go-between n intermediary, mediator, middleman, medium, agent, broker, dealer, factor, liaison, contact, contact person, pander, panderer.

goblet n wineglass, chalice, beaker, tumbler, cup; *Scots* tass.

goblin n hobgoblin, gnome, dwarf, imp, elf, sprite.

God n God Almighty, the Almighty, the Godhead, the Divine Being, the Deity, the Holy One, God the Father, Our Father, the Creator, Our Maker, the Lord, Jehovah, Allah.

god n **1** *tribal gods* deity, divine being, divinity, spirit, genius, numen. **2** *false gods* idol, graven image, icon, golden calf.

God-forsaken adj *a God-forsaken place* desolate, dismal, dreary, bleak, wretched, miserable, gloomy, deserted, abandoned, forlorn, neglected, remote, in the back of beyond, backward.

godless adj **1** *churchgoers pitying godless people* atheistic, agnostic, sceptical, faithless, nullifidian. **2** *missionaries converting godless people* heathen, pagan, ungodly, impious, irreligious, unrighteous, unprincipled, sinful, wicked, evil, depraved.

godlike adj **1** *godlike forgiveness* godly, divine, celestial, heavenly, sacred, holy, saintly. **2** *a godlike beauty* divine, deific, deiform, transcendent, superhuman.

godly adj God-fearing, devout, pious, religious, pietistic, believing, righteous, moral, virtuous, good, holy, saintly.

godsend n boon, blessing, benediction, benison, stroke of luck, piece of good fortune, windfall, bonanza.

goggle v stare, gape, gaze, ogle; *inf* gawk, rubberneck.

goings-on npl *strange goings-on at the bank* misconduct, misbehaviour, conduct, behaviour, mischief, pranks; *inf* funny business, monkey business, hanky-panky.

gold n **1** *gold is more precious than silver* gold pieces, gold nugget, bullion, gold ingot, gold bar. **2** *misers counting their gold* money, wealth, treasure, fortune, riches.

golden adj **1** *golden hair* gold-coloured, blond, blonde, yellow, yellowish, fair, flaxen, tow-coloured, bright, gleaming, resplendent, brilliant, shining. **2** *a golden future* successful, prosperous, flourishing, thriving, rosy, bright, brilliant, rich. **3** *golden memories* happy, joyful, delightful, glorious, precious, treasured. **4** *golden opportunities* fine, superb, excellent, favourable, opportune, promising, rosy, advantageous, profitable, fortunate, providential, auspicious, propitious. **5** *the golden boy of athletics* talented, gifted, special, favourite, favoured, cherished, beloved, pet, acclaimed, applauded, praised, lauded; *inf* blue-eyed.

good adj **1** *a good person* virtuous, moral, ethical, righteous, right-minded, right-thinking, honourable, honest, upright, high-minded, noble, worthy, admirable, estimable, exemplary. **2** *a good child* well-behaved, obedient, well-mannered, manageable, tractable, malleable. **3** *that's good* satisfactory, acceptable, good enough, passable, tolerable, adequate, fine, excellent; *inf* great, OK, hunky-dory. **4** *a good thing to do* right, correct, proper, fitting, suitable, appropriate, decorous, seemly. **5** *a good driver* competent, capable, able, accomplished, efficient, skilful, adept, proficient, dexterous, expert, excellent, first-class, first-rate; *inf* A1, tiptop, top-notch. **6** *good brakes/friends* reliable, dependable, trustworthy.

7 *in good condition* fine, healthy, sound, robust, strong, vigorous. **8** *a good party* enjoyable, pleasant, agreeable, pleasing, pleasurable, amusing, cheerful, convivial, congenial, sociable, satisfying, gratifying, to one's liking. **9** *good of you to come* kind, kindly, kind-hearted, good-hearted, friendly, obliging, well-disposed, charitable, gracious, sympathetic, benevolent, benign, altruistic. **10** *come at a good time* convenient, fitting, suitable, favourable, advantageous, fortunate, lucky, propitious, auspicious. **11** *milk is good for you* wholesome, health-giving, healthful, nutritional, beneficial, salubrious, salutary. **12** *is this cheese still good?* fit to eat, eatable, edible, untainted, fresh. **13** *the food is good here* delicious, tasty, appetizing; *inf* scrumptious, yummy. **14** *a good reason for going* valid, genuine, authentic, legitimate, sound, bona fide. **15** *wait a good hour* full, entire, whole, complete, solid, not less than. **16** *a good number came* considerable, substantial, goodly, sizeable, large, sufficient, ample; *inf* tidy. **17** *good friends* close, intimate, bosom, fast, dear, valued, treasured. **18** *wear her good clothes* best, finest, newest, nicest, smartest, special, party, Sunday. **19** *good weather* fine, fair, mild, clear, bright, cloudless, sunshiny, sunny, calm, balmy, tranquil, clement, halcyon. **make good 1** *make good the damage* compensate for, make recompense for, make amends for, make restitution for, pay for, reimburse for. **2** *make good a promise* fulfil, carry out, effect, discharge, live up to. **3** *make good a statement* substantiate, back up, demonstrate the truth of, confirm, prove, validate, authenticate. **4** *he made good in America* be successful, succeed, do well, get ahead, reach the top, set the world/Thames/heather on fire.

good n **1** *for your own good* benefit, advantage, behalf, gain, profit, interest, well-being, welfare, usefulness, avail, service. **2** *tell good from bad* virtue, goodness, morality, ethics, righteousness, rightness, rectitude, honour, honesty, uprightness, integrity, probity, worth, merit. **for good** for always, forever, permanently, never to return, *sine die*.

good interj fine, very well, all right; *inf* okay, OK, okey-dokey.

goodbye interj farewell, au revoir, adieu; *inf* bye, cheerio, cheers, see you later, see you, so long, toodle-oo, ciao; *inf* bye-bye, ta-ta.

good-for-nothing adj *a good-for-nothing son* useless, of no use, no-good, lazy, idle, slothful, feckless.

good-for-nothing n *a real good-for-nothing* ne'er-do-well, waster, wastrel, black sheep, layabout, idler, loafer, sluggard.

good-humoured adj amiable, affable, easygoing, genial, cheerful, cheery, happy, pleasant, good-tempered.

good-looking adj attractive, handsome, pretty, lovely, beautiful, personable, comely, well-favoured, fair.

goodly adj *a goodly amount* considerable, substantial, sizeable, significant, large, great, ample, sufficient; *inf* tidy.

good-natured adj kind, kindly, kind-hearted, warm-hearted, generous, benevolent, charitable, friendly, helpful, accommodating, amiable, tolerant.

goodness n **1** *the goodness of the saint* virtue, virtuousness, morality, righteousness, rectitude, honour, honesty, uprightness, integrity, probity, nobility, worthiness, merit. **2** *she had the goodness to stay* kindness, kindliness, kind-heartedness, warmheartedness, generosity, obligingness, benevolence, beneficence, friendliness, goodwill, compassion, graciousness, charitableness, unselfishness. **3** *the goodness in the food* nourishment, nutritional value, nutrition, wholesomeness. *see* GOOD adj 11.

goods npl *all her goods and chattels* belongings, possessions, property, effects, gear, things, paraphernalia, chattels, movables, appurtenances, trappings, accoutrements; *inf* stuff.

goodwill n *full of goodwill* friendliness, friendship, kindness, kindliness, benevolence, compassion, amity.

gorge n *the stream at the foot of the gorge* chasm, canyon, ravine, abyss, defile, pass, cleft, crevice, rift, fissure.

gorge v **1** *gorge oneself on ice-cream* stuff, cram, fill, glut, satiate, surfeit, overeat. **2** *gorge the food* bolt, gobble, guzzle, gulp down, wolf, devour, stuff down, gormandize, raven; *inf* shovel.

gorgeous adj **1** *a gorgeous sight* magnificent, splendid, superb, grand, resplendent, stately, impressive, imposing, sumptuous, luxurious, elegant, opulent, dazzling, brilliant, glittering, breath-taking. **2** *we had a gorgeous time* wonderful, marvellous, firstrate, delightful, enjoyable, entertaining, excellent; *inf* glorious, terrific. **3** *a gorgeous blonde* attractive, beautiful, lovely, good-looking, sexy; *inf* stunning.

gory adj **1** *a gory film* bloody, bloodthirsty, sanguinary, violent, murderous, brutal, savage, horror-filled, horrific; *inf* blood-and-thunder, blood-and-guts. **2** *a gory garment* bloody, blood-stained, blood-soaked.

gospel n **1** *studying the Gospel* Christian doctrine, Christ's teaching, the New Testament, the writings of the evangelists. **2** *believing in the gospel of hard work* principle, tenet, doctrine, ethic, belief, creed, credo. **3** *she's gone and that's gospel* the truth, the whole truth, a certainty, a fact, actual fact, verity.

gossamer n cobweb, spider's web, silky substance, gauze, tissue, chiffon, thistledown, feather.

gossamer adj *a scarf of gossamer material* gossamery, cobwebby, silky, gauzy, chiffony, feathery, light, fine, delicate, frail, flimsy, insubstantial, airy, diaphanous, sheer, transparent, see-through, translucent.

gossip n **1** *have you heard the gossip about her?* rumours, scandal, tittle-tattle, tattle, idle talk, hearsay, smear campaign, whispering campaign; *inf* mud-slinging, dirt. **2** *have a gossip with the neighbours* chat, blather, blether, conversation, talk, prattle; *inf* chit-chat, chin-wag, jaw, yackety yack. **3** *he's just a gossip* gossip-monger, scandal-monger, busybody, blether, blatherskite, tittle-tattler, babbler, chatterer, prattler.

gossip v **1** *gossiping about her colleagues* spread gossip/rumours, circulate rumours, spread stories. **2** *spend too much time gossiping* chat, chit-chat, blather, blether, talk, tattle, babble, gabble, prattle, prate; *inf* chin-wag, jaw, yack.

govern v **1** *govern the country* rule, reign over, be in power over, exercise control over, hold sway over, preside over, administer, lead, be in charge of, control, command, direct, order, guide, manage, conduct, oversee, supervise, superintend, steer, pilot. **2** *govern one's passions* control, restrain, keep in check, check, curb, hold back, keep back, bridle, rein in, subdue, constrain, contain, arrest. **3** *the weather will govern our decision* determine, decide, sway, rule, influence, have an influence on, be a factor in.

government n **1** *the country's government is weak* administration, regime, parliament, congress, ministry, council, executive, the powers that be. **2** *their government of the country has been criticized* rule, administration, leadership, command, direction, control, guidance, management, conduct, supervision, superintendence. **3** *the government of one's emotions* control, restraint, checking, curbing, bridling, constraint, discipline.

gown n dress, frock, garment, costume, garb, habit; evening gown, ball-gown, dinner-gown.

grab v **1** *grab his collar* grasp, clutch, grip, clasp, lay hold of, catch hold of, take hold of, fasten upon, collar. **2** *grab the money from him* seize, snatch, pluck, snap up, appropriate, capture; *inf* bag, nab.

grab n clutch, grasp, firm hold; hug, embrace. **up for grabs** available, accessible, obtainable, to be had, up for sale.

grace n **1** *the grace of the ballerina* gracefulness, suppleness, fluidity of movement, smoothness, ease, elegance, agility; *inf* poetry in motion. **2** *admire the grace of the women* elegance, refinement, finesse, culture, cultivation, polish, suaveness, good taste, taste, tastefulness, charm, attractiveness, beauty, loveliness, comeliness. **3** *have the grace to apologize* manners, mannerliness, courtesy, courteousness, decency, consideration, tact, tactfulness, breeding, decorum, propriety, etiquette. **4** *fall from grace* favour, goodwill, preferment. **5** *acquire a house by grace of the king* favour, good will, generosity, kindness, kindliness, benefaction, beneficence, indulgence. **6** *beg the king's grace* mercy, mercifulness, compassion, pardon, reprieve, forgiveness, leniency, lenity, clemency, indulgence, charity, quarter. **7** *ask for a year's grace* delay, postponement, deferment, deferral. **8** *say grace* blessing, benediction, thanks, thanksgiving, prayer.

grace v **1** *paintings gracing the room* adorn, decorate, ornament, embellish, enhance, beautify, prettify, set off, deck, enrich, garnish. **2** *grace the gathering with his presence* dignify, distinguish, add distinction to, honour, favour, glorify, elevate.

graceful adj **1** *graceful ballerinas* supple, fluid, flowing, smooth, easy, elegant, agile, nimble. **2** *graceful women* elegant, refined, cultured, cultivated, polished, suave, having good taste, charming, appealing, attractive, beautiful, lovely, comely.

gracious adj **1** *a gracious lady* kind, kindly, kind-hearted, warm-hearted, benevolent, friendly, amiable, affable, pleasant, cordial, courteous, considerate, polite, civil, chivalrous, well-mannered, charitable, indulgent, obliging, accommodating, beneficent, benign. **2** *a gracious room | gracious way of life* elegant, tasteful, comfortable, luxurious. **3** *gracious God* merciful, compassionate, gentle, mild, lenient, humane, clement.

grade n **1** *what grade did he reach?* degree of proficiency/quality/merit, level, stage, echelon, rank, standing, station, position, order, class. **2** *all belonging to the same grade* category, class, classification, type, brand. **3** *progress one grade at a time* stage, step, rung, notch. **4** *a steep grade* gradient, slope, incline, hill, rise, bank, acclivity, declivity.

make the grade pass, pass muster, measure up, measure up to expectation, come up to standard, come up to scratch, succeed, be successful, come through with flying colours, win through, qualify, get through.

grade v *grade the vegetables* classify, class, categorize, sort, group, order, brand, size, rank, evaluate, rate, value, range, graduate.

gradient n slope, incline, hill, rise, rising ground, bank, acclivity, declivity, grade.

gradual adj **1** *a gradual improvement* step-by-step, degree-by-degree, progressive, successive, continuous, systematic, regular, steady, even, moderate, slow, measured, unhurried. **2** *a gradual slope* gentle, not steep, moderate.

gradually adv *gradually improve* bit by bit, little by little, by degrees, step by step, inch by inch, piece by piece, drop by drop, slowly, progressively, successively, continuously, constantly, regularly, at a regular pace, steadily, evenly, moderately.

graduate v **1** *graduated last summer* take an academic degree, receive one's degree, become a graduate. **2** *graduate a scale* mark off, measure off, divide into degrees, grade, calibrate. **3** *graduate income tax bands* arrange in order, order, group, classify, class, categorize, rank. **4** *graduate to a more senior post* move up, progress, advance, gain promotion, be promoted.

graft[1] n **1** *a plant graft* shoot, bud, scion, slip, new growth, sprout, splice. **2** *a skin graft* transplant, implantation, implant. **3** *succeed by sheer graft* hard work, work, toil, effort, labour, industry, the sweat of one's brow.

graft[1] v **1** *graft a shoot on to a stock* insert, engraft, affix, slip, join. **2** *graft skin* transplant, implant.

graft[2] n *get ahead in business by graft* bribery, illegal means, unlawful practices, underhand means, payola; *inf* palm-greasing.

grain n **1** *farmers growing grain* cereal, cereal crops; corn, wheat, barley, rye, maize, oats. **2** *a grain of corn* kernel, seed, grist. **3** *grains of sand* particle, granule, bit, piece, scrap, crumb, fragment, morsel, mote, speck, mite, iota, molecule, atom. **4** *not a grain of truth in it* iota, trace, hint, suggestion, suspicion, soupçon, spark, scintilla. **5** *the grain of wood/cloth* texture, intertexture, surface,

fabric, weave, nap, fibre, pattern. **6** *a man of a different grain* disposition, character, nature, make-up, humour, temperament, temper, inclination.

grand adj **1** *grand houses* impressive, magnificent, imposing, splendid, striking, superb, palatial, stately, large, monumental, majestic. **2** *a grand feast* splendid, luxurious, sumptuous, lavish, magnificent, glorious, opulent, princely. **3** *bow down before the grand people in the land* great, noble, aristocratic, distinguished, august, illustrious, eminent, esteemed, elevated, exalted, celebrated, pre-eminent, prominent, leading, notable, renowned, famous. **4** *make a grand gesture* ostentatious, showy, pretentious, lordly, ambitious, imperious. **5** *the grand total* complete, comprehensive, total, all-inclusive, inclusive, exhaustive, final. **6** *the grand hall/master* principal, main, chief, leading, head, supreme. **7** *have a grand time* very good, excellent, wonderful, marvellous, splendid, first-class, first-rate, outstanding, fine, enjoyable, admirable; *inf* superb, terrific, great, super, smashing.

grandeur n **1** *the grandeur of the houses* impressiveness, magnificence, splendour, splendidness, superbness, stateliness, largeness, majesty. **2** *the grandeur of the feast* splendour, luxuriousness, luxury, sumptuousness, lavishness, magnificence, opulence. **3** *the grandeur of the ruling classes* greatness, nobility, illustriousness, eminence, elevation, exaltation, prominence, pre-eminence, renown, fame.

grandfather n **1** *a little girl playing with her grandfather* inf grandad, grandpa, grandpop; *Amer inf* gramps, grand daddy. **2** *writing the history of their grandfathers* forefather, ancestor, forebear, progenitor, father.

grandiloquent adj *grandiloquent speech/writing* pompous, pretentious, ostentatious, high-flown, wordy, bombastic, magniloquent, euphuistic, periphrastic, orotund, fustian.

grandiose adj **1** *grandiose plans* ambitious, over-ambitious, extravagant, high-flown, high-sounding, pompous, pretentious, flamboyant; *inf* over-the-top, OTT. **2** *grandiose buildings* grand, impressive, magnificent, imposing, splendid, striking, superb, stately, majestic.

grandmother n *inf* grandma, granny, gran, nan.

grant v **1** *grant them an interview* agree to, consent to, give one's assent to, assent to, accede to, permit, give one's permission for, allow, concede, accord, vouchsafe.

2 *grant them an award* bestow, confer, give, impart, award, present, donate, contribute, provide, endow, furnish, supply, allocate, allot, assign. **3** *I grant you that you may be right* admit, acknowledge, concede, go along with, yield, cede. **4** *grant property to his heirs* transfer, convey, transmit, pass on, hand on, assign, bequeath.

grant n *a grant for studying* award, endowment, donation, contribution, allowance, subsidy, allocation, allotment, bursary, gift, present.

granule n grain, particle, crumb, fragment, bit, scrap, mite, molecule, atom, iota, jot.

graph n grid, chart, diagram, histogram, bar chart.

graphic adj **1** *a graphic description of the events* vivid, striking, expressive, descriptive, illustrative, lively, forcible, detailed, well-defined, well-delineated, well-drawn, telling, effective, cogent, clear, lucid, explicit. **2** *a graphic representation* diagrammatic, representational, pictorial, illustrative, drawn, delineative.

grapple v **1** *grapple with the enemy* wrestle with, fight with, struggle with, tussle with, clash with, close with, engage with, combat with, battle with, brawl with. **2** *grapple with a problem* tackle, face, cope with, deal with, confront, address oneself to, attack, get down to, come to grips with. **3** *grapple the thief* seize, grab, lay hold of, take hold of, grip, clench, hold, grasp, clasp. **4** *grapple the boat* secure, fasten, make fast, hook, pin.

grasp v **1** *grasp his hand* grip, clutch, clasp, hold, clench, take/latch on to, lay hold of, catch, seize, grab, snatch, catch at, grapple. **2** *grasp the point* understand, comprehend, follow, see, take in, realize, perceive, apprehend; *inf* get, get the picture, get the drift, catch on.

grasp n **1** *take a firm grasp of the rail* grip, hold, clutch, clasp, clench. **2** *beyond the grasp of her enemy* clutches, power, control, command, mastery, dominion, rule. **3** *well within your grasp* capacity, reach, scope, limits, range, compass. **4** *have a good grasp of the subject* understanding, comprehension, perception, apprehension, awareness, grip, realization, knowledge, ken, mastery.

grasping adj *a grasping old miser* avaricious, greedy, acquisitive, rapacious, grabbing, covetous, mean, miserly, parsimonious, niggardly, stingy, penny-pinching, tight-fisted, hoarding, selfish, possessive; *inf* grabby.

grate v **1** *grate cheese/onions* shred, rub into pieces, pulverize, mince, grind, granulate, triturate. **2** *the knife grated against the metal surface* rasp, scrape, jar, scratch, grind, creak, rub, grit. **3** *his voice/behaviour grates on me* irritate, set someone's teeth on edge, rub someone up the wrong way, jar on, irk, annoy, vex, gall, nettle, peeve, rankle with, anger, rile, exasperate, chafe, fret, get someone down; *inf* get on someone's nerves, aggravate.

grateful adj **1** *grateful to you* thankful, filled with gratitude, indebted, obliged, obligated, under obligation, beholden. **2** *a grateful letter* thankful, appreciative. **3** *a grateful rest* pleasant, agreeable, pleasing, pleasurable, satisfying, gratifying, cheering, refreshing, welcome, acceptable, nice.

gratify v **1** *their appreciation gratified her* please, give pleasure to, make happy, make content, delight, make someone feel good, gladden, satisfy, warm the cockles of the heart, thrill. **2** *gratify their desires* fulfil, indulge, humour, comply with, pander to, cater to, pacify, appease, give in to.

grating adj **1** *a grating noise* rasping, scraping, jarring, scratching, grinding, creaking. **2** *a grating voice* harsh, raucous, strident, screeching, piercing, shrill, squawking, squawky, squeaky, discordant, hoarse, croaky. **3** *a grating personality* irritating, jarring, annoying, vexatious, irksome, galling, exasperating, offensive, disagreeable, unpleasant.

gratis adv free of charge, free, without charge, for nothing, at no cost, without paying, without payment, on the house, freely, gratuitously; *inf* for free.

gratitude n gratefulness, thankfulness, thanks, thanksgiving, appreciation, indebtedness, recognition, acknowledgement, sense of obligation.

gratuitous adj **1** *gratuitous work* free, gratis, complimentary, voluntary, unpaid, unrewarded, unasked-for, free of charge, without charge, for nothing, at no cost, without payment, on the house; *inf* for free. **2** *gratuitous insults/violence* unjustified, unprovoked, groundless, ungrounded, causeless, without cause, without reason, unfounded, baseless, uncalled-for, unwarranted, unmerited, needless, unnecessary, superfluous.

gratuity n tip, perquisite, fringe benefit, bonus, gift, present, donation, reward, recompense, largesse, benefaction, boon, *pourboire*, *douceur*, baksheesh; *inf* perk.

grave n burying place, tomb, sepulchre, vault, burial chamber, burial pit, mausoleum, crypt, last home, last resting place, long home.

grave adj **1** *a grave expression/mood* solemn, earnest, serious, sober, sombre, severe, unsmiling, long-faced, stone-faced, grim-faced, grim, gloomy, preoccupied, thoughtful, pensive, subdued, muted, quiet, sedate, dignified, staid, dour. **2** *grave matters* serious, important, all-important, significant, momentous, weighty, urgent, pressing, of great consequence, vital, crucial, critical, acute, pivotal, life-and-death, exigent, perilous, hazardous, dangerous, threatening, menacing.

graveyard n cemetery, burial ground, churchyard, memorial park, necropolis, charnel house; *inf* boneyard; *Amer* potter's field; *lit* God's acre, golgotha.

gravitate v **1** *gravitate to the bottom of the sea* sink, fall, drop, descend, precipitate, be precipitated, settle. **2** *gravitate towards the attractive girl* move towards, head towards, be drawn to, be pulled towards, be attracted to, drift towards, lean towards, incline towards.

gravity n **1** *the gravity of her expression/mood* solemnity, earnestness, seriousness, sobriety, sombreness, severity, grimness, thoughtfulness, pensiveness, sedateness, dignity, staidness, dourness. *see* GRAVE adj 1. **2** *the gravity of the situation* seriousness, importance, significance, momentousness, moment, weightiness, consequence, vitalness, crucialness, criticalness, acuteness, exigence, perilousness, peril, hazard, danger. *see* GRAVE adj 2.

graze[1] v *sheep grazing* feed, crop, browse, ruminate.

graze[2] v **1** *the car grazed the wall* brush, brush against, touch, touch lightly, rub lightly, shave, glance off, skim, kiss. **2** *graze his knee* scrape, abrade, skin, scratch, chafe, bark, bruise, contuse.

graze[2] n *he has a graze on his knee* scrape, abrasion, scratch, bruise, contusion.

greasy adj **1** *greasy food* fatty, fat, oily, buttery, oleaginous, adipose, sebacious. **2** *greasy roads* slippery, slippy, slimy. **3** *a greasy fellow* unctuous, oily, slimy, smooth-tongued, smooth, glib, suave, slick, fawning, ingratiating, grovelling, sycophantic, toadying, flattering, gushing; *inf* smarmy.

great adj **1** *a great expanse of forest* large, big, extensive, vast, immense, unlimited, boundless, spacious, huge, enormous, gigantic, colossal, mammoth, monstrous, prodigious, tremendous, stupendous. **2** *describe in great detail* considerable, sub-stantial, pronounced, exceptional, inordinate, sizeable. **3** *the great thing is to keep your temper* important, salient, essential, significant, crucial, critical, vital, momentous, weighty, dominant, consequential. **4** *the great cities of the world* major, main, most important, leading, chief, principal, capital, paramount, primary. **5** *a great occasion* grand, impressive, magnificent, imposing, splendid, majestic, glorious, sumptuous. **6** *the great people of the land* prominent, eminent, pre-eminent, distinguished, august, illustrious, celebrated, noted, notable, noteworthy, famous, famed, renowned, leading, top, high, high-ranking, noble. **7** *a great thinker* gifted, talented, outstanding, remarkable, exceptional, first-rate, incomparable. **8** *a great tennis player* expert, skilful, skilled, able, masterly, adept, adroit, proficient, good; *inf* crack, ace, A1. **9** *a great film-goer* enthusiastic, eager, keen, zealous, devoted, active. **10** *we had a great time* enjoyable, excellent, marvellous, wonderful, first-class, first-rate, admirable, fine, very good; *inf* terrific, tremendous, fantastic, fabulous, fab. **11** *he's a great fool* absolute, utter, out-and-out, downright, thoroughgoing, total, complete, perfect, positive, arrant, unmitigated, unqualified, consummate, egregious; *inf* thundering.

greatly adv *greatly admired/superior* very much, much, by a considerable amount, considerably, to a great extent, extremely, exceedingly, enormously, vastly, immensely, tremendously, hugely, markedly, mightily, remarkably, abundantly.

greatness n **1** *the greatness of the forest* largeness, bigness, boundlessness, extensiveness, vastness, immensity, hugeness, enormity, spaciousness, prodigiousness, magnitude, size, bulk, mass, length. **2** *the greatness of the occasion* grandness, grandeur, impressiveness, magnificence, pomp, splendour, gloriousness, sumptuousness, majesty. **3** *the greatness of the leaders* eminence, distinction, lustre, illustriousness, celebrity, noteworthiness, fame, renown, nobility. **4** *admire the greatness of the players* talent, expertness, expertise, skill, skilfulness, adeptness, proficiency.

greed, greediness n **1** *appalled at the greed of the eaters* gluttony, gormandizing, gourmandism, voraciousness, voracity, ravenousness, insatiability, omnivorousness, edaciousness, edacity; *inf* hoggishness, piggishness, gutsiness, swinishness; *lit* esurience. **2** *the greed of the miser* avarice, acquisitiveness, graspingness, rapacity, covetousness, cupidity, miserliness, tight-fistedness, parsimony. **3** *greed for knowledge* avidity, eagerness, desire, hunger, craving, longing, enthusiasm, impatience.

greedy adj **1** *a fat, greedy man* gluttonous, gormandizing, gourmand, voracious, ravenous, ravening, insatiable, insatiate, omnivorous, gannet-like, edacious; *inf* hoggish, piggish, gutsy, swinish; *lit* esurient. **2** *a greedy miser* avaricious, acquisitive, grasping, rapacious, grabbing, covetous, cupidinous, hoarding, miserly, niggardly, tight-fisted, close-fisted, parsimonious; *inf* grabby, money-grubbing. **3** *greedy for knowledge* avid, eager, hungry, desirous, craving, longing, enthusiastic, anxious, impatient.

green adj **1** *green clothes* greenish, viridescent, virescent, glaucous; sea-green, aquamarine, aqua, eau-de-Nil, olive-green, pea-green, emerald-green, sage-green, acid-green. **2** *green land* verdant, grass-covered, grassy, leafy, verdurous. **3** *green plums* unripe, not ripe, immature. **4** *green wood* unseasoned, not aged, unfinished, pliable, supple. **5** *green tobacco/tea/bacon* raw, fresh, undried, unfermented, unsmoked. **6** *a green old age* flourishing, vigorous, strong, sturdy, sound, healthy. **7** *keep memories of her green* fresh, flourishing, remembered, unforgotten. **8** *a green apprentice* inexperienced, untrained, inexpert, unqualified, ignorant, unversed, new, raw, immature, simple, unsophisticated, unpolished, naïve, innocent, ingenuous, callow, credulous, gullible, wet behind the ears. **9** *feel green on seeing his new bike* envious, jealous, covetous, grudging, resentful. **10** *look/go green* greenish, pale, wan, pallid, ashen, ill, sick, sickly, unhealthy, nauseous. **11** *green issues | Green politicians* environmentalist, conservationist, preservationist; environmentally sound/friendly, ecologically sound.

green n *cows grazing on the green* village green, common, grassy area, grass, lawn, greensward, sward, turf.

greenhouse n hothouse, glasshouse, conservatory.

green light n *give the plans the green light* permission, approval, assent, consent, authorization, sanction, leave, warranty, confirmation, imprimatur, blessing; *inf* OK, okay, go-ahead, thumbs up.

greens npl **1** *eat up your greens* vegetables, leaf vegetables; *inf* veg, veggies. **2** *the greens/ Greens won more votes* environmentalists, conservationists, preservationists, ecologists.

greet v **1** *greet his neighbour in the street* say hello to, address, salute, hail, nod to, wave to, raise one's hat to, acknowledge the presence of, accost. **2** *the hostess greeted the guests at the door* receive, meet, welcome.

greeting n **1** *return his neighbour's greeting* hello, hallo, salute, salutation, address, nod, wave, acknowledgement. **2** *receive a birthday greeting* message, tidings.

greetings npl *send birthday greetings* good wishes, best wishes, regards, kind regards, congratulations, compliments, respects.

gregarious adj sociable, social, company-loving, companionable, convivial, outgoing, friendly, affable, cordial, hospitable, hail-fellow-well-met.

grey adj **1** *a grey dress* greyish, silvery; silver-grey, pearl-grey, pearly, gun-metal grey, smoke-grey. **2** *invalids looking grey* ashen, wan, pale, pallid, colourless, bloodless, anaemic, livid. **3** *a grey day* cloudy, overcast, dull, dark, sunless, gloomy, dim, dreary, dismal, drab, cheerless, depressing, misty, foggy, murky. **4** *grey people* characterless, colourless, dull, uninteresting, neutral, anonymous. **5** *a grey area* doubtful, unclear, uncertain, indistinct, mixed. **6** *the grey vote* grey-haired, elderly, old, aged, ancient, hoary, venerable.

grief n *grief at his death* sorrow, mourning, mournfulness, bereavement, lamentation, misery, sadness, anguish, pain, distress, agony, affliction, suffering, heartache, heartbreak, broken-heartedness, heaviness of heart, trouble, woe, tribulation, trial, desolation, despondency, dejection, despair, remorse, regret. **come to grief** fail, miscarry, meet with failure, meet with disaster; *inf* come unstuck, come a cropper, go phut.

grievance n **1** *answer the workers' grievances* complaint, charge, protest, moan, axe to grind, bone to pick; *lit* plaint; *inf* grouse, gripe, beef; *Amer inf* crow to pluck. **2** *workers claiming a grievance* wrong, injustice, unjust act, unfairness, injury, damage, hardship, offence, affront, insult.

grieve v **1** *the widow is still grieving | grieving for/over/about his dead wife* mourn, lament, be sorrowful, sorrow, be sad, weep and wail, cry, sob, suffer, ache, be in anguish, be distressed, eat one's heart out; bewail, bemoan. **2** *his behaviour grieved her* hurt, wound, pain, sadden, break someone's heart, upset, distress, cause suffering to, crush. **3** *grieve the loss of her dog* bewail, bemoan, regret, rue, deplore, take to heart.

grievous adj **1** *a grievous injury* painful, agonizing, hurtful, afflicting, wounding, damaging, injurious, severe, sharp, acute. **2** *grievous news* calamitous, disastrous, distressing, sorrowful, mournful, sad, crushing. **3** *grievous sins/crimes* heinous, flagrant, glaring, outrageous, shocking, appalling, atrocious, gross, dire, iniquitous, nefarious, grave, deplorable, shameful, lamentable, dreadful, egregious, flagitious. **4** *a grievous sound* grief-stricken, anguished, agonized, mournful, sorrowful, tragic, pitiful, heart-rending.

grim adj **1** *teachers looking grim* stern, forbidding, formidable, fierce, ferocious, threatening, menacing, harsh, sombre, cross, churlish, crabbed, morose, surly, sour, ill-tempered, implacable, cruel, ruthless, merciless. **2** *grim determination* resolute, determined, firm, decided, obstinate, adamant, unyielding, unwavering, unfaltering, unshakeable, obdurate, inflexible, unrelenting, relentless, inexorable, strong-willed, dead set. **3** *a grim sight/accident* dreadful, dire, ghastly, horrible, horrendous, horrid, terrible, awful, appalling, frightful, shocking, unspeakable, harrowing, grisly, gruesome, hideous, macabre.

grimace v *grimace behind her back* make a face, make faces, pull a face, scowl, frown, mouth, sneer, pout.

grimace n *make a grimace* scowl, frown, sneer, face, wry face, distorted expression, pout, mouth, moue.

grime n dirt, smut, soot, dust, mud, filth; *inf* muck, gunge, yuck, crud.

grimy adj begrimed, dirty, dirt-encrusted, grubby, soiled, stained, smutty, sooty, dusty, muddy, muddied, filthy, besmirched, besmeared; *inf* mucky, gungy, yucky, cruddy.

grin v *she grinned at him | grin like a Cheshire cat* smile broadly, smile/grin from ear to ear.

grind v **1** *grind coffee beans/nuts* crush, pound, pulverize, mill, powder, granulate, grate, crumble, mash, smash, comminute, triturate, kibble, levigate. **2** *grind knives* sharpen, file, whet, smooth, polish, sand. **3** *grind one's teeth* gnash, grit, grate, scrape, rasp. **4** *grind down the poor* oppress, persecute, tyrannize, afflict, maltreat, ill-treat, scourge, torture, torment, molest, harass, harry. **5** *grind away at the task* labour, toil, slog, slave, drudge, plod, sweat; *inf* plug.

grind n *he regards his job as a grind* drudgery, chore, slog, travail, toil, hard work, labour, slavery, forced labour, exertion; *inf* fag, sweat.

grip n **1** *lose his grip of the railing* hold, grasp, clutch, clasp, clench. **2** *have a firm grip* handgrip, handshake, hand-clasp, clasp. **3** *have her in a grip* hold, hug, embrace; *inf* clinch. **4** *have a grip of the problem* grasp, understanding, comprehension, perception, awareness, apprehension. *see* GRASP n 4. **5** *in the grip of an addiction | the tyrant's grip* clutches, control, domination, dominion, command, power, mastery, influence, hold, possession, rule. **6** *pack a grip* bag, holdall, overnight bag, travelling bag, flight bag, kitbag, Gladstone bag, valise.
come/get to grips with *come to grips with his opponent | must get to grips with the problem* face, face up to, meet head on, confront, encounter, deal with, cope with, handle, tackle, grasp, undertake, take on, grapple with, close with, contend with.

grip v **1** *grip the railing* grasp, clutch, clasp, clench, hold, grasp/take/lay hold of, latch on to, grab, seize, catch, catch at. **2** *the actor/speech gripped the audience* absorb, engross, rivet, spellbind, hold spellbound, entrance, fascinate, enthrall, hold, catch, compel, mesmerize.

gripe v *griping about money* complain, grumble, moan, groan, protest, whine; *inf* grouse, bellyache, beef, bitch, grouch, whinge.

gripe n *listen to their gripes* complaint, grumble, moan, groan, grievance, objection, protest, whine; *inf* grouse, bellyaching, beefing, beef, bitching, grouching, whinging.

gripping adj *a gripping story* riveting, spellbinding, compulsive, compelling, absorbing, engrossing, entrancing, fascinate, enthralling, thrilling, exciting; *inf* unputdownable.

grisly adj *a grisly sight/story* gruesome, ghastly, frightful, horrid, horrifying, horrible, horrendous, grim, awful, dreadful, terrible, fearful, hideous, disgusting, repulsive, repugnant, revolting, repellent, macabre, spine-chilling, sickening, shocking, appalling, abominable, loathsome, abhorrent, odious.

grit n **1** *put grit on icy roads* gravel, pebbles, sand, dust, dirt. **2** *he has no grit* pluck, mettle, mettlesomeness, backbone, spirit, strength of character, nerve, gameness, courage, bravery, valour, fortitude, stamina, toughness, hardiness, determination, resolution, doggedness, tenacity, perseverance, endurance; *inf* gumption, guts, spunk, bottle.

grit v *grit one's teeth* grate, grind, gnash, scrape, rasp.

gritty adj **1** *a gritty substance* sandy, grainy, granular, gravelly, pebbly, powdery, dusty. **2** *a gritty fighter* plucky, mettlesome, spirited, game, courageous, brave, hardy, tough, determined, resolute, dogged, tenacious, enduring; *inf* gutsy, spunky.

groan n **1** *a groan of pain* moan, cry, sigh, murmur, whine, whimper. **2** *make a list of their groans* complaint, grumble, objection, protest, grievance, moan; *inf* grouse, gripe, beefing, bellyaching, bitching. **3** *the groan of the gate* creak, grating, squeak, screech.

groan v **1** *groan in pain* moan, cry, call out, sigh, murmur, whine, whimper. **2** *groaning about working conditions* complain, grumble, object, moan, lament; *inf* grouse, gripe, beef, bellyache, bitch. **3** *the gate groaned* creak, grate, squeak, screech.

groggy adj dazed, stunned, stupefied, in a stupor, muzzy, dizzy, faint, befuddled, muddled, confused, bewildered, punch-drunk, shaky, staggering, reeling, unsteady, wobbly; *inf* woozy, woolly-headed.

groom n **1** *the groom brushing the horse* stable boy/stable girl, stable hand/lad, equerry. **2** *her groom was late* bridegroom, husband-to-be, newly-married man, newly-wed.

groom v **1** *groom one's hair | groom oneself* arrange, fix, adjust, do, dress, put in order, tidy, make tidy, brush, comb, smooth, spruce up, smarten up, preen, primp, freshen up. **2** *groom the horses* curry, brush, rub, rub down, clean. **3** *groom the pupils for university* train, coach, prepare, prime, make ready, ready, instruct, tutor, drill, teach, educate, school.

groove n **1** *a groove in the ground* furrow, channel, trench, trough, canal, gouge, hollow, indentation, rut, gutter, cutting, cut, score, rabbet, rebate. **2** *tired of being in a groove* rut, routine, habit, treadmill; *inf* daily grind.

grope v **1** *grope one's way* feel, fumble, pick, move blindly. **2** *grope for one's keys* fumble for, fish for, scrabble for, cast about for, search for, hunt for, look for, grabble for.

gross adj **1** *he's grown gross* obese, massive, immense, huge, colossal, corpulent, overweight, bloated, bulky, hulking, fat, big, large, lumpish, cumbersome, unwieldy. **2** *gross jokes* coarse, crude, vulgar, obscene, rude, ribald, lewd, bawdy, dirty, filthy, earthy, smutty, blue, risqué, indecent, indelicate, improper, impure, unseemly, offensive, sensual, sexual, pornographic. **3** *her brother is gross* boorish, loutish, oafish, coarse, crass, vulgar, ignorant, unrefined, unsophisticated, uncultured, uncultivated,

undiscriminating, tasteless, insensitive, unfeeling, imperceptive, callous; *inf* yobbish. **4** *a gross error* flagrant, blatant, glaring, outrageous, shocking, serious, egregious, manifest, obvious, plain, apparent. **5** *gross income* total, whole, entire, aggregate, before deductions, before tax.

gross v *he grosses £20,000 per annum* earn, make, bring in, take; *inf* rake in.

grotesque adj **1** *a grotesque costume/sight* bizarre, weird, outlandish, freakish, strange, odd, peculiar, unnatural, fantastic, fanciful, whimsical, ridiculous, ludicrous, absurd, incongruous, preposterous, extravagant. **2** *a grotesque shape* misshapen, distorted, twisted, deformed, malformed, misproportioned.

ground n **1** *fall to the ground* earth, terra firma, floor; *inf* deck. **2** *the ground is wet* earth, soil, dirt, land, terrain, clay, loam, turf, clod, mould, sod, dust. **3** *players going to the ground* stadium, pitch, field, arena, park. *see* GROUNDS.

ground v **1** *ground his suspicions on her behaviour* base, found, establish, set, settle. **2** *ground the pupil in maths* teach, instruct, coach, tutor, train, drill, educate, school, prepare, initiate, familiarize with, acquaint with, inform.

groundless adj *groundless fears* without basis, baseless, without foundation, unfounded, unsupported, imaginary, illusory, false, unsubstantiated, unwarranted, unjustified, unjustifiable, uncalled-for, unprovoked, without cause/reason/justification, unreasonable, irrational, illogical, empty, idle, chimerical.

grounds npl **1** *a house set in large grounds* surroundings, land, property, estate, acres, tract of land, lawns, gardens, park, parkland, area, domain, holding, territory. **2** *grounds for concern* reason, cause, basis, base, foundation, call, justification, rationale, argument, premise, occasion, factor, excuse, pretext, motive, inducement. **3** *coffee grounds* dregs, lees, deposit, sediment, precipitate, settlings, grouts.

groundwork n foundation, base, basis, cornerstone, footing, underpinning, fundamentals, basics, ABC, elements, essentials, preliminaries, preparations, spadework.

group n **1** *divide the books into groups* category, classification, class, set, lot, batch, family, species, genus, bracket. **2** *a group of people* band, company, party, body, gathering, congregation, assembly, collection, cluster, crowd, flock, pack, troop, gang, batch; *inf* bunch. **3** *belong to the radical group on the committee* clique, coterie, faction, circle, set. **4** *she joined a sewing group* society, association, league, guild, circle, club, work party. **5** *a group of trees* clump, cluster.

group v **1** *group pupils according to ability* classify, class, categorize, sort, grade, rank, bracket. **2** *group the children for a photograph* assemble, collect, gather together, arrange, organize, marshal, range, line up, dispose. **3** *the police grouped round the prisoner* collect, gather, assemble, cluster. **4** *they grouped together to form a club* get together, band together, associate, consort.

grouse v *grouse about the weather* complain, grumble, moan, groan, protest; *inf* gripe, bellyache, beef, bitch, grouch, whinge.

grouse n *tired of their grouses* complaint, grumble, moan, groan, grievance, objection, protest; *inf* gripe, bellyaching, beefing, beef, bitching, grouching, whinging.

grovel v **1** *grovel to the boss* abase oneself, humble oneself, kowtow, bow and scrape, toady, fawn, fawn upon, lick someone's boots, curry favour, curry favour with, flatter; *inf* crawl, butter someone up, be all over someone, suck up to, bootlick. **2** *grovel before the tyrant* crawl, creep, slither, kneel, fall on one's knees, prostrate oneself, throw oneself at someone's feet.

grow v **1** *the child/pile grew* get taller, get bigger, get larger, stretch, heighten, lengthen, enlarge, extend, expand, spread, thicken, widen, fill out, swell, increase, multiply. **2** *the plants are growing* shoot up, spring up, develop, sprout, burgeon, bud, germinate, pullulate, flourish, thrive. **3** *her fear grows from her insecurity* arise, originate, stem, spring, issue. **4** *the business is growing* flourish, thrive, prosper, succeed, progress, make progress, make headway, advance, improve, expand. **5** *grow prettier* become, come to be, get to be, get, turn, wax. **6** *grow corn* cultivate, produce, farm, propagate, raise.

growl v snarl, howl, yelp, bark.

grown-up n adult, grown man, man, grown woman, woman, mature man, mature woman.

grown-up adj adult, mature, of age, fully-grown, full-grown, fully-developed.

growth n **1** *the growth in population | the growth of the town* augmentation, increase, proliferation, multiplication, enlargement, expansion, extension, development, evolution, aggrandizement, magnification, amplification, growing, deepening, heightening, widening, thickening, broadening, swelling. **2** *the growth of the plants* development, maturation, germination, shooting

up, springing up, burgeoning, pullulation, sprouting, blooming, vegetation. **3** *the growth of the industry* expansion, rise, progress, success, advance, advancement, improvement, headway. **4** *find a growth on her body* tumour, lump, excrescence, intumescence, tumefaction.

grub v **1** *grub up plants/hedgerows* dig up, unearth, disinter, root out, uproot, root up, deracinate, pull out, tear out. **2** *grub in the ground* dig, spade, delve, excavate, burrow. **3** *grub out information* search out, ferret out, root out, uncover, unearth, disinter. **4** *grub among the old papers* search, hunt, rummage, scour, probe, root around; *inf* rootle around. **5** *grub away at the task* grind, labour, toil, drudge, slog, slave, plod, sweat; *inf* plug.

grub n **1** *grubs developing* larva, caterpillar, maggot. **2** *cheap grub* food, meals, sustenance, victuals, rations; *inf* eats, nosh.

grubby adj dirty, unwashed, grimy, begrimed, filthy, messy, soiled, smutty, besmeared, scruffy, shabby, untidy, unkempt, slovenly, slatternly, sordid, squalid; *inf* mucky, gungy, cruddy.

grudge n *nurse a grudge* resentment, spite, malice, bitterness, ill-will, pique, umbrage, grievance, hard feelings, rancour, malevolence, venom, hate, hatred, dislike, aversion, animosity, antipathy, antagonism, enmity, animus.

grudge v **1** *grudge her a piece of the cake* begrudge, give unwillingly, give reluctantly, give stintingly. **2** *grudge her her success* resent, mind, take ill, begrudge, envy, be jealous of.

gruelling adj *a gruelling five-hour walk* exhausting, tiring, fatiguing, wearying, taxing, demanding, trying, arduous, laborious, back-breaking, strenuous, punishing, crushing, draining, difficult, hard, harsh, severe, stiff, grinding, brutal, relentless, unsparing, inexorable.

gruesome adj *gruesome details of the murder | gruesome sight* grisly, ghastly, frightful, horrid, horrible, horrifying, horrendous, awful, grim, dreadful, terrible, fearful, hideous, disgusting, repulsive, repugnant, revolting, repellent, spine-chilling, macabre, sickening, shocking, appalling, abominable, loathsome, abhorrent, odious.

gruff adj **1** *a gruff voice* hoarse, harsh, rough, throaty, husky, croaking, rasping, low, thick, guttural. **2** *a gruff old man* surly, churlish, brusque, curt, blunt, abrupt, grumpy, crotchety, crabby, crabbed, cross, bad-tempered, ill-natured, crusty, tetchy, bearish, sullen, sour, uncivil, rude, unmannerly, impolite, discourteous, ungracious; *inf* grouchy.

grumble v **1** *always grumbling about the weather* complain, moan, groan, protest, object, find fault with, carp, whine; *inf* grouse, gripe, bellyache, beef, bitch, grouch, whinge. **2** *stomach was grumbling* rumble, gurgle, murmur, growl, mutter, roar.

grumble n **1** *listen to their grumbles* complaint, moan, groan, protest, grievance, objection, whine; *inf* grouse, gripe, bellyaching, beefing, beef, bitching, grouching, whinging. **2** *the grumble of his stomach* rumble, gurgle, murmur, growl, muttering, roar.

grumpy adj *grumpy first thing in the morning* bad-tempered, surly, churlish, crotchety, crabby, tetchy, crusty, bearish, ill-natured; *inf* grouchy.

guarantee n **1** *get a guarantee that the goods are perfect* warranty, warrant, contract, covenant, bond, guaranty. **2** *give his guarantee that he will return* pledge, promise, assurance, word, word of honour, oath, bond. **3** *the house acts as a guarantee for a loan* collateral, security, surety, earnest, guaranty. **4** *her father is the guarantee of the loan* guarantor, warrantor, underwriter, voucher, sponsor, supporter, backer; *Law* bondsman.

guarantee v **1** *guarantee a loan* put up collateral for, give earnest money for, provide surety for, provide security for, underwrite, sponsor, vouch for, support, back. *see* GUARANTEE n 3, 4. **2** *I guarantee that I shall return* promise, pledge, give a pledge, give an assurance, give assurances, give one's word, swear, swear to the fact.

guarantor n guarantee, warrantor, underwriter. *see* GUARANTEE n 4.

guard v **1** *guard the town* stand guard over, protect, watch over, cover, patrol, police, defend, shield, safeguard, preserve, save, conserve, secure, screen, shelter. **2** *guard the prisoners* keep under guard, keep under surveillance, keep watch over, mind, supervise, restrain. **3** *guard against losing your bag | guard against thieves* beware, keep watch, be alert, take care, keep an eye out for, be on the alert, be on the qui vive, be on the lookout; *inf* keep one's eyes peeled/ skinned.

guard n **1** *volunteer as castle guards* protector, defender, guardian, guarder, bodyguard, custodian, sentinel, sentry, watchman, night-watchman, scout, lookout, watch, picket, garrison. **2** *prison guards* warder, jailer, keeper; *inf* screw. **3** *act as a guard*

for the precious load escort, convoy, patrol. **4** *soldiers on guard* watch, close watch, watchfulness, vigilance, caution, heed, attention, care, wariness. **5** *a guard for a machine* safety guard, safety device, safeguard, protective device, shield, bulwark, screen, fence, fender, bumper, buffer, cushion, pad. **off one's guard, off guard** *the question/enemy caught him off his guard* unprepared, unready, unalert, unwatchful, napping, with one's defences down. **on one's guard** *keep on your guard* on the alert, vigilant, wary, watchful, cautious, careful, heedful, circumspect, on the lookout, on the qui vive, prepared, ready.

guarded adj *a guarded reply* careful, cautious, circumspect, wary, chary, reluctant, noncommittal, reticent, restrained, reserved, discreet, prudent; *inf* cagey.

guardian n *the guardian of the castle | guardians of public morals* guard, protector, defender, preserver, champion, custodian, warden, keeper, curator, caretaker, steward, trustee.

guerrilla n freedom fighter, underground fighter, terrorist, member of the resistance, partisan, irregular soldier, irregular.

guess v **1** *guess the weight* make a guess at, conjecture, surmise, estimate, reckon, fathom, hypothesize, postulate, predict, speculate; *inf* guesstimate. **2** *I guess that you're right* conjecture, surmise, reckon, hazard a guess, suppose, believe, think, imagine, judge, consider, feel, suspect, dare say, fancy, divine, deem.

guess n *my guess was wrong* conjecture, surmise, estimate, guesswork, hypothesis, theory, reckoning, judgement, supposition, feeling, assumption, inference, prediction, speculation, notion; *inf* guesstimate.

guesswork n guessing, conjecture, surmise, estimate, supposition, hypothesis, theory, presupposition, assumption, presumption, prediction, suspicion, speculation; *inf* guesstimate.

guest n **1** *the hostess welcoming guests* visitor, caller, company, visitant. **2** *a guest in the hotel* boarder, lodger.

guidance n **1** *under the guidance of the headmaster* direction, leadership, auspices, management, control, handling, conduct, government, charge, rule, teaching, instruction. **2** *career guidance* counselling, counsel, advice, direction, recommendation, suggestion, tip, hint, pointer, intelligence, information, instruction.

guide v **1** *guide them to their seats* lead, lead the way to, conduct, show, usher, shepherd, direct, show the way to, pilot, steer, escort, accompany, convoy, attend. **2** *guide the firm through its problems* control, direct, steer, manage, command, be in charge of, govern, rule, preside over, superintend, supervise, handle, regulate, manipulate, manoeuvre. **3** *guide young school leavers* give counselling to, counsel, give advice to, advise, give direction to, make recommendations to, make suggestions to, give someone tips/hints/pointers, inform, give information/intelligence to, instruct.

guide n **1** *a tourist guide* leader, conductor, director, courier, pilot, usher, escort, attendant, convoy, chaperon, cicerone. **2** *act as a career guide* counsellor, adviser, mentor, confidant, tutor, teacher, guru, therapist. **3** *a light as a guide to shipping* marker, indicator, pointer, mark, landmark, guiding light, sign, signal, beacon, lodestar, signpost, key, clue. **4** *use that essay as a guide* model, pattern, example, exemplar, standard, criterion, touchstone, measure, benchmark, yardstick, gauge, norm, archetype, prototype, paradigm, ideal, precedent, guiding principle. **5** *read a guide to Paris* guidebook, tourist guide, travelogue, directory, handbook, manual, ABC, instructions, key, catalogue, vade-mecum.

guideline n guiding principle, criterion, measure, standard, gauge, yardstick, benchmark, touchstone, rule, regulation.

guild n association, society, club, union, league, federation, organization, company, fellowship, order, lodge, brotherhood, fraternity, sisterhood, sorority, alliance, combine, corporation, consortium, syndicate, trust.

guile n cunning, duplicity, craftiness, craft, artfulness, art, artifice, wiliness, wiles, foxiness, slyness, deception, deceit, underhandedness, double-dealing, trickery, trickiness, sharp practice, treachery, chicanery, skulduggery, fraud, gamesmanship, knavery.

guileless adj ingenuous, artless, open, sincere, genuine, naïve, simple, innocent, unsophisticated, unworldly, trustful, trusting, honourable, frank, candid.

guilt n **1** *prove/admitted his guilt* guiltiness, culpability, blame, blameworthiness, censurableness, wrongdoing, wrong, wrongfulness, criminality, unlawfulness, misconduct, delinquency, sin, sinfulness, iniquity. **2** *haunted by guilt* guiltiness, feelings of guilt, guilty conscience, bad conscience, remorse, regret, contrition, contriteness, repentance, penitence, compunction, conscience, self-accusation, self-

reproach, self-condemnation, shame, disgrace, dishonour, stigma.

guiltless adj free from guilt, innocent, blameless, free from blame, unblamable, uncensurable, unimpeachable, inculpable, irreproachable, above reproach, clear, pure, sinless, faultless, spotless, stainless, immaculate, unsullied, uncorrupted, undefiled, untainted, unblemished, untarnished, impeccable.

guilty adj **1** *found guilty of the crime* to blame, blameworthy, blamable, culpable, at fault, responsible, censurable, criminal, convicted; reproachable, condemnable, erring, errant, wrong, delinquent, offending, sinful, wicked, evil, unlawful, illegal, illicit, reprehensible, felonious, iniquitous. **2** *feel guilty* conscience-stricken, remorseful, ashamed, shamefaced, regretful, contrite, compunctious, repentant, penitent, rueful, sheepish, hangdog.

guise n **1** *in the guise of a witch* external appearance, likeness, costume, clothes, outfit, dress, habit, style. **2** *under the guise of friendship* pretence, disguise, show, external appearance, outward form, screen, cover, blind.

gulf n **1** *ships sailing into the gulf* bay, cove, inlet, bight. **2** *a gulf opened up by an earthquake* chasm, abyss, hollow, pit, hole, opening, rift, cleft, fissure, split, crevice, gully, canyon, gorge, ravine. **3** *a gulf has developed between husband and wife* chasm, abyss, rift, split, wide difference, area of difference, division, gap, separation.

gullet n oesophagus, throat, pharynx, crop, craw.

gullible adj credulous, trustful, overtrustful, easily deceived, easily taken in, unsuspecting, unsuspicious, ingenuous, naïve, innocent, simple, inexperienced, green, foolish, silly, wet behind the ears.

gully n ravine, canyon, gorge, valley, gulf, chasm, abyss; *Amer* gulch. *see* GULF 2.

gulp v **1** *gulp a drink* swallow, quaff, swill, toss off; drain one's glass; *inf* swig, knock back. **2** *gulp one's food* bolt, wolf, gobble, guzzle, devour; *inf* tuck into. **3** *gulp back the tears* fight back, suppress, stifle, smother, choke back, strangle.

gulp n *take a gulp of the water* swallow, mouthful, draught; *inf* swig.

gum n *stick the page/wood together with gum* glue, adhesive, fixative, paste, cement, mucilage, resin, synthetic/epoxy resin.

gum v *gum the pieces together* stick, glue, paste, affix, cement. **gum up 1** *gum up the mechanism* clog, choke up, stop up, obstruct. **2** *gum up the works* obstruct, impede, hinder, interfere with, bring to a halt.

gumption n *hasn't got much gumption* initiative, resourcefulness, enterprise, cleverness, astuteness, shrewdness, acumen, common sense, wit, mother wit, discernment, sagacity, native ability, spirit, forcefulness, backbone, pluck, mettle, nerve, courage; *inf* get-up-and-go, grit, spunk, nous, savvy, horse sense.

gun n pistol, revolver, automatic, repeater, six-shooter, handgun, rifle, shotgun, sawn-off shotgun, musket, flintlock, blunderbuss, field gun, cannon, mortar, machine-gun, howitzer, Gatling gun; *inf* shooter.

gunman n hold-up man, armed robber, sniper, gangster, terrorist, assassin, murderer, liquidator, bandit; *inf* gunslinger, hitman, gun, hired gun, trigger man, stick-up man, hatchet man, hood, mobster. *Amer* gunfighter, shootist.

gurgle v **1** *water gurgling* bubble, ripple, murmur, babble, burble, tinkle, lap, splash, plash, purl. **2** *babies gurgling* crow, burble, babble, chuckle, laugh.

gurgle n **1** *the gurgle of water* bubbling, ripple, babble, tinkle. *see* GURGLE v 1. **2** *the gurgle of babies* crowing, burbling, chuckle. *see* GURGLE v 2.

guru n teacher, spiritual teacher, tutor, sage, swami, maharishi, guiding light, mentor, leader, master, authority.

gush v **1** *water gushing from the pipe* stream, rush forth, spout, spurt, surge, jet, well out, pour forth, burst forth, cascade, flood, flow, run, issue, emanate. **2** *she gushed about the beautiful room* be effusive, effuse, overenthuse, enthuse, wax enthusiastic, wax lyrical, effervesce, bubble over, get carried away, fuss, babble, prattle, jabber, gabble, blather, chatter, make too much, overstate the case.

gush n *a gush of water* stream, outpouring, spurt, jet, spout, burst, rush, surge, cascade, flood, torrent, spate, freshet.

gust n **1** *a gust of wind blew the hat away* blast, flurry, puff, blow, rush, squall, breeze, gale. **2** *a gust of laughter/temper* outburst, burst, outbreak, eruption, explosion, gale, fit, paroxysm, storm, surge.

gust v *wind gusting* blast, blow, puff, rush, squall.

gusto n *perform/eat with gusto* relish, zest, enthusiasm, zeal, fervour, verve, enjoyment, delight, exhilaration, pleasure, appreciation, liking, fondness, appetite, savour, taste.

gut n **1** *a sore gut* stomach, belly, abdomen, bowels, colon; *inf* insides, innards; *Med* solar plexus. **2** *remove the guts from the animal* intestines, entrails vital organs, vital parts, viscera; *inf* insides, innards.

gut v **1** *gut the fish/rabbit* eviscerate, disembowel, draw, dress, clean, exenterate. **2** *thieves/fire gutted the empty house* ransack, strip, empty, plunder, loot, rob, rifle, ravage, sack, clear out, destroy, devastate, lay waste.

gut adj *a gut reaction* instinctive, intuitive, involuntary, spontaneous, unthinking, natural, basic, emotional, heartfelt, deepseated.

guts npl courage, bravery, valour, backbone, nerve, fortitude, pluck, mettle, mettlesomeness, gameness, spirit, boldness, audacity, daring, hardiness, toughness, forcefulness, stamina, will-power, tenacity; *inf* grit, gumption, spunk, bottle.

gutter n *water running in the gutter* drain, sewer, sluice, culvert, conduit, pipe, duct, channel, trough, trench, ditch, furrow, cloaca.

guttersnipe n street urchin, street Arab, ragamuffin, waif, gamin, mudlark.

guttural adj *guttural voice/accent* throaty, husky, gruff, gravelly, croaking, harsh, rasping, deep, low, rough, thick.

guy n **1** *who is that guy?* man, male, fellow, lad; *inf* chap, bloke, customer. **2** *burn a guy* effigy, figure, representation.

guy v *guy the poor old man* ridicule, make fun of, poke fun at, make game/sport of, mock, sneer at, caricature; *inf* send up, rib, rag, take off.

guzzle v **1** *guzzle food* gulp, gobble, bolt, wolf, devour; cram oneself, stuff oneself, gormandize; *inf* tuck into, scoff, put away. **2** *guzzle beer* gulp down, swallow greedily, quaff, swill, toss off; *inf* knock back, swig.

gypsy n Romany, tzigane, didicoi, traveller, rover, roamer, wanderer, rambler; *derog* transient, vagrant, vagabond, tinker.

gyrate v rotate, revolve, wheel round, turn round, circle, whirl, pirouette, twirl, swirl, spin, swivel.

gyration n rotation, circumrotation, revolution, wheeling, turning around, circling, convolution, circumconvolution, whirling, pirouetting, twirling, swirling, spinning, swivelling.

Hh

habit n **1** *it was his habit to go for a morning walk* custom, practice, procedure, wont, way, routine, matter of course, style, pattern, convention, policy, mode, rule. **2** *he had a habit of peering* tendency, propensity, predisposition, proclivity, penchant, leaning, bent, inclination, custom, practice, quirk. **3** *a cheerful habit of mind* disposition, temper, temperament, nature, character, make-up, constitution, humour, frame of mind. **4** *get into the habit of smoking* addiction, dependence, weakness, fixation, obsession. **5** *a riding habit* | *his old-fashioned habit* costume, dress, garb, attire, apparel, clothes, clothing, garments, livery, uniform; *inf* gear, togs, rig-out, rags.

habitable adj inhabitable, livable-in, fit to live in, fit to occupy, tenantable, fit to lodge/reside in.

habitat n **1** *the animal's natural habitat* environment, natural environment, natural setting/background/element, home, abode. **2** *the habitat of students* home, abode, residence, residency, dwelling, dwelling-place, habitation, location, situation, address.

habitation n **1** *fit for habitation* occupancy, occupation, tenancy, residence, residency, living, dwelling, housing, inhabitance, inhabitancy, inhabitation, lodging, lodgement, domiciliation, billeting, quartering. **2** *settled into a new habitation* home, house, residence, residency, dwelling, dwelling-place, abode, domicile, lodging, lodging-place, quarters, living quarters, rooms, apartment, flat, accommodation, housing, roof over one's head; *inf* pad, digs. **3** *the habitation of the flat* occupancy, occupation, inhabitance, inhabiting, tenancy, tenure.

habitual adj **1** *taking his habitual route/place* customary, accustomed, regular, usual, normal, set, fixed, established, routine, wonted, common, ordinary, familiar, traditional. **2** *their habitual grumbling* persistent, constant, continual, recurrent, repeated, perpetual, non-stop, continuous, frequent. **3** *a habitual smoker* by habit, confirmed, addicted, chronic, inveterate, hardened, ingrained.

habituate v *habituate oneself to a hot climate* accustom, make used to, adapt, acclimatize, condition, break in, inure, harden, season, train, school, discipline, familiarize, make familiar with.

habitué n frequenter, frequent visitor, regular visitor, regular customer, regular patron/client, constant visitor, familiar face.

hack v **1** *hack down the tree* cut down, chop down, fell, hew, saw down. **2** *hack one's way through the jungle* cut, hew, slash, clear. **3** *hack the carcass* gash, cut, chop, mangle, mutilate, lacerate, shatter, fracture. **4** *children hacking away* cough, rasp, choke; *inf* bark.

hack n **1** *a farmer with just an old hack* horse, hired horse, tired-out horse, worn-out horse, jade; *inf* nag, crock. **2** *no specialist staff, just hacks* drudge, labourer, menial, slave, factotum, toiler, plodder; *inf* skivvy. **3** *newspapers just employing hacks* literary drudge, penny-a-liner, scribbler, Grub Street writer.

hack adj *using hack phrases* banal, trite, overused, tired, worn-out, stale, stereotyped. *see* HACKNEYED.

hackle n **make someone's hackles rise** anger, annoy, enrage, vex; *inf* make someone see red, get someone's dander up, rile.

hackneyed adj *using hackneyed phrases* hack, banal, trite, overused, overworked, tired, worn-out, time-worn, stale, stereotyped, clichéd, platitudinous, unoriginal, unimaginative, commonplace, common, pedestrian, prosaic, run-of-the-mill, stock, conventional; *inf* played-out, corny, old-hat.

hag n crone, witch, gorgon, harridan, fury, ogress, hellcat, harpy, shrew, virago, vixen, termagant; *inf* battleaxe, old bat.

haggard adj drawn, gaunt, pinched, hollow-cheeked, hollow-eyed, ghastly, ghostlike, deathlike, wan, pallid, cadaverous, peaked, drained, careworn, emaciated, wasted, thin.

haggle v **1** *haggle over the price* bargain, drive a hard bargain, beat down, chaffer, higgle, patter; *Amer* dicker. **2** *children haggling* wrangle, squabble, bicker, quarrel, argue, dispute.

hail¹ v **1** *hail a friend* salute, greet, say hello to, nod to, wave to, smile at, lift one's hat to, acknowledge. **2** *hail a taxi* signal, make a sign to, flag, flag down, wave down, call, shout to, sing out to, halloo, accost. **3** *hail the king* acclaim, applaud, cheer, praise, sound the praises of, laud, extol, pay tribute to, pay homage to, exalt, glorify. **4** *hail from England* come from, be a native of, be born in, originate in, have one's roots in.

hail¹ n give a hail call, cry, shout, signal, greeting, salutation, salute, hello, acknowledgement.

hail² n **1** *hail falling* hailstones, sleet, frozen rain. **2** *a hail of bullets/protest* shower, rain, storm, volley, barrage, bombardment, pelting.

hail² v *hail stones/curses down on them | stones hailed down on him* shower, rain, rain down, pelt, pepper, batter, bombard, volley; beat down upon.

hair n **1** *she has beautiful hair* head of hair, locks, tresses, shock, mop. **2** *animal's hair* coat, fur, pelt, hide, wool, fleece, mane. **by a hair, by a hair's breadth** by the narrowest of margins, by a narrow margin, by the skin of one's teeth, by a split second; *inf* by a whisker. **let one's hair down** throw off one's inhibitions, relax, be informal; *inf* hang loose, let it all hang out; *Amer inf* chill out. **not turn a hair** remain calm; *inf* keep one's cool, keep one's hair on, not bat an eyelid. **split hairs** quibble, argue over nothing, fuss over trifles, niggle, cavil, pettifog; *inf* nit-pick.

hair-raising adj spine-chilling, blood-curdling, terrifying, petrifying, horrifying, frightening, alarming, shocking, exciting, thrilling; *inf* scary, creepy.

hairy adj hair-covered, hirsute, woolly, shaggy, bushy, furry, fleecy, fuzzy, bearded, unshaven, bewhiskered, stubbly; *Tech* pilose, pileous, pappose.

halcyon adj **1** *halcyon weather* mild, calm, still, tranquil, quiet, serene, pleasant, moderate, temperate, gentle, placid, peaceful, windless, stormless. **2** *halcyon days of youth* carefree, happy, blissful, golden, joyful, joyous, contented, flourishing, thriving, prosperous, palmy.

hale adj healthy, in good health, well, fit, bursting with good health, flourishing, blooming, in excellent shape, in fine fettle, strong, robust, vigorous, hardy, sturdy, hearty, full of vim, able-bodied, lusty; *inf* in the pink, fit as a fiddle, in tip-top condition.

half n *take a half* equal part/portion/section/division, fifty percent, hemisphere, semisphere. **by half** *too smart by half* excessively, far, to too great an extent, by an excessive amount, considerably, very much. **by halves** *do something by halves* inadequately, insufficiently, incompletely, imperfectly, scrappily, skimpily.

half adj **1** *half orange* halved, divided in two, in two equal parts, bisected, hemispherical. **2** *half measures | a half smile* partial, incomplete, limited, moderate, slight, inadequate, insufficient.

half adv **1** *half-cooked | she half smiled* partly, partially, in part, part, incompletely, inadequately, insufficiently, slightly, barely. **2** *half inclined to agree* nearly, very nearly, to a certain extent, to a considerable extent, all but, almost. **not half 1** *not half good enough | not half bad* not at all, not in any way, not nearly. **2** *he didn't half lose his temper* to a great extent, to a considerable extent, certainly, indeed.

half-baked adj **1** *half-baked plans* ill-conceived, poorly-planned, unplanned, not thought through, premature, undeveloped, unformed, ill-judged, short-sighted, injudicious, impractical; *inf* crackpot. **2** *a half-baked young man* foolish, stupid, silly, brainless, senseless, ignorant, inexperienced, immature, callow, green, credulous, wet behind the ears; *inf* half-witted, dim-witted, dopey.

half-hearted adj *plan received a half-hearted welcome* lukewarm, unenthusiastic, apathetic, indifferent, uninterested, unconcerned, cool, listless, lacklustre, dispassionate, unemotional, cursory, perfunctory, superficial, passive, neutral.

halfway adv **1** *go halfway* midway, to/in the middle, to/at the midpoint. **2** *halfway finished* almost, nearly, just about, in part, partly, part, to a certain degree/ extent, in some measure. **meet someone halfway** reach a compromise with, come to terms with, strike a balance with, find a happy medium with, establish a middle ground with, give and take with; *inf* go fifty-fifty with.

halfway adj *the halfway point* midway, equidistant, mid, middle, intermediate, central, mean, medial, median.

halfwit n simpleton, idiot, dolt, blockhead, dunderhead, dullard, dunce, fool, numbskull; *inf* nitwit, moron, dim-wit, imbecile, crackpot, nut.

halfwitted adj *you halfwitted fool! | halfwitted plans* simple-minded, feeble-minded, simple, stupid, idiotic, doltish, dull-witted, foolish, silly, half-baked; *inf* dim-witted, crazy, moronic, barmy, batty, nutty, cracked, nitwitted, crackpot.

hall n **1** *concerts held in the main hall* auditorium, assembly room, chamber; assembly hall, conference hall, concert hall, church hall, town hall. **2** *hostesses greeting their guests in the hall* entrance hall, vestibule, hallway, entry, lobby, foyer, passageway, passage.

hallmark n **1** *the hallmark on silver* assay mark, stamp of authenticity, authentication seal, endorsement of authentication. **2** *good craftsmanship is his hallmark* mark, trademark, stamp, sign, sure sign, telltale sign, badge, device, symbol, indicator, indication, index.

hallucinate v *certain drugs can make you hallucinate* have/experience hallucinations, see visions, have a vision, fantasize, imagine things, dream, be delirious; *inf* see things, be on a trip.

hallucination n *this drug causes hallucinations* illusion, figment of the imagination, imagining, vision, mirage, false conception, fantasy, apparition, dream, delirium, phantasmagoria; *inf* trip.

halo n nimbus, aureole, aureola, aura, gloriole, ring of light, crown of light, radiance, corona, halation.

halt[1] v **1** *halt at the traffic lights* come to a halt, stop, come to a stop, come to a standstill, pull up, draw up, wait. **2** *halt for the day* stop, finish, cease, break off, call it a day, down tools, desist, discontinue, rest; *inf* knock off. **3** *work has halted* stop, finish, cease, come to an end, be at an end, draw to a close, run its course. **4** *halt progress* bring to a halt/stop, arrest, check, block, curb, stem, terminate, end, put an end to, put a stop to, bring an end to, crush, nip in the bud, frustrate, baulk, obstruct, impede, hold back.

halt[1] n **1** *a halt in the work* stop, stopping, stoppage, cessation, close, end, desistance, discontinuation, discontinuance, standstill, pause, interval, interlude, intermission, break, hiatus, rest, respite, breathing-space, time out; *inf* breather. **2** *come/draw/grind to a halt* stop, standstill.

halt[2] v **1** *keep halting when speaking* falter, hesitate, stammer, stutter, stumble, flounder, fumble for words. **2** *halting between going and staying* hesitate, waver, vacillate, dither, be unsure, be undecided, be in doubt, have qualms/misgivings; *Scots* swither.

halter n bridle, harness; *Amer* headstall.

halting adj **1** *walk with a halting gait* limping, hobbling, stumbling, unsteady, awkward. **2** *speak in halting tones* faltering, hesitating, stammering, stuttering, stumbling, laboured.

halve v *halved the orange with a knife* | *try to halve imports* cut in half, divide into two equal parts, divide in two, divide equally, split in two, sever in two, share equally, dichotomize, reduce by fifty per cent.

halves npl **by halves** see HALF n by halves .

hammer n *workmen using hammers* claw-hammer, sledgehammer, mallet, beetle, gavel.

hammer v **1** *hammer out a horseshoe* | *hammer it on the anvil* beat out, shape, form, mould, forge, fashion, make, fabricate. **2** *a bully hammering little boys* beat, batter, pound, pummel, hit, strike, slap, cudgel, bludgeon, club; *inf* wallop, clobber. **3** *hammer the opposition* trounce, defeat utterly, inflict heavy damage on, bring someone to their knees, beat, thrash, worst, drub, give a drubbing to; *inf* clobber, beat hollow. **4** *hammer facts into the pupils* drum into, din into, drive into, teach over and over again, drub into. **5** *hammer away at the problem* persevere, persist; work, pound away, keep on, plod/slog away, labour, grind away, drudge, peg away; *inf* stick, beaver away, plug away. **6** *hammer out a solution* | *still hammering out the detail* thrash out, work out, resolve, form a resolution about, sort out, settle, negotiate, bring about, bring to a satisfactory conclusion, bring to a finish, come to decision on, complete, accomplish, produce, carry through, effect.

hamper v *hamper progress* hinder, obstruct, impede, hold back, inhibit, retard, slow down, hold up, restrain, block, check, frustrate, baulk, thwart, foil, curb, interfere with, cramp, restrict, bridle, handicap, stymie, hamstring, shackle, fetter, encumber, cumber, trammel; *inf* throw a spanner in the works.

hamper n *a picnic/Christmas hamper* basket, creel, pannier, wickerwork box, box, container, holder.

hamstring v **1** *hamstring the athlete* cripple, lame, injure, disable, hock. **2** *hamstring the opposition's plans* frustrate, thwart, baulk, foil, check, curb, hamper, ruin, prevent, stop. see HAMPER V.

hand n **1** *large hands* palm, fist; *inf* paw, mitt, duke; *Scots* nieve. **2** *the hand of a clock* dial pointer, indicator, needle. **3** *give the workers a hand* helping hand, help, assistance, aid, support, succour, relief. **4** *sack a number of hands* worker, workman, work person, employee, operative, hired hand, hired man, hired person, hired help, labourer, artisan, crewman, crew. **5** *have a* *neat hand* writing, handwriting, penmanship, script, calligraphy, chirography. **6** *try your hand at baking* ability, skill, art, artistry, craftsmanship. **7** *give a big hand to the singer* applause, round of applause, clapping of hands, clap, handclap, ovation. **at hand, to hand 1** *help is at hand* | *keep the book to hand* readily available, available, at one's disposal, handy, ready, within reach, accessible, close, close at hand, near, nearby; *inf* on tap. **2** *your big moment is at hand* close at hand, imminent, approaching, coming, about to happen, impending. **by hand** *make it by hand* manually, with one's hands, using one's hands. **from hand to mouth** *live from hand to mouth* in poverty, meagrely, scantily, skimpily, precariously, uncertainly, insecurely, improvidently; *inf* on the breadline. **hand in glove** *working hand in glove with the enemy* in partnership, in league, in close association, in collusion; *inf* in cahoots. **hand in hand 1** *walking hand in hand* holding hands, clasping hands, with hands clasped. **2** *working hand in hand* together, closely, side by side, in close association, in partnership, conjointly, concurrently. **in hand 1** *the matter is in hand* receiving attention, being dealt with, under control, under way. **2** *have money in hand* ready, available, available for use, in reserve, put by. **to hand** *see* HAND n at hand. **try one's hand** try, make an attempt, attempt, essay; *inf* have/take a shot, have a go.

hand v **1** *hand the book to her* give, pass, pass over, hand over, deliver, present. *see* HAND v hand over. **2** *hand her out of the car* | *hand an old lady across the road* help, assist, aid, give someone a helping hand, guide, convey, lead. **hand down/on** *hand down/on the family jewels* pass down, pass on, give, transfer, transmit, bequeath, will. **hand out** *hand out food supplies* distribute, give out, pass out, deal out, dole out, mete out, dispense, apportion, disseminate, disburse; *inf* dish out. **hand over** *hand over the money* give, give up, pass, pass over, present, turn over, deliver, surrender, yield, release; *inf* fork out.

handbag n bag, shoulder-bag, clutch bag, evening bag, flight bag, travelling bag; *Amer* purse.

handbill n circular, advertisement, notice, pamphlet, leaflet, brochure, bulletin; *inf* junk mail; *Amer* flyer.

handbook n guide, guidebook, travel guide, tourist guide, manual, instruction manual, instructions, book of directions, directory, vade-mecum, Baedeker, ABC.

handcuff v put handcuffs on, manacle, fetter, shackle.

handcuffs npl manacles, fetters, shackles; *inf* cuffs, bracelets, darbies.

handful n **1** *a handful of people* few, small number, small amount, small quantity, sprinkling. **2** *the child is a handful* nuisance, pest, bother, irritant, source of annoyance, thorn in the flesh, bugbear; *inf* pain, pain in the neck.

handicap n **1** *pupils suffering from a handicap* physical/mental disability, physical/mental disadvantage, physical/mental abnormality, impairment. **2** *her poverty was a handicap in her career* disadvantage, impediment, hindrance, obstruction, obstacle, encumbrance, check, block, curb, trammel, barrier, stumbling block, constraint, restriction, limitation, drawback, shortcoming.

handicap v *handicapped by his slight build* put at a disadvantage, disadvantage, impede, hinder, impair, hamper, obstruct, check, block, encumber, curb, trammel, bridle, hold back, constrain, restrict, limit.

handicraft n *go to handicraft classes* craft, handiwork, craftsmanship, workmanship, artisanship, art, skill.

handiwork n **1** *admire the handiwork at the crafts exhibition* handicraft, craft, craftsmanship. *see* HANDICRAFT. **2** *this is the handiwork of a maniac* action, achievement, work, doing, creation, design, product, production, result.

handle n *held the handle of the tool/sword* shaft, grip, handgrip, hilt, haft, knob, stock, helve.

handle v **1** *handle the goods* touch, feel, finger, hold, grasp, grip, pick up, lift, pat, caress, stroke, fondle, poke, maul; *inf* paw. **2** *handle difficult pupils* cope with, deal with, treat, manage, control. **3** *handle their business affairs* be in charge of, control, manage, administer, direct, guide, conduct, supervise, take care of. **4** *handle a car* drive, steer, operate, manoeuvre. **5** *his paper handled the story well* deal with, treat, discuss, discourse on. **6** *dealers handling grain* deal in, traffic in, trade in, market, sell, stock, carry.

handout n **1** *beggars waiting for handouts* alms, charity, gifts of food/money/clothes, dole. **2** *read the handout* press release, circular, advertising leaflet, brochure, pamphlet, bulletin, notice, literature. **3** *accept the handouts from reps* free sample; *inf* freebie.

hand-picked adj *hand-picked team of negotiators* select, specially-selected, élite, choice, specially-chosen, elect.

hands npl *in the hands of the enemy* possession, keeping, clutches, grasp, charge, care, power, authority, command, management, control, custody, guardianship, supervision, disposal, jurisdiction. **hands down** *win hands down* easily, with no trouble, effortlessly, without effort; *inf* no sweat.

handsome adj **1** *a handsome man* good-looking, attractive, personable; *inf* dishy. **2** *a handsome woman* good-looking, attractive, personable, elegant, fine, well-formed, well-proportional, stately, dignified. **3** *a handsome gift* generous, magnanimous, liberal, lavish, bounteous, considerable, sizeable, large, ample, abundant, plentiful.

handwriting n writing, hand, penmanship, script, calligraphy, chirography; *inf* scrawl, scribble, fist.

handy adj **1** *is the book handy?* to hand, at hand, available, within reach, accessible, near, nearby, close, at one's fingertips, convenient; *inf* on tap. **2** *a handy instrument* useful, helpful, practicable, practical, serviceable, functional, expedient, easy-to-use, neat, convenient. **3** *a handy person* dexterous, deft, nimble-fingered, adroit, adept, proficient, skilful, skilled, expert, clever/good with one's hands.

hang v **1** *mobiles hanging from the ceiling* hang down, be suspended, dangle, swing, sway, be pendent. **2** *hang the picture* suspend, put up, put on a hook. **3** *hang the prisoner* send to the gallows, put the noose on, send to the gibbet, gibbet, execute; *inf* string up. **4** *hang wallpaper* stick on, attach, fix, fasten on, append, paste, glue, cement. **5** *a hall hung with tapestries* decorate, adorn, ornament, deck, drape, cover, furnish. **6** *hawks hanging in the air* hover, float, be poised, flutter, flit, drift, remain static. **hang about/around 1** *hang about, he won't be long* hold on, wait, wait a minute, linger, loiter, tarry, dally, waste time; *inf* hang on. **2** *hang about bars* frequent, be a regular visitor to, be a regular client of, haunt; *inf* hang out in. **3** *hang about with thugs* associate with, keep company with, be a friend/companion of; *inf* hang out with. **hang back** *hang back when volunteers were asked for* hold back, stay back, stay in the background, be reluctant, hesitate, demur, recoil, shrink back. **hang down** *with her skirt hanging down* droop, trail, sag. **hang fire** *they're hanging fire until prices rise* delay, hang back, hold back, procrastinate, stall, adopt Fabian tactics. **hang on 1** *hang on to*

her mother's hand hold, hold fast to, cling to, cling on to, grip, clutch, grasp, cleave to. **2** *everything hangs on the financial position* depend, be dependent on, turn on, hinge on, rest on, be conditional on, be contingent upon, be determined by, be conditioned by. **3** *hang on his every word* listen closely to, be very attentive to, concentrate hard on, be rapt by, give ear to; be all ears for. **4** *hang on till things improve* hold out, hold on, persevere, persist, go on, carry on, continue, remain, endure. **5** *hang on, I'll get him* hold on, wait, wait a minute, stop, stay, remain, hold the line. **hang over 1** *trees hanging over the fence* lean over, bend over, bend downwards, bend forwards, bow, droop. **2** *the threat of redundancy is hanging over them* loom, be imminent, impend, menace, threaten, approach, draw near; *inf* be just around the corner. **get the hang of** get the knack of, acquire the technique of, catch on, grasp, comprehend, understand.

hangdog adj *looked at him with a hangdog expression* shamefaced, ashamed, embarrassed, guilty-looking, sheepish, abashed, abject, cowed, cringing, downcast, crestfallen, browbeaten, defeated, intimidated, wretched.

hanger-on n follower, henchman, retainer, appendage, dependant, parasite, minion, lackey, vassal, flunkey, camp-follower, sycophant, fawner, sponger, leech; *inf* groupie, freeloader.

hangover n after-effects, effects of alcohol, crapulence, crapulousness; *inf* morning after feeling.

hang-up n **1** *a hang-up about French films* preoccupation, fixation, obsession, phobia, bee in one's bonnet, idée fixe; *inf* thing. **2** *she has a hang-up about maths* mental block, psychological block, block, inhibition, difficulty, problem; *inf* thing.

hank n *hanks of coloured wool* skein, coil, loop, twist, length, roll, piece.

hanker v **hanker after/for** *hanker after/for a holiday abroad* long for, have a longing for, yearn for, crave, desire, hunger for, thirst for, be bent on, covet, want, wish for, set one's heart on, pine for, be itching for, lust after; *inf* be dying for, have a yen for.

hankering n longing, yearning, craving, desire, hunger, thirst, want, wish, urge, itch, lust; *inf* yen.

haphazard adj unplanned, random, unsystematic, unorganized, unmethodical, orderless, aimless, indiscriminate, undirected, irregular, slapdash, thrown together, careless, casual, hit-or-miss.

hapless adj *the hapless child began to cry* unlucky, luckless, out of luck, unfortunate, ill-starred, forlorn, wretched, woebegone, unhappy; *inf* down on one's luck.

happen v 1 *the accident happened at dawn* take place, occur, come about, come to pass, present itself, arise, materialize, appear, come into being, chance, arrive, transpire, crop up, develop, supervene, eventuate; *inf* come off. 2 *what happened to her?* become of, befall, betide. 3 *I happened to meet her* chance, have the good/bad fortune to, be someone's fortune/misfortune to. 4 *happen upon hidden treasure* chance upon, stumble on, discover unexpectedly, find, meet by chance, encounter.

happening n occurrence, event, incident, occasion, affair, circumstance, action, case, phenomenon, eventuality, episode, experience, adventure, scene, proceedings, chance.

happily adv 1 *I shall happily go* with pleasure, gladly, delightedly, willingly, freely, contentedly, enthusiastically, with all one's heart and soul. 2 *children playing happily* cheerfully, merrily, gaily, light-heartedly, joyfully, blithely. *see* HAPPY 1. 3 *happily, it turned out all right* luckily, fortunately, as luck would have it, providentially.

happiness n cheerfulness, cheeriness, merriness, gaiety, good spirits, high spirits, light-heartedness, joy, joyfulness, joviality, glee, blitheness, carefreeness, enjoyment, gladness, delight, exuberance, elation, ecstasy, bliss, blissfulness, euphoria, transports. *see* HAPPY 1.

happy adj 1 *happy children* cheerful, cheery, merry, gay, in good spirits, in high spirits, light-hearted, joyful, joyous, jovial, gleeful, buoyant, blithe, blithesome, carefree, untroubled, smiling, glad, delighted, exuberant, elated, ecstatic, blissful, euphoric, overjoyed, thrilled, in seventh heaven, over the moon, floating/walking on air; *inf* on cloud nine, on top of the world. 2 *happy to see you* glad, pleased, delighted, contented, satisfied, gratified, thrilled. 3 *by a happy chance* lucky, fortunate, favourable, advantageous, beneficial, helpful, opportune, timely, convenient, propitious, auspicious. 4 *a happy choice* apt, appropriate, fitting, fit, good, right, proper, seemly.

happy-go-lucky adj *he's always so happy-go-lucky | has such a happy-go-lucky manner* carefree, light-hearted, devil-may-care, blithe, free and easy, easygoing, nonchalant, casual, untroubled, unworried, unconcerned, insouciant, heedless, irresponsible, improvident.

harangue n lecture, tirade, diatribe, speech, talk, sermon, exhortation, declamation, oration, address, homily, peroration; *inf* spiel.

harass v 1 *children harassing their mother* bother, pester, annoy, exasperate, worry, fret, disturb, agitate, provoke, badger, hound, torment, plague, persecute, harry, tease, bait, nag, molest, bedevil; *inf* hassle, give someone a hard time, drive someone up the wall. 2 *troops harassing the enemy* harry, attack repeatedly, raid, beleaguer, press hard, oppress.

harassed adj *harassed parents* distraught, under pressure, stressed, under stress, strained, worried, careworn, troubled, vexed, agitated, fretting; *inf* hassled.

harbinger n herald, forerunner, precursor, usher, announcer, *avant-courier*, sign, portent, omen, augury.

harbour n 1 *ships in harbour* port, anchorage, haven, dock, harbourage, marina. 2 *a safe harbour for refugees* place of safety, refuge, shelter, haven, sanctuary, retreat, asylum, sanctum, covert.

harbour v 1 *harbour criminals* give shelter to, shelter, house, lodge, put up, take in, billet, provide refuge for, shield, protect, conceal, hide, secrete. 2 *harbour resentment* nurse, nurture, maintain, hold on to, cherish, cling to, retain, entertain, brood over.

hard adj 1 *hard ground* firm, solid, solidified, compact, compacted, condensed, close-packed, compressed, dense, rigid, stiff, unyielding, resistant, unmalleable, inflexible, unpliable, tough, strong, stony, rock-like. 2 *hard physical work* arduous, strenuous, heavy, tiring, fatiguing, exhausting, back-breaking, laborious, rigorous, exacting, formidable, tough, difficult, uphill, toilsome, Herculean. 3 *a hard problem* difficult, complicated, complex, involved, intricate, puzzling, perplexing, baffling, knotty, thorny, bewildering, enigmatic, insoluble, insolvable, unfathomable, incomprehensible. 4 *a hard master* harsh, hard-hearted, severe, stern, cold, cold-hearted, unfeeling, unsympathetic, grim, ruthless, oppressive, tyrannical, pitiless, merciless, unrelenting, unsparing, lacking compassion, callous, cruel, vicious, implacable, obdurate, unyielding, unjust, unfair. 5 *hard living conditions* difficult, grim, harsh, unpleasant, disagreeable, uncomfortable, intolerable, unendurable, unbearable, insupportable, distressing, painful, disastrous, calamitous. 6 *a hard blow/knock* forceful, violent, heavy, strong, powerful, sharp, fierce, harsh. 7 *a hard* *worker* hard-working, energetic, industrious, diligent, assiduous, conscientious, sedulous, keen, enthusiastic, zealous, earnest, persevering, persistent, unflagging, untiring, indefatigable. **8** *hard words* | *no hard feelings* angry, acrimonious, bitter, antagonistic, hostile, resentful, rancorous. **9** *the hard facts* actual, definite, undeniable, indisputable, verifiable, plain, cold, bare, bold, harsh, unvarnished, unembellished. **10** *hard liquor* alcoholic, strong, spiritous. **11** *hard drugs* addictive, habit-forming, harmful, noxious, injurious.

hard adv **1** *push hard* strenuously, energetically, powerfully, heavily, with all one's might, with might and main, heartily, vigorously, with vigour, forcefully, with force, forcibly, with great effort, fiercely, intensely. **2** *work hard* energetically, industriously, diligently, assiduously, conscientiously, enthusiastically, sedulously, with application, earnestly, with perseverance, persistently, indefatigably; *inf* like billy-oh. *see* HARD adj 7. **3** *our victory was hard won* with difficulty, with effort, laboriously, after a struggle, painfully. **4** *her death hit him hard* badly, intensely, violently, forcefully, harshly, distressingly, painfully, agonizingly. **5** *it was raining hard* heavily, steadily, cats and dogs, buckets. **6** *look hard at* keenly, sharply, carefully, closely, painstakingly. **7** *they followed hard on his heels* close, near. **hard by** *living hard by the motorway* right by, beside, near to, nearby, close to, close by, not far from, a step away from, within a stone's throw of. **hard up** poor, short of money/cash, in financial difficulties, penniless, impoverished, impecunious, bankrupt, in the red, without means of support, on one's beam-ends; *inf* broke, stony-broke, cleaned out, bust, strapped, on one's uppers, skint. **hard-and-fast** adj *hard-and-fast rules* binding, set, strict, stringent, inflexible, rigorous, immutable, unalterable, uncompromising, incontestable, incontrovertible.

hard-bitten adj *hard-bitten journalists* hardened, case-hardened, hardened, inured, toughened by experience, tough, cynical, down-to-earth.

hard-boiled adj *hard-boiled young women* cynical, unsentimental, lacking sentiment, tough, down-to-earth, world-weary.

hard-core adj **1** *hard-core socialists* die-hard, dyed-in-the-wool, staunch, steadfast, dedicated, intransigent, uncompromising, obstinate, stubborn, extreme. **2** *hard-core pornography* explicit, blatant, obscene; *inf* full-frontal.

harden v **1** *the cement hardened* become hard, solidify, set, stiffen, bake, anneal, cake, freeze, congeal, clot, coagulate. *see* HARD adj 1. **2** *harden one's heart* toughen, make insensitive/unfeeling, deaden, numb, benumb. **3** *life had hardened him* make tough, toughen, case-harden, make unfeeling, brutalize, make callous, indurate. **4** *harden to cold* accustom, habituate, acclimatize, inure. **5** *harden one's defences* strengthen, fortify, reinforce, buttress, brace, gird.

hardened adj *a hardened criminal* habitual, accustomed, chronic, inured, seasoned, inveterate, incorrigible, irredeemable, reprobate, impenitent, unregenerate, shameless.

hard-headed adj *hard-headed businessmen* shrewd, astute, sharp, sharp-witted, tough, unsentimental, hard-bitten, practical, pragmatic, realistic, level-headed, cool-headed, sensible, rational, with one's feet on the ground.

hard-hearted adj *mother could be so hard-hearted* hard, heartless, unfeeling, unsympathetic, uncompassionate, lacking compassion, without sentiment, cold, cold-hearted, uncaring, unconcerned, indifferent, unmoved, unkind, cruel, callous, inhuman, merciless, pitiless, stony-hearted, stony. *see* HARD adj 4.

hard-hitting adj *a hard-hitting report* tough, uncompromising, unsparing, strongly worded, vigorous, pulling no punches, straight-talking, blunt, frank, critical.

hardihood n **1** *the hardihood of the soldiers* bravery, courage, valour, boldness, intrepidity, heroism. *see* HARDY 2. **2** *the hardihood of the children in defying the teacher* audacity, rashness, foolhardiness, impudence. *see* HARDY 3.

hardiness n *the hardiness of the children* healthiness, strength, robustness, sturdiness, toughness, ruggedness, vigour. *see* HARDY 1.

hard-line adj *hard-line members of the party* extreme, tough, uncompromising, inflexible, unyielding, intransigent, not giving an inch.

hardly adv *hardly able to walk* | *can hardly see* | *hardly alive* scarcely, barely, only just, just, almost not, with difficulty, with effort.

hard-pressed adj **1** *the retreating army was hard-pressed* closely pursued, hotly pursued, harried, hounded, under attack, in a tight corner. **2** *hard-pressed workers* overloaded, overburdened, overworked, overtaxed, under pressure, harassed, in difficulties, with one's back to the wall; *inf* pushed, up against it.

hardship n *suffer great hardship* adversity, deprivation, privation, want, need, destitution, poverty, austerity, desolation, misfortune, distress, suffering, affliction, pain, misery, wretchedness, tribulation, trials, trials and tribulation, burdens, calamity, catastrophe, disaster, ruin, ruination, oppression, persecution, torment, torture, travail.

hard-wearing adj *hard-wearing shoes/carpet* durable, strong, tough, stout, rugged, made to last, resilient, well-made.

hard-working adj *many hard-working pupils* diligent, industrious, conscientious, assiduous, sedulous, energetic, keen, enthusiastic, zealous, busy, with one's shoulder to the wheel.

hardy adj **1** *hardy children* healthy, fit, strong, robust, sturdy, tough, rugged, vigorous, lusty, stalwart, hale and hearty, sound in body and limb, fit as a fiddle, in fine fettle, in good kilter, in good condition. **2** *hardy men defying death* brave, courageous, valiant, bold, valorous, intrepid, fearless, heroic, stout-hearted, daring, plucky, mettlesome. **3** *hardy children defying the teacher* audacious, rash, reckless, foolhardy, impetuous, daredevil, brazen, impudent.

hare-brained adj **1** *a hare-brained scheme* foolish, foolhardy, rash, reckless, madcap, wild, ridiculous, half-baked, ill-thought-out, ill-conceived; *inf* crackpot. **2** *a hare-brained young girl* foolish, silly, empty-headed, scatterbrained, feather-brained, brainless, giddy, dizzy, whimsical, capricious, flighty; *inf* half-witted.

hark v *hark! the birds are singing* harken, listen, pay attention, pay heed, give ear. **hark back** *hark back to subjects previously discussed* go back, turn back, look back, think back, revert, regress, retrovert, remember, recall, recollect.

harlequin n *dressed as a harlequin* jester, fool, buffoon, zany.

harlequin adj *a harlequin pattern* chequered, variegated, varicoloured, particoloured, multicoloured, many-coloured, motley.

harlot n whore, prostitute, call-girl, streetwalker, loose woman, fallen woman, woman of the night, *fille de joie*, madam, procuress, bawd; *inf* tart, pick-up girl, pro, tramp, scrubber, hooker; *lit* strumpet.

harm n **1** *inflict harm on* hurt, injury, pain, suffering, trauma, adversity, disservice, abuse, damage, mischief, detriment, defacement, defilement, impairment, destruction, loss, ruin, havoc. **2** *men full of harm* badness, evil, wrongdoing, wrong, wickedness, vice, iniquity, sin, sinfulness, immorality, nefariousness.

harm v *harm the child/building | try not to harm their relationship* hurt, injure, wound, inflict pain/suffering/trauma on, abuse, maltreat, ill-treat, ill-use, molest, do violence to, damage, do mischief to, deface, defile, impair, spoil, mar, blemish, destroy.

harmful adj **1** *harmful effects* hurtful, injurious, wounding, abusive, detrimental, deleterious, disadvantageous, destructive, dangerous, pernicious, noxious, baneful, toxic. **2** *a harmful influence* bad, evil, malign, wicked, corrupting, subversive.

harmless adj **1** *a harmless substance* innocuous, innoxious, safe, non-dangerous, non-toxic, non-irritant, mild. **2** *a harmless old man* innocuous, inoffensive, unoffending, innocent, blameless, gentle.

harmonious adj **1** *a harmonious musical piece* melodious, tuneful, musical, harmonizing, sweet-sounding, mellifluous, dulcet, euphonious, symphonious, rhythmic, consonant. **2** *a harmonious atmosphere/relationship* peaceful, peaceable, friendly, amicable, cordial, amiable, agreeable, congenial, united, in harmony, in rapport, in tune, attuned, in accord, compatible, sympathetic. **3** *a harmonious collection of colours/buildings* compatible, congruous, coordinated, concordant, well-matched, matching.

harmonize v **1** *the colours harmonize well* be harmonious, go together, fit together, be compatible, blend, mix well, be congruous, be consonant, be well-coordinated, match. **2** *their stories/thoughts harmonize* be in accord, agree, be in assent, correspond, coincide, tally, be in unison, be congruent, be of one mind. **3** *harmonize relations* restore harmony to, settle differences, reconcile, patch up, make peaceful, negotiate peace between, heal the breach, pour oil on troubled waters.

harmony n **1** *working in harmony* agreement, assent, accord, accordance, concordance, concurrence, cooperation, unanimity, unity, unison, oneness, amity, amicability, good will, affinity, rapport, sympathy, likemindedness, friendship, fellowship, comradeship, peace, peacefulness. **2** *the harmony of the colours* compatibility, congruity, consonance, concord, coordination, blending, balance, symmetry, suitability. **3** *enjoy the harmony at the concert* tune, melody, tunefulness, melodiousness, mellifluousness, euphony, euphoniousness.

harness n *horse's harness* tackle, tack, equipage, equipment, gear, accoutrement, trappings, yoke, bridle. **in harness** working, at work, employed, in occupation, in action, active, busy.

harness v **1** *harness the horses* put in harness, saddle, yoke, bridle, hitch up, couple. **2** *harness the sun's rays | must harness her energies* control, utilize, put to use, render useful, make productive, turn to good account, apply, exploit, channel, mobilize, capitalize on.

harp n *playing the harp* lyre; aeolian/wind harp, jew's harp, Celtic harp, clarsach. **harp on** *harp on his untidiness* dwell on, persist in talking about, repeat complaints about, nag about, press/labour the point about; *inf* go on and on about.

harridan n shrew, harpy, virago, termagant, vixen, scold, nag, fishwife, witch, hellcat, tartar, spitfire, fury, hag, gorgon; *inf* old bag, battleaxe.

harrowing adj *harrowing cries/sight/experience* distressing, agonizing, excruciating, traumatic, heart-breaking, heart-rending, painful, racking, afflicting, chilling, disturbing, vexing, alarming, perturbing, unnerving, horrifying, terrifying.

harry v **1** *invaders harrying the villagers* plunder, rob, raid, sack, pillage, devastate, ravage, despoil, lay waste to. **2** *children harrying their mother* harass, annoy, bother, pester, disturb, worry, badger, chivvy, plague, vex, torment, tease, molest, persecute, bedevil; *inf* hassle, drive someone up the wall.

harsh adj **1** *a harsh noise* grating, jarring, grinding, rasping, strident, jangling, raucous, ear-piercing, discordant, dissonant, unharmonious. **2** *a harsh voice* rough, coarse, guttural, hoarse, croaking, raucous, strident, gravelly, gruff. **3** *harsh colours* gaudy, garish, glaring, over-bold, bold, loud, flashy, showy, crass, crude, vulgar. **4** *harsh conditions/countryside* grim, severe, desolate, stark, austere, barren, rough, bleak, bitter, wild, inhospitable, comfortless, Spartan. **5** *a harsh winter* severe, hard, bitter, bitterly cold, freezing, arctic, Siberian. **6** *a harsh reply* abrupt, brusque, blunt, curt, gruff, short, surly, concise, clipped, impolite, discourteous, uncivil, ungracious. **7** *a harsh ruler* cruel, brutal, savage, barbarous, hard-hearted, despotic, tyrannical, ruthless, uncompassionate, unfeeling, merciless, pitiless, relentless, unrelenting, inhuman. **8** *harsh rules/measure* stern,

severe, grim, stringent, austere, uncompromising, inflexible, punitive, Draconian.

harum-scarum adj reckless, rash, wild, impetuous, daredevil, madcap, harebrained, foolhardy, thoughtless, careless, heedless, frivolous.

harvest n **1** *celebrate the end of the harvest* harvest time, harvest tide, harvesting, reaping, ingathering, harvest home. **2** *a good harvest of wheat/apples* crop, yield, produce, vintage. **3** *the squirrels have a harvest of nuts* store, supply, stock, stockpile, hoard, cache, accumulation. **4** *the harvest of hard work* product, fruits, return, effect, result, consequence.

harvest v **1** *harvest the crop* gather in, gather, reap, glean, pick, pluck, collect. **2** *squirrels harvesting nuts* collect, amass, accumulate, hoard, garner. **3** *harvest benefits from his experience* acquire, gain, obtain, get, derive, procure, secure, net.

hash¹ n **make a hash of** make a mess of, botch, bungle, mishandle, mismanage, muddle up, mix up, get into a jumble; *inf* screw up.

hash² n hashish, marijuana, marihuana, cannabis, ganja, hemp; *inf* grass, pot.

hassle n **1** *tired of all the hassle* inconvenience, trouble, bother, annoyance, nuisance, trials and tribulation, harassment, badgering, difficulty, problem, struggle. **2** *a hassle at the pub last night* fight, quarrel, squabble, argument, disagreement, dispute, altercation, wrangle, tussle, struggle; *inf* set-to, barney, fisticuffs, argy-bargy.

hassle v *stop hassling him* annoy, badger, harass, hound, pester, bother, trouble, worry, torment, plague; *inf* give someone a hard time.

haste n **1** *fulfil the order with haste* speed, swiftness, rapidity, rapidness, quickness, fastness, alacrity, promptness, promptitude, dispatch, expeditiousness, expedition, celerity, fleetness, briskness, immediateness, urgency. **2** *haste causes carelessness* hastiness, hurriedness, hurry, rushing, hustling, impetuosity, recklessness, rashness, foolhardiness, precipitateness, impulsiveness, heedlessness, carelessness.

hasten v **1** *you must hasten to get there on time* make haste, hurry, hurry up, go fast, move faster, go quickly, dash, rush, speed up, run, race, sprint, fly, tear along, bolt, scurry, scamper, scuttle; *inf* get a move on, step on it, hotfoot it, hightail it. **2** *hasten the growth/work* speed up, accelerate, hurry on, quicken, advance, push forward, urge on, facilitate, precipitate, aid, assist, help, boost, increase, step up.

hasty adj **1** *with hasty steps* swift, rapid, quick, fast, speedy, hurried, hurrying, running, prompt, expeditious, fleet, brisk, urgent. **2** *a hasty visit/glance* quick, short, rapid, brief, rushed, short-lived, fleeting, transitory, cursory, perfunctory, superficial, slight. **3** *a hasty decision* hurried, rushed, impetuous, reckless, rash, foolhardy, precipitate, impulsive, headlong, heedless, thoughtless, careless, ill-conceived. **4** *a hasty temper/nature* hot-headed, quick-tempered, irascible, irritable, impatient, fiery, excitable, volatile, choleric, snappish, snappy, brusque.

hat n cap, bonnet, beret, tam-o'-shanter, tammy, hard hat, soft hat, trilby, bowler, top hat, deerstalker, homburg, stetson, straw hat, boater, panama, toque, cloche, pillbox, helmet, beaver, turban, fez, skull-cap, yarmulke.

hatch v **1** *hatch eggs* incubate, brood, sit on, cover. **2** *hatch chicks* bring forth. **3** *hatch a scheme* devise, concoct, contrive, plan, scheme, design, invent, formulate, originate, conceive, dream up, think up; *inf* cook up.

hatchet n axe, cleaver, pickaxe, poleaxe, chopper, mattock, machete, tomahawk.

hate v **1** *hate his rival/job* loathe, detest, abhor, dislike, abominate, despise, execrate, have an aversion to, feel hostile towards, be unable to abide/bear/stand, view with dislike, be sick of, be tired of, shudder at, be repelled by, recoil from. **2** *I hate to upset her* be reluctant, be loath, be unwilling, feel disinclined, be sorry, dislike, not have the heart, shy away from, flinch from, shrink from.

hate n *see* HATRED.

hateful adj loathsome, detestable, abhorrent, abominable, despicable, execrable, odious, revolting, repugnant, repellent, disgusting, obnoxious, offensive, insufferable, horrible, unpleasant, nasty, disagreeable, foul, vile, heinous.

hatred n hate, loathing, detestation, abhorrence, dislike, abomination, execration, aversion, hostility, ill-will, enmity, animosity, antagonism, antipathy, animus, revulsion, repugnance, odium, rancour, grudge.

haughty adj *she is so haughty | had a haughty expression* proud, arrogant, conceited, self-important, egotistical, vain, swollen-headed, overweening, overbearing, presumptuous, supercilious, condescending, lofty, patronizing, snobbish, scornful,

imperious, lordly, high-handed; *inf* on one's high horse, snooty, high and mighty, stuck-up, hoity-toity, uppity, uppish.

haul v **1** *haul the body out of the water* drag, draw, pull, tug, heave, trail, lug, tow, take in tow, hale. **2** *haul merchandise* transport, convey, move, cart, carry, convoy, ship.

haunt v **1** *ghosts haunting the castle* walk, roam, visit; *inf* spook. **2** *haunt bars* frequent, be a regular client of, visit regularly, spend all one's time in; *inf* hang out in, hang about/around. **3** *thoughts of guilt haunted him* obsess, prey on the mind of, prey on, torment, plague, beset, harry, disturb, trouble, worry, oppress, burden, weigh on, recur to, come back to, stay with.

haunt n *the local pub was one of his haunts* stamping-ground, frequented place, favourite spot, resort, rendezvous, meeting-place; *inf* hang-out, local, watering-hole.

haunting adj **1** *haunting music* evocative, poignant, atmospheric, wistful, disturbing, nostalgic. **2** *haunting memories* persistent, recurring, recurrent, indelible, unforgettable.

have v **1** *we have two cars* own, possess, keep, keep for one's use, use, hold, retain, occupy. **2** *we had three cups of tea* get, be given, receive, accept, obtain, acquire, procure, secure, gain. **3** *the flat has five rooms* contain, include, comprise, embrace, embody, comprehend, take in, incorporate. **4** *she had a lot of trouble with him* experience, undergo, go through, encounter, meet, find, be subjected to, submit to, suffer from, endure, tolerate, put up with. **5** *have a good time* experience, enjoy. **6** *have doubts/misgivings* feel, entertain, have/keep/bear in mind, harbour, foster, nurse, cherish. **7** *have the impudence to answer back* show, display, exhibit, demonstrate, manifest, express. **8** *they had her doing all their work* make, cause, oblige, require, force, coerce, induce, prevail upon, talk into, persuade. **9** *I'll have the engineer repair the telephone* ask, request, bid, tell, give orders to, order, command, direct, enjoin. **10** *she won't have such behaviour* permit, allow, put up with, tolerate, stand, brook, support, endure, abide. **11** *she had a baby daughter* give birth to, bear, deliver, be delivered of, bring into the world, bring forth, beget. **12** *they certainly had you* fool, trick, take in, dupe, outwit, deceive, cheat, swindle; *inf* do, diddle. **13** *he boasted that he had had all the woman there* have sexual intercourse with, have sex with, make love to/with, copulate with,

have carnal knowledge of; *inf* bed, lay.
have had it 1 *he won't win now, he's had it*
have no chance, have no chance of success,
have no hope, be finished, be out, be
defeated, have lost. **2** *you've had it when your
mother finds you* be about to be punished, be
going to be chastised, be in for a scolding;
inf be for it. **have on 1** *she had on a blue
dress* wear, be wearing, be dressed in, be
clothed in. **2** *I have something on today* have
planned, have arranged, be committed to,
have on the agenda. **3** *have someone on*
tease, joke with, play a joke on, trick, play
a trick on, pull someone's leg; *inf* kid. **4** *the
police have something on him* have information about, have evidence against, know
something bad/incriminating about. **have
to** *have to clean the floor* must, have got to,
be bound to, be obliged to, be under an
obligation to, be forced to, be compelled to.

haven n **1** *ships entering a haven* harbour,
harbourage, port, anchorage, moorage,
dock, cove, bay. **2** *refugees seeking a safe
haven* refuge, shelter, sanctuary, asylum,
retreat, sanctum, sanctum sanctorum,
covert.

haversack n knapsack, rucksack, backpack, satchel, kitbag.

havoc n **1** *forest fires causing/wreaking havoc*
devastation, destruction, damage, ruina-
tion, ruin, rack and ruin, despoliation, ravaging, waste, wreckage, gutting,
desolation, extermination, disaster, catastrophe, cataclysm. **2** *the havoc in the room
when the children left* chaos, disorder, confusion, disruption, disorganization, mayhem;
inf shambles.

hawk v peddle, sell, market, vend, doorstep,
cry, tout; *Amer* bark.

hawker n pedlar, door-to-door salesman,
travelling salesman, barrow boy, huckster,
vendor, crier, colporteur.

hay n straw, pasturage, fodder, forage, feed.
make hay while the sun shines make the
most of an opportunity, capitalize on an
advantageous situation, exploit an opportune occasion, strike while the iron is hot,
carpe diem, seize the day.

haywire adj **go haywire** go wrong, go out
of control, become disorganized, cease to
function properly.

hazard n **1** *face hazards on the journey* danger, peril, risk, jeopardy, threat, menace.
2 *a game of hazard* chance, accident, luck,
contingency, fortuity, fortuitousness.

hazard v **1** *hazard a guess* venture, put forward, proffer, offer, submit, advance, volunteer. **2** *hazard his life* risk, put at risk,

endanger, expose to danger, imperil, put in
jeopardy, jeopardize.

hazardous adj **1** *a hazardous journey* dangerous, danger-filled, risky, perilous, fraught
with danger/risk/peril, precarious, unsafe,
insecure, threatening, menacing; *lit* par-
lous; *inf* dicey, hairy. **2** *a hazardous venture*
open to chance, chancy, risky, uncertain,
unpredictable, precarious, speculative.

haze n **1** *a haze covered the town* mist, film of
mist, mistiness, fog, cloud, cloudiness,
smog, vapour. **2** *her mind is in a state of haze*
vagueness, confusion, muddle, befuddlement, bewilderment, obscurity, dimness,
indistinctness.

hazy adj **1** *a hazy day* misty, foggy, cloudy,
smoggy, overcast. **2** *hazy memories* vague,
indefinite, blurred, fuzzy, muzzy, faint,
confused, muddled, unclear, obscure, dim,
indistinct, ill-defined.

head n **1** *hurt his head* skull, cranium, poll,
sconce; *inf* pate, nut, noddle, conk, bonce.
2 *he has a good head | use your head* mind,
intellect, intelligence, brain, brains, mentality, wit, wits, wisdom, sense, reasoning,
rationality, understanding; *inf* loaf, upper
storey, grey matter. **3** *a head for business*
mind, brain, aptitude, ability, capacity,
flair, talent, faculty. **4** *the head of the organi-
zation/team/school/nation* leader, chief, commander, director, chairman, managing
director, manager, superintendent, controller, administrator, supervisor, captain,
principal, headmaster, headmistress, head
teacher, governor, president, premier,
prime minister, headman. **5** *at the head of
the firm* top, command, control, controls,
charge, leadership, headship, directorship.
6 *at the head of the hill* top, summit, peak,
crest, crown, tip, brow, apex, vertex. **7** *at
the head of the queue* front, fore, forefront,
van, vanguard. **8** *matters coming to a head*
climax, culmination, crisis, critical point,
turning-point, crossroads. **9** *at the head of
the stream* origin, source, fountain-head,
fount, well-head, well-spring, headwater.
10 *a head on the beer* froth, foam, lather,
suds. **11** *standing on the head looking out to
sea* headland, promontory, point, cape,
foreland. **12** *the material is listed under various heads* heading, category, class, classification. *see* HEADING 1. **13** *rushed to the head to
be sick* toilet, lavatory, WC, bathroom,
water-closet, latrine; *inf* loo, bog; *Amer inf*
john, can. **go to one's head 1** *the wine has
gone to my head* make intoxicated, intoxicate, make dizzy, make someone's head
spin; *inf* make woozy. **2** *their praise went to
her head* make conceited/arrogant/boastful,
puff up. **head first 1** *fall head first down-*

stairs on one's head, head foremost, headlong, head on, diving, plunging. **2** *rush into things head first* without thinking, rashly, recklessly, precipitately, carelessly, heedlessly. *see* HEADLONG 2. **head over heels** *head over heals in love* utterly, completely, thoroughly, full, wholeheartedly, intensely, passionately, fervently, fervidly, uncontrollably; *inf* madly. **keep one's head** *keep one's head in a crisis* keep calm, keep cool, remain unruffled, maintain one's equilibrium, keep control of oneself; *inf* keep one's cool. **lose one's head** panic, lose control of oneself, lose control of the situation, get flustered/confused, get angry, get excited, get hysterical; *inf* lose one's cool, blow one's top, freak out, fly off the handle.

head adj *the head gardener/teacher/priest* chief, leading, main, principal, first, prime, premier, foremost, topmost, supreme, cardinal.

head v **1** *head the expedition* be at the head/front of, lead, be the leader of, lead the way for, go/be first, precede. **2** *head the firm* be at the head of, be in charge of, be in command of, command, be in control of, control, run, lead, be the leader of, manage, direct, administer, supervise, rule, govern, guide. **3** *a tower headed by a spire* crown, top, surmount, cap, tip. **4** *head for town* make for, go to, go in the direction of, direct one's steps towards, point oneself towards, aim for, set out for, start out for, go/turn towards, steer towards, make a beeline for. **head off** **1** *head off the charging bull* divert, deflect, turn aside, intercept, stop in mid-course, block off, cut off. **2** *head off disaster* ward off, fend off, forestall, avert, prevent, parry, baulk, check, stop.

headache n **1** *she is susceptible to headaches* sore head, pain in the head, migraine; *Med* cephalagia. **2** *her nephew is nothing but a headache to her* nuisance, bother, pest, trouble, vexation, bane, bugbear, worry, inconvenience; *inf* pain, pain in the neck.

heading n **1** *materials listed under various headings* head, category, class, classification, subject, topic, division, section, branch, department. **2** *put the headings on the illustrations/articles* title, caption, headline, name, rubric, banner headline.

headlong adv **1** *fall headlong into the bushes* head first, on one's head, head foremost, head on. *see* HEAD n head first. **2** *rush headlong into a decision* hastily, in haste, hurriedly, impetuously, impulsively, unrestrainedly, impatiently, without think-

ing, rashly, recklessly, wildly, prematurely, precipitately, carelessly, heedlessly.

head-on adj **1** *a head-on collision* direct, front-to-front. **2** *a head-on confrontation* direct, directly opposing/opposite, straight-on, face-to-face; *inf* eyeball-to-eyeball, full-frontal.

headquarters npl HQ, main office, head office, main branch, centre of operations, home base, command post.

headstone n gravestone, tombstone, stone, monument, memorial.

headstrong adj stubborn, stubborn as a mule, obstinate, obdurate, mulish, inflexible, intransigent, intractable, pigheaded, unyielding, self-willed, refractory, recalcitrant, ungovernable, wayward, contrary, wilful, perverse, unruly, wild, reckless, heedless, rash.

headway n **make headway** make progress, make way, progress, advance, get ahead, get on, proceed, develop, gain ground, go forward by leaps and bounds, make strides.

heady adj **1** *a heady drink* intoxicating, inebriating, inebriant, potent, strong, spirituous. **2** *she was heady with success* exhilarated, excited, overjoyed, thrilled, overwhelmed, euphoric, ecstatic, overpowered, in seventh heaven, over the moon; *inf* on cloud nine. **3** *the heady days of youth* exhilarating, exciting, stimulating, rousing, arousing, invigorating, thrilling, galvanizing, electrifying. **4** *a heady person/action* impetuous, rash, reckless, wild, foolhardy, thoughtless, heedless, imprudent, incautious, impulsive, precipitate.

heal v **1** *heal the wound* cure, make well, make better, remedy, treat, mend, restore, regenerate. **2** *the skin began to heal* get better, get well, be cured, mend, be on the mend, be restored, improve, show improvement. **3** *heal the breach* conciliate, reconcile, patch up, settle, set right, put right, make good, harmonize. **4** *heal the sorrow* alleviate, appease, mitigate, ameliorate, assuage, allay, palliate, soften.

health n **1** *full of health* healthiness, fitness, well-being, good condition, good trim, good shape, fine fettle, soundness, robustness, strength, vigour, salubrity, good kilter. **2** *his health is not good* state of health, constitution, physical state, physical health, physical shape, condition, form, tone.

healthy adj **1** *a healthy young man* in good health, fit, physically fit, in good condition/trim/shape/kilter, in fine fettle, in fine/top form, robust, strong, vigorous, hardy, flourishing, hale and hearty, hale, hearty, bursting with health, blooming, active; *inf* in the pink. **2** *a healthy climate* health-giving, salubrious, invigorating, bracing, stimulating, refreshing, tonic. **3** *a healthy diet* health-giving, healthful, good for one, nutritious, nourishing, wholesome, beneficial.

heap n **1** *a heap of rubbish* pile, stack, mass, mound, mountain, stockpile, accumulation, collection, lot, assemblage, amassment, aggregation, agglomeration, conglomeration, hoard, store, stock, supply. **2** *a heap of trouble* a lot, lots, a great deal, an abundance, plenty, a superabundance; *inf* loads, tons. **3** *lost a heap of money | earn heaps of money* a lot, lots, a great deal, abundance, considerable quantities, huge quantities, plenty, a mint; *inf* oodles, loads, tons, pots, stacks, lashings.

heap v **1** *heap up leaves/money* pile up, stack, amass, stockpile, mound, accumulate, collect, assemble, hoard, store, store up, stock up, set aside, lay by. **2** *heap praise/insults on him* bestow, confer, shower, give, grant, assign, load, burden.

hear v **1** *he does not hear* have the sense of hearing, perceive sound, have the faculty of hearing, have the auditory faculty. **2** *I listened but I didn't hear what he said* catch, take in, overhear; *inf* get, latch on to. **3** *we heard that he was dead | how did you hear of his appointment?* be informed, be told, be made aware, receive information, find out, discover, learn, gather, pick up, be given to understand, hear tell, get wind. **4** *the chief judge heard the case* try, judge, pass judgement on, ajudicate, examine, investigate, inquire into, consider.

hearing n **1** *his hearing is poor* power of hearing, faculty/sense of hearing, ability to hear, aural faculty, auditory perception. **2** *give someone a hearing* chance to speak, opportunity to express one's point of view, opportunity to be heard, chance to put one's side of the story, interview, audience. **3** *they were within hearing* earshot, hearing distance/range, reach, carrying range, range of one's voice, auditory range. **4** *present at the hearing* inquiry, trial, inquest, investigation, inquisition, review, examination.

hearsay n *according to hearsay, he is a thief* rumour, gossip, tittle-tattle, tattle, common talk, common knowledge, idle talk, mere talk, report, talk of the town, word of mouth, *on dit*; *inf* buzz, grapevine.

heart n **1** *his heart isn't right* inf ticker. **2** *love her with all his heart* passion, love, affection, emotions, feelings. **3** *he has no heart* tender feelings, tenderness, warm emotions, compassion, sympathy, empathy, responsiveness to others, humanity, fellow feeling, concern for others, pathos, goodwill, humanitarianism, benevolence, kindness, kindliness, brotherly love. **4** *I don't have the heart to go on holiday* spirit, enthusiasm, keenness, eagerness, liveliness. **5** *heroes with great heart* courage, bravery, valour, intrepidity, fearlessness, heroism, stout-heartedness, boldness, pluck, mettle, backbone, nerve, fortitude, purpose, resolution, determination; *inf* guts, spunk, gumption. **6** *the heart of the matter/universe* centre, central part, core, nucleus, middle, kernel, essential part, hub, quintessence, essence, crux, marrow, pith, substance, sum and substance. **after one's own heart** *a person/ holiday after my own heart* of the kind that one likes, to one's liking, attractive to one, favoured by one, desirable. **at heart** *at heart he is a kind man* basically, fundamentally, at bottom, in essence, essentially, intrinsically, innately, in reality, really, in fact, actually, truly, in truth. **by heart** *learn by heart* off by heart, by rote, word for word, pat, off pat, by memory, parrot-fashion. **do one's heart good** do someone good, give someone pleasure, please, gladden, make happy, cheer, delight, gratify, satisfy. **eat one's heart out** *jilted lovers eating their hearts out* sorrow, grieve, mourn, ache, suffer, agonize, pine, mope, fret, regret, brood, repine, be filled with envy. **from the bottom of one's heart** *apologize from the bottom of my heart* with all one's heart, profoundly, deeply, sincerely, devoutly, heartily, fervently, passionately. **have a change of heart** *they had a change of heart about moving* change one's mind, change one's tune, have a rethink. **have a heart** *have a heart and let them off* be kind, be merciful, be lenient, be compassionate, be sympathetic, be considerate. **have one's heart set on** *the little girl had her heart set on the doll* long for, yearn for, desire, be desirous of, wish for, want badly, crave. **heart and soul** *devote oneself heart and soul to the project* enthusiastically, eagerly, zealously, wholeheartedly, gladly, with open arms, thoroughly, completely, entirely, absolutely. **lose one's heart to** *she lost her heart to a soldier* fall in love with, fall for, take a liking/fancy to, become infatuated with. **take heart** *take heart from the fact that you did better than many others* cheer up, brighten up, be heartened, be encouraged, be comforted, perk up, revive, derive comfort/satisfaction from; *inf* buck up. **with one's heart in one's mouth** *she* looked into the dark space with her heart in her mouth in fear, fearfully, with apprehension, apprehensively, with fear and trembling, with alarm, with trepidation, with bated breath.

heartache n sorrow, grief, sadness, anguish, pain, hurt, agony, suffering, misery, wretchedness, despair, desolation, despondency, woe; lit dolour.

heartbreaking adj heartbreaking cries/tale heart-rending, sad, pitiful, poignant, tragic, painful, agonizing, distressing, desolating, affecting, grievous, bitter, cruel, harsh, harrowing, tear-jerking, excruciating.

heartbroken adj broken-hearted, heartsick, miserable, sorrowful, sad, anguished, suffering, grieving, grieved, dejected, dispirited, disheartened, downcast, disconsolate, crestfallen, disappointed, crushed, desolate, despondent, in low spirits.

heartburn n dyspepsia, indigestion, brash; Med pyrosis.

hearten v cheer, cheer up, raise the spirits of, invigorate, revitalize, energize, animate, revivify, exhilarate, uplift, elate, comfort, encourage, buoy up, pep up; inf buck up, give a shot in the arm to.

heartfelt adj sends his heartfelt sympathy deepfelt, deeply felt, deep, profound, wholehearted, sincere, honest, devout, genuine, unfeigned, earnest, ardent, fervent, passionate, kindly, warm, cordial, enthusiastic, eager.

heartily adv 1 thanked/welcomed them heartily warmly, cordially, feelingly, from the bottom of one's heart, deeply, profoundly, wholeheartedly, sincerely, genuinely, unfeignedly. 2 eat heartily with eagerness, eagerly, with enthusiasm, enthusiastically, zealously, earnestly, vigorously, energetically, resolutely. 3 dislike him heartily | am heartily sick of this weather very much, completely, totally, absolutely, thoroughly.

heartless adj unfeeling, unsympathetic, uncompassionate, unkind, uncaring, unmoved, untouched, cold, cold-hearted, cold-blooded, hard-hearted, cruel, harsh, stern, hard, brutal, merciless, pitiless, ruthless.

heart-rending adj heartbreaking, sad, pitiful, painful, distressing, affecting, harrowing, tear-jerking. see HEARTBREAKING.

heartsick adj sick at heart, heavy-hearted, heartsore, dejected, downcast, dispirited, depressed, despondent, disappointed.

heart-to-heart adj a-heart-to-heart talk intimate, personal, unreserved, candid, frank, open.

heart-to-heart n have a heart-to-heart tête-à-tête, cosy chat.

heart-warming adj 1 a heart-warming story touching, moving, affecting, warming, cheering, cheerful, gladdening, encouraging, uplifting. 2 a heart-warming job gratifying, satisfying, rewarding, pleasing.

hearty adj 1 a hearty welcome enthusiastic, eager, warm-hearted, warm, cordial, jovial, friendly, affable, unreserved, uninhibited, ebullient, exuberant, effusive. 2 a hearty dislike wholehearted, complete, total, absolute, thorough, genuine, unfeigned. 3 a hearty young/old man strong, robust, hardy, vigorous, stalwart, healthy, sound, sturdy, active, energetic, hale, hale and hearty. 4 a hearty meal substantial, solid, abundant, ample, sizeable, filling, nutritious, nourishing.

heat n 1 the heat melted the ice hotness, warmth, warmness, calefaction, torridness. 2 the heat of summer hotness, warmth, sultriness, torridness, torridity, swelter, heatwave, hot spell, dog days. 3 the heat of the child frightened her high temperature, fever, feverishness, febrility, febricity, flush; Med pyrexia. 4 speak with heat warmth, passion, vehemence, intensity, ardour, fervour, fervency, fervidness, zeal, eagerness, enthusiasm, animation, earnestness, excitement, agitation.

heat v 1 heat up the milk warm, warm up, make hot, make warm, reheat, cook; inf hot, hot up. 2 the day heated up grow hot, grow warm, become hotter/warmer, get hotter/warmer. 3 the argument heated up grew passionate/vehement/fierce/angry. see HEATED 1. 4 the subject seemed to have heated him arouse, rouse, excite, inflame, stimulate, stir, animate, anger, make angry, enrage.

heated adj 1 a heated argument passionate, vehement, fierce, angry, furious, stormy, tempestuous, frenzied, raging, intense, impassioned, violent. 2 both parties were rather heated excited, roused, animated, inflamed, angry, furious, enraged.

heater n electric heater, gas heater, convector heater, fan heater, storage heater, radiator, brazier; car heater, water heater, immersion heater.

heathen n 1 missionaries converting heathens unbeliever, infidel, pagan, idolater/idolatress, atheist, disbeliever, agnostic, sceptic, heretic. 2 lands invaded by heathens barbarian, savage.

heathen adj 1 converting a heathen tribe heathenish, infidel, pagan, godless, irreligious, idolatrous, atheistic, agnostic, heretical.

2 *invaded by heathen tribes* barbarian, barbarous, savage, uncivilized, brutish.

heave v **1** *heaving heavy weights* lift, haul, pull, tug, raise, hoist, upheave. **2** *heave the hammer in the games* throw, cast, toss, fling, hurl, let fly, pitch, send; *inf* sling, chuck. **3** *heave a sigh* give, utter, let out, pant, gasp, blow, puff, breathe, sigh, sob. **4** *people heaving as the ship sailed* vomit, be sick, spew, retch, gag; *inf* throw up.

heaven n **1** *children were told their granny was in heaven* abode of God, abode of the angels, Kingdom of God, paradise, bliss, next life, life to come, next world, the hereafter, Abraham's bosom, Zion, nirvana, Valhalla, Elysium, Elysian Fields, empyrean, Avalon, the Isles of the Blessed, happy hunting-ground. **2** *she was in heaven when she heard the news* ecstasy, bliss, sheer bliss, transports, rapture, supreme happiness, supreme joy, perfect contentment, seventh heaven, paradise, Eden, utopia, dreamland, fairyland. **3** *the heavens opened* sky, skies, firmament, ether, empyrean, aerosphere, vault of heaven, the blue; *lit* welkin.

heavenly adj **1** *heavenly concerns* cosmic, extraterrestrial, unearthly, extramundane, not of this world, other-worldly, celestial, paradisical, empyrean, empyreal, Elysian. **2** *heavenly beings* celestial, divine, angelic, seraphic, cherubic, blessed, blest, beatific, beatified, holy, godlike, immortal, superhuman, paradisical. **3** *a heavenly party* delightful, pleasurable, enjoyable, marvellous, gratifying, wonderful, blissful, rapturous, sublime; *inf* glorious, divine. **4** *a heavenly dress* beautiful, exquisite, perfect, superb, ravishing, alluring, enchanting, entrancing, ideal; *inf* divine.

heavily adv **1** *walking heavily* with difficulty, slowly, laboriously, painfully, awkwardly, clumsily, ponderously. **2** *heavily defeated* utterly, completely, thoroughly, absolutely, decisively, roundly, soundly. **3** *drink heavily* excessively, to too great an extent, to a great extent, too much, very much, a great deal, copiously. **4** *ground heavily packed* compactly, densely, closely, hard, thick, thickly.

heavy adj **1** *a heavy log/load* weighty, bulky, hefty, big, large, substantial, massive, enormous, mighty, colossal, ponderous, unwieldy, cumbersome, burdensome, awkward, unmanageable. **2** *a heavy responsibility* onerous, burdensome, difficult, oppressive, unbearable, intolerable. **3** *a heavy task* hard, difficult, arduous, laborious, demanding, exacting, irksome, troublesome, trying. **4** *a heavy blow* hard, forceful, strong, severe, grievous, harsh, intense, sharp, stinging,

penetrating, overwhelming. **5** *a heavy man* large, bulky, hulking, stout, overweight, fat, obese, corpulent, portly, tubby, paunchy, lumbering. **6** *a heavy mist* dense, thick, solid. **7** *heavy ground* difficult, muddy, sticky, considerable, miry, boggy, clayey, clogged. **8** *heavy traffic/losses/crop* very much/great, large, considerable, considerable quantities of, abundant, copious, profuse, superabundant, huge numbers of. **9** *heavy fighting* severe, intense, serious, grave. **10** *heavy newspapers* serious, grave, deep, sombre, profound. **11** *heavy reading* difficult, dull, over-serious, tedious, boring, uninteresting, dry, wearisome, dry as dust. **12** *feeling heavy after dinner* sleepy, drowsy, sluggish, inactive, indolent, inept, idle, apathetic, listless, torpid. **13** *heavy of heart* sad, sorrowful, downcast, dejected, disconsolate, disheartened, despondent, downhearted, depressed, crestfallen, disappointed, grieving, gloomy, melancholy. **14** *heavy with child* burdened, encumbered, weighted down, laden, loaded, oppressed. **15** *heavy seas/waves* rough, wild, stormy, tempestuous, turbulent, squally, boisterous, violent. **16** *heavy day/skies* cloudy, overcast, grey, dark, dull, gloomy, dreary, leaden, louring. **17** *heavy features* coarse, ungraceful, broad, wide, jowly.

heavy on *heavy on the petrol/butter* using a lot of, using too much, overusing, extravagant with, lavish with.

heavy-handed adj **1** *heavy-handed and always breaking things* clumsy, awkward, maladroit, bungling, blundering, unhandy, inept, unskilful, inexpert, graceless, ungraceful, like a bull in a china shop; *inf* ham-handed, ham-fisted. **2** *too heavy-handed to deal with the bereaved* insensitive, tactless, thoughtless, inept. **3** *a heavy-handed father* harsh, hard, stern, severe, oppressive, domineering, overbearing, tyrannical, despotic, autocratic, ruthless, merciless.

heckle v shout down, shout at, interrupt, disrupt, barrack, jeer, taunt, badger, bait, harass, give trouble to, pester; *inf* give someone a hard time.

hectic adj *a hectic day/life* very busy, very active, frantic, frenetic, frenzied, bustling, flustering, flurried, fast and furious, turbulent, tumultuous, confused, exciting, excited, wild.

hector v bully, torment, intimidate, ride roughshod over, browbeat, cow, coerce, bulldoze, steamroller, strong-arm, badger, bait, harass, plague, provoke, threaten, menace; *inf* bulldoze, ballyrag.

hedge n **1** *planted a hedge round the garden* hedgerow, row of bushes, quickset. **2** *grow a hedge against the wind* barrier, screen, protection, wind-break. **3** *a hedge against inflation* safeguard, guard, protection, shield, cover, insurance, insurance cover.

hedge v **1** *the trees hedge in the garden* surround, enclose, encircle, circle, border, edge, skirt. **2** *hedged in by petty restrictions* hem in, confine, restrict, limit, hinder, obstruct, impede. **3** *she hedged when questioned* equivocate, prevaricate, be vague/ambivalent, be noncommital, dodge the question/issue, sidestep the issue, hum and haw, beat about the bush, pussyfoot around, temporize, quibble; *inf* beg/duck the question, waffle. **4** *hedge yourself against inflation* safeguard, guard, protect, cover, shield, take out insurance, take out insurance cover, insure oneself.

heed n *pay no heed* heedfulness, attention, attentiveness, notice, note, regard, regardfulness, mindfulness, mind, respect, consideration, thought, care, caution, watchfulness, wariness, chariness.

heed v *heed what they say* pay heed to, be heedful of, pay attention to, attend to, take notice of, take note of, notice, note, pay regard to, bear in mind, be mindful of, mind, mark, consider, take into account/consideration, be guided by, follow, obey, adhere to, observe, take to heart, be on guard for, be alert to, be cautious of, watch out for.

heedful adj *heedful of advice* attentive, careful, mindful, cautious, prudent, circumspect, wary, chary, observant, watchful, vigilant, alert, on guard, on the alert, on one's toes, on the qui vive.

heedless adj unheeding, inattentive, careless, incautious, unmindful, disregardful, regardless, unnoticing, unthinking, thoughtless, improvident, unwary, oblivious, unobservant, unwatchful, unvigilant, negligent, neglectful, rash, reckless, foolhardy, precipitate.

heel n **1** *the heel of a shoe* heelpiece, wedge, wedge heel, stiletto, stiletto heel, platform heel. **2** *the heel of the loaf* crust, end, remnant, remainder, tail-end, stump, butt, rump. **3** *he's an utter heel* scoundrel, cad, blackguard; *inf* rat, swine, rotter, bounder. **Achilles' heel** weak spot, weakness, vulnerable spot, soft underbelly, downfall, undoing. **down at heel** shabby, shabbily-dressed, poorly-dressed, out-at-elbows, seedy, run-down, slovenly, slipshod. **take to one's heels** run away, run off, take flight, flee, escape; *inf* show a clean pair of heels, skedaddle, hightail it, hotfoot it, split, vamoose.

heel v *ships heeling over* cant, tilt, list, tip, lean, lean over, keel over, incline, careen.

heft v *heft the load* lift, lift up, raise, raise up, hoist, hike up, heave, throw up, boost, boost up.

hefty adj **1** *hefty young man* heavy, bulky, hulking, big, large, stout, massive, huge, muscular, brawny, strapping, solidly-built, powerfully-built, sturdy, rugged, stalwart, beefy. **2** *a hefty blow* hard, forceful, heavy, powerful, vigorous, mighty. **3** *a hefty load* heavy, weighty, big, large, massive, tremendous, immense, bulky, awkward, unwieldy, cumbersome, ponderous. **4** *a hefty price/bill* substantial, sizeable, expensive, huge, colossal, overpriced.

height n **1** *measure the height* highness, altitude, loftiness, elevation, distance/extent upwards. **2** *3 metres in height* tallness, highness, stature. **3** *on the mountain height* top, mountain-top, hilltop, summit, crest, crown, pinnacle, peak, apex, vertex, apogee. **4** *at the height of his powers* culmination, crowning point, high point, peak, zenith, climax, consummation, perfection, apex. **5** *the height of fashion/rudeness* utmost degree, uttermost, ultimate, acme, *ne plus ultra*, very limit, limit, extremity, maximum, ceiling. **6** *afraid of heights | the heights above the town* high ground, high places, rising ground, hill, mountain, cliff, precipice, summit.

heighten v **1** *heighten the ceiling* make higher, raise, lift, elevate. **2** *heighten their status* magnify, ennoble, exalt, enhance. **3** *heighten the tension* make greater, intensify, raise, increase, add to, augment, build up, boost, strengthen, amplify, magnify, aggravate, enhance, improve.

heinous adj *heinous crimes/criminal* atrocious, abominable, abhorrent, odious, detestable, loathsome, hateful, execrable, wicked, monstrous, horrible, ghastly, shocking, flagrant, contemptible, reprehensible, despicable.

heir, heiress n beneficiary, legatee, inheritor, inheritress, inheritrix, successor, next in line, scion.

helix n spiral, screw, corkscrew, whorl, twist, coil, loop, volute, curl, curlicue.

hell n **1** *wicked spirits in hell* infernal regions, inferno, hellfire, eternal fire, fire and brimstone, nether world, lower world, abode of evil spirits, abode of the damned, perdition, abyss, bottomless pit, Hades, Acheron, Tartarus, Erebus, Gehenna. **2** *it* *was hell in the battle* purgatory, torment, torture, misery, suffering, affliction, anguish, agony, ordeal, wretchedness, nightmare, woe, tribulation, trials and tribulations. **3** *get hell from the teacher* upbraiding, scolding, castigation, vituperation, reprimand, censure, criticism, disapprobation; *inf* what for. **hell for leather** as fast/quickly/rapidly/speedily/swiftly as possible, very fast/quickly/rapidly/speedily/swiftly/hurriedly, pell-mell, post-haste, at the double, helter-skelter, headlong, full tilt, hotfoot; *inf* like a bat out of hell. **raise hell 1** *partygoers raising hell* party, carouse, revel, make a noise, cause a disturbance, cause a commotion, be loud and noisy, raise the roof, raise Cain. **2** *his father raised hell* be very angry, be furious, be enraged, protest, expostulate, complain, object, remonstrate, raise the roof, raise Cain.

hellish adj **1** *hellish spirits* diabolical, fiendish, demonic, demoniac, demoniacal, devilish, satanic, infernal, hell-born. **2** *a hellish slavemaster* brutal, brutish, barbarous, barbaric, savage, murderous, bloodthirsty, cruel, wicked, inhuman, ferocious, vicious, ruthless, relentless, detestable, abominable, accursed, execrable, nefarious. **3** *a hellish day* unpleasant, nasty, disagreeable; *inf* horrible, horrid, awful.

hellish adv *hellish cold/expensive* very, to a great extent, extremely, excessively; *inf* awfully, jolly, ever so.

helm n *the captain of the ship at the helm* wheel, tiller, rudder, steering gear, automatic pilot. **at the helm** *the managing director at the helm of the firm* in charge, in command, in control, directing, in authority, in the seat of authority, at the wheel, in the driving seat, in the saddle.

help v **1** *help the old lady off the bus* assist, aid, lend a helping hand, lend a hand, guide, be of service to, be useful to, succour, befriend. **2** *help the charity* assist, aid, contribute to, support, back, promote, boost, give a boost to, uphold. **3** *help the pain/situation* soothe, relieve, ameliorate, alleviate, mitigate, assuage, remedy, cure, heal, improve, ease, facilitate, restore. **4** *can I help you?* serve, be of assistance/help, give help. **5** *he helped himself to my books* take, appropriate, take possession of, commandeer, steal, make free with; *inf* pinch, walk off with, nick. **cannot help** *he cannot help it/snoring* be unable to prevent/stop/cease/halt/avoid/abstain from/refrain from/keep from/forbear from/break the habit of.

help n **1** *give the old lady some help* assistance, aid, helping hand, service, use, guidance, benefit, advantage, avail, support, backing, succour. **2** *no help for the condition* relief, amelioration, alleviation, mitigation, assuagement, remedy, cure, healing, improvement, ease, restorative, corrective, balm, salve. **3** *ask the help for assistance* helper, assistant, employee, worker, hired help, maid, domestic help, servant, daily.

helper n **1** *the jumble sale helpers gathered together* assistant, aider, aid worker. **2** *the chief and his helper* assistant, subsidiary, aide, adjutant, deputy, second, second-in-command, auxiliary, right-hand man/woman, henchman, girl/man Friday; *inf* sidekick. **3** *the author and his helpers* colleague, associate, co-worker, helpmate, helpmeet, partner, ally, collaborator.

helpful adj **1** *a helpful suggestion* useful, of use, of service, beneficial, advantageous, valuable, profitable, instrumental, constructive, practical, productive. **2** *helpful people* supportive, friendly, kind, obliging, accommodating, cooperative, sympathetic, considerate, caring, neighbourly, charitable, benevolent.

helping n *a second helping of potatoes* serving, portion, ration, piece, plateful, bowlful, spoonful.

helpless adj **1** *a helpless invalid* weak, feeble, disabled, impotent, incapable, infirm, debilitated, powerless, dependent, unfit, invalid, bed-ridden, paralysed; *inf* laid-up. **2** *troops left helpless in the wilderness* defenceless, unprotected, vulnerable, exposed, abandoned, forlorn, destitute, desolate.

helpmate n associate, partner, companion, helper, helpmeet.

helter-skelter adv *run helter-skelter* hastily, hurriedly, as fast/quickly/rapidly/speedily as possible, pell-mell, headlong, rashly, recklessly, precipitately, impetuously, impulsively, carelessly, heedlessly, wildly.

hem n *the decorative hem on a skirt* border, edge, edging, trim, trimming, fringe, frill, flounce, valance.

hem v **1** *hem the dress* put a hem on, bind, edge, trim, fringe. **2** *trees hemming the lake* border, edge, skirt, surround, encircle, circle, enclose, encompass. **3** *feel hemmed in by trees/restrictions* close in, shut in, hedge in, pen in, keep within bounds, confine, constrain, restrain, restrict, limit, trap.

hence adv *hence my decision not to go* therefore, thus, on that account, because of that, for this reason, consequently, ergo.

henceforth adv *henceforth you will arrive on time* from now on, from this day/time on, from this day forth/forward, hereafter, in future, in the future, hence, henceforward, hereinafter, subsequently, in time to come, after this.

henchman n assistant, aide, supporter, follower, right-hand man/woman, girl/man Friday, adjutant, subordinate, underling, lackey, flunkey, toady, hired killer/assassin; *inf* sidekick, hit man, hatchet man, hood.

henpecked adj *henpecked husbands* bullied, dominated, browbeaten, nagged, subjugated, led by the nose, without a mind of one's own, cringing, cowering, meek, timid, docile; *inf* under the thumb.

herald n **1** *news announced by the court herald* messenger, crier, announcer, bearer of tidings, courier. **2** *a herald of things to come* forerunner, precursor, harbinger, usher, sign, omen, portent, indication, augury.

herald v **1** *companies heralding their new products* announce, make public, make known, proclaim, broadcast, publicize, advertise, promote, promulgate, trumpet, beat the drum about. **2** *prototypes heralding major new inventions* usher in, pave the way for, show in, harbinger, precede, be the forerunner/precursor of, portend, indicate, augur, presage, promise, foreshadow, forebode, foretoken.

herculean adj *a herculean task* arduous, laborious, back-breaking, onerous, strenuous, difficult, hard, tough, formidable, huge, massive, uphill.

herd n **1** *a herd of cattle* drove, collection, assemblage, flock, pack, cluster. **2** *flocks tended by a herd* shepherd, cowherd, cattleman, cowman, herdsman, herder, drover. **3** *a herd of people* crowd, horde, multitude, mob, mass, host, throng, swarm, press. **4** *ignore the tastes of the herd* the masses, the mob, the populace, the rabble, the riff-raff, the hoi polloi, peasants; *inf* plebs, proles, the great unwashed.

herd v **1** *herd the sheep into the pens* drive, round up, shepherd, guide, lead, force, urge, goad. **2** *people herding together in the hall* assemble, gather, collect, congregate, flock, rally, muster, huddle, get together. **3** *shepherds herding the sheep* look after, take care of, watch, stand guard over, guard, tend.

here adv **1** *bring it here | he died here* to/at/in this place/spot/location, hither, to here. **2** *here I must pause* now, at this point, at this point in time, at this time, at this juncture.

hereafter adv *hereafter to be called the author* after this, from now on, from this day/time on, from this day forth/forward, in future, in the future, hence, henceforth, henceforward. *see* HENCEFORTH.

hereafter n *believe in the hereafter* life after death, the after-life, life to come, the afterworld, next world, the beyond, immortality, heaven, paradise.

hereditary adj **1** *hereditary characteristics* genetic, genetical, congenital, innate, inborn, inherent, inbred, family, transmissible, transferrable. **2** *hereditary property* inherited, handed down, obtained by inheritance, bequeathed, willed, transferred, transmitted, family, ancestral.

heredity n *this disorder is the result of heredity* passing on of genetic characteristics.; genetics, genetic make-up, genes, congenital characteristics/traits.

heresy n apostasy, dissent, dissension, dissidence, unbelief, scepticism, agnosticism, atheism, nonconformity, unorthodoxy, separatism, sectarianism, free thinking, heterodoxy, recusancy, schism, revisionism, idolatry, paganism.

heretic n apostate, dissenter, dissident, unbeliever, sceptic, agnostic, atheist, nonconformist, separatist, sectarian, free thinker, renegade, recusant, schismatic, revisionist, idolater, pagan.

heretical adj *heretical beliefs/views* dissident, sceptical, agnostic, atheistical, nonconformist, separatist, sectarian, free-thinking, heterodox, unorthodox, renegade, recusant, schismatic, revisionist, idolatrous, pagan.

heritage n **1** *proud of his country's heritage* history, tradition, background. **2** *proud of his family heritage* ancestry, lineage, descent, extraction, family, dynasty, bloodline, heredity, birth. **3** *receive a heritage from his father* inheritance, legacy, bequest, endowment, estate, patrimony, portion, birthright, lot.

hermit n recluse, solitary, anchorite/anchoress, ancress, eremite, stylite, pillarist, pillar-saint, ascetic.

hermitage n retreat, refuge, haven, shelter, sanctuary, sanctum, sanctum sanctorum, asylum, hideaway.

hero n **1** *the hero of the battle/hour* champion, conquering hero, victor, conqueror, brave man, man of courage, great man, man of the hour, celebrity, lion, cavalier, paragon, shining example, exemplar, paladin, knight, *beau idéal*. **2** *the teacher was the girl's hero* idol, ideal, ideal man/woman, popular

figure; *inf* heart-throb. **3** *the hero of the play/
opera* principal male character/role, lead
actor, leading man, male lead, male star/
superstar, male protagonist.

heroic adj **1** *heroic soldier/deeds* brave, courageous, valiant, valorous, intrepid, fearless,
gallant, stout-hearted, lion-hearted, bold,
daring, undaunted, dauntless, doughty,
manly, virile, chivalrous. **2** *read tales of
heroic characters/myths* classic, classical,
Homeric, mythological, legendary, fabulous. **3** *heroic language* epic, epical, Homeric,
grandiloquent, high-flown, high-sounding,
extravagant, grandiose, bombastic, rhetorical, pretentious, turgid, magniloquent, orotund, elevated.

heroine n **1** *declared a heroine for saving the
child* brave woman, woman of courage,
great woman, woman of the hour,
celebrity, paragon, shining example. **2** *the
heroine of the play/opera* principal female
character/role, lead actress, leading lady,
female lead, female star/superstar, prima
donna, diva, female protagonist.

heroism n bravery, courage, courageousness, valour, valiance, intrepidity, fearlessness, gallantry, stout-heartedness,
lion-heartedness, boldness, daring, dauntlessness, doughtiness, manliness, virility,
mettle, spirit, fortitude, chivalry.

hero worship n idolization, putting on a
pedestal, adulation, worship, adoration,
glorification, exaltation, idealization, admiration, high esteem, veneration.

hesitancy n **1** *hesitancy when making decisions* uncertainty, unsureness, doubt,
doubtfulness, scepticism, irresolution,
indecision, indecisiveness, vacillation,
oscillation, shilly-shallying, stalling, cunctation. **2** *show hesitancy about interfering*
reluctance, unwillingness, disinclination,
demurral, scruples, misgivings, qualms.

hesitant adj **1** *hesitant when making decisions*
hesitating, uncertain, unsure, doubtful,
dubious, sceptical, irresolute, indecisive,
vacillating, wavering, oscillating, shilly-
shallying, hanging back, stalling, delaying,
cunctatory, disinclined, unwilling, half-
hearted, lacking confidence, diffident,
timid, shy. **2** *hesitant about giving advice*
reluctant, unwilling, disinclined, diffident,
having scruples/misgivings/qualms about.

hesitate v **1** *always hesitate before making a
decision* pause, delay, hang back, wait, be
uncertain, be unsure, be doubtful, be indecisive, vacillate, oscillate, waver, dither,
shilly-shally, dally, stall, temporize; *inf*
dilly-dally; *Scots* swither. **2** *she hesitates to
interfere* be reluctant, be unwilling, be dis-

inclined, shrink from, hang back from,
think twice about, baulk at, demur from,
scruple to, have misgivings/qualms about,
be diffident about. **3** *he hesitates a lot when
giving a speech* stammer, stumble, stutter,
falter, hum and haw, fumble for words, be
halting, halt.

hesitation n **1** *they never acted without some
hesitation* pause, delay, cunctation, hanging
back, waiting, waiting period, uncertainty,
unsureness, doubt, doubtfulness, dubiousness, scepticism, irresolution, indecisiveness, vacillation, wavering, oscillation,
shilly-shallying, stalling, temporizing; *inf*
dilly-dallying; *Scots* swithering. **2** *feel some
hesitation about interfering* reluctance,
unwillingness, disinclination, demurral,
scruples, misgivings, qualms. **3** *complain
about his hesitation when speaking publicly*
stammering, stumbling, stuttering, faltering, humming and hawing, fumbling for
words, haltingness.

hew v **1** *hew down a tree* chop, chop down,
hack, hack down, axe, cut/saw down, fell.
2 *hew off branches* lop, cut off, chop off,
sever, trim, prune. **3** *hew a piece of wood into
a figure* carve, sculpt, sculpture, shape,
fashion, form, model, whittle, chip, hammer, chisel, rough-hew.

heyday n prime, prime of life, bloom, full
flowering, flowering, peak, peak of perfection, pinnacle, culmination, crowning
point, salad days.

hiatus n **1** *a hiatus in the manuscript* gap,
break, lacuna, blank, discontinuity, interruption. **2** *an anatomical hiatus* opening,
aperture, cavity, hole, fissure, cleft, fora-
men, breach. **3** *a hiatus in the programme*
interval, intermission, pause, lull, rest,
break, suspension, abeyance.

hibernate v sleep, winter, overwinter, lie
dormant, be idle, lie low, stagnate, vegetate; *inf* hole up.

hidden adj **1** *hidden treasure* concealed,
unrevealed, secret, unseen, out of sight,
not visible, not on view, covered, masked,
shrouded. **2** *a hidden meaning/motive* secret,
concealed, obscure, indistinct, indefinite,
unclear, vague, cryptic, mysterious, covert,
under wraps, abstruse, arcane, recondite,
clandestine, ulterior, unfathomable, inexplicable, occult, mystical.

hide v **1** *prisoners hiding from the police* go
into hiding, conceal oneself, take cover,
find a hiding-place, lie low, keep out of
sight, secrete oneself, go to ground, go
underground, cover one's tracks; *inf* hole
up. **2** *hide the jewels* secrete, conceal, put in
a hiding-place, store away, stow away,

stash, lock up. **3** *clouds hiding the sun* obscure, cloud, darken, block, eclipse, obstruct. **4** *hide one's motives* keep secret, conceal, keep dark, withhold, suppress, hush up, mask, veil, shroud, camouflage, dissemble, disguise; *inf* keep mum, keep under one's hat.

hide n *an animal's hide* skin, pelt, coat, fur, fleece.

hideaway n hiding-place, den, lair, retreat, shelter, refuge, hermitage, cache; *inf* hide-out, hidey-hole.

hidebound adj *hidebound officials/ideas* narrow-minded, narrow, intolerant, conventional, fixed in one's views, set in one's opinions/ways, intractable, uncompromising, rigid, prejudiced, bigoted, conservative, ultra-conservative, reactionary, orthodox, fundamentalist, strait-laced.

hideous adj **1** *a hideous sight* ugly, unsightly, grotesque, monstrous, repulsive, repellent, revolting, gruesome, disgusting, grim, ghastly, macabre. **2** *a hideous crime* horrible, horrific, horrendous, horrifying, frightful, shocking, dreadful, outrageous, monstrous, appalling, terrible, terrifying, heinous, abominable, foul, vile, odious, loathsome, contemptible, execrable.

hide-out n hiding-place, hideaway, retreat, shelter. *see* HIDEAWAY.

hiding n *got a good hiding from his father* beating, thrashing, whipping, caning, spanking, flogging, drubbing, thumping, battering; *inf* walloping, licking, tanning, whaling, lathering, larruping.

hie v hurry, hasten, go quickly, speed, rush, run, dash, scamper, scuttle, dart, tear.

hierarchy n ranking, grading, social order, class system, pecking order.

hieroglyphics npl code, cipher, cryptogram, cryptograph, shorthand; *inf* scribble, scrawl.

high adj **1** *a high building* tall, lofty, elevated, soaring, towering, steep. **2** *a high official* high-ranking, leading, top, ruling, powerful, important, principal, chief, main, prominent, eminent, influential, distinguished, notable, exalted, illustrious. **3** *high ideals* high-minded, noble, virtuous, moral, lofty. **4** *a high wind* intense, extreme, strong, forceful, vigorous, powerful, potent, sharp, violent. **5** *high prices* dear, top, excessive, stiff, inflated, exorbitant, extortionate, high-priced, expensive, costly; *inf* steep. **6** *a high lifestyle* high-living, extravagant, luxurious, lavish, rich, grand, prodigal, sybaritic. **7** *have a high opinion of them* good, favourable, approving, admiring, flattering. **8** *the children are high before the holidays* overexcited, excited, boisterous, in high spirits, high-spirited, ebullient, bouncy, elated, ecstatic, euphoric, exhilarated, joyful, merry, happy, cheerful, jolly; *inf* high as a kite. **9** *high on drugs* drugged, drug-affected, intoxicated, inebriated, delirious, hallucinating; *inf* stoned, turned on, on a trip, tripping, hyped up, freaked out, spaced out. **10** *high voice/notes* high-pitched, acute, high-frequency, soprano, treble, piping, shrill, sharp-toned, piercing, penetrating. **11** *the meat/cheese is high* going bad, going off, rotting, smelling, tainted; *inf* ponging, niffy, whiffy. **high and dry** *ships/wives left high and dry* stranded, marooned, abandoned, helpless, destitute, bereft. **high and mighty** *high and mighty people looking down on the poor* haughty, arrogant, self-important, proud, conceited, egotistic, overweening, overbearing, snobbish, condescending, disdainful, supercilious, imperious; *inf* stuck-up, uppity, highfalutin. **In high dudgeon** in indignation, indignant, in anger, angrily, angry, with resentment, resentful, offended, vexed, in a huff; *inf* peeved.

high adv *flying high in the sky* high up, far up, way up, at a great height, at altitude, aloft. **high and low** *look high and low* everywhere, all over, far and near, far and wide, in every nook and cranny, extensively, exhaustively.

high n **1** *profits/temperatures reached a new high* high level, height, record, record level, peak, summit, top, zenith, apex. **2** *he's on a high with drugs* intoxication, delirium, ecstasy, euphoria, transports; *inf* trip, freak-out.

high-born adj noble, noble-born, of noble birth, well-born, aristocratic, patrician, blue-blooded.

highbrow n intellectual, scholar, savant, mastermind, genius; *inf* egghead, brain, brainbox, bookworm; *Amer* Brahmin.

highbrow adj *highbrow person/programme/pursuits* intellectual, scholarly, bookish, cultured, cultivated, educated, sophisticated; *inf* brainy.

high-class adj superior, luxurious, de luxe, select, choice, élite, top-flight, first-rate, elegant, posh, upper-class, up-market; *inf* tiptop, A1, super, super-duper, classy.

highfalutin adj pompous, pretentious, affected, supercilious, condescending, grandiose, lofty, magniloquent, bombastic; *inf* swanky.

high-flown adj *uses very high-flown language* high-sounding, bombastic, grandiloquent, magniloquent, overdone, overdrawn, ornate, exaggerated, elaborate, extravagant, flowery, florid, pretentious, overblown.

high-handed adj *high-handed person/manner* arbitrary, autocratic, dictatorial, despotic, tyrannical, domineering, oppressive, peremptory, imperious, overbearing, arrogant, haughty, lordly; *inf* bossy.

highland n plateau, tableland, ridge, heights, hill, hilly country, mountain, mountainous region, uplands.

highlight n *this is the highlight of the day/show/tour* outstanding feature, main feature, feature, high point, high spot, best part, climax, peak, memorable part, focal point, focus, centre of interest, cynosure.

highlight v *a programme highlighting famine* give prominence to, call attention to, bring to the fore, focus attention on, feature, place emphasis on, give emphasis to, emphasize, accentuate, accent, stress, underline, spotlight, bring home, point up.

highly adv **1** *highly entertaining/inflammable* very, very much, to a great extent, greatly, extremely, decidedly, certainly, exceptionally, tremendously, vastly, immensely, eminently, supremely, extraordinarily. **2** *speak highly of* approvingly, favourably, well, warmly, appreciatively, admiringly, with approbation, enthusiastically.

highly strung adj *highly strung artist/racehorse* nervous, nervy, easily upset/agitated, on edge, edgy, excitable, tense, taut, stressed, temperamental, neurotic, irritable, overwrought, restless, wound up.

high-minded adj *high-minded intellectuals/ideals* noble-minded, moral, virtuous, ethical, upright, righteous, principled, honourable, good, fair, pure, lofty, elevated.

high-powered adj *high-powered executives* dynamic, aggressive, assertive, energetic, driving, ambitious, go-ahead, effective, enterprising, vigorous, forceful; *inf* gogetting.

high-pressure adj *high-pressure salesmen | used high-pressure sales techniques* aggressive, insistent, persistent, intensive, forceful, high-powered, importunate, bludgeoning, coercive, compelling, persuasive, not taking no for an answer; *inf* pushy.

high-priced adj expensive, dear, costly, exorbitant, extortionate, excessive, stiff; *inf* pricey, steep.

high-sounding adj *high-sounding language/phrases* high-flown, bombastic, grandiloquent, magniloquent, elaborate, pretentious. *see* HIGH-FLOWN.

high-spirited adj spirited, lively, full of life, animated, vibrant, vital, dynamic, active, energetic, full of vim, vigorous, boisterous, bouncy, frolicsome, effervescent, buoyant, cheerful, exuberant, ebullient, exhilarated, vivacious, joyful, full of fun.

high spirits npl liveliness, animation, vitality, dynamism, boisterousness, bounciness, cheerfulness, exuberance, vivacity, joy, *joie de vivre*. *see* HIGH-SPIRITED.

hijack v commandeer, seize, expropriate, take over, skyjack.

hike v **1** *hike over the hills* walk, march, tramp, trek, trudge, plod, ramble, wander, backpack; *inf* hoof it, leg it, take shanks's pony. **2** *he hiked up his trousers/load* hitch up, pull up, jack up, lift, raise. **3** *they've hiked up the prices* raise, increase, put up, add to; *inf* jack up.

hike n *go on a hike* walk, march, tramp, trek, ramble, trudge, wander.

hilarious adj **1** *a hilarious play/story* very funny, extremely amusing, humorous, entertaining, comical, uproarious, side-splitting. **2** *a hilarious party* amusing, entertaining, uproarious, merry, jolly, mirthful, animated, vivacious, sparkling, exuberant, boisterous, noisy, rowdy.

hilarity n *the joke provoked great hilarity* amusement, comedy, mirth, laughter, merriment, levity, glee, high spirits.

hill n **1** *the hills behind the town* elevation, heights, high land, hillock, hilltop, knoll, hummock, mound, rising ground, tor, mount, fell, ridge; *Scots* brae. **2** *cars going slowly up the hill* slope, rise, incline, gradient, acclivity; *Scots* brae. **3** *a hill of rubbish* mountain, heap, pile, mound, stack, drift.

hillock n knoll, barrow, knob, hummock, monticule; *dial* knap.

hilt n handle, haft, handgrip, grip, shaft, hold, helve. **to the hilt** *back the leader to the hilt* completely, fully, wholly, entirely, totally, to the maximum extent, all the way.

hind adj *horse's hind legs* rear, back, hinder, posterior, caudal.

hinder v *hinder their efforts/progress* hamper, impede, hold back, interfere with, delay, hold up, slow down, retard, obstruct, inhibit, handicap, hamstring, block, interrupt, check, trammel, forestall, curb, baulk, thwart, frustrate, foil, baffle, stymie, stop, bring to a halt, arrest, abort, defer, prevent, debar.

hindmost adj *hindmost wagon in the train* last, furthest behind, furthest back, rearmost, rear, nearest the rear, endmost, most remote.

hindrance n *prove a hindrance to their plans* impediment, obstacle, interference, obstruction, handicap, block, restraint, interruption, check, bar, barrier, drawback, snag, difficulty, stumbling-block, encumbrance, curb, stoppage, trammel, deterrent, prevention, debarment.

hinge v *plans hinge on finance* depend on, turn on, be contingent on, hang on, pivot on, revolve around, rest on, centre on.

hint n **1** *give a hint that he was leaving* inkling, clue, suggestion, innuendo, tip-off, insinuation, implication, indication, mention, allusion, intimation, whisper, a word to the wise. **2** *write gardening hints* tip, pointer, advice, help, suggestion; *inf* wrinkle. **3** *just a hint of garlic* suspicion, suggestion, trace, touch, dash, soupçon, speck, sprinkling, tinge, whiff, breath, taste, scent.

hint v *he hinted that he was leaving* give a clue, suggest, give someone a tip-off, insinuate, imply, indicate, mention, allude to the fact, make an allusion, intimate, let it be known, signal, make a reference to the fact, refer to the fact.

hippy n beatnik, flower person/child, bohemian; *inf* drop-out.

hire v **1** *hire a boat/car/dress* rent, lease, charter, engage. **2** *hire staff* appoint, sign on, take on, engage, employ, secure the services of, enlist, contract with.

hire n **1** *worthy of their hire* pay, salary, wage, earnings, remuneration, fee, charge, stipend, price. **2** *the hire will cost £100* rent, rental, lease.

hiss n **1** *the hiss of the snake/kettle* hissing, sibilation, sibilance, buzz, whistle, wheeze. **2** *the hisses of the audience* boo, jeer, shout of derision, catcall, hoot, whistle, clamour, scoffing; *inf* raspberry.

hiss v **1** *snake/kettle was hissing* sibilate, buzz, whistle, wheeze. **2** *the audience is hissing* boo, jeer, cry/howl down, shout one's disapproval, deride, catcall, utter catcalls, hoot, scoff at, scorn, mock, taunt, decry, ridicule, revile; *inf* blow raspberries.

historian n chronicler, annalist, archivist, recorder, historiographer, palaeographer, biographer, antiquarian.

historic adj *historic event/house* famous, famed, notable, celebrated, renowned, momentous, significant, important, consequential, red-letter, memorable, remarkable, outstanding, extraordinary, epoch-making.

historical adj **1** *a historical rather than a legendary account* factual, recorded, documented, chronicled, archival, authentic, actual, attested, verified, confirmed. **2** *in historical times* old, past, former, prior, bygone, ancient; *lit* of yore.

history n **1** *the history of the times* annals, chronicles, records, public records, account, study, story, tale, saga, narrative, recital, reports, memoirs, biography, autobiography. **2** *what is the young man's history?* life story, background, antecedents, experiences, adventures, fortunes. **3** *that is history now* the past, former times, bygone days, yesterday, the old days, the good old days, days of old, time gone by, antiquity; *lit* days of yore, olden days/times, yesteryear.

hit v **1** *his father hit him* strike, slap, smack, buffet, punch, box, cuff, beat, thump, batter, pound, pummel, thrash, hammer, bang, knock, swat; *inf* whack, wallop, bash, belt, clout, clip, clobber, sock, biff, swipe. **2** *the car hit the lorry* run into, bang into, smash into, crash into, knock into, bump, collide with, meet head-on. **3** *her death hit him hard* affect, have an effect on, make an impression on, influence, make an impact on, leave a mark on, impinge on, move, touch, overwhelm, devastate, damage, hurt; *inf* knock back, knock for six. **4** *hit the right tone in his speech | hit the bull's-eye* achieve, accomplish, reach, attain, arrive at, gain, secure, touch, strike. **hit home** *his remarks hit home* have the intended effect, reach the target, strike home, hit the mark. **hit it off** *the children hit it off right away* get on, get on well, be/get on good terms with, become friends, take to each other, warm to each other, find things in common; *inf* be on the same wavelength. **hit on/upon** *hit on the solution* stumble on, chance on, light on, come upon, blunder on, discover, uncover, arrive at, think of, come up with. **hit out at** *hit out at his enemies* lash out at, attack, assail, strike out at, rail against, inveigh against, denounce, revile, condemn, castigate, censure, vilify.

hit n **1** *the hit from his father* blow, slap, smack, buffet, punch, box, cuff, beating, thump, thumping, battering, bang; *inf* whack, wallop, bashing, belting, clout, clobbering, swipe. *see* HIT v 1. **2** *a nasty hit at her hair* gibe, taunt, jeer, piece of sarcasm; *inf* dig.

hitch v **1** *hitch the trailer to the car* fasten, connect, attach, join, couple, unite, tie, tether, bind, harness, yoke. **2** *hitching up their skirts/socks* pull up, hike up, jerk up; *inf* yank up. **3** *hitching in France* hitch-hike, hitch a lift, thumb a lift.

hitch n *what's the hitch?* hindrance, hold-up, delay, impediment, obstacle, obstruction, barrier, stoppage, stumbling-block, block, check, snag, catch, difficulty, problem, trouble.

hither adv *he came hither* here, to here, over here, to this place, near, nearer, close, closer.

hitherto adv *hitherto he was unemployed* until now, up until now, till now, up to now, so far, previously, thus far, heretofore, before, beforehand.

hit-or-miss adj *a hit-or-miss attempt/method* haphazard, random, aimless, undirected, disorganized, indiscriminate, careless, casual, offhand, cursory, perfunctory.

hoar n hoar-frost, frost, rime, rime frost, verglas, Jack Frost.

hoard n *a hoard of food/money* store, stockpile, supply, reserve, reservoir, fund, cache, accumulation, heap, pile, mass, amassment, aggregation, conglomeration, treasure house, treasure trove; *inf* stash.

hoard v *hoard food/money* store, store up, stock up, stockpile, put by, put away, lay by, lay in, set aside, pile up, stack up, stow away, husband, save, buy up, accumulate, amass, heap up, collect, gather, garner, squirrel away; *inf* stash away.

hoarder n collector, saver, miser, niggard, magpie, squirrel.

hoarse adj *a hoarse voice* croaking, croaky, throaty, harsh, rough, gruff, husky, gravelly, grating, rasping, guttural, raucous, discordant, cracked.

hoary adj **1** *hoary hair/head* grey, grey-haired, white, white-haired, silvery, silvery-haired, grizzled, grizzly. **2** *hoary gentleman* old, elderly, aged, at an advanced age, venerable, time-honoured. **3** *hoary jokes* old, antiquated, ancient, antique, old as the hills, hackneyed, trite.

hoax n *the telephone call was a hoax* practical joke, joke, jest, prank, trick, ruse, deception, fraud, imposture, cheat, swindle; *inf* con, fast one, spoof, scam.

hoax v *hoax the old woman* play a practical joke on, play a joke/jest on, play a prank on, trick, fool, deceive, bluff, hoodwink, delude, dupe, take in, cheat, swindle, defraud, pull the wool over someone's eyes, gull; *inf* con, pull a fast one on, take someone for a ride, put one over on someone, spoof; *lit* cozen.

hobble v walk with difficulty, limp, walk with a limp, walk lamely, walk haltingly, falter, move unsteadily, shuffle, totter, stagger, reel; *Scots* hirple.

hobby n leisure activity, leisure pursuit, leisure interest, pastime, diversion, recreation, relaxation, divertissement, sideline, entertainment, amusement, sport, game.

hobgoblin n goblin, imp, elf, gnome, dwarf, bogey, bogeyman, evil spirit.

hobnob v *hobnobbing with journalists* fraternize, associate, socialize, mingle, mix, keep company, go around, consort; *inf* hang around, hang out.

hocus-pocus n **1** *accuse the salesman of hocus-pocus* trickery, chicanery, deception, deceit, artifice, stratagem, sleight of hand, legerdemain, ruse, hoax, sham, delusion, pretence, imposture. **2** *the hocus-pocus spoken by the magician* spell, mumbo-jumbo, abracadabra, magic words, magic formula, incantation, chant, invocation, charm.

hodgepodge n *see* HOTCHPOTCH.

hog n **1** *farmer raising hogs* pig, boar, swine, porker, grunter. **2** *hogs at the table* glutton, gourmand, gormandizer, cormorant, wolf, big eater, trencherman, trencherwoman; *inf* pig, gannet.

hogwash n *talking hogwash* nonsense, rubbish, gibberish, twaddle, drivel, balderdash, humbug, bunkum, trash; *inf* gobbledook, piffle, bunk, bosh, tosh, bilge, tripe, rot, tommy-rot, crap, hooey.

hoi polloi n the common people, the populace, the masses, the many, the proletariat, the peasants, the commons, the commonality, the lower orders, the third estate, the rabble, the riffraff, the herd, the common herd, the mob, ragtag and bobtail; *inf* plebs, proles, the great unwashed.

hoist v *hoist the load on to the lorry* lift, raise, upraise, heave, jack up, hike up, elevate, erect.

hoist n *need a hoist for the heavy load* crane, winch, tackle, capstan, pulley, jack, elevator, lift.

hold v **1** *hold his hand* hold on to, clasp, clutch, grasp, grip, seize, clench, cling to; *lit* cleave to. **2** *hold his sweetheart in his arms* embrace, hug, enfold, clasp, cradle, fondle. **3** *hold the relevant documents* have, possess, own, retain, keep. **4** *hold pleasant memories* cherish, harbour, treasure, retain. **5** *will it hold his weight* bear, carry, take, support, hold up, keep up, sustain, prop up, buttress, brace, suspend. **6** *police are holding the suspect* detain, confine, hold in custody, impound, constrain, keep under constraint, lock up, imprison, put behind bars, incarcerate. **7** *you cannot hold him from going* hold back, restrain, impede, check, bar, curb, stop, retard, delay, prevent. **8** *hold the* *interest of the audience* keep, maintain, occupy, engage, involve, absorb, engross, immerse, monopolize, arrest, catch, spellbind, fascinate, rivet. **9** *he holds a well-paid post* hold down, be in, occupy, fill, maintain, continue in, enjoy, boast. **10** *the bottle holds one litre | the hall holds 400 people* contain, have a capacity for, accommodate, take, comprise. **11** *we hold that he is guilty* maintain, think, believe, consider, regard, deem, judge, assume, presume, reckon, suppose, esteem. **12** *will the good weather hold?* go on, carry on, remain, continue, stay, persist, last, endure, keep up, persevere. **13** *the old rule still holds* hold good, stand, apply, be in force, be in operation, operate, remain valid, remain, exist, be the case. **14** *hold you responsible* make, think, consider, regard as, view, treat as. **15** *hold a meeting* call, convene, assemble, conduct, run, preside over, officiate at. **hold back 1** *hold back a laugh* keep back, suppress, repress, stifle, smother. **2** *hold back progress* prevent, impede, obstruct, hinder, check, curb, inhibit, restrain, control. **3** *hold back from hitting him* keep, desist, forbear, stop oneself, restrain oneself. **4** *hold back information* withhold, not disclose, suppress, refuse to disclose. **hold down 1** *hold down the people* oppress, repress, tyrannize, dominate. **2** *hold down prices* keep low, keep down, keep at a low level. **3** *hold down a job* hold, be in, occupy, fill, continue in. *see* HOLD v 9. **hold forth 1** *hold forth about politics* speak at length, speak, talk, declaim, discourse, lecture, harangue, preach, orate, speechify, sermonize, perorate; *inf* spout, spiel. **2** *hold forth the hand of friendship* hold out, extend, proffer, offer. *see* HOLD v *hold out*. **hold off 1** *the storm held off* not occur, not happen, be delayed. **2** *hold off the attack* keep off, keep at bay, fend off, stave off, ward off, repel, repulse, rebuff. **3** *hold off making a decision* delay, postpone, put off, defer, keep from, refrain from, avoid. **hold on 1** *hold on to his hand* clasp, clutch, grasp. *see* HOLD v 1. **2** *if the survivors can hold on* survive, last, carry on, keep going, continue; *inf* hang on. **3** *hold on to the house* keep, keep/retain possession of, retain ownership of, not sell/give away, keep for oneself. **hold one's own 1** *they held their own in the battle* stand firm, stand fast, stand one's ground, maintain one's position, stay put, not be defeated. **2** *the patient is holding his own* survive, be still alive, not lose strength, do well. **hold out 1** *hold out the hand of friendship* extend, proffer, offer, present, hold forth. **2** *hold out against the attack* stand fast, stand firm, resist, withstand, endure, carry on, persist, persevere, fight

to the end, fight to the last man; *inf* hang on. **3** *as long as supplies hold out* last, continue, remain. **hold over** *hold the matter over until the next meeting* put off, postpone, defer, delay, defer, adjourn, suspend, waive. **hold up 1** *hold up progress* delay, hinder, impede, obstruct, retard, slow, slow down, set back, stop, bring to a halt, prevent. **2** *hold up his weight* hold, bear, carry, support, sustain. *see* HOLD v 5. **3** *hold up the flag | she held up her father as an example* display, exhibit, show, put on show, present, flaunt, brandish. **4** *hold up a bank/train | they held up travellers* rob, commit armed robbery on, hold to ransom, waylay, mug; *inf* stick up. **5** *will his story hold up* survive investigation, be convincing, be verifiable, be provable, bear examination, hold water. **hold with** *he doesn't hold with modern education trends* approve of, agree with, be in favour of, support, give support to, subscribe to, countenance, take kindly to.

hold *n* **1** *keep a firm hold of the child's hand* grasp, grip, clutch, clasp. **2** *lose his hold on the cliff* foothold, footing, toe-hold, anchorage, purchase, leverage, prop, stay. **3** *government tightened its hold on the country* grip, power, control, dominion, authority, ascendary. **4** *he has a hold over the younger boy* influence, mastery, dominance, sway; *inf* pull, clout. **5** *put it on hold* pause, delay, postponement, deferment.

holder *n* **1** *ticket-holder | the present holder of the title* owner, possessor, bearer, proprietor, keeper, custodian, purchaser, incumbent, occupant. **2** *cigarette-holder* container, case, casing, receptacle, stand, cover, covering, housing, sheath.

hold-up *n* **1** *a hold-up on the motorway* delay, wait, stoppage, obstruction, bottleneck, traffic jam, hitch, snag, set-back, trouble, problem. **2** *a bank hold-up* robbery, theft, burglary, mugging; *inf* stick-up.

hole *n* **1** *a hole in the wall/material* opening, aperture, orifice, gap, space, breach, break, fissure, crack, rift, puncture, perforation, cut, incision, split, gash, rent, slit, vent, notch. **2** *a hole in the ground* excavation, pit, crater, shaft, mine, dug-out, cave, cavern, pothole, cavity, chamber, hollow, scoop, pocket, depression, dent, dint, dip. **3** *an animal's hole* burrow, lair, den, covert, earth, set, nest, retreat, shelter, recess. **4** *they took us to a real hole for a meal* slum, hovel; *inf* dump, dive, joint. **5** *the captives were thrown into a black hole* dungeon, prison, cell, oubliette. **6** *spot the hole in their argument* flaw, fault, defect, loophole, crack, inconsistency, discrepancy, error, fallacy. **7** *they are in a financial hole* predicament, mess, plight, difficulty, trouble, corner, tight corner, spot, tight spot, quandary, dilemma, muddle, tangle, imbroglio; *inf* fix, jam, scrape, pickle, hot water. **pick holes in** find fault with, criticize, pull to pieces, run down, cavil at, carp at, disparage, denigrate; *inf* slag off, slate.

hole v *rocks holed the ship* make a hole in, puncture, perforate, pierce, spike, stab, lacerate, gash, split, rent. **hole up 1** *the animals have holed up for the winter* hibernate, retire, go to sleep, lie dormant. **2** *the thieves have holed up somewhere* hide, hide out, lie low, conceal oneself, go underground.

hole-and-corner adj *hole-and-corner affair/method* secret, secretive, in secret, furtive, stealthy, surreptitious, underhand, clandestine, backstair; *inf* sneaky.

holiday n **1** *go on holiday | take a holiday* vacation, break, time off, leave, leave of absence, furlough, sabbatical, day/week/month off, breathing-space. **2** *celebrate a holiday* festival day, saint's day, feast day, holy day, day of observance, festival, festivity, fête, gala day, carnival day, celebration, anniversary, public holiday, bank holiday.

holier-than-thou adj sanctimonious, self-righteous, unctuous, pietistic, pietistical, religiose, pharisaic, priggish, smug, self-satisfied; *inf* goody-goody; *Scots* unco guid.

holiness n sanctity, sanctitude, saintliness, sacredness, divineness, divinity, godliness, blessedness, spirituality, religiousness, piety, righteousness, goodness, virtue, virtuousness, purity.

hollow adj **1** *a hollow vessel* empty, unfilled, vacant, void, not solid, hollowed out. **2** *hollow cheeks/marks* sunken, deep-set, dented, indented, depressed, concave, caved-in, incurvate, cavernous. **3** *a hollow sound* muffled, muted, low, dull, deep, rumbling, flat, toneless, dead, sepulchral. **4** *a hollow victory/triumph* valueless, worthless, useless, of no use, of no avail, unavailing, empty, fruitless, profitless, unprofitable, pointless, meaningless, insignificant, specious, pyrrhic. **5** *hollow compliments/condolences* insincere, hypocritical, feigned, artificial, false, dissembling, deceitful, sham, counterfeit, spurious, untrue, unsound, flimsy, faithless, treacherous, two-faced. **6** *feeling hollow* empty, hungry, famished, starving, starved, half-starved, ravenous. **beat someone hollow** trounce, thrash, rout, worst, defeat soundly, beat, overcome, overwhelm, outdo, surpass; *inf* hammer.

hollow n **1** *hollows in the ground* depression, indentation, concavity, dent, dint, dip, dimple, hole, crater, cavern, pit, cavity,

well, trough, basin, cup, bowl, niche, nook, cranny, recess. **2** *picnic in the hollow* valley, dell, dingle, dale, glen, gorge, ravine.

hollow v *river banks hollowed out by water* scoop out, gouge out, dig out, excavate, furrow, groove, channel, indent, dent.

holocaust n fire, inferno, conflagration, destruction, devastation, demolition, ravaging, annihilation, massacre, mass murder, carnage, slaughter, butchery, extermination, genocide, ethnic cleansing.

holy adj **1** *a holy person* God-fearing, godly, pious, pietistic, devout, spiritual, religious, righteous, good, virtuous, moral, saintly, saintlike, sinless. **2** *a holy place* blessed, blest, sanctified, consecrated, hallowed, sacred, sacrosanct, dedicated, venerated, divine, religious.

home n **1** *where is his home?* house, abode, domicile, residence, dwelling, dwelling-place, habitation. **2** *live a long way from home* home town, birthplace, homeland, native land, fatherland, motherland, mother country, country of origin. **3** *she comes from a good home* family, family background, family circle, household. **4** *estate agents advertising homes* house, flat, apartment, bungalow, terraced house, semi-detached house, detached house, cottage, accommodation; *inf* pad, semi. **5** *private home for the elderly* residential home, institution, shelter, refuge, hostel, hospice, retirement home, nursing home, convalescent home/hospital, children's home, old people's home. **6** *the home of the buffalo/ancient tribes had their home here* abode, habitat, natural habitat, environment, natural element, natural territory, original habitation, home ground, stamping-ground, haunt, domain. **at home 1** *is Jane at home?* in, present, available. **2** *at home in the academic world* familiar with, used to, comfortable, at ease, relaxed, in one's element, on familiar territory, on home ground. **3** *at home with computers* familiar with, proficient in, conversant with, skilled in, competent at, well-versed in; *inf* well up in, up on. **4** *Lady Travers is at home* entertaining, receiving guests, giving a party. **bring home** *the programme brought home the tragedy of famine | bring home to her the risk she is taking* drive home, press home, make someone aware of, make someone conscious of, emphasize, stress, impress upon someone, underline, highlight. **nothing to write home about** nothing important, nothing worth mentioning, nothing to comment on, nothing out of the ordinary.

home adj **1** *home issues, as opposed to international* domestic, internal, interior, local, national, native. **2** *home produce* home-grown, home-made, home-bred.

home v **home in on** *home in on the main issue* aim at, focus on, focus attention on, concentrate on, pinpoint, zero in on, zoom in on.

homeland n native land, fatherland, motherland, mother country, country of origin.

homeless adj of no fixed abode, down-and-out, destitute, derelict, without a roof over one's head, vagrant; *inf* dossing.

homelike adj homely, homey, homy, comfortable, cosy, snug, cheerful, welcoming, friendly, congenial, hospitable, informal, relaxed, intimate; *inf* comfy; *Amer* down-home, homestyle.

homely adj **1** *homely atmosphere/place* homelike, comfortable, cosy, snug, welcoming, informal, relaxed. *see* HOMELIKE. **2** *a homely but friendly place* plain, simple, modest, unsophisticated, natural, everyday, ordinary, unaffected, unassuming, unpretentious. **3** *a homely girl* plain, plain-featured, plain-looking, unattractive, ill-favoured, ugly; *inf* not much to look at, short on looks.

homespun adj *homespun advice/philosophy* plain, simple, homely, modest, natural, artless, unsophisticated, unpolished, unrefined, inelegant, coarse, rough, rude, rustic.

homicidal adj *homicidal maniac | has homicidal tendencies* murderous, death-dealing, mortal, deadly, lethal, violent, maniacal, berserk.

homicide n **1** *found guilty of homicide* murder, manslaughter, killing, slaying, slaughter, assassination, patricide, matricide, infanticide. **2** *a convicted homicide* murderer, killer, slayer, assassin, patricide, matricide, infanticide; *inf* hitman.

homily n *gave a short homily on forgiveness* sermon, preaching, lecture, discourse, lesson, talk, speech, address, oration.

homogeneous adj **1** *consisting of homogeneous parts* identical, alike, all alike, of the same kind, all the same, the same, all one, all of a piece, uniform, unvaried, unvarying, consistent. **2** *homogeneous substances* similar, kindred, akin, comparable, analogous, corresponding, parallel, correlative, cognate.

homogenize v make uniform, combine, coalesce, fuse, merge, blend, emulsify.

homogenous adj *see* HOMOGENEOUS.

homosexual adj **1** *homosexual men* gay, homoerotic, homophile; *inf derog* bent, queer, camp, poofy. **2** *homosexual women* gay, lesbian, homoerotic, homophile; *inf derog* butch.

homosexual n **1** *he's a homosexual* gay, homophile; *inf derog* queer, poof, queen; *Amer inf derog* faggot, fag. **2** *she's a homosexual* gay, lesbian, homophile; *inf derog* butch, dyke.

honest adj **1** *honest people* upright, honourable, moral, ethical, principled, righteous, right-minded, virtuous, good, worthy, decent, law-abiding, high-minded, upstanding, just, fair, incorruptible, truthful, true, veracious, trustworthy, trusty, reliable, conscientious, scrupulous, reputable, dependable, loyal, faithful. **2** *an honest reply* truthful, sincere, candid, frank, direct, forthright, straightforward, open, genuine, plain-speaking, matter-of-fact, unconcealed, blunt, undisguised, unfeigned, unequivocal. **3** *an honest mistake* real, true, genuine, authentic, actual, above-board, bona fide, proper, straight, fair and square; *inf* on the level, honest-to-goodness. **4** *an honest judgement* fair, just, equitable, even-handed, impartial, objective, balanced, unprejudiced, disinterested, unbiased.

honestly adv **1** *earn his living honestly* fairly, by fair means, by just means, lawfully, legally, legitimately, honourably, decently, ethically, morally, without corruption; *inf* on the level. **2** *honestly, I tell you he's not going | she told me honestly she was leaving* to be honest, speaking truthfully, truthfully, speaking frankly, in all sincerity, candidly, frankly, openly, plainly, in plain language, to someone's face, straight out, without dissembling, without shilly-shallying; *inf* straight up, Scouts' honour.

honesty n **1** uprightness, honourableness, honour, integrity, morals, morality, ethics, principle, high principles, righteousness, rectitude, virtue, goodness, probity, worthiness, justness, fairness, incorruptibility, truthfulness, truth, veracity, trustworthiness, reliability, conscientiousness, reputability, loyalty, faithfulness, fidelity. *see* HONEST 1. **2** *the honesty of his reply* truthfulness, truth, sincerity, candour, frankness, forthrightness, openness, genuineness, bluntness. *see* HONEST 2. **3** *the honesty of his judgement* fairness, justness, justice, equitability, even-handedness, impartiality, objectiveness, lack of prejudice, lack of bias, balance.

honorarium n remuneration, recompense, fee, salary, pay, emolument, reward.

honorary adj *made an honorary member* nominal, in name/title only, titular, unofficial, *ex officio*, complimentary, unpaid.

honour n **1** *a man of honour* honesty, uprightness, integrity, ethics, morals, high principles, righteousness, rectitude, virtue, goodness, decency, probity, worthiness, worth, fairness, justness, justice, truthfulness, trustworthiness, reliability, dependability, faithfulness, fidelity. **2** *the honour of winning the battle* fame, renown, glory, prestige, illustriousness, noble reputation, esteem, distinction, notability, credit; *inf* kudos. **3** *his honour is at stake* reputation, good name, name. **4** *protecting a lady's honour* chastity, virginity, virtue, purity, innocence, modesty. **5** *treat the hero with honour* acclaim, acclamation, applause, accolades, tributes, homage, praise, compliments, lauding, eulogy, paeans, adoration, reverence, veneration, adulation, exaltation, glorification. **6** *it was an honour to serve him* privilege, source of pleasure/pride/satisfaction, pleasure, joy, compliment, favour.

honour v **1** *all his pupils honour him* hold in honour, have a high regard for, hold in esteem, esteem, respect, admire, defer to, reverence, revere, venerate, worship, idolize, value, prize. **2** *the crowd honoured the victor* acclaim, applaud, give accolades to, pay homage to, pay tribute to, lionize, praise, cheer, compliment, laud, eulogize, sing paeans to, panegyrize. **3** *honour the agreement/guarantee* fulfil, discharge, carry out, observe, keep, be true to, be faithful to, live up to. **4** *honour the cheque* cash, pay out money for, clear, accept, take, pass.

honourable adj **1** *honourable men* honest, upright, ethical, moral, principled, high-principled, upstanding, righteous, right-minded, virtuous, good, decent, worthy, fair, just, true, truthful, trustworthy, trusty, reliable, dependable, faithful. **2** *an honourable victory* famous, renowned, glorious, prestigious, distinguished, esteemed, notable, noted, great, eminent, noble, illustrious, creditable. **3** *an honourable member of the community* worthy, respected, respectable, reputable, decent, venerable.

honours npl *honours given to the victor* rewards, awards, prizes, decorations, titles, distinctions, laurels, laurel wreaths, bays.

hood n head covering, cowl, head scarf.

hoodlum n **1** *hoodlums vandalizing telephone kiosks* ruffian, hooligan, thug, rowdy, delinquent, vandal, mugger; *inf* tough, rough, yob, yobbo. **2** *hoodlums killing policemen* gangster, mobster, gunman, murderer, assassin, terrorist; *inf* hit man, hatchet man; *Amer inf* hood.

hoodwink v deceive, delude, dupe, outwit, fool, befool, trick, get the better of, cheat, take in, hoax, mislead, defraud, swindle, gull, pull the wool over someone's eyes; *inf* con, bamboozle, lead up the garden path, pull a fast one on, put one over on, take for a ride, make a sucker of; *lit* cozen.

hook n **1** *a harvest hook* billhook, scythe, sickle, falchion, scimitar, sabre, cutlass. **2** *hang your coat on the hook* peg, holder. **3** *the hook of the dress is broken* hook-and-eye, fastener, catch, clasp, clip, link. **4** *animals caught in hooks* snare, trap, noose, springe. **5** *a hook in the river* crook, angle, loop, curve, bend, bow, arc, dog-leg, horseshoe bend, oxbow, hairpin turn/bend. **by hook or by crook** by any means whatsoever, by any means, by fair means or foul, no matter how, somehow or other, somehow, in one way or another. **hook, line and sinker** *believe the story hook, line and sinker* completely, entirely, thoroughly, wholly, totally, utterly, through and through. **off the hook 1** *her evidence got him off the hook* acquitted, cleared of the charge, exonerated, in the clear, let off, vindicated. **2** *her brother's taking his mother to the airport - she's off the hook* under no obligation, uncommitted, not bound, free.

hook v **1** *hook the dress/necklace* fasten, secure, fix, close the clasp. **2** *hook the animals* snare, ensnare, trap, entrap, enmesh.

hooked adj **1** *a hooked nose* hook-shaped, hooklike, aquiline, curved, bent, bowed, angular; *Med* falcate, falciform. **2** *been hooked for years | they're hooked on drugs/television/gambling* dependent, addicted, addicted to, devoted to, given to.

hooligan n ruffian, thug, rowdy, delinquent, vandal, mugger, hoodlum; *inf* tough, rough, yob, yobbo.

hoop n ring, band, circle, circlet, loop, wheel, girdle.

hoot n **1** *the owl's hoot* call, screech, whoop, cry, tu-whit, tu-whoo. **2** *the hoots of the audience* boo, hiss, jeer, catcall, yell, shout of derision, whistle; *inf* raspberry. **3** *the woman/story is a hoot* somebody/something very funny; *inf* scream, laugh, card, caution.

hoot v **1** *the owls hooted* call, screech, whoop, tu-whit-tu-whoo, tu-whoo. **2** *the audience hooted at the comedian* boo, hiss, jeer, catcall, cry/howl down, deride, mock, taunt, decry, ridicule, condemn, shout, yell; *inf* blow raspberries.

hop v *frogs hopping* jump, leap, bound, spring, vault, bounce, skip, caper, dance, frisk.

hop n **1** *get there in one hop* jump, leap, bound, spring, vault, bounce, skip. **2** *a quick hop over the Channel* flight, short flight, plane trip, trip, quick trip, jaunt. **3** *a hop in the local hall* dance, disco, party, social.

hope n *full of hope that we shall win* hopefulness, expectation, expectancy, anticipation, desire, longing, wish, wishing, craving, yearning, aspiration, ambition, dream, belief, assurance, assumption, confidence, conviction, faith, trust, optimism.

hope v *hope to win | hope for a victory* be hopeful of, expect, anticipate, look forward to, await, contemplate, foresee, desire, long, wish, crave, yearn, aspire, be ambitious, dream, believe, feel assured, assume, have confidence, be convinced, rely on, count on, trust in.

hopeful adj **1** *hopeful candidates | hopeful of winning* full of hope, expectant, anticipating, anticipative, looking forward to, optimistic, confident, assured, buoyant, sanguine. **2** *hopeful news/signs* promising, encouraging, heartening, gladdening, optimistic, reassuring, auspicious, favourable, propitious, cheerful, bright, pleasant, rosy.

hopefully adv **1** *travelling hopefully* with hope, full of hope, expectantly, with anticipation, optimistically, confidently, with assurance, buoyantly, sanguinely. **2** *hopefully he will win* it is to be hoped that, with luck, all being well, if all goes well, if everything turns out all right, probably, conceivably, feasibly.

hopeless adj **1** *feeling hopeless* without hope, despairing, in despair, desperate, pessimistic, defeatist, dejected, downhearted, despondent, demoralized, disconsolate, downcast, wretched, woebegone, forlorn, suicidal. **2** *a hopeless case* beyond hope, despaired of, lost, beyond remedy, irremediable, remediless, beyond recovery, past cure, incurable, beyond repair, irreparable, irreversible, incorrigible, serious, grave, fatal, deadly. **3** *a hopeless task/ situation* impossible, impracticable, futile, useless, vain, pointless, worthless, forlorn, no-win, unattainable, unachievable. **4** *she's hopeless at maths* poor, incompetent, ineffective, ineffectual, inadequate, inferior; *inf* no good, useless.

horde n *hordes of people/penguins on the beach* crowd, mob, throng, mass, large group, multitude, host, army, pack, gang, troop, drove, crew, band, flock, swarm, gathering, assemblage, press.

horizon n **1** *disappearing over the horizon* skyline, range of vision, field of view, view, vista. **2** *broaden the child's horizon* scope, range of experience, area of knowledge, perspective, perception, prospect, outlook, compass, sphere, purview.

horizontal adj flat, flat as a pancake, plumb, level, supine, prone, flush.

horrendous adj **1** *a horrendous sight* dreadful, awful, horrid. *see* HORRIBLE 1. **2** *a horrendous child* nasty, disagreeable, unpleasant. *see* HORRIBLE 2.

horrible adj **1** *a horrible sight/accident* dreadful, awful, horrid, terrible, horrifying, terrifying, frightful, fearful, horrendous, shocking, appalling, hideous, grim, ghastly, harrowing, gruesome, disgusting, revolting, repulsive, loathsome, abhorrent, detestable, hateful, abominable. **2** *horrible child/weather/food/picture/mess* nasty, disagreeable, unpleasant, mean, unkind, obnoxious, odious; *inf* horrid, awful, dreadful, terrible, beastly, ghastly, frightful, fearful, horrendous, shocking, appalling, hideous, revolting, abominable.

horrid adj **1** *a horrid sight* dreadful, awful, horrifying, terrible, frightful, hideous, grim, ghastly, revolting, abhorrent, abominable. *see* HORRIBLE 1. **2** *a horrid child* horrible, nasty, disagreeable, unpleasant, mean, unkind, obnoxious. *see* HORRIBLE 2.

horrify v **1** *the apparition horrified the children* terrify, terrorize, intimidate, frighten, frighten out of one's wits, alarm, scare, scare to death, startle, panic, throw into a panic, make someone's blood run cold; *inf* make someone's hair stand on end, make someone's hair curl, scare stiff, scare the living day lights out of. **2** *his attitude horrifies me* shock, appal, outrage, scandalize, disgust, revolt, repel, nauseate, sicken, offend, dismay; *inf* turn off.

horror n **1** *full of horror at the sight of the ghost* terror, fear, fear and trembling, fearfulness, fright, alarm, dread, awe, panic, trepidation, apprehensiveness, uneasiness, nervousness, dismay, consternation. **2** *view his attitude with horror* abhorrence, abomination, loathing, hate, detestation, repulsion, revulsion, disgust, distaste, aversion, hostility, antipathy, animosity.

horse n mount, steed, hack, pony, Shetland pony, cob, palfrey, nag, racehorse, filly, jade, draught-horse, cart-horse, packhorse, hunter, bay, sorrel, pinto, piebald; foal, colt, stallion, mare; *inf* gee-gee.

horseman, horsewoman n rider, equestrian, horse-soldier, cavalier, dragoon, jockey; cavalryman, cowboy/cowgirl.

horseplay n clowning, fooling, fooling around, tomfoolery, buffoonery, pranks, practical jokes, antics, capers, high jinks, rough-and-tumble, romping, skylarking; *inf* rough-housing, shenanigans, monkey business.

horse sense n common sense, sense one is born with, mother wit, judgement, soundness of judgement, practicality; *inf* nous, gumption, savvy.

horticulture n cultivation of gardens, gardening, floriculture, arboriculture.

hosanna n shout of praise, alleluia, song of praise, paean, laudation, glorification, hurrah, huzzah, cheer.

hose n 1 *a rubber hose* tube, tubing, pipe, siphon, conduit, channel, outlet. 2 *wearing red hose* socks, stockings, tights, hosiery.

hosiery n leg-covering, hose, socks, stockings, tights, knee socks, ankle socks, leggings.

hospitable adj welcoming, sociable, convivial, generous, liberal, bountiful, open-handed, congenial, friendly, neighbourly, warm, warm-hearted, cordial, kind, kindly, kind-hearted, amicable, well-disposed, amenable, helpful.

hospital n medical centre, clinic, infirmary, sanatorium.

hospitality n hospitableness, welcome, sociability, conviviality, generosity, liberality, bountifulness, open-handedness, friendliness, neighbourliness, warmth, warm-heartedness, cordiality, kindness, kind-heartedness, amicability, amenability, helpfulness.

host¹ n 1 *the host of the pub* proprietor, proprietress, landlord, landlady, innkeeper, hotel-keeper, hotelier. 2 *the host greeting his guests* party-giver, entertainer. 3 *the host of the radio/TV show* presenter, compère, master of ceremonies, MC, anchorman, anchorwoman; *inf* emcee.

host¹ v 1 *host a party* to be the host/hostess of, give. 2 *host a radio/TV show* present, introduce, compère; *inf* emcee.

host² n *a host of people gathered for the march* multitude, crowd, throng, horde, mob, army, legion, crush, herd, pack, flock, swarm, troop, band, mass, assemblage, assembly, array, myriad.

hostage n pawn, gage, security, surety, pledge, captive, prisoner.

hostile adj 1 *hostile to the idea* antagonistic, opposed, averse, opposite, ill-disposed, against, inimical; *inf* anti. 2 *hostile weather conditions* adverse, unfavourable, unpropitious, disadvantageous, inauspicious. 3 *a hostile crowd* belligerent, bellicose, aggressive, warlike, warring, militant, antagonistic, unfriendly, unkind, unsympathetic, malevolent, malicious, spiteful, wrathful, angry.

hostilities npl war, warfare, fighting, conflict, militancy, strife, action, battles.

hostility n 1 *their hostility to the idea* antagonism, opposition, aversion, animosity, ill-will, enmity, inimicalness. 2 *the hostility of the crowd* belligerence, bellicosity, aggression, warlikeness, militancy, antagonism, unfriendliness, unkindness, malevolence, malice, spite, wrath, anger.

hot adj 1 *hot food straight from the oven* heated, very warm, boiling, boiling hot, piping, piping hot, scalding, red-hot, sizzling, steaming, scorching, roasting, searing. 2 *a hot day* very warm, boiling hot, boiling, blazing hot, sweltering, parching, scorching, roasting, searing, blistering, baking, oven-like, torrid, sultry. 3 *the curry is very hot* peppery, spicy, pungent, piquant, fiery, sharp, biting, acrid. 4 *the child is hot* feverish, fevered, febrile, flushed, red, pyretic. 5 *hot on the idea of free speech* ardent, eager, enthusiastic, keen, fervent, fervid, zealous, vehement, passionate, animated, excited. 6 *hot with anger* inflamed, furious, infuriated, seething, raging, fuming, wrathful, angry, indignant. 7 *hot young men* randy, sexually excited, sex-hungry, lustful, lascivious, lecherous, libidinous; *inf* horny. 8 *a hot temper/argument* heated, violent, furious, fierce, ferocious, stormy, tempestuous, savage. 9 *hot from the presses/warehouses* new, fresh, recent, late, brand-new, just out, just released, just issued. 10 *this brand of trainers is hot with children* popular, in vogue, in demand, sought-after, in favour, well-liked, well-loved. 11 *hot on their heels* close, following closely, near. 12 *hot goods* stolen, illegally obtained, smuggled, wanted.

hot air n empty talk, nonsense, bombast, verbiage, wind, blather, blether, claptrap; *inf* gas, bunkum, guff, bosh.

hotbed n *the place is a hotbed of vice/crime* breeding-ground, forcing-house, seed-bed, nursery, cradle, nest, womb.

hot-blooded adj 1 *hot-blooded young lovers* passionate, impassioned, ardent, sensual, sex-hungry, lustful, libidinous, randy; *inf* horny. 2 *hot-blooded people quarrelling* excitable, temperamental, fiery, spirited, impulsive, rash, wild, quixotic.

hotchpotch n hodgepodge, mixture, jumble, mishmash, miscellany, medley, *mélange*, mess, clutter, odds and ends, potpourri, farrago, gallimaufry, olio, olla podrida.

hotel n inn, tavern, pub, hostelry, motel, boarding-house, guest-house.

hotfoot adv *ran hotfoot to the river* posthaste, pell-mell, helter-skelter, hurriedly, hastily, speedily, quickly, fast, rapidly, swiftly.

hotheaded adj hot-tempered, shorttempered, quick-tempered, fiery, hasty, excitable, volatile, rash, impetuous, impulsive, reckless, foolhardy, wild, unruly.

hothouse n greenhouse, glasshouse, conservatory.

hothouse adj *hothouse children* overprotected, pampered, coddled, overindulged, spoiled, spoonfed, sheltered, shielded, delicate, frail, fragile, sensitive, dainty.

hound n 1 *she breeds hounds* bloodhound, foxhound, wolfhound, greyhound, dog, hunting dog. 2 *he's a mean hound* scoundrel, cad, blackguard, rascal, rogue, villain, miscreant, knave, scallywag; *inf* rotter, bounder, wrong'un.

hound v 1 *police hounding the criminal* chase, give chase to, pursue, follow, hunt, hunt down, stalk, track, trail, follow on the heels of, shadow; *inf* tail. 2 *hound him to do as they wished* nag, bully, browbeat, pester, harass, harry, keep after, urge, badger, goad, prod, provoke, impel, force, pressure, pressurize.

house n 1 *new estate of 200 houses | his house is over there* abode, residence, domicile, home, habitation; bungalow, cottage; *inf* semi. 2 *how many are in the house?* household, family, family circle, home, ménage. 3 *the House of Stewart* family, clan, family tree, line, lineage, dynasty, ancestry, ancestors, kindred, blood, race, strain, tribe. 4 *a publishing house* firm, business, company, concern, corporation, enterprise, organization; *inf* outfit. 5 *the lower House* legislative body, legislative assembly, parliament, congress, chamber. 6 *a large house for the event* audience, gathering, assembly, congregation, listeners, spectators. 7 *a house owned by the brewery* inn, pub, public house, tavern, hotel, hostelry. **on the house** free, for nothing, gratis, without payment.

house v 1 *the building houses 20 people* accommodate, lodge, put up, take in, have room for, have space/capacity for, sleep, shelter, harbour. 2 *the box houses the machinery* cover, sheathe, protect, shelter, guard, contain, keep.

household n *how many are in the household?* family, family circle, house, home, ménage.

household adj *household articles/bleach* domestic, family, ordinary, everyday, common, usual, run-of-the-mill.

householder n home-owner, resident, occupant, occupier, tenant.

housekeeping n household management, home economics, housecraft, domestic science, housewifery.

housing n 1 *a shortage of housing* accommodation, houses, dwellings, homes, shelter, habitations. 2 *housing for machinery* case, casing, cover, covering, sheath, container, enclosure, jacket, capsule, holder.

hovel n shack, shanty, hut; *inf* dump, hole; *Scots* bothy.

hover v 1 *kites hovering in the air* be suspended, hang, fly, flutter, float, drift, be wafted. 2 *students hovering by the notice-board* linger, hang about, wait near, stay near. 3 *hovering between going and staying* waver, vacillate, fluctuate, oscillate, alternate, seesaw; *Scots* swither.

however adv *however, you will have to go* nevertheless, be that as it may, nonetheless, notwithstanding, anyway, anyhow, regardless, despite that, still, yet, just the same, though.

however conj *however he approached the problem* whatever way, regardless of how.

howl v 1 *dogs howling* bay, yowl, yelp, ululate, quest. 2 *children howling* yell, wail, bawl, scream, shriek, bellow, roar, shout, caterwaul, yelp, cry, weep, ululate; *Amer inf* holler. 3 *howling at the clown's antics* laugh loudly, roar with laughter, split one's sides; *inf* fall about.

howl n 1 *the howls of the dogs* bay, yowl, yelp, ululation, questing. 2 *children's howls* yell, wail, bawl, bellow, roar, caterwauling, crying. see HOWL v 2.

howler n mistake, error, blunder, gaffe, malapropism; *inf* bloomer, boo-boo, clanger.

hub n 1 *the hub of a wheel* pivot, axis, nave. 2 *the hub of the firm* centre, centre of activity, middle, core, heart, nerve centre, focus, focal point.

huddle v 1 *huddle into the hall* crowd, press, throng, flock, pack, cram, herd, squeeze, bunch up, cluster, gather, congregate. 2 *huddle up under her coat* curl up, snuggle, cuddle, nestle, hunch up.

huddle n 1 *a huddle of people* crowd, throng, press, pack, cluster, gathering. 2 *a huddle of objects* heap, jumble, confusion, muddle, tangle, mess. **3** *people going into a huddle* conference, discussion, consultation, meeting, powwow; *inf* confab.

hue¹ n **1** *a blue hue* colour, tone, shade, tint, tinge, dye. **2** *political opinions of every hue* complexion, cast, aspect, light.

hue² n **hue and cry** outcry, uproar, commotion, racket, clamour, furore, brouhaha, hullabaloo, much ado. *see* HULLABALOO.

huff n **in a huff** in a bad mood, sulky, having a sulk, having a fit of the sulks, peeved; *inf* miffed.

hug v **1** *hug his wife* embrace, cuddle, take in one's arms, hold close, enfold in one's arms, clasp/press to one's bosom, squeeze. **2** *hug the shore* keep close to, stay near to, follow closely, follow the course of. **3** *hug his memories* cling to, hold onto, cherish, harbour, nurse, keep close.

hug n *give the child a hug* embrace, cuddle, squeeze, hold, clasp, bear-hug; *inf* clinch.

huge adj enormous, immense, great, massive, colossal, vast, prodigious, gigantic, giant, gargantuan, mammoth, monumental, monstrous, elephantine, extensive, bulky, mountainous, titanic, Herculean, Brobdingnagian; *inf* jumbo.

hulk n **1** *the hulk of a ship* wreck, shipwreck, derelict, ruin, shell, skeleton, hull, frame. **2** *a clumsy great hulk* oaf, lout, lump, lubber, bull in a china shop; *inf* lummox; *Amer* klutz.

hulking adj **1** *a hulking great wardrobe* cumbersome, unwieldy, bulky, weighty, massive, ponderous. **2** *a hulking boy* clumsy, awkward, ungainly, lumbering, lumpish, loutish, large, overgrown.

hull n **1** *the hull of a ship* body, framework, frame, skeleton, structure, casing, covering. **2** *the hull of fruit* rind, skin, peel, shell, husk, pod, shuck, capsule, integument, pericarp.

hull v *hull fruit* peel, pare, skin, trim, shell, husk, shuck.

hullabaloo n uproar, commotion, roar, racket, din, noise, clamour, disturbance, hubbub, outcry, furore, brouhaha, hue and cry, pandemonium, tumult, turmoil, fuss, to-do, much ado, bedlam, babel, hurlyburly; *inf* rumpus, ruction; *Amer* ruckus.

hum v **1** *bees/machines humming* drone, murmur, vibrate, throb, thrum, buzz, whirr, purr. **2** *humming a tune* sing, croon, whisper, mumble. **3** *things are humming* be busy, be active, bustle, move quickly, vibrate, pulsate, buzz.

hum n *the hum of bees/machines* drone, murmur, vibration, throb, thrum, buzz, whirr, purr.

human adj **1** *a human creature* anthropoid, mortal. **2** *human frailty/weaknesses* mortal, physical, bodily, fleshly, carnal, corporal. **3** *a very human person* kind, kindly, considerate, understanding, sympathetic, compassionate, approachable, accessible, humane. *see* HUMANE. **4** *they're only human* mortal, flesh and blood, fallible, weak, frail, vulnerable, erring.

human n *animals and humans* human being, mortal, member of the human race, individual, living soul, soul; man, woman, child; *inf* body.

humane adj *a humane ruler | humane to animals* kind, kindly, kind-hearted, good, good-natured, compassionate, considerate, understanding, sympathetic, forgiving, merciful, lenient, forbearing, gentle, tender, mild, clement, benign, benevolent, charitable, generous, magnanimous, approachable, accessible.

humanitarian adj **1** *humanitarian enemy soldiers* humane, kind, good, compassionate, sympathetic, merciful, lenient, gentle, magnanimous. *see* HUMANE. **2** *interested in humanitarian issues* philanthropic, altruistic, welfare, charitable.

humanitarian n philanthropist, altruist, benefactor, good Samaritan, social reformer, do-gooder.

humanities npl classics, classical studies, classical languages, classical literature, liberal arts, literae humaniores.

humanity n **1** *bombs bringing the end of humanity* humankind, human race, the human species, mankind, man, people, mortals, Homo sapiens. **2** *err because of their humanity* humanness, human nature, mortality, flesh and blood. **3** *monks noted for their humanity* kindness, kind-heartedness, goodness, good-heartedness, benevolence, compassion, sympathy, understanding, pity, mercy, mercifulness, gentleness, tenderness, leniency, tolerance, goodwill, brotherly love, fellow-feeling, generosity, magnanimity, charity, philanthropy.

humble adj **1** *brilliant but humble* modest, unassuming, self-effacing, unassertive, unpretentious, unostentatious, meek. **2** *the villagers are humble people* plain, common, ordinary, simple, poor, of low birth, lowborn, of low rank, low-ranking, low, lowly, inferior, plebeian, proletarian, base, mean, unrefined, vulgar, unimportant, insignificant, inconsequential, undistinguished, ignoble. **3** *hate his humble attitude to the boss* servile, submissive, obsequious, subservient, deferential, over-respectful, slavish, sycophantic.

humble v **1** *humble them by his criticism* humiliate, mortify, bring down, bring low, subdue, chasten, shame, put to shame, abash, abase, degrade, make someone eat humble pie, take down a peg or two. *see* HUMILIATE. **2** *feel humbled in the presence of the great man* belittle, demean, deflate, depreciate, disparage. **3** *humble the enemy* crush, trounce, rout, break, conquer, vanquish, defeat, utterly overwhelm, smash, bring to one's knees.

humbug n **1** *taken in by the humbug* hoax, trick, trickery, cheat, cheating, bluff, ruse, wile, stratagem, fraud, swindle, deceit, deception, imposture, pretence, sham, delusion; *inf* con. **2** *the salesman's a humbug* charlatan, imposter, fake, sham, fraud, cheat, trickster, swindler, mountebank, quack, deceiver, dissembler; *inf* con-man, phoney. **3** *he talks a lot of humbug* nonsense, rubbish, balderdash, twaddle, bunkum; *inf* rot, tommy-rot, bunk, boloney, bosh, tosh, hogwash, crap.

humdrum adj *humdrum life/routine* commonplace, run-of-the-mill, routine, unvaried, unvarying, ordinary, everyday, mundane, uneventful, monotonous, repetitious, dull, uninteresting, banal, boring, tedious, tiresome, wearisome.

humid adj *humid atmosphere/day* muggy, sticky, steamy, clammy, close, sultry, damp, moist, dank, wet, wettish, soggy, misty.

humidity n humidness, mugginess, stickiness, steaminess, clamminess, closeness, sultriness, dampness, damp, moistness, dankness, moisture, wetness, sogginess.

humiliate v mortify, humble, shame, bring low, put to shame, make ashamed, disgrace, embarrass, discomfit, chasten, subdue, abash, abase, debase, degrade, crush, make someone eat humble pie, take down a peg or two; *inf* put down; *Amer inf* make someone eat crow.

humiliation n mortification, humbling, loss of pride, shame, disgrace, loss of face, dishonour, indignity, discredit, ignoring, embarrassment, discomfiture, affront, abasement, debasement, degradation, submission, humble pie; *inf* put-down.

humility n **1** *the winner showed humility* lack of pride, humbleness, modesty, modestness, meekness, self-effacement, unpretentiousness, unobtrusiveness, diffidence. **2** *dislike his humility towards the boss* servility,

submissiveness, obsequiousness, subservience, deference, sycophancy.

humorist n comic writer, writer of comedy, cartoonist, caricaturist, comic, comedian, comedienne, joker, jokester, clown, jester, wag, wit, funny man.

humorous adj **1** *a humorous story* funny, comic, comical, witty, jocular, amusing, laughable, hilarious, side-splitting, rib-tickling, facetious, farcical, ridiculous, ludicrous, absurd, droll. **2** *a humorous person* funny, amusing, entertaining, witty, jocular, facetious, waggish, whimsical.

humour n **1** *not to see the humour of the situation* funny side, funniness, comic side, comical aspect, comedy, laughableness, facetiousness, farcicalness, farce, jocularity, hilarity, ludicrousness, absurdness, absurdity, drollness. **2** *entertain them with his humour* comedy, jokes, joking, jests, jesting, gags, wit, wittiness, witticisms, waggishness, pleasantries, buffoonery; *inf* wisecracks. **3** *what humour is she in today?* mood, temper, temperament, frame of mind, state of mind, disposition, spirits. **4** *change one's actions according to his humours* whim, caprice, fancy, whimsy, propensity, inclination, bent, vagary, quirk, kink, idiosyncrasy, eccentricity, crotchet.

humour v **1** *humour the child* indulge, pamper, spoil, cosset, coddle, mollify, soothe, placate, gratify, satisfy, pander to, go along with, accommodate. **2** *humour their fantasies* adapt to, make provision for, give in to, yield to, go along with, acquiesce in, indulge, pander to, tolerate, permit, allow, suffer.

hump n *a hump on his back | hump in the tree* protuberance, protrusion, projection, bulge, swelling, lump, bump, knob, hunch, mass, nodule, node, intumescence, tumefaction. **give someone the hump** depress, bring low, give someone the blues; *inf* bring down. **over the hump** *we were doing badly but we're over the hump* over the worst part, over the worst of it, out of the woods, in the clear, on the road to recovery, getting better, on the way up, making progress.

hump v **1** *stop humping your back* hunch, arch, curve, crook, curl up. **2** *hump the luggage to the train* lug, heave, carry, lift, shoulder, hoist; *Scots* humph.

hunch n **1** *a hunch on his back* hump, protuberance, protrusion, bulge, swelling, bump, intumescence. *see* HUMP n. **2** *have a hunch that she will win* feeling, presentiment, premonition, intuition, sixth sense, suspicion, inkling, impression, idea.

hunch v **1** *hunching his back* hump, arch, curve. *see* HUMP v 1. **2** *hunch oneself up over one's books* crouch, stoop, bend, huddle, squat.

hunger n **1** *suffering from hunger* hungriness, need for food, lack of food, emptiness, ravenousness, famishment, starvation, famine, voracity, greed, greediness, edacity, esurience. **2** *a hunger for knowledge/travel* craving, longing, yearning, desire, want, need, thirst, appetite, appetence, pining, itch, lust, hankering; *inf* yen.

hunger v **1** *hungering for/after knowledge* crave, have a craving for, long for, yearn for, have a yearning for, desire, want, need, thirst for, have an appetite for, pine for, lust after, itch for, hanker after; *inf* have a yen for. **2** *hunger for food* be hungry, feel hunger, be ravenous, be famished, be starving.

hungry adj **1** *hungry children | the people are hungry* in need of food, empty, hollow, ravenous, famished, famishing, starving, starved, half-starved, sharp-set, greedy, voracious; *inf* peckish. **2** *hungry for knowledge* craving, in need/want of, eager/keen for, desirous of, covetous of, longing/yearning/pining for. *see* HUNGER v 1.

hunk n **1** *a hunk of cheese* large piece, block, chunk, lump, mass, slab, wedge, square, gobbet, dollop, portion; *inf* wodge; *Scots* dod. **2** *the film star is a hunk* he-man, muscle-man, Adonis.

hunt v **1** *hunt stags/criminals* chase, give chase, pursue, stalk, track, trail, follow, shadow, hunt down, hound; *inf* tail. **2** *hunt for her keys* search for, look for, look high and low for, seek, try to find, scour for, forage for, fish for, rummage for, scrabble for, ferret for.

hunt n **1** *the hunt for foxes/hares/stags/criminals* chase, pursuit, course, coursing, stalking, tracking, trailing, shadowing; *inf* tailing. **2** *the hunt for her keys* search, quest, rummage; seeking, foraging, scrabbling, ransacking. *see* HUNT v 2.

hurdle n **1** *runners clearing hurdles* fence, railing, rail, wall, hedge, hedgerow, bar, barrier, barricade. **2** *a hurdle in the way of their plans* barrier, obstacle, hindrance, impediment, obstruction, stumbling-block, snag, complication, difficulty, handicap.

hurl v *hurl stones/insults* throw, fling, pitch, cast, toss, heave, fire, launch, let fly, shy, propel, project, dart, catapult; *inf* sling, chuck.

hurly-burly n commotion, hubbub, bustle, tumult, turmoil, turbulence, pandemonium, bedlam, furore, uproar, upheaval, disorder, confusion, chaos, unrest, agitation, disruption, trouble.

hurricane n typhoon, cyclone, tornado, windstorm, storm, gale, tempest, squall, whirlwind; *Amer inf* twister.

hurried adj **1** *with hurried steps* quick, fast, swift, rapid, speedy, hasty, breakneck, posthaste. **2** *a hurried glance* hasty, quick, swift, rapid, rushed, cursory, superficial, perfunctory, offhand, passing, fleeting, transitory.

hurry v **1** *hurry or we'll be late* hurry up, move quickly, be quick, make haste, hasten, speed, speed up, lose no time, press on, push on, run, dash, rush, go hell for leather; *inf* get a move on, put one's foot down, step on it, get cracking, shake a leg, fly, race, scurry, scamper, put a spurt on, go like a bat out of hell, hightail it, hotfoot it. **2** *hurry them on* speed up, quicken, hasten, accelerate, expedite, urge on, drive on, push on, goad, prod, hustle.

hurry n **1** *surprised at the hurry of the crowd* speed, quickness, fastness, swiftness, rapidity, haste, celerity, expedition, dispatch, promptitude. **2** *what's all the hurry?* haste, urgency, rush, flurry, bustle, hubbub, hurry-scurry, turmoil, agitation, confusion, commotion.

hurt v **1** *my foot hurts* be sore, be painful, cause pain, ache, smart, nip, sting, throb, tingle, burn. **2** *he has hurt his leg* injure, cause injury to, wound, cause pain to, bruise, cut, scratch, lacerate, maim, mutilate, damage, disable, incapacitate, debilitate, impair. **3** *his cruel words hurt her* upset, sadden, cause sorrow, cause suffering, grieve, wound, distress, pain, cut to the quick, sting, cause anguish, offend, give offence, discompose. **4** *that will not have hurt his reputation* harm, damage, spoil, mar, blight, blemish, impair.

hurt n **1** *the hurt in his hand was acute* pain, soreness, ache, smarting, stinging, throbbing, suffering, pangs, discomfort. **2** *a hurt on his leg* sore, wound, injury, bruise, cut, scratch, laceration. **3** *the hurt he caused her* upset, sadness, sorrow, suffering, grief, distress, pain, misery, anguish, affliction. **4** *the hurt caused to his reputation* harm, damage, injury, detriment, blight, loss, disadvantage, mischief.

hurt adj **1** *a hurt leg* wounded, injured, bruised, cut, lacerated, sore, painful, aching, smarting, throbbing. *see* HURT v 1, 2. **2** *a hurt child/expression* upset, sad, sorrowful, grieving, grief-stricken, aggrieved, distressed, anguished, offended, piqued. *see* HURT v 3.

hurtful adj **1** *hurtful remarks* upsetting, wounding, injurious, distressing, unkind, nasty, mean, malicious, spiteful, cutting, cruel, mischievous, offensive. **2** *actions hurtful to his career* harmful, damaging, injurious, detrimental, disadvantageous, deleterious, destructive, prejudicial, ruinous, inimical.

husband n spouse, consort, partner, groom, bridegroom; *inf* hubby, old man, the other half; *dial* man.

husband v *husband resources* conserve, preserve, save, save for a rainy day, put aside, put by, reserve, store, hoard, use sparingly, use economically, manage thriftily, budget.

husbandry n **1** *men engaged in husbandry* farming, agriculture, farm management, land management, agronomy, agronomics, agribusiness, cultivation, tillage; animal husbandry. **2** *practise husbandry with the available resources* budgeting, economy, good housekeeping, careful management, thrift, frugality, sparingness, saving.

hush v **1** *hush the children* silence, quieten, quieten down, shush; *inf* shut up. **2** *they suddenly hushed* fell silent, became silent, quieten, quieten down; *inf* pipe down, shut up. **3** *hush their fears* still, quieten, calm, soothe, allay, assuage, pacify, mollify, compose. **hush up** *hush up the scandal* suppress, conceal, cover up, keep secret, keep dark, smother, stifle, squash.

hush n *a hush fell over the room* quiet, quietness, silence, stillness, still, soundlessness, peacefulness, peace, calm, tranquillity.

hush-hush adj *hush-hush information* top secret, secret, confidential, classified, restricted.

husk n hull, shell, covering, pod, shuck, rind, skin, peel, integument, pericarp.

husky adj **1** *a husky voice* throaty, gruff, deep, gravelly, hoarse, coarse, croaking, croaky, rough, thick, guttural, harsh, rasping. **2** *a husky young man* brawny, well-built, strapping, muscular, big and strong, rugged, powerfully-built, burly, sturdy, thickset; *inf* beefy.

hussy n minx, seductress, trollop, slut, loose woman, jade; *inf* vamp, tramp, floozy, tart, scrubber, *lit* wanton, strumpet.

hustle v **1** *hustle them out of the way* push, shove, thrust, crowd, jostle, elbow, nudge, shoulder. **2** *hustle them into making a decision* force, coerce, impel, pressure, badger, pester, prompt, urge, goad, prod, spur, propel, egg on. **3** *have to hustle to get there on time* hurry, be quick, hasten, make haste,

move quickly, dash, rush, fly; *inf* get a move on, put one's foot down, step on it.

hustle n *tired of the hustle of life* activity, hurry, rushing, hurry-scurry, haste, flurry, hurly-burly, bustle, hubbub, tumult, fuss.

hut n shed, lean-to, shack, cabin, shanty, hovel; *Scots* bothy.

hybrid n cross-breed, cross, mixed-breed, half-breed, half-blood, mixture, conglomerate, composite, compound, amalgam.

hygiene n cleanliness, personal hygiene, personal cleanliness, public health, environmental health, sanitation, sanitary measures.

hygienic adj *kitchens must be hygienic* sanitary, clean, germ-free, disinfected, sterilized, aseptic, sterile, unpolluted, uncontaminated, healthy, pure.

hymn n psalm, anthem, carol, religious song, paean, song of praise, chant, plainsong, spiritual.

hype n *a lot of hype for the new film* publicity, promotion, advertising, puff, puffery, ballyhoo; *inf* plug, plugging, razzmatazz.

hyperbole n exaggeration, overstatement, excess, overkill.

hypercritical adj overcritical, captious, fault-finding, carping, cavilling, over-exacting, over-censorious, hair-splitting, niggling, quibbling, pedantic, over-rigorous, over-strict; *inf* nit-picking.

hypnosis n hypnotic suggestion, autosuggestion, mesmerism.

hypnotic adj *hypnotic drugs/effect* mesmeric, mesmerizing, sleep-inducing, sleep-producing, soporific, somniferous, somnific, numbing, sedative, stupefactive.

hypnotize v **1** *hypnotize the patient* put under, put out, send into a trance, mesmerize, put to sleep. **2** *they were hypnotized by her beauty* fascinate, bewitch, entrance, beguile, spellbind, magnetize.

hypochondria n valetudinarianism, imagined ill-health, hypochondriasis, health obsession.

hypochondriac adj hypochondriacal, valetudinarian, malingering, obsessed with one's health, preoccupied with ill-health.

hypocrisy n sanctimoniousness, sanctimony, pietism, false goodness, Pharisaism, insincerity, falseness, falsity, deceptiveness, deceit, deceitfulness, deception, dishonesty, dissembling, duplicity, imposture, cant, two-facedness, double-dealing, pretence, speciousness; *inf* phoneyness.

hypocrite n Pharisee, pietist, canter, tartuffe, Holy Willie, whited sepulchre,

hypocritical · hysterical

deceiver, dissembler, impostor, pretender, charlatan, mounteback, quack; *inf* phoney, creeping Jesus.

hypocritical adj sanctimonious, pietistic, Pharisaical, canting, unctuous, insincere, false, fraudulent, deceitful, deceptive, dishonest, untruthful, lying, dissembling, duplicitous, two-faced, double-dealing, untrustworthy, perfidious, specious, spurious; *inf* phoney.

hypothesis n **1** *a working hypothesis* theorem, thesis, proposition, theory, postulate, axiom, premise. **2** *impossible to deduce anything from his hypothesis* supposition, assumption, presumption, conjecture, speculation.

hypothetical adj *to take a hypothetical case* supposed, assumed, presumed, putative, theoretical, conjectured, imagined, speculative, notional, academic.

hysteria n hysterics, loss of control, frenzy, outburst/fit of agitation, panic attack, loss of reason, fit of madness, delirium; *inf* the screaming habdabs.

hysterical adj **1** *hysterical at the news of his death* frenzied, in a frenzy, frantic, out of control, berserk, beside oneself, distracted, distraught, overwrought, agitated, in a panic, mad, crazed, delirious, out of one's mind/wits, raving. **2** *hysterical play/game* very funny, wildly amusing, hilarious, uproarious, side-splitting, comical, farcical, screamingly funny.

ice n **1** *ships encountering ice* frozen water; frost, rime, icicle, iceberg, glacier. **2** *ice in a drink* ice cubes, crushed ice; *inf* rocks. **3** *an ice for dessert* ice-cream, sorbet, water ice, sherbet. **4** *you could feel the ice in her greeting* coldness, coolness, frigidity, stiffness, aloofness, distance, unresponsiveness, reserve, reticence, constraint, restraint. **on ice** *our project is on ice for the moment* in abeyance, in reserve, awaiting attention, pending.

ice v **1** *the lake has iced over* freeze, freeze over, harden, solidify. **2** *ice drinks* add ice to, cool, chill, refrigerate. **3** *ice the cake* cover with icing, frost, add frosting, glaze.

icing n *icing on the birthday cake* frosting, glaze, sugar paste; royal icing, butter icing, glacé icing, fondant icing.

icon n image, idol, likeness, representation, figure, statue.

icy adj **1** *icy winds/weather* freezing, frigid, chill, chilly, chilling, frosty, biting, bitter, raw, arctic, glacial, Siberian, polar, gelid. **2** *icy roads* frozen over, ice-bound, frosty, rimy, glassy, like a sheet of glass, slippery; *inf* slippy. **3** *an icy welcome* cold, cool, frigid, frosty, stiff, aloof, distant, unfriendly, unwelcoming, unresponsive, uncommunicative, reserved, reticent, constrained, restrained.

idea n **1** *the idea of death scares her* concept, conception, conceptualization, thought, image, abstraction, perception, notion. **2** *tell him your ideas on the subject* thought, theory, view, viewpoint, opinion, feeling, outlook, belief, judgement, conclusion. **3** *I had an idea that he was dead* thought, understanding, belief, impression, feeling, notion, suspicion, fancy, inkling. **4** *could you give me some idea of the cost?* estimation, approximation, guess, surmise; *inf* guesstimate. **5** *our idea is to open a new shop* plan, design, scheme, aim, intention, objective, object, purpose, end, goal, target. **6** *she's not my idea of a good mother* notion, vision, archetype, ideal example, exemplar, pattern.

ideal n **1** *she never married; she had her mind set on an ideal* standard of perfection/excellence, epitome, peak of perfection, paragon, nonpareil. **2** *an ideal at which we can aim* archetype, prototype, model, pattern, exemplar, example, paradigm, criterion, yardstick. **3** *a man of high ideals* principle, standard, moral value; morals, ethics.

ideal adj **1** *ideal beauty* perfect, consummate, supreme, absolute, complete, flawless, exemplary, classic, archetypal, model, quintessential. **2** *confusing ideal and concrete matters* abstract, conceptual, intellectual, mental, philosophical, theoretical, hypothetical. **3** *she dreams of an ideal world* unattainable, Utopian, unreal, impracticable, ivory-towered, imaginary, romantic, visionary, fanciful.

idealist n **1** *an idealist who does not accept second-best* perfectionist. **2** *idealist dreaming of a perfect world* Utopian, visionary, romanticist.

idealistic adj Utopian, perfectionist, visionary, romantic, quixotic, unrealistic, impracticable, castle-building.

ideally adv *ideally, everyone should have enough to live on* in a perfect world, in a Utopia, all things being equal, theoretically, hypothetically, in theory.

identical adj **1** *that is the identical dress that she wore last night* the same, the very same, one and the same, selfsame. **2** *they have identical personalities* alike, like, similar, much the same, indistinguishable, corresponding, matching, twin.

identification n **1** *witnesses helping in the identification of the criminal* recognition, singling out, spotting, pointing, pinpointing, naming; *Amer inf* fingering. see IDENTIFY 1. **2** *the identification of the best method* establishment, finding out, ascertainment, diagnosis, selection, choice. **3** *show the doorman his identification* ID card, ID, badge, letter of introduction; papers, credentials. **4** *her identification with her fellow patient* empathy, rapport, fellow feeling, bond of sympathy, sympathetic cord, sympathy; *inf* good vibes.

identify v **1** *identify the criminal* recognize, single out, pick out, spot, point out, pinpoint, discern, distinguish, name; *inf* put the finger on; *Amer inf* finger. **2** *identify the problem* establish, find out, ascertain, diagnose, select, choose. **3** *I identify her with my youth* associate, connect, think of in con-

nection with. **4** *she identifies with all struggling artists* empathize, have a rapport with,
relate to, respond to. *see* IDENTIFICATION 4.

identity n **1** *the identity of the criminal has not
been established* name, specification. **2** *felt
that he lost his identity on emigrating* personality, self, selfhood, ego, individuality, distinctiveness, singularity, uniqueness,
differentness. **3** *a case of mistaken identity*
identification, recognition, naming. *see*
IDENTIFICATION 1. **4** *the identity of their interests*
identicalness, sameness, selfsameness,
indistinguishability, interchangeability,
likeness, alikeness, similarity, closeness,
accordance.

ideology n doctrine, creed, credo, teaching,
dogma, theory, thesis; tenets, beliefs, opinions.

idiocy n **1** *the idiocy of their actions* stupidity,
stupidness, foolishness, senselessness,
inanity, absurdity, fatuity, fatuousness,
asinity, lack of intelligence, lunacy, craziness, insanity; *inf* dumbness, daftness.
2 *tired by their idiocies* stupid actions, inane
remarks; foolish talk, absurdity. **3** *the idiocy
of the youngest child* feeble-mindedness,
weak-mindedness, imbecility.

idiom n **1** *unable to think of a clever idiom*
turn of phrase, set phrase, fixed expression, phrase, expression, locution. **2** *adopt
the modern idiom* language, mode of expression, phraseology, style of speech, speech,
talk, usage, parlance, vernacular, jargon,
patois; *inf* lingo.

idiosyncrasy n peculiarity, individual/per-
sonal trait, singularity, oddity, eccentricity,
mannerism, quirk, habit, characteristic,
speciality, quality, feature.

idiot n **1** *the idiots stole the car* blockhead,
nitwit, dunderhead, dolt, dunce, halfwit,
fool, ass, booby, nincompoop, ninny, ignoramus, cretin, moron; *inf* numskull, dim-
wit. **2** *the village idiot* mentally
handicapped/retarded person, retardate,
moron, halfwit, imbecile.

idiotic adj *an idiotic idea/action* stupid, foolish, senseless, inane, absurd, fatuous, asinine, unintelligent, halfwitted,
hare-brained, lunatic, crazy, insane,
moronic; *inf* dumb, daft.

idle adj **1** *an idle fellow* lazy, indolent, slothful, shiftless, sluggish, loafing, do-nothing,
dronish. **2** *machines lying idle* not in operation, not operating, inoperative, not working, inactive, out of action, unused, not in
use, mothballed. **3** *the building workers are
idle just now* not working, unemployed, out
of work, jobless, out of a job, redundant;
inf on the dole. **4** *pass away the idle hours*

unoccupied, empty, vacant, unfilled. **5** *idle
rumours* groundless, without grounds, baseless, foundationless, lacking foundation.
6 *idle remarks* unimportant, trivial, trifling,
shallow, foolish, insignificant, superficial,
without depth, inane, fatuous, senseless,
meaningless, purposeless, unnecessary.
7 *idle threats* useless, in vain, vain, worthless, futile, ineffective, ineffectual, inefficacious, unproductive, fruitless, pointless,
meaningless. **8** *idle pleasures* frivolous, trivial, trifling, shallow, insubstantial, worthless, nugatory.

idle v **1** *idle away the hours* while, laze, loaf,
lounge, loiter, dawdle, dally, fritter, potter,
waste, fool away. **2** *stop idling and work* do
nothing, sit back and do nothing, laze,
loaf, be inactive, mark time, shirk, slack,
vegetate; *inf* take it easy, rest on one's oars.
3 *idle down to the shops* saunter, stroll, dawdle, potter, drift, move slowly. **4** *the engine
idling* tick over.

idol n **1** *pagans worshipping idols* icon, god,
false god, effigy, image, graven image,
fetish, likeness. **2** *the singer is the idol of
teenagers* hero, heroine, favourite, darling,
beloved, pet, apple of one's eye, blue-eyed
boy/girl, star, superstar; *inf* pin-up.

idolatrous adj **1** *idolatrous tribes of old* idol-
worshipping, idolistic, icon-worshipping,
fetishistic, pagan, heathen, heretical. **2** *idolatrous fans of the singer* hero-worshipping,
idolizing, worshipping, worshipful, adulatory, adoring, lionizing, reverential, glorify-
ing.

idolatry n **1** *the idolatry of non-Christian tribes*
idolism, idolization, idolatrism, idol-wor-
ship, fetishism, iconolatry, icon-worship,
paganism, heathenism. **2** *the idolatry of the
singer's fans* idolization, idolizing, worshipping, hero-worshipping, adulation, adoring, loving, admiring, doting, lionization,
lionizing, reverence, glorification.

idolize v **1** *idolize false gods* worship, bow
down before, glorify, exalt, revere, deify.
2 *idolize the pop singer* hero-worship, worship, adulate, adore, love, look up to,
admire, dote upon, lionize, reverence,
revere, venerate.

idyll n **1** *poets writing idylls* pastoral, eclogue,
georgic, rural poem. **2** *enjoying an idyll* won-
derful/perfect/romantic time, moment of
bliss, honeymoon, paradise, heaven on
earth, Garden of Eden, Shangri-La.

if conj **1** *if you go he will go* on condition that,
provided, providing, supposing, assuming,
on the assumption that, allowing. **2** *I don't
know if he will come* whether, whether or

not. **3** *a boring if well-paid job* although, even, though, however, yet.

if n *the situation is full of ifs* doubt, uncertainty, hesitation, condition, stipulation.

iffy adj **1** *the situation is a bit iffy* doubtful, uncertain, unsure, undecided, unsettled, indeterminate, unresolved; *inf* up in the air. **2** *I'm a bit iffy about going* doubtful, dubious, unsure, uncertain, undecided, hesitant, tentative.

ignite v **1** *ignite the fire* light, set fire to, set on fire, set alight, fire, kindle, inflame, touch off; *inf* set/put a match to. **2** *the fire ignited* catch/take fire, catch, burst into flames, burn up, burn, flame up, kindle.

ignominious adj **1** *an ignominious defeat* shameful, dishonourable, disgraceful, humiliating, mortifying, discreditable, disreputable, undignified, infamous, ignoble, inglorious, scandalous, abject, sorry, base. **2** *his ignominious behaviour* contemptible, despicable, offensive, revolting, wicked, vile, base, low.

ignominy n **1** *the ignominy of defeat* shame, dishonour, disgrace, humiliation, mortification, discredit, stigma, disrepute, infamy, ignobleness, scandal, opprobrium, obloquy, abjectness. **2** *behave with ignominy* contemptibleness, dishonour, wickedness, baseness, vileness, dishonesty, treachery.

ignorance n **1** *ignorance of the law* unawareness, unfamiliarity, unconsciousness, lack of enlightenment, lack of knowledge/information, inexperience, greenness, innocence; *lit* nescience. **2** *appalled at the ignorance of the pupils* lack of education/knowledge, illiteracy, lack of intelligence, unintelligence, stupidity, thickness, denseness, unenlightenment, benightedness.

ignorant adj **1** *ignorant of legal procedure* unaware of, unfamiliar with, unconversant with, unacquainted with, unconscious of, uninformed about, unenlightened about, inexperienced in, blind to, uninitiated in, unschooled in, naïve about, innocent about; *inf* in the dark about; *lit* nescient of. **2** *ignorant pupils* unscholarly, uneducated, untaught, unschooled, untutored, untrained, illiterate, unlettered, unlearned, unread, uninformed, unknowledgeable, unintelligent, stupid, unenlightened, benighted; *inf* thick, dense, dumb. **3** *ill-mannered, ignorant louts* rude, crude, coarse, vulgar, gross, insensitive.

ignore v **1** *ignore their nasty remarks* disregard, pay no attention/heed to, take no notice of, brush aside, pass over, shrug off, push aside, shut one's eyes to, be oblivious to, turn a blind eye to, turn a deaf ear to.

2 *ignore her former friend* slight, spurn, cold-shoulder, look right through, look past, turn one's back on, send to Coventry; *inf* give someone the brush-off, pass up, cut dead, cut. **3** *just ignore the first question* set aside, pay no attention to, take no account of, omit, leave out, overlook, neglect; *inf* skip.

ill adj **1** *the patient has been ill for some time | feeling rather ill* not well, unwell, ailing, poorly, sick, sickly, on the sick list, off-colour, afflicted, infirm, indisposed, out of sorts, diseased, bedridden, invalided, weak, feeble, valetudinarian; *inf* under the weather, laid up, seedy, dicky, queasy, queer, funny. **2** *the ill feeling/will in the firm* hostile, antagonistic, acrimonious, belligerent, bellicose, unfriendly, unkind, spiteful, rancorous, resentful, malicious, malevolent, bitter. **3** *his ill temper* fractious, irritable, irascible, cross, cantankerous, crabbed, surly, snappish, gruff, sullen. **4** *an ill wind | suffering ill luck* adverse, unfavourable, unadvantageous, unlucky, unfortunate, unpropitious, inauspicious, unpromising, ominous, infelicitous. **5** *the ill-effects of the medicine/accident* harmful, detrimental, deleterious, hurtful, damaging, pernicious, destructive, ruinous. **6** *a person of ill repute* bad, infamous, low, wicked, nefarious, vile, evil, foul, sinful, iniquitous, sinister, corrupt, depraved, degenerate. **7** *ill manners* rude, unmannerly, impolite, objectionable, boorish. **8** *ill management* unsatisfactory, unacceptable, inadequate, deficient, faulty, poor, unskilful, inexpert. **ill at ease** adj uncomfortable, uneasy, awkward, embarrassed, self-conscious, out of place, strange, unsure, uncertain, unsettled, hesitant, faltering, restless, unrelaxed, disquieted, unquiet, disturbed, discomfited, troubled, anxious, on edge, edgy, nervous, tense, on tenterhooks, apprehensive, distrustful; *inf* on pins and needles.

ill n **1** *she meant him no ill* harm, hurt, injury, mischief, pain, trouble, unpleasantness, misfortune. **2** *the ills of life* pain, misfortune, suffering, misery, woe, affliction, damage, disaster, tribulation; troubles, problems, trials. **3** *bodily ills* illness, ill/poor health; ailment, disorder, complaint, sickness, disease, malady, infirmity, indisposition, infection, contagion.

ill adv **1** *speak ill of them* badly, unfavourably, with disfavour, with disapproval, with hostility, hostilely, unkindly, maliciously, spitefully. **2** *it went ill with them* badly, hard, adversely, unsuccessfully, unfortunately, unluckily, inauspiciously. **3** *we could ill afford it* barely, scarcely, hardly, with difficulty. **4** *ill-adapted to country life* badly, poorly, insufficiently, inadequately, unsatisfactorally, faultily.

ill-advised adj unwise, ill-considered, imprudent, incautious, injudicious, ill-judged, impolitic, misguided, foolish, wrong-headed, foolhardy, rash, hasty, over-hasty, short-sighted, uncircumspect, thoughtless, careless, reckless.

ill-assorted adj mismatched, incongruous, unsuited, incompatible, inharmonious, uncongenial.

ill-bred adj ill-mannered, bad-mannered, unmannerly, rude, impolite, discourteous, uncivil, ungentlemanly, unladylike, boorish, churlish, loutish, vulgar, coarse, crass, uncouth, crude, unrefined, uncivilized, ungallant, indelicate, indecorous, unseemly.

ill-defined adj indistinct, unclear, blurred, fuzzy, vague, nebulous, shadowy, dim.

ill-disposed adj hostile, opposing, opposed, antagonistic, unfriendly, unsympathetic, averse, contrary, antipathetic, inimical; *inf* anti, down on.

illegal adj unlawful, illegitimate, illicit, lawless, criminal, actionable, felonious, unlicensed, unauthorized, unsanctioned, unwarranted, unofficial, outlawed, banned, forbidden, barred, prohibited, interdicted, proscribed, contraband, black-market, under the counter, bootleg.

illegible adj unreadable, hard to read, indecipherable, undecipherable, unintelligible, scrawled, scribbled, hieroglyphic, squiggly, crabbed, faint, obscure; *inf* clear as mud.

illegitimate adj **1** *illegitimate use of property* illegal, unlawful, illicit, lawless, criminal, unlicensed, unauthorized, unsanctioned. *see* ILLEGAL. **2** *an illegitimate child* natural, love, born out of wedlock, born on the wrong side of the blanket, fatherless, bastard. **3** *an illegitimate deduction* illogical, wrongly inferred/deduced, unsound, spurious, incorrect, invalid. **4** *illegitimate language usage* irregular, non-standard, substandard, ungrammatical, dialectal, colloquial, informal.

ill-fated adj unlucky, luckless, unfortunate, hapless, unhappy, doomed, blighted, starcrossed, ill-starred, ill-omened.

ill-favoured adj plain, ugly, ugly looking, hideous, unsightly, unlovely, unattractive; *Amer* homely.

ill feeling n ill will, bad blood, hostility, enmity, hatred, no love lost, antipathy, aversion, dislike, antagonism, acrimony, animus, indignation, anger, wrath,

unfriendliness, unkindness, spite, spitefulness, rancour, grudge, resentment, bitterness, dissatisfaction, malice, malevolence, belligerence, bellicosity; hard feelings.

ill-founded adj baseless, groundless, without foundation, foundationless, unjustified, unsupported, unsubstantiated, unproven, unverified, unauthenticated, unreliable.

ill humour n ill temper, bad temper, temper, bad mood, huff, pet, fit of pique, rage; moodiness, irritability, irascibility, peevishness, crossness, crabbedness, testiness.

illicit adj illegal, unlawful, illegitimate, lawless, criminal, unlicensed, unauthorized, unsanctioned, unofficial, outlawed, banned, forbidden, prohibited. *see* ILLEGAL.

illiteracy n illiterateness, inability to read; lack of education, ignorance, unenlightenment, benightedness; *lit* nescience.

illiterate adj unable to read; uneducated, untaught, unschooled, untutored, uninstructed, unlearned, unlettered, ignorant; *lit* nescient.

ill-judged adj ill-advised, ill-considered, unwise, imprudent, injudicious, misguided, foolish, foolhardy, rash, hasty, short-sighted. *see* ILL-ADVISED.

ill-mannered adj unmannerly, mannerless, rude, impolite, discourteous, uncivil, insolent, impertinent, badly behaved, ill-behaved, boorish, loutish, oafish, uncouth, coarse, gross, ill-bred.

ill-natured adj ill-tempered, bad-tempered, ill-humoured, moody, irritable, irascible, surly, peevish, petulant, cross, crabbed, testy, grouchy, disagreeable, perverse, mean, nasty, disobliging, spiteful, malicious.

illness n ailment, sickness, disorder, complaint, malady, disease, affliction, attack, disability, indisposition, infection, contagion; ill health, poor health.

illogical adj unsound, unreasonable, unreasoned, irrational, faulty, spurious, fallacious, fallible, unproved, untenable, specious, unscientific, sophistic, casuistic, inconclusive, inconsistent, incorrect, invalid, wrong, absurd, preposterous, meaningless, senseless.

ill-starred adj ill-fated, unlucky, unfortunate, hapless, doomed, blighted, ill-omened. *see* ILL-FATED.

ill-tempered adj ill-humoured, cross, bad-tempered, irritable, irascible, peevish, crabbed, choleric, cantakerous, grumpy, grouchy, crusty, splenetic.

ill-timed adj inopportune, inconvenient, awkward, inappropriate, untimely, mis-timed, badly timed, unwelcome, unfavourable, unfortunate, inept.

ill-treat v treat badly, abuse, harm, injure, damage, handle roughly, mishandle, ill-use, maltreat, misuse; *inf* knock about.

illuminate v **1** *lights illuminating the hall* light, light up, throw/cast light upon, brighten, shine on, irradiate; *lit* illumine. **2** *illuminate the problem* clarify, make clear, clear up, shed/cast light on, elucidate, explain, make explicit, explicate, expound. **3** *illuminate a manuscript* adorn, decorate, ornament, embellish, enhance, illustrate.

illuminating adj *an illuminating talk* instructive, informative, enlightening, explanatory, revealing, helpful.

illumination n **1** *the illumination of the hall* lighting, lighting up, brightening, irradiation. *see* ILLUMINATE 1. **2** *see the illumination in the dark* light, beam/ray/shaft of light, radiance, gleam, glitter, effulgence; lights. **3** *the illumination of the problem* clarification, elucidation, explanation, explication. *see* ILLUMINATE 2. **4** *illumination coming to savage tribes* enlightenment, understanding, awareness, insight, learning, education, instruction, information, knowledge, revelation.

illusion n **1** *create the illusion of depth* false/deceptive appearance, deception, faulty perception, misperception. **2** *under the illusion that he was her first love* delusion, misapprehension, misconception, deception, false/mistaken impression, fallacy, error, misjudgement, fancy. **3** *see an illusion* hallucination, figment of the imagination, phantom, spectre, mirage, phantasm, fantasy, will-o'-the-wisp, ignis fatuus.

illusive, illusory adj deceptive, delusory, delusional, delusive, illusionary, false, fallacious, mistaken, erroneous, misleading, untrue, specious, unreal, imagined, imaginary, fancied, non-existent, fanciful, notional, chimerical, dreamlike.

illustrate v **1** *illustrate the story* add pictures/drawings/sketches to, provide artwork for, adorn, decorate, ornament, embellish. **2** *illustrate his point* exemplify, demonstrate, point up, show, instance, make plain/clear, clarify, bring home, emphasize, interpret.

illustration n **1** *the illustration in the child's book* picture, drawing, sketch, plate, figure; artwork, adornment, decoration, ornamentation, embellishment. **2** *interesting illustrations explaining his theory* example, typical case, case in point, instance, specimen, sample, exemplar, analogy. **3** *appreciate the illustration of his theory* exemplification, demonstration, pointing up, showing, instancing, clarification, emphasis, interpretation.

illustrative adj exemplifying, explanatory, elucidative, explicative, expository, interpretative, interpretive.

illustrious adj renowned, famous, famed, well-known, celebrated, acclaimed, noted, notable, distinguished, esteemed, honoured, prominent, pre-eminent, splendid, brilliant, remarkable, great, noble, glorious, exalted, venerable.

ill will n ill feeling, bad blood, hostility, enmity, hatred, antipathy, antagonism, acrimony, animus, unfriendliness, spite, rancour, resentment, malice; hard feelings. *see* ILL FEELING.

image n **1** *images of the saints* likeness, representation, resemblance, effigy, figure, figurine, doll, statue, statuette, sculpture, bust, idol, icon, fetish, graven image, false god, painting, picture, portrait. **2** *the image formed by the camera/telescope* reproduction, optical representation, reflection; picture, facsimile, photograph, snapshot, photo. **3** *an image of what the new country would be like* mental picture/representation, vision, concept, conception, idea, perception, impression, fancy, thought. **4** *he is the image of his father* double, living image, replica, clone, copy, reproduction, counterpart, similitude, doppelganger; *inf* very spit, spitting image, chip off the old block, ringer, dead ringer. **5** *politicians trying to improve their images* public impression/perception/conception. **6** *he is the image of goodness* emblem, symbol, archetype, perfect example, embodiment, incarnation. **7** *the use of images in poetry* figure of speech, conceit, trope, figurative expression.

imaginable adj thinkable, conceivable, supposable, believable, credible, comprehensible, possible, within the bounds of possibility, probable, likely, plausible, feasible.

imaginary adj fanciful, fancied, fantastic, unreal, non-existent, illusory, illusive, visionary, dreamy, dreamlike, shadowy, unsubstantial, chimerical, figmental, notional, assumed, supposed, suppositious, fictitious, fictional, legendary, mythical, mythological, made up, invented, hallucinatory, phantasmal, phantasmic, spectral, ghostly, ideal, idealistic, Utopian, romantic.

imagination n **1** *the poem shows imagination | handling the project needs imagination* imaginative faculty, creative power, creativity, vision, inspiration, power of fancy, fancifulness, insight, inventiveness, originality, invention, innovation, resourcefulness, ingenuity, enterprise, cleverness, wit. **2** *I thought I saw her but it was only my imagination* mental image, illusion, fancy, figment of the imagination, vision, dream, chimera, shadow, phantom, conceptualization, unreality.

imaginative adj *an imaginative writer/cook/ planner* creative, visionary, inspired, fanciful, inventive, original, innovative, resourceful, ingenious, enterprising, clever, whimsical.

imagine v **1** *he imagines a bright future for himself* picture, see in the mind's eye, visualize, envisage, envision, conjure up, dream about, dream up, fantasize about, conceptualize, think up, conceive, think of, plan, project, scheme. **2** *I imagine he'll be late* assume, presume, suppose, think, believe, be of the opinion that, take it, gather, fancy, judge, deem, infer, deduce, conjecture, surmise, guess, reckon, suspect, realize.

imbecile n **1** *imbeciles unable to look after themselves* mental defective, retardate, halfwit, idiot. **2** *that child is an imbecile* fool, idiot, dolt, halfwit, nitwit, dunce, dunderhead, dullard, simpleton; *inf* thickhead, dim-wit, dope.

imbecile adj **1** *an imbecile patient* mentally defective/retarded, feeble-minded, simple. **2** *that imbecile child has got the wrong key* stupid, foolish, idiotic, doltish, halfwitted, witless, dull; *inf* dense, thickheaded, dim-witted, dopey. **3** *what an imbecile thing to do* foolish, stupid, silly, idiotic, senseless, absurd, crazy, mad, fatuous, inane, asinine.

imbed v *see* EMBED V.

imbibe v **1** *imbibe some water* drink, quaff, swallow, consume; *inf* swig, knock back, sink. **2** *he doesn't imbibe any more* drink, drink alcohol, take strong drink. **3** *imbibe the fresh air* drink in, breathe in, inhale. **4** *imbibe ideas* assimilate, absorb, take in, digest, learn, acquire, gain, pick up. **5** *imbibe moisture* absorb, soak up, blot up, sop up, suck up, draw up, take up.

imbroglio n **1** *cannot sort out the imbroglio in the office* complicated situation, complication, complexity, problem, difficulty, trouble, entanglement, confusion, muddle, mess, quandary. **2** *an imbroglio of papers* confused heap, jumble, muddle, mess. **3** *people involved in an imbroglio in the bar* disagreement, conflict, altercation, argument, quarrel, fight, row, commotion, disturbance, turmoil, fracas.

imbue v *he imbues his sermons with topicality* fill, impregnate, inject, inculcate, instil, ingrain, inspire, permeate, charge.

imitate v **1** *imitate the language of Shakespeare | imitate his elder brother in everything* copy, emulate, take as a model/pattern, follow the example of, follow as an example, take after, follow, follow suit, take a page from someone's book, tread in the steps of, walk in the footsteps of, echo. **2** *cruel children imitating the crippled man* mimic, ape, impersonate, do an impression of, parody, mock, caricature, burlesque, travesty; *inf* send up, take off, spoof, do; *Amer inf* make like. **3** *the stage set imitated a street market* look like, simulate, echo, mirror. **4** *imitate the portrait* copy, reproduce, replicate, duplicate, counterfeit, forge, fake.

imitation n **1** *the house was built in imitation of Robert Adam* emulation, resemblance. *see* IMITATE 1. **2** *the cruel imitation of the crippled man* mimicking, mimicry, aping, impersonation, impression, parody, mocking, mockery, caricature, burlesque, travesty; *inf* send-up, take-off, spoof. **3** *a bad imitation of the portrait* copy, reproduction, counterfeit, forgery, fake.

imitation adj *imitation leather/antiques* artificial, synthetic, simulated, man-made, ersatz, mock, sham, fake, reproduction, repro; *inf* pseudo, phoney.

imitative adj **1** *an imitative style | a style imitative of Dickens* in imitation of, copying, copied, emulating, emulated, derivative, unoriginal, mimicking, mimetic, echoic, parrot-like, plagiarized, second-hand; *inf* copycat. **2** *an imitative word* onomatopoeic, echoic.

imitator n copier, copyist, emulator, follower, mimic, echo, impersonator, epigone, plagiarist, counterfeiter, forger, ape, parrot.

immaculate adj **1** *immaculate white sheets | immaculate rooms* clean, spotless, unsoiled, unstained, snowy-white, whiter than white, speckless, spick and span, neat, neat as a new pin, spruce, trim. **2** *of immaculate character* flawless, faultless, stainless, unblemished, spotless, pure, perfect, above reproach, innocent, virtuous, incorrupt, guiltless, sinless, unsullied, undefiled, untarnished, uncontaminated, unpolluted.

immaterial adj **1** *it's immaterial what he thinks* unimportant, inconsequential, of no matter/moment, of little account, irrelevant, insignificant, trivial, petty, slight, inappreciable. **2** *immaterial as ghosts* not material, incorporeal, bodiless, unembodied, disembodied, discarnate, intangible, impalpable, ethereal, unsubstantial, airy, aerial, spiritual, ghostly, transcendental, unearthly, supernatural.

immature adj **1** *immature fruit/plans* unripe, undeveloped, unformed, imperfect, unfinished, incomplete, half-grown, crude, raw, green, unmellowed, unfledged, untimely. **2** *an immature young man* adolescent, childish, babyish, infantile, juvenile, puerile, jejune, callow, inexperienced, green, unsophisticated; *inf* wet behind the ears.

immaturity n **1** *the immaturity of the fruit/plans* unripeness, imperfection, lack of completion, crudeness, crudity, rawness, greenness. *see* IMMATURE 1. **2** *the immaturity of the young men* adolescence, childishness, babyishness, infantileness, juvenility, puerility, lack of experience, inexperience. *see* IMMATURE 2.

immeasurable adj not measurable, measureless, limitless, boundless, unbounded, illimitable, infinite, incalculable, unfathomable, fathomless, undeterminable, indeterminate, inestimable, extensive, vast, innumerable, countless, numberless, endless, never ending, interminable, inexhaustible, bottomless.

immediate adj **1** *an immediate reaction* instant, instantaneous, on the spot, prompt, swift, speedy, sudden, abrupt. **2** *his immediate neighbour* near, nearest, next, next door, close, closest, adjacent, adjoining, abutting, contiguous, proximate. **3** *the immediate cause of his failure* direct, primary. **4** *in the immediate past* recent. **5** *our immediate plans* present, current, existing, existent, actual, extant, urgent, pressing. **6** *get immediate experience* direct, firsthand, hands on, in service, in the field, on the job.

immediately adv **1** *he went away immediately* right away, right now, straight away, at once, instantly, now, this/that very minute, this/that instant, directly, promptly, forthwith, without delay, without hesitation, unhesitatingly, *tout de suite*; *inf* before you can/could say Jack Robinson, pronto. **2** *he was immediately behind us* right, directly, closely, at close quarters. **3** *I heard the news immediately from the victim* directly, at first hand, without intermediary.

immemorial adj ancient, age-old, timeless, dateless, archaic, of yore, rooted in the past, long-standing, time-honoured, ancestral, traditional.

immense adj huge, vast, massive, enormous, gigantic, colossal, giant, great, very large, extensive, infinite, immeasurable, illimitable, monumental, tremendous,

prodigious, elephantine, monstrous, titanic, Brobdingnagian; *inf* ginormous, mega.

immerse v **1** *immerse the cloth in the dye* submerge, plunge, dip, dunk, duck, sink, douse, souse, soak, drench, imbue, saturate. **2** *immerse the Christian converts* baptise, christen, purify, lustrate. **3** *immerse oneself in one's work* absorb, engross, occupy, engage, preoccupy, involve, engulf; *inf* lose oneself in.

immigrant n non-native, settler, incomer, newcomer, new arrival, migrant, naturalized citizen, expatriate.

imminent adj impending, at hand, fast-approaching, close, near, approaching, coming, forthcoming, on the way, about to happen, upon us, in the offing, on the horizon, in the air, brewing, threatening, menacing, looming.

immobile adj immobilized, without moving, unmoving, motionless, unable to move, immovable, still, static, at rest, stationary, at a standstill, stock-still, dormant, rooted, fixed to the spot, rigid, frozen, stiff, riveted, like a statue, as if turned to stone, immotile, immotive.

immobilize v bring to a standstill/halt, halt, stop, put out of action, render inactive, inactivate, paralyse, make inoperative, freeze, transfix, disable, cripple.

immoderate adj excessive, extreme, intemperate, lavish, undue, inordinate, extravagant, unreasonable, unjustified, unwarranted, uncalled for, outrageous, egregious, unrestrained, unrestricted, uncontrolled, unlimited, unbridled, uncurbed, self-indulgent, overindulgent, prodigal, profligate, wanton, dissipative.

immoderation n excess, excessiveness, intemperateness, inordinateness, lavishness, lack of restraint, self-indulgence, overindulgence, profligacy, wantonness, dissipation. *see* IMMODERATE.

immodest adj forward, bold, brazen, impudent, unblushing, shameless, wanton, indecorous, improper, indecent; *inf* fresh, cheeky.

immoral adj bad, wrongdoing, unprincipled, dishonest, unethical, wicked, evil, sinful, impure, iniquitous, corrupt, depraved, vile, base, degenerate, debauched, abandoned, dissolute, villainous, nefarious, miscreant, reprobate, perverted, indecent, lewd, licentious, pornographic, unchaste, of easy virtue, bawdy.

immorality n badness, dishonesty, unethicalness, wickedness, evil, impurity, sinfulness, sin, iniquity, corruption, depravity, vileness, vice, turpitude, degeneracy, debauchery, dissolution, perversion, indecency, lewdness, licentiousness, bawdiness. *see* IMMORAL.

immortal adj **1** *immortal beings/love* never dying, undying, deathless, eternal, ever living, everlasting, never ending, endless, imperishable, perdurable, timeless, indestructible, unfading, undecaying, perennial, evergreen, perpetual, lasting, enduring, constant, abiding, immutable, indissoluble; *lit* sempiternal. **2** *immortal poets* famous, celebrated, remembered, commemorated, honoured, lauded, glorified.

immortal n **1** *mythological immortals* god, goddess, Olympian. **2** *the immortals of poetry* great, hero, genius, celebrity.

immortality n **1** *angels blessed with immortality* eternal life, deathlessness, everlastingness, endlessness, imperishability, timelessness, unfadingness, evergreenness, perpetuality, constancy. *see* IMMORTAL adj 1. **2** *the immortality of the poet* fame, renown, repute, celebrity, commemoration, honour, glory.

immortalize v commemorate, memorialize, eternalize, eternize, perpetuate, exalt, laud, glorify.

immovable adj **1** *immovable concrete pillars* set firm/fast, fast, firm, fixed, secure, stable, rooted, riveted, moored, anchored, stuck, jammed, stiff, unbudgeable. **2** *the spectators stood immovable* motionless, unmoving, stationary, still, stock-still, at a standstill, dead still, statue-like. **3** *the planning committee were immovable* adamant, firm, steadfast, unwavering, unswerving, resolute, determined, tenacious, stubborn, dogged, obdurate, inflexible, unyielding, unbending, uncompromising, unshakable, inexorable.

immune adj not subject to, not liable to, protected from, safe from, unsusceptible to, secure against, exempt from, clear of, free from, freed from, absolved from, released from, excused from, relieved of, spared from, excepted from, exempted from, unaffected by, resistant to, proof against; *inf* let off.

immunity n **1** *immunity from the disease* non-susceptibity to, resistance to, protection from, immunization/inoculation against. **2** *immunity from tax* non-liability (for), exemption, exception, freedom, release. **3** *diplomatic immunity* indemnity, privilege, prerogative, special treatment, right, charter, liberty, licence, permission. **4** *immunity from religious observance* indemnity, dispensation, absolution, exoneration, excusal.

immunize v inoculate, vaccinate, protect, shield, safeguard; *inf* give a jab to.

imp n **1** *devils and imps* little devil, demon, hobgoblin, goblin, elf, sprite, puck, gnome, dwarf. **2** *the child's a little imp* scamp, rogue, rascal, minx, mischief-maker, troublemaker, prankster, brat, gamin, urchin, tearaway.

impact n **1** *the impact of the two cars* collision, contact, crash, smash, striking, clash, bump, bang, knock, jolt, thump, whack, thwack, slam, smack, slap. **2** *the impact of his talk* influence, effect, impression; results, consequences, repercussions. **3** *he took the full impact of the blow* force, full force, shock, brunt, impetus, pressure.

impair v weaken, lessen, decrease, reduce, blunt, diminish, deteriorate, enfeeble, debilitate, enervate, damage, mar, spoil, injure, harm, hinder, disable, cripple, impede, undermine, vitiate.

impale v transfix, pierce, stab, prick, stick, spear, spike, run through, disembowel.

impalpable adj **1** *if there is a lump in the abdomen it is impalpable* intangible, imperceptible to the touch. **2** *find his conclusions impalpable* abstruse, obscure, unclear, indiscernible, tenuous, esoteric, recondite.

impart v **1** *impart the good news* pass on, convey, communicate, transmit, relate, tell, make known, report, disclose, reveal, divulge, proclaim, broadcast. **2** *his age imparts wisdom to his words* bestow, confer, give, grant, lend, accord, afford, assign, offer, yield, contribute, dispense.

impartial adj unbiased, unprejudiced, disinterested, detached, objective, neutral, equitable, even-handed, fair, fair-minded, just, open-minded, without favouritism, free from discrimination, non-partisan, with no axe to grind, without fear or favour.

impartiality n lack of bias/prejudice, disinterest, detachment, objectivity, neutrality, even-handedness, fairness, justness, open-mindedness. *see* IMPARTIAL.

impassable adj **1** *impassable roads* unnavigable, untraversable, impenetrable, closed, blocked, obstructed, pathless, trackless. **2** *impassable obstacles* insurmountable, insuperable, unconquerable.

impasse n deadlock, dead end, stalemate, checkmate, standstill, full/dead stop; *Amer* stand-off.

impassioned adj passionate, amorous, ardent, fervent, fervid, perfervid, vehement, intense, violent, fiery, burning, inflamed, emotional, emotive, zealous, eager, enthusiastic, animated, excited, aroused, feverish, frantic.

impatience n **1** *wait with impatience for the doors to open* restlessness, restiveness, impetuosity, eagerness, avidity, excitability, anxiety, agitation, nervousness, edginess, fretfulness, jitteriness, fluster, disquiet, disquietude. **2** *answer with impatience* abruptness, brusqueness, shortness, curtness, irascibility, irritability, testiness, snappiness, querulousness, peevishness, intolerance.

impatient adj **1** *an impatient crowd* restless, restive, impetuous, eager, excitable, anxious, agitated, nervous, edgy. **2** *an impatient answer* abrupt, brusque, short, terse, curt, short-tempered, quick-tempered, irritated, angry, testy, snappy, querulous, peevish, intolerant. **3** *impatient to see her boyfriend* anxious, eager, keen, avid, desirous, yearning, longing.

impeach v **1** *impeach his neighbour for breaking his fence* charge, accuse, bring a case/charge against, indict, inculpate, implicate, blame, censure, hold accountable for, denounce, arraign. **2** *they impeached his honour* challenge, question, call into question, cast doubt on, impugn, attack, assail, revile, discredit, deprecate, cast slurs/aspersions on, malign, slander.

impeccable adj **1** *impeccable behaviour|speak impeccable French* perfect, faultless, flawless, unblemished, exemplary, correct, exact, precise, ideal. **2** *an impeccable young woman* virtuous, innocent, chaste, pure, pure as the driven snow, sinless, upright, irreproachable, unimpeachable, blameless, above suspicion, incorrupt.

impecunious adj penniless, insolvent, poor, poor as a church mouse, without a penny, without a sou, hard up, impoverished, poverty-stricken, destitute, unable to make ends meet, needy, indigent, penurious; *inf* broke, flat/stony broke, strapped for cash, cleaned out; skint.

impede v hinder, obstruct, hamper, handicap, block, check, bar, curb, hold back, hold up, delay, interfere with, disrupt, retard, slow, slow down, brake, restrain, thwart, frustrate, baulk, stop; *inf* put a spanner in the works.

impediment n **1** *an impediment to our plans* hindrance, obstruction, obstacle, handicap, block, stumbling-block, check, encumbrance, bar, barrier, curb, brake, restraint, drawback, difficulty, snag, set-back, clog. **2** *she has an impediment so has to speak slowly*

stammer, stutter, speech defect, hesitancy, faltering.

impedimenta npl equipment, gear, baggage, luggage; effects, possessions, belongings, goods, movables, traps, accoutrements, odds and ends, things; *inf* stuff.

impel v **1** *impel him to go* urge, press, exhort, force, oblige, constrain, necessitate, require, demand, make, apply pressure, pressure, pressurize, spur, prod, goad, incite, prompt, chivvy, persuade, inspire. **2** *impel the vehicle* actuate, set in motion, get going, get moving, propel.

impending adj imminent, at hand, approaching, coming, forthcoming, close, near, nearing, on the way, about to happen, upon us, in the offing, on the horizon, in the air/wind, brewing, looming, threatening, menacing.

impenetrable adj **1** *impenetrable containers* impervious, impermeable, solid, dense, thick, hard, closed, sealed, hermetically sealed, tight, resistant, waterproof, unpierceable, puncture-proof. **2** *impenetrable forests* impassable, unpassable, inaccessible, thick, dense, overgrown, jungly, pathless, trackless, untrodden. **3** *impenetrable jargon* incomprehensible, unintelligible, indiscernible, baffling, puzzling, abstruse, obscure, hidden, inexplicable, unfathomable, recondite, inscrutable, enigmatic. **4** *impenetrable ignorance* stupid, senseless, obtuse, gross, prejudiced, bigoted, biased, narrow-minded.

impenitent adj unrepentant, unrepenting, uncontrite, remorseless, obdurate, unfeeling, uncaring, abandoned.

imperative adj **1** *it is imperative that you stay* important, vital, essential, of the essence, crucial, critical, necessary, indispensable, required, mandatory, obligatory, exigent, pressing, urgent. **2** *an imperative tone of voice* imperious, authoritative, peremptory, commanding, lordly, masterful, autocratic, dictatorial, domineering, overbearing, magisterial.

imperceptible adj unnoticeable, unobtrusive, unapparent, slight, small, gradual, subtle, faint, fine, inappreciable, inconsequential, tiny, minute, miniscule, microscopic, infinitesimal, undetectable, indistinguishable, indiscernible, invisible, indistinct, unclear, obscure, vague, indefinite, shadowy, inaudible, muffled, impalpable.

imperceptibly adv unnoticeably, unobtrusively, unseen, gradually, slowly, subtly, inappreciably, undetectably, infinitesimally, little by little, bit by bit.

imperfect adj **1** *imperfect goods sold cheaply* faulty, flawed, defective, blemished, damaged, impaired, broken. **2** *an imperfect set of books* incomplete, not whole/entire, deficient, broken, partial. **3** *imperfect knowledge of the subject* deficient, inadequate, insufficient, lacking, rudimentary, limited, patchy, sketchy. **4** *imperfect plants* undeveloped, immature, premature.

imperfection n **1** *an imperfection in the vase* fault, flaw, defect, deformity, blemish; crack, break, scratch, cut, tear, stain, spot. **2** *the imperfection of the set* incompleteness, deficiency, partialness. **3** *an imperfection in his character* failing, flaw, foible, deficiency, weakness, weak point, shortcoming, fallibility, frailty, infirmity, peccadillo.

imperial adj **1** *his/her imperial majesty* royal, sovereign, regal, monarchal, kingly, queenly, princely, majestic, imperatorial. **2** *he has an imperial carriage* majestic, magnificent, grand, great, lofty, imposing, august, stately, splendid, glorious, exalted. **3** *the imperial ruler of the region* supreme, absolute, dominant, predominant, paramount, chief. **4** *very imperial in her manner* commanding, lordly, masterful, authoritative, imperious, peremptory, domineering. *see* IMPERIOUS.

imperil v endanger, expose to danger, put in danger/jeopardy, put at risk, risk, jeopardize, hazard, gamble with, take a chance with.

imperious adj peremptory, overbearing, overweening, domineering, high-handed, assertive, authoritative, commanding, lordly, masterful, dictatorial.

impermanent adj not permanent, nonpermanent, temporary, transient, transitory, passing, fleeting, momentary, short-lived, ephemeral, evanescent, volatile.

impersonal adj **1** *an impersonal assessment of the candidates* detached, objective, disinterested, dispassionate, neutral, unbiased, unprejudiced, unswayed, fair, equitable, even-handed. **2** *an impersonal manner* cold, cool, frigid, aloof, formal, stiff, rigid, wooden, starchy, stilted, stuffy, matter-of-fact, businesslike, bureaucratic.

impersonate v imitate, mimic, personate, mock, ape, parody, caricature, burlesque, masquerade as, pose as, pass oneself off as; *inf* take off, do.

impersonation n imitation, mimickry, impression, personation, mockery, parody, caricature, burlesque, travesty; *inf* take-off.

impertinence n **1** *the impertinence of the young woman* insolence, impudence, cheek, rudeness, impoliteness, unmannerliness, lack of civility, discourtesy, boldness, brazenness, audacity, effrontery, presumptuousness, brashness; *inf* brass neck, nerve, sauce, lip, gall. *see* IMPERTINENT 1. **2** *impertinence of the information* irrelevance, inapplicability, inappositeness, unrelatedness. *see* IMPERTINENT 2.

impertinent adj **1** *an impertinent youth/act* insolent, impudent, cheeky, rude, impolite, unmannerly, ill-mannered, uncivil, coarse, crude, uncouth, discourteous, disrespectful, bold, brazen, audacious, presumptuous, forward, pert, brash, shameless; *inf* brass-necked, saucy, fresh, flip. **2** *this document is impertinent to the case* irrelevant, inapplicable, inapposite, immaterial, unrelated, unconnected, not germane; beside the point.

imperturbable adj composed, collected, self-possessed, calm, cool, calm and collected, tranquil, serene, inexcitable, unflappable, even-tempered, easygoing, unperturbed, at ease, unruffled, untroubled, undismayed, unmoved, nonchalant.

impervious adj **1** *impervious to arguments* unmoved by, unaffected by, proof against, immune to, invulnerable to, unreceptive to, untouched by, unswayable by, closed to. **2** *impervious containers* impenetrable, impermeable, sealed, hermetically closed. *see* IMPENETRABLE 1.

impetuous adj **1** *an impetuous action* hasty, precipitate, headlong, impulsive, spontaneous, impromptu, spur-of-the-moment, unthinking, unplanned, unthought out, ill-conceived, ill-considered, unreasoned, reckless, rash, foolhardy, heedless. **2** *an impetuous person* impulsive, hasty, spontaneous, eager, enthusiastic, impatient, excitable, ardent, passionate, zealous, headstrong, rash, reckless, foolhardy, wild, uncontrolled. **3** *an impetuous wind* violent, forceful, powerful, vigorous, vehement, raging, rampant, unrestrained, uncontrolled, unbridled.

impetus n **1** *the car lost impetus on the steep slope* momentum, propulsion, impelling force, continuing motion, energy, force, power. **2** *the student needs some impetus to start studying* stimulus, instigation, actuation, moving force, motivation, incentive, inducement, inspiration, encouragement, influence, push, urging, pressing, spur, goading, goad.

impiety n **1** *churchgoers offended at his impiety* godlessness, ungodliness, unholiness, irre-

ligion, sinfulness, unrighteousness, sacrilege, irreverence, disrespect, profaneness,
scoffing, derision, apostasy, atheism,
agnosticism, paganism, heathenism.
2 *appalled at their impieties* sin, vice, wrongdoing, evildoing, transgression, desecration, profanity, blasphemy.

impinge v **impinge on 1** *impinge on other
people's rights* encroach on, infringe, intrude
on, invade, trespass on, obtrude into, make
inroads into, violate, usurp. **2** *impinge on
her consciousness* affect, have an effect/bear-
ing on, impress, touch, exert influence on,
bear upon. **3** *the rain impinging on the roof*
strike, hit, dash/crash/smash against, collide with.

impious adj godless, ungodly, unholy, irreligious, sinful, unrighteous, sacrilegious,
profane, blasphemous, irreverent, disrespectful, apostatic, atheistic, agnostic,
pagan, heathen.

impish adj **1** *impish little boys* mischievous,
mischief-making, full of mischief, rascally,
roguish, prankish, unruly, troublemaking,
devilish, sportive. **2** *an impish smile* elfin,
pixyish, puckish, mischievous, roguish.

implacable adj unplacatable, unappeasable, unpacifiable, not to be appeased/
pacified, unmollifiable, rancorous, grudge-
holding, unforgiving, inexorable, adamant,
unyielding, uncompromising, unrelenting,
relentless, ruthless, remorseless, merciless,
pitiless, heartless, cruel, hard.

implant v **1** *implant radical ideas in her head*
inculcate, instil, insinuate, inject, inseminate, sow, infuse, introduce. **2** *implant the
posts in the ground* embed, fix firmly, fix,
place, plant, root, set. **3** *implant hormone pellets under the skin* insert, place, put in place.
4 *implant skin tissue from a different part of
the body* graft, engraft.

implausible adj not likely, unlikely,
improbable, hard to believe, incredible,
unbelievable, unimaginable, inconceivable,
debatable, questionable, doubtful.

implement n **1** *garden/kitchen implements*
tool, utensil, appliance, instrument, device,
apparatus, contrivance, gadget; *inf* gismo.
2 *use her faith as an implement of peace* agent,
medium, channel, expedient; means.

implement v *implement their instructions* fulfil, carry out, execute, perform, discharge,
accomplish, achieve, realize, put into
effect/action, bring about, effect, enforce.

implementation n *the implementation of
their instructions* fulfilment, execution, discharge, accomplishment, realization,
effecting, enforcement. *see* IMPLEMENT V.

implicate v **1** *try to implicate his friend when
he was accused* incriminate, compromise,
inculpate, accuse, charge, blame, impeach,
involve, entangle. **2** *he was not implicated in
the events* involve, concern, include, associate, connect, embroil, entangle; be a part
of, tie up with.

implication n **1** *resent the implication that he
was lying* suggestion, inference, insinuation, innuendo, hint, allusion, reference,
assumption, presumption. **2** *the implication
of his friend in the charge* incrimination,
inculpation, blame. *see* IMPLICATE 1. **3** *their
implication in the events* involvement, concern, association, connection, entanglement. *see* IMPLICATE 2.

implicit adj **1** *there was implicit criticism in his
voice* implied, indirect, inferred, deducible,
unspoken, unexpressed, undeclared,
unstated, tacit, understood, hinted, suggested. **2** *implicit in the argument was a lack
of confidence in management* implied, inherent, latent, taken for granted. **3** *have
implicit trust in the doctor* absolute, complete, entire, total, wholehearted, perfect,
sheer, utter, unqualified, unconditional,
unreserved, positive, unshaken, unshakable, unhesitating, unquestioning, firm,
steadfast, constant.

implicitly adv *trust the doctor implicitly*
absolutely, completely, totally, wholeheartedly, utterly, unconditionally, unreservedly, without reservation, positively,
unhesitatingly, unquestioningly, firmly. *see*
IMPLICIT 3.

implied adj *their implied criticism* implicit,
indirect, inferred, deducible, unspoken,
unexpressed, tacit, hinted, suggested. *see*
IMPLICIT 1.

implore v *implored her to come* | *implore for-
giveness* appeal to, beg, entreat, plead with,
beseech, pray, ask, request, solicit, supplicate, importune, press; crave, plead for,
appeal for.

imply v **1** *he implied that all was not well*
insinuate, say indirectly, hint, suggest,
infer, intimate, give to understand, signal,
indicate. **2** *being a civil servant implies discretion* involve, entail, presuppose, presume,
assume. **3** *war implies bloodshed* signify,
mean, indicate, denote, connote, betoken,
point to.

impolite adj unmannerly, ill-mannered,
bad-mannered, rude, discourteous, uncivil,
ill-bred, ungentlemanly, unladylike, ungracious, ungallant, disrespectful, inconsiderate, boorish, churlish, loutish, rough,
crude, unrefined, indelicate, indecorous,
insolent, impudent, impertinent.

impolitic adj injudicious, ill-judged, undiplomatic, unwise, imprudent, ill-advised, misguided, ill-considered, short-sighted, uncircumspect, indiscreet, incautious, maladroit, inexpedient, untimely.

import n **1** *exports and imports* imported commodity/service, foreign commodity, non-domestic commodity. **2** *did you get the import of what he said?* gist, drift, sense, essence, meaning, purport, message, thrust, implication, pith, core, sum and substance. **3** *men of import in the town* importance, significance, consequence, moment, magnitude, substance, weight.

importance n **1** *the importance of the talks* significance, momentousness, seriousness, graveness, urgency, gravity, weightiness, value. see IMPORTANT 1. **2** *people of importance* prominence, eminence, pre-eminence, note, notability, noteworthiness, influence, power, high rank, status, prestige, standing, mark.

important adj **1** *important talks* of import, consequential, significant, of great import/consequence, far-reaching, critical, crucial, pivotal, momentous, of great moment, serious, grave, urgent, substantial, weighty, valuable. **2** *the important points to remember* significant, salient, chief, main, principal, major. **3** *it is important to the project that he is there* of concern, of interest, relevant, of value, valuable, necessary, essential. **4** *the important people in the town* prominent, eminent, pre-eminent, leading, foremost, outstanding, distinguished, esteemed, notable, noteworthy, of note, of import, influential, of influence, powerful, power-wielding, high-ranking, high-level, top-level, prestigious.

importunate adj persistent, insistent, pertinacious, dogged, earnest, unremitting, continuous, pressing, urgent, demanding, exigent, exacting, clamorous, entreating, solicitous, suppliant, imploratory, imprecatory.

importune v **1** *importune him for money* beg, beseech, entreat, implore, plead with, appeal to, call upon, supplicate, solicit, petition, harass, beset, press, dun. **2** *importune men in the street* solicit, make sexual advances towards.

impose v **1** *impose a tax* enforce, apply, exact, levy, charge, put on, lay on, set, establish, fix, decree, ordain, institute, introduce, promulgate. **2** *impose her views on the group* force, foist, inflict, thrust, obtrude. **3** *impose a new leader on them* appoint, superimpose, superpose; *inf* sad-

dle with. **4** *impose herself on the company* force/foist/thrust oneself, intrude, break in, obtrude, interlope, trespass; *inf* gatecrash, crash, butt in, horn in. **5** *not wishing to impose on your good nature* take advantage of, abuse, exploit, play on, be a burden on. **6** *impose fake antiques on the public* palm off, foist, pass off, fob off.

imposing adj impressive, striking, splendid, grand, majestic, august, lofty, stately, dignified.

imposition n **1** *the imposition of new taxes* enforcement, application, exacting, levying, fixing, decreeing, institution. see IMPOSE 1. **2** *new impositions on tax payers* tax, levy, charge, tariff, toll, tithe. **3** *unfair impositions on the poor* burden, load, charge, onus, encumbrance. **4** *the imposition of her on the company* intrusion, obtrusion, interlopement, trespassing; *inf* gatecrashing, butting in, horning in. see IMPOSE 4.

impossible adj **1** *an impossible task* not possible, beyond the bounds of possibility, out of the question, unthinkable, unimaginable, inconceivable, beyond the realm of reason, impracticable, unattainable, unachievable, unobtainable, beyond one, hopeless. **2** *an impossible story* unbelievable, incredible, absurd, ludicrous, ridiculous, preposterous, outlandish, outrageous. **3** *an impossible child* unmanageable, intractable, recalcitrant, wayward, objectionable, intolerable, unbearable. **4** *life became impossible for the homeless* unbearable, intolerable, unendurable, hopeless.

imposter, impostor n masquerader, pretender, deceiver, fake, fraud, sham, charlatan, quack, mountebank, hoodwinker, bluffer, trickster, deluder, duper, cheat, cheater, swindler, defrauder, exploiter, confidence man/woman, rogue; *inf* phoney, con man, con artist.

imposture n misrepresentation, pretence, deceit, fraudulence, deception, fraud, charlatanry, quackery, trickery, duping, cheating, swindling.

impotence n **1** *helpers angry at their impotence* powerlessness, lack of power, helplessness, inability, incapability, incapacity, incompetence. **2** *the impotence of the defeated army* powerlessness, helplessness, weakness, feebleness, exhaustion, enervation, debilitation. see IMPOTENT 2. **3** *the impotence of their attempts* ineffectiveness, ineffectualness, inefficiency, inadequacy, uselessness, futility, unsuccessfulness. see IMPOTENT 3.

impotent adj **1** *impotent to help* powerless, helpless, unable, incapable, incapacitated, incompetent. **2** *the defeated general and his* *impotent forces* powerless, helpless, enfeebled, weak, feeble, frail, worn out, exhausted, spent, enervated, debilitated, prostrate, crippled, paralysed, infirm. **3** *make impotent attempts to help* ineffective, ineffectual, inefficient, inadequate, inept, useless, worthless, vain, futile, unavailing, unsuccessful, profitless.

impound v **1** *impound stray animals* shut up/in, pen up/in, fence in, coop up, hem in, tie up, cage, enclose, confine, imprison, incarcerate, immure. **2** *impound legal documents* appropriate, take possession of, seize, commandeer, expropriate; *Law* distrain; *Scots* poind.

impoverished adj **1** *impoverished homeless people* poverty-stricken, destitute, penurious, beggared, indigent, impecunious, penniless, poor, needy, in distressed/reduced/straitened circumstances, down and out, bankrupt, insolvent, ruined; *inf* broke, flat/stony broke, on one's uppers. **2** *impoverished soil* exhausted, depleted, diminished, weakened, drained, used up, spent, played out. **3** *impoverished region/landscape* barren, bare, arid, desolate, empty, dead, waste, denuded.

impracticable adj *an impracticable plan* not feasible, impossible, out of the question, unworkable, unachievable, unattainable, unrealizable, unsuitable.

impractical adj **1** *an impractical solution* unworkable, useless, ineffective, ineffectual, inefficacious, unrealistic, impossible, non-viable, inoperable, inoperative, unserviceable. **2** *his work is too impractical for a civil engineer* theoretical, abstract, academic, speculative. **3** *an impractical young woman* unrealistic, unbusinesslike, idealistic, romantic, starry-eyed, visionary, quixotic.

imprecation n **1** *under an imprecation* curse, malediction, execration. **2** *embarrassed by his imprecations* swearing, cursing, blaspheming, blasphemy, foul language.

imprecise adj **1** *an imprecise estimate of the cost* inexact, approximate, estimated, rough, inaccurate, incorrect. **2** *an imprecise account of the incident* vague, loose, indefinite, inexplicit, hazy, blurred, indistinct, woolly, confused, ambiguous, equivocal.

impregnable adj **1** *an impregnable castle* impenetrable, unattackable, unassailable, inviolable, secure, strong, stout, invulnerable, invincible, unconquerable, unbeatable, indestructible. **2** *an impregnable argument* irrefutable, indisputable, incontestable, unquestionable, flawless, faultless.

impregnate v **1** *impregnate the cloth with dye* permeate, suffuse, imbue, penetrate, pervade, fill, infuse, soak, steep, saturate, drench, inundate. **2** *impregnate the young woman* make pregnant, inseminate; *inf* put in the family way, put in the club. **3** *impregnate the ovum* fertilize, fecundate.

impresario n organizer, manager, producer; director, conductor, maestro, precentor, ballet master.

impress v **1** *impress the crowd with his speech* make an impression/impact on, move, sway, bend, influence, affect, affect deeply, stir, rouse, excite, inspire, galvanize; *inf* grab. **2** *impress upon them the need for speed* emphasize, stress, bring home, establish, fix deeply, instil, inculcate, urge. **3** *impress one's name on a metal strip* stamp, imprint, print, mark, engrave, emboss. **4** *she's always trying to impress* make an impression, draw attention to oneself, show off, cut a good figure, cut a dash.

impression n **1** *make an impression on the crowd* effect, influence, sway, impact, hold, power, control. **2** *the impression where his head lay | the impression made by the ring* mark, indentation, dent, hollow, outline, stamp, stamping, imprint, impress. **3** *I have the impression that he is bored* feeling, vague feeling, sense, sensation, awareness, perception, notion, idea, thought, belief, opinion, conviction, fancy, suspicion, inkling, intuition, hunch; *inf* funny feeling. **4** *his impression of the politician* impersonation, imitation, mimicry, parody, caricature, burlesque, travesty; *inf* send-up, take-off. **5** *the impression sold out* print run, printing, imprinting, issue, edition.

impressionable adj susceptible, suggestible, persuadable, receptive, responsive, sensitive, open, gullible, ingenuous, pliable, malleable, mouldable.

impressive adj moving, affecting, touching, stirring, rousing, exciting, powerful, inspiring.

imprint n *the imprint of his feet* impression, print, mark, indentation, stamp, sign.

imprint v **1** *imprint a seal on wax* stamp, print, impress, mark, engrave, emboss. **2** *imprint the details on his mind* fix, establish, stamp, impress, etch.

imprison v put in prison, send to prison, jail, lock up, take into custody, put under lock and key, put away, incarcerate, intern, confine, detain, constrain, immure; *inf* send down.

imprisonment n custody, incarceration, internment, confinement, detention, duress; *inf* porridge.

improbable adj unlikely, highly unlikely, doubtful, dubious, questionable, implausible, far-fetched, unconvincing, unbelievable, incredible, ridiculous.

impromptu adj *an impromptu speech* ad lib, unrehearsed, unprepared, extempore, extemporized, extemporaneous, spontaneous, improvised, unscripted, unstudied, unpremeditated; *inf* off the cuff.

impromptu adv *she spoke impromptu* ad lib, without preparation/rehearsal, extempore, spontaneously, on the spur of the moment; *inf* off the cuff, off the top of one's head.

improper adj **1** *improper behaviour* unseemly, indecorous, unbecoming, unfitting, unladylike, ungentlemanly, impolite, indiscreet, injudicious. **2** *an improper remark* indecent, risqué, off-colour, indelicate, suggestive, blue, smutty, obscene, lewd, pornographic. **3** *draw an improper inference* inaccurate, incorrect, wrong, erroneous, false. **4** *an improper tool for the job* inappropriate, unsuitable, unsuited, unfitting, inapt, inapplicable, incongruous.

impropriety n **1** *guilty of impropriety* incorrectness, indecorum, indecorousness, unseemliness, indiscretion, bad taste, immodesty, indecency. **2** *appalled at her improprieties* improper act, improper remark. *see* IMPROPER 1, 2.

improve v **1** *try to improve conditions* make better, better, ameliorate, amend, mend, reform, rehabilitate, set/put right, correct, rectify, help, advance, upgrade, revamp, modernize; *inf* give a face-lift to, gentrify. **2** *things are improving* get/grow better, make headway, advance, come along, develop, progress, make progress, pick up, rally, perk up; *inf* look up, take a turn for the better, take on a new lease of life. **3** *she was ill but she's improving now* recover, get better/well, recuperate, convalesce, gain strength; *inf* be on the mend, turn the corner. **4** *can you improve on your offer* increase, make larger, raise, put up; *inf* jack up.

improvement n **1** *the improvement of conditions* betterment, amelioration, reform, rehabilitation, rectifying, rectification, advance, upgrading, revamp; *inf* face-lift, gentrification. *see* IMPROVE 1. **2** *there has been an improvement in the economy* betterment, change for the better, advance, development, rally, recovery, upswing, comeback; progress, growth.

improvident adj **1** *improvident people left penniless in old age* thriftless, unthrifty, spendthrift, wasteful, prodigal, extravagant, squandering, unfrugal, uneconomical, shiftless. **2** *improvident troops* incautious,

unobservant, unwatchful, unwary, unvigilant, unalert, heedless, careless, inattentive; *inf* asleep on the job, asleep at the wheel.

improvise v **1** *if you haven't prepared anything you'll have to improvise* ad lib, extemporize, make it up as you go along; *inf* speak off the cuff, play it by ear. **2** *you'll have to improvise a shelter* throw/put together, devise, contrive, concoct, rig, jury rig.

improvised adj **1** *improvised entertainment* impromptu, ad lib, unrehearsed, extempore, spontaneous; *inf* off the cuff. *see* IMPROMPTU adj. **2** *an improvised shelter* thrown together, makeshift, devised, rigged, jury-rigged.

imprudent adj indiscreet, ill-considered, thoughtless, unthinking, incautious, unwary, improvident, irresponsible, foolish, injudicious, ill-judged, unwise, ill-advised, impolitic, careless, hasty, overhasty, rash, reckless, heedless, foolhardy.

impudence n impertinence, insolence, cheek, boldness, effrontery, audacity, brazenness, pertness, sauciness, presumption, bumptiousness, rudeness, shamelessness; bad/ill manners; *inf* brass neck, face, nerve, lip, sauce. *see* IMPUDENT.

impudent adj impertinent, insolent, cheeky, bold, audacious, brazen, brazenfaced, pert, saucy, presumptuous, forward, bumptious, impolite, rude, disrespectful, ill-mannered, bad-mannered, unmannerly, ill-bred, shameless, immodest; *inf* fresh, cocky, brass-necked.

impugn v *impugn his motives* challenge, call into question, question, dispute, query, cast aspersions on, look askance at, attack, assail, berate, criticize, denounce, censure.

impulse n **1** *the impulse driving the machine* impetus, propulsion, impulsion, momentum, force, thrust, push, surge. **2** *the literary impulse* stimulus, inspiration, stimulation, incitement, incentive, inducement, motivation, urge. **3** *buy the coat on impulse* sudden desire/fancy, spur of the moment, notion, whim, caprice. **4** *suppress sexual impulse* drive, urge, instinct, appetite, proclivity.

impulsive adj **1** *an impulsive action* hasty, impromptu, snap, spontaneous, extemporaneous, sudden, quick, precipitate, impetuous, ill-considered, unplanned, unpremeditated, thoughtless, rash, reckless. **2** *an impulsive person* hasty, spontaneous, impetuous, instinctive, intuitive, passionate, emotional, rash, reckless, madcap, devil-may-care, foolhardy.

impunity n *played truant with impunity* exemption/freedom from punishment/retribution/harm, immunity, indemnity, excusal, non-liability, licence, dispensation, pardon, reprieve, stay of execution.

impure adj **1** *impure chemicals* adulterated, alloyed, mixed, admixed, combined, blended, debased. **2** *impure water* contaminated, polluted, tainted, infected, foul, dirty, filthy, unclean, feculent, sullied, defiled, unwholesome, poisoned. **3** *impure women* unchaste, unvirginal, immoral, loose, promiscuous, wanton, immodest, shameless, corrupt, dissolute, depraved, licentious, lascivious, prurient, lustful, lecherous, lewd. **4** *impure thoughts* lewd, lustful, lecherous, obscene, dirty, indecent, ribald, risqué, smutty, pornographic, improper, crude, vulgar, coarse, gross.

impurity n **1** *the impurity of the chemical* adulteration, admixture, debasement. *see* IMPURE 1. **2** *the impurity of the water* contamination, pollution, foulness, filthiness, unwholesomeness. *see* IMPURE 2. **3** *impurities in the chemicals/water* foreign body, contaminant, pollutant, adulterant; dross, dirt, filth, grime, scum; bits. **4** *the impurity of the women* unchasteness, unchastity, immorality, looseness, promiscuity, wantonness, immodesty, lasciviousness, lust, lechery, lewdness. *see* IMPURE 3. **5** *the impurity of their thoughts* lewdness, lustfulness, obscenity, ribaldry, smut, smuttiness, impropriety, crudity, vulgarity. *see* IMPURE 4.

impute v *impute the crime to him* ascribe, attribute, assign, credit, accredit; connect with, associate with.

in adj **1** *short skirts were in then* fashionable, in fashion, in vogue, voguish, stylish, in style; *inf* trendy, all the rage. **2** *she seems to be in with the teacher* in favour, favoured, liked; *inf* in someone's good books.

in n **ins** and **outs** *the ins and outs of the situation* intricacies, particulars, facts, details, features, characteristics, traits, particularities, peculiarities, idiosyncracies.

inability n incapability, incapableness, incapacity, incompetence, ineptitude, inaptitude, unfitness, ineffectiveness, powerlessness, uselessness, inefficacy, ineligibility, unqualifiedness.

inaccessible adj *houses inaccessible in the winter* unreachable, out of reach, beyond reach, unapproachable, impenetrable, unattainable, out of the way, remote, back of beyond, God-forsaken; *inf* unget-at-able.

inaccuracy n **1** *the inaccuracy of the results* incorrectness, erroneousness, wrongness, mistakenness, fallaciousness, faultiness, inexactness, inexactitude, imprecision. **2** *the accounts were full of inaccuracies* error, mistake, miscalculation, erratum, corrigendum, slip, fault, blunder, defect; *inf* slip-up, howler, bloomer, boo-boo. **3** *a document full of inaccuracies* error, mistake, slip, slip of the pen, printer's error, literal; *inf* typo.

inaccurate adj **1** *your calculation is inaccurate* incorrect, wrong, erroneous, faulty, inexact, imprecise, out. **2** *the report is inaccurate* incorrect, wrong, erroneous, fallacious, false, not true, not right, imperfect, flawed, defective, unsound, unreliable, wide of the mark; *inf* full of holes.

inactive adj **1** *he hates to be inactive but he has to stay in bed* immobile, motionless, inert, stationary. **2** *all the machines lying inactive* idle, inoperative, non-functioning, not working, out of service, unused, out of use, not in use, unoccupied, unemployed, inert, mothballed. **3** *a former sportsman now completely inactive* idle, inert, slow, sluggish, indolent, lazy, lifeless, slothful, lethargic, stagnant, vegetating, vegetant, dilatory, torpid; *inf* low-key. **4** *an inactive volcano* dormant, quiescent, latent, passive.

inadequacy n **1** *the inadequacy of the food supply* inadequateness, insufficiency, dearth, deficiency, meagreness, scantness, scarcity, paucity. *see* INADEQUATE 1. **2** *war brought food inadequacies* shortage, deficit, lack, dearth, scarcity. **3** *the inadequacy of the present staff* incompetence, incapability, unfitness, ineffectiveness, ineffectuality, inefficiency, inefficacy, inexpertness, lack of skill/proficiency, inaptness, ineptness. **4** *show up his inadequacies as a manager* shortcoming, fault, failing, flaw, defect, imperfection, weakness, foible.

inadequate adj **1** *inadequate food supplies* insufficient, not enough, too little, too few, lacking, found wanting, deficient, short, in short supply, meagre, scanty, scant, niggardly, scarce, sparse, skimpy, scrimpy, sketchy, incomplete. **2** *an inadequate teacher* incompetent, incapable, not able, unfit, ineffective, ineffectual, inefficient, inefficacious, unskilful, inexpert, unproficient, inapt, inept; *inf* not up to scratch.

inadmissible adj *inadmissible evidence* not allowable, unallowable, prohibited, precluded, unacceptable, improper, inappropriate, inapposite, irrelevant, immaterial, impertinent, not germane, beside the point.

inadvertent adj **1** *an inadvertent omission* accidental, unintentional, chance, unpremeditated, unplanned, uncalculated, unconscious, unwitting, involuntary. **2** *an* *inadvertent driver* inattentive, careless, negligent, thoughtless, heedless, unheeding, unmindful, unobservant.

inadvisable adj ill-advised, unwise, injudicious, ill-judged, imprudent, impolitic, inexpedient, foolish.

inalienable adj *inalienable rights* untransferable, unforfeitable, inherent, unchallengable, inviolable, sacrosanct.

inane adj silly, foolish, stupid, idiotic, absurd, ridiculous, ludicrous, fatuous, trifling, frivolous, senseless, nonsensical, unintelligent, mindless, puerile, asinine, futile, worthless, vacuous, vapid; *inf* daft.

inanimate adj 1 *inanimate objects* lifeless, without life, exanimate, dead, inert, insentient, insensate, extinct, defunct. 2 *inanimate people* spiritless, apathetic, lazy, inactive, phlegmatic, listless, lethargic, sluggish, torpid.

inapplicable adj *rules inapplicable to the situation* irrelevant, immaterial, not germane, inapposite, not pertinent, impertinent, inappropriate, unrelated, unconnected, beside the point.

inapposite adj irrelevant, immaterial, not germane, not pertinent, impertinent, inapplicable. *see* INAPPLICABLE.

inappreciable adj imperceptible, microscopic, infinitesimal, miniscule, minute, tiny, slight, small, insignificant, negligible, petty, trivial, trifling, paltry; *inf* piddling.

inappropriate adj 1 *inappropriate behaviour* unsuitable, unfitting, unseemly, unbecoming, indecorous, improper, ungentlemanly, unladylike, ungenteel. 2 *inappropriate dress* unsuitable, inapposite, incongruous, out of place/keeping. 3 *it would be inappropriate to comment* unsuitable, inexpedient, inadvisable, injudicious, infelicitous, untimely.

inapt adj 1 *an inapt remark* inappropriate, unsuitable, unsuited, unfitting, out of place, inapposite, inapplicable, not pertinent, impertinent, not germane, incongruous, out of keeping, unrelated, unconnected. 2 *an inapt tradesman* inept, incompetent, unadept, incapable, unskilful, inexpert, clumsy, awkward, maladroit, undexterous, heavy-handed; *inf* cack-handed.

inarticulate adj 1 *inarticulate cries/sounds* unintelligible, incomprehensible, incoherent, unclear, indistinct, blurred, muffled, mumbled, muttered. 2 *inarticulate children* non-eloquent, uneloquent, poorly spoken, non-fluent, faltering, hesitating, halting, stumbling, stuttering, stammering. 3 *inarticulate emotion* unspoken, unuttered, unexpressed, unvoiced, wordless, silent, mute, dumb, speechless, voiceless, soundless, taciturn, tongue-tied.

inattention n 1 *pupils guilty of inattention* inattentiveness, distraction, preoccupation, absent-mindedness, daydreaming, reverie, wool-gathering, mental wandering, lack of concentration/application, staring into space; brown study. 2 *inattention to duty* neglect, negligence, remissness, forgetfulness, carelessness, thoughtlessness, heedlessness, disregard, indifference, unconcern, inconsideration.

inattentive adj 1 *inattentive pupils* distracted, *distrait*, preoccupied, absentminded, daydreaming, wool-gathering, lost in thought, off in a world of one's own, lacking concentration/application, in a brown study, with one's head in the clouds; *inf* miles away. 2 *inattentive to duty | inattentive guards* neglectful, negligent, remiss, forgetful, careless, thoughtless, heedless, disregarding, indifferent, unconcerned, inconsiderate.

inaudible adj not heard, hard to hear, hard to make out, indistinct, imperceptible, out of earshot, faint, muted, soft, low, muffled, stifled, dull, whispered, muttered, murmured, mumbled.

inaugural adj first, initial, introductory, opening, maiden, dedicatory.

inaugurate v 1 *inaugurate the conference proceedings* initiate, begin, start, commence, launch, start off, set in motion, get going, get underway, ring up the curtain on, get off the ground. 2 *inaugurate the new chancellor of the university* install, instate, induct, invest, ordain. 3 *inaugurate the new building* open, open officially, dedicate.

inauspicious adj unpropitious, unpromising, unlucky, unfortunate, infelicitous, unhappy, unfavourable, ill-omened, ominous, ill-fated, ill-starred, untoward, untimely.

inborn adj innate, inherent, inherited, congenital, hereditary, in the family, in the blood/genes, inbred, connate, ingrained, constitutional, structural.

inbred adj inherent, innate, ingrained, deep-seated.

incalculable adj 1 *the distance/number is incalculable* immeasurable, measureless, inestimable, uncountable, incomputable, not to be reckoned, endless, without end, infinite, boundless, limitless, fathomless, bottomless, innumerable, countless, without number, numberless, multitudinous, enormous, immense, vast. 2 *an incalculable* *risk* unpredictable, indeterminable, unforeseeable.

incandescent adj white-hot, intensely hot, red-hot, bright, brilliant, dazzling, shining, gleaming, glowing, aglow.

incantation n chant, chanting, invocation, conjuration, spell, magic formula/word; abracadabra, open sesame.

incapable adj **1** *tired of employing incapable people* lacking ability, incompetent, ineffective, ineffectual, inefficacious, inadequate, unfit, unfitted, unqualified, inept, inapt, unable, useless, feeble; *inf* not up to scratch. **2** *fell down incapable* helpless, powerless, impotent. **3** *incapable of doing good* unable to, not capable of, lacking experience to, lacking the ability to. **4** *problems incapable of solution* not admitting, not open to, impervious to, resistant to, not susceptible to.

incapacitated adj *incapacitated and unable to play football* disabled, debilitated, unfit, immobilized, crippled, indisposed, *hors de combat*; *inf* laid up, out of action.

incapacity n **1** *his incapacity to do a job well* inability, incapability, incompetence, incompetency, inadequacy, unfitness, ineffectiveness, ineffectuality, inefficiency, powerlessness, impotence. **2** *legal incapacity* lack of entitlement, lack of legal ability, inability, disqualification.

incarcerate v imprison, jail, put in prison/jail, throw in prison/jail, lock up, put under lock and key, intern, impound, take captive, put into detention, detain, clap in irons, confine, shut away, shut in, coop up, immure, restrain, restrict; *inf* send down.

incarceration n imprisonment, internment, captivity, detention, bondage, confinement, restraint.

incarnate adj **1** *the devil incarnate* in bodily/human form, in the flesh, made manifest, embodied, corporeal, fleshly. **2** *tactlessness incarnate* embodied, personified, typified.

incarnation n **1** *in another incarnation* life, bodily form, manifestation, embodiment. **2** *she is the incarnation of motherliness* embodiment, personification, exemplification, type, avatar.

incautious adj **1** *incautious guards not spotting the enemy* unwary, unchary, unwatchful, unvigilant, unalert, off-guard, inattentive, unobservant, inadvertent; *inf* asleep on the job, asleep at the wheel. **2** *incautious of him to trust her* unwise, imprudent, ill-advised, ill-judged, injudicious, uncircumspect, improvident, thoughtless, careless, impetuous, hasty, precipitate, rash, reckless, foolhardy.

incendiary adj **1** *an incendiary bomb* combustible, flammable, fire-producing, fire-raising. **2** *an incendiary speech* inflammatory, incensing, inciting, instigating, arousing, stirring, provocative, rabble-rousing, seditious, subversive.

incendiary n **1** *buildings deliberately set alight by incendiaries* arsonist, fire-raiser, fire-setter, pyromaniac; *inf* firebug. **2** *crowds driven to rioting by incendiaries* demagogue, agitator, *agent provocateur*, rabble-rouser, instigator, inciter, insurgent, firebrand, revolutionary.

incense v *the naughty children incensed the teacher* anger, enrage, infuriate, exasperate, irritate, madden, provoke, rile, inflame, agitate, nettle, vex, irk, get one's hackles up; *inf* make one's blood boil, make one see red, get in one's hair, get one's dander up.

incense n *sweet-smelling incense* perfume, fragrance, scent, aroma, bouquet, redolence, balm.

incentive n inducement, incitement, stimulus, stimulant, impetus, encouragement, motivation, inspiration, impulse, goad, spur, lure, bait; *inf* carrot.

inception n beginning, commencement, start, starting point, outset, opening, debut, inauguration, initiation, institution, birth, dawn, origin, rise; *inf* kick-off.

incessant adj ceaseless, unceasing, nonstop, endless, unending, never-ending, everlasting, eternal, constant, continual, perpetual, continuous, uninterrupted, unbroken, ongoing, unremitting, persistent, recurrent.

incidence n rate, frequency, prevalence, occurrence, amount, degree, extent.

incident n **1** *unhappy incidents in her life* event, happening, occurrence, episode, adventure, experience, proceeding, occasion, circumstance, fact, matter. **2** *the police were called to an incident in the bar* disturbance, commotion, row, scene, fracas, contretemps, skirmish, clash, conflict, confrontation, brush.

incidental adj **1** *her part in the event was incidental* accidental, by chance, chance, fortuitous, random. **2** *travel incidental to her job* related (to), connected (with), associated (with), accompanying, attendant, concomitant, contingent, by the way. **3** *her social engagements are incidental upon her job* ancillary (to), subordinate (to), subsidiary (to), secondary (to). **4** *incidental expenses* minor, trivial, trifling, petty, small, meagre.

incidentally adv **1** *incidentally, I'm leaving tomorrow* by the way, by the by, in passing, *en passant*, speaking of, on the subject of, apropos of. **2** *she helped quite incidentally* accidentally, by chance, fortuitously, by a fluke, as luck would have it.

incinerate v burn, burn up, reduce to ashes, carbonize, cremate.

incipient adj beginning, commencing, starting, inceptive, initial, inchoative, original, inaugural, nascent, newborn, embryonic, embryonal, germinal, rudimentary, developing.

incise v **1** *incise the skin* cut, cut into, make an incision in, slit, slit open, gash, slash, notch, nick, furrow. **2** *incise the stone* engrave, etch, sculpt, sculpture, carve.

incision n cut, opening, slit, gash, slash, notch, nick.

incisive adj **1** *an incisive mind* keen, acute, sharp, penetrating, astute, shrewd, perspicacious, clever, smart, quick. **2** *an incisive turn of phrase* caustic, acid, sharp, biting, cutting, stinging, tart, trenchant, mordant, sarcastic, sardonic.

incite v **1** *incite a rebellion* instigate, provoke, foment, whip up, stir up, prompt. **2** *incite them to rebel* egg on, encourage, urge, goad, spur on, prod, stimulate, drive on, excite, arouse, agitate, inflame, stir up, provoke.

incitement n *incitement to action* encouragement, urging, goading, spurring, prodding, stimulation, agitation, provocation, instigation; spur, impetus.

incivility n bad/ill manners; unmannerliness, impoliteness, discourtesy, discourteousness, rudeness, disrespect, boorishness.

inclement adj **1** *inclement weather* rough, stormy, squally, blustery, severe, bitter, raw, foul, nasty, harsh. **2** *inclement judges* harsh, unmerciful, pitiless, unpitying, ruthless, remorseless, hard-hearted, hard, cruel, inexorable, unrelenting, callous, severe, rigorous, Draconian.

inclination n *he has an inclination to overeat* | *an inclination towards overeating* tendency, leaning, propensity, proclivity, proneness, liableness, disposition, predisposition, subjectability, weakness. **2** *an inclination for blondes* penchant, predilection, predisposition, partiality, preference, affinity, attraction, fancy, liking, fondness, affection, love. **3** *an inclination of the head* bow, bowing, bend, bending, nod, lower-

ing, stooping. **4** *an inclination in the terrain* slope, slant, gradient, bank, ramp, lift, tilt, acclivity, rise, ascent, declivity, descent, drop, dip, sag, cant, bevel, angle.

incline v **1** *the land inclines towards the shore* curve, bend, slope, slant, bank, cant, bevel, tilt, lean, tip, list, deviate. **2** *he inclines towards the left in politics* tend, lean, swing, veer, have a preference/penchant for, be attracted to, have an affinity for. **3** *that inclines me to believe you* | *I'm inclined to believe you* predispose, dispose, influence, bias, prejudice, sway, make willing, persuade, bend. **4** *the door is inclined to bang* have a tendency, be liable/likely. **5** *incline the head* bow, bend, nod, lower, stoop, cast down.

include v **1** *the group includes representatives from all countries* contain, hold, take in, admit, incorporate, embrace, encompass, comprise, embody, comprehend, subsume. **2** *remember to include them on the invitation list* allow for, add, insert, put in, enter, introduce, count in, take account of, build in, number, incorporate.

including prep *everyone is going including me* counting, inclusive of.

inclusion n *the inclusion of new material* addition, insertion, incorporation, introduction.

inclusive adj **1** *an inclusive price* all-in, all-embracing, comprehensive, with everything included, *in toto*. **2** *the total inclusive of VAT* including, taking into account/consideration, counting, taking account/cognizance of. **3** *from Monday to Friday inclusive* including the limits stated, encompassed.

incognito adj/adv under an assumed name, with one's identity concealed, in disguise, disguised, in masquerade, camouflaged, unrecognized, unidentified, sailing under false colours.

incognizant adj unaware, unconscious, ignorant, unknowing, unsuspecting, unknowledgeable, unenlightened.

incoherent adj *incoherent speech* unconnected, disconnected, disjointed, disordered, confused, mixed-up, muddled, jumbled, scrambled, rambling, wandering, discursive, illogical, unintelligible, inarticulate, mumbled, muttered, stuttered, stammered.

incombustible adj noncombustible, uninflammable, non-flammable, flameproof, fireproof, unburnable, unignitable, flame-retardant, flame-resistant.

income n salary, pay, remuneration, revenue; earnings, wages, receipts, takings, profits, gains, proceeds, means.

incoming adj **1** *the incoming tide/train* coming, coming in, approaching, entering, arriving. **2** *the incoming president* new, succeeding.

incomparable adj beyond compare, inimitable, unequalled, without equal, matchless, nonpareil, paramount, unrivalled, peerless, unparalleled, unsurpassed, transcendent, superior, superlative, supreme.

incomparably adv beyond compare, by far, far and away, easily, immeasurably.

incompatible adj **1** *he and his wife are incompatible* inharmonious, unsuited, mismatched, ill-assorted, uncongenial, incongruous, like day and night, uncomplementary, conflicting, antagonistic, antipathetic, dissentient, disagreeing, discordant, like cat and dog. **2** *incompatible colours* inharmonious, discordant, clashing, jarring, uncomplementary. **3** *views incompatible with his behaviour* differing from, contrary to, at odds with, inconsistent with, in opposition to, diametrically opposed to. *see* INCONGRUOUS 1.

incompetent adj **1** *incompetent to do the task* unable, incapable, unfitted, unfit, unsuitable, unqualified, inapt, inept, inefficient, ineffectual, ineffective, inadequate, deficient, insufficient, useless. **2** *an incompetent performance* unskilful, inexpert, inept, bungling, botched, awkward, maladroit, clumsy, gauche, floundering.

incomplete adj **1** *an incomplete task* unfinished, unaccomplished, partial, undone, unexecuted, unperformed, undeveloped. **2** *an incomplete set of books* deficient, lacking, wanting, defective, imperfect, not entire, not total, broken. **3** *an incomplete text* deficient, shortened, curtailed, abridged, expurgated, bowdlerized.

incomprehensible adj **1** *incomprehensible writing* illegible, unintelligible, indecipherable, unreadable. **2** *an incomprehensible theory* unintelligible, inapprehensible, too difficult, too hard, complicated, complex, involved, intricate; *inf* over one's head, tough. **3** *his motives are incomprehensible* beyond comprehension, unfathomable, impenetrable, profound, deep, inexplicable, puzzling, enigmatic, mysterious, abstruse, recondite.

inconceivable adj unimaginable, unthinkable, incomprehensible, incredible, unbelievable, implausible, impossible, out of the question, preposterous, ridiculous, ludicrous.

inconclusive adj indefinite, indecisive, indeterminate, undetermined, still open to question, open to doubt, vague, unestab-

lished, unsettled, ambiguous; *inf* up in the air.

incongruity n incompatibility, inconsistency, inappropriateness, unsuitability, inaptness, inharmoniousness, discordancy, disparity, discrepancy.

incongruous adj **1** *behaviour incongruous with his principles* incompatible with, inconsistent with, out of keeping/place with, differing from, contrary to, inappropriate to, unsuited to, at odds with, in opposition to, diametrically opposed to, conflicting with, irreconcilable with. **2** *modern furniture seeming incongruous in the old-fashioned setting* out of place/keeping, strange, odd, absurd, unsuitable, inappropriate, incompatible, inharmonious, discordant, clashing, jarring.

inconsequential adj *his influence is inconsequential* insignificant, negligible, inappreciable, unimportant, of minor importance, of little/no account, trivial, trifling, petty; *inf* piddling.

inconsiderable adj *a not inconsiderable sum of money* insignificant, negligible, trifling, petty, small, slight, niggling, minor, inappreciable; *inf* piddling.

inconsiderate adj thoughtless, unthinking, unthoughtful, uncaring, heedless, unmindful, regardless, undiscerning, insensitive, unsolicitous, tactless, uncharitable, unkind, unbenevolent, ungracious, selfish, self-centred, egotistic.

inconsistent adj **1** *actions inconsistent with his politics* incompatible with, out of keeping with, out of place with, differing from, contrary to, at odds with, at variance with, in opposition to, conflicting with, in conflict with, irreconcilable, discordant with, discrepant with. **2** *inconsistent character/actions* inconstant, unstable, unsteady, changeable, variable, erratic, irregular, unpredictable, capricious, fickle, whimsical, mercurial, volatile.

inconsolable adj grief-stricken, brokenhearted, heartbroken, sick at heart, bowed down, miserable, wretched, woebegone, disconsolate, desolate, despairing, forlorn, unhappy, sad, upset.

inconspicuous adj **1** *an inconspicuous house* unnoticeable, unobtrusive, indistinct, ordinary, plain, run-of-the-mill, unremarkable, undistinguished, unostentatious, unimposing, hidden, camouflaged. **2** *try to be as inconspicuous as possible* unnoticeable, unobtrusive, insignificant, unostentatious, quiet, retiring, in the background; *inf* lowkey.

inconstant adj **1** *inconstant quantities* not constant, changeable, variable, mutable, unstable, unsteady, unsettled, unfixed. **2** *inconstant friends* changeable, fickle, capricious, volatile, mercurial, faithless, unfaithful.

incontestable adj indisputable, incontrovertible, undeniable, irrefutable, unquestionable, beyond dispute/question/doubt, indubitable, unshakable, beyond a shadow of a doubt, conclusive, decisive, definite, established, sure, certain, positive.

incontinent adj **1** *incontinent desires* unrestrained, unbridled, unchecked, uncurbed, ungoverned, uncontrolled, uncontrollable. **2** *incontinent young men* licentious, lascivious, lustful, lecherous, lewd, libidinous, promiscuous, randy, debauched, dissolute, dissipated, loose, degenerate, wanton. **3** *incontinent old people* lacking bladder/bowel control.

incontrovertible adj incontestable, indisputable, undeniable, irrefutable, unquestionable, beyond question/doubt, indubitable, conclusive, decisive, positive. *see* INCONTESTABLE.

inconvenience n **1** *not wishing to cause you any inconvenience* trouble, bother, disruption, disturbance, vexation, worry, annoyance, disadvantage, difficulty, embarassment. **2** *their arrival was an inconvenience* trouble, bother, source of disruption/vexation/annoyance, nuisance, burden, hindrance; *inf* pain, drag, bore. **3** *the inconvenience of the furniture* awkwardness, unwieldiness, cumbersomeness, unhandiness.

inconvenience v disturb, bother, trouble, worry, disrupt, put out, impose upon, burden, distract, annoy, discommode.

inconvenient adj **1** *call at an inconvenient time* awkward, unsuitable, inappropriate, inopportune, inexpedient, disadvantageous, disturbing, troublesome, bothersome, tiresome, vexatious, annoying, embarrassing, ill-timed, untimely, unseasonable. **2** *an inconvenient size of wardrobe* awkward, unwieldy, cumbersome, unmanageable, unhandy, difficult.

incorporate v **1** *incorporate the various ingredients to form a whole* merge, coalesce, fuse, blend, mix, amalgamate, combine, unite, integrate, unify, compact. **2** *the document incorporates all our thoughts* embody, include, comprise, embrace, absorb, subsume, assimilate.

incorrect adj **1** *incorrect answers* not right, wrong, inaccurate, erroneous, wide of the mark. **2** *an incorrect account of what happened* not right, inaccurate, mistaken, faulty, inexact, untrue, fallacious, non-factual, flawed; *inf* full of holes. **3** *incorrect behaviour* improper, lacking in propriety, unbecoming, unseemly, indecorous, unsuitable, inappropriate, unladylike, ungentlemanly.

incorrigible adj *an incorrigible criminal* hardened, incurable, inveterate, unreformable, irreformable, unreformative, irredeemable, hopeless, beyond hope/redemption, impenitent, uncontrite, unrepentant.

incorruptible adj **1** *incorruptible members of society* virtuous, upright, high-principled, honourable, honest, moral, ethical, trustworthy, straight, unbribable, untemptable. **2** *incorruptible materials* imperishable, indestructible, non-biodegradable, not decaying, indissoluble, indissolvable, everlasting.

increase v **1** *demand has increased* grow, grow greater/larger/bigger, expand, extend, multiply, intensify, heighten, mount, escalate, snowball, mushroom, swell, wax. **2** *increase the demand* add to, boost, enhance, build up, augment, enlarge, expand, extend, spread, heighten, raise, intensify, strengthen, magnify, proliferate, inflate; *inf* step up.

increase n *the increase in size/demand* growth, rise, enlargement, expansion, extension, increment, addition, development, intensification, heightening, escalation, snowballing, mushrooming, boost, augmentation, strengthening, magnification, inflation; *inf* stepping-up, step-up. *see* INCREASE V.

increasingly adv *he is increasingly annoying* more and more, progressively.

incredible adj **1** *find his story incredible* unbelievable, hard to believe, beyond belief, far-fetched, inconceivable, unimaginable, unthinkable, impossible, implausible, highly unlikely, quite improbable, absurd, preposterous, questionable, dubious, doubtful, fictitious, mythical. **2** *an incredible athletic performance* extraordinary, supreme, great, wonderful, marvellous, tremendous, prodigious, astounding, amazing, astonishing, awe-inspiring, awesome, superhuman; *inf* magic, fab, fantastic.

incredulity n *view his story with incredulity* incredulousness, disbelief, unbelief, scepticism, distrust, mistrust, doubt, dubiousness, dubiety, suspicion.

incredulous adj *incredulous listeners to his tale* disbelieving, unbelieving, sceptical, cynical, distrusting, distrustful, mistrusting, mistrustful, doubtful, doubting, dubious, unconvinced, suspicious.

increment n **1** *an increment in salary* increase, gain, addition, augmentation, supplement, addendum, adjunct, accretion, accrual, accrument, profit. **2** *appalled by the increment in quantities/prices* enlargement, expansion, extension, escalation, mushrooming; *inf* step-up. *see* INCREASE n.

incriminate v charge, accuse, indict, impeach, arraign, blame, implicate, inculpate, involve, inform against, blacken the name of, stigmatize; *inf* point the finger at, stick/pin the blame on, grass on, rat on.

inculcate v *inculcate Latin into schoolchildren* instil, implant, fix, ingrain, infuse, imbue, impress, imprint, indoctrinate, teach, hammer, din.

inculpate v charge, accuse, indict, impeach, arraign, incriminate, blame. *see* INCRIMINATE.

incumbent adj **1** *incumbent on you to be present* binding, obligatory, mandatory, necessary, compulsory, compelling. **2** *the invalid incumbent on the couch* lying, reclining, reposing, resting, lounging.

incumbent n *the incumbent of the office* office-holder, official, functionary, occupier.

incur v *incur his wrath | incurred huge debts* bring upon oneself, expose oneself to, lay oneself open to, provoke, be liable/subject to, contract, meet with, experience.

incurable adj **1** *an incurable illness* beyond cure, cureless, unhealable, terminal, fatal, untreatable, inoperable, irremediable. **2** *an incurable romantic* inveterate, dyed in the wool, incorrigible, hopeless, beyond hope.

incursion n *the enemy's midnight incursion* raid, foray, sortie, attack, assault, onslaught, invasion, onset, sally.

indebted adj *indebted to you for your help* in someone's debt, beholden, under an obligation, obliged, obligated, grateful, thankful, appreciative.

indecency n **1** *the indecency of the remark* suggestiveness, indelicacy, improperness, impurity, risquéness, ribaldry, bawdiness, foulness, vulgarity, grossness, crudity, dirtiness, smuttiness, smut, coarseness, obscenity, blueness, lewdness. *see* INDECENT 1. **2** *the indecency of the haste* impropriety, unseemliness, indecorum, indecorousness, unsuitableness, inappropriateness, bad taste, tastelessness, unacceptability, offensiveness. *see* INDECENT 2.

indecent adj **1** *an indecent suggestion/joke* suggestive, indelicate, improper, impure, risqué, off-colour, ribald, bawdy, foul, vulgar, gross, crude, dirty, smutty, coarse, obscene, blue, lewd, lascivious, licentious, salacious, pornographic, scatalogical; *inf* raunchy. **2** *marry with indecent haste after the funeral* improper, unseemly, indecorous, unbecoming, unsuitable, inappropriate, unfitting, unbefitting, in bad taste, tasteless, unacceptable, offensive, outrageous.

indecipherable adj illegible, unreadable, unclear, indistinct, unintelligible, cramped, crabbed.

indecision n *his indecision lost him the job* indecisiveness, irresolution, irresoluteness, vacillation, fluctuation, hesitancy, hesitation, tentativeness, ambivalence, doubt, shilly-shallying, uncertainty. *see* INDECISIVE 1.

indecisive adj **1** *an indecisive person* irresolute, vacillating, wavering, fluctuating, hesitant, tentative, faltering, ambivalent, doubtful, in two minds, shilly-shallying, undecided, indefinite, uncertain, unresolved, undetermined, sitting on the fence; *inf* blowing hot and cold. **2** *an indecisive ballot* inconclusive, open, indeterminate, undecided, unsettled, indefinite, unclear; *inf* up in the air.

indecorous adj unbecoming, unseemly, improper, unsuitable, inappropriate, impolite, unladylike, ungentlemanly, ill-bred, ill-mannered, in bad taste, crude.

indecorum n unbecomingness, unseemliness, impropriety, improperness, unsuitability, inappropriateness, impoliteness, bad taste, crudeness. *see* INDECOROUS.

indeed adv **1** *he is indeed her brother* in fact, in point of fact, in truth, truly, actually, really, in reality, certainly, surely, for sure, to be sure, positively, absolutely, doubtlessly, undoubtedly, without doubt, undeniably, veritably. **2** *indeed I shall come | very pleased indeed* yes, certainly, emphatically.

indefatigable adj *indefatigable workers* tireless, untiring, never-tiring, unwearied, unflagging, persistent, tenacious, dogged, assiduous, industrious, indomitable, relentless, unremitting.

indefensible adj **1** *indefensible behaviour* inexcusable, unjustifiable, unpardonable, unforgivable, inexpiable. **2** *an indefensible theory* untenable, unarguable, insupportable, unmaintainable, unwarrantable, flawed, faulty, specious, implausible. **3** *indefensible buildings* defenceless, vulnerable, exposed, pregnable, unfortified, unguarded, unprotected, unshielded, unarmed.

indefinable adj *an indefinable atmosphere in the room* indescribable, inexpressible, nameless, obscure, unanalysable.

indefinite adj **1** *the venue for the meeting is as yet indefinite* undecided, unfixed, undetermined, unsettled, inconclusive, undefined, unknown, uncertain, unspecific, unexplicit, imprecise, inexact, vague, doubtful. **2** *an indefinite shape in the distance* ill-defined, indistinct, blurred, fuzzy, hazy, dim, vague, obscure. **3** *an indefinite answer* vague, unclear, imprecise, inexact, ambiguous, ambivalent, equivocal, confused, evasive, abstruse. **4** *she's a bit indefinite about whether she's going or not* undecided, indecisive, irresolute, vacillating, wavering, hesitant, tentative, uncertain. *see* INDECISIVE 1. **5** *an indefinite number/amount* indeterminate, unspecified, unlimited, limitless, infinite, immeasurable, boundless.

indefinitely adv *suspended indefinitely* for an unspecified time/period, for an unlimited time/period, without a fixed limit, *sine die*.

indelible adj *indelible marks/memories* inerasable, ineradicable, unobliterable, ineffaceable, unexpungeable, indestructible, permanent, lasting, enduring, inextirpable, ingrained, unfading, imperishable.

indelicate adj **1** *indelicate manners/behaviour* vulgar, coarse, rough, unrefined, uncultivated, tasteless, unmannerly, unseemly, unbecoming, indecorous, immodest, boorish, churlish, loutish, offensive. **2** *indelicate jokes* indecent, impure, risqué, ribald, bawdy, vulgar, gross, crude, dirty, smutty, obscene, blue, lewd. *see* INDECENT 1.

indemnify v **1** *indemnify them for their loss* reimburse, compensate, make restitution/amends to, recompense, repay, pay, pay back, remunerate. **2** *indemnify travellers against transport problems* insure, underwrite, guarantee, protect, secure, make secure, give security to, endorse.

indemnity n **1** *receive indemnity for losses sustained* reimbursement, compensation, restitution, reparation, redress, requital, atonement, payment, repayment, remuneration, recompense; amends. **2** *take out indemnity against lost luggage* insurance, assurance, protection, security, endorsement; guarantee, safeguard. **3** *receive diplomatic indemnity for his crimes* legal exemption, immunity, diplomatic immunity, privilege, prerogative, impunity.

indent[1] v *indent for a new uniform* ask for, request, order, requisition.

indent[2] v **1** *the sea had indented the coastline* notch, nick, make notches/nicks in, scallop, serrate, pink. **2** *indent the line* move right, move further from the margin/edge.

indenture n contract, written agreement, compact, covenant, certificate, deed, document, lease, warranty, bond, written commitment.

independence n **1** *states seeking independence* self-government, self-rule, home rule, self-legislation, self-determination, sovereignty, autonomy, freedom, non-alignment, separation, autarchy. **2** *financial independence* self-sufficiency, self-reliance. **3** *independence of spirit* individualism, boldness, liberation, unconstraint, unrestraint, lack of constraint/restraint. *see* INDEPENDENT 5.

independent adj **1** *an independent state* self-governing, self-ruling, self-legislating, self-determining, sovereign, autonomous, autonomic, free, absolute, non-aligned, autarchic. **2** *two independent units making up the desk* separate, individual, free-standing, self-contained. **3** *the two firms are quite independent of each other* separate, unconnected, unrelated, unattached, distinct, individual. **4** *independent people not requiring financial help* self-sufficient, self-supporting, self-reliant; *inf* standing on one's own feet. **5** *an independent spirit* free-thinking, individualistic, unconventional, bold, liberated, unconstrained, unrestrained, unfettered, untrammelled.

indescribable adj undescribable, inexpressible, undefinable, beyond words/description, surpassing/beggaring description, incommunicable, ineffable, unutterable, incredible, extraordinary, remarkable, prodigious.

indestructible adj durable, enduring, unbreakable, infrangible, imperishable, inextinguishable, undecaying, perennial, deathless, undying, immortal, endless, everlasting.

indeterminate adj **1** *an indeterminate number of people are expected* undetermined, unfixed, indefinite, unspecified, unstipulated, unknown, uncertain, unpredictable, uncounted, uncalculated. **2** *an indeterminate reply* vague, hazy, unclear, obscure, ambiguous, ambivalent, equivocal, inconclusive, inexact, imprecise, inexplicit, ill-defined.

index n **1** *an index to the information* guide, key, directory, catalogue; table of contents, thumb index, card index. **2** *his untidy appearance was an index to his disorderly mind* mark, token, sign, symptom, indication, clue, hint. **3** *the index on the compass* pointer, indicator, needle, hand. **4** *injure his index* index finger, forefinger, first finger.

indicate v **1** *his lack of concentration indicates his distress* point to, show, evince, manifest, reveal, be a sign/symptom of, be symptomatic of, mark, signal, denote, bespeak, betoken, connote, suggest, imply. **2** *he indicated the right direction* point to/out, designate, specify. **3** *he indicated his displeasure* show, demonstrate, exhibit, display, manifest, evince, express, make known, tell, state, reveal, disclose, register, record.

indication n **1** *his tiredness is an indication of his overwork* sign, symptom, mark, manifestation, signal, omen, augury, portent, warning, hint. **2** *the indication of the right direction* pointing out, designation, specification. **3** *he frowned as an indication of his displeasure* show, demonstration, exhibition, display, manifestation, evincement, revelation, disclosure, register, record.

indicative adj *his behaviour is indicative of his attitude* indicatory, demonstrative, suggestive, symptomatic, typical, characteristic, symbolic, emblematic. see INDICATE 1.

indicator n **1** *the indicator on the dial* pointer, needle, marker, index. **2** *a temperature indicator* gauge, meter, display. **3** *an economic indicator* index, guide, mark, sign, signal, signpost, symbol.

indict v accuse, charge, arraign, impeach, prosecute, bring to trial, put on trial, cite, summons, incriminate, inculpate.

indictment n accusation, charge, arraignment, impeachment, prosecution, citation, summons, incrimination, inculpation.

indifference n **1** *the indifference of the spectators* apathy, lack of concern, unconcernedness, heedlessness, disregard, lack of interest, aloofness, detachment, coldness, coolness, impassivity, lack of passion/emotion/feeling. see INDIFFERENT 1. **2** *the indifference of the players* mediocrity, adequacy, averageness, ordinariness, lack of distinction. see INDIFFERENT 2. **3** *the indifference of the issues* unimportance, insignificance, inconsequence, triviality, slightness, pettiness, irrelevance. see INDIFFERENT 3. **4** *the indifference of the judges* impartiality, disinterest, lack/absence of bias, non-partisanship, neutrality, objectivity, dispassionateness, dispassion, detachment, justness, justice, equitability, even-handedness, fairness, fair-mindedness.

indifferent adj **1** *totally indifferent spectators | kidnappers totally indifferent to the pain of their victims* apathetic, unconcerned, careless, heedless, regardless, uncaring, uninterested, unimpressed, aloof, detached, dis-

tant, cold, cool, impassive, dispassionate, unresponsive, passionless, unemotional, emotionless, unmoved, unexcited, unfeeling, unsympathetic, uncompassionate, callous. **2** *an indifferent player* mediocre, middling, moderate, medium, fair, not bad, passable, adequate, barely adequate, average, ordinary, commonplace, undistinguished, uninspired; *inf* OK, so-so. **3** *an indifferent issue* unimportant, insignificant, inconsequential, of no importance/consequence, minor, trivial, trifling, slight, of no matter, petty, irrelevant, immaterial. **4** *an indifferent judge* impartial, disinterested, unbiased, non-discriminatory, neutral, unprejudiced, non-partisan, uninvolved, objective, dispassionate, detached, just, equitable, even-handed, fair, fair-minded.

indigenous adj native, original, aboriginal, autochthonous, autochthonal.

indigent adj poverty-stricken, impoverished, penniless, penurious, impecunious, poor, beggared, destitute, in want, in need, needy, in distress, in financial/dire straits, down and out; *inf* broke, stony broke, hard up, on one's uppers, strapped for cash, skint.

indigestion n dyspepsia, dyspepsy, hyperacidity, acidity, heartburn, waterbrash, pyrosis; upset stomach, gastric upset.

indignant adj angry, angered, irate, incensed, furious, infuriated, annoyed, wrathful, enraged, exasperated, heated, riled, in a temper, in high dudgeon, provoked, piqued, disgruntled, in a huff; *inf* fuming, livid, aggravated, mad, seeing red, up in arms, peeved, huffy, miffed, narked.

indignation n anger, fury, rage, wrath, exasperation, pique, disgruntlement, umbrage, offence, resentment, ire. see INDIGNANT.

indignity n affront, insult, abuse, mistreatment, injury, offence, outrage, slight, snub; humiliation, aspersion, disrespect, discourtesy, dishonour, obloquy; *inf* slap in the face.

indirect adj **1** *an indirect route* roundabout, circuitous, deviant, divergent, wandering, meandering, winding, curving, tortuous, zigzag. **2** *an indirect way of giving the news* oblique, discursive, digressive, long-drawn-out, rambling, circumlocutory, periphrastic, allusive. **3** *an indirect insult* backhanded, left-handed, devious, insidious, deceitful, underhand, surreptitious; *inf* sneaky. **4** *an indirect result of the talks* incidental, accidental, unintended, secondary, subordinate, ancillary, collateral, contingent.

indirectly adv **1** *hear the information indirectly* second-hand, in a roundabout way. **2** *tell them the news indirectly* by implication, obliquely, circumlocutorily, periphrastically.

indiscernible adj **1** *an indiscernible difference in attitude* imperceptible, unperceivable, unnoticeable, unapparent, hidden, indistinguishable, inappreciable, impalpable, subtle, minute, minuscule, microscopic. **2** *indiscernible to the naked eye* invisible, imperceivable, undetectable, indistinct, indefinite, obscure, shadowy, unclear, dim.

indiscreet adj **1** *an indiscreet course of action | an indiscreet remark* unwise, imprudent, injudicious, impolitic, ill-advised, ill-considered, ill-thought-out, ill-judged, ill-gauged, foolish, incautious, careless, unwary, hasty, rash, reckless, impulsive, precipitate, foolhardy, tactless, untactful, insensitive, undiplomatic. **2** *indiscreet behaviour* immodest, indelicate, indecorous, unseemly, indecent, shameless, brazen, bold.

indiscretion n **1** *guilty of indiscretion* imprudence, injudiciousness, foolishness, folly, lack of caution, carelessness, hastiness, rashness, tactlessness, lack of diplomacy. *see* INDISCREET 1. **2** *embarrassed by her indiscretions* gaffe, *faux pas*, breach of etiquette, slip, blunder, lapse, mistake, error; *inf* slip-up, bloomer. **3** *the indiscretion of her behaviour* immodesty, indelicacy, indecorum, indecorousness, unseemliness, indecency, shamelessness, brazenness, boldness.

indiscriminate adj **1** *indiscriminate reading habits | indiscriminate choice of clothes* undiscriminating, unselective, unparticular, uncritical, undifferentiating, aimless, careless, haphazard, random, unsystematic, unmethodical, broad-based, wholesale, general, sweeping; *inf* hit-or-miss. **2** *an indiscriminate collection of furniture* jumbled, mixed, haphazard, motley, miscellaneous, diverse, varied, mongrel, confused, chaotic, thrown together; *inf* higgledy-piggledy.

indispensable adj essential, of the essence, vital, crucial, imperative, key, necessary, requisite, required, needed, needful, important, of the utmost importance, urgent, pressing, high-priority, fundamental.

indisposed adj **1** *indisposed and so unable to be present* ill, unwell, sick, ailing, confined to bed, incapacitated; *inf* on the sick list, under the weather, poorly, out of sorts/ commission, laid up. **2** *indisposed to believe him* unwilling, disinclined, reluctant, hesitant, loath, averse, not in favour of.

indisposition n **1** *absent owing to indisposition* illness, sickness, ill health; ailment, complaint, disorder, malady, disease. **2** *his indisposition towards modernizing the factory* unwillingness, disinclination, reluctance, hesitation, hesitancy, loathness, aversion, dislike, distaste.

indisputable adj incontestable, incontrovertible, undeniable, irrefutable, unquestionable, indubitable, beyond dispute/ question/doubt, beyond the shadow of a doubt, unassailable, certain, sure, positive, definite, absolute, final, conclusive.

indistinct adj **1** *indistinct figures in the distance* blurred, fuzzy, out of focus, bleary, hazy, misty, shadowy, dim, obscure, indefinite, indistinguishable, barely perceptible, undefined. **2** *indistinct writing* undecipherable, illegible, unreadable, unintelligible, pale, faded. **3** *indistinct noises* muffled, low, muted, muttered, mumbled.

indistinguishable adj **1** *the twins/views are indistinguishable* identical, alike, very similar; *inf* as like as two peas in a pod. **2** *his identity was indistinguishable in the dark* indiscernible, imperceptible, hard to make out, indefinite, unnoticeable, obscure, camouflaged, invisible.

individual adj **1** *each individual flower/house* single, separate, sole, lone, solitary, distinct, distinctive, particular, specific, peculiar, detached, isolated. **2** *an individual style* characteristic, distinctive, particular, peculiar, typical, personal, personalized, own, private, special, especial, singular, original, unique, exclusive, idiosyncratic.

individual n **1** *several individuals arrived late | a most unpleasant individual* person, personage, human being, creature, mortal, living soul, body, character, type. **2** *she's very much an individual* individualist, free spirit, nonconformist, original, eccentric, bohemian, maverick, egocentric, *rara avis*, rare bird, rarity, loner, lone wolf.

individualist n individual, free spirit, nonconformist, eccentric, egocentric. *see* INDIVIDUAL n 2.

individualistic adj *an individualistic way of dealing with things* free-thinking, independent, nonconformist, unorthodox, unconventional, original, eccentric, bohemian, maverick, strange, odd, egocentric.

individuality n *works of individuality* distinctiveness, distinction, originality, uniqueness, singularity, peculiarity, personality, character.

individually adv *tutor each student individually* one at a time, one by one, singly, separately, independently, apart; personally; *lit* severally.

indoctrinate v *indoctrinate the pupils with his political ideas* instruct, teach, drill, ground, initiate, inculcate, impress on, instil in, imbue, impregnate, brainwash, propagandize, proselytize.

indolent adj lazy, idle, slothful, do-nothing, sluggish, lethargic, slow, slow-moving, slack, shiftless, languid, lackadaisical, apathetic, listless, impassive, inactive, inert, torpid, fainéant.

indomitable adj invincible, unconquerable, undefeatable, unbeatable, unassailable, impregnable, unyielding, unsubmissive, stalwart, stout-hearted, lion-hearted, staunch, resolute, firm, steadfast, determined, intransigent, inflexible, adamant, unflinching, courageous, brave, valiant, heroic, intrepid, fearless.

indubitable adj beyond doubt, beyond the shadow of a doubt, indisputable, unarguable, beyond dispute/question, unquestionable, undeniable, irrefutable, incontestable, incontrovertible, certain, sure, positive, definite, absolute, conclusive.

induce v **1** *induce them to go* persuade, talk into, get, prevail upon, prompt, move, inspire, instigate, influence, exert influence on, press, urge, incite, encourage, impel, actuate, motivate, inveigle, coax, wheedle. **2** *induce a reaction* bring about, bring on, cause, produce, effect, create, give rise to, generate, originate, engender, occasion, set in motion, develop, lead to.

inducement n **1** *offer a salary increase as an inducement* incentive, attraction, encouragement, bait, lure, reward, incitement, stimulus, spur, goad, impetus, motive, provocation; *inf* carrot, come-on. **2** *gave in to their inducement to go* persuasion, prompting, urging, incitement, encouragement, inveigling. *see* INDUCE 1.

indulge v **1** *indulge one's appetites* give way to, yield to, pander to, cater to, satisfy, gratify, fulfil, satiate, appease. **2** *indulge in a bout of self-pity* give oneself up to, give rein to, give free rein to, wallow in, luxuriate in, revel in. **3** *indulge the child* pamper, spoil, coddle, mollycoddle, cosset, pander to, humour, go along with, baby, pet. **indulge oneself** treat oneself, give oneself a treat, splurge; *inf* have a spree, paint the town red, go on the town.

indulgence n **1** *the indulgence of one's appetites* satisfaction, gratification, fulfilment, satiation, appeasement. **2** *lead a life of indulgence* self-gratification, dissipation, dissoluteness, intemperance, immoderation, immoderateness, debauchery, excess, lack of restraint, unrestraint, prodigality, extravagance. **3** *travelling is his only indulgence* extravagance, luxury, treat. **4** *I was allowed the indulgence of going on board ship* privilege, courtesy, favour, treat. **5** *treat the prisoners with indulgence* tolerance, forbearance, compassion, humanity, kindness, understanding, sympathy, liberalness, liberality, forgiveness, leniency, mercy, clemency. **6** *dislike indulgence of the children* pampering, spoiling, coddling, mollycoddling, cosseting, humouring, partiality. *see* INDULGE 3.

indulgent adj **1** *indulgent judges* tolerant, forbearing, compassionate, humane, kind, kindly, understanding, sympathetic, liberal, forgiving, lenient, merciful, clement. **2** *indulgent parents* permissive, easygoing, compliant, fond, doting, pampering, spoiling, mollycoddling, cosseting, humouring.

industrial adj manufacturing.

industrialist n manufacturer, producer, captain of industry, magnate, tycoon, business/manufacturing baron, capitalist, financier.

industrious adj hard-working, diligent, assiduous, sedulous, conscientious, steady, laborious, busy, busy as a bee, active, bustling, energetic, on the go, vigorous, determined, dynamic, indefatigable, tireless, persistent, pertinacious, zealous, productive.

industry n **1** *involved in heavy industry* manufacturing, production, fabrication, construction. **2** *employed in the publishing industry* business, trade, commercial enterprise, field, line, craft, métier. **3** *work with industry* industriousness, diligence, assiduity, application, sedulousness, sedulity, conscientiousness, concentration, intentness, steadiness, laboriousness, busyness, activity, energy, vigour, effort, determination, dynamism, tirelessness, persistence, pertinacity, zeal, productiveness.

inebriated adj intoxicated, inebriate, drunk, drunken, blind drunk, drunk as a lord, the worse for drink, in one's cups, tipsy, merry, befuddled; *inf* tight, one over the eight, under the influence, half-cut, half-seas-over, three sheets to the wind, plastered, stoned, loaded, blotto, pickled, paralytic, out of it, under the table, legless, pie-eyed, smashed, sloshed, well-oiled, well-lubricated, stewed to the gills, tanked up, bevvied, pissed, pissed as a newt; *Scots* stotious, fou.

inedible adj unedible, uneatable, not fit to eat, unconsumable, unwholesome, off, rotten, bad, putrid, poisonous.

ineffable adj 1 *ineffable joy/cheek* inexpressible, unutterable, beyond words, indescribable, undefinable. 2 *the ineffable name of Jehovah* not to be uttered, unutterable, not to be spoken, unmentionable, taboo.

ineffective adj 1 *ineffective attempts to hold back the water* ineffectual, vain, to no avail, unavailing, useless, worthless, unsuccessful, futile, fruitless, unproductive, profitless, abortive, inadequate, inefficient, inefficacious, powerless, impotent, idle, feeble, weak, incompetent, inept, lame, barren, sterile. 2 *ineffective people* ineffectual, unproductive, inadequate, inefficient, inefficacious, powerless, impotent, incompetent, inept, feeble, weak.

ineffectual adj 1 *ineffectual efforts* ineffective, vain, unavailing, useless, worthless, futile, fruitless, unproductive, abortive, inadequate, inefficient, inefficacious, lame, inept. *see* INEFFECTIVE 1. 2 *ineffectual people* ineffective, inadequate, inefficient, inefficacious, powerless, impotent, inept. *see* INEFFECTIVE 2.

inefficient adj 1 *inefficient people* ineffective, badly organized, disorganized, incompetent, inept, incapable, unprepared, ineffectual, inefficacious. 2 *an inefficient method of procedure* incompetent, unskilful, inexpert, wasteful, uneconomical, negligent, lax, slipshod, sloppy, slack.

inelegant adj 1 *inelegant manners* unrefined, uncultured, uncultivated, unpolished, unsophisticated, unfinished, gauche, crude, uncouth, ill-bred, coarse, vulgar. 2 *sit in an inelegant position* awkward, clumsy, ungainly, ungraceful, graceless.

ineligible adj 1 *ineligible candidates* unqualified, unfitted, unfit, unequipped, unsuitable, unacceptable, undesirable, ruled out, legally disqualified; *Law* incompetent. 2 *ineligible suitors* unmarriageable, unsuitable, undesirable, unacceptable.

inept adj 1 *an inept tradesman* incompetent, unadept, incapable, unskilful, unskilled, inexpert, clumsy, awkward, maladroit, undexterous, heavy-handed; *inf* cack-handed. 2 *an inept attempt* incompetent, unadept, unskilful, inadequate, bungling, awkward, maladroit, unproductive, unsuccessful, ineffectual; *inf* cack-handed. 3 *an inept remark in the circumstances* out of place, badly timed, inapt, inappropriate, unsuitable, infelicitous. 4 *always doing inept things* absurd, foolish, silly, stupid, inane, non-

sensical, senseless, farcical, ridiculous, ludicrous, asinine, crazy; *inf* screwy.

inequality n 1 *inequality of salaries/opportunity* unequalness, disparity, imparity, imbalance, lack of balance, unevenness, disproportion, discrepancy, nonconformity, variation, variability, difference, dissimilarity, contrast. 2 *treat women with inequality* bias, prejudice, discrimination, preferentiality. 3 *the inequality of the surface* unevenness, irregularity, roughness.

inequitable adj unjust, unfair, partial, prejudiced, biased, partisan, discriminatory, preferential, one-sided, intolerant, bigoted.

inequity n *the inequity of the sentence/treatment* unfairness, injustice, unjustness, partisanship, partiality, bias, preferentialism, discrimination.

inert adj 1 *inert bodies lying around* inactive, unmoving, motionless, immobile, still, stock-still, stationary, static, lifeless, inanimate, unconscious, passive, out cold, comatose, dormant, dead. 2 *inert members of the company* inactive, idle, indolent, slack, lazy, slothful, dull, sluggish, lethargic, stagnant, languid, lackadaisical, listless, torpid, otiose, fainéant.

inertia n inertness, inactivity, inaction, inactiveness, motionlessness, immobility, unemployment, stagnation, stasis, passivity, idleness, indolence, laziness, sloth, slothfulness, dullness, sluggishness, lethargy, languor, listlessness, torpor, fainéance.

inescapable adj unavoidable, inevitable, unpreventable, inexorable, assured, certain, bound/sure to happen, ineludible, ineluctable.

inestimable adj *of inestimable value* immeasurable, measureless, incalculable, priceless, beyond price, precious, invaluable, worth its weight in gold, worth a king's ransom, unparalleled, supreme, superlative.

inevitable adj unavoidable, unpreventable, inexorable, inescapable, fixed, settled, irrevocable, fated, destined, predestined, ordained, decreed, out of one's hands, assured, certain, sure, bound/sure to happen, for sure, necessary, ineluctable.

inexact adj not accurate, not exact, imprecise, approximate, incorrect, erroneous, wrong, false, fallacious, wide of the mark.

inexcusable adj unexcusable, unpardonable, unforgivable, unatonable, inexpiable, unjustifiable, unwarrantable, indefensible, blameworthy, censurable, reprehensible, outrageous.

inexhaustible adj **1** *a seemingly inexhaustible supply of ammunition* unlimited, limitless, illimitable, infinite, boundless, endless, never-ending, unrestricted, bottomless, measureless, copious, abundant. **2** *inexhaustible workers* indefatigable, tireless, untiring, unwearying, weariless, unfaltering, unfailing, unflagging, unwavering, unremitting, persevering, persistent, dogged.

inexorable adj **1** *the inexorable march of progress* relentless, unavoidable, inescapable, inevitable, unpreventable, irrevocable, fated, destined, certain. *see* INEVITABLE. **2** *inexorable tyrants* adamant, obdurate, unbending, unyielding, immovable, intransigent, implacable, unappeasable, unforgiving, uncompromising, inflexible, strict, severe, iron-handed, stringent, harsh, exacting, rigorous, Draconian, cruel, ruthless, relentless, pitiless, merciless, remorseless.

inexpedient adj impolitic, ill-advised, unadvisable, injudicious, ill-judged, unwise, imprudent, ill-considered, thoughtless, wrong-headed, foolish, detrimental, harmful.

inexpensive adj low-cost, low-price, low-priced, reasonably priced, reasonable, economical, cheap, budget, reduced, sale-price, half-price, marked-down, discount, discounted, cut-rate, bargain, bargain-basement.

inexperienced adj lacking experience, untrained, untutored, undrilled, unqualified, unpractised, amateur, unskilled, uninitiated, uninformed, ignorant, unacquainted, unversed, naïve, unsophisticated, unfledged, untried, unseasoned, new, callow, immature, fresh, green, raw; *inf* wet behind the ears.

inexpert adj unskilled, unskilful, amateur, amateurish, unprofessional, untrained, unpractised, unqualified, incompetent, maladroit, inept, clumsy, awkward, bungling, bumbling, blundering; *inf* cackhanded.

inexplicable adj unexplainable, inexplainable, unaccountable, incomprehensible, beyond comprehension/understanding, unintelligible, unfathomable, baffling, puzzling, perplexing, mystifying, insoluble, bewildering, mysterious, strange, weird, abstruse, enigmatic, inscrutable.

inexpressible adj indescribable, undescribable, beyond words/description, unutterable, undefinable, unspeakable, incommunicable, ineffable.

inexpressive adj expressionless, blank, vacant, empty, deadpan, dead, lifeless, poker-faced, inscrutable, emotionless, impassive, inanimate, bland, cold, stony.

inextinguishable adj unquenchable, ever-burning, unsuppressible, irrepressible, indestructible, imperishable, undying, enduring, lasting, eternal.

inextricable adj **1** *an inextricable situation* inescapable. **2** *the two family histories are inextricable* entangled, tangled, ravelled, inseparable, mixed up, confused. **3** *an inextricable problem* complicated, knotty, convoluted, intricate, involved, complex, perplexing, puzzling, baffling, labyrinthine, mazelike.

infallible adj **1** *an infallible remedy* unfailing, without failure, foolproof, dependable, trustworthy, reliable, sure, certain; *inf* sure-fire. **2** *an infallible memory* error-free, unerring, unfailing, faultless, flawless, impeccable, unimpeachable, perfect.

infamous adj **1** *an infamous robber* notorious, disreputable, ill-famed, of ill-repute, iniquitous, ignominious, dishonourable, discreditable, villainous, bad, wicked, vile, odious, nefarious. **2** *guilty of infamous conduct* abominable, outrageous, shocking, monstrous, disgraceful, dishonourable, shameful, atrocious, heinous, detestable, loathsome, hateful, wicked, vile, base, iniquitous, criminal, odious, nefarious, scandalous, egregious, flagitious.

infancy n **1** *die in infancy* babyhood, early childhood. **2** *the infancy of space science* start, commencement, beginning, origin, rise, emergence, outset, onset, dawn, birth, cradle, conception, genesis; beginnings, early stages.

infant n **1** *die when an infant* babe, baby, little child, tot, little one, neonate; *Scots* bairn, wean. **2** *an infant in the publishing industry* beginner, novice, newcomer, learner, apprentice, trainee, new recruit, tiro, new boy/girl, initiate, novitiate, neophyte, *ingénue*, innocent, child, mere child, babe in arms; *inf* greenhorn, rookie, fresher.

infant adj *an infant industry* emergent, developing, dawning, nascent.

infantile adj babyish, childish, puerile, immature, juvenile.

infantry n infantrymen, foot soldiers, ranks; rank and file, cannon fodder; *inf* Tommies; *Amer* GIs.

infatuated adj *they're infatuated | he's infatuated with her* in love, head over heels in love, hopelessly in love; enamoured, besotted, captivated, bewitched, beguiled, spellbound, fascinated, enraptured, carried away, obsessed, swept off one's feet; taken with, under the spell of; *inf* smitten, sweet on, keen on, mad about, wild about, crazy about, nuts about, stuck on, turned on by.

infatuation n passing fancy, fancy, passion, obsession, fixation, craze, mania; *inf* puppy/calf love, crush, thing, hang-up, pash.

infect v 1 *infect the wound* cause infection/disease in, make septic, contaminate, poison, ulcerate. 2 *infect the others with the germs* pass/transmit infection to, pass on to, spread to. 3 *infect the air/water* contaminate, pollute, taint, make foul, blight, spoil, mar, impair. 4 *infect others with his wickedness* influence, corrupt, pervert, debauch, debase, degrade, vitiate. 5 *infect others with his enthusiasm/laughter* influence, affect, imbue, infuse, excite, inspire, stimulate, animate.

infection n 1 *an infection in the wound* septicity, septicaemia, contamination, poison, ulceration; germs, bacteria. 2 *the infection of the air/water* contamination, pollution, tainting, fouling, spoiling, blighting. *see* INFECT 3. 3 *catch an infection of the lungs* disease, disorder, virus, contagion; *inf* bug.

infectious adj 1 *an infectious disease* infective, communicable, transmittable, transmissible, catching, spreading; contagious. 2 *infectious material* germ-laden, contaminating, polluting, pestilential, septic, toxic, noxious, virulent, poisonous. 3 *her laughter/enthusiasm is infectious* catching, spreading, contagious, communicable, irresistible, compelling.

infer v 1 *from the evidence they inferred that he was guilty* deduce, reason, conclude, gather, understand, presume, conjecture, surmise, read between the lines, theorize, hypothesize; *inf* figure, suss, guesstimate. 2 *his conduct inferred a guilty conscience* indicate, point to, signal, signify, demonstrate, show, bespeak, evidence. 3 *she inferred in her speech that he was a coward* imply, insinuate, hint, suggest, intimate.

inference n 1 *dispute the inference from the evidence* deduction, conclusion, ratiocination, presumption, conjecture, surmise, reasoning, theorizing. *see* INFER 1. 2 *resent her inference that he was a coward* implication, insinuation, suggestion, intimation.

inferior adj 1 *in an inferior position* lower, lesser, subordinate, junior, secondary, subsidiary, ancillary, second-class, second-fiddle, minor, subservient, lowly, humble, servile, menial. 2 *inferior goods* imperfect,

faulty, defective, substandard, low-quality, low-grade, shoddy, cheap, reject, gimcrack; *inf* grotty. 3 *an inferior teacher* second-rate, indifferent, mediocre, incompetent, poor, bad, awful.

inferior n *despise his inferiors* subordinate, junior, underling, menial.

inferiority n 1 *the inferiority of the goods* imperfection, faultiness, deficiency, shoddiness, cheapness; *inf* grottiness. *see* INFERIOR adj 2. 2 *the inferiority of the teaching* second-rateness, indifference, mediocrity, incompetence, poorness. *see* INFERIOR adj 3. 3 *conscious of his inferiority* inferior status/position, lowliness, subordination, subservience.

infernal adj 1 *the infernal regions* lower, nether, hellish, Hadean, Plutonic, Plutonian, Stygian, Styxian, Acherontal, Tartarean, Avernal, chthonic. 2 *infernal wickedness/crimes* hellish, diabolical, devilish, demonic, demoniac, fiendish, satanic, malevolent, malicious, heinous, vile, atrocious, execrable, unspeakable, outrageous. 3 *the infernal car won't start* damned, damnable, accursed, cursed, pestilential, wretched.

infertile adj 1 *infertile soil* barren, unfruitful, unfructuous, sterile, unproductive, non-productive, arid. 2 *infertile women* barren, sterile, infecund, childless, unprolific.

infest v overrun, spread through, take over, overspread, pervade, permeate, penetrate, infiltrate, invade, swarm over, crawl over, beset, pester, plague.

infidel n unbeliever, disbeliever, heathen, heretic, pagan, agnostic, atheist, irreligionist.

infidelity n 1 *discovering the spouse's infidelity* unfaithfulness, adultery, cuckoldry; affair, liaison, intrigue, amour; *inf* fooling/playing around, cheating, hanky-panky. 2 *the servant's infidelity to his master* breach of trust, faithlessness, unfaithfulness, treachery, perfidy, perfidiousness, disloyalty, falseness, traitorousness, treason, double-dealing, duplicity.

infiltrate v 1 *water infiltrated the roof* pervade, penetrate, filter through, percolate, seep into/through, soak into. 2 *they infiltrated the enemy's meeting* slip into, sneak into, creep into, insinuate oneself into, worm one's way into, invade, intrude on.

infinite adj 1 *infinite space* boundless, unbounded, unlimited, limitless, without limit/end, extensive, vast. 2 *infinite numbers of insects* countless, without number, numberless, innumerable, immeasurable, incalculable, untold, uncountable, inestimable, indeterminable, vast, enormous, stupendous, prodigious. **3** *infinite depths* limitless, boundless, measureless, immeasurable, fathomless, bottomless. **4** *infinite patience* unlimited, boundless, endless, unending, no end of, never-ending, inexhaustible, interminable, absolute, total.

infinitesimal adj minute, tiny, microscopic, minuscule, very small, teeny, wee, Lilliputian, inappreciable, insignificant, inconsiderable, trifling; *inf* piddling.

infinity n *the infinity of space | stare into infinity* boundlessness, limitlessness, unlimitedness, endlessness, infinitude, infiniteness; infinite distance, space.

infirm adj **1** *infirm old people* feeble, enfeebled, weak, frail, debilitated, decrepit, disabled, in poor/declining health, failing, ailing, doddering, doddery, tottering, wobbly, lame, crippled. **2** *of infirm judgement* indecisive, irresolute, wavering, vacillating, fluctuating, faltering. **3** *infirm furniture* rickety, unsteady, shaky, wobbly, unsound, flimsy, tumble-down, jerry-built, on its last legs, decayed.

infirmity n **1** *suffering from an infirmity* ailment, illness, malady, disease, disorder, sickness. **2** *moral infirmities* fault, failing, defect, flaw, weakness, imperfection, foible. **3** *the infirmity of the old people* feebleness, weakness, frailty, debilitation, impairment, decrepitude, disability, dodderiness. *see* INFIRM 1. **4** *the infirmity of his judgement* indecision, irresoluteness, irresolution, vacillation. *see* INFIRM 2. **5** *the infirmity of the furniture* ricketiness, wobbliness, unsoundness, flimsiness. *see* INFIRM 3.

inflame v **1** *inflame the passions of the crowd* incite, excite, arouse, rouse, stir up, work up, whip up, agitate, fire, ignite, kindle, foment, impassion, provoke, stimulate, actuate. **2** *inflame the onlookers with his cruelty to the child* enrage, incense, infuriate, exasperate, anger, madden, provoke, rile. **3** *inflame the feud* aggravate, intensify, make worse, exacerbate, fan, fuel. **4** *her face inflamed with anger* redden, flush, suffuse, make glow, make hot.

inflamed adj **1** *an inflamed arm* red, hot, angry-looking, swollen, sore, infected, festered, septic. **2** *inflamed passions* excited, aroused, roused, stirred, kindled, impassioned. *see* INFLAME 1.

inflammable adj flammable, burnable, combustible, ignitable, ignitible, incendiary, deflagrable.

inflammation n *treat the inflammation on his leg* redness, hotness, heat, swelling, soreness, sore, painfulness, tenderness, infection, festering, eruption, suppuration, septicity.

inflammatory adj **1** *an inflammatory reaction to the drug* red, hot, swollen, sore, painful, tender, eruptive, allergic. *see* INFLAMMATION. **2** *an inflammatory speech* inflaming, inciting, arousing, rousing, stirring, fiery, passionate, impassioned, provocative, provoking, instigative, actuating, fomenting, rabble-rousing, demagogic, rebellious, revolutionary, insurgent, seditious, mutinous, anarchic. *see* INFLAME 1.

inflate v **1** *inflate the rubber dinghy | inflate one's cheeks* blow up, pump up, aerate, puff up, puff out, dilate, distend, swell. **2** *his cheeks inflated* puff up, puff out, dilate, distend, swell. **3** *every time he tells the story he inflates the element of danger* increase, extend, amplify, augment, expand, intensify, exaggerate. **4** *please do not inflate his self-importance* add to, boost, augment, intensify, magnify, escalate, aggrandize. **5** *inflate prices* increase, boost, raise, escalate, step up.

inflated adj **1** *inflated rubber toys* blown up, pumped up, dilated. **2** *inflated prices* increased, raised, escalated, stepped-up. **3** *an inflated sense of his own importance* exaggerated, magnified, aggrandized. **4** *inflated prose style* high-flown, extravagant, pretentious, pompous, rhetorical, grandiloquent, bombastic, orotund.

inflection n **1** *the inflection of the line* curving, curvature, bending, turning; curve, bend, turn, bow, crook, angle, arc, arch. **2** *the inflection of his voice* change of pitch/tone/timbre, flow, modulation, accentuation, emphasis, stress, cadence, rhythm. **3** *a language with inflections* conjugation, declension.

inflexible adj **1** *an inflexible substance* nonflexible, rigid, stiff, unbendable, unyielding, taut, hard, firm, inelastic, unmalleable. **2** *inflexible rules* unalterable, unchangeable, immutable, unvarying, firm, fixed, hard and fast, unbendable, uncompromising, stringent, rigorous, inexorable. **3** *inflexible people/attitudes* adamant, firm, immovable, unadaptable, dyed in the wool, unaccommodating, uncompliant, stubborn, obdurate, obstinate, intractable, unbending, intolerant, relentless, merciless, pitiless, uncompromising, inexorable, steely, iron-willed.

inflict v administer, deal out, mete out, serve out, deliver, apply, lay on, impose, levy, exact, wreak.

infliction n **1** *the infliction of punishment*
administering, administration, dealing out,
meting out, delivering, application, imposition, levying, exaction, wreaking. **2** *recover-*
ing from his infliction trouble, worry,
suffering, affliction, hurt, torture, torment,
tribulation, punishment, penalty.

influence n **1** *have a good/bad influence on*
them effect, impact; control, sway, ascendancy, power, mastery, agency, guidance,
domination, rule, supremacy, leadership,
direction, pressure. **2** *under the influence of*
drugs effect, control, hold, sway, power.
3 *he has influence on the board* power, authority, sway, prestige, standing, footing; good
offices, connections; *inf* clout, pull.

influence v **1** *his illness influenced his behav-*
iour affect, have an effect on, impact on,
sway, bias, incline, motivate, actuate,
determine, guide, control, change, alter,
transform. **2** *he tried to influence the jury*
affect, sway, bias, bring pressure to bear
on; *inf* pull strings with, pull rank on. **3** *he*
influenced her not to go persuade, induce,
impel, incite, manipulate, prompt.

influential adj **1** *an influential member of the*
board powerful, important, leading, authoritative, controlling, dominant, predominant, prestigious. **2** *money was an influential*
issue in his decision to go instrumental, guiding, significant, important, persuasive,
telling, meaningful.

influx n inrush, rush, inflow, inundation,
flood, invasion, intrusion, incursion,
ingress, convergence.

inform v **1** *inform him of the facts* tell, let
know, apprise, advise, notify, announce to,
impart to, relate to, communicate to,
acquaint, brief, instruct, enlighten, make
conversant, make knowledgeable, send
word to; *inf* put in the picture, fill in, clue
in/up, put wise, spill the beans to, tip off,
tip the wink to, give the low-down to, give
the inside story to. **2** *inform on his accom-*
plices betray, denounce, incriminate, inculpate, blab on; *inf* grass on, rat on, squeal
on, tell tales about, tell on, blow the whistle on, spill the beans about, put the finger
on, sell down the river, nark, snitch on,
peach; *Scots inf* clype on. **3** *optimism informs*
her writing characterize, typify, pervade,
permeate, suffuse, infuse, imbue, instil.
4 *her love of God informed her* inspire, animate, arouse, fire, kindle.

informal adj **1** *an informal party* | *informal*
dress non-formal, casual, unceremonious,
unofficial, simple, unpretentious, everyday,
relaxed, easy. **2** *informal language* colloquial, vernacular, non-literary, simple, natural, everyday, unofficial, unpretentious;
inf slangy.

informality n non-formality, casualness,
lack of ceremony, unceremoniousness,
unofficialness, simplicity, naturalness,
unpretentiousness, ease, relaxedness.

information n **1** *the information has been*
recorded data, facts. **2** *what information do*
you have? | *has she sent any information?*
knowledge, intelligence, news, notice,
word, advice, counsel, instruction, enlightenment; tidings; message, report, communiqué, communication; *inf* info, gen,
low-down, dope, inside story, bumf, dirt.

informative adj instructive, illuminating,
enlightening, edifying, educational, revealing, telling, communicative, chatty, newsy,
gossipy.

informed adj knowledgeable, well-briefed,
abreast of the facts, well-posted, primed,
well-versed, up-to-date, *au courant, au fait.*

informer n informant, betrayer, traitor,
Judas; *inf* grass, rat, squealer, snout, stool
pigeon, tell-tale, whistle-blower, canary,
nark, snitch, peacher; *Scots inf* clype.

infraction n breach, violation, transgression, contravention, infringement, intrusion, encroachment, invasion.

infrequent adj few and far between, rare,
occasional, sporadic, irregular, uncommon,
unusual, exceptional.

infringe v **1** *infringe the law* break, disobey,
violate, contravene, transgress, breach,
infract, disregard, take no notice of.
2 *infringe on his neighbour's land* encroach,
impinge, intrude, trespass.

infringement n **1** *an infringement of the rules*
breaking, violation, contravention, breach,
transgression, infraction, non-observance,
non-compliance. **2** *an infringement on his*
property encroachment, impingement,
intrusion, trespass.

infuriate v enrage, incense, inflame, madden, exasperate, anger, provoke, rile, make
one's blood boil, make one's hackles rise,
annoy, irritate, vex, pique; *inf* aggravate,
make one see red, get one's back up, get
one's goat, bug, get one.

infuriating adj maddening, exasperating,
provoking, annoying, irritating, vexing,
vexatious, galling; *inf* aggravating.

ingenious adj *an ingenious person* | *an ingen-*
ious course of action clever, shrewd, astute,
smart, sharp, bright, brilliant, talented,
masterly, resourceful, inventive, creative,
original, subtle, crafty, wily, cunning, skilful, adroit, deft, capable; *inf* on the ball.

ingenuous adj *too ingenuous to lie* open, sincere, honest, frank, candid, direct, forthright, artless, guileless, simple, naïve, innocent, genuine, undeceitful, undeceptive, undissembling, undissimulating, above-board, trustful, truthful, unsuspicious; *inf* on the level.

inglorious adj disgraceful, shameful, dishonourable, ignominious, discreditable, disreputable, humiliating, mortifying, unheroic, ignoble, blameworthy, culpable.

ingrained adj **1** *ingrained dirt* fixed, infixed, planted, implanted, rooted, deep-rooted, permanent, built-in. **2** *ingrained stupidity* inbred, inherent, intrinsic, hereditary, inherited, in the blood/family.

ingratiate v **ingratiate oneself** *ingratiate herself with the director* seek the favour of, curry favour with, toady to, crawl to, grovel to, fawn over, play up to, be a yes man/woman to, be a sycophant to; *inf* suck up to, rub up the right way, lick the boots of.

ingratiating adj sycophantic, toadying, fawning, unctuous, obsequious, servile, overhumble, crawling, flattering, wheedling, cajoling; *inf* bootlicking.

ingratitude n ungratefulness, thanklessness, unthankfulness, lack of appreciation, unappreciativeness, non-recognition.

ingredient adj constituent, component, element, part, unit, item, feature.

ingress n **1** *find the ingress to the castle* way in, entrance, entry, approach. **2** *that ticket gives you ingress to the concert* admission, admittance, access, right of entry.

inhabit v live in, dwell in, reside in, occupy, tenant, lodge in, make one's home in, settle in, settle, people, populate.

inhabitant n resident, resider, dweller, occupant, occupier, habitant, settler.

inhale v breathe in, draw in, suck in, sniff in, gasp, gulp, inspire.

inharmonious adj **1** *inharmonious sounds* unharmonious, unmelodious, unmusical, tuneless, discordant, dissonant, harsh, jarring, jangling, raucous, strident. **2** *holding inharmonious views* conflicting, incompatible, contradictory, irreconcilable, antagonistic, antipathetic, dissentient. **3** *an inharmonious relationship* quarrelsome, argumentative, disputatious.

inherent adj **1** *an inherent tendency to high blood pressure* inborn, inbred, innate, hereditary, inherited, in the blood/family, congenital, familial. **2** *an inherent part of the boat's design* intrinsic, innate, built-in,

inseparable, essential, basic, fundamental, ingrained.

inherit v **1** *inherit a fortune/estate* become/fall heir to, be bequeathed, be left, be willed, come into/by. **2** *inherit the title* succeed to, accede to, assume, take over, be elevated to.

inheritance n **1** *value their inheritance* legacy, bequest, endowment, birthright, heritage, patrimony. **2** *his inheritance of the title* accession, succession, assumption, elevation. *see* INHERIT 2.

inhibit v **1** *inhibit progress* hold back, impede, hinder, hamper, interfere with, obstruct, curb, check, restrict, restrain, constrain, bridle, rein in, baulk, frustrate, arrest, prevent, stop. **2** *inhibit them from going* forbid, prohibit, ban, bar, debar, vet, interdict, proscribe.

inhibited adj *feel inhibited in the presence of parents* shy, reticent, self-conscious, reserved, constrained, repressed, embarrassed, tongue-tied, subdued, withdrawn; *inf* uptight.

inhibition n **1** *regret the inhibition of progress* holding back, impediment, hindrance, hampering, interference, obstruction, curb, check, restriction, restraint, constraint, bridling, baulking, frustration, arrest, prevention, stopping. **2** *suffer from inhibition in the presence of parents* shyness, reticence, reserve, self-consciousness, constraint, repression, embarrassment, subduedness, withdrawnness.

inhospitable adj **1** *an inhospitable host/welcome* unwelcoming, unsociable, unsocial, antisocial, unfriendly, uncivil, discourteous, ungracious, uncongenial, ungenerous, cool, cold, chilly, aloof, unkind, unsympathetic, ill-disposed, hostile, inimical, xenophobic. **2** *an inhospitable landscape* uninviting, unwelcoming, barren, bleak, bare, uninhabitable, sterile, desolate, lonely, empty, forbidding, hostile, inimical.

inhuman adj **1** *an inhuman cry* non-human, non-mortal, animal, ghostly. **2** *inhuman people* unkind, unkindly, inconsiderate, uncompassionate, unsympathetic, unapproachable, inhumane. *see* INHUMANE.

inhumane adj unkind, unkindly, inconsiderate, uncompassionate, unfeeling, unsympathetic, unforgiving, cold-blooded, heartless, hard-hearted, pitiless, merciless, ruthless, remorseless, brutal, cruel, harsh, savage, vicious, barbaric, barbarous, bestial, fiendish, diabolical.

inhumanity n unkindness, lack of compassion/feeling/sympathy, cold-bloodedness, heartlessness, hardheartedness, pitilessness, mercilessness, ruthlessness, remorselessness, brutality, cruelty, harshness, savagery, viciousness, barbarity, bestiality, fiendishness.

inimical adj **1** *an inimical atmosphere* hostile, unfriendly, unkind, inhospitable, unwelcoming, unfavourable, cold, unsociable, adverse, opposed, antagonistic, contrary, antipathetic, ill-disposed. **2** *inimical to their survival* harmful, injurious, detrimental, deleterious, hurtful, damaging, dangerous, pernicious, destructive, noxious, toxic, virulent.

inimitable adj matchless, unmatched, incomparable, unparalleled, unrivalled, unsurpassed, unsurpassable, unique, superlative, supreme, model, faultless, perfect, consummate, ideal, unexampled, nonpareil, peerless.

iniquitous adj **1** *an iniquitous action* wicked, sinful, evil, immoral, villainous, criminal, heinous, vile, foul, base, odious, abominable, execrable, atrocious, malicious, outrageous, monstrous, shocking, scandalous, reprehensible, unjust. **2** *an iniquitous robber* wicked, evil, criminal, lawless, crooked, dishonourable, unprincipled, blackguardly, degenerate, corrupt, reprobate, immoral, dissolute.

iniquity n **1** *his falling into iniquity* wickedness, sin, sinfulness, vice, evil, ungodliness, godlessness, wrong, wrongdoing, badness, villainy, knavery, lawlessness, crime, baseness, heinousness. **2** *appalled at his iniquities* sin, vice, offence, crime, transgression, injury, violation, atrocity, outrage.

initial adj *the initial stages of the enterprise* first, beginning, commencing, starting, opening, early, prime, primary, elementary, foundational, introductory, inaugural, inceptive, incipient, inchoate.

initial v *initial the document* put one's initials on, sign, undersign, countersign; endorse.

initially adv in/at the beginning, at first, at the start/outset, to begin/start with, originally, in the early stages.

initiate v **1** *initiate the proceedings* begin, start off, commence, open, institute, inaugurate, get under way, set in motion, lay the foundations of, lay the first stone of, launch, actuate, instigate, trigger off, originate, pioneer, sow the seeds of; start the ball rolling. **2** *initiate the pupil in science* teach, instruct, coach, tutor, school, train, drill, prime, familiarize, indoctrinate, inculcate. **3** *initiate the new member into the organization* admit, introduce, induct,

install, instate, incorporate, ordain, invest, enlist, enrol, sign up.

initiate n **1** *train the initiates in the organization* beginner, new boy/girl, newcomer, learner, trainee, apprentice, probationer, new/raw recruit, greenhorn, novice, tiro, novitiate, neophyte; *inf* rookie. **2** *longstanding initiate of the organization* member, card-carrier, enlistee, enrolee.

initiation n **1** *the initiation of the proceedings* beginning, starting, commencement, opening, institution, inauguration, launch, actuation, instigation. *see* INITIATE v 1. **2** *an initiation ceremony* admission, admittance, introduction, induction, installation, ordination, investment, enlistment, enrolment, baptism.

initiative n **1** *take the initiative* first step, first move, first blow, lead, gambit, opening move/gambit, beginning, start, commencement. **2** *promotion for those with initiative* enterprise, inventiveness, resourcefulness, resource, originality, creativity, drive, dynamism, ambition, ambitiousness, verve, dash, leadership; *inf* get-up-and-go, zing, push, pep, zip.

inject v **1** *inject the child/arm* syringe, inoculate, vaccinate; *inf* jab. **2** *inject fluid into the patient | inject heroin* introduce, intromit, insert, syringe; *inf* shoot up, mainline. **3** *inject some enthusiasm into the class* introduce, instil, bring in, infuse, imbue.

injection n **1** *a tetanus injection* inoculation, vaccination, vaccine, shot, booster; *inf* jab; *inf* fix, hit. **2** *the injection of some enthusiasm* introduction, instilment, instilling, infusion, imbuing.

injudicious adj imprudent, unwise, inadvisable, ill-considered, ill-judged, ill-advised, impolitic, inexpedient, unrecommendable, misguided, incautious, undesirable, indiscreet, inappropriate, unsuitable, wrongheaded, wrong, hare-brained, foolish, hasty, rash; *inf* dumb.

injunction n command, instruction, order, ruling, direction, directive, dictum, dictate, mandate, ordainment, enjoinment, admonition, precept, ultimatum.

injure v **1** *injure his foot* hurt, harm, damage, wound, maim, cripple, lame, disable, mutilate, deform, mangle. **2** *injure his health* harm, damage, impair, weaken, enfeeble. **3** *injure his reputation by his conduct* ruin, spoil, mar, damage, blight, blemish, besmirch, tarnish, undermine. **4** *guilty of injuring his fellow citizens* do an injury to, wrong, do an injustice to, offend against, abuse, maltreat, defame, vilify, malign; *inf* do the dirty on.

injured adj **1** *his injured leg* hurt, wounded, broken, fractured, sore, maimed, crippled, lame. *see* INJURE 1. **2** *the injured party* wronged, offended, abused, maltreated, illtreated, defamed, vilified, maligned. **3** *give him an injured look* reproachful, hurt, wounded, upset, cut to the quick, put out, unhappy, disgruntled, displeased, condemnatory, censorious.

injurious adj *injurious to health* harmful, hurtful, damaging, deleterious, detrimental, disadvantageous, unfavourable, destructive, pernicious, ruinous, disastrous, calamitous, malignant.

injury n **1** *dangerous machines bound to cause injury* harm, hurt, wounding, damage, impairment, affliction. **2** *his injuries taking long to heal* wound, sore, bruise, cut, gash, laceration, abrasion, lesion, contusion, trauma. **3** *do an injury to his neighbours by his conduct* injustice, wrong, ill, offence, disservice, grievance, evil.

injustice n **1** *the injustice of the verdict* unjustness, unfairness, inequitableness, inequity, bias, prejudice, favouritism, partiality, one-sidedness, discrimination, partisanship. **2** *infamous for his injustices done to others* unfairness, unjustness, inequity, wrong, injury, offence, evil, villainy, iniquity.

inkling n **1** *they gave no inkling of their intentions* hint, clue, intimation, suggestion, indication, whisper, suspicion, insinuation, innuendo. **2** *have no inkling of how best to proceed* idea, vague idea, notion, glimmering; knowledge, slight knowledge; *inf* foggiest idea, the foggiest.

inky adj *inky nights* black, pitch-black, coalblack, jet-black, sable, ebony, dark.

inlaid adj inset; veneered, enamelled, ornamented, enchased, tesselated, mosaic, studded, lined, tiled.

inland adj *inland towns* interior, inshore, internal, up-country.

inlet n cove, bay, arm/armlet of the sea, bight, creek, fjord, sound; *Scots* firth, sea loch.

inmate n **1** *hospital inmates* patient, hospital case. **2** *prison inmates* prisoner, convict, captive, jailbird.

inmost *see* INNERMOST.

inn n public house, pub, tavern, bar, hotel.

innate adj **1** *an innate tendency* inborn, inbred, connate, congenital, hereditary, inherited, in the blood/family, inherent, intrinsic, ingrained, natural, native, indigenous. **2** *an innate part of the plan* essential, basic, fundamental, quintessential, organic, radical. **3** *an innate capacity* instinctive, intuitive, spontaneous, unlearned, untaught.

inner adj **1** *the inner rooms* interior, inside, central, middle, further in. **2** *the inner political circle* restricted, privileged, confidential, intimate, private, exclusive, secret. **3** *the inner meaning* unapparent, veiled, obscure, esoteric, hidden, secret, unrevealed. **4** *man's inner life* spiritual, emotional, mental, psychological, psychic.

innermost, inmost adj **1** *the innermost section* furthest in, deepest within, central, middle. **2** *innermost beliefs* intimate, private, personal, deep, deepest, profound, secret, hidden.

innkeeper n publican, landlady, landlord, mine host, bar-keeper, hotelier.

innocence n **1** *the innocence of the prisoners* guiltlessness, blamelessness, freedom from guilt/blame, unblameworthiness, inculpability, unimpeachability, irreproachability, clean hands. **2** *the innocence of their play* harmlessness, innocuousness, safety, lack of danger/malice, inoffensiveness, innoxiousness. *see* INNOCENT adj 2. **3** *the innocence of the young girls* virtuousness, virtue, purity, lack of sin, sinlessness, morality, decency, righteousness, chastity, virginity, immaculateness, impeccability, spotlessness. *see* INNOCENT adj 3. **4** *the innocence of the new army recruits* simpleness, ingenuousness, naïvety, lack of sophistication, artlessness, guilelessness, frankness, openness, credulity, inexperience, gullibility. *see* INNOCENT adj 5.

innocent adj **1** *innocent prisoners* not guilty, guiltless, blameless, clear, in the clear, above suspicion, unblameworthy, inculpable, unimpeachable, irreproachable, cleanhanded. **2** *innocent fun* harmless, innocuous, safe, non-injurious, unmalicious, unobjectionable, inoffensive, innoxious, playful. **3** *innocent young girls* virtuous, pure, sinless, moral, decent, righteous, upright, chaste, virginal, virgin, immaculate, impeccable, pristine, spotless, stainless, unblemished, unsullied, incorrupt, uncorrupted. **4** *innocent of guile* free from, without, lacking, empty of, clear of, unacquainted with, ignorant of, unaware of, unfamiliar with, nescient of, untouched by. **5** *too innocent for the world of business* simple, ingenuous, naïve, unsophisticated, artless, guileless, childlike, frank, open, unsuspicious, trustful, trusting, credulous, inexperienced, unworldly, green, gullible; *inf* wet behind the ears. **6** *innocent tumours* benign, non-cancerous, non-malignant.

innocent n *an innocent in the business world* child, babe, babe in arms, *ingénue*, novice, greenhorn.

innocuous adj **1** *an innocuous substance* harmless, unhurtful, uninjurious, safe, danger-free, non-poisonous. **2** *an innocuous person* harmless, inoffensive, unobjectionable, unexceptionable, unoffending, mild, peaceful, bland, commonplace, run-of-the-mill, insipid.

innovation n new method/device/measure, introduction, modernism, modernization, novelty, change, alteration, variation, transformation, metamorphosis, renovation, restyling, recasting, remodelling, coining, neology, neologism.

innuendo n insinuation, implication, suggestion, hint, overtone, allusion, inkling, imputation, aspersion.

innumerable adj very many, numerous, countless, untold, incalculable, numberless, unnumbered, beyond number, infinite, myriad; *inf* umpteen, masses, oodles.

inoculate v immunize, vaccinate; *inf* give shots/jabs.

inoculation n immunization, vaccination, injection, shot; *inf* jab.

inoffensive adj **1** *an inoffensive substance* harmless, innocuous, unhurtful, safe, danger-free. *see* INNOCUOUS 1. **2** *an inoffensive person* harmless, innocuous, unobjectionable, unexceptionable, mild, peaceful.

inoperative adj **1** *inoperative machines* not operative, not in operation, not working, out of order, out of service/commission/action, non-active, broken, broken-down, defective, faulty; *inf* kaput, knackered. **2** *an inoperative system* useless, ineffectual, ineffective, inefficient, inadequate, worthless, valueless, futile, unproductive, abortive.

inopportune adj inconvenient, ill-timed, badly timed, mistimed, untimely, unseasonable, inappropriate, unsuitable, inapt, ill-chosen, infelicitous, unfavourable, unfortunate, unpropitious, inauspicious.

inordinate adj excessive, immoderate, over-abundant, extravagant, unrestrained, unrestricted, unlimited, unwarranted, uncalled for, undue, unreasonable, disproportionate, exorbitant, extreme, outrageous, preposterous, unconscionable.

inquest n inquiry, investigation, inquisition, probe.

inquire v **1** *inquire into the cause of the fire* make inquiries, conduct an inquiry, question, query, investigate, research, look into, examine, explore, probe, scan, search, scrutinize, study, inspect, reconnoitre.

2 *inquire about the weather* | *inquire his name* ask, make inquiries about; quiz, interogate; *inf* grill.

inquiring adj *an inquiring mind* questioning, investigative, curious, interested, analytical, probing, exploring, searching, scrutinizing, inquisitive.

inquiry n **1** *conduct an inquiry into the murder* investigation, examination, exploration, sounding, probe, search, scrutiny, scrutinization, study, inspection, reconnoitring, interrogation. **2** *reply to her inquiry* question, query.

inquisition n *subject the suspects to an inquisition* interrogation, cross-examination, examination, investigation, quizzing, questioning, inquiry, inquest; *inf* grilling, third degree.

inquisitive adj *inquisitive neighbours* inquiring, questioning, probing, scrutinizing, curious, burning with curiosity, interested, over-interested, intrusive, meddlesome, prying, snooping, snoopy, peering, spying; *inf* nosy, nosy-parker.

inroad n **1** *enemy inroads* invasion, raid, foray, attack, assault, onslaught, charge, offensive, sally, sortie. **2** *object to the inroads on her time* encroachment, intrusion, incursion, infringement, trespassing.

insane adj **1** *insane people in hospital* mad, severely mentally disordered, of unsound mind, deranged, demented, *non compos mentis*, out of one's mind, unhinged, crazed, crazy. **2** *he's insane to take that job* extremely foolish, mad, mad as a hatter, raving mad, out of one's/mind, unhinged, not all there, crazy; *inf* bonkers, cracked, crackers, barmy, batty, bats, cuckoo, loony, loopy, nuts, nutty, screwy, bananas, off one's rocker/heads/chump/nut, out of one's head, round the bend/twist, off one's trolley. **3** *an insane idea* very foolish, mad, crazy, idiotic, stupid, senseless, nonsensical, irrational, impracticable, pointless, absurd, ridiculous, ludicrous, bizarre, fatuous; *inf* daft.

insanitary adj unsanitary, unsanitized, unhygienic, impure, unclean, dirty, dirtied, filthy, contaminated, polluted, foul, feculent, infected, septic, infested, disease-ridden, germy, unhealthy, insalubrious, noxious.

insanity n **1** *patients suffering from insanity* madness, severe mental disorder, mental derangement, dementia, frenzy, delirium. **2** *the insanity of the idea* folly, foolishness, madness, craziness, idiocy, stupidity, senselessness, irrationality, absurdity. *see* INSANE 3.

insatiable adj insatiate, unappeasable, unquenchable, greedy, hungry, craving, voracious, ravening, gluttonous, omnivorous, avid, desirous, eager.

inscribe v **1** *inscribe one's name on the book/ stone* imprint, write, stamp, impress, mark, brand, engrave, etch, carve, cut. **2** *inscribe the candidates in the book* enter, register, record, write, list, enrol, enlist, engross. **3** *inscribe his novel to his son* dedicate, address.

inscription n **1** *read the inscription on the gravestone* engraving, writing, etching, lettering, legend, epitaph, epigraph; words. **2** *the inscription on the book* dedication, address, message.

inscrutable adj **1** *an inscrutable expression* enigmatic, unreadable, impenetrable, cryptic, deadpan, sphinxlike; *inf* poker-faced. **2** *an inscrutable situation* mysterious, inexplicable, unexplainable, incomprehensible, beyond comprehension/understanding, unintelligible, puzzling, baffling, unfathomable, arcane.

insecticide n insect spray, insect powder, fly-spray, pesticide, insect killer.

insecure adj **1** *insecure children* unconfident, lacking confidence, diffident, timid, uncertain, unsure, doubtful, hesitant, anxious, fearful, apprehensive, worried. **2** *insecure fortresses* vulnerable, open to attack, defenceless, unprotected, ill-protected, unguarded, unshielded, exposed, in danger, dangerous, perilous, hazardous. **3** *insecure fitments* loose, flimsy, frail, fragile, infirm, weak, unsubstantial, jerry-built, rickety, wobbly, shaky, unsteady, unstable, unsound, decrepit.

insecurity n **1** *the insecurity of the children* lack of confidence/security, diffidence, timidity, uncertainty, anxiety, apprehension, worry. *see* INSECURE 1. **2** *the insecurity of the fortresses* vulnerability, defencelessness, lack of protection, unguardedness, danger, peril, perilousness. *see* INSECURE 2. **3** *the insecurity of the fitments* looseness, flimsiness, frailty, fragility, infirmity, ricketiness, wobbliness, shakiness, unsteadiness, instability, decrepitude. *see* INSECURE 3.

insensible adj **1** *try to rouse the insensible man* unconscious, insensate, senseless, insentient, anaesthetized, comatose, knocked out, inert, stupefied; *inf* out, out cold, out for the count, zonked. **2** *insensible fingers and toes* numb, benumbed, numbed, lacking feeling/sensation. **3** *insensible of their danger* unaware of, ignorant of, without knowledge of, unconscious of, unmindful of, oblivious to. **4** *insensible to their*

suffering indifferent to, impervious to, deaf to, unmoved by, untouched by, unaffected by, unresponsive to, inured to. **5** *a passionate person among insensible people* apathetic, dispassionate, cool, passionless, emotionless, detached, indifferent, aloof, hard, hard-hearted, tough, cruel, callous. **6** *an insensible difference in their views* imperceptible, unnoticeable, indiscernible, indistinguishable, negligible, slight, minute, minuscule.

insensitive adj **1** *insensitive to pain/cold* impervious to, immune to, proof against, insusceptible to, unaffected by, nonreactive to, unreactive to. **2** *insensitive to the demands of the public* unresponsive to, impervious to, indifferent to, unaffected by, unmoved by, oblivious to, unappreciative of. **3** *insensitive people laughing at the funeral* heartless, unfeeling, callous, tactless, thick-skinned, uncaring, unconcerned, uncompassionate, unsympathetic.

insentient adj inanimate, lifeless, inert, vegetative, insensate, numb, anaesthetized, comatose.

inseparable adj **1** *inseparable parts* unseparable, inseverable, indivisible, undividable, indissoluble. **2** *inseparable companions* constant, devoted, close, intimate, bosom.

insert v **1** *insert a nail in the wall* put in/into, place in, press in, push in, stick in, thrust in, drive in, work in, slide in, slip in, tuck in; *inf* pop in. **2** *insert a sentence into the paragraph* put in, introduce, enter, interpolate, inset, interpose, interject, implant, infix.

insert n *an insert in the magazine* insertion, inset, supplement, circular, advertisement; *inf* ad.

inside n **1** *the inside of the book* interior, inner part/side/surface; contents. **2** *a sore inside | sore insides* stomach, abdomen, gut; internal organs, intestines, viscera, entrails, bowels, bodily/vital organs; *inf* belly, tummy, guts, bread basket.

inside adv **1** *go/stand inside* indoors; in/into the interior, in/into the house, in/into the building, within. **2** *inside she felt frightened* emotionally, in her thoughts/feelings, intuitively, instinctively.

inside adj **1** *the inside part* interior, inner, internal, inward, on/in the inside, inmost, innermost, intramural. **2** *have inside information* confidential, classified, restricted, reserved, privileged, private, internal, privy, secret, exclusive, esoteric.

insidious adj stealthy, subtle, surreptitious, sneaky, sneaking, cunning, crafty, designing, intriguing, Machiavellian, artful, guileful, sly, wily, tricky, slick, deceitful, deceptive, underhand, double-dealing, duplicitous, dishonest, insincere, disingenuous, treacherous, perfidious; *inf* crooked.

insight n **1** *a person of insight* intuition, perception, awareness, discernment, understanding, penetration, acumen, perspicacity, perspicaciousness, discrimination, judgement, shrewdness, sharpness, acuteness, flair, vision. **2** *give an insight into country life* awareness, understanding, realization, revelation, observance; *inf* eye-opener.

insignia n/npl **1** *insignia of office* badge, decoration, medallion, ribbon, crest, emblem, symbol, sign, mark, seal, signet. **2** *politeness is meant to be the insignia of the firm* mark of distinction, trademark, label, trait, characteristic.

insignificant adj **1** *insignificant details* unimportant, of minor/no importance, of little importance/import, trivial, trifling, negligible, inconsequential, of no consequence/account, of no moment/matter, inconsiderable, not worth mentioning, nugatory, meagre, paltry, scanty, petty, insubstantial, unsubstantial, flimsy, irrelevant, immaterial; *Amer inf* dinky. **2** *insignificant members of the government* unimportant, uninfluential, powerless, small-fry.

insincere adj lacking sincerity, not candid, not frank, disingenuous, dissembling, dissimulating, pretended, devious, hypocritical, deceitful, deceptive, duplicitous, dishonest, underhand, double-dealing, false, faithless, disloyal, treacherous, two-faced, lying, untruthful, mendacious, evasive, shifty, slippery.

insinuate v **1** *he insinuated that she was dishonest* imply, hint, whisper, suggest, indicate, convey the impression, intimate, mention. **2** *insinuate doubts into their minds* infiltrate, implant, instil, introduce, inculcate, infuse, inject. **insinuate oneself** *insinuate herself into his affections* worm oneself into, work one's way into, ingratiate oneself with, curry favour with; *inf* get in with.

insinuation n **1** *resent the insinuation that he was dishonest* implication, suggestion, hint, innuendo, intimation, mention, reference, allusion, aspersion, slur. **2** *the insinuation of doubts* infiltration, implanting, instilling, instillation, introduction. *see* INSINUATE 2. **3** *their insinuation into her affections* worming, ingratiation. *see* INSINUATE, INSINUATE ONESELF.

insipid adj **1** *an insipid person* lacking personality, colourless, anaemic, drab, inanimate, spiritless, jejune, vapid, dull, uninteresting, boring, unentertaining. **2** *insipid prose* unimaginative, characterless, flat, bland, vapid, uninteresting, dull, prosaic, boring, monotonous, tedious, wearisome, dry, dry as dust, humdrum, run-of-the mill, trite, banal, hackneyed, stale. **3** *insipid soup* tasteless, flavourless, savourless, bland, thin, watery, watered-down, unappetizing, unpalatable; *Scots* wersh.

insist v **1** *if they refuse you must insist* stand firm, be firm, stand one's ground, make a stand, be resolute, be determined, be emphatic, not take no for an answer, brook no refusal. **2** *insist that they go* demand, require, command, importune, entreat, urge, exhort. **3** *she insists that she is innocent* maintain, assert, declare, hold, contend, pronounce, proclaim, aver, propound, avow, vow, swear, be emphatic, emphasize, stress, repeat, reiterate.

insistence n **1** *her insistence that they go* requirement, command, importuning, entreaty, urging, exhortation; demands. **2** *her insistence that she is innocent* maintenance, assertion, declaration, contention, avowal, emphasis, stress. *see* INSIST 3. **3** *the insistence of the demands* persistence, doggedness, incessantness, urgency, coercion, exigency. *see* INSISTENT 2. **4** *the insistence of the call of the birds* constancy, incessantness, repetition, recurrence. *see* INSISTENT 3.

insistent adj **1** *she is insistent that you go* emphatic, determined, resolute, tenacious, importunate, persistent, unyielding, obstinate, dogged, unrelenting, inexorable. **2** *insistent demands for payment* persistent, determined, dogged, incessant, urgent, pressing, compelling, high-pressure, pressurizing, coercive, demanding, exigent. **3** *the insistent call of the bird* constant, incessant, iterative, repeated, repetitive, recurrent.

insolence n impertinence, impudence, cheek, cheekiness, ill-manneredness, rudeness, disrespect, incivility, insubordination, contempt, abuse, offensiveness, contumely, audacity, boldness, brazenness, brashness, pertness, forwardness, effrontery; insults; *inf* gall, back-chat, sauce; *Amer inf* chutzpah.

insolent adj impertinent, impudent, cheeky, rude, ill-mannered, disrespectful, insubordinate, contemptuous, insulting, abusive, offensive, audacious, bold, brazen, brash, pert, forward; *inf* fresh.

insoluble adj **1** *an insoluble substance* not soluble, indissoluble, indissolvable, undissolvable. **2** *insoluble problems/puzzles/situations* insolvable, unsolvable, baffling, unfathomable, indecipherable, complicated, perplexing, intricate, involved, impenetrable, inscrutable, enigmatic, obscure, mystifying, inexplicable, incomprehensible, mysterious.

insolvency n bankruptcy, indebtedness, liquidation, financial ruin, default, pennilessness, impoverishedness, penury, impecuniousness, beggary.

insolvent adj bankrupt, indebted, in debt, liquidated, ruined, defaulting, in the hands of the receivers, penniless, impoverished, penurious, impecunious; *inf* gone bust, gone to the wall, on the rocks, in the red, in queer street, broke, hard up, strapped for cash.

insomnia n sleeplessness, wakefulness, insomnolence, restlessness.

insouciant adj carefree, nonchalant, untroubled, unworried, unconcerned, heedless, casual, easygoing, free and easy, happy-go-lucky, indifferent, frivolous, capricious.

inspect v examine, check, go over, look over, survey, scrutinize, vet, audit, study, pore over, view, scan, observe, investigate, assess, appraise; *inf* give the once-over.

inspection n examination, check, check-up, look-over, survey, scrutiny, vetting, view, scan, observation, investigation, probe, assessment, appraisal; *inf* once-over, going-over, look-see. *see* INSPECT.

inspector n examiner, checker, scrutinizer, scrutineer, vetter, auditor, surveyor, scanner, observer, investigator, overseer, supervisor, assessor, appraiser, critic.

inspiration n **1** *acts as an inspiration to his work* stimulus, stimulation, motivation, fillip, encouragement, influence, muse, goad, spur, incitement, arousal, rousing, stirring. **2** *his pictures lack inspiration* creativity, originality, inventiveness, genius, insight, vision, afflatus. **3** *have a sudden inspiration* bright idea, brilliant/timely thought, revelation; illumination, enlightenment.

inspire v **1** *inspire the artist | inspire the artist's work* stimulate, motivate, encourage, influence, inspirit, animate, fire the imagination of. **2** *ambition inspired him to work* rouse, stir, spur, goad, energize, galvanize. **3** *her beauty inspired love in many men* arouse, excite, quicken, inflame, touch off, spark off, ignite, kindle, give rise to, produce, bring about, prompt, instigate.

inspired adj **1** *an inspired operatic performance* brilliant, outstanding, supreme, superlative, dazzling, exciting, thrilling,

enthralling, wonderful, marvellous, memorable; *inf* out of this world. **2** *an inspired guess* intuitive, instinctive.

instability n **1** *instability of human relationships* impermanence, unendurability, temporariness, transience, inconstancy. **2** *the instability of his physical condition* unsteadiness, uncertainty, precariousness, fluidity, fluctuation. **3** *the instability of the furniture* unsteadiness, unsoundness, shakiness, ricketiness, wobbliness, frailty, flimsiness, unsubstantiality. **4** *children leading lives of instability* insecurity, precariousness, unpredictability, unreliability; *inf* chanciness, uncertainty. **5** *upset by her instability* changeableness, variability, capriciousness, volatility, flightiness, vacillation, wavering, fitfulness, oscillation.

install v **1** *install kitchen units* put in, insert, put in place, position, place, emplace, fix, locate, situate, station, lodge. **2** *install him as rector* induct, instate, institute, inaugurate, invest, ordain, introduce, initiate, establish. **3** *install themselves in the best seats* ensconce, position, settle.

installation n **1** *the installation of kitchen units* putting in, insertion, positioning, placing, fixing, situating. *see* INSTALL 1. **2** *the installation of the rector* induction, instatement, inauguration, investiture, ordination, initiation. *see* INSTALL 2. **3** *factory installations* machinery, plant, equipment. **4** *military installations* base, camp, station, post, establishment.

instalment n **1** *pay for goods by instalment* part/partial payment, hire purchase, HP. **2** *issue the novel in instalments* part, portion, section, segment, chapter, division, episode.

instance n **1** *an instance of his insolence* case, case in point, example, illustration, exemplification, occasion, occurrence. **2** *in the first instance* stage, step. **3** *they went away at his instance* behest, instigation, urging, demand, insistence, request, prompting, solicitation, entreaty, importuning, pressure.

instance v *the teacher instanced several examples* give, cite, mention, name, specify, quote, adduce.

instant n **1** *gone in an instant* moment, minute, second, split second, trice, twinkling, twinkling of an eye, flash, flash of lightning; *inf* jiffy, shake, two shakes of a lamb's tail. **2** *at this instant I am not sure* moment, time, present time, this minute, this very minute, particular/specific time, moment in time, juncture, point. **on the**

instant now, right away, immediately, instantly, forthwith, without delay.

instant adj **1** *instant recognition* instantaneous, immediate, on-the-spot, prompt, rapid, sudden, abrupt. **2** *instant whip/coffee/potato* pre-prepared, ready-prepared, ready-mixed, pre-cooked, fast, easy/quick to prepare, easy/quick to make. **3** *at his instant request* urgent, pressing, earnest, importunate, exigent, imperative.

instantaneous adj *death was instantaneous* instant, immediate, on the spot, direct, prompt, expeditious, rapid, sudden, abrupt.

instantaneously adv right away, straight away, immediately, at once, now, instantly, on the instant, forthwith, then and there, quick as lightning, in a trice, in less than no time, in a fraction of a second, in the twinkling of an eye, before you can say Jack Robinson, before you can turn around; *inf* in a jiffy.

instate v install, induct, inaugurate, invest, ordain, initiate.

instead adv *I'll have a chocolate ice cream instead* as an alternative/substitute/replacement, for preference. **instead of** *I'll have chocolate instead of strawberry ice cream* as an alternative to, as a substitute/replacement for, in place/lieu of, in preference to, rather than.

instigate v **1** *instigate legal proceedings | instigate a rebellion* bring about, start, initiate, actuate, generate, incite, provoke, inspire, foment, kindle, stir up, whip up. **2** *instigate them to rebel* incite, encourage, egg on, urge, prompt, goad, prod, induce, impel, constrain, press, persuade, prevail upon, sway, entice.

instigation n *the proceedings/rebellions were at his instigation* initiation, actuation, incitement, encouragement, urging, inducement, persuasion, enticement. *see* INSTIGATE.

instigator n prime mover, inciter, motivator, agitator, fomenter, troublemaker, *agent provocateur*, ringleader, leader.

instil v **1** *instil water into the substance* add gradually, introduce, infuse, inject. **2** *instil common sense into the children* introduce, insinuate, infuse, inculcate, implant, teach, drill, arouse. **3** *instil the children with common sense* infuse, imbue, permeate, inculcate.

instinct n **1** *birds migrate by instinct | she found the way here by instinct* inborn/inherent tendency, natural feeling, innate inclination, intuition, sixth sense, inner prompting. **2** *he has an instinct for poetry* talent, gift, ability, capacity, faculty, aptitude, knack, bent, trait, characteristic.

instinctive adj **1** *birds' instinctive behaviour pattern* inborn, inherent, innate, inbred, natural, intuitive, intuitional, involuntary, untaught, unlearned. **2** *his instinctive reaction was to hide* automatic, reflex, mechanical, spontaneous, involuntary, impulsive, intuitive, unthinking, unpremeditated.

institute v **1** *institute legal proceedings* begin, start, commence, set in motion, put into operation, initiate. **2** *institute new organizations | institute reforms* found, establish, start, launch, bring into being, bring about, constitute, set up, organize, develop, create, originate, pioneer. **3** *institute the new rector* install, instate, induct, invest, ordain, introduce, initiate, appoint.

institute n **1** *start an educational institute* institution, organization, foundation, society, association, league, guild, consortium. **2** *build an institute for research* foundation, institution, academy, school, college, conservatory, seminary, seat of learning. **3** *legal/local institutes* law, rule, regulation, decree, tenet, principle, precedent, institution, custom, tradition, convention, practice.

institution n **1** *the institution of legal proceedings* starting, commencement, initiation. *see* INSTITUTE v 1. **2** *the institution of new organizations* foundation, establishment, setting up, creation, origination, pioneering. *see* INSTITUTE v 2. **3** *the institution of the new rector* installation, instatement, induction, investiture. *see* INSTITUTE v 3. **4** *start educational institutions* institute, organization, society, association. *see* INSTITUTE n 1. **5** *a research institution* institute, foundation, academy, college. *see* INSTITUTE n 2. **6** *in an institution for life* hospital, mental hospital, children's home, prison, reformatory, detention centre. **7** *local institutions* institute, law, rule, custom, tradition, convention, practice. *see* INSTITUTE n 3. **8** *the old man was an institution in the village* regular/prominent feature, familiar sight.

institutional adj **1** *institutional methods* organized, established, bureaucratic, accepted, orthodox, conventional, customary, formal, systematic, methodical, orderly; *inf* establishment. **2** *institutional food* uniform, same, unvarying, unvaried, unchanging, regimented, monotonous, bland, dull, insipid. **3** *an institutional atmosphere in the building* cold, cheerless, clinical, dreary, drab, unwelcoming, uninviting, impersonal, formal, forbidding.

instruct v **1** *instruct the messenger to take a reply* tell, direct, order, command, bid, charge, enjoin, demand, require. **2** *instruct the pupils in science* teach, educate, tutor, coach, train, school, drill, ground, prime, prepare, guide, inform, enlighten, edify, discipline. **3** *instruct them that I shall be late* inform, tell, notify, acquaint, make known to, advise, apprise. **4** *instruct one's lawyer* give the facts to, give information to, brief.

instruction n **1** *get good instruction in the arts* teaching, education, tutoring, tutelage, coaching, training, schooling, drilling, grounding, priming, preparation, guidance, information, enlightenment, edification, discipline; lessons, classes, lectures. **2** *his instruction was to leave at once* direction, directive, briefing, order, command, charge, injunction, requirement, ruling, mandate.

instructions npl **1** *his instructions are to leave now* directions, orders, commands, requirements. see INSTRUCTION 2. **2** *read the instructions to find out* directions; key, book of rules, guide.

instructive adj instructional, informative, informational, educational, educative, enlightening, illuminating, useful, helpful, edifying, cultural, uplifting, academic, didactic, doctrinal.

instructor n teacher, schoolteacher, schoolmaster, schoolmistress, educator, lecturer, professor, pedagogue, tutor, coach, trainer, adviser, counsellor, guide, mentor, demonstrator.

instrument n **1** *dental instruments* implement, tool, appliance, apparatus, mechanism, utensil, gadget, contrivance, device, aid; *inf* contraption. **2** *musicians tuning their instruments* musical instrument; piano, violin, viola, cello, double bass, horn, trombone, tuba, piccolo, flute, oboe, clarinet, saxophone, drum. **3** *the ships' instruments* measuring device, gauge, meter. **4** *her information was the instrument which led to his arrest | the instrument of his downfall* agency, agent, prime mover, catalyst, cause, factor, channel, medium, force, mechanism, instrumentality, vehicle, organ; means. **5** *he was just the king's instrument* pawn, puppet, tool, cat's paw, dupe, minion, creature, flunkey; *inf* stooge.

instrumental adj *she was instrumental in catching the thief* helpful, of help/assistance, useful, of use/service, contributory, active, involved, influential, significant, important.

insubordinate adj rebellious, mutinous, insurgent, seditious, insurrectional, riotous, disobedient, non-compliant, defiant, refractory, recalcitrant, contumacious, undisciplined, ungovernable, uncontrollable, unmanageable, unruly, disorderly.

insubordination n rebelliousness, rebellion, mutinousness, mutiny, insurgence, sedition, insurrection, riotousness, rioting, defiance, non-compliance, disobedience, refractoriness, recalcitrance, contumacy, ungovernability, unruliness. see INSUBORDINATE.

insubstantial adj **1** *insubstantial buildings/furniture* flimsy, fragile, frail, weak, feeble, jerry-built. **2** *an insubstantial argument* weak, feeble, thin, slight, tenuous, insignificant, inconsequential. **3** *insubstantial shapes* unsubstantial, unreal, illusory, illusive, delusive, hallucinatory, phantom, phantasmal, spectral, ghostlike, intangible, impalpable, incorporeal, visionary, imaginary, imagined, fanciful, chimerical, airy, vaporous.

insufferable adj intolerable, unbearable, unendurable, insupportable, not to be borne, past bearing, too much to bear, impossible, too much, more than one can stand, more than flesh and blood can stand, enough to try the patience of Job, enough to test the patience of a saint, unspeakable, dreadful, excruciating, grim, outrageous.

insufficient adj inadequate, deficient, in short supply, scarce, meagre, scant, scanty, too small/little/few, not enough, lacking, wanting, at a premium.

insular adj **1** *country people leading insular lives* isolated, detached, separate, segregated, solitary, insulated, self-sufficient. **2** *have insular ideas* narrow, narrow-minded, illiberal, prejudiced, biased, bigoted, provincial, parochial, parish-pump, blinkered, inward-looking, limited, restricted.

insulate v **1** *insulate pipes/wires/walls* make non-conducting; heatproof, soundproof, make shockproof, cover, wrap, enwrap, encase, envelop, pad, cushion, seal. **2** *long-term hospital patients are insulated from the world* segregate, separate, isolate, detach, cut off, keep/set apart, sequester, exclude, protect, shield.

insult v *insult him by calling him lazy | insult his honour* offend, give/cause offence to, affront, slight, hurt the feelings of, hurt, abuse, injure, wound, mortify, humiliate, disparage, discredit, depreciate, impugn, slur, revile.

insult n *upset by their insults about his character* affront, slight, gibe, snub, barb, slur; abuse, disparagement, depreciation, impugnment, revilement, insolence, rudeness, contumely; aspersions; *inf* dig.

insulting adj *insulting behaviour* offensive, affronting, slighting, abusive, injurious, wounding, mortifying, humiliating, disparaging, discrediting, depreciating, deprecatory, impugning, reviling, scurrilous, snubbing, insolent, rude, contumacious.

insuperable adj *insuperable difficulties* insurmountable, impassable, overwhelming, invincible, unconquerable, unassailable.

insupportable adj **1** *insupportable pain* insufferable, intolerable, unbearable, unendurable, more than flesh and blood can stand. *see* INSUFFERABLE. **2** *insupportable claims* unjustifiable, indefensible, untenable, unmaintainable, implausible, specious.

insurance n **1** *take out travel insurance* assurance, financial protection, indemnity, indemnification, surety, security, cover, coverage, guarantee, warranty, warrant, provision. **2** *he took an umbrella as an insurance against it raining* safeguard, precaution, protection, provision, preventive measure.

insure v **1** *insure her life/jewels* protect against death/loss/damage, assure, indemnify, cover, underwrite, guarantee, warrant. **2** *insured against fire/theft* take out insurance, protect, guarantee.

insurgent n *insurgents rising against the king* rebel, revolutionary, revolutionist, revolter, mutineer, rioter, insurrectionist, insurrectionary, seditionist, malcontent.

insurgent adj *insurgent forces fighting the king* rebellious, revolutionary, revolting, mutinying, mutinous, rioting, lawless, insurrectionist, insurrectionary, seditious, factious, subversive, insubordinate, disobedient.

insurmountable adj insuperable, invincible, unconquerable, impassable, overwhelming, unassailable, hopeless, impossible.

insurrection n rebellion, revolt, revolution, uprising, rising, riot, mutiny, sedition, coup, *coup d'état*, putsch; insurgency, insurgence.

intact adj whole, complete, entire, perfect, all in one piece, sound, unbroken, unsevered, undamaged, unscathed, uninjured, unharmed, unmutilated, inviolate, unviolated, undefiled, unblemished, unsullied, faultless, flawless.

intangible adj **1** *intangible things* impalpable, untouchable, not perceptible by touch, incorporeal, phantom, spectral, ghostly. **2** *an intangible air of sadness* indefinable,

indescribable, vague, subtle, unclear, obscure, mysterious.

integral adj **1** *an integral part of the organization* essential, necessary, indispensable, requisite, basic, fundamental, inherent, intrinsic, innate. **2** *integral parts of the machine* constituent, component, integrant. **3** *an integral design/concept* entire, complete, whole, total, full, intact, unified, integrated, undivided.

integrate v **1** *integrate the various parts* unite, join, combine, amalgamate, consolidate, blend, incorporate, coalesce, fuse, merge, intermix, mingle, commingle, assimilate, homogenize, harmonize, mesh, concatenate. **2** *integrate school districts* desegregate, open up.

integrated adj **1** *integrated parts* united, joined, amalgamated, consolidated, assimilated, concatenated. *see* INTEGRATE 1. **2** *integrated schools* desegregated, non-segregated, unsegregated, racially mixed, racially balanced.

integration n *the integration of the parts into a whole* unification, amalgamation, consolidation, incorporation, coalescing, fusing, assimilation, homogenizing, homogenization, concatenation.

integrity n **1** *doubt the integrity of the council* uprightness, honesty, rectitude, righteousness, virtue, probity, morality, honour, goodness, decency, truthfulness, fairness, sincerity, candour; principles, ethics. **2** *challenge the integrity of the empire* unity, unification, wholeness, entirety, completeness, totality, cohesion.

intellect n **1** *a person of little intellect* intelligence, reason, understanding, comprehension, mind, brain, thought, sense, judgement. **2** *leave the decisions to the intellects* intellectual, genius, thinker, mastermind; *inf* brain, mind, egghead, Einstein.

intellectual adj **1** *an intellectual exercise* mental, cerebral, academic. **2** *an intellectual family* intelligent, academic, well-educated, well-read, erudite, learned, bookish, donnish, highbrow, scholarly, studious. **3** *using only intellectual considerations* mental, cerebral, rational, logical, clinical, unemotional, non-emotional.

intellectual n **1** *one of the great intellectuals of our time* intellect, genius, thinker, mastermind; *inf* egghead. *see* INTELLECT 2. **2** *disapprove of the intellectuals on the club* academic, academician, man of letters, don, bluestocking, pundit, highbrow, bookworm, pedant; *inf* egghead, walking encyclopedia.

intelligence n **1** *people of great intelligence* intellect, mind, brain, brain-power, mental capacity/aptitude, reason, understanding, comprehension, acumen, wit, cleverness, brightness, brilliance, sharpness, quickness of mind, alertness, discernment, perception, perspicacity, penetration, sense, sagacity; brains; *inf* grey matter, nous. **2** *the intelligence came too late to save him* information, news, notification, notice, account, knowledge, advice, rumour; facts, data, reports, tidings; *inf* gen, low-down, dope. **3** *he's in military intelligence* information collection, enemy investigation, surveillance, observation, spying.

intelligent adj **1** *intelligent children* clever, bright, brilliant, sharp, quick, quick-witted, smart, apt, discerning, thinking, perceptive, perspicacious, penetrating, sensible, sagacious, well-informed, educated, enlightened, knowledgeable; *inf* brainy. **2** *is there intelligent life on the planet?* rational, reasoning, higher-order.

intelligentsia npl intellectuals, academics, literati, cognoscenti, illuminati, highbrows, pedants; the enlightened. *see* INTELLECTUAL n 2.

intelligible adj *a scarcely intelligible message* understandable, comprehensible, clear, lucid, plain, explicit, unambiguous, legible, decipherable.

intemperate adj **1** *an intemperate indulgence of the appetites* immoderate, self-indulgent, excessive, inordinate, extreme, extravagant, unreasonable, outrageous. **2** *intemperate drinkers* immoderate, excessive, drunken, drunk, intoxicated, inebriated, alcoholic, sottish; *inf* boozy. **3** *intemperate rages* uncontrolled, unrestrained, uncurbed, unbridled, ungoverned, tempestuous, violent. **4** *lead an intemperate life* immoderate, dissolute, dissipated, debauched, profligate, prodigal, loose, wild, wanton, licentious, libertine.

intend v **1** *he intends to go* mean, plan, have in mind/view, propose, aim, resolve, be resolved, be determined, expect, purpose; contemplate, think of. **2** *they intended the bullet for the leader* mean, aim, destine, purpose, plan, scheme, devise.

intense adj **1** *intense heat/cold* acute, fierce, severe, extreme, harsh, strong, powerful, potent, vigorous, great, profound, deep, concentrated, consuming. **2** *an intense desire to learn* earnest, eager, ardent, keen, enthusiastic, zealous, excited, impassioned, passionate, fervent, fervid, burning, consuming, vehement, fanatical. **3** *an intense person* nervous, nervy, tense,

fraught, overwrought, highly strung, emotional.

intensify v **1** *her indifference intensified his love* heighten, deepen, strengthen, increase, reinforce, magnify, enhance, fan, whet. **2** *intensify the quarrel* aggravate, exacerbate, worsen, inflame; *inf* add fuel to the flames. **3** *intensify their efforts to find the child* increase, extend, augment, boost, escalate, step up.

intensity n **1** *the intensity of the heat* acuteness, fierceness, severity, extremeness, extremity, harshness, strength, power, powerfulness, potency, vigour, greatness, concentration. *see* INTENSE 1. **2** *the intensity of their desire* ardour, keenness, enthusiasm, zeal, excitement, passion, fervour, fervency, vehemence, fanaticism. **3** *her intensity frightens people* nervousness, tenseness, fraughtness, emotionalism, emotion. *see* INTENSE 3.

intensive adj *an intensive search | intensive revision* in-depth, concentrated, exhaustive, all-out, thorough, thorough-going, total, all-absorbing.

intent adj **1** *an intent expression* concentrated, concentrating, fixed, steady, steadfast, absorbed, attentive, engrossed, occupied, preoccupied, extreme, enrapt, wrapped up, focused, observant, watchful, alert, earnest, committed, intense. **2** *intent on getting their own way* set on, bent on, committed to, firm about; determined to, resolved to; *inf* hell-bent on.

intent n *it was their intent to win* intention, purpose, aim, objective, goal, end, plan. *see* INTENTION 1. **to all intents and purposes** virtually, in practical terms, practically, as good as.

intention n **1** *it is his intention to be leader* aim, purpose, intent, goal, objective, end, end in view, target, aspiration, ambition, wish, plan, design, resolve, resolution, determination. **2** *he assaulted the old man without intention* premeditation, preconception, design, plan, calculation.

intentional adj *an intentional crime* intended, deliberate, meant, done on purpose, wilful, purposeful, purposed, planned, calculated, designed, premeditated, preconceived, predetermined, prearranged, preconcerted, considered, weighed up, studied.

intentionally adv *she damaged the toy intentionally* deliberately, on purpose, purposefully, by design, wilfully.

inter v bury, consign to the grave, entomb, lay to rest, inhume, inearth, inurn, ensepulchre, sepulchre.

intercede v *intercede in the strike* | *intercede for the child with her parents* mediate, negotiate, arbitrate, intervene, interpose, step in, plead for, petition for.

intercept v **1** *intercept the ball* stop, cut off, deflect, head off, seize, expropriate, commandeer, catch. **2** *intercept the train* check, arrest, block, obstruct, impede, cut off, deflect, head off.

intercession n mediation, negotiation, arbitration, mediatorship, intervention, interposition, pleading, petition, entreaty, supplication; good offices. *see* INTERCEDE.

interchange v **1** *interchange ideas* exchange, trade, trade off, swap, barter, bandy, reciprocate. **2** *interchange the simpleton with the young prince* substitute, change, cause to change places, switch, replace, supplant.

interchange n **1** *the interchange of ideas* exchange, trading, trade, trade-off, swap, barter, bandying, give and take, reciprocation, reciprocity, interplay, crossfire. **2** *the interchange of babies* substitution, change, switch, replacement, supplanting. **3** *a car crash at the interchange* junction, intersection. *see* INTERSECTION 2.

interchangeable adj exchangeable, transposable, equivalent, corresponding, correlative, reciprocal, comparable.

intercourse n **1** *business intercourse* dealings; trade, traffic, commerce, communication, intercommunication, association, connection, contact, correspondence, communion, congress. **2** *have intercourse with a minor* sex, sexual intercourse, sexual relations, coitus, coition, copulation, carnal knowledge, intimacy, love-making, sexual congress, congress.

interdict n *under an interdict preventing him from visiting* prohibition, ban, injunction, restraining order, embargo, veto, proscription, preclusion, exclusion order.

interdict v *interdict him from going* prohibit, forbid, ban, embargo, veto, proscribe, disallow, preclude, exclude, prevent.

interest n **1** *look with interest at the new product* attentiveness, attention, undivided attention, absorption, engrossment, heed, regard, notice, scrutiny, curiosity, inquisitiveness. **2** *an object of interest* curiosity, attraction, appeal, fascination, charm, allure. **3** *a matter of interest to all of us* concern, importance, import, consequence, moment, significance, note, relevance, seriousness, weight, gravity, priority, urgency.

4 *his interests include reading and music* leisure activity, pastime, hobby, diversion, amusement, pursuit, relaxation; *inf* thing, scene. **5** *have an interest in the business* share, stake, portion, claim, investment, involvement, participation; stock, equity. **6** *you must declare your interest in the case* involvement, partiality, partisanship, preference, one-sidedness, favouritism, bias, prejudice, discrimination. **7** *his commercial interests are in trouble* concern, business, matter, care; affairs. **8** *earn interest on investments* dividend, profit, return, percentage, gain. **9** *it is in their interests to go* benefit, advantage, good, profit, gain. **In the interests of** for the sake/benefit of, to the advantage of, in the furtherance of.

interest v **1** *the book interests her* attract/ hold/engage the attention of, attract, absorb, engross, fascinate, rivet, grip, captivate, amuse, intrigue, arouse curiosity in. **2** *the outcome of the war interests us all* affect, have an effect/bearing on, concern, involve. **3** *can I interest you in this computer?* arouse one's interest, persuade to buy, sell.

interested adj **1** *the interested children* attentive, intent, absorbed, engrossed, curious, fascinated, riveted, gripped, captivated, intrigued. **2** *interested parties waiting in the lawyer's office* concerned, involved, implicated. **3** *no interested person can judge the contest* involved, partial, partisan, one-sided, biased, prejudiced, discriminative, discriminating.

interesting adj absorbing, engrossing, fascinating, riveting, gripping, compelling, compulsive, spell-binding, captivating, appealing, engaging, amusing, entertaining, stimulating, thought-provoking, diverting, exciting, intriguing.

interfere v **1** *emotional problems interfering with his work* hinder, inhibit, impede, obstruct, get in the way of, check, block, hamper, handicap, cramp, trammel, frustrate, thwart, baulk. **2** *interfere in other people's business* meddle with, butt into, pry into, tamper with, intrude into, intervene in, get involved in, intercede in; *inf* poke one's nose in, horn in, stick one's oar in; *Amer inf* kibitz on.

interference n **1** *his work suffered from the interference of his emotional problems* hindrance, impediment, obstruction, handicap, baulk. **2** *resent her interference in their affairs* meddling, meddlesomeness, prying, intrusion, unwelcome intervention, intercession.

interim adj *an interim appointment* | *interim measures* temporary, provisional, pro tem, stopgap, caretaker, acting, intervening, makeshift, improvised.

interim n *in the interim we shall choose a new leader* meantime, meanwhile, intervening time, interval, interregnum.

interior adj **1** *the interior part of the building* inner, inside, on the inside, internal, inward. **2** *the interior parts of the country* inland, non-coastal, central, up-country, remote. **3** *the country's interior affairs* home, domestic, civil, local. **4** *his interior motivation* instinctive, intuitive, impulsive, involuntary, spontaneous; *inf* gut. **5** *his interior self* inner, spiritual, mental, psychological, emotional, private, personal, intimate, secret, hidden.

interior n **1** *the interior of the building* inside, inner part/side/surface, centre, middle, nucleus, core, heart. **2** *the interior of the country* centre, heartland, hinterland.

interject v *interject light-hearted remarks into a serious conversation* throw in, insert, introduce, interpolate, interpose, insinuate, add, mingle, intersperse.

interjection n **1** *the interjection of jokes into the script* insertion, introduction, interpolation, interposition, insinuation, intermixing, intermingling, interspersion. **2** *he gave an interjection of pain* cry, exclamation, ejaculation, utterance.

interloper n unwanted visitor/guest, trespasser, invader, intruder, encroacher, gate-crasher.

interlude n interval, intermission, break, recess, pause, respite, rest, breathing-space, halt, stop, stoppage, hiatus, delay, wait.

intermediary n mediator, go-between, broker, agent, middleman, negotiator, arbitrator.

intermediate adj in-between, halfway, in the middle, middle, mid, midway, medial, median, intermediary, intervening, interposed, transitional.

interment n burial, burying, entombment, inhumation, sepulture, funeral; funeral rites, exequies.

interminable adj **1** *an interminable road* seemingly endless, never-ending, without end, everlasting, ceaseless, incessant. **2** *an interminable talk* seemingly endless, never-ending, uninterrupted, monotonous, tedious, wearisome, boring, long-winded, wordy, loquacious, prolix, verbose, rambling. **3** *interminable supplies of food from his benefactor* seemingly endless, unlimited, boundless, infinite, countless, untold,

numberless, innumerable, unmeasured, incalculable, indeterminable.

intermingle v mingle, mix, commingle, intermix, commix, blend, fuse, amalgamate, merge, combine, compound, interweave.

intermission n interval, interlude, interim, entr'acte, break, recess, rest, pause, respite, lull, stop, stoppage, halt, cessation, suspension; *inf* let-up, breather, time out.

intermittent adj fitful, spasmodic, irregular, sporadic, occasional, periodic, cyclic, recurrent, recurring, broken, discontinuous, on again and off again, on and off.

intern v confine, hold in custody, imprison, impound, detain.

internal adj **1** *internal wall* interior, inside, inner, inward. **2** *the country's/firm's internal affairs* home, domestic, civil, interior, in-house, in-company. **3** *his internal opinion* mental, psychological, emotional, subjective, private, intimate.

international adj cosmopolitan, global, universal, worldwide, intercontinental.

interpolate v insert, interject, intercalate, interpose, introduce, insinuate, add, inject, put in, work in.

interpolation n insert, insertion, interjection, intercalation, introduction, addition, injection.

interpose v **1** *interpose a barrier between the speaker and the audience* place between, put between. **2** *interpose a few jokes in the script* insert, interject, introduce, insinuate, add. **3** *interpose in the quarrel* intervene, intercede, step in, mediate, arbitrate, interfere, intrude, obtrude, butt in, meddle; *inf* barge in, horn in, muscle in.

interpret v **1** *interpret the difficult text for the pupils* explain, elucidate, expound, explicate, clarify, make clear, illuminate, shed light on, gloss, simplify, spell out. **2** *interpreted her silence as consent* understand, understand by, construe, take, take to mean, read. **3** *interpret the hieroglyphics* decode, decipher, crack, solve, untangle, unravel. **4** *interpret for the foreign ambassador* translate, transcribe, transliterate, paraphrase. **5** *dancers interpreting the ballet* portray, depict, present, perform, execute, enact.

interpretation n **1** *the interpretation of the difficult text* explanation, elucidation, expounding, explication, clarification, exegesis. see INTERPRET 1. **2** *his interpretation of her silence as consent* understanding, construal, reading. **3** *the interpretation of the coded message* decoding, deciphering. see

INTERPRET 3. **4** *the scientist's interpretation of the results* analysis, reading, diagnosis. **5** *her instant interpretation of the foreign ambassador's speech* translation, transcription, transliteration; paraphrase. **6** *the dancer's interpretation of the ballet* portrayal, depiction, presentation, performance, execution, rendering, rendition, enactment.

interpreter n **1** *foreign language interpreter* translator, transcriber. **2** *a skilful interpreter of the dance* portrayer, performer, exponent. **3** *an interpreter of the world situation* commentator, annotator, scholiast.

interrogate v question, put/pose questions to, inquire of, examine, cross-examine, cross-question, quiz, pump, grill, give the third degree to, probe, catechize; *inf* put the screws on.

interrogation n **1** *give way under interrogation | a long interrogation* questioning, quizzing, investigation, examination, cross-examination, cross-questioning, pumping, grilling, third degree, probing, inquisition, catechization; inquiry, catechism. **2** *complain about the policeman's interrogations* question, query, enquiry, poser.

interrogative adj questioning, quizzing, quizzical, inquiring, curious, inquisitive, investigative, grilling, third-degree, inquisitorial, probing, catechistic.

interrupt v **1** *interrupt his speech | she continuously interrupted* cut in (on), break in (on), barge in (on), intrude (on), disturb, heckle, interfere (with); *inf* butt in (on), chip in (on), chime in (on), horn in (on), muscle in (on). **2** *interrupt the talks for a time* suspend, discontinue, break the continuity of, break, break off, hold up, delay, lay aside, leave off, postpone, stop, put a stop to, halt, bring to a halt/standstill, cease, end, cancel, sever. **3** *only a few trees interrupted the flatness of the landscape* break, break up, punctuate. **4** *the huge office block interrupts our view* obstruct, impede, block, interfere with, cut off.

interruption n **1** *resent his interruption* cutting in, interference, disturbance, intrusion, obtrusion; *inf* butting in, homing in. *see* INTERRUPT 1. **2** *the interruption of the talks* suspension, discontinuance, breaking off, delay, postponement, stopping, halt, cessation. *see* INTERRUPT 2. **3** *there was an interruption of half an hour in the talks* intermission, interval, interlude, break, pause, recess, gap, hiatus.

intersect v **1** *the motorway would intersect an agricultural area* cut across/through, cut in two/half, divide, bisect. **2** *the lines intersect* cross, criss-cross, meet, connect.

intersection n **1** *the intersection of the lines* crossing, criss-crossing, meeting. **2** *a car crash at the intersection* road junction, junction, interchange, crossroads, roundabout; *inf* spaghetti junction.

intersperse v **1** *intersperse flowers among the trees* scatter, distribute, disperse, spread, strew, dot, sprinkle, pepper. **2** *intersperse drawings in the text* insert, interpose, interpolate, incorporate, intercalate. **3** *intersperse the text with illustrations* vary, diversify, variegate.

intertwine v entwine, interwind, interweave, interlace, twist together, coil, twirl, convolute.

interval n **1** *in the interval before the next meeting* interim, interlude, intervening time, time, period, meantime, meanwhile, wait, space. **2** *drinks served in the theatre during the interval* intermission, break, half-time, pause, lull, respite, breather, breathing-space, gap, hiatus, delay. **3** *the intervals between the trees* distance, space, gap, interspace. **4** *children in the playground during the interval* break, recess, playtime.

intervene v **1** *in the years that intervened* come/occur between, come to pass, occur, befall, happen, arise, take place, ensue, supervene, succeed. **2** *intervene in the dispute* intercede, mediate, arbitrate, negotiate, step in, involve oneself, come into, interpose, interfere, intrude.

intervention n *his intervention in the dispute* intercession, mediation, arbitration, negotiation, agency, involvement, interposing, interposition, interference, intrusion.

interview n **1** *candidates nervous at the interview* conference, discussion, meeting, talk, dialogue, evaluation. **2** *the prime minister giving an interview to the press* audience, question and answer session, exchange, dialogue, colloquy, interlocution.

interview v talk to, have a discussion/dialogue with, hold a meeting with, confer with, question, put questions to, sound out, examine, interrogate, cross-examine, evaluate.

interviewer n **1** *the interviewer of candidates* evaluator, assessor, examiner, questioner, interrogator. **2** *the television interviewer* questioner, reporter, correspondent.

interweave v **1** *interweave strands of various fabrics* weave, intertwine, twine, twist, interlace, braid, plait. **2** *their financial affairs are interwoven* intermingle, mingle, interlink, intermix, mix, blend, fuse, interlock, knit, connect, associate.

intestinal adj abdominal, enteric, visceral, coeliac, stomachic, gastric, duodenal.

intestines npl entrails, viscera; small intestine, large intestine, bowel, colon, gut; inf guts, insides, innards.

intimacy n 1 *an intimacy between them* closeness, close association/relationship, familiarity, confidentiality, close friendship, comradeship, amity, affection, warmth, understanding. 2 *guilty of intimacy with a minor* sex, intercourse, sexual intercourse/relations, coition, coitus, carnal knowledge, love-making.

intimate adj 1 *intimate friends* close, near, dear, nearest and dearest, cherished, bosom, familiar, confidential, warm, friendly, comradely, amicable; inf thick; Amer inf buddy-buddy. 2 *in an intimate atmosphere* informal, warm, cosy, friendly, comfortable, snug, tête-à-tête; inf comfy. 3 *a diary giving intimate details* personal, private, confidential, secret, privy. 4 *his intimate views* private, innermost, inmost, inner, inward, intrinsic, deep-seated, inherent. 5 *an intimate knowledge of the law* experienced, deep, in-depth, profound, detailed, thorough, exhaustive, personal, first-hand, direct, immediate. 6 *have intimate relations with a minor* sexual, carnal, fornicatory, unchaste.

intimate n close/best/bosom friend, constant companion, confidant, confidante, close associate, mate, crony, *alter ego*, Achates; inf chum, pal, buddy, mucker.

intimate v 1 *intimate to the crowd that they should go* announce, make known, state, tell, inform, communicate, impart. 2 *in his speech he intimated that he would like to be chairman* imply, suggest, let it be known, hint, insinuate, give an inkling that, indicate, signal; inf tip someone the wink that.

intimation n 1 *receive the intimation of his resignation* announcement, statement, information, communication, notice. 2 *the intimation that he wished the chairmanship* implication, suggestion, hint, insinuation, inkling, indication, signal, reference, allusion.

intimidate v frighten, terrify, scare, alarm, terrorize, overawe, awe, cow, subdue, daunt, domineer, browbeat, bully, tyrannize, coerce, compel, bulldoze, pressure, pressurize, threaten; inf push around, lean on, twist someone's arm.

intimidation n 1 *the intimidation of shopkeepers by gangs* frightening, terrorization, subduing, domineering, bullying, tyrannization, coercion, threatening; inf arm-twisting. see INTIMIDATE. 2 *leave his premises out of intimidation* fear, terror, alarm, awe, trepidation.

intolerable adj unbearable, unendurable, beyond endurance, insufferable, insupportable, not to be borne, more than one can stand, impossible, painful, excruciating, agonizing.

intolerance n 1 *the intolerance of the village inhabitants* bigotry, illiberalism, narrow-mindedness, parochialism, provincialism, insularity, prejudice, bias, partisanship, one-sidedness; chauvinism, jingoism, racism, xenophobia, sexism, ageism, homophobia. see INTOLERANT 1. 2 *his intolerance to/of the sun* sensitivity, hypersensitivity, allergy.

intolerant adj 1 *intolerant citizens objecting to incomers* bigoted, illiberal, narrow-minded, narrow, parochial, provincial, insular, small-minded, prejudiced, biased, partial, partisan, one-sided, warped, twisted, fanatical; chauvinistic, jingoistic, racist, xenophobic, sexist, ageist, homophobic. 2 *intolerant of sun* sensitive to, hypersensitive to, allergic to.

intonation n 1 *a characteristic northern intonation* pitch, tone, timbre, cadence, lilt, inflection, accentuation, emphasis, stress. 2 *listen to the intonation of the monks* chant, chanting, incantation, invocation.

intone v 1 *the choir intoned a psalm* chant/sing/recite in a monotone. 2 *the headmaster intoned his speech slowly and with emphasis* utter, speak, say, articulate, voice, enunciate, pronounce, deliver.

intoxicate v 1 *the cocktails intoxicated them* inebriate, make drunk, befuddle, fuddle, stupefy. see INTOXICATED. 2 *the sunny weather intoxicated them* exhilarate, elate, thrill, invigorate, animate, enliven, excite, arouse, inflame, enrapture.

intoxicated adj inebriated, inebriate, drunk, drunken, drunk as a lord, blind/dead drunk, the worse for drink, under the influence, tipsy, merry, befuddled, stupefied, staggering; inf one over the eight, half-seas-over, three sheets to/in the wind, tight, pickled, soused, under the table, sloshed, plastered, stewed, well-oiled, canned, loaded, stoned, bombed out of one's mind, lit up, tanked up, smashed, paralytic; Scots inf stotious, fou.

intoxicating adj 1 *intoxicating drinks* intoxicant, alcoholic, strong, spiritous, inebriant. 2 *intoxicating news* exhilarating, heady, elating, thrilling, animating, exciting.

intoxication n 1 *suffering from the effects of intoxication* drunkenness, inebriation, inebriety, insobriety, alcoholism, dipsomania, tipsiness, befuddledment, stupefaction; *inf* tightness. **2** *intoxication following the good news* exhilaration, elation, ecstasy, euphoria, thrill, invigoration, animation, excitement, rapture, delirium.

intractable adj unmanageable, ungovernable, uncontrollable, uncompliant, stubborn, obstinate, obdurate, perverse, disobedient, unsubmissive, indomitable, refractory, recalcitrant, insubordinate, rebellious, wild, unruly, rowdy.

intransigent adj uncompromising, irreconcilable, implacable, relentless, unrelenting, inexorable, unbending, unyielding, hardline, die-hard, immovable, inveterate, rigid, tough, tenacious, stubborn, obdurate.

intrench *see* ENTRENCH.

intrenched *see* ENTRENCHED.

intrepid adj fearless, unafraid, undaunted, dauntless, undismayed, unalarmed, unflinching, bold, daring, audacious, adventurous, dashing, rash, reckless, brave, courageous, valiant, valorous, stout-hearted, lion-hearted, gallant, manly, stalwart, plucky, game, spirited, mettlesome, doughty; *inf* gutsy, spunky.

intricate adj **1** *intricate patterns* tangled, entangled, ravelled, twisted, knotty, convoluted, involute, mazelike, labyrinthine, winding, serpentine, circuitous, sinuous, roundabout, fancy, elaborate, ornate, Byzantine, rococo. **2** *intricate problems* complex, complicated, difficult, involved, perplexing, puzzling, thorny, mystifying, enigmatic, obscure.

intrigue v **1** *your behaviour intrigues me | intrigued by the new play* interest, absorb, arouse one's curiosity, attract, draw, pull, rivet one's attention, rivet, fascinate, charm, captivate, divert, pique, titillate. **2** *they are intriguing to kill the king* plot, conspire, scheme, connive, complot, manoeuvre, machinate, devise. **3** *intriguing without her husband's knowledge* have an affair, philander, commit adultery; *inf* carry on.

intrigue n **1** *involved in an intrigue to kill the king* plot, conspiracy, collusion, complot, conniving, cabal, scheme, ruse, stratagem, wile, dodge, artifice, manoeuvre, machination, trickery, sharp practice, double-dealing. **2** *her husband found out about the intrigue* love affair, affair, liaison, amour; adultery; *inf* carrying on.

intriguer n plotter, conspirator, conniver, collaborator, machinator, Machiavelli.

intriguing adj *intriguing news | an intriguing play* interesting, absorbing, compelling,

attractive, appealing, riveting, fascinating, captivating, diverting, titillating, tantalizing.

intrinsic adj inherent, inborn, inbred, congenital, natural, native, indigenous, constitutional, built-in, engrained, implanted, basic, fundamental, elemental, essential, true, genuine, real, authentic.

introduce v **1** *introduce his friends to each other* present, present formally, make known, acquaint, make acquainted. **2** *introduce the speaker* present, announce, give an introduction to. **3** *introduce his talk with a short biography* preface, precede, lead into, commence, start off, begin. **4** *introduce a new method of teaching* bring in, bring into being, originate, launch, inaugurate, institute, initiate, establish, found, set in motion, organize, develop, start, begin, commence, usher in, pioneer. **5** *introduce his ideas* propose, put forward, suggest, broach, advance, bring up, set forth, submit, moot, air, ventilate. **6** *introduce a note of solemnity to the party* insert, inject, interject, interpose, interpolate, intercalate, add, bring, infuse, instil.

introduction n **1** *the introduction of friends/ speakers* presentation, formal presentation. **2** *an informative introduction to the book* foreword, preface, front matter, preamble, prologue, prelude, prolegomenon, proem, exordium, lead-in; *inf* intro, prelims. **3** *the introduction of new teaching methods* origination, launch, inauguration, institution, establishment, development, start, commencement, pioneering. *see* INTRODUCE 4. **4** *his introduction to a new way of life* baptism, initiation, inauguration, debut, first acquaintanceship. **5** *the course provides an introduction to the subject* basics, rudiments, fundamentals; groundwork. **6** *the introduction of a serious note to the party* insertion, injection, interjection, interposition, interpolation, intercalation, addition, infusion. *see* INTRODUCE 6.

introductory adj **1** *the speaker's introductory remarks | the introductory section of the book* prefatory, preliminary, precursory, lead-in, initiatory, opening, initial, starting, commencing. **2** *an introductory course* preparatory, elementary, basic, basal, rudimentary, fundamental, initiatory.

introspective adj inward-looking, inner-directed, introverted, self-analysing, self-examining, subjective, contemplative, reflective, meditative, musing, pensive, brooding, preoccupied.

introverted adj inward-looking, inner-directed, introspective, self-absorbed, contemplative, withdrawn, shy, reserved.

intrude v **1** *not wish to intrude* interrupt, push/thrust oneself in, gatecrash, barge in, encroach, butt in, interfere, obtrude. **2** *intrude on their grief* encroach on, invade, impinge on, infringe on, trespass on, obtrude on, violate.

intruder n **1** *police found an intruder in the house/grounds* burglar, housebreaker, thief, raider, invader, prowler, trespasser. **2** *the strangers were regarded as intruders at the party* unwelcome guest/visitor, gatecrasher, interloper, infiltrator.

intrusion n *resent the intrusion* interruption, gatecrashing, interference, encroachment, invasion, infringement, trespass, obtrusion, violation.

intrusive adj **1** *intrusive neighbours* intruding, interrupting, interfering, invasive, obtrusive, trespassing, meddlesome, inquisitive; *inf* pushy, nosy. **2** *intrusive music* interrupting, invasive, disturbing, annoying, irritating, irksome, unwanted.

intuition n **1** *knew by intuition where the child was* instinct, sixth sense, divination, presentiment, clairvoyance, second sight, extrasensory perception, ESP. **2** *I had an intuition that the child was there* feeling, feeling in one's bones, hunch, inkling, presentiment, foreboding.

intuitive adj intuitional, instinctive, instinctual, innate, inborn, inherent, untaught, unlearned, involuntary, spontaneous, automatic.

intumescence n swelling, distention, bloating, dilatation, tumefaction, turgescence, turgidity.

inundate v **1** *the river inundating the town* flood, deluge, overflow, overrun, swamp, submerge, engulf, drown, cover, saturate, soak. **2** *inundated with correspondence* overwhelm, overpower, overburden, swamp, bog down, glut.

inundation n **1** *people lost in the inundation* flood, deluge, torrent, overflow, tidal wave, flash flood, spate. **2** *not coping with the inundation of work* flood, deluge, overabundance, superabundance, plethora, excess, superfluity, surplus; *inf* tons, heaps.

inure v harden, toughen, indurate, season, temper, habituate, familiarize, accustom, naturalize, acclimatize.

invade v **1** *the enemy invaded the city* march into, overrun, occupy, storm, take over, descend upon, make inroads on, attack, assail, assault, raid, plunder. **2** *invade their privacy* interrupt, intrude on, obtrude on, encroach on, infringe on, trespass on, burst in on, violate. **3** *doubts invaded his*

mind assail, permeate, pervade, fill, spread over.

invader n **1** *enemy invaders of the town* attacker, assailant, assaulter, raider, plunderer. **2** *invaders of their privacy* interrupter, intruder, obtruder, encroacher, infringer, trespasser, violator.

invalid[1] adj *his invalid mother* ill, sick, ailing, unwell, infirm, bed-ridden, valetudinarian, disabled, frail, feeble, weak, debilitated; *inf* poorly.

invalid[1] n *doctors visiting invalids* ill/infirm person, valetudinarian, sufferer, patient, convalescent.

invalid[2] adj **1** *the bye-law is now invalid* inoperative, legally void, null, null and void, void, not binding, nullified, revoked, rescinded, abolished. **2** *an invalid assumption/argument* baseless, unfounded, groundless, unjustified, unsubstantiated, unwarranted, untenable, illogical, irrational, unscientific, false, faulty, fallacious, spurious, unacceptable, inadequate, unconvincing, ineffectual, unsound, weak, useless, worthless.

invalidate v **1** *invalidate the contract* render invalid, void, nullify, annul, cancel, quash, veto, negate, revoke, rescind, abolish, terminate, repeal, repudiate. **2** *invalidate the argument* weaken, undermine, disprove, refute, rebut, negate, discredit, debase.

invaluable adj priceless, beyond price, inestimable, precious, costly, worth its weight in gold, worth a king's ransom.

invariable adj unchanging, changeless, unchangeable, constant, unvarying, unvaried, invariant, unalterable, immutable, fixed, stable, set, steady, unwavering, static, uniform, regular, consistent.

invariably adv *he invariably arrives last* always, every/each time, on every occasion, at all times, without fail/exception, regularly, consistently, repeatedly, habitually, unfailingly, infallibly, inevitably.

invasion n **1** *the invasion of the city* overrunning, occupation, incursion, offensive, attack, assailing, assault, raid, foray, onslaught, plundering. **2** *the invasion of privacy* interruption, intrusion, obtrusion, encroachment, infringement, breach, infraction, trespass, violation.

invective n vituperation, railing, fulmination, berating, upbraiding, castigation, reproval, admonition, denunciation, disparagement, censure, recrimination, abuse, contumely, obloquy; tirade, diatribe, philippic, harangue, tongue-lashing, reprimand, reproach, rebuke, billingsgate.

inveigh v *inveigh against the decision* rail, protest, complain vehemently, fulminate, harangue; denounce, censure, condemn, criticize, disparage, denigrate, revile, abuse, vilify, impugn.

inveigle v ensnare, delude, persuade, talk into, cajole, wheedle, coax, sweet-talk, beguile, tempt, decoy, lure, allure, entice, seduce, deceive.

invent v **1** *invent a new machine/word* originate, create, innovate, discover, design, devise, contrive, formulate, think up, conceive, come up with, hit upon, compose, frame, coin. **2** *he invented that story* make up, fabricate, concoct, hatch, trump up, forge; *inf* cook up.

invention n **1** *the invention of the zip | invention of new words* origination, creation, innovation, discovery, design, devising, contriving, coining, coinage. *see* INVENT 1. **2** *his most famous invention* origination, creation, innovation, discovery, design, contrivance, construction, coinage; *inf* brainchild. **3** *an artist of great invention* inventiveness, originality, creativity, creativeness, imagination, artistry, inspiration; ingenuity, resourcefulness, genius, skill. **4** *his account of the event was pure invention* fabrication, concoction, fiction, falsification, forgery, fake, deceit, myth, fantasy, romance, illusion, sham. **5** *they refused to believe his obvious invention* fabrication, lie, untruth, falsehood, fib, piece of fiction, figment of one's imagination, yarn, story; *inf* tall story.

inventive adj *an inventive artist* original, creative, innovational, imaginative, artistic, inspired, ingenious, resourceful, innovative, gifted, talented, skilful, clever.

inventor n originator, creator, innovator, discoverer, author, architect, designer, deviser, developer, initiator, coiner, father, prime mover, maker, framer, producer.

inventory n list, listing, checklist, catalogue, record, register, tally, account, description, statement.

inverse adj *the inverse side* opposite, converse, contrary, reverse, counter, reversed, inverted, transposed, retroverted.

inverse n *look at the inverse of the coin* opposite side, converse side, obverse side, other side; *inf* flip side.

inversion n **1** *the inversion of the boat* overturn, overturning, upturning, capsizing. *see* INVERT 1, 2. **2** *the inversion of their previous relationship* reverse, turning about, transposal, transposition, contrary, antithesis, converse.

invert v **1** *invert the eggcup/pullover* turn upside down, upturn, turn inside out. **2** *the boat inverted* turn upside down, overturn, upturn, turn turtle, capsize, upset. **3** *invert the printed picture* reverse, interpose, retrovert. **4** *their previous relationship of bully and victim has been inverted* reverse, transpose, turn about/around.

invest v **1** *invest in the business* put/sink money into, lay out money on, provide capital for, fund, subsidize. **2** *invest money/energy in the venture* spend, expend, lay out, put in, use up, devote, contribute, donate, give. **3** *invest power in the king's eldest son* vest, endow, confer, bestow, grant, entrust; give, place. **4** *the rector/king will be invested tomorrow* install, induct, inaugurate, instate, ordain, initiate, swear in, consecrate, crown, enthrone. **5** *he invested his bride in silk* clothe, attire, dress, garb, robe, gown, drape, swathe, adorn, deck. **6** *the enemy army invested the city* besiege, lay siege to, beleaguer, beset, surround, enclose.

investigate v research, probe, explore, inquire into, make inquiries about, go/look into, search, scrutinize, study, examine, inspect, consider, sift, analyse; *inf* check out, suss out.

investigation n research, probe, exploration, inquiry, fact-finding, search, scrutinization, scrutiny, study, survey, review, examination, inspection, consideration, sifting, analysis, inquest, hearing, questioning, inquisition.

investigator n **1** *the investigator of the complaints* researcher, prober, explorer, inquirer, fact-finder, searcher, scrutinizer, scrutineer, reviewer, examiner, inspector, analyser, questioner, inquisitor. **2** *hire a private investigator to find the criminal* detective, private eye; *inf* dick, sleuth, Sherlock; *Amer inf* gumshoe.

investiture n *the investiture of the rector/king* investment, installation, inauguration, instatement, ordination, induction, initiation, swearing in, consecration, crowning, enthroning.

investment n **1** *his business is not a safe investment* venture, speculation, risk. **2** *his investment amounts to £3,000* stake, money/capital invested; *inf* ante. **3** *the investment of the rector* installation, inauguration, instatement, ordination. *see* INVESTITURE.

inveterate adj **1** *an inveterate conservative/drinker* confirmed, habitual, inured, hardened, chronic, die-hard, deep-dyed, dyed-in-the-wool, long-standing, addicted, hard-core, incorrigible. **2** *an inveterate habit* ingrained, deep-seated, deep-rooted, deep-set, entrenched, long-established, ineradicable, incurable.

invidious adj **1** *make invidious comparisons* discriminatory, unfair, prejudicial, slighting, offensive, objectionable, deleterious, detrimental. **2** *it put her in an invidious position* unpleasant, awkward, unpopular, repugnant, hateful.

invigorate v revitalize, energize, fortify, strengthen, put new strength/life/heart in, brace, refresh, rejuvenate, enliven, liven up, animate, exhilarate, pep up, perk up, stimulate, motivate, rouse, excite, wake up, galvanize, electrify.

invincible adj **1** *an invincible opponent* unconquerable, undefeatable, unbeatable, unassailable, invulnerable, indestructible, impregnable, indomitable, unyielding, unflinching, dauntless. **2** *an invincible hurdle* insuperable, unsurmountable, overwhelming, overpowering.

inviolable adj *inviolable rights/oaths* inalienable, untouchable, unalterable, sacrosanct, sacred, holy, hallowed.

inviolate adj *a treaty still inviolate | purity still inviolate* intact, unbroken, whole, entire, complete, untouched, undamaged, unhurt, unharmed, unscathed, unmarred, unspoiled, unsullied, unstained, undefiled, unpolluted, pure, virgin.

invisible adj **1** *invisible to the passers-by* unseeable, out of sight, undetectable, imperceivable, indiscernible, indistinguishable, unseen, unnoticed, unobserved, hidden, concealed. **2** *invisible hairnets* inconspicuous, unnoticeable, imperceptible.

invitation n **1** *reject their invitation to lunch* asking, bidding, call; *inf* invite. **2** *accept their invitation to apply for the post* request, call, appeal, petition, solicitation, supplication, summons. **3** *he regarded her friendliness as a sexual invitation* welcome, encouragement, provocation, overture, attraction, draw, allurement, lure, bait, enticement, temptation, tantalization; *inf* come-on, glad eye.

invite v **1** *they invited him to dinner* ask, bid, summon; request someone's company/ presence at. **2** *invite applications* ask for, request, call for, solicit, look for, seek, appeal for, petition, summon. **3** *invite disaster* cause, bring on, bring upon oneself, draw, make happen, induce, provoke. **4** *she invited his advances* welcome, encourage, foster, attract, draw, allure, entice, tempt, court, lead on.

inviting adj *an inviting prospect* attractive, appealing, pleasant, agreeable, delightful, engaging, tempting, enticing, alluring, winning, beguiling, fascinating, enchanting, entrancing, bewitching, captivating, intriguing, irresistible, ravishing, seductive.

invocation n *an invocation for God's help* call, prayer, request, supplication, entreaty, solicitation, beseeching, imploring, importuning, petition, appeal.

invoice n *receive the invoice for building alterations* bill, account, statement of charges, itemization.

invoke v **1** *invoke God's help* call for, call up, pray for, request, supplicate, entreat, solicit, beseech, beg, implore, importune, call on, petition, appeal to. **2** *invoke the amendment to the constitution* apply, implement, call into use, put into effect/use, resort to, use, have recourse to, initiate.

involuntary adj **1** *an involuntary reaction* reflexive, reflex, automatic, mechanical, unconditioned, spontaneous, instinctive, instinctual, unconscious, unthinking, unintentional, uncontrolled. **2** *their cooperation was involuntary* unwilling, against one's will/wishes, reluctant, unconsenting, grudging, disinclined, forced, coerced, coercive, compelled, compulsory, obligatory.

involve v **1** *his new job involves total discretion* entail, imply, mean, denote, betoken, connote, require, necessitate, presuppose. **2** *try to involve everyone in the party preparations* include, count in, cover, embrace, take in, number, incorporate, encompass, comprise, contain, comprehend. **3** *the criminal tried to involve others in the crime* implicate, incriminate, inculpate, associate, connect, concern. **4** *try to introduce the pupils to something that involves them* interest, be of interest to, absorb, engage, engage/hold/rivet the attention of, rivet, grip, occupy, preoccupy, engross. **5** *the situation was further involved by the police activity* complicate, perplex, confuse, mix up, confound, entangle, tangle, embroil, enmesh.

involved adj **1** *very involved situation/problem/ politics* complicated, difficult, intricate, complex, elaborate, confused, confusing, mixed up, jumbled, tangled, entangled, convoluted, knotty, tortuous, labyrinthine, Byzantine. **2** *involved parties should declare themselves* implicated, incriminated, inculpated, associated, concerned, participating, taking part.

invulnerable adj **1** *she seemed invulnerable against emotional or physical abuse* unwoundable by, unhurtable by, proof against, insensitive to, insusceptible to, indestructible by. **2** *invulnerable fortresses* impenetrable, impregnable, unassailable, unattackable, inviolable, invincible, undefeatable, secure, safe, safe and sound.

inward, inwards adv *proceed inward* inside, towards the inside, within.

inward adj **1** *the inward section* interior, inside, internal, inner, innermost. **2** *his inward thoughts* private, personal, intimate, hidden, secret, confidential, privy.

inwardly adv *he smiled, but inwardly he hated her* at heart, deep down/within, in one's heart, inside, privately, secretly.

inwards see INWARD adv.

iota n bit, mite, speck, atom, jot, whit, particle, fraction, morsel, grain; *inf* smidgen.

irascible adj irritable, quick-tempered, short-tempered, thin-skinned, snappy, snappish, testy, touchy, edgy, surly, cross, crusty, crabbed, grouchy, crotchety, cantankerous, querulous, captious, fractious.

irate adj angry, very angry, wrathful, infuriated, furious, indignant, annoyed, irritated, vexed, incensed, enraged, raging, fuming, ireful, ranting, raving, mad, in a frenzy; *inf* foaming at the mouth.

ire n anger, wrath, rage, fury, indignation, annoyance, exasperation, irritation, hot temper, resentment, choler, spleen.

iridescent adj shimmering, shimmery, glittering, sparkling, dazzling, kaleidoscopic, multicoloured, rainbow-like, variegated, shot.

irk v irritate, annoy, provoke, vex, pique, peeve, nettle, exasperate, ruffle, discountenance, anger, infuriate, incense, try one's patience; *inf* get one's goat, get one's back up.

irksome adj irritating, annoying, vexing, vexatious, exasperating, infuriating, tiresome, wearisome, tedious, trying, troublesome, boring, uninteresting, disagreeable.

iron v *iron their shirts* press, smooth. **iron out 1** *iron out the problems* straighten out, sort out, clear up, settle, solve, resolve, unravel. **2** *iron out their differences* get rid of, eliminate, eradicate, erase, harmonize, reconcile, smooth over.

ironic adj **1** *an ironic remark/wit* satirical, mocking, scoffing, ridiculing, derisory, derisive, scornful, sneering, sardonic, wry, double-edged, sarcastic. **2** *ironic that he died immediately after he won the money* paradoxical, incongruous.

irons npl fetters, chains, shackles, bonds, manacles.

irony n **1** *the irony of his wit* | *use irony* satire, mockery, ridicule, derision, scorn, wryness, sarcasm. **2** *it was an irony that he died soon after winning money* paradox, incongruity, incongruousness.

irradiate v **1** *beacons irradiating the coastline* illuminate, light up, light, brighten, cast light upon, illumine. **2** *irradiate young minds* enlighten, inform, instruct, teach, tutor, give insight to, illumine, edify, inspire. **3** *irradiate tumours/food* treat with radiation, expose to radiation, X-ray.

irrational adj **1** *irrational fears* illogical, unreasonable, groundless, invalid, unsound, implausible, absurd, ridiculous, silly, foolish, senseless, nonsensical, ludicrous, preposterous, crazy. **2** *an irrational person* illogical, unthinking, unintelligent, stupid, brainless, mindless, senseless, confused, muddled, muddle-headed, demented, insane, crazy, unstable.

irreconcilable adj **1** *irreconcilable points of view* incompatible, at odds, at variance, opposite, contrary, incongruous, opposing, conflicting, clashing, discordant. **2** *irreconcilable enemies* implacable, unappeasable, uncompromising, inexorable, intransigent, hard line, inflexible.

irrecoverable adj unrecoverable, unregainable, unreclaimable, irretrievable, irredeemable, unsavable, unsalvageable, irreparable, lost, lost and gone, gone for ever.

irrefutable adj incontrovertible, incontestable, indisputable, undeniable, unquestionable, beyond question, indubitable, beyond doubt, conclusive, decisive, definite, certain, sure, positive, definitive, fixed, final, irrefragable, apodictic.

irregular adj **1** *an irregular coastline* asymmetric, unsymmetric, without uniformity, non-uniform, uneven, broken, jagged, ragged, serrated, crooked, curving, craggy. **2** *an irregular road surface* uneven, unlevel, rough, bumpy, lumpy, knotty, pitted. **3** *an irregular pulse* uneven, unsteady, shaky, fitful, variable, erratic, spasmodic, wavering, fluctuating, aperiodic. **4** *an irregular attender at meetings* inconsistent, erratic, sporadic, variable, inconstant, desultory, haphazard, intermittent, occasional, unpunctual, unsystematic, capricious, unmethodical. **5** *irregular periods of employment* disconnected, sporadic, fragmentary, haphazard, patchy, intermittent, occasional, random, fluctuating, coming and going. **6** *his appointment was most irregular* out of order, contrary, perverse, against the rules, unofficial, unorthodox, unconventional, abnormal. **7** *an irregular result* anomalous, aberrant, deviant, abnormal, unusual, uncommon, freak, extraordinary, exceptional, odd, peculiar, strange, eccentric, bizarre, queer. **8** *lead an irregular life* immoral, dissolute, dissipated, intemperate, immoderate, lascivious, licentious, degenerate, wanton, improper, indecent, lawless, wild, unruly, disorderly. **9** *an irregular army* guerrilla, underground, resistance, mercenary.

irregular n *irregulars shot dead by the army* guerrilla, underground/resistance fighter, mercenary.

irregularity n **1** *the irregularity of the coastline* lack of symmetry, asymmetry, unsymmetricalness, non-uniformity, unevenness, jaggedness. *see* IRREGULAR adj 1. **2** *the irregularity of the road surface* unevenness, unlevelness, roughness, bumpiness, pittedness. *see* IRREGULAR adj 2. **3** *the irregularities on the surface* roughness, bump, lump, pit, hole. **4** *the irregularity of the pulse* unevenness, unsteadiness, shakiness, fitfulness, fluctuation. *see* IRREGULAR adj 3. **5** *the irregularity of their attendance* inconsistency, inconstancy, desultoriness, haphazardness, intermittence, patchiness. *see* IRREGULAR adj 4, 5. **6** *the irregularity of his appointment* unorthodoxy, unconventionality. *see* IRREGULAR adj 6. **7** *the irregularity of the result* anomaly, anomalousness, aberrance, aberrancy, deviation, abnormality, unusualness, freakishness. *see* IRREGULAR adj 7. **8** *spot the irregularities in the result* anomaly, aberration, deviation, abnormality. **9** *the irregularity of his life* immorality, dissoluteness, dissipation, intemperance, immoderation, degeneracy, lawlessness, wildness, unruliness. *see* IRREGULAR adj 8.

irrelevant adj inapposite, inapt, inapplicable, impertinent, non-germane, immaterial, unrelated, unconnected, inappropriate, extraneous, beside the point, not to the point, out of place, nothing to do with it, neither here nor there.

irreligious adj **1** *make irreligious remarks* impious, irreverent, heretical, sacrilegious, ungodly, blasphemous, profane. **2** *trying to preach the gospel to irreligious people* atheistic, unbelieving, non-believing, agnostic, sceptical, infidel, heathen, pagan, unenlightened.

irreparable adj *irreparable damage to his reputation* beyond repair, past mending, irreversible, irrevocable, irretrievable, irrecoverable, irremediable, incurable, ruinous.

irreplaceable adj priceless, invaluable, inestimably precious, unique, worth its weight in gold, rare.

irrepressible adj **1** *irrepressible optimism* unrestrainable, uncontainable, insuppressible, uncontrollable, unstoppable, unquenchable, unreserved, unchecked, unbridled. **2** *irrepressible children playing* bubbling over, buoyant, effervescent, ebullient, vivacious, animated, spirited, lively.

irreproachable adj beyond reproach, blameless, unblameworthy, unblamable, faultless, flawless, guiltless, sinless, innocent, unimpeachable, inculpable, irreprehensible, impeccable, immaculate, unblemished, stainless, pure.

irresistible adj **1** *an irresistible impulse* overwhelming, overpowering, compelling, unsuppressible, irrepressible, forceful, potent, imperative, urgent. **2** *an irresistible fate* unavoidable, inevitable, inescapable, unpreventable, ineluctable, inexorable, relentless. **3** *an irresistible beauty/gateau* fascinating, alluring, enticing, seductive, captivating, enchanting, ravishing, tempting, tantalizing.

irresolute adj uncertain, unsure, doubtful, dubious, undecided, undecisive, unresolved, undetermined, unsettled, vacillating, wavering, hesitant, hesitating, tentative, in two minds, oscillating.

irrespective adj **irrespective of** regardless of, without regard/reference to, setting aside, discounting, ignoring, notwithstanding.

irresponsible adj **1** *irresponsible people* undependable, unreliable, untrustworthy, careless, reckless, rash, flighty, giddy, scatterbrained, erratic, hare-brained, feather-brained, immature; *inf* harum-scarum. **2** *irresponsible actions* thoughtless, ill-considered, unwise, injudicious, careless, reckless, immature.

irretrievable adj irrecoverable, unregainable, unsalvageable, unsavable, irreclaimable, irredeemable, irreparable, lost, hopeless.

irreverent adj **1** *children irreverent to their parents* disrespectful, unrespectful, impertinent, insolent, impudent, rude, cheeky, discourteous, impolite, uncivil; *inf* flip. **2** *irreverent remarks about God* impious, irreligious, heretical, sacrilegious, ungodly, blasphemous, profane.

irreversible adj *irreversible damage/decisions* unalterable, irreparable, unrectifiable, irrevocable, unrepealable, final.

irrevocable adj *irrevocable decisions/fate* unalterable, unchangeable, irreversible, unreversible, fixed, settled, fated, immutable, predetermined, predestined.

irrigation n watering, wetting, spraying, sprinkling, moistening, soaking, flooding, inundating.

irritable adj bad-tempered, ill-tempered, ill-humoured, irascible, cross, snappish, snappy, edgy, testy, touchy, crabbed, peevish, petulant, cantankerous, grumpy, grouchy, crusty, dyspeptic, choleric, splenetic.

irritate v **1** *the children irritate the old man* annoy, vex, provoke, irk, nettle, peeve, get on one's nerves, exasperate, infuriate, anger, enrage, incense, make one's hackles rise, ruffle, disturb, put out, bother, pester, try one's patience; *inf* aggravate, rub up the wrong way, get one's goat, get one's back up, get up one's nose, drive up the wall, drive one bananas. **2** *the rough cloth irritated her skin* chafe, fret, rub, pain, hurt, inflame, aggravate.

irritating adj *irritating habits/people* annoying, vexing, provoking, irksome, exasperating, infuriating, maddening, disturbing, bothersome, troublesome, pestering; *inf* aggravating. *see* IRRITATE 1.

irritation n **1** *snap in irritation* irritability, annoyance, impatience, vexation, exasperation, indignation, crossness, ill-temper, anger, fury, rage, wrath, displeasure, ire; *inf* aggravation. **2** *the child is an irritation to her* source of annoyance, annoyance, irritant, pest, nuisance, tease, thorn in the flesh; *inf* pain in the neck, pain.

island n isle, islet.

isolate v set apart, segregate, cut off, separate, detach, abstract, quarantine, keep in solitude, sequester, insulate.

isolated adj **1** *feeling isolated far from her friends* alone, solitary, lonely, separated, segregated, exiled, forsaken, forlorn. **2** *an isolated place* remote, out of the way, off the beaten track, outlying, secluded, hidden, unfrequented, lonely, desolate, God-forsaken. **3** *an isolated example | an isolated case of polio* single, solitary, unique, random, unrelated, unusual, uncommon, exceptional, abnormal, atypical, untypical, anomalous, freak.

isolation n **1** *the isolation of the patients was necessary* segregation, separation, detachment, abstraction, quarantine, sequestration, insulation. *see* ISOLATE. **2** *the country girl's isolation in the city* lack of contact, separation, segregation, exile, forlornness, aloneness, solitariness, loneliness. **3** *the iso-*lation of the village depressed her* remoteness, seclusion, loneliness, desolation. *see* ISOLATED 2.

issue n **1** *debate the issue for hours* matter, matter in question, point at issue, question, subject, topic, affair, problem, bone of contention, controversy, argument. **2** *the issue is still in doubt* result, outcome, decision, upshot, end, conclusion, consequence, termination, effect, denouement. **3** *the next issue of the magazine* edition, number, printing, print run, impression, copy, instalment, version. **4** *the issue of the new stamps/paper/shares* issuing, issuance, publication, circulation, distribution, supplying, supply, dissemination, sending out, delivery. **5** *Abraham and his issue* offspring, progeny, children; heirs, scions, descendants; *inf* brood. **6** *the issue of the stream* outflow, effusion, discharge, debouchment, emanation. **at issue** *the matters at issue* to be discussed, under discussion, for debate, in dispute, to be decided, unsettled. **take issue** *take issue with management over pay* disagree with, dispute with, raise an objection with/about, make a protest about, challenge, oppose.

issue v **1** *issue new stamps | issue a news statement* put out, give out, deal out, send out, distribute, circulate, release; disseminate, announce, proclaim, broadcast. **2** *smoke issuing from the chimney | liquid issuing from the machine* emit, exude, discharge, emanate, gush, pour forth, seep, ooze. **3** *people issued from the building* emerge, come out, come forth, appear; leave. **4** *his knowledge issues from a love of books* derive, arise, stem, proceed, spring, originate, result; be a result/consequence of.

itch v **1** *her head itches* be itchy, tingle, prickle, tickle, be irritated. **2** *itch for a new car* long, have a longing, yearn, hanker, pine, ache, burn, hunger, thirst, lust, pant, desire greatly, crave.

itch n **1** *have an itch in the head* itchiness, tingling, prickling, tickling, irritation, burning; *Med* formication, paraesthesia. **2** *have an itch for a new car* great desire, longing, yearning, craving, hankering, ache, burning, hunger, thirst, lust; *inf* yen.

itching adj **1** *an itching head* itchy, tingling, prickling. *see* ITCH n 1. **2** *itching to go/know* longing, yearning, craving, aching, burning, avid, agog, keen, eager, impatient, raring, dying.

itchy adj itching, tingling, prinkling. *see* ITCH n 1.

item n **1** *three items for sale* article, thing, piece of merchandise; goods. **2** *several items* *to be discussed* point, detail, matter, consideration, particular, feature, circumstance, aspect, component, element, ingredient. **3** *items in an account* entry, record. **4** *a news item* piece of news/information, piece, story, bulletin, article, account, report, feature, dispatch. **5** *Jim and Jane are an item now* couple, recognized couple; partners.

itemize v *itemize the house contents* list, inventory, record, set out, document, register, tabulate, detail, particularize, specify, instance, enumerate, number.

iterate v repeat, restate, dwell on, hammer away at, harp on about, press one's point about, emphasize, stress, underscore.

itinerant adj travelling, peripatetic, journeying, wandering, roaming, roving, rambling, wayfaring, unsettled, nomadic, migratory, vagabond, vagrant, gypsy.

itinerary n **1** *his itinerary takes him through France* route, planned route, travel plan, course of travel, journey. **2** *the travel agent gave her her itinerary* travel plan/schedule, schedule, timetable, programme; travel arrangements. **3** *keep an itinerary of foreign journeys* diary, journal, logbook, daybook, log, record. **4** *a considerable number of itineraries are in publication* guidebook, travel guide/book, guide.

jab v *jab in the ribs/nose* poke, prod, dig, nudge, elbow, thrust, stab, bump, tap, punch, box; *inf* sock, biff.

jab n *a jab in the ribs/nose* poke, prod, dig, nudge, stab, punch. *see* JAB v.

jabber v chatter, gibber, prattle, babble, gabble, prate, blather, clack, rattle, ramble.

jack v **jack up 1** *jack up the car* lift, lift up, hoist, raise, elevate, uprear, hike up, haul up. **2** *shopkeepers jacking up prices* raise, put up, push up, make higher, increase, boost, inflate, escalate.

jacket n **1** *wearing a jacket and matching trousers* sports coat, short coat, blazer, anorak, parka, cardigan; *inf* cardi. **2** *a jacket for a machine | a jacket for a hot-water tank* casing, case, encasement, sheath, sheathing, envelope, cover, covering, wrapping, wrapper, wrap.

jackpot n kitty, pool, pot, bank, first prize, main prize, prize, winnings, reward, bonanza. **hit the jackpot** win a large prize, win a lot of money, strike it rich/lucky, have a great success, be very successful; *inf* make a killing.

jaded adj **1** *a jaded appetite* satiated, sated, allayed, surfeited, glutted, gorged, dulled, blunted. **2** *feel jaded after the week's work* tired, wearied, weary, fatigued, worn out, exhausted, spent; *inf* played out, done, done in, bushed, pooped, fagged out.

jagged adj *the jagged edge of the broken window* serrated, toothed, notched, indented, denticulate, nicked, pointed, snaggy, spiked, barbed, uneven, rough, ridged, ragged, craggy, broken, cleft.

jail, gaol n *sent to jail for theft* prison, lock-up, detention centre; *inf* nick, clink, inside, stir, slammer, cooler, jug, quod, choky, can; *Amer* jailhouse, penitentiary; *Amer inf* pen.

jail, gaol v *they jailed him for life* send to prison, imprison, clap in prison, send down, lock up, put away, incarcerate, confine, detain, intern, impound, immure.

jailer, gaoler n prison warder, warder, prison warden, warden, guard, keeper, captor; *inf* screw.

jam¹ v **1** *jam something in the door to keep it closed* wedge, sandwich, insert, force, ram, thrust, push, stick, press, cram, stuff. **2** *the ushers jammed too many people into the hall* cram, pack, crowd, squeeze, crush. **3** *the broken-down vehicles jammed the roads* obstruct, block, clog, close off, congest. **4** *the machine has jammed* become stuck, stick, stall, halt, stop.

jam¹ n **1** *a jam of people* crowd, throng, mass, multitude, horde, herd, swarm, mob, pack, crush, press. **2** *caught in a jam on the motorway* traffic jam, hold-up, obstruction, congestion, bottleneck, stoppage; *Amer* gridlock. **3** *in a financial jam* predicament, plight, straits, trouble, quandary; *inf* fix, pickle, spot of bother, hole, spot, tight spot, scrape.

jam² n *spread jam on bread* preserve, preserves, conserve, jelly, marmalade, confiture.

jamb n doorjamb, doorpost, upright, post, pillar.

jamboree n gathering, rally, party, get-together, celebration, festivity, festival, fête, carnival, jubilee, revelry, merrymaking, carouse, spree; *inf* do, beanfeast, shindig, blow-out, bash, rave-up.

jangle v **1** *the chains jangled* clank, clink, clang, clash, clatter, rattle, vibrate, chime. **2** *the noise jangled his nerves* jar on, grate on, irritate, disturb.

jangle n *the jangle of chains* clank, clink, clang, clangour, clash, clatter, rattle, cacophony, din, dissonance, stridor, reverberation, jarring.

janitor n caretaker, concierge, doorkeeper, doorman, custodian; *Scots* school caretaker.

jar n *store rice in a jar* glass container, container, receptacle, vessel, carafe, flagon, flask, pitcher, jug, vase, urn, pot; jamjar.

jar v **1** *the knife jarred against the metal surface* grate, rasp, scratch, squeak, screech. **2** *he jarred his neck in the crash* jolt, jerk, shake, vibrate. **3** *the sound jarred his nerves | her manner jarred on him* grate (on), jangle, irritate, disturb, upset, discompose, irk, annoy, nettle, vex. **4** *his views jarred with hers* clash, conflict, be inharmonious, be in opposition, be at variance, be at odds.

jargon n **1** *the jargon of street traders* cant, slang, argot, idiom, usage, vernacular, dialect, patois; *inf* lingo. **2** *technical jargon* specialized language; computerese, legalese, bureaucratese, journalese, buzz word, gobbledegook, psychobabble.

jaundiced adj **1** *jaundiced skin | his jaundiced face* yellow, yellowish, yellow-tinged, yellow-skinned, sallow. **2** *a jaundiced view of life* cynical, pessimistic, sceptical, distrustful, suspicious, misanthropic, bitter, resentful, jealous, envious, narrow-minded, bigoted, prejudiced.

jaunt n *went on a jaunt to the seaside* trip, outing, short drive, short excursion, short expedition, short tour, mini-holiday, short break, airing, stroll, ramble.

jaunty adj **1** *in a jaunty mood* sprightly, bouncy, buoyant, lively, breezy, perky, frisky, merry, blithe, carefree, joyful. **2** *a jaunty outfit* smart, stylish, spruce, trim, dapper, fancy, flashy; *inf* natty.

javelin n spear, shaft, bolt, pike, assegai, dart.

jaw n **1** *break one's jaw* jawbone, mandible, maxilla. **2** *have a jaw about old times* chat, gossip, conversation, talk, blether, blather; *inf* natter, chinwag.

jaw v *jaw about old times | the speaker jawed on* chat, chatter, gossip, talk, converse, babble, lecture, drone; *inf* natter.

jaws n pl *the jaws of the cave | the jaws of Hell* mouth, maw, opening, entrance, entry, ingress, orifice, aperture, abyss.

jazz n **1** *listen to jazz* ragtime, swing, jive, bebop; hot jazz, cool jazz, traditional jazz. **2** *her performance needs a bit of jazz* liveliness, animation, vivacity, spark, spirit, zest; *inf* pizazz. **3** *can't be bothered with formal invitations and all that jazz* things like that, stuff, rigmarole, paraphernalia. **jazz up** v *jazz up her performance | jazz up the living room* brighten up, liven up, enliven, put some spirit into, put some animation into, add some colour to, enhance.

jazzy adj *jazzy car/clothes* flashy, fancy, stylish, smart, gaudy; *inf* flash, snazzy.

jealous adj **1** *jealous of her beauty* begrudging, grudging, resentful, envious, green with envy, green-eyed, covetous, desirous, emulous. **2** *a jealous lover* suspicious, distrustful, mistrustful, doubting, insecure, apprehensive of rivals, possessive. **3** *jealous of her chastity* protective, vigilant, watchful, heedful, mindful, careful, solicitous, on guard, wary.

jealousy n **1** *show jealousy at her rival's success* grudgingness, resentment, resentfulness, ill-will, bitterness, spite, envy, covetousness; green-eyed monster. **2** *the jealousy of* her husband suspicion, suspiciousness, distrust, mistrust, doubt, insecurity, apprehension about rivals, possessiveness. **3** *guard his honour with jealousy* vigilance, watchfulness, heedfulness, attentiveness, care.

jeans n pl blue jeans, denims; *Trademark* Levis.

jeer v *crowds jeering the politician | he jeered at authority* mock, ridicule, deride, taunt, gibe, scorn, contemn, flout, cry down, tease, hector, barrack, boo, hiss; scoff at, laugh at, sneer at; *inf* knock.

jeer n *the jeers of the crowd* mockery, ridicule, derision; banter, scoffing, teasing, hectoring, barracking; sneer, taunt, gibe, boo, hiss, catcall, abuse; *inf* knocking.

jejune adj **1** *a jejune person* naïve, simple, unsophisticated, immature, inexperienced, ignorant, uninformed; *inf* wet behind the ears. **2** *jejune behaviour* childish, immature, juvenile, puerile, silly, senseless, inane. **3** *jejune prose* insipid, uninteresting, dull, vapid, arid, dry, trite, banal, boring, tedious.

jell v **1** *let the dessert jell* set, stiffen, solidify, harden, thicken, congeal, coagulate. **2** *ideas beginning to jell* take shape, take form, form, crystallize, come together.

jeopardize v put in jeopardy, put at risk, risk, expose to risk, expose to danger, lay open to danger, endanger, imperil, threaten, menace, take a chance with, gamble with.

jeopardy n risk, danger, endangerment, peril, hazard, precariousness, insecurity, vulnerability, threat, menace.

jerk v **1** *jerk him inside by the arm* pull, yank, tug, wrench, tweak, pluck. **2** *the car jerked along* jolt, lurch, bump, jump, bounce, jounce. **3** *his arm was jerking* twitch, shake, tremble, be in convulsion. **4** *jerk a reply | 'yes,' he jerked* snap, say curtly, utter brusquely.

jerk n **1** *pull it out with a jerk* pull, yank, tug, wrench, tweak. **2** *the car stopped with a jerk* jolt, lurch, bump, start, jar. **3** *he's a complete jerk* fool, idiot, rogue, scoundrel; *inf* nerd, twit, dimwit, dope, creep, heel.

jerky adj **1** *a jerky movement of the limbs* spasmodic, fitful, convulsive, twitchy, shaking, shaky, tremulous, uncontrolled. **2** *the jerky motion of the car* jolting, lurching, jumpy, bumpy, bouncy, jouncing, rough.

jerry-built adj *the sports centre is jerry-built* badly built, carelessly built, thrown together, gimcrack, improvised, insubstantial, flimsy, unstable, rickety, ramshackle, defective, faulty, flawed, cheap, cheapjack, shoddy.

jersey n sweater, pullover, jumper, top; *inf* woolly.

jest n **1** *tell jests* joke, witticism, gag, quip, sally, *bon mot*; *inf* crack, wisecrack, funny. **2** *play a jest on someone* joke, prank, hoax, practical joke, trick, jape; *inf* leg-pull, lark. **3** *they did it in jest* fun, sport, play, banter. **4** *they made a jest of him* laughing-stock, butt, fool, Aunt Sally; *inf* stooge, fall guy.

jest v **1** *they joked and jested all evening* joke, tell jokes, crack jokes, quip, banter; *inf* wisecrack. **2** *she took them seriously but they were jesting* fool, fool around, tease, play a prank, play a practical joke, hoax, play a hoax, pull someone's leg; *inf* kid, have someone on.

jester n **1** *her uncle's a jester* joker, comic, comedian, humorist, wag, wit, quipster, prankster, hoaxer. **2** *the jesters in Shakespeare's plays* fool, court fool, clown, zany, buffoon, merry-andrew, harlequin, pantaloon, wearer of the motley.

jet n **1** *a jet of water* stream, gush, spurt, spout, spray, rush, fountain, spring. **2** *put a jet on the hose* nozzle, spout, nose, sprinkler, sprinkler head, spray, rose, atomizer. **3** *travel in a jet* jetplane, jetliner, turbojet, ramjet, jumbo jet.

jet v **1** *water jetted out of the hose* shoot, gush, spurt, spout, well, rush, spray, squirt, spew, stream, surge, flow, issue. **2** *jet off to Spain* fly, travel by plane, zoom.

jet adj *a jet cat* jet-black, black, pitch-black, pitch, ebony, ink-black, ink, sooty, coal-black, sable, raven, sloe-black.

jettison v **1** *jettison heavy goods from a ship* throw overboard, throw over the side, unload, eject. **2** *jettison unwanted clothes* throw out, throw away, discard, get rid of, toss out, scrap, dump.

jetty n *tie the boat to the jetty* pier, wharf, quay, harbour, dock, breakwater, mole, groyne.

jewel n **1** *a crown set with priceless jewels* gem, gemstone, precious stone, stone, brilliant, *bijou*; *inf* sparkler, rock. **2** *she wore a jewel on her dress* piece of jewellery, trinket, ornament. **3** *the jewel of his collection* choicest example, pearl, flower, pride, pride and joy, cream, *crème de la crème*, plum, boast. **4** *his wife is an absolute jewel* treasure, one in a million, saint, paragon; *inf* one of a kind.

jeweller n lapidary, gemmologist.

jewellery n jewels, gems, precious stones, treasure, regalia, trinkets, ornaments; costume jewellery.

Jezebel n loose woman, wanton, scarlet woman, *femme fatale*, temptress, vamp, woman of easy virtue, whore, prostitute, harlot, strumpet, jade, hussy, trollop; *inf* tart, scrubber.

jib v **1** *jib at taking his money* balk at, recoil from, shrink from, stop short of, refuse. **2** *the horse jibbed at the fence* balk at, stop short at, retreat from, refuse.

jiffy n moment, second, split second, minute, instant, flash, trice, twinkling of an eye; *inf* two shakes of a lamb's tail.

jig v *children jigging up and down* bob up and down, bounce, jump about, leap up and down, skip, hop, prance, caper, jounce.

jilt v reject, cast aside, discard, throw over, drop, leave, forsake; *inf* ditch, dump, give the brush-off, give the heave-ho, give the elbow.

jingle v **1** *money jingling* clink, chink, jangle, rattle, clank. **2** *the bell jingled* tinkle, ding, go ding-dong, go ting-a-ling, ring, chime, tintinnabulate.

jingle n **1** *the jingle of money* clink, chink. see JINGLE v **1**. **2** *the jingle of the bell* tinkle, tinkling, ding, ding-dong, ting-a-ling, ringing, tintinnabulation, chime. **3** *sing a little jingle* ditty, chorus, refrain, short song, limerick, piece of doggerel, carol, melody, tune, catchy tune.

jingoism n patriotism, excessive patriotism, blind patriotism, nationalism, chauvinism, flag-waving.

jinx n curse, malediction, spell, plague, affliction; black magic, voodoo, evil eye, bad luck, evil fortune; *Amer* hex.

jinx v curse, cast a spell on, put a voodoo spell on, bewitch; *Amer* hex.

jitter v *she's jittering* be jittery, be nervous, be nervy, be uneasy, be anxious, be agitated, be on edge, be jumpy, tremble, shake, fidget. **the jitters** n *it gives me the jitters* nervousness, nerves, fit of the nerves, uneasiness, anxiety, agitation, trembling, shaking, fidgeting, jumpiness; *inf* the willies, the heebie-jeebies.

jittery adj nervous, nervy, uneasy, anxious, agitated, trembling, quivering, shaking, shaky, fidgety, jumpy.

job n **1** *this job will take hours* work, piece of work, task, undertaking, chore, assignment, venture, enterprise, activity, business, affair. **2** *what is his job?* occupation, profession, trade, employment, vocation, calling, career, field of work, means of livelihood, *métier*, pursuit, position, post, situation, appointment. **3** *it is his job to open the mail* duty, task, chore, errand, responsibility, concern, function, role, charge, office, commission, capacity, contribution. **4** *we must get this job off to the distributors* work, product, batch, lot, consignment. **5** *I had a job to get here* difficult task, problem, trouble, bother, hard time, trial, tribulation. **6** *the police arrested him for the job* crime, felony, burglary, break-in, theft.

jobber n broker, dealer, agent, middleman.

jobless adj unemployed, without paid employment, out of work, without work, workless, idle, inactive, unoccupied.

jockey n rider, horse-race rider, horseman/horsewoman, equestrian.

jockey v **1** *jockey for position* | *jockey oneself into position* | *jockey him into lending money* manoeuvre, manipulate, engineer, elbow, insinuate, ingratiate, wheedle, coax, cajole; *inf* finagle. **2** *jockey the old lady* cheat, swindle, dupe, hoodwink, trick, deceive, take in, exploit, bamboozle, delude, hoax; *inf* con.

jocular adj *a jocular mood* | *a jocular person* humorous, funny, witty, comic, comical, facetious, joking, jesting, playful, roguish, waggish, whimsical, droll, jocose, teasing, sportive, amusing, entertaining, diverting, hilarious; farcical, laughable.

jocund adj cheerful, cheery, merry, happy, gay, blithe, light-hearted, carefree, buoyant, jolly, jovial, in high spirits, smiling, laughing.

jog v **1** *she jogs for exercise* go jogging, run slowly, dogtrot, jogtrot, trot, canter, lope. **2** *they know they won't win but they are jogging along* trudge, plod, tramp, lumber, stump, pad. **3** *she jogged him in the ribs* nudge, prod, poke, push, elbow, tap. **4** *the sight jogged her memory* stimulate, activate, stir, arouse, prompt. **5** *his backpack jogged up and down on his back* bounce, bob, joggle, jiggle, jounce, jolt, jerk, shake.

join v **1** *join the pieces of string/wood/metal together* fasten, attach, tie, bind, couple, connect, unite, link, splice, yoke, knit, glue, cement, fuse, weld, solder. **2** *the two clubs have joined together* join forces, amalgamate, merge, combine, unify, ally, league, federate. **3** *we joined them in their venture* join forces with, team up with, band together with, cooperate with, collaborate with, affiliate with. **4** *join the Army* | *join a sports club* enlist, sign up, enrol; become a member of, enlist in, sign up for, enrol in. **5** *join the search party* join in, participate in, take part in, partake in, contribute to, lend a hand with. **6** *his land joins ours* adjoin, conjoin, abut on, border, border on, touch, meet, verge on, reach to, extend to.

joint n **1** *reinforce the pipes at the joint* join, junction, juncture, intersection, nexus, knot, seam, coupling; coupler, dovetail joint. **2** *drinking in some joint* club, nightclub, bar. **3** *what a filthy joint* place, dwelling, house, establishment; *inf* hole. **4** *smoke a joint* marijuana cigarette; *inf* reefer, stick.

joint adj *a joint interest* common, shared, joined, mutual, combined, collective, cooperative, allied, united, concerted, consolidated.

joint v *joint a carcass* cut, carve, cleave, chop, hew, hack, sever, segment, divide, dismember, disjoint.

jointly adv *decide jointly* together, in combination, in conjunction, as one, mutually, in partnership, cooperatively, in cooperation, in league, in collusion; *inf* in cahoots.

joke n **1** *tell a joke* jest, witticism, quip, gag, yarn, pun, sally; *inf* wisecrack, crack, funny. **2** *play a joke on him* practical joke, prank, trick, hoax, jape; *inf* leg-pull, lark. **3** *we did it for a joke* fun, sport, play, banter, whimsy. **4** *he is the joke of the class* laughingstock, butt, figure of fun, target, fair game, jest, Aunt Sally.

joke v **1** *they joked and jested all evening* tell jokes, crack jokes, jest, banter, quip; *inf* wisecrack. **2** *she took them seriously but they were joking* fool, fool around, tease, pull someone's leg; *inf* kid, have someone on.

joker n **1** *her uncle's a joker* comic, stand-up comic, comedian, humorist, funny man/woman, jester, wag, wit, quipster, banterer, prankster, practical joker, hoaxer, trickster; *inf* kidder, wisecracker. **2** *take no account of jokers that might spoil the plan* unexpected factor, catch, hitch, drawback, pitfall, trap, snare, hindrance, impediment. **3** *who's that joker?* person, man/woman, fellow; *inf* chap, guy, bloke.

jolly adj merry, gay, joyful, joyous, jovial, happy, glad, mirthful, gleeful, cheerful, cheery, carefree, buoyant, lively, bright, light-hearted, blithe, jocund, sprightly, elated, exuberant, exhilarated, jubilant, high-spirited, sportive, playful.

jolt v **1** *people in the crowd jolting each other* bump against, knock against, bump into, bang into, collide with, jostle, push, shove, elbow, nudge, jar. **2** *the car jolted along* bump, bounce, jounce, start, jerk, lurch, jar. **3** *the accident jolted him* upset, disturb, perturb, shake, shake up, shock, stun, disconcert, discompose, disquiet, startle, surprise, astonish, amaze, stagger.

jolt n **1** *one of the crowd gave him a jolt* bump, knock, bang, hit, push, shove, nudge, jar. **2** *the car moved in jolts* bump, bounce, jounce, shake, jerk, lurch, start, jar. **3** *her death came as a jolt* shock, bombshell, blow, upset, setback, surprise, bolt from the blue, thunderbolt.

jostle v **1** *people jostling each other* bump against, knock against, bump into, bang into, collide with, jolt, push, shove, elbow. **2** *jostle her way through* push, thrust, shove, press, squeeze, elbow, force.

jot n *not care a jot* iota, whit, little bit, bit, scrap, fraction, atom, grain, particle, morsel, mite, speck, trace, trifle, tinge; *inf* smidgen, tad.

jot v *jot down the details* write down, note, note down, make a note of, take down, put down, mark down, list, make a list of, register, record, chronicle.

journal n **1** *keep a journal on his travels* diary, daybook, notebook, commonplace-book, log, logbook, chronicle, record, register. **2** *publish medical journals* periodical, magazine, trade magazine, review, publication, professional organ. **3** *the proprietor of several national journals* newspaper, paper, daily newspaper, daily, weekly newspaper, weekly, gazette.

journalism n **1** *have a job in journalism* the press, the newspaper business, the newspaper world, print media, the fourth estate, Fleet Street; radio journalism, television journalism. **2** *do not admire their style of journalism* reporting, newspaper writing, feature writing, news coverage, broadcasting.

journalist n reporter, newspaperman/newspaperwoman, newsman/newswoman, newshound, pressman/presswoman, feature writer, columnist, correspondent, contributor, commentator, reviewer, editor, sub-editor; broadcaster; *inf* stringer, sub.

journey n *go on a long/short journey* trip, expedition, excursion, travels, tour, trek, voyage, cruise, safari, peregrination, roaming, roving, globe-trotting, odyssey, pilgrimage, outing, jaunt.

journey v *journey to India* go, travel, go on a trip, go on an expedition, go on an excursion, tour, voyage, sail, cruise, fly, hike, trek, roam, rove, ramble, wander, meander, peregrinate, globe-trot.

jovial adj *jovial person/comment/mood/gathering* jolly, jocular, jocose, jocund, happy, cheerful, cheery, glad, in good spirits, merry, gay, mirthful, blithe, buoyant, animated, convivial, sociable, cordial.

joy n **1** *receive the gift with joy* delight, pleasure, gladness, enjoyment, gratification, happiness, rapture, glee, bliss, ecstasy, elation, rejoicing, exultation, jubilation, euphoria, ravishment, transport, felicity. **2** *their daughter is a joy* source of joy, treasure, prize, gem, jewel, pride and joy, delight. **3** *it is a joy to see you* pleasure, delight, treat, thrill. **4** *we had no joy from the bank* success, satisfaction, good fortune, luck, achievement.

joyful adj **1** *joyful at the news* overjoyed, elated, beside oneself with joy, thrilled, delighted, pleased, gratified, happy, glad, blithe, gleeful, jubilant, ecstatic, exultant, euphoric, enraptured, over the moon, in seventh heaven, on cloud nine; *inf* tickled pink. **2** *we heard the joyful news* glad, happy, good, pleasing, cheering, gratifying, heartwarming. **3** *a joyful occasion/song* joyous, happy, cheerful, merry, gay, festive, celebratory.

joyless adj **1** *a joyless existence/place* gloomy, dreary, drab, dismal, bleak, depressing, cheerless, grim, desolate, comfortless. **2** *joyless children* unhappy, sad, miserable, wretched, downcast, dejected, depressed, despondent, melancholy, mournful.

joyous adj joyful, happy, cheerful, merry. *see* JOYFUL 1, 3.

jubilant adj *his jubilant family welcomed him home* rejoicing, overjoyed, exultant, triumphant, elated, thrilled, euphoric, ecstatic, enraptured, rhapsodic, transported, exuberant, on top of the world, walking on air, over the moon, in seventh heaven, on cloud nine; *inf* tickled pink.

jubilation n exultation, triumph, elation, joy, euphoria, ecstasy, rapture, transport, exuberance.

jubilee n celebration, commemoration, anniversary, holiday, feast day, festival, gala, carnival, fête, festivity, revelry.

judge v **1** *judge the murder case* try, hear evidence, sit in judgement, give a verdict, pronounce a verdict, pass sentence, pronounce sentence, sentence, decree. **2** *judge the contest* adjudicate, adjudge, umpire, referee, arbitrate, mediate. **3** *judge the entries/judge his conduct for yourself* assess, appraise, evaluate, weigh up, size up, gauge, examine, review, criticize, diagnose. **4** *judge the distance to be three miles* estimate, assess, reckon, guess, surmise; *inf* guesstimate. **5** *I judge that he is not honest/judge him to be dishonest* consider, believe, think, form the opinion, deduce, gather, conclude.

judge n **1** *the judge pronounced sentence* magistrate, sheriff, his/her honour; *inf* beak, m'lud; high-court judge. **2** *the flower-show judge* appraiser, assessor, evaluator, critic, expert. **3** *the contest judge* adjudicator, umpire, referee, arbiter, arbitrator, mediator.

judgement n **1** *he has no judgement* discernment, acumen, shrewdness, common sense, good sense, sense, perception, perspicacity, percipience, penetration, discrimination, wisdom, judiciousness, prudence, sagacity, understanding, intelligence, powers of reasoning. **2** *the adjudicator/magistrate gave his judgement* verdict, decision, adjudication, ruling, finding, opinion, conclusion, decree, sentence. **3** *in my judgement he is dishonest* opinion, view, belief, conviction, estimation, evaluation, assessment, appraisal. **4** *the Day of Judgement/Judgement Day* damnation, doom, fate, punishment, retribution, sentence.

judicial adj **1** *judicial process/review* judiciary, juridical, judicatory, legal. **2** *a judicial mind* judgelike, impartial, unbiased, critical, analytical, discriminating, discerning, perceptive.

judicious adj *a judicious course of action* wise, prudent, politic, sagacious, shrewd, astute, sensible, common-sense, sound, well-advised, well-considered, well-judged, considered, thoughtful, expedient, practical, discerning, discriminating, informed, intelligent, smart, clever, enlightened, logical, rational, discreet, careful, cautious, circumspect, diplomatic.

jug n pitcher, ewer, crock, carafe, decanter, jar, urn, vessel, receptacle, container.

juggle v *juggle the figures* change around, alter, tamper with, falsify, fake, manipulate, manoeuvre, rig, massage; *inf* fix, doctor, cook.

juice n extract, sap, secretion, liquid, liquor, fluid, serum; *orange juice, meat juice.*

juicy adj **1** *juicy fruit* succulent, moist, lush, sappy, watery, wet, flowing. **2** *a juicy tale* racy, risqué, spicy, sensational, thrilling, fascinating, colourful, exciting, vivid.

jumble v *jumble up the toys* disarrange, disorganize, disorder, dishevel, muddle, confuse, tangle, shuffle, mix, mix up, mingle, put in disarray, make a shambles of, throw into chaos.

jumble n *a jumble of toys* clutter, muddle, confusion, litter, mess, hodgepodge, hotchpotch, mishmash, confused heap, miscellany, motley collection, mixture, medley, gallimaufry, farrago.

jumbo adj *jumbo packet/sausages* giant, gigantic, immense, huge, extra-large, over-sized.

jump v **1** *jump around* spring, leap, bound, hop, bounce, skip, caper, gambol, frolic, frisk, cavort. **2** *jump over the rope* high-jump, leap over, vault, pole-vault, hurdle, clear, go over, sail over. **3** *she jumped when she heard the noise* start, flinch, jerk, recoil, twitch, quiver, shake, wince; *inf* jump out of one's skin. **4** *jump a piece of text* skip, miss, omit, leave out, cut out, pass over, overlook, disregard, ignore. **5** *jump the traffic lights* overshoot, drive through, disregard, ignore. **6** *prices jumped* rise, go up, leap up, increase, mount, escalate, surge. **7** *retailers jumping prices* raise, put up, up, increase, escalate, hike up, advance, boost, elevate, augment; *inf* jack up. **8** *youths jumped the old man* pounce on, set upon, fall on, swoop down on, attack, assault; *inf* mug. **jump at** *jump at the opportunity* grab, snatch, accept eagerly, go for enthusiastically, show enthusiasm for. **jump the gun** *jump the gun by applying for a job not yet advertised* act prematurely, be too soon, act too soon, be previous, be ahead of time, anticipate.

jump n **1** *with one jump* spring, leap, vault, bound, hop, bounce, skip. **2** *the jumps in the race* hurdle, fence, rail, hedge, obstacle, barrier, gate. **3** *a jump in the sequence* gap, break, hiatus, interruption, space, lacuna, breach, interval. **4** *she gave a jump at the sight* start, flinch, jerk, twitch, quiver, shake, wince. **5** *the car started with a jump* start, jolt, jerk, lurch, bump, jounce, jar. **6** *a jump in prices* rise, increase, upturn, upsurge, escalation, hike, boost, advance, elevation, augmentation.

jumper n sweater, pullover, jersey, top; *inf* woolly.

jumpy adj **1** *feeling jumpy waiting for news* nervous, nervy, edgy, on edge, jittery, agitated, fidgety, anxious, uneasy, restive, tense, alarmed, apprehensive, panicky. **2** *the jumpy movements of the car* jolting, fitful, convulsive, jerky, lurching, bumpy, jouncing, jarring.

junction n **1** *reinforcement at the junction of the pipes* join, joint, juncture, link, bond, connection, seam; joining, coupling, linking, welding, union. **2** *cars stop at the junction* crossroads, crossing, intersection, interchange; motorway junction, railway junction.

juncture n **1** *at this juncture we should vote* point, point in time, time, stage, period, critical point, crucial moment, moment of truth, turning-point, crisis, crux, extremity. **2** *reinforcement at the juncture of the pipes* junction, join, joint, coupling, union. *see* JUNCTION 1.

jungle n **1** *wild animals in the thick jungle* forest, tropical forest, rain forest, wilderness, wilds, the bush. **2** *a jungle of paperwork/facts* jumble, tangle, disarray, confusion, hotchpotch, hodgepodge, heap, mass, mess, mishmash, motley selection, gallimaufry, farrago. **law of the jungle** survival of the fittest, each man for himself, dog-eat-dog, cutthroat competition.

junior adj **1** *the junior member* younger. **2** *the junior position* subordinate, lesser, lower, minor, secondary, inferior.

junk n *clear up all this junk* rubbish, refuse, litter, scrap, waste, garbage, trash, debris, leavings, leftovers, remnants, cast-offs, rejects, odds and ends, bric-à-brac, oddments.

junk v *junk unwanted things* throw out, throw away, discard, get rid of, dispose of, scrap; *inf* dump.

junket n *have a junket on his birthday* feast, festivity, revelry, party, picnic, celebration, spree, excursion; *inf* do, bash, thrash, beanfeast.

junket v *junketing to celebrate victory* feast, eat, drink and be merry, throw a party, entertain, party, picnic, celebrate, go on a spree, go on an excursion.

jurisdiction n **1** *under the governor's jurisdiction* authority, control, administration, command, leadership, power, dominion, sovereignty, rule, mastery, sway, say, influence. **2** *living in adjoining jurisdictions* territory, district, province, domain, principality, realm, area, zone. **3** *the jurisdiction of his authority* extent, range, scope, bounds, compass, sphere, area, field, orbit.

just adj **1** *a just judge* fair, fair-minded, equitable, even-handed, impartial, unbiased, objective, neutral, disinterested, unprejudiced, open-minded. **2** *a just man* upright, honourable, upstanding, honest, righteous, ethical, moral, virtuous, principled, good, decent, straight, truthful, sincere. **3** *just criticism* valid, sound, well-founded, well-grounded, justified, justifiable, warrantable, defensible, reasonable. **4** *just desserts* deserved, well-deserved, merited, earned, rightful, due, proper, fitting, appropriate, apt, suitable, condign. **5** *the just heir* lawful, legitimate, legal, licit, rightful, genuine; *inf* kosher. **6** *a just account of the events* true, truthful, accurate, correct, factual, exact, precise, close, faithful, strict.

just adv **1** *I just saw him* only now, a moment ago, a second ago, a short time ago, recently, lately, not long ago. **2** *the house is just right* exactly, precisely, absolutely, completely, totally, entirely, perfectly. **3** *we just made it* only just, barely, scarcely, hardly, by a narrow margin, by a hair's breadth; *inf* by the skin of one's teeth. **4** *she's just a child* only, merely, simply, but, nothing but, no more than. **5** *I just told him what I thought of him* really, indeed, truly, actually, certainly. **just about 1** *I've got just about every one of his books* all but, almost, nearly, practically, well-nigh, not quite. **2** *we lost it just about here* near, around, close to, in the vicinity of.

justice n **1** *expect justice from the courts* justness, fairness, fair play, fair-mindedness, equitableness, equity, even-handedness, impartiality, impartialness, lack of bias, objectivity, neutrality, disinterestedness, lack of prejudice, open-mindedness. *see* JUST adj 1. **2** *a man of justice* justness, uprightness, integrity, honour, honesty, righteousness, ethics, morals, virtue, principle, decency, propriety. *see* JUST adj 2. **3** *see the justice of his criticism* validity, justification, soundness, reasonableness. *see* JUST adj 3. **4** *the justice of his heirdom* lawfulness, legitimacy, legality, licitness. *see* JUST adj 5. **5** *demand justice* amends, recompense, redress, compensation, reparation, requital, retribution, penalty, punishment. **6** *the justice was passing sentence* judge, magistrate, sheriff.

justifiable adj valid, sound, well-founded, lawful, legitimate, legal, tenable, right, defensible, supportable, sustainable, warrantable, vindicable, reasonable, within reason, sensible, acceptable, plausible.

justification n **1** *give as the justification of his behaviour* grounds, reason, just cause, basis, explanation, rationalization, defence. *see* JUSTIFY 1. **2** *the justification of his crime* substantiation, proof, establishment, verification, legalization. *see* JUSTIFY 2. **3** *outline the justification for our fears* warranty, substantiation, reasonableness, confirmation. *see* JUSTIFY 3. **4** *the justification of the accused* acquittal, absolution, exoneration, exculpation, pardon, excusing. *see* JUSTIFY 4.

justify v **1** *justify his behaviour* give grounds for, give reasons for, show just cause for, explain, give an explanation for, rationalize, defend, stand up for, uphold, sustain. **2** *he had to justify his claim* substantiate, prove, establish, verify, certify, vindicate, legalize, legitimize. **3** *his conduct justified our* *worries* warrant, substantiate, bear out, show to be reasonable, prove to be right, confirm. **4** *the accused was finally justified* declare innocent, pronounce not guilty, acquit, clear, absolve, exculpate, exonerate, pardon, excuse.

justly adv **1** *justly proud* justifiably, rightfully, with reason, with good reason. **2** *behave justly* fairly, equitably, impartially, without bias, objectively, without prejudice, disinterestedly. **3** *describe the incident* justly accurately, correctly, truthfully, faithfully.

jut v stick out, project, protrude, poke out, bulge out, overhang, beetle.

juvenile adj **1** *juvenile entrants* young, junior, minor. **2** *a juvenile attitude* childish, puerile, infantile, jejune, immature, inexperienced, callow, green, unsophisticated, naïve; *inf* wet behind the ears.

juxtapose v place/set side by side, place parallel, put adjacent, compare.

Kk

kaleidoscopic adj **1** *a kaleidoscopic pattern* many-coloured, variegated, motley, rainbowlike, many-splendoured, psychedelic. **2** *a kaleidoscopic scene* changeable, everchanging, variable, varying, mutable, protean, ever-moving, fluid, mobile, unstable, unsteady, labile. **3** *a kaleidoscopic set of facts* complex, complicated, intricate, convoluted, confused, disordered, disarranged, jumbled, muddled, chaotic.

keel n **1** *the keel of a boat* bottom, bottom side, underside. **2** *admiring the keels sailing on the sea* boat, ship, vessel, craft.

keel v *the boat suddenly keeled* keel over, turn over, overturn, turn upside down, turn turtle, capsize, topple over, upset. **keel over 1** *the boat keeled over* turn over, overturn, capsize. **2** *a member of the crowd keeled over* faint, fall down in a faint, collapse, lose consciousness, pass out, black out.

keen adj **1** *a keen edge to the blade* sharp, sharp-edged, sharpened, fine-edged, razorsharp. **2** *a keen sense of smell* sharp, acute, discerning, perceptive, sensitive, discriminating. **3** *a keen mind* sharp, astute, quickwitted, sharp-witted, shrewd, perceptive, penetrating, perspicacious, clever, bright, smart, intelligent, brilliant, wise, canny, sagacious, sapient; *inf* brainy. **4** *be the butt of her keen wit* acerbic, acid, biting, caustic, tart, pointed, mordant, trenchant, incisive, razor-like, razor-sharp, finely honed, cutting, stinging, scathing, sardonic, satirical. **5** *keen pupils* willing, eager, enthusiastic, avid, earnest, intent, diligent, assiduous, conscientious, zealous, fervent, fervid, impatient. **6** *keen on learning/girls* fond of, devoted to, eager for, hungry for, thirsty for. **7** *keen to learn* eager to, longing to, yearning to, impatient to, itching to; *inf* rarin' to. *see* KEEN adj 5.

keen v *keen over the dead body* wail, lament, weep, sob, cry, ululate, howl, moan, groan, mourn, sorrow, grieve.

keenness n **1** *the keenness of the blade* sharpness, razor-sharpness. *see* KEEN adj 1. **2** *the keenness of her sense of smell* sharpness, acuteness, perceptiveness, sensitivity. *see* KEEN adj 2. **3** *the keenness of his mind* sharpness, astuteness, quick-wittedness, sharpwittedness, perspicacity, shrewdness, cleverness, brightness, intelligence, canni-

ness. *see* KEEN adj 3. **4** *the keenness of her wit* acerbity, acidity, causticity, tartness, mordancy, trenchancy, incisiveness, sardonicism, satire. *see* KEEN adj 4. **5** *the keenness of the pupils* willingness, eagerness, enthusiasm, avidity, intentness, diligence, assiduity, zeal, fervour, devotion, impatience. *see* KEEN adj 5, 6 *and* 7.

keep v **1** *keep going* carry on, continue, maintain, persist, persevere. **2** *he kept the ring which she gave him* hold on to, keep hold of, retain, retain in one's possession; *inf* hang on to. **3** *he keeps all his old newspapers* save up, accumulate, store, hoard, amass, pile up, collect, garner. **4** *keep the memory of her* preserve, conserve, keep alive, keep fresh. **5** *does the grocer keep string?* sell, stock, have in stock, carry, deal in, trade in. **6** *he is responsible for keeping the estate* look after, keep in good order, tend, mind, maintain, keep up, manage, superintend. **7** *the boy keeps the sheep* tend, care for, look after, mind, guard, safeguard, protect, watch over, shield, shelter. **8** *he could not keep a wife and children on his salary* provide for, support, maintain, sustain, subsidize, feed, nurture, provide board for. **9** *keep it from her* keep secret, keep hidden, hide, conceal, keep dark, withhold, hush, hush up, not breathe a word of, suppress, censor. **10** *keep one's promise/word* keep to, abide by, comply with, fulfil, carry out, effectuate, keep faith with, stand by, honour, obey, observe. **11** *keep the Sabbath* observe, hold, celebrate, commemorate, respect, ritualize, solemnize, ceremonialize. **12** *what kept you?* keep back, hold back, hold up, delay, detain, retard, hinder, obstruct, impede, hamper, constrain, check, block, hamstring, prevent. **keep at 1** *we'll finish in time if we keep at it* persist, persevere, be persistent, be pertinacious, carry on, keep going, continue, work away, see it through; *inf* stick at it, stay the distance, hang on in there, slave away, peg away. **2** *the teacher kept at us to work* keep on at, keep after, go on at, chivvy, badger, harp on at, nag, harass. **keep back 1** *what kept you back?* hold, back, hold up, delay, detain. *see* KEEP v 12. **2** *keep back information* withhold, keep secret, keep hidden, hide, conceal, suppress. *see* KEEP v 9. **keep from 1** *keep myself from falling* prevent, stop, restrain, check, halt. **2** *keep him from harm* keep safe, preserve, protect, guard, safeguard, shield, shelter. **keep off 1** *keep off his property* keep away from, stay away from, stay off, remain at a distance from, not go near, not approach, not stand on, not walk on, not touch, not trespass on. **2** *keep off the subject* avoid, steer clear of, not mention, not refer to, not allude to, abstain from, evade, dodge, shun, eschew. **3** *keep off chocolate/wine/cigarettes* refrain from, abstain from, give up, quit, renounce, turn aside from; *inf* swear off. **4** *the rain kept off* stay away, not start, not begin. **keep on 1** *keep on going* go on, carry on, continue, persist, persevere. **2** *the boss decided to keep the man on* continue to employ, keep employing, retain the services of, not to dismiss; *inf* not to sack. **3** *keep on about his faults* keep talking, go on, go on and on, refer to again and again, dwell on, repeat oneself, ramble on, rant on; *inf* witter on. **4** *keep on at* keep at, keep after, go on at, chivvy, badger, nag. *see* KEEP v *at* 2. **keep to 1** *keep to his word* keep, abide by, comply with, stand by, honour. *see* KEEP v 10. **2** *keep to the path/subject* not stray from, not wander from, stay with; *inf* stick with. **keep under** *the poor were kept under by the authorities* suppress, oppress, tyrannize, tyrannize over, keep in submission, keep down, keep under one's thumb, quell, squelch. **keep up 1** *keep up the payments/progress* maintain, continue with, go on with, carry on with, keep going. **2** *try to keep up in the race* keep pace, keep abreast, not fall behind, not lag behind. **3** *keep up with the rest* keep pace with, keep abreast of, compete with, vie with, rival. **4** *keep up with latest developments* keep pace with, keep abreast of, keep informed about, learn about, retain an interest in. **5** *keep up with old friends* stay in touch with, keep in contact with, remain in correspondence with, be in communication with, keep alive one's friendship with, remain acquainted with.

keep n **1** *pay for their/its keep* maintenance, support, board, board and lodging, subsistence, sustenance, food, nourishment, living, livelihood, upkeep. **2** *enemies storming the keep* donjon, dungeon, tower, stronghold, fastness, citadel, fortress, fort, castle. **for keeps** forever, for always, for good, once and for all.

keeper n **1** *prisoners escaping their keeper* jailer, gaoler, warder, warden, guard, custodian, sentry; *inf* screw. **2** *a museum/lighthouse keeper* curator, conservator, attendant, caretaker, steward, superinten-

dent, overseer, administrator. **3** *his brother's keeper* guardian, escort, bodyguard, chaperon, chaperone, nursemaid, nurse.

keeping n **1** *children/property in the keeping of the grandfather* keep, guardianship, protection, protectorship, trusteeship, trust, safe keeping, safeguard, care, charge, custody, possession, auspices, aegis, patronage. **2** *behaviour in keeping with their beliefs* agreement, harmony, accordance, accord, concurrence, conformity, consistency, correspondence, congruity, compliance, proportion.

keepsake n memento, souvenir, remembrance, reminder, token of remembrance, relic, favour.

keg n *don't like keg beer* barrel, cask, vat, tun, butt, drum, hogshead, firkin, container, vessel.

kernel n **1** *grown from a kernel* grain, seed, germ, stone, nut. **2** *the kernel of the problem* nub, nucleus, core, centre, heart, marrow, pith, substance, essence, essential part, gist, quintessence; *inf* nitty-gritty, nuts and bolts, brass tacks.

key n **1** *key in the lock* latchkey, passkey, master-key, skeleton key. **2** *the key to the problem* answer, solution, explanation, guide, clue, cue, pointer, gloss, interpretation, explication, annotation, clarification, exposition, translation. **3** *musical key* tone, pitch, timbre, tonality, tone colour. **4** *a poem in a mournful key* mood, humour, vein, style, character, spirit.

keynote n **1** *musical keynote* tonic, leading note. **2** *the keynote of the speech* theme, gist, salient point, substance, essence, pith, centre, heart, core, nucleus, marrow, policy line.

keystone n **1** *the keystone of the pillar* central stone, cornerstone, quoin. **2** *the keystone of the theory* principle, basis, foundation, linchpin.

kibosh v **put the kibosh on** stop, bring to an end, put an end to, put a stop to, check, curb, nip in the bud, quell, quash, suppress, crack down on.

kick v **1** *kick the ball* boot, put one's boot to, punt. **2** *the gun kicked* recoil, spring back. **3** *kick against the rules* protest against, resist, oppose, rebel against, spurn, object to, complain about, grumble about; *inf* gripe about, grouse about, beef about, bitch about. **4** *kick the habit* give up, stop, abandon, quit, leave off, desist from. **kick around 1** *kick around the poor people* abuse, mistreat, maltreat, push around. **2** *kick around ideas* discuss, talk over, debate, thrash out, argue the pros and cons. **kick off** *kick off the proceedings* start, begin, commence, open, get under way, get going, start the ball rolling, initiate. **kick out** throw out, eject, expel, get rid of, force out, turn out, oust, evict, dismiss, discharge, give someone his marching orders; *inf* send packing, show the door to, sack, fire, give the boot to, boot out, give the axe to, throw out on one's ear, give the bum's rush to.

kick n **1** *gave the ball a kick* boot, punt. **2** *she steals for kicks* thrill, excitement, stimulation, fun, pleasure, enjoyment, amusement, gratification; *inf* buzz. **3** *the drink has quite a kick* strength, potency, tang, zip, alcoholic effect; *inf* punch, zing. **4** *there's no kick left in the firm* vigour, force, forcefulness, energy, vitality, vivacity, liveliness, verve, animation, enthusiasm, zest, zip; *inf* punch, zing.

kick-off n start, beginning, commencement, outset, opening, initiation.

kid n *an adult and three kids* child, young one, young person, youngster, little one, baby, toddler, tot, infant, boy/girl, adolescent, juvenile, teenager, youth; *inf* kiddie; *Scots* bairn.

kid v **1** *he was only kidding* tease, joke, jest, fool, fool around, pull someone's leg, chaff, be facetious; *inf* have someone on. **2** *don't kid yourself you won't win* deceive, delude, fool, trick, cozen, gull, hoodwink, hoax, beguile, bamboozle.

kidnap v abduct, seize, snatch, capture, hold to ransom, take as hostage.

kill v **1** take someone's life, slay, murder, do away with, do to death, slaughter, butcher, massacre, assassinate, liquidate, wipe out, destroy, erase, eradicate, exterminate, dispatch, put to death, execute, hang, behead, guillotine, send to the electric chair; *inf* bump off, do in, knock off, top. **2** *kill all his hopes* destroy, put an end to, ruin, extinguish, scotch, quell. **3** *kill time* pass, spend, expend, while away, fill up, occupy, use up. **4** *the walk will kill you* exhaust, overtire, tire out, fatigue, wear out, fag out, debilitate, enervate, prostrate, tax, overtax, strain. **5** *these shoes are killing me | my feet were killing me* hurt, cause pain, cause discomfort, be uncomfortable, be painful. **6** *kill the information in the file* cancel, delete, remove, erase, cut out, eradicate, expunge, obliterate; *inf* zap. **7** *kill the parliamentary bill* defeat, veto, vote down, reject, overrule. **8** *wall-linings killing the noise* deaden, muffle, dull, dampen, smother, stifle. **9** *kill the bottle of wine* consume, drink up, drain, empty, finish; *inf* knock back. **10** *his jokes kill me* overwhelm with laughter, amuse greatly, make someone laugh; *inf* have people rolling in the aisles, make someone crack up.

killer n slayer, murderer, slaughterer, butcher, assassin, liquidator, destroyer, exterminator, executioner, gunman, homicide, patricide, matricide, infanticide, fratricide, sororicide, regicide; *inf* hit man.

killing n **1** *guilty of killing* slaying, murder, manslaughter, homicide, slaughter, butchery, massacre, bloodshed, carnage, assassination, liquidation, destruction, extermination, execution, patricide, matricide, infanticide. *see* KILL 1 *and* KILLER. **2** *make a killing on the stock market | she made a killing in the sales* financial success, bonanza, fortune, windfall, gain, profit, booty, piece of good luck, coup; *inf* bomb, clean-up.

killing adj **1** *a killing blow* fatal, lethal, mortal, death-dealing, murderous, homicidal. **2** *a killing walk/task* exhausting, tiring, fatiguing, debilitating, enervating, prostrating, taxing, punishing. **3** *a killing joke* hilarious, uproarious, rib-tickling, comical, amusing, laughable, absurd, ludicrous, outrageous; *inf* screamingly funny.

killjoy n spoilsport, dampener, damper; *inf* wet blanket, party-pooper.

kilter n condition, state, shape, fettle, trim, fitness, repair, order, working order.

kin n *no kin living in the area* relatives, relations, family, connections, folks, people, kindred, kith and kin, kinsfolk, kinsmen/kinswomen.

kind adj *kind people/invitation* kind-hearted, kindly, generous, charitable, giving, benevolent, bounteous, magnanimous, big-hearted, warm-hearted, altruistic, philanthropic, humanitarian, humane, tender-hearted, soft-hearted, gentle, mild, lenient, merciful, clement, pitying, forbearing, patient, tolerant, sympathetic, compassionate, understanding, considerate, helpful, thoughtful, good, nice, decent, pleasant, benign, friendly, genial, congenial, amiable, amicable, cordial, courteous, gracious, good-natured, warm, affectionate, loving, indulgent, obliging, accommodating, neighbourly.

kind n **1** *different kinds of paper/creatures* sort, type, variety, brand, class, category. **2** *different kinds of plant* genus, species, family, strain. **3** *human kind* race, species. **4** *a difference in kind rather than degree* nature, character, manner, aspect, disposition, humour, style, stamp, mould.

kindle v **1** *kindle a fire* light, set alight, set on fire, set fire to, ignite, start, torch. **2** *kindle interest* stimulate, rouse, arouse, excite, stir, awaken, inspire, inflame, incite, induce, provoke, actuate, activate, touch off.

kindly adj **1** *a kindly old lady | a kindly expression on her face* kind, kind-hearted, generous, charitable, magnanimous, warm-hearted, humane, gentle, sympathetic, compassionate, understanding, considerate, helpful, thoughtful, good, nice, decent, polite, friendly, genial, pleasant, amiable, amicable, cordial. **2** *a kindly climate* pleasant, agreeable, mild, gentle, benign, favourable, beneficial, advantageous.

kindness n **1** *the kindness of the people* kindheartedness, kindliness, generosity, charitableness, charity, good will, benevolence, magnanimity, hospitality, philanthropy, warm-heartedness, altruism, humanitarianism, humaneness, tender-heartedness, gentleness, mildness, leniency, clemency, patience, tolerance, sympathy, compassion, fellow-feeling, understanding, considerateness, consideration, helpfulness, thoughtfulness, goodness, niceness, decency, pleasantness, friendliness, geniality, congeniality, amiability, cordiality, graciousness, warmth, affection, lovingness, love, indulgence, neighbourliness. *see* KIND adj. **2** *do the neighbours a kindness* kind act, good deed, good turn, favour, help, service, aid.

kindred n **1** *have no living kindred* kin, relatives, relations, family, people. *see* KIN. **2** *he did not know of the kindred between them* kinship, relationship, blood ties, family ties, consanguinity. *see* KINSHIP 1. **3** *there is a definite kindred between them* kinship, affinity, similarity, likeness, correspondence. *see* KINSHIP 2.

kindred adj **1** *kindred members of the wedding party* related, connected, of the same blood, of the same family, consanguineous, cognate. **2** *kindred spirits enjoying the same things* like, similar, resembling, corresponding, matching, congenial, allied.

king n **1** *crowned king of Sweden* monarch, sovereign, ruler, crowned head, majesty, royal personage, emperor, overlord, prince. **2** *king of jazz* leading light, luminary, star, superstar, kingpin; *inf* big wheel, mogul.

kingdom n **1** *the ruler's kingdom* realm, empire, domain, country, land, nation, state, province, territory. **2** *the plant kingdom* division, grouping, group, classification, class, category, family, genus, kind. **3** *the headmaster's kingdom stops at the school gates* sphere/field of influence, area of power, dominion, province, territory.

kink n **1** *a kink in the rope* twist, bend, coil, corkscrew, curl, twirl, knot, tangle, entanglement. **2** *a kink in one's hair* curl, wave, crimp, frizz, crinkle. **3** *a kink in the neck* crick, spasm, twinge, tweak, stab of pain. **4** *a few kinks in the plan* flaw, defect, imperfection, hitch, snag, difficulty, complication. **5** *a person full of kinks* quirk, whim, whimsy, caprice, vagary, eccentricity, foible, idiosyncrasy, crotchet, fetish, deviation.

kinky adj **1** *a kinky rope* twisted, bent, coiled, curled. *see* KINK 1. **2** *kinky hair* curly, wavy, crimped, frizzy, frizzed, crinkled. **3** *kinky ideas* quirky, peculiar, odd, strange, queer, bizarre, eccentric, idiosyncratic, weird, outlandish, unconventional, unorthodox, whimsical, capricious, fanciful; *inf* way-out, far out. **4** *kinky sexual habits* perverted, warped, deviant, deviative, unnatural, abnormal, depraved, degenerate, lascivious, licentious, lewd, sadistic, masochistic.

kinsfolk n kin, relatives, relations, family, kindred. *see* KIN.

kinship n **1** *kinship was thought more of than friendship* blood relationship, relationship, blood ties, family ties, consanguinity, common ancestry, common lineage, kindred. **2** *a kinship between the friends | kinship between their interests* affinity, similarity, likeness, correspondence, kindred, concordance, alliance, association, equivalence, parallelism, symmetry.

kiosk n booth, stand, news-stand, stall, bookstall; telephone kiosk, refreshments kiosk.

kismet n destiny, fate, fortune, providence, portion, lot, one's lot in life, what is to come, what is written in the stars, the writing on the wall, God's will, predestination, preordination, predetermination, doom.

kiss v **1** *friends/lovers kissing | she kissed him | he kissed her hand* salute/greet with the lips, brush the lips against, blow a kiss to, osculate; *inf* peck, give a peck to, give a smacker to, smooch, canoodle, neck, snog. **2** *the branches kissed the lake* caress, brush lightly against, brush against, touch gently, graze, glance off.

kiss n **1** *exchange kisses* salutations/greetings with the lips, hand kiss, osculation; *inf* peck, smacker, smooch, snog. **2** *the kiss of the flowers against her cheeks* light/gentle touch, brush, graze, glance.

kit n **1** *a plumber's kit | bicycle repair kit* equipment, apparatus, set of tools, tools, implements, instruments, utensils, gear, tackle, supplies, paraphernalia, accoutrements, effects, stuff, trappings, appurtenances; *inf* things, the necessary. **2** *football kit* outfit, clothing, dress, uniform, colours; *inf* rig-out, gear, strip. **3** *build furniture from a kit* set of parts, set of components; DIY kit, do-it-yourself kit.

kit v **kit out** *kit out the children with sports equipment* equip, supply, provide, fit out, fix up, furnish, outfit, deck out, rig out, arm, accoutre.

kitchen n kitchenette, galley, cookhouse, bakehouse, scullery.

kittenish adj playful, frolicsome, frisky, cute, coquettish, coy.

knack n talent, aptitude, aptness, gift, flair, bent, forte, ability, capability, capacity, expertise, expertness, skill, skilfulness, genius, facility, propensity, dexterity, adroitness, readiness, quickness, ingenuity, proficiency, competence, handiness.

knave n scoundrel, blackguard, villain, rogue, reprobate, miscreant, cheat, swindler, rascal, wrongdoer, evil-doer, wretch, cur, louse, devil, dastard; *inf* rotter, bounder.

knavery n knavishness, villainy, baseness, roguery, unscrupulousness, cheating, swindling, duplicity, double-dealing, chicanery, deceit, deception, fraud, trickery, rascality, wrong-doing, evil-doing, corruption.

knead v *knead the dough | the masseur kneaded his body* work, manipulate, press, squeeze, massage, rub, form, shape.

kneel v *knelt before the altar* get down on one's knees, fall to one's knees, genuflect, bow, bow down, stoop, make obeisance, kowtow.

knell n **1** *hear the knell of the church bells* toll, tolling, ring, ringing, peal, chime, sound, resounding, death-knell. **2** *the knell of their way of life* death-knell, end, beginning of the end, presage of the end.

knell v **1** *funeral bells knelling* toll, ring, peal, chime, sound, resound. **2** *the drawing of the curtains knelled the end of the day* herald, announce, proclaim, augur.

knickers n pl pants, panties, briefs, bikini briefs, underpants, drawers, bloomers, underwear, lingerie, Directoire knickers, camiknickers; *inf* smalls.

knick-knack n showy ornament, piece of bric-à-brac, trifle, trinket, bauble, gewgaw, gimcrack, bagatelle, kickshaw, bibelot, plaything.

knife n *stab the victim with a knife* blade, cutting tool, dagger, dirk, skean-dhu, machete, kukri, poniard, stiletto, scalpel; *Trademark* Swiss Army knife, Stanley knife; cook's knife, cooking knife, table knife, steak-knive, penknife, pocket knife, bowie knife, sheath knife, flick-knife, jackknife.

knife v *knife the victim to death* stab, pierce, run through, impale, bayonet, transfix, cut, slash, lacerate, wound.

knight n *knights went off to the Crusades* horseman, equestrian, cavalryman, gallant, knight errant, Sir Galahad; lord.

knit v **1** *knit wool into a sweater* purl, loop, weave, interweave, crochet. **2** *knit one's brows* wrinkle, crease, furrow, gather, draw in, contract. **3** *the tragedy knitted the community together* join, link, bind, unite, draw together, ally. **4** *the wound is knitting* draw together, heal, mend, become whole.

knit n *wearing a brightly coloured knit* sweater, jumper, pullover, jersey, cardigan; *inf* cardi, woolly.

knob n **1** *turn the knob on the door/machine* doorknob, handle, door-handle, switch, on/off switch. **2** *iron knobs on the saddle* stud, boss, protuberance, knop. **3** *knobs on the tree* knot, knar, knur, knurl, gnarl, excrescence, protuberance. **4** *knobs on the backs of her hands* bump, bulge, swelling, lump, knot, node, nodule, pustule, growth, tumour, protuberance, tumescence. **5** *a knob of coal* lump, nub, nubble.

knock v **1** *knock on/at the door* tap, rap, bang, pound, hammer. **2** *knock his head with her fist* strike, hit, slap, smack, box, punch, cuff, buffet, thump, thwack, batter, pummel; *inf* clip, clout, wallop. **3** *knock against the sideboard* knock into, bang into, bump into, collide with, run into, crash into, crash against, smash into, dash against, jolt. **4** *knock the play* criticize, find fault with, take apart, take to pieces, pick holes in, run down, shoot down, carp at, cavil at, deprecate, belittle, disparage, minimize, censure, condemn; *inf* slam, lambaste, pan.

knock about/around 1 *men knocking their wives around* strike, hit, beat, beat up, batter, maul, punch, mistreat, maltreat, illtreat, abuse, manhandle, hurt, cause injury to, injure, bruise, wound, damage. **2** *knock about the countryside for a while* travel, wander, roam, ramble, rove, range, saunter, stroll, jaunt, gallivant, traipse, gad. **knock down 1** *knock down the buildings* demolish, pull down, level, raze. **2** *knock down the trees* fell, cut down, hew. **3** *knock down his opponent* knock to the floor, floor, throw to the ground. **4** *knock down the prices/goods* lower, bring down, put down, decrease, reduce, slash. **knock into 1** *knock into his car* knock against, bang into, bump into, collide with, run into, crash into, crash against, smash into, dash against, jolt. **2** *I knocked into her yesterday* run into, meet by chance, come across, encounter, chance upon, happen upon, stumble upon; *inf* bump into. **knock off 1** *they knock off at 5 o'clock* stop work, finish work, finish working, finish the working day, clock off, close shop, shut down; *inf* call it a day. **2** *knock off smoking | knock it off!* stop, finish, give up, terminate, conclude, bring to an end. **3** *knock off his rival* kill, slay, murder, assassinate, do away with, get rid of, dispose of, finish off; *inf* do in, bump off, top. **4** *knock off goods from the lorry* steal, rob, thieve, filch, pilfer, purloin; *inf* pinch, nick, lift. **knock out 1** *knock him out with the blow* render unconscious, floor, prostrate; *inf* KO, kayo, knock cold, put out cold. **2** *knock out his opponent in the first round* eliminate, defeat, beat, vanquish, overthrow. **3** *the storm knocked out the electrical supply* make inoperative, put out of order, destroy, damage. **4** *walking that far knocked her out* knock up, exhaust, wear out, tire out, tire, overtire, fatigue, weary, enervate, fag out, debilitate, make ill; *inf* do in, poop. **5** *they were knocked out by her performance* overwhelm, dazzle, amaze, astound, impress, affect deeply; *inf* bowl over. **knock up 1** *knock up some food/shelves* put together quickly, prepare hastily, build rapidly, improvise, devise, jerry-build. **2** *the hard work knocked him up* knock out, exhaust, wear out, tire out, fatigue, enervate, debilitate. *see* KNOCK v knock out 4. **3** *we knocked up 1000 miles on the journey* achieve, reach, make, attain; *inf* clock up. **4** *the housekeeper knocked up the maids in the morning* wake up, call, awaken, rouse, get up, get out of bed. **5** *he was accused of knocking up the young girl* make pregnant, impregnate, get with child, inseminate; *inf* get in the club, put up the spout/stick/duff, put one in the oven of. **6** *they're knocking up before the tennis match* practise, have a practice game, warm up, hit a ball around.

knock n **1** *a knock at the door* tap, rap, rat-tat, rat-tat-tat, bang. *see* KNOCK v 1. **2** *a knock on the ear* slap, smack, blow, box, punch, cuff, buffet, thump, thwack; *inf* clip, clout, wallop. *see* KNOCK v 2. **3** *the knock damaged the car* collision, crash, bang, bump, smash, thud, jolt. *see* KNOCK v 3. **4** *the knocks of the reviewers* criticism, strictures, fault-finding, carping, cavilling, deprecation, disparagement, censure, condemnation; *inf* slamming, lambasting, panning. *see* KNOCK v 4.

5 *receive many knocks in her life* set-back, reversal, rebuff, rejection, misfortune, bad luck, defeat, failure.

knockout n **1** *win the boxing match by a knockout* finishing blow, *coup de grâce*; *inf* KO, kayo. *see* KNOCK v knock out 1. **2** *take part in a knockout* elimination contest/competition. *see* KNOCK v knock out 2. **3** *her outfit/performance was a knockout* sensation, hit, smash hit, success, triumph, winner, attraction, coup, master stroke.

knoll n hillock, hill, hummock, elevation, mound, hump, knob, barrow.

knot n **1** *a knot in the string/tie* loop, twist, bend, intertwinement, interlacement, ligature, joint; slip knot, reef knot, Windsor knot. **2** *a knot in the wood* lump, knob, node, nodule, protuberance, knur, knurl, knar, gnarl. **3** *a knot of trees* clump, cluster. **4** *a knot of people* group, cluster, bunch, band, circle, ring, gathering, company, throng, crowd, flock, gang, assemblage, mob, pack.

knot v *knot the rope to the pier* tie, loop, bind, secure, tether, lash, leash; tie.

knotty adj **1** *a knotty problem* difficult, complicated, intricate, complex, Byzantine, thorny, perplexing, baffling, mystifying, obscure, unfathomable. **2** *a knotty piece of wood* knotted, gnarled, knurled, lumpy, bumpy, nodose, nodular, rough, coarse. **3** *a knotty piece of thread* knotted, tangled, entangled, twisted, ravelled.

know v **1** *know what they are saying* be aware of, notice, perceive, realize, be conscious of, be cognizant of, sense, recognize; *inf* latch on to. **2** *know the rules* have knowledge of, understand, comprehend, apprehend, be conversant with, be familiar with, be acquainted with, have memorized, have learned by heart. **3** *have known tragedy* be familiar with, acquainted with, experience, undergo, go through. **4** *do you know her husband? | get to know one's neighbours* have met, be acquainted with, have dealings with, associate with, be friends with, socialize with, fraternize with, be intimate with, be close to, be on good terms with; *inf* be thick with; *Scots* ken. **5** *know one brand from another* distinguish, differentiate, tell, tell which is which, identify, make out, discern.

know-how n *savoir faire*, knowledge, expertise, expertness, skill, skilfulness, proficiency, adeptness, dexterity, adroitness, aptitude, ability, capability, competence, faculty, knack, talent, gift, flair, bent, ingenuity.

knowing adj **1** *give a knowing look* astute, shrewd, perceptive, meaningful, well-informed, significant, eloquent, expressive. **2** *a knowing little girl* aware, astute, shrewd, perceptive, sophisticated, worldly, worldly-wise. **3** *a knowing infringement of rules* conscious, intentional, intended, deliberate, wilful, purposeful, calculated, on purpose, by design.

knowingly adv *would not knowingly hurt them* consciously, willingly, intentionally, deliberately, wilfully, purposefully, on purpose, by design, calculatedly.

knowledge n **1** *be taught by people of knowledge* learning, erudition, scholarship, letters, education, enlightenment, wisdom. **2** *his knowledge of the subject* understanding, grasp, comprehension, apprehension, cognition, adeptness, skill, expertise, proficiency, know-how, *savoir faire*. **3** *his knowledge of the area* acquaintanceship, familiarity, conversance. **4** *where do you acquire the knowledge?* information, facts, intelligence, data, news, reports, rumours.

knowledgeable adj **1** *knowledgeable people* well-informed, informed, educated, learned, erudite, scholarly, well-read, cultured, cultivated, enlightened. **2** *knowledgeable about the workings of the machine* having a knowledge of, acquainted with, familiar with, experienced in, expert in, conversant with, having an understanding of.

known adj *a known fact* recognized, acknowledged, admitted, declared, proclaimed, avowed, confessed, published, revealed.

kowtow v **1** *slaves kowtowing to their masters* bow, kneel, genuflect, prostrate oneself, throw oneself at the feet of, humble oneself to. **2** *he's always kowtowing to management* grovel, fawn, pay court, curry favour, bow and scrape, toady; *inf* suck up to, lick the boots of.

kudos n prestige, glory, acclaim, acclamation, praise, extolment, approbation, tribute, honour.

label n **1** *put a label on the luggage/goods* identification tag, ID tag, tag, ticket, tab, sticker, marker, docket. **2** *he resented his label of "four eyes"* epithet, name, nickname, title, sobriquet, designation, denomination, description, characterization. **3** *goods sold under the label of a famous department store* brand, brand name, tradename, trademark, proprietary name, logo.

label v **1** *label the specimens* attach labels to, tag, tab, ticket, stamp, mark, put stickers on, docket. **2** *label him a liar* describe, designate, identify, classify, class, categorize, brand, call, name, term, dub.

laborious adj **1** *a laborious task* hard, heavy, difficult, arduous, strenuous, fatiguing, tiring, wearying, wearisome, tedious. **2** *laborious students* painstaking, careful, meticulous, diligent, assiduous, industrious, hard-working, scrupulous, persevering, pertinacious, zealous. **3** *the laborious style of the writer* laboured, strained, forced. *see* LABOURED 2.

labour n **1** *paid well for his labour* work, employment, job, toil, exertion, effort, industry, industriousness, hard work, hard labour, travail, drudgery, slog, donkeywork, sweat of one's brow, menial work; *inf* grind, sweat. **2** *the labours of Hercules* task, job, chore, undertaking, commission, assignment, charge, venture. **3** *a lack of labour in the area* potential employees, employees, workers, workmen, workforce, working people, hands, labourers. **4** *in labour for many hours having the child* childbirth, birth, parturition, child delivery, delivery, birth contractions, contractions, labour pains, labour pangs, labour throes, travail.

labour v **1** *labour for little reward* work hard, work away, toil, slave away, drudge, grub away, plod on/away, grind/sweat/away, struggle, strive, drudge away, exert oneself, overwork, travail, work like a slave, work one's fingers to the bone, work like a Trojan; *inf* kill oneself, plug away. **2** *labour the point* belabour, overemphasize, lay too much emphasis on, overdo, strain, overelaborate, dwell on, expound on, expand. **3** *labour to finish on time/labour for victory* strive, struggle, endeavour, work, make every effort, do one's best, do one's

utmost. **4** *labour under universal disapproval | labouring under a delusion* suffer from, be a victim of, be burdened by, be overburdened by, be disadvantaged by. **5** *ships labouring on heavy seas* roll, pitch, heave, toss, turn.

laboured adj **1** *laboured breathing* difficult, strained, forced, heavy, awkward. **2** *a laboured style of writing* contrived, affected, studied, stiff, strained, stilted, forced, unnatural, artificial, overdone, overworked, heavy, ponderous, ornate, elaborate, overelaborate, intricate, convoluted, complex, laborious.

labourer n worker, workman, navvy, working man, hand, manual worker, unskilled worker, blue-collar worker, drudge, menial.

labyrinth n **1** *a labyrinth in the grounds | the office is a labyrinth of passages* maze, warren, network, circuitous course, winding, coil, convolution, twisting and turning, meander, meandering, entanglement. **2** *the plot of the book was a labyrinth* entanglement, tangle, jungle, snarl, intricacy, confusion, perplexity, complication, puzzle, riddle, enigma, problem.

labyrinthine adj **1** *labyrinthine paths* mazelike, meandering, winding, wandering, twisting, circuitous, tangled. **2** *labyrinthine plots* intricate, complicated, complex, involved, tortuous, convoluted, tangled, entangled, confusing, puzzling, perplexing, mystifying, bewildering, baffling.

lace n **1** *a covering made of lace* filigree, meshwork, openwork, tatting, netting. **2** *fasten the shoes/bodice with laces* shoelace, bootlace, lacing, string, cord, thong, twine, tie.

lace v **1** *lace the shoes/bodice* lace up, do up, fasten, secure, close, bind, tie, twine, thread, string. **2** *lace their fingers* interweave, twine, intertwine. **3** *lace her into a corset* compress, confine, constrict, squeeze. **4** *the sunset lacing the sky with colour* streak, stripe, striate, band. **5** *lace the coffee with brandy* mix, blend, flavour, fortify, strengthen, stiffen; *inf* spike. **lace into 1** *lace into the members of the other gang* set about, set upon, fall upon, attack, assault, assail, beat, strike, thrash, thresh, tear into; *inf* lay into, sail into, belt. **2** *lace into* *the child for unpunctuality* scold, chide, berate, upbraid, castigate, condemn, harangue, rant at, rave at; *inf* pitch into, lambaste.

lacerate v **1** *lacerate her hand on barbed wire* tear, gash, slash, cut, cut open, rip, rend, mangle, mutilate, hurt, wound, injure, maim. **2** *the parting lacerated her feelings* hurt, wound, distress, harrow, torture, torment, afflict, crucify.

laceration n **1** *the laceration of her hand* tearing, gashing, slashing. *see* LACERATE 1. **2** *a bleeding laceration on the animal's back* tear, gash, slash, cut, rip, rent, mutilation, wound, injury.

lachrymose adj tearful, weeping, crying, sobbing, with tears in the eyes, close to tears, on the verge of tears, sad, mournful, woeful, lugubrious, dolorous; *inf* weepy.

lack n *a lack of food/talent* absence, want, need, deprivation, deficiency, privation, dearth, insufficiency, shortage, shortness, scarcity, scarceness, paucity.

lack v *they lack food* be lacking, be without, have need of, need, stand in need of, require, want, feel the want of, be short of, be deficient in, miss.

lackadaisical adj apathetic, listless, languid, languorous, lethargic, limp, sluggish, enervated, spiritless, unanimated, indifferent, half-hearted, lukewarm, uninterested, unenthusiastic, idle, lazy, indolent, inert.

lackey n **1** *rich men and their lackeys* toady, sycophant, flatterer, fawner, flunkey, minion, doormat, stooge, hanger-on, parasite, camp-follower, tool, puppet, instrument, pawn, creature, cat's-paw; *inf* yes-man, bootlicker. **2** *tales of the emperor and his lackeys* flunkey, footman, manservant, valet, liveried servant, steward, equerry.

lacklustre adj **1** *lacklustre prose* bland, insipid, vapid, dull, flat, dry, prosaic, run-of-the-mill, commonplace, matter-of-fact, unimaginative, uninspired, uninteresting, boring, tedious, wearisome. **2** *lacklustre people* dull, uninteresting, boring, unimaginative, apathetic, spiritless, unanimated, dull-witted, vacuous.

laconic adj **1** *a laconic reply* brief, concise, terse, succinct, short, economical, elliptical, crisp, pithy, to the point, incisive, abrupt, blunt, curt. **2** *a laconic person* of few words, untalkative, uncommunicative, reticent, reserved, taciturn, quiet, silent.

lad n **1** *when he was just a lad* boy, schoolboy, youth, juvenile, youngster, stripling, young man; *inf* kid, little shaver; *Scots* laddie.

2 *who's that lad over there?* boy, man, fellow; *inf* chap, guy, bloke.

ladder n **1** *climb the ladder to the loft* stepladder, set of steps; kitchen steps, loft ladder, folding ladder, rope ladder, Jacob's ladder. **2** *the social/career ladder* hierarchy, scale, set of stages, stratification, pecking order.

laden adj *women laden with shopping* loaded, burdened, heavily-laden, weighed down, weighted, fully charged, encumbered, hampered, oppressed, taxed.

ladle n *a soup ladle* spoon, scoop, dipper, bailer.

ladle v *ladle out the soup/water* spoon out, scoop out, dish up/out, bail out.

lady n **1** *give that lady your seat* woman, female; young woman, old woman. **2** *the lady and her servants* noblewoman, gentlewoman, duchess, countess, peeress, viscountess, baroness.

ladylike adj genteel, refined, well-bred, cultivated, polished, decorous, proper, correct, respectable, well-mannered, courteous, polite, civil, gracious.

lag v **1** *lag behind in the race* fall behind, fall back, trail, not keep pace, bring up the rear. **2** *stop lagging and keep up* loiter, linger, dally, straggle, dawdle, hang back, delay, move slowly, drag one's feet; *inf* dilly-dally. **3** *their efforts were lagging* flag, wane, ebb, fall off, diminish, decrease, ease up, let up, slacken, abate, fail, falter, grow faint.

laggard n loiterer, lingerer, dawdler, straggler, sluggard, snail, delayer, idler, slowcoach, loafer, lounger; *inf* lazybones.

lagoon n pool, pond, lake, reservoir, tarn; *Scots* loch; *Amer* bayou.

laid-back adj relaxed, at ease, easy, leisurely, unhurried, casual, easygoing, free and easy, informal, nonchalant, unexcitable, unperturbable; *inf* unflappable.

laid up adj *mother's been laid up for ten days* bed-ridden, ill in bed, housebound, immobilized, incapacitated, disabled, ill, sick, ailing, on the sick-list, out of action.

lair n **1** *the animal's lair* den, hole, earth, covert, burrow, form, sett, tunnel, dugout, hollow, cave, haunt. **2** *retreat to his lair in the house* retreat, hideaway, refuge, sanctuary, sanctum, sanctum sanctorum, study, den, snug; *inf* hide-out.

laissez-faire n *believe in laissez-faire* free enterprise, private enterprise, individualism, free trade, non-intervention, non-interference, non-involvement, indifference.

laissez-faire adj *a laissez-faire attitude* non-interventional, non-interfering, non-restrictive, uninvolved, indifferent, lax, loose, permissive, live-and-let-live.

lake n pond, tarn, pool, reservoir, lagoon; *Scots* loch; *dial* lough; *Amer* bayou.

lambaste v **1** *cruel masters lambasting the slaves* beat, thrash, flog, lash, drub, strike, thump, thwack, batter, hammer, pummel; *inf* wallop, clout, paste, lace into. **2** *lambaste the children for being late* scold, reprimand, rebuke, chide, reprove, admonish, berate, upbraid, rail at, rant at; *inf* lace into, pitch into.

lame adj **1** *a lame man/leg* limping, hobbling, halting, crippled, game, disabled, incapacitated, defective; *inf* gammy. **2** *a lame excuse* weak, feeble, thin, flimsy, unconvincing, unsatisfactory, inadequate, insufficient, deficient, defective, ineffectual.

lament v **1** *widows lamenting* mourn, grieve, sorrow, wail, moan, groan, weep, cry, sob, complain, keen, ululate, howl, beat one's breast. **2** *lamenting the lack of sports facilities* complain about, bemoan, bewail, deplore.

lament n **1** *the laments of the bereaved* wail, wailing, lamentation, moan, moaning, groan, weeping, crying, sob, sobbing, complaint, keening, ululation, howl. **2** *play/recite a lament* dirge, requiem, elegy, monody, threnody; *Scots* coronach.

lamentable adj **1** *a lamentable state of affairs* deplorable, regrettable, tragic, terrible, wretched, woeful, sorrowful, distressing, grievous. **2** *a lamentable salary* miserable, pitiful, poor, meagre, low, unsatisfactory, inadequate; *inf* measly.

lamentation n lament, wail, wailing, moaning, weeping, keening. *see* LAMENT n 1.

lamp n **1** *all the lamps were lit* light, lantern; table lamp, standard lamp, night-light, fog-lamp, oil-lamp, gas lamp, light-bulb. **2** *see the lamps of a car* headlight, headlamp, sidelight, fog light, fog-lamp, tail-light, brake light.

lampoon n satire, burlesque, travesty, parody, skit, caricature, pasquinade, squib, take-off; *inf* send-up.

lampoon v satirize, parody, caricature, ridicule, mock, make fun of, burlesque, pasquinade, take off, do a take-off of; *inf* send up.

lance n **1** *a knight's lance* spear, pike, javelin. **2** *a doctor's lance* scalpel, knife, lancet.

lance v *lance the boil* cut, cut open, slit, incise, puncture, prick, stab.

land n **1** *glad to be back on land* dry land, ground, solid ground, earth, terra firma. **2** *the land is fertile there* soil, earth, loam, dirt. **3** *prefer working on the land to working in town* farmland, agricultural land, country, countryside, rural areas. **4** *houses with plenty of land around them* ground, fields, open space, open area, expanse, stretch, tract, unbuilt land, green area, green belt. **5** *he owns all the land here* property, ground, acres, estate, realty, real property. **6** *born in a far land* country, nation, fatherland, motherland, state, realm, province, territory, district, region, area, domain.

land v **1** *the plane landed* touch down, alight, make a landing, come in to land. **2** *the pilot landed the plane* make a landing, bring down, put down, take down. **3** *the ship landed at Dover* berth, dock, reach the shore. **4** *we landed at Dover* berth, dock, reach the shore, go ashore, disembark, debark. **5** *how did we land up here?* arrive, get, reach, find oneself, end up, turn up; *inf* wind up. **6** *his behaviour landed him in jail* bring, lead, cause to go to, cause to arrive in. **7** *land a good job* get, acquire, obtain, procure, secure, gain, net, win, carry off. **8** *land a blow* deal, deliver, deposit, give, catch; *inf* fetch.

landlady, landlord n **1** *the landlord of the pub* publican, pub-owner, innkeeper, hotel-keeper, hotelier, host, mine host. **2** *the landlord of the rented flats* owner, proprietor, lessor, householder, freeholder.

landmark n **1** *one of the landmarks of the town* distinctive feature, prominent feature, feature, monument. **2** *a landmark in the town's history* milestone, watershed, turning-point, turning, critical point, crisis, historic event. **3** *landmarks dividing the two estates* marker, demarcator, boundary line, boundary fence, pale, picket. **4** *landmarks indicating the distance* milepost, milestone, guidepost, cairn.

landscape n countryside, scene, scenery, outlook, view, aspect, prospect, vista, panorama, perspective.

landslide n **1** *killed in a landslide* avalanche, landslip, rockfall. **2** *win an election by a landslide* decisive victory, runaway victory, overwhelming majority.

lane n **1** *travel through the lanes* narrow road, narrow way, passageway, passage, alley, path, pathway, footpath, track. **2** *traffic lanes* track, course, road-division.

language n **1** *children acquiring language* speech, speaking, talking, words, vocabulary, utterance, verbal expression, verbalization, vocalization, communication, conversation, converse, discourse, interchange. **2** *the French language* tongue, speech, parlance, mother tongue, native tongue; *inf* lingo. **3** *various forms of language found throughout the country/world* speech, dialect, vernacular, regionalism, provincialism, localism, rhyming slang, patois, lingua franca, barbarism, vulgarism, colloquialism, informal language, slang, idiom, idiolect, jargon, patter, cant, legalese, medicalese, journalese, newspeak, bureaucratese, pidgin English; *inf* lingo, gobbledegook. **4** *admire the language of the speaker/writer* vocabulary, terminology, wording, phrasing, phraseology, style, diction, expression, manner of writing/speaking, rhetoric.

languid adj **1** *a languid young woman* languishing, listless, languorous, lackadaisical, spiritless, vigourless, lacking energy, lethargic, torpid, idle, inactive, inert, indolent, lazy, sluggish, slow-moving, unenthusiastic, apathetic, indifferent. **2** *feeling languid after her illness* weak, weakly, sickly, faint, feeble, frail, limp, flagging, drooping, fatigued, enervated, debilitated. **3** *a languid response* apathetic, lukewarm, half-hearted, unenthusiastic, bored, passive.

languish v **1** *she languished after his departure* droop, flag, wilt, wither, fade, fail, weaken, decline, go into a decline, waste away; *inf* go downhill. **2** *people languishing away in institutions* waste away, rot, decay, wither away, be abandoned, be neglected, be forgotten, be disregarded. **3** *languish for her lover* pine for, yearn for, long for, sigh for, hunger for, desire, want, mope for, repine for, grieve for, mourn for.

languor n **1** *feeling full of languor in the heat* listlessness, lethargy, torpor, idleness, inactivity, inertia, indolence, laziness, sluggishness, sleepiness, drowsiness, somnolence, dreaminess, relaxation. **2** *disturb the languor of the atmosphere* stillness, tranquillity, calm, calmness, lull, silence, windlessness.

lank adj **1** *lank hair* lifeless, lustreless, limp, straggling, straight, long. **2** *lank youths* tall, thin, lean, lanky, skinny, spindly, gangling, gangly, scrawny, scraggy, angular, bony, gaunt, raw-boned, gawky, rangy; *inf* weedy.

lap[1] n **1** *sit on mother's lap* knee, knees. **2** *live in the lap of luxury* security, secureness, safety, protection, refuge, comfort. **3** *the arrangements are in your lap* responsibility, charge, task, job, obligation.

lap[2] n **1** *three laps of the stadium* circuit, circle, loop, orbit, round, compass, ambit. **2** *the last lap of the journey* round, tour, section, stage.

lap[2] v **1** *lap blankets around her* wrap, wind, fold, twist. **2** *lap her in blankets* wrap, swathe, cover, envelop, enfold, encase, wind, swaddle.

lap[3] v **1** *water lapping against the shore* wash, splash, beat, swish, slap, plash, slosh. **2** *cats lapping milk* drink up, drink, lick up, sip, sup.

lapse n **1** *forgive his occasional lapse* slip, error, mistake, blunder, failing, fault, failure, omission, oversight, negligence, dereliction; *inf* slip-up. **2** *after a lapse of time* interval, gap, pause, intermission, interlude, lull, hiatus, break, passage. **3** *a lapse in standards* decline, downturn, fall, falling, falling-away, slipping, drop, deterioration, worsening, degeneration, backsliding. **4** *the lapse of her season ticket* expiry, voiding, invalidity, termination. **5** *lapse of faith* abandonment, forsaking, relinquishment, defection, renunciation, repudiation, rejection, disavowal, denial, abjuration, apostasy.

lapse v **1** *standards have lapsed* decline, fall, fall off, drop, deteriorate, worsen, degenerate; *inf* go downhill, go to pot. **2** *our friendship lapsed when we left school* cease, end, come to an end, stop, terminate. **3** *the season ticket has lapsed* become void, become invalid, expire, run out, terminate, become obsolete. **4** *lapse into silence/sleep* slide, slip, drift, sink, subside, submerge. **5** *time has lapsed* elapse, pass, go by, go on, roll on, glide by, run its course.

lapsed adj **1** *lapsed season tickets* void, invalid, expired, run out, out of date, terminated. **2** *lapsed traditions* obsolete, old, former, past, bygone, forgotten, extinct, outworn, abandoned. **3** *lapsed Christians* non-practising, lacking faith, backsliding, recidivist, apostate.

larceny n theft, stealing, robbery, pilfering, purloining, burglary, misappropriation; *inf* filching, nicking.

larder n pantry, storage room, storeroom, store, still-room, cooler, scullery.

large adj **1** *large buildings/sums* big, great, of considerable size, sizeable, substantial, goodly, tall, high, huge, immense, enormous, colossal, massive, mammoth, vast, prodigious, gigantic, giant, monumental, stupendous, gargantuan, man-size, king-size, giant-size, outsize, considerable; *inf* jumbo, whopping. **2** *a large man/woman* big, burly, heavy, bulky, thickset, powerfully built, heavyset, chunky, strapping, hulking, hefty, ample, fat, obese, corpulent. **3** *a large supply* abundant, copious, plentiful, ample, liberal, generous. **4** *take the large* *view | officials with large powers* wide, wide-ranging, large-scale, broad, extensive, far-reaching, sweeping, comprehensive, exhaustive. **at large 1** *wild animals are at large | some prisoners at large* at liberty, free, unconfined, unrestrained, roaming, on the loose, on the run, fugitive. **2** *society at large* as a whole, as a body, generally, in general, in the main. **3** *a report given at large* in detail, with full details, exhaustively, at length. **by and large** *by and large we are better off* on the whole, generally, in general, all things considered, taking everything into consideration, for the most part, in the main, as a rule.

largely adv *he is largely to blame* to a large extent, to a great degree, chiefly, for the most part, mostly, mainly, in the main, principally, in great measure.

large-scale adj **1** *a large scale police search* extensive, wide-reaching, wide-ranging, sweeping, wholesale, global. **2** *large-scale prints* enlarged, blown-up, magnified.

largesse n **1** *known for her largesse* generosity, kindness, liberality, open-handedness, munificence, bounty, bountifulness, beneficence, benefaction, altruism, charity, philanthropy, alms-giving. **2** *distributing largesse* gift, present, contribution, donation, hand-out, endowment, grant, aid, alms.

lark¹ n *larks singing* skylark, meadowlark, songbird.

lark² n *tired of the children's larks* prank, horseplay, trick, fooling, antic, mischief, escapade, fun, cavorting, caper, play, game, romp, frolic, sport, rollicking, gambol, jape, fling, skylark.

lark² v *children larking about* play pranks, indulge in horseplay, play tricks, fool about, make mischief, have fun, cavort, caper, play, romp, frolic, sport, rollick, gambol, disport, skylark.

lascivious adj **1** *lascivious old men leering at girls* lewd, lecherous, lustful, licentious, promiscuous, libidinous, prurient, salacious, lubricious, concupiscent, debauched, depraved, degenerate, dissolute, dissipated. **2** *lascivious magazines/talk* lewd, blue, obscene, smutty, gross, bawdy, dirty, salacious; *inf* raunchy.

lash n **1** *produce a lash to beat the slaves* whip, horsewhip, bullwhip, scourge, flagellum, cat-o'-nine-tails, cat. **2** *six lashes with a whip | with one lash of his fist* stroke, stripe, blow, hit, strike, bang, thwack, thump; *inf* swipe, wallop, whack.

lash v **1** *lash the children with a whip/belt* whip, horsewhip, scourge, birch, switch,

flog, flail, flagellate, thrash, beat, strike, batter, hammer; *inf* wallop, whack, lam, lambaste. **2** *waves lashing the ship* buffet, pound, batter, beat against, dash against, smack against, strike, knock. **3** *lash him for his behaviour* berate, upbraid, castigate, scold, rebuke, chide, reprove, reproach, harangue, rant at, fulminate against, attack, censure, criticize, condemn, flay; *inf* bawl out, pitch into, lambaste. **4** *lions lashing their tails* flick, wag, wave, whip, switch. **5** *lash the crowd to a frenzy* provoke, incite, arouse, excite, agitate, stir up, whip up, work up, egg on, goad. **6** *lash the boat to the side of the ship* fasten, bind, tie, tether, hitch, attach, join, rope, strap, leash, make fast, secure. **lash out 1** *lash out at his critics* speak out against, burst into angry speech at, shout at, lose one's temper at, attack verbally, attack physically, denounce, harangue, rant at, fulminate against, criticize, condemn, censure; *inf* pitch/lace into. **2** *lash out on a new dress* spend lavishly, be extravagant, spend a lot of money; *inf* push the boat out, go on a spending spree, go on a shopping binge.

lass n girl, young woman, young lady, schoolgirl, maid, maiden, miss; *inf* bird; *Scots* lassie; *Irish* colleen.

last¹ adj **1** *the last runner arrived* hindmost, rearmost, at the end, at the back, final, aftermost. **2** *his last words* final, closing, concluding, ending, finishing, terminating, ultimate, terminal. **3** *our last chance* final, only remaining, only one left. **4** *the last thing she would want* least likely, most unlikely, least suitable, least wanted, least favourite. **5** *last Thursday* latest, most recent. **the last word 1** *that is the chairman's last word on the subject* final statement, summation, ultimatum, final decision, definitive statement. **2** *have the last word in an argument* final remark, final say, closing statement, concluding remark. **3** *the last word in sports cars* most fashionable, most-up-to-date, latest, newest, peak, best, epitome, quintessence, acme of perfection, cream, crème de la crème, ne plus ultra, dernier cri.

last¹ adv *come last* at the end, at the rear, in the rear, behind, after.

last¹ n *stay to the last* end, ending, finish, close, conclusion, completion, finale, termination, the bitter end. **at last** in the end, finally, eventually, at length, ultimately, in conclusion.

last² v **1** *how long will the symptoms last?* continue, go on, carry on, remain, persist, keep on. **2** *how long will the climbers last in* *the snow?* survive, exist, live, subsist, hold on, hold out. **3** *those shoes won't last* last long, wear well, stand up to wear, keep, endure. **4** *the heartache won't last* be permanent, be constant, last long.

last³ n *shoemaker's last* mould, model, pattern, form, matrix.

last-ditch adj *a last-ditch attempt* desperate, frantic, frenzied, wild, struggling, straining, final, last-chance, last-minute, last-gasp, all-out.

lasting adj *a lasting peace* long-lasting, enduring, long-lived, lifelong, abiding, continuing, long-term, surviving, persisting, permanent, deep-rooted, durable, constant, eternal, undying, everlasting, perennial, perpetual, unending, never-ending, immortal, ceaseless, unceasing, interminable, imperishable, indestructible.

lastly adv *lastly I want to thank you all* finally, in conclusion, to conclude, to sum up, in drawing things to a close.

latch n *the latch on the door* catch, fastening, hasp, hook, bar, bolt, lock; *Scots* sneck, snib.

latch v *latch the door* fasten, secure, make fast, bar, bolt, lock; *Scots* sneck, snib.

late adj **1** *she's always late* unpunctual, behind time, behind schedule, behind, behindhand, not on time, tardy, overdue, delayed, dilatory, slow. **2** *her late husband* deceased, dead, departed, defunct, nonextant. **3** *the late government* former, previous, preceding, past, prior. **4** *some late news* recent, fresh, new, last-minute, up-to-date, up-to-the-minute.

late adv **1** *he arrived late* unpunctually, behind time, behindhand, belatedly, tardily, at the last minute, at the tail end, dilatorily, slowly. **2** *we worked late yesterday* past the usual finishing/stopping/closing time, after hours. **3** *get home late from the dance* late at night, in the early hours of the morning; *inf* in the wee small hours. **of late** lately, recently, latterly, in the past few days, in the last couple of weeks, in recent times.

lately adv of late, recently. *see* LATE adv of late.

latent adj *latent talent* dormant, quiescent, inactive, passive, hidden, unrevealed, concealed, unapparent, indiscernible, imperceptible, invisible, covert, undeveloped, unrealized, potential, possible.

later adj *the later bus* subsequent, next, following, succeeding, successive, sequential.

later adv **1** *I can't come today but I'll come later* later on, at a later time, at a later date, at a

future time/date, at some point in the future, in the future, in time to come. **2** *he arrived and she came later* later on, after, afterwards, subsequently, by and by, in a while, after a bit.

lateral adj sidewise, sideways, sidelong, sideward, edgewise, edgeways, indirect, oblique, slanting, askance.

latest adj *the latest news/style* most recent, newest, up-to-date, up-to-the-minute, current, modern, fashionable, in fashion, in vogue, in; *inf* with-it.

lather n **1** *soap not producing much lather* suds, soapsuds, foam, froth, bubbles. **2** *horses covered in lather* sweat, perspiration. **3** *getting in a lather over the exams* nervous state, state of agitation, state of anxiety, fluster, flutter, fret, fuss, frenzy, fever, pother; *inf* flap, sweat, tizzy, dither, twitter, state, stew.

latitude n **1** *on the same latitude as Moscow* parallel, meridian, grid line. **2** *give his staff a great deal of latitude in decision-making | children given too much latitude* scope, scope for initiative, freedom of action, freedom from restriction, freedom, unrestrictedness, liberty, free play, *carte blanche*, leeway, elbowroom, licence, indulgence, laxity.

latter adj **1** *the latter is the better* last-mentioned, second-mentioned, second of the two, second. **2** *the latter part of the year/process* later, hindmost, closing, end, concluding, final. **3** *the technology of latter times* recent, latest, modern.

latter-day adj *latter-day missionaries* modern, present-day, present-time, current, contemporary.

latterly adv **1** *the old man was in a coma latterly* towards the end, at the end, finally. **2** *latterly management has been more reasonable* recently, lately, of late.

lattice n lattice-work, fretwork, open framework, openwork, trellis, network, mesh, web, tracery, reticulation, grating, grid, grille.

laud v **1** *laud their efforts* praise, sing the praises of, extol, hail, applaud, acclaim, commend, admire, approve of, make much of, cheer, celebrate, eulogize, panegyrize. **2** *laud the Creator* glorify, worship, magnify, exalt, pay tribute to, pay homage to, honour, adore, revere, venerate.

laudable adj *laudable behaviour/actions* praiseworthy, commendable, admirable, worthy of admiration, meritorious, deserving, creditable, worthy, estimable, of note, noteworthy, exemplary, excellent.

laudation n extolment, applause, praise, acclaim, acclamation, commendation, admiration, approval, approbation, eulogy, panegyric, paean, encomium.

laudatory adj praising, extolling, acclamatory, commendatory, admiring, approving, approbatory, complimentary, adulatory, celebratory, eulogizing, eulogistic, panegyric, panegyrical, encomiastical.

laugh v chuckle, chortle, guffaw, giggle, titter, snigger, ha-ha, tee-hee, burst out laughing, roar/hoot with laughter, shake with laughter, be convulsed with laughter, split one's sides, be rolling in the aisles, be doubled up; inf be in stitches, die laughing, be creased up, fall about, crack up, break up. **laugh at 1** laugh at the beggar mock, ridicule, deride, scoff at, jeer at, sneer at, make fun of, poke fun at, make a fool of, make one's butt, lampoon, satirize, taunt, tease; inf send up, take the mickey out of. **2** laugh at danger laugh off, belittle, make light of, close one's eyes to, refuse to acknowledge, discount, rule out, ignore, dismiss, disregard, reject the possibility of, shrug off, brush aside, scoff at, pooh-pooh. **laugh off** laugh off danger laugh at, belittle, make light of, discount, shrug off. see LAUGH v LAUGH AT 2. **laugh on the other side of one's face** you'll be laughing on the other side of your face when the police catch up with you show sudden disappointment, be dejected, be disheartened, be downcast, eat one's words, get a taste of one's own medicine; inf get one's comeuppance.

laugh n **1** give a laugh chuckle, chortle, guffaw, giggle, titter, snigger, roar/hoot of laughter, peal of laughter, belly-laugh. **2** her uncle's such a laugh comedian, comic, joker, humorist, wag, wit, entertainer, clown; inf card, case, caution, hoot, scream. **3** we didn't mean to hurt her, it was just a laugh joke, jest, prank, lark, trick, piece of fun, bit of mischief.

laughable adj **1** a laughable business proposition ludicrous, ridiculous, absurd, derisory, derisive, risible, preposterous, outrageous. **2** children finding the entertainment laughable amusing, funny, humorous, hilarious, uproarious, comical, comic, entertaining, diverting, farcical, droll, mirthful, side-splitting.

laughing stock n figure of fun, dupe, butt, fool, everybody's fool, stooge, fair game, everybody's target, victim, Aunt Sally; inf fall guy.

laughter n **1** hear the laughter laughing, chuckling, chortling, guffawing, giggling, tittering, sniggering, cachinnation; inf hooting. **2** a source of laughter amusement, entertainment, humour, mirth, merriment, gaiety, hilarity, glee, light-heartedness, blitheness.

launch v **1** launch the ship set afloat, float. **2** launch a rocket/missile fire, discharge, propel, project, send forth, throw, cast, hurl, let fly. **3** launch a search/project set in motion, get going, begin, start, commence, embark upon, initiate, instigate, institute, inaugurate, establish, set up, organize, introduce, usher in, start the ball rolling. **4** launch out into criticism burst into, start, begin.

launder v sheets were freshly laundered wash, wash and iron, wash and press, clean, dry-clean.

laundry n **1** put the laundry into the washing machine washing, dirty washing, wash, dirty clothes, clothes to be cleaned. **2** take the washing to a laundry launderette, dry cleaner's, laundry room, public wash-house, Chinese laundry; Amer laundromat.

laurels n pl honours, awards, trophies, prizes, rewards, tributes, bays, praises, laudation, acclaim, acclamation, commendation, credit, glory, honour, distinction, fame, renown, prestige, recognition; inf kudos.

lavatory n toilet, WC, water-closet, bathroom, public convenience, ladies, gents, cloakroom, powder-room, privy, latrine; inf loo, bog; Amer washroom, rest room; Amer inf can, john, head; humorous little girls' room, little boys' room.

lavish adj **1** a lavish supply copious, abundant, superabundant, plentiful, profuse, prolific, unlimited. **2** too lavish in her catering extravagant, excessive, immoderate, wasteful, squandering, profligate, prodigal, thriftless, improvident, intemperate, unrestrained, dissolute, wild. **3** a lavish hostess generous, liberal, bountiful, open-handed, unstinting, free, munificent, overgenerous, extravagant. **4** a lavish display of flowers luxuriant, lush, gorgeous, sumptuous, costly, opulent, pretentious, showy.

lavish v lavish presents/praises on his children heap, shower, pour, deluge, give freely, give generously, give unstintingly, bestow freely, waste, squander, dissipate.

law n **1** the law of the land system of laws, body of laws, constitution, code, legal code, charter, rules and regulations, jurisprudence. **2** parliament issuing laws rule, regulation, statute, enactment, act, decree, edict, command, order, ordinance, commandment, directive, pronouncement, covenant. **3** obey the laws of the game rule, regulation,

principle, direction, instruction, guideline.
4 *moral laws* rule, principle, precept, standard, criterion, formula, tenet, doctrine,
canon. **5** *law of nature* generalization, general truth, axiom, maxim, truism. **6** *go to
law* litigation, legal action, legal proceedings, lawsuit. **7** *a career in the law* legal profession, bar. **8** *the law has arrived* police,
officers of the law; *inf* fuzz, the Old Bill,
pigs, bobbies, boys in blue.

law-abiding adj lawful, righteous, honest,
honourable, upright, upstanding, good, virtuous, orderly, peaceable, peace-keeping,
peaceful, dutiful, duteous, obedient, compliant, complying.

lawbreaker n criminal, felon, wrongdoer,
miscreant, offender, delinquent, culprit,
transgressor, violator, convict, jailbird; *inf*
crook, baddy.

lawful adj **1** *lawful actions* legal, legitimate,
licit, just, valid, permissible, allowable,
rightful, proper, constitutional, legalized,
sanctioned, authorized, warranted,
approved, recognized. **2** *a lawful person* law-
abiding, righteous, honourable, orderly. *see*
LAW-ABIDING.

lawless adj **1** *a lawless country* without law
and order, anarchic, disorderly,
ungoverned, unruly, insurrectionary,
insurgent, revolutionary, rebellious, insubordinate, riotous, mutinous, seditious, terrorist. **2** *lawless actions* unlawful, illegal,
law-breaking, illicit, illegitimate, criminal,
felonious, wrongdoing, miscreant, transgressing, violating. **3** *lawless rage* unbridled,
unrestrained, unchecked, uncontrolled,
immoderate, intemperate, wild.

lawsuit n suit, case, legal action, action,
legal proceedings, proceedings, litigation,
trial, bringing to book, bringing of charges,
indictment.

lawyer n solicitor, legal practitioner, legal
adviser, criminal lawyer, civil lawyer, barrister, advocate, counsel, Queen's Counsel,
QC, defending counsel, prosecuting counsel; *inf* brief; *Amer* attorney.

lax adj **1** *lax about discipline in the school*
slack, slipshod, negligent, neglectful,
remiss, careless, heedless, unmindful, inattentive, casual, easygoing, lenient, permissive, indulgent, overindulgent,
complaisant, overtolerant. **2** *a lax description* loose, inexact, inaccurate, imprecise,
unrigorous, vague, indefinite, non-specific,
broad, general. **3** *lax flesh* slack, flabby, flaccid, limp, yielding, sagging, drooping,
droopy, hanging.

laxative n purgative, aperient, cathartic,
senna, ipecacuanha, castor oil.

lay v **1** *lay the parcel on the table* put, place,
set, deposit, plant, settle, posit. **2** *lay the
carpet* position, set out, arrange, dispose.
3 *lay charges* put forward, bring forward,
advance, submit, present, prefer, offer,
lodge. **4** *lay the blame at his door* attribute,
assign, ascribe, allocate, allot, impute. **5** *lay
bets* wager, bet, gamble, stake, give odds,
hazard, risk, chance. **6** *lay plans* devise,
arrange, contrive, make, prepare, work
out, hatch, concoct, design, plan, plot. **7** *lay
the burden on him* impose, inflict, encumber,
saddle, tax, charge, burden, apply. **8** *lay
eggs* deposit, produce, bear, oviposit. **9** *lay
him with a blow* lay low, lay out, floor, fell,
knock down, prostrate. **10** *lay their fears*
allay, assuage, soothe, calm, still, quiet,
relieve, ease, alleviate, mitigate, palliate,
suppress. **11** *lay his unruly hair* flatten,
smooth, level. **12** *lay the woman/man* have
sex with, have intercourse with, have sexual relations with, copulate with, go to bed
with, sleep with; *inf* bed. **lay aside 1** *lay
aside the dress for the customer* put aside, put
to one side, keep, save, store. **2** *lay aside
one's studies* abandon, cast aside, forsake,
reject, renounce, repudiate, discard. **3** *lay
aside evil thoughts* set aside, put aside, dismiss, disregard, put out of one's mind,
ignore, forget, shelve. **lay bare** *lay bare
one's secret thoughts* reveal, make known,
disclose, divulge, show, expose, exhibit,
uncover, unveil, unmask. **lay down 1** *lay
down their weapons* surrender, relinquish,
give up, yield, cede, turn over. **2** *it is laid
down that candidates must be interviewed* set
down, stipulate, formulate, prescribe,
order, command, ordain, postulate,
demand, proclaim, assert, maintain. **3** *lay
down wine* store, put into store, keep for
future use, keep, save. **lay hands on 1** *if I
ever lay hands on the thief* lay hold of, get
hold of, catch, seize. *see* LAY vlay hold of. **2** *I
just can't lay hands on that book* find, locate,
unearth, bring to light, run to earth, discover, acquire, turn up. **3** *priests laying
hands on members of the congregation* bless,
consecrate, confirm, ordain. **lay hold of** *lay
hold of the thief* get hold of, get one's hands
on, catch, seize, grab, snatch, clutch, grip,
grasp, lay hands on. **lay in** *lay in a supply of
logs* stock up with/on, stockpile, store,
accumulate, amass, heap up, hoard, collect.
lay into 1 *lay into their attackers* set about,
set upon, assail, attack, hit out at, strike
out at, let fly at; *inf* lace/sail/pitch into,
lambaste. **2** *lay into the child for being late*
scold, rebuke, chide, berate, upbraid,
reproach, reprove, castigate, punish, criticize, censure, condemn, rant at, rave at,
harangue; *inf* pitch into, lambaste. **lay it**

on *he's laying it on to charm his mother-in-law* exaggerate, stretch the truth, overdo it, flatter, pay extravagant compliments, give fulsome praise, overpraise, soft-soap; *inf* pile it on, lay it on thick, lay it on with a trowel, sweet-talk. **lay off 1** *lay off half of the workforce* let go, make redundant, dismiss, discharge, pay off; *inf* sack, fire. **2** *lay off hitting him* stop, cease, desist from, refrain from, give up, discontinue, leave off, finish; *inf* give over; *Amer* quit. **3** *lay off alcohol* desist from, refrain from, give up, leave alone, leave off, not touch. **lay on** *lay on refreshments* provide, supply, furnish, give.

lay out 1 *lay out the plans* spread out, set out, arrange, display, exhibit. **2** *lay out a garden* set out, arrange, plan, design. **3** *lay out a lot of money* spend, expend, pay, disburse, contribute, give, invest; *inf* shell out, fork out. **4** *lay out his opponent* knock out, knock unconscious, knock down, fell, floor, flatten, prostrate; *inf* KO, kayo, knock for six.

lay *adj* **1** *a lay preacher* laic, laical, secular, non-clerical, non-ordained. **2** *a lay member of the club* non-professional, amateur, non-specialist, dilettante.

layabout *n* good-for-nothing, ne'er-do-well, do-nothing, idler, loafer, lounger, shirker, wastrel, fainéant, sluggard, laggard; *inf* skiver, waster.

layman, lay person *n* *he's a dealer; I'm just an interested layman* amateur, non-professional, dilettante.

lay-off *n* *many lay-offs at the factory* redundancy, dismissal, discharge; *inf* sacking, firing.

layout *n* **1** *the layout of the house* arrangement, geography, plan. **2** *the magazine's layout* arrangement, design, format, formation.

lay person *see* LAYMAN.

laze *v* *lazing all day in the garden* idle, do nothing, loaf, lounge, lounge about, loll around, waste time, fritter away time.

laziness *n* idleness, indolence, slothfulness, sloth, inactivity, inertia, lethargy, languor, remissness, laxity. *see* LAZY.

lazy *adj* idle, indolent, slothful, work-shy, inactive, inert, sluggish, lethargic, languorous, listless, torpid, slow-moving, remiss, negligent, lax.

lead¹ *v* **1** *lead him to the right spot* guide, show someone the way, conduct, lead the way, usher, escort, steer, pilot. **2** *the evidence led him to believe he was guilty* cause, induce, prompt, move, incline, dispose, predispose, persuade, sway, influence, pre-

vail, bring round. **3** *his action led to disaster* cause, result in, bring on, call forth, provoke, contribute to. **4** *lead the procession* be at the head of, be at the front of, head. **5** *lead the country/discussion* command, direct, govern, rule, manage, be in charge of, regulate, preside over, head, supervise, superintend, oversee; *inf* head up. **6** *he was leading after the first lap* be in the lead, be in front, be out in front, be ahead, be first, come first, precede. **7** *leading the field* be at the front of, be ahead of, outdistance, outrun, outstrip, leave behind, outdo, excel, exceed, surpass, outrival, outshine, eclipse, transcend. **8** *lead a happy life* have, live, pass, spend, experience, undergo. **lead off** *lead off the dance* begin, start, start off, commence, open; *inf* kick off. **lead on** *he won't marry her; he's just leading her on* deceive, mislead, delude, hoodwink, dupe, trick, beguile, tempt, entice, lure, tantalize, inveigle, seduce; *inf* string along. **lead the way 1** *he led the way to the spot* guide, conduct, show the way. **2** *the scientist led the way in space development* initiate things, take the first step, make a start, break ground, blaze a trail, lay the foundation, lay the first stone. **lead up to** *lead up to asking them for money* prepare the way for, pave the way for, open the way for, do the groundwork for, work round/up to, make overtures about, make advances about, hint at, approach the subject of, introduce the subject of.

lead¹ *n* **1** *the runner in the lead* leading position/place, first place, advance position, van, vanguard. **2** *take the lead in the market* first position, head place, forefront, primacy, pre-eminence, supremacy, advantage, edge, precedence. **3** *a lead of half a lap* margin, gap, interval. **4** *prefects should act as a lead to others* example, model, pattern, standard of excellence. **5** *she's in the lead in the new play* leading role, star/starring role, star part, title role, principal part. **6** *she's/he's the lead in the play* star, principal character, male lead, female lead, leading man, leading lady, hero, heroine. **7** *a dog's lead* leash, tether, rein, cord, rope, chain. **8** *we have no leads in the murder hunt* clue, pointer, guide, hint, tip, suggestion, indication, intimation, tip-off.

lead¹ *adj* *in the lead position* leading, first, top, foremost, front, head, chief, principal, main, most important, premier, paramount, prime, primary.

lead² *n* **1** *sink a lead to test the depth* weight, sinker, plummet, plumb, bob. **2** *remove the lead from the wound* lead pellet, shot, ammunition.

leaden adj **1** *leaden limbs* heavy, weighty, burdensome, cumbersome, inactive, inert. **2** *leaden steps* heavy, laboured, lumbering, plodding, sluggish. **3** *leaden prose* heavy, unimaginative, uninspired, uninteresting, dull, boring, tedious, monotonous, insipid, vapid. **4** *leaden skies* grey, greyish, grey-coloured, cloudy, gloomy, overcast, louring, oppressive, dark, dreary, dismal, bleak.

leader n **1** *the leader of the country/committee/team* ruler, head, chief, commander, director, governor, principal, captain, skipper, manager, superintendent, supervisor, overseer, foreman, kingpin; *inf* boss, number one; *Amer inf* honcho. **2** *a leader of fashion* pace-setter, pacemaker, trend-setter, front runner. **3** *a leader in the field of genetics* front runner, innovator, pioneer, trail-blazer, pathfinder, ground-breaker, originator.

leadership n **1** *under the leadership of a responsible person* rule, command, headship, directorship, direction, governorship, administration, captaincy, management, supervision, control, guidance, authority, superintendency. **2** *he is competent but has no leadership qualities* authority, control, direction, guidance, initiative, influence.

leading adj **1** *play the leading role* chief, main, most important, principal, foremost, supreme, paramount, dominant, superior, ruling, directing, guiding, controlling; *inf* number-one. **2** *one of the leading writers* chief, most important, foremost, greatest, best, outstanding, pre-eminent, supreme, principal, top-rank, of the first rank, first-rate. **3** *the leading runner* front, first, in first place.

leaf n **1** *a leaf from the tree/plant* frond, foliole, blade, bract, flag, needle, pine needle, pad, lily-pad; *Tech* cotyledon. **2** *a leaf missing from the book* page, sheet, folio, flyleaf. **turn over a new leaf** *she turned over a new leaf after she was punished* reform, improve, mend one's ways, become a new person, change completely, make a fresh start.

leaf v **1** *leafing through a book* flick, skim, browse, glance. **2** *trees leafing* bud, put out leaves, burst into leaves, turn green, foliate.

leaflet n pamphlet, booklet, brochure, handbill, bill, circular; *inf* advert; *Amer* flyer.

league n **1** *a league of nations* alliance, confederation, confederacy, federation, union, association, coalition, combine, consortium, affiliation, guild, corporation, conglomerate, cooperative, partnership, fellowship, syndicate, band, group. **2** *sign a league* pact, compact, covenant, treaty, concordat, contract, agreement, settlement. **3** *a football league* group, band, association. **4** *he is not in the same league as his brother* ability group, level of ability, level, class, category. **in league with** *he was in league with the other crook* in alliance with, allied with, cooperating with, collaborating with, leagued with, linked with, hand in glove with, in collusion with; *inf* in cahoots with.

league v *they leagued together to promote their interests* ally, join forces, unite, form an association, band together, combine, amalgamate, form a federation, confederate, collaborate.

leak n **1** *see a leak in the bucket* hole, opening, crack, crevice, chink, fissure, puncture, cut, gash, slit, rent, break, rift. **2** *a water/gas leak* drip, leaking, leakage, escape, seeping, seepage, oozing, percolation, discharge. **3** *a leak of secret information to a newspaper* disclosure, divulgence, revelation, uncovering.

leak v **1** *water/gas leaking* escape, drip, seep out/through, ooze out, exude, discharge, issue, gush out. **2** *leak information to the press* disclose, divulge, reveal, make known, make public, tell, impart, pass on, relate, give away, let slip, let the cat out of the bag; *inf* spill the beans about, take the lid off.

lean v **1** *the ladder leaning against the wall | his wife leaning on his arm* rest, be supported, be propped up, recline, repose. **2** *the pole/ship is leaning* incline, bend, slant, tilt, be at an angle, slope, bank, list, heel, careen. **3** *she leans towards anarchy* incline towards, tend towards, have a tendency towards, have a propensity for, have a proclivity for, have a preference for, be attracted to, have a liking for, gravitate towards, have an affinity with. **4** *she leans on her husband* depend on, be dependent on, rely on, count on, pin one's faith on, have faith in, trust, have every confidence in.

lean adj **1** *lean and hungry people/animals* thin, slender, slim, spare, lank, skinny, scrawny, scraggy, bony, gaunt, emaciated, skin and bones, raw-boned, rangy, gangling. **2** *lean meat* non-fat, low-fat, unfatty. **3** *a lean harvest* meagre, scanty, sparse, poor, inadequate, insufficient. **4** *lean years for art* unproductive, unfruitful, arid, barren, bare, non-fertile.

leaning n *a leaning towards anarchy* tendency, inclination, bent, proclivity, propensity, penchant, predisposition, predilection, proneness, partiality, preference, bias, attraction, liking, fondness, taste.

leap v **1** *children leaping around* jump, bound, bounce, hop, skip, romp, caper, spring, frolic, frisk, cavort, gambol, dance. **2** *leap to one's feet* jump, jump up, spring. **3** *leap the obstacle* jump, jump over, high-jump, vault over, vault, spring over, bound over, hurdle, clear, cross over, sail over. **4** *leap to help* jump, hurry, hasten, rush, hurtle. **5** *leap to conclusions* arrive at hastily, reach hurriedly, come to overhastily, form hastily. **6** *prices have leapt* increase rapidly, soar, rocket, sky-rocket, shoot up, escalate, mount. **7** *leap to stardom* rocket, sky-rocket, advance/mount/ascend rapidly, climb the ladder. **leap at** *leap at the chance* accept eagerly, grasp, grasp with both hands, grab, take advantage of.

leap n **1** *clear the obstacle at the first leap* jump, vault, spring, bound, hop, skip. **2** *a leap in the number of jobless* rapid increase, sudden rise, escalation, soaring, surge, upsurge, upswing. **by leaps and bounds** *progress by leaps and bounds* rapidly, swiftly, quickly, speedily, at an amazing rate.

learn v **1** *learn French* acquire a knowledge of, gain an understanding of, acquire skill in, become competent in, grasp, master, take in, absorb, assimilate, pick up. **2** *learn the poem* learn by heart, get by heart, memorize, commit to memory, become word-perfect in, get off pat. **3** *we learned that he had gone* discover, find out, detect, become aware of, gather, hear, be informed, have it brought to one's attention, understand, ascertain, discern, perceive. **4** *learn of his departure* find out about, hear of, get word of, be informed of, have brought to one's attention, get wind of.

learned adj *learned professors/journals* erudite, scholarly, well-educated, knowledgeable, well-read, widely read, well-versed, well-informed, lettered, cultured, intellectual, academic, literary, bookish, studious, pedantic, sage, wise; *inf* highbrow.

learner n beginner, trainee, apprentice, pupil, student, novice, tiro, neophyte, initiate, greenhorn, learner driver.

learning n **1** *a man of learning* erudition, scholarship, knowledge, education, letters, culture, intellect, academic attainment, booklearning, information, pedantry, sageness, wisdom. **2** *happy to leave learning behind* study, studying, education, schooling, tuition, teaching, instruction.

lease v **1** *lease a house/car from an agency* rent, hire, charter. **2** *lease their house to visitors from Canada* rent, rent out, let, let out, hire, hire out, sublet.

lease n *sign a lease for the house/car* rental agreement, hire agreement, charter, contract.

leash n **1** *a dog's leash* lead, rein, tether, rope, cord, chain. **2** *keep a tight leash on his anger* rein, curb, control, check, restraint, hold. **straining at the leash** *straining at the leash to get out in the sunshine* impatient, eager, anxious, enthusiastic, itching, dying.

leash v **1** *leash the dog* put the leash/lead on, fasten, hitch up, tether, tie up, secure. **2** *leash one's anger* curb, control, keep under control, check, restrain, hold back, suppress.

leather n *jackets made of leather | leather gloves* skin, hide, kid, doeskin, pigskin, suede, imitation leather, leatherette.

leather v *leather the guilty child* strap, belt, beat, thrash, flog, whip, lash, scourge; *inf* wallop, lather.

leathery adj **1** *leathery skin* wrinkled, wizened, weather-beaten, rough, rugged, coriaceous. **2** *leathery meat* tough, hard, hardened, coriaceous.

leave v **1** *leave hurriedly* depart, go away, go, withdraw, retire, take oneself off, exit, take one's leave, make off, pull out, quit, be gone, decamp, disappear, say one's farewells/goodbyes; *inf* push off, shove off, cut, do a bunk, split, vamoose. **2** *leave for France* set off, set sail. **3** *leave his wife* abandon, desert, forsake, discard, turn one's back on, leave in the lurch. **4** *has left his job* give up, quit, abandon, move from. **5** *leave his gloves at the hotel* leave behind, forget, mislay. **6** *leave the job to them* assign, allot, consign, hand over, give over, refer, commit, entrust. **7** *he left the estate to his nephew* bequeath, will, endow, hand down, transfer, convey; *fml* demise, devise. **8** *the quarrel left feelings of resentment* leave behind, cause, produce, generate, result in. **leave in the lurch** *leave the firm in the lurch by walking out* let down, leave in trouble, leave helpless, leave stranded, leave high and dry, abandon, desert, forsake. **leave off** *leave off talking* stop, cease, finish, halt, end, desist from, break off, give up, discontinue, refrain from; *inf* give over, knock off; *Amer* quit. **leave out** *leave out a sentence* miss out, omit, omit by accident, fail to include, overlook. **2** *please leave him out of the invitation list* exclude, omit, except, eliminate, count out, disregard, ignore, reject, repudiate.

leave n **1** *get leave to be absent* permission, consent, authorization, sanction, warrant, dispensation, concession, indulgence. **2** *going on leave for three weeks* holiday, vacation, break, time off, furlough, sabbatical, leave of absence; *inf* hols, vac. **3** *they took their leave* leaving, leave-taking, departure, parting, withdrawal, exit, farewell, goodbye, adieu.

leaven n **1** *add leaven to the dough* leavening, ferment, barm, raising agent, yeast, baking powder. **2** *the children added some leaven to the solemn occasion* transformer, modifier, catalyst, enlivening influence, lightening effect.

leaven v **1** *leaven the dough* raise, make rise, ferment, work, lighten. **2** *leaven the atmosphere of formality* permeate, infuse, pervade, penetrate, imbue, suffuse, transform, modify, lighten, enliven, stimulate.

leavings npl residue, remainder, remains, remnants, leftovers, scraps, oddments, odds and ends, fragments, junk, waste, dregs, refuse, rubbish, debris, sweepings.

lecher n libertine, womanizer, lady-killer, seducer, adulterer, fornicator, pervert, debauchee, rake, roué, Don Juan, Casanova, Lothario; *inf* dirty old man, DOM, lech, flasher.

lecherous adj lustful, promiscuous, randy, carnal, sensual, licentious, lascivious, lewd, salacious, libertine, libidinous, lubricious, concupiscent, debauched, dissolute, wanton, intemperate, dissipated, degenerate, depraved; *inf* horny, raunchy.

lechery n lust, lustfulness, promiscuity, randiness, carnality, sensualness, sensuality, licentiousness, lasciviousness, lewdness, salaciousness, salacity, libertinism, libidinousness, lubricity, concupiscence, debauchery, dissoluteness, wantonness, intemperance, dissipation, degeneracy, depravity; *inf* horniness, raunchiness.

lecture n **1** *attend a lecture on the environment* talk, speech, address, discourse, disquisition, lesson, sermon, homily, harangue. **2** *children given a lecture for being late* scolding, chiding, reprimand, rebuke, reproof, reproach, remonstration, upbraiding, berating, tirade, diatribe; *inf* dressing-down, telling-off, talking-to.

lecture v **1** *lectured on local politics* give a lecture, give a talk, talk, give a speech, make a speech, speak, give an address, address, discourse, expound, hold forth, give a sermon, sermonize, harangue; *inf* spout, jaw. **2** *he lectures in philosophy* teach, tutor in, instruct in, give instruction in, give lessons in. **3** *lecture the children for being late* scold, chide, reprimand, rebuke, reprove, reproach, remonstrate with, upbraid, berate, castigate, haul over the coals, give a tirade to, give a diatribe to; *inf* lambaste,

give a dressing-down to, give a talking-to to, tell off.

lecturer n **1** *the lecturer gave a talk on villages* speaker, public speaker, speech-maker, orator, preacher. **2** *he is a lecturer in French* university teacher, college teacher, tutor, reader, instructor, academic, academician.

ledge n shelf, sill, mantel, mantelpiece, mantelshelf, projection, protrusion, overhang, ridge, step.

ledger n account book, record book, register, registry, log.

lee n *in the lee of the hill* shelter, protection, cover, refuge.

leech n *I can't get rid of her; she's such a leech* clinger, hanger-on, parasite, barnacle, constant appendage, sycophant, toady, bloodsucker, extortioner, sponger; *inf* scrounger, freeloader.

leer v ogle, look lasciviously at, look suggestively at, give sly looks to, eye, wink at, watch, stare, goggle, sneer, smirk, grin; *inf* give someone the glad eye, give someone the once-over.

leer n lascivious look, lecherous glance, suggestive look, sly glance, wink, stare, sneer, smirk, grin; *inf* the glad eye, the once-over.

leery adj wary, chary, cautious, careful, guarded, on one's guard, suspicious, distrustful, mistrusting.

lees npl *emptied the lees from a wine glass* dregs, sediment, deposit, grounds, settlings, residue, remains; *Tech* precipitate, sublimate.

leeway n *the tight budget leaves little leeway for design costs* room to manoeuvre, room to operate, scope, latitude, elbow-room, slack, space, margin, play.

left adj **1** *the left side* left-hand, sinistral, sinister, sinistrous; port, starboard. **2** *a left politician* left-wing, leftist, socialist, radical, progressive, liberal, communist, communistic.

left-handed adj **1** *left-handed writers* sinistral; *inf* cack-handed, southpaw. **2** *a left-handed compliment* back-handed, ambiguous, equivocal, double-meaning, double-edged, dubious, indirect, enigmatic, cryptic, paradoxical, ironic, sardonic. **3** *a left-handed attempt at putting things right* awkward, clumsy, fumbling, unskilful, gauche, maladroit; *inf* cack-handed.

leftover n *a leftover from a bygone age* survivor, residue, legacy.

leftover adj *leftover food* remaining, excess, surplus, extra, uneaten, unused, unwanted.

leftovers npl *give the leftovers to the dogs* remainder, excess, surplus, leavings, uneaten food, unused supplies, scraps, odds and ends. see LEAVINGS.

leg n **1** *her injured leg* lower limb, limb, member, shank; *inf* stump, peg, pin. **2** *the legs of the tripod | chair legs* support, upright, prop, brace, underpinning. **3** *the final leg of the journey* part, portion, segment, section, bit, stretch, stage, lap. **give someone a leg up to** *give him a leg up onto the wall | give her a leg up in her career* act as someone's support to, support, help up, help, give someone assistance, assist, lend someone a helping hand, come to someone's aid, aid, give someone a boost, boost, advance. **not have a leg to stand on** *after his accomplice confessed, he did not have a leg to stand on* have nothing to support one's story/opinion etc, lack support, lack validity, lack credence, be vulnerable, be defenceless. **on its last legs 1** *this furniture is on its last legs* about to break, about to collapse, dilapidated, worn out, rickety. **2** *the firm's on its last legs* about to fail, about to go bankrupt, failing, near to ruin, going to the wall; *inf* going bust. **on one's last legs** *she's on her last legs after the long journey* exhausted, worn out, fatigued, fagged out, about to collapse, about to break down, about to die, dying, at death's door; *inf* all in, done in, shattered. **pull someone's leg** *we didn't mean to upset her; we were just pulling her leg* tease, chaff, rag, make fun of, trick, hoax, fool, deceive; *inf* kid, have on, rib; *Amer inf* put on. **stretch one's legs** *stop the car and stretch one's legs* go for a walk, take a walk, go for a stroll, move about, promenade, get some exercise, get some air, take the air.

leg v **leg it** *having missed the bus we had to leg it | let's leg it out of here* walk, go on foot, hurry; *inf* hightail it, go on Shanks's pony, hotfoot it.

legacy n **1** *willed a legacy of several thousand pounds* bequest, inheritance, heritage, bequeathal, endowment, gift, patrimony, heirloom; *fml* devise. **2** *a legacy of Celtic culture | this is the legacy of unemployment* inheritance, heritage, tradition, hand-me-down, residue.

legal adj **1** *legal behaviour* lawful, legitimate, licit, legalized, valid, right, proper, sound, permissible, permitted, allowable, allowed, above-board, admissible, acceptable, authorized, sanctioned, warranted, licensed; *inf*

legit. **2** *legal processes/adviser* judicial, juridical, jurisdictive, forensic.

legality n *dispute the legality of their actions* lawfulness, legitimacy, legitimateness, validity, rightness, rightfulness, soundness, permissibility, admissibility.

legalize v *legalize soft drugs* make legal, decriminalize, legitimize, legitimatize, legitimate, validate, ratify, permit, allow, admit, accept, authorize, sanction, warrant, license.

legate n *a papal legate* envoy, emissary, agent, ambassador, representative, commissioner, nuncio, messenger.

legatee n *the chief legatees mentioned in the will* beneficiary, recipient, inheritor, heir, heiress.

legation n **1** *part of the French legation in Britain* mission, diplomatic mission, embassy, consulate, ministry, delegation, deputation, representation, envoys. **2** *the address of the British legation* embassy, consulate, diplomatic establishment, ministry.

legend n **1** *a book of Scandinavian legends* myth, saga, epic, folk-tale, folk-story, traditional story, tale, story, narrative, fable, romance. **2** *Greta Garbo became a legend* famous person, celebrity, star, superstar, luminary. **3** *the legends under the photographs | legends on coins* caption, inscription, dedication, motto, device. **4** *the legends accompanying the tables* key, code, cipher, explanation, table of symbols.

legendary adj **1** *legendary figures in Icelandic saga* mythical, heroic, traditional, fabled, fictitious, fictional, story-book, romantic, fanciful, fantastical, fabulous. **2** *a legendary actor* celebrated, acclaimed, illustrious, famous, famed, renowned, well-known, popular, remembered, immortal.

legerdemain n **1** *stage magicians practising legerdemain* sleight of hand, juggling, conjuring, prestidigitation, trickery, hocus-pocus, thaumaturgy. **2** *a politician noted for his legerdemain* trickery, cunning, artfulness, craftiness, craft, wiles, deceit, deception, dissimulation, double-dealing, artful argument, specious reasoning, sophistry.

legibility n readability, readableness, ease of reading, decipherability, clearness, clarity, plainness, neatness.

legible adj easily read, easy to read, readable, decipherable, clear, distinct, plain, carefully written, neat.

legion n **1** *legions of soldiers* army, brigade, regiment, battalion, company, troop, division, unit, force. **2** *legions of people arrived for the festival* horde, host, throng, multitude, crowd, drove, mass, mob, gang, swarm, flock, herd.

legislate v **1** *it is parliament's task to legislate* make laws, pass laws, enact laws, formulate laws, establish laws, codify laws. **2** *they must legislate for more council houses* pass laws, decree, order, ordain, prescribe, authorize, make provision for.

legislation n **1** *his office is in charge of legislation* law-making, law enactment, law formulation, codification, prescription. **2** *dislike the new legislation* law, body of laws, constitution, rules, regulations, acts, bills, statutes, enactments, charters, ordinances, measures, canon, code.

legislative adj *legislative assembly/powers* law-making, law-giving, judicial, juridical, jurisdictive, parliamentary, congressional, senatorial.

legislator n law-maker, law-giver, parliamentarian, congressman, senator, politician.

legitimate adj **1** *legitimate actions* legal, lawful, licit, within the law, going by the rules; *inf* legit. **2** *the legitimate heir* lawful, rightful, genuine, authentic, real, true, proper, correct, authorized, sanctioned, warranted, acknowledged, recognized, approved; *inf* legit, kosher. **3** *a legitimate reason for being late* valid, sound, admissible, acceptable, well-founded, justifiable, reasonable, plausible, credible, believable, reliable, logical, rational.

legitimize v legitimate, legalize, pronounce lawful, declare legal, decriminalize, validate, permit, warrant, authorize, sanction, license, give the stamp of approval to.

leisure n *seek a hobby for periods of leisure | leisure pursuits* free time, spare time, spare moments, time to spare, idle hours, inactivity, time off, relaxation, recreation, freedom, holiday, vacation, breathing space, breathing spell, respite; *inf* time to kill. **at one's leisure** *you can do this work at your leisure* at one's convenience, when it suits one, in one's own good time, when one can fit it in, without need for haste, without haste, unhurriedly, without hurry, when one gets round to it.

leisurely adj *at a leisurely pace* unhurried, relaxed, easy, easygoing, gentle, comfortable, restful, slow, lazy, lingering; *inf* laidback.

lend v **1** *lend him a book* loan, give someone the loan of, let someone have the use of, advance. **2** *the flowers lend beauty to the room* impart, add, give, bestow, confer, provide, supply, furnish. **3** *lend his professional skill to the venture* give, contribute, donate, grant. **lend an ear** *lend an ear to what the teacher is saying* listen, pay attention to, take notice of, heed, pay heed to, give ear to. **lend a hand** *lend a hand with the preparations* help, help out, give a helping hand, assist, give assistance, aid, make a contribution; *inf* pitch in. **lend itself to** *the house does not lend itself to being divided* be suitable for, be suited to, be appropriate for, be adaptable to, have the right characteristics for.

length n **1** *what length is the cloth?* distance lengthwise, distance, extent lengthwise, extent, linear measure, span, reach. **2** *he's been here for quite a length of time* period, stretch, duration, term, span. **3** *a length of cloth* piece, portion, section, measure, segment, swatch. **4** *a speech noted for its length* longness, lengthiness, extensiveness, protractedness, elongation, prolixity, prolixness, wordiness, verbosity, verboseness, long-windedness, tediousness, tedium. **at length 1** *speak at length* for a long time, for ages, for hours, on and on, interminably, endlessly. **2** *deal at length with the problem* fully, to the fullest extent, in detail, in depth, thoroughly, exhaustively, completely. **3** *at length he agreed to accept* after a long time, after a considerable time, finally, at last, at long last, eventually, in the end, ultimately, in time. **go to any length(s)** *she would go to any lengths to save her child* do absolutely anything, go to any extreme, go to any limits, observe no limits.

lengthen v **1** *lengthen a skirt* make longer, elongate, let down. **2** *the days are lengthening* grow longer, get longer, draw out, stretch. **3** *lengthen the time taken | lengthened his speech* make longer, prolong, increase, extend, expand, protract, stretch out, draw out.

lengthy adj **1** *a lengthy affair* long, very long, long-lasting, prolonged, extended, protracted, long-drawn-out. **2** *a lengthy speech* long, very long, over-long, protracted, long-drawn-out, diffuse, discursive, verbose, wordy, prolix, long-winded, tedious.

lenience, leniency n **1** *the leniency of the judge* mercy, mercifulness, clemency, lenity, humanity, tolerance, compassion, indulgence, gentleness. *see* LENIENT 1. **2** *the leniency of the sentence* mildness, mercifulness, lenity, moderateness, lack of severity.

lenient adj **1** *a lenient judge* merciful, clement, sparing, moderate, compassionate, humane, forbearing, tolerant, liberal, magnanimous, indulgent, kind, gentle, easygoing. **2** *a lenient sentence* mild, merciful, moderate, non-severe.

leper n *a social leper* social outcast, outcast, pariah, untouchable, *persona non grata*.

leprechaun n elf, sprite, fairy, gnome; little people.

lesbian n homosexual, gay, homoerotic, Sapphic, tribade; *derog inf* lezzy, butch; dyke.

lesbian adj homosexual, gay, homoerotic, Sapphic, tribadic; *inf* queer.

lesion n *lesions on her face after the accident* wound, injury, sore, abrasion, scratch, scrape, cut, gash, laceration, trauma.

less adj *of less importance* smaller, slighter, not so much, not so great.

less n *have less than they have* smaller amount, not so much.

less adv *she reads less now* to a lesser degree, to a smaller extent, not so much.

less prep *£100 less the deposit* minus, subtracting, excepting, without.

lessen v **1** *the wind/pain lessened* grow less, abate, decrease, diminish, subside, moderate, slacken, die down, let up, ease off, tail off, ebb, wane. **2** *the tablets lessened the pain* relieve, soothe, allay, assuage, alleviate, palliate, ease, dull, deaden, blunt, take the edge off. **3** *his behaviour lessened him in their eyes* diminish, lower, reduce, minimize, degrade, discredit, devalue, belittle, humble.

lesser adj **1** *one of his lesser works* less important, minor, slighter, secondary, inferior. **2** *lesser people had to stand* subordinate, minor, inferior.

lesson n **1** *have a music lesson* class, period of instruction/teaching/coaching/tutoring/schooling. **2** *children doing lessons* exercise, schoolwork, homework, assignment, school task. **3** *reading the lesson in church* Bible passage, Bible reading, scripture, text. **4** *punished as a lesson to others* example, warning, deterrent, message, moral, precept. **5** *hardship taught him valuable lessons* knowledge, wisdom, enlightenment, experience, truths.

lest conj *lest we forget* in case, in order to avoid, for fear that.

let v **1** *let them play there* allow, permit, give permission to, give leave to, authorize, sanction, grant, warrant, license, assent to, consent to, agree to, give the go-ahead to, give the thumbs up to; *inf* give the green light to. **2** *let the people through* allow to go, permit to pass. **3** *let it be known* cause, make, enable. **4** *he let his house* let out, rent,

rent out, lease, hire, hire out, sublet. **let down 1** *they felt he had let them down* fail to support, fail, fall short of expectation, disappoint, disillusion, forsake, abandon, desert, leave stranded, leave in the lurch, betray. **2** *let down the skirt* lengthen, make longer. **let fly 1** *let fly a large stone* hurl, fling, throw, propel, pitch, lob, toss, heave, launch, shoot; *inf* chuck. **2** *she just let fly at him* lose one's temper, explode, erupt with anger, let someone have it, give free reign to one's emotions, keep nothing back, give vent to one's emotions, lash out at. **let in** *let the dog in* allow to enter, admit, open the door to, grant entrance to, give access to, give right of entry to, receive, welcome, greet. **let in for** *let them in for a lot of expense* involve, draw into, implicate. **let in on** *let them in on the deal* include, count in, admit, allow to share in, let participate in, take in. **let off 1** *let off the firework* explode, detonate. **2** *letting off fumes* give off, discharge, emit, release, exude, leak. **3** *let the guilty man off* acquit, release, discharge, reprieve, absolve, exonerate, pardon, forgive, exempt, spare. **let on 1** *don't let on that you know him* reveal, make known, tell, disclose, divulge, let out, let slip, give away, leak. **2** *he let on that he was deaf* pretend, feign, affect, make out, make believe, simulate, fake. **let out 1** *let the animals out of the cage* allow to leave, open the door for, grant exit to, let go, free, set free, release, liberate. **2** *let out a scream* emit, utter, give vent to, produce. **3** *she let out that she knew him* reveal, make known, tell, disclose. *see* LET, LET ON 1. **let up 1** *the storm finally let up* lessen, abate, decrease, diminish, subside, moderate, slacken, die down, ease off, tail off, ebb, wane. **2** *if you don't let up you'll have a breakdown* do less, relax one's efforts, relax, stop. **3** *please let up on the child* treat less severely, be more lenient with, be kinder to; *inf* go easy on.

let-down n *the match was a let-down* disappointment, disillusionment, non-success, fiasco, anticlimax; *inf* wash-out.

lethal adj *a lethal blow/dose | potentially lethal set of circumstances* fatal, deadly, mortal, death-dealing, murderous, poisonous, toxic, dangerous, virulent, noxious, destructive, disastrous, calamitous, ruinous.

lethargic adj sluggish, inactive, slow, slothful, torpid, phlegmatic, listless, languid, apathetic, passive, weary, enervated, fatigued, sleepy, narcotic. *see* LETHARGY.

lethargy n sluggishness, inertia, inactivity, slowness, sloth, idleness, torpor, torpidity, lifelessness, dullness, listlessness, languor, languidness, phlegm, apathy, passivity, weariness, lassitude, fatigue, sleepiness, drowsiness, somnolence, narcosis.

letter n **1** *written in bold letters | letter of the alphabet* character, alphabetical character, sign, symbol. **2** *send a letter* written message, message, written communication, communication, note, line, business letter, missive, epistle, dispatch, love-letter, billet-doux, fan letter, letter of thanks, thank-you letter, bread-and-butter letter, reply, acknowledgement; *inf* Dear John letter. **to the letter** *follow our instructions to the letter* with strict attention to detail, strictly, precisely, exactly, accurately, literally, word for word, verbatim. **the letter of the law** *interpret agreements according to the letter of the law* exact wording, literal interpretation, form of words.

lettered adj *a lettered person* learned, erudite, academic, well-educated, educated, well-read, widely read, cultured, cultivated, scholarly, literary; *inf* highbrow.

letters npl *a man of letters* learning, scholarship, erudition, education, culture, cultivation, literature, humanities, belles-lettres.

let-up n *no let-up in the hostilities* lessening, abatement, decrease, diminishing, diminution, subsidence, moderation, slackening, dying down, easing off, tailing off, ebbing, waning.

level adj **1** *a level surface* flat, smooth, even, uniform, plane, flush, horizontal. **2** *keep the temperature level* even, uniform, regular, consistent, constant, stable, steady, unchanging, unvarying, unfluctuating. **3** *the two teams are level* equal, on a level, in a position of equality, close together, neck and neck, level-pegging, side by side, on a par, with nothing to choose between them; *inf* even-Steven. **4** *hang the pictures level with each other* on the same level, on a level, at the same height, aligned, in line, balanced. **5** *have a level temper* even, even-tempered, equable, steady, stable, calm, serene, tranquil, composed, unruffled.

level n **1** *at eye-level* height, highness, altitude, elevation, distance upward. **2** *what level is he in the firm?* level of achievement, position, rank, standing, status, station, degree, grade, stage, standard. **3** *what level of expense have you in mind?* extent, amount, quantity, measure, degree, volume, size. **4** *glad to be back on the level after mountaineering* flat surface, flat, horizontal, plane, plain. **5** *levels of rock* layer, stratum, bed. **6** *what level do you live on?* floor, storey. **on the level** *are you sure your partner's on the level?* honest, above-board, straight, fair, genuine, true, sincere, open, straightforward; *inf* upfront, kosher.

level v **1** *level the surface* level out, make level, even off, even out, make flat, flatten, smooth, smooth out, plane. **2** *level the buildings* raze, raze to the ground, pull down, knock down, tear down, demolish, flatten, bulldoze, lay waste, destroy. **3** *level the trees* fell, cut down, chop down, hew down. **4** *level his opponent* knock down, knock to the ground, throw to the ground, lay out, prostrate, flatten, floor, fell, knock out; *inf* KO, kayo. **5** *his goal levelled the score* make level, equalize, make equal, even, even up. **6** *level his gun at the target* aim, point, direct, train, sight, focus, beam, zero in on, draw a bead on. **7** *he's not levelling with you* be honest, be above-board, tell the truth, tell all, be frank, be open, hide nothing, keep nothing back, be straightforward, put all one's cards on the table; *inf* be upfront.

level-headed adj sensible, full of common sense, prudent, circumspect, shrewd, wise, reasonable, rational, sane, composed, calm, cool, collected, cool calm and collected, cool-headed, balanced, self-possessed, unruffled, even-tempered, imperturbable; *inf* unflappable, together.

lever n **1** *use a lever to prise the lid off* bar, crowbar, handspike, jemmy. **2** *release the lever to operate the machine* handle, grip, pull, switch.

lever v *lever the lid open | lever the load up* prise, force, move, jemmy, raise, lift, hoist, purchase; *Amer* pry.

leverage n **1** *not enough leverage to move the load* purchase, force, strength. **2** *not have the leverage to win over the committee* power, influence, authority, weight, ascendancy, rank; *inf* pull, clout.

levitate n *people claiming to be able to levitate* rise into the air, float, hover, be suspended, glide, fly.

levity n **1** *showing levity at a solemn occasion* light-heartedness, carefreeness, light-mindedness, humour, facetiousness, fun, jocularity, hilarity, frivolity, flippancy, triviality, silliness, giddiness, skittishness. **2** *the levity of her nature* fickleness, inconstancy, instability, unsteadiness, variability, changeability, unreliability, undependability, inconsistency, flightiness.

levy n **1** *the levy of taxes* collection, gathering, raising, imposition, exaction, assessment. *see* LEVY v 1. **2** *unable to pay the levy* tax, taxation, tariff, toll, excise, customs, duty, dues, imposition, impost, assessment. **3** *inspect the levy* conscripts, troops, forces, armed forces, army, militia, guard.

levy v **1** *levy taxes* collect, gather, raise, impose, exact, demand, charge, tax. **2** *levy troops* conscript, call up, enlist, muster, mobilize, rally, press; *Amer* draft.

lewd adj **1** *a lewd old man* lecherous, lustful, licentious, lascivious, promiscuous, carnal, sensual, randy, prurient, salacious, lubricious, libidinous, concupiscent, debauched, dissipated, dissolute, profligate, unchaste, wanton. **2** *lewd literature* obscene, pornographic, blue, bawdy, salacious, suggestive, ribald, indecent, vulgar, crude, smutty, dirty, coarse, gross, foul, vile; *inf* raunchy.

lewdness n **1** *the lewdness of the old man* lechery, lust, lustfulness, licentiousness, lasciviousness, promiscuity, carnality, sensuality, randiness, prurience, pruriency, salaciousness, salacity, lubricity, libidinousness, concupiscence, debauchery, dissipation, dissoluteness, profligacy, unchasteness, wantonness. **2** *the lewdness of the literature* obscenity, blueness, bawdiness, salaciousness, salacity, suggestiveness, ribaldry, indecency, vulgarity, crudeness, smut, smuttiness, dirtiness, coarseness, grossness, foulness, vileness; *inf* raunchiness.

liability n **1** *admit liability for the lost goods* responsibility, legal responsibility, accountability, answerability, blame, blameworthiness, culpability, amenableness. **2** *meet his financial liabilities* obligation, financial obligation, debt, indebtedness, debit, arrears, dues. **3** *don't take her brother with you - he will just be a liability* hindrance, encumbrance, burden, impediment, handicap, nuisance, inconvenience, drawback, drag, disadvantage, millstone round one's neck, stumbling-block, cross to bear. **4** *dislike her liability to burst into tears* aptness, likelihood, inclination, tendency, disposition, predisposition, proneness.

liable adj **1** *husbands liable for their wives' debts | hotels are not liable for customers' lost property* responsible, legally responsible, accountable, answerable, chargeable, blameworthy, at fault, censurable, amenable. **2** *liable to injury* exposed, open, subject, susceptible, vulnerable, in danger of, at risk of, pregnable. **3** *liable to burst into tears* apt, likely, inclined, tending, disposed, predisposed, prone.

liaison n **1** *no liaison between the departments* communication, contact, connection, interchange, link, linkage, tie-up. **2** *he acts as liaison between the departments* intermediary, contact man/woman/person, linkman, linkwoman, linkperson, go-between. **3** *his wife found out about his liaison* affair, love affair, relationship, romance, intrigue, amour, amorous/romantic entanglement, entanglement, flirtation; *inf* hanky-panky.

liar n teller of lies, teller of untruths, fibber, fibster, perjurer, falsifier, false witness, fabricator, equivocator, prevaricator, deceiver, spinner of yarns; *inf* storyteller.

libation n **1** *offer a libation to the gods* liquid offering, offering, tribute, oblation, sacrifice. **2** *in need of a libation after the long walk* drink, liquid refreshment, beverage, alcoholic drink, dram, bracer; *inf* tincture.

libel n *a writer found guilty of libel* defamation of character, defamation, denigration, vilification, disparagement, derogation, aspersions, calumny, slander, false report, traducement, obloquy, abuse, slur, smear, smear campaign.

libel v *his biographer libelled him* defame, vilify, give someone a bad name, blacken someone's name, denigrate, disparage, derogate, cast aspersions on, asperse, calumniate, slander, write false reports about, traduce, abuse, revile, malign, slur, smear, fling mud at, drag someone's name through the mud/mire.

libellous adj *published libellous remarks* defamatory, denigratory, vilifying, disparaging, derogatory, aspersive, calumnious, calumniatory, slanderous, false, misrepresentative, traducing, abusive, reviling, malicious, maligning, scurrilous, slurring, smearing, muckraking.

liberal adj **1** *a liberal supply of food* abundant, copious, ample, plentiful, lavish, profuse, munificent, bountiful, rich, handsome, generous. **2** *hosts liberal with their hospitality* generous, magnanimous, open-handed, unsparing, unstinting, ungrudging, lavish, munificent, bountiful, bounteous, beneficent, big-hearted, kind-hearted, kind, philanthropic, charitable, altruistic, unselfish. **3** *people of liberal ideas who are against discrimination of any kind* tolerant, unprejudiced, unbiased, unbigoted, impartial, non-partisan, disinterested, broad-minded, enlightened, catholic, indulgent, permissive. **4** *a liberal interpretation of the law* broad, loose, flexible, non-restrictive, free, general, non-literal, not strict, not close, inexact, imprecise. **5** *liberal in his politics* advanced, forward-looking, progressive, reformist, radical, latitudinarian. **6** *a liberal education* wide-ranging, broad-based, general, humanistic.

liberate v *liberate prisoners | liberate the occupied country* set free, free, release, let out, let go, discharge, set loose, unshackle, unfetter, unchain, deliver, rescue, emancipate, manumit, unyoke.

liberation n **1** *the liberation of the prisoners* freeing, release, discharge, unshackling, deliverance, emancipation, manumission. see LIBERATE. **2** *women seeking liberation* freedom, equality, equal rights, non-discrimination, emancipation, enfranchisement.

liberator n rescuer, saviour, deliverer, freer, emancipator, manumitter.

libertine adj *disapprove of their libertine ways* licentious, lustful, lecherous, lascivious, dissolute, dissipated, debauched, immoral, wanton, decadent, depraved, profligate, rakish, sensual, promiscuous, unchaste, impure, sinful, intemperate, abandoned, corrupt.

libertine n *seduced by a libertine* lecher, seducer, debauchee, profligate, rake, roué, wanton, loose liver, sensualist, reprobate, womanizer, adulterer, Don Juan, Lothario, Casanova; *inf* lech.

liberty n **1** *countries which have always had liberty* freedom, independence, autonomy, sovereignty, self-government, self-rule. **2** *prisoners gaining their liberty* freedom, liberation, release, discharge, deliverance, emancipation, manumission. **3** *have the liberty to choose* freedom, free will, volition, latitude, option, choice, non-compulsion, non-coercion. **4** *given the liberty to leave the grounds* right, prerogative, privilege, permission, sanction, authorization, licence, *carte blanche*, dispensation, exemption. **5** *sacked because of the liberties he took | was guilty of taking liberties* overfamiliarity, familiarity, disrespect, impropriety, indecorum, breach of etiquette, impertinence, insolence, impudence, presumptuousness, presumption, forwardness, audacity. **at liberty 1** *the thief/animal is still at liberty* free, loose, on the loose, at large, unconfined. **2** *you are at liberty to do as you wish* free, permitted, allowed, entitled.

libidinous adj lustful, lecherous, lascivious, lewd, carnal, sensual, salacious, prurient, concupiscent, lubricious, dissolute, debauched, degenerate, decadent, wanton, immoral, unchaste, impure, intemperate, randy; *inf* horny.

libido n *has a high/low libido* sexual desire, sex drive, sexual appetite, sexiness, sexual passion, lust, lustfulness, randiness; *inf* horniness.

licence n **1** *be given licence to sell their wares* permission, leave, liberty, freedom, consent, authority, authorization, sanction, approval, warranty, certification, accreditation, entitlement, privilege, prerogative,

right, dispensation, exemption. **2** *they have the licence to do as they please* freedom, liberty, free will, latitude, choice, option, independence, self-determination. **3** *have a driving licence* permit, certificate, credential, document, documentation, pass. **4** *appalled at the licence at the all-night party* licentiousness, dissoluteness, dissipation, debauchery, immorality, decadence, profligacy, immoderation, intemperateness, indulgence, self-indulgence, excess, excessiveness, lack of restraint, lack of control, irresponsibility, abandon, disorderliness, unruliness, lawlessness, anarchy.

license v **1** *license them to sell alcohol* grant a licence to, give a licence to, give a permit to, authorize, give authorization to, grant the right to, warrant, certify, accredit, charter, franchise. **2** *license them to ride the horses at weekends* give permission to, permit, allow, grant leave to, entitle, give the freedom to, sanction, give one's approval to, empower.

licentious adj dissolute, lustful, lecherous, lascivious, dissipated, debauched, immoral, wanton, decadent, depraved, profligate, sensual, promiscuous, unchaste, impure, intemperate, abandoned.

licit adj *declared a licit action* legal, lawful, legitimate, permissible, admissible, allowable, acceptable.

lick v **1** *lick the ice-cream* pass the tongue over, touch with the tongue, tongue, taste, lap. **2** *flames licking the walls* touch, play over, flick over, dart over, ripple over. **3** *lick the opponents* defeat, beat, conquer, trounce, thrash, rout, vanquish, overcome, overwhelm, overpower, drub; *inf* wipe the floor with. **4** *lick his son* beat, thrash, flog, whip, strike, hit, thwack, slap, spank; *inf* wallop, whack, lambaste. **5** *lick the problem* get the better of, overcome, solve, find an answer to, find a solution to.

licking n **1** *the team gave their opponents a good licking* defeat, beating, trouncing, thrashing, drubbing. **2** *the boy received a licking from his father* beating, thrashing, flogging, whipping, slapping, spanking; *inf* walloping, hiding, tanning.

lid n cover, top, cap, cork, stopper, plug. **put the lid on** *when the teacher found out it put the lid on their plans* be the end of, put an end to, put a stop to, ruin, put paid to, destroy. **take the lid off** *take the lid off the scandal* expose, reveal, bring to light, make known, make public, bring into the open.

lie[1] n *witness found to be telling lies* untruth, falsehood, barefaced lie, fib, white lie, little white lie, fabrication, made-up story, trumped-up story, invention, piece of fiction, fiction, falsification, falsity, fairystory, cock-and-bull story, dissimulation, prevarication, departure from the truth; *inf* terminological inexactitude, tall tale, whopper. **give the lie to** *the historical evidence gave the lie to his theory* disprove, contradict, negate, deny, refute, rebut, challenge, gainsay.

lie¹ v *the witness was lying* tell a lie, tell an untruth, tell a falsehood, perjure oneself, fib, tell a white lie, fabricate, invent/make up a story, falsify, dissemble, dissimulate, prevaricate, depart from the truth, be economical with the truth, bear false witness; *inf* tell a terminological inexactitude.

lie² v **1** *he was lying not sitting* recline, be recumbent, be prostrate, be supine, be prone, be stretched out, sprawl, rest, repose, relax, lounge, loll. **2** *the town lies on the other side of the hill* be, be situated, be located, be placed, be positioned, be found. **3** *two poets lie there* be buried, be interred. **4** *lie dormant* remain, continue, stay, be. **5** *his guilt lies heavily on him* press down, weigh down, be a great weight on, be a burden to, oppress. **lie in** *their strength lies in their faith* consist, be inherent, inhere, be present, exist, reside. **lie low** *they lay low during the police search* hide, go into hiding, hide out, conceal oneself, keep out of sight, keep a low profile, take cover, go to earth, go to ground, go underground; *inf* hole up.

liege n liege lord, lord, feudal lord, overlord, suzerain, master, chief, chieftain, superior.

lieutenant n *the gang-leader and his lieutenant* assistant, aide, deputy, second-in-command, right-hand man/woman, henchman, henchwoman, subordinate; *inf* sidekick.

life n **1** *is there life in the body?* existence, being, animation, aliveness, viability. **2** *is there life on Mars?* | *no sign of life* living things, living beings, living creatures, human/animal/plant life, fauna, flora, human activity. **3** *many lives were lost in the war* person, human being, individual, mortal, soul. **4** *worked hard all her life* lifetime, days, duration of life, course of life, lifespan, time on earth, existence, career; *inf* one's born days. **5** *the life of a battery* duration, active life, functioning period, period of effectiveness, period of usefulness. **6** *modern conveniences make life easier* course of life, living, activities, conduct, behaviour. **7** *he should really have won but that's life* the human condition, the way of the world, the world, the times we live in, the usual state of affairs. **8** *he leads/has a very*

affluent life way of life, way of living, manner of living, lifestyle, situation, position. **9** *he wrote a life of the poet* | *she is writing her life* biography, autobiography, life story, memoirs, history, career, diary, journal, confessions. **10** *children full of life* | *put some life in the party* animation, vivacity, liveliness, vitality, verve, high spirits, sparkle, exuberance, buoyancy, effervescence, enthusiasm, energy, vigour, dynamism, go, brio; *inf* oomph, pizazz, pep, zing. **11** *he was the life of the firm* life force, vital spirit, spirit, vital spark, animating spirit, moving force, lifeblood, very essence, essence, heart, core, soul, *élan vital*. **come to life** **1** *the town comes to life at night* become active, come alive, become lively, wake up, awaken, show signs of life. **2** *toys come to life in the play* become animate, come alive, become a living creature. **for dear life, for dear life's sake** *they ran for dear life* | *they banged the door for dear life's sake* as fast/hard etc as possible, for all one is worth, in desperation, with urgency, urgently, with as much vigour as possible, like the devil. **give one's life** **1** *he gave his life for his friend* die for, sacrifice oneself for, die to save. **2** *give one's life to teaching* dedicate oneself, devote oneself, give oneself, pledge oneself, surrender oneself.

life-and-death adj *a life-and-death decision* vital, of vital importance, crucial, critical, urgent, momentous, important, serious.

lifeblood n *manufacturing is the lifeblood of the economy* life, life-force, animating spirit, moving force, driving force, vital spark, inspiration, animus, essence, heart, core.

life-giving adj vitalizing, animating, vivifying, energizing, invigorating, enlivening, stimulating.

lifeless adj **1** *the boy was lifeless on being pulled from the water* dead, deceased, gone, cold, defunct. **2** *prefer lifeless statues to people* inanimate, without life, abiotic. **3** *lifeless stretches of country* barren, sterile, bare, desolate, stark, arid, unproductive, uncultivated, empty, uninhabited, unoccupied. **4** *a lifeless performance* spiritless, lacking vitality, unspirited, lacklustre, apathetic, uninspired, colourless, dull, flat, stiff, wooden, tedious, uninspiring.

lifelike adj *a lifelike portrait* true-to-life, realistic, photographic, speaking, faithful, authentic, exact, vivid, graphic, natural.

lifelong adj *a lifelong commitment* for all one's life, lifetime's, lasting, constant, enduring, abiding, permanent.

lifestyle n *an affluent lifestyle* way of life, way of living, manner of living, life.

lifetime n **1** *many technological advances in his lifetime* life, life-span, existence. *see* LIFE 4. **2** *what is the lifetime of the average battery?* life, duration, functioning period. *see* LIFE 5. **3** *wait a lifetime for him to change his ways* all one's life, a very long time; *inf* ages, an age.

lift v **1** *lift the sack* pick up, uplift, hoist, upheave, raise, raise up, upraise, heft. **2** *lift the flag* raise high, hold up, bear aloft. **3** *your visit lifted his spirits* raise, buoy up, boost, elevate. **4** *the new player lifted their game* improve, boost, enhance, make better, ameliorate, upgrade. **5** *the mist lifted* rise, disperse, dissipate, disappear, vanish, be dispelled. **6** *lift the ban* raise, remove, withdraw, revoke, rescind, cancel, annul, void, countermand, relax, end, stop, terminate. **7** *lift the potatoes* dig up, pick, pull up, take up. **8** *lift food to the famine region* airlift, transport by air, transport, move, transfer. **9** *lift one's voice* raise, make louder, louden, amplify. **10** *lift the passage from a critic* plagiarize, pirate, copy, abstract; *inf* crib. **11** *someone's lifted my purse* steal, thieve, rob, pilfer, purloin, filch, pocket, take, appropriate; *inf* pinch, nick, swipe.

lift n **1** *give the child a lift up* hoist, heave, push, thrust, shove, help, a helping hand. **2** *the visitors gave the patient a lift* boost, fillip, pick-me-up, stimulus; *inf* shot in the arm. **3** *the new player gave their game a lift* boost, improvement, enhancement, upgrading, amelioration. **4** *give the children a lift to school* car ride, ride, run, drive, transportation. **5** *go up in the lift | goods lift* elevator, hoist.

light¹ n **1** *see by the light of the sun/fire* illumination, luminescence, luminosity, shining, gleaming, brightness, brilliance, glowing, blaze, glare, incandescence, effulgence, refulgence, lambency, radiance, lustre, sunlight, moonlight, starlight, lamplight, firelight, electric light, gaslight, ray of light, shaft of light, beam of light. **2** *bring the light over here* lamp, torch, flashlight, lantern, candle, taper, beacon. **3** *strike a light* flame, spark, match, lighter. **4** *we like to travel in the light, not the dark* daylight, daylight hours, daytime, day, hours of sunlight. **5** *we shall leave at light* first light, dawn, crack of dawn, daybreak, sunrise, cockcrow, morning. **6** *see things in a different light | things appeared in a new light* aspect, angle, slant, approach, viewpoint, point of view. **7** *light finally dawned and I solved the problem* enlightenment, illumination, understanding, comprehension, awareness, knowledge, elucidation, explanation. **8** *he was one of the lights in the theatre group* leading lights, luminary, star, guiding light,

expert, authority. **9** *he did his best; he acted according to his lights | by her own lights she knew* mental powers, intelligence, intellect, knowledge, understanding, talent. **bring to light** *the search brought to light new evidence* reveal, disclose, expose, uncover, show up, unearth, bring to notice. **come to light** *new evidence came to light* be discovered, be uncovered, be unearthed, appear, come out, turn up, transpire. **in light of** *in light of his previous convictions* taking into consideration, considering, taking into account, bearing in mind, keeping in mind, mindful of, taking note of, in view of. **shed/throw light on** *can you shed any light on this matter?* elucidate, clarify, clear up, explain, offer an explanation for.

light¹ adj **1** *a light room* full of light, bright, well-lit, well-lighted, well-illuminated, sunny. **2** *wearing light clothes* light-coloured, light-toned, pale, pale-coloured, pastel, pastel-coloured, whitish, faded, bleached. **3** *she had light hair* light-coloured, fair, blond.

light¹ v **1** *light the fire* set burning, set fire to, set a match to, ignite, kindle. **2** *fireworks lit up the sky* illuminate, brighten, lighten, irradiate, flood with light, floodlight; *lit* illumine. **3** *a smile lit up her face* irradiate, brighten, animate, make cheerful, cheer up, enliven. **4** *light them to their seats* direct, guide, usher, escort.

light² adj **1** *the suitcases are light* non-heavy, easy to carry, portable. **2** *small, light children* slight, thin, slender, skinny, underweight, small, tiny. **3** *wearing light clothes* light-weight, thin, flimsy, insubstantial, delicate, floaty, gossamer. **4** *a light tap on the shoulder | heard a light knock* gentle, slight, delicate, soft, weak, faint, indistinct. **5** *light tasks* moderate, easy, simple, undemanding, untaxing, unexacting, effortless, facile; *inf* cushy. **6** *light music/reading/entertainment* non-serious, readily-understood, light-hearted, entertaining, diverting, recreative, pleasing, amusing, humorous, funny, frivolous, superficial, trivial, trifling. **7** *a light attack of flu | a light sentence* non-severe, mild, moderate, slight. **8** *this is no light matter* unimportant, insignificant, trivial, trifling, petty, inconsequential. **9** *a light meal* non-heavy, non-rich, non-large, easily digested, small, modest, scanty, skimpy, frugal. **10** *with light heart* light-hearted, carefree, cheerful, cheery, happy, gay, merry, blithe, sunny, untroubled. **11** *with light fingers | was light of foot* nimble, deft, agile, supple, lithe, spry, sprightly, graceful, light-footed. **12** *feeling light in the head* light-headed, giddy, dizzy, vertiginous, faint, unsteady; *inf* woozy. **13** *light in character* frivolous, giddy, skittish, flighty, fickle, erratic, mercurial, volatile, capricious. **14** *of light morals* non-chaste, loose, promiscuous, licentious, dissolute, dissipated, wanton. **15** *light soil* non-dense, porous, crumbly, friable.

light² v **light into** *light into their attackers* attack, assault, set upon, fall upon, strike, beat, tear into; *inf* lay into, let someone have it, lambaste, lace into. **light upon** *light upon treasure* | *lit upon the truth* come across, chance upon, happen upon, stumble upon, hit upon, find, discover, encounter.

lighten¹ v **1** *the sky lightened* become lighter, grow brighter, brighten. **2** *the flames lightened* blaze, glow, gleam, flicker, sparkle. **3** *it was lightening this morning* emit lightning, flash lightning, fulgurate. **4** *the larger windows lightened the room* make lighter, make brighter, brighten, light up, illuminate, shed light on, cast light on, irradiate. **5** *the sun had lightened the colours* whiten, bleach, pale.

lighten² v **1** *lighten the horse's load* make lighter, lessen, reduce, ease. **2** *lighten his burden of pain* lessen, reduce, ease, alleviate, mitigate, allay, relieve, assuage, ameliorate. **3** *the good news lightened his mood* brighten, cheer up, gladden, hearten, buoy up, perk up, lift, uplift, enliven, elate, inspire, revive, restore.

light-fingered adj *shopkeepers on the watch for light-fingered people* thieving, thievish, stealing, pilfering, filching, shop-lifting, pocket-picking, dishonest; *inf* crooked.

light-footed adj light of foot, spry, sprightly, light on one's feet, graceful, nimble, agile, lithe.

light-headed adj **1** *feeling light-headed at the top of the ladder* giddy, dizzy, vertiginous, faint, unsteady, light in the head; *inf* woozy. **2** *light-headed young girls* giddy, scatterbrained, feather-brained, hare-brained, flighty, dizzy, frivolous, superficial, empty-headed, vacuous, flippant, shallow, light-minded, silly, inane; *inf* birdbrained.

light-hearted adj carefree, cheerful, cheery, happy, glad, gay, merry, playful, jolly, joyful, jovial, gleeful, frolicsome, effervescent, in good spirits, blithe, sunny, untroubled; *inf* chirpy, upbeat.

lighthouse n light-tower, warning light, guiding light, beacon, suitor's landmark, pharos.

lightly adv **1** *snow falling lightly* slightly, thinly, softly, gently. **2** *salt the food lightly* sparingly, sparsely, slightly. **3** *get off lightly* easily, without severe punishment,

leniently. **4** *jump lightly over the fence* easily, nimbly, agilely, lithely, spryly, gracefully. **5** *dismiss the subject lightly* airily, carelessly, heedlessly, uncaringly, indifferently, thoughtlessly, flippantly, frivolously, slightingly; *inf* breezily.

lightweight adj **1** *lightweight clothes* light, thin, flimsy. see LIGHT² adj 3. **2** *lightweight prose* | *he's a lightweight writer* insignificant, of no account, unimportant, of no consequence, inconsequential, insubstantial, trivial, trifling, paltry, petty, of no merit, of no value, valueless, worthless.

likable see LIKEABLE.

like adj *like people are attracted to each other* | *houses of like design* similar, much the same, more or less the same, not unlike, comparable, corresponding, resembling, analogous, parallel, equivalent, of a kind, identical, matching, akin.

like prep **1** *he paints like Picasso* in the same way as, in the manner of, in a similar way to, after the fashion of, along the lines of. **2** *it was like him to be generous* typical of, characteristic of, in character with.

like n *not see his like again* equal, match, counterpart, fellow, twin, mate, parallel, peer, compeer.

like v **1** *they like each other* be fond of, have a liking for, be attracted to, be keen on, love, adore, have a soft spot for. **2** *he likes swimming* enjoy, be keen on, find/take pleasure in, love, adore, find agreeable, delight in, relish, revel in; *inf* get a kick from. **3** *we should like you to go* wish, want, desire, prefer, had sooner, had rather. **4** *how would you like it if it happened to you?* feel about, regard, think about, appreciate.

likeable, likable adj pleasant, nice, friendly, agreeable, amiable, genial, charming, engaging, pleasing, appealing, winning, attractive, winsome, lovable, adorable.

likelihood n *very little likelihood of his winning* likeliness, probability, good chance, chance, prospect, good prospect, reasonable prospect, possibility, distinct possibility, strong possibility.

likely adj **1** *it is likely that he will go* probable, distinctly possible, to be expected, on the cards, odds-on, possible. **2** *it is likely to rain at this time of year* apt, inclined, tending, disposed, liable, prone. **3** *he gave a likely enough reason* reasonable, plausible, feasible, acceptable, believable, credible, tenable, conceivable. **4** *that's a likely story! who would believe that?* unlikely, implausible, unacceptable, unbelievable, incredible, untenable, inconceivable. **5** *a likely place for a picnic* suitable, appropriate, fit, fitting, acceptable, proper, right, qualified, relevant, reasonable. **6** *the most likely young people in the firm* likely-to-succeed, promising, talented, gifted; *inf* up-and-coming.

likely adv *he'll very likely refuse* probably, in all probability, no doubt, doubtlessly; *inf* like enough, like as not.

liken v *liken his work to that of Picasso* show the resemblance/similarity between, compare, equate, analogize, draw an analogy between, draw a parallel between, parallel, correlate, link, associate.

likeness n **1** *there is a distinct likeness in the faces of the two friends* alikeness, resemblance, similarity, sameness, similitude, correspondence, analogy, parallelism. **2** *appear in the likeness of Santa Claus* guise, semblance, appearance, outward form, form, shape, character. **3** *he will draw a likeness of your child* picture, drawing, sketch, painting, portrait, photograph, study, representation, image, bust, statue, statuette, sculpture, icon.

likewise adv **1** *she left early and he did likewise* in like manner, in the same way, similarly, in similar fashion, the same. **2** *we enjoyed the food and likewise the company* in addition, also, too, besides, moreover, furthermore, into the bargain, as well.

liking n fondness, love, affection, desire, preference, partiality, penchant, bias, weakness, weak spot, soft spot, appreciation, taste, predilection, fancy, inclination, bent, leaning, affinity, proclivity, propensity, proneness, tendency.

lilt n *a lilt in her voice* rise and fall, cadence, inflection, upswing, rhythm.

limb n **1** *injure a limb* arm, leg, wing, member, extremity, appendage. **2** *cut down limbs from the tree* branch, bough. **3** *a limb of a mountain* spur, projection. **4** *the society is a limb of an international organization* branch, section, member, offshoot. **out on a limb** **1** *he put himself out on a limb when he voted against the bill* isolated, stranded, segregated, set apart, separate, solitary, sequestered. **2** *you will be out on a limb if you challenge the headmaster's authority* in a precarious position, vulnerable, in a risky situation.

limber v **limber up** warm up, loosen up, stretch, exercise, get ready.

limbo n **1** *souls in limbo* abode of unbaptized infants. **2** *slaves sentenced to limbo* imprisonment, incarceration, confinement, internment, detention, captivity, bondage, prison. **in limbo** *the proposals are in limbo* abeyance, suspended, in a state of suspension, in a state of uncertainty, in a state of neglect, up in the air, hanging fire, awaiting action; *inf* on the back-burner.

limelight n *people in the limelight* | *those seeking the limelight* focus of attention, public attention, public notice, public eye, public recognition, publicity, glare of publicity, fame, renown, celebrity, stardom, notability, eminence, prominence, spotlight.

limit n **1** *outside the 200-mile fishing limit* boundary, boundary line, bound, bounding line, partition line, demarcation line, endpoint, cut-off point, termination. **2** *push his patience to the limit* extremity, utmost, greatest extent, ultimate, breaking-point, end-point, the bitter end. **3** *cross the limits of his land* boundary, border, bound, frontier, edge, perimeter, confines, periphery. **4** *impose a speed/spending limit* maximum, ceiling, limitation, restriction, curb, check, restraint. **the limit** *his latest action is the limit* the last straw, the straw that broke the camel's back, enough, more than enough; *inf* the end, it.

limit v **1** *limit their expenditure* place a limit on, restrict, curb, check, keep within bounds, hold in check, restrain, confine, control, ration, reduce. **2** *the long skirt limited her freedom to move freely* restrict, curb, restrain, constrain, hinder, impede, hamper, check, trammel. **3** *the extent of their land is limited by high fencing* demarcate, define, delimit, delimitate, mark off, stake out, encircle, encompass, bound, circumscribe.

limitation n **1** *the new rules imposed a limitation on their freedom* restriction, curb, restraint, constraint, qualification, control, check, hindrance, impediment, obstacle, obstruction, bar, barrier, block, deterrent. **2** *you must recognize your own limitations* inability, incapability, incapacity, defect, frailty, weakness. **3** *the new plan has its limitations* weak point, weakness, drawback, snag, defect.

limited adj **1** *committees having only limited powers* restricted, curbed, checked, controlled, restrained, constrained. **2** *provide limited accommodation* restricted, scanty, sparse, cramped, basic, minimal, inadequate. **3** *of limited experience* restricted, little, narrow, scanty, basic, minimal, inadequate, insufficient. **4** *he's a hard worker but he's a bit limited* unintelligent, slow, slow-witted, not very bright, dull-witted, stupid, dense, unimaginative, stolid.

limitless adj **1** *a limitless expanse of forest* infinite, endless, never-ending, interminable, immense, vast, extensive, measureless. **2** *limitless optimism/enthusiasm* unlimited, boundless, unbounded, illimitable, infinite, endless, never-ending, unceasing, interminable, inexhaustible, constant, perpetual.

limp v **1** *he still limps after the injury* walk with a limp, walk with a jerk, hobble, shuffle, shamble. **2** *the damaged ship limped into harbour* move slowly, crawl, drag.

limp n *walk with a pronounced limp* lameness, hobble, jerk, uneven gait, shuffle.

limp adj **1** *limp leaves/flesh* lacking firmness, floppy, drooping, droopy, soft, flaccid, flabby, loose, slack. **2** *feeling limp after the long illness* without energy, tired, fatigued, weary, exhausted, worn-out, lethargic, enervated, feeble, frail, puny, debilitated. **3** *he's rather a limp character* weak, characterless, ineffectual, insipid, wishy-washy, vapid, jejune; *inf* wet.

limpid adj **1** *limpid water/eyes* clear, crystal-clear, transparent, glassy, glass-like, translucent. **2** *limpid prose* lucid, clear, plain, understandable, intelligible, comprehensible, coherent, explicit, unambiguous. **3** *limpid seas/days* calm, still, serene, tranquil, placid, peaceful, unruffled, unperturbed.

line¹ n **1** *draw lines* rule, bar, score, underline, underscore, stroke, slash. **2** *lines of white through the black material* band, stripe, strip, belt, seam. **3** *lines on her face* furrow, wrinkle, crease, crow's-foot, groove, scar. **4** *admire the lines of the sculpture | the line of her dress/figure* outline, contour, configuration, shape, figure, delineation, silhouette, profile, cameo. **5** *the ball went over the line | the state line* boundary, boundary line, limit, border, borderline, frontier, demarcation line, edge, margin, perimeter, periphery. **6** *the line of the march | our line of flight* course, route, track, channel, path, way, road, lane, trajectory. **7** *his line of thought* direction, course, drift, tack, tendency, trend, bias, tenor. **8** *taking a tough line | the line of least resistance* course of action, course, procedure, technique, way, system, method, *modus operandi*, policy, practice, scheme, approach, avenue, position. **9** *what line is he in?* line of work, line of business, business, field, area, trade, occupation, employment, profession, work, job, calling, career, pursuit, activity, province, specialty, forte; *inf* line of country, game. **10** *he is stocking a new line of cosmetics* brand, kind, sort, type, variety. **11** *a line of figures*

row, column, series, sequence, succession, progression. **12** *a line of people* row, queue, procession, column, file, string, chain, array; *inf* crocodile. **13** *behind enemy lines* formation, position, disposition, front, front line, firing-line. **14** *he comes from a noble line* lineage, descent, ancestry, parentage, family, extraction, heritage, stock, strain, race, breed. **15** *hang the washing on the line | a clothes-line | a fishing-line* rope, string, cord, cable, wire, thread, twine, strand, filament. **16** *drop her mother a line* note, letter, card, postcard, message, word, communication. **17** *give his usual line about having no money* spiel, story, patter, piece of fiction, fabrication. **draw the line** *draw the line at lending him money* stop short of, bar, proscribe, set a limit at; *inf* put one's foot down about. **in line 1** *stand in line to be served* in a row, in a queue, in a column, in a file. **2** *are the two pipes in line?* in alignment, aligned, straight, plumb, true. **3** *their views are very much in line* in agreement, in accord, in harmony, in step, in conformity, in rapport. **4** *keep the junior staff in line* under control, in order, in check, obedient, conforming with the rules. **in line for** *in line for the post of manager* a candidate for, in the running for, on the short list for, being considered for, next in succession for. **lay it on the line** *lay it on the line to him that he would be sacked if he was late again* speak frankly, state openly, be direct with, speak honestly, pull no punches; *inf* give it to someone straight. **lay/put on the line** *put his job on the line* risk, put at risk, set at risk, put in danger, endanger, imperil. **toe the line** *pupils who do not toe the line are asked to leave* conform, obey the rules, comply with the rules, observe the rules, abide by the rules, submit, yield.

line¹ v **1** *grief had lined her face* mark with lines, cover with lines, furrow, wrinkle, crease. **2** *trees lined the driveway* border, edge, fringe, bound, skirt, hem, rim, verge. **line up 1** *line the children up* arrange in a line, arrange in lines, put in rows, arrange in columns, group, marshal. **2** *the children lined up* form a line, form lines, get into rows/columns, file, form a queue, queue up, group together, fall in; *inf* form a crocodile. **3** *line up entertainment for the party* get together, organize, prepare, assemble, lay on, get, obtain, procure, secure, produce, come up with.

line² v *line a skirt | have lined the drawers with paper* put a lining in, back, interline, face, panel, inlay, paper.

lineage n line, descent, ancestry, family, extraction. *see* LINE¹ n 14.

lineament n distinctive feature, feature, features, distinguishing characteristic, outline, line, contour, configuration, physiognomy, profile, face, countenance, visage.

lined adj **1** *lined paper* ruled, feint. **2** *a lined face* furrowed, wrinkled, creased. **3** *lined skirt/drawers* interlined, faced. *see* LINE².

liner n **1** *travel to Australia by liner* ocean liner, ship, boat, passenger vessel, aeroplane, aircraft, airliner; *inf* plane. **2** *eyeshadow and liner* eye-liner, eyebrow pencil, eye pencil, lip-liner.

lines npl *forget her lines* words, speech, script, part.

line-up n **1** *the line-up for tonight's show/game* list of performers/players, list, team, selection, array. **2** *the line-up for the inspection parade* line, row, queue.

linger v **1** *linger after the others went* stay, remain, wait around, hang around, delay, dawdle, loiter, dally, take one's time, tarry; *inf* dilly-dally. **2** *the infection lingered* persist, continue, remain, stay, hang around, be protracted, endure. **3** *dying man is lingering | customs which linger on* die slowly, stay alive, survive, last, stay around, continue.

lingerie n underwear, underclothes, underclothing, undergarments, nightwear, nightclothes; *inf* undies, smalls, frillies.

lingering adj **1** *lingering doubts* remaining, surviving, persistent. **2** *a lingering illness* persistent, protracted, long-drawn-out.

lingo n language, tongue, speech, jargon, terminology, phraseology, idiom, dialect, patter, vernacular, lingua franca.

linguistic adj semantic, lingual, semasiological.

lining n *a skirt/drawer lining* backing, interlining, facing, inlay.

link n **1** *a link in the metal chain* ring, loop, connection, connective, coupling, joint, knot. **2** *one of the links in the organization* component, constituent, element, part, piece, member, division. **3** *a link between smoking and cancer* connection, relationship, relatedness, association, tie-up. **4** *strong family links* bond, tie, attachment, connection, relationship, association, affiliation, mutual interest.

link v **1** *the joint linking the two pieces* join, connect, fasten, together, attach, bind, unite, couple, yoke. **2** *the press linking their names together* join, connect, associate, relate, bracket.

lion n **1** *lions with their cubs* big cat, lioness. **2** *a lion in the battle* lion-heart, lion-hearted man/woman/person, hero, heroine, man/woman/person of courage, brave man/woman/person, conqueror, champion, warrior, knight. **3** *photographing the lions at the party* celebrity, person of note, dignitary, notable, VIP, public figure, luminary, star, superstar, big name, leading light, idol; *inf* big shot, bigwig, big noise, somebody.
beard the lion in his den defy danger, face up to danger, brave danger, confront danger, defy danger, court destruction, tempt providence.

lion-hearted adj brave, courageous, valiant, gallant, intrepid, valorous, fearless, bold, daring, dauntless, stout-hearted, stalwart, heroic.

lionize v *team captain was lionized wherever he went* make much of, treat as a celebrity, glorify, exalt, magnify, acclaim, sing the praises of, praise, extol, laud, eulogize, fête, pay tribute to, put on a pedestal, hero-worship, worship, idolize, adulate, aggrandize.

lip n **1** *the lip of a cup/crater* edge, rim, brim, margin, border, verge, brink. **2** *punish the child for lip* cheek, impertinence, impudence, insolence, rudeness, audacity, effrontery; *inf* sauce, backchat. **keep a stiff upper lip** keep control of oneself, not show emotion, appear unaffected, bite one's lip; *inf* keep one's cool. **lick one's lips** show enjoyment, show pleasure/anticipation, drool, slaver.

liquid n fluid, liquor, solution, juice, sap.

liquid adj **1** *liquid substances* fluid, flowing, running, runny, watery, aqueous, liquefied, melted, molten, dissolved, hydrous. **2** *liquid eyes* clear, transparent, limpid, unclouded, bright, shining, brilliant, glowing, gleaming. **3** *liquid notes* clear, pure, smooth, flowing, fluent, fluid, mellifluent, mellifluous, dulcet, sweet, soft, melodious. **4** *liquid assets* convertible, negotiable.

liquidate v **1** *liquidate debts* pay, pay in full, pay off, settle, clear, discharge, square, make good, honour. **2** *liquidate a firm/partnership* close down, wind up, dissolve, break up, disband, terminate, annul. **3** *liquidate assets* convert to cash, convert, cash, cash in, sell off, sell up, realize. **4** *liquidate an enemy* kill, murder, put to death, do away with, assassinate, put an end to, eliminate, get rid of, dispatch, finish off, destroy, annihilate, obliterate; *inf* do in, bump off, rub out, wipe out.

liquidize v blend, crush, purée, pulverize, process.

liquor n **1** *addicted to liquor* spirits, alcohol, alcoholic drink, strong drink, drink, intoxicant, inebriant; *inf* booze, hard stuff, juice, grog; *Amer inf* the sauce, hooch. **2** *cooking liquor* liquid, stock, broth, bouillon, juice, gravy, infusion, extract, concentrate.

list¹ n *a list of purchases/films* catalogue, inventory, record, register, roll, file, index, directory, listing, enumeration, table, tabulation, schedule, syllabus, calendar, programme, series.

list¹ v *list the purchases* make a list of, note down, write down, record, register, set down, enter, itemize, enumerate, catalogue, file, tabulate, schedule, chronicle, classify, alphabetize.

list² v *vessels listing* lean, lean over, tilt, tip, heel, heel over, careen, cant, incline, slant, slope.

listen v **1** *listen to the speaker/speech* pay attention to, be attentive to, attend, hark, concentrate on hearing, give ear to, lend an ear to; hang on someone's words, keep one's ears open, prick up one's ears; *inf* be all ears, pin back one's ears. **2** *if you'd listened to your teacher you would have passed* pay attention, take heed, heed, give heed, take notice, mind, obey, do as one is told by, believe. **listen in** *listen in to someone's conversation* eavesdrop, overhear, tap, wiretap; *inf* bug.

listless adj languid, lethargic, languishing, enervated, lackadaisical, spiritless, unenergetic, lifeless, inactive, inert, indolent, apathetic, passive, dull, heavy, sluggish, slothful, limp, languorous, torpid, supine, indifferent, uninterested, impassive.

litany n **1** *church litany* prayer, invocation, petition, supplication, devotion; *lit* orison. **2** *a litany of complaints* recital, recitation, catalogue, list, listing, enumeration.

literacy n reading ability, reading proficiency, learning, book learning, education, culture, knowledge, scholarship, erudition, learnedness, enlightenment, articulateness, articulacy.

literal adj **1** *a literal translation* word-for-word, verbatim, line-for-line, letter-for-letter, exact, precise, faithful, close, strict, undeviating, true, accurate. **2** *a literal account* true, accurate, genuine, authentic, veritable, plain, simple, unexaggerated, unvarnished, unembellished, undistorted. **3** *rather a literal person* literal-minded, down-to-earth, prosaic, factual, matter-of-fact, unimaginative, colourless, commonplace, tedious, boring, dull, uninspiring, prosy.

literally adv **1** *translated literally* word for word, verbatim, line for line, letter for letter, exactly, precisely, faithfully, closely,

strictly, strictly speaking, to the letter, accurately. **2** *literally thousands of people* actually, really, truly, honestly, certainly, surely, positively, absolutely.

literary adj **1** *literary works* written, published, printed, in print. **2** *a literary man* well-read, widely-read, educated, well-educated, scholarly, learned, intellectual, cultured, erudite, bookish, studious, lettered; *inf* highbrow. **3** *a literary word* formal, poetic.

literate adj **1** *scarcely literate* able to read and write, educated, schooled. **2** *book-buying literate people* educated, well-educated, well-read, scholarly, learned, intellectual, erudite, cultured, cultivated, knowledgeable, well-informed. **3** *literate prose* well-written, stylish, polished, articulate, lucid, eloquent.

literature n **1** *study English literature* written works, writings, printed works, published works, letters, belles-lettres. **2** *receive literature about the course* printed matter, brochure, leaflet, pamphlet, circular, information, data, facts; *inf* bumf.

lithe adj agile, flexible, supple, limber, loose-limbed, pliant, pliable, lissome.

litigant n litigator, opponent in law, opponent, contestant, contender, disputant, plaintiff, claimant, complainant, petitioner.

litigation n lawsuit, legal case, case, legal dispute, legal contest, legal action, legal proceedings, suit, suit at law.

litigious adj *litigious neighbours* argumentative, disputatious, quarrelsome, contentious, belligerent, aggressive, pugnacious, combative.

litter n **1** *litter lying on the grass* rubbish, debris, refuse, junk, odds and ends, fragments, detritus, flotsam; *Amer* trash. **2** *a litter of books everywhere* disorder, untidiness, clutter, jumble, confusion, mess, disarray, disorganization, disarrangement; *inf* shambles. **3** *a litter of pups/piglets* brood, young, offspring, progeny, family, issue. **4** *invalids carried in litters* stretcher, portable bed/couch, palanquin. **5** *strew litter in the barn* animal bedding, bedding, straw, floor covering.

litter v **1** *litter the place up with rubbish* make untidy, mess up, make a mess of, clutter up, throw into disorder, disarrange; *inf* make a shambles of. **2** *litter papers about* scatter, strew, throw around.

little adj **1** *a little man* small, short, slight, petite, tiny, wee, miniature, mini, diminutive, minute, infinitesimal, microscopic, minuscule, dwarf, midget, pygmy, bantam;

inf teeny, teeny-weeny, pint-sized. **2** *she died when he was little* small, young, junior. **3** *after a little period* short, brief, fleeting, short-lived, momentary, transitory, ephemeral. **4** *exaggerate little difficulties* unimportant, insignificant, minor, trivial, trifling, petty, paltry, inconsequential, negligible, nugatory. **5** *gain little advantage* hardly any, small, scant, meagre, skimpy, sparse, insufficient, exiguous; *inf* piddling. **6** *nasty little minds* mean, narrow, narrow-minded, small-minded, base, cheap, shallow, petty, illiberal, provincial, parochial, insular. **7** *pretty little rooms* pleasingly small, sweet, nice, dear, cute, appealing; *inf* dinky.

little adv **1** *little known as an artist* hardly, barely, scarcely, not much, only slightly, only just. **2** *little seen around* hardly ever, hardly, scarcely ever, scarcely, not much, rarely, seldom, infrequently. **little by little** gradually, slowly, bit by bit, by degrees, step by step, progressively.

little n **1** *add just a little* small amount, bit, touch, trace, hint, soupçon, trifle, dash, taste, pinch, dab, spot, sprinkling, speck, modicum, grain, fragment, snippet. **2** *he'll go in a little* short time, little while, minute, moment, second, bit, before you can say Jack Robinson.

liturgy n ritual, worship, service, ceremony, rite, observance, celebration, office, sacrament.

live v **1** *when dinosaurs lived* be alive, have life, be, have being, breathe, draw breath, exist, walk the earth. **2** *invalids/customs not expected to live* remain/stay alive, survive, last, endure, persist, abide, continue, stay around. **3** *live quietly* pass/spend one's life, have a life/lifestyle, conduct oneself, lead one's life, behave, comport oneself. **4** *he lives by begging* keep alive, survive, make a living, earn one's living, subsist, support oneself, maintain oneself, make ends meet, keep body and soul together. **5** *live on vegetables* live off, subsist, feed, rely for nourishment on, thrive. **6** *live in the city* dwell, reside, have one's home, have one's residence, inhabit, lodge, be settled; *inf* hang out, hang one's hat; *Scots* stay. **7** *he really lived when he was young* enjoy life, enjoy oneself, have fun, be happy, make the most of life, flourish, prosper, thrive. **live it up** live extravagantly, live in clover, live in the lap of luxury; *inf* go on a spree, push the boat out, paint the town red, have a ball, make whoopee.

live adj **1** *live bodies* alive, living, having life, breathing, animate, vital, existing, exis-

tent; *inf* in the land of the living. **2** *a real live tiger* actual, in the flesh, not imaginary, true-to-life, genuine, authentic. **3** *a live show* unpre-recorded, unedited, with an audience. **4** *live coals* glowing, aglow, burning, alight, flaming, aflame, blazing, hot, smouldering. **5** *live electric wires* charged, connected, active, switched on. **6** *live bombs* unexploded, explodable, explosive. **7** *a live issue* current, topical, active, prevalent, important, of interest, lively, vital, pressing, burning, pertinent, controversial, debatable, unsettled. **live wire** person of energy, self-starter, self-motivator; *inf* ball of fire, human dynamo, life and soul of the party, go-getter, whiz-kid, mover and shaker, hustler.

livelihood n **1** *earn a livelihood* living, subsistence, means of support, income, keep, maintenance, sustenance, upkeep. **2** *a poorly paid livelihood* job, work, employment, occupation, trade, profession, career.

livelong adj *the livelong day* whole, entire, total, complete, full, unbroken, undivided.

lively adj **1** *lively young people* full of life, active, animated, energetic, alive, vigorous, alert, spirited, high-spirited, vivacious, enthusiastic, keen, cheerful, buoyant, sparkling, bouncy, perky, sprightly, spry, frisky, agile, nimble; *inf* chirpy, go-go, chipper, peppy. **2** *maintain a lively pace* brisk, quick, rapid, swift, speedy, vigorous. **3** *a lively discussion* animated, spirited, stimulating, heated, enthusiastic, forceful, interesting, eventful. **4** *a lively scene at the beach* busy, crowded, bustling, hectic, swarming, teeming, astir, buzzing, thronging. **5** *lively writing/decoration* vivid, colourful, bright, striking, graphic, stimulating, exciting, effective, imaginative. **6** *things got lively in the war area* eventful, exciting, busy, dangerous; *inf* hairy.

liven v **1** *liven the party up* enliven, put some life into, brighten up, cheer up, perk up, put some spark into, add some zest to, give a boost to, animate, vitalize, vivify; *inf* pep up, hot up. **2** *do liven up* cheer up, brighten up, waken up, perk up; *inf* buck up.

livery n uniform, regalia, costume, dress, attire, habit, garb, clothes, clothing, suit, garments, apparel, ensemble, vestments; *inf* get-up, gear, togs.

livid adj **1** *a livid patch on his forehead* discoloured, bruised, black-and-blue, purplish, bluish, greyish-blue. **2** *the livid faces of the dying* ashen, deathly pale, pale, pallid, white, greyish, bloodless, ghastly. **3** *livid with his son* furious, infuriated, fuming, seething, beside oneself, incensed, enraged, exasperated, angry, indignant, wrathful, ireful; *inf* mad, boiling.

living adj **1** *living creatures* alive, live, having life, breathing, animate, vital, existing, existent; *inf* in the land of the living. **2** *living languages* current, in use, extant, existing, existent, contemporary, operating, active, ongoing, continuing, surviving, persisting. **3** *a living likeness* exact, close, faithful, true-to-life, authentic, genuine.

living n **1** *earn a living* livelihood, subsistence, means of support, income, keep, maintenance, sustenance, upkeep. **2** *lose his living* job, work, employment, occupation, trade, profession, career. **3** *high living* way of life, lifestyle, manner/way/mode of living, life, conduct, behaviour.

living-room n sitting-room, drawing-room, lounge, parlour, family room.

load n **1** *the lorry's/aircraft's load* cargo, freight, charge, burden, lading, contents, consignment, shipment, lorryload, shipload, containerload, busload. **2** *the heavy load of single parents* burden, onus, weight, responsibility, duty, charge, obligation, tax, strain, trouble, worry, encumbrance, affliction, oppression, handicap, trial, tribulation, cross, millstone, albatross, incubus.

load v **1** *load the lorry/cart* fill, fill up, lade, freight, charge, pack, pile, heap, stack, stuff, cram. **2** *load the staff with responsibility* burden, weigh down, weight, saddle, charge, tax, strain, encumber, hamper, handicap, overburden, overwhelm, oppress, trouble, worry. **3** *load a gun* prime, charge, fill. **4** *load a dice* weight, add weight to, bias, rig.

loaded adj **1** *a loaded lorry/basket* full, filled, laden, freighted, charged, packed, stacked. *see* LOAD v 1. **2** *a loaded gun/camera* primed, charged, filled, containing ammunition, ready to fire, ready for use. **3** *loaded dice* weighted, biased, rigged. **4** *loaded questions* manipulative, cunning, insidious, artful, crafty, tricky, trapping. **5** *loaded tourists* rich, wealthy, well off, well-to-do, affluent, moneyed; *inf* well-heeled, rolling in it, flush, on easy street. **6** *loaded when leaving the pub* drunk, intoxicated, inebriated; *inf* sozzled, plastered, stoned, smashed, legless. *see* DRUNK adj.

loaf n **1** *sugar loaf* | *two sliced loaves* block, cake, slab, brick, lump, hunk. **2** *use your loaf* head, mind, common sense, sense, brains; *inf* chump, gumption.

loaf v *loafing around at home* laze, lounge, do nothing, idle, lie around, hang about, waste time, fritter away time, take things

easy, twiddle one's thumbs, sit on one's hands.

loan n *a loan from the bank* lending, money-lending, advancing; advance, credit, mortgage.

loan v *loan money* | *loaned a painting* lend, advance, give credit, give on loan, let out.

loath adj *loath to go* reluctant, unwilling, disinclined, not in the mood, against, averse, opposed, resisting.

loathe v *asked why he loathes her so* hate, detest, abhor, despise, abominate, have an aversion to, not be able to bear, dislike, shrink from, recoil from, feel repugnance towards, be unable to stomach, execrate.

loathing n hatred, hate, detestation, abhorrence, aversion, abomination, repugnance, disgust, revulsion, odium, antipathy, dislike, ill will, enmity, execration.

loathsome adj hateful, detestable, abhorrent, odious, repugnant, disgusting, repulsive, revolting, nauseating, abominable, vile, nasty, obnoxious, horrible, offensive, disagreeable, despicable, contemptible, reprehensible, execrable; *inf* horrid, yucky.

lob v *lobbed the sack over the wall* throw, toss, fling, pitch, shy, hurl, loft, heave, flip; *inf* chuck.

lobby n **1** *a pram in the lobby* porch, hall, hallway, entrance-hall, entrance, vestibule, foyer, corridor, passage, passageway, ante-room, antechamber. **2** *the animal rights lobby* pressure group, interest group, ginger group, lobbyists, supporters.

lobby v **1** *lobby MPs* seek to influence, try to persuade, bring pressure to bear on, urge, press, pressure, solicit. **2** *lobby for animal rights* press for, campaign for, push for, promote, drum up support for; *inf* pull strings for.

local adj **1** *local politics* community, district, neighbourhood, regional, city, town, municipal, provincial, village, parish, parish-pump. **2** *our local store* in the area, nearby, near, at hand, close by, neighbourhood. **3** *the pain being local* | *administer a local anaesthetic* confined, restricted, contained, limited, circumscribed, delimited, specific.

local n **1** *locals disliking change* local person, native, inhabitant, resident, parishioner; *derog inf* local yokel. **2** *drinking in his local* pub, public house, bar, inn, tavern; *inf* boozer, watering-hole.

locale n *a suitable locale for the conference* place, site, spot, position, location, venue, area, neighbourhood, locality, setting, scene.

locality n **1** *the murderer was still in the locality of the crime* vicinity, surrounding area, area, neighbourhood, district, region, environs, locale; *fml* locus. **2** *identify the locality of the car* location, position, place, whereabouts, bearings; *fml* locus. *see* LOCATION 1.

localize v *succeed in localizing the infection* confine, restrict, contain, limit, circumscribe, delimit, delimitate.

locate v **1** *locate the source of infection* find, find out, discover, identify, pinpoint, detect, uncover, track down, run to earth, unearth, hit upon, come across, reveal, pin down, define. **2** *factories located near the sea* situate, site, position, place, put, build, establish, station, set, fix, settle.

location n **1** *identify the location of the ship* position, place, situation, whereabouts, bearings, site, spot, point; *fml* locus. **2** *a pleasant location for a house* position, place, situation, site, spot, scene, setting, venue, locale.

lock¹ v **1** *lock the door* bolt, fasten, bar, secure, make secure, padlock. **2** *pieces of the puzzle locking together* interlock, engage, mesh, join, link, unite. **3** *wheels locked* jam, become immovable, become rigid. **4** *locked in each other's arms | locked in combat* clasp, clench, entangle, entwine, embrace, hug, squeeze. **lock in** *a town locked in by hills* enclose, encircle, surround, shut in, hem in. **lock out** v *lock out late arrivals* keep out, shut out, refuse entrance to, deny admittance to, exclude, bar, debar, ban, ostracize. **lock up** *lock up prisoners* shut up, shut in, confine, imprison, jail, incarcerate, put behind bars, put under lock and key, cage, coop up, fence in, pen in, wall in.

lock¹ n *force the lock* bolt, catch, fastener, clasp, bar, hasp, padlock, security lock, mortise lock.

lock² n *a lock of hair* strand, tuft, tress, curl, ringlet, kiss-curl, lovelock.

locker n cupboard, compartment, cabinet, cubicle, storeroom, storage room.

lock-up n **1** *prisoners in the lock-up* prison, jail, cell, police cell; *inf* cooler, slammer, jug, can, stir, clink, quod, choky. **2** *hire a lock-up* garage, store, storeroom, storage/space.

locomotion n movement, motion, moving, action, travel, travelling, walking, perambulation, progress, progression, headway.

lodestar n *his father's career was a lodestar to him* guiding star, guide, guiding principle, standard, model, pattern.

lodge n **1** *retired nanny living at the lodge* gatehouse. **2** *a shooting/ski lodge* house, cottage, cabin, chalet. **3** *the Masonic lodge* branch, chapter, section, association, society, club, group, fraternity, sorority. **4** *an animal's lodge* lair, den, hole, retreat, haunt, shelter.

lodge v **1** *he's lodging at the Smiths'* stay, board, have lodgings, put up, reside, dwell, sojourn, stop; *inf* have digs; *Amer* room. **2** *the Smiths can lodge all of the children* house, provide accommodation for, accommodate, put up, billet, shelter, harbour, entertain. **3** *lodge money* deposit, put in, bank, reposit. **4** *lodge a complaint* register, submit, put forward, place, file, lay, put on record, record. **5** *the bullet lodged in his brain* become fixed, become embedded, become implanted, stick, become caught, come to rest. **6** *lodge power in the governor* place, put, lay, vest, entrust, transfer, consign, deliver.

lodger n boarder, paying guest, PG, guest, tenant; *Amer* roomer.

lodging n **1** *gave them lodging for the night* accommodation, shelter, board, housing, a roof over one's head. **2** *move to new lodgings* accommodation, rooms, place, residence, dwelling, abode, habitation; *inf* digs.

lofty adj **1** *lofty peaks* towering, soaring, tall, high, elevated, sky-high, sky-scraping. **2** *lofty contempt* arrogant, haughty, proud, self-important, conceited, overweening, disdainful, supercilious, condescending, patronizing, lordly, snobbish, scornful, contemptuous, insulting, cavalier; *inf* high-and-mighty, stuck-up, snooty, toffee-nosed, uppity. **3** *lofty thoughts/ideals* noble, exalted, grand, sublime, imposing, esoteric. **4** *lofty members of the community* eminent, leading, noted, notable, well-known, distinguished, famous, renowned, illustrious, esteemed, celebrated, noble, aristocratic.

log n **1** *logs of wood* block, piece, chunk, billet, stump, trunk, branch, bole. **2** *a ship's log* logbook, record, register, journal, diary, day-book, chart, account, tally.

log v **1** *log details of the voyage* set down, make a note of, note/write down, jot down, register, record, book down, file, chart, tabulate, catalogue. **2** *log 50 miles a day* achieve, attain, make, do, go, cover, travel, traverse.

loggerheads npl **at loggerheads** in conflict, at war, quarrelling, at daggers drawn, fighting, wrangling, feuding, in disagreement, at odds, at variance, in opposition, estranged; *inf* at each other's throats.

logic n **1** *studying logic* science of reasoning, science of deduction, science of thought, dialectics, argumentation, ratiocination. **2** *her logic was flawed* line of reasoning, chain of reasoning, process of reasoning, reasoning, argument, argumentation. **3** *no logic in her actions* reason, sound judgement, judgement, wisdom, sense, good sense, common sense, rationale, relevance, coherence; *inf* horse sense.

logical adj **1** *a logical argument* reasoned, well-reasoned, rational, sound, cogent, coherent, well-organized, clear, consistent, relevant. **2** *the logical thing to do* rational, reasonable, sensible, intelligent, wise, judicious. **3** *the logical outcome* most likely, likeliest, plausible, obvious. **4** *not a logical person* reasoning, thinking, straight-thinking, rational, consistent.

logistics npl *the logistics of combining two schools* organization, strategy, tactics, planning, plans, management, masterminding, direction, orchestration, engineering, coordination, execution, handling.

logo n trade mark, emblem, company emblem, device, symbol, design, seal, stamp, logotype.

loiter v **1** *loiter at street corners* hang around, hang about, linger, wait, skulk, loaf, lounge, idle, waste time; *lit* tarry. **2** *loiter along the road* dawdle, go slowly, take one's time, go at a snail's pace, dally, stroll, saunter, delay, loll; *inf* dilly-dally.

loll v **1** *lolling on the sofa* lounge, slump, flop, sprawl, relax, recline, rest, lie around, lean against, repose on. **2** *loll around the house* lounge, loaf, idle, loiter, hang about/around, vegetate, languish. **3** *with his tongue lolling* hang down, hang, hang out, hang loosely, dangle, droop, sag, flap, flop.

lone adj **1** *a lone yachtsman* by oneself, alone, single, solitary, sole, unaccompanied, without companions, companionless, lonely. **2** *a lone parent* single, unmarried, separated, divorced, unattached, without a partner/husband/wife, partnerless, husbandless, wifeless. **3** *a lone landscape* lonely, desolate, barren, isolated, remote, deserted, uninhabited. *see* LONELY 3.

loneliness n **1** *the loneliness of people living alone* friendlessness, lonesomeness, forlornness, isolation, sadness, despondency. *see* LONELY 1. **2** *the loneliness of his existence* aloneness, solitariness. *see* LONELY 2. **3** *the loneliness of the landscape* desolation, isolation, remoteness, seclusion, desertedness. *see* LONELY 3.

lonely adj **1** *lonely people at Christmas/feeling lonely* friendless, companionless, lonesome, forlorn, forsaken, abandoned, rejected, isolated, outcast, sad, unhappy, despondent. **2** *lead a lonely existence* lone, by oneself, alone, single, solitary, sole, companionless.

see LONE 1. **3** *a lonely landscape* desolate, barren, isolated, out-of-the-way, remote, secluded, off the beaten track, deserted, uninhabited, unfrequented, unpopulated, God-forsaken, lone.

loner n lone wolf, recluse, hermit, solitary, anchorite, eremite.

lonesome adj lonely, friendless, forlorn, isolated, sad. *see* LONELY 1.

long adj **1** *three metres long* in length, lengthways, lengthwise. **2** *a long road/way/time* lengthy, extended, extensive, stretched out, spread out. **3** *a long speech | ten long years* lengthy, prolonged, protracted, overlong, extended, long-drawn-out, long-drawn, spun out, dragged out, seemingly endless, interminable, long-winded, verbose, prolix, tedious. **before long** soon, shortly, in a short time, in a minute, in a moment, before you know it, any minute now.

long v *long for peace* wish for, desire, want, yearn for, crave, hunger for, thirst for, itch for, covet, lust after, hope for, dream of, pine for, eat one's heart out over, have a fancy for, hanker for/after; *inf* have a yen for.

long-drawn-out adj lengthy, prolonged, protracted, over-long, long-drawn, interminable, tedious. *see* LONG adj 3.

longing n *a longing for peace* wish, desire, wanting, yearning, craving, hunger, thirst, itch, covetousness, lust, hope, dream, aspiration, pining, fancy, urge, hankering; *inf* yen.

longing adj *a longing look* wishful, desirous, yearning, craving, covetous, hopeful, wistful, avid.

long-lasting adj *long-lasting friendship* long-lived, long-running, long-established, long-standing, abiding, enduring, established.

long-lived adj long-lasting, enduring, durable, old; *fml* longevous.

long-standing adj *long-standing invitation/arrangement* long-established, well-established, established, fixed, time-honoured, time-hallowed, abiding, enduring.

long-suffering adj *his long-suffering wife* patient, having the patience of Job, forbearing, tolerant, uncomplaining, stoical, resigned, easygoing, indulgent, charitable, forgiving.

long-winded adj *long-winded speaker/speech* verbose, wordy, garrulous, prolix, discursive, diffuse, rambling, repetitious, lengthy, over-long, prolonged, protracted, long-drawn-out, tedious.

look v **1** *look over there!* see, take a look, glance, fix one's gaze, focus, observe, view, regard, eye, take in, watch, examine, study, inspect, scan, scrutinize, survey, check, contemplate, consider, pay attention to, run the eyes over, peep, peek, glimpse, gaze, stare, gape, ogle; *inf* take a dekko, take a butcher's, take a gander, give someone/something the once-over, take a shufti, have a squint, gawp, rubberneck; *Amer inf* eyeball. **2** *she looks ill* | *he looked a fool* seem, seem to be, appear, appear to be, give every appearance/indication of being, look to be, present as being, strike someone as being. **3** *the room looks east* | *the house looks onto the sea* face, overlook, front, front on, give onto. **look after** take care of, care for, attend to, tend, mind, keep an eye on, watch, sit with, nurse, take charge of, supervise, protect, guard. **look at** take a look at, observe, view, eye, watch, examine, study, inspect, scan, scrutinize, survey, check, contemplate, consider, pay attention to, run one's eyes over. *see* LOOK v 1. **look back** *look back on/over her life* reflect on, think about, recall, bring to mind, muse on, brood on, ponder on, reminisce about. **look down on** regard with contempt, treat with contempt, scorn, disdain, hold in disdain, sneer at, spurn, disparage, pooh-pooh, despise; *inf* look down one's nose at, turn up one's nose at. **look for 1** *look for the lost glove* search for, hunt for, seek, look around for, cast about for, forage for. **2** *look for some improvement* anticipate, expect, await, count on, reckon on, hope for, look forward to. **look forward to** anticipate, await with pleasure, wait for, be unable to wait for, count the days until, long for, hope for. **look into** investigate, explore, research, probe, search into, go into, inquire about, make inquiries about, ask questions about, ask about, delve into, dig into, examine, study, scrutinize, check, follow up on; *Amer* check out. **look like** resemble, bear a resemblance to, have a look of, have the appearance of, put someone in mind of, make someone think of, take after, be the image of; *inf* be the spitting image of, be the spit of, be a dead ringer for, favour. **look on** *with a crowd looking on* watch, observe, spectate, be a spectator, view, witness. **look on/upon** *look on it as a favour* | *look upon him as a brother* regard, consider, think of, deem, judge, see, take, reckon. **look out** *you'll drop it if you don't look out* watch out, beware, be on guard, be alert, be wary, be vigilant, be careful, pay attention, take heed, keep one's eyes open, keep one's eyes peeled/skinned, keep an eye out, be on

the qui vive. **look over** look through, inspect, examine, check, monitor, read through, scan, run through, cast an eye over, flick through, give something/someone the once-over, take stock of, view, peruse; *inf* take a dekko at; *Amer* check out; *Amer inf* eyeball. **look to 1** *look to the future* consider, give thought to, think about, turn one's thoughts to, take heed of, pay attention to. **2** *look to the family for support* turn to, resort to, have recourse to, fall back on, avail oneself of, make use of. **look up 1** *look up the information* search for, seek out, research, hunt for, track down, find, locate. **2** *look up a reference book* consult, refer to, turn to. **3** *look them up in London* visit, pay a visit to, call on, go to see, look in on; *inf* drop in on. **4** *things are looking up* get better, improve, show improvement, pick up, come along/on, make progress, make headway, shape up, perk up, ameliorate. **look up to** *look up to his brother* admire, hold in admiration, have a high opinion of, think highly of, hold in high regard, regard highly, respect, hold in esteem, esteem, revere, idolize, worship, hero-worship, put on a pedestal, lionize.

look n **1** *one look at the evidence* | *gave him a worried look* sight, glance, observation, view, examination, study, inspection, scan, survey, peep, peek, glimpse, gaze, stare, gape, ogle; *inf* eyeful, dekko, butcher's, gander, look-see, once-over, squint, shufti. **2** *an angry look* expression, face, countenance, features, mien. **3** *houses having a dilapidated/Scandinavian look* | *she has a depressed look about her* appearance, air, aspect, bearing, cast, demeanour, features, semblance, guise, façade, impression, effect. **4** *miniskirts are the look this year* fashion, style, latest style, vogue, trend, fad, craze, rage.

look-alike n double, twin, exact likeness, image, living image, exact match, replica, clone, duplicate, *doppelganger*; *inf* spitting image, spit, spit and image, ringer, dead ringer.

lookout n **1** *on the lookout for danger* watch, guard, vigil, alertness, qui vive. **2** *lookouts located along the coast* observation post, lookout point, lookout station, lookout tower, watch-tower, tower, coastguard station. **3** *the lookout was killed* guard, sentry, sentinel, watchman, vedette. **4** *it's a poor lookout* prospect, future, outlook, view of the future, chances. **5** *it's your own lookout if you're penniless* business, concern, affair, responsibility, worry; *inf* pigeon, funeral.

loom v **1** *a shape loomed out of the darkness* appear, emerge, become visible, take shape, materialize, reveal itself, appear indistinctly, take on a threatening shape. **2** *cliffs loomed above them* tower, soar, rise, rise up, mount, overhang, hang over, dominate. **3** *exams are looming* be imminent, impend, be close, be ominously close, threaten, menace.

loop n **1** *loops of ribbon* coil, hoop, noose, circle, ring, oval, spiral, curl, twirl, whorl, twist, convolution. **2** *a loop in the road* bend, curve, kink, arc.

loop v **1** *loop the string* coil, form a hoop with, form hoops with, make a circle with, make circles with, bend into spirals/whorls. **2** *the estate loops around the castle* encircle, form a ring round, surround, encompass. **3** *loop the sections together* fasten, tie, join, connect. **4** *the creature looped along the path | the aircraft looped upwards* coil, wind, circle, twist, spiral, bend, curl, curve, turn.

loophole n **1** *a loophole in the law* let-out, let-out clause, means of evasion/avoidance, means of escape, escape clause, escape route, ambiguity, omission. **2** *a loophole in the wall* hole, gap, opening, slot, aperture.

loose adj **1** *cows loose in the street* at large, at liberty, free, on the loose, unconfined, untied, unchained, untethered, unsecured, unshackled, unfastened, unrestricted, unbound, freed, let go, liberated, released, set loose. **2** *the handle is loose* wobbly, not secure, insecure, rickety, unsteady, movable. **3** *loose hair* untied, unpinned, unbound, hanging free, flowing, floppy. **4** *loose clothes* loose-fitting, easy-fitting, generously cut, slack, baggy, bagging, sagging, sloppy. **5** *a loose translation* inexact, imprecise, vague, indefinite, ill-defined, broad, general, non-specific, diffuse, unrigorous, unmeticulous. **6** *loose women/morals* immoral, disreputable, dissolute, corrupt, fast, promiscuous, debauched, dissipated, degenerate, wanton, whorish, unchaste, licentious, lascivious, lustful, libertine, abandoned, profligate, reprobate, careless, thoughtless, negligent, rash, heedless, unmindful. **7** *be/hang loose* relaxed, informal, uninhibited, unreserved, frank, open, unceremonious, unconstrained. **at a loose end** with nothing to do, unoccupied, at leisure, idle, twiddling one's thumbs. **break loose** escape, make one's escape, run off, run away, flee, take to one's heels, make off. **let loose 1** *let the cows loose* set free, unloose, turn loose, set loose, loose, untie, unchain, untether, unfasten, detach, unleash, let go, release, free, liberate. **2** *let loose a cry of pain* give, emit, burst out with, give forth, send forth, shout, yell, bellow.

on the loose *cows on the loose* at liberty, free at large, unconfined.

loose v **1** *loose the dogs* let loose, set free, unloose, turn loose, set loose, untie, unchain, untether, unleash, detach, let go, release. *see* LOOSE adj LET LOOSE 1. **2** *loose her grip | persuade them to loose their control* loosen, relax, slacken, weaken, lessen, reduce, diminish, moderate, soften. **3** *loose a missile* discharge, shoot, loose off, fire off, eject, catapult.

loose-limbed adj supple, agile, limber, lithe, lissom, flexible, pliant, pliable.

loosen v **1** *loosen a nut* slacken, slack, unstick. **2** *the nut loosened* become loose, work loose, work free. **3** *loosen a belt | loosened his trousers* slacken, let out, undo, unfasten, unhook. **4** *loosen her grip | try to loosen government control* loose, relax, slacken, weaken, lessen, moderate. *see* LOOSE v 2. **5** *don't be so tense—loosen up* relax, ease up/off; *inf* let up, hang loose, lighten up.

loot n booty, spoils, spoil, plunder, haul, stolen goods, pillage, prize; *inf* swag, the goods, hot goods, boodle.

loot v *looting unoccupied property* plunder, pillage, rob, burgle, steal from, ransack, sack, maraud, ravage, despoil, spoliate.

lop v **1** *lop off several branches* cut off, chop, chop off, hack off, prune, sever, clip, dock, crop, remove, detach. **2** *lop hundreds of pounds from the costs* cut, cut back, slash, axe, remove, take off, trim, prune, dock, eliminate.

lope v bound, stride, spring, gallop, canter, lollop, leap, jump.

lopsided adj asymmetrical, unsymmetrical, unevenly balanced, uneven, unbalanced, off-balance, unequal, askew, squint, tilting, crooked, out of true, out of line, awry.

loquacious adj talkative, overtalkative, garrulous, voluble, long-winded, wordy, verbose, effusive, chatty, gossipy, chattering, babbling, blathering, gibbering; *inf* having the gift of the gab, yacking, big-mouthed, gabby, gassy.

loquacity n talkativeness, overtalkativeness, garrulousness, garrulity, volubility, long-windedness, wordiness, verbosity, effusiveness, logorrhoea, chattiness, gossipiness, chattering, babble, blathering, gibbering; *inf* gift of the gab, yackety-yack, yacking, big mouth, blah-blah, gabbiness, gassiness.

lord n **1** *swear allegiance to their lord | lord of all he surveys* master, lord and master, ruler, leader, chief, monarch, sovereign, king, emperor, prince, governor, commander, captain, overlord, suzerain, baron, potentate, liege. **2** *the lords in disagreement with the king* noble, nobleman, peer, aristocrat, feudal lord, landowner, lord of the manor, seigneur; duke, earl, viscount. **3** *believe in the Lord* God, the Almighty, God the Father, the Deity, Our Maker, Jehovah, the King of Kings, Jesus, Jesus Christ, Christ, Christ the Lord, the Redeemer, the Saviour.

lord v **lord it 1** *arrogant people lording it* put on airs, be overbearing, swagger around, play the lord; *inf* act big. **2** *lord it over the juniors* order about/around, domineer, dictate to, pull rank on, tyrannize; *inf* boss about/around.

lordly adj **1** *a lordly disregard for others* imperious, arrogant, haughty, high-handed, overbearing, overweening, overconfident, dictatorial, authoritarian, peremptory, autocratic, tyrannical, supercilious, disdainful, condescending, patronizing; *inf* high-and-mighty, bossy, stuck-up, snooty, uppity, hoity-toity, toffee-nosed. **2** *lordly beings/splendour* noble, aristocratic, lofty, exalted, majestic, grand, regal, princely, kingly, masterful, imperial, stately, dignified, magnificent, grandiose.

lore n **1** *researching Gypsy lore* traditions, folklore, beliefs, superstitions, legends. **2** *bird lore* knowledge, learning, wisdom, know-how, skill.

lorry n truck, wagon, juggernaut, pick-up, van.

lose v **1** *has lost his keys* mislay, misplace, fail to keep/retain, fail to keep sight of, drop, forget. **2** *losing a lot of blood* be deprived of, suffer the loss of. **3** *trying to lose their pursuers* leave behind, outdistance, outstrip, outrun. **4** *lose the police in the crowd* escape from, evade, elude, dodge, give someone the slip, shake off, throw off, throw off the scent, duck, get rid of. **5** *lose the way | lose track of* stray from, wander from, fail to keep to, fail to keep in sight. **6** *lose the opportunity* fail to grasp/take, fail to take advantage of, let pass, miss, forfeit, neglect; *inf* pass up, lose out on. **7** *hope to win but expect to lose | lost the contest/battle* suffer defeat, be defeated, be the loser, be worsted, get/have the worst of it, be beaten, be conquered, be vanquished, be trounced, come off second-best, fail, come to grief, meet one's Waterloo; *inf* lose out, come a cropper. **8** *lose time/effort* waste, squander, dissipate, spend, expend, consume, deplete, exhaust, use up. **lose out 1** *the poor lose out | he lost out on the profits* be unsuccessful, be defeated, be the loser, be

disadvantaged, fail to take advantage of, fail to benefit from; *inf* miss out on. **2** *lose out to a more experienced applicant* be defeated by, be beaten by, be beaten into second place by, be replaced by.

loser n runner-up, also-ran, the defeated, the vanquished, failure, born loser; *inf* flop, dud, non-starter, no-hoper, wash-out, lemon, two-time loser.

loss n **1** *report the loss of the keys* mislaying, misplacement, dropping, forgetting. **2** *loss of blood/life/prestige/money* losing, deprivation, privation, forfeiture, bereavement, disappearance, waste, squandering, dissipation. **3** *families/firms suffering loss* deprivation, privation, detriment, disadvantage, damage, injury, impairment, harm, hurt, ruin, destruction, undoing, incapacitation, disablement. **4** *regret the civilian losses* casualty, fatality, dead, death toll, number killed/dead/wounded. **5** *firms making a loss | the company has made significant losses* deficit, debit, debt, lack of profit, deficiency, losing, depletion, minus sum of money. **at a loss** *we are at a loss to understand his motives* baffled, nonplussed, mystified, stumped, stuck, puzzled, perplexed, bewildered, ignorant, lost, at one's wit's ends, confused; *inf* clueless.

lost adj **1** *lost children/books* missing, strayed, gone missing/astray, mislaid, misplaced, vanished, disappeared, forgotten. **2** *lost travellers/ships* stray, astray, off-course, off-track, disorientated, having lost one's bearings, adrift, going round in circles, at sea. **3** *lost opportunities* missed, passed, forfeited, neglected, wasted, squandered, dissipated, frittered, gone by the board; *inf* down the drain. **4** *lost tribes/traditions* extinct, dead, bygone, lost and gone, lost in time, past, vanished, forgotten, unremembered, unrecalled, consigned to oblivion. **5** *lost ships/towns/armies* destroyed, ruined, wiped out, wrecked, finished, perished, demolished, obliterated, effaced, exterminated, eradicated, annihilated, extirpated. **6** *lost souls* damned, fallen, irredeemable, irreclaimable, irretrievable, past hope, hopeless, past praying for. **7** *lost to all shame* impervious, immune, closed, unreceptive, unaffected by, unmoved by, untouched by. **8** *lost in thought | she was lost in a book* engrossed in, absorbed in, preoccupied by, taken up by, spellbound by, distracted by, entranced by, rapt, abstracted, dreamy, distrait, absent-minded, somewhere else, not there, not with us. **9** *we are lost to understand the motive* at a loss, baffled, nonplussed, mystified, puzzled, perplexed, ignorant. *see* LOSS, AT A LOSS.

lot n **1** *a lot of people | lots of books* many, a great many, a good/great deal, a deal, a great quantity, quantities, a considerable number, numerous, a large amount, an abundance, plenty, masses, scores; *inf* loads, loadsa, heaps, piles, oodles, stacks, scads, reams, wads, oceans, miles; *Amer inf* gobs. **2** *smile a lot* much, a good/great deal, to a great extent, often, frequently, many times. **3** *draw lots* slip of paper, number, straw, counter, die, pebble. **4** *decided by lot* chance, luck, lottery, drawing lots, gamble, hazard, accident, serendipity, fortuity. **5** *his lot in life* fate, destiny, fortune, doom, situation, circumstances, portion, plight. **6** *the brothers' lots* share, portion, quota, ration, allowance, percentage, part, piece; *inf* cut. **7** *sold as a lot* set, batch, collection, load, group, bundle, consignment, quantity, assortment, parcel. **8** *a lot of land | parking lots* allotment, piece of ground, plot, patch of ground, tract of land, building lot. **draw lots** toss a coin, toss, throw a dice, draw straws, cut straws, decide on the toss of a coin, decide on the throw of a dice, decide on the drawing of straws. **throw in one's lot with** join forces with, join up with, form an alliance with, ally with, align oneself with, link up with, go into league with, combine with, join fortunes with, make common cause with.

lotion n cream, salve, ointment, moisturizer, balm, emollient, lubricant, unguent, liniment, embrocation, pomade, hand lotion, body lotion.

lottery n **1** *take part in a lottery* draw, raffle, sweepstake, game of chance, gamble, drawing of lots, bingo, tombola. **2** *life is a lottery* gamble, game of chance, risk, hazard, venture.

loud adj **1** *loud music/noises* blaring, booming, noisy, deafening, resounding, reverberant, sonorous, stentorian, roaring, thunderous, tumultuous, clamorous, head-splitting, ear-splitting, ear-piercing, piercing, strident, harsh, raucous. **2** *loud behaviour* noisy, rowdy, boisterous, rough, rollicking. **3** *loud young women* brash, brazen, bold, loud-mouthed, vociferous, raucous, aggressive, coarse, crude, rough, crass, vulgar, brassy; *inf* pushy. **4** *loud demands* vociferous, clamorous, insistent, vehement, emphatic, urgent, importunate, demanding. **5** *loud colours/wallpaper* garish, gaudy, flashy, bold, flamboyant, lurid, glaring, showy, obtrusive, vulgar, tawdry, tastless, meretricious; *inf* flash, naff, kitsch, camp, tacky.

loudly adv **1** *speak/play loudly* at full/top volume, at the top of one's voice, boomingly, noisily, deafeningly, tumultuously, clamorously, piercingly, raucously. *see* LOUD 1. **2** *behave loudly* noisily, rowdily, boisterously, roughly, brashly, aggressively, coarsely, crassly. *see* LOUD 2, 3.

loud-mouth n **1** *loud-mouths showing off* braggart, brag, boaster, blusterer, swaggerer, braggadocio; *inf* windbag, bigmouth, blowhard, gasbag. **2** *loud-mouths discussing neighbours' affairs* blabbermouth, blabber, gossip, gossipmonger, scandalmonger, busybody, chatterer, prattler; *inf* gasbag.

loud-mouthed adj **1** *disturbed by loud-mouthed spectators* noisy, vociferous, bragging, boasting, swaggering; *inf* big-mouthed. **2** *upset by loud-mouthed neighbours* blabbing, tactless, gossiping, indiscreet, undiplomatic.

loudspeaker n speaker, speaker unit, speaker system, public address system, PA system, loud hailer, megaphone, microphone; *inf* mike.

lounge v **1** *lounge around on deckchairs* laze, lie, lie around, recline, relax, take it easy, sprawl, slump, loll, repose. **2** *lounge around at street corners* loaf, idle, loiter, hang about, linger, skulk, waste time; *inf* hang out.

lounge n **1** *have tea in the lounge* sitting-room, drawing-room, living-room, parlour. **2** *the lounge of a hotel* public room, sitting-room, cocktail lounge.

lour, lower v **1** *an old man louring at the children* scowl, frown, look sullen, glower, glare, give someone black looks, look daggers; *inf* give someone dirty looks. **2** *skies louring* cloud over, look black, darken, blacken, become overcast, be gloomy, appear threatening/menacing.

lousy adj **1** *a lousy player/parent* very bad, poor, incompetent, inadequate, unsatisfactory, inferior, careless, second-rate, terrible, miserable; *inf* rotten, no-good, duff, poxy. **2** *a lousy trick to play* dirty, low, mean, base, despicable, contemptible, low-down, hateful, detestable, loathesome, vile, wicked, vicious; *inf* rotten. **3** *lousy bedclothes* lice-infested, lice-ridden, lice-infected, pedicular. **lousy with** *places lousy with tourists* full of, covered in, well-supplied with, crowded with, overrun by, swarming with, teeming with, alive with, crawling with.

lout n boor, oaf, dolt, churl, bumpkin, yahoo, gawk, lubber, barbarian; *inf* yob, yobbo, slob, clodhopper, clod; *Amer inf* lummox.

loutish adj boorish, oafish, doltish, churlish, awkward, inept, blundering, maladroit, gawky, lubberly; inf yobbish, slobbish, clodhopping.

lovable adj adorable, dear, sweet, cute, charming, lovely, likeable, attractive, delightful, captivating, enchanting, engaging, bewitching, pleasing, appealing, winsome, winning, taking, endearing, affectionate, warm-hearted, cuddly.

love v 1 *he loves her* care for, be in love with, be fond of, feel affection for, be attracted to, be attached to, hold dear, adore, think the world of, dote on, worship, idolize, treasure, prize, cherish, be devoted to, desire, want, be infatuated with, lust after, long for, yearn for, adulate; inf fancy, have a crush on, have a pash on, lech after, have the hots for, be soft on. 2 *she loves chocolate* like, have a liking for, have a weakness for, be partial to, have a soft spot for, be addicted to, enjoy, find enjoyment in, relish, savour, appreciate, take pleasure in, delight in; inf get a kick out of, have a thing about. 3 *couples loving each other on the grass* embrace, cuddle, hug, caress, fondle, pet, make love, kiss; inf neck, canoodle, smooch.

love n 1 *the couple's love for each other* affection, fondness, care, concern, attachment, regard, warmth, intimacy, devotion, adoration, passion, ardour, desire, lust, yearning, infatuation, adulation. 2 *her love of chocolate* liking for, weakness for, partiality for, enjoyment of, appreciation of, delight in, relish, passion for. 3 *love for one's fellow men* care, caring, regard, solicitude, sympathy, warmth, friendliness, friendship, rapport, brotherhood, kindness, charity. 4 *be brave, my love* beloved, loved one, true love, love of one's life, dear, dearest, dear one, darling, sweetheart, sweet, sweet one, angel, lover, inamorato/inamorata. 5 *their love was short-lived* love affair, affair, romance, relationship, liaison. see LOVE AFFAIR. **fall in love with** become sexually attracted to, form an attachment to, develop a fondness for, become infatuated with, become smitten with; inf develop a crush on. **in love with** attracted to, sexually attracted to, infatuated with, enamoured of, smitten by, besotted with, devoted to, having a passion for, consumed with desire for, lusting after; inf leching after, having the hots for.

love affair n affair, romance, relationship, meaningful relationship, liaison, amour, intrigue, affair of the heart, *affaire de coeur*.

lovelorn adj lovesick, unrequited in love, crossed in love, spurned, jilted, ill-starred, miserable, unhappy, pining, moping.

lovely adj 1 *a lovely girl* beautiful, pretty, attractive, good-looking, glamorous, comely, handsome, sweet, fair, charming, adorable, enchanting, engaging, bewitching, winsome, seductive, ravishing. 2 *a lovely surprise* delightful, pleasant, nice, agreeable, pleasing, marvellous, wonderful; inf terrific, fabulous, fab.

lovemaking n sexual intercourse, intercourse, act of love, sexual relations, intimate relations, intimacy, copulation, coitus, coition, sexual union/congress, congress, carnal knowledge, mating; inf sex, it, the other, nooky, rumpy-pumpy, humping.

lover n 1 *left her husband for her lover* boyfriend, girlfriend, man friend, woman friend, mistress, lady-love, paramour, other man, other woman, beau, loved one, beloved, sweetheart, inamorato/inamorata; inf bit on the side, bit of fluff, toy boy, fancy man, fancy woman. 2 *a lover of antiques/Italy* admirer, devotee, fan, enthusiast, aficionado; inf buff, freak.

loving adj *a loving daughter/kiss* affectionate, fond, devoted, caring, adoring, doting, solicitous, demonstrative, tender, warm, warm-hearted, friendly, kind, sympathetic, charitable, cordial, amiable, amorous, ardent, passionate.

low adj 1 *a low table* short, small, little, squat, stubby, stunted, truncated, dwarfish, knee-high. 2 *low land* low-lying, ground-level, sea-level, flat, sunken, depressed, subsided, nether. 3 *of low birth | low members of society* lowly, humble, low-born, low-bred, low-ranking, plebeian, peasant, poor, common, ordinary, simple, plain, unpretentious, inferior, subordinate, obscure. 4 *supplies are low* sparse, meagre, scarce, scanty, scant, few, little, deficient, inadequate, paltry, measly, trifling, reduced, depleted, diminished. 5 *a low hum* soft, quiet, muted, subdued, muffled, hushed, quietened, whispered, murmured, gentle, dulcet, indistinct, inaudible. 6 *feeling low* low-spirited, down, depressed, dejected, despondent, disheartened, downhearted, downcast, gloomy, glum, unhappy, sad, miserable, blue, fed up, morose, moody, heavy-hearted, forlorn; inf down in the mouth, down in the dumps, brassed off, cheesed off. 7 *in a low state of health | invalids getting low* weak, weakly, feeble, enfeebled, debilitated, frail, delicate, fragile, infirm, ill, ailing, unhealthy, poorly, helpless, powerless, stricken, prostrate, failing, declining, sinking, fading, dying. **8** *of low intelligence* low-grade, inferior, substandard, below par, second-rate, deficient, defective, wanting, lacking, inadequate, mediocre, unacceptable, worthless. **9** *low expectations* lowly, simple, plain, ordinary, commonplace, run-of-the-mill, modest, unambitious, unpretentious, unaspiring. **10** *have a low opinion of them* unfavourable, poor, bad, adverse, hostile, negative. **11** *a low thing to do* mean, nasty, foul, bad, wicked, evil, vile, vicious, despicable, contemptible, heinous, villainous, base, dishonourable, unprincipled, dastardly, ignoble, sordid. **12** *low creatures* mean, nasty, foul, vile, despicable, contemptible, base, villainous, hateful, loathsome, reprehensible, depraved, debased, wretched, miserable, sorry. **13** *low comedy/humour* vulgar, crude, coarse, obscene, indecent, gross, ribald, smutty, bawdy, pornographic, blue, rude, rough, unrefined, indelicate, improper, offensive. **14** *low prices/wages* cheap, inexpensive, moderate, reasonable, modest, bargain-basement.

low v *cattle lowing* moo, bellow.

low-down n information, data, facts, facts and figures, intelligence, inside information; *inf* info, gen, dope.

lower¹ adj **1** *of lower status* lesser, lower-level, lower-grade, subordinate, junior, inferior, minor, secondary. **2** *her lower lip* under, underneath, nether. **3** *lower prices/wages* cheaper, reduced, decreased, lessened, cut, slashed, curtailed, pruned.

lower¹ v **1** *lower the flag/weight* let down, take down, haul down, drop, let fall, let sink. **2** *lower one's voice/lower the volume* modulate, soften, quieten, hush, tone down, muffle, turn down, mute. **3** *will only lower him in her eyes* degrade, debase, demean, downgrade, discredit, devalue, dishonour, disgrace, belittle, humble, humiliate, disparage. **4** *lower the temperature/prices* reduce, bring down, decrease, lessen, cut, slash, curtail, prune. **5** *the winds lowered* abate, die down, subside, let up, moderate, slacken, dwindle, lessen, ebb, fade away, wane, taper off, lull.

lower² v *see* LOUR.

low-grade adj poor-quality, inferior, substandard, below standard, not up to scratch, second-rate, bargain-basement, poor, bad; *Amer inf* two-bit.

low-key adj restrained, muted, subtle, quiet, understated, played down, toned down, relaxed, downbeat, easygoing, modulated, softened; *inf* laid-back.

lowly adj **1** *of lowly birth/lowly members of society* low, humble, low-born, low-ranking, plebeian, peasant, poor, common, ordinary, inferior, subordinate. *see* LOW adj 3. **2** *feeling lowly before God* humble, meek, submissive, dutiful, docile, mild, gentle, modest, unassuming. **3** *lowly ambitions* low, simple, plain, ordinary, commonplace, run-of-the-mill, modest, unambitious, unpretentious, unaspiring.

low-spirited adj low, down, depressed, dejected, despondent, gloomy, unhappy, miserable, blue; *inf* down in the mouth, down in the dumps. *see* LOW adj 6.

loyal adj faithful, true, true-hearted, tried and true, trusted, trustworthy, trusty, true-blue, steadfast, staunch, dependable, reliable, devoted, dutiful, patriotic, constant, unchanging, unwavering, unswerving, firm, stable.

loyalty n faithfulness, fidelity, fealty, allegiance, trueness, true-heartedness, trustiness, trustworthiness, steadfastness, staunchness, dependability, reliability, devotion, duty, patriotism, constancy, stability. *see* LOYAL.

lozenge n tablet, pastille, cough sweet, cough drop, gum, gumdrop, jujube; *Med* troche.

lubber n oaf, dolt, boor, gawk; *inf* yob, yobbo, slob; *Amer inf* lummox.

lubberly adj awkward, clumsy, blundering, bumbling, lumbering, inept, maladroit, ungainly, gawky, oafish, doltish, boorish, lumpish, lumpen, like a bull in a china shop, all fingers and thumb, heavy-handed; *inf* yobbish, slobbish, clodhopping, butter-fingered.

lubricant n lubricator, oil, grease, emollient, lard, fat, moisturizer, lotion, unguent.

lubricate v **1** *lubricate the machinery* oil, grease, make slippery, moisturize. **2** *lubricate the planning process* make smooth, smooth the way for, oil the wheels for.

lucid adj **1** *a lucid description* clear, clear-cut, crystal clear, comprehensible, intelligible, understandable, plain, simple, direct, straightforward, graphic, explicit, obvious, evident, apparent, distinct, transparent, overt, cogent. **2** *an old man who is scarcely lucid* sane, rational, in one's right mind, in possession of one's faculties, of sound mind, *compos mentis*, sensible, clear-headed; *inf* all there, with all one's marbles. **3** *lucid pools* clear, crystal clear, transparent, limpid, translucent, glassy, pellucid. **4** *lucid* *stars* bright, shining, gleaming, luminous, radiant, lustrous.

luck n **1** *as luck would have it* fate, fortune, destiny, predestination, the stars, chance, fortuity, accident, hazard, serendipity. **2** *wishing you luck* good luck, good fortune, success, successfulness, prosperity, advantage, advantageousness, felicity; *inf* lucky break. **in luck** lucky, fortunate, blessed with good luck, favoured, born under a lucky star, advantaged, successful, prosperous, happy. **out of luck** unlucky, unfortunate, luckless, cursed with ill-luck, unsuccessful, disadvantaged, miserable.

luckily adv *luckily he survived* fortunately, by good luck, by good fortune, happily, providentially, as luck would have it, propitiously.

luckless adj *luckless competitors* unlucky, unfortunate, unsuccessful, out of luck, down on one's luck, jinxed, hapless, ill-starred, ill-fated, unhappy, miserable, wretched, forlorn, star-crossed.

lucky adj **1** *lucky people* fortunate, blessed with good luck, favoured, born under a lucky star, charmed; successful, prosperous, happy; advantaged, born with a silver spoon in one's mouth. **2** *a lucky guess* fortunate, fortuitous, providential, advantageous, timely, opportune, expedient, auspicious, propitious.

lucrative adj profitable, profit-making, moneymaking, paying, high-income, well-paid, high-paying, gainful, remunerative, productive, fat, fruitful, rewarding, worthwhile.

lucre n money, cash, profit, profits, gain, proceeds, winnings, pay, remuneration, earnings, income, yield, revenue; *inf* dosh, dough, bread, the ready.

ludicrous adj absurd, ridiculous, laughable, risible, derisible, comic, comical, farcical, silly, funny, humorous, droll, amusing, diverting, hilarious, crazy, zany, nonsensical, odd, outlandish, eccentric, incongruous, preposterous.

lug v **1** *lugging a heavy suitcase* carry, bear, tote, transport; *inf* hump; *Scots* humph. **2** *lugging a handcart behind him* haul, drag, heave, trail, tug, tow.

luggage n bags, baggage, bag and baggage, cases, suitcases, trunks, things, gear, belongings, kit, effects, goods and chattels, impedimenta, paraphernalia, accoutrements.

lugubrious adj mournful, doleful, melancholy, dismal, gloomy, sombre, funereal, sorrowful, morose, miserable, joyless, woebegone, woeful, dirgelike, elegaic.

lukewarm adj **1** *lukewarm water* tepid, warm, blood-hot, blood-warm, at room temperature, at skin temperature. **2** *lukewarm about going to the party* indifferent, cool, cold, half-hearted, apathetic, unenthusiastic, uninterested, unconcerned, impassive, dispassionate, unresponsive, sluggish, phlegmatic, Laodicean.

lull v **1** *lull the child to sleep* rock to sleep, lullaby, soothe, quiet, hush. **2** *lull their fears* soothe, quiet, silence, calm, hush, still, quell, assuage, allay, ease, alleviate, pacify, mitigate. **3** *the storm lulled* abate, die down, subside, let up, moderate, slacken, lessen, dwindle, decrease, diminish, ebb, fade away, wane, taper off, lower.

lull n **1** *a lull in the proceedings* pause, respite, interval, break, hiatus; *inf* let-up. **2** *the lull before the storm* calm, calmness, stillness, quiet, quietness, tranquillity, silence, hush.

lullaby n cradle-song, *berceuse*.

lumber[1] n *lumber in the attic* jumble, clutter, junk, rubbish, odds and ends, cast-offs, rejects, trash, refuse, white elephant.

lumber[1] v *lumber him with her jobs* burden, load, saddle, encumber, impose upon; *inf* land.

lumber[2] v *heard him lumbering around upstairs* clump, stump, plod, trudge, stamp, shuffle, shamble, stumble, waddle, lump along.

lumbering adj awkward, clumsy, heavy-footed, blundering, bumbling, inept, maladroit, ungainly, like a bull in a china shop, ungraceful, lumpish, hulking, ponderous, stolid, lubberly; *inf* clodhopping.

luminary n *a luminary of the council* leading light, guiding light, star, superstar, megastar, leader, notable, dignitary, VIP, celebrity, big name, household name, somebody, name, important personage, lion; *inf* bigwig, big shot, big cheese, biggie, celeb.

luminous adj **1** *luminous stars/colours* lighted, lit, illuminated, shining, bright, brilliant, radiant, dazzling, glowing, effulgent, luminescent, phosphorescent, vivid, resplendent. **2** *a luminous account* lucid, clear, crystal clear, comprehensible, intelligible, plain, simple, direct, straightforward, graphic, obvious, distinct, apparent. *see* LUCID 1.

lump[1] n **1** *a lump of putty* chunk, wedge, hunk, piece, mass, cake, nugget, ball, dab, pat, clod, gob, gobbet, wad, clump, cluster, mound. **2** *a lump on his head* bump, swelling, bruise, bulge, protuberance, protrusion, growth, carbuncle, hump, tumour, tumescence, node.

lump¹ v *often lump together* put together, combine, group, unite, pool, mix together, blend, merge, mass, fuse, conglomerate, coalesce, consolidate.

lump² v *like it or lump it | you'll have to lump the situation* put up with, bear, endure, take, stand, tolerate, suffer, brook; *Scots* thole.

lumpish adj **1** *a lumpish young woman* heavy, stolid, lumbering, ponderous, elephantine, awkward, clumsy, ungainly, gawky, hulking, lethargic, bovine, vegetable-like, pudding-like. **2** *lumpish children* stupid, dull-witted, slow-witted, slow, doltish, oafish; *inf* thick, dumb, dopey.

lumpy adj **1** *a lumpy mattress* bumpy, knobbly, bulging, uneven. **2** *lumpy custard* curdled, clotted, granular, grainy.

lunacy n **1** *suffering from lunacy* insanity, insaneness, madness, mental illness/derangement, dementia, dementedness, loss of reason, unsoundness of mind, mania, frenzy, psychosis; *inf* craziness. **2** *the sheer lunacy of the decision* madness, insanity, foolishness, folly, foolhardiness, stupidity, idiocy, irrationality, illogicality, senselessness, absurdity, absurdness, silliness, inanity, ludicrousness; *inf* craziness, daftness.

lunatic n *driving like a lunatic* maniac, madman, madwoman, imbecile, idiot, psychopath; *inf* loony, nut, nutter, nutcase, head case, basket case, headbanger, screwball, psycho.

lunatic adj *a lunatic idea | it was a lunatic thing to do* mad, insane, foolish, stupid, foolhardy, idiotic, crack-brained, irrational, unreasonable, illogical, senseless, nonsensical, absurd, silly, inane, asinine, ludicrous, imprudent, preposterous; *inf* crazy, daft.

lunch n luncheon, midday meal, brunch; *dial* dinner.

lunge n **1** *make a lunge towards the open door* spring, jump, leap, bound, dash, charge, pounce, dive. **2** *take a lunge at his attacker* stab, jab, poke, thrust, swing, pass, cut, feint; *inf* swipe.

lunge v **1** *lunge towards the door* spring, jump, leap, bound, dash, charge, pounce, dive. **2** *lunge at his attacker* stab, jab, poke, thrust at, pitch into, lash out at, take a swing at, aim a blow at; *inf* take a swipe at.

lurch v **1** *drunks lurching home* stagger, sway, reel, weave, stumble, totter. **2** *ships lurching*

in the storm list, roll, pitch, toss, sway, veer, swerve.

lure v *lure them into a trap | lured by greed* entice, attract, induce, inveigle, decoy, draw, lead, allure, tempt, seduce, beguile, ensnare, magnetize, cajole.

lure n *use sweets as a lure to the children* enticement, attraction, inducement, decoy, draw, allurement, temptation, bait, magnet, drawing card, carrot; *inf* come-on.

lurid adj **1** *lurid colours/sunsets* overbright, brilliant, glaring, flaming, dazzling, glowing, intense, vivid, showy, gaudy, fiery, blood-red, burning. **2** *lurid descriptions of their affair* sensational, melodramatic, exaggerated, extravagant, graphic, explicit, unrestrained, shocking, startling; *inf* full-frontal. **3** *lurid details of the murder* gruesome, gory, grisly, macabre, repugnant, revolting, disgusting, ghastly. **4** *lurid complexions* pale, pallid, ashen, colourless, chalk-white, white, wan, sallow, ghostly, ghastly.

lurk v skulk, lie in wait, lie low, hide, conceal oneself, take cover, crouch, sneak, slink, prowl, steal, tiptoe.

luscious adj **1** *luscious fruit* delicious, juicy, sweet, succulent, mouth-watering, tasty, appetizing, delectable, palatable, toothsome, nectar-like; *inf* scrumptious, yummy. **2** *luscious blondes* voluptuous, sensuous, sexy, gorgeous, beautiful, attractive.

lush adj **1** *lush vegetation* luxuriant, abundant, profuse, exuberant, dense, thick, riotous, overgrown, prolific, rank, teeming, jungle-like, flourishing, verdant, green. **2** *lush fruits* juicy, succulent, fleshy, pulpy, ripe, soft, tender, fresh. **3** *lush drawing-rooms* luxurious, sumptuous, grand, palatial, opulent, lavish, elaborate, extravagant; *inf* plush, ritzy.

lush n alcoholic, heavy/hard drinker, problem drinker, drinker, drunk, drunkard, toper, sot, dipsomaniac; *inf* alky, boozer, dipso, tosspot, soak.

lust n **1** *satisfy his lust* sexual desire, sexual appetite, sexual longing, sexual passion, libido, sex drive, sexuality, biological urge, randiness. **2** *guilty of lust* lechery, lecherousness, lasciviousness, lewdness, carnality, licentiousness, salaciousness, salacity, prurience, concupiscence, wantonness, randiness; *inf* horniness, raunchiness, the hots. **3** *a lust for gold* greed, greediness, desire, craving, covetousness, avidness, avidity, cupidity, longing, yearning, hunger, thirst, appetite, passion.

lust v *lust after girls | lusting for power/revenge* be consumed with desire for, desire, crave, covet, want, need, long for, yearn for, hunger for, thirst for, ache for; *inf* have the hots for, lech after.

lustful adj lecherous, lascivious, lewd, libidinous, licentious, salacious, prurient, concupiscent, wanton, unchaste, hot-blooded, passionate, sensual, sexy, randy; *inf* horny, raunchy.

lustily adv *children crying lustily* loudly, vigorously, heartily, at the top of one's voice, with might and main, powerfully, forcefully.

lustre n **1** *admire the lustre of the table* sheen, gloss, shine, burnish, glow, gleam, sparkle, shimmer. **2** *the lustre of the stars* brilliance, brightness, dazzle, luminousness, radiance, refulgence, lambency. **3** *bring lustre to the school* honour, glory, credit, merit, prestige, renown, fame, distinction, notability.

lustreless adj dull, flat, matt, unburnished, unpolished, tarnished, dingy, dim, dark, drab, gloomy, colourless, washed out, faded.

lustrous adj shiny, shining, glossy, gleaming, glowing, bright, burnished, polished, dazzling, sparkling, glistening, twinkling, shimmering, luminous.

lusty adj **1** *lusty young men* healthy, strong, vigorous, robust, hale and hearty, hearty, energetic, lively, blooming, rugged, sturdy, tough, stalwart, brawny, hefty, husky, burly, solidly built, powerful, virile, red-blooded. **2** *a lusty cry* loud, vigorous, hearty, powerful, forceful.

luxuriant adj **1** *luxuriant vegetation* lush, abundant, profuse, exuberant, dense, thick, riotous, overgrown, prolific, teeming, verdant. *see* LUSH adj **1**. **2** *luxuriant prose* florid, flowery, ornate, elaborate, fancy, adorned, decorated, embellished, embroidered, extravagant, flamboyant, ostentatious, showy, high-flown, baroque, rococo.

luxuriate v **1** *luxuriate in a hot bath* bask in, revel in, delight in, enjoy, wallow in, savour, appreciate; *inf* get a kick out of, get a charge from. **2** *plants luxuriating* thrive, flourish, bloom, prosper, do well, burgeon, spring up, sprout, shoot up, mushroom. **3** *luxuriating after a life of poverty* live in lux-ury, live in the lap of luxury, live off the fat of the land, be in clover, take it easy, relax, have the time of one's life, lead the life of Riley.

luxurious adj **1** *luxurious surroundings* opulent, affluent, sumptuous, expensive, rich, costly, de luxe, lush, grand, splendid, magnificent, lavish, well-appointed, comfortable, extravagant, ornate, fancy; *inf* plush, posh, ritzy, swanky. **2** *luxurious habits* self-indulgent, sensual, pleasure-loving, comfort-seeking, epicurean, hedonistic, sybaritic.

luxury n **1** *live in luxury* luxuriousness, opulence, affluence, sumptuousness, richness, grandeur, splendour, magnificence, lavishness, lap of luxury, bed of roses. **2** *the luxury of independence* boon, benefit, advantage, delight, bliss, comfort. **3** *one of life's luxuries* extra, non-essential, frill, extravagance, indulgence, treat, refinement.

lying n *accused of lying* untruthfulness, fabrication, fibbing, perjury, white lies, little white lies, falseness, falsity, dishonesty, mendacity, lack of veracity, story-telling, dissimulation, dissembling, prevarication, deceit, guile, crookedness, double-dealing.

lying adj *lying witnesses* untruthful, fabricating, false, dishonest, mendacious, dissimulating, dissembling, prevaricating, deceitful, guileful, crooked, double-dealing, two-faced.

lynch v put to death, execute, hang, kill, murder, slay; *inf* string up.

lyric adj **1** *lyric poetry* songlike, musical, melodic, melodious, expressive, deep-felt, personal, subjective, passionate, lyrical. **2** *lyric voices* light, silvery, clear, lilting, flowing, dulcet, sweet, mellifluous, mellow, lyrical.

lyrical adj **1** *lyrical verse* lyric, songlike, musical, melodic, expressive, personal. *see* LYRIC **1**. **2** *lyrical voices* light, silvery, clear, flowing, sweet. *see* LYRIC **2**. **3** *lyrical about her success* enthusiastic, rhapsodic, effusive, rapturous, ecstatic, euphoric, carried away, emotional, impassioned.

lyrics npl *the lyrics of the song* words, libretto, book, text.

Mm

macabre adj gruesome, grisly, grim, gory, morbid, grim, ghastly, hideous, horrific, horrible, horrifying, horrid, horrendous, terrifying, frightening, frightful, fearsome, shocking, dreadful, appalling, loathsome, repugnant, repulsive, sickening.

mace n staff, club, cudgel, bludgeon, bastinado.

macerate v pulp, mash, squash, soften, liquefy, soak, steep.

machete n knife, cutlass, cleaver, kukri.

machiavellian adj devious, cunning, crafty, artful, wily, sly, scheming, designing, conniving, expedient, opportunistic, insidious, treacherous, perfidious, two-faced, double-dealing, unscrupulous, deceitful, dishonest.

machinations npl schemes, plot, intrigues, conspiracies, complots, designs, plans, devices, ploys, ruses, trick, wiles, stratagems, tactics, manoeuvres, contrivances, expedients.

machine n 1 *the cutting machine broke down* appliance, apparatus, instrument, tool, device, contraption, gadget, mechanism, engine, motor. 2 *the competitor's machine* vehicle, car, bicycle, motor cycle, aeroplane; *inf* bike, motor bike, plane. 3 *machines took over from men* robot, automaton, mechanical man, zombie, puppet. 4 *the party machine* organization, system, structure, agency, machinery, council, cabal, clique; *inf* set-up.

machinery n 1 *factory machinery* equipment, apparatus, mechanism, gear, tackle, instruments, gadgetry. 2 *the machinery of local government* workings, organization, system, structure, agency, channel, vehicle; *inf* set-up, nuts and bolts, brass tacks, nitty-gritty.

machinist n machine-operator, operator, operative, worker.

machismo n masculinity, manliness, virility, toughness, chauvinism, male chauvinism, sexism.

macrocosm n 1 *exploration of the macrocosm* universe, cosmos, world, wide world, globe, creation, solar system. 2 *society and other macrocosms* complete system, system, total structure, structure, totality, entirety.

mad adj 1 *gone mad with grief* stark mad, insane, deranged, demented, of unsound mind, crazed, lunatic, *non compos mentis*, unbalanced, unhinged, unstable, distracted, manic, frenzied, raving, distraught, frantic, hysterical, delirious, psychotic, not quite right, mad as a hatter, mad as a March hare, foaming at the mouth; *inf* crazy, off one's head, out of one's mind, off one's nut, nuts, nutty, off one's rocker, round the bend, round the twist, raving mad, barmy, batty, bonkers, crackers, crackpot, cuckoo, loopy, loony, bananas, loco, dippy, screwy, with a screw loose, out of one's tree, off one's trolley, off the wall, not all there, not the full shilling, not the full pound note, not right upstairs. 2 *mothers mad at their children* flaming mad, blazing mad, angry, furious, infuriated, irate, raging, enraged, fuming, blazing, in a towering rage, incensed, wrathful, seeing red, cross, indignant, exasperated, irritated, berserk, out of control, beside oneself; *inf* livid, wild, ape, in a wax, with guns blazing. 3 *a mad scheme/idea* insane, foolish, stupid, lunatic, foolhardy, idiotic, crack-brained, irrational, unreasonable, illogical, senseless, nonsensical, absurd, impractical, silly, inane, asinine, ludicrous, wild, unwise, imprudent, preposterous; *inf* crazy, daft. 4 *mad about jazz* wildly enthusiastic, passionate, impassioned, avid, eager, keen on, ardent, zealous, fervent, fanatical, devoted to, infatuated with, in love with; *inf* crazy, nuts, dotty, hooked on, wild, gone on. 5 *mad, passionate love* wild, unrestrained, uncontrolled, abandoned, excited, frenzied, frantic, frenetic, ebullient, energetic, boisterous. **like mad 1** *run like mad* furiously, as fast as possible, as fast as one's legs can carry one, fast, hurriedly, quickly, rapidly, speedily, hastily, energetically; *inf* like billy-oh. 2 *love her like mad* madly, enthusiastically, unrestrainedly, wildly, passionately, intensely, ardently, fervently, to distraction, devotedly.

madcap adj daredevil, impulsive, wild, reckless, rash, hotheaded, daring, adventurous, heedless, thoughtless, incautious, imprudent, indiscreet, ill-advised, hasty, foolhardy, foolish, senseless, impractical, hare-brained, crack-brained; *inf* crazy, crackpot.

madcap n daredevil, hothead, tearaway, adventurer/adventuress, wild man/woman.

madden v 1 *maddened by their behaviour* anger, infuriate, send into a rage, enrage, incense, exasperate, irritate, inflame, annoy, provoke, upset, agitate, vex, irk, pique, gall, make one's hackles rise, raise one's hackles, make one's blood boil, make one see red, get one's back up; *inf* aggravate, get up one's nose, nark, bug, make one livid. 2 *in a mental hospital maddened by grief* drive mad/insane, derange, unhinge, unbalance; *inf* drive off one's head, send round the bend. *see* MAD 1.

maddening adj infuriating, exasperating, irritating, annoying, provoking, upsetting, vexing, irksome, unsettling, disturbing, troublesome, vexatious, galling.

made-up adj 1 *a made-up story* invented, fabricated, trumped-up, concocted, devised, manufactured, fictional, false, untrue, unreal, sham, specious, spurious, imaginary, mythical. 2 *made-up young women* painted, done up, powdered, rouged. 3 *cabinets already made up* put together, built, constructed, finished, ready, prepared, fixed.

madhouse n 1 *certified and in a madhouse* mental hospital, mental institution, psychiatric hospital, asylum, lunatic asylum; *inf* nut-house, funny farm, loony bin. 2 *it was a madhouse with the wedding preparations* bedlam, babel, chaos, pandemonium, uproar, turmoil, wild, disarray, scene of confusion, disorder, three-ring circus.

madly adv 1 *behaving madly* insanely, dementedly, distractedly, frenziedly, maniacally, frantically, hysterically, deliriously, wildly; *inf* crazily. 2 *rushing around madly like mad*, furiously, fast, hurriedly, quickly, speedily, hastily, energetically. *see* MAD, LIKE MAD 1. 3 *love her madly* enthusiastically, unrestrainedly, wildly, intensely, fervently, to distraction. *see* MAD, LIKE MAD 2. 4 *madly expensive* extremely, very, exceedingly, excessively, absurdly, ridiculously.

madman n maniac, lunatic, imbecile, psychopath; *inf* loony, nut, nutter, nutcase, head case, basket case, headbanger, screwball, psycho.

madness n 1 *madness caused by grief* insanity, insaneness, dementia, mental illness/derangement, dementedness, instability of mind, unsoundness of mind, lunacy, distraction, mania, frenzy, psychosis; *inf* craziness. 2 *concealing her madness at the children's behaviour* anger, fury, rage, infuriation, irateness, wrath, ire, crossness, indignation, exasperation, irritation; *inf* lividness,

wildness. 3 *amazed at the madness of the decision* insanity, folly, foolishness, stupidity, lunacy, foolhardiness, idiocy, irrationality, unreasonableness, illogicality, senselessness, nonsense, nonsensicalness, absurdness, absurdity, silliness, inanity, ludicrousness, wildness, imprudence, preposterousness; *inf* craziness, daftness. *see* MAD 3. 4 *known for her madness about jazz* enthusiasm, passion, impassionedness, avidness, eagerness, keenness, ardour, zeal, fervour, fanaticism, infatuation. *see* MAD 4.

maelstrom n 1 *ships destroyed in a maelstrom* whirlpool, vortex, eddy, swirl, Charybdis. 2 *the maelstrom of war* turbulence, tumult, uproar, commotion, disorder, disarray, chaos, confusion, upheaval, pandemonium, bedlam.

maestro n master, expert, virtuoso, genius; *inf* ace, whiz.

magazine n periodical, journal, publication, supplement, colour supplement; *inf* glossy, book.

magenta adj fuchsia, reddish-purple, purplish-red, crimson, mauvish-crimson, carmine.

magic n 1 *believers in magic* sorcery, witchcraft, wizardry, enchantment, spell-working, necromancy, the supernatural, occultism, the occult, black magic, black art, voodoo, hoodoo, sortilege, thaumaturgy. 2 *the magic of the conjuror* sleight of hand, legerdemain, conjuring, illusion, prestidigitation, deception, trickery, juggling; *inf* jiggery-pokery. 3 *the magic of the stage* allure, allurement, enchantment, entrancement, fascination, charm, glamour, magnetism, enticement.

magic adj 1 *a magic place* magical, enchanting, entrancing, spellbinding, fascinating, captivating, charming, glamorous, magnetic, irresistible, hypnotic. 2 *the tennis game was magic* marvellous, wonderful, excellent; *inf* brilliant, terrific, brill, fabulous, fab.

magician n 1 *frightened by the magician in the story* sorcerer, sorceress, witch, wizard, warlock, enchanter, enchantress, spellworker, spell-caster, necromancer, thaumaturge. 2 *the magician at the children's party* illusionist, conjuror, legerdemainist, prestidigitator, juggler. 3 *he is a magician at the piano* genius, master, virtuoso, expert, marvel, wizard, maestro; *inf* ace, whiz.

magisterial adj imperious, peremptory, authoritative, masterful, lordly, domineering, dictatorial, autocratic, overbearing, overweening, high-handed, arrogant, haughty, supercilious, patronizing; *inf* bossy.

magnanimity n generosity, charitableness, charity, benevolence, beneficence, open-handedness, big-heartedness, kindness, munificence, bountifulness, largesse, altruism, philanthropy, unselfishness, selflessness, self-sacrifice, mercy, leniency. *see* MAGNANIMOUS.

magnanimous adj generous, generous to a fault, charitable, benevolent, beneficent, open-handed, big-hearted, great-hearted, kind, kindly, munificent, bountiful, liberal, altruistic, philanthropic, noble, unselfish, selfless, self-sacrificing, ungrudging, unstinting, forgiving, merciful, lenient, indulgent.

magnate n *a business magnate* tycoon, captain of industry, baron, industrialist, entrepreneur, financier, top executive, chief, leader, VIP, notable, nabob, grandee; *inf* big shot, bigwig, big wheel, fat cat, mogul.

magnet n **1** *a magnet attracting iron filings* lodestone, magnetite, field magnet, bar magnet, electromagnet, solenoid. **2** *the refreshment tent was the magnet at the fair* focus, focal point, centre of attraction, cynosure. **3** *her beauty was a magnet to all* lure, allurement, attraction, fascination, captivation, enticement, draw, appeal, charm, temptation.

magnetic adj alluring, attractive, fascinating, captivating, entrancing, enchanting, enthralling, appealing, charming, engaging, tempting, tantalizing, seductive, inviting, irresistible, magic, bewitching, charismatic, hypnotic, mesmeric.

magnetism n *the leader has great magnetism* allure, attraction, fascination, captivation, enchantment, appeal, draw, drawing power, pull, charm, temptation, seductiveness, magic, spell, charisma, hypnotism, mesmerism.

magnification n **1** *the magnification of the specimen* increase, augmentation, enlargement, extension, expansion, intensification, heightening, enhancement, aggrandizement. *see* MAGNIFY 1. **2** *the magnification of their troubles* exaggeration, overstatement, overemphasis, overplaying, dramatization, embroidery, embellishment, enhancement. *see* MAGNIFY 2.

magnificence n splendour, splendidness, resplendence, grandeur, impressiveness, imposingness, glory, majesty, nobility, pomp, pomp and circumstance, stateliness, sumptuousness, opulence, luxuriousness, luxury, lavishness, richness, brilliance,

radiance, elegance, gorgeousness, éclat; *inf* ritziness, poshness. *see* MAGNIFICENT 1.

magnificent adj **1** *magnificent processions/apartments* splendid, resplendent, grand, grandiose, impressive, imposing, striking, glorious, superb, majestic, august, noble, stately, exalted, awe-inspiring, royal, regal, kingly, princely, sumptuous, opulent, luxurious, lavish, rich, brilliant, radiant, elegant, gorgeous; *inf* splendiferous, ritzy, posh. **2** *a magnificent performance/game* excellent, masterly, skilful, virtuoso, splendid, impressive, fine, marvellous, wonderful; *inf* terrific, glorious, superb, brilliant, out of this world.

magnify v **1** *bacteria visible when magnified* increase, augment, enlarge, extend, expand, amplify, intensify, heighten, deepen, broaden, widen, dilate, boost, enhance, aggrandize. **2** *magnifying their troubles* exaggerate, overstate, overdo, overemphasize, overplay, dramatize, colour, embroider, embellish, enhance, inflate, make a mountain out of a molehill, draw the long bow; *inf* make a big thing out of, blow up, blow up out of all proportion.

magniloquence n grandiloquence, loftiness, grandiosity, pompousness, pretentiousness, bombast, rhetoric, orotundity, fustian, boastfulness, braggadocio. *see* MAGNILOQUENT.

magniloquent adj grandiloquent, high-sounding, high-flown, lofty, grandiose, pompous, pretentious, bombastic, rhetorical, declamatory, sonorous, orotund, fustian, stilted, turgid, boastful, bragging, braggart; *inf* highfalutin.

magnitude n **1** *estimate the magnitude of the explosion* size, extent, measure, proportions, dimensions, volume, weight, quantity, mass, bulk, amplitude, capacity. **2** *amazed at the magnitude of the epidemic* size, extent, greatness, largeness, bigness, immensity, vastness, hugeness, enormity, enormousness, expanse. **3** *underestimate the magnitude of his problem/rank* importance, significance, weight, moment, consequence, mark, notability, note, greatness, distinction, eminence, fame, renown. **of the first magnitude** of the utmost importance, of the greatest significance, very important, of importance, of significance, of note, of moment, of consequence.

maid n **1** *employ a maid* maidservant, housemaid, serving maid, lady's maid, chambermaid, maid-of-all-work, servant, domestic, girl, au pair. **2** *two lads and a maid* maiden, girl, young lady, lass, miss, nymph, slip of a girl, wench; *lit* damsel; *Scots* lassie. **3** *no longer a maid* virgin, vestal virgin. *see* MAIDEN n 2.

maiden n **1** *lads and maidens* maid, girl, lass; *lit* damsel. *see* MAID 2. **2** *no longer a maiden* virgin, chaste girl, unmarried girl, celibate, vestal virgin.

maiden adj **1** *maiden aunt* unmarried, spinster, unwed, unwedded, single, husbandless, spouseless, celibate. **2** *maiden voyage/speech* first, initial, inaugural, introductory, initiatory. **3** *maiden territory* virgin, intact, undefiled, untrodden, untapped, unused, untried, untested, fresh, new.

maidenhood n virginity, maidenhead, celibacy.

maidenly adj maidenlike, virginal, chaste, pure, undefiled, virtuous, unsullied, vestal, demure, reserved, retiring, decorous, seemly, decent, gentle.

mail¹ n **1** *collect the mail* post, letters, packages, parcels, correspondence, communications, airmail, registered mail. **2** *criticizing the mail* post, postal system, postal service, post office.

mail¹ v *mail the letter/package* post, send by mail/post, send, dispatch, airmail.

mail² n *knights wearing mail* armour, coat of mail, chain-mail, chain-armour, plate armour.

maim v wound, injure, hurt, cripple, disable, put out of action, lame, incapacitate, impair, mar, mutilate, disfigure, mangle.

main adj **1** *the main office/road/issue* head, chief, principal, leading, foremost, most important, central, prime, premier, primary, supreme, predominant, pre-eminent, paramount, cardinal, crucial, vital, critical, pivotal, urgent. **2** *by main force* sheer, pure, utter, downright, mere, plain, brute, stark, absolute, out-and-out, direct.

main n **in the main** for the most part, on the whole, mainly, mostly, by and large, all in all, effectively.

mainly adv *the people are mainly visitors* for the most part, mostly, in the main, on the whole, largely, by and large, to a large extent, to a great degree, predominantly, chiefly, principally, substantially, overall, in general, generally, usually, commonly, as a rule.

mainspring n *jealousy was the mainspring of the crime* motive, motivation, driving force, incentive, impulse, cause, prime mover, reason, origin, root, generator, basis.

mainstay n *the mainstay of the family | she is the mainstay of the theatre company* chief sup-

port, prop, linchpin; pillar, pillar of strength, bulwark, buttress, backbone, anchor, foundation, base.

maintain v **1** *maintain friendly relations | must maintain efficiency* continue, keep going, keep up, keep alive, keep in existence, carry on, preserve, conserve, prolong, perpetuate, sustain. **2** *maintain the houses/roads* keep in good condition, keep in repair, keep up, conserve, preserve, keep intact, care for, take good care of, look after. **3** *maintain a family* support, provide for, keep, finance, feed, nurture, nourish, sustain. **4** *maintain his innocence | he maintains that he is innocent* insist on, hold to, declare, assert, state, announce, affirm, aver, avow, profess, claim, allege, contend, asseverate. **5** *maintain a position* uphold, defend, fight for, stand by, take up the cudgels for, argue for, champion, support, back, advocate.

maintenance n **1** *the maintenance of friendly relations* continuation, continuance, keeping up, carrying on, preservation, conservation, prolongation, perpetuation. *see* MAINTAIN 1. **2** *pay for the maintenance of the property* upkeep, repairs, preservation, conservation, care. *see* MAINTAIN 2. **3** *the maintenance of a family is costly* supporting, keeping, upkeep, financing, feeding, nurture. *see* MAINTAIN 3. **4** *pay maintenance to his children* aliment, alimony, support, allowance, keep, upkeep, subsistence.

majestic adj regal, royal, kingly, queenly, princely, imperial, noble, lordly, august, exalted, awesome, elevated, lofty, stately, dignified, distinguished, magnificent, grand, splendid, resplendent, glorious, impressive, imposing, marvellous, superb, proud.

majesty n **1** *the majesty of the procession* regalness, royalty, royalness, kingliness, queenliness, nobility, nobleness, augustness, exaltation, awesomeness, awe, loftiness, stateliness, dignity, magnificence, grandeur, grandness, splendour, resplendence, glory, impressiveness, superbness, pride. *see* MAJESTIC. **2** *the majesty invested in him* sovereignty, authority, power, dominion, supremacy.

major adj **1** *the major part is complete* larger, bigger, greater, main. **2** *one of our major poets* greatest, best, most important, leading, foremost, chief, main, outstanding, first-rate, notable, eminent, pre-eminent, supreme. **3** *a major issue | a matter of major importance* important, significant, crucial, vital, great, weighty, paramount, utmost, prime. **4** *major surgery* serious, radical, complicated.

majority n **1** *the majority of the people/audience* larger part/number, greater part/number, most, more than half, bulk, mass, main body, preponderance, lion's share. **2** *their majority was halved* winning margin, winning difference, superiority of numbers/votes. **3** *young people reaching their majority* legal age, coming-of-age, seniority, adulthood, manhood, womanhood, maturity, age of consent.

make v **1** *make sandcastles/furniture* build, construct, assemble, put together, put up, erect, manufacture, produce, fabricate, create, form, fashion, model, mould, shape, forge. **2** *make them pay* force to, compel to, coerce into, press into, drive into, pressure into, pressurize into, oblige to, require to, prevail upon to, dragoon into, impel to, constrain to, urge to; *inf* railroad into, put the heat on, put the screws on, use strong-arm tactics on. **3** *make a noise/scene* cause, create, give rise to, produce, bring about, generate, engender, occasion, effect. **4** *make a bow* perform, execute, do, accomplish, carry out, effect, practise, engage in, prosecute. **5** *make him chairman* create, appoint, designate, name, nominate, select, elect, vote in, install, invest, ordain, assign. **6** *make a will/film* compose, put together, frame, formulate, prepare, write, direct. **7** *make money | he's making a profit | can't make a good wage* gain, acquire, obtain, get, realize, secure, win, earn, net, gross, clear, bring in, take home, pocket. **8** *make tea* prepare, get ready, make arrangements for, put together, concoct, cook; *inf* whip up; *Amer inf* fix. **9** *make laws* draw up, frame, form, formulate, enact, lay down, establish, institute, found, originate. **10** *that makes £100* come to, add up to, total, amount to. **11** *what do you make the total?* estimate, calculate, compute, gauge, reckon. **12** *what do you make of him?* look upon, view, regard, consider, think of, judge, deem, evaluate, adjudge. **13** *make a decision* come to, settle on, determine on, conclude, establish, seal. **14** *make a speech* give, deliver, utter, give voice to, enunciate, recite, pronounce. **15** *make a great leader | the sofa makes a good bed* be, act as, serve as, constitute, perform the function of, play the part of, represent, embody. **16** *make the first eleven* achieve, attain, get into, gain access to, gain a place in. **17** *make the bus/ party* catch, arrive in time for, arrive at, reach, get to, succeed in attending. **18** *boasting about making girls* seduce, have sexual intercourse with, make love to, go to bed with, sleep with; *inf* have sex with. **make as if/though** *make as if to run away |*

made as if he was mad act as if/though, pretend, feign, give the impression, make a show of, affect, feint; *inf* put it on. **make away with 1** *make away with his bags/money/wife* make off with, run away with, abscond with, steal, purloin, kidnap, abduct; *inf* nick, swipe, nab. *see* MAKE v make off with. **2** *make away with the evidence* do away with, destroy, dispose of, get rid of, eliminate; *inf* dump. **3** *make away with his enemy* do away with, kill, murder, assassinate, put to death, slaughter, execute, eliminate; *inf* bump off, do in. **make believe** pretend, fantasize, indulge in fantasy, daydream, build castles in the air, build castles in Spain, dream, imagine, romance, play-act, act, enact. **make do 1** *we have very little but we make do* get by on few resources, get by, get along, scrape by, manage, cope, survive, muddle through, make the best of a bad job. **2** *make do with what you have* get by with/on, make the best of, put to the best use, make the most of, improvise. **make for 1** *make for a safe place* go towards, head for, aim for, make one's way towards, proceed towards, direct one's footsteps towards, steer a course towards, be bound for. **2** *this will make for a good relationship* contribute to, be conducive to, promote, facilitate, further, advance, forward, favour. **make off** *on seeing the police they made off* run away/off, take to one's heels, leave, take off, beat a hasty retreat, flee, bolt, fly, make a getaway, make one's getaway, make a quick exit, abscond, decamp; *inf* clear off, beat it, make tracks, split, cut and run, do a runner, leg it, skedaddle, vamoose, hightail it. **make off with** *make off with his bags/money/wife* make away with, run off/away with, abscond with, steal, purloin, appropriate, kidnap, abduct; *inf* nick, swipe, nab, waltz off with, filch. **make out 1** *make out a figure in the distance* discern, see, distinguish, espy, behold, perceive, descry, notice, observe, recognize, pick out, detect, discover. **2** *unable to make out what she says* understand, comprehend, follow, grasp, fathom, work out, figure out, interpret. **3** *unable to make out the handwriting* decipher, work out, figure out, understand, interpret. **4** *they made out that he was violent* assert, declare, affirm, aver, allege, claim, suggest, imply, pretend. **5** *how did you make out?* get on, get along, fare, do, get by, proceed, go, progress, manage, survive. **6** *how do you make that out?* prove, show to be true, establish, demonstrate, substantiate, verify, validate, authenticate, corroborate. **7** *make out an application form* fill out, fill in, complete, write out, inscribe. **make over 1** *make over his property* *to his son* transfer, sign over, turn over, hand over, transmit, assign, convey. **2** *make over the old house* renovate, remodel, redo, restore, redecorate, brighten up, improve, upgrade, gentrify; *inf* do up. **make up 1** *the children's statements make up the case for the prosecution* comprise, form, compose, constitute. **2** *make up the balance* supply, furnish, provide. **3** *extra people required to make up the full complement* complete, round off, meet, finish. **4** *children making up for their previous rudeness* make amends for, atone for, compensate for, make recompense for, make reparation for, make redress for, offset. **5** *kiss and make up* be friends again, bury the hatchet, declare a truce, make peace, forgive and forget, shake hands, become reconciled, settle differences, mend fences, call it quits. **6** *make up a medicine/prescription* prepare, mix, concoct, put together. **7** *make up an excuse* invent, fabricate, concoct, hatch, coin, trump up, dream up, think up, devise, manufacture, formulate, frame, construct; *inf* cook up. **8** *make up a short story* compose, write, create, originate, devise. **9** *make up her face* use make-up on, apply cosmetics to, powder, rouge; *inf* put on one's face, do one's face, paint one's face, tart oneself up, do oneself up, apply one's warpaint. **make up one's mind** come to a decision, make/reach a decision, decide, determine, resolve, settle on a plan of action, choose/determine/resolve/settle one's course of action, reach a conclusion. **make up to 1** *making up to their boss* curry favour with, fawn on, toady to, lick someone's boots, truckle to, flatter; *inf* butter up, play up to, be all over. **2** *making up to her friend's husband* flirt with, make romantic advances to, court, woo; *inf* chat up, make eyes at, make sheep's eyes at, give the come-on to. **make way** *make way for the king* clear the way for, make a space for, make room for, stand back for, allow to pass, allow through.

make *n* **1** *different makes of car | buy the store's own make* brand, label, trademark, sort, type, variety, style, mark, marque. **2** *a burly make of dog | a clumsy make of machine* build, form, frame, structure, construction, shape. **3** *a man of a different make from his brother* character, nature, temperament, temper, disposition, humour. *see* MAKE-UP 3.

make-believe *n* pretence, fantasy, daydreaming, dreaming, imagination, romancing, fabrication, play-acting, charade, masquerade. *see* MAKE V MAKE BELIEVE.

make-believe *adj a make-believe world/friend* pretended, feigned, made-up, fantasy, fantasized, dream, imagined, imaginary, unreal, fictitious, mock, sham; *inf* pretend.

maker *n the maker of the machines | clock-makers* manufacturer, builder, constructor, producer, creator, fabricator, author, architect, framer.

Maker *n* God, God the Father, the Creator, the Almighty, God Almighty.

makeshift *adj* stopgap, make-do, provisional, temporary, rough and ready, substitute, improvised, stand-by, jerry-built, thrown-together.

make-up *n* **1** *girls putting on their make-up | actors applying make-up* cosmetics, greasepaint, maquillage, foundation, powder, blusher, rouge, eye make-up, eye-liner, eyeshadow, eyebrow pencil, lipstick, lip gloss; *inf* warpaint, face paint. **2** *the make-up of the machines varies* structure, composition, constitution, formation, form, format, configuration, construction, assembly, arrangement, organization. **3** *family backgrounds which contribute to the make-up of individuals* character, nature, temperament, temper, personality, disposition, humour, make, stamp, mould, kidney, cast of mind, frame of mind; *inf* what makes someone tick.

making *n the making of the cars | image-making* manufacture, manufacturing, building, construction, production, creation, fabrication, forming, moulding, forging. **in the making** budding, burgeoning, coming, emergent, growing, developing, nascent.

makings *npl* **1** *have the makings of a leader* potential, potentiality, promise, capacity, capability, qualities, characteristics, ingredients, materials, essentials, beginnings, basics. **2** *his makings are less than his outgoings* income, earnings, pay, wages, salary, returns, takings, proceeds, profits, revenue.

maladjusted *adj* disturbed, unstable, illadjusted, neurotic, alienated from society, muddled, confused; *inf* mixed-up, screwedup, untogether.

maladroit *adj* awkward, clumsy, inept, bungling, bumbling, incompetent, unskilful, unhandy, ungainly, inelegant, graceless, gauche, all fingers and thumbs, like a bull in a china shop; *inf* butter-fingered, ham-fisted, cack-handed.

malady *n* disease, disorder, illness, sickness, ailment, affliction, complaint, infection, indisposition, infirmity.

malaise *n* lassitude, listlessness, languour, enervation, weakness, feebleness, infirmity, illness, sickness, unease, discomfort, anxiety, angst, disquiet, melancholy, depression, despondency, dejection, weariness, ennui.

malapropism n wrong word, misuse, misusage, misapplication, infelicity.

malcontent n *young malcontents resenting the adults* grumbler, complainer, moaner, fault-finder, carper, agitator, troublemaker, mischief-maker, rebel, dissentient; *inf* grouser, griper, nit-picker, bellyacher, beefer, stirrer.

malcontent adj *a malcontent mood in the crowd* discontented, dissatisfied, disgruntled, disaffected, restive, unhappy, grumbling, complaining, fault-finding, carping, resentful, troublemaking, rebellious, dissentious, factious; *inf* nit-picking, bellyaching. see MALCONTENT n.

male adj *male bird/plant/characteristics* masculine, manlike, manly, virile.

male n **1** *two males and a female* man, gentleman, boy, lad, youth; *inf* chap, fellow, bloke, guy. **2** *animals which are males* | *male has brighter plummage* dog, tomcat, bull, ram, stallion, buck, stag, boar, billy-goat, cock, gander, drake.

malediction n curse, imprecation, execration, anathema, voodoo; damning, damnation.

malefactor n criminal, lawbreaker, felon, convict, offender, wrongdoer, evil-doer, villain, miscreant, delinquent, sinner, reprobate, transgressor, outlaw, trespasser; *inf* crook.

malevolence n malignance, malignity, malice, maleficence, ill nature, ill will, animosity, hostility, hatred, hate, spite, spitefulness, vindictiveness, rancour, revengefulness, viciousness. see MALEVOLENT.

malevolent adj malign, malignant, malicious, maleficent, evil-intentioned, evil-minded, ill-natured, hostile, unfriendly, spiteful, baleful, vindictive, revengeful, rancorous, vicious, pernicious, cruel, fierce.

malformation n deformity, distortion, crookedness, misshapenness, disfigurement, misproportion.

malformed adj deformed, distorted, crooked, twisted, misshapen, disfigured, misproportioned.

malfunction v *the computer is malfunctioning* develop a fault, go wrong, break down, break, fail, cease to function/work, stop working; *inf* conk out, go kaput.

malfunction n **1** *detect a malfunction in the machine* fault, defect, flaw, impairment; *inf* glitch. **2** *complain about the malfunction of the*

machine breakdown, failure, collapse; *inf* conking out.

malice n malevolence, maliciousness, malignity, malignance, evil intentions, ill will, ill feeling, animosity, animus, hostility, enmity, bad blood, hatred, hate, spite, spitefulness, vindictiveness, rancour, bitterness, grudge, venom, spleen, harm, destruction, defamation; *inf* bitchiness, cattiness.

malicious adj malevolent, malign, malignant, evil, evil-intentioned, ill-natured, hostile, spiteful, baleful, vindictive, rancorous, bitter, venomous, pernicious, harmful, hurtful, destructive, defamatory; *inf* bitchy, catty.

malign v slander, libel, defame, smear, run a smear campaign against, blacken someone's name/character, calumniate, vilify, speak ill of, spread lies about, accuse falsely, cast aspersions on, misrepresent, traduce, denigrate, disparage, slur, derogate; *inf* bad-mouth, run down, drag through the mud.

malignant n **1** *a malignant old woman* | *has malignant intentions* malevolent, malign, malicious, evil, evil-intentioned, hostile, spiteful, vindictive, rancorous, venomous, pernicious, harmful, hurtful, destructive. **2** *a malignant growth* cancerous, nonbenign. **3** *a malignant disease* dangerous, virulent, uncontrollable, deadly, fatal, life-threatening, lethal.

malinger v feign/fake illness, pretend to be ill, pretend to be an invalid, have a fake illness, shirk, pretend; *inf* put it on, skive.

mall n shopping centre, shopping plaza, shopping precinct, shopping complex.

malleable adj **1** *malleable substances* workable, shapable, mouldable, plastic, pliant, ductile, tractile. **2** *malleable people being bullied* pliable, compliant, easily influenced, accommodating, adaptable, impressionable, susceptible, amenable, biddable, tractable, manageable, governable.

malnutrition n undernourishment, poor diet, inadequate diet, unhealthy diet, lack of food, starvation, famine, anorexia.

malodorous adj foul-smelling, evil-smelling, fetid, smelly, stinking, reeking, rank, noisome, mephitic; *inf* niffing, nitty, pongy, stinking to high heaven.

malpractice n *doctors guilty of malpractice* unprofessional conduct, unprofessionalism, dereliction, negligence, carelessness, breach of ethics, unethical behaviour, misconduct, wrongdoing.

maltreat v treat badly, ill-treat, ill-use, mis-treat, misuse, abuse, handle/treat roughly, mishandle, manhandle, maul, bully, injure, harm, hurt, molest; *inf* beat up, rough up, do over.

maltreatment n ill-treatment, ill use, mis-treatment, abuse, rough handling, mishan-dling, manhandling, bullying, injury, harm. *see* MALTREAT.

mammoth adj huge, enormous, giant, gigantic, vast, immense, mighty, colossal, massive, gargantuan, prodigious, monu-mental, stupendous, mountainous, ele-phantine, king-size, Brobdingnagian; *inf* whopping, ginormous, humongous.

man n **1** *three men and a woman* male, adult male, gentleman; *inf* chap, fellow, bloke, guy. **2** *no man is perfect* human being, human, mortal, person, individual, one, personage. **3** *Man is more intelligent than ani-mals* Homo sapiens, mankind, the human race, the human species, humankind, human beings, humans, people. **4** *employ a man to do the garden* workman, worker, labourer, helper, hand. **5** *the nobleman and his man* valet, manservant, gentleman's gentleman, batman, attender, retainer, page, footman, flunkey, Jeeves. **6** *his sister and her man* husband, spouse, boyfriend, partner, lover, common-law husband, escort, beau, live-in lover, significant other, cohabitee; *inf* toy boy. **to a man** with no exceptions, without exception, bar none, one and all, everyone, each and everyone, unanimously, as one.

man v **1** *man the bar/fort* supply with men/people/staff, furnish with men/people/staff, staff, crew. **2** *man the pumps* work, operate, use, utilize, service.

manacles npl handcuffs, chains, irons, hand shackles/fetters; *inf* cuffs, bracelets, darbies.

manage v **1** *manage the team/organization* be in charge of, run, be head of, head, direct, control, preside over, lead, govern, rule, command, superintend, supervise, oversee, administer, organize, conduct, handle, guide, be at the helm of; *inf* head up. **2** *manage to survive* succeed in, contrive, engineer, bring about/off, achieve, accom-plish, effect. **3** *will you manage?* cope, deal with the situation, get along/on, carry on, survive, make do, be/fare all right, weather the storm; *inf* make out, get by. **4** *can you manage the dog/children?* cope with, deal with, handle, control, master, influence. **5** *manage a weapon* wield, use, operate, work, ply, handle, manipulate, brandish, flourish.

manageable adj **1** *manageable tasks* easy, doable, practicable, possible, feasible, attainable, viable. **2** *manageable children/peo-ple* controllable, governable, tamable, tractable, pliant, compliant, docile, accom-modating, amenable, yielding, submissive. **3** *manageable tools* handy, easy, user-friendly.

management n **1** *the workers' dispute with management* managers, employers, owners, proprietors, directors, board of directors, board, directorate, executives, administra-tion; *inf* bosses, top brass. **2** *responsible for the management of the firm* running, charge, care, direction, leadership, control, govern-ing, ruling, command, superintendence, supervision, overseeing, administration, organization, conduct, handling, guidance.

manager n **1** *managers and workers* employer, director, executive, head of department, administrator, superinten-dent, supervisor; *inf* boss, gaffer. **2** *the team's manager* organizer, controller, comp-troller.

mandate n *by mandate of the electorate/king* authority, bidding, direction, instruction, authorization, sanction, warrant, order, command, directive, ruling, decree, edict, dictate, charge, injunction, statute, law, ordinance, fiat, ukase.

mandatory adj obligatory, compulsory, binding, required, requisite, essential, imperative, necessary.

manful adj manly, brave, courageous, gal-lant, heroic, intrepid, valiant, bold, stout, stout-hearted. *see* MANLY 1.

manfully adv bravely, courageously, gal-lantly, heroically, intrepidly, valiantly, boldly, stoutly, stout-heartedly, stalwartly, hard, strongly, vigorously, with might and main, like a Trojan, with all one's strength, to the best of one's abilities, as best one can, determinedly, resolutely, desperately, with desperation, with all the stops out.

mange n scabies, scab, itch, rash, eruption, skin infection.

manger n trough, feeding trough, fodder rack.

mangle v **1** *mangle the captured animals* | *had mangled the enemy* mutilate, hack, cut about, lacerate, maul, tear at, rend, butcher, disfigure, deform. **2** *mangle the piece of music* spoil, ruin, mar, bungle, mess up, make a mess of; *inf* murder.

mangy adj **1** *mangy animals* scabby, scaly, diseased. **2** *mangy carpets/flats* shabby, scruffy, moth-eaten, worn, shoddy, dirty, mean, squalid, filthy, seedy; *inf* grotty.

3 *he's a mangy individual* contemptible, despicable, hateful, odious, nasty, mean, base, low.

manhandle v **1** *accused of manhandling prisoners* handle roughly, push, pull, shove, maul, mistreat, ill-treat, abuse, injure, damage, beat, batter; *inf* knock about, beat up, rough up. **2** *having to manhandle the huge parcels* move/carry/lift manually, heave, haul, push, shove, pull, tug, manoeuvre; *inf* hump.

manhood n **1** *reach manhood* adult maleness, maturity, sexual maturity, puberty. **2** *insult his manhood* maleness, masculinity, masculineness, manliness, virility, machismo. **3** *soldiers demonstrating their manhood* manliness, bravery, courage, heroism, intrepidity, valour, boldness, mettle, spirit, fortitude. *see* MANLINESS 1.

mania n **1** *the mania phase of the manic depressive illness | suffering from mania* frenzy, franticness, violence, wildness, hysteria, raving, derangement, dementia. **2** *a mania for collecting old china* obsession, compulsion, fixation, fetish, fascination, preoccupation, passion, enthusiasm, desire, urge, craving, craze, fad; *inf* thing.

maniac n *murder committed by a maniac* madman, madwoman, mad person, deranged person, psychopath, lunatic; *inf* loony, nutcase, nut, nutter, psycho, screwball.

manifest v **1** *manifest strange symptoms* display, show, exhibit, demonstrate, present, evince, express, reveal, indicate, make plain, declare. **2** *manifest his guilt* prove, be evidence of, establish, show, evidence, substantiate, corroborate, verify, confirm, settle.

manifest adj *a manifest disinterest in the proceedings* obvious, clear, plain, apparent, patent, noticeable, perceptible, visible, transparent, conspicuous, unmistakable, distinct, blatant, glaring.

manifestation n **1** *a manifestation of solidarity* display, show, exhibition, demonstration, presentation, exposition, illustration, exemplification, indication, declaration, expression, profession. **2** *produce manifestations of their presence* evidence, proof, testimony, substantiation, sign, indication, mark, symbol, token, symptom.

manifesto n proclamation, pronouncement, declaration, declaration of political policies, announcement, statement, publication, notification.

manifold adj multifarious, multiple, multifold, numerous, many, several, multitudinous, various, varied, diverse, assorted, sundry, copious, abundant.

manikin n dwarf, midget, little man, homunculus, pygmy, Tom Thumb.

manipulate v **1** *manipulate the tool/weapon* handle, wield, ply, work, operate, use, employ, utilize, exercise. **2** *manipulate his colleagues | has manipulated the situation* influence, control, use to one's advantage, exploit, manoeuvre, engineer, steer, direct, guide, pull the strings. **3** *manipulate the figures* juggle, massage, falsify, doctor, tamper with, fiddle with, tinker with; *inf* cook.

manipulator n **1** *the manipulator of the tools* handler, wielder, operator. *see* MANIPULATE 1. **2** *don't trust him—he is a manipulator* exploiter, manoeuvrer, conniver, intriguer, puller of strings, puppet-master. *see* MANIPULATE 2.

mankind n man, *Homo sapiens*, the human race, the human species, humankind, human beings, humans, people.

manliness n **1** *show their manliness in battle* manhood, bravery, braveness, courage, courageousness, heroism, intrepidity, valour, boldness, fearlessness, stout-heartedness, dauntlessness, mettle, spirit, fortitude. *see* MANLY 1. **2** *his thinness contrasting with his brother's manliness* masculinity, virility, strength, robustness, muscularity, powerfulness, ruggedness, toughness. *see* MANLY 2.

manly adj **1** *exhibiting manly characteristics* manful, brave, courageous, gallant, heroic, intrepid, valiant, valorous, bold, fearless, stout, stout-hearted, dauntless; *inf* macho, Ramboesque. **2** *a manly figure* masculine, all-male, virile, strong, robust, vigorous, muscular, powerful, well-built, strapping, sturdy, rugged, tough; *inf* macho.

man-made adj manufactured, synthetic, artificial, imitation, ersatz, plastic.

manner n **1** *do the work in an efficient manner* way, means, method, system, approach, technique, procedure, process, methodology, routine, practice, fashion, mode, style, habit, custom. **2** *have an unfriendly manner* look, air, appearance, demeanour, aspect, mien, bearing, cast, deportment, behaviour, conduct. **3** *what manner of person is he?* kind, sort, type, variety, form, nature, breed, brand, stamp, class, category.

mannered adj affected, unnatural, artificial, stilted, theatrical, posed, stagy, pretentious, put-on; *inf* pseudo.

mannerism n habit, characteristic, characteristic gesture, trait, idiosyncrasy, quirk, foible, peculiarity.

mannerly adj well-mannered, well-behaved, polite, courteous, civil, gentlemanly, lady-like, genteel, decorous, respectful, well-bred, refined, polished, civilized, cultivated, gracious, chivalrous.

manners npl **1** *it is bad manners to stare* social behaviour, behaviour, conduct, way of behaving, social habit. **2** *it is manners to remain seated* correct behaviour, etiquette, good form, protocol, politeness, decorum, propriety, social graces, formalities, *politesse*; *inf* the done thing.

mannish adj masculine, manlike, unfeminine, unwomanly, unladylike, Amazonian; *inf* butch, dyke.

manoeuvre n **1** *manoeuvre of troops* movement, deployment, operation, exercise. **2** *park the vehicle in one manoeuvre* skilful movement/move, movement, move, clever stroke, stroke, skilful measure/handling. **3** *get the promotion by a series of manoeuvres* trick, stratagem, tactic, machination, manipulation, artifice, subterfuge, device, dodge, ploy, ruse, scheme, plan, plot, intrigue; *inf* wangle.

manoeuvre v **1** *manoeuvre the car* move, work, negotiate, steer, guide, direct, manipulate. **2** *manoeuvres things to suit himself* manage, manipulate, contrive, engineer, devise, plan, plot; *inf* wangle. **3** *he is manoeuvring for the leadership* scheme, intrigue, plot, use trickery/artifice, machinate, pull strings.

manse n vicarage, parsonage, rectory, deanery.

mansion n imposing residence, manor-house, manor, hall, stately home, house, abode, seat.

manslaughter n killing, slaying, murder, homicide, patricide, matricide, fratricide, infanticide, regicide.

mantle n **1** *ladies wearing mantles of red* cloak, cape, shawl, wrap, poncho, pelisse. **2** *a mantle of snow/darkness* covering, cover, blanket, curtain, canopy, cloud, pall, envelope, veil, cloak, shroud, screen, mask.

mantle v *fields mantled in snow* | *houses mantled in darkness* cover, blanket, curtain, envelop, veil, cloak, wrap, shroud, cloud, conceal, hide, disguise, mask.

manual adj **1** *manual work* with one's hands, labouring, physical. **2** *manual gear-change* hand-operated, done by hand, by hand, non-automatic.

manual n *an instruction manual* handbook, set of instructions, instructions, guidebook, guide; *inf* bible, book of words.

manufacture v **1** *manufacture cars* make, produce, mass-produce, build, construct, assemble, put together, create, fabricate, turn out, process, form, fashion, model, mould, shape, forge. **2** *manufacture an excuse* make up, invent, fabricate, concoct, hatch, coin, trump up, dream up, think up, devise, formulate, frame, construct; *inf* cook up.

manufacture n *the manufacture of cars* making, production, mass-production, construction, assembly, creation, fabrication, processing. *see* MANUFACTURE v 1.

manufacturer n maker, producer, builder, constructor, creator, fabricator, factory-owner, industrialist, captain/baron of industry.

manure n *farmyard manure*, dung, animal excrement, muck, guano, droppings, ordure, fertilizer.

many adj *many people/books/times* numerous, innumerable, a large/great number of, countless, scores of, myriad, great quantities of, multitudinous, multiple, copious, abundant, various, sundry, diverse, several, frequent; *inf* a lot of, umpteen, lots of, masses of, scads of, heaps of, piles of, bags of, tons of, oodles of, an army of, zillions of.

many n *many were killed* | *so many have been thrown out* many people, many things, scores, large numbers, great quantities, a large number, a host, a horde, a crowd, a multitude, a mass, an accumulation, an abundance, a profusion, plenty; *inf* lots, a lot, umpteen, armies, scads, heaps, piles, bags, tons, masses, oodles, a thousand and one, zillions. **the many** *have to listen to the wishes of the many* the majority, the people, the masses, the multitude, the rank and file, the crowd, hoi polloi.

map n chart, plan, plot, guide, street guide, town plan, road-map, atlas, gazetteer.

map v *map the surface of the moon* chart, plot, delineate, depict, portray. **map out** *map out the conference programme* set out, lay out, detail, draw up, sketch out, plan, plot out.

mar v *marred her beauty/career/happiness* spoil, detract from, impair, damage, ruin, wreck, disfigure, blemish, scar, deface, harm, hurt, injure, deform, mutilate, maim, mangle, tarnish, taint, contaminate, pollute, sully, stain, blot, debase, vitiate; *inf* foul up.

maraud v **1** *maraud around the countryside* foray, raid, go on forays/raids, forage, plunder, go looting, pirate, freeboot; *Scots* reive. **2** *tribes marauding the neighbouring villages* raid, plunder, loot, pillage, foray, ransack, forage, ravage, harry, sack, despoil.

marauder n raider, plunderer, pillager, looter, ravager, robber, pirate, freebooter, buccaneer, corsair, rover, bandit, brigand, rustler, highwayman; *Scots* reiver, cateran.

march v **1** *armies marching* walk, step, pace, tread, stride, footslog, tramp, hike, trudge, stalk, strut, parade, file. **2** *time marches on* move forward, advance, progress, forge ahead, make headway, go on, continue on, roll on, develop, evolve.

march n **1** *soldiers/scouts on a march* route march, walk, footslog, tramp, trek, hike, parade. **2** *a quick/slow march* step, pace, stride, gait. **3** *a march against pit closures* demonstration, parade, procession; *inf* demo. **4** *the march of time/progress* advance, progress, progression, passage, headway, continuance, development, evolution.

marches npl *lives in the Welsh marches* boundary, border, borderland, frontier, limits, confines.

margin n **1** *the margin of the lake* edge, side, verge, border, perimeter, boundary, limits, periphery, brink, brim. **2** *the margin between the countries* border, borderland, boundary, boundary line, frontier, bounding line, demarcation line. **3** *little margin for error* leeway, latitude, scope, room, room for manoeuvre, space, allowance, extra, surplus. **4** *win by a narrow margin | a margin of one vote* measure of difference, degree of difference, difference, amount.

marginal adj **1** *marginal areas* border, boundary, on the edge, peripheral. **2** *the difference is marginal* slight, small, tiny, minute, low, minor, insignificant, minimal, negligible.

marijuana n cannabis, hashish, bhang, hemp, kef, kif, charas, ganja, sinsemilla; *inf* drugs, dope, hash, grass, pot, stuff, mary jane, tea, the weed.

marinade v marinate, soak, steep, immerse.

marine adj **1** *marine life* sea, aquatic, salt-water, sea-water, oceanic, pelagic, thalassic. **2** *marine careers* maritime, nautical, naval, seafaring, seagoing.

mariner n sailor, seaman, seafarer, seafaring man, sea dog, salt, Jack tar, bluejacket; *inf* tar, limey, matelot.

marital adj *marital vows/bliss* matrimonial, marriage, wedding, conjugal, connubial, nuptial, spousal, married, wedded.

maritime adj **1** *maritime careers* naval, marine, nautical, seafaring, seagoing. **2** *maritime areas* coastal, seaside, littoral.

mark n **1** *marks left on the table* stain, blemish, blot, smear, trace, spot, speck, dot, blotch, smudge, splotch, bruise, scratch, scar, dent, pit, pock, chip, notch, nick, line, score, cut, incision, gash. **2** *the marks on a horse/cow* marking, blaze, spot, speckle, stripe, brand, earmark. **3** *question mark | proofreader's marks* exclamation mark, symbol, sign, character, question mark, quotation marks. **4** *marks showing the way* marker, guide, pointer, landmark, direction post, signpost, milestone, waymark. **5** *mark of respect* sign, symbol, indication, symptom, feature, token, badge, emblem, evidence, proof, clue, hint. **6** *recognize the king's/firm's mark* seal, stamp, signet, symbol, emblem, device, badge, motto, monogram, hallmark, trade mark, logo, watermark, label, tag, flag. **7** *put one's mark on the document* cross, X, scribble, squiggle, signature, autograph, initials, imprint. **8** *marks left by the thief* print, fingerprint, thumbprint, footprint, imprint, track, trail, trace, vestige. **9** *war left its mark on him* impression, imprint, traces, vestiges, remains, effect, impact, influence. **10** *have the mark of an honest man* characteristic, feature, trait, attribute, quality, stamp, peculiarity. **11** *the bullet/insult missed its mark* target, goal, aim, bull's-eye, objective, object, end, purpose, intent, intention. **12** *work falling below the mark* standard, required standard, norm, par, level, criterion, gauge, yardstick, rule, measure, scale. **13** *a person of mark* distinction, importance, consequence, eminence, pre-eminence, prominence, note, notability, fame, repute, greatness, prestige, celebrity, glory, standing, rank. **14** *nothing of mark occurred* note, noteworthiness, importance, consequence. **make one's mark** *by 30 he had made his mark in the financial world* be successful, gain success, be a success, succeed, prosper, get on, make good, achieve recognition; *inf* make it. **wide of the mark 1** *his observations were wide of the mark* irrelevant, inapplicable, inapposite, inappropriate, not to the point, beside the point. **2** *his answers were wide of the mark* inaccurate, incorrect, wrong, erroneous, inexact, off-target, fallacious.

mark v **1** *mark the table* stain, smear, smudge, scratch, scar, dent, chip, notch, score, cut, gash. *see* MARK n **1**. **2** *mark your property* put one's name on, name, initial, put one's seal on, label, tag, stamp, flag, hallmark, watermark, brand, earmark. **3** *mark the places on a map* name, indicate, write down, tag, label, flag. **4** *mark essays* correct, assess, evaluate, appraise; *Amer* grade. **5** *mark the goods at £10* price, put a price-tag on, cost. **6** *the children marked his displeasure* see, notice, observe, take note of, discern, descry, spot, recognize; *inf* get a load of. **7** *you should mark his words* take heed of, pay heed to, heed, take notice of, pay attention to, attend to, note, mind, bear in mind, give a thought to, take into consideration. **8** *a day marked by misfortune* characterize, distinguish, identify, denote, brand, signalize. **9** *mark his birthday* celebrate, commemorate, honour, observe, recognize, acknowledge, solemnize. **10** *marked for greatness* designate, choose, select, nominate. **mark down 1** *mark down the prices* reduce, decrease, lower, cut, put down, take down, slash. **2** *mark down the goods* reduce, lower the price of, make cheaper, sell at a give-away price; *Amer* put on sale. **mark out 1** *mark out the football pitch* mark off, mark the boundaries/limits of, measure out, demarcate, delimit. **2** *his honesty marked him out from the rest of the gang* set apart, separate, single out, differentiate, distinguish. **mark up 1** *mark up the price* raise, increase, put up, up, hike up, escalate; *inf* jack up. **2** *mark up the goods* increase/raise the price of.

marked adj pronounced, decided, striking, clear, glaring, blatant, unmistakable, remarkable, prominent, signal, conspicuous, noticeable, noted, distinct, pointed, salient, recognizable, identifiable, distinguishable, obvious, apparent, evident, manifest, open, patent, written all over one.

markedly adv decidedly, strikingly, remarkably, unmistakably, conspicuously, noticeably, pointedly, distinctly, recognizably, obviously, clearly, plainly, apparently, evidently, manifestly, to a marked extent, to a great extent. *see* MARKED.

market n **1** *shopping at the market* marketplace, mart, shopping centre, bazaar, souk, retail outlet. **2** *no market for such expensive goods* demand, call, want, desire, need. **3** *the market is sluggish* trade, business, commerce, buying and selling, dealing. **in the market for** wishing to buy, in need of, wanting, lacking, wishing for, desiring. **on the market** on sale, up for sale, for sale, purchasable, available, obtainable.

market v *market furniture* sell, retail, offer for sale, put up for sale, vend, peddle, hawk.

marksman, markswoman n sharpshooter, good shot; *inf* crack shot, dead shot.

maroon v abandon, forsake, leave behind, leave, desert, strand, leave stranded, turn one's back on, leave isolated.

marriage n **1** *their marriage lasted 20 years | join in marriage* married state, matrimony, holy matrimony, wedlock, conjugal bond, union, match. **2** *invited to their marriage* marriage ceremony, wedding, wedding ceremony, nuptials. **3** *the marriage of their skills* alliance, union, merger, unification, amalgamation, combination, affiliation, association, connection, coupling; *inf* hook-up.

married adj **1** *married couple* wedded, wed, joined in marriage, united in wedlock; *inf* spliced, hitched. **2** *married bliss* marital, matrimonial, connubial, conjugal, nuptial, spousal.

marrow n *marrow of his statement* core, kernel, nucleus, pith, heart, centre, soul, spirit, essence, quintessence, gist, substance, sum and substance, meat, stuff; *inf* nitty-gritty, nuts and bolts.

marry v **1** *the couple married last year* be married, wed, be wed, become man and wife, become espoused; *inf* tie the knot, walk down the aisle, take the plunge, get spliced, get hitched, get yoked. **2** *he married her | she married him* wed, take to wife/husband, espouse. **3** *marry their skills* join, join together, unite, ally, merge, unify, amalgamate, combine, affiliate, associate, link, connect, fuse, weld, couple.

marsh n marshland, bog, peatbog, swamp, swampland, morass, mire, quagmire, quag, slough, fen, fenland, bayou.

marshal v **1** *marshal the pupils | tried to marshal his thoughts* gather together, assemble, collect, muster, draw up, line up, align, set/put in order, arrange deploy, dispose, rank. **2** *marshal the guests to their seats* usher, guide, escort, conduct, lead, shepherd, take.

marshy adj boggy, swampy, muddy, squelchy, miry, quaggy, fenny, paludal.

martial adj **1** *martial exploits* military, soldierly, army. **2** *martial arts* militant, warlike, combative, belligerent, bellicose, aggressive, pugnacious.

martial arts npl judo, ju-jitsu, aikido, karate, kung fu, t'ai chi chu'an, tae kwon do.

martinet n disciplinarian, stickler for discipline, hard taskmaster.

martyr n sufferer, victim, Christian martyr, early martyr.

martyr v **1** *martyr them for their beliefs* make a martyr of, martyrize, put to death, burn at the stake, immolate, throw to the lions, crucify. **2** *the invading army martyred the villagers* persecute, torture, inflict agony on.

martyrdom n persecution, ordeal, torture, torment, suffering, agony, anguish.

marvel v *marvel at their exploits* be amazed by, be filled with amazement at, be awed by, be full of wonder at, wonder at, stare at, gape at, goggle at, not believe one's eyes/ears at.

marvel n *his desserts are a marvel* wonder, wonderful thing, amazing thing, prodigy, sensation, spectacle, phenomenon, miracle; *inf* something else, something to shout about, something to write home about, eye-opener.

marvellous adj **1** *his solo climb was marvellous* amazing, astounding, astonishing, awesome, breathtaking, sensational, remarkable, spectacular, stupendous, phenomenal, wondrous, prodigious, miraculous, extraordinary. **2** *he's a marvellous singer* excellent, splendid, wonderful; *inf* magnificent, superb, glorious, super, great, smashing, fantastic, terrific, fabulous, fab, brill, awesome, ace, mean, bad, wicked; *Amer inf* boffo.

masculine adj **1** *that's a masculine trait* male, manly, manlike, virile, of men, man's, men's, male-oriented. **2** *she likes masculine men* manly, all-male, virile, robust, vigorous, muscular, strapping, rugged; *inf* macho. *see* MANLY 2. **3** *he has all the masculine virtues* manful, brave, courageous, gallant, heroic, valiant, bold, fearless, stout-hearted; *inf* macho, Ramboesque. *see* MANLY 1. **4** *masculine woman* mannish, manlike, unfeminine, unwomanly, Amazonian; *inf* butch, dyke.

masculinity n **1** *admire the masculinity of his physique* manliness, virility, robustness, vigour, muscularity, ruggedness. *see* MANLINESS 2. **2** *show their masculinity in battle* manliness, manhood, bravery, courage, courageousness, heroism, intrepidity, mettle, fortitude. *see* MANLINESS 1.

mash v *mash the potatoes* crush, pulp, purée, smash, squash, pound, beat.

mash n *feed the mash to the dogs* pulp, mush, paste, purée, slush, pap.

mask n **1** *wearing masks to the party* false face, domino, visor. **2** *wearing masks for protection* protective mask, swimming mask, snorkel mask, gas mask, safety goggles, fencing mask, skier's mask, surgical mask, visor. **3** *under the mask of being a tourist* disguise, guise, concealment, cover, cover-up, cloak, camouflage, veil, screen, front, false front, façade, blind, semblance, false colours, pretence.

mask v *mask her identity/feelings* disguise, hide, conceal, cover up, obscure, cloak, camouflage, veil, screen.

mass n **1** *a mass of wood/cloud* concretion, lump, block, chunk, hunk, piece; *inf* wodge. **2** *gathered in a mass | a mass of fibres* concentration, conglomeration, aggregation, amassment, assemblage, collection. **3** *men in the mass* total, totality, whole, entirety, aggregate. **4** *a mass of people | masses of people/toys* many, a large number, an abundance, a profusion, numerous, countless, myriad, a multitude, group, crowd, mob, horde, throng, host, troop; *inf* a lot, lots, scads, piles, heaps, bags, tons. *see* MANY adj, n. **5** *the mass of people voted against* majority, greater part, major part, most, bulk, main body, preponderance, almost all, lion's share. **6** *measure the mass of the body* size, magnitude, bulk, dimension, capacity, greatness, bigness.

mass adj *mass hysteria/suicide | the mass media* wholesale, universal, widespread, general, large-scale, extensive, pandemic, popular.

mass v **1** *clouds massing* amass, accumulate, assemble, gather, collect, draw together, join together. **2** *generals massing their troops* assemble, gather together, marshal, muster, rally, round up, mobilize.

massacre n mass slaughter, wholesale slaughter, slaughter, wholesale/indiscriminate killing, mass murder, mass homicide, mass slaying, mass execution, mass destruction, carnage, butchery, blood bath, annihilation, extermination, liquidation, decimation, pogrom, genocide, ethnic cleansing, holocaust.

massacre v slaughter, butcher, slay, murder, kill, annihilate, exterminate, liquidate, decimate, eliminate, kill off, wipe out, mow down, cut down, cut to pieces.

massage n *have a massage to relieve aches and pains* rub, rub-down, rubbing, kneading, pummelling, palpation, manipulation; refloxology, acupressure, shiatsu, aromatherapy.

massage v *massage stiff limbs* rub, rub down, knead, pummel, palpate, manipulate.

masses npl the common people, the populace, the proletariat, the multitude, the commonality, the crowd, the mob, the rabble, *hoi polloi*, the *canaille*; *inf* the great unwashed.

massive adj huge, immense, enormous, vast, mighty, extensive, gigantic, colossal, mammoth, monumental, elephantine, mountainous, gargantuan, king-size, monstrous, prodigious, titanic, hulking, bulky, weighty, hefty, solid, substantial, big, large, great; *inf* ginormous, whopping, humongous.

mast n **1** *a ship's mast* spar, boom, yard, gaff, foremast, mainmast, topmast, mizzenmast, mizzen. **2** *the mast on top of the building* flagpole, flagstaff, pole, post, support, upright.

master n **1** *master of the household/hunt | the dog's master* lord and master, lord, overlord, ruler, overseer, superintendent, director, manager, controller, governor, commander, captain, chief, head, headman, principal, owner, employer; *inf* boss, top dog, big cheese; *Amer inf* honcho. **2** *master of the ship* captain, skipper, commander. **3** *pupils being taught by the master* schoolmaster, headmaster, teacher, schoolteacher, tutor, instructor, pedagogue, preceptor. **4** *a master of innuendo | a tennis master* expert, adept, professional, authority, pundit, genius, master-hand, maestro, virtuoso, prodigy, pastmaster, grand master, wizard; *inf* ace, pro, dab hand; *Amer inf* maven. **5** *students/ followers sitting at the feet of the master* guru, teacher, spiritual leader, guide, swami, Roshi.

master adj **1** *master craftsmen* masterly, expert, adept, proficient, skilled, skilful, deft, dexterous, practised, experienced; *inf* crack. **2** *master spirit/plan* controlling, ruling, directing, commanding, dominating. **3** *master bedroom* chief, main, principal, leading, prime, predominant, foremost, great, most important.

master v **1** *master one's horse/emotions* conquer, vanquish, defeat, overcome, overpower, triumph over, subdue, subjugate, govern, quell, quash, suppress, control, curb, check, bridle, tame. **2** *master the technique* learn, learn thoroughly, become proficient in, acquire skill in, grasp; *inf* get the hang of, get clued up about.

masterful adj **1** *masterful men marrying meek women* dominating, authoritative, powerful, controlling, domineering, tyrannical, despotic, dictatorial, overbearing, overweening, imperious, peremptory, highhanded, arrogant, haughty. **2** *masterful handling of the situation* masterly, expert, consummate, clever, adept, adroit, skilful, skilled, proficient, deft, dexterous, accomplished, polished, excellent, superlative, first-rate, fine, talented, gifted; *inf* crack, ace.

masterly adj *masterly handling of the situation* masterful, expert, consummate, adept, skilful, deft, dexterous, accomplished, polished, excellent, superlative, first-rate, talented, gifted; *inf* crack, ace. *see* MASTERFUL 2.

mastermind v *mastermind the project* direct, manage, plan, organize, arrange, engineer, conceive, devise, forge, originate, initiate, think up, come up with, have the bright idea of; *inf* be the brains behind.

mastermind n *the mastermind behind the plan* genius, intellect, author, architect, engineer, director, planner, organizer, deviser, originator, manager, prime mover; *inf* brain, brains, brainbox.

masterpiece n *magnum opus*, master-work, *chef-d'oeuvre*, work of art, creation, *pièce de résistance*.

master-stroke n stroke of genius, *tour de force*, *coup de maître*, successful manoeuvre, feat of triumph, triumph, victory, complete success.

mastery n **1** *gain mastery over the enemy | master over his emotions* control, domination, command, ascendancy, supremacy, superiority, triumph, victory, the upper hand, the whip hand, rule, government, power, authority, jurisdiction, dominion, sovereignty. **2** *admire his mastery of the language* command, grasp, knowledge, familiarity with, understanding, comprehension, expertise, skill, prowess, proficiency, ability, capability; *inf* know-how.

masticate v chew, munch, champ, chomp, crunch, eat.

masturbation n auto-eroticism, onanism, self-abuse, self-gratification; *inf* playing with oneself.

mat n **1** *wipe one's feet on the mat* doormat, welcome mat, rug, carpet. **2** *a mat of hair* mass, tangle, knot, mesh.

mat v *the blood had matted her hair* tangle, entangle, knot, ravel.

match n **1** *a tennis/boxing match* contest, competition, game, tournament, bout, event, test, trial, meet. **2** *she's no match for the champion* equal, equivalent, peer, counterpart, rival, competitor. **3** *this glove is a match for that one* mate, fellow, companion, twin, counterpart, pair, complement. **4** *the new one is an exact match for the previous one* look-alike, double, twin, duplicate, copy, replica; *inf* spitting image, spit and image, spit, dead spit, ringer, dead ringer. **5** *make a good match* marriage, union, partnership, pairing, alliance, affiliation, combination.

match v **1** *curtains which match the walls | their stories match each other* complement, blend with, harmonize with, go with, tone with, coordinate with, team with, tally with, correspond to, accord with. **2** *these socks don't match* be a pair, be a set, be the same. **3** *her strength matches his* be equal to, be a match for, measure up to, rival, vie with, compete with, compare with, parallel, be in the same category as, keep pace with, keep up with. **4** *match him with one of her friends* | *match the socks* marry, pair up, mate, couple, unite, join, combine, link, ally; *inf* hitch up, yoke.

matching adj corresponding, equivalent, complementing, parallel, analogous, complementary, harmonizing, blending, toning, coordinating, the same, paired, twin, coupled, double, duplicate, identical, like.

matchless adj unmatched, incomparable, beyond compare, unequalled, without equal, unrivalled, unparalleled, unsurpassed, inimitable, peerless, unique, consummate, perfect, transcendent.

matchmaker n marriage broker, go-between, marriage bureau, dating agency.

mate n **1** *his mates gave him a leaving present* workmate, fellow worker, co-worker, associate, colleague, companion, compeer. **2** *he goes out with his mates on Saturdays* friend, companion, comrade, crony; *inf* pal, chum, buddy; *dial* marrow. **3** *he/she is looking for a mate* husband, wife, spouse, partner, companion, helpmate, live-in lover; *inf* significant other, POSSLQ (= person of the opposite sex sharing living quarters), other half, better half. **4** *where's the mate of this sock?* fellow, twin, match, companion, pair, one of a pair, other half, equivalent. **5** *a plumber's mate* assistant, helper, apprentice, subordinate.

mate v **1** *animals mating* breed, copulate, couple. **2** *mate the animals* bring together, pair, couple, join.

material n **1** *organic/nuclear material* matter, substance, stuff, medium, constituent elements. **2** *clothes of strong material* fabric, cloth, stuff, textile. **3** *enough material for a book* data, information, facts, facts and figures, evidence, details, notes; *inf* info, gen.

material adj **1** *the material, rather than the spiritual, world* corporeal, physical, bodily, fleshly, tangible, substantial, concrete. **2** *material pleasures* non-spiritual, physical, bodily, fleshly, worldly, earthly, temporal. **3** *material facts* important, of consequence, consequential, momentous, weighty, vital, essential, indispensable, key, significant, meaningful. **4** *material evidence* relevant, applicable, pertinent, apposite, germane, apropos.

materialize v **1** *our plans did not materialize* come into being, happen, occur, come about, come to pass, take place; *inf* shape up. **2** *the guests did not materialize* appear, turn up, become visible, come into view, come into sight, show oneself/itself, present oneself/itself, reveal oneself/itself, come to light, emerge.

materially adv *not materially affected by the plans* significantly, much, greatly, to a great extent, considerably, substantially, essentially, fundamentally, seriously, gravely.

maternal adj **1** *maternal feelings* motherly, protective. *see* MOTHERLY. **2** *his maternal grandparents* on one's mother's side, on the distaff side.

maternity n motherhood, motherliness.

mathematical adj **1** *mathematical problems* arithmetical, numerical, statistical, algebraic, geometrical, trigonometrical. **2** *with mathematical care* precise, exact, rigorous, unerring, correct, strict, meticulous, scrupulous, careful.

matrimonial adj *matrimonial home/dispute* marital, marriage, wedding, conjugal, connubial, nuptial, spousal, married, wedded.

matrimony n holy matrimony, marriage, wedlock, union.

matted adj tangled, entangled, knotted, tousled, dishevelled, uncombed.

matter n **1** *organic/waste matter* material, substance, stuff, medium. **2** *concentrate on the matter, not the style* content, subject matter, text, argument, substance, sense, thesis. **3** *no laughing matter* affair, business, proceeding, situation, circumstance, event, happening, occurrence, incident, episode, occasion, experience. **4** *discuss important matters* subject, topic, issue, question, point, case, concern, theme. **5** *issues of little matter* importance, consequence, significance, note, import, moment, weight. **6** *wounds full of matter* pus, suppuration, purulence, discharge; *Tech* sanies. **as a matter of fact** actually, in actual fact, in fact, in point of fact, really, in truth, to tell the truth, truly. **no matter** it does not matter, it makes no difference/odds, it is unimportant, never mind, don't worry about it. **the matter** *is anything the matter?* | *what is the matter?* | *there is nothing the matter* trouble, upset, distress, worry, problem, difficulty, complication.

matter v *your lateness/wealth doesn't matter* be of importance, be of consequence, make a difference, make any difference, signify, be relevant, carry weight, count.

matter-of-fact adj factual, literal, prosaic, down-to-earth, straightforward, plain, mundane, unembellished, unvarnished, unimaginative, uncreative, unemotional, unsentimental, deadpan, flat, dull, dry, pedestrian, lifeless, humdrum.

mature adj **1** *mature human beings* adult, grown-up, grown, fully grown, full-grown, of age. **2** *young people becoming very mature* sensible, responsible, wise, discriminating, shrewd, practical, sagacious. **3** *mature fruits/ cheese* ripe, ripened, mellow, ready, seasoned. **4** *our plans are now mature* complete, finished, finalized, developed, prepared, ready.

mature v **1** *when the children have matured* grow up, develop fully, become adult, reach adulthood, be fully grown, be fullgrown, come of age. **2** *when the young people have matured* become sensible/responsible/ wise/discriminating. *see* MATURE adj 2. **3** *when the fruit/cheese has matured* ripen, grow ripe, become ripe, become mellow, mellow, maturate. **4** *our plans gradually matured* be complete, be finished, be fully developed, maturate. *see* MATURE adj 4.

maturity n **1** *children reaching maturity* matureness, adulthood, manhood/womanhood, puberty, full growth, majority, coming-of-age. **2** *the maturity of the young people* matureness, sensibleness, sense of responsibility, responsibleness, wisdom, discrimination, shrewdness, practicality, sagacity. **3** *the maturity of the fruit/cheese* matureness, ripeness, mellowness. **4** *the maturity of our plans* matureness, completion, finalization, developed state, preparedness, readiness.

maudlin adj mawkish, sentimental, oversentimental, sickeningly sentimental, tearful, lachrymose; *inf* weepy, soppy, mushy, slushy, schmaltzy.

maul v **1** *mauled by a lion* tear to pieces, claw, lacerate, mutilate, mangle. **2** *mauling the women present* handle roughly, handle clumsily, manhandle, paw, molest. **3** *fathers mauling children* beat, batter, thrash, illtreat; *inf* belt, wallop, clobber, rough up, kick about. **4** *his book was mauled by the critics* censure, condemn, find fault with, give a bad press to, take to pieces; *inf* knock, slate, slam, pan, lambaste.

mausoleum n tomb, sepulchre, crypt, charnel-house.

maverick n nonconformist, rebel, dissenter, dissident, individualist, bohemian, eccentric; *inf* trend-setter.

mawkish adj maudlin, oversentimental, sickeningly sentimental, lachrymose; *inf* mushy, slushy, schmaltzy. *see* MAUDLIN.

maxim n aphorism, proverb, adage, saw, saying, axiom, precept, epigram, gnome.

maximum n *reach its maximum* most, utmost, uttermost, extremity, upper limit, height, ceiling, top, summit, peak, pinnacle, crest, apex, vertex, apogee, acme, zenith.

maximum adj *the maximum amount* highest, greatest, biggest, largest, topmost, most, utmost, supreme, maximal.

maybe adv perhaps, it could be that, possibly; *dial* happen; *lit* peradventure.

mayhem n havoc, disorder, confusion, chaos, bedlam, destruction, violence, trouble, disturbance, commotion, tumult, pandemonium.

maze n **1** *a maze in the castle grounds* labyrinth, network of paths. **2** *a maze of regulations* network, mesh, web, jungle, tangle, confusion, snarl, imbroglio.

meadow n field, grassland, pasture, paddock, lea.

meagre adj **1** *meagre supplies* paltry, sparse, scant, scanty, spare, inadequate, insufficient, insubstantial, exiguous, short, little, small, slight, slender, poor, puny, skimpy, scrimpy, miserly, niggardly, stingy, pathetic; *inf* measly, as scarce as hens' teeth. **2** *meagre bodies* thin, lean, emaciated, skinny, spare, scrawny, scraggy, bony, gaunt, starved, underfed.

meagreness n paltriness, sparseness, scarcity, scantiness, inadequacy, insufficiency, exiguity, shortness, slightness, skimpiness, miserliness, stinginess; *inf* measliness. *see* MEAGRE.

meal n repast, collation, banquet, feast, picnic, barbecue, buffet; *inf* blow-out.

mean¹ v **1** *what do the words mean?* indicate, signify, betoken, express, convey, denote, designate, spell out, show, stand for, represent, symbolize, portend, connote, imply, purport, suggest, allude to, intimate, hint at, insinuate, drive at. **2** *not mean to break it* intend, have in mind, have in view, contemplate, think of, purpose, plan, have plans, set out, aim, aspire, desire, want, wish. **3** *meant to be used | not meant for the army* intend, made, design, destine, predestine, fate. **4** *this will mean war* involve, entail, lead to, result in, give rise to, bring about cause, engender, produce. **5** *this means a lot to her* have importance, have significance, matter. **6** *dark clouds meaning rain* presage, portend, foretell, augur, promise, foreshadow.

mean² adj **1** *a mean old man* miserly, niggardly, parsimonious, tight-fisted, close-fisted, penny-pinching, penurious, grasping, greedy, avaricious, ungenerous, illiberal, close, near; *inf* stingy, tight, mingy, cheap. **2** *a mean creature* base, dishonourable, ignoble, disreputable, vile, sordid, foul, nasty, despicable, contemptible, abominable, odious, hateful, horrible. **3** *of mean understanding/intellect* inferior, poor, limited, restricted, meagre, scant. **4** *a mean hovel* shabby, poor, wretched, dismal, miserable, squalid, sordid, seedy, mangy, broken-down, run-down, dilapidated, down-at-heel; *inf* scruffy, grungy. **5** *a mean act | a mean old woman* nasty, disagreeable, unpleasant, unfriendly, offensive, obnoxious, cross, ill-natured, bad-tempered, irritable, churlish, surly, cantankerous, crotchety, crabbed, crabby, grumpy; *inf* grouchy. **6** *of mean birth | mean peasants* low, lowly, low-born, humble, modest, common, ordinary, base, proletarian, plebeian, obscure, undistinguished, ignoble.

mean³ n *find a mean between frankness and rudeness* mid-point, middle, median, norm, average, middle course, middle way, happy medium, golden mean.

mean³ adj *the mean temperature* middle, median, medial, average, normal, standard, medium, middling.

meander v **1** *meander about in the sunshine* wander, roam, ramble, rove, stroll, amble, drift; *inf* mosey/tootle along. **2** *rivers meandering through the country* wind, zigzag, snake, curve, turn, bend.

meandering adj **1** *meandering crowds* wandering, roaming, rambling. *see* MEANDER 1. **2** *meandering streams* winding, zigzag, snaking, serpentine, tortuous. **3** *meandering prose* rambling, tortuous, circuitous, indirect, roundabout, convoluted, anfractuous.

meaning n **1** *understand the meaning of what he said* signification, sense, message, import, drift, gist, essence, substance, purport, connotation, denotation, implication, significance, thrust. **2** *what is the meaning of the word?* definition, explanation, interpretation, elucidation, explication. **3** *it was not our meaning to delay him* intention, purpose, plan, aim, goal, end, object, objective, aspiration, desire, want, wish. **4** *his life has no meaning* significance, point, value, worth, consequence, account. **5** *a glance full of meaning* significance, implication, allusion, intimation, insinuation, eloquence, expression.

meaning adj meaningful, significant, pointed, eloquent. *see* MEANINGFUL 3.

meaningful adj **1** *a meaningful statement/ remark* significant, important, relevant,

material, valid, worthwhile. **2** *a meaningful relationship* significant, important, serious, sincere, in earnest. **3** *a meaningful glance* significant, pointed, suggestive, eloquent, expressive, pregnant.

meaningless adj **1** *meaningless babble* senseless, unintelligible, incomprehensible, incoherent. **2** *a meaningless act of violence* senseless, pointless, purposeless, motiveless, irrational, inane. **3** *lead meaningless lives* empty, futile, pointless, aimless, valueless, worthless, trivial, insignificant, inconsequential.

meanness n **1** *the meanness of the old man* miserliness, niggardliness, parsimony, parsimoniousness, tight-fistedness, penny-pinching, penury; *inf* stinginess, cheapness, tightness, minginess. *see* MEAN² 1. **2** *the meanness of the creature* baseness, vileness, sordidness, foulness, nastiness, contemptibility, abominableness, odiousness. *see* MEAN² adj 2. **3** *the meanness of his intellect* poorness, limitations, meagreness. *see* MEAN² 3. **4** *the meanness of the hovel* shabbiness, wretchedness, dismalness, misery, squalor, sordidness, seediness, dilapidation; *inf* grunginess. *see* MEAN² 4. **5** *an act of such meanness | the meanness of the old woman* nastiness, disagreeableness, unpleasantness, unfriendliness, crossness, bad temper, irritability, surliness, cantankerousness. *see* MEAN² 5. **6** *the meanness of her birth* lowness, lowliness, humbleness, commonness, baseness, obscurity, ignobility. *see* MEAN² 6.

means npl **1** *a means of getting there* way, method, expedient, process, mode, manner, agency, medium, instrument, channel, avenue, course. **2** *a man of means* money, capital, wealth, riches, affluence, substance, fortune, property. **3** *haven't the means to buy it* money, resources, capital, finance, funds, wherewithal; *inf* dough, bread, lolly. **by all means** of course, certainly, definitely, surely, absolutely. **by means of** *get the money by means of borrowing* through, by dint of, with the help of, with the aid of. **by no means** *by no means poor* in no way, not at all, not in the least, not in the slightest, not the least bit.

meantime adv **1** meanwhile, in the meantime, for the time being, for now. *see* MEANWHILE 1. **2** *meantime back at the ranch* at the same time. *see* MEANWHILE 2.

meanwhile adv **1** *meanwhile I shall wait* meantime, in the meantime, for the time being, for now, for the moment, in the intervening period, in the interim, in the interval, in the meanwhile. **2** *meanwhile* *back at the ranch* at the same time, simultaneously, concurrently, coincidentally.

measurable *adj* **1** *a measurable quantity of sand* assessable, gaugeable, estimable, appraisable, computable, quantifiable, fathomable. **2** *a measurable improvement* significant, appreciable, noticeable, visible, perceptible, obvious, striking, material.

measure *n* **1** *find the measure of the material* size, dimension, proportions, magnitude, amplitude, mass, bulk, volume, capacity, quantity, weight, extent, expanse, area, range. *see* MEASUREMENT 2. **2** *use a linear measure* system, standard, units, scale. **3** *use a measure to check the size* rule, ruler, tape-measure, gauge, meter, scale, level, yardstick. **4** *receive a measure of her father's estate* share, portion, division, allotment, part, piece, quota, lot, ration, percentage; *inf* rake-off. **5** *have a measure of wit* quantity, amount, certain amount, degree. **6** *sales are the measure of the company's success* yardstick, test, standard, touchstone, criterion, benchmark. **7** *take drastic measures* action, act, course, course of action, deed, proceeding, procedure, step, means, expedient, manoeuvre. **8** *announce measures to control crime* statute, act, bill, law, resolution. **9** *do what you like within measure* moderation, limit, limitation, bounds, control, restraint. **10** *poetic measure* metre, cadence, rhythm. **beyond measure** immeasurably, incalculably, infinitely, limitlessly, immensely, extremely, vastly, excessively. **for good measure** as a bonus, as an extra, into the bargain, to boot, in addition, besides, as well.

measure *v* **1** *measure the material/quantity* calculate, compute, estimate, quantify, weigh, size, evaluate, rate, assess, appraise, gauge, measure out, determine, judge, survey. **2** *measure one's words* choose carefully, select with care, consider, think carefully about, plan, calculate. **3** *measure one's work to one's time* adapt, adjust, fit, tailor. **4** *measure his strength against his brother's* pit, set, match, test, put into competition with. **measure out** mete out, measure, deal out, dole out, share out, divide out, parcel out, allocate, allot, apportion, assign, distribute, administer, dispense, issue. **measure up** **1** *measure up the windows for curtains* measure, take the measurements of, estimate the size of. **2** *he was sacked because he didn't measure up* come up to standard, fulfil expectations, fit/fill the bill, pass master, be capable, be adequate, be suitable; *inf* come up to scratch, make the grade, cut the mustard, be up to snuff. **3** *didn't mea-*

sure up to the requirements meet, come up to, be equal to, match, be on a level with.

measured *adj* **1** *measured amounts* measured out, calculated, computed, quantified. *see* MEASURE V 1. **2** *measured tread* regular, steady, even, rhythmical, slow, dignified, stately, sedate, leisurely, unhurried. **3** *measured words* carefully chosen, selected with care, well-thought-out, studied, calculated, planned, premeditated, considered, deliberate, reasoned.

measurement *n* **1** *the measurement of the quantity* calculation, computation, estimation, quantification, quantifying, weighing, sizing, evaluation, assessment, appraisal, gauging. *see* MEASURE V 1. **2** *take the first measurement at noon | the measurements of the carpet are wrong* size, dimension, proportions, magnitude, amplitude, mass, bulk, volume, capacity, extent, expanse, amount, quantity, area, length, height, depth, weight, width, range.

meat *n* **1** *vegetarians don't eat meat* flesh, animal flesh; beef, pork, lamb, mutton, veal, venison. **2** *meat and drink* food, nourishment, sustenance, provisions, rations, fare, viands, victuals, comestibles, provender, feed; *inf* grub, eats, chow, nosh, scoff. **3** *the meat of the matter* substance, pith, marrow, heart, kernel, core, nucleus, nub, essence, essentials, gist, fundamentals, basics; *inf* nitty-gritty, nuts and bolts.

meaty *adj* **1** *a meaty stew* meat-filled, fleshy. **2** *a meaty discussion/book* giving food for thought, substantial, pithy, meaningful, profound, deep, involved, interesting, significant.

mechanical *adj* **1** *a mechanical device* automated, automatic, machine-driven, motor-driven, power-driven. **2** *mechanical gestures* automatic, machine-like, unthinking, unconscious, unfeeling, unemotional, cold, involuntary, instinctive, routine, habitual, perfunctory, cursory, lacklustre, lifeless, unanimated, dead, casual, careless, inattentive, negligent.

mechanism *n* **1** *a mechanism for folding paper* machine, apparatus, appliance, tool, device, instrument, contraption, contrivance, gadget, structure, system. **2** *the mechanism of the car* motor, workings, works, gears, components; *inf* innards, guts. **3** *the mechanism for complaints* process, procedure, system, operation, method, technique, workings, means, medium, agency, channel.

meddle *v* interfere, butt in, intrude, intervene, interlope, pry, nose; *inf* stick one's nose in, horn in, snoop.

meddlesome adj meddling, interfering, intrusive, prying; *inf* snooping, nosy. *see* MEDDLE.

mediate v **1** *mediate between the warring factions* act as mediator, act as go-between, act as middleman/intermediary, arbitrate, negotiate, conciliate, intervene, intercede, interpose, moderate, umpire, referee, act as peacemaker, reconcile differences, restore harmony, make peace, bring to terms, step in. **2** *mediate a difference of opinion* settle, arbitrate, umpire, reconcile, resolve, mend, clear up, patch up. **3** *mediate a peace settlement* bring about, effect, effectuate, make happen, negotiate.

mediation n arbitration, negotiation, intervention, intercession, interposition, good offices, conciliation, reconciliation.

mediator n arbitrator, arbiter, negotiator, go-between, middle-man, intermediary, honest broker, peacemaker, intervenor, interceder, moderator, umpire, referee, judge, conciliator, reconciler.

medicinal adj *medicinal herbs|for medicinal purposes* medical, therapeutic, curative, healing, remedial, restorative, health-giving, analeptic.

medicine n **1** *given medicine* medication, medicament, drug, remedy, cure, physic. **2** *study medicine* medical science, practice of medicine, healing art. **take one's medicine** accept one's punishment, take the consequences of one's actions; *inf* get what is coming to one, take the rap, take it on the chin.

medieval adj **1** *medieval history* of the Middle/Dark Ages, Middle-Age, Dark-Age, Gothic. **2** *his attitude is medieval* antiquated, archaic, antique, obsolete, antediluvian, primitive, outmoded, outdated, old-fashioned, *passé*, unenlightened; *inf* out of the ark.

mediocre adj **1** *her work is mediocre* indifferent, average, middle-of-the-road, middling, ordinary, commonplace, pedestrian, run-of-the-mill, tolerable, passable, adequate, uninspired, undistinguished, unexceptional; *inf* so-so, fair-to-middling, nothing to write home about, no great shakes. **2** *mediocre goods/actors* inferior, second-rate, second-class, low-grade, poor, shabby, minor.

mediocrity n **1** *the mediocrity of her work* mediocreness, indifference, ordinariness, commonplaceness, passableness, lack of inspiration, unexceptionalness. *see* MEDIOCRE 1. **2** *the mediocrity of the goods* inferiority, second-rateness, poorness, shabbiness. *see* MEDIOCRE 2. **3** *they are mediocrities* nonentity, nobody, nothing, lightweight, cipher, second-rater; *inf* no-hoper.

meditate v **1** *he's meditating on/upon the past* engage in contemplation about, be in a thoughtful state about, contemplate, think about/over, muse on/about, ponder on/over, consider, concentrate on, reflect on, deliberate about/on, ruminate about/on/over, brood over, mull over, be in a brown study over; *inf* put on one's thinking cap about. **2** *he's meditating leaving/revenge* think about, consider, have in mind, intend, plan, project, design, devise, scheme, plot.

meditation n contemplation, thought, musing, pondering, consideration, reflection, deliberation, rumination, brooding, mulling over, reverie, brown study, concentration.

medium n **1** *find the medium between two extremes* mean, median, mid-point, middle, centre point, average, norm, standard, middle way, middle course, middle ground, compromise, happy medium, golden mean. **2** *through the medium of television|want to use wood as an artistic medium* means of communication, means/mode of expression, means, agency, channel, avenue, vehicle, organ, instrument, instrumentality. **3** *organisms growing in their natural medium* habitat, element, environment, surroundings, milieu, setting, conditions, atmosphere. **4** *visit a medium to contact the dead* spiritualist, spiritist, necromancer.

medium adj **1** *in the medium position* middle, mean, medial, median, midway, mid-point, intermediate. **2** *of medium height* average, middling.

medley n assortment, miscellany, mixture, *mélange*, variety, collection, motley collection, pot-pourri, conglomeration, jumble, confusion, mishmash, hotchpotch, hodge-podge, pastiche, patchwork, farrago, gallimaufry, olio, salmagundi, mixed bag, mix; *inf* omnium gatherum.

meek adj **1** *meek, Christian people* patient, long-suffering, forbearing, resigned, gentle, peaceful, docile, modest, humble, unassuming, unpretentious. **2** *meek people being bullied by the strong* submissive, yielding, unresisting, compliant, acquiescent, deferential, weak, timid, frightened, spineless, spiritless; *inf* weak-kneed.

meekness n **1** *Christian meekness* patience, forbearance, resignation, gentleness, peacefulness, docility, modesty, humility, humbleness. *see* MEEK 1. **2** *the meekness of the pupils faced by bullies* submissiveness, lack of resistance, compliance, acquiescence, deference, weakness, timidity, fearfulness, spinelessness, lack of spirit.

meet v **1** *meet friends for tea | met an old friend on the train* encounter, come face to face with, make contact with, run into, run across, come across, come upon, chance upon, happen upon, light upon; *inf* bump into. **2** *where the land and sea meet* come together, abut, adjoin, join, link up, unite, connect, touch, converge, intersect. **3** *the committee met on Saturday* gather, assemble, come together, forgather, congregate, convene, convoke, muster, rally. **4** *meet the proposal with hostility* deal with, handle, treat, cope with, approach, answer. **5** *meet the demands of the job* satisfy, fulfil, measure up to, come up to, comply with. **6** *meet one's responsibilities* carry out, perform, execute, discharge, take care of. **7** *meet the cost* pay, settle, honour, square. **8** *meet death bravely* face, encounter, undergo, experience, go through, bear, suffer, endure. **9** *meet the enemy at dawn* encounter, confront, engage, engage in battle with, join battle with, clash with, fight with.

meeting n **1** *the meeting of the two friends/ lovers* encounter, contact, assignation, rendezvous, tryst. **2** *address the meeting* gathering, assembly, conference, congregation, convention, convocation, conclave; *inf* get-together. **3** *the meeting of land and sea* abutment, junction, conjunction, union, convergence, confluence, concourse, intersection. **4** *crowds flocking to the meeting* meet, race-meeting, athletics meeting, sports meeting.

melancholic, melancholy adj despondent, dejected, depressed, down, downhearted, downcast, disconsolate, glum, gloomy, sunk in gloom, miserable, dismal, dispirited, low, in low spirits, in the doldrums, blue, mournful, lugubrious, woeful, woebegone, doleful, sorrowful, unhappy, heavy-hearted, low-spirited, sombre, pensive, defeatist, pessimistic; *inf* down in the dumps, down in the mouth.

melancholy n despondency, dejection, depression, gloom, gloominess, misery, low spirits, doldrums, blues, woe, sadness, sorrow, unhappiness, pensiveness, defeatism, pessimism, melancholia; *inf* dumps.

mélange n assortment, miscellany, mixture, medley, variety, motley collection, conglomeration, jumble, mishmash, hotchpotch, hodgepodge, farrago, mixed bag. *see* MEDLEY.

mêlée n fight, quarrel, fracas, affray, fray, rumpus, commotion, tumult, brawl, scuf-fle, struggle, skirmish, free-for-all, tussle; *inf* set-to, shindy, shindig.

mellifluous adj *speak in mellifluous tones* sweet, sweet-sounding, sweet-toned, dulcet, honeyed, mellow, soft, soothing, smooth, silvery, euphonious, musical.

mellow adj **1** *mellow fruit* ripe, mature, well-matured, soft, juicy, tender, luscious, sweet, full-flavoured, flavoursome. **2** *a mellow, tuned voice* dulcet, sweet, sweet-sounding, tuneful, euphonious, melodious, mellifluous, smooth, full, rich, well-rounded. **3** *a mellow old man* gentle, easygoing, pleasant, kindly, kind-hearted, amicable, amiable, good-natured, affable, gracious. **4** *in a mellow mood* genial, jovial, jolly, cheerful, happy, merry. **5** *feeling mellow after two glasses of wine* tipsy; *inf* happy, merry.

melodious adj melodic, musical, tuneful, harmonious, lyrical, dulcet, sweet, sweet-sounding, sweet-toned, silvery, silvery-toned, euphonious.

melodramatic adj theatrical, stagy, overdramatic, histrionic, oversensational, extravagant, overdone, over-emotional; *inf* actressy, camp, hammy.

melody n **1** *composing melodies* tune, air, strain, music, refrain, theme, song. **2** *not much melody in this music* melodiousness, tunefulness, musicality, harmony, lyricism, sweetness, euphony.

melt v **1** *solids melting* liquefy, dissolve, deliquesce, thaw, unfreeze, defrost, soften, fuse. **2** *the crowd melted away* disperse, vanish, vanish into thin air, fade away, disappear, dissolve, evaporate, evanesce. **3** *her charm melted the old lady | her charm melted the old lady's heart* soften, touch, disarm, mollify.

member n **1** *a member of the club* card-carrying member, adherent, associate, fellow. **2** *many victims had injured members* part of the body, organ, limb, appendage, extremity, arm, leg. **3** *a member of the mathematical set* element, constituent, component, part, portion.

membrane n sheet, layer, film, skin, tissue, pellicle, integument.

memento n souvenir, keepsake, reminder, remembrance, token, memorial, trophy, relic, vestige.

memoir n *write a memoir on World War II* account, historical account, monograph, record, chronicle, essay, narrative.

memoirs npl *write one's memoirs* autobiography, life story, life, memories, recollections, personal recollections, reminiscences, experiences, journal, diary.

memorable adj **1** *a memorable event/person* unforgettable, not to be forgotten, signal, momentous, significant, historic, notable, noteworthy, important, consequential, remarkable, outstanding, extraordinary, striking, impressive, distinctive, distinguished, famous, celebrated, illustrious. **2** *a memorable tune* unforgettable, catchy, striking.

memorandum n reminder, note, message, minute, *aide-mémoire; inf* memo.

memorial n **1** *install a memorial to him* monument, statue, plaque, cairn, shrine, tombstone. **2** *this will serve as a memorial of him* remembrance, memento, souvenir.

memorial adj *memorial service* remembrance, commemorative, commemorating, monumental.

memorize v commit to memory, remember, learn by heart, get by heart, learn off, learn, learn by rote.

memory n **1** *my memory of the events is faint | her memory is poor* remembrance, recollection, powers of recall, recall, reminiscence, powers of retention, retention. **2** *build a statue in memory of him* remembrance, commemoration, honour, tribute. **3** *a computer's memory* memory bank, storage bank, store, information store.

menace n **1** *an atmosphere full of menace* threat, ominousness, intimidation, warning, ill-omen, commination. **2** *he/it is a menace to the residents* threat, danger, peril, risk, hazard, jeopardy, source of apprehension/dread/fright/fear/terror. **3** *the child next door is a menace* nuisance, pest, source of annoyance, annoyance, plague, torment, troublemaker, mischief-maker.

menace v **1** *older boys menacing the young* threaten, intimidate, issue threats to, frighten, scare, alarm, terrify, bully, browbeat, cow, terrorize. **2** *bad weather menacing* loom, impend, lour, be in the air, be in the offing.

menacing adj **1** *a menacing look/silence* threatening, ominous, intimidating, frightening, terrifying, alarming, forbidding, minatory, minacious. **2** *a menacing storm* looming, louring, impending.

mend v **1** *mend the furniture* repair, fix, put back together, patch up, restore, rehabilitate, renew, renovate, make whole, make well, cure, heal. **2** *mend socks | mend a hole in the sweater* sew, stitch, darn, patch. **3** *the invalid will soon mend* get better, recover, recuperate, improve, be well, be cured, be

all right. **4** *try to mend matters/the situation* put right, set straight, rectify, put in order, correct, amend, emend, improve, make better, better, ameliorate, reform.

mendacious adj **1** *mendacious people* lying, untruthful, dishonest, deceitful, dissembling, insincere, disingenuous, hypocritical, fraudulent, unveracious, economical with the truth. **2** *mendacious tales* lying, untrue, false, fraudulent, fictitious, falsified, fabricated, invented, made up.

mendicant adj begging, cadging; *inf* scrounging, sponging; *Amer inf* mooching.

mendicant n beggar, beggarman/woman, tramp, vagrant, vagabond, cadger; *inf* scrounger, sponger; *Amer* hobo; *Amer inf* moocher, bum.

menial adj *menial duties/jobs* lowly, humble, low-grade, low-status, unskilled, routine, humdrum, boring, dull.

menial n servant, domestic servant, domestic, drudge, maid of all work, labourer, slave, underling, vassal, lackey, flunkey; *inf* dogsbody, skivvy, gofer.

menstruation n period, menses, menstrual cycle, monthly flow; *inf* the curse, monthlies, the usual.

mental adj **1** *mental work* intellectual, cerebral, brain. **2** *mental hospital/nurse* psychiatric. **3** *he's completely mental* mad, insane, deranged, disturbed, mentally unbalanced, mentally ill, mentally unstable, psychotic, lunatic; *inf* crazy, off one's head, off one's trolley, out to lunch.

mentality n **1** *of a slightly twisted mentality* cast of mind, frame of mind, turn of mind, way of thinking, way one's mind works, mind, psychology, mental attitude, outlook, character, disposition, make-up. **2** *of low-grade mentality* intellect, intellectual capabilities, intelligence, IQ (= intelligence quotient), brainpower, brains, mind, comprehension, understanding, wit, rationality, powers of reasoning; *inf* grey matter.

mentally adv in the mind, in the brain, in the head, intellectually, psychologically.

mention v **1** *he only mentioned it* allude to, refer to, touch on, speak briefly of, hint at. **2** *he mentioned your name* say, state, name, cite, quote, call attention to, adduce. **3** *don't mention this to anyone* tell, speak about/of, utter, communicate, let someone know, disclose, divulge, reveal, intimate, whisper, breathe a word of; *inf* let on about. **don't mention it** don't apologize, it doesn't matter, don't worry. **not to mention** not counting, not including, to say nothing of, aside from, as well as, besides, in addition to.

mention n **1** *made no mention of your request* | *a mention in the book* reference, allusion, observation, remark, statement, announcement, indication. **2** *a mention in dispatches* honourable mention, acknowledgement, citation, recognition, tribute.

mentor n guide, advisor, counsellor, therapist, guru, spiritual leader, confidant, teacher, tutor, coach, instructor.

menu n bill of fare, tariff, *carte du jour*; *inf* what's on.

mercantile adj commercial, trade, trading, marketable.

mercenary adj **1** *mercenary people interested only in money* money-oriented, grasping, greedy, acquisitive, avaricious, covetous, bribable, venal; *inf* money-grubbing. **2** *mercenary soldiers* hired, paid, bought, professional, venal.

mercenary n professional soldier, hired soldier, soldier of fortune; free lance, *condottiere*, galloglass.

merchandise n *damaged merchandise* goods, wares, stock, commodities, produce, vendibles.

merchandise v **1** *merchandise a wide range of goods* market, sell, retail, buy and sell, distribute, deal in, trade in, traffic in, do business in, vend. **2** *merchandise the new range* promote, advertize, publicize, push, puff, give a puff to, beat the drum for; *inf* hype, plug.

merchant n **1** *a fruit merchant* trader, dealer, trafficker, wholesaler, broker, seller, salesman/woman/person, vendor, retailer, shopkeeper, distributor. **2** *speed merchants* enthusiast, fan; *inf* freak, buff.

merciful adj lenient, clement, compassionate, pitying, forgiving, forbearing, sparing, humane, mild, soft-hearted, tender-hearted, kind, sympathetic, liberal, tolerant, generous, beneficent, benignant.

merciless adj unmerciful, ruthless, relentless, inexorable, harsh, pitiless, uncompassionate, unforgiving, unsparing, unpitying, implacable, barbarous, inhumane, inhuman, hard-hearted, heartless, callous, cruel, unsympathetic, unfeeling, illiberal, intolerant, rigid, severe, stern.

mercurial adj *mercurial child/temperament* volatile, capricious, temperamental, fickle, changeable, unpredictable, variable, erratic, quicksilver, inconstant, unstable, unsteady, fluctuating, wavering, vacillating, flighty, impulsive.

mercy n **1** *the mercy of the judge* leniency, clemency, compassion, compassionateness, pity, charity, forgiveness, forbearance, quarter, humanity, humaneness, mildness, soft-heartedness, tender-heartedness, kindness, sympathy, liberality, tolerance, generosity, beneficence, benignancy. **2** *thankful for small mercies* boon, favour, piece of luck, blessing, godsend. **at the mercy of 1** *at the mercy of the tyrant* in the power of, under/in the control of, in the clutches of. **2** *at the mercy of the storm* threatened by, prey to, open to, exposed to, defenceless against, unprotected against, vulnerable to.

mere adj *a mere child* nothing more than, no better than, no more important than, just a, only a, pure and simple.

merge v **1** *the two firms merged* join together, join forces, amalgamate, unite, combine, incorporate, coalesce, team up. **2** *merge the firms* join, amalgamate, unite, combine, incorporate, coalesce. **3** *the colours merged* blend, fuse, mingle, mix, intermix, homogenize. **4** *caused her personality to merge into his* run into, melt into, become assimilated into/in, become lost in, be swallowed up by, be buried in, be submerged in.

merger n amalgamation, combination, union, fusion, coalition, alliance, incorporation.

merit n **1** *the merit of his work* excellence, goodness, quality, high quality, worth, worthiness, value. **2** *the merits of the scheme* good point, strong point, advantage, asset, plus. **3** *receive his merits* what one deserves, desert, just deserts, due, right, reward, recompense.

merit v *merit a prize* deserve, be deserving of, earn, be worthy of, be worth, be entitled to, have a right to, have a claim to, warrant, rate, incur.

meritorious adj praiseworthy, laudable, commendable, admirable, estimable, creditable, excellent, exemplary, good, worthy, deserving.

merriment n cheerfulness, gaiety, high-spiritedness, high spirits, blitheness, buoyancy, carefreeness, levity, frolicsomeness, sportiveness, joy, joyfulness, joyousness, rejoicing, jolliness, jollity, jocundity, conviviality, festivity, merry-making, revelry, mirth, mirthfulness, glee, gleefulness, laughter, hilarity, amusement, fun.

merry adj **1** *merry children playing* cheerful, cheery, gay, in good spirits, high-spirited, blithe, blithesome, light-hearted, buoyant, carefree, frolicsome, sportive, joyful, joyous, rejoicing, jolly, jocund, convivial, festive, mirthful, gleeful, happy, glad, laughing. **2** *a merry tale* comical, comic, amusing, funny, humorous, facetious, hilarious. **3** *slightly merry after the party* tipsy, mellow; *inf* happy, tiddly, squiffy. **make merry** have fun, have a good time, enjoy oneself, have a party, party, celebrate, carouse, revel, rejoice; *inf* have a ball, make whoopee.

mesh n **1** *wire mesh | purse made of fine silk mesh* network, netting, net, tracery, web, lattice, latticework, lacework, trellis, reticulation, plexus. **2** *caught in the mesh of political intrigue* net, tangle, entanglement, web, snare, trap.

mesh v **1** *gears meshing* be engaged, connect, interlock. **2** *our ideas do not mesh* harmonize, fit together, go together, coordinate, match, be on the same wavelength, dovetail. **3** *mesh the prey* net, snare, ensnare, entangle, enmesh, trap, catch.

mesmerize v **1** *hypnotists mesmerizing people* hypnotize, put into a trance, put under. **2** *he was mesmerized by her beauty* hold spellbound, spellbind, entrance, enthral, bewitch, captivate, enchant, fascinate, grip, magnetize, hypnotize.

mess n **1** *clear up the mess in the kitchen* disorder, untidiness, disarray, dirtiness, filthiness, clutter, shambles, litter, jumble, muddle, chaos, confusion, disorganization, turmoil. **2** *have to get out of this mess* plight, predicament, tight spot, tight corner, difficulty, trouble, quandary, dilemma, muddle, mix-up, confusion, imbroglio, fine kettle of fish; *inf* jam, fix, pickle, stew, hole. **3** *what a mess he made of the project* muddle, botch, bungle; *inf* hash, muck, foul-up, screw-up, cock-up. **4** *cat's mess* dirt, excrement, faeces, excreta.

mess v **1** *mess up the kitchen* dirty, befoul, litter, besmirch, pollute, clutter up, disarrange, throw into disorder, dishevel. **2** *mess up the project* botch, bungle, muff, make a mess of, mar, spoil, ruin; *inf* make a hash of, make a muck of, muck up, foul up, screw up, cock-up. **3** *mess with the cutlery* fiddle, play, tinker, toy. **mess about, mess around** potter about, amuse oneself, pass the time, do nothing very much, fiddle about, play about, fool about; *inf* muck about.

message n **1** *leave a message | there's a telephone message for you* communication, piece of information, news, word, tidings, note, memorandum, letter, missive, bulletin, communiqué, dispatch; *inf* memo. **2** *the message of the sermon* meaning, import, idea, point, purport, intimation, theme, moral. **3** *be sent on a message* errand, task, job,

commission, mission. **get the message** get the point, get the drift, understand, comprehend, take the hint; *inf* understand what's what, catch on, get it, get the picture.

messenger n message-bearer, message-carrier, courier, errand-boy/girl, runner, envoy, emissary, agent, go-between, herald, harbinger.

messy adj untidy, disordered, dirty, filthy, grubby, slovenly, cluttered, littered, muddled, in a muddle, chaotic, confused, disorganized, in disarray, disarranged, dishevelled, unkempt; *inf* sloppy, shambolic.

metallic adj **1** *metallic goods* metal, made of metal, metal-like, iron, steel, stainless-steel. **2** *metallic sounds* grating, harsh, jarring, jangling, dissonant, raucous. **3** *metallic colours/paint* shiny, gleaming, lustrous, polished, burnished.

metamorphosis n transformation, transfiguration, change, alteration, conversion, change-over, mutation, transmutation, sea change; *inf* transmogrification.

metaphor n figure of speech, image, trope, allegory, analogy, symbol, emblem.

metaphorical adj non-literal, figurative, allegorical, symbolic, emblematic, emblematical.

mete v *mete out* deal out, dole out, measure out, divide out, allocate, allot, apportion, assign, distribute, administer, dispense, issue. *see* MEASURE v measure out.

meteoric adj *meteoric rise to fame* lightning, rapid, swift, fast, quick, speedy, overnight, sudden, dazzling, brilliant, spectacular, flashing, momentary, fleeting, transient, ephemeral, evanescent, brief, short-lived.

method n **1** *use old-fashioned methods* procedure, technique, system, practice, *modus operandi*, process, approach, way, course of action, scheme, plan, rule, arrangement, form, style, manner, mode. **2** *method in his madness* order, orderliness, sense of order, organization, arrangement, structure, form, system, planning, plan, design, purpose, pattern, regularity.

methodical adj **1** *a methodical approach* orderly, well-ordered, organized, systematic, structured, logical, well-regulated, planned, efficient, businesslike. **2** *a methodical person* organized, systematic, efficient, businesslike, meticulous, punctilious.

meticulous adj **1** *a meticulous proofreader* conscientious, careful, ultra-careful, scrupulous, punctilious, painstaking, demanding, exacting, thorough, perfectionist, fastidious, particular. **2** *a meticulous report* careful, exact, precise, detailed, thorough, rigorous, painstaking.

metropolis n capital, city, chief town.

mettle n **1** *men of a different mettle* calibre, character, disposition, nature, temperament, temper, personality, make-up, stamp, kind, sort, variety, mould, kidney. **2** *soldiers of mettle* courage, courageousness, bravery, gallantry, valour, intrepidity, fearlessness, boldness, daring, hardihood, grit, pluck, nerve, gameness, backbone, spirit, fortitude, indomitability; *inf* guts, bottle, spunk.

microscopic adj invisible to the naked eye, scarcely perceptible, infinitesimal, minuscule, tiny, minute.

midday n noon, twelve noon, twelve midday, twelve o'clock, high noon, noontide, noontime, noonday, twelve hundred, twelve hundred hours, one-two-double-O.

middle adj **1** *the middle point between two extremes* mid, mean, medium, medial, median, midway, halfway, central, equidistant. **2** *the middle ranks* intermediate, intermediary, intermedial.

middle n **1** *the middle of the line/scale* mean, median, mid-point, halfway point, centre, dead centre. **2** *in the middle of the crowd* midst, heart, centre, thick. **3** *have a thickening middle* midriff, waist, waistline.

middleman n intermediary, go-between, broker, distributor.

middling adj average, medium, ordinary, fair, moderate, adequate, passable, tolerable, mediocre, indifferent, run-of-the-mill, unexceptional, unremarkable; *inf* fair-to-middling, so-so.

midget n *midgets in circuses* dwarf, homunculus, manikin, gnome, pygmy, Tom Thumb; *inf* shrimp.

midget adj **1** *midget species of plants* dwarf, miniature, baby. **2** *midget beings/dogs* tiny, minute, very small, pocket, toy, pygmy.

midnight n twelve o'clock, twelve midnight, twelve at night, dead of night, the middle of the night, the witching hour.

midst n middle, centre, heart, bosom, core, kernel, nucleus, nub, interior, depths, thick.

midway adv halfway, in the middle, at the mid-point, in the centre, betwixt and between.

mien n look, appearance, aspect, aura, expression, countenance, demeanour, air, manner, bearing, carriage, deportment.

miffed adj annoyed, displeased, offended, aggrieved, piqued, nettled, vexed, irked, upset, hurt, put out, resentful, in a huff; *inf* narked.

might n force, power, strength, mightiness, powerfulness, forcefulness, potency, toughness, robustness, sturdiness, muscularity, vigour, energy, stamina, stoutness. **with might and main** with all one's strength, with everything one has got, as hard as one can, as hard as possible, with maximum force, full force, full blast, forcefully, powerfully, strongly, vigorously.

mighty adj **1** *a mighty figure of a man* | *struck a mighty blow* forceful, powerful, strong, lusty, manful, potent, tough, robust, sturdy, muscular, strapping, vigorous, energetic, stout. **2** *a mighty structure/mountain* huge, massive, vast, enormous, colossal, giant, gigantic, prodigious, monumental, mountainous, towering, titanic.

migrant adj migrating, migratory, travelling, roving, roaming, wandering, drifting, nomadic, itinerant, peripatetic, vagrant, gypsy, transient, unsettled, on the move.

migrant n vagrant, nomad, itinerant, traveller, gypsy, transient, rover, wanderer, drifter.

migrate v **1** *migrate to another place* emigrate, move, resettle, relocate, go abroad, go overseas. **2** *tramps migrating* travel, voyage, journey, trek, hike, rove, roam, wander, drift.

migratory adj migrant, migrating, travelling, roving, wandering, nomadic, itinerant, vagrant, transient, unsettled. *see* MIGRANT adj.

mild adj **1** *of a mild disposition* tender, gentle, soft, soft-hearted, tender-hearted, sensitive, sympathetic, warm, warm-hearted, compassionate, humane, forgiving, conciliatory, forbearing, merciful, lenient, clement, placid, meek, docile, calm, tranquil, serene, peaceful, peaceable, pacific, good-natured, amiable, affable, genial, easy, easygoing, mellow. **2** *mild winds* gentle, soft, moderate, warm, balmy. **3** *mild food* bland, spiceless, non-spicy, insipid, tasteless.

mildness n **1** *the mildness of her disposition* tenderness, gentleness, softness, sensitivity, warmness, compassion, meekness, docility, calmness, tranquillity, placidity, serenity, amiability, affability, geniality, mellowness. *see* MILD 1. **2** *the mildness of the winds* softness, moderation. *see* MILD 2. **3** *mildness of the food* blandness, lack of spiciness, insipidness, tastelessness.

milieu n environment, surroundings, background, setting, scene, location, sphere, element.

militant adj **1** *militant members of the organization* aggressive, assertive, vigorous, active, ultra-active, combative, pugnacious; *inf* pushy. **2** *militant groups/armies* fighting, warring, combating, contending, in conflict, clashing, embattled, in arms, belligerent, bellicose.

militant n **1** *militants in the party* activist, partisan. **2** *militants meeting on the battlefield* fighter, fighting man, soldier, warrior, combatant, belligerent, aggressor.

military adj *military forces* army, service, soldierly, soldierlike, armed, martial.

military n army, forces, armed forces, services, militia, soldiery, navy, air force, marines.

militate v **militate against** *his attitude will militate against him* operate against, go against, count against, tell against, weigh against, be detrimental to, be disadvantageous to, be to the disfavour of, be counter to the interests of, conflict with the interests of.

milk v **1** *milk sap from a tree* | *milk money from shopkeepers* draw, draw off, express, siphon, tap, drain, extract. **2** *milk the poor people* exploit, take advantage of, impose on, bleed, suck dry.

milksop n coward, weakling, namby-pamby; *inf* mummy's boy, sissy, pansy, wimp, scaredy-cat; *Amer inf* fraidy-cat.

milky adj *milky skin* white, milk-white, snow-white, whitish, creamy, pearly, nacreous, ivory, alabaster, off-white, clouded, cloudy.

mill n *workers employed at the mill* factory, plant, foundry, works, workshop, shop, industrial centre.

mill v *mill coffee/grain* grind, pulverize, pound, crush, powder, crunch, granulate, comminute, triturate. **mill around** *people milling around everywhere* move around, wander around, amble, meander, crowd, swarm, throng.

millstone n *a millstone round our necks* load, burden, weight, dead weight, onus, duty, tax, obligation, responsibility, trouble, misfortune, affliction, cross to bear, cross, albatross round one's neck.

mime n *take part in a mime* dumb show, mummery, pantomime.

mime v *mime his intentions* use gestures to indicate, gesture, indicate by dumb show, indicate by sign language.

mimic v **1** *mimic his friend* impersonate, give an impersonation of, imitate, copy, ape, caricature, parody; *inf* take off. **2** *the monkey's actions mimicked those of man* resemble, look like, have/take on the appearance of, echo, mirror, simulate.

mimic n mimicker, impersonator, impressionist, imitator, parodist, copyist, parrot, ape.

mince v **1** *finely minced beef* chop/cut into tiny pieces, grind, crumble, hash. **2** *she minces along, head in the air* walk affectedly, take tiny/baby steps, strike a pose, attitudinize, pose, posture, put on airs, be affected.

mincing adj affected, pretentious, overdone, over-dainty, effeminate, niminy-piminy, foppish, precious; *inf* sissy, la-di-da.

mind n **1** *be all in the mind* brain, head, seat of intellect, psyche, ego, subconscious. **2** *have an active mind* brainpower, powers of thought, intellect, intellectual capabilities, mentality, intelligence, powers of reasoning, brain, brains, wits, understanding, comprehension, sense, ratiocination; *inf* grey matter, brainbox. **3** *my mind was wandering* thoughts, thinking, concentration, attention, application, absorption. **4** *bring thoughts of him to mind* memory, recollection, remembrance. **5** *be of the same mind* opinion, way of thinking, thoughts, outlook, view, viewpoint, point of view, belief, judgement, attitude, feeling, sentiment. **6** *have a mind to go home* inclination, desire, wish, urge, will, notion, fancy, intention, intent, aim, purpose, design. **7** *of unsound mind* mental balance, sanity, senses, wits, reason, reasoning, judgement. **8** *one of the great minds* genius, intellect, intellectual, thinker; *inf* brain, egghead. **be in two minds** be undecided, be uncertain, be unsure, be hesitant, hesitate, waver, vacillate, dither, shilly-shally; be on the horns of a dilemma. **bear/keep in mind** remember, be mindful of, do not forget, take into consideration, consider, take cognizance of, take note of. **cross one's mind** occur to one, come to one, enter in one's mind/head, come into one's consciousness. **keep in mind** *see* MIND n bear in mind. **put in mind** remind, call up, conjure up, suggest. **to one's mind** in one's opinion, according to one's way of thinking, to one's way of thinking, from one's standpoint, in one's estimation, in one's judgement.

mind v **1** *didn't seem to mind their rudeness/smoking* be offended by, take offence at, object to, care about, be bothered by, be upset by, be affronted by, resent, dislike, disapprove of, look askance at. **2** *mind what the teacher says* take heed of, heed, pay heed to, be heedful of, pay attention to, attend to, concentrate on, listen to, note, take notice of, mark, observe, have regard for, respect, obey, follow, comply with, adhere to. **3** *mind your own business* attend to, pay attention to, concentrate on, apply oneself to, have regard for. **4** *mind the step | mind you don't cut yourself* be careful of, be cautious of, beware of, be on one's guard for, be wary of, be watchful of, watch out for, look out for, keep one's eyes open for, take care. **5** *mind you go* make sure, be sure, ensure that, take care, take care that; remember to, be sure to. **6** *mind the house/shop/baby* look after, take care of, attend to, tend, have charge of, keep an eye on, watch. **mind out** be careful, be cautious, beware, be on one's guard, be wary, be watchful, watch out, look out, keep one's eyes open, take care. **never mind** *never mind about the cost* do not bother about, pay no attention to, do not worry about, disregard, forget, do not take into consideration, do not give a second thought to.

mindful adj *mindful of her feelings* paying attention to, heedful of, watchful of, careful of, wary of, chary of, regardful of, taking into account, cognizant of, aware of, conscious of, alert to, alive to, sensible of.

mindless adj **1** *a mindless idiot* stupid, foolish, brainless, senseless, witless, empty-headed, unintelligent, dull, slow-witted, obtuse, weak-minded, feather-brained; *inf* birdbrained, dumb, dopey, moronic. **2** *mindless actions/violence* unthinking, thoughtless, careless, ill-advised, negligent, neglectful, brutish, barbarous, barbaric, gratuitous. **3** *mindless tasks* mechanical, automatic, routine.

mine n **1** *work in a mine* colliery, pit, excavation, well, quarry, lode, vein, deposit, coalmine, gold-mine, diamond-mine. **2** *the librarian/book is a mine of information* source, reservoir, quarry, repository, store, storehouse, abundant supply, wealth, mint; *inf* gold-mine. **3** *blown up by a mine* explosive, land-mine, depth charge. **4** *mines built under fortifications* tunnel, trench, sap.

mine v **1** *mine coal* excavate, quarry for, dig for, dig up, extract, unearth. **2** *armies mining* lay mines. **3** *mine a fortification* dig a mine/tunnel/trench/sap under, undermine, weaken.

miner n coalminer, collier, pitman, gold-miner.

mingle v **1** *mingle the water and wine | mingle the two colours* mix, blend, combine, compound, homogenize, merge, unite, join, amalgamate, fuse. **2** *the colours mingle* intermingle, mix, intermix, coalesce, blend, fuse, merge, unite, commingle. **3** *guests mingling at the party* circulate, socialize, hobnob, fraternize, associate with others, meet people.

miniature adj small-scale, scaled-down, mini, midget, baby, toy, pocket, dwarf, Lilliputian, reduced, diminished, small, tiny, wee, minute, minuscule, microscopic; *inf* pint-sized.

minimal adj minimum, least, least possible, smallest, littlest, slightest, nominal, token.

minimize v **1** *minimize the costs/work* keep at/to a minimum, reduce, decrease, curtail, cut back on, prune, slash. **2** *minimize the size* reduce, decrease, diminish, abbreviate, attenuate, shrink, miniaturize. **3** *minimize his achievement* belittle, make light of, decry, discount, play down, deprecate, depreciate, underestimate, underrate.

minimum n *reduce to the minimum* lowest level, bottom level, bottom, depth, nadir, least, lowest, slightest.

minimum adj *the minimum amount* minimal, lowest, smallest, littlest, least, least possible, slightest.

minion n **1** *the nobleman and his minions* lackey, flunkey, henchman, creature, toady, sycophant, flatterer, fawner, lickspittle, underling, hireling, servant, dependant, hanger-on, parasite, leech; *inf* yes-man, bootlicker. **2** *the queen's minion* favourite, pet, darling, jewel, apple of one's eye.

minister n **1** *government ministers* cabinet member, secretary, department chief. **2** *ministers saying prayers* minister of religion, clergyman, cleric, ecclesiastic, churchman, preacher, priest, vicar, parson, pastor, rector, curate, chaplain, padre. **3** *the British minister in Egypt* ambassador, diplomat, consul, plenipotentiary, envoy, emissary, legate, delegate, representative, chargé d'affaires, chargé.

minister v *minister to the patient | he ministered to their needs* administer to, attend to, tend, look after, take care of, see to, cater to, serve, accommodate, be solicitous of, pander to.

ministration n aid, help, assistance, succour, relief, support, backing, cooperation, service.

ministry n **1** *work for the ministry* government, cabinet, administration. **2** *go in for the ministry* Church, priesthood, holy

517

orders, pulpit. **3** *the ministry for foreign affairs* department, office, bureau.

minor adj **1** *a minor poet* little-known, unknown, lesser, insignificant, unimportant, inconsequential, inferior, lightweight, subordinate. **2** *suffer minor discomfort* slight, small, insignificant, unimportant, inconsequential, trivial, negligible, trifling. **3** *Smith minor* junior, younger.

minstrel n musician, singer, bard, troubadour; *lit* jongleur.

mint n **1** *earn a mint* fortune, small fortune, vast sum of money, millions, king's ransom; *inf* pile, stack, heap, packet, bundle, bomb. **2** *he is a mint of ideas* mine, source, reservoir, storehouse, wealth, gold-mine. *see* MINE n 2.

mint adj *in mint condition* brand-new, as new, unused, perfect, unblemished, undamaged, unmarred, untarnished, fresh, first-class; *inf* spanking new.

mint v **1** *mint coins* stamp, stamp out, punch, die, cast, strike, coin, monetize, make, manufacture, produce. **2** *mint new words* coin, invent, make up, fabricate, think up, dream up, hatch up, devise, fashion, forge, produce.

minute n **1** *I'll only be a minute | please wait a minute* moment, short time, second, instant; *inf* tick, jiffy. **2** *the minute he appeared* moment, instant, point, point in time, time, juncture, stage. **in a minute** in a short time, shortly, very soon, in a moment/second/trice/flash, in an instant, in the twinkling of an eye; *inf* in a tick/jiffy, in two shakes, in two shakes of a lamb's tail. **up to the minute** up to date, ultramodern, modern, fashionable, modish, stylish, in vogue, voguish, chic, in, all the rage; *inf* bang up to date, trendy, with it, now.

minute adj **1** *a minute creature* tiny, minuscule, microscopic, miniature, diminutive, Lilliputian, little, small; *inf* knee-high to a grasshopper. **2** *a minute difference* infinitesimal, negligible, trifling, trivial, paltry, petty, insignificant, inconsequential, unimportant, slight, minimal. **3** *in minute detail* detailed, exhaustive, meticulous, punctilious, painstaking, close, strict, exact, precise, accurate.

minutely adv *minutely dissected/discussed* in detail, exhaustively, meticulously, punctiliously, painstakingly, closely; *inf* with a fine tooth comb.

minutes npl record, proceedings, transactions, notes, transcript.

minutiae npl subtleties, niceties, finer points, particulars, minute detail, minor details, trivia, trifles, non-essentials.

miracle n wonder, marvel, prodigy, phenomenon, act of thaumaturgy.

miraculous adj **1** *Jesus performing miraculous feats* inexplicable, unaccountable, preternatural, superhuman, supernatural, fantastic, magical, thaumaturgic, phenomenal, prodigious, wonderful, wondrous, remarkable. **2** *it is miraculous that you have finished* amazing, astounding, remarkable, extraordinary, incredible, unbelievable; *inf* fantastic.

mirage n optical illusion, illusion, hallucination, phantasmagoria, phantasm.

mire n **1** *stuck in a mire* marsh, marshland, bog, peatbog, swamp, swampland, morass, quagmire, quag, slough, fen, fenland, bayou. **2** *mire all over their shoes* mud, slime, dirt, filth; *inf* muck. **in the mire** *in the mire over money* in difficulties, in trouble, having problems, in dire straits, in a mess; *inf* in a fix/hole.

mire v **1** *cars mired in the swamp* sink, sink down, bog down, stick in the mud. **2** *they are mired in financial problems* entangle, catch up, involve, bog down. **3** *children mired from playing outside* make muddy/dirty, cake with dirt/soil, begrime, besmirch.

mirror n **1** *the mirror on the wall* looking-glass, glass, reflector, reflecting surface; cheval-glass, rear-view mirror, wing mirror. **2** *he is a mirror of his father* reflection, twin, double, exact likeness, image, replica, copy, clone, match; *inf* spitting image, spit, dead ringer for.

mirror v *children mirroring his actions/statements* reflect, imitate, emulate, simulate, copy, follow, mimic, echo, ape, parrot, impersonate.

mirth n gaiety, merriment, high spirits, cheerfulness, cheeriness, hilarity, glee, laughter, jocularity, levity, buoyancy, blitheness, light-heartedness, joviality, joyousness, fun, enjoyment, amusement, pleasure, merry-making, jollity, festivity, revelry, frolics, sport.

mirthful adj gay, high-spirited, cheerful, cheery, hilarious, gleeful, laughter-filled, jocular, buoyant, carefree, blithe, light-hearted, jovial, joyous, fun-filled, enjoyable, amusing, pleasurable, merry, jolly, festive, frolicsome, sportive, playful.

misadventure n **1** *lost it through misadventure* accident, misfortune, bad luck, ill fortune, ill luck, poor/hard luck, mischance.

2 *be involved in a misadventure* accident, mishap, setback, disaster, tragedy, calamity, catastrophe, contretemps, debacle.

misanthropist n misanthrope, hater of mankind, recluse, hermit.

misapprehend v misunderstand, be mistaken, misinterpret, misconstrue, misread, miscalculate, get the wrong idea, get it wrong, receive a false impression, be under a delusion, get the wrong end of the stick, be barking up the wrong tree.

misapprehension n misunderstanding, mistake, error, mix-up, misinterpretation, misconstruction, misreading, misjudgement, misconception, misbelief, miscalculation, the wrong idea, a false impression, delusion.

misappropriate v **1** *misappropriate the firm's money* embezzle, steal, thieve, swindle, pocket, peculate, help oneself to; *inf* nick, pinch, lift. **2** *misappropriate the tools* misuse, misapply, misemploy, put to a wrong use.

misbegotten adj **1** *the king's misbegotten child* illegitimate, bastard, natural, born out of wedlock, born on the wrong side of the blanket. **2** *a misbegotten scoundrel* contemptible, disreputable, dishonourable, dishonest, base, wretched. **3** *their misbegotten plans* abortive, ill-conceived, ill-advised, ill-made, badly planned, badly thought-out, hare-brained.

misbehave v behave badly, be bad, be naughty, be disobedient, get up to mischief, misconduct oneself, be guilty of misconduct, be bad-mannered, show bad/poor manners, be rude, fool around; *inf* carry on, act up.

misbehaviour n misconduct, bad behaviour, disorderly conduct, badness, naughtiness, disobedience, mischief, mischievousness, delinquency, misdeed, misdemeanour, bad/poor manners, rudeness, fooling around; *inf* carrying on, acting up, shenanigans.

misbelief n **1** *religious misbelief* false belief, unorthodoxy, heresy. **2** *guilty of misbelief* wrong belief, delusion, illusion, fallacy, error, mistake, misconception, misapprehension.

miscalculate v *the answer is wrong—you have miscalculated* calculate wrongly, make a mistake, go wrong, err, blunder, be wide of the mark; *inf* slip up, make a booboo, boob.

miscarriage n **1** *the woman had a miscarriage* spontaneous abortion. **2** *the miscarriage of our plans* unsuccessfulness, failure, aborting, foundering, ruination, non-fulfil-

ment, misfiring. *see* MISCARRY 2. **3** *miscarriage of justice* failure, breakdown, mismanagement, perversion, thwarting, frustration.

miscarry v **1** *the woman miscarried* have a miscarriage, abort, have a spontaneous abortion, lose the baby. **2** *our plan miscarried* go wrong, go awry, go amiss, be unsuccessful, fail, misfire, abort, be abortive, founder, come to nothing, come to grief, meet with disaster, fall through, be ruined, fall flat; *inf* bite the dust, go up in smoke, go phut.

miscellaneous adj varied, assorted, mixed, diverse, sundry, variegated, diversified, motley, multifarious, jumbled, confused, indiscriminate, heterogeneous, farraginous.

miscellany n assortment, mixture, *mélange*, variety, collection, motley collection, medley, pot-pourri, conglomeration, jumble, confusion, mix, mishmash, hotchpotch, hodgepodge, pastiche, patchwork, farrago, gallimaufry, olio, salmagundi, mixed bag; *inf* omnium gatherum.

mischance n **1** *we lost it by mischance* accident, misfortune, bad luck, ill fortune, ill luck, poor luck, misadventure. **2** *a life full of mischances* misfortune, mishap, misadventure, setback, failure, disaster, tragedy, calamity, catastrophe, contretemps, debacle.

mischief n **1** *children getting up to mischief* mischievousness, naughtiness, badness, bad behaviour, misbehaviour, misconduct, pranks, wrongdoing, delinquency; *inf* monkey tricks, monkey business, shenanigans, goings-on. **2** *with mischief in her eyes* impishness, roguishness, rascality, devilment. **3** *do mischief to them | did mischief to their property* harm, hurt, injury, impairment, damage, detriment, disruption, trouble.

mischievous adj **1** *mischievous child* full of mischief, naughty, bad, badly behaved, misbehaving, disobedient, troublesome, vexatious, playful, frolicsome, rascally, roguish, delinquent. **2** *a mischievous smile* playful, teasing, impish, roguish, waggish, arch. **3** *mischievous gossip* malicious, spiteful, malignant, vicious, wicked, evil. **4** *with mischievous intent* hurtful, harmful, injurious, damaging, detrimental, deleterious, destructive, pernicious.

misconception n misapprehension, misunderstanding, mistake, error, misinterpretation, the wrong idea, a false impression, delusion. *see* MISAPPREHENSION.

misconduct n **1** *children guilty of misconduct* misbehaviour, bad behaviour, disorderly conduct, badness, mischief, naughtiness, misdeed, misdemeanour, wrongdoing, delinquency, rudeness. *see* MISBEHAVIOUR. **2** *doctors guilty of misconduct* professional misconduct, unprofessional behaviour, unethical behaviour, malpractice, impropriety, immorality. **3** *the misconduct of the affair* mismanagement, mishandling, misgovernment, misdirection.

misconstrue v misinterpret, put a wrong interpretation on, misunderstand, misapprehend, misread, misjudge, get it wrong, get the wrong idea, receive a false impression, take the wrong way, get the wrong end of the stick.

miscreant n villain, wrongdoer, criminal, evil-doer, sinner, scoundrel, wretch, reprobate, blackguard, rogue, rascal.

misdeed n wrongdoing, evil deed, crime, criminal act, misdemeanour, offence, error, peccadillo, transgression, sin.

misdemeanour n misdeed, wrongdoing, crime, offence, error, transgression. *see* MISDEED.

miser n skinflint, penny-pincher, niggard, cheese-parer, Scrooge; *inf* money-grubber, cheapskate, tightwad.

miserable adj **1** *feeling miserable* unhappy, sorrowful, dejected, depressed, downcast, down-hearted, down, despondent, disconsolate, desolate, wretched, glum, gloomy, dismal, blue, melancholy, low-spirited, mournful, woeful, woebegone, sad, doleful, forlorn, crestfallen; *inf* down in the mouth, down in the dumps. **2** *a miserable hovel* wretched, mean, poor, shabby, squalid, filthy, foul, sordid, seedy, dilapidated. **3** *miserable wretches* poverty-stricken, needy, penniless, impoverished, beggarly, destitute, indigent, down at heel, out at elbow. **4** *miserable scoundrels* contemptible, despicable, base, mean, low, vile, sordid, scurvy. **5** *miserable salaries/supplies* meagre, paltry, scanty, low, poor, niggardly, pathetic. **6** *miserable weather/conditions* unpleasant, disagreeable, displeasing, uncomfortable, wet, rainy, stormy.

miserly adj mean, niggardly, parsimonious, tight-fisted, close-fisted, penny-pinching, cheese-paring, penurious, grasping, greedy, avaricious, ungenerous, illiberal, close, near; *inf* stingy, mingy, tight, money-grabbing; *Amer* cheap.

misery n **1** *suffer/undergo misery* distress, wretchedness, hardship, suffering, affliction, anguish, torment, torture, agony, pain, discomfort, deprivation, poverty, grief, sorrow, heartbreak, heart-brokenness, despair, depression, dejection, desolation, gloom, melancholy, woe, sadness,

unhappiness. **2** *endure untold miseries* trouble, misfortune, adversity, affliction, ordeal, pain, sorrow, burden, load, blow, trial, tribulation woe, torment, catastrophe, calamity, disaster. **3** *he's a real old misery* killjoy, spoilsport, pessimist, prophet of doom, complainer, moaner; *inf* sourpuss, grouch, wet blanket, doom-merchant.

misfire v miscarry, go wrong, go awry, go amiss, fail, fall through; *inf* bite the dust, go up in smoke, go phut. *see* MISCARRY 2.

misfit n fish out of water, square peg in a round hole, nonconformist, eccentric, maverick; *inf* oddball, weirdo.

misfortune n **1** *by misfortune we got lost* bad luck, ill luck, ill fortune, poor/hard luck, accident, misadventure, mischance. **2** *endure many misfortunes* trouble, setback, reverse, adversity, reverse of fortune, misadventure, mishap, stroke of bad luck, blow, failure, accident, disaster, tragedy, affliction, sorrow, misery, woe, trial, tribulation, catastrophe, calamity.

misgiving n qualm, doubt, reservation, second thoughts, suspicion, distrust, anxiety, apprehension, unease, uncertainty, hesitation.

misguided adj **1** *their action was misguided* mistaken, deluded, erroneous, fallacious, wrong, unwarranted, uncalled-for, misplaced, ill-advised, unwise, injudicious, imprudent, foolish. **2** *misguided people believed him* misled, misdirected, misinformed, labouring under a delusion/misapprehension, deluded, ill-advised, foolish.

mishandle v **1** *mishandle the project* mismanage, misdirect, misgovern, misconduct, maladminister, bungle, botch, muff, make a mess of; *inf* make a hash of, make a pig's ear of, foul up, screw up. **2** *mishandle the prisoners* handle roughly, treat roughly, mistreat, maltreat, manhandle; *inf* rough up. *see* MALTREAT.

mishap n **1** *without further mishap* misfortune, ill luck, ill fortune, bad luck, poor/hard luck, accident, misadventure, mischance. **2** *after a series of mishaps* accident, trouble, setback, reverse, adversity, misadventure, misfortune, stroke of bad luck, blow, disaster, trial, tribulation, catastrophe, calamity.

mishmash n hotchpotch, hodgepodge, jumble, scramble, tangle, confusion, miscellany, mixture, medley, assortment, *mélange*, variety, collection, pot-pourri, pastiche, farrago, gallimaufry, olio, salmagundi, mixed bag; *inf* omnium gatherum.

misinform v give someone wrong information, mislead, misdirect, misguide, put on the wrong track; *inf* give someone a bum steer.

misinterpret v put a wrong interpretation on, misconstrue, misunderstand, misapprehend, misread, get something wrong, *inf* get the wrong end of the stick. *see* MISCONSTRUE.

misjudge v have a wrong opinion about, be wrong about, get the wrong idea about, get the wrong end of the stick about.

mislay v lose, misplace, put in the wrong place, lose track of, miss, be unable to find, be unable to lay one's hands on, forget the whereabouts of, forget where one has put something.

mislead v misinform, misguide, misdirect, delude, take in, deceive, fool, hoodwink, lead astray, throw off the scent, send on a wild-goose chase, pull the wool over someone's eyes; *inf* lead up the garden path, take for a ride.

misleading adj confusing, deceptive, deceiving, delusive, evasive, ambiguous, equivocal, fallacious, spurious, illusory, casuistic, sophistical.

mismanage v misdirect, mishandle, misgovern, misconduct, maladminister, bungle, botch, muff, make a mess of; *inf* make a hash of, make a pig's ear of, mess up, foul up, screw up.

misogynist n woman-hater, anti-feminist, male chauvinist, chauvinist; *inf* male chauvinist pig, MCP.

misplace v put in the wrong place, mislay, lose, be unable to find, be unable to lay one's hands on, *see* MISLAY.

misprint n printing error, typographical error, typing error, mistake, literal, corrigendum, erratum; *inf* typo.

misquote v *misquoted the president/speech/figures* misstate, misreport, misrepresent, distort, twist, falsify, garble, muddle.

misrepresent v give a false account of, give a false idea of, misstate, misreport, misquote, misinterpret, falsify, distort, garble.

misrule n **1** *accuse the government of misrule* bad government, misgovernment, mismanagement, misdirection, maladministration, negligence. **2** *misrule descended on the country* lawlessness, disorder, chaos, anarchy.

miss[1] v **1** *miss a shot* let go, bungle, botch, muff, fail to achieve. **2** *miss the bus* fail to catch/get, be too late for. **3** *miss the meeting* fail to attend, be too late for, absent oneself from, be absent from, play truant from, take French leave from; *inf* skip. **4** *miss an opportunity* fail to seize/grasp, let slip, let go, pass up, overlook, disregard. **5** *I'm sorry, I missed what you said* fail to hear/catch, fail to take in, mishear, misunderstand. **6** *did they miss their father* regret the absence/loss of, feel the loss of, feel nostalgic for, long to see, long for, pine for, yearn for, ache for. **7** *we did not miss the children until darkness fell* notice the absence of, find missing. **8** *try to miss the traffic* avoid, evade, escape, dodge, sidestep, steer clear of, give a wide berth to.

miss[1] n *one hit and three misses* failure, omission, slip, blunder, error, mistake, fiasco; *inf* flop.

miss[2] n girl, schoolgirl, young lady, lass, maiden, maid, damsel.

misshapen adj out of shape, deformed, malformed, ill-proportioned, misproportioned, twisted, distorted, contorted, warped, curved, crooked, wry, bent, hunchbacked.

missile n projectile, rocket, ballistic missile, weapon for throwing.

missing adj lost, mislaid, misplaced, nowhere to be found, absent, not present, gone, gone astray, unaccounted for.

mission n **1** *accomplish his mission* assignment, commission, task, job, errand, work, chore, business, undertaking, operation, duty, charge, trust, goal, aim, purpose. **2** *her mission in life is to heal the sick* vocation, calling, pursuit, quest, undertaking. **3** *a trade mission* delegation, deputation, task force, legation.

missionary n evangelist, converter, apostle, proselytizer, preacher, minister, priest.

missive n communication, message, letter, note, memorandum, bulletin, communiqué, report, dispatch; *inf* memo.

misspent adj dissipated, wasted, squandered, thrown away, prodigal.

mist n haze, fog, smog, cloud, vapour, condensation, steam, film; *dial* haar; *inf* peasouper.

mist v **mist over, mist up** become cloudy, cloud, cloud over, become hazy, haze over, become foggy, fog over, fog up, become blurred; steam up.

mistake n error, fault, inaccuracy, slip, blunder, miscalculation, misunderstanding, oversight, gaffe, *faux pas*, solecism, misapprehension, misreading; *inf* slip-up, bloomer, boob, booboo, howler, clanger.

mistake v **1** *mistake his meaning* get wrong, misunderstand, misapprehend, misinterpret, misconstrue, misread. **2** *mistake him for his brother* take someone for, mix someone up with, confuse someone with, misinterpret something as. **be mistaken** *you are mistaken* be wrong, be in error, be at fault, be under a misapprehension, be misinformed, be misguided, be wide of the mark, be barking up the wrong tree, get the wrong end of the stick.

mistaken adj *mistaken impressions/idea* wrong, erroneous, inaccurate, incorrect, false, fallacious, unsound, unfounded, misguided, misinformed, wide of the mark.

mistakenly adv by mistake, wrongly, in error, erroneously, incorrectly, falsely, fallaciously, misguidedly.

mistreat v maltreat, treat badly, ill-treat, ill-use, misuse, abuse, mishandle, harm, hurt, molest; *inf* beat up, rough up. *see* MALTREAT.

mistress n lover, live-in lover, girlfriend, partner, lady-love, paramour, kept women, concubine, inamorata.

mistrust v **1** *mistrust him | I mistrust his motives* feel mistrustful of, distrust, feel distrustful of, have doubts about, be suspicious of, suspect, have reservations about, have misgivings about, be wary of. **2** *mistrust his ability* have no confidence in, question, doubt, lack faith in.

mistrustful adj distrustful, doubtful, dubious, suspicious, chary, wary, uncertain, cautious, hesitant, sceptical; *inf* leery.

misty adj **1** *misty weather* hazy, foggy, cloudy. **2** *a misty shape* hazy, blurred, fuzzy, dim, indistinct, vague. **3** *a misty idea of what it is like* hazy, vague, obscure, nebulous.

misunderstand v misapprehend, misinterpret, misconstrue, misread, get the wrong idea, receive a false impression, get the wrong end of the stick, be barking up the wrong tree. *see* MISAPPREHEND.

misunderstanding n **1** *his misunderstanding of the statement* misapprehension, mistake, error, mix-up, misinterpretation, misconstruction, misreading, misconception, misbelief, the wrong idea, a false impression; *inf* the wrong end of the stick. *see* MISAPPREHENSION. **2** *the friends have had a misunderstanding* disagreement, difference, difference of opinion, clash of views, dispute, quarrel, argument, tiff, squabble, conflict; *inf* falling-out, spat, scrap.

misuse v **1** *misuse their talents/money* put to wrong use, misapply, misemploy, abuse, squander, waste, dissipate. **2** *misuse the chil-*

dren maltreat, mistreat, treat badly, ill-treat, ill-use, abuse, mishandle, manhandle, harm, hurt, bully, molest; *inf* beat up, rough up. *see* MALTREAT.

misuse n **1** *the misuse of their talents/money* wrong use, misapplication, misemployment, abuse, squandering, waste, dissipation. **2** *this misuse of the verb* misusage, malapropism, barbarism, catachresis. **3** *misuse of the children* maltreatment, mistreatment, ill-treatment, ill use, abuse, rough handling, mishandling, manhandling, bullying, injury, harm, molesting.

mitigate v alleviate, reduce, diminish, lessen, weaken, attenuate, allay, assuage, palliate, appease, soothe, relieve, ease, soften, temper, mollify, lighten, still, quieten, quiet, tone down, moderate, modify, extenuate, calm, lull, pacify, placate, tranquillize.

mitigating adj extenuating, exonerative, justificatory, justifying, vindicatory, vindicating, exculpatory, palliative, qualifying, modifying, tempering.

mix v **1** *mix cement | mix the water and the wine* admix, blend, put together, combine, mingle, compound, homogenize, alloy, merge, unite, join, amalgamate, fuse, coalesce, interweave. **2** *the two of them together just don't mix* be compatible, get along/on, be in harmony, be like-minded, be of the same mind; *inf* be on the same wavelength. **3** *he doesn't mix* socialize, mingle, associate with others, meet people. **4** *she mixes with all sorts* associate, mingle, have dealings, fraternize, hobnob. **mix up 1** *mix up the medicine* mix, blend, combine. **2** *mix up the dates* confuse, get confused, muddle, muddle up, get muddled up, get jumbled up, scramble, mistake. **3** *hush or you'll mix me up* confuse, throw into confusion, muddle, muddle up, fluster, upset, disturb. **4** *he is mixed up in the crime* involve, implicate, entangle, embroil, draw into, incriminate.

mix n mixture, blend, combination, compound, alloy, merger, union, amalgamation, fusion, coalition.

mixed adj **1** *a mixed collection* assorted, varied, miscellaneous, diverse, diversified, motley, heterogeneous. **2** *of mixed breed* hybrid, cross-bred, interbred, mongrel. **3** *have mixed reactions* ambivalent, equivocal, unsure, uncertain.

mixed-up adj *a mixed-up kid* maladjusted, ill-adjusted, disturbed, confused, muddled; *inf* screwed-up, untogether.

mixer n **1** *put it in the mixer* blender, food processor, liquidizer. **2** *she's shy but he's a* *mixer* socializer, mingler, social butterfly; *inf* life and soul of the party, party person.

mixture n **1** *pour out the mixture* compound, blend, mix, brew, combination, concoction, alloy. **2** *a mixture of objects* assortment, variety, *mélange*, collection, motley collection, medley, pot-pourri, conglomeration, jumble, mix, mishmash, hotchpotch, pastiche, farrago, mixed bag. *see* MISCELLANY. **3** *the dog is a mixture* cross, cross-breed, mongrel, hybrid.

mix-up n confusion, muddle, jumble, misunderstanding, mistake.

moan n **1** *the moans of the injured man* groan, lament, lamentation, wail, whimper, whine. **2** *the moan of the wind* groan, sigh, sough, murmur, whisper. **3** *tired of his moans* moans and groans, complaint, complaining, whine, whining, carping; *inf* grouse, grousing, gripe, griping, grouch, grouching, whinge, whingeing. beef, beefing.

moan v **1** *the injured man moans* groan, wail, whimper, whine. **2** *the wind moaning* groan, sigh, sough, murmur, whisper. **3** *always moaning about the weather* complain, whine, carp; *inf* grouse, gripe, grouch, whinge, beef.

mob n **1** *police tried to move the mob of spectators on* crowd, horde, multitude, rabble, mass, body, throng, host, pack, press, gang, drove, herd, flock, gathering, assemblage. **2** *despising the mob* the common people, the masses, the populace, the multitude, the commonality, the proletariat, the crowd, the rabble, *hoi polloi, the canaille*; *inf* the great unwashed. **3** *those gatecrashers left but another mob arrived* lot, group, set, troop, company; *inf* gang.

mob v **1** *mob the royal car* | *fans mobbed the football team* crowd around, swarm around, surround, besiege, jostle. **2** *mob the theatre* crowd into, cram full, fill to overflowing, fill, pack, throng. **3** *prisoners mobbing the murderer* set upon, attack, harass, fall upon, assault.

mobile adj **1** *the patient is mobile* able to move, able to move around, moving, walking, motile, ambulatory. **2** *a mobile face* expressive, animated, ever-changing, changeable. **3** *mobile shops* | *set up a mobile missile launcher* movable, transportable, portable, travelling, peripatetic, locomotive. **4** *socially mobile* moving, on the move, flexible, adaptable, adjustable.

mobilize v **1** *mobilize the troops* call up, call to arms, muster, rally, marshal, assemble, organize, make ready, prepare, ready.

2 *mobilize for action* get ready, prepare, ready oneself.

mock v **1** *rich children mocking the peasants* ridicule, jeer, at, sneer at, deride, treat with contempt, treat contemptuously, scorn, make fun of, poke fun at, laugh at, laugh to scorn, tease, taunt, twit, chaff, gibe at, insult, flout; *inf* rag, kid, rib, take the mickey out of. **2** *children mocking the crippled woman* | *they mocked their teacher's mannerisms* imitate, mimic, parody, ape, caricature, satirize, lampoon, burlesque; *inf* take off, send up. **3** *the wind mocked their attempts to proceed* defy, set at naught, thwart, frustrate, foil, disappoint.

mock adj *mock leather/money* imitation, artificial, simulated, synthetic, ersatz, so-called, fake, sham, false, spurious, bogus, counterfeit, forged, pseudo, pretended; *inf* pretend.

mockery n **1** *a note of mockery in his voice* ridicule, jeering, sneer, derision, contempt, scorn, disdain, teasing, taunting, gibe, insult, contumely; *inf* ribbing. **2** *the trial was a mockery* laughing-stock, farce, parody, travesty, caricature, lampoon, burlesque; *inf* take-off, send-up, spoof. **3** *his attempt to run was a mockery* travesty, inanity, act of stupidity, futile act, joke, laugh, apology, poor specimen.

mocking adj *a mocking smile* sneering, derisive, derisory, contemptuous, scornful, disdainful, sardonic, insulting, satirical.

mocks npl mock examinations/exams, trial examinations/exams, preliminary exams; *inf* prelims.

model n **1** *a model of a train* replica, representation, mock-up, copy, dummy, imitation, facsimile, image. **2** *this is the model of the projected sculpture/building* prototype, protoplast, archetype, type, mould, original, pattern, design, paradigm, sample, example, exemplar. **3** *this is the model of car I want* style, design, mode, form, mark, version, type, variety, kind, sort. **4** *she was a model as a teacher* | *a model of tact* ideal, paragon, perfect example, perfect specimen, exemplar, the epitome of something, *beau ideaal*, nonpareil, acme, *crème de la crème*; *inf* pick of the bunch. **5** *he used his wife as a model* artist's model, photographic model, sitter, poser, subject. **6** *she is a model in Paris* fashion model, mannequin; *inf* clothes-horse. **7** *this dress is a model* original design, original.

model adj **1** *the model building* prototypical, prototypal, archetypal, illustrative. **2** *a model teacher* ideal, perfect. *see* MODEL n **4**.

moderate adj **1** *moderate views* non-extreme, middle-of-the-road, non-radical, non-reactionary. **2** *moderate demands* non-excessive, reasonable, within reason, within due limits, fair, just. **3** *moderate behaviour* not given to excesses, restrained, controlled, temperate, sober, steady. **4** *moderate winds* temperate, calm, equable, mild. **5** *moderate work/success* average, middle-of-the-road, middling, ordinary, fair, fairish, modest, tolerable, passable, adequate, indifferent, mediocre, run-of-the-mill; *inf* so-so, fair-to-middling. **6** *moderate amount/prices* reasonable, within reason, acceptable, average, fair, fairish, modest, lowish.

moderate v **1** *the wind has moderated* die down, abate, let up, calm down, lessen, decrease, diminish, slacken. **2** *moderate the force/pain* lessen, decrease, diminish, mitigate, alleviate, allay, appease, assuage, ease, palliate, soothe, soften, calm, modulate, pacify. **3** *moderate his anger* curb, check, keep in check, keep in control, temper, regulate, restrain, subdue, repress, tame. **4** *moderating the assembly* arbitrate, mediate, referee, judge, chair, take the chair of, preside over.

moderately adv **1** *moderately expensive* quite, rather, somewhat, fairly, reasonably, to a certain degree, to some extent, within reason, within limits. **2** *the work is moderately good | she did moderately well in the test* fairly, tolerably, passably.

moderation n **1** *the moderation of their behaviour | moderation in all things* moderateness, restraint, self-restraint, control, self-control, temperateness, temperance, non-indulgence. *see* MODERATE adj 1-5. **2** *the moderation of the force/pain* lessening, decrease, mitigation, allaying, appeasement, assuagement, soothing, calming, modulation, pacification. *see* MODERATE v 1-3. **3** *the moderation of the assembly* arbitration, mediation, refereeing, chairing, presiding over. *see* MODERATE v 4. **in moderation** moderately, within reason, within due limits.

modern adj **1** *in modern times* contemporary, present-day, present-time, present, current, twentieth-century, existing, existent. **2** *her clothes/ideas are very modern* up-to-date, up to the minute, fashionable, in fashion, in, in style, in vogue, voguish, modish, the latest, new, newfangled, fresh, modernistic, ultra-modern, advanced, progressive; *inf* trendy, with-it.

modernize v **1** *modernize the machinery/methods* make modern, update, bring up to date, bring into the twentieth century, renovate, remodel, remake, redo, refresh,

revamp, rejuvenate; *inf* do over. **2** *the industry must modernize* get up to date, move with the times; *inf* get in the swim, drag oneself into the twentieth century, get on the ball, get with it.

modest adj **1** *he was modest about his achievements* self-effacing, self-deprecating, humble, unpretentious, unassuming, free from vanity, keeping one's light under a bushel. **2** *children too modest to speak* shy, bashful, self-conscious, diffident, reserved, retiring, reticent, quiet, coy, embarrassed, blushing, timid, fearful, meek. **3** *modest behaviour/clothes* decorous, decent, seemly, demure, proper, discreet, delicate, chaste, virtuous. **4** *modest demands/improvement* moderate, fair, tolerable, passable, adequate, satisfactory, acceptable, unexceptional, small, limited. **5** *a modest gift/house* unpretentious, simple, plain, humble, inexpensive, low-cost.

modesty n **1** *admire his modesty* lack of vanity, humility, self-effacement, lack of pretension, unpretentiousness. *see* MODEST 1. **2** *her modesty prevented her speaking* shyness, bashfulness, self-consciousness, reserve, reticence, timidity, meekness. *see* MODEST 2. **3** *modesty of her behaviour/clothes* decorum, decorousness, seemliness, demureness, propriety, chasteness. *see* MODEST 3. **4** *the modesty of their demands* moderation, fairness, passableness, adequacy, satisfactoriness, acceptability, smallness. *see* MODEST 4. **5** *the modesty of the gift/house* lack of pretension, unpretentiousness, simplicity, plainness, inexpensiveness, lack of extravagance. *see* MODEST 5.

modicum n small amount, little, little bit, bit, particle, iota, jot, atom, whit, grain, speck, scrap, crumb, fragment, shred, mite, dash, drop, dab, pinch, ounce, inch, touch, tinge, trifle; *inf* teeny bit.

modification n **1** *the modification of the punishment* lessening, reduction, decrease, abatement, mitigation, restriction. *see* MODIFY 1. **2** *the modification of the design* altering, alteration, adjusting, adjustment, adaptation, refashioning, refining, refinement. *see* MODIFY 2. **3** *the modifications made to the plans* alteration, change, adjustment, adaptation, variation, revision, refinement, transformation.

modify v **1** *modify the punishment* lessen, reduce, decrease, diminish, lower, abate, soften, mitigate, restrict, limit, moderate, temper, blunt, dull, tone down, qualify. **2** *modify the design* alter, make alterations to, change, adjust, make adjustments to, adapt, vary, revise, recast, reform, reshape, refashion, rework, remould, redo, revamp, reorganize, refine, transform.

modulate v **1** *modulate the proportions* regulate, adjust, moderate, temper. **2** *modulate one's voice* adjust/vary/adapt/modify the tone of.

mogul n notable, VIP, magnate, tycoon, baron, captain, lord; *inf* bigwig, big noise, big shot, big cheese, big gun, big wheel.

moist adj **1** *moist weather* wet, wettish, damp, dampish, clammy, humid, dank, rainy, drizzly, drizzling, dewy, dripping, soggy. **2** *a moist cake* succulent, juicy, soft, spongy.

moisten v make wet/wettish, wet, dampen, damp, water, soak, bedew, humidify, irrigate.

moisture n water, liquid, wetness, wet, dampness, damp, humidity, dankness, wateriness, rain, dew, drizzle, perspiration, sweat.

moisturize v *moisturize the skin* apply lotion/cream to, keep supple.

mole n spot, blemish, mark, blotch, discoloration, freckle.

molecule n *not a molecule of politeness* particle, iota, jot, atom, whit, grain, speck, scrap, crumb, shred, ounce, modicum. *see* MODICUM.

molest v **1** *children molesting their mother* pester, annoy, nag, chivvy, plague, torment, harass, badger, harry, persecute, bother, worry, trouble, needle, provoke, vex, agitate, disturb, upset, fluster, ruffle, irritate, exasperate, tease; *inf* bug, hassle. **2** *accused of molesting children* abuse, sexually abuse, interfere with, sexually assault, rape, ravish, assault, attack, injure, hurt, harm, mistreat, maltreat, ill-treat, manhandle.

mollify v *mollify his mother | tried to mollify her anger* calm, calm down, pacify, placate, appease, soothe, still, quiet, tranquillize.

mollycoddle v pamper, coddle, cosset, spoil, overindulge, indulge, baby, featherbed, wait on hand and foot, nanny.

moment n **1** *only lasted a moment* minute, short time, second, instant; *inf* tick, jiffy. **2** *the very moment he came* minute, instant, point, point in time, time, juncture, stage. **3** *matters of no great moment* importance, import, significance, value, consequence, prominence, eminence, note, weight, mark, concern, interest, gravity, seriousness. **in a moment** in a short time, shortly, very soon, in a minute/second/trice/flash, in an instant, in the twinkling of an eye; *inf* in a tick/jiffy, in two shakes, in two shakes of a lamb's tail.

momentarily adv briefly, temporarily, just for a moment/second/instant/minute, for a short time.

momentary adj brief, short, short-lived, fleeting, passing, transient, transitory, ephemeral, evanescent, fugitive, temporary, impermanent.

momentous adj crucial, critical, vital, decisive, pivotal, serious, grave, weighty, important, significant, consequential, of moment, of importance, of consequence, fateful, historic; *inf* earth-shaking, earth-shattering.

momentum n impetus, impulse, propulsion, thrust, push, driving-power, drive, power, energy, force.

monarch n sovereign, ruler, crowned head, potentate, king, queen, emperor, empress.

monarchy n **1** *abolish the monarchy* absolutism, absolute power, autocracy, monocracy, kingship, royalism, sovereignty, despotism. **2** *the country is a monarchy* kingdom, sovereign state, realm, principality, empire.

monastery n religious house, religious community; friary, abbey, convent, nunnery, priory.

monastic adj monastical, cloistered, cloistral, monachal, coenobitic, conventual, canonical, ascetic, celibate, contemplative, meditative, sequestered, secluded, withdrawn, reclusive, recluse, eremitic, hermit-like, anchoritic.

monetary adj money, cash, financial, capital, pecuniary, fiscal, budgetary.

money n **1** *not enough money to buy the business* cash, hard cash, ready money, finance, capital, funds, banknotes, currency, coin, coinage, silver, copper, legal tender, specie; *inf* wherewithal, dough, lolly, bread, dosh, brass, loot, the necessary, the needful, the ready, readies, shekels, spondulicks, tin, dibs, gelt, mazuma, moolah, rhino, filthy lucre, pelf; *Amer inf* the green stuff. **2** *he is a man of money* affluence, wealth, riches, prosperity. **in the money** moneyed, well-to-do, well-off, affluent, rich, wealthy, prosperous, in clover; *inf* rolling in it, loaded, stinking rich, well-heeled, flush, made of money, on Easy Street.

moneyed adj well-to-do, well-off, affluent, rich, wealthy, prosperous; *inf* in the money, rolling in it, loaded, well-heeled. *see* MONEY, IN THE MONEY.

money-making adj profitable, lucrative, gainful, paying, remunerative, successful, thriving, going.

mongrel n *the dog is a mongrel* cross-breed, cross, half-breed, mixed breed, hybrid, cur.

mongrel adj *a mongrel bitch* cross-bred, of mixed breed, hybrid.

monitor n **1** *monitors watching shoppers/workers* detector, scanner, recorder, security system, security camera, observer, watchdog, overseer, supervisor, invigilator. **2** *elected class monitor* prefect, head girl/boy, head pupil.

monitor v *monitor his movements/condition* observe, scan, record, survey, follow, keep an eye on, keep track of, check, oversee, supervise, invigilate.

monk n brother, monastic, religious, friar, abbot, prior.

monkey n **1** *monkeys in the jungle* primate, simian, ape, baboon. **2** *the child is a little monkey* rascal, scamp, imp, rogue, mischief-maker, devil. **make a monkey of** make a fool of, make someone look a fool, make someone look foolish, make a laughing-stock of, ridicule, deride, make fun of.

monkey v monkey about, monkey around fool about/around, play about/around, potter about; *inf* muck about, mess about. **monkey with** fiddle with, play with, tinker with, tamper with, interfere with, meddle with, fool with, trifle with, mess with.

monkey business n **1** *children up to monkey business* mischief, naughtiness, pranks, clowning, skylarking; *inf* monkey tricks, carrying-on, shenanigans, goings-on. **2** *there's been some monkey business in the accounts department* dishonesty, trickery, misconduct, misdemeanour, chicanery, skulduggery; *inf* funny business, hanky-panky.

monkey tricks npl mischief, pranks; *inf* monkey business. *see* MONKEY BUSINESS 1.

monologue n soliloquy, speech, address, lecture, oration, sermon.

monopolize v **1** *monopolize the market* exercise a monopoly of, corner, control, take over, have sole rights in. **2** *monopolize the conversation* dominate, take over, not let anyone else take part in, not let anyone else get a word in edgeways. **3** *monopolize his wife* keep to oneself, take up all the attention of, not allow to associate with others.

monotonous adj **1** *a monotonous job* unvarying, lacking/without variety, unchanging, repetitious, all the same, uniform, routine, humdrum, run-of-the-mill, commonplace, mechanical, uninteresting, unexciting, prosaic, wearisome, dull, boring, tedious, tiresome; *inf* samey. **2** *a monotonous voice* flat, unvarying, toneless, uninflected, droning, soporific.

monotony n **1** *the monotony of the job* lack of variety, lack of variation, repetition, repetitiveness, sameness, uniformity, routine, routineness, humdrumness, lack of interest, lack of excitement, prosaicness, wearisomeness, dullness, boredom, tedium, tiresomeness; *inf* sameyness. **2** *the monotony of her voice* flatness, tonelessness, lack of inflection, drone.

monster n **1** *frightened by the monster in the myth* fabulous creature, mythical creature, dragon, troll, werewolf, sea-monster, behemoth. **2** *the step-parents are monsters* fiend, beast, brute, barbarian, savage, villain, ogre, devil, demon. **3** *the foetus was a monster* monstrosity, miscreation, malformation, abortion, freak, freak of nature, mutant, teratism, *lusus naturae*. **4** *a monster of a man/building* giant, mammoth, colossus, titan, behemoth, leviathan, Brobdingnagian.

monster adj *a monster lorry/tower* huge, enormous, massive, vast, immense, colossal, gigantic, monstrous, stupendous, prodigious, tremendous, giant, mammoth, gargantuan, titanic, Brobdingnagian; *inf* jumbo, whopping, ginormous.

monstrosity n **1** *a monstrosity of a building* enormity, horror, eyesore, carbuncle. **2** *the monstrosity of the attack* monstrousness, outrageousness, outrage, scandalousness, atrocity, heinousness, horror, hideousness, foulness, vileness, odiousness, viciousness, cruelty, savagery, brutishness, fiendishness, devilishness. *see* MONSTROUS 3. **3** *the foetus is a monstrosity* monster, miscreation, abortion, freak, mutant. *see* MONSTER n 3.

monstrous adj **1** *monstrous creatures being born* miscreated, malformed, unnatural, abnormal, grotesque, gruesome, repellent, freakish, mutant, teratoid. **2** *monstrous lorries* huge, enormous, massive, vast, immense, colossal, gigantic, tremendous, giant. *see* MONSTER adj. **3** *it was a monstrous thing to do* outrageous, shocking, disgraceful, scandalous, atrocious, heinous, evil, abominable, terrible, horrible, dreadful, hideous, foul, vile, nasty, ghastly, odious, loathsome, intolerable, contemptible, despicable, vicious, cruel, savage, brutish, bestial, barbaric, inhuman, fiendish, devilish, diabolical, satanic.

monument n **1** *build a monument to the dead soldiers* memorial, statue, shrine, reliquary, sepulchre, mausoleum, cairn, pillar, col-

umn, obelisk, dolmen, cromlech, megalith.
2 *place a monument on the grave* gravestone,
headstone, tombstone. **3** *travel scholarships
as a monument to his talent* memorial, commemoration, remembrance, reminder, testament, witness, token.

monumental adj **1** *a monumental effort*
great, huge, enormous, immense, vast,
exceptional, extraordinary, tremendous,
stupendous, prodigious, staggering. **2** *a
monumental error* huge, enormous, terrible,
colossal, egregious, catastrophic, staggering, unforgivable, indefensible; *inf* whopping. **3** *a monumental work of art* massive,
impressive, striking, remarkable, magnificent, awe-inspiring, marvellous, majestic,
stupendous, prodigious, historic, epoch-
making, classic, memorable, unforgettable,
enduring, permanent, immortal. **4** *monumental tributes* commemorative, celebratory,
in memory, recalling to mind.

mood n **1** *in a happy mood* humour, temper,
disposition, frame of mind, state of mind,
spirit, tenor, vein. **2** *he's in a mood* bad
mood, bad temper, fit of bad/ill temper, fit
of irritability, fit of pique, low spirits, fit of
melancholy, depression, sulk, the sulks,
bout of moping, doldrums, blues; *inf* the
dumps. **in the mood for/to** *in the mood for
dancing | in the mood to dance* feeling like,
inclined to, disposed towards, minded to,
interested in, keen on/to, eager to, having
enthusiasm for, willing to.

moody adj **1** *teenagers are often moody* temperamental, changeable, unpredictable,
volatile, mercurial, unstable, unsteady,
erratic, fitful, impulsive, capricious. **2** *don't
say anything—he's moody today* in a mood, in
a bad mood, bad-tempered, ill-tempered,
ill-humoured, short-tempered, irritable,
irascible, crabbed, crabby, cantankerous,
cross, crotchety, crusty, testy, touchy, petulant, in a pique, sullen, sulky, moping,
gloomy, glum, depressed, dejected, despondent, melancholic, doleful, lugubrious,
introspective, in a huff, huffed, huffy; *inf*
down in the dumps, down in the mouth.

moon n satellite. **many moons ago** a long
time ago, ages ago; *inf* yonks ago. **once in
a blue moon** hardly ever, almost never,
rarely, very seldom. **over the moon** ecstatic, euphoric, elated, rapturous, thrilled,
jubilant, overjoyed, transported, in seventh
heaven; *inf* on cloud nine.

moon v languish, idle, mope, daydream, be
in a reverie, be in a brown study; *inf*
mooch.

moor n moorland, heath, grouse-moor, fell.

moor v *moored the boat at the quayside* secure,
fix firmly, fasten, make fast, tie up, lash,
anchor, berth.

moot adj *a moot point* debatable, open to
debate, open to discussion, questionable,
open to question, open, doubtful, disputable, arguable, contestable, controversial, unresolved, undecided.

moot v *moot the question of money* broach,
bring up, mention, introduce, put forward,
propose, suggest, propound.

mop n **1** *clean the floor with a kitchen mop*
swab, squeegee, sponge. **2** *a mop of hair*
shock, thatch, mane, tangle, mass, mat.

mop v **1** *mop the floor* clean, wipe, wash,
swab, sponge. **2** *mop one's face* wipe, clean,
dry. **mop up 1** *mop up the spilt water* soak
up, absorb, sponge, clean, wipe. **2** *mop up
all the profits* absorb, use up, exhaust, consume, swallow up. **3** *mop up the last bits of
work* finish off, make an end of, clear up,
eliminate, dispatch. **4** *mop up the enemy territory* complete the occupation of, take
over, secure. **5** *mop up resisting soldiers* kill
off, eliminate, dispose of, make away with.

mope v **1** *she's moping because her friend's
gone* be miserable, be sad, be despondent,
pine, fret, grieve, brood, sulk. **2** *mope about
the place* wander, idle, languish, droop,
moon; *inf* mooch.

moral adj **1** *moral issues* ethical. **2** *a moral
man/woman* ethical, good, virtuous, right-
eous, upright, upstanding, high-minded,
principled, honourable, honest, just,
decent, chaste, pure, blameless. **3** *moral act/
behaviour* good, virtuous, honourable, right,
proper, fit, decent, decorous. **4** *moral support* psychological, emotional, mental.

moral n *the moral of the story* lesson, teaching, message, meaning, significance, point.

morale n self-confidence, confidence, heart,
spirit, hope, hopefulness, optimism, determination, zeal.

moral fibre n strength of character, firmness of purpose, resolution, toughness of
spirit.

morality n **1** *the morality of abortion* ethics,
rights and wrongs. **2** *a man/woman of morality* ethics, goodness, virtue, righteousness,
rectitude, uprightness, integrity, principles, honour, honesty, justness, decency,
chasteness, chastity, purity, blamelessness.
3 *discuss morality* morals, moral code, moral
standards, ethics, principles of right and
wrong, standards/principles of behaviour.

morals npl ethics, moral code, principles of
right and wrong, principles, moral behav-
iour/conduct, standards/principles of

behaviour, standards, morality, sense of morality, scruples, mores.

morass n **1** *in a morass of detail* confusion, muddle, tangle, entanglement, mix-up, jumble, clutter. **2** *get stuck in a morass* marsh, marshland, bog, peatbog, swamp, quagmire, slough, fen.

moratorium n suspension, postponement, stay, halt, freeze, embargo, ban, standstill, respite.

morbid adj **1** *morbid thoughts/details* gruesome, grisly, macabre, hideous, dreadful, horrible, unwholesome. **2** *a morbid person* death-orientated, death-obsessed, death-fixated. **3** *don't be so morbid* gloomy, glum, dejected, melancholy, lugubrious, pessimistic, given to looking on the black side. **4** *a morbid condition* diseased, infected, sickly, ailing. **5** *a morbid growth* malignant, deadly, pathological.

mordant adj **1** *mordant wit/remarks* acid, caustic, trenchant, cutting, incisive, stinging, biting, acerbic, stringent, bitter, sarcastic, virulent, vitriolic, venomous, waspish. **2** *a mordant solution* acid, acidic, caustic, corrosive, vitriolic.

more adj *require more space* additional, supplementary, further, added, extra, increased, spare, fresh, new.

more adv *concentrate more* to a greater extent, further, longer, some more.

more n *need more* additional amount/number, greater quantity/part, addition, supplement, extra, increase, incrementation.

moreover adv besides, furthermore, further, more than that, what is more, in addition, also, as well, to boot.

morgue n mortuary, charnel-house, funeral parlour; *Amer* funeral home.

moribund adj **1** *moribund old men* dying, on one's deathbed, near death, near the end, breathing one's last, fading fast, failing rapidly, having one foot in the grave, on one's last legs, *in extremis*. **2** *moribund customs* dying, declining, on the decline, waning, on the way out, obsolescent, on its last legs.

morning n forenoon, a.m., early part of the day, dawn, daybreak, sunrise; *lit* morn.

moron n *he's a complete moron* fool, dolt, dunce, dullard, blockhead, dunderhead, ignoramus, numskull, nincompoop; *inf* idiot, imbecile, nitwit, halfwit, dope, dimwit, dummy; *Amer inf* schmuck.

morose adj sullen, gloomy, glum, sombre, sober, saturnine, lugubrious, mournful, depressed, dour, melancholy, melancholic,

doleful, blue, down, low, moody, taciturn, pessimistic, sour, scowling, sulky, surly, churlish, crabbed, crabby, cross.

morsel n mouthful, bite, nibble, bit, crumb, grain, particle, fragment, piece, scrap, segment, soupçon, taste.

mortal adj **1** *mortal beings | the mortal world* temporal, transient, ephemeral, passing, impermanent, perishable, human, earthly, worldly, corporeal, fleshly. **2** *a mortal blow* death-dealing, deadly, fatal, lethal, killing, murderous, terminal, destructive. **3** *mortal enemies* deadly, to the death, sworn, out-and-out, irreconcilable, bitter, implacable, unrelenting, remorseless. **4** *mortal pain/fear* terrible, awful, intense, extreme, severe, grave, dire, very great, great, unbearable, agonizing. **5** *of no mortal use* conceivable, imaginable, perceivable, possible.

mortal n *mortals must die* human being, human, earthling, person, man/woman, being, body, individual.

mortality n **1** *humans subject to mortality* temporality, transience, ephemerality, impermanence, perishability, humanity, earthliness, worldliness. see MORTAL adj 1. **2** *appalled at the wartime mortality* bloodshed, death, loss of life, fatalities, killing, slaying, carnage, slaughter.

mortification n **1** *their mortification at their failure* humiliation, disgrace, shame, dishonour, abasement, discomfiture, embarrassment. see MORTIFY 1. **2** *her mortification at their remarks* hurt, affront, offence, annoyance, displeasure, vexation, discomfiture, embarrassment. see MORTIFY 2. **3** *the mortification of the flesh* subduing, control, controlling, restraint, suppression, disciplining, chastening. **4** *the mortification of flesh* gangrene, festering, necrosis, putrefaction.

mortify v **1** *they were mortified by their failure* humiliate, humble, cause to eat humble pie, bring low, disgrace, shame, dishonour, abash, fill with shame, put to shame, chasten, degrade, abase, deflate, crush, discomfit, embarrass, take down a peg or two. **2** *their remarks mortified her* hurt, wound, affront, offend, annoy, displease, vex, embarrass. **3** *mortify the flesh | mortify such fleshly pleasures* subdue, get under control, control, restrain, suppress, discipline, chasten. **4** *flesh mortifying* become gangrenous, fester, necrose, putrefy.

mortuary n morgue, charnel-house. *see* MORGUE.

most n *most did not vote* majority, greatest number, greatest quantity/part, nearly all, almost all, bulk, mass.

mostly adv **1** *they were mostly young* for the most part, on the whole, in the main, largely, mainly, chiefly, predominantly. **2** *mostly we eat at home* for the most part, usually, generally, in general, as a general rule, as a rule, ordinarily, normally, commonly.

mot n **bon mot**, witticism, quip, pun, epigram, aphorism, maxim, saw, saying, proverb, adage, axiom.

mother n female parent, materfamilias, matriarch, earth mother, foster mother, biological mother, birth mother, adoptive mother, surrogate mother; *inf* mum, mummy, mumsy, ma, mam, mamma, mammy, mater, old lady; *Amer inf* mom.

mother adj inborn, innate, connate, native, natural.

mother v **1** *mother the orphans* look after, care for, tend, raise, rear, foster, cherish, fuss over, indulge, spoil. **2** *she mothered twins | countries which have mothered geniuses* be the mother of, give birth to, bear, produce, bring forth.

motherly adj maternal, protective, comforting, caring, loving, affectionate, fond, warm, tender, gentle, kind, kindly.

motion n **1** *the motion made her sick | vehicles in motion* motility, mobility, locomotion, movement, moving, changing place/position, travel, travelling, going, progress, passing, passage, flow, action, activity, course. **2** *a motion with her hand* movement, gesture, gesticulation, signal, sign, wave, nod. **in motion** *trains in motion* moving, going, travelling, not at rest, on the move, under way. **set/put in motion** *set the process in motion* get going, get under way, get in operation, get working/functioning, start, begin, commence.

motion v *motioned to me to step forward* gesture, gesticulate, signal, sign, wave, nod.

motionless adj unmoving, still, stock-still, at a standstill, stationary, immobile, immovable, static, at rest, halted, stopped, paralysed, transfixed, frozen, inert, lifeless.

motivate v **1** *that motivated him to write* move, cause, lead, persuade, prompt, actuate, drive, impel, spur, induce, provoke, incite, inspire. **2** *trying to motivate the pupils/children* give incentive to, stimulate, inspire, arouse, excite, stir, spur, goad.

motivation n **1** *he has no motivation* ambition, drive, inspiration. **2** *you must give the children some motivation to succeed* incentive, stimulus, inspiration, inducement, incitement, spur, goad, motive.

motive n motivation, reason, rationale, thinking, grounds, cause, basis, occasion, incentive, inducement, incitement, influence, lure, attraction, inspiration, persuasion, stimulus, spur, goad, pressure; *inf* what makes one tick.

motley adj **1** *motley collection of old clothes* assorted, varied, miscellaneous, mixed, diverse, diversified, variegated, heterogeneous. **2** *a motley coat* many-coloured, multicoloured, particoloured, many-hued, variegated, kaleidoscopic, prismatic.

mottled adj blotched, blotchy, splotchy, speckled, spotted, streaked, marbled, flecked, freckled, dappled, stippled, variegated, piebald, pied, brindled, tabby.

motto n **1** *'waste not, want not' should be your motto* maxim, aphorism, adage, saying, saw, axiom, truism, precept, epigram, proverb, byword, gnome. **2** *the club's motto* slogan, watchword, cry. **3** *cracker mottoes* joke.

mould[1] n **1** *set the mixture in a mould* cast, die, form, matrix, shape. **2** *the mould of history* shape, form, figure, cast, outline, line, configuration, formation, format, structure, frame, construction, build, cut, style, model, pattern, type, kind, brand, make. **3** *objects constructed on a mould* frame, framework, template. **4** *people of heroic mould* character, nature, calibre, kind, sort, stamp, type, kidney.

mould[1] v **1** *mould plastic into pipes* cast. **2** *mould the model from clay* shape, form, fashion, model, construct, frame, make, create, design, carve, sculpt, chisel, forge. **3** *mould children's minds* influence, affect, direct, shape, form, make.

mould[2] n *mould covered the woodwork* mouldiness, fungus, mildew, blight, must, mustiness, dry rot, wet rot.

mouldy adj mildewed, blighted, musty, fusty, decaying, rotting, rotten, bad, spoiled.

mound n **1** *a mound of leaves* heap, pile, stack. **2** *flat country broken by mounds* hillock, hill, knoll, rise, hummock, tump, embankment, bank, dune. **3** *Pictish mounds* barrow, tumulus.

mount v **1** *mount the stairs* ascend, go up, climb up, clamber up, make one's way up, scale. **2** *mount the bus* get on to, climb on to, jump on to. **3** *he mounted the horse* get on to, get astride, get on the back of. **4** *costs mounting up* accumulate, accrue, pile up, grow, multiply. **5** *prices/fear mounting* increase, grow, escalate, intensify. **6** *mount a picture* frame, set, dispose. **7** *mount an* *exhibition* stage, put on, install, prepare, organize, arrange, set in motion; *inf* get up.

mount n **1** *choose a quiet mount* horse, steed. **2** *a plain mount for the gem/picture* setting, fixture, frame, support, stand, base, backing, foil.

mountain n **1** *rocky mountains* peak, height, elevation, eminence, pinnacle, fell, alp, Munro; *Scots* ben; *lit* mount. **2** *mountains of clothes* heap, pile, mound, stack, abundance; *inf* ton. **3** *a butter mountain* surplus, surfeit, excess, overabundance.

mountainous adj **1** *mountainous regions* hilly, high, highland, high-reaching, steep, lofty, towering, soaring, alpine, rocky. **2** *mountainous athletes* huge, enormous, immense, massive, vast, gigantic, mammoth, hulking, mighty, monumental, colossal, ponderous, prodigious, Brobdingnagian.

mourn v **1** *the widow is still mourning* grieve, sorrow, keen, lament, wail, wear mourning, wear black, wear widow's weeds. **2** *mourn for her dead husband* grieve for, sorrow over, weep for, regret/deplore the loss of, bewail, bemoan.

mournful adj **1** *mournful music* sad, sorrowful, doleful, gloomy, sombre, melancholy, lugubrious, funereal, elegaic. **2** *had such a mournful expression* | *looked so mournful* sad, doleful, dejected, depressed, downcast, disconsolate, melancholy, gloomy, miserable, lugubrious, woeful, unhappy, heavyhearted, sombre.

mourning n **1** *the mourning of the bereaved* grief, grieving, sorrowing, lamentation, keening, wailing, weeping, moaning. **2** *wear mourning* black clothes, black, widow's weeds, weeds, sackcloth and ashes.

mousy adj **1** *a mousy person* timid, fearful, timorous, self-effacing, unobtrusive, unassertive, withdrawn, shy. **2** *mousy hair/colours* brownish-grey, greyish, grey, dun-coloured, colourless, neutral, drab, dull, lacklustre.

mouth n **1** *open their mouths* lips, jaws, maw, muzzle; *inf* gob, trap, chops, kisser. **2** *mouth of the cave/trumpet* opening, entrance, entry, inlet, door, doorway, gateway, portal, hatch, aperture, orifice, vent, cavity, crevice, rim, lips. **3** *the mouth of the river* river mouth, estuary, outlet, embouchure. **4** *he's all mouth and no action* empty talk, idle talk, babble, claptrap, boasting, bragging, braggadocio; *inf* hot air, gas. **5** *don't take any mouth from her* impudence, cheek, insolence, impertinence, rudeness, incivility, effrontery, audacity; *inf* lip, backchat, neck. **down in the mouth** down, down-

hearted, dejected, downcast, low in spirits, depressed, dispirited, discouraged, disheartened, disconsolate, crestfallen, miserable, unhappy; *inf* down in the dumps.

mouthful n bite, swallow, spoonful, forkful, nibble, sip, sup, taste, drop, bit, piece, morsel, sample.

mouthpiece n **1** *he is his company's mouthpiece* spokesman, spokeswoman, spokesperson, negotiator, intermediary, mediator, agent, representative. **2** *he publishes the mouthpiece of the union* organ, journal, periodical, publication.

movable adj mobile, transportable, transferable, portable, portative.

move v **1** *men moving slowly* go, walk, march, proceed, progress, advance. **2** *move objects* carry, transport, transfer, transpose, change over, shift, switch. **3** *time moves fast* progress, advance, pass. **4** *the government must move soon* take action, act, do something, get moving. **5** *our neighbours are moving* move house, relocate, change house, change jobs, move away, leave, go away. **6** *she was moved by the performance* affect, touch, impress, upset, disturb, disquiet, agitate; make an impression on, have an impact on, tug on someone's heartstrings. **7** *the sight moved her to tears* provoke, incite, actuate, rouse, excite, urge, incline, stimulate, motivate, influence, persuade, lead, prompt, cause, impel, induce. **8** *as the spirits moves him* | *she was moved to act* activate, get going, propel, drive, push, shift, motivate. **9** *nothing can move him on that* | *she will not move on this issue* change, budge, change someone's mind; *inf* do an about-turn, do a U-turn. **10** *move that he be sacked* propose, put forward, advocate, recommend, urge, suggest. **11** *the goods are not moving* sell, be sold, move from the shelf, retail, be marketed.

move n **1** *birds frightened by the man's slightest move* movement, motion, moving, action, activity, gesture, gesticulation. **2** *arrange our move* removal, change of house/address/job, relocation, transfer; *Scots* flit, flitting. **3** *plan our next move* action, act, deed, measure, step, tack, manoeuvre, tactic, stratagem, ploy, ruse, trick. **4** *it's your move in the game* turn, go; *inf* shot. **get a move on** hurry up, make haste, speed up, move faster, get moving; *inf* get cracking, make it snappy, step on it, shake a leg. **make a move** take action, act, do something. **on the move 1** *cars/birds on the move* moving, in motion, going, travelling, journeying, under way, on the wing. **2** *things are on the* *move* progressing, making progress, advancing, moving/going forward.

movement n **1** *the movement of the furniture* moving, carrying, transportation, transferral, shifting. **2** *make a sudden movement* moving, move, motion, action, activity, gesture, gesticulation. **3** *the movement of time* progress, progression, advance, passing, passage. **4** *the clock's movement* mechanism, machinery, works, workings, action, wheels; *inf* innards, guts. **5** *form a peace movement* group, party, organization, faction, wing, coalition, front. **6** *mount a peace movement* campaign, crusade, drive. **7** *play the first movement* part, section, passage. **8** *a movement towards better government* trend, tendency, drift, swing, current. **9** *no movement in the stock market* rise/fall, change, variation, fluctuation. **10** *some movement has been made in the situation* progress, advance, improvement, step forward, breakthrough.

moving adj **1** *a moving story* affecting, touching, emotive, emotional, poignant, pathetic, stirring, arousing, upsetting, disturbing. **2** *moving parts* movable, mobile, motile, unfixed. **3** *the moving force behind the scheme* driving, dynamic, impelling, motivating, stimulating, inspirational.

mow v cut, trim, crop, clip, scythe, shear. **mow down** *armies mowing down the townspeople* slaughter, massacre, butcher, cut to pieces, cut down, decimate.

much adj *not much time | too much trouble* a great/large amount of, a great number of, a great deal of, plenty of, ample, copious, abundant; *inf* a lot of, lots of.

much adv **1** *I much regret it* greatly, to a great extent/degree, exceedingly, considerably, decidedly, indeed; *inf* a lot. **2** *he's not here much* often, frequently; *inf* a lot. **much of a muchness** much the same, more or less the same, very similar, almost alike, practically identical, practically indistinguishable.

much n *he doesn't know much* a good deal, a great deal; *inf* a lot, lots.

muck n **1** *clear the muck from the barn* dung, manure, ordure, excrement, guano, droppings, faeces. **2** *clean the muck from the car* dirt, grime, filth, mud, slime, sludge, scum, mire; *inf* gunk, gunge. **make a muck of** botch, bungle, muff, make a mess of, mess up, mar, spoil, ruin; *inf* make a hash of, foul up, screw up.

muck v **muck up** *see* MUCK, MAKE A MUCK OF.

mud n sludge, clay, silt, mire, dirt, soil.

muddle v **1** *muddle the dates | he's muddled up the situation* confuse, get confused, mix up, jumble, jumble up, scramble, disarrange, disorganize, throw into disorder, get into a tangle, make a mess of, mess up. **2** *numbers muddle her* confuse, disorientate, bewilder, befuddle, daze, perplex, puzzle, baffle, nonplus, confound.

muddle n **1** *files in a muddle* chaos, disorder, disarray, confusion, disorganization, jumble, mix-up, mess, clutter, tangle. **2** *she's in such a muddle | her mind's in a muddle* state of confusion, disorientation, bewilderment, perplexity, puzzlement, bafflement.

muddled adj **1** *muddled files* chaotic, in disorder, in disarray, disorganized, jumbled, mixed-up, scrambled, tangled; *inf* higgledy-piggledy. **2** *muddled people trying to cope* confused, disorientated, at sea, befuddled, bewildered, dazed, perplexed. *see* MUDDLE V 2. **3** *muddled thinking/logic* confused, jumbled, incoherent, unclear, woolly, muddied, loose.

muddy adj **1** *a muddy substance* mucky, miry, oozy, slushy, slimy. **2** *muddy ground/ field* marshy, boggy, swampy. **3** *muddy shoes* mud-caked, dirty, filthy, grubby, grimy. **4** *muddy stream/liquid/colours* cloudy, murky, smoky, dingy, dull, turbid, opaque, brownish-green. **5** *muddy thinking* confused, jumbled, incoherent, woolly. *see* MUDDLED 3.

muddy v **1** *muddy the waters | muddied his hands* dirty, begrime, soil. **2** *muddy the issue* make unclear, cloud, confuse, mix up, jumble, scramble, get into a tangle.

muffle v **1** *muffle oneself up against the cold* wrap up, cover up, swathe, swaddle, envelop, cloak. **2** *muffle the sound* deaden, dull, dampen, stifle, smother, suppress, soften, quieten, hush, mute, silence.

muffled adj *muffled sound* faint, indistinct, unclear, dull, muted, dampened, stifled, smothered, suppressed.

mug n **1** *a mug of cocoa | beer mug* beaker, cup, tankard, pot, glass, toby jug. **2** *he's a mug to believe her* fool, simpleton, innocent; *inf* sucker, muggins, soft touch. **3** *he has an ugly mug* face, countenance, visage, features; *inf* clock, phiz, phizog.

mug v assault, attack, beat up, knock down, rob; *inf* rough up, do over.

muggy adj close, stuffy, sultry, oppressive, airless, humid, clammy, sticky.

mull v **mull over** think over, think about, consider, ponder, reflect on, contemplate, meditate on, deliberate about/on, muse on, ruminate over/on, weigh up, have one's mind on, examine, study, review.

multifarious adj many, multiple, numerous, legion, sundry, diverse, diversified, varied, variegated, manifold, different, miscellaneous, assorted.

multiple adj several, many, numerous, various, collective, manifold.

multiply v **1** *people multiplying in great numbers* breed, reproduce. **2** *troubles are multiplying* increase, grow, accumulate, augment, proliferate, spread.

multitude n **1** *a multitude of people came* crowd, assembly, throng, host, horde, mass, mob, legion, army; *inf* a lot, lots. **2** *he despises the multitude* the common people, the masses, the populace, the commonality, the proletariat, the mob, the crowd, the rabble, *hoi polloi*, the *canaille*; *inf* the great unwashed.

munch v chew, champ, chomp, masticate, crunch, eat.

mundane adj **1** *mundane issues/prose* common, ordinary, everyday, workaday, usual, prosaic, pedestrian, routine, customary, regular, normal, typical, commonplace, banal, hackneyed, trite, stale, platitudinous. **2** *mundane not spiritual matters* worldly, earthly, terrestrial, secular, temporal, fleshly, carnal, sensual.

municipal adj civic, civil, city, metropolitan, urban, town, borough, community, public.

munificence n **1** *the munificence of the host* bounty, bountifulness, bounteousness, liberality, generosity, charity, charitableness, magnanimity, magnanimousness, largesse. *see* MUNIFICENT 1. **2** *the munifence of the supplies* abundance, copiousness, profusion. *see* MUNIFICENT 2.

munificent adj **1** *he is a munificent provider* bountiful, bounteous, liberal, generous, free, open-handed, charitable, hospitable, big-hearted, beneficent, benevolent, ungrudging, magnanimous, philanthropic. **2** *munificent supplies of food* plentiful, ample, abundant, copious, lavish, profuse, princely.

murder n **1** *commit murder|guilty of murder* killing, slaying, manslaughter, homicide, slaughter, assassination, butchery, carnage, massacre, patricide, matricide, fratricide, sororicide, infanticide, genocide, regicide. **2** *driving there was murder* an ordeal, a trial, a frustrating/unpleasant/difficult/dangerous experience, a misery, agony; *inf* hell, hell on earth.

murder v **1** *murder his brother* kill, slay, put to death, do to death, take the life of, shed the blood of, slaughter, assassinate, butcher, cut to pieces, massacre; *inf* bump off, do in, eliminate, hit, rub out, blow

away. **2** *murder the song* mangle, mutilate, ruin, make a mess of, spoil, mar, destroy. **3** *they murdered our team* trounce, beat soundly, beat decisively, thrash, defeat utterly, give a drubbing to; *inf* slaughter, hammer, make mincemeat of.

murderer n killer, slayer, homicide, slaughterer, cutthroat, assassin, butcher, patricide, matricide, fratricide. *see* MURDER n 1.

murderous adj **1** *a murderous blow* fatal, lethal, deadly, mortal, death-dealing, homicidal, savage, barbarous, brutal, bloodthirsty, bloody. **2** *a murderous climb* arduous, difficult, strenuous, exhausting, formidable, harrowing, dangerous; *inf* killing, hellish.

murky adj **1** *murky streets/shadows* dark, dim, gloomy. **2** *murky weather* foggy, misty, cloudy, louring, overcast, dull, grey, dismal, dreary, cheerless. **3** *murky pools* dirty, muddy, dingy, dull, cloudy, turbid, opaque. **4** *a murky past* dark, questionable, doubtful, obscure, enigmatic, nebulous, mysterious, hidden, secret.

murmur n **1** *the murmur of the stream* babble, burble, whisper, purl, rustle, buzzing, drone, sigh; *inf* whoosh. **2** *tell him in a murmur* whisper, undertone, mutter, mumble. **3** *have heard murmurs against his presidency* mutter, grumble, moan, complaint, carping, whisper; *inf* grouse, gripe, beef, bitch.

murmur v **1** *streams murmuring* babble, burble, whisper, purl, rustle, buzz, drone, sigh; *inf* whoosh. **2** *murmured that she wished to leave* whisper, speak in an undertone, speak *sotto voce*, mutter, mumble. **3** *murmur against the king* mutter, grumble, moan, complain, carp; *inf* grouse, gripe, beef, bitch.

muscle n **1** *strain a muscle* muscular tissue, sinew, tendon, ligament, thew; biceps, calf, sartorius. **2** *she likes a man with muscle* muscularity, brawn; *inf* beef. **3** *the new chairman has no muscle* power, potency, force, forcefulness, might, strength, weight, influence; *inf* clout, pull.

muscle v **muscle in on** *trust him to muscle in on our trip* push/force one's way in to, elbow one's way in to, impose oneself on, invite oneself to; *inf* butt in on.

muscular adj **1** *muscular tissue/pain* sinewy, fibrous. **2** *muscular men doing weight-lifting* brawny, strapping, powerfully built, solidly built, hefty, stalwart, sturdy, rugged, burly; *inf* beefy, husky. **3** *a muscular character/attempt* vigorous, potent, powerful, strong, energetic, active, dynamic, aggressive, determined, resolute.

muse v **1** *stand and muse* think, meditate, be lost in contemplation/thought, be in a brown study, reflect, deliberate, day dream, be in a reverie. **2** *muse over the situation* think over, think about, consider, ponder, reflect on, contemplate, meditate on, deliberate about/on, mull over, ruminate over/on, weigh up, have one's mind on, examine, study, review. **3** *"I wonder," he mused* say thoughtfully/reflectively/meditatively.

muse n *the poetic muse is silent* inspiration, afflatus, creative influence, stimulus, stimulation.

mushroom n *gather/cook mushrooms* fungus; field mushroom, chanterelle, morel, inkcap, Chinese mushroom.

mushroom v *new towns mushrooming* spring up, shoot up, sprout, burgeon, burst forth, grow/develop rapidly, boom, thrive, flourish, prosper.

music n melody, tune, air, rhythm, harmonization, orchestration.

musical adj tuneful, melodic, melodious, harmonious, lyrical, sweet-sounding, mellifluous, dulcet, euphonious.

musing n thinking, meditation, contemplation, deliberation, pondering, reflection, rumination, day dreaming, reverie, brown study, wool-gathering.

muss v dissarrange, misarrange, put out of place, make untidy, make a mess of, mess up, rumple, dishevel, tousle.

must[1] n *the new show is a must* something not to be missed, essential, necessity, necessary thing, imperative, requirement, requisite, prerequisite.

must[2] n *a smell of must* mould, mustiness, mouldiness, mildew, fungus.

muster v **1** *muster the soldiers* assemble, bring together, call/gather together, call up, summon, rally, mobilize, round up, marshal, collect, convoke. **2** *we must muster at dawn* assemble, gather together, come together, meet, congregate, convene. **3** *muster one's courage* call up, gather together, summon, rally, screw up.

muster n *soldiers present for the muster* assembly, assemblage, rally, mobilization, call-up, round-up, convocation, meeting, congregation, convention. **pass muster** measure up, come up to scratch, be acceptable, qualify; *inf* make the grade, fill/fit the bill.

musty adj **1** *musty books/food/rooms* mouldy, mildewed, mildewy, fusty, decaying, stale, stuffy, airless, damp, dank. **2** *musty ideas* antiquated, obsolete, ancient, antediluvian,

out-of-date, outdated, old-fashioned, out-of-fashion, out-of-style, behind the times, passé, hoary, moth-eaten, worn-out, threadbare, hackneyed, trite, clichéd.

mutable adj changeable, variable, alterable, convertible, adaptable, modifiable, transformable, transmutable, inconstant, unsteady, unstable, vacillating, wavering, unsettled, inconsistent, volatile, capricious.

mutation n **1** *undergo genetic mutation* change, variation, alteration, modification, transformation, metamorphosis, evolution, transmutation, transfiguration. **2** *the creature is a genetic mutation* mutant, deviant, anomaly, freak.

mute adj **1** *mute with surprise* silent, speechless, wordless, unspeaking, taciturn, uncommunicative; *inf* mum. **2** *animals born mute* dumb, voiceless, speechless, aphasic, aphonic. **3** *a mute appeal* silent, dumb, wordless, unexpressed, unspoken.

mute v **1** *mute the sound* deaden, dull, dampen, muffle, stifle, smother, suppress, soften, quieten, soft-pedal, turn down. **2** *mute the colour scheme* soften, subdue, tone down, make less intense.

muted adj *muted colours* soft, softened, subdued, subtle, discreet, toned down, quiet, understated.

mutilate v **1** *mutilate the bodies* dismember, tear limb from limb, amputate limbs from, cut to pieces, cut up, lacerate, hack up, butcher, mangle, cripple maim, lame, disable, disfigure. **2** *mutilate a limb* cut off, chop off, hack off, lop off, tear off, pull off, damage, injure, impair. **3** *mutilate a text* mar, spoil, ruin, damage, butcher, mangle, distort, cut, hack, censor, bowdlerize, expurgate.

mutinous adj rebellious, insurgent, insurrectionary, revolutionary, anarchistic, subversive, seditious, traitorous, insubordinate, disobedient, riotous, rioting, unruly, disorderly, restive, contumacious, refractory, out of control, uncontrollable, ungovernable, unmanageable; *inf* bolshie.

mutiny n rebellion, revolt, insurrection, insurgence, insurgency, uprising, rising, riot, revolution, resistance, disobedience, defiance, insubordination, protest, strike.

mutiny v rebel, revolt, take part in an insurrection/insurgence/uprising, riot, rise up, resist/oppose authority, defy authority, be insubordinate, protest, strike.

mutter v **1** *going along muttering* talk under one's breath, talk to oneself, whisper, speak in an undertone, speak *sotto voce*, mumble, murmur. **2** *mutter against the king* murmur, grumble, moan, complain, carp; *inf* grouse, gripe, beef, bitch.

muzzle n **1** *the dog's muzzle is wet with blood* mouth, jaw, maw. **2** *the dog pushed its muzzle into the bucket* nose, snout. **3** *put a muzzle on the dangerous dog* gag, guard, restraint, bridle.

muzzle v **1** *muzzle the dog* put a muzzle on, gag, bridle. **2** *attempts to muzzle the press* silence, impose silence on, censor, suppress, stifle, inhibit, restrain, check, fetter.

myopic adj **1** *myopic guests peering across the table* short-sighted, near-sighted, purblind. **2** *a board full of myopic people* narrow, narrow-minded, short-sighted, insular, parochial, provincial, limited, prejudiced, unimaginative, uncreative.

myriad n *a myriad of butterflies in the sky* a great number/quantity, scores, multitude, host, horde, army, legion, mass, throng, swarm, sea; *inf* millions, thousands, oodles, zillions, a lot.

myriad adj *myriad colours* innumerable, countless, incalculable, immeasurable, numerous, multitudinous, multifarious, manifold, multiple, several, many, various, sundry, diverse.

mysterious adj **1** *God moves in mysterious ways* enigmatic, inscrutable, impenetrable, incomprehensible, inexplicable, unexplainable, unfathomable, unaccountable, insoluble, obscure, arcane, abstruse, cryptic, unknown, recondite, secret, preternatural, supernatural, uncanny, mystical, peculiar, strange, weird, curious, bizarre, undisclosed, mystifying, baffling, puzzling, perplexing, bewildering, confounding. **2** *he was being very mysterious about his whereabouts* secretive, reticent, non-committal, discreet, evasive, furtive, surreptitious.

mystery n **1** *his death remains a mystery* enigma, puzzle, secret, unsolved problem, problem, riddle, conundrum, question, question mark, closed book, unexplored ground, *terra incognita*. **2** *his whereabouts are clothed in mystery* secrecy, concealment, obscurity, obscuration, vagueness, nebulousness, inscrutability, inexplicability.

mystic, mystical adj **1** *a mystic experience* spiritual, paranormal, transcendental, other-worldly, supernatural, preternatural, non-rational, occult, metaphysical. **2** *mystic rites* symbolic, representational, allegorical, metaphorical, emblematic, emblematical, non-literal. **3** *mystical events* obscure, cryptic, enigmatic, abstruse, arcane, recondite, inscrutable, inexplicable, unfathomable, mysterious.

mystify v confuse, bewilder, confound, perplex, baffle, nonplus, puzzle, elude, escape; *inf* stump, beat, bamboozle.

myth n **1** *read ancient myths* legend, saga, tale, story, fable, folk tale, allegory, parable, fairy story/tale, bestiary. **2** *her having a rich father was just a myth* fantasy, delusion, figment of the imagination, invention, fabrication, untruth, lie; *inf* story, fairy story/tale, tall story.

mythical adj **1** *a mythical creature* legendary, mythological, fabled, chimerical, imaginary, imagined, fabulous, fantastical, fairytale, story-book, fictitious, allegorical. **2** *a mythical rich uncle* fantasy, imagined, imaginary, pretended, make-believe, unreal, fictitious, invented, fabricated, made-up, untrue; *inf* pretend.

mythology n body of myths, myths, legend, lore, folklore, folk tales, stories.

Nn

nadir n the lowest point, the lowest level, the bottom, rock-bottom, the depths, all-time low, as low as one can get, zero; *inf* the pits.

nag¹ v **1** *parents nagging children* scold, carp, pick on, keep on, harp on at, be on someone's back, henpeck, bully, upbraid, berate, chivvy, criticize, find fault with, complain to, grumble to; *inf* go on at. **2** *children nagging mothers about buying toys* badger, pester, plague, torment, harry, goad, worry, vex, harass, irritate; *inf* hassle, drive up the wall.

nag¹ n *his nag of a wife* shrew, scold, harpy, termagant, fault-finder, carper, caviller, complainer, grumbler; *inf* grouser.

nag² n *ride an old nag* broken-down old horse, jade, hack, Rosinante; *inf* bag of bones, plug.

nagging adj **1** *a nagging wife* scolding, carping, cavilling, criticizing, fault-finding, complaining, grumbling. *see* NAG¹ v 1. **2** *a nagging pain* persistent, continuous, aching, painful, distressing.

naiad n water nymph, water sprite, undine.

nail n **1** *drive a nail into the wood* pin, brad, tack, sprig, rivet. **2** *cut one's nails | the animal's nails* fingernail, toenail, claw, talon, nipper, pincer.

nail v **1** *nail the pieces together* pin, tack, hammer, fix, fasten, secure, join, attach. **2** *nail the headmaster at the meeting* get hold of, grab, get the attention of, make someone commit himself/herself, pin down. **3** *nail his lies | nailed the myth* expose, reveal, detect, uncover, unmask, bare, unearth, dig out. **4** *nail the thief* catch, seize, capture, apprehend, arrest, take into custody; *inf* collar, nab, pinch.

naive adj **1** *naive young girls* innocent, artless, childlike, simple, ingenuous, guileless, trusting, unsophisticated, unworldly, jejune, natural, unaffected, unpretentious, frank, open, candid. **2** *unbelievably naive employees* gullible, overtrusting, overtrustful, credulous, unsuspicious, unsuspecting, deceivable, dupable, callow, raw, green, immature, inexperienced; *inf* wet behind the ears.

naiveté, naivety n **1** *the young girl's naiveté* innocence, artlessness, childlikeness, simplicity, ingenuousness, guilelessness, lack of guile, unsophistication, lack of sophistication, unworldliness, naturalness, candour. *see* NAIVE 1. **2** *their unbelievable naiveté* gullibility, credulousness, credulity, overtrustfulness, lack of suspicion, callowness, greenness, immaturity. *see* NAIVE 2.

naked adj **1** *naked bodies/men* stark naked, nude, in the nude, bare, stripped, exposed, unclothed, undressed, uncovered, undraped, disrobed, *au naturel*; *inf* without a stitch on, starkers, in one's birthday suit, in the raw, in the altogether, in the buff, naked as the day one was born, mother naked; *Amer inf* buck naked. **2** *naked landscapes/rooms* bare, barren, stark, uncovered, denuded, stripped, treeless, grassless, unfurnished. **3** *the naked truth* undisguised, unqualified, unadorned, stark, bald, unvarnished, unveiled, unmitigated, unexaggerated, plain, simple, open, patent, evident, apparent, obvious, manifest, overt, unmistakable, blatant, glaring, flagrant. **4** *naked flames/sword* exposed, unprotected, unguarded, uncovered, unsheathed, unwrapped. **5** *feeling naked in an alien country* defenceless, unprotected, vulnerable, exposed, helpless, weak, powerless.

nakedness n **1** *embarrassed at his nakedness* nudity, bareness, undress, state of undress. *see* NAKED 1. **2** *the nakedness of the landscape* bareness, barrenness, starkness. *see* NAKED 2. **3** *her feeling of nakedness in the alien country* defencelessness, vulnerability, exposure, helplessness. *see* NAKED 5.

namby-pamby adj over-sentimental, sentimental, mawkish, maudlin, insipid, colourless, anaemic, feeble, weak, vapid, spineless, effeminate, womanish, effete, prim, prissy, mincing, simpering; *inf* wet, wishy-washy, wimpish, weedy.

name n **1** *the name of the person/family/plant/tree/book* appellation, designation, cognomen, denomination, sobriquet, title, style, label, tag, epithet, first/second name, Christian/given name, surname, family name, maiden name, nickname, pet name, stage name, pseudonym, alias, *nom de guerre, nom de plume*; *inf* moniker, handle. **2** *he's a name in the theatre* big name, celebrity, luminary, star, dignitary, VIP, lion; *inf* celeb, megastar, big noise/shot, bigwig. **3** *make his name in films* reputation, fame, renown, repute, note, distinction, eminence, prominence, honour, esteem, prestige.

name v **1** *name the child/plant* baptize, christen, give a name to, call, entitle, label, style, term, title, dub, denominate. **2** *name the criminal* | *name the most suitable day* identify, specify, mention, cite, give. **3** *name his successor* appoint, choose, select, pick, nominate, designate.

named adj **1** *a girl named Anne* called, by the name of, under the name of, baptized, christened, entitled, styled. *see* NAME v 1. **2** *named individuals/articles* identified, specified, mentioned, cited, given.

nameless adj **1** *nameless graves* unnamed, untitled, unlabelled, untagged, innominate. **2** *nameless poets/benefactors* unnamed, anonymous, unidentified, undesignated, unspecified. **3** *nameless fears/vices* unspeakable, unutterable, inexpressible, unmentionable, indescribable, abominable, horrible, horrific.

namely adv viz, that is to say, i.e., to wit, specifically.

nap[1] v *children napping in the afternoon* take a nap, catnap, doze, sleep lightly, rest, lie down, drowse; *inf* drop off, nod off, snooze, snatch forty winks, get some shut-eye, have a kip, zizz, get some zizz.

nap[1] n *have a nap* catnap, doze, light sleep, rest, lie-down; *inf* snooze, forty winks, shut-eye, kip, zizz.

nap[2] n *the nap on velvet/carpets* pile, down, surface, shag, weave, grain, fibre.

narcissism n self-admiration, self-love, conceit, self-conceit, vanity, egotism.

narcissistic adj self-admiring, self-loving, in love with oneself, conceited, vain, egotistic.

narcotic adj *narcotic substances* opiate, sleep-inducing, soporific, somnolent, hypnotic, anaesthetic, stupefying, stupefacient, painkilling, pain-dulling, analgesic, anodyne, numbing, calming, tranquillizing, sedative.

narcotic n drug, opiate, sleeping-pill, anaesthetic, painkiller, analgesic, anodyne, tranquillizer, sedative, soporific.

narrate v tell, relate, recount, recite, unfold, give an account of, give a report of, set forth, chronicle, describe, detail, portray, sketch out, rehearse, repeat.

narration n **1** *a fascinating narration* account, story, story-telling, tale, telling, relation, recital, reciting, report, chroni-cling, chronicle, description, portrayal, sketch, rehearsal, repetition. **2** *do the narration for the film* voice-over, voice, spoken part.

narrative n account, statement, report, chronicle, history, story, tale.

narrator n **1** *spellbound by the narrator* recounter, relater, reporter, describer, chronicler, annalist, storyteller, taleteller, teller of tales, raconteur, anecdotist, author, writer. **2** *the film's narrator* voice-over.

narrow adj **1** *narrow roads/waists* not wide, not broad, narrow-gauged, slender, thin, slim, slight, spare, attenuated, tapering. **2** *narrow spaces* confined, confining, constricted, tight, cramped, close, restricted, limited, incommodious, pinched, straitened, squeezed, meagre, scant, scanty, spare, scrimped, exiguous. **3** *a narrow range* limited, restricted, select, exclusive. **4** *a narrow interpretation* literal, exact, precise, close, faithful. **5** *a narrow old woman* narrow-minded, intolerant, illiberal, prejudiced, bigoted, parochial, provincial, insular, small-minded. *see* NARROW-MINDED.

narrowly adv **1** *narrowly escaped with his life* barely, scarcely, just, only just, just and no more, by a hair's breadth; *inf* by a whisker. **2** *look at her opponent narrowly* closely, carefully, scrutinizingly, attentively.

narrow-minded adj intolerant, illiberal, unliberal, over-conservative, conservative, hidebound, dyed-in-the-wool, reactionary, close-minded, unreasonable, prejudiced, bigoted, biased, discriminatory, warped, twisted, jaundiced, parochial, provincial, insular, small-minded, petty-minded, petty, mean-spirited, prudish, strait-laced.

narrows npl strait, sound, channel, passage.

nascent adj beginning, budding, embryonic, incipient, young, growing, developing, evolving, burgeoning, forming.

nastiness n **1** *appalled by the nastiness of the sight/mess/taste/smell* unpleasantness, disagreeableness, vileness, foulness, loathsomeness, ugliness, offensiveness, squalor, filthiness, filth, pollution, unsavouriness, smelliness, stink; *inf* yuckiness, yukkiness, yuck, grottiness. *see* NASTY 1. **2** *the nastiness of the situation* dangerousness, danger, seriousness. *see* NASTY 2. **3** *the nastiness of his temper* ill temper, ill nature, ill humour, bad-temperedness, crossness, unpleasantness, viciousness, spitefulness; *inf* grouchiness. *see* NASTY 3. **4** *the nastiness of the weather* disagreeableness, foulness, wetness. *see* NASTY 4. **5** *the nastiness of the videos* obscenity,

pornography, indecency, foulness, smuttiness, vulgarity, lewdness. see NASTY 5.

nasty adj **1** *a nasty sight/mess/taste/smell*
unpleasant, disagreeable, distasteful, horrible, vile, foul, hateful, loathsome, revolting, disgusting, odious, obnoxious,
repellent, repugnant, ugly, offensive, objectionable, noisome, squalid, dirty, filthy,
impure, polluted, tainted, unpalatable,
unsavoury, unappetizing, evil-smelling,
foul-smelling, smelly, stinking, rank, fetid,
malodorous, mephitic; *inf* yucky, yukky,
grotty, niffing. **2** *a nasty illness/situation* dangerous, serious, critical, crucial, severe,
alarming, threatening. **3** *a nasty old man |
was so nasty to his mother* ill-tempered, ill-
natured, ill-humoured, bad-tempered,
cross, surly, unpleasant, disagreeable,
vicious, spiteful, malicious, mean; *inf*
grouchy. **4** *nasty weather* unpleasant, disagreeable, foul, wet, rainy, stormy, foggy.
5 *nasty jokes/videos* obscene, pornographic,
indecent, foul, vile, blue, off colour,
smutty, bawdy, vulgar, ribald, risqué, lewd,
lascivious, licentious.

nation n country, land, state, kingdom,
empire, realm, republic, confederation,
union of states, commonwealth, people,
race, tribe, society, community, population.

national adj **1** *national not local issues* state,
public, federal, governmental, civic, civil.
2 *national as opposed to international problems*
domestic, internal, indigenous, native. **3** *a
national strike/search* nationwide, country-
wide, state, coast-to-coast, widespread,
overall, comprehensive, general.

national n *a national of this country* citizen,
subject, native, resident, inhabitant.

nationalism n patriotism, loyalty/alle-
giance/fealty to one's country, chauvinism,
jingoism, xenophobia.

nationalistic adj patriotic, loyal to one's
country, pro one's country, chauvinistic,
jingoistic, xenophobic.

nationality n nation, race, ethnic group,
tribe.

nationwide adj national, country-wide,
state, coast-to-coast, widespread, overall,
comprehensive, all-embracing, general,
extensive.

native adj **1** *native instinct* inborn, inherent,
innate, connate, built-in, intrinsic, instinctive, intuitive, natural, natural-born, congenital, hereditary, inherited, in the blood,
in the family, inbred, ingrained. **2** *native/
plants/produce* indigenous, original, home-
grown, home-made, domestic, local.

3 *native tongue* mother, vernacular. **4** *native
peoples* original, indigenous, aboriginal,
autochthonous.

native n *a native of France | natives of other con-
tinents* inhabitant, dweller, resident, citizen, national, aborigine, autochthon.

nativity n birth, childbirth, delivery, parturition.

natter v *nattering away to her neighbour* chat,
chatter, gossip, talk idly, prattle, blather,
blether, prate, gabble, jabber, palaver; *inf*
rabbit on, witter on, jaw.

natter n *having a natter with her friend* chat,
gossip, talk, conversation, tête-à-tête,
blather, blether, palaver; *inf* chin-wag, jaw.

natty adj dapper, trim, spruce, well-turned-
out, well-dressed, smart, stylish, fashionable, chic, elegant; *inf* snazzy, trendy.

natural adj **1** *in the natural course of events*
usual, normal, regular, common, ordinary,
everyday, typical, routine, run-of-the-mill.
2 *her natural instincts* native, native-born,
inborn, inherent, innate, connate, built-in,
intrinsic, instinctive, intuitive, natural,
natural-born, congenital, hereditary, inherited, ingrained. **3** *natural charm* artless,
ingenuous, candid, open, frank, genuine,
real, authentic, simple, unsophisticated,
unaffected, unpretentious, spontaneous,
relaxed, unstudied. **4** *natural produce*
organic, pure, unrefined, unpolished,
unbleached, unmixed, whole, plain, real,
chemical-free, additive-free.

naturalist n botanist, biologist, zoologist,
ecologist, natural historian.

naturalistic adj realistic, real-life, true-to-
life, lifelike, factual, graphic, representational; *inf* kitchen-sink, warts and all.

naturalize v **1** *people wishing to be naturalized*
endow with rights of citizenship, confer
citizenship on, enfranchise. **2** *plants becoming naturalized* introduce, acclimatize,
domesticate; *Amer* acclimate. **3** *new words
having been naturalized* adopt, accept, take
in, assimilate, absorb, incorporate, homogenize.

naturally adv **1** *behave naturally* artlessly,
ingenuously, candidly, unaffectedly, unpretentiously, spontaneously. see NATURAL 3.
2 *naturally, he is going* of course, certainly,
as might be expected, as you/one would
expect, as was anticipated.

naturalness n **1** *the naturalness of her charm*
artlessness, ingenuousness, openness, genuineness, simplicity, unsophistication, lack
of sophistication, lack of affectation,
unpretentiousness, spontaneity. see NATURAL
3. **2** *the naturalness of the produce* purity,

pureness, wholeness, lack of chemicals, lack of additives.

nature n **1** *it is in the nature of man* character, characteristic, essence, essential qualities/attributes/features/traits, constitution, make-up, complexion, stamp, personality, identity. **2** *communing with nature* Mother Nature, natural forces, creation, the environment, the earth, mother earth, the world, the universe, the cosmos; landscape, scenery. **3** *things of this nature* kind, sort, type, variety, description, category, class, classification, species, style. **4** *he has a pleasant nature* temperament, temper, personality, disposition, humour, mood, outlook.

naught n nothing, nought, nil, zero, love, nothingness; *inf* zilch.

naughty adj **1** *a naughty child* bad, mischievous, badly behaved, misbehaving, disobedient, defiant, unruly, roguish, wayward, delinquent, undisciplined, unmanageable, ungovernable, fractious, refractory, perverse, errant, sinful, wicked, evil. **2** *naughty films* blue, risqué, smutty, off-colour, indecent, improper, vulgar, bawdy, ribald, lewd, licentious.

nausea n **1** *travellers overcome by nausea* sickness, vomiting, retching, gagging, biliousness, queasiness, faintness, seasickness, carsickness, airsickness, motion sickness, morning sickness; *inf* throwing-up. **2** *horror films causing feelings of nausea* disgust, revulsion, repugnance, distaste, aversion, loathing, abhorrence, detestation, odium.

nauseate v make sick, sicken, make one's gorge rise, turn one's stomach, revolt, disgust, repel, repulse, offend; *inf* make someone want to throw up; *Amer inf* gross out.

nauseous adj **1** *nauseous food* nauseating, sickening, sickly, disgusting, revolting; *inf* sick-making. **2** *a nauseous sight* disgusting, revolting, repulsive, repellent, repugnant, offensive, loathsome, abhorrent, odious. **3** *feeling nauseous* nauseated, sick, queasy, green, unwell, off colour, indisposed, seasick, carsick, airsick; *inf* green about the gills, under the weather, below par.

nautical adj maritime, naval, marine, seagoing, seafaring, yachting, boating, sailing.

navel n **1** *the baby's navel* umbilicus; *lit* omphalos; *inf* belly-button, tummy-button. **2** *the navel of the organization* central point, centre, middle, hub.

navigable adj **1** *navigable rivers* negotiable, passable, traversable, clear, unobstructed. **2** *navigable vessels* steerable, sailable, seaworthy, watertight.

navigate v **1** *the captain/passenger navigated* direct the course, plan/plot the course, give directions, map-read. **2** *navigate the craft* steer, pilot, manoeuvre, guide, direct, handle, drive, skipper. **3** *navigate the Atlantic* sail, sail across, cross, traverse, cruise, journey, voyage.

navigation n **1** *the navigation of the craft* steering, pilotage, manoeuvring, guidance, directing. *see* NAVIGATE 2, 3. **2** *study navigation* seamanship, pilotage, helmsmanship, chart-reading, map-reading.

navigator n pilot, helmsman, seaman, mariner.

navvy n labourer, manual worker, workman.

navy n *watch the arrival of the navy* fleet, flotilla, armada.

nay adv *impressive, nay, magnificent* and indeed, or rather, and even, and more than that.

near adj **1** *the shop's very near* close, close by, nearby, alongside, at close range/quarters, accessible, within reach, close/near at hand, at hand, handy, not far off/away, a stone's throw away, neighbouring, adjacent, adjoining, bordering, contiguous, proximate; *inf* within spitting distance. **2** *the time is near* | *the near future* close/near at hand, next, approaching, coming, imminent, forthcoming, in the offing, impending, looming, proximate, immediate. **3** *near relatives* closely related, related, connected, akin, allied, close, intimate, familiar, dear. **4** *a near escape* close, narrow, by a hair's breath; *inf* by a whisker. **5** *the old man's so near* mean, close, miserly, tight-fisted, close-fisted, niggardly, parsimonious, ungenerous, grasping; *inf* tight; *Amer* cheap. **near miss** near thing, narrow escape; *inf* close shave.

near adv *they live near* close, nearby, close by, alongside, close/near at hand, at hand, within reach, within close range, within earshot, within sight, not far off/away, a stone's throw away; *inf* within spitting distance.

near prep *near the house* close to, close by, in the neighbourhood of, next to, adjacent to, alongside, bordering on, contiguous to, adjoining, within reach of, a stone's throw away from; *inf* within spitting distance of.

near v *we are nearing our destination* get near to, draw near to, get close to, approach, come close to, come towards, move towards, lean towards.

nearly adv *nearly all gone* almost, all but, as good as, virtually, next to, close to, well-nigh, about, just about, practically, roughly, approximately, not quite; *inf* pretty nearly/much/well.

nearness n **1** *the nearness of the shops* closeness, accessibility, handiness, proximity, propinquity. *see* NEAR adj 1. **2** *the nearness of the wedding day* closeness, imminence, immediacy. *see* NEAR adj 2. **3** *the nearness of the relatives* closeness, intimacy, familiarity. *see* NEAR adj 3. **4** *the nearness of the old man* meanness, miserliness, tight-fistedness, niggardliness, parsimony, parsimoniousness. *see* NEAR adj 5.

near-sighted adj short-sighted, myopic, purblind.

neat adj **1** *a neat house* neat and tidy, neat as a new pin, tidy, orderly, well-ordered, straight, in good order, shipshape and Bristol fashion, in apple-pie order, spick and span. **2** *a neat person/dresser* tidy, spruce, trim, smart, dapper, well-groomed, well-turned-out, dainty, fastidious, organized, well-organized, methodical, systematic; *inf* natty. **3** *wearing neat clothes* simple, plain, unadorned, unornamented, unpretentious, unassuming. **4** *a neat saying* elegant, well-put, well-expressed, well-turned, clever, witty, pithy, apt, felicitous. **5** *neat footwork/movements* adroit, skilful, expert, practised, dexterous, deft, accurate, precise, nimble, agile, graceful, stylish, effortless, easy. **6** *neat drinks* straight, undiluted, unmixed, pure.

neatly adv **1** *neatly dressed* tidily, smartly, simply, plainly. *see* NEAT 2, 3. **2** *neatly put* aptly, cleverly, wittily, pithily. *see* NEAT 4. **3** *neatly executed steps* adroitly, skilfully, expertly, deftly, precisely, nimbly, agilely, gracefully, effortlessly. *see* NEAT 5.

neatness n **1** *the neatness of the room* tidiness, orderliness, straightness. *see* NEAT 1. **2** *the neatness of her dress* tidiness, spruceness, trimness, smartness, fastidiousness, simplicity, plainness. *see* NEAT 2, 3. **3** *the neatness of the remark* elegance, cleverness, wit, pithiness, aptness, felicity. **4** *the neatness of her movements* adroitness, deftness, precision, nimbleness, grace, gracefulness, ease, effortlessness. *see* NEAT 5.

nebulous adj **1** *nebulous figures in the distance* shapeless, unformed, amorphous, shadowy, dim, indistinct, indefinite, vague, unclear, obscure, misty, cloudy, hazy, fuzzy. **2** *nebulous ideas about his future career* uncertain, indefinite, indeterminate, imprecise, vague, hazy, unformed, abstract, muddled, confused, ambiguous.

necessarily adv **1** *plans which are necessarily vague* of necessity, by force of circum-

stance, willy-nilly, like it or not, perforce. **2** *he won't necessarily have to go* certainly, definitely, undoubtedly, inevitably, unavoidably, inescapably, automatically, incontrovertibly, inexorably.

necessary adj **1** *a necessary reduction in expenditure* needed, needful, essential, required, requisite, vital, indispensable, imperative, mandatory, obligatory, compulsory, *de rigueur*. **2** *a necessary evil* certain, sure, inevitable, unavoidable, inescapable, inexorable, ineluctable, fated, preordained.

necessitate v require, make necessary, demand, call for, entail, involve, exact, oblige, compel, impel, force, leave no choice but to.

necessities npl *food and clothing are basic necessities* needs, essentials, requisites, requirements, indispensables, fundamentals, necessaries, exigencies.

necessitous adj needy, in need, in want, poor, badly off, impoverished, poverty-stricken, penniless, impecunious, penurious, destitute, indigent, disadvantaged, underprivileged, unable to make ends meet, in straitened circumstances.

necessity n **1** *silence is a necessity* essential, requisite, requirement, prerequisite, necessary, fundamental, *sine qua non*, desideratum. **2** *she left out of necessity* need, needfulness, call, force/pressure of circumstance, exigency, obligation. **3** *necessity made them steal* need, neediness, want, poverty, deprivation, privation, penury, destitution, indigence. **4** *a logical necessity that night follows day* certainty, inevitability, inescapability, inexorability, ineluctability, fate, destiny.

necromancer n spiritualist, spiritist, medium, magician, wizard, warlock, witch, sorcerer/sorceress, enchanter/enchantress, wonder-worker, thaumaturgist.

necromancy n spiritualism, magic, black magic, black art, wizardry, witchcraft, witchery, sorcery, enchantment, spell-casting, spell-weaving, wonder-working, thaumaturgy, demonology, voodooism.

necropolis n cemetery, graveyard, churchyard, burial-ground, burial place, garden of remembrance, memorial park, God's Acre.

née adj born, formerly, previously, heretofore.

need v **1** *it needs work on it* have need of, require, necessitate, demand, call for, have occasion for, want, lack, be without. **2** *he needs her* miss, desire, yearn for, pine for, crave for. **3** *I didn't need to go* have to, be under an obligation to, be obliged to, be compelled to, be under a compulsion to.

need n **1** *their needs are few* requirement, want, wish, demand, prerequisite, requisite, essential, desideratum. **2** *he has need of a coat* want, lack, shortage, requirement. **3** *no need to be frightened | there is no need to go* necessity, call, force of circumstance, exigency, obligation. **4** *people in need* neediness, want, poverty, deprivation, privation, penury, destitution, indigence. **5** *in one's hour of need* crisis, emergency, urgency, distress, trouble, extremity, exigency.

needful adj *do what is needful* needed, requisite, required, stipulated, necessary, essential, vital, indispensable.

needle n **1** *sharp-pointed steel needles* sewing needle, darner, bodkin, knitting-needle, hypodermic needle. **2** *the needle on the dial* arrow, pointer, indicator. **3** *pricked by a needle in the wood* pine needle, thorn, prickle, bramble, briar, bristle, spine.

needle v **1** *needle them into action* goad, spur, prod, prick, sting, press, nag, persuade. **2** *the boys were deliberately needling the teacher* provoke, bait, harass, annoy, anger, irritate, vex, irk, nettle, ruffle, taunt, pester; *inf* aggravate, rile, niggle, get to.

needless adj unnecessary, uncalled for, gratuitous, undesired, unwanted, pointless, useless, dispensable, expendable, inessential.

needlework n needlecraft, sewing, stitching, embroidery, petit point, gros point, tapestry, crocheting.

needy adj necessitous, poor, poverty-stricken, deprived, disadvantaged, penurious, impecunious, impoverished, penniless, destitute, indigent, on the breadline, in straitened circumstances.

ne'er-do-well n good-for-nothing, wastrel, black sheep, loafer, idler, layabout, shirker, sluggard, drone; *inf* skiver, waster.

nefarious adj wicked, evil, sinful, iniquitous, villainous, criminal, heinous, atrocious, vile, foul, base, abominable, odious, horrible, horrendous, dreadful, terrible, detestable, loathsome, execrable, depraved, shameful, scandalous, monstrous, outrageous, flagitious.

negate v **1** *facts negating your theory* nullify, render null and void, annul, void, invalidate, cancel, revoke, rescind, abrogate, repeal, retract, countermand, disestablish, reject, disprove, explode, overrule. **2** *try to negate the existence of God* deny, dispute, call in/into question, gainsay, contradict, disprove, refute, discredit, disclaim, repudiate, renounce, oppose.

negation n **1** *the negation of the theory* nullification, voiding, cancellation, revocation, rescinding, abrogation, repeal, retraction. *see* NEGATE 1. **2** *the attempted negation of the existence of God* denial, contradiction, disproval, disclaiming, repudiation. *see* NEGATE 2. **3** *anarchy is the negation of government* opposite, reverse, antithesis, contrary, converse, want, lack, absence, deficiency. **4** *a life full of negation* nothingness, nothing, nullity, blankness, void, non-existence, vacuity, nonentity.

negative adj **1** *negative replies* in the negative, saying 'no', rejecting, refusing, dissenting, contradictory, contradicting, contrary, opposing, opposite, opposed, denying, gainsaying. **2** *rather a negative young man* unenthusiastic, uninterested, lackadaisical, colourless, anaemic, insipid, vapid, weak, spineless, purposeless. **3** *a negative reaction* pessimistic, defeatist, gloomy, gloom-laden, cynical, jaundiced, critical, fault-finding, complaining, unhelpful, unconstructive, uncooperative.

negative n *reply in the negative* rejection, refusal, dissension, opposite, denial, contradiction.

negative v **1** *negative a request/application* turn down, refuse, assent to, reject, veto, forbid, prohibit, give the thumbs down to, give the red light to, nullify, negate. **2** *negative his theory/statement* disprove, give the lie to, belie, show to be false, invalidate, refute, contradict, deny, negate, gainsay, discredit, explode, squash. **3** *negative the effect* neutralize, counteract, cancel out, offset, balance, equalize.

neglect v **1** *neglect their children* fail to look after, fail to provide for, abandon, forsake, leave alone. **2** *neglect his work* let slide, skimp on, shirk, be remiss about, be lax about, pay little/no attention to, not attend to, leave undone, procrastinate about. **3** *neglect to lock the door* omit, fail, forget, not remember. **4** *neglect his warning* disregard, ignore, pay no attention/heed to, overlook, disdain, scorn, slight, spurn, rebuff.

neglect n **1** *parents/workers guilty of neglect* negligence, neglectfulness, lack of proper care and attention, remissness, carelessness, heedlessness, lack of concern, unconcern, slackness, laxity, laxness, failure to act, dereliction, default. **2** *his neglect of her warning* disregard, ignoring, inattention to, heedlessness, indifference to, disdain, scorn, slight, spurning, rebuff.

neglected adj **1** *neglected children* uncared for, unkempt, mistreated, abandoned, forsaken. **2** *neglected gardens* untended, derelict, overgrown. **3** *neglected opportunities/warnings* disregarded, ignored, spurned, unappreciated, underestimated.

neglectful adj negligent, remiss, lax, careless, inattentive, heedless, thoughtless, unmindful, forgetful, indifferent, uncaring.

negligence n neglect, lack of proper care and attention, remissness, laxity, laxness, dereliction, dereliction of duty, carelessness, inattention, inattentiveness, heedlessness, thoughtlessness, unmindfulness, forgetfulness, inadvertence, oversight, omission, failure, disregard, default, shortcoming, indifference, slackness, sloppiness, slipshodness, procrastination.

negligent adj neglectful, remiss, lax, careless, inattentive, heedless, thoughtless, neglectful, unmindful, uncaring, forgetful, disregardful, indifferent, offhand, cursory, slack, sloppy, slapdash, slipshod, procrastinating, dilatory.

negligible adj *a negligible amount* trivial, trifling, insignificant, of no account, not worth bothering about, paltry, petty, tiny, minute, small, minor, inconsequential, inappreciable, imperceptible.

negotiable adj **1** *pay is negotiable* open to discussion, discussable, debatable, subject to bargaining, transactional. **2** *negotiable cheques* transferable. **3** *negotiable roads* passable, navigable, crossable, traversable, penetrable, unblocked, unobstructed.

negotiate v **1** *negotiate a deal/settlement* work out, thrash out, arrange, reach an agreement on, agree on, settle, come to terms about, conclude, pull off, bring off, contract, complete, transact, execute, fulfil, orchestrate, engineer. **2** *unions and managements negotiate* bargain, drive a bargain, hold talks, confer, debate, discuss, discuss terms, discuss a settlement, consult together, parley, haggle, wheel and deal, dicker. **3** *negotiate the hurdles | careful negotiating the icy roads* clear, get over, get through, pass over, make it over, cross, get past, get round, surmount.

negotiation n **1** *the negotiations went on all day* bargaining, conference, debate, talks, discussion, consultation, parleying, haggling, wheeling and dealing, dickering. **2** *the negotiation of the settlement* working out, thrashing out, discussing the terms of, settlement, pulling off, transaction. *see* NEGOTIATE 1, 2.

negotiator n bargainer, parleyer, haggler, wheeler-dealer, dickerer.

neighbourhood n **1** *move to a different neighbourhood* district, area, region, locality, part, quarter, precinct, community; *inf* stamping-ground, neck of the woods. **2** *he doesn't live here but somewhere in the neighbourhood* vicinity, surrounding district, environs, proximity, purlieus. **in the neighbourhood of** *in the neighbourhood of £5000* around, about, approximately, roughly, nearly, almost, close to, just about.

neighbouring adj *neighbouring village/families* adjacent, adjoining, bordering, abutting, contiguous, next, nearby, nearest, closest, near, very near, close/near at hand, not far away, in the vicinity.

neighbourly adj friendly, cordial, kind, helpful, obliging, generous, hospitable, companionable, sociable, amiable, affable, genial, well-disposed, civil, easy to get along with.

neither adj *neither sister* not either, not the one nor the other.

nemesis n **1** *nemesis won the day* fate, destiny, retribution, vengeance. **2** *meet his nemesis* downfall, undoing, ruin, destruction, Waterloo.

neologism n neology, new word, new term, new phrase, new expression, coinage, newly coined word, made-up word, nonce-word, portmanteau word, vogue word; *inf* buzz-word.

neophyte n **1** *neophytes in the religious community* novice, noviciate, convert, proselyte, catechumen. **2** *introducing the neophytes to the club* beginner, newcomer, new member, new entrant, new recruit, raw recruit, initiate, novice, noviciate, tiro, greenhorn, learner, trainee, apprentice, probationer, pupil, student; *inf* rookie.

ne plus ultra n the ultimate, the last word, acme, culmination, perfection, the uttermost degree.

nepotism n favouritism, patronage, partisanship, partiality, preferential treatment; *inf* the old boy network.

nerve n **1** *rock-climbing requires nerve* courage, courageousness, bravery, valour, intrepidity, fearlessness, daring, coolness, cool-headedness, boldness, pluck, gameness, hardihood, mettle, spirit, backbone, fortitude, endurance, firmness of purpose, stout-heartedness, resolution, determination, tenacity, steadfastness; *inf* grit, guts, spunk, bottle. **2** *she had the nerve to ask for more* temerity, impudence, impertinence, effrontery, cheek, insolence, audacity, boldness, presumption, gall, brazenness; *inf* neck, face, brass neck, brass, neck, sauce, chutzpah.

nerve v *soldiers nerved by his presence* embolden, encourage, hearten, steel, fortify. **nerve oneself** *nerve oneself to climb up* brace oneself, steel oneself, summon/gather/screw up one's courage; *inf* psych oneself up.

nerve-racking adj stressful, worrying, anxious, disquieting, tense, harrowing, frightening, distressing, difficult, trying, harassing; *inf* nail-biting.

nerves npl nervousness, strain, nervous tension, tenseness, tension, stress, anxiety, worry, apprehensiveness, apprehension; *inf* butterflies in the stomach, collywobbles, the jitters, the willies.

nervous adj 1 *a nervous person | she is of a nervous disposition* easily frightened, timid, timorous, fearful, apprehensive, anxious, edgy, highly-strung, tense, strained, excitable, jumpy, hysterical; *inf* nervy. 2 *feeling nervous about the interview* on edge, edgy, tense, strained, anxious, agitated, worried, fretful, uneasy, disquieted, restless, impatient, excitable, jumpy, on tenterhooks, fidgety, ruffled, flustered, apprehensive, perturbed, fearful, frightened, scared, with one's heart in one's mouth, quaking, trembling, shaking, shaking in one's shoes, shaky; *inf* nervy, with butterflies in one's stomach, jittery, twitchy, in a state, uptight, wired.

nervous breakdown n breakdown, mental breakdown, nervous collapse, personal crisis, clinical depression; *inf* crack-up.

nervousness n 1 *given to nervousness* timidity, timorousness, fearfulness, anxiety, tenseness. *see* NERVOUS 1. 2 *a feeling of nervousness about the interview* edginess, tension, nervous tension, tenseness, strain, stress, anxiety, agitation, worry, uneasiness, disquiet, restlessness, impatience, jumpiness, apprehensiveness, apprehension, perturbation, fearfulness, trembling; *inf* nerviness, jitteriness, twitchiness. *see* NERVOUS 2.

nervy adj 1 *a nervy kind of person* nervous, timid, timorous, fearful, anxious, highly-strung, tense, excitable. *see* NERVOUS 1. 2 *feeling nervy about the outcome* edgy, on edge, tense, anxious, worried, fretful, uneasy, restless, impatient, on tenterhooks, apprehensive, shaky, jumpy; *inf* jittery, uptight. *see* NERVOUS 2.

nescient adj ignorant, unaware, unconscious, unenlightened, benighted, uneducated, illiterate, unschooled, unknowledgeable.

nest n 1 *birds/creatures building nests* bird's nest, eyrie, wasps' nest, ants' nest, lair, den, drey, lodge, burrow, set, form. 2 *a love-nest | a thieves' nest* retreat, hideaway, hiding-place, shelter, refuge, snuggery, resort, den, haunt; *inf* hide-out, hidey-hole. 3 *a nest of tables* set, cluster, assemblage, group, series.

nest egg n life savings, savings, reserve funds, reserve, money/something for a rainy day, cache.

nestle v snuggle, curl up, huddle together, cuddle up, nuzzle.

net¹ n 1 *trim a dress with net | net curtains | ball hit the net* netting, tulle, fishnet, meshwork, mesh, latticework, lattice, openwork, webbing, tracery, reticulum. 2 *fishermen casting their nets* fishing net, drag, drag-net, drift, drift-net, seine, seine-net. 3 *fall into the enemy's net* trap, booby trap, snare, mesh, pitfall, stratagem.

net¹ v *net the animal/runaway* catch, take captive, trap, snare, ensnare, entangle, enmesh, bag; *inf* nab, collar.

net², nett adj 1 *their net salary* take-home, after-tax, after-deductions, bottom-line, clear. 2 *the net result* final, ultimate, concluding, conclusive, closing, actual.

net², nett v *was netting £200 per week* take home, clear, earn, make, bring in, get, pocket, receive, gain, obtain, realize; *inf* pull in.

nether adj 1 *in the nether part of the store* lower, low, low-level, bottom, under, basement, underground. 2 *myths about the nether regions* infernal, hellish, underworld, Hadean, Plutonian, Stygian, Avernal.

nettle v irritate, provoke, ruffle, try someone's patience, annoy, incense, exasperate, irk, vex, pique, bother, pester, harass, torment, plague; *inf* aggravate, rile, peeve, rub up the wrong way, get under someone's skin, get in someone's hair, get someone's goat, get to.

nettled adj irritated, irritable, provoked, ruffled, annoyed, incensed, irked, vexed, piqued, harassed; *inf* riled, peeved. *see* NETTLE.

network n 1 *a pattern consisting of a network of lines* meshwork, latticework, openwork, mesh, lattice, webbing, tracery, filigree, fretwork. 2 *a network of old friends | the old boy network* interconnection, nexus, system, complex, organization, structure, arrangement, formulation. 3 *a network of roads | the electricity network* interconnection, grid, circuitry, plexus.

neurosis n mental illness, mental disorder, psychological disorder, mental disturbance, mental derangement, mental/emotional instability, psychological maladjustment, psychoneurosis, psychopathy, obsession, phobia, fixation.

neurotic adj **1** *treating neurotic patients* mentally ill, mentally disturbed, mentally deranged, unstable, maladjusted, psychopathic, obsessive, phobic. **2** *his wife is completely neurotic* suffering from nerves, over-anxious, obsessive, phobic, fixated, compulsive, over-sensitive, hysterical, irrational.

neuter adj *neuter organisms* asexual, sexless, unsexed.

neuter v **1** *neuter a tom-cat/bull* castrate, geld, emasculate, dress; *inf* cut, fix, doctor. **2** *neuter a bitch* spay, dress; *inf* fix, doctor.

neutral adj **1** *referees must be neutral* impartial, unbiased, unprejudiced, open-minded, non-partisan, without favouritism, even-handed, disinterested, non-aligned, dispassionate, objective, detached, uninvolved, uncommitted. **2** *neutral countries during the war* non-combatant, non-combative, non-fighting, non-participating, non-aligned, unallied, uninvolved, non-interventionist. **3** *he's rather a neutral character* indefinite, indeterminate, unremarkable, ordinary, commonplace, average, run-of-the-mill, everyday, bland, uninteresting, colourless, insipid, dull. **4** *curtains of a neutral colour* beige, greige, stone-coloured, stone, pale, colourless, uncoloured, achromatic, achromic.

neutrality n **1** *challenge the neutrality of the referee* impartiality, lack/absence of bias/prejudice, open-mindedness, objectivity, even-handedness, disinterestedness, detachment. *see* NEUTRAL 1. **2** *the neutrality of the countries* non-combativeness, non-alignment, non-participation, non-involvement, non-intervention, non-interventionism.

neutralize v **1** *neutralize the poison* counteract, cancel, nullify, negate, annul, undo, invalidate, frustrate, be an antidote to. **2** *her warmth neutralizing their hostility* offset, counterbalance, counteract, compensate for, make up for, cancel out, negate.

never adv not ever, at no time, not at any time, not once, not at all, certainly not, not in any circumstances, under no circumstances, on no account; *lit* ne'er; *inf* no way, not on your life, not in a million years, not on your nelly.

never-ending adj **1** *a seemingly never-ending saga* endless, unending, without end, perpetual, everlasting, interminable, without ceasing, ceaseless, unceasing, incessant, non-stop, continuous, continual, uninterrupted, unbroken, unremitting, relentless, persistent; *inf* eternal. **2** *a never-ending supply of books* endless, infinite, limitless, boundless. **3** *their never-ending love* endless, without end, perpetual, everlasting, infinite, eternal, lasting, enduring, abiding, constant, unchanging, unwavering, unfaltering.

never-never n hire-purchase, HP, instalment system.

nevertheless adv none the less, even so, however, still, yet, be that as it may, for all that, just the same, though, in any event, notwithstanding, regardless.

new adj **1** *new techniques* modern, recent, advanced, state-of-the-art, contemporary, present-day, current, latest, up-to-date, up-to-the-minute, new-fashioned, modish, brand new, newly arrived, modernist, ultra-modern, avant-garde, futuristic, newfangled; *inf* way-out, far-out. **2** *in need of new ideas* modern, state-of-the-art, up-to-date, new-fashioned, novel, original, fresh, unhackneyed, imaginative, creative, experimental. **3** *a new rather than a second-hand book* pristine, fresh, mint, in mint condition, virgin, unused. **4** *new people next door | starting a new job* unfamiliar, unknown, strange, different, unaccustomed, untried. **5** *a new bit on the house* additional, added, extra, supplementary, further, another. **6** *feel like a new person* refreshed, renewed, improved, restored, reinvigorated, regenerated, reborn, remodelled.

newborn adj just born, new-fledged, neonatal.

newcomer n **1** *newcomers to the town* new arrival, arrival, incomer, immigrant, settler, stranger, outsider, foreigner, alien, intruder, interloper; *inf* johnny-come-lately. **2** *a newcomer to the game* beginner, novice, learner, trainee, probationer, new recruit, raw recruit, tiro, greenhorn, initiate, neophyte.

newfangled adj *dislike newfangled methods/ machines* modern, ultra-modern, state-of-the-art, contemporary, fashionable, new-fashioned, gimmicky.

newly adv just, just recently, lately, of late.

news n information, facts, data, report, story, news item, news flash, account, statement, announcement, press release, communication, communiqué, message, bulletin, dispatch, disclosure, revelation, word, talk, the latest, gossip, tittle-tattle, rumour, scandal, exposé; *inf* gen, info.

newspaper n paper, gazette, journal, tabloid, broadsheet, daily paper, daily, evening paper, weekly paper, weekly, scandal sheet; *inf* rag.

next adj **1** *the next patient/day* following, succeeding, successive, subsequent, later, ensuing. **2** *the next house* neighbouring, adjacent, adjoining, bordering, contiguous, closest, nearest, proximate.

next adv *next we went to the zoo* then, later, at a later time, after, afterwards, thereafter, subsequently, at a subsequent time, after this/that, after that time.

nibble v take small bites from, bite, gnaw, peck at, pick at, pick over, eat, munch, eat between meals; *inf* snack on.

nibble n **1** *have a nibble of the cheese* bite, gnaw, peck, munch, taste, crumb, piece, morsel, soupçon. **2** *party nibbles* snack, titbit, canapé, hors-d'oeuvre.

nice adj **1** *have a nice time* good, pleasant, enjoyable, pleasurable, agreeable, delightful, amusing, satisfying, gratifying, marvellous. **2** *a nice lady/friend* pleasant, agreeable, likable, charming, delightful, amiable, friendly, kindly, genial, gracious, sympathetic, understanding, compassionate, good. **3** *nice manners/behaviour* polite, courteous, civil, refined, cultivated, polished, genteel, elegant, seemly, decorous, proper, fitting, suitable, appropriate, respectable, good, virtuous. **4** *a nice distinction* fine, ultra-fine, subtle, minute, precise, exact, accurate, strict, close, careful, meticulous, rigorous. **5** *it's a nice day* fine, dry, sunny, warm, pleasant, agreeable. **6** *she is too nice to eat with her fingers* fastidious, delicate, refined, dainty, particular, discriminating, over-refined, over-particular, fussy, finicky; *inf* pernickety.

nicely adv **1** *children behaving nicely* well, politely, courteously, decorously, properly, fittingly, suitably, respectably, virtuously. *see* NICE 3. **2** *distinguishing nicely between the possibilities* fine, subtly, precisely, exactly, strictly, closely, carefully, meticulously, rigorously. *see* NICE 4.

niceness n **1** *appreciate their neighbour's niceness* pleasantness, agreeableness, friendliness, geniality. **2** *the niceness of the children's behaviour* politeness, courtesy, refinement, civility, gentility, respectability. **3** *they laugh at the niceness of her table manners* fastidiousness, delicacy, over-refinement, fussiness, finickiness, pernicketiness.

nicety n **1** *the niceties of meaning* finer point, subtlety, nuance, detail. **2** *the nicety of the judgement* precision, accuracy, exactness, meticulousness, rigour.

niche n **1** *vases placed in a niche in the wall* alcove, recess, nook, cranny, cubbyhole. **2** *his niche in life* calling, vocation, place, position, job; *inf* slot.

nickname n pet name, family name, familiar name, diminutive; *inf* moniker, handle.

nifty adj **1** *a nifty piece of footwork* agile, nimble, deft, adroit, skilful, neat. **2** *wearing rather nifty clothes* smart, stylish, elegant, chic; *inf* natty.

niggardly adj **1** *a niggardly old man* mean, miserly, stingy, tight-fisted, parsimonious, penny-pinching, cheese-paring, avaricious; *Amer inf* tight-assed. **2** *a niggardly supply of food* meagre, paltry, skimpy, scanty, measly, inadequate, insubstantial, miserable; *inf* piddling.

niggle v **1** *he was always niggling about money* fuss, nag, carp, criticize, cavil; *inf* nit-pick. **2** *many doubts were niggling him* irritate, annoy, worry, trouble, rankle.

night n night-time, darkness, dark, hours of darkness. **night and day** all the time, around the clock, ceaselessly, incessantly, continuously.

nightfall n sunset, sundown, dusk, evening, twilight; *lit* eventide, crepuscule, gloaming.

nightly adj at night, night-time, nocturnal.

nightmare n **1** *I have had nightmares since the accident* bad dream, incubus, phantasmagoria. **2** *the interview was a nightmare* ordeal, horror, torment, torture.

nihilism n **1** *former believers are turning to nihilism* rejection, repudiation, renunciation, denial, abnegation; disbelief, scepticism; negativism, cynicism, pessimism. **2** *they lapsed into political nihilism* anarchy, lawlessness, disorder, chaos. **3** *he felt himself to be in a state of nihilism* nihility, nothingness, non-existence, void.

nil n nought, zero, love, duck; nothing, naught, none; *inf* zilch.

nimble adj **1** *nimble gymnasts/movements* agile, lithe, sprightly, spry, lively, quick, quick-moving, graceful, skilful, deft. **2** *nimble of wit* quick-thinking, clever, bright, quick, quick-witted, alert.

nip v **1** *nip his arm* pinch, tweak, squeeze, grip, bite, nibble. **2** *nip off the withered shoots* snip, cut off, lop, dock. **3** *frost nipping her cheeks* sting, bite, hurt. **4** *I'm nipping off to the shops* dart, hurry, rush, scurry, scamper. **nip in the bud** *her plans were nipped in the bud* stop, quash, quell, check, thwart, frustrate.

nipple n teat, udder, dug, mamilla, papilla; *dial* pap.

nippy adj icy, chilly, bitter, raw, piercing, stinging.

nirvana n enlightenment, oblivion; paradise, heaven; bliss, joy, peace, serenity, tranquillity.

nit-picking adj captious, hair-splitting, quibbling, fault-finding, ultra-critical, critical, cavilling, pedantic.

nitty-gritty n crux, gist, substance, essence, quintessence; core, heart, centre, kernel, nucleus; essentials, basics, facts; *inf* brass-tacks, nuts and bolts.

nitwit n fool, ninny, idiot, nincompoop, dolt, dunce, ignoramus, noodle, donkey; *inf* dope, chump, twit, dimwit, wally, nerd, jerk, pillock.

no adv no indeed, absolutely not, under no circumstances, by no means, never; *inf* not on your life, no way; *Amer inf* nope, no siree.

nobble v **1** *nobble the jury* influence, bribe, win over, secure the support of; *inf* get at. **2** *nobble the racehorse* tamper with, interfere with, disable, incapacitate, weaken. **3** *nobble the firm's profits* steal, rob, embezzle; *inf* pinch, nick, swipe. **4** *nobble the thief* grab, seize, capture; *inf* nab, collar.

nobility n **1** *the nobility are not always wealthy* lords, peers, peers of the realm, aristocracy, high society, the élite, the upper class; *inf* nobs. **2** *the nobility of his deed* magnanimity, generosity, selflessness, honour, integrity, bravery. **3** *the nobility of thoughts* loftiness, grandness. *see* NOBLE adj 3. **4** *he admired the nobility of the setting* impressiveness, splendour, magnificence, stateliness, grandeur. **5** *the nobility of the breed* excellence, prime quality.

noble n nobleman, noblewoman, lord, lady, peer, peer of the realm, aristocrat.

noble adj **1** *the noble people of the land* aristocratic, patrician, blue-blooded, titled, landed, born with a silver spoon in one's mouth. **2** *noble deeds* noble-minded, magnanimous, generous, self-sacrificing, honourable, virtuous, brave. **3** *noble thoughts* lofty, grand, exalted, elevated. **4** *of noble appearance* impressive, magnificent, striking, awesome, stately, grand, dignified. **5** *horses of a noble strain* first-rate, prime, choice, prize, quality; *inf* A1, top-notch.

nod v **1** *nod one's head* incline, bob, bow, dip, duck. **2** *nod a greeting* signal, gesture, motion, sign, indicate. **3** *the audience began to nod* doze off, drop off, fall asleep, nap, slumber. **4** *even Homer nods* make a mistake, err, blunder, slip up.

node n protuberance, swelling, lump, growth, excrescence, knob, knot, nodule, bump, bulge.

noise n sound, loud sound, din, hubbub, clamour, racket, row, uproar, tumult, commotion, rumpus, pandemonium.

noisome adj disgusting, repugnant, revolting, repulsive, obnoxious; offensive, nauseating; unpleasant, disagreeable, horrible, detestable, loathsome.

noisy adj **1** *noisy neighbours* rowdy, clamorous, boisterous, obstreperous, turbulent; *inf* rackety. **2** *noisy music* loud, blaring, blasting, deafening, ear-splitting.

nomad n itinerant, traveller, migrant, wanderer, roamer, rover; transient, vagabond, vagrant, tramp.

nominal adj **1** *the nominal head* in name only, titular, formal; theoretical, self-styled; purported, supposed. **2** *a nominal sum* token, symbolic; minimal, trivial, insignificant.

nominate v **1** *they nominated several candidates* name, propose, put forward, submit, present, recommend; *inf* put up. **2** *he nominated his successor* name, designate, appoint, assign, select, choose.

non-aligned adj neutral, uncommitted, impartial, uninvolved, unallied.

non-believer n atheist, agnostic, sceptic, doubter, doubting Thomas, unbeliever, disbeliever, cynic, infidel, pagan, heathen.

nonce n **for the nonce** for the present, for the moment, for the present moment, for the time being, for now, for just now.

nonchalance n composure, self-possession, sang-froid, equanimity, imperturbability, calm, coolness, unconcern, indifference, dispassionateness, detachment, detachedness, apathy, casualness, carefreeness, insouciance, carelessness; *inf* cool.

nonchalant adj composed, self-possessed, imperturbable, unexcitable, calm, cool, collected, cool calm and collected, cool as a cucumber, unconcerned, indifferent, unemotional, blasé, dispassionate, detached, apathetic, casual, offhand, carefree, insouciant, easygoing, careless; *inf* laid-back.

non-combatant adj non-combative, non-fighting, non-belligerent, pacifist, civilian, neutral, non-aligned, non-participating.

non-committal adj cautious, guarded, circumspect, wary, careful, discreet, politic, tactful, diplomatic, prudent, playing one's cards close to one's chest, giving nothing away, sitting on the fence, unrevealing, temporizing, evasive, equivocal, vague, reserved.

non compos mentis adj of unsound mind, mentally deranged, mentally unbalanced, mentally ill, insane, mad; *inf* crazy.

nonconformist n *the nonconformists of society* radical, dissenter, dissentient, protester, rebel, seceder, maverick, individualist, deviant, misfit, fish out of water, eccentric, iconoclast, outsider; *inf* drop-out, hippie, freak, oddball.

nondescript adj indefinite, indeterminate, unclassifiable, indescribable, indistinguishable, vague, blending into the background, unremarkable, featureless, undistinguished, ordinary, commonplace, average, mediocre, unexceptional, unmemorable, uninteresting, uninspiring, dull, colourless, anaemic, insipid, bland; *inf* common-or-garden.

none pron **1** *we expected several people but none came* no one, nobody, not one, not a one, never a one, not a soul, not a single person. **2** *she expected presents but none came* nothing, nothing at all, not a thing, not a single thing, not a one, nil, zero. **3** *none of this concerns me* not any, not a part, not a bit.

none adv *none the wiser* not at all, not a bit, in no way, to no extent.

nonentity n nobody, person of no account, person of no importance, cipher, nonperson; *inf* nothing, small beer, small fry, lightweight.

non-essential adj inessential, unessential, unnecessary, needless, unneeded, unrequired, superfluous, redundant, dispensable, expendable, peripheral, unimportant, insignificant, inconsequential, irrelevant, inapplicable, inapposite, extraneous.

nonetheless adv nevertheless, even so, however, still, yet, be that as it may, for all that, just the same, though, in any event, notwithstanding, regardless.

non-existent adj unreal, hypothetical, suppositional, fictional, fictitious, imagined, imaginary, fancied, fanciful, mythical, legendary, fantasy, illusory, delusive, illusionary, hallucinatory, insubstantial, inexistent, missing, unreal.

non-intervention n *laissez-faire*, neutrality, non-participation, non-interference, non-involvement, inaction, passivity.

non-observance n *non-observance of the rules* ignoring, non-compliance, disobedience, unruliness, infringement, violation.

nonpareil adj *his artistic work is nonpareil | as a writer he is nonpareil* unparalleled, unri-

valled, without rival, incomparable, peerless, matchless, unmatched, without equal, unequalled, unsurpassed, unique, unbeatable, supreme.

nonpareil n *the nonpareils of the art world* nonesuch, *crème de la crème*, élite, jewel, jewel in the crown, gem, paragon.

nonplus v take aback, stun, dumbfound, confound, astound, astonish, amaze, surprise, disconcert, discomfit, dismay, make one halt in one's tracks, puzzle, perplex, baffle, mystify, stump, confuse, bewilder, embarrass, fluster; *inf* faze, flummox, floor.

nonsense n **1** *talk nonsense* rubbish, balderdash, drivel, gibberish, twaddle, blather, stuff and nonsense; *inf* tommy-rot, bunkum, trash, tripe, tosh, bosh, double Dutch, gobbledegook, mumbo-jumbo, poppycock, flannel, waffle, claptrap, bilge, bull. **2** *tired of their nonsense* foolishness, folly, silliness, senselessness, stupidity, ridiculousness, ludicrousness, inanity, fatuity, joking, jesting, clowning, buffoonery, drollery.

nonsensical adj **1** *nonsensical remarks* meaningless, incomprehensible, unintelligible, senseless, incongruous. **2** *a nonsensical scheme* foolish, absurd, silly, inane, senseless, stupid, ridiculous, ludicrous, preposterous, hare-brained, irrational, idiotic, insane; *inf* crazy, crackpot, nutty, wacky.

non-stop adj *non-stop commentaries/nagging* incessant, unceasing, ceaseless, constant, continuous, continual, without interruption, unbroken, unfaltering, steady, unremitting, relentless, persistent, endless, never-ending, unending, interminable; *inf* eternal.

non-stop adv *talk non-stop* incessantly, unceasingly, constantly, continuously, continually, steadily, unremittingly, relentlessly, persistently, endlessly. *see* NON-STOP adj.

nook n **1** *a room full of nooks and crannies* corner, cranny, recess, alcove, niche, opening, cavity, crevice, gap, cubbyhole, inglenook. **2** *find a quiet nook to be alone* hideaway, retreat, refuge, shelter, den; *inf* hide-out, hidey-hole.

noon n midday, twelve noon, twelve midday, twelve o'clock, high noon, noontime, noontide, noonday, twelve hundred, twelve hundred hours, one-two-double-O.

no one pron nobody, not a one, not anyone, not a person, not a single person, never a one, not a soul.

norm n **1** *measured against the norm* standard, criterion, measure, gauge, yardstick, benchmark, touchstone, scale, rule, pattern, model, type. **2** *six hours a day is the norm* average, mean, normal rate, the usual, the rule.

normal adj **1** *the normal temperature/method* usual, standard, average, common, ordinary, natural, general, commonplace, conventional, typical, regular, routine, run-of-the-mill, everyday, accustomed, habitual, prevailing, popular, accepted, acknowledged; *inf* common-or-garden. **2** *of normal size* average, medium, middling, standard, mean. **3** *the patient isn't normal* well-adjusted, well-balanced, rational, compos mentis, sane.

normality n **1** *return to normality | the normality of his surroundings* usualness, commonness, ordinariness, naturalness, commonplaceness, conventionality, regularity, routine, accustomedness, habitualness. *see* NORMAL 1. **2** *question the normality of the patient* balance, rationality, sanity.

normally adv **1** *behave normally* as usual, ordinarily, naturally, conventionally, routinely, typically, regularly. **2** *normally, we eat late* usually, ordinarily, as a rule, as a general rule, generally, in general, mostly, commonly, habitually.

north adj *north winds* northern, northerly, northwardly, Arctic, polar, boreal.

north adv *go north* northwards, northward, northwardly.

nose n **1** *have a large nose* proboscis, bird's bill/beak, animal's snout/muzzle, elephant's trunk; *inf* beak, snout, conk, snoot, schnozzle, hooter, snitch; *dial* neb. **2** *have a good nose* sense of smell, olfactory sense. **3** *a nose for a good story* instinct, sixth sense, intuition, insight, perception, gift for discovering/detecting. **4** *admire the wine's nose* bouquet, aroma, fragrance, perfume, scent, smell. **by a nose** *win by a nose* by a hair's breadth, by the narrowest of margins, by a narrow margin, narrowly, by the skin of one's teeth; *inf* by a whisker. **on the nose** *£200 on the nose | arrive at 6 pm on the nose* exactly, precisely, promptly, prompt, on time, on target; *inf* on the dot, spot on, on the button.

nose v **1** *dogs nosing out the thieves* smell out, sniff out, follow the scent of, scent out, search for, detect, run to earth/ground. **2** *dogs were nosing his arm* nudge, push, nuzzle. **3** *nose around the room* pry, search, peer, prowl, have a good look; *inf* snoop. **4** *nose into someone's business* pry into, interfere in, meddle in, inquire into; *inf* poke one's nose into. **5** *nose the car forward* ease, inch, move, run.

nosedive n **1** *the plane/parachutist took a nosedive* dive, plunge, swoop. **2** *the nosedive taken by prices* fall, drop, plunge, decline.

nosedive v **1** *the plane nosedived out of the sky* dive, plunge, swoop, drop, plummet. **2** *the prices situation nosedived after the news* fall, drop, plunge, plummet, go down, decline, worsen, get worse.

nosegay n bouquet, posy, spray, bunch of flowers.

nosh n food, fare, sustenance, meal, repast, snack, victuals, viands, comestibles, provisions, aliment; *inf* grub, scoff, chow.

nostalgia n longing/yearning/pining for the past, regret, regretfulness, reminiscence, remembrance, recollection, wistfulness, homesickness.

nostalgic adj longing/yearning/pining for the past, regretful, reminiscing, remembering, recollecting, wistful, sentimental, emotional about the past, maudlin, homesick.

nostrum n **1** *prescribing nostrums for patients* patent medicine, medicine, medication, drug, potion, pill, quack remedy, elixir, remedy, cure, panacea, sovereign remedy, magic bullet. **2** *claiming to have a nostrum for the country's problems* remedy, cure, cure-all, panacea, solution, perfect solution, answer, magic bullet, magic formula, recipe for success.

nosy adj prying, inquisitive, quizzing, probing, eavesdropping, curious, interfering, meddlesome, intrusive; *inf* snooping, snoopy.

notability n **1** *the notability of his achievements* noteworthiness, importance, significance, momentousness, memorability, impressiveness, extraordinariness. *see* NOTABLE adj 1. **2** *the notability of the members of council* eminence, pre-eminence, distinction, illustriousness, greatness, prestige, fame, renown, reputation, acclaim, consequence. *see* NOTABLE adj 2. **3** *the notabilities of the university/theatre* dignitary, notable, celebrity, luminary star, superstar, VIP, personage, worthy, lion; *inf* somebody, celeb, megastar, big shot, big gun.

notable adj **1** *a notable achievement* noteworthy, remarkable, outstanding, important, significant, momentous, memorable, unforgettable, pronounced, marked, striking, impressive, uncommon, unusual, particular, special, extraordinary, conspicuous, rare, signal. **2** *notable people in the town* noted, of note, distinguished, eminent, pre-eminent, well-known, prominent, illustrious, great, famous, famed, renowned, celebrated, acclaimed.

notable n *the notables of the university* nota-bility, dignitary, celebrity, luminary, star, VIP; *inf* celeb, megastar. *see* NOTABILITY 3.

notably adv *notably successful* remarkably, outstandingly, significantly, markedly, strikingly, impressively, uncommonly, unusually, particularly, especially, extraor-dinarily, conspicuously, signally.

notation n system of symbols, symbols, signs, code, cipher, hieroglyphics, short-hand, musical notation.

notch n **1** *make a notch in the wood* indenta-tion, dent, nick, groove, gouge, cut, mark, incision, score, scratch, gash, slit, cleft. **2** *her singing is several notches up from the rest of the choir* degree, grade, gradation, level, step, stage, rung.

notch v *notch the wood* indent, make an indentation in, dent, nick, gouge, cut, mark, score, scratch, gash, slit. *see* NOTCH n 1. **notch up** *notch up another success* score, achieve, attain, gain, make, register, record.

note n **1** *always kept a note of her purchases* record, account. **2** *there is a note in the regis-ter* entry, item, notation, record, comment, jotting, inscription. **3** *leave him a note* letter, message, memorandum; *inf* memo. **4** *drop them a note* letter, epistle, missive, commu-nication, thank-you note, bread-and-butter letter. **5** *read the notes in the book* footnote, annotation, commentary, gloss, margina-lia, explanation, explication, exposition, exegesis. **6** *exchange notes for coins* banknote, bill, paper money; *inf* fiver, tenner. **7** *wor-thy of note* notice, attention, attentiveness, heed, observation, consideration, thought, regard, care, mindfulness. **8** *people of note* distinction, eminence, pre-eminence, illus-triousness, greatness, prestige, fame, renown, reputation, acclaim, consequence. **9** *a note of amusement in her voice* tone, into-nation, inflection, sound, indication, hint, element.

note v **1** *note the date in your diary* write down, put down, jot down, mark down, enter, mark, record, register. **2** *note his com-ments in your report* mention, make mention of, refer to, allude to, touch on, indicate, point out, make known, state. **3** *he noted their concern* take note of, take notice of, see, observe, perceive, behold, detect, take in.

notebook n notepad, memorandum book, exercise book, jotter, scratch pad, register, logbook, log, diary, journal, commonplace book, record book, personal organizer; *Trademark* Filofax; *inf* memo pad.

noted adj *a noted artist* of note, notable, dis-tinguished, eminent, pre-eminent, well-known, prominent, illustrious, great, famous, famed, renowned, celebrated, acclaimed.

notes npl *make/take notes on the conference | his notes for the screenplay* jottings, record, report, commentary, chronicle, transcript, minutes, observations, impressions, synop-sis, précis, sketch, outline.

noteworthy adj *a noteworthy achievement* notable, remarkable, outstanding, impor-tant, significant, marked, striking, impres-sive, unusual, conspicuous, rare, signal. *see* NOTABLE adj 1.

nothing n **1** *nothing to declare* not anything, nothing at all, nought, naught, nil, not a thing, not a single thing; *inf* zilch, sweet Fanny Adams. **2** *write nothing in the right-hand column* nought, zero, cipher, 0. **3** *the wound is a mere nothing* trifling matter, piece of trivia, matter of no importance/consequence, bagatelle; *inf* no big deal. **4** *they treat her like a nothing* nobody, person of no account, nonentity, cipher; *inf* small beer, lightweight. **5** *pass into nothing* noth-ingness, non-existence, non-being, nullity. *see* NOTHINGNESS 1. **for nothing 1** *work for nothing* free, for free, gratis, without charge, without payment, gratuitously. **2** *do all that studying for nothing* in vain, to no avail, to no purpose, futilely, needlessly. **nothing but** *nothing but a miracle can save us* only, solely, simply, purely, merely.

nothingness n **1** *pass into nothingness* noth-ing, non-existence, non-life, non-being, nihility, nullity, oblivion, void, vacuum, blankness. **2** *aware of the nothingness of his work* insignificance, unimportance, trivial-ity, worthlessness, valuelessness, pointless-ness, uselessness, meagreness.

notice n **1** *escape my notice* attention, atten-tiveness, heed, note, observation, cog-nizance, regard, consideration, interest, thought, mindfulness, watchfulness, vigi-lance. **2** *see the notice on the board* informa-tion sheet, bulletin, poster, handbill, bill, circular, leaflet, pamphlet, advertisement. **3** *receive notice of the planning request* notifi-cation, appraisal, announcement, intima-tion, information, intelligence, news, communication, advice, instruction, order, warning. **4** *workers have received their notice* notice to quit, redundancy notice, dis-missal; *inf* marching orders, the sack, the boot. **5** *plays receiving poor notices* review, write-up, critique.

notice v see, note, take note of, observe, perceive, discern, detect, behold, descry, spot, distinguish, make out, take heed of, heed, pay attention to, take notice of, mark, regard.

noticeable adj *no noticeable improvement | was it noticeable?* observable, visible, discernible, perceptible, detectable, distinguishable, distinct, evident, obvious, apparent, manifest, patent, plain, clear, conspicuous, unmistakable, pronounced, striking, blatant.

notification n **1** *the notification of the tenants* informing, telling, warning, alerting. *see* NOTIFY 1. **2** *the notification of his intentions* disclosure, divulgence, announcement, declaration, publishing. *see* NOTIFY 2. **3** *receive a notification* notice, announcement, statement, declaration, communication, message, information, advice.

notify v **1** *notify the tenants* inform, tell, advise, acquaint, apprise, warn, alert, caution. **2** *notify his intentions to the tenants* make known, disclose, reveal, divulge, announce, declare, broadcast, publish, communicate.

notion n **1** *have strange notions about children* idea, belief, opinion, thought, impression, view, conviction, concept, conception, conceptualization, assumption, presumption, hypothesis, theory, postulation, abstraction, apprehension, understanding. **2** *a notion to go to the sea* impulse, inclination, fancy, whim, wish, desire, caprice.

notional adj hypothetical, theoretical, suppositional, speculative, conceptual, abstract, imaginary, fanciful, fancied, unreal, illusory, unsubstantiated, ideal.

notoriety n infamy, ill/evil repute, bad reputation/name, disrepute, dishonour, scandal, opprobrium, obloquy.

notorious adj **1** *a notorious murderer/liar* infamous, of ill repute, having a bad reputation/name, ill-famed, disreputable, dishonourable. **2** *a notorious murder | in a notorious accident black spot* well-known, infamous, prominent, scandalous, opprobrious, obloquial, legendary.

notwithstanding adv *notwithstanding, we must go* nevertheless, nonetheless, even so, however, still, yet, be that as it may, for all that, just the same, through, in any event, regardless.

notwithstanding prep *notwithstanding the delay* despite, in spite of, regardless of.

nought n nothing, naught, nil, zero, love, nothingness; *inf* zilch.

nourish v **1** *nourish the children* feed, nurture, provide for, care for, take care of, tend, attend to, bring up, rear. **2** *nourish*

growth encourage, promote, foster, stimulate, boost, further, advance, forward, contribute to, be conducive to, assist, help, aid. **3** *nourish hopes of success* cherish, entertain, harbour, foster, hold, have.

nourishing adj nutritious, nutritive, wholesome, healthy, health-giving, healthful, beneficial, good for one.

nourishment n food, nutriment, nutrition, sustenance, subsistence, aliment, provisions, provender, meat, fare, viands, victuals, daily bread; *inf* grub, scoff, chow.

nouveau riche n new-rich, parvenu, *arriviste*, *arrivé*, upstart.

novel adj new, fresh, different, original, unusual, uncommon, unfamiliar, rare, unique, singular, imaginative, unhackneyed, unconventional, creative, innovative, ground-breaking, trail-blazing, modern, ultra-modern, advanced, futuristic.

novel n book, story, tale, narrative, work of fiction, romance.

novelist n novel writer, author/authoress, writer, writer of fiction, fiction-writer, creative writer, fictionist.

novelty n **1** *the novelty of the idea/approach* newness, freshness, difference, originality, unusualness, uniqueness, rareness, imaginativeness, creativity. *see* NOVEL adj. **2** *a stall selling novelties* memento, souvenir, knick-knack, trinket, bauble, trifle, gimmick, curiosity, gimcrack.

novice n **1** *novices to the work* beginner, newcomer, apprentice, trainee, learner, probationer, student, pupil, new recruit, raw recruit, tiro, initiate, noviciate, neophyte, greenhorn; *inf* rookie. **2** *welcoming the novices to the convent* novitiate, postulant, neophyte.

noviciate n **1** *undertaking their noviciate* apprenticeship, traineeship, training, probation, trial period, test period, initiation, indoctrination. **2** *noviciates in the convent* novice, postulant, neophyte.

now adv **1** *we do not have any now* just now, right now, at present, at the present time, at this time, at the moment, at this moment in time, for the time being, currently; *Amer* presently. **2** *you must go now* right away, right now, immediately, at once, straight away, instantly, promptly, without delay. **now and again/then** occasionally, on occasions, sometimes, from time to time, at times, once in a while, every once in a while, at intervals, periodically.

nowadays adv **1** *nowadays there is unemployment* at the present time, in these times, in this day and age, today, just now, now, at the moment, at present. **2** *I never see her nowadays* these days, any more, now.

noxious adj *noxious fumes/chemical* nocuous, noisome, harmful, hurtful, injurious, damaging, destructive, ruinous, pernicious, malignant, detrimental, deleterious, prejudicial, menacing, threatening, unwholesome, unhealthy, insalubrious, poisonous, toxic.

nuance n *nuances of colour/meaning* shade, shading, gradation, subtlety, fine distinction, nicety, refinement, degree.

nucleus n core, kernel, centre, heart, nub, basis, pith, meat, marrow, focus, pivot.

nude adj *in the nude*, naked, stark naked, bare, stripped, exposed, unclothed, undressed, uncovered, *au naturel*; *inf* without a stitch on, starkers, in one's birthday suit, in the raw, in the altogether, in the buff, naked as the day one was born, mother naked; *Amer inf* buck naked.

nudge v poke, jab, prod, dig, jog, elbow, bump, touch, push, shove.

nudge n poke, jab, prod, dig, jog, dig in the ribs, elbow, bump, touch, push, shove.

nudity n nakedness, bareness, bare skin, undress, state of undress.

nugget n chunk, lump, piece, mass, clump, wad, hunk; *inf* wodge; *Scots* dod.

nuisance n pest, bother, plague, irritant, source of annoyance, annoyance, vexation, trouble, burden, weight, problem, difficulty, worry, affliction, trial, tribulation, bore, inconvenience, disadvantage, handicap, thorn in the side/flesh; *inf* drag.

null adj **1** *render the ruling null* null and void, void, invalid, annulled, nullified, cancelled, abolished, revoked, rescinded, repealed. **2** *the null effects of the trade embargo* ineffectual, useless, in vain, worthless, futile, powerless, unproductive, non-existent, negative. **3** *null expressions* | *such null young people* blank, expressionless, vacuous, characterless, colourless, insipid, vapid, inane, senseless, foolish.

nullify v render null and void, declare null and void, annul, disannul, void, invalidate, cancel, abolish, set aside, revoke, rescind, repeal, reverse, abrogate, discontinue, retract, withdraw, renounce, repudiate, countermand, veto, negate, terminate, dissolve, cast aside, do away with, bring to an end, obliterate.

nullity n **1** *the nullity of the document* invalidity, non-validity, illegality. **2** *the nullity of* their attempts* ineffectualness, uselessness, worthlessness, futility, powerlessness, non-existence. **3** *the nullity of the expressions/people* blankness, expressionlessness, vacuity, characterlessness, insipidity, vapidity, inanity.

numb adj *numb fingers* | *she was feeling numb with grief/cold* benumbed, dead, without feeling, sensationless, deadened, insensible, insensate, torpid, dull, anaesthetized, drugged, dazed, stunned, stupefied, in shock, paralysed, immobilized, frozen, chilled.

numb v *cold numbing her fingers* | *grief numbing her* benumb, deaden, dull, anaesthetize, drug, daze, stun, stupefy, paralyse, immobilize, freeze, chill.

number n **1** *add up the numbers* figure, digit, numeral, cipher, character, symbol, unit, integer, whole number, cardinal number, ordinal number, Roman number, Arabic number. **2** *the number of accidents has increased* total, aggregate, score, tally, count, sum, summation. **3** *a large number of people* quantity, amount, group, collection, company, crowd. **4** *the latest number of the magazine* edition, issue, printing, imprint, copy.

number v **1** *number the items/reasons* enumerate, count, add up, total, calculate, compute, reckon, tell, estimate, assess, take stock of. **2** *number the accounts* assign a number to, categorize by number, specify by number. **3** *number them among my friends* count, include, reckon. **4** *his days are numbered* limit, limit in number, restrict, fix.

numberless adj *on numberless occasions* innumerable, countless, multitudinous, myriad, numerous, many, untold, infinite, more than one can count, immeasurable, abundant, copious.

numbing adj benumbing, deadening, dulling, anaesthetizing, dazing, paralysing, freezing. *see* NUMB V.

numbness n lack of feeling, lack of sensation, deadness, insensibility, torpor, dullness, stupefaction, paralysis, immobility, chill.

numeral n number, figure, digit, cipher, character, symbol, unit, integer, Roman numeral, Arabic numeral.

numerous adj many, very many, innumerable, myriad, multitudinous, several, quite a few, various, diverse; *inf* a lot of, lots of.

nuncio n envoy, legate, messenger, ambassador.

nuptial adj matrimonial, marriage, marital, wedding, conjugal, connubial, bridal, spousal, hymeneal, married, wedded.

nuptials npl wedding, wedding ceremony, marriage ceremony, marriage.

nurse v **1** *nurse the patient* take care of, care for, look after, tend, attend to, minister to, treat, doctor. **2** *a mother nursing her baby* suckle, breast-feed, feed, wet-nurse. **3** *nurse her career* nurture, encourage, promote, boost, further, advance, contribute to, assist, help. *see* NOURISH 2. **4** *nurse feelings of resentment* harbour, have, hold, entertain, foster, cherish, nourish.

nurture v **1** *nurture the children* feed, nourish, provide for, care for, take care of, tend, attend to, bring up, rear. **2** *nurture the pupils* educate, school, train, tutor, coach. **3** *nurture growth | nurtured her career* encourage, promote, foster, stimulate, develop, cultivate, boost, further, advance, forward, contribute to, be conducive to, assist, help, aid.

nurture n **1** *provide nurture* food, nutrition, nutriment, sustenance, subsistence. **2** *the nurture of the children* feeding, tending, rearing. *see* NURTURE v 1. **3** *the nurture of the pupils* education, schooling, training, discipline. *see* NURTURE v 2. **4** *the nurture of her career/ hopes* encouragement, promotion, fostering, development, cultivation, boosting, furtherance, advancement, assistance. *see* NURTURE v 3.

nut n **1** *squirrels eating nuts* kernel, store, seed, stone; peanut, hazelnut, walnut, Brazil, cob-nut. **2** *a cinema nut* fan, enthusiast, aficionado, devotee, follower; *inf* buff, freak, fiend. **3** *he was attacked by a nut* madman, lunatic, psychopath; *inf* maniac, nutcase, loony, weirdo, oddball, crackpot, screwball.

nutrition n nourishment, nutriment, food, sustenance, subsistence, aliment, provisions, provender, victuals, daily bread; *inf* grub, scoff, chow. *see* NOURISHMENT.

nutritious adj nourishing, nutritive, wholesome, health-giving, healthy, healthful, beneficial, good for one.

nuts adj mad, insane, deranged, demented, irrational, non compos mentis, lunatic, psychopathic; *inf* nutty, crazy, bananas, loony, loopy, batty, barmy, out of one's mind, off one's head, not the full shilling/ pound, with a screw loose, out to lunch.

nuts and bolts npl fundamentals, basics, practicalities, essentials; *inf* nitty-gritty.

nuzzle v **1** *dogs nuzzling their masters* nose, nudge, prod, push. **2** *nuzzle up to her mother* snuggle, cuddle, nestle, lie close to, curl up.

nymph n **1** *the nymphs of legend* wood nymph, water nymph, sylph, sprite, water sprite, undine, naiad, dryad, hamadryad, oread. **2** *nymphs dancing with the boys* girl, lass, damsel, maiden, maid.

Oo

oaf n **1** *that oaf tripped me up* lout, gawk, lubber, blunderer, bungler, boor, churl, bumpkin, yokel, brute, gorilla, bull in a china shop; *inf* clodhopper, lummox, galoot. **2** *the oaf doesn't understand* fool, dolt, blockhead, numskull, dunderhead, dunce, dullard, nincompoop, ninny, simpleton, booby; *inf* idiot, moron, imbecile, sap, dummy, bonehead, thickie, thickhead, nitwit, dim-wit, halfwit, chump, clod, clot, goon, zombie; *Amer inf* schmuck.

oafish adj **1** *oafish boys trying to dance* clumsy, awkward, loutish, gawkish, gawky, lumbering, lubberly, blundering, heavy, bungling, boorish, churlish, brutish; *inf* clodhopping. **2** *oafish children looking blank* dull, stupid, blockish, doltish, blockheaded, dunderheaded, slow-witted, obtuse; *inf* dim, dense, thick, moronic, dim-witted, halfwitted, dumb, slow on the uptake, boneheaded, thickheaded.

oasis n **1** *an oasis in the desert* watering-hole, fertile spot. **2** *an oasis among all the noise* refuge, haven, retreat, sanctuary, sanctum, hiding-place, hideaway; *inf* hideout.

oath n **1** *take an oath to tell the truth|on my oath* sworn statement, vow, promise, pledge, avowal, affirmation, attestation, bond, word of honour, word, troth. **2** *oaths uttered by the man* curse, swear-word, expletive, blasphemy, profanity, imprecation, malediction, obscenity, bad/foul language, strong language, epithet, four-letter word, dirty word, bad word, naughty word; *inf* cuss.

obdurate adj **1** *obdurate children|he was obdurate about not going* stubborn, obstinate, headstrong, wilful, adamant, firm, fixed, dogged, unyielding, unbending, inflexible, unshakeable, unmalleable, intractable, unimpressible, pigheaded, mulish, iron-willed, hard-hearted. **2** *obdurate criminals* hardened, case-hardened, cold-blooded, tough, unresponsive, unfeeling, insensitive, impenitent, unrepenting, uncontrite, shameless.

obedience n dutifulness, duteousness, duty, sense of duty, observance of the law/rules, conformity, conformability, deference, respect, compliance, acquiescence, tractability, amenability, malleability, yielding, submission, docility, meekness. *see* OBEDIENT.

obedient adj biddable, dutiful, duteous, law-abiding, rule-abiding, conforming, deferential, respectful, compliant, acquiescent, tractable, amenable, malleable, governable, under control, well-trained, yielding, submissive, docile, meek, subservient, obsequious, servile.

obeisance n **1** *make obeisance to the emperor* bow, curtsy, bob, kneel, genuflection, stoop, salaam, kowtow. **2** *pay obeisance to the emperor* homage, worship, adoration, reverence, respect, veneration, honour, submission.

obelisk n monolith, column, pillar, shaft, needle, monument.

obese adj overweight, fat, plump, stout, ample, chubby, tubby, portly, rotund, corpulent, podgy, paunchy, fleshy, big, heavy, on the heavy side, large, bulky, chunky, outsize, massive, gross, Falstaffian.

obesity n fatness, corpulence, plumpness, stoutness, rotundness, rotundity, portliness, chubbiness, tubbiness, podginess, fleshiness, bigness, largeness, bulk, grossness, weight problem, *embonpoint*.

obey v **1** *obey the rules* abide by, comply with, adhere to, observe, conform to, respect, acquiesce in, consent to, agree to, follow. **2** *obey orders* perform, carry out, execute, put into effect, fulfil, act upon. **3** *you must obey your mother* be dutiful to, do as/what someone says, follow the orders of, carry out the orders of, heed, be regulated by, be governed by.

obfuscate v **1** *obfuscate the issue* confuse, obscure, blur, muddle, jumble, complicate, make abstruse/unclear, garble, scramble, muddy, cloud, conceal, hide, veil. **2** *the brightest of people obfuscated by the problem* puzzle, perplex, baffle, confound, bemuse, bewilder, mystify, nonplus; *inf* stump, beat, bamboozle.

obituary n death notice; *inf* obit.

object n **1** *wooden objects* thing, something, anything, body, entity, phenomenon, article, item, device, gadget; *inf* thingumajig, thingumabob, doodad, whatsit, what's-its-name, what-d'you-call-it, thingy. **2** *the object of our discussion* subject, subject matter, substance, issue, concern. **3** *the object of their affection/abuse* focus, target, recipient, butt, victim. **4** *our object is to win* objective, aim, goal, target, end, end in view, ambition, purpose, design, intent, intention, idea, point. *see* OBJECTIVE n.

object v **1** *they were successful but many people objected* raise objections, protest, lodge a protest, demur, beg to differ, be in opposition, remonstrate, expostulate, take exception. **2** *object to the plan* raise objections to, protest against, lodge a protest against, argue against, oppose, be in opposition to, remonstrate against, expostulate about, take exception to, complain about.

objection n **1** *their objection to the plan is understandable* protest, protestation, demurral, opposition, remonstration, remonstrance, expostulation, complaining about, dissatisfaction with, disapproval of. **2** *lodge/name their objections* argument, counterargument, demurral, opposition, remonstrance, remonstration, expostulation, doubt, complaint, grievance, scruple, qualm; *inf* niggle.

objectionable adj *objectionable people/behaviour/smells* offensive, obnoxious, unpleasant, disagreeable, unacceptable, nasty, disgusting, repulsive, repellent, abhorrent, repugnant, revolting, loathsome, nauseating, hateful, detestable, reprehensible, deplorable, insufferable, intolerable, despicable, contemptible, odious, vile, obscene, foul, horrible, horrid, noxious.

objective adj *referees must be objective* unbiased, bias-free, unprejudiced, prejudice-free, impartial, neutral, uninvolved, non-partisan, disinterested, detached, dispassionate, unswayed, even-handed, equitable, fair, just, open-minded.

objective n *our objective is to win* object, aim, goal, target, end, end in view, ambition, aspiration, intent, intention, purpose, idea, point, desire, hope, design, plan, scheme, plot.

objectively adv *look at the issue objectively* with objectivity, without bias, without prejudice, impartially, disinterestedly, with detachment, dispassionately, equitably, even-handedly, fairly, justly, open-mindedly, with an open mind, without fear or favour.

objectivity n absence of bias/prejudice, impartiality, disinterest, detachment, dispassion, dispassionateness, equitability, even-handedness, fairness, justness, justice, open-mindedness.

obligate v *we felt obligated to attend* oblige, compel, require, necessitate, impel, force, constrain, press, pressure, pressurize.

obligation n **1** *the obligations specified by the contract* requirement, pre-requisite, demand, necessity, command, order, constraint, compulsion; *inf* must. **2** *fulfil/discharge one's obligations* duty, function, chore, task, job, assignment, commission, business, burden, charge, onus, trust, liability, responsibility, accountability, indebtedness, debt, engagement. **3** *we attended only from a sense of obligation* duty, compulsion, necessity, enforcement, duress, pressure. **4** *the obligation is still binding* contract, agreement, deed, covenant, compact, bond, treaty, deal, pact, understanding, transaction. **under an obligation** *under an obligation to them* obliged to, beholden to, owing someone a favour, indebted to, in someone's debt, owing someone a debt of gratitude, duty-bound to, honour-bound to, be grateful to, owing someone thanks.

obligatory adj **1** *the agreement is obligatory* binding, valid, legal, in force, effective. **2** *maths/attendance is obligatory* compulsory, enforced, prescriptive, mandatory, necessary, essential, required, requisite, imperative, de rigueur, unavoidable, unescapable.

oblige v **1** *ties of friendship oblige me to go* put under an obligation, leave someone no option, require, necessitate, obligate, compel, call for, force, constrain, press, pressure, pressurize, impel. **2** *will you oblige me by going?* do someone a favour, do someone a kindness, do someone a service, serve, accommodate, meet the wants/needs of, help accommodate, put oneself out for, indulge, gratify the wishes of, help, assist.

obliging adj helpful, eager to help/please, accommodating, willing, complaisant, indulgent, friendly, kind, generous, considerate, cooperative, neighbourly, agreeable, pleasant, good-natured, amiable, civil, courteous, polite.

oblique adj **1** *an oblique line* slanting, slanted, sloping, sloped, inclined, at an angle, angled, tilted, listing, diagonal; *Amer* cater-cornered. **2** *an oblique compliment | oblique references to the crime* indirect, implied, roundabout, circuitous, circumlocutory, ambagious, evasive, backhanded.

oblique n *words separated by an oblique* oblique line/stroke, solidus, slanting line, slant, slash, back slash.

obliquely adv **1** *the line runs obliquely* at an angle, slantwise, aslant, diagonally. **2** *refer obliquely to the matter* indirectly, in a roundabout way, not in so many words, not out-right, circuitously, evasively.

obliterate v **1** *obliterate all traces of blood | had obliterated all memories of her* erase, eradicate, efface, blot out, rub out, wipe out, expunge, sponge out, delete, cross out, strike out, blue-pencil, remove, cancel. **2** *the army/village was obliterated* destroy, exterminate, annihilate, wipe out, eliminate, eradicate, extirpate, decimate, liquidate, demolish.

obliteration n **1** *the obliteration of the stains/ memories* erasing, eradication, effacement, rubbing out, blotting out, expunging, deletion, striking out, removal, cancellation. *see* OBLITERATE 1. **2** *the obliteration of the army/village* destruction, extermination, annihilation, wiping out, elimination, eradication, extirpation, decimation, liquidation, demolition.

oblivion n **1** *sitting in a state of oblivion as people shouted* obliviousness, heedlessness, unmindfulness, unawareness, unconsciousness, insensibility, inattentiveness, disregard, disregardfulness, forgetfulness, absent-mindedness, amnesia, unconcern, abstraction, preoccupation, absorption. *see* OBLIVIOUS. **2** *the old traditions have sunk into oblivion* neglect, disuse, non-existence, abeyance, suspension. **3** *oblivion came when he hit his head* blackness, darkness, blankness, unconsciousness, insensibility, senselessness, stupor, coma.

oblivious adj *he was completely oblivious of/to his surroundings | she is oblivious to danger* unheeding, heedless of, unmindful of, unaware of, unconscious of, insensible of, ignorant of, blind to, unobservant of, deaf to, inattentive to, disregardful of, neglectful of, forgetful of, absent-minded, careless of, unconcerned with, abstracted, *distrait*, preoccupied, absorbed, far away.

obloquy n **1** *bring obloquy on the family* discredit, shame, dishonour, disgrace, humiliation, loss of face, ignominy, disfavour, disrepute, ill repute, infamy, scandal, odium. **2** *undergo the obloquy of the crowd* abuse, attack, opprobrium, censure, criticism, condemnation, denunciation, reproach, castigation, reproof, upbraiding, invective, railing, tirade, defamation, denigration, vilification, slander, libel, insult, aspersions, calumny, contumely.

obnoxious adj *obnoxious man/behaviour/smell* offensive, objectionable, unpleasant, disagreeable, unacceptable, nasty, disgusting, repulsive, repellent, abhorrent, repugnant, revolting, loathsome, nauseating, sickening, hateful, detestable, reprehensible,

deplorable, insufferable, intolerable, despicable, contemptible, odious, vile, obscene, foul, horrible, horrid, noxious.

obscene adj **1** *obscene publications/jokes* indecent, pornographic, blue, off-colour, risqué, lewd, salacious, smutty, lecherous, lascivious, licentious, prurient, lubricious, ribald, scatalogical, scabrous, bawdy, suggestive, vulgar, dirty, filthy, foul, coarse, gross, vile, nasty, offensive, immoral, impure, immodest, shameless, unchaste, improper, unwholesome, erotic, carnal, sexy; *inf* raunchy. **2** *the murder was an obscene act* atrocious, heinous, vile, foul, outrageous, shocking, repugnant, repulsive, revolting, nauseating, sickening, wicked, evil, odious.

obscenity n **1** *the obscenity of the publication* indecency, lewdness, salaciousness, smuttiness, lechery, lasciviousness, licentiousness, prurience, lubricity, ribaldry, scatalogy, scabrousness, bawdiness, suggestiveness, vulgarity, dirt, dirtiness, filth, filthiness, foulness, coarseness, grossness, vileness, nastiness, immorality, impurity, immodesty, shamelessness, unchasteness, impropriety, unwholesomeness, eroticism, carnality, sexiness. **2** *the obscenity of the crime* atrocity, heinousness, vileness, foulness, repugnance, wickedness, evil. *see* OBSCENE 2. **3** *a stream of obscenities came from him* curse, oath, swear-word, expletive, imprecation, blasphemy, bad/foul language, strong language, epithet, profanity, four-letter word, dirty word, bad word, naughty word; *inf* cuss.

obscure adj **1** *obscure references* unclear, indeterminate, opaque, abstruse, recondite, unexplained, concealed, hidden, arcane, enigmatic, deep, cryptic, mysterious, puzzling, perplexing, confusing, intricate, involved, unfathomable, incomprehensible, impenetrable, vague, indefinite, hazy, uncertain, doubtful, dubious, ambiguous, equivocal. **2** *obscure shapes looming out of the mist* indistinct, vague, shadowy, hazy, blurred, fuzzy, cloudy. **3** *obscure parts of the forest* dark, dim, black, unlit, murky, sombre, gloomy, shady, shadowy. **4** *obscure villages* unknown, unheard-of, out-of-the-way, off the beaten track, remote, hidden, secluded, God-forsaken. **5** *obscure poets* little-known, unknown, unheard-of, undistinguished, insignificant, inconspicuous, minor, unimportant, unrenowned, unrecognized, unhonoured, unsung, inglorious.

obscure v **1** *obscure the main issue* confuse, blur, muddle, complicate, make abstruse, obfuscate, garble, cloud, muddy, conceal, hide, veil. **2** *clouds obscure the sun* hide, con-

obscurity · obsessive

ceal, cover, veil, screen, mask, cloak, shroud, block, block out, eclipse, adumbrate. **3** *clouds obscured the sky* darken, blacken, dim, bedim.

obscurity n **1** *the obscurity of the reference* lack of clarity, unclearness, opaqueness, reconditeness, arcaneness, enigma, deepness, abstruseness, mystery, puzzle, confusion, intricacy, involvement, incomprehensibility, impenetrability, vagueness, uncertainty, doubtfulness, ambiguity, equivocalness. see OBSCURE adj 1. **2** *the obscurity of the village* remoteness, seclusion. see OBSCURE adj 4. **3** *the obscurity of the poet* insignificance, inconspicuousness, unimportance, lack of fame/renown/honour/recognition, ingloriousness. **4** *a text full of obscurities* difficulty, problem, complication, intricacy, opacity, enigma, puzzle, perplexity, mystery, ambiguity.

obsequies npl funeral rites, funeral service, funeral, burial ceremony, burial, last offices, exequies.

obsequious adj servile, subservient, submissive, slavish, menial, abject, fawning, grovelling, cringing, toadying, truckling, sycophantic, ingratiating, unctuous, oily, Uriah Heepish; *inf* bootlicking.

observable adj noticeable, visible, perceptible, perceivable, detectable, discernible, recognizable, obvious, evident, apparent, manifest, patent, clear, distinct, plain, unmistakable, appreciable.

observance n **1** *the observance of laws* observation of, keeping of, obeying, obedience to, adherence to, abiding by, compliance with, heeding. **2** *observance of duty/rites* carrying out, performance, execution, discharge, fulfilment, honouring. **3** *religious observances* rite, ritual, ceremony, ceremonial, celebration, festival, practice, tradition, custom, formality, form, service, office.

observant adj **1** *an observant boy spotted the thief* alert, sharp-eyed, sharp, eagle-eyed, attentive, vigilant, wide-awake, watchful, heedful, on the qui vive, on the lookout, on guard, mindful, intent, aware, conscious, with one's eyes peeled/skinned; *inf* not missing a thing/trick, on the ball. **2** *observant members of the community/faith* dutiful, obedient, conforming, law-abiding, orthodox, practising.

observation n **1** *our observation of the man upset him* seeing, noticing, watching, viewing, eyeing, witnessing. see OBSERVE 1. **2** *keep the thief/patient under observation* scrutiny, scrutinization, watch, watching, monitoring, surveillance, inspection, attention,

consideration, study, review, examination. **3** *record your observations on the experiment* findings, results, information, data, remarks, comments, notes, annotation, report, description, opinion, thoughts, reflections. **4** *make a sarcastic observation* remark, comment, statement, utterance, pronouncement, declaration. **5** *observation of the law/rules/customs* observance of, keeping of, obedience to, adherence to, compliance with, heeding. see OBSERVANCE 1.

observe v **1** *we observe him go into the bank* see, catch sight of, notice, note, perceive, discern, detect, espy, behold, watch, view, spot, witness; *inf* get a load of. **2** *police observe the house* keep under observation, watch, keep watch on, look at, keep under surveillance, keep in sight, keep in view, spy upon, monitor, reconnoitre, scan; *inf* keep an eye on, keep tabs on. **3** *doctors observe the patient* keep under observation, keep under scrutiny, watch, monitor, keep under surveillance, inspect, study, review, examine, check. **4** *"a good try," he observed* say, remark, comment, state, utter, enunciate, exclaim, announce, declare, pronounce. **5** *observe the rules* keep, obey, adhere to, abide by, heed, follow, comply with, conform to, acquiesce in, consent to, accept, respect, defer to. **6** *observe one's duty* carry out, perform, execute, discharge, fulfil. **7** *observe Christmas* celebrate, keep, recognize, commemorate, mark, remember, solemnize.

observer n watcher, looker-on, onlooker, witness, eyewitness, spectator, bystander, beholder, viewer, commentator, reporter, sightseer, spotter; *inf* rubberneck.

obsess v *her memory obsesses him* | *memories which obsess his mind* preoccupy, haunt, monopolize, have a hold on, possess, consume, engross, have a grip on, grip, dominate, rule, control, be on one's mind, be uppermost in one's mind, prey on, plague, torment, hound, bedevil. **be obsessed by** be preoccupied with, be haunted by, be possessed by, be beset by, be consumed with, be gripped by, be dominated by, be plagued by, be bedevilled by; *inf* have a bee in one's bonnet about, have a thing about, be hung up on.

obsession n preoccupation, fixation, *idée fixe*, ruling/consuming passion, mania, enthusiasm, infatuation, compulsion, phobia, complex, fetish, craze; *inf* bee in one's bonnet, hang-up, thing.

obsessive adj *an obsessive concern for hygiene* excessive, overdone, consuming, compulsive, besetting, gripping, haunting.

obsolescent adj going out of use, going out of fashion, dying out, on the decline, declining, waning, on the wane, disappearing, past its prime, ageing, moribund; *inf* on the way out.

obsolete adj *obsolete machinery/words* no longer in use, in disuse, disused, outworn, discarded, discontinued, extinct, bygone, outmoded, *démodé, passé*, antiquated, out of date, outdated, out, superannuated, old-fashioned, out of fashion, out of style, behind the times, old, dated, antique, archaic, ancient, antediluvian, time-worn, past its prime, having seen better days; *inf* old-hat, out of the ark.

obstacle n bar, barrier, obstruction, impediment, hindrance, hurdle, barricade, blockade, stumbling-block, block, blockage, curb, check, stop, stoppage, deterrent, baulk, snag, difficulty, catch, drawback, hitch, interference, interruption, fly in the ointment.

obstinacy n stubbornness, mulishness, pig-headedness, wilfulness, perversity, refractoriness, recalcitrance, contumaciousness, firmness, steadfastness, inflexibility, immovability, intransigence, intractability, persistence, pertinacity, tenacity, doggedness, single-mindedness, relentlessness.

obstinate adj *obstinate woman/resitance* stubborn, stubborn as a mule, mulish, pigheaded, headstrong, wilful, self-willed, strong-minded, perverse, refractory, recalcitrant, contumacious, unmanageable, firm, steadfast, unyielding, inflexible, unbending, immovable, intransigent, intractable, uncompromising, persistent, persevering, pertinacious, tenacious, dogged, single-minded, relentless, unrelenting.

obstreperous adj *obstreperous person/behaviour* unruly, disorderly, turbulent, rowdy, boisterous, rough, riotous, out of control, uncontrolled, out of hand, wild, rampaging, undisciplined, unrestrained, unbridled, ungoverned, unmanageable, noisy, loud, clamorous, raucous, vociferous; *inf* stroppy, bolshie.

obstruct v **1** *logs obstruct the road/river* block, barricade, bar, cut off, shut off, choke, clog, dam up. **2** *floods obstructing traffic* hold up, bring to a standstill, stop, halt, block, prohibit. **3** *obstructing our efforts/progress* hinder, impede, hamper, block, interfere with, interrupt, hold up, frustrate, thwart, baulk, inhibit, curb, brake, bridle, hamstring, encumber, restrain, slow, retard, delay, arrest, check, stop, halt, restrict, limit.

obstruction n obstacle, impediment, hindrance, bar, barrier, barricade, hurdle, block, blockage, stumbling-block, blockade, curb, check, stop, stoppage, deterrent, baulk, snag, difficulty, catch, drawback, restriction, hitch, fly in the ointment.

obstructive adj **1** *obstructive measures/tactics* blocking, delaying, hindering, stalling, inhibiting, interrupting, restrictive, preventative, preventive. **2** *obstructive people* unhelpful, uncooperative, awkward.

obtain v **1** *obtain tickets/promotion* get, get hold of, acquire, come by, procure, secure, gain, earn, achieve, attain, take possession of, get one's hands on, seize, grab, pick up. **2** *new rules obtain* be in force, be in use, be effective, exist, stand, prevail, hold, be the case, reign, rule, hold sway.

obtainable adj *no tickets obtainable* available, to be had, procurable, achievable, attainable, at hand, ready; *inf* on tap.

obtrusive adj **1** *obtrusive colours/music* noticeable, conspicuous, obvious, unmistakable, blatant, flagrant, bold, audacious, intrusive. **2** *obtrusive behaviour* forward, interfering, meddling, prying, intrusive, officious, importunate; *inf* pushy, nosy.

obtuse adj *too obtuse to understand* stupid, dull, dull-witted, slow-witted, slow, uncomprehending, unintelligent, imperceptive, bovine, stolid, insensitive, thick-skinned; *inf* dim, dense, thick, dim-witted, slow on the uptake, boneheaded, dumb, dopey.

obvious adj clear, clear-cut, crystal-clear, plain, visible, noticeable, perceptible, discernible, detectable, recognizable, evident, apparent, manifest, distinct, palpable, patent, conspicuous, unconcealed, overt, pronounced, transparent, prominent, unmistakable, indisputable, undeniable, as plain as a pikestaff, as plain as the nose on one's face, staring someone in the face; *inf* sticking out like a sore thumb, sticking out a mile.

obviously adj **1** *obviously pregnant* clearly, plainly, visibly, noticeably, discernibly, evidently, manifestly, distinctly, patently, unmistakably, undeniably. *see* OBVIOUS. **2** *obviously, we must go* of course, certainly, undoubtedly, clearly.

occasion n **1** *we met on one or two occasions* time, juncture, point, situation, instance, case, circumstance. **2** *it was a sad occasion* event, incident, occurrence, happening, episode, affair, experience. **3** *we met at a college occasion* function, party, affair, celebration; *inf* get-together, do. **4** *if the occasion arises* opportunity, golden opportunity, chance, opening, contingency. **5** *have occa-*

sion to believe reason, cause, grounds, justification, call, excuse, inducement.

occasion v *occasion much grief* cause, give rise to, bring about, result in, lead to, prompt, provoke, produce, create, generate, engender, originate, effect.

occasional adj *an occasional meeting/letter* infrequent, intermittent, irregular, sporadic, odd, rare, casual, incidental.

occasionally adv now and then, now and again/then, from time to time, sometimes, at times, every so often, once in a while, on occasion, periodically, at intervals, irregularly, sporadically, infrequently, intermittently, on and off, off and on.

occult adj supernatural, magic, magical, mystical, mystic, preternatural, transcendental, unrevealed, secret, hidden, concealed, invisible, obscure, recondite, arcane, abstruse, esoteric, inexplicable, unfathomable, mysterious, cryptic, enigmatic.

occult n **the occult** the supernatural, magic, black magic, witchcraft, sorcery, wizardry, the black arts, diabolism, devil worship, supernaturalism, mysticism.

occupancy n occupation, tenancy, tenure, residence, residency, inhabitancy, inhabitance, inhabitation, habitation, habitancy, living, possession, possessorship, holding, owner-occupancy.

occupant n occupier, owner-occupier, tenant, renter, lease-holder, lessee, inhabitant, resident, dweller, householder, addressee, incumbent, inmate.

occupation n **1** *what is his occupation?* job, work, profession, business, employment, employ, career, calling, *métier*, vocation, trade, craft, line, field, province, area. **2** *occupation of the house* occupancy, tenancy, tenure, residence, inhabitancy, habitation, possession, holding. *see* OCCUPANCY. **3** *suffer the occupation of their land* possession, foreign rule, invasion, seizure, take-over, conquest, capture, overthrow, subjugation, subjection.

occupational adj employment, work, professional, business, career, vocational.

occupied adj **1** *everyone is occupied just now* busy, engaged, working, at work, employed; *inf* tied up, hard at it. **2** *all the rooms are occupied* full, engaged, taken, in use, unavailable. **3** *the houses are all occupied* inhabited, lived-in, tenanted, settled.

occupy v **1** *occupy the lower flat* live in, inhabit, reside in, dwell in, be the tenant of, tenant, have one's residence/abode in, make one's home in; *Scots* stay in. **2** *occupy*

her time | *will occupy too much space* fill, fill up, take up, use up, utilize, cover. **3** *occupy a top post* hold, be in, fill, have; *inf* hold down. **4** *occupy oneself* engage, employ, absorb, engross, preoccupy, immerse, interest, involve, entertain, divert, amuse, beguile. **5** *the invading army occupied their country* take possession of, invade, overrun, seize, take over, capture, garrison.

occur v **1** *the accident/promotion occurred last year* happen, take place, come about, come to pass, materialize, transpire, arise, crop up, turn up, befall, eventuate. **2** *the disease occurs in the tropics* be found, be met with, be, present, exist, have its being, obtain, appear, present itself, show itself, manifest itself, arise, spring up. **3** *an idea occurs to me* | *didn't it occur to you to telephone?* come to mind, spring to mind, come to one, enter one's head, cross one's mind, strike one, hit one, dawn on, suggest itself.

occurrence n **1** *robbery is an everyday occurrence* happening, event, incident, circumstance, affair, episode, proceedings, adventure. **2** *the occurrence of the disease is nationwide* existence, appearance, manifestation, materialization, springing up.

odd adj **1** *an odd woman* | *she's becoming odd* strange, eccentric, queer, peculiar, idiosyncratic, unconventional, outlandish, droll, weird, bizarre, offbeat, freakish, whimsical; *inf* wacky, freaky, kinky, off-the-wall. **2** *rather an odd happening* unusual, uncommon, irregular, strange, peculiar, funny, curious, queer, abnormal, atypical, different, out-of-the-ordinary, exceptional, rare, extraordinary, remarkable, singular, deviant, aberrant, freak, freakish, bizarre, weird. **3** *do odd jobs* occasional, casual, temporary, part-time, seasonal, periodic, irregular, miscellaneous, various, varied. **4** *at odd moments* occasional, random, irregular, periodic, haphazard, chance, fortuitous, fragmentary, various, sundry. **5** *an odd sock* unmatched, unpaired, left-over, spare, remaining, surplus, superfluous, lone, single, solitary, sole. **odd man out** exception, outsider, nonconformist, misfit, maverick, individualist, fish out of water; *inf* freak.

oddity n **1** *comment on the oddity of his behaviour* strangeness, eccentricity, queerness, peculiarness, peculiarity, weirdness, freakishness; *inf* wackiness. *see* ODD 1. **2** *the oddity of the happening* unusualness, uncommonness, peculiarness, peculiarity, abnormality, rarity, rareness, bizarreness. *see* ODD 2. **3** *the house is an oddity* | *this is a grammatical oddity* curiosity, rarity, anomaly, aberration, irregularity, phenomenon. **4** *he is an* *oddity* eccentric, crank, original, misfit, fish out of water, *rara avis*; *inf* character, card, oddball, weirdo, crackpot, nut, screwball, freak, odd/queer fish. **5** *her character oddities* peculiarity, idiosyncrasy, eccentricity, mannerism, quirk, twist, kink, crotchet.

oddment n **1** *oddments of material* scrap, remnant, leftover, fragment, snippet, offcut, bit, piece, end, shred, sliver, stub, tailend; *inf* fag-end. **2** *shops selling oddments* miscellanea, odds and ends, sundry, knickknack, notion, novelty, souvenir, keepsake, memento.

odds npl **1** *the odds are in his favour* advantage, lead, edge, superiority, supremacy, ascendancy. **2** *the odds are that he will win* likelihood, probability, chances, balance. **3** *against heavy odds* difference, disparity, unevenness, inequality, discrepancy, variation, dissimilarity. **at odds 1** *at odds with each other* in conflict, in disagreement, on bad terms, at daggers drawn, at loggerheads. **2** *at odds with his principles* out of keeping, not in keeping, in opposition to, at variance. **odds and ends** bits and pieces, bits, pieces, oddments, fragments, remnants, scraps, offcuts, cuttings, snippets, miscellanea, leftovers, leavings, debris.

odious adj abhorrent, repugnant, disgusting, repulsive, repellent, revolting, foul, vile, unpleasant, disagreeable, loathsome, detestable, hateful, despicable, contemptible, objectionable, offensive, horrible, horrid, abominable, heinous, atrocious, execrable.

odium n abhorrence, repugnance, disgust, revulsion, loathing, detestation, hatred, dislike, disapproval, antipathy, contempt.

odour n **1** *the odour of baking | a strong odour of bad drains* aroma, smell, scent, perfume, fragrance, bouquet, redolence, essence, stench, stink; *inf* niff, pong. **2** *an odour of ill will about the place* atmosphere, air, ambience, aura, spirit, quality, flavour, emanation.

odyssey n journey, voyage, trek, quest, peregrination, crusade, pilgrimage, journeying.

off adj **1** *the teacher is taking a day off* away, absent. **2** *the match is off* cancelled, postponed, shelved. **3** *chips are off* unavailable, unobtainable, finished. **4** *these answers are off* incorrect, inaccurate, wrong, in error, erroneous. **5** *the food/milk is off* bad, rotten, decomposed, mouldy, high, sour, rancid, turned.

off adv *feeling rather off* ill, unwell, sick, poorly; *inf* under the weather, below par.

off and on on and off, sporadically, irregularly, intermittently, at intervals, periodically, once in a while, every so often, now and then, now and again, from time to time, occasionally.

offbeat adj eccentric, unconventional, unorthodox, idiosyncratic, unusual, strange, bizarre, weird, freakish, outlandish, *outré*, Bohemian, hippie, freaky; *inf* kinky, way-out, far-out, off-the-wall.

off-colour adj **1** *feeling off-colour* ill, unwell, sick, queasy, poorly, out of sorts, not oneself, run-down, peaky, washed out; *inf* not up to par, below par, under the weather. **2** *off-colour jokes* risqué, racy, blue, vulgar, indecent, smutty, dirty, ribald, obscene, bawdy, pornographic; *inf* raunchy.

offence n **1** *commit an offence* crime, illegal act, breaking of the law, breach/violation/infraction of the law, wrongdoing, wrong, misdemeanour, act of misconduct, misdeed, peccadillo, sin, transgression, act of dereliction, shortcoming, fault, lapse; *Law* malfeasance. **2** *an offence against society* affront, injury, hurt, source of harm, outrage, atrocity, insult, injustice, indignity, slight, snub. **3** *her behaviour causes offence* annoyance, anger, indignation, exasperation, wrath, ire, displeasure, disapproval, dislike, animosity, resentment, pique, vexation, umbrage, antipathy, aversion, opposition, enmity. **4** *the enemy's offence* attack, assault, act of aggression, aggression, onslaught, offensive, thrust, charge, sortie, sally, invasion, incursion. **take offence** *take offence at his remarks* be offended at/by, be affronted at/by, take umbrage at, feel upset at/by, get annoyed at, get angry at, feel piqued at/by, feel resentment at, resent, get/go into a huff; *inf* be miffed.

offend v **1** *his behaviour offended them* give offence to, hurt the feelings of, wound, be an affront to, affront, upset, displease, annoy, anger, incense, exasperate, vex, pique, put out, gall, irritate, provoke, ruffle, disgruntle, rankle with, outrage, insult, slight, humiliate; *inf* rile, miff, rattle, put someone's back up, tread on someone's corns/toes. **2** *offend his ear | will offend her sense of taste | guaranteed to offend art-lovers* cause offence to, be offensive to, displease, upset, be disagreeable to, put someone off, be distasteful to, repel, disgust, revolt, nauseate; *inf* turn someone off. **3** *apologize for having offended* commit a crime, break the law, do wrong, sin, go astray, fall from grace, err, transgress.

offended adj hurt, wounded, affronted, upset, displeased, annoyed, angered,

incensed, exasperated, vexed, piqued, put
out, irritated, ruffled, disgruntled, resentful, outraged, insulted, in a huff, huffy; *inf*
riled, miffed, rattled. *see* OFFEND 1.

offender n wrongdoer, culprit, criminal,
lawbreaker, miscreant, delinquent, sinner,
transgressor, malefactor.

offensive adj **1** *an offensive remark/person*
hurtful, wounding, abusive, affronting, displeasing, annoying, exasperating, vexing,
galling, irritating, provocative, provoking,
objectionable, outrageous, insulting,
humiliating, rude, discourteous, uncivil,
impolite, unmannerly, impertinent, insolent, disrespectful. **2** *an offensive smell/sight*
disagreeable, unpleasant, nasty, foul, vile,
objectionable, odious, abominable,
detestable, loathsome, repugnant, disgusting, obnoxious, repulsive, repellent, nauseating, sickening, unpalatable, distasteful,
unsavoury, noisome; *inf* horrid, yucky.
3 *the offensive army* attacking, on the attack,
assaulting, invading, invasive, aggressive,
combative, martial, warlike, belligerent,
bellicose, hostile; *inf* on the warpath.

offensive n *many killed in the offensive* attack,
assault, onslaught, drive, invasion, push,
thrust, charge, sortie, sally, act of war,
incursion. **be on the offensive** attack,
begin to attack, attack first, be aggressive,
strike the first blow, start a war/battle/
quarrel; *inf* be on the warpath.

offer v **1** *offer a suggestion* put forward, propose, advance, submit, propound, suggest,
recommend, make a motion of, put to the
motion, move. **2** *offer to help* volunteer
one's services, volunteer, offer one's service, offer assistance/help, be at someone's
service, be at someone's disposal, make
oneself available, show readiness/willing-
ness to help. **3** *the job offers good career
prospects* afford, provide, supply, give, furnish, make available, present, give an
opportunity for. **4** *offer the house for sale at
£100,000* put up for sale, put on the market,
put under the hammer, ask for bids for.
5 *he has offered for the house* put in an offer
for, bid for, put in a bid for, offer to buy,
tender for. **6** *offer his son to the gods* | *a goat
was offered to the goddess* offer up, offer as a
sacrifice, sacrifice. **7** *as opportunities offer*
arrive, appear, happen, occur, come on the
scene, present itself, show itself. **8** *offer vio-
lence/resistance* attempt, try, essay, show,
give.

offer n **1** *offers of help* proposal, proposition,
suggestion, submission, approach, over-
ture. **2** *accept the highest offer* bid, bidding

price. **3** *counteract their offers of resistance*
attempt, endeavour, essay.

offering n **1** *collecting offerings from the members* contribution, donation, subscription,
gift, present, alms, charity, hand-out.
2 *offerings to the gods* sacrifice, oblation,
immolation.

offhand adj *an offhand manner* | *her behaviour
was very offhand* casual, unceremonious,
cavalier, careless, indifferent, perfunctory,
cursory, uninterested, unconcerned, blasé
curt, abrupt, terse, brusque, discourteous,
uncivil, impolite, rude; *inf* off, couldn't-
care-less, take-it-or-leave-it.

offhand adv **1** *always acts very offhand* casually, unceremoniously, cavalierly, perfunctorily, cursorily, unconcernedly, curtly,
abruptly, discourteously, rudely. *see* OFFHAND
adj. **2** *I cannot say offhand* extempore,
impromptu, ad lib, extemporaneously,
without preparation, without consideration, without rehearsal, spontaneously; *inf*
off the cuff, off the top of one's head, just
like that.

office n **1** *his office is near his home* place of
business, base, workplace, workroom,
room. **2** *he has the office of treasurer* post,
position, appointment, role, place, situation, station. **3** *the office of administrator is
demanding* | *to hold high office* work, employ-
ment, business, duty, function, responsibility, obligation, charge, tenure. **4** *perform
their domestic offices* job, work, task, chore,
duty, assignment, commission, routine.

officer n **1** *an officer in charge of the men* military officer, army officer, naval officer, air
force officer, commissioned officer, non-
commissioned officer. **2** *the officer in charge
of the investigation* police officer, policeman/
policewoman, PC/WPC, officer of the law/
peace, constable, detective; *inf* copper, cop,
bobby, pig, dick, gumshoe. **3** *the officers of
the society* office-holder, office-bearer, official, committee member, board member,
administrator, executive, functionary,
bureaucrat. **4** *courts sending out officers* representative, agent, deputy, messenger,
envoy.

offices npl *through the good offices of* assistance, help, aid, support, backing, patronage, aegis, auspices, intervention,
intercession, mediation, advocacy, recommendation, word.

official adj **1** *official permission* | *his appoint-
ment is now official* authorized, accredited,
approved, validated, authenticated, certified, endorsed, sanctioned, licensed, recognized, accepted, legitimate, legal, lawful,
bona fide, proper, *ex cathedra*; *inf* kosher.

2 *an official function* formal, ceremonial, solemn, conventional, ritualistic, pompous; *inf* stuffed-shirt.

official n **1** *club/party officials* officer, office-holder, office-bearer, administrator, executive. *see* OFFICER 3. **2** *officials of the court* officer, representative, agent. *see* OFFICER 4.

officiate v **1** *who will officiate in the absence of the chairman?* take charge, be in charge, preside, take the chair. **2** *officiate at the service/proceedings* be in charge of, be responsible for, chair, preside over, manage, oversee, superintend, conduct, run, operate.

officious adj *officious bureaucrats/behaviour* over-zealous, over-busy, bustling, interfering, intrusive, meddlesome, meddling, prying, inquisitive, importunate, forward, obtrusive, self-important, opinionated, dictatorial, domineering; *inf* pushy, nosy.

offing n **in the offing** *a salary increase is in the offing* on the way, coming soon, coming up, close at hand, near, imminent, in prospect, on the horizon, on the cards, in the wings.

offload v *offload the cargo/responsibility* unload, unburden, disburden, jettison, get rid of, discharge, transfer, shift; *inf* dump.

off-putting adj *had a rather off-putting manner* discouraging, disheartening, dispiriting, daunting, disconcerting, discomfiting, dismaying, upsetting, unsettling, unnerving, intimidating, frightening, fearsome, formidable.

offset v *weights offsetting each other | this year's profits offset last year's loss* counterbalance, counterpoise, counteract, countervail, balance, balance out, cancel out, neutralize, compensate for, make up for, make good, indemnify.

offshoot n **1** *plant offshoots* side-shoot, shoot, offset, branch, bough, limb, sucker, tendril, runner, scion. **2** *he is an offshoot of a noble family* descendant, scion, relation, relative, kin. **3** *his business an offshoot of the family firm* branch, subsidiary, adjunct, appendage. **4** *his attitude is an offshoot of his war experiences* result, outcome, aftermath, consequence, upshot, product, by-product, spin-off, ramification.

offspring n **1** *the couple have no offspring* children, family, progeny, young, issue, descendants, heirs, successors, spawn; *inf* kids. **2** *he/she is the offspring of the headmaster* child, son, daughter, descendant, heir, successor; *inf* kid.

often adv frequently, many a time, on many occasions, repeatedly, again and again, time and again, time and time again, time after time, over and over, over and over again, day in day out; *lit* oft, oft-times; *inf* a lot.

ogle v *ogle the girl at the next table* stare at, gaze at, eye amorously, look flirtatiously at, leer at, make eyes at, make sheep's eyes at; *inf* give someone the glad eye, give someone the once-over, eye up, undress with one's eyes, give someone the come-on.

ogre/ogress n **1** monster, giant/giantess, troll, bogeyman, bogey, bugbear, demon, devil. **2** *the teacher's an ogre* frightening person, monster, harridan, shrew, termagant, harpy, tartar, fury, gorgon; *inf* battleaxe.

oil n **1** *use oil to lubricate the surface/skin* lubricant, grease, petroleum jelly, penetrating oil, baby oil, bath oil; *Trademark* Vaseline. **2** *fry in oil not lard* cooking oil, vegetable oil; sunflower oil, corn oil, olive oil, peanut oil, rape-seed oil, walnut oil.

oil v *oil the surface/lock* lubricate, grease, smear with oil, make slippery/smooth, anoint.

oily adj **1** *oily fish* oil-containing, oleaginous. **2** *oily food* greasy, fatty, buttery, swimming in oil/fat. **3** *oily charm/remarks* smooth, over-smooth, smooth-talking, honey-tongued, flattering, fulsome, glib, suave, urbane, unctuous, subservient, servile, oleaginous.

ointment n medicated cream/lotion, emollient, salve, balm, liniment, embrocation, unguent, gel.

OK, okay interj *okay, I'll go* yes, all right, right, very well, very good; *inf* right you are, righto.

OK, okay n *give the OK to* agreement, consent, assent, permission, authorization, endorsement, sanction, approval, seal of approval, approbation, the thumbs up, the go-ahead; *inf* the green light, say-so.

OK, okay adj *an okay bloke/job | the film was OK* all right, reasonable, acceptable, tolerable, passable, satisfactory, adequate, middling; *inf* not bad, so-so, fair-to-middling.

OK, okay v *OK the project* give one's consent to, consent to, say yes to, agree to, give one's approval to, approve, pass, authorize, sanction, give something thumbs up, give something go-ahead, give something the nod, rubber-stamp; *inf* give something the green light, give something one's say-so.

old adj **1** *old people* older, mature, elderly, aged, advanced in years, up in years, getting on, grey-haired, grizzled, hoary, past one's prime, ancient, decrepit, senescent, senile, venerable, senior; *inf* past it, over

the hill, long in the tooth. **2** *old clothes*
worn, worn-out, cast-off, shabby, torn, tattered, ragged, old-fashioned, out-of-date,
outmoded, *démodé*. **3** *old farm buildings*
dilapidated, broken-down, run-down, tumbledown, ramshackle, decaying, crumbling,
disintegrating. **4** *old ideas* out-of-date, outdated, old-fashioned, outmoded, *passé*,
archaic, obsolete, extinct, antiquated, antediluvian, superannuated; *inf* old-hat, out of
the ark. **5** *in the old days* of old, olden,
bygone, past, early, earlier, earliest,
primeval, primordial, prehistoric. **6** *old customs* age-old, long-standing, long-lived,
long-established, time-honoured, enduring,
lasting. **7** *old cars* antique, veteran, vintage.
8 *old for her years* | *he's an old hand* mature,
wise, sensible, experienced, knowledge-
able, well-versed, practised, skilled, skilful,
adept. **9** *an old girlfriend* ex-, former, previous, one-time, sometime, erstwhile; *lit*
quondam. **old age** oldness, elderliness,
age, agedness, declining years, advanced
years, winter/autumn of one's life, senes-
cence, senility, dotage. **old man** elderly
man, senior citizen, old-age pensioner,
OAP, grandfather, old fogy; *lit* greybeard;
inf gaffer, oldie, wrinkly, oldster, old
codger, old boy, old geezer, old-stager, old-
timer.

older adj *the older child* | *she's older than me*
elder, more advanced in years, senior.

old-fashioned adj old, former, out of fashion, outmoded, *démodé*, unfashionable, out
of style, out of date, outdated, dated, out,
dead, old-time, behind the times, past,
bygone, *passé*, archaic, obsolescent, obsolete, ancient, antiquated, superannuated,
antediluvian, old-fogyish, old-fangled; *inf*
old-hat, not with it.

old-time adj *old-time customs/dancing* old, former, past, bygone, old-fashioned, archaic,
ancient.

old-world adj **1** *old-world charm* old, archaic,
old-fashioned, quaint, traditional, ceremonious, chivalrous, gallant, courtly. **2** *old-
world cottages* old, old-fashioned,
traditional, quaint, picturesque.

omen n portent, sign, token, foretoken,
harbinger, premonition, forewarning,
warning, foreshadowing, prediction, forecast, prophesy, augury, straw in the wind,
writing on the wall, auspice, presage, presentiment, feeling, vague feeling, foreboding, misgiving; *inf* funny feeling, feeling in
one's bones.

ominous adj **1** *ominous clouds* | *the future was
looking ominous* threatening, menacing,
minatory, black, dark, gloomy, heavy, sinis-

ter, bad, unpromising, unpropitious, pessimistic, inauspicious, unfavourable,
unlucky, ill-fated. **2** *ancients believing in ominous signs* oracular, augural, divinatory,
prophetic, premonitory, prognostic, sibyl-
lic.

omission n **1** *the omission of his name from
the list* leaving out, exclusion, exception,
non-inclusion, deletion, erasure, elimination, expunction. **2** *guilty of a sin of omission*
neglect, neglectfulness, negligence, dereliction, forgetfulness, oversight, disregard,
non-fulfilment, default, failure. **3** *note several omissions from the list* exclusion, oversight, gap, lacuna.

omit v **1** *omit his name from the list* leave out,
exclude, except, miss out, miss, fail to
mention, pass over, drop, delete, erase,
eliminate, expunge, rub out, cross out; *inf*
give something a miss. **2** *omit to close the
door* forget to, neglect to, fail to, leave
undone, overlook, skip.

omnipotence n all-powerfulness, almighti-
ness, supremacy, pre-eminence, invincibil-
ity, supreme power, absolute/unlimited
power, undisputed sway, divine right.

omnipotent adj all-powerful, almighty,
supreme, pre-eminent, invincible.

omnipresent adj all-present, present everywhere, ubiquitous, all-pervasive, infinite,
boundless.

omniscient adj all-knowing, all-wise, all-
seeing, all-perceiving.

omnivorous adj all-devouring, eating anything, pantophagous, indiscriminate.

on adv **on and off** *came on and off for three
years* off and on, sporadically, irregularly,
intermittently, at, intervals, periodically,
every so often, now and then. *see* OFF adv,
OFF AND ON. **on and on** *talked/rambled on and
on* at great length, incessantly, constantly,
continuously, endlessly, interminably,
unremittingly, relentlessly.

once adv **1** *they were friends once* at one time,
once upon a time, previously, formerly, in
the past, in times gone by, in times past, in
the old days, long ago. **2** *I saw him only once*
on one occasion, one time, one single time.
3 *he did not once help* ever, at any time, on
any occasion. **at once 1** *you must leave at
once* immediately, right away, right now,
this moment, now, straight away,
instantly, directly, forthwith, without
delay; *inf* before you can say Jack Robinson.
2 *they both arrived at once* at the same time,
at one and the same time, at the same
instant/moment, together, simultaneously.
once and for all 1 *you must decide once and*

for all decisively, conclusively, finally, positively, determinedly. **2** *he has gone once and for all* for always, for good, forever, permanently, finally. **once in a while** every now and again/then, now and again/then, occasionally, on the odd occasion, on occasion, at times, from time to time; *inf* once in a blue moon.

once conj *he'll be all right once she's gone* as soon as, when, after, the minute.

oncoming adj *oncoming traffic* approaching, advancing, nearing, onrushing, forthcoming, imminent.

one adj **1** *one person* a single, a solitary, a sole, a lone. **2** *one day they'll come* some. **3** *they are now one* united, allied, joined, unified, bound, wedded, married.

onerous adj burdensome, heavy, crushing, back-breaking, oppressive, weighty, arduous, strenuous, difficult, hard, formidable, laborious, exhausting, tiring, exigent, taxing, demanding, exacting, wearing, wearisome, fatiguing.

oneself pron the id, the self, ego; *inf* number one, numero uno. **by oneself 1** *stay by oneself* alone, all alone, on one's own, in a solitary state, unaccompanied, companionless, unattended; *inf* on one's tod. **2** *do the work by oneself* alone, all alone, on one's own, by one's own efforts, unaided, without help, without assistance, independently.

one-sided adj **1** *one-sided opinions* biased, prejudiced, partisan, partial, discriminatory, coloured, inequitable, unfair, unjust, narrow-minded, bigoted. **2** *a one-sided game/discussion* uneven, unequal, unbalanced, lopsided.

one-time adj *one-time journalist* ex-, former, previous, sometime, erstwhile; *lit* quondam.

ongoing adj **1** *ongoing projects* in progress, current, extant, progressing, advancing, successful, developing, evolving, growing. **2** *the work in the factory is ongoing* continuous, continual, uninterrupted, unbroken, non-stop, incessant, unending, constant.

onlooker n looker-on, eyewitness, witness, observer, spectator, watcher, viewer, bystander, sightseer; *inf* rubberneck.

only adv **1** *only enough for two* just, at most, not more than, barely, scarcely. **2** *he's only saying that* just, merely, simply, purely.

only adj **1** *their only son* single, one and only, solitary, sole, lone. **2** *the only place to eat* only possible, individual, unique, exclusive.

onomatopoeic adj imitative, echoic.

onset n **1** *the onset of the invading army* onslaught, assault, attack, charge, onrush. *see* ONSLAUGHT. **2** *the onset of trouble* start, beginning, commencement, inception, outbreak; *inf* kick-off.

onslaught n assault, attack, charge, onrush, onset, storming, sortie, sally, raid, foray, push, thrust, drive, blitz.

onus n burden, weight, load, responsibility, liability, obligation, duty, charge, encumbrance, cross to bear, millstone round one's neck, albatross.

ooze v **1** *pus oozing from the wound* flow, discharge, exude, seep, trickle, drip, dribble, filter, filtrate, percolate, excrete, escape, leak, drain, bleed, sweat. **2** *she was positively oozing charm* exude, pour forth, send out, let loose, display, exhibit, manifest.

ooze n **1** *the ooze of pus* flow, discharge, exudation, seeping, trickling, leak. *see* OOZE v. **2** *the ooze at the bottom of the river* deposit, alluvium, silt, mude, slime, mire, muck.

opacity n **1** *the opacity of the glass* non-transparency, non-translucence. **2** *the opacity of the windscreen* cloudiness, filminess, haziness, dirtiness, muddiness, griminess. *see* OPAQUE 2. **3** *the opacity of the text* abstruseness, obscurity, unclearness, lack of clarity, enigma, unintelligibility, incomprehensibility. *see* OPAQUE 3.

opalescent adj multicoloured, many-hued, prismatic, rainbow-like, kaleidoscopic, iridescent, opaline, milky, pearly, nacreous.

opaque adj **1** *opaque glass* non-transparent, non-translucent, non-see-through. **2** *opaque windscreens* cloudy, filmy, blurred, smeared, hazy, misty, dirty, dingy, muddy, muddied, grimy; *inf* smeary. **3** *a piece of opaque prose* abstruse, obscure, unclear, cryptic, enigmatic, unfathomable, unintelligible, incomprehensible, baffling, perplexing.

open adj **1** *open doors* not shut, not closed, unlocked, unbolted, unlatched, unbarred, unfastened, unsecured, ajar, wide open, agape, gaping, yawning. **2** *open boxes/drains* uncovered, coverless, unlidded, topless, unsealed. **3** *open spaces/countryside* unenclosed, unfenced, exposed, unsheltered, wide, wide open, extensive, broad, spacious, sweeping, airy, uncrowded, uncluttered, undeveloped, unbuilt-up. **4** *open roads* unobstructed, unblocked, clear, passable, navigable. **5** *maps open on the table* spread out, unfolded, unfurled, unrolled, straightened out, extended, stretched out. **6** *open material/fabric* openwork, holey, full of holes, honeycombed, lacy, filigree, airy, cellular, porous, spongy. **7** *quite open about her dislike* frank, candid, honest, forthright, direct, blunt, plain-spoken, downright. **8** *the shop/theatre is open* open to the public, open for business, admitting customers/visitors. **9** *an open meeting/competition* public, general, non-exclusive, accessible, non-restrictive, unrestricted, non-discriminatory. **10** *the job is still open* vacant, available, unfilled, unoccupied, free. **11** *open hostility* obvious, clear, noticeable, visible, apparent, evident, manifest, overt, conspicuous, patent, unconcealed, unhidden, undisguised, blatant, flagrant. **12** *three courses open to us* available, on hand, obtainable, accessible. **13** *the system is open to abuse* wide open to, allowing of, permitting, vulnerable to, exposed to, susceptible to, liable to, at the mercy of, an easy target for. **14** *the subject is still open* open to debate, open for discussion, yet to be decided, undecided, unresolved, unsettled, arguable, debatable, moot. **15** *keep an open mind* unbiased, prejudice-free, unprejudiced, non-partisan, impartial, non-discriminatory, objective, disinterested, dispassionate, detached. **16** *have an open disposition* frank, honest, artless, natural, simple, guileless, ingenuous, innocent. **17** *open hosts* open-handed, generous, liberal, bountiful, munificent.

open v **1** *open the door* throw open, unlock, unbolt, unlatch, unbar, unfasten. **2** *open the parcel* unwrap, undo, untie, unseal. **3** *open the bottle* uncork, broach, crack. **4** *open out the map* spread out, unfold, unfurl, unroll, straighten out, extend, stretch out. **5** *the crack opened* open up, come apart, split, separate, rupture. **6** *we open tomorrow* open for business, be ready for customers/visitors, admit customers, begin business, set up shop, put up one's plate, have a launch, start, begin, commence, start the ball rolling; *inf* kick off. **7** *open his heart* lay bare, bare, uncover, expose, exhibit, disclose, divulge, pour out.

open-air adj outdoor, out-of-doors, outside, alfresco.

open-handed adj generous, liberal, lavish, free, bountiful, bounteous, munificent.

opening n **1** *an opening in the fence/wall* gap, aperture, space, hole, orifice, vent, slot, break, breach, crack, split, fissure, cleft, crevice, chink, interstice, rent, rupture. **2** *an opening in the new office* vacancy, position, job, opportunity, chance; *inf* break, lucky break. **3** *the opening of the match* beginning, start, commencement, outset, inception, launch, birth, dawn; *inf* kick-off. **4** *present at the gallery's opening* opening ceremony, official opening, launch.

openly adv **1** *she told him quite openly* frankly, candidly, honestly, forthrightly, directly, bluntly, unreservedly, straight from the shoulder, with no holds barred. **2** *conduct their affair openly* publicly, in public, in full view of people, blatantly, flagrantly, brazenly, with no attempt at concealment, overtly, unashamedly, shamelessly, unabashed, wantonly, immodestly.

open-minded adj **1** *open-minded judges* unbiased, unprejudiced, prejudice-free, non-partisan, impartial, non-discriminatory, objective, disinterested, dispassionate, detached, tolerant, liberal, broad-minded, undogmatic. **2** *writers should be open-minded* receptive, open to suggestions, open to new ideas, amenable.

operate v **1** *the machine ceased to operate* work, function, go, run, perform, act, be in action. **2** *he can operate the machine* work, make go, run, use, utilize, employ, handle, manipulate, manoeuvre, ply, manage, be in charge of. **3** *operate on the accident victim* perform an operation, perform surgery; *inf* put under the knife.

operation n **1** *the operation of the machine is crucial* working, functioning, running, performance. *see* OPERATE 1. **2** *his operation of the machine* working, using, handling, manipulation. *see* OPERATE 2. **3** *when the building was evacuated the operation went smoothly* activity, exercise, affair, business, undertaking, enterprise, task, job. **4** *operations on the stock exchange* transaction, business, deal, proceedings. **5** *military operations* manoeuvre, exercise, campaign, assault. **6** *an operation to remove the appendix* surgery, major surgery, minor surgery. **In operation** *rules/machines not yet in operation* operative, in force, effective, in use, functioning, working, valid. *see* OPERATIVE adj 1, 2.

operational adj *machines now operational* operative, workable, in operation, working, in working order, functioning, functional, going, in use, usable, in action, ready for action.

operative adj **1** *the rules are operative now* in operation, in force, effective, valid. **2** *the machines are now operative* operational, workable, working, functioning, functional, usable. *see* OPERATIONAL. **3** *"might" is the operative word* key, relevant, significant, crucial, vital, important, essential.

operative n **1** *factory operatives* worker, workman, machinist, operator, mechanic, factory hand/employee. **2** *a foreign power's operatives* agent, secret agent, undercover agent, spy, double agent; *inf* spook, mole.

3 *employ a private operative* detective, private detective, private investigator, sleuth; *inf* private eye, dick, gumshoe.

operator n **1** *machine operators* operative, machinist, machine-handler, mechanic, practitioner. **2** *transport operators* driver, bus-driver, taxi-driver, lorry-driver, truck-driver, haulier, hauler; *inf* cabby, trucker. **3** *a smart operator* manoeuvrer, manipulator, machinator, mover, wheeler-dealer; *inf* punter.

opiate n drug, narcotic, sedative, tranquillizer, depressant, bromide, soporific, morphine, opium, laudanum; *inf* downer.

opinion n point of view, view, viewpoint, belief, thought, thinking, way of thinking, standpoint, theory, judgement, estimation, feeling, sentiment, impression, notion, assumption, conception, conviction, persuasion, creed, dogma. **a matter of opinion** *how he should be punished is a matter of opinion* open to/for discussion, open to debate, debatable, a debatable point, open to question, a moot point, up to the individual.

opinionated adj dogmatic, of fixed views, of preconceived ideas, pontifical, doctrinaire, dictatorial, self-assertive, positive, confident, assured, cocksure, pompous, self-important, adamant, obstinate, stubborn, pigheaded, headstrong, wilful, single-minded, inflexible, uncompromising, bigoted.

opponent n *the two opponents shook hands* | *an opponent of the government* opposer, the opposition, rival, adversary, fellow-contestant, fellow-competitor, enemy, foe, antagonist, contender, dissenter, disputant.

opportune adj *wait for an opportune moment* advantageous, favourable, auspicious, propitious, good, lucky, happy, timely, well-timed, fortunate, providential, felicitous, convenient, expedient, suitable, apt, fitting, relevant, applicable, pertinent.

opportunism n exploitation, expediency, taking advantage, unscrupulousness, exploitation, striking while the iron is hot, making hay while the sun shines, making the best of a bad job.

opportunity n lucky chance, chance, good time, golden opportunity, favourable time/occasion/moment, right set of circumstances, appropriate time/moment; *inf* break.

oppose v **1** *oppose the proposals* dislike, disapprove of, be hostile to, take a stand against, be/stand against, stand up to, stand up and be counted against, take

issue with, take on, contradict, counter, argue against, counterattack, confront, resist, withstand, defy, fight, put up a fight against, combat, fly in the face of. **2** *oppose memory and imagination* compare, contrast, juxtapose, offset, balance, counterbalance, set against, pit against, parallel. **be opposed to** *be opposed to the plans* | *am opposed to going to war* be against, be in opposition to, dislike, be in disagreement with, disagree with, be averse to, be hostile to, be antagonistic to, be inimical to; *inf* be anti.

opposing adj **1** *hold opposing opinions* opposite, differing, different, contrary, contradictory, conflicting, clashing, incompatible, at variance, irreconcilable. *see* OPPOSITE adj 2. **2** *on opposing sides* opposite, rival, competitive, enemy, warring, fighting, contending, combatant.

opposite adj **1** *people/houses opposite each other* facing, face to face with; *inf* eyeball to eyeball with. **2** *hold opposite opinions* diametrically opposite, opposing, differing, different, unlike, contrary, reverse, contradictory, conflicting, clashing, discordant, dissident, at variance, incompatible, irreconcilable, antipathetical, poles apart. **3** *on opposite sides* opposing, rival, competitive, enemy, warring, fighting, contending, combatant.

opposite n reverse, contrary, antithesis, converse, inverse, contradiction, the other extreme, the other side of the coin.

opposition n **1** *express their opposition to the plans* dislike, disapproval, hostility, resistance, defiance. *see* OPPOSE 1. **2** *back the opposition* opponent, opposing side, other side, other team, rival, adversary, competition, antagonist, enemy, foe.

oppress v **1** *the invading army oppressed the people* overwhelm, overpower, subjugate, enslave, suppress, crush, subdue, quash, quell, bring someone to his/her knees. **2** *the tyrant oppressed the citizens* tyrannize, crush, suppress, repress, abuse, maltreat, persecute, rule with a rod of iron, trample on, trample underfoot, ride roughshod over. **3** *oppressed by grief* weigh down, lie heavy on, weigh heavy on, burden, crush, depress, dispirit, dishearten, take the heart out of, discourage, sadden, make despondent, deject, desolate.

oppressed adj **1** *the oppressed citizens/children* tyrannized, subjugated, enslaved, crushed, subdued, repressed, persecuted, abused, maltreated, misused, browbeaten, downtrodden, disadvantaged, underprivileged. **2** *oppressed, grief-stricken widows* weighed down, depressed, dispirited, despondent, dejected, desolate. *see* OPPRESS 3.

oppression n 1 *the oppression of the people by the invading army* overwhelming, subjugation, subduing. *see* OPPRESS 1. 2 *the tyrant's oppression of the people* tyranny, suppression, abuse, persecution. *see* OPPRESS 2. 3 *people suffering from oppression for generations* tyranny, despotism, abuse, maltreatment, persecution, cruelty, brutality, injustice, ruthlessness, harshness, hardship, misery, suffering, wretchedness. 4 *oppression brought on by grief* depression, despondency, dejection, desolation. *see* OPPRESS 3.

oppressive adj 1 *an oppressive regime* tyrannical, despotic, Draconian, iron-fisted, high-handed, repressive, domineering, harsh, crushing, cruel, brutal, ruthless, relentless, merciless, pitiless, inexorable, unjust, undemocratic. 2 *oppressive weather* muggy, close, airless, stuffy, stifling, suffocating, sultry, torrid.

oppressor n tyrant, despot, autocrat, subjugator, persecutor, bully, iron hand, slavedriver, hard taskmaster, scourge, dictator, tormentor, torturer.

opprobrium n *bring opprobrium on his family* disgrace, shame, dishonour, ignominy, discredit, loss of face, disrepute, ill repute, infamy, notoriety, odium, obloquy.

opt v **opt for** *opt for a red one* choose, select, pick, decide on, settle on, plump for, prefer; *inf* go for.

optimistic adj 1 *an optimistic person* disposed to look on the bright side, always expecting the best, inclined to look through rose-coloured spectacles, hopeful, full of hope, Pollyannaish, Panglossian. 2 *feeling optimistic about the future | was in optimistic mood* positive, sanguine, hopeful, confident, bullish, cheerful, buoyant; *inf* upbeat.

optimum adj 1 *the optimum time to choose* most favourable, best, most advantageous, most appropriate, ideal, perfect. 2 *plants in optimum condition* peak, top, best, perfect, ideal, flawless, superlative, optimal; *inf* tiptop, A1.

option n 1 *have little option* choice, freedom of choice, power to choose, right to choose. 2 *have no other option* choice, alternative, other possibility, preference.

optional adj *attendance/tipping is optional* non-compulsory, not required, voluntary, up to the individual, discretionary, at one's discretion, elective.

opulence n 1 *the opulence of the family* affluence, wealth, richness, riches, money, fortune, prosperity. 2 *the opulence of the house/furnishings* luxury, luxuriousness, sumptuousness, lavishness; *inf* plushiness, ritziness. 3 *the opulence of the vegetation* abundance, superabundance, copiousness, plentifulness, profuseness, prolificness, luxuriance, cornucopia.

opulent adj 1 *opulent families* affluent, wealthy, rich, well-off, well-to-do, moneyed, prosperous; *inf* well-heeled, rolling in it. 2 *opulent houses* luxurious, sumptuous, lavishly appointed; *inf* plush, plushy, ritzy. 3 *opulent vegetation* abundant, superabundant, copious, plentiful, profuse, prolific, luxuriant.

opus n work, composition, *oeuvre*, piece, creation, production.

oracle n 1 *the oracles of classical times* prophet/prophetess, seer, soothsayer, sibyl, augur, wise man/woman, sage. 2 *he regards himself as an oracle on architecture* authority, expert, mastermind, specialist, connoisseur, pundit, guru, mentor, adviser.

oracular adj 1 *his statement proved oracular* prophetic, prescient, augural, divinatory, mantic. 2 *his answers are always rather oracular* ambiguous, equivocal, two-edged, obscure, enigmatic, cryptic, abstruse, arcane, puzzling, perplexing, baffling.

oral adj spoken, verbal, vocal, uttered, said.

oral n oral examination, interview, viva voce; *inf* viva.

oration n *delivered an oration* speech, lecture, address, homily, sermon, discourse, declamation, harangue, tirade; *inf* spiel.

orator n speaker, public speaker, speechmaker, lecturer, declaimer, haranguer, rhetorician, Cicero. *see* ORATION.

oratorical adj *oratorical style* rhetorical, grandiloquent, magniloquent, high-flown, high-sounding, bombastic, grandiose, orotund, declamatory, Ciceronian.

orb n sphere, globe, ball, round, circle, ring.

orbit n 1 *the planet's orbit* revolution, circle, circuit, cycle, rotation, circumgyration, path, course, track, trajectory. 2 *subjects within his orbit of responsibility* sphere, sphere of influence, range, reach, scope, ambit, sweep, domain.

orbit v *orbit the earth* revolve round, circle round, go/sail/fly round, encircle, circumnavigate.

orchestrate v 1 *orchestrate the piece of music* arrange, score. 2 *orchestrate the event* organize, arrange, put together, set up, man-

age, stage-manage, mastermind, coordinate, integrate.

ordain v **1** *ordain a new priest* appoint, confer holy orders on, frock, induct, install,
invest, anoint, consecrate. **2** *his lack of success seems to have been ordained* fate, predestine, predetermine, preordain. **3** *parliament
ordained that taxes be increased* decree, legislate, rule, order, command, enjoin, dictate,
prescribe, pronounce. **4** *ordain new laws*
decree, enact, lay down, establish, set out.

ordeal n trial, test, tribulation, painful/dis-
turbing experience, suffering, affliction,
distress, agony, anguish, torture, torment,
calamity, trouble, nightmare.

order n **1** *restore order to the room* orderliness, neatness, tidiness, trimness, har-
mony, apple-pie order. **2** *no sense of order in
the filing system* method, organization, system, plan, uniformity, regularity, symmetry, pattern. **3** *everything is in good/working
order* condition, state, shape, situation.
4 *arrange in alphabetical/numerical order*
arrangement, grouping, system, systemiza-
tion, organization, form, structure, disposition, classification, categorization,
codification, series, sequence, progression,
succession, layout, set-up. **5** *give orders to
fire | must obey the king's orders* command,
direction, directive, instruction, behest,
decree, edict, injunction, law, rule, regulation, mandate, ordinance, stipulation, dictate, say-so. **6** *lack of order in the land* law,
lawfulness, law and order, discipline, control, peace, calm, quiet, quietness, peace
and quiet, tranquillity. **7** *place an order for
bread/tickets* request, call, requirement,
requisition, demand, booking, reservation,
commission, notification, application. **8** *the
lower orders of society* rank, class, caste,
grade, level, degree, position, station. **9** *the
social order* grouping, grading, ranking, system, class system, caste system, hierarchy,
pecking order. **10** *work of a high order* kind,
sort, type, variety, genre, nature. **11** *botani-
cal/biological orders* taxonomic group, class,
subclass, family, species, breed. **12** *a religious order* brotherhood, sisterhood, community. **13** *they all belong to some order*
lodge, society, secret society, guild, club,
association, league, union, fellowship, fraternity, confraternity, sorority, brotherhood, sisterhood, sodality. **14** *raise a point
of order* procedure, correct procedure, standard procedure, ruling. **in order 1** *the
library books are in order* in sequence, in
series, in alphabetical order, in numerical
order, in order of merit, in order of seniority, classified, categorized. **2** *the room is in
order* orderly, tidy, neat, trim, shipshape,

shipshape and Bristol fashion, in apple-pie
order. **3** *is it in order for her to attend?* acceptable, all right, fitting, suitable, appropriate,
right, correct; *inf* OK. **out of order** *the
machine is out of order* broken, broken-down,
not working, unserviceable, not in working
order, not functioning, non-functional,
inoperative, in disrepair, out of commission; *inf* bust, kaput, gone phut, on the
blink, wonky, gone haywire, US; *Amer inf*
on the fritz.

order v **1** *order them to fire* give the order to,
command, give the command to, instruct,
direct, bid, enjoin. **2** *the king has ordered that
tomorrow be a holiday* decree, ordain, rule,
legislate, enjoin, prescribe, pronounce.
3 *order bread/tickets* put in an order for,
place an order for, request, call for, requisition, make one's requirements/demands
known, book, reserve, contract for, apply
for, send away for. **4** *order the files better |
thought it was time to order his life* put in
order, set in order, organize, systematize,
methodize, arrange, dispose, lay out, marshal, group, classify, catalogue, codify,
tabulate, put/set to rights, sort out, tidy
up, regulate.

orderly adj **1** *an orderly room* in order, neat,
tidy, trim, shipshape, shipshape and Bristol
fashion, in apple-pie order. **2** *an orderly
business/person* organized, well-organized,
well-regulated, methodical, systematic, systematized, efficient, businesslike. **3** *an
orderly class of pupils* well-behaved, law-
abiding, non-violent, disciplined, quiet,
peaceful, controlled, restrained.

ordinarily adv *ordinarily he is well-behaved* as
a rule, generally, as a general rule, in general, in the general run of things, usually,
normally, habitually, customarily, commonly.

ordinary adj **1** *our ordinary procedure* usual,
normal, standard, typical, stock, common,
customary, habitual, accustomed, wonted,
everyday, quotidian, regular, routine,
established, settled, fixed, prevailing, hum-
drum. **2** *we lead very ordinary lives | ordinary
houses* run-of-the-mill, common, conventional, standard, typical, average, commonplace, workaday, humdrum, unremarkable,
unexceptional, unmemorable, pedestrian,
prosaic, unpretentious, modest, plain, simple, humble; *inf* common or garden. **3** *a
very ordinary piece of writing | the dress is too
ordinary* average, run-of-the-mill, pedestrian, prosaic, uninteresting, dull, uninspired, unimaginative, hackneyed, stale,
undistinguished, unexceptional, unremarkable, mediocre, indifferent, second-rate.

ordinary n **out of the ordinary** *want something out of the ordinary* unusual, uncommon, atypical, non-standard, exceptional, extraordinary, rare, unique, remarkable, striking, noteworthy, memorable, distinguished, impressive, outstanding, special, exciting, imaginative, creative, inspired.

organ n **1** *he plays the organ* pipe-organ, reed-organ, electric organ, electronic organ, barrel-organ, hand-organ, mouth-organ, harmonica; *inf* hurdy-gurdy. **2** *vital organs* biological structure, part, part of the body, component, constituent, element. **3** *the organ of the trade union* newspaper, paper, journal, periodical, magazine, newsletter, gazette, bulletin, publication, means of communication, mouthpiece, voice, forum.

organic adj **1** *organic ingredients* natural, non-chemical, pesticide-free, chemical-free, additive-free. **2** *organic matter* living, live, animate, biotic, biological. **3** *the music in the play is organic not incidental* fundamental, basic, structural, integral, inherent, innate, intrinsic, vital, essential, indispensable. **4** *society is an organic whole* structured, organized, systematic, systematized, ordered, methodical, methodized.

organism n **1** living entity, living thing, living structure, being, something, creature, animal, plant. **2** *the computer company is a complex organism* structure, system, organization, set-up.

organization n **1** *the organization of the firm/files/party* establishment, development, assembly, arrangement, regulation, coordination, systematization, methodization, categorization, administration, running, management. *see* ORGANIZE. **2** *the human body is a complex organization* structure, system, whole, unity, organism, set-up. **3** *he is now head of the organization* company, firm, concern, operation, corporation, institution, group, consortium, conglomerate, combine, syndicate, federation, confederation, association, body.

organize v establish, set up, form, lay the foundations of, found, institute, create, originate, begin, start, develop, build, frame, construct, assemble, structure, shape, mould, put together, arrange, dispose, regulate, marshal, put in order, put straight, coordinate, systematize, methodize, standardize, collocate, group, sort, sort out, classify, categorize, catalogue, codify, tabulate, be responsible for, be in charge of, take care of, administrate, run, manage, lick/knock into shape, see to.

orgy n **1** *a drunken orgy* drunken bout, drunken party, wild party, carousal, debauch, revel, revels, revelry, bacchanalia, saturnalia; *inf* spree, binge, jag, bender, love-in; *Amer inf* toot. **2** *a spending orgy | go on an orgy of killing* bout, overindulgence, excess, surfeit; *inf* spree, splurge, binge.

orientate v **1** *difficult to orientate oneself in the fog* get/find one's bearings, get the lie of the land, establish one's location. **2** *orientate himself to his new life* adapt, adjust, accommodate, familiarize, acclimatize, find one's feet. **3** *orientate students towards science subjects* direct, guide, lead, point someone in the direction of, turn. **4** *orientate the course towards beginners* aim, direct, slant, angle, intend for, design for.

orientation n **1** *orientation is difficult in the dark* getting one's bearings. *see* ORIENTATE 1. **2** *his orientation to his new way of life* adaptation, adjustment, accommodation, familiarization, acclimatization. **3** *establish one's orientation* bearings, location, position, direction. **4** *the orientation of students* directing, direction, guiding. *see* ORIENTATE 3. **5** *the orientation of the course towards beginners* aiming, directing, designing. *see* ORIENTATE 4.

orifice n opening, hole, vent, aperture, gap, space, breach, break, rent, slot, slit, cleft, cranny, fissure, crevice, rift, crack, chink.

origin n **1** *the origin of the word* source, derivation, root, roots, provenance, etymology, genesis, aetiology. **2** *the origins of life* source, basis, base, well-spring, spring, well-head, fountain-head, fountain, genesis, *fons et origo*. **3** *the origin of the age of steam* birth, dawn, dawning, beginning, start, commencement, emergence, inception, launch, creation, early stages, inauguration, foundation. **4** *explore the family's origin(s)* descent, ancestry, pedigree, lineage, heritage, parentage, extraction, beginnings.

original adj **1** *the original inhabitants* aboriginal, indigenous, early, earliest, first, initial, primary, primordial, primal, primeval, primitive, autochthonal, authochthonous. **2** *his work is original* innovative, innovatory, inventive, new, novel, fresh, creative, imaginative, resourceful, individual, ingenious, unusual, unconventional, unorthodox, unprecedented, ground-breaking. **3** *this painting is original* not copied, genuine, authentic, archetypal, prototypical, master.

original n **1** *this is the original, not a copy* original work/painting, archetype, prototype, master. **2** *he really is an original* eccentric, oddity, crank, nonconformist; *inf* oddball, queer fish, nut, character, card, case, screwball, weirdo; *Amer inf* wacko.

originality n *admire the originality of his work* innovativeness, innovation, inventiveness, newness, novelty, break with tradition, freshness, creativity, imaginativeness, resourcefulness, individuality, unusualness, unconventionality, unprecedentedness.

originally adv *originally he was unwilling* at first, in the beginning, to begin with, at the start, at the outset, initially.

originate v **1** *the spring originates in the mountains* arise, rise, flow from, emanate from, issue from. **2** *the quarrel originated from a misunderstanding* have its origin in, arise, stem, spring, result, derive, start, begin, commence. **3** *he originated the idea* give birth to, be the father/mother of, set in motion, set up, invent, dream up, conceive, discover, initiate, create, formulate, inaugurate, pioneer, introduce, establish, found, evolve, develop, generate.

originator n father/mother, inventor, discoverer, initiator, architect, author, prime mover, founder, pioneer, establisher, developer. *see* ORIGINATE 3.

ornament n **1** *a house full of ornaments* knick-knack, trinket, bauble, gewgaw, accessory, decoration, frill, furbelow, whatnot, doodah. **2** *the beautiful house/dress needs little ornament* decoration, adornment, embellishment, trimming, garnish, garnishing. **3** *the ornament of the company's range* jewel, jewel in the crown, gem, treasure, pride, flower, leading light, *crème de la crème*.

ornamental adj *ornamental pool/plates* decorative, decorating, adorning, embellishing, ornamenting, embroidering.

ornate adj **1** *ornate furnishings* elaborate, overelaborate, decorated, embellished, adorned, ornamented, fancy, fussy, busy, ostentatious, showy, baroque, rococo; *inf* flash. **2** *ornate prose/speeches* elaborate, overelaborate, flowery, florid, flamboyant, laboured, strained, stilted, pretentious, high-flown, high-sounding, grandiose, pompous, orotund, magniloquent, grandiloquent, oratorical, bombastic; *inf* highfalutin.

orotund adj **1** *orotund voices* strong, powerful, full, rich, deep, sonorous, resonant, ringing, reverberating, booming. **2** *orotund speeches* ornate, overelaborate, laboured, strained, pretentious, high-flown, grandiose, pompous, magniloquent, bombastic; *inf* highfalutin. *see* ORNATE 2.

orthodox adj **1** *hold orthodox religious beliefs | an orthodox Jew* conformist, doctrinal, of the faith, of the true faith, sound, conservative, correct, faithful, true, true-blue, devoted, strict, devout. **2** *orthodox behaviour* conventional, accepted, approved, correct, proper, conformist, established, traditional, prevailing, customary, usual, regular, standard, *comme il faut, de rigueur*.

orthodoxy n **1** *the orthodoxy of his religious beliefs* conformism, conformity, doctrinalism, conservatism, soundness, correctness, faithfulness, devotion, devoutness, strictness. **2** *the orthodoxy of his behaviour* conventionality, conventionalism, correctness, properness, propriety, traditionalism. *see* ORTHODOX 2.

oscillate v **1** *the pendulum oscillating* swing, move back and forth, move backwards and forwards, move to and fro; *inf* wigwag. **2** *oscillate between feeling hot and cold* swing, sway, fluctuate, see-saw, waver, vacillate, vary, hesitate, yo-yo.

oscillation n **1** *the oscillation of the pendulum* swing, swinging, moving backwards and forwards. *see* OSCILLATE 1. **2** *his oscillation between courses of action* fluctuation, wavering, vacillation, yo-yoing. *see* OSCILLATE 2.

ossify v **1** *material ossifying with age* harden, solidify, stiffen, become rigid, fossilize, petrify. **2** *beliefs have ossified into rigid dogma* become rigid, become unyielding/obdurate, become inflexible, grow unprogressive, become unreceptive, harden, solidify.

ostensible adj outward, apparent, seeming, professed, alleged, claimed, purported, pretended, feigned, specious, supposed.

ostensibly adv apparently, allegedly, supposedly. *see* OSTENSIBLE.

ostentation n showiness, show, conspicuousness, obtrusiveness, loudness, extravagance, flamboyance, gaudiness, flashiness, pretentiousness, affectation, flaunting, exhibitionism, vulgarity, bad taste; *inf* showing-off, flashness, swank. *see* OSTENTATIOUS.

ostentatious adj *ostentatious jewellery/manner* showy, conspicuous, obtrusive, loud, extravagant, flamboyant, gaudy, flashy, pretentious, affected, overdone, overelaborate, vulgar, kitsch; *inf* flash, over-the-top, OTT, swanky.

ostracism n the cold shoulder, exclusion, barring, shunning, avoidance, boycotting, repudiation, rejection, banishment, exile. *see* OSTRACIZE.

ostracize v cold-shoulder, give someone the cold shoulder, send to Coventry, exclude, shut out, bar, keep at arm's length, shun, spurn, avoid, boycott, repudiate, cast out, reject, blackball, blacklist, black, banish, exile, expel, excommunicate, debar, leave out in the cold; *inf* hand someone the frozen mitt.

other adj **1** *use other means* different, unlike, variant, dissimilar, disparate, distinct, separate, alternative. **2** *need a few other examples* more, additional, further, extra, supplementary.

otherwise adv **1** *hurry, otherwise we'll be late* or else, or, if not. **2** *he's too young, otherwise he's fine* in other respects, in other ways, apart from that. **3** *he could not have acted otherwise* in any other way, differently.

ounce n *not to have an ounce of courage* iota, whit, trace, particle, atom, speck, scrap, shred, crumb, grain, drop.

oust v *ousted from his post* drive out, force out, thrust out, expel, eject, put out, evict, throw out, dispossess, dismiss, dislodge, displace, depose, unseat, topple, disinherit; *inf* fire, sack.

out adv **1** *the manager's out just now* not in, not here, not at home, gone away, away, elsewhere, absent, away from one's desk. **2** *the children have gone out* outside, outdoors, out of doors. **3** *tire them out* completely, thoroughly, entirely, wholly. **4** *the fire is out* not burning, extinguished, quenched, doused, dead. **5** *the boxer is completely out* out cold, unconscious, knocked out, senseless; *inf* KO'd, flaked out. **6** *your secret is out* revealed, disclosed, divulged, in the open, out in the open, known, exposed, common knowledge, public knowledge. **7** *the flowers are out* open, in bloom, in full bloom, blooming. **8** *long hair is out this year* unfashionable, out-of-fashion, dated, out-of-date, not in, behind the times, *démodé*, *passé*; *inf* old-hat. **9** *that idea is out* inappropriate, unsuitable, irrelevant, not worth considering.

out-and-out adj absolute, complete, utter, downright, thorough, thoroughgoing, total, perfect, unmitigated, unqualified, consummate, inveterate, dyed-in-the-wool, true-blue.

outbreak n *outbreak of disease* eruption, flare-up, upsurge, outburst, sudden appearance, start, rash.

outburst n *an outburst of anger/laughter* burst, explosion, eruption, outbreak, flare-up, access, attack, fit, spasm, paroxysm.

outcast n *social outcast* pariah, *persona non grata*, leper, untouchable, castaway, exile, displaced person, refugee, evictee, evacuee.

outclass v surpass, be superior to, be better than, outshine, eclipse, overshadow, outdistance, outstrip, outdo, outplay, outrank, outrival, trounce, beat, defeat; *inf* be a cut above, be head and shoulders above, run rings round, leave standing, outfox.

outcome n consequence, result, end result, sequel, upshot, issue, product, conclusion, after-effect, aftermath, wake; *inf* pay-off.

outcry n clamour, howls of protest, protest, complaints, objections, fuss, outburst, commotion, uproar, tumult, hue and cry, hullaballoo, ballyhoo, racket.

outdated adj out of date, out of style, out of fashion, old-fashioned, unfashionable, outmoded, dated, *démodé*, *passé*, behind the times, antiquated, archaic; *inf* old-hat, not with it.

outdistance v outstrip, outrun, outpace, leave behind, overtake, pass, shake off, lose; *inf* leave standing.

outdo v surpass, top, exceed, excel, get the better of, outstrip, outshine, eclipse, overshadow, transcend, outclass, outdistance, overcome, beat, defeat, outsmart, outmanoeuvre; *inf* be a cut above, be head and shoulders above, run rings round, outfox.

outdoor adj out-of-doors, outside, open-air, alfresco.

outer adj **1** *pierce the outer layer* outside, outermost, outward, exterior, external, surface, superficial. **2** *the outer areas of the estate* outlying, distant, remote, far-away, peripheral, fringe, perimeter.

outfit n **1** *wearing a smart outfit* clothes, dress, ensemble, suit, costume, garb, kit, accoutrements, trappings; *inf* rig-out, get-up, gear, togs. **2** *a car repair outfit* kit, equipment, tools, tackle, apparatus, paraphernalia. **3** *a small publishing outfit* organization, set-up, company, firm, business, unit, group, team, coterie, clique.

outfit v equip, kit out, fit out, rig out, supply, furnish with, provide with, stock with, provision, accoutre, attire.

outfitter n clothier, tailor, dressmaker, couturier, costumier, modiste; *Amer* haberdasher.

outflow n outflowing, outpouring, outrush, rush, discharge, issue, spurt, jet, gush, leakage, drainage, outflux, effluence, efflux.

outgoing adj **1** *outgoing people* extrovert, unreserved, demonstrative, affectionate, warm, friendly, genial, cordial, affable, hail-fellow-well-met, sociable, communicative, open, expansive, talkative, gregarious, approachable, easygoing, easy. **2** *the outgo-*

ing president retiring, departing, leaving, withdrawing, ex-, former, past, late.

outgoings npl costs, expenses, expenditure, outlay, overheads.

outing n trip, excursion, jaunt, expedition, pleasure trip, tour, mystery tour, airing; *inf* spin.

outlandish adj strange, unfamiliar, unknown, unheard-of, odd, unusual, extraordinary, peculiar, queer, curious, singular, eccentric, quaint, bizarre, grotesque, preposterous, fantastic, *outré*, weird; *inf* freaky, wacky, far-out, off-the-wall.

outlaw n fugitive, outcast, exile, pariah, bandit, desperado, brigand, criminal, robber; *inf* villain.

outlaw v **1** *outlaw the thief* banish, exile, cast out, expel, send away, repudiate, put a price on someone's head. **2** *outlaw the sale of liquor* ban, bar, prohibit, forbid, embargo, make illegal, disallow, proscribe, interdict.

outlay n expenditure, expenses, spending, outgoings, money spent, cost, price, charge, payment, disbursement.

outlet n **1** *water outlets* way out, exit, vent, vent-hole, outfall, valve, safety-valve, duct, blow-hole, channel, trench, culvert, cut, conduit. **2** *an outlet for her emotion/creativity* means of expression, release, means of release, release mechanism, safety-valve. **3** *an outlet for their farm produce* retail outlet, market, market-place, selling-place, shop, store.

outline n **1** *an outline of our plans* draft, rough draft, rough, sketch, tracing, skeleton, framework, layout, diagram, plan, design, schema. **2** *give an outline of what happened* thumbnail sketch, rough idea, quick run-down, abbreviated version, summary, synopsis, résumé, précis, main points, bones, bare bones. **3** *draw an outline of the building* contour, silhouette, profile, lineaments, delineation, configuration, perimeter, circumference.

outline v **1** *outline the shape* sketch, delineate, trace, silhouette. **2** *outline your ideas* sketch out, give a thumbnail sketch of, give a rough idea of, give a quick run-down on, summarize, précis.

outlook n **1** *a gloomy outlook on life* view, point of view, viewpoint, perspective, attitude, frame of mind, standpoint, slant, angle, interpretation, opinion. **2** *the house has a pleasant outlook* view, vista, prospect, panorama, aspect.

outlying adj outer, outermost, out-of-the-way, remote, distant, far-away, far-flung, peripheral, isolated, inaccessible, off the beaten track, backwoods. *see* OUT OF THE WAY 1.

outmoded adj old-fashioned, unfashionable, out of fashion, out of style, outdated, out of date, dated, *passé*, *démodé*, behind the times, antiquated, archaic, obsolete; *inf* old-hat.

out of date adj **1** *out-of-date clothes* outdated, dated, old-fashioned, out of fashion, behind the times, archaic, obsolete. *see* OUTMODED. **2** *the licence is out of date* expired, lapsed, elapsed, invalid, void, null and void.

out of the way adj **1** *out-of-the-way places* outlying, outer, outermost, remote, distant, far-away, far-flung, peripheral, isolated, lonely, inaccessible, obscure, off the beaten track, unfrequented, backwoods. **2** *I don't find his methods out of the way* uncommon, unusual, odd, peculiar, abnormal, strange, curious, extraordinary, out of the ordinary, outlandish.

out of work adj *an out-of-work actor | he is out of work* unemployed, jobless, out of a job, redundant, laid off, idle; *inf* on the dole, signing on.

outpouring n outflow, effluence, efflux, flux, outflux, debouchment, cascade, deluge, spate, stream, spurt, jet, torrent.

output n production, product, amount/quantity produced, productivity, yield, harvest, achievement, accomplishment.

outrage n **1** *outrages committed by the soldiers* atrocity, act of violence, evil, act of wickedness, crime, horror, enormity, brutality, barbarism, inhumane act. **2** *the sacking of the men was an outrage | the building is an outrage* offence, affront, insult, injury, abuse, indignity, scandal, desecration, violation. **3** *arouse outrage in the citizens* anger, fury, rage, indignation, wrath, annoyance, shock, resentment, horror, amazement.

outrage v **1** *outrage the community* anger, infuriate, enrage, incense, madden, annoy, shock, horrify, amaze, scandalize, offend. **2** *outrage the churches/women* abuse, maltreat, misuse, injure, desecrate, defile, profane, rape, ravage, ravish, violate.

outrageous adj **1** *his outrageous behaviour when drunk* intolerable, insufferable, insupportable, unendurable, unbearable, impossible, exasperating, offensive, provocative, maddening, distressing. **2** *commit outrageous acts* atrocious, heinous, abominable, wicked, vile, foul, monstrous, horrible, horrid, dreadful, terrible, horrendous, hideous, ghastly, unspeakable, gruesome. **3** *outrageous prices* immoderate, excessive, exorbitant, unreasonable, preposterous, scandalous, shocking; *inf* steep, over the top, OTT.

outré adj unconventional, eccentric, odd, outlandish, strange, extraordinary, unusual, bizarre, freakish, freaky, queer, weird; *inf* rum, offbeat, off-the-wall, wacky, way-out, far-out.

outright adj **1** *an outright fool* out-and-out, absolute, complete, downright, utter, thorough, thoroughgoing, perfect, total, unmitigated. *see* OUT-AND-OUT. **2** *the outright winner* definite, unequivocal, unqualified, incontestable, undeniable, unmistakable.

outright adv **1** *reject the proposal outright* completely, entirely, wholly, totally, categorally, absolutely. **2** *killed outright* instantly, instantaneously, immediately, at once, straight away, there and then, on the spot. **3** *tell her outright* openly, candidly, frankly, honestly, forthrightly, directly, plainly, explicitly, unreservedly.

outset n start, starting point, beginning, commencement, dawn, birth, inception, opening, launch, inauguration; *inf* kick-off.

outshine v surpass, eclipse, put in the shade, overshadow, be superior to, be better than, outclass, outstrip, outdistance, outdo, top, tower above, dwarf, transcend, upstage; *inf* be head and shoulders above, be a cut above, leave standing.

outside adj **1** *outside layers* outer, outermost, outward, exterior, external. **2** *outside furniture/toilet* outdoor, out-of-doors. **3** *an outside chance* unlikely, improbable, slight, slender, slim, small, faint, negligible, marginal, remote, distant, vague.

outside adv *go outside* outdoors, out of doors, out of the house.

outside n **1** *brown on the outside* outer side, exterior, surface, outer surface, case, skin, shell, sheath. **2** *the outside of the building* exterior, front, face, façade.

outsider n odd man out, alien, stranger, foreigner, outlander, immigrant, emigrant, émigré, incomer, newcomer, parvenu, *arriviste*, interloper, intruder, gatecrasher, outcast, misfit.

outskirts npl vicinity, neighbourhood, environs, edges, outlying districts, fringes, margin, periphery, borders, boundary, suburbs, suburbia, purlieus, *faubourgs*.

outsmart v get the better of, outwit, outmanoeuvre, outperform, outplay, be cleverer than, steal a march on, trick, dupe, make a fool of; *inf* outfox, put one over on, pull a fast one on, give someone the runaround, run rings round.

outspoken adj candid, frank, forthright, direct, straightforward, straight-from-the-shoulder, plain, plain-spoken, explicit, blunt, brusque, unequivocal, unreserved, unceremonious.

outstanding adj **1** *an outstanding painter* pre-eminent, eminent, well-known, notable, noteworthy, distinguished, important, famous, famed, renowned, celebrated, great, excellent, remarkable, exceptional, superlative. **2** *the painting is outstanding* striking, impressive, eye-catching, arresting, memorable, remarkable. **3** *outstanding debts* unpaid, unsettled, owing, due. **4** *work outstanding* to be done, unfinished, remaining, pending, ongoing.

outward adj **1** *outward layers* outer, outside, outermost, exterior, external, surface, superficial. **2** *no outward sign of his grief* external, superficial, visible, observable, noticeable, perceptible, discernible, apparent, evident, obvious.

outwardly adv **1** *outwardly visible* externally, on the outside. **2** *outwardly he seems all right* on the surface, superficially, on the face of it, to all appearances, to the eye, as far as one can see, to all intents and purposes, apparently, evidently.

outweigh v be greater than, exceed, be superior to, take precedence over, have the edge on/over, preponderate.

outwit v get the better of, be cleverer than, outsmart, outmanoeuvre, steal a march on, trick, dupe, make a fool of; *inf* outfox, put one over on, pull a fast one on. *see* OUTSMART.

outworn adj *outworn ideas/traditions* outdated, out of date, old-fashioned, out of fashion, outmoded, behind the times, ancient, archaic, antiquated, obsolescent, obsolete, disused, abandoned, cast out, rejected, discredited, tired, exhausted, stale, hackneyed, superannuated; *inf* old-hat, out of the ark.

oval adj egg-shaped, ovoid, ovate, oviform, elliptical, ellipsoidal.

ovation n applause, hand-clapping, clapping, cheering, cheers, acclaim, acclamation, praise, plaudits, laurels, tribute, accolade, laudation, extolment; *inf* bouquets.

oven n stove, kitchen stove, microwave oven, haybox, kiln.

over adv **1** *fly over* overhead, above, on high, aloft. **2** *the relationship is over* ended, at an end, finished, concluded, terminated, no more, extinct, gone, dead, a thing of the past, ancient history. **3** *have food over* left over, left, remaining, unused, surplus, superfluous, in excess, extra, in addition. **over and over** again and again, over and over again, repeatedly, time and again, time and time again, ad nauseam.

over prep **1** *earn over £20,000* more than, above, in excess of, exceeding. **2** *he has three people over him* above, superior to, higher up than, more powerful than. **3** *all over the world/place* throughout, all through, throughout the extent of, everywhere in, in all parts of, around. **over and above** *over and above the sum mentioned* in addition to, on top of, plus, as well as, besides, not to mention, let alone.

overact v exaggerate; *inf* ham, camp it up, pile it on, lay it on.

overall adj *an overall plan/improvement* comprehensive, universal, all-embracing, inclusive, all-inclusive, general, sweeping, complete, blanket, umbrella, global.

overall adv *overall, things have improved* on the whole, in general, generally speaking.

overawe v intimidate, daunt, disconcert, abash, dismay, frighten, alarm, scare, terrify, terrorize.

overbalance v lose one's balance, lose one's footing, fall over, topple over, tip over, keel over, capsize, overturn, turn turtle.

overbearing adj domineering, autocratic, tyrannical, despotic, oppressive, highhanded, lordly, officious, dogmatic, dictatorial, pompous, peremptory, arrogant, haughty, cocksure, proud, over-proud, overweening, presumptuous, supercilious, disdainful, contemptuous; *inf* bossy, throwing one's weight about, cocky.

overblown adj **1** *an overblown piece of writing* overwritten, extravagant, florid, pompous, overelaborate, over-flowery, pretentious, high-flown, turgid, bombastic, grandiloquent, magniloquent, euphuistic, fustian, aureate; *inf* over the top, OTT. **2** *overblown roses/beauty* past its/one's prime, past its/one's best, fading.

overcast adj cloudy, clouded, clouded over, overclouded, sunless, darkened, dark, murky, misty, hazy, foggy, grey, leaden, louring, threatening, heavy, promising rain, dismal, dreary.

overcharge v **1** *overcharge the customers* charge too much, cheat, swindle, fleece, short change; *inf* rip off, sting, diddle, do, rook, clip. **2** *overcharge the description* overwrite, overdraw, overdo, overstate, exaggerate, hyperbolize, overcolour, overembroider, embroider, embellish; *inf*

pile it on, lay it on thick, lay it on with a trowel.

overcoat n coat, topcoat, winter coat, greatcoat, raincoat, mackintosh, anorak, parka, frock-coat, ulster.

overcome v **1** *overcome the enemy | must overcome her resistance* conquer, defeat, vanquish, beat, be victorious over, gain a victory over, prevail over, get the better of, triumph over, best, worst, trounce, rout, gain mastery over, master, overpower, overwhelm, overthrow, subdue, subjugate, quell, quash, crush; *inf* lick, clobber, whip, wipe the floor with, tank, blow out of the water. **2** *overcome one's disability* conquer, get the better of, triumph over, master, surmount, rise above.

overcome adj *too overcome to react* overwhelmed, emotional, moved, affected, speechless, at a loss for words; *inf* bowled over.

overconfident adj cocksure, swaggering, blustering, self-assured, self-assertive, brash, overbearing, overweening, presumptuous, egotistic, riding/heading for a fall; *inf* cocky.

overcritical adj hypercritical, fault-finding, captious, carping, cavilling, quibbling, hairsplitting, niggling, hard to please, overparticular, fussy, finicky, over-exacting; *inf* nit-picking, pernickety.

overcrowded adj overfull, full to overflowing, crammed full, packed as tight as sardines, congested, overloaded, overpopulated, overpeopled, overrun, thronged, swarming, teeming; *inf* full to the gunwales, jam-packed, like the Black Hole of Calcutta.

overdo v **1** *overdo the comic scenes* overact, overplay, exaggerate, do to death; *inf* ham up, camp up, go overboard over. **2** *overdo the sympathy* do to excess, carry too far, carry to extremes, exaggerate, belabour, stretch/strain a point over, overstate, overemphasize, hyperbolize, not know when to stop, do to death; *inf* pile on, lay on thick, lay on with a trowel, make a production of, make a big deal out of. **3** *overdo the meat* overcook, overbake, burn, burn to a crisp; *inf* burn to a frazzle. **overdo it** do too much, overwork, work too hard, strain oneself, do too much, overtax oneself, overtax one's strength, overburden oneself, overload oneself, drive oneself too hard, push oneself too far/hard, wear oneself out, burn the candle at both ends, have too many irons in the fire, have too many balls in the air, burn oneself out, bite off more than one can chew; *inf* knock oneself out, work/run oneself into the ground.

overdone adj **1** *the flattery/sympathy was overdone* excessive, too much, undue, immoderate, inordinate, disproportionate, beyond the pale, extravagant, overenthusiastic, effusive, over-effusive, gushing, fulsome; *inf* at bit much, over the top, OTT, hyped up, laid on with a trowel. **2** *overdone food* overcooked, overbaked, dried out, burnt, burnt to a cinder/crisp; *inf* burnt to a frazzle.

overdue adj **1** *our arrival/visit is overdue* late, not on time, behind schedule, behindhand, delayed, belated, tardy, unpunctual. **2** *overdue bills* unpaid, owed, owing, outstanding, unsettled, in arrears.

overeat v eat too much, eat like a horse, gorge oneself, stuff oneself, overindulge, overindulge oneself, surfeit, guzzle, gormandize; *inf* binge, stuff one's face, pack it away, make a pig of oneself, pig out.

overemphasize v place/put too much emphasis on, overstress, put/lay too much stress on, exaggerate, attach too much importance/weight to, make too much of, overdo, overdramatize, make something out of nothing, make a mountain out of a molehill, belabour the point; *inf* blow up out of all proportion.

overflow v **1** *the water was overflowing* flow over, run over, spill over, brim over, well over, pour forth, stream forth, discharge, surge, debouch. **2** *water overflowed the land* flood, deluge, inundate, submerge, cover, swamp, engulf, drown, soak, drench, saturate. **overflowing with 1** *overflowing with people* full of, crowded with, thronged with, swarming with, teeming with, abounding in. **2** *hearts overflowing with kindness* full of, very full of, filled with, filled to the brim with, brimful of, abounding in.

overflow n **1** *the overflow from the cistern* excess water, overspill, spill, spillage, flood, flooding, inundation. **2** *the overflow of the meeting* surplus, additional people/things, extra people/things.

overhang v stand out, stick out, extend, project, protrude, jut, jut out, beetle, bulge out, loom, cantiliver.

overhaul v **1** *overhaul the engine* check, check out, check over, give something a check-up, investigate, inspect, examine, service, repair, mend, recondition, renovate, revamp, fix up, patch up. **2** *overhaul the other runners* overtake, pass, get ahead of, outdistance, outstrip, gain on, catch up with, draw level with.

overhead adv *clouds overhead* | *bird flew overhead* above, up above, high up, up in the sky, on high, aloft.

overheads npl expenses, expenditure, outlay, disbursement, running costs, operating costs.

overindulge v **1** *overindulge and have a hangover* drink/eat too much, be immoderate, be intemperate, overdo it, drink/eat/go to excess, not know when to stop; *inf* binge, go on a binge, paint the town red, push the boat out, go overboard, live it up, make a pig of oneself. **2** *overindulge the children* give in to, spoil, cosset, pamper, mollycoddle, feather-bed; *inf* spoil rotten.

overjoyed adj full of joy, joyful, elated, jubilant, thrilled, delighted, euphoric, ecstatic, in raptures, rapturous, enraptured, in transports, transported, delirious with happiness, on top of the world; *inf* tickled pink, over the moon, on cloud nine, in seventh heaven.

overlay v **1** *overlay the floor with carpet* cover, overspread, carpet, blanket. **2** *overlay the table with gold* inlay, laminate, veneer, varnish, gild, decorate, ornament.

overload v overburden, weigh down, encumber, overcharge, overtax, oppress, impose strain on, strain; *inf* saddle with.

overlook v **1** *he overlooked a mistake on the first page* fail to notice/observe/spot, miss, leave, neglect to notice, leave unnoticed; *inf* slip up on. **2** *overlook tasks* leave undone, ignore, disregard, omit, neglect, forget. **3** *decide to overlook his crime* deliberately to ignore, not to take into consideration, disregard, take no notice of, let something pass, turn a blind eye to, wink at, blink at, excuse, pardon, forgive, condone, let someone off with; *inf* let something ride. **4** *the house overlooks the sea* look over, look onto, front onto, give over, open out over, have a view of, afford a view of, command a view of.

overly adv *not overly concerned* too, to too great an extent/degree, unduly, excessively, inordinately, immoderately.

overpower v **1** *overpower the enemy* gain control over, overwhelm, overcome, get the upper hand over, gain mastery over, master, best, worst, conquer, defeat, vanquish, trounce, rout, subjugate, quell, quash, crush; *inf* whip. **2** *his charm overpowered her* overcome, overwhelm, move, stir, affect, touch, impress, take aback; *inf* bowl over, knock/hit for six, get to.

overpowering adj **1** *overpowering grief* overwhelming, burdensome, weighty, unbearable, unendurable, intolerable, shattering; *inf* mind-blowing. **2** *an overpowering smell* overstrong, suffocating, stifling, nauseating. **3** *overpowering evidence* compelling, forceful, telling, irrefutable, undeniable, unquestionable, indisputable, incontestable, incontrovertible.

overrate v *overrated him* | *overrate his chances* overestimate, overvalue, overprize, exaggerate the worth of, think too much of, attach too much importance to, expect too much of.

overreach v *overreach the enemy* get the better of, outsmart, outwit; *inf* outfox, steal a march on, trick, make a fool of, pull a fast one on. *see* OUTSMART. **overreach oneself** overestimate one's ability, try to do too much, go too far, try to be too clever/smart, defeat one's own ends, have one's scheme backfire on one, be hoist with one's own petard, bite off more than one can chew.

overreact v get overexcited, get upset over nothing, act irrationally, lose one's sense of proportion, make something out of nothing, make a mountain out of a molehill; *inf* go over the top, press the panic button.

override v **1** *his career overrides all other considerations* be more important than, take priority over, take precedence over, supersede, outweigh. **2** *override her objections* trample on, ride roughshod over, set aside, ignore, disregard, discount, pay no heed to, take no account of, close one's mind to, turn a deaf ear to.

overriding adj *the overriding consideration* most important, predominant, principal, primary, paramount, chief, main, major, foremost, central, focal, pivotal; *inf* number one.

overrule v *overrule their objections* rule against, disallow, override, veto, set aside, overturn, cancel, reverse, rescind, repeal, revoke, repudiate, annul, nullify, declare null and void, invalidate, void, abrogate.

overrun v **1** *the enemy army was overrunning their country* invade, march into, penetrate, occupy, beseige, storm, attack, assail. **2** *rats overrunning the warehouses* swarm over, surge over, inundate, overwhelm, permeate, infest. **3** *weeds overrunning the garden* spread over, spread like wildfire over, grow over, cover, choke, clog; *inf* run riot over. **4** *the lecture overran* exceed the allotted time, go/run over the allotted time, be too long.

overseer n supervisor, superintendent, foreman, manager/manageress, master, boss; *inf* gaffer, super; *Amer inf* honcho.

overshadow v **1** *that runner overshadows the others* | *the achievement of the others is overshadowed* outshine, eclipse, put in the shade, surpass, be superior to, outclass, outstrip, outdo, top, transcend, tower above, dwarf, upstage; *inf* be head and shoulders above, be a cut above. **2** *his death overshadowed the family gathering* cast gloom over, blight, take the pleasure out of, bring a note of sadness to, take the edge off, mar, spoil, ruin. **3** *clouds overshadowing the sun* | *many trees overshadowed the garden* cloud, darken, bedim, dim, conceal, obscure, eclipse, screen, shroud, veil.

oversight n **1** *done in oversight* carelessness, inattention, neglect, inadvertence, laxity, dereliction, omission. **2** mistake, error, blunder, gaffe, fault, omission, slip, lapse; *inf* slip-up, bloomer, goof, boob, booboo. **3** *have oversight of the workforce* supervision, surveillance, superintendence, charge, care, administration, management, direction, control, handling.

overt adj *overt hostility* obvious, noticeable, observable, visible, undisguised, unconcealed, apparent, plain, plainly seen, plain to see, manifest, patent, open, public, blatant, conspicuous.

overtake v **1** *cars/runners overtaking each other* pass, get past, go past, go by, overhaul, leave behind, outdistance, outstrip, go faster than. **2** *misfortune overtook them* befall, happen to, come upon, hit, strike, fall upon, overwhelm, engulf, take by surprise, surprise, catch unawares, catch unprepared, catch off guard.

overthrow v **1** *overthrow the government* cause the downfall of, remove from office, overturn, depose, oust, unseat, dethrone, disestablish. **2** *overthrow the army of occupation* conquer, vanquish, defeat, beat, rout, trounce, best, worst, subjugate, crush, quash, quell, overcome, overwhelm, overturn, overpower. **3** *kids overthrowing cars* throw over, turn over, overturn, tip over, topple over, upset, capsize, knock over, upturn, upend, invert.

overthrow n **1** *the overthrow of the government* downfall, deposition, ousting. *see* OVERTHROW v 1. **2** *the overthrow of the army* defeat, vanquishing, rout, subjugation, crushing, overwhelming, overturning. *see* OVERTHROW v 2.

overtone n hidden meaning, secondary meaning, implication, innuendo, hint, suggestion, insinuation, association, connotation, undercurrent, nuance, flavour, colouring, vein.

overture n **1** *miss the overture* musical introduction/opening, prelude. **2** *the enemy making peace overtures* advances, move, opening move, conciliatory move, approach, proposal, proposition, offer, suggestion, motion.

overturn v **1** *the boat overturned* capsize, keel over, overbalance, tip over, topple over. **2** *boys overturning cars* upturn, turn over, throw over, overthrow, tip over, topple over, upset, knock over, upend, invert. **3** *overturn the previous decision* overrule, override, veto, set aside, cancel, reverse, rescind, repeal, revoke, repudiate, annul, nullify, invalidate, void, abrogate. **4** *overturn the government* overthrow, cause the downfall of, depose, oust, unseat. *see* OVERTHROW V 1. **5** *overturn the army of occupation* conquer, vanquish, defeat, trounce, worst, subjugate, crush, quash, quell, overcome. *see* OVERTHROW V 2.

overweening adj arrogant, haughty, proud, vain, vainglorious, conceited, self-important, egotistical, high-handed, domineering, presumptuous, lordly, peremptory, pompous, officious, blustering, self-confident, cocksure, self-assertive, opinionated, bold, forward, insolent, supercilious, disdainful, patronizing; *inf* cocky, high and mighty, throwing one's weight about/around.

overweight adj obese, fat, plump, stout, ample, chubby, tubby, corpulent, rotund, portly, podgy, paunchy, heavy, on the heavy side, big, hefty large, bulky, chunky, outsize, massive, gross, Falstaffian; *inf* well-padded, well-upholstered, roly-poly.

overwhelm v **1** *the generous present overwhelmed her* overcome, move, make emotional, daze, dumbfound, shake, take aback, leave speechless, stagger; *inf* bowl over, knock for six, blow one's mind, flabbergast. **2** *they were overwhelmed with work/mail* inundate, flood, deluge, engulf, submerge, swamp, bury, overload, overburden, snow under. **3** *overwhelm the army of occupation* overcome, overpower, conquer, vanquish, defeat, subjugate, quell, quash, crush. *see* OVERCOME V 1.

overwhelming adj **1** *an overwhelming desire to laugh* uncontrollable, irrepressible, irresistible, overpowering. **2** *an overwhelming amount of mail* profuse, enormous, immense, inordinate, massive, huge, stupendous, prodigious, staggering, shattering; *inf* mind-boggling, mind-blowing. **3** *the*

overwhelming majority vast, massive, great, large.

overwork v **1** *the staff are all overworking* work too hard, do too much, overdo it, work like a Trojan, work like a horse/slave, work day and night, burn the midnight oil, drive/push oneself too hard, overtax oneself, sweat, work one's fingers to the bone; *inf* work one's tail off, work/run oneself into the ground. **2** *the factory owner overworks the men* exploit, sweat, be a hard taskmaster, overburden, oppress, be a slave driver; *inf* drive into the ground. **3** *overwork certain words* overuse, overemploy.

overworked adj *overworked employees* stressed, under stress, stress-ridden, strained, overtaxed, overburdened, exhausted, fatigued, worn-out.

overwrought adj **1** *overwrought mothers* tense, agitated, nervous, on edge, edgy, keyed-up, highly strung, overexcited beside oneself, distracted, jumpy, frantic, frenzied, hysterical; *inf* nervy, in a state, in a tizzy, uptight, twitchy, strung-up, wound-up. **2** *overwrought decoration/designs* overornate, overelaborate, overembellished, overblown, overcharged, florid, busy, fussy, strained, contrived, overworked, baroque, rococo.

owe v be in debt to, be indebted to, be in arrears to, be under an obligation to, be obligated to, be beholden to.

owing adj owed, outstanding, unpaid, payable, due, overdue, in arrears. **owing to** because of, as a result of, on account of.

own adj personal, individual, particular, private.

own n **hold one's own 1** *she can hold her own against the men in the firm* maintain/keep one's position, stick up for oneself, look after one's interests; *inf* fight one's corner. **2** *the patient is holding his own* be in a stable condition, be stable, be surviving, have a chance of survival. **on one's own 1** *live/go on one's own* alone, all alone, by oneself, unaccompanied; *inf* on one's tod. **2** *be on one's own* single, unmarried, unattached, footloose and fancy-free. **3** *build the business on her own* all by herself, independently, unaided, unassisted, by one's own efforts, standing on one's own two feet, off one's own bat.

own v **1** *they own three cars* possess, have in one's possession, have, keep, retain, maintain, hold, enjoy. **2** *I own that he is right* admit, allow, concede, grant, accept, acknowledge, recognize, agree. **own up** *won't own up | own up to the crime* confess to, confess everything, admit to, acknowledge that, tell the truth about, make a clean breast of it; *inf* come clean.

owner n **1** *the owner of the car* possessor, holder, keeper. **2** *the owner of the hotel* proprietor/proprietress/proprietrix, landlord, landlady. **3** *the dog's owner* master/mistress, keeper.

ownership n possession, right of possession, proprietorship, proprietary rights, title.

ox n bull, bullock, steer.

Pp

pace n **1** *take one pace towards her* step, stride. **2** *walk with an ambling pace* gait, walk, tread. **3** *runners unable to keep up with the pace of the race* speed, swiftness, fastness, quickness, rapidity, velocity, tempo; *inf* clip, lick. **4** *the fast/slow pace of life there* rate of progress, tempo, momentum, measure.

pacific adj **1** *make pacific overtures* peace-making, placatory, placating, conciliatory, propitiatory, appeasing, mollifying, calming, mediatory, mediating, diplomatic, irenic. **2** *a pacific nation* peace-loving, peaceable, pacifist, non-violent, non-aggressive, non-belligerent, non-combative, mild, gentle, dovelike, dovish. **3** *pacific waters* calm, still, motionless, smooth, tranquil, peaceful, at peace, placid, unruffled, undisturbed.

pacifist n conscientious objector, passive resister, peace-lover, peacemaker, peacemonger, dove, satyagrahi; *inf* conchie.

pacify v *pacify the angry woman* calm, calm down, placate, conciliate, propitiate, appease, mollify, sooth, tranquillize, quieten.

pack n **1** *carry his goods in a pack* bundle, parcel, bale, truss; *lit* fardel. **2** *carry a pack on his back* bag, backpack, rucksack, knapsack, kitbag. **3** *buy a pack of cigarettes* packet, container, package, carton. **4** *a pack of animals* herd, drove, flock, troop. **5** *a pack of thieves* gang, crowd, mob, group, band, company, troop, set, clique; *inf* crew, bunch. **6** *a pack of lies* great deal, collection, parcel, assortment, mass, assemblage, bunch; *inf* load, heap.

pack v **1** *pack a suitcase* fill, load, bundle, stuff, cram. **2** *pack clothes in a suitcase* put, place, store, stow. **3** *pack the glass in straw* package, parcel, wrap, wrap up, box, bale, cover, protect. **4** *young people packing the stadium* fill, crowd, throng, mob, cram, jam, press into, squeeze into. **5** *snow packed by the wind against the wall* compact, compress, press, tamp, ram. **pack in 1** *also* **pack into** *everyone was packing into the small car* crowd, cram, jam, squeeze, press. **2** *a show that has been packing them in for years* draw in, pull in, attract, fill the theatre etc with. **3** *pack in one's job* resign, leave, give up, abandon; *inf* chuck, jack in. **pack off** *pack the children*

off *to bed* send off, dispatch, dismiss, put away, bundle off; *inf* send packing. **pack up 1** *pack up one's equipment for the night* put away, tidy up/away, clear up, store. **2** *decided to pack up for the day* finish, leave off, halt, stop, cease; *inf* call it a day, pack/jack it in. **3** *his car packed up on the motorway* break down, stop working, cease to function, fail, give out, stall, come to a halt; *inf* conk out, go kaput.

package n **1** *a Christmas package | sweets in a brightly-coloured package* parcel, packet, container, box, carton. **2** *you cannot select individual sections of the deal you must go for the whole package* package deal, whole, unit, lot, entity, combination.

package v *package the gift and send it* pack, pack up, parcel, parcel up, wrap, wrap up, gift-wrap, box.

packaging n *low-cost goods in expensive packaging* wrapping, wrappers, packing, covering, container, packet, presentation.

packed adj *theatre groups playing to packed halls* full, filled, filled to capacity, crowded, thronged, mobbed, crammed, jammed, packed like sardines, overfull, overloaded, brimful, chock-full, chock-a-block, full to the gunwales; *inf* jam-packed.

packet n **1** *buy a packet of cigarettes/sweets* pack, carton, box, container, package, bag. **2** *received a packet by post* parcel, package, container, padded bag.

pact n *sign a pact with the opposing side* agreement, treaty, deal, contract, bargain, settlement, compact, covenant, bond, concordat, entente, protocol.

pad n **1** *a pad to prevent friction* padding, wadding, wad, stuffing, buffer. **2** *a pad to rest one's head on* cushion, pillow, bolster. **3** *a pad to absorb the blood* gauze pad, piece/wad of cotton wool, dressing, compress. **4** *write one's notes in a pad* note-pad, writing-pad, notebook, jotter; *inf* memo-pad. **5** *the animal's injured pad* paw, foot, sole.

pad v *pad the package with tissue paper/cotton wool* pack, stuff, line, cushion, protect. **pad out** *pad out a few facts with a lot of detail* fill out, expand, augment, amplify, increase, add to, stretch out, eke out, flesh out, lengthen, spin out, protract, elaborate.

padding n **1** *use padding to prevent the china being damaged* packing, stuffing, filling, filler, wadding, cushioning, lining, wrapping. **2** *an essay with few facts and too much padding* filling-out, wordiness, verbiage, verbosity, verboseness, prolixity, prolixness; *inf* waffle, hot air.

paddle[1] n *use the paddles to row ashore* oar, scull, sweep.

paddle[1] v *paddle one's way to the shore* row, pull, oar, scull, pole, punt.

paddle[2] v **1** *paddle one's hands/feet in cold water* dabble, splash, plunge, plash. **2** *children paddling at the seaside* wade, splash about.

paddock n *horses grazing in the paddock* field, meadow, enclosure, yard, pen, pound, corral.

padlock n *renew the padlock on the gate* lock, catch, latch, fastening, fastener.

padre n *soldiers asking the padre for advice* minister, priest, parson, vicar, pastor, rector, reverend, chaplain, clergyman, cleric, man of God, man of the cloth.

paean n **1** *paeans to God* song of praise, praise, hymn, psalm, anthem, exaltation, glorification, magnification. **2** *the retiring chairman had received paeans from the board-members | films receiving paeans of praise* praise, eulogy, encomium, panegyric, compliment, bouquet.

pagan n *missionaries trying to convert pagans* unbeliever, non-believer, disbeliever, heathen, infidel, idolater, pantheist, atheist, polytheist.

pagan adj *missionaries trying to cope with pagan beliefs* paganistic, paganish, heathen, heathenish, heathenistic, infidel, idolatrous, pantheistic, atheistic, polytheistic.

page[1] n **1** *a report 20 pages long* sheet, side, leaf, folio, recto, verso. **2** *his bravery will be recorded in the pages of history* report, account, anecdote, book, volume, writing. **3** *one of the glorious pages of British history | a glorious page in this distinguished writer's life* chapter, event, episode, incident, time, period, stage, phase, epoch, era, point.

page[1] v *page the report/book* number, give a number to, paginate, foliate.

page[2] n **1** *employed by the hotel as a page* page-boy, messenger-boy; *Amer* bellboy, bellhop; *inf* buttons. **2** *the king's pages* page-boy, servant boy, serving boy, attendant, train-bearer, squire.

page[2] v *page a hotel guest* call, ask for, summon, send for.

pageant n *a pageant was part of the centenary festival* display, spectacle, extravaganza, show, parade, scene, representation, tableau, tableau vivant.

pageantry n *all the pageantry of a coronation* pageant, display, spectacle, magnificence, pomp, splendour, grandeur, glamour, flourish, glitter, theatricality, show, showiness; *inf* pizazz.

pain n **1** *a pain in her leg* soreness, hurt, ache, aching, throb, throbbing, smarting, twinge, pang, spasm, cramp, discomfort, irritation, tenderness. **2** *invalids enduring pain all their lives* suffering, physical suffering, agony, affliction, torture, torment. **3** *the pain of losing a loved one* suffering, mental suffering, emotional suffering, hurt, sorrow, grief, heartache, brokenheartedness, sadness, unhappiness, distress, misery, wretchedness, anguish, affliction, woe, agony, torment, torture. **4** *that child is a pain* nuisance, pest, bother, vexation, source of irritation, worry, source of aggravation; *inf* pain in the neck, drag. see PAINS.

pain v **1** *her foot is still paining* cause pain, be painful, hurt, be sore, ache, throb, smart, twinge, cause discomfort, be tender. **2** *the memory of the event still pains her* hurt, grieve, sadden, distress, make miserable/wretched, cause anguish to, afflict, torment, torture. **3** *it pained her to tell him to go* worry, distress, trouble, hurt, vex, embarrass.

pained adj *wear a pained expression* hurt, aggrieved, reproachful, offended, insulted, vexed, piqued, upset, unhappy, distressed, wounded; *inf* miffed.

painful adj **1** *a painful arm* sore, hurting, aching, throbbing, smarting, cramped, tender, inflamed, irritating, agonizing, excruciating. **2** *endure a painful experience* disagreeable, unpleasant, nasty, distressing, disquieting, disturbing, miserable, wretched, agonizing, harrowing. **3** *a painful climb* arduous, laborious, strenuous, rigorous, demanding, exacting, trying, hard, tough, difficult. **4** *it was painful to watch him work so slowly* irksome, tedious, annoying, vexatious.

painfully adv **1** *a leg that is painfully swollen* achingly, agonizingly, excruciatingly. **2** *become painfully thin* distressingly, alarmingly, worryingly, excessively; *inf* terribly, dreadfully. **3** *it was painfully obvious that he was incompetent* embarrassingly, uncomfortably, disconcertingly, markedly, woefully.

painkiller n *take painkillers for headaches* analgesic, anodyne, palliative, lenitive.

painless adj **1** *a painless medical procedure* pain-free, without pain. **2** *getting rid of him proved painless* easy, simple, trouble-free, effortless, plain sailing; *inf* as easy as pie, as easy as falling off a log, as easy as ABC, a piece of cake, child's play, a cinch.

pains npl *childbirth pains* contractions, labour, birth-pangs. **be at pains** *they were at pains to put him at ease* try hard, make every effort, take care, put oneself out.

painstaking adj **1** *a painstaking investigation* careful, thorough, assiduous, conscientious, meticulous, punctilious, sedulous, scrupulous, searching. **2** *a painstaking student* careful, thorough, assiduous, attentive, diligent, industrious, hard-working, conscientious, meticulous, punctilious, sedulous, scrupulous, persevering, pertinacious.

paint n **1** *buy paint for the walls* colouring, colourant, tint, dye, stain, pigment, emulsion, emulsion paint, gloss, gloss paint, distemper, wash, whitewash. **2** *the paint required for his picture* colourant, tint, pigment, water-colour, oil, oil-paint, oil-colour. **3** *apply paint to her face* make-up, cosmetic, greasepaint, *maquillage*; *inf* warpaint.

paint v **1** *paint the walls* apply paint to, decorate, colour, tint, dye, stain, distemper, whitewash. **2** *paint slogans on the walls* daub, smear, plaster, spray-paint. **3** *paint his mother | painted the scene from her window* portray, depict, delineate, draw, sketch, represent, catch a likeness of. **4** *paint a story of great happiness/misery* tell, recount, narrate, unfold, describe, depict, portray, evoke, conjure up. **paint the town red** *paint the town red at the end of the exams* celebrate; *inf* go out on the town, whoop it up, make whoopee, have a night on the tiles; *Amer* step out.

painting n picture, illustration, portrayal, depiction, delineation, representation, likeness, drawing, sketch, portrait, landscape, seascape, still life, oil-painting, water-colour; *inf* oil.

pair n **1** *the pair walked down the road* twosome, two, two people, couple, duo. **2** *a pair of pheasants* brace, two, couple. **3** *a pair of gloves* matched set, matching set. **4** *a coach and pair* team, yoke, span, two horses. **5** *the happy pair after their wedding* married couple, couple, man and wife, husband and wife, partners, lovers.

pair v **pair off** *pair off the children for games* arrange/group in pairs, pair up, put together. **pair up** *we paired up to go on holiday | if you pair up to do the work* get together, join up, link up, team up, unite, form a partnership.

pal n *they're best pals* friend, mate, companion, crony, comrade; *inf* chum, buddy.

palace n *the king's summer palace* royal residence, castle, château.

palatable adj **1** *chefs providing palatable dishes* tasty, appetizing, pleasant-tasting, flavourful, flavoursome, delicious, delectable, mouth-watering, savoury, luscious, toothsome; *inf* scrumptious, yummy, moreish. **2** *unlikely to find the truth palatable* agreeable, pleasant, pleasing, pleasurable, nice, attractive, acceptable, satisfactory.

palate n **1** *a sore palate* roof of the mouth, hard palate, soft palate. **2** *have no palate for food after witnessing the accident* appetite, stomach. **3** *have a good palate | dry wines that suit her palate* sense of taste, taste, taste buds. **4** *have no palate for that style of prose* taste, liking, appreciation, enjoyment, relish, enthusiasm.

palatial adj *palatial residences* luxurious, de luxe, imposing, splendid, grand, magnificent, stately, majestic, opulent, sumptuous, plush; *inf* plushy, posh.

palaver n **1** *always a lot of palaver when guests come to stay* fuss, fuss and bother, commotion, fluster, flurry, agitation, stir. **2** *a palaver in the boardroom* conference, discussion, meeting, talks, colloquy; *inf* confab, pow-wow, gassing.

pale adj **1** *a pale complexion | pale with fear* white, whitish, white-faced, colourless, anaemic, wan, drained, pallid, pasty, peaky, ashen, ashy, waxen, green, as white as a sheet/ghost, deathly pale. **2** *pale colours/shades* light, light-coloured, pastel, muted, low-key, restrained, faded, bleached, whitish, washed-out, etiolated. **3** *the pale light of dawn* dim, faint, weak, feeble, thin.

pale v **1** *she paled at the gruesome sight* grow pale, become pale, go/turn white, blanch, lose colour. **2** *other problems paled beside their financial difficulties* pale into insignificance, fade, dim, diminish, lessen, decrease in importance, lose significance.

pale n **beyond the pale** *his behaviour at the party was considered beyond the pale* unacceptable, unseemly, improper, indiscreet, unsuitable, irregular, unreasonable, out-of-line.

pall v *the pleasures of sunbathing began to pall* lost its/their etc interest, lose attraction, cloy, become tedious, become boring, grow tedious, grow tiresome.

pall n **1** *the pall over the coffin* funeral cloth, coffin covering. **2** *a pall of smoke/darkness* dark covering, shroud, mantle, cloak. **3** *the news cast a pall over the gathering* cloud, shadow, gloom, depression, melancholy, sombreness, gravity.

palliate v **1** *palliate the pain* relieve, ease, soothe, alleviate, mitigate, assuage, abate, allay, dull, take the edge off, blunt. **2** *palliate an offence* extenuate, minimize, make light of, tone down, play down, downplay, make allowances for, excuse, whitewash.

pallid adj **1** *pallid faces* | *invalids looking pallid* pale, white, whitish, white-faced, colourless, anaemic, wan, drained, pasty, peaky, ashen, ashy, waxen, sickly, ghostly, ghastly, lurid, green, as white as a sheet/ ghost, deathly pale, like death; *inf* like death warmed up. **2** *a pallid performance* colourless, uninteresting, dull, boring, tedious, unimaginative, lifeless, uninspired, spiritless, bloodless, bland, vapid.

pallor n *the pallor of the invalid* paleness, whiteness, colourlessness, wanness, pallidness, pastiness, peakiness, ashenness, sickliness, ghastliness, luridness.

palm¹ v **palm off** *palm off a broken-down car on him* foist, fob, pass off, offload, thrust, get rid of; *inf* unload. **grease someone's palm** bribe, buy off, give money to, corrupt, suborn; *inf* give a backhander to, give a sweetener to, square. **have in the palm of one's hand** have control over, have power over, have at one's mercy, have in one's clutches.

palm² n *win the palm* victory, triumph, success, honour, glory, fame, prize, trophy, award, crown, wealth, laurels, bays.

palmist n *get my future told by a palmist* palm-reader, fortune-teller, clairvoyant.

palmy adj *in the palmy days of the firm* prosperous, thriving, flourishing, golden, glorious, happy, halcyon.

palpable adj **1** *a palpable swelling* tangible, feelable, touchable, solid, concrete. **2** *a palpable error* obvious, apparent, clear, plain, evident, manifest, visible, conspicuous, patent, blatant, glaring, definite, unmistakable.

palpitate v **1** *with her heart palpitating* beat rapidly, pulsate, pulse, throb, flutter, quiver, vibrate, pound, thud, thump, pump. **2** *she was palpitating with fear* tremble, quiver, quake, quaver, shake.

paltry adj **1** *a paltry sum of money* small, meagre, trifling, minor, insignificant, trivial, derisory; *inf* piddling. **2** *a paltry excuse/ trick* mean, low, base, worthless, despic-

able, contemptible, miserable, wretched, sorry, puny.

pamper v *pamper oneself* | *does pamper her husband* spoil, cosset, indulge, overindulge, humour, coddle, mollycoddle, baby, wait on someone hand and foot, cater to someone's every whim, feather-bed.

pamphlet n *a pamphlet giving advice on Aids* leaflet, booklet, brochure, circular.

pan¹ n **1** *pans simmering on the stove* saucepan, pot, frying-pan, preserving pan, fish-kettle, pressure-cooker, casserole, wok; *Amer* skillet. **2** *bedpan/dustpan* container, vessel, receptacle. **3** *salt-pans* depression, dip, indentation, hollow, crater, cavity.

pan¹ v **1** *pan for gold* search for, look for, sift for. **2** *critics panning the play* criticize, censure, find fault with, flay, roast, take to pieces; *inf* slate, slam, knock, rubbish. **pan out** *see how things pan out* work out, turn out, come out, fall out.

pan² v *cameras panning the strikers' march* scan, sweep, follow, track, traverse.

panacea n *a panacea for the economic ills* cure-all, cure for all ills, universal cure, universal remedy, elixir, nostrum.

panache n *open the village fête with panache* | *dress with panache* dash, flourish, flamboyance, *élan*, style, verve, zest, brio, éclat; *inf* pizazz.

pancake n crêpe, drop scone, blini, tortilla.

pandemic adj *diseases pandemic in the African continent* widespread, universal, global, extensive, prevalent, wholesale, rife, rampant.

pandemonium n *pandemonium reigned when the pop concert was cancelled* uproar, tumult, turmoil, commotion, clamour, din, hullaballoo, hubbub, hue and cry, chaos, confusion, disorder, bedlam.

pander v *pander to her every whim* | *pander to the taste of the majority* give in to, gratify, indulge, humour, please, satisfy, cater for.

panegyric n **1** *a panegyric on the hero's achievements* eulogy, paean, encomium, extolment, laudation, accolade, testimonial, tribute, exaltation, glorification. **2** *a talk full of panegyric* eulogy, praise, adulation, acclamation, extolment, laudation, exaltation, glorification.

pang n **1** *hunger pang* pain, sharp pain, shooting pain, twinge, spasm, ache. **2** *feel a pang of remorse* twinge, qualm, misgiving, scruple, regret, feeling of uneasiness.

panic n *feel panic at the sight of the smoke* alarm, fright, fear, terror, horror, trepidation, nervousness, agitation, hysteria, perturbation, dismay, disquiet.

panic v **1** *panic at the sight of the smoke* be alarmed, take fright, be filled with fear, be scared, be terrified/horrified, be nervous, be agitated, be hysterical, lose one's nerve, overreact, be perturbed, be filled with dismay, go to pieces; *inf* lose one's cool, get the jitters, get into a tizzy/tiz-woz, get the wind up, run around like a headless chicken. **2** *be panicked into jumping from the window* alarm, frighten, scare, terrify, petrify, startle, agitate, unnerve; *inf* put the wind up someone.

panic-stricken adj panicky, alarmed, frightened, scared, terrified, terror-stricken, petrified, horror-stricken, horrified, aghast, nervous, agitated, hysterical, perturbed, dismayed, disquietened; *inf* in a tizzy, in a tiz-woz.

panoply n *the full panoply of a royal wedding* array, trappings, display, show, splendour.

panorama n **1** *the panorama from the top of the tower* wide view, aerial view, bird's-eye view, view, vista, spectacle. **2** *present a panorama of the political events of the decade* survey, overview, perspective, appraisal.

panoramic adj **1** *a panoramic view from the tower* wide, extensive, sweeping, bird's-eye. **2** *a panoramic presentation of the events of the decade* wide, wide-ranging, extensive, comprehensive.

pant v **1** *panting after climbing the hill* breathe heavily, puff, huff and puff, blow, gasp, wheeze. **2** *panting for a drink | she was panting for some new clothes* long for, yearn for, crave, pine for, ache for, hunger for, thirst for, lust after, burn for, sigh for; *inf* have a yen for. **3** *with his heart panting* throb, palpitate, pulsate, pulse, pound, thump, beat rapidly.

pant n *disturbed by the pants from the dog* puff, gasp, wheeze.

pantry n *pies stolen from the pantry* larder, cold-room, still-room, buttery, storeroom.

pants npl **1** *he wears brightly-patterned pants* underpants, briefs, boxer shorts, Y-fronts. **2** *she wears frilly pants* knickers, briefs, panties; *Amer* underpants. **3** *wear old pants for gardening* trousers, slacks, jeans; *inf* strides.

pap n **1** *prepare pap for the baby/invalid* baby food, soft food, mush, pulp; *inf* goo. **2** *prefer pap to serious novels* trivia, drivel, rubbish, trash, pulp.

paper n **1** *go for the morning paper* newspaper, magazine, journal, gazette, broadsheet, tabloid, scandal sheet, daily, weekly;

inf rag. **2** *lose the papers relating to the house ownership* legal paper, document, certificate, record, deeds, instrument, assignment. **3** *write a paper on child development* essay, article, work, dissertation, treatise, thesis, monograph, study, report, analysis. **4** *put striped paper on the bedroom walls* wallpaper, wall-covering, anaglypta, lining paper. **on paper 1** *put your objections on paper* in writing, written down, in black and white. **2** *on paper the scheme looked fine but in practice it was a disaster* in theory, theoretically, hypothetically, in the abstract.

paper v *paper the walls* wallpaper, line, hang wallpaper on, decorate. **paper over** *paper over the firm's difficulties* hide, conceal, draw a veil over, disguise, camouflage, cover up, gloss over, whitewash.

papers npl **1** *sign the adoption papers* legal paper, document, certificate. *see* PAPER n 2. **2** *escape using forged papers* identification papers, identification documents, identity card, ID. **3** *go through her papers after her death* personal papers, personal documents, letters, records, files.

papery adj *papery clothes/walls* paper-thin, ultra-thin, flimsy, insubstantial, fragile, frail.

par n *up to par* average, mean, standard, normal, norm. **below par 1** *work that is below par* below average, substandard, inferior, lacking, wanting, second-rate, poor; *inf* not up to scratch, not up to snuff. **2** *feeling below par since having flu* slightly unwell/unhealthy, unfit, off colour, poorly, indisposed, out of sorts; *inf* not oneself, under the weather. **on a par with** *modern novels which are on a par with those of the great classical writers* equal to, a match for, on a level with, on an equal footing with, of the same standard as, as good as. **par for the course** *his behaviour does not surprise me - it's par for the course* usual, normal, standard, typical, predictable, what one would expect. **up to par** *work no longer up to par* up to the mark, satisfactory, acceptable, good enough, adequate, passable; *inf* up to scratch, up to snuff.

parable n *the parable of/about the prodigal son* allegory, moral story, moral tale, story with a moral, fable.

parade n **1** *watch the parade of the soldiers | parade of children in fancy dress* march, procession, progression, cavalcade, spectacle, pageant, array. **2** *make a parade of their wealth* display, exhibition, show, spectacle, flaunting, ostentation, demonstration; *inf* showing-off.

parade v **1** *soldiers/children parading during the centenary celebrations* march, process, go in columns, file by. **2** *parade their wealth/knowledge* display, exhibit, show, demonstrate, air, make a show of, flaunt; *inf* show off. **3** *parade up and down in her new hat* strut, swagger; *inf* swank.

paradigm n *a paradigm for others to copy* example, pattern, model, standard, gauge, criterion, archetype, prototype, paragon, exemplar.

paradise n **1** *believe in paradise after death* heaven, heavenly kingdom, kingdom of heaven, abode of the saints, Elysium, the Elysian Fields. **2** *Adam and Eve in paradise* the Garden of Eden, Eden. **3** *think the holiday island a paradise* Eden, fairyland, utopia, Shangri-La. **4** *thinking it was paradise in her arms* heaven, bliss, ecstasy, supreme joy, seventh heaven.

paradox n *a paradox that there is so much poverty in such a rich country* contradiction, self-contradiction, inconsistency, incongruity, anomaly, enigma, puzzle, absurdity, oxymoron.

paradoxical adj *it is paradoxical that there is so much poverty in such a rich country* contradictory, self-contradictory, inconsistent, incongruous, anomalous, enigmatic, puzzling, absurd.

paragon n *a paragon of good behaviour* perfect example, good example, ideal, model, pattern, exemplar, nonpareil, paradigm, standard, criterion, archetype, prototype, quintessence, epitome, apotheosis, acme, jewel, flower.

paragraph n **1** *the essay should be divided into paragraphs* section, subdivision, segment. **2** *a paragraph in the local paper about the death* article, item, piece, notice, note.

parallel adj **1** *parallel lines* side by side, equidistant, collateral. **2** *the judge considering a parallel case | cases parallel to each other* similar, like, resembling, analogous, comparable, equivalent, corresponding, matching, duplicate. **3** *parallel processes* concurrent, coexistent, coexisting.

parallel n **1** *find a parallel for the case* analogue, counterpart, equivalent, correspondent, match, duplicate, equal. **2** *draw a parallel between the two cases* similarity, likeness, resemblance, analogy, correspondence, comparison, equivalence, symmetry.

parallel v **1** *the case parallels the murder of her neighbour* be similar to, be like, resemble, bear a resemblance to, be analogous to, be an analogy with, correspond to, compare with, be comparable/equivalent to. **2** *his*

account of the incident parallels the policeman's match, correspond to, agree with, be in harmony with, conform to. **3** *his rowing feat has never been paralleled* match, equal, rival, emulate.

paralyse v **1** *paralysed legs* immobilize, render/make powerless, numb, deaden, dull, obtund, incapacitate, debilitate, disable, cripple. **2** *he was paralysed in the accident* immobilize, incapacitate, debilitate, disable, cripple. **3** *paralyse the transport system* immobilize, bring to a halt, bring to a complete stop, bring to a grinding halt, bring to a standstill, freeze, put out of order/commission. **4** *paralysed with fear at the sight* immobilize, render motionless, freeze, unnerve, terrify, shock, stun, stagger.

paralysis n **1** *suffer from paralysis of the legs* immobility, powerlessness, lack of feeling, numbness, palsy, incapacity, debilitation; *Med* paresis. **2** *lead to paralysis of the rail network* immobilization, breakdown, shutdown, stopping, stoppage, halt, standstill.

paralytic adj **1** *paralytic limbs* immobile, immobilized, powerless, numb, dead, palsied, incapacitated, debilitated, disabled, crippled. **2** *completely paralytic after the party* drunk, inebriated, intoxicated; *inf* legless, sloshed, smashed, stoned, plastered, pie-eyed, steaming, stewed.

parameter n *within the parameters of the budget* limit, limitation, limiting factor, restriction, constant, specification, guidelines, framework.

paramount adj *financial considerations are paramount* most important, of greatest importance, of prime importance, of supreme importance, of greatest significance, uppermost, supreme, predominant, foremost, first and foremost, pre-eminent, outstanding.

paramour n **1** *his wife found out about his paramour* mistress, lover, girlfriend, kept woman, inamorata; *inf* fancy woman, bit on the side. **2** *preferring her paramour to her husband* lover, boyfriend, inamorato; *inf* fancy man, toy boy, bit on the side.

paranoid adj *paranoid about what everyone was saying about her* suspicious, mistrustful, distrustful, fearful, insecure.

parapet n **1** *the parapet of a balcony* wall, railing, handrail, fence, barrier. **2** *soldiers sheltering behind the parapet* fortification, barricade, rampart, bulwark, bank, embankment.

paraphernalia npl **1** *all the artist's paraphernalia* equipment, gear, stuff, apparatus, implements, tools, materials, accoutrements, trappings, appurtenances, appointments. **2** *loaded with her suitcase and all her paraphernalia* baggage, bags and baggage, luggage, personal belongings, belongings, possessions, things, impedimenta; *inf* clobber.

paraphrase v *paraphrase the complicated instructions* reword, put in other words, rephrase, restate, rehash, interpret, gloss.

paraphrase n *a simple paraphrase of the instructions* rewording, rephrasing, restatement, restating, rehash, interpretation, gloss.

parasite n *a parasite on society | a parasite totally dependent on others* hanger-on, sponger, cadger, leech, bloodsucker, passenger, drone; *inf* scrounger, freeloader.

parcel n **1** *tie the parcel with string* package, packet, pack, bundle. **2** *a parcel of land* plot, tract, piece, lot, patch. **3** *a parcel of thieves* band, pack, gang, group, company, collection, crowd, mob, troop; *inf* crew, bunch. **4** *a parcel of lies* pack, great deal, collection, assortment, mass, assemblage, bunch; *inf* heap, load.

parcel v *parcel up the goods* pack, pack up, package, wrap, wrap up, gift-wrap, tie up, do up, box, bundle up. **parcel out** *parcel out the food to the needy* distribute, divide out, share out, hand out, deal out, dole out, dispense, allocate, allot, portion out, apportion, mete out, carve up; *inf* divvy up.

parched adj **1** *parched ground/grass* dried up, dried out, dry, baked, burned, scorched, seared, desiccated, dehydrated, withered, shrivelled. **2** *parched from walking in the heat* thirsty, dehydrated; *inf* dry.

pardon n **1** *seek their pardon* forgiveness, forbearance, indulgence, condonation, clemency, lenience, leniency, mercy. **2** *the accused received a pardon* free pardon, reprieve, release, acquittal, absolution, amnesty, exoneration, exculpation.

pardon v **1** *begged her to pardon him | pardon me | could never pardon such an offence* forgive, excuse, condone, let off. **2** *the accused man was pardoned* reprieve, release, acquit, absolve, exonerate, exculpate.

pardonable adj *a pardonable error* forgivable, excusable, allowable, condonable, understandable, minor, slight, venial.

parent n **1** *resemble one of his parents* mother/father; *inf* old man/old woman, old lady. **2** *the parent of all his misfortune* source, root, origin, originator, well-spring, fountain, cause, author, architect.

parent v *parent three sons* be the parent of, bring into the world, produce, procreate, look after, rear, bring up, raise.

parentage n *a successful man of humble parentage* family, birth, origins, extraction, ancestry, lineage, descent, heritage, pedigree.

pariah n *a social pariah* outcast, leper, *persona non grata*, untouchable, undesirable.

parish n **1** *local administrators of the parish* community, district, commune, canton. **2** *the parish choosing a new minister* parishioners, churchgoers, congregation, flock, fold.

parity n *workers having parity of status/salary* equality, levelness, identity, sameness, unity, uniformity, evenness, equivalence, parallelism, correspondence.

park n **1** *children playing in the park* public park, public garden, recreation ground, playground, play area. **2** *park surrounding the mansion-house* parkland, grassland, lawns, grounds. **3** *few players left on the park* field, playing-field, stadium, arena.

park v **1** *park the car on a yellow line* stop, pull up, leave, station. **2** *park the baby in his pram* put, place, set, seat, leave, plonk.

parlance n *fail to understand the parlance of the young* speech, language, talk, vocabulary, phraseology, idiom, vernacular, jargon, patter, argot, patois; *inf* lingo.

parliament n *the parliaments of different countries* legislative assembly, lawmaking body, congress, senate, chamber, house, convocation, diet.

Parliament n *the Queen recalling Parliament* the Houses of Parliament, the House of Commons/Lords, the Commons, the Lords, the House, the Lower/Upper House, Westminster.

parliamentary adj **1** *parliamentary assemblies* legislative, legislatorial, lawmaking, lawgiving, governmental, congressional, senatorial, democratic, representative. **2** *parliamentary behaviour/language* orderly, proper, seemly, by the rules, according to the rule book.

parlour n **1** *have tea in the parlour* sitting-room, front-room, best room, drawing-room, lounge. **2** *a beauty parlour* salon, shop, establishment, store.

parochial adj *a parochial attitude to life* provincial, small-town, parish-pump, insular, inward-looking, narrow, narrow-minded, petty, small-minded, limited, restricted.

parody n **1** *a parody of a gothic novel* burlesque, lampoon, satire, pastiche, caricature, mimicry, take-off; *inf* spoof, send-up. **2** *trial was a parody of justice* travesty, poor imitation, misrepresentation, perversion, corruption.

parody v *parody an operatic aria* burlesque, lampoon, satirize, caricature, mimic, take off; *inf* send up.

paroxysm n *a paroxysm of coughing/rage* fit, attack, convulsion, spasm, seizure, outburst, outbreak, eruption.

parrot v *children parroting the teacher's words* repeat, echo, copy, imitate, mimic, ape, take off.

parry v **1** *parry a blow* ward off, fend off, stave off, turn aside, avert, deflect, block, rebuff, repel, repulse, hold at bay. **2** *parry awkward questions* avoid, dodge, evade, elude, steer clear of, sidestep, circumvent, fight shy of; *inf* duck.

parsimonious adj mean, miserly, niggardly, tight-fisted, close-fisted, close, near, grasping, money-grubbing, Scrooge-like, scrimping, skimping, penny-pinching, cheese-paring, penurious, ungenerous; *inf* stingy, tight, mingy.

parsimony n meanness, miserliness, niggardliness, closeness, tight-fistedness, close-fistedness; *inf* stinginess, tightness. *see* PARSIMONIOUS.

parson n priest, vicar, rector, minister, reverend, pastor, clergyman, cleric, chaplain, ecclesiastic, churchman, man of the cloth, man of God, preacher, divine.

part n **1** *the early part of her life | part of an orange* portion, division, section, segment, bit, piece, fragment, scrap, slice, fraction, chunk, wedge. **2** *spare parts* component, bit, constituent, element, module. **3** *body parts | parts of the body* organ, member, limb. **4** *an unknown part of the country* section, area, region, sector, quarter, territory, neighbourhood. **5** *a book/play in several parts* volume, book, section, episode. **6** *his part in the project* function, role, job, task, work, chore, responsibility, capacity, participation, duty, charge. **7** *play the part of Hamlet* role, character. **8** *learn his part* lines, words. **9** *a man of many parts* talent, gift, ability, capability, capacity, skill, attribute. **for the most part** *for the most part they are reliable* on the whole, in the main, by and large, all in all, generally, to all intents and purposes, mostly. **in good part** *take the teasing in good part* good-naturedly, good-humouredly, without offence, cheerfully, well. **in part** *success due in part to good luck* partly, partially, to a certain extent/degree,

to some extent/degree, somewhat, in some measure. **on the part of** *an error on the part of the headmaster | on his part* made by, done by, carried out by, caused by, by. **take part in** *take part in the protest* participate in, join in, engage in, play a part in, contribute to, be associated with, associate oneself with, be involved in, share in, have a hand in, have something to do with, partake in.

take someone's part, take the part of *take his mother's part in the quarrel | take the part of weaker candidates* take the side of, side with, support, back, back up, abet, aid and abet.

part v **1** *the crowd parted to let the police through* divide, divide in two, separate, split, split in two, break up, sever, disjoin. **2** *the police parting the crowd* divide, separate, split up, break up, sever, cleave. **3** *couples deciding to part* separate, seek/get a separation, split up, break up, part company, go their etc separate ways, divorce, get divorced, seek/get a divorce. **4** *exchange kisses before parting* take one's departure, take one's leave, leave, go, go away, say goodbye/farewell/adieu, say one's goodbyes, separate; *inf* split, push off, hit the road. **part with** *part with her last few pounds* give up, relinquish, forgo, surrender, let go of, renounce, sacrifice, yield, cede.

part adj **1** *in part payment* partial, half. **2** *a part-conversion of the building* partial, half, semi-, demi-.

partake v **1** *partake in the protest* take part in, participate in, join in, engage in, play a part in, contribute to, be associated with, associate oneself with, be involved in, share in, have a hand in, have something to do with. **2** *partake of Christmas cheer* consume, eat, take, receive, drink, share in. **3** *their manner partook of insolence* suggest, have the qualities/attributes of, hint at, evidence, demonstrate, exhibit, show.

partial adj **1** *a partial solution/eclipse* part, in part, limited, incomplete, imperfect, fragmentary. **2** *a partial judgement/judge* biased, prejudiced, partisan, coloured, one-sided, discriminatory, preferential, interested, unjust, unfair, inequitable. **be partial to** *partial to dark chocolate | always been partial to holidays in the sun* have a liking for, like, love, have a fondness for, be fond of, be keen on, have a weakness/taste for, have a soft spot for, be taken with, care for, have a predilection/proclivity/penchant for.

partiality n **1** *condemn the partiality of the judge* bias, prejudice, partisanship, discrimination, preference, favouritism, unjustness, unfairness, inequity. **2** *their partiality* *for chocolate | has always had a partiality for holidays in the sun* liking, love, fondness, keenness, taste, weakness, soft spot, inclination, predilection, proclivity, penchant.

partially adv *partially paralysed* partly, in part, not wholly, not fully, half, somewhat, to a certain extent/degree, to some extent/degree, in some measure, fractionally, slightly.

participant n *participants in the protest/concert* participator, member, contributor, associate, sharer, partaker.

participate v *participate in the protest* take part in, join in, engage in, play a part in, contribute to, be associated with, associate oneself with, be involved in, share in, have a hand in, have something to do with, partake in.

participation n *their participation in the protest/concert* part, contribution, association, involvement, partaking. *see* PARTICIPATE.

particle n 1 *particles of dust* tiny bit, tiny piece, speck, spot, atom, molecule. 2 *not a particle of common sense* iota, jot, whit, grain, bit, scrap, shred, morsel, mite, atom, hint, touch, trace, suggestion, tittle.

particular adj 1 *in this particular case* specific, individual, single, distinct, precise. 2 *take particular care | a matter of particular importance* special, especial, singular, peculiar, exceptional, unusual, uncommon, notable, noteworthy, remarkable, outstanding. 3 *particular about hygiene | he is so particular about what he eats* fastidious, discriminating, selective, fussy, painstaking, meticulous, punctilious, nice, exacting, demanding, critical, over-particular, overfastidious, finicky; *inf* pernickety, choosy, picky. 4 *require a particular account of the incident* detailed, exact, precise, faithful, close, thorough, blow-by-blow, itemized, circumstantial, painstaking, meticulous, punctilious, minute.

particular n **in particular** 1 *have someone in particular in mind* specific, special, distinct, precise. 2 *the desserts in particular were delicious* particularly, specifically, especially, specially.

particularize v *particularize your reasons for leaving* specify, be specific about, detail, itemize, list, enumerate, spell out, cite.

particularly adv 1 *a film that is particularly good* especially, specially, singularly, peculiarly, distinctly, markedly, exceptionally, unusually, uncommonly, notably, remarkably, outstandingly, surprisingly. 2 *ask for him particularly* in particular, specifically, explicitly, expressly, specially, especially.

parting n 1 *the parting of the crowd* division, dividing, separation, separating, splitting, breaking up, severance, disjoining, detachment, partition. 2 *sad at the parting of his parents* separation, splitting up, breakup, breaking up, divorce, split, rift, rupture. 3 *partings taking place at the railway station* departure, leave-taking, goodbye, farewell, adieu, valediction.

parting adj *a parting handshake* departing, leaving, goodbye, farewell, valedictory, last, final.

partisan n 1 *a partisan of the breakaway party* supporter, adherent, devotee, backer, champion, upholder, follower, disciple, fan, votary. 2 *partisans fighting against the ruling power* guerrilla, resistance fighter, underground fighter.

partisan adj *a partisan attitude to the legal dispute* biased, prejudiced, coloured, one-sided, discriminatory, preferential, partial, interested, unjust, unfair, inequitable.

partition n 1 *the partition of India* division, dividing, subdivision, separation, segregation, splitting-up, breaking-up, break-up, severance. 2 *erect a partition to divide the room* room-divider, divider, dividing wall, separator, screen, barrier, wall, fence.

partition v 1 *partition India* divide up, separate, segregate, split up, break up, sever. 2 *partition the room to make two sleeping areas* divide, divide up, subdivide, separate, separate off, screen off, wall off, fence off.

partly adv *partly responsible for the mistake* in part, partially, not wholly, not fully, half, somewhat, to a certain extent/degree, to some extent/degree, in some measure, fractionally, slightly.

partner n 1 *his partner in business* associate, colleague, co-worker, team-mate, co-operator, collaborator, ally, comrade, companion, consociate. 2 *his partner in crime* accomplice, confederate, accessory, collaborator, fellow-conspirator; *inf* sidekick. 3 *invite workers and partners to the party* wife/husband, spouse, mate, girlfriend/boyfriend, consort, helpmate, helpmeet.

partnership n 1 *work in partnership with his brother* association, cooperation, collaboration, alliance, union, fellowship, companionship, consociation. 2 *a partnership in crime* collaboration, collusion, connivance, conspiracy. 3 *the partnership formed by the brothers was bought out* company, firm, corporation, cooperative, conglomerate, combine, syndicate.

parturition n childbirth, labour.

party n **1** *invite guests to a party* social gathering, social function, gathering, function, reception, celebration, festivity, at-home, soirée, orgy, bacchanal; *inf* get-together, do, bash, shindig, knees-up, rave-up. **2** *a shooting/search party* group, band, company, body, squad, team, crew, contingent, detachment, unit; *inf* bunch. **3** *belong to a left-wing party* political party, alliance, affiliation, association. **4** *both parties declared they were right* side, grouping, faction, camp, set, caucus. **5** *a certain party who shall be nameless* person, individual, human being, somebody, someone; *inf* character. **6** *the judge speaking to both parties* litigant, plaintiff, defendant.

parvenu n *villagers suspicious of parvenus* arrivé, arriviste, nouveau riche, intruder, upstart.

pass[1] v **1** *traffic passing along the road* go, move, proceed, progress, drive, run, travel, roll, flow, course. **2** *pass her hand over her forehead* move, cross. **3** *cars passing us | other runners passing them* go past, move past, go ahead of, get ahead of, go by, overtake, outstrip, outdistance. **4** *pass the frontier/barrier* go over, go across, get across, get through, cross, traverse. **5** *pass the butter* hand over, reach, let someone have, give, transfer. **6** *the title passes to his eldest son* be passed on, be transferred, be made over, be turned over, be signed over, go, devolve. **7** *time passed slowly* go by, proceed, progress, advance, roll by, slip by, glide by, flow by, elapse. **8** *how to pass the time* spend, occupy, fill, take up, use, employ, while away, beguile. **9** *pass all understanding* exceed, surpass, transcend. **10** *let the matter pass* go, go unheeded, go unnoticed, go unremarked, go undisputed, go uncensored. **11** *students passing their exams* gain a pass in, get through, be successful in, succeed in, meet the requirements of, pass muster in; *inf* come up to scratch in, come up to snuff in. **12** *the examiners passed everyone | all the material was passed* let through, declare acceptable/adequate/satisfactory, declare successful, accept, approve. **13** *pass the bill/motion* vote for, accept, approve, adopt, authorize, ratify, sanction, validate, legalize. **14** *pass judgement/sentence* pronounce, utter, express, deliver, declare. **15** *after all that has passed* happen, occur, take place, come about, befall, supervene. **16** *the storm/anger passed* blow over, run its course, ebb, die out, fade, fade away, evaporate, draw to a close, disappear, finish, end, terminate. **17** *pass urine | was passing blood in the faeces* discharge, excrete, eliminate, evacuate, expel, emit. **come to pass**

it came to pass that the old man died come about, happen, occur, befall, arise. **pass for** *she could pass for 30 | pass for a much younger woman* be taken for, be regarded as, be accepted as, be mistaken for. **pass off 1** *the demonstration passed off without incident* take place, happen, occur, be completed, be brought to a conclusion. **2** *the pain gradually passed off* pass, fade, fade away, disappear, vanish, die down, ebb, come to an end. **3** *pass him off as her husband* present as genuine, present with intent to deceive, give a false identity, have accepted as genuine. **pass out 1** *old ladies passing out in the heat* faint, collapse, lose consciousness, black out, keel over, swoon; *inf* flake out. **2** *pass out the exam papers* hand out, distribute, give out, deal out, dole out, allot, allocate. **pass over 1** *pass over the interruption and proceed* ignore, disregard, overlook, forget, pay no attention to, gloss over, take no notice of, close one's eyes to, turn a deaf ear to, turn a blind eye to. **2** *he was passed over for promotion* overlook, ignore, disregard, forget, neglect, not take into consideration, omit. **pass up** *pass up an opportunity for promotion* fail to take advantage of, waive, reject, refuse, decline, neglect, let slip, ignore, brush aside, forgo.

pass[1] n **1** *gain a pass in the French exam* success, victory. **2** *soldiers requiring a pass to go out for the evening* warrant, permit, authorization, licence, passport, visa, safe conduct, exeat. **3** *old-age pensioners receiving a bus pass | a press pass* warrant, permit, free ticket, free admission, complimentary ticket, reduced ticket; *inf* freebie. **4** *object to his passes* sexual advance, advance, sexual overture, sexual approach/suggestion; *inf* proposition. **come to a pretty pass** *things have come to a pretty pass when they had to sell the house* reach a critical state, reach a crucial juncture, come to a difficult state of affairs, be in a worrying predicament, be in a sad plight, be in troubled circumstances, be in dire straits; *inf* be in a pickle/hole. **make a pass at** *make a pass at his friend's wife* make sexual advances to, make sexual overtures to, make a sexual approach/suggestion to; *inf* make a play for, make a proposition to, proposition.

pass[2] n *a mountain pass* narrow road, gap, gorge, defile, col, canyon.

passable adj **1** *work that is passable | a passable knowledge of the subject* adequate, all right, tolerable, fair, acceptable, satisfactory, mediocre, middling, ordinary, average, run-of-the-mill, moderately good, not too bad, unexceptional, indifferent; *inf* so-so, OK, nothing to write home about.

2 *roads scarcely passable in the snow* crossable, traversable, navigable, unblocked, unobstructed, open, clear.

passage n **1** *the passage of time* passing, progress, advance, process, flow, course. **2** *our passage through life | their passage through foreign lands* journey, voyage, transit, trek, crossing, trip, tour. **3** *denied passage to the country* access, entry, admission, leave to travel in, permission to pass through, safe conduct, warrant, passport, visa. **4** *his passage from boyhood to manhood | the passage from liquid to solid* change, change-over, transformation, transition, conversion, shift, switch. **5** *a passage through the mountains | underground passages* road, route, path, way, track, trail, lane, channel, course, conduit. **6** *bicycles left in the passage* passageway, corridor, hall, hallway, entrance hall, entrance, vestibule, lobby. **7** *read aloud passages from the novel* extract, excerpt, quotation, citation, section, verse. **8** *the passage of the bill by Parliament* acceptance, approval, adoption, authorization, ratification, sanction, validation, enactment, legalization.

passé adj *ideas that are passé* out of date, outdated, dated, outmoded, outworn, old-fashioned, out of fashion, out of style, obsolete, obsolescent, archaic, antiquated, antediluvian; *inf* old-hat, fuddy-duddy.

passenger n **1** *bus/train passengers* rider, fare-payer, traveller, fare. **2** *just a passenger in the firm* drone, idler, parasite, hanger-on; *inf* freeloader.

passer-by n *passers-by helped the accident victim* bystanders, onlooker, witness, spectator; *inf* rubberneck.

passing n **1** *the passing of time* passage, progress, advance, process, flow, course. **2** *regret the passing of old customs | mourn his aunt's passing* disappearance, fading, demise, death, end, termination, expiry, loss. **3** *the passing of the bill by Parliament* acceptance, approval, adoption, enactment. *see* PASSAGE 8. **in passing** *mention in passing that he was leaving* en passant, incidentally, by the by, by the way, parenthetically, in the course of conversation.

passing adj **1** *a passing interest in local history* fleeting, transient, transitory, ephemeral, brief, short-lived, short, temporary, momentary. **2** *a passing glance told her everything* brief, quick, hasty, hurried, cursory, superficial, casual.

passion n **1** *do everything with great passion* intensity, fervour, fervidness, ardour, zeal, vehemence, fire, emotion, feeling, zest, enthusiasm, eagerness, excitement, animation. **2** *fly into a passion* rage, blind rage, fit of rage, fit of anger, fit of temper, temper, towering rage, outburst of anger, tantrum, fury, frenzy, paroxysm. **3** *his passion for her* love, sexual love, desire, sexual desire, lust, concupiscence, ardour, infatuation, adoration. **4** *his passion for motor bikes* enthusiasm, fascination, keen interest, obsession, fixation, craze, mania. **5** *one of the passions of his life* idol, hero/heroine, heart's desire, obsession, preoccupation, hobby-horse.

passionate adj **1** *a passionate entreaty/performance* impassioned, intense, fervent, fervid, ardent, zealous, vehement, fiery, emotional, heartfelt, zestful, enthusiastic, eager, excited, animated. **2** *a passionate lover* ardent, aroused, desirous, hot, sexy, amorous, sensual, erotic, lustful; *inf* turned-on. **3** *a very passionate person* intense, emotional, ardent, vehement, fiery. **4** *break the vase in a passionate fit* enraged, furious, angry, hot-tempered, frenzied, violent, wild, tempestuous.

passionless adj **1** *a passionless creature* cold, emotionless, frigid, passive, unfeeling, unresponsive, undemonstrative, unfeeling, withdrawn, unapproachable, aloof, detached, distant, dispassionate, remote. **2** *a passionless performance* emotionless, spiritless, lifeless, flat, zestless, insipid, lacklustre, colourless, anaemic, vapid.

passive adj **1** *play a passive role in the marriage/firm* inactive, non-active, inert, non-participating, uninvolved. **2** *a passive attitude to their invaders* unresisting, non-resistant, unassertive, yielding, submissive, compliant, pliant, acquiescent, quiescent, resigned, obedient, tractable, malleable. **3** *look on with a passive expression | rather a passive person* impassive, emotionless, unmoved, unresponsive, undemonstrative, dispassionate, detached, distant, remote, aloof, indifferent.

passport n **1** *show passports at the border* travel document, travel papers, papers, travel permit, visa, identity card, ID. **2** *his passport to happiness* means of access, avenue, access, entry, entrée, admission, admittance, open sesame.

password n *give the password to gain entry* watchword, key word, word of identification, signal, word, open sesame, shibboleth.

past adj **1** *in times past* gone by, gone, bygone, elapsed, over, over and done with, ended, former, long ago. **2** *the past few months* recent, preceding, last, latter, foregone. **3** *past achievements/chairmen* former, previous, prior, foregoing, late, erstwhile, one-time, sometime, ex-.

past n **in the past** *we used to go there in the past* in days gone by, in bygone days, in former times, formerly, previously, before.

past prep **1** *walk past the shop* in front of, by, beyond. **2** *past retirement age* beyond the limits of, beyond, in excess of.

past adv *drive/hurried past* by, on, further on.

paste n **1** *stick cuttings on the page/wall with paste* adhesive, glue, gum, cement. **2** *mix to a paste* mixture, blend, compound, pulp, mush, pap; *inf* goo. **3** *fish paste* spread, pâté, purée.

paste v *paste cuttings into a book* stick, fasten, glue, gum, cement.

pastel adj *pastel colours* pale, soft, delicate, muted, subdued, faint, low-key.

pastiche n *a work that is a pastiche of various styles* medley, mélange, miscellany, blend, mixture, pot-pourri, mosaic, patchwork, hotchpotch, hodgepodge, jumble, mishmash, gallimaufry, farrago.

pastille n *suck a pastille* lozenge, sweet, drop, gum, gumdrop, jujube, tablet, pill, troche.

pastime n *take up snooker as a pastime* hobby, leisure activity, sport, game, recreation, diversion, amusement, entertainment, distraction, relaxation.

past master n *a past master at disguise* expert, virtuoso, wizard, genius, artist, old hand; *inf* dab hand.

pastor n *listen to the pastor preaching* minister, vicar, parson, priest, rector, reverend, clergyman, churchman, ecclesiastic, cleric, divine.

pastoral adj **1** *a pastoral scene* rural, country, rustic, simple, idyllic, innocent, Arcadian, agricultural, bucolic, georgic. **2** *his pastoral duties* ministerial, vicarial, parsonical, priestly, rectorial, ecclesiastical, clerical.

pastry n *buy pastries for tea* tart, tartlet, pie, pasty, patty, vol-au-vent, quiche, Danish pastry; *inf* Danish.

pasture n *cows in the pasture* pasturage, pasture land, grassland, grass, field, grazing land, grazing, meadow.

pat v **1** *pat the child on the head | pat the dog* stroke, clap, caress, fondle, pet. **2** *pat the mixture* tap, slap, dab. **pat oneself on the back, pat someone on the back** *pat himself on the back for bringing off the deal* congratulate, praise, commend, compliment, applaud, throw bouquets at.

pat n **1** *a pat on the cheek* light blow, stroke, clap, caress. **2** *flatten the mixture with a pat* light blow, tap, slap, dab. **3** *a pat of butter* dab, lump, cake, portion. **give oneself a pat on the back, give someone a pat on the back** *see* PAT V.

patch n **1** *put a patch over the hole* piece of cloth, piece of material. **2** *a patch over the eye* cover, covering, pad, shield. **3** *a cabbage patch | patch of ground* plot, area, piece, ground, land, lot, tract, parcel. **4** *encounter a bad patch* period, time, spell, stretch, interval, term.

patch v **1** *patch the trousers* put a patch on, cover, mend, repair, sew, sew up, stitch, stitch up. **2** *patch the roof* repair/fix hastily, do a makeshift repair on, repair/fix clumsily, repair/fix temporarily. **patch up 1** *patch up the roof* repair/fix hastily. **2** *patch up the quarrel* make up, settle, resolve, set right.

patchwork n *work that was a patchwork of different styles* hotchpotch, hodgepodge, mishmash, jumble, medley, mélange, miscellany, pot-pourri, mosaic, blend, mixture. *see* PASTICHE.

patchy adj *a patchy knowledge of the subject* sketchy, bitty, uneven, varying, variable, erratic, random.

patent n *take out a patent for his invention* licence, copyright, registered trademark.

patent adj **1** *it was patent to everyone that she was lying | her patent dislike of him* obvious, clear, plain, evident, apparent, manifest, transparent, conspicuous, blatant, glaringly obvious, unmistakable, unconcealed. **2** *patent medicine* patented, proprietary, licensed, branded, brand-name.

paternal adj **1** *take a paternal interest in the boy* fatherly, fatherlike, patriarchal, protective, concerned, solicitous, kindly, benevolent. **2** *his paternal grandfather* patrilineal, patrimonial, on the father's side.

paternity n **1** *dispute paternity* fatherhood. **2** *of unknown paternity* descent, extraction, lineage, parentage, family.

path n **1** *a path through the forest* pathway, footpath, footway, track, jogging track, trail, tow-path, walk. **2** *the moon's path round the earth* course, route, circuit, track, orbit, trajectory. **3** *unable to predict the path he will take* course of action, route, procedure, direction, approach, method, system, strategy. **4** *the path to success* way, road, avenue, route.

pathetic adj **1** *children in rags were a pathetic sight* pitiful, pitiable, piteous, to be pitied, moving, touching, poignant, affecting, distressing, heartbreaking, heart-rending, sad, wretched, mournful, woeful. **2** *a pathetic attempt/performance* pitiful, lamentable, deplorable, miserable, wretched, feeble, woeful, sorry, poor, contemptible, inadequate, unsatisfactory, worthless.

pathological adj **1** *a pathological condition* morbid, diseased. **2** *a pathological liar* irrational, compulsive, obsessive, unreasonable, illogical.

pathos n *the pathos in the dying girl's speech* poignancy, pitifulness, pitiableness, piteousness, sadness, plaintiveness.

patience n **1** *wait in the long queue with patience* calmness, composure, even temper, even-temperedness, equanimity, equilibrium, serenity, tranquillity, restraint, self-restraint, imperturbability, inexcitability, tolerance, long-suffering, indulgence, forbearance, endurance, resignation, stoicism, fortitude; *inf* unflappability, cool. **2** *a task requiring patience* perseverance, persistence, endurance, tenacity, assiduity, diligence, staying power, indefatigability, doggedness, singleness of purpose.

patient adj *children told to be patient when waiting for Christmas | have to be patient about delayed flights* uncomplaining, serene, calm, composed, even-tempered, tranquil, restrained, imperturbable, inexcitable, tolerant, accommodating, long-suffering, forbearing, indulgent, resigned, stoical; *inf* unflappable, cool.

patient n *doctors examining patients* sick person, invalid, case, sufferer.

patio n *deck-chairs on the patio* terrace, courtyard, veranda; *Amer* deck, piazza.

patois n *visitors unable to understand the local patois* local speech, vernacular, dialect, local parlance; *inf* lingo.

patrician n *Roman patricians | patricians looking down on the peasants* aristocrat, noble, nobleman, lord; *inf* nob.

patrician adj *a patrician family* aristocratic, noble, well-born, high-born, blue-blooded.

patriot n *patriots dying for their country* nationalist, loyalist, chauvinist, flag-waver, jingoist, jingo.

patriotic adj *patriotic people singing the national anthem* nationalist, nationalistic, loyalist, loyal, chauvinistic, flag-waving, jingoistic.

patrol v *soldiers patrolling the border area* make the rounds of, perform sentry-duty on, walk the beat of, pound the beat of, range, police, keep watch on, guard, keep guard on, keep a vigil on, monitor.

patrol n **1** *make regular patrols of the border area* patrolling, round, sentry-duty, beat-pounding, policing, watch, guard, vigil, monitoring. **2** *report the matter to the patrol* patrolman/patrolwoman, sentinel, sentry, garrison, guard, watchman, watch, security man, night-watchman, policeman/policewoman.

patron n **1** *a patron of the theatre/arts* sponsor, backer, benefactor/benefactress, promoter, friend, helper, supporter, upholder, champion, protector; *inf* angel. **2** *regular patrons of the salon | car park for patrons only* customer, client, frequenter, shopper, buyer, purchaser; *inf* regular.

patronage n **1** *customers taking their patronage elsewhere* trade, custom, business, commerce, trafficking, shopping, buying, purchasing. **2** *their patronage of the arts | a festival under the patronage of local firms* sponsorship, backing, funding, financing, promotion, help, aid, assistance, support, encouragement, championship, protection. **3** *a post under the patronage of the Queen* power of appointment, right of appointment. **4** *treat his staff with patronage* patronizing, condescension, disdain, scorn, contempt, snobbery, snobbishness.

patronize v **1** *patronize those less well-off than she is* look down on, talk down to, condescend to, treat condescendingly, treat with condescension, treat like a child, treat as inferior, treat with disdain, treat scornfully/contemptuously, be snobbish to. **2** *patronize the new salon* be a customer of, be a client of, frequent, shop at, buy from, do business with, deal with, trade with. **3** *patronize the arts | wants to patronize the new theatre* be a patron of, sponsor, back, fund, finance, promote, help, aid, assist, support, encourage, champion, protect.

patronizing adj *a patronizing attitude to younger people* condescending, supercilious, superior, haughty, lofty, lordly, disdainful, scornful, contemptuous, snobbish; *inf* uppity, snooty, toffee-nosed.

patter[1] v **1** *mice pattering across the attic floor* scurry, scuttle, trip. **2** *rain pattering on the window* pitter-patter, tap, drum, beat, pound, pelt, rat-a-tat, go pit-a-pat, pit-a-pat.

patter[1] n **1** *the patter of mice on the floor above* pattering, scurrying, scuttling, tripping. **2** *the patter of rain on the window* pitter-patter, pattering, tap, tapping, drumming, beat, beating, pounding, pelting, rat-a-tat, pit-a-pat.

patter[2] n **1** *the salesman's patter* spiel, glib talk, monologue, harangue; *inf* sales pitch, line. **2** *can't understand the young people's pat-*

ter speech, language, jargon; *inf* lingo. *see*
PARLANCE.

pattern n **1** *the pattern on the wallpaper*
design, decoration, motif, marking, ornament, ornamentation, device, figure.
2 *study the rats' behaviour pattern* system,
order, arrangement, method, sequence. **3** *a
knitting pattern* design, guide, blueprint,
model, plan, template, stencil, instructions. **4** *a pattern of elegance* model, ideal,
exemplar, paradigm, example, archetype,
prototype, paragon, criterion, standard,
gauge, norm, guide, yardstick, touchstone,
benchmark. **5** *a book of textile patterns* sample, swatch, specimen.

pattern v *pattern himself on his father* model/
mould/style/form/shape oneself on.

patterned adj *patterned carpets/china* decorated, ornamented, figure.

paucity n *a paucity of evidence* scarcity,
sparseness, sparsity, dearth, shortage,
insufficiency, deficiency, lack, want, meagreness, paltriness.

paunch n **1** *developing quite a paunch* fat/pro-
truding stomach/belly/abdomen, pot-belly,
pot; *inf* beer-belly, corporation. **2** *a belt
round his paunch* stomach, belly, abdomen.

pauper n *once a rich person, now a pauper*
poor person, penniless person, bankrupt
person, bankrupt, insolvent person, beggar, mendicant, down-and-out, homeless
person.

pause n *a pause in the fighting* break, halt,
cessation, stoppage, interruption, lull,
respite, stay, discontinuation, gap, interlude, intermission, interval, rest, delay,
hesitation; *inf* let-up, breather.

pause v *pause for thought* stop, halt, cease,
discontinue, break, take a break, desist,
rest, hold back, delay, hesitate, waver; *inf*
let up, take a breather.

pave v *pave the front path* concrete, asphalt,
flag, tile, tar, macadamize, floor. **pave the
way for** *pave the way for radical change* prepare for, prepare the way for, clear the way
for, make preparations for, make provision
for, get ready for, lay the foundations/
groundwork for, put things in order for,
set the scene for.

pavement n *a car mounting the pavement*
footpath, paved path, pedestrian way,
walkway; *Amer* sidewalk.

paw n *an animal's paw* foot, pad, forepaw,
hind paw.

paw v *accused of pawing the female staff*
molest, maul; *inf* touch up, goose.

pawn v *pawn her necklace to pay the rent*
deposit with a pawnbroker, put in pawn,
give as security, pledge, mortgage; *inf* pop;
inf esp Amer hock, put in hock.

pawn n *members of staff who were pawns in the
struggle for power in the firm* tool, cat's-paw,
instrument, puppet, dupe; *inf* stooge.

pay v **1** *pay him for work done* give payment
to, settle up with, remunerate, reimburse,
recompense, reward, indemnify, requite.
2 *pay hundreds of pounds for his services* pay
out, spend, expend, lay out, part with, disburse, hand over, remit, render; *inf* dish
out, shell out, fork out, cough up. **3** *pay his
debts* pay off, pay in full, settle, discharge,
meet, clear, square, honour, liquidate.
4 *pay the bill* settle, foot, defray, square, discharge. **5** *the business/work does not pay* make
money, be profitable, make a profit, be
remunerative, make a return. **6** *investments
paying large sums of money* pay out, yield,
return, produce, bring in; *inf* rake in. **7** *it
would pay you to listen to his advice* repay, be
advantageous to, be of advantage to, be of
benefit to, be beneficial to, be profitable to,
be worthwhile to. **8** *pay compliments* give,
bestow, extend, offer, proffer, render. **9** *pay
him for what he did* pay back, punish, avenge
oneself on, get revenge on. **pay back 1** *pay
back the loan* repay, pay off, give back,
return, reimburse. **2** *pay her back for her
treatment of him* pay, repay, punish, avenge
oneself on, get revenge on, retaliate
against, settle a score with, get even with.
pay for 1 *pay for their services/meal* foot the
bill for, settle up for, defray the cost of; *inf*
shell out for, fork out for, cough up for.
2 *make him pay for his mistakes* be punished
for, pay a penalty for, suffer for, atone for,
make atonement for, pay the price for, get
one's deserts for, take one's medicine for;
inf get one's comeuppance for. **pay off
1** *pay off his debts* pay, pay in full, settle, discharge, meet, clear, square, honour, liquidate. **2** *pay off some workers* make/declare
redundant, dismiss, discharge, lay off, let
go; *inf* sack, fire. **3** *his hard work paid off*
meet with success, be successful, be effective, work, get results, be profitable. **pay
out** *pay out a lot of money on the mortgage*
pay, spend, expend, lay out, part with,
hand over, remit; *inf* dish out, shell out,
fork out, cough up. **pay up** *pay up or be sued*
pay, make payment, settle up, pay in full,
meet one's obligations.

pay n *get one's pay at the end of the month* payment, salary, wages, earnings, fee, remuneration, recompense, reimbursement,
reward, stipend, emoluments.

payable adj *a bill that is payable now* due, to be paid, owed, owing, outstanding, unpaid.

payment n **1** *receive payment for his services* pay, salary, wages, earnings, fee, remuneration, recompense. *see* PAY n. **2** *in payment of the account* settlement, discharge, clearance, squaring, liquidation. **3** *make twelve monthly payments* instalment, premium, amount, remittance.

peace n **1** *the peace of the countryside* peace and quiet, peacefulness, tranquillity, restfulness, calm, calmness, quiet, quietness, stillness, still. **2** *a mind seeking peace* peacefulness, tranquillity, serenity, calm, calmness, composure, placidity, rest, repose, contentment. **3** *hope for peace between the countries* peacefulness, peaceableness, harmony, harmoniousness, accord, concord, amity, amicableness, goodwill, friendship, cordiality, non-aggression, non-violence, cease-fire. **4** *sign the peace* | *the Peace of Versailles* treaty, truce, agreement, armistice, cessation of hostilities.

peaceable adj **1** *a peaceable person/temperament* peace-loving, non-aggressive, nonbelligerent, non-violent, non-combative, unwarlike, easygoing, placid, gentle, mild, good-natured, even-tempered, amiable, amicable, pacific, pacifist, pacifistic, dovelike, dovish, irenic. **2** *a peaceable set of negotiations* peaceful, strife-free, harmonious, amicable, amiable, friendly, cordial.

peaceful adj **1** *in a peaceful setting* tranquil, restful, quiet, calm, still, undisturbed. **2** *a peaceful mind* at peace, tranquil, serene, calm, composed, placid, at rest, in repose, reposeful, undisturbed, untroubled, unworried, anxiety-free. **3** *peaceful conditions between the two countries* peaceable, at peace, on good terms, strife-free, harmonious, amicable, friendly, cordial, non-violent, unwarlike.

peacemaker n *call in a third party as a peacemaker* conciliator, mediator, arbitrator, pacifier, appeaser, peacemonger.

peak n **1** *snow on the mountain peaks* top, summit, crest, pinnacle. **2** *climb several peaks* mountain, hill, height, alp. **3** *the peak of a cap* brim, visor, projection. **4** *at the peak of his career as a singer* height, high point, climax, culmination, zenith, acme, meridian, apogee, prime, heyday, *ne plus ultra*.

peak v **1** *prices peaking just before Christmas* reach its/their etc height, reach the highest point. **2** *the political party's popularity peaked too soon* reach its/their etc height, reach the highest point, culminate, reach the high point, reach a climax, reach the zenith.

peaky adj *looking rather peaky this morning* peaked, pale, wan, drained, drawn, pallid, pasty, white, whitish, anaemic, whey-faced, ill-looking, sickly-looking.

peal n **1** *hear the peal of the church bells* ring, ringing, chime, clang, resounding, reverberation, tintinnabulation. **2** *bell-ringers ringing a peal* carillon, chime. **3** *the peal of laughter* ring, ringing, tinkle, roar, boom, resounding, reverberation. **4** *the peal of thunder* roar, boom, rumble, crash, clap, resounding, reverberation.

peal v **1** *bells pealing* ring, ring out, chime, clang, resound, reverberate. **2** *thunder pealed around us* roar, boom, rumble, crash, resound, reverberate.

peasant n **1** *peasants driving cows to market* small farmer, agricultural worker, rustic, son of the soil. **2** *refusing to sit with people he called peasants* lout, boor, churl, yokel, provincial.

peccadillo n *treat his peccadilloes as major crimes* misdemeanour, minor offence, petty offence, indiscretion, lapse, misdeed, error, infraction; *inf* slip-up.

peck v **1** *birds pecking the wood* bite, strike, hit, tap, rap, jab. **2** *peck her on the cheek* kiss, plant a kiss on, give someone a peck. **3** *chickens pecking at the corn* pick at, pick up, eat. **4** *children pecking at their food* nibble, pick at, eat sparingly of.

peculiar adj **1** *a peculiar smell* strange, odd, queer, funny, curious, unusual, abnormal. **2** *peculiar clothes/appearance* strange, odd, queer, funny, curious, unusual, abnormal, eccentric, unconventional, bizarre, weird, quaint, outlandish, out-of-the-way, grotesque, freakish, offbeat, droll, comical; *inf* far-out, way-out. **3** *have a peculiar walk* characteristic, distinctive, distinct, individual, individualistic, distinguishing, special, unique, idiosyncratic, conspicuous, notable, remarkable. **4** *feel rather peculiar* unwell, poorly, ill, below par, strange, indisposed; *inf* funny, under the weather.
peculiar to *peculiar to that period of history* belonging to, characteristic of, typical of, representative of, indicative of, exclusive to.

peculiarity n **1** *the peculiarity of the smell* peculiarness, strangeness, oddness, queerness, abnormality. *see* PECULIAR 1. **2** *the peculiarity of her clothes/appearance* peculiarness, strangeness, oddness, queerness, eccentricity, unconventionality, bizarreness, weirdness, outlandishness, grotesqueness, freakishness, drollness. *see* PECULIAR 2. **3** *a geographical peculiarity of the region* | *a peculiarity of the breed* characteristic, feature, quality, property, trait, attribute, mark, stamp, hallmark. **4** *peculiarities of dress/ behaviour* abnormality, eccentricity, oddity, idiosyncrasy, quirk, foible.

pecuniary adj *of no pecuniary advantage* financial, monetary, fiscal.

pedagogic adj *pedagogic considerations* educational, teaching, academic, scholastic.

pedagogue n **1** *children taking notes from a pedagogue* teacher, schoolmaster/ schoolmistress, tutor, lecturer, instructor, educator, educationalist. **2** *a pedagogue without inspiration* dogmatist, pedant.

pedant n **1** *pedants insisting on the rules being interpreted literally* precisionist, perfectionist, formalist, dogmatist, literalist, quibbler, hair-splitter, casuist, sophist, pettifogger; *inf* nit-picker. **2** *pedants displaying their knowledge* intellectual, academic, pedagogue, highbrow, bluestocking; *inf* egghead.

pedantic adj **1** *a pedantic interpretation of the rules* precise, precisionist, exact, scrupulous, overscrupulous, punctilious, meticulous, over-nice, perfectionist, formalist, dogmatic, literalist, literalistic, quibbling, hair-splitting, casuistic, casuistical, sophistic, sophistical, pettifogging; *inf* nit-picking. **2** *a pedantic display of knowledge* intellectual, academic, scholastic, didactic, bookish, pedagogic, donnish, highbrow, pretentious, pompous; *inf* egghead. **3** *a pedantic account of the incident* formal, stilted, stiff, stuffy, unimaginative, uninspired, rhetorical, bombastic, grandiloquent, high-flown, euphuistic; *inf* highfalutin.

pedantry n **1** *his pedantry in interpreting the rules* precision, precisionism, exactness, scrupulousness, punctiliousness, meticulousness, over-niceness, over-nicety, perfectionism, formalism, dogmatism, literalism, quibbling, hair-splitting, casuistry, sophistry, pettifogging; *inf* nit-picking. **2** *an audience tired of the speaker's pedantry* intellectualism, scholasticism, didacticism, bookishness, pedagogism, donnishness, pretentiousness, pomposity, pompousness. **3** *the pedantry of his prose* formality, stiltedness, stiffness, stuffiness, unimaginativeness, lack of inspiration, rhetoric, bombast, grandiloquence, euphuism.

peddle v **1** *peddle goods round the doors* hawk, sell, sell from door to door, tout, market, vend; *inf* flog, push. **2** *peddle his political views to his workmates* present, offer, introduce, spread, promote, advocate, recommend.

pedestal n *a bust of Shakespeare on a pedestal* base, support, stand, foundation, pillar, column, plinth. **put on a pedestal** *put his father on a pedestal* idealize, exalt, glorify, adulate, worship, deify.

pedestrian n *areas for pedestrians only* person on foot, walker, foot-traveller, hiker, footslogger.

pedestrian adj **1** *pedestrian traffic* on foot, walking. **2** *pedestrian precincts in the city* pedestrianized, for pedestrians, for pedestrians only. **3** *piece of pedestrian prose* plodding, unimaginative, uninspired, unexciting, dull, flat, prosaic, turgid, stodgy, mundane, humdrum, banal, run-of-the-mill, commonplace, ordinary, mediocre; *inf* nothing to write home about.

pedigree n **1** *proud of his aristocratic pedigree* ancestry, descent, lineage, line, extraction, heritage, parentage, birth, family, strain, stock, blood, stirps. **2** *draw up the son's/dog's pedigree* genealogy, family tree, ancestral record, line of descent.

pedigree adj *a pedigree spaniel* pedigreed, pure-bred, thoroughbred, pure-blooded, full-blooded.

peek v *peek into the Christmas package before Christmas* take a secret look, take a sly/ stealthy look, peep, glance, cast a brief look, look hurriedly, look; *inf* sneak a look, take a gander, have a look-see.

peek n *take a peek into the Christmas package before Christmas* secret look, sly look, stealthy look, sneaky look, peep, glance, glimpse, brief/hurried look, look; *inf* gander, look-see.

peel v **1** *peel the skin from the fruit* pare, strip, remove, take off. **2** *peel the fruit* pare, skin, decorticate. **3** *skin peeling after getting sunburnt* flake, scale off, come off in layers, desquamate. **4** *peel off his wet clothes* strip off, cast off, remove, doff. **keep one's eyes peeled** *keep one's eyes peeled for the lost kitten* keep one's eyes skinned, keep a sharp look-out, be on the look-out, look out, watch closely, be alert, be on guard.

peel n *the peel of the fruit* rind, skin, covering, zest, shell, husk, epicarp.

peep[1] v **1** *peep through the keyhole* take a secret look, take a sly look, peek; *inf* sneak a look. *see* PEEK V. **2** *snowdrops peeping through the hard winter ground* appear, show, come into view, become visible, emerge, spring up, pop up.

peep[1] n *take a peep at the secret document* secret look, sly look, stealthy look, sneaky look, peek, glance. *see* PEEK N.

peep[2] v *fledglings peeping in the nest* cheep, chirp, chirrup, tweet, twitter, pipe, squeak.

peep² n **1** *the peep of a fledgling from the nest* cheep, chirp, chirrup, tweet, twitter, piping, squeak. **2** *not a peep out of the children* sound, noise, cry, utterance, word; *inf* cheep. **3** *we expected a protest but there was not a peep out of the opposition* complaint, grumble, moan, groan, word; *inf* gripe, grouse.

peep-hole n *look through the peep-hole in the door to see who's there* aperture, opening, spyhole, judas, slit, crack, clink, crevice, fissure.

peer v *peer at the faded handwriting | peer through the mist* look closely, try to see, look through narrowed eyes, narrow one's eyes, screw up one's eyes, squint.

peer n **1** *one of the peers of the realm | a life peer* noble, nobleman, aristocrat, lord, titled man, patrician, duke, marquess, marquis, earl, viscount, baron. **2** *look older than his peers | be a cleverer child than his peers* compeer, fellow, equal, match, like, co-equal, confrère.

peerage n **1** *elevated to the peerage* nobility, aristocracy. **2** *the peerage voted on the bill* nobility, aristocracy, peers and peeresses, lords and ladies, upper classes, the House of Lords, the Lords.

peerless adj *a peerless performance* incomparable, beyond compare, matchless, unmatched, unrivalled, unsurpassed, unequalled, without equal, unparalleled, superlative, second to none, nonpareil.

peeve v *his behaviour really peeved her* irritate, annoy, anger, vex, provoke, upset, exasperate, irk, pique, nettle, get on someone's nerves, rub up the wrong way; *inf* aggravate, miff, rile, get under someone's skin, get in someone's hair.

peevish adj *the children were tired and peevish | peevish old men* irritable, fractious, fretful, cross, crabbed, crabby, petulant, complaining, querulous, sulky, moody, in a bad mood, grumpy, ill-tempered, ill-natured, ill-humoured, surly, churlish, touchy, testy, snappish, snappy, crusty, splenetic; *inf* ratty, whingeing.

peg n *fasten the pieces of wood with a peg* pin, nail, dowel, spike, skewer, brad, screw, bolt, post, clothes-peg. **take down a peg or two** *feel like taking the conceited young fool down a peg or two* humble, humiliate, mortify, bring down, bring low; *inf* settle someone's hash.

peg v **1** *peg the clothes to the line | peg a tent to the ground* pin, attach, fasten, fix, secure, make fast. **2** *peg prices at last year's level* fix, set, control, freeze, limit. **peg away at** *peg away at their studies* apply oneself to, work hard at, work away at, persevere at, persist in, keep at, hammer away at; *inf* beaver away at, plug away at, stick at, stick with.

pejorative adj *always making pejorative remarks* derogatory, disparaging, deprecatory, slighting.

pellet n **1** *a paper pellet | a pellet of bread* ball, little ball. **2** *firing pellets at birds* bullet, shot, lead shot, buckshot. **3** *take pellets for indigestion* pill, tablet, capsule, lozenge, bolus.

pell-mell adv **1** *children rushing pell-mell from the school* helter-skelter, headlong, impetuously, recklessly, hurriedly, hastily. **2** *books lying pell-mell around the room* in disorder, in confusion, in a muddle, in disarray, untidily, in a mess, anyhow.

pellucid adj **1** *pellucid water* transparent, translucent, clear, crystal clear, glassy, limpid. **2** *pellucid prose* clear, lucid, coherent, articulate, intelligible, understandable, comprehensible, straightforward, simple.

pelt v **1** *pelt the strikebreakers with stones* bombard, shower, attack, assail, batter, pepper. **2** *rain came pelting down* pour, teem, bucket down, rain cats and dogs, come down like stair-rods. **3** *pelt along the road | came pelting down the hill* race, run, sprint, dash, rush, speed, charge, career, hare; *inf* belt, tear, whiz.

pelt n *a fox's/beaver's pelt* skin, hide, fleece, coat, fur, fell.

pen¹ n *bring pen and paper* fountain-pen, ball-point, ball-point pen, felt-tip, felt-tip pen, marker; *Trademark* Biro.

pen¹ v *pen a note* write, write down, jot down, scribble, pencil, compose, draft, commit to paper.

pen² n *put animals in a pen* enclosure, fold, sheepfold, coop, hen-coop, pound, compound, corral.

pen² v **pen in, pen up** *pen in the animals for the night* shut up, enclose, confine, fence in, coop up, mew up, corral.

penal adj **1** *a penal institution* disciplinary, punitive, corrective, retributive. **2** *a penal offence* punishable, indictable, chargeable, impeachable.

penalize v **1** *penalized for arriving late* punish, discipline, castigate, correct. **2** *people penalized for being poor* handicap, inflict a handicap on, disadvantage, put at a disadvantage.

penalty n **1** *have to pay a penalty for his crime* punishment, punitive action, retribution, castigation, penance, fine, forfeit, sentence, mulct. **2** *one of the penalties of living in* *the city* handicap, disadvantage, drawback, snag, obstacle.

penance n **1** *a penance imposed by the priest* punishment, penalty. **2** *carry out a penance for one's sins* self-punishment, atonement, reparation, amends, mortification.

penchant n *a penchant for bright colours | has a penchant for spicy food* liking, fondness, preference, taste, partiality, soft spot, inclination, bent, proclivity, predilection, love, passion, desire, fancy, whim, weakness.

pencil n **1** *pencil and paper* lead pencil, propelling pencil. **2** *a pencil of light* ray, beam, shaft, finger.

pencil v **1** *pencil a note* write, write down, jot down, scribble, pen, compose, draft, commit to paper. **2** *pencil a likeness of the child* sketch, outline, draw, trace.

pendant n *wear a silver pendant* necklace, locket, medallion.

pendent adj *a pendent light* hanging, suspended, dangling.

pending prep **1** *receive bail pending trial* awaiting, waiting for, until. **2** *no action pending negotiations* during, throughout, in the course of, for the time/duration of.

pending adj **1** *the lawsuit then pending* undecided, unsettled, unresolved, uncertain, awaiting action, undetermined, hanging fire, up in the air; *inf* on the back burner. **2** *a decision is pending* imminent, impending, on the way, coming, approaching, forthcoming, near, nearing, close, close at hand, in the offing.

penetrate v **1** *penetrate the skin* pierce, bore, perforate, stab, prick, gore, spike. **2** *penetrate the dense forest* go into, get in, enter, make one's way into/through, infiltrate. **3** *terror penetrated her whole being* permeate, pervade, fill, imbue, suffuse, seep through, saturate. **4** *we explained, but it didn't penetrate* be understood, be comprehended, be taken in, be grasped, register. **5** *the explanation did not seem to penetrate his mind* get through to, be understood/comprehended by, register on, make an impression on, have an impact on. **6** *unable to penetrate the mystery* understand, comprehend, apprehend, fathom, get to the bottom of, make out, solve, resolve, work out, figure out, unravel, decipher; *inf* crack.

penetrating adj **1** *a penetrating wind* sharp, keen, biting, stinging, harsh. **2** *a penetrating voice* shrill, loud, strong, carrying, piercing, ear-piercing, ear-splitting, intrusive. **3** *a penetrating mind* keen, sharp, sharp-witted, discerning, perceptive, percipient, intelligent, clever, smart, incisive, astute,

shrewd, acute, discriminating. **4** *ask penetrating questions* penetrative, searching, sharp, incisive, inquisitive, analytic, in-depth.

penetration n **1** *the penetration of the skin* piercing, perforation, pricking. *see* PENETRATE 1. **2** *the penetration of the forest* entry, infiltration. *see* PENETRATE 2. **3** *the penetration of her being with terror* permeation, pervasion, imbuing, suffusion. *see* PENETRATE 3. **4** *the penetration of the mystery is taking a lot of time* understanding, comprehension, apprehension, fathoming, resolution; *inf* cracking. *see* PENETRATE 6. **5** *impressed by the penetration of their minds* keenness, sharpness, sharp-wittedness, discernment, perception, perceptiveness, intelligence, cleverness, smartness, incisiveness, astuteness, shrewdness, acuteness, acuity, discrimination. **6** *admire the penetration of the questions* searchingness, sharpness, incisiveness. *see* PENETRATING 4.

penitence n *show penitence for his sins* repentance, contrition, compunction, regret, remorse, remorsefulness, ruefulness, self-reproach, self-accusation, shame, sorrow.

penitent adj *feel penitent about his sin | penitent pupils apologizing* repentant, contrite, regretful, remorseful, sorry, apologetic, conscience-stricken, rueful, ashamed, abject, sorrowful.

pen-name n pseudonym, *nom de plume*, *nom de guerre*, assumed name, allonym, alias.

pennant n *pennants flying in the breeze* banner, banderole, streamer, flag, ensign, colours, bunting.

penniless adj without a penny, without a penny to one's name, impecunious, penurious, impoverished, indigent, poor, as poor as a church mouse, poverty-stricken, destitute, bankrupt, in reduced circumstances, in straitened circumstances, hard up; *inf* broke, stony-broke, flat broke, skint, cleaned-out, strapped for cash, strapped.

penny n *it costs one penny* pence; *inf* p; *Amer* cent. **a bad penny** undesirable, *persona non grata*, rascal, scoundrel, rogue, good-for-nothing; *inf* bad egg, bad news. **a pretty penny** *will cost a pretty penny* considerable sum of money; *inf* lot of money, heaps of money, a mint, a bundle, a packet.

penny-pinching adj *penny-pinching people refusing to give to charity* mean, miserly, parsimonious, niggardly, tight-fisted, close-fisted, cheese-paring, penurious, scrimping, skimping, close, near, grasping, money-grubbing, Scrooge-like, ungenerous; *inf* stingy, tight, mingy.

pension n **1** *draw one's pension at 60* retirement pension, old-age pension, superannuation. **2** *a disability pension* allowance, benefit, support, welfare.

pensioner n retired person, old-age pensioner, OAP, senior citizen.

pensive adj *in pensive mood* thoughtful, thinking, reflective, contemplative, musing, meditative, pondering, cogitative, ruminative, absorbed, preoccupied, serious, solemn, dreamy, dreaming, wistful, melancholy, sad.

pent-up adj *pent-up feelings* bottled-up, repressed, suppressed, restrained, constrained, held in, kept in check, curbed, bridled.

penurious adj **1** *penurious homeless people* penniless, without a penny, impecunious, impoverished, indigent, poor, poor as a church mouse, poverty-stricken, destitute, bankrupt, in reduced circumstances, in straightened circumstances, hard up; *inf* broke, stony-broke, flat broke, skint, cleaned-out, strapped for cash, strapped. **2** *a penurious old skinflint* mean, miserly, parsimonious, niggardly, tight-fisted, cheese-paring, penurious, scrimping, skimping, close, Scrooge-like, ungenerous; *inf* stingy, tight, mingy. *see* PENNY-PINCHING.

penury n *formerly wealthy but now reduced to penury* extreme poverty, pennilessness, impecuniousness, impoverishment, indigence, need, want, neediness, destitution, privation, pauperism, beggarliness, beggary, bankruptcy, insolvency, reduced circumstances, straightened circumstances.

people n **1** npl *too many people in the hall/country* persons, individuals, human beings, humans, mortals, living souls, men women and children. **2** *a warlike people* race, tribe, clan, nation, country, population, populace. **3** npl *issue to be decided by the people* the common people, the ordinary people, ordinary citizens, the general public, the public, the populace, electorate, the masses, the rank and file, commonalty, the mob, the multitude, the *hoi polloi*, the rabble, the herd; *inf* the plebs. **4** npl *her people live far away* family, relatives, relations, folk, kinsfolk, kin, kith and kin; *inf* folks.

pep n *full of pep after the holidays | a performance without pep* spirit, liveliness, animation, life, sparkle, effervescence, verve, ebullience, vivacity, fire, dash, zest, exuberance, élan, vigour, vim, brio; *inf* zip.

pepper n **1** *season the soup with pepper* white pepper, black pepper, peppercorns, cayenne pepper, cayenne. **2** *stuffed peppers* capsicum, red pepper, green pepper, yellow pepper.

pepper v **1** *pepper the soup/sauce* add pepper to, season, flavour, spice, spice up. **2** *pepper his speech with quotations* sprinkle, intersperse, dot, bespatter, bestrew. **3** *pepper the new boy with paper pellets* pelt, bombard, shower, attack, assail, batter.

peppery adj **1** *peppery food* peppered, hot, spicy, spiced, highly-seasoned, pungent, fiery. **2** *a peppery old man* irascible, hot-tempered, fiery, quick-tempered, irritable, touchy, testy, crabbed, crabby, crusty, splenetic, dyspeptic. **3** *give a peppery speech to the wrongdoers* caustic, acerbic, astringent, trenchant, cutting, sarcastic, stinging, biting, sharp.

perceive v **1** *perceive someone walking down the hill* see, catch sight of, spot, observe, glimpse, notice, make out, discern, behold, espy, detect, witness, remark. **2** *perceive the difference between right and wrong* discern, appreciate, recognize, be cognizant of, be aware of, be conscious of, know, grasp, understand, comprehend, apprehend, figure out, see, sense.

perceptible adj *a perceptible change in her appearance | no perceptible improvement* perceivable, discernible, noticeable, detectable, distinguishable, appreciable, visible, observable, distinct, clear, plain, evident, apparent, obvious, manifest, conspicuous, patent, palpable, tangible.

perception n **1** *his perception of the magnitude of the problem* discernment, appreciation, recognition, cognizance, awareness, consciousness, knowledge, grasp, understanding, comprehension, apprehension, notion, conception, idea, sense. **2** *show great perception in his performance | his analysis shows great perception* perspicacity, discernment, perceptiveness, understanding, discrimination, insight, intuition, feeling, sensitivity.

perceptive adj **1** *the fire noticed by the most perceptive* sharp-eyed, sharp-sighted, keen-sighted, observant, alert, vigilant. **2** *one of the more perceptive theatre critics* discerning, perspicacious, percipient, shrewd, understanding, discriminating, intuitive, responsive, sensitive. **3** *a perceptive analysis of the problem* discerning, perspicacious, percipient, penetrating, astute, shrewd.

perch n *birds sitting on a perch* pole, rod, branch, roost, rest.

perch v *birds perching on a branch* sit, rest, roost, settle, alight, land.

perchance adv **1** *if perchance he arrives on time* by chance, by any chance, fortuitously. **2** *perchance we shall find the right book* perhaps, maybe, possibly, for all one knows; *lit* peradventure.

percipient adj **1** *a percipient commentator* perceptive, discerning, perspicacious, astute, shrewd, understanding, discriminating, intuitive, responsive, sensitive. **2** *a percipient summing-up of the situation* perceptive, discerning, perspicacious, penetrating, astute, shrewd.

percolate v **1** *liquid percolating through the strainer* filter, filtrate, drain, drip, ooze, seep, leach. **2** *percolate the coffee/liquid* strain, filter, filtrate, sieve, sift. **3** *coffee percolating in the pot* brew, bubble; *inf* perk. **4** *information finally percolating through the department* go through, pass through, filter through, permeate, pervade.

percussion n *instruments based on percussion* impact, collision, bang, clash, crash, striking, beating.

perdition n *cursed to perdition* damnation, hell-fire, hell, spiritual destruction.

peremptory adj **1** *receive a peremptory request from the boss* imperious, high-handed, urgent, pressing, imperative, high-priority. **2** *behave in a peremptory manner to shop assistants* imperious, high-handed, overbearing, dogmatic, autocratic, dictatorial, domineering, arbitrary, tyrannical, despotic, arrogant, overweening, supercilious, lordly. **3** *a peremptory judgement* incontrovertible, irreversible, binding, absolute, final, conclusive, decisive, definitive, categorical, irrefutable.

perennial adj **1** *a subject of perennial interest | perennial favourite* perpetual, everlasting, eternal, unending, never-ending, endless, undying, ceaseless, abiding, enduring, lasting, persisting, permanent, constant, unfailing, unchanging. **2** *tired of their perennial complaining* constant, continual, continuous, continuing, uninterrupted, ceaseless, persistent, recurrent, chronic, never-ending; *inf* eternal.

perfect adj **1** *a perfect set of antique dinner plates* complete, full, whole, entire. **2** *this piece of work is now perfect* perfected, completed, finished. **3** *a perfect fool/disaster* absolute, complete, out-and-out, thorough, thoroughgoing, downright, utter, sheer, consummate, unmitigated, unqualified. **4** *a perfect performance | a perfect piece of work* flawless, faultless, unmarred, ideal, impeccable, consummate, immaculate, exemplary, superb, superlative, supreme, excellent, wonderful. **5** *a perfect mother/pupil* ideal, model, without fault, faultless, flawless, consummate, exemplary, excellent, wonderful. **6** *a perfect evening* superb, exquisite, superlative, excellent, wonderful, marvellous; *inf* out of this world, terrific, fantastic, fabulous. **7** *a perfect copy* exact, precise, accurate, faithful, correct, right, close, true, strict; *inf* spot on. **8** *the perfect present* ideal, just right, right, appropriate, fitting, fit, suitable, apt.

perfect v *perfect the technique* make perfect, render faultless/flawless, improve, better, polish, refine, elaborate, complete, consummate, put the finishing touches to.

perfection n **1** *working on the perfection of their technique* perfecting, improvement, betterment, polishing, refinement, completion, consummation. *see* PERFECT V. **2** *try to achieve perfection in his work* perfectness, flawlessness, faultlessness, consummation, impeccability, immaculateness, exemplariness, superbness. *see* PERFECT adj 4. **3** *as a singer she was perfection* paragon, one in a million; *inf* the tops. **4** *the meal was perfection* ideal, acme, crown, peak of perfection.

perfectionist n *writers who are perfectionists* stickler for perfection, precisionist, precisian, purist, formalist.

perfectly adv **1** *perfectly happy/miserable* absolutely, utterly, completely, altogether, entirely, wholly, totally, thoroughly, fully. **2** *the cake turned out perfectly | he played perfectly* to perfection, flawlessly, faultlessly, without blemish, ideally, impeccably, immaculately, superbly, exquisitely, superlatively, wonderfully.

perfidious adj *betrayed by perfidious allies* treacherous, traitorous, treasonous, false, untrue, disloyal, faithless, unfaithful, deceitful, double-dealing, duplicitous, dishonest, two-faced.

perfidy n *captured because of the perfidy of his allies* perfidiousness, treachery, traitorousness, falseness, infidelity, disloyalty, faithlessness, unfaithfulness, deceitfulness, deceit, double-dealing, duplicity, dishonesty, two-facedness.

perforate v **1** *perforate the skin* pierce, puncture, prick, stab, gore, bore, penetrate, spike. **2** *perforate paper* put holes in, make holes in, hole, punch holes in, punch, honeycomb.

perform v **1** *perform acts of charity | could perform feats of skill* do, carry out, execute, discharge, conduct, effect, bring about, bring off, accomplish, achieve, fulfil, complete. **2** *perform in Hamlet* act, play, appear. **3** *perform a new symphony* play, execute. **4** *a car* *performing well* function, work, operate, run, go.

performance n **1** *faithful in the performance of his duty | performance of acts of charity* carrying out, execution, discharge, conducting, effecting, accomplishment, achievement, fulfilment. **2** *watch a musical performance* show, production, entertainment, act, presentation; *inf* gig. **3** *his performance of Hamlet* acting, playing, representation, staging.

performer n **1** *applaud the performers* actor/actress, player, entertainer, artist, artiste, Thespian, trouper, musician, singer, dancer. **2** *performers of acts of charity | a performer of strange feats* doer, executor, worker, operator, architect, author.

perfume n **1** *the perfume of roses | love the perfume of new-mown hay* scent, fragrance, aroma, smell, bouquet, redolence. **2** *buy some French perfume* scent, fragrance, eau de toilette, toilet water, eau-de-Cologne, cologne.

perfunctory adj *take a perfunctory look at the contract* cursory, superficial, desultory, mechanical, automatic, routine, sketchy, brief, hasty, hurried, rapid, fleeting, quick, fast, offhand, casual, indifferent, careless, inattentive, negligent.

perhaps adv *perhaps we may meet him on the way* it may be, maybe, possibly, it is possible that, conceivably, feasibly, for all one knows; *lit* peradventure.

peril n *abducted children in great peril* danger, jeopardy, risk, hazard, menace, threat.

perilous adj *a perilous journey through the mountains* dangerous, fraught with danger, menacing, risky, precarious, hazardous, chancy, threatening, unsafe.

perimeter n **1** *the perimeter of a circle* circumference. **2** *guards patrolling the perimeter of the estate* boundary, border, frontier, limits, outer limits, confines, edge, margin, fringe, periphery.

period n **1** *during periods of peace | over a period of several years* time, space, spell, interval, term, stretch, span. **2** *absent for a period* time, while, spell. **3** *the post-war period | the period of the French Revolution* time, days, age, era, epoch, aeon. **4** *he's going, period* finis, end, finish, conclusion, stop, halt, and that's that. **5** *put a period at the end of a sentence* full stop, full point, point, stop. **6** *irregular periods* menstruation, menstrual flow, monthly flow, menses; *inf* the curse.

periodic adj *periodic inspections | has periodic attacks of dizziness* periodical, at fixed intervals, recurrent, recurring, repeated, cycli-

cal, cyclic, regular, intermittent, occasional, infrequent, sporadic, every once in a while, every so often.

periodical n *consult a specialist periodical* journal, publication, magazine, review, organ, quarterly, monthly, weekly; *inf* book, glossy.

peripatetic adj **1** *peripatetic tribes* itinerant, travelling, wandering, roving, roaming, nomadic, migrant, migratory. **2** *peripatetic teachers* itinerant, travelling, mobile.

peripheral adj **1** *peripheral zones of the city* outer, on the edge/outskirts, surrounding, neighbouring. **2** *waste time discussing peripheral matters* minor, lesser, secondary, subsidiary, ancillary, unimportant, superficial, irrelevant, beside the point.

periphery n **1** *on the periphery of the town* outskirts, boundary, border, limits, outer limits, edge, margin, fringe, perimeter. **2** *on the periphery of the group* edge, fringe, margin.

periphrastic adj *a periphrastic style of prose* circumlocutory, redundant, tautological, pleonastic, roundabout, indirect, rambling, wandering, ambagious.

perish v **1** *soldiers perishing in battle* die, lose one's life, be killed, lay down one's life, meet one's death, breathe one's last, draw one's last breath; *inf* bite the dust, kick the bucket. **2** *the old theories/values having perished* come to an end, die away, disappear, vanish, disintegrate, go under, be destroyed. **3** *food perishing in the heat* go bad, go off, go sour, rot, decay, decompose.

perjure v *perjure oneself* *found guilty of contempt of court for perjuring herself* commit perjury, lie under oath, give false evidence/testimony, bear false witness.

perjury n **1** *witnesses found guilty of perjury | committed perjury* lying under oath, violation of oath, giving false evidence/testimony, bearing false witness, false swearing. **2** *repeated her perjury* false oath, false statement, wilful/deliberate falsehood.

perk v **perk up 1** *children perking up at the promise of a treat* cheer up, become cheerful, brighten up, feel happy, be gladdened, take heart; *inf* buck up, pep up. **2** *invalids perking up after treatment* brighten up, recover, recuperate, rally, revive. **3** *the holiday perked them up* cheer up, brighten up, raise someone's spirits, give someone heart, give someone a boost/lift; *inf* buck up, pep up.

perk n see PERQUISITE.

permanence n **1** *the permanence of their separation/disability* everlastingness, perpetuity, perpetualness, permanency, eternalness, eternality, endurance, constancy, persistence, endlessness, immutability, inalterability. *see* PERMANENT 1. **2** *the permanence of the job/relationship* stability, lastingness, long-lastingness, fixedness, soundness, firmness.

permanent adj **1** *the couple's separation is permanent | left with a permanent disability* everlasting, perpetual, eternal, enduring, perennial, lasting, abiding, constant, persistent, unending, endless, never-ending, immutable, unchangeable, inalterable, invariable. **2** *a permanent job/relationship* lasting, long-lasting, stable, fixed, established, sound, firm.

permanently adv *permanently separated/disabled* everlastingly, perpetually, eternally, perennially, lastingly, constantly, persistently, unendingly, endlessly, immutably, inalterably, invariably, for all time, for good, for good and all, for ever and ever, for ever, evermore, for evermore, till the end of time, time without end; *inf* till the cows come home, till hell freezes over.

permeate v **1** *cooking smells permeating the whole house* spread through, be disseminated through, pass through, pervade, fill, diffuse through, be diffused through, extend throughout, imbue, penetrate, infiltrate, percolate through. **2** *water permeating the soil* spread through, pass through, penetrate, soak through, seep through, leak through, infiltrate, percolate through, leach through, saturate.

permissible adj *driving with more than the permissible amount of alcohol* permitted, allowable, admissible, acceptable, tolerated, authorized, sanctioned, legal, lawful, legitimate, licit, within bounds; *inf* legit.

permission n *enter without permission | act with the permission of her mother* authorization, sanction, leave, licence, dispensation, empowerment, allowance, consent, assent, acquiescence, go-ahead, thumbs up, agreement, approval, approbation, tolerance, sufferance; *inf* green light.

permissive adj *a permissive parent/upbringing* liberal, tolerant, broad-minded, open-minded, easygoing, forbearing, latitudinarian, indulgent, lenient, unrestricted, overindulgent, lax, unprescriptive.

permit v **1** *parents not permitting the children to go | not permit talking in class* give permission, allow, let, authorize, give leave, sanction, grant, license, empower, enable, consent to, assent to, acquiesce in, give the go-ahead to, give the thumbs up to, agree to, approve of, tolerate, countenance, suf-

fer, brook; *inf* give the green light to. **2** *if time permits* allow, make possible, allow the possibility of, give an opportunity.

permit n *a permit to have a market stall* licence, authorization, warrant, sanction, pass, passport.

permutation n *the system allows for permutation* variation, alteration, change, shift, transformation, transposition, transmutation.

pernicious adj *a pernicious influence on society* destructive, ruinous, injurious, damaging, harmful, hurtful, detrimental, deleterious, deadly, lethal, fatal, wicked, evil, bad, malign, malevolent, malignant, noxious, poisonous, venomous.

pernickety adj difficult to please, difficult, fussy, punctilious, finicky, over-fastidious, fastidious, over-particular, particular, nice, over-nice; *inf* nit-picking, choosy, picky.

peroration n **1** *give a peroration at the end of a speech* closing remarks, conclusion, summation, summing-up, recapitulation; *inf* recapping. **2** *students wearying of the lecturer's peroration* lengthy talk/lecture/speech/ address, rhetorical speech, bombastic oration, harangue, declamation, diatribe.

perpendicular adj **1** *the perpendicular supports* upright, vertical, on end, standing, straight. **2** *a line perpendicular to another* at right angles to, at 90 degrees to. **3** *perpendicular cliffs* steep, sheer, precipitous, abrupt.

perpetrate v *perpetrate a crime | has perpetrated an indiscretion* commit, carry out, perform, execute, do, effect, effectuate, bring about, be guilty of, be to blame for, be responsible for; *inf* pull off.

perpetual adj **1** *a state of perpetual bliss | the perpetual snow of the Arctic* everlasting, eternal, never-ending, unending, endless, undying, perennial, permanent, perdurable, lasting, abiding, persisting, enduring, constant, unfailing, unchanging, unvarying, invariable. **2** *work with perpetual noise* incessant, unceasing, ceaseless, unending, endless, never-stopping, nonstop, continuous, uninterrupted, unbroken, unremitting. **3** *tired of their perpetual complaints* interminable, persistent, frequent, continual, recurrent, repeated; *inf* eternal

perpetuate v **1** *perpetuate the myth that he was a hero* keep alive, keep going, keep up, preserve, conserve, sustain, maintain, continue. **2** *perpetuate his memory with a statue* memorialize, commemorate, immortalize, eternalize, eternize.

perpetuity n in perpetuity land given in perpetuity to the family by the King perpetually, permanently, perennially, for ever, for ever and ever, for all time, until the end of time, for good, eternally, for eternity, everlastingly.

perplex v 1 her behaviour perplexed him puzzle, baffle, mystify, stump, keep someone guessing, bewilder, confound, confuse, nonplus, disconcert, dismay, dumbfound; inf bamboozle. 2 issues which perplex the situation complicate, confuse, make involved, muddle, mix up, jumble, entangle, tangle, snarl up; inf foul up.

perplexed adj explain the situation to her perplexed family | give a perplexed look puzzled, baffled, mystified, bewildered, confused, nonplussed, disconcerted, dumbfounded; inf bamboozled.

perplexing adj 1 her perplexing behaviour puzzling, baffling, mystifying, mysterious, bewildering, confusing, disconcerting, unaccountable, strange, weird. 2 a perplexing problem complicated, involved, intricate, complex, difficult, thorny, knotty, taxing, trying, vexing.

perplexity n 1 filled with perplexity at her behaviour puzzlement, bafflement, incomprehension, mystification, bewilderment, confusion, disconcertion, disconcertment, dismay; inf bamboozlement. 2 a problem of much perplexity complication, involvement, intricacy, complexity, difficulty, muddle, jumble, entanglement. see PERPLEXING 2. 3 the perplexities of the murder case complication, intricacy, complexity, difficulty, mystery, puzzle, enigma, paradox.

perquisite n a perquisite of the job fringe benefit, benefit, advantage, bonus, dividend, extra, plus; inf perk, freebie.

persecute v 1 persecute people for their beliefs oppress, tyrannize, abuse, mistreat, maltreat, ill-treat, molest, afflict, torment, torture, victimize, martyr. 2 film stars persecuted by the press harass, pester, hound, badger, vex, bother, worry, annoy; inf hassle.

perseverance n to start with he wasn't very good but perseverance brought success persistence, tenacity, pertinacity, determination, resolve, resolution, resoluteness, purposefulness, obstinacy, insistence, intransigence, patience, application, diligence, assiduity.

persevere v 1 persevere in his attempts to win persist, go on, keep on, keep at, keep going, continue, carry on, struggle, work, hammer away, be tenacious, be persistent, be pertinacious, be resolute, be purposeful,

be obstinate, be insistent, be intransigent, be patient, be diligent; inf plug away. 2 when you fail you must persevere persist, go on, keep on, keep going, continue, carry on, be tenacious, be persistent, be pertinacious, be determined, be resolute, stand one's ground, stand fast, not give up; inf stick to one's guns, stick at it.

persist v 1 persist in his efforts to win persevere, go on, keep on, keep going, continue, carry on; inf plug away. see PERSEVERE 1. 2 you must persist, not give up persevere, keep going, carry on, be resolute, stand one's ground; inf stick to one's guns, stick at it. see PERSEVERE 2. 3 the cold weather persisted carry on, keep on, keep up, continue, last, remain, linger, hold.

persistence n with persistence he got a job tenacity, determination, purposefulness, insistence, intransigence, patience, application. see PERSEVERANCE.

persistent adj 1 persistent people refusing to give up in their attempts persevering, tenacious, pertinacious, determined, resolute, purposeful, obstinate, stubborn, insistent, intransigent, obdurate, intractable, patient, diligent. 2 matches called off because of persistent rain constant, continual, continuous, continuing, interminable, incessant, unceasing, endless, unremitting, unrelenting, relentless. 3 a persistent cough chronic, frequent, repetitive, repititious.

person n not a person was left alive individual, human being, human, creature, living soul, soul, mortal; inf character.

persona n seen to take on the persona of his dead brother character, personality, role, part, public face.

personable adj a personable young man pleasant, agreeable, amiable, affable, likeable, charming, nice, attractive, good-looking, presentable.

personage n events attended by royal personages person, public figure, dignitary, notable, person of note, celebrity, personality, VIP, famous name, household name, luminary, worthy; inf big shot, big noise, big gun, celeb.

personal adj 1 his reasons for leaving are personal individual, private, confidential, secret, one's own business. 2 a personal style of prose | a personal interpretation of the music personalized, individual, idiosyncratic, characteristic, unique, peculiar. 3 a personal letter to her boss private, confidential, intimate. 4 receive the personal attention of the manager in person, individual, special. 5 make personal remarks insulting, slighting, derogatory, disparaging, pejorative, offensive.

personality n **1** *of an unassuming personality* nature, disposition, character, temperament, temper, make-up, traits, psyche. **2** *an unassuming man with little personality* strength of personality, force of personality, personal identity, character, charisma, magnetism, powers of attraction, charm. **3** *several personalities attending charity events* celebrity, VIP, famous name, household name, dignitary, notable, person of note, personage, luminary, worthy. *see* PERSONAGE.

personalize v **1** *he tends always to personalize issues* regard as personal, take personally, regard subjectively, be subjective about, interpret in terms of oneself. **2** *personalize his luggage | personalized number-plate* give a personal touch to, have one's initials engraved on, initial, monogram, customize.

personally adv **1** *deal with the matter personally* in person, oneself/herself/themselves etc. **2** *personally speaking, I am opposed to the idea* for my etc part, for my etc own part, for myself etc, from my etc own point of view, as far as I etc am concerned. **take something personally** take as an insult, regard as a slight, take offence at, be offended by.

personification n *he is the personification of politeness* embodiment, incarnation, epitome, quintessence, essence, symbol, representation, image, portrayal, likeness, semblance.

personify v *personify all that was good about the country* embody, body forth, be the incarnation of, epitomize, typify, exemplify, symbolize, represent, mirror.

personnel n *factory managers in charge of personnel* staff, employees, workers, workforce, labour force, manpower, human resources, liveware.

perspective n **1** *young people have a different perspective of such matters* outlook, view, viewpoint, point of view, standpoint, vantage point, stand, stance, angle, slant, attitude, frame of mind. **2** *get a perspective of the whole valley from the tower* view, vista, bird's-eye view, prospect, scene, outlook, panorama, aspect, sweep.

perspicacious adj *perspicacious of him to recognize her distress* discerning, perceptive, penetrating, percipient, sharp, sharp-witted, quick-witted, keen-witted, alert, clear-sighted, shrewd, acute, clever, intelligent, smart, judicious, wise, sagacious, sensitive, intuitive, understanding.

perspicacity n *admire his perspicacity in recognizing her distress* discernment, perception, perceptiveness, percipience, sharpness, sharp-wittedness, quick-wittedness, keen-wittedness, alertness, clear-sightedness, shrewdness, acuteness, acuity, cleverness, intelligence, smartness, judiciousness, sagacity, wisdom, sensitivity, intuition, intuitiveness, insight, understanding.

perspiration n *perspiration running down his face* sweat, moisture; *Tech* sudor.

perspire v *perspire in the heat* sweat, be dripping with sweat, be pouring with sweat, swelter, glow.

persuade v *persuade her to go despite her disinclination* prevail upon, win over, talk someone into, bring round, induce, convince, influence, sway, prompt, coerce, inveigle, cajole, wheedle; *inf* sweet-talk, soft-soap.

persuasion n **1** *their successful persuasion of the children to go* persuading, prevailing, winning over, inducement, convincing, coercion, inveiglement, cajolery, wheedling; *inf* sweet-talking, soft-soaping. **2** *use their powers of persuasion* persuasiveness, inducement, influence, coercion, inveiglement, cajolery, wheedling, suasion. **3** *it is his persuasion that the decision was a mistake* belief, opinion, view, point of view, conviction. **4** *churchmen of different persuasions* denomination, belief, creed, credo, faith, school of thought, philosophy, sect, affiliation, camp, side, faction.

persuasive adj *persuasive arguments* effective, effectual, convincing, cogent, plausible, compelling, forceful, eloquent, weighty, influential, telling.

pert adj **1** *a pert young girl* impudent, impertinent, saucy, forward, presumptuous, audacious, bold, brash, brazen, bumptious. **2** *a pert little hat* jaunty, stylish, chic, trim, smart, spruce; *inf* natty, saucy.

pertain v **1** *evidence which does not pertain to the case* be connected with, relate to, be relevant to, have relevance to, concern, apply to, be pertinent to, have reference to, have a bearing upon. **2** *the manor-house and the land pertaining to it* belong to, be a part of, be an adjunct of, go along with, be included in. **3** *the feeling of rebellion pertaining to youth* be appropriate to, be suited to, befit, fit in with, appertain to.

pertinacious adj **1** *pertinacious people refusing to give up* persistent, persevering, tenacious, resolute, determined, purposeful, insistent, stubborn, obstinate, obdurate, strong-willed, headstrong, inflexible, intransigent, wilful, mulish, pig-headed, bull-headed, intractable, refractory, perverse. **2** *make pertinacious attempts to succeed* persistent, persevering, resolute, determined, dogged, purposeful, insistent.

pertinent adj *make a few pertinent comments* relevant, appropriate, suitable, fitting, fit, apt, apposite, to the point, applicable, material, germane, to the purpose, apropos, *ad rem*.

perturb v **1** *news of the war perturbed the King* disturb, make anxious, worry, alarm, trouble, upset, disquiet, discompose, disconcert, vex, bother, agitate, unsettle, fluster, ruffle, harass. **2** *perturb the smooth running of the office* throw into confusion, confuse, throw into disorder, disarrange, throw into disarray, muddle, jumble.

perturbed adj *feel perturbed at the news | try to calm the perturbed people* disturbed, anxious, worried, alarmed, troubled, upset, disquieted, discomposed, disconcerted, vexed, agitated, unsettled, flustered, ruffled, harassed.

peruse v **1** *peruse the document before signing* read carefully, read thoroughly, scrutinize, study, pore over, inspect, examine, scan. **2** *peruse the leaflets in the waiting-room* browse through, look through, glance through, leaf through, run an eye over, scan, skim through.

pervade v *cooking smells pervaded the entire house | terror pervaded his whole being* spread through, be disseminated through, permeate, fill, pass through, extend throughout, suffuse, diffuse through, be diffused through, imbue, infuse, penetrate, infiltrate, percolate.

pervasive adj *pervasive cooking smells | pervasive feelings of terror* pervading, permeating, prevalent, suffusive, extensive, ubiquitous, omnipresent, rife, widespread, universal.

perverse adj **1** *perverse children | old people can be perverse* contrary, wayward, troublesome, unruly, difficult, awkward, unreasonable, disobedient, unmanageable, uncontrollable, rebellious, wilful, headstrong, capricious, stubborn, obstinate, obdurate, pertinacious, mulish, pig-headed, bull-headed, wrong-headed, querulous, fractious, intractable, refractory, intransigent, contumacious; *inf* bolshie, stroppy. **2** *take a perverse delight in annoying her* contradictory, unreasonable, irrational, illogical, senseless, abnormal, deviant, excessive, undue, immoderate, inordinate, outrageous.

perversion n **1** *a perversion of the truth* distortion, misuse, misrepresentation, falsification, misinterpretation, misconstruction. **2** *the treatment of his sexual perversion* deviation, aberration, abnormality, irregularity, unnaturalness, corruption, debauchery, depravity, vice, wickedness; *inf* kinkiness. **3** *such sexual perversions are very rare* deviation, aberration, abnormality, irregularity, depravity, vice, kink.

perversity n **1** *the perversity of the children | the old man's perversity* perverseness, contrariness, troublesomeness, unruliness, difficulty, awkwardness, unreasonableness, disobedience, unmanageableness, unmanageability, rebelliousness, wilfulness, stubbornness, obstinacy, obduracy, pertinacity, mulishness, pig-headedness, querulousness, fractiousness, intractability, refractoriness, intransigence, contumaciousness. *see* PERVERSE 1. **2** *appalled at the perversity of his behaviour* unreasonableness, irrationality, abnormality, deviation, excessiveness, immoderateness, outrageousness. *see* PERVERSE 2.

pervert v **1** *pervert the course of justice* turn aside, divert, deflect, avert, subvert. **2** *pervert common English expressions out of ignorance* misapply, misuse, distort, garble, warp, twist, misinterpret, misconstrue. **3** *pervert young minds* lead astray, corrupt, warp, deprave, debauch, debase, degrade, vitiate.

pervert n *a sexual pervert* deviant, deviate, degenerate, debauchee; *inf* perv, weirdo.

perverted adj *a perverted old man abusing children | a perverted interest in young boys* corrupt, corrupted, depraved, debauched, debased, vitiated, deviant, abnormal, aberrant, warped, distorted, twisted, sick, unhealthy, immoral, evil, wicked, vile; *inf* kinky.

pessimism n *his pessimism made everyone gloomy* looking on the black side, expecting the worst, lack of hope, hopelessness, gloom, gloominess, gloom and doom, cynicism, defeatism, fatalism, distrust, doubt, suspicion, resignation, depression, dejection, despair.

pessimist n *pessimists forecasting disaster* prophet of doom, cynic, defeatist, fatalist, alarmist, doubter, doubting Thomas; *inf* doom merchant, gloom merchant, doomster.

pessimistic adj *a pessimistic outlook on life* hopeless, gloomy, gloom-ridden, cynical, defeatist, fatalistic, distrustful, alarmist, doubting, suspicious, bleak, resigned, depressed, dejected, despairing.

pest n *regard the child as a pest* nuisance, bother, source of annoyance/irritation, vexation, irritant, thorn in the flesh, problem, trouble, worry, inconvenience, trial, tribulation, the bane of one's life; *inf* pain, pain in the neck, aggravation.

pester v *photographers pestering the film star | beggars pestering tourists for money* badger, hound, irritate, annoy, bother, irk, nag, fret, worry, harass, chivvy, get on someone's nerves, torment, plague, bedevil, harry; *inf* get at, bug, hassle.

pestilence n **1** *villagers dying from a/the pestilence* plague, bubonic plague, Black Death, epidemic, pandemic, disease, contagion, sickness. **2** *the pestilence of marauding neighbours* bane, blight, affliction, scourge, curse, torment.

pestilential adj **1** *a pestilential infection* plague-like, contagious, communicable, catching, epidemic, dangerous, injurious, harmful, destructive, virulent, pernicious, toxic, venomous, malign, fatal, deadly. **2** *a pestilential creature wreaking havoc in their lives* annoying, irritating, irksome, vexatious, troublesome, bothersome, tiresome.

pet[1] n *teacher's pet | she was a pet of the King* favourite, darling, idol, apple of one's eye; *inf* blue-eyed boy/girl; *Amer. inf* fair-haired boy/girl.

pet[1] adj **1** *a pet lamb* domesticated, domestic, tame, tamed, house-trained, housebroken. **2** *a pet theory/charity* favourite, favoured, cherished, prized, dear to one's heart, preferred, particular, special. **pet name** *call her daughter/husband by a pet name* affectionate name, term of endearment, endearment, nickname.

pet[1] v **1** *pet the cat* stroke, caress, fondle, pat, clap. **2** *young people petting in public* make love, kiss, cuddle, embrace, caress; *inf* canoodle, neck, smooch, snog, bill and coo.

pet[2] n *in a pet at not getting her own way* sulk, the sulks, tantrum, bad mood, mood, bad temper, ill temper, temper, ill humour, fit of pique; *inf* huff, paddy.

peter v **peter out** *great enthusiasm which petered out* fade, die away, melt away, evaporate, wane, ebb, diminish, taper off, come to nothing, die out, fail, fall through, come to a halt, come to an end.

petition n **1** *sign a petition to save the building from destruction* protest document, list of protesters, appeal, round robin. **2** *make a petition to God | made several petitions for mercy to the King* entreaty, supplication, plea, prayer, appeal, request, application, suit.

petition v *petition God | petitioned the King for mercy* entreat, beg, beseech, plead with,

make a plea to, pray, appeal to, request, ask, apply to, call upon, press, adjure, present one's suit to, sue.

petrify v **1** *the thought of speaking in public petrified her | petrified at the strange sight* terrify, strike terror into, horrify, frighten, make terror-stricken, fill with fear, panic, alarm, scare out of his/her etc wits, appal, paralyse, stun, stupefy, transfix. **2** *age had petrified the plant life* turn to stone, fossilize, calcify, ossify.

petticoat n *a frilly petticoat* slip, underskirt, undergarment.

petty adj **1** *waste time discussing petty matters/ details* trivial, trifling, minor, small, slight, unimportant, inessential, inconsequential, inconsiderable, negligible, paltry, fiddling; *inf* piffling. **2** *indulge in petty behaviour | do it out of petty spite* narrow-minded, narrow, small-minded, mean-minded, mean, ungenerous, grudging.

petulant adj *petulant children squabbling | children making petulant demands* querulous, complaining, peevish, fretful, impatient, cross, irritable, moody, crabbed, crabby, snappish, crotchety, touchy, bad-tempered, ill-tempered, ill-humoured, irascible, sulky, sullen; *inf* ratty.

phantom n **1** *imagine he saw phantoms in the graveyard* ghost, apparition, spectre, shade, spirit, revenant, wraith, shadow, phantasm; *inf* spook. **2** *dreams haunted by phantoms of evil* vision, hallucination, illusion, figment of the imagination, chimera.

phase n **1** *the various phases of the reconstruction process | an exciting phase in history* stage, part, step, chapter, point, period, time, juncture. **2** *children going through a difficult phase* stage, time, period, spell. **3** *changing phases of the moon* aspect, facet, shape, form.

phase v **phase in** *phase in new teaching methods* introduce gradually, incorporate by stages, begin using, ease in, start using. **phase out** *phase out the old machinery* withdraw/remove gradually, dispose of gradually, get rid of by stages, stop using, ease off, run down, wind down, wind up.

phenomenal adj *enjoying phenomenal success* extraordinary, remarkable, exceptional, singular, uncommon, unheard-of, unique, unparalleled, unprecedented, amazing, astonishing, astounding, unusual, marvellous, prodigious, sensational, miraculous; *inf* fantastic, fabulous, mind-boggling, mind-blowing.

phenomenon n **1** *a social phenomenon peculiar to our times* circumstances, fact, experience, occurrence, happening, event, incident, episode. **2** *the child is really a phe-nomenon | the child's compositions are regarded as something of a musical phenomenon* marvel, prodigy, rarity, wonder, sensation, miracle, nonpareil.

philander v *always philandering | accused of philandering with the girls in the office* flirt, have an affair, have a love affair, dally with, womanize, trifle/toy with the affec-tions of, play around, fool around, coquet with.

philanderer n *marry a philanderer who would never be faithful* Casanova, Don Juan, wom-anizer, woman-chaser, ladies' man, flirt, Lothario, dallier, trifler; *inf* lady-killer, wolf, stud.

philanthropic adj **1** *a philanthropic concern for his fellow-men | charity work stemming from philanthropic motives* humanitarian, humane, public-spirited, socially-con-cerned, solicitous, unselfish, selfless, altru-istic, kind-hearted. **2** *a philanthropic millionaire/organization* benevolent, benefi-cent, benignant, charitable, alms-giving, generous, kind, munificent, bountiful, bounteous, liberal, open-handed, giving, helping.

philanthropist n **1** *philanthropists showing concern for their fellow-men* humanitarian, altruist. **2** *charitable organizations funded by philanthropists* alms-giver, benefactor, patron, sponsor, giver, donor, contributor, backer, helper.

philanthropy n **1** *look after his neighbours out of philanthropy* humanitarianism, humanity, humaneness, public-spiritedness, social concern, unselfishness, selflessness, altru-ism, kind-heartedness, brotherly love. **2** *organizations dependent on the philanthropy of the townspeople* benevolence, beneficence, benignity, charity, charitableness, alms-giving, generosity, kindness, munifence, bounty, bountifulness, bounteousness, lib-erality, open-handedness, patronage, spon-sorship, giving, backing, help.

philippic n *deliver a philippic against the state* diatribe, invective, tirade, harangue, verbal onslaught, fulmination, vituperation.

philistine adj *a philistine attitude to the arts* uncultured, uncultivated, uneducated, unenlightened, unread, lowbrow, anti-intellectual, ignorant, bourgeois, boorish, barbaric.

philosopher n **1** *the Greek philosopher* philos-ophizer, scholar, metaphysicist, metaphysi-cian, sage, wise man, guru, pundit, seeker after truth. **2** *a philosopher rather than a man of action* philosophizer, thinker, theorist, theorizer.

philosophical adj **1** *read philosophical works of philosophy,* philosophic, metaphysical. **2** *in a philosophical mood* thoughtful, reflec-tive, pensive, meditative, contemplative. **3** *remain philosophical in the face of failure* calm, composed, cool, collected, cool calm and collected, self-possessed, serene, tran-quil, stoical, impassive, phlegmatic, unper-turbed, imperturbable, dispassionate, unruffled, patient, resigned, rational, logi-cal, realistic, practical.

philosophy n **1** *the philosophy of Aristotle | studying philosophy* thought, thinking, rea-soning, logic, wisdom, metaphysics, moral philosophy. **2** *his philosophy of life* beliefs, convictions, ideology, ideas, doctrine, tenets, values, principles, attitude, view, viewpoint, outlook. **3** *admire their philosophy when disaster struck* philosophicalness, calm-ness, calm, coolness, composure, equanim-ity, aplomb, self-possession, serenity, tranquillity, stoicism, impassivity, phlegm, imperturbability, dispassion, dispassionate-ness, patience, resignation, rationality, logic, realism, practicality; *inf* cool.

phlegm n **1** *coughing up phlegm* mucus, catarrh. **2** *no crisis disturbs his phlegm* calm-ness, calm, coolness, composure, equanim-ity, serenity, tranquillity, placidity, placidness, impassivity, imperturbability, dispassionateness, philosophicalness; *inf* cool. **3** *tire of the phlegm of most of her pupils* apathy, indifference, lack of interest, impassivity, sluggishness, lethargy, listless-ness, languor, dullness, indolence, inertia, inactivity, stolidness, bovineness.

phlegmatic adj **1** *a phlegmatic disposition | a phlegmatic attitude to every crisis* calm, cool, composed, cool calm and collected, serene, tranquil, placid, impassive, imperturbable, dispassionate, philosophical. **2** *tired of the lack of interest of her phlegmatic pupils* apa-thetic, indifferent, uninterested, impassive, sluggish, lethargic, listless, languorous, dull, indolent, inert, inactive, stolid, placid, bovine.

phobia n *a phobia about/towards rats | has a phobia about spiders* aversion, abnormal fear, irrational fear, obsessive fear, fear, dread, horror, terror, dislike, hatred, loathing, detestation, distaste, antipathy, revulsion, repulsion; *inf* thing, hang-up.

phone n **1** *a public phone | spend hours on the phone* telephone, mobile phone, car phone, radio-telephone; *inf* blower. **2** *give her a quick phone* phone call, telephone call, call, ring; *inf* buzz, tinkle, bell.

phone v *phone her mother for a chat* tele-phone, call, make/place a call to, give someone a call, ring, ring up, give someone a ring; *inf* buzz, give someone a buzz/ tinkle/bell, get on the blower to.

phoney adj **1** *old people taken in by phoney workmen* bogus, sham, fake, fraudulent, pseudo; *inf* cod. **2** *phoney documents* bogus, sham, counterfeit, imitation, spurious, mock, ersatz, fake, forged, feigned, simulated, make-believe, false, fraudulent. **3** *a phoney American accent* bogus, sham, counterfeit, imitation, fake, feigned, assumed, simulated, affected, contrived, false, mock, pseudo; *inf* cod.

phoney n **1** *the doctor's a phoney* impostor, pretender, sham, fraud, fake, faker, charlatan, mountebank; *inf* quack. **2** *the diamond's a phoney* counterfeit, fake, forgery, imitation, sham.

photocopy n *take a photocopy of the documents* copy, photostat, facsimile, fax; *Trademark* Xerox.

photograph n *show them a photograph of his children* | *take a photograph of the house* photo, snap, snapshot, picture, likeness, shot, print, slide, transparency.

photograph v *photograph the film star* take a photograph/photo of, take a snapshot/snap of, snap, take a picture of, take a shot of, take a likeness of, shoot, capture on film.

photographic adj **1** *a photographic record* pictorial, in photographs. **2** *a photographic description* detailed, graphic, exact, accurate, precise.

phrase n **1** *in phrases and sentences* word group, group of words. **2** *a few well-chosen phrases* expression, idiomatic expression, idiom, remark, saying, utterance, witticism, tag. **3** *an elegant turn of phrase* phrasing, phraseology, way of speaking/writing, manner of speaking/writing, style of speech/writing, style, mode of speech/writing, usage, choice of words, idiom, language, diction, parlance.

phrase v *phrase the instruction differently* put into words, put, word, express, formulate, couch, frame.

phraseology n **1** *admire the writer's phraseology* way of speaking/writing, manner of speaking/writing, style of speech/writing, style, mode of speech/writing, phrasing, usage, idiom, language, diction, parlance. **2** *express it in simple phraseology* phrasing, wording, words, choice of words, language, vocabulary, terminology.

physical adj **1** *physical and mental pain* | *physical well-being* bodily, non-mental, corporeal, corporal, somatic. **2** *the physical not spiritual considerations* non-spiritual, unspiritual,

material, earthly, corporeal, carnal, fleshly, mortal. **3** *everything physical in the universe* material, substantial, solid, concrete, tangible, palpable, visible, real.

physician n *treated by his own physician at home* doctor, doctor of medicine, medical practitioner, medical man, general practitioner, GP, specialist, consultant; *inf* doc, medic, medico, quack.

physique n *gymnasts having splendid physiques* body, body structure, build, shape, frame, form, figure.

pick v **1** *pick a new television set from the range* | *pick him for the team* pick out, choose, select, opt for, plump for, single out, handpick, decide upon, settle upon, fix upon, sift out, prefer, favour, elect. **2** *get a job picking apples* harvest, gather, collect, take in, pluck, pull, cull. **3** *pick a safe* break into, break open, force open, prise open, crack. **pick at** *children picking at their food after eating sweets* nibble at, peck at, toy with, play with, eat like a bird, show no appetite for, eat sparingly of. **pick off** *soldiers picked off by a sniper* shoot, shoot down, gun down, fire at, hit, take out. **pick on** *a teacher accused of picking on a child* punish repeatedly, blame regularly, constantly find fault with, criticize, badger. **pick out 1** *picked out from a huge list of applicants* pick, choose, select, single out, hand-pick. *see* PICK v 1. **2** *pick out his face in the crowd* make out, distinguish, tell apart, discriminate, recognize, notice. **pick up 1** *pick up the case and leave* lift, take up, raise, hoist. **2** *business starting to pick up* improve, get better, recover, be on the road to recovery, rally, make a comeback, perk up, be on the mend, make headway, make progress, take a turn for the better. **3** *manage to pick up a first edition* find, discover, locate, come across, stumble across, happen upon, unearth, obtain, get, acquire, purchase, buy. **4** *pick up tomorrow where we left off today* take up, begin, begin again, start, start again, carry on, go on, continue. **5** *pick them up on the way to the station* collect, go to get, call for, fetch, give someone a lift, give someone a ride. **6** *picked up by the police for questioning* take into custody, arrest, apprehend; *inf* collar, nab, run/pull in, nick, pinch. **7** *pick up a girl at the party* strike up an acquaintance with, take up with, fall in with, strike up a casual friendship with, strike up a sexual friendship with. **8** *pick up the basic skills* | *pick up the local language* learn, get to know, acquire a knowledge of, master; *inf* get the hang of. **9** *pick up malaria abroad* catch, contract, get, become infected with, become ill with, go/come down with. **10** *pick up some interesting news* learn, hear, get to know, glean.

pick n **1** *early purchasers have the pick of the range* choice, selection, option, preference. **2** *the pick of the crop/bunch* best, choicest, prime, cream, flower, prize, élite, *créme de la créme*.

picket n **1** *line of pickets outside the factory* picketer, demonstrator, protester, objector, rebel, dissident. **2** *part of a picket on the lookout for the enemy* sentry, watch, guard, lookout, patrol, sentinel. **3** *drive pickets into the ground* stake, post, paling, pale, peg, upright, pike, stanchion, palisade.

picket v **1** *picket the factory to keep out non-strikers* | *picket the laboratory in protest at research on animals* form a picket at, go on a picket line at, man the picket-line at, demonstrate at, launch a demonstration at, protest at, form a protest group at, blockade. **2** *picket the walls of the castle* form a sentry at, be part of the watch at, guard, patrol, form a sentinel at. **3** *picket the area where the animals were kept* enclose, fence off, box in, stake off, secure, rail off, palisade. **4** *picket the dog by the front door* tether, tie up, secure, fasten.

pickle n **1** *serve pickle with the cold meat* relish, chutney. **2** *pickle in which vegetables are preserved* marinade, brine, vinegar. **3** *what a financial pickle to be in!* plight, predicament, mess, trouble, problem, straits, crisis, tight corner; *inf* jam, fix, scrape, hole, hot water, tight spot, spot, pretty kettle of fish.

pickle v *pickle vegetables* marinade, preserve, conserve.

pick-me-up n **1** *invalids in need of a pick-me-up* tonic, restorative, energizer, bracer; *Med* roborant. **2** *the visit to the theatre was a real pick-me-up* boost, boost to the spirits, reviver, stimulus, invigoration; *inf* shot in the arm.

pickpocket n *a wallet snatched by a pickpocket* thief, purse-snatcher, petty thief; *inf* dip.

picnic n **1** *have a birthday picnic* | *a picnic on the mountainside/beach* outdoor meal, outdoor party, alfresco meal. **2** *persuading her to go was no picnic* easy task, child's play, walk-over; *inf* piece of cake, pushover, cinch, doddle, breeze.

pictorial adj **1** *a pictorial record of the holiday* in pictures, in picture form, in photographs, photographic, in snapshots. **2** *a pictorial calendar* illustrated, with illustrations, with pictures, with sketches.

picture n **1** *paint a picture of the house* | *looked at the picture of the happy scene* painting,

drawing, sketch, oil-painting, water-colour, print, canvas, delineation, portrait, portrayal, illustration, likeness, representation, similitude, semblance. **2** *take pictures at the wedding* | *keep her picture in his wallet* photograph, photo, snapshot, shot, snap, slide, print, still. **3** *his report painted a bleak picture* scene, view, image, impression, representation, vision, concept. **4** *write a graphic picture of his despair* description, portrayal, account, report, narrative, narration, story, tale, recital. **5** *the picture of health/happiness* personification, embodiment, epitome, essence, perfect example, model, exmplar, archetype. **6** *the child is the picture of his father* image, living image, double, exact likeness, duplicate, replica, carbon copy, twin; *inf* spitting image, spit and image, spit, very/dead spit, ringer, dead ringer. **7** *see a picture starring Abbot and Costello* film, motion picture; *inf* movie, flick. **put someone in the picture** *put him in the picture about the financial state of the firm* fully inform, give information to, give details to, explain the situation to, explain the circumstances to, describe the state of affairs to, bring up to date, update; *inf* clue in/up. **the pictures** *have a night out at the pictures* cinema; *inf* movies, flicks.

picture v **1** *I can picture them still* see in one's mind, see in one's mind's eye, conjure up a picture of, conjure up an image of, imagine, call to mind, visualize, see, evoke. **2** *in the drawing they were pictured against a snowy background* paint, draw, sketch, depict, delineate, portray, illustrate, reproduce, represent. **3** *film stars pictured at a charity ball* photograph, snap, show. *see* PHOTOGRAPH V.

picturesque adj **1** *a picturesque old village* | *a picturesque setting* beautiful, pretty, lovely, attractive, scenic, charming, quaint, pleasing, delightful. **2** *write a picturesque description of the events* | *use picturesque language* vivid, graphic, colourful, impressive, striking.

piddling adj **1** *ignore the piddling details* trivial, trifling, minor, small, unimportant, insignificant, petty, paltry, worthless, useless, fiddling; *inf* piffling. **2** *a piddling some of money* meagre, trifling, paltry, derisory, negligible, small; *inf* measly, piffling, Mickey Mouse.

pie n *savoury and sweet pies* pastry, tart, tartlet, pasty, quiche. **pie in the sky** *their dreams of travel are pie in the sky* false hopes, illusions, delusions, unrealizable dreams, pipedreams, daydreams, castles in the air, castles in Spain.

piebald adj *piebald horses* pied, skewbald, black and white, brown and white, dappled, brindled, spotted, mottled, speckled, flecked, variegated; *Amer* pinto.

piece n **1** *a wardrobe delivered in several pieces* part, bit, section, segment, unit. **2** *a vase broken to pieces | a dress torn to pieces* bit, fragment, smithereens, shard, shred. **3** *buy a large piece of cheese/wood* bit, section, slice, chunk, lump, hunk, wedge. **4** *a piece of cloth* length, bit, remnant, scrap, snippet. **5** *a piece of his fortune | get a piece of the action* share, slice, portion, allotment, allocation, quota, percentage, fraction, quantity. **6** *a fine piece of early Victorian furniture* example, specimen, sample, instance, illustration, occurrence. **7** *write a piece on modern theatre | disagree with his latest piece* article, item, story, report, essay, review, paper, column. **8** *one of the finest pieces by the composer* musical work, work, composition, creation, opus. **9** *one of the artist's finest pieces* work of art, work, painting, canvas, composition, creation, opus. **all in one piece** *find the vase/car/child all in one piece* unbroken, undamaged, unhurt, uninjured, safe, sound, safe and sound. **fall/go to pieces** *people going to pieces in an emergency* panic, become agitated, lose control, lose one's head, fall apart, break down; *inf* crack up.

piece v *piece together the torn parts of the page | trying to piece together all the evidence* put together, assemble, join up, fit together, unite.

pièce de résistance n *the pièce de résistance of the theatre group's performances* masterpiece, master-work, *chef d'oeuvre*, showpiece, jewel, jewel in the crown.

piecemeal adv *put the story together piecemeal* piece by piece, bit by bit, gradually, in stages, in steps, little by little, by degrees, in fits and starts.

pied adj *pied horses* piebald, black and white, dappled, brindled, spotted. *see* PIEBALD.

pier n **1** *stand on the pier to watch the boats* jetty, quay, wharf, dock, landing-stage, landing-place, landing, promenade. **2** *the piers of the bridge damaged by storms* support, upright, pillar, post, column, pile, piling, buttress.

pierce v **1** *arrows which pierced the skin | spear had pierced his shoulder* penetrate, puncture, perforate, prick, stab, spike, enter, pass through, transfix. **2** *pierce the leather to make a belt* make holes in, perforate, bore, drill. **3** *a heart pierced by the suffering of others* wound, hurt, pain, cut to the quick, affect, move, sting. **4** *torches piercing the darkness* penetrate, pass through, percolate, filter

through, light up. **5** *shrill sounds piercing the air* penetrate, pervade, permeate, fill.

piercing adj **1** *a piercing glance* penetrating, sharp, keen, searching, alert, shrewd, perceptive, probing. **2** *a piercing shriek* penetrating, shrill, ear-piercing, ear-splitting, high-pitched, loud, air-rending. **3** *a piercing intelligence* perceptive, percipient, perspicacious, discerning, quick-witted, sharp, sharp-witted, shrewd, keen, acute, astute. **4** *a piercing pain* penetrating, sharp, stabbing, shooting, intense, severe, fierce, excruciating, agonizing, exquisite. **5** *frostbitten in the piercing cold* biting, numbing, bitter, raw, keen, freezing, frigid, arctic.

piety n **1** *a family noted for their piety* piousness, religiousness, religion, holiness, godliness, devoutness, devotion to God, devotion, veneration, reverence, faith, religious duty, spirituality, sanctity, religious zeal. **2** *children noted for their filial piety* obedience, duty, dutifulness, respect, respectfulness, deference, veneration.

pig n **1** *farmers keeping pigs* hog, boar, sow, porker, grunter, swine, piglet; *inf* piggy. **2** *pigs who left hardly any food for the others* glutton, guzzler; *inf* greedy pig, hog, greedy hog, greedy guts, guts. **3** *her boss is a real pig* boor, brute, swine, animal, monster; *inf* bastard, beast, louse.

pigeon n **1** *feeding the pigeons* squab, homing pigeon, carrier pigeon. **2** *con men swindling pigeons* dupe, fool, simpleton, victim; *inf* sucker, sap, sitting duck, sitting target, soft touch, pushover. **3** *sorting the problem out's your pigeon* responsibility, business, concern, worry, province; *inf* look-out, baby.

pigeon-hole n **1** *put the papers into the students' pigeon-holes* compartment, locker, cubby-hole, niche. **2** *apt to put people in pigeon-holes* compartment, category, class, classification, slot.

pigeon-hole v **1** *pigeon-hole plans for reconstruction* postpone, put off, defer, shelve; *inf* put on ice, put on the back burner. **2** *pigeon-hole her before she even started work* compartmentalize, categorize, classify, characterize, label, tag, slot.

pigheaded adj *too pigheaded to take advice* obstinate, stubborn, stubborn as a mule, mulish, bull-headed, obdurate, tenacious, dogged, single-minded, inflexible, uncompromising, adamant, intractable, intransigent, unmalleable, headstrong, self-willed, wilful, perverse, contrary, stiff-necked.

pigment n *use a red pigment for the wallpaint | natural pigments are used to dye the fab-*

ric colouring matter, colouring agent, colourant, colour, tint, dye.

pile[1] n **1** *a pile of clothes/logs/coins* heap, bundle, stack, mound, mass, accumulation, collection, assemblage, store, stockpile, hoard, load, mountain. **2** *a pile of work to do* great deal, quantity, abundance, mountain; *inf* a lot, lots, heap, ocean, stacks, oodles, scuds. **3** *make a/his pile on the black market* fortune, money, wealth; *inf* mint, packet, bomb, pots of money, stacks of money, tidy sum. **4** *the owner of a historical pile* edifice, impressive building/structure/erection.

pile[1] v **1** *pile up the tins of vegetables* heap, stack. **2** *pile up logs for the winter* accumulate, amass, collect, gather, stockpile, hoard, store up, assemble, lay by/in. **3** *snow piled up by the roadsides* form piles, form heaps, heap up, amass, accumulate. **4** *pile his plate with food* heap, full, load, stock. **5** *commuters piling on to the train* crowd, charge, tumble, stream, flock, flood, pack, squeeze, crush, jam. **pile it on** *it was a sad case but he really piled it on* exaggerate, overstate the case, overdraw the situation, make a mountain of a molehill, build up out of all proportion; *inf* lay it on, lay it on with a trowel, blow up out of all proportion.

pile[2] n *the piles supporting the bridge collapsed* pillar, column, support, post, foundation, piling, pier, buttress, upright.

pile[3] n **1** *the pile of the carpet* soft surface, surface, nap. **2** *pile blocking up the vacuum cleaner* hair, fur, down, wool, fluff.

pile-up n *a pile-up on the motorway* crash, multiple crash, collision, multiple collision, smash, smash-up, accident, road accident.

pilfer v *pilfer money from the petty cash* steal, thieve, rob, take, filch, purloin, embezzle, misappropriate; *inf* walk off/away with, pinch, swipe, nick, lift, knock off, snaffle, snitch.

pilgrim n *pilgrims going to Bethlehem/Mecca* worshipper, devotee, shrine-visitor, traveller, palmer, hajji.

pilgrimage n *make a pilgrimage to Bethlehem/ Mecca* religious expedition, holy expedition, excursion, hajj.

pill n **1** *take a pill for a headache* tablet, capsule, pellet, lozenge, bolus. **2** *she's a real pill* nuisance, pest, bore, trial; *inf* pain, pain in the neck, drag.

pillage v *rival tribes invading and pillaging* plunder, rob, raid, loot, maraud, sack, ransack, ravage, lay waste, despoil, spoil, spoliate, depredate, rape.

pillage n *invaders guilty of pillage* pillaging, plunder, plundering, robbery, robbing, raiding, looting, marauding, sacking, ransacking, ravaging, rapine, despoiling, laying waste, spoliation, depredation.

pillar n **1** *pillars supporting the temple* column, post, pole, support, upright, pile, piling, pilaster, stanchion, peristyle. **2** *a pillar of the community* mainstay, backbone, strength, tower of strength, support, upholder, rock.

pillory n *put in the pillory for theft* stocks.

pillory v *pilloried in the press for his treatment of children* brand, stigmatize, cast a slur on, denounce, show up, hold up to shame, hold up to ridicule, expose to ridicule, ridicule, heap scorn on.

pillow n *lay one's head on the pillow* cushion, bolster, headrest.

pilot n **1** *the pilot at the aircraft's controls* airman/airwoman, aviator, aeronaut, captain, commander, copilot, first/second officer; *inf* flyer. **2** *the pilot directing the ship into the harbour* navigator, guide, steersman, helmsman. **3** *act as his pilot through life* guide, leader, conductor, director.

pilot v **1** *pilot the aircraft* fly, drive, operate, control, handle, manoeuvre. **2** *pilot the ship into the harbour* navigate, guide, steer. **3** *pilot the bill through Parliament* guide, steer, conduct, direct, shepherd.

pilot adj *pilot scheme* trial, test, experimental, model.

pimple n *put ointment on a pimple* spot, pustule, boil, swelling, papule; *inf* whitehead, zit.

pin v **1** *pin the pieces of cloth together* fasten, join, attach, secure. **2** *pin the notice to the board* attach, fasten, affix, fix, stick, tack, nail. **3** *pinned under the fallen tree* | *pinned against the wall* pinion, hold, press, restrain, constrain, hold fast, immobilize. **pin down 1** *bullies pinned the boy down* | *pinned down by the weight of the car* pinion, hold down, press down, restrain, constrain, hold fast, immobilize. **2** *he won't choose a date but you must pin him down* force, compel, make, pressure, put pressure on, pressurize, constrain, nail down. **3** *there's something I dislike about him but I can't pin it down* define, put one's finger on, put into words, put words to, express in words, express, designate, name, specify, identify, home in on. **pin something on someone** *try to pin the burglary on him* blame, blame something on someone, blame someone for something, lay the blame for something on someone, place the blame for something on someone, fix the responsibility for something on someone, attribute something to someone, impute something to someone, ascribe something to someone.

pin n **1** *fasten the hem with a pin* dressmaking pin, safety pin. **2** *a broken pin in the machine* peg, bolt, rivet, screw, dowel, post.

pinch v **1** *pinch her little brother's arm* nip, tweak, squeeze, compress. **2** *shoes pinching her feet* hurt, cause pain to, pain, crush, squeeze, cramp, confine. **3** *have to pinch and scrape to live* scrimp, skimp, stint, be sparing, be frugal, be economical, economize, be niggardly/tight-fisted/close; *inf* be stingy, be tight, be mingy. **4** *pinch money from her mother's purse* steal, thieve, rob, take, pilfer, filch, purloin, embezzle, misappropriate; *inf* walk away/off with, swipe, nick, lift, knock off, snaffle, snitch. **5** *burglars pinched by the police* arrest, take into custody, apprehend; *inf* pick up, pull in, run in, nick, nab, collar, bust, do.

pinch n **1** *give her arm a pinch* nip, tweak, squeeze. **2** *a pinch of salt* small quantity, bit, touch, trace, soupçon; *inf* smidgen, tad. **at a pinch** *at a pinch we could accommodate five people if necessary*, in case of necessity, if need be, in an emergency, just possibly. **feel the pinch** *feel the pinch during a recession* be short of money, have less money, suffer hardship, suffer poverty, suffer adversity. **if it comes to the pinch** *if it comes to the pinch, he'll have to sell the car* if it comes to the push, in an emergency, in a crisis, if things get bad, in times of hardship, if one is in difficulty, in time of need, in case of necessity, if necessary.

pinched adj *individuals looking pinched and tired* drawn, haggard, gaunt, worn, peaky, pale.

pine v **1** *pine away with grief* decline, go into a decline, lose strength, weaken, waste away, wilt, fade, languish, droop. **2** *pine for her old way of life* long for, yearn for, ache for, sigh for, hunger for, thirst for, hanker for/after, crave, covet, lust after.

pinion v **1** *pinion him to the ground* pin down, hold down, press down, restrain, constrain, hold fast, immobilize. **2** *pinion his arms to the wall* bind, tie, fasten, shackle, fetter, chain, manacle.

pink adj **1** *pink dresses* rose, rose-coloured, salmon, salmon-pink, shell-pink, flesh-coloured, pale red. **2** *pink cheeks* rosy, flushed, blushing.

pink n *the pink of condition* peak, best, height, culmination, acme, pinnacle, zenith, summit. **in the pink** *feeling in the pink after his holiday* in perfect health, in good health, very healthy, very well, hale and hearty, bursting with health, in rude health, bursting with rude health, in fine fettle.

pink v **1** *pink the leather* pierce, punch, perforate, prick, stab, bore, drill. **2** *pink the edge of the cloth* scallop, serrate, notch, crenellate.

pinnacle n **1** *the pinnacle of her success* peak, height, culmination, high point, acme, zenith, climax, crowning point, meridian, summit, apex, vertex, apogee. **2** *snow-covered pinnacles* peak, summit, top, crest, mountain, hill. **3** *pinnacles on the temple* turret, spire, obelisk, pyramid, cone.

pinpoint v *pinpoint the cause of the trouble* identify, discover, distinguish, locate, spot, home in on, put one's finger on.

pioneer n **1** *the pioneers of the Wild West* settler, colonist, colonizer, frontiersman/frontierswoman, explorer. **2** *the pioneers of television | a pioneer of cancer research* developer, innovator, ground-breaker, trailblazer, front-runner, founder, founding father, architect.

pioneer v *pioneer cancer research | pioneered the use of the drug* lay the groundwork for, lead the way for, prepare the way for, lay the foundations of, develop, introduce, launch, instigate, initiate, take the initiative in, institute, originate, set the ball rolling, create, open up, blaze a trail, break new ground.

pious adj **1** *pious members of the community attending church regularly* religious, holy, godly, spiritual, devout, devoted, dedicated, reverent, God-fearing, righteous, faithful, dutiful. **2** *dislike being patronized by pious do-gooders* sanctimonious, hypocritical, self-righteous, unctuous, pietistic, religiose; *inf* holier-than-thou, goody-goody. **3** *pious children performing filial duties* obedient, dutiful, respectful, reverent, righteous.

pipe n **1** *lay pipes under the street* tube, cylinder, conduit, main, duct, channel, conveyor, pipeline, drainpipe. **2** *smoke a pipe* brier, meerschaum, clay pipe, tobacco-pipe, peace-pipe, calumet, hookah. **3** *playing a pipe* whistle, penny-whistle, flute, recorder, fife, wind instrument. **pipes** npl *playing the pipes* bagpipes, pan-pipes.

pipe v **1** *pipe the oil to the stove* convey, duct, channel, transmit, bring in, siphon. **2** *listen to him piping* play on a pipe, play the pipes, tootle. **3** *birds piping* tweet, cheep, chirp, chirrup, peep, twitter, sing, warble, whistle, squeak. **4** *'why?' the little girl piped* chirp, shrill, squeal, squeak. **pipe down** *children told to pipe down* be quiet, quieten down, be silent, hush, hold one's tongue; *inf* shut up, button up one's lip, belt up.

pipedream n *have pipedreams of winning the pools* fantasy, illusion, daydream, castle in the air, castle in Spain, pie in the sky, delusion.

pipeline n *lay the pipeline under the street* pipe, conduit, main, duct, channel, conveyor. **in the pipeline** *price rises in the pipeline* on the way, under way, coming, imminent, about to happen, in preparation, being prepared.

piquancy n **1** *the piquancy of the sauce/flavour* spice, spiciness, pepperiness, tang, pungency, sharpness, edge, tartness, zest, zip; *inf* zing, kick, punch. *see* PIQUANT 1. **2** *the piquancy of the gossip* stimulation, intrigue, interest, fascination, allurement, raciness, saltiness, provocativeness. **3** *the piquancy of her wit* liveliness, sparkle, animation, spiritedness, sharpness, cleverness, quickness, raciness, saltiness.

piquant adj **1** *a piquant sauce/flavour* spicy, highly-seasoned, flavoursome, peppery, tangy, pungent, sharp, tart, zesty, stinging. **2** *a piquant piece of gossip* stimulating, intriguing, interesting, fascinating, alluring, racy, salty, provocative. **3** *a piquant wit* lively, sparkling, animated, spirited, sharp, clever, quick, racy, salty.

pique v **1** *her lack of interest piqued him* irritate, annoy, anger, displease, affront, put out, offend, irk, peeve, vex, nettle, gall, wound; *inf* aggravate, miff, rile. **2** *pique her curiosity* arouse, rouse, awaken, excite, stimulate, kindle, stir, whet.

pique n *full of pique at his behaviour* irritation, annoyance, anger, displeasure, affront, offence, resentment, grudge, umbrage, vexation, gall.

piracy n **1** *piracy on the high seas* buccaneering, freebooting. **2** *publishers guilty of piracy* copyright infringement, plagiarism.

pirate n **1** *pirates boarded the ship* buccaneer, rover, sea rover, sea robber, corsair, freebooter. **2** *tapes/music/poems issued by pirates* copyright infringer, plagiarist, plagiarizer.

pirate v *pirate his music/poetry* infringe the copyright of, plagiarize, illegally reproduce, copy, poach; *inf* crib, lift.

pit[1] n **1** *fall down a pit* abyss, chasm, crater, hole, cavity, excavation, quarry, coalmine, mine, diggings, working. **2** *pits in her skin* depression, hollow, dent, dint, indentation, dimple, pock-mark, pock, mark.

pit[1] v *the disease had pitted her skin* depress, dent, dint, dimple, mark, pock-mark, scar.

pit against *pit her wits against her enemy's*

set against, match against, put in opposition to, oppose against.

pit[2] n *remove the pits from the cherries* stone, pip, seed, kernel.

pitch[1] v **1** *pitch a stone in the water | pitch the bales on to the lorry* throw, cast, fling, hurl, toss, heave, launch; *inf* chuck, lob, bung. **2** *pitch a tent* put up, set up, erect, raise. **3** *trip and pitch forwards into the lake* fall headlong, fall, tumble, topple, plunge, dive. **4** *ships pitching in the storm* lurch, roll, reel, sway, rock, flounder, keel, list, make heavy weather. **pitch in 1** *everyone pitched in to finish the work* help, assist, lend a hand, join in, participate, play a part, do one's bit, cooperate, collaborate. **2** *everyone pitched in to buy a leaving present* contribute, make a contribution, make a donation, put money in; *inf* chip in.

pitch[1] n **1** *players leaving the pitch* field, ground, park, stadium, arena, sports field, playing-field. **2** *excitement reached such a pitch* level, point, degree, height, extent, intensity. **3** *the pitch of the roof* angle, slope, slant, tilt, cant, dip, inclination. **4** *get the right musical pitch* tone, timbre, sound, tonality, modulation. **5** *with one pitch* throw, cast, fling, hurl, toss, heave; *inf* chuck, lob. **6** *the pitch of the ship* pitching, lurch, roll, reeling, swaying, rocking, keeling, list. **7** *taken in by the salesman's pitch* spiel, sales talk, patter; *inf* line. **8** *the street vendor's pitch* place, station; *Scots* stance.

pitch[2] n *use pitch to make the barrels watertight* bitumen, asphalt, tar.

pitch-black adj *pitch-black nights/eyes* pitch, pitch-dark, jet-black, jet, coal-black, inky, ebony, raven, sable.

pitcher n *a pitcher of water* jug, ewer, jar, crock.

piteous adj *hear a piteous cry/tale* pitiful, to be pitied, pitiable, pathetic, distressing, affecting. *see* PITIFUL 1.

pitfall n *the pitfalls of running a small business* trap, snare, catch, stumbling-block, hazard, peril, danger, difficulty.

pith n **1** *the pith of the argument* essence, essential part, main point, point, quintessence, gist, salient point, crux, heart, heart of the matter, nub, core, meat, kernel, marrow. **2** *make a speech that lacks pith* substance, weight, moment, significance, importance, import, depth, force, vigour, power, strength, cogency.

pithy adj *a pithy remark | wrote a pithy piece of prose* terse, succinct, concise, condensed, compact, summary, epigrammatic, to the point, pointed, significant, meaningful, expressive, incisive, forceful.

pitiful adj **1** *in a pitiful condition | a pitiful sight* to be pitied, pitiable, piteous, pathetic, wretched, distressing, affecting, moving, sad, woeful, deplorable, heart-rending, heartbreaking, poignant, emotional, emotive. **2** *a pitiful excuse/coward* contemptible, despicable, poor, sorry, miserable, inadequate, worthless, base, shabby; *inf* pathetic.

pitiless adj *a pitiless tyrant* merciless, ruthless, relentless, cruel, severe, harsh, heartless, callous, brutal, inhuman, inhumane, cold-hearted, hard-hearted, unfeeling, uncaring, unsympathetic.

pittance n *earn a pittance* insufficient amount, tiny amount; *inf* peanuts, chickenfeed.

pity n **1** *show pity for her situation* commiseration, condolence, sympathy, compassion, fellow-feeling, understanding, forbearance, distress, sadness, emotion, mercy, clemency, kindness, charity. **2** *it's a pity that he left* shame, crying shame, misfortune, unfortunate thing, sad thing, sin; *inf* crime. **take pity on** *take pity on the homeless child* show compassion towards, be compassionate towards, be sympathetic/charitable towards, show sympathy for, show charity/mercy to, help.

pity v *pity the poor orphans* feel pity for, feel sorry for, weep for, grieve for, commiserate with, feel sympathy for, be sympathetic towards, sympathize with, have compassion for, be compassionate towards, feel for, show understanding towards, show forbearance towards, show mercy to, be merciful towards.

pivot n **1** *the machine turning on a pivot* axis, fulcrum, axle, swivel, spindle, central shaft. **2** *his job was the pivot of his life* central point, centre, focal point, focus, hub, heart, raison d'être. **3** *he was the pivot of the firm* key person, kingpin, key player, cornerstone, linchpin.

pivot v **1** *the machine pivots on a central shaft* turn, revolve, rotate, spin, swivel, twirl. **2** *his whole future pivots on their decision* turn on, revolve around, depend on, hinge on, hang on, rely on, be contingent on.

pixie n *children dressed up as pixies* elf, fairy, sprite, brownie.

placard n *placards showing pictures of the wanted men* poster, notice, public notice, bill, sticker, advertisement; *inf* advert.

placate v *placate the angry customer* calm, calm down, pacify, soothe, appease, conciliate, propitiate, mollify, win over.

place n **1** *the place where the accident happened* location, spot, scene, setting, position, site, situation, venue, area, region, whereabouts, locus. **2** *a sore place on her arm* spot, area, bit, part. **3** *the names of all the places in the region | visit a different place abroad each year* town, city, village, hamlet, district, locality, neighbourhood, quarter, country, state, area, region. **4** *have a place in town* house, flat, apartment, residence, home, accommodation, abode, dwelling, domicile, property, pied-à-terre; *inf* pad. **5** *occupy a lowly place in the film | win first place* position, status, grade, rank, station, standing, footing, role, niche. **6** *find a place in a law firm* position, post, job, appointment, situation, office. **7** *children asked to go back to their places* seat, position, space. **8** *put the book back in its place* position, correct position, place. **9** *not your place to criticize* function, job, role, task, duty, responsibility, charge, concern, affair, prerogative. **in place** *everything must be in place before the meeting* in position, in order, set up, arranged. **in place of** *her sister went in place of her* instead of, in lieu of, in someone's place, in someone's stead, taking the place of, as a substitute for, as an alternative for, in exchange for. **out of place 1** *with not a hair out of place* out of position, out of order, in disorder, disarranged, in disarray, disorganized, in a mess, topsy-turvy. **2** *her remarks were quite out of place* inappropriate, unsuitable, inapposite, out of keeping, unseemly, improper, unfit. **3** *feel out of place at the party* out of one's element, uncomfortable, ill-at-ease, uneasy, like a fish out of water. **put someone in his/her place** *he was trying to flirt with her but she put him in his place* take down a peg or two, humble, humiliate, mortify, make someone eat humble pie; *inf* cut down to size, settle someone's hash. **take place** *where did the murder take place?* happen, occur, come about, transpire, crop up, befall, come to pass. **take the place of** *trying to take the place of her mother* replace, substitute for, be a substitute for, act for, stand in lieu of, cover for.

place v **1** *place the books on the shelves* put, put down, position, set down, lay down, deposit, rest, stand, install, establish, settle, station, situate. **2** *place the children according to their marks in the exam* order, rank, grade, group, arrange, sort, class, classify, categorize, bracket. **3** *place her trust in him* put, lay, set, invest, consign. **4** *I know* *his face but I can't place him* identify, recognize, know, remember, put one's finger on, locate. **5** *try to place school-leavers in local firms* find employment for, find a job for, find a home for, accommodate, find accommodation for, appoint, assign, allocate.

placid adj **1** *the placid waters of the lake* still, calm, peaceful, at peace, pacific, tranquil, motionless, smooth, unruffled, undisturbed. **2** *remain placid throughout the disturbance | of a placid temperament* calm, cool, cool-headed, cool calm and collected, composed, self-possessed, serene, tranquil, equable, even-tempered, peaceable, easygoing, unmoved, undisturbed, unperturbed, imperturbable, unexcited, unexcitable, unruffled, unemotional.

plagiarize v *plagiarize part of his colleague's work* copy, pirate, poach, borrow, reproduce, appropriate; *inf* rip off, crib, lift.

plague n **1** *villagers dying from a/the plague* bubonic plague, Black Death, contagious disease, contagion, disease, pestilence, sickness, epidemic, pandemic. **2** *a plague of locusts ate the crops* huge number, miltitude, host, swarm, influx, infestation. **3** *famine and other plagues* affliction, evil, scourge, curse, blight, bane, calamity, disaster, trial, tribulation, torment, visitation. **4** *that boy's a real plague* pest, nuisance, thorn in the flesh, problem, bother, source of annoyance/irritation, irritant, the bane of one's life; *inf* pain, pain in the neck, aggravation.

plague v **1** *plagued with/by poor health* afflict, cause suffering to, torture, torment, bedevil, trouble. **2** *plagued by her little brother* annoy, irritate, bother, disturb, worry, pester, vex, harass, torment, tease; *inf* hassle, bug.

plain adj **1** *it was plain that he was guilty* clear, clear as crystal, crystal-clear, obvious, evident, apparent, manifest, transparent, patent, unmistakable. **2** *plain indications of his guilt* clear, clear-cut, obvious, evident, apparent, manifest, visible, discernible, perceptible, distinct, transparent, patent, noticeable, pronounced, marked, striking, unmistakable, conspicuous. **3** *a plain statement of the facts* clear, clear-cut, simple, straightforward, uncomplicated, comprehensible, intelligible, understandable, lucid, unambiguous. **4** *live on a plain diet | have a plain lifestyle* simple, austere, stark, severe, basic, ordinary, unsophisticated, Spartan. **5** *the plain furnishings | a plain style of decoration* restrained, muted, simple, austere, stark, bare, basic, unadorned, undecorated, unembellished,

unornamented, unpatterned, Spartan. **6** *rather a plain child* unattractive, illfavoured, ugly, unprepossessing, unlovely; *Amer* homely. **7** *a plain man* simple, straightforward, ordinary, average, typical, unpretentious, unassuming, unaffected, artless, guileless, sincere, honest, plainspeaking, plain-spoken, frank, candid, blunt, outspoken, forthright, direct, downright.

plain adv *that was just plain stupid* downright, utterly, completely, totally, thoroughly, positively, incontrovertibly, unquestionably, undeniably, simply.

plain n *corn growing on the plain* flatland, lowland, grassland, prairie, steppe, tundra.

plain-spoken adj *pride himself on being plainspoken* plain-speaking, frank, candid, blunt, outspoken, forthright, direct, downright, unequivocal, unambiguous.

plaintive adj *the plaintive cries of the lost* mournful, doleful, melancholy, sad, sorrowful, unhappy, disconsolate, wretched, woeful, grief-stricken, heartbroken, broken-hearted, pathetic, pitiful, piteous.

plan n **1** *draw up an escape plan | think up a plan to make money* plan of action, scheme, system, procedure, method, programme, schedule, project, way, means, strategy, tactics, formula. **2** *our plan is to emigrate* idea, scheme, proposal, project, intention, intent, aim, hope, aspiration, ambition. **3** *look at the architect's plan for the new building* drawing, scale drawing, blueprint, layout, sketch, diagram, chart, map, illustration, representation, delineation.

plan v **1** *plan a picnic for tomorrow* arrange, organize, line up, schedule, programme. **2** *plan the reconstruction of the company* devise, design, plot, formulate, frame, outline, sketch out, draft, prepare, develop, shape, build, concoct, contrive, think out. **3** *plan a garden* draw up a plan of, design, make a drawing of, draw up a layout of, sketch out, make a chart of, map out, make a representation of. **4** *we're planning to emigrate* make plans, intend, aim, propose, mean, purpose, contemplate, envisage, foresee.

plane n **1** *objects standing on a plane* flat surface, level surface, the flat. **2** *on a different intellectual plane* level, stratum, stage, degree, position, rank, footing. **3** *planes taking off from the airport* aeroplane, aircraft, jet, jumbo jet; *Amer* airplane.

plane adj *require a plane surface* flat, level, horizontal, even, flush, smooth, regular, uniform.

plane v **1** *aircraft/seagulls planing through the air* glide, float, drift, volplane. **2** *boats planing across the water* glide, skim, skate.

plant n **1** *buy plants for the garden | grow house-plants* flower, vegetable, herb, shrub, weed. **2** *invest in new plant* machinery, equipment, apparatus, gear. **3** *work in the office, not the plant* factory, works, foundry, mill, workshop, shop, yard.

plant v **1** *plant sweet peas in the spring to flower in the summer* put in the ground, implant, set out, sow, scatter. **2** *plant his feet firmly on the ground* place, position, set, situate. **3** *plant an idea in his head* put, place, fix, establish, lodge, imbed, insert. **4** *plant a microphone in his bedroom* place secretly, hide, conceal, secrete.

plaque n *a plaque on the wall where the hero died* plate, stone plate, metal plate, panel, slab, tablet, sign, brass.

plaster n **1** *wait till the plaster is dry before painting the walls* stucco, plasterwork. **2** *ceiling decorations made of plaster | a broken leg in plaster* plasterwork, plaster of Paris, gypsum. **3** *put a plaster on the child's grazed knee* sticking-plaster, adhesive dressing; *Trademark* Elastoplast, Band-Aid.

plaster v *plaster her face with make-up* cover thickly, spread, coat, smear, overlay, bedaub. **plaster down** *plaster down his hair with gel* flatten, smooth down, sleek down.

plastic adj **1** *plastic substances such as clay* mouldable, shapable, ductile, fictile, pliant, pliable, supple, flexible, soft. **2** *the plastic minds/personalities of young children* impressionable, responsive, receptive, malleable, mouldable, ductile, pliable, supple, flexible, compliant, tractable, manageable, controllable, docile. **3** *a plastic charm* false, artificial, synthetic, spurious, sham, bogus, assumed, superficial, specious, meretricious, pseudo; *inf* phoney.

plate n **1** *serve food on plates* dish, platter, dinner plate, side plate. **2** *serve generous plates* plateful, helping, portion, serving. **3** *a plate on the church-wall commemorating his heroism* plaque, tablet, sign, brass. **4** *a children's book with many coloured plates* illustration, picture, photograph, print, lithograph. **5** *steel plates used in shipbuilding* sheet, panel, slab.

plateau n **1** *stand on the plateau to view the valley below* elevated plain, highland, upland, tableland. **2** *prices reaching a plateau after a period of high inflation* quiescent period, resting/flat period, quiet time, let-up, break, respite, lull.

platform n **1** *deliver a speech from the platform* dais, rostrum, podium, stage, stand. **2** *fight the election on a platform of improved welfare services* programme, policy, manifesto, party line, plan, plan of action, objectives, principles, tenets.

platitude n *write in platitudes rather than in creative prose* cliché, truism, hackneyed expression, commonplace, stock expression, trite phrase, banal phrase, banality, stereotyped phrase, bromide, inanity.

platitudinous adj *tired of his platitudinous remarks* hackneyed, overworked, clichéd, commonplace, stock, trite, banal, stereotyped, set, stale, well-worn, tired, vapid, inane; *inf* corny.

platonic adj *a platonic relationship* non-romantic, non-sexual, non-physical, friendly, spiritual, intellectual.

platoon n *the officer in charge of the platoon* squadron, squad, company, patrol, group.

platter n *serve the meal on a platter* serving-plate, salver, plate, dish, tray.

plaudits npl *receive the plaudits of his colleagues* praise, acclaim, acclamation, applause, ovation, congratulations, compliments, cheers, bouquets, approval, approbation, commendation, accolade, pat on the back.

plausible adj *an excuse that was far from plausible | put forward a plausible argument* tenable, cogent, reasonable, believable, credible, convincing, persuasive, likely, probable, conceivable, imaginable.

play v **1** *time to play rather than work* amuse oneself, entertain oneself, enjoy oneself, have fun. **2** *children playing in the park* play games, frolic, frisk, gambol, romp, cavort, sport, disport oneself. **3** *play a musical instrument* perform on. **4** *play Ophelia in Hamlet* play the part of, act, act the part of, perform, portray, represent, execute. **5** *play a trick on* perform, carry out, execute, do, accomplish, discharge, fulfill. **6** *play football* take part in, participate in, engage in, be involved in. **7** *play against the neighbouring team* compete against, contend against, oppose, take on, challenge, vie with, rival. **8** *sunlight playing on the water | a smile playing on her lips* move lightly, dance, flit, dart. **play around** *accuse her husband of playing around* philander, womanize, have an affair, have a love affair, fool around; *inf* mess about. **play at** *play at being a businesswoman* pretend to be, give the appearance of, assume/affect the role of; *inf* make like. **play ball** *want to do business but they refused to play ball* cooperate, collaborate, play along, go along with the plan, show willing, be willing. **play down** *play down his part in the crime* make light of, make little of, gloss over, minimize, diminish, set little store by, underrate, underestimate, undervalue, think little of; *inf* soft-pedal. **play for time** *try to play for time while his friend got away* stall, temporize, gain time, hang back, hang fire, procrastinate, delay, filibuster, stonewall. **play it by ear** *we have no plans - we're going to play it by ear* improvise, extemporize, ad lib, take it as it comes. **play on** *friends playing on his weakness for beautiful blondes* exploit, take advantage of, turn to one's account, profit by, capitalize on, impose on, trade on, milk, abuse, misuse; *inf* walk all over. **play the fool** *always playing the fool even in serious situations* act the fool, fool about/around, monkey about/around, clown, clown around, act the clown, horse around; *inf* act the goat, lark around, mess about/around. **play the game** *being honourable himself he expects everyone else to play the game* play fair, be fair, play by the rules, abide by the rules, follow the rules, be a good sport, toe the line. **play up 1** *this played up his eyes which are his best feature* emphasize, put/lay emphasis on, accentuate, bring/draw/call attention to, point up, underline, underscore, highlight, spotlight, give prominence to, bring to the fore, stress. **2** *children playing up when they have a new teacher* misbehave, be misbehaved, be naughty, be mischievous, be disobedient, be awkward, give trouble; *inf* be stroppy, be bolshie. **3** *children playing the teacher up* be naughty/mischievous/disobedient/troublesome to, annoy, irritate, vex, be a nuisance to, be a thorn in the flesh/side of; *inf* be a pain to, be a pain in the neck to. **4** *his injured leg was playing up* cause trouble, be painful, hurt, be sore, cause pain; *inf* give someone gyp. **5** *the car is playing up* be not working properly, be malfunctioning, malfunction; *inf* be on the blink, be wonky. **play up to** *she's always playing up to the boss so as to get her own way* flatter, ingratiate oneself with, try to get on the good side of, curry favour with, fawn over, toady to; *inf* soft-soap, suck up to, butter up, be all over, lick someone's boots. **play with 1** *children told not to play with their pencils* fiddle with, toy with, fidget with, fool about/around with; *inf* mess about/around with. **2** *he's only playing with her affections and isn't at all serious about their relationship* trifle with, toy with, dally with, amuse oneself with.

play n **1** *children at play | prefer play to work* amusement, entertainment, recreation, diversion, leisure, enjoyment, fun, merry-

making, revelry. **2** *appear in a play by a local dramatist* drama, stage play, stage show, radio play, television play, teleplay, comedy, tragedy, farce. **3** *the play of supernatural forces* action, activity, operation, agency, working, functioning, exercise, interaction, interplay. **4** *need more play on the fishing-line* movement, freedom of movement, free motion, slack; *inf* give. **5** *give full play to her emotions* scope, range, latitude, liberty, licence, freedom, indulgence, free rein. **6** *injure the child accidentally in play* fun, jest, joking, sport, teasing.

playboy n *just a playboy without any interest in work* pleasure-seeker, man-about-town, socialite, rake, roué, womanizer, philanderer, ladies' man, lady-killer; *inf* gay dog.

player n **1** *one of the players in the tennis/football match* competitor, contestant, participant, team-member, sportsman/sportswoman. **2** *one of the players in the theatre company* actor/actress, performer, entertainer, artist, artiste, trouper, Thespian. **3** *several of the players in the orchestra* performer, musician, instrumentalist, artist, artiste, virtuoso.

playful adj **1** *playful kitten | in playful mood* fun-loving, full of fun, high-spirited, frisky, skittish, coltish, frolicsome, sportive, mischievous, impish, puckish. **2** *a playful remark* in fun, in jest, joking, jesting, humorous, fun, facetious, waggish, tongue-in-cheek, arch, roguish.

playground n *take the children to the playground* play area, park, playing-field, recreation ground.

playwright n *plays written by various playwrights* dramatist, dramaturge, dramaturgist.

plea n **1** *make a plea to the King to save his mother's life* appeal, entreaty, imploration, supplication, petition, prayer, request, solicitation, suit, invocation. **2** *enter a plea of guilty | her plea was not guilty* answer, statement. **3** *produce evidence in support of his plea against the accused* allegation, case, suit, action, claim. **4** *ignore her pleas of another engagement* excuse, pretext, claim, vindication.

plead v **1** *plead with the judge to show mercy* appeal to, beg, entreat, beseech, implore, petition, make supplication to, supplicate, importune, pray to, solicit, request, ask earnestly, present one's suit to. **2** *plead insanity as the reason for his crime* put forward, state, assert, argue, claim, allege.

pleasant adj **1** *a pleasant experience* pleasing, pleasurable, agreeable, enjoyable, entertaining, amusing, delightful, satisfying, gratifying, nice, good, fine, welcome, acceptable; *inf* lovely. **2** *a pleasant person/ manner* agreeable, friendly, amiable, affable, genial, likeable, nice, good-humoured, charming, engaging, winning, delightful; *inf* lovely.

pleasantry n **1** *exchange pleasantries with his neighbour every morning* good-natured remark, polite remark. **2** *try to laugh at the speaker's pleasantries* joke, jest, quip, witticism, *bon mot*, sally; *inf* wisecrack.

please v **1** *try to find a show that will please his mother* give pleasure to, be agreeable to, make pleased/happy/glad etc, gladden, delight, cheer up, charm, divert, entertain, amuse, tickle, satisfy, gratify, fulfil, content, suit; *inf* tickle pink. **2** *do as one pleases* want, wish, see fit, will, like, desire, be inclined, prefer, opt.

pleased adj *give a pleased smile* happy, glad, cheerful, delighted, thrilled, elated, contented, satisfied, gratified, fulfilled, over the moon, as pleased as Punch; *inf* on cloud nine.

pleasing adj **1** *a pleasing experience* pleasant, pleasurable, agreeable, enjoyable, entertaining, amusing, delightful, satisfying, gratifying, nice, good, fine, welcome, acceptable; *inf* lovely. **2** *he had/was a pleasing personality* pleasant, agreeable, friendly, amiable, affable, genial, likeable, nice, good-humoured, charming, engaging, winning, delightful; *inf* lovely.

pleasure n **1** *events which bring pleasure* happiness, gladness, delight, joy, enjoyment, entertainment, amusement, diversion, satisfaction, gratification, fulfilment, contentment. **2** *one of his pleasures was to play the piano* source of pleasure, delight, joy, enjoyment, diversion, recreation. **3** *the pursuit of pleasure* delight, joy, enjoyment, diversion, recreation. **4** *what is your pleasure?* wish, desire, will, inclination, preference, choice, option, purpose.

plebeian adj **1** *of plebeian origins* lower-class, low-class, low, low-born, working-class, proletarian, common, peasant, mean, ignoble. **2** *have plebeian tastes* uncultivated, uncultured, unrefined, coarse, common, base; *inf* plebby.

plebeian n *aristocrats looking down on the plebeians* common person, commoner, man/ woman/person in the street, proletarian, working peasant; *inf* pleb, prole.

pledge n **1** *give his pledge to look after the children* promise, word, word of honour, vow, assurance, undertaking, oath, covenant, warrant. **2** *give his watch as a pledge that he would repay the loan* security, surety, guar-

antee, collateral, bond, earnest, gage, deposit, pawn. **3** *give her a ring as a pledge of his love* token, symbol, sign, mark, testimony, proof, evidence. **4** *drink a pledge to colleagues who were retiring* toast, health.

pledge v **1** *he pledged that he would support the children* promise, give one's word, vow, give one's assurance, give an undertaking, undertake, take an oath, swear, swear an oath, vouch, engage, contract. **2** *pledge one's house as security for a personal loan* mortgage, put up as collateral, guarantee, plight, pawn. **3** *pledge the bride and groom* drink to the health of, drink to, toast.

plentiful adj *plentiful supplies of food* abundant, copious, ample, profuse, lavish, liberal, generous, large, huge, bumper, infinite.

plenty n *the years of plenty* plentifulness, plenteousness, affluence, prosperity, wealth, opulence, luxury, abundance, copiousness, fruitfulness, profusion. **plenty of** *have plenty of money* enough, sufficient, a good deal of, a great deal of, masses of; *inf* lots of, heaps of, stacks of, piles of.

plethora n *a plethora of good advice* overabundance, superabundance, excess, superfluity, surplus, surfeit, glut.

pliable adj **1** *a pliable substance* flexible, bendable, bendy, pliant, elastic, supple, stretchable, ductile, plastic. **2** *expect women to be pliable* malleable, yielding, compliant, docile, biddable, tractable, manageable, governable, controllable, amenable, adaptable, flexible, impressionable, influenceable, persuadable.

plight n *the plight of the homeless | the plight they're in* unfortunate situation, sorry condition, predicament, trouble, difficulty, dire straits, extremity, tight corner; *inf* hole, pickle, spot, jam.

plod v *plod along the road* walk heavily, trudge, clump, stomp, lumber, tramp, drag oneself along, plough. **plod away** *plod away at/with one's work* toil away at, labour at, soldier on with, slog away at, drudge away at, persevere with, peg away at, grind away at; *inf* plug away at.

plot n **1** *grow vegetables in a plot* piece of ground, patch, allotment, lot, parcel. **2** *nobels planning a plot against the King* conspiracy, intrigue, secret plan, secret scheme, stratagem. **3** *the plot of the novel/ play* action, theme, subject, story line, story, scenario, thread.

plot v **1** *plot the escape route | plot the new construction site* map out, make a plan/drawing of, draw, draw a diagram of, draw the layout of, make a blueprint/chart of, sketch out, outline. **2** *plot the battle-sites on the map* mark, chart, map. **3** *nobles plotting against the King* take part in a plot, scheme, conspire, participate in a conspiracy, intrigue, form an intrigue. **4** *plot the King's downfall* plan, hatch, scheme, construe, concoct, devise, frame, think up, dream up, conceive; *inf* cook up.

plough v *plough the field* till, work, cultivate, break up, turn up. **plough into** *the car ploughed into a crowd of people on the pavement* plunge into, lunge into, career into, crash into, smash into, bulldoze into, hurtle into, drive into. **plough through** *plough through the mud* plod through, trudge through, clump through, push one's way through, forge one's way through, wade through, flounder through.

ploy n *a ploy to distract the teacher's attention* dodge, ruse, scheme, trick, stratagem, manoeuvre, move.

pluck v **1** *pluck a rose from the bush | pluck the burning paper from the fire* pull, pull off/out, remove, extract. **2** *pluck flowers to make perfume | pluck blackberries for jam* gather, collect, harvest, take in, pull, cull. **3** *sit plucking nervously at his hair | plucking at her mother's skirt* tug at, pull at, clutch at, snatch at, catch at, tweak; *inf* yank. **4** *pluck the string of the guitar* finger, strum, pick, plunk, thrum, twang.

pluck n *require a lot of pluck to go into the jungle alone* courage, bravery, valour, heroism, intrepidity, fearlessness, mettle, nerve, backbone, determination, boldness, daring, spirit, audacity; *inf* gumption, grit, guts, spunk, bottle.

plucky adj *the plucky young man saved his friend from drowning* courageous, brave, valiant, valorous, heroic, intrepid, fearless, mettlesome, gritty, determined, bold, daring, spirited, audacious; *inf* gutsy, spunky.

plug n **1** *put a plug in to prevent the water/oil escaping* stopper, bung, cork, stopple, seal. **2** *a plug of tobacco* cake, chew, twist, quid, wad. **3** *give him a free plug for his book on the television programme* publicity, advertisement, commercial, promotion, puff, push, mention; *inf* advert, ad, hype.

plug v **1** *plug the hole to prevent the water/oil escaping* stop up, close off, bung, cork, dam up, block, stopper, stopple, seal off, pack, stuff. **2** *arrested for plugging his enemy* shoot, shoot down, gun down, put a bullet in, hit, take out, pick off, pot. **3** *plug his new book on a television show* publicize, promote, give publicity to, advertise, give a puff to, puff up, push, give a push to, give a mention to,

write up, build up; *inf* hype, hype up. **plug away** *plug away at the investigation | must keep plugging away at his work* toil away at, labour at, soldier on with, slog away at, plod away at, drudge away at, persevere with, peg away at, grind away at.

plum adj *get a plum job* prize, first-class, choice, best, excellent.

plumb adv **1** *cliffs rising up plumb from the sea* vertically, perpendicularly, straight up, straight up and down. **2** *placed plumb in the centre* exactly, precisely, right, dead, slap; *inf* bang, spot on. **3** *plumb crazy* utterly, absolutely, completely, totally, entirely, wholly, quite, stark.

plumb v *plumb the mysteries of computer technology* probe, search out, delve into, explore, scrutinize, investigate, inspect, examine, sound out, go into, fathom, unravel. **plumb the depths of** *plumb the depths of despair | jokes which plumb the depths of bad taste* reach the lowest possible level of, reach the lowest point, reach the nadir of.

plummet v **1** *the plane plummeted to the ground* fall perpendicularly, fall headlong, plunge, hurtle, nosedive, dive, drop. **2** *prices plummeted* fall steeply, plunge, tumble, nosedive, take a nosedive, drop rapidly, go down.

plump adj *plump little girls | plump people trying to slim* chubby, round, rounded, well-rounded, of ample proportions, rotund, buxom, stout, fat, fattish, obese, corpulent, fleshy, portly, tubby, dumpy, podgy, roly-poly, well-covered; *inf* well-upholstered, beefy.

plump v **1** *plump down into a chair* fall, drop, flop, plonk, sink, collapse. **2** *plump the dish down on the table* set down, deposit, plonk, dump. **3** *children plumping for a day at the sea* decide on, choose, pick, select, opt for, vote for.

plunder v **1** *enemy forces plundering the villages* rob, pillage, loot, raid, ransack, rifle, strip, fleece, ravage, lay waste, despoil, spoil, spoliate, depredate, harry, maraud, sack, rape. **2** *plunder food* steal, thieve, rob, purloin, filch, make off with; *inf* walk away/off with, snaffle.

plunder n **1** *the plunder of the village* plundering, robbery, robbing, pillaging, looting, raiding, ransacking, despoiling, laying waste, harrying, marauding, rapine. *see* PLUNDER V 1. **2** *take their plunder back to their camp* stolen goods, loot, booty, spoils, prize, pillage, ill-gotten gains; *inf* swag.

plunge v **1** *plunge the dagger into his back* thrust, stick, jab, push, drive. **2** *the man on the deck plunged into the sea* dive, nosedive, jump, plummet, drop, fall, fall headlong, swoop down, descend. **3** *plunge the house into darkness* throw, cast, pitch. **4** *plunge his burnt hand into cold water* immerse, sink, dip, douse. **5** *the car plunged forward|plunge into matrimony* charge, lurch, rush, dash, hurtle, career. **6** *house prices plunged during the recession* fall steeply, drop rapidly, go down, plummet, tumble, nosedive, take a nosedive.

plunge n **1** *witness his plunge into the sea* dive, nosedive, jump, fall, drop, swoop, descent. **2** *the car's sudden plunge forward* charge, lurch, rush, dash. **3** *an unexpected plunge in house prices* fall, drop, tumble, nosedive.

plus prep **1** *3 plus 3 makes 6* and, added to. **2** *we have to get four people plus their luggage into the car* as well as, in addition to, added to, and, coupled with, with.

plus n *he likes the job - it's a plus that it's well paid* bonus, extra, added advantage, additional benefit, fringe benefit, perquisite; *inf* perk.

plush adj *plush furnishings* luxurious, luxury, de luxe, sumptuous, lavish, gorgeous, opulent, rich, costly; *inf* ritzy, classy.

plutocrat n *plutocrats with plenty of money to spend* rich person, person of means, capitalist, tycoon, magnate, millionaire, billionaire, Midas, Croesus; *inf* fat cat, moneybags.

ply v **1** *a woodman plying his saw|plying the oars* wield, use, operate, work, utilize, employ, manipulate, handle. **2** *ply his trade as a street-merchant* carry on, practise, work at, engage in, pursue, follow, occupy oneself with, busy oneself with. **3** *ply them with questions* bombard, assail, besiege, beset, harass, importune; *inf* hassle. **4** *ply them with food and drink* supply, provide, lavish, shower, load, heap. **5** *ships plying between England and France|buses plying between two cities* travel regularly, go regularly, ferry, shuttle.

poach v **1** *poach rabbits/pheasants* hunt illegally, take illegally, kill illegally, trap illegally, steal. **2** *poach on his neighbour's property/territory* trespass on, encroach on, infringe on, intrude on. **3** *poach his friend's ideas* steal, appropriate, misappropriate, copy, pirate; *inf* lift, rip off.

pocket n **1** *pockets on the side of the suitcase* pouch, compartment, receptacle. **2** *luxury goods beyond his pocket* budget, means, resources, finances, funds, capital, assets. **3** *isolated pockets of resistance to the govern-* ment small area, small region, small district, small zone.

pocket adj *a pocket edition of the reference book* small, little, miniature, compact, concise, abridged, potted.

pocket v *shop assistants pocketing part of the takings* take for oneself, appropriate, misappropriate, steal, thieve, purloin, filch; *inf* lift, nick, swipe, snaffle.

pod n *pea-pod|bean-pod* shell, husk, hull, shuck.

podgy adj **1** *a podgy man with a long thin woman* small and fat/obese/corpulent, short and stout, round, rotund, roly-poly, dumpy, squat, stubby, stumpy, chubby, tubby; *inf* pudgy. **2** *podgy fingers* short and fat, plump, fleshy, stubby, stumpy.

podium n *deliver an address from the podium* platform, stage, dais, rostrum, stand.

poem n *have a poem published in an anthology* verse composition, verse, verselet, ode, sonnet, ballad, song, lyric, lay, elegy, rhyme, limerick, haiku, jingle.

poet n *an amateur poet* verse-maker, versifier, rhymer, rhymester, sonneteer, balladmonger, balladeer, lyricist, bard, minstrel.

poetic adj **1** *write poetic works* of poetry, poetical, metrical, rhythmical, lyrical, elegaic. **2** *poetic language* imaginative, creative, figurative, symbolic, flowery. **3** *a poetic rendering of the symphony* aesthetic, artistic, tasteful, graceful, elegant, sensitive.

poetry n *write poetry rather than prose* poems, verse, verses, versification, metrical composition, rhythmical composition, rhymes, rhyming.

pogrom n *a pogrom ordered by the invading tyrant* massacre, wholesale, slaughter, general slaughter, mass killing, mass murder, mass homicide, carnage, blood bath, genocide, ethnic cleansing, megadeath.

poignancy n **1** *the poignancy of the farewell| the poignancy of her emories* tenderness, emotionalness, emotion, sentiment, feeling, pathos, sadness, sorrowfulness, tearfulness, evocativeness. *see* POIGNANT 1. **2** *the poignancy of the sight of the two orphans* pitifulness, piteousness, pathos, sadness, sorrow, misery, pain, distress, tragedy.

poignant adj **1** *poignant farewell/memories* moving, affecting, touching, tender, emotional, sentimental, heartfelt, heart-moving, sad, sorrowful, tearful, evocative. **2** *the poignant sight of the weeping orphans* moving, affecting, touching, pitiful, piteous, pitiable, pathetic, sad, sorrowful, mournful, wretched, miserable, painful, distressing, upsetting, heart-moving, tragic.

point n **1** *the point of the spear/tool* sharp end, tapered end, tip, top, extremity, prong, spike, tine. **2** *points at the end of sentences* full stop, full point, stop, period. **3** *ships sailing round the point* promontory, headland, head, foreland, cape, bluff. **4** *found dead at a point near her home* place, position, location, situation, site, spot, area, locality. **5** *abrupt to the point of rudeness* extent, degree, stage. **6** *reach an important point in her life* stage, position, circumstance, condition. **7** *have to die at some point* point/moment in time, time, juncture, stage, period, moment, instant. **8** *when it came to the point he couldn't face her* critical point, decisive point, crux, moment of truth, point of no return. **9** *explain the situation point by point* detail, item, particular. **10** *get to the point | the point of the question* main point, central point, essential point, focal point, salient point, keynote, heart of the matter, essence, nub, core, pith, marrow, meat, crux. **11** *miss the point of the story* meaning, significance, signification, import, essence, gist, substance, drift, thrust, burden, theme, tenor, vein. **12** *raise various points during the discussion* subject, subject under discussion, issue, topic, question, matter, item. **13** *arguments that lack point* effectiveness, cogency, force, power, potency. **14** *the various points of the argument* part, element, constituent, component, ingredient. **15** *the point of the exercise is to make some money | what is the point of it?* aim, purpose, object, objective, goal, intention, reason for, use, utility. **16** *kindness is one of his strong points* characteristic, trait, attribute, quality, feature, property, predisposition, streak, peculiarity, idiosyncrasy. **17** *have more points than the other team* mark, score. **beside the point** *it's beside the point what he thinks - he's not on the deciding committee* irrelevant, immaterial, incidental, not to the point, not germane, not to the purpose. **in point of fact** *people think he's stupid but in point of fact he's brilliant* in fact, as a matter of fact, really, in reality, in truth, truly. **point of view 1** *listen to everyone's point of view before making a decision* view, viewpoint, opinion, belief, attitude, feeling, sentiment, stand, standpoint, stance, position. **2** *look at the situation from a different point of view* viewpoint, angle, slant, perspective, standpoint, outlook. **to the point** *his remarks were very much to the point* pertinent, relevant, germane, applicable, apropos, apposite, appropriate, apt, fitting, suitable. **up to a point** *I*

agree with you up to a point to some extent, to some degree, in part, partly.

point v *point the gun at his victim* direct, aim, level, train. **point out** *point out the disadvantages of the proposal* call attention to, draw attention to, indicate, show, specify, designate, identify, mention, allude to. **point to** *all the evidence points to the fact that he is the murderer* indicate, show, signify, suggest, be evidence of, evidence. **point up** *point up the difference between them* emphasize, put/lay emphasis on, stress, lay stress on, accentuate, underline, underscore, give prominence to, highlight, spotlight, play up, bring to the fore.

point-blank adv **1** *shoot his victim point-blank* at close range, close up, close to. **2** *ask him point-blank for his reasons | refuse point-blank to go* directly, plainly, straight, straightfowardly, frankly, candidly, forthrightly, bluntly, openly, explicitly, unequivocally, unambiguously.

pointed adj **1** *the pointed end of the stick* sharp, sharp-edged, edged, cuspidate, acicular. **2** *a pointed remark* cutting, trenchant, biting, incisive, penetrating, forceful, telling, significant. **3** *treat her with a pointed indifference* obvious, evident, conspicuous, striking, emphasized, unmistakable.

pointer n **1** *the pointer on the speedometer* indicator, needle, hand. **2** *indicate the relevant place on a map with a pointer* stick, rod, cane. **3** *the older players will give the trainee a few pointers* tip, hint, piece of advice, suggestion, guideline, recommendation. **4** *some pointers to the likely text of the chairman's speech* indication, indicator, clue, sign.

pointless adj **1** *it is pointless to try to go on in this bad weather* futile, useless, in vain, unavailing, to no purpose, valueless, unproductive, senseless, absurd, foolish, nonsensical, stupid, silly. **2** *a few pointless remarks* meaningless, insignificant, vague, empty, worthless, irrelevant, senseless, fatuous, foolish, nonsensical, stupid, silly, absurd, inane.

poise n **1** *admire her poise in difficulties* composure, equanimity, self-possession, aplomb, presence of mind, self-assurance, self-control, calmness, coolness, collectedness, serenity, dignity, imperturbability, suaveness, urbanity, elegance; *inf* cool. **2** *admire the poise of the ballet dancers* balance, equilibrium, control, grace, gracefulness.

poise v **1** *poise a jug of water on her head* balance, steady, position, support. **2** *poise one-*

self to jump steady, get into position, brace, get ready, prepare. **3** *the hawk poised in mid-air ready to attack* hang, hang suspended, float, hover.

poised adj **1** *a very poised young woman* composed, serene, self-possessed, self-assured, self-controlled, calm, cool, cool calm and collected, dignified, imperturbable, unperturbed, unruffled, suave, urbane, elegant; *inf* unflappable. **2** *soldiers poised ready to attack | the deputy was poised ready to take over the president's job* ready, prepared, all set, standing by, waiting, waiting in the wings.

poison n **1** *kill the woman by means of poison* venom, toxin. **2** *a poison in our society* blight, bane, contagion, cancer, canker, malignancy, corruption, pollution.

poison v **1** *a nurse who poisoned her patient* administer poison to, give poison to, kill by poison, murder by poison. **2** *his wound became poisoned* infect, make septic. **3** *poison the environment/soil* contaminate, pollute, blight, spoil. **4** *poison their minds* corrupt, warp, pervert, deprave, defile, debauch.

poisonous adj **1** *poisonous snakes* venomous. **2** *poisonous plants/chemicals* toxic, venomous, deadly, fatal, lethal. **3** *a poisonous influence on society* cancerous, malignant, corrupting, polluting, harmful, injurious, noxious, pernicious, spiteful, malicious, rancorous, malevolent, vicious, vindictive, slanderous, libellous, defamatory.

poke v **1** *poke him in the ribs* jab, prod, dig, elbow, nudge, butt. **2** *poke a pencil in his eye* jab, push, thrust, shove, stick. **poke around** *poke around among his possessions* rummage around, forage, rake around, ransack, nose around, pry into. **poke fun at** *children poking fun at the strangely dressed old woman* make fun of, laugh at, mock, jeer at, ridicule, deride, tease, chaff, taunt; *inf* take the mickey out of, send up, rib, rag. **poke one's nose into** *poke one's nose into other people's affairs* pry into, interfere in, nose around in, intrude on, butt into, meddle with, tamper with; *inf* snoop into. **poke out** *a letter poking out from her bag* stick out, jut out, protrude, project, extend.

poke n **1** *give him a poke in the ribs* jab, prod, dig, nudge, elbow, butt. **2** *a poke in the eye with a stick* jab, push, thrust, shove.

poky adj *a poky room* confined, cramped, narrow, cell-like, small, little, tiny.

polar adj **1** *polar conditions* Arctic, Antarctic, frozen, freezing, icy, glacial, cold. **2** *polar political ideals* opposite, opposed, diametrically opposed, contrary, antithetical, antagonistic, conflicting.

polarity n *the growing polarity between their political views* difference, separation, opposition, contrariety, antithesis, antagonism, conflict.

pole[1] n **1** *poles supporting the bridge* post, upright, pillar, stanchion, standard, support, prop, rod, shaft, mast. **2** *jump over the pole* bar, rod, stick.

pole[2] n *our points of view are at opposite poles* extremity, extreme, limit. **be poles apart** *be poles apart in their attitudes* be completely different, be widely separated, be incompatible, be worlds apart, be at opposite extremes, be like night and day.

polemics npl *skilled in polemics* argument, argumentation, dispute, disputation, discussion, controversy, wrangling.

police n *send for the police | wanted by the police* police force, the law, constabulary; *inf* the cops, the fuzz, the boys in blue, the Old Bill, the rozzers, the pigs.

police v **1** *police the school buildings looking for intruders* patrol, make the rounds of, guard, keep guard over, keep watch on, protect. **2** *police the football match* keep in order, control, keep under control, regulate.

policeman, policewoman n *a policeman directing the traffic | a policewoman arresting a criminal* police officer, PC, WPC; *inf* bobby, copper, cop, rozzer, pig.

policy n *the government's educational policy | not company policy* plan, scheme, programme, schedule, code, system, approach, procedure, guideline, theory.

polish v **1** *polish the table* wax, buff, rub up, burnish, shine. **2** *polish one's French/etiquette* perfect, refine, improve, brush up, touch up, finish off. **polish off** *polish off his meal quickly* finish, eat up, consume, devour, eat greedily, wolf down, down, bolt.

polished adj **1** *a polished table* waxed, buffed, burnished, shining, shiny, glossy, gleaming, lustrous, glassy, slippery. **2** *polished manners* refined, cultivated, civilized, well-bred, polite, well-mannered, genteel, courtly, urbane, suave, sophisticated. **3** *give a polished performance at the concert* expert, accomplished, masterly, skilful, proficient, adept, impeccable, flawless, faultless, perfect, consummate, exquisite, outstanding, remarkable.

polite adj **1** *teaching children to be polite | polite children giving up their seats in buses to elderly people* well-mannered, mannerly, courteous, civil, respectful, deferential, well-behaved, well-bred, genteel, polished, tactful, diplomatic. **2** *things not done in polite* *society* well-bred, civilized, cultured, refined, polished, genteel, urbane, sophisticated, elegant, courtly.

politic adj *decide on the most politic action | think it politic to leave | a politic young man* wise, prudent, sensible, advisable, judicious, well-judged, sagacious, expedient, shrewd, astute, discreet, tactful, diplomatic.

political adj **1** *hold a political position in the country* governmental, ministerial, public, civic, administrative, bureaucratic. **2** *dismissed from the firm for political reasons* factional, partisan, bipartisan, power, status.

politician n *politicians accused of running the country badly* Member of Parliament, MP, statesman, legislator, lawmaker, public servant; *Amer* senator, congressman; *inf* politico.

politics n **1** *a career in politics* government, local government, affairs of state, party politics. **2** *study politics* political science, civics, statecraft, statesmanship. **3** npl *what are his politics?* party politics, political alliance, politic belief. **4** npl *resigned because the firm was full of politics* power struggle, manipulation, manoeuvring, jockeying for position, machiavellianism, opportunism, realpolitik.

poll n **1** *organize a poll to decide on the best candidate* vote, ballot, vote-casting, canvass, headcount, show of hands, straw vote/poll. **2** *a heavy poll in favour of the present administration* voting figures, returns, count, tally. **3** *conduct a poll to investigate people's eating habits* opinion poll, Gallup poll, survey, market research, sampling.

poll v **1** *poll more votes than his opponent* register, record, return, get, gain. **2** *poll one hundred people in a survey of eating habits* ballot, canvass, question, interview, survey, sample.

pollute v **1** *pollute the water/soil with chemicals | pollute the environment* contaminate, adulterate, infect, taint, poison, befoul, foul, make dirty, make filthy. **2** *pollute the minds of the young* corrupt, poison, warp, pervert, deprave, defile, debauch. **3** *pollute the good name of the family* besmirch, sully, taint, blacken, tarnish, dishonour, debase, vitiate, desecrate.

pollution n **1** *chemicals involved in the pollution of our water* contaminating, contamination, adulteration, adulterating, infecting, tainting, befouling, fouling, dirtying. *see* POLLUTE 1. **2** *environmentalists trying to prevent pollution* contamination, adulteration, infection, impurity, foulness, dirtiness, filthiness; *inf* muckiness. **3** *the pollution of young minds* corruption, corrupting, poisoning, warping, depraving. *see* POLLUTE 2. **4** *the pollution of their good name* besmirching, sullying, tainting, blackening. *see* POLLUTE 3. **5** *concerned about the pollution in our society* corruption, poison, blight, contagion, cancer, canker, malignancy, bane.

pomp n **1** *the pomp expected at a coronation ceremony* ceremoniousness, ritual, display, pageantry, pageant, show, spectacle, splendour, grandeur, magnificence, majesty, glory, brilliance, flourish, style. **2** *only interested in pomp rather than in the reason for the celebration* ostentation, exhibitionism, grandiosity, glitter, show, showiness, pomposity, vainglory, fanfaronade.

pomposity n **1** *irritated by the pomposity of the official* pompousness, presumption, self-importance, presumptuousness, imperiousness, grandiosity, affectation, airs, pretentiousness, pretension, arrogance, vanity, haughtiness, pride, conceit, egotism, superciliousness, condescension, patronization; *inf* uppishness. **2** *the pomposity of the language* pompousness, bombast, turgidity, portentousness, grandiloquence, magniloquence, euphuism, pedantry, stiltedness, fustian.

pompous adj **1** *a pompous official who kept quoting the rules* self-important, presumptuous, imperious, overbearing, grandiose, affected, pretentious, arrogant, vain, haughty, proud, conceited, egotistic, supercilious, condescending, patronizing; *inf* uppity, uppish. **2** *pompous language* high-sounding, high-flown, bombastic, turgid, grandiloquent, magniloquent, euphuistic, portentous, pedantic, stilted, fustian.

pond n pool, puddle, lake, tarn, mere, millpond, duck pond, fish-pond, fish-pool.

ponder v **1** *take time to ponder his previous behaviour* think about, give thought to, consider, reflect on, mull over, contemplate, meditate on, deliberate about/on, dwell on, brood on/over, ruminate about/on/over, puzzle over, cogitate about/on, weigh up, review. **2** *sit in the dark and ponder* think, consider, reflect, meditate, contemplate, deliberate, brood, ruminate, cogitate, cerebrate.

ponderous adj **1** *ponderous movements* heavy, slow, awkward, clumsy, lumbering, heavy-footed. **2** *a ponderous style | a piece of ponderous prose* heavy, awkward, clumsy, lumbering, heavy-footed, laboured, forced, stilted, turgid, stodgy, lifeless, plodding, dull, boring, uninteresting, tedious, monotonous, dry, dreary, pedantic, verbose.

pontificate v *pontificate about the rights and wrongs of the situation* hold forth, expound, declaim, preach, lay down the law, sound off, dogmatize, sermonize; *inf* preachify.

pony n Shetland pony, Iceland pony, Welsh pony, pit pony, polo pony.

pooh-pooh v *pooh-pooh their attempts to raise money* ridicule, deride, disregard, brush aside, dismiss, make light of, belittle, hold up to scorn, treat with contempt, scoff at, sneer at.

pool[1] n **1** *pools of water in the fields after the rain* pond, water hole, puddle, fish-pool, lake, tarn, mere. **2** *a pool of blood* puddle. **3** *have a pool behind their house | go to the pool every day in summer* swimming-pool, swimming-baths, baths.

pool[2] n **1** *a pool of parents to drive children to school | a pool of typists for the whole office | typing pool* consortium, syndicate, collective, combine, group, team. **2** *a pool of cars for use by all the firm's reps* common supply, supply, reserve. **3** *the pool in a gambling game* stakes, bank, kitty, purse, jackpot, ante, fund.

pool[2] v *pool their resources/ideas* put together, combine, amalgamate, merge, share.

poor adj **1** *poor people with very few belongings | live in poor circumstances* badly off, poverty-stricken, penniless, hard up, needy, deprived, in need, needful, in want, indigent, impoverished, impecunious, destitute, penurious, beggared, in straitened circumstances, as poor as a church mouse, in the red, on one's beam ends; *inf* broke, stony-broke, flat broke, on one's uppers, on the rocks, skint. **2** *live in poor surroundings* humble, lowly, mean, modest, plain. **3** *a poor diet/performance* inadequate, deficient, insufficient, unsatisfactory, below standard, below par, inferior, imperfect, bad, low-grade. **4** *a poor crop of apples* sparse, scanty, meagre, scarce, skimpy, reduced, at a premium, paltry, miserable, exiguous. **5** *a diet poor in nutrients* deficient in, lacking in, wanting, insufficient in. **6** *poor furniture | goods of poor quality* unsatisfactory, defective, faulty, imperfect, below standard, inferior, low-grade, second-rate, third-rate, jerry-built, rubbishy. **7** *poor soil* unproductive, barren, unyielding, unfruitful, uncultivatable, bare, arid, sterile, infecund, unfecund. **8** *you poor thing* wretched, pitiable, pitiful, unfortunate, unlucky, luckless, unhappy, hapless, ill-fated, ill-starred. **9** *a poor specimen of a man* miserable, sad, sorry, spiritless, mean, low, base, disgraceful, despicable, contemptible, abject, pathetic.

poorly adj *too poorly to go to school* ill, unwell, sick, ailing, indisposed, below par, off colour, out of sorts; *inf* under the weather, seedy.

poorly adv *perform poorly in the competition* badly, inadequately, unsatisfactorily, unsuccessfully, incompetently, inexpertly.

pop v *champagne corks popped | guns were popping* explode, go off, go off with a bang, go bang, bang, crack, burst, detonate. **pop in 1** *pop a coin in the phone box | popped the ticket into her handbag* insert, put in, place in, slip in, slide in, push in, stick in. **2** *pop in to see his mother on his way to work* visit, call in, go in, stop by; *inf* drop in/by, nip in. **pop out, pop off** *just popping out to get a newspaper* go out quickly/briefly, leave quickly/briefly; *inf* nip out/off. **pop up** *snowdrops popping up all over the garden | a new case popped up every few weeks* appear, appear suddenly/abruptly, occur suddenly/abruptly, crop up.

pop n **1** *champagne opening with a pop | balloons bursting with a pop* bang, crack, boom, burst, explosion, report, detonation. **2** *serve biscuits and pop to the children* soft drink, fizzy drink, lemonade, cola, carbonated drink; *Amer* soda.

pope n *an audience with the Pope in the Vatican* pontiff, Bishop of Rome, Holy Father, Vicar of Christ.

populace n **1** *the government seeking the view of the populace by a referendum* the general public, the public, the people, population, the common people, common folk, the masses, commonalty, the mob, the multitude, the rabble, the rank and file, the hoi polloi; *inf* the plebs. **2** *populace of the city* population, inhabitants, residents.

popular adj **1** *a popular choice/teacher | teachers popular with the pupils | entertainers popular with the audience* well-liked, liked, favoured, in favour, favourite, well-received, approved, admired, accepted. **2** *the goods have proved so popular that we have run out* well-liked, liked, in favour, well-received, sought-after, in demand, desired, wanted, fashionable, in fashion, in vogue, in. **3** *popular film stars* well-known, famous, celebrated, renowned. **4** *for the popular market | a range of popular cars* inexpensive, budget, low-budget, low-priced, cheap, reasonably-priced, reasonable, moderately-priced, modestly-priced; *inf* down-market. **5** *popular literature/music/science | the popular press* middle-of-the-road, middlebrow, lowbrow, accessible, simple, understandable, readily understood, easy to understand, readily comprehensible; *inf* pop. **6** *issues of popular concern* public, general, civic. **7** *popular* *beliefs/myths* current, prevalent, prevailing, accepted, recognized, widespread, universal, general, common, customary, usual, standard, stock, conventional.

popularity n **1** *teachers gaining in popularity | teachers winning popularity with the pupils* favour, approval, approbation, admiration, acceptance. **2** *the popularity of their recent line of goods* demand, fashionableness, vogue. **3** *ideas gaining popularity | myths losing popularity* currency, prevalence, prevalency, recognition. **4** *the popularity of the film stars | film stars winning popularity* fame, renown, acclaim, esteem, repute.

popularize v **1** *popularize classical music* simplify, give mass appeal to, make mass-market, make accessible to all. **2** *help to popularize the belief that the world was flat* give currency to, give credence to, universalize, generalize, spread, disseminate.

popularly adv *it was popularly believed that every strange old woman was a witch | the EC, once popularly known as the Common Market* widely, generally, universally, commonly, usually, regularly, customarily, ordinarily, traditionally.

populate v **1** *nomadic tribes populate the area | an area largely populated by nomadic tribes* inhabit, dwell in, occupy, people. **2** *newly discovered areas of the continent gradually populated by people from other countries* settle, colonize, people.

population n **1** *the entire population of the town was affected by the closure of the factory* inhabitants, residents, community, people, citizenry, populace, society. **2** *the working population | the elderly population* people, folk, society. **3** *populations decreasing in rural areas* population count, numbers of inhabitants, census, headcount.

populous adj *the populous urban areas of the country* densely populated, heavily populated, thickly populated, crowded.

porch n *leave wellingtons in the porch* vestibule.

pore v **pore over 1** *students poring over their books before the exams | poring over the map* study closely, read intently, peruse closely, be absorbed in, scrutinize, examine closely. **2** *sitting alone poring over his problem* meditate on, brood on/over, go over, ponder, reflect on, deliberate on, mull over, muse on, think about, contemplate.

pore n *perspiration oozing from every pore | sap oozing through the plant's pores* opening, orifice, hole, outlet.

pornographic adj *pornographic magazine/ videos* obscene, blue, salacious, lewd, pruri-

ent, erotic, indecent, dirty, smutty, filthy; *inf* porn, porno.

pornography n **1** *make his money from pornography* obscenity, salaciousness, lewdness, prurience, erotica, indecency, smut, filth; *inf* porn, porno, sexploitation. **2** *a shop selling pornography* pornographic literature, pornographic films/videos, erotica; *inf* porn, hard porn, soft porn, porno, girlie magazines.

porous adj **1** *porous soil | clothe made of porous material* absorbent, permeable, penetrable, pervious. **2** *a chunk of porous material* sponge-like, spongy, sieve-like, honeycomb, honeycombed, holey.

port n **1** *ships seeking a port in a storm* harbour, harbourage, haven, anchorage, roads, roadstead. **2** *ports along the south coast* seaport.

portable adj *portable radios/typewriters* transportable, movable, conveyable, easily carried, lightweight, compact, handy, manageable.

portend v *the grey, angry sky portending a storm | his silence portends trouble* be a sign of, be a warning of, be an indication of, be a presage of, point to, be an omen of, herald, bode, augur, presage, forebode, foreshadow, foretell.

portent n **1** *dark skies can be a portent of a storm | his silence was a portent of trouble* sign, indication, presage, warning, omen, harbinger, foreshadowing, augury. **2** *the lavish building was considered one of the portents of the modern world* marvel, wonder, prodigy, phenomenon, spectacle.

portentous adj **1** *portentous events indicating that trouble was inevitable* ominous, warning, threatening, menacing, foreboding, foreshadowing, ill-omened. **2** *a portentous monument* marvellous, remarkable, prodigious, phenomenal, spectacular, wondrous, amazing, astounding. **3** *a portentous speech* pompous, pontifical, ponderous, solemn.

porter[1] n *porters struggling with heavy baggage* carrier, bearer, baggage-carrier, stretcher-bearer, stretcher-carrier.

porter[2] n *the porter refused to tell him which flat she lived in* door-keeper, doorman, door-attendant, commissionaire, caretaker, janitor, concierge.

portion n **1** *serve generous portions at the restaurant | children's portions available* helping, serving, piece, quantity. **2** *give a portion of his estate to each of his children* share, division, quota, part, bit, allocation, allotment, piece; *inf* cut, whack. **3** *ask for three portions of cheese at the delicatessen* bit, section, segment, slice, wedge, lump, chunk, hunk. **4** *her portion in life to serve others* lot, fate, destiny, fortune, luck.

portion v *portion the estate among his children* share, divide, split, partition, carve up, parcel out; *inf* divvy up. **portion out** *portion out pieces of cake to the children* distribute, dispense, hand out, deal out, dole out, divide out, share out, allocate, apportion, allot, parcel out, mete out; *inf* divvy up.

portly adj stout, plump, fat, corpulent, obese, tubby, of ample build, stocky.

portrait n **1** *portraits of his ancestors hung on the walls* painting, picture, drawing, sketch, portrayal, representation, likeness, image, study, portraiture, canvas. **2** *have the photographer take a portrait of his daughter* photograph, photo, picture, studio portrait, study, shot, snapshot, snap, still. **3** *the writer's portrait of his childhood* description, portrayal, depiction, account, story, chronicle, thumbnail sketch, vignette, profile.

portray v **1** *the artist portrayed the girl in a simple blue dress* paint a picture of, paint, draw a picture of, draw, sketch, depict, represent, delineate. **2** *portray a scene of abject poverty in his novel* describe, depict, characterize, paint a word-picture of, paint in words, put into words. **3** *portray Hamlet's mother in the production* play, act the part of, play the part of, act, perform, represent, execute.

portrayal n **1** *his portrayal of the girl in riding-habit* painting, portrait, picture, drawing, sketch, representation, depiction, delineation, study. **2** *the writer's portrayal of scenes of poverty* description, depiction, characterization, word-picture, word-painting. **3** *her portrayal of the role of Hamlet's mother* acting, performance, representation, interpretation.

pose v **1** *ask him to pose for a portrait* sit, model, take up a position. **2** *carefully pose the subjects for his still life* arrange, position, lay out, set out, dispose, place, put, locate, situate. **3** *she was always posing to try and impress the boys* strike an attitude, posture, put on an act, act, play-act, attitudinize, put on airs, show off. **4** *pose a question relating to finance* put forward, put, submit, set, advance, propound, posit. **5** *traffic conditions pose problems for drivers* present, set, create, cause, give rise to. **pose as** *the thief posed as a social worker* pretend to be, impersonate, pass oneself off as, masquerade as, profess to be, feign the identity of.

pose n **1** *models asked to adopt a provocative pose for the swimsuit commercial* posture, stance, position, attitude, bearing, carriage.

2 *her shyness is only a pose, she's really brazen* act, play-acting, pretence, façade, front, masquerade, posture, attitudinizing, affectation, airs.

poser n **1** *how we're going to cope with him is a real poser* difficult question, awkward problem, vexed question, enigma, dilemma, puzzle, mystery, conundrum; *inf* brainteaser, facer. **2** *posers in the nude* model, sitter, subject. **3** *he's a real poser see* POSEUR.

poseur n *he's not genuine - he's just a poseur* poser, attitudinizer, posturer, play-actor.

posh adj **1** *a posh hotel* luxurious, luxury, de luxe, sumptuous, opulent, lavish, rich, elegant, ornate, fancy, plush; *inf* plushy, ritzy, swanky. **2** *a posh accent* upper-class, aristocratic, fancy; *inf* up-market, upper-crust.

position n **1** *a house in an isolated position | plants in a sunny position* situation, location, site, place, spot, area, locality, locale, scene, setting. **2** *identify the ship's position* location, bearings, whereabouts. **3** *sitting/ standing in an uncomfortable position | in an upright position* posture, stance, attitude, pose, bearing. **4** *in an unfortunate financial position* situation, state, condition, circumstance, predicament, plight, pass. **5** *several people jockeying for position in the race* advantageous position, favourable position, pole position, primacy, the upper hand, the edge, the whip hand. **6** *have to declare their position on privatization | speak from a position of knowledge* point of view, viewpoint, opinion, way of thinking, outlook, attitude, stand, standpoint, stance. **7** *apply for the vacant position of manager | his position as captain* post, job, situation, appointment, role, office, place, capacity, duty. **8** *what is his position in the class* place, level, grade, grading, rank, status, standing. **9** *people of position in society* rank, status, stature, standing, social standing, prestige, influence, reputation, importance, consequence.

position v *position the building so that it faces south | position the soldiers in rows* place, locate, situate, put, arrange, set, settle, dispose, array.

positive adj **1** *a set of positive rules | given positive instructions* clear, clear-cut, definite, precise, categorical, direct, explicit, express, firm. **2** *no positive proof of his guilt* real, actual, absolute, concrete, conclusive, unequivocal, incontrovertible, indisputable, undeniable, incontestable, unmistakable. **3** *they are positive that they have the solution* certain, sure, assured, confident, convinced. **4** *the results of the blood test are positive* affirmative. **5** *positive criticism/propos-*

als constructive, productive, helpful, practical, useful, beneficial. **6** *a positive attitude to his work* | *positive thinking* confident, optimistic, assured, assertive, firm, forceful, determined, resolute, emphatic, dogmatic. **7** *positive developments have been made* | *positive progress* good, favourable, effective, promising, encouraging, heartening. **8** *he's a positive fool* | *it's a positive disgrace* utter, complete, absolute, perfect, out-and-out, outright, thoroughgoing, thorough, downright, sheer, consummate, unmitigated, rank.

positively adv **1** *she assured us positively that he had gone* | *they were positively convinced that they were right* with certainty, definitely, emphatically, firmly, categorically, absolutely, without qualification, confidently, dogmatically. **2** *they were positively furious* absolutely, really, indeed, extremely, to a marked degree.

possess v **1** *they possess two cars* own, be the owner of, have, be the possessor of, be the proud possessor of, count among one's possessions, have to one's name, hold, be blessed with, enjoy. **2** *possess a good mind* have, be endowed with, be gifted with. **3** *the invaders set out to possess all the castles* seize, take into possession, take possession of, take over, occupy. **4** *devils seemed to have possessed her* | *what possessed her?* influence, control, dominate, have mastery over, bewitch, enchant, put under a spell, obsess; *inf* get into someone.

possessed adj **1** *like someone possessed* bewitched, enchanted, under a spell, obsessed, haunted, bedevilled, crazed, mad, demented, berserk, frenzied. **2** *a very possessed young woman* self-possessed, poised, self-controlled, self-assured, self-confident, confident, calm, cool, composed, even-tempered, imperturbable; *inf* unflappable.

possession n **1** *her possession of the jewels* ownership, proprietorship, possessorship. **2** *their possession of the land/house* occupancy, occupation, holding, tenure, tenancy. **3** *a possession of which she was very fond* thing/article/item owned, asset. see POSSESSIONS.

possessions npl *thrown out of the flat with all her possessions* belongings, things, property, luggage, baggage, bags and baggage, personal effects, goods and chattels, accoutrements, paraphernalia, appendages, assets, impedimenta.

possessive adj **1** *children possessive of their toys* | *a possessive attitude to toys* | *possessive children* acquisitive, greedy, grasping, covetous, selfish; *inf* grabby. **2** *possessive parents*

over-protective, clinging, controlling, dominating, jealous.

possibilities npl *the cottage is dilapidated but it has possibilities* | *see the possibilities of the run-down farm* | *have possibilities as an actress* potential, potentiality, promise, prospects, capability. see POSSIBILITY.

possibility n **1** *beyond the bounds of possibility* | *discuss the possibility of the plan working* feasibility, practicability, attainability, likelihood, potentiality, conceivability, probability. see POSSIBLE. **2** *buying a smaller house is one possibility* likelihood, prospect, chance, hope, probability. **3** *a possibility of more violence* likelihood, prospect, chance, risk, hazard. see POSSIBILITIES.

possible adj **1** *it is not humanly possible to get there on time* | *a dream that is not possible* feasible, able to be done, practicable, doable, attainable, achievable, realizable, within reach; *inf* on. **2** *one of several possible outcomes* likely, potential, conceivable, imaginable, probable, credible, tenable, odds-on.

possibly adv **1** *he may possibly arrive tomorrow* perhaps, maybe, it may be, for all one knows, very likely; *lit* peradventure. **2** *he will arrive if he possibly can* | *you can't possibly carry all that* conceivably, by any means, by any chance, at all.

post[1] n **1** *put up the posts for the fence* | *posts supporting the wooden bridge* stake, upright, pole, shaft, prop, support, column, stanchion, standard, stock, picket, pillar, pale, palisade, baluster, newel. **2** *first past the post* finishing post, finishing tape. **3** *left at the post* starting post, finishing post.

post[1] v **1** *post notices on the walls of the building* put up, stick, stick up, pin, pin up, tack, tack up, attach, affix, hang, display. **2** *details of the exams will be posted later* announce, make known, advertise, publish, publicize, circulate, broadcast.

post[2] n **1** *send the goods by post* postal service, mail. **2** *what time is the post?* postal delivery/collection, mail delivery/collection. **3** *got a lot of post this morning* mail, letters, correspondence. **4** *take the letters to the post* postbox, letter-box, pillar-box, post office, post room; *Amer* mailbox, mailroom.

post[2] v **1** *post the parcel early in the morning* send by post, dispatch by post, mail, transmit. **2** *post today's sales in the ledger* enter, write in, fill in, record, register, note. **keep someone posted** *the boss asked us to keep him posted while he was away* keep informed, keep briefed, brief, advise, notify, report to; *inf* keep someone in the picture, keep someone up to date, fill someone in.

post[3] n **1** *advertise the post | three possible candidates for the post of manager* position, job, appointment, situation, place, office. **2** *soldiers at their posts* station, position, beat.

poster n *posters advertising the amateur production | stick posters up all over his bedroom walls* placard, bill, notice, public notice, sticker, advertisement, announcement, bulletin, *affiche*; *inf* advert.

posterity n **1** *conserve the rain forests for posterity* future generations, succeeding generations. **2** *wish to keep his estate intact for posterity* descendants, heirs, successors, issue, offspring, progeny, children, seed.

post-mortem n PM, autopsy, necropsy.

postpone v defer, put off, put back, delay, hold over, adjourn, shelve, table, pigeonhole; *inf* put on ice, put on the back burner.

postponement n deferment, deferral, delay, adjournment, moratorium, stay. *see* POSTPONE.

postscript n **1** *add a postscript to her letter* PS, subscript, afterthought. **2** *add a postcript to the essay* subscript, afterword, addendum, appendix, codicil, appendage, supplement.

postulate v *postulate that the population will decrease by 10%* assume, presuppose, suppose, presume, take for granted, posit, hypothesize, theorize.

posture n **1** *in a reclining posture* position, pose, attitude. **2** *have an elegant posture | stand with a hunched posture* carriage, bearing, stance. **3** *the parents adopted a critical posture towards the new educational policy* attitude, position, point of view, viewpoint, opinion, way of thinking, outlook, stand, standpoint, stance, angle, slant.

posture v *posturing in front of the mirror admiring himself | girls posturing to attract the boys* pose, strike an attitude, put on an act, act, play-act, attitudinize, put on airs, show off.

potency n **1** *the potency of the drugs* powerfulness, power, strength, effectiveness, efficacy. **2** *the potency of his influence in the land* power, powerfulness, force, forcefulness, strength, vigour, might, mightiness, influence, authoritativeness, authority, dominance, energy; *lit* puissance. *see* POTENT 2. **3** *admire the potency of their arguments* power, powerfulness, force, forcefulness, strength, effectiveness, cogency, conviction, persuasiveness, impressiveness. *see* POTENT 3.

potent adj **1** *potent drugs* powerful, strong, effective, efficacious. **2** *he was a potent force in the land* powerful, forceful, strong, vigorous, mighty, influential, authoritative, commanding, dominant, energetic, dynamic; *lit* puissant. **3** *a potent argument* powerful, forceful, strong, effective, cogent, compelling, convincing, persuasive, eloquent, impressive, telling.

potentate n *the potentate of the neighbouring country* ruler, monarch, king/queen, emperor/empress, sovereign, mogul.

potential adj **1** *a potential star* budding, embryonic, developing, promising, prospective, likely, possible, probable. **2** *his potential musical ability* latent, dormant, inherent, embryonic, developing, promising. **3** *a potential disaster* likely, possible, probable.

potential n **1** *recognize the potential of the young singer* promise, capability, capacity, ability, aptitude, talent, flair. **2** *recognize the potential of the broken-down house* possibilities, promise, potentiality.

potion n drink, beverage, brew, concoction, mixture, draught, elixir, philtre.

pot-pourri n *a pot-pourri of children's poems and drawings* medley, miscellany, *mélange*, pastiche, collage, blend, mixture, hotchpotch, hodgepodge, mishmash, jumble, gallimaufry, farrago, olio, olla podrida.

potter v *potter down the road* dawdle, loiter, dally, dilly-dally; *inf* tootle. **potter about, potter around** *spend the weekend pottering about/around* mess about/around, dabble, fritter, tinker about/around, fiddle about/around.

pottery n ceramics, earthenware, stoneware, terracotta.

pouch n *carry money/tobacco in a pouch* bag, purse, wallet, container.

pounce v **1** *the hawk pounced when it spied its prey* swoop down, drop down, descend. **2** *the fox pounced on the hen | the robbers pounced on the men carrying the gold* swoop on, spring on, lunge at, leap at, jump at/on, bound at, make a grab for, take by surprise, take unawares, attack suddenly.

pounce n *the fox grabbed the hen at one pounce* swoop, spring, lunge, leap, jump, bound, grab, attack.

pound[1] v **1** *pound the solid to powder | pound the garlic to a paste* crush, beat, pulverize, smash, mash, grind, comminute, triturate. **2** *pound his opponent with his fists* beat, batter, pummel, strike, belabour, hammer, pelt, thump. **3** *pound the streets* tramp, tread heavily on, trudge, walk heavily on, stomp along, clump along. **4** *with heart pounding* beat heavily, pulsate, pulse, throb, thump, pump, palpitate, go pit-a-pat.

pound² n **1** *a pound of apples* pound avoirdupois, lb, pound troy, t. **2** *the cost in pounds* pound sterling, pound coin, pound note; *inf* quid.

pound³ n *stray dogs in a pound* | *cars in a pound* compound, enclosure, pen, yard.

pour v **1** *she poured cream over the fruit* let flow, decant, splash, spill. **2** *water poured from the burst pipe* | *blood poured from the gunshot wound* gush, rush, stream, flow, course, spout, jet, spurt. **3** *it was pouring* | *it poured rain heavily/hard*, come down in torrents/ sheets, rain cats and dogs, bucket, be bucketing, sheetdown, come down like stair-rods. **4** *people poured from the burning cinema* | *letters poured in* stream, swarm, crowd, throng, flood.

pout v **1** *pout her lips provocatively/sullenly* push forwards, purse. **2** *pouting because she did not get her own way* sulk, look sullen, look petulant, scowl, glower, lour, make a moue.

poverty n **1** *appalled at the poverty of the homeless people* pennilessness, neediness, need, want, hardship, deprivation, indigence, impoverishment, impecuniousness, destitution, penury, privation, beggary, pauperism, straitened circumstances. **2** *the poverty of their surroundings* humbleness, lowliness, meanness, modesty, plainness. **3** *poverty of resources* | *the poverty of their imagination* deficiency, dearth, shortage, scarcity, paucity, insufficiency, lack, want, meagreness. **4** *the poverty of the soil/land* poorness, barrenness, unfruitfulness, bareness, aridity, aridness, sterility, infecundity.

powder n *lumps of sugar crushed to powder* | *dry snow like powder* dust, fine grains, face-powder, talcum powder, talc, dusting powder, baby powder, soap powder, baking-powder, sleeping-powder, stomach-powder, pounce.

powder v **1** *powder her face* | *powdered the baby* dust/sprinkle with powder, dredge/strew/ scatter with powder. **2** *powder the coffee beans* crush, pound, pulverize, grind, granulate, comminute, triturate.

powdery adj **1** *powdery snow* powder-like, fine, dry, dusty, chalky, floury, friable, granulated, ground, crushed, pulverized. **2** *her powdery face and reddened lips* powder-covered, powdered.

power n **1** *the power to corrupt/inspire* ability, capability, capacity, potential, potentiality. **2** *lose the power of speech* ability, capability, faculty, competence. **3** *the power behind the blow* | *the sheer power of his arms* powerfulness, strength, force, forcefulness, might,

weight, vigour, energy, potency. **4** *have him in her power* | *she fell into his power* control, authority, mastery, domination, dominance, rule, command, ascendancy, supremacy, dominion, sway, sovereignty, influence. **5** *have the power to veto the rule* authority, authorization, warrant, licence, right, prerogative. **6** *different kinds of power used for heating* energy, electrical power, nuclear power, solar power. **7** *the power of her oratory/argument* powerfulness, potency, strength, force, forcefulness, eloquence, effectiveness, cogency, conviction, persuasiveness.

powerful adj **1** *of powerful build* | *two powerful boxers* strong, sturdy, strapping, stout, stalwart, robust, vigorous, tough, mighty. **2** *powerful members of the committee* | *a country afraid of its powerful neighbours* influential, controlling, dominant, authoritative, commanding, forceful, strong, vigorous, potent, puissant. **3** *a powerful argument against leaving* forceful, strong, effective, cogent, compelling, convincing, persuasive, eloquent, impressive, telling. **4** *have powerful advertising appeal* strong, great, weighty, influential.

powerless adj **1** *formerly influential members of the committee now totally powerless* without power, impotent. **2** *legs powerless after the accident* without power, without strength, paralysed, diasbled, incapacitated, debilitated, weak, feeble. **3** *powerless to give them any assistance* helpless, unfit, impotent, ineffectual, inadequate.

practicability n *question the practicability of the scheme* feasibility, possibility, viability, workability, achievability, attainability. *see* PRACTICABLE.

practicable adj *find a practicable scheme* feasible, possible, within the bounds of possibility, within the realms of possibility, viable, workable, doable, achievable, attainable, accomplishable.

practical adj **1** *practical tradesmen rather than graduates with academic qualifications* hands-on, active, trained, seasoned, experienced, skilled, practised, accomplished, proficient. **2** *a practical rather than theoretical knowledge* applied, empirical, pragmatic, workaday, hands-on; *inf* nuts and bolts. **3** *practical clothing for hillwalking* | *the furniture is attractive but not very practical* functional, useful, utilitarian, sensible. **4** *he has a lot of theories but she is very practical* businesslike, sensible, down-to-earth, pragmatic, realistic, hard-headed; *inf* hard-nosed. **5** *find a practical solution* pragmatic, matter-of-fact, down-to-earth, hard-headed, sensible, businesslike, realistic, utilitarian, expedient. **6** *a practical atheist* | *in practical control* virtual, effective, in effect, essential.

practically adv **1** *practically every day* | *practically unknown* almost, nearly, very nearly, wellnigh, virtually, all but, in effect; *inf* pretty nearly/well. **2** *behave practically* sensibly, with common sense, realistically, reasonably, pragmatically.

practice n **1** *put the plan into practice* | *it would never work in practice* action, operation, application, effect, exercise, use. **2** *go to tennis practice* training, preparation, study, exercise, drill, work-out, rehearsal. **3** *it is standard practice for shops to close on Wednesday afternoons* procedure, method, system, usage, tradition, convention. **4** *it was his practice to visit his mother on Sundays* habit, custom, routine, wont. **5** *he engaged in the practice of law/medicine* profession, career, business, work, pursuit. **6** *buy a medical/legal practice* firm, business.

practise v **1** *to practise economy/self-control* carry out, perform, do, execute, follow, pursue, observe. **2** *practise her tennis strokes* | *practising a musical piece* work at, go through, run through, go over, rehearse, polish, refine. **3** *she must practise before the match/test* train, study, prepare, exercise, drill. **4** *practise medicine/law* work at, have a career in, pursue a career in, engage in, specialize in.

practised adj *a practised liar* experienced, seasoned, skilled, skilful, accomplished, expert, proficient, able, adept, adroit.

pragmatic adj *he has a lot of theories but she is very pragmatic* | *a pragmatic approach to the problem* | *a pragmatic solution* practical, matter-of-fact, down-to-earth, hard-headed, sensible, businesslike, realistic, utilitarian; *inf* hard-nosed, nuts and bolts.

praise v **1** *praise the musician's performance* | *praise him for his contribution* express approval of, express admiration for, applaud, acclaim, cheer, compliment someone on, congratulate someone on, pay tribute to, extol, laud, sing the praises of, eulogize about, cry up, throw bouquets at; *inf* crack up. **2** *praise God* worship, glorify, honour, exalt, adore, laud, pay tribute to, give thanks to.

praise n **1** *express praise for his efforts* | *work worthy of praise* | *receive praise for his efforts* approval, approbation, applause, acclaim, acclamation, cheers, compliments, congratulations, commendation, tributes, accolades, plaudits, eulogy, panegyric, encomium, extolment, laudation, ovation,

bouquets. **2** *praise to God* worship, glory, honour, devotion, exaltation, adoration, tribute, thanks.

praiseworthy adj commendable, laudable, admirable, honourable, estimable, creditable, deserving, meritorious, worthy, excellent, exemplary, sterling, fine.

prance v **1** *horses prancing round the field* leap, spring, jump, skip, cavort, caper, frisk, gambol. **2** *prancing along in her new shoes* parade, skip, cavort, strut, swagger; *inf* swank.

prank n *a childish prank* | *play a prank on his friend* trick, practical joke, joke, hoax, caper, stunt; *inf* lark.

prattle v *prattle on about the details of her wedding* chatter, jabber, babble, twitter, blather, blether, gabble, run on, rattle on; *inf* rabbit on, witter on.

pray v **1** *pray every night before going to bed* say one's prayers. **2** *pray to God* offer prayers to, say prayers to, commune with. **3** *pray the emperor to spare her husband's life* appeal to, call upon, beseech, entreat, ask earnestly, request, implore, beg, petition, solicit, plead with, importune, supplicate, sue, invoke, crave, adjure. **4** *pray for mercy* appeal for, call for, ask earnestly for, request earnestly, beg for, beg, petition for, solicit, plead for, crave, crave for, clamour for.

prayer n **1** *say a prayer to God* | *say evening prayers* devotion, communion, litany, collect. **2** *prayers for mercy answered by the emperor* appeal, plea, beseeching, entreaty, petition, solicitation, supplication, suit, invocation, adjuration. *see* PRAY 3.

preach v **1** *ministers preaching in Church on Sunday* give a sermon, deliver a sermon, sermonize, spread the gospel, evangelize. **2** *preach the word of God* make known, proclaim, teach, spread. **3** *preach economy* advocate, recommend, advise, urge, exhort. **preach at** *tired of being preached at by her father* lecture, moralize, admonish, harangue, sermonize.

preacher n **1** *preachers giving sermons from the pulpit* minister, parson, clergyman, churchman, cleric, missionary, revivalist, evangelist, televangelist. **2** *preachers of economy* advocate, adviser, urger, exhorter. **3** *tired of preachers telling other people how to lead their lives* moralizer, sermonizer, homilist.

preaching n **1** *inspired by the minister's preaching* sermon, homily, pulpitry, evangelism. **2** *tired of her father's preaching about her lifestyle* lecturing, moralizing, harangue sermon, sermonizing, homily; *inf* preachify.

preamble n *begin his lecture without any preamble | a historical novel with a long preamble* opening statement, opening remarks, introduction, prefatory remarks, preface, prologue, front matter, forward matter, foreword, prelude, exordium, proem, prolegomenon; *inf* prelims.

precarious adj **1** *earn rather a precarious living | a precarious way of earning a living* uncertain, unsure, unpredictable, undependable, unreliable, risky, hazardous, chancy, doubtful, dubious, unsettled, insecure, unstable; *inf* dodgy, dicey. **2** *sitting in rather a precarious position at the edge of the cliff | in rather a precarious legal position* risky, hazardous, insecure, unstable, shaky, tricky, perilous, dangerous, on a slippery slope, touch-and-go; *inf* dicey, hairy.

precaution n **1** *take a few precautions to avoid being burgled* preventive measure, preventative measure, safety measure, safeguard, provision. **2** *a situation which demands precaution* foresight, foresightedness, farsightedness, forethought, anticipation, prudence, circumspection, caution, care, attentiveness, chariness, wariness.

precede v **1** *his father preceded him as chairman* go before, be the predecessor of. **2** *she preceded him into the room* go before, come before, go/come ahead of, lead, usher in. **3** *the events that preceded the murder/triumph* go before, go in advance of, antedate, antecede, lead to, lead up to, usher in, herald, pave the way for. **4** *precede her lecture with a few informal remarks* preface, prefix, introduce, begin, open, launch.

precedence n *a list of the nobles in order of precedence* rank, seniority, superiority, preeminence, eminence, supremacy, primacy, transcendence, ascendancy. **take precedence over** *educational considerations should take precedence over financial considerations* come before, take priority over, be considered more important/urgent than, take antecedence over.

precedent n *is there a precedent for such a severe punishment? | the judge's ruling has created a precedent* previous case, prior case, previous instance, prior instance, pattern, model, example, exemplar, paradigm, criterion, yardstick, standard.

preceding adj **1** *as stated in the preceding paragraph above*, foregoing, previous, earlier, prior, antecedent, anterior. **2** *on the preceding day* previous, earlier, prior.

precept n **1** *follow the precepts of one's religion/contract* rule, guideline, principle,

working principle, code, law, tenet, canon, ordinance, statute, command, order, decree, mandate, dictate, dictum, directive, direction, instruction. **2** *precepts that her grandmother used to quote* maxim, axiom, saying, saw, adage, aphorism.

precinct n **1** *the cathedral/college precinct* close, enclosure, court, courtyard, quadrangle. **2** *a pedestrian/shopping precinct* quarter, sector, zone, district, region.

precincts npl **1** *the cottages within the precincts of his estate* boundary, bounds, limits, confines. **2** *visit the old city and its precincts* surrounding area, surroundings, environs, neighbourhood, vicinity, purlieus.

precious adj **1** *precious metals* valuable, high-priced, costly, expensive, dear, priceless, rare, choice. **2** *precious souvenirs/memories* valued, cherished, prized, treasured, favourite, dear, beloved, adored, revered, venerated. **3** *poetry full of precious images | her manners are too precious for words* affected, artificial, chichi, overrefined, effete; *inf* twee.

precipice n cliff face, rock-face, steep cliff, sheer drop, cliff, crag, bluff.

precipitate v **1** *precipitate the crisis* hasten, accelerate, expedite, speed up, push forward, bring on, trigger. **2** *the collision precipitated the car into the river | precipitated into economic disaster* hurl headlong, hurl, throw headlong, fling, thrust, heave, propel.

precipitate adj **1** *his precipitate dash from the room* hurried, rapid, swift, speedy, headlong, abrupt, sudden, unexpected, breakneck, violent, precipitous. **2** *it was precipitate of him to act like that | his precipitate action landed him in trouble* hasty, hurried, rash, heedless, reckless, impetuous, impulsive, precipitous, hare-brained.

precipitous adj **1** *a precipitous cliff face* steep, sheer, perpendicular, abrupt, high. **2** *his precipitous exit from the room* precipitate, hurried, rapid, headlong, abrupt, sudden, violent. *see* PRECIPITATE adj 1. **3** *precipitous of him to act like that | his precipitous action landed him in trouble* precipitate, hasty, rash, heedless, impetuous. *see* PRECIPITATE *adj* 2.

précis n *a précis of the report* summary, synopsis, résumé, abridgement, abstract, outline, sketch, run-down, digest, epitome, compendium.

précis v *précis the monthly report* summarize, sum up, abridge, condense, shorten, compress, abstract, outline.

precise adj **1** *a precise record of events* exact, literal, actual, close, faithful, strict, express, minute, accurate, correct. **2** *at that precise moment she saw him | articles found at the precise spot where they were left* exact, very, actual, particular, specific, distinct. **3** *she's a very precise person | precise attention to detail* careful, exact, meticulous, scrupulous, conscientious, punctilious, particular, methodical, fastidious, finicky, rigid, strict, rigorous.

precisely adv **1** *at 6 o'clock precisely* exactly, sharp, on the dot, dead, dead on; *inf* bang on, spot on; *Amer* on the button. **2** *write out instructions very precisely* exactly, literally, strictly, minutely. *see* PRECISE 1.

precision n **1** *admire the precision of his prose* carefulness, exactness, meticulousness, scrupulousness, conscientiousness, punctiliousness, methodicalness, rigour. **2** *the precision of the mechanism* accuracy, exactness, reliability, regularity.

preclude v **1** *the rules of the club preclude women from joining | the owners are precluded from altering the front of the house* prevent, prohibit, debar, interdict, block, bar, hinder, impede. **2** *the police findings preclude any doubt as to his guilt* make impossible, rule out, eliminate. .

precocious adj *precocious children in need of special schooling* advanced, ahead, far ahead, forward, ahead of one's peers, gifted, brilliant, ultra-bright, quick, smart, adult-like.

preconception n *have a preconception that the solicitor would be a man* preconceived idea, preconceived notion, assumption, presupposition, presumption, prejudgement, prejudice, bias.

precondition n *a degree in an appropriate subject is a precondition of the post* prerequisite, essential condition, requirement, necessity, essential, *sine qua non*; *inf* must.

precursor n **1** *the sporadic attacks proved to be the precursors of a full-scale war* forerunner, prelude, harbinger, herald, curtain-raiser. **2** *his precursor in the post* predecessor, former/previous holder of the post etc, forerunner, antecedent. **3** *a machine that was the precursor of the modern computer* predecessor, forerunner, ancestor, forebear, antecedent, progenitor, pioneer.

predatory adj **1** *predatory birds* of prey, hunting, predacious, rapacious, raptorial. **2** *predatory tribes invading the country* plundering, pillaging, marauding, ravaging, looting, robbing, thieving, rapacious. **3** *her predatory relatives have left her without any money* exploitative, exploiting, imposing, greedy, acquisitive, rapacious, vulturine.

predecessor n **1** *the success of the department is the result of the efforts of his predecessor* former/previous holder of the post etc, precursor, forerunner, antecedent. **2** *collect information on his predecessors for a family tree* ancestor, forefather, forebear, progenitor, antecedent.

predestine v *he seemed predestined to lead a life of poverty | her success seemed predestined* preordain, foreordain, predetermine, fate, destine, predestinate.

predetermined adj *everyone acted on a predetermined signal* prearranged, pre-agreed, predecided, preplanned, agreed, settled, fixed, set.

predicament n difficult situation, problematic situation, corner, plight, tight corner, mess, emergency, crisis, dilemma, quandary, trouble; *inf* jam, sticky situation, hole, fix, pickle, scrape, tight spot, spot.

predict v *predict future events | predict that something terrible would happen* forecast, foretell, prophesy, foresee, divine, prognosticate, forewarn, forebode, portend, presage, augur.

predictable adj *a predictable reaction* foreseeable, to be expected, expected, anticipated, probable, likely, certain, sure; *inf* on the cards.

prediction n prophecy, forecast, divination, prognostication, forewarning, augury, soothsaying.

predilection n *a predilection for spicy food | his predilection for intelligent women* liking, fondness, preference, love, partiality, taste, weakness, soft spot, fancy, inclination, leaning, bias, propensity, bent, proclivity, proneness, penchant, predisposition.

predispose v **1** *his poverty-stricken childhood predisposed him to save* move, incline, dispose, persuade, influence, sway, induce, prompt. **2** *the child is predisposed to asthma* make susceptible to, make liable to, make subject to, make prone to, make vulnerable to, make open to.

predisposed adj *before meeting her he was predisposed to believe her story* inclined, of a mind to, willing, biased, prejudiced.

predisposition n **1** *a predisposition towards rheumatism/meanness* susceptibility, proneness, tendency, inclination, vulnerability, *see* PREDISPOSE. **2** *have a predisposition towards fast cars* predilection, inclination, leaning, bias, propensity, bent, proclivity, proneness, penchant. *see* PREDILECTION.

predominance n **1** *try to avoid the predominance of one group over another in the alliance* dominance, control, ascendancy, leadership, mastery, supremacy, upper hand, edge, preponderance. **2** *a predominance of men on the staff | a predominance of blue in the room's colour-scheme* preponderance, dominance, prevalence, greater/greatest number/amount, majority, bulk.

predominant adj **1** *the predominant member of the alliance* dominant, controlling, in control, ascendant, ruling, leading, principal, chief, main, supreme, more/most powerful, more/most important, superior, in the ascendancy. **2** *idleness is the predominant characteristic in that family* chief, main, principal, preponderant, most obvious, most noticeable, most prominent, prevailing, prevalent.

predominate v **1** *the largest country predominates in the policy-making of the alliance* be dominant, be in control, rule, hold ascendancy, hold sway, have the upper hand, carry most weight. **2** *male members of staff predominate in the firm | blue predominates in the room's colour-scheme* be predominant, be greater/greatest in amount/number, be prevalent, preponderate, be most prominent. *see* PREDOMINANT 2.

pre-eminence n *his pre-eminence as a poet* excellence, distinction, prestige, prominence, eminence, importance, fame, renown, supremacy, superiority, transcendence.

pre-eminent adj *a pre-eminent scientist | a scientist pre-eminent in his field* outstanding, leading, foremost, chief, excellent, distinguished, prominent, eminent, important, famous, renowned, supreme, superior, unrivalled, unsurpassed, transcendent.

pre-empt v **1** *pre-empt the sale of the building by buying it themselves* forestall, prevent, invalidate. **2** *the invading army pre-empted all the houses for their own use* take over, appropriate, acquire, commandeer, take possession of, occupy, seize, arrogate.

preen v *birds preening their feathers with their beaks* clean, smooth, arrange, plume. **preen oneself 1** *preening himself in front of the mirror* groom oneself, tidy oneself up, spruce oneself up, smarten oneself up, beautify oneself, prettify oneself, primp, primp oneself up, prink, prink oneself up, plume oneself; *inf* titivate oneself, doll oneself up, tart oneself up. **2** *preen oneself on winning the prize* give oneself a pat on the back, congratulate oneself, be pleased with oneself, pride oneself, be proud of oneself.

preface n *the preface explaining how to use the book* introduction, foreword, front matter, forward matter, preamble, prologue, prel-

ude, proem, exordium, prolegomenon; *inf* prelims, intro.

preface v *preface her speech with a short introduction* precede, prefix, introduce, begin, open, launch.

prefatory adj *made a few prefatory remarks before reading his poem* preliminary, introductory, opening, precursory, initial, preparatory.

prefer v **1** *prefer cheese to dessert* like better, favour, be more partial to, incline towards, choose, select, pick, opt for, go for, plump for, single out; *inf* fancy. **2** *prefer to go by bus* like better, would rather, would sooner, favour, choose, opt, elect, wish, want. **3** *prefer a proposal to the committee | prefer charges* put forward, proffer, present, offer, propose, tender, lodge, file, press. **4** *hope to be preferred in the near future* promote, upgrade, advance, move up, elevate, aggrandize.

preferable adj *find going by train preferable to going by car* better, superior, more desirable, more suitable.

preferably adv *looking for a cottage preferably a thatched one | preferably we would like to be paid in cash* for preference, by preference, from choice, by choice, much rather, rather, much sooner, sooner.

preference n **1** *her preference is for a flat rather than a bungalow* choice, first choice, first option, liking, fancy, desire, wish, inclination, partiality, predilection, leaning, bias, bent. **2** *here are the cakes, what is your preference?* choice, selection, option, pick. **3** *applicants with experience will be given preference | show preference to members of her own family* preferential treatment, favoured treatment, favour, precedence, priority, advantage.

preferential adj *preferential travel rates given to members of the group | members of the manager's family get preferential treatment* special, better, advantageous, favoured, privileged, partial, partisan.

preferment n *hope for preferment in the firm* promotion, upgrading, advancement, moving up, elevation, aggrandizement.

pregnancy n gestation, gravidity, parturiency.

pregnant adj **1** *discover that she was pregnant* having a baby/child, expectant, with child, heavy with child, gravid, *enceinte*; *inf* expecting, in the family way, preggers, in a delicate condition, in a certain condition, in the club, in the pudding club, in trouble, with a bun in the oven. **2** *a speech pregnant with menace | a situation pregnant with*

danger | an event pregnant with joy full of,
filled with, charged with, fraught with,
abounding in, replete with, rich in. **3** *a
pregnant pause following her surprise announcement* meaningful, significant, eloquent,
expressive, suggestive, loaded, charged,
pointed, telling.

prehistoric adj **1** *prehistoric man* primeval,
primordial, primitive, earliest. **2** *prehistoric
attitudes to women | wear prehistoric clothes* out
of date, old-fashioned, ancient, antiquated,
superannuated; *inf* out of the ark.

prejudice n **1** *have a prejudice against young
people | forget his prejudices against people from
other countries* bias, partiality, jaundiced
eye, preconceived idea, preconceived
notion, preconception, prejudgement, predetermination. **2** *employers showing prejudice
towards older people | found guilty of racial prej-
udice* bias, discrimination, partisanship,
partiality, preference, one-sidedness, chauvinism, bigotry, intolerance, narrow-
mindedness, unfairness, unjustness,
racism, sexism, ageism, heterosexism.
3 *without prejudice to any future judgement |
without prejudice to his claim* detriment, disadvantage, damage, injury, harm, hurt,
loss.

prejudice v **1** *wonder whether newspaper articles had prejudiced the attitude of the jury* bias,
make partial, make partisan, colour, poison, jaundice, influence, sway, predispose.
2 *his conviction may prejudice his chances* be
prejudicial to, be detrimental to, be deleterious, be disadvantageous to, damage,
injure, harm, hurt, mar, spoil, impair,
undermine. *see* PREJUDICIAL.

prejudiced adj *have a prejudiced attitude to
others of a different race | be prejudiced against
young people* biased, discriminatory, partisan, partial, one-sided, jaundiced, chauvinistic, bigoted, intolerant, narrow-minded,
unfair, unjust, racist, sexist, ageist.

prejudicial adj *his conviction will be prejudi-
cial to his chances of getting a job | actions preju-
dicial to the country's economy* detrimental,
deleterious, disadvantageous,
unfavourable, damaging, injurious, harmful, hurtful, inimical.

preliminary adj **1** *preliminary training | a few
preliminary remarks* introductory, prefatory,
prior, precursory, opening, initial, beginning, preparatory, initiatory. **2** *preliminary
heats/rounds/interviews* prior, precursory,
qualifying, eliminating. **3** *preliminary experiments* introductory, early, exploratory,
pilot, test, trial.

preliminary n *dispense with the preliminaries
and get on with the meeting | tired of prelimi-*

*nary after preliminary before their appeal was
heard* preliminary measure, preliminary
action, preparation, groundwork, first
round, introduction, preamble, prelude,
opening.

prelims npl **1** *got high marks in the prelims
but not in the actual exam* preliminary
exams, mock exams; *inf* mocks. **2** *read the
prelims at the start of the reference book* preliminary material, front matter, forward
matter, introductory material, introduction, prefatory material, foreword, preface,
preamble, proem, prolegomenon,
exordium.

prelude n **1** *the military skirmishes were a prelude to full-scale war* precursor, forerunner,
curtain-raiser, harbinger, herald, preliminary, introduction, start, beginning. **2** *the
prelude to the narrative poem* introduction,
preface, prologue, preamble, proem,
exordium, prolegomenon; *inf* intro. **3** *the
prelude to the fugue* overture, introductory
movement, voluntary.

premature adj **1** *his premature death/birth |
the premature closing of the play because of lack
of support* too soon, too early, early,
untimely. **2** *it was premature of him to
announce his plans* too soon, hasty, over-
hasty, precipitate, impulsive, impetuous,
rash. **3** *announce premature plans* incomplete, undeveloped, immature, embryonic.

prematurely adv **1** *leave prematurely* too
soon, too early, before the usual time.
2 *announce his plans prematurely* too soon,
too early, overhastily, precipately.

premeditated adj *premeditated murder*
planned, preplanned, prearranged, intentional, intended, deliberate, calculated, wilful.

premier n *an international meeting of premiers*
head of government, prime minister, PM.

premier adj *the country's premier computer
firm | a firm with a premier position in the com-
puter industry* leading, foremost, chief, principal, head, top-ranking, top, prime, first,
highest, main.

première n *the première of the play/film* first
night, first performance, first showing,
opening, opening night, début.

premise, premiss n *financial advice based
on the premise that the recession was over*
hypothesis, thesis, assumption, presupposition, presumption, argument, postulation.

premises npl *the firm has moved to new
premises* building, property, establishment.

premiss *see* PREMISE.

premium n **1** *monthly premiums for life insurance* insurance payment, insurance instal-

ment. **2** *paid a premium of £3 on their invest- ment* bonus, bounty. **3** *pay a premium for early delivery* additional payment, additional fee, surcharge. **4** *the boys received a premium for working late* reward, recompense, remu- neration, perquisite, prize; *inf* perk. **at a premium** *parking spaces are at a premium in the city centre* rare, hard to come by, in short supply, scarce, in great demand, like gold dust, not to be had; *inf* not to be had for love or money. **put a premium on 1** *the tutor puts a premium on creative work* set great store by, put a high value on, regard as valuable, hold in high regard, appreciate greatly, attach great importance to. **2** *the risk of disease puts a premium on hygiene* make invaluable, make valuable, put a high value on, make essential, make important.

premonition n **1** *had a premonition that something terrible was going to happen* fore- boding, presage, presentiment, intuition, feeling, hunch, suspicion, sneaking suspi- cion, misgiving, apprehension, fear, feeling in one's bones, funny feeling. **2** *given a pre- monition that all was not well in the firm* fore- warning, warning, sign, pre-indication, indication, omen, portent.

preoccupation n **1** *in his preoccupation he failed to notice her* abstraction, absorption, engrossment, concentration, brown study, deep thought, musing, pensiveness, reverie, absent-mindedness, absence of mind, distraction, inattentiveness, heed- lessness, oblivion, daydreaming, wool- gathering. **2** *DIY is his major preoccupation* chief concern, obsession, fixation, hobby- horse, pet subject, bee in one's bonnet, *idée fixe*; *inf* hang-up.

preoccupied adj *she seemed rather preoccu- pied* lost in thought, deep in thought, immersed in thought, in a brown study, absorbed, engrossed, pensive, absent- minded, distracted, abstracted, *distrait*, oblivious, far-away, rapt.

preoccupy v *his financial worries were preoc- cupying him* absorb, engross, take up one's whole attention, take up all one's time, distract, obsess.

preparation n **1** *the preparation of their plans* making ready, arrangement, development, assembling, assembly, drawing up, produc- tion, construction, composing, composi- tion, fashioning. see PREPARE 1. **2** *often preparations finalize their preparations for bat- tle* arrangement, provision, preparatory measure, necessary step, groundwork, spadework. **3** *the preparation of the students for the exam/contest* coaching, training,

grooming, priming. **4** *a preparation used as a tranquillizer* mixture, compound, concoc- tion, composition, tincture. **5** *children com- plaining at doing preparation* homework, schoolwork; *inf* prep.

preparatory adj *a great deal of preparatory work to be done before the store opens* prelimi- nary, introductory, prefatory, precursory, basic, elementary, fundamental, rudimen- tary, preparative. **preparatory to** *much to be done preparatory to the opening of the store* in preparation for, in advance of, before, prior to, in anticipation of, leading up to.

prepare v **1** *prepare their plans* get ready, make ready, arrange, develop, put together, assemble, draw up, produce, con- struct, compose, concoct, fashion, work up. **2** *prepare for trouble* make preparations, get ready, arrange things, make provision, get everything set, take the necessary steps, lay the groundwork, do the spadework; *inf* gear oneself up, psych oneself up, gird up one's loins. **3** *prepare for the sports event* train, get into shape for, practise, exercise, warm up. **4** *prepare for the exam* do prepara- tion, revise, study, do homework; *inf* swot. **5** *prepare the students for the exam/contest* coach, train, groom, prime. **6** *prepare her/ oneself for a shock* make ready, brace, steel. **7** *prepare a meal* cook, make, put together, assemble; *Amer inf* fix.

prepared adj **1** *everything is prepared for the wedding* ready, in readiness, arranged, in order, set, all set, fixed, planned, primed. **2** *they are prepared to make peace* ready, dis- posed, predisposed, willing, inclined, of a mind, minded.

preponderance n **1** *a preponderance of men over women on the staff | a preponderance of red in the room's decor* predominance, domi- nance, prevalence, greater number/ quantity, majority, bulk. **2** *the prepon- derance of the group in the alliance* domi- nance, predominance, control, ascendancy, leadership, mastery, supremacy, upper hand, edge.

prepossessing adj *a prepossessing child/man- ner* attractive, beautiful, pretty, handsome, good-looking, fetching, striking, pleasing, agreeable, appealing, likeable, lovable, ami- able, charming, engaging, winning, win- some, taking, enchanting, captivating, bewitching, fascinating.

preposterous adj *what a preposterous idea!* absurd, ridiculous, foolish, ludicrous, farci- cal, asinine, senseless, unreasonable, irra- tional, outrageous, shocking, astonishing, unbelievable, incredible, unthinkable; *inf* crazy, insane.

prerequisite adj *tolerance is prerequisite when bringing up children* necessary, needed, required, called for, essential, requisite, vital, indispensable, imperative, obligatory, mandatory.

prerequisite n *patience is a prerequisite for parenthood* requirement, requisite, necessity, essential, precondition, condition, *sine qua non*; *inf* must.

prerogative n *it's a woman's prerogative to change her mind | he thinks it's his prerogative to make all the decisions* right, birthright, privilege, due, entitlement, liberty, authority, licence, *carte blanche*.

presage v **1** *clouds presaging a storm* be a sign of, be an indication of, be a presage of, be an omen of, be a warning of, give a warning of, portend, augur. **2** *she presaged that something terrible would happen* forecast, foretell, prophesy, predict, foresee, divine, prognosticate, forewarn.

prescribe v **1** *the doctor prescribed antibiotics* write a prescription for, order, advise, direct. **2** *prescribe a holiday to cure her depression* advise, recommend, commend, suggest. **3** *the law prescribes strict penalties for drunk driving | school regulations prescribe that everyone must wear the uniform* lay down, require, direct, stipulate, specify, impose, decree, order, command, ordain, enjoin.

prescription n **1** *the prescription of drugs is part of a doctor's job* prescribing, ordering, advising. *see* PRESCRIBE 1. **2** *the doctor wrote a prescription for antibiotics* instruction, order, direction. **3** *his prescription for long life was hard work* recipe, formula, direction, advice. **4** *ask the chemist to make up the prescription* medicine, drug, remedy, preparation, mixture.

presence n **1** *the presence of too much acid in the soil | detect the presence of poison in the drink* existence, being. **2** *demand his presence at the meeting* attendance, company, companionship. **3** *they feel inadequate in the presence of such a great man* company, propinquity, proximity, neighbourhood, vicinity, closeness, nearness. **4** *a woman of presence* magnetism, aura, charisma, personality, attraction, poise, self-assurance, self-possession, self-confidence. **5** *impressed by her presence* dignified bearing, impressive carriage, dignified air/demeanour, dignity. **6** *she felt a presence in the castle* manifestation, apparition, supernatural being, spirit, ghost, spectre, wraith. **presence of mind** aplomb, level-headedness, sang-froid, phlegm, self-assurance, self-possession, composure, calmness, calm, coolness,

imperturbability, alertness, quickness, quick-wittedness; *inf* unflappability.

present¹ adj **1** *establish that poison was present in the drink* existing, existent, extant. **2** *in the present climate* present-day, existing, current, contemporary. **3** *a doctor had to be present* in attendance, here, there, near, nearby, available, at hand, ready.

present¹ n *forget the past and think about the present* today, now, here and now, the present moment, the time being. **at present** *at present he's unavailable* just now, right now, at the moment, at this time, for the moment, at the present time, currently, at this moment in time; *Amer Scots* presently. **for the present** *for the present we must economize* for the moment, for the time being, for now, in the meanwhile, in the meantime. **the present day** *the old man is shocked by the morals of the present day* the present age/time, modern times, nowadays.

present² v **1** *present a gift to the retiring chairman* give, hand over, confer, bestow, donate, award, grant, accord. **2** *present his proposals to the committee* submit, set forth, put forward, proffer, offer, tender, advance. **3** *present his apologies/greetings* give, offer, send, tender. **4** *may I present my daughter?* introduce, make known. **5** *present their new product to the trade/public* show, put on show, exhibit, display, put on display, demonstrate, introduce, launch. **6** *present a performance of Hamlet* put on, produce, perform, stage, mount. **7** *present a radio/television programme* be the presenter of, introduce, host, compère; *inf* emcee. **present oneself 1** *you must present yourself for interview at 11 a.m. tomorrow morning* be present, make an appearance, appear, attend, turn up. **2** *if the opportunity presents itself* occur, arise, happen, transpire, come about, appear.

present² n *a birthday present | the money was a present* gift, donation, offering, contribution, gratuity, hand-out, presentation, largesse, award, premium, bounty, boon, benefaction; *inf* pressie, freebie.

presentable adj *make yourself presentable for the interview | go to school looking presentable* well-groomed, smartly-dressed, tidily-dressed, tidy, spruce, of smart appearance, fit to be seen.

presentation n **1** *the presentation of his retirement gift* presenting, giving, handing over, conferral, bestowal, donation, award, granting, according. **2** *hand over a presentation to mark his retirement* gift, present, donation, offering, contribution, gratuity. *see* PRESENT² n. **3** *the presentation of their pro-*

posals to the committee submission, proffering, offering. *see* PRESENT[2] v 2. **4** *the presentation of his fiancée to his family* introduction, making known, acquainting. **5** *attend the presentation of their new product* launch, launching, show, exhibition, display, demonstration. **6** *attend the drama club's presentation of Hamlet* production, performance, staging, mounting, showing, rendition. **7** *improve the presentation of his material* arrangement, organization, ordering, disposition, layout, scheme, system, structure.

presentiment n *a presentiment of impending doom* foreboding, premonition, presage, intuition, feeling, hunch, suspicion, sneaking suspicion, misgiving, fear, apprehension, feeling in one's bones, funny feeling.

presently adv *he'll be here presently* soon, shortly, in a short time, in a short while, directly, in a moment, in a minute, before long, before you can say Jack Robinson; *inf* in a jiffy, in a mo, in two shakes of a lamb's tail; *Amer* momentarily.

preservation n **1** *the preservation of the wood* conservation, protection. *see* PRESERVE v 1. **2** *the preservation of the town from danger* protection, defence, guarding, safeguarding, safe keeping, safety, security, salvation, shielding. *see* PRESERVE v 2. **3** *the preservation of old traditions* conservation, keeping alive, maintenance, continuation, upholding, perpetuation. *see* PRESERVE v 4. **4** *preservation of financial resources* conservation, keeping, saving, putting away. *see* PRESERVE v 5.

preserve v **1** *find a substance to preserve the wood* conserve, protect, safeguard, care for. **2** *preserve the town from danger* keep, protect, defend, guard, safeguard, secure, shelter, shield. **3** *preserve his work for posterity* conserve, save, keep, safeguard, maintain, perpetuate. **4** *preserve the old traditions* conserve, keep up, keep alive, keep going, maintain, continue with, uphold, prolong, perpetuate. **5** *preserve their financial resources until a rainy day* conserve, keep, save, retain, put away, put aside, store, hoard. **6** *preserve food* cure, smoke, dry, pickle, salt, marinate, kipper.

preserve n **1** *an animal preserve* sanctuary, reserve, reservation, game reserve. **2** *he regards the family finances as his preserve* area, domain, field, sphere, realm; *inf* thing. **3** *she usually makes strawberry preserve* jam, jelly, confiture, marmalade, conserve.

preside v **1** *the committee members elected him to preside* chair, be in the chair, be chairman/chairwoman/chairperson, officiate. **2** *preside over a huge firm* be in charge of, be

at the head/helm of, head, manage, administer, be in control of, control, be responsible for, direct, run, conduct, supervise, govern, rule, be boss of, head up, be in the driver's seat, be in the saddle, pull the strings, call the shots.

president n **1** *terrorists have assassinated the president of a neighbouring country* chief of state, head of state. **2** *the president of the society* head, chief, director, leader, captain.

press v **1** *press the button/accelerator* press down, depress, push down, force down, bear down on. **2** *press grapes* crush, squeeze, compress, mash, reduce. **3** *press trousers* iron, smooth out, put creases in, calender, mangle. **4** *press flowers | press the soil down* flatten, make flat, smooth out. **5** *press the child to her bosom* clasp, enfold, hold close, clutch, grasp, embrace, hug, cuddle, squeeze, crush. **6** *press her hand/arm affectionately* squeeze, give something a squeeze, pat, caress. **7** *they are pressing him to make a decision* urge, entreat, exhort, implore, put pressure on, use pressure on, pressurize, force, compel, coerce, constrain. **8** *they are pressing for quick decision* call for, demand, insist on, clamour for. **9** *press a claim* plead, urge, push forward, advance insistently. **10** *press round the board to see the results* crowd, surge, cluster, mill, flock, gather, swarm, throng. **11** *the enemy are pressing our army* harass, besiege, attack, assail, beset, worry, torment. **be pressed for** *we are pressed for time | they are pressed for cash just now* be short of, have barely enough of, have too little of, have an insufficiency of; *inf* be strapped for. **be pressing** *other matters are pressing* be urgent, demand attention, require attention, call for action. **press on** *we must press on to reach the summit tonight | press on with the work* push on, make haste, hasten, hurry, proceed, continue, put one's nose to the grindstone, put one's shoulder to the wheel.

press n **1** *usually the press the freedom of the press | advertise in the press* newspapers, papers, news media, journalism, the newspaper world, the media, Fleet Street, the fourth estate, newspapermen, newspaper women, reporters, pressmen, presswomen, gentlemen of the press. **2** *get a good/bad press* press treatment, press coverage, press reporting, newspaper articles, newspaper write-ups. **3** *go to press | the presses are running* printing-press, printing-machine. **4** *he has set up a small press* printing firm, publishing firm, publishing house. **5** *children getting lost in the press leaving the cinema* crowd, throng, multitude, mob, troop, horde, swarm, herd, flock, pack, crush.

6 *the press of modern life* pressure, strain, stress, urgency, demands, hurry, hustle, hustle and bustle, flurry.

pressing adj **1** *have a pressing engagement* urgent, vital, crucial, critical, demanding, important, high-priority, exigent, pivotal. **2** *a pressing invitation to dinner* insistent, persistent, determined, importunate, repeated, repetitive.

pressure n **1** *have to exert pressure on the door to open it | the pressure of the crowd against the barriers* force, weight, heaviness. **2** *kill him by applying pressure to his neck and strangling him* compression, compressing, squeezing, crushing. **3** *parents exerting pressure to get her to marry him* force, compulsion, coercion, constraint, duress. **4** *have a breakdown because of the pressures of modern life | unable to cope with the pressure of work* strain, stress, tension, burden, load, weight, trouble; *inf* hassle. **5** *find it difficult to work under pressure* adversity, difficulty, urgency, strain, stress, tension.

pressure, pressurize v *pressure him into taking the job* put pressure on, use pressure on, press, force, compel, coerce, constrain, bulldoze, dragoon.

prestige n *suffer a loss of prestige in the community when he lost his job* status, kudos, standing, stature, importance, reputation, fame, renown, esteem, influence, authority, supremacy, eminence, superiority, predominance.

prestigious adj **1** *a prestigious school* reputable, respected, esteemed, eminent, distinguished, of high standing, well-known, celebrated, illustrious, renowned, famous. **2** *a prestigious job* conferring prestige, important, prominent, impressive, high-ranking, influential, glamorous.

presumably adv *presumably he'll get the job* it is to be presumed, in all probability, probably, in all likelihood, all things being equal, all things considered, on the face of it, as likely as not; *inf* as like as not.

presume v **1** *I presume that your new partner is honest | presumed innocent until proved guilty* assume, take for granted, take it, take as read, suppose, presuppose, believe, think, imagine, judge, guess, surmise, conjecture, hypothesize, infer, deduce. **2** *don't presume to offer advice to a more experienced person* have the temerity, have the audacity, be so bold as, make so bold as, have the effrontery, go so far as, dare, venture. **presume on** *presume on his good nature* take advantage of, take unfair advantage of, exploit, take liberties with.

presumption n **1** *she was infuriated by his presumption in booking a seat next to her* confidence, arrogance, egotism, boldness, audacity, forwardness, insolence, impudence, bumptiousness, temerity, effrontery. **2** *our presumption is that he has run away* assumption, supposition, presupposition, belief, thought, guess, surmise, conjecture, hypothesis, premise, premiss, inference, deduction. *see* PRESUME 1. **3** *the presumption for their hypothesis* grounds, ground, basis, reason, evidence.

presumptive adj **1** *the police lack any presumptive evidence* reasonable, plausible, feasible, likely, credible, believable, which holds water. **2** *the heir presumptive | the presumptive heir* probable, likely, assumed, supposed, expected.

presumptuous adj *it was presumptuous of him to offer advice to someone of her age and experience | a presumptuous, overbearing young woman* presuming, ultra-confident, super-confident, overconfident, cocksure, self-confident, self-assured, arrogant, egotistical, conceited, overbold, bold, audacious, forward, insolent, impudent, bumptious, self-assertive, overbearing, overweening, haughty; *inf* big-headed, swollen-headed, too big for one's boots, pushy.

presuppose v **1** *they cannot presuppose the accuracy of his alibi* presume, assume, take for granted, take it, take as read, suppose. **2** *does their approval of the plan presuppose that funding is available* require, imply, assume, presume, take for granted.

presupposition n *in the absence of evidence to the contrary their presupposition must be that he is innocent* presumption, assumption, preconception, supposition, thesis, theory, premise, premiss.

pretence n **1** *she's not ill—it's just pretence* putting on an act, acting, dissembling, shamming, faking, dissimulation, make-believe, invention, imagination, posturing. *see* PRETEND 1. **2** *not taken in by their pretence of grief* false show, show, semblance, false appearance, appearance, false front, guise, façade, masquerade, mask, veneer, cover, charade. **3** *on the pretence that he was dying* pretext, false excuse, guise, sham, ruse, wile, trickery, lie, falsehood. *see* PRETEXT. **4** *make no pretence to expertness | I have no pretence to being expert* claim, aspiration, purporting, profession. **5** *lead humble lives without pretence* pretentiousness, display, ostentation, affectation, showiness, flaunting, posturing.

pretend v **1** *she's not ill—she's only pretending* put on an act, act, play-act, put it on, dissemble, sham, feign, fake, fake it, dissimulate, make believe, put on a false front, posture, go through the motions. **2** *she is pretending that she knows nothing about the situation* make believe, affect, profess, make out, fabricate. **3** *pretend illness* sham, feign, fake, simulate, put on. **4** *pretend to the throne/title* claim, lay claim to, make a claim to, aspire to. **5** *pretend to be her friend* claim, profess, purport.

pretended adj **1** *a pretended affection* alleged, avowed, professed, purported, spurious, insincere, sham, bogus, fake, faked, counterfeit, affected, put-on, pseudo; *inf* phoney. **2** *a pretended friend* alleged, so-called, professed, ostensible, in name only, supposed, bogus, pseudo; *inf* pretend.

pretender n *a pretender to the throne* claimant, claimer, aspirant.

pretension n **1** *make no pretensions to being an expert* | *a writer with pretensions to literary greatness* claim, aspiration, pretence, profession, purporting. **2** *dislike the pretension of her style* | *a life full of pretension* pretentiousness, affectation, ostentation, ostentatiousness, showiness, pomposity, floweriness, extravagance, flamboyance, grandiloquence, magniloquence, bombast. *see* PRETENTIOUS 1. **3** *the pretension of their lifestyle* affectation, ostentation, ostentatiousness, showiness, flaunting, flamboyance.

pretentious adj **1** *a pretentious style of writing* affected, ostentatious, showy, overambitious, pompous, artificial, mannered, high-flown, high-sounding, flowery, grandiose, elaborate, extravagant, flamboyant, grandiloquent, magniloquent, bombastic, orotund; *inf* highfalutin. **2** *a pretentious lifestyle* affected, ostentatious, showy, flaunting, flamboyant.

preternatural adj *preternatural powers/experience* extraordinary, out of the ordinary, exceptional, unusual, uncommon, singular, abnormal, supernatural, paranormal.

pretext n *the thief got into the old lady's house on the pretext of reading the gas meter* | *find a pretext for getting into the house* pretence, false excuse, excuse, ostensible reason, alleged reason, alleged plea, supposed grounds, cover, guise, sham, ruse, wile, trickery, red herring, lie, falsehood, misrepresentation.

pretty adj **1** *a pretty child* attractive, lovely, good-looking, nice-looking, comely, personable, prepossessing, appealing, charming, delightful, nice, engaging, pleasing, winning, winsome, cute, as pretty as a picture;

Scots bonny. **2** *a pretty pattern* attractive, lovely, appealing, pleasant, pleasing, charming, delightful, nice; *Scots* bonny. **3** *a pretty turn of phrase* fine, neat, clever. **4** *cost a pretty penny* | *make a pretty profit* considerable, large, sizeable, substantial, appreciable, fair, tolerable, goodly, goodish; *inf* tidy.

pretty adv **1** *a pretty large sum of money* moderately, reasonably, fairly. **2** *feeling pretty secure* quite, rather, somewhat; *inf* kind of.

prevail v **1** *in the end common sense prevailed* win, win out, win through, triumph, be victorious, be the victor, carry the day, prove superior, conquer, overcome, gain mastery, gain ascendancy, take the crown, gain the palm, rule. **2** *the economic conditions prevailing at the time* exist, be in existence, obtain, occur, be prevalent, be current, be widespread, abound, hold sway, predominate, preponderate. **prevail on, prevail upon** *try to prevail upon him to speak at the conference* persuade, induce, talk someone into, bring someone round, convince, sway, prompt, influence, urge, exhort, pressure, bring pressure to bear on, pressurize, cajole, coax; *inf* sweet-talk.

prevailing adj **1** *the prevailing attitude towards prisoners* | *the prevailing fashion in hats* prevalent, current, usual, common, general, widespread, set, established, accepted, popular, fashionable, in fashion, in style, in vogue. **2** *the prevailing political party* prevalent, dominant, predominant, predominating, preponderant, most influential, ruling, governing, ascendant, principal, chief, main, supreme. **3** *the prevailing wind in the area* most frequent, most common, commonest, most usual.

prevalence n **1** *the prevalence of sexism in the firm* | *the prevalence of short skirts* currency, frequency, commonness, pervasiveness, universality, popularity, fashionableness. **2** *the prevalence of malaria in the region* commonness, universality, extensiveness, ubiquity, ubiquitousness, frequency, rifeness. **3** *the prevalence of the right wing of the party* dominance, predominance, preponderance, ascendancy, mastery, supremacy.

prevalent adj **1** *the prevalent opinion in the country is against the war* prevailing, current, frequent, usual, common, general, widespread, pervasive, universal, set, established, accepted, popular, fashionable, in fashion, in style, in vogue. **2** *malaria is prevalent there* common, usual, endemic, widespread, universal, extensive, frequent, ubiquitous, rampant, rife. **3** *the prevalent political party* prevailing, dominant, predominant, predominating, preponderant, ruling, governing. *see* PREVAILING 2.

prevaricate v *they tried to get him to commit himself to a course of action but he prevaricated* hedge, fence, beat about the bush, be evasive, shilly-shally, hum and haw, dodge the issue, dodge, sidestep the issue, sidestep, equivocate, quibble, tergiversate; *inf* beg the question.

prevarication n hedging, fencing, beating about the bush, evasion, evasiveness, shilly-shallying, humming and hawing, dodging, sidestepping, equivocation, quibbling, tergiversation. *see* PREVARICATE.

prevent v **1** *prevent the spread of the fire | prevent further progress* stop, put a stop to, halt, arrest, avert, nip in the bud, fend off, turn aside, stave off, ward off, block, check, hinder, impede, hamper, obstruct, baulk, foil, thwart, frustrate, forestall, inhibit, hold back, restrain, prohibit, bar, deter. **2** *prevent his daughter from leaving school* stop, hinder, impede, hamper, obstruct, inhibit, hold back, restrain, prohibit, bar.

prevention n *the prevention of the spread of the fire | the prevention of crime* stopping, halting, halt, arresting, staving off, warding off, checking, hindrance, hampering, obstruction, baulking, foiling, frustration, restraint, prohibition, barring, deterrence. *see* PREVENT 1.

preventive, preventative adj **1** *preventive/preventative measures against crime* precautionary, protective, deterrent. **2** *preventive medicine* prophylactic, disease-preventing, precautionary, protective.

preventive, preventative n **1** *a preventive/preventative against crime* preventive measure, precautionary/protective measure, safeguard, protection, deterrent, hindrance, obstruction. **2** *a preventive/preventative against disease* preventive, preventative drug, precautionary measure, prophylactic medicine, prophylactic device, prophylactic.

previous adj **1** *the previous holder of the post* former, ex-, preceding, foregoing, past, sometime, one-time, quondam, erstwhile, antecedent, precursory. **2** *in previous paragraph* preceding, foregoing, earlier, prior, above, precursory, antecedent, anterior. **3** *on a previous occasion* prior, earlier, former, preceding. **4** *it was rather previous of him to assume he was in charge | you're rather previous in assuming you're in charge* premature, precipitate, hasty, overhasty, impetuous, too early, too soon, untimely, presumptuous; *inf* ahead of oneself. **previous to** *previous to this everything was fine*

before, prior to, until, up to, earlier than, preceding.

previously adv **1** *they now live locally but previously they lived in London* formerly, earlier on, before, until now, hitherto, heretofore, once, at one time, in the past, in years gone by. **2** *at that point he was a teacher but previously he had been in banking* formerly, earlier on, before, until then, once, at one time, in the past, in years gone by.

prey n **1** *lions looking for prey* quarry, game, kill. **2** *a conman looking for prey | a prey for any dishonest salesman* victim, target, dupe; *inf* sitting duck, sitting target, fall guy, mug.

prey v **prey on 1** *lions preying on deer | hawks preying on small birds* live on, live off, eat, devour, hunt, catch, seize. **2** *unscrupulous conmen preying on old women* use as a victim, victimize, exploit, take advantage of, fleece, attack, terrorize, blackmail, bleed; *inf* con. **3** *his crime preyed on his mind* weigh down on, weigh upon, weigh heavily on, lie heavy on, oppress, burden, be a burden on, hang over, trouble, worry, distress, haunt.

price n **1** *what is the price of the table in the window? | with prices rising | charge a high price* cost, asking price, charge, fee, payment, rate, amount, figure, value, valuation, outlay, expenses, expenditure, bill. **2** *the price of breaking the law | being constantly photographed is the price that famous people have to pay* consequence, result, cost, penalty, sacrifice, forfeit, forfeiture, punishment. **3** *outlaws with a price on their heads* reward, bounty, premium, recompense, compensation. **at a price** *during the war most things were available on the black market—at a price* at a high price, at an expensive price, at a dear price, at a high cost, for a great deal of money, at considerable cost. **at any price** *they want that house at any price | the country wants peace at any price* whatever the price, whatever the cost, at whatever cost, no matter what the price, no matter the cost, cost what it may, cost what it might, expense no object, regardless. **beyond price 1** *jewels/souvenirs beyond price* priceless, without price, of incalculable value, of incalculable worth, of inestimable value, invaluable, precious, rare, expensive, costly, irreplaceable, treasured, prized. *see* PRICELESS 1. **2** *a virtue beyond price* priceless, without price, of incalculable worth, of inestimable value, invaluable, precious, cherished. *see* PRICELESS 2.

price v *price the items at £10 each* fix the price of, set the price of, cost, value, rate, evaluate, assess, estimate, appraise, assay.

priceless adj **1** *priceless jewels* beyond price, without price, of incalculable value, of incalculable worth, of inestimable value, of inestimable worth, invaluable, precious, rare, incomparable, expensive, costly, rich, dear, irreplaceable, treasured, prized, worth its weight in gold, worth a king's ransom. **2** *honesty is a priceless virtue* beyond price, without price, of incalculable worth/value, of inestimable value/worth, invaluable, precious, rare, treasured, prized, cherished, worth its weight in gold, worth a king's ransom. **3** *his jokes are priceless* hilarious, extremely amusing, very funny, comic, riotous, side-splitting, rib-tickling; *inf* killingly funny, a scream, a hoot. **4** *looking priceless in that hat* absurd, ridiculous, comical, hilarious, extremely amusing, very funny; *inf* a scream, a hoot, killingly funny.

prick n **1** *give his finger a prick with a sharp needle* jag, jab, stab, nick, wound. **2** *see the prick on the surface* puncture, perforation, hole, pinhole, nick, wound. **3** *feel a prick on the surface of the skin* prickle, sting, smarting, tingle, tingling, pain. **4** *the pricks of his conscience* pricking, pang, twinge, gnawing. **5** *a stick with a prick* | *rose-bushes with pricks* spike, thorn, barb, spine, prong, tine.

prick v **1** *prick the balloon with a needle* | *prick the boil with a sterilized needle* pierce, puncture, perforate, make a hole in, put a hole in, stab, nick, gash, slit, bore, spike. **2** *she pricked her finger on a needle* | *thorns pricked her bare legs* jag, jab, stab, nick, wound. **3** *his eyes began to prick in the smoke* sting, smart, tingle. **4** *his conscience began to prick him* distress, cause distress to, trouble, worry, gnaw at, cause pain to. **5** *ambition pricked him on to greater effort* goad, prod, urge, spur, prompt, incite, push, propel.

prickle n **1** *the prickles on the branches of the rose-tree* thorn, needle, barb, spike, point, spine, spur. **2** *feel a prickle on her skin* prickling sensation, tingle, tingling sensation, tingling, sting, stinging, smarting, itching, creeping sensation, goose-pimples, formication, paraesthesia, pins and needles.

prickle v **1** *his scalp began to prickle* tingle, sting, smart, itch, have a creeping sensation, have goose-pimples, have pins and needles. **2** *the rough wool prickled his skin* make something, tingle, sting, make something smart, make something itch.

prickly adj **1** *a prickly branch* spiky, spiked, thorny, barbed, bristly, spiny, pronged. **2** *a*

prickly feeling in his scalp prickling, tingling, stinging, smarting, itching, itchy, creeping, crawling. **3** *the old man's rather a prickly character* cantankerous, irascible, irritable, bad-tempered, touchy, edgy, fractious, tetchy, peevish, grumpy, snappish, snappy; *inf* ratty, stroppy, shirty. **4** *prickly issues* | *prickly problems* difficult, troublesome, vexatious, tough, complicated, complex, intricate, involved, knotty, thorny, ticklish, tricky.

pride n **1** *his pride was hurt by her comments on his lack of ability* self-esteem, self-respect, ego, *amour propre*, self-worth, self-image, self-identity, feelings, sensibilities. **2** *guilty of pride* | *puffed with pride at his achievement* conceit, vanity, arrogance, haughtiness, self-importance, self-conceit, self-love, self-glorification, egotism, presumption, hauteur, superciliousness, disdain; *inf* big-headedness, swollen-headedness. **3** *take/have pride in his work* satisfaction, gratification, pleasure, joy, delight. **4** *since she won the singing competition she is the pride of the school* pride and joy, prize, jewel, jewel in the crown, flower, gem, treasure, glory.

pride v **pride oneself on** *she prided herself on her punctuality* be proud of oneself for, take pride in, take satisfaction in, congratulate oneself on, flatter oneself on, preen oneself on, give oneself a pat on the back for, revel in, glory in, exult in, boast about, brag about, crow about.

priest n clergyman, minister, vicar, ecclesiastic, cleric, churchman, churchwoman, man/woman of the cloth, man/woman of God, father, padre.

prig n prude, puritan, killjoy, Mrs Grundy, Grundy; *inf* goody-goody, Goody Two-Shoes, holy Joe, holy Willie.

priggish adj prudish, puritanical, prim, strait-laced, stuffy, starchy, self-righteous, sanctimonious, narrow-minded, censorious; *inf* holier-than-thou, goody-goody, Grundyish.

prim adj *too prim and proper to join in the fun of the party* proper, demure, formal, precise, stuffy, starchy, strait-laced, prudish, prissy, old-maidish, priggish, puritanical; *inf* school-marmish, schoolmistressy.

prima donna n diva, leading lady, star.

primarily adv *his role is primarily an administrative one* basically, essentially, in essence, fundamentally, in the first place, first and foremost, chiefly, mainly, in the main, principally, mostly, for the most part, on the whole, predominantly, predominately.

primary adj **1** *the children's welfare is our primary consideration* prime, chief, main, principal, leading, predominant, most important, paramount. **2** *finding food to eat is a primary need* basic, fundamental, elemental, rudimentary, essential, prime. **3** *the primary stages of development | the primary stages of the disease* earliest, original, initial, beginning, first, opening, introductory. **4** *the primary stage of civilization* first, earliest, prehistoric, primitive, primeval, primal, primordial, autochthonal, pristine.

prime adj **1** *his prime motive was self-interest* chief, main, principal, leading, predominant, most important, major, paramount. **2** *the prime cause of the trouble* basic, fundamental, elemental, rudimentary, essential, primary. **3** *of prime quality | a prime site | prime meat* top-quality, highest, top, best, first-class, high-grade, grade A, superior, choice, select; *inf* A1. **4** *a prime example of what's wrong with modern society* classic, ideal, excellent, typical, standard.

prime n **1** *in the prime of his life* best part, peak, pinnacle, best days, height, zenith, acme, culmination, apex, heyday, full flowering. **2** *flowers in their prime* perfection, peak, full flowering, blossoming.

prime v **1** *prime the machines for use* prepare, make ready, get ready, equip. **2** *prime the investigating officer* brief, give information to, inform, supply with facts; *inf* clue in, clue up, give the low-down to, fill in, gen up. **3** *the solicitor was accused of priming the witness* instruct beforehand, coach, give information to, prepare. **4** *prime the travellers with food and drink* supply, provide, equip, furnish, provision, accommodate.

primeval adj *primeval rocks* ancient, earliest, prehistoric, primitive, primordial, primal, autochthonal, pristine.

primitive adj **1** *in primitive times | the primitive church* ancient, earliest, primeval, primordial, primal, autochthonal, pristine. **2** *primitive farming tools* crude, simple, rudimentary, undeveloped, unrefined, rough, unsophisticated, rude. **3** *primitive tribes* uncivilized, barbarian, barbaric, savage, wild. **4** *primitive art* simple, natural, unsophisticated, naive, undeveloped, childlike. **5** *primitive artists* unsophisticated, naive, untaught, untrained, untutored.

primp v *primp one's hair/clothes* groom, tidy, smarten, spruce, prink; *inf* titivate. **primp oneself** groom oneself, tidy oneself up, smarten oneself up, spruce oneself up, preen oneself, prink, prink oneself up, plume oneself; *inf* titivate oneself, doll oneself up, tart oneself up.

prince v *the prince of a neighbouring state* ruler, lord, sovereign, potentate.

princely adj **1** *a princely procession/array* regal, royal, stately, imposing, dignified, august, magnificent, majestic. **2** *give princely gifts | a princely sum of money* magnanimous, munificent, bounteous, bountiful, lavish, generous, open-handed, liberal.

principal adj **1** *the principal members of the organization* chief, leading, pre-eminent, foremost, most important, most influential, dominant, controlling, ruling, in charge. **2** *the principal issues on the agenda | the principal points to be considered* chief, main, major, most important, leading, key, primary, prime, paramount. **3** *the principal cities of the world* capital, main, leading, major.

principal n **1** *the principals in the firm* chief, head, director, leader, manager, boss, ruler, controller; *inf* honcho. **2** *the principal of the school* head teacher, headmaster, headmistress, head, rector. **3** *the principal of the college* head, master, dean, director, rector. **4** *the principals in the play* leading player, leading performer, leading man/ lady, lead, star. **5** *lend him the principal to start up the firm* capital, capital sum, capital funds, working capital, financial resources.

principally adv *he is interested principally in higher education* chiefly, above all, first and foremost, mainly, in the main, primarily, for the most part, mostly, particularly, especially.

principle n **1** *the basic principles of geometry | understand the principles of monetarism* truth, philosophy, idea, theory, basis, fundamental, essence, assumption. **2** *believe in the principle of equal opportunity* rule, golden rule, law, canon, tenet, code, maxim, axiom, dictum, postulate. **3** *a woman of principle | a woman without principle* morals, ethics, integrity, uprightness, righteousness, probity, rectitude, sense of honour, honour, conscience, scruples. *see* PRINCIPLES. **in principle 1** *there is no reason in principle why such a machine could not be built* in theory, theoretically. **2** *they agree in principle to the plan* in essence, in general.

principles npl *it is against his principles to lie | have no principles* moral code, code of ethics, code, morals, ethics, beliefs, credo. *see* PRINCIPLE 3.

print v **1** *print books/newspapers* set in print, send to press, run off, put to bed. **2** *they have printed thousands of copies* publish, issue. **3** *print a design on the cloth* imprint, stamp, mark. **4** *events printed forever on her* *memory* imprint, impress, engrave, etch, stamp, mark.

print n **1** *see the story in print | the print is too small to be legible* type, letters, lettering, typeface, newsprint. **2** *buy a print of one of Monet's works* copy, reproduction, replica. **3** *buy a set of prints showing the castles of Britain* picture, design, engraving, lithograph. **4** *get enlarged prints* photograph, photo, snap, snapshot. **5** *chairs covered in a print* printed material/cloth, patterned material/cloth, chintz. **6** *leave prints* fingerprint, footprint, mark, impression. **in print 1** *she will believe it only if she sees it in print | likes to see his name in print* printed, in black and white, on paper. **2** *are her novels still in print?* published, printed, available in bookshops, obtainable in the shops, on the market. **out of print** *looking for a biography which is out of print* o.p., no longer published/printed, not on the market, unavailable, unobtainable.

prior adj *a prior claim | no prior knowledge required* earlier, previous, anterior. **prior to** *prior to the conference they had never met before*, until, up to, earlier than, preceding.

priority n **1** *making sure the children are safe must be their priority | decide on a list of priorities* first/prime concern, most important thing/act, most pressing thing/act. **2** *give priority to homeless people* precedence, preference, urgency, highest place, top place. **3** *in terms of length of service he has priority* precedence, seniority, superiority, supremacy, paramountcy, prerogative. **4** *drive on—you have priority* right of way.

priory n religious house, abbey, cloister, monastery, friary, convent, nunnery.

prise v *prise the lid off* lever, force, pull; *inf* yank; *Amer* pry.

prison n jail, gaol, lock-up, penal institution, place of detention, place of confinement, dungeon; *inf* clink, nick, cooler, quod, slammer, choky, stir, can, jug; *Amer* penitentiary; *Amer inf* pen.

prisoner n **1** *prisoners let out on parole* convict, jailbird; *inf* con, lag, lifer. **2** *the kidnappers refused to release their prisoner | the invading army took many prisoners* prisoner of war, POW, hostage, captive, detainee, internee.

pristine adj **1** *a pristine copy of the book* unmarked, unblemished, unspoilt, spotless, immaculate, clean, in mint condition, in perfect condition. **2** *pristine snow* unmarked, spotless, clean, fresh, virgin. **3** *remains of some pristine era* early, ancient, prehistoric, primeval, primordial, primal, primitive, autochthonal.

privacy n **1** *enjoy the privacy of his study | the privacy of their walled garden* privateness, seclusion, solitude, isolation, retirement, sequestration, quietness, peace, lack of disturbance, lack of interruption, freedom from interference. **2** *accuse the press of invading her privacy* right to privacy, right to privateness, privateness, freedom from interference.

private adj **1** *for her private use* personal, individual, own, particular, especial, special, exclusive. **2** *hold private talks | her private opinion* confidential, strictly confidential, not for publication, not to be made public, not to be disclosed, secret, unofficial, off-the-record, in camera, closet, privileged; *inf* hush-hush. **3** *her private thoughts* personal, intimate, secret. **4** *a private place where the lovers meet* secluded, sequestered, quiet, secret, remote, out-of-the-way, withdrawn, retired. **5** *trespassing on private property* privately-owned, not open to the public, off-limits. **6** *wish to be private* undisturbed, without disturbance, uninterrupted, without interruption, alone, solitary. **7** *a private person* reserved, retiring, self-contained, uncommunicative, non-communicative, non-committal, diffident, secretive. **8** *the queen on a private visit* unofficial, non-official, non-public, personal. **9** *private industry/education/medicine* non-state, non-state-controlled, private-enterprise, privatized, independent.

private n *privates in the British army* private soldier, infantryman; *Amer* enlisted man; *inf* Tommy, squaddie. **in private** *the talks were held in private | the legal case was heard in private* privately, in camera, in secret, secretly, in secrecy, behind closed doors, in confidence, confidentially, *sub rosa*.

privately adv **1** *the talks were held privately* in private, in camera, in secret, behind closed doors. *see* PRIVATE n, IN PRIVATE. **2** *privately she thought he was doing the wrong thing* personally, secretly, unofficially. **3** *they required somewhere to meet privately* out of public view, in seclusion, in solitude, alone, without being disturbed, without being interrupted.

privation n *children suffering a life of privation* deprivation, want, need, neediness, disadvantage, poverty, penury, hardship, distress, indigence, destitution.

privilege n **1** *parking in that area is the privilege of local residents* right, birthright, prerogative, entitlement, due, sanction, advantage, benefit. **2** *enjoy parliamentary privilege* immunity, exemption, dispensation, concession, liberty, freedom. **3** *has* *always led a life of privilege* advantage, social advantage, advantageousness, favour, favourable circumstances, superior situation. **4** *he felt that it had been a privilege to meet her* honour, special benefit.

privileged adj **1** *coming from a privileged background* advantaged, socially advantaged, favoured, élite, indulgent, spoilt, protected, sheltered. **2** *that is certainly the law but MPs are privileged* immune, exempt, excepted. **3** *punished for revealing privileged information* confidential, private, not for publication, off-the-record, secret, top secret; *inf* hush-hush.

privy adj **privy to** *not privy to the plans of management* acquainted with, aware of, in on, informed of, apprised of, cognizant of; *inf* in the know about, genned up on, clued in on.

prize n **1** *win a prize in the lottery* winnings, jackpot, stakes, purse. **2** *win first prize in the track race | get second prize in the horticultural competition* trophy, medal, award, accolade, reward, premium, honour, laurels, palm, bays. **3** *he is studying for further qualifications with a higher salary the prize* goal, aim, desire, hope. **4** *the prizes of war* spoils, booty, plunder, loot, pillage, pickings, trophy, capture.

prize adj *wind destroyed his prize roses* prize-winning, award-winning, winning, champion, best, top, choice, select, first-class, first-rate, excellent; *inf* top-notch, A1.

prize v *prize his few remaining possessions | she prizes his freedom* value, set a high value on, set great store by, treasure, cherish, hold dear, appreciate greatly, attach great importance to, esteem, hold in high regard.

prized adj *have his prized stamp collection stolen* valued, treasured, cherished, precious, beloved.

probability n **1** *what is the probability of the government losing the election? | there is little probability that we will be able to go* likelihood, likeliness, prospect, expectation, chance, chances, odds, possibility. **2** *snow at Christmas is a distinct probability* probable event, likelihood, prospect, possibility, reasonable bet.

probable adj *the probable result is a win for the home team | it is probable that we will arrive late* likely, most likely, odds-on, expected, to be expected, anticipated, predictable, forseeable, on the cards, credible, quite possible, possible.

probably adv *they will probably win* in all probability, likely, most likely, in all likeli-

hood, as likely as not, it is to be expected that, perhaps, maybe, it may be, possibly; *inf* as like as not; *lit* peradventure.

probation n *new trainees must do a three-month period of probation* trial, trial period, test period, try-out, experimental period. **on probation 1** *young offenders on probation* under official supervision. **2** *trainees on probation* on trial, on a trial period.

probe n *order a probe into the company's accounting procedures* investigation, scrutiny, scrutinization, close inquiry, inquest, exploration, examination, study, research, analysis.

probe v **1** *probing the patient's stomach looking for a lump | probe the tooth with his tongue* feel, feel around, prod, poke, explore, check. **2** *probe the financial state of the company* investigate, conduct an investigation into, scrutinize, inquire into, conduct an inquiry into, carry out an inquest into, examine, subject to an examination, study, research, analyse.

problem n **1** *face a seemingly impossible problem* difficulty, difficult situation, vexed question, complication, trouble, mess, predicament, plight, dilemma, quandary; *inf* pickle, can of worms, facer. **2** *he has business problems | the car's mechanical problems* difficulty, difficult situation, trouble, complication. **3** *he and his wife have had a few problems* difficulty, dispute, subject of dispute, point at issue, bone of contention. **4** *solve the arithmetical problems | be baffled by the word problems* question, puzzle, poser, enigma, riddle, conundrum; *inf* teaser, brain-teaser. **5** *the child's a real problem* source of trouble, source of difficulty, bother, nuisance, pest, vexation; *inf* hassle, aggravation.

problem adj *a problem child* difficult, troublesome, delinquent, unmanageable, unruly, uncontrollable, intractable, recalcitrant, nuisance.

problematic adj **1** *a problematic situation* problematical, difficult, troublesome, complicated, puzzling, knotty, thorny, ticklish, tricky; *inf* dodgy. **2** *the likely result is still problematic* doutful, open to doubt, uncertain, unsettled, questionable, open to question, debatable, arguable.

procedure n **1** *the usual office procedure | pay due attention to procedure* course of action, line of action, plan of action, policy, system, method, methodology, *modus operandi*, technique, means, practice, operation, strategy, way, routine, wont, custom. **2** *essential procedures for setting up the new sys-*

tem action, step, process, measure, move, operation, transaction.

proceed v **1** *proceed along the platform with all possible haste | proceed upstairs slowly* make one's way, go, go on, go forward, go ahead, advance, carry on, move on, press on, progress. **2** *proceed to question him | how shall we proceed?* act, take action, take steps, take measures, go ahead, move, make a start, progress, get under way. **3** *noise proceeding from the floor below | the tragedy that proceeded from a family feud* arise, originate, spring, stem, come, derive, result, follow, ensue, emanate, issue, flow. **proceed against** *he decided to proceed against his employers for unfair dismissal* take proceedings against, begin an action against, start an action against, take to court, sue. **proceed with** *proceed with their work* go on with, continue with, continue, get on with, get ahead with.

proceeding n *such a proceeding will have to be carefully considered* action, course of action, step, measure, move, manoeuvre, act, deed, operation, transaction, venture, procedure, process.

proceedings npl **1** *the evening's proceedings begin at 7 p.m. | the prize-giving proceedings were interrupted by someone fainting* activities, events, action, process, business, affairs, doings, happenings. **2** *the proceedings against him are likely to last several weeks* legal proceedings, legal action/case, case, lawsuit, litigation, trial. **3** *the proceedings of the meeting were made available to all society members* minutes, report, account, record, transactions.

proceeds npl *donate the proceeds of/from the fête to charity* takings, profits, returns, receipts, gain, income, earnings.

process n **1** *damaged during the manufacturing process* operation, action, activity, steps, stages. **2** *develop a new process for cleaning old stone buildings* method, system, technique, means, practice, way, procedure. **3** *the ageing process* development, evolution, changes, stages, steps. **4** *in the process of time* course, advance, progress. **5** *legal processes can be very slow* proceedings, legal action, legal case, case, lawsuit, trial. **in the process of** *we are in the process of cataloguing our books* in the midst of, in the course of, in the performance of, in the execution of, at the stage of.

procession n **1** *a torchlight procession as part of the town's centenary celebration* parade, march, column, file, train, cortège. **2** *a procession of decorated lorries* cavalcade, motorcade. **3** *a seemingly endless procession of house-guests* stream, steady stream, string, succession, series, sequence, run.

proclaim v **1** *proclaim the news of a royal birth | proclaim a public holiday* announce, declare, make known, give out, notify, circulate, advertise, publish, broadcast, promulgate, pronounce, blazon, trumpet, shout something from the rooftops. **2** *proclaim him king* pronounce, announce, declare someone to be. **3** *her accent proclaimed that she was French* indicate, show, reveal, testify.

proclamation n **1** *hear the proclamation of a royal birth* announcement, declaration, notification, circulation, advertisement, publishing, broadcasting, promulgation, pronouncement, blazoning. *see* PROCLAIM 1. **2** *the king's proclamation was posted in each town* announcement, declaration, pronouncement, decree, edict, order, command, rule, manifesto.

proclivity n *a proclivity towards outbursts of rage | have peculiar sexual proclivities* tendency, inclination, leaning, propensity, bent, bias, proneness, penchant, predisposition, weakness.

procrastinate v *procrastinate in the hope that someone else would do the work* delay, postpone action, defer action, be dilatory, use delaying tactics, stall, temporize, play for time, play the waiting game, dally, dillydally, drag one's feet/heels.

procreation n *marriage regarded as being purely for procreation* sexual reproduction, generation, propagation, multiplication.

procure v **1** *procure a copy of the book from the library* obtain, acquire, get, pick up, find, come by, get hold of, secure, get possession of, lay one's hands on, get one's hands on, gain. **2** *somehow procure the dismissal of his colleague* bring about, cause, contrive, manage, manipulate, rig; *inf* fix. **3** *the police found that he was procuring* pimp, pander.

prod v **1** *prod him in the ribs when pushing past* poke, jab, dig, nudge, elbow, butt, push, shove, thrust. **2** *try to prod the child into doing some work* urge, encourage, rouse, move, motivate, stimulate, incite, spur on, impel, actuate, goad.

prod n **1** *get a prod in the ribs from someone in the crowd* poke, jab, dig, nudge, elbow, butt, push, shove, thrust. **2** *use a prod to get the cows to go back to the farm* goad, stick, spike. **3** *giving the child a prod to get him to do some work* encouragement, prompting, prompt, motivation, stimulus, incitement, spur, goad.

prodigal adj **1** *a government accused of being prodigal | her prodigal catering* extravagant, spendthrift, squandering, improvident, imprudent, immoderate, profligate, excessive, wasteful, reckless, wanton. **2** *a philanthropist prodigal of his gifts to the poor | prodigal of compliments* lavish with, liberal with, generous with, bountiful with, bounteous with, abundant in, abounding in.

prodigious adj **1** *a prodigious achievement* amazing, astonishing, astounding, staggering, stupendous, marvellous, wonderful, phenomenal, miraculous, impressive, striking, startling, extraordinary, remarkable, exceptional, unusual; *inf* fantastic, fabulous, flabbergasting. **2** *children frightened by the prodigious creatures on the screen* enormous, huge, colossal, gigantic, giant, mammoth, immense, massive, vast, monumental, tremendous, inordinate, monstrous, grotesque, abnormal. **3** *charge a prodigious amount of money* huge, large, colossal, immense, massive, considerable, substantial, sizeable; *inf* vast, tremendous.

prodigy n **1** *the child musician is a prodigy* genius, child genius, wonder child, wonderkind, gifted child, mastermind; *inf* Einstein. **2** *the pyramids are among the prodigies of the world* wonder, marvel, phenomenon, sensation, miracle. **3** *the saint is a prodigy of patience* classic example, example, model, paragon, paradigm, epitome, exemplar, ideal.

produce v **1** *a country which produces more goods than it can sell | a factory producing high-quality work* make, manufacture, create, construct, build, fabricate, put together, assemble, turn out. **2** *produce great works of art* compose, create, originate, prepare, develop, frame, fashion, turn out. **3** *produce new evidence* bring forward, set forth, present, offer, proffer, advance, show, exhibit, demonstrate, disclose, reveal. **4** *soil producing good crops | cows producing very little milk* yield, bear, give, bring forth, supply, provide, furnish. **5** *sows producing large litters of piglets* give birth to, bring forth, bear, breed, give life to, bring into the world, procreate. **6** *his speech produced an angry reaction* cause, give rise to, evoke, bring about, set off, occasion, generate, engender, induce, initiate, start, spark off. **7** *produce plays for television* mount, stage, put on, present, direct.

produce n *organically-grown produce* crops, fruit and vegetables, fruit, vegetables, greengrocery, greens.

producer n **1** *a country which is a major producer of cars | a factory noted as a producer of* high-quality work maker, manufacturer, creator, builder. *see* PRODUCE v 1. **2** *producers of fine fruit and vegetables* grower, farmer. **3** *the producer of several major films* backer, impresario, casting-director, schedule-director; *inf* angel. **4** *a producer of television/radio/amateur plays* director, stage-manager.

product n **1** *a factory specializing in electronic products* commodity, artefact, manufactured item/article/thing. **2** *necessary for the firm to improve the image of its product* goods, wares, merchandise. **3** *good health is the product of good nutrition | he is a typical product of a Victorian upbringing* result, outcome, effect, consequence, upshot, fruit, spin-off, legacy.

production n **1** *speed up the production of cars* producing, making, manufacture, manufacturing, creation, construction, building, fabrication, assembly. **2** *his production of great works of literature/work* composition, creation, origination, preparation, development, framing, fashioning. **3** *the production of new evidence* presenting, offering, proffering, advancement, exhibition, demonstration, disclosure. *see* PRODUCE v 3. **4** *there has been a fall/increase in production* output, yield. **5** *go and see a production of Hamlet in modern dress* performance, staging, mounting. **6** *several productions staged by the company* play, film, concert, show, performance, presentation, piece. **7** *this is the writer's latest production* work, publication, book, volume, tome, novel, story, composition, piece, creation, opus. **8** *artist's latest production* work, work of art, painting, picture, piece, creation.

productive adj **1** *productive soil* fertile, fruitful, fecund, rich, high-yielding. **2** *a productive worker* prolific, energetic, vigorous, efficient. **3** *not a very productive day's work* profitable, gainful, valuable, fruitful, useful, constructive, effective, worthwhile, beneficial, rewarding. **4** *an attitude scarcely productive of good labour relations* producing, causing, resulting in.

productivity n **1** *the productivity of the soil* productiveness, fertility, fecundity, fruitfulness, richness. **2** *improve the productivity of the workers/factory* productiveness, workrate, output, yield, production, capacity, efficiency.

profane adj **1** *their profane behaviour in setting fire to the altar* blasphemous, sacrilegious, impious, idolatrous, irreligious, ungodly, godless, irreverent, disrespectful. **2** *old ladies shocked by the man's profane language* blasphemous, obscene, foul, vulgar, crude, filthy, coarse. **3** *profane, not church* *music* lay, secular, non-religious, temporal, worldly.

profanity n **1** *the profanity of drinking and brawling in church* profaneness, blasphemy, sacrilege, impiety, idolatry, irreligiousness, irreverence, disrespectfulness, disrespect. **2** *issue a stream of profanities* oath, swearword, swearing, curse, obscenity, four-letter word, execration, imprecation.

profess v **1** *profess satisfaction with his work* declare, announce, proclaim, assert, state, utter, affirm, avow, aver. **2** *professed undying love | he professed total ignorance of the situation but no one believed him* claim, lay claim to, allege, pretend, feign, make out, sham, fake, dissemble. **3** *profess one's Christian faith* declare publicly, make a public declaration of, avow, confess, confirm, declare one's allegiance to, acknowledge publicly.

professed adj **1** *see through her professed love for children | deserted by her professed supporters* claimed, alleged, ostensible, supposed, so-called, pretended, feigned, sham, fake, would-be. **2** *he is a professed Christian/pacifist* declared, avowed, confessed, self-confessed, self-acknowledged, confirmed.

profession n **1** *a teacher by profession | seek a profession in medicine* career, calling, vocation, occupation, line of work, line of employment, position, situation, post, job, office, appointment, métier. **2** *in the medical/legal profession* sphere of work, line of work, area of work, walk of life, business. **3** *they were relieved by his professions of satisfaction with their work* declaration, announcement, proclamation, assertion, statement, affirmation, avowal, averment. **4** *were not taken in by his profession of ignorance | believed his profession of undying love* claim, allegation, pretence, feigning, shamming, faking, dissembling. **5** *his profession of his Christian faith* declaration, public declaration, avowal, confession, public acknowledgement, testimony.

professional adj **1** *he is a professional man* white-collar. **2** *a very professional worker* skilled, skilful, proficient, expert, adept, competent, efficient, experienced. **3** *a very professional piece of work | such a professional performance* skilful, expert, adept, masterly, excellent, fine, polished, finished. **4** *a professional tennis player* non-amateur, paid. **5** *conduct that was hardly professional* ethical, fitting.

professional n **1** *accommodation sought for young professionals* professional worker, white-collar worker. **2** *this tennis player is a professional now* professional player, non-amateur, paid player. **3** *the singer/tailor is a*

real professional expert, skilled person, master, past master, adept, authority; *inf* pro, dab hand.

professor n **1** *professor of French at the local university* head of faculty, head of department, holder of a chair, chair, Regius professor. **2** *encouraged by the professors of satisfaction* declarer, proclaimer, asserter. *see* PROFESS 1. **3** *not deceived by the professors of total loyalty* claimant, alleger, pretender, dissembler. *see* PROFESS 2.

proffer v *proffer assistance | decide to proffer one's resignation* offer, tender, present, extend, give, submit, volunteer, suggest.

proficiency n *their proficiency in keyboarding | acquired proficiency in the art of public speaking* skill, skilfulness, adeptness, aptness, expertise, expertness, adroitness, deftness, excellence, ability, ableness, capability, competence, experience, effectiveness, accomplishment, talent.

proficient adj *a proficient keyboarder/ swimmer | proficient at swimming | proficient in French* skilful (at), skilled (at/in), adept (at/ in), apt (at), expert (at/in), adroit (at/in), deft (at), able (at), capable (at), competent (at/ in), experienced (in/at), effective (at), accomplished (in/at), talented (at), gifted (at/in).

profile n **1** *draw her profile | look better in profile* side-view, outline. **2** *the profile of the church against the sky* silhouette, outline, contour, lines, shape, form, figure. **3** *write a profile of the winner of the Booker prize* short biography, potted biography, sketch, thumbnail sketch, portrait, vignette.

profit n **1** *the profit made from the sale of the house | the builder's annual profit* takings, proceeds, gain, yield, return, receipts, income, earnings, winnings. **2** *you could, with profit, take her advice | seem to gain little profit from the experience* gain, benefit, advantage, good, value, use, avail.

profit v *it will not profit you to be openly critical of the firm* benefit, be of benefit to, be of advantage to, be advantageous to, be of use/value to, be of service to, serve, do someone good, help, be helpful to, assist, aid, stand someone in good stead. **profit from** *profit from his advice | try to profit from the experience* derive benefit from, benefit from, reap the benefit of, gain from, derive advantage from, put to good use, learn from; *inf* cash in on.

profitable adj **1** *a profitable venture* profit-making, money-making, commercial, gainful, remunerative, paying, lucrative. **2** *a profitable company* profit-making, money-making, sound, solvent, in the black. **3** *find* it a profitable experience | think the conference profitable beneficial, advantageous, rewarding, helpful, productive, useful, worthwhile, valuable.

profligacy n **1** the profligacy of her housekeeping | the profligacy of people who are always in debt extravagance, improvidence, prodigality, immoderateness, recklessness, wastefulness. see PROFLIGATE adj 1. **2** tired of her husband's profligacy dissoluteness, dissipation, debauchery, corruption, degeneracy, depravity, immorality, promiscuity, looseness, wantonness, licentiousness, lasciviousness, lechery.

profligate adj **1** a profligate housekeeper | a profligate young woman who is always in debt extravagant, spendthrift, improvident, prodigal, immoderate, squandering, reckless, wasteful. **2** a profligate cad dissolute, dissipated, debauched, abandoned, corrupt, degenerate, depraved, reprobate, unprincipled, immoral, promiscuous, loose, wanton, licentious, lascivious, lecherous.

profligate n **1** the profligate soon got through his inheritance spendthrift, prodigal, squanderer, wastrel, waster. **2** he was a real profligate but he has reformed debauchee, degenerate, reprobate, roué, lecher.

profound adj **1** a profound treatise/thinker discerning, penetrating, thoughtful, philosophical, deep, weighty, serious, learned, erudite, wise, sagacious. **2** unable to understand such profound doctrine learned, erudite, serious, deep, difficult, complex, abstract, abstruse, esoteric, impenetrable. **3** a profound love for his country deep, intense, keen, great, extreme, sincere, heartfelt. **4** a profound silence deep, pronounced, total, absolute, complete, utter. **5** profound changes taking place far-reaching, radical, extensive, exhaustive, thoroughgoing.

profoundly adv **1** speak very profoundly on the poet's philosophy discerningly, penetratingly, thoughtfully, philosophically, weightily, seriously, learnedly, eruditely, wisely, sagaciously. **2** profoundly disturbed by the news deeply, extremely, greatly, very, thoroughly, intensely, keenly, sincerely.

profuse adj **1** give profuse apologies/thanks lavish, liberal, unstinting, generous, fulsome, extravagant, inordinate, immoderate, excessive. **2** a profuse harvest | profuse blossom on the trees abundant, copious, ample, plentiful, bountiful, luxuriant.

profusion n a profusion of roses on the bushes abundance, superabundance, copiousness, quantities, scores, masses, multitude, plethora, wealth, plenitude, cornucopia; inf

heaps, stacks, piles, loads, mountains, tons, oodles.

progeny n **1** the parents and all their progeny sitting round the table children, offspring, young ones, family, issue. **2** the progeny of William the Conqueror descendants, successors, lineage, scions, seed, posterity.

programme n **1** what's on the programme for the first day of the conference? agenda, calendar, schedule, syllabus, list of events, order of the day. **2** buy a programme at the theatre list of performers, list of players, list of artistes. **3** the orchestra played a varied programme list of items, series of items. **4** watch several television programmes | listen to a radio programme production, presentation, show, performance, broadcast. **5** get the programme for the session's academic courses syllabus, prospectus, schedule, list, curriculum, literature. **6** organize a programme of financial investment schedule, scheme, plan, plan of action, project.

programme v **1** a school trip programmed for next week schedule, plan, line up, map out, arrange, prearrange, organize. **2** programme the heating to come on at dawn set, fix, arrange.

progress n **1** climbers making rapid progress towards the summit | drivers making slow progress on the icy roads forward movement, headway, advance, going, passage, advancement, advance, progression. **2** the company has made very little progress in the past few years advance, advancement, headway, steps forward, progression, improvement, betterment, upgrading, development, growth. **in progress** work in progress under way, going on, ongoing, happening, occurring, taking place, proceeding, being done, being performed.

progress v **1** the climbers progressed up the mountain go forward, move forward/on, make one's way, advance, go on, continue, proceed, make progress, make headway, push forward, go/forge ahead. **2** the talks are progressing | science progresses all the time make progress, move forward, advance, make headway, take steps forward, make strides, develop, get better, improve. **3** the patient is progressing make progress, get better, improve, recover, recuperate.

progression n **1** the progression from primary to secondary school | the progression from tea-boy to managing director progress, forward movement, upward movement, passage, advancement, advance, development. **2** a progression of unsuitable applicants | had a progression of dreary jobs succession, sequence, series, string, stream, steady stream, parade, chain, train.

progressive adj **1** *progressive movement* forward, onward, advancing. **2** *a progressive improvement in the crime rate* | *a progressive amount of violence on the streets* | *a progressive disease* increasing, growing, intensifying, accelerating, escalating. **3** *a progressive firm* | *a progressive office system* modern, advanced, forward-looking, forward-thinking, go-ahead, enlightened, enterprising, up-and-coming, innovative, avant-garde. **4** *progressive ideas on education* | *progressive political views* radical, reforming, innovative, revolutionary, revisionist.

prohibit v **1** *a regulation to prohibit smoking in hospitals* forbid, ban, bar, disallow, proscribe, veto, interdict, outlaw. **2** *low salaries prohibit them from buying a house* | *the high cost of the medicine prohibits its universal use* prevent, stop, rule out, preclude, make impossible, hinder, impede, hamper, obstruct, restrict, constrain.

prohibition n **1** *vote for the prohibition of smoking in hospitals* forbidding, banning, barring, disallowing, proscription, vetoing, interdiction, outlawing. **2** *introduce a prohibition on the sale of cigarettes to children* ban, bar, interdict, veto, embargo, injunction, proscription.

prohibitive adj **1** *introduce prohibitive measures on the employment of children* prohibitory, forbidding, banning, barring, disallowing, proscriptive, restrictive, suppressive, vetoing, interdicting, outlawing. **2** *the prohibitive cost of housing in that area of the city* exorbitant, extortionate, excessive, preposterous, high-priced, high-cost, sky-high; *inf* steep.

project n *a local authority project to build a community hall* | *initiate a project to conserve the environment* scheme, plan, programme, enterprise, undertaking, venture, activity, operation, campaign.

project v **1** *they are projecting a visit to India* | *a projected new cinema complex* plan, propose, map out, devise, design, outline. **2** *project missiles into space* launch, discharge, propel, hurl, throw, cast, fling, shoot. **3** *a balcony that projects over the garden* jut, jut out, protrude, extend, stick out, stand out, hang over, bulge out, beetle, obtrude. **4** *project sales figures for next year* extrapolate, calculate, estimate, gauge, reckon, forecast, predict, predetermine.

projectile n missile, rocket, shell, grenade, bullet.

projection n **1** *a projection of rock* overhang, ledge, shelf, ridge, protuberance, protru-

sion, jut, bulge. **2** *their sales projection for next year* extrapolation, calculation, computation, estimate, estimation, gauge, reckoning, forecast, prediction.

proletariat n workers, working class, wage-earners, labouring classes, the common people, the ordinary people, the commonalty, lower classes, lower orders, the rank and file, the masses, the mob, the rabble, the *hoi polloi*; *inf* the plebs, the proles, the great unwashed.

proliferate v *the number of houses in the area has proliferated beyond belief* increase, grow rapidly, multiply, extend, expand, burgeon, accelerate, escalate, rocket, snowball, mushroom.

proliferation n *the proliferation of new houses in the area* increase, growth, multiplication, spread, expansion, extension, burgeoning, acceleration, escalation, build-up, rocketing, snowballing, mushrooming.

prolific adj **1** *prolific vegetation* fertile, fruitful, fecund, luxuriant, abundant, profuse, copious, rank. **2** *a prolific writer* productive.

prolix adj over-long, lengthy, long-winded, long-drawn-out, prolonged, protracted, verbose, wordy, discursive, digressive, rambling, wandering, circuitous, ambagious, pleonastic.

prologue n *the prologue to the play/poem/novel* introduction, foreword, preface, preamble, prelude, preliminary, exordium, proem, prolegomenon.

prolong v *mechanical problems with the car prolonged the journey by three hours* lengthen, make longer, elongate, extend, stretch out, draw out, drag out, protract, spin out.

prominence n **1** *the prominence of her cheek-bones/eyes* protruding, protrusion, protuberance, protrusiveness, jutting out, standing out. see PROMINENT 1. **2** *a prominence on the flat countryside* protuberance, projection, jutting, swelling, bulge. **3** *a prominence overhanging the beach* promontory, pinnacle, projection, height, crest, cliff, crag. **4** *the prominence of the tower on the skyline* conspicuousness, obviousness, obtrusiveness. see PROMINENT 2. **5** *newspapers giving prominence to the political scandal* importance, weight, conspicuousness, precedence, top billing. **6** *men of prominence in the community* importance, eminence, pre-eminence, distinction, note, prestige, stature, illustriousness, celebrity, fame, renown, acclaim.

prominent adj **1** *prominent cheek-bones/eyes* protruding, protuberant, protrusive, jutting, jutting out, projecting, standing out, sticking out, bulging. **2** *a prominent feature of the landscape* easily seen, conspicuous, noticeable, obvious, unmistakable, obtrusive, eye-catching, striking. **3** *a prominent member of the local community* leading, outstanding, chief, foremost, main, top, important, eminent, pre-eminent, distinguished, notable, noted, illustrious, celebrated, well-known, famous, renowned, acclaimed.

promiscuity n promiscuousness, dissoluteness, dissipation, licentiousness, looseness, profligacy, immorality, debauchery, wantonness.

promiscuous adj *promiscuous people contracting sexually-transmitted diseases* sexually indiscriminating, dissolute, dissipated, fast, licentious, loose, profligate, abandoned, immoral, debauched, wanton, of easy virtue, unchaste.

promise v **1** *promise that he will be present | promise to go | but you promised* give one's word (that), give an undertaking (that/to), give one's assurance (that), swear (that/to), vow that/to, take an oath (that/to), pledge that/to, contract that/to. **2** *skies which promise good weather | it promises well for him that he has got an interview* augur, indicate, denote, signify, be a sign of, show signs of, hint at, suggest, betoken, presage.

promise n **1** *give a promise that he would be there* word, word of honour, undertaking, assurance, guarantee, commitment, vow, oath, pledge, bond, contract, covenant. **2** *a promise of spring in the air* indication, hint, suggestion, sign. **3** *a young musician of promise* talent, potential, flair, ability, aptitude, capability, capacity.

promising adj **1** *their first reactions to the scheme are promising | it is promising that you have a second interview* encouraging, hopeful, favourable, auspicious, propitious, optimistic, bright. **2** *a promising young writer* with potential, talented, gifted, able, apt; *inf* up-and-coming.

promontory n headland, point, cape, head, foreland, bluff, cliff, precipice, overhang, height, projection, prominence.

promote v **1** *the boss had promoted him | she has been promoted to sales manager* give promotion to, upgrade, give a higher position to, give a higher rank to, place in a higher rank, elevate, advance, move up, prefer, aggrandize. **2** *he promoted the cause of peace by his actions* advance, further, assist, aid, help, contribute to, foster, boost. **3** *the local council promotes equal rights for all* advocate, recommend, urge, support, back, endorse, champion, sponsor, espouse. **4** *companies*

promoting their new products advertise, publicize, push, puff, puff up, beat the drum for; *inf* plug, give a plug to, hype, hype up.

promotion n **1** *get promotion to a managerial post* upgrading, move up, elevation, advancement, preferment, aggrandizement. **2** *his promotion of peace by his actions* advancement, furtherance, furthering, assistance, aid, help, contribution to, fostering, boosting. **3** *the council's promotion of equal rights for all* advocacy, recommendation, urging, support, backing, endorsement, championship, sponsoring, espousal. **4** *the company's promotion of their new products* advertising, advertising campaign, publicity, publicizing, push, pushing, hard sell, puff, puffing; *inf* plug, plugging, hype, hyping.

prompt adj **1** *receive a prompt reply* immediate, instant, instantaneous, swift, rapid, speedy, quick, fast, expeditious, early, punctual, in good time, timely. **2** *she is prompt to offer assistance* swift, rapid, speedy, quick, fast, ready, willing, eager.

prompt adv *arrive at 9 a.m. prompt* sharp, exactly, precisely, on the dot, dead, dead on, promptly, punctually; *inf* bang on, spot on; *Amer inf* on the button.

prompt v **1** *what prompted them to join the party?* cause, make, encourage, move, induce, urge, incite, impel, spur on, motivate, stimulate, inspire, provoke. **2** *his actions provoked an angry response* cause, give rise to, induce, call forth, occasion, elicit, evoke, provoke. **3** *he forgot what he was going to say and she prompted him* remind, jog someone's memory, refresh someone's memory, cue, give someone a cue, help out.

promptly adv **1** *arrive promptly* punctually, on time, on the dot; *inf* bang on, spot on; *Amer inf* on the button. **2** *reply to the letter promptly* at once, directly, immediately, by return, instantly, instantaneously, swiftly, rapidly, speedily, quickly, fast, expeditiously; *inf* pronto.

promptness n **1** *the promptness of his reply* immediacy, immediateness, instantaneousness, swiftness, rapidity, speediness, alacrity, quickness, fastness, expeditiousness, expedition, earliness, punctuality. **2** *the promptness of her offer to help* swiftness, rapidity, speediness, alacrity, quickness, fastness, readiness, willingness, eagerness.

promulgate v **1** *promulgate the information about the project to the townspeople* make known, make public, publicize, announce, spread, communicate, disseminate, circulate, broadcast. **2** *promulgate the new law* proclaim, announce, declare, herald, blazon, trumpet.

prone adj **1** *suffocate on his pillow after lying prone* face down, face downwards, in a prone position, procumbent. **2** *after the party the place was full of people in a prone position | people lying prone on the battlefield* lying down, flat, horizontal, full-length, supine, prostrate, stretched out, recumbent, procumbent. **3** *prone to lose his temper* inclined, given, likely, liable, apt, disposed, predisposed. **4** *prone to headaches* inclined, liable, subject, susceptible, disposed, predisposed.

prong n point, tip, spike, tine.

pronounce v **1** *pronounce the words wrongly | have difficulty in pronouncing the letter 's'* enunciate, articulate, say, utter, sound, voice, vocalize. **2** *pronounce judgement | pronounce the patient out of danger* announce, declare, proclaim, assert, affirm, rule, decree.

pronounced adj **1** *have a pronounced lisp* marked, noticeable, obvious, evident, conspicuous, striking, distinct, unmistakable. **2** *have pronounced views on the subject* decided, definite, clear, strong, positive, distinct.

pronouncement n *wait for the consultant's pronouncement on the patient's chances of survival* formal statement, declaration, announcement, judgement, decree, proclamation, assertion, dictum.

pronunciation n *have difficulty with the pronunciation of certain words* enunciation, articulation, saying, uttering, utterance, sounding, voicing, vocalization.

proof n **1** *produce proof of your identity* evidence, certification, verification, authentication, validation, confirmation, attestation. **2** *produce proof of his guilt* evidence, demonstration, substantiation, corroboration, confirmation, attestation, testimony. **3** *send the novelist proofs of her book* galley proof, galley, page proof, pull, trial print.

proof adj *roofing material proof against heavy winds* impervious, impenetrable, resistant, repellent, waterproof, windproof, bulletproof, soundproof, childproof.

prop n **1** *clothes prop | a prop holding up the side of the house* support, upright, brace, buttress, stay, bolster, stanchion, truss, column, post, rod, pole, shaft. **2** *a prop of the amateur theatrical society* pillar, mainstay, anchor, rock, backbone, supporter, upholder, sustainer.

prop v *prop his bike/ladder against the wall* lean, rest, set, lay, stand, balance, steady.

prop up **1** *prop up the wall of the garage* hold up, shore up, bolster up, buttress, support, brace, underpin, reinforce, strengthen. **2** *prop up a firm in difficulties* support, give support to, bolster up, shore up, maintain, fund, finance, subsidize, underwrite.

propaganda n *party members trying to recruit people by means of their propaganda* publicity material, publicity information, publicity, promotion, advertising, advertisement, information, agitprop; *inf* hype.

propagate v **1** *propagate plants/animals* grow, breed, multiply. **2** *animals propagating* reproduce, multiply, proliferate, breed, procreate. **3** *propagate new political ideas* spread, communicate, circulate, disseminate, transmit, distribute, broadcast, publish, publicize, proclaim, promulgate.

propel v *propel the boat by means of oars | ambition propelling him to work long hours* move, set in motion, push forward, drive, thrust forward, force, impel.

propensity n *a propensity to lie | a propensity for getting into trouble* tendency, inclination, leaning, bent, bias, disposition, predisposition, proneness, proclivity, penchant, susceptibility, weakness.

proper adj **1** *the proper equipment for the sport | the proper qualifications for the job* right, suitable, fitting, appropriate, apt. **2** *the proper way to do things | doesn't know the proper way to address the queen* right, correct, precise, accepted, acceptable, established, orthodox, conventional, formal, *comme il faut*. **3** *put the books in their proper place* right, correct, own, individual, particular, respective, special, specific. **4** *have a very proper upbringing* seemly, decorous, respectable, decent, refined, genteel, gentlemanly/ladylike, formal, conventional, orthodox, strict, punctilious, sedate. **5** *have a proper holiday* real, actual, genuine, true. **6** *make a proper mess of things* real, actual, complete, thorough, thoroughgoing, utter.

property n **1** *the books were her personal property* possessions, belongings, things, goods, effects, chattels, assets, resources. **2** *put his money in property* real estate, buildings, land, estates, acres. **3** *herbs with healing properties | the antiseptic properties of the substance* quality, attribute, characteristic, feature, power, peculiarity, idiosyncrasy, quirk.

prophecy n **1** *her prophecy came true* prediction, forecast, prognostication, divination, augury. **2** *the gift of prophecy* prediction, foretelling the future, forecasting the future, fortune-telling, second sight, prognostication, divination, augury, soothsaying.

prophesy v *the old woman prophesied his death* predict, foretell, forecast, foresee, forewarn of, presage, prognosticate, divine, augur.

prophet n seer, soothsayer, fortune-teller, diviner, clairvoyant, forecaster of the future, prognosticator, prophesier, oracle, augur, sibyl, Cassandra. **prophet of doom** pessimist, Cassandra; *inf* doom merchant, gloom merchant, doomster.

prophetic adj *her pessimistic remarks proved prophetic—we did indeed fail* predictive, foretelling, forecasting, presaging, prognostic, divinatory, oracular, sibylline.

prophylactic adj *prophylactic medicine* preventive, preventative, precautionary, protective, disease-preventing.

prophylaxis n *advocate prophylaxis in medicine* prevention, protection.

propinquity n **1** *dislike the propinquity of the two houses/families* closeness, nearness, proximity, adjacency, contiguity. **2** *the families have a propinquity with each other* close relationship, close kinship, blood ties, family connection, proximity, consanguinity.

propitiate v *propitiate his angry mother* appease, conciliate, placate, mollify, pacify, soothe.

propitious adj *not a propitious time to try to sell one's house* auspicious, favourable, promising, optimistic, bright, advantageous, fortunate, lucky, happy, rosy, beneficial, opportune, suitable, timely.

proponent n *a proponent of socialism* advocate, supporter, upholder, adherent, backer, promoter, endorser, champion, defender, sponsor, espouser, friend, well-wisher.

proportion n **1** *the proportion of women to men on the staff* ratio, distribution, relative amount/number, relationship. **2** *give a large proportion of his income to the poor* portion, part, segment, share, quota, division, percentage, fraction, measure; *inf* cut, whack. **3** *the pleasing proportions of the room | her features are in perfect proportion to each other* balance, symmetry, harmony, correspondence, congruity, agreement.

proportional adj *have more work to do with a proportional increase in salary* proportionate, in proportion to, corresponding, commensurate, equivalent, comparable.

proportions npl *a man of huge proportions* dimensions, size, measurements, mass, bulk, expanse, magnitude, extent, width, breadth.

proposal n **1** *the proposal of new terms of employment* putting forward, advancing, offering, proffering, presentation, submitting. *see* PROPOSE 1. **2** *study their proposals for expansion | draw up a financial proposal* scheme, plan, project, programme, motion, bid, proposition, presentation, suggestion, recommendation, tender, terms.

propose v **1** *propose changes in legislation | propose that changes be made in the legislation* put forward, advance, offer, proffer, present, submit, tender, propound, suggest, recommend, advocate. **2** *they are proposing to leave now* intend, have the intention, mean, plan, have in mind, aim, purpose. **3** *propose his cousin as president of the society* put forward, put up, nominate, name, suggest, recommend. **4** *propose to his girlfriend* offer marriage to, ask for someone's hand in marriage to, pay suit to; *inf* pop the question to.

proposition n **1** *an attractive business proposition* proposal, scheme, plan, project, programme, motion, bid. *see* PROPOSAL 2. **2** *getting into the building unnoticed is not an easy proposition | it's a tough proposition* task, job, undertaking, venture, problem. **3** *make a proposition to the girl at the bar* sexual advance, sexual overture, indecent proposal, improper suggestion; *inf* come-on.

proposition v *proposition the girl/man at the bar* make sexual advances to, make sexual overtures to, make an indecent proposal to, make an improper suggestion to, accost; *inf* make a proposition to, make a pass at.

propound v *propound the theory that all men are equal* put forward, advance, offer, proffer, present, submit, tender, suggest, postulate, propose, advocate.

proprieties npl *expected to observe the proprieties* etiquette, social conventions, social graces, social niceties, protocol, civilities, formalities, rules of conduct, accepted behaviour, good manners, good form, the done thing, punctilio.

proprietor n owner, possessor, title-holder, deed-holder, landowner, landlord/landlady.

propriety n **1** *behave with propriety* seemliness, decorum, respectability, decency, correctness, appropriateness, good manners, courtesy, politeness, civility, refinement, gentility, breeding, conventionality, orthodoxy, formality, etiquette, protocol. **2** *question the propriety of your decision | I am uncertain of the propriety of the way he treats his staff* rightness, correctness, fitness, suitability, suitableness, appropriateness, aptness.

propulsion n *fuel used for propulsion | jet propulsion* motive force, propelling force, drive, driving force, thrust, push, momentum, power.

prosaic adj **1** *a prosaic style of writing | a prosaic decription of her experiences abroad* unimaginative, uninspired, matter-of-fact, dull, dry, humdrum, mundane, pedestrian, lifeless, spiritless, stale, bland, vapid, banal, hackneyed, trite, insipid, monotonous, flat. **2** *lead rather a prosaic life* ordinary, everyday, usual, common, routine, humdrum, commonplace, workaday, pedestrian, mundane, dull, tedious, boring, uninspiring, monotonous.

proscribe v **1** *proscribe the sale of alcohol on Sundays* prohibit, forbid, ban, bar, disallow, embargo, interdict, outlaw. **2** *he was proscribed for his part in the conspiracy* outlaw, exile, expel, expatriate, deport, boycott, blackball, ostracize, send to Coventry.

proscription n **1** *the proscription of the sale of alcohol on Sundays* prohibiting, prohibition, forbidding, banning, barring, embargo, interdicting. *see* PROSCRIBE 1. **2** *the proscription of her brother for his part in the conspiracy* outlawing, exiling, expelling, expulsion, expatriation, deporting. *see* PROSCRIBE 2. **3** *a proscription placed on the sale of alcohol* prohibition, ban, bar, embargo, interdict.

prosecute v **1** *he was prosecuted for dangerous driving* bring a charge against, bring a criminal charge against, charge, prefer charges against, bring an action against, try, bring to trial, put on trial, sue, bring a suit against, interdict, arraign. **2** *prosecute an inquiry into the murder* carry on, conduct, direct, engage in, work at, proceed with, continue with. **3** *prosecute his prescribed tasks* accomplish, complete, finish, carry through, discharge, bring to an end.

proselyte n convert, neophyte.

prospect n **1** *there is little prospect of success* likelihood, likeliness, hope, expectation, anticipation, chance, chances, odds, probability, possibility. *see* PROSPECTS. **2** *the prospect of being unemployed frightens him* thought, idea, contemplation, outlook. **3** *admire the prospect from the hill* view, vista, outlook, perspective, panorama, scene, spectacle. **in prospect** *there are no jobs in prospect* in store, in the offing, on the horizon, on the cards, in the wind.

prospect v *prospect an area for diamonds* explore, search, inspect, survey, examine, check out. **prospect for** *prospect for gold* search for, look for, seek, go after.

prospective adj **1** *her prospective father-in-law* future, to-be, soon-to-be, intended, expected. **2** *attract prospective customers* would-be, potential, possible, likely, hoped-for, looked-for, awaited, anticipated. **3** *her prospective date with her friend's brother* coming, to come, approaching, about to be, forthcoming, imminent.

prospects npl *a job with few prospects* potential, promise, possibilities, expectations, scope.

prospectus n *the prospectus from the college* brochure, literature, syllabus, programme.

prosper v *the family/business is prospering* do well, get on well, thrive, flourish, be successful, succeed, get ahead, progress, advance, get on in the world, make headway, make good, become rich, be in clover; *inf* be on Easy Street, live the life of Riley.

prosperity n *go from poverty to prosperity* prosperousness, success, good fortune, ease, plenty, affluence, wealth, riches, the good life, luxury, life of luxury.

prosperous adj *prosperous young men working in the city* thriving, flourishing, successful, well-off, well-to-do, affluent, wealthy, rich, moneyed, opulent, in clover; *inf* well-heeled, in the money, on Easy Street.

prostitute n call-girl, whore, woman of the streets, streetwalker, loose woman, woman of ill repute, fallen woman, courtesan, *fille de joie*, bawd; *inf* tart, pro, hooker, hustler, moll.

prostitution n whoredom, whoring, streetwalking, the oldest profession, Mrs Warren's profession; *inf* the game, hustling.

prostrate adj **1** *people found prostrate on the floor after the fire* prone, lying down, flat, stretched out, horizontal, full-length, procumbent. **2** *prostrate before the emperor* bowed low, humbled. **3** *prostrate with grief* overcome by/with, overwhelmed by, overpowered by, brought to one's knees by, crushed by, helpless with, paralysed by, laid low by/with, impotent with. **4** *a country left prostrate after years of war | the old lady was prostrate after the long journey* worn out, exhausted, fatigued, tired out, dog-tired, spent, drained; *inf* all in, done, fagged out, bushed, whacked, pooped.

prostrate v **1** *the blow prostrated him* knock flat, flatten, knock down, floor, level. **2** *the heat prostrated them | prostrated by pain* overcome, overwhelm, overpower, bring to one's knees, crush, make helpless, paralyse, lay low, make powerless, make impotent. **3** *the long war prostrated the country | she was prostrated by the long journey* wear out, exhaust, tire out, fatigue, weary, drain, sap; *inf* fag out, poop.

protagonist n **1** *the protagonist in the new play* chief character, central character, leading/main character, principal, hero/heroine, leading man/lady, title role, lead. **2** *a protagonist of feminism* leader, leading supporter, prime mover, moving spirit, standard-bearer, mainstay, spokesman/woman/person, advocate, supporter, upholder, adherent, backer, proponent, promoter, champion, exponent.

protean adj ever-changing, variable, changeable, mutable, kaleidoscopic, mercurial, volatile, labile, versatile.

protect v **1** *protect the child from would-be kidnappers | protect the house from burglars* keep safe, save, safeguard, shield, preserve, defend, shelter, secure. **2** *soldiers protecting the castle* guard, mount/stand guard on, defend, secure, watch over, look after, take care of. **3** *protect the surface of the table with a plastic sheet* preserve, shield, cover, cover up, conceal, mask.

protection n **1** *provide protection against violence* safe keeping, safety, shield, preservation, defence, security. **2** *under the protection of the police* safe keeping, care, charge, keeping, defence, protectorship. **3** *wear warm clothes as a protection against the cold | use a sun-block as a protection against the sun* safeguard, shield, barrier, buffer, screen, cover.

protective adj **1** *wear a protective cream on her face in the sun | cyclists wearing protective headgear* protecting, safeguarding, shielding, covering. **2** *protective mother/parents* careful, watchful, vigilant, paternal/maternal, fatherly/motherly, over-protective, possessive, jealous, clinging.

protector n **1** *his elder brother acted as his protector* defender, champion, bodyguard, guardian, knight in shining armour, guardian angel. **2** *wear shin protectors* guard, shield, pad, cushion.

protégé/protégée n pupil, student, ward, dependant, charge.

protest v **1** *protest at his treatment of his staff | protest against the government's economic police | protest about their low wages* make a protest at/against/about, object to, raise objections to, oppose, express opposition to, take issue about/on/over, make/take a stand against, put up a fight against, take exception to, complain about, express disapproval of, express disagreement with, demur at, remonstrate about, make a fuss about, demonstrate against; *inf* kick up a fuss about, gripe about, grouse about, beef about, bitch about. **2** *protest his innocence*

declare, announce, profess, proclaim, assert, affirm, argue, attest, testify to, maintain, insist on, aver, avow.

protest n **1** *register a protest at/against/about his treatment of the children* objection, opposition, exception, complaint, disapproval, disagreement, dissent, demurral, remonstration, fuss, outcry, demonstration, protestation. **2** *listen to his protests that he was innocent* protestation, declaration, announcement, profession, assertion, affirmation, attestation, assurance, avowal, proclamation.

protestation n **1** *not to believe his protestations of innocence/loyalty* protest, declaration, announcement, assertion, affirmation. *see* PROTEST n 2. **2** *his protestations against his treatment in prison* protest, objection, opposition, exception, complaint. *see* PROTEST n 1.

protester n *a crowd of protesters gathered outside the embassy* objector, opposer, opponent, complainer, demonstrator, dissenter, dissident, rebel, protest marcher, striker, agitator.

protocol n *observe the protocol associated with royal visits | guilty of a breach of protocol* etiquette, rules of conduct, code of behaviour, conventions, formalities, customs, propriety, proprieties, decorum, manners, courtesies, civilities, good form, *politesse*.

prototype n *the prototype of the flying machine* original, first example, first model, pattern, paradigm, archetype.

protract v *loves to talk at meetings and protract the discussions* prolong, extend, stretch out, draw out, lengthen, make longer, drag out, spin out, keep something going, continue.

protracted adj *tired of the protracted discussions* prolonged, extended, stretched out, drawn out, long-drawn-out, lengthened, lengthy, long, over-long, dragged out, spun out, interminable, never-ending, endless.

protrude v *a piece of rock protruding from the cliff face | protruding front teeth* jut, jut out, stick out, stand out, project, extend, beetle, obtrude, bulge.

protrusion n **1** *the protrusion of a piece of rock from the cliff face* jutting, sticking out, projection, projecting, obtrusion, obtruding. *see* PROTRUDE. **2** *rocky protrusions on the face of the cliff* projection, swelling, bulge, protuberance, lump, bump, knob.

protuberance n *a protuberance on the trunk of the tree* swelling, bulge, lump, bump, protrusion, projection, knob, growth, outgrowth, tumour, excrescence.

protuberant adj *protuberant stomach/eyes* bulging, swelling, swollen, jutting, jutting out, protruding, protrusive, prominent, bulbous, gibbous.

proud adj **1** *proud parents | parents proud of their daughter's achievement* pleased (with), glad (about/at), happy (about/at/with), satisfied (with), gratified (at), content (at), appreciative (of). **2** *they were poor but proud* self-respecting, dignified, independent. **3** *he used to stop and speak to all the villagers but he has become very proud and passes them by* arrogant, conceited, vain, self-important, egotistical, boastful, haughty, disdainful, scornful, supercilious, snobbish, imperious, overbearing, lordly, presumptuous, overweening, high-handed; *inf* high-and-mighty, stuck-up, uppity, snooty, toffee-nosed, highfalutin. **4** *it was a proud day when they won the cup* gratifying, satisfying, happy, memorable, notable, red-letter, glorious, marvellous. **5** *the ship was a proud sight sailing into harbour* magnificent, splendid, grand, noble, stately, imposing, majestic, august.

prove v **1** *prove that he was the murderer* produce/submit proof, produce/submit evidence, establish evidence, determine, demonstrate, show beyond doubt, substantiate, corroborate, verify, validate, authenticate, confirm. **2** *prove the new drug | young people having to prove themselves* put to the test, test, try out, put to trial. **3** *the rumour proved to be correct* be found, turn out. **be proved** *she was proved the winner* emerge, come out, end up.

proverb n saying, adage, maxim, saw, axiom, aphorism, gnome, dictum, apophthegm.

proverbial adj *in view of her proverbial meanness, we did not ask her for a contribution to the charity* legendary, notorious, infamous, famous, famed, renowned, well-known, acknowledged, accepted, traditional, time-honoured.

provide v **1** *provide food and drink for the travellers | provide them with a car for their holiday* supply, furnish, equip, accommodate, provision, outfit. **2** *the job provides ample scope for promotion | the novel provides an insight into the problems of the age* give, bring, afford, present, offer, accord, yield, impart, lend. **3** *the contract provides that the tenants are responsible for house repairs* stipulate, lay down, give as a condition, require, state, specify. **provide against** *provide against a power cut by buying stocks of candles* make provision for, take precautions against, take steps/measures against, guard against,

forearm oneself against. **provide for 1** *provide for his wife and children* support, maintain, keep, sustain, take care of, care for, look after. **2** *the organizers of the fête tried to provide for every eventuality* allow for, prepare for, make preparations for, be prepared for, anticipate, arrange for, make arrangements for, get ready for, plan for, make plans for.

provided, provided that conj *we are going on holiday, provided we have enough money | the party will be held out of doors, provided that it is not raining* providing that, on condition that, if, as long as, given, with the provision/proviso that, contingent upon, on the assumption that.

providence n **1** *just have to trust in providence* God's will, divine intervention, destiny, fate, fortune. **2** *lack of providence has brought him to his present state* foresight, forethought, far-sightedness, prudence, judgement, judiciousness, shrewdness, circumspection, wisdom, sagacity, caution, care, carefulness, good management, careful budgeting, thrift, thriftiness, economy, canniness, frugality.

provident adj *it was provident of them to take out accident insurance | provident people providing for their old age* far-sighted, prudent, judicious, shrewd, circumspect, wise, sagacious, cautious, careful, thrifty, canny, economical, frugal.

providing, providing that conj provided, provided that, on condition that, if. *see* PROVIDED.

province n **1** *the administrative centre of the province* state, territory, region, area, district. **2** *that part of the business is not my province | its outside my province* area of responsibility, sphere of action, area of activity, field, business, line of business, line, charge, concern, duty; *inf* pigeon. **3** *in the province of English literature* discipline, field, speciality, area.

provincial adj **1** *provincial rather than national/central government* state, regional. **2** *provincial newspapers/issues* non-national, local, parish-pump. **3** *live in the city and look down on provincial areas* non-metropolitan, non-city, outlying, small-town, rural, country, rustic, backwood, backwater; *inf* one-horse, hick. **4** *she regards herself as sophisticated and most of her colleagues as provincial* unsophisticated, parochial, limited, small-minded, insular, inward-looking, illiberal, narrow, narrow-minded, inflexible, bigoted, prejudiced, intolerant.

provincial n *city people looking down on people they regard as provincials* country cousin, rustic, yokel, peasant.

provision n **1** *the provision of conference facilities | the provision of nursery schools* providing, supplying, supply, furnishing, equipping, outfitting, accommodation, giving, affording. **2** *make provision for their old age | make provision for a hard winter* preparation, plan, prearrangement, arrangement, precaution, precautionary steps/measures. **3** *the housing policy makes no provision for single people* arrangement, allowance, concession. **4** *under the provisions of his will his children inherit all his estate* term, requirement, specification, stipulation. **5** *the contract document has the provision that it must be reviewed annually* proviso, condition, stipulation, clause, rider, qualification, restriction, reservation, limitation, strings.

provisional adj *a provisional contract | get provisional permission* provisory, temporary, interim, stopgap, transitional, to be confirmed, conditional, tentative, contingent; *inf* pro tem.

provisions npl *stock up with provisions for the Christmas holiday* supplies, food supplies, stores, groceries, food, food and drink, foodstuffs, staples, rations, provender, eatables, edibles, victuals, comestibles, viands.

proviso n *they agreed to the change with the proviso that an investigation be held* condition, stipulation, provision, clause, rider, qualification, restriction, reservation, limitation, strings.

provocation n **1** *the children's provocation of their mother* annoying, angering, incensing, enraging, irritating, irritation, exasperating, exasperation, infuriating, infuriation, maddening, vexing, harassing, harassment, irking; *inf* riling, aggravation. see PROVOKE 1. **2** *hit him under provocation* incitement, rousing, stirring, stimulation, stimulus, motivation, prompting, inducement, goading. see PROVOKE 2. **3** *the provocation of the crowd's anger | the provocation of the audience's laughter* evocation, causing, occasioning, eliciting, inducement, inspiration, kindling, production, generation, instigation, precipitation, promotion. see PROVOKE 3. **4** *tired of his provocations | react to the slightest provocation* annoyance, irritation, vexation, harassment, affront, insult.

provocative adj **1** *the fight was started by a provocative remark* provoking, annoying, irritating, exasperating, infuriating, maddening, vexing, galling, affronting, insulting, inflaming, goading; *inf* aggravating. see PROVOKE 1, PROVOKE 1, 2. **2** *a provocative pout | wear a provocative, low-cut dress* sexually arousing, sexually exciting, alluring, seductive, sexy, tempting, suggestive, erotic, titillating.

provoke v **1** *he's very irascible—don't provoke him | that child would provoke anyone* annoy, make angry, anger, incense, enrage, irritate, exasperate, infuriate, madden, pique, nettle, vex, harass, irk, gall, affront, insult; *inf* rile, needle, make someone's blood boil, aggravate. **2** *provoke her into shouting at them* incite, rouse, stir, move, stimulate, motivate, excite, inflame, work/fire up, prompt, induce, spur, goad, prod, egg on. **3** *his speech provoked anger | his act provoked laughter* evoke, cause, give rise to, occasion, call forth, draw forth, elicit, induce, inspire, excite, kindle, produce, generate, engender, instigate, lead to, precipitate, promote, prompt.

prow n *the prow of the ship* bow, bows, nose, stem, fore, forepart, front, head.

prowess n **1** *admire his prowess as a yachtsman | envied her prowess with a tennis-racket* skill, skilfulness, expertise, expertness, facility, ability, capability, talent, genius, adroitness, adeptness, aptitude, dexterity, deftness, competence, proficiency, know-how, *savoir faire*. **2** *the prowess of the soldiers in battle* courage, bravery, gallantry, valour, valiance, heroism, intrepidity, fearlessness, mettle, pluck, pluckiness, gameness, nerve, boldness, daring, fortitude, steadfastness, stoutness, sturdiness; *inf* grit, guts, bottle, spunk.

prowl v *prowling around the grounds looking for a way into the building* roam, range, move stealthily, slink, skulk, steal, sneak, stalk; *inf* snoop.

proximity n *live in proximity to a motorway | disturbed by the proximity of the railway to the house* closeness, nearness, propinquity, adjacency, contiguity.

proxy n *send a proxy to vote at the annual general meeting* representative, deputy, substitute, agent, delegate, surrogate.

prude n puritan, prig, Mrs Grundy, Grundy, old maid; *inf* goody-goody, Miss Prim.

prudence n **1** *question the prudence of his action* wisdom, judgement, good judgement, judiciousness, sagacity, shrewdness, common sense, sense, circumspection, farsightedness, foresight, forethought. **2** *behave with prudence rather than rashness* caution, cautiousness, care, carefulness, discretion, wariness, vigilance, heedfulness. **3** *her prudence as a housewife* providence, good management, careful budgeting, thrift, thriftiness, economy, canniness, sparingness, frugality.

prudent adj **1** *a prudent decision* wise, well-judged, judicious, sagacious, sage, shrewd, sensible, circumspect, far-sighted, politic. **2** *rash people always being advised to be prudent* cautious, careful, discreet, wary, vigilant, heedful. **3** *a prudent housewife* provident, thrifty, economical, canny, sparing, frugal.

prudery n *the prudery of the Victorian age* prudishness, puritanism, puritanicalness, priggishness, primness, strait-lacedness, prissiness, stuffiness, starchiness, Grundyism, old-maidishness; *inf* schoolmarmishness.

prudish adj *a prudish attitude towards sex* puritan, puritanical, priggish, prim, strait-laced, prissy, stuffy, starchy, Victorian, Grundyish, old-maid, old-maidish; *inf* goody-goody, school-marmish, schoolmistressy.

prune v **1** *prune the roses* trim, thin, thin out, cut back, shape. **2** *prune branches from the bushes* cut, lop, chop, clip, snip, remove. **3** *prune the expenses budget* | *prune the overlong manuscript* cut back on, cut back, pare down, make cut-backs in, cut, trim, reduce, shorten, make reductions in, retrench, curtail.

prurient adj *demonstrating a prurient interest in the details of the sex crimes* lascivious, lecherous, lustful, lewd, salacious, licentious, lubricious, libidinous.

pry v *she was trying to help but they thought she was prying* be inquisitive, interfere, meddle, intrude, mind other people's business, be a busybody; *inf* stick/poke one's nose in, stick one's oar in, snoop. **pry into 1** *pry into her private affairs* be inquisitive about, nose into, inquire impertinently into, interfere in, meddle in; *inf* be nosy about, stick/poke one's nose into, stick one's oar into, snoop into. **2** *pry into her possessions* peer into, peek into, scrutinize, probe into, ferret about in, nose into, nose around in, spy on; *inf* stick/poke one's nose into, snoop into.

prying adj *tired of their prying neighbours* inquisitive, curious, interfering, meddling, meddlesome, intrusive, probing, spying, impertinent; *inf* nosy, snooping, snoopy.

psalm n hymn, sacred song, song of praise, paean, religious song, chant, anthem.

pseudo adj *his intellectualism is pseudo* | *a pseudo interest in the arts* feigned, pretended, simulated, imitation, false, artificial, ersatz, quasi-, spurious, fake, bogus, sham, mock, fraudulent, counterfeit, forged; *inf* phoney.

pseudonym n *the pseudonym of the writer/ actor* nom de plume, pen-name, stage name, professional name, assumed name, alias, allonym, false name, sobriquet, nickname, nom de guerre.

psych v **psych out** *try to psych out his opponent* unsettle, upset, agitate, disturb, make nervous, put off, put off balance, put off one's stroke, intimidate, frighten. **psych up** *have to psych himself up before the competition/interview* steel oneself, prepare, get ready, gird one's loins, get in the mood, get in the right frame of mind.

psyche n *a disturbed psyche* soul, spirit, mind, intelligence, anima, self, essential nature, inner ego, man/woman, personality.

psychiatrist n psychopathologist, psychotherapist, therapist, psychoanalyst, psychoanalyser; *inf* shrink, head-shrinker, trick cyclist; *Amer* alienist.

psychic adj **1** *people thought to be psychic* clairvoyant, telepathic, telekinetic, spiritualistic. **2** *psychic powers/influences/research* supernatural, supernormal, preternatural, preternormal, extrasensory, other-worldly, paranormal, occult. **3** *psychic analysis/disorder* spiritual, mental, psychological, psychogenic.

psychological adj **1** *psychological studies* mental, of the mind, cerebral, psychic, psychical. **2** *her inability to work is thought to be psychological* in the mind, all in the mind, psychosomatic, emotional, irrational, imaginary, subconscious, unconscious.

psychology n **1** *studying psychology* science of the mind, science of the personality, study of the mental processes. **2** *the psychology of the typical burglar* mind, mind-set, mental processes, thought processes, way of thinking, attitude, make-up; *inf* what makes one tick.

psychopathic adj *murders carried out by psychopathic people* severely mentally ill, disturbed, insane, mad, maniac, maniacal, deranged, sociopathic, psychotic.

psychosomatic adj *psychosomatic illnesses* stress-induced, stress-related, in the mind, all in the mind, psychological.

pub n public house, bar, tavern, inn; *inf* local, boozer.

puberty n *young people reaching puberty* pubescence, sexual maturity, adolescence, young adulthood, teenage years, teens.

public adj **1** *public health services* | *public law* state, national, civic, civil, social. **2** *public sentiment is against it* | *increase public awareness* popular, general, common, universal, widespread. **3** *public places/parks* not private, not exclusive, accessible to all, open to the public, of free access. **4** *make his views public* known, widely known, acknowledged, overt, in circulation, published, publicized, plain, obvious. **5** *scandals about public figures* in the public eye, prominent, well-known, important, eminent, respected, influential, prestigious, famous, celebrated, illustrious.

public n **1** *the public has/have a right to know about the claims* people, everyone, population, country, nation, community, citizens, populace, the ordinary people, the masses, commonalty, the multitude, the mob, the *hoi polloi*, electorate, voters. **2** *actors/authors worrying about what their public think* audience, spectators, readers, followers, following, fans, admirers, patrons, clientele. **in public** *refuse to appear in public after the scandal* publicly, openly, for all to see, in full view of the public.

publication n **1** *the publication of the book/newspaper* publishing, production, issuing, issuance. **2** *a widely-read publication* book, newspaper, magazine, periodical, journal, daily, weekly, monthly, quarterly, booklet, brochure, leaflet, pamphlet, handbill. **3** *the publication of the committee's findings* publishing, announcement, notification, reporting, declaration, communication, imparting, proclamation, disclosure, divulgence, broadcasting, publicizing, distribution, spreading, dissemination, promulgation, issuance.

publicity n **1** *film stars marrying amid a blaze of publicity* public attention, public interest, public notice. **2** *the publicity associated with the launch of the book* promotion, advertising, puff, push; *inf* plug, hype, build-up.

publicize v **1** *publicize a description of the wanted man* make public, make known, bring to public notice/attention, announce, publish, broadcast, distribute, disseminate, promulgate. **2** *publicize her new book* give publicity to, promote, advertise, give a puff to, puff, puff up, push, beat the drum for; *inf* hype, plug.

publish v **1** *a firm publishing reference books* produce, issue, print, bring out. **2** *publish the results | publish the committee's findings* make public, make known, announce, notify, report, declare, communicate, impart, proclaim, disclose, divulge, broadcast, publicize, distribute, spread, disseminate, promulgate.

pucker v **1** *a dress puckered at the waist* gather, shirr, pleat, ruck, ruffle, wrinkle, crease. **2** *the unhappy child's face puckered |*

pucker her brows screw up, wrinkle, crease, furrow, knit, crinkle, corrugate.

puckish adj *a puckish sense of humour* mischievous, mischief-making, impish, implike, roguish, playful, arch, waggish.

pudding n *soup, meat and pudding* dessert, sweet, sweet course/dish; *inf* afters, pud.

puddle n *puddles of water/blood* pool.

puerile adj *puerile behaviour | has a puerile sense of humour | piece of writing is so puerile* childish, immature, infantile, juvenile, adolescent, foolish, silly, inane, asinine.

puff n **1** *a puff of wind* gust, blast, whiff, breath, flurry, draught. **2** *part of the puff given to his new book* promotion, publicity, advertising, advertisement, push; *inf* hype, plug, build-up. **3** *give his new book a puff in her literary column* favourable mention, favourable review, good word, commendation, praise.

puff v **1** *puffing while climbing the hill* breathe heavily/loudly/rapidly, pant, blow, gasp, gulp. **2** *the drug seemed to have puffed him up* swell, distend, inflate, dilate, bloat. **3** *publishers puffing the latest works of their authors* promote, give publicity to, publicize, advertise, push, give a puff to, puff up; *inf* hype, plug.

puffy adj *puffy cheeks/eyes* puffed up, swollen, distended, inflated, dilated, bloated, bulging, oedematous.

pugilist n boxer, fighter, prizefighter; *inf* bruiser.

pugnacious adj *a drunk in a pugnacious mood* belligerent, bellicose, combative, fighting, battling, aggressive, antagonistic, quarrelsome, argumentative, disputatious, hostile, threatening, ill-tempered, bad-tempered, irascible.

pull v **1** *the child was pulling a toy behind him* haul, drag, draw, trail, tow, tug. **2** *pull the rope to straighten it* haul, tug, jerk; *inf* yank. **3** *pull flowers* pluck, pick, gather, collect, cull. **4** *pull teeth* pull out, draw out, take out, extract, remove, root out. **5** *pull a muscle/ligament | has a pulled muscle* strain, sprain, wrench, stretch, tear, dislocate, damage. **6** *a new play that is pulling the audiences* pull in, draw, bring in, attract, lure, catch the eye of, entice. **pull apart 1** *children pulling apart their toys* take/pull to pieces, take/pull to bits, demolish, destroy, break. **2** *critics pulled apart her latest novel* take apart, take to pieces, criticize severely, find fault with, pick holes in, attack; *inf* slate, pan, slam. **pull back** *the army pulled back after the defeat* withdraw, retreat, draw back, fall back. **pull down** *pull down old* *buildings to make way for new* take down, knock down, demolish, raze to the ground, level, destroy, bulldoze, dismantle. **pull in 1** *the car pulled in to the kerb* drive in, draw in, draw up, stop, park. **2** *plays pulling in large audiences* pull, draw, bring in, attract, lure, catch the eye of, entice. **3** *policeman pulling known criminals in for questioning* detain, take into custody, arrest; *inf* run in, pinch, nab, collar, nail. **4** *he pulls in £50,000 a year* earn, take home, bring in, make, clear, net, gross, pocket. **pull off 1** *pull the top off the can* remove, detach, tear off, rip off, wrench off; *inf* yank off. **2** *pull off the export deal* bring off, carry out, accomplish, execute, succeed in. **pull oneself together** regain one's composure/calm, get a grip on oneself; *inf* snap out of it. **pull out 1** *pull out a gun* draw out, take out, bring out, withdraw. **2** *pull out of the agreement/contest* withdraw, retreat from, leave, quit, abandon, give up, stop participating in, renege on. **pull someone's leg** *she was upset but he was only pulling her leg* tease, make fun of, poke fun at, joke with, rag, chaff, twit; *inf* rib, take the mickey out of. **pull through** *she was very ill but pulled through* get better, recover, rally, survive, come through, recuperate. **pull up 1** *pull up the weeds* root out, uproot, dig up, grub up, extract; *inf* yank out. **2** *buses pulling up at the stop* stop, come to a stop, halt, come to a halt, brake. **3** *pull up the children for being cheeky* rebuke, scold, reprimand, admonish, reprove, take to task, castigate; *inf* tell off, give someone a telling-off/dressing-down, tick off, give someone a ticking-off, carpet, give someone a carpeting.

pull n **1** *give a pull at the bell-rope* tug, haul, yank, jerk; *inf* yank. **2** *the pull of the current* tug, force, forcefulness, power, exertion, effort. **3** *the pull of the sea to sailors* attraction, lure, enticement, drawing power, draw, magnetism, influence. **4** *he could get you a job—he has a lot of pull with the boss | hasn't got much pull in the firm* influence, weight, leverage, muscle; *inf* clout.

pulp n **1** *the pulp of the fruit* soft part, fleshy part, flesh, marrow. **2** *reduce the mixture of vegetables to a pulp* paste, purée, mush, mash, pap, triturate. **3** *make a fortune out of writing pulp* pulp fiction, rubbish, trash, trivia, drivel, pap.

pulp v *pulp the fruit to make jam* crush, squash, mash, purée, pulverize, triturate.

pulp adj *pulp fiction* rubbishy, trashy, sensational, lurid.

pulsate v *with hearts pulsating | loud music pulsating throughout the building* beat, throb,

vibrate, pulse, palpitate, pound, thud, thump, drum.

pulse n *the compelling pulse of the music* beat, rhythm, throb, throbbing, vibration, pulsation, pounding, thudding, thud, thumping, thump, drumming.

pulse v *loud music pulsing throughout the building* beat, throb, vibrate, pulsate, palpitate, pound, thud, thump, drum.

pulverize v **1** *pulverize the solid foods* grind, crush, pound, crumble, powder, crunch, squash, pulp, purée, liquidize, mash, comminute, triturate. **2** *pulverize his opponent in the boxing ring* defeat utterly, overwhelm, trounce, rout, flatten, crush, smash, vanquish, destroy, annihilate; *inf* hammer.

pump v **1** *pump the bicycle tyres* pump up, blow up, inflate. **2** *pump blood through the body* drive, force, push, send. **3** *pump the child for information about his father* question closely, quiz, interrogate, cross-examine, give someone the third degree; *inf* grill.

pun n *amused by his puns* play on words, double entendre, paronomasia, calembour.

punch[1] v *punch his opponent in the face* strike, hit, knock, thump, thwack, box, jab, cuff, slug, smash, bash, slam, batter, pound, pummel; *inf* sock, biff, bop, wallop, whack, clout, plug.

punch[1] n **1** *give his opponent a punch in the jaw/face* blow, hit, knock, thump, thwack, box, jab, cuff, slug, smash, bash, slam; *inf* sock, biff, bop, wallop, whack, clout, plug. **2** *a speech which lacked punch* strength, vigour, vigorousness, force, forcefulness, verve, drive, impact, bite, effectiveness; *inf* oomph, pizazz.

punch[2] v *punch the paper/ticket/metal* make a hole in, put/punch holes in, perforate, puncture, pierce, prick, drill, bore, hole.

punctilio n **1** *draw the organizers' attention to a punctilio relating to the coronation ceremony* fine point, nicety, detail, subtlety. **2** *observe the punctilio required by a royal visit* etiquette, conventions, formalities, code, protocol, proprieties, rules of conduct. **3** *organize the royal vist with punctilio | behave at the ceremony with punctilio* conformity, scrupulousness, meticulousness, conscientiousness, exactitude, precision, strictness, nicety.

punctilious adj *a punctilious attention to detail | a punctilious observance of the convention* careful, scrupulous, meticulous, conscientious, exact, precise, particular, strict, nice, finicky, fussy; *inf* pernickety.

punctual adj *they were always punctual at meetings | punctual arrivals* on time, on the dot, prompt, in good time, when expected, timely, well-timed, early.

punctuality n *require punctuality of his employees* promptness, punctualness, promptitude, timeliness, earliness.

punctuate v **1** *punctuate the piece of writing* put punctuation marks in, mark with punctuation marks. **2** *his speech was punctuated with coughs | punctuated his speech with thumps on the table* interrupt with/by, intersperse with, pepper with, sprinkle with.

puncture n **1** *the puncture of the tyre* puncturing, holing, perforation, piercing, pricking, spiking, rupturing, cutting, nicking, slitting. **2** *get/mend a puncture in the tyre* hole, perforation, prick, rupture, cut, nick, slit, leak. **3** *get/mend a puncture* flat tyre; *inf* flat.

puncture v **1** *the piece of glass punctured the tyre* make a hole in, hole, perforate, pierce, bore, prick, spike, penetrate, rupture, cut, nick, slit. **2** *the news punctured his feeling of joy | puncture his conceit* prick, deflate, flatten, reduce.

punctured adj *two punctured tyres* flat, deflated.

pundit n *pundits disagreeing on the implications of the election results* expert, authority, master, guru, sage, highbrow.

pungent adj **1** *a pungent smell* sharp, acrid, acid, sour, biting, stinging, burning, smarting, irritating. **2** *a pungent taste* sharp, acid, sour, biting, bitter, tart, tangy, spicy, highly-flavoured, aromatic, piquant, peppery, hot, fiery. **3** *pungent remarks/wit* caustic, acid, biting, cutting, sharp, incisive, piercing, penetrating, scathing, pointed, acrimonious, trenchant, mordant, stringent.

punish v **1** *punish the children* mete out punishment to, discipline, subject to discipline, take disciplinary action against, teach someone a lesson, penalize, castigate, chastise, smack, slap, beat, cane, whip, flog, lash, scourge. **2** *the boxer really punished his opponent* batter, thrash, beat up, knock about, thump, pummel, trounce; *inf* wallop, bash, hammer, rough up. **3** *punish the car's engine by driving too fast* maltreat, mistreat, abuse, manhandle, damage, harm.

punishing adj *a punishing exercise routine | journey was extremely punishing* arduous, demanding, taxing, strenuous, hard, exhausting, fatiguing, wearing, tiring, gruelling, uphill, back-breaking.

punishment n **1** *the punishment of the children* punishing, disciplining, penalizing, castigation, castigating, chastising, chas-

tisement, smacking, slapping, beating, caning, whipping, flogging, lashing, scourging. **2** *children receiving a severe punishment* discipline, penalty, castigation, retribution, chastisement, smack, slap, beating, caning, whipping, flogging, lashing, scourging; *inf* come-uppance. **3** *the punishment of his opponent in the ring* battering, thrashing, beating, thumping, pummelling, trouncing; *inf* walloping, bashing, hammering, roughing up. **4** *the punishment given to the engine* maltreatment, mistreatment, abuse, manhandling, damage, harm.

punitive adj **1** *take punitive measures against the culprits* punishing, penalizing, disciplinary, corrective, castigating, castigatory, chastising. **2** *punitive rates of taxation* harsh, severe, stiff, taxing, cruel, savage.

punning n *there is a great deal of punning in the first scene* wordplay, playing on words.

puny adj **1** *puny young men unable to do labouring work* weak, weakly, frail, feeble, undersized, underdeveloped, stunted, small, slight, little, dwarfish, pygmy. **2** *a puny contribution* paltry, petty, trifling, trivial, insignificant, inconsequential, minor, meagre; *inf* piddling.

pupil n **1** *all pupils wearing school uniform* schoolboy/girl, schoolchild, scholar, student. **2** *a pupil of Picasso* student, disciple.

puppet n **1** *puppets amusing children* marionette, string-puppet, glove-puppet, finger-puppet. **2** *accused of being a puppet of management* tool, instrument, cat's-paw, pawn, poodle, creature, dupe, mouthpiece.

purchase v **1** *purchase a new dress/car | purchased some shares* buy, pay for, acquire, pick up, obtain, invest in, put money into. **2** *purchase victory with young lives* attain, achieve, gain, win.

purchase n **1** *carry her purchases home | proud of her new purchase* buy, acquisition, investment. **2** *difficult to get any purchase on the slippery cliff face* grip, hold, foothold, footing, toe-hold, support, grasp, leverage, advantage.

pure adj **1** *pure gold* unalloyed, unmixed, unadulterated, uncontaminated, flawless, perfect, genuine, real, true. **2** *pure air/water/food* clean, clear, fresh, unpolluted, untainted, unadulterated, uncontaminated, uninfected, wholesome, natural. **3** *insist on his bride being pure* virgin, virginal, chaste, maidenly, virtuous, undefiled, unsullied. **4** *clerics expected to be pure* uncorrupted, non-corrupt, moral, righteous, honourable, virtuous, honest, upright, decent, good, worthy, noble, blameless, guiltless, pious, sinless. **5** *of pure* *morals/character* stainless, spotless, unsullied, unblemished, impeccable, immaculate, blameless, sinless. **6** *pure madness* sheer, utter, absolute, downright, out-and-out, complete, total, perfect, unmitigated, unqualified. **7** *pure science of mathematics* theoretical, abstract, conceptual.

purely adv *find out purely by accident* entirely, completely, totally, wholly, solely, only, simply, just, merely.

purge v **1** *purge their souls of sin* cleanse, clear, purify, make pure, shrive, lustrate. **2** *purge the party of dissidents* rid, clear, empty. **3** *purge the dissidents from the party* remove, clear out, expel, eject, dismiss, oust, depose, eradicate, root out, weed out. **4** *purge him of the charge* clear, absolve, pardon, forgive, exonerate, expiate.

purge n **1** *the purge of their souls* purging, cleansing, purification. *see* PURGE V 1. **2** *the purge of the dissidents from the party* removal, expulsion, ejection, dismissal, ousting, deposal, deposition, eradication, rooting out, weeding out. **3** *take a purge* purgative, aperient, laxative, enema, dose of salts.

purify v **1** *purify the water* make pure, clean, cleanse, decontaminate, depollute, filter, filtrate. **2** *purify the air* make pure, clean, cleanse, freshen, deodorize, decontaminate, depollute, refine. **3** *purify the hospital after the cholera epidemic* make pure, clean, cleanse, decontaminate, depollute, disinfect, sterilize, sanitize, fumigate. **4** *purify their souls* purge, cleanse, clear, absolve, shrive, lustrate.

purist n *purists disliking loose use of language* precisionist, formalist, stickler, dogmatist, pedant.

puritan n *puritans who object to sex scenes in television plays* moral zealot/fanatic, moralist, pietist, prude, Mrs Grundy, Grundy; *inf* goody-goody.

puritanical adj *a puritanical view of life | her puritanical attitude to entertainment* puritan, ascetic, austere, strait-laced, narrow-minded, rigid, stiff, prudish, prim, priggish, prissy, Grundyish; *inf* goody-goody.

purity n **1** *test the purity of the gold* pureness, flawlessness, perfection, genuineness. *see* PURE 1. **2** *comment on the purity of the water* pureness, cleanness, clearness, freshness, lack of pollution, untaintedness, lack of contamination, wholesomeness. *see* PURE 2. **3** *formerly bridegrooms insisted on the purity of their brides* pureness, virginity, chasteness, chastity, virtue, virtuousness. *see* PURE 3. **4** *purity expected in churchmen* pureness, lack of corruption, righteousness, rectitude, morality, honour, virtuousness, honesty,

integrity, uprightness, decency, goodness, worthiness, nobility, blamelessness, guiltlessness, piety, sinlessness. **5** *the purity of their morals* pureness, stainlessness, spotlessness, impeccableness, immaculateness, blamelessness, sinlessness.

purport v **1** *he purports to be his firm's official representative | this report purports to be an official statement* claim, allege, profess, assert, proclaim, pretend, feign, pose as. **2** *the document purports that changes are to be made to the administration* mean, signify, indicate, denote, suggest, imply, state, convey, express, show, betoken.

purport n **1** *the purport of his message is that he has gone permanently* gist, substance, drift, implication, meaning, import, tenor, thrust. **2** *his purport is to embarrass them* aim, intention, intent, object, objective, goal, plan, scheme, design, purpose.

purpose n **1** *the purpose of his visit* reason, point, basis, motivation, cause, justification. **2** *his only purpose in life* aim, intention, object, objective, goal, end, target, ambition, aspiration, desire, wish, hope. **3** *their approach to the project lacks purpose* determination, resoluteness, resolution, resolve, firmness, steadfastness, single-mindedness, persistence, perseverance, tenacity, doggedness. **4** *to little purpose | not to much purpose* benefit, advantage, use, usefulness, value, gain, profit, avail, result, outcome, effect. **on purpose** *the driver hit our car on purpose* purposely, intentionally, deliberately, by design, wilfully, wittingly, knowingly, consciously.

purpose v *they purposed to reach the summit that night* intend, have the intention, mean, decide, resolve, determine, plan, aim, have a mind, propose, set one's sights on, aspire.

purposeful adj *attack the problem in a purposeful way* determined, resolute, resolved, firm, steadfast, single-minded, persistent, persevering, tenacious, dogged, unfaltering, unwavering.

purposely adv *damage the car purposely* on purpose, intentionally, deliberately, by design, wilfully, wittingly, knowingly, consciously.

purse n **1** *have her purse stolen* wallet, money, pouch. **2** *paid for from the public purse* funds, resources, money, coffers, exchequer. **3** *a purse of £50,000 won by the boxer* prize, award, reward, gift, present.

purse v *purse her lips in disapproval* press together, compress, tighten, pucker.

pursuance n *in the pursuance of his duties* execution, discharge, performance, carrying out, doing, pursuing, prosecution, following.

pursue v **1** *the detective pursued the thief* go after, run after, follow, chase, give chase to, hunt, stalk, track, trail, shadow; *inf* tail. **2** *decide not to pursue the line of inquiry* follow, go on with, proceed with, keep/carry on with, continue with, continue, persist in. **3** *pursue a career in science | a life in science* follow, engage in, be engaged in, be occupied in, work at, practise, prosecute, conduct, ply, apply oneself to. **4** *pursue his goal of happiness | pursue his ambition to be a doctor* strive towards, push towards, work towards, seek, search for, be intent on, aim at, have as a goal, have as an objective, aspire to. **5** *she pursued every eligible young man | he pursued all rich young women* chase after, chase, run after, woo, court, pay court to, pay suit to, make up to, set one's cap at.

pursuit n **1** *take part in the pursuit of the thief* pursuing, chasing, chase, hunt, stalking, tracking; *inf* tailing. *see* PURSUE 1. **2** *give up the pursuit of that line of inquiry* pursuing, following, proceeding, continuance, persistence. *see* PURSUE 2. **3** *his pursuit of a life of crime | determined on his pursuit of a career in medicine* following, engagement, occupation, work, practising, prosecution, conducting, plying. *see* PURSUE 3. **4** *his pursuit of happiness | their pursuit of their ambitions* striving towards, search, aim, goal, objective, aspiration. *see* PURSUE 4. **5** *her relentless pursuit of eligible young men* chase, wooing, courting, suit, making up to. *see* PURSUE 5.

purvey v **1** *purvey meat to the local schools* provide, supply, furnish, sell, retail, deal in. **2** *purvey information to the public about the drought* provide, supply, furnish, make available, pass on, spread, circulate, communicate, make known, publicize, publish, broadcast, disseminate.

pus n *pus oozing from the wound* matter, suppuration, discharge; *Med* sanies.

push v **1** *push his friend into the swimming pool* shove, thrust, propel, drive, ram, jolt, butt, jostle. **2** *push one's way through the crowd* shove, thrust, force, press, squeeze, jostle, elbow, shoulder. **3** *push the bell press*, push down, press down, depress, exert pressure on. **4** *push him into applying for the job* encourage, prompt, press, urge, egg on, spur on, prod, goad, incite, impel, dragoon, force, coerce, constrain, browbeat, strongarm. **5** *firms pushing their latest products* give a push to, promote, advertise, publicize,

give a puff to, puff, puff up, boost, beat the drum for; *inf* plug, hype. **push around** *older boys pushing him around* bully, ride roughshod over, trample on, tread on, browbeat, tyrannize, intimidate, domineer. **push off** *they told him to push off* go away, leave, depart, get out; *inf* shove off, make oneself scarce, beat it, get lost, skedaddle, hit the road.

push n **1** *the children gave his friend a push* shove, thrust, ram, jolt, butt, jostle. **2** *the general launched a big push* attack, assault, advance, onslaught, onset, charge, sortie, sally. **3** *looking for sales staff with push* drive, force, ambition, enterprise, initiative, energy, vigour, vitality, spirit, verve, enthusiasm, go, vim; *inf* get-up-and-go, gumption, pizazz. **if it comes to the push** *see* PINCH n IF IT COMES TO THE PINCH.

pushover n **1** *the task was a pushover* easy task, something easy, child's play, walkover; *inf* piece of cake, picnic, doddle, cinch, breeze. **2** *he'll lend you the money—he's a pushover* fool, dupe; *inf* sucker, mug, soft touch, soft mark, easy mark, easy touch, walk-over, sap.

pushy adj pushing, assertive, self-assertive, aggressive, forceful, forward, bold, brash, bumptious, presumptuous, cocksure, loud, obnoxious.

pusillanimous adj cowardly, timorous, timid, fearful, faint-hearted, lily-livered, chicken-hearted, spineless, craven; *inf* yellow, chicken, gutless.

pussyfoot v **1** *pussyfoot around the house so as not to wake people* creep, tiptoe, pad, steal, sneak, prowl, slink, tread warily. **2** *pussyfoot around instead of saying what he thought* equivocate, be evasive, evade the issue, dodge/sidestep the issue, prevaricate, hedge, fence, hum and haw, hem and haw, beat about the bush, sit on the fence, tergiversate.

pustule n boil, spot, blister, pimple, abscess, papule; *inf* whitehead, zit.

put v **1** *put the books on the shelf | put him in a difficult situation* place, lay, lay down, set down, deposit, position, rest, stand, locate, situate, settle, emplace, install, posit. **2** *put them in the top grade* place, assign to, consign to, allocate to, rate, rank, grade, classify, categorize, catalogue, bracket. **3** *put the blame on the father/weather* place, attribute to, impute to, impose, fix, attach to, assign to, allocate to, lay, pin. **4** *put a tax on all travellers* impose, levy, demand, require, apply to, assign to, inflict, force, exact from. **5** *put into English* translate, transcribe, turn, render, construe, transliterate, interpret. word, express, phrase, frame, formulate, couch, say, utter, voice, speak, state, pronounce, proclaim. **7** *put to good use | put them to work* set, apply, employ, use, utilize, assign, allocate, devote. **8** *put to death* commit, consign, subject, condemn, sentence, convict, doom. **9** *I'd put it at five acres | put its worth at £500* assess, evaluate, value, estimate, calculate, reckon, guess, measure, establish, fix, place, set; *inf* guesstimate. **10** *put money on a horse* place, bet, wager, gamble, stake, risk, chance, hazard. **11** *put it to the committee* set before, lay before, present, bring forward, forward, submit, tender, offer, proffer, put forward, set forth, advance, posit. **12** *put the shot* throw, toss, fling, pitch, cast, hurl, heave, lob, let fly, shy. **13** *put his fist through the window* thrust, drive, plunge, stick, push, force, lunge, knock, bang, smash, bash. **put about 1** *put a rumour about | put it about that he's bankrupt* spread, bandy about, circulate, disseminate, make public, make known, give out, publicize, broadcast, propagate, announce, bruit. **2** *ships putting about* come/ go about, change course, alter course, change direction, turn round. **put across, put over** *successfully put across the message* get across/over, convey, communicate, make clear, explain, express, spell out, make understood, clarify. **put one across/over on** *succeed in putting one across on his rival* trick, deceive, hoodwink, mislead, delude, fool, take in, dupe, lead on, outwit, bamboozle, steal a march on; *inf* pull a fast one on, con, make a sucker of. **put aside 1** *put aside food/money for a rainy day* put/lay by, put away, set/lay aside, save, reserve, keep in reserve, keep, put/lay down, store, stockpile, hoard, deposit, stow away, salt away, squirrel away. **2** *put aside the newspaper* set/lay aside, put to one side, move to one side, cast aside, discard, abandon, dispense with, drop. **3** *put aside their differences* set/lay aside, forget, disregard, ignore, forget, discount, bury, consign to oblivion. **put away 1** *put away food/money for a rainy day* put/lay aside, put/lay by, set/ lay aside, save, keep in reserve, store, stockpile. **2** *put away the books* put back, replace, set back, return to its/their place, tidy away, tidy up, clear away. **3** *put away all thoughts of him* set/put/lay aside, discard, cast aside, forget, disregard, get rid of, rid oneself of, jettison, consign to oblivion. **4** *put the criminal/mental patient away* put in prison/mental hospital, confine, lock up, shut away/up, commit, imprison, hospitalize, institutionalize, certify; *inf* bang up. **5** *put away quantities of food* consume, eat, eat up, swallow, gulp down, devour, down,

get down, gobble up, bolt, wolf; *inf* tuck away/into. **6** *put away the enemy | the injured dog had to be put away* kill, do away with, murder, slaughter, slay, dispatch, finish off, destroy, put down, put to sleep, put out of its misery; *inf* bump off, wipe out. **put down 1** *put down a rebellion* crush, suppress, quash, quell, stamp out, stop, repress, smash, extinguish. **2** *put their names down* write down, put in writing, note down, make a note of, jot down, take down, set down, enter, list, record, register, log. **3** *put it down to experience* mark down, set down, attribute, ascribe, impute, chalk up to, blame on. **4** *put down cases of port* lay down/aside, put aside, set aside, save, store. **5** *put down the sick animal* put to sleep, put out of its misery, destroy, put away, do away with, kill. **6** *always putting down his wife* snub, disparage, deprecate, belittle, denigrate, deflate, slight, humiliate, crush, mortify. **put forward** *put forward a theory | his name was put forward for a life peerage* lay before, set before, submit, present, suggest, advance, tender, propose, move, introduce, offer, proffer, recommend, suggest, nominate, name. **put off 1** *put off the meeting* postpone, put back, defer, delay, adjourn, hold over, reschedule, shelve; *inf* put on ice, put on the back burner. **2** *put off by his surly behaviour | the smell put her off* discourage, dissuade, dishearten, distress, dismay, discomfit, nonplus, daunt, repel, offend, disgust, revolt, sicken, nauseate. **3** *don't put the driver off* distract, divert the attention of, disturb the concentration of, draw away, sidetrack. **put it on** *he's not hurt—he's putting it on* pretend, play-act, make believe, exaggerate. **put on 1** *put on her new suit* dress in, get dressed in, clothe oneself in, change into, slip into, don. **2** *put on the light* switch on, turn on. **3** *put on transport for travellers to go to the airport* lay on, provide, supply, furnish, make available. **4** *put on a production of Hamlet* stage, mount, present, produce. **5** *she's not sad—she's putting on the grief* feign, fake, sham, simulate, affect. **6** *put money on a horse* place, lay, bet, wager. **put out 1** *she is easily put out* annoy, anger, irritate, exasperate, infuriate, provoke, irk, vex, gall, disturb, perturb, disconcert, agitate, harass. **2** *we don't want to put you out by staying to dinner | don't put yourself out* inconvenience, put (someone) to trouble, trouble, bother, impose upon, discommode, incommode. **3** *put out the fire* extinguish, quench, douse, stamp out. **4** *put out the candle* extinguish, blow out, snuff out, douse. **5** *put out a news report on the king's health* bring out, issue, circulate, release, disclose, make known, make public, publish, broadcast, publicize. **put up 1** *put up new houses/blocks of flats* build, construct, erect, raise. **2** *put up his friends for the night* give accommodation to, accommodate, provide with board and lodging, house, give a roof to, give a bed to, entertain. **3** *put up proposals for the expansion of the firm* put forward, propose, present, submit, recommend. **4** *put his friend up for chairman* put forward, nominate, propose, recommend. **5** *put up the money for the campaign* provide, supply, furnish, give, donate, pay, advance, pledge. **6** *put up prices* raise, increase; *inf* jack up. **7** *put up notices advertising the event* stick up, post, display, exhibit. **put (someone) up to** *put his friend up to breaking into the house* egg on to, urge, encourage, persuade, incite, goad, spur. **put up with** endure, tolerate, bear, stand, abide, suffer, take, stomach, brook, accept, swallow. **put upon** *she is so obliging that she gets put upon* take advantage of, impose upon, take for granted, exploit, overwork, overburden, saddle.

putative adj **1** *the putative father of the baby* supposed, assumed, presumed, presumptive, acknowledged, accepted, recognized, commonly believed, commonly regarded, alleged, reputed.

put-down n *regard his remark as a gross put-down* snub, rebuff, slight, disparagement, sneer, humiliation.

puzzle v *he was puzzled by her behaviour* perplex, baffle, stump, beat, mystify, confuse, bewilder, nonplus, stagger, dumbfound, daze, confound; *inf* flummox. **puzzle over** *puzzling over what she had said | puzzling over her motives* rack one's brains about, cudgel one's brains about, think hard about, give much thought to, mull over, muse over, ponder, brood about, wonder about. **puzzle out** *puzzle out the solution* find the answer to, work out, think out, think through, figure out, reason out, solve, resolve, decipher, find the key to, unravel; *inf* crack.

puzzled adj *the puzzled audience looked in amazement at the magician's tricks | despite all the information the police are still puzzled* perplexed, baffled, stumped, nonplussed, beaten, mystified, confused, bewildered, confounded, staggered, dumbfounded, dazed, at a loss, at sea; *inf* flummoxed.

puzzling adj *a puzzling situation* difficult, hard, unclear, perplexing, knotty, baffling, enigmatic, abstruse, nonplussing, mystifying, bewildering, unfathomable, inexplicable, incomprehensible, beyond one, above one's head.

pygmy n **1** *insultingly call the small man a pygmy* small man/woman/person, midget, dwarf; *inf* shrimp, pint-sized person, Tom Thumb. **2** *a pygmy among intellectual giants* cipher, nonentity, nobody, lightweight; *inf* pipsqueak.

pyromaniac n arsonist, fire-raiser, incendiary; *inf* firebug.

Qq

quack n **1** *quacks selling fake medicines* charlatan, mountebank, impostor, fraud, fake, confidence trickster, pretender, humbug; *inf* con man, phoney. **2** *get the quack to examine you* doctor, medical/general practitioner; *inf* GP, doc, medic.

quack adj *a quack cure for colds* fake, fraudulent, counterfeit, sham; *inf* phoney.

quaff v drink, swallow, gulp down, imbibe; *inf* guzzle, swig.

quagmire n **1** *birds on the quagmire* quag, bog, peat bog, marsh, swamp, morass, mire, slough, fen. **2** *in a quagmire with no place to live* difficulty, quandary, dilemma, predicament, plight, tight corner, muddle, entanglement, involvement, imbroglio, impasse, stalemate; *inf* jam, scrape, pickle, fix, hot water, stew.

quail v flinch, shrink, recoil, shy away, pull back, draw back, cower, cringe, shudder, shiver, tremble, shake, quake, blench, blanch.

quaint adj pleasantly old-fashioned, old-fashioned, old-world, attractively unusual, unusual, droll, curious, whimsical, attractive, charming, sweet.

quake v shake, tremble, quiver, shiver, shudder, rock, vibrate, pulsate, throb.

qualification n **1** *qualification to be a teacher* certification, training, competence, competency, accomplishment, eligibility, acceptability, suitableness, preparedness, fitness, proficiency, skilfulness, adeptness, capability, aptitude; skill, ability, attribute, endowment. **2** *say what you mean without qualification* modification, limitation, restriction, reservation, stipulation, allowance, adaptation, adjustment; condition, proviso, provision, caveat.

qualified adj **1** *a qualified doctor* certificated, trained, fitted, fit, equipped, prepared, competent, accomplished, proficient, skilled, skilful, adept, practised, experienced, expert, capable, able. **2** *a qualified approval* modified, limited, conditional, restricted, bounded, contingent, confined, circumscribed, reserved, guarded, equivocal, stipulated, adapted, adjusted.

qualify v **1** *he qualified as a doctor* gain certification/qualifications, train, take instruction. **2** *his training qualifies him to teach*

certify, license, empower, authorize, allow, permit, sanction, warrant, fit, equip, prepare, arm, make ready, ground, train, educate, coach, teach, instruct. **3** *qualify her statement* modify, limit, make conditional, restrict. **4** *qualify her criticism* modify, temper, soften, modulate, mitigate, reduce, lessen, diminish. **5** *not qualify as poetry* be characterizable as, meet the requirement of, be eligible, be designated.

quality n **1** *the material is of poor quality* degree of excellence, standard, grade, level, make, sort, type, kind, variety. **2** *his quality has been recognized* excellence, superiority, merit, worth, value, calibre, talent, talentedness, distinction, eminence, pre-eminence. **3** *they have many good qualities* feature, trait, attribute, characteristic, aspect, property, peculiarity. **4** *differences in the quality of the two personalities* character, nature, constitution, make-up. **5** *the quality are not necessarily wealthy* aristocracy, nobility, upper class, gentry.

qualm n **1** *have some qualms about going* doubt, misgiving, hesitation, hesitancy, reluctance, disinclination, anxiety, apprehension, disquiet, uneasiness, concern. **2** *have no qualms about having hurt them* pang/twinge of conscience, scruple, compunction, remorse.

quandary n awkward situation, difficulty, dilemma, predicament, plight, tight corner/spot, cleft stick, state of uncertainty/perplexity, muddle, impasse; *inf* jam, pickle, fix.

quantity n **1** *what quantity of books/paper do you need?* number, amount, total, aggregate, sum, quota, weight. **2** *a quantity of books/paper has gone missing* number, quite a number, good number/few, several, numerous, many, amount, large amount, considerable amounts; *inf* lot, lots. **3** *estimate the quantity* property, aspect; size, capacity, mass, volume, bulk, extent, length, area, time.

quarrel n **1** *the lovers have had a quarrel* argument, row, fight, disagreement, difference of opinion, dispute, disputation, squabble, altercation, wrangle, tiff, misunderstanding, feud, vendetta; *inf* spat, scrap. **2** *a quarrel developed in the pub* argument, row, fight, tussle, disturbance, altercation, clash, conflict, affray, fracas, fray, brawl, rumpus, brouhaha, commotion, uproar, tumult, scrimmage; *inf* dust-up, set-to, shindig. **3** *I have no quarrel with him* bone of contention, complaint, grievance, resentment.

quarrel v **1** *the lovers quarrelled* argue, have a row/fight, row, fight, dispute, squabble, bicker, spar, wrangle, have a misunderstanding; *inf* fall out. **2** *I cannot quarrel with his logic* find fault with, fault, criticize, object to, take exception to, complain about, cavil, carp; *inf* pick holes in, nit-pick.

quarrelsome adj argumentative, belligerent, disputatious, contentious, pugnacious, combative, ready for a fight, bellicose, litigious, hot-tempered, irascible, choleric, irritable.

quarry n *huntsmen stalking their quarry* prey, victim, prize.

quarter n **1** *live in the Latin quarter of the city* district, area, region, part, side, neighbourhood, locality, zone, territory, province. **2** *accept help from any quarter* direction, place, point, spot, location. **3** *receive no quarter from the tyrant* mercy, leniency, clemency, lenity, compassion, pity, forgiveness, indulgence.

quarter v *soldiers quartered in the town* put up, house, board, billet, accommodate, lodge, install, put a roof over someone's head.

quarters npl lodgings, rooms, chambers, barracks; accommodation, billet, residence, abode, dwelling, domicile, habitation, cantonment; *inf* digs, pad.

quash v **1** *quash the jail sentence* annul, declare null and void, nullify, invalidate, void, cancel, overrule, override, overthrow, reject, set aside, reverse, revoke, rescind, repeal. **2** *quash the rebellion* crush, put down, squash, quell, subdue, suppress, repress, quench, extinguish, stamp out, put a stop to, end, terminate, defeat, destroy.

quasi- pfx **1** *quasi-scientific evidence* supposedly, seemingly, apparently, nominally, pseudo. **2** *a quasi-friend* supposed, so-called, would-be, pretended, pretend, sham, fake, pseudo.

quaver v *his voice quavered* quiver, vibrate, tremble, shake, waver.

queasy adj sick, nauseated, ill, indisposed, dizzy; *Amer* sick to one's stomach; *inf* under the weather.

queen n **1** *the queen reigned for 50 years* monarch, sovereign, ruler, king's consort. **2** *she was the queen of Wimbledon/pop* star, prima donna, idol, ideal, doyenne.

queer adj **1** *a queer fellow* | *queer behaviour* odd, strange, unusual, extraordinary, funny, curious, peculiar, weird, outlandish, singular, eccentric, unconventional, unorthodox, atypical, abnormal, irregular, anomalous, deviant, *outré*, offbeat; *inf* off-the-wall. **2** *it's a queer story* | *something queer going on* strange, peculiar, suspicious, suspect, irregular, questionable, dubious, doubtful; *inf* fishy, shady. **3** *feel a bit queer* ill, unwell, sick, queasy, faint, dizzy, giddy, light-headed.

queer v *queer one's chances* spoil, damage, impair, mar, wreck, ruin, injure, harm, hurt, jeopardize, threaten, put at risk, endanger, imperil.

quell v **1** *quell the rebellion* | *quell rebellious forces* quash, defeat, conquer, vanquish, overpower, overcome, overwhelm, rout, crush, suppress, subdue, extinguish, stamp out, put down. **2** *quell their fears* allay, lull, put at rest, quiet, silence, calm, soothe, appease, assuage, abate, deaden, dull, pacify, tranquillize, mitigate, palliate.

quench v **1** *quench one's thirst* satisfy, slake, sate, satiate. **2** *quench the candle* extinguish, put out, snuff out, blow out, douse. **3** *quench their desire* suppress, extinguish, stamp out, smother, stifle.

query n **1** *raise a query* question, enquiry. **2** *his behaviour raises a query as to his sanity* question, question mark, doubt, uncertainty, reservation, suspicion; scepticism.

query v **1** *"where are we?" he queried* ask, enquire, question. **2** *he queried their fitness for the job* call into question, question, raise/entertain doubts about, throw doubt on, doubt, have/harbour suspicions about, suspect, feel uneasy about, express reservations about, challenge, raise objections to.

quest n **1** *in quest of a better life* search, seeking, pursuit, chase, hunt. **2** *their quest was the holy grail* goal, aim, objective, purpose, quarry, prey. **3** *knights setting out on a quest* adventure, expedition, journey, voyage, exploration, crusade.

question n **1** *answer her questions* query, enquiry, interrogation. **2** *there is no question that he is ill* doubt, dubiety, dubiousness, dispute, argument, debate, controversy, reservation. **3** *there is the question of safety* issue, point at issue, problem, matter, point, subject, topic, theme, bone of contention. **beyond question** beyond doubt, without doubt, undoubtedly, undisputably, incontestably, incontrovertibly. **in question** *the matter in question* being discussed, under discussion/consideration, at issue, on the agenda. **out of the question** impossible, inconceivable, unthinkable, unimaginable, absurd, ridiculous, preposterous.

question v **1** *question the witnesses* ask questions of, interrogate, cross-examine, cross-question, quiz, catechize, interview, sound out, examine, give the third degree to; *inf* grill, pump. **2** *question his motives* call into question, query, raise doubts about, throw doubt on, have suspicions about, express reservations about, challenge, raise objections to. *see* QUERY v 2.

questionable adj *his motive/ability is questionable* open to question/doubt, doubtful, dubious, uncertain, debatable, in dispute, arguable, controversial, controvertible.

queue n *join the queue | a queue of lorries* line, row, column, file, chain, string, train, succession, sequence, series, concatenation.

quibble n **1** *raise quibbles over the cost* petty criticism/complaint, protest, trivial objection, niggle, cavil, nicety; *inf* nit-picking. **2** *introduce the issue as a quibble* evasion, avoidance, equivocation, prevarication, dodge, hedging, fudging.

quibble v **1** *quibble about a minor detail* raise petty objections (to), cavil, carp, pettifog, split hairs, chop logic; *inf* nit-pick. **2** *he quibbles so that it is difficult to get a straight answer* be evasive, equivocate, avoid the issue, prevaricate, hedge, fudge, be ambiguous; *inf* beat about the bush.

quick adj **1** *a quick runner/worker/reader* fast, rapid, speedy, swift, fleet, express. **2** *a quick response* prompt, without delay, immediate, instantaneous, expeditious. **3** *a quick look at the map* brief, brisk, fleeting, momentary, hasty, hurried, cursory, perfunctory. **4** *the child is very quick* quick-witted, sharp-witted, alert, intelligent. *see* QUICK-WITTED. **5** *quick of temper* irascible, irritable. *see* QUICK-TEMPERED.

quicken v **1** *his pulse quickened* become/grow faster, speed up, accelerate. **2** *they quickened their steps/progress* speed up, accelerate, expedite, hasten, hurry, hurry up, precipitate. **3** *the film quickened his interest in wild life* stimulate, stir up, arouse, rouse, incite, instigate, whet, inspire, kindle, fan, refresh, strengthen, revive, revitalize, resuscitate, revivify.

quickly adv **1** *run quickly* fast, rapidly, speedily, swiftly, with all speed, at speed, with all possible haste, at the double, posthaste; *inf* at a rate of knots, hell for leather, like a bat out of hell, like an arrow from a bow. **2** *respond quickly* promptly, without delay, immediately, instantaneously, expeditiously. **3** *read the letter quickly* rapidly, briskly, hastily, hurriedly, cursorily, perfunctorily.

quick-tempered adj irascible, irritable, hot-tempered, fiery, hasty, impatient, touchy, testy, snappish, quarrelsome, petulant, choleric, splenetic, volatile; *inf* on a short fuse.

quick-witted adj quick, sharp-witted, nimble-witted, alert, intelligent, bright, lively, smart, perceptive, discerning, shrewd; *inf* quick on the uptake.

quid pro quo n exchange, substitution, trading, trade-off, barter, compensation, recompense, requital, reprisal, retaliation.

quiescent adj inert, dormant, passive, inactive, idle, still, stagnant, torpid.

quiet adj **1** *the house was quiet* silent, hushed, noiseless, soundless, peaceful. **2** *a quiet voice* soft, low, inaudible. **3** *she's a quiet person* calm, serene, composed, placid, untroubled, peaceful, tranquil, gentle, mild, temperate, unexcitable, restrained, phlegmatic, imperturbable, moderate, reserved, uncommunicative, taciturn, silent. **4** *quiet colours/clothes* unobtrusive, unostentatious, restrained, muted, understated, subdued, subtle, conservative, sober, modest, demure. **5** *live in a quiet village* peaceful, sleepy, undisturbed, unfrequented, private, secluded, sequestered, retired, isolated, out of the way; *inf* off the beaten track. **6** *the shop/business is quiet today* inactive, not busy, sluggish. **7** *have a quiet word with him* private, confidential, secret, discreet, unofficial, off the record; *inf* hush-hush. **8** *we kept his presence quiet* secret, unrevealed, undisclosed, uncommunicated; *inf* hush-hush.

quiet n *in the quiet of the evening* quietness, stillness, silence, hush, noiselessness, soundlessness, peace, peacefulness, calmness, tranquillity, serenity.

quieten v **1** *quieten the noisy children* silence, hush, shush, quiet; *inf* shut up. **2** *the children soon quieten* become quiet, grow silent, settle down; *inf* shut up. **3** *quieten the frightened horse* calm, calm down, soothe, tranquillize. **4** *quieten their fears* allay, soothe, calm, tranquillize, appease, lull, pacify, mollify, palliate, suppress, quell, stifle, dull, deaden.

quietly adv **1** *speak quietly* softly, in a low voice, in low/hushed tones, in a whisper, in an undertone, inaudibly. **2** *creep out quietly* silently, noiselessly, soundlessly. **3** *tell him quietly that he must leave* privately, confidentially, secretly, discreetly. **4** *she is quietly confident* calmly, patiently, placidly, serenely, undemonstratively, unemotionally. **5** *dress quietly* unobtrusively, unostentatiously, with restraint, conservatively, soberly, modestly, demurely.

quilt n eiderdown, duvet, continental quilt.

quintessence n **1** *the novel captures the quintessence of youth* essence, essentialness, core, heart, soul, spirit, quiddity. **2** *he is the quintessence of a gentleman* embodiment, personification, exemplar, perfect example, ideal, *beau idéal*.

quip n *make witty quips* witticism, sally, wisecrack, joke, jest, *bon mot*, epigram, aphorism; *inf* one-liner, crack.

quirk n *it is one of his quirks to polish his car everyday* idiosyncrasy, peculiarity, oddity, eccentricity, foible, whim, vagary, caprice, kink, mannerism, habit, characteristic, trait, feature, obsession, passion, mania, fetish, *idée fixe*; *inf* hang-up.

quit v **1** *quit smoking* give up, stop, cease, discontinue, drop, leave off, abandon, abstain from, desist from. **2** *quit his job* leave, depart from, vacate, walk out on. **3** *he has decided to quit* leave, depart, go away, take off; *inf* call it a day, call it quits, pack it in.

quite adv **1** *he has quite recovered* completely, fully, entirely, totally, wholly, absolutely, in all respects. **2** *he is quite talented but not as good as his brother* fairly, relatively, moderately, reasonably, to some extent/degree, to a certain extent, rather, somewhat.

quiver v *quiver with fear* tremble, shiver, vibrate, quaver, quake, shudder, pulsate, convulse, palpitate.

quiver n *a quiver of fear* tremble, tremor, shiver, vibration, quaver, shudder, pulsation, convulsion, palpitation, throb, spasm, tic.

quiz n **1** *take part in a television quiz* test of knowledge, knowledge test. **2** *police subjecting them to a quiz* questioning, interrogation, cross-examination, cross-questioning, catechism, examination, third degree; *inf* grilling, pumping.

quiz v *quiz them about their movements* question, ask, interrogate, cross-examine, cross-question, catechize; *inf* pump, grill.

quizzical adj *a quizzical look/smile* questioning, puzzled, perplexed, baffled, mystified, mocking, teasing.

quota n share, allowance, allocation, portion, ration, part, slice, measure, proportion; *inf* cut, whack.

quotation n **1** *full of quotations from Shakespeare* citation, reference, allusion, excerpt, extract, selection, passage, line; *inf* quote. **2** *give them a quotation for the work* estimate, estimated price, cost, charge, figure; *inf* quote.

quote v **1** *quote verses from the Bible* repeat, iterate, recite, reproduce. **2** *he could not quote them an example of what he meant* cite, give, name, instance, mention, refer to, make reference to, allude to. **3** *quote for the job* estimate for, price, set a price for.

rabble n **1** *a rabble gathered round the accident* mob, horde, swarm, crowd, throng. **2** *noblemen despising the rabble* common people, populace, commonality, the mob, rank and file, peasantry, *hoi poloi*, riff-raff, *canaille*; the masses, lower classes, dregs of society; *inf* great unwashed.

rabid adj **1** *rabid dogs* rabies-infected, mad, foaming at the mouth, hydrophobic. **2** *rabid socialists/conservatives* fanatical, extreme, overzealous, overenthusiastic, fervent, perfervid, unreasonable, irrational, intolerant, bigoted, narrow-minded, narrow. **3** *rabid hatred/enemies* violent, wild, frenzied, frenetic, frantic, raging, raving, maniacal, distracted, beside oneself, berserk.

race¹ n **1** *the competitors for the race* speed contest, competition, chase, pursuit, relay. **2** *the race for the presidency* contest, competition, rivalry, contention. **3** *drowned in the mill-race* channel, waterway, watercourse, sluice, spillway.

race¹ v **1** *horses racing at Doncaster* run, take part in a race, contend, compete. **2** *race each other in the Olympics* run against, compete against, be pitted against. **3** *race to the finishing line* run, sprint, dash, dart, bolt, make a dash/bolt for, speed, hare, fly, tear, zoom, accelerate, career. **4** *you'll have to race to get there on time* hurry, hasten, make haste, rush; *inf* get cracking, get a move on, step on it.

race² n **1** *humankind divided into races* racial division, people, ethnic group. **2** *discrimination on grounds of race* racial type, blood, bloodline, stock, line, lineage, breed, strain, stirps, extraction, ancestry, parentage. **3** *sailors are a race apart* group, type, class, species.

racial adj race-related, ethnic, ethnological.

racism n racialism, racial discrimination, racial prejudice/bigotry, apartheid.

racist n racialist, bigot, illiberal.

racist adj racialist, discriminatory, prejudiced, bigoted, intolerant, illiberal.

rack n **1** *a clothes/luggage rack* frame, framework, stand, form, trestle, structure, holder, shelf. **2** *prisoners on the rack* instrument of torture, stretching instrument. **on the rack** in pain, in agony, in distress, suffering, in torture.

rack v **1** *he was racked with pain* torture, agonize, afflict, torment, persecute, plague, distress, rend, tear, harrow, crucify, convulse. **2** *rack one's back/ankle* strain, wrench, rick, pull, stretch, put out of joint, disjoint, throw out, twist, sprain.

racket n **1** *a racket coming from next door* noise, din, row, commotion, disturbance, uproar, hubbub, hullabaloo; clamour, pandemonium, tumult, shouting, yelling. **2** *he's involved in a drugs racket* criminal activity, illegal scheme/enterprise, fraud, fraudulent scheme, swindle. **3** *what racket is he in?* business, line of business, line, occupation, profession, job; *inf* game.

raconteur n storyteller, teller of tales, spinner of yarns, narrator, relater, romancer.

racy adj **1** *a racy prose style* vigorous, lively, spirited, energetic, dynamic, animated, vivacious, enthusiastic, buoyant, sparkling, fast-moving, exciting, stimulating, entertaining, fascinating; *inf* sexy, peppy. **2** *his racy jokes* risqué, suggestive, off-colour, ribald, bawdy, vulgar, coarse, crude, rude, smutty, dirty, blue, indecent, indelicate, immodest, naughty; *inf* spicy, near the bone/knuckle. **3** *a racy wine/sauce* strong, strong-flavoured, distinctive, full-flavoured, flavoursome, tasty, rich, pungent, well-flavoured, piquant, spicy, tangy, peppery.

raddled adj haggard, coarsened, the worse for wear, dishevelled, unkempt, dilapidated, run-down, broken-down, worn-out.

radiance n **1** *the radiance of the sun* light, shining, brightness, brilliance, luminosity, effulgence, incandescence, glow, gleam, glitter, sparkle, shimmer, glare. **2** *the radiance of the bride* joyfulness, joy, elation, rapture, bitheness, happiness, delight, pleasure, gaiety, warmth. **3** *the radiance of her beauty* resplendence, splendour, dazzlingness.

radiant adj **1** *the radiant sun/light* irradiant, shining, bright, illuminated, brilliant, luminous, luminescent, lustrous, lucent, effulgent, refulgent, incandescent, beaming, glowing, gleaming, glittering, sparkling, shimmering, glaring. **2** *the bride was radiant* joyful, elated, in raptures, ecstatic, blissfully happy, delighted, pleased, gay, happy, glowing; *inf* in seventh heaven, on cloud nine. **3** *her radiant beauty* splendid, resplendent, magnificent, dazzling, glowing, vivid, intense.

radiate v **1** *radiating heat/light* send out/ forth, scatter, diffuse, spread, shed, give off/out, emit, emanate. **2** *radiate joy/hope* transmit, emanate, show, exhibit, demonstrate; *inf* be the picture of. **3** *lines radiating* branch out, spread out, diverge, divaricate, issue.

radiation n **1** *the radiation of light/X-rays* emission, emanation, propagation, transmission. **2** *ultraviolet/infrared radiation* waves, rays; transmitted energy.

radical adj **1** *radical issues/errors* fundamental, basic, rudimentary, elementary, elemental, constitutional. **2** *radical change needed* thorough, complete, total, entire, absolute, utter, comprehensive, exhaustive, sweeping, far-reaching, profound, drastic, stringent, violent. **3** *radical views/actions* extremist, extreme, immoderate, revolutionary, rebel, rebellious, militant, fanatic, leftist, left-wing.

raffish adj **1** *he has a raffish air* rakish, bohemian, jaunty, dashing, devil-may-care, casual, careless, disreputable, dissolute, dissipated, debauched, decadent, degenerate. **2** *raffish bars/decoration* tawdry, flashy, gaudy, loud, garish, showy, vulgar, tasteless, gross, coarse, meretricious; *inf* flash.

raffle n lottery, draw, sweepstake, sweep, tombola.

rag[1] n **1** *a rag of cloth* remnant, fragment, worn/frayed piece. **2** *hand me the oil rag* cloth, duster.

rag[2] n **1** *students holding a rag* fund-raising event, charity event, charitable event. **2** *just having a rag* prank, lark, caper, romp, joke, practical joke.

rag[2] v *other children ragging him* tease, poke fun at, make fun of, make a fool of, taunt; *inf* rib, send up.

ragamuffin n urchin, street arab, guttersnipe.

ragbag n jumble, hotchpotch, mishmash, mixed bag, miscellany, medley, motley collection, pot-pourri, gallimaufry, salmagundi; *inf* mix, omnium gatherum.

rage n **1** *be filled with rage* fury, anger, wrath, ire, high dudgeon, frenzy, madness, raving. **2** *fly into a rage* fit of rage/fury, frenzy, tantrum, paroxysm of rage/anger, rampage. **3** *the rage of the storm* violence, turbulence, tumult, fire and fury. **all the**

rage ultra-fashionable, ultra-popular, in demand; *inf* trendy, latest thing/craze.

rage v **1** *the teacher is raging* be furious, be infuriated, be angry, seethe, be beside oneself, lose one's temper, boil over, rant, rave, rant and rave, storm, fume, fulminate; *inf* foam at the mouth, blow one's top, blow up, blow a fuse/gasket, hit the ceiling, flip one's lid, freak out. **2** *rage against the new rules* fulminate, complain vociferously, storm, inveigh against, rail. **3** *the storm is raging* be violent, be at its height, be turbulent, be tempestuous.

ragged adj **1** *ragged clothes* tattered, in tatters, torn, rent, in holes, holey, worn to shreds, falling to pieces, threadbare, frayed, the worse for wear. **2** *ragged children* in rags, shabby, unkempt, down and out, down at heel, poor, destitute, indigent. **3** *a ragged coastline* jagged, notched, serrated, saw-toothed, craggy, rugged, uneven, irregular. **4** *a ragged prose style* rough, crude, unpolished, unrefined, faulty, imperfect, irregular, uneven. **5** *a ragged band of soldiers* in disarray, straggling, straggly, disorganized, fragmented.

raging adj **1** *met by a raging teacher* enraged, furious, angry, infuriated, wrathful, incensed, seething, fuming, ranting, raving, mad. *see* RAGE v 1. **2** *a raging storm* violent, strong, wild, stormy, turbulent, tempestuous, blustery. **3** *a raging toothache* agonizing, excruciating, painful, throbbing, aching, sore. **4** *a raging thirst* extreme, excessive, severe, very great, inordinate.

rags npl *dressed in rags* tatters, tattered/old clothes; torn clothing.

raid n **1** *make a raid on the enemy* surprise attack, assault, onset, onslaught, invasion, incursion, foray, charge, thrust, sortie, sally. **2** *a bank raid* robbery, break-in; *inf* smash and grab. **3** *a police raid* surprise search; *inf* bust.

raid v **1** *raid the enemy lines* make a raid on, attack, assault, invade, charge, assail, storm, rush, set upon, descend upon, swoop upon; *dial* reive. **2** *raid the enemy supplies* | *raid the fridge* plunder, pillage, loot, rifle, forage, ransack, steal from. **3** *raid a bank* rob, break into. **4** *police raiding a house* make a raid on, search thoroughly, make a search of; *inf* bust.

raider n **1** *the enemy raiders* attacker, assaulter, invader, pillager, plunderer, marauder, ransacker, sacker; *dial* reiver. **2** *the bank raiders* | *the raiders of the supplies* robber, burglar, thief; *inf* crook.

rail v *rail against the new rules* inveigh against, declaim against, rage against, protest strongly, complain bitterly, criticize severely, censure, condemn, castigate; *inf* lambaste.

railing n rails; balustrade, fencing, paling, barrier.

raillery n banter, badinage, teasing, joking, japing, persiflage; *inf* kidding, ragging, ribbing.

rain n **1** *soaked in the rain* rainfall, precipitation, raindrops, drizzle, shower, rainstorm, cloudburst, torrent, downpour, deluge, thunderstorm. **2** *a rain of arrows* shower, hail, deluge, volley.

rain v **1** *it is raining* pour, pour/come down, precipitate, shower, drizzle, rain hard, rain heavily; *inf* rain cats and dogs, come down in buckets. **2** *contents rained from the suitcase* | *arrows rained down* fall, pour out/down, drop, shower. **3** *rain gifts on them* lavish, pour, give generously, bestow.

rainy adj wet, showery, drizzly, damp.

raise v **1** *raise one's eyes/hat* | *raise the ship* lift, lift up, raise aloft, elevate, uplift, upthrust, hoist, heave up. **2** *raise the fence* set up, set upright, put up, stand, up-end, stand on end. **3** *raise his offer/prices* increase, put up, escalate, inflate; *inf* step up, hike, jack up. **4** *raise the volume/temperature* increase, heighten, augment, amplify, intensify; *inf* step up. **5** *raise a block of flats* | *raise a statue* construct, build, erect, put up. **6** *raise money/troops* get/gather together, collect, assemble, muster, levy, accumulate, amass, scrape together. **7** *raise objections* put forward, introduce, advance, bring up, broach, suggest, moot, present. **8** *raise doubts/hopes* cause, set going, bring into being, engender, create, set afoot, kindle, arouse, awaken, excite, summon up, provoke, activate, evoke, incite, stir up, foment, whip up, instigate. **9** *raise three children* bring up, rear, nurture, educate. **10** *raise chickens* breed, rear. **11** *raise crops* grow, farm, cultivate, propagate, till, produce. **12** *raise him to captain/manager* promote, advance, upgrade, elevate, exalt. **13** *raise bread* cause to rise, leaven, puff up. **14** *raise a siege* end, bring to an end, put an end to, terminate, abandon, lift. **15** *raise the barriers* remove, get rid of, take away. **16** *raise a ghost* cause to appear, call up, call forth, summon up, conjure up. **17** *she must be away—we can't raise her* get hold of, reach, contact, communicate with. **18** *fail to raise him for work* awaken, wake, arouse, rouse, stir.

rake v **1** *rake the dead leaves* scrape up, collect, gather. **2** *rake the soil* smooth, smooth out, level, even out, flatten. **3** *rake through*

her things search, hunt, ransack, rummage, rifle, comb, turn upside down, scour. **4** *soldiers raking the line of prisoners with gunfire* sweep, enfilade, pepper. **5** *rake the side of the car* scratch, scrape, graze, bark. **rake in** *rake in money* gather in, earn, pull in, haul in, pile up, amass, accumulate. **rake up** *rake up the past* | *rake up old memories* revive, call to mind, reminisce about, recollect.

rake n roué, debauchee, dissolute man, playboy, libertine, profligate.

rake-off n share, cut, dividend, commission, half, portion, part.

rakish adj **1** *a rakish young man in a sports car* | *at a rakish angle* dashing, jaunty, devil-may-care, sporty, breezy, debonair, smart, dapper, spruce; *inf* natty. **2** *a rakish drunk* dissolute, debauched, dissipated, profligate, wanton, degenerate, depraved.

rally v **1** *rally to support the king* come/get together, assemble, group, band together, convene, unite. **2** *rally the forces* call/bring together, assemble, summon, round up, muster, marshall, mobilize. **3** *they were defeated but they rallied* regroup, reassemble, re-form, reunite. **4** *she was very ill but she rallied* recover, recuperate, revive, get better/well, improve, perk up, regain one's strength, pull through, take a turn for the better, turn the corner, be on the mend, get one's second wind.

rally n **1** *a political rally* mass meeting, meeting, gathering, assembly, assemblage, convention, conference, congregation, convocation. **2** *a rally on the stock exchange* recovery, recuperation, improvement, revival, rehabilitation, comeback, resurgence.

ram v **1** *ram the tobacco into the pipe* | *ram clothes into the case* force, cram, stuff, compress, jam, squeeze, thrust, tamp. **2** *ram piles into a river bed* drive, hammer, pound, beat, hit. **3** *his car rammed ours* strike, hit, dash against, run into, crash into, collide with, bump, slam.

ramble v **1** *ramble through the countryside* take a walk, go for a walk, walk, hike, wander, stroll, saunter, amble, roam, range, rove, traipse, jaunt. **2** *the speaker rambled on* | *that writer rambles* digress, wander, speak/write discursively, go off at tangents, talk aimlessly, maunder, gibber, blather, blether, babble, chatter, gabble, rattle on; *inf* rabbit on, witter on.

ramble n walk, hike, wander, stroll, saunter, amble, roam, traipse, jaunt, trip, excursion, tour.

rambler n walker, hiker, stroller, saunterer, wanderer, roamer, rover, drifter, traveller, wayfarer.

rambling adj 1 *rambling holiday-makers* walking, hiking, strolling, roaming. *see* RAMBLE V 1. 2 *rambling speeches/writings* digressive, wandering, roundabout, circuitous, diffuse, periphrastic, disconnected, disjointed, maundering, long-winded, verbose, wordy, prolix. 3 *rambling suburbs* sprawling, spreading, unsystematic. 4 *rambling plants* straggling, trailing.

ramification n 1 *the action had many ramifications* consequence, aftermath, outcome, result, upshot, issue, sequel, complication, implication. 2 *the ramifications of the structure* subdivision, offshoot, branch, outgrowth, limb, scion.

ramp n *a ramp for wheelchairs* slope, sloping surface, incline, inclined plane, gradient, acclivity, rise; access ramp.

rampage v 1 *animals/children rampaging about the woods* rush/run wildly, run riot, run amuck, charge, tear. 2 *parents rampaging at their children's behaviour* rage, rave, rant, rant and rave, storm, go berserk.

rampage n uproar, furore, mayhem, turmoil. **on the rampage** running amuck, going berserk, out of control, rampaging.

rampant adj 1 *rampant disease/crime* uncontrolled, out of control/hand, unrestrained, unchecked, unbridled, widespread, pandemic, epidemic, spreading like wildfire. 2 *rampant foliage* luxuriant, exuberant, rank, profuse, lavish. 3 *lion rampant* rearing, standing, upright, erect. 4 *rampant militancy* aggressive, vehement, violent, wild, fanatical.

rampart n 1 *castle/town ramparts* embankment, earthwork, parapet, fortification, fort, stronghold, bulwark, bastion, barbican. 2 *a rampart against infection* protection, defense, guard, shield, barrier, buffer.

ramshackle adj tumbledown, brokendown, run-down, dilapidated, derelict, gone to rack and ruin, falling to pieces, decrepit, neglected, crumbling, rickety, shaky, unsteady, tottering, unsafe, flimsy, jerry-built.

rancid n 1 *rancid butter* sour, turned, overripe, high, gamy, rotten, bad, off, tainted, putrid. 2 *a rancid smell* rank, sour, stale, fusty, musty, foul, stinking, malodorous, evil-smelling, fetid, offensive, obnoxious, noxious, noisome.

rancorous adj resentful, malicious, spiteful, hateful, malevolent, malignant, antipathetic, hostile, acrimonious, venomous, vindictive.

rancour n resentment, malice, spite, ill will, hatred, malevolence, malignance, animosity, antipathy, enmity, hostility, acrimony, venom, vindictiveness.

random adj haphazard, chance, accidental, fortuitous, serendipitous, adventitious, arbitrary, hit-or-miss, indiscriminate, sporadic, stray, spot, casual, unsystematic, unmethodical, orderless, disorganized, unarranged, unplanned, unpremeditated. **at random** 1 *chose numbers at random* randomly, haphazardly, arbitrarily, leaving things to chance, without method, without conscious choice, without pre-arrangement. 2 *trees planted at random* unsystematically, unmethodically, erratically, indiscriminately, sporadically, every now and then.

range n 1 *range of vision | the range of his influence | range of ability* scope, compass, radius, span, scale, gamut, reach, sweep, extent, area, field, orbit, province, domain, latitude; limits, bounds, confines. 2 *a range of mountains* row, line, file, rank, string, chain, series, sequence, succession, tier. 3 *a stock range of goods | a wide range of people* assortment, variety, kind, sort, type, class, rank, order, genus, species. 4 *cooking on the range* stove, cooking stove, oven; Trademark Aga. 5 *animals on the range* pasture, pasturage, grass, grassland, grazing land.

range v 1 *range from very hot to freezing | range from brilliant to poor* extend, stretch, reach, cover, go, run, pass, fluctuate between, vary between. 2 *range the goods on the shelves | soldiers ranged along the battlements* line up, align, draw up, put/set in order, order, place, position, arrange, dispose, array, rank. 3 *range the pupils according to ability* classify, class, categorize, bracket, group, grade, catalogue, file, pigeon-hole. 4 *children/sheep ranging over the hills* roam, rove, ramble, traverse, travel over, wander, meander, amble, stroll, stray, drift.

rank n 1 *salary according to rank* grade, level, stratum, class, status, position, station, standing. 2 *persons of rank* nobility, aristocracy, high birth, eminence, distinction, influence, power, prestige, weight, importance. 3 *what is his rank in the organization?* grade, position, gradation, point on the scale, mark, echelon, rung on the ladder. 4 *a rank of people waiting/rank of mountains* line, file, column, row, range, series, succession, queue, string, train, procession. 5 *break rank* array, alignment, order,

arrangement, organization. **rank and file**
1 *the officers separated from the rank and file*
other ranks, ordinary/private soldiers, soldiers, men, troops. **2** *directors/governments*
ignoring the wishes of the rank and file ordinary members, non-office bearers; ordinary
people, public, general public. **3** *the aristoc-*
racy despising the rank and file common people, populace, commonality, rabble; the
masses, lower classes. *see* RABBLE 2.

rank v **1** *he ranks above a captain | rank with*
the best have a rank, be graded, be placed,
be positioned, have a status. **2** *rank their*
achievements | rank him a champion classify,
class, categorize, grade. **3** *rank the goods on*
the shelves | soldiers along the field range, line
up, align, set in order, place, arrange, dispose, array. *see* RANGE V 2.

rank adj **1** *rank vegetation* lush, luxuriant,
abundant, dense, profuse, flourishing, exuberant, vigorous, productive, spreading,
overgrown, jungly. **2** *a rank smell* strong,
strong-smelling, pungent, acrid, malodorous, foul-smelling, evil-smelling, stinking,
rancid, putrid, fetid, unpleasant, disagreeable, offensive, revolting, sickening, obnoxious, noxious, noisome, mephitic.
3 *condemn his rank behaviour/language* indecent, immodest, indecorous, coarse, gross,
vulgar, shocking, outrageous, lurid, crass,
scurrilous, abusive, nasty, foul, filthy, vile,
obscene, smutty, risqué, profane, porno-
graphic. **4** *a rank outsider | rank disobedience*
utter, complete, total, absolute, out and
out, downright, thorough, thoroughgoing,
sheer, unqualified, unmitigated, arrant,
flagrant, blatant, glaring, gross, egregious.

rankle v *their insults still rankle* fester, cause
resentment, cause annoyance, annoy,
anger, irk, vex, peeve, irritate, rile, chafe,
fret, gall, embitter; *inf* get one's goat.

ransack v **1** *raiders ransacking the area* plunder, pillage, raid, rob, loot, despoil, rifle,
strip, fleece, sack, ravage, harry, maraud,
devastate, depredate. **2** *ransack the house*
looking for the will search, rummage
through, rake through, scour, look all over,
go through, comb, explore, turn inside out,
turn over.

ransom n **1** *pay the kidnappers a ransom* pay-
off, payment, price. **2** *obtain the kidnapped*
child's ransom release, freedom, deliverance,
liberation, rescue, redemption, restoration.

ransom v **1** *succeed in ransoming the kid-*
napped child exchange for a ransom, buy
the freedom of, release, free, deliver, liberate, rescue, redeem, restore to freedom.
2 *the kidnappers have ransomed the child*
exchange for a ransom, release for money,

release, free, set free, deliver, liberate, set
loose.

rant v *actors ranting | parents ranting with rage*
declaim, hold forth, go on and on, bluster,
harangue, vociferate, shout, yell, roar, bellow, bawl, rave, rant and rave; *inf* spout.

rant n *tired of the actor's rant | his parents' rants*
bombast, rhetoric, oration, declamation,
discourse, harangue, tirade, diatribe,
philippic, lecture, shouting, yelling, raving.

rap¹ n **1** *a rap on the knuckles* tap, hit, blow,
whack, bang, cuff, clip, clout. **2** *hear a rap*
at the door knock, knocking, tap, bang,
hammering, battering, ratatat. **3** *take/get*
the rap for the accident blame, responsibility,
accountability, punishment, penalty, castigation.

rap¹ v **1** *rap him on the knuckles* tap, hit,
strike, whack, bang, cuff, clip, clout, batter; *inf* bash. **2** *rap at the door* knock, tap,
bang, hammer, batter. **3** *rap him for his mis-*
take criticize, censure, reproach, scold,
chide, castigate.

rap² n *not care/give a rap* little bit, whit, iota,
jot; *inf* damn.

rapacious adj **1** *rapacious moneylender* grasping, acquisitive, greedy, avaricious, covetous, insatiable, predatory, usurious.
2 *rapacious invaders* plundering, pillaging,
robbing, marauding, looting, piratical.

rape n **1** *commit rape on the girl* sexual
assault, ravishment, violation; date rape.
2 *the rape of their neighbour's territory* plundering, pillaging, ravaging, foraging, raiding, despoilment, despoliation, spoliation,
marauding, sacking, sack, ransacking, rapine. **3** *the rape of the Sabine women* abduction, carrying off, kidnapping, seizure,
capture. **4** *the rape of democracy* violation,
abuse, defilement, desecration.

rape v **1** *he raped the girl* sexually assault,
ravish, violate. **2** *they rape their neighbour's*
territory plunder, pillage, ravage, forage,
raid, despoil, spoliate, maraud, ransack,
sack. **3** *the Romans raped the Sabine women*
abduct, carry off, kidnap, seize, capture.
4 *terrorists rape a national institution* violate,
abuse, defile, desecrate.

rapid adj quick, fast, swift, speedy, fleet,
hurried, hasty, expeditious, express, brisk,
lively, prompt, precipitate.

rapidity n quickness, fastness, swiftness,
speed, speediness, fleetness, hurriedness,
haste, hastiness, rush, expeditiousness,
alacrity, dispatch, velocity, celerity,
promptness, promptitude, precipateness.

rapidly adv quickly, fast, swiftly, speedily,
at speed, hurriedly, in a hurry, hastily, in

haste, in a rush, expeditiously, briskly, promptly, precipitately, hotfoot, at full tilt; *inf* before one can say Jack Robinson, before the ink is dry on the page, like a bat out of hell, like greased lightning.

rapport n affinity, bond, empathy, harmony, sympathy, understanding, close/special relationship, link.

rapt adj **1** *rapt in thought | rapt attention* absorbed, engrossed, preoccupied, intent, concentrating, pensive, meditative. **2** *rapt by the music | a rapt smile* enraptured, enchanted, entranced, spellbound, bewitched, captivated, fascinated, charmed, thrilled, transported, blissful, ecstatic, ravished.

rapture n joy, ecstasy, elation, exaltation, exhilaration, bliss, euphoria, transport, rhapsody, ravishment, enchantment, delight, delectation, happiness, enthusiasm; *inf* cloud nine, seventh heaven.

rapturous adj joyful, joyous, ecstatic, elated, blissful, euphoric, transported, in transports, rhapsodic, ravished, enchanted, delighted, happy; *inf* on cloud nine, in seventh heaven.

rara avis n rarity, rare person/thing, anomaly, aberration, freak, freak of nature, wonder, marvel, nonpareil, nonsuch, one of a kind.

rare adj **1** *a rare specimen* unusual, uncommon, out of the ordinary, exceptional, atypical, singular, remarkable, phenomenal, strange, recherché, unique. **2** *make a rare appearance* infrequent, few and far between, scarce, sparse, sporadic, scattered, thin on the ground. **3** *exhibit a rare skill* outstanding, superior, first-rate, special, choice, excellent, very fine, incomparable, unparalleled, peerless, matchless; *inf* A1, top-notch.

rarely adv *she rarely visits* on rare occasions, seldom, infrequently, hardly/scarcely ever, hardly, scarcely, almost never, little, once in a while, only now and then, not often; *inf* once in a blue moon.

rarity n **1** *the rarity of the specimen* rareness, unusualness, uncommonness, singularity, strangeness, uniqueness. see RARE 1. **2** *the rarity of the occurrences* infrequency, scarcity, sparseness, sporadicness. see RARE 2. **3** *the rarity of his skill* superiority, excellence, incomparability. see RARE 3. **4** *that book is a rarity* rare person/thing, rara avis, anomaly, freak, wonder, marvel, one of a kind. see RARA AVIS.

rascal n **1** *the child's a little rascal* imp, scamp, scallywag, mischief-maker, little devil. **2** *that man is a real rascal* scoundrel, villain, rogue, blackguard, ne'er-do-well, good-for-nothing, wastrel, reprobate, cad; *inf* rotter, bounder, creep, rat.

rash adj **1** *a rash young woman* reckless, impetuous, hasty, impulsive, madcap, over-adventurous, adventurous, overbold, audacious, brash, daredevil, foolhardy, harum-scarum, devil-may-care, headstrong, hot-headed, incautious, careless, heedless, thoughtless, imprudent. **2** *a rash act* reckless, impetuous, hasty, impulsive, incautious, careless, unthinking, ill-advised, ill-considered, foolish, imprudent, injudicious, hare-brained, unwary, unguarded.

rash n **1** *a rash on his face* skin eruption, outbreak, breaking out; erythema, hives, heat rash, nettle rash, nappy rash. **2** *a rash of burglaries* outbreak, spate, torrent, flood, wave, plague, epidemic, succession, series, run.

rasp n *the rasp of knives against plates* grating, grinding, scraping, scratching.

rasp v **1** *rasp the surface smooth* abrade, file, sand, sandpaper, scrape, scratch. **2** *"go away," he rasped* screech, shrill, squawk, croak, stridulate. **3** *his behaviour really rasps | it rasps my nerves* grate (upon), jar (upon), irritate, irk, set one's teeth on edge, rub one up the wrong way.

rasping adj *a rasping noise/voice* grating, scratchy, jarring, discordant, creaky, harsh, rough, gravelly, croaking, croaky, gruff.

rate n **1** *rate of interest* percentage, ratio, proportion, scale, degree, standard. **2** *the rate per day* pay, payment, fee, remuneration, price, cost, charge, rent, tariff; *inf* damage. **3** *walk at a great/swift rate* pace, stride, gait, motion, speed, tempo, velocity, measure. **at any rate** in any case, anyhow, anyway, nevertheless, at all events, in any event, no matter what happens.

rate v **1** *how would you rate his performance?* adjudge, judge, assess, appraise, evaluate, value, put a value on, measure, weigh up, grade, rank, classify, class, categorize. **2** *I rate him as a complete fool* regard as, consider, count, deem, reckon, account, esteem. **3** *he rates respect* be worthy of, deserve, merit, be entitled to. **4** *I don't really rate him as a player* regard as good/talented, think highly of, hold in esteem, esteem, value, admire.

rather adv **1** *I would rather not go* sooner, preferably, by preference, from choice, more willingly, more readily. **2** *she is tactless rather than rude* more, more truly. **3** *a leaflet rather than a book* correctly/strictly speaking, to be exact/precise. **4** *he is rather outspo-*

ken quite, fairly, a bit, a little, slightly, somewhat, relatively, to some degree/extent; *inf* sort of, kind of, pretty. **5** *he's not poor, rather he's very wealthy* on the contrary, instead.

ratify v confirm, endorse, sign, countersign, corroborate, sanction, warrant, approve, authorize, authenticate, certify, validate, agree to, accept, consent to, uphold, bear out.

rating n **1** *rating the competitors* adjudging, assessing, evaluating, grading, ranking, classifying. *see* RATE v **1**. **2** *his rating as a player has diminished* assessment, evaluation, value, appraisal, grading, grade, ranking, rank, classification, class, categorization, designation, standing, status, placing, position.

ratio n proportion, comparative size/extent, correlation, correspondence, percentage, fraction, quotient.

ration n *your ration of food/books/money for the week* allowance, quota, allotment, portion, share, measure, part, lot, amount, helping, proportion, percentage, budget.

ration v **1** *ration the amount per person* limit, restrict, control, conserve, budget. **2** *ration out the week's supplies* distribute, issue, allocate, allot, divide out, apportion, give out, share out, deal out, hand out, pass out, dole out, measure out, mete out, parcel out.

rational adj **1** *based on purely rational considerations* thinking, cognitive, mental, cerebral, reasoning, logical, analytical, conceptual. **2** *it seemed a rational decision | a rational course of action* sensible, reasonable, logical, sound, intelligent, wise, judicious, sagacious, prudent, circumspect, politic, astute, shrewd, perceptive, well-advised, well-grounded. **3** *the invalid does not always seem rational* able to think/reason, in sound mind, in one's right mind, *compos mentis*, lucid, coherent, well-balanced, sane, normal; *inf* all there.

rationale n theory, hypothesis, thesis, exposition, logic, philosophy, reason, *raison d'être*; grounds.

rationalize v **1** *rationalize his behaviour* explain away, account for, make excuses/allowances for, make plausible, try to vindicate/justify. **2** *rationalize our research plans* apply logic/reasoning to, reason out, think through, elucidate, clarify, make consistent. **3** *rationalize workforce/work methods* streamline, trim, make more efficient/economic, make cuts in, cut back on, retrench on.

rations npl provisions, stores, supplies, victuals, commons; food, provender.

rattle v **1** *the windows rattled* bang, clatter, clang, clank, jangle, clink. **2** *rattle the door-knocker* bang, knock, rap, clatter, clank. **3** *the car rattled along* bounce, bump, jiggle, jounce, shake, jolt, vibrate, jar. **4** *he rattled off their names* reel off, list/recite rapidly, run through. **5** *he rattled on about his job* go on, chatter, babble, gabble, prattle, jabber, gibber, blether, blather, prate; *inf* rabbit, witter, yak, yakkety-yak. **6** *she was rattled by the experience* disconcert, disturb, fluster, upset, shake, perturb, discompose, discomfit, discountenance, put off one's stroke, frighten, scare; *inf* faze.

raucous adj strident, shrill, screeching, piercing, ear-piercing, harsh, sharp, grating, rasping, scratching, discordant, dissonant, jarring.

ravage v devastate, lay waste, leave desolate, lay/leave in ruins, ruin, wreak havoc on, destroy, level, raze, demolish, wreck, shatter, damage, pillage, plunder, despoil, harry, maraud, ransack, sack, loot.

ravages npl *the ravages of war* devastation, desolation, ruination, ruin, havoc, destruction, demolition, depredation, wreckage, damage, pillaging, plunder, spoliation, ransacking, looting.

rave v **1** *the invalid is raving* talk wildly, be delirious, babble, ramble. **2** *her parents raved at her* rant and rave, rage, deliver a tirade/harangue, storm, fulminate, explode in anger, lose one's temper, lose control, go into a frenzy, run amuck; *inf* fly off the handle, flip one's lid. **3** *rave about her performance | rave over his car* go into raptures over, rhapsodize over, enthuse about, praise extravagantly, praise to the skies, gush over, express delight over, acclaim, cry up; *inf* go wild about, be mad about, throw bouquets at. **4** *going to rave after the exams* enjoy oneself with abandon, have a wild/good time, have a party, paint the town red; *inf* let one's hair down.

rave n **1** *receive a rave for her performance* lavish praise, acclaim, applause, encomium, rapturous welcome; *inf* bouquets. **2** *teenagers attending a rave* warehouse party, Acid House party. **3** *have a rave to celebrate the wedding* party, celebration; *inf* do, bash, beanfeast, blow-out, knees-up. **4** *flared trousers are all the rave* fashion, vogue, trend, fad; *inf* craze, rage.

rave adj *rave reviews* rapturous, ecstatic, enthusiastic, laudatory, praising, excellent, favourable.

ravenous adj **1** *ravenous after the day's march* very hungry, starving, starved, famished. **2** *a ravenous appetite* greedy, gluttonous, voracious, insatiable, insatiate, ravening, wolfish.

ravine n chasm, gorge, canyon, abyss, gulf, gully, gulch, defile, pass, gap.

raving adj **1** *raving patients* delirious, out of one's mind, irrational, frenzied, in a frenzy, deranged, hysterical, frantic, berserk, unbalanced, demented, insane, mad, crazed, wild; *inf* crazy. **2** *a raving beauty* very great, considerable, remarkable, extraordinary, singular, striking, outstanding, stunning.

ravings npl *kept awake by his ravings* wild talk, babbling, rambling, gibberish.

ravish v **1** *ravish the young girl* rape, sexually assault/abuse, violate. **2** *they were ravished by his performance* enchant, entrance, enthrall, captivate, bewitch, spellbind, fascinate, charm, enrapture, delight, transport, overjoy.

ravishing adj beautiful, lovely, stunning, gorgeous, dazzling, radiant, enchanting, bewitching, charming.

raw adj **1** *raw food* uncooked, fresh. **2** *raw sugar/silk* unrefined, crude, green, coarse, unprocessed, unprepared, untreated, unfinished, unmanufactured. **3** *raw recruits* inexperienced, untrained, unskilled, untutored, unschooled, unpractised, untried, untested, unseasoned, undisciplined, new, callow, immature, green, ignorant, naïve, unsophisticated; *inf* wet behind the ears. **4** *raw flesh/wounds* excoriated, skinned, grazed, abraded, scratched, chafed, open, exposed, unhealed, sore, tender. **5** *a raw day/raw weather* damp, wet, cold, chilly, chilling, chill, freezing, bitter, biting, nippy, nipping, piercing, penetrating. **6** *a raw literary style* unrefined, unpolished, unsophisticated, crude, rough, coarse. **7** *a raw portrayal of the miner's life* realistic, frank, candid, forthright, straightforward, blunt, outspoken, unembellished, unvarnished, naked, bare, brutal.

ray n **1** *rays of light* beam, shaft, streak, stream, gleam, glint, flash, glimmer, flicker, twinkle. **2** *a ray of hope* flicker, glimmer, spark, trace, hint, indication, suggestion

raze v tear down, pull down, take down, knock down, knock to pieces, fell, level, lay low, bulldoze, flatten, demolish, ruin, wreck.

reach v **1** *he reached out / reach out a hand* stretch, stretch out, outstretch, extend, hold out, thrust out, stick out. **2** *reach for the book* get hold of, grasp, seize, catch at, grab at, clutch at. **3** *reach one's destination* get as far as, get to, arrive at, come to, set foot on, land at/on. **4** *reach perfection* attain, achieve, gain, accomplish, make, get to. **5** *his land reaches ours* extend to, go as far as, stretch to, neighbour, touch, border on, abut. **6** *we could not reach him that day* contact, get in touch with, get hold of, get through to, communicate with. **7** *reach me that book* hand, pass, give.

reach n **1** *the rope was beyond her reach / within reach of safety* grasp, stretch, spread, extension, extent, span, distance. **2** *within the reach of his influence* scope, range, compass, latitude, ambit, orbit, sphere, area, field, territory, authority, jurisdiction, sway, control, command.

react v **1** *react to the drug* have a reaction/ response to, respond, change/behave in response to. **2** *how did she react on hearing the news?* behave, act, conduct oneself, proceed, operate, function, cope. **3** *react against the new bill* rebel against, oppose, revolt against, rise up against.

reaction n **1** *receive a reaction to their proposal* response, answer, reply, feedback. **2** *his harsh regime was a reaction to total disorder* counteraction, counterbalance, counterpoise, recoil, reversion, retroversion, reversal. **3** *they are people of political reaction* ultraconservatism, conservatism, obscurantism, the right, the right wing, the extreme right.

reactionary adj ultraconservative, conservative, obscurantist, Colonel Blimp, diehard, rightist, right-wing.

read v **1** *read the words/book* peruse, study, scan, pore over, scrutinize, run one's eye over, look at, refer to, browse through; *inf* wade through, dip into. **2** *read his silence as consent* interpret, construe, take to mean, decipher, deduce, understand, comprehend. **3** *the thermometer is reading zero* register, record, display, show, indicate. **4** *read the future* foresee, foretell, predict, forecast, prophesy, divine. **read into** *read too much into their statement/relationship* assume from, infer from, interpolate from, read between the lines.

read n *a quick read of the book* perusal, study, scan, scrutiny, browse, reference.

readable adj **1** *readable exam papers* legible, easy to read, decipherable, clear, intelligible, understandable, comprehensible. **2** *readable works of fiction* enjoyable, entertaining, interesting, gripping, enthralling, stimulating.

readily adv **1** *he will readily help you* willingly, without hesitation, gladly, happily, cheerfully, with pleasure, eagerly. **2** *the sofa readily converts into a bed* easily, with ease, without difficulty, effortlessly.

readiness n **1** *the readiness of the troops for battle* preparedness, fitness. **2** *their readiness to help* willingness, inclination, aptness, eagerness, keenness, gladness; *inf* gameness. *see* READY 3. **3** *the readiness of resources* availability, accessibility, handiness, convenience. *see* READY 4. **4** *the readiness of her answers* promptness, quickness, rapidity, swiftness, speed, speediness, punctuality, timeliness. **5** *the readiness of his wit/skill* alertness, resourcefulness, smartness, sharpness, astuteness, shrewdness, keenness, acuteness, discernment, cleverness, intelligence, brightness, aptness, adroitness, deftness, dexterity, skill, skilfulness. **in readiness** *reserves in readiness* ready, at the ready, available, on hand, accessible, handy, at one's fingertips, prepared, primed; *inf* on tap.

reading n **1** *his reading of the document* perusal, study, scan, scanning, scrutinization, scrutiny, browsing. *see* READ V 1. **2** *a man of reading* book learning, learning, scholarship, knowledge, attainment, enlightenment, education, edification. **3** *his reading of the statement/situation* interpretation, construction, deciphering, deduction, understanding, comprehension, grasp, impression. **4** *several readings of the play in existence* version, edition, text, rendering. **5** *what's the reading on the gas meter?* measurement, indication.

ready adj **1** *dinner is ready* prepared, completed, finished, organized. **2** *ready for battle|ready to go* prepared, equipped, organized, all set, in a fit state, fit. **3** *ready to help* willing, inclined, disposed, predisposed, minded, apt, prone, given, agreeable, eager, keen, happy, glad; *inf* game. **4** *a ready source of income* within reach, available, on hand, present, near, near at hand, accessible, handy, convenient, on call, at one's fingertips; *inf* on tap. **5** *a ready answer* prompt, quick, rapid, swift, speedy, punctual, timely. **6** *a ready wit/skill* alert, resourceful, smart, sharp, astute, shrewd, keen, acute, perceptive, discerning, clever, intelligent, bright, apt, adroit, deft, dexterous, skilful. **7** *ready to collapse* about to, on the verge/brink/edge of, in danger of, liable to, likely to. **8** *ready for anything* prepared, eager, enthusiastic, anxious, keen; *inf* psyched up, geared up.

real adj **1** *the real world|real fears/illnesses* actual, existent, occurring, factual, unimaginary, non-fictitious. **2** *real leather* authentic, genuine, *bona fide*, veritable, valid, legal, licit. **3** *real emotion/feelings* sincere, heartfelt, earnest, fervent, unfeigned, unpretended, unaffected, honest, truthful.

realistic adj **1** *be realistic as to your prospects* practical, pragmatic, rational, down-to-earth, matter-of-fact, sensible, commonsensical, level-headed, hard-headed, business-like, hard-boiled, sober, unromantic, unsentimental, unidealistic; *inf* with both feet on the ground, no-nonsense. **2** *a realistic model of a dinosaur* lifelike, true-to-life, true, faithful, close, representational, graphic, naturalistic, authentic, genuine.

reality n **1** *come back to reality* real/actual world, actuality, physical existence, corporeality, substantiality, materiality. **2** *the reality of his work* verisimilitude, lifelikeness, authenticity, genuineness, validity. *see* REALISTIC 2. **3** *the harsh realities of life|in reality the picture's a fake* fact, actuality, truth.

realization n **1** *come to the realization that he is mad* understanding, awareness, consciousness, cognizance, appreciation, recognition, perception, discernment. **2** *the realization of one's hopes* fulfilment, achievement, accomplishment, fruition, consummation, effecting, actualization. *see* REALIZE 2. **3** *the realization of profits* making, clearing, obtaining. *see* REALIZE 3, 4.

realize v **1** *realize that they are rich* understand clearly, grasp, take in, know, comprehend, apprehend, become aware, be conscious/cognizant of the fact, appreciate, recognize, perceive, discern, conceive; *inf* twig, latch on. **2** *realize one's hopes/dreams* fulfil, achieve, accomplish, make happen, bring about, bring off, bring to fruition, consummate, effect, effectuate, perform, execute, actualize, reify. **3** *realize one's assets* convert into money. **4** *realize a profit* make, clear, acquire, gain, bring in, obtain, earn.

really adv **1** *the comedienne is really a man* in reality, actually, in actuality, in fact, in truth. **2** *this is really useful* certainly, surely, truly, undoubtedly, without a doubt, indubitably, assuredly, unquestionably, indeed, absolutely, categorically. **3** *a really charming person* very, extremely, thoroughly, truly, decidedly. **4** *his career is really over* to all intents and purposes, virtually, for all practical purposes, just about, almost.

realm n **1** *when the Tudors ruled the realm* kingdom, country, land, state, province, empire, domain, monarchy, principality. **2** *the realm of the imagination|the realm of sci-*

ence world, field, sphere, area, department, region, province, orbit, zone.

reap v **1** *reap the corn* cut, crop, harvest, gather in, bring in, take in. **2** *reap the benefits of an education* realize, receive, obtain, get, acquire, secure, procure.

rear n **1** *at the rear of the garage* back, back part, hind part, back end. **2** *at the rear of the queue* rear end, back end, end, tail, tail end.

rear v **1** *rear three children* bring up, raise, care for, nurture, parent, educate, train, instruct. **2** *rear chickens* breed, keep, tend. **3** *rear plants* grow, cultivate. **4** *rear one's head* raise, lift up, hold up, hoist, elevate, upraise. **5** *rear a ladder* set up, stand up, make upright, stand on end, up-end. **6** *rear a tower* erect, build, put up, construct. **7** *mountains rearing in the distance* tower, soar, loom, rise up.

reason n **1** *the reason for his behaviour* grounds; ground, cause, basis, motive, motivation, impetus, actuation, instigation, inducement. **2** *give a reason for your absence* explanation, exposition, justification, argument, case, defence, vindication, apologia, rationalization, excuse, apology. **3** *follow reason not emotion* reasoning, intellect, intelligence, intellectuality, mind, judgement, logic, rationality, thought, understanding, apprehension, comprehension, ratiocination; brains. **4** *he has lost his reason* sanity, mind, soundness of mind; senses. **5** *keep a sense of reason in your expenditure* reasonableness, common sense, sense, good sense, practicality, practicability, shrewdness, wisdom, sagacity, moderation, propriety. **within reason** *have anything you like within reason* in moderation, within reasonable/sensible limits, within limits/bounds.

reason v **1** *unable to reason when upset* use reason, think, think straight, use one's mind, use one's brain/head, analyse, cogitate, cerebrate, intellectualize, ratiocinate; *inf* put on one's thinking cap. **2** *try reasoning with him* use logic on, apply argument to, argue with, debate with, dispute with, try to persuade, plead with. **3** *he reasoned that two could live as cheaply as one* deduce, infer, conclude, work out, reckon, be of the opinion, think, surmise. **4** *reason him out of that course of action | reason her into it* argue, persuade, talk, urge, coax. **5** *reason things out* think out, think through, consider, deliberate, analyse, come to a conclusion about.

reasonable adj **1** *he's quite a reasonable man* open to reason, moderate, fair, just, equitable, impartial, dispassionate, unbiased,

disinterested, above-board. **2** *it seemed a reasonable idea/plan* logical, practical, rational, sensible, intelligent, wise, sound, judicious, advisable, well-thought-out, admissible, tenable, plausible. **3** *reasonable prices* moderate, inexpensive, low, modest, cheap, within one's means. **4** *his work is reasonable* tolerable, passable, acceptable, average; *inf* OK.

reasoned adj *reasoned arguments* logical, rational, well-thought-out, clear, systematic, methodical, organized, well-expressed, well-presented.

reasoning n **1** *let reasoning not emotion dictate your actions* reason, thinking, thought, logic, rationalization, deduction, analysis, cerebration, ratiocination. **2** *his reasoning is faulty* argument, rationale, case, hypothesis, interpretation.

reassure v put one's mind at rest, put at ease, settle doubts, restore/give confidence to, encourage, hearten, buoy up, cheer up, inspirit.

rebate n refund, partial refund, repayment, deduction, discount, allowance, reduction, decrease.

rebel n **1** *the government acting against the rebels* revolutionary, revolutionist, insurrectionist, insurgent, revolter, mutineer, seditionist, agitator, freedom/resistance fighter, anarchist, traitor. **2** *rebels not obeying rules/fashion* dissenter, nonconformist, heretic, apostate, schismatic, recusant.

rebel v **1** *the troops are rebelling* mutiny, riot, revolt, rise up, rise up in arms, take to the streets. **2** *rebel against authority* defy, disobey, refuse to obey/follow. **3** *his stomach rebelled at the thought of food* recoil from, shrink from, flinch from, shy away from, pull back from, show repugnance/revulsion for/at.

rebel adj **1** *the rebel troops* revolutionary, insurrectionary, insurgent, mutinous, mutinying. *see* REBEL n 1. **2** *rebel schoolgirls* rebellious, defiant, disobedient, resistant, dissentient, recalcitrant, unmanageable.

rebellion n **1** *troops putting down a rebellion* revolt, revolution, insurrection, insurgence, insurgency, uprising, rising, mutiny, riot, civil disobedience, resistance. **2** *rebellion against rules/fashion* defiance, disobedience, resistance, dissent, nonconformity, heresy, apostasy, schism, recusancy.

rebellious adj **1** *rebellious tribes/schoolchildren* unruly, ungovernable, unmanageable, turbulent, disorderly, intractable, recalcitrant, incorrigible, contumacious. **2** *the rebellious group were imprisoned* rebelling, revolutionary, insurrectionary, insurgent, mutinous, mutinying, rioting. **3** *the rebellious pupils were expelled* defiant, disobedient, resistant, dissentient, nonconformist.

rebound v **1** *the ball rebounded off the wall* bounce, bounce back, spring back, recoil, ricochet, boomerang. **2** *the plan rebounded on her* misfire, backfire, have an adverse effect, come back on, redound on.

rebound n **1** *the rebound of the ball* bounce, recoil, ricochet. see REBOUND V 1. **2** *the rebound of her plans* misfiring, backfiring, kickback, repercussion.

rebuff n **1** *the rebuff of her suitor/request* rejection, refusal, spurning, repudiation, repulsion, cold shouldering, discouragement. **2** *upset by her rebuffs* snub, slight, repulse, cut, check, thumbs down; *inf* brush-off, knock-back, put-down, slap in the face.

rebuff v *rebuff their advances | rebuff them* reject, refuse, decline, turn down, turn away, spurn, repudiate, repel, discourage, fend off, stave off, snub, slight, cold shoulder, cut, give the thumbs down to; *inf* brush off, knock back, put down.

rebuke v *rebuke the children for their naughtiness* reprimand, scold, chide, admonish, reproach, reprove, remonstrate with, lecture, reprehend, censure, find fault with, berate, upbraid, castigate, take to task; *inf* tell off, carpet, lambaste, haul over the coals, tear a strip off, tick off, bawl out.

rebuke n *deliver a rebuke to the disobedient children/troops* reprimand, scolding, admonition, reproach, reproof, reproval, remonstration, lecture, censure, upbraiding, castigation; *inf* telling-off, carpeting, lambasting, dressing-down, ticking-off, bawling-out, wigging.

rebut v *rebut the charge/evidence* refute, disprove, negate, invalidate, deny, confute, contradict, discredit, give the lie to, drive a coach and horses through, explode; *inf* shoot full of holes.

recalcitrant adj intractable, refractory, unmanageable, ungovernable, disobedient, insubordinate, defiant, contrary, wayward, wilful, headstrong, perverse, contumacious, rebellious, mutinous, obstinate, obdurate.

recall v **1** *recall parliament* summon back, call back, bring back. **2** *unable to recall his name* call to mind, remember, recollect, think of. **3** *sit recalling the old days* remember, recollect, reminisce about, look back on/to, think back on/to, hark back to. **4** *the sight of her recalled the old days* call/bring to mind, call up, summon up, evoke, put one

in mind of. **5** *recall the verdict* revoke, retract, countermand, take back, withdraw, repeal, rescind, veto, overrule, override, invalidate, annul, nullify, cancel, recant.

recall n **1** *the recall of parliament* summoning back. see RECALL V 1. **2** *have total recall* memory, recollection, remembrance. **3** *the recall of the verdict | beyond recall* revocation, retracting, countermanding, withdrawal, repeal, rescinding, vetoing, veto, invalidation, anulment, cancellation. see RECALL V 5.

recant v **1** *recant his former beliefs* disavow, disclaim, disown, deny, renounce, relinquish, abjure, forswear, repudiate, renege on. **2** *he was a Catholic but he has recanted* change one's mind, apostatize, tergiversate, defect, renege. **3** *recant his evidence* recall, revoke, retract, countermand, take back, repeal, rescind, annul, cancel. see RECALL V 5.

recapitulate v restate, resay, repeat, reiterate, go over, run over, summarize, sum up; *inf* recap.

recede v **1** *the water receded* go back, move back, move further off, move away, retreat, withdraw, fall back, ebb, abate, subside. **2** *the coastline receded as we rowed* grow less visible, become distant, become far off, fade into the distance, begin to disappear. **3** *danger receded in time* grow less, lessen, fade, diminish, decrease, dwindle, shrink, wane, fall off, taper off, peter out. **4** *his chin recedes* slope backwards, slant, fall away.

receipt n **1** *the receipt of the goods | receipt of his apology* receiving, recipience, acceptance, getting, obtaining, taking. see RECEIVE 1, 2. **2** *get a receipt for the goods* till receipt, sales slip/ticket, proof of purchase, slip, stub, counterfoil, voucher. **3** *make a list of receipts for the tax inspector* money/payment received, financial return, income; takings, proceeds, profits, gains, earnings.

receive v **1** *he did receive the goods* be in receipt of, accept delivery of, accept, take into one's possession. **2** *receive many benefits | receive good news* get, obtain, acquire, come by, gain, take, gather, collect. **3** *he received the news at home | received the news with fortitude* heard, be told, find out about, learn about, gather, be informed of, be notified of, take, react to. **4** *receive bad treatment* undergo, experience, meet with, encounter, go through, sustain, be subjected to, bear, suffer. **5** *the room/container will receive 20 people/tonnes* hold, contain, accommodate, admit, take. **6** *receive guests* welcome, greet, entertain, be at home to.

recent adj **1** *recent developments* new, fresh, novel, latest, late, modern, contemporary, latter-day, current, up to date, up to the minute. **2** *his recent illness* occurring/appearing recently, not long past.

recently adv *recently developed* newly, freshly, lately, not long ago, of late.

receptacle n container, holder, repository.

reception n **1** *the reception of the goods* receiving, acceptance. *see* RECEIVE 1. **2** *the reception of the guests* welcoming, greeting, entertaining. **3** *the celebrity/show/news receiving a warm/cool reception* acceptance, response, acknowledgement, recognition, reaction, treatment, welcome. **4** *a wedding/graduation reception* party, formal party, function, social occasion, entertainment, soirée; *inf* do, bash, beanfeast.

receptive adj open, open to suggestions/ideas, flexible, willing, perceptive, sensitive, alert, bright, quick, keen.

recess n **1** *books arranged in a recess* alcove, niche, nook, corner, cavity, bay, oriel. **2** *in the recesses of my memory* remote/secret/dark place, interior, heart, retreat, refuge, sanctum; depths; *inf* innards. **3** *the children's recess | the parliamentary recess* break, respite, rest, interval, intermission, holiday, time off, vacation, closure, cessation of work/business; *inf* breather, time out.

recession n **1** economic decline, downturn, depression, slump; hard times. **2** *the recession of flood waters* receding, retreat, withdrawal, ebbing, abatement. *see* RECEDE 1.

recipe n **1** *follow the recipe for pancakes* directions, instructions; guide, cooking procedure. **2** *his suggestions are a recipe for a disaster* method, technique, system, procedure, *modus operandi*, process, means, way, formula, prescription.

reciprocal adj **1** *a reciprocal favour* return, in return, returned, requited, retaliated. **2** *reciprocal affection* mutual, shared, common, reciprocative, reciprocatory, exchanged, give-and-take, complementary, corresponding, correlative.

reciprocate v **1** *reciprocate his affection* return, requite, feel/give in return, repay, give back. **2** *I will take part if she reciprocates* respond, respond in kind, return the favour/compliment, do the same. **3** *reciprocate their ideas* interchange, exchange, give and take/receive, swap, barter, trade, bandy.

recital n **1** *the recital of the poem* saying, rendering, declaiming, reading. *see* RECITE 1. **2** *the recital of the disasters* enumeration,

detailing, itemizing, specification. *see* RECITE 3. **3** *a piano recital* musical performance, performance, solo performance, concert, show. **4** *listen to his recital of the events* account, report, recounting, telling, relation, description, detailing, rendering, narrative, record, story, tale, chronicle.

recitation n **1** *the recitation of passages from John Donne* recital, saying, rendering, rendition, declaiming, reading. *see* RECITE 1. **2** *excellently chosen recitations* verse, poem, reading, passage, piece.

recite v **1** *recite a poem/passage* say, repeat, read aloud, deliver, declaim, speak, render. **2** *ask the child to recite* say a poem, read a passage; *inf* do one's party piece. **3** *recite a list of disasters* enumerate, detail, list, itemize, reel off, rattle off, specify, particularize, describe, recount, relate, narrate, recapitulate.

reckless adj rash, careless, thoughtless, incautious, heedless, unheeding, inattentive, regardless, daredevil, devil-may-care, madcap, harum-scarum, wild, precipitate, headlong, hasty, irresponsible, harebrained, foolhardy, overventuresome, ill-advised, imprudent, unwise, indiscreet, mindless, negligent, temerarious.

reckon v **1** *he reckoned that she was lying* be of the opinion, think, believe, suppose, assume, surmise, conjecture, imagine, fancy, guess. **2** *she was reckoned a good painter* regard as, consider, judge, hold to be, think of as, look upon as, account, deem, rate, evaluate, gauge, count, estimate, appraise. **3** *reckon the cost* count, calculate, add up, compute, total, tally, put a figure on, give a figure to. **4** *reckon in the cost of the furnishings* count in, include, take into account. **5** *reckon on it being fine* count on, rely on, depend on, bank on, take for granted, trust. **6** *he will have her father to reckon with* cope with, deal with, contend with, handle, face. **7** *we did not reckon with his father's needs | we reckoned without the cost of the trip* anticipate, foresee, take into account/consideration, allow for, take cognizance of, take note of, bear in mind, not lose sight of; fail to anticipate, disregard, overlook.

reckoning n **1** *according to my reckoning the total is wrong* counting, calculation, addition, computation, working out, total, tally, summation, score. **2** *according to their reckoning she is the best* opinion, judgement, evaluation, estimation, appraisal. **3** *deal with the reckoning of the account* settlement, paying, payment, discharging, defrayal, squaring, clearance. **4** *ask for the reckoning* bill, account, tally, amount due; *Amer* check; *Amer inf* tab. **5** *the day of reckoning* settlement, retribution, judgement, fate, doom.

reclaim v **1** *reclaim one's property* have returned, get back, take back, regain, retrieve, recover. **2** *reclaim the land from wilderness* retrieve, regain, reinstate, save, rescue, salvage. **3** *reclaim the criminals from vice* redeem, reform, regenerate, save, rescue.

recline v lie, lie down, lean, be recumbent, rest, repose, loll, lounge, sprawl, stretch out, drape oneself over.

recluse n hermit, anchorite, ascetic, eremite, monk, nun, solitary, lone wolf, loner.

recognition n **1** *recognition of the criminal | recognition of an old friend* knowing, identification, spotting, recollection. *see* RECOGNIZE 1. **2** *his recognition of his defects/mistake* realization, awareness, consciousness, perception, appreciation, understanding, acknowledgement, acceptance, granting. *see* RECOGNIZE 2. **3** *their recognition of his claim* acknowledgement, acceptance, admittance, granting, endorsement, sanctioning, approval, validation, ratification. *see* RECOGNIZE 3. **4** *receive recognition as an artist* acknowledgement, appreciation, reward, honour, homage, applause; *inf* bouquets.

recognize v **1** *recognize the criminal | recognize an old friend* know, know again, identify, place, spot, recall, recollect, remember, call to mind. **2** *recognize his own defects/mistake | recognized that he was wrong* realize, see, be aware/conscious of, perceive, discern, appreciate, understand, apprehend, acknowledge, accept, admit, concede, allow, grant, confess, own. **3** *recognize his claim* acknowledge, accept, admit, concede, allow, grant, endorse, sanction, put the seal of approval on, approve, validate, ratify, uphold. **4** *recognize his achievement* show appreciation of, reward, honour, pay homage to, salute, applaud.

recoil v **1** *recoil from him in terror/disgust* draw back, jump back, pull back, shrink, shy away, flinch, start, wince, cower, quail. **2** *recoil from/at the idea* feel revulsion at, baulk at, shrink from, shy away from, hesitate at, falter at. **3** *the spring recoiled* spring back, fly back, rebound, resile. **4** *the plan recoiled on the instigator* rebound, come back on, redound on, misfire, backfire, go wrong, have an adverse effect, boomerang. **5** *the gun recoiled* kick back, jerk back.

recoil n **1** *recoil of a gun* kickback, kick. **2** *the recoil from their plans* rebound, backlash; reaction; repercussions.

recollect v **1** *as far as I recollect* remember, recall. **2** *I cannot recollect his name* remember, succeed in remembering, recall, call to mind, think of, summon up, place; *inf* put one's finger on.

recollection n **1** *the recollection of his name* remembering, recalling, calling to mind. *see* RECOLLECT 1. **2** *the photographs brought back happy recollections* memory, remembrance, reminiscence, mental image, impression. **3** *my recollection is that he was tall* memory, remembrance, power of recall.

recommend v **1** *recommend this as a cure* advocate, commend, put in a good word for, speak favourably of, look with favour on, endorse, approve, vouch for, suggest, offer, put forward, propose, advance. **2** *I recommend caution | recommend that you go home* advise, counsel, guide, urge, exhort, enjoin. **3** *his plan has much to recommend it | his honesty recommended him to the board* make appealing/attractive/interesting, endow with appeal/attraction/interest, give an advantage to.

recommendation n **1** *the recommendation of the cure* advocacy, commendation, endorsement. *see* RECOMMEND 1. **2** *the recommendation of caution* advising, counselling, urging. *see* RECOMMEND 2. **3** *accept your recommendation as to the wine* commendation, endorsement, suggestion, tip, hint, proposal, good word, favourable mention, praise; *inf* plug. **4** *accept the judge's recommendation as to how to act* advice, counsel, guidance, exhortation, enjoinder. **5** *cheapness is the restaurant's only recommendation* good point, advantage, favourable aspect, benefit, blessing, boon.

reconcile v **1** *mother and daughter have been reconciled | try to reconcile the feuders* make friendly gestures/overtures, reunite, bring together, restore harmony between, make peace between, resolve differences between, bring to terms, pacify, appease, placate, propitiate, mollify. **2** *reconcile themselves to her death | become reconciled to the unfortunate situation* come to accept, accept, accommodate, get used, resign, submit, yield, make the best of, grin and bear it. **3** *reconcile their differences* settle, resolve, square, put to rights, mend, remedy, patch up, heal, cure, rectify. **4** *reconcile his philosophy and his actions* harmonize, make compatible, put in agreement, adjust, attune, make coincide, make congruent.

reconciliation n **1** *the reconciliation of the feuders* reuniting, bring together, pacification, placating, propitiation, mollification. *see* RECONCILE 1. **2** *the reconciliation of differences* settling, settlement, resolving, resolution, mending, remedying. *see* RECONCILE 3. **3** *bring about a reconciliation* peace, end of hostilities, harmony, concord, amity. **4** *a reconciliation between his philosophy and his actions* harmonizing, adjustment. *see* RECONCILE 4.

recondite adj *recondite information/texts* obscure, esoteric, abstruse, abstract, cryptic, incomprehensible, inscrutable, arcane, deep, profound, difficult, complex, involved, mysterious, dark.

reconnaissance n preliminary survey, survey, spying, exploration, scouting, probe, investigation, scrutiny, scan, inspection, observation; *inf* recce.

reconnoitre v survey, find out the lie of the land, see how the land lies, spy out, take stock of, explore, scout, investigate, scrutinize, scan, inspect, observe; *inf* recce, case, check out.

reconsider v *I ask you to reconsider your decision | please reconsider* think over, rethink, review, re-examine, re-evaluate, reassess, think better of; think again, think twice, have second thoughts, change one's mind.

reconstruct v **1** *reconstruct the house* rebuild, remake, reassemble, refashion, recreate, remodel, revamp, renovate, recondition. **2** *reconstruct the scene* recreate, re-enact, piece together, build up, build up a picture/impression of. **3** *reconstruct society | reconstruct the firm* reorganize, rearrange, make over, redo, do over, overhaul, re-establish, reform.

record n **1** *the records are missing* official document, register, log, logbook, file, official report/account, chronicle, diary, journal; documentation; documents, minutes, notes, annals, archives. **2** *play a record* gramophone record, disc, album, single, recording, release; vinyl; *inf* platter. **3** *what do you know of his record?* employment/work history, employment/work performance, career to date, past performance, curriculum vitae, life history, history, background, reputation; *inf* track record. **4** *does he have a record?* police/criminal record, history of crime; previous convictions. **5** *his jump was a record* best/star performance. **6** *this is a record of his achievement* memorial, remembrance, souvenir, token, testimony, testimonial, witness, trace; documentation, evidence. **7** *climate records* information, collected information; data, reports, accounts.

off the record *this information is off the record* confidential, in confidence, unofficial, not for publication/circulation, private, secret, *sub rosa*. **on record 1** *the wettest winter on record* recorded, registered, documented, officially noted. **2** *he is on record as promising improvements* recorded, officially noted, documented, publicly known.

record v **1** *record the details* put on record, set down, write down, put in writing, take down, put down, enter, make a note of, document, minute, register, chronicle, file, put on file, docket, list, log, catalogue, inscribe, transcribe. **2** *record a very low temperature* register, read, indicate, show, display. **3** *record a song | record the wedding* make a record/recording of. **4** *record a disc/video* make, produce, cut, tape, videotape, video.

recorder n **1** *purchase a recorder* tape recorder, video recorder. **2** *the documents compiled by the recorder* keeper of records, record keeper, registrar, archivist, annalist, chronicler, historian. **3** *the recorder noted down the details* scribe, clerk, secretary.

recording n disc, record, gramophone record, tape recording, tape, video recording, video; vinyl, compact disc; *inf* CD.

recount v **1** *recount a tale* narrate, tell, relate, unfold, repeat. **2** *recount the events of the day* describe, detail, enumerate, list, specify, itemize, cite, particularize, catalogue.

recoup v **1** *recoup the lost property* get back, win back, regain, recover, retrieve, repossess, redeem. **2** *recoup her for her losses* reimburse, pay back, repay, recompense, compensate, indemnify.

recourse n **1** *their recourse to him was a last chance* resorting, turning to, looking to, appealing. *see* RESORT v 1. **2** *their only recourse was private medicine* resort, way out, place/person to turn to, source of assistance, available resource, choice, option, possibility, alternative, expedient.

recover v **1** *recover their stolen possessions* get back, win back, regain, recoup, retrieve, reclaim, repossess, redeem, recuperate, recapture. **2** *the invalid will recover in time* get better, get back to normal, get well, recuperate, convalesce, heal, get back on one's feet, feel oneself again, improve, mend, pick up, rally, revive, pull through, bounce back; *inf* perk up. **3** *recover land from the sea | recover usable substances from waste* reclaim, retrieve, salvage, save, rescue, redeem, restore, recycle.

recovery n **1** *the recovery of their goods* recouping, regaining, retrieval, reclamation, repossession, recapture. **2** *the invalid's* *recovery is slow* return to normal/health, recuperation, convalescence, healing, rallying, revival. *see* RECOVER 2. **3** *the recovery of the economy* improvement, betterment, amelioration, upturn, upswing. **4** *the recovery of land from the sea | recovery of material from waste* reclamation, retrieval, salvaging, rescue, recycling. *see* RECOVER 3.

recreation n **1** *for recreation he rows* relaxation, refreshment, restoration, leisure, amusement, entertainment, distraction, diversion, pleasure, enjoyment, fun, play, sport. **2** *his recreations are all sport-based* leisure activity, pastime, hobby, diversion, distraction.

recriminate v counter-accuse, counter-charge, counter-attack, make mutual accusations, retaliate, take reprisals, exact retribution.

recrimination n counter-accusation, countercharge, counter-attack, retaliation, reprisal, retribution, vengeance; mutual accusations.

recruit v **1** *recruit soldiers | recruit new members* enlist, enrol, sign up, draft, conscript, levy, engage, obtain, acquire, procure, take on, round up, muster. **2** *recruit an army* form, raise, gather/put together, muster, assemble. **3** *recruit his finances/membership* replenish, augment, increase, enlarge, add to, build up, strengthen, reinforce, fortify, shore up; *inf* beef up.

recruit n **1** *army recruits* enlistee, draftee, conscript. **2** *new recruits to the society/industry* new member, new entrant, newcomer, initiate, beginner, learner, trainee, apprentice, novice, tiro, neophyte, proselyte; *inf* rookie, greenhorn.

rectify v put/set right, right, correct, amend, emend, remedy, repair, fix, make good, redress, reform, improve, better, ameliorate, adjust, square.

rectitude n **1** *appoint a man of rectitude* righteousness, virtue, moral virtue, morality, honour, integrity, principle, probity, uprightness, good character, decency, honesty, upstandingness, scrupulousness, incomparability. **2** *the rectitude of the judgement/results* correctness, accuracy, exactness, precision, soundness, verity.

recuperate v **1** *he is recuperating after an illness* recover, convalesce, get better, get back to normal, get well, regain one's strength/health, improve, mend, pick up, rally, revive, pull through, bounce back; *inf* perk up. *see* RECOVER 2. **2** *recuperate costs* recover, recoup, get back, regain, retrieve, reclaim.

recur v reoccur, happen/occur again, come back, return, reappear, be repeated, repeat itself, happen repeatedly.

recurrent adj recurring, repeated, repetitive, reiterative, periodic, cyclical, regular, habitual, continual, frequent, intermittent, chronic.

recycle v reuse, reprocess, salvage, save.

red adj **1** *red dresses/wallpaper/flowers* reddish, crimson, scarlet, vermilion, cherry, ruby, cardinal, carmine, ruby-coloured, maroon, wine, wine-coloured, claret, claret-coloured, russet, coral, salmon-pink, pink, cochineal, rose. **2** *she had a red face* flushed, blushing, florid, ruddy, rubicund, roseate. **3** *with red eyes* bloodshot, red-rimmed, inflamed. **4** *red hair | horses with red coats* reddish, flaming-red, flame-coloured, auburn, Titian, chestnut, carroty, sandy, foxy, bay. **5** *soldiers with red hands* bloody, bloodstained, gory. **6** *red beliefs* Communist, ultra-left-wing, leftist; *inf* commie, lefty.

red n **1** *colour the walls with red* red colour/pigment. **2** *wearing red* red clothes/garments. **3** *suspecting them of being reds* Communist, socialist, leftist; *inf* commie, lefty. **in the red** overdrawn, insolvent, in debt, in debit, owing money, showing a loss, bankrupt, in arrears; *inf* on the rocks. **see red** be furious, be incensed, be infuriated, lose one's temper, become enraged, get mad, boil, seethe; *inf* hit the roof, blow one's top, lose one's rag.

redden n **1** *redden her lips* make/colour red. *see* RED adj 1. **2** *she reddened in embarrassment* go red, blush, flush, colour, colour up, crimson.

redeem v **1** *redeemed her gloves | redeem pawned goods* reclaim, get back, regain, recover, retrieve, repossess, recoup, buy back, repurchase. **2** *redeem the vouchers* exchange, give in exchange, cash in, convert, turn in, trade in. **3** *Christ/missionaries redeeming sinners* free/save/deliver from sin, turn from sin, convert, purge/absolve of sin. **4** *his generosity redeems his bad temper* make up for, compensate for, atone for, offset, redress, outweigh. **5** *the wicked man redeemed himself by helping his neighbour* save/free from blame, vindicate, absolve, remove guilt from. **6** *redeem the slaves/hostages* free, set free, liberate, release, emancipate, ransom, rescue, save. **7** *redeem his promise/obligations* fulfil, discharge, make good, carry out, execute, keep, hold to, adhere to, abide by, obey, be faithful to, meet, satisfy.

redemption n **1** *the redemption of possessions* reclamation, recovery, retrieval, recoupment, repurchase. *see* REDEEM 1. **2** *the redemption of his faults by his generosity* compensation, atonement, redress. *see* REDEEM 4. **3** *his redemption of himself by good works* freeing/saving from blame, vindication, absolution. **4** *the redemption of the slaves/hostages* freeing, liberation, release, emancipation, ransom, rescue, saving. **5** *the redemption of his promise/obligations* fulfilment, discharge, making good, execution, adherence, meeting, satisfying. *see* REDEEM 7.

redolent adj **1** *films redolent of another age* evocative, suggestive, reminiscent. **2** *a room redolent of roses | breath redolent of garlic* smelling (of), scented (with), reeking (of). **3** *redolent flower gardens* sweet-smelling, fragrant, scented, perfumed, aromatic.

redoubtable adj formidable, awe-inspiring, fearsome, mighty, powerful, dreadful, terrible, awful.

redound v **1** *his action redounded to his credit* contribute to, conduce to, be conducive to, have an effect on, affect. **2** *your wicked actions will redound on you one day* come back on, recoil on, rebound on.

redress v **1** *redress a wrong* rectify, remedy, put/set right, make amends for, compensate for, make up for, make reparation/restitution for, recompense for, atone for. **2** *redress the balance of power* put right, even up, regulate, adjust, correct.

redress n **1** *make redress for the wrong* amends; compensation, reparation, restitution, recompense, atonement. **2** *the redress of wrongs* rectification, remedying, putting right, amending. *see* REDRESS V 1.

reduce v **1** *reduce the size of the garden | reduce the volume/speed/strength* make smaller, make less, lessen, lower, decrease, diminish, cut, curtail, contract, shorten, abbreviate, moderate, dilute, mitigate, alleviate, abate. **2** *they were reduced to tears/begging* bring to, bring to the point of, force to, drive to. **3** *they were reduced to a lower form/rank* demote, downgrade, lower, lower in rank/status, humble. **4** *reduced yesterday's stock* lower/cut in price, lower, make cheaper, cheapen, cut, mark down, slash, discount, put on sale. **5** *she is trying to reduce* get thinner, slim, slim down, lose/shed weight, go/be on a diet, diet, lose some inches, shed some pounds; *Amer* slenderize. **6** *the army finally reduced the enemy/city* conquer, vanquish, overpower, subdue, subjugate, overcome, overrun. **7** *they have been reduced by the recession* bankrupt, make penniless/poor, impoverish, ruin, break.

reduction n **1** *the reduction in size/volume/length/speed/strength* lessening, lowering,

decrease, diminution, cut, contraction, abbreviation, moderation, dilution, alleviation, abatement. *see* REDUCE 1. **2** *their reduction to lower classes/ranks* demotion, downgrading, lowering, humbling. **3** *the reduction of goods* cheapening, discounting. *see* REDUCE 4. **4** *the reduction of the enemy/city* conquering, vanquishing, overpowering, subjugation, overrunning. *see* REDUCE 6. **5** *what reduction did you get on the car?* discount, deduction, cut, concession, allowance. **6** *the museum has some reductions of the artist's work* smaller copy, miniature, model.

redundant adj **1** *his presence was redundant | redundant supplies* surplus to requirements, not required, unnecessary, inessential, unwanted, *de trop*, surplus, supernumerary, excessive, in excess, extra; *inf* needed like a hole in the head. **2** *redundant passages/writings* unnecessary, inessential, padded, wordy, verbose, tautological, periphrastic, diffuse, pleonastic. **3** *declared redundant | redundant people seeking jobs* sacked, dismissed, disemployed, unemployed, jobless.

reel v **1** *drunks reeling down the street* stagger, lurch, sway, stumble, totter, wobble, falter, waver, pitch, roll. **2** *she was reeling from the blow* feel giddy/dizzy, feel confused, be shaken, be in shock, be upset. **3** *her mind was reeling | the room seemed to reel* go round, go round and round, whirl, spin, revolve, swirl, twirl, swim.

refer v **1** *refer to a dictionary | refer to his notes* consult, turn to, look at, look up, seek information from, have recourse to. **2** *refer the question/person to a higher court* pass, hand on, send on, transfer, remit, direct. **3** *he referred to her death in his speech* mention, make mention of, make reference to, allude to, touch on, speak of, cite, advert to, hint at. **4** *these figures refer to last year* apply to, be relevant to, have relevance to, concern, relate to, belong to, pertain to, have a bearing on.

referee n **1** *football referee | send the disputed matter to a referee* umpire, judge, adjudicator, arbitrator, arbiter, mediator; *inf* ref. **2** *act as referee for his job application* character witness, commender, upholder, advocate, backer.

referee v **1** *referee the match* umpire, judge, adjudicate. **2** *referee in the dispute* arbitrate, mediate, act as arbitrator/negotiator, intercede.

reference n **1** *a reference to her death in his speech* mention, allusion, citation, hint. **2** *with reference to yesterday's meeting* regard, respect, relation, bearing, applicability, application, relevance, pertinence, connection, correlation. **3** *give a list of your references for the book* source, information source, citation, authority; bibliography. **4** *the teacher gave her a reference* character reference, testimonial, recommendation, good word; credentials.

referendum n public vote, plebiscite, popular vote, poll.

refine v **1** *refine sugar/flour* purify, rarefy, clarify, clear, cleanse, strain, sift, filter, distil, process. **2** *school refined her to some extent* civilize, make cultivated, polish, improve, make elegant. **3** *refine the art of conversation* improve, perfect, consummate, elaborate, hone, fine-tune, complete.

refined adj **1** *refined sugar/flour* purified, pure, rarefied, clarified, clear, filtered, distilled, processed. **2** *a refined lady/gentleman* cultivated, cultured, polished, civilized, civil, gracious, stylish, elegant, sophisticated, urbane, courtly, well-mannered, well-bred, gentlemanly, ladylike, genteel. **3** *refined tastes/manners* discriminating, discerning, tasteful, sophisticated, fastidious.

refinement n **1** *the refinement of sugar* purification, processing. *see* REFINE 1. **2** *a person of refinement* cultivation, culture, taste, discrimination, polish, finish, civility, grace, graciousness, style, elegance, finesse, sophistication, urbanity, courtliness, good breeding, politeness, gentility, politesse; good manners. **3** *refinements of logic/language* subtlety, nicety, nuance, fine point.

reflect v **1** *the surface reflects heat/light* throw back, cast back, send back, give back, scatter, diffuse. **2** *their faces reflected in the pool* mirror, image. **3** *reflect sound* send back, bounce back, echo, re-echo. **4** *their/a complexion reflecting his state of health* indicate, express, bespeak, communicate, show, display, demonstrate, exhibit, reveal, manifest, bear out, result from. **5** *it will reflect on the school if he does badly* discredit, put in a bad light, damage, damage the reputation of, detract from. **6** *reflect on her problems* think about, consider, give thought/consideration to, mull over, contemplate, deliberate over, ponder, meditate about, muse about, ruminate about, cogitate about, cerebrate, dwell on, brood about.

reflection n **1** *the reflection of heat/sound/images* throwing back, sending back, echoing, mirroring. *see* REFLECT 1, 2, 3. **2** *look at her reflection* image, mirror image. **3** *his complexion is a reflection of the state of his health* indication, expression, display, demonstration, manifestation, result. **4** *his behaviour is a reflection on the school* imputation, slur,

aspersion, source of discredit, derogation. **5** *on reflection, he decided to go* thought, thinking, consideration, contemplation, deliberation, meditation, rumination, cogitation, cerebration. **6** *write down your reflections on the subject* thought, opinion, view, idea, impression, comment; findings.

reflex adj *a reflex action* automatic, involuntary, spontaneous; *inf* knee-jerk.

reform v **1** *reform the system* improve, make better, better, ameliorate, amend, mend, rectify, correct, rehabilitate, change, revise, revolutionize, reorganize, reconstruct, rebuild, refashion, remodel, remake, make over, revamp, renovate. **2** *he has reformed since you knew him* mend one's ways, change for the better, turn over a new leaf, improve; *inf* go straight, get back on the straight and narrow.

reform n *the reform of the system* improvement, betterment, amelioration, amendment, rectification, correction, rehabilitation, change, revision, reorganization, reconstruction, rebuilding, refashioning, remodelling, renovation.

refractory adj intractable, recalcitrant, unmanageable, ungovernable, disobedient, insubordinate, defiant, contrary, wayward, wilful, headstrong, perverse, contumacious, rebellious, mutinous, obstinate, obdurate.

refrain v *refrain from drinking* desist, abstain, hold back, forbear, forgo, do without, avoid, eschew, cease, stop, give up, leave off, quit, renounce.

refresh v **1** *refreshed by a long walk* freshen, invigorate, revitalize, revive, brace, fortify, enliven, stimulate, energize, exhilarate, reanimate, resuscitate, revivify, rejuvenate, regenerate, breathe new life into, inspirit; *inf* perk up. **2** *refresh one's memory* stimulate, prompt, prod, jog, activate, rouse, arouse.

refreshing adj **1** *a refreshing breeze* freshening, invigorating, revitalizing, reviving, bracing, stimulating, exhilarating, energizing. *see* REFRESH 1. **2** *a refreshing piece of writing | refreshing attitude* fresh, new, novel, original, different.

refreshment n **1** *the refreshment of their system/ideas* freshening, invigoration, revitalizing, revival, stimulation, energizing, exhilarating, reanimation, rejuvenation. **2** *the guests took some refreshment | refreshments were avaialble* food, food and drink, drink, sustenance; snacks, drinks; *inf* eats, grub, nosh, chow.

refrigerate v keep cold, cool, chill, freeze.

refuge n **1** *seek refuge from the elements/danger* shelter, safety, security, protection, asylum, sanctuary. **2** *regard their house as a refuge* place of safety, safe house, shelter, haven, retreat, bolt-hole, sanctuary, harbour. **3** *borrowing money was his last refuge* resort, recourse, expedient, stopgap, tactic, stratagem, strategy.

refugee n displaced/stateless person, émigré, exile, fugitive, escapee.

refund v *refund her deposit* give back, return, repay, pay back, reimburse, make good, restore, replace.

refund n *give the disappointed audience a refund* repayment, reimbursement.

refurbish v renovate, revamp, make over, overhaul, redecorate, spruce up, recondition, refit, re-equip, remodel, repair, mend; *inf* do up, fix up.

refusal n **1** *the refusal of her invitation* turning down, declining, rejecting, spurning. *see* REFUSE v 1. **2** *four acceptances and one refusal to the invitation* non-acceptance, dissent, no, demurral, negation, thumbs down, rebuff; regrets; *inf* knock-back, brush-off. **3** *you can have first refusal* option, choice, consideration, opportunity.

refuse v **1** *refuse an invitation/offer* turn down, decline, say no to, reject, spurn, rebuff, repudiate; *inf* pass up, knock back. **2** *refuse to go* decline, be unwilling, baulk at, demur at, avoid, resist, protest at. **3** *refuse permission to go* withhold, not grant.

refuse n rubbish, waste, debris, litter, dross; dregs, leavings, sweepings; *Amer* garbage, trash; *inf* junk.

regain v **1** *regain one's property/composure* get back, win back, recover, recoup, retrieve, reclaim, repossess, redeem, recuperate, take back, retake, recapture. **2** *regain the shore* get back to, return to, reach again, reattain.

regal adj royal, majestic, noble, proud, stately, magnificent, sumptuous; kingly, queenly, princely, fit for a king/queen/prince/princess.

regale v **1** *regale their guests* entertain lavishly/sumptuously, ply with food and drink, wine and dine, feast, fête. **2** *regale his friends with stories of his travels* entertain, amuse, divert, delight, fascinate, captivate.

regard v **1** *the security officer regarded them closely* watch, look at, gaze at, keep an eye on, stare at, observe, view, study, scrutinize, eye, mark, behold. **2** *he seldom regards her advice* heed, pay attention to, attend to, listen to, mind, take notice of, take into consideration/account. **3** *regard the prospect with horror* look upon, view, consider, contemplate, think of, weigh up, mull over, reflect on, deliberate on. **4** *his work/aunt is well/poorly regarded* judge, adjudge, rate, value, estimate, gauge, appraise, assess, account, deem, consider, look upon, hold. **5** *these figures do not regard to the present project* apply to, relate to, concern, be relevant to, refer to, belong to, pertain to, have a bearing on.

regard n **1** *she was aware of his steady regard* look, gaze, stare; observation, scrutiny. *see* REGARD v 1. **2** *pay no regard to his warning* heed, attention, notice, consideration, thought, mind. **3** *looked upon with regard in the firm* respect, esteem, admiration, approval, approbation, appreciation, favour, deference, affection, love. **4** *in this regard I disagree with you | consider from all regards* respect, aspect, point, particular, detail, item, feature. **5** *this has no regard to the matter in question* application, relation, relationship, connection, relevance, reference, pertinence, bearing.

regarding prep with/in regard to, as regards, as to, with reference to, on the subject/matter of, apropos, concerning, about, respecting.

regardless adj **regardless of** without regard to, disregarding, unmindful of, heedless of, without consideration of, indifferent to, negligent of.

regardless adv *he decided to go, regardless* anyway, anyhow, in any case, nevertheless, nonetheless, despite everything, for all that, no matter what.

regards npl *send her my regards* best/good wishes, greetings, salutations, respects, compliments, remembrances.

regenerate v **1** *he felt regenerated after his holiday* renew, breathe new life into, restore, invigorate, refresh, revitalize, revive, stimulate, energize, exhilarate, revivify, rejuvenate, uplift, inspirit. **2** *regenerate the political party* breathe new life into, change radically, improve, amend, reorganize, reconstruct, overhaul.

regime n government, system of government, rule, reign, control, command, administration, establishment, direction, management, leadership.

regiment v *regiment tourists into groups | regimented school classes* organize/order rigidly, systematize, methodize, control strictly, discipline, keep a tight rein on, bring into line, run a tight ship, rule with a rod of iron.

region n **1** *the western region of the country* area, province, territory, division, section, sector, zone, tract, part, quarter, locality. **2** *the lumbar region of the body* part, place, section, locality, site. **3** *work in the region of metaphysics* field, sphere, orbit, ambit, realm, domain, world. **in the region of** in *the region of 500 people/tonnes* approximately, about, roughly, more or less, in the area/ neighbourhood of.

regional adj **1** *regional distinctions shown on the map* geographical, topographical, zonal, territorial. **2** *organized on a regional rather than a national basis* local, localized, district, provincial, parochial.

register n **1** *sign the register | be on the medical register* official list, listing, roll, roster, index, directory, catalogue. **2** *historians consulting old parish registers* record, chronicle, diary, journal, log; annals, archives, files. **3** *the register of her voice* range, compass, scope, scale, gamut, reach, sweep, spectrum.

register v **1** *register a birth | record the date of arrival* record, put on record, enter, set down, chronicle, enrol, inscribe, write down, put in writing, take down, note, minute, list, catalogue. **2** *the speedometer registered 50 miles per hour* read, record, indicate, show, display. **3** *her face registered surprise* show, express, display, exhibit, evince, betray, reveal, manifest, demonstrate, reflect. **4** *his death/danger did not register* make an impression, get through, sink in, penetrate, have an effect.

regress v *he had improved but he has now regressed* retrogress, revert, relapse, lapse, backslide, fall away, go backwards, degenerate, retrograde, recidivate.

regret v **1** *she regrets her action* feel sorry/ contrite about, feel remorse about, wish undone, have a conscience about, repent, rue. **2** *she regrets their going | regretting lost opportunities* feel sorry about, lament, bemoan, be upset/disappointed about, mourn, grieve over, weep over, fret about, pine over, deplore.

regret n **1** *she looks upon her actions with regret* sorrow, remorse, contrition, repentance, pangs of conscience, compunction, ruefulness, self-reproach, penitence. **2** *she regarded their going with regret | regret at her lost opportunities* sorrow, disappointment, lamentation, grief, mourning, pining.

regretful adj sorry, apologetic, remorseful, contrite, repentant, conscience-stricken, rueful, penitent.

regrettable adj deplorable, reprehensible, disgraceful, blameworthy, unfortunate, unwelcome, distressing, ill-advised.

regular adj **1** *his regular route to work* usual, normal, customary, habitual, routine, typical, everyday, daily, unvarying, common, average, commonplace. **2** *regular breathing* rhythmic, periodic, steady, even, uniform, constant, unchanging. **3** *trees placed at regular intervals* even, uniform, consistent, orderly, systematic, fixed. **4** *build on a regular surface* level, smooth, flat, uniform. **5** *apply through the regular channels* official, established, fixed, stated, conventional, formal, proper, orthodox, approved, sanctioned, bona fide, standard, usual, traditional, classic, time-honoured. **6** *insist on regular office procedures* methodical, systematic, well-organized, orderly, efficient, smooth-running, streamlined. **7** *he's a regular charmer/hero* real, thorough, absolute, utter, complete.

regulate v **1** *regulate one's expenditure/ lifestyle | regulate the traffic* control, direct, guide, govern, rule, manage, order, administer, handle, arrange, organize, conduct, run, supervise, oversee, superintend, monitor. **2** *regulate the clock/mechanism* adjust, balance, set, synchronize, modulate.

regulation n **1** *the regulation of expenditure/ lifestyles/traffic* control, direction, guidance, government, rule, management, administration, organization, conducting, handling, supervision, monitoring. *see* REGULATE 1. **2** *the regulation of the clocks/mechanisms* adjustment, balancing, synchronization, modulation. **3** *new government/school regulations* rule, ruling, order, directive, act, law, decree, statute, edict, ordinance, pronouncement, dictum, command, procedure, requirement, prescription, precept.

regulation adj *regulation dress* official, prescribed, mandatory, required, set, fixed, standard, normal, usual, customary.

rehabilitate v **1** *rehabilitate the wounded soldiers* restore to health/normality, get back to health/normality, reintegrate, readapt, retrain. **2** *rehabilitate slum areas/houses* restore, redevelop, recondition, renovate, renew, refurbish, redecorate, mend, repair, fix up, rebuild, reconstruct. **3** *rehabilitate the disgraced minister* reinstate, restore, bring back, re-establish.

rehearsal n **1** *a rehearsal of the play/concert* practice, practice session, trial performance, run-through, going-over. **2** *weary of his rehearsal of the events* account, relating, recounting, narration, repeating, reiteration. *see* REHEARSE 4. **3** *listen to the rehearsal of* *their grievances* enumeration, listing, itemization, specification; list, catalogue. *see* REHEARSE 5.

rehearse v **1** *rehearse the play/speech* practise, try out, run through, go over. **2** *actors rehearsing* practise, have a practice session, prepare, try out, have a trial performance, go through one's paces. **3** *rehearse the actors/children* drill, train, prepare. **4** *rehearse his adventures* relate, recount, narrate, describe, delineate, repeat, reiterate, recapitulate, go over. **5** *rehearse their grievances on paper* enumerate, list, itemize, detail, spell out, catalogue, recite.

reign v **1** *the king/queen reigned for thirty years* be king/queen, be monarch/sovereign, sit on the throne, occupy the throne, wear the crown, wield the sceptre. **2** *the present committee has reigned for years* be in power, govern, be in government, rule, be in command/charge/control, administer, hold sway; *inf* be at the helm. **3** *chaos reigned* prevail, predominate, obtain, hold sway, be supreme, be rife, be rampant.

reign n **1** *during the reign of the king/queen* monarchy, sovereignty. **2** *under the reign of the present government* power, government, rule, command, control, administration, charge, influence, sway, ascendancy, dominion, supremacy.

rein n *act as a rein on their expenditure* check, curb, restraint, constraint, restriction, limitation, control, bridle, brake.

rein v *try to rein in his impatience | rein your expenditure* check, curb, restrain, constrain, hold back, restrict, control, bridle, put the brakes on, slow down.

reinforce v **1** *reinforce the bridge | reinforce his argument* strengthen, fortify, bolster up, shore up, buttress, prop up, brace, support, back up, uphold, stress, underline, emphasize. **2** *reinforce the troops* augment, increase, add to, supplement.

reinforcement n **1** *the reinforcement of the bridge/argument* strengthening, fortification, bolstering, propping up, supporting, stressing, emphasizing. *see* REINFORCE 1. **2** *the reinforcement of the troops* augmentation, increasing, supplementing. **3** *act as a reinforcement of his argument* fortification, buttress, prop, brace, support, emphasis.

reinforcements npl *armies sending for reinforcements* additional troops/supplies, supplementaries, reserves; support.

reiterate v repeat, repeat/go over and over, say again, belabour, dwell on, harp on, hammer away at.

reject v **1** *reject an offer/invitation* refuse, turn down, decline, say no to, give the thumbs down to, spurn, rebuff, repudiate, veto, deny; *inf* pass up, knock back. **2** *reject the bill | reject his wife* cast out, cast aside, discard, jettison, renounce, abandon, forsake, scrap, exclude, eliminate.

reject n **1** *a reject from the factory* substandard article, discard, second. **2** *one of society's rejects* failure, outcast, derelict; *inf* drop-out.

rejection n **1** *the rejection of their offer/invitation* refusal, turning down, declining, spurning; *inf* knock-back, brush-off. *see* REJECT V 1. **2** *the rejection of the bill | rejection of his wife* casting out, discarding, jettisoning, renunciation. *see* REJECT V 2. **3** *receive a rejection* refusal, non-acceptance, no, demurral, negation, thumbs down; *inf* knock-back, brush-off.

rejoice v **1** *people rejoicing on hearing the good news* be joyful, be happy, be pleased, be glad, be delighted, be elated, be overjoyed, be jubilant, be euphoric, jump for joy, exult, glory, triumph, celebrate, revel, make merry, feast. **2** *rejoice in her new baby* take delight/pleasure in, find joy in.

rejoicing n happiness, pleasure, gladness, delight, elation, jubilation, euphoria, exultation, glory, triumph, celebration, revelry, merry-making, feasting.

rejoinder n answer, response, reply, riposte, retort; *inf* comeback.

relapse v **1** *the firm improved but then relapsed* lapse, regress, retrogress, revert, backslide, fall away, go backwards, slip back, degenerate, retrograde, recidivate. **2** *the patient relapsed* have/suffer a relapse, get ill/worse again, worsen, take a turn for the worse, sicken, deteriorate, sink.

relapse n **1** *the firm had a relapse after its improvement* lapse, regression, retrogression, reversion, backsliding, recidivism. **2** *the patient suffered a relapse* reoccurence of illness, worsening of condition, turn for the worse, set-back, deterioration.

relate v **1** *relate the story of the accident* recount, tell, narrate, describe, of, report, impart, communicate, recite, rehearse, present, detail, delineate, chronicle, set forth. **2** *it is sometimes difficult to relate cause and affect* connect, associate, link, correlate, ally, couple, join. **3** *this information does not relate to the matter in hand* apply to, be relevant to, have relevance to, concern, refer to, have reference to, belong to, pertain to, bear on.

related adj **1** *related issues* connected, interconnected, associated, linked, correlated, allied, affiliated, accompanying, concomitant, akin. **2** *related through marriage* connected, akin, kindred, agnate, cognate, consanguineous.

relation n **1** *the relation of the story* recounting, recountal, telling, narrating, narrative, description, reporting, rehearsal, reciting. *see* RELATE 1. **2** *the relation between cause and effect* connection, association, linking, tie-in, correlation, alliance, bond, interdependence. **3** *have no relation to the problem in hand* applicability, application, relevance, reference, pertinence, bearing. **4** *have relations in America* relative, member of the family, kinsman, kinswoman, connection; kin.

relations npl **1** *have business relations* connections, dealings, associations, communications; contact, interaction. **2** *suspected of having relations with each other* sexual intercourse, intimacy; sexual relationship, affair, liaison; *inf* sex. **3** *have no relations in this country* family, kin, kinsfolk, kindred; connections, folks.

relationship n **1** *the relationship between cause and effect* connection, association, link, correlation, alliance, bond, tie-up, parallel, correspondence, conjunction. **2** *enter in a new relationship* friendship, love affair, affair, liaison. **3** *I don't think there is a relationship between the families* family/blood ties, kinship.

relative adj **1** *consider the relative merits of the candidates* comparative, comparable, respective, correlative, parallel, corresponding. **2** *the salary scale is relative to production* proportionate (to), in proportion/ratio (to), based (on). **3** *facts relative to the issue* applicable, relevant, pertaining, pertinent, germane, material, apposite, appropriate, apropos, appurtenant.

relative n *a relative of his wife* relation, member of the family, kinsman, kinswoman, connection; kin, parent, sibling, grandparent; mother, father, brother, sister, son, daughter, stepmother, stepfather, stepchild, stepbrother, stepsister, aunt, uncle, niece, nephew, cousin, grandfather, grandmother.

relatively adv **1** *for a car of this size it is relatively roomy* comparatively, in comparison, by comparison, proportionately. **2** *although ill he is relatively cheerful* quite, rather, reasonably, somewhat.

relax v **1** *relax one's grip* loosen, slacken, weaken, untighten, lessen, let up, reduce, diminish. **2** *let her muscles relax* become less tense/stiff/rigid, loosen, slacken, untighten. **3** *relax the rules* moderate, make less strict/formal, soften, ease. **4** *relax one's efforts* lessen, reduce, diminish, decrease, ease off, slacken off, let up on, abate. **5** *tense people learning to relax* loosen up, ease up/off; *inf* unwind, take it easy, let it all hang out, hang loose. **6** *this will relax you* loosen up, make less tense/uptight, calm, calm down, tranquillize, soothe, pacify; *inf* unwind. **7** *he relaxes by playing the piano* be at leisure, take time off, enjoy oneself, amuse oneself, entertain oneself, rest; *inf* let one's hair down. **8** *relax by the pool* rest, lounge, repose, take one's ease, idle, put one's feet up.

relaxation n **1** *the relaxation of his grip* loosening, slackening, weakening, letting-up. *see* RELAX 1. **2** *the relaxation of her muscles* loosening, slackening, untightening. *see* RELAX 2. **3** *relaxation of rules* moderation, softening, easing. *see* RELAX 3. **4** *relaxation of one's efforts* lessening, reduction, easing-off, abatement. *see* RELAX 4. **5** *tense people learning relaxation* loosening up. *see* RELAX 5. **6** *the relaxation of the patients* calming, tranquillization, soothing, pacification. *see* RELAX 6. **7** *for relaxation he plays the piano* leisure, recreation, enjoyment, amusement, entertainment, fun, pleasure, rest, refreshment.

relay v *relay the information* pass on, hand on, communicate, send, transmit, broadcast, spread, circulate.

release v **1** *release the prisoners* set free, free, let go, set/turn loose, let out, liberate, deliver, emancipate, manumit. **2** *release those who had been tied up* set free, free, untie, undo, unloose, unbind, unchain, unfetter, unshackle, extricate. **3** *release her from her promise/engagement* let off, let go, excuse, absolve, acquit, exonerate, exempt. **4** *release the news|release a bulletin* make public, make known, issue, break, announce, reveal, divulge, unveil, present, disclose, publish, broadcast, put out, circulate, disseminate, distribute, spread.

release n **1** *the release of the prisoners* freeing, liberation, deliverance, emancipation, manumission. *see* RELEASE v 1. **2** *prisoners obtaining their release* freedom, liberation, deliverance, emancipation, manumission. **3** *the release of the bound victims* freeing, untying, unbinding, unchaining, extrication. *see* RELEASE v 2. **4** *the release from her promise* excusing, absolution, acquittal, dispensation, exemption; *inf* let-off. *see* RELEASE v 3. **5** *the release of the news* issuing, breaking, announcement, divulging, publishing, publication, broadcasting, circulation. *see* RELEASE v 4. **6** *write a press release* announce-

ment, bulletin, publication, proclamation.
7 *the artist's latest release* record, disc,
album, book, film.

relent v **1** *the tyrant relented and released the
child's mother* soften, become merciful/
lenient, show mercy/pity, give quarter,
melt, capitulate, yield, give way, give in,
unbend, come round, forbear, change
one's mind; *inf* do a U-turn. **2** *the pace/wind
relented* let up, ease, slacken, relax, abate,
drop, fall off, die down, weaken.

relentless adj **1** *a relentless tyrant* unrelenting, ruthless, merciless, uncompassionate,
pitiless, remorseless, unforgiving, implacable, inexorable, cruel, grim, harsh, hard,
cold-hearted, fierce, strict, obdurate,
unyielding, unflexible, unbending. **2** *a
relentless urge/ambition* unrelenting,
unremitting, undeviating, persistent,
unswerving, persevering, unflagging, punishing, unfaltering, unstoppable, incessant,
unceasing, non-stop, unabated, unbroken.

relevant adj applicable, pertinent, apposite,
material, appurtenant, to the point/pur-
pose, germane, admissible, appropriate,
apt, fitting.

reliable adj **1** *a reliable friend* dependable,
trustworthy, trusty, true, tried and true/
tested, faithful, devoted, steady, steadfast,
constant, unfailing, infallible, certain, sure,
responsible. **2** *reliable evidence* dependable,
trustworthy, well-founded, well-grounded,
authentic, genuine, credible, sound. **3** *a
reliable firm* dependable, trustworthy, reputable, established, safe, stable.

reliance n **1** *place no reliance on what she says*
confidence, trust, faith, belief, conviction.
2 *his total reliance on his colleagues* dependence, leaning.

relic n **1** *relics on view in the museum* ancient/
historical object, artefact, antique, heirloom. **2** *a tradition that is a relic of another
age* vestige, trace, survivor, remnant.
3 *regard the ring as a relic of a former relationship* souvenir, memento, keepsake, remembrance, reminder.

relics npl **1** *looking for Roman relics* remains,
reliquiae, fragments, shards. **2** *exhume the
relics* corpse, dead body; remains.

relief n **1** *the relief of the pain* relieving, alle-
viating, mitigating, assuaging, allaying,
soothing, easing, dulling, lessening, reduction. *see* RELIEVE 1. **2** *the medicine brought relief*
alleviation, mitigation, assuagement, palliation, ease, appeasement, abatement. **3** *the
relief of the starving people/city* aiding, assisting, rescuing, saving. *see* RELIEVE 2. **4** *bring
relief to the starving people* aid, help, assistance, succour. **5** *bring relief from the monot-*

ony respite, remission, interruption, break,
variation, diversion, lightening, brightening; *inf* let-up. **6** *the soldier's/doctor's relief*
replacement, substitute, stand-in, fill-in,
locum, understudy. **7** *details bringing the
story out in sharp relief* contrast, distinctness,
vividness, intensity. **8** *relief from his burden*
freedom, release, liberation, deliverance,
exemption, extrication, discharge. *see*
RELIEVE 5.

relieve v **1** *relieve his pain/distress* alleviate,
mitigate, assuage, allay, soothe, soften, palliate, appease, ease, dull, abate, reduce,
lessen, diminish. **2** *relieve the starving people/
city* bring aid to, aid, help, assist, rescue,
save, succour. **3** *relieve the monotony* bring
respite to, interrupt, break up, vary,
lighten, brighten. **4** *relieve the soldier on
guard* take over from, take the place of,
stand in for, substitute for. **5** *relieve them of
their burdens* free, release, liberate, deliver,
exempt, extricate, discharge, unburden,
disburden, disencumber, disembarrass.

religious adj **1** *religious festivals/discussions*
church, holy, divine, theological, doctrinal,
spiritual, sectarian. **2** *religious people*
churchgoing, God-fearing, godly, pious,
devout. **3** *pay religious attention to detail*
scrupulous, conscientious, meticulous,
zealous, strict, rigid, rigorous, exact,
unfailing, unswerving, undeviating.

relinquish v **1** *relinquish her right to the title*
give up, renounce, resign, abdicate, surren-
der, sign away. **2** *relinquish his position*
depart from, leave, quit, vacate, pull out of,
abandon, forsake. **3** *relinquish the habit* give
up, discontinue, stop, cease, drop, abstain
from, forbear from, forgo, desist from.
4 *relinquish her grip* release, let go, loosen,
unloose.

relish n **1** *eat/play with relish* enjoyment,
delight, pleasure, satisfaction, gratification,
appreciation, liking, zest, gusto. **2** *food with
relish* flavour, taste, tang, piquancy, spiciness. **3** *serve relishes with the meat* condiment, sauce, chutney, pickle.

relish v **1** *the children relish a visit to the sea*
enjoy, delight in, like, love, adore, appreciate, revel in, luxuriate in. **2** *they don't relish
a visit from the doctor* look forward to, fancy,
savour.

reluctance n unwillingness, disinclination,
hesitance, hesitancy, lack of enthusiasm,
loathness, aversion, disrelish, distaste.

reluctant adj **1** *a reluctant bride* unwilling,
disinclined, hesitant, unenthusiastic,
grudging. **2** *reluctant to go* unwilling, disinclined, loath, averse, slow, chary.

rely v **1** *you can rely on him to help* depend on, count on, bank on, trust, be confident/sure of, swear by. **2** *he relies on his parents too much* depend on, lean on.

remain v **1** *only a handful remained* be left, be left over, stay behind, survive, last, abide, endure, prevail. **2** *remain at home | remain in hospital* stay, wait, linger, tarry; *inf* stay put. **3** *remain calm* stay, continue, persist in being.

remainder n remnant, residue, residuum, balance, surplus, excess, superfluity; remains, remnants, relics, vestiges, leavings, dregs.

remains npl **1** *the remains of a meal* remnants, leftovers, leavings, scraps; residue, debris, detritus. **2** *Roman remains* relics, reliquiae, fragments, shards. **3** *take his remains to the cemetery* corpse, dead body, body, cadaver, carcass.

remark v **1** *she remarked that she had been ill* mention, say, state, declare, pronounce, assert, observe. **2** *she remarked on his appearance* comment on, pass comment on, mention. **3** *remark his resemblance to his father* note, notice, observe, mark, perceive, discern.

remark n **1** *ignore his nasty remarks* comment, statement, utterance, declaration, pronouncement, observation, reference, opinion. **2** *a performance worthy of remark* comment, attention, mention, notice, observation, heed, acknowledgement, recognition.

remarkable adj **1** *a remarkable achievement* out of the ordinary, extraordinary, unusual, uncommon, conspicuous, singular, signal, rare, exceptional, outstanding, striking, impressive, considerable, notable, noteworthy, memorable, pre-eminent, significant, important, momentous, phenomenal, wonderful. **2** *he is remarkable for his calmness* noteworthy, notable, conspicuous, distinctive, unusual, uncommon, peculiar.

remedy n **1** *given a remedy for asthma* cure, treatment, medicine, medication, medicament, therapy, antidote, specific, restorative, nostrum, panacea. **2** *find a remedy for the situation/problem* corrective, solution, redress, panacea.

remedy v **1** *unable to remedy her condition* cure, heal, treat, counteract, control. **2** *remedy the situation/problem* rectify, solve, set to rights, put right, redress, fix, sort out.

remember v **1** *I cannot remember his name* recall, call to mind, recollect, think of. **2** *remember to go | remember that it's raining* keep/bear in mind, not forget. **3** *sit remembering | sit remembering the past* recall, recollect, reminisce; reminisce about, look/think back on, hark back to, summon up. **4** *remember the waiter* tip, reward, recompense. **5** *remember me to your parents* send greetings from, send one's regards/compliments to.

remembrance n **1** *their remembrance of times past* remembering, recalling, recollecting, recollection, reminiscing. **2** *I have a remembrance of seeing him once* memory, recollection. **3** *give her a remembrance of their meeting* keepsake, souvenir, momento, token, commemoration, memorial. **4** *send my remembrances to your parents* greetings, regards, best wishes, compliments.

remind v **1** *remind me to go* cause one to remember, jog/refresh one's memory, prompt. **2** *the village reminds me of home* cause one to remember, awake one's memories of.

reminisce v **1** *sit and reminisce* remember, recollect, think back, look back, dwell on the past. **2** *reminisce about the past* remember, recall, recollect, call to mind, exchange memories.

reminiscences npl **1** *listen to her reminiscences about the old days* memories, recollections, anecdotes; review, retrospection. **2** *publish her reminiscences* memoirs, remembrances.

reminiscent adj *reminiscent of an Italian village* evocative, suggestive, redolent.

remiss adj negligent, neglectful, lax, slack, slipshod, careless, forgetful, inattentive, heedless, thoughtless, unthinking, unmindful, culpable, delinquent; *inf* sloppy.

remission n **1** *the remission of the penalty* cancellation, revocation, repeal, rescinding. **2** *receive a remission for good behaviour* reduction in sentence, reduced sentence. **3** *no remission of our efforts* relaxation, slackening, weakening, lessening, reduction, decrease, diminution, dwindling, cessation, stopping, halt. **4** *the remission of the storm/pain* easing, moderation, abatement, lessening, decrease, dwindling, wane, waning, ebb, ebbing, subsidence. **5** *the remission of payment* sending, dispatch, forwarding, transmission, posting, mailing. **6** *the remission of the matter to a committee* referral, passing on, transfer, direction. *see* REMIT 5. **7** *the remission of the meeting/decision* postponement, deferral, shelving, delay, suspension. *see* REMIT 6. **8** *given a remission for his offences/sins* pardon, absolution, exoneration, forgiveness, indulgence.

687

remit v **1** *remit a punishment/penalty* cancel, revoke, repeal, rescind, stop, halt. **2** *remit our efforts* relax, slacken, weaken, lessen, reduce, decrease, diminish, cease, stop, halt, desist from. **3** *the storm/pain remitted* ease, moderate, abate, lessen, decrease, dwindle, wane, ebb, subside. **4** *remit payment* send, dispatch, forward, transmit, post, mail. **5** *remit the matter to a committee | remit the case to another court* refer, pass on, hand on, send on, transfer, direct. **6** *remit the meeting/decision* postpone, defer, put off, shelve, delay, hold off, suspend, prorogue, reschedule. **7** *remit the offence/sin* pardon, forgive, excuse, overlook, pass over.

remittance n payment, fee, allowance.

remnant n **1** *the remnant of the army* remainder, residue, balance; remains, vestiges. **2** *a remnant of material* piece, fragment, scrap, cut-off.

remonstrate v **1** *remonstrate with them* take issue with, argue with, dispute with, protest to, complain to, expostulate with. **2** *remonstrate against cruelty to children* argue against, protest against, object to, complain about, take a stand against, oppose.

remorse n regret, sorrow, sorriness, contriteness, compunction, penitence, repentance, bad/guilty conscience, guilt, shame, self-reproach, ruefulness; pangs of conscience.

remorseful adj sorry, regretful, contrite, apologetic, penitent, repentant, guilt-ridden, conscience-stricken, ashamed, chastened, rueful.

remote adj **1** *the remote past | places remote from each other* distant, far, far-off, far-away, far-removed. **2** *in remote mountain villages* out of the way, outlying, inaccessible, off the beaten track, isolated, secluded, lonely, God-forsaken. **3** *remarks remote from the subject* irrelevant, non-pertinent, inapposite, immaterial, unrelated, unassociated, unconnected, inappropriate, inapt. **4** *a remote possibility* outside, unlikely, improbable, implausible, negligible, insignificant, doubtful, dubious, meagre, inconsiderable, slight, slender, slim, small, poor. **5** *she is rather remote, although he is friendly* aloof, distant, detached, withdrawn, reserved, uncommunicative, unapproachable, stand-offish, cool, haughty, uninvolved, indifferent, unconcerned.

removal n **1** *the removal of dishes from the table to the sink* taking away, moving, shifting, conveying, conveyance, transfer, carrying away, transporting. **2** *his removal from office* dismissal, eviction, ejection, expulsion, ousting, dislodgement, deposition. *see* REMOVE 2. **3** *the removal of privileges* taking away, withdrawal, deprivation, abolition. **4** *removal of errors* deletion, elimination, erasure, effacing, obliteration. *see* REMOVE 5. **5** *the removal of weeds/opposition* uprooting, eradication, extirpation, destruction, extermination, annihilation. **6** *the removal of a limb/branch* cutting off, amputation, excision. *see* REMOVE 7. **7** *their removal to France* move, transfer, relocation; *Scots* flitting. **8** *the removal of a gang member by a rival* disposal, elimination, killing, murder, assassination, liquidation. *see* REMOVE 9.

remove v **1** *remove the dishes from the table | remove them to the sink* take away, carry away, move, shift, convey, transfer, transport. **2** *remove him from office* get rid of, dismiss, evict, eject, expel, cast out, oust, throw out, thrust out, dislodge, relegate, unseat, depose, displace; *inf* sack, fire. **3** *remove their coats/hats* take off, doff, pull off. **4** *remove their privileges* take away, withdraw, do away with, abolish. **5** *remove the errors* delete, eliminate, erase, rub out, cross out, strike out, blue-pencil, efface, obliterate. **6** *remove the weeds/opposition* take out, pull out, uproot, eradicate, extirpate, destroy, exterminate, annihilate. **7** *remove a limb/branch* cut off, amputate, lop off, chop off, excise. **8** *remove to France* move, move house to, transfer, relocate; *Scots* flit. **9** *hire an assassin to remove him* get rid of, dispose of, do away with, eliminate, kill, murder, assassinate, liquidate; *inf* bump off, do in.

remuneration n payment, pay, salary, fee, emolument, stipend, honorarium, income, profit, reward, recompense, reimbursement; wages, earnings.

remunerative adj profitable, money-making, paying, lucrative, gainful, financially rewarding, rich.

renaissance, renascence n rebirth, reappearance, re-emergence, resurgence, renewal, reawakening, revival, resurrection, rejuvenation, regeneration.

render v **1** *render them helpless* make, cause to be/become, leave. **2** *pay for services rendered* give, contribute, make available, provide, supply, furnish. **3** *render good for evil | render insult for insult* give, exchange, trade, swap, return. **4** *render obedience* show, display, exhibit, evince, manifest. **5** *render an account* present, send in, submit, tender. **6** *the artist rendered her in a wistful mood* paint, portray, depict, represent. **7** *render the role of Macbeth* act, perform, play. **8** *the piano solo was well rendered* play, execute, perform, interpret. **9** *render the passage into Russian* translate, transcribe, construe, put, express. **10** *they rendered their land to the emperor* give, hand over, deliver, turn over, give up, yield, cede, surrender, relinquish. **11** *render the lands to the original owners* give back, return, restore.

rendezvous n **1** *have a rendezvous with her lover* appointment, date, engagement, meeting, assignation. **2** *their rendezvous is the river-bank* meeting-place, venue, place of assignation.

rendezvous v *we shall rendezvous at dawn* meet, come/gather together, gather, assemble.

renegade n defector, deserter, turncoat, betrayer, traitor, dissenter, apostate, renouncer, recanter, revolutionary, rebel, mutineer.

renege v go back on one's word, break one's promise, default, back out, pull out; *inf* cop out, welsh.

renounce v **1** *renounce his claim* give up, relinquish, resign, abdicate, abnegate, surrender, sign away, waive, forego. **2** *renounce his son* repudiate, disown, cast off, discard, reject, disinherit, wash one's hands of, spurn, shun. **3** *renounce strong drink* give up, abstain from, desist from, swear off, eschew. **4** *renounce one's friendship/religion* give up, abandon, forsake, renege on, turn one's back on, abjure.

renovate v modernize, recondition, refurbish, rehabilitate, overhaul, restore, revamp, remodel, repair, redecorate, refit; *inf* do up, fix up.

renown n fame, repute, acclaim, celebrity, distinction, illustriousness, eminence, pre-eminence, prominence, mark, note, consequence, prestige.

renowned adj famous, famed, well-known, of repute, acclaimed, celebrated, distinguished, illustrious, eminent, pre-eminent, prominent, noted, notable, of note, of consequence, prestigious.

rent¹ n *what is the rent of the house/boat?* rental, tenant's payment, hire fee.

rent¹ v **1** *rent a house/boat from the owner* lease, hire, charter. **2** *they rent out houses/boats* let, lease, hire, hire/let out, farm out.

rent² n *a rent in the material* tear, rip, split, gash, slash, hole, perforation, break, crack, fracture, crevice, fissure, cleft.

renunciation n **1** *the renunciation of his claim* relinquishment, resignation, abdication, abnegation, surrender, waiving. **2** *the renunciation of his son* repudiation, disowning, discarding, rejecting, disinheriting, spurning. *see* RENOUNCE 2. **3** *the renunciation of strong drink* giving up, abstention. *see*

RENOUNCE 3. **4** *the renunciation of their friendship/religion* abandonment, forsaking, reneging, abjuration.

repair¹ v **1** *repair the machine* mend, fix, put right, restore, restore to working order, service, adjust, regulate, overhaul. **2** *repair the torn clothes* mend, darn, sew, patch. **3** *repair the rift in their friendship* mend, fix, patch up, heal, cure. **4** *repair the omission* make reparation for, put right, make good, rectify, correct, redress, compensate for.

repair¹ n **1** *the repair of the car* mending, fixing, restoration, servicing, overhaul. *see* REPAIR ¹ v 1. **2** *you won't notice the repair* mend, darn, patch. **3** *the furniture/car is in good repair* condition, state, form, fettle, kilter; *inf* shape, nick.

repair² v *repair to the library* go to, withdraw to, head for, betake oneself to, take off for, leave for, depart for.

reparation n *demand reparation for wrongs* redress, atonement, restitution, satisfaction, compensation, recompense, indemnity; amends, damages.

repartee n witty conversation, badinage, banter, raillery, wordplay, lively exchange.

repast n meal, collation, refection, snack, feast; food, nourishment; *inf* spread, feed.

repay v **1** *repay him the money owed* pay back, refund, reimburse, recompense, remunerate, square accounts with, settle up with, indemnify. **2** *repay the money owed* pay back, give back, refund. **3** *repay him for the crime against her family* get back at, hit back, retaliate against, get even with, settle the score with; *inf* get one's own back on, give just deserts, give comeuppance. **4** *repay the wrong* avenge, revenge, make reprisal for.

repeal v *repeal the act/bill* revoke, rescind, abrogate, annul, nullify, declare null and void, make void, void, invalidate, quash, set aside, cancel, countermand, retract, withdraw, recall, abjure, overrule, override, reverse.

repeal n *the repeal of the act/bill* revocation, rescinding, rescission, abrogation, annulment, disannulment, nullification, voiding, invalidation, quashing, setting aside, cancellation, countermanding, retraction, withdrawal, recall, abjuration, overruling, overriding, reversal.

repeat v **1** *repeat the statement/story* say again, restate, retell, iterate, recite, rehearse, recapitulate; *inf* recap. **2** *she repeated his words* say again, restate, echo, parrot, quote, duplicate, copy, reproduce. **3** *repeat the task* do again, redo, duplicate. **4** *repeat the film/tape* rerun, replay. **repeat**

itself *history repeated itself* occur again, reoccur, happen again, reappear.

repeat n 1 *a repeat of his statement/story* repetition, restatement, retelling, iteration, recapitulation; *inf* recap. 2 *a repeat of his words/actions* repetition, restatement, echoing, parroting, duplication, copy, reproduction. 3 *watch a repeat of the comedy* rerun, replay, rebroadcast.

repeated adj recurrent, frequent, continual, incessant, constant, endless.

repeatedly adv again and again, over and over, time and time again, time after time, frequently, often, many times.

repel v 1 *repel attackers/invaders* repulse, drive back, push back, thrust back, force back, beat back, hold off, ward off, fend off, stave off, parry, keep at bay, keep at arm's length, foil, check, frustrate, put to flight. 2 *repel their advances* repulse, reject, decline, turn down, rebuff. 3 *the sight of blood repels her* revolt, disgust, sicken, nauseate, make one sick, turn one's stomach, be repugnant to, make one's flesh creep, put one off, offend, shock; *inf* turn one off, give one the creeps/heebie-jeebies.

repellent adj repulsive, revolting, disgusting, sickening, nauseating, distasteful, repugnant, abhorrent, offensive, obnoxious, loathsome, off-putting, hateful, vile, nasty, shocking, despicable, reprehensible, contemptible, odious, abominable, horrible, horrid, foul, heinous, obscene.

repent v regret, feel remorse for, rue; be penitent, be sorry, see the error of one's ways, be regretful, be contrite, feel remorse/remorseful, be conscience-stricken, reproach oneself, be ashamed, be guilt-ridden; *inf* see the light.

repentance n penitence, sorrow, sorriness, regret, contrition, contriteness, remorse, conscience, self-reproach, ruefulness, shame, guilt.

repentant adj penitent, sorrowful, apologetic, regretful, contrite, remorseful, conscience-stricken, rueful, ashamed, guilt-ridden.

repercussion n 1 *the repercussions of his action* effect, result, consequence, reverberation, backlash. 2 *he heard/felt the repercussion* echo, reverberation, reflection, recoil, rebound.

repetition n 1 *a repetition of the statement/story* restatement, retelling, iteration, recital, rehearsal, recapitulation; *inf* recap. 2 *her repetition of his words* repeating, restatement, echoing, parroting, quoting, copying. 3 *a repetition of his previous actions*

repeat, redoing, duplication. 4 *a lot of repetition in the essay* repetitiousness, redundancy, tautology.

repetitive adj *repetitive tasks/work* recurrent, unchanging, unvaried, undiversified, monotonous, tedious, boring, mechanical, automatic; *inf* samey.

replace v 1 *replace the book on the shelf* put back, return, restore. 2 *he will replace the retired teacher* take the place of, succeed, supersede, follow after, come after, supplant, substitute for, stand in for, act for, fill in for, cover for, act as locum for, understudy. 3 *replace the broken vase* give in place of, give as a replacement for, give in return/exchange for.

replacement n *find a replacement for the retired teacher* successor, substitute, stand-in, fill-in, locum, understudy, proxy, surrogate.

replenish v 1 *replenish one's glass/plate* refill, top up, fill up, recharge, reload. 2 *replenish stocks of food* stock up, fill up, make up, replace, renew.

replete adj 1 *guests feeling replete* full, full up, full to bursting, satiated, sated, glutted, gorged, stuffed, well-fed. 2 *replete shelves* full, well-stocked, well-provided, brimful, brimming, chock-full, jam-packed, crammed, teeming.

replica n copy, carbon copy, duplicate, facsimile, model, reproduction, imitation.

reply v 1 *reply to his question/letter* answer, make answer, respond to, acknowledge, write back. 2 *"not likely," she replied* answer, respond, rejoin, retort, return, riposte, come back, counter.

reply n answer, response, acknowledgement, rejoinder, retort, return, riposte, come back.

report n 1 *a report of the accident* account, statement, record, exposition, delineation. 2 *newspaper/television reports* article, piece, account, story, write-up, communication, communiqué, dispatch, bulletin. 3 *a company's financial report* formal statement, record, register, chronicle. 4 *according to report he is a miser* rumour, hearsay, talk, gossip, tittle-tattle; *inf* the grapevine. 5 *a person of good report* reputation, repute, regard, character, name. 6 *the report of a gun/explosion* bang, boom, crack, crash, rumble, reverberation, noise, sound, echo.

report v 1 *report the latest findings* bring word about, announce, pass on, communicate, relay, relate, tell, recount, give an account of, set forth, document, narrate, describe, delineate, detail, divulge, disclose, circulate. **2** *journalists reporting on events in Russia* write, write an account of, broadcast. **3** *report the child for cheating* tell on, inform on, accuse, make a charge/complaint against; *inf* grass on, squeal on, rat on. **4** *they will report at noon* present oneself, be present, appear, arrive, come, turn up, clock on/in; *inf* show up. **5** *report the proceedings of the conference* record, document, minute, write up, chronicle, write down, take down.

reporter n journalist, newsman, newswoman, pressman, correspondent, writer, broadcaster, announcer, presenter, news commentator; *inf* newshound, hack.

repose n **1** *seek repose after work* rest, relaxation, leisure, ease, inactivity, respite, time off, breathing-space, sleep, slumber. **2** *a place of repose in the mountains* quiet, quietness, quietude, calm, calmness, tranquillity, peace, peacefulness, stillness, silence, hush. **3** *her face looked sad in repose* relaxation, inactivity, stillness, idleness.

repose v **1** *workers reposing after their labours* rest, relax, take one's ease, take a break, sleep, slumber; *inf* take it easy. **2** *reposing on couches* lie, lie down, recline, stretch out, sprawl.

repository n store, storehouse, storeroom, reservoir, bank, safe, cache, receptacle, container.

reprehensible adj blameworthy, blamable, reproachable, censurable, condemnable, reprovable, culpable, erring, errant, wrong, bad, shameful, disgraceful, discreditable, dishonourable, ignoble, objectionable, odious, opprobrious, unpardonable, indefensible, unjustifiable, inexcusable.

represent v **1** *X represents the larger number | the tent represents home for them* stand for, correspond to, be the counterpart of, equal, be equivalent to, symbolize, mean, betoken. **2** *John Bull represents the spirit of Britain* stand for, symbolize, personify, epitomize, typify. **3** *the old man represents their idea of a Frenchman* embody, incorporate, typify, exemplify, be a sample/specimen of. **4** *the saint is usually represented as a young child* depict, portray, delineate, illustrate, picture, denote, paint, draw, sketch, exhibit, shown, display, evoke. **5** *he represents Hamlet in the play* act, enact, portray, appear as, perform as. **6** *they represented Twelfth Night in Stratford* present, produce, put on, show, stage. **7** *he represented the children at the hearing* act for, appear for, speak for, be spokesperson for, be the representative of. **8** *he represents the constituency/ward* be the councillor/MP for, have the vote of.

9 *he represented himself as a qualified doctor* describe as, pass off as, pose as, pretend to be. **10** *represent their grievances to the committee* present, put/bring forward, set forth, state.

representation n **1** *the representation of the saint as a young child* depiction, portrayal, portrait, delineation, illustration, picture, painting, drawing, sketch, image, model. **2** *their representation of Twelfth Night* presentation, production, performance, show, play, spectacle. **3** *have the best representation at the court/conference* spokesman, spokeswoman, spokesperson, representative, agent, deputy, ambassador, envoy, delegate; delegation, deputation. **4** *make representations to the court* statement, account, report, declaration, allegation, argument, protestation, remonstrance, expostulation.

representative adj **1** *a representative specimen | a specimen representative of its genus* typical, archetypal, exemplary, characteristic, indicative, illustrative. **2** *John Bull is representative of Britain* emblematic, symbolic, evocative. **3** *a representative body* elected, elective, chosen, delegated, ambassadorial, authorized, accredited, official.

representative n **1** *a typical representative of its class* example, exemplification, exemplar, specimen, type, archetype, illustration, epitome, embodiment. **2** *he is the society's representative* spokesman, spokeswoman, spokesperson, agent, deputy, proxy. **3** *he is a sales representative* commercial traveller, travelling salesman, traveller, agent; *inf* rep. **4** *our country's representative at the conference* delegate, commissioner, ambassador, envoy. **5** *the town's representative in Parliament | our representative on the council* Member of Parliament, MP, Member, deputy, councillor.

repress v **1** *tyrants repressing the people* subjugate, conquer, vanquish, overpower, overcome, crush, master, dominate, domineer, bully, intimidate, oppress, tyrannize. **2** *repress a rebellion* put down, quell, quash, squash, subdue, suppress, extinguish, stamp out, stop, put an end to. **3** *repress a laugh | repress his desire* hold/keep back, hold in, bite back, restrain, suppress, keep in check, check, inhibit, bottle up, silence, muffle, stifle, smother.

repressed adj **1** *a repressed people* subjugated, oppressed, tyrannized. *see* REPRESS 1. **2** *a repressed laugh* restrained, suppressed, muffled, smothered. **3** *a repressed child* inhibited, withdrawn, restrained.

repression n **1** *the repression of the people* subjugation, domination, oppression, tyrannization. *see* REPRESS 1. **2** *the repression of the rebellion* quelling, quashing, suppression. *see* REPRESS 2. **3** *a regime of repression* tyranny, despotism, oppression, dictatorship, authoritarianism, domination, coercion, suppression, subjugation. **4** *the repression of a laugh* holding back, biting back, restraint, suppression, smothering. *see* REPRESS 3.

repressive adj *a repressive regime* repressing, tyrannical, despotic, dictatorial, authoritarian, dominating, oppressive, coercive, suppressive, harsh, severe, strict, cruel.

reprieve v **1** *reprieve the condemned man* postpone/delay punishment of, remit/cancel punishment of, grant a stay of execution to, let off, pardon; *inf* let off the hook. **2** *the building has been reprieved for a while* give a respite to, save, rescue.

reprieve n *the condemned man has had a reprieve* postponement of punishment, remission/cancellation of punishment, stay of execution, pardon; *inf* let-off.

reprimand n *receive a reprimand from the teacher* rebuke, scolding, chiding, reproach, reproof, reproval, lecture, admonition, berating, upbraiding, castigation, tongue-lashing; *inf* row, talking-to, telling-off, ticking-off, dressing-down, wigging, bawling-out.

reprimand v *reprimand the pupils* rebuke, scold, chide, reproach, reprove, lecture, admonish, berate, upbraid, castigate, take to task, haul over the coals, blame, censure, check; *inf* give a row to, give a talking-to, tell off, tick off, give a dressing-down/wigging to, bawl out.

reprisal n retaliation, revenge, vengeance, retribution, redress, requital, recrimination, an eye for an eye, tit for tat.

reproach v *reproach the government/pupils for their actions* criticize, find fault with, censure, blame, admonish, condemn, reprehend, disparage, abuse, reprimand, scold, chide, reprove, berate, upbraid, castigate, take to task, haul over the coals; *inf* give a dressing-down to.

reproach n **1** *words of reproach* criticism, fault-finding, censuring, admonition, condemnation, abuse, reprimand, scolding, reproof, reproval, upbraiding. *see* REPROACH v. **2** *the ugly building is a reproach to the town* discredit, disgrace, shame, source of shame, stigma, blemish, stain, slur. **3** *her behaviour brought reproach to the family* discredit, disgrace, shame, dishonour, disrepute, ignominy, scorn, contempt, opprobrium, odium, obloquy.

reproachful adj disapproving, disappointed, critical, censorious, admonitory, condemnatory, disparaging, reproving, castigatory.

reproduce v **1** *the copier can reproduce colour photographs* copy, make a copy of, duplicate, replicate, photocopy, xerox, mimeograph, print, transcribe, clone. **2** *reproduce the effect* repeat, recreate, redo, remake, imitate, follow, emulate, echo, mirror, parallel, match, mimic, ape. **3** *the animals seem unable to reproduce* breed, procreate, bear young, produce offspring, give birth, multiply, propagate, proliferate, spawn.

reproduction n **1** *the reproduction of colour photographs* copying, duplicating, photocopying, xeroxing, printing. *see* REPRODUCE 1. **2** *a reproduction of the painting* copy, duplicate, replica, facsimile, imitation, print. **3** *a reproduction of the photograph* copy, duplicate, facsimile, fax, photocopy, mimeograph, print; *Trademark* Xerox. **4** *animal reproduction* breeding, procreation, producing young, multiplying, propagation, proliferation.

reproof n **1** *without a word of reproof* reproval, disapproval, disapprobation, reproach, admonition, castigation, criticism, censure, blame, condemnation. **2** *ignore their reproofs* rebuke, scolding, chiding, reproach, lecture, admonition, berating, upbraiding, castigation, criticism, fault-finding, censure.

reprove v *reprove the pupils* rebuke, scold, chide, reproach, reprove, lecture, admonish, berate, upbraid, castigate, take to task, haul over the coals, criticize, check, censure, blame, condemn; *inf* give a row to, give a talking-to, tell off, tick off, give a dressing-down to, bawl out.

repudiate v **1** *repudiate one's son/faith* disown, cast off, cut off, abandon, forsake, desert, discard, reject, renounce, disavow, abjure, turn one's back on, have nothing to do with, wash one's hands of. **2** *repudiate a charge/claim* deny, contradict, gainsay, disclaim, disavow. **3** *repudiate a treaty* reject, rescind, revoke, cancel, set aside, overrule, override, disregard, ignore, flout, spurn, dishonour, disobey.

repugnance n abhorrence, aversion, revulsion, repulsion, disgust, nausea, distaste, antipathy, dislike, loathing, hatred, reluctance, contempt, odium.

repugnant adj abhorrent, revolting, repulsive, repellent, disgusting, sickening, nauseating, disagreeable, distasteful, offensive, objectionable, obnoxious, loathsome, off-putting, hateful, despicable, reprehensible, contemptible, abominable, horrible, horrid, foul, nasty, vile, ugly, odious, heinous.

repulsive adj abhorrent, revolting, repellent, disgusting, sickening, nauseating, disagreeable, distasteful, offensive, objectionable, obnoxious, loathsome, off-putting, hateful, despicable, reprehensible, contemptible, abominable, horrible, foul, nasty, vile, ugly, odious, heinous.

reputable adj of repute, of good repute, respectable, respected, well-thought-of, esteemed, estimable, worthy, creditable, reliable, dependable, conscientious, trustworthy, honest, honourable, above-board, legitimate, upright, virtuous, good, excellent.

reputation n **1** *have an honest/dishonest reputation* name, estimation, character, repute, standing, position, status, station, rank. **2** *she has lost her reputation* good name, good character, good standing, respect, respectability, repute, esteem, fame, celebrity, renown. **3** *the shop has lost its reputation as a good restaurant* name, standing, position, status, stature.

repute n **1** *a house of ill repute* reputation, name, character. *see* REPUTATION 1. **2** *they are firms of repute* good reputation, good name, high standing, stature, esteem, fame, renown, celebrity, distinction. *see* REPUTATION 2.

repute v *he is reputed to be a good player | reputed to be the father* think, believe, consider, held, suppose, reckon, judge, assume, presume.

reputedly adv *he is reputedly the father* supposedly, allegedly, apparently, seemingly.

request n **1** *come at his request* asking, entreaty, solicitation, petitioning, application, imploration, begging, pleading, behest, supplication, demand, summons, requisition. **2** *make several requests* entreaty, appeal, petition, plea, behest, demand, call, suit.

request v *request a favour* ask for, solicit, seek, apply for, put in for, call for, entreat, beseech, beg for, plead for, pray for, petition, implore, sue for, supplicate for, requisition, demand, desire.

require v **1** *we require peace and quiet* need, have need of, stand in need of, lack, be short of, be deficient in, want, wish, desire, crave, miss. **2** *absolute obedience is required* demand, order, command, call for, insist on, ask for, request. **3** *they required him to go* order, instruct, command, oblige, enjoin, bid, compel. **4** *the job requires patience* call for, demand, necessitate, involve, take.

required adj *required reading* compulsory, obligatory, mandatory, prescribed, recommended, set, essential, necessary, vital.

requirement n **1** *list your travel requirements* need, want, lack, must, necessity, necessary/essential item, demand. **2** *what are the requirements for the job?* prerequisite, requisite, precondition, specification, qualification, *sine qua non*, stipulation.

requisite adj *the requisite amount* required, prerequisite, needed, necessary, essential, indispensable, vital, called-for, demanded, obligatory, mandatory.

requisite n **1** *list your holiday requisites* requirement, need, want. *see* REQUIREMENT 1. **2** *what are the requisites for the job?* requirement, prerequisite, precondition, specification, qualification. *see* REQUIREMENT 2.

requisition n **1** *put in a requisition for supplies* application, order, claim, request, call, demand, summons. **2** *the requisition of their farm building* commandeering, appropriation, possession, occupation, seizure, confiscation.

requisition v **1** *requisition for more books* apply for, order, put in a claim for, request, call for, demand. **2** *soldiers requisitioned the farm buildings* commandeer, appropriate, take over, take possession of, occupy, seize, confiscate.

rescind v repeal, revoke, reverse, abrogate, retract, countermand, overturn, annul, disannul, nullify, declare null and void, void, quash, invalidate, cancel, set aside.

rescue v save, save/deliver from danger, save the life of, come to the aid of, free, set free/loose, release, liberate, emancipate, get out, extricate, redeem, salvage, relieve.

rescue n rescuing, saving, deliverance, delivery, freeing, release, liberation, emancipation, extrication, redemption, salvage, relief. *see* RESCUE V.

research n *carry out medical research* investigation, experimentation, fact-finding, testing, exploration, analysis, examination, scrutiny; experiment, assessment, study, review, inquiry, probe, inspection; tests.

research v *research the new drug* do tests on, investigate, inquire into, look into, probe, explore, analyse, study, examine, scrutinize, review, inspect, experiment with, assess.

resemblance n **1** *the resemblance between them* likeness, alikeness, similarity, similitude, semblance, identicalness, sameness, uniformity, correspondence, comparability, comparison, parallelism, parity, analogy, affinity, closeness, nearness, agreement, congruity, concurrence, conformity. **2** *this is a resemblance of their father* likeness, representation, image; photograph, painting.

resemble v *he resembles his brother|his work resembles hers* be like, look like, bear a resemblance to, be similar to, put one in mind of, remind one of, take after, echo, mirror, parrot, duplicate, parallel; *inf* favour.

resent v feel aggrieved at, take offence/ umbrage at, take exception to, take amiss, be annoyed/angry at, begrudge, feel bitter about, dislike.

resentful adj aggrieved, offended, indignant, irritated, displeased, annoyed, angry, irate, incensed, piqued, in high dudgeon, grudging, bitter, embittered, wounded; *inf* huffed, huffy, in a huff, miffed, peeved.

resentment n offense, indignation, irritation, displeasure, annoyance, anger, ire, pique, grudgingness, bitterness, animosity, hostility; hard feelings.

reservation n **1** *the reservation of some supplies* putting aside, conservation, saving, retention, storing. *see* RESERVE v 1. **2** *the reservation of a room* booking, engaging, prearranging. *see* RESERVE v 2. **3** *make a reservation* advance booking, booking, engagement, prearrangement; charter/hire arrangements. **4** *have reservations concerning the plan|go ahead with some reservation* qualification, proviso, provision, condition, stipulation, limitation, qualm, scruple; hesitancy, doubt, demur. **5** *an American Indian reservation* reserve, preserve, enclave, sanctuary, tract, area, territory.

reserve v **1** *reserve some food for later* put/set/ lay aside, put away, keep back, keep, withhold, conserve, save, retain, store, hoard, stockpile; *inf* hang on to. **2** *reserve a room* book, engage, arrange for, prearrange for, bespeak, charter, hire. **3** *reserve judgement* put off, postpone, defer, delay, withhold. **4** *reserve the right to refuse* keep, retain, secure; *inf* hang on to.

reserve n **1** *we have reserves of steel* store, stock, supply, reservoir, pool, cache, fund, stockpile, accumulation, backlog, hoard. **2** *agree with some reserve* reservation, qualification, proviso, condition, limitation, stipulation, qualm, scruple. *see* RESERVATION 4. **3** *her reserve puts people off* self-restraint, restraint, self-control, constraint, aloofness, detachment, distance, remoteness, formality, coolness, coldness, frigidity, reticence, unapproachability, uncommunicativeness, unresponsiveness, shyness, diffidence, secretiveness, taciturnity, silence. **4** *a nature reserve* preserve, reserva-

tion, sanctuary, park, tract, territory, area. **in reserve** available, at hand, to hand, obtainable, accessible, at one's disposal, on tap.

reserve adj *a reserve player* in reserve, spare, extra, auxiliary, substitute, alternate.

reserved adj **1** *reserved supplies* conserved, stored, stockpiled. *see* RESERVE n 1. **2** *the table is reserved|reserved rooms* booked, engaged, prearranged, taken, spoken for, chartered, hired. **3** *she is reserved but he is outgoing* self-restrained, aloof, detached, remote, formal, unemotional, undemonstrative, cool, cold, frigid, reticent, unapproachable, uncommunicative, unsociable, unfriendly, unresponsive, unforthcoming, shy, retiring, diffident, secret, secretive, taciturn, silent.

reservoir n **1** *picnic by the reservoir* water source/supply; lake, loch, pool, pond. **2** *pour liquid into the reservoir* container, receptacle, holder, tank, cask, bowl, basin. **3** *reservoir of supplies/knowledge* reserve, store, stock, supply, pool, cache, fund, stockpile. *see* RESERVE n 1.

reside v **1** *he resides in London* live in, dwell in, stay in, sojourn in, inhabit, occupy, be settled in, lodge in; *inf* hang out in. **2** *the strength residing in his personality* be inherent in, be intrinsic to, be contained/present in, rest in, lie in, dwell in, abide in, exist in. **3** *the authority residing in him* vested in, bestowed on, conferred on.

residence n **1** *his residence is in London* house, home, place, dwelling, domicile, habitation; quarters, lodgings. **2** *take up residence tomorrow|a residence of five years* occupation, occupancy, habitation, inhabitation, tenancy, stay, sojourn.

resident n *all residents pay taxes* inhabitant, occupant, occupier, householder, dweller, resider, sojourner, tenant, local, denizen.

resident adj **1** *a resident housekeeper* live-in, living-in. **2** *the resident population* inhabiting, dwelling, neighbourhood, local.

residue n residuum, remainder, remnant, rest, surplus, extra, excess, balance; remains, leftovers, dregs, lees.

resign v **1** *he resigned yesterday* give notice, hand in one's notice, leave, quit. **2** *resigned from his post* give up, leave, quit, vacate, retire from. **3** *resign his right to the title* renounce, relinquish, give up, abdicate, surrender, cede. **4** *resign oneself to losing* reconcile oneself. *see* RESIGNED 1.

resignation n **1** *his resignation from his post* leaving, quitting, vacating, retirement. **2** *the resignation of his claim* renunciation, relinquishment, abdication. *see* RESIGN 3.

3 *hand over his resignation* letter of resignation, notice, notice to quit. **4** *accept the decision with resignation* resignedness, acceptance, compliance, non-resistance, submission, passivity, patience, forbearance, sufferance, toleration, endurance.

resigned adj **1** *resigned to the fact that he would fail* reconciled, acquiescent, submitting, yielding, bowing, acceding. **2** *give a resigned shrug | take a resigned attitude* complaint, unresisting, non-resistant, unprotesting, passive, submissive, subdued, docile, patient, long-suffering, forbearing, tolerant, enduring, stoical.

resilient adj **1** *a resilient material* elastic, springy, rubbery, whippy, flexible, pliant, supple, pliable, plastic. **2** *children are resilient after upsets* quick to recover, quick to bounce back, difficult to keep down, irrepressible, tough, strong, hardy.

resist v **1** *material resisting the action of the rain* withstand, be proof against, repel. **2** *resist the march of progress* stop, halt, prevent, check, stem, curb, obstruct, hinder, impede, block, thwart, frustrate, inhibit, restrain. **3** *resist smoking* abstain from, refrain from, keep from, forbear from, desist from, forgo, avoid. **4** *resist the invading army* fight, battle against, stand up to, withstand, stand one's ground against, hold out against, defy, oppose, confront, struggle against, contend with.

resistance n **1** *their resistance to progress* curb, obstruction, hindrance, impediment, block. *see* RESIST 2. **2** *their resistance against the invaders* fight, battle, opposition, stand, defiance, confrontation, struggle, contention.

resistant adj *material resistant to water | diseases resistant to drugs* proof against, impervious to, unaffected by, unsusceptible to, immune to.

resolute adj determined, resolved, decided, firm, fixed, set, intent, steadfast, constant, earnest, staunch, bold, courageous, serious, purposeful, deliberate, inflexible, unyielding, unwavering, unfaltering, unhesitating, unswerving, unflinching, obstinate, obdurate, strong-willed, dogged, persevering, persistent, tenacious, relentless, unshakable, dedicated.

resolution n **1** *admire the resolution of the competitors* resolve, determination, firmness, intentness, steadfastness, constancy, staunchness, boldness, courage, seriousness, purpose, purposefulness, obstinacy, obdurateness, obduracy, will-power, doggedness, perseverance, persistence, tenacity, staying power, dedication. *see* RESOLUTE. **2** *it is our resolution to proceed* resolve, decision, aim, intent, intention, purpose, object, plan, design, aspiration. **3** *the committee/court passed a resolution* motion, declaration, decree, verdict, judgement. **4** *the resolution of the problem/question will take time* resolving, solving, solution, answer, sorting out, working out, unravelling, disentanglement, cracking.

resolve v **1** *he resolved to leave* decide, make up one's mind, determine, settle on, undertake. **2** *resolve the problem* solve, answer, sort out, work out, clear up, fathom, unravel, disentangle, crack. **3** *resolve their doubts* dispel, remove, banish, clear up. **4** *resolve the compound* break down, break up, separate, divide, disintegrate, reduce, dissolve, analyse, anatomize, dissect.

resolve n **1** *their resolve is to win* resolution, decision, aim, intent, intention, purpose. *see* RESOLUTION 2. **2** *set out with resolve* resolution, determination, firmness of purpose, staunchness, boldness, courage, purposefulness, obstinacy, perseverance, dedication. *see* RESOLUTION 1.

resort v **1** *resort to force* fall back on, turn to, have recourse to, look to, make use of, use, utilize, avail oneself of, bring into play/service, exercise. **2** *tourists resorting to the beaches* head for, go to, repair to, visit, frequent, haunt.

resort n **1** *a beautiful resort | holiday/health resort* holiday/tourist centre, haunt, centre, spot, retreat. **2** *your only resort is to ask the police* recourse, source of help, expedient, measure, alternative, choice, possibility, hope. **3** *without resort to violence* recourse, turning to, utilizing. *see* RESORT v 1.

resound v **1** *caves resounding with the noise of waves* reverberate, resonate, echo, ring. **2** *her fame/discovery resounded throughout Europe* be talked about, be made known, spread, circulate, be proclaimed, be famed, be celebrated, be glorified.

resounding adj **1** *resounding tones* reverberating, resonating, resonant, echoing, ringing, sonorous, vibrant. **2** *the fête was a resounding success* very great, emphatic, striking, impressive, outstanding, notable, noteworthy.

resource n **1** *use any resource to find help* expedient, resort, course, way, device; means. **2** *draw on one's coal resources* reserve, reservoir, store, stock, supply, pool, fund, stockpile, accumulation, hoard. **3** *person of resource* resourcefulness, initiative, ingenuity, inventiveness, quick-wittedness, cleverness, native wit, talent, ability, capability.

4 *rely on their country's resources* assets, reserves, materials; wealth.

resourceful adj ingenious, inventive, creative, imaginative, quick-witted, clever, bright, sharp, talented, gifted, able, capable.

respect n **1** *their respect for their teacher* esteem, high regard, regard, high opinion, admiration, approbation, approval, appreciation, veneration, reverence, deference, honour, praise, homage. **2** *treat the old lady with respect* deference, consideration, thoughtfulness, attentiveness, politeness, courtesy, civility. **3** *without any respect for/to rhythm* heed, regard, consideration, attention, notice. **4** *correct in all respects* aspect, facet, feature, way, sense, characteristic, particular, point, detail, matter. **5** *with respect to the matter in hand* reference, relevance, regard, relation, connection, bearing.

respect v **1** *they respect their teacher* esteem, have a high opinion of, think highly of, admire, approve of, appreciate, venerate, revere, honour, praise. **2** *they respect his judgement* think highly of, have a high opinion of, value, set store by. **3** *respect other people's privacy | respect the environment* show consideration/regard for, take into consideration, take cognizance of, observe, pay heed/attention to. **4** *respect her wishes | respect the treaty* heed, observe, comply with, follow, abide by, adhere to, obey.

respectable adj **1** *a respectable woman/background* reputable, of good repute, upright, honest, honourable, trustworthy, aboveboard, worthy, decent, good, virtuous, admirable, well-bred, proper, decorous. **2** *a respectable effort* reasonable, fair, passable, tolerable, adequate, satisfactory; *inf* not bad. **3** *earn a respectable salary* reasonable, fairly good, fair, considerable, ample, sizable, substantial; *inf* not to be sneezed at.

respective adj individual, separate, personal, own, particular, specific, various.

respects npl *send/pay one's respects* greetings, regards, best wishes, compliments, remembrances.

respite n **1** *a respite from work* rest, break, breathing spell, interval, intermission, recess, lull, pause, hiatus, halt; relief, relaxation; *inf* breather, let-up. **2** *a respite from the penalty* remission, reprieve, stay, stay of execution, suspension, postponement, adjournment, deferment, delay, moratorium.

respond v **1** *respond to his question/letter* answer, reply to, say in response to, acknowledge. **2** *"No," she responded* say in response, answer, reply, rejoin, retort, return, riposte, come back, counter. **3** *they responded to his action by hitting him* react to, act in response to.

response n **1** *the children gave no response to the question* answer, reply, acknowledgement, rejoinder, retort, return, riposte, comeback. **2** *receive a good response to their questionnaire* reply, reaction, feedback; *inf* comeback.

responsibility n **1** *it is his responsibility to get us there* charge, duty, onus, task, role, liability, accountability, answerability. **2** *the confusion was his responsibility* blame, fault, guilt, culpability. **3** *people of responsibility* maturity, adultness, reason, sanity, sense, common sense, soundness, stability, reliability, dependability, trustworthiness, competence, conscientiousness. *see* RESPONSIBLE 4. **4** *a post of responsibility* authority, control, power.

responsible adj **1** *he is responsible for the production department* in charge/control of, accountable for, liable for; *inf* at the helm of. **2** *who is responsible for the confusion?* accountable, answerable, to blame, blameworthy, at fault, guilty, culpable. **3** *he is responsible to the president* answerable to, accountable to. **4** *the children are very responsible* mature, adult, rational, sane, reasonable, sensible, level-headed, sound, stable, reliable, dependable, trustworthy, competent, conscientious, hard-working, industrious. **5** *a responsible position* authoritative, executive, decision-making, powerful, high, important.

responsive adj *a responsive audience* quick to react, reactive, receptive, forthcoming, sensitive, perceptive, sympathetic, susceptible, impressionable, open, alive, awake, aware, sharp.

rest[1] n **1** *seek rest after work* repose, relaxation, leisure, ease, inactivity, respite, time off, breathing-space, sleep, slumber. **2** *have a rest after work* sleep, nap, doze, slumber, siesta; *inf* breather, snooze, forty winks, lie-down. **3** *go away for a rest* break, breathing-space, interval, interlude, intermission, lull, pause, holiday, vacation; time off. **4** *a place of rest in the mountains* repose, quiet, quietness, quietude, calm, calmness, tranquillity, peace, peacefulness, stillness, silence, hush. **5** *a rest for the vase* stand, base, holder, support, prop, shelf.

rest[1] v **1** *invalids resting* take a rest, put one's feet up, relax, sit down, lie down, go to bed, sleep, take a nap, nap, catnap, doze, slumber; *inf* take it easy, snooze. **2** *she rested her hands on the table* support, prop, steady, lie, place, position. **3** *the shelf rests on bricks* be supported by, be propped up by, lie on, be laid on, recline on, stand on, sit on. **4** *the result rests on the decision of the jury* depend, rely, hang, hinge, be based, be founded.

rest² n *some will go; the rest will stay* remainder, residue, residuum, balance, remnant, surplus, excess, rump; those left, others, remains, leftovers.

rest² v **1** *you may rest assured* remain, stay, continue, be left. **2** *the arrangements rest with you* be the responsibility of, be down to, lie, reside.

restful adj **1** *a restful effect* calming, relaxing, soothing, tranquillizing. **2** *a restful place* quiet, calm, tranquil, relaxed, peaceful, placid, still, languid, undisturbed, unhurried, sleepy.

restitution n reparation, redress, atonement, recompense, compensation, indemnification, indemnity, requital, retribution, remuneration, reimbursement, repayment; amends.

restive adj **1** *restive children on a Friday afternoon* restless, fidgety, fidgeting. **2** *the crowd grew restive* uneasy, ill at ease, edgy, on edge, tense, worked up, nervous, agitated, unquiet; *inf* jittery, uptight. **3** *police trying to cope with restive demonstrators* unruly, unmanageable, uncontrollable, refractory, recalcitrant.

restless adj **1** *pass a restless night* sleepless, wakeful, tossing and turning, fitful. **2** *the crowd grew restive*, ill at ease, on edge, agitated. *see* RESTIVE 2. **3** *the restless sea* moving, in motion, on the move, changeable, changing. **4** *restless bands of people* unsettled, roaming, roving, wandering, itinerant travelling, nomadic, peripatetic. **5** *restless children* restless, fidgety, fidgeting.

restoration n **1** *the restoration of the building* renovation, repair, reconditioning, rehabilitation, refurbishment, rebuilding. *see* RESTORE 1. **2** *the invalid's restoration* recovery, resuscitation, revitalization. *see* RESTORE 2. **3** *the restoration of democracy* reinstitution, re-establishment, reinstatement, reinstallation. *see* RESTORE 5.

restore v **1** *restore the building* renovate, repair, fix, mend, set to rights, recondition, rehabilitate, refurbish, rebuild, reconstruct, remodel, revamp, redecorate, touch up; *inf* do up, fix up. **2** *a rest will help to restore him* build up, resuscitate, revitalize, refresh, revive, revivify. **3** *restore the dog to its owner* return, give back, hand back, send back. **4** *restore the vase to the shelf* put back, return, replace, reinstate. **5** *restore democ-*

racy re-establish, reinstitute, reinstate, reinstall, reinforce, reimpose.

restrain v **1** *restrain the unruly children/crowd* control, keep under control, hold in check, curb, keep within bounds, subdue. **2** *restrain one's anger* control, check, suppress, repress, contain, smother, stifle, bottle up, rein in; *inf* keep the lid on. **3** *restrain the boy from jumping* prevent, hold back, hinder, impede, obstruct, delay, inhibit. **4** *restrain the thieves* tie up, bind, chain up, fetter, pinnion, confine, lock up, imprison, detain, arrest.

restrained adj **1** *he's very restrained but she is outgoing* self-restrained, self-controlled, controlled, unemotional, undemonstrative, calm, reticent. **2** *restrained colours* muted, subdued, discreet, subtle, quiet, unobtrusive, understated, tasteful.

restraint n **1** *he acts as a restraint on their impulsiveness* constraint, check, curb, barrier, block, hindrance, impediment, deterrent, inhibition. **2** *behave with restraint* self-restraint, self-control, self-discipline, moderation, temperateness, prudence, judiciousness. **3** *her restraint puts people off* self-restraint, self-control, self-possession, reserve, lack of emotion, coldness, formality, aloofness, detachment, reticence, uncommunicativeness. **4** *put the thieves under restraint* confinement, detention, imprisonment, incarceration, bondage, strait-jacket; bonds, chains, fetters, manacles. **5** *furnished with restraint* mutedness, discretion, subtlety, understatedness, taste, tastefulness, discrimination.

restrict v **1** *restrict movement* hinder, impede, hamper, retard, handicap, cramp. **2** *restrict your food consumption* limit, set/impose limits on, keep within bounds, keep under control, regulate, control, moderate. **3** *restrict the prisoners* restrain, confine, lock up, imprison, wall up, hem in.

restricted adj **1** *a restricted space* cramped, confined. **2** *a restricted intake* limited, controlled, regulated, moderate. **3** *a restricted area* out of bounds, off limits; private, closed off.

restriction n **1** *impose currency restrictions* constraint, limitation, control, check, curb, regulation, condition, provision, proviso, stipulation, qualification, demarcation. **2** *the restriction of the space* confinement, crampedness, constraint. **3** *restriction of movement* hindrance, impediment, handicap.

result n **1** *pleased with the result of the talks* outcome, consequence, issue, upshot, sequel, effect, reaction, repercussion, event, end, conclusion, termination, aftermath, product, by-product; fruits. **2** *the wrong result to the addition* answer, solution.

result v **1** *a fight resulted from the discussion* follow, ensue, issue, develop, stem, arise, evolve, emerge, emanate, occur, happen, come about, eventuate. **2** *it resulted in a draw* end in, culminate in, finish in, terminate in.

resume v **1** *resume after lunch* take up, carry on, continue, proceed, go on, recommence, restart, start/begin again. **2** *resume negotiations* take up, carry on, continue, recommence, begin again, reopen, reinstitute. **3** *resume one's seat* take up again, reoccupy, occupy again. **4** *resume ownership* take up again, take back, recover, assume again.

résumé n *present a résumé of the events* summary, précis, synopsis, abstract, epitome, outline, sketch, abridgement, digest.

resurrect v **1** *Jesus was resurrected* raise from the dead, restore to life, bring back to life. **2** *resurrect old plans/practices* revive, breathe new life into, give new life to, bring back, restore, resuscitate, revitalize, reintroduce, reinstall, re-establish; *inf* give the kiss of life to.

resurrection n **1** *the resurrection of Jesus* raising from the dead, rising/return from the dead. **2** *the resurrection of old practices* revival, rebirth, renaissance, restoration, resuscitation, reintroduction, reinstallation, re-establishment, comeback.

resuscitate v **1** *resuscitate him after his collapse* give artificial respiration to, bring round, revive, save; *inf* give the kiss of life to. **2** *resuscitate old practices* revive, resurrect, breathe new life into, bring back, restore, reintroduce; *inf* give the kiss of life to. *see* RESURRECT 2.

retain v **1** *retain his job | retain the title* keep, keep possession/hold of, hold on/fast to; *inf* hang on to. **2** *retain the old system* keep, maintain, continue, preserve, reserve. **3** *retain the facts* keep/bear in mind, memorize, remember, call to mind, recall, recollect. **4** *retain a gardener* hire, employ, engage, commission, pay.

retainer n **1** *pension off old retainers* attendant, servant, domestic; valet, footman. **2** *pay him a retainer in the holidays* retaining fee, partial payment, fee, deposit, advance.

retaliate v return like for like, give tit for tat, give as good as one gets, get one's own back, get back at, make reprisal(s), take/exact/wreak revenge, avenge oneself, exact retribution, reciprocate, get even with, even the scores, settle a score.

retard v slow down, slow up, hold back, set back, hold up, delay, hinder, hamper, obstruct, impede, decelerate, put a brake on, check, arrest, interfere with, interrupt, thwart, frustrate.

retch v gag, heave, dry-heave, vomit, be sick, spew; *Amer* keck; *inf* throw up, puke.

reticence n reserve, restraint, diffidence, uncommunicativeness, secretiveness, quietness, taciturnity, silence. *see* RETICENT.

reticent adj reserved, restrained, diffident, uncommunicative, unforthcoming, secretive, tight-lipped, close-mouthed, quiet, taciturn, silent; *inf* mum.

retire v **1** *he retires at 65* give up work, stop working, be pensioned off; *inf* be put out to grass. **2** *the jury retired* withdraw, go away, go out, depart, exit, take oneself off, leave, absent oneself. **3** *they retire at midnight* go to bed, go to one's room; *inf* turn in, call it a day, hit the hay/sack. **4** *the troops retired, defeated* withdraw, pull back, fall back, pull out, give ground/way, retreat, decamp.

retirement n **1** *happy in his retirement* retired years, post-work years. **2** *the retirement of the jury* withdrawal, exit. *see* RETIRE 2. **3** *they chose to live in retirement from the world* retreat, seclusion, solitude, loneliness, privacy, obscurity.

retiring adj *a very retiring young woman* shy, diffident, bashful, self-effacing, shrinking, unassuming, unassertive, reserved, reticent, timid, timorous, nervous, modest, demure, coy, meek, humble.

retract v **1** *retract their horns | retracted his fishing line* draw in, pull in, pull back. **2** *retract one's statement* take back, withdraw, revoke, repeal, rescind, annul, cancel, abrogate, disavow, abjure, renounce, recant, disclaim, backtrack on, renege on, do an about-turn on.

retreat v **1** *the army retreated* withdraw, pull back, fall back, back off, give way/ground, decamp, depart, leave, flee, take flight, turn tail, beat a retreat, beat a hasty retreat. **2** *the tide retreated* go back, recede, ebb.

retreat n **1** *the retreat of the army* withdrawal, pulling back, decamping, departure, flight evacuation. *see* RETREAT v 1. **2** *he has a retreat in the mountains* refuge, haven, shelter, den, sanctuary, sanctum sanctorum, hideaway, resort, asylum. **3** *seek retreat from the world* retirement, seclusion, solitude, privacy, sanctuary.

retrench v **1** *the firm must retrench* cut back, make cut-backs/savings/economies, economize, reduce expenditure, tighten one's belt, husband one's resources; *inf* draw in one's horns. **2** *costs must be retrenched* curtail, limit, pare, prune, reduce, decrease, diminish.

retribution n punishment, justice, nemesis, what is coming to one, reckoning, reprisal, requital, retaliation, revenge, vengeance, an eye for an eye, tit for tat, measure for measure, redress, reparation, recompense, restitution; just deserts.

retrieve v **1** *retrieve one's property* get back, recover, regain, win back, recoup, redeem, reclaim, repossess, recapture, salvage, rescue. **2** *dogs retrieving sticks* fetch, bring back. **3** *difficult to retrieve the situation* set right, set/put to rights, repair, mend, remedy, rectify, redress, make good.

retrograde adj **1** *retrograde motion* backwards, directed backwards, retreating, retrogressive, reverse. **2** *retrograde policy* worsening, deteriorating, declining, on the downgrade/wane.

retrospect n **in retrospect** on looking/ thinking back, on reflection, with hindsight.

return v **1** *they returned at dawn* | *the symptoms returned* go back, come back, reappear, reoccur, come again, come round again. **2** *the ball/boomerang returned* rebound, recoil, boomerang. **3** *return milk bottles* | *return his love letters* give back, send back, take back, carry back, remit. **4** *return the books to the shelves* put back, replace, restore, reinstate, reinstall. **5** *return her greetings* reciprocate, repay, requite, send/ give in response to. **6** *the firm returned a profit* yield, bring in, earn, made, net. **7** *"No, I won't,"* *he returned* retort, reply, answer, respond, rejoin, riposte; *Amer* come back. **8** *return the ball* hit back, send back, throw back. **9** *return him as their candidate* elect, vote in, chose, select, pick. **10** *return a guilty verdict* bring in, deliver, announce, submit.

return n **1** *look forward to their return* homecoming, reappearance, reoccurrence. *see* RETURN v 1. **2** *the return of the ball/boomerang* rebound, recoil. **3** *the return of the books to the shelf* replacement, restoration, reinstatement, reinstallment. **4** *there have been several returns from the bookshops* thing returned, returned article, reject. **5** *the return on the investment* profit, yield, gain, income, revenue, interest, benefit. **6** *fill in a tax return* | *the school attendance return* statement, report, account, summary, form. **7** *he gave a haughty return* retort, reply, answer, response, rejoinder, riposte; *inf* comeback.

8 *done in return for your help* reciprocation, repayment, response, exchange.

reveal v **1** *the coat blew back to reveal a red dress* show, display, exhibit, expose to view. **2** *examination revealed a deep cut* bring to light, uncover, expose to view, lay bare, unearth, unveil, unmask. **3** *reveal the details of the affair* disclose, divulge, tell, let out, let on, let slip, give away, give out, leak, betray, make known/public, broadcast, publicize, publish, proclaim.

revel v **1** *party-goers revelling all night* celebrate, make merry, have a party, party, carouse, roister; *inf* live/whoop it up, go on a spree, have a fling, rave, paint the town red, push the boat out. **2** *revel in her victory* delight in, take pleasure in, bask in, rejoice in, relish, savour, gloat over, luxuriate in, wallow in.

revel n *noisy revels* celebration, festivity, jollification, merrymaking, carousal, carouse, bacchanal; *inf* spree, rave, bash, beanfeast, jag.

revelation n **1** *the revelation of the dress beneath* show, display, exhibition, exposure. **2** *the revelation of a deep cut* bringing to light, uncovering, unearthing. *see* REVEAL 2. **3** *the revelation of the details* disclosure, divulgence, telling, leak, betrayal, broadcasting, publicizing, communication, publishing, proclamation. *see* REVEAL 3. **4** *amazed at his revelations* disclosure, divulgence; private/ confidential information.

reveller n celebrator, party-goer, merry-maker, pleasure-seeker, carouser.

revelry n celebrations, festivities; jollification, merrymaking, carousal.

revenge n **1** *seek revenge* vengeance, retaliation, retribution, reprisal, requital, redress, satisfaction, eye for an eye, tit for tat, measure for measure. **2** *a heart full of revenge* vengefulness, vindictiveness, spite, spitefulness, malice, maliciousness, ill will, animosity, hostility, hate, hatred, venom, rancour, bitterness.

revenge v *revenge an injustice* | *revenge oneself* take revenge for, avenge, make retaliation for, retaliate, exact retribution for, take reprisals for, requite, get redress/satisfaction for.

revenue n income, return, yield, interest, gain; profits, returns, receipts, proceeds, takings, rewards.

reverberate v resound, echo, ring, vibrate.

revere v look up to, think highly of, admire, respect, esteem, defer to, honour, reverence, venerate, worship, pay homage to, adore, hold in awe, exalt, put on a pedestal, idolize.

reverence n *regard the leader with reverence* high esteem, admiration, respect, deference, honour, veneration, worship, homage, adoration, devotion, awe, exaltation.

reverence v *reverence the leader* revere, admire, respect, defer to, venerate, worship, adore, exalt, idolize. *see* REVERE.

reverent adj reverential, admiring, respectful, deferential, worshipping, adoring, loving, devoted, awed, submissive, humble, meek.

reversal n **1** *policy reversal* turn-round, turnabout, about-turn, about-face, volte-face, change of heart, tergiversation; *inf* U-turn. **2** *the reversal of roles* change, exchange, trading, trade-off, swapping. **3** *the reversal of the decision/verdict* overturn, overthrow, revocation, repeal, rescinding, annulment, invalidation. *see* REVERSE v 5. **4** *firms/families/armies suffering reversal* failure, misfortune, adversity, vicissitude; reverse, upset, set-back, check, defeat. *see* REVERSE n 3.

reverse v **1** *reverse the collar* turn round, put back to front. **2** *reverse the barrel* turn upside down, up-end, up-turn, invert. **3** *reverse the car* move/direct backwards, back. **4** *reverse roles* change, change round, exchange, trade, swap. **5** *reverse the decision* alter, change, countermand, undo, set aside, upset, overturn, overthrow, revoke, repeal, rescind, annul, nullify, declare null and void, void, invalidate, quash.

reverse adj **1** *a reverse trend* opposite, contrary, converse, counter, inverse, contrasting, antithetical. **2** *in reverse order* reversed, backwards, inverted, transposed, turned round.

reverse n **1** *the reverse is the case* opposite, contrary, converse, antithesis. **2** *write on the reverse* other side, back, rear, underside, wrong side, flip side, verso. **3** *the firm/family/army has suffered reverses* reversal, upset, set-back, check, non-success, failure, misfortune, mishap, misadventure, blow, disappointment; adversity, hardship, affliction, vicissitude, defeat, rout.

review n **1** *a review of the whole situation* survey, study, analysis, examination, scrutiny, assessment, appraisal. **2** *the salary structure is under review | undertake a salary review* reconsideration, re-examination, reassessment, re-evaluation, reappraisal, revision, rethink, another look, fresh look. **3** *the queen conducting a military review* inspection, parade, display, procession, march past. **4** *his review of the play* criticism, critique,

notice, assessment, evaluation, study, judgement, rating. **5** *publish a learned review* journal, periodical, magazine.

review v **1** *review the situation from their point of view* survey, study, analyse, examine, scrutinize, assess, appraise. **2** *it is more than time to review salaries* reconsider, rethink, re-examine, re-evaluate, reassess, reappraise, revise. **3** *review the past* remember, recall, recollect, reflect on, look back on, call to mind, summon up, evoke. **4** *review the troops* inspect, view, scrutinize. **5** *review the play/book* criticize, evaluate, assess, appraise, judge, weigh up, discuss. *see* REVIEW n 4.

reviewer n critic, literary/arts critic, commentator.

revise v **1** *revise the text* amend, emend, correct, alter, change, edit, rewrite, redraft, rework, update, revamp. **2** *revise our plans/opinions* reconsider, review, reassess, alter, change. **3** *revise the term's work* go over, reread, run through, study; *inf* swot/bone up on.

revision n **1** *the revision of the text* amendation, emendation, correction, alteration, editing, updating. *see* REVISE 1. **2** *the revision of our plans/opinions* reconsideration, alteration. **3** *get down to revision before the exam* studying; *inf* swotting. *see* REVISE 3.

revival n **1** *the revival of the collapsed man* resuscitation. *see* REVIVE 1. **2** *the revival of old traditions* resurrection, rebirth, renaissance, restoration, resuscitation, reintroduction, reinstallation, re-establishment; *inf* comeback.

revive v **1** *revive the man who collapsed* bring round, resuscitate, give artificial respiration to, save, restore to health; *inf* give the kiss of life to. **2** *the man soon revived* come round, recover consciousness, recover. **3** *a cup of tea revived her* refresh, restore, cheer up, comfort, enliven, revitalize. **4** *revive old traditions* revive, breathe new life into, give a new lease of life to, bring back, restore, resuscitate, resurrect, revitalize, reintroduce, reinstall, re-establish.

revoke v repeal, rescind, abrogate, countermand, annul, nullify, declare null and void, make void, void, invalidate, quash, set aside, cancel, retract, withdraw, recall, abjure, overrule, override, reverse.

revolt v **1** *the citizens revolted against the army* rise up, rise, take to the streets, take up arms, rebel, mutiny, show resistance (to). **2** *the filthy sight revolted me* repel, disgust, sicken, nauseate, make sick, turn one's stomach, be repugnant to, make one's flesh creep, put one off, offend, shock; *inf* turn one off, give one the creeps/heebie-jeebies.

revolting adj repulsive, repellent, disgusting, sickening, nauseating, distasteful, repugnant, abhorrent, offensive, obnoxious, loathsome, off-putting, hateful, foul, vile, nasty, shocking, abominable, despicable, reprehensible, contemptible, odious, heinous, obscene.

revolution n **1** *the French Revolution* rebellion, revolt, insurrection, uprising, rising, insurgence, mutiny, riot, coup, *coup d'état*, putsch. **2** *a revolution in the fashion industry* drastic change, radical alteration, complete shift, metamorphosis, sea change, upheaval, upset, transformation, innovation, reformation, cataclysm. **3** *a revolution of the wheel* rotation, single turn, whirl, round, spin, wheel. **4** *revolution of the planets round the sun* orbital motion; orbit.

revolutionary adj **1** *revolutionary troops* rebellious, insurgent, insurrectionary, insurrectionist, mutinous, seditious, factious, insubordinate, subversive, extremist. **2** *revolutionary changes in education* | *revolutionary fashion* progressive, radical, innovative, new, novel, avant-garde, experimental, different, drastic.

revolutionary n rebel, insurgent, insurrectionist, mutineer.

revolve v **1** *the wheel revolved slowly* go round, turn round, rotate, spin, whirl, wheel. **2** *revolve round the sun* circle, orbit, gyrate, whirl. **3** *revolve the problem in her mind* turn over, think over, think about, deliberate, consider, reflect on, mull over, ponder, muse over, meditate, ruminate. **4** *her life revolves round her children* be concerned/preoccupied with, focus on, concentrate on.

revulsion n repulsion, disgust, nausea, distaste, aversion, repugnance, recoil, abhorrence, loathing, hate, hatred, detestation, contempt.

reward n **1** *a reward for your efforts* | *a reward for finding the wallet* recompense, payment, remuneration, bonus, bounty, present, gift, tip, gratuity, prize; *inf* cut. **2** *the criminal got his just reward* punishment, penalty, retribution, requital, retaliation; just deserts, deserts; *inf* comeuppance.

reward v *reward them for their efforts* recompense, pay, remunerate, give a bounty/present to, tip.

rewarding adj *taking the children out was a rewarding experience* satisfying, worthwhile, fulfilling, enriching, edifying, beneficial, profitable, advantageous, productive, valuable.

rhetoric n **1** *the use of rhetoric to win over the crowd* oratory, eloquence, power of speech, delivery. **2** *the literary work was spoiled by rhetoric* bombast, grandiloquence, magniloquence, hyperbole, pomposity, verbosity, long-windedness, wordiness, prolixity, turgidity, extravagant language, purple prose, fustian.

rhetorical adj **1** *rhetorical language/passages* extravagant, pretentious, ostentatious, pompous, high-flown, flamboyant, showy, flowery, florid, oratorical, declamatory, bombastic, grandiloquent, magniloquent, hyperbolic, verbose, long-winded, wordy, prolix, turgid, periphrastic. **2** *rhetorical skills* oratorical, linguistic, verbal, stylistic.

rhyme n *a nursery rhyme* verse, ditty, poem, song, ode.

rhythm n **1** *musical rhythm* beat, cadence, tempo, pulse, throb, lilt. **2** *poetic rhythm* flow, cadence, metre. **3** *disturb the rhythm of their lives* flow, pattern, tempo, harmony.

ribald adj bawdy, risqué, blue, smutty, broad, vulgar, coarse, earthy, off-colour, rude, naughty, racy, suggestive, indecent, indelicate, offensive, filthy, gross, lewd, salacious, licentious, concupiscent; *inf* near the bone/knuckle.

rich adj **1** *rich and powerful people* wealthy, affluent, well off, well-to-do, prosperous, moneyed, propertied; *inf* well-heeled, filthy rich, loaded, made of money, rolling in it/money, flush, worth a packet/bundle, on Easy Street. **2** *rich furnishings/surroundings* opulent, expensive, costly, precious, valuable, priceless, beyond price, lavish, luxurious, lush, sumptuous, palatial, splendid, superb, resplendent, elegant, fine, exquisite, magnificent, grand, gorgeous. **3** *rich in oil/talent* well-provided, well-supplied, well-stocked, abounding, overflowing, replete, rife. **4** *rich supplies of minerals/ideas* copious, abundant, ample, plentiful, plenteous, bountiful. **5** *a rich soil* fertile, productive, fecund, fruitful, lush. **6** *rich food* creamy, fatty, heavy, spicy, highly spiced. **7** *rich wines* full-bodied, heavy. **8** *rich colours* strong, deep, intense, vivid, brilliant, warm, vibrant. **9** *rich voices/music* full, sonorous, resonant, deep, mellow, mellifluous, melodious. **10** *"that's rich, coming from you"* preposterous, outrageous, ridiculous, laughable, risible. **11** *rich jokes* amusing, comical, funny, humorous, hilarious, side-splitting.

riches npl **1** *amass riches* money, gold, capital, property, treasure; assets, resources.

2 *a man of riches* wealth, affluence, opulence, prosperity.

richly adv **1** *richly dressed/furnished* expensively, lavishly, luxuriously, sumptuously, palatially, splendidly, superbly, resplendently, magnificently. *see* RICH 2. **2** *an award/punishment richly deserved* fully, in full measure, well, thoroughly, completely, amply, utterly.

rid v *rid the child/place of the pests* clear, cleanse, purge, purify, free, make free, relieve, deliver, unburden. **get rid of** dispose of, do away with, throw away, remove, dispense with, eliminate, dump, unload, jettison, expel, eject, weed out.

riddle n puzzle, poser, conundrum, brainteaser, Chinese puzzle, problem, enigma, mystery.

ride v **1** *ride a horse* sit on, mount, be mounted on, bestride, manage, control. **2** *ride on a bus | ride in a car* travel, go, move, progress.

ride n *a ride in a car | go for a ride* trip, outing, journey, jaunt; *inf* spin.

ridicule n *treat the old man with ridicule* derision, mockery, laughter, scorn, jeering, gibing, teasing, taunting, chaff, banter, badinage, raillery, satire, sarcasm, irony; *inf* kidding, ribbing, ragging.

ridicule v *ridicule the new pupil* deride, mock, laugh at, scoff at, scorn, jeer at, gibe at, make/poke fun at, make a fool of, tease, taunt, chaff, banter; *inf* kid, rib, rag, take the mickey out of, send up.

ridiculous adj **1** *wearing a ridiculous hat | telling ridiculous jokes* absurd, comical, funny, laughable, hilarious, humorous, droll, farcical, facetious, ludicrous, risible, derisory. **2** *what a ridiculous thing to do* pointless, senseless, foolish, inane, fatuous, nonsensical, mindless. **3** *it is ridiculous that he got away with it* unreasonable, illogical, unbelievable, incredible, outrageous, preposterous, shocking, monstrous.

rife adj **1** *disease is rife* prevalent, predominant, widespread, common, general, extensive, ubiquitous, universal, global, rampant. **2** *the territory is rife with disease/vermin* abounding, overflowing, alive, swarming, teeming.

riff-raff n rabble, mob, commonality, hoi poloi, canaille, scum; dregs of society, undesirables.

rifle v **1** *rifle through her belongings* ransack, rummage through, go through, rake through, search. **2** *rifle the contents of the safe* steal, rob, burgle, thieve. **3** *raiders rifling*

their neighbour's goods plunder, pillage, loot, despoil, sack, ransack.

rift n **1** *a rift in the rock* fault, split, break, breach, fissure, cleft, crevice, gap, crack, cranny, slit, chink, cavity, opening, space, hole, aperture. **2** *a rift between family members* breach, division, estrangement, schism, split, alienation, quarrel, disagreement, fight, row, altercation, conflict, feud; *inf* falling-out.

rig v **1** *rig the yacht with sails* equip, supply, furnish, provide, make ready. **2** *rigged out in silk* clothe, dress, attire, accoutre, array, deck, bedeck, drape, trick out. **3** *rig up a shelter* put together, erect/assemble hastily, throw together, cobble together, improvise. **4** *rig the results of the vote* falsify, fake, tamper with, doctor, engineer, manipulate, juggle, arrange, massage; *inf* fix.

right adj **1** *his actions were not right* just, fair, equitable, impartial, good, upright, righteous, virtuous, proper, moral, ethical, honourable, honest, principled, lawful, legal. **2** *the right answer/procedure/way* correct, accurate, without error, unerring, exact, precise, valid; *inf* spot on, on the mark. **3** *he is the right owner—the other is a fraud* rightful, true, genuine, authentic, lawful, legal, legitimate; *inf* legit. **4** *the right person for the job* suitable, appropriate, fitting, fit, proper, desirable, preferable, ideal. **5** *he came at the right moment* opportune, favourable, convenient, suitable, appropriate, propitious. **6** *in his right mind* sane, sound, rational, lucid, sensible, reasonable, clear-thinking; *inf* all there. **7** *he was ill but he is all right now | the engine does not sound right* fine, healthy, in good health, well, fit, normal, sound, unimpaired, up to par; *inf* up to scratch, in the pink. **8** *make a right mess* real, complete, thorough, thoroughgoing, absolute, utter, out-and-out. **9** *his politics are right but hers are left* Conservative, Tory, reactionary.

right adv **1** *go right on* straight, directly, in a straight line, as the crow flies. **2** *he'll be right down* immediately, instantly, promptly, quickly, straightaway, without delay. **3** *sink right to the bottom | come right off its hinges* all the way, completely, entirely, totally, wholly, altogether, utterly, quite. **4** *right in the middle* bang, exactly, precisely, just, squarely; *inf* slap bang. **5** *if I remember right* aright, accurately, correctly, properly, exactly, precisely. **6** *you must behave/treat them right* justly, fairly, properly, righteously, virtuously, honourably, honestly, morally, ethically. **7** *it will come out right* well, for the better/best, favourably, advantageously, to one's advantage, beneficially.

right away at once, immediately, right now, now, straight away, this instant, instantly, promptly, directly, forthwith, without delay/hesitation; *inf* straight off.

right n **1** *know the difference between right and wrong* lawfulness, legality, goodness, righteousness, virtue, virtuousness, integrity, rectitude, propriety, morality, truth, truthfulness, honesty, honour, honourableness, justice, justness, fairness, equity, equitableness, impartiality; ethics. **2** *his position gives him the right to dismiss people* prerogative, privilege, authority, power, licence, permission, warrant, sanction, entitlement. **by right/rights** in fairness, with justice, properly. **put to rights** right, put/set right, sort out, straighten out, rectify, fix, put in order, tidy up, repair.

right v **1** *he righted himself | right the pole* stand/set upright. **2** *right the situation* put to rights, sort out, straighten out, rectify, fix, put in order, tidy up, repair. **3** *right a wrong* set/put right, rectify, compensate for, redress, vindicate.

righteous adj **1** *righteous people outnumbering wrongdoers* good, virtuous, upright, moral, ethical, law-abiding, honest, innocent, faultless, honourable, blameless, guiltless, pure, noble, God-fearing. **2** *righteous indignation* rightful, justifiable, well-founded, defensible, admissible, allowable, reasonable.

righteousness n goodness, virtue, virtuousness, uprightness, integrity, rectitude, probity, morality, ethicalness, honesty, honour, honourableness, innocence, purity; ethics. *see* RIGHTEOUS 1.

rigid adj **1** *a rigid substance* stiff, hard, taut, inflexible, non-flexible, unbendable, unbending, unyielding, inelastic, non-pliant, unmalleable. **2** *a rigid schedule* fixed, set, firm, inflexible, unalterable, unchangeable, unvarying, invariable, hard and fast. **3** *a man of rigid principles* strict, severe, stern, stringent, rigorous, austere, Spartan, harsh, inflexible, intransigent, uncompromising.

rigorous adj **1** *a rigorous regime | rigorous discipline* strict, severe, stern, stringent, austere, Spartan, tough, hard, harsh, rigid, inflexible, intransigent, uncompromising, demanding, exacting. **2** *rigorous attention to detail | a rigorous search* meticulous, punctilious, painstaking, thorough, laborious, scrupulous, conscientious, nice, exact, precise, accurate. **3** *rigorous weather* harsh, severe, bad, bleak, extreme, inclement.

rigour n **1** *the rigour of the regime* strictness, severity, sternness, stringency, austerity,

toughness, hardness, harshness, rigidity, inflexibility, intransigence. *see* RIGOROUS 1. **2** *this job must be tackled with rigour* meticulousness, punctiliousness, thoroughness, exactness, exactitude, precision, accuracy. *see* RIGOROUS 2. **3** *the rigours of winter* hardship; adversity, harshness, severity.

rim n **1** *the rim of a cup* brim, edge, lip, circumference. **2** *the rim of a lake* edge, border, verge, margin, brink, circumference.

rind n outer layer, peel, skin, husk, crust, integument, epicarp.

ring¹ n **1** *a wedding ring | she didn't wear a ring* band, gold band; wedding ring, marriage token. **2** *a ring round the moon* circle, circlet, round, loop, circuit, halo, disc. **3** *a circus/boxing ring* arena, enclosure, area. **4** *a ring of people stood around* circle, group, knot, gathering. **5** *a spy ring* gang, syndicate, cartel, mob, organization, confederacy, association, society, combine, alliance, league, fraternity, clique, cabal, junta.

ring¹ v *a fence ringed the area | ring the correct answer* circle, encircle, circumscribe, encompass, loop, gird, enclose, surround, hem in, fence in, seal off.

ring² n **1** *the ring of the bells* ringing, tolling, peal, pealing, knell, chime, clang, tinkle. *see* RING² v 1,2. **2** *give her a ring* call, telephone call; *inf* phone call, buzz.

ring² v **1** *ring the bells* toll, sound. **2** *the bells rang out* toll, peal, sound, chime, ding, ding-dong, clang, tinkle. **3** *the halls rang with music* resound, reverberate, resonate, echo, re-echo. **4** *bells ringing in the new year | ring in a new regime* herald, signal, announce, usher in. **5** *I shall ring you* call, telephone; *inf* phone, buzz.

rinse v *rinse the clothes by hand | rinse out the teapot* wash, wash out, wash lightly, clean.

riot n **1** *there was a riot when he was arrested* rebellion, revolt, uprising, insurrection, insurgence, street fight, commotion, disturbance, uproar, tumult, mêlée, row, scuffle, fracas, fray, brawl, free-for-all. **2** *the young people's riot brought the police in* revelry, celebration, partying, merrymaking, festivity, jollification; revels; *inf* high jinks, rave. **3** *the garden was a riot of colour* lavish display, splash, extravagance, flourish, show, exhibition. **run riot 1** *children running riot* rampage, run/go wild, run amok, go berserk; *inf* raise hell. **2** *flowers running riot in the wilderness* grow profusely, spread uncontrolled.

riot v **1** *crowds rioting in the streets* rebel, revolt, mutiny, take to the streets, run riot, rampage, go on the rampage, run wild/

amok, go berserk, fight, brawl. **2** *young peo-ple rioting* celebrate, party, make merry, revel, carouse, roister; *inf* paint the town red, go on a spree/binge, let one's hair down, rave.

riotous adj **1** *a riotous assembly* rebellious, mutinous, unruly, disorderly, uncontrol-lable, ungovernable, unmanageable, insub-ordinate, rowdy, wild, violent, brawling, lawless, anarchic. **2** *a riotous party* loud, noisy, boisterous, uproarious, rollicking, orgiastic. **3** *a riotous show* hilarious, uproari-ous, side-splitting, too funny for words; *inf* screamingly funny.

ripe adj **1** *ripe fruit/grain/cheese* mature, fully developed, full grown, ready to eat, ready, mellow, seasoned, tempered. **2** *our plans are now ripe* ready, all ready/set, developed, pre-pared, arranged, complete, finished. **3** *ripe in years* advanced, far on, old. **4** *sites ripe for development* ready, fit, suitable, right. **5** *the time is ripe* suitable, convenient, opportune, favourable, advantageous, auspicious.

ripen v **1** *fruit ripening on the trees* grow ripe, mature, come to maturity, mellow. **2** *ripen the fruit/cheese* make ripe, mature, bring to maturity, make mellow, season. **3** *our plans are ripening* develop, be in preparation, come to fruition.

riposte n retort, rejoinder, answer, reply, response, return, sally; *inf* comeback.

riposte v retort, rejoin, answer, reply, respond, return; *Amer* come back.

rise v **1** *the sun rose | a hand rose from the lake* arise, come/go up, move up, ascend, climb up. **2** *mountains rising above the town* rise up, tower, soar, loom, rear up. **3** *prices rose* go up, get higher, increase, soar, rocket, esca-late. **4** *standards have risen* go up, get higher/better, improve, advance. **5** *her voice rose | noise levels rose* get higher, grow, increase, become louder, swell, intensify. **6** *the children rose on the arrival of the guest* stand up, get to one's feet, get up, jump up, leap up, spring up, become erect. **7** *he rose at dawn* arise, get up, get out of bed, wake up; *inf* rise and shine, surface. **8** *the court rose at midday* adjourn, break off, be suspended, take a break. **9** *rise from the ranks | rise up the social ladder* climb, make progress, advance, get on, make/work one's way, be promoted. **10** *she won't rise to the bait* react to, respond to, take. **11** *Christ rose again* come to life, come back from the dead, be resurrected. **12** *dough rising* swell, expand, enlarge. **13** *citizens rising against the troops* rebel, revolt, mutiny, stage an insur-rection, take up arms, mount the barri-cades. **14** *the river rises in the mountains*

originate, begin, start, commence, issue from, spring from, flow from, emanate from. **15** *her spirits rose* become more cheer-ful, grow buoyant, become optimistic/hope-ful. **16** *the ground rises here* slope/slant upwards, go uphill, climb, mount, get steeper.

rise n **1** *the rise of the sun* rising, ascent. *see* RISE v 1. **2** *the rise in prices* increase, upsurge, upswing. *see* RISE v 3. **3** *a rise in standards* improvement, amelioration, advance, upturn. *see* RISE v 4. **4** *his rise to power | his rise from the ranks* climb, progress, progression, advancement, promotion, aggrandizement. **5** *a rise in the ground | climb the rise* incline, elevation, upward slope, acclivity, rising ground, hillock, hill. **6** *workers seeking a rise* pay increase, salary/wage increase, incre-ment; *Amer* raise.

risk n **1** *there is a risk of fire* chance, possibil-ity. **2** *put lives at risk* danger, peril, jeopardy. **3** *take a risk | an element of risk in the game* chance, hazard, uncertainty, speculation, venture.

risk v **1** *risk his life* put at risk, endanger, imperil, jeopardize. **2** *risk getting wet* take the risk of, chance, venture; *inf* grin and bear. **3** *risk £5 on the bet* gamble, hazard, chance, venture.

risky adj dangerous, fraught with danger, hazardous, perilous, unsafe, precarious, touch-and-go, tricky, uncertain; *inf* chancy, dodgy, dicey.

risqué adj off-colour, indecent, indelicate, improper, suggestive, naughty, rude, coarse, earthy, crude, bawdy, smutty, dirty, spicy, racy, salacious, licentious, lewd, rib-ald.

rite n ritual, ceremony, ceremonial, obser-vance, service, sacrament, celebration, per-formance, act, practice, tradition, convention, formality, procedure, usage.

ritual n **1** *the ritual of the Japanese tea cere-mony* rite, ceremony, ceremonial, obser-vance, celebration, act, practice, tradition, convention, procedure. *see* RITE. **2** *dislike ritual in public occasions* ceremony, tradition, convention, protocol, custom, habit, proce-dure, routine, stereotype.

rival n **1** *he defeated his rival | they are rivals for her love* opponent, opposition, adversary, antagonist, contestant, competitor, chal-lenger, vier, contender. **2** *in tennis she has no rival* equal, match, equivalent, fellow, peer.

rival v *rival the south of France* compete with, vie with, match, equal, emulate, measure up to, compare with, bear comparison with, parallel.

rival adj *rival teams* opposed, opposing, competing, in competition, contending, in conflict, conflicting.

rivalry n *rivalry between brothers* opposition, competition, competitiveness, vying, contention, conflict.

road n **1** *well-lit roads* street, thoroughfare, highway. **2** *this is the road to London* way, route, direction. **3** *ships in roads* roadstead, anchorage.

roam v **1** *children/animals roaming around* wander, rove, ramble, meander, drift. **2** *roam the hills* wander through, range, travel, walk, tramp, traverse, trek, peregrinate.

roar v **1** *the lion roared | the teacher roared at the children* bellow, yell, bawl, shout, howl, thunder, shriek, scream, cry, bay. **2** *roar at the comedian's jokes* roar/howl with laughter, laugh heartily, guffaw, hoot; *inf* spilt one's sides, roll in the aisles.

roar n **1** *the lion's/teacher's roar | the roar of the wind* bellow, growl, yell, bawl, shout, howl, rumble, shriek, scream, cry. **2** *his act was greeted with roars of laughter* guffaw, howl, hoot.

rob v **1** *rob a bank* steal from, burgle, burglarize, hold up, break into. **2** *rob an old lady* steal from, mug; *inf* rip off, jump. **3** *rob them of their savings* defraud, swindle, cheat, mulct, dispossess; *inf* diddle, bilk, do out of. **4** *rob them of peace of mind* deprive.

robber n burglar, thief, mugger, stealer, pilferer, housebreaker, looter, raider, bandit, brigand, pirate, highwayman.

robbery n **1** *commit robbery* burglary, theft, thievery, stealing, housebreaking, larceny, pilfering, filching, embezzlement, misappropriation, swindling, fraud. **2** *a robbery at the bank* mugging, hold-up, break-in, raid; *inf* rip-off.

robe n **1** *wearing coronation robes* vestment, habit, costume, gown. **2** *wearing a robe over pyjamas* dressing-gown, housecoat, wrapper, peignoir.

robot n automaton, android, machine.

robust adj **1** *robust young athletes* healthy, strong, vigorous, hale and hearty, energetic, muscular, powerful, powerfully built, tough, rugged, sturdy, stalwart, strapping, brawny, burly. **2** *a robust sense of humour* earthy, crude, coarse, rough, raw, unsubtle, indecorous, unrefined. **3** *a robust attitude to life* sensible, common-sense, no-nonsense, down-to-earth, practical, realistic, pragmatic, hard-headed.

rock n **1** *rocks dislodged from the cliff* boulder, stone. **2** *that department is the rock on which the firm is built* foundation, cornerstone, support, prop, mainstay. **3** *he is her rock in an uncertain world* bulwark, anchor, tower of strength, protection, security.

rock v **1** *the cradle/boat was rocking* move to and fro, swing, sway, roll, lurch, pitch, reel, wobble, undulate, oscillate. **2** *the world was rocked by his death* stun, shock, stagger, astound, astonish, amaze, dumbfound, surprise, shake, take aback, bewilder.

rocket v **1** *it rocketed into the air* shoot up, take off, soar, zoom. **2** *prices have rocketed* soar, increase rapidly, escalate; *inf* go through the ceiling, sky-rocket.

rocky¹ adj **1** *a rocky shore* rock-strewn, stony, pebbly, rough.

rocky² adj *he's a bit rocky after his illness* unsteady, unstable, shaky, tottering, teetering, wobbly, wobbling. **2** *their marriage is rather rocky* unsteady, unstable, uncertain, unsure; *inf* iffy.

rod n **1** *rods of iron* bar, stick, pole, baton, staff. **2** *spare the rod and spoil the child* cane, stick, birch, switch, wand.

rogue n **1** *rogues who steal from their friends* villain, scoundrel, rascal, reprobate, swindler, fraudster, cheat, deceiver, confidence trickster, charlatan, mountebank, sharper, wretch, cad, blackguard, ne'er-do-well, wastrel, good-for-nothing; *inf* rotter, bounder, con man, crook. **2** *the child's a rogue* scamp, imp, rascal, little devil, mischief-maker.

role n **1** *play the role of King Lear* part, character, representation, portrayal. **2** *in his role as headmaster* capacity, function, position, place, situation, job, post, task.

roll v **1** *the wheels rolled round* go round, turn, turn round, rotate, revolve, spin, whirl, wheel. **2** *roll up a newspaper* furl, coil, fold. **3** *as time rolls by | the bus rolled along* pass, go, flow, travel. **4** *roll the lawn/pastry* flatten, level, smooth, even, press down, crush. **5** *ships rolling on the ocean* toss, rock, pitch, lurch, sway, reel. **6** *waves rolling* billow, toss, tumble. **7** *drunks rolling him home* lurch, stagger, reel, sway, waddle, wobble.

roll n **1** *a roll of the wheel* turn, rotation, revolution, spin, whirl. **2** *a roll of film/tape* spool, reel, bobbin, cylinder. **3** *buy rolls for lunch* bread roll, bun, bap. **4** *on the electoral roll* register, list, file, index, roster, directory, catalogue. **5** *a roll of drums* boom, reverberation, thunder, rumble. **6** *the roll of the sea* undulation, billowing, swell, tossing, pitching, rocking.

romance n **1** *live in a world of romance, not the real world* fantasy, fancy, whimsy, fabrication, glamour, mystery, legend, fairy tale, idyll. **2** *their romance is over* love affair, affair, liaison, attachment, intrigue, courtship, amour. **3** *write romances* love story; romantic fiction, melodrama; *inf* tear-jerker. **4** *tired of the child's romances* lie, falsehood, fabrication, invention, trumped-up story, piece of fiction, fairy tale, flight of fancy, exaggeration; *inf* tall story.

romance v **1** *the young woman was romancing* fantasize, daydream. **2** *the child is romancing* lie, tell a lie, invent a story, exaggerate. **3** *he is romancing the girl next door* court, woo, go out with; *inf* go steady with, date.

romantic adj **1** *present a romantic picture of life today* unrealistic, idealistic, visionary, utopian, starry-eyed, optimistic, hopeful. **2** *romantic words* loving, amorous, passionate, fond, tender, sentimental; *inf* soppy, mushy, sloppy. **3** *a romantic figure in black* fascinating, mysterious, glamorous, exotic, exciting. **4** *tell a romantic tale of his adventures* fantastic, fanciful, imaginative, extravagant, exaggerated, fictitious, improbable, unlikely, implausible.

romantic n *they are romantics but their child is practical* romanticist, dreamer, visionary, idealist, utopian.

room n **1** *take up a lot of room* space, area, territory, expanse, extent, volume, elbow-room. **2** *room for improvement* scope, capacity, margin, leeway, latitude, occasion, opportunity. **3** *she has a room in that building* bedroom, apartment, office, bedsitting room; *inf* bedsit.

room v *room in the same building* have rooms, lodge, board, stay, dwell, reside.

rooms npl lodgings, quarters; apartment, residence, dwelling, abode; accommodation.

roomy adj spacious, commodious, capacious, voluminous, ample, generous, sizable, large, broad, wide, extensive.

root n **1** *the plant's roots* radicle, radix, rhizome, tuber, tap root. **2** *the root of the problem* source, origin, fountain-head, starting-point, basis, foundation, fundamental, seat, nucleus, kernel, nub, cause, reason, rationale, occasion, motivation; beginnings. **root and branch** completely, entirely, thoroughly, wholly, totally, utterly, radically.

root v **1** *the seeds/idea rooted* take root, grow roots, become established, set. **2** *rooted to the spot|her fear was deeply rooted* fix, establish, embed, implant, entrench. **root around** *root around in the drawers* rummage, rifle, forage, search, shuffle through, ran-

sack. **root out 1** *root out the weeds* uproot, tear up by the roots. **2** *root out the evil* extirpate, weed out, eradicate, get rid of, remove, do away with, eliminate, abolish, destroy, erase, put an end to. **3** *root out the cause* dig out, unearth, turn up, dredge up, bring to light, discover.

rope n *tie the logs with a rope|pin the clothes on a rope* cord, cable, line, strand, hawser.

rope v *rope the logs together* bind, tie, fasten, lash, tether, pinion. **rope in** *rope us in to help* enlist, engage, inveigle, persuade, talk into, involve.

roster n list, listing, rota, roll, register, schedule, agenda, calendar, directory, index, table.

rostrum n dais, platform, stage, podium.

rosy adj **1** *rosy cheeks* pink, pinkish, red, reddish, ruddy, rubicund, blushing, glowing, healthy looking. **2** *a rosy future* optimistic, promising, auspicious, hopeful, encouraging, bright, favourable, cheerful, happy, sunny.

rot v **1** *the material is rotting* decompose, decay, crumble, disintegrate, corrode, perish. **2** *the food is rotting* go bad, spoil, go sour, moulder, putrefy, fester; *inf* go off. **3** *moral standards are rotting away* degenerate, deteriorate, decline, break down, waste away, wither away.

rot n **1** *material suffering from rot* decomposition, decay, disintegration, corrosion, putrefaction mould, blight. *see* ROT v 1. **2** *it was a thriving society but rot has set in* degeneracy, deterioration, decline, dissoluteness. **3** *talk rot* rubbish, nonsense, stuff and nonsense, bunkum, claptrap, twaddle, drivel, moonshine; *inf* bosh, bunk, tommy-rot, gobbledegook, codswallop, hogwash, poppycock, guff, tosh.

rotary adj rotating, rotational, revolving, turning, gyrating, gyratory, spinning, whirling.

rotate v **1** *the wheels are rotating* go round, move round, turn, turn round, revolve, spin, whirl, swivel, reel, wheel, gyrate. **2** *the two doctors rotate|the directorship rotates* alternate, take turns, work/act in sequence, take place in rotation.

rotation n **1** *the rotation of the wheel* revolving, spinning, whirling, gyration. *see* ROTATE 1. **2** *one rotation of the wheel* turn, revolution, spin, whirl, orbit. **3** *do the work in rotation* alternation, sequence, cycle. *see* ROTATE 2.

rotten adj **1** *rotten food* bad, mouldy, mouldering, spoiled, tainted, sour, rancid, rank, decaying, decomposed, putrid, putrescent, festering, fetid, stinking; *inf* off. **2** *rotten* *material* decomposing, decaying, crumbling, disintegrating, corroding, perishing. **3** *rotten teeth* decaying, crumbling, carious. **4** *he's a rotten creep* corrupt, dishonourable, dishonest, untrustworthy, immoral, unprincipled, unscrupulous, villainous, bad, wicked, evil, sinful, iniquitous, vicious, debauched, degenerate, dissolute, dissipated, perverted, wanton; *inf* crooked, bent. **5** *that was a rotten thing to do* nasty, foul, mean, bad, dirty, filthy, contemptible, despicable, base, scurrilous. **6** *we had a rotten time* miserable, unpleasant, disagreeable, disappointing, regrettable, unfortunate, unlucky. **7** *it's a rotten idea* ill-considered, ill thought out, ill-advised, injudicious. **8** *what a rotten selection of goods* poor, inadequate, inferior, substandard, unsatisfactory, unacceptable; *inf* lousy, crummy. **9** *feeling rotten with the flu* ill, sick, unwell, unhealthy, below par, off colour; *inf* under the weather, poorly, rough, ropy.

rotter n bad lot, blackguard, cad, swine; *inf* bounder, creep, rat, louse.

rotund adj **1** *rotund and jolly* plump, chubby, buxom, roly-poly, tubby, well-rounded, portly, stout, corpulent, podgy, fat, obese, heavy, fleshy. **2** *rotund vowels/speech* sonorous, full-toned, round, canorous, rich, mellow, resonant, orotund, magniloquent, grandiloquent.

rough adj **1** *rough surfaces* uneven, irregular, bumpy, broken, stony, rugged, jaggy, craggy, lumpy, nodulous. **2** *dogs with a rough coat* shaggy, hairy, bushy, fuzzy, bristly, hirsute. **3** *get involved in some rough play* boisterous, rowdy, disorderly, wild, violent, savage. **4** *rough seas* turbulent, tumultuous, choppy. **5** *rough weather* inclement, stormy, squally, wild, tempestuous, wintry. **6** *he's a rough character* coarse, crude, uncouth, vulgar, unrefined, uncultured, loutish, boorish, churlish, brutish, ill-bred, ill-mannered, unmannerly, impolite, discourteous, uncivil, brusque, blunt, curt. **7** *a few rough words to say to him* curt, sharp, harsh, stern, unfeeling, insensitive. **8** *have a rough time | receive rough treatment* harsh, severe, hard, tough, difficult, unpleasant, disagreeable, nasty, cruel. **9** *had rough luck* unfortunate, undeserved. **10** *he was rough on his son* harsh, hard, stern, unrelenting, merciless, unfeeling, unfair, unjust. **11** *rough wood/flour* crude, raw, unpolished, undressed, uncut, rough-hewn, unrefined, unprocessed. **12** *rough voices* husky, gruff, hoarse, harsh. **13** *rough sounds* discordant, inharmonious, cacophonous, harsh, grating, jarring, strident, raucous. **14** *rough wines* harsh, sharp,

unrefined. **15** *a rough sketch* rough-and-ready, hasty, quick, sketchy, cursory, crude, incomplete, rudimentary, basic, unpolished, unrefined. **16** *a rough estimate* approximate, inexact, imprecise, vague, hazy. **17** *feeling rather rough* ill, sick, unwell, unhealthy, below par, off colour; *inf* hungover, under the weather, poorly, rotten, ropy.

rough n **1** *make a rough of your plan* draft, sketch, outline, mock-up, model. **2** *mugged by a gang of roughs* ruffian, thug, bully-boy; *inf* tough, roughneck, bruiser, bovver boy.

rough v roughen, make rough. **rough out** *rough out your ideas* draft, sketch out, outline, block out, adumbrate. **rough up** *the children were roughed up by their father | old men roughed up by muggers* maltreat, mistreat, abuse, manhandle, batter, beat up, knock about; *inf* bash.

rough-and-tumble n horseplay; scuffle, struggle, fight, brawl, fracas, mêlée; *inf* scrap, dust-up, rough house.

round adj **1** *a round shape* circular, ring-shaped, hooplike, annular, cycloid, discoid, disklike, cylindrical, spherical, spheroid, ball-shaped, globelike, globular, globate, globose, orblike, orbicular, orbiculate, bulb-shaped, balloon-like, convex, curved. **2** *a round dozen* complete, entire, whole, full, undivided, unbroken. **3** *a round figure* well-rounded, ample, rotund, chubby, buxom, roly-poly, tubby, portly, stout, corpulent, podgy, fat, obese. **4** *use round language | she was round with him* blunt, candid, outspoken, frank, direct, plain, straightforward; *inf* not pulling any punches. **5** *the round tones of the singer* sonorous, resonant, rich, full, mellow, flowing, orotund.

round n **1** *shaped in a round | cut it in rounds* circle, circlet, ring, hoop, band, disk, cylinder, sphere, ball, globe, orb. **2** *a round of parties* succession, sequence, series, cycle. **3** *the milkman's/ doctor's round* circuit, course, ambit, beat, routine, schedule. **4** *two rounds left in the gun* bullet, cartridge, shell. **5** *the first round of the competition* stage, level, division, lap, heat, game.

round v *round Cape Horn* go round, move round, travel round, sail round, circumnavigate. **round off 1** *round off the evening | round off his career* finish off, crown, cap, top off, complete, conclude, close, bring to a close/end, end, terminate. **2** *round off the edges* smooth, plane, level, sand. **round on** *she suddenly rounded on her tormentor* attack, set upon; *inf* lay into, light into, lace into, tear into, lambaste. **round up** bring together, gather together, drive together, assemble, collect, group, muster, marshal, rally.

roundabout adj **1** *a roundabout route* indirect, circuitous, meandering, winding, tortuous. **2** *a roundabout way of saying it* indirect, circuitous, discursive, oblique, circumlocutory, periphrastic.

rouse v **1** *rouse the sleeping children* wake, wake up, call, get up. **2** *he finds it difficult to rouse* wake up, awaken, get up, get out of bed, rise. **3** *rouse the crowds to protest | rouse himself to participate* stir up, bestir, excite, incite, egg on, induce, impel, inflame, agitate, whip up, galvanize, stimulate. **4** *the teacher was really roused* anger, annoy, infuriate, incense, exasperate, work up. **5** *rouse feelings of guilt* stir up, kindle, touch off, provoke, induce, evoke, call up, conjure up.

rousing adj **1** *a rousing speech* inspiring, stimulating, exciting, stirring, inflammatory, moving, exhilarating, inspiriting, encouraging, vigorous, energetic, lively, spirited, enthusiastic, fervent. **2** *three rousing cheers* hearty, vigorous, loud, strong, great, tremendous.

rout n **1** *troops put to rout* disorderly retreat, retreat, flight, headlong flight. **2** *suffer a rout at the hands of the enemy/opponents* crushing defeat, defeat, drubbing, trouncing, conquest, subjugation, overthrow, beating, thrashing; *inf* licking, pasting.

rout v **1** *they routed the enemy troops and chased them* put to rout/flight, drive off, dispel, scatter. **2** *they easily routed their enemy/opponents* defeat, drub, trounce, worst, conquer, subjugate, overthrow, crush, beat, thrash; *inf* lick, give a pasting to.

route n course, way, itinerary, road, path.

routine n **1** *he hates to upset his routine* pattern, procedure, practice, custom, habit, wont, programme, schedule, formula, method, system, order, way. **2** *have heard the comic's routine before* act, performance, piece, line; *inf* spiel.

routine adj **1** *carry out routine procedure* usual, normal, everyday, workaday, common, ordinary, typical, customary, habitual, wonted, scheduled, conventional, standard. **2** *he finds the work too routine* boring, tedious, tiresome, monotonous, humdrum, run-of-the-mill, hackneyed, predictable, unexciting, uninspiring.

row¹ n **1** *a row of people* line, column, queue, procession, chain, string; *inf* crocodile. **2** *a row of vegetables* line, column, sequence, series. **3** *a row of seats* line, tier, rank, bank.

row² n **1** *the two brothers had a row* argument, dispute, disagreement, controversy, quarrel, squabble, tiff, fight, conflict, altercation, brawl, affray, wrangle, scuffle, free-for-all, fracas, mêlée; *inf* falling-out, set-to, scrap. **2** *the row coming from the party* noise, din, clamour, commotion, rumpus, uproar, tumult, hubbub, babel, pandemonium. **3** *the children got a row* reprimand, reproof, scolding, chiding, lecture, castigation; *inf* dressing-down, telling-off, ticking-off, talking-to, rollicking, flea in one's ear, bawling-out.

row² v *the brothers are rowing again* argue, quarrel, squabble, fight, wrangle, brawl; *inf* scrap.

rowdy adj *rowdy drunks* unruly, disorderly, noisy, boisterous, loud, obstreperous, wild, rough, unrestrained, lawless.

rowdy n *police arresting rowdies* ruffian, thug, hooligan, troublemaker, brawler; *inf* tearaway, tough, rough.

royal adj **1** *a royal wave* kingly, queenly, kinglike, queenlike, princely, regal, monarchical, sovereign. **2** *royal surroundings* majestic, magnificent, impressive, glorious, splendid, imposing, grand, superb. **3** *have a royal time* excellent, fine, first-rate, first-class, marvellous, wonderful.

rub v **1** *rub her sore neck* massage, knead, embrocate. **2** *rub the cat's back* stroke, caress, fondle, pat. **3** *rub the silver lamp* polish, buff up, burnish. **4** *rub the dirty mark/floor* scrub, scour, wipe, clean. **5** *rub in the ointment* apply, put on, smear, spread, work in. **6** *rub off/out the message* erase, wipe off, efface, obliterate, expunge, remove, cancel, delete.

rub n **1** *give her neck a rub* massage, kneading, embrocation, friction. **2** *give the cat's back a rub* stroke, caress. *see* RUB v 2. **3** *give the lamp a rub* polish, buffing, burnishing. **4** *give the floor a rub* scrub, scour, wipe, clean. **5** *there's the rub* difficulty, problem, trouble, drawback, snag, hitch, hindrance, obstacle, obstruction, impediment.

rubbish n **1** *put the rubbish in bins* waste, refuse, litter, lumber, junk, debris, detritus, dross, rubble, scrap, flotsam and jetsam; sweepings, leavings, dregs, offscourings, odds and ends; *Amer* garbage, trash. **2** *talking rubbish* nonsense, stuff and nonsense, drivel, gibberish, balderdash, bunkum, twaddle, moonshine; *Scots* havers; *inf* rot, tommy-rot, bunk, gobbledegook, bosh, piffle, hogwash, codswallop, guff, tosh.

ruddy adj **1** *a ruddy complexion* red, reddish, pink, pinkish, rosy, rosy-cheeked, rubicund, flushed, blushing, glowing, fresh, healthy. **2** *what a ruddy cheek!* damnable, abominable, diabolical, flaming; *inf* bloody.

rude adj **1** *rude children | being rude to old people* ill-mannered, bad-mannered, mannerless, impolite, discourteous, impertinent, insolent, impudent, cheeky, uncivil, disrespectful, churlish, curt, brusque, blunt, offhand, short, offensive. **2** *rude tools* primitive, crude, rudimentary, rough, rough-hewn, simple. **3** *rude peasants* simple, artless, uncivilized, uneducated, untutored, ignorant, illiterate, uncultured, unrefined, rough, coarse, uncouth, oafish, loutish. **4** *rude jokes* vulgar, coarse, indelicate, smutty, dirty, naughty, risqué, blue, ribald, bawdy, licentious. **5** *a rude awakening* sudden, abrupt, sharp, violent, startling, harsh, unpleasant, disagreeable, nasty.

rudimentary adj **1** *rudimentary arithmetic* elementary, basic, fundamental, introductory, early. **2** *rudimentary tools* primitive, crude, rough, simple. **3** *a rudimentary organ* undeveloped, immature, incomplete, vestigial.

rudiments npl basics, fundamentals, beginnings, elements, essentials; foundation; *inf* nuts and bolts.

rue v *live to rue her actions* regret, be sorry about, feel apologetic/remorseful about, feel remorse for.

rueful adj regretful, apologetic, sorry, remorseful, contrite, repentant, penitent, conscience-stricken, self-reproachful, woebegone, woeful, plaintive.

ruffian n thug, villain, scoundrel, hoodlum, hooligan, rogue, rascal, miscreant; *inf* rough, tough, rowdy.

ruffle v **1** *ruffle feathers* disarrange, discompose, disorder, derange, rumple, dishevel, tousle, tangle, mess up; *inf* muss up. **2** *she gets ruffled in a crisis* annoy, irritate, irk, vex, nettle, rile, anger, exasperate, fluster, agitate, harass, upset, disturb, discompose, perturb, unsettle, disconcert, worry, alarm, trouble, confuse; *inf* rattle, shake up, hassle.

rugged adj **1** *rugged terrain* rough, uneven, irregular, bumpy, rocky, stony, broken up, jagged, craggy, precipitous. **2** *rugged features* wrinkled, furrowed, lined, gnarled, irregular, weather-beaten, leathery. **3** *rugged manners | a rugged beauty* unrefined, unpolished, uncultured, crude, unsophisticated, graceless, inelegant. **4** *you have to be rugged to survive there* tough, hardy, robust, sturdy, strong, vigorous, stalwart, hale and hearty, muscular, brawny, solid, mighty, burly, well-built; *inf* husky, beefy. **5** *a rugged way of life* tough, harsh, austere,

Spartan, exacting, taxing, demanding, difficult, hard, arduous, rigorous, strenuous, onerous.

ruin n **1** *cities in a state of ruin | his plans in ruin* ruination, destruction, devastation, havoc, wreckage, demolition, disintegration, dilapidation, desolation, decay, disrepair. **2** *the ruin of the army | the ruin of his hopes* ruination, downfall, overthrow, defeat, undoing, conquest, elimination, termination, end. **3** *firms facing ruin* ruination, loss, failure, bankruptcy, insolvency, financial failure, deprivation, penury, impoverishment, indigence, destitution, calamity, disaster. **4** *castle ruins | the ruins of our hopes* remains, relics, remnants, vestiges; wreckage, wreck, remainder, debris, detritus.

ruin v **1** *the rain ruined the crops/dresses | it ruined our plans* damage, spoil, wreak havoc on, mar, injure, wreck, botch, make a mess of, mess up, smash, shatter. **2** *the recession ruined him* bring to ruin, bankrupt, make insolvent, impoverish, pauperize. **3** *invading armies ruining cities | decisions ruining our hopes | armies leaving ruined cities* destroy, devastate, lay waste, raze, demolish, crush.

ruinous adj **1** *a ruinous agreement | ruinous expenses* disastrous, devastating, calamitous, catastrophic, cataclysmic, dire, injurious, damaging, crippling, destructive. **2** *ruinous old buildings* in ruins, ruined, dilapidated, decaying, in disrepair, derelict, ramshackle, broken-down, decrepit.

rule n **1** *obey the rules of the realm/society* ruling, law, by-law, regulation, statute, ordinance, tenet, canon, order, court order, decree, commandment, directive, guideline. **2** *it is a good rule to wait for others to speak* principle, precept, standard, axiom, truth, truism, maxim, aphorism, motto. **3** *as a general rule children are not allowed* practice, procedure, routine, custom, habit, wont, convention, standard, form. **4** *under the rule of the Tudors | the rule of the present government* reign, dominion, sovereignty, kingship, queenship, regime, government, administration, jurisdiction, authority, control, direction, mastery, leadership, command, ascendancy, supremacy, power, sway, influence. **as a rule** generally, in general, usually, normally, ordinarily, for the most part, on the whole, mainly.

rule v **1** *the king/president/administration rules over a wide area* preside over, govern, control, have control of, dominate, direct, administer, manage, regulate. **2** *the king ruled for ten years* reign, sit on the throne, wear the crown, wield the sceptre. **3** *the last administration ruled for only a few months* be in power, be in control, be in authority, be in command, be in charge, govern; *inf* be at the helm. **4** *the judge ruled that he be released* order, decree, direct, pronounce, make a judgement, judge, adjudge, adjudicate, lay down, decide, determine, resolve, settle, establish. **5** *let common sense rule* prevail, obtain, hold sway, predominate, preponderate. **rule out** *rule out the possibility of arson* preclude, exclude, eliminate, reject, dismiss, disregard, ignore.

ruler n sovereign, monarch, king, queen, emperor, empress, head of state, head, governor, president, overlord, chief, chieftain, lord, commander, leader.

ruling n judgement, adjudication, finding, verdict, resolution, decree, pronouncement.

ruling adj **1** *the ruling monarch* reigning, regnant, on the throne. **2** *the ruling classes* dominant, controlling, governing, commanding, leading, in charge, upper. **3** *the ruling theory* prevalent, predominant, main, chief, principal, widespread, general, popular, universal.

ruminate v **1** *sit and ruminate* | *ruminating on her problems* think, contemplate, deliberate, ponder, broad, meditate, muse, cogitate; think about, think over, give thought to, consider, mull over, brood about, chew over; *inf* put on one's thinking cap. **2** *cows ruminating* chew the cud.

rummage v *rummage through drawers/papers* search through, hunt through, forage through, rifle, ransack, turn over, pry into.

rumour n **1** *rumour has it that he has gone* gossip, hearsay, talk; *inf* the grapevine. **2** *hear a rumour that he has gone* report, story, whisper, canard; information, word, news; tidings; *inf* buzz.

rumour v *it is rumoured that they are wealthy* | *they are rumoured to be wealthy* say, report, think, give out, put about, circulate, spread, pass around, noise abroad, disseminate, gossip, hint, suggest.

rumple v **1** *rumple clothes* crumple, crease, wrinkle, crush, crinkle. **2** *rumple hair* disarrange, tousle, dishevel, ruffle, mess up; *inf* muss up.

rumpus n disturbance, row, uproar, commotion, brouhaha, fracas, brawl, free-for-all, mêlée, riot.

run v **1** *she ran to catch the bus* race, rush, hasten, hurry, dash, sprint, bolt, dart, gallop, career along, tear along, charge along, speed along, jog along, scurry, scamper, scramble; *inf* scoot, hare, step on it, get a move on, hotfoot it, stir one's stumps.

2 *the prisoners ran from the camp* abscond, flee, take flight, take oneself off, make off, decamp, bolt, beat a retreat, make a run for it, show a clean pair of heels, clear out, make one's getaway, escape; *inf* beat it, scarper, vamoose, skedaddle, split, cut and run, do a runner, hightail it. **3** *trains run on tracks* move, go, get along, travel. **4** *the river runs by* glide, course, roll, slide. **5** *leave the engine running* go, operate, function. **6** *the lease runs for 20 years* operate, be in operation, be valid, be current, continue. **7** *the play is running at the Empire Theatre* be staged, be presented, be performed, be on, be put on. **8** *the road runs along the coast* | *the path runs from the lake to the village* go, continue, proceed, extend, stretch. **9** *prices/tempers are running high* get, go, reach, stretch. **10** *he has decided not to run in a race* compete, take part, enter, be in the race. **11** *run for president* stand for, stand for election as, stand as candidate for, be a contender for, put oneself forward for. **12** *water running* flow, issue, stream, pour, gush, cascade, spurt, jet, trickle, leak. **13** *walls running with water* be wet with, stream with, flow with, drip with, be flooded by. **14** *run the water* turn on, switch on. **15** *ink ran over the surface* spread, spread over, be diffused, extend, stretch. **16** *the dye from the shirt ran on to the trousers* spread, be diffused, bleed, mix with. **17** *the butter ran* melt, dissolve, liquefy, thaw. **18** *he'll never run the course* travel, traverse, go over, complete, finish. **19** *run an errand* go on, do, carry out, perform, fulfil, execute. **20** *the newspaper ran a story about the accident* publish, print, feature, carry. **21** *run a business* | *run the firm* own, operate, conduct, carry on, direct, manage, administer, be in charge/control of, control, head, lead, look after, organize, coordinate, supervise, superintend, oversee; *inf* boss. **22** *run a car* drive, own, possess, have. **23** *run the children to school* drive, transport, convey. **24** *run guns* smuggle, traffic in, deal in, bootleg. **25** *run them out of town* chase, drive, propel, hunt, put to flight. **26** *ideas running through my mind* go, pass, dart, flow, slide. **27** *run your eye over the page* pass, slide, flick. **28** *tights/stockings running* ladder, unravel, tear, be snagged. **29** *her eyes are running because of the cold* stream, exude/secrete/ooze liquid. **run across** *run across an old friend* run into, come across, chance upon, stumble upon; *inf* bump into.

run away 1 *the prisoners have run away* abscond, flee, make off, bolt, decamp, clear out, escape. *see* RUN V 2. **2** *he tries to run away from the problems* avoid, evade, disregard, ignore, take no notice of, pay no attention to, put to the back of one's mind, turn one's back on. **run away with 1** *run away with his daughter* run off with, elope with, abduct, make off with. **2** *run away with the firm's takings* run off with, make off with, abscond with, snatch, steal, purloin; *inf* pinch, nick, swipe. **3** *run away with the race* win easily; *inf* win hands down, win by a mile, walk it. **run down 1** *the driver ran down an old woman* knock down, knock over, knock to the ground. **2** *run down the workforce* cut back on, cut, curtail, pare down, trim, reduce, decrease. **3** *my watch has run down* stop, halt, cease to function/operate. **4** *the British manufacturing industry has been running down for years* decline, wane, diminish, dwindle, become less effective; *inf* lose steam. **5** *she finally ran down the book in a second-hand shop* run to earth, unearth, track down, ferret out, hunt out, dredge up, find, discover, locate. **6** *she's always running down her neighbour* speak ill/badly of, disparage, denigrate, criticize, decry, belittle, revile, vilify; *inf* knock. **run high** *feelings are running high* be strong, be vehement, be fervent/fervid, be passionate. **run in 1** *run in a new car* drive gently/slowly, break in. **2** *the police finally ran him in* arrest, apprehend, take into custody, jail; *inf* pull in, collar, nab, nick, bust. **run into 1** *another car ran into ours* bump into, knock into, collide with, crash into, hit, strike, ram. **2** *I ran into an old friend* run across, chance on; *inf* bump into. *see* RUN V run across. **3** *the cost runs into thousands of pounds* reach, extend to, be as high/much as. **run low** *supplies are running low* dwindle, diminish, get less, become depleted, become exhausted. **run off 1** *the children/dog ran off* run away, flee, make off, bolt, beat a retreat, show a clean pair of heels, make one's getaway, clear out, escape; *inf* beat it, scarper, hightail it. **2** *run off several copies* copy, duplicate, xerox, mimeograph. **run off with 1** *run off with her daughter* run away with, elope. *see* RUN V run away with 1. **2** *run off with the takings* run away with, abscond with, snatch, steal. *see* RUN V run away with 2. **run on 1** *I hope the meeting will not run on into the afternoon* go on, continue, carry on, keep going, last. **2** *she does run on* talk a lot, talk incessantly, chatter on, ramble on; *inf* rabbit on, witter on, natter on. **run out** *supplies have run out|run out of food* be finished, give out, dry up, fail, be exhausted; exhaust. **run out on** *he has run out on his wife* desert, abandon, forsake, jilt; *inf* leave high and dry, leave in the lurch, leave holding the baby, rat on. **run over 1** *run over a rabbit* run down, knock down, knock over, hit. **2** *the bath water's running*

over overflow, overbrim, spill over. **3** *run over a speech|run over the figures for tomorrow* run through, look over, go over, go through. **4** *could you run over yesterday's work?* run through, go over, repeat, iterate, recapitulate; *inf* recap. **run through 1** *run through the speech/figures for tomorrow* run over, go over, look over, look through. **2** *could you run through yesterday's work?* run over, go over, repeat, recapitulate. **3** *run through money* go through, squander, fritter away, dissipate, waste; *inf* blow. **4** *an air of sadness runs through the book* go through, pervade, permeate, suffuse. **5** *the knight ran through his enemy with his spear* pierce, transfix, stab. **run to 1** *the cost runs to thousands* run into, reach, extend to, be as high/much as. **2** *we can't run to a new car* afford, have/be sufficient for. **3** *the family runs to fat* tend to, be disposed/inclined to.

run n **1** *go for a run|break into a run* jog, sprint, dash, gallop, canter, headlong rush, scamper. *see* RUN V 1. **2** *go for a run in the car/bus* drive, ride, trip, outing, excursion, jaunt, short journey; *inf* spin, tootle. **3** *the train-driver operates on the Edinburgh to London run* route, way, course, itinerary. **4** *a run of fine weather|a run of luck/disasters* period, spell, stretch, streak, chain, string, round, cycle, sequence, series, succession. **5** *a run on sterling/ice-cream* demand, rush, clamour. **6** *different from the general run of applicants* kind, variety, type, sort, class, category, order. **7** *against the run of play|the recent run of events* tendency, trend, tide, course, direction, movement, drift, current, stream. **8** *the chickens' run* enclosure, pen, coop. **9** *a run in her tights* ladder, rip, tear, snag. **in the long run** *he will have to pay in the long run* eventually, in the end, ultimately, when all is said and done, in the final analysis. **on the run** *prisoners on the run* running away, fleeing, in flight, bolting, escaping.

runaway n *runaways from the children's home* absconder, deserter, escapee, fugitive, truant.

runaway adj **1** *a runaway horse* escaped, loose, on the loose, uncontrolled, out of control, wild. **2** *runaway children from the home* absconding, escaping, fugitive. **3** *a runaway victory* effortless, easy; *inf* peasy, easy as pie.

rundown n **1** *been a rundown in the workforce* cut, curtailment, reduction, decrease. *see* RUN V run down 2. **2** *a rundown in British industry* decline, waning, diminution. *see* RUN V run down 4. **3** *give them the rundown on/of the situation* analysis, briefing, brief, review, summary, résumé, sketch, outline; *inf* low-down.

run-down adj **1** *run-down property* dilapidated, tumbledown, ramshackle, broken-down, decaying, decayed, in ruins, ruined, gone to wrack and ruin, seedy, shabby, slummy. **2** *feel run-down after an illness* debilitated, out of condition, below par, drained, exhausted, fatigued, tired, enervated, worn-out, unhealthy; *inf* not oneself, under the weather, pooped.

runner n **1** *twenty runners in the field* racer, sprinter, hurdler, harrier, jogger, athlete. **2** *runners from the plant* branch, shoot, offshoot, tendril. **3** *give the message to the runner* messenger, courier, dispatch rider, bearer, errand boy/girl.

running n **1** *take part in the running* racing, race, sprinting, sprint, jogging. **2** *his running of the firm* direction, administration, controlling, organization, coordination, supervision. *see* RUN v 21. **3** *the smooth running of the business* operation, working, functioning, performance. **4** *out of the running for the job* competition, contest, contention.

running adj **1** *a running battle* continuous, unceasing, incessant, ceaseless, uninterrupted, constant, perpetual. **2** *three weeks running* in a row, in succession, in sequence, one after the other; *inf* on the trot. **3** *running water* flowing, streaming, gushing. *see* RUN v 12.

run-of-the-mill adj ordinary, average, common, middling, mediocre, commonplace, everyday, undistinguished, unexceptional, passable, tolerable, acceptable, fair, not bad; *inf* common or garden, nothing special, so-so.

rupture n **1** *a rupture in the defences* break, fracture, crack, split, burst, rent, tear, rift, fissure. **2** *the rupture of the defences/artery* breaking, fracture, cracking, splitting, bursting. *see* RUPTURE v1. **3** *there has been a rupture in their relationship | ruptures exist within the party* rift, estrangement, schism, break-up, division, alienation, variance, disagreement, quarrel, feud; *inf* falling-out. **4** *an operation for a rupture* hernia.

rupture v **1** *rupture the defences | rupture an organ* break, fracture, crack, split, breach, burst, rend, tear, puncture. **2** *rupture East-West relations* sever, cut off, break off, disrupt, breach.

rural adj country, countryside, pastoral, rustic, agricultural, agrarian, Arcadian.

ruse n trick, stratagem, subterfuge, artifice, device, wile, dodge, ploy, machination, manoeuvre, tactic, deception, hoax, blind.

rush v **1** *rush to the door* hurry, make haste, hasten, run, race, dash, sprint, bolt, dart, gallop, career, tear, charge, speed, scurry, scamper; *inf* step on it, get a move on, hotfoot it. **2** *rush the enemy* attack, assault, charge, storm, take by storm, capture, seize. **3** *rush the job through* hurry, hasten, expedite, speed up, accelerate, advance, hustle, press, push.

rush n **1** *make a rush on the enemy* onslaught, attack, assault, charge. **2** *a rush of water/blood* surge, flow, gush, stream, flood. **3** *no rush for the goods* hurry, haste, speed, swiftness, rapidity, dispatch. **4** *a rush for toys* demand, clamour, run (on). **5** *the Christmas rush* activity, bustle, hubbub, flurry.

rushed adj *a rushed job* hurried, hasty, speedy, quick, fast, swift, rapid, expeditious, prompt.

rustic adj **1** *rustic scenes* country, countryside, rural, pastoral, agricultural, agrarian, Arcadian, bucolic. **2** *rustic pleasures* unsophisticated, plain, simple, homely, homespun. **3** *rustic peasants* artless, plain, simple, homely, unassuming, guileless, naïve, ingenuous, unsophisticated, uncultured, unrefined, unpolished, homespun, coarse, rough, indelicate, uncouth, graceless, awkward, clumsy, inept, maladroit, blundering, lumbering, clodhopping, churlish, boorish.

rustic n countryman, countrywoman, countryperson, peasant, son/daughter of the soil, country cousin/bumpkin, yokel; *Amer inf* hill-billy, hayseed.

rustle v **1** *silk rustling | trees rustling in the wind* swish, whisper, whoosh. **2** *rustle cattle* steal, purloin, filch, plunder, abduct, kidnap.

rusty adj **1** *rusty parts on the car* rusted, rust-covered, corroded, oxidized. **2** *a rusty dress* rust-coloured, reddish, reddish-brown, russet, brick-red, brick. **3** *his French is a bit rusty* deficient, impaired, diminished, weak, below par, unpractised, out of practice, neglected, not what it was. **4** *his voice is a bit rusty* hoarse, croaking, cracked.

rut n **1** *farm roads full of ruts* furrow, groove, track, crack, hollow, hole, pothole, trough, gutter, ditch. **2** *in a rut in his job* humdrum existence, routine job, boring routine; *inf* daily grind, treadmill, dead end.

ruthless adj merciless, unmerciful, pitiless, compassionless, relentless, unrelenting, remorseless, unforgiving, unsparing, inexorable, implacable, heartless, unfeeling, hard, harsh, severe, stern, grim, cruel, vicious, brutal, barbarous, callous, savage, fierce, ferocious.

S s

sable adj black, jet-black, jet, pitch-black, pitch, black as pitch, raven, ink-black, inky, black as ink, coal-black, black as coal, black as night.

sabotage n **1** *the fire at the factory was an act of sabotage* deliberate destruction/damage/wrecking, impairment/incapacitation, subversive destruction, vandalism **2** *the sabotage of our plans* disruption, spoiling, ruining, wrecking; *inf* fouling up

sabotage v **1** *sabotage the factory machinery* deliberately destroy/damage/wreck, impair, incapacitate, cripple, vandalize; *inf* foul up **2** *sabotage our plans* disrupt, spoil, ruin, wreck; *inf* throw a spanner in the works of, put the kibosh on, foul up

saccharine adj **1** *saccharine desserts* oversweet, cloying **2** *saccharine words of farewell | saccharine novels* mawkish, maudlin, sentimental; *inf* soppy, mushy, schmaltzy.

sack ¹ n **1** *sacks of coal/flour* bag, pack. **2** *get the sack* dismissal, discharge, redundancy, termination of employment; *inf* one's cards, one's marching orders, the boot, the old heave-ho, the push, the chop, the axe. **3** *longing for one's sack after a hard day* bed, bunk; *inf* pit, kip. **hit the sack** go to bed, retire, go to sleep; *inf* turn in, hit the hay, go to one's pit, go to one's kip.

sack¹ v *sack workers for stealing* discharge, dismiss, terminate someone's employment, declare redundant, give the sack; *inf* kick out, give someone his/her cards, give someone his/her marching orders, boot out, give the boot to, give someone the old heave-ho, give someone the push/chop/axe.

sack ² v *enemy soldiers sacking the city* plunder, ransack, raid, loot, strip, rob, rifle, pillage, maraud, harry, forage, lay waste, wreak havoc on, destroy, ruin, devastate, ravage, vandalize, despoil, rape.

sack² n *the sack of the city* plunder, ransack, raid, looting, stripping, robbing, pillage, marauding, harrying, destruction, ruin, devastation, ravaging, vandalization, vandalism, despoliation, rape, rapine. *see* SACK ² v.

sackcloth n **1** *aprons of sackcloth* sacking, hopsacking, ginny, burlap. **2** *wearing sackcloth* mourning, funeral garments, penitential garments. **In sackcloth and ashes**

penitent, penitential, repentant, contrite, sorry, remorseful, regretful, conscience-stricken, guilt-ridden, ashamed, chastened, compunctious.

sacred adj **1** *a sacred place* holy, blessed, blest, hallowed, consecrated, sanctified. **2** *sacred music* religious, spiritual, devotional, church, churchly, ecclesiastical. **3** *sacred beings* godly, divine, deified, supreme, venerated. **4** *in Hinduism the cow is sacred* sacrosanct, inviolable, inviolate, unimpeachable, invulnerable, protected, defended, secure, safe, unthreatened.

sacrifice n **1** *the job wasn't worth the sacrifice of her principles* giving up, renunciation, abandonment, surrender, relinquishment, yielding, ceding, forfeiture. **2** *make many sacrifices to educate their children* renunciation, relinquishment, loss, self-sacrifice. **3** *give the goat as a sacrifice to their god* offering, gifts, oblation, burnt offering **4** *the sacrifice of the goat to their god* offering, immolations, hecatomb.

sacrifice v **1** *sacrifice her principles for the job* give up, forgo, renounce, abandon, surrender, relinquish, yield, cede, forfeit. **2** *sacrifice the goat to the god* offer up, offer, immolate.

sacrilege n *sacrilege to vandalize the cross* desecration, profanity, profaneness, profanation, blasphemy, impiety, irreverence, irreligion, godlessness, disrespect.

sacrilegious adj profane, blasphemous, impious, irreverent, irreligious, godless, disrespectful.

sad adj **1** *feeling/looking sad about his departure* unhappy, miserable, sorrowful, gloomy, melancholy, blue, mournful, woebegone, wretched, dejected, downcast, despondent, in low spirits, low-spirited, low, downhearted, depressed, doleful, glum, cheerless, dispirited, disconsolate, heart-broken, broken-hearted, sick at heart, grief-stricken, grieving; *inf* down, down in the dumps, down in the mouth, in the pits. **2** *the sad events of the past* unhappy, unfortunate, sorrowful, miserable, sorry, depressing, upsetting, distressing, dispiriting, heart-breaking, heart-rending, pitiful, pitiable, grievous, tragic, disastrous, calamitous. **3** *the country is in a sad state* sorry, wretched, deplorable, lamentable, regrettable, unfortunate, pitiful, pitiable, pathetic, shameful, disgraceful.

sadden v cast down, deject, depress, down-hearten, dispirit, dampen one's spirits, cast a gloom upon, desolate, upset, distress, grieve, break one's heart, make one's heart bleed. *see* SAD 1.

sadness n *she was full of sadness* unhappiness, misery, sorrow, gloom, melancholy, wretchedness, dejection, despondency, low spirits, depression, dolefulness, glumness, cheerlessness, disconsolateness, broken-heartedness, heartache, grief. *see* SAD 1.

safe adj 1 *the children are safe in bed | the jewels are safe in the bank* safe and sound, secure, protected, sheltered, guarded, defended, free from harm/danger, out of harm's way. 2 *the kidnapped children are safe* unharmed, all right, alive and well, well, unhurt, uninjured, unscathed, undamaged, out of danger; *inf* OK, out of the woods. 3 *the place/building is quite safe* secure, sound, risk-free, riskless, impregnable, unassailable. 4 *he's a safe person to leave the children with* reliable, dependable, responsible, trustworthy, tried and true, reputable, upright, honest, honourable. 5 *he's a safe driver | on the safe side* reliable, cautious, circumspect, prudent, unadventurous, conservative, timid, unenterprising. 6 *these drugs are quite safe for children* harmless, innocuous, non-toxic, non-poisonous, wholesome.

safe n *put money/jewellery in the safe* strong deposits, safety-deposit box, safe-deposit box, cash-box, repository, depository, locker, vault, crypt.

safeguard n *they need to have some safeguard against fraud* protection, defence, preventive, precaution, security, surety.

safeguard v *you must safeguard your investment in the firm* protect, look after, defend, guard, preserve, secure.

safekeeping n *leave the children in her safekeeping* protection, care, charge, keeping, surveillance, custody, guardianship, trusteeship, wardship.

safety n 1 *worry about the safety of the children/jewels* safeness, security, secureness. *see* SAFE adj 1. 2 *worry about the safety of the place/building* security, secureness, soundness, riskiness, impregnability, assailability. 3 *check her safety as a baby-sitter* reliability, dependability, responsibility, trustworthiness, reputableness. *see* SAFE adj 4. 4 *ships/refugees reaching safety* shelter, sanctuary, refuge. ·

sag v 1 *the ceiling sags | the cake sags in the middle* sink, subside, curve down, slump. 2 *the hem of the skirt sags* hang unevenly, droop. 3 *his spirits sagged as the bus passed him by* fall, flag, fail, wilt, falter, weaken, languish. 4 *industrial production has sagged* fall, decline, decrease, diminish, sink, plummet, tumble; *inf* take a nose-dive.

saga n epic, chronicle, legend, history, romance

sage adj 1 *give sage advice* wise, judicious, prudent, sensible, shrewd, politic. 2 *he's a sage old man* wise, sagacious, learned, intelligent, acute, shrewd, discerning, perspicacious; *lit* sapient.

sage n wise man/woman, learned man/woman, man/woman of letters, philosopher, thinker, savant, pundit, authority, expert, guru.

sail v 1 *learn to sail* bout, cruise, yacht, ride the waves, go by water, go on a sea voyage, voyage. 2 *we sail tonight* set sail, embark, put to sea, leave port/dock, hoist sail, raise sail, put off, shove off. 3 *he is sailing the ship* steer, captain, pilot, navigate. 4 *swans/clouds sailing by* glide, drift, float, slide, sweep, skim. 5 *sail into the air* soar, wing, fly. **sail into** *he really sailed into the driver of the other car* attack, set about, fall upon, belabour; *inf* lay into, lambaste. **sail through** *sail through the exams* pass easily, gain success in easily; *inf* walk.

sailor n seaman, seafaring man, seafarer, mariner, marine, salt, sea dog, boatman, yachtsman/woman; *inf* tar, Jack Tar, matelot.

saintly adj saintlike, sainted, holy, godly, pious, God-fearing, religious, devout, blessed, virtuous, righteous, good, moral, ethical, unworldly, innocent, sinless, blameless, pure, angelic.

sake n 1 *pardon her for her mother's sake* good, wellbeing, welfare, behalf, benefit, advantage, interest, gain, profit, consideration, regard, concern, account, respect. 2 *for the sake of peace we agreed* cause, reason, purpose, aim, end, objective, object, goal, motive.

salacious adj 1 *salacious literature* lewd, obscene, pornographic, crude, ribald, blue, smutty, filthy, dirty, indecent, indelicate. 2 *he's a salacious young rascal* lustful, lecherous, randy, libidinous, licentious, lascivious, promiscuous, loose, wanton.

salary n pay, earnings, remuneration, fee, emolument, stipend, honorarium.

sale n 1 *not concerned in the actual sale of the cars* selling, vending, bargaining. 2 *she gets* *commission on all sales* deal, transaction. **3** *a ready sale for high-quality furniture* markets, outlet, demand, buyers, purchasers, customers, consumers. **for sale** *cars/flowers for sale* on sale, on offer, to be bought/purchased, purchasable. **on sale 1** *videos on sale now* for sale, in stock, on the market, purchasable, available, obtainable. **2** *end-of-season clothes on sale* reduced, marked down, discounted.

salient adj *discuss the salient points* important, main, prominent, conspicuous, striking, noticeable, obvious, remarkable, pronounced, signal, arresting.

sallow adj *looking rather sallow in the winter* yellowish, jaundiced-looking, pallid, wan, pale, waxen, anaemic, colourless, pasty, pasty-faced, unhealthy-looking, sickly-looking.

sally n **1** *enemy troops making a sally into our territory* charge, sortie, foray, thrust, offensive, drive, attack, raid, assault, onset, rush, onrush. **2** *taking a quick sally to the seaside* trip, excursion, expedition, outing, jaunt, visit, tour, airing. **3** *coming out with a series of quick sallies* witticism, smart remark, *bon mot*, quip, joke, jest, barb; *inf* wisecrack, crack.

salon n *a hairdressing salon* shop, small shop, boutique.

salt n **1** *salt added to the dish* sodium chloride, table salt, sea salt, rock salt. **2** *conversation in need of a little salt* spice, spiciness, flavour, piquancy, pungency, zest, bite, liveliness, vigour; *inf* zing, zip, zap. **3** *old salts sitting by the harbour* sailor, seaman, mariner, seafarer; *inf* tar, limey, matelot. **with a grain/pinch of salt** with reservations, sceptically, cynically, doubtfully, suspiciously, disbelievingly.

salt adj *salt water* salted, salty, saline, briny, brackish.

salty adj **1** *salty water* salted, saline, briny, brackish. **2** *a salty after-dinner speech* spicy, piquant, pungent, biting, zestful, tangy, lively, vigorous.

salubrious adj *living in a not very salubrious place/climate* healthy, health-giving, healthful, beneficial, good for one's health, wholesome, salutary, refreshing, invigorating, bracing.

salutary adj **1** *learn a salutary lesson* good, beneficial, good for one, advantageous, profitable, helpful, useful, valuable, practical, timely. **2** *salutary conditions* healthy, health-giving, healthful, wholesome. *see* SALUBRIOUS.

salutation n greeting, salute, address, welcome.

salute n **1** *raise his hat as a friendly salute* greeting, salutation, address, welcome. **2** *in salute of his services to the country* tribute, testimonial, honour, homage, recognition, acknowledgement.

salute v **1** *salute one's neighbour in passing* greet, address, hail, acknowledge, pay one's respects to. **2** *salute the old man's achievement* pay tribute to, pay homage for honour, recognize, acknowledge; *inf* take one's hat off to.

salvage n **1** *the salvage of the ship* rescue, save, recovery, reclamation, salvation. **2** *council workers collecting salvage for recycling* waste material, waste paper, scraps, remains.

salvage v **1** *succeed in salvaging the ship* rescue, save, recover. **2** *salvage valuable articles from the fire | salvage her pride* rescue, save, recover, retrieve, reclaim, get back.

salvation n **1** *the salvation of sinners* redemption deliverance, saving, rescue. **2** *regard his work as his salvation* lifeline, preservation, conservation.

same adj **1** *the same person I saw yesterday* identical, the very same, selfsame, one and the same, the very. **2** *family members having the same mannerisms* identical, alike, duplicate, twin, indistinguishable, interchangeable, corresponding, equivalent. **3** *this same man later died* selfsame, aforesaid, aforementioned. **4** *the same old food/story* unchanging, unchanged, changeless, unvarying, unvaried, invariable, unfailing, constant, consistent, uniform. **all the same 1** *all the same, I've got to go* nevertheless, nonetheless, still, yet, be that as it may, in any event, anyhow, nothwithstanding. **2** *all the same to them whether he stays or goes* immaterial, irrelevant, of no importance, important, of no consequence, inconsequential.

sameness n *complain about the sameness of the work* monotony, lack of variety, identicalness, similarity, uniformity, tedium, tediousness, routine, humdrum, predictability, repetition.

sample n **1** *a sample of his handwriting* specimen, example, instance, illustration, exemplification, representative type, model, pattern. **2** *the votes of a sample of the population* cross-section, sampling, test.

sample v *sample the wine* try, try out, test, examine, inspect, taste, partake of.

sample adj **1** *a sample section of people* representative, illustrative, typifying. **2** *a sample size of perfume bottle* test, trials, pilot.

sanctify v **1** *sanctify the building* consecrate, make holy/sacred, bless, hallow, set apart, dedicate. **2** *sanctify sinners* free from sin, absolve, purify, cleanse, wash someone's sins away. **3** *a practice sanctified by tradition* sanction, ratify, confirm, warrant, legitimize, legitimatize.

sanctimonious adj self-righteous, holier-than-thou, over-pious, pietistic, unctuous, smug, mealy-mouthed, hypocritical, simon pure, pharisaic, Tartuffian; *inf* too good to be true, goody-goody, pi.

sanction n **1** *receive the sanction of the church/ authorities* authorization, warrant, accreditation, licence, endorsement, permission, consent, approval, seal of approval, stamp of approval, go-ahead, approbation, acceptance, thumbs up; *inf* backing, support; *inf* the green light, OK. **2** *laws receiving sanction* ratification, validation, confirmation. **3** *sanctions imposed against certain crimes* penalty, punishment, penalization, penance, sentence. **4** *impose trade sanctions on the enemy country* embargo, ban, boycott.

sanction v **1** *unwilling to sanction the sale* authorize, warrant, accredit, license, endorse, permit, allow, consent to, approve, accept, give the thumbs up to, back, support; *inf* give the green light to, OK. **2** *sanction the new law* ratify, validate, confirm.

sanctity n **1** *the sanctity of the altar | the sanctity of marriage* sacredness, holiness, inviolability. **2** *the sanctity of the priest* holiness, godliness, saintliness, spirituality, religiosity, piety, devoutness, devotion, righteousness, goodness, virtue, purity.

sanctuary n **1** *priests standing in the sanctuary* holy place, church, temple, shrine, altar, sanctum. **2** *find a sanctuary from his pursuers* refuge, haven, shelter, retreat, hide-out, hiding place. **3** *seek sanctuary in the church* safety, safe-keeping, protection, shelter, security, immunity. **4** *a bird sanctuary* preserve, reserve, wildlife reserve, reservation.

sane adj **1** *patients not absolutely sane* of sound mind, in one's right mind, *compos mentis*, rational, lucid, in possession of one's faculties; *inf* all there. **2** *a sane decision | a sane course of action* sensible, reasonable, sound, balanced, level-headed, judicious, responsible, prudent, wise, politic, advisable.

sang-froid n composure, coolness, calmness, self-possession, self-control, presence of mind, poise, equanimity, equilibrium, aplomb, nerve, imperturbability, unflappability.

sanguine adj **1** *not sanguine of their chances of success* optimistic, confident, assured, hopeful, buoyant, cheerful, spiral. **2** *a sanguine complexion* florid, ruddy, red, rubicund.

sanitary adj *scarcely sanitary conditions in the hotel kitchens* hygienic, clean, germ-free, antiseptic, aseptic, sterile, unpolluted, salubrious, healthy.

sanity n **1** *question the patient's sanity* saneness, soundness of mind, mental health, reason, rationality, lucidness. **2** *acknowledge the sanity of the decision* sense, sensibleness, common sense, good sense, reasonableness, rationality, soundness, judiciousness, prudence, wisdom, advisability.

sap n **1** *of the sap rising in the plants* vital fluids, life fluid, juice. **2** *people full of sap and ready to go* vigour, energy, vitality, vivacity, enthusiasm, spirit; *inf* pep, zip, oomph. **3** *a poor sap taking all the blame* fool, idiot, simpleton, nincompoop, ninny; *inf* twit, nitwit, chump, jerk, drip, wet.

sap v **1** *completely sapped by the heat* drain, enervate, exhaust, weaken, enfeeble, debilitate, devitalize. **2** *sap their confidence* erode, wear away, deplete, impair, drain, bleed.

sarcasm n decision, scorn, mockery, ridicule, sneering, scoffing, gibing, taunting, irony, satire, lampoon, causticness, trenchancy, acerbity, acrimony, asperity, mordancy, bitterness, spitefulness.

sarcastic adj derisive, derisory, scornful, mocking, sneering, jeering, scoffing, taunting, ironic, sardonic, satirical, caustic, trenchant, acerbic, acrimonious, mordant, bitter, spiteful; *inf* sarky.

sardonic adj dry, wry, derisory, scornful, mocking, cynical, sneering, jeering, scoffing, contemptuous, ironic, sarcastic, caustic, trenchant, acerbic, mordant, bitter, spiteful.

Satan n the Devil, the Evil One, Old Nick, Prince of Darkness, Lord of the Flies, Lucifer, Beelzebub, Moloch, Belial, Apollyon.

satanic adj diabolical, fiendish, devilish, demonic, demoniac, demoniacal, hellish, infernal, accursed, wicked, evil, sinful, iniquitous, malevolent, vile, foul.

satellite n **1** *launch a satellite into space* spacecraft, space capsule, space station, communications satellite, weather satellite. **2** *satellites requesting independence* protectorate, dependency, colony, dominion.

3 *the star and his satellites have arrived* hench-man, hanger-on, lackey, flunkey, minion, underling, toady, sycophant, follower, dependent, retainer, dependant.

satellite adj *a satellite state* dependent, tributary, subordinate, puppet, vassal.

satiate v *satiated with food/pleasure* sate, fully satisfy, overfill, surfeit, stuff, glut, gorge, cloy.

satire n **1** *write a satire* burlesque, parody, travesty, caricature, lampoon, skit, pasquinade; *inf* take-off, spoof, send-up. **2** *treat them with satire* mockery, ridicule, irony, sarcasm.

satirical adj mocking, ridiculing, taunting, ironic, sarcastic, sardonic, caustic, biting, cutting, stinging, trenchant, mordant, ascerbic, pungent, critical, censorius, cynical.

satirize v mock, ridicule, hold up to ridicule, deride, make fun of, poke fun at, parody, lampoon, burlesque, travesty, criticize, censure; *inf* take off, send up.

satisfaction n **1** *derive satisfaction* fulfilment, gratification, pleasure, enjoyment, delight, happiness, pride, comfort, content, contentment, smugness. **2** *the satisfaction of her desires/demands* fulfilment, gratification, appeasement, assuagement, achievement. **3** *demand satisfaction for the trouble caused* damages, compensation, recompense, amends, reparation, redress, indemnity, restitution, requital, atonement, reimbursement, remuneration, payment.

satisfactory adj adequate, all right, acceptable, fine, good enough, sufficient, competent, up to standard, up to the mark, up to par, up to scratch, passable, average; *inf* OK, okay.

satisfied adj **1** *satisfied* fulfilled, gratified, appeased, assuaged. **2** *satisfied with the results of their work* pleased, happy, content, smug; *inf* like the cat that swallowed the cream/canary. **3** *satisfied that he is telling the truth* convinced, persuaded, sure, positive, certain, easy in one's mind.

satisfy v **1** *satisfy their appetites/thirst* satiate, sate, slake, quench. **2** *satisfy their desires/ demands* fulfil, gratify, appease, assuage, meet, indulge. **3** *satisfy the heating needs* solve, resolve, answer, be the answer to, meet, serve the purpose of, be sufficient/ adequate/good enough for. **4** *satisfy the qualification requirements* fulfil, meet, comply with, answer. **5** *satisfy a debt* pay, settle, discharge, square up. **6** *satisfy old scores* make reparation for, atone for, compensate for, recompense. **7** *satisfy the police that he is*

innocent convince, persuade, assure, reassure, remove/dispel doubts, put one's mind at rest.

satisfying adj **1** *a satisfying job* fulfilling, gratifying, pleasing, enjoyable, pleasurable. **2** *give a satisfying reason* satisfactory, reasonable, convincing, reassuring.

saturate v **1** *saturate the garment* wet through, wet, soak, souse, steep, douse. **2** *the rain saturated us* wet through, soak, drench. **3** *bodies saturated with sunshine* permeate, imbue, pervade, suffuse. **4** *saturate the mark* overfill, surfeit, glut, satiate, sate.

saturated adj wet through, soaked, soaked to the skin, soaking, soaking wet, drenched, sodden, dripping wet, wringing wet.

sauce n **1** *salt and sauce | a red-wine sauce* relish, dressing, condiment, flavouring. **2** *annoyed at the sauce of the girl* impudence, cheek, impertinence, insolence, rudeness, disrespect, audacity, presumption, temerity, boldness, brazenness, gall, pertness, brashness; *inf* sauciness, brass, lip, freshness, backchat.

saucy adj **1** *older people complaining about saucy girls* impudent, cheeky, impertinent, insolent, rude, disrespectful, audacious, presumptuous, bold, brazen, pert, brash; *inf* fresh. **2** *hats worn at a saucy angle* jaunty, dashing, rakish, sporty, gay, dapper; *inf* natty.

saunter v stroll, amble, wander, meander, walk, ramble, roam, promenade; *inf* mosey.

saunter n stroll, amble, wander, meander, walk, ramble, turn, roam, airing, promenade, constitutional.

savage adj **1** *a savage blow | savage criticism* vicious, ferocious, fierce, brutal, cruel, bloody, murderous, bloodthirsty, inhuman, harsh, grim, terrible, merciless, ruthless, pitiless, sadistic, barbarous, fell. **2** *a savage animal* fierce, ferocious, wild, untamed, undomesticated, feral. **3** *attacked by a savage gang* fierce, ferocious, wild, rough, rugged, uncivilized, barbarous, barbaric. **4** *explorers encountering savage tribes in the jungle* primitive, uncivilized, uncultivated, wild.

savage n **1** *sailors attacked by island savages* barbarians wild man/woman, native, primitive, heathen. **2** *calling the children savages* barbarian, boor, churl, yahoo; *inf* yobbo. **3** *her attacker was a savage* brute, beast, monster, barbarian, ogre.

savage v **1** *lambs savaged by a wild dog* maul, lacerate, mangle, tear to pieces, attack. **2** *plays savaged by critics* criticize severely, tear to pieces, take apart; *inf* knock, slate, slam.

save v **1** *save the children from death/danger* rescue, free, set free, liberate, deliver, snatch, bail out, salvage, redeem. **2** *save them from their sinful desires* protect, safeguard, guard, keep, keep safe, shield, screen, preserve, conserve. **3** *save a lot of trouble* prevent, obviate, forestall, spare, make unnecessary, rule out. **4** *save some money/supplies* put aside, set aside, put by, put away, lay by, keep, reserve, conserve, salt away, stockpile, store, hoard. **5** *time to save not spend* economise, practise, economy, be thrifty, be frugal, budget, husband one's resources, cut costs, cut expenditure, draw in one's horns.

savings npl capital, assets, resources, reserves, funds, nest-egg.

saviour n *rescued children thanking their saviour* rescuer, liberator, deliverer, emancipator, champion, knight in shining armour, Good Samaritan, friend in need.

Saviour n *worshipping the Saviour* Christ, Jesus, Jesus Christ, the Redeemer, the Messiah, Our Lord.

savoir faire n finesse, poise, aplomb, social graces, social skill, adroitness, accomplishment, style, tact, tactfulness, diplomacy, discretion, smoothness, urbanity, suaveness; *inf* savvy.

savour n **1** *the savour of fresh raspberries in her mouth* taste, flavour, tang, relish, smack. **2** *the savour of freshly-baked bread in the air* smell, aroma, fragrance, scent, perfume, bouquet, odour. **3** *a smile with a savour of menace | politics with a savour of fanaticism* hint, suggestion, touch, vein, tone. **4** *a life deprived of some of its savour* enjoyment, joy, excitement, interest, zest, spice, piquancy.

savour v **1** *savour the taste of home-made soup | savour the joys of freedom* taste, enjoy, enjoy to the full/to the hilt, appreciate, delight in, take pleasure in, relish, revel in, smack one's lips over, luxuriate in. **2** *a situation savouring of dishonesty* smack of, show signs of, exhibit traces of, suggest, be suggestive of, be indicative of, bear the hallmark of.

savoury adj **1** *savoury smells from the kitchen | tables laden with savoury delights* appetizing, mouth-watering, fragrant, flavoursome, palatable, tasty, delicious, delectable, luscious, toothsome; *inf* scrumptious. **2** *preferring savoury snacks to sweets* salty, piquant, tangy, spicy.

saw n *a book of old saws* saying, proverb, maxim, aphorism, axiom, adage, epigram,

dictum, gnome, apothegm, platitude, cliché.

say v **1** *refuse to say his name* speak, utter, mention, voice, pronounce, put into words, give utterance to, give voice to, vocalize. **2** *"It's too expensive", he said* state, remark, announce, affirm, assert, maintain, declare, aver, allege, profess, avow; *lit* opine; *inf* come out with. **3** *finding it difficult to say how one feels* express, put into words, tell, phrase, articulate, communicate, make known, convey, reveal, divulge, disclose. **4** *say a short poem* recite, repeat, deliver, declaim, orate, read, perform, rehearse. **5** *What do the instructions say?* indicate, specify, designate, tell, give information, suggest. **6** *I would say it's four miles from here* estimate, judge, guess, hazard a guess, predict, speculate, conjecture, surmise, imagine, assume, suppose, presume. **7** *old people said to be dying* state, suggest, allege, claim, put about, report, rumour, bruit, noise abroad. **8** *much to be said in favour of the idea* propose, advance, bring forward, offer, introduce, adduce, plead.

say n **1** *everyone being entitled to a say* opinion, view, right to speak, chance to speak, turn to speak, vote, voice; *inf* twopence worth. **2** *people having no say in the decision* share, part, influence, sway, weight, input. **that is to say** *a fortnight, that is to say fourteen days* in other words, to put it another way, to rephrase it. **to say the least** *to say the least he is not a good worker* to put it mildly, without any exaggeration, at the very least.

saying n *old sayings about the weather* proverb, maxim, aphorism, axiom, adage, saw, epigram, dictum, gnome, apothegm, platitude, cliché. **it goes without saying** *it goes without saying that he will pay* of course, naturally, it is taken for granted, it is understood/assumed, it is taken as read, it is accepted, it is unquestionable.

scaffold n **1** *painters standing on a scaffold* scaffolding, frame, framework, gantry. **2** *murderers going to the scaffold* gallows, gibbet.

scale[1] n **1** *scales on a fish* lamella, lamina, plate, squama. **2** *a disease causing scales on the skin* flake, scurf, furfur. **3** *scale on a kettle* coating, coat, crust, incrustation, covering.

scale[2] n *weigh it on the scale* scales, weighing-machines, balance.

scale[3] n **1** *on the Richter scale | social scale* graduated system, calibrated system, measuring system, progression, succession, sequence, series, ranking, register, ladder, hierarchy; *inf* pecking order. **2** *a scale of a* hundred miles to the centimetre ratio, proportion. **3** *entertain on the grand scale* extent, scope, range, degree, reach.

scale v *scale the high wall* climb, ascend, go up, clamber, mount, clamber up, escalade. **scale down** *scale down the extent of the alterations* reduce, cut down, cut back on, decrease, lessen, lower, trim.

scaly adj **1** *scaly creatures* squamate, squamose, squamous. **2** *scaly patches on the skin* flaky, scurfy, rough, scabrous, furfuraceous.

scamp n rascal, rogue, imp, devil, monkey, wretch, scallywag, mischief-maker, troublemaker, prankster, miscreant, tyke, scapegrace.

scamper v scurry, scuttle, dart, run, rush, dash, race, sprint, hurry, hasten, scramble; *inf* scoot.

scan v **1** *scan the horizon/evidence* study, examine, scrutinize, survey, inspect, take stock of, search, scour, sweep. **2** *scan the pages of the document* skim, look over, have a look at, glance over, run one's eye over, read through, leaf through, thumb through, flick through, flip through

scandal n **1** *corruption scandals destroying political careers* wrongdoing, impropriety, misconduct, offence, transgression, crime, sin. **2** *caused a scandal in the village* outrage, disgrace, embarrassment. **3** *bring scandal on the family* disgrace, shame, dishonour, disrepute, discredit, odium, opprobrium, censure, obloquy. **4** *spread scandal about the politician* scandalmongering, slander, libel, calumny, defamation, aspersion, gossip, malicious rumours, dirt, muck-raking, smear campaign. **5** *his treatment of her was a scandal* disgrace, shame, pity, crying shame.

scandalize v *scandalized by their unethical behaviour* shock, appal, outrage, horrify, affront, disgust, offend, insult, cause raised eyebrows.

scandalous adj **1** *public figures, guilty of scandalous behaviour* disgraceful, shameful, dishonourable, outrageous, shocking, monstrous, disreputable, improper, unseemly, discreditable, infamous, opprobrious. **2** *spread scandalous rumours* slanderous, libellous, defamatory, scurrilous, malicious, gossiping.

scant adj *pay scant attention* little, minimal, limited, barely sufficient, insufficient, inadequate, deficient.

scanty adj *scanty supplies of food* meagre, scant, sparse, small, paltry, slender, negligible, skimpy, thin, poor, insufficient, inad-

equate, deficient, limited, restricted, exiguous.

scapegoat n whipping-boy; *inf* fall guy.

scar n **1** *a scar left by the knife-wound* mark, blemish, blotch, discolouration, cicatrix, disfigurement, defacement. **2** *child abuse leaving a permanent emotional scar* damage, trauma, shock, injury, suffering, upset.

scar v **1** *scarred for life by the knife attack* mark, blemish, blotch, discolour, disfigure, deface. **2** *emotionally scarred for life* damage, traumatize, shock, injure, upset.

scarce adj **1** *money being scarce* in short supply, short, meagre, scant, scanty, sparse, paltry, not enough, too little, insufficient, deficient, inadequate, lacking, at a premium, exiguous. **2** *red squirrels being scarce* rare, infrequent, few and far between, seldom seen/found, sparse, uncommon, unusual.

scarcely adv **1** *I scarcely know them* hardly, barely, only just. **2** *I can scarcely expect them to believe that* hardly, certainly not, definitely not, surely not, not at all, on no account, under no circumstances, by no means.

scarcity n **1** *scarcity of money in the recession* dearth, shortage, undersupply, paucity, meagreness, scantness, sparseness, insufficiency, deficiency, inadequacy, lack, exiguity. **2** *the scarcity of red squirrels* rarity, rareness, infrequency, sparseness, uncommonness, unusualness.

scare v fright, make afraid, alarm, startle, make fearful, make nervous, terrify, terrorize, petrify, horrify, appal, shock, intimidate, daunt, awe, cow, panic, put the fear of God into, scare stiff, make one's blood run cold, make one's flesh creep, make one's hair stand on end; *inf* put the wind up one, scare the living daylights out of, scare the pants off.

scare n *children recovering from a scare* fright, alarm, start, fearfulness, nervousness, terror, horror, shock, panic.

scared adj *scared children running away* frightened, afraid, alarmed, shaken, fearful, nervous, terrified, petrified, horrified, cowed, panic-stricken, panicky.

scarf n muffler, neckerchief, kerchief, cravat, bandanna, headscarf.

scary adj *a scary experience* scaring, frightening, alarming, startling, nerve racking, terrifying, petrifying, hair-raising, horrifying, appalling, daunting.

scathing adj *scathing criticism* virulent, savage, fierce, ferocious, brutal, stinging, biting, mordant, trenchant, caustic, vitriolic, withering, scornful, harsh, severe, stern.

scatter v **1** *scatter seed | scatter breadcrumbs for birds* disseminate, diffuse, spread, sow, sprinkle, strew, broadcast, fling, toss, throw. **2** *the crowd scattered | police scattered the crowd* break up, disperse, disband, separate, dissolve.

scatter-brained adj irresponsible, forgetful, dreamy, wool-gathering, with one's head in the clouds, feather-brained, harebrained, erratic, giddy.

scavenge v *scavenging on the beach for food* search, look for, hunt, forage for, rummage for, scrounge.

scavenger n *scavengers looking for goods in dustbins* forager, rummager, scrounger.

scenario n **1** *discuss the scenario with the producer* plot, outline, synopsis, summary, précis, rundown, story-line, structure, scheme, plan. **2** *predict a depressing scenario* sequence of events, future situation.

scene n **1** *the scene of the accident* place, location, site, position, spot, setting, locate, whereabouts, arena, stage. **2** *against a scene of confusion* background, backdrop, setting, set, *mise en scène*. **3** *witnessing scandalous scenes* event, incident, happening, situation, episode, affair, moment, proceeding. **4** *look out on beautiful rural scenes* scenery, view, outlook, landscape, vista, panorama, prospect. **5** *the embarrassing scene created by his wife* fuss, exhibition, outburst, commotion, to-do, row, upset, tantrum, furore, brouhaha. **6** *football not being his scene* area of interest, field of interest, field, interest, sphere, world, milieu. **7** *appearing in every scene of the play* division.

scenery n **1** *tourists admiring the scenery* view, outlook, landscape, vista, panorama, prospect. **2** *helping to shift/paint the scenery* set, stage set, setting, background, backdrop, *mise en scène*.

scenic adj **1** *the scenic route* picturesque, pretty, beautiful, pleasing. **2** *the scenic advantages of the area* landscape, panoramic.

scent n **1** *the scent of new-mown hay* aroma, perfume, fragrance, smell, bouquet, redolence, odour. **2** *dogs losing the scent of the fox* track, trail, spoor. **3** *a scent of scandal about the affair* hint, suggestion, whiff, implication. **4** *wearing an expensive scent* perfume, fragrance, toilet water; *eau de Cologne*.

scent v **1** *dogs scenting the fox* smell, sniff, be on the track/trail of, track, trail. **2** *scenting danger/redundancy* detect, discern, recognize, become aware of, sense, get wind of, sniff out, nose out.

scented adj *scented paper* perfumed, sweet-smelling, fragrant, aromatic.

sceptic n **1** *supporters of his theories arguing with the sceptics* questioner, doubter, doubting Thomas, disbeliever, dissenter, scoffer, cynic. **2** *ministers of the church challenging sceptics* agnostic, unbeliever, doubter, doubting Thomas.

sceptical adj *trying to convince sceptical opponents* doubting, doubtful, dubious, questioning, distrustful, mistrustful, suspicious, hesitant, disbelieving, misbelieving, incredulous, unconvinced, scoffing, cynical, pessimistic, defeatist.

scepticism n **1** *persist in the face of scepticism* doubt, doubtfulness, dubiety, distrust, mistrust, suspicion, hesitancy, disbelief, misbelief, incredulity, scoffing, cynicism, pessimism, defeatism. **2** *religious scepticism* agnosticism, unbelief, doubt.

schedule n **1** *projects going according to schedule* timetable, plan, scheme, programme. **2** *a busy schedule* appointment list, list of appointments, diary, calendar, social calendar, itinerary, agenda. **3** *a schedule of services/equipment* list, catalogue, syllabus, inventory.

schedule v *schedule the meeting for tomorrow* time, timetable, arrange, organize, plan, programme, book, slot in.

scheme n **1** *a scheme for recycling paper* plan, programme, project, course of action, line of action, system, procedure, strategy, design, device, tactics, contrivance. **2** *an attractive colour scheme* arrangement, system, organization, disposition, schema. **3** *produce the scheme for the new shopping centre* outline, blueprint, design, delineation, diagram, layout, sketch, chart, map, schema. **4** *police discovering his little scheme* plot, ruse, ploy, stratagem, manoeuvre, machinations, subterfuge, intrigue, conspiracy; *inf* game, racket.

scheme v *rebels scheming to overthrow the government* plot, conspire, intrigue, manoeuvre, plan, lay plans.

scheming adj calculating, designing, conniving, wily, crafty, cunning, sly, tricky, artful, foxy, slippery, underhand, duplicitous, devious, Machiavellian.

schism n division, breach, split, rift, break, rupture, separation, splintering, disunion, scission, severance, detachment, discord, disagreement.

scholar n **1** *scholars giving expert opinions on texts* man/woman of letters, learned person, academic, intellectual, pundit, savant; *inf* bookworm, egghead, highbrow. **2** *quick* *scholars | a school of 500 scholars* learner, student, pupil, schoolboy, schoolgirl.

scholarly adj learned, erudite, academic, well-read, intellectual, scholastic, literary, studious, bookish, lettered; *inf* egghead, highbrow.

scholarship n **1** *works showing scholarship* learning, book-learning, knowledge, education, erudition, letters. **2** *people of great scholarship* learning, book-learning, letters, erudition, education, academic achievement/attainment/accomplishment. **3** *on a scholarship to the school/college* bursary, fellowship, endowment, grant.

scholastic adj *her scholastic record* academic, educational, school.

school n **1** *attend the local school* educational institution, nursery school, primary school, secondary school, comprehensive school, grammar school, high school, academy, seminary, public school, private school. **2** *the music school at the university* department, faculty, division. **3** *belonging to the Impressionist school of art* group, set, proponents, adherents, devotees, circle, class, sect, clique, faction, followers, following, disciples, admirers, votaries, pupils, students. **4** *teachers belonging to the old school* school of thought, outlook, persuasion, opinion, point of view, belief, faith, creed, credo, doctrine, stamp, way of life.

school v **1** *schooled locally* educate, teach, instruct. **2** *school a horse | school oneself to be patient* train, coach, instruct, drill, discipline, direct, guide, prepare, prime, verse.

schooling n **1** *refuse to continue with his schooling* education, instruction, teaching, tuition, learning, book-learning. **2** *the schooling of a horse* training, coaching, instruction, drill, discipline. *see* SCHOOL v 2.

schoolteacher n schoolmaster/mistress, instructor, tutor, pedagogue.

science n **1** *the science of the universe* body of knowledge/information/facts, branch of knowledge, area of study, discipline. **2** *study science rather than the arts* physical science, physics, chemistry, biology. **3** *pursuits requiring a certain science* skill, art, expertise, expertness, proficiency, dexterity, deftness, facility.

scientific adj **1** *scientific discoveries* chemical, biological, medical, technical, technology. **2** *requiring a scientific approach* systematic, methodical, orderly, regulated, controlled, exact, precise, mathematical.

scintillate v **1** *diamonds scintillating* sparkle, twinkle, flash, gleam, glitter, glint, glisten, coruscate. **2** *scintillating at the dinner party*

be sparkling, be vivacious, be lively, be witty. *see* SCINTILLATING.

scintillating adj *scintillating companions/conversation* sparkling, dazzling, vivacious, effervescent, lively, animated, ebullient, bright, brilliant, witty, exciting, stimulating, invigorating.

scion n **1** *a scion of a noble family* descendent, heir, offspring, issue, child. **2** *planting scions* shoot, offshoot, cutting, graft.

scoff[1] v *upset by other children scoffing at his size* jeer at, mock at, sneer at, gibe at, taunt, laugh at, ridicule, poke fun at, make a fool of, make sport of, rag, revile, deride, belittle, pooh-pooh, scorn; *inf* knock.

scoff[2] v *scoff all the biscuits* guzzle, gulp down, devour, finish off.

scold v **1** *children scolded for being late* rebuke, reprimand, chide, reprove, reproach, remonstrate with, upbraid, berate, censure, lecture, castigate, haul over the coals, read the riot act to, rap over the knuckles, bring to book; *inf* tell off, give a telling-off to, give a talking-to to, give a dressing-down to, tick off, give a ticking-off to, carpet, give a carpeting to, bawl out. **2** *a wife always scolding* nag, lay down the law, rail, carp, criticize, find fault, complain; *inf* go on.

scold n *married to a scold* nag, shrew, termagant; *inf* battleaxe.

scolding n rebuke, reprimand, chiding, reproach, upbraiding, lecture, rap over the knuckles; *inf* telling-off, talking-to, ticking-off, row, carpeting, bawling-out, wigging.

scoop n **1** *a scoop of ice-cream* ladle, spoon, dipper. **2** *reporters getting a scoop* exclusive story, revelation, exposé.

scoop v **1** *scoop out the hole* hollow out, gouge out. **2** *scoop out the earth from the site* hollow out, gouge out, dig, excavate. **3** *scoop up the leaves* gather up, pick up, lift.

scope n **1** *within the scope of the inquiry* extent, range, sphere, area, field, realm, compass, orbit, reach, span, sweep, confine, limit. **2** *a job with much scope | scope for improvement* opportunity, freedom, latitude, capacity, room to manoeuvre, elbow-room.

scorch v **1** *scorched by an iron* burn, singe, char, sear, discolour. **2** *grass scorched by the sun* burn, dry up, wither, discolour, brown.

scorching adj **1** *a scorching day* very hot, unbearably hot, sweltering, torrid; *inf* boiling, broiling, sizzling, baking. **2** *scorching criticism* stringent, scathing, caustic, mordant, trenchant, biting, harsh, severe.

score n **1** *enter their score* number of points/ goals, record of points/goals, total. **2** *a score of five-nil* result, outcome. **3** *rejected on several scores* basis, grounds, reason, account, count. **4** *a score on the table/wall* notch, mark, scratch, scrape, groove, cut, nick, chip, gouge, incision, slit, gash. **5** *money to pay the score* bill, tally, reckoning, amount, due, debt, obligation; *inf* tab. **6** *a score to settle* dispute, grievance, grudge, injury, a bone to pick, a bone of contention. **know the score** be aware of the situation, be aware of the facts, know the truth of the matter, know the true state of affairs; *inf* know what's what.

score v **1** *score a point/goal* win, gain, achieve; *inf* chalk up, notch up. **2** *yet to score* win a point/goal, gain a point. **3** *scoring for the two teams* keep count, keep a record, keep a tally. **4** *least likely to score* achieve success, win, triumph, gain an advantage, make an impression; *inf* be a hit. **5** *score the paintwork* notch, make a notch in, mark, scratch, scrape, make a groove in, cut, nick, chip, gouge, slit, gash. **score off** *score points off his opponent in public* get the better of, humiliate, make a fool of, have the last laugh; *inf* be one up on. **score out/through** *score out his name* cross out, strike out, put a line through, delete, obliterate.

scores npl *scores of people at the concert* crowds, throngs, multitudes, droves, swarms, armies, legions.

scorn n *treat the poor with scorn* contempt, contemptuousness, disdain, haughtiness, disparagement, derision, mockery, contumely.

scorn v **1** *scorn their attempts at playing* be contemptuous, hold in contempt, look down on, disdain, disparage, slight, deride, mock, scoff at, sneer at. **2** *scorn his invitation/advice* rebuff, spurn, shun, refuse, reject, turn down.

scornful adj contemptuous, disdainful, haughty, supercilious, disparaging, slighting, scathing, derisive, mocking, scoffing, sneering, contumelious.

scoundrel n villain, rogue, rascal, miscreant, reprobate, scapegrace, cad, good-for-nothing, ne'er-do-well, wastrel; *inf* rotter, bounder.

scour v **1** *scour the bath* scrub, rub, clean, cleanse, abrade, wash, wipe, polish, buff, burnish. **2** *scour the countryside/scour the newspaper* search, comb, go over, look all over, ransack, hunt through, rake through, rummage through, leave no stone unturned.

scourge n **1** *her employer/backache regarded as the scourge of her life* bane, curse, affliction, plague, trial, trial and tribulation, torment, torture, suffering, burden, cross to bear, thorn in one's flesh/side, nuisance, pest, punishment, penalty, visitation. **2** *punished with a scourge* whip, horsewhip, bullwhip, switch, lash, cat o' nine tails, thong, flail, strap, birch.

scourge v **1** *scourge the offenders* whip, horsewhip, flog, lash, strap, birch, cane, thrash, beat, leather; belt, wallop, lambaste, tan someone's hide. **2** *scourge by guilt* curse, afflict, plague, torment, torture, suffer from, burden, punish.

scout n **1** *scouts returning with no information* advance guard, vanguard, look-out man/ woman, outrider, spy. **2** *a scout in the audience* talent scout, talent spotter, recruiter.

scout v **1** *scout for information* search for, search out, look for, seek, hunt for, look around for, cast around for, ferret around for. **2** *scout out the territory* reconnoitre, make a reconnaissance of, spy out, survey, make a survey of, inspect, investigate, examine, scan, study, observe; *inf* check out, case, make a recce of.

scowl v *old men scowling at the noisy children* frown, glower, glare, lower, look daggers at, look angry/disapproving, give black looks, give dirty looks.

scowl n frown, glower, glare, black look, dirty look.

scraggy adj scrawny, thin, thin as a rake, skinny, gaunt, bony, angular, raw-boned.

scramble v **1** *scramble over the fence* clamber, climb/crawl. **2** *scramble to get there on time* hastily struggle, hurry, hasten, rush, race, scurry. **3** *scramble for a place in the final* jockey, struggle, jostle, strive, contend, compete, vie. **4** *sewing things scrambled together* mix up, jumble, tangle, throw into confusion, disorganize.

scramble n **1** *go for a scramble over the hills* clamber, climb, trek. **2** *a scramble to get there on time* hurry, rush, race, scurry. **3** *a scramble to get/reach the final* jockeying, struggle, tussle, jostle, competition, vying.

scrap[1] n **1** *a scrap of material* fragment, piece, bit, snippet, remnant, tatter. **2** *a scrap of food* piece, bit, morsel, particle, sliver, crumb, bite, mouthful. **3** *not a scrap of truth in it* bit, grain, iota, trace, whit, snatch. **4** *collect scrap* waste, junk, rubbish, scrap metal.

scrap[1] v *scrap the van/plans* throw away, get rid of, discard, toss out, abandon, jettison, dispense with, shed; *inf* ditch, junk, throw on the scrap-heap.

scrap² n *children having a scrap* fight, row, quarrel, argument, squabble, wrangle, tiff, fracas, brawl, scuffle, disagreement, clash; *inf* set-to, dust-up, run-in, barney.

scrap² v *children scrapping* fight, row, quarrel, bicker, argue, squabble, wrangle, brawl, disagree; *inf* fall out, have a set-to/dust-up.

scrape v **1** *scrape the surface to level it* scour, rub, scrub, file, sandpaper. **2** *scrape food from the pans* clean, remove, erase. **3** *a child scraping a knife across metal* grate, rasp, grind, scratch. **4** *gates scraping in the wind* creak, grate, squeak, screech, set one's teeth on edge. **5** *fall and scrape one's knee* graze, scratch, abrade, skin, cut, lacerate, bark. **6** *scrape the side of a car* damage, deface, spoil, mark. **scrape by/along** *scrape by on his earnings* barely manage to live, barely have enough to live on, keep the wolf from the door, scrape a living. **scrape through** *scrape through exams* just pass, pass and no more, pass by a narrow margin, just succeed, narrowly achieve.

scrape n **1** *the scrape of a knife on metal* grating, rasping, grinding, scratching, creaking, squeaking. **2** *wash the scrape on the child's knee* graze, scratch, abrasion, cut, laceration, wound. **3** *a scrape on the paintwork* scratch, mark, defacement. **4** *getting into scrapes at school* trouble, mischief. **5** *in a bit of a financial scrape* trouble, difficulty, straits, distress, mess, muddle, predicament, plight, tight spot, tight corner; *inf* fix.

scraps npl leftovers, leavings, scrapings, remains, residue, bits and pieces, odds and ends.

scratch v **1** *skin scratched by rose bushes* graze, scrape, abrade, skin, cut, lacerate, bark. **2** *scratch an itchy part* rub, scrape, tear at. **3** *scratch a knife over metal* scrape, grate, rasp, grind. **4** *scratch his name from the list* cross out, strike out, delete, erase, remove, eliminate. **5** *runners scratching from the race* withdraw, pull out, stand down. **scratch about/around** *scratch about for proof* search, hunt, cast about, rummage around, forage about, poke about.

scratch n **1** *a scratch on the skin* graze, scrape, abrasion, cut, laceration, wound. **2** *a scratch on the paint-work* scrape, mark, line, defacement. **up to scratch** up to standard, up to par, satisfactory, acceptable, passable, sufficient, adequate, competent; *inf* OK.

scrawl v *scrawl his name* scribble, scratch, dash off.

scrawl n *unable to read his scrawl* scribble, illegible handwriting.

scrawny adj scraggy, thin, skinny. *see* SCRAGGY.

scream n **1** *a scream of pain* shriek, howl, shout, yell, cry, screech, yelp, squeal, wail, squawk, bawl; *inf* holler. **2** *the entertainer's a scream* comedian, comic, joker, laugh, wit, clown; *inf* hoot, riot, barrel of laughs, card, caution.

scream v **1** *scream in pain* shriek, howl, shout, cry out, call out, yell, screech, yelp, squeal, wail, squawk, bawl; *inf* holler. **2** *the true facts screamed at one* be obvious, be glaringly obvious, be blatant, be apparent. **3** *the colours screamed* clash, not to go together, jar.

screech n *a screech of fright* shriek, howl, shout, yell, squeal, squawk, ball; *inf* holler.

screech v *screeching in pain* shriek, howl, shout, yell. *see* SCREECH n.

screen n **1** *washing facilities behind a screen* partition, room-divider. **2** *a screen on a window* mesh, net, netting, curtain, blind. **3** *act as a screen from the wind/sun* shelter, shield, protection, guard, safeguard, buffer. **4** *the shop was a screen for his drug-dealing* concealment, cover, cloak, veil, mask, camouflage, disguise, façade, front, blind. **5** *coal put through a screen* sieve, riddle, strainer, colander, filter, winnow.

screen v **1** *screen off the washing area* partition off, divide off, conceal, hide. **2** *screen them from the wind* shelter, shield, protect, guard, safeguard. **3** *their activities screened by darkness* conceal, hide, cover, cloak, veil, mask, camouflage, disguise. **4** *employees screened by the security service* vet, check, test. **5** *screen people for cancer* check, test, examine, investigate, scan. **6** *screen coal* sieve, riddle, sift, strain, filter, winnow.

screw n **1** *loose screws in the door* bolt, pin, fastener. **2** *tighten with two or three screws* turn, twist, twirl. **put the screws on** *put the screws on them to get the money* put pressure on, pressurize, bring force to bear on, force, coerce, compel, constrain, hold a pistol to someone's head.

screw v **1** *screw in the nail* tighten, turn, twist, work in. **2** *screw the planks down* fasten, clamp, rivet, batten. **3** *screw money out of her* force, extort, extract, wrest, bleed, wring. **screw up 1** *screw up one's face in the sun* wrinkle up, pucker, crumple, contort, distort, twist. **2** *screw up a business deal* make a mess of, bungle, botch, make a botch of, ruin, spoil.

scribble v *scribble a note* dash off, jot down, scrawl.

scribble n *unable to read the scribble* scrawl, illegible handwriting.

scribe n **1** *scribes taking dictation* amanuensis, copyist, transcriber, secretary, recorder. **2** *describes himself as a scribe* writer, author, journalist, reporter.

scrimp v skimp, economize, be frugal, be thrifty, husband one's resources, tighten one's belt, draw in one's horns.

script n **1** *written in a careful script* handwriting, writing, hand, pen, calligraphy. **2** *read over the script of the play* text, book, libretto, score, lines, words, manuscript.

Scripture n Holy Writ, the Bible, the Holy Bible, the Gospel, the Good Book, the Word of God, the Book of Books.

scrounge v *scrounge money* cadge, beg, borrow; *inf* sponge, bum.

scrounger n cadger, beggar, borrower, parasite; *inf* sponger, freeloader.

scrub v **1** *scrub the floor/bath* rub, scour, clean, cleanse, wash, wipe. **2** *scrub the plans* cancel, drop, discontinue, abandon, call off, give up, do away with, discard, forget about, abort.

scrub n *land covered in scrub* brushwood, brush, copse, coppice, thicket.

scruffy adj untidy, unkempt, dishevelled, ungroomed, ill-groomed, shabby, down-at-heel, ragged, tattered, slovenly, messy, slatternly, sluttish.

scrumptious adj delicious, tasty, mouth-watering, palatable, delectable, delightful.

scruple v *not scruple about lying* have qualms about, hesitate, to stick at, think twice about, balk at, demur about, boggle at, be reluctant to, recoil from, shrink from, waver about, vacillate about.

scruples npl *have no scruples about stealing food* qualms, twinge of conscience, compunction, hesitation, second thoughts, doubt, misgivings, uneasiness, reluctance, restraint, wavering, vacillation.

scrupulous adj **1** *pay scrupulous attention to detail | a scrupulous inspection* meticulous, careful, painstaking, thorough, rigorous, strict, conscientious, punctillious, exact, precise, fastidious. **2** *scrupulous in his business dealings* honest, honourable, upright, righteous, right-minded, moral, ethical.

scrutinize v examine, study, inspect, survey, scan, look over, investigate, go over, peruse, probe, inquire into, sift, analyse, dissect.

scrutiny n examination, study, inspection, survey, scan, perusal, investigation, exploration, probe, inquiry, analysis, dissection.

scuffle n *involved in a bar-room scuffle* struggle, fight, tussle, row, quarrel, fracas, brawl, clash, affray, rumpus, disturbance, brouhaha, commotion; *inf* scrap, set-to, dust-up, barney, ruction.

scuffle v *arrested for scuffling in the street* struggle, fight, exchange blows, come to blows, tussle, row, brawl, clash; *inf* scrap, have a set to/dust-up.

sculpture n *purchase a sculpture of Churchill* statue, statuette, bust, figure, figurine.

sculpture v *sculpture his head in bronze* sculpt, sculp, chisel, model, fashion, shape, cast, carve, cut, hew.

scum n **1** *scum forming on coffee* film, layer, froth, foam. **2** *scum forming on a pond* film, crust, algae, filth, dirt. **3** *regard his neighbours as scum* lowest of the low, dregs of society, riffraff, rabble, *canaille*, rubbish.

scupper v **1** *scupper a ship* sink, submerge. **2** *scupper their plans* ruin, defeat, demolish, wreck, smash.

scurrilous adj *a scurrilous attack on her character* abusive, vituperative, insulting, offensive, disparaging, defamatory, slanderous, gross, foul, scandalous.

scurry v *scurry home in the rain* hurry, hasten, make haste, rush, race, dash, run, sprint, scuffle, scamper, scramble.

scurry n *the scurry of the homeward-bound crowds* hurry, haste, rush, bustle, racing, dashing, scuttling, scampering. *see* SCURRY V.

sea n **1** *sail on the sea* ocean, brine; *lit* the deep, main; *inf* the brink, the drink. **2** *experience rough seas* waves, swell, breakers, rollers, billows. **3** *a sea of daffodils* expanse, sheet, mass, multitude, host, profusion, abundance, plethora. **at sea** *at sea as to the cause of their behaviour* confused, perplexed, bewildered, puzzled, baffled, at a loss, mystified.

seal n **1** *carry the king's seal* emblem, symbol, insignia, badge, crest, token, mark, monogram. **2** *the seal round the bath* sealant, sealer, adhesive. **3** *receive their seal of approval* assurance, attestation, confirmation, ratification, guarantee, proof, authentication, warrant, warranty.

seal v **1** *seal the parcel* fasten, secure, shut, close up. **2** *seal the jars* seal up, make airtight, make watertight, close, shut, cork, stopper, stop up. **3** *seal off the area* close off, shut off, cordon off, fence off. **4** *seal the bargain* secure, clinch, settle, decide, complete. **5** *seal his appointment* confirm, guarantee, ratify, validate.

seam n **1** *the seam between the lengths of material/wood* joint, join, junction. **2** *seams of coal* layer, stratum, vein, lode. **3** *seams on her brows* furrow, line, ridge, wrinkle, scar.

sear v **1** *cloth seared by an iron* burn, singe, scorch, char. **2** *grass seared by the sun* burn, dry up, wither, discolour, brown. **3** *a soul seared by an unhappy love affair* anguish, torture, torment, wound, distress, harry.

search v **1** *search the house* go through, look through, hunt through, rummage through, forage through, rifle through, scour, ransack, comb, go through with a fine-tooth comb, sift through, turn upside down, turn inside out, leave no stone unturned in. **2** *search for clues* look for, seek, hunt for, look high and low for, cast around for, ferret about for, scout out. **3** *search one's soul* examine, explore, investigate, inspect, survey, study, pry into. **4** *search the prisoner* examine, inspect, check; *inf* frisk. **search me!** I don't know, how should I know?, why ask me?, it beats me, it's a mystery.

search n **1** *conduct a search of the house* hunt, rummage, forage, rifling, scour, ransacking. *see* SEARCH v 1. **2** *a search for truth* exploration, pursuit, quest, probe. **in search of** *in search of happiness* looking for, on the lookout for, seeking, hunting for, in pursuit of, on the track of, questing after.

searching adj **1** *a searching look* penetrating, piercing, discerning, keen, alert, sharp, observant, intent. **2** *searching questions* probing, penetrating, analytic, quizzical, inquiring, inquisitive.

season n *in the warm season of the year* period, time, time of year, spell, term. **in season** *when strawberries are in season* available, obtainable, readily available/obtainable, common, plentiful.

season v **1** *season the sauce* flavour, add flavouring to, add salt/pepper/herbs to, spice, add spices to, pep up; *inf* add zing to. **2** *letters seasoned with gossip* enliven, leaven, add spice to, pep up; *inf* add zest/zing to. **3** *season the wood* mature, mellow, prime, prepare. **4** *season one's language* temper, moderate, qualify, tone down.

seasonable adj **1** *seasonable weather* usual, appropriate to the time of year. **2** *seasonable advice* opportune, timely, well-timed, appropriate, suitable, apt.

seasoned adj *seasoned travellers* experienced, practised, well-versed, established, habituated, long-serving, time-served, veteran, hardened, battle-scarred.

seasoning n *add seasoning to the sauce* flavouring, salt and pepper, herbs, spices, condiments, dressing, relish.

seat n **1** *enough seats for the audience/spectators* chair, bench, settle, stool, stall. **2** *the seat of government* headquarters, location, site, whereabouts, place, base, centre, hub, heart. **3** *fall on one's seat* bottom, buttocks, posterior, rump, hindquarters; *inf* behind, backside, bum; *Amer inf* butt, tail, fanny; *vulg* arse. **4** *the seat of his anxiety* grounds, cause, reason, basis, source, origin. **5** *the family seat in Suffolk* family residence, ancestral home, mansion, stately home.

seat v **1** *seat them next to each other* place, position, put, situate, deposit. **2** *the hall seats 500* hold, take, have room for, accommodate.

seating n seats, room, places, chairs, accommodation.

secede v *secede from the organization* withdraw from, break away from, break with, separate oneself from, sever relations with, quit, split with, resign from, pull out of, drop out of, have nothing more to do with, turn one's back on, repudiate, reject, renounce.

secluded adj *a secluded place* sheltered, concealed, hidden, private, unfrequented, solitary, lonely, sequestered, retired, out-of-the-way, remote, isolated, off-the-beaten-track, tucked-away, cut-off.

seclusion n *former filmstars now living in seclusion* privacy, solitude, retreat, retirement, withdrawal, sequestration, isolation, concealment, hiding, secrecy.

second[1] adj **1** *on the second day of the trial* next, following, subsequent, succeeding. **2** *a second helping/a second pair of boots* additional, extra, further. **3** *take a second pair of climbing boots* extra, additional, other, alternative, back-up, substitute. **4** *move from the second team to the first* secondary, lower, subordinate, lesser, lower-grade, inferior. **5** *regarded as a second Churchill* other, duplicate, replicate. **second to none** *as a player he is second to none* unparalleled, without parallel, unequalled, without equal, unmatched, unique, in a class of one's own.

second[1] n *act as second to the boxer/duellist* assistant, attendant, helper, supporter, backer, right-hand man/woman.

second[1] v **1** *seconded in his research by a student* assist, help, aid, support. **2** *second the proposal* formally support, give one's support to, back, approve, give one's approval to, endorse, promote.

second² v *second staff to another department* transfer, move, shift, assign.

second³ n *I'll be with you in a second | disappear in a second* moment, minute, instant, trice, twinkling, twinkling of an eye; *inf* sec, jiffy, jif, tick, mo, two shakes of a lamb's tail, two shakes.

secondary adj **1** *ignore the secondary issues* lesser, subordinate, minor, ancillary, subsidiary, non-essential, unimportant. **2** *patients with secondary infectionss* non-primary, derived, derivative, indirect, resulting, resultant. **3** *a secondary line of action* second, back-up, reserve, relief, auxiliary, extra, alternative, subsidiary.

second-class adj *treated as second-class citizens* second-rate, low-class, inferior, lesser, unimportant.

second-hand adj *second-hand/goods/clothes* used, worn, nearly-new, handed-down; *inf* hand-me-down, reach-me-down.

second hand adv *hear the news second hand* at second hand, indirectly; *inf* on the grapevine, on the bush telegraph.

second-in-command n deputy, number two, substitute, subordinate, right-hand man/woman.

secondly adv second, in the second place, next.

second-rate adj **1** *regarded as second-rate citizens* second-class, low-class, inferior, lesser, unimportant. **2** *try to give us second-rate goods* inferior, sub-standard, poor-quality, low-quality, low-grade, shoddy, rubbishy, tawdry; *inf* tacky.

seconds npl **1** *children asking for seconds* second helping, further helping, more. **2** *a shop selling seconds* rejects, imperfect goods, faulty/flawed goods, inferior goods.

secrecy n **1** *the secrecy of the information* confidentiality, privateness. *see* SECRET adj 1. **2** *the secrecy of their love affair* clandestineness, furtiveness, surreptitiousness, stealth, covertness. *see* SECRET adj 3. **3** *appreciate the secrecy of their meeting-place* seclusion, concealment, privacy, solitariness, retirement, sequestration, remoteness. *see* SECRET 5.

secret adj **1** *keep the matter secret* confidential, private, unrevealed, undisclosed, under wraps, unpublished, untold, unknown; *inf* hush-hush. **2** *a secret drawer in the table* hidden, concealed, camouflaged, disguised. **3** *a secret love affair | secret political activities* hidden, clandestine, furtive, conspiratorial, undercover, surreptitious,

stealthy, cloak-and-dagger, covert; *inf* hole-and-corner, closet. **4** *a secret code/message* hidden, mysterious, cryptic, abstruse, recondite, arcane. **5** *a secret place* secluded, concealed, hidden, sheltered, private, unfrequented, solitary, lonely, sequestered, retired, out-of-the-way, remote, tucked-away. *see* SECLUDED. **6** *a secret person* secretive, reticent, uncommunicative. *see* SECRETIVE.

secret n **1** *unable to keep a secret* confidential matter, confidence, private affair. **2** *the secrets of nature* mystery, enigma, puzzle, riddle. **3** *the secret of their success* recipe, formula, key, answer, solution. **in secret** **1** *talks held in secret* secretly, behind closed doors, in camera. *see* SECRET adj 1. **2** *conduct their love affair in secret* privately, discretely, furtively, stealthily, covertly.

secrete v **1** *secrete a watery discharge* discharge, emit, excrete, exude, ooze, leak, give off, send out. **2** *secrete the package in a hidden drawer* hide, conceal, cover up, stow away, sequester, cache; *inf* stash away.

secretion n discharge, emission, excretion, exudate, oozing, leakage.

secretive adj *a secretive person/nature* secret, reticent, uncommunicative, unforthcoming, reserved, taciturn, silent, quiet, tight-lipped, close-mouthed, close, playing one's cards close to one's chest, clamlike; *inf* cagey.

secretly adv **1** *committees meeting secretly* married secretly/in secret, confidentially, privately, behind closed doors, in camera, sub rosa. **2** *conducting their love affair secretly* in secret, clandestinely, furtively, conspiratorially, surreptitiously, stealthily, on the sly, covertly; *inf* on the q.t. **3** *secretly she admired him* privately, in one's heart, in one's innermost thoughts.

sect n **1** *a strange religious sect* religious cult, religious group, religious denomination, religious order. **2** *the organization split by warring sects* faction, camp, splinter group, wing, division.

sectarian adj *sectarian groups in conflict | sectarian views* doctrinaire, partisan, bigoted, prejudiced, narrow-minded, insular, hide-bound, extreme, fanatic, fanatical.

section n **1** *divide the wood/fruit/material into sections* part, segment, division, component, piece, portion, bit, slice, fraction, fragment. **2** *the various sections of the book* part, division, component, chapter. **3** *the reference section of the library* part, division, department, branch.

sector adj **1** *the manufacturing sector of the economy* part, division, area, branch, category, field. **2** *forbidden to enter the military sector* zone, quarter, district, area, region.

secular adj *secular music/matters* lay, non-religious, non-spiritual, non-church, laical, temporal, worldly, earthly.

secure adj **1** *the children/jewels will be quite secure there* safe, free from danger, out of harm's way, invulnerable, unharmed, undamaged, protected, sheltered, shielded. **2** *the windows are quite secure* fastened, closed, shut, locked, sealed. **3** *secure steps leading to the attic* stable, fixed, steady, strong, sturdy, solid. **4** *children feeling secure | feeling secure in his job* safe, unworried, at ease, comfortable, confident, assured. **5** *look forward to a secure future* safe, reliable, dependable, settled, fixed, established, solid.

secure v **1** *secure the building from attack* make safe, make sound, fortify, strengthen, protect. **2** *secure the doors and windows* fasten, close, shut, lock, bolt, chain, seal. **3** *secure the boat* tie up, moor, anchor. **4** *secure their rights* assure, ensure, insure, guarantee, underwrite, confirm, establish. **5** *finally secure all they needed* acquire, obtain, gain, get, get hold of, procure, get posession of, come by; *inf* get one's hands on, land.

security n **1** *the security of the children/jewels* safety, freedom from danger, invulnerability, protection, safe-keeping, shielding. *see* SECURE adj 1. **2** *seek security from their pursuers* protection, refuge, sanctuary, asylum, safety. **3** *children losing their feelings of security* safety, lack of worry/anxiety, freedom from doubt, certainty, feeling of ease, confidence, assurance. **4** *the security of the future/job* safety, reliability, dependability. *see* SECURE adj 5. **5** *tight security for the queen's visit* safety measures, safeguards, guards, surveillance, defence, protection. **6** *use one's house as security for a loan* collateral, surety, guarantee, pledge, gage.

sedate adj **1** *too sedate a way of life for the teenagers* calm, tranquil, placid, dignified, formal, decorous, proper, demure, sober, earnest, staid, stiff. **2** *sedate old ladies untroubled by the excitement* calm, composed, tranquil, placid, serene, unruffled, imperturbable, unflappable. **3** *move at a sedate pace* slow, slow-moving, leisurely, measured, deliberate, dignified, staid.

sedate v *sedate the patient* give a sedative to, put under sedation, calm down, tranquillize.

sedative n tranquillizer, calmative, depressant, sleeping pill, narcotic, opiate; *inf* downer.

sedative adj *drugs/voices with a sedative effect* calming, tranquillizing, soothing, calmative, relaxing, assuaging, lenitive, soporific, narcotic.

sedentary adj *sedentary workers/people* sitting, seated, desk-bound, desk, inactive.

sediment n lees, dregs, grounds, deposit, residue, precipitate, settlings.

sedition n **1** *speakers accused of sedition* incitement to riot/rebellion, agitation, rabble-rousing, fomentation. **2** *advocating sedition* civil disorder, rebellion, insurrection, insurgence, uprising, mutiny, rioting, subversion, treason.

seditious adj **1** *a seditious speech* inciting, rabble-rousing, agitating, fomenting. **2** *a seditious element at court* rebellious, insurrectionist, insurgent, mutinous, subversive, dissident, disloyal, treasonous.

seduce v **1** *men seducing young girls* lead astray, corrupt, deflower, ravish, violate. **2** *seduced into the industry by high salaries* attract, allure, lure, tempt, entice, beguile, ensnare.

seductive adj **1** *seductive smiles/dresses* attracting, alluring, tempting, provocative, exciting, arousing, sexy. **2** *seductive music/salaries* attractive, appealing, inviting, alluring, tempting, enticing, beguiling.

see v **1** *I can see the house* make out, catch sight of, glimpse, spot, notice, observe, view, perceive, discern, espy, descry, distinguish, identify, recognize. **2** *see that man over there* look at, regard, note, observe, heed, mark, behold, watch; *inf* get a load of. **3** *see the comedy programme last night* watch, look at, view. **4** *see what they mean* understand, grasp, get, comprehend, follow, take in, know, realize, get the drift of, make out, fathom; *inf* latch on to. **5** *go and see what he wants* find out, discover, learn, ascertain, determine, ask, enquire, make enquiries, investigate. **6** *we'll have to see* think, consider, reflect, deliberate, give thought, have a think. **7** *see that the door is locked* see to it, take care, mind, make sure, make certain, ensure, guarantee. **8** *see trouble ahead* foresee, predict, forecast, anticipate, envisage, imagine, picture, visualize. **9** *see an old friend in the street* meet, encounter, run into, stumble upon, chance upon, recognize. **10** *see the doctor* visit, pay a visit to, consult, confer with. **11** *they see each other from time to time* meet, have meetings, arrange to meet, meet socially. **12** *he's seeing someone else now* go out with, take out, keep company with, court; *inf* go steady with, date. **13** *see her to her car* escort, accompany, show, lead, take, usher, attend. **see about 1** *see about travel arrangements* see to, deal with, attend to, cope with, look after, take care of. *see* SEE, SEE TO. **2** *see about what's happening* look into, investigate, enquire about, make enquiries about, ask about. **see over** *see over the house* see round, look round, have a look around, go on a tour of, tour, inspect. **see through 1** *see through his disguise | see through their attempts to charm* be undeceived by, not be taken in by, be wise to, get the measure of, fathom, penetrate; *inf* not fall for, have someone's number. **2** *see the job through* keep at, persevere with, persist with; *inf* stick out. **3** *see a friend through misfortune* support, help, assist, back up, stand by, stick by. **see to** *see to the travel arrangements* see about, deal with, arrange, organize, attend to, cope with, look after, take care of, be in charge of, be responsible for.

seed n **1** *growing plants from seeds* ovule, germ. **2** *issue of his seed* sperm, spermatic fluid, semen, spermatozoa. **3** *the seed of her discontent* source, origin, root, cause, reason, grounds, basis, motivation, motive. **4** *seed of the royal house* child, offspring, progeny, issue, descendants, scions. **go/ run to seed** *the farm has gone to seed* deteriorate, decline, degenerate, decay, go to rack and ruin, become dilapidated; *inf* go downhill, go to pot, go to the dogs.

seedy adj **1** *seedy little hotels* shabby, scruffy, shoddy, run-down, dilapidated, squalid, mean, sleazy, sordid, tatty; *inf* crummy. **2** *feeling rather seedy* unwell, ill, poorly, out of sorts, off-colour, indisposed; *inf* under the weather.

seek v **1** *seek up-to-date information* search for, try to find, look for, be on the look-out for, be after, hunt for, be in quest of, be in pursuit of. **2** *seek help from a counsellor* ask for, request, solicit, entreat, beg for. **3** *seek to please* try to, attempt to, endeavour to, strive to, aim to, aspire to.

seem v *seem a pleasant place* appear, appear to be, have the appearance of being, give the impression of being, look, look like, look to be, have the look of.

seeming adj *his seeming charm* apparent, ostensible, outward, external, surface, superficial, pretended, feigned, assumed, supposed.

seemly adj *seemly behaviour/dress* decorous, proper, decent, becoming, fitting, suitable, appropriate, apt, apposite, meet, *comme il faut*, in good taste.

seep v *pus seeping from the wound* ooze, leak, exude, drip, drain, percolate.

seer n prophet, soothsayer, augur, sibyl.

seesaw v *emotions seesawing* fluctuate, go from one extreme to the other, swing, oscillate.

seethe v **1** *liquid seething in the pan* boil, bubble, fizz, foam, froth, ferment, churn. **2** *seething at the lateness of the bus* be furious, be livid, be incensed, be in a rage, rant and rave, storm, fume, foam at the mouth, breathe fire.

segment n *divide the fruit into segments* section, part, division, component, piece, portion, slice, wedge.

segregate v separate, set apart, isolate, dissociate, cut off, sequester, ostrucize, discriminate against.

segregation n separation, setting apart, isolation, dissociation, sequestration, discrimination, apartheid, partition. *see* SEGREGATE.

seize v **1** *a drowning man seizing an overhanging branch* grab, grab hold of, take hold of, grasp, take a grip of, grip, take hold of, clutch at. **2** *police seizing a haul of drugs* confiscate, impound, commandeer, appropriate, take possession of, sequester, sequestrate. **3** *criminals seizing a child/van* snatch, abduct, take captive, kidnap, hijack. **4** *police seizing the criminals* catch, arrest, apprehend, take into custody, take prisoner; *inf* collar, nab. **5** *seize upon the meaning of the message* grasp, understand, comprehend, discern, perceive, get the drift of.

seizure n **1** *the police's seizure of the drug haul* confiscation, commandeering, appropriation, sequestration. *see* SEIZE 2. **2** *the seizure of the child/van* snatching, abduction, kidnapping, hijacking. **3** *the seizure of the criminals* arrest, apprehension; *inf* collaring, nabbing. *see* SEIZE 4.

seldom adv rarely, hardly ever, scarcely ever, infrequently, only occasionally, not ever; *inf* once in a blue moon.

select v choose, pick, hand-pick, single out, opt for, decide on, settle on, prefer, favour.

select adj **1** *a select range of goods* choice, hand-picked, prime, first-rate, first-class, finest, best, high-quality, top-quality, supreme, superb, excellent. **2** *a select club* exclusive, elite, limited, privileged, cliquish; *inf* posh.

selection n **1** *offer a wide selection of goods* choice, pick, option. **2** *publish a selection of his works* choice, anthology, variety, assortment, miscellany, collection, range.

selective adj *able to be selective about houses* particular, discriminating, discriminatory, discerning, fussy, careful, cautious; *inf* choosy, picky.

self-assurance n self-confidence, confidence, assertiveness, positiveness.

self-centred adj egocentric, egotistic, egotistical, self-absorbed, self-seeking, wrapped up in oneself, selfish, narcissistic.

self-confidence n self-assurance, confidence, self-reliance, self-dependence, self-possession, poise, aplomb, composure, *sang froid*.

self-conscious adj awkward, shy, diffident, bashful, blushing, timorous, nervous, timid, retiring, shrinking, ill-at-ease, embarrassed, uncomfortable.

self-control n self-restraint, restraint, self-discipline, willpower, strength of will.

self-denial n self-discipline, ascetism, self-abnegation, self-deprivation, abstemiousness, temperance, abstinence, self-sacrifice, selflessness, unselfishness, altruism.

self-esteem n self-respect, self-regard, pride in oneself/one's abilities, faith in oneself, *amour-propre*.

self-important adj pompous, vain, conceited, arrogant, swollen-headed, egotistical, presumptuous, overbearing, overweening, haughty, swaggering, strutting.

self-indulgence n self-gratification, lack of self-restraint, unrestraint, intemperance, immoderation, excess, pleasure-seeking, pursuit of pleasure, sensualism, dissipation.

selfish adj self-seeking, self-centred, egocentric, egotistic, egoistic, self-interested, self-regarding, self-absorbed; *inf* looking out for number one.

selfless adj unselfish, altruistic, generous, self-sacrificing, self-denying, magnanimous, liberal, ungrudging.

self-possessed adj self-assured, confident, sure of oneself, composed, cool, cool as a cucumber, cool, calm and collected; *inf* together.

self-respect n self-esteem, self-regard, pride in oneself, pride in one's abilities, belief in one's worth, faith in oneself, *amour-propre*.

self-righteous adj santimonious, holier-than-thou, over-pious, pietistic, too good to be true, pharisaic, unctuous, mealy-mouthed; *inf* goody-goody.

self-sacrifice n self-denial, selflessness, self-abnegation, unselfishness, altruism.

self-satisfied adj pleased with oneself, well-pleased, proud of oneself, flushed with success, self-approving, complacent, smug, like the cat that swallowed the cream/canary.

self-seeking adj self-interested, opportunistic, looking out for oneself, ambitious, mercenary, out for what one can get, fortune-hunting, gold-digging; *inf* on the make, looking for number one.

self-styled adj would-be, so-called, self-named, self-titled.

self-willed adj wilful, contrary, perverse, uncooperative, wayward, recalcitrant, refractory, intractable, stubborn, pig-headed, mulish, intransigent, difficult, disobedient; *inf* cussed.

sell v **1** *sell their house* put up for sale, put on sale, dispose of, vend, auction off, trade, barter. **2** *traders selling fruit and vegetables* trade in, deal in, be in the business of, traffic in, stock, carry, offer for sale, market, handle, peddle, hawk. **3** *goods selling well* be bought, be purchased, go, go like hotcakes, move, be in demand. **4** *selling for £5* retail, go for, be, be found for. **5** *sell the idea of self-support* get acceptance for, win approval for, get support for, get across, promote. **6** *you won't sell the workforce that* persuade of, convince of, talk someone into, bring someone round to, induce to, win someone over to. **7** *You've been sold!* sell down the river, betray, cheat, swindle, defraud, fleece, deceive, trick, double-cross, bilk, gull; *inf* diddle, con, stab someone in the back. **sell out 1** *bakers sold out of bread* be out of stock of, run out of, dispose of, have none left. **2** *supplies of tickets all sold out* be bought up, be depleted, be exhausted. **3** *he used to have principles but he sold out for a huge salary* prostitute oneself, sell one's soul, betray one's cause/ideals, go over to the other side, play false.

seller n vendor, retailer, salesman/woman/person, shopkeeper, trader, tradesman, merchant, dealer, agent, representative, traveller, commercial traveller; *inf* rep.

selling n **1** *the selling of property* vending, trading. *see* SELL. **2** *a career in selling* sales, salesmanship, marketing, merchandising.

semblance n *only a semblance of honesty* appearance, outward appearance, show, air, guise, pretence, façade, front, veneer, mask, cloak, disguise, camouflage, pretext.

send v **1** *send a letter* dispatch, forward, mail, post, remit. **2** *send a message* transmit, convey, communicate, broadcast, televise, telecast, radio. **3** *send a stone skimming over the water* throw, fling, hurl, cast, let fly, propel, project. **4** *send one mad* drive, make, cause one to be/become. **5** *the music sent him* excite, stimulate, titillate, rouse, stir, thrill, intoxicate, enrapture, enthrall, ravish, charm, delight; *inf* turn one on. **send for** *send for a doctor/plumber* call for, summon, request, order. **send off** *send off evil-smelling fumes* give off, discharge, emit, exude.

senile adj doddering, decrepit, failing, in one's dotage, in one's second childhood, mentally confused.

senior adj **1** *senior officer* high-ranging, higher-ranking, superior. **2** *the senior of the staff/James Black senior* older, elder.

sensation n **1** *awake with a sensation of fear* feeling, sense, awareness, consciousness, perception, impression. **2** *their affair caused a sensation* stir, excitement, agitation, commotion, furore, scandal. **3** *the new show's a sensation* great success; *inf* hit, smash hit, wow.

sensational adj **1** *a sensational news story* spectacular, stirring, exciting, startling, staggering, dramatic, amazing, shocking, scandalous, lurid. **2** *looking sensational in the evening dress* marvellous, superb, excellent, exceptional, remarkable; *inf* fabulous, fab, out of this world.

sense n **1** *a sense of touch* feeling, sensation, faculty, sensibility. **2** *detect a sense of hostility* feeling, atmosphere, impression, aura. **3** *a sense of guilt* feeling, sensation, awareness, consciousness, perception. **4** *a sense of humour* appreciation, awareness, understanding, comprehension. **5** *have the sense to keep quiet* common sense, practicality, wisdom, sagacity, sharpness, discernment, perception, wit, intelligence, cleverness, understanding, reason, logic, brain, brains; *inf* gumption, nous. **6** *a word with several senses* meaning, definition, import, signification, significance, implication, nuance, drift, gist, purport, denotation. **7** *no sense in what she said/did* intelligibility, coherence, comprehensibility, logic, rationality, purpose, point.

sense v *sense their hostility* feel, get the impression of, be aware of, be conscious of, observe, notice, perceive, discern, grasp, pick up, suspect, divine, intuit; *inf* have a feeling about.

senseless adj **1** *a senseless act/comment* nonsensical, stupid, foolish, silly, inane, idiotic, mindless, unintelligent, unwise, irrational, illogical, meaningless, pointless, absurd, ludicrous, fatuous, asinine, moronic, imbecilic, mad; *inf* daft. **2** *knocked senseless by the*

blow unconscious, insensible, out cold, out, cold, stunned, numb, numbed, insensate.

sensibilities npl *offend older people's sensibilities* moral sense, finer feelings, susceptibilities, sense of outrage.

sensibility n *a coarse man without sensibility* sensitivity, sensitiveness, finer feelings, delicacy, taste, discrimination, discernment.

sensible adj **1** *a sensible person/approach* practical, realistic, down-to-earth, wise, prudent; judicious, sagacious, sharp, shrewd, discerning, perceptive, far-sighted, intelligent, clever, reasonable, rational, logical; *inf* brainy. **2** *a sensible rise in temperature* perceptible, discernible, appreciable, noticeable, visible, observable, tangible, palpable. **3** *sensible of his inadequacies* aware of, conscious of, mindful of, sensitive to, alive to, cognizant of, acquainted with.

sensitive adj **1** *sensitive to unfriendly atmospheres* responsive to, easily affected by, susceptible to, reactive to, sentient of. **2** *sensitive skin* delicate, fine, soft, easily damaged, fragile. **3** *sensitive rather than coarse people* responsive, receptive, perceptive, discerning, discriminatory, sympathetic, understanding, empathetic. **4** *too sensitive for a competitive industry* oversensitive, easily upset, thin-skinned, touchy, temperamental. **5** *a sensitive issue* delicate, difficult, problematic, ticklish.

sensitivity n **1** *the sensitivity of her skin* sensitiveness, delicacy, fineness, softness, fragility. **2** *the sensitivity of the artist* sensitiveness, responsiveness, receptiveness, perceptiveness, discernment, discrimination. *see* SENSITIVE 3. **3** *unable to cope with her sensitivity* over-sensitivity, touchiness. *see* SENSITIVE 4.

sensual adj **1** *sensual rather than spiritual pleasures* physical, carnal, bodily, fleshly, animal, voluptuous, non-spiritual, epicurean, sybaritic. **2** *sensual curves/lips* voluptuous, sexual, sexy, erotic.

sensuous adj *sensuous music | the sensuous feel of satin* aesthetic, pleasing, pleasurable, gratifying.

sentence n **1** *listen to the judge delivering the sentence* judgement, verdict, pronouncement, ruling, decision, decree. **2** *serve a three-year sentence* prison sentence, jail sentence, penal sentence, prison term; *inf* time, porridge.

sentence v **1** *hear the judge sentencing the prisoners* impose a sentence on, pass judgement on, mete out punishment to, punish.

2 *sentenced to a life of pain* condemn, doom, punish, penalize.

sentientious adj **1** *always making sentientious remarks about their neighbour's behaviour* moralistic, moralizing, judgemental, sanctimonious, canting, pompous. **2** *a sentientious style of prose* concise, succinct, terse, compact, epigrammatic, pithy, axiomatic, aphoristic.

sentiment n **1** *no room for sentiment in business* emotion, emotionalism, finer feelings, tender feelings, tenderness, softness. **2** *a revolutionary sentiment obvious in her writings* feelings, attitude, belief, opinion, view, point of view. *see* SENTIMENTS. **3** *romantic novels full of sentiment* sentimentality, emotionalism, over-emotionalism, mawkishness. *see* SENTIMENTALITY.

sentimental adj **1** *singing sentimental love songs* emotional, overemotional, romantic, mawkish, maudlin, soppy; *inf* mushy, slushy, soppy, schmaltzy, corny. **2** *a sentimental attachment to the town* emotional, nostalgic, affectionate, loving, tender, warm.

sentimentality n *criticizing the sentimentality of the novels* emotionalism, overemotionalism, romanticism, mawkishness, soppiness; *inf* mush, slush, soppiness, corniness.

sentiments npl *my sentiments exactly* feeling, attitude, belief, thoughts, way of thinking, opinion, view, point of view, idea, judgement, persuasion.

sentry n guard, lookout, watch, watchman, sentinel.

separate adj **1** *have separate residences* individual, distinct, discrete, particular, autonomous, independent. **2** *the problems being quite separate* unconnected, unattached, distinct, different, disconnected, unrelated, detached, divorced, divided, discrete.

separate v **1** *separate the joined pieces of wood* disconnect, detach, sever, uncouple, divide, disjoin, sunder. **2** *old pipes separating at the joints* come apart, come away, break off, divide, disunite. **3** *the fence separating the two gardens* divide, come between, stand between, keep apart, partition. **4** *the roads separated at the foot of the hill* part, part company, go their separate ways, go different ways, diverge, split, divide. **5** *the couple separated last year* officially separate, obtain an official separation, break up, split up, part, become estranged, divorce. **6** *a splinter group separating from the society* break away from, break with, secede from, withdraw from, sever relations with. **7** *separate the items according to size* divide, sort, sort out,

classify, categorize. **8** *separate the naughty children from the rest* set apart, segregate, single out, put to one side, isolate.

separately adv **1** *all four living separately* apart, individually, independently, autonomously. **2** *the members of the group left separately* individually, one by one, one at a time, singly, severally, independently.

separation n **1** *the separation of the pieces* disconnection, detachment, severance, uncoupling, division, disjunction, disunion, dissociation, segregation. **2** *upset by her parent's separation* break-up, split-up, split, parting, estrangement, parting of the ways, rift, divorce.

septic adj infected, festering, pussy, poisoned, putrefying, putrefactive, putrid.

sepulchre n tomb, vault, burial place, grave.

sequel n *an unfortunate sequel of/to the party* follow-up, development, result, consequence, outcome, issue, upshot, end, conclusion.

sequence n *sequence of events/movements/numbers* chain, course, cycle, series, progression, succession, set, arrangement, order, pattern.

sequester v **1** *nuns sequestered from the world* isolate, seclude, withdraw, retire, cut off, set apart, segregate, shut off. **2** *sequester a debtor's funds* sequestrate, confiscate, take possession of, seize, appropriate, expropriate, impound, commandeer.

seraphic adj **1** *seraphic beings* angelic, celestial, heavenly, holy. **2** *a seraphic smile* blissful, beatific, rapt, joyful, serene.

serendipity n chance, mere chance, happy chance, luck, good fortune, fortuity, fortuitousness, accident, coincidence.

serene adj **1** *remain serene throughout the trouble* calm, composed, tranquil, peaceful, placid, still, quiet, unperturbed, imperturbable, undisturbed, unruffled, unworried, unexcited, unexcitable, unflappable. **2** *a serene sky* cloudless, unclouded, clear, bright, sunny.

serenity n **1** *admire her serenity in face of trouble* calm, calmness, composure, tranquillity, peace, peacefulness, peace of mind, placidity, placidness, stillness, quietness, quiet, quietude, imperturbability. **2** *the serenity of the sky* cloudlessness, clearness, brightness, sunniness.

series n *a series of events/people/numbers* succession, progression, sequence, chain, course, string, train, run, cycle, set, row, arrangement, order.

serious adj **1** *serious expressions* solemn, earnest, unsmiling, unlaughing, thoughtfully, preoccupied, pensive, grave, sombre, sober, long-faced, dour, stern, grim, poker-faced. **2** *serious problems/trouble* important, significant, consequential, of consequence, momentous, of moment, weighty, far-reaching, urgent, pressing, crucial, vital, life-and-death. **3** *serious injuries* acute, grave, bad, critical, alarming, grievous, dangerous, perilous. **4** *serious about reforming* earnest, in earnest, sincere, honest, genuine, firm, resolute, resolved, determined, fervent.

seriously adv **1** *nodding seriously* solemnly, earnestly, unsmilingly, with a straight face, thoughtfully, pensively, gravely, sombrely, soberly, dourly, sternly, grimly. **2** *seriously injured* severely, acutely, gravely, badly, critically, alarmingly, grievously, dangerously, perilously. **3** *seriously, you'll like it here* to be serious, without joking, no joking, truthfully, I mean it.

seriousness n **1** *the seriousness of their expressions* solemnity, solemness, thoughtfullness, preoccupation, pensiveness, graveness, gravity, sombreness, soberness, sobriety, dourness, sterness, grimness. **2** *the seriousness of the problem* importance, significance, consequence, momentousness, moment, weightiness, weight, urgency, crucialness, vitalness. **3** *the seriousness of the injuries* severity, severeness, acuteness, gravity, graveness, badness, criticalness, grievousness, danger, dangerousness, peril, perilousness. **4** *acknowledge their seriousness about reforming* sincerity, earnestness, honesty, genuineness, firmness, resolution, resolve, determination, fervour.

sermon n **1** *sermons from the pulpit* preaching, teaching, speech, homily, address, oration. **2** *she listened to a sermon on lateness by her father* lecture, moralizing, declamation, trade, harangue, ranting, diatribe, reprimand, reproof, remonstrance, castigation; *inf* talking to, dressing-down.

serrated adj serrate, serrulate, serrulated, serriform, saw-toothed, notched, jagged.

servant n *kitchen servants* domestic, help, domestic help, helper, maid, charwoman, char, handyman, menial, drudge; scullion, slave, vassal, serf, retainer, attendant, lackey, flunky; *inf* Mrs Mop.

serve v **1** *serve two masters* be in the service of, work for, be employed by, have a job with. **2** *willing to serve his fellow men* be of service for, be of use to, help, give help to, assist, give assistance to, aid, lend a hand to, do a good turn to, benefit, support, foster, minister to, succour. **3** *serve on the committee* have/hold a place on, be on, perform duties, carry out duties, fulfil duties. **4** *sofas serving also as beds* act as, do duty as, function as, fulfil the function of, do the work of, be suitable for. **5** *Will the car serve us for another year?* be useful, be all right, be good, be adequate, suffice, serve a purpose, meet requirements; *inf* fill the bill, do. **6** *serve three years as an apprentice/prisoner* spend, go through, carry out, fulfill, complete, discharge. **7** *serve food* dish up, give out, distribute, set out, present, provide. **8** *serve at table* wait, act as waiter/waitress, distribute food/refreshments, deal out food. **9** *serve a customer* attend to, attend to the wants of, look after, take care of, assist. **10** *it has served them well* treat, act towards, behave towards, conduct oneself towards, deal with, handle.

service n **1** *conditions of service in the factory* work, employment, labour, duty, business. **2** *retire after fifty years' service* work, employment, period of employment, labour, duties. **3** *do him a service by telling him* good turn, assistance, help, advantage, benefit. **4** *wedding service | service of baptism* ceremony, ritual, rite, sacrament. **5** *cars due for a service* servicing, overhaul, check, maintenance check, repair. **6** *pay extra for service in a restaurant* serving, waiting at table, waiting, waitressing, serving food and drink. **7** *have had good service from it* treatment, behaviour, conduct, handling.

service v *service the washing machine* check, go over, overhaul, give a maintenance check to, repair.

serviceable adj **1** *serviceable rather than fashionable shoes* functional, utilitarian, practical, non-decorative, plain, useful, durable, hard-wearing, tough, strong. **2** *machinery no longer serviceable* usable, of use, functioning, operative, repairable.

services npl **1** *go into the services* armed services, forces, armed forces. **2** *require the services of a lawyer* work, labour, duties, assistance, ministrations.

servile adj **1** *made to do servile tasks* menial, low, lowly, humble, mean, base. **2** *a rich man surrounded by servile employees* subservient, obsequious, sycophantic, fawning, toadying, grovelling, submissive; *inf* bootlicking.

serving n *dish up six servings of soup* helping, portion, plateful.

servitude n slavery, enslavement, thraldom, subjugation, subjection, domination, bondage, bonds, chains, fetters, shackles, serfdom, vassalage.

session n **1** *a recording session* period, time, spell, stretch; *inf* get-together. **2** *the afternoon sessions of the summit talks* meeting, sitting, assembly, conference, discussion. **3** *pupils at the start of the session* school year, school term, term; *Amer* semester.

set v **1** *set the books down there | a house set in parkland* put, put down, place, lay, lay down, deposit, position, rest, locate, lodge, situate, station, posit; *inf* stick, park, plonk. **2** *set the post in the ground | set a jewel in the ring* fix, embed, insert, lodge, mount, arrange, install. **3** *set pen to paper* put, apply, lay, place, bring into contact with, touch. **4** *set your mind to it* apply, direct, aim, turn, address, focus, concentrate, zero in on. **5** *set one's watch* adjust, regulate, synchronize, coordinate, harmonize, collimate, callibrate, rectify, set right. **6** *set the machine to start* fix, make ready, prepare, arrange, organize. **7** *set the table* lay, make ready, prepare, arrange. **8** *set her hair* fix, style, arrange, curl, wave. **9** *the sky set with stars | a dress set with sequins* decorate, adorn, ornament, deck, bedeck, embellish, furbish, bejewel. **10** *set things in motion | set it on fire* put, cause to be, start, actuate, instigate. **11** *the jelly/concrete won't set* solidify, stiffen, thicken, jell, harden, cake, congeal, coagulate, crystallize, gelatinate. **12** *the sun setting* go down, sink, dip below the horizon, vanish, disappear, subside, decline. **13** *set them thinking* set off, start, begin, motivate, cause. **14** *set a new record* set up, establish, fix, create, bring into being, bring into existence, institute. **15** *set a date/time for the meeting* fix, fix on, settle, agree on, appoint, decide on, name, specify, stipulate, determine, designate, select, choose, arrange, schedule, confirm. **16** *set down rules* lay down, impose, establish, define, determine, stipulate, prescribe, ordain, allot. **17** *set them tasks* assign, allocate, allot, give, give out, distribute, dispense, mete out, deal out, dole out, prescribe. **18** *set her services at naught* evaluate, valuate, valve, assess, price, rate, estimate, reckon, calculate. **19** *faces/footsteps set towards home* direct, steer, orientate, point, incline, bend, train, aim. **set about 1** *set about clearing up* begin, start, make a start on, commence, set to, get to work, get down to, get going, tackle, undertake, address oneself to, attack, enter upon, put the wheels in motion, set in motion, set the ball rolling, lead off, put into execution, put one's shoulder to the wheel, put one's hand to the plough; *inf* get cracking, get weaving, sail into, wade into. **2** *set about the intruders with a stick* attack,

assault, assail, belabour; *inf* sail into. **set apart 1** *behaviour setting him apart from the rest* differentiate, mark off, distinguish, single out, demarcate, characterize. **2** *set apart some logs for winter* lay aside, put aside, reserve. **set aside 1** *set aside money/food for later* lay aside, lay by, put away, put aside, set apart, save, reserve, keep in reserve, keep, put down, store, stockpile, hoard, deposit, stow away, salt away, squirrel away; *inf* stash away **2** *set aside the newspaper* put aside, put to one side, move to one side, cast aside, discard, abandon, dispense with, drop. **3** *set aside our differences for now* put aside, forget, disregard, ignore, discount, bury, consign to oblivion. **4** *set aside the judge's ruling* overrule, overturn, reverse, nullify, render null and void, annul, quash, dismiss, reject, repudiate, abrogate. **set back** *set back their progress* hinder, impede, obstruct, hold up, delay, slow down, retard, check, thwart. **set down 1** *set down a list of requirements* write down, write out, put in writing, commit to writing, put down, mark down, jot down, note down, record, register, tabulate, catalogue. **2** *set his incompetence down to inexperience* put down, attribute, ascribe, assign, lay at the door of, charge. **set forth 1** *set forth for the city* set out, start out, depart. *see* SET V SET OUT 1. **2** *set forth their demands* declare, state, expound, describe, detail, delineate, submit, present, bring forward, advance. **set in** *winter has set in* begin, start, commence, arrive, come, come into being. **set off 1** *set off for the city* set out, start out, set forth, depart. *see* SET V SET OUT 1. **2** *set off a bomb* detonate, explode, blow up, ignite, light. **3** *set off a flurry of selling on the stock market* cause, begin, start, commence, initiate, set in motion, prompt, touch off, incite, stimulate, encourage. **4** *a dress setting off the blue of her eyes* enhance, bring out, heighten, intensify, increase, emphasize, show off, throw into relief. **set on** *thugs setting on the old man* attack, assault, strike, beat, beat up, fall upon, pounce on, go for, fly at; *inf* mug, sail into. **set out 1** *set out for the city early* set off, set forth, start out, depart, leave, take one's departure, get under way, embark, sally forth; *inf* hit the road. **2** *didn't set out to hurt them* intend to, have the intention of, aim to, have the aim of, mean to, have in mind, set one's sights on, aspire to. **3** *set out goods on a counter* lay out, arrange, dispose, present, exhibit, display, array, expose to view. **4** *set out their demands* set forth, declare, state, describe, detail, submit, present. *see* SET V SET FORTH 2 **set up. 1** *set up a statue in his memory* put up, erect, raise, elevate, construct, build, assemble.

2 *set up a business/scholarship* establish, institute, found, create, bring into being, start, begin, initiate, inaugurate, institute, organize, set going, get going, lay the foundations of. **3** *set up a meeting* arrange, prearrange, organize, prepare, plan, devise, fix. **4** *the country air will soon set the invalid up* make better, make stronger, strengthen, build up, restore, invigorate, energize, fortify, rehabilitate.

set n **1** *a set of articles for sale* collection, group, assemblage, series, batch, arrangement, array, succession, progression, assortment, selection. **2** *the golfing set* circle, crowd, clique, group, gang, coterie, faction, group, band, company, sect; *inf* crew. **3** *the set of his shoulder/eyes* bearing, carriage, cast, posture, position, altitude, turn, inclination. **4** *paint the set* stage set, stage setting, setting, stage scene, scene, scenery, backdrop, wings, flats, *mise en scène*.

set adj **1** *set texts/meals* fixed, prescribed, scheduled, specified, predetermined, prearranged, determined, arranged, appointed, established, decided, agreed. **2** *her set routine* customary, regular, normal, usual, habitual, accustomed, everyday, common. **3** *give a set speech* stock, standard, habituals, routine, rehearsed, unspontaneous, hackneyed, conventional, stereotyped. **4** *people of set opinions | set in their ways* fixed, firm, rooted, immovable, deepseated, ingrained, entrenched, rigid, inflexible, hidebound. **5** *all set for the journey* ready, prepared, equipped, primed, fit. **6** *set on getting his own way* intent, resolved, determined, bent on, resolute about, earnest about.

setback n *their progress/plans suffered a setback* reversal, reverse, upset, check, stumbling block, hitch, hold-up, hindrance, impediment, obstruction, disappointment, misfortune, blow.

setting n **1** *houses in rural settings | animals in their natural settings* environment, surroundings, milieu, background, location, place, site. **2** *a modern setting for the play* stage setting, set, scene, stage, scenery, back-drop, back-cloth, flats, *mise en scène*. **3** *an unusual setting for the jewel* mounting, frame.

settle v **1** *settle in America* make one's home, set up home, take up residence, put down roots, establish oneself, go to live, move to, emigrate to. **2** *an area settled by Scots* establish/found a colony, colonize, occupy, people, inhabit, populate. **3** *the children will not settle after the excitement* calm down, quieten down, be quiet, be still,

relax. **4** *the sedative will settle her* calm, calm down, tranquillize, quieten, quiet, soothe, compose, pacify, lull, sedate, quell. **5** *settle the patients for the night* make comfortable, bed down, tuck in. **6** *a butterfly settling on the leaf* alight, light, land, come down, descend, repose, rest. **7** *settle on a date* decide on, agree on, determine, confirm, arrange, fix, choose, appoint, select. **8** *settle a dispute* resolve, clear up, make peace, patch up, reconcile, conclude, bring to an end. **9** *settle one's affairs* put in order, order, arrange, set to rights, straighten out, organize, regulate, adjust, clear up, systematize. **10** *settle for a smaller sum* compromise on, submit to, accept, agree to, accede to, acquiesce in, assent to. **11** *settle one's bills/debts* pay, discharge, square, clear, liquidate. **12** *dregs settled at the foot of the cup* sink, subside, fall, gravitate.

settlement n **1** *the settlement of the area* establishing, founding, pioneering, peopling, colonization. *see* SETTLE 2. **2** *a remote settlement* community, colony, village, hamlet, encampment, outpost. **3** *the settlement of the dispute* resolution, patching up, reconciliation, conclusion. *see* SETTLE 8. **4** *reach a financial settlement with management* agreement, contract, pact, compact. **5** *the settlement of his financial affairs* ordering, arrangement, organization, regulation, adjustment, systematization. *see* SETTLE 9. **6** *in settlement of debts* payment, discharge, defrayal, liquidation. *see* SETTLE 11.

settler n colonists, colonizer, pioneer, frontiersman/woman, immigrant.

set-to n argument, quarrel, row, disagreement, fight, squabble, wrangle, fracas; *inf* dust-up, scrap, slanging-match, spat, barney.

set-up n system, organization, structure, arrangement, framework, format, composition, procedure.

sever v **1** *sever a limb/branch* cut off, chop off, lop off, hack off, break off, tear off. **2** *sever the log in two pieces* divide, split, cleave, rive, dissect, halve. **3** *sever relations with them* break off, discontinue, suspend, dissolve, end, bring to an end, terminate, stop, cease, conclude.

several adj **1** *several people came* some, a number of, a few. **2** *go their several ways* separate, different, diverse, disparate, divergent, respective, individual, own, particular, specific, various, sundry.

severe adj **1** *severe criticism/punishment* harsh, hard, stringent, rigorous, unsparing, relentless, merciless, ruthless, painful, sharp, caustic, biting, cutting, scathing, serious, extreme. **2** *a severe regime* harsh, hard, stern, rigorous, stringent, strict, grim, inflexible, uncompromising, inexorable, implacable, relentless, unrelenting, merciless, pitiless, ruthless, brutal, inhuman, cruel, savage, hard-hearted, iron-fisted, iron-handed, autocratic, tyrannical, despotic. **3** *a severe shortage of food* extreme, very bad, serious, grave, acute, critical, dire, dangerous, perilous. **4** *severe storms/headaches* fierce, strong, violent, intense, powerful, forceful, very bad. **5** *a severe test of their stamina* demanding, taxing, exacting, tough, difficult, hard, fierce, arduous, rigorous, punishing, onerous, burdensome. **6** *a severe expression* stern, grim, cold, chilly, austere, forbidding, dour, disapproving, tight-lipped, unsmiling, sombre, grave, sober, serious. **7** *a severe style of decoration* austere, stark, ultra-plain, spartan, ascetic, plain, simple, modest, bare, blank, unadorned, undecorated, unembellished, restrained, functional, classic. **8** *a severe winter* harsh, extreme, inclement, cold, freezing, frigid.

severely adv **1** *treat the culprits severely | speak severely to them* harshly, stringently, unsparingly, relentlessly, painfully, sharply, with an iron hand, with a rod of iron, caustically, scathingly. *see* SEVERE 1. **2** *injured severely* very badly, extremely badly, seriously, gravely, acutely, critically. **3** *severely dressed* austerely, starkly, spartanly, plainly, simply, without adornment, restrainedly, classically. *see* SEVERE 6.

severity n **1** *the severity of the criticism* harshness, stringency, rigorousness, relentlessness, painfulness, sharpness, causticness. *see* SEVERE 1. **2** *the severity of the regime* harshness, hardness, sternness, rigorousness, stringency, strictness, inflexibility, relentlessness, pitilessness, ruthlessness, brutality, cruelty, savagery, tyranny, despotism. *see* SEVERE 2. **3** *the severity of the storm/pain* fierceness, strength, violence, intensity. *see* SEVERE 4. **4** *the severeness of her expression* sternness, graveness, gravity. *see* SEVERE 6. **5** *the severity of the decoration* austerity, starkness, spartanism, asceticism, plainness, simplicity, bareness, lack of adornment, restraint, functionalism. *see* SEVERE 7. **6** *the severity of the winter* severeness, harshness, extremity, inclemency, coldness.

sew v stitch, machine stitch, seam, embroider, mend, darn.

sex n **1** *identify the sex of the animal* gender. **2** *attraction based on sex* sexuality, sexual attraction, sexual chemistry, sexual desire, desire, sex drive, sexual appetite, libido. **3** *lessons in sex | sex education* facts of life,

sexual reproduction, reproduction; *inf* the birds and the bees. **4** *have sex with him | a relationship without sex* intimacy, coitus, coition, coupling, copulation, carnal knowledge, mating, fornication.

sexuality n **1** *differences based on sexuality* sex, gender, sexual characteristics. **2** *famous for her sexuality* sexual desire, sexual appetite, sexiness, carnality, physicalness, eroticism, lust, sensuality, voluptuousness; sexual orientation, sexual preferences.

sexy adj **1** *sexy films* erotic, titillating, suggestive, arousing, exciting, stimulating. **2** *sexy clothes* titillating, arousing, provocative, seductive, sensuous, slinky. **3** *sexy women/men* sexually attractive, alluring, seductive, shapely. **4** *a sexy new project* exciting, stimulating, stirring, interesting, intriguing, trendy, fashionable.

shabby adj **1** *shabby furniture/houses* dilapidated, broken-down, run-down, tumbledown, ramshackle, in disrepair, scruffy, dingy, seedy, squalid, tatty, slum-like, slummy; *inf* tacky. **2** *shabby clothes* worn, worn-out, threadbare, ragged, frayed, tattered, faded, scruffy, tatty, the worse for wear. **3** *shabby treatment of the old lady* contemptible, despicable, dishonourable, disreputable, mean, base, low, dirty, odious, shameful, ignoble, unworthy, cheap, shoddy; *inf* rotten, low-down.

shackle v **1** *shackle the prisoner* chain, fetter, put in irons, manacle, tie up, bind, tether, hobble, handcuff. **2** *no longer shackled by convention* deter, restrain, restrict, limit, impede, hinder, hamper, obstruct, encumber, check, curb, constrain, tie the hands of.

shackles npl **1** *prisoners in shackles* chains, fetters, bonds, irons, manacles, tethers, ropes, handcuffs; *inf* cuffs. **2** *throw off the shackles of convention* deterrent, restraint, impediment, hindrance, obstruction, obstacle, check, curb, constraint.

shade n **1** *sit in the shade of a tree* shadiness, shadow, shadowiness, shadows, shelter, cover. **2** *in the shade of evening* dimness, dusk, semi-darkness, twilight, gloaming, darkness, gloom, gloominess, murkiness, murk. **3** *a darker shade for the carpets* colour, hue, tone, tint, tinge. **4** *act as a shade against the light* screen, shield, curtain, blind, canopy, veil, cover, covering. **5** *in the shade compared to his brother* obscurity, shadow, inconspicuousness, unrecognition. **6** *a word with several shades of meaning* nuance, degree, gradation, difference, variety. **7** *imagined he saw the shade of his father* ghost, spectre, phantom, apparition, spirit, manes. **a shade** *a shade better* a little, a bit, a trace, a touch, a dash, a modicum, a soupçon, slightly, marginally. **put one in the shade** *her dress put all the others in the shade* outshine, outclass, overshadow, eclipse, surpass, excel, transcend, cap, top, outstrip, outdo, outrival, put to shame. **shades of** *shades of Napoleon* reminder, memories of, intimations of, suggestions of, hints of.

shade v **1** *trees shading the garden* shut out the light from, block off light to, cast a shadow over, screen, darken, dim. **2** *shading the light* cover, obscure, mute, hide, conceal, veil, curtain.

shadow n **1** *sit in the shadow of the building* shade, shadowiness, shadows. *see* SHADE n 1. **2** *in the shadow of evening* dimness, dusk, semi-darkness, twilight, gloaming, darkness, gloom. *see* SHADE n 2. **3** *their shadows on the wall* silhouette, outline, shape. **4** *cast a shadow on their happiness* gloom, gloominess, cloud, blight, sadness, unhappiness. **5** *her younger sister was her shadow* constant companion, inseparable companion, close friends, bosom friend, intimate, alter ego; *lit* Achates; *inf* sidekick. **6** *the policewoman acting as a shadow* watch, follower, detective; *inf* tail. **a shadow of 1** *not a shadow of a doubt* a little, a bit, a shade, a trace, a touch, a dash, a modicum, a soupçon, slightly, marginally. **2** *a shadow of a smile* a trace, a hint, a suggestion, a suspicion, a ghost. **3** *a shadow of his former self* a ghost, a spectre, a phantom, a remnant, a poor imitation.

shadowy adj **1** *shadowy parts of the garden/house* shady, shaded, dim, dark, gloomy, murky, crepuscular, tenebrous, tenebrious. **2** *shadowy shapes on the horizon* indistinct, indeterminate, indefinite, unclear, vague, nebulous, ill-defined, indistinguishable, unsubstantial, ghostly, phantom, spectral.

shady adj **1** *shady parts of the garden* shaded, shadowy, screened, sheltered, covered, dim, dark, leafy, bowery, umbrageous, tenebrous, tenebrious. **2** *shady character* disreputable, of dubious character, suspicious, suspect, questionable, dishonest, dishonourable, untrustworthy, devious, shifty, slippery, tricky, underhand, unscrupulous; *inf* crooked, fishy.

shaft n **1** *the shafts of the mine* passage, duct, tunnel, well, flue. **2** *shafts of light* ray, beam, gleam, streak, pencil. **3** *the shaft of a spade* pole, stick, rod, staff, shank, stem, handle, upright. **4** *his cruel shafts of sarcasm* barb,

gibe, thrust, dart, sting, cutting remark, cut.

shaggy adj hairy, hirsute, long-haired, rough, coarse, matted, tangled, unkempt, untidy.

shake v **1** *the cart shaking on the rough roads* rock, bump, jolt, bounce, roll, sway, swing, oscillate, wobble, rattle, vibrate, jar, jerk, judder, joggle, jounce. **2** *children shaking with fear/cold* shiver, tremble, quiver, quake, shudder. **3** *shake the can of coins* jiggle, joggle, jolt, jerk, rattle, agitate, jounce. **4** *people shaken by the accident/news* agitate, upset, distress, shock, alarm, disturb, perturb, fluster, unsettle, discompose, disquiet, disconcert, unnerve, ruffle, jolt, flurry, confuse, muddle; *inf* rattle. **5** *shake her confidence* undermine, weaken, lessen, impair, harm, hurt, injure. **6** *shake a fist/stick at them* brandish, wave, flourish, swing, wield, raise. **shake off** *shake off their pursuers* escape, elude, get away from, leave behind, give the slip to, throw off, get rid of, rid oneself of, extricate oneself from; *inf* get shot of. **shake up 1** *shake up the dressing/cocktail* mix, churn up, agitate. **2** *passengers shaken up by the accident* shake, agitate, upset, disturb, unsettle, discompose. **3** *shake up the system/firm* reorganize, rearrange, revolutionize, rouse, stir up.

shake n **1** *upset by the shakes of the cart on the rough road* shaking, rocking, bump, jolt, bounce, roll, swaying, rattle, vibration, jarring, jerk. *see* SHAKE v 1. **2** *the children had the shakes* shaking, shivering, trembling, tremor, quiver, quivering, convulsion. *see* SHAKE v 2. **3** *with one shake of the can* jiggle, joggle, jolt, jerk, rattle. *see* SHAKE v 3. **4** *get quite a shake from the accident/news* upset, shock, jolt. *see* SHAKE v 4. **5** *with a shake of his fist/stick* brandish, wave, flourish, swing.

shaky adj **1** *with shaky limbs* shaking, trembling, tremulous, quivering, quivery, tremulous, unsteady, wobbly, weak. **2** *take a few shaky steps* shaking, unsteady, faltering, wobbly, tottering, teetering, doddering, staggering. **3** *still a bit shaky after the illness* infirm, unsound, unwell, ill, below par, indisposed; *inf* under the weather. **4** *rather shaky reasoning/grounds* questionable, dubious, tenuous, unsubstantial, flimsy, weak, nebulous, unsound, unreliable, undependable, ungrounded, unfounded. **5** *shaky bits of furniture* rickety, wobbly, flimsy, ramshackle, dilapidated, gimcrack, jerry-built.

shallow adj **1** *a shallow person* frivolous, foolish, unintelligent, unthinking, trivial, insincere, superficial. **2** *shallow ideas/atti-*

tudes/remarks frivolous, superficial, unsubstantial, trifling, trivial, petty, empty, meaningless.

sham v **1** *sham illness* fake, pretend, feign, counterfeit, put on, simulate, affect, imitate. **2** *he's only shamming* fake, feign, pretend, counterfeit, dissemble, malinger, make believe.

sham n **1** *his charm is only a sham* fake, pretence, feign, feigning, counterfeit, imposture, simulation. **2** *he's not a doctor – he's a sham* impostor, fake, fraud, pretender, masquerader, dissembler, wolf in sheep's clothing, charlatan; *inf* phoney, pseudo. **3** *the document's a sham* counterfeit, fake, forgery, imposture, copy, imitation, hoax.

sham adj **1** *sham sympathy* pretended, pretend, feigned, fake, contrived, put-on, simulated, affected, artificial, insincere, ungenuine, false, bogus, spurious; *inf* phoney, pseudo. **2** *sham gold watches* fake, counterfeit, imitation, simulated, artificial, synthetic, ersatz; *inf* phoney, pseudo.

shamble v shuffle, hobble, limp, falter, totter, dodder, toddle.

shambles npl chaos, muddle, mess, confusion, disorder, disarray, disorganization, anarchy; *inf* disaster area.

shame n **1** *feel shame at being imprisoned* humiliation, ignominy, mortification, loss of face, remorse, guilt, compunction, shamefacedness, embarrassment, discomfort, discomposure. **2** *bring shame on the family* disgrace, dishonour, scandal, discredit, degradation, ignominy, disrepute, infamy, odium, opprobrium, condemnation, reproach. **3** *he's a shame to the family* disgrace, discredit, blot, smirch, stain, blemish, stigma. **4** *a shame he couldn't be there* pity, misfortune, bad luck, ill luck, source of regret. **put to shame** *put their efforts to shame* outshine, outclass, overshadow, eclipse, surpass, excel, outstrip, outdo, outrival, put in the shade.

shamefaced adj **1** *too shamefaced to appear after his crime* ashamed, embarrassed, guilty, conscience-stricken, remorseful, contrite, penitent, regretful, humiliated, mortified, shamed. **2** *shamefaced children hiding behind their mothers* shy, bashful, timid, timorous, shrinking, coy, sheepish.

shameful adj **1** *shameful behaviour/secrets* disgraceful, base, mean, low, vile, outrageous, shocking, dishonourable, unbecoming, unworthy, discreditable, deplorable, despicable, contemptible, reprehensible, scandalous, atrocious, heinous. **2** *shameful secrets* shaming, humiliating, mortifying, embarrassing; *inf* blush-making.

shameless adj **1** *shameless about his prison sentence* unashamed, without shame, unabashed, uncontrite, unpenitent, impenitent, unregretful. **2** *the shameless behaviour of the girls* brazen, impudent, bold, brash, forward, audacious, immodest, unseemly, improper, unbecoming, indecorous, wanton, abandoned, indecent.

shape n **1** *clouds of different shapes | pieces of plastic in all shapes and sizes* form, figure, configuration, formation, conformation, contours, outline, silhouette, profile, outward form, external appearance. **2** *in the shape of the devil* form, guise, appearance, likeness, look, semblance, image, aspect. **3** *business in poor shape | athletes in good shape* condition, state, health, trim, fettle, kilter. **4** *make out shapes in the distance* figure, form, outline, shadow, body, apparition. **5** *jelly/cement in a shape* mould, frame. **6** *dress-making shapes* pattern, model.

shape v **1** *shape the clay into a figure* form, fashion, make, create, design, mould, model, cast, create, frame, block, carve, sculpt, sculpture. **2** *attitudes shaped by childhood experiences* form, fashion, mould, create, produce, influence, guide, determine, define. **3** *shape a secret plan* plan, devise, prepare, develop, organize, line up. **4** *shape the dress to her figure* adjust, adapt, accommodate, alter, modify, tailor. **shape up 1** *new recruits shaping up* improve, show improvement, get better, make progress, progress, make headway, show promise. **2** *plans shaping up* take form, take shape, develop, crystallize, fall into place, come along, go forward, progress, make headway.

shapeless adj **1** *shapeless hunks of plastic* amorphous, formless, unformed, unshaped, unfashioned, undeveloped, embryonic. **2** *shapeless clothes* formless, badly cut, sack-like, ill-proportioned, inelegant. **3** *shapeless old hats* mis-shapen, battered, deformed.

shapely adj *shapely legs* well-formed, well-shaped, well-proportioned, elegant, curvaceous, curvy.

shard n fragment, piece, particle, scrap, bit, chip, sliver, splinter, paring, shaving, remnant.

share n *each receiving a fair share* division, quota, allowance, ration, allocation, allotment, portion, part, lot, measure, helping, serving; *inf* cut, whack, rake-off, piece of the cake, piece of the action.

share v **1** *share a job/costs* divide, split, use/have in common, go halves in; *inf* go fifty-fifty in, go Dutch. **2** *share the profits* divide, distribute, apportion, parcel out, deal out, dole out, give out. **3** *everyone sharing in their good fortune* have a share in, have a part in, participate in, take part in, partake of, have a percentage of, have a stake in.

sharp adj **1** *a sharp utensil* cutting, serrated, knife-like, edged, razor-edged, keen. **2** *a sharp length of metal* pointed, needle-like, spear-shaped, barbed, spiky. **3** *a sharp drop to the sea* steep, sheer, abrupt, precipitous, vertical. **4** *come to a sharp stop* sudden, abrupt, rapid, unexpected. **5** *a sharp difference between the two* clear, clear-cut, distinct, marked, well-defined, crisp. **6** *a sharp pain* intense, acute, keen, piercing, cutting, extreme, severe, stabbing, shooting, stinging. **7** *a sharp taste* pungent, biting, bitter, acid, sour, tart, vinegary. **8** *a sharp smell* acrid, pungent, burning. **9** *a sharp noise* piercing, shrill, high-pitched, ear-splitting, harsh, strident. **10** *exchange sharp words* harsh, curt, brusque, bitter, hard, cutting, scathing, caustic, biting, barbed, acrimonious, trenchant, sarcastic, sardonic, venomous, malicious, vitriolic, hurtful, unkind, cruel. **11** *a sharp pupil* sharp-witted, intelligent, bright, clever, quick. **12** *sharp intelligence/wits* keen, acute, quick, ready, smart, knowing, comprehending, shrewd, discerning, perceptive, penetrating. **13** *sharp practices|a sharp customer* unscrupulous, dishonest, cunning, wily, crafty, artful; *inf* fly. **14** *move at a sharp pace* brisk, rapid, quick, fast, swift, vigorous, spirited, animated. **15** *a sharp dresser* smart, stylish, fashionable, chic, elegant; *inf* dressy, snappy, natty.

sharp adj **1** *arrive at 9 a.m. sharp* promptly, punctually, on time, on the dot; *inf* on the nose. **2** *pull up sharp* abruptly, suddenly, all of a sudden, unexpectedly, without warning.

sharpen v put an edge on, edge, whet, hone, strop, grind.

shatter v **1** *shatter the windscreen* smash, smash to smithereens, break, break into pieces, splinter, fracture, shiver, pulverize, crush, crack; *inf* bust. **2** *shatter one's hopes/dreams* destroy, demolish, wreck, ruin, dash, blight, wipe out, overturn, blast, bring to nought, devastate, torpedo. **3** *shattered by their betrayal* break one's heart, devastate, crush, upset, distress, dumbfound; *inf* knock the stuffing out of.

shave v **1** *shave his beard* cut off, trim, snip off, crop. **2** *shave off pieces of wood* pare, plane, shear. **3** *shave the fence with his car* brush, graze, touch, scrape, rub.

sheath v **1** *a sheath from a sword* scabbard, case. **2** case, casing, cover, covering, envelope, wrapper. **3** *a contraceptive sheath* condom, contraceptive; *Amer* rubber.

shed n *a garden shed* hut, outhouse, lean-to, shack.

shed v **1** *trees shedding their leaves* let fall, drop. **2** *snakes shedding their skins* cast off, slough off. **3** *shed clothes* take off, remove, strip off, doff. **4** *shed blood* pour forth, let flow, spill, discharge, exude. **5** *shed light* diffuse, send forth, radiate, disperse, scatter. **6** *companies shedding workers* discard, get rid of, dispense with, drop, declare/make redundant, dismiss; *inf* sack, fire.

sheen n shine, lustre, gleam, sparkle, gloss, burnish, polish, patina.

sheepish adj embarrassed, uncomfortable, ashamed, shamefaced, blushing, abashed, shy, bashful, diffident, foolish, silly.

sheer adj **1** *sheer folly/magic* utter, complete, thoroughgoing, total, absolute, veritable, downright, out-and-out, unqualified, unconditional, unmitigated, unalloyed, unadulterated. **2** *a sheer cliff/drop to the sea* steep, abrupt, sharp, precipitous, vertical, perpendicular. **3** *sheer silk* diaphanous, transparent, see-through, translucent, filmy, gossamer, gauzy, ultra-fine, fine, thin.

sheer v **1** *ships sheering* swerve, change course, slew, veer, drift, yaw. **2** *sheer away from the topic* turn away from, change the subject from, avoid, evade, dodge, deviate from.

sheet n **1** *sheets and blankets* bed-sheet, bed-linen. **2** *a sheet of lacquered veneer on the table* layer, statum, overlay, surface, lamina, covering, coating, coat, facing, veneer, film. **3** *sheets of glass/plastic* piece, pane, panel, plate, slab. **4** *sheet of paper* piece of paper, leaf, page, folio. **5** *sheets of water* expanse, stretch, span, reach, sweep, covering, blanket, carpet.

shelf n **1** *putting books/cards on shelves* ledge, bracket, mantelshelf, mantelpiece. **2** *shelves in the sea* sandbank, sand bar, reef, shoal.

shell n **1** *the shell of a crab* carapace, case. **2** *the shell of a nut* casing, case, husk, pod, integument. **3** *shells in the army* magazine bullet, grenade, shot, shrapnel. **4** *the shell of a car/ship under construction* framework, frame, structure, chassis, hull, skeleton.

shell v **1** *shell peas* husk, shuck. **2** *troops shelling the city* bomb, bombard, blitz, torpedo, strafe, fire on, open fire on. **shell out** *shell out money* pay out, spend, lay out, disburse, squander; *inf* fork out.

shelter n **1** *provide shelter from danger/cold* protection, shield, cover, screen, safety, security, defence, refuge, sanctuary, asylum. **2** *a shelter for battered wives* refuge, sanctuary, retreat, haven, harbour.

shelter v **1** *shelter them from the weather* protect, provide protection from, shield, cover, screen, safeguard. **2** *shelter the criminal from the police* protect, shield, screen, safeguard, provide refuge/sanctuary from, guard, harbour, conceal, hide. **3** *shelter from the elements/pursuers in a barn* take shelter, take refuge, seek protection, seek refuge/sanctuary.

sheltered adj **1** *a sheltered spot for the picnic* shady, shaded, protected, screened, shielded, secluded. **2** *lead a sheltered life* secluded, quiet, withdrawn, retired, isolated, protected, cloistered, reclusive.

shelve v *shelve expansion plans* put to one side, lay aside, put off, postpone, defer, delay, suspend, mothball, pigeonhole, put on ice, put in cold storage, put on the back-burner; *Amer* table.

shepherd v *shepherd the children to their classes* escort, conduct, usher, convoy, guide, marshal, steer.

shield v **1** *using his shield to fend off blows* buckler; *lit* targe; *Herald* escutcheon. **2** *act as a shield against bullies* protection, defence, guard, safeguard, support, bulwark, screen, protector.

shield v *shield one's eyes from the dust | shield the child from the facts* protect, screen, defend, guard, safeguard, shelter.

shift v **1** *shift the furniture from the house to the van* move, carry, transfer, switch, transpose, relocate, reposition, rearrange. **2** *shift one's position on the new project* change, alter, vary, modify, reverse, do an about-turn; *inf* do a U-turn. **3** *unable to shift the stain* remove, take out, get rid of, budge. **shift for oneself** manage by oneself, manage without help/assistance, make it on one's own, fend for oneself, take care of oneself, make do, get by, scrape by; *inf* stand on one's own two feet, paddle one's own canoe.

shift n **1** *a shift of people from the country areas* move, movement, transference, switch, transposition, relocation, repositioning. **2** *a shift in public opinion* change, alteration, variation, modification, about-turn, reversal, sea-change; *inf* U-turn. **3** *an eight-hour shift* work period, stint, spell of work. **4** *resort to dubious shifts to make money* expedient, scheme, strategy, stratagem, device, plan, subterfuge, dodge, trick, ruse, wile, artifice, deception.

shiftless adj lazy, idle, indolent, slothful, inefficient, unambitious, unenterprising, worthless, good-for-nothing, ne'er-do-well.

shifty adj evasive, slippery, devious, duplicitous, deceitful, underhand, untrustworthy, double-dealing, dishonest, wily, crafty, artful, sly, scheming, contriving.

shilly-shally v be indecisive/irresolute, vacillate, waver, hesitate, hem and haw, oscillate, fluctuate; *inf* blow hot and cold.

shimmer v *light shimmering on the water* glisten, glint, flicker, twinkle, sparkle, gleam, glow, scintillate, dance.

shimmer n *the shimmer of light on water* glistening, glint, flicker, twinkle, sparkle, gleam, glow, lustre, iridescence, scintillation.

shine v **1** *the sun/torch shining* emit light, give off light. **2** *with shoes/glasses shining* gleam, sparkle, glisten. **3** *lights shining in the distance* gleam, glow, glint, sparkle, twinkle, flicker, glitter, glisten, shimmer, flash, dazzle, beam, radiate, illuminate, luminesce, incandesce. **4** *with face shining* glow, beam, radiate, bloom, look healthy, look good. **5** *shine the shoes* polish, burnish, buff, wax, gloss, brush, rub up. **6** *shine at tennis* excel, be expert, be brilliant, be very good, be outstanding. **7** *shine in a crowd* stand out, be outstanding, be conspicuous, be pre-eminent, excel, dominate, star.

shine n **1** *the shine of the street lights* light, brightness, gleam, glow, glint, sparkle, twinkle, flicker, glitter, glisten, shimmer, flash, dazzle, glare, beam, radiance, illumination, luminescence, luminosity, lambency, effulgence. **2** *put a shine on the polished table* polish, burnish, gleam, gloss, lustre, sheen, patina.

shining adj **1** *shining lights* gleaming, glowing, glinting, sparkling, twinkling, flickering, glittering, flashing, dazzling, incandescent, effulgent. *see* SHINE v 3. **2** *with shining, happy faces* glowing, beaming, radiant, blooming, healthy. **3** *a shining example | shining stars in the theatre* outstanding, pre-eminent, leading, illustrious, brilliant, splendid. **4** *shining tables/glasses* shiny, polished, burnished, gleaming, glossy, satiny, lustrous; *lit* nitid.

shiny adj *shiny tables/glasses* shining, polished, burnished, gleaming, glossy, satiny, lustrous; *lit* nitid.

shirk v *shirk work* avoid, evade, dodge, sidestep, shrink from, shun, get out of, slide out of, play truant from; *inf* funk, skive off.

shirker n dodger, slacker, truant, habitual, absentee, malinger, layabout, loafter, idler; *inf* skiver.

shiver [1] v *shiver with cold/fear* tremble, quiver, shake, shudder, quaver, quake, vibrate.

shiver [1] n *give a shiver of fear* tremble, quiver, shake, quaver, shudder.

shiver [2] n *cut by a shiver of glass* splinter, sliver, fragment, shard, shaving.

shiver [2] v *the window shivered into thousands of pieces* shatter, smash, splinter, fragment, explode, crack, break.

shivery adj *feeling shivery in the cold | be shivery from the fever* trembling, trembly, quivering, quivery, shaking, shaky, shuddering, quavering, quaking.

shock [1] n **1** *the shock of the two cars hitting each other* impact, blow, collision, crash, clash, jolt, bump, jar, jerk, shake. **2** *the news of the murder came as a shock | he gave the villagers a shock* blow, upset, disturbance, state of agitation/perturbation, source of distress, source of amazement, consternation, revelation, bolt from the blue, bombshell, eye-opener. **3** *suffering from shock after the accident* state of shock, trauma, traumatism, prostration, stupor, stupefaction, collapse.

shock [1] v *shocked by the housing conditions | shocked by the battle-scenes* appal, horrify, scandalize, outrage, repel, revolt, disgust, nauseate, sicken, offend, traumatize, make one's blood run cold, distress, upset, perturb, disturb, disquiet, unsettle, discompose, agitate, astound, dumbfound, stagger, amaze, astonish, stun, flabbergast, stupefy, overwhelm, bewilder.

shock [2] n *a shock of red hair* mass, mop, mane, thatch.

shocking adj *shocking conditions | a shocking sight* appalling, horrifying, horrific, dreadful, awful, frightful, terrible, horrible, scandalous, outrageous, vile, disgraceful, abominable, ghastly, foul, monstrous, unspeakable, abhorrent, hideous, atrocious, repellent, revolting, odious, repulsive, repugnant, disgusting, nauseating, sickening, grisly, loathsome, offensive, distressing, upsetting, perturbing, disturbing, disquieting, unsettling, agitating, astound, staggering, amazing, astonishing, stupefying, overwhelming, bewildering.

shoddy adj poor-quality, inferior, second-rate, cheapjack, tawdry, rubbishy, trashy, junky, gimcrack, jerry-built; *inf* tacky, tatty.

shoot v **1** *shoot a deer* hit, wound, injure, shoot down, bring down, pick off, bag, fell,

kill, slay; *inf* pump full of lead, plug, zap. **2** *shoot at the fugitives* fire at, open fire on, aim at, snipe at, shell. **3** *shoot a round of bullets/arrows* fire, discharge, launch, let off, let fly, send forth, emit. **4** *athletes shooting past* race, dash, sprint, bound, charge, dart, fly, hurtle, bolt, streak, flash, whisk, run, speed, hurry, hasten; *inf* scoot. **5** *plants shooting* put forth buds, bud, burgeon, sprout, germinate, appear, spring up. **6** *shooting animal scenes* film, photograph, take photographs of.

shoot n *shoots of a plant/tree* bud, offshoot, slip, scion, sucker, sprout, branch, twig, sprig, cutting, graft.

shop n **1** *purchase goods at a shop* store, retail outlet, trading post. **2** *cars worked on at the shop* workshop, plant, factory.

shop v **1** *shop for essential goods* go shopping, look to buy, be in the market for. **2** *shop his fellow bank-raiders* inform against, tell tales on, impeach; *inf* grass on, rat on, blow the whistle on, put the finger on, squeal on, peach on, sing about.

shore n seashore, seaside, beach, coast, seaboard, waterside, foreshore, strand.

shore v *shore up the broken wall* prop up, support, hold up, underpin, strengthen, brace, buttress.

short adj **1** *short people* small, little, slight, petite, tiny, squat, stubby, dwarfish, diminutive, dumpy, Lilliputian; *Scots* wee; *inf* pint-sized, pocket-sized, knee-high to a grasshopper. **2** *short bushes* low, stubby, miniature; *Scots* wee. **3** *a short piece of string* small, little, tiny, miniscule. **4** *a short report* brief, concise, succinct, to the point, compact, terse, summary, crisp, pithy, epigrammatic, abridged, abbreviated, condensed, summarized, contracted, curtailed, truncated. **5** *a short affair* brief, momentary, temporary, short-lived, impermanent, short-term, cursory, fleeting, passing, transitory, transient, ephemeral, fugacious, evanescent, meteoric. **6** *the short route* direct, straight. **7** *money/food is a bit short* deficient, lacking, wanting, insufficient, inadequate, scarce, scanty, meagre, sparse, unplentiful, tight, low. **8** *he was short with her | give rather a short reply* curt, sharp, abrupt, blunt, brusque, terse, gruff, surly, testy, tart, rude, discourteous, uncivil, impolite. **9** *short pastry* short-crust, crumbly, crispy, crisp, brittle, friable.

short adv *stop short* abruptly, suddenly, all of a sudden, unexpectedly, without warning, out of the blue. **cut short** shorten, curtail, truncate, abbreviate, reduce, bring to an untimely end, terminate, end, stop,

halt, arrest, cut off, interrupt, break up.
fall short be deficient, be insufficient, be
inadequate, disappoint, fail, not to fulfil
expectations; *inf* not come up to scratch. **in
short** briefly, to put it briefly, in a word, in
a nutshell, in essence, to cut a long story
short, to come to the point. **sell short**
1 *always selling herself short* undervalue,
underrate, underestimate, disparage, deprecate, belittle, detract from, derogate.
2 *shopkeepers selling people short* cheat, swindle, defraud, fleece, short-change, overcharge. **short of 1** *short of eggs/brains*
deficient in, lacking, wanting, in need of,
low on, missing. **2** *short of killing him how
will you get rid of him?* other, than, apart
from, aside from, besides, except, without,
excluding, leaving out, not counting, disregarding.

shortage n dearth, scarcity, lack, deficiency, insufficiency, paucity, deficit, inadequacy, shortfall, want, poverty.

shortcoming n *forgive his shortcomings*
defect, fault, flaw, imperfection, failing,
drawback, weakness, weak point, foible,
frailty, infirmity.

shorten v **1** *shorten the text* abbreviate, condense, abridge, cut, cut down, contract,
compress, reduce, lessen, decrease, diminish, curtail, duck, trim, pare down. **2** *the
days are shortening* get shorter, grow
shorter, grow less.

short-lived adj *short-lived happiness* brief,
momentary, temporary, impermanent,
fleeting, transitory, ephemeral. *see* SHORT
adj 5.

shortly adv **1** *she will be with you shortly*
soon, in a short while, in a little while,
presently, before long, directly; *inf* before
you know it, before you can say Jack Robinson. **2** *he replied shortly* curtly, sharply,
abruptly, bluntly, brusquely, tersely,
gruffly, surlily, testily, tartly, rudely, discourteously, uncivilly, impolitely.

short-sighted adj **1** *wear spectacles because of
being short-sighted* myopic, near-sighted. **2** *a
short-sighted attitude to business* lacking foresight, uncircumspect, ill-considered,
unwary, imprudent, injudicious, unwise,
ill-advised, thoughtless, unthinking, heedless, rash, incautious.

short-staffed adj under-staffed, short-
handed, undermanned, below strength.

short-tempered adj quick-tempered, hot-
tempered, irascible, touchy, testy, fiery,
peppery, choleric; *inf* on a short fuse, ratty.

shot n **1** *hear a shot* gun-fire, report of a
gun, crack, bang, blast, explosion. **2** *shot for*
the guns pellet, bullet, slug, projectile,
ammunition. **3** *hit the target with one shot*
throw, lob, fling, hurl, put shot. **4** *a better
shot than his brother* shooter, marksman,
rifleman. **5** *take a shot of the house* photograph, photo, film, snap, snapshot. **6** *have a
shot at getting there* attempt, try, effort,
endeavour, essay; *inf* go, stab, crack, bash,
whack. **7** *it's your shot now* turn, chance,
opportunity; *inf* go. **8** *have shots before going
to the tropics* injection, vaccination. **9** *a
nasty/cheap shot* comment, remark, statement, utterance; *inf* crack. **a shot in the
arm** *a shot in the arm for the tourist industry*
boost, filip, lift, encouragement, stimulus.
a shot in the dark *her answer was right but
it was a shot in the dark* wild guess, random
guess, guess, pure conjecture. **like a shot**
he would take the job like a shot without hesitation, unhesitatingly, very willingly,
eagerly, immediately, instantly, right away,
at once, like a flash. **not by a long shot** by
no means, not at all, not in the least, on
no account, under no circumstances.

shot adj *shot silk* variegated, multicoloured,
many-coloured, varicoloured.

shoulder n **1** *shoulder a heavy burden/respon-
sibility* bear, carry, support, be responsible
for, take on, take upon oneself, take on.
2 *shoulder his way to the front* push, shove,
thrust, jostle, elbow, force. **give someone
the cold shoulder** ostracize, shun, snub,
ignore, rebuff, send someone to Coventry;
inf cut, cut dead. **put one's shoulder to
the wheel** apply oneself, exert oneself, get
down to work, set to work, make an effort,
strive; *inf* buckle down, give it one's best
shot. **rub shoulders with** associate with,
mix with, socialize with, consort with, fraternize with, hobnob with. **shoulder to
shoulder** side by side, cheek by jowl,
together, united, jointly, in partnership, in
cooperation, in unity, in unison, as one.
straight from the shoulder directly,
frankly, candidly, forthrightly, bluntly,
plainly, explicitly, outspokenly, unequivocally, unambiguously; *inf* pulling no
punches, with no holds barred.

shout v *"Help", he shouted* cry out, call out,
yell, roar, howl, bellow, scream, bawl, call
at the top of one's voice, raise one's voice;
inf holler.

shout n **1** *a shout of pain* cry, call, yell, roar,
howl, bellow, scream, bawl; *inf* holler.
2 *your shout* turn to pay, round, treat.

shove v *shove forward | shove her out of the way*
push, thrust, drive, force, shoulder, elbow,
jostle, jolt.

shove n *give the child a shove* push, thrust, jostle, jolt.

shovel n *move coal with a shovel* spade, scoop.

shovel v *shovel coal* scoop up, spade, dig, excavate.

show v **1** *grey hairs beginning to show* be visible, be seen, be in view, appear, put in an appearance. **2** *show the toys to the children* exhibit, display, present, demonstrate, set forth, uncover, reveal. **3** *show his grief* indicate, express, manifest, reveal, make known, make plain, make obvious, evince, evidence, disclose, betray, divulge. **4** *show them the new procedures* demonstrate, point out, explain, expound, clarify, elucidate, teach, instruct in, give instructions in, tutor in, indoctrinate in. **5** *show them to their seats* escort, accompany, usher, conduct, attend, guide, lead, direct, steer. **6** *he didn't show* appear, put in an appearance, make an appearance, turn up, come, arrive, be present. **show off 1** *models showing off the dresses* show to advantage, display, exhibit, demonstrate, parade, flaunt. **2** *children showing off about their new clothes* put on airs, give oneself airs, boast, brag, swagger around. **show up 1** *sunshine showing up the dust* expose, reveal, bring to light, lay bare, make visible, make obvious, highlight, pinpoint, put the spotlight on. **2** *the red showing up well against the grey* be visible, be obvious, be conspicuous, stand out, catch the eye. **3** *show him up in front of his rich friends* expose, show in a bad light, shame, put to shame, mortify, humiliate, embarrass. **4** *the guest didn't show up* appear, make an appearance, put in an appearance, turn up, come, get here/there, be present; *inf* show

show n **1** *a brilliant show of flowers* display, array, arrangement, exhibition, presentation, exposition, spectacle. **2** *a clothes show* exhibition, demonstration, display, exposition, presentation; *inf* expo. **3** *put on a musical show* performance, public performance, theatrical performance, production; *inf* gig. **4** *a show of courage although terrified* appearance, outward appearance, air, guise, semblance, pretence, illusion, pose, affectation, profession, parade. **5** *only doing it for show* display, ostentation, affectation, window dressing. **6** *run the show* organization, establishment, undertaking, enterprise, business, venture. **steal the show** be the main attraction, be the centre of attraction, get all the attention, have all eyes upon one, be the cynosure.

showdown n confrontation, open conflict, clash, face-off, moment of truth, crisis, culmination, climax.

shower n **1** *a shower of rain/snow* fall, drizzle, flurry, sprinkling. **2** *a shower of arrows* volley, raining, barrage, fusillade. **3** *a shower of gifts* abundance, profusion, plethora, flood, deluge.

shower v **1** *arrows showered on them* rain, fall. **2** *shower them with gifts* deluge, inundate, overwhelm. **3** *shower gifts on them* lavish, pour, load, heap.

showing n **1** *a private showing* show, exhibition, display, exposition; *inf* expo. **2** *on the firm's/employee's present showing* performance, track record, record, results.

show-off n exhibitionist, extrovert, swagger, bragger, braggart, boaster, braggadocio; *inf* blow-hard.

showy adj *showy clothes/lifestyle* ostentatious, flamboyant, elaborate, fancy, pretentious, overdone, glittering.

shred n **1** *shreds of material* scrap, fragment, wisp, sliver, bit, piece, remnant, snippet, tatter. **2** *not a shred of evidence* scrap, bit, iota, whit, particle, atom, modicum, trace, speck.

shred v *shred paper/cabbage* cut up, tear up, rip up, grate.

shrew n *married to a real shrew* virago, termagant, fury, harpy, nag.

shrewd adj **1** *a shrewd businessman* astute, sharp, clever, intelligent, smart, alert, quick-witted, discerning, perspicacious, perceptive, discriminating, wise, sagacious, far-seeing, canny, cunning, artful, crafty, wily, calculating; *inf* with all one's wits about one. **2** *a shrewd plan* astute, clever, wise, judicious, far-sighted, cunning, artful, crafty, wily, calculated.

shrewdness n acumen, astuteness, sharpness, cleverness, smartness, alertness, quick-wittedness, discernment, perspicacity, perceptiveness, wisdom, sagacity, canniness, cunning, artfulness, craftiness, wiliness, calculation, calculatedness.

shriek v *shriek with laughter/terror* scream, screech, squeal, yell, howl, shout, cry out, call out, whoop, wail; *inf* holler.

shriek n *a shriek of laughter/terror* scream, screech, squeal, yell, howl, shout, cry, call, whoop, wail; *inf* holler.

shrill adj high-pitched, high, sharp, piercing, ear-piercing, penetrating, ear-splitting, screeching, shrieking.

shrine n **1** *a shrine in memory of the dead soldiers* memorial, monument, cenotaph.

2 *worship in the shrine* holy place, temple, church. **3** *the relics of the saint in a shrine* reliquary, burial chamber, tomb, sepulchre.

shrink v **1** *shirts shrinking in the wash* get smaller, become/grow smaller. **2** *markets shrinking* get smaller, become/grow smaller, contract, diminish, lessen, reduce, dwindle, narrow, decline, fall off, drop off, shrivel. **3** *children shrinking from the bully | shrink from admitting the truth* draw back, pull back, start back, back away, shy away, recoil, retreat, withdraw, flinch, cringe, wince.

shrivel v *leaves shrivelled by the sun* dry up, wither, dessicate, dehydrate, wrinkle, pucker up.

shrivelled adj *shrivelled leaves/skins* dried up, withered, desiccated, dehydrated, wrinkled, puckered, wizened; *lit* sere.

shroud n **1** *corpses in shrouds* winding-sheet, grave-clothes, burial clothes, cerements. **2** *a shroud of mist over the hills* cover, covering, pall, cloak, mantle, blanket, cloud, veil, screen.

shroud v *hills shrouded in mist* cover, enshroud, swathe, envelop, cloak, blanket, cloud, veil, screen, conceal, hide.

shrug v *shrug off failure* disregard, take no notice of, not trouble about, dismiss, gloss over, play down, make light of, minimize.

shudder v *shudder in horror* shake, shiver, tremble, quiver, quaver, quake, convulse.

shudder n *a shudder of horror* shake, shiver, tremor, tremble, quiver, quaver, convulsion, spasm.

shuffle v **1** *shuffle along the road* shamble, hobble, limp, drag one's feet, scuff one's feet. **2** *the audience shuffling their feet* scrape, scuff, drag. **3** *shuffle cards/papers* mix, intermix, shift about, rearrange, reorganize, jumble. **4** *shuffling and refusing to give a straight answer* edge, equivocate, be evasive, prevaricate, fence, parry, beat about the bush, beg the question; *inf* pussyfoot around.

shun n *shun the ex-convict/publicity* avoid, evade, eschew, steer clear of, shy away from, recoil from, keep away from, keep one's distance from, cold-shoulder, give a wide berth to.

shut v *shut the doors* draw to, pull to, close, fasten, bar, lock, secure, seal. **shut down 1** *shut down the factory* close, close down. **2** *the factory has shut down* close, close down, cease productions, come to halt, cease operating, go on strike. **3** *shut down the machinery* switch off, stop, halt. **shut in** *shut in the dogs/prisoners* lock in, keep in, hem

in, fence in, corral. **shut out 1** *shut out intruders* lock out, keep out. **2** *shut him out of their negotiations/club* exclude, leave out, omit, keep out, bar, debar, ostracize, blackball, banish, exile, outlaw. **3** *shut out the light* keep out, block out, screen, cover up.

shut up 1 *shut the child up in a wardrobe* lock in, confine, imprison, coop up, box in, cage in. **2** *criminals shut up for life* imprison, jail, incarcerate, intern, immure. **3** *children asked to shut up* keep quiet, be quiet, keep silent, fall silent; *inf* hold one's tongue, keep one's lips sealed, keep mum, pipe down, keep one's trap shut. **4** *shut the children up* quieten, silence, hush, shush, gag; *inf* button the lip of.

shutter n blind, shade.

shuttle v *shuttle between the two cities* go back and forth between, alternate between, commute between, shunt between, ply between.

shy adj bashful, diffident, reserved, reticent, retiring, self-effacing, shrinking, withdrawn, timid, timorous, fearful, nervous, hesitant, wary, suspicious, chary, unconfident, self-conscious, embarrassed, abashed, modest.

shy v *shy a stone at the tree* throw, fling, cast, pitch, toss, hurl, propel; *inf* chuck. **fight shy of** *fight shy of getting involved* shy away from, recoil from, flinch from, back away from. *see* SHY V SHY AWAY FROM. **shy away from** *shy away from trouble* fight shy of, shrink from, recoil from, flinch from, balk at, quail at, draw back from, back away from.

shyness n bashfulness, diffidence, reserve, reservedness, reticence, timidity, timorousness, fearfulness, nervousness, hesitancy, hesitation, wariness, suspicion, chariness, lack of confidence, self-consciousness, embarrassment, modesty. *see* SHY adj.

sick adj **1** *off work sick* unwell, ill, ailing, indisposed, poorly, below par, out of sorts, laid up; *inf* under the weather, on the sick list. **2** *feel sick on a boat* nauseated, queasy, bilious; *inf* green about the gills. **3** *be sick on the boat* vomit, retch; *Amer* be sick to one's stomach; *inf* throw up, puke. **4** *sick of that music* tired, weary, bored, jaded, surfeited, satiated, glutted; *inf* fed up, have had something up to here. **5** *be sick about losing* angry, annoyed, displeased, disgruntled, distressed, disgusted; *inf* fed up, cheesed off. **6** *a sick joke | sick humour* morbid, macabre, ghoulish, gruesome, sadistic, perverted, cruel.

sicken v **1** *sickened by the sight of the mangled corpse* make sick, nauseate, turn one's stomach, make one's gorge rise, revolt, disgust, repel, shock, appal. **2** *sicken for something/flu* show symptoms of, take ill with, become ill with, fall ill with, become infected with, contract, be stricken with; *inf* come down with. **3** *begin to sicken of that type of music* tire, weary, become bored with/of, feel jaded with, have a surfeit of, be satiated with, have a glut of; *inf* be fed up with, have had something up to here.

sickening adj *the sickening sight of the mangled corpse* nauseating, nauseous, revolting, disgusting, repellent, repulsive, loathsome, off-putting, distasteful, stomach-turning, stomach-churning, shocking, appalling, offensive, vile, foul.

sickly adj **1** *a sickly child* unhealthy, in poor health, chronically ill, delicate, frail, weak, feeble, puny. **2** *look sickly | a sickly complexion* pale, wan, pallid, peaky, anaemic, bloodless, languid, listless; *inf* washed-out. **3** *sickly love songs* sentimental, cloying, mawkish, maudlin, slushy, mushy, syrupy; *inf* soppy, schmaltzy. **4** *sickly colours* pallid, insipid, wan, pale, washed-out, faded; *inf* bilious.

sickness n **1** *suffering from a terminal sickness* illness, disease, disorder, ailment, complaint, affliction, malady, infirmity, indisposition; *inf* bug. **2** *a bout of sickness* vomiting, retching, upset stomach, stomach upset; *inf* throwing up, puking. **3** *a feeling of sickness on the swaying boat* nausea, queasiness, biliousness.

side n **1** *by the side of the lake/road* edge, border, verge, boundary, margin, rim, fringe, skirt, flank, brink, brim, periphery. **2** *on the east side of the city* part, quarter, section, sector, neighbourhood. **3** *the upper side of the paper/wood* surface, face, part, facet. **4** *both sides of the question/problem* aspect, angle, facet, point of view, viewpoint, view, opinion, standpoint, position, slant. **5** *on the chairman's side in the dispute* camp, faction, caucus, party, wing, splinter, group, sect. **6** *left out of the football side* team, squad, line-up. **7** *no side about the aristocratic family* airs, airs and graces, pretentiousness, arrogance, superciliousness; *inf* snootiness. **side by side** *walk/fight side by side* close together, together, alongside each other, shoulder to shoulder, cheek by jowl, arm in arm. **take the side of** *take the side of the likely winner* side with, take the part of, support, give one's support to, favour.

side adj **1** *on the side position of the battle* lateral, wing, flank. **2** *a side issue/road* minor, lesser, secondary, subordinate, subsidiary,

ancillary, marginal. **3** *a side look* sidelong, oblique, indirect. *see* SIDELONG.

side v *side with his brother against his sister* take the side of, be on the side of, take the part of, support, give one's support to, back, give one's backing to, ally with, associate oneself with, join with, favour.

sidelong adj side, sideways, oblique, indirect, covert.

sidestep v *sidestep the problematic issue* avoid, skirt round, evade, dodge, circumvent, bypass, steer clear of; *inf* duck.

sidetrack v *get sidetracked from the main issue* divert, deflect, distract, lead away from.

sideways adv **1** *walk sideways* crabwise, to the side. **2** *bring the table in sideways* side first, edgeways, edgewise. **3** *look sideways at her* obliquely, indirectly, sidelong.

sideways adj *a sideways glance* sidelong, side, oblique, indirect.

siege n blockade, besiegement, beleaguerment, investment.

siesta n nap, sleep, rest, catnap, doze; *inf* forty winks, snooze.

sieve n *use a sieve to strain the mixture* strainer, sifter, filter, colander, riddle, screen.

sieve v **1** *sieve the mixture* strain, sift, filter, riddle, screen. **2** *sieve the lumps from the sauce* separate out, remove, winnow.

sift v **1** *sift the flour* filter, strain, riddle, screen. **2** *sift flour onto a board* shake, sprinkle, distribute, scatter, strew. **3** *sift the lumps from the flour* separate out, remove, winnow. **4** *sift through the evidence* examine, scrutinize, study, pore over, investigate, analyse, screen, review, probe. **5** *sift through the debris* search through, look through, rummage through, ransack.

sigh v **1** *sigh with tiredness/boredom* breathe out, exhale. **2** *the wind sighing through the trees* whisper, rustle. **3** *sigh for times past* yearn for, pine for, long for, weep for, mourn for.

sight n **1** *have excellent sight* eyesight, vision, eyes, faculty of sight, power of sight. **2** *within sight of her father* range of vision, field of vision, view. **3** *our first sight of the building* view, glimpse, seeing, glance at. **4** *in her father's sight she was perfect* opinion, view, point of view, judgement, estimation, feeling, observation, perception. **5** *on a tourist sight | the town's historic sight* spectacle, scene, display, show, exhibition, curiosity, rarity, marvel; *inf* something to write home about. **6** *a sight in those clothes* spectacle, eyesore, monstrosity, mess; *inf* fright, blot on the landscape. **catch sight of** glimpse, get a glimpse of, see, spot, sight, descry, espy, set eyes on, have sight of. **set one's sights on** aim at/for, aspire to, strive towards, work towards, be after, seek.

sight v *sight land* catch sight of, see, behold, spot, make out, descry, espy, perceive, observe, discern.

sign n **1** *a sign of weakness/strength* indication, symptom, hint, suggestion, face, mark, clue, manifestation, token, evidence, proof. **2** *signs indicating the various shops in the complex* signpost, notice, placard, board, marker. **3** *make a sign to follow him* gesture, signal, motion, movement, wave, gesticulation. **4** *mathematical signs|signs instead of language* symbol, mark, cipher, code, hieroglyph, hieroglyphics. **5** *look for a sign that the Messiah will come* omen, portent, warning, forewarning, augury, presage.

sign v **1** *sign one's name* write, inscribe. **2** *sign the letter* write one's name on, autograph, initial. **3** *sign the agreement* write one's name on, initial, endorse, certify, validate, authenticate. **4** *sign to her to follow* signal, indicate, beckon, gesture, motion, gesticulate, wave, nod. **sign on/up 1** *soldier signing on for five years* enlist, join up, join the services. **2** *sign on for music classes* enrol, register, put one's name down for, enlist, become a member of. **3** *sign on new employees* employ, take on, engage, hire, recruit, take into one's employ. **sign over** *sign over the estate to his son* transfer, make over, hand over, turn over, assign, consign.

signal n **1** *the signal to stop|a signal that someone was coming* sign, indicator, cue. **2** *a signal that winter was coming* sign, indication, token, evidence, hint. **3** *the arrival of the star was the signal for applause* incentive, impetus, stimulus, motive, cause, reason.

signal v **1** *signal to her to follow* sign, give a sign to, indicate, beckon, gesture, motion, gesticulate, nod. **2** *signal his displeasure with silence* indicate, show, express, communicate. **3** *the sudden cold weather signalled the start of a hard winter* be a sign of, mark, signify, designate.

signal adj *a signal achievement* exceptional, conspicuous, notable, noteworthy, significant, memorable, outstanding, striking, remarkable, distinguished, eminent.

significance n **1** *not comprehend the significance of his remark* meaning, sense, import, signification, purport, point, gist, essence, implications. **2** *the significance of the medical discovery* importance, consequence, moment, momentousness, weight, weighti-

ness, magnitude, impressiveness, seriousness.

significant adj **1** *a significant few words* meaningful, eloquent, expressive, indicative, pregnant, knowing. **2** *make significant progress* important, of importance, of consequence, momentous, of moment, weighty, material, impressive, serious, vital, critical.

signify v **1** *dark clouds signifying rain* be a sign of, indicate, mean, denote, betoken, suggest, point to, portend. **2** *What do the symbols signify?* mean, denote, represent, symbolize, stand for. **3** *signify one's agreement* indicate, show, exhibit, express, communicate, intimate, announce, proclaim, declare, pronounce. **4** *his opinion doesn't signify* matter, be of importance, be of consequence, be important, be significant, be of significance, carry weight, count.

silence n **1** *in the silence of the night* still, stillness, quiet, quietness, hush, peace, peacefulness, tranquillity, noiselessness, soundlessness. **2** *their behaviour reduced him to silence* speechlessness, wordlessness, voicelessness, dumbness, muteness, taciturnity, reticence, uncommunicativeness. **3** *the need for silence about their whereabouts* secrecy, secretiveness, concealment, reticence, taciturnity, uncommunicativeness.

silence v **1** *silence the noisy children* quiet, quieten, hush, still, calm, pacify, subdue, quell. **2** *silence the noise of the engine* muffle, deaden, abate, extinguish. **3** *silence their complaints* put an end to, put a stop to, cut short, gag, prevent.

silent adj **1** *in their silent surroundings* still, quiet, hushed, peaceful, tranquil, noiseless, soundless. **2** *silent in the face of the opposition* speechless, unspeaking, wordless, voiceless, dumb, mute, taciturn, reticent, uncommunicative, mum, tight-lipped, tongue-tied; *inf* struck dumb. **3** *silent criticism* unspoken, wordless, unvoiced, unsaid, unexpressed, unpronounced, tacit, implicit, understood, implied.

silhouette n *see her silhouette on the wall* outline, contour, profile, delineation, form, shape.

silhouette v *silhouetted against the sky* outline, stand out, etch, delineate.

silky adj silken, smooth, sleek, velvety, diaphanous.

silly adj **1** *a silly person* foolish, stupid, unintelligent, idiotic, brainless, witless, unwise, imprudent, thoughtless, reckless, foolhardy, irresponsible, mad, erratic, unstable, scatter-brained, feather-brained, flighty, frivolous, giddy, fatuous, inane, immature, childish, shallow, naive; *inf* daft, crazy, dotty, scatty, loopy, screwy. **2** *silly actions* foolish, stupid, unintelligent, senseless, mindless, idiotic, unwise, imprudent, inadvisable, injudicious, ill-considered, misguided, unsound, impractical, pointless, meaningless, purposeless, inappropriate, illogical, irrational, unreasonable, thoughtless, reckless, foolhardy, irresponsible, erratic, hare-brained, absurd, ridiculous, ludicrous, laughable, risible, farcical, preposterous, fatuous, asinine; *inf* half-baked, daft, crazy, dotty, loopy, screwy, for the birds. **3** *knocked silly by the blow* dazed, in a daze, stunned, stupefied, groggy, muzzy, benumbed.

silly n *accused of being a silly* fool, ninny, nincompoop, idiot, simpleton, dolt, halfwit, scatter-brain; *inf* nitwit, twit, clot, dope, goose, silly-billy.

similar adj **1** *have similar houses* like, alike, much the same, comparable, corresponding, analogous, parallel, equivalent, kindred, approximate. **2** *ideas similar to his* resembling, like, much the same as, comparable to, corresponding to, close to.

similarity n *a degree of similarity* resemblance, likeness, sameness, similitude, comparability, correspondence, closeness, analogy, parallel, parallelism, equivalence, approximation, affinity, kinship.

similarly adv likewise, in the same way, in like matter, correspondingly, by the same token.

similitude n *a marked degree of similitude in their views* resemblance, likeness, similarity, sameness, comparability, correspondence, closeness, analogy. *see* SIMILARITY.

simmer v **1** *a stew simmering on the stove* cook gently, boil gently, bubble, stew, poach, seethe. **2** *simmering with rage* fume, seethe, smoulder, chafe, smart, be angry, be furious.

simple adj **1** *a simple task* easy, uncomplicated, straightforward, uninvolved, effortless, manageable, elementary, facile; *inf* like falling off a log, a piece of cake, a cinch, easy-peasy, no sweat. **2** *simple instructions | in simple language* clear, plain, intelligible, comprehensible, understandable, lurid, direct, straightforward, uncomplicated, uninvolved. **3** *simple clothes* plain, classic, clean-cut, unelaborate, unadorned, undecorated, without ornament/ornamentation, unembellished, unfussy, uncluttered, austere, stark, Spartan, unpretentious, restrained, natural, casual, informal. **4** *simple chemical substances* non-

complex, non-compound, uncompounded, uncombined, unmixed, unblended, unalloyed, pure, basic, single, elementary, fundamental. **5** *the simple truth/facts* plain, straightforward, frank, direct, candid, honest, sincere, absolute, unqualified, unvarnished, bald, stark, unadorned, unembellished. **6** *a simple country girl* unsophisticated, natural, unaffected, wholesome, innocent, artless, guileless, childlike, naive, ingenuous, gullible, inexperienced; *inf* green. **7** *lead a simple life* ordinary, commonplace, unpretentious, modest, homely, humble, lowly, rustic. **8** *too simple to have committed the crime* simple-minded, feeble-minded, mentally retarded, retarded, backward, slow-witted, slow, dull-witted.

simpleton n idiot, half-wit, daft, fool, ninny, nincompoop; *inf* nitwit, twit, clot, dope.

simplicity n **1** *the simplicity of the task* simpleness, easiness, lack/absence of complication, straightforwardness, effortlessness, elementariness, facility. *see* SIMPLE 1. **2** *the simplicity of the directions/language* simpleness, clarity, clearness, plainness, intelligibility, lucidity, lucidness, directness, straightforwardness; *inf* calling a spade a spade, telling like it is. *see* SIMPLE 2. **3** *the simplicity of the clothes* simpleness, classic lines, clean lines, non-elaborateness, lack/absence of adornment/decoration/ornament/ornamentation/embellishment, unfussiness, plainness, lack/absence of clutter, austereness, starkness, unpretentiousness, restraint, naturalness, casualness, informality. **4** *the simplicity of the statement* simpleness, plainness, straightforwardness, frankness, directness, candidness, candour, honesty, sincerity, baldness, starkness, lack of embellishment. **5** *the simplicity of their lifestyle* ordinariness, unpretentiousness, modesty, homeliness, humbleness, lowliness.

simplify v **1** *simplify the complicated instructions* make simple/simpler, make easy/easier, make plainer, clarify, decipher, disentangle, explain, paraphrase, translate, abridge, shorten, condense. **2** *simplify the procedure/method* make simple/simpler, make easy/easier, streamline, reduce to essentials.

simplistic adj *a simplistic solution/attitude* oversimple, oversimplified, facile, shallow, superficial, naive.

simply adj **1** *try to express oneself simply* clearly, plainly, intelligibly, lucidly, directly, straightforwardly. **2** *dress simply* plainly, classically, unelaborately, without adornment/decoration/ornament/ornamentation/embellishment, unfussily, without clutter, austerely, starkly, spartanly, with restraint, naturally, casually, informally. **3** *live simply* unpretentiously, modestly, humbly. **4** *break windows simply to gain attention* purely, solely, merely, only, just. **5** *simply the best painting he had ever seen* absolutely, unreservedly, positively, certainly, unconditionally, categorically, utterly, completely, altogether, totally, wholly.

simulate v **1** *simulate grief* feign, pretend, fake, sham, affect, fake the appearance of. **2** *simulate flight landing conditions* reproduce, mimic, parallel, do a mock-up of.

simultaneous adj *simultaneous disasters in different parts of the country* concurrent, contemporaneous, concomital, coinciding, coincident, synchronous, coexistent, parallel.

simultaneously adj *twins giving birth simultaneously | scream simultaneously* at the same time, concurrently, concomitantly, together, all together, in unison, in concert, in chorus.

sin n **1** *commit a sin in the eyes of the church* wrong, wrongdoing, act of evil/wickedness/badness, crime, offence, misdeed, misdemeanour, transgression, error, lapse, fall from grace; *lit* trespass. **2** *guilty of sin* wrongdoing, wrong, evil, evildoing, wickedness, badness, iniquity, crime, immorality, transgression, error, unrighteousness, ungodliness, irreligiousness, irreverence, profanity, blasphemy, impiety, sacrilege.

sin v **1** *sin against the church/family* commit a sin, do wrong, commit a crime, offend, commit an offence, transgress. **2** *punish people who sin* commit a sin, do wrong, commit a crime, commit an offence, break the law, misbehave, transgress, go astray, stray from the straight and narrow, go wrong, fall from grace.

sincere adj **1** *sincere affection/beliefs* genuine, real, true, honest, unfeigned, unaffected, *bona fide*, honest, wholehearted, heartfelt, serious, earnest, fervent. **2** *sincere people* honest, above-board, trustworthy, frank, candid, straightforward, plain-dealing, nononsense, genuine, undeceitful, artless, guileless, ingenuous; *inf* up-front.

sincerely v **1** *thank them sincerely* with all sincerity, wholeheartedly, with all one's heart, earnestly, fervently. **2** *mean it most sincerely* genuinely, really, truly, in truth, without pretence, without feigning, honestly, in good faith.

sincerity n **1** *doubt the sincerity of his affections/beliefs* genuineness, truth, honesty, good faith, wholeheartedness, seriousness, earnestness, fervour. **2** *misled by their seeming sincerity* openness, honesty, trustworthiness, frankness, candour, candidness, straightforwardness, genuineness, lack of deceit, artlessness, guilelessness, ingenuousness.

sinecure n easy job, soft option, cinch; *inf* cushy number, money for old rope, money for jam, picnic, gravy train.

sinewy adj muscular, brawny, burly, powerfully-built, stalwart, strapping.

sinful adj **1** *sinful deeds/thoughts* wrong, evil, wicked, bad, iniquitous, criminal, immoral, corrupt, unrighteous, ungodly, irreligious, irreverent, profane, blasphemous, impious, sacrilegious. **2** *sinful people* wrongdoing, evil, evildoing, wicked, bad, criminal, erring, immoral, dissolute, corrupt, depraved.

sing v **1** *children singing happily* carol, trill, warble, pipe, quaver, croon, chant, yodel. **2** *birds singing* trill, warble, chirp. **3** *sing to the police* inform, act as informer, tell tales, rat; *inf* grass, squeal, blow the whistle, spill the beans, fink, peach. **sing out** *"We're here," he sang out* call, call out, cry, cry out, shout, yell, bellow; *inf* holler.

singe v *singe the cloth/bread* scorch, burn, sear, char, blacken.

singer n vocalist, soloist, songster, songstress, chorister, crooner, warbler, *chanteuse*, minstrel; ballad-singer, opera-singer, diva, pop singer.

single adj **1** *a single apple on the tree | send a single rose* one, one only, sole, lone, solitary, unique, isolated, by itself, unique, exclusive. **2** *the single most important event | remove every single item* individual, particular, separate, distinct. **3** *men preferring to remain single* unmarried, unwed, unwedded, wifeless/husbandless, spouseless, partnerless, a bachelor, a spinster, unattached, free. **single out** *single out the best/worst pupil* separate out, set apart, put to one side, pick, choose, select, fix on, decide on, winnow.

single-handedness adv *sail the Atlantic single-handed* by oneself, alone, on one's own, solo, independently, unaided, unassisted, without help.

single-minded adj *too single-minded to be distracted from their aim* unswerving, unwavering, undeviating, set, fixed, devoted, dedicated, committed, determined, dogged, tireless, purposeful, obsessive, monomaniacal.

singly adv *guests arriving singly* one by one, one at a time, individually, separately, by oneself.

singular adj **1** *a singular talent* extraordinary, exceptional, rare, unusual, unique, remarkable, outstanding, notable, noteworthy, striking, conspicuous, distinctive. **2** *singular occurrences happening in the village* strange, unusual, odd, peculiar, curious, queer, bizarre, weird, abnormal, atypical.

sinister adj **1** *a sinister figure* evil-looking, wicked-looking, villainous, malevolent, menacing, threatening, frightening, terrifying. **2** *sinister motives* evil, wicked, bad, criminal, base, vile, vicious, cruel, malicious, malign. **3** *sinister signs* ominous, ill-omened, inauspicious, portentous.

sink v **1** *sink to one's knees* | *watch the sun sinking* fall, drop, descend, go down, go lower, plunge, plummet, slump. **2** *ships sinking* go under, submerge, founder, capsize. **3** *feel the ground sinking* collapse, cave in, fall in. **4** *empires/invalids sinking rapidly* decline, fade, fail, deteriorate, weaken, grow weak, flag, degenerate, decay; *inf* go downhill. **5** *would not sink to that level* stoop, lower oneself, debase oneself, be reduced to. **6** *voices sinking* lower, become/get lower, drop, become softer. **7** *sink a well/shaft* dig, bore, drill, excavate. **8** *sink posts in the earth* drive, place, put down, plant, position. **9** *sink hopes of winning* | *sink the opposition's plans* destroy, ruin, cause the downfall of, be the ruin/ruination of, demolish, devastate; *inf* put the kibosh on, scupper, put the skids under. **10** *having sunk their savings in the venture* invest, put into, venture, risk. **11** *sink their differences* overlook, disregard, ignore, forged.

sinner n wrongdoer, evildoer, criminal, offender, miscreant, transgressor, reprobate; *lit* trespasser.

sinuous adj winding, curving, twisting, turning, bending, curling, coiling, undulating, serpentine.

sip v *sip the drink* drink slowly, sup, taste, sample.

sip n *take a sip of the drink* mouthful, swallow, drink, drop, thimbleful, sup, taste.

siren n **1** *police sirens* alarm, alarm bell, warning bell, danger signal, tocsin. **2** *attracted by the siren at the bar* seductress, temptress, *femme fatale*; *lit* Circe, Lorelei; *inf* vamp.

sit v **1** *children asked to sit* sit down, take a seat, settle down, be seated; *inf* take the load/weight off one's feet. **2** *the books sitting on the mantelpiece* be placed, be positioned, be situated, rest, perch. **3** *sit the package on the table* set down, place, put, deposit, rest, position, situate. **4** *tables sitting twelve people* seat, have spare for, have room for, accommodate, hold. **5** *committees sitting until midnight* be convened, meet, assemble, be in session. **6** *sit for her neighbours* babysit, babymind, childmind.

site n **1** *the site of the battle* location, situation, position, place, locality, setting, scene. **2** *the building side* ground, plot, lot.

site v *site the garage to the right of the house* place, put, install, position, situate, locate.

sitting n *during a sitting of the council* meeting, session, assembly, hearing.

situate v *companies situating their headquarters out of town* | *schools situated near the city centre* place, position, locate, site.

situation n **1** *houses in a rural situation* place, position, location, site, setting, milieu, environment. **2** *their financial situation* circumstances, affairs, state, state of affairs, condition, case, predicament, plight; *inf* kettle of fish, ball-game. **3** *from a lowly situation in life* status, station, standing, footing, rank, degree. **4** *apply for a situation in the new firm* post, position, place, job, employment.

size n *the size of his feet/car* dimensions, measurements, proportions, bigness, largeness, magnitude, vastness, bulk, area, expanse, extent.

size v *size the eggs* sort, categorize, classify.

size up *size up the opposition* appraise, assess, judge, evaluate, gauge, estimate, rate.

skeleton n **1** *the skeleton of the building/car* framework, frame, structure, shell, chassis, support. **2** *give the skeleton of the argument* outline, sketch, bones, bare bones, draft, rough draft, plan, blueprint.

skeleton adj *skeleton staff* minimum, minimal, essential.

sketch n **1** *draw a rough sketch of the house* drawing, preliminary drawing, outline, diagram, plan, representation, delineation. **2** *give a sketch of his plans* outline, summary, abstract, précis, résumé, sketch, skeleton, bones, bare bones, draft, plan. **3** *the theatre company performing a comic sketch* short play, skit, act, scene.

sketch v **1** *sketch the subject of the portrait* draw, rough out, outline, pencil, represent, delineate, depict. **2** *sketch out his plans* outline, rough-out, give a summary of, summarize, give an abstract/précis/résumé of, précis, draft.

sketchy adj **1** *plans still a bit sketchy* preliminary, provisional, unfinished, unrefined, unpolished, rough, crude. **2** *sketchy, knowledge/information* slight, superficial, cursory, perfunctory, meagre, scrappy, skimpy, bitty, insufficient, inadequate, imperfect, incomplete, deficient, defective.

skilful adj **1** *a skilful performer* skilled, able, good, accomplished, adept, competent, efficient, adroit, deft, dexterous, masterly, expert, first-rate, experienced, trained, practised, professional, talented, gifted, clever, smart. **2** *a skilful performance* skilled, able, accomplished, competent, masterly, deft, expert, first-rate, talented, clever.

skill n *the skill of the performer/performance* skilfullness, ability, accomplishment, adeptness, competence, efficiency, adroitness, deftness, dexterity, aptitude, expertise, expertness, art, finesse, experience, professionalism, talent, cleverness, smartness.

skilled adj **1** *a skilled performer* skilful, able, good, accomplished, adept, competent, masterly, expert, talented. *see* SKILFUL 1. **2** *a skilled performance* skilful, able, accomplished, competent, masterly, expert, first-rate. *see* SKILFUL 2. **3** *jobs for skilled workers* trained, qualified, expert, experienced, practised.

skim v **1** *skim the milk* cream. **2** *skim the greasy liquid* scum, despumate. **3** *birds skimming the surface of the lake* glide over, move lightly over, brush, graze. **4** *skim pebbles across the lake* throw, pitch, skip, bounce. **5** *time only to skim through the report* read quickly, glance at, scan, run-one's eye over, flip through, leaf through, thumb through.

skimp v **1** *skimp on food/material* be sparing with, be economical with, economize on, be sparing with, be frugal with, be mean with, be parsimonious, be niggardly with, scrimp on, stint on, cut corners with, limit; *inf* be stingy with. **2** *skimp a piece of work* do hastily, do carelessly, dash off, cut corners with.

skimpy adj **1** *skimpy meals* small, meagre, scanty, insubstantial, insufficient, inadequate, sketchy, paltry. **2** *skimpy dresses* short, brief, scanty, insubstantial, sketchy.

skin n **1** *damage the skin* integument, epidermis, cuticle, corium, derma. **2** *fair skins* complexion, colouring. **3** *animal skin* hide, pelts, fleece, fell, integument, tegument. **4** *banana/orange skin* peel, rind, hull, husk. **5** *a skin forming on the coffee* film, coating, coat, layer, crust. **6** *the skin of a rocket* casing, cover, covering, pod. **by the skin of one's teeth** *catch the train by the skin of one's*

teeth only just, narrowly, barely, by a hair's-breadth; *inf* by a whisker. **get under one's skin 1** *noisy neighbours getting under her skin* irritate, annoy, irk, vex, grate on, rub up the wrong way, chafe, gall, nettle; *inf* needle. **2** *computer games getting under children's skins* interest, absorb, engross, rivet, grip, attract, charm, enchant, mesmerize, hypnotize. **no skin off one's nose** *it's no skin off my nose if they leave* of no concern to, of no importance to, of no relevance to, of no interest to.

skin v **1** *skin the fruit* peel, pare, hull, decorticate. **2** *skin one's knee* scrape, graze, abrade, cut, bark, excoriate.

skinflint n miser, niggard, penny-pincher, Scrooge.

skinny adj thin, thin as a rake, lean, scraggy, scrawny, emaciated, skeletal; *inf* skin and bone.

skip v **1** *children skipping along in the sunshine* bound, jump, leap, spring, hop, bounce, dance, caper, prance, trip, cavort, gambol, frisk, bob. **2** *skip from subject to subject/city to city* move quickly, go rapidly, pass quickly, flit, dart, zoom. **3** *skip the more boring parts of the text* omit, leave out, miss out, pass over, by-pass, skim over. **4** *skip lectures* play truant from, miss, not attend, dodge; *inf* cut, play hookey from, skive off from, wag.

skirmish n battle, fight, clash, conflict, encounter, confrontation, engagement, combat, contest, tussle, scrimmage, fracas, affray, melée, quarrel, altercation, argument, dispute; *inf* set-to, scrap, dust-up.

skirmish v *skirmishing with the enemy* fight, engage with, combat with, clash, collide, have a confrontation, come to blows, tussle, quarrel, argue, have a dispute.

skirt n **1** *growing round the skirt of the lake* edge, border, boundary, margin, fringe, rim. **2** *on the skirts of the town* outskirts, outer area, outer limits, outlying districts, periphery, suburbs, purlieus.

skirt v **1** *flowers skirting the lake* border, edge, flank. **2** *people skirting the lake* go round, move round, walk round, circle, circumnavigate. **3** *skirt the issue* evade, avoid, dodge, steer clear of, sidestep, circumvent, bypass.

skit n burlesque, parody, travesty; *inf* spoof, take-off, send-up.

skittish adj **1** *get skittish on a few drinks* playful, lively, frolicsome, frisky, sportive, mischievous, flirtatious. **2** *skittish horses* highly-strung, nervous, restive, jumpy, fidgety, excitable.

skulk v lurk, loiter, prowl, creep, sneak, slink, steal, sidle.

sky n *fly off into the sky* upper atmosphere, heaven, the firmament, the blue, the blue yonder; *lit* welkin, the ether. **to the skies** *praise them to the skies* unreservedly, without reserve, very much, very greatly, highly, profusely, fulsomely, extravagantly, inordinately, excessively, immoderately.

slap n **1** *a slab of cake/cheese* hunk, chunk, lump, slice, wedge, piece, portion. *inf* wodge. **2** *a slab of wood/stone* plank, hunk, chunk, lump, piece.

slack adj **1** *slack clothes* not tight, loose, baggy, bagging, easy, hanging, flapping. **2** *slack muscles* not taut, relaxed, limp, flaccid, flabby. **3** *a slack rope* not taut, not rigid, relaxed, flexible, pliant. **4** *business a bit slack/not busy* slow, quiet, inactive, sluggish. **5** *rather slack about punctuality* lax, negligent, remiss, neglectful, careless, inattentive, offhand, slapdash, slipshod, sloppy, disorderly, disorganized, tardy.

slack n **1** *take up the slack of the rope* looseness, play; *inf* give. **2** *no more slack left in the staffing situation* surplus, excess, inessentials, leeway.

slack v *workers slacking when the boss is away* idle, shirk, be inactive, be lazy, be indolent, be neglectful; *inf* skive. **slack off 1** *business slacks off in the winter* get less, lessen, fall off, drop off, tape off, let up, decrease, dwindle, ebb, recede, wane. **2** *children slacking off after the exams* relax, let up, take things easy, be less active. **3** *drivers slackening off at the corner* slow down, slow, decelerate, drop speed.

slacker n idler, shirker, loafer, dawdler, dallier, layabout, work-dodger, malingerer, good-for-nothing; *inf* clock-watcher, skiver.

slake v *slake one's thirst/desire* satisfy, quench, assuage, relieve, take the edge off, gratify, satiate.

slam v **1** *slam the door | the door slammed* bang, shut/close with a bang, shut/close with a crash, shut/close noisily, shut/close with force. **2** *slam the money on the table* slap, bang, thump, crash, smash, dash, hurl, fling, throw. **3** *a play slammed by the critics* criticize, attack, pillary, villify, damn; *inf* slate, pan, lambaste, shout down, blast. **4** *slam the opposition* defeat, utterly, rout, trounce, thrash, vanquish, conquer, crush, overwhelm, give a drubbing to; *inf* wipe the floor with, clobber, slaughter, hammer.

slander n *gossips guilty of slander* defamation, misrepresentation, calumny, libel, aspersion, villification, verbal abuse, muck-raking, smear campaigning, backbiting, obloquy, disparagement, denigration.

slander v *slander his neighbour by lying about her being in prison* defame, blacken the name of, libel, cast aspersions on, malign, villify, verbally abuse, muck-rake about, smear, slur, backbite, caluminate, disparage, denigrate, decry, run down.

slanderous adj defamatory, damaging, libellous, abusive, muck-raking, malicious, backbiting, calumnious, disparaging, denigrating.

slang n **1** *use slang rather than formal language* colloqualism, informal language, lingo. **2** *outsiders failing to understand the technicians' slang* jargon, cant, argot; *inf* gobbledegook, technospeak, mumbo-jumbo.

slant v **1** *the old floor/picture on the wall slants* slope, tilt, be askew, lean, dip, shelve, list. **2** *accuse the newspaper of slanting the news* give a slant to, give a bias to, bias, angle, distort, twist.

slant n **1** *the slant of the floor/picture* slope, tilt, dip, leaning, inclination, shelving, listing. **2** *accused of giving a political slant to the news* bias, leaning, one-sidedness, prejudice, angle, distortion, twist. **3** *require a woman's slant on the new product* angle, point of view, view, opinion, attitude.

slanting adj slanted, aslant, at an angle, sloping, oblique, tilting, tilted, askew, leaning, dipping, shelving, listing, diagonal.

slap n *a slap across the ears* smack, blow, hit, whack, thump, cuff, punch, spank, buffed, rap, bang; *inf* wallop, clout, clip, biff, swipe, belt, sock. **a slap in the face** *giving the job to his assistant was a slap in the face to him* snub, insult, rebuff, put-down, repulse, humiliation, blow to one's pride.

slap v **1** *slap the man's face* smack, strike, hit, whack, cuff, spank, bang; *inf* wallop, clout, biff, swipe, belt, sock. **2** *slap the money on the table* plonk, plop, slam, bang, fling, hurl, toss, throw. **3** *slap paint on* daub, plaster, spread. **slap down** *slap down the protesters* squash, put down, bring to heel, put someone in his/her place, rebuke, reprimand. **slap on** *slap on a service charge* put on, add, append, tack on.

slap adv *run slap into the policeman* smack, headlong, right, straight, directly, exactly, precisely, suddenly, bang. plumb; *inf* slap-bang.

slapdash adj careless, slipshod, sloppy, untidy, messy, hasty, hurried, cursory, perfunctory, disorganized, slipshod, offhand, thoughtless, heedless, negligent, neglectful, remiss.

slash v **1** *slash the cloth* cut, gash, lacerate, hack, rip, rend, slit, score, knife. **2** *slash prices* reduce/lower/decrease drastically, cut/drop/mark down greatly.

slash n *the slashes in the garment* cut, gash, laceration, hacks, rip, rent, slit, score, incision.

slate n *critics slating the performance* criticize harshly/severely; *inf* tear to pieces/shreds, pan, slam, hammer, lambaste.

slaughter v **1** *slaughter animals for food* kill, butcher. **2** *slaughter the enemy soldiers* massacre, murder, butcher, kill, put to death, do to death, put to the sword, slay, assassinate, liquidate, exterminate, annihilate. **3** *slaughter the opposition* defeat utterly, rout, trounce, thrash, vanquish, conquer, crush, overwhelm, give a drubbing to; *inf* wipe the floor with, clobber, slam, hammer.

slaughter n **1** *the slaughter of the innocent children* massacre, murder, butchery, killing, putting to death, slaying, liquidation, extermination, annihilation. **2** *a scene of slaughter* massacre, murder, bloodshed, carnage.

slaughterhouse n abattoir, butchery, shambles.

slave n **1** *the master and his slaves* bondsman/bondswoman, bondservant, serf, vassal. **2** *slaves in the kitchen* drudge, labourer, menial worker, servant; *lit* scullion; *inf* skivvy.

slave v *slave away at the stove* toil, drudge, slog, labour, grind, work one's fingers to the bone, work day and night, work like a Trojan.

slaver v slobber, drool.

slavery n **1** *sold into slavery* enslavement, bondage, servitude, subjugation, thraldom, thrall, serfdom, vassalage. **2** *working there is sheer slavery* drudgery, toil, slog, hard labour, grind.

slavish adj **1** *slavish followers/admiration* servile, subservient, obsequious, sycophantic, deferential, grovelling, fawning, cringing, menial, abject. **2** *slavish imitation* imitative, unoriginal, uninspired, unimaginative.

slay v **1** *slay his enemy* kill, murder; slaughter, put to death, do to death, assassinate, do away with; *inf* rub out. **2** *the comedian's act slayed them* convulse with mirth/laughter, amuse greatly, entertain greatly; *inf* have one rolling in the aisles, be a hit with, wow.

sleek adj **1** *sleek hair* smooth, glossy, shiny, lustrous, silken, silky, satiny, burnished.

2 *sleek businessmen* well-fed, thriving, prosperous, well-groomed; *inf* well-heeled.

sleep v *sleep for a few hours* be asleep, slumber, doze, nap, drowse; *lit* rest in the arms of Morpheus; *inf* snooze, have forty winks, be in the land of Nod.

sleep n *have a short sleep* slumber, doze, nap, rest, siesta, drowse; *inf* snooze, forty winks, a bit of shut-eye.

sleepiness n drowsiness, tiredness, somnolence, somnolency, languor, languidness, lethargy, sluggishness, inactivity, heaviness, lethargy, lassitude, torpor, torpidity, comatoseness.

sleepless adj **1** *sleepless nights* without sleep, wakeful, restless, disturbed. **2** *sleepless people* unsleeping, wakeful, insomniac.

sleeplessness n *suffer from sleeplessness* insomnia, wakefulness.

sleepwalking n somnabulism, somnambulation, noctambulism, noctambulation.

sleepy adj **1** *feeling sleepy | sleepy children* drowsy, tired, somnolent, languid, languorous, lethargic, sluggish, inactive, heavy, torpid, comatose. **2** *sleepy little villages* inactive, quiet, peaceful, slow-moving, slumberous.

slender adj **1** *slender figures* slim, thin, slight, lean, narrow, svelte, willowy, sylphlike. **2** *people of slender means* slight, small, little, meagre, scanty, paltry, insubstantial, inadequate, insufficient, deficient, negligible, trifling. **3** *a slender hope of success* small, slight, slim, faint, remote, feeble, flimsy, tenuous, fragile.

sleuth n detective, private detective, investigator, private investigator; *inf* private eye, dick, gumshoe.

slice n **1** *a slice of cake* piece, portion, segment, sliver, wedge, chunk, hunk; *inf* wodge. **2** *a slice of the action* share, part, proportion, allotment, allocation.

slice v **1** *slice the cake/apple/meat* cut up, cut through, carve, divide, segment. **2** *slice a piece from the apple* cut, sever, separate.

slick adj **1** *a slick presentation* smooth, smooth-running, well-organized, streamlined, efficient, polished. **2** *a slick reply* smooth, glib, fluent, plausible, specious. **3** *a slick performer/operator* smooth, efficient, skilful, deft, adroit, masterly, professional, smart, sharp, shrewd. **4** *slick businessman* suave, urbane, sophisticated, polished, smooth-speaking, glib, smarmy, unctuous.

slick v *slick one's hair down* smooth, flatten, plaster down.

slide v **1** *slide on the ice* slip, skid, slither, skate, glissade. **2** *drawers sliding in easily* slip, glide, slither. **3** *they slid from the room* pass/move quickly, slip, steal, slink. **let slide** *let the housework slide* neglect, forget, ignore, pass over, gloss over, push to the back of one's mind.

slight adj **1** *a slight change* small, little, tiny, minute, inappreciable, imperceptible, subtle, modest. **2** *of slight importance* little, minor, unimportant, petty, inconsiderable, insignificant, inconsequential, negligible, irrelevant, trivial, trifling, paltry, meagre, scant. **3** *a slight girl/figure* slightly-built, slim, slender, small, spare, delicate, frail. **4** *a slight structure* fragile, frail, flimsy, rickety, jerry-built.

slight v *slight him by not inviting him* snub, insult, affront, rebuff, treat disrespectfully, give the cold shoulder to, cold-shoulder, keep at arm's length, disregard, ignore, neglect, take no notice of, disdain, scorn.

slight n *upset by her slights* snub, insult, affront, rebuff, cold-shouldering, disregard, neglect, inattention, scorn, disdain; *inf* a slap in the face.

slighting adj *a slighting remark* snubbing, insulting, disrespectful, uncomplimentary, abusive, offensive, disparaging, belittling, derogatory, disdainful, scornful.

slightly adj *slightly hurt* a little, a bit, somewhat, rather, to some degree.

slim adj **1** *slim girls/ankles* slender, thin, slight, lean, narrow, svelte, willowy, sylphlike. **2** *slim hopes of success* slight, small, slender, faint, remote, feeble, flimsy, tenuous, fragile.

slim v *trying to slim* lose weight, shed weight, lose pounds, reduce, diet, go on a diet.

slime n sludge, muck, ooze, mud; *inf* goo, gunk.

slimy adj **1** *slimy surfaces* sludgy, mucky, oozy, muddy, slippery, sticky, viscous, mucous. **2** *distrust the slimy creature* oily, unctuous, obsequious, sycophantic, toadying, ingratiating, servile, grovelling, forelock-tugging, creeping; *inf* smarmy.

sling v **1** *sling it into the rubbish bag* toss, fling, throw, cast, hurl, heave, pitch, shy, lob; *inf* chuck. **2** *sling it from a hook* hang, suspend, dangle, swing.

sling n *have one's arm in a sling* support bandage, support, bandage, strap.

slink v **1** *culprits slinking from the room* steal, sneak, creep, slip, slide. **2** *strange figures slinking around in the garden* skulk, lurk, sneak, creep.

slip[1] v **1** *slip on the ice* slip, skid, slither, lose one's footing, lose one's balance. **2** *slip from her hands* fall, slide, drop. **3** *slip from the room unnoticed* steal, slide, creep, sneak, slink. **4** *officials having slipped up* make a mistake, blunder, make a blunder, miscalculate, err, go wrong; *inf* boob, make a bloomer, make a boo-boo, slip my mind, screw up. **5** *slip through the police net* break free from, escape, get away from, break away from, evade, dodge. **6** *slip the knot* untie, unfasten, undo, unbind, untangle, unsnarl. **7** *slip on a jersey* put on, pull on, don. **8** *the value of the pound slipped* go down, decline, decrease, lessen, depreciate, sink, slump, plummet. **9** *the standard of the students work slipped* drop, fall off, decline, deteriorate, escape, degenerate; *inf* go downhill, go to the dogs. **let slip** *let slip the secret* let out, reveal, disclose, divulge, give away, leak, blurt out, come out with.

slip[1] n **1** *one slip and she fell* slide, skid, slither. **2** *an accountant accused of making a slip* slip-up, mistake, error, blunder, miscalculation, oversight; *inf* boob, bloomer, boo-boo. **3** *a silk slip* underskirt, petticoat. **give the slip** *the pickpocket eventually gave the policeman the slip* escape from, get away from, get free from, break away from, lose, evade, dodge, elude, shake off, get rid of, outwit.

slip[2] n **1** *written on a slip* slip of paper, piece of paper, paper, note, card; *Trademark* Post-it note. **2** *a slip from the plant* cutting, offshoot, scion, sprout, sprig. **a slip of a** *a slip of a girl* small, slender, delicate, young.

slipper n **1** *housecoat and slippers* bedroom slipper, mule, houseshoe, moccasin. **2** *evening slippers* pump, soft shoe.

slipperiness n **1** *the slipperiness of the surface* greasiness, oiliness, sliminess, iciness; *inf* slippiness. *see* SLIPPERY 1. **2** *the slipperiness of the criminal* shiftiness, deviousness, deceit, deceitfulness, duplicitousness, craftiness, cunning, sneakiness, treachery, dishonesty, untrustworthiness. *see* SLIPPERY 2.

slippery adj **1** *slippery surfaces* greasy, oily, slimy, icy, glassy, smooth, soapy; *inf* slippy, skiddy. **2** *a slippery customer/creature* shifty, devious, deceitful, duplicitous, crafty, cunning, foxy, tricky, sneaky, treacherous, perfidious, two-faced, dishonest, false, unreliable, untrustworthy.

slipshod adj *slipshod methods* careless, slovenly, untidy, sloppy, slapdash, disorganized, unsystematic, unmethodical.

slip-up n slip, mistake, error, blunder. *see* SLIP[1] n 2.

slit v *slit the material* cut, split open, slash, gash, rip, make an incision in, tear, rend, pierce, knife, lance.

slit n *make a slit in the material* cut, split, slash, gash, rip, incision, tear, rent, fissure, opening.

slither v *slither about on the ice* slide, slip, skid.

sliver n chip, flake, splinter, shred, fragment, scrap.

slobber v slaver, drool, dribble, splutter.

slog v **1** *slog his opponent* hit, strike, thump, whack; *inf* hit for six, slug, wallop, sock, slosh. **2** *slog away at homework* work, labour, toil, slave, drudge, plough. **3** *slog up the hill* trudge, tramp, hike, plod, trek.

slog n **1** *knock out his opponent with one slog* hit, stroke, thump, whack; *inf* slug, wallop, sock. **2** *regard homework as a slog* labour, Herculean task, hard task. **3** *a slog up the hill* trudge, tramp, hike, plod, trek.

slogan n motto, logo, catchword, jingle, rallying cry, shibboleth.

slop v *water slopping over* spill, overflow, splash, slosh, splatter, spatter.

slope v *gardens sloping down to the river* | *handwriting sloping* drop away, fall way, slant, incline, lean, tilt, dip. **slope off** *pupils sloping off before the class* go away, slip away, steal away, slink off; *inf* make oneself scarce.

slope n **1** *floors on a slope* slant, inclination, angle, skew, tilt, dip, gradient. **2** *grassy slopes* hill, hillside, hillock, bank, rise, scarp, mountain.

sloping adj slanting, oblique, leaning, inclining, inclined, angled, askew, tilting, dipping.

sloppy adj **1** *a sloppy mixture* watery, wet, soggy, splashy, slushy, sludgy. **2** *sloppy work* careless, slapdash, slipshod, disorganized, unmethodical, untidy, messy, slovenly, hasty, hurried, offhand. **3** *sloppy verses* sentimental, overemotional, mawkish, maudlin, gushing, gushy, effusive, banal, trite; *inf* soppy, mushy, wet, schmaltzy.

slot n **1** *money in the slot* slit, crack, hole, opening, aperture, groove, notch. **2** *a slot in the programme* place, position, niche, space, opening, time, period.

sloth n laziness, indolence, idleness, sluggishness, inertia, inactivity, lethargy, langour, slothfulness, torpor, torpidity, faineance.

slothful adj lazy, indolent, idle, workshy, sluggish, inert, inactive, lethargic, languorous, torpid, faineant.

slouch v slump, hunch, stoop, droop, bend.

slovenly adj **1** *of slovenly appearance* slattenly, untidy, dirty, unclean, messy, unkempt, dishevelled, bedraggled, tousled, rumpled. **2** *slovenly methods* careless, sloppy, slapdash, slipshod, disorganized, unmethodical.

slow adj **1** *at a slow pace* slow-moving, unhurried, leisurely, measured, deliberate, ponderous, creeping, dawdling, loitering, lagging, laggard, sluggish, snail-like, tortoise-like. **2** *slow pupils* backward, retarded, slow-witted, dull-witted, dull, unintelligent, stupid, thick, dense; *inf* dumb, dopey; slow on the uptake. **3** *the service being a bit slow* slow-moving, delayed, dilatory, unpunctual, tardy. **4** *a slow process* long-drawn-out, drawn-out, time-consuming, protracted, prolonged, interminable. **5** *a slow play* dull, uninteresting, tedious, boring, tiresome, wearisome, monotonous, uneventful. **6** *a slow part of the world* sleepy, unprogressive, behind-the-times, backward, stagnant; *inf* not with it, one-horse, dead-and-alive. **7** *business being slow* not busy, slack, quiet, sluggish, slow-moving, dead. **slow to** *slow to anger* reluctant, hesitant, loath, unwilling, disinclined, averse.

slow v **1** *slow down at the corner* reduce speed, decelerate, relax speed, put the brakes on. **2** *weather slowed the runners down* hold back, keep back, delay, detain, restrain. **3** *businessmen told to slow down* take it easy, easy up, relax; *inf* let up.

slowly adv **1** *walk slowly* at a slow pace, without hurrying, unhurriedly, at a leisurely pace, steadily, ploddingly, taking one's time, in one's own good time, with heavy steps, at a snail's pace. **2** *improve slowly* at a slow pace, gradually, bit by bit, by degrees.

sluggish adj **1** *feeling sluggish with a hangover* inactive, inert, heavy, lifeless, apathetic, listless, lethargic, languid, languorous, torpid, phlegmatic, indolent, lazy, slothful, drowsy, sleepy. **2** *business being sluggish* slow, slow-moving, slack, inactive, stagnant.

sluggishness n **1** *sluggishness caused by overeating* inactivity, inertia, heaviness, lifelessness, apathy, listlessness, lethargy, languidness, languor, lassitude, torpidity, torpor, indolence, laziness, sloth, slothfulness, drowsiness, sleepiness, somnolence. **2** *the sluggishness of business* slowness, slackness, inactivity, stagnation.

slumber v sleep, be asleep, doze, nap, drowse; *inf* rest in the arms of Morpheus;

753

inf snooze, have forty winks, be in the land of Nod.

slumber n sleep, doze, nap, rest, siesta, drouse; *inf* snooze, forty winks, a bit of shut-eye.

slump n *a slump in share prices* plummeting, plunge, nosedive, collapse, fall, falling-off, drop, downturn, downswing, slide, decline, decrease, lowering, devaluation, depreciation, depression.

slump v **1** *slump into a chair* collapse, sink, fall, subside. **2** *prices slumped* plummet, plunge, nosedive, fall, drop, go down, slide, decline, decrease, devalue. **3** *standards slumped* plummet, plunge, nosedive, fall, drop, decline, deteriorate, degenerate; *inf* go downhill, go to the dogs.

slur v *slur his words* mumble, stumble over, stammer, drawl.

slur n **1** *upset by the slurs made by the opposition on her character* insult, slight, aspersion, imputation, slanderous statement, libellous statement, misrepresentation, smear, stain, stigma. **2** *avoid all suggestion of a slur* insult, affront, defamation, slander, libel, calumny.

slush n **1** *slush thrown up by cars* melting snow, muck, mud. **2** *the slush of romantic songs* sentimentality, overemotionalism, mawkishness, maudlinism, effusiveness, banality, triteness; *inf* sloppiness, soppiness, mush, mushiness, schmaltz.

slut n **1** *a slut who rarely washes* slattern, sloven, trollop. **2** *a slut seducing men* loose woman, hussy, wanton; prostitute, harlot, whore, street-walker; *inf* tart, floozie, hooker.

sly adv **1** *a sly creature* cunning, crafty, wily, artful, foxy, tricky, conniving, scheming, devious, underhand, shrewd, smart, astute. **2** *in a sly manner* furtive, insidious, underhand, shifty, stealthy, sneaky, secret, surreptitious, covert, under-cover, clandestine. **3** *a sly smile* roguish, impish, mischievous, playful, arch, knowing. **on the sly** *have another job on the sly* in secret, secretly, furtively, stealthily, sneakily, surreptitiously, covertly, under cover, clandestinely.

smack¹ n **1** *a smack on the face* slap, blow, hit, whack, thump, cuff, punch, spank, buffet, rap, bang; *inf* wallop, clout, clip, biff, swipe, belt, sock. **2** *the object hit the car with a smack* thud, thump, bang, wham; *inf* wallop. **a smack in the eye** rebuff, repulse, snub, setback, slight, cold shoulder; *inf* brush-off.

smack¹ v *smack the child* slap, hit, strike, whack, thump, cuff, punch, rap, bang; *inf* wallop, clout, clip, biff, swipe, belt, sock.

smack¹ adv *run smack into the police* slap, headlong, right, straight, directly, bang, plumb, exactly, precisely, suddenly.

smack² v **1** *a sauce smacking of garlic* taste of, have the flavour of. **2** *actions smacking of treachery* suggest, hint at, have overtones of, have the hallmark of, resemble, seem like, have the air of.

smack² n **1** *dishes having a smack of garlic* taste, flavour, savour. **2** *have a smack of treachery* suggestion, hint, trace, tinge, touch, overtones, hallmark, resemblance, air.

small adj **1** little, tiny, teeny, teeny-weeny, petite, slight, minute, miniature, mini, miniscule, diminutive, under-sized, puny; *inf* pocket-size, pint-sized, teensy-weensy; *Scots* wee. **2** *a small change/mistake* slight, minor, unimportant, trifling, trivial, insignificant, inconsequential, inappreciable. **3** *from small beginnings* humble, modest, lowly, simple, unpretentious, poor, inferior. **4** *a small mind/man* narrow, narrow-minded, mean, petty.

small-minded adj narrow-minded, bigoted, prejudiced, intolerant, hidebound, rigid, ungenerous, illiberal.

small-time adj *small-time crooks* petty, minor, unimportant, insignificant, of no account, of no consequence, inconsequential.

smart adj **1** *wedding-guests looking smart* well-dressed, well turned-out, fashionably-dressed, fashionable, stylish, modish, elegant, chic, neat, spruce, trim; *inf* natty, snappy, out of a bandbox. **2** *smart children* clever, bright, intelligent, gifted, sharp, quick-witted, nimble-witted, shrewd, ingenious. **3** *at a smart pace* brisk, quick, fast, swift, lively, energetic, spirited, vigorous, jaunty; *inf* cracking, spanking.

smart v *eyes smarting with the smoke* sting, nip, burn, bite, pain.

smash v **1** *smash the crockery* break, shatter, crash, shiver, pulverize, splinter, crack. **2** *smash the crash* smash, collide, wreck. **3** *smash their hopes* destroy, ruin, shatter, devastate.

smash n **1** *hear the smash of crockery* breaking, shattering, crashing, crack. **2** *involve in a smash* car smash, car crash, car accident, traffic accident, collision; *inf* pile-up. **3** *survive the smash of their plans* destruction, ruin, ruination, failure, shattering, devastation.

smashing adj *a smashing time at the fair* marvellous, magnificent, sensational, stupendous, superb, wonderful, excellent, first-rate; *inf* terrific, fantastic, super, great, fabulous, fab.

smattering n *a smattering of French* bit, modicum, dash, rudiments, elements.

smear v **1** *children smearing paint on the walls* spread, daub, slap, plaster. **2** *smear the windows* smudge, streak, blur. **3** *smear his reputation* sully, tarnish, blacken, taint, stain, slur, defame, defile, vilify, slander, libel, calumniate.

smear n **1** *a smear of paint on the walls* daub, spot, patch, splotch. **2** *smears on the windows* smudge, streak. **3** *the smears on their reputation* taint, stain, slur, blot.

smell v **1** *smell something rotten* pleasant, scent, sniff, get a sniff of, get a whiff of, nose. **2** *drains smelling* have a bad smell, stink, be stinking, reek, be malodorous; *inf* stink to high heaven, pong, hum.

smell n **1** *the smells of the countryside* odour, scent, whiff. **2** *the smell of new-mown hay* scent, aroma, perfume, fragrance, bouquet, redolence. **3** *What a smell from the drains!* stink, stench, reek; *inf* pong, hum.

smelly adj *smelly drains* smelling, evil-smelling, foul-smelling, stinking, high, malodorous, fetid, mephitic; *lit* noisome; *inf* ponging, humming, whiffy.

smirk v leer, sneer, simper, grin.

smitten adj **1** *smitten with flu* suffering from, affected by, laid low with, struck down with, afflicted by. **2** *smitten with the pretty girl/the new fashion* taken with, infatuated with, enamoured of, attracted by, charmed by, captivated by, enchanted by, bewitched by, beguiled by; *inf* bowled over by, swept off one's feet by.

smog n haze, fog, pollution.

smoke v **1** *fires smoking* smoulder, reek. **2** *smoke the salmon* cure, dry, preserve.

smoky adj **1** *a smoky atmosphere* smoke-filled, reeky, hazy, foggy, smoggy, murky. **2** *smoky walls* begrimed, grimy, smoke-stained, smoke-darkened, sooty. **3** *smoky glass* dark, grey, black.

smooth adj **1** *paint smooth surfaces* even, level, flat, plane, flush, unrough, unwrinkled. **2** *smooth hair/table-tops* glossy, shiny, sleek, silky, satiny, velvety, polished, burnished. **3** *smooth sea* calm, still, tranquil, flat, glassy, mirrorlike. **4** *smooth progress* easy, effortless, trouble-free, simple, plain sailing. **5** *the smooth running of the machine* steady, regular, rhythmic, uninterrupted, flowing, fluid. **6** *smooth sounds* soft, soothing, mellow, dulcet, mellifluous, melodious, musical. **7** *smooth face* clean-shaven, smooth, shaven, hairless. **8** *smooth young men* smooth-tongued, suave, urbane, sophisticated, courteous, gracious, glib, persuasive, slick, oily, ingratiating, unctuous; *inf* smarmy.

smooth v **1** *smooth the surface* level, even, flatten, plane, press down, steamroll. **2** *smooth the troubled situation* ease, soothe, pacify, calm, tranquillize, alleviate, assuage, appease, palliate. **3** *smooth out/away the difficulties* get rid of, remove, eliminate. **4** *smooth his promotion* ease, make easy/easier, facilitate, clear the way for, pave the way for, open the door for, expedite, assist, aid, help, help along.

smoothness n **1** *the smoothness of the road surfaces* evenness, levelness, flatness. *see* SMOOTH adj 1. **2** *the smoothness of her hair* glossiness, gloss, shininess, sleekness, silkiness. *see* SMOOTH adj 2. **3** *the smoothness of the sea* calmness, stillness, tranquillity, flatness. *see* SMOOTH adj 3. **4** *the smoothness of the progress* ease, easiness, effortlessness, simplicity. *see* SMOOTH adj 4. **5** *the smoothness of the engine's running* steadiness, regularity, rhythm, fluidity. *see* SMOOTH adj 5. **6** *the smoothness of the sounds* softness, mellowness, mellifluousness, melodiousness. *see* SMOOTH adj 6. **7** *the smoothness of his face* clean-shavenness, smooth-shavenness, hairlessness. **8** *the smoothness of the salesman* suaveness, urbaneness, urbanity, sophistication, courteousness, glibness, slickness; *inf* smarminess. *see* SMOOTH adj 8.

smother v **1** *smother the old woman with a pillow* suffocate, stifle, asphyxiate, choke. **2** *smother them with kindness* overwhelm, shower, inundate, envelop, surround, cocoon. **3** *smother the pudding in cream* cover, pile with, heap with. **4** *smother a fire* extinguish, dampen, damp down, put out, snuff out, stamp out. **5** *smother a laugh* stifle, muffle, repress, suppress, keep back, conceal, hide.

smoulder v **1** *fires smouldering* smoke, reek. **2** *hate smouldering in her* burn, seethe, simmer, fester. **3** *she was smouldering with resentment* seethe, fume, burn, boil, foam, rage, smart.

smudge n *smudges on the walls* dirty mark, mark, spot, smear, streak, stain, blotch, blot, blur, smut, splotch.

smudge v **1** *walls smudged with children's finger marks* mark, dirty, soil, blacken, smear, streak, daub, stain, besmirch. **2** *smudge the wet paint/lipstick* smear, streak, blur.

smug adj self-satisfied, complacent, content, pleased with oneself, superior, proud of oneself, conceited.

smuggler n contrabandist, runner; *inf* bootlegger.

snack n *a snack between meals* light meal, refreshments, bite, nibbles, titbit; *inf* elevenses, bite to eat, little something.

snack v *snack between meals* eat between meals, nibble, munch; *inf* graze.

snag n **1** *discover a snag about the seemingly attractive job* catch, drawback, hitch, stumbling-block, obstacle, disadvantage, inconvenience, unseen problem, problem, complication. **2** *a snag in her tights* rip, tear, run, hole.

snag v *snag one's tights* catch, rip, tear.

snap v **1** *the rod/rope snapped* break, break into two, fracture, splinter, separate, come apart, crack. **2** *suddenly snap after years of being abused* have a nervous break down, break down, collapse, lose one's mind, lose one's reason, go mad, go insane. **3** *snap one's fingers* crack, click, crackle. **4** *dogs snapping* bite, gnash the teeth. **5** *snapping irritably at the children* speak sharply/brusquely/curtly/abruptly/angrily, bark, snarl, growl, lash out at; *inf* jump down the throat of, fly off the handle at. **6** *snap into action* hurry, hasten, rush, race. **7** *snap the children at play* take a snap of, photograph, take a photograph, take a shot of, film, capture. **snap out of it** *she's been miserable but she's snapped out of it* get over it, recover, get better, cheer up, become cheerful, perk up; *inf* pull oneself together, get a grip on oneself, become one's old self. **snap up** *snap up the bargain* offers snatch at, accept eagerly, take advantage of, grab, seize, grasp, pounce upon, swoop down upon; *inf* nab.

snap n **1** *with a snap of one's fingers* crack, click, crackle. **2** *with a snap of its teeth* bite, gnashing, clenching. **3** *a snap of cold weather* spell, period, time, stretch, interval. **4** *put a bit of snap into the production* liveliness, animation, sparkle, verve, vitality, vivacity, spirit, vigour, sprightliness, zest; *inf* pizzazz, zip, zing, pep, oomph. **5** *a snap of the children at play* photo, photograph, picture.

snappy adj **1** *a snappy mood/reply* irritable, irascible, ill-tempered, cross, touchy, testy, crabbed, crotchety, grumpy, grouchy, peppery. **2** *a snappy dresser* smart, fashionable, up-to-date, stylish, chic, up-to-the-minute, modish, dapper; *inf* natty, trendy. **look snappy/make it snappy** hurry up, be quick, make haste, look lively; *inf* get a move on, get one's skates on, step on it, move it, buck up.

snare v **1** *snare rabbits* trap, entrap, catch, springe, net. **2** *snare a rich husband* ensnare, trap, catch, get hold of, seize, captivate.

snare n **1** *rabbits caught in a snare* trap, gin, springe, net, noose. **2** *unaware of the snares set by the opposition* trap, pitfall, trick, catch, danger, hazard, peril.

snarl[1] v **1** *dogs snarling* show one's teeth, growl. **2** *snarling at everyone first thing in the morning* snap, growl, bark, lash out at; *inf* jump down the throat of, fly off the handle at.

snarl[2] v **1** *ropes getting snarled up* tangle, entangle, entwine, ravel, twist, knot. **2** *snarl up plans for reorganization* complicate, confuse, muddle, jumble; *inf* mess up.

snatch v **1** *snatch the last sandwich from the plate* seize, grab, take hold of, pluck. **2** *snatch the old lady's handbag* grab, steal, make off with, appropriate; *inf* nab, swipe. **3** *snatch the millionaire's child* kidnap, abduct, grab, hold to ransom, take as hostage. **4** *snatch victory towards the end of the game* pluck, wrest, wring, seize, secure. **snatch at 1** *a drowning man snatching at the branch* grab at, make a grab for, grasp at, catch at, clutch at, grope for, reach for. **2** *snatch at the bargain/opportunity* snap up, accept eagerly, grab, seize, pounce upon. *see* SNAP V SNAP UP.

snatch n **1** *at one snatch* grab, pluck, grip, clutch. **2** *a snatch of song/a broadcast* fragment, snippet, bit, scrap, piece, part. **3** *a snatch of sleeplessness* spell, period, time, fit, bout.

sneak v **1** *sneak out of the lecture* steal, creep, slip, slide, slink, sidle. **2** *hear people sneaking around outside* creep, skulk, lurk, prowl, pad. **3** *sneak a quick look* snatch, take, catch. **4** *sneak on friends* tell tales on, inform on, report; *inf* tell on, grass on, squeal on, blow the whistle on, peach on.

sneak n informer, tell-tale; *inf* grass, squealer, whistle-blower, snitch.

sneak adj *a sneak look* secret, stealthy, furtive, clandestine, surprise.

sneaking adj *a sneaking desire to be chairman* secret, private, hidden, concealed, unexpressed, unvoiced, undisclosed, undivulged, unconfessed, unavowed.

sneer v **1** *sneering rather than smiling* curl one's lip, smirk, snicker, snigger. **2** *sneer at their unsuccessful attempts* scoff at, scorn, be contemptuous of, hold in contempt, disdain, mock, jeer at, gibe at, ridicule, deride, taunt, insult, slight.

sneer n **1** *give a sneer* smirk, snicker.
2 *endure the sneers of her enemies* jeer, jibe,
taunt, insult, slight.

sneeze v *not to be sneezed at* a salary not
to be sneezed at be taken seriously, not be
taken lightly, not be scoffed at, not be
laughed at.

snicker v snigger, sneer, smirk, titter, giggle, chortle.

snicker n snigger, sneer, smirk.

sniff n **1** *people with colds sniffing* snuffle,
inhale, breathe in. **2** *sniff the aroma of newly
made bread* smell, detect the smell of, catch
the scent of, scent, get a whiff of. **sniff at**
sniffing superiorly at their ragged children scoff
at, show contempt for, scorn, mock, disdain, turn up one's nose at, look down
one's nose at, look down on.

sniff n **1** *the sniffs of people with colds* snuffle.
2 *take a sniff of the sea air* smell, scent,
whiff.

snip v **1** *snip the piece of cloth* cut, cut into,
nick, slit, notch, incise, snick. **2** *snip off a
lock of hair* cut, clip, dock, trim, crop,
prune.

snip n **1** *cut it with one snip* cut, nick, slit,
notch, incision, snick. **2** *snips of cloth* scrap,
cutting, bit, piece, fragment, remnant, tatter. **3** *the dress was a snip* bargain, good,
buy, cheap buy; *inf* giveaway, steal. **4** *the job
was a snip* easy task, child's play; *inf* picnic,
cinch, pushover.

snippet n *snippets of information* bit, piece,
scrap, fragment, particle, shred, snatch.

snivel v **1** *children snivelling with disappointment* weep, cry, sob, whimper; *inf* blub,
blubber. **2** *children snivelling with colds* sniffle, snuffle, run at the nose, have a runny/
running nose.

snobbery n snobbishness, social arrogance,
pride, airs, airs and graces, condescension,
haughtiness, superiority, disdain, disdain-
fulness, superciliousness; *inf* snootiness,
uppishness, side.

snobbish adj snobby, arrogant, proud, condescending, haughty, disdainful, supercilious, patronizing; *inf* snooty, uppity,
stuck-up, hoity-toity, toffee-nosed.

snoop v *snoop into another's affairs* pry into,
spy on, interfere with, meddle with; *inf*
poke one's nose into.

snoop n **1** *a snoop into another's affairs* pry,
poke. **2** *accused of being a snoop* snooper,
pryer, interferer, meddler; *inf* nosy parker,
sticky beak, Paul Pry.

snooze v *snooze in front of the fire* doze, nap,
catnap, drowse, sleep, slumber; *inf* take
forty winks, have a kip, kip.

snooze n *a snooze after lunch* doze, nap, catnap, siesta, sleep, slumber; *inf* forty winks,
kip.

snub v *snub him in public* ignore, disregard,
take no notice of, shun, rebuff, repulse,
spurn, slight, give the cold shoulder to,
cold-shoulder, insult, affront; *inf* cut dead,
give the brush-off to, give a slap in the face
to, give the go-by, put down.

snub n *embarrassed by the snub* rebuff,
repulse, slight, insult, affront; *inf* brush-off,
slap in the face, put-down.

snug adj **1** *a snug little house* cosy, comfortable, warm, homelike, homely, sheltered;
inf comfy. **2** *a snug fit* close-fitting, tight,
skin-tight.

snuggle v nestle, cuddle, curl up, nuzzle.

soak v **1** *soaked by the rain* drench, wet
through, saturate, make sopping. **2** *soak the
soiled dress in soapy water* steep, immerse,
souse. **3** *ink soaking through the paper* permeate, penetrate, infuse, imbue.

soaking adj *dry off the soaking children/soak-
ing wet clothes* soaked, soaked to the skin,
wet through, drenched, sodden, saturated,
sopping wet, dripped wet, wringing wet,
streaming wet.

soar v **1** *birds/planes soaring into the air* fly,
take flight, take off, ascend, climb, rise,
mount. **2** *prices soaring* rise, go up, increase,
climb, rapidly, spiral.

sob v *sobbing at the funeral* weep, cry, shed
tears, blubber, snivel, howl, bawl; *Scots*
greet; *inf* boohoo.

sober adj **1** *he was drunk but now he is sober*
not drunk/intoxicated, abstemious, tee-
total, abstinent, temperate, moderate; *inf*
on the wagon, dry, having signed the
pledge. **2** *both sober and light-hearted people*
serious, solemn, thoughtful, grave, earnest,
calm, composed, sedate, staid, dignified,
steady, level-headed, self-controlled, strict,
puritanical. **3** *discuss sober matters* serious,
solemn, grave, important, crucial, weighty,
ponderous. **4** *a sober account* factual, low-
key, dispassionate, objective, rational, logical, circumspect, well-considered, lucid,
clear. **5** *wearing sober clothes/colours* dark,
dark-coloured, sombre, quiet, restrained,
drab, severe, austere. **sober up 1** *sober up
after the party* become sober, become clear-
headed, be cured of one's hangover; *inf* dry
out. **2** *sober him up after all the excitement*
make sober, make serious, subdue, calm
down, quieten, make reflective/pensive,

make one stop and think, give pause for thought.

sobriety n **1** *impressed by the sobriety of the former drunks* soberness, teetotalism, abstemiousness, abstinence, nonindulgence, temperance, moderation, moderateness. **2** *his sobriety and studiousness* soberness, seriousness, solemnness, solemnity, thoughtfulness, gravity, graveness, earnestness, calmness, composure, sedateness, staidness, dignity, dignifiedness, steadiness, level-headedness, practicality, practicalness, self-control, self-restraint, strictness, puritanism. **3** *the sobriety of the subject* soberness, seriousness, solemnness, solemnity, gravity, graveness, importance, crucialness, weightiness, ponderousness. **4** *the sobriety of the account* soberness, factualness, dispassionateness, objectivity, rationality, logicality, circumspection, lucidity, clarity. **5** *the sobriety of the clothes/colours* soberness, darkness, sombreness, quietness, restraint, drabness, severity, austerity.

so-called adj **1** *so-called professional people* self-styled, professed, *soi-disant*. **2** *so-called friendship* supposed, alleged, ostensible, pretended.

sociability n friendliness, affability, cordiality, neighbourliness, companionably, gregariousness, convivialness, conviviality. *see* SOCIABLE.

sociable adj social, friendly, affable, cordial, neighbourly, companionable, gregarious, convivial, communicative, conversable, genial, outgoing, approachable, accessible.

social adj **1** *social problems* community, civil, civic, public, societal. **2** *social clubs/evenings* entertainment, recreational, amusement. **3** *not a very social person* friendly, affable, cordial, companionable, gregarious, convivial, communicative. *see* SOCIABLE.

socialize v *lonely people not socializing with colleagues* be social, be sociable, mix, mingle, keep company, fraternize, consent, hobnob, get together, get out and about.

society n **1** *enemies of society* mankind, humanity, civilization, the public, the general public, the people, the population, the world at large, the community. **2** *urban and rural societies* community, group, culture, civilization. **3** *leaders of society | marry into society* high society, polite society, aristocracy, gentry, nobility, upper classes, the elite, the smart set, beau monde, haut monde; *inf* privileged classes, the upper crust, the top drawer, toffs, nobs, swells.

4 *enjoy the society of friends* company, companionship, fellowship, friendship, camaraderie. **5** *join a society* association, club, group, band, circle, body, fraternity, brotherhood, sisterhood, league, union, alliance, federation.

sodden adj **1** *sodden clothes* soaked, soaking wet, drenched, saturated, sopping, dripping, wringing wet. **2** *sodden ground* saturated, sopping, soggy, boggy, swampy, miry, waterlogged.

soft adj **1** *soft clay/mud* mushy, squashy, pulpy, doughy, spongy; *inf* gooey. **2** *soft ground* spongy, swampy, boggy, miry, quaggy. **3** *pieces of a soft substance* pliable, pliant, supple, elastic, flexible, ductile, malleable, plastic. **4** *the soft surface of the curtains* smooth, velvety, cushiony, fleecy, downy, leathery, furry, silky, silken, satiny; *inf* like a baby's bottom. **5** *soft winds blowing* gentle, light, mild, moderate, calm, balmy, delicate. **6** *soft lights* low, faint, dim, shaded, subdued, muted, mellow. **7** *soft colours* pale, light, pastel, subdued, muted, understated, restrained, dull. **8** *he spoke in soft tones* hushed, whispered, murmured, stifled, inaudible, low, faint, quiet, mellow, melodious, mellifluous. **9** *soft outlines* vague, blurred, fuzzy, ill-defined, indistinct, flowing, fluid. **10** *soft words* sympathetic, kind, gentle, soothing, tender, affectionate, loving, warm, sweet, sentimental, romantic; *inf* mushy, slushy, schmaltzy. **11** *teachers too soft with the pupils* easygoing, tolerant, forgiving, forbearing, lenient, indulgent, permissive, liberal, lax. **12** *too soft to kill the chicken* tender-hearted, docile, sensitive; spineless, feeble; *inf* soppy. **13** *soft muscles* flabby, flaccid, limp, out of condition. **14** *lead a soft life* easy, comfortable, cosy; pampered, privileged, indulged; *inf* cushy. **15** *soft in the head* feeble-minded, simple, silly; *inf* daft, nutty.

soften v **1** *soften the blow* ease, cushion, temper, mitigate, assuage. **2** *the winds softened* abate, moderate, lessen, diminish, calm down. **3** *they softened their harsh approach* modify, moderate, temper, tone down. **soften up** *soften him up until he agrees* work on, persuade, win over, disarm.

soggy adj soft, soaking, saturated, sodden, sopping wet, boggy, swampy, miry, waterlogged, over-moist.

soil n **1** *plant in a light soil* earth, ground, clay, dirt. **2** *on British soil* land, country, terra firma.

soil v **1** *soil her white gloves* dirty, stain, muddy, spot, smear, splash, smudge. **2** *soil* *his reputation* sully, stain, taint, besmirch, blot, smear.

sojourn n stay, visit, stop, stopover; holiday, vacation.

solace n **1** *bring solace to the bereaved* comfort, consolation, condolence, support. **2** *solace for their pain* mitigation, alleviation, assuagement, amelioration.

soldier n fighter, warrior, trooper, warmonger; *inf* cannon fodder. **soldier on** *soldier on through hard times* persevere, keep going; *inf* plug away, stick it out.

solecism n **1** *an essay full of solecisms* mistake, error, blunder; *inf* howler, boob. **2** *she was embarrassed by her solecism at the dinner party* breach of etiquette, inappropriate behaviour, impropriety, social indiscretion, *faux pas.*

solemn adj **1** *a solemn occasion* serious, grave, important, profound; formal. **2** *a solemn procession* dignified, ceremonious, stately, majestic, imposing, impressive, grand. **3** *a solemn child* serious, sombre, unsmiling; pensive, thoughtful; gloomy, glum, grim; *inf* moody, blue. **4** *a solemn promise* earnest, sincere, honest, genuine, committed, heartfelt.

solemnity n **1** *the solemnity of the occasion* solemness, graveness, gravity; dignity, formality. **2** *the solemnity of the procession* formality, ceremoniousness, dignity, stateliness, majesty. **3** *the solemnity of the child* solemness, gravity, thoughtfulness, sombreness, gloominess. **4** *the solemnity of his promise* seriousness, formality, earnestness, sincerity, fervour. **5** *attend the coronation solemnities* ceremony, proceedings, rite, ritual, formalities, celebration.

solicit v **1** *solicit information/assistance* ask for, request, apply for, seek, beg, plead for, crave. **2** *solicit him for financial help* ask, beg, beseech, implore, entreat, petition, importune, supplicate. **3** *women soliciting in the streets* work as a prostitute, engage in prostitution, accost people, make sexual advances; *inf* hustle.

solicitous adv **1** *solicitous enquiries about his health | solicitous about your health* concerned, caring, attentive, considerate, anxious, worried, nervous, uneasy, apprehensive. **2** *solicitous to be successful* eager, keen, anxious, desirous, enthusiastic, avid, zealous.

solicitude adv *show solicitude for his sick wife | solicitude for her health* concern, care, caringness, regard, attentiveness, consideration, considerateness, anxiety, worry, nervousness, uneasiness, apprehensiveness.

solid adj **1** *a solid rather than liquid substance* firm, hard, thick, dense, concrete, compact, compressed, condensed. **2** *made of solid silver* complete, pure, unalloyed, unmixed, unadulterated, genuine. **3** *solid houses* sound, substantial, strong, sturdy, stout, durable, well-built, well-constructed, stable. **4** *solid arguments* sound, well-founded, well-grounded, concrete, valid, reasonable, logical, cogent, weighty, authoritative, convincing, plausible, reliable. **5** *a solid friendship* reliable, dependable, trustworthy, stable, steadfast. **6** *solid citizens* sensible, level-headed, down-to-earth, decent, law-abiding, upright, upstanding, worthy. **7** *good solid work* sound, worthy, staid, unexciting, unimaginative, uninspired. **8** *a solid company* financially sound, sound, solvent, creditworthy, in good standing, in the black, secure. **9** *a solid line of people | a solid hour* continuous, uninterrupted, unbroken, undivided. **10** *political support that remained solid* unanimous, united, undivided, of one mind, of the same mind, in unison, consentient.

solidarity n *the success of the strike relies on the solidarity of the workers* unity, unification, union, unanimity, singleness of purpose, like-mindedness, team spirit, camaraderie, harmony, esprit de corps.

solidify v *leave the jelly/toffee mixture to solidify* harden, go hard, set, jell, congeal, cake.

solitary adj **1** *forced to lead a solitary life* lonely, lonesome, companionless, friendless, antisocial, unsocial, unsociable, withdrawn, reclusive, cloistered, introverted, hermitical. **2** *seek a solitary spot for holidays* loney, remote, out-of-the-way, isolated, secluded, hidden, concealed, private, unfrequented, unvisited, sequestered, retired, desolate. **3** *a solitary tree on the horizon* lone, single, sole, alone, by oneself/itself.

solitary n *a solitary living in the forest* loner, lone wolf, introvert, recluse, hermit, eremite, anchorite, stylite, cenobite.

solitude n **1** *the solitude of the place* loneliness, remoteness, isolation, seclusion, privacy, retirement, desolation. *see* SOLITARY adj 1. **2** *few solitudes left* wilderness, desert, vast expanse.

solution n **1** *the solution to the mathematical problem* answer, result, key, resolution. **2** *the solution of the problem will take years* solving, resolving, explanation, clarification, elucidation, unravelling, unfolding. **3** *a solution of brine* suspension, emulsion, mixture, mix, blend, compound.

solve v *solve the problem* find the solution to, answer, find the answer to, resolve, work out, figure out, fathom, find the key to, decipher, clear up, get to the bottom of, unravel, disentangle, unfold; *inf* crack.

solvent adj financially sound, debt-free, creditworthy, in the black.

sombre adj **1** *dress in sombre clothes* dark, dark-coloured, dull, dull-coloured, drab, dingy. **2** *in a sombre mood | a sombre expression* gloomy, depressed, sad, melancholy, dismal, doleful, mournful, joyless, cheerless, lugubrious, funereal, sepulchral.

somebody n *her father's a somebody on the local council* VIP, person of note, notable figure, notable, public figure, dignitary, celebrity, name, luminary, personage, household name; *inf* bigwig, big noise, big shot, big wheel, big cheese.

someday adv *they'll get there someday* sometime, one day, one of these days, at some time in the future, at a future time/date, one of these fine days, sooner or later, by and by, eventually, ultimately.

somehow adv *get thee somehow* by some means, in some way, in one way or other, no matter how, come what may, be fair means or foul, by hook or by crook; *inf* come hell or high water.

sometime adv *we must visit her sometime* someday, one day, one of these days, at some time in the future, at a future time/date, by and by. *see* SOMEDAY.

sometimes adv *we see her sometimes* occasionally, on occasion, on occasions, now and then, now and again, from time to time, once in a while, every so often, off and on.

somnolent adj **1** *feeling somnolent* sleepy, drowsy, half-asleep, heavy-eyed, dozy, groggy, comatose; *inf* dopey. **2** *a somnolent drug* soporific, sleep-inducing.

song n **1** *a beautiful song* ballad, popular song, pop song, ditty, chorus, shanty, carol, anthem, hymn, psalm, chant, canticle, lay. **2** *the song of the birds* warble, chirp, trill, whistle, pipe.

sonorous adj **1** *the sonorous tones of the minister* deep, rich, full, round, resonant, resounding, booming, ringing, reverberating, vibrating, pulsating. **2** *a sonorous style of prose* impressive, imposing, majestic, lofty, high-sounding, grandiloquent, declamatory, orotund, euphuistic, fustian.

soon adv **1** *be there soon* shortly, in a short time, in a little while, before long, in a minute, in a moment, any minute, in the near future, in a twinkling, in the twinkling of an eye; *inf* before you know it, before you can say Jack Robinson, pronto,

in two shakes of a lamb's tale. **2** *How soon can you get here?* quickly, promptly, speedily, punctually, early.

soothe v **1** *soothe the baby* quieten, quiet, calm, calm down, pacify, settle, settle down, hush, lull, tranquillize, mollify. **2** *soothe the pain* ease, assuage, alleviate, allay, moderate, mitigate, temper, palliate, soften, lessen, reduce.

soothsayer n seer, augur, prophet, diviner, sibyl.

sophisticated adj **1** *sophisticated city-dwellers* worldly-wise, worldly, experienced, seasoned, suave, urbane, cultured, cultivated, polished, refined, elegant, stylish, cosmopolitan, blasé. **2** *sophisticated production techniques* advanced, highly-developed, ultra-modern, complex, complicated, elaborate, intricate.

sophistication n *the sophistication of the city-dwellers* worldliness, experience, suaveness, urbanity, urbaneness, culture, refinement, elegance, poise, finesse, *savoir faire*.

sophistry n casuistry, quibbling, equivocation, fallaciousness, fallacy.

soporific adj *soporific drugs* sleep-inducing, somnolent, sedative, tranquillizing, narcotic, opiate, somniferous.

soporific n *given a soporific* sleeping potion, sleeping pill, sedative, tranquillizer, narcotic, opiate.

soppy adj **1** *soppy love films* mawkish, maudlin, sentimental, oversentimental, overemotional, slushy, mushy, sloppy; *inf* schmaltzy, corny. **2** *boys thinking girls soppy* silly, foolish; *inf* daft, wet, soft. **3** *soppy about the boy next door* infatuated with, in love with, enamoured of, smitten with, keen on; *inf* sweet on, wild about, crazy about, stuck on.

sorcerer n magician, wizard, enchanter, warlock, necromancer, magus, thaumaturgist.

sorceress n magician, witch, enchantress, necromancer, thaumaturgist.

sorcery n black magic, magic, witchcraft, witchery, wizardry, necromancy, black art, enchantment, thaumaturgy.

sordid adj **1** *sordid hovels* filthy, dirty, foul, unclean, grimy, sooty, soiled, stained, mucky, squalid, shabby, seedy, seamy, slummy, sleazy. **2** *a sordid creature* vile, foul, base, low, debased, degenerate, dishonourable, disreputable, despicable, ignominious, ignoble, abhorrent, abominable. **3** *sordid money-lenders* mean, greedy, avaricious, covetous, grasping, mercenary, miserly, niggardly, stingy; *inf* grubby.

sore adj **1** *a sore leg* painful, in pain, aching, hurting, tender, inflamed, raw, smarting, stinging, burning, irritated, bruised, wounded, injured. **2** *feel sore about her treatment of him* distressed, upset, resentful, vexed, aggrieved, offended, hurt, pained, annoyed, angry, irritated, irked, nettled; *inf* peeved. **3** *in sore need of some food* dire, urgent, pressing, desperate, critical, acute, extreme.

sore n *a sore on his leg* wound, scrape, abrasion, cut, laceration, graze, boil, abscess, swelling, gathering.

sorrow n **1** *the sorrow of the widow* sadness, unhappiness, grief, misery, distress, heartache, heartbreak, anguish, suffering, pain, woe, affliction, wretchedness, dejection, heaviness of heart, desolation, depression, disconsolateness, mourning. **2** *one of the great sorrows of his life* trouble, worry, woe, misfortune, affliction, trial, tribulation.

sorrow v **1** *children sorrowing at the departure of their mother* be sad, feel sad, be miserable, suffer, be wretched, be dejected, be heavy of heart, pine, weep. *see* SORROW n 1. **2** *the bereaved sorrowing* grieve, mourn, lament, wail.

sorrowful adj **1** *sorrowful expressions* sad, unhappy, tearful, heartbroken, wretched, woebegone, miserable, dejected, desolated, depressed, disconsolate, mournful, doleful, melancholy, lugubrious. **2** *a sorrowful sight before their eyes* sorry, wretched, miserable, pitiful, piteous, pitiable, moving, affecting, pathetic, heart-rending, deplorable, lamentable.

sorry adj **1** *sorry for his actions* regretful, apologetic, repentant, penitent, remorseful, contrite, ashamed, conscience-stricken, guilt-ridden, in sackcloth and ashes, compunctious. **2** *feel sorry for the child* sympathetic, pitying, full of pity, compassionate, moved, commiserative, empathetic. **3** *sorry to hear about his accident* sad, unhappy, distressed, grieved, regretful, sorrowful, miserable, wretched. **4** *a sorry sight* wretched, miserable, pitiful, piteous. *see* SORROWFUL 2.

sort n **1** *a new/different sort of plant/car* kind, type, variety, class, category, style, variety, group, set, genre, genus, family, order, breed, make, brand, stamp. **2** *a good sort* person, individual, soul; *inf* fellow, chap, bloke, guy, character, customer. **out of sorts 1** *having been out of sorts with a bad cold* unwell, unhealthy, sick, ill, indisposed, off colour, poorly, below par, not up to the mark; *inf* sedy, under the weather. **2** *avoid his father when he's out of sorts* in a bad

mood, in a bad temper, ill-tempered, irritable, cross, crabbed, touchy, testy, crotchety, grumpy, snappish. **3** *out of sorts after her broken engagement* in low spirits, dejected, depressed, downcast, gloomy, glum, melancholy, unhappy, miserable, wretched; *inf* down, down in the mouth, down in the dumps.

sort v **1** *sort the potatoes according to size | sort out the books in piles* classify, class, categorize, catalogue, grade, rank, group, divide, arrange, order, put in order, organize, assort, systematize, methodize. **2** *teachers asked to sort out the problem/mess* clear up, tidy up, put straight, put in order, deal with. **sort out 1** *sort the books out into piles* sort, classify, class, categorize, grade, arrange, organize. **2** *sort out the weaker plants and dispose of them* separate out, put to one side, segregate, sift, pick out, select. **3** *sort out the problem* sort, clear up, put straight, put right, solve, find a solution to.

sortie n *a sortie into enemy territory* sully, foray, charge, rush, onrush, raid, attack.

so-so adj mediocre, average, indifferent, unexceptional, undistinguished, uninspiring, tolerable, passable; *inf* fair to middling, no great shakes, nothing to write home about.

soul n **1** *the soul as opposed to the body* spirit, psyche, inner self, true being, vital force, animating principle. **2** *the soul of discretion* personification, embodiment, incarnation, essence, epitome. **3** *not a soul in sight* person, human being, being, individual, creature. **4** *the life and soul of the party* essential part, essence, heart, core, centre, vital force, driving force. **5** *play the piece without soul* feeling, emotion, intensity, fervour, ardour, vitality, animation, vivacity, energy, inspiration.

sound[1] n **1** *not a sound was heard* noise. **2** *she made not a sound* utterance, cry. **3** *the sound of the flute* noise, music; note, chord. **4** *they do not like the sound of her plans* impression, idea, thought, concept. **5** *within the sound of the church bells* hearing, distance, earshot, range.

sound[1] v **1** *sound the trumpet/bugle* play, blow. **2** *the trumpet sounded* resound, reverberate, resonate. **3** *sound the alarm* operate, set off, ring. **4** *sound the letter "f" or "t"* pronounce, utter, voice, enunciate, articulate, vocalize. **5** *it sounds as though he's mad* appear, look, seem, give/create the impression that, strike one that, have every indication that. **6** *sound a word of warning* utter, express, voice, pronounce, declare, announce.

sound¹ adj **1** *sound lungs | sound in limb* healthy, in good health, in good condition, physically fit, disease-free, hale and hearty, undamaged, uninjured, unimpaired, in good shape, in fine fettle. **2** *sound rafters in the building* solid, substantial, sturdy, well-constructed, intact, whole, undamaged, unimpaired. **3** *sound policies/arguments* solid, well-founded, well-grounded, concrete, valid, reasonable, logical, cogent, weighty, authoritative, convincing, plausible, reliable, orthodox. **4** *a sound judge of character* reliable, dependable, trustworthy, fair, good, sensible, intelligent, wise, judicious, sagacious, astute, shrewd, perceptive, foresighted. **5** *sound business* solvent, creditworthy, in good financial standing, in the black, solid, secure. **6** *a sound sleep* deep, undisturbed, unbroken, uninterrupted, untroubled, peaceful. **7** *a sound thrashing/telling-off* thorough, complete, without reserve, unqualified, out-and-out, drastic, severe.

sound² v **1** *sound the river depths* plumb, fathom, probe. **2** *sound the patient's chest* examine, do tests on, investigate, inspect.
sound out *sound out popular opinion* investigate, carry out an investigation of, conduct a survey of, research, carry out research into, explore, look into, examine, probe, canvass.

sour adj **1** *sour substances* acid, acidy, acid-like, acetic, aciduous, tart, bitter, sharp, vinegary, vinegarlike, unpleasant, distasteful, pungent. **2** *sour milk/butter* turned, curdled, fermented, give off, rancid, bad. **3** *a sour old man* embittered, nasty, unpleasant, disagreeable, bad-tempered, ill-tempered, ill-natured, sharp-tongued, irritable, crotchety, cross, crabbed, testy, touchy, snappish, peevish, churlish, grumpy; *inf* grouchy.

sour v *people soured by his treatment of them* embitter, make bitter, disenchant, alienate; *inf* turn off.

source n **1** *the source of the river* wellspring, wellhead, headspring. **2** *the source of the rumour* original, derivation, commencement, beginning, start, rise, cause, wellspring, fountainhead, provenance, author, originator, begetter. **3** *sources listed in the essay* reference, authority, informant.

souse v **1** *souse the herring* pickle, marinade, soak, steep. **2** *souse the garment in the dye solution* plunge, immerse, dip, submerge, sink, dusk, dunk, soak, steep, douse, drench, saturate. **3** *set out to get his friend soused* become drunk, intoxicate, inebriate, befuddle.

souvenir n memento, keepsake, token, reminder, relic, memorabilia.

sovereign n ruler, monarch, supreme ruler, king, queen, emperor, empress, tsar, crowned head, potentate.

sovereign adj **1** *sovereign power* supreme, absolute, unlimited, chief, paramount, principle, dominant, predominant, ruling. **2** *a sovereign state* independent, self-ruling, self-governing, autonomous. **3** *our sovereign lord* ruling, kingly, queenly, princely, royal, regal, majestic, noble. **4** *a sovereign remedy* efficient, effective, efficacious, effectual, excellent, outstanding.

sovereignty n **1** *hold sovereignty over adjoining states* supremacy, dominion, power, ascendancy, jurisdiction, control, sway. **2** *an island sovereignty* kingdom, realm, country.

sow v **1** *sow seed* scatter, disperse, strew, bestrew, disseminate, distribute, spread, broadcast. **2** *sow a field with wheat* plant. **3** *sow doubt in their minds* implant, plants, lodge, initiate, instigate, foster, promote, foment, invite.

space n **1** *houses taking up a lot of space | not enough space for them all* room, expanse, capacity, area, extent, volume, amplitude, spaciousness, scope, elbow-room, latitude, margin, leeway. **2** *a large space between houses* interval, gap, opening, interstice, break. **3** *write your name in the space provided* blank, empty space, gap. **4** *no spaces left in the theatre* empty seat, seat, place, berth, accommodation. **5** *green spaces at the edge of the city* unoccupied area, empty area, expanse, stretch, sweep. **6** *within the space of three hours* time, duration, period, span, stretch, interval. **7** *staring into space* empty space, the blue, vacuum, void. **8** *travel in space* outer space, the universe, the galaxy, the solar system; infinity.

space v **1** *space the trees out around the garden* place at intervals, arrange, line up, range, order. **2** *space out the plans* interspace, set apart.

spacious adj **1** *a spacious house* roomy, comodious, capacious, sizable, large, big, ample. **2** *spacious grounds* extensive, broad, wide, expansive, ample, large, vast.

span n **1** *the span of the bird's wings* length, extent, reach, stretch, spread, distance. **2** *within a short span of time* time, duration, period, space, stretch, interval.

span v **1** *a life spanning almost a century | knowledge spanning many areas* extend over, stretch across, cover, range over. **2** *bridges spanning the Thames | planks spanning the river* bridge, cross, traverse, pass over, arch over, vault over.

spank v smack, slap, put over one's knee; *inf* tan someone's hide, give someone a hiding, warm someone's bottom, wallop, belt, give someone a licking.

spar v *children who are always sparring* argue, bicker, squabble, wrangle, fight, quarrel, skirmish, have a tiff; *inf* fall out, have a spat.

spare adj **1** *a spare blanket* extra, additional, reserve, supplementary, auxiliary, surplus, supernumerary. **2** *have little spare time* free, leisure, unoccupied. **3** *a spare figure | of spare build* lean, thin, slim, slender, without an ounce of fat, skinny, wiry, lank; *inf* skin and bones. **4** *a spare helping* meagre, frugal, scanty, skimpy, modest. **5** *spare with money* sparing, economical, frugal. *see* SPARING **to spare** *a few plants to spare* left over, superfluous, surplus, surplus to requirement; *inf* going a-begging. **go spare** *father going spare at the damage* go into a rage, lose one's temper, be furious, be angry; *inf* go mad, have a fit, blow one's top, hit the ceiling/roof, go up the wall, do one's nut.

spare v **1** *Can you spare a few pounds for charity?* afford, part with, give, provide. **2** *no staff to spare* dispense with, do without, manage without, get along without. **3** *spare the culprit* be merciful to, show mercy to, be lenient to, deal leniently with, pardon, leave unpunished; *inf* let off, unhurt, go easy on, uninjured. **4** *spare the tree from destruction* save, protect, guard, defend.

sparing adj *be sparing with money/food* economical, frugal, thrifty, careful, saving, prudent, cautious, parsimonious, niggardly; *inf* stingy, tight-fisted.

spark n **1** *sparks of light* flicker, flash, flare, glint. **2** *not a spark of interest* bit, flicker, glimmer, trace, scrap, vestige, touch, hint, suggestion, suspicion, jot, whit, iota. **3** *require some spark in his employees* sparkle, vivacity, liveliness, animation, energy, spirit, enthusiasm, wit. *see* SPARKLE n 2.

spark v *spark off* *incidents sparking off wars* set off, start off, trigger off, touch off, precipitate, provoke, stir up, incite.

sparkle v **1** *lights/diamonds sparkling* twinkle, flicker, shimmer, flash, glitter, glint, blink, wink, dance, shine, gleam, glow, coruscate. **2** *people sparkling at the party* be sparkling, be vivacious, be lively, be animated, be ebullient, be effervescent, be witty, be brilliant. **3** *wine sparkling* bubble, give off bubbles, effervesce.

sparkle n **1** *the sparkle of lights on the river* twinkle, flicker, shimmer, flash, glitter, glint, blinking, winking, dancing, shining, gleam, glow, coruscation. **2** *require employees with some sparkle* vivacity, liveliness, life, animation, energy, vitality, spirit, enthusiasm, dash, élan, panache; *inf* pizzazz, vim, zip, zing.

sparse adj *a sparse population | sparse coverage of the news* scanty, meagre, slight, thinly distributed.

spartan n *a spartan life* austere, harsh, frugal, stringent, rigorous, strict, severe, bleak, grim, ascetic, abstemious, self-denying.

spasm n **1** *stomach spasms* contraction, convulsion, cramp, twitch. **2** *a spasm of coughing/laughter* fit, paroxysm, convulsion, attack, bout, seizure, outburst, access.

spasmodic adj *spasmodic fits of repentance* intermittent, fitful, irregular, sporadic, erratic, periodic, recurring, recurrent.

spate n *a spate of burglaries* rush, flood, deluge, torrent, outpouring, outbreak, cluster.

spatter v *cars spattering mud up on pedestrians* bespatter, splash, spray, shower, daub.

spawn n *governments spawning committees* create, bring into being, give rise to, cause, originate.

speak v **1** *speak the truth* utter, voice, express, say, pronounce, articulate, enunciate, state, tell. **2** *she spoke to him angrily* address, talk to, converse with, communicate with, have a discussion with, chat with, have a chat with, have a word with, accost, apostrophise; *inf* have a confab with, have a chinwag with, chew the fat/rag with, pass the time of day with. **3** *the lecturer spoke for two hours* give a speech, give a talk, talk, lecture, deliver an address, hold forth, discourse, orate, harangue, sermonize; *inf* spout, spiel, speechify. **4** *speak volumes | actions speak louder than words* mean, convey, signify, impart, suggest, denote, indicate, demonstrate. **speak for 1** *a lawyer speaking for the accused* represent, act for, act on behalf of, intercede for, act as spokesman/woman/person. **2** *speak for the motion* support, uphold, defend, stand up for, advocate. **speak of** *speak of his faults* talk about, discuss, mention, make mention of, refer to, make reference to, allude to, comment on, advert to. **speak out/up 1** *speak out/up to be heard in the crowd* speak loudly, speak clearly, raise one's voice, make oneself heard, make oneself audible. **2** *speak out/up against the cruelty* speak boldly, speak frankly, speak openly, speak one's mind, sound off, stand up and be counted. **speak to 1** *speaking angrily to him* address, talk to, converse with, communicate with. **2** *speak to the naughty children* reprimand, rebuke, scold, lecture, admonish; *inf* tell off, give a telling-off, talk to, give a talking to, give a dressing-down to, tick off, give a ticking-off to, carpet. **3** *speak to the motion* comment on, give information about, say something about, say a word about, touch upon, remark on.

speaker n *an accomplished speaker* public speaker, speech-maker, lecturer, orator, declaimer, haranguer, demagogue; *inf* tub-thumper, spieler.

spearhead n *the spearhead of the opposition to the plan* vanguard, van, forefront, driving force.

spearhead v *spearhead the opposition to the plan* lead, head, be in the van/vanguard of, set in motion, initiate, launch, pioneer.

special adj **1** *have a special talent | be a special person* exceptional, remarkable, unusual, rare, out-of-the-ordinary, extraordinary, singular, distinctive, notable, outstanding, unique. **2** *words with a special meaning* specific, particular, individual, distinctive, exact, precise, definite. **3** *take special care of it* especial, extra special, particular, exceptional, out-of-the ordinary. **4** *a special occasion* significant, momentous, memorable, festive, gala, red-letter. **5** *a special tool* specific, particular, custom-built. **6** *his special interest/subject* particular, chief, main, major, primary.

specialist n *a specialist in electronics* expert, authority, professional, consultant, master.

speciality n **1** *many specialities in the field of medicine* specialty, area of specialization, field of study. **2** *putting people at ease is her speciality* distinctive feature, forte, métier, talent, gift, pièce de resistance, claim to fame. **3** *the restaurant's speciality* speciality of the house, house special, specialité de la maison, chef's special, particular product.

species n *a species of plant* sort, kind, type, variety, class, category, group, genus, breed, genre.

specific adj **1** *give very specific instructions* well-defined, clear-cut, unambiguous, unequivocal, exact, precise, explicit, express, detailed. **2** *for a specific purpose* particular, specified, fixed, set, determined, distinct, definite.

specification n **1** *the specification of your housing requirements* stating, statement, naming, itemizing, designation, detailing, cataloguing. see SPECIFY. **2** *a house built to their specifications* instructions, description,

details, delineation, conditions, stipulations.

specify v *specify your housing requirements* state, mention, name, stipulate, define, set out, itemize, designate, detail, list, spell out, enumerate, particularize, catalogue, be specific about.

specimen n *collect specimens of the soil | dry plant specimens* sample, representative, example, illustration, exemplification, exemplify, instance, type, exhibit.

specious adj *arguments found to be specious* plausible, seemingly correct, misleading, deceptive, fallacious, unsound, casuistic, sophistic.

speck v **1** *specks of soot on the white sheets* spot, fleck, dot, speckle, stain, mark, smudge, blemish. **2** *not a speck of food left* particle, bit, piece, atom, iota, grain, trace.

speckled adj *speckled eggs/birds* mottled, flecked, spotted, dotted, dappled, brindled, stippled.

spectacle n **1** *the spectacle of brilliantly-clad skiers against the snow* sight, vision, scene, picture. **2** *spectacles organized as part of the celebrations* display, show, exhibition, pageant, parade, extravaganza. **3** *a drunk making a spectacle of himself* laughing stock, fool, curiosity.

spectacles n glasses, eye-glasses; *inf* specs.

spectacular adj **1** *a spectacular display/view* striking, picturesque, impressive, magnificent, splendid, eye-catching, breathtaking, glorious, dazzling, sensational, stunning, dramatic; *inf* out of this world. **2** *a spectacular victory* striking, impressive, remarkable, outstanding, extraordinary, sensational, dramatic, astonishing, singular.

spectacular n *a Christmas spectacular* extravaganza, display, exhibition, performance.

spectator n watcher, beholder, viewer, observer, onlooker, looker-on, witness, eye-witness, bystander; *inf* rubber-neck.

spectre n apparition, ghost, phantom, wraith, spirit, shade, vision, revenant, manes; *inf* spook.

speculate v **1** *speculate on their chances of success | speculate that he left unwillingly* conjecture about, theorize about, hypothesize about, guess about, take a guess about, surmise about, muse on, reflect on, mediate about, deliberate about, cogitate about, consider, think about. **2** *speculate on the stock market* gamble, take a risk on, venture on, take a venture on; *inf* have a flutter on.

speculation n **1** *much speculation about the creation of the universe* conjecture, theorizing, hypothesizing, supposition, guessing, surmising, musing, reflection, meditation, cogitation. *see* SPECULATE 1. **2** *unfounded speculation* conjecture, theory, hypothesis, supposition, guess, guesswork, surmise, opinion, reflection, meditation, deliberation, cogitation. **3** *his speculation on the stock market* gambling, gamble, venture, risk; *inf* flutter.

speculative adj **1** *conclusions which are purely speculative* conjectural, theoretical, hypothetical, suppositional, notional, academic, tentative, unproven, vague, indefinite. **2** *speculative dealings on the stock market* gambling, risky, hazardous; *inf* chancy, dicey.

speech n **1** *the power of speech | express opinions in speech* communication, talk, conversation, discussion, dialogue, colloquy. **2** *slurred speech* diction, articulation, enunciation, pronunciation. **3** *give an after-dinner speech* talk, lecture, address, discourse, oration, sermon, harangue, diatribe, tirade, philippic. **4** *the speech of Southern Germany* language, tongue, idiom, dialect, parlance; *inf* lingo. **5** *given to obscene speech* utterance, remarks, comments, observations, declarations, assertions.

speechless adj **1** *speechless with rage* rendered speechless, struck dumb, dumbstruck, dumbfounded, astounded, thunderstruck. **2** *speechless with modesty* tongue-tied, inarticulate, dumb, struck dumb. **3** *speechless disappointment* silent, unspoken, unexpressed, unsaid, unvoiced, tacit.

speed n *move with great speed* rapidity, swiftness, quickness, fastness, haste, hurry, hurriedness, expeditiousness, expedition, alacrity, promptness, fleetness, celerity, velocity.

speed v **1** *workers speeding homewards* hurry, hasten, make haste, rush, race, dash, sprint, scurry, scamper, charge; *inf* tear, scout. **2** *drivers speeding* drive too fast, break the speed limit, exceed the speed limit; *inf* put one's foot down, step on it. **3** *speed their recovery* expedite, hasten, hurry up, accelerate, advance, further, forward, facilitate, promote, boast, aid, assist. **speed up 1** *need to speed up to win the race* make haste, hurry up, rush, increase speed, accelerate; *inf* get moving, get a move on, step on it. **2** *speed up the process* speed, expedite, hasten, hurry, accelerate. *see* SPEED v 3.

speedy adj **1** *a speedy form of transport* rapid, swift, quick, fast, expeditious, fleet, high-speed. **2** *a speedy reply* rapid, swift, quick, fast, prompt, immediate, express.

spell[1] v *the storm spelt disaster for farmers* mean, signify, amount to, add up to, signal, denote, result in, cause, bespeak, portend, augur, presage. **spell out** *spell out their reasons for leaving* specify, set out, itemize, detail, enumerate, particularize, stipulate, make clear, make plain, elucidate, clarify.

spell[1] n **1** *recite a spell* incantation, conjuration, charm, abracadabra. **2** *put under a spell* trance, state of enchantment, entrancement, enthrallment, bewitchment. **3** *fall under the spell of an evil man* irresistible influence, fascination, magnetism, allure, charm, attraction, pull, draw, enticement, beguilement.

spell[2] n **1** *a spell of warm weather* time, period, interval, stretch, course, extent, span, patch. **2** *a spell of coughing* bout, fit, access. **3** *do a spell at the wheel* turn, stint, term, stretch, shift.

spellbinding adj *a spellbinding tale* riveting, entrancing, enthralling, bewitching, fascinating, captivating, mesmerizing, mesmeric, hypnotic.

spellbound adj *an audience spellbound by the actor's performance* riveted, entranced, enthralled, enraptured, transported, rapt, bewitched, fascinated, captivated, mesmerized, hypnotized; *inf* hooked.

spend v **1** *spend a great deal of money on clothes* pay out, lay out, expend, disburse; *inf* fork out, shell out, dish out, splash out, splurge. **2** *spend hours on the task* occupy, fill, take up, use up, pass, while away. **3** *spend a lot of effort* use, use up, employ, put in, apply, devote. **4** *the storm spent its force | soldiers having spent all their ammunition* use up, consume, exhaust, finish off, deplete, drain.

spendthrift n *spendthrifts getting into debt* squanderer, prodigal, profligate, wastrel; *inf* big spender.

spendthrift adj *spendthrift habits* extravagant, thriftless, squandering, prodigal, profligate, wasteful, improvident.

spent adj **1** *a spent force/talent* used up, consumed, exhausted, finished, depleted, drained, emptied; *inf* played-out, burnt-out. **2** *feeling spent after the long walk* exhausted, worn-out, tired out, fatigued, weary, wearied, weakened; *inf* all in, done in, dead beat, dead on one's feet, shattered, knackered, bushed, whacked, fagged out, had it.

spew v **1** *passengers spewing up on the sea voyage* vomit, be sick, retch, heave; *inf* puke, throw up. **2** *lava spewing from the volcano* gush, pour, spurt, issue, discharge, spout, rush.

sphere n **1** *ornaments in the shape of glass spheres* globe, bull, orb, globule. **2** *spheres in the sky* planet, star, moon, celestial body. **3** *a limited sphere of influence* area, field, range, scope, extent, compass, jurisdiction. **4** *in the sphere of economics* field, area of interest, area of study, discipline, speciality, specialty, domain, realm, province. **5** *marry out of his sphere* social class, social level, social stratum, station, rank, status, social circumstances, walk of life.

spherical adj *spherical ornaments* globe-shaped, globular, globoid, round, orb-like, orbicular.

spice n **1** *add spices to food* flavouring, seasoning, herb, condiment, relish. **2** *add a bit of spice to food* spiciness, flavouring, flavour, seasoning, piquancy, pungency, relish, tang, bite, zest, savoir; *inf* punch, kick. **3** *add spice to life* excitement, interest, colour, piquancy, zest, gusto, pep; *inf* zip, zing, zap.

spicy adj **1** *spicy sauces* spiced, seasoned, flavoursome, well-seasoned, sharp, tart, hot, peppery, piquant, pungent. **2** *spicy stories about her colleagues* lively, spirited, suggestive, risqué, racy, off-colour, improper, indecent, offensive; *inf* raunchy.

spike n *spikes on top of a fence* prong, barb, stake, spine, point, projection.

spike v **1** *spike one's foot on a nail* pierce, penetrate, prick, impale, injure. **2** *spike their drinks* lace, adulterate, contaminate, drug. **3** *spike their efforts to win* frustrate, foil, check, thwart, balk, hinder, obstruct, defeat, crush, destroy, eradicate.

spill v **1** *milk spilling from the jug* pour, pour out, flow, overflow, brim over, run over, slop over, well over. **2** *spill the scandalous details* reveal, disclose, divulge, leak, make known; *inf* let out, blab.

spill n *take a spill from a horse* fall, tumble, accident; *inf* header, nosedive, cropper.

spin v **1** *wheels spinning* revolve, rotate, turn, turn round, circle, whirl, gyrate. **2** *spin around to face him* wheel, whirl, twirl, turn, twist, swivel, pirouette. **3** *spin the plate* revolve, rotate, turn, whirl. **4** *spin a yarn about his successes* tell, unfold, relate, narrate, recount, concoct, make up, invert, fabricate. **5** *her head was spinning* go round, whirl, reel, swim, be giddy. **spin out** *have to spin out his lecture* protract, draw out,

stretch out, drag out, prolong, extend, expand, enlarge, fill out, pad out.

spin n **1** *a spin of the coin* turn, revolution, rotation, whirl, gyration. **2** *a spin in the car* drive, ride, trip, run, jaunt, journey, outing, turn; *inf* joyride, tool. **in a flat spin** agitate, flustered, in a panic, overwrought, in a dither, frantic, frenzied; *inf* in a flap, in a state, in a tizz, in a tiz-woz.

spine n **1** *injure his spine* spinal column, vertebrae, vertebral column, backbone, dorsum. **2** *a weak man lacking spine* mettle, grit, pluck, pluckiness, spirit, firmness of purpose, determination, resolution, fortitude, courage, braveness, valour, manliness. **3** *the hedgehog's/shrub's spines* needle, spike, barb, quill, rachis.

spine-chilling adj terrifying, horrifying, blood-curdling, hair-raising; *inf* scary, spooky.

spineless adj *spineless people not fighting back* weak, weak-willed, feeble, spiritless, irresolute, indecisive, cowardly, timorous, timid, submissive, unmanly, lily-livered, white-livered; *inf* chicken, yellow, yellow-bellied, gutless.

spiral adj *spiral staircases* | *spiral columns of smoke* coiled, corkscrew, winding, twisting, whorled, helical, cochlear, cochleate, voluted.

spiral n *a spiral of smoke* coil, twist, whorl, corkscrew, wreathe, curlicue, helix, volute.

spiral v **1** *smoke spiralling from the chimney* coil, wind, twist, swirl, wreathe. **2** *prices spiralling* soar, rocket, rise, go up, mount, increase.

spire n **1** *a church spire* steeple, belfry. **2** *mountain spires* peak, pinnacle, crest, top, tip.

spirit n **1** *a healthy body but a troubled spirit* soul, psyche, inner self, ego. **2** *the spirit of nature* breath of life, vital spark, animating principle, life force. **3** *haunted by spirits* apparition, ghost, phantom, spectre, wraith, shade, revenant, manes; *inf* spook. **4** *a person of determined spirit* character, temperament, temper, disposition, humour, complexion, quality, constitution, make-up. **5** *take the criticism in the wrong spirit* attitude, way, state of mind, mood, frame of mind, point of view, reaction, feeling, humour. **6** *the spirit of the age* prevailing tendency, motivating force, animating principle, dominating characteristic, ethos, essence, quintessence, embodiment, personification, quiddity. **7** *lack the spirit to carry out the task* courage, bravery, braveness, valour, mettle, pluck, grit, pluckiness, willpower, motivation, backbone, stout-heartedness, manliness, vigour, energy, determination, firmness of purpose, resoluteness; *inf* guts, spunk. **8** *play the song with spirit* animation, liveliness, vivacity, enthusiasm, fervour, fire, passion, energy, verve, zest, dash, élan; *inf* pizzazz, zing, zip, zap. **9** *the spirit of the new rule* implication, underlying message, essence, gist, tenor, drift, meaning, sense, purport. *see* SPIRITS. **spirit away** *spirit away the pop star from the photographers* whisk away, carry off, steal away with, make off with, snatch, seize.

spirited adj **1** *put up a spirited defence* courageous, brave, valiant, valorous, heroic, mettlesome, plucky, gritty, determined, resolute. **2** *a spirited playing of the song* animated, lively, vivacious, enthusiastic, fervent, fiery, passionate, energetic.

spiritless adj **1** *spiritless creatures putting up no defence* weak, feeble, spineless, irresolute, indecisive, cowardly, timorous, timid, submissive, unmanly, lily-livered, white-livered; *inf* chicken, yellow, yellow-bellied, gutless. **2** *a spiritless performance* lacklustre, dull, colourless, passionless, bland, insipid, vapid, indifferent, prosaic. **3** *seeming spiritless after their defeat* depressed, dejected, disconsolate, downcast, listless, languid, lethargic, sluggish, inert, lifeless.

spirits npl **1** *in low spirits | raise one's spirits* mood, humour, temperament, temper, feelings, morale, frame of mind. **2** *wine and spirits* liquor, strong liquor; *inf* hard stuff, hooch, fire-water.

spiritual adj **1** *spiritual needs* nonmaterial, incorporeal, ethereal, intangible, otherworldly, unworldly. **2** *spiritual music* religious, sacred, divine, holy, nonsecular, churchly, ecclesiastic, devotional, devout.

spit[1] v **1** *not allowed to spit in public* expectorate, hawk. **2** *spit blood* discharge, issue, eject. **3** *"Get out", he spat* hiss, rasp, snort.

spit[1] n *clean the spit from the floor* spittle, saliva, sputum. **the spit/the very spit** the spitting image, exact likeness, the very image, mirror image, clone, identical twin, duplicate, copy; *inf* ringer, dead ringer.

spit[2] n *cook the meat on a spit* turnspit, roasting rod, skewer, rotisserie.

spite n *say it out of spite* malice, maliciousness, ill-will, malevolence, venom, malignance, hostility, evil, resentment, resentfulness, snideness, rancour, grudgingness, envy, hate, hatred, vengeance, vengefulness, vindictiveness. **in spite of**

happy in spite of being poor despite, despite the fact, notwithstanding, regardless of.

spite v *do it to spite her sister* injure, harm, hurt, wound, annoy, harass, irritate, vex, offend, provoke, peeve, pique, thwart, foil, frustrate.

spiteful adj *spiteful comments/behaviour* malicious, ill-natured, malevolent, venomous, poisonous, malignant, malign, hostile, resentful, snide, rancorous, grudging, envious, vengeful, vindictive, splenetic; *inf* bitchy, catty.

splash v **1** *splash water/paint around* spatter, sprinkle, spray, shower, splatter, squirt, slosh, slop, splodge. **2** *splash clothes with mud* spatter, bespatter, spray, shower, splatter. **3** *waves splashing against the rocks* dash, beat, batter, buffet, break, wash, surge. **4** *children splashing about in water* paddle, wade, wallow, dabble. **5** *his name splashed across the newspapers* blazon, display, exhibit, plaster, publicize, broadcast, headline, flaunt, trumpet. **splash out** *splash out on new clothes after being paid* be extravagant, go on a spending spree, splurge, spare no expense; *inf* last out, push the boat out.

splash n **1** *the splash of water against the rocks* splashing, dashing, beating, battering. **2** *splashes of mud on the walls* spot, splotch, daub, smudgy, smear, murk, stain. **3** *the scandal made a front-page splash* display, exhibition, splurge, sensation, impact. **4** *a splash of colour* patch, burst, streak. **make a splash** *make a splash with her first novel* cause a sensation, cause a stir, cut a dash, attract attention, get noticed.

spleen n *vent one's spleen on the innocent* bad temper, ill-temper, ill-nature, ill-humour, irritability, irascibility, peevishness, petulance, pique, querulousness, crossness, crabbedness, testiness, touchiness, cantankerousness, moodiness, sullenness, resentment, spite, spitefulness, bitterness, hostility, rancour, malice, maliciousness, malevolence, malignity, acrimony, animosity, bile.

splendid adj **1** *splendid furnishings* magnificent, imposing, superb, grand, sumptuous, resplendent, opulent, luxurious, plush, deluxe, rich, costly, lavish, ornate, gorgeous, glorious, dazzling, brilliant, showy, elegant, handsome. **2** *a splendid reputation* distinguished, impressive, glorious, illustrious, brilliant, notable, noted, remarkable, outstanding, eminent, celebrated, renowned, noble, venerable. **3** *splendid colours* glorious, brilliant, bright, gleaming, glowing, lustrous, radiant, dazzling, refulgent. **4** *a splendid meal/holiday* excellent, fine, first-class, first-rate, marvellous, wonderful; *inf* fantastic, terrific, great, fabulous, fab.

splendour n **1** *the splendour of the furnishings* magnificence, grandeur, sumptuousness, opulence, luxury, luxuriousness, richness, lavishness, gloriousness, elegance. *see* SPLENDID 1. **2** *the splendour of his reputation* illustriousness, brilliance, notability, eminence, renown, venerableness. *see* SPLENDID 2. **3** *the splendour of the colours* gloriousness, brilliance, brightness, gleam, glow, lustre, radiance. *see* SPLENDID 3.

splice v **1** *splice the rope ends* interweave, braid, plait, intertwine, interlace, join, unite, connect, bind, fasten. **2** *splice the tapes* join, unite, connect, overlap. **get spliced** *get spliced in a registry office* get married, marry, get wed, wed, become man and wife, tie the knot.

splinter n *splinters of wood* sliver, fragment, shiver, shard, chip, shaving, shred, piece, bit.

splinter v *the glass splintered* break into pieces, break into fragments, break into smithereens, shatter, shiver, fracture, split, disintegrate, crumble.

split v **1** *split the material in two* break, chop, cut, hew, lop, cleave, rend, rip, tear, slash, slit, splinter, snap, crack, rive. **2** *split the party in two* divide, separate, sever, sunder, bisect, partition. **3** *split up the twins at birth* divide, separate, set apart, disunite. **4** *split the money/profits* share, divide, halve, apportion, distribute, dole out, parcel out, allot, allocate, carve up, slice up; *inf* divvy. **5** *the road splits over the hill* divide in two, divide, fork, bifurcate. **6** *split with his partner* break up with/from, separate from, part from, part company with, reach the parting of the ways, dissociate oneself from. **7** *the couple split up* break up, separate, part, part company, become estranged, reach the parting of the ways, divorce, get a divorce. **8** *her husband split* leave, depart, take off, decamp, exit; *inf* push off, shove off. **9** *children splitting on their friends* inform on, tell tales on, report, give away; *inf* grass on, squeal on, blow the whistle on, rat on, peach on.

split n **1** *a split in the material* break, cut, rent, rip, tear, slash, slit, crack, fissure, breach. **2** *a split in the political party* division, rift, schism, rupture, division, partition, separation, break-up, alienation, estrangement.

split-up n *after the split-up of her parents* break-up, separation, parting, estrangement, divorce.

spoil v **1** *spoil the material by washing it* damage, impair, mar, blemish, disfigure, deface, injure, harm, ruin, destroy, wreck. **2** *spoil our plans* upset, mess up, disorganize, ruin, destroy, wreck. **3** *spoil her little boy* pamper, overindulge, mollycoddle, cosset, coddle, baby, spoonfeed, featherbed, wait on hand and foot, kill with kindness. **4** *the food will spoil* go bad, turn, go sour, become rotten, rot, become tainted, decompose, decay; *inf* go off. **spoiling for** *spoiling for a fight* eager for, anxious for, keen to have, desirous of, bent on, longing for, on the lookout for.

spoils npl **1** *the spoils of high rank* benefit, advantage, gain, profit. **2** *divide up the spoils from the burglary* booty, loot, plunder, pickings, pillage; *inf* swag, boodle.

spoilsport n killjoy, damper, dog in the manger; *inf* wet blanket, party-pooper, misery.

spoken adj *spoken judgement* oral, verbal, uttered, voiced, expressed, by word of mouth, unwritten.

spokesman n spokeswoman, spokesperson, mouthpiece, voice, negotiator, mediator, representative.

sponge v *sponge the walls* clean, wash, wipe, mop, rub, swab. **sponge off/on** live off, impose on, be a parasite on, scrounge from, beg from, borrow from; *inf* freeload on, cadge from, mooch from; *Amer inf* bum from.

sponger n parasite, hanger-on, scrounger, beggar, borrower; *inf* free-loader, cadger, moocher; *Amer inf* bum.

spongy adj *spongy material/ground* soft, cushiony, squashy, springy, resilient, elastic, porous, absorbent.

sponsor n *a sponsor of the new art gallery* patron, backer, promoter, subsidizer, guarantor, supporter; *inf* angel.

sponsor v *companies sponsoring the sports meeting* be a patron of, back, put up the money for, fund, finance, promote, subsidize, act as guarantor of, support, lend one's name to.

spontaneous adj **1** *spontaneous offers of help* voluntary, unforced, unconstrained, uncompelled, unprompted. **2** *a spontaneous vote of thanks* unplanned, unpremeditated, unrehearsed, impromptu, extempore, spur-of-the-moment, extemporaneous; *inf* off-the-cuff. **3** *a spontaneous smile* natural, instinctive, involuntary, automatic, impulsive, impetuous.

spoonfeed v pamper, mollycoddle, cosset, coddle, featherbed, wait on hand and foot, kill with kindness, overindulge, spoil.

sporadic adj *sporadic showers* irregular, intermittent, scattered, random, infrequent, occasional, on and off, isolated, spasmodic.

sport n **1** *the world of sport* physical activity, physical exercise, physical recreation, athletics. **2** *play a variety of sports* physical activity, competitive game, pastime. **3** *torment the animal for sport* amusement, entertainment, diversion, play, fun, pleasure, enjoyment. **make sport of** *children making sport of the new boy* make fun of, laugh at, poke fun at, mock, jeer at, ridicule, taunt, gibe at, sneer at.

sport v **1** *children sporting in the water* play, have fun, amuse oneself, entertain oneself, divert oneself, frolic, gambol, frisk, romp, cavort, caper, disport oneself. **2** *sport a new tie* wear, exhibit, display, have on show, show off.

sporting adj *a sporting gesture* sportsmanlike, fair, just, honourable, generous.

sportive adj *students in sportive mood* playful, frolicsome, high-spirited, sprightly, jaunty, rollicking, frisky, skittish, mischievous, waggish, prankish, gamesome.

spot n **1** *black spots on the white cloth* mark, dot, speck, speckle, fleck, smudge, stain, blotch, splotch, patch. **2** *a spot on her face* pimple, pustule, papule, boil, pock, whitehead, blackhead, blemish. **3** *a black spot on her reputation* stain, taint, blemish, defect, flaw, brand, stigma. **4** *a picnic spot* area, place, site, location, scene, locate, setting, situation. **5** *a regular spot on the programme* place, position, niche. **6** *a spot of lunch* little, bit, morsel, smidgen, bite. **7** *a spot of whisky* little, splash, smidgen. **8** *in rather a spot* difficulty, mess, trouble, plight, predicament, quandary, tight corner; *inf* hot water, fix, jam.

spot v **1** *spot someone following him* catch sight of, see, notice, observe, espy, discern, descry, detect, make out, pick out, recognize, identify. **2** *the material spots easily* mark, stain. **3** *the mud spotted her dress* mark, stain, dirty, soil, spatter, besmirch. **4** *spot her reputation* stain, sully, blacken, taint, blemish.

spotless adj **1** *spotless sheets/houses* clean, ultra-clean, snowy-white, whiter-than-white. **2** *spotless houses* clean, ultra-clean, spick-and-span, immaculate, shining,

gleaming. **3** *of spotless character* pure, flawless, faultless, blameless, unstained, unsullied, untainted, unblemished, unimpeachable, above reproach.

spotlight n *celebrities always in the spotlight* limelight, public eye, glare of publicity, publicity, public attention, public interest.

spotlight v *a report which spotlights the financial problems* highlight, point up, draw attention to, focus on, zero in on, accentuate, underline, stress, emphasize, give prominence to, bring to the fore.

spotted adj **1** *a spotted dog/horse* dappled, mottled, pied, piebald, speckled. **2** *a spotted dress* polka-dot, spotty, flecked.

spotty adj **1** *a spotty face/youth* pimply, acned. **2** *a spotty dog* spotted, dappled, mottled. *see* SPOTTED 1. **3** *a spotty dress* spotted, polka-dot, flecked. **4** *the standard of the quality being spotty* patchy, irregular, non-uniform.

spouse n husband/wife, partner, mate, companion, consort, helpmate; *inf* better half, old man/woman/lady, missis.

spout v **1** *oil spouting from the well* spurt, gush, spew, squirt, jet, spray, emit, erupt, disgorge, pour, stream, flow, spray. **2** *tired of politicians spouting* declaim, orate, hold forth, ramble, rant, harangue, speechify, sermonize; *inf* spiel.

sprawl v **1** *people sprawling on the sofa* stretch out, lounge, lie around, repose, recline, slump, flop, loll, slouch. **2** *suburbs sprawling out into the countryside* spread, stretch, spill over, ramble, straggle, trail.

spray[1] n **1** *a spray from the sea* shower, jet, mist, drizzle, spindrift, foam, froth. **2** *buy a deodorant spray* atomizer, vaporizer, aerosol, sprinkler, sprinkling can.

spray[1] v **1** *spray scent/insecticide* disperse, disseminate, sprinkle, shower. **2** *water sprayed from the sea* jet, spout, gush.

spray[2] n *a spray of flowers* sprig, posy, bouquet, nosegay, corsage, wreath, garland.

spread v **1** *spread its wings | spread the map out* stretch, extend, open out, unfurl, unroll. **2** *the town is spreading out* stretch out, extend, enlarge, grow bigger, widen, broaden, grow, develop, branch out. **3** *the view spread out before them* stretch out, unfold, be on display, be exhibited, be on show, uncover, be unveiled, be revealed. **4** *spread manure on the fields* lay on, put on, apply, smear on; *inf* plaster on. **5** *spread the bread with butter* cover, coat, layer. **6** *the disease/influence is spreading* mushroom, extend, increase, advance, proliferate, escalate. **7** *spread rumours* disseminate, circulate, transmit, make public, make known, broadcast, publicize, propagate, promulgate, bruit. **8** *spread a table* set, lay, arrange, order.

spread n **1** *measure the spread of the bird's wings* extent, stretch, span, reach, compass, sweep. **2** *a spread of three decades* period, time, term. **3** *the spread of the disease* increase, advance, expansion, mushrooming, proliferation, escalating, diffusion. **4** *the spread of rumours* dissemination, circulation, transmission, broadcasting, publicizing, propagation. *see* SPREAD V 7. **5** *a brightly-coloured spread* bedspread, bedcover, cover, counterpane, coverlet, throw. **6** *lay on a birthday spread* feast, banquet, repast; *inf* blow-out.

spree n **1** *go out on a spree to celebrate* enjoyable outing, fling, revel, junketing, jollification, drinking bout, orgy, debauch, bacchanal, bacchanalia; *inf* binge, bender, jag. **2** *a shopping spree* buying orgy; *inf* shopping splurge.

sprig n *a sprig of lilac* spray, branch, bough, twig, shoot.

sprightly adj *sprightly elderly people* spry, lively, energetic, active, agile, nimble, supple, animated, vivacious, spirited, brisk, vital, light-hearted, cheerful, merry, jolly, blithe, jaunty, perky, frisky, frolicsome, playful, sportive.

spring v **1** *springing to his feet | cats springing from the trees* jump, leap, bound, vault, hop. **2** *her family springs from a relative of Queen Anne* be described from, descend from, have its/their origins in, originate in, derive from, issue from. **3** *disapproval springs from ignorance* originate, have its origins in, derive from, stem from, arise in, emanate from, proceed from, arise in, start from. **4** *Where did you spring from?* appear, come into view, crop up; *inf* pop up. **5** *spring his resignation on them* present unexpectedly, introduce suddenly, reveal suddenly, announce without warning. **spring back** *the branch sprang back* rebound, recoil, fly back. **spring up** *new houses springing up everywhere* appear, make a sudden appearance, come into being, come into existence, shoot up, develop quickly, mushroom, burgeon.

spring n **1** *reach her in one spring* jump, leap, bound, vault, hop. **2** *injured by the spring of the branch* rebound, recoil. **3** *a mattress with little spring* springiness, bounciness, elasticity, resilience, flexibility, stretch, stretchiness, tensility. **4** *put a spring in his step* bounce, bounciness, buoyancy, liveliness, light-heartedness, merriment. **5** *get married in the spring* springtime, springtide. **6** *mineral springs* well, wellspring, source. **7** *the springs of their behaviour* origin, source, cause, root, basis.

spring adj *spring weather* springlike, vernal.

springy adj **1** *springy mattresses* bouncy, elastic, resilient, flexible, stretchy, tensile. **2** *a springy step* bouncy, lively, light-hearted, merry.

sprinkle v **1** *sprinkle water on the grass* spray, shower, splash, trickle, spatter. **2** *sprinkle icing sugar on the cake* scatter, strew. **3** *sprinkle the cake with icing sugar* dust, powder, dredge.

sprinkling n **1** *a sprinkling of snow on the ground* scattering, dusting. **2** *only a sprinkling of people in the audience* few, handful, trickle.

sprint v *sprinting for the bus* run, race, rush, dash, hotfoot it, put on a turn/burst of speed; *inf* scoot, tear, hare.

sprite n fairy, elf, pixie, nymph, dryad, imp, goblin, kelpie, leprechaun.

sprout v **1** *deer sprouting antlers* send forth, put forth, grow, develop. **2** *potatoes sprouting* bud, germinate, put forth shoots. **3** *weeds sprouting up everywhere* shoot up, spring up, grow, develop, appear, mushroom, proliferate.

spruce adj neat, well-groomed, well-turned-out, smart, trim, dapper, elegant, chic, looking as though one has just stepped out of a bandbox; *inf* natty.

spry adj sprightly, lively, energetic, active, agile, nimble, quick.

spume n foam, froth, head, lather, surf, spindrift.

spunk n courage, bravery, valour, pluck, pluckiness, mettle, gameness, daring, spirit, backbone; *inf* guts.

spur n **1** *the use of spurs to speed up the animals* goad, prick, prod. **2** *act as a spur to his ambition* stimulus, stimulant, incentive, inducement, encouragement, impetus. **on the spur of the moment** *make his decision on the spur of the moment* impulsively, on impulse, impetuously, impromptu, on the spot, unpremeditatedly, without thinking, without planning, suddenly, all of a sudden, unexpectedly, out of the blue.

spur v **1** *spur the animal to go faster* goad, prick, prod. **2** *his early success spurred him on to try hard* stimulate, give the incentive to, induce, encourage, motivate, prompt, urge, impel.

spurious adj *spurious excuses/research* counterfeit, fraudulent, fake, bogus, sham, mock, feigned, pretended, make-believe, imitation, contrived, fictitious, deceitful, specious; *inf* phoney, pseudo.

spurn v *spurn her lover/his advances* reject, turn away, repulse, rebuff, repudiate, snub, slight, cold-shoulder, treat with contempt, disdain, look down one's nose at, scorn, despise, condemn; *inf* kick in the teeth, give the go-by.

spurt v *oil/water spurting from the well* gush, squirt, shoot, surge, well, jet, spring, pour, stream, flow, issue, emanate.

spurt n **1** *a spurt of oil/water* gush, surge, jet, spray, outpouring. **2** *a sudden spurt of energy/speed* burst, outburst, fit, surge, access. **3** *put on a spurt at the end* burst of speed, turn of speed, increase of speed, burst of energy, sprint, rush.

spy n *government documents stolen by an enemy spy* enemy agent, foreign agent, secret agent, undercover agent, secret service agent, intelligence agent, double agent, fifth columnist; *inf* mole, spook.

spy v *spy someone on the horizon* catch sight of, spot, see, notice, observe, glimpse, make out, discern, descry, espy. **spy on** *spy on the rival firm* | *spy on his neighbours* keep under surveillance, watch, keep a watch on, keep an eye on, observe, keep under observation, follow, shadow, trail; *inf* tail.

squabble n *a squabble over money* quarrel, fight, row, dispute, argument, difference of opinion, dispute, tiff, wrangle, brawl; *inf* scrap, set-to, dust-up, barney, run-in, spat.

squabble v *children squabbling constantly* quarrel, fight, row, argue, bicker, have a dispute/difference of opinion, have a tiff, have words, wrangle, brawl; *inf* fall out, scrap.

squad n **1** *a squad of soldiers* company, platoon, troop, unit. **2** *a squad of workmen* gang, band, group.

squalid adj **1** *squalid hovels* dirty, filthy, dingy, grubby, grimy, mucky, slummy, slumlike, foul, vile, low, wretched, mean, nasty, seedy, sordid, sleazy, slovenly, repulsive, disgusting, neglected, dilapidated, ramshackle, broken-down, tumble down; *inf* grungy, grotty. **2** *squalid tales of corruption* sordidly, vile, nasty, repulsive, horrible, disgraceful, shameful, abominable, odious, filthy, indecent, depraved.

squalor n *the squalor of slums* squalidness, dirt, dirtiness, filth, filthiness, dinginess, grubbiness, grime, griminess, muckiness, foulness, vileness, lowness, wretchedness, meanness, nastiness, seediness, sordidness, dilapidation; *inf* grunge, grottiness.

squander v *squander his savings on alcohol* waste, misspend, dissipate, fritter away, run through, lavish, splurge, be prodigal with, spend like water, pour down the drain; *inf* blow.

square n **1** *a band playing in the square* town square, village square, market square, quadrangle. **2** *regard parents as old squares* fogy, old fogy, conservative, traditionalists, conventionalist, die-hard, conformist; *inf* stick-in-the-mud, fuddy-duddy.

square adj **1** *the teams are all square* equal, even, level-pegging, drawn; *inf* even-steven. **2** *a businessman square in all his dealings* fair, just, equitable, honest, straight, upright, above board, ethical; *inf* on the level. **3** *a square refusal* direct, straight, straightforward, explicit, unequivocal. **4** *regard her parents as being square* old-fashioned, behind the times, conservative, ultra-conservative, traditionalist, conventional, conformist, bourgeois, strait-laced, stuffy, unadventurous; *inf* fuddy-duddy.

square v **1** *the two accounts do not square with each other* tally, agree, be consistent with, correspond, fit, conform, be in harmony with, harmonize, be congruous with. **2** *square the score* level, even, make equal. **3** *square the bill* settle, settle up, pay, pay in full, discharge, make good. **4** *square the doorman to let them in* bribe, suborn, corrupt; *inf* buy off. **5** *square matters before we go* straighten out, set straight, set right, put in order, arrange.

squash v **1** *squash the beetle with his foot* | *squash the berries with a wooden spoon* crush, squeeze, flatten, compress, press, smash, pulp, mash, pulverize, macerate. **2** *the audience were squashed into the hall* crowd, crush, cram, pack tight, pack like sardines, jam, squeeze, wedge. **3** *squash him in front of the class* humiliate, mortify, deflate, repress, put in his/her place, take the wind out of someone's sails, take down a peg or two, intimidate, bully; *inf* put down. **4** *squash the rebellion* put down, quash, quell, crush, suppress, scotch, squelch, nip in the bud; *inf* put the kibosh on.

squashy adj pulpy, mushy, spongy, squishy, oozy, pappy.

squat v *squat behind the hedge* crouch, sit on one's haunches, sit on one's heels.

squat adj *a squat figure* dumpy, stubby, chunky, thickset, stocky, short.

squawk n **1** *the squawk of the hens* screech, cackle, shriek, scream, yelp. **2** *squawking about the high prices* complain, protest, grumble, moan; *inf* grouse, kick up a fuss, gripe, beef, bitch, bellyache.

squeak n *the squeak of the mice* squeal, peep, pipe, yelp, whimper.

squeak v **1** *mice squeaking* squeal, peep, pipe, yelp, whimper. **2** *gates squeaking in the wind* creak, scrape, grate.

squeal n *the squeals of the children* shriek, yell, scream, screech, howl, shout, cry, wail.

squeal v **1** *children squealing with pain/excitement* shriek, yell, scream, howl, shout, cry, shrill, wail. **2** *the burglar squealing on his associates* inform, tell tales on; *inf* grass, blow the whistle on, rat, peach, snitch, put the finger on. **3** *squealing about the prices* complain, protest, grumble, moan; *inf* grouse, kick up a fuss, gripe, beef, bitch, squawk, bellyache.

squeamish adj **1** *feeling squeamish on the sea voyage* queasy, nauseous, sickish, sick, queer. **2** *squeamish with regard to etiquette and morals* fastidious, particular, punctilious, finicky, fussy, scrupulous, prudish, straight-laced; *inf* pernickety, prissy.

squeeze v **1** *squeeze the sweater to remove moisture* wring, twist, press. **2** *squeeze the water from the sweater | squeeze the juice from the orange* extract, press, force, express. **3** *squeeze the oranges* compress, crush, squash, mash, pulp. **4** *squeeze his arm* grip, clutch, pinch, press, compress. **5** *the audience were squeezed into the hall* crowd, crush, cram, pack tight, pack like sardines, jam, squash, wedge. **6** *squeeze his fiancée* embrace, hug, cuddle, clasp, hold tight. **7** *squeeze money out of them* extort, wring, wrest, extract, tear from, milk; *inf* bleed. **8** *squeeze them for money* bring pressure to bear on, pressure, pressurize, strong-arm, blackmail; *inf* put the squeeze on, lean on, bleed, put the screws on, put the bite on.

squeeze n **1** *give his fiancée a squeeze* embrace, hug, cuddle, clasp, hold. **2** *give her hand a squeeze* clasp, grip, grasp, clutch. **3** *it was a bit of a squeeze in the hall* crowd, crush, jam, squash, press, congestion. **4** *a squeeze of lemon juice* drop, droplet, dash, spot, bit.

squire n *country squires* landowner, landholder, country gentleman.

squire v *squire her to the dance* escort, accompany, be someone's partner, be someone's companion, attend, usher, guide, conduct, lead.

squirm v *squirm in their seats | squirm in embarrassment* wriggle, wiggle, writhe, twist, turn, shift.

squirt v **1** *squirt water from a water pistol* discharge, expel, shoot, spurt. **2** *water squirting from the water pistol* eject, emit, discharge, spew out, spurt, spout, jet, stream, spray, gush, surge, pour, flow, issue. **3** *squirting people with water* splash, wet, spray, bespatter, shower, sprinkle, besprinkle.

squirt n **1** *a squirt of water/cream* jet, stream, spray, flow. **2** *a nasty little squirt* insignificant person; *inf* pipsqueak, twerp.

stab v *stab him in the heart* knife, pierce, puncture, run through, stick, skewer, gash, slash, wound, injure. **stab in the back** betray, break faith with, be a traitor to, play false, double-cross, sell out, give a Judas kiss; *inf* sell down the river.

stab n **1** *receive a stab in the leg* puncture, gash, slash, incision, wound, injury. **2** *feel a stab of pain in the chest* pain, shooting pain, pang, twinge, ache, throb, spasm. **3** *have a stab at writing a novel* try, attempt, endeavour, essay, effort, venture; *inf* go, shut, crack.

stability n **1** *the stability of the structures* firmness, solidity, steadiness, secureness, strength, fastness, stoutness, sturdiness. *see* STABLE 1. **2** *the stability of their relationship* secureness, solidity, strength, steadiness, firmness, sureness, durability, constancy, permanence, reliability, dependability. *see* STABLE 2. **3** *question her stability* soundness, sense, responsibility, self-control, sanity. *see* STABLE 3.

stable adj **1** *stable structures* firm, solid, steady, secure, fixed, strong, fast, stout, sturdy, moored, anchored, immovable. **2** *a stable relationship* secure, solid, strong, steady, firm, sure, steadfast, unwavering, unfaltering, unswerving, established, long-lasting, long-lived, deep-rooted, well-founded, well-grounded, abiding, durable, enduring, lasting, constant, permanent, reliable, dependable, true. **3** *a stable person* well-balanced, balanced, sound, mentally sound, steady, reasonable, sensible, responsible, equable, self-controlled, sane.

stack n **1** *a stack of logs* heap, pile, mass, accumulation, collection, hoard, store, stock, stock-pile, mound, mountain. **2** *put hay into stacks* haystack, rick, hayrick, cock, shock. **3** *a stack of money | stacks of money* abundance, amplitude; *inf* a great deal, a lot, lots, bags, loads, heaps, tons, oodles, scads.

stack v *stack logs* heap, pile, pile up, amass, accumulate, collect, hoard, store, stockpile.

stadium n *sports stadium* arena, sports field, athletic field, football field, football pitch.

staff n **1** *the lame man leaning on a staff* walking-stick, stick, cane, crook, crutch, prop.

2 *hit him with a staff* stick, cane, rod, pole, baton, truncheon. **3** *the staff of office* rod, mace, sceptre. **4** *reduce staff in the office* employees, workers, workforce, personnel.

staff v *staff the factory with school-leavers* man, people, equip, fit out, supply, furnish, provide.

stage n **1** *a stage in the development* point, period, step, juncture, time, division, level. **2** *the last stage of a race/journey* lap, leg, phase, step. **3** *stand on a stage in the theatre* platform, dais, rostrum, podium. **4** *the stage for many international meetings* setting, scene, site, arena, background, backdrop. **the stage** *a career connected with the stage* the theatre, drama, show business, the footlights, the boards.

stage v **1** *stage a production of Shakespeare* put on, produce, direct, perform, mount, present. **2** *stage a protest rally* arrange, organize, engineer, orchestrate, put together, lay on.

stagger v **1** *stagger drunkenly up the road* reel, sway, teeter, totter, wobble, lurch, pitch, roll. **2** *staggered by the price of the toys* amaze, astound, dumbfound, astonish, flabbergast, shock, shake, confound, nonplus, take aback, take one's breath away, stupefy, stun; *inf* strike dumb. **3** *stagger the lines of bricks* alternate, step.

stagnant adj **1** *stagnant water* still, unflowing, motionless, standing, foul, stale, dirty, filthy, polluted, putrid, putrefied, brackish. **2** *stagnant business/economy* sluggish, slowmoving, quiet, inactive, dull, static.

stagnate v **1** *water stagnating in weed-covered pools* stand, vegetate; become stagnant/still/foul/stale/dirty/filthy; fester, putrefy. *see* STAGNANT 1. **2** *businesses/economies stagnating* become stagnant, do nothing, be sluggish, lie dormant, be inert. *see* STAGNANT 2. **3** *stagnating waiting for a job to turn up* vegetate, idle, be idle, laze, loaf, hang about, languish.

staid adj *staid old gentleman/ladies* sedate, quiet, serious, serious-minded, grave, solemn, sombre, sober, proper, decorous, formal, prim, demure, stiff, starchy; *inf* stuffy, stick-in-the-mud.

stain v **1** *material permanently stained with blood/rust* soil, mark, discolour, dirty, spot, blotch, blemish, smudge, smear, besmirch, begrime. **2** *stain her reputation* blacken, tarnish, sully, blemish, damage, mar, injure, defame, denigrate, dishonour, besmirch, defile, taint, blot, slur. **3** *stain the wood* varnish, dye, paint, colour.

stain n **1** *unable to remove the stains made by the blood* mark, spot, blotch, blemish, smudge, smear. **2** *stains on her character* blemish, damage, injury, taint, blot, slur, stigma. **3** *use a brown stain on the wood* varnish, dye, paint, colourant.

stake[1] n *stakes for plants to grow up* post, pole, stick, upright, rod, spike, pale.

stake[1] v **1** *stake the rose bushes* support, prop up, hold up, brace, tether. **2** *stake off his garden with posts* mark off, mark out, separate off, demarcate, define, delimit, bound, circumscribe. **3** *stake a claim to part of the estate* establish, declare, state, lay claim to.

stake[2] n **1** *card-players laying down £50 stakes each* wager, bet, ante. **2** *have a stake in the firm* financial interest, interest, share, investment, involvement, concern.

stake[2] v *stake £10 on the race | stake his life on the outcome* wager, bet, place a bet of, put on, gamble, pledge, chance, venture, risk, hazard.

stakes npl *the stakes in a horse-race* prizemoney, purse, winnings.

stale adj **1** *stale bread/cheese* unfresh, dry, dried-out, hard, hardened, mouldy, decayed. **2** *stale air* unfresh, stuffy, close, musty, fusty. **3** *stale beer* flat, sour, turned, spoiled; *inf* off. **4** *stale jokes* hackneyed, tired, worn-out, threadbare, banal, trite, stock, stereotyped, clichéd, run-of-the-mill, commonplace, platitudinous, unoriginal, unimaginative, uninspired, flat, insipid, vapid; *inf* old hat.

stalemate n *reach stalemate in their talks* dead-lock, impasse, standstill, stand-off.

stalk n *the stalk of a plant* stem, branch, shoot, twig.

stalk v **1** *hunters stalking deer* pursue, chase, give chase to, follow, shadow, trail, track down, creep up on, hunt; *inf* tail. **2** *stalk haughtily out of the room* stride, march, flounce, strut, prance. **3** *raiders stalking the land* move threateningly through, pervade, permeate.

stall n **1** *stalls in a market* booth, stand, table, counter. **2** *animals in their stalls* pen, coop, sty, corral, compartment, cubicle.

stall v **1** *stall until he thinks of the answer* play for time, use delaying tactics, delay, beat about the bush, hem and haw; *inf* drag one's feet. **2** *stall his creditors* hold off, stave off, keep at bay, keep at arm's length, evade, avoid.

stalwart adj **1** *healthy stalwart young men* strong, sturdy, robust, hardy, muscular, brawny, strapping, powerfully built, burly, rugged, lusty; *inf* husky. **2** *stalwart adventurers* brave, courageous, valiant, valorous, intrepid, fearless, manly, heroic, indomitable, bold, daring, plucky, spirited, adventurous; *inf* gutsy.

stamina n endurance, staying power, indefatigability, resistance, resilience, fortitude, strength, vigour, energy, staunchness, robustness, toughness; *inf* grit, guts.

stammer v *stammer nervously* stutter, stumble, mumble, splutter, hesitate, falter, pause.

stammer n *have a stammer when he's nervous* stutter, speech impediment, speech defect.

stamp v **1** *stamp on the poisonous insect* trample, step on, tread on, trample on, crush, squash. **2** *stamp his name on the book* imprint, inscribe, engrave, emboss, mark, sign. **3** *her last words stamped on her mind* imprint, impress, fix. **4** *he was stamped as a criminal* brand, characterize, designate, identify, categorize, style, term, label, dub, name, tag. **stamp out** *stamp out the rebellion* quash, suppress, put down, quell, crush, squelch, extinguish, scotch, put an end to, eradicate, eliminate.

stamp n **1** *have the stamp of genius* mark, hallmark, label, brand, tag, characteristics, quality. **2** *a man of a different stamp* kind, sort, type, variety, class, classification, form, breed, kidney, mould, cast, cut.

stampede n *run over by the stampede of the cattle* charge, rush, flight, scattering.

stampede v *the animals stampeded in fear | the shoppers stampeded to the sales* charge, rush, flee, take flight, dash, race, run.

stance n *take up a liberal stance on the issue* stand, standpoint, position, line, policy, attitude, angle, slant, viewpoint, point of view, opinion.

stand v **1** *ask the children to stand* be upright, be erect, rise, rise to one's feet, get to one's feet, get up. **2** *a village once stood there* be situated, be located. **3** *stand the ladder against the wall* set, place, put, position. **4** *stand and listen* stop, halt, come to a halt, come to a standstill. **5** *their offer/orders stand* remain/be in force, remain/be valid, remain/be effective, hold, hold good, obtain, prevail, be the case. **6** *unable to stand his attitude* put up with, tolerate, bear, take, endure, abide, suffer, brook, countenance, cope with, handle; *inf* stomach, wear. **stand by 1** *stand by his friend* stand up for, support, be supportive of, back, uphold, be loyal to, defend, come to the defence of, stick up for, champion, take someone's part, take the side of, side with. **2** *stand by his word* adhere to,

hold for, stick to, observe. **3** *soldiers asked to stand by* wait, be prepared, be ready for action. **stand for 1** *What do the initials stand for?* represent, mean, signify, denote, indicate, betoken, imply, symbolize, exemplify, illustrate. **2** *he stands for all that is good* advocate, favour, support, back, uphold, promote, argue for, speak in favour of, subscribe to. **3** *refuse to stand for her behaviour* put up with, tolerate, bear, take, endure, suffer, brook, countenance; *inf* stomach, wear. **stand in for** *stand in for the headmaster when he was ill | stand in for the leading lady* deputize for, act as deputy for, take the place of, replace, act as substitute for, do duty for, cover for, hold the fort for, act as understudy, understudy, act as locum for. **stand out 1** *sculptures standing out from the building* project, jut out, protrude, extend, stick out, poke out. **2** *in that dress she stood out in the crowd* be noticeable, be noticed, be conspicuous, be striking, be distinctive, be prominent, attract attention, catch the eye; *inf* stick out a mile, stick out like a sore thumb. **stand up 1** *that argument will not stand up in court* be valid, be sound, have force, be well-founded, be well-grounded, be effective, be plausible. **2** *stand her up on a date* fail to meet, fail to keep an appointment with, fail to turn up for, let down. **stand up for 1** *stand up for his friend in his trouble* stand by, support, be supportive of, defend, come to the defence of, stick up for, champion. *see* STAND V STAND BY 1. **2** *stand up for what one believes* uphold, promote, argue for, speak in favour of. **stand up to** *stand up to the bully* confront, face up to, oppose openly, show resistance to, brave, defy, challenge.

stand n **1** *come to a stand* standstill, halt, stop, stoppage, rest. **2** *take up a stand against the new policies* firm stand, defensive position, resistance, opposition. **3** *take a liberal stand* stance, standpoint, position, line, policy, attitude. *see* STANCE. **4** *stands in the market-place* stall, booth, table, counter. **5** *put books in stands* display case, shelf, rack, frame, base. **6** *give a speech from the stand in the hall* platform, stage, staging, dais, rostrum. **7** *a taxi stand* rank, station, place.

standard n **1** *a standard by which quality is judged* yardstick, benchmark, gauge, measure, criterion, guide, guideline, norm, touchstone, model, pattern, example, exemplar, paradigm, ideal, archetype, specification, requirement, rule, principle, law, canon. **2** *works of a low standard* level, grade, quality, evaluation, worth, merit. **3** *raise the battle standard* flag, banner, pennant, streamer, ensign, colours. **4** *trees supported by standards* support, prop, post, pole, cane, upright. **5** *maintain old-fashioned standards* principle, code of behaviour, code of honour, morals, ethics, ideals.

standard adj **1** *standard behaviour* | *standard shoe sizes* usual, ordinary, average, normal, habitul, common, regular, stock, set, fixed, conventional. **2** *the standard work on Shakespeare* definitive, established, classic, recognized, approved, accepted, authoritative, official.

standardize v *standardize procedures* make uniform, regulate, systematize, normalize, homogenize, regiment, bring into line.

stand-in n *act as a stand-in for the teacher/actor/doctor* representative, deputy, substitute, second, proxy, understudy, locum, right-hand man/woman/person.

standing n **1** *his standing in the community* status, rank, ranking, social position, position, station, footing, place, circumstances. **2** *people of standing in the community* reputation, good reputation, repute, eminence, prominence, note, noteworthiness. **3** *her husband of many years standing* duration, length of time, existence, continuance, endurance.

standing adj **1** *standing stones* upright, erect, vertical, upended, perpendicular; *Herald* rampant. **2** *standing water* still, stagnant, static, motionless. **3** *a standing army/invitation* permanent, fixed, regular, perpetual, constant.

stand-off n *the two sides have reached a stand-off* deadlock, impasse, stalemate.

standoffish adj aloof, distant, cold, cool, reserved, withdrawn, remote, detached, unapproachable, unfriendly, unsociable, haughty, disdainful.

standpoint n *from the standpoint of the customer* point of view, viewpoint, opinion, perspective, angle, slant, frame of reference.

standstill adj *factories/talks coming to a standstill* halt, stop, dead stop, stoppage, rest, pause, cessation, stand.

staple adj *staple foods* chief, primary, main, principal, foremost, leading, basic, fundamental, essential, indispensable, necessary, important, vital.

star n **1** *stars in the sky* heavenly body, celestial body, planet, planetoid, asteroid. **2** *born under a lucky star* astral influence, destiny, fate, fortune, lot. **3** *read his stars* horoscope, forecast, augury. **4** *one of the stars of the film* principal, leading lady, leading man, lead, name, superstar. **5** *some of the stars on the* local council celebrity, dignitary, notable, name, somebody, VIP; *inf* bigwig, big shot, big cheese, big wheel.

star adj *one of her star pupils* brilliant, great, talented, gifted, celebrated, illustrious, renowned, famous, distinguished, prominent, eminent, pre-eminent, principal, chief, leading, major.

stare v **1** *stare into space* gaze, gape, goggle, look; *inf* gawp, gawk. **2** *the solution was staring them in the face* be conspicuous, be obvious, be blatant, stand out, be prominent, stick out, glare.

stark adj **1** *in stark contrast* sharp, sharply delineated, sharply defined, obvious, evident, clear, clear-cut. **2** *a stark landscape* desolate, bare, barren, arid, vacant, empty, forsaken, bleak, dreary, depressing, grim, harsh; *lit* drear. **3** *stark attire* austere, severe, plain, simple, unadorned, unembellished, undecorated. **4** *stark madness* sheer, utter, absolute, downright, out-and-out, outright, total, complete, thorough, thoroughgoing, pure, unmitigated, unqualified, consummate, unmissable, patent, palpable, rank, arrant. **5** *the stark facts* bald, bare, simple, blunt, straightforward, unadorned, unembellished, harsh, grim. **6** *the stark figure of a man* naked, nude, bare, stark naked. *see* STARK adv STARK NAKED.

stark adv *stark staring mad* completely, totally, entirely, wholly, altogether, utterly, absolutely, quite. **stark naked** naked, nude, in the nude, bare, stripped, undressed, unclad, as naked as the day one was born, in a state of nature; *inf* in the buff, in the altogether, in the raw, in one's birthday suit, starkers.

start v **1** *events starting in the morning* begin, commence, get underway, get going; *inf* kick off. **2** *when her illness started* commence, get underway, get going, begin, commence, appear, come into being, come into existence, arise, originate, crop up, first see the light of day. **3** *have to start now to finish the job in time* begin, commence, make a start, make a beginning, get going, go ahead, set things moving, buckle to/down, turn to, put one's shoulder to the wheel, put one's hand to the plough, start the ball rolling; *inf* get moving, get down to it, get down to business, get one's finger out, get the show on the road, take the plunge, kick off, pitch in, get off one's backside. **4** *start now to be there by tonight* start out, set out, set off, depart, leave, make a start; *inf* hit the road, hit the trail, push off, get the show on the road. **5** *start the machine* set in motion, set moving, turn on, start functioning, start operating, activate. **6** *the machine started up* begin working, start functioning, start operating. **7** *start the campaign* | *start up the business* set up, establish, found, lay the foundations of, lay the corner-stone of, create, institute, initiate, launch, get going, originate, pioneer, organize. **8** *start in pain* jump, leap up, jerk, twitch, recoil, shrink, flinch, blench, wince, shy. **9** *animals suddenly starting out of the bushes* jump, leap, spring, bound, dart.

start n **1** *present at the start of the event* beginning, commencement, opening, inception, inauguration, dawn, birth; *inf* kick-off. **2** *at the start of her illness* beginning, commencement, onset, emergence, first appearance. **3** *the start of the trouble* origin, source, root, basis, derivation, wellspring. **4** *at the start of the campaign* establishment, foundation, institution, launch, origination. *see* START v 7. **5** *get a start in the race* head start, advantage, advantageous position. **6** *get a start in life* good start, advantageous beginnings, opening, opportunity, chance, helping hand, encouragement, introduction, embarking, sponsorship, patronage; *inf* break. **7** *give a start in pain* jump, leap, jerk, twitch, flinch, blench, wince, spasm, convulsion.

startle v *a loud noise startled the children* | *startled by the news* make one jump, disturb, agitate, perturb, unsettle, scare, frighten, alarm, surprise, astonish, shock; *inf* give one a turn.

startling adj *some starling news* | *a startling result* disturbing, unsettling, alarming, surprising, unexpected, unforeseen, astonishing, amazing, staggering, shocking, extraordinary, remarkable.

starvation n extreme hunger, lack of food, death from lack of food, fasting, famine, undernourishment, malnourishment.

starving adj starved, famished, ravenous, very hungry, faint from lack of food, dying from lack of food, fasting; *inf* able to eat a horse.

state n **1** *in a state of readiness* | *in its previous state* condition, shape, situation, circumstances, state of affairs, position, predicament, plight. **2** *in a calm/nervous state* condition, mood, humour, spirits, frame of mind, attitude. **3** *she often gets into a state* state of agitation, anxiety, nerves, panic, distressed state, fluster, pother; *inf* flap, tizzy, tiz-woz. **4** *look at the state of this room* untidy state, untidiness, mess, chaos, disorder, disarray, disorganization, confusion, clutter. **5** *a meeting of the world's states* country, nation, land, realm, kingdom, republic,

territory, federation, commonwealth, body politic. **6** *feel the state is too powerful* government, parliament, the administration, the establishment. **7** *occasions of state* pomp, ceremony, display, dignity, majesty, grandeur, glory, splendour.

state v *state one's objections* express, voice, utter, say, tell, declare, set out, lay down, affirm, assert, announce, make known, reveal, disclose, divulge, pronounce, articulate, aver, proclaim, present, expound, promulgate.

stated adj *at the stated times* set, settled, fixed, agreed, declared, determined, approved, authorized, ruled, ordained, accredited, official.

stately adj *stately occasions* ceremonial, dignified, solemn, majestic, royal, regal, magnificent, grand, glorious, splendid, elegant, imposing, impressive, august, lofty, pompous; slow-moving, measured, deliberate.

statement n *a statement of one's views* declaration, account, recitation, report, affirmation, assertion, announcement, revelation, disclosure, divulgence, pronouncement, articulation, averment, proclamation, presentation, expounding, promulgation.

static adj *static house prices/pressure* unmoving, unvarying, undeviating, changeless, constant, stable, steady, stationary, motionless, at a standstill, frozen.

station n **1** *trains stopping at several stations* stop, stopping-place. **2** *get the bus at the bus station* terminus, terminal, depot. **3** *police station* depot, base, office, headquarters, seat. **4** *security staff at their appointed stations* post, place, position, location, site. **5** *from different stations in life* class, level, rank, grade, standing, status, caste.

stationary adj **1** *stationary traffic* unmoving, motionless, at a standstill, parked. **2** *stationary price patterns* changeless, unchanging, constant, unvarying, invariable, undeviating.

statue n statuette, sculpture, effigy, figure, figurine, representation, likeness, image, bust, head.

statuesque adj *statuesque figures/woman* dignified, stately, majestic, noble, magnificent, splendid, imposing, impressive, regal, well-proportioned, handsome, beautiful.

stature n **1** *ill-developed in stature* height, tallness, size, altitude. **2** *post demanding people of stature* status, importance, import, standing, consequence, eminence, pre-eminence, prominence, note, fame, renown.

status n *of uncertain social status* standing, rank, level, grade, degree, position, importance, reputation, consequence.

staunch adj *staunch supporters* loyal, faithful, dependable, reliable, steady, constant, stable, firm, steadfast, unswerving, unwavering, unhesitating, unfaltering.

stave v **stave in** *stave in the side of door* break in, smash in, put a hole in, push in, cave in, splinter, shiver, fracture. **stave off** *stave off their attack* ward off, fend off, evade, avert, avoid, dodge, keep at bay, keep at arm's length, repel, repulse, rebuff.

stay v **1** *stay there till we call you* remain, wait, stay put, continue, linger, pause, rest, delay, tarry. **2** *stay loyal to him* remain, continue, go on. **3** *stay at a hotel | stay with her mother for a few days* lodge at, take a room at, put up at, be accommodated at, sojourn at, visit, reside at, take up residence, dwell at, live at. **4** *stay judgement until tomorrow* put off, postpone, suspend, adjourn, defer, hold over, hold in abeyance, delay, prorogue. **5** *stay the progress of the disease* check, curb, arrest, stop, delay, hold, prevent, hinder, impede, obstruct.

stay n **1** *a brief stay at a hotel* visit, sojourn, stop, stopover, holiday, vacation. **2** *a stay of judgement* postponement, suspension, adjournment, deferment, delay. **3** *a stay in his old age* prop, underprop, support, brace, bolster, buttress.

staying power n endurance, stamina, resistance, resilience, fortitude, strength, vigour, energy, staunchness, robustness, toughness; *inf* grit, guts.

steadfast adj **1** *a steadfast friend* faithful, loyal, true, constant, devoted, dedicated, trustworthy, dependable, reliable, staunch. **2** *a steadfast refusal to help | steadfast in his views* steady, firm, determined, resolute, unchanging, unwavering, unfaltering, unswerving, unyielding, inflexible, uncompromising, relentless, implacable. **3** *a steadfast gaze* steady, fixed, intent, immovable, unwavering, unfaltering.

steady adj **1** *make the posts steady* firmly fixed, firm, fixed, stable, secure, immovable. **2** *a steady hand* still, unshaking, motionless, unmoving, sure. **3** *a steady gaze* steadfast, fixed, immovable, unwavering, unfaltering. **4** *a steady faith* constant, unchanging, changeless, unvarying, invariable, undeviating, continuous, continual, unceasing, ceaseless, perpetual, persistent, unremitting, unwavering, unfaltering, unfluctuating, undying, unending, endless. **5** *walk at a steady pace* uniform, even, regular, rhythmic, consistent. **6** *a steady boyfriend* regular, habitual, usual, customary. **7** *a steady young man* well-balanced, balanced, sensible, level-headed, rational, settled, down-to-earth, calm, equable, imperturbable, reliable, dependable, serious-minded, serious.

steady v **1** *steady the ladder* make steady, hold steady, stabilize, secure, balance, support. **2** *steady one's nerves* calm, calm down, settle, compose, tranquillize, control, get a grip on.

steal v **1** *steal money from the old lady* thieve, take, appropriate, misappropriate, pilfer, purloin, filch, walk off with, embezzle, pocket, abstract, shoplift, peculate; *inf* pinch, nick, snitch, swipe, lift, rip off. **2** *steal someone else's work* plagiarize, copy, pirate, appropriate, poach; *inf* lift, crib. **3** *steal a child* kidnap, snatch, abduct, carry off, make off with, seize, shanghai. **4** *steal a kiss | steal a few hour's sleep* snatch, obtain stealthily, get surreptitiously. **5** *steal out of the room* slip, slide, tiptoe, sneak, creep, slink, slither, flit, glide.

steal n **1** *taking that money was a steal* theft, robbery, misappropriation, pilfering, larceny; embezzlement, peculation; *inf* pinching, nicking. *see* STEAL v 1. **2** *her new dress was a steal* bargain buy, bargain, good buy, cheap buy; *inf* giveaway. **3** *getting into the house secretly was a steal* easy job, simple task; *inf* cinch, piece of cake, child's play, picnic, pushover.

stealing n **1** *found guilty of stealing* theft, thieving, thievery, robbery, larceny, burglary, appropriation, misappropriation, pilfering, pilferage, purloining, filching, embezzlement, shoplifting, peculation; *inf* pinching, nicking, swiping. *see* STEAL v 1. **2** *guilty of the stealing of other people's work* plagiarizing, copying, piracy, appropriation, poaching; *inf* lifting, cribbing. **3** *the stealing of children* kidnapping, snatching, abduction, seizure, shanghaiing. *see* STEAL v 3.

stealth n *get into the house by stealth* stealthiness, secrecy, furtiveness, surreptitiousness, slyness, sneakiness, clandestineness, covertness, shadiness.

stealthy adj *stealthy movements/manoeuvres* secret, furtive, surreptitious, sly, sneaky, clandestine, covert, shady, underhand, undercover.

steam n **1** *boiling water giving off steam* vapour, fume, smoke, exhalation. **2** *run out of steam | have no steam left* energy, vigour, vigourousness, vitality, stamina, power, force. **let off steam** use up energy, release surplus energy, give vent to one's feelings, lose one's inhibitions, let oneself go; *inf* let it all hang out. **under one's own steam** *get the job under one's own steam* unaided, unassisted, without help, by oneself, by one's own efforts, on one's own two feet.

steam v *steaming along the road to the bus stop* rush, race, run, dash, charge, sprint, hurry, speed, hasten; *inf* tear, zoom, zip. **get all steamed up** get agitated, get excited, get flustered, get hot and bothered, get angry, get annoyed, get furious; *inf* lose one's cool. **steam up** *windscreens steaming up* become misty/misted, become blurry/blurred, become cloudy/clouded.

steamy adj **1** *a steamy atmosphere* humid, muggy, sticky, moist, damp, sweltering, boiling, like a Turkish bath, like a sauna. **2** *steamy love scenes in the film* erotic, sexy, passionate, tempestuous, sensuous, lustful, wanton.

steel n **1** *men of steel* strength, fortitude, hardiness, courage, bravery, valour, intrepidity, pluck, mettle, nerve; *inf* grit, guts. **2** *a grip of steel* firmness, solidness, hardness. **steel oneself** *steel herself to have the operation* brace oneself, harden oneself, nerve oneself, get up courage, screw up courage, screw one's courage to the sticking point.

steely adj **1** *a steely colour* steel-coloured, grey, blue-grey, steel-grey, iron-grey. **2** *steely eyes* hard, harsh, severe, unfeeling, unsympathetic, cruel, ruthless, pitiless. **3** *steely determination* firm, determined, resolute, undaunted, unyielding, inflexible, unwavering, unfaltering.

steep adj **1** *steep cliffs* sheer, abrupt, precipitous, sudden, sharp, perpendicular, vertical, declivitous, acclivitous. **2** *a steep rise in share prices* sharp, rapid, sudden, precipitate. **3** *prices at that restaurant are a bit steep* high, dear, costly, expensive, unreasonable, excessive, exorbitant; *inf* over the top, OTT. **4** *demands considered too steep* unreasonable, excessive, exorbitant, immoderate, inordinate, unwarranted; *inf* over the top, OTT.

steep v **1** *steep the stained clothes in cold water* soak, saturate, immerse, submerge, wet through, drench, souse, macerate. **2** *steep the meat in wine* marinade, marinate, soak, souse. **3** *a family steeped in misery* imbue, permeate, pervade, infuse, suffuse, fill. **4** *they were steeped in the classics* submerge, immerse, saturate, make thoroughly conversant with, make closely acquainted with.

steeple n spire, tower, church tower, bell tower, campanile, turret, minaret.

steer v **1** *steer the car/boat* guide, navigate, drive, pilot, be in the driver's seat of, be at the wheel of. **2** *steer the guests to the garden* | *steer the conversation back to the subject* guide, lead, direct, conduct, usher. **steer clear of** *steer clear of his ex-wife* keep away from, keep one's distance from, keep at arm's length, give a wide berth to, avoid, evade, dodge, eschew, shun.

stem n **1** *the stem of a bush* trunk, stock, peduncle. **2** *flowers/foliage on a stem* stalk, shoot, branch, twig. **stem from** *troubles stemming from poverty* arise from, originate from, have its origins in, be rooted in, derive from, spring from, emanate from, issue from, proceed from, be caused by, be brought about by.

stem v *stem the flow of blood* check, stop, halt, hold back, contain, curb, dam, staunch.

stench n stink, foul smell, foul odour, reek, mephitis; *lit* noisomeness; *inf* pong, whiff, niff.

stentorian adj stentorious, booming, roaring, thundering, thunderous, trumpeting, ear-splitting, resonant, vibrant, powerful, loud, strong, full.

step n **1** *reach her in one step* stride, pace. **2** *hear steps on the stairs* footstep, footfall, tread, tramp. **3** *police examining steps in the mud* footstep, footprint, print, impression, track. **4** *walk with a cheerful step* walk, gait, bearing, carriage. **5** *live just a step away* short distance, pace, stone's throw, spitting distance. **6** *the steps of a ladder* rung, tread. **7** *take a foolish step* course of action, move, act, action, deed, measure, manoeuvre, procedure, expedient, effort. **8** *another step towards international peace* step forward, advance, advancement, development, progression, stage, move. **9** *another step in his promotion* stage, level, grade, rank, degree. **in step** *in step with the views of the committee* in agreement, in accord with, in harmony with, in line with, in concurrence with, in conformity with, in consensus with, in unison with. **mind/watch one's step 1** *mind/watch your step on the broken pavement* step carefully, walk carefully, tread cautiously. **2** *mind/watch your step when doing business with him* be careful, be cautious, be wary, be circumspect, be chary, take care, take heed, be attentive, be on one's guard, look out, have one's wits about one, mind how one goes. **out of step** *out of step with modern thinking* in disagreement with, at odds with, out of line with, at variance with, in opposition to, at loggerheads with. **step by step** *follow the instructions step by step* by stages, by degrees, progressively, through all the gradations, gradually, bit by bit, slowly. **take steps** *take steps to control expenditure* take action, take measures, act, take the initiative, prepare, get ready.

step v *step lightly down the street* walk, tread, stride, pace, move, advance, proceed; *inf* hoof it. **step down** *step down to make way for a younger person* resign, give up one's post/job, retire, abdicate. **step in** *the police had to step in to prevent a murder* intervener, intercede, become involved, act, take action, take measures, take a hand; *inf* clip on. **step on** *step on dog dirt* walk on, tread on, tramp on, trample on. **step up 1** *police stepping up their efforts* increase, boost, augment, intensify, escalate. **2** *step up the pace of production* increase, speed up, accelerate, raise up.

stereotype n *the stereotype of a sergeant major* conventional type, received idea, standardized image, hackneyed conception, cliché.

stereotype v *stereotype librarians as being serious people* typecast, pigeonhole, conventionalize, standardize, label, tag, categorize.

stereotyped adj *stereotyped images of a woman's role* typecast, conventional, conventionalized, standardized, hackneyed, clichéd, banal, trite, platitudinous.

sterile adj **1** *sterile women* infertile, barren, infecund, unprolific. **2** *sterile soil/land* infertile, unproductive, unfruitful, unyielding, arid, dry, barren, unprolific. **3** *sterile discussions* unproductive, unfruitful, fruitless, useless, futile, vain, idle, unsuccessful, ineffectual, ineffective, worthless, abortive, unprofitable, unrewarding. **4** *sterile conditions in the operating theatre* sterilized, germ-free, germless, antiseptic, disinfected, aseptic, uninfected, uncontaminated, unpolluted, pure, clean.

sterility n **1** *the sterility of the woman* sterileness, infertility, barrenness, infecundity, unprolificness. **2** *the sterility of the soil/land* sterileness, infertility, non-productivity, unproductiveness, unfruitfulness, aridness, aridity. *see* STERILE 2. **3** *the sterility of the discussions* sterileness, unproductiveness, unfruitfulness, fruitlessness, uselessness, futility, unsuccessfulness, ineffectualness, ineffectiveness, worthlessness, abortiveness. *see* STERILE 3. **4** *the sterility of the operating theatre* sterileness, freedom from germs, asepticism, lack of infection/contamination/pollution, purity, cleanliness.

sterilize v **1** *sterilize surgical instruments* disinfect, purify, fumigate. **2** *sterilize a woman* make infertile, make barren, make infecund. **3** *sterilize a man* make infertile, castrate, vasectomize. **4** *sterilize male animals* castrate, geld, neuter, emasculate; *inf* fix. **5** *sterilize female animals* make infertile, spay; *inf* fix.

sterling adj **1** *have done sterling service* excellent, first-rate, first-class, exceptional, outstanding, splendid, superlative; *inf* A1. **2** *sterling friends* genuine, real, true, reliable, dependable, trustworthy, faithful, loyal.

stern adj **1** *stern treatment | a stern regime* strict, harsh, hard, severe, rigorous, stringent, rigid, exacting, demanding, cruel, relentless, unsparing, inflexible, unyielding, authoritarian, tyrannical, despotic, Draconian. **2** *look very stern | a stern expression* severe, forbidding, frowning, unsmiling, sombre, sober, austere.

stern n *the stern of the ship* back, rear, tail, poop.

stew v **1** *stew the meat* simmer, boil, casserole, fricassee. **2** *be stewing waiting for the results* be anxious, be nervous, be agitated, worry, fret, agonize, get in a panic, get worked up, get overwrought; *inf* get in a flap, get in a tizz, get in a tiz-woz. **3** *people stewing in the heat* swelter, be very hot, perspire, sweat; *inf* be boiling.

stew n **1** *make a beef stew* casserole, ragout, fricassee. **2** *get in a stew about the lost document* state of agitation, nervous state, fluster, panic, dither, pother; *inf* flap, tizz, tiz-woz.

steward n **1** *air stewards* cabin attendant, member of cabin staff. **2** *stewards at the horse show* official, functionary, organizer. **3** *club/bar stewards* caterer, catering manager/manageress, house-keeper, major-domo, butler. **4** *the steward of the estate* property manager, agent, bailiff, caretaker; *Scots* factor.

stick n **1** *throw a stick for the dog | burn sticks and leaves from the garden* piece of wood, branch, twig, switch. **2** *old men leaning on sticks* walking stick, cane, crutch, staff, crook, alpenstock. **3** *sticks supporting plants* cane, pole, post, stake, upright. **4** *punish the boy with a stick* cane, birch, switch, rod. **5** *mug the old man with a stick* cosh, cudgel, truncheon, baton. **6** *get stick for his handling of the situation* criticism, abuse, blame, censure, reproach, reproof, condemnation. **7** *get stick from the headmaster* punishment, chastisement, discipline, beating. **the sticks** *bored with living in the sticks* remote area, rural districts, backwoods, hinterland, backwater; *inf* the middle of no-where, boondock.

stick v **1** *stick a fork in the potato* thrust, push, insert, jab, poke. **2** *stick his head out the window* thrust, push, poke. **3** *a nail sticking into the tyre | a needle sticking into his finger* pierce, penetrate, puncture, prick, spear, stab. **4** *stick him through with a sword* stab, speaar, run through, transfix, impale. **5** *stick the pictures to a sheet of paper* glue, paste, gum, tape, sellotape, fasten, attach, fix, pin, tack. **6** *events which stick in the mind* remain, stay, linger, dwell, lodge, persist, continue. **7** *the car stuck in the mud* become bogged down, become embedded, become lodged, become clogged up, be mixed, become immobilized, be unable to move. **8** *machines sticking* jam, become jammed, come to a stand still, stop, halt, come to a halt, cease to work, become inoperative. **9** *stick the books over there* put, set down, place, lay, deposit, drop, position, locate, site, plant; *inf* plonk, stuff. **10** *make the accusation stick* be valid, be sound, be well-founded, be well-grounded, be convincing, be cogent, be persuasive, be relevant. **11** *she can't stick his behaviour* put up with, tolerate, bear, stand, take, abide, endure, stomach. **stick at 1** *you'll have to stick at it to finish the job today* keep at, persist with, persevere with, work at; *inf* put one's back into. **2** *he would stick at walking out* draw back from, recoil from, shrink from, balk at, demur, have scruples about. **stick by** *stick by his friend in his misfortune* stand by, be loyal to, remain faithful to, support, be supportive of, back, defend. **stick it out** *the work's hard but he'll stick it out* see it through, see it through to the end, last out, put up with it, endure it, grin and bear it, soldier on; *inf* take it, hang in there, tough it out. **stick out 1** *sculptures sticking out from the wall* stand out, jut out, project, extend, protrude, poke out, bulge. **2** *she stuck out in the crowd* stand out, be noticeable, be obvious, be obtrusive.

sticky adj **1** *sticky tape* adhesive, adherent, gummy, gluey, tacky. **2** *sticky substances* gluey, treacly, glutinous, viscous, viscoid; *inf* gooey. **3** *a sticky summer day* close, humid, muggy, clammy, sultry, sweltering, oppressive. **4** *a sticky situation* awkward, difficult, tricky, ticklish, delicate, thorny, touch-and-go, embarrassing; *inf* hairy.

stiff adj **1** *stiff cardboard/substance* rigid, inflexible, unyielding, inelastic, firm, hard, hardened, brittle. **2** *stiff muscles* unsupple, tight, tense, taut, aching, arthritic, rheumatic; *inf* creaky. **3** *a stiff climb/task* difficult, hard, arduous, tough, laborious, exacting, demanding, formidable, challenging, tiring, fatiguing, exhausting, Herculean. **4** *a stiff penalty* severe, harsh, hard, stringent, rigorous, drastic, strong, heavy, Draconian. **5** *put up a stiff resistance* strong, vigorous, determined, resolute, dogged, tenacious, unflagging, stubborn, obdurate. **6** *a stiff occasion* formal, ceremonial, ceremonious, dignified, proper, decorous, pompous. **7** *stiff behaviour* formal, unrelaxed, prim, punctilious, chilly, cold; *inf* starchy. **8** *a stiff drink* strong, potent, alcoholic. **9** *a stiff breeze* strong, vigorous, powerful, brisk, fresh.

stiffen v **1** *the mixture needs time to stiffen* become stiff, thicken, set, jell, solidify, harden, congeal, coagulate. **2** *need something to stiffen their resolve* strengthen, harden, fortify, brace, steel, reinforce. **3** *his muscles have stiffened* tighten, become stiff, tense, become taut, begin to ache, become arthritic/rheumatic; *inf* become creaky.

stifle v **1** *stifle a yawn* smother, check, restrain, keep back, hold back, hold in, withhold, choke back, muffle, suppress, curb, silence, prevent. **2** *stifle a rebellion* suppress, quash, quell, put an end to, put down, stop, extinguish, stamp out, crush, subdue, repress. **3** *stifle the old lady with a pillow* suffocate, smother, asphyxiate, choke. **4** *it's stifling in here* suffocating, very hot, sweltering, airless, close.

stigma n *the stigma formerly associated with illegitimacy* shame, disgrace, dishonour, slur, stain, taint.

still adj **1** *completely still bodies | asked to be still* motionless, unmoving, without moving, immobile, unstirring, inert, lifeless, stock-still, stationary, static. **2** *the house was completely still at night* quiet, silent, hushed, soundless, soundfree, noiseless, undisturbed. **3** *a still evening* calm, mild, tranquil, peaceful, serene, restful, windless, windfree, halcyon. **4** *a still pool/sea* calm, stagnant.

still n *in the still of the night* quietness, quiet, silence, hush, soundlessness, noiselessness, calmness, calm, tranquillity, peace, peacefulness, serenity.

still adv **1** *they are still here* at this time, yet, up to this time, even now, until now. **2** *he was badly injured but he's still getting better* nevertheless, however, in spite of that, notwithstanding, for all that.

still v **1** *try to still her fears* quiet, quieten, calm, settle, lull, pacify, soothe, allay, assuage, appease, silence, hush, subdue. **2** *the wind stilled* abate, die down, grow less, lessen, moderate, slacken, weaken.

stilted · stitch

stilted adj **1** *a stilted manner | a stilted way of speaking* stiff, unnatural, wooden, forced, laboured, constrained, unrelaxed, awkward. **2** *stilted prose* pompous, pretentious, high-flown, high-sounding, grandiloquent, pedantic, bombastic.

stimulant n **1** *act as a stimulant to the system* tonic, restorative, reviver, energizer, excitant, analeptic; *inf* pep-pill, upper, pick-me-up, bracer. **2** *act as a stimulant to further economic growth* stimulus, incentive, impetus, fillip, spur. *see* STIMULUS.

stimulate v *stimulate economic activity* act as a stimulus/incentive/impetus/fillip/spur, encourage, prompt, spur on, activate, stir up, excite, whip up, kindle, incite, instigate, foment, fan.

stimulating adj **1** *a stimulating drug* tonic, restoring, restorative, reviving, energizing, analeptic; *inf* pick-me-up. **2** *a stimulating lecture* interesting, exciting, stirring, thought-provoking, inspiring, exhilarating, rousing, intriguing, provoking, provocative.

stimulus n *act as a stimulus to economic growth* stimulant, incentive, fillip, spur, push, drive, encouragement, inducement, incitement, goad, jog, jolt; *inf* shot in the arm.

sting n **1** *get a sting from a nettle* prick, inflamed area, wound, injury. **2** *take the sting out of the burns* irritation, smarting, tingling, tingle, pain, hurt. **3** *the sting of unrequited love* pain, hurt, distress, anguish, agony, torture, torment. **4** *a sharp sting in his wit* sharpness, bite, edge, pungency, causticness, acrimony, malice, spite, venom. **5** *crooks bringing off a sting* swindle, fraud, cheating, fleecing; *inf* rip-off. *see* STING V 5.

sting v **1** *stung by a nettle/jelly-fish* prick, wound, injure, hurt. **2** *wounds stinging from the antiseptic solution | eyes stinging in the smoke* smart, tingle, burn, be irritated by. **3** *parents stung by their son's treatment of them* hurt, wound, distress, grieve, vex, pain, anguish, torture, torment, harrow. **4** *stung to shout about his rudeness* provoke, incense, anger, annoy, vex, rouse, stir up, drive, spur on, goad, move, motivate. **5** *stung by the dishonest dealer* swindle, defraud, cheat, fleece, gull, overcharge; *inf* do, rip off, take for a ride.

stingy adj mean, miserly, parsimonious, niggardly, tight-fisted, cheese-paring, penny-pinching; *inf* tight, cheap.

stink v **1** *the rotten meat stinks* smell bad, give off a bad smell, reek; *inf* smell to high heaven. **2** *his behaviour stinks* be very bad, be unpleasant, be nasty, be vile, be foul, be abhorrent, be despicable, be dishonest, be corrupt. **3** *his name stinks around here* be disreputable, be in disrepute, have a bad reputation, be in disgrace, be infamous, be tainted.

stink n **1** *rotten meat giving off a stink* bad smell, foul smell, stench, reek, malodour, malodorousness. **2** *the parents raised a stink about the teacher's behaviour* row, fuss, trouble, to-do, commotion, outcry, uproar, brouhaha; *inf* dust-up.

stint v *not to stint on the wine* skimp on, limit, restrict, hold back on, be sparing with, be economical with, be frugal with, be mean with, be parsimonious with, be niggardly with; *inf* be stingy with, be mingy with.

stipulate v *stipulate a delivery date as part of the argument* specify, set down, lay down, state clearly, demand, require, insist upon, make a condition of, make a point of, make a precondition/proviso of.

stipulation n *make several stipulations before signing the contract* specification, demand, requirement, condition, precondition, provision, proviso, prerequisite.

stir v **1** *stir the mixture* mix, blend, beat, whip. **2** *the child stirred in his sleep* move, quiver, tremble, twitch. **3** *the wind stirring the leaves* move, disturb, agitate, rustle. **4** *refuse to stir from the fireside* move, move an inch, budge, get up, leave, depart from. **5** *everyone stirring early on Christmas Day* get up, get out of bed, rise, rouse oneself, bestir oneself, move about, be up and about, be active; *inf* be up and doing, shake a leg, look lively. **6** *stir his imagination* stimulate, excite, rouse, awaken, waken, kindle, quicken, electrify, inspire. **7** *speakers stirring the men to action* stir up, rouse, incite, provoke, inflame, guard, spur, egg on, urge, encourage, motivate, drive, impel.

stir n *their arrival caused quite a stir in the village* excitement, commotion, disturbance, fuss, uproar, to-do, bustle, flurry, ferment, brouhaha.

stirring adj *a stirring tale of adventure* exciting, dramatic, thrilling, gripping, riveting, spirited, rousing, stimulating, moving, lively, animated, heady, passionate, impassioned.

stitch n *get a stitch after running* sharp pain, stabbing pain, stab of pain, shooting pain, pang, twinge, spasm.

stitch v **1** *stitch the cloth* sew, baste, seam. **2** *stitch the tear* sew, sew up, repair, mend, darn. **stich up** *stitched up by his fellow crimi-*

nals betray, cheat, trick, deceive, hoodwink, defraud, cozen, swindle.

stock n **1** *a stock of goods for sale* store, supply, range, selection, assortment, variety, collection, quantity. **2** *run out of stock before Christmas* supplies, goods, merchandise, wares, items/articles for sale, commodities. **3** *lay in a stock of wood for the winter* store, supply, stockpile, reserve, reservoir, accumulation, pile, heap, load, hoard, amassment, cache. **4** *rolling stock* equipment, apparatus, machinery, implements, appliances. **5** *employed to look after the farm stock* farm animals, livestock, cattle, cow, beasts, herds, sheep, flocks, pigs. **6** *the stock of the business* capital, funds, assets. **7** *have stock in the company* shares, investment, holding, money. **8** *his stock in the company is rising* standing, status, reputation, repute, position. **9** *of good peasant stock* descent, line of descent, lineage, ancestry, extraction, family, parentage, relatives, pedigree, genealogy, strain, breed, background. **10** *stock for soup/stews* bouillon. **11** *the stock of a tree* trunk, tree-trunk, stalk, stem, caudex. **12** *the stock of an implement* handle, haft, grip, shaft, shank. *see* STOCKS. **in stock** *a range of goods always in stock* for sale, on sale, available. **take stock of** *take stock of the situation before proceeding* review, weigh up, appraise, make an appraisal of; see how the land lies; *inf* size up.

stock adj **1** *stock sizes of clothes* standard, regular, average, readily available, widely available. **2** *stock items in a kitchen cupboard* regular, common, customary, staple, basic, fundamental, necessary, essential, indispensable. **3** *stock responses to his requests | stock jokes* usual, routine, run-of-the-mill, commonplace, conventional, traditional, stereotyped, clichéd, hackneyed, overused, worn-out, banal, trite.

stock v **1** *shops stocking children's clothes* sell, trade in, deal in, market, handle, supply, keep. **2** *stock the factory with modern machinery* equip, fit, outfit, kit out, furnish, accoutre, supply, provide. **stock up 1** *stock up the shelves* fill, fill up, load, replenish. **2** *stock up with logs for the winter* get in supplies of, obtain a store of, buy up, collect, gather, accumulate, amass, lay in, put away, put down, deposit, store up, stockpile, hoard; *inf* squirrel away, salt away.

stockings npl hosiery, hose, nylons.

stockpile v *stockpile logs for the winter* collect, gather, accumulate, amass, pile up, store, lay in, put away, put down, deposit; *inf* put away for a rainy day, squirrel away, salt away, stash.

stocks npl *a ship still on the stocks* supporting structure, support, framework, frame, timbers. **on the stocks** *the car he designed is still on the stocks* in preparation, under construction.

stock-still adv *stand stock-still* motionless, unmoving, without moving, immobile, immobilized, inert.

stocky adj heavy-set, thick-set, dumpy, stubby, stumpy, squat, chunky, solid, sturdy, mesomorphic.

stodgy adj **1** *stodgy food* heavy, solid, substantial, filling, starchy, leaden, indigestible. **2** *a stodgy young man* dull, uninteresting, boring, staid, sedate, stuffy; *inf* fuddy-duddy. **3** *stodgy prose* dull, dull as ditchwater, uninteresting, boring, tedious, dry, wearisome, heavy-going, unimaginative, uninspired, monotonous, laboured, wooden, turgid.

stoical adj *remain stoical in misfortune | stoical attitude to misfortune* impassive, dispassionate, unimpassioned, unemotional, self-controlled, self-disciplined, forbearing, patient, long-suffering, resigned, philosophical, fatalistic, imperturbable, calm, cool, unexcitable, unflappable, phlegmatic.

stoicism n *admire his stoicism in misfortune* impassivity, dispassion, self-control, self-discipline, forbearing, patience, long suffering, fortitude, endurance, resignation, acceptance, fatalism, philosophicalness, imperturbability, calmness, coolness, cool, phlegm.

stolid adj *difficult to engage the interest of the stolid child* impassive, unemotional, apathetic, uninterested, unimaginative, indifferent, dull, stupid, bovine, lumpish, wooden, doltish, thick, dense.

stomach n **1** *a pain in the stomach* abdomen, belly, paunch, potbelly; *inf* tummy, gut, insides, pot, corporation, bread-basket. **2** *have no stomach for rich food* appetite, taste, hunger. **3** *have no stomach for the battle* appetite, inclination, desire, liking, fancy, mind, taste, fondness, relish, zest, gusto.

stomach v **1** *unable to stomach rich food* eat, digest, swallow, find palatable. **2** *unable to stomach his arrogance* stand, put up with, bear, take, tolerate, abide, endure, suffer, swallow, submit to; *inf* weather.

stone n **1** *throwing stones on the road before* pebble, rock, boulder. **2** *an engagement ring set with three stones* precious stone, jewel, gem, brilliant; *inf* rock. **3** *erect a stone in his memory* tombstone, gravestone, headstone, memorial stone, monument. **4** *remove the* *stones from the fruit before cooking* kernel, pit, nut, seed, pip.

stony adj **1** *stony ground* rocky, pebbly, gravelly, shingly, gritty, rough, hard. **2** *a stony stare* cold, chilly, frosty, icy, frigid, hard, stern, severe, rigid, fixed, expressionless, blank, poker-faced, deadpan, sphinxlike. **3** *a stony heart* | *a stony attitude to the poor* unfeeling, uncaring, unsympathetic, insensitive, callous, heartless, tough, unmoved, unemotional, dispassionate, unresponsive, stern, severe, harsh, hard, cruel, coldhearted, merciless, pitiless, ruthless, unforgiving, inflexible, unbending, unyielding, adamant, obdurate.

stooge n **1** *the comedian's stooge* butt, foil. **2** *he gets his stooges to do all the work* dogsbody, underling, subordinate, assistant, deputy, right-hand man/woman, girl/man Friday; *inf* sidekick, skivvy.

stoop v **1** *stoop to pick something up* bend down, lean over, lean down, crouch down. **2** *stoop his head to get into the car* bend, bend down, bow, lower, duck. **3** *very tall people often stoop* walk with a stoop, be roundshouldered, hunch one's shoulders, bend one's head forward. **4** *never stoop to talk to her inferiors* condescend, deign, lower oneself to, humble oneself to, demean oneself to. **5** *refuse to stoop to crime* sink to, descend to, lower oneself to, demean oneself to, resort to.

stoop n **1** *with a slight stoop of her head* bending, bow, lowering, ducking. **2** *have a scholarly stoop* round-shoulderedness, hunch, droop/sag of the shoulders.

stop v **1** *stop the fight* bring to a stop, halt, bring to a halt, end, bring to an end, put an end to, finish, bring to a close, terminate, bring to a standstill, wind up, discontinue, cut short, interrupt, nip in the bud. **2** *unable to stop laughing* discontinue, cease from, refrain from, desist from, leave off, break off, quit, forbear from, abandon; *inf* knock off, pack in. **3** *work has stopped for the day* come to a stop, come to a halt, end, come to an end, finish, come to a close, be over, cease, conclude, terminate, come to a standstill, pause. **4** *stop the crooks from getting away* prevent, hinder, obstruct, impede, block, check. **5** *stop their getaway flight* prevent, hinder, obstruct, impede, hamper, block, check, curb, frustrate, thwart, foil, stall, restrain, bar; *inf* put the kibosh on. **6** *stop up a leak* plug, seal, block, bung, staunch, stem. **7** *stop off/over at York on the way to London* break one's journey, stay, remain, sojourn, put up, lodge, rest.

stop n **1** *come to a stop* halt, end, finish, close, cessation, conclusion, termination, standstill, stoppage, discontinuation, discontinuance. **2** *there are ten stops on the bus route* stopping-place, halt, stage, fare-stage, terminus, terminal, depot. **3** *stops on the railway line* stopping-place, station, halt, terminus, terminal, depot. **4** *put a stop at the end of the sentence* full stop, period, point. **5** *a stop in the leaking pipe* plug, bung, cork, stopper. **6** *aim for a stop at York* journeybreak, break, stop-off, stop-over, stay, sojourn, overnight, rest.

stopgap n temporary substitute, substitution, fill-in, makeshift, improvisation, expedient, last resort.

stop-over n *a stop-over halfway through the journey* stop, break, stop-off, stay. *see* STOP n 6.

stoppage n **1** *the stoppage of some forms of welfare benefit* stopping, halting, end, discontinuation, discontinuance, finish, cessation, termination. **2** *another stoppage at the factory* strike, walk-out, industrial action, shut-down. **3** *a stoppage in the pipe* blockage, obstruction, occlusion. **4** *a stoppage in the supply* obstruction, obstacle, impediment, check, snag. **5** *stoppages from their salaries* deduction, charge, subtraction.

stopper n **1** *the stopper in a bottle* cork, lid, cap, top. **2** *put a stopper in the leak* stop, plug, bung, cork.

store n **1** *a store of logs for the winter* supply, stock, stockpile, reserve, accumulation, pile, heap, load, amassment, cache, deposit, reservoir. *see* STORES. **2** *get supplies from the store* store-room, store-house, warehouse, repository, depository. **3** *build new houses and stores* shop, department store, chain store, supermarket, retail outlet, emporium. **set store by** think highly of, hold in regard, hold in high regard, hold in high esteem, admire, appreciate, value, prize, esteem.

store v **1** *store food in case of a shortage* stock up with, get in supplies of, stockpile, collect, gather, accumulate, amass, lay in, put away, put down, deposit, hoard; *inf* put away for a rainy day, squirrel away, salt away, stash. **2** *store furniture* put into storage, put in store.

stores npl *get low on stores* supplies, provisions, rations, food, provender.

storm n **1** *ships damaged in the storm* | *children soaked in the storm* gale, hurricane, cyclone, tempest, squall, cloudburst, downpour, torrent. **2** *a storm of protest at the decision* outcry, outburst, commotion, furore, brouhaha, clamour, tumult, row, disturbance, fight, trouble; *inf* to-do, rumpus, dust-up. **3** *engage in a storm on the castle* assault, attack, offensive, onslaught, charge, raid, foray, sortie, siege. **4** *a storm of missiles* shower, spray, deluge, volley, salvo, discharge.

storm v **1** *storm the castle* attack, conduct an offensive on, make an onslaught on, charge, rush, make a raid/foray/sortie on, take by storm. **2** *storm out of the room* charge, rush headlong, flounce, stake, stride, stamp; *inf* stomp. **3** *storming at the children because of their behaviour* rage, rant, rave, rant and rave, fume, bellow, thunder, shout, fly into temper; *inf* fly off the handle, blow one's top, blow up, raise the roof, raise hell.

stormy adj *stormy weather* | *a stormy day* blustery, blustering, windy, gusty, squally, rainy, wild, tempestuous, turbulent.

story n **1** *have a story published* | *read the children a story* short story, tale, fairy tale, fable, myth, legend, anecdote, novel, novella, romance, narrative, chronicle; *inf* yarn. **2** *their stories of the accident did not tally* account, report, recital, record. **3** *the novel's complicated story* story-line, plot, plot development. **4** *journalists looking for a story* news item, news report, article, feature; *inf* scoop. **5** *told a story when she was caught* lie, white lie, untruth, falsehood, fib, piece of fiction; *inf* terminological inexactitude.

stout adj **1** *stout people advised to lose weight* fat, fattish, plump, portly, tubby, obese, corpulent, rotund, big, heavy, thick-set, overweight, bulky, burly, brawny, fleshy; *inf* beefy. **2** *a stout stick* strong, heavy, solid, substantial, sturdy. **3** *a stout defender of the city* stout-hearted, brave, courageous, valiant, valorous, gallant, fearless, unafraid, intrepid, bold, plucky, manly, heroic, lion-hearted, daring, tough, doughty; *inf* gutsy, spunky. **4** *put up a stout resistance* firm, determined, resolute, staunch, steadfast, unyielding, unbending, unfaltering, unswerving, unwavering. **5** *launch a stout attack on the enemy* vigorous, forceful, spirited, energetic, strenuous.

stout-hearted adj *stout-hearted defenders of the city* stout, courageous, valiant, valorous, gallant, fearless, plucky. *see* STOUT 3.

stove n oven, range, furnace, cooker.

stow v *stow one's hand luggage in the rack* place, deposit, put, put away, pack, store, load, bundle, stuff. **stow away** *stow away on the yacht* travel secretly, hide, conceal oneself, secrete oneself.

straddle v **1** *straddle the fence/horse* bestraddle, sit/stand astride of. **2** *the town straddles*

the border be situated on both sides of, lie on each side of. **3** *straddle an issue* be undecided about, be noncommittal about, equivocate about, vacillate about, waver about, sit on the fence about, hem and haw about.

strafe v **1** *the enemy strafing the city* bombard, bomb, shell, fire on, open fire on, shout at, machine-gun, rake with gun-fire. **2** *children getting strafed for their wicked behaviour* punish/chastise/discipline severely, reprimand/scold/upbraid harshly; *inf* carpet.

straggle v **1** *sheep straggling across the moors* wander, ramble, stray, roam, meander, rove, range, spread out. **2** *some of the runners are straggling* trail behind, fall behind, lag, string out, linger, loiter. **3** *hair straggling to her shoulders* grow untidily, be messy, be dishevelled, be unkempt.

straight adj **1** *in a straight line/course* direct, undeviating, unswerving, uncurving, unbent, straight as an arrow. **2** *three straight wins* successive, consecutive, in a row, running, uninterrupted, solid, non-stop. **3** *Is the picture straight?* level, symmetrical, even, true, in line, aligned. **4** *get the room/things straight* in order, orderly, neat, tidy, spruce, shipshape, in place, organized, arranged, sorted out; *inf* shipshape and Bristol fashion. **5** *a straight answer* direct, honest, faithful, sincere, frank, candid, forthright, straightforward, plain-spoken, plain-speaking, plain, matter-of-fact, outspoken, straight from the shoulder, unequivocal, unambiguous, unqualified, unmodified. **6** *incapable of straight thinking* logical, rational, sound, intelligent, unemotional, dispassionate. **7** *a straight and valued colleague* respectable, upright, upstanding, honourable, honest, sincere, decent, fair, just, righteous, right-minded, law-abiding, conventional, orthodox. **8** *straight spirits* unmixed, undiluted, unadulterated, pure, neat.

straight adv **1** *go straight there* directly, by a direct route, without deviating; without delay. **2** *tell them straight* straight out, directly, honestly, frankly, candidly, outspokenly, plainly, straight from the shoulder, with no holds barred, unequivocally, unambiguously; *inf* pulling no punches. *see* STRAIGHT adj 5. **3** *not thinking straight* logically, rationally, intelligently, unemotionally, dispassionately. **straight away, straightaway** *the work must be done straight away* right away, immediately, at once, instantly, without delay, without hesitation, straight off; *inf* pronto, PDQ (= pretty damned quickly). **straight out** *tell him*

straight out that he is disliked straight,
directly, honestly, frankly, candidly, outspoken.

straighten v **1** *straighten the carpet* make
straight, adjust, arrange, put in order,
make tidy, tidy up, neaten, put to rights.
2 *have her hair straightened* uncurl, untangle.
straighten out *straighten out the mess his
affairs are in* put in order, put right, sort
out, clear up, tidy up, settle, resolve, regulate, rectify, disentangle, unsnarl.
straighten up *she was bending down but she
suddenly straightened up* stand up, stand up
straight, stand upright, become erect,
straighten one's back.

straightened adj *live in straightened circumstances* poverty-stricken, poor, destitute,
impoverished, penniless, impecunious,
penurious, beggared, pauperized; *inf* on
one's uppers.

straightforward adj **1** *a straightforward
answer* straight, direct, honest, frank, candid, forthright, plain-speaking, unambiguous, straight from the shoulder. *see* STRAIGHT
adj 5. **2** *a straightforward task* uncomplicated, easy, simple, elementary, effortless,
undemanding, unexacting, routine; *inf*
easy as falling of a log, easy as pie.

strain[1] v **1** *strain a rope till it snaps* draw
tight, tighten, make taut, tauten, stretch,
extend, elongate, distend. **2** *strain a muscle*
pull, wrench, twist, sprain, rick, wrick,
injure, hurt, damage, weaken, impair.
3 *strain one's eyes by reading too much | strain
every nerve* tax, overtax, exert to the limit,
exert something excessively, overwork,
push to the limit, fatigue, tire. **4** *strain to
win* make every effort, make a supreme
effort, strive one's utmost, push/drive oneself to the limit, struggle, labour; *inf* pull
out all the stops, go all out, give it one's
all. **5** *strain at the rope* pull, tug, heave, haul,
jerk; *inf* yank. **6** *an account which strained the
truth* distort, falsify, garble, misrepresent,
invert, stretch, exaggerate, embroider,
overdraw. **7** *his account strained the credulity
of his listeners* tax, overtax, be too much for,
go beyond the limit of, exceed the range/
scope of, overstep. **8** *strain the coffee* sieve,
filter, percolate. **9** *strain the mixture* sieve,
sift, screen, riddle, separate. **10** *strain her to
his bosom* clasp, press, clutch, embrace,
hug, squeeze, enfold, envelop.

strain[1] n **1** *the rope snapped under the strain*
tightness, tautness, tension, tensity, disten-
sion. **2** *his injury is just a strain | suffer muscle
strain* wrench, twist, sprain, rick. *see* STRAIN
v 2. **3** *the strain of his job* demands, exer-
tions, burdens, pressure, stress, tension.

4 *suffer from strain* stress, pressure of work,
tension, overwork, exhaustion, anxiety.

strain[2] n **1** *people coming from a hardy strain*
stock, descent, lineage, ancestry, family,
extraction, blood, breed. **2** *a new strain of flu*
variety, kind, type, sort. **3** *a strain of madness in the family* trait, disposition, characteristic, tendency, susceptibility,
propensity, proclivity, proneness, inclination. **4** *a strain of cruelty in an otherwise
kindly man* streak, vein, element, strand,
trace, indication, suggestion, suspicion.
5 *the speaker went on in the same strain for
more than an hour* vein, way, tone, style,
manner. **6** *the strains of a boys' choir* music,
tone, melody, air, song. **7** *remember a strain
of an old poem* snatch, line, snippet, fragment, scrap, bit.

strained adj **1** *a strained smile/laugh* forced,
artificial, unnatural, false, constrained,
laboured, wooden, stiff, self-conscious. **2** *a
strained silence* awkward, embarrassed,
uneasy, uncomfortable, tense, unrelaxed.
3 *strained relations | relations between them are
strained* under a strain, tense, troubled,
uneasy, hostile.

strainer n *put the food through a strainer*
sieve, colander, filter, sifter, screen, riddle.

strait n *the boat crossing the strait* sound, narrows, channel, inlet, arm of the sea. *see*
STRAITS.

strait-laced adj puritanical, prudish, prim,
proper, priggish, moralistic, narrow, narrow-minded, stuffy; *inf* fuddy-duddy.

straits npl *in dire straits* predicament,
plight, difficulty, trouble, crisis, mess,
pretty kettle of fish; *inf* tight corner, hot
water, jam, hole, scrape, stew.

strand[1] n **1** *the strands of the wool/rope*
thread, fibre, filament, length. **2** *curling
strands of hair* lock, wisp, tress. **3** *the last volume drawing together the strands of the trilogy*
element, component, strain, story-line,
theme.

strand[2] n *walk on the strand* shore, seashore, foreshore, beach, coast, seaside,
waterfront.

stranded adj **1** *left stranded when her purse
was stolen* left helpless, without help/assis-
tance, left penniless, in dire straits, in difficulties, left in the lurch, left high and dry,
abandoned, forsaken. **2** *stranded ships*
grounded, beached, shipwrecked, wrecked,
marooned.

stranger n **1** *he was a complete stranger to her*
unknown person, alien. **2** *strangers not being
welcome in the village* new person, new
arrival, newcomer, incomer, foreigner.

a stranger to *a stranger to the area* unfamiliar with, unacquainted with, unaccustomed to, new to, fresh to, unused to, inexperienced in, unpractised in, unversed in, unconversant with.

strangle v **1** *he strangled his victim with a scarf* throttle, choke, strangulate, garrotte. **2** *strangle artistic expression* suppress, inhibit, repress, check, restrain, hold back, curb, stifle, gag.

strap n *straps fastening the trunk* band, belt, thong, cord, tie.

strap v **1** *strap the trunk with leather thongs* fasten, secure, tie, bind, lash, truss, pinion. **2** *strap her strained ankle* bind, bandage. **3** *strap the naughty children* flog, lash, whip, scourge, beat; *inf* belt.

stratagem n *only win by means of a stratagem* trick, ruse, plot, cunning/crafty plan, scheme, manoeuvre, plan, tactic, artifice, machination, wile, subterfuge, dodge, deception.

strategic adj **1** *strategic schemes* tactical, diplomatic, politic, calculated, planned, plotted, cunning, wily. **2** *strategic bases in the war* crucial, key, vital, critical, essential, important.

strategy n **1** *the government's economic strategy* policy, approach, programme, scheme, plan of action, master plan, schedule, blueprint, game plan. **2** *the general's strategy* art of war, martial art, military science, military tactics.

stratum n **1** *the top stratum of rock* layer, tier, scum, vein, lode. **2** *belong to the same stratum of society* class, level, grade, status, station, gradation.

stray v **1** *children straying from home | cows straying from the field* wander, roam, rove, go astray from. **2** *walkers straying over the hills* wander, roam, ramble, meander, drift, range, stroll, amble, saunter, straggle. **3** *stray from the point* digress from, wander from, deviate from, get off the subject of, get sidetracked from, go off at a tangent from, lose the thread of. **4** *good children who strayed in later life* go astray, go wrong, do wrong, stray from the straight and narrow, err, sin, transgress, go down the primrose path.

stray n *give strays a home* homeless animal, stray dog/cat, homeless person, waif, foundling.

stray adj **1** *a stray dog* strayed, gone astray, lost, homeless, wandering, vagrant, abandoned, unclaimed. **2** *a stray customer or two | a stray bullet* odd, random, isolated, scattered, occasional, incidental, accidental, chance, freak.

streak n **1** *a streak of light in the dark sky* line, band, strip, stripe, slash, smear. **2** *a streak of cowardice in him* strain, vein, element, trace, touch, dash. **3** *a streak of lightning* bolt, flash, beam. **4** *streaks on the windows when he cleaned them* smear, smudge, mark. **5** *on a winning streak* spell, period, course, stretch, series.

streak v **1** *a blue sky streaked with white* band, stripe, mark, slash, striate, fleck, daub, smear. **2** *dirty cloths streaking the glass* smear, smudge, mark. **3** *runners streaking past* race, rush, speed, dash, sprint, hurtle, scurry, fly, flee, flash, whistle, zoom, zip; *inf* tear, whiz, go hell for leather.

stream n **1** *mountain streams* river, brook, rivulet, rill, freshet; *dial* beck; *Scots* burn; *Amer* creek. **2** *a stream of blood* flow, rush, gush, surge, jet, outpouring, efflux, current, cascade. **3** *people going with the stream* flow, current, tide, course, drift.

stream v **1** *water streaming from the pipe | tears streaming down his face* flow, run, pour, course, spill, gush, surge, flood, cascade, well. **2** *wound streaming blood* emit, issue, shed, spill. **3** *hair/flags streaming in the breeze* flow, float, swing, flap, flutter. **4** *people streaming out of the building* surge, pour, crowd.

streamer n flag, pennant, banner, standard, ensign, gonfalon.

streamlined adj **1** *streamlined cars* smooth, sleek, elegant. **2** *streamlined production methods* efficient, smooth-running, well-run, modernized, rationalized, slick.

street n **1** *lighted streets* road, thoroughfare. **2** *live in a suburban street* road, terrace, avenue, drive, row, crescent.

strength n **1** *men of great physical strength | the strength to break the door* power, might, force, brawn, muscle, muscularity, sturdiness, robustness, vigour, toughness, stamina. **2** *regain his strength* health, healthiness, robustness, vigour. **3** *adversity gave him inner strength* fortitude, courage, bravery, pluck, firmness, stamina, backbone; *inf* grit, guts. **4** *test the strength of the castle doors* solidity, toughness, resistance, impregnability. **5** *the strength of the feeling against him* force, forcefulness, intensity, vehemence, ardour, fervency. **6** *the strength of their argument* cogency, potency, weight, effectiveness, efficacy, soundness, validity. **7** *workers who are the strength of the firm* mainstay, chief support, tower of strength, anchor, foundation stone. **8** *the firm's reliability is its main strength* advantage, asset, strong point, forte. **9** *the strength of the workforce* size, extent, magnitude, bigness, largeness, greatness. **on the strength of** *he got the job on the strength of his qualifications* on the basis of, based on, because of, on the grounds of.

strengthen v **1** *strengthen children's bones* make strong, make stronger, give strength to, make healthy, nourish, build up. **2** *the wind strengthened* grow strong, grow stronger, gain strength, intensify, heighten. **3** *strengthen their determination* make stronger, give strength to, fortify, give a boost to, harden, stiffen, toughen, steel. **4** *his evidence strengthened their argument* give strength to, reinforce, support, back up, bolster, authenticate, confirm, substantiate, corroborate.

strenuous adj **1** *a strenuous task* arduous, laborious, taxing, demanding, difficult, hard, tough, uphill, heavy, weighty, burdensome, exhausting, tiring, fatiguing. **2** *make strenuous efforts to reach the top* energetic, active, vigorous, forceful, strong, spirited, bold, determined, resolute, tenacious, earnest, keen, zealous.

stress n **1** *the stress of his new job* | *suffer from stress* strain, pressure, tension, worry, anxiety. **2** *in times of stress* worry, anxiety, trouble, difficulty, distress, trauma. **3** *place stress on education* emphasis, priority, importance, weight, significance, value, worth, merit. **4** *place stress on the first syllable* emphasis, accent, accentuation. **5** *wire unable to bear stress* strain, tension, tensity, tightness, tautness, stretching.

stress v **1** *stress the importance of education* lay stress on, emphasize, place emphasis on, give emphasis to, accentuate, underline, underscore, point up, highlight, spotlight, press home, dwell on, harp on, belabour. **2** *stress the first syllable* lay stress on, emphasize, place emphasis on, give emphasis to, place the accent on, accentuate. **3** *discover that the workers have been stressed for years* subject to stress/strain/tension, tax, overtax, pressurize, overwork, overstretch, overburden, push to the limit, push too far.

stretch v **1** *the material stretches* be stretchy, be elastic, be tensile. **2** *stretch the piece of elastic/rope* extend, elongate, lengthen, expand, draw out, pull out. **3** *sweaters stretching in the wash* get larger, get bigger, enlarge, expand, pull out of shape. **4** *stretched a hand out* reach out, hold out, put forth, proffer, offer. **5** *stretch one's arms* unbend, extend, elongate. **6** *the forests stretched for miles* extend, spread, unfold,

cover, range. **7** *a job that will stretch her* be a challenge to, challenge, extend, tax, push to the limit. **8** *stretch the truth* strain, overstrain, exaggerate, overdraw, push too far. **9** *stretch out on the sofa* lie down, recline, sprawl, lounge.

stretch n **1** *stretches of forest* expanse, area, tract, extent, spread, sweep. **2** *a four-hour stretch* period, time, spell, term, space, run, stint.

strict adj **1** *a strict interpretation of the rules* precise, exact, close, faithful, true, accurate, scrupulous, meticulous, conscientous, punctilious. **2** *a strict regime/upbringing* | *strict parents* stringent, rigorous, severe, harsh, hard, stern, authoritarian, rigid, narrow, austere, illiberal, inflexible, unyielding, uncompromising. **3** *in strict confidence* absolute, utter, complete, total, perfect. **4** *strict members of the religious sect* orthodox, fundamentalist.

stricture n **1** *pass strictures on the children's behaviour* criticism, censure, blame, condemnation; *inf* flak. **2** *be able to do what they like without strictures* restriction, limitation, control, constraint, restraint, curb, check. **3** *a stricture in the wind-pipe* narrowing, constriction, strangulation.

stride v *stride along swinging their arms* step, pace, walk, stalk.

stride n *take huge strides* long/large step, pace.

strident adj *strident music/voices* harsh, raucous, rough, grating, discordant, rasping, jarring, shrill, loud, screeching, unmelodious, unmusical, stridulous, stridulant, stridulatory.

strife n *a country suffering from industrial strife* conflict, friction, discord, disagreement, dissension, dispute, argument, quarrelling, wrangling, bickering, controversy, contention, ill feeling, hostility, animosity.

strike v **1** *strike the gong at lunch-time* bang, beat, hit, pound, batter. **2** *strike the child for misbehaving* hit, slap, smack, beat, batter, thrash, thump, thwack, punch, cuff, box, knock, rap, buffet, smite, cane, lash, whip; *inf* wallop, belt, tan someone's hide, clout, whack, bash, clobber, bop, biff, lambaste, sock, plug. **3** *the ship struck a rock* run into, knock into, bang into, bump into, smash into, collide with, be in collision with, dash against. **4** *strike the ball a good distance* hit, drive, propel; *inf* swipe. **5** *strike his arm away* push, thrust, shove, force. **6** *strike a match* light, ignite. **7** *the enemy struck our army at dawn* attack, launch an attack upon, charge, make an assault on, assault, storm, set upon, fall upon. **8** *disease struck the* *town | disaster struck the family* hit, come upon, affect, afflict, smite. **9** *strike a balance* reach, achieve, arrive at, find, attain, effect. **10** *strike a bargain* agree on, come to an agreement on, settle on, sign, endorse, ratify, sanction. **11** *strike a dramatic pose* assume, adopt, take on, affect, feign. **12** *strike oil/gold | strike a new source of information* discover, find, come upon, light upon, chance upon, happen upon, stumble upon, unearth, uncover, turn up. **13** *an idea struck him* occur to, come to, come to the mind of, dawn on, hit. **14** *the house strikes me as unfriendly* seem, appear, impress, affect, have an impact on. **15** *workers striking for higher wages* go on strike, take industrial action, down tools, walk out. **16** *strike a tent* take down, pull down, knock down, level, take apart. **17** *strike a flag* lower, take down, let down, bring down. **18** *strike north* go, make one's way, set out, direct one's footsteps. **strike out** *strike out the disputed clause* delete, cross out, erase, rub out, obliterate. **strike up** **1** *the band struck up* begin/start/commence playing, begin/start to play. **2** *he struck up an acquaintance with his fellow-passenger* begin, start, commence, embark on, set going, initiate.

strike n **1** *kill the boy with one strike* hit, slap, smack, thump, thwack, punch, cuff, box, knock; *inf* wallop, clout, whack, bop, biff, plug. *see* STRIKE v 2. **2** *a lucky strike* discovery, find, unearthing, uncovering. **3** *killed during an enemy strike* air strike, air attack, attack, assault, bombing, blitz. **4** *workers on strike | declare a strike* industrial action, walk-out.

striking adj **1** *a striking resemblance* noticeable, obvious, conspicuous, evident, visible, distinct, prominent, clear-cut, unmistakable, remarkable, extraordinary, incredible, amazing. **2** *a striking floral display* impressive, imposing, grand, splendid, magnificent, superb, marvellous, wonderful, dazzling; *inf* great, smashing. **3** *married to a striking woman* attractive, good-looking, beautiful, glamorous, stunning, gorgeous.

string n **1** *tie the package with string* twine, cord, yarn, rope, cable, line. **2** *own a string of shops/houses* chain, series, succession. **3** *a string of people waiting to get in* queue, line, row, procession, file, column, stream, succession, sequence. **4** *a string of coloured beads* strand, necklace.

string v **1** *string decorations from the branches of the tree* hang, suspend, sling. **2** *string the washing line from pole to pole* stretch, sling, run, fasten, tie, secure together. **3** *string the beads* thread. **string along 1** *she won't marry*

him – she's just stringing him along make use of, take advantage of, mislead, deceive, make a fool of, fool, lead up the garden path. **2** *string along with them for want of anything else to do* go along, go with, accompany, join up with. **string out 1** *string out the seats across the lawn* spread out, space out, set apart, place at intervals. **2** *speakers stringing out their material as much as possible* draw out, stretch, protract, spin out. **string up** *his fellow prisoners decided to string him up* hang, lynch; *inf* make swing.

stringent adj **1** *a stringent ban on smoking* strict, firm, rigid, rigorous, severe, harsh, tough, tight, exacting, demanding, inflexible, hard and fast, uncompromising. **2** *stringent economic conditions* difficult, tight, hard, harsh, tough.

strings npl *she got the job but there were strings attached* conditions, qualifications, provisions, provisos, stipulations, contingencies, limitations.

stringy adj **1** *stringy hair* lank, straggly, straggling. **2** *stringy young men* lanky, gangling, spindly, skinny, wiry. **3** *stringy meat* tough, fibrous, gristly, leathery.

strip v **1** *they stripped and got into dry clothes* strip naked, undress, take one's clothes off, remove one's clothes, disrobe. **2** *strip the soaking wet child* undress, unclothe. **3** *strip the bark from the tree* peel, pare, skin, excoriate. **4** *strip paint from the doors* remove, take off, peel off, flake off. **5** *strip him of his rank/ honours* take away, dispossess of, deprive of, confiscate. **6** *strip a machine* dismantle, take to pieces, take to bits, take apart. **7** *the burglars stripped the house* clear out, empty out, clean out, plunder, ransack, rob.

strip n *strips of paper* piece, bit, band, belt, ribbon, stripe, bar, swathe, slip, fillet.

stripe n *a white stripe on a black background* strip, band, belt, bar.

striped adj *wear a striped dress* stripy, banded, barred, striated, variegated.

stripling n *his father died when he was just a stripling* youth, adolescent, youngster, boy, lad, teenager, child, juvenile, minor, young man; *inf* kid, young'un.

strive v **1** *strive to succeed* try, try hard, attempt, endeavour, make an effort, make every effort, exert oneself, do one's best, do all one can, do one's utmost, labour, toil, strain, struggle, bend over backwards; *inf* go all out, give it one's best shot. **2** *had to strive all his life against poverty/oppression* struggle, fight, battle, combat, contend with, grapple with.

stroke n **1** *kill him with one stroke* blow, hit, slap, smack, thump, thwack, punch, cuff, box, knock, rap, buffet, smite; *inf* wallop, clout, whack, bop, biff. **2** *swimming/rowing strokes* movement, action, motion. **3** *a stroke of genius/diplomacy* accomplishment, achievement, feat, attainment, coup. **4** *with one stroke of the pen/brush* movement, action, mark, line. **5** *put the finishing strokes to the plan* touch, detail, bit, addition. **6** *hear five strokes of the church bell* striking, peal, ring, knell, ding-dong, boom. **7** *in hospital since he had a stroke* thrombosis, embolism, cerebral vascular accident, CVA, seizure, shock, apoplexy.

stroke v *stroke the cat* caress, fondle, pat, touch, rub, massage, soothe.

stroll v *stroll along in the sunshine* saunter, amble, wander, meander, ramble, dawdle, promenade, go for a walk, take a walk, stretch one's legs, take the air; *inf* mosey along.

stroll n *go for a stroll in the sunshine* saunter, walk, amble, wander, turn, airing, constitutional, promenade, perambulation.

strong adj **1** *strong men lifting heavy weights* powerful, mighty, brawny, muscular, well-built, strapping, sturdy, burly, robust, vigorous, tough, rugged, stalwart, hardy, lusty, Herculean, strong as an ox/horse/lion. **2** *invalids becoming strong again* healthy, well, robust, vigorous, hale and hearty. **3** *strong enough to refuse the black-mailer's demands* courageous, brave, plucky, firm, resolute, strong-minded; *inf* gutsy. **4** *nervous of strong women* determined, forceful, high-powered, self-assertive, tough, formidable, aggressive, redoubtable. **5** *strong castle doors* solid, well-built, heavy, tough, secure, well-fortified, well-defended, well-protected, impregnable, impenetrable. **6** *strong material* heavy-duty, solid, sturdy, durable, hard-wearing, long-lasting, enduring. **7** *a strong interest in local history* keen, eager, deep, acute, dedicated, passionate, fervent, zealous. **8** *arouse strong feelings against him* forceful, intense, vehement, passionate, fervent. **9** *a strong supporter of the local team* keen, eager, enthusiastic, dedicated, staunch, loyal, steadfast, passionate, fierce, fervent. **10** *a strong argument* powerful, cogent, potent, weighty, compelling, convincing, plausible, effective, efficacious, sound, valid, well-founded. **11** *a strong resemblance* marked, pronounced, distinct, definite, clear-cut, obvious, evident, unmistakable, notable, remarkable. **12** *strong colours* deep, intense, vivid, graphic. **13** *in strong light* bright, brilliant, intense, radiant, gleaming, dazzling, glaring. **14** *strong measures required to reduce crime* firm, energetic, active, forceful, severe, drastic, extreme, Draconian. **15** *strong coffee* concentrated, undiluted, highly flavoured. **16** *strong drink* alcoholic, spiritous, intoxicating, heady. **17** *strong cheese/garlic/sauces* highly flavoured, sharp, pungent, biting, spicy.

strongbox n *put the jewels in the strongbox* safe, safety-deposit box, vault.

stronghold n **1** *launch an assault on the enemy stronghold* fortress, fort, castle, keep, citadel, fastness. **2** *a conservative stronghold at the last election* bastion, centre, refuge, hotbed.

strong-minded adj *strong-minded enough to give up smoking* determined, firm, resolute, resolved, self-disciplined, uncompromising, unyielding, unbending.

strong-willed adj *too strong-willed to take others' advice* determined, resolute, stubborn, obstinate, headstrong, self-willed, inflexible, intractable, recalcitrant, refracting.

structure n **1** *wooden structures* building, edifice, construction, erection, pile, complex. **2** *the structure of the body/firm/sentence* construction, form, configuration, conformation, shape, constitution, composition, make-up, organization, system, arrangement, design, frame, framework.

structure v *structure the timetable to suit the students* construct, build, put together, assemble, shape, design, organize, arrange, order.

struggle v **1** *struggle to obtain power* strive, try hard, endeavour, make every effort, exert oneself, do one's best, do all one can, do one's utmost, battle, labour, toil, strain, bend over backwards; *inf* go all out, give it one's best shot. **2** *boys struggling with each other* fight, grapple, wrestle, scuffle, brawl; *inf* scrap. **3** *rivals struggling with each other for supremacy* fight, compete, contend, vie, clash, lock horns, cross swords. **4** *struggling up the hill* make one's way with difficulty, battle, battle one's way, fight one's way.

struggle n **1** *his struggles to obtain power* striving, battle, endeavour, effort, exertion, labour, toiling, pains. **2** *boys engaging in a struggle in the playground* fight, wrestling match, wrestling-bout, scuffle, brawl, tussle; *inf* scrap, set-to, dust-up. **3** *opposing armies engaged in a struggle* battle, fight, combat, conflict, contest, hostilities, clash, skirmish, brush. **4** *a struggle on the committee for supremacy* battle, fight, competition, contention, vying, rivalry. **5** *a struggle just to survive* battle, fight, trial, labour, problem, trouble; *inf* grind, hassle.

strumpet n **1** *earn a living as a strumpet* prostitute, sex worker, call girl, street-walker; *derog* harlot, whore; *derog inf* tart, hooker. **2** *the nobleman's strumpet* mistress, paramour, kept woman, concubine, courtesan.

strut v *strutting around in his new suit* swagger, prance, parade, flounce, peacock; *Amer* sashay.

stub n **1** *cigarette stubs* end, butt, tail-end, remnant; *inf* dog-end, fag-end. **2** *ticket stubs* counterfoil. **3** *the stub of a tree* stump, remnant.

stubborn adj obstinate, headstrong, wilful, strong-willed, pig-headed, mulish, dogged, persistent, adamant, inflexible, uncompromising, unbending, unyielding, unmalleable, obdurate, adamant, intractable, refractory, recalcitrant, contumacious.

stubby adj *clothes making her look stubby* dumpy, squat, stumpy, stocky, chunky, thickset, chubby.

stuck adj **1** *posters stuck to the wall* glued, fixed, fastened. **2** *stuck in the mud* immovable, immobile, fast, fixed, rooted. **3** *she cannot solve the problem – she's stuck* baffled, beaten, stumped, at a loss, perplexed, nonplussed, at one's wits ends; *inf* up against a brick wall. **get stuck into** *get stuck into some work* get down to, make a start on, make a beginning on, set about, tackle. **stuck on** *he's stuck on the new girl* attracted to, infatuated with, keen on, enthusiastic about, fond of, in love with, obsessed by; *inf* mad about, wild about, hung up on. **be stuck with** *he was stuck with his young sister for the day* left with, made responsible for, lumbered with.

stuck-up adj conceited, proud, arrogant, haughty, condescending, disdainful, patronizing, snobbish; *inf* high-and-mighty, snooty, uppity, uppish, big-headed, swollen-headed, toffee-nosed, hoity-toity.

student n **1** *college students* undergraduate. **2** *students at the high school* pupil, schoolboy, schoolgirl. **3** *nursing students on the wards* trainee, apprentice, probationer.

studied adj *with studied indifference* deliberate, wilful, conscious, calculated, purposeful, studious, contrived, affected, forced, feigned, artificial.

studio n *the artist's studio* workshop, workroom, atelier.

studious adj **1** *a studious pupil* scholarly, academic, intellectual, bookish, book-loving, serious, earnest. **2** *the studious checking of detail* diligent, careful, attentive, industrious, assiduous, painstaking, thorough, meticulous, punctilious, zealous, sedulous. **3** *with studious indifference* deliberate, wilful, conscious, calculated, purposeful, contrived. *see* STUDIED.

study n **1** *a life devoted to study* learning, scholarship, education, academic work, research, book work, reading; *inf* swotting, cramming. **2** *make a study of rural transport* investigation, inquiry, research, examination, analysis, review, survey, scrutiny. **3** *writing in his study* office, workroom, studio, library. **4** *write a study on/of Shakespeare's late plays* paper, work, essay, review. **in a brown study** lost in thought, in a reverie, thinking, reflecting, pondering, contemplating, deliberating, ruminating.

study v **1** *study hard before the exams* apply oneself, revise, burn the midnight oil; *inf* swot, cram, mug up. **2** *study history* learn, read up on, read, work at; *inf* mug up on. **3** *study the effects of sleeplessness* investigate, inquire into, research, conduct research into, look into, examine, analyse, review, survey, conduct a survey of, scrutinize. **4** *study the suspect's movements* watch, keep watch on, look at, observe, keep an eye on, keep under surveillance.

stuff n **1** *make out of hard-wearing stuff* material, fabric, matter, substance. **2** *get rid of the stuff in the hall* things, objects, articles, items. **3** *leave your stuff in the left-luggage office* things, luggage, baggage, belongings, possessions, goods, goods and chattels, paraphernalia. **4** *know one's stuff* facts, information, data, subject, discipline; *inf* onions. **stuff and nonsense** nonsense, rubbish, twaddle, balderdash, bunkum; *inf* poppycock, rot, tummy-rot, tripe, bunk, piffle, bosh.

stuff v **1** *stuff a pillow* fill, pack, pad. **2** *too much furniture stuffed into the room* pack, load, cram, squeeze, crowd, stow, press, force, compress, jam, wedge. **3** *stuff the money into his wallet* thrust, shove, push, ram. **4** *stuff themselves with turkey* fill, gorge, overindulge, satiate; *inf* make a pig of oneself. **5** *his nostrils are stuffed because of the cold* block, stop up, bung up, obstruct, choke.

stuffing n **1** *stuffing for cushions* filling, filler, packing, padding, wadding. **2** *stuffing for the duck* filling, forcemeat, farcemeat, farce.

stuffy adj **1** *a stuffy atmosphere* airless, close, muggy, fuggy, stifling, suffocating, musty, stale. **2** *a stuffy young man* dull, boring, dreary, staid, sedate, stiff, formal, pompous, starchy, prim, priggish, strait-laced, conventional, conservative, stodgy; *inf* fuddy-duddy, square. **3** *a stuffy nose* stuffed up, blocked, bunged-up.

stultify v **1** *stultify their efforts to escape* thwart, frustrate, foil, impede, obstruct, hamper, suppress, repress, nullify, negate. **2** *a mind stultified by a boring job* dull, numb, benumb, stupefy, make bored.

stumble v **1** *stumble and fall* trip, lose one's balance, slip. **2** *drunks stumbling home* blunder, lumber, lurch, stagger, reel. **3** *stumble a little when giving her speech* stammer, stutter, hesitate, falter; *inf* fluff one's lines.
stumble upon *stumble upon an unpublished work of the novelist* chance upon, happen upon, light upon, hit upon, come across, run across, find, discover, encounter.

stump n **1** *a tree stump* end, stub, remnant, remains. **2** *a pencil stump* end, tail-end, butt, remnant.

stump v **1** *the last question stumped him* baffle, be too much for, put at a loss, nonplus, mystify, outwit, foil, perplex, puzzle, confound, bewilder; *inf* flummox, stymie. **2** *stumping around in a bad temper* clomp, clump, stamp, stomp, lumber, blunder.
stump up *stump up his share of the bill* pay up, pay, hand over, part with, contribute, donate; *inf* fork out, shell out, come across with, cough up, chip in.

stun v **1** *the blow stunned him* daze, stupefy, knock senseless, knock unconscious, knock out, lay out, knock stupid. **2** *stunned by the news of his death* shock, astound, dumbfound, stupefy, overwhelm, overcome, overpower, devastate, stagger, amaze, astonish, take one's breath away, confound, bewilder, confuse; *inf* flabbergast, knock for six, hit one like a ton of bricks.

stunning adj **1** *a stunning range of electronic equipment* impressive, imposing, remarkable, extraordinary, staggering, incredible, amazing, astonishing, marvellous, splendid; *inf* mind-boggling, mind-blowing. **2** *looking stunning in a new evening dress* sensational, ravishing, dazzling, wonderful, marvellous, magnificent, glorious, exquisite, impressive, splendid, beautiful, lovely; *inf* gorgeous, out of this world, fabulous, smashing.

stunt v *stunt the child's growth* retard, slow, impede, hamper, hinder, check, curb, restrict, arrest, stop.

stunt n *children amazed at the acrobat's stunts* feat, exploit, trick, *tour de force*, act, action, deed.

stunted adj *a stunted tree* dwarf, dwarfish, undersized, diminutive, tiny, small, little, baby.

stupefaction n **1** *stupefaction caused by a blow to the head* daze, senselessness, state of unconsciousness, insensibility, oblivion, black-out, coma. **2** *his stupefaction at the news of his redundancy* shock, devastation, amazement, astonishment, bewilderment, confusion.

stupefy v **1** *a boxer stupefied by the first blow* stun, daze, knock senseless, knock unconscious, knock out, lay out. **2** *stupefied by the news of his redundancy* stun, shock, astound, dumbfound, overwhelm, shake, devastate, stagger, amaze. *see* STUN 2.

stupendous adj **1** *a stupendous achievement* amazing, astounding, astonishing, extraordinary, remarkable, wonderful, prodigious, phenomenal, staggering, breath-taking; *inf* fantastic, mind-boggling, mind-blowing. **2** *a stupendous beast* colossal, immense, vast, gigantic, massive, huge, enormous, mighty.

stupid adj **1** *a stupid fellow* unintelligent, foolish, dense, brainless, mindless, dull-witted, dull, slow witted, slow, duncelike, doltish, simple-minded, half-witted, gullible, naive; *inf* thick, dim, dumb, dopey, dozy, crazy, moronic, imbecilic, cretinous. **2** *stupid error* foolish, silly, unintelligent, idiotic, brainless, mindless, crackbrained, nonsensical, senseless, irresponsible, unthinking, ill-advised, ill-considered, inept, unwise, injudicious, indiscreet, short-sighted, inane, absurd, ludicrous, ridiculous, laughable, fatuous, asinine, pointless, meaningless, futile, fruitless, mad, insane, lunatic; *inf* crazy, cock-eyed. **3** *knocked stupid by the blow* dazed, stupefied, unconscious.

stupidity n **1** *the unbelievable stupidity of the fellow* lack of intelligence, unintelligence, foolishness, denseness, brainlessness, mindlessness, dull-wittedness, dullness, slow-wittedness, slowness, doltishness; *inf* thickness, dimness, dumbness, dopiness, doziness, craziness. *see* STUPID 1. **2** *the stupidity of his actions* foolishness, folly, silliness, idiocy, brainlessness, senselessness, irresponsibility, injudiciousness, ineptitude, inaneness, inanity, absurdity, ludicrousness, ridiculousness, fatuousness, fatuity, asininity, pointlessness, meaningfulness, futility, fruitlessness, madness, insanity, lunacy; *inf* craziness. *see* STUPID 2.

stupor n *in a drunken stupor* daze, state of stupefaction/senselessness/unconsciousness, insensibility, oblivion, coma, black-out.

sturdy adj **1** *sturdy young men* well-built, well-made, muscular, athletic, strong, strapping, brawny, powerfully built, powerful, solid, substantial, robust, vigorous, tough, hardy, stalwart, mighty, lusty. **2** *put up a sturdy resistance* strong, vigorous, stalwart, firm, determined, resolve, tenacious, staunch, steadfast, unyielding, unwavering, uncompromising.

stutter v *stutter nervously as she gave the speech* stammer, stumble, speak haltingly, hesitate, falter, splutter.

style n **1** *an unusual style of house* kind, type, variety, sort, design, pattern, genre. **2** *try to copy the style of her favourite novelist* technique, method, methodology, approach, manner, way, mode, system. **3** *launch the new product in/with style* stylishness, smartness, elegance, polish, suaveness, urbanity, chic, flair, dash, panache, élan; *inf* pizzazz, ritziness. **4** *used to living in style* comfort, elegance, chic, affluence, wealth, luxury. **5** *styles popular in the 1920s* fashion, trend, vogue, mode. **6** *criticize both the content and style of the novel* mode of expression, phraseology, wording, language.

style v **1** *style the clothes to suit a warm climate* design, fashion, tailor, make, produce. **2** *he styled himself professor* designate, call, term, name, entitle, dub, address, denominate, label, tag.

stylish adj **1** *stylish clothes* fashionable, smart, elegant, chic, modish, à la mode, voguish, modern, up-to-date; *inf* trendy. **2** *a stylish dresser* fashionable, smart, elegant, chic; *inf* dressy, trendy, natty, classy, nifty, ritzy, snazzy, snappy, with it.

suave adj smooth, smooth-tongued, glib, bland, sophisticated, urbane, worldly, charming, polite, civil, courteous, affable, tactful, diplomatic, civilized, polished, worldly.

subconscious adj *subconscious images/fears* subliminal, latent, suppressed, repressed, hidden, underlying, innermost, deep, intuitive, instinctive.

subdue v **1** *subdue the rebel forces* conquer, defeat, vanquish, get the better of, overpower, overcome, overwhelm, subjugate, master, gain the upper hand at, triumph over, crush, quash, quell, tame, hold in check. **2** *subdue one's desire to hit him* control, curb, restrain, check, hold back, inhibit, rein in, repress, suppress.

subdue v **1** *subdue the rebel forces* conquer, vanquish, defeat, crush, quell, quash, get the better of, overpower, overcome, bring under control, get the upper hand over, subjugate, gain mastery over, gain ascendancy of, tame, break, humble, bring to his/her knees. **2** *succeed in subduing his rage* control, keep control of, keep a rein on,

curb, keep in check, check, repress, suppress, restrain, stifle.

subdued adj **1** *subdued lighting* dim, muted, toned down, softened, soft, lowered, shaded, low-key, subtle, unobtrusive. **2** *a subdued atmosphere in the hall* quiet, hushed, noiseless, soundless, silent, still, calm. **3** *children seeming very subdued* low-spirited, downcast, dejected, depressed, down in the mouth, restrained, repressed, inactive, spiritless, lifeless, dull, passive, unexcited, unemotional, unresponsive.

subject n **1** *the subject of the talk/discussion* subject matter, topic, theme, question, substance, gist, text, thesis. **2** *subjects studied at university* branch of study, branch of knowledge, course of study, course, discipline. **3** *a suitable subject for hypnosis* case, client, patient, participant; *inf* guinea pig. **4** *his disappearances was the subject of much speculation* occasion, basis, grounds, source. **5** *a British subject* citizen, national. **6** *the king's subjects* liege, liegeman, subordinate, underling, vassal.

subject adj **subject to 1** *the house is yours, subject to the contract being signed* conditional upon, contingent upon, dependent on. **2** *children subject to colds in the winter* susceptible to, liable to, prone to, apt/likely to suffer from, in danger of, vulnerable to. **3** *subject to the laws of the land* bound by, constrained by, answerable to, accountable to.

subject v *subject prisoners of war to torture* submit, put through, expose to, lay open to, treat one to.

subjective adj *present a highly subjective view of the situation* personal, personalized, individual, biased, prejudiced, bigoted.

subjugate v *subjugate a people* gain mastery over, gain ascendancy over, gain control of, bring one to his/her knees, bring to heel, bring under the yoke, conquer, vanquish, defeat, crush, quell, quash, overpower, overcome, subdue, tame, break, humble, tyrannize, oppress, enslave.

sublime adj **1** *sublime devotion/beauty* noble, exalted, lofty, awe-inspiring, majestic, imposing, glorious, supreme, grand, great, virtuous, high-principled. **2** *a sublime meal* excellent, outstanding, first-rate, first-class, superb, perfect, ideal, wonderful, marvellous; *inf* fantastic, fabulous, fab. **3** *a sublime lack of concern for the truth* supreme, total, complete, utter, arrogant.

submerge v **1** *watch the submarines submerging* go under water, dive, sink, plummet. **2** *submerge the dress in soapy water* immerse, dip, plunge, duck, dunk. **3** *flood water sub-*

merged the streets flood, inundate, deluge, engulf, swamp, overflow. **4** *submerged in a backlog of correspondence* overwhelm, inundate, deluge, swamp, bury, engulf. **5** *submerge his true feelings* hide, conceal, veil, cloak, repress, suppress.

submission n **1** *despise their submission to his demands* yielding, capitulation, agreement, acceptance, consent, accession, compliance. *see* SUBMIT 1. **2** *the submission of our army to the enemy forces* surrender, yielding, laying down one's arms. *see* SUBMIT 2. **3** *resent their submission to discipline* observance, adherence, regulation, subjection. *see* SUBMIT 3. **4** *the submission of a planning proposal* presentation, presenting, proffering, tendering, proposal, proposing, tabling, introduction. *see* SUBMIT 4. **5** *reject his submission for planning permission* presentation, tender, proposal, suggestion. **6** *the submission of his claim* sending in, entry, referral. *see* SUBMIT 5. **7** *accept his submission that his client was innocent* argument, assertion, contention, statement, averment, claim. **8** *he expects submission from women* submissiveness, yielding, compliance, malleability, acquiescence, tractability, manageability, unassertiveness, nonresistance, passivity, obedience, biddability, dutifulness, docility, meekness, patience, resignation, humility, self-effacement, deference, subservience, obsequiousness, servility, subjection, self-abasement; *inf* boot-licking.

submissive adj *he expects women to be submissive* yielding, compliant, malleable, acquiescent, accommodating, tractable, manageable, unassertive, nonresisting, passive, obedient, biddable, dutiful, docile, meek, patient, resigned, subdued, humble, self-effacing, deferential, obsequious, servile, self-abasing; *inf* boot-licking.

submit v **1** *refuse to submit to his demands* give in to, yield to, give way to, bow to, capitulate to, defer to, agree to, accept, consent to, accede to, acquiesce in, comply with, conform to. **2** *submit to the enemy forces* surrender to, give in to, yield to, lay down one's arms to, raise/show the white flag to, knuckle under to, humble oneself to, bend the knee to. **3** *submit to discipline* observe, adhere, abide by, be governed by, be regulated by, be subject to. **4** *submit a planning proposal* put forward, present, proffer, tender, advance, propose, suggest, table, introduce, move. **5** *submit a claim* put in, send in, hand in, enter, refer. **6** *submit that his client was innocent* argue, assert, contend, state, claim, aver, propound.

subnormal adj **1** *subnormal temperatures* below normal, below average, too low, very low. **2** *educationally subnormal | subnormal pupils* slow, retarded, backward, of low intelligence.

subordinate adj **1** *his subordinate officers* lower-ranking, junior, lower, lesser, inferior. **2** *subordinate issues* lesser, minor, secondary, subsidiary, ancillary, auxilliary, subservient.

subordinate n *be patronizing to his subordinates* junior, assistant, second, deputy, aide, subaltern, underling, inferior, second fiddle; *inf* sidekick.

sub rosa adv *the discussion was sub rosa* in secret, secret, private, in confidence, confidential, behind closed doors, in camera.

subscribe v **1** *subscribe to several learned journals* pay a subscription to, buy regularly, take regularly, contract to buy. **2** *subscribe to several charities* make a subscription to, make a donation to, donate to, give to, give money to, make a contribution to, contribute towards; *inf* chip into. **3** *subscribe to the theory that he was murdered* agree with, be in agreement with, accede to, consent to, accept, believe in, endorse, back, support. **4** *subscribe one's name to the petition* sign, initial, write, inscribe, undersign, add, append.

subscription n **1** *pay one's annual subscription to the club* fee, membership fee, dues, annual payment. **2** *make a subscription to the charity* donation, contribution, offering. **3** *his subscription on the document* signature, initials, undersigning, addition, appendage. **4** *his subscription to an old-fashioned theory* subscribing, agreement with, acceding to, consent to, acceptance of, belief in, endorsement of, backing for, support of.

subsequent adj *on subsequent visits to the house* following, ensuing, succeeding, later, future. **subsequent to** *subsequent to his illness* following, after, in the wake of.

subservient adj **1** *a powerful man surrounded by subservient people* servile, submissive, deferential, obsequious, sycophantic, grovelling, fawning, ingratiating, toadying, unctuous, truckling; *inf* boot-licking. **2** *workers regarded as being subservient to profits* subordinate to, secondary to, subsidiary to, less important than, of lesser importance than, ancillary to. **3** *his friendship with the manager was subservient to his promotion* conducive to, instrumental to, contributory to, helpful to, useful to, advantageous to, beneficial to, valuable to.

subside v **1** *storms subsiding* abate, let up, moderate, quieten down, calm, slacken, die out, peter out, taper off, recede, lessen, diminish, dwindle. **2** *water levels subsiding* go down, get lower, sink, fall back, recede. **3** *houses subsiding* sink, settle. **4** *land near old mines subsiding* sink, cave in, fall in, collapse.

subsidiary adj *discuss subsidiary issues after the main one* subordinate, secondary, ancillary, auxiliary, lesser, minor, subservient, supplementary, additional.

subsidize v *ask the local council to subsidize the project* pay a subsidy to, give a grant to, contribute to, make a contribution to, give money to, back, support, invest in, sponsor, finance, fund, underwrite, foot the bill for; *inf* pick up the tab for.

subsidy n *government subsidies for the arts* grant, contribution, backing, support, aid, investment, sponsorship, finance, funding, subvention.

subsist v **1** *subsist on bread and water* live on, exist on, eke out an existence on, survive on. **2** *old customs still subsist | animals thought to be extinct still subsisting* be in existence, exist, be alive, live, survive, continue, last. **3** *her attractiveness subsists in her personality* lie in, reside in, have its being in, be attributable to, be ascribable to.

subsistence n **1** *their subsistence on bread and water* existence, survival. *see* SUBSIST 1. **2** *be unaware of the subsistence of such old customs* existence, survival, continuance. *see* SUBSIST 2. **3** *contribute to the child's subsistence* keep, support, maintenance, livelihood; sustenance, provisions, food, aliment.

substance n **1** *a hard substance* matter, material, stuff, medium, mass, fabric. **2** *he saw ghostly figures with no substance* solidity, body, corporeality, reality, actuality, materiality, concreteness, tangibility. **3** *an argument with little substance* solidity, meaningfulness, significance, weight, power, soundness, validity, pith. **4** *a person of very little substance* character, backbone, mettle, strength of character. **5** *the substance of the novel as opposed to the style* subject matter, subject, theme, topic, content, text, burden, essence, gist, sense, import. **6** *born poor, he became a man of substance* wealth, affluence, prosperity, money, capital, means, resources, assets, property.

substantial adj **1** *confuse the substantial world with the world of the imagination* real, true, actual, existing, material, concrete. **2** *make a substantial contribution to the project* real, material, weighty, sizeable, considerable, meaningful, significant, important, notable, major, marked, valuable, useful, worthwhile. **3** *pay substantial damages* sizeable, considerable, significant, large, ample, goodly; *inf* tidy. **4** *substantial houses*

solid, sturdy, stout, strong, well-built, durable. **5** *a substantial figure of a man* large, big, solid, sturdy, stout, hefty, bulky. **6** *put forward a substantial argument* solid, meaningful, significant, weighty, powerful, sound, valid, pithy. **7** *run a substantial business | a substantial businessman* successful, profit-making, prosperous, wealthy, affluent, moneyed, well-to-do. **8** *in substantial agreement* essential, basic, fundamental.

substantially adv **1** *standards have improved substantially* considerably, significantly, greatly, to a great extent, to a marked extent, markedly. **2** *a report that is substantially accurate* largely, for the most part, by and large, in the main, in essence, essentially, materially, basically, fundamentally.

substantiate v *substantiate their accusation against him* give substance to, prove, support, uphold, back up, bear out, validate, corroborate, verify, authenticate, confirm.

substitute n *act as a substitute for the manager/actor/doctor* replacement, deputy, relief, proxy, reserve, surrogate, fill-in, stand-in, stand-by, locum, locum tenens, stopgap.

substitute v **1** *substitute sparkling wine for champagne* use as a replacement for, replace with, use instead of, exchange, switch; *inf* swap. **2** *she substituted for him when he was ill* take the place of, replace, deputize for, act as deputy for, relieve, fill in for, act as stand-in for, cover for, take over from, act as locum for, hold the fort for. *see* SUBSTITUTE n.

substitute adj acting, replacement, deputy, relief, reserve, surrogate, fill-in, stand-in, temporary, stand-by, locum, stopgap.

subterfuge n **1** *think of a subterfuge to get past the doorman* trick, ruse, wile, ploy, stratagem, artifice, dodge, manoeuvre, pretext, expedient, intrigue, scheme, deception. **2** *use subterfuge to gain entry* trickery, intrigue, deviousness, evasion, deception, duplicity.

subtle adj **1** *a subtle flavour* elusive, delicate, faint, understated, low-key, muted, toned down. **2** *a subtle distinction* fine, fine-drawn, nice, slight, minute, tenuous, indistinct, indefinite. **3** *a subtle intelligence* perceptive, discerning, sensitive, discriminating, penetrating, astute, keen, acute, shrewd, sagacious. **4** *subtle devices to trap the unwary* clever, ingenious, skilful, adroit, complex, intricate, strategic, cunning, crafty, wily, artful, devious.

subtlety n **1** *the subtlety of the flavour* subtleness, elusiveness, delicacy, delicateness, faintness, understatedness, understatement, mutedness. *see* SUBTLE 1. **2** *the subtlety* *of the distinction* subtleness, fineness, niceness, nicety, slightness, minuteness, tenuousness, indistinctness, indefiniteness, lack of definition. **3** *the subtlety of his mind* perceptiveness, perception, discernment, sensitivity, discrimination, astuteness, keenness, acuteness, shrewdness, sagacity. **4** *the subtlety of the devices* cleverness, ingenuity, skilfulness, adroitness, complexity, intricacy, cunning, guile, craftiness, wiliness, artfulness, deviousness.

subtract v *subtract 5 from 20* take away, take from, deduct; *inf* knock off.

suburb n *a suburb of Glasgow* outlying district, residential area, dormitory area, purlieus.

suburban adj *suburban housewives/attitudes* provincial, unsophisticated, parochial, insular.

subversive adj *spread subversive rumours about the abilities of his boss* undermining, discrediting, destructive, disruptive, trouble-making, inflammatory, seditious, revolutionary, treasonous.

subvert v **1** *subvert the government* overthrow, overturn, wreak havoc on, sabotage, ruin, destroy, demolish, wreck, upset, disrupt, undermine, weaken. **2** *subverted by gifts from the enemy* corrupt, pervert, warp, deprave, contaminate, vitiate.

subway n **1** *cross the road by the subway* underground road, pedestrian tunnel. **2** *go by subway* underground railway, underground, metro; *inf* tube.

succeed v **1** *succeed in his endeavour/ambition* be successful, gain success, accomplish, achieve, bring off, carry out, attain, reach, arrive at, complete, fulfil, realize, be victorious in, triumph in. **2** *he succeeded in life* achieve success, be successful, do well, make good, prosper, flourish, thrive, triumph; *inf* make it, do all right for oneself, arrive. **3** *plans that succeed* be successful, turn out well, work, work out; *inf* pan out, do the trick. **4** *as day succeeded day* come after, follow, follow after. **5** *he succeeded him as chairman* come after, follow, replace, take the place of, supplant, supersede. **6** *succeed to the throne* accede to, inherit, assume, take over, come into, be elevated to.

succeeding adj *grow weaker in the succeeding days* subsequent, following, ensuing, next.

success n **1** *gain success in his endeavour/aim* accomplishment, achievement, attainment, fulfilment, victory, triumph. *see* SUCCEED 1. **2** *plans meeting with success* successful outcome, favourable result, positive result, victory. **3** *envy his success* prosperity, affluence,

wealth, life of ease, fame, eminence. **4** *the book/play was a success* best-seller, winner; *inf* hit, sensation. **5** *the play was a success* box-office success, winner, sell-out, triumph; *inf* hit, box-office hit, smash-hit, sensation. **6** *a former pupil who was a success* celebrity, big name, somebody, VIP, star.

successful adj **1** *successful in his endeavour/ aim* victorious, triumphant. **2** *envying successful people* prosperous, affluent, wealthy, well-to-do, famous, eminent, at the top, top. **3** *a successful business* flourishing, thriving, booming, profitable, profit-making, money-making, lucrative.

succession n **1** *a succession of events leading to disaster* sequence, series, progression, course, cycle, chain, train, run, continuation. **2** *his succession to the throne* accession, inheritance, assumption, elevation. *see* SUCCEED 6. **3** *the succession is through his eldest son* line of descent, descent, ancestral, line, dynasty, lineage. **in succession** *several firms closed in quick succession* successively, running, one after the other, one behind the other; *inf* on the trot.

successor n **1** *the successor to the throne* heir, heir apparent, next-in-line. **2** *select the chairman's successor* heir, replacement, supplanter.

succinct adj *a succinct report* short, brief, concise, compact, condensed, crisp, terse, tight, to the point, pithy, summary, short and sweet, in a few well-chosen words.

succour n *give succour to the wounded/ bereaved* assistance, aid, help, comfort, relief, support.

succour v *succour the wounded* give assistance to, render assistance to, assist, aid, bring aid to, help, give help to, minister to, comfort, bring comfort to, bring relief to, support.

succulent adj *succulent fruit/steak* juicy, moist, luscious, mouthwatering.

succumb v **1** *succumb to temptation* give in to, give way to, yield to, submit to, surrender to, capitulate to, be overcome by, be overwhelmed by, fall victim to. **2** *succumb to his injuries* die from/of, pass away as a result of, be a fatality of.

suck v **suck in 1** *suck in one's cheeks* draw in, pull in. **2** *material sucking in liquid* suck up, draw up, absorb, soak up, blot up. **3** *sucked in to the whirlpool* draw in, pull in, engulf, swallow up, swamp, drown. **4** *sucked into the conspiracy against his will* draw in, involve, implicate; *inf* mix up. **suck up 1** *materials sucking up liquid* suck in, absorb. **2** *sucking up to the teacher* toady to, fawn upon, be obsequious/servile/sycophantic to; inf boot-lick.

suckle v *mothers suckling their young* feed, breast-feed, nurse, give suck to.

sudden adj **1** *a sudden change in the temperature* immediate, instantaneous, abrupt, unexpected, unforeseen, unanticipated, unlooked-for, without warning. **2** *his sudden rise to fame* rapid, swift, speedy, fast, quick, meteoric.

suddenly adv *suddenly it began to rain* all of a sudden, all at once, instantaneously, abruptly, unexpectedly, without warning; inf out of the blue.

suds npl *soap suds* foam, lather, froth, bubbles.

sue v **1** *sue him for libel* take one to court, take legal action against, bring an action against, prefer/bring charges against, charge, bring a suit against, prosecute, bring to trial, summons, indict; inf have the law on. **2** *sue for peace* petition for, appeal for, solicit, request, ask for, beg for, plead for, entreat for, beseech.

suffer v **1** *she suffered greatly before she died* be in pain, feel pain, be racked with pain, endure agony, hurt, ache. **2** *children who suffer when parents divorce* be distressed, be in distress, experience hardship, be upset, be miserable, be wretched, be hurt, hurt, be handicapped. **3** *suffer from headaches* be affected by, be afflicted by, be troubled with. **4** *suffer loss* experience, undergo, sustain, encounter, meet with, endure. **5** *his work suffered because of emotional problems* be impaired, deteriorate, fall off, decline, get worse. **6** *she cannot suffer his arrogance* put up with, tolerate, bear, stand, abide, endure, stomach, support. **7** *suffer them to approach* allow, permit, let, give leave to, sanction.

suffering n **1** *distressed by the suffering of the dying woman* pain, agony, torment, torture, hurting. **2** *children who endure suffering when parents divorce* distress, hardship, misery, wretchedness, hurt, pain, anguish.

suffice v **1** *a sandwich will suffice for lunch* be enough, be sufficient, be adequate, do, serve, meet requirements, satisfy demands, answer/fulfil/meet one's needs; inf fill the bill, hit the spot. **2** *two will suffice* be enough/sufficient/adequate for, do, satisfy, meet the requirements of, answer/fulfil/ meet the needs of.

sufficient adj *sufficient stocks of food* enough, adequate, plenty of, ample; inf plenty.

suffocate v **1** *kill the child by suffocating him* smother, stifle, asphyxiate. **2** *she was suffo-*

cating in the heat be suffocating, be stifling, be breathless, be short of air, be too hot.

suffrage n right to vote, voting rights, franchise.

suffuse v *a blush suffusing her cheeks | the evening sky suffused with crimson* spread over, cover, bathe, mantle, permeate, pervade, imbue.

sugary adj **1** *sugary tea* sugared, sweet, over-sweet. **2** *sugary love songs* oversweet, syrupy, sentimental, maudlin, mawkish, sloppy, slushy, mushy; inf schmaltzy.

suggest v **1** *suggest that they go by bus | suggest him as a replacement* propose, put forward, move, submit, recommend, advocate; inf throw out. **2** *an aroma suggesting home-baked cakes* put one in mind of, bring to mind, evoke. **3** *an appearance suggesting that he lived rough* indicate, lead to believe, give the impression, give the idea. **4** *a letter suggesting that he is lying* insinuate, hint, imply, intimate.

suggestion n **1** *put forward a suggestion that we leave* proposal, proposition, plan, motion, submission, recommendation. **2** *a suggestion of a French accent in her speech* hint, trace, touch, suspicion. **3** *object to the suggestion that he was making* insinuation, hint, implication, intimation.

suggestive adj *make suggestive remarks* provocative, titillating, sexual, sexy, indecent, indelicate, improper, off-colour, smutty, dirty, ribald, bawdy, racy, blue, risqué, lewd, salacious. **suggestive of** *an aroma suggestive of newly cut grass* redolent of, indicative of, evocative of, reminiscent of.

suicide n self destruction, *felo de se*, hara-kiri, suttee; inf topping oneself.

suit n **1** *a woman wearing a blue suit* set of clothes, outfit, costume, ensemble. **2** *bring a suit against his employers* lawsuit, court case, action, proceedings, prosecution. **3** *take one's suit to the king* petition, appeal, request, plea, entreaty. **4** *pay suit to his friend's sister* courtship, wooing, addresses, attentions.

suit v **1** *a colour which suits her* become, look attractive on, enhance the appearance of, go well with, look right on. **2** *the suggested date does not suit him* be suitable for, be convenient for, be acceptable to, meet requirements, satisfy demands, be in line with the wishes of. **3** *rich food does not suit him* be agreeable to, agree with, be good for, be healthy for. **4** *suit your speech to the occasion* make appropriate to, make fitting to, tailor, fashion, accommodate, adjust, adapt, modify.

suitable adj **1** *find a suitable date* convenient, acceptable, satisfactory. **2** *wear suitable shoes|shoes suitable for dancing* right, appropriate, fitting, apt. **3** *a speech suitable for the occasion* suited to, befitting, appropriate to, relevant to, pertinent to, apposite to, in keeping with, in character with, tailor-made for. **4** *not suitable behaviour* appropriate, fitting, becoming, seemly, decorous, proper. **5** *a suitable candidate for the post* right, appropriate, fitting, apt, well qualified, ideal.

suitcase n case, travel bag, travelling-bag, holdall, grip, valise, overnight case, vanity case.

suite n **1** *reserve a suite at a central hotel* suite of rooms, set of rooms, apartment. **2** *the suite of the king* retinue, entourage, train, escort, attendants, retainers, followers.

suitor n **1** *unable to choose among her suitors* admirer, beau, wooer, boyfriend; *lit* follower. **2** *the king giving audience to several suitors* petitioner, supplicant, beseecher, plaintiff, appellant.

sulk v *sulking after losing the contest* mope, pout, be sullen, have a long face, be in a bad mood, be put out, be out of sorts, be out of humour, be grumpy; *inf* be in a huff.

sulk n *have a sulk|be in the sulks* pout, bad mood, bad humour, ill humour, pique; *inf* huff.

sulky adj *a sulky young woman|sulky because of losing* moping, pouting, moody, sullen, piqued, disgruntled, ill-humoured, out of humour, bad-tempered, grumpy, churlish, glowering.

sullen adj *difficult to communicate with the sullen girl* morose, unresponsive, uncommunicative, unsociable, resentful, sulky, sour, glum, gloomy, dismal, cheerless, surly, cross, angry, frowning, glowering, grumpy.

sultry adj **1** *a sultry day/atmosphere* close, airless, stuffy, stifling, suffocating, oppressive, muggy, humid, sticky, hot, sweltering. **2** *a sultry singer* sensual, sexy, voluptuous, seductive, provocative, alluring, tempting, passionate, erotic.

sum n **1** *find the sum of the line of figures* sum total, grand total, tally, aggregate, answer. **2** *a large sum of money* amount, quantity. **3** *get the children to do sums* arithmetical problem, problem, calculation, reckoning, tally. **4** *look at the problem in its sum* entirety, totality, total, whole; *inf* whole shebang, whole caboodle, whole shooting match.

sum up 1 *when the judge sums up* give a summing-up, summarize the evidence, review the evidence, summarize the argument. **2** *sum up the situation* form an opinion of, form an impression of, make one's mind up about, get the measure of, form a judgement of; *inf* size up. **3** *sum up the facts of the situation* give a summary of, summarize, précis, give an abstract of, encapsulate, put in a nutshell.

summarily adv *summarily dismissed when caught stealing* immediately, instantly, right away, straight away, at once, on the spot, directly, forthwith, promptly, speedily, swiftly, rapidly, without delay, suddenly, abruptly, peremptorily, without discussion, without formality.

summarize v *summarize the plot of the novel in a short essay|summarize recent events* give/make a summary of, sum up, give a synopsis of, précis, give a précis of, give a résumé of, give an abstract of, abridge, condense, epitomize, outline, sketch, give the main points, give a rundown of, review.

summary n *give a summary of the plot of the novel* synopsis, précis, résumé, abstract, abridgement, digest, epitome, outline, sketch, rundown, review, summing-up.

summary adj **1** *summary dismissal/justice* immediate, instant, instantaneous, direct, prompt, speedy, swift, rapid, without delay, sudden, abrupt, hasty, peremptory, without discussion, without formality. **2** *a summary account of the long debate* abridged, abbreviated, shortened, condensed, short, brief, concise, succinct, thumbnail, cursory.

summerhouse n pavilion, gazebo, arbour, bower, pergola.

summit n **1** *the summit of the mountain* top, peak, crest, crown, apex, vertex, apogee. **2** *the summit of her stage career* peak, height, pinnacle, culmination, climax, crowning-point, zenith, acme.

summon v **1** *summoned by the headmaster* send for, call for, bid, request the presence of, demand the presence of. **2** *summon a committee meeting* order, call, convene, assemble, convoke, muster, rally. **3** *summon a witness* summons, serve with a summons, cite, serve with a citation, serve with a writ, subpoena. **summon up 1** *summon up the courage to act* gather, collect, muster, rally, call into action, mobilize. **2** *summon up half-forgotten memories* call to mind, bring to mind, call up, conjure up, evoke, recall, revive. **3** *summon up evil spirits by magic* call up, conjure up, invoke, rouse up.

summons n **1** *a summons to give evidence in court* citation, writ, subpoena. **2** *obey the headmaster's summons to attend* order, directive, command, instruction, dictum, demand.

summons v *summons him to appear in court* serve with a summons, summon, serve with a citation/writ, subpoena.

sumptuous adj *sumptuous furnishings* lavish, luxurious, deluxe, opulent, magnificent, gorgeous, splendid, rich, costly, expensive, dear, extravagant; *inf* plush, ritzy.

sunburnt adj **1** *soothe her sunburnt shoulders* sunburned, burnt, peeling, burned, inflamed, blistering. **2** *showing off her sunburnt arms* suntanned, tanned, brown, bronzed.

sunder v *sunder the beam* separate, divide, split, sever, cleaver, rend.

sundry adj **1** *sundry items* several, various, varied, miscellaneous, assorted, diverse. **2** *on sundry occasions* several, some, various, different.

sunken adj **1** *a sunken terrace* at a lower level, below ground level, lowered. **2** *the sunken cheeks of the invalid* hollow, hollowed, concave, drawn, haggard.

sunless adj **1** *a sunless day* overcast, dark, grey, gloomy, murky. **2** *a sunless spot* dark, shady, shadowy, dim, gloomy, murky, bleak.

sunlight n *sunlight does not penetrate the forest* sun, sunshine, light, daylight, light of day.

sunny adj **1** *a sunny day* sunshiny, sunlit, bright, clear, fine, cloudless, unclouded, without a cloud in the sky. **2** *a sunny nature* happy, cheerful, cheery, light-hearted, bright, glad, gay, merry, joyful, buoyant, bubbly, blithe. **3** *look on the sunny side* bright, cheerful, hopeful, optimistic.

sunrise n dawn, crack of dawn, daybreak, morning, cock-crow; *lit* peep of day, aurora; *Amer* sunup.

sunset n nightfall, close of day, evening, twilight, dusk, gloaming; *Amer* sundown.

sunshine n **1** *sit and enjoy the sunshine* sun, sunlight, sun's rays. **2** *a life devoid of sunshine* happiness, laughter, cheerfulness, gladness, gaiety, merriment, joy, joyfulness, blitheness.

superannuated adj **1** *superannuated ex-employees* pensioned, pensioned off, retired, elderly. **2** *a superannuated bicycle* old, old-fashioned, antiquated, obsolete, broken-down; *inf* clapped-out.

superb adj **1** *dancers giving a superb performance* superlative, excellent, first-rate, first-

class, of the first water, outstanding, remarkable, dazzling, brilliant, marvellous, magnificent, wonderful, splendid, exquisite; *inf* fantastic, fabulous, A1. **2** *superb furnishings* magnificent, gorgeous, splendid, sumptuous, opulent, lavish, luxurious, de luxe; *inf* plush, ritzy.

supercilious adj arrogant, haughty, conceited, proud, vain, disdainful, scornful, condescending, superior, patronizing, imperious, overbearing, lofty, lordly, snobbish, snobby; *inf* hoity-toity, high-and-mighty, uppity, snooty, stuck-up, toffee-nosed.

superficial adj **1** *superficial damage/wounds only* surface, exterior, external, outer, outside, peripheral, slight. **2** *a superficial examination* cursory, perfunctory, hasty, hurried, casual, sketchy, desultory, slapdash. **3** *a superficial similarity* outward, apparent, evident, ostensible. **4** *rather a superficial person* shallow, empty-headed, trivial, frivolous, silly. **5** *a superficial book* lightweight, sketchy, slight, insignificant, trivial.

superfluous adj **1** *sell off the superfluous furniture* spare, to spare, surplus, surplus to requirements, extra, unneeded, unrequired, excess, in excess, supernumerary. **2** *their presence was superfluous* unnecessary, needless, unneeded, inessential, uncalled-for, unwarranted, gratuitous.

superhuman adj **1** *require a superhuman effort* herculean, phenomenal, prodigous, stupendous, heroic, extraordinary. **2** *superhuman intervention* divine, god-like, holy. **3** *a cry that seemed superhuman* supernatural, preternatural, preterhuman, paranormal, otherworldly.

superintend v *superintend the factory* be in charge of, be in control of, preside over, direct, administer, manage, run, look after, supervise, oversee.

superintendent n director, administrator, manager, supervisor, overseer, controller, boss, chief; *inf* honcho.

superior adj **1** *the superior player* better, greater, better-class, more expert, more skilful, more advanced. **2** *hold a superior position* higher, higher-ranking, higher-up. **3** *of superior quality* better, higher-grade, greater, surpassing. **4** *goods of superior leather* good-quality, high-quality, first-rate, top-quality, high-grade, of the first water, of the first order, choice, select, prime, fine, up-market. **5** *live in a superior area* high-class, up-market, select, exclusive, snobby. **6** *act superior* | *give her a superior look* haughty, disdainful, condescending, supercilious, patronizing, lofty, lordly, snobbish, snobby; *inf* high-and-mighty, hoity-toity, uppity, snooty, stuck-up, toffee-nosed.

superior n *get a warning from his superior* boss, manager, chief, supervisor, foreman.

superiority n **1** *the superiority of their performance* better quality, supremacy. **2** *their superiority in numbers* advantage, lead, dominance.

superlative adj *superlative players* | *of superlative quality* best, greatest, supreme, consummate, first-rate, first-class, of the first water, of the first order, of the higher order, brilliant, excellent, magnificent, outstanding, unsurpassed, unparalleled, unrivalled, peerless, matchless, transcendent; *inf* crack, ace.

supernatural adj **1** *supernatural beings* otherworldly, unearthly, spectral, ghostly, phantom, magical, mystic, unreal. **2** *supernatural powers* paranormal, supernormal, hypernormal, psychic, miraculous, extraordinary, uncanny.

supersede v **1** *workers superseded by machines* take the place of, replace, take over from, displace, supplant, oust, usurp. **2** *supersede him as chairman* replace, take the place of, take over from, succeed. **3** *the office equipment was superseded when it became obsolete* discard, cast aside, throw out, dispose of, abandon, jettison; *inf* chuck out.

supervise v **1** *supervise the factory* superintend, be in charge of, direct, administer, manage, run. *see* SUPERINTEND. **2** *supervise the work of trainees/the trainees* oversee, keep an eye on, watch, observe, inspect, be responsible for, guide.

supervision n **1** *the supervision of the factory* administration, management, direction, control, charge, superintendence. **2** *children playing under supervision* observation, inspection, guidance.

supervisor n **1** *the supervisor of the factory* director, administrator, manager, overseer, controller, boss, chief, superintendent; *inf* honcho. **2** *the supervisors of the children/ trainees* overseer, observer, inspector, guide, advisor.

supine adj **1** *supine on the floor* flat on one's back, prone, prostrate, horizontal. **2** *rather a supine individual* weak, feckless, spineless, idle, inactive, indolent, lazy, slothful, languid, apathetic, indifferent; *inf* laid-back.

supper n **1** *invite guests to supper* dinner, evening meal. **2** *have toasted cheese for supper* evening snack.

supplant v *a nobleman plotting to supplant the king* take the place of, take over from,

replace, displace, supersede, oust, usurp, overthrow, remove, unseat.

supple adj **1** *supple gymnasts* lithe, loose-limbed, limber. **2** *supple leather* pliant, pliable, flexible, bendable, stretchable, elastic.

supplement adj **1** *dietary supplement* addition, supplementation, additive, extra, add-on. **2** *add a supplement to the book/document* appendix, addendum, end-matter, tailpiece, codicil, rider. **3** *a newspaper supplement* pull-out, insert, special-feature section, magazine section.

supplement v *supplement his salary with an evening job* add to, augment, increase, top up, complement.

supplementary adj **1** *a supplementary payment* supplemental, additional, extra, add-on, complementary. **2** *a supplementary section* added, appended, attached, extra.

suppliant n *suppliants asking the king for mercy* supplicant, petitioner, pleader, beseecher, applicant, suitor, beggar, appellant.

supplicate v *supplicate for a pardon* plead, entreat, beseech, beg, implore, petition, appeal, solicit, ask, request, pray, invoke.

supplication n *ignore the poor man's supplication* plea, pleading, entreaty, beseeching, begging, imploration, petition, appeal, solicitation, request, prayer, invocation.

supplies n *army supplies running out* provisions, stores, rations, food, victuals, provender.

supply v **1** *supply the necessary money* provide, give, furnish, contribute, donate, grant, come up with; *inf* fork out, shell out. **2** *supply him with food/tools* provide, furnish, equip, kit out, outfit. **3** *supply all their needs* satisfy, meet, fulfil.

supply n **1** *difficult to organize the supply of wood* supplying, providing, provision, furnishing. **2** *build up a supply of logs* stock, store, reserve, reservoir, stockpile, heap, pile, mass, hoard, cache. *see* SUPPLIES.

supply adj *a supply teacher* substitute, stand-in, fill-in, locum, temporary, stopgap.

support v **1** *beams supporting the roof* bear, carry, hold up, prop up, bolster up, brace, keep up, shore up, underpin, buttress. **2** *work to support his family* maintain, provide for, provide sustenance for, sustain, take care of, look after. **3** *support him in his hour of need* give moral support to, give strength to, be a source of strength to, comfort, help, sustain, encourage, buoy up, hearten, fortify; *inf* buck up. **4** *bring evidence to support his argument* back up, substantiate, give force to, bear out, corroborate, confirm, verify, validate, authenticate, endorse, ratify. **5** *support several charities/new enterprises* back, contribute to, give a donation to, give money to, subsidize, fund, finance. **6** *support the youngest candidate* back, champion, give help to, help, assist, aid, be on the side of, side with, vote for, stand behind, stand up for, take one's part, take up the cudgels for; *inf* stick up for. **7** *support conservation of the countryside* back, advocate, promote, further, champion, be on the side of, espouse, espouse the cause of, be in favour of, recommend, defend. **8** *cannot support his behaviour* bear, put up with, tolerate, stand, abide, suffer, stomach, brook.

support n **1** *the supports of the bridge* base, foundations, pillar, post, prop, underprop, underpinning, substructure, brace, buttress, abutment, bolster, stay. **2** *pay towards his family's support* keep, maintenance, sustenance, food and accommodation, subsistence, aliment. **3** *in need of support in his hour of need* moral support, friendship, strengthening, strength, encouragement, buoying up, heartening, fortification; *inf* bucking up. **4** *give support to charities/enterprises* backing, contribution, donation, money, subsidy, funding, funds, finance, capital. **5** *give his support to the youngest candidate* backing, help, assistance, aid, votes. *see* SUPPORT v 6. **6** *in support of conservation of the countryside* backing, advocacy, promotion, championship, espousal, recommendation. **7** *he was a great support to his widowed mother* help, assistance, comfort, tower of strength, prop, backbone, mainstay.

supporter n **1** *supporters of the charity* backer, contributor, donor, sponsor, patron, friend, well-wisher. **2** *the candidate's supporters* backers, helper, adherent, follower, ally, voter, apologist. **3** *supporters of the cause of animals* backer, adherent, advocate, promoter, champion, defender, apologist. **4** *football supporter* fan, follower.

supportive adj *need supportive friends when in trouble* helpful, encouraging, caring, sympathetic, understanding.

suppose v **1** *I suppose you're right* dare say, assume, take for granted, take as read, presume, expect, imagine, believe, think, fancy, suspect, guess, surmise, reckon, conjecture, theorize, opine. **2** *suppose we arrive late* take as a hypothesis, hypothesize, postulate, posit. **3** *creation supposes a creator* presuppose, require, imply.

supposed adj *his supposed brother* presumed, assumed, believed, professed, so-called,

alleged, putative, reputed. **be supposed to** *they are not supposed to know* meant, intended, expected.

supposition n **1** *his suppositions proved correct* assumption, presumption, suspicion, guess, surmise, conjecture, speculation, theory. **2** *on the supposition that he is right* assumption, hypothesis, postulation.

suppress v **1** *suppress the rebellion* conquer, vanquish, put an end to, crush, quell, squash, stamp out, extinguish, put out, put an end to, crack down on, clamp down on. **2** *suppress his anger/laughter* restrain, keep a rein on, hold back, control, keep under control, check, keep in check, curb. **3** *suppress the information/truth* keep secret, conceal, hide, keep hidden, keep silent about, withhold, cover up, smother, stifle, muzzle.

suppression n **1** *the suppression of the rebellion* conquering, crushing, extinction, crackdown, clampdown. *see* SUPPRESS 1. **2** *the suppression of his anger* restraint, holding back, curbing. *see* SUPPRESS 2. **3** *the suppression of the information/truth* concealment, withholding, cover-up, smothering, stifling, muzzling. *see* SUPPRESS 3.

suppurate v fester, matter, maturate, gather, come to a head, discharge.

supremacy n **1** *a country holding supremacy over its neighbours* ascendancy, predominance, paramountcy, dominion, sway, authority, mastery, control, power, rule, sovereignty, lordship. **2** *challenge her supremacy as top tennis player* pre-eminence, dominance, superiority, ascendancy, incomparability, inimitability, matchlessness, peerlessness.

supreme adj **1** *the supreme commander* highest-ranking, highest, leading, chief, foremost, principal. **2** *supreme bravery | a supreme effort* extreme, greatest, utmost, uttermost, maximum, extraordinary, remarkable. **3** *the supreme sacrifice/judgement* final, last, ultimate. **reign supreme** *the athlete still reigns supreme* be superlative, be unsurpassed, be the best, be the greatest, be unrivalled, be matchless, be peerless, be pre-eminent, be excellent, be first-rate.

sure adj **1** *we cannot be sure that he is honest* certain, definite, positive, convinced, confident, decided, assured, free from doubt, unhesitating, unwavering, unfaltering, unvacillating. **2** *sure of success* assured of, certain of, confident of, with no doubts about. **3** *a sure success/failure* assured, certain, guaranteed, inevitable, irrevocable; *inf* in the bay. **4** *in the sure knowledge* true, certain, undoubted, absolute, categorical, well-grounded, well-founded, proven, unquestionable, indisputable, incontestable, irrefutable, incontrovertible, undeniable. **5** *a sure remedy* certain, unfailing, infallible, never-failing, reliable, dependable, trustworthy, tested, tried and true, foolproof, effective, efficacious; *inf* sure-fire. **6** *sure friend* true, reliable, dependable, trusted, trustworthy, trusty, loyal, faithful, steadfast. **7** *with a sure hand* firm, steady, stable, secure, confident, unhesitating, unfaltering, unwavering. **be sure of** *be sure to arrive on time* be certain to, be careful to, take care to, remember to.

surely adv **1** *they will surely fail* for certain, certainly, definitely, assuredly, undoubtedly, without doubt, beyond the shadow of a doubt, indubitably, unquestionably, incontestably, irrefutably, incontrovertibly, undeniably, without fail, inevitably, unavoidably. **2** *walk slowly but surely* firmly, steadily, confidently, unhesitatingly.

surety n **1** *use the house as surety for the loan* security, indemnity, collateral, guarantee, pledge, bond. **2** *he acted as surety for her loan* guarantor, sponsor.

surface n **1** *the surface of the wood* outside, exterior, top. **2** *look beneath the surface to appreciate his vulnerability* outward appearance, superficial appearance, façade. **on the surface** *on the surface the firm seems profitable* at first glance, to the casual eye, outwardly, to all appearances, apparently, superficially.

surface adj *a surface scratch* superficial, external, exterior, outward.

surface v **1** *the submarine surfaced* come to the surface, come up, come to the top. **2** *the old rumours have surfaced again* reappear, appear, come to light, come up, emerge, crop up. **3** *he won't surface till lunchtime* get up, get out of bed, rise, wake, awaken.

surfeit n **1** *a surfeit of food and drink* excess, surplus, oversupply, superabundance, superfluity, glut, too much. **2** *ill from a surfeit of chocolates* overindulgence, satiety, satiation.

surfeit v *be surfeited with food/pleasure* satiate, gorge, overfeed, overfill, glut, cram, stuff, overindulge.

surge n **1** *a surge of water* gush, rush, outpouring, stream, flow, sweep, efflux. **2** *a sudden surge in prices* upsurge, increase, rise, upswing, escalation. **3** *the surge of the sea* rise, swell, swelling, heaving, billowing, rolling, eddying, swirling.

surge v **1** *the water surged from the broken pipe* | *crowds surging from the hall* gush, rush, stream, flow. **2** *the sea surged in the storm* rise, swell, heave, billow, roll, eddy, swirl.

surly adj bad-tempered, ill-natured, crabbed, grumpy, crotchety, grouchy, cantankerous, irascible, testy, crusty, gruff, abrupt, brusque, churlish, uncivil, morose, sullen, sulky.

surmise v *she surmised that he was lying* guess, conjecture, suspect, deduce, assume, presume, gather, feel, be of the opinion, think, believe, imagine.

surmount v **1** *many problems/obstacles to surmount* get over, overcome, conquer, triumph over, prevail over, get the better of, beat. **2** *climbers struggling to surmount the mountain* climb, ascend, scale, mount. **3** *snow surmounting the hills* top, cap, crown. **4** *mountains surmounting the houses* rise above, tower above, overtop, dominate.

surname n last name, family name, patronymic.

surpass v *her beauty/work surpasses that of the others* be greater than, be better than, beat, exceed, excel, transcend, outdo, outshine, outstrip, overshadow, eclipse.

surpassing adj exceptional, extraordinary, remarkable, outstanding, striking, phenomenal, rare, supreme, incomparable, inimitable, unrivalled, matchless.

surplus n *get rid of the surplus after the sale* excess, remainder, residue, surfeit.

surplus adj *surplus food going to waste* excess, in excess, superfluous, left over, unused, remaining, extra, spare.

surprise v **1** *their sudden appearance surprised him* astonish, amaze, nonplus, take aback, startle, astound, stun, flabbergast, stagger, leave open-mouthed, take one's breath away; *inf* bowl over, blow one's mind. **2** *surprise the burglars opening the safe* take by surprise, catch unawares, catch off guard, catch red-handed, catch in the act, catch napping, burst in on, spring upon, catch with his/her trousers down, catch on the hop.

surprise n **1** *look up in surprise* astonishment, amazement, incredulity, wonder. **2** *it was a surprise when she left* shock, bolt from the blue, bombshell, revelation.

surprised adj *a surprised look* | *the surprised children* astonished, amazed, nonplussed, startled, astounded, stunned, flabbergasted, staggered, open-mouthed, speechless, thunderstruck. *see* SURPRISE v 1.

surprising adj astonishing, amazing, startling, astounding, staggering, incredible, extraordinary, remarkable; *inf* mind-blowing.

surrender v **1** *surrender his right to the title* give up, relinquish, renounce, forgo, forsake, cede, abdicate, waive. **2** *surrender the keys of the car* hand over, give up, deliver up, part with, let go of, relinquish. **3** *surrender to the enemy* give in, give oneself up, yield, submit, capitulate, lay down one's arms, raise/show the white flag, throw in the towel, throw in the sponge. **4** *surrender to his old habits* give way to, yield to, succumb to, capitulate to. **5** *surrender all hope* give up, abandon, leave behind, lose.

surrender n **1** *the surrender of his title* surrendering, relinquishment, renunciation, forgoing, ceding, cession, abdication. *see* SURRENDER v 1. **2** *witness their surrender to the enemy* yielding, capitulation, submission. *see* SURRENDER v 3.

surreptitious adj *find the information by surreptitious means* stealthy, clandestine, secret, sneaky, sly, cunning, furtive, underhand, undercover, covert.

surround v *a fence surrounds the lake* go around, encircle, enclose, encompass, ring, gird, girdle, fence in, hem in, confine.

surrounding adj *the surrounding countryside* neighbouring, nearby.

surroundings npl *brought up in squalid surroundings* environment, setting, milieu, element, background.

surveillance n *under surveillance* observation, watch, scrutiny, spying, espionage.

survey v **1** *survey the burnt building* look at, take a look at, observe, view, contemplate, regard, examine, inspect. **2** *survey the evidence* look at, look over, scan, study, consider, review, examine, inspect, scrutinize, take stock of; *inf* size up. **3** *survey a building* make a survey of, value, carry out a valuation of, estimate the value of, appraise, assess, prospect, triangulate.

survey n **1** *undertake a survey of the evidence* study, consideration, review, overview, examination, inspection, scrutinization, scrutiny. *see* SURVEY v 2. **2** *carry out a survey of the building* valuation, appraisal. *see* SURVEY v 3. **3** *carry out a survey into TV viewing habits* investigation, inquiry, research, study, review, probe, questionnaire.

survive v **1** *old customs surviving in the village* live on, be extant, continue, remain, last, persist, endure, exist, be. **2** *fathers surviving their sons* outlive, outlast, live after, remain alive after. **3** *people surviving in the freezing conditions* remain alive, live, hold out, pull through, cling to life.

susceptibility n **1** *the young woman's susceptibility* impressionability, credulity, credulousness, gullibility, defencelessness, vulnerability, responsiveness, sensitivity, emotionalism. *see* SUSCEPTIBLE. **2** *their susceptibility to his charm* openness, responsiveness, receptiveness, vulnerability, defencelessness. **3** *their susceptibility to colds* liability, proneness, predisposition, propensity. *see* SUSCEPTIBLE.

susceptible adj *protect susceptible young girls* impressionable, likely to be taken in, credulous, gullible, innocent, defenceless, vulnerable, easily led, responsive, sensitive, thin-skinned, highly-strung, emotional. **susceptible to 1** *susceptible to his charm* open to, responsive to, receptive to, vulnerable to, defenceless against. **2** *susceptible to colds/disease* subject to, liable to, prone to, inclined to, predisposed to, disposed.

suspect v **1** *I suspect you could be right* feel, have a feeling, be inclined to think, fancy, surmise, guess, conjecture, have a suspicion that, speculate, have a hunch, suppose, believe, think, conclude. **2** *suspect the truth of his statement* doubt, have doubts about, harbour suspicions about, have misgivings about, be sceptical about, distrust, mistrust. *see* SUSPICION 1. **3** *police suspect her brother* regard as guilty, regard as a wrongdoer.

suspend v **1** *suspend a light from the tree* hang, put up, swing, dangle, sling. **2** *suspend the proceedings* adjourn, interrupt, cut short, bring to an end, cease, discontinue, break off, arrest, put off, postpone, delay, defer, shelve, pigeonhole, table, put on the back burner; *inf* put on ice. **3** *suspend him from his job/membership* debar, shut out, exclude, keep out, remove.

suspense n *in a state of suspense about the outcome* uncertainty, doubt, doubtfulness, anticipation, expectation, expectancy, excitement, tension, anxiety, nervousness, apprehension, apprehensiveness.

suspension n **1** *the suspension of talks* adjournment, interruption, cessation, postponement, delay, deferment, shelving. *see* SUSPEND 2. **2** *his suspension from office* debarment, exclusion, removal, temporary removal.

suspicion n **1** *have suspicions about his motives* doubts, misgivings, qualms, wariness, chariness, scepticism, distrust, mistrust; *inf* funny feeling. **2** *his suspicion is that she will appear* feeling, surmise, guess, conjecture, speculation, hunch, supposition, belief, notion, idea, conclusion; *inf* gut feeling. **3** *a suspicion of liqueur in the dessert* trace, touch, suggestion, hint, soupçon, tinge, shade.

suspicious adj **1** *give him suspicious looks* doubtful, unsure, wary, chary, sceptical, distrustful, mistrustful, disbelieving. **2** *police observing a suspicious character* guilty-looking, dishonest-looking, strange-looking, queer-looking, funny-looking; *inf* shifty, shady. **3** *suspicious circumstances* questionable, doubtful, odd, strange, irregular, queer, funny; *inf* fishy, shady.

sustain v **1** *beams sustaining the weight of the roof* bear, support, carry, keep something up, prop up, shore up. **2** *sustain one's courage* keep something up, keep something going, continue, carry on, maintain, prolong, protract. **3** *sustain him in his hour of need* support, give strength to, be a source of strength to, be a tower of strength to, comfort, help, assist, encourage, buoy up, cheer up, hearten; *inf* buck up. **4** *not enough to sustain her* keep alive, keep going, maintain, continue, preserve. **5** *enough food to sustain them* feed, nourish, keep going, nurture. **6** *sustain defeat/injury* experience, undergo, go through, suffer, endure. **7** *the court sustained his claim* uphold, validate, ratify, vindicate. **8** *evidence sustaining his allegations* confirm, verify, corroborate, substantiate, bear out, prove, authenticate, validate.

sustained adj *a sustained interest in the firm* continuing, steady, continuous, constant, prolonged, perpetual, unremitting.

sustenance n **1** *enough money to buy sustenance for his family* food, nourishment, daily bread, provisions, victuals, rations, aliment, comestibles; *lit* provender; *inf* grub, chow, scoff. **2** *try to earn enough for sustenance* living, livelihood, means of support, maintenance, support, subsistence.

swagger v **1** *swagger down the street in his new coat* strut, parade, prance. **2** *swaggering about his recent victory* boast, bray, bluster; *inf* show off, swank.

swagger n **1** *walk with a swagger* strut, parading, prancing. **2** *tired of his swagger* boasting, bragging, bluster, swashbuckling, braggadocio, vainglory; *inf* showing-off, swank.

swallow v **1** *swallow the meat with difficulty* gulp down, eat, consume, devour, ingest; *inf* scoff. **2** *swallow two drinks in quick succession* gulp down, drink, swill down; *inf* swig. **3** *unable to swallow her treatment of him* put up with, tolerate, endure, stand, bear, suffer, abide, stomach, brook. **4** *expect him to swallow their story* believe, accept; *inf* fall for, buy. **5** *swallow one's pride/anger* repress,

restrain, hold back, choke back, control, rein in. **swallow up 1** *the waves swallowed him up* engulf, swamp, flood over, overwhelm. **2** *big companies swallowing up small ones* engulf, take over, absorb, assimilate, overrun, overwhelm, swamp.

swamp n *get stuck in a swamp* marsh, bog, quagmire, mire, morass, fen, quag.

swamp v **1** *heavy rains swamping the town* flood, inundate, deluge, wash out, soak, drench, saturate. **2** *swamped with applications* inundate, flood, deluge, overwhelm, engulf, snow under, overload, overburden, weight down, besiege, beset.

swampy adj marshy, boggy, soggy, soft, spongy, waterlogged, miry, fenny, quaggy.

swap v **1** *children swapping toys with each other* exchange, interchange, trade, barter, switch. **2** *swap jokes/insults* exchange, trade, bandy.

swarm n **1** *a swarm of bees* hive, flight. **2** *a swarm of people* crowd, multitude, horde, host, mob, throng, stream, mass, body, army, flock, herd, pack, drove.

swarm v **1** *shoppers swarming to the sales* flock, crowd, throng, stream, surge. **2** *rats swarming all over the floor* run, crawl, crowd. **be swarming with** be crowded with, be thronged with, be overrun with, abound in, be teeming with, be bristling with, be alive with, be crawling with, be infested with.

swarthy adj dark, dark-coloured, dark-skinned, dark-complexioned, dusky, tanned.

swashbuckling adj swaggering, dashing, daring, adventurous, bold, gallant.

swathe v *swathed in bandages* wrap, envelop, bind, swaddle, bandage, bundle up, muffle up, cover, shroud, drape.

sway v **1** *trees swaying in the breeze* swing, shake, bend, lean, incline. **2** *drunks swaying on their way home* roll, stagger, wobble, rock. **3** *swaying her hips* swing, oscillate, shake. **4** *swaying between emigrating and staying* waver, hesitate, fluctuate, vacillate, oscillate. **5** *swayed by their arguments* influence, affect, persuade, prevail on, bring round, win over, induce. **6** *swayed by ambition* rule, govern, dominate, control, direct, guide.

sway n **1** *countries under the sway of Rome* jurisdiction, rule, government, sovereignty, dominion, control, command, power, authority, ascendancy, domination, mastery. **2** *under the sway of her husband* control, domination, power, authority, influence, guidance, direction. **hold sway** *the same* *political power still holds sway* be most powerful, hold power, rule, be in control, predominate, have ascendance, have the greatest influence.

swear v **1** *swear to take care of the child | swear that he would take care of the child* promise, promise under oath, solemnly promise, pledge oneself, vow, give one's word, take an oath, swear on the Bible. **2** *he swore that he was fit to drive* vow, insist, be emphatic, pronounce, declare, assert, maintain, contend, aver. **3** *he swore when he hit his finger | swear at the other driver* curse, blaspheme, be blasphemous, utter profanities, be foul-mouthed, use bad language, take the Lord's name in vain, swear like a trooper; *inf* cuss, turn the air blue. **swear by 1** *swear by Almighty God* call as one's witness, appeal to, invoke. **2** *swear by her remedy for colds* have confidence in, have faith in, have trust in, place reliance on, depend on, believe in.

swearing n *disapprove of swearing* cursing, blaspheming, profanity, imprecation, bad language.

sweat n **1** *sweat pouring from his brow* perspiration; *Tech* sudor, diaphoresis. **2** *in a sweat until the results came through* fluster, fret, dither, fuss, panic, state of anxiety/agitation/nervousness/worry; *inf* tizwoz, stew, lather. **3** *it was a sweat to finish on time* labour, effort, chore, back-breaking task.

sweat v **1** *sweating in the heat* perspire, exude perspiration, drip with perspiration/sweat, break out in a sweat. **2** *they were sweating until the results came through* be flushed, fret, dither, fuss, panic, be on tenterhooks, be in a state of anxiety/agitation/nervousness, worry, agonize, lose sleep; *inf* be on pins and needles, be in a state of anxiety/agitation/nervousness, worry, agonize, lose sleep, be in a state/flap/tiz-woz/stew/lather. **3** *sweat to get the work done* work hard, work like a Trojan, labour, toil, slog.

sweaty adj *sweaty hands* sweating, perspiring, clammy, sticky.

sweep v **1** *sweep the floor* brush, vacuum, clean. **2** *sweep up the dust* brush up, clean up, clear up, remove. **3** *sweep aside the rest of the queue* push, thrust, shove, force, elbow, jostle, make a path through. **4** *sweep away/aside their objections* cast aside, discard, disregard, ignore, take no notice of, dismiss. **5** *swept away by the waves* carry, pull, drag, drive. **6** *sweep from the room* glide, sail, stride, flounce. **7** *fire sweeping through the building* race, hurtle, streak, whip, spread

like lightning; *inf* tear. **8** *cars sweeping up the drive* glide, sail, zoom, swoop.

sweep n **1** *with one sweep of her hand* gesture, movement, move, action, stroke, wave. **2** *the sweep of the road* curve, curvature, bend, arc. **3** *within the sweep of his power* range, scope, span, compass, reach. **4** *a sweep of pasture-lands* stretch, expanse, extent, vastness.

sweeping adj **1** *sweeping reforms* extensive, wide-ranging, global, broad, wide, comprehensive, all-inclusive, all-embracing, thorough, radical, far-reaching. **2** *make sweeping statements* blanket, wholesale, over-general, unqualified, indiscriminate. **3** *a sweeping victory* decisive, overwhelming, thorough, complete, total, absolute, out-and-out, thoroughgoing.

sweet adj **1** *sweet types of food* sweetened, sugary, sugared, honeyed, syrupy, saccharine. **2** *sweet fruit* ripe, mellow, luscious. **3** *the sweet smell of roses* sweet-smelling, fragrant, aromatic, perfumed, scented, balmy. **4** *the sweet sound of children's voices* sweet-sounding, musical, tuneful, dulcet, mellifluous, soft, harmonious, euphonious, silvery, silver-toned. **5** *sweet foodstuffs* not sour, not rotten, wholesome, palatable, pure. **6** *the sweet sight of home* pleasant, pleasing, agreeable, delightful, welcome. **7** *have a sweet nature* good-natured, amiable, pleasant, agreeable, friendly, kindly, charming, likeable, appealing, engaging, winning, winsome, taking. **8** *sweet girls* attractive, beautiful, lovely, comely, glamorous. **9** *his sweet wife* dear, dearest, darling, beloved, loved, cherished, precious, treasured. **sweet on** *sweet on the boy next door* fond of, taken with, in love with, enamoured of, infatuated with, keen on; *inf* gone on, made about.

sweet n **1** *have fruit for sweet* sweet course, dessert, pudding; *inf* afters. **2** *suck a sweet* bonbon, sweetmeat; *Amer* candy; *inf* sweetie.

sweeten v **1** *sweeten the tea* make sweet, add sugar to, sugar, add honey to, add sweetener to. **2** *sweeten an unpleasant situation* make agreeable, soften, ease, alleviate, relieve, mitigate. **3** *sweeten her father before asking for a loan* soften, soften up, mellow, pacify, appease, mollify. **4** *sweeten the air* purify, fresh, ventilate, deodorize.

sweetheart n **1** *his teenage sweetheart* girlfriend, boyfriend, lover, suitor, admirer, beau, paramour, inamorato, inamorata; *lit* swain, follower; *inf* steady, flame. **2** *goodbye, sweetheart* dear, dearest, darling, love, beloved; *inf* honey, sweetie, sugar, baby.

swell v **1** *his stomach/ankle swelled up* expand, bulge, distend, become distended, inflate, become inflated, dilate, become bloated, blow up, puff up, balloon, tumefy, intumesce. **2** *the numbers have swelled* increase, grow larger, grow greater, rise, mount, escalate, accelerate, step up, snowball, mushroom. **3** *the music swelled* grow loud, grow louder, intensify, heighten.

swell n **1** *the swell of the sea* billowing, undulation, surging. **2** *a swell in numbers* increase, rise, escalation, acceleration, stepping-up, snowballing, mushrooming. **3** *think himself a bit of a swell* dandy, fop, beau; *inf* fashion plate, trend-setter, nob.

swell adj **1** *have a swell time* enjoyable, marvellous, wonderful, first-rate, excellent. **2** *a swell hotel* expensive, luxurious, deluxe, fashionable, elegant, grand; *inf* posh, plush, ritzy.

swelling n *treat the swelling on his head* bump, lump, bulge, blister, inflammation, protuberance, tumescence.

sweltering adj *a sweltering day | sweltering conditions* too hot, hot, torrid, tropical, stifling, suffocating, humid, sultry, sticky, muggy, clammy, close, stuffy; *inf* boiling, baking.

swerve v *swerve to avoid an oncoming car* change direction, go off course, veer, turn aside, skew, deviate, sheer, twist.

swift adj **1** *a swift runner* fast, rapid, quick, speedy, fleet-footed, fleet, swift as an arrow; *inf* nippy. **2** *at a swift pace* fast, rapid, quick, brisk, lively, speedy, expeditious, express; *inf* spanking, nippy. **3** *a swift change of plan* rapid, sudden, abrupt, hasty, hurried, meteoric. **4** *a swift reply* rapid, prompt, immediate, instantaneous.

swiftness n **1** *the swiftness of the runners* fastness, rapidity, rapidness, quickness, speediness, fleetness; *inf* nippiness. **2** *the swiftness of the race* fastness, rapidity, rapidness, quickness, briskness, liveliness, speed, speediness, expeditiousness. **3** *the swiftness of the change of plan* rapidity, rapidness, suddenness, abruptness, haste, hastiness, hurriedness. **4** *the swiftness of the reply* rapidity, rapidness, promptness, immediateness, immediacy, instantaneousness.

swill v *swill pints of beer* gulp down, drink, quaff, swallow, down, drain, guzzle; *inf* swig, knock off. **swill out** *swill out the stables* sluice, wash down, wash out, clean out, flush out, rinse out.

swill n **1** *take a swill from the beer-mug* gulp, drink, swallow; *inf* swig. **2** *remove the swill from the pigsties* pigswill, waste matter, waste, slop, refuse, scourings.

swim v **1** *children swimming in the pond* float, tread water. **2** *food swimming in grease* be saturated in, be drenched in, be soaked in, be steeped in, be immersed in.

swimmingly adv *things going swimmingly* very well, smoothly, effortlessly, like clockwork, with no hitch, without difficulty, as planned; *inf* like a dream.

swindle v *swindle the old lady* defraud, cheat, trick, fleece, dupe, deceive, rook, exploit; *inf* do, con, diddle, rip off, take for a ride, pull a fast one on, bilk.

swindle n *get the money through a swindle* fraud, trick, deception, exploitation, sharp practice; *inf* con-trick, con, diddle, rip-off, fiddle.

swindler n *done out of her money by a swindler* fraudster, cheat, trickster, rogue, mountebank, exploiter; *inf* con-man, con artist, shark, bilker.

swing v **1** *lights swinging from the roof* hang, be suspended, dangle, be pendent. **2** *the pendulum swings* move back and forth, sway, oscillate, wag. **3** *the road swings to the right* curve, veer, turn, lean, incline, wind, twist. **4** *swing down the road* march, stride, stroll. **5** *he swings from optimism to despair* change, fluctuate, oscillate, waver, seesaw, yo-yo. **6** *manage to swing an interview with the chairman* achieve, obtain, acquire, get, manoeuvre.

swing n **1** *the swing of the pendulum* swaying, oscillation, wagging. **2** *music with a swing* rhythm, beat, pulse. **3** *a swing to the left at the election* move, change, variation, turnaround.

swirl v *water swirling round and round* whirl, eddy, circulate, revolve, spin, twist, churn, swish.

switch n **1** *a switch from a tree* shoot, twig, branch. **2** *hit the child with a switch* cane, rod, stick, whip, thong, cat-o'-nine-tails. **3** *a sudden switch in direction* change, change of direction, shift, reversal, turnaround, about-turn, swerve, U-turn. **4** *the switch from one method to another* change, changeover, transfer, conversion. **5** *get a new book in a switch with his friend* exchange, trade; *inf* swap.

switch v **1** *switch the naughty child* cane, whip, lash, birch, scourge, flagellate. **2** *switch directions* change, shift, reverse. **3** *switch cars* exchange, interchange, trade, barter; *inf* swap.

swollen adj *a swollen stomach* expanded, bulging, distended, inflated, dilated, bloated, blown-up, puffed-up, puffy, tumescent.

swoop v *hawks swooping on their prey* pounce, dive, descend, sweep down on, drop down on. **swoop up** *swoop up the baby in her arms* take up, lift up, pick up, scoop up, seize, snatch, grab.

sword n blade, steel; *lit* brand. **cross swords** fight, do battle, quarrel, have a dispute, engage in conflict, wrangle, bicker, lock horns; *inf* have a dust-up, have a scrap, have a barney. **put to the sword** *put the traitor to the sword* put to death, execute, kill, slay, murder.

sybaritic adj *sybaritic tastes* luxurious, self-indulgent, pleasure-seeking, sensual, voluptuous, hedonistic, epicurean, debauched, dissolute.

sycophant n *a great man surrounded by sycophants* toady, fawner, flatterer, truckler, Uriah Heep; *inf* boot-licker, yes-man.

sycophantic adj servile, subservient, obsequious, toadying, fawning, flattering, ingratiating, unctuous, truckling, Uriah Heepish; *inf* boot-licking.

syllabus n *introduce a new syllabus to the schools* course of study, educational programme, course outline.

symbol n **1** *the dove is the symbol of peace* emblem, token, sign, badge, representation, figure, image, type. **2** *mathematical/chemical symbol* sign, character, mark. **3** *the symbol of the firm* stamp, emblem, badge, trademark, logo, logotype, monogram.

symbolic adj **1** *the dove being symbolic of peace* emblematic, representative, typical. **2** *a symbolic dance* representative, illustrative, emblematic, figurative, allegorical.

symbolize v *the dove symbolizing peace* be a symbol of, stand for, be a sign of, represent, personify, exemplify, typify, betoken, denote, signify, mean.

symmetrical adj **1** *symmetrical features* balanced, well-proportioned, proportional, in proportion, regular, even, harmonious. **2** *the two sides of the building must be symmetrical* regular, even, uniform, consistent, in agreement.

symmetry n **1** *the symmetry of her features* balance, proportions, regularity, evenness of form, harmony. **2** *the symmetry of the two sides of the building* regularity, evenness, uniformity, consistency, congruity, conformity, agreement, correspondence.

sympathetic adj **1** *be sympathetic when she lost | give the losers a sympathetic look* compassionate, commiserating, commiserative,

pitying, condoling, consoling, comforting, supportive, caring, concerned, solicitous, considerate, kindly, kind, kind-hearted, warm, warm-hearted, understanding, charitable, empathetic. **2** *she's a very sympathetic person/character* pleasant, agreeable, likeable, congenial, friendly, sociable, companionable, neighbourly, easy to get along with; *inf* simpatico. **3** *not very sympathetic to their cause* in sympathy with, well-disposed to, favourably disposed to, favourable to, in favour of, approving of, pro, on the side of, supporting of, encouraging of.

sympathize v **1** *sympathize with the bereaved* show sympathy for, be sympathetic towards, show compassion for, be compassionate towards, commiserate with, pity, offer condolences to, console, offer consolation to, comfort, be supportive of, show understanding to, empathize with. **2** *sympathize with their cause/aims* be in sympathy with, be sympathetic towards, be in favour of, be well-disposed to, approve of, commend, back, side with, support, encourage.

sympathizer n **1** *the bereaved being comforted by sympathizers* commiserater, condoler, consoler, comforter, empathizer. **2** *sympathizers of their cause* advocate, supporter, backer, well-wisher, ally, partisan, fellow-traveller.

sympathy n **1** *express their sympathy to the bereaved* compassion, commiseration, pity, condolence, consolation, comfort, solace, support, caring, concern, solicitude, solicitousness, consideration, kindness, kind-heartedness, warmth, warm-heartedness, charity, charitableness, understanding, empathy. **2** *a bond of sympathy between them* affinity, empathy, rapport, fellow-feeling, harmony, accord, compatibility, closeness, friendship. **3** *show sympathy for their cause* favour, approval, approbation, good will, commendation, support, encouragement.

symptom n **1** *a symptom of the disease* sign, indication, signal, warning, mark, characteristic, feature. **2** *his bad behaviour was a symptom of his unhappiness* expression, sign, indication, signal, mark, token, evidence, demonstration, display.

symptomatic adj *pains symptomatic of heart disease* indicative of, signalling, characteristic of, suggesting, suggestive of.

synthesis n **1** *the synthesis of several elements into a whole* combination, combining, union, unification, merging, amalgamation, fusion, coalescence, integration. **2** *a synthesis of two substances* combination, union, amalgam, blend, compound, fusion, coalescence.

synthetic adj *synthetic leather* manufactured, man-made, fake, artificial, mock, ersatz.

syrupy adj **1** *syrupy desserts* over-sweet, sugary, sweet, honeyed, saccharine, sticky; *inf* gooey. **2** *syrupy love stories* sentimental, over-sentimental, mawkish, maudlin, mushy, slushy, sloppy; *inf* soppy, schmaltzy.

system n **1** *the railway/digestive system* structure, organization, order, arrangement; *inf* set-up. **2** *a new system for teaching languages* method, methodology, technique, process, procedure, approach, practice, line, attack, means, way, modus operandi. **3** *absolutely no system in his accounting methods* systematization, methodicalness, orderliness, planning, logic, tightness, routine.

systematic adj *a systematic approach to the problem* structured, organized, methodical, orderly, well-ordered, planned, systematized, logical, efficient, business-like.

tab n *hang the jacket up by the tab* loop, flap, tag.

table n **1** *put the plates on the table* counter, bar, buffet, bench, stand. **2** *provide an excellent table* food, fare, diet, board; meals, victuals; *inf* spread, nosh, grub, chow. **3** *terrain characterized by tables* tableland; plateau, elevated plain, flat, mesa, steppe. **4** *a table of contents | table of geographical data* list, catalogue, tabulation, inventory, digest, itemization, index. **5** *leave room in the scientific text for tables* chart, diagram, figure, graph, plan.

table v *table a question/motion* submit, put forward, propose, suggest, move, enter.

tableau n **1** *paint evocative tableaux of village life* picture, painting, representation, portrayal, illustration. **2** *the children's tableau was part of the show* human representation, tableau vivant, pageant. **3** *admire the tableau below from the mountain top* spectacle, scene, sight.

tablet n **1** *the dedication inscribed on the stone tablet* slab, panel, stone. **2** *prescribed tablets for headaches* pill, capsule, lozenge. **3** *a tablet of soap* bar, cake.

taboo adj *such practices are taboo | taboo language* forbidden, prohibited, banned, proscribed, vetoed, ruled out, outlawed, not permitted, not acceptable, frowned on, beyond the pale.

taboo n *such practices are subject to taboo* prohibition, proscription, veto, interdiction, non-acceptance; interdict, ban.

tabulate v tabularize, chart, systematize, systemize, arrange, order, dispose, organize, catalogue, list, classify, class, codify, group, range, grade.

tacit adj *by tacit agreement* implicit, understood, implied, taken for granted, unstated, undeclared, unspoken, unexpressed, unmentioned, unvoiced, silent, wordless.

taciturn adj unforthcoming, uncommunicative, reticent, untalkative, tight-lipped, close-mouthed, quiet, silent, mute, dumb, reserved, withdrawn, antisocial, unsociable, distant, aloof, cold, detached, dour, sullen.

tack n **1** *attach the notice to the wall with a tack* drawing pin, nail, pin, staple, rivet. **2** *try a different tack if that one is unsuccessful* course/line of action, method, approach, process, way, policy, tactic, plan, strategy, attack.

tack v **1** *tack the picture to the wall | tack the carpet to the floor* nail, pin, staple, fix, fasten, affix, put up/down. **2** *tack up the hem* stitch, baste, sew. **3** *in politics it is necessary to know when to tack* change course/direction, alter one's approach, change one's mind/attitude, have a change of heart, do an about-turn; *inf* do a U-turn. **4** *tack a postscript on the letter | tack a conservatory to the house* add, attach, append, tag, annex.

tackle n *fishing tackle* gear, equipment, apparatus, outfit; tools, implements, accoutrements, paraphernalia, trappings; *inf* things, stuff.

tackle v **1** *tackle the task/problem* undertake, attempt, apply/address oneself to, get to grips with, set/go about, get to work at, busy oneself with, embark on, set one's hand to, take on, engage in. **2** *tackle the intruder* grapple with, seize, take hold of, confront, face up to; *inf* have a go at. **3** *tackle him on the subject of his lateness* speak to, confront, accost, waylay, remonstrate with.

tacky[1] adj *the paint/surface is tacky* sticky, gluey, gummy; *inf* gooey.

tacky[2] adj *tacky souvenirs on sale* tawdry, tasteless, kitsch, vulgar, crude, garish, gaudy, flashy; *inf* flash.

tact n diplomacy, discretion, *savoir faire*, sensitivity, understanding, thoughtfulness, consideration, delicacy, subtlety, finesse, skill, adroitness, dexterity, discernment, perception, judgement, prudence, judiciousness; *inf* savvy.

tactful adj diplomatic, politic, discreet, sensitive, understanding, thoughtful, considerate, delicate, subtle, skilful, adroit, discerning, perceptive, prudent, judicious.

tactic n *try a different tactic to achieve success* manoeuvre, expedient, device, stratagem, trick, scheme, plan, ploy, course/line of action, method, approach, tack; means. *see also* TACTICS.

tactical adj *effect the take over by tactical means* strategic, politic, planned, shrewd, skilful, adroit, clever, smart, cunning, artful.

tactics npl *military tactics | his clever tactics secured the take-over bid* strategy, campaign, policy; plans, battle/game plans, manoeuvres.

tactless adj undiplomatic, impolitic, indiscreet, insensitive, inconsiderate, indelicate, unsubtle, rough, crude, unskilful, clumsy, awkward, inept, bungling, maladroit, gauche, undiscerning, imprudent, injudicious.

tag n **1** *a tag showing the price* label, ticket, sticker, docket. **2** *hang the jacket up by its tag* tab, loop, flap. **3** *tags of wool at the end of the sleeves* end, snippet, tatter, rag, remnant, shred, clipping. **4** *Latin tags* quotation, stock phrase, platitude, cliché, epithet.

tag v **1** *tag the items* label, put a ticket/sticker on, mark. **2** *tag him Lanky* name, call, nickname, title, entitle, label, dub, term, style, christen. **3** *tag a postscript to the letter* add, attach, append, affix, tack. **4** *children tagging along with their parents* go with, accompany, follow, trail behind, tread on the heels of, dog.

tail n **1** *the tail of the animal* brush, scut, dock; *Tech* cauda. **2** *hurt one's tail* bottom, rump; buttocks; *inf* backside, rear, btm, situpon, arse. **3** *the tail of the queue* rear, end, back, extremity. **4** *the tail of the shirt* bottom, lowest part, extremity. **5** *a tail of traffic stretching from the accident* tailback, queue, line, file, train. **6** *at the tail of the storm* tail-end, close, end, conclusion, termination. **7** *the pursuers are on his tail* track, trail, scent. **8** *put a tail on the crook* detective, investigator, private investigator, shadow; *inf* sleuth, private eye; *Amer inf* gumshoe. **turn tail** run away, flee, retreat, take to one's heels, cut and run; *inf* skedaddle, vamoose.

tail v *detectives tailing the crooks* follow, shadow, stalk, trail, track, dog the footsteps of, keep under surveillance. **tail off/away** *business tails off in the winter* dwindle, decrease, drop off, fall away, peter out, fade, wane, die away, die out, come to an end.

tailor n outfitter, dressmaker, couturier, clothier, costumier.

tailor v *tailor the holiday to your needs* fit, suit, fashion, style, mould, shape, adapt, adjust, modify, convert, alter, accommodate.

taint v **1** *the water/meat had become tainted* contaminate, pollute, adulterate, infect, blight, befoul, spoil. **2** *taint his reputation* tarnish, sully, blacken, stain, besmirch, smear, blot, blemish, muddy, damage, injure, harm.

taint n **1** *food poisoning caused by the taint of the water* contamination, pollution, adulteration, infection, contagion. **2** *a taint on his character* stain, smear, blot, blemish, stigma. **3** *a taint of insanity in the family* trace, touch, suggestion, hint.

take v **1** *take the book from the woman* get/lay hold of, get into one's hands, grasp, grip, clutch. **2** *take first prize* get, receive, obtain, gain, acquire, secure, precure, come by, win, earn. **3** *take several prisoners* seize, catch, capture, arrest, carry off, abduct. **4** *who took my pen/savings?* remove, appropriate, make off with, steal, filch, pilfer, purloin, pocket; *inf* pinch, swipe, nick. **5** *take a pound of apples* buy, purchase, pay for. **6** *take a single room | take a boat for the day* reserve, book, engage, rent, hire, lease. **7** *she showed me several dresses but I took the blue one* pick, choose, select, decide on, settle on, opt for. **8** *take the bus/motorway* use, make use of, utilize. **9** *take some bread and wine* consume, eat, devour, swallow; drink, imbibe. **10** *the vaccination did not take* be effective, have/take effect, be efficacious, work, operate, succeed. **11** *the journey takes three hours* use, use up, require, call for, need, necessitate. **12** *take the box home with you* carry, fetch, bring, bear, transport, convey, cart, ferry; *inf* tote. **13** *will you take his sister home?* escort, accompany, conduct, guide, lead, usher, convoy. **14** *take measles* catch, become infected/ill with. **15** *take fright | take pleasure in acting* experience, be affected by, undergo. **16** *take the child's temperature* find out, discover, ascertain, determine, establish. **17** *I take it that you agreed | she took his silence to mean agreement* understand, interpret as, grasp, gather, comprehend, apprehend, assume, believe, suppose, consider, presume. **18** *take the news badly* receive, deal with, cope with. **19** *she took him for a fool* regard as, consider as, view as, look upon as. **20** *take the offer* accept, receive, adopt. **21** *take a course of study* enter upon, undertake, begin, set about. **22** *take French at school* study, learn, be taught, take up, pursue. **23** *take an oath/look* perform, execute, effect, do, make, have. **24** *take a nap* engage in, occupy oneself in. **25** *the bucket takes three litres* hold, contain, have the capacity for, have space/room for, accommodate. **26** *I cannot take his rudeness* bear, tolerate, stand, put up with, stomach, brook. **27** *the machine takes its name from the inventor* derive, obtain, come by. **28** *the passage is taken from Hamlet* extract, quote, cite, excerpt, derive. **29** *take three from five* subtract, deduct, remove. **30** *we were quite taken with the little girl* | *taken by her beauty* captivate, enchant, charm, delight, please, attract, win over, fascinate. **31** *do you think the idea will take?* catch on, become popular, gain popularity, be successful, succeed. **take after** resemble, look like, be like, favour; *inf* be a chip off the old block, be the spitting image of. **take against** take a dislike to, feel hostile towards, view with disfavour. **take back** **1** *take back the accusing statement* retract, withdraw, renounce, disclaim, unsay, disavow, recant. **2** *take the book back to its owner* carry back, bring back, fetch back, return. **3** *his stories took me back to my youth* awaken/ evoke one's memories of, put one in mind of, remind one of. **4** *the shop won't take the goods back* accept back, give a refund for, exchange, trade, swap. **5** *his wife has taken him back* accept back, welcome, forgive. **6** *take back the land won by the enemy* get back, regain, repossess, reclaim, recapture, reconquer. **take down** **1** *take down the details* write down, note down, make a note of, jot down, set down, record, put on record, commit to paper, document, minute. **2** *take down the marquee/scaffolding/ fence* remove, dismantle, disassemble, take apart, take to pieces, demolish, tear down, level, raze. **3** *take down the flag* | *took down his trousers* pull down, let down, haul down, lower, drop. **4** *that should take him down a bit* humble, deflate, humiliate, mortify, take down a peg or two; *inf* put down. **take in** **1** *take in the homeless child* | *take in paying guests* take, admit, let in, receive, welcome, accommodate, board. **2** *take the skirt in* make smaller/narrower, reduce in size. **3** *he didn't seem to take the news in* grasp, understand, comprehend, absorb, assimilate. **4** *the child said nothing but took everything in* observe, see, notice, take note of, note, perceive, regard. **5** *the old lady was completely taken in by the con man* deceive, delude, hoodwink, mislead, trick, dupe, fool, cheat, defraud, swindle, gull; *inf* con, bilk, pull the wool over someone's eyes, do. **6** *the school catchment area takes in these three districts* include, encompass, embrace, contain, comprise, cover. **7** *try to take in a concert/film when you are there* go to, go to see, attend, visit. **take off** **1** *take the lid off the jar* remove, detach, pull off. **2** *take off one's clothes* remove, discard, strip off, peel off, throw off, divest oneself of, doff. **3** *take the show off after three weeks* remove, withdraw, retract. **4** *take money off the bill for poor service* deduct, subtract, take away. **5** *the chil-*

dren took off when they saw the police | *she took off for Australia* run away, take to one's heels, flee, decamp, disappear, leave, go, depart; *inf* split, beat it, skedaddle, vamoose, hightail it. **6** *the child takes off the teacher very cleverly* mimic, impersonate, imitate, parody, mock; *inf* send up, spoof. **7** *the plane took off* become airborne, leave the ground, lift off. **8** *the business/scheme has really taken off* succeed, do well, become popular, catch on. **9** *it's time I took myself off* take one's leave, make one's departure. **take on** **1** *take on extra work* undertake, accept, tackle, turn one's hand to; *inf* have a go at. **2** *take on extra staff* employ, engage, hire, enroll, enlist; *inf* take on board. **3** *take him on at chess* compete against, oppose, challenge, face, pit/match oneself against, contend with, vie with, fight. **4** *suddenly his words/situation took on a new meaning* acquire, come to have, assume. **5** *don't take on so* get upset, make a fuss, break down, get excited, overreact; *inf* lose one's cool, get in a tizzy. **take out** **1** *take out a tooth* remove, extract, pull out, yank out. **2** *take out the girl next door* go out with, escort; *inf* date. **take over** *take over the business* | *take over the running of the household* take/assume/ gain control of, take charge/command of, assume responsibility for. **take to 1** *she's taken to smoking* begin, start, commence, make a habit of, resort to. **2** *he didn't take to her friend* develop a liking for, like, get on with, become friendly with. **3** *he has really taken to swimming* become good at, develop an ability/aptitude for, develop a liking for, like, enjoy, become interested in. **take up** **1** *take up the carpets/pen* lift up, raise. **2** *take up surfing* become involved/interested in, engage in, begin, start, commence. **3** *practising the piano takes up a great deal of time* use, use up, occupy, fill, consume, absorb, cover, extend over. **4** *take up the story where they left off* resume, recommence, restart, begin again, carry on, continue, pick up. **5** *take up an offer* accept, say yes to, agree to, accede to, adopt. **6** *take up a skirt/hem* shorten, make shorter; raise. **7** *take up with the wrong sort of people* become friendly/ friends (with), go around (with); *inf* knock about (with), hang around (with).

take *n* **1** *fishermen/hunters assessing the take* catch, haul, bag. **2** *counting the take after the sale/match* takings, proceeds, returns, receipts, profits, winnings, pickings, earnings; gain, income, revenue.

take-off *n* **1** *the take-off of the plane* taking-off, lift-off, departure, ascent, climbing, mounting, soaring, flying. **2** *admire his take-off of the celebrity* mimicry, impersonation, imitation, parody, mockery; *inf* send-up, spoof.

taking adj *a taking child* captivating, enchanting, beguiling, bewitching, fascinating, charming, delightful, pleasing, engaging, attractive, winning, lovable, winsome, prepossessing; *inf* fetching.

takings npl proceeds, returns, receipts, earnings, winnings, pickings; profit, gain, income, revenue.

tale n **1** *a fairy tale* story, short story, narrative, anecdote, legend, fable, myth, parable, allegory, epic, saga; *inf* yarn. **2** *hear tales of her wild behaviour* talk, rumour, gossip, hearsay; report, allegation. **3** *the child didn't see the burglar—that was a tale* lie, fib, falsehood, untruth, fabrication, piece of fiction; *inf* story, tall story, cock-and-bull story, whopper, terminological inexactitude.

talent n gift, flair, aptitude, facility, knack, bent, ability, capacity, faculty, aptness, endowment, strong point, forte, genius.

talented adj gifted, accomplished, able, capable, apt, deft, adept, proficient, brilliant, expert, artistic.

talk v **1** *talk incessantly* speak, give voice/utterance, chat, chatter, gossip, natter, prattle, prate, gibber, jabber, babble, rattle on, gabble; *inf* rabbit, yak, witter, gab. **2** *talk rubbish* speak, say, utter, voice, express, articulate, pronounce, enunciate, verbalize. **3** *they don't talk any more* communicate, converse, speak to each other, discuss things, confer, consult each other, have negotiations, have a tête-à-tête, parley, palaver, confabulate; *inf* have a confab, chew the fat/rag, jaw, rap. **4** *If you tell her your secret she'll talk* tell, reveal all, tell tales, give the game away, open one's mouth, let the cat out of the bag; *inf* blab, squeal, spill the beans, grass, sing. **5** *people will talk if they live together* gossip, spread rumours, pass comment, make remarks, criticize. **6** *the professor is talking tonight* give a talk, give/make/deliver a speech, speak, lecture, discourse. **7** *after years of silence the spy has decided to talk* speak, speak out, speak up, give voice, tell the facts, divulge information, reveal all. **talk back** *children reprimanded for talking back to their parents* answer defiantly/impertinently, answer back. **talk big** brag, boast, crow, exaggerate; *inf* blow one's own trumpet, shoot one's mouth. **talk down 1** *hecklers talking down the speaker* out-talk, drown, silence, override. **2** *talk down to young people* speak condescendingly to, condescend to, speak haughtily to, patronize. **3** *talk the pilot down* give landing instructions to, bring to land.

talk into *talk him into buying the car* persuade to, cajole to, coax into, influence. **talk of** *they talked of going away* speak about, discuss, mention, make mention of, refer to, make reference to. **talk out of** dissuade from, persuade against, discourage from, deter from, stop.

talk n **1** *their noisy talk kept me awake* talking, speaking, chatter, chatting, gossiping, nattering, prattling, gibbering, jabbering, babbling, gabbling; *inf* rabbiting, yakking, wittering, gabbing. *see* TALK v 1. **2** *baby/seamen's talk* words; speech, language, dialect, jargon, cant, slang, idiom, idiolect, patois; *inf* lingo. **3** *have a talk about their future* conversation, chat, discussion, tête-à-tête; dialogue; *inf* confab, jaw, rap. **4** *give a talk to the society* lecture, speech, address, discourse, oration, sermon, disquisition. **5** *there is talk of a merger* gossip, rumour, hearsay, tittle-tattle. **6** *the talk in the pub was of the footballer's accident* chat, conversation, discussion, gossip, subject, theme.

talkative adj loquacious, garrulous, voluble, chatty, gossipy, conversational, long-winded, gushing, effusive; *inf* gabby, mouthy, big-mouthed.

talker n **1** *the talker bored the audience* speaker, speech-maker, lecturer, orator. **2** *the child is a good talker* speaker. **3** *they are a family of talkers* conversationalist, chatter, chatterbox, gossip.

talking-to n *give the naughty children a talking-to* lecture, scolding, row, reprimand, rebuke, reproof, reproach; *inf* telling-off, ticking-off, wigging, carpeting.

talks npl *talks to try stop the war* conference, summit, meeting, consultation, discussion, dialogue, negotiation, symposium, seminar, conclave, colloquy, palaver, parley, confabulation; *inf* pow-wow.

tall adj **1** *tall people* big, colossal, gigantic, lanky, rangy, gangling. **2** *three feet tall* in height, high. **3** *tall buildings* high, lofty, towering, soaring, sky-high, sky-scraping. **4** *a tall story* exaggerated, unlikely, incredible, far-fetched, implausible. **tall order** demanding/exacting/difficult task, unreasonable demand/request.

tally n **1** *keep a tally of the number of visitors* count, record, running total, reckoning, enumeration, register, roll, census, poll. **2** *what was the tally at the end of the game?* score, count, result, total, sum. **3** *produce as a tally for identification* ticket, label, sticker, stamp, tab. **4** *his tally in the other team | the glove's tally* counterpart, match, mate, duplicate.

tally v *the two accounts don't tally* | *his story doesn't tally with hers* agree, accord, concur, coincide, conform, correspond, match, fit, harmonize.

tame adj **1** *tame animals* domesticated, not wild, not fierce, gentle, used to humans. **2** *find the supposedly rebellious children quite tame* subdued, docile, submissive, compliant, meek, obedient, tractable, amenable, manageable, unresisting. **3** *we have a tame joiner* available, willing, amenable. **4** *the horror film turned out to be quite tame* unexciting, uninteresting, uninspired, dull, bland, flat, insipid, vapid, run-of-the-mill, mediocre, prosaic, humdrum, boring, tedious, wearisome.

tame v **1** *tame the wild cat* domesticate, break, train, gentle. **2** *tame the unruly element in the class/party* subdue, discipline, curb, control, master, bring to heel, overcome, suppress, repress, humble.

tamper v **tamper with 1** *tamper with the exam papers* meddle with, interfere with, monkey around with, mess about with, tinker with, fiddle with, alter/change/adjust illegally; *inf* fool about with, muck about with, poke one's nose into, stick one's oar into. **2** *tamper with the jury* influence, get at, rig, manipulate, bribe, corrupt; *inf* fix.

tan adj *tan shoes* yellowish-brown, brownish-yellow, light brown, pale brown, tawny.

tan v **1** *they tan easily* become suntanned, take a suntan/tan, brown, go brown. **2** *the hot sun tanned their skins* suntan, brown, turn brown, darken. **3** *the father tanned his son* beat, thrash, wallop, whip, lash, leather, lambaste.

tang n **1** *the tang of orange* flavour, taste, savour. **2** *the tang of the sea* smell, odour, aroma. **3** *add some tang to the food/occasion* spice, spiciness, piquancy, relish, sharpness, zest; *inf* ginger, punch, zip.

tangible adj **1** *tangible changes to the skin* touchable, palpable, tactile, visible. **2** *tangible proof* concrete, real, actual, solid, substantial, hard, well-documented, well-defined, definite, clear, clear-cut, distinct, unmistakable, positive, discernible.

tangle v **1** *her hair became tangled in the rose bush* | *the rain had tangled her hair* entangle, intertwine, intertwist, twist, snarl, ravel, knot, mat. **2** *don't tangle with the authorities* become involved, come into conflict, have a dispute, dispute, argue, quarrel, fight, row, wrangle, squabble, contend, cross swords, lock horns.

tangled adj **1** *tangled wool/hair* entangled, twisted, snarled, ravelled, knotted, knotty,

matted, tousled, messy; *inf* mussed-up. **2** *tangled affairs* confused, jumbled, mixed-up, messy, chaotic, complicated, involved, convoluted, complex.

tank n **1** *water tank* container, receptacle, vat, cistern. **2** *soldiers in tanks* armoured car, combat vehicle.

tantalize v *tantalize them with a sight of the unobtainable gold* tease, torment, torture, frustrate, disappoint, thwart, make one's mouth water, lead on, entice, titillate, allure, beguile.

tantamount adj *his statement was tantamount to a confession* equivalent (to), equal (to), as good (as), synonymous (with).

tantrum n fit of temper/rage, fit, outburst, flare-up, pet, paroxysm; *inf* paddy, wax.

tap¹ n **1** *turn the tap off* spigot, stopcock, valve; *Amer* faucet. **2** *put a tap on their telephone* listening device; *inf* bug, bugging device. **on tap 1** *beer on tap* on draught, not bottled/canned. **2** *extra supplies on tap* at/on hand, available, ready, in reserve, standing by.

tap¹ v **1** *tap cider from a cask* draw off, siphon off, drain, bleed. **2** *tap a cask* draw liquid from, broach, open, pierce. **3** *tap sources of information* use, make use of, put to use, utilize, draw on, exploit, milk. **4** *tap mineral resources* extract, obtain, exploit, open up, explore, probe. **5** *tap their telephone* wire tap; *inf* bug. **6** *tap their telephone calls* wire tap, listen in to, eavesdrop on; *inf* bug, get on record.

tap² n **1** *give a tap at the window* knock, rap, beat. **2** *give a tap on the shoulder* touch, pat, light blow/slap.

tap² v **1** *tap on the window* | *tap the table* knock, rap, strike, beat, drum. **2** *tap him on the shoulder* touch, pat, strike/slap lightly.

tape n **1** *tie a tape round the parcel* band, strip, string, ribbon. **2** *use tape to repair the crack/tear* adhesive tape, insulating tape, masking tape, parcel tape; *Trademark* Sellotape. **3** *play a tape* tape recording, cassette, videotape, video cassette, video, audiotape, audiocassette.

tape v **1** *tape the pieces together* bind, tie, fasten, stick, seal, secure; *Trademark* Sellotape. **2** *tape the concert/conversation* record, tape-record, video-record, video. **3** *tape off the area* seal, mark with tape. **have taped** *have the situation/patient taped* understand fully, know all about, have all the details of, know the ins and outs of.

taper v **1** *the candles taper at the top* narrow, thin, become narrow/thinner, come to a point. **2** *sales tend to taper off at this time of* *year* dwindle, diminish, lessen, decrease, reduce, subside, die off, die away, fade, peter out, wane, ebb, wind down, slacken off, thin out.

target n **1** *fail to hit the target in the shooting-gallery* mark, bull's-eye. **2** *the injured bird was an easy target* prey, quarry, game. **3** *our target is £50,000 | their target is the European market* objective, goal, object, aim, end, intention, desired result. **4** *she is the target of their jokes* butt, victim, scapegoat.

tariff n **1** *the tariff is on display* price list/schedule, list of charges. **2** *ask the waitress for the tariff* menu, bill of fare. **3** *pay a tariff on imports* tax, duty, toll, excise, levy, impost.

tarnish v **1** *time had tarnished the brass* dull, dim, discolour, rust. **2** *silver tarnishes easily* lose its shine/lustre, become dull, discolour, rust. **3** *tarnish his reputation* sully, besmirch, blacken, stain, blemish, blot, taint, befoul, drag through the mud.

tarnish n **1** *remove the tarnish from the silver* discoloration, oxidation, rust. **2** *survive the tarnish on his reputation* black mark, slur, stain, blemish, blot, taint, stigma.

tart¹ n *a fruit/meat tart* pastry, tartlet, pie, quiche, strudel.

tart² n **1** *he picked up a tart* prostitute, whore, call girl, harlot, streetwalker, fallen woman, woman of easy virtue, woman of the night, *fille de joie; inf* hooker. **2** *his wife's just a tart* loose woman, slut, trollop, wanton.

tart² v **tart up 1** *tart oneself up* dress (oneself) up, make (oneself) up, smarten (oneself) up. **2** *tart up the old café* renovate, refurbish, redecorate, modernize, smarten up.

tart³ adj **1** *rather a tart apple/dessert* sharp, sharp-tasting, sour, tangy, piquant, pungent, bitter, acid, acidulous, vinegary. **2** *a tart remark/wit* astringent, caustic, sharp, biting, cutting, stinging, mordant, trenchant, incisive, piercing, acrimonious, barbed, scathing, sarcastic, sardonic.

task n job, duty, chore, charge, odd job, piece of work/business, assignment, commission, mission, engagement, occupation, undertaking, exercise, errand, quest. **take to task** rebuke, reprimand, reprove, reproach, upbraid, scold, berate, lecture, castigate, censure, criticize, blame; *inf* tell off.

taste n **1** *the taste of fresh raspberries* flavour, savour, relish, tang. **2** *have a taste of the pudding/sauce* bit, morsel, bite, mouthful, spoonful, sample, sip, drop, swallow, touch, soupçon. **3** *have a taste for the unknown | expensive tastes* liking, love, fondness, fancy, desire, preference, penchant, predilection, inclination, partiality, leaning, bent, hankering, appetite, palate, thirst, hunger. **4** *furnish the house with taste* discrimination, discernment, judgement, cultivation, culture, refinement, polish, finesse, elegance, grace, stylishness. **5** *her remark lacked taste* decorum, propriety, correctness, etiquette, politeness, tact, tactfulness, diplomacy, delicacy, nicety, discretion.

taste v **1** *taste the pudding while cooking it* sample, test, try, nibble, sip. **2** *I can't taste the garlic* make out, perceive, discern, distinguish, differentiate. **3** *not to taste food for days* eat, partake of, consume, devour. **4** *taste of onions* have a flavour of, savour of, smack of. **5** *taste success/defeat* experience, undergo, encounter, meet, come face to face with, come up against, know.

tasteful adj **1** *a tasteful display/room* in good taste, aesthetic, artistic, harmonious, pleasing, elegant, graceful, beautiful, pretty, charming, handsome, discriminating, refined, restrained. **2** *tasteful behaviour/manners* decorous, proper, seemly, correct, polite, fitting, fit, appropriate, refined, cultured, cultivated.

tasteless adj **1** *tasteless food* flavourless, unflavoured, savourless, bland, insipid, watery, watered-down, weak, thin, unappetizing, uninteresting, vapid. **2** *tasteless decorations* vulgar, crude, tawdry, garish, gaudy, loud, flashy, showy, cheap, gross, meretricious. **3** *tasteless behaviour* indecorous, improper, unseemly, incorrect, impolite, rude, unfitting, inappropriate, unrefined, uncultured, uncultivated. **4** *tasteless remarks* vulgar, crude, low, gross, indelicate, uncouth, crass, tactless, undiplomatic, indiscreet.

tasty adj flavoursome, flavourful, full-flavoured, appetizing, palatable, toothsome, delectable, delicious, luscious, mouth-watering, piquant, pungent, spicy; *inf* scrumptious, yummy, finger-licking.

tatter n rag, torn/ragged piece. **in tatters 1** *clothes in tatters* ragged, torn, in shreds, in bits. **2** *his career/argument in tatters* in ruins, ruined, destroyed, demolished.

tattle v *tattling about their friend's affairs* gossip, tittle-tattle, chatter, natter, prattle, prate, babble, rattle on; *inf* rabbit on, witter on, gab.

taunt n *ignore the taunts of the opposition* gibe, jeer, sneer, insult, barb, catcall, brickbat;

teasing, provocation, ridiculing, derision, mockery, sarcasm; *inf* dig, put-down.

taunt v *rich children taunting the poor* gibe at, jeer at, sneer at, insult, chaff, tease, torment, provoke, ridicule, deride, mock, poke fun at.

taut adj **1** *taut ropes* tight, tightly stretched, stretched, rigid. **2** *taut muscles* tightened, flexed, tensed. **3** *a taut expression* tense, strained, stressed, drawn; *inf* uptight. **4** *run a taut ship* in good order/condition, orderly, in order, shipshape, tight, trim, neat, well-ordered, well-regulated, tidy, spruce, smart.

tautology n repetition, repetitiveness, repetitiousness, reiteration, redundancy, pleonasm, wordiness, long-windedness, verbosity, prolixity.

tawdry adj showy, gaudy, flashy, garish, loud, tasteless, cheap, cheapjack, shoddy, meretricious, Brummagem; *inf* flash, tatty, tacky, kitsch.

tax n **1** *income tax* | *charge a tax on imports* levy, charge, duty, toll, excise, tariff, impost, tribute; customs. **2** *they became a tax on her health/resources* burden, load, weight, encumbrance, strain, pressure, stress, drain.

tax v **1** *tax his salary at source* | *tax imports* levy a tax on, impose a toll on, charge duty on. **2** *work taxing his strength* make demands on, weigh heavily on, weigh down, burden, load, encumber, overload, push, push too far, stretch, strain, try, wear out, exhaust, sap, drain, enervate, fatigue, tire, weary, weaken. **3** *tax him with his unpunctuality* confront, call to account, charge, blame, censure, accuse, impeach, indict, arraign.

taxing adj *a taxing job* demanding, exacting, burdensome, onerous, difficult, hard, tough, heavy, tiring, exhausting, enervating, draining, sapping, stressful, wearing, trying, punishing.

teach v **1** *teach children* give lessons to, instruct, educate, school, tutor, coach, train, drill, ground, enlighten, edify. **2** *teach French to children* give lessons/instruction in, instil, inculcate. **3** *teach them how to ride a bike* instruct, train, show, guide.

teacher n schoolteacher, schoolmaster, schoolmistress, master, mistress, instructor, educator, tutor, coach, trainer, lecturer, professor, don, pedagogue, guide, mentor, guru.

team n **1** *a team of workers/players* group, band, bunch, company, party, gang, crew, troupe, set, squad, side, line-up. **2** *a team of horses* pair, span, yoke.

team v *team up with his friend to do the project* join (with), get come/band together (with), work together (with), unite (with), cooperate (with), form an alliance (with).

tear¹ n **1** *a tear in the material* rip, split, hole, rent, run, rupture. **2** *bandage the tear in his arm* laceration, gash, slash, scratch, cut, mutilation, injury, wound.

tear¹ v **1** *tear the paper/cloth* rip, pull apart, pull to pieces, split, rend, sever, rive, sunder, rupture. **2** *tear the flesh* lacerate, gash, slash, pierce, stab, scratch, cut, claw, mangle, mutilate, hack, injure, wound. **3** *tear the painting from the wall* | *tear off the cover* rip, pull, wrench, yank, wrest, extract, peel, snatch, pluck, grab, seize. **4** *torn between going and staying* divide, split, rend, disrupt, break apart. **5** *torn by guilt* disrupt, distress, upset, harrow, torture, torment. **6** *children tearing down the street* run, race, sprint, gallop, rush, dash, bolt, career, dart, fly, shoot, hurry, speed, hasten; *inf* belt, hotfoot it, whiz, zoom, zip, zap.

tear² n **1** *tears ran down her cheeks* tear-drop. **2** *tears of perspiration/resin* drop, droplet, globule, bead. **in tears** tearful, crying, weeping, sobbing, blubbering, wailing; upset.

tearful adj **1** *in a tearful state* in tears, crying, weeping, sobbing, blubbering, snivelling, whimpering, wailing; emotional, upset, distressed; *inf* weepy, blubbing. **2** *a tearful parting/event* emotional, upsetting, distressing, heartbreaking, heart-rending, sad, sorrowful, piteous, pitiful, pitiable, pathetic, poignant, mournful, melancholy, lamentable, dolorous.

tease v **1** *tease the cat* | *tease the new boy* torment, provoke, badger, bait, goad, needle, pest, bother, worry, vex, irritate, annoy, gibe, mock, ridicule, poke fun at; *inf* aggravate. **2** *he didn't mean to upset her; he was only teasing her* joke (with), fool (with), chaff, rag, twit; *inf* kid, rib, have on.

technical adj **1** *technical training/applications* mechanical, practical, scientific, applying science, non-theoretical. **2** *technical terms* specialist, specialized, scientific.

technique n **1** *new business techniques* method, method of working, *modus operandi*, system, procedure, style of approach, manner, way, course of action, mode, fashion; means. **2** *admire the violinist's technique* execution, performance, skill, skilfulness, proficiency, expertise, expertness, mastery, artistry, art, craftsmanship, craft, ability, adroitness, deftness, dexterity, knack. **3** *admire his technique in dealing with management* skill, ability, capability, proficiency, capacity, aptitude, expertise, knack, talent, gift, genius; *inf* know-how.

tedious adj wearisome, wearying, tiresome, tiring, fatiguing, soporific, long-drawn-out, overlong, long-winded, prolix, dull, deadly dull, boring, uninteresting, dry, dreary, drab, unexciting, lifeless, uninspired, flat, banal, vapid, insipid, monotonous, unvaried, prosaic, humdrum, run-of-the-mill, routine.

tedium n tediousness, wearisomeness, tiresomeness, prolixity, dullness, boredom, ennui, uninterestingness, dryness, lifelessness, dreariness, drabness, flatness, banality, vapidity, insipidity, monotony, sameness.

teem v **1** *fish teem in these waters* abound, be abundant, be plentiful, be copious. **2** *rivers teeming with fish | teeming with ideas* abound, swarm, crawl, bristle, seethe, brim.

teenage adj adolescent, youthful, young, juvenile.

teenager n young person, adolescent, youth, minor, juvenile; *inf* teeny-bopper.

teeter v **1** *teeter down the street on high heels* totter, wobble, stagger, stumble, reel, sway, roll, lurch. **2** *teeter between accepting and refusing* waver, vacillate, fluctuate, oscillate, dither, hesitate, shilly-shally, seesaw.

teetotalism n abstinence, abstention, temperance, sobriety, Rechabitism.

teetotaller n abstainer, non-drinker, Rechabite.

telegram n telemessage, cable, telex; *inf* wire.

telepathy n thought transference, mind-reading, extrasensory perception, ESP, psychometry.

telephone n **1** *speak on the telephone* telephone set; car phone, cellular telephone, cellphone, cordless telephone, videophone; *inf* phone, blower. **2** *lift the telephone* handset, receiver.

telephone v *I'll telephone you tomorrow* call, call up, ring up, ring; *inf* phone, give someone a ring/tinkle/buzz, get on the blower, buzz.

telescope n glass, spyglass, reflector, refractor; radio telescope/dish, infrared/X-ray telescope.

telescope v **1** *the two parts of the instrument telescope* slide into each other, slide together. **2** *the front two carriages were telescoped together in the crash* concertina, crush, squash, squeeze, compress, compact. **3** *telescope the long novel into a one-act play* reduce,

condense, boil down, compress, compact, consolidate, shorten, abbreviate, abridge, truncate, curtail, cut, trim.

television n television set; *inf* TV, telly, the box, gogglebox, small screen, the tube, idiot box, talking head.

tell v **1** *tell the news to everyone | tell the truth* make known, impart, communicate, announce, proclaim, broadcast, divulge, reveal, disclose, declare, state, mention, utter, voice, say, speak. **2** *tell a story* narrate, relate, recount, give an account of, report, chronicle, recite, rehearse, describe, portray, sketch, delineate. **3** *tell them tomorrow that you are going* inform, let know, make aware, apprise, notify. **4** *he's guilty, I tell you* assure, promise, guarantee, warrant. **5** *tell them to go home* instruct, bid, order, give orders, command, direct, charge, enjoin, dictate to, call upon, require. **6** *he knows her secret but he promised not to tell* talk, tell tales, blab, give the game away, open one's mouth, let the cat out of the bag; *inf* squeal, spill the beans, grass, sing, rat. **7** *his friend told on him* report (on), inform (on); *inf* squeal (on), rat (on), grass (on), blow the whistle (on), pull the plug (on). **8** *his expression told how he felt* reveal, disclose, show, display, exhibit, indicate. **9** *unable to tell his reaction from his expression* deduce, make out, discern, perceive, see, identify, recognize, discover, understand, comprehend. **10** *unable to tell one from the other* distinguish, differentiate, discriminate. **11** *breeding tells* have an effect, make its presence felt, count, carry weight, have influence/force, register; *inf* have clout. **12** *the strain told on him* have an effect on, affect, take its toll of. **13** *tell the votes* count, calculate, tally, estimate, compute, number, reckon.

telling adj *make a telling contribution | telling evidence* marked, significant, substantial, considerable, sizeable, solid, weighty, important, striking, impressive, potent, powerful, forceful, effective, effectual, cogent, influential, decisive.

tell-tale n *the tell-tale reported his friend to the teacher/authorities* talebearer, blabbermouth, blabber; *inf* loud mouth, squealer, grass.

tell-tale adj *children stealing raspberries with tell-tale signs round their mouths* revealing, revelatory, suggestive, meaningful, significant, indicative; *inf* give-away.

temerity n *have the temerity to call him a liar* effrontery, impudence, audacity, cheek, gall, presumption, presumptiveness, brazenness, rashness, recklessness, foolhardiness.

temper n **1** *he is of an equable temper* temperament, disposition, nature, humour, mood, character, frame of mind, cast of mind, mind, attitude, stamp. *see* TEMPERAMENT. **2** *the temper of the times* tenor, tone, attitude, vein. **3** *he is in a temper* bad mood, ill humour, fury, rage, passion, fit of temper/pique, tantrum; *inf* paddy, wax. **4** *a display of temper* ill humour, anger, annoyance, fury, rage, irritation, irritability, irascibility, hot-headedness, petulance, peevishness, resentment, surliness, churlishness. **5** *lose one's temper* composure, equanimity, self-control, coolness, calm, calmness, tranquillity, good humour; *inf* cool.

temper v **1** *temper the metal* toughen, anneal, harden, strengthen, fortify. **2** *temper justice with mercy* moderate, soften, tone down, modify, mitigate, alleviate, allay, palliate, mollify, assuage, lessen, weaken.

temperament n **1** *of an equable/nervous temperament* disposition, nature, humour, mood, character, personality, make-up, constitution, complexion, temper, spirit, mettle, frame of mind, cast of mind, mind, attitude, outlook, stamp, quality. **2** *actors often are people of temperament* excitability, emotionalism, volatility, mercurialness, capriciousness, moodiness, oversensitivity, touchiness, hot-headedness, impatience, petulance; moods.

temperamental adj **1** *temperamental differences between them | a temperamental dislike of parties* constitutional, inherent, innate, inborn, congenital, deep-rooted, ingrained. **2** *actors are often temperamental people* excitable, emotional, volatile, mercurial, oversensitive, capricious, erratic, touchy, moody, hot-headed, explosive, impatient, petulant.

temperance n **1** *now leading a life of temperance after his excesses* moderation, self-restraint, self-control, abstemiousness, continence, abstinence, austerity, self-denial. **2** *former alcoholics now practising temperance* teetotalism, abstinence, abstention, sobriety, prohibition.

temperate adj **1** *lead a temperate life* moderate, self-restrained, restrained, abstemious, self-controlled, continent, austere, self-denying. **2** *the temperate members of the party* teetotal, abstinent, sober. **3** *temperate winds/climates* moderate, mild, gentle, clement, balmy, pleasant, agreeable.

tempest n **1** *ships/houses buffeted by the tempest* storm, gale, hurricane, squall, cyclone, tornado, typhoon, whirlwind. **2** *a tempest broke out when the star lost her necklace* storm, uproar, commotion, furore, disturbance, tumult, turmoil, upheaval.

tempestuous adj **1** *tempestuous weather* stormy, turbulent, blustery, squally, windy, gusty, breezy. **2** *a tempestuous affair* stormy, turbulent, boisterous, violent, wild, uncontrolled, unrestrained, passionate, impassioned, emotional, intense, fierce, heated, feverish, hysterical, frenetic.

temple n place of worship, holy place, shrine, sanctuary.

tempo n **1** *the lively tempo of the music* beat, rhythm, cadence, throb, pulse, pulsation. **2** *the tempo of life today* pace, rate, speed, measure.

temporal adj **1** *temporal affairs* secular, non-spiritual, worldly, material, earthly, carnal. **2** *temporal measurements* of time, time-related.

temporarily adv **1** *temporarily out of order* for the time being, for the moment, for now, for the nonce, pro tem. **2** *he was temporarily in love with her* briefly, fleetingly, for a short time, for a little while, momentarily, transiently.

temporary adj **1** *just a temporary job* short-term, impermanent, interim, provisional, pro tem, *pro tempore*. **2** *a temporary infatuation* brief, fleeting, passing, momentary, short-lived, here today and gone tomorrow, transient, transitory, ephemeral, fugitive, evanescent, fugacious.

tempt v **1** *tempt him to break the law by bribing him | she is tempted to run away* try to persuade, entice, incite, induce, egg on, urge, goad, prompt, sway, influence, persuade, cajole, coax. **2** *rows of glamorous gifts to tempt buyers* allure, lure, entice, attract, whet the appetite of, make one's mouth water, captivate, appeal to, beguile, inveigle, woo, seduce, tantalize. **3** *tempt fate* fly in the face of, risk, bait, provoke.

temptation n **1** *subject the jury to temptation* enticement, incitement, inducement, urging, influence, persuasion, cajolery, coaxing. **2** *sweets acting as a temptation to children* allurement, lure, attraction, draw, bait, pull, enticement, inducement, invitation, decoy, snare; *inf* come-on. **3** *the temptation of the array of sweets* allure, attractiveness, appeal, fascination, tantalization.

tempting adj *a tempting array of goods* alluring, enticing, attractive, captivating, appealing, beguiling, fascinating, tantalizing, appetizing, mouth-watering.

tenable adj **1** *tenable theories/objections* justifiable, defensible, defendable, arguable, maintainable, supportable, plausible, credible, reasonable, rational, sound, viable. **2** *positions tenable only for a year* holdable, occupiable, available.

tenacious adj **1** *the eagle held its prey in a tenacious grip* clinging, firm, fast, tight, strong, forceful, powerful, unshakable, iron. **2** *we tried to get rid of her but she's so tenacious | tenacious efforts* persistent, pertinacious, determined, dogged, resolute, firm, steadfast, purposeful, unshakable, unswerving, relentless, inexorable, unyielding, inflexible, stubborn, obstinate, intransigent, obdurate, strong-willed, contumacious. **3** *a tenacious memory* retentive, retaining, remembering, unforgetful. **4** *tenacious clay* sticky, gluey, adhesive, clinging.

tenacity n **1** *the tenacity of its grip* firmness, fastness, tightness, strength, force, forcefulness, power. **2** *admire her tenacity in seeing it through until the end* persistence, pertinacity, determination, doggedness, resolution, resoluteness, resolve, firmness, steadfastness, purposefulness, purpose, strength of purpose, application, diligence, relentlessness, inexorableness, inflexibility, stubbornness, obstinacy, intransigence, obduracy, strong will. *see* TENACIOUS 2. **3** *the tenacity of his memory* retentiveness. **4** *the tenacity of the clay* stickiness, gluiness, adhesiveness.

tenancy n **1** *disapprove of his tenancy of the flat* occupancy, occupation, residence, habitation, inhabitance, renting, leasing, lease, holding, possession. **2** *his tenancy is for three years* period of occupancy/occupation, lease, tenure.

tenant n occupier, occupant, resident, inhabitant, renter, leaseholder, lessee, holder, possessor.

tend¹ v **1** *he tends to lose his temper easily* have/show a tendency to, inclined towards, be apt/disposed/liable to, be likely to. **2** *the graph tends upwards* move, go, head, point, gravitate.

tend² v *tend the sick/cows* look after, take care of, care for, attend to, minister to, see to, cater to, nurse, wait on, watch over, watch, guard, keep an eye on, keep.

tendency n **1** *he has a tendency to dishonesty* inclination, disposition, predisposition, proclivity, propensity, proneness, aptness, bent, leaning, penchant, susceptibility, liability. **2** *the upward tendency of the graph* movement, direction, course, drift, bias, trend.

tender adj **1** *tender meat* not tough, easily chewed, succulent, juicy, soft. **2** *tender blossoms/shoots* easily damaged, breakable, frag-

ile, frail, delicate, sensitive, slight, feeble. **3** *they are still of tender years | a tender youth* young, youthful, early; immature, callow, inexperienced, green, raw. **4** *have a tender heart* compassionate, soft-hearted, kind, kindly, sympathetic, warm, caring, humane, gentle, solicitous, generous, benevolent, sentimental, emotional, susceptible, vulnerable. **5** *have tender feelings for her* fond, loving, affectionate, warm, emotional, amorous. **6** *awake tender memories* warm, fond, emotional, touching, moving, poignant, evocative. **7** *a tender spot on her arm* sore, painful, aching, smarting, throbbing, inflamed, irritated, red, raw, bruised. **8** *a tender subject requiring tact* delicate, sensitive, difficult, tricky, ticklish, risky.

tender v **1** *tender assistance | tender a proposal* offer, proffer, present, extend, give; volunteer, put forward, propose, suggest, advance, submit. **2** *tender for the job* put in a bid, bid, give an estimate, propose a price.

tenderness n **1** *the tenderness of the meat* succulence, softness. *see* TENDER adj 1. **2** *the tenderness of the blossoms/shoots* fragility, frailness, frailty, delicacy, sensitivity, sensitiveness, slightness, feebleness. *see* TENDER adj 2. **3** *the tenderness of their years* youthfulness, immaturity, callowness, inexperience, greenness. *see* TENDER adj 3. **4** *the tenderness of her heart* compassion, compassionateness, soft-heartedness, kindness, kindliness, sympathy, warmth, humaneness, gentleness, solicitousness, generosity, benevolence, sentimentality, emotionalism, vulnerability. **5** *the tenderness of his feelings for her* fondness, love, affection, affectionateness, warmth, emotion, amorousness. **6** *the tenderness of the topic* delicacy, delicateness, sensitivity, sensitiveness, difficulty, trickiness, ticklishness, riskiness. **7** *the tenderness of the wounded area* soreness, pain, painfulness, ache, aching, smarting, throbbing, inflammation, irritation, redness, rawness, bruising.

tenet n doctrine, creed, credo, principle, belief, conviction, persuasion, view, opinion, theory, thesis, hypothesis, postulation.

tenor n **1** *the tenor of his speech* drift, gist, essence, import, vein, meaning, purport, intent. **2** *follow the even tenor of his ways* settled course, prevailing trend, movement, current, flow, direction, drift.

tense adj **1** *tense ropes* pulled tight, tight, taut, rigid, stretched, strained. **2** *feeling tense about the interview* strained, under a strain, under pressure, nervous, keyed up, worked up, overwrought, distraught, anxious, uneasy, worried, apprehensive, agitated, jumpy, edgy, on edge, restless, jittery, fidgety; *inf* uptight, wound up, strung up. **3** *there were some tense moments in the negotiations/film* nerve-racking, stressful, worrying, fraught, exciting, cliff-hanging.

tension n **1** *the tension of the ropes* tightness, tautness, rigidity, stretching, straining. **2** *the tension of waiting for the interview* strain, stress, stressfulness, suspense, pressure, anxiety, unease, disquiet, worry, apprehensiveness, agitation, jumpiness, edginess, restlessness; nerves; *inf* butterflies in the stomach. **3** *the tension between the two sides grew* strain, unease, ill feeling, hostility, enmity.

tentative adj **1** *a tentative proposal/plan* speculative, conjectural, experimental, exploratory, trial, provisional, test, pilot, untried, unproven, unconfirmed, unsettled, indefinite. **2** *take a few tentative steps* hesitant, hesitating, faltering, wavering, uncertain, unsure, doubtful, cautious, diffident, timid.

tenterhooks npl **on tenterhooks** in suspense, on edge, edgy, jumpy, jittery, keyed up, overwrought, anxious, apprehensive, uneasy, worried; *inf* uptight, waiting for the axe to fall.

tenuous adj **1** *a tenuous connection between the two events* slight, flimsy, weak, insubstantial, shaky, sketchy, doubtful, dubious, nebulous, hazy, vague, unspecific, indefinite. **2** *a tenuous thread* fine, thin, slender.

tepid adj **1** *tepid water* lukewarm, warmish. **2** *he's rather tepid about the idea | a tepid reaction* unenthusiastic, apathetic, half-hearted, indifferent, cool.

term n **1** *fail to understand the technical term* word, expression, phrase, name, title, denomination, appellation, designation. **2** *the chairman's term of office* period, time, spell, interval, stretch, span, duration, space. **3** *a pregnancy reaching term | a life cut off before its natural term* fruition, culmination, limit, termination, close, end, conclusion.

term v *what do they term the process?* call, name, entitle, style, dub, label, tag, designate, denominate.

terminal adj **1** *a terminal illness* fatal, deadly, mortal, lethal, killing, incurable. **2** *a terminal patient* dying, on one's deathbed, near death, in the throes of death, incurable. **3** *terminal markers* boundary, bounding, limiting, confining, end, ending.

terminal n **1** *the terminals of the estate* extremity, end, boundary, bound, limit, edge. **2** *the terminal of the railway line* termi-

nus, last stop, depot. *see* TERMINUS. **3** *collect one's luggage at the terminal* air/sea terminal. **4** *seated at the computer terminal* workstation, visual display unit, input/output device; *inf* VDU.

terminate v **1** *terminate the meeting as soon as you can* bring to a close/end/conclusion, close, end, conclude, finish, stop, wind up, discontinue. **2** *the meeting terminated at midnight* come to a close/end, close, end, conclude, finish, stop. **3** *they terminated his contract* end, bring to an end, stop, cease, discontinue, cancel. **4** *the match terminated in a draw* end, finish, conclude, result. **5** *his contract terminated last week* end, come to an end, stop, cease, expire, run out, lapse. **6** *terminate a pregnancy* abort, end, put an end to, stop.

termination n **1** *the termination of the meeting* closing, close, ending, end, conclusion, finish, stopping, winding-up, discontinuance; *inf* wind-up. **2** *the termination of his contract* end, stopping, cessation, discontinuance, expiry, lapse, cancellation. **3** *the termination of the match was a draw* end, finish, conclusion, result, issue, denouement. **4** *the pregnant woman underwent a termination* abortion.

terminology n *legal terminology* language, phraseology, vocabulary, nomenclature, jargon, cant, argot; terms, expressions, words; *inf* lingo.

terminus n *the bus/railway terminus* last stop, depot, garage, station, end of the line.

terms npl **1** *tell them in no uncertain terms* words, phrases, expressions; language, mode of expression, manner of speaking. **2** *be on good/friendly/unfriendly terms with their neighbours* relations; standing, footing, relationship. **3** *under the terms of the will/ treaty* stipulations, specifications, conditions, provisions, provisos, particulars, premises, details, points, clauses. **4** *offer reduced terms in the winter* prices, rates, charges, costs, fees. **come to terms 1** *they finally came to terms with the neighbours about the dividing wall* reach agreement, come to an agreement/understanding, reach a compromise. **2** *come to terms with her loss* become reconciled, reach an acceptance (of), learn to live (with). **in terms of** *in terms of worldly wealth he is poor* with regard to, as regards, regarding, with reference to, as to, in respect of.

terrible adj **1** *he's a terrible bore/flirt* great, extreme, incorrigible, outrageous; *inf* awful, dreadful, frightful, impossible. **2** *he's a terrible tennis player* bad, poor, incompetent, useless, talentless; *inf* rotten, duff.

3 *hostages enduring terrible experiences* dreadful, terrifying, frightening, frightful, horrifying, horrible, horrific, horrendous, terrific, harrowing, hideous, grim, unspeakable, appalling, awful, gruesome. **4** *the terrible heat/pain* extreme, severe, harsh, unbearable, intolerable, insufferable. **5** *what's that terrible smell?* | *he's a terrible creature* nasty, foul, offensive, odious, obnoxious, vile, revolting, repulsive, abhorrent, loathsome, hateful, unpleasant, disagreeable; *inf* dreadful, awful, horrible, horrid.

terribly adv *terribly good/sad* very, extremely, exceedingly, decidedly, thoroughly; *inf* awfully, dreadfully, frightfully, terrifically.

terrific adj **1** *a terrific bang/speed* tremendous, great, very great, very big, huge, sizeable, considerable, intense, extreme, extraordinary, excessive. **2** *she's a terrific singer* very good, excellent, superb, remarkable, magnificent, wonderful, marvellous, great, super, sensational; *inf* fantastic, fabulous, fab, A1, ace, wizard, unreal, awesome. **3** *there's been a terrific accident* dreadful, frightful, horrible, horrific, hideous, grim, appalling, awful.

terrified adj terror-stricken, terror-struck, terrorized, frightened out of one's wits/skin, frightened to death, frightened, scared stiff, scared, petrified, horrified, horror-struck, alarmed, panic-stricken, intimidated, dismayed, appalled, shocked, paralysed with fear; *inf* spooked.

terrify v terrorize, frighten to death, frighten, scare stiff, scare, petrify, horrify, make one's blood run cold, make one's flesh creep, make one's hair stand on end, alarm, panic, intimidate, dismay, appal, shock, paralyse with fear, put the fear of God into; *inf* spook.

territory n **1** *territories governed by the same ruler* country, state, domain, county, district. **2** *an unexplored territory* region, area, terrain, tract. **3** *the financial affairs of the firm are her father's territory* area, area of concern/activity, province, field, sector, department. **4** *a salesman's territory* area, section, route, beat, ambit. **5** *an animal defending its territory* area, domain, space.

terror n **1** fright, fear, fear and trembling, dread, alarm, panic, intimidation, dismay, consternation, shock, horror; *inf* heebie-jeebies. **2** *imagining all manner of terrors* bogeyman, bugbear, monster, demon, fiend, devil. **3** *that child's a little terror* hooligan, ruffian, hoodlum, villain, rogue, rascal, troublemaker; *inf* holy terror.

terrorize v **1** *terrorize the children* strike terror in/into, terrify, frighten to death, scare stiff, petrify, horrify. *see* TERRIFY. **2** *terrorize them into leaving their homes* coerce, browbeat, bully, intimidate, menace, threaten; *inf* bulldoze, strong-arm.

terse adj **1** *a terse description of the event* concise, succinct, compact, brief, short, to the point, crisp, pithy, elliptical, epigrammatic. **2** *she sounded terse on the phone* abrupt, curt, brusque, laconic, short, clipped, blunt.

test n **1** *a test to distinguish the competent from the incompetent* examination, check, assessment, evaluation, appraisal, investigation, inspection, analysis, scrutinization, scrutiny, study, probe, exploration. **2** *take the bike out for a test* trial, try-out, try, probation, assay. **3** *the children are sitting a test tomorrow* exam, examination, quiz, set of questions, questionnaire. **4** *the test of a good cake* | *the test by which a good cake is judged* criterion, touchstone, yardstick, standard, measure, model, pattern.

test v **1** *test the children's knowledge of local history* put to the test, examine, check, assess, evaluate, appraise, investigate, scrutinize, study, probe. **2** *their behaviour really tested his patience* try, tax, strain, put a strain on. **3** *test the bike for oneself* try, try out, put to the test. **4** *test the water for pollution* analyse, assay, check, investigate, scrutinize, explore, probe.

testament n **1** *left her his estate by testament* will. **2** *the sculpture was a testament to his skill* attestation, testimony, evidence, proof, witness; demonstration, indication, exemplification, tribute.

testify v **1** *asked to testify in court* give evidence, bear witness, attest, be a witness. **2** *she testified to his honesty* swear to, attest to, corroborate, substantiate, verify, vouch for, endorse, support, back up, uphold. **3** *testify that she had witnessed the accident* swear, declare, assert, affirm, state, allege, pledge, profess, avow. **4** *tears that testified to her guilt* be evidence/proof of, confirm, corroborate, bear out, prove, show, demonstrate, establish, indicate.

testimonial n **1** *a testimonial from his previous employer* reference, character reference, recommendation, letter of recommendation, commendation, credential, endorsement, certificate of competence. **2** *given as a testimonial to him* gift, tribute, trophy, memento, souvenir.

testimony n **1** *challenge the testimony of the witness* evidence, attestation, sworn statement, deposition, affidavit. **2** *he stuck to his testimony that he had seen her before* statement, declaration, assertion, protestation, affirmation, profession, submission, allegation. **3** *her academic record was a testimony to her ability* proof, evidence, verification, corroboration, support; demonstration, manifestation, indication.

testy adj tetchy, touchy, irritable, irascible, petulant, cross, ill-tempered, crotchety, crabbed, snappish, querulous. *see* TETCHY.

tetchy adj touchy, irritable, irascible, petulant, peevish, cross, ill-tempered, crotchety, grouchy, grumpy, crabbed, testy, cantankerous, crusty, peppery, snappish, querulous, fractious.

tête-à-tête n chat, dialogue, conversation, duologue; *inf* confab, rap.

tether n *the goat broke free from its tether* rope, cord, chain, lead, leash, line.

tether v *tether the goat to a stake* tie, tie up, fasten, secure, chain, rope.

text n **1** *references in the text of the book to the index* main body, content, main matter. **2** *responsible for the text of the book, not for the illustrations* words; wording. **3** *the speaker took covetousness as his text* theme, subject matter, subject, matter, topic, issue, point, motif. **4** *the texts chosen for the funeral service* passage, verse, paragraph. **5** *familiarize yourself with some of the texts before term begins* textbook, book, set book.

texture n **1** *the texture of her skin* feel, touch, appearance, surface, grain. **2** *fabrics of varying texture* weave, structure, composition, constitution, constituency.

thank v *thank them for their present/help* offer/ extend thanks to, express/show gratitude to, show appreciation to.

thankful adj **1** *she was thankful to reach home safely* grateful, appreciative, pleased, relieved. **2** *she was thankful to them for taking her in* grateful, indebted, obliged, under an obligation, beholden.

thankless adj **1** *thankless children* ungrateful, unthankful, unappreciative, ungracious, unmannerly. **2** *thankless tasks* unappreciated, unrewarded, unrewarding, unacknowledged, vain, in vain, fruitless, useless.

thanks npl *express thanks for their help* gratitude, gratefulness, appreciation, acknowledgement, recognition. **thanks to** *thanks to his late arrival we missed the bus* as a result of, because of, owing to, due to, through, by reason of.

thanks interj thank you, many thanks, thank you kindly, much obliged, much appreciated; *inf* ta, cheers.

thaw v **1** *the frozen juice thawed* defrost, unfreeze, melt, soften, liquefy. **2** *at first she was very aloof but she soon thawed* become friendly/genial/sociable, relax, loosen up, become responsive.

theatre n **1** *study theatre at college* drama, dramatic art, dramaturgy, the stage, show business, thespian art; *inf* show biz. **2** *the lecture theatre* hall, room. **3** *the theatre of war | the theatre of civil discord* scene, field, place of action.

theatrical adj **1** *theatrical performances/ careers* dramatic, stage, dramaturgical, show-business, thespian; *inf* show-biz. **2** *theatrical gestures* dramatic, melodramatic, histrionic, emotional, exaggerated, overdone, ostentatious, showy, affected, mannered, stilted, unreal, forced, stagy; *inf* hammy.

theft n *done for theft | a theft at the bookshop* stealing, robbery, thieving, thievery, burglary, larceny, misappropriation, pilfering, purloining, shoplifting, embezzlement, swindling, fraud; *inf* swiping, nicking, rip-off, knocking-off.

theme n **1** *the theme of the speech* topic, subject, subject matter, matter, thesis, text, argument, burden, idea, keynote. **2** *play the theme from the TV series* theme song, melody, tune, air, leitmotif. **3** *the theme of the fancy dress ball* motif, leitmotif, unifying idea. **4** *students writing themes in French* essay, composition, paper, dissertation.

then adv **1** *we went home then* at that point, at that time/moment, on that occasion. **2** *from then on he was ill* that point, that time/moment, that occasion. **3** *she went and then he went* next, after that, afterwards, subsequently, later. **4** *she has the washing to do and then there's the cooking* in addition, also, besides, as well, moreover. **5** *you're tired? then you must go home* in that case, that being the case, that being so, under those circumstances. **6** *our hero then received the hand of the princess* so, therefore, thus, consequently.

theological adj religious, scriptural, divine, holy, ecclesiastical, doctrinal, dogmatic.

theoretical adj **1** *theoretical sciences* not practical, conceptual, abstract. **2** *a theoretical situation* hypothetical, conjectural, suppositional, speculative, notional, postulatory, assumed, presumed.

theorize v form/evolve a theory, speculate, conjecture, suppose, hypothesize.

theory n **1** *one of my pet theories* hypothesis, thesis, conjecture, supposition, speculation, guess, notion, postulation, assumption, presumption, opinion, view. **2** *all very well in theory* abstract knowledge, speculative thought, hypothetical situation, the abstract. **3** *scientific theory* system, scheme, philosophy.

therapeutic adj curative, curing, healing, restorative, remedial, health-giving, sanative, reparative, corrective, ameliorative, beneficial, good, advantageous, salutary.

therapy n **1** *limbs responding to therapy* treatment, remedy, cure. **2** *receiving therapy for depression* psychotherapy, psychoanalysis.

thereabouts adv **1** *it's over there or thereabouts* about there, near there, around there, around that place. **2** *we'll need two hundred or thereabouts* about that, approximately that number/quantity, roughly that number/quantity.

thereafter adv afterwards, after that, then, next, subsequently.

therefore adv and so, so, then, thus, accordingly, consequently, as a result, for that reason.

thesis n **1** *his thesis is that the territory is uninhabited* theory, hypothesis, contention, argument, proposal, proposition, premiss, postulation, opinion, view, idea. **2** *present a thesis for his doctorate* dissertation, paper, treatise, disquisition, essay, composition, monograph.

thick adj **1** *walls/concrete/trees a metre thick* across, in extent/diameter, wide, broad, deep; of great extent/diameter. **2** *thick legs* broad, wide, large, big, bulky, solid, substantial, fat; *inf* beefy. **3** *the ground thick with ants | thick with dust* teeming, swarming, crawling, alive, abounding, overflowing, covered. **4** *the room thick with smoke* full (of), filled; *inf* chock-full. **5** *a thick forest* dense, close-packed, concentrated, crowded, condensed, compact, impenetrable, impassable. **6** *thick cream* clotted, coagulated, heavy, firm. **7** *thick mists* dense, heavy, opaque, smoggy, soupy, murky, impenetrable. **8** *he's too thick to understand* stupid, dense, unintelligent, dull-witted, dull, slow-witted, slow, doltish, blockish; *inf* dim, dim-witted, boneheaded, woodenheaded. **9** *a thick voice | a voice thick with emotion* husky, hoarse, throaty, guttural, rough, indistinct, muffled. **10** *a thick accent* broad, pronounced, marked, strong, rich, obvious, distinct, decided, very great, extreme. **11** *those two are very thick these days* friendly, on friendly/good terms, intimate, close, devoted, hand-in-glove, inseparable, familiar; *inf* pally, palsy-walsy, chummy, matey, well in. **a bit thick** excessive, unreasonable, unfair, unjust.

thicken v **1** *the jelly/cream would not thicken* set, gel, solidify, congeal, clot, coagulate, cake. **2** *the plot thickens* deepen, get more profound, become more involved/complicated/intricate.

thicket n dense growth, tangle, copse, grove, wood.

thickness n **1** *two metres in thickness* width, breadth, depth, diameter, extent. **2** *the thickness of their legs* breadth, broadness, width, wideness, largeness, bigness, bulkiness, solidness, fatness; *inf* beefiness. **3** *the thickness of the mist* denseness, heaviness, opacity, opaqueness, soupiness, murkiness, impenetrability. **4** *his thickness is unbelievable* stupidity, denseness, dull-wittedness, dullness, slow-wittedness, doltishness, blockishness; *inf* dimness, dim-wittedness, boneheadedness, wooden-headedness. **5** *the thickness of her voice* huskiness, hoarseness, throatiness, gutturalness, roughness, gravelliness, indistinctness. **6** *the thickness of his accent* broadness, pronouncedness, markedness, richness, obviousness, decidedness.

thickset adj **1** *thickset countrymen* heavily/solidly built, powerfully built, well-built, heavy, burly, brawny, muscular, bulky, sturdy, stocky; *inf* beefy. **2** *a thickset hedge/forest* dense, close-packed, crowded, compact.

thick-skinned adj insensitive, unfeeling, tough, unsusceptible, impervious, invulnerable, hardened, case-hardened, callous; *inf* hard-boiled.

thief n robber, burglar, housebreaker, larcenist, pilferer, stealer, purloiner, filcher, shoplifter, pickpocket, embezzler, bandit, swindler, fraudster; *inf* mugger, swiper, nicker.

thieve v steal, rob, pilfer, purloin, shoplift, filch, run off with, embezzle, swindle; *inf* swipe, nick, rip off, knock off, lift, snitch.

thin adj **1** *thin lines* narrow, fine, attenuated. **2** *thin materials* fine, light, delicate, flimsy, diaphanous, gossamer, unsubstantial, sheer, transparent, see-through, gauzy, filmy, translucent. **3** *trying to be thin | models have to be thin* slim, slender, lean, slight, svelte, light, spare. **4** *thin and ill-looking* thin as a rake, skinny, spindly, lank, lanky, scrawny, scraggy, bony, skeletal, wasted, emaciated, shrunken, anoxeric, undernourished, underweight. **5** *thin hair* sparse, scanty, wispy, skimpy. **6** *the audience was rather thin* sparse, scarce, scanty, meagre, paltry, scattered. **7** *a thin mixture* dilute, diluted, weak, watery, runny; *inf* wishy-washy. **8** *a thin voice* weak, small, low, soft, faint, feeble. **9** *a thin excuse* flimsy, unsubstantial, weak, feeble, lame, poor, shallow, unconvincing, inadequate, insufficient.

thin v **1** *she has thinned down a lot* become thinner/slimmer, slim down, lose weight, reduce. **2** *thin down the mixture* dilute, water down, weaken. **3** *thin out the plants/population* reduce in number, lessen, decrease, diminish. **4** *the mist/traffic thinned out* become less dense, decrease, diminish, dwindle.

thing n **1** *people matter more than things* object, article. **2** *a few things to buy* item, article. **3** *where did you get that thing?* object; *inf* what-d'you-call-it, what's-its-name, what's-it, thingummy, thingumabob, thingumajig. **4** *what a silly/difficult thing to do* action, act, deed, exploit, feat, undertaking, task, job, chore. **5** *what a silly thing to think* idea, thought, notion, concept, theory, conjecture. **6** *say silly things* statement, remark, comment, declaration, utterance, pronouncement. **7** *a terrible thing to happen* event, happening, occurrence, incident, episode. **8** *patience is a useful thing* quality, characteristic, attribute, property, trait, feature. **9** *the poor/little thing has no home* poor soul, creature, wretch. **10** *there's another thing you should know* fact, point, detail, particular, aspect. **11** *have a thing about spiders* phobia, fear, dislike, aversion, horror, obsession, fixation; *inf* hang-up. **12** *have a thing about champagne* liking, love, fancy, predilection, penchant, preference, taste, particularity, inclination, obsession, fixation, *idée fixe*. **13** *the latest thing in swimwear* style, fashion, specimen, example. **the thing 1** *the thing is to avoid annoying him* aim, intention, idea, objective, object, purpose. **2** *I've found just the thing for a wedding present* something ideal/appropriate/desirable, something necessary, right thing, very thing. **3** *the thing is that he has no money* fact, fact of the matter, point, issue, problem.

things npl **1** *put on dry things | take night things* clothing, attire, apparel; clothes, garments; *inf* gear, togs, clobber. **2** *I'll watch your things while you get a ticket* belongings, possessions, paraphernalia; *inf* stuff, bits and pieces. **3** *her painting things* equipment, apparatus, gear, tackle; implements, tools. **4** *things are getting worse* matters, affairs, circumstances, conditions, relations; state of affairs, situation.

think v **1** *I think they will come* believe, suppose, expect, imagine, surmise, conjecture, guess, fancy. **2** *he is thought to be clever* consider, deem, hold, reckon, regard as, assume, presume, estimate. **3** *he is sitting thinking* ponder, meditate, deliberate, con-

template, muse, cogitate, ruminate, cerebrate, concentrate, brood, rack one's brains, be lost in thought, be in a brown study. **4** *he is thinking about his career* contemplate, consider, deliberate about, muse on, mull over, reflect on, weigh up, review. **5** *she's thinking about her youth* think back to, call to mind, recall, remember, recollect. **6** *he's thinking about what it would be like to be wealthy* imagine, picture, visualize, envisage, dream. **7** *I think I'll go* have a mind to, consider possible, intend possibly. **8** *who'd have thought she would be there* expect, anticipate, imagine, surmise. **think better of** have second thoughts about, reconsider, change one's mind about, decide against. **think nothing of** regard as quite usual/normal, consider routine, take in one's stride. **think over** *think over the implications* contemplate, consider, deliberate about, muse over, mull over, ponder, reflect on, weigh up, consider the pro's and cons of. **think up** *think up an advertising slogan* dream up, come up with, devise, invent, create, concoct.

think n *have a think about the situation* consideration, contemplation, deliberation, muse, reflection.

thinker n *among the world's great thinkers* philosopher, scholar, sage, theorist; *inf* intellect, brain.

thinking n *what's the latest thinking on the effects of the drug?* view, opinion, outlook, judgement, assessment, appraisal, evaluation, position, theory, reasoning; conclusions, thoughts.

thinking adj *a thinking person* rational, reasoning, logical, sensible, intelligent, philosophical, contemplative, reflective, meditative.

thin-skinned adj sensitive, oversensitive, hypersensitive, supersensitive, easily offended/hurt, touchy, temperamental.

third-rate adj inferior, poor-quality, low-quality, low-grade, poor, bad, shoddy, mediocre; *inf* duff, ropy.

thirst n **1** *dying of thirst in the desert* thirstiness, dryness, parchedness, dehydration. **2** *a thirst for knowledge/novelty* desire, craving, longing, hankering, yearning, avidity, keenness, eagerness, hunger, lust, appetite, passion, covetousness; *inf* yen.

thirst v **1** *thirsting for a drink* feel/have a thirst. **2** *thirsting for revenge | thirsted after knowledge* desire, crave, long for, hanker after, yearn for, hunger after, lust after, covet.

thirsty adj **1** *thirsty people* having a thirst, parched, dehydrated; *inf* dry. **2** *thirsty land* dry, droughty, parched, dehydrated. **3** *thirsty for knowledge* thirsting, avid, keen, eager, hungry, greedy, covetous. *see* THIRST n 2.

thong n strip, belt, strap, cord, lash, rope, tie, tether.

thorn n prickle, spike, barb, spine, bristle.

thorny adj **1** *thorny branches* prickly, spiky, barbed, spiny, spined, spinose, bristly, sharp, pointed. **2** *a thorny situation/issue* problematic, awkward, ticklish, difficult, tough, troublesome, bothersome, trying, taxing, irksome, vexatious, worrying, harassing, complicated, convoluted, involved.

thorough adj **1** *a thorough investigation* in-depth, exhaustive, complete, comprehensive, full, intensive, extensive, widespread, sweeping, all-embracing, all-inclusive, detailed. **2** *he is slow but thorough* meticulous, scrupulous, assiduous, conscientious, painstaking, punctilious, methodical, careful. **3** *he's a thorough villain* thoroughgoing, out and out, utter, downright, sheer, absolute, unmitigated, unqualified, complete, total, perfect.

thoroughbred adj **1** *thoroughbred horses* pure-bred, pure, pure-blooded, full-blooded, pedigreed, pedigree. **2** *thoroughbred young women* well-bred, high-born, aristocratic, blue-blooded, elegant, graceful, refined, cultivated; *inf* classy.

thoroughfare n **1** *police directing traffic on the thoroughfare* road, roadway; main road, motorway, street; *Amer* highway, freeway, throughway. **2** *no thoroughfare* passageway, passage, way, access.

thoroughly adv **1** *search the place thoroughly | investigate the matter thoroughly* exhaustively, from top to bottom, completely, comprehensively, fully, intensively, extensively, meticulously, scrupulously, assiduously, conscientiously, painstakingly, methodically, carefully, in detail, detailedly. **2** *she is thoroughly spoilt* completely, utterly, absolutely, totally, entirely, unreservedly, positively, dead.

though conj **1** *he went though he did not want to* although, despite the fact that, in spite of the fact that, notwithstanding that. **2** *he will go though he has to walk* even if, even supposing, despite the possibility that.

though adv *you'll probably be right; I'll find out though* even so, however, but, still, yet, be that as it may, for all that, nonetheless, all the same, notwithstanding.

thought n **1** *incapable of thought* powers of thinking, faculty of reason, power of reasoning. **2** *lost in thought* thinking, reasoning, pondering, meditation, deliberation, cogitation, rumination, musing, mulling, reflection, introspection, contemplation, consideration, cerebration. **3** *a thought came to me as to how we should proceed* idea, notion, line of thinking, theory, opinion. **4** *I had no thought of going* intention, plan, design, purpose, aim. **5** *what are your thoughts on the matter?* judgement, conclusion, appraisal, assessment, estimation, opinion, point of view, position, stance, stand, feeling, sentiment, belief, conviction. **6** *act without thought | give the matter thought* consideration, attention, heed, regard, scrutiny, care, carefulness. **7** *give up all thought of winning* expectation, anticipation, hope, prospect, aspiration, dream. **8** *he has no thought for his widowed mother* thoughtfulness, consideration, care, regard, concern, solicitude, kindness, kindliness, compassion, tenderness. **9** *he could be a thought more helpful* little, touch, bit, dash, jot, tinge, trace; *Amer inf* tad.

thoughtful adj **1** *he seems thoughtful | in a thoughtful mood* pensive, reflective, introspective, meditative, contemplative, ruminative, cogitative, absorbed, rapt/lost in thought, in a brown study. **2** *a thoughtful book/essay* profound, deep, serious, pithy, meaty, weighty. **3** *every action he takes is thoughtful* considered, circumspect, prudent, careful, cautious, heedful, wary, guarded. **4** *he is a thoughtful son | thoughtful acts* considerate, attentive, caring, solicitous, helpful, kind, kindly, compassionate, tender, charitable.

thoughtless adj **1** *she is a very thoughtless person | thoughtless remarks* tactless, undiplomatic, indiscreet, insensitive, inconsiderate, careless, selfish, impolite, rude. **2** *his thoughtless actions* unthinking, heedless, careless, unmindful, absent-minded, injudicious, ill-advised, ill-considered, imprudent, unwise, foolish, silly, stupid, reckless, rash, precipitate, negligent, neglectful, remiss.

thrash v **1** *masters thrashing boys* beat, whip, horsewhip, flog, lash, birch, cane, flagellate, scourge, leather, spank, chastise, belt, wallop, lambaste; *inf* tan, give a hiding/ pasting to. **2** *the home team thrashed the opposition* trounce, rout, vanquish, drub, give a drubbing to, defeat, beat, worst, crush; *inf* beat hollow, lick, clobber, hammer, slaughter, wipe the floor with. **3** *thrashing around unable to get to sleep* thresh, flail, toss and turn, jerk, twitch, squirm, writhe. **thrash**

out *thrash out their differences* discuss, talk over, debate, air, argue out, resolve, settle.

thread n **1** *embroidered with gold thread* | *needles and thread* yarn, cotton, filament, fibre. **2** *a thread of white through the dark background* strand, line, streak, strip, seam. **3** *lose the thread of the story* train of thought, story line, drift, theme, plot, subject, subject matter, motif, tenor.

thread v **1** *thread film into a projector* pass, string, ease. **2** *thread beads* string. **3** *she threaded her way through the crowds* inch, wind, push, squeeze, shoulder, elbow.

threadbare adj **1** *threadbare clothes/upholstery* worn, frayed, tattered, ragged, holey, shabby; *inf* tatty. **2** *threadbare imagery/jokes/ arguments* hackneyed, tired, stale, worn-out, trite, banal, platitudinous, clichéd, cliché-ridden, stock, stereotyped; *inf* old-hat, corny, played-out.

threat n **1** *issue threats* threatening remark, warning, menace, menacing, intimidating remark; *lit* commination. **2** *a threat of rain in the air* | *under threat of war* warning, menace, risk, danger, omen, foreboding, portent. **3** *she is a threat to the smooth running of the company* menace, danger, risk, hazard.

threaten v **1** *bullies threatening younger children* make threats, menace, intimidate, browbeat, bully, pressurize; *inf* lean on. **2** *threaten to tell* announce one's intention. **3** *rain is threatening* be imminent, impend, hang over, loom, foreshadow. **4** *a sky threatening rain* warn of, give warning of, presage, portend, augur. **5** *pollution threatening the environment* be a threat to, menace, endanger, imperil, put at risk, put in jeopardy, jeopardize.

threatening adj **1** *make threatening gestures* menacing, warning, intimidating, bullying, minacious, minatory. **2** *threatening signs of a storm* ominous, inauspicious, foreboding.

threesome n trio, triumvirate, triad, trinity, troika, triune; triplets.

threshold n **1** *guests standing on the threshold* doorway, doorstep, entrance, entry. **2** *on the threshold of a new era* beginning, commencement, start, outset, inception, opening, dawn, brink, verge, debut; *inf* kick-off. **3** *threshold of pain* lower limit, minimum.

thrift n thriftiness, good husbandry, economy, economicalness, economizing, carefulness, frugality, frugalness, sparingness, scrimping, parsimony, penny-pinching, miserliness.

thrifty adj economical, economizing, careful, frugal, sparing, scrimping, parsimonious, penny-pinching, miserly.

thrill n **1** *seeing his hero gave him a thrill* feeling of excitement/stimulation, sensation of joy, wave of pleasure, glow, tingle; *inf* buzz, charge, kick. **2** *it was a thrill to see the baby take her first steps* thrilling experience, joy, delight, pleasure, adventure. **3** *a thrill of terror ran through him* throb, tremble, tremor, quiver, flutter, shudder, vibration.

thrill v **1** *seeing the air display thrilled him* excite, stimulate, arouse, stir, electrify, move, give joy/pleasure to; *inf* give a buzz/ charge/kick. **2** *she thrilled to hear the music* tingle, be excited, feel joy; *inf* get a buzz/ charge/kick. **3** *his body thrilled with fear* throb, tremble, quiver, shiver, flutter, shudder, vibrate.

thrilling adj **1** *a thrilling experience* exciting, stirring, stimulating, electrifying, rousing, moving, gripping, riveting, joyful, pleasing; *inf* hair-raising. **2** *a thrilling sensation through the body* throbbing, trembling, tremulous, quivering, shivering, fluttering, shuddering, vibrating.

thrive v **1** *the business/family is thriving* flourish, prosper, do/go well, boom, burgeon, succeed, advance, get ahead, make progress. **2** *plants thriving* flourish, burgeon, grow vigorously, do well, shoot up.

thriving adj **1** *a thriving business* flourishing, prosperous, prospering, booming, burgeoning, successful, advancing, progressing; *inf* going strong. **2** *thriving plants* flourish, burgeoning, growing, healthy, luxuriant, lush, prolific.

throat n gullet, oesophagus.

throb v *his pulse throbbed rapidly* | *her wound throbbed* beat, pulse, pulsate, palpitate, pound, vibrate, go pit-a-pat, thump.

throb n *the throb of her pulse/wound* beating, beat, pulse, pulsating, palpitation, pounding, vibration, pit-a-pat, pitter-patter, thumping.

throes npl **1** *the throes of childbirth* | *death throes* agony, suffering, excruciation, pain, torture, distress; pangs. **2** *in the throes of moving house* turmoil, upheaval, disruption, tumult, hurly-burly, confusion, chaos, pandemonium.

throne n **1** *a golden throne* royal seat, seat of state. **2** *succeed to the throne* sovereignty, rule, command, dominion.

throng n *a throng of fans* crowd, horde, mob, mass, host, multitude, swarm, flock, pack, herd, drove, press, assemblage, gathering, congregation.

throng v **1** *people thronged to see the play* | *they thronged forward* flock, troop, swarm. **2** *fans thronging round the star* crowd round, press round, mill around, congregate round, converge round, hem in, jostle. **3** *fans thronging the stadium* pack, cram, jam, fill.

throttle v **1** *the attacker throttled him* choke, strangle, strangulate, garrotte. **2** *governments trying to throttle opposition* gag, muzzle, silence, stifle, suppress, control, inhibit.

through prep **1** *go through the building* into and out of, to the other/far side of, from one side to the other of, from end to end of. **2** *he got the job through an advertisement/friend* by means/way of, through the agency of, via, using, with the help/aid/assistance of, under the aegis of, by virtue of, as a result/consequence of, on account of, owing to, because of. **3** *he worked through the night* throughout, during, until the end of. **4** *Monday through Friday* up to and including.

through adv **1** *just walk through* from one end to another, from end to end. **2** *the baby slept through | we worked through* all the time, without a break, without an interruption, non-stop. **3** *it was a struggle but we got through* to the end/finish/termination, to the completion, to the culmination. **through and through** *he's a villain through and through* thoroughly, completely, utterly, altogether, totally, to the core, entirely, wholly, fully, unreservedly, out and out.

through adj **be through 1** *I'm through and I'm going home* finished, finished work, reached the end. **2** *the job is through now* completed, done, finished, ended, terminated; *inf* washed-up. **3** *she says she's through with acting/boyfriends* finished with, no longer involved with, tired of.

throughout prep **1** *throughout the world/house* all over, all round, in every part of, everywhere in. **2** *working throughout the night* through, all through, for the duration of, until the end of.

throughout adv **1** *the house is carpeted throughout | they painted the house throughout* all through, right through, in every part, all over, everywhere. **2** *we loved the performance; we were riveted throughout* all the time, until the end, for the duration.

throw v **1** *throw a brick* hurl, toss, cast, sling, pitch, shy, lob, propel, launch, project, send; *inf* heave, chuck. **2** *throw his arms in the air* move quickly/suddenly, turn quickly/suddenly. **3** *throw a shadow* cast, project, send. **4** *throw a glance/smile at him* cast, send, dart, bestow on, give. **5** *the wrestler threw his opponent* throw/hurl to the ground, fell, floor, prostrate. **6** *the horse threw his rider* unseat, dislodge. **7** *his question threw me* disconcert, discomfit, disturb, confound, astonish, surprise, dumbfound, discountenance. **8** *threw the lever* operate, switch on, move. **9** *throw a vase* shape, form, mould, fashion. **10** *she threw on her clothes* pull on, put on quickly, don quickly, slip into. **throw away 1** *throw away his textbooks* throw out, discard, get rid of, dispose of, jettison, scrap, reject, dispense with; *inf* dump, ditch. **2** *throw away a good opportunity | actresses throwing away their lines* fail to exploit, make poor use of, waste, squander, fritter away, lose; *inf* blow. **throw off 1** *throw off their shackles* cast off, discard, shake off, drop, jettison, free/rid oneself of, abandon. **2** *threw off one's pursuers* shake off, outdistance, outrun, evade, escape from, get away from, elude, give someone the slip, lose, leave behind. **throw out 1** *throw out old letters* throw away, discard, get rid of, dispose of, jettison, scrap. **2** *throw the drunk out of the house* eject, evict, expel, show the door to, put out; *inf* kick out, turf out. **3** *throw out a proposal* reject, give the thumbs down to, turn down, dismiss, disallow. **4** *fires throwing out heat* emit, radiate, give off, diffuse, disseminate.

throw n **1** *hit the coconut in the fair at one throw* hurl, toss, cast, sling, pitch, shy, lob; *inf* heave, chuck. **2** *jackets at £50 a throw* each, apiece, per item, for one.

thrust v **1** *thrust the money at the taxi-driver* push, shove, ram. **2** *thrust open the door* push, shove, drive, press, prod, propel. **3** *thrust responsibility on him* force, impose, push, press, urge. **4** *thrust him through the heart* stab, pierce, stick, jab, lunge at. **5** *thrust their way through the crowd* push, shove, press, force, shoulder, elbow, jostle.

thrust n **1** *with one thrust of his fist* push, shove, ram, drive, press, prod. **2** *killed by his opponent's thrust* stab, jab, lunge. *see* LUNGE n. **3** *surprised by the enemy's sudden thrust* advance, push, drive, attack, offensive, assault, charge, onslaught, incursion, raid. **4** *upset by her nasty thrust* verbal attack/assault, criticism, censure, hostile remark. **5** *a man with thrust* drive, push, force, impetus, energy, assertiveness, aggression, ambition; *inf* get-up-and-go. **6** *the thrust of the engine | the thrusts in the bridge* motive force, propulsive force, force, pressure. **7** *they failed to grasp the thrust of the speech* gist, drift, substance, essence, theme, subject, thesis.

thrusting adj *a thrusting young salesman* forceful, pushing, forward, energetic, assertive, aggressive, insistent, ambitious; *inf* pushy.

thud n *fall with a thud* thump, clunk, clonk, crash, smack, wham, bang, wallop.

thud v **1** *thudding around in heavy boots* thump, clump, clunk, clonk, crash. **2** *branches thudding against the window* thump, clunk, clonk, crash, smack, knock, bang.

thug n ruffian, tough, rough, hoodlum, bully-boy, hooligan, villain, gangster, robber, bandit, murderer, killer, assassin; *inf* heavy, bovver boy, hit-man.

thumb n *an injured thumb* pollex. **all thumbs** clumsy, awkward, maladroit, inept; *inf* butter-fingered, cack-handed, ham-fisted. **thumbs down** rejection, refusal, no, negation, rebuff, disapproval. **thumbs up** acceptance, affirmation, yes, approval, encouragement; *inf* go-ahead, OK, green light.

thumb v **1** *thumb through the book* leaf through, flick through, flip through, riffle through, browse, skim, scan. **2** *thumb a book badly* soil, mark, make dog-eared. **3** *thumb a lift* signal for, obtain; *inf* hitch.

thumbnail adj *a thumbnail sketch* succinct, concise, compact, short, brief, pithy, quick, rapid.

thump v **1** *he thumped the girl's attacker* strike, hit, punch, thwack, wallop, smack, slap, batter, beat, cudgel, knock, thrash; *inf* whack, belt, clout, lambaste. **2** *my heart/head is thumping* pound, thud, pulse, pulsate, throb, palpitate. **3** *thumping on the table* bang, batter, beat, crash, knock, rap.

thump n **1** *give the attacker a thump* blow, punch, thwack, wallop, smack, slap; *inf* whack, belt, clout, lambasting. **2** *give the table a thump* bang, knock, rap. **3** *the shoe landed with a thump* thud, clunk, clonk, crash, smack, wham, bang, wallop.

thumping adj **1** *hear a thumping noise* thudding, clunking, clonking, crashing, banging. **2** *a thumping lie/majority* huge, massive, enormous, immense, vast, colossal, gigantic, mammoth, monumental, great, tremendous, impressive, extraordinary; *inf* whopping, thundering.

thumping adv *a thumping great house/present* extremely, very, extraordinarily, remarkably, uncommonly; *inf* thundering.

thunder n **1** *we could hear thunder* thunder crack, thunder clap. **2** *the thunder of guns/applause* boom, booming, rumble, rumbling, outburst, roar, roaring.

thunder v **1** *his voice thundered in my ear* boom, rumble, roar, blast, resound, reverberate. **2** *workers thundering against management* fulminate against, rail against,

denounce, curse, threaten. **3** *"get back," he thundered* roar, bellow, bark, declaim, yell, shout.

thundering adj *a thundering lie/majority* huge, massive, enormous, immense, vast, colossal, great, tremendous; *inf* thumping. *see* THUMPING adj 2.

thundering adv *a thundering great house/present* extremely, very, extraordinarily; *inf* thumping.

thunderous adj *thunderous voices/applause* booming, rumbling, roaring, resounding, reverberating, deafening, ear-splitting, loud, noisy, tumultuous.

thunderstruck adj amazed, astonished, dumbfounded, astounded, speechless, struck dumb, open-mouthed, at a loss for words, aghast, stunned, staggered, startled, taken aback, surprised, disconcerted, shocked, nonplussed, bewildered; *inf* flabbergasted, bowled over, knocked for six, floored, flummoxed.

thus adv **1** *hold the apparatus thus* like this, in this way, so, like so. **2** *he is the eldest son and thus inherits the estate* so, that being so, therefore, accordingly, hence, consequently, as a result, for this/that reason, on this/that account, ergo. **3** *having come thus far* so, to this extent.

thwack v *thwack the child | thwack his attacker* hit, strike, slap, smack, wallop, thump, punch, box, knock, beat, batter, pound, pummel; *inf* whack, belt, clout, bush, bop, slug, lambaste.

thwack n *give the child/attacker a thwack* hit, slap, smack, wallop, thump, punch, box, knock; *inf* whack, clout, bop, slug. *see* THWACK V.

thwart v *thwart their plans | he was thwarted in his aims* frustrate, foil, baulk, check, block, stop, prevent, defeat, impede, obstruct, hinder, hamper, stymie.

tic n *a tic in his eye/face* twitch, spasm, jerk.

tick n **1** *the tick of a clock/taximetre* ticking, click, beat, tap, tapping, tick-tock. **2** *I'll be there in a tick* moment, second, instant, minute, flash, trice, in no time at all, twinkling, the twinkling of an eye; *inf* sec, jiffy, shake, two shakes of a lamb's tail, half a mo. **3** *put a tick at the correct answer* affirmative mark, stroke, mark, dash, line.

tick v **1** *the clock/metre was ticking* click, beat, tap, sound, tick-tock. **2** *tick the items you want | tick the items present* put a tick at, mark, mark off, check off, indicate. **tick off 1** *tick off the items present* put a tick at, mark, mark off, check off, indicate. **2** *she ticked the children off for being late* scold, reprimand, chide, rebuke, lecture, reproach, reprove, upbraid, berate, censure, take to task; *inf* tell off, give a dressing-down to, haul over the coals, carpet, tear into.

ticket n **1** *show your ticket to enter* pass, token, stub, coupon, card. **2** *there's no price ticket on this label,* tag, tally.

tickle v **1** *tickle the child under the chin* stroke, pet, touch. **2** *tickle the fancy* interest, excite, stimulate, arouse, captivate, please, gratify, delight. **3** *we were tickled by the antics of the children* amuse, entertain, divert, cheer, gladden.

ticklish adj *a ticklish situation* difficult, problematic, awkward, delicate, sensitive, tricky, thorny, knotty, touchy, risky, uncertain, precarious; *inf* sticky.

tide n **1** *sailing times dependent on the tide* tidal flow, tidewater, tide race, ebb, current, stream. **2** *the tide of events* course, movement, direction, trend, current, drift, run, tendency, tenor.

tide v **tide over** *the extra money will tide us over until pay day* help out, assist, aid, keep one going, see one through, keep one's head above water, keep the wolf from the door.

tidings npl *good tidings | hear tidings of his death* news, notification, word, communication, information, intelligence, advice; reports; *inf* info, low-down, dope.

tidy adj **1** *a tidy room/garden* neat, trim, orderly, in order, in good order, well-ordered, spruce, shipshape, well-kept, clean, spick and span. **2** *children looking tidy* neat, well-groomed, spruce. **3** *people who are tidy by nature* neat, orderly, organized, well-organized, methodical, systematic, business-like. **4** *leave a tidy sum* considerable, sizeable, substantial, goodly, handsome, generous, ample, largish, large, respectable, fair, decent, healthy.

tidy v **1** *tidy up the living room | tidy your desk* clean, clean up, put to rights, put in order, straighten, make shipshape. **2** *tidy oneself up for the interview* spruce up, groom, smarten, neaten, brush down.

tie v **1** *tie the dog to the tree | the boat was tied fast to the jetty* tie up, fasten, attach, fix, bind, secure, tether, moor, lash, join, connect, link, couple, rope, chain. **2** *tie the string/knot* knot, make a bow/knot in. **3** *having a young child rather tied her* tie down, restrict, confine, curb, limit, constrain, restrain, hamper, hinder, impede, cramp. **4** *the two teams tied* draw, be equal, be even, be neck and neck. **tie in** *her evidence doesn't tie in with that of other people | the new evidence*

just does not tie in fit in with, correspond to, tally with, concur with, conform with, dovetail with. **tie down** *children/petty rules tied her down* tie, restrict, confine, curb, limit, constrain, hinder. **tie up 1** *tie up the dog/boat* fasten, attach, bind, secure, tether, moor, connect, rope, chain. *see* TIE v 1. **2** *the robbers tied up the guard* bind, truss up. **3** *tie up the parcel* wrap, wrap up, bind, truss. **4** *his capital is tied up* invest, commit. **5** *the meeting will tie him up all morning* occupy, engage, keep busy, engross, take up one's attention. **6** *we should tie up the meeting/arrangements/contract* finalize, conclude, bring to a conclusion, wind up, complete, finish off; *inf* wrap up.

tie n **1** *rubbish bags fastened with a tie* bond, ligature, link, fastening, fastener, clip, catch. **2** *men wearing ties* necktie, bow-tie, cravat, neckerchief. **3** *family/business ties* bond, connection, relationship, kinship, affiliation, allegiance, liaison, friendship. **4** *owning a restaurant can be a tie* restriction, curb, limitation, constraint, restraint, hindrance, impediment, encumbrance. **5** *the game ended in a tie* draw, dead heat, deadlock, stalemate. **6** *the team have two ties this week* fixture, game, match, contest.

tier n **1** *tiers of seats* row, rank, bank, line. **2** *the tiers of a wedding cake* layer, level. **3** *the tiers of the underground garage* level, storey. **4** *the tiers of the hierarchy in the firm* layer, level, echelon, rank.

tight adj **1** *keep a tight grip* fast, secure, fixed, clenched, clinched. **2** *tight ropes/muscles* taut, rigid, stiff, tense, stretched, strained. **3** *a tight skirt rather than a full one* tight-fitting, close-fitting, figure-hugging, narrow. **4** *a tight mass of fibres* compact, compacted, compressed. **5** *space was a bit tight with so many people* cramped, restricted, limited, constricted. **6** *the box must be tight* impervious, impenetrable, sound, sealed, hermetic; watertight, airtight. **7** *money is a bit tight just now* scarce, scant, sparse, in short supply, limited, insufficient, inadequate. **8** *security was tight at the president's talk* strict, rigorous, stringent, tough, rigid, uncompromising, exacting. **9** *in a tight situation* problematic, difficult, precarious, hazardous, dangerous, perilous, tricky, ticklish, worrying, delicate; *inf* sticky. **10** *a piece of tight prose* concise, succinct, terse, crisp, straightforward, pithy, epigrammatic. **11** *it was a tight race* close, even, evenly matched, neck and neck. **12** *he got tight at the party* drunk, intoxicated, inebriated, tipsy; *inf* tiddly, under the influence, bevvied, plastered, smashed, legless, paralytic, wasted, wrecked, pickled, sozzled, steaming, stewed, out of it, blotto, pie-eyed, half-cut, three sheets to the wind, pissed. **13** *the old man's so tight he won't buy food* tight-fisted, mean, miserly, parsimonious, stingy, niggardly.

tighten v **1** *she tightened her grip* secure, make fast, make more secure. **2** *tighten the rope* tauten, make tight/taut, stretch, make rigid, rigidify, stiffen, tense. **3** *tighten the lid* screw on, close. **4** *tighten security* increase, make stricter, make rigorous/stringent/rigid. *see* TIGHT 8. **5** *his throat tightened* narrow, constrict, contract.

till prep **1** *he played till six o' clock* | *playing till they went home* until, up to, as late as, up to the time that/of. **2** *we hadn't seen him till then* before, prior to, previous to, earlier than.

till n *money in the till* cash register, cash box, cash drawer, strong box.

till v *till the soil/field* cultivate, work, farm, plough, dig, turn over.

tilt v **1** *the building tilts a bit* lean, list, slope, slant, incline, tip, cant. **2** *tilt at the other knight* charge against, rush at, run at. **3** *tilt with the other knight* joust with, clash with, contend with, fight with.

tilt n **1** *the building/picture is at a tilt* | *with a tilt of his head* angle, slant, slope, incline, inclination, cant. **2** *knights taking part in a tilt* joust, tournament, tourney, combat, contest, fight, duel; lists. **at full tilt** at full speed/pelt, at breakneck speed, headlong, very rapidly/quickly/swiftly, with great force.

timber n **1** *timber for building the house* wood; *Amer* lumber. **2** *the ceiling/ship's timbers* beam, spar, pole. **3** *timber for the fire* wood, firewood; logs.

time n **1** *in the time of the dinosaurs* age, era, epoch, period. **2** *he worked there for a time* while, spell, stretch, span, period, term. **3** *the last time I saw him* occasion, point, juncture. **4** *now is the time to act/leave* moment, point, instant, stage. **5** *the house will last his time* lifetime, life, life span, allotted span. **6** *have a hard time* | *endure hard times* conditions, circumstances; situation, experience. **7** *beat time* | *in waltz time* rhythm, measure, tempo, beat, metre. **8** *he never has any time to himself* freedom, leisure, leisure time, spare time; moments, odd moments. **ahead of time** early, earlier than expected, in good time, with time to spare. **all the time 1** *they chattered all the time he was speaking* throughout, for the duration. **2** *he works all the time* constantly, always, at all times, perpetually, continu-

ously, continually. **at one time 1** *at one time he worked there* at one point, once, time was when, in the past, previously, formerly, hitherto. **2** *several matches going on at one time* simultaneously, concurrently, at once, at the same time, together. **at the same time 1** *they arrived at the same time* simultaneously, together, concurrently. **2** *he's wealthy; at the same time he lives frugally* nevertheless, nonetheless, however, but, still, yet, just the same. **at times** from time to time, every now and then, periodically, on occasion, occasionally. **behind time** late, running late, behind schedule. **behind the times** old-fashioned, out of date/fashion, dated, outmoded, obsolete, *passé*, antiquated; *inf* old hat. **for the time being** for now, for the moment/present, in the meantime, meantime, meanwhile, temporarily, pro tem. **from time to time** now and then, every so often, once in a while, at times, periodically, on occasion, occasionally, sometimes. **in no time 1** *your mum will be here in no time* very soon, any moment/minute now, before one knows it, in a trice; *inf* in a jiffy. **2** *he did the job in no time* very rapidly/quickly/swiftly, speedily, at great speed, expeditiously, with dispatch. **in good time** punctually, on time, early, ahead of time, with time to spare. **in time 1** *he didn't reach the station in time* early enough, punctually, in good time, at the appointed/right time, on schedule. **2** *they will forget in time* eventually, ultimately, as time goes on/by, by and by, one day, someday, sooner or later, in the long run. **many a time** often, frequently, many times, on many occasions. **on time** punctually, early enough, in good time, sharp; *inf* on the dot. **time after time** again and again, many times over, repeatedly, time and again, time and time again, recurrently, frequently, often, on many occasions.

time v **1** *time the meeting for the afternoon* schedule, fix, set, arrange, timetable, programme. **2** *time his progress* | *time the race* clock, measure, calculate, regulate, count. **3** *time the film exposure* | *time his entrance* regulate, adjust, set, synchronize.

timeless adj ageless, enduring, lasting, permanent, abiding, unending, ceaseless, undying, deathless, eternal, everlasting, immortal, changeless, immutable, indestructible.

timely adj *their timely intervention* opportune, well-timed, at the right time, convenient, appropriate, seasonable, felicitous.

timetable n *bus timetables* | *the timetable for the conference* schedule, programme, calendar, list, agenda.

timetable v *timetable the appointment for tomorrow* schedule, fix, set, programme.

timid adj **1** *too timid to stand up to the bully* easily frightened, timorous, fearful, apprehensive, afraid, frightened, scared, fainthearted, cowardly, pusillanimous; *inf* chicken, yellow, lily-livered. **2** *too timid to speak to strangers* shy, diffident, bashful, reticent, unselfconfident, timorous, shrinking, retiring, coy, demure.

timorous adj **1** *too timorous to fight* easily frightened, timid, fearful, apprehensive, afraid, frightened, scared, cowardly; *inf* chicken. *see* TIMID 1. **2** *too timorous to introduce herself* timid, shy, diffident, bashful, reticent, retiring, coy. *see* TIMID 2.

tincture n **1** *tincture of iodine* solution, suspension, infusion. **2** *a tincture of pink in the material* tint, colour, shade, tinge. **3** *a tincture of garlic* flavour, taste, smell, aroma, trace. **4** *a tincture of heresy in their attitude* hint, suggestion, trace, touch, dash, soupçon.

tinge v **1** *wallpapers tinged with silver* colour, tint, shade, dye, stain, suffuse, imbue. **2** *admiration slightly tinged with envy* affect by, flavour with, colour with, suffuse, imbue.

tinge n **1** *a tinge of silver in the wallpaper* colour, tint, shade, tone, tincture, cast, dye, stain, wash. **2** *a tinge of sadness in her attitude* hint, suggestion, trace, touch, bit dash, tincture, soupçon.

tingle v *my fingers were tingling* prickle, prick, tickle, itch, sting, quiver, tremble.

tingle n **1** *the tingle in her fingers* tingling, prickling, pricking, tickle, itch, quiver, trembling; *inf* pins and needles. **2** *feel a tingle of excitement* quiver, tremor, thrill, throb.

tinker v *tinker with the engine* | *tinker at computers* fiddle with, play with, toy with, tamper with, fool around with, mess about with.

tinkle v *the bell tinkled* ring, chime, peal, ding, jingle.

tinkle n **1** *the tinkle of the doorbell* ring, chime, peal, ding, jingle. **2** *give her a tinkle* telephone call, call; *inf* phone, phone call, ring, buzz, bell. **3** *go for a tinkle* urination; *inf* pee.

tinsel n **1** *Christmas trees decorated with tinsel* metallic yarn, spangle, clinquant. **2** *dislike the tinsel of the occasion* ostentation, showiness, flashiness, pretentiousness, display, glitter, ornateness, flamboyance, gaudiness, garishness, tawdriness, meretriciousness.

tinsel adj *tinsel clothes/furnishings/occasions* ostentatious, showy, flashy, pretentious, glittering, ornate, flamboyant, gaudy, garish, trashy, meretricious, tawdry; *inf* flash.

tint n **1** *several tints to chose from* shade, colour, tone, tinge, cast, tincture. **2** *strong colours contrasting with tints* pastel, pale colour, soft colour. **3** *a hair tint* dye, colourant, colouring, wash.

tiny adj minute, diminutive, miniature, mini, miniscule, infinitesimal, microscopic, dwarfish, midget, pocket-sized, Lilliputian, wee, *petite*, small, little, insignificant, trifling, negligible, inconsequential; *inf* teeny, teeny-weeny, itsy-bitsy, pint-sized.

tip[1] n **1** *the tip of an iceberg* | *the mountain tip* point, peak, top, summit, apex, crown. **2** *the tip of the fingers* end, extremity. **3** *the tip of an umbrella* point, end. **4** *the chair legs have rubber tips* cap, cover.

tip[1] v *they tipped the cigarettes with filters* | *warriors tipping their spears with poison* cap, top, crown.

tip[2] n *take the rubbish to the tip* rubbish dump, dump, refuse dump, rubbish heap; *dial* midden.

tip[2] v **1** *the wardrobe tends to tip* tilt, lean, list, cant, slant. **2** *the chair/boat tipped over* topple, overturn, fall over, turn topsyturvy, capsize. **3** *he tipped over the rubbish bin* upset, overturn, topple, upend, capsize. **4** *tip the water into the bath* | *tip rubbish onto the dump* pour, empty, unload, dump.

tip[3] n **1** *give the waiter a tip* gratuity, *pourboire*, baksheesh. **2** *tips on how to take out stains* hint, suggestion, piece of advice; advice. **3** *a tip for the 3.30* racing tip, recommendation.

tip[3] v **1** *tip the waiter* give a tip to, reward, remunerate. **2** *tip the grey horse* | *the older candidate to win* recommend, back.

tip[4] v *the ball tipped the edge of the racket* touch, tap, strike/hit lightly.

tip-off n *the police received a tip-off about the murderer's whereabouts* warning, forewarning, hint, clue; advice, information, notification.

tipple v **1** *began to tipple on his wife's death* drink, take alcohol regularly, have a drink problem; *inf* indulge, booze. **2** *tipple whisky* drink, sip, swig, quaff, imbibe.

tipple n *what's your tipple?* regular/usual drink, favourite drink; *inf* poison.

tippler n drinker, hard/problem drinker, drunk, drunkard, inebriate, toper, sot, imbiber; *inf* boozer, soak, lush.

tipsy adj drunk, intoxicated, inebriated; *inf* tiddly, tight, under the influence, merry, bevvied, half-cut.

tirade n diatribe, harangue, stream of abuse, verbal onslaught, lecture, upbraiding, denunciation, obloquy, philippic; invective, vituperation, fulmination, censure, vilification.

tire v **1** *climbing the mountain tired him* tire out, fatigue, wear out, weary, exhaust, drain, enervate, debilitate, jade; *inf* fag out, take it out of, whack, bush, knacker, poop. **2** *he tires easily* get/grow/become tired, get fatigued, flag, droop. **3** *their constant boasting tires me* bore, weary, irk, irritate, get on one's nerves, annoy, exasperate; *inf* get to. **4** *he never tires of hearing the story | she tired of her lover* grow bored, become weary, be fed up; *inf* be sick (of).

tired adj **1** *feel tired after the climb* fatigued, worn out, weary, wearied, exhausted, drained, enervated, debilitated, jaded; *inf* fagged, done, done in, all in, dead beat, dog-tired, whacked, bushed, knackered, pooped, dead on one's feet, ready to drop. **2** *tired children anxious for bed* sleepy, drowsy, weary; *inf* asleep on one's feet. **3** *tired jokes* stale, hackneyed, familiar, worn-out, outworn, well-worn, clichéd, stock, platitudinous, trite, banal; *inf* corny. **4** *made tired by their chatter* bored, wearied, irked, irritated, annoyed, exasperated. **5** *tired of listening to the story* bored, weary, wearied, fed up; *inf* sick.

tireless adj *tireless workers/efforts* untiring, unwearied, unflagging, indefatigable, energetic, industrious, vigorous, determined, resolute, dogged.

tiresome adj **1** *tiresome work* wearisome, laborious, wearing, tedious, boring, monotonous, dull, uninteresting, unexciting, humdrum, routine. **2** *she's a tiresome child* troublesome, irksome, vexatious, irritating, annoying, exasperating, trying.

tiring adj *a tiring journey/job* wearying, wearing, fatiguing, exhausting, draining, enervating, arduous, laborious, strenuous, exacting, taxing, tough.

tissue n **1** *coverings made of tissue* gauze, gossamer, netting, webbing. **2** *wrap the china in tissue* tissue paper. **3** *pass the child a tissue* paper handkerchief, disposable handkerchief, paper towel; *Trademark* Kleenex. **4** *a tissue of lies* web, network, nexus, mass, conglomeration, set, series, chain.

titbit n **1** *keep some titbits for the children/dogs* tasty morsel, treat, snack, delicacy, dainty, *bonne bouche*; *inf* goody. **2** *neighbours passing on titbits* piece of gossip, bit of scandal, juicy/spicy scrap.

titillate v *titillated by the pornographic film* excite, arouse, stimulate, provoke, thrill, interest, fascinate, tantalize, seduce; *inf* turn on.

titillating adj *titillating pictures* exciting, arousing, stimulating, provocative, thrilling, interesting, fascinating, tantalizing, suggestive, seductive, erotic.

titivate v *titivate herself to go out* groom, smarten up, spruce up, make up, prink, preen, primp; *inf* doll up, do up, tart up.

title n **1** *what is the title of the book/musical?* name. **2** *picture/illustration titles* credit, caption, legend, inscription, heading. **3** *what is the title of the queen's niece?* form of address, designation, appellation, name, denomination, epithet, sobriquet, style; *inf* moniker, handle. **4** *disputing his title to the land* entitlement, right, claim, ownership, proprietorship, possession, holding. **5** *lose the titles to the land* title-deed, deed, ownership document, proof of ownership. **6** *boxers contending for the title* championship, first place, crown; laurels.

title v *they titled the book Sunburst* entitled, name, call, designate, label, tag, style, term.

titter n snicker, snigger, giggle, tee-hee, laugh, chuckle, cackle; *inf* chortle.

tittle-tattle n *you shouldn't listen to tittle-tattle* gossip, idle talk, chit-chat, prattle, hearsay.

titular adj **1** *a titular description* naming, designative, appellative, denominative, identifying, labelling. **2** *the titular head of state* nominal, in title/name only, so-called, self-called, self-styled, *soi-disant*, token, puppet, putative.

toady n *the boss and a couple of his toadies* sycophant, fawner, flatterer, groveller, kowtower, lackey, flunkey, minion, lickspittle, truckler, hanger-on, parasite, leech, jackal, spaniel; *inf* yes-man, crawler, bootlicker.

toady v *he toadies to his superiors* bow and scrape to, be obsequious to, fawn on, flatter, grovel to, kowtow to, curry favour with, truckle to; *inf* butter up, fall all over, suck up to.

toast v **1** *toast the bread/crumpets* brown, crisp. **2** *toast oneself at the fire* warm, warm up, heat, heat up. **3** *toast the winner* drink the health of, drink to, pledge, salute.

toast n **1** *drink/make a toast to the winner* health, pledge, salutation, salute, tribute; compliments, greetings. **2** *she was the toast* *of the town* celebrity, darling, favourite, heroine, hero.

today n **1** *today is his birthday* this day, this very day. **2** *today is all that matters to the young* the present, the present time, now, the here and now, this moment, this time, this period, this age.

toddle v **1** *children toddling down the road* totter, teeter, wobble, falter, dodder. **2** *we must be toddling off* go, leave, depart.

to-do n commotion, fuss, fuss and bother, bother, trouble, disturbance, uproar, tumult, hurly-burly, brouhaha, bustle, hustle and bustle.

together adv **1** *friends who work together* with each other, in conjunction, jointly, conjointly, in cooperation, as one, in unison, side by side, hand in hand, hand in glove, shoulder to shoulder, cheek by jowl. **2** *they arrived/shouted together* simultaneously, concurrently, at the same time, at once, all at once, in unison, with one accord, synchronously. **3** *it rained for days together* in a row, in succession, successively, consecutively, on end, one after the other, continuously, without a break, without interruption. **4** *they've got it/things together at last* organized, sorted out, straight, to rights, settled, fixed, arranged.

together adj *she seems very together* composed, calm, cool, well-balanced, stable, well-adjusted, well-organized, efficient.

toil v **1** *they toiled away on the land | toiling at their books* labour, slog, slave, push oneself, drive oneself, strive, drudge, work, work doggedly, work like a dog/slave/Trojan; *inf* work one's fingers to the bone, sweat, grind, graft. **2** *they toiled up the hill* labour, struggle, drag oneself; *inf* sweat, make heavy weather.

toil n *years of toil wore him out* hard/heavy work, labour, slog, slaving, donkey-work, drudgery, striving, application, industry, effort, exertion, travail, sweat of one's brow; *inf* elbow-grease, grind, graft.

toilet n **1** *public toilets* lavatory, bathroom, ladies' room, powder room, convenience, urinal, latrine, privy, outhouse; *Amer* washroom; *inf* loo, bog, gents, ladies, WC; *Amer inf* john, can. **2** *attending to his toilet* bathing, washing, grooming, dressing; ablutions.

toils npl *caught in the toils of the law* net, snare, trap.

token n **1** *a white flag being a token of surrender | a token of friendship* symbol, sign, emblem, badge, representation, indication, mark, manifestation, expression, demon-

stration, recognition, index; evidence. **2** *keep the menu as a token of the celebration* memento, souvenir, keepsake, remembrance, reminder, memorial. **3** *slot machine tokens* disc, substitute, substitute coin. **4** *book tokens* voucher, coupon.

token adj **1** *a token strike to emphasize union solidarity* symbolic, emblematic. **2** *offer token resistance* perfunctory, superficial, nominal, minimal, slight, hollow.

tolerable adj **1** *the pain/noise level was scarcely tolerable* endurable, bearable, sufferable, supportable, brookable, acceptable. **2** *his work was tolerable but far from brilliant* fairly good, fair, all right, passable, adequate, satisfactory, good enough, average, mediocre, middling, fair to middling, ordinary, run-of-the-mill, indifferent, unexceptional; *inf* not bad, OK, so-so, nothing to write home about.

tolerance n **1** *treat the young with tolerance* toleration, open-mindedness, lack of prejudice/bias, broad-mindedness, liberalism, forbearance, patience, magnanimity, understanding, charity, lenience, lenity, indulgence, permissiveness, complaisance, laxness. **2** *his tolerance of pain | accept the situation with tolerance* toleration, endurance, sufferance, acceptance, fortitude, stamina, hardiness, resilience, toughness.

tolerant adj *tolerant people accepting the beliefs of others | tolerant of the views of others* open-minded, unprejudiced, unbiased, unbigoted, broad-minded, liberal, catholic, forbearing, patient, long-suffering, magnanimous, sympathetic, understanding, charitable, lenient, indulgent, permissive, free and easy, easygoing, complaisant, lax.

tolerate v **1** *tolerate opposition | tolerate other people's views* permit, allow, admit, sanction, warrant, countenance, brook, recognize, acknowledge. **2** *unable to tolerate the pain/noise* endure, bear, suffer, take, stand, put up with, abide, accept, stomach, submit to. **3** *able to tolerate the new drug/treatment* take, receive, be treated with.

toleration n **1** *treat the young with toleration* tolerance, open-mindedness, lack of prejudice/bias, broad-mindedness, liberalism, patience, understanding, charity, indulgence. *see* TOLERANCE 1. **2** *his toleration of the noise levels | accept it with toleration* tolerance, endurance, sufferance, acceptance, fortitude, stamina, hardiness. *see* TOLERANCE 2. **3** *countries which do not practise religious toleration* freedom of worship, religious freedom, freedom of conscience.

toll n **1** *pay a toll to use the bridge/road* charge, fee, payment, levy, tariff. **2** *the fever took a* *heavy toll of her health | the death toll* cost, damage, loss; inroads.

toll v **1** *bells tolling in the distance* sound, ring, peal, knell, clang. **2** *toll the bells* sound, ring. **3** *bells tolling for his death | tolling the outbreak of war* announce, herald, signal, warn of. **4** *clocks tolling 6 o'clock* strike, chime.

tomb n grave, burial place/chamber, sepulchre, vault, crypt, catacomb, mausoleum.

tombstone n headstone, gravestone, grave marker, memorial, monument.

tome n volume, book, work, opus.

tomfool adj *what a tomfool thing to do* foolish, stupid, idiotic, silly, insane, mad, irresponsible.

tomfoolery n *children told to stop their tomfoolery* horseplay, mischief, fooling, foolery, clowning, skylarking, buffoonery, nonsense; pranks, tricks, capers, antics, larks; *inf* shenanigans, monkey tricks.

tone n **1** *the pleasant tone of the flute* sound, sound quality, tone, colour, pitch, timbre, tonality. **2** *speak in an angry tone | whisper in soft tones* tone of voice, mode of expression, expression, intonation, inflection, modulation, accentuation. **3** *the tone of his letter was optimistic* mood, air, attitude, character, manner, spirit, temper, tenor, vein, drift, gist. **4** *lower the tone of the place* style, quality, high quality. **5** *decorated in tones of pink* tint, shade, tinge, cast, tincture.

tone v *the curtains tone with the bedspread* harmonize with, go with, go well with, blend with, match, suit. **tone down 1** *tone down the brightness of the wall colours* soften, lighten, subdue, mute. **2** *tone down your aggressive approach* moderate, soften, modulate, play down, temper, subdue, dampen, restrain, soft-pedal.

tongue n **1** *speak in a foreign tongue* language, speech, parlance, dialect, idiom, patois, vernacular; *inf* lingo. **2** *he has a glib tongue* way of speaking, mode of expression.

tongue-tied adj *tongue-tied in the presence of her hero* at a loss for words, wordless, speechless, bereft of speech, struck dumb, dumb, silent, mute, taciturn, inarticulate.

tonic n **1** *prescribe a tonic for the invalid* restorative, stimulant, analeptic, pick-me-up. **2** *the good news was a tonic to the depressed woman* stimulant, boost, fillip, pick-me-up; *inf* shot in the arm.

too adv **1** *the dog came too | think, too, of her age* as well, also, in addition, besides, furthermore, moreover, to boot. **2** *she is too busy* excessively, overly, unduly, inordi-

nately, unreasonably, extremely, very; *inf* too-too.

tool n **1** *the tools of his trade | kitchen tools* implement, instrument, utensil, device, apparatus, gadget, appliance, machine, contrivance, contraption, aid. **2** *he is the manager's tool* creature, cat's-paw, puppet, pawn, minion, lackey, flunkey, henchman, toady; *inf* stooge.

tool v **1** *tool leather* shape, work, cut, chase, decorate, ornament. **2** *tooling along the motorway* bowl, drive, ride, motor.

top n **1** *the top of the mountain/hill* highest point/part, summit, peak, pinnacle, crest, crown, tip, apex, vertex, apogee. **2** *he's at the top of his career* height, high point, peak, pinnacle, zenith, acme, culmination, climax, crowning point, prime, meridian. **3** *the top of the table/milk* upper part, upper surface, upper layer. **4** *put the top on the bottle/jar* cap, lid, stopper, cork, cover. **5** *she wore a blue top* sweater, jumper, jersey, sweat shirt, T-shirt, blouse, shirt. **6** *turnip tops* leaves, shoots; stem, stalk. **over the top** *his criticism of the play was over the top | her budget/dress for the party was over the top* excessive, inordinate, immoderate, over the limit, exaggerated, too much, uncalled-for, going too far; *inf* a bit much, OTT.

top adj **1** *the top drawer/floor* topmost, uppermost, highest. **2** *top scientists* foremost, leading, principal, pre-eminent, greatest, finest; *inf* top-notch. **3** *the top men/positions in the firm* leading, chief, principal, main, highest, ruling, commanding. **4** *top goods* top-quality, top-grade, best, finest, prime, choicest, quality, excellent; *inf* A1, top-notch. **5** *at top speed* maximum, maximal, greatest, utmost.

top v **1** *icecream topped with chocolate sauce* cap, cover, finish, garnish. **2** *top the list of candidates* head, lead, be first in. **3** *donations have topped the £1,000 mark | topped our expectations | he topped his previous record* surpass, exceed, go beyond, transcend, better, best, beat, excel, outstrip, outdo, outshine, eclipse. **4** *top the mountain* reach the top of, climb, scale, ascend, mount, crest.

topcoat n overcoat, greatcoat.

topic n subject, subject matter, theme, issue, matter, point, question, argument, thesis, text.

topical adj *write about topical issues* newsworthy, in the news, current, up to date, up to the minute, contemporary, popular.

topmost adj **1** *the topmost drawer* top, uppermost, highest. **2** *the topmost authority on the subject* top, foremost, leading, principal, pre-eminent. *see* TOP adj 2. **3** *the topmost people/positions in the organization* leading, chief, principal, highest, ruling. *see* TOP adj 3.

top-notch adj first-rate, top-grade, excellent, choice, superior, superb; *inf* A1, ace, crack, top-hole, tiptop, wizard.

topple v **1** *the load was unstable and toppled* fall over, tip over, keel over, overturn, overbalance, capsize. **2** *his kick toppled the dustbin* upset, knock over, push over, tip over, capsize. **3** *the rebels toppled the tyrant* overthrow, oust, unseat, overturn, bring down, bring low.

topsy-turvy adv/adj **1** *children turning topsy-turvy on the climbing frame* upside down, wrong side up, head over heels. **2** *turn the house topsy-turvy looking for the documents* in disorder, in confusion, in a muddle, in a jumble, in chaos, in disarray, in a mess, upside down.

torment n **1** *endure torment at the hands of his captors* agony, suffering, torture, pain, excruciation, anguish, hell, misery, distress, affliction, wretchedness. **2** *the ill-behaved children were a torment to him* scourge, curse, plague, bane, affliction, thorn in the flesh, irritation, irritant, vexation, annoyance, worry, nuisance, bother, trouble, pest; *inf* pain in the neck.

torment v **1** *he was tormented by his captors/wound/conscience* cause agony/suffering/pain to, inflict anguish on, afflict, harrow, plague, torture, distress, worry, trouble. **2** *the children tormented the new teacher* tease, irritate, vex, annoy, pester, harass, badger, plague, worry, be a nuisance to, bother, trouble, be a pest to.

torn adj **1** *torn clothes* ragged, tattered, ripped, split, slit, cut, lacerated, rent. **2** *I am torn between the two dresses* divided, split, wavering, vacillating, irresolute, uncertain, unsure, undecided.

tornado n cyclone, whirlwind, wind storm, storm, hurricane, gale, squall, typhoon; *Amer inf* twister.

torpid adj sluggish, slow-moving, slow, dull, lethargic, heavy, inactive, stagnant, inert, somnolent, sleepy, languorous, languid, listless, apathetic, passive, slothful, indolent, lazy.

torpor n torpidity, sluggishness, slowness, dullness, lethargy, heaviness, inactivity, stagnation, inertia, somnolence, sleepiness, languor, languidness, listlessness, apathy, passivity, sloth, slothfulness, indolence, laziness.

torrent n **1** *torrents of flood water pouring down the streets* flood, deluge, inundation, spate, cascade, rush, stream, current. **2** *get soaked in the torrent* downpour, deluge, rainstorm. **3** *a torrent of abuse* outburst, stream, volley, outpouring, barrage, battery.

torrid adj **1** *the torrid conditions in the desert* hot, arid, sweltering, scorching, boiling, parching, sultry, stifling. **2** *torrid love scenes* passionate, impassioned, ardent, fervent, fervid, amorous, erotic; *inf* steamy.

tortuous adj **1** *a tortuous mountain path* twisting, winding, curving, curvy, sinuous, undulating, coiling, serpentine, snaking, snaky, zigzag, convoluted, meandering, spiralling, anfractuous. **2** *a tortuous description of the incident* convoluted, roundabout, circuitous, indirect, unstraightforward, involved, complicated, ambiguous. **3** *his tortuous policy* devious, cunning, tricky, deceitful, deceptive, guileful.

torture n **1** *use torture to extract a confession* persecution, pain, suffering, abuse, ill-treatment, punishment, torment. **2** *the torture of toothache | the torture of watching his friend die* torment, agony, suffering, pain, excruciation, anguish, misery, distress. *see* TORMENT n 1.

torture v **1** *torture the hostages* persecute, inflict pain/suffering on, abuse, ill-treat, punish, torment; *inf* work over. **2** *he was tortured by the pain of his wound | tortured by his conscience* torment, rack, cause agony/suffering/pain to, inflict anguish on, afflict, harrow, plague, distress, worry, trouble.

toss v **1** *toss the book over here* throw, hurl, cast, sling, pitch, shy, lob, propel, launch, project; *inf* heave, chuck. **2** *tossing and turning restlessly | tossing around unable to sleep* thrash, wriggle, writhe, squirm, roll, tumble. **3** *ships tossing around on the waves* rock, roll, sway, undulate, pitch, lurch, heave. **4** *toss one's head* throw back, throw up, jerk, jolt.

tot n **1** *mothers and tots* baby, infant, toddler, child, little one, mite. **2** *a tot of whisky* measure, dram, nip, slug; *inf* shot, finger.

tot v **1** *tot up the costs* add, count, calculate, total, sum, reckon, tally. **2** *it's surprising how the costs tot up* add up, mount up. **tot up to** *the bill tots up to £2000* amount to, total, come to.

total n *the total of those figures is 500 | score a total of six goals* sum, sum total, aggregate, whole, entirety, totality.

total adj **1** *the total number of votes | the total amount spent* complete, entire, whole, full, comprehensive, combined, aggregate, composite, integral. **2** *he's a total idiot* | *it was a total disaster* complete, thorough, thorough-going, all-out, utter, absolute, downright, out and out, outright, sheer, rank, unmitigated, unqualified.

total v **1** *these figures total more than £1000* add up to, come to, tot up to, amount to. **2** *total these figures rapidly* add up, sum, count up, count, reckon, tot up. **3** *total a car* wreck, crash, destroy, demolish, write off.

totalitarian adj *totalitarian government* one-party, monocratic, undemocratic, autocratic, authoritarian, absolute, despotic, dictatorial, tyrannical, oppressive, fascist.

totality n **1** *the grant in its totality will not cover the expense* entirety, entireness, wholeness, fullness, completeness, inclusiveness. **2** *the totality was less than expected* total, sum, aggregate, whole, entirety; all, everything.

totally adv *totally blind* | *forget totally* completely, entirely, wholly, fully, thoroughly, utterly, absolutely, quite.

totter v **1** *babies tottering about* | *women tottering on high heels* teeter, wobble, stagger, stumble, reel, sway, roll, lurch. **2** *tables/buildings tottering in the explosion* shake, sway, rock, lurch, shudder, judder. **3** *the regime is tottering* be unstable, be unsteady, be shaky, be on the point of collapse, falter.

touch v **1** *the wires are touching* be in contact, come into contact, come together, meet, converge, be contiguous, adjoin, abut. **2** *he touched her arm* press lightly, tap, brush, graze, feel, stroke, pat, fondle, caress. **3** *don't touch her things* handle, hold, pick up, move, play with, toy with, fiddle with, interfere with. **4** *she didn't touch her meal* | *never touch alcohol* eat, consume, drink, take, partake of. **5** *they were touched by the child's sad plight* affect, move, make an impression on, have an impact on, influence, upset, disturb, make sad, arouse sympathy; *inf* get to. **6** *the recession did not touch him* have an effect on, affect, concern, involve, have a bearing on, be relevant/pertinent to. **7** *they wouldn't touch anything illegal* be associated with, concern/involve oneself in, have dealings with, deal with, handle, be a party to. **8** *no-one can touch him at tennis* come near, come up to, compare with, be on a par with, equal, match, be a match for, be in the same league as, parallel, rival; *inf* hold a candle to. **9** *their speed touched 100 miles per hour* | *they touched rock bottom* reach, get up/down to, attain, arrive at, come to. **10** *touch his father for money*

ask, beg, borrow from. **touch down** *the plane touched down at midnight* land, alight, arrive. **touch off 1** *touch off the explosive* set alight, set off, ignite, trigger, explode, detonate. **2** *the statement touch off a storm of protest* set off, start, begin, set in motion, initiate, instigate, trigger off, launch.

touch on/upon 1 *touch on the financial situation in his speech* refer to, mention, comment on, remark on, allude to, bring in, speak of, talk about, write about, deal with. **2** *his actions touched on treason* come close to, verge on, incline to, be tantamount to. **touch up 1** *touch up the paintwork of the house* patch up, fix up, repair, refurbish, renovate, revamp, give a face-lift to. **2** *touch up a photograph* improve, enhance. **3** *accused of touching up women* fondle, molest.

touch n **1** *feel a touch on his arm* pressure, tap, strike, hit, blow, brush, stroke, pat, caress. **2** *sense its presence by touch* feel, feeling, sense of touch, tactile sense, tactility. **3** *the material has a velvety/steely touch* feel, texture, grain, finish, surface, coating. **4** *a touch of garlic/professionalism* | *a touch downhearted* small amount, bit, trace, dash, taste, spot, drop, pinch, speck, smack, suggestion, hint, soupçon, tinge, tincture, whiff, suspicion. **5** *admire the player's/artist's touch* craftsmanship, workmanship, artistry, performance, dexterity, deftness, skill, virtuosity, adroitness. **6** *the room needs a few extra touches* detail, feature, addition, accessory, fine point. **7** *I think the teacher is losing his touch* skill, skilfulness, expertise, technique, knack, adeptness, ability, talent, flair. **8** *the house needs a woman's touch* influence, effect, hand, handling, direction, management, technique, method. **9** *be/get in touch with old friends* | *lose touch* contact, communication, correspondence.

touch-and-go adj *a touch-and-go situation* | *it was touch-and-go whether he got the job* uncertain, precarious, risky, hazardous, dangerous, critical, suspenseful, cliff-hanging, hanging by a thread.

touched adj **1** *he was touched by their thoughtfulness* moved, impressed, affected, softened, warmed. **2** *he must be a bit touched to do that* unbalanced, unhinged, deranged, demented, crazed, mad, insane; *inf* daft, barmy, batty, dotty, nutty, screwy.

touching adj **1** *a touching act of kindness* moving, impressive, affecting, warming, heart-warming. **2** *a touching story of a sad childhood* affecting, moving, emotive, stirring, upsetting, disturbing, saddening, pitiful, piteous, poignant, pathetic, heartbreaking, heart-rending.

touchstone n criterion, yardstick, benchmark, norm, standard, gauge, guide, exemplar, model, pattern.

touchy adj **1** *he's very touchy about his lack of height/results* sensitive, oversensitive, hypersensitive, easily offended, thin-skinned; tetchy, testy, irascible, irritable, grouchy, grumpy, peevish, querulous, bad-tempered, captious, crabbed, cross, surly. **2** *a touchy situation* tricky, ticklish, delicate, precarious, chancy, risky, uncertain.

tough adj **1** *a tough substance* strong, durable, resistant, resilient, sturdy, firm, solid, hard, rigid, stiff. **2** *tough meat* chewy, leathery, gristly, stringy, fibrous, sinewy. **3** *explorers/children have to be tough to survive those conditions* hardy, strong, fit, sturdy, rugged, stalwart, vigorous, strapping, robust, resilient. **4** *it's a tough job managing the firm* difficult, hard, arduous, onerous, heavy, uphill, laborious, strenuous, exacting, taxing, stressful. **5** *teachers getting tough with the children | police getting tough with criminals* firm, strict, stern, severe, harsh, hard-hitting, adamant, inflexible. **6** *tough exam questions* difficult, hard, knotty, thorny, baffling, perplexing, ticklish. **7** *a tough way of life* hard, harsh, austere, rugged, bleak, grim, dire, rough, taxing, exacting. **8** *led astray by tough kids* rough, rowdy, unruly, disorderly, violent, wild, lawless, lawbreaking, criminal. **9** *it was tough that he had to lose* unfortunate, unlucky, hard, regrettable; *inf* too bad.

tough n *set on by a gang of toughs* ruffian, rowdy, thug, hoodlum, hooligan, bully; *inf* hard man, roughneck, bruiser.

toughen v **1** *toughen the glass* strengthen, fortify, reinforce, harden, rigidify. **2** *toughen the laws* stiffen, tighten, make stricter, make severe; *inf* beef up.

tour n **1** *a world tour | a coach tour through France* trip, excursion, journey, expedition, jaunt, outing, peregrination. **2** *give the visitors a tour of the new building* guided tour, walk round, visit, inspection. **3** *on a golfing tour* circuit, ambit, round, course, beat. **4** *troops doing a tour in Northern Ireland* tour of duty, duty, stint, stretch, turn.

tour v **1** *touring the world | touring France* travel round/through, journey through, explore, holiday in. **2** *tour the new building/estate* go round, walk/drive round, visit, sightsee, inspect.

tourist n visitor, sightseer, holiday-maker, traveller, tripper, excursionist, journeyer; *inf* globe-trotter.

tournament n **1** *a tennis tournament* competition, contest, series, meeting, event,

match. **2** *knights competing in a tournament* joust, jousting, tourney; lists.

tousled adj *tousled hair* rumpled, dishevelled, uncombed, unkempt, disordered, disarranged, untidy, messy; *inf* mussed up.

tout v **1** *tout for business* ask for, solicit, seek, petition for, appeal for, beg for. **2** *tout customers* solicit, seek, petition, importune, accost, approach; *inf* hustle. **3** *tout their wares/tickets* hawk, peddle, sell, offer for sale.

tow v *towing a car/sledge* pull, draw, drag, haul, tug, trail, lug.

tow n *gave the car a tow* towing, haul. *see* TOW v. **in tow** *he had the family/girlfriend in tow* in attendance, by one's side, in one's charge, under one's protection.

towards prep **1** *walk towards the door/town* in the direction of, to, on the way to, en route for. **2** *his attitude towards her success* with regard to, as regards, regarding, with respect to, respecting, in relation to, concerning, about, apropos. **3** *working towards a degree* for, with the aim of, in order to obtain/achieve. **4** *the money will go towards the hospital appeal fund* as a contribution, for, to help, to assist. **5** *towards the end of the day/journey* near, nearing, around, close to, coming to, getting on for, just before, shortly before.

tower n **1** *the tower at the top of the church/castle* steeple, spire, belfry, bell tower, turret, column, pillar, obelisk, minaret. **2** *soldiers manning the tower* fortress, fort, citadel, stronghold, fortification, keep, castle.

tower v **1** *mountains towering into the skies | he towers above the children* soar, rise, ascend, mount, rear, reach/stand high. **2** *he towers above the rest of the modern poets | his writing towers above the rest* surpass, excel, outshine, outclass, overshadow, cap, top, transcend, eclipse, be head and shoulders above, put in the shade; *inf* run circles around.

towering adj **1** *towering mountain peaks | towering skyscrapers* high, tall, lofty, elevated, sky-high. **2** *in a towering rage* extreme, mighty, fierce, terrible, intense, violent, vehement, passionate, frenzied, frantic. **3** *one of the towering intellects of his age* outstanding, extraordinary, pre-eminent, surpassing, superior, great, incomparable, unrivalled, peerless.

town n borough, municipality, township, urban area.

toxic adj poisonous, venomous, virulent, noxious.

toy n **1** *children's toys* plaything, game. **2** *the rich woman surrounds herself with toys* trinket, bauble, knick-knack, gewgaw, trifle, triviality.

toy adj **1** *a toy car | toy soldiers* model, miniature, imitation, make-believe. **2** *toy breeds of dog* small, tiny, miniature, diminutive.

toy v **1** *he's just toying with the girl* amuse oneself with, play around with, flirt with, dally with, sport with, trifle with. **2** *the child was toying with his food* play around with, fiddle with, fool around with, mess about with. **3** *he's toying with the idea of leaving* play with, think idly about, have thoughts about.

trace n **1** *there was no trace left of the picnic* mark, sign, vestige, indication; evidence; remains, remnants, relics. **2** *traces of poison in the drink | no trace of emotion in his voice* bit, touch, hint, suggestion, suspicion, trifle, drop, dash, tinge, tincture, shadow, jot, iota. **3** *follow the burglar's/bear's traces* track, trail, spoor, scent; marks, tracks, prints, imprints, footprints, footmarks, footsteps.

trace v **1** *unable to trace the letter* find, discover, detect, unearth, uncover, track down, turn up, dig up, ferret out, hunt down. **2** *trace the bear to the forest* follow, pursue, track, trail, tail, shadow, stalk, dog. **3** *trace the river back | trace his ancestry back* find the origins/source/roots of. **4** *trace out the route they would take | trace out the policies for the year* draw, draw up, sketch, draft, outline, mark out, delineate, rough out, map, chart, record, indicate, show, depict.

track n **1** *follow the tracks of the burglar/bear/motor-bike* marks, traces, impressions, prints, imprints, footprints, footmarks, footsteps; trail, spoor, scent. **2** *follow in the track of the great explorers* trail, path, pathway, way, course, route. **3** *the track of the hurricane/satellite* path, line, course, orbit, route, trajectory, flight path. **4** *follow the track through the forest* path, trail, route, way. **5** *the train left the track* rail, line; railway line, tramline; rails. **6** *run round the track* course; running track, racetrack. **keep track of** keep up with, follow, monitor, record. **lose track of** forget about, be unaware of, misplace, lose/cease contact with.

track v *track the bear to the forest* follow, pursue, trail, trace, tail, shadow, stalk, dog. **track down** *track down the necessary information* hunt down, hunt out, run to earth, unearth, uncover, turn up, dig up, ferret out, nose out, bring to light, expose, discover, find out, detect.

tract[1] n *tracts of forest/desert* area, region, zone, stretch, expanse, extent, plot.

tract[2] n *religious tracts* pamphlet, booklet, leaflet, brochure, monograph, essay, treatise, disquisition, dissertation, thesis, lecture, homily, sermon.

tractable adj malleable, controllable, manageable, governable, amenable, complaisant, compliant, submissive, yielding, docile, dutiful, obedient.

trade n **1** *he's in the export trade* commerce, buying and selling, dealing, traffic, trafficking, business, marketing, merchandizing; transactions. **2** *what trade is his father in?* line of work/business, line, occupation, job, career, profession, craft, vocation, calling, *métier*; work, employment. **3** *I'll do a trade of my car with yours* swap, trade-off, exchange, switch, barter.

trade v **1** *the firm is trading at a loss* do business, deal, run, operate. **2** *they trade in diamonds | they trade with France* buy and sell, deal, traffic, market, merchandize. **3** *he traded his stamp collection for the collection of comics* swap, exchange, switch, barter. **trade on** *he trades on his father's reputation | trading on her kind nature* take advantage of, make use of, exploit, capitalize on, profit from; *inf* cash in on.

trade mark n **1** *a trade mark for a kind of cleaner* stamp, symbol, logo, sign, emblem, badge, crest, trade name, brand name, proprietary name. **2** *killing dogs is the burglar's trade mark* characteristic, speciality, feature, trait, penchant, proclivity, peculiarity, idiosyncrasy.

trader n merchant, dealer, buyer, seller, buyer and seller, marketer, merchandizer, broker.

tradesman, tradeswoman n **1** *high-street tradesmen protesting against a sales tax* shopkeeper, retailer, storekeeper, vendor, merchant, dealer. **2** *require skilled tradesmen to renovate the old house* workman, craftsman, skilled worker, artisan.

tradition n **1** *keep up the old traditions* custom, belief, practice, convention, ritual, observance, habit, institution, usage, praxis. **2** *handed on by tradition* historical convention, unwritten law, oral history, lore, folklore.

traditional adj **1** *traditional Christmas fare* customary, accustomed, conventional, established, ritual, ritualistic, habitual, set, fixed, routine, usual, wonted, old, time-honoured, historic, folk, familial, ancestral. **2** *keeping alive traditional customs* handed-down, folk, unwritten, oral.

traduce v *accused of traducing his neighbour* defame, slander, speak ill/evil of, misrepresent, malign, vilify, calumniate, blacken the name of, cast aspersions on.

traffic n **1** *noisy traffic rushing past* vehicles, cars. **2** *a move to attract traffic to the railways from the roads* transport, transportation, movement of goods/people, freight, conveyancing. **3** *the traffic in diamonds has decreased | drug traffic* trafficking, trade, trading, dealing, commerce, business, peddling, smuggling, boot-legging. **4** *he has little traffic with his neighbours* contact, communication, intercourse; dealings, relations.

traffic v *arrested for trafficking in drugs* trade in, deal in, do business in, peddle, smuggle.

tragedy n **1** *some tragedy had blighted his youth* disaster, calamity, catastrophe, misfortune, misadventure, affliction, adversity, sad event, serious accident, shock, blow. **2** *the play was a tragedy* tragic drama; lit buskin.

tragic adj **1** *a tragic accident | a tragic end to the day* disastrous, calamitous, catastrophic, fatal, terrible, dreadful, appalling, dire, awful, miserable, wretched, unfortunate. **2** *listen to her tragic tale* sad, unhappy, pathetic, moving, distressing, disturbing, pitiful, piteous, melancholy, doleful, mournful, dismal, gloomy. **3** *it is tragic what they have done to the village* dreadful, terrible, awful, deplorable, lamentable, regrettable.

trail n **1** *follow the trail left by the leader | police on the trail of the criminal* track, scent, spoor; traces, marks, signs, footprints, footmarks. **2** *follow the trail through the forest* path, beaten path, pathway, footpath, track, road, route. **3** *the rock star had a trail of young admirers* line, queue, train, file, column, procession, following, entourage. **4** *leave a trail of disaster behind them* train, chain, series, sequence, aftermath. **5** *vapour trail* stream, tail, appendage.

trail v **1** *the child trailed the toy behind him* tow, pull, drag, draw, haul. **2** *her long skirt trailing on the floor* drag across, sweep, dangle, hang down, droop. **3** *children trailing along | trailing behind their parents* trudge, plod, drag oneself, dawdle, straggle, loiter, linger, lag, fall behind. **4** *plants/creatures trailing along the ground* creep, crawl, slide, slink. **5** *they trailed him to his lair* follow, pursue, track, trace, tail, shadow, stalk, dog. **6** *the team is trailing by five points* lose, be down, be behind. **7** *their enthusiasm gradually trailed off | his voice trailed away* fade, fade away/out, disappear, vanish, peter out, die away, melt away.

train n **1** *the dress had a long train* tail, appendage. **2** *leaving a train of vapour* trail, stream, track, path, wake, wash. **3** *a train of disasters followed* trail, chain, string, series, sequence, set, progression, order, concatenation. **4** *a train of people climbing the mountain* procession, line, file, column, convoy, caravan. **5** *having to accommodate the princess and her train* retinue, entourage, cortège, following, staff, household, court; followers, attendants.

train v **1** *train the young pupils in reading/musical skills* instruct, teach, coach, tutor, give lessons to, school, educate, drill, prepare, ground, guide, indoctrinate, inculcate. **2** *she is training to be a teacher* study, qualify, learn, prepare. **3** *athletes having to train each night* exercise, do exercises, work out, practise, prepare. **4** *train the football team | train the horse for the race* coach, drill, exercise. **5** *train the gun/binoculars on the distant figure* aim, point, focus, direct, level, line up.

trainer n *the trainer of the team* coach, instructor.

trainers npl *wearing trainers* training/sports shoes.

training n **1** *pupils getting training in the social skills* instruction, teaching, coaching, tutoring, schooling, education, drilling, preparation, grounding, guidance, indoctrination, inculcation; lessons. **2** *undergo training for the race* exercise, working out, body-building, practice, preparation; exercises, physical exercises.

trait n *one of her annoying/endearing traits* characteristic, attribute, feature, quality, property, idiosyncrasy, peculiarity, quirk.

traitor n betrayer, back-stabber, turncoat, double-crosser, double-dealer, renegade, defector, deserter, apostate, Judas, quisling, fifth columnist; *inf* snake in the grass, two-timer.

traitorous adj treacherous, back-stabbing, double-crossing, double-dealing, disloyal, faithless, unfaithful, perfidious, false-hearted, false, untrue, renegade, seditious, apostate; *inf* two-timing.

trajectory n path, track, line, course, orbit, route, flight path.

trammel n *coping with the trammels of ill health* restraint, constraint, obstacle, bar, block, curb, check, barrier, hindrance, handicap, impediment, drawback, snag, stumbling-block; shackles, fetters, bonds.

trammel v *mothers trammelled by young children* restrict, restrain, constrain, shackle, fetter, curb, check, hinder, handicap, impede, obstruct, thwart, frustrate.

tramp v **1** *hear him tramping upstairs | workmen tramping in and out of the kitchen* trudge, march, plod, stamp, stump, stomp; *inf* traipse. **2** *spend the day tramping over the hills* trek, trudge, hike, march, slog, footslog, plod, walk, ramble, roam, range, rove; *inf* traipse, yomp. **3** *tramp down the corn* trample, tread on, step on, stamp on, squash, crush, flatten.

tramp n **1** *tramps sleeping rough* vagrant, vagabond, derelict, down-and-out, itinerant, drifter; *Amer* hobo; *inf* dosser. **2** *hear the tramp of the soldiers approaching* heavy step, footstep, footfall, tread, stamp, stomping. **3** *go for a tramp over the hills* trek, hike, march, walk, ramble, roam, wander, range; *inf* traipse, yomp. **4** *she's just a tramp* loose woman, slut, wanton, trollop, prostitute, whore; *inf* tart.

trample v **1** *trample on the corn | people trampled to death* tramp on, tread on, walk over, stamp on, squash, crush, flatten. **2** *trample on other people | trample on other people's feelings/rights* ride roughshod over, treat with contempt, disregard, set at naught, show no consideration, encroach on, infringe.

trance n daze, stupor, hypnotic state, half-conscious state, dream, reverie, brown study.

tranquil adj **1** *a tranquil life* peaceful, restful, reposeful, calm, quiet, still, serene, placid, undisturbed. **2** *she's a tranquil person* calm, placid, pacific, composed, cool, calm, cool and collected, serene, even-tempered, unexcitable, unflappable, unruffled, unperturbed.

tranquillity n **1** *love the tranquillity of the place* peace, peacefulness, restfulness, reposefulness, calm, calmness, quiet, quietness, quietude, stillness, serenity, placidity. **2** *her tranquillity is never disturbed* calm, calmness, placidity, composure, coolness, serenity, equanimity, even-temperedness, unexcitability, unflappability.

tranquillize v *tranquillize the excited animal/anxious woman* sedate, calm, calm down, soothe, quiet, quieten down, pacify, compose, settle someone's nerves, lull, relax.

tranquillizer n sedative, opiate; *inf* downer.

transact v *transact business in private* carry out, conduct, do, perform, execute, enact, manage, handle, negotiate, take care of, see to, conclude, discharge, accomplish, settle.

transaction n **1** *the transaction took less than an hour* business, deal, undertaking, affair, bargain, negotiation; proceedings. **2** *the transaction of business in private* conducting, performance, execution, enactment, handling, negotiation, conclusion, discharge, settlement. *see* TRANSACT.

transactions npl *publish the transactions of the Royal Society* records, proceedings, affairs, concerns, dealings; *inf* doings, goings-on.

transcend v **1** *transcend human belief* go beyond, exceed, overstep, rise above. **2** *her performance transcended that of her opponents* surpass, excel, be superior to, outdo, outstrip, leave behind, outrival, outvie, outrank, outshine, eclipse, overshadow, throw into the shade.

transcendence, transcendency n *acknowledge his transcendence* excellence, greatness, magnificence, superiority, supremacy, predominance, pre-eminence, ascendency, paramountcy, incomparability, matchlessness.

transcendent adj *his transcendent talent* excellent, excelling, great, magnificent, superior, supreme, consummate, predominant, pre-eminent, ascendent, paramount, unsurpassed, incomparable, matchless, unrivalled, unequalled, unparalleled.

transcendental adj *a transcendental experience* mystical, mystic, mysterious, preternatural, supernatural, otherworldly, transmundane.

transcribe v **1** *students transcribing rough notes* copy out, write out, copy/write in full, type/print out. **2** *transcribe the symbols* interpret, translate, transliterate, render. **3** *transcribe the performance | now transcribed to compact disc* record, rerecord, transfer.

transcript n *a transcript of the trial* written/recorded copy, copy, record, written/printed version, documentation.

transfer v **1** *transfer the material from the house to the garage* convey, move, shift, remove, take, carry, transport. **2** *transfer the pupils to a different school* move, shift, remove, change, relocate. **3** *transfer his property/share to his son* make over, turn over, sign over, hand on, hand down, pass on, transmit, convey, devolve, assign, delegate.

transfer n **1** *teachers/footballers asking for a transfer* move, shift, relocation, change. **2** *the property transfer has been drawn up* transfer document, conveyance; papers, deeds.

transfix v **1** *a fish transfixed with a harpoon* run through, pierce, transpierce, impale, stab, spear, prick, stick, spike, skewer. **2** *the onlookers were transfixed with/in terror* root to the spot, paralyse, petrify, stop dead, hypnotize, mesmerize, rivet, spellbind, fascinate, engross, stun, astound.

transform v *transform the girl's appearance | transform his outlook on life* change, alter, convert, metamorphose, revolutionize, transfigure, remodel, redo, reconstruct, rebuild, reorganize, rearrange, renew, translate, transmute; *inf* transmogrify.

transformation n change, radical change, alteration, conversion, metamorphosis, sea change, revolutionization, revolution, transfiguration, remodelling, reconstruction, reorganization, renewal, transmutation; *inf* transmogrification. *see* TRANSFORM.

transgress v **1** *transgress the bounds of decency | transgress the laws of the land* go beyond, overstep, exceed, infringe, breach, break, contravene, violate, defy, disobey. **2** *they transgressed and were punished* do wrong, go astray, misbehave, break the law, err, lapse, fall from grace, stray from the straight and narrow, sin, trespass.

transgression n **1** *their transgression of the bounds of taste | transgression of the law* overstepping, infringement, breach, breaking, contravention, violation, defiance, disobedience. **2** *punished for their transgressions* wrong, misdemeanour, misdeed, lawbreaking, crime, offence, lapse, fault, sin; wrongdoing, misbehaviour.

transgressor n *transgressors will be punished* wrongdoer, law-breaker, criminal, miscreant, delinquent, villain, felon, offender, culprit, sinner, trespasser, malefactor.

transience n short-livedness, transitoriness, impermanence, temporariness, brevity, briefness, shortness, evanescence, momentariness, fugitiveness, mutability. *see* TRANSIENT.

transient adj transitory, short-lived, short-term, impermanent, temporary, brief, short, ephemeral, evanescent, momentary, fleeting, flying, passing, fugitive, fugacious, mutable, here today and gone tomorrow.

transit n **1** *troop transit* movement, travel, journeying, passage, transfer, crossing. **2** *city councils budgeting for modern transit* transport, transportation, conveyance, haulage, freightage. **in transit** *goods lost in transit* en route, on the journey, on the way, on the road, during transport.

transition n *the transition from childhood to adulthood | the transition to foreign currency* move, passage, change, transformation, conversion, change-over, metamorphosis,

shift, switch, jump, leap, progression, gradation, development, evolution, transmutation.

transitional adj **1** *the transitional period* transition, changing, change-over, conversion, developmental, evolutionary, intermediate, fluid, unsettled. **2** *the transitional government* transition, provisional, temporary.

transitory adj transient, short-lived, short-term, impermanent, temporary, brief, short, ephemeral, evanescent, momentary, fleeting, flying, passing, fugitive, fugacious, mutable, here today and gone tomorrow.

translate v **1** *translate the French passage into English* construe, interpret, render, convert, transcribe, transliterate. **2** *translate the legal jargon into plain English* render, paraphrase, reword, convert, decipher, decode, explain, elucidate. **3** *translate his silence as agreement* interpret, take, construe, understand, read, judge, deem. **4** *translate ideas into action* turn, change, convert, transform, alter, metamorphose, transmute; *inf* transmogrify. **5** *translate the children from the country to the city* transfer, move, remove, shift, relocate, convey, transport.

translation n **1** *the translation of the French passage into English* interpretation, construing, rendering, rendition, conversion, transcription, transliteration. **2** *unable to follow the rough translation* interpretation, rendition, transcription, transliteration. **3** *the translation of the legal jargon into plain English* rendering, rendition, paraphrasing, rewording, conversion, deciphering, decoding, explanation, elucidation. **4** *the translation of ideas into action* change, conversion, transformation, alteration, metamorphosis, transmutation; *inf* transmogrification. **5** *the translation of the children from the country to the city* transfer, transferral, move, removal, shift, relocation, conveyance, transportation.

transmission n **1** *the transmission of mail* sending, conveyance, transport, dispatch, remission. **2** *the transmission of information/ disease* transference, transferral, passing on, communication, imparting, dissemination, spreading. *see* TRANSMIT 2. **3** *the transmission of late-night programmes* broadcasting, relaying, sending out. **4** *a live transmission* broadcast, programme.

transmit v **1** *transmit the package by air* send, convey, transport, dispatch, forward, remit. **2** *transmit information/disease to others* transfer, pass on, hand on, communicate, impart, disseminate, spread, carry, diffuse.

3 *transmit late-night programmes* broadcast, relay, send out, put on air.

transparency n **1** *the transparency of the plastic/streams* clarity, clearness, translucency, lucidity, pellucidity, limpidness, limpidity, glassiness, transpicuousness. **2** *the transparency of the material* sheerness, diaphanousness, diaphaneity, filminess, gauziness. **3** *the transparency of his lies* obviousness, patentness, unmistakableness, clearness, plainness, distinctness, apparentness, perceptibility, discernibility. *see* TRANSPARENT 3. **4** *appreciate her transparency* frankness, openness, candidness, directness, forthrightness, ingenuousness, artlessness. **5** *the transparency of the prose* clarity, clearness, lucidity, straightforwardness, plainness, explicitness, unambiguousness. **6** *transparencies of their holiday* slide, photograph.

transparent adj **1** *transparent plastic/streams* clear, see-through, translucent, lucid, pellucid, crystal-clear, crystalline, limpid, glassy, transpicuous. **2** *blouses made of transparent material* see-through, sheer, diaphanous, filmy, gauzy. **3** *his transparent dishonesty* obvious, patent, manifest, undisguised, unmistakable, clear, plain, visible, noticeable, recognizable, distinct, evident, apparent, perceptible, discernible. **4** *preferring transparent people to dissembling people* frank, open, candid, direct, forthright, plain-spoken, straight, ingenuous, artless. **5** *a transparent account of the events* clear, lucid, straightforward, plain, explicit, unambiguous, unequivocal.

transpire v **1** *it transpired that he had been married before* become known, be revealed, be disclosed, come to light, emerge, come out. **2** *tell me what transpired at the meeting* come about, take place, happen, occur, turn up, arise, chance, befall.

transplant v **1** *transplant seedlings* replant, repot, relocate. **2** *transplant organs* transfer, graft. **3** *he hated being transplanted to a different region* transfer, move, remove, shift, relocate.

transport v **1** *transport the goods to the warehouse* convey, take, transfer, move, shift, bring, fetch, carry, bear, haul, lug, cart, run, ship. **2** *transport criminals to an island* banish, exile, deport, drive away, expatriate. **3** *she was transported by his piano-playing* enrapture, entrance, enchant, enthrall, captivate, bewitch, fascinate, spellbind, charm, overjoy, thrill, delight, ravish, carry away.

transport n **1** *road and rail transport* transportation, conveyance, transit, carriage,

freight. **2** *our transport has not yet arrived* transportation, conveyance, vehicle, car, carriage. **3** *a transport of joy/rage* strong emotion. *see* TRANSPORTS.

transports npl **1** strong emotion, intense feeling, passion, fervour, vehemence. **2** *in transports over her engagement/promotion* rapture, ecstasy, elation, exaltation, exhilaration, euphoria, bliss, seventh heaven, heaven, paradise; *inf* cloud nine.

transpose v *transpose the middle letters of the word* interchange, exchange, switch, swap, transfer, reverse, invert, rearrange, reorder, change, alter, convert, move.

transverse adj *transverse beams* crosswise, crossways, cross, athwart.

trap n **1** *rabbits caught in a trap* snare, net, mesh, gin, springe, ambush, pitfall, booby trap. **2** *the question was a trap to get him to confess* stratagem, play, artifice, ruse, wile, trick, device, deception, subterfuge. **3** *lay a trap for the criminal* ambush, lure, decoy, bait. **4** *regard marriage as a trap* snare, net, cage, prison.

trap v **1** *trap the rabbits* snare, ensnare, enmesh, entrap, catch, corner. **2** *trapped into making a confession* trick, dupe, deceive, lure, inveigle, beguile. **3** *they were trapped in the burning building* cut off, corner, confine, imprison.

trappings npl *all the trappings necessary for the coronation | the trappings of power* accoutrements, appurtenances, appointments, trimmings, paraphernalia, fittings, things; equipage, equipment, apparatus, gear, livery, adornment, ornamentation, decoration, finery, frippery; panoply.

trash n **1** *talk trash* rubbish, garbage, nonsense, drivel, balderdash, bunkum, twaddle; *inf* rot, tommy-rot, bunk, tripe, bilge, poppycock. **2** *empty out the trash* rubbish, waste, refuse, litter, garbage. **3** *he regards his neighbours as trash* riff-raff, scum, rabble, canaille, vermin; dregs, good-for-nothings.

trauma n **1** *the trauma caused by the accident/surgery* injury, wound, lesion. **2** *suffering from trauma after the attack | the trauma of divorce* shock, disturbance, disorder, distress, pain, anguish, suffering.

traumatic adj **1** *a traumatic injury/attack* painful, agonizing, shocking, scarring, disturbing, distressing, damaging, injurious, harmful. **2** *a traumatic journey home* unpleasant, disagreeable, irksome, troublesome, vexatious, irritating, distressing.

travel v **1** *he travels a lot in connection with his work | she plans to travel after she retires* use transport, journey, take a trip, tour, voyage, sightsee. **2** *light travels faster than sound* | *news travels fast* proceed, progress, advance, be transmitted, carry. **3** *travel the length of the country* journey, cross, traverse, cover, wander, ramble, roam, rove, range, wend, make one's way over. **4** *the driver/car was certainly travelling* speed, go fast/rapidly, drive fast, go at breakneck speed; *inf* go hell for leather, go like a bat out of hell, tear up the miles. **5** *he travels in perfume* sell, be a representative/agent for; *inf* rep for.

travel n *the cost of travel* travelling, journeying, touring.

traveller n **1** *holiday/foreign travellers* journeyer, tripper, tourer, tourist, excursionist, explorer, passenger, voyager, holiday-maker, sightseer, globe-trotter. **2** *have a job as a traveller* sales representative, agent, travelling salesman, commercial traveller; *inf* rep, sales rep. **3** *travellers moving from camp to camp* gypsy, nomad, migrant, wanderer, wayfarer, tramp, vagrant; travelling people/folk.

travelling adj **1** *a travelling circus* itinerant, peripatetic, moving, mobile. **2** *a travelling people/tribe* itinerant, peripatetic, nomadic, migratory, migrating, wandering, roaming, roving, wayfaring, unsettled, restless, on the move/go.

travels npl *she wrote about her travels* journey, journeying, trip, tour, expedition, excursion, voyage, sightseeing, exploration, wandering, roaming, ramble, rambling, peregrination, *inf* globe-trotting.

traverse v **1** *traversing the desert* cross, go across, travel over, journey over, make one's way across, pass over, wander, roam, range. **2** *beams traversing the ceiling* go across, lie across, stretch across, extend across, cross, cut across, bridge. **3** *traverse all aspects of the subject* consider, examine, check, study, review, investigate, inspect, scrutinize, look into, look over, scan, pore over, take stock of.

travesty n *the trial was a travesty of justice* misrepresentation, distortion, perversion, corruption, poor imitation, mockery, parody, caricature, sham, burlesque, satire, lampoon, take-off; *inf* send-up, spoof.

travesty v *travesty the solemn occasion* misrepresent, distort, pervert, mock, ridicule, deride, make fun of, parody, caricature, burlesque, satirize, lampoon, take off; *inf* send up, spoof.

treacherous adj **1** *betrayed by a treacherous follower* traitorous, back-stabbing, double-crossing, double-dealing, disloyal, faithless, unfaithful, perfidious, duplicitous, deceit-

ful, false-hearted, false, untrue, untrustworthy, unreliable, undependable; *inf* two-timing. **2** *the weather conditions can be treacherous* precarious, unreliable, undependable, unstable, unsafe, risky, hazardous, dangerous, perilous, deceptive; *inf* dicey. **3** *roads which are treacherous in winter* hazardous, dangerous, unsafe; flooded, icy, ice-covered, slippery.

treachery n *the treachery of his best friend* traitorousness, back-stabbing, double-crossing, double-dealing, disloyalty, faithlessness, unfaithfulness, perfidy, perfidiousness, treason, duplicity, deceit, deceitfulness, deception, false-heartedness, falseness, untrustworthiness; *inf* two-timing.

tread v **1** *tread softly so as not to wake the baby* walk, step, go, pace, march, tramp. **2** *tread the long road home* walk, hike, tramp, stride, step out, trek, march, trudge, plod. **3** *tread grapes* | *tread the corn down* trample, tramp on, step on, stamp on, squash, crush, flatten, press down. **4** *tread mud into the carpet* trample, tramp, stamp, press. **5** *aristocrats tread on the villagers* ride roughshod over, oppress, repress, suppress, subdue, subjugate, quell, crush.

tread n *walk with a heavy/soft tread* | *hear the tread of the people upstairs* step, footstep, footfall, walk, tramp.

treason n *high treason;* betrayal, traitorousness, treachery, disloyalty, faithlessness, perfidy, disaffection, sedition, subversion, mutiny, rebellion, lese-majesty.

treasonable adj traitorous, treacherous, disloyal, faithless, perfidious, seditious, subversive, mutinous, rebellious.

treasure n **1** *find buried treasure* | *a miser gloating over his treasure* riches, valuables; wealth, fortune, hoard; jewels, gems, coins, gold, money, cash. **2** *art treasures* valuable, masterpiece. **3** *she's her father's treasure* darling, pride and joy, apple of one's eye, jewel, jewel in the crown, gem, pearl, precious, prize, paragon. **4** *advertising for a treasure* paragon, household/domestic help, housekeeper.

treasure v **1** *she treasures their friendship* value, place great value on, prize, set great store by, think highly of, hold dear. **2** *she treasures her children* adore, cherish, love, worship, revere, venerate, dote on, prize, hold dear. **3** *treasure the souvenirs of holidays* value, prize, save, collect, accumulate, hoard, store up, lay by, stow away, squirrel away, salt away; *inf* stash away.

treat n **1** *think of a treat for her birthday* surprise, celebration, entertainment, amusement, diversion, party, feast, banquet. **2** *grandmother bringing a treat for the child* gift, present, titbit, delicacy; *inf* goodie. **3** *it was a treat to see her again* pleasure, delight, thrill, joy, gratification, satisfaction; fun. **4** *the drinks are his treat* gift, present, one's turn to pay; *inf* shout.

treat v **1** *treat his wife badly* | *treat his car recklessly* act towards, behave towards, deal with, handle, cope with, contend with, manage, use. **2** *treat his remarks as jokes* regard, consider, view, look upon, deal with. **3** *treat the sick patient* give treatment to, medicate, doctor, nurse, care for, attend to, minister to, cure, heal. **4** *treat the wood with creosote* | *treat the stain with chemicals* apply to, put on, use on, ply with. **5** *treat them to dinner* pay for, buy for, pay/foot the bill for, stand, finance, entertain, take out. **6** *we were treated to the unusual sight of him letting his hair down* entertain, amuse, divert, cheer, gratify, delight, regale. **7** *the general treating with the enemy* have talks with, talk with, confer with, negotiate with, parley with, bargain with, make terms with, come to terms with. **8** *she treats the question of incest in her books* | *her essay treats of religious doubt* deal with, discuss, go into, write/speak/talk about, discourse upon, be concerned with, touch upon, refer to, consider, study, review, analyse.

treatise n discourse, exposition, disquisition, dissertation, thesis, study, essay, paper, monograph, tract, pamphlet, work, piece of writing.

treatment n **1** *his treatment was cruel* action, behaviour, conduct, handling, management, use; dealings. **2** *patients/wounds responding to treatment* medical care, medication, medicament, therapy, doctoring, nursing, first aid, care, ministration; cure, remedy; drugs, therapeutics.

treaty n agreement, pact, deal, compact, covenant, bargain, pledge, contract, alliance, concordat, convention, entente.

trek v *trek across the rough terrain* trudge, tramp, hike, march, slog, footslog, plod, walk, ramble, roam, range, rove, travel, journey; *inf* traipse, yomp.

trek n *a trek across the desert* | *it's quite a trek to the village* expedition, trip, journey, trudge, tramp, hike, march, slog, walk, odyssey.

trellis n lattice, network, mesh, fret, grille, grid, grating.

tremble v **1** *fingers trembling with excitement* shake, quiver, shiver, quake, twitch, wiggle. **2** *buildings trembling in the earthquake* shake, shudder, judder, teeter, totter, wobble, rock, vibrate, oscillate, rattle. **3** *she*

trembles for the safety of her children fear, be afraid, be fearful, be frightened, be apprehensive, worry, be anxious.

tremendous adj **1** *animals of a tremendous size* | *people of tremendous girth* great, huge, enormous, immense, massive, vast, colossal, prodigious, stupendous, gigantic, gargantuan, mammoth, giant, titanic; *inf* whopping. **2** *it made a tremendous difference to his lifestyle* great, huge, enormous, immense, colossal, prodigious, stupendous; *inf* whopping. **3** *there was a tremendous noise* loud, deafening, ear-splitting, booming, thundering, roaring, resounding, crashing. **4** *she's a tremendous player/cook* excellent, very good, great, marvellous, remarkable, extraordinary, exceptional, wonderful, incredible; *inf* fabulous, fantastic, terrific, super, ace, wizard.

tremor n **1** *notice the tremor of her hands* | *a tremor of fear* tremble, trembling, shake, shaking, shiver, quiver, quaver, vibration, twitch, judder, spasm, paroxysm. **2** *villages damaged by a tremor* earth tremor, earthquake; *inf* quake.

tremulous adj **1** *a tremulous voice* trembling, shaking, shaky, quivering, quavering, vibrating, nervous, weak. **2** *with tremulous hands* trembling, shaking, shaky, quivery, twitching, twitchy, jittery, shuddering, juddering, jerky, spasmodic. **3** *give a tremulous look* timid, diffident, shy, timorous, fearful, frightened, scared, nervous, anxious, apprehensive, alarmed, cowardly.

trench n ditch, excavation, earthwork, furrow, duct, trough, channel, conduit, cut, drain, waterway, moat, fosse.

trenchant adj **1** *a trenchant wit/criticism* incisive, cutting, pointed, sharp, biting, pungent, caustic, piercing, penetrating, razor, razor-edged, mordant, scathing, acrid, acid, tart, acidulous, acerbic, astringent, sarcastic. **2** *trenchant divisions between the political parties* clear, clear-cut, distinct, defined, well-defined, sharp, crisp, unequivocal, unambiguous.

trend n **1** *an upward trend in prices* | *votes showing a trend towards the right* tendency, drift, course, direction, bearing, current, inclination, bias, leaning, bent, swing. **2** *teenagers like to follow the trend* fashion, vogue, style, mode, look, craze; *inf* fad.

trend v *prices trending upwards* | *political opinions trending to the left* move, go, tend, head, drift, turn, incline, lean, shift, veer, swing.

trepidation n fear, fearfulness, alarm, fright, apprehensiveness, apprehension, terror, panic, anxiety, worry, uneasiness, disquiet, unrest, agitation, trembling, nervousness, jumpiness, perturbation, discomposure, dismay, consternation; *inf* butterflies, cold feet, jitters, cold sweat, blue funk, heebie-jeebies, willies.

trespass v **1** *trespass on his land/privacy* intrude on, encroach on, infringe on, poach on, invade, obtrude on. **2** *trespass on their hospitality* take advantage of, impose upon, exploit, abuse, make use of. **3** *punished for having trespassed* do wrong, err, go astray, fall from grace, stray from the straight and narrow, sin, transgress. **4** *punished for trespassing against his neighbours* do wrong to, wrong.

trespass n **1** *the laws of trespass | found guilty of trespass* unlawful entry, intrusion, encroachment, infringement, invasion, obtrusion. **2** *forgive their trespasses* wrongdoing, wrong, misdemeanour, misdeed, crime, offence, transgression, sin, malefaction.

trespasser n **1** *trespassers will be prosecuted* intruder, interloper, unwelcome visitor, encroacher, infringer, invader, obtruder. **2** *trespassers asking for forgivance* wrongdoer, evildoer, criminal, offender, transgressor, sinner, malefactor.

tresses npl hair; locks, curls, ringlets, braids, plaits.

trial n **1** *the murder trial lasted several days* court case, case, hearing, inquiry, tribunal, litigation, judicial examination, legal investigation. **2** *give the applicant a trial* trial period, probation, test, test/testing period, audition. **3** *put a car through safety trials* test, testing, try-out, trial/test run, check, assay, experiment; *inf* dry run. **4** *climb the mountain at the third trial* try, attempt, endeavour, effort, venture; *inf* go, shot, stab, crack. **5** *she's a trial to her mother* nuisance, pest, bother, worry, vexation, annoyance, irritant, irritation, bane, affliction, curse, burden, cross to bear, thorn in one's flesh; *inf* pain in the neck, hassle, plague. **6** *the trials of life* trouble, worry, anxiety, vexation, load, burden, cross to bear, blow, affliction, tribulation, adversity, hardship, ordeal, pain; suffering, distress, misery, wretchedness, unhappiness, sadness, woe, grief. **7** *football trials* selection contest, preliminary match, audition. **8** *motorbike/sheepdog trials* contest, competition.

trial adj *trial period* testing, experimental, pilot, probationary, provisional.

tribe n **1** *the tribes of Israel* ethnic group, family, dynasty, clan, sept. **2** *meet a tribe of doctors at the conference* group, crowd, company, party, band, number, gang, assembly, collection; *inf* bunch.

tribulation n trouble, worry, anxiety, vexation, load, burden, cross to bear, blow, affliction, trial, adversity, hardship, ordeal, pain; suffering, distress, misery, wretchedness, unhappiness, sadness, woe, grief.

tribunal n **1** *members of a rent tribunal* court, forum, arbitration board. **2** *hold a tribunal* hearing, court case, judicial examination.

tributary n *tributaries of the Thames* branch, feeder, confluent.

tribute n **1** *give tributes to the heroes* gift, present, accolade, commendation, testimonial, paean, eulogy, panegyric, encomium; gratitude, applause, praise, homage, honour, exaltation, laudation, extolment, glorification; congratulations, compliments; *inf* bouquets. **2** *the success is a tribute to their hard work* acknowledgement, recognition, testimonial, indication, manifestation; evidence, proof. **3** *kings paying tributes to the emperor* homage; payment, contribution, offering, gift, donation, charge, tax, duty, levy, tariff, ransom.

trick n **1** *he got the job by a trick* stratagem, ploy, artifice, ruse, dodge, wile, device, manoeuvre, trick of the trade, deceit, deception, subterfuge, swindle, fraud; *inf* con. **2** *a trick of the light* illusion, mirage. **3** *he has trick of making guests feel welcome* knack, art, gift, talent, technique, ability, skill, expertise; *inf* know-how. **4** *play tricks on the old man | tired of the children's tricks* hoax, practical joke, joke, prank, jape, antic, caper, frolic, lark, gambol; *inf* legpull, gag, put-on. **5** *artists demonstrating their tricks* sleight of hand, legerdemain; juggling, prestidigitation. **6** *he has an annoying trick of repeating himself* idiosyncracy, habit, mannerism, quirk, peculiarity, foible, eccentricity, characteristic, trait, practice.

trick v *he wasn't a policeman—you've been tricked* deceive, delude, mislead, take in, cheat, hoodwink, fool, outwit, dupe, hoax, gull, cozen, defraud, swindle; *inf* con, pull a fast one on, put one over on; *Amer inf* shaft. **trick out** *they were tricked out in their finery* dress up, deck out, array, attire, adorn, decorate, embellish, ornament.

trickery n *use trickery to get the job* guile, artifice, wiliness, deceit, deception, cheating, subterfuge, craft, craftiness, chicanery, pretence, dishonesty, fraud, swindling, imposture, double-dealing, duplicity; *inf* conning, monkey/funny business, hankypanky, jiggery-pokery.

trickle v **1** *water trickled from the tap | blood trickled from the wound* drip, dribble, leak, ooze, seep, exude, percolate. **2** *information* *trickled out | people trickled into the meeting* come/go/pass gradually.

trickster n cheat, swindler, fraud, fraudster, defrauder, confidence man, deceiver, deluder, dissembler, hoodwinker, hoaxer, phoney, charlatan, rogue, scoundrel; *inf* con man.

tricky adj **1** *a tricky situation* difficult, problematic, awkward, delicate, sensitive, ticklish, thorny, knotty, touchy, risky, uncertain, precarious; *inf* sticky. **2** *he's a tricky character* cunning, crafty, wily, artful, devious, scheming, foxy, sly, slippery, subtle, deceitful, deceptive.

tried adj *tried remedies | friends who are tried and true* tried out, tested, put to the test, proved, proven, established, sure, certain, true, dependable, reliable, trustworthy, reputable.

trifle n **1** *her mind is occupied with trifles* trivia, inessentials; triviality, unimportant thing, thing of no consequence, bagatelle, nothing. **2** *buy a few trifles for Christmas* bauble, trinket, knick-knack, gimcrack, gewgaw, toy, doodah, whatnot. **3** *I paid a mere trifle for it* next to nothing, hardly anything, pittance; *inf* piddling amount, row of beans. **4** *he's a trifle confused* bit, small amount, touch.

trifle v **1** *stop trifling and do some work* idle, do nothing, potter about, fiddle about, fool about, mess around, hang around, loiter, waste time, fritter away one's time. **2** *he's just trifling with the young woman | trifle with her affections* amuse oneself with, toy with, play around with, flirt with, dally with, sport with. **3** *he's not a man to be trifled with* treat lightly, deal with casually, treat in a cavalier fashion, dismiss.

trifling adj **1** *discuss trifling matters* petty, trivial, unimportant, insignificant, inconsequential, shallow, superficial, frivolous, silly, idle, foolish, empty. **2** *cost a trifling amount* trivial, small, tiny, miniscule, infinitesimal, negligible, insignificant, paltry, nominal, worthless, valueless; *inf* piddling.

trigger v *it triggered the riot | her behaviour triggered off his fit of rage* set off, set in motion, spark off, activate, give rise to, generate, start, cause, bring about, prompt, provoke.

trim adj **1** *looking trim in her uniform* neat, tidy, neat and tidy, smart, spruce, well-groomed, well-dressed, well-turned-out, dapper, elegant, soigné/soignée; *inf* natty. **2** *trim gardens* neat, tidy, orderly, in good order/condition, well-maintained, shipshape, well-looked-after, well-cared-for, spick and span. **3** *have a trim figure | keep*

trim slim, slender, lean, svelte, streamlined, willowy, lissom, sleek, shapely, in good shape, fit, physically fit.

trim v **1** *trim one's hair/beard* cut, clip, snip, shear, prune, pare, even up, neaten, tidy up. **2** *trim the fat from the meat | trim the branches from the tree* cut, chop, hack, remove, take off. **3** *trim the annual budget* cut down, decrease, reduce, diminish, cut back on, curtail, dock, retrench. **4** *trim the Christmas tree | trim her evening dress* decorate, adorn, ornament, embellish, trick out, festoon. **5** *trim the dress with lace* decorate, adorn, ornament, embellish, edge, pipe, border, fringe, embroider, bespangle. **6** *the father trimmed his son* scold, chide, rebuke, reprimand, reproach, reprove, admonish; *inf* give a dressing-down to, tell off. **7** *schoolmasters were not allowed to trim pupils* beat, thrash, leather, cane, whip, flog, spank; *inf* tan someone's hide, thump, lambaste. **8** *they trimmed them at football* trounce, rout, give a drubbing to, worst, vanquish, conquer, defeat thoroughly, beat soundly.

trim n **1** *admire the trim on the dress* trimming, decoration, adornment, ornamentation, embellishment, edging, piping, border, fringe, frill, embroidery. **2** *have a trim at the hairdressers* haircut, cut, clip, snip, shearing, pruning, paring, tidy-up. **3** *the old man's still in trim* good health, good condition, in good shape/form, fine fettle, shape.

trimming n *admire the trimming on the dress* trim, decoration, adornment, ornamentation, edging, piping, fringe, fringing, frill, embroidery. *see* TRIM n 1.

trimmings npl **1** *turkey with all the trimmings* accompaniments, frills, extras, accessories, accoutrements, trappings, paraphernalia; garnishing, garnish. **2** *hedge/pastry trimmings* cuttings, clippings, parings, shavings.

trinket n *buy a trinket as a souvenir* bauble, ornament, knick-knack, trifle, gimcrack, gewgaw, piece of bric-à-brac, bibelot, doodah, whatnot.

trio n threesome, triumvirate, triad, trine, trinity, triune, triple, trilogy, triptych; triplets.

trip n **1** *go on a trip to China/town* excursion, tour, expedition, voyage, jaunt, outing, run. **2** *just one trip crippled her for life* stumble, misstep, false step, slip, slide, fall, tumble, spill. **3** *one more trip and you're sacked* mistake, error, blunder, slip, lapse, *faux pas*, indiscretion, oversight, bungle, botch; *inf* slip-up, booboo, boob. **4** *have a* *bad trip* hallucination, drug experience, vision.

trip v **1** *she tripped on the broken pavement* stumble, lose one's footing/balance, stagger, totter, slip, slide, misstep, fall, tumble. **2** *she tripped up when she tried to alter the accounts* make a mistake, blunder, go wrong, err, lapse, bungle, botch; *inf* slip up, boob. **3** *the defending lawyer tripped the witness up* catch out, trap, outwit, outsmart, put off one's stride, confuse, disconcert, unsettle, discountenance; *inf* throw, wrongfoot. **4** *she tripped upstairs* skip, dance, hop, prance, bound, spring, gambol, caper, frisk, cavort, waltz. **5** *he trips at least once a week* hallucinate; *inf* get stoned/high.

tripe n *he's talking tripe* nonsense, rubbish, drivel, twaddle, bunkum, balderdash; *inf* rot, tommy-rot, poppycock, claptrap, bunk, garbage, trash, hogwash, guff.

triple adj **1** *a triple alliance* three-way, threefold, tripartite. **2** *a triple whisky | at triple the recommended speed* three times, three times as much as, threefold, treble.

triple n trio, threesome, triumvirate, triad, trine, trinity, triune.

tripper n tourist, holiday-maker, sightseer, excursionist, traveller, journeyer, voyager.

trite adj hackneyed, banal, commonplace, ordinary, common, platitudinous, clichéd, stock, stereotyped, overused, overdone, stale, worn-out, threadbare, unimaginative, unoriginal, uninspired, dull, pedestrian, run-of-the-mill, routine, humdrum.

triumph n **1** *his triumph over his opponent* conquest, victory, win, ascendancy, mastery, success; *inf* walk-over. **2** *it was a triumph of British engineering* coup, *tour de force*, feat, master-stroke, achievement, attainment, accomplishment, supreme example, sensation; *inf* hit. **3** *expressions of triumph on their faces* exultation, jubilation, jubilance, elation, rejoicing, joy, joyfulness, pride.

triumph v **1** *the better team triumphed* win, succeed, come first, be the victor, be victorious, gain a victory, carry the day, take the honours/prize/crown. **2** *triumph over his opponent/disability* beat, defeat, conquer, vanquish, best, worst, overcome, overpower, get the better of, gain ascendancy over, gain mastery of, prevail against. **3** *the defeated team watching the winners triumph* exult, rejoice, jubilate, celebrate, revel, glory, gloat, swagger, brag, boast.

triumphant adj **1** *the triumphant team took a bow* winning, victorious, successful, undefeated, unbeaten, prize-winning, trophy-winning. **2** *wearing triumphant expressions |*

giving triumphant shouts exultant, jubilant, elated, rejoicing, joyful, joyous, proud, cock-a-hoop, gloating, boastful.

trivia npl *ignore the trivia and address the main issue* petty details, details, minutiae, trivialities, trifles, technicalities.

trivial adj **1** *raise trivial objections* unimportant, insignificant, inconsequential, flimsy, insubstantial, petty, minor, of no account/matter, negligible, paltry, trifling, foolish, worthless; *inf* piddling. **2** *he's a trivial young man* frivolous, small-minded, feather-brained, giddy, silly.

triviality n **1** *the triviality of the objections* unimportance, insignificance, inconsequence, flimsiness, insubstantiality, pettiness, paltriness, foolishness, worthlessness. **2** *the triviality of the young man* frivolousness, small-mindedness, feather-brainedness, giddiness, silliness. **3** *do not wish to discuss trivialities* petty/mere detail, thing of no importance, trifle, technicality.

troop n *a troop of people surged forward* band, group, company, assemblage, gathering, body, crowd, throng, multitude, horde, host, mob, squad, pack, drove, flock, swarm, stream; *inf* gang, crew.

troop v *the audience trooped out* flock, stream, swarm, surge, crowd, throng, mill.

troops npl *call in the troops* armed forces, army, military, services, soldiers, soldiery, fighting men/women.

trophy n **1** *win the sports trophy* cup, prize, award; laurels. **2** *trophies of his time as a hunter* spoil;, booty; souvenir, memento, keepsake, relic.

tropical adj *tropical weather* hot, torrid, sweltering, boiling, sultry, steamy, humid, sticky.

trouble n **1** *his car is causing him trouble | having trouble with the computer* worry, bother, anxiety, disquiet, unease, irritation, vexation, inconvenience, annoyance, agitation, harassment, difficulty, distress; problems. **2** *there has been a lot of trouble in her life* difficulty, misfortune, adversity, hardship, bad luck, ill luck, burden, distress, pain, suffering, affliction, torment, woe, grief, unhappiness, sadness, heartache; problems. **3** *please don't go to any trouble | our hostess went to a lot of trouble* bother, inconvenience, disturbance, fuss, effort, exertion, work, labour, attention, care, thoughtfulness; *inf* hassle. **4** *the girl was no trouble | it was no trouble to collect the mail* nuisance, bother, inconvenience, problem, pest; *inf* headache, pain in the neck, pain. **5** *the trouble with her is she's too old-fashioned | his trouble* *is he's too nice* problem, difficulty, failing, weakness, shortcoming, fault, imperfection, defect, blemish. **6** *he has stomach trouble* disorder, disease, illness, dysfunction. **7** *the barman doesn't want any trouble* disturbance, disorder, unrest, fighting, rowing, strife, conflict, tumult, commotion, turbulence, law-breaking. **in trouble 1** *he's in trouble financially | in trouble with the police* in difficulty, having problems, in dire straits, in a predicament; *inf* in a tight corner, in hot water, in a jam/pickle, in a mess/spot. **2** *the girl's in trouble* pregnant while unmarried, having a baby; *inf* expecting.

trouble v **1** *he's troubled by neighbours/finances* worry, bother, disturb, annoy, irritate, vex, irk, fret, pester, torment, plague, inconvenience, upset, perturb, agitate, discompose, harass, distress; *inf* hassle. **2** *don't trouble to see me out* take the trouble/time (to), bother, make the effort (to), exert/disturb oneself, go out of one's way. **3** *he is troubled by back pain* afflict, oppress, weigh down, burden, incapacitate. **4** *I'm sorry to trouble you but may I use your phone* bother, disturb, inconvenience, put out, impose upon, discommode, incommode.

troublemaker n mischief-maker, inciter, agitator, instigator, *agent provocateur*, rabble-rouser, demagogue, storm petrel.

troublesome adj *troublesome neighbours/problems* worrying, worrisome, bothersome, tiresome, disturbing, annoying, irritating, irksome, upsetting, perturbing, harassing, distressing, difficult, problematic, demanding, taxing.

trough n **1** *animals feeding from a trough* feeding box, feedbox, manger, rack, crib. **2** *troughs to drain away water* channel, conduit, duct, flume, gutter, drain, culvert, trench, ditch, furrow, groove, depression.

trounce v **1** *they trounced the other team* defeat utterly, beat soundly, rout, drub, thrash, crush, overwhelm; *inf* make mincemeat of, walk all over, wipe the floor with, hammer, clobber, slaughter, give a pasting to. **2** *the father trounced his son for breaking the window* thrash, beat, whip, flog, lash, birch, cane, leather, spank, chastise; *inf* belt, wallop, lambaste, give a hiding to, tan the hide of.

troupe n *a troupe of artistes* company, band, cast.

trousers npl slacks, jeans, flannels; *Amer* pants.

truancy n absenteeism, absence, French leave, shirking, malingering; *inf* skiving, bunking-off.

truant n absentee, dodger, malingerer, shirker, deserter.

truant v play truant, dodge, malinger, shirk; *inf* skive, play hooky, bunk off, be AWOL.

truce n cease-fire, armistice, suspension/cessation of hostilities, peace, respite, moratorium, lull; *inf* let-up.

truck[1] n *trucks racing down the motorway* lorry, articulated lorry, heavy goods vehicle, van; *inf* HGV.

truck[2] n *refuse to have any truck with them* association, contact, communication, connection, business, trade; dealings, relations.

truculent adj aggressive, antagonistic, belligerent, pugnacious, bellicose, combative, contentious, hostile, obstreperous, violent, fierce, defiant, sullen, surly, cross, bad-tempered, ill-natured.

trudge v *trudge through the deep snow* plod, lumber, shuffle, drag one's feet, clump, slog, footslog, trek, tramp, hike; *inf* yomp.

true adj **1** *what you say is true | it's true that he's dead | a true account* truthful, accurate, correct, right, valid, factual, exact, precise, faithful, genuine, reliable, veracious, honest. **2** *a true witchdoctor* real, genuine, authentic, actual, *bona fide*, valid, legitimate; *inf* honest-to-goodness. **3** *a true friend* loyal, faithful, trustworthy, trusty, reliable, dependable, staunch, firm, fast, steady, constant, unswerving, unwavering, devoted, sincere, dedicated, supportive, dutiful. **4** *give a true picture of Victorian times* exact, precise, perfect, faithful, close, accurate, correct, unerring; *inf* spot-on.

true adv **1** *tell me true* truly, truthfully, honestly, sincerely, candidly, veraciously. **2** *the arrow flew true* accurately, unerringly, unswervingly, without deviating, on target; *inf* spot on.

truly adv **1** *she is truly his daughter* in truth, really, in reality, actually, in fact, genuinely, certainly, surely, definitely, decidedly, positively, absolutely, unquestionably, undoubtedly, beyond doubt/question, indubitably, beyond the shadow of a doubt. **2** *tell me truly what you think* truthfully, honestly, frankly, candidly, openly; *inf* with no punches pulled. **3** *truly, I did not know* honestly, truthfully, genuinely, really, indeed, veritably. **4** *they are truly grateful* really, genuinely, sincerely, very, extremely, exceptionally. **5** *the old man served his master truly* loyally, faithfully, reliably, staunchly, firmly, steadily, constantly, unswervingly, devotedly, with all one's heart, sincerely, dedicatedly, dutifully. **6** *the novel does not truly depict the era* exactly, precisely, faithfully, closely, accurately, correctly, unerringly.

trump v *she trumped her sister's record/rival* surpass, outperform, outdo. **trump up** *trump up an excuse for not going* invent, make up, fabricate, devise, concoct, hatch, contrive, fake; *inf* cook up.

trumpery n *wanton women in their trumpery* cheap finery, flashy ornamentation; baubles, trinkets, gewgaws.

trumpery adj *trumpery decorations/furnishings* worthless, valueless, showy, flashy, tawdry, shoddy, meretricious, Brummagem; *inf* flash.

trumpet v **1** *trumpet in rage* bellow, roar, bay, shout, yell, cry out, call out. **2** *trumpet the news of his appointment* proclaim, announce, herald, broadcast, promulgate, noise abroad.

truncate v *truncate the time allotted | truncate the length/essay* shorten, reduce, diminish, decrease, cut short, prune, trim, lop, curtail, abbreviate.

truncheon n club, baton, cudgel, staff, stick.

trunk n **1** *the trunk of a tree* main stem, bole. **2** *find the trunk of the murdered man* torso. **3** *the animal's trunk* proboscis, snout. **4** *put the linen in a trunk* chest, case, portmanteau, crate, storage box, box, coffer.

truss v **1** *truss a fowl* tie up, wrap up, bind up, bundle up. **2** *the thieves trussed up the guard* tie up, bind, tether, chain up, secure.

truss n **1** *the truss of the bridge* support, brace, prop, strut, buttress. **2** *a truss for a hernia* support, pad. **3** *a truss of hay* bundle, bunch, bale.

trust n **1** *have trust in the surgeon | take it on trust* faith, confidence, belief, conviction, credence, assurance, certainty, reliance, hope, expectation. **2** *a position of trust* responsibility, duty, obligation, commitment. **3** *the money is kept in trust for her* trusteeship, guardianship, safe keeping, protection, charge, care, custody.

trust v **1** *I do not trust him | trust his judgement* put/place one's trust in, have faith/confidence in, be convinced by, pin one's hopes on. **2** *you can trust him to behave well* rely on, depend on, bank on, count on, be sure of, swear by. **3** *I trust you will come | trust everything is all right* hope, assume, presume, expect, believe, suppose. **4** *he trusted his son to her | trust them with his life* entrust, put in the hands of, turn over, assign, consign, commit, delegate.

trustful adj trusting, unsuspicious, unguarded, unwary, unsuspecting, unquestioning, credulous, gullible, ingenuous, naïve, innocent.

trustworthy adj *trustworthy employees* reliable, dependable, stable, staunch, loyal, faithful, trusty, responsible, sensible, level-headed, honest, honourable, upright, ethical, righteous, principled, virtuous.

trusty adj *his trusty steed/valet* trustworthy, reliable, dependable, staunch, faithful, loyal, responsible. *see* TRUSTWORTHY.

truth n **1** *no truth in what she says* truthfulness, accuracy, correctness, rightness, validity, fact, factualness, factuality, genuineness, veracity, verity, honesty. **2** *truth is stranger than fiction* reality, actuality, factuality. **3** *he is a man of truth* truthfulness, honesty, integrity, uprightness, righteousness, honour, honourableness, sincerity, candour. **4** *cite an old truth* truism, axiom, maxim, proverb, adage, aphorism, saw.

truthful adj **1** *a truthful child* honest, trustworthy, veracious, candid, frank, open, forthright, straight. **2** *a truthful account* true, accurate, correct, right, valid, factual, exact, faithful, precise, genuine, reliable, veracious, honest.

try v **1** *try to do well* attempt, aim, endeavour, make an effort, exert oneself, undertake, strive, assay, seek, struggle, do one's best; *inf* have a go/shot/crack/stab. **2** *try a new brand | try something new* try out, test, put to the test, experiment with, assay, investigate, examine, appraise, evaluate, assess, experience, sample; *Amer* check out. **3** *the children try her patience* tax, strain, make demands on, sap, drain, exhaust. **4** *she has been sorely tried by the children* trouble, bother, irk, vex, annoy, irritate, harass, afflict, nag, pester, plague, torment; *inf* drive mad. **5** *try the case* hear, adjudge, adjudicate, examine. **try out** *try out a new product/restaurant* try, test, put to the test, experiment with, appraise, evaluate, sample; *Amer* check out. *see* TRY 2.

trying adj **1** *the children were very trying* troublesome, bothersome, tiresome, irksome, vexatious, annoying, irritating, exasperating. **2** *have a trying day* taxing, demanding, stressful, difficult, arduous, hard, tough, tiring, fatiguing, exhausting, upsetting.

tuck v **1** *tuck the shirt into the skirt* gather, push, ease, insert, stuff. **2** *tuck the material* gather, fold, ruck, ruffle, pleat. **tuck in/ into 1** *tuck the child in* tuck up, cover up, wrap up, put to bed, make snug/comfortable. **2** *tuck into a large meal* eat heartily, gobble up, wolf down, *inf* get stuck into.

tuck away *houses tucked away under the mountain* hide, conceal, secrete, stow away.

tuck n **1** *tucks in the fabric* gather, fold, ruck, ruffle, pleat. **2** *children asking for tuck* food; victuals, comestibles; *inf* eats, grub, nosh, scoff.

tug v **1** *tug the rope hard | tug her hair* pull, jerk, yank, wrench, wrest. **2** *the dog was tugging him along the road* pull, draw, drag, haul, tow, trail.

tug n *give the gate a good tug* pull, jerk, yank, wrench, haul.

tuition n teaching, instruction, coaching, education, schooling, training, drill, direction, guidance.

tumble v **1** *the toddler tumbled suddenly* fall over, fall down, fall headlong, topple, fall head over heels, fall end over end, lose one's footing/balance, stumble, stagger, trip up. **2** *acrobats tumbling* somersault, go head over heels. **3** *share prices have tumbled* plummet, plunge, slump, dive, drop, slide, fall, decrease, decline. **4** *ships tumbling about on the waves* roll, toss, pitch, heave, thrash about. **5** *tumble out of bed | tumble into the car* fall headlong, move hurriedly, blunder, stumble. **6** *the wind had tumbled her hair* tousle, dishevel, ruffle, disarrange, disorder, mess up, rumple; *inf* muss up. **7** *suddenly tumble to what he meant | tumble to his motive* grasp, realize, understand, comprehend, apprehend, perceive; *inf* latch on to, suss.

tumble n **1** *the toddler took a tumble* fall, stumble, trip, spill; *inf* nosedive, header. **2** *the tumble of the share index* plummeting, plunge, slump, dive, drop, fall, decline, failure, collapse. **3** *acrobats demonstrating tumbles* somersault, acrobatic feat. **4** *clothes in a tumble on the floor* jumble, clutter, mess, confusion; chaos, disorder, disarray.

tumbledown adj dilapidated, ramshackle, crumbling, disintegrating, falling to pieces/bits, decrepit, ruined, in ruins, rickety, shaky, tottering, teetering.

tumid adj *limbs looking tumid* swollen, enlarged, puffy, puffed up, bloated, distended, tumescent, turgid, oedematose.

tumour n **1** *benign tumours* lump, growth, swelling, excrescence, protuberance, tumefaction, intumescence. **2** *die of a lung tumour* cancerous/malignant growth, carcinoma, cancer, malignancy.

tumult n **1** *we cannot hear you above the tumult* din, uproar, commotion, racket, hubbub, hullabaloo, clamour, shouting, yelling, pandemonium, babel, bedlam, noise. **2** *the meeting ended in tumult* disorder, disarray, disturbance, confusion, chaos, upheaval, uproar. **3** *police sent to deal with a tumult* riot, protest, insurrection, rebellion, breach of the peace, row, brawl, fight, quarrel, altercation, affray, fracas, mêlée, brouhaha; *inf* ruction, free-for-all. **4** *emotions in tumult* turmoil, upheaval, confusion, ferment.

tumultuous adj **1** *tumultous applause* loud, noisy, clamorous, ear-shattering, deafening, ear-piercing, blaring, uproarious, unrestrained, boisterous. **2** *a tumultuous crowd* rowdy, unruly, boisterous, disorderly, disturbed, restless, agitated, excited, fierce, obstreperous, wild, violent, lawless, vociferous, noisy, rioting. **3** *tumultous emotions* passionate, vehement, fervent, violent, raging, unrestrained, uncontrolled, frenzied, in turmoil, turbulent.

tune n **1** *play a folk tune* melody, air, song, theme, strain, motif. **2** *his ideas are not in tune with modern thinking* agreement, accord, accordance, harmony, correspondence, congruence, conformity, sympathy. **3** *changed his tune* mind, attitude, view, opinion.

tune v *tune the instrument* adjust, regulate, pitch, bring into harmony, attune.

tuneful adj melodious, melodic, musical, rhythmical, mellifluous, sweet-sounding, dulcet, euphonious, lyrical, harmonious, pleasant, agreeable, catching, foot-tapping, easy on the ear.

tunnel n **1** *miners crawling along the tunnel* underground/subterranean passage, underpass, subway. **2** *moles/rabbits making tunnels* burrow, underground passage.

tunnel v **1** *prisoners tunnelling under the prison* dig, excavate, burrow, mine. **2** *tunnel a way out* dig, excavate, cut, scoop out.

turbulence n **1** *the turbulence of the seas* tempestuousness, storminess, roughness, choppiness, agitation. **2** *experience turbulence on the flight* irregular atmospheric motion, uneven air movement, rough air currents. **3** *the turbulence of the crowds* rowdiness, unruliness, disorderliness, restlessness, agitation, wildness, violence, noisiness. *see* TURBULENT 2. **4** *the turbulence of her emotions* agitation, instability, troubledness, turmoil.

turbulent adj **1** *turbulent seas* tempestuous, stormy, raging, foaming, rough, choppy, agitated. **2** *turbulent crowds* rowdy, unruly, boisterous, disorderly, restless, agitated, obstreperous, wild, violent, lawless, noisy. *see* TUMULTUOUS 2. **3** *affected by turbulent emotions/moods* disturbed, agitated, unsettled, unstable, troubled, distraught, in turmoil.

turf n **1** *lay new turf in the garden* grass, patch of grass, lawn, green; *lit* sward. **2** *replace a damaged turf* divot, clod, sod. **3** *he is a fan of the turf* racing, horse-racing; racecourses.

turf v *turf the garden* lay grass, grass. **turf out 1** *turf out old clothes* throw out, fling out, dispose of, get rid of, discard, scrap; *inf* chuck out, dump. **2** *turf out the intruder* throw out, fling out, eject, evict, oust, dismiss, discharge, expel; *inf* chuck out, bounce, show someone the door, sack, fire.

turgid adj **1** *turgid ankles* swollen, enlarged, puffy, puffed up, bloated, distended, tumescent, oedematose. **2** *turgid prose* bombastic, high-flown, high-sounding, rhetorical, oratorical, grandiloquent, magniloquent, extravagant, pretentious, pompous, flowery, fulsome, orotund, fustian.

turmoil n *the house was in turmoil just before the wedding* agitation, ferment, confusion, disorder, disarray, upheaval, chaos, pandemonium, bedlam, tumult; disturbance, bustle, flurry, commotion.

turn v **1** *the wheel is turning* go round, rotate, revolve, circle, roll, spin, wheel, whirl, twirl, gyrate, swivel, pivot. **2** *he turned in the driveway | they turned for home* turn round, change direction/course, go back, return, reverse direction, make a U-turn. **3** *the tide is turning* change direction/course. **4** *he turned towards her* change position, veer, wheel round, swing round. **5** *turn the meat* turn over, reverse, invert, flip over, turn topsy-turvy. **6** *turn the hose on them* aim, direct, point, train, level, focus. **7** *his expression turned from amusement to horror* change, alter, transform, metamorphose, mutate. **8** *turn to the next task* turn one's attention to, attend to, address/apply/devote oneself to, set about, take up, undertake. **9** *he turned nasty* become, come to be, get, go. **10** *the milk/butter turned* go/turn sour, sour, curdle, become rancid, go bad; *inf* go off. **11** *the heat turned the milk/butter* turn sour, sour, curdle, make rancid, spoil, taint. **12** *my stomach is turning* be nauseated, be upset, be unsettled. **13** *the sight turned my stomach* nauseate, sicken, upset, unsettle. **14** *my head is turning* go round, spin, feel dizzy/giddy. **15** *turn the corner* go/come round, round, pass round, negotiate, take. **16** *turn 40 | turn 5 o'clock* become, reach, get to, pass. **17** *turn on/off/out the light* put, switch. **18** *turn somersaults* perform, execute, do, carry out. **19** *turn a profit* make, bring in, gain, acquire, obtain, get, procure, secure. **20** *turn a pot* shape, mould, fashion, form, cast, construct. **21** *he used to*

be a loyal follower but he turned change sides, go over, defect, desert, renege, turn renegade, break faith, apostatize, tergiversate.

turn against 1 *he suddenly turned against his old friend* become unfriendly/hostile to, take a dislike to. **2** *he turned her against her old friend* set against, make hostile to, cause to be unfriendly, prejudice against, influence against. **turn away** *turn away the beggar | turn away those without tickets* send away, refuse admittance/entrance to, reject, rebuff, repel, cold-shoulder; *inf* give the brush-off to. **turn back** *turn back if the weather is bad* go back, retrace one's steps, return, retreat. **turn down 1** *he turned down the applicant/proposal* reject, decline, give the thumbs down to, rebuff, repudiate, spurn, veto; *inf* give the red light to. **2** *turn down the volume/gas* lessen, lower, reduce, decrease, diminish. **turn in 1** *turn in your homework/uniform before you leave* hand in, give in, submit, tender, hand over, deliver, return, give back, surrender. **2** *they turned in high scores* register, record, reach, achieve, attain. **3** *it's time to turn in* go to bed, retire, call it a day, go to sleep; *inf* hit the hay/sack. **4** *her feet turn in* curve in, bend in/inwards. **5** *turn him in to the police* hand over, turn over, deliver, inform on, betray; *inf* grass on, squeal on, blow the whistle on, rat on, finger, put the finger on. **turn off 1** *turn off the electricity/heater* put off, turn out, switch off, shut off, flick off, unplug. **2** *the driver suddenly turned off the main road* branch off, leave, quit, depart from, deviate from. **3** *she turned off before the town* branch off, take a side road, take another road. **4** *he was turned off geography by the boring lessons | she was turned off by his table manners* put off, turn against; disenchant, alienate, repel, disgust, nauseate, sicken. **turn on 1** *turn on the electricity/heater* put on, switch on, flick on, plug in, operate. **2** *she turned on her husband when he criticized her friend | the dog turned on his master* attack, launch an attack on, fall on, round on, set upon, become hostile to; *inf* lay into, tear into, light into, lace into. **3** *the result turns on the number of people voting* depend on, hang on, hinge on, pivot on, rest on, be contingent on, be decided by. **4** *she is turned on by muscular men* arouse, sexually arouse, excite, titillate, stimulate, thrill, attract, please. **turn out 1** *turn her out of her house* put out, throw out, kick out, eject, evict, oust; *inf* chuck out, turf out, bounce. **2** *turn her out of her job* eject, dismiss, discharge, axe; *inf* fire, sack, give the sack to, boot out. **3** *turn out the light/gas* turn off, put off, switch off, shut off, flick off, unplug. **4** *turn out thousands of books/toys* *per year* bring out, put out, produce, make, manufacture, fabricate, yield, process. **5** *turn out the cupboards* clear out, clean out, empty. **6** *a big crowd turned out to hear him go*, come, be present, attend, put in an appearance, appear, turn up, arrive, assemble, gather; *inf* show up, show. **7** *as it turned out we were safe | it turned out that she was right* happen, occur, come about, end up, prove to be the case, emerge, eventuate; *inf* transpire, pan out. **8** *she turned out a beautiful girl* become, grow/come/get to be, develop into, end up, emerge as. **turn over 1** *the boat turned over* overturn, topple, upturn, capsize, keel over, turn turtle. **2** *they turned the boat over* overturn, upturn, upend, capsize, upset. **3** *turn over the pages* flick over, flip over, leaf over. **4** *turn over the pros and cons* consider, think about, ponder, reflect on, mull over, muse on, ruminate about. **5** *turn over the estate to his brother* hand over, transfer, consign, assign, commit. **turn to 1** *turn to drink* have recourse to, resort to, take to. **2** *turn to him for help* look, apply to, approach, appeal to, have recourse to. **3** *arrived and soon turned to* set about one's work/task. **turn up 1** *turn up the volume* increase, raise, amplify, make louder, intensify. **2** *turn up some interesting information* uncover, unearth, discover, bring to light, find, hit upon, dig up, ferret out, root out, expose. **3** *he's mislaid the book but it'll turn up* be found, be located, come to light. **4** *they didn't turn up at the party* arrive, appear, put in an appearance, present oneself, be present; *inf* show up, show. **5** *he hopes a job will turn up* present itself, occur, happen, crop up, pop up, arise, come on the scene, come to light, manifest itself; *inf* transpire. **6** *turn up the garment* take up, raise, shorten.

turn n **1** *give the wheel a few turns* rotation, revolution, circle, spin, whirl, twirl, gyration, swivel. **2** *take a turn to the left* change of direction/course, deviation, divergence, veer. **3** *a road full of turns* turning, bend, curve, corner, twist, winding. **4** *dislike the turn of events* trend, tendency, bias, leaning, direction, drift. **5** *a turn for the better/worse* change, alteration, variation, difference, deviation, divergence, shift. **6** *he is of an academic turn of mind* bent, tendency, inclination, bias, propensity, affinity, leaning, aptitude, talent, gift, flair, knack. **7** *it is your turn to play* time, opportunity, chance, stint, spell, move, try, attempt; *inf* go, shot, crack. **8** *take a turn in the park* walk, stroll, saunter, amble, airing, constitutional, promenade, drive, ride, outing, excursion, jaunt; *inf* spin. **9** *a comedy turn in the show* performance, act, routine, appearance, show. **10** *do him a good/bad turn* act, action, deed, service, gesture, favour. **11** *you gave me quite a turn* shock, start, surprise, fright, scare. **12** *it served my turn* purpose, objective, object, aim, end.

turning-point n *the turning-point in their fortunes* crossroads, crisis, crisis point, critical period, crux, decisive point, moment of truth/decision.

turnout n **1** *there was a good turnout at the meeting* number, gathering, crowd, assembly, assemblage, audience, attendance, gate. **2** *dressed in a smart turnout* outfit, costume, ensemble, attire; *inf* rig-out, get-up, gear.

turnover n **1** *the company's annual turnover is two million dollars* gross revenue, volume of business, business, financial flow; sales figures. **2** *aim for a quick turnover in the shop* buying and selling, movement of goods. **3** *the turnover of staff is very high* change, coming and going, movement, replacement.

tussle n **1** *in the tussle to get the gun from him* struggle, wrestle, conflict, fight, battle, skirmish, scuffle, affray, brawl; *inf* set-to, scrap. **2** *we had a tussle to finish the work on time* struggle, effort, exertion, labour, toil, strain.

tutor n *tutors marking exams* teacher, instructor, coach, lecturer, educator.

tutor v *tutor him in maths* teach, instruct, coach, educate, school, train, drill, direct, guide.

TV n television set, television; *inf* telly, the box, gogglebox, small screen, the tube, idiot box, talking head.

twaddle n nonsense, rubbish, garbage, trash, drivel, blather, balderdash, bunkum, hogwash, gibberish, gobbledegook; *inf* hot air, waffle, bunk, tosh, bosh, poppycock, piffle.

tweak v *tweak the child's ear* twist, pinch, nip, twitch, squeeze, pull, jerk.

tweak n *give his ear a tweak* twist, pinch, nip, twitch, squeeze, pull, jerk.

twig n branch, stick, offshoot, shoot, spray, stem.

twilight n **1** *walk home at twilight* dusk, late afternoon, early evening; *lit* crepuscule; *Scots* gloaming. **2** *scarcely able to see her in the twilight* half-light, semidarkness, dimness. **3** *in the twilight of his career* decline, ebb, waning, closing years.

twin n **1** *he and his brother are twins* identical twin, non-identical twin. **2** *where is the twin* *of that glove?* mate, fellow, match, counter-part, complement. **3** *she's an absolute twin for the queen* double, look-alike, likeness, image, duplicate, clone; *inf* spitting image, spit, dead spit, ringer, dead ringer.

twin v *twin the two firms* join, link, couple, pair, yoke.

twine n **1** *a ball of twine* cord, string, yarn, thread. **2** *vines in a twine* coil, spiral, whorl, convolution, twist, tangle.

twine v **1** *the plant had twined itself round the tree* entwine, coil, twist, wind, weave, wrap. **2** *twine a garland* weave, plait, braid, twist. **3** *the path twines up the mountain* twist, twist and turn, wind, curve, zigzag, meander, snake, worm.

twinge n **1** *a twinge of rheumatism* stab of pain, spasm, pain, pang, ache, throb, tweak, tingle, cramp, stitch. **2** *a twinge of conscience* pang, uneasiness, discomfort, qualm, scruple, misgiving.

twinkle v **1** *stars twinkling* glitter, glint, sparkle, flicker, shimmer, glimmer, gleam, dazzle, flash, wink, blink, shine, scintillate, coruscate. **2** *her eyes twinkled with amusement* sparkle, gleam, shine. **3** *her feet twinkled upstairs* dart, glide, dance, flit.

twinkle n **1** *the twinkle of stars* twinkling, glitter, glint, sparkle, flicker, shimmer, glimmer, gleam, dazzle, flash, wink, blink, shining, scintillation, coruscation. **2** *with a twinkle of her eyes* sparkle, gleam, shining. **3** *the twinkle of her feet* darting, gliding, dancing, flitting. **4** *she'll be with you in a twinkle* twinkling, instant, second, moment, flash. *see* TWINKLING.

twinkling n **1** *the twinkling of the stars* twinkle, glitter, glint, sparkle, flicker, shimmer. *see* TWINKLE n 1. **2** *I'll be there in a twinkling* twinkle, instant, second, split second, moment, flash; *inf* jiffy, tick, shake, two shakes of a lamb's tail.

twirl v **1** *twirl the cane* spin, whirl, twist. **2** *she twirled round to the music* spin, whirl, turn, pirouette, wheel, gyrate, revolve, rotate, pivot. **3** *twirl a curl of hair round her finger* twist, coil, wind, curl.

twirl n **1** *give the cane a twirl* spin, whirl, twist. **2** *a series of twirls round the room* spin, whirl, turn, pirouette, gyration, revolution, rotation. **3** *a twirl of chocolate* twist, coil, whorl, curl.

twist v **1** *twist the metal rod* | *twist it off the wall* bend, warp, misshape, deform, con-tort, distort; wrench, wrest. **2** *his face twisted in agony* contort, screw up. **3** *he twisted his ankle* wrench, turn, sprain, rick. **4** *the plant had twisted itself round the tree*

twine, entwine, coil, wind, weave, wrap. **5** *twist a garland* twine, weave, plait, braid. **6** *twist a curl of hair round her finger* twirl, coil, wind, curl. **7** *the path twisted round the mountain* wind, curve, bend, twine, zigzag, meander, snake, worm. **8** *the child twisted out of his grasp* wriggle, writhe, squirm, wig-gle. **9** *twist their words* distort, pervert, warp, garble, misrepresent, falsify, mis-quote, misreport, change, alter. **10** *she twisted her head round* swivel, screw, turn, rotate. **11** *she twisted round to look at him* swivel, turn, spin, pivot, rotate, revolve.

twist n **1** *with a twist of his arm* wrench, wrest, turn, contortion, pull, jerk, yank. **2** *try to repair the twist in the metal bar* bend, warp, kink, deformity, contortion, distor-tion, defect, flaw, imperfection. **3** *a painful twist of the ankle* wrench, turn, sprain, rick. **4** *a twist of hair* coil, twirl, curl, braid. **5** *a twist of tobacco* roll, plug, quid. **6** *the twists in the mountain path* bend, turn, curve, wind-ing, arc, zigzag, meander, undulation. **7** *a slight twist to his character* aberration, pecu-liarity, quirk, oddity, eccentricity, idiosyn-cracy, foible. **8** *upset by the twist of events* development, turn, change, alteration, variation, slant.

twit n fool, idiot, ass, blockhead, nincom-poop, ninny, simpleton, clown; *inf* chump, halfwit, dope.

twitch v **1** *with limbs twitching* move spas-modically, jerk, jump, quiver, shiver, qua-ver. **2** *her eye twitched* blink, flutter, jump. **3** *twitch the rug into place* | *twitch at his tie* pull, tug, pluck; *inf* yank.

twitch n **1** *his leg gave a twitch* spasm, jerk, jump, quiver, tremor, shiver, quaver. **2** *a twitch in her eye* blink, flutter, jump, tic. **3** *adjust the rug with a twitch* pull, tug; *inf* yank.

twitter v **1** *birds twittering* chirrup, cheep, tweet, trill, warble, whistle, sing. **2** *stand twittering in the bus queue* chatter, jabber, prattle, babble, gossip.

twitter n **1** *the twitter of the birds* trill, chirrup, cheep, tweet, warble, whistle, song. **2** *in a twitter about her exam results* flutter, flurry, state of excitement/agita-tion; *inf* tizzy, state, dither.

two-edged adj *a two-edged remark* double-edged, ambiguous, equivocal, ambivalent.

two-faced adj hypocritical, insincere, deceitful, deceiving, dissembling, dupli-citous, false, untrustworthy, treacherous, perfidious, double-dealing, Janus-faced.

tycoon n magnate, baron, big business-man, captain of industry, industrialist, financier, merchant prince, mogul; *inf* fat cat.

type n **1** *a nasty type of person* | *a rare type of plant* kind, sort, variety, form, class, classification, category, group, order, set, genre, strain, species, genus; *inf* ilk. **2** *he's a nasty type* person, individual, specimen, character. **3** *they regard her as the very type of womanhood* example, exemplar, model, pattern, essence, personification, epitome, quintessence, archetype, prototype. **4** *set in a different kind of type* print, fount, face, character.

typhoon n cyclone, tornado, tropical storm, hurricane, squall, tempest.

typical adj **1** *a typical English pub* representative, classic, standard, stock, orthodox, conventional, true-to-type, quintessential, archetypal. **2** *what would be your typical day?* normal, average, ordinary, regular, general, customary, habitual, routine, run-of-the-mill. **3** *it is typical of him to be rude* characteristic, in character, in keeping, to be expected, usual, normal.

typify v **1** *he typifies the self-made man* exemplify, characterize, personify, epitomize, symbolize, embody, sum up, incarnate. **2** *they have tried to typify the various sectors of society* exemplify, represent, indicate, illustrate, denote.

tyrannical adj despotic, autocratic, dictatorial, absolute, arbitrary, authoritarian, high-handed, imperious, oppressive, coercive, domineering, bullying, harsh, strict, severe, cruel, brutal, unjust, unreasonable.

tyrannize v *tyrannize over the peasants* | *tyrannize the children* rule despotically, rule with a rod of iron; oppress, suppress, repress, crush, subjugate, dominate, domineer, order around, browbeat, intimidate, bully, ride roughshod over, lord it over.

tyranny n **1** *the tyranny of the country's/school's regime* despotism, absolutism, authoritarianism, arbitrariness, high-handedness, imperiousness, oppressiveness, oppression, coercion, bullying, harshness, strictness, severity, cruelty, brutality, unjustness, unreasonableness. **2** *government by tyranny rather than democracy* despotism, autocracy, dictatorship, absolute power, authoritarianism.

tyrant n despot, autocrat, dictator, absolute ruler, authoritarian, oppressor, martinet, slave-driver, bully.

ubiquitous adj everywhere, omnipresent, ever-present, in all places, all-over, all over the place, pervasive, universal.

ugly adj 1 *ugly people/buildings* ill-favoured, hideous, plain, unattractive, unlovely, unprepossessing, unsightly, displeasing; *Amer* homely; *inf* not much to look at. 2 *an ugly sight met their eyes* hideous, horrible, horrid, frightful, terrible, disagreeable, unpleasant, foul, nasty, vile, shocking, distasteful, disgusting, revolting, repellent, repugnant, loathsome, hateful, nauseating, sickening. 3 *he is an ugly character* horrible, disagreeable, unpleasant, nasty, objectionable, offensive, obnoxious, foul, vile, base, dishonourable, dishonest, rotten. 4 *an ugly situation* threatening, menacing, ominous, sinister, dangerous, nasty, unpleasant, disagreeable. 5 *the crowd grew ugly* nasty, angry, bad-tempered, ill-natured, hostile, surly, sullen, mean, sour. 6 *gave them ugly looks* dark, threatening, menacing, hostile, spiteful, malevolent, evil.

ulcer n ulceration, sore, open sore, abscess, gathering, boil, carbuncle, pustule.

ulterior adj *an ulterior motive* hidden, concealed, unrevealed, undisclosed, undivulged, unexpressed, secret, covert, unapparent.

ultimate adj 1 *the ultimate outcome | take ultimate responsibility* last, final, eventual, concluding, conclusive, terminal, end, furthest. 2 *ultimate truths* basic, fundamental, primary, elemental, radical. 3 *the ultimate gift/luxury* topmost, utmost, maximum, supreme, superlative, paramount, greatest, highest, unsurpassed, unrivalled.

ultimate n *the ultimate in luxury* last word, utmost, height, peak, culmination, perfection, epitome, nonpareil.

ultimately adv 1 *he is bound to win ultimately* in the end, in the long run, eventually, finally, sooner or later. 2 *ultimately he is an honourable person* basically, fundamentally, at heart, deep down.

ultramodern adj ahead of its/one's time, futuristic, avant-garde, modernistic, advanced, progressive, forward-looking.

umbrage n offence, pique, chagrin, vexation, irritation, exasperation, indignation, annoyance, anger, ire, high dudgeon, hurt, resentment, bitterness; *inf* huff.

umbrella n *under the umbrella of the parent organization* agency, aegis, cover, protection, support, patronage, backing.

umpire n *the umpire in the dispute/match* adjudicator, arbitrator, arbiter, judge, moderator, referee; *inf* ref.

umpire v *umpire in the dispute | umpire the match* adjudicate, arbitrate, judge, moderate, referee; *inf* ref.

umpteen adj countless, numerous, very many, ever so many.

unable adj *unable to get about | unable to reach the standard* not able, incapable, powerless, impotent, not up/equal to, inadequate, ineffectual, incompetent, unfit, unfitted, unqualified.

unabridged adj uncut, unshortened, unreduced, uncondensed, unexpurgated, fulllength, complete, entire, whole, intact.

unacceptable adj 1 *unacceptable terms of agreement* unsatisfactory, inadmissible, unsuitable. 2 *unacceptable behaviour* insupportable, intolerable, objectionable, offensive, obnoxious, undesirable, disagreeable, distasteful, improper.

unaccompanied adj *go unaccompanied | unaccompanied people* alone, on one's own, by oneself, partnerless, unescorted, solo, lone, solitary, single.

unaccomplished adj 1 *unaccomplished tasks* unfinished, uncompleted, incomplete, undone, half-done, unperformed, unexecuted. 2 *unaccomplished players* inexpert, unskilful, unskilled, without finesse, blundering, talentless, amateur, dilettante.

unaccountable adj 1 *an unaccountable increase in births | for some unaccountable reason* inexplicable, unexplainable, insoluble, unsolvable, incomprehensible, beyond comprehension/understanding, unfathomable, puzzling, baffling, mysterious, inscrutable, peculiar, unusual, curious, strange, queer, bizarre, extraordinary, astonishing; *inf* weird. 2 *she is unaccountable for the error* not responsible, not answerable, not liable, free, clear, exempt, immune.

unaccustomed adj **1** *unaccustomed to public speaking* unused (to), not used (to), new (to), unpractised, unfamiliar, inexperienced, unversed. **2** *the unaccustomed luxury* unusual, unfamiliar, uncommon, unwonted, new, exceptional, out of the ordinary, extraordinary, special, remarkable, singular, rare, surprising, strange.

unaffected adj **1** *unaffected by the events* unchanged, unaltered, uninfluenced, untouched, unmoved, unimpressed, proof (against), impervious, unresponsive. **2** *unaffected young girls* artless, guileless, ingenuous, naïve, unsophisticated, unassuming, unpretentious, down-to-earth, without airs, natural, plain, simple. **3** *unaffected sincerity* unfeigned, unpretended, genuine, real, sincere, honest, true, candid, frank; *inf* up-front.

unanimity n **1** *the unanimity of the committee* agreement, accord, concord, unity, consensus, like-mindedness. **2** *the unanimity of the vote* solidity, concertedness, consensus, uniformity, consistency, congruence.

unanimous adj **1** *the committee was unanimous* in complete agreement/accord, of one mind, like-minded, totally in harmony, at one, of a piece, with one voice, united, concordant. **2** *a unanimous vote* solid, united, concerted, uniform, consistent, congruent.

unanswerable adj **1** *an unanswerable case* irrefutable, inarguable, undisputable, undeniable, incontestable, incontrovertible, conclusive, absolute, positive. **2** *unanswerable questions* insoluble, unsolvable, insolvable, unresolvable, unexplainable, inexplicable. **3** *unanswerable for the error* not answerable, not responsible, unaccountable. *see* UNACCOUNTABLE 2.

unapproachable adj **1** *unapproachable places* inaccessible, remote, out of the way, out of reach, unreachable; *inf* off the beaten track, unget-at-able. **2** *the new head teacher is unapproachable* aloof, standoffish, distant, remote, detached, reserved, withdrawn, uncommunicative, unresponsive, unfriendly, unsociable, cool, chilly, frigid.

unarmed adj without arms/weapons, weaponless, open to attack, defenceless, unprotected, vulnerable, exposed, pregnable.

unassailable adj **1** *an unassailable stronghold* impregnable, invulnerable, invincible, secure, well-defended. **2** *their unassailable right to vote* indisputable, undeniable, unquestionable, incontestable, incontrovertible, irrefutable, conclusive, absolute, positive, proven.

unassuming adj modest, self-effacing, humble, meek, retiring, demure, restrained, reticent, diffident, shy, bashful, unassertive, unobtrusive, unostentatious, unpretentious, unaffected, natural, genuine, simple, artless, ingenuous.

unattached adj **1** *is she still unattached* unmarried, unwed, unwedded, unengaged, unbetrothed, wifeless, husbandless, spouseless, uncommitted, free, available, footloose and fancy free, partnerless, single, on one's own, by oneself, unescorted. **2** *the firm is still unattached to any other organization* independent of, unaffiliated, unassociated, autonomous, non-aligned, self-governing, self-ruling.

unattended adj **1** *an unattended garden* untended, neglected, ignored, disregarded, forgotten, forsaken, abandoned. **2** *an unattended vehicle* by itself, left alone, unguarded, unwatched. **3** *unattended young women* unaccompanied, alone, lone, on one's own, by oneself, partnerless, unescorted. *see* UNACCOMPANIED.

unauthorized adj uncertified, unaccredited, unlicensed, unofficial, unsanctioned, unwarranted, unapproved, disallowed, prohibited, forbidden, illegal.

unavailing adj vain, futile, useless, ineffective, ineffectual, unsuccessful, failed, fruitless, unproductive, pointless, to no avail/purpose, abortive, for nought.

unavoidable adj inescapable, inevitable, bound to happen, inexorable, ineludible, ineluctable, certain, fated, predestined, necessary, compulsory, required, obligatory, mandatory.

unaware adj **1** *unaware of what is going on | unaware that they have gone* unknowing, unconscious, ignorant, heedless, unmindful, oblivious, uninformed (about), unenlightened (about); *inf* in the dark. **2** *politically unaware* not perceptive, undiscerning, incognizant, nondiscriminating, unresponsive.

unawares adv **1** *come upon him unawares* unexpectedly, by surprise, without warning, suddenly, abruptly, unprepared, off-guard; *inf* with one's trousers down. **2** *I must have dropped my keys unawares* unknowingly, unwittingly, unintentionally, unconsciously, inadvertently, without noticing, accidentally, by accident, by mistake, mistakenly.

unbalanced adj **1** *unbalanced since the death of her husband* unstable, of unsound mind, mentally ill, deranged, demented, crazed, distracted, insane, mad, lunatic; *inf* crazy, not all there, off one's head. **2** *an unbal-*

anced report of the events one-sided, biased, prejudiced, partisan, partial, inequitable, unjust, unfair.

unbearable adj intolerable, insufferable, unsupportable, unendurable, unacceptable, more than flesh and blood can stand; *inf* too much, enough to try the patience of a saint.

unbeatable adj invincible, indomitable, unconquerable, unstoppable, unsurpassable, excelling.

unbecoming adj 1 *an unbecoming hat* unflattering, unattractive, unsightly. 2 *behaviour unbecoming in a young girl | unbecoming behaviour* unfitting, inappropriate, unsuitable, inapt, improper, indecorous, unseemly, unladylike, ungentlemanly, indelicate, tasteless.

unbelief n non-belief, atheism, disbelief, incredulity, scepticism, doubt, agnosticism.

unbelievable adj beyond belief, incredible, unconvincing, far-fetched, implausible, improbable, inconceivable, unthinkable, unimaginable, impossible, astonishing, astounding, staggering, preposterous.

unbeliever n non-believer, atheist, disbeliever, infidel, sceptic, doubter, doubting Thomas, agnostic.

unbend v 1 *unbend the twisted pole* straighten, align, flatten. 2 *she unbent enough to smile* relax, become less formal, become informal, unwind, loosen up, let oneself go; *inf* let one's hair down, let up, let it all hang out, hang loose.

unbending adj 1 *an unbending material* rigid, stiff, inflexible, unpliable, inelastic, unmalleable. 2 *she is a very unbending old lady* formal, stiff, aloof, reserved; *inf* up-tight. 3 *an unbending regime* inflexible, hard-line, uncompromising, tough, harsh, strict, stern, severe, firm, resolute, determined, unrelenting, relentless, inexorable.

unbiased adj impartial, unprejudiced, non-partisan, neutral, objective, disinterested, dispassionate, detached, even-handed, open-minded, equitable, fair, fair-minded, just.

unbidden adj 1 *unbidden guests* unasked, uninvited, unrequested, unwanted, unwelcome. 2 *memories coming unbidden to mind* spontaneous, voluntary, unprompted, unforced, uncompelled.

unbind v 1 *unbind the hostages* release, free, set free/loose, liberate, untie, unchain, unfetter. 2 *unbind the ropes* untie, unfasten, undo, loosen, unloose.

unborn adj 1 *her unborn child* expected, awaited, *in utero*, embryonic. 2 *unborn gen-*

erations future, to come, coming, subsequent, hereafter.

unbounded adj boundless, unlimited, limitless, illimitable, infinite, unrestrained, unconstrained, uncontrolled, unchecked, unbridled, vast, immense, immeasurable.

unbreakable adj non-breakable, shatterproof, infrangible, indestructible, toughened.

unbridled adj unrestrained, unconstrained, uncontrolled, unchecked, uncurbed, ungoverned, rampant, excessive, intemperate.

unbroken adj 1 *unbroken china/sets* intact, whole, undamaged, unimpaired, complete, entire. 2 *an unbroken horse* untamed, unsubdued. 3 *an unbroken series* uninterrupted, continuous, unremitting, ceaseless, unceasing, endless, incessant, constant, non-stop. 4 *unbroken sleep* uninterrupted, undisturbed, untroubled, sound. 5 *unbroken records* unbeaten, unsurpassed, unrivalled.

unburden v 1 *unburden the horse* unload, disburden, unpack, disencumber. 2 *unburden one's sins/guilt* confess, confide, acknowledge, disclose, reveal, divulge, expose, lay bare, make a clean breast of; *inf* come clean.

uncalled-for adj 1 *uncalled-for advice* unsought, unasked, unsolicited, unrequested, unprompted, unwelcome, gratuitous. 2 *uncalled-for rudeness* unnecessary, needless, undeserved, unmerited, unjustified, unreasonable, inappropriate.

uncanny adj 1 *uncanny happenings in the old house* strange, mysterious, odd, queer, weird, eerie, unnatural, preternatural, supernatural, unearthly, ghostly; *inf* creepy, spooky. 2 *bear an uncanny resemblance to the king* remarkable, striking, extraordinary, exceptional, astounding, astonishing, incredible.

unceremonious adj 1 *his unceremonious departure* abrupt, sudden, hasty, hurried, undignified, rude, impolite, uncivil, discourteous, unmannerly. 2 *an unceremonious occasion* informal, without ritual, casual, simple, relaxed, easy.

uncertain adj 1 *the outcome is uncertain* unknown, undetermined, unsettled, pending, in the balance, up in the air. 2 *feel uncertain about what to do* unsure, doubtful, dubious, undecided, unresolved, indecisive, irresolute, hesitant, wavering, vacillating, equivocating, vague, hazy, unclear, ambivalent, in two minds. 3 *the future is uncertain* unpredictable, unforeseeable, incalculable, speculative, unreliable, untrustworthy, undependable, risky, chancy. **4** *uncertain weather* changeable, variable, irregular, fitful, unpredictable, unreliable. **5** *in an uncertain voice* hesitant, hesitating, tentative, halting, unsure, unconfident.

uncertainty n **1** *full of uncertainty about the future* unsureness, indecision, irresolution, hesitancy, vacillation, equivocation, doubt, doubtfulness, vagueness, ambivalence. *see* UNCERTAIN 2. **2** *the uncertainty of the future* unpredictability, unreliability, riskiness, chanciness. *see* UNCERTAIN 3. **3** *give voice to a few uncertainties* doubt, qualm, misgiving, quandary, dilemma. **4** *the uncertainty of the weather* changeableness, variability, irregularity, fitfulness, unpredictability, unreliability. **5** *the uncertainty in her voice* | *uncertainty of the baby's steps* hesitancy, tentativeness, unsureness, lack of confidence.

unchangeable adj changeless, immutable, unalterable, incommutable, invariable, firm, fixed, established, permanent, deep-rooted, enduring, abiding, lasting, indestructible, unfading, constant, perpetual, eternal.

uncharitable adj *uncharitable in judging other's faults* harsh, severe, stern, hard, hardhearted, censorious, uncompromising, inflexible, unforgiving, merciless, ruthless, uncompassionate, unsympathetic, ungenerous, unfeeling, unkind, unchristian.

uncharted adj *uncharted territory* unmapped, unsurveyed, unexplored, unresearched, unplumbed, unfamiliar, unknown, strange.

uncivil adj discourteous, rude, impolite, unmannerly, bad-mannered, ill-bred, ungallant, unchivalrous, ungracious, disrespectful, brusque, curt, gruff, surly, boorish, churlish, uncouth.

uncivilized adj **1** *uncivilized tribes* barbarian, barbarous, barbaric, primitive, savage, wild. **2** *some of their friends are so uncivilized* uncouth, coarse, rough, boorish, vulgar, philistine, uneducated, uncultured, uncultivated, unsophisticated, unrefined, unpolished.

unclean adj **1** *unclean water* dirty, filthy, polluted, fouled, impure, adulterated, tainted. **2** *unclean hands/houses* dirty, filthy, grubby, grimy, stained, besmirched, smeared, unwashed. **3** *unclean people corrupting the innocent* unchaste, impure, lustful, licentious, lewd, corrupt, sullied, degenerate, bad, wicked, evil, sinful. **4** *unclean food* forbidden, impure.

uncomfortable adj **1** *uncomfortable chairs/shoes/houses* not comfortable. **2** *feel uncomfortable in their presence* uneasy, ill-at-ease, nervous, tense, edgy, self-conscious, awkward, embarrassed, discomfited, disturbed, troubled, worried, anxious apprehensive. **3** *an uncomfortable silence* awkward, uneasy, unpleasant, disagreeable, painful, distressing, disturbing.

uncommitted adj **1** *uncommitted young people* unpledged, unpromised, unengaged, unbetrothed, unmarried, free, available, unattached, single. **2** *uncommitted politically* non-aligned, non-partisan, neutral, undecided, floating, undeclared, sitting on the fence.

uncommon adj **1** *an uncommon name* unusual, rare, uncustomary, unfamiliar, strange, odd, curious, out of the ordinary, novel, singular, peculiar, queer, bizarre; *inf* weird. **2** *those birds are uncommon here* rare, scarce, infrequent, few and far between, occasional. **3** *an uncommon resemblance/appetite* remarkable, extraordinary, exceptional, singular, outstanding, notable, noteworthy, distinctive, striking.

uncommonly adv *uncommonly talented* unusually, remarkably, extraordinarily, exceptionally, singularly, particularly, strikingly, extremely, inordinately, incredibly, amazingly.

uncommunicative adj taciturn, reserved, shy, retiring, diffident, reticent, quiet, unforthcoming, unconversational, untalkative, silent, tight-lipped, secretive, unresponsive, close, distant, remote, aloof, withdrawn, standoffish, unsociable, antisocial.

uncompromising adj rigid, stiff, inflexible, unbending, unyielding, hard-line, tough, immovable, firm, determined, dogged, obstinate, obdurate, tenacious, relentless, implacable, inexorable, intransigent.

unconcern n indifference, apathy, lack of interest, uninterestedness, nonchalance, insouciance, lack of involvement, passivity, dispassionateness, detachment, aloofness, remoteness.

unconcerned adj **1** *unconcerned with political issues* indifferent, apathetic, uninterested, uninvolved, dispassionate (about), detached (from), aloof (from), remote (from). **2** *she is completely unconcerned despite her difficulties* unworried, untroubled, unperturbed, unruffled, unanxious, insouciant, nonchalant, carefree, blithe, without a care in the world, serene, relaxed, at ease.

unconditional adj complete, total, entire, full, plenary, outright, absolute, downright, out and out, utter, all-out, thoroughgoing, unequivocal, conclusive, definite, positive, indubitable, incontrovertible, categorical, unqualified, unlimited, unreserved, unrestricted.

unconnected n **1** *the two houses are unconnected* unjoined, detached, independent, separate. **2** *the two events are unconnected* unassociated, unrelated, separate. **3** *his prose style is unconnected | unconnected prose* disconnected, disjointed, rambling, diffuse, ununified, disorderly, haphazard, disorganized, incoherent, meaningless.

unconscionable adj **1** *an unconscionable criminal* amoral, immoral, unethical, unprincipled, unscrupulous, dishonourable, dishonest, corrupt. **2** *an unconscionable length of time* excessive, unwarranted, uncalled-for, unreasonable, inordinate, immoderate, undue, outrageous, preposterous, inexcusable.

unconscious adj **1** *fall unconscious* senseless, insensible, comatose, knocked out, stunned, dazed; *inf* blacked out, KO'd, out like a light, laid out, flaked-out, out cold, out. **2** *unconscious of the noise* unaware, heedless, ignorant, in ignorance, incognizant, oblivious, insensible. **3** *deliver an unconscious insult* unintentional, unintended, accidental, unthinking, unwitting, inadvertent, unpremeditated. **4** *unconscious prejudice* instinctive, automatic, reflex, involuntary, inherent, innate, subliminal, subconscious, latent.

uncontrollable adj **1** *uncontrollable children* out of control, unmanageable, ungovernable, wild, unruly, disorderly, restive, recalcitrant, refractory, intractable, incorrigible, contumacious. **2** *uncontrollable rages* ungovernable, unrestrained, wild, violent, frantic, frenzied, raging, raving, mad.

unconventional adj unorthodox, irregular, informal, unusual, uncommon, uncustomary, unwonted, rare, out of the ordinary, atypical, singular, individual, individualistic, different, original, idiosyncratic, nonconformist, bohemian, eccentric, odd, strange, bizarre; *inf* offbeat, freakish, way-out.

uncoordinated adj *uncoordinated people always dropping things* clumsy, awkward, inept, maladroit, bungling, blundering, bumbling, lumbering, heavy-footed, clodhopping, graceless, ungainly; *inf* butterfingered, all thumbs, like a bull in a china shop; *Amer inf* klutzy.

uncouth adj rough, coarse, uncivilized, uncultured, uncultivated, unrefined, unpolished, unsophisticated, provincial, crude, gross, loutish, boorish, oafish, churlish, uncivil, rude, impolite, discourteous,

unmannerly, bad-mannered, ill-bred, vulgar.

uncover v **1** *uncover the wound/food* expose, lay bare, bare, reveal, unwrap. **2** *uncover a plot against the president* discover, detect, unearth, dig up, expose, bring to light, unmask, unveil, reveal, lay bare, make known, divulge, disclose.

unctuous adj **1** *unctuous followers at court | unctuous behaviour* sycophantic, ingratiating, obsequious, fawning, servile, toadying, insincere, flattering, honey-tongued, gushing, effusive, suave, urbane, glib, smooth. **2** *unctuous substance* oily, oleaginous, greasy, soapy, saponaceous.

undaunted adj undismayed, unalarmed, unafraid, unflinching, unfaltering, indomitable, resolute, unflagging, intrepid, bold, valiant, brave, courageous, heroic, doughty, plucky; *inf* spunky.

undeceive v *undeceive her of the error* put right, set straight, disabuse, enlighten, be honest with, disillusion, disenchant.

undecided adj **1** *the result is as yet undecided* uncertain, unsettled, unresolved, indefinite, unknown, unestablished, unascertained, pending, in the balance, up in the air. **2** *they are undecided as to what to do* unsure, uncertain, doubtful, dubious, unresolved, indecisive, irresolute, hesitant, wavering, vacillating, equivocating, dithering, vague, hazy, unclear, ambivalent, in two minds.

undefined adj **1** *an undefined reason/plan* unexplained, non-specific, unspecified, indeterminate, unclear, vague, imprecise, inexact. **2** *undefined shapes* indefinite, indistinct, vague, hazy, nebulous, dim, obscure, blurred, shadowy, formless.

undemonstrative adj unemotional, impassive, restrained, self-contained, reserved, uncommunicative, unresponsive, stiff, reticent, aloof, distant, remote, withdrawn, cool, cold, unaffectionate.

undeniable adj indisputable, indubitable, unquestionable, beyond doubt/question, inarguable, incontrovertible, incontestable, irrefutable, unassailable, certain, sure, definite, positive, proven, clear, obvious, evident, manifest, patent.

under prep **1** *under the tree* below, beneath, underneath, at the foot/bottom of. **2** *prices under £5 | numbers under 20* below, less than, lower than, smaller than. **3** *ranks under major* below, lower than, inferior to, subordinate to, junior to, secondary to, subservient to, reporting to, subject to, controlled by, at the mercy of, under the heel of. **4** *under repair* undergoing, receiving, in the process of. **5** *under water* submerged by, immersed in, sunk in, engulfed by, inundated by, flooded by, drowned by. **6** *it is under his mother's name* listed under, classified under, categorized under, placed under, positioned under, included under, subsumed under. **7** *living under threat* subject to, liable to, bound by.

under adv **1** *if you cannot go over the bridge go under* below, beneath, underneath. **2** *his father kept him under* down, in an inferior position, in a subordinate position; *inf* under someone's thumb. **3** *the swimmer went under* underwater, to the bottom, downward.

underclothes npl undergarments; underclothing, underwear, lingerie, underlinen; *inf* underthings, undies, smalls, unmentionables.

undercover adj **1** *an undercover operation | undercover behaviour* secret, hidden, concealed, masked, veiled, shrouded, private, confidential, covert, clandestine, underground, surreptitious, furtive, stealthy, sly, underhand; *inf* hush-hush. **2** *undercover agents* spying, espionage.

undercurrent n **1** *boats affected by the undercurrent* undertow, underflow. **2** *an undercurrent of discontent in the firm* undertone, overtone, hint, suggestion, implication, whisper, murmur, atmosphere, aura, tenor, flavour; vibrations; *inf* vibes.

undercut v **1** *undercut their competitors* charge less than, undersell. **2** *undercut the ore vein* cut out, cut away, gouge out, scoop out, hollow out, excavate. **3** *laws undercutting democracy* undermine, weaken, impair, damage, injure, sap, threaten, subvert, sabotage.

underdog n weaker party, loser, victim, prey, scapegoat; *inf* little fellow, fall guy, stooge.

underestimate v **1** *underestimate the cost* miscalculate, misjudge, set too low. **2** *underestimate the opposition* underrate, rate too low, undervalue, set little store by, not do justice to, misprize, minimize, hold cheap, belittle, disparage, look down on, deprecate, depreciate; *inf* sell short.

undergo v *undergo surgery/hardship* go through, experience, sustain, be subjected to, submit to, endure, bear, tolerate, stand, withstand, put up with, weather.

underground adv **1** *animals going underground* below ground, below the surface. **2** *criminals going underground* into secrecy,

into seclusion, into hiding, behind closed doors.

underground adj **1** *underground shelters* subterranean, subterrestrial, below-ground, buried, sunken, hypogean. **2** *an underground organization* secret, clandestine, surreptitious, covert, undercover, concealed, hidden. **3** *underground literature* unconventional, unorthodox, experimental, avant-garde, alternative, radical, revolutionary, subversive.

underground n **1** *go round London by underground* metro, subway; *inf* tube. **2** *the army executing members of the underground* resistance, opposition; partisans.

undergrowth n underwood, thicket, brushwood, brush, scrub; *Amer* underbrush, underbush.

underhand adj deceitful, devious, crafty, cunning, scheming, sneaky, furtive, secret, clandestine, surreptitious, covert, dishonest, dishonourable, unethical, immoral, unscrupulous, fraudulent, dirty, unfair, treacherous, double-dealing, below the belt, two-timing; *inf* crooked.

underline v **1** *underline the word* underscore, emphasize. **2** *underline the importance of seat belts* emphasize, stress, highlight, point up, accentuate, call attention to, give prominence to.

underling n subordinate, deputy, junior, inferior, minion, lackey, flunky, menial, retainer, hireling, servant.

underlying adj **1** *underlying issues* basic, basal, fundamental, primary, prime, root, elementary, elemental. **2** *an underlying hostility amid all the friendliness* latent, lurking, concealed, hidden, veiled, masked.

undermine v **1** *undermine their authority* weaken, impair, damage, injure, sap, threaten, subvert, sabotage; *inf* throw a spanner in the works of, queer the pitch of, foul up. **2** *undermine the foundations* tunnel under, dig under, burrow under, excavate. **3** *undermine the river banks* wear away, erode, eat away at.

underprivileged adj disadvantaged, deprived, in need, needy, in want, destitute, in distress, poor, impoverished, impecunious, badly off.

underrate v underestimate, undervalue, set little store by, rate too low, not do justice to, belittle, disparage; *inf* sell short. *see* UNDERESTIMATE.

undersized adj undersize, underdeveloped, stunted, atrophied, dwarf, dwarfish, pygmy, runtish, short, small, little, tiny, miniscule, stubby, squat; *inf* pint-sized, pocket-sized, knee-high to a grasshopper.

understand v **1** *understand his meaning* | *understand what he says* comprehend, apprehend, grasp, see, take in, perceive, discern, make out, glean, recognize, appreciate, get to know, follow, fathom, get to the bottom of, penetrate, interpret; *inf* get the hang/ drift of, catch on, latch on to, tumble to, twig, figure out. **2** *I understand your feelings/ position* appreciate, accept, commiserate with, feel compassionate towards, sympathize with, empathize with. **3** *I understand that he has left* gather, hear, be informed, learn, believe, think, conclude.

understanding n **1** *it depends on your understanding of his meaning* comprehension, apprehension, grasp, perception, discernment, appreciation, interpretation. *see* UNDERSTAND 1. **2** *his powers of understanding are limited* | *use your understanding* intelligence, intellect, mind, brainpower; brains, powers of reasoning; *inf* grey matter. **3** *it is my understanding that he has gone* belief, perception, view, notion, idea, fancy, conclusion, feeling. **4** *treat the difficult problem with understanding* compassion, sympathy, empathy, insight. **5** *we have an understanding although not a signed contact* agreement, gentleman's agreement, arrangement, bargain, pact, compact, contract.

understanding adj *an understanding boss to give him time off* compassionate, sympathetic, sensitive, considerate, kind, thoughtful, tolerant, patient, forbearing, lenient, merciful, forgiving.

understate v *understate the difficulties* downplay, play down, make light of, minimize, de-emphasize; *inf* soft-pedal.

understudy n substitute, replacement, reserve, stand-in, fill-in, locum, backup, relief.

undertake v *undertake the job/responsibility* take on, set about, tackle, shoulder, assume, enter upon, begin, start, commence, embark on, venture upon, attempt, try.

undertaker n funeral director; *Amer* mortician.

undertone n **1** *speak in an undertone* low tone/voice, murmur, whisper. **2** *undertones of unrest in their seemingly peaceful life* undercurrent, hint, suggestion, intimation, inkling, insinuation, trace, tinge, touch, atmosphere, aura, tenor, flavour.

undervalue v underestimate, underrate, set little store by, rate too low, think too little

of, not do justice to, belittle, disparage; *inf* sell short. *see* UNDERESTIMATE.

underwater adj submarine, subaqueous, undersea, submerged, immersed.

underwear n underclothes, undergarments; underclothing, lingerie, underlinen; *inf* underthings, undies, smalls, unmentionables.

underworld n **1** *police trying to arrest members of the underworld* | *the underworld revenged his death* criminal world, world of crime, organized crime; criminals, gangsters; *inf* gangland, mob. **2** *Orpheus in the underworld* abode of the dead, nether/infernal regions, hell, Hades, Avernus.

underwrite v **1** *underwrite the official document* sign, countersign, endorse, initial. **2** *underwrite the agreement* agree to, approve, sanction, confirm, ratify, validate; *inf* okay, OK. **3** *underwrite the new project fund*, finance, back, support, sponsor, subsidize, contribute to, insure.

undesirable adj **1** *the undesirable side-effects of the drug* unpleasant, disagreeable, nasty, unacceptable, unwanted, unwished-for. **2** *he's a most undesirable character* unpleasant, disagreeable, nasty, foul, objectionable, offensive, obnoxious, disliked, hateful, repugnant, repellent, distasteful, unsavoury.

undisciplined adj **1** *undisciplined pupils* unruly, disorderly, disobedient, obstreperous, recalcitrant, refractory, uncontrolled, unrestrained, wild, wilful, wayward, capricious, unsteady, untrained, unschooled. **2** *undisciplined office methods* unsystematic, unmethodical, disorganized, unorganized, erratic, lax.

undisguised adj *undisguised envy* open, obvious, evident, patent, manifest, transparent, overt, unconcealed, unhidden, unmistakable.

undisputed adj uncontested, unchallenged, unquestioned, not in question, undoubted, not in doubt, certain, accepted, acknowledged, recognized, incontestable, unquestionable, indubitable, incontrovertible, irrefutable.

undistinguished adj ordinary, common, plain, simple, commonplace, everyday, mediocre, run-of-the-mill, pedestrian, prosaic, unexceptional, indifferent, unimpressive, unremarkable, unnoticeable, inconspicuous; *inf* nothing special, no big deal, no great shakes, nothing to write home about.

undo v **1** *undo buttons/laces/bonds/locks* unfasten, unhook, unbutton, untie, unlace, unbind, unfetter, unshackle, loosen, loose, disentangle, release, free, open, unlock. **2** *undo the arrangement/agreement* cancel, annul, nullify, invalidate, revoke, repeal, rescind, reverse, set aside, wipe out. **3** *undo all his work/hopes* destroy, ruin, wreck, smash, shatter, annihilate, eradicate, obliterate, defeat, conquer, overthrow, overturn, topple, upset, quash, squelch, crush.

undoing n **1** *the undoing of all his work/hopes* destruction, ruin, ruination, downfall, defeat, overthrow, collapse. *see* UNDO 3. **2** *his drunkenness was his undoing* fatal flaw, weakness, blight, misfortune, affliction, trouble, curse.

undone adj *leave tasks undone* not done, unfinished, incomplete, unaccomplished, unperformed, unfulfilled, unattended to, omitted, neglected, passed over, disregarded, ignored, left, outstanding.

undoubted adj undisputed, not in doubt, uncontested, unquestioned, not in question, certain, unquestionable, indubitable, incontrovertible, irrefutable. *see* UNDISPUTED.

undoubtedly adv indubitably, doubtless, doubtlessly, beyond a doubt, unquestionably, beyond question, undeniably, positively, absolutely, certainly, with certainty, decidedly, definitely, assuredly, of course.

undress v **1** *they undressed quickly* take off one's clothes, remove one's clothes, strip, disrobe; *inf* peel off. **2** *undress her daughter* unclothe, take off clothes from, remove clothes from, strip.

undress n *a state of undress* nakedness, nudity, *déshabillé*.

undue adj unwarranted, unjustified, unreasonable, inappropriate, unsuitable, unseemly, unbecoming, improper, ill-advised, excessive, immoderate, disproportionate, inordinate, fulsome, superfluous, too much, too great, uncalled-for, unneeded, unnecessary, non-essential, unrequired.

unduly adv *not unduly worried* excessively, overly, over-much, disproportionately, out of all proportion, immoderately, inordinately, unnecessarily, unreasonably, unjustifiably.

undying adj deathless, immortal, eternal, infinite, perpetual, unending, never ending, never dying, unceasing, ceaseless, incessant, permanent, lasting, endurable, abiding, continuing, constant, unfading, undiminished, imperishable, indestructible, undestroyed, inextinguishable.

unearth v **1** *dogs unearthing bones* dig up, excavate, exhume, disinter, unbury.

2 *unearth new evidence* uncover, discover, find, come across, hit upon, bring to light, reveal, expose, turn up, root up, dredge up, ferret out.

unearthly adj **1** *unearthly manifestations/sounds/happenings* otherworldly, not of this world, supernatural, preternatural, ghostly, spectral, phantom, haunted, uncanny, eerie, strange; *Scots* eldritch; *inf* spooky, creepy. **2** *come home at an unearthly hour* unreasonable, preposterous, abnormal, extraordinary, absurd, ridiculous; *inf* ungodly, unholy.

uneasy adj **1** *feel uneasy about what was happening* ill at ease, troubled, worried, anxious, apprehensive, alarmed, disturbed, agitated, nervous, on edge, edgy, restive, restless, unsettled, discomposed, discomfited, perturbed, upset; *inf* jittery, nervy. **2** *an uneasy peace* strained, constrained, tense, awkward, precarious, unstable, insecure. **3** *an uneasy suspicion that all was not well* worrying, alarming, dismaying, disturbing, perturbing, disquieting, unsettling, upsetting.

uneconomic adj *uneconomic industries | uneconomic to sell goods at that price* unprofitable, non-profit-making, non-paying, unremunerative, non-viable, loss-making.

unemotional adj undemonstrative, passionless, cold, frigid, cool, reserved, restrained, self-controlled, unfeeling, unresponsive, unexcitable, unmoved, impassive, apathetic, indifferent, phlegmatic, detached.

unemployed adj jobless, out of work, out of a job, workless, redundant, laid off, idle; *inf* on the dole.

unending adj endless, never ending, interminable, perpetual, ceaseless, incessant, unceasing, non-stop, uninterrupted, continuous, continual, constant, unremitting, relentless.

unenviable adj *an unenviable task* undesirable, unpleasant, disagreeable, nasty, painful, thankless.

unequal adj **1** *unequal in size/talent/difficulty* different, differing, dissimilar, unlike, unalike, disparate, unidentical, varying, variable, not uniform, unmatched. **2** *unequal to the task* not up to, inadequate, insufficient, found wanting. **3** *the sides of the box are unequal* uneven, asymmetrical, unsymmetrical, unbalanced, lopsided, irregular, disproportionate, not matching. **4** *unequal contest* unfair, unjust, inequitable, uneven, one-sided, ill-matched.

unequalled adj without equal, peerless, unmatched, unrivalled, unparalleled, without parallel, unsurpassed, incomparable, beyond compare, inimitable, perfect, supreme, paramount, second to none, nonpareil, unique.

unequivocal adj *an unequivocal statement/demand* unambiguous, clear, clear-cut, crystal clear, unmistakable, plain, well-defined, explicit, unqualified, categorical, outright, downright, direct, straightforward, blunt, point-blank, straight from the shoulder, positive, certain, decisive.

unethical adj immoral, unprincipled, unscrupulous, dishonourable, dishonest, disreputable, dirty, unfair, underhand, bad, wicked, evil, sinful, iniquitous, corrupt, depraved; *inf* shady.

uneven adj **1** *uneven surfaces* rough, bumpy, lumpy. **2** *his work is uneven* variable, varying, changeable, irregular, fluctuating, erratic, patchy. **3** *the sides of the box are uneven* unequal, asymmetrical, unsymmetrical, unbalanced, lopsided, irregular, disproportionate, not matching. **4** *an uneven contest* unequal, unfair, unjust, inequitable, one-sided, ill-matched.

uneventful adj unexciting, uninteresting, monotonous, boring, dull, tedious, routine, unvaried, ordinary, run-of-the-mill, pedestrian, commonplace, everyday, unexceptional, unremarkable, unmemorable; *inf* common or garden.

unexceptional adj ordinary, usual, regular, normal, average, typical, common, everyday, run-of-the-mill, mediocre, pedestrian, unremarkable, undistinguished, unimpressive; *inf* nothing special, nothing to write home about.

unexpected adj unforeseen, unanticipated, unlooked-for, unpredicted, not bargained for, sudden, abrupt, surprising, startling, astonishing, out of the blue, chance, fortuitous.

unfair adj **1** *an unfair judgement/receive unfair treatment* unjust, inequitable, partial, partisan, prejudiced, biased, one-sided, unequal, uneven, unbalanced. **2** *the punishment was unfair* undeserved, unmerited, uncalled-for, unreasonable, unjustifiable, unwarrantable, out of proportion, disproportionate, excessive, extreme, immoderate. **3** *unfair play* foul, unsporting, unsportsmanlike, dirty, below-the-belt, underhand, unscrupulous, dishonourable; *inf* crooked.

unfaithful adj **1** *unfaithful friends* disloyal, false, false-hearted, faithless, perfidious, treacherous, traitorous, untrustworthy, unreliable, undependable, insincere.

2 *unfaithful spouses* faithless, adulterous, fickle, untrue, inconstant; *inf* cheating, two-timing.

unfamiliar adj **1** *an unfamiliar face/this work is unfamiliar* unknown, new, strange, alien, unaccustomed, uncommon. **2** *I am unfamiliar with this method* unacquainted, unused to, unaccustomed, unconversant, unpractised, inexperienced, unskilled, uninformed, uninitiated.

unfashionable adj out of fashion/date, old-fashioned, outmoded, démodé, outdated, dated, behind the times, passé, archaic, obsolete, antiquated.

unfasten v undo, open, loose, detach, disconnect, untie, unwrap, unbind, unlace, unhitch, untether, unlock, unbolt.

unfavourable adj **1** *an unfavourable report/unfavourable reviews* adverse, critical, hostile, inimical, unfriendly, negative, discouraging, poor, bad. **2** *unfavourable circumstances* disadvantageous, adverse, unfortunate, unhappy, detrimental. **3** *come at an unfavourable moment* inconvenient, inopportune, untimely, untoward.

unfeeling adj *unfeeling people ignoring the poor* uncaring, unsympathetic, hard-hearted, hard, harsh, heartless, apathetic, cold, callous, cruel, pitiless, inhuman.

unfit adj **1** *she is unfit for the task* unsuited, ill-suited, unsuitable, unqualified, ineligible, unequipped, unprepared, untrained, incapable, inadequate, incompetent, not up to, not equal to; *inf* not cut out for. **2** *food unfit for human consumption* unsuitable, inappropriate, not good enough. **3** *unfit people taking up sport* out of condition, in poor condition/shape, out of kilter, flabby, unhealthy, debilitated, weak.

unflattering adj **1** *unflattering remarks* uncomplimentary, critical, blunt, candid, honest, straight from the shoulder. **2** *an unflattering hat* unbecoming, unattractive, unsightly.

unfold v **1** *unfold the map* open out, spread out, stretch out, flatten, straighten out, unfurl, unroll, unravel. **2** *unfold a tale of horror/unfold the events of the night* narrate, relate, recount, tell, reveal, make known, disclose, divulge, present. **3** *when our plans unfold* develop, evolve, grow, mature, bear fruit.

unforeseen adj unpredicted, unexpected, unanticipated, unlooked-for, not bargained for, sudden, abrupt, surprising, startling, astonishing, out of the blue.

unforgettable adj memorable, impressive, striking, outstanding, extraordinary, exceptional, remarkable.

unforgivable adj inexcusable, unpardonable, unwarrantable, unjustifiable, indefensible, reprehensible, deplorable, despicable, contemptible, disgraceful, shameful.

unfortunate adj 1 *unfortunate circumstance* adverse, disadvantageous, unfavourable, unlucky, untoward, unpromising, hostile, inimical, disastrous, calamitous. 2 *the unfortunate girl* unlucky, out of luck, luckless, ill-starred, star-crossed, hapless, wretched, miserable, unhappy, poor. 3 *an unfortunate remark* regrettable, deplorable, ill-advised, inappropriate, unsuitable, inapt, tactless. *see* UNHAPPY 4.

unfounded adj *unfounded rumours* without basis/foundation, groundless, baseless, unsubstantiated, unproven, unsupported, uncorroborated, speculative, conjectural, spurious.

unfriendly adj 1 *unfriendly neighbours/looks* unamicable, uncongenial, unsociable, inhospitable, unneighbourly, unkind, unsympathetic, aloof, cold, cool, distant, disagreeable, unpleasant, surly, sour, hostile, inimical, antagonistic, aggressive, quarrelsome. 2 *an unfriendly climate/atmosphere* unfavourable, disadvantageous, unpropitious, inauspicious, hostile, inimical, alien.

ungainly adj awkward, clumsy, ungraceful, graceless, inelegant, gawky, gangling, maladroit, inept, bungling, bumbling, lumbering, uncoordinated, hulking, lubberly.

ungodly adj 1 *ungodly people/acts* godless, irreligious, impious, blasphemous, profane, immoral, sinful, wicked, iniquitous. 2 *come home at an ungodly hour* unreasonable, preposterous, outrageous, abnormal, extraordinary, absurd, ridiculous; *inf* unholy, unearthly.

ungrateful adj unthankful, unappreciative, impolite, uncivil, rude.

unguarded adj 1 *an unguarded comment* careless, ill-advised, ill-considered, incautious, thoughtless, rash, foolhardy, indiscreet, imprudent, unwise, uncircumspect, undiplomatic. 2 *in an unguarded moment* off guard, unwary, inattentive, unobservant, unmindful, unheeding, heedless, distracted, absent-minded. 3 *unguarded fortresses* undefended, unprotected, defenceless, vulnerable, open to attack.

unhappy adj 1 *feeling unhappy* sad, miserable, sorrowful, dejected, despondent, disconsolate, broken-hearted, down, downcast, dispirited, crestfallen, depressed, melancholy, blue, gloomy, glum, mournful, woebegone, long-faced, joyless, cheerless. 2 *an unhappy girl* unfortunate, unlucky, luckless, hapless, ill-starred, ill-fated, star-crossed, wretched, miserable. 3 *unhappy circumstances* unfortunate, disadvantageous, unlucky, adverse, miserable, wretched. 4 *an unhappy choice of phrase* unfortunate, regrettable, inappropriate, unsuitable, inapt, tactless, untactful, ill-advised, injudicious, awkward, clumsy.

unhealthy adj 1 *unhealthy children* in poor health, unwell, ill, ailing, sick, sickly, poorly, indisposed, unsound, weak, feeble, frail, delicate, debilitated, infirm. 2 *an unhealthy diet/climate* unwholesome, unnourishing, detrimental, injurious, damaging, deleterious, noxious, insalubrious. 3 *show an unhealthy interest in death* unwholesome, morbid, undesirable.

unheard-of adj 1 *unheard-of authors* unknown, little-known, undiscovered, obscure, nameless, unsung. 2 *unheard-of levels of radiation* unprecedented, unexampled, exceptional, extraordinary, out of the ordinary, uncommon, unusual, unparalleled, unrivalled, unmatched, unequalled, singular, unique, unbelievable, inconceivable.

unheeded adj disregarded, ignored, neglected, overlooked, unobserved, unnoted.

unhinged adj unbalanced, deranged, demented, out of one's mind, crazed, mad, insane; *inf* crazy.

unholy adj 1 *unholy people/acts* ungodly, godless, irreligious, impious, blasphemous, profane, immoral, sinful, wicked, iniquitous. 2 *an unholy row* unreasonable, preposterous, outrageous, appalling, shocking, dreadful; *inf* ungodly.

unhoped-for adj unexpected, unanticipated, unlooked-for, undreamed of, beyond one's wildest dreams, like a dream come true.

unhurried adj leisurely, leisured, easy, slow, slow-moving, slow-going, slow and steady, deliberate, sedate, lingering, loitering.

unidentified adj *an unidentified donor/spot* nameless, unnamed, unknown, anonymous, incognito, obscure, unmarked, undesignated, unclassified.

unification n union, junction, merger, fusion, alliance, amalgamation, coalition, combination, consolidation, confederation.

uniform adj 1 *a uniform temperature* constant, consistent, invariable, unvarying, unvaried, unchanging, undeviating, stable, regular, even, equal, equable. **2** *all of uniform length* same, alike, like, selfsame, identical, similar, equal.

uniform n livery, regalia, habit, suit, dress, costume, garb; regimentals.

uniformity n **1** *the uniformity of the temperature is important* constancy, consistency, lack of variation/change, stability, regularity, evenness, equality, equability. **2** *uniformity of length of all the garments* sameness, likeness, identicalness, similarity, equalness, equality. **3** *tired of the uniformity of the days* sameness, monotony, tedium, dullness, drabness.

unify v unite, bring together, merge, fuse, amalgamate, coalesce, combine, blend, mix, bind, link up, consolidate.

unimaginable adj unthinkable, inconceivable, incredible, unbelievable, unheard-of, unthought-of, implausible, improbable, unlikely, impossible, undreamed of, fantastic, beyond one's wildest dreams; *inf* mindboggling, mind-blowing.

unimaginative adj *an unimaginative description* unoriginal, uninspired, uncreative, commonplace, pedestrian, mundane, matter-of-fact, ordinary, usual, routine, humdrum, prosaic, stale, hackneyed, derived, dull, monotonous, lifeless, vapid, insipid, bland, dry; *inf* common or garden.

unimportant adj of little/no importance, insignificant, of little/no consequence, inconsequential, of no account/moment, non-essential, immaterial, irrelevant, not worth mentioning, not worth speaking of, minor, slight, trifling, trivial, petty, paltry, insubstantial, inferior, worthless, nugatory; *inf* small-fry, no great shakes; *Amer inf* dinky.

uninhabited adj *uninhabited houses/places* vacant, empty, unoccupied, untenanted, unpopulated, unpeopled, unsettled, abandoned, deserted, forsaken, unfrequented, barren, desert, desolate.

uninhibited adj **1** *her sister is completely uninhibited* unreserved, unrepressed, unconstrained, unselfconscious, spontaneous, free and easy, relaxed, informal, open, candid, outspoken. **2** *uninhibited behaviour* unrestrained, unrestricted, unrepressed, unconstrained, uncontrolled, uncurbed, unchecked, unbridled.

unintelligible adj **1** *unintelligible ramblings* incomprehensible, meaningless, unfathomable, incoherent, indistinct, inarticulate, confused, muddled, jumbled. **2** *unintelligible handwriting* illegible, undecipherable.

unintentional adj unintended, accidental, inadvertent, unplanned, unpremeditated, uncalculated, chance, fortuitous, unconscious, involuntary, unwitting, unthinking.

uninterested adj **1** *uninterested in other people's problems* indifferent, unconcerned, uninvolved, apathetic, blasé, unresponsive, impassive, dispassionate, aloof, detached, distant. **2** *uninterested in the lecture* bored, incurious.

uninteresting adj unexciting, dull, unentertaining, boring, tiresome, wearisome, tedious, dreary, flat, monotonous, humdrum, uneventful, commonplace, dry, pedestrian, prosaic, hackneyed, stale.

uninterrupted adj unbroken, undisturbed, continuous, continual, constant, steady, sustained, non-stop, unending, endless, ceaseless, unceasing, incessant, interminable, unremitting.

uninviting adj unappealing, untempting, undesirable, unattractive, unappetizing, unpleasant, disagreeable, distasteful, unpalatable, repellent, revolting, repugnant, sickening, nauseating, offensive; *inf* off-putting.

union n **1** *the union of three firms into one* joining, junction, merging, merger, fusion, amalgamating, amalgamation, blend, mixture, coalition, combining, combination, consolidation, confederation. **2** *the union is made up of several organizations* association, alliance, league, coalition, consortium, syndicate, guild, confederation, federation, confederacy. **3** *the union of the man and the woman* marriage, wedding, coupling, intercourse, coition, coitus, copulation. **4** *we are all in union about the plans* agreement, accord, concurrence, unity, unison, unanimity, harmony, concord.

unique adj **1** *a unique specimen* only, one and only, single, sole, lone, solitary, *sui generis*, exclusive, in a class by itself. **2** *a unique opportunity/beauty* unequalled, without equal, unparalleled, unexampled, unmatched, matchless, peerless, unsurpassed, unexcelled, incomparable, beyond compare, inimitable, second to none.

unison n *the committee was in unison* agreement, accord, harmony, concord.

unit n **1** *the family regarded as a unit* entity, whole. **2** *the course is divided into units* component, part, section, element, constituent, subdivision, portion, segment, module, item, member. **3** *a unit of length* measurement, measure, quantity.

unite v **1** *unite the two parties/firms* join, link, connect, combine, amalgamate, fuse, weld.

2 *unite the two substances* combine, mix, commix, admix, blend, mingle, homogenize. **3** *unite this man and this woman* marry, wed, join in wedlock, tie the knot between; *inf* splice. **4** *they united to fight the common enemy* join together, join forces, combine, amalgamate, band/club together, ally, cooperate, work/act/pull together, work side by side, pool resources.

united adj **1** *a united force/effort* combined, amalgamated, allied, cooperative, concerted, collective, pooled. *see* UNITE 4. **2** *united in their opinion of the plan* in agreement, agreed, in unison, of the same opinion/mind, of like mind, like-minded, at one, in accord, unanimous.

unity n **1** *detract from the unity of the painting* oneness, singleness, wholeness, entity, integrity. **2** *their strength lies in their unity* union, unification, amalgamation, coalition, alliance, cooperation, undividedness. **3** *strive for political unity | live in unity* agreement, harmony, accord, concord, concurrence, unanimity, consensus, concert, togetherness, solidarity.

universal adj general, all-embracing, all-inclusive, comprehensive, across the board, worldwide, global, widespread, common, predominant, preponderate, omnipresent, ubiquitous, catholic.

universally adv without exception, in all instances/cases, everywhere, comprehensively, uniformly, invariably.

universe n **1** *the wonders of the universe* cosmos, totality, whole world, Creation. **2** *the achievements of the universe* mankind, humankind, human race, humanity, people, society.

unjust adj **1** *an unjust verdict* unfair, inequitable, prejudiced, biased, partisan, partial, one-sided. **2** *an unjust accusation* unfair, wrongful, wrong, undue, undeserved, unmerited, unwarranted, uncalled-for, unreasonable, unjustifiable.

unjustifiable adj **1** *unjustifiable behaviour* indefensible, inexcusable, unforgivable, unpardonable, uncalled-for, blameworthy, culpable, unwarrantable. **2** *unjustifiable fears/accusations* groundless, unfounded, without foundation, baseless, without basis, unsupported, unsubstantiated, unreasonable.

unkempt adj *unkempt hair/people* untidy, dishevelled, disordered, disarranged, tousled, rumpled, windblown, uncombed, ungroomed, messy, messed up, scruffy, slovenly; *inf* sloppy; *Amer inf* mussed up.

unkind adj **1** *unkind people/remarks* unkindly, unfriendly, unamiable, uncharitable, unchristian, inhospitable, ungenerous, nasty, mean, cruel, vicious, spiteful, malicious, malevolent, harsh, pitiless, ruthless, unsympathetic, unfeeling, hard-hearted, heartless, cold-hearted. **2** *an unkind climate* inclement, harsh, intemperate.

unknown adj **1** *the results of the test are as yet unknown* untold, unrevealed, undisclosed, undivulged, undetermined, undecided, unestablished, unsettled, unascertained, in the balance, up in the air. **2** *the donor is unknown* unidentified, unnamed, nameless, anonymous, incognito. **3** *unknown territory* unfamiliar, unexplored, uncharted, untravelled, undiscovered. **4** *unknown poets* unheard-of, little-known, obscure, undistinguished, unrenowned, unsung.

unlawful adj against the law, illegal, illicit, illegitimate, criminal, felonious, actionable, prohibited, banned, outlawed, proscribed, unauthorized, unsanctioned, unwarranted, unlicensed.

unlike adj unalike, dissimilar, different, distinct, disparate, contrastive, contrasted, contrary, diverse, divergent, incompatible, ill-matched, incongruous; *inf* like chalk and cheese.

unlike prep not like, not typical of, differently from.

unlikely adj **1** *an unlikely chance of success* improbable, doubtful, dubious, faint, slight, remote. **2** *it is unlikely that he will win* not likely, improbable, unexpected. **3** *an unlikely excuse* improbable, implausible, questionable, unconvincing, incredible, unbelievable, inconceivable, unimaginable.

unlimited adj **1** *unlimited freedom | unlimited room for manoeuvre* unrestricted, unconstrained, uncontrolled, unrestrained, unchecked, unhindered, unhampered, unimpeded, unfettered, untrammelled. **2** *unlimited power* unrestricted, absolute, total, unqualified, unconditional. **3** *unlimited supplies of money* limitless, illimitable, boundless, unbounded, immense, vast, great, extensive, immeasurable, incalculable, untold, infinite, endless.

unload v *unload the horse/lorry* unburden, unlade, empty, unpack.

unlock v unbolt, unlatch, unbar, undo, unfasten.

unlooked-for adj unforeseen, unexpected, unanticipated, not bargained for, unhoped for, undreamed of, unpredicted, sudden, abrupt, surprise, surprising, startling, astonishing, out of the blue.

unloved adj unbeloved, uncared-for, uncherished, unwanted, unpopular, forsaken, rejected, jilted, disliked, hated, detested, loathed.

unlucky adj **1** *an unlucky young man* luckless, out of luck, down on one's luck, unfortunate, hapless, ill-fated, ill-starred, star-crossed, wretched, miserable. **2** *an unlucky attempt* unsuccessful, failed, ill-fated. **3** *an unlucky set of circumstances* adverse, disadvantageous, unfavourable, unfortunate, untoward, unpromising, inauspicious, unpropitious, doomed, ill-fated, ill-omened.

unmanageable adj **1** *an unmanageable load* unwieldy, unmanoeuvrable, awkward, inconvenient, cumbersome, bulky, incommodious. **2** *unmanageable children* unruly, disorderly, uncontrollable, ungovernable, out of hand, wild, difficult, refractory, recalcitrant, intractable, obstreperous, wayward, incorrigible, contumacious; *inf* stroppy.

unmanly adj **1** *an unmanly way of walking* effeminate, womanish; *inf* sissy. **2** *too unmanly to fight* timid, timorous, fearful, cowardly, craven, pusillanimous; *inf* yellow.

unmannerly adj ill-mannered, mannerless, impolite, uncivil, discourteous, disrespectful, rude, ill-bred, uncouth.

unmarried adj single, unwed, unwedded, spouseless, partnerless, divorced, unattached, bachelor, celibate; husbandless, wifeless.

unmistakable adj *the unmistakable noise of a train* clear, plain, obvious, evident, manifest, apparent, patent, palpable, distinct, distinctive, conspicuous, well-defined, pronounced, striking, glaring, blatant, undoubted, indisputable, indubitable, beyond a doubt, unquestionable, beyond question.

unmitigated adj *an unmitigated disaster* absolute, unqualified, unconditional, categorical, complete, total, thorough, thoroughgoing, downright, utter, out and out, veritable, perfect, consummate.

unmoved adj **1** *unmoved furniture* in place, in position, unchanged. **2** *unmoved from their purpose* firm, steadfast, unshaken, staunch, unwavering, unswerving, undeviating, determined, resolute, decided, resolved. **3** *unmoved by the sad sight* unaffected, untouched, unstirred, unconcerned, uncaring, indifferent, impassive, unfeeling, impervious.

unnatural adj **1** *his face turned an unnatural colour* unusual, uncommon, extraordinary, strange, queer, odd, bizarre, preternatural. **2** *unnatural mothers* inhuman, heartless, uncaring, unconcerned, unfeeling, soulless, cold, hard, hard-hearted, callous, cruel, brutal, merciless, pitiless, remorseless, evil, wicked. **3** *an unnatural laugh | unnatural behaviour* affected, artificial, feigned, false, self-conscious, contrived, forced, laboured, studied, strained, insincere, theatrical, stagy, mannered.

unnecessary adj **1** *it is unnecessary to come early* needless, inessential. **2** *unnecessary expense/supplies* needless, unneeded, inessential, non-essential, uncalled-for, unrequired, gratuitous, useless, dispensable, expendable, redundant, superfluous.

unnerve v unman, discourage, dishearten, dispirit, deject, demoralize, daunt, alarm, frighten, dismay, disconcert, discompose, perturb, upset, throw off balance, unsettle, disquiet, fluster, agitate, shake; *inf* rattle.

unobtrusive adj **1** *an unobtrusive person* self-effacing, retiring, unassuming, modest, quiet, meek, humble, unaggressive, unassertive, low-profile. **2** *unobtrusive decorations/colours* low-key, restrained, subdued, quiet, unostentatious, unshowy, inconspicuous, unnoticeable.

unoccupied adj **1** *unoccupied houses* vacant, empty, uninhabited, untenanted, tenantless. **2** *unoccupied territory* uninhabited, unpopulated, unpeopled, depopulated, deserted, forsaken, desolate, God-forsaken. **3** *he is unoccupied just now* not busy, at leisure, idle, inactive, unemployed.

unofficial adj **1** *an unofficial meeting* informal, casual, unauthorized, unsanctioned, unaccredited, wildcat. **2** *an unofficial rumour* unconfirmed, unauthenticated, uncorroborated, unsubstantiated.

unorthodox adj **1** *unorthodox beliefs* heterodox, uncanonical, heretical, nonconformist. **2** *unorthodox methods* unconventional, unusual, uncommon, uncustomary, unwonted, out of the ordinary, nonconformist, unconforming, irregular, abnormal, divergent, aberrant, anomalous.

unpalatable adj *unpalatable food/suggestions* unsavoury, unappetizing, uneatable, inedible, undelectable, nasty, disgusting, repugnant, revolting, nauseating, sickening, distasteful, disagreeable, unpleasant, offensive, obnoxious, unattractive, repulsive, repellent.

unparalleled adj without parallel, unequalled, without equal, matchless, unmatched, peerless, unrivalled, unprecedented, unsurpassed, unexcelled, incomparable, beyond compare, singular, unique.

unperturbed adj calm, composed, cool, collected, serene, tranquil, self-possessed, placid, unruffled, unflustered, unexcited, undismayed, untroubled, unworried; *inf* laid-back.

unpleasant adj **1** *an unpleasant taste* disagreeable, unpalatable, unsavoury, unappetizing, disgusting, repugnant, revolting, nauseating, sickening. **2** *an unpleasant smell* disagreeable, offensive, obnoxious, foul, smelly, stinking. **3** *unpleasant person/personality* disagreeable, unlikable, unlovable, unattractive, nasty, ill-natured, cross, bad-tempered. **4** *an unpleasant task* disagreeable, irksome, troublesome, annoying, irritating, vexatious.

unpopular adj disliked, unliked, unloved, friendless, unwanted, unwelcome, avoided, ignored, rejected, shunned, out in the cold, cold-shouldered, unattractive, undesirable, out of favour, not in the swim; *inf* sent to Coventry.

unprecedented adj unparalleled, unequalled, unmatched, unheard-of, extraordinary, uncommon, out of the ordinary, unusual, exceptional, abnormal, singular, anomalous, atypical, remarkable, novel, original, unique; *inf* one of a kind.

unpredictable adj **1** *unpredictable results* unforeseeable, undivinable, doubtful, dubious, uncertain, unsure, in the balance, up in the air; *inf* iffy. **2** *unpredictable people/behaviour* erratic, fickle, capricious, whimsical, mercurial, volatile, unstable, undependable, unreliable.

unpremeditated adj unplanned, unarranged, unprepared, unintentional, extempore, impromptu, ad lib, spontaneous, spur of the moment, on the spot, impulsive, hasty; *inf* off the cuff.

unpretentious adj **1** *an unpretentious house/lifestyle* simple, plain, modest, ordinary, humble, unostentatious, unshowy, unimposing, homely. **2** *an unpretentious person* unassuming, modest, unaffected, natural, straightforward, honest.

unprincipled adj immoral, amoral, unethical, dishonourable, dishonest, unprofessional, deceitful, devious, unscrupulous, corrupt, crooked, bad, wicked, evil, villainous.

unproductive adj **1** *an unproductive exercise* fruitless, futile, vain, idle, useless, worthless, valueless, ineffective, ineffectual, inefficacious, unprofitable, unremunerative,

unrewarding. **2** *unproductive soil* barren, sterile.

unprofessional adj **1** *unprofessional methods/conduct* unethical, unprincipled, improper, unseemly, indecorous, lax, negligent. **2** *unprofessional workers* amateur, amateurish, unskilled, inexpert, untrained, unqualified, inexperienced, incompetent.

unpromising adj *unpromising prospects* unfavourable, adverse, unpropitious, inauspicious, gloomy, black, discouraging, portentous, ominous.

unqualified adj **1** *unqualified teachers* uncertificated, unlicensed, untrained. **2** *unqualified to do the job | unqualified to comment* ineligible, unfit, incompetent, incapable, unequipped, unprepared, not equal/up to, not cut out. **3** *unqualified approval* unconditional, unreserved, without reservations, categorical, unequivocal, positive, unmitigated, complete, absolute, thorough, thoroughgoing, total, utter, outright, out and out, perfect, consummate.

unquestionable adj *his honesty is unquestionable* beyond question/doubt, indubitable, undoubted, indisputable, undeniable, irrefutable, uncontestable, incontrovertible, certain, sure, definite, positive, conclusive, self-evident, obvious.

unravel v **1** *unravel knots* untangle, disentangle, straighten out, separate out, unknot, undo. **2** *unravel the problem* solve, resolve, work out, clear up, puzzle out, get to the bottom of, fathom; *inf* figure out.

unreal adj *unreal characters/situation* imaginary, make-believe, fictitious, mythical, fanciful, fantastic, fabulous, hypothetical, non-existent, illusory, chimerical, phantasmagoric.

unrealistic adj **1** *an unrealistic plan* impractical, impracticable, unworkable, unreasonable, irrational, illogical, improbable, foolish, wild, absurd, quixotic; *inf* half-baked. **2** *an unrealistic model* unreal-looking, unlifelike, non-naturalistic.

unreasonable adj **1** *unreasonable demands* excessive, immoderate, undue, inordinate, outrageous, extravagant, preposterous, unconscionable. **2** *unreasonable prices* exorbitant, extortionate, expensive; *inf* steep. **3** *unreasonable people* irrational, illogical, opinionated, biased, prejudiced, blinkered, obstinate, obdurate, wilful, headstrong, temperamental, capricious. **4** *unreasonable behaviour* unacceptable, preposterous, outrageous, ludicrous, absurd, irrational, illogical.

unrefined · unshakable

unrefined adj **1** *unrefined flour* crude, raw, unpurified, unprocessed, untreated. **2** *unrefined guests/manners* uncultured, uncultivated, unsophisticated, inelegant, ungraceful, boorish, loutish, coarse, vulgar, rude, uncouth.

unrelenting adj **1** *unrelenting demands/rain* relentless, unremitting, continuous, continual, constant, incessant, unceasing, nonstop, endless, unending, perpetual, unabating. **2** *unrelenting judge* relentless, merciless, pitiless, unforgiving, unsparing, ruthless, implacable, inexorable, inflexible, rigid, hard, strict, harsh, stern.

unreliable adj **1** *unreliable friends* undependable, irresponsible, untrustworthy, erratic, fickle, inconstant. **2** *unreliable evidence* suspect, questionable, open to question/doubt, doubtful, unsound, implausible, unconvincing, fallible, specious.

unrepentant adj impenitent, unrepenting, unremorseful, shameless, unregenerate, abandoned.

unreserved adj **1** *unreserved seats* unbooked, unhired, unchartered. **2** *unreserved young women* uninhibited, extrovert, outgoing, unrestrained, demonstrative, bold, communicative, outspoken, frank, open. **3** *unreserved approval* without reservations, unqualified, unconditional, categorical, unequivocal, positive, unmitigated, absolute, complete, thorough, thoroughgoing, wholehearted, total, utter, outright, out and out, perfect, consummate.

unresolved adj undecided, to be decided, unsettled, undetermined, pending, unsolved, unanswered, debatable, open to debate/question, doubtful, in doubt, moot, up in the air; *inf* iffy.

unrest n *industrial unrest* dissatisfaction, discontent, discontentment, unease, disquiet, dissension, dissent, discord, strife, protest, rebellion, agitation, turmoil, turbulence.

unrestricted adj *unrestricted access* unlimited, open, free, unhindered, unchecked, unbounded; *inf* free for all, with no holds barred.

unrivalled adj unparalleled, unequalled, without equal, matchless, unmatched, peerless, unsurpassed, unexcelled, incomparable, beyond compare, singular, unique.

unruly adj disorderly, unmanageable, uncontrollable, rowdy, wild, irrepressible, obstreperous, refractory, recalcitrant, intractable, contumacious, disobedient, rebellious, mutinous, insubordinate, defiant, wayward, wilful, headstrong.

unsaid adj unspoken, unvoiced, unpronounced, unuttered, unstated, unmentioned, untold, untalked-of, tacit, suppressed, unrevealed.

unsavoury adj **1** *unsavoury food/smell* unpalatable, unappetizing, unpleasant, disagreeable, disgusting, loathsome, repugnant, revolting, nauseating, sickening. **2** *unsavoury characters* unpleasant, disagreeable, nasty, objectionable, offensive, obnoxious, repellent, repulsive, disreputable, degenerate, coarse, gross, vulgar, boorish, churlish, rude, uncouth.

unscrupulous adj unprincipled, unethical, amoral, immoral, conscienceless, shameless, corrupt, dishonest, dishonourable, deceitful, devious, exploitative, wrongdoing, bad, evil, wicked; *inf* crooked.

unseat v **1** *unseat the MP/king* depose, oust, remove from office, dislodge, discharge, dethrone; *inf* drum out. **2** *the horse unseated the rider* throw, dismount, unsaddle, unhorse.

unseemly adj unbecoming, unfitting, unbefitting, indecorous, improper, unsuitable, inappropriate, undignified, unrefined, indelicate, tasteless, in poor taste, coarse, crass.

unselfish adj altruistic, self-sacrificing, selfless, self-denying, open-handed, generous, liberal, unsparing, kind, ungrudging, unstinting, charitable, philanthropic.

unsettle v **1** *the move unsettled the children* upset, disturb, discompose, throw off balance, confuse, perturb, discomfit, disconcert, trouble, bother, agitate, ruffle, shake; *inf* rattle. **2** *unsettle the smooth workings of the firm* throw into confusion/disorder, disorder, disorganize, disarrange, derange.

unsettled adj **1** *the children are unsettled* restless, restive, fidgety, flustered, agitated, ruffled, uneasy, anxious, edgy, on edge, tense, troubled, perturbed, shaken; *inf* thrown, rattled. **2** *the weather is unsettled* changeable, changing, variable, inconstant, erratic, undependable, unreliable, uncertain, unpredictable. **3** *several issues are still unsettled* undecided, to be decided, unresolved, undetermined, pending, open to debate/question, doubtful, in doubt, moot, up in the air; *inf* iffy. **4** *unsettled accounts* unpaid, payable, outstanding, owing, due, in arrears. **5** *unsettled territories* uninhabited, unpopulated, unpeopled, unoccupied.

unshakable adj firm, steadfast, resolute, staunch, constant, unswerving, unwavering, unfaltering.

unsightly adj ugly, unattractive, unprepossessing, hideous, horrible, repulsive, revolting, offensive, distasteful.

unskilled adj untrained, unqualified, inexpert, inexperienced, amateurish, unprofessional.

unsociable adj unfriendly, unamiable, unaffable, uncongenial, unneighbourly, inhospitable, reclusive, solitary, misanthropic, uncommunicative, unforthcoming, reticent, withdrawn, aloof, distant, remote, standoffish, cold, cool, chilly.

unsolicited adj unsought, unasked-for, unrequested, undemanded, uncalled-for, unrequired, uninvited, unwelcome, gratuitous, volunteered, voluntary, spontaneous.

unsophisticated adj **1** *unsophisticated country girls* unworldly, naïve, simple, innocent, inexperienced, childlike, artless, guileless, ingenuous, natural, unaffected, unpretentious, unrefined, unpolished, gauche, provincial. **2** *unsophisticated tools* crude, unrefined, basic, rudimentary, primitive, undeveloped, homespun. **3** *unsophisticated methods | unsophisticated approach to the problem* simple, straightforward, uncomplicated, uninvolved, unspecialized.

unsound adj **1** *in unsound health* unhealthy, unwell, ailing, delicate, weak, frail. **2** *of unsound mind* disordered, diseased, deranged, demented, unbalanced, unhinged. **3** *unsound furniture* defective, disintegrating, broken, broken-down, rotten, rickety, flimsy, shaky, wobbly, tottery, insubstantial, unsafe, unreliable, dangerous. **4** *unsound reasoning* flawed, defective, faulty, ill-founded, weak, shaky, unreliable, illogical, unfounded, ungrounded, untenable, specious, spurious, false, fallacious, erroneous.

unspeakable adj **1** *unspeakable joy* beyond words, inexpressible, unutterable, indescribable, undefinable, beggaring description, ineffable, unimaginable, inconceivable, unthinkable, unheard-of, overwhelming, marvellous, wonderful. **2** *an unspeakable scoundrel/crime* indescribable, indescribably bad/wicked/evil, unmentionable, appalling, shocking, horrible, frightful, terrible, dreadful, abominable, deplorable, despicable, contemptible, repellent, loathsome, odious, monstrous, heinous, execrable.

unspoilt adj **1** *unspoilt countryside* preserved, intact, as good as new/before, perfect, unblemished, unimpaired, undamaged, untouched, unaffected, unchanged. **2** *unspoilt young girls | unspoilt despite her success* innocent, wholesome, natural, simple,

artless, unaffected, pure, uncorrupted, undefiled, unblemished.

unspoken adj **1** *unspoken criticism* unexpressed, unstated, undeclared, not spelt out, tacit, implicit, implied, understood, taken for granted. **2** *unspoken plea for mercy* mute, silent, wordless, unuttered.

unstable adj **1** *unstable chairs* unsteady, infirm, rickety, shaky, wobbly, tottery, unsafe, unreliable, insecure, precarious. **2** *unstable people likely to kill* unbalanced, unhinged, irrational, deranged, mentally ill, crazed, insane, mad. **3** *emotionally unstable* unbalanced, volatile, moody, mercurial, capricious, giddy, erratic, unpredictable. **4** *unstable prices* changeable, variable, unsettled, fluctuating, inconstant, unpredictable.

unstudied adj *unstudied grace* natural, unaffected, unpretentious, without airs, artless, guileless, informal, casual, spontaneous, impromptu.

unsubstantial adj **1** *unsubstantial furniture* insubstantial, flimsy, fragile, frail, slight, puny, inadequate, insufficient; *inf* jerry-built. **2** *unsubstantial arguments/evidence* insubstantial, flimsy, tenuous, weak, lame, poor, unsound, faulty, ungrounded, groundless, unfounded, baseless, unsupported. **3** *unsubstantial figures* insubstantial, imaginary, unreal, impalpable, incorporeal, illusory, chimerical, hallucinatory, phantom, ghostly.

unsubstantiated adj unconfirmed, uncorroborated, unproven, not validated, unestablished, questionable, open to question, disputable.

unsuccessful adj **1** *an unsuccessful attempt* without success, failed, vain, unavailing, futile, useless, worthless, abortive, nugatory, ineffective, ineffectual, inefficacious, fruitless, unproductive, unprofitable, baulked, frustrated, thwarted, foiled. **2** *an unsuccessful businessman* failed, losing, unprosperous, unlucky, luckless, out of luck, unfortunate, ill-starred, ill-fated.

unsuitable adj inappropriate, inapt, inapposite, unfitting, unbefitting, incompatible, incongruous, out of place/keeping, inelegible, unacceptable, unbecoming, unseemly, indecorous, improper.

unsung adj unacclaimed, unapplauded, uncelebrated, unhonoured, unpraised, unlauded, unhailed, unacknowledged, unrecognized, unrenowned, neglected, disregarded, unknown, anonymous, nameless.

unsure adj **1** *he was a bit unsure at first | unsure of himself* lacking self-confidence, unselfconfident, not confident, not self-assured, lacking assurance, insecure, hesitant, diffident. **2** *unsure what to do* undecided, irresolute, in two minds, in a dilemma/quandary, ambivalent. **3** *unsure about his motive* uncertain, unconvinced, dubious, doubtful, sceptical, distrustful, suspicious.

unsuspecting adj unsuspicious, unwary, off guard, trusting, trustful, overtrustful, gullible, credulous, ingenuous, naïve, innocent, dupable, exploitable.

unsympathetic adj **1** *unsympathetic parents* unsympathizing, unkind, uncompassionate, compassionless, unpitying, pitiless, uncommiserating, uncaring, unfeeling, insensitive, unconcerned, indifferent, unresponsive, apathetic, unmoved, untouched, heartless, cold, hard-hearted, stony-hearted, hard, harsh, callous, cruel. **2** *unsympathetic to his cause* disapproving of, opposed to, against, anti.

untangle v **1** *untangle the knotted wool* disentangle, unravel, unsnarl, straighten out. **2** *untangle the complications* straighten out, sort out, clear up.

untenable adj indefensible, undefendable, insupportable, unmaintainable, unsustainable, refutable, unsound, weak, flawed, defective, faulty, implausible, specious, groundless, unfounded, baseless, unacceptable, unadmissible.

unthinkable adj **1** *it is unthinkable that the territory is unexplored* inconceivable, unimaginable, unbelievable, beyond belief, impossible, beyond the bounds of possibility, implausible. **2** *it is unthinkable that he should represent us* not to be considered, out of the question, absurd, preposterous, outrageous; *inf* not on.

unthinking adj **1** *hurt by an unthinking remark* thoughtless, inconsiderate, tactless, undiplomatic, injudicious, indiscreet, insensitive, blundering, careless, rude. **2** *an unthinking kick of the ball* inadvertent, unintentional, unintended, mechanical, automatic, instinctive, involuntary.

untidy n **1** *untidy children* dishevelled, unkempt, bedraggled, rumpled, messy, slovenly, slatternly; *inf* mussed up, sloppy. **2** *untidy desks/rooms* disordered, disorderly, disarranged, disorganized, chaotic, confused, muddled, jumbled, topsy-turvy, at sixes and sevens; *inf* higgledy-piggledy, like a dog's breakfast, every which way.

untie v undo, loose, unbind, unfasten, unwrap, unlace, untether, unhitch, unknot.

untimely adj **1** *an untimely visit* ill-timed, mistimed, inconvenient, inopportune, inappropriate, inapt, awkward, unsuitable, infelicitous. **2** *his untimely death* premature, early.

untiring adj tireless, indefatigable, unfailing, unfaltering, unwavering, unflagging, unremitting, constant, incessant, unceasing, dogged, determined, resolute, steady, persistent, staunch.

untold adj **1** *her untold story | untold secrets* unrecounted, unrelated, unnarrated, unreported, unmentioned, unstated, unspoken, unrevealed, undisclosed, undivulged, unpublished, secret. **2** *the untold horrors of the war | untold joy* unspeakable, indescribable, inexpressible, unutterable, ineffable, unimaginable, inconceivable. **3** *untold millions/damage* countless, innumerable, myriad, incalculable, immeasurable, measureless.

untoward adj **1** *untoward developments delayed us* unfortunate, inconvenient, inopportune, untimely, awkward, annoying, troublesome, vexatious. **2** *do their best in untoward circumstances* unfortunate, unlucky, adverse, disadvantageous, inauspicious, unpropitious, hostile, inimical. **3** *see nothing untoward in his reaction* unusual, uncommon, abnormal, atypical, out of the way, out of place. **4** *find nothing untoward in his behaviour at the party | the teacher's treatment of the child was untoward* unsuitable, inappropriate, unbefitting, unseemly, improper, indecorous.

untroubled adj unperturbed, undisturbed, unworried, unruffled, unagitated, unbothered, unconcerned, calm, cool, collected, composed, serene.

untrue adj **1** *untrue stories/accounts* false, fallacious, fictitious, fabricated, erroneous, in error, wrong, incorrect, inaccurate, economical with the truth, inexact, flawed, unsound, distorted, misleading. **2** *untrue friends* disloyal, faithless, unfaithful, false, treacherous, perfidious, deceitful, untrustworthy, double-dealing, insincere, unreliable, inconstant. **3** *his aim was untrue* inaccurate, wide of the mark, wide, off, out of true.

untrustworthy adj treacherous, not to be trusted, two-faced, double-dealing, duplicitous, deceitful, dishonest, dishonourable, unreliable, undependable; *inf* slippery.

untruth n **1** *a story full of untruth* lying, falsehood, falsity, fiction, fabrication, mendacity, inaccuracy; lies. **2** *tell an untruth* lie, falsehood, piece of fiction, fabrication, fib, white lie; *inf* whopper, terminological inexactitude.

untruthful adj **1** *an untruthful account* false, fictitious, fabricated, fallacious, erroneous, wrong, economical with the truth, inaccurate, inexact, flawed, unsound. **2** *an untruthful person* lying, mendacious, dishonest, deceitful.

unusual adj **1** *unusual behaviour/reactions* uncommon, out of the ordinary, atypical, abnormal, rare, singular, odd, strange, curious, queer, bizarre, surprising, unexpected, different, unconventional, uncustomary, unwonted, unorthodox, irregular; *inf* weird. **2** *an unusual talent* extraordinary, exceptional, singular, rare, remarkable, outstanding.

unutterable adj **1** *unutterable joy* unspeakable, inexpressible, indescribable, beyond words/description, ineffable, unimaginable, inconceivable, overwhelming. *see* UNSPEAKABLE 1. **2** *unutterable cad* indescribable, indescribably bad, appalling, shocking, frightful, dreadful, deplorable. *see* UNSPEAKABLE 2.

unveil v *unveil the facts | unveiled their plans* uncover, reveal, lay open/bare, expose, bring to light, disclose, divulge, make known/public.

unwarranted adj **1** *an unwarranted entry into the palace | unwarranted market traders* unauthorized, uncertified, unaccredited, unlicensed, unsanctioned, unapproved. **2** *unwarranted behaviour | an unwarranted intrusion into our affairs* unjustifiable, unjustified, indefensible, inexcusable, unforgivable, unpardonable, uncalled-for, gratuitous.

unwelcome adj **1** *unwelcome visitors* unwanted, undesired, uninvited, unpopular. **2** *unwelcome news | the unwelcome truth* unpleasant, disagreeable, unpalatable, displeasing, distasteful, undesirable.

unwell adj ill, sick, sickly, ailing, in poor health, unhealthy, off-colour, run-down, below par; *inf* out of sorts, poorly, under the weather.

unwieldy adj cumbersome, unmanageable, unmanoeuvrable, awkward, clumsy, massive, hefty, bulky, ponderous; *inf* hulking.

unwilling adj **1** *an unwilling guest | their unwilling presence* reluctant, disinclined, unenthusiastic, grudging, involuntary, forced. **2** *unwilling to go* reluctant, disinclined, averse, loth, opposed, not in the mood.

unwind v **1** *unwind the balls of wool | unwind the roll of bandage* undo, unravel, uncoil,

unroll, untwine, untwist, disentangle. **2** *unwind by watching television* wind down, relax, calm down, slow down; *inf* loosen up, let oneself go, take it easy, let one's hair down.

unwise adj imprudent, injudicious, inadvisable, ill-considered, ill-judged, ill-advised, impolitic, indiscreet, short-sighted, irresponsible, foolhardy, rash, reckless, foolish, silly, unintelligent, mindless.

unwitting adj **1** *an unwitting offender* unknowing, unconscious, unaware, ignorant. **2** *an unwitting slight* unintentional, unintended, inadvertent, unmeant, unplanned, accidental, chance.

unwonted adj unusual, uncommon, uncustomary, out of the ordinary, exceptional, atypical, abnormal, irregular, anomalous.

unworldly adj **1** *unworldly considerations* spiritual, spiritualistic, non-material, religious. **2** *too unworldly to cope on her own* naïve, inexperienced, green, raw, uninitiated, unsophisticated, gullible, ingenuous, trusting, credulous, idealistic. **3** *unworldly beings* other-worldly, unearthly, extraterrestrial, ethereal, ghostly, spectral, phantom, preternatural, supernatural.

unworthy adj **1** *conduct unworthy of a teacher | unworthy conduct* unsuitable in, inappropriate in, unbefitting, unfitting, unseemly in, improper in, incompatible with, incongruous in, inconsistent with, out of keeping with, out of character, out of place in, degrading, discreditable. **2** *he is unworthy of her | she is unworthy of the honour conferred on her* not worthy, not good enough for, undeserving, ineligible for, unqualified for. **3** *an unworthy cause* worthless, inferior, second-rate, undeserving, ignoble, disreputable; *inf* lousy, crappy. **4** *an unworthy wretch* disreputable, dishonourable, base, contemptible, reprehensible.

upbraid v scold, rebuke, reproach, reprove, chide, reprimand, berate, remonstrate with, castigate, criticize, censure.

upbringing n bringing up, rearing, raising, nurture, care, tending, training.

upgrade v **1** *upgrade the facilities/building* improve, better, ameliorate, reform, enhance, touch up, rehabilitate, refurbish. **2** *upgrade the teacher | upgrade him to a higher position* promote, advance, elevate, raise.

upheaval n disruption, disturbance, revolution, disorder, confusion, turmoil, chaos, cataclysm.

uphill adj **1** *an uphill path* upward, ascending, climbing, mounting, rising. **2** *an uphill job* arduous, difficult, laborious, strenuous, hard, tough, burdensome, onerous, taxing, punishing, gruelling, exhausting, wearisome, Herculean, Sisyphean.

uphold v **1** *uphold the committee's decision* | *uphold his right to refuse* confirm, endorse, support, back up, stand by, champion, defend. **2** *uphold the old traditions* maintain, sustain, hold to, keep.

upkeep n **1** *pay for the upkeep of the house* maintenance, running, preservation, conservation; repairs. **2** *pay for the child's upkeep* keep, maintenance, support, subsistence, sustenance. **3** *the upkeep is deducted from his salary* outlay, running/operating costs, costs, overheads, expenses.

uplift v **1** *uplift the load* raise, upraise, lift, hoist up, heave up, elevate. **2** *uplift his spirits* raise, improve, edify, inspire.

upper adj **1** *the upper shelf/storey* higher, further up, loftier. **2** *the upper ranks* superior, higher-ranking, elevated, greater.

upper-class adj aristocratic, noble, highborn, patrician, blue-blooded; *inf* topdrawer.

upper hand n advantage, edge, whip hand, ascendancy, superiority, supremacy, sway, control, mastery, dominance, command.

uppermost adj **1** *the uppermost shelf/floor* highest, furthest up, loftiest, top, topmost. **2** *the uppermost consideration* | *uppermost in our minds* foremost, greatest, predominant, dominant, principal, chief, main, paramount, major.

uppish adj conceited, arrogant, overweening, self-important, self-assertive, presumptuous, supercilious, snobbish, disdainful, hoity-toity; *inf* uppity, high and mighty, stuck-up, toffee-nosed.

upright adj **1** *upright posts* erect, on end, vertical, perpendicular, standing up, rampant. **2** *upright members of the community* honest, honourable, upstanding, decent, respectable, worthy, reputable, good, virtuous, righteous, law-abiding, ethical, moral, high-principled, of principle, high-minded.

uprising n rising, rebellion, revolt, insurrection, insurgence, mutiny, riot, revolution, coup, *coup d'état*, overthrow, putsch; fighting in the streets.

uproar n **1** *the place was in uproar* tumult, turmoil, turbulence, disorder, confusion, commotion, mayhem, pandemonium, bedlam; din, noise, clamour, hubbub, racket. **2** *there was an uproar when he was dismissed* outburst, row, rumpus, brouhaha, hullabaloo, affray, furore, fracas, brawl, scuffle, conflict, struggle, free-for-all; howls of protest; *inf* ruckus.

uproarious adj **1** *an uproarious party* noisy, loud, rowdy, disorderly, unruly, boisterous, wild, unrestrained, rollicking. **2** *an uproarious show* hilarious, hysterically/riotously funny, side-splitting; *inf* killingly funny, killing, too funny for words, too much, riproaring, rib-tickling.

upset v **1** *upset the bucket/boat* overturn, knock over, push over, upend, tip over, topple, capsize. **2** *upset the old lady* perturb, disturb, discompose, unsettle, disconcert, dismay, disquiet, trouble, worry, bother, agitate, fluster, ruffle, shake, frighten, alarm, anger, annoy, distress, hurt, grieve. **3** *upset the smooth running of the firm* disturb, throw into disorder/confusion, disorganize, disarrange, mess up, mix up, jumble, turn topsy-turvy. **4** *upset Napoleon's army* defeat, beat, conquer, vanquish, rout, overthrow, overcome, triumph over, be victorious over, get the better of, worst, thrash, trounce.

upset n **1** *cause a great deal of upset* | *emotional upset* perturbation, discomposure, dismay, disquiet, trouble, worry, bother, agitation, fluster, alarm, distress, hurt. *see* UPSET v 2. **2** *cause upset to the running of the firm* | *an upset of our plans* disturbance, disorder, confusion, disorganization, disarrangement. *see* UPSET v 3. **3** *a stomach upset* disorder, disturbance, complaint, ailment, illness, sickness, disease, malady; *inf* bug. **4** *the upset of the army* defeat, conquering, rout, overthrow, worsting. *see* UPSET v 4.

upset adj **1** *the upset bucket* overturned, upturned, up-ended, toppled, capsized, upside down. **2** *the old lady was upset by the attack/news* perturbed, disturbed, discomposed, unsettled, disconcerted, dismayed, disquieted, troubled, worried, bothered, anxious, agitated, flustered, ruffled, shaken, frightened, alarmed, angered, annoyed, distressed, hurt, saddened, grieved. **3** *an upset stomach* | *feeling upset in the boat* disordered, disturbed, queasy, ill, sick; *inf* gippy. **4** *our upset plans* disturbed, disordered, in disorder, confused, in confusion, disarranged, in disarray, jumbled up, messed up, chaotic, in chaos, topsy-turvy; *inf* at sixes and sevens, higgledy-piggledy.

upshot n result, outcome, conclusion, issue, end, end result, denouement, effect, repercussion, reaction; *inf* pay-off.

upside down adj **1** *the bucket was upside down* upturned, up-ended, bottom up, wrong side up, inverted. **2** *the house is upside down* | *our plans are upside down* in disorder, in disarray, jumbled up, in a muddle, messed up, chaotic, in chaos, topsy-turvy; *inf* at sixes and sevens, higgledy-piggledy.

upstanding adj **1** *ask the congregation to be upstanding* in a standing position, on one's feet, erect, vertical. **2** *a fine upstanding young man* healthy, hale and hearty, strong, sturdy, robust, vigorous, hardy, stalwart, well-made, well-built. **3** *upstanding members of the community* upright, honest, honourable, decent, worthy, respectable, good, virtuous, righteous, law-abiding. *see* UPRIGHT 2.

upstart n parvenu, parvenue, would-be, social climber, status seeker, nouveau riche, *arriviste*.

up-to-date adj *up-to-date clothes* | *she's so up to date* modern, current, prevalent, prevailing, present-day, recent, up to the minute, fashionable, in fashion, in vogue, voguish; *inf* all the rage, in the swim, trendy, with it, now.

upturn n **1** *an upturn in sales* upswing, increase, rise, upsurge, boost, acceleration, escalation; *inf* step-up. **2** *an upturn in the economy* upswing, improvement, advancement, betterment, recovery, revival.

upward adj *the upward slope/trend* rising, climbing, mounting, ascending, on the rise.

upward, upwards adv **1** *going upward* up, uphill, to the top, straight up. **2** *prices spiralling upward* towards a higher level/standing. **upwards of** *upwards of 100 miles* more than, above, over, beyond.

urban adj city, cityish, citified, inner-city, town, townish, metropolitan, municipal, civic, oppidan.

urbane adj suave, debonair, sophisticated, smooth, worldly, elegant, cultivated, cultured, civilized, polished, refined, gracious, charming, agreeable, affable, courtly, civil, polite, courteous, well-mannered, mannerly.

urbanity n suaveness, sophistication, smoothness, worldliness, cultivation, culture, polish, refinement, graciousness, charm, affability, courtliness, civility, politeness, mannerliness.

urchin n street Arab, ragamuffin, gamin, guttersnipe, waif, stray, imp, rogue, brat.

urge v **1** *urge the horses on* | *urge the children up the hill* push, drive, propel, impel, force, hasten, hurry, speed up. **2** *urge the contestants to greater effort* spur, incite, stir up, stimulate, prod, goad, egg on, encourage, prompt; *inf* psych up. **3** *urged him to go* | "Go," he urged entreat, exhort, implore, appeal, beg, beseech, plead. **4** *urge caution*

upon them advise, counsel, advocate, recommend, suggest, support, endorse, back, champion.

urge n *a sudden urge to travel* | *sexual urge* desire, need, compulsion, longing, yearning, wish, fancy, impulse, itch; *inf* yen.

urgency n **1** *a matter of urgency* imperativeness, exigency, top priority, importance, necessity, seriousness, gravity, extremity, hurry, haste. **2** *the urgency in her voice* importunateness, insistence, clamorousness, earnestness, pleading, begging.

urgent adj **1** *it is urgent that we operate* imperative, vital, crucial, critical, essential, exigent, top-priority, high-priority, important, necessary. **2** *urgent matters* vital, crucial, exigent, top-priority, high-priority, important, pressing, serious, grave. **3** *an urgent whisper/demand* importunate, insistent, clamorous, earnest, pleading, begging.

urinate v pass water, micturate; *inf* spend a penny, pee, wee-wee, wee, have a tinkle/ slash, take a leak.

usable adj for use, to be used, utilizable, available, ready/fit for use, in working order, functional.

usage n **1** *damaged by rough usage* use, treatment, handling, management, running, operation, manipulation, manoeuvring. **2** *old usages now forgotten* custom, practice, habit, way, procedure, method, mode, form, tradition, convention. **3** *study English usage* manner of speaking/writing, mode of expression, phraseology, phrasing, idiom, idiolect.

use v **1** *use tools* make use of, utilize, employ, work, operate, wield, ply, manoeuvre, manipulate, avail oneself of, put to use, put into service. **2** *use tact* employ, exercise, apply. **3** *use him roughly* treat, handle, deal with, act/behave towards. **4** *he just uses people for his own ends* make use of, exploit, manipulate, take advantage of, impose upon, abuse; *inf* walk all over, play for a sucker. **5** *have you used any eggs?* | *we have used up all the food* consume, get through, exhaust, deplete, expend, spend, waste, fritter away. **used to** accustomed to, familiar with, at home with, in the habit of, given to, prone to, wont to, habituated to, addicted to, inured to.

use n **1** *for external use* usage, application, utilization, employment, operation, manipulation, manoeuvring. **2** *fall to pieces from use* using, usage, wear, wear and tear. **3** *he has the use of the garden* right, privilege, prerogative, usufruct. **4** *his use of other people for his own ends* exploitation, manipulation. *see* USE v 4. **5** *what use is this to you?* usefulness, good, advantage, benefit, service, help, gain, profit, avail. **6** *established by long use* usage, practice, custom, habit, wont. **7** *we have no use for this machine* need, necessity, call, demand, purpose, reason.

used adj *used car/clothing* second-hand, nearly new, cast-off; *inf* hand-me-down.

useful adj **1** *a useful tool* of use, functional, utilitarian, of service, practical, convenient. **2** *a useful experience* beneficial, advantageous, of help, helpful, worthwhile, profitable, rewarding, productive, valuable. **3** *he's a useful player* effective, efficacious, effectual, competent, capable, able.

useless adj **1** *a useless attempt | useless meetings* vain, in vain, to no avail/purpose, unavailing, unsuccessful, futile, purposeless, ineffectual, inefficacious, fruitless, unprofitable, unproductive, abortive. **2** *he's a useless player/salesman* worthless, ineffective, ineffectual, incompetent, incapable, inadequate; *inf* no good.

usher n escort, guide, attendant.

usher v **1** *usher the people to their seats* escort, show, conduct, direct, guide, lead. **2** *usher in new methods* herald, precede, pave the way for, give notice of, announce, introduce, bring in, get going, get under way, launch.

usual adj **1** *his usual route* habitual, customary, accustomed, wonted, normal, regular, routine, everyday, established, set, familiar. **2** *not usual behaviour* common, typical, ordinary, average, run-of-the-mill, expected, standard, stock, regular.

usually adv *usually he works late* generally, as a rule, normally, by and large, in the main, mainly, mostly, for the most part, on the whole.

usurp v *usurp the throne/position* take over, seize, expropriate, take possession of, appropriate, commandeer, lay claim to, assume.

utilitarian adj practical, functional, useful, to the purpose.

utility n use, usefulness, service, serviceableness, advantageousness, benefit, helpfulness, profitability, convenience, practicality, practicability, effectiveness, efficacy.

utilize v use, put to use, make use of, employ, avail oneself of, have recourse to, resort to, take advantage of, turn to account.

utmost adj **1** *have the utmost confidence in them* maximum, supreme, paramount, greatest, highest, most. **2** *the utmost ends of the earth* uttermost, furthest, farthest, remotest, outermost, extreme, ultimate.

utmost n *to the utmost* maximum, most, uttermost, top, pinnacle, peak, best, finest.

utter adj *an utter cad | feel utter happiness* absolute, complete, total, thorough, thoroughgoing, positive, downright, out and out, sheer, unmitigated, categorical, unqualified, unconditional, perfect, consummate.

utter v **1** *utter a sound* emit, let out, give. **2** *utter threats* voice, say, speak, pronounce, express, put into words, enunciate, articulate, verbalize, vocalize.

utterance n **1** *give utterance to his thoughts* voice, expression, articulation, enunciation, verbalization, vocalization. **2** *his prophetic utterances* remark, word, comment, statement, opinion.

utterly adv *utterly delightful* absolutely, completely, totally, entirely, thoroughly, positively, extremely, categorically, perfectly, consummately, to the core.

Vv

vacancy n **1** *the vacancy of the place* emptiness, voidness. **2** *a vacancy in the firm* opening, position, post, job, opportunity, slot. **3** *no vacancies in the hotel* unoccupied room, room. **4** *the vacancy of his expression* blankness, lack of expression, expressionlessness, lack of emotion/interest, emotionlessness, vacuousness. **5** *his vacancy is unbelievable* lack of thought/intelligence, brainlessness, denseness, thickness, vacuousness, vacuity, inaneness, inanity, stupidity.

vacant adj **1** *a vacant space* empty, void, without contents. **2** *a vacant position* unoccupied, unfilled, free, empty, available. **3** *a vacant seat* empty, unoccupied, free, unengaged, not in use, unused, available; *inf* up for grabs. **4** *a vacant house* empty, unoccupied, uninhabited, untenanted, tenantless, to let, abandoned, deserted. **5** *how to spend his vacant time* free, leisure, idle, unemployed. **6** *a vacant expression/countenance* blank, expressionless, inexpressive, deadpan, poker-faced, emotionless, uninterested, vacuous, inane. **7** *he seems to be completely vacant* without thought, unintelligent, brainless, dense, dull-witted, thick, vacuous, inane, stupid.

vacate v *vacate the house/post* leave, quit, depart from, evacuate, abandon, desert.

vacation n **1** *take a vacation* holiday, break, recess, furlough, rest, respite; leave, time off. **2** *the vacation of the post* quitting, departure, evacuation. *see* VACATE.

vacillate v shilly-shally, waver, dither, be irresolute/indecisive, hesitate, equivocate, hem and haw, keep changing one's mind, beat about the bush; *inf* blow hot and cold.

vacuous adj **1** *a vacuous expression* vacant, blank, expressionless, deadpan, inane. *see* VACANT 6. **2** *he seems to be completely vacuous* unintelligent, brainless, vacant, inane, stupid. *see* VACANT 7.

vacuum n **1** *create a vacuum* emptiness, void, empty, space, nothingness, vacuity. **2** *a vacuum in his life* gap, empty space, lacuna, vacuity, hollowness, need, want. **3** *plug in the vacuum* vacuum cleaner; *Trademark* Hoover.

vagabond n *vagabonds living rough* wanderer, itinerant, nomad, wayfarer, trav-

eller, rover, tramp, vagrant, derelict, beachcomber, down-and-out, beggar, person of no fixed address, knight of the road, bird of passage, rolling stone; *Amer* hobo; *Amer inf* bum.

vagabond adj *a vagabond existence* wandering, nomadic, itinerant, peripatetic, travelling, journeying, roving, roaming, vagrant, drifting, unsettled, transient, footloose.

vagary n caprice, whim, whimsy, fancy, notion, crotchet.

vagrancy n nomadism, peripateticism, itineracy, vagabondism, wandering, roving, roaming, drifting, homelessness.

vagrant n *vagrants sleeping rough* tramp, beggar, person of no fixed address, itinerant, nomad, wanderer, vagabond; *Amer* hobo; *Amer inf* bum. *see* VAGABOND n.

vagrant adj *a vagrant existence* tramplike, itinerant, nomadic, peripatetic, wandering, roving, vagabond, homeless. *see* VAGABOND adj.

vague adj **1** *a vague shape* indistinct, indeterminate, ill-defined, unclear, nebulous, amorphous, shadowy, hazy, dim, fuzzy, foggy, blurry, bleary, out of focus. **2** *a vague description* imprecise, inexact, unexplicit, non-specific, loose, generalized, ambiguous, equivocal, hazy, woolly. **3** *have only a vague idea of what is involved* imprecise, ill-defined, hazy, nebulous. **4** *she is rather vague about her plans* uncertain, unsure, hesitant, wavering, shilly-shallying; *inf* blowing hot and cold. **5** *her plans are rather vague* uncertain, undecided, indefinite, indeterminate, doubtful, open, speculative, conjectural; *inf* up in the air. **6** *she is rather vague* absent-minded, abstracted, dreamy, vacuous; *inf* with one's head in the clouds.

vaguely adv **1** *she looks vaguely familiar* in a general way, in a way, somehow, slightly, obscurely. **2** *point vaguely in her direction* approximately, roughly, imprecisely. **3** *smiling vaguely* absent-mindedly, abstractedly, vacantly, vacuously.

vain adj **1** *vain people* conceited, self-loving, self-admiring, narcissistic, peacockish, egotistical, proud, haughty, arrogant, boastful, swaggering, imperious, overweening, cocky, affected; *lit* vainglorious; *inf* stuck-up, big-headed, swollen-headed. **2** *vain tri-*

umphs worthless, futile, insignificant, pointless, meaningless, nugatory, valueless, meritless, empty, hollow, insubstantial, idle, vapid. **3** *vain attempts* futile, unsuccessful, useless, unavailing, to no avail, ineffective, inefficacious, fruitless, unproductive, abortive, unprofitable, profitless. **in vain 1** *try in vain to save him* unsuccessfully, without success, to no avail/ purpose, ineffectually, with no result, fruitlessly. **2** *his efforts were in vain* unsuccessful, unavailing, to no avail/purpose, ineffectual.

valedictory adj farewell, parting, final.

valiant adj brave, courageous, valorous, heroic, stout-hearted, lion-hearted, gallant, manly, intrepid, fearless, undaunted, undismayed, bold, daring, audacious, staunch, stalwart, indomitable, resolute, determined.

valid adj **1** *valid reasons/objections* sound, well-founded, well-grounded, substantial, reasonable, logical, justifiable, defensible, vindicable, authentic, bona fide, effective, cogent, powerful, convincing, credible, forceful, weighty. **2** *the ruling is still valid* lawful, legal, licit, legitimate, legally binding, binding, contractual, in force, in effect, effective.

validate v **1** *validate the contract | validate his appointment* ratify, legalize, legitimize, authorize, sanction, warrant, license, approve, endorse, set one's seal to. **2** *validate a statement* verify, prove, authenticate, substantiate, confirm, corroborate, justify.

valley n dale, dell, hollow, coomb, vale, depression; *Scots* glen, strath.

valour n bravery, courage, heroism, stoutheartedness, gallantry, manliness, intrepidity, fearlessness, boldness, daring, staunchness, fortitude.

valuable adj **1** *a valuable watch* costly, highpriced, expensive, priceless, precious. **2** *a valuable contribution/lesson* useful, helpful, beneficial, advantageous, worthwhile, worthy, important.

valuables npl treasures, costly articles.

value n **1** *place a value on the ring* monetary value, face value, price, market price, cost. **2** *the value of a healthy diet | his advice is of great value* worth, merit, usefulness, advantage, benefit, gain, profit, good, avail, importance, significance.

value v **1** *value the watch | value his worth to the firm* set a price on, price, evaluate, assess, appraise. **2** *we value his contribution greatly* rate highly, appreciate, esteem, hold in high regard, think highly of, set store by, respect, admire, prize, cherish, treasure.

valued adj *a valued contribution/friendship* esteemed, highly regarded, respected, prized, cherished, treasured.

values npl *moral values* code of behaviour; principles, ethics, morals, standards.

vamp[1] v *vamp up old property* renovate, restore, rehabilitate, recondition, refashion, repair, mend, patch up.

vamp[2] v *girls trying to vamp older men* seduce, tempt, lure, beguile, flirt with, make up to.

vamp[2] n *vamps seducing men in bars* seductress, siren, temptress, loose woman, adventuress.

van[1] n *drive a van* lorry, truck, pantechnicon, camper.

van[2] n *in the van of the new fashion* vanguard, forefront, front, front line, leading position. *see* VANGUARD.

vanguard n advance guard, forefront, front, front line, front rank, leading position, van; leaders, spearheads, trail-blazers, trendsetters.

vanish v **1** *she vanished in the mist* disappear, be lost to sight/view, be/become invisible, evaporate, dissipate, disperse, fade, fade away, evanesce, melt away, recede from view, withdraw, depart, leave. **2** *a way of life that has vanished | hopes of success have vanished* cease to exist/be, pass away, die out, come to an end, end, be no more, become extinct/obsolete.

vanity n **1** *his vanity about his looks/achievements* conceit, conceitedness, self-conceit, self-admiration, self-love, narcissism, egotism, pride, haughtiness, arrogance, boastfulness, braggadocio, pretension, affectation, ostentation, show, vainglory; airs; *inf* stuck-upness, big-headedness, swollen-headedness, showing-off. **2** *the vanity of human triumphs* worthlessness, futility, futileness, insignificance, pointlessness, meaninglessness, emptiness, hollowness, insubstantiality, vapidity. *see* VAIN 2.

vanquish v conquer, defeat, triumph over, beat, overcome, best, worst, master, subdue, subjugate, put down, quell, quash, repress, rout, overwhelm, overrun, overthrow, crush, trounce, thrash, drub; *inf* clobber.

vapid adj insipid, flat, lifeless, colourless, bland, dull, trite, uninteresting, zestless.

variable adj varying, variational, changeable, changeful, changing, mutable, chameleonic, protean, shifting, fluctuating, wavering, vacillating, inconstant, unsteady, unstable, fitful, capricious, fickle; *inf* blowing hot and cold.

variance n *an obvious variance between statements* discrepancy, disagreement, diverging. **at variance** *they are at variance about his suitability* in disagreement, in dissent, in opposition, in conflict, at odds.

variant adj *variant spellings* alternative, divergent, derived, modified.

variant n *a variant of the normal spelling* variation, alternative, derived form, development, modification, mutant.

variation n **1** *subject to variation* change, alteration, modification, diversification. **2** *noted for its variation* variability, changeability, fluctuation, vacillation, vicissitude. **3** *a variation in sizes* varying, difference, dissimilarity. **4** *show variation from the norm* deviation, divergence, departure, difference. **5** *a variation on a theme* diversification, innovation, novelty.

varied adj *a varied selection* diversified, diverse, assorted, miscellaneous, mixed, motley, heterogeneous.

variegated adj multicoloured, particoloured, prismatic, rainbow-like, kaleidoscopic, marbled, streaked, striated, mottled, speckled, flecked.

variety n **1** *introduce variety into your selection* variation, diversification, diversity, multifariousness, many-sidedness, change, difference. **2** *a variety of flowers were exhibited* assortment, miscellany, range, mixture, medley, motley, collection, multiplicity. **3** *a variety of rose/humour* strain, breed, kind, type, sort, class, category, classification, brand, make.

various adj **1** *come in various shapes* varying, diverse, different, differing, dissimilar, unlike, disparate, many, assorted, mixed, miscellaneous, variegated, heterogeneous. **2** *for various reasons* numerous, many, several, varied, sundry, divers.

varnish v **1** *varnish the table* lacquer, japan, shellac, enamel, glaze, veneer. **2** *varnish the truth* embellish, smooth over, cover up, gloss over, mask, disguise.

varnish n *apply a varnish to the surface* coating, lacquer, shellac, enamel, glaze, veneer.

vary v **1** *they tend to vary in size* differ, be different, be unlike, be dissimilar. **2** *the sky varies constantly* change, be transformed, alter, metamorphose, suffer a sea change, vacillate, fluctuate. **3** *our opinions vary* be at variance, disagree, be in disagreement, differ, conflict, clash, be at odds, be in opposition, diverge. **4** *vary the speed/appearance* change, alter, modify, transform, permutate. **5** *vary from the norm* deviate, diverge, depart, differ.

vast adj **1** *a vast shape loomed* immense, huge, enormous, massive, bulky, tremendous, colossal, prodigious, gigantic, monumental, elephantine, Brobdingnagian; *inf* hulking. **2** *vast forests* immense, extensive, broad, wide, expansive, boundless, limitless, infinite.

vault n **1** *look up at the vault* arched roof/ceiling, arch. **2** *hide in the vault* cellar, basement, underground chamber, tomb. **3** *valuables stored in the vault* strongroom, repository, depository. **4** *take a vault over the fence* jump, leap, spring, bound.

vault v *vault the fence* jump, leap, jump over, leap over, spring over, bound over.

vaunt v *always vaunting his achievements* boast about, brag about, make much of, crow about, give oneself airs about, exult in; *inf* show off about.

veer v change course/direction, shift direction, turn, swerve, swing, sidestep, sheer, tack, be deflected.

vegetate v **1** *vegetating at home without a job* do nothing, idle, be inactive, laze around, lounge around, loaf around, languish, stagnate, moulder; *inf* go to seed. **2** *plants vegetating* grow, sprout, shoot up, burgeon, flourish.

vegetation n plant life, herbage, greenery, verdure; plants, flora.

vehemence n passion, ardour, fervour, strength, force, forcibleness, forcefulness, emphasis, vigour, intensity, violence, earnestness, keenness, enthusiasm, zeal, zealousness, spirit, spiritedness, gusto, verve.

vehement adj passionate, ardent, impassioned, fervent, fervid, strong, forceful, forcible, powerful, emphatic, vigorous, intense, violent, earnest, keen, enthusiastic, zealous, spirited.

vehicle n **1** *park the vehicle* means of transport, transportation, conveyance; car, bus, lorry. **2** *a vehicle for their propaganda* channel, medium, means, means of expression, agency, instrument, mechanism, organ, apparatus.

veil n **1** *her face covered by a veil* face covering, mantilla, yashmak, purdah. **2** *a veil of mist covered the mountain | under a veil of secrecy* covering, cover, screen, curtain, film, mantle, cloak, mask, blanket, shroud, canopy, cloud.

veil v **1** *try to veil his contempt | did not veil his threats* hide, conceal, cover up, camouflage, disguise, mask, screen. **2** *mist veiling the mountains* cover, envelop, mantle, cloak, blanket, shroud, canopy.

veiled adj *thinly veiled threats* hidden, concealed, covert, disguised, camouflaged, masked, suppressed.

vein n **1** *sever a vein* blood vessel. **2** *a vein of ore* lode, seam, stratum. **3** *veins of blue in the white marble* streak, stripe, line, thread, marking. **4** *there was a vein of wickedness in him* streak, strain, trait, dash, hint. **5** *he was in humorous vein* humour, mood, temper, temperament, disposition, frame of mind, attitude, inclination, tendency, tenor, tone.

velocity n speed, swiftness, fastness, quickness, rapidity, celerity.

venal adj corrupt, corruptible, bribable, open to bribery, purchasable, buyable, mercenary, greedy, avaricious, grasping, rapacious.

vendetta n feud, blood feud, quarrel, war, conflict, rivalry, enmity.

vendor n seller, salesperson, dealer, trader, merchant, pedlar, hawker.

veneer n **1** *a veneer of mahogany* facing, covering, coat, finishing coat, finish. **2** *a veneer of politeness* façade, front, false front, show, outward display, appearance, semblance, guise, mask, pretence, camouflage.

venerable adj *venerable scientist/traditions* venerated, respected, revered, reverenced, worshipped, honoured, esteemed, hallowed.

veneration n respect, reverence, worship, adoration, honour, esteem.

vengeance n revenge, retribution, requital, retaliation, reprisal, an eye for an eye, tit for tat, measure for measure, blow for blow, quid pro quo. **with a vengeance 1** *the rain came down with a vengeance* forcefully, violently, vehemently, furiously, wildly. **2** *go at the job with a vengeance* to the utmost, to the greatest extreme, to the full, to the limit, all out, flat out.

venial adj *a venial offence* pardonable, forgivable, excusable, allowable, tolerable, slight, minor, unimportant, insignificant, trivial.

venom n **1** *suck the venom of the snake bite* poison, toxin, toxicant. **2** *speak with venom about his rival* spite, spitefulness, rancour, vindictiveness, malice, malevolence, malignity, ill will, animosity, bitterness, resentment, grudgingness, acrimony, virulence, antagonism, hostility, enmity, hatred, viciousness.

venomous adj **1** *a venomous snake/bite* poisonous, toxic, lethal, deadly, fatal, noxious. **2** *a venomous remark/look* spiteful, rancorous, vindictive, malicious, malevolent, malignant, baleful, bitter, resentful, grudging, virulent, antagonistic, hostile, hate-filled, vicious.

vent n **1** *an air vent* opening, outlet, aperture, hole, gap, orifice, duct, flue. **2** *give vent to his anger* outlet, free passage, expression, release.

vent v *vent his anger on his children* give vent/expression to, express, air, utter, voice, verbalize, let out, release, pour out, emit, discharge, come out with.

ventilate v **1** *ventilate a room* aerate, oxygenate, air, air-condition, freshen, cool, purify. **2** *ventilate one's views* air, give an airing to, bring into the open, discuss, debate, talk over, give expression to, express.

venture n **1** *explorers engaged in a new venture* adventure, exploit, mission, risky undertaking. **2** *a business venture* enterprise, undertaking, project, speculation, fling, plunge, gamble.

venture v **1** *venture to voice an opinion* dare, take the liberty of, make so bold as to, presume to. **2** *venture an opinion* volunteer, advance, put forward, chance, risk. **3** *venture his life for her* risk, put at risk, endanger, hazard, put in jeopardy, jeopardize, imperil, chance, gamble. **4** *it's now possible to venture out/forth* go, set forth, embark (on).

veracious adj **1** *a veracious person* truthful, honest, sincere, frank, candid, honourable, upright, upstanding, ethical, moral, righteous, virtuous, decent, good. **2** *a veracious statement* true, truthful, accurate, exact, precise, factual, literal, realistic.

verbal adj **1** *a verbal account* oral, spoken, said, uttered, articulated. **2** *a verbal translation* word for word, verbatim, literal, close, faithful, exact, precise.

verbatim adj *a verbatim translation* word for word, literal, exact. *see* VERBAL 2.

verbatim adv *translate his statement verbatim* word for word, literally, to the letter, closely, faithfully, exactly, precisely.

verbose adj wordy, loquacious, garrulous, long-winded, prolix, diffuse, pleonastic, circumlocutory, periphrastic, tautological.

verbosity n verboseness, wordiness, loquacity, garrulity, long-windedness, logorrhoea, verbiage, prolixity, diffuseness, circumlocution, periphrasis, tautology.

verdict n decision, judgement, adjudication, finding, conclusion, ruling, opinion.

verge n **1** *the verges of the lake* edge, border, margin, rim, limit, boundary, end, extremity. **2** *on the verge of a breakdown/discovery* brink, threshold.

verge v *it verges on the ridiculous* approach, incline to/towards, tend towards, border on, come near.

verification n *ask for verification of his statement* confirmation, substantiation, corroboration, attestation, validation, authentication, endorsement, accreditation, ratification; evidence, proof.

verify v **1** *ask the witness to verify his statement* confirm, substantiate, prove, corroborate, attest to, testify to, validate, authenticate, endorse, accredit, ratify. **2** *our suspicions were verified* bear out, justify, give credence to, confirm, prove, substantiate.

vernacular n everyday/spoken language, colloquial/native speech, conversational language, common parlance, non-standard language, jargon, cant, patois; *inf* lingo, patter.

versatile adj **1** *a versatile member of staff* adaptable, flexible, all-round, multifaceted, resourceful, ingenious, clever. **2** *a versatile tool* adaptable, adjustable, multipurpose, all-purpose, handy.

verse n **1** *write verse rather than prose* poetry; poems. **2** *a poem in several verses* stanza, strophe, canto, couplet. **3** *read out a verse about the countryside* poem, lyric, sonnet, ode, limerick, piece of doggerel, ditty, song, lay, ballad.

version n **1** *tell us your version of the events* account, report, story, rendering, interpretation, construction, understanding, reading, impression, side. **2** *published in several versions* adaptation, interpretation, translation. **3** *there are several versions of the song going around* variant, variation, form, copy, reproduction.

vertical adj upright, erect, on end, perpendicular.

vertigo n dizziness, giddiness, light-headedness, loss of balance/equilibrium; *inf* wooziness.

verve n enthusiasm, vigour, force, energy, vitality, vivacity, liveliness, animation, sparkle, spirit, life, élan, dash, brio, fervour, gusto, passion, zeal, feeling, fire; *inf* zing, zip, vim, punch, get-up-and-go, pizzazz.

very adv *very pretty* | *done very easily* extremely, exceedingly, to a great extent, exceptionally, uncommonly, unusually, decidedly, particularly, eminently, remarkably, really, truly; *inf* awfully, terribly, jolly.

very adj **1** *his very words* actual, exact, precise, unqualified. **2** *that is the very thing for the task* ideal, perfect, appropriate, suitable, fitting, right, just right. **3** *its very simplicity appeals* sheer, utter, simple, pure, plain,

mere. **4** *at the very beginning* extreme, absolute.

vessel n **1** *a sea-going vessel* ship, boat, yacht, craft; *lit* barque. **2** *pour the milk into several vessels* container, receptacle.

vest v *he has the power to execute vested in him* bestow, confer, endow, entrust, invest, lodge, place, put in the hands of.

vestibule n entrance hall, hall, porch, portico, foyer, lobby, anteroom.

vestige n **1** *see vestiges of a pack of wolves* trace, mark, sign, indication, print, imprint, impression, track. **2** *vestiges of a lost civilization* remains, relics; evidence. **3** *not a vestige of proof* scrap, hint, suggestion, touch, tinge, suspicion, soupçon, inkling, drop, dash, jot, iota.

vestigial adj **1** *vestigial signs of an extinct civilization* remaining, surviving. **2** *a vestigial tail* rudimentary, non-functional, undeveloped.

vet v *vet their qualifications* | *vet the staff* check, check out, investigate, examine, appraise, look over, review, scrutinize; *inf* give the once-over, size up.

veteran n *veterans of the acting profession* old hand, old-timer, old stager, past master, master; *inf* pro, warhorse.

veteran adj *a veteran member of the committee* long-serving, seasoned, old, adept, expert; *inf* battle-scarred.

veto v *veto the tax cuts* | *veto the candidate for membership* reject, turn down, give the thumbs down to, prohibit, forbid, interdict, proscribe, disallow, outlaw, embargo, ban, bar, preclude, rule out; *inf* kill, put the kibosh on.

veto n *the right of veto* | *have a veto over any proposal* rejection, prohibition, interdict, proscription; embargo, ban.

vex v anger, annoy, irritate, incense, irk, enrage, infuriate, exasperate, pique, provoke, nettle, disturb, upset, perturb, discompose, put out, try one's patience, try, bother, trouble, worry, agitate, pester, harass, fluster, ruffle, hound, nag, torment, distress, tease, fret, gall, molest; *inf* peeve, miff, bug, hassle, aggravate, rile, get one's goat, drive up the wall, get to.

vexation n **1** *her vexation at his behaviour* anger, annoyance, irritation, rage, fury, exasperation, pique, provocation, perturbation, discomposure, worry, agitation, harassment, gall. *see* VEX. **2** *the child is a vexation to them* nuisance, pest, problem, trouble, worry, bother, irritant, thorn in one's flesh; *inf* headache, pain, pain in the neck.

vexatious adj annoying, irritating, irksome, infuriating, exasperating, provoking, upsetting, perturbing, bothersome, troublesome, worrying, worrisome, trying, distressing; *inf* aggravating.

vexed adj **1** *vexed about his behaviour | his vexed parents* annoyed, irritated, incensed, irked, enraged, infuriated, exasperated, upset, perturbed, bothered, trouble, worried, agitated, harassed, flustered, distressed; *inf* aggravated, peeved, miffed. *see* VEX. **2** *the vexed question* disputed, in dispute, contested, in contention, debated, controversial, moot.

viable adj *a viable plan/operation* workable, sound, feasible, practicable, applicable, usable.

vibrant adj **1** *vibrant pendulums* vibrating, vibratory, oscillating, swinging. **2** *vibrant music* throbbing, pulsating, resonant, reverberating, ringing, echoing. **3** *vibrant with excitement* trembling, quivering, shaking, shivering. *see* VIBRATE 3. **4** *a vibrant personality* lively, energetic, spirited, vigorous, animated, sparkling, vivacious, dynamic, electrifying. **5** *vibrant colours* vivid, bright, strong, striking.

vibrate v **1** *the pendulum vibrated* oscillate, swing, move to and fro. **2** *the noise vibrated through the house* throb, pulsate, resonate, resound, reverberate, ring, echo. **3** *vibrating with excitement* pulsate, tremble, quiver, shake, quaver, shiver, shudder.

vibration n **1** *the vibration of the pendulum* oscillation, swinging. **2** *the musical vibration* throb, pulsation, resonance, reverberation. *see* VIBRATE 2. **3** *the vibration of the engine | vibration of the bird's wings* pulsating, trembling, tremble, quivering, quiver, shake, shaking, quaver, shiver, shivering; *inf* judder.

vicar n minister, parson, priest, clergyman, cleric, churchman, ecclesiastic.

vicarious adj *vicarious pleasure from another's joy* indirect, second-hand, surrogate, by proxy, at one remove.

vice n **1** *vice is rampant* sin, sinfulness, wrong, wrongdoing, wickedness, badness, immorality, iniquity, evil, evildoing, venality corruption, depravity, degeneracy. **2** *enumerate his vices* sin, wrongdoing, transgression, offence, misdeed, error, violation. **3** *chocolate/shopping is one of her vices* failing, flaw, defect, imperfection, weakness, foible, shortcoming.

vice versa adv conversely, inversely, the other way round, contrariwise.

vicinity n **1** *he lives in the vicinity* surrounding district, neighbourhood, locality, area, district; environs, precincts, purlieus; *inf* this neck of the woods. **2** *the village's vicinity to London* nearness, closeness, proximity, propinquity. **in the vicinity** *in the vicinity of £3000* in the neighbourhood (of), near (to), close (to).

vicious adj **1** *attacked by vicious dogs* fierce, ferocious, savage, dangerous, ill-natured, bad-tempered, surly, hostile. **2** *vicious gossip/remarks* malicious, malevolent, malignant, spiteful, vindictive, venomous, catty, backbiting, rancorous, caustic, mean, cruel, defamatory, slanderous; *inf* bitchy. **3** *a vicious attack* violent, savage, brutal, fierce, ferocious, inhuman, barbarous, fiendish, sadistic, monstrous, heinous, atrocious, diabolical. **4** *fall in with a vicious band of people* corrupt, degenerate, depraved, debased, wicked, evil, sinful, bad, wrong, immoral, unprincipled, abandoned, unscrupulous, disreputable, dissolute, dissipated, debauched, profligate, libertine, vile, infamous, notorious.

vicissitude n *the vicissitudes of a writer's life* change, alteration, transformation, inconstancy, instability, uncertainty, unpredictability, chanciness, fickleness; ups and downs.

victim n **1** *victims of the attack* injured party, casualty, sufferer. **2** *they were victims of his sales patter* dupe, easy target/prey, fair game, sitting target, everybody's fool; *inf* sitting duck, sucker, sap, fall guy, pushover. **3** *track down their victims* prey, quarry, game, the hunted, target. **4** *a sacrificial victim for the gods* offering, sacrifice, scapegoat.

victimize v **1** *bullies victimizing young children* persecute, pick on, discriminate against, punish unfairly; *inf* have it in for, have a down on. **2** *unscrupulous men victimize old ladies* exploit, prey on, take advantage of, swindle, dupe, cheat, trick, hoodwink.

victor v conqueror, vanquisher, winner, champion, prizewinner, conquering hero; *inf* champ, top dog, number one.

victorious adj conquering, vanquishing, triumphant, winning, champion, successful, prizewinning, top, first.

victuals npl food, food and drink; eatables, foodstuffs, viands, comestibles, food supplies, provisions, rations, stores; *inf* eats, grub, nosh.

vie v *vie with her for first place* compete, contend, contest.

view n **1** *come into view* sight, field/range of vision, vision, eyeshot. **2** *the view from the mountain* outlook, prospect, scene, spectacle, vista, panorama; landscape, seascape. **3** *his view is that we should wait | have radical views* point of view, viewpoint, opinion, belief, judgement, way of thinking, thinking, thought, notion, idea, conviction, persuasion, attitude, feeling, sentiment, impression. **4** *a private view of the exhibition* viewing, sight, look, contemplation, observation, study, survey, inspection, scrutiny, scan. **in view of** *in view of his political opinions* considering, taking into consideration, bearing in mind, taking into account, in the light of. **on view** *pictures on view* on display, on exhibition, on show.

view v **1** *view the birds through binoculars* look at, watch, observe, contemplate, regard, behold, scan, survey, inspect, gaze at, stare at, peer at. **2** *view the house* see over, be shown over, survey, examine, scrutinize, take stock of. **3** *view the prospect with dismay* look on, consider, contemplate, think about, reflect on, ponder. **4** *view himself as an upright man* see, consider, judge, deem.

viewer n television watcher, watcher, spectator, onlooker, member of the audience.

viewpoint n point of view, way of thinking, frame of reference, perspective, angle, slant, standpoint, position, stance, vantage point.

vigilance n watchfulness, observation, surveillance, attentiveness, attention, alertness, guardedness, carefulness, caution, wariness, circumspection, heedfulness, heed.

vigilant adj watchful, on the lookout, observant, sharp-eyed, eagle-eyed, attentive, alert, on the alert, on the qui vive, awake, wide awake, unsleeping, on one's guard, careful, cautious, wary, circumspect, heedful.

vigorous adj **1** *vigorous children brought up in the country* robust, healthy, in good health, hale and hearty, strong, sturdy, fit, in good condition/shape/kilter, tough. **2** *feel much more vigorous after a holiday* energetic, lively, active, spry, sprightly, vivacious, animated, dynamic, full of life, sparkling. **3** *a vigorous attempt at winning* powerful, potent, strenuous, forceful, forcible, spirited, mettlesome, plucky, determined, resolute, aggressive, eager, keen, enthusiastic, zealous, ardent, fervent, vehement, intense, passionate. **4** *use vigorous arguments* strong, forceful, effective, cogent, valid, pointed, to the point, striking, graphic, vivid.

vigorously adv *defend himself vigorously | argue vigorously* strongly, powerfully, strenuously, forcefully, energetically, aggressively, eagerly, enthusiastically, with might and main, all out, with a vengeance, hammer and tongs; *inf* like mad.

vigour n **1** *the natural vigour of country children* robustness, healthiness, strength, sturdiness, fitness, toughness. **2** *return to work with renewed vigour* energy, activity, liveliness, spryness, sprightliness, vitality, vivacity, verve, animation, dynamism, sparkle, zest, dash, *élan*, gusto, pep; *inf* zip, zing, oomph, vim.

vile adj **1** *a vile taste/smell* foul, nasty, unpleasant, disagreeable, horrid, horrible, offensive, obnoxious, odious, repulsive, repellent, revolting, repugnant, disgusting, distasteful, loathsome, hateful, nauseating, sickening. **2** *he's a vile creature | a vile thing to do* base, low, mean, wretched, foul, nasty, horrible, horrid, dreadful, disgraceful, appalling, shocking, ugly, abominable, monstrous, wicked, evil, iniquitous, sinful, vicious, corrupt, depraved, perverted, debased, reprobate, degenerate, debauched, dissolute, contemptible, despicable, reprehensible. **3** *vile weather* foul, nasty, unpleasant, disagreeable.

vilify v defame, run down, impugn, revile, berate, denigrate, disparage, speak ill of, cast aspersions at, criticize, decry, denounce, fulminate against, malign, slander, libel, conduct a smear campaign against, blacken the name/reputation of, calumniate, traduce; *inf* badmouth, do a hatchet job on, pull to pieces, throw mud at, drag through the mud.

villain n **1** *he pretends to be honest but he's a real villain* rogue, scoundrel, blackguard, wretch, cad, reprobate, evildoer, wrongdoer, ruffian, hoodlum, hooligan, miscreant; *inf* baddy, crook, rat, louse. **2** *the police chasing the villains* criminal, miscreant, jailbird; *inf* crook. **3** *the child's a little villain* rascal, rogue, imp, monkey, scamp, brat; *inf* scallywag.

villainous adj **1** *a villainous attack* wicked, evil, iniquitous, sinful, nefarious, vile, foul, monstrous, shocking, outrageous, atrocious, abominable, reprehensible, hateful, detestable, horrible, heinous, diabolical, fiendish, vicious. **2** *a villainous wretch* wicked, evil, sinful, bad, base, dishonourable, dishonest, unscrupulous, scoundrelly, unprincipled, criminal, lawless, corrupt, degenerate, reprobate, depraved, dissolute; *inf* crooked.

villainy n wickedness, badness, evil, sin, iniquity, wrongdoing, roguery, rascality, vice, criminality, delinquency, vileness, viciousness, degeneracy, depravity, turpitude; crime, offence, misdeed.

vindicate v **1** *he was vindicated when his alibi was proved* acquit, clear, absolve, free from blame, exonerate, exculpate. **2** *time vindicated his suspicions* justify, warrant, substantiate, testify to, verify, confirm, corroborate. **3** *vindicate his claim* defend, support, back, fight for, champion, uphold, maintain, sustain, stand by.

vindictive adj vengeful, out for revenge, revengeful, avenging, unforgiving, grudge-bearing, resentful, ill-disposed, implacable, unrelenting, unconciliative, spiteful, rancorous, venomous, malicious, malevolent, malignant.

vintage n **1** *the vintage was ruined by storms* grape harvest, grape gathering, grape crop. **2** *what vintage is this wine?* year. **3** *the furniture is of 18th century vintage* era, epoch, period, time. **4** *his parents are of the same vintage as mine* generation, period, time.

vintage adj **1** *vintage wines* high-quality, quality, prime, choice, select, superior, best. **2** *vintage comedy* classic, ageless, enduring. **3** *this is vintage Sharon* characteristic, most typical, supreme, at his/her/its best.

violate v **1** *violate a law/treaty* break, breach, infringe, contravene, infract, transgress, disobey, disregard, ignore. **2** *violate a grave* desecrate, profane, defile, blaspheme. **3** *violate their privacy* disturb, disrupt, intrude on, interfere with, encroach on, invade. **4** *violate the peace* disturb, disrupt, break into, upset, shatter, destroy. **5** *he was accused of violating his niece* rape, ravish, indecently assault, abuse, deflower, molest, seduce.

violence n **1** *the violence of his temper* strength, forcefulness, lack of control/restraint, wildness, passion. *see* VIOLENT 1. **2** *the violence of the blow* forcefulness, powerfulness, might, savagery, ferocity, destructiveness, brutality. **3** *the violence of the storm* wildness, tempestuousness, turbulence. *see* VIOLENT 4. **4** *the violence of his dislike* strength, intensity, vehemence. *see* VIOLENT 5. **5** *the violence of the pain* sharpness, acuteness, intensity. *see* VIOLENT 6. **6** *use violence to get his way* force, brute force, roughness, ferocity, brutality, savagery; strong-arm tactics.

violent adj **1** *a violent temper* strong, powerful, forceful, uncontrolled, unrestrained, unbridled, uncontrollable, ungovernable, wild, passionate, raging. **2** *he's a violent person* brutal, vicious, destructive, savage, fierce, wild, intemperate, hot-headed, hot-tempered, bloodthirsty, homicidal, murderous, maniacal. **3** *a violent blow* forceful, powerful, mighty, savage, ferocious, destructive, damaging, brutal. **4** *a violent storm* wild, blustery, boisterous, raging, tempestuous, turbulent, tumultuous. **5** *a violent dislike* strong, great, intense, extreme, vehement, inordinate, excessive. **6** *a violent pain/toothache* sharp, acute, intense, excruciating, agonizing, biting.

virgin adj **1** *virgin snow/territory* pure, immaculate, unblemished, spotless, stainless, unused, untouched, untainted, unspoilt, untarnished, unadulterated. **2** *virgin young girls. see* VIRGINAL.

virginal adj *virginal young girls* pure, chaste, virtuous, uncorrupted.

virile adj **1** *a virile man* manly, all-male, strong, vigorous, robust, powerfully built, muscular, rugged, strapping, sturdy, red-blooded; *inf* macho. **2** *virile enough to procreate* young sexually potent. **3** *virile rather than feminine/effeminate* manly, masculine, male.

virility n **1** *the virility of the body-building enthusiasts* manliness, strength, vigour, robustness, muscularity, ruggedness; *inf* machismo. *see* VIRILE 1. **2** *impaired virility* sexual potency, potency, sexuality. **3** *question his virility* manliness, masculinity, maleness, manhood.

virtual adj **1** *traffic at a virtual standstill* more or less, near, effective, in effect, tantamount to, for all practical purposes. **2** *he is the virtual manager* in all but name, functioning as, operating as, for all practical purposes.

virtually adv *traffic virtually at a standstill | he is virtually in charge* more or less, nearly, practically, as good as, effectively, in effect, essentially, in essence, for all practical purposes, to all intents and purposes, in all but name.

virtue n **1** *admire the virtue of the hard-working men* goodness, righteousness, morality, ethicalness, uprightness, upstandingness, integrity, rectitude, honesty, honourableness, honour, incorruptibility, probity, decency, respectability, worthiness, worth, trustworthiness. **2** *admire virtue in a young girl* virginity, celibacy, purity, pureness, chastity, chasteness, innocence, modesty. **3** *generosity is one of her virtues | reliability is one of the car's virtues* good quality/point, merit, asset, credit, attribute, advantage, benefit, strength; *inf* plus. **4** *there is no virtue in the use of such drugs* merit, advantage, benefit, usefulness, efficacy, efficaciousness, power, potency. **by virtue of** *win by virtue of his talent* by reason of, by dint of, on account of, as a result of, owing to, thanks to.

virtuosity n skill, skilfulness, mastery, expertise, prowess, excellence, craftsmanship, flair, finish, polish, panache, brilliance, éclat, wizardry.

virtuoso n *a virtuoso on the piano* master, genius, expert, artist, maestro, wizard.

virtuoso adj *a virtuoso performance* skilful, masterly, impressive, outstanding, dazzling, bravura.

virtuous adj **1** *virtuous hard-working people* good, righteous, moral, ethical, upright, upstanding, honest, honourable, incorruptible, decent, respectable, worthy, trustworthy. **2** *virtuous young girls* virginal, celibate, pure, chaste, innocent, modest.

virulent adj **1** *using virulent substances as weed-killers* poisonous, toxic, venomous, deadly, lethal, fatal, noxious, harmful. **2** *a virulent form/strain of the disease* severe, extreme, violent, rapidly spreading, highly infectious/contagious, harmful, lethal. **3** *a virulent attack | virulent forms of abuse* hostile, spiteful, venomous, vicious, vindictive, malicious, malevolent, malignant, bitter, rancorous, acrimonious, abusive, aggressive, violent.

visible adj **1** *hills scarcely visible in the mist* in view, perceptible, perceivable, discernible, detectable, seeable. **2** *his distress was visible to all* apparent, evident, noticeable, observable, detectable, recognizable, manifest, plain, clear, obvious, patent, palpable, unmistakable, unconcealed, undisguised, conspicuous, distinct, distinguishable.

vision n **1** *have good vision* eyesight, sight, power of seeing; eyes. **2** *the saint saw a vision* apparition, spectre, phantom, ghost, wraith, phantasm, chimera, revelation. **3** *see his late mother in one of his visions* dream, hallucination, chimera, optical illusion, mirage, illusion, delusion, figment of the imagination. **4** *have visions of a juicy steak* dream, daydream, pipe-dream, fantasy, image, mental picture. **5** *artists must have vision* perception, perceptiveness, insight, intuition, imagination. **6** *in need of political vision* foresight, far-sightedness, prescience, breadth of view, discernment. **7** *she was a vision in white* dream, spectacle, picture, feast for the eyes, beautiful sight; *inf* sight for sore eyes.

visionary adj **1** *too visionary to make a success of business* idealistic, impractical, unrealistic, utopian, romantic, quixotic, dreamy, dreaming; *inf* starry-eyed. **2** *visionary artists*

perceptive, intuitive. *see* VISION 5. **3** *visionary politicians* far-sighted, discerning, wise. *see* VISION 6. **4** *visionary figures* unreal, imaginary, imagined, fanciful, fancied, illusory, delusory, figmental, phantasmal, phantasmagoric, spectral, ghostly, wraithlike. **5** *visionary schemes* impractical, unrealistic, unworkable, unfeasible, theoretical, hypothetical, idealistic, utopian.

visionary n **1** *ancient visionaries* mystic, seer, prophet. **2** *too much of a visionary to run a business* dreamer, daydreamer, idealist, romantic, romanticist, fantasist, theorist, utopian.

visit v **1** *visit his aunt | visit a friend in hospital* pay a visit to, go/come to see, pay a call on, call on, call/look in on, stop by; *inf pop/* drop in on, look up. **2** *he is visiting his aunt this week* stay with, be the guest of. **3** *inspectors visiting the school* pay a call on, inspect, survey, examine. **4** *a city visited with the plague* attack, assail, afflict, smite, descend on, trouble, harrow, torture.

visit n **1** *pay a visit to the new tenants* call, social call. **2** *their visit lasted three days* stay, sojourn, stopover.

visitation n **1** *school inspectors making their annual visitation* official visit, inspection, tour of inspection, survey, review, scrutiny, examination. **2** *the peasants regarded the earthquake as a divine visitation* affliction, scourge, plague, pestilence, blight, disaster, tragedy, calamity, catastrophe, cataclysm.

visitor n **1** *a visitor to the house* caller, guest. **2** *a visitor to the country* tourist, traveller, pilgrim.

visual adj **1** *visual problems* seeing, optical, ocular. **2** *have visual appeal | the visual arts* to be seen, seeable, perceivable, discernible.

visualize v conjure up, envisage, picture in the mind's eye, picture, envision, imagine, conceive.

vital adj **1** *the heart performs a vital function | the vital organs* life-giving, life-preserving, life-sustaining, basic, fundamental, essential. **2** *matters of vital importance* essential, necessary, needed, indispensable, key, important, significant, imperative, urgent, critical, crucial, life-and-death. **3** *such a vital person* lively, animated, spirited, vivacious, vibrant, zestful, dynamic, energetic, vigorous, forceful. **4** *a vital error* deadly, lethal, fatal, fateful.

vitality n *children full of vitality* life, liveliness, animation, spirit, spiritedness, vivacity, vibrancy, zest, zestfulness, dynamism, energy, vigour, forcefulness.

vitriolic adj *vitriolic criticism* caustic, mordant, acrimonious, bitter, acerbic, astringent, acid, acidulous, acrid, trenchant, virulent, spiteful, venomous, malicious, scathing, withering, sarcastic, sardonic; *inf* bitchy.

vituperate v revile, rail against, inveigh against, fulminate against, condemn, denounce, upbraid, berate, reprimand, castigate, chastise, rebuke, scold, chide, censure, find fault with, take to task, abuse, vilify, denigrate; *inf* slate.

vituperation n revilement, invective, condemnation, denunciation, blame, reprimand, admonition, castigation, chastisement, rebuke, scolding, fault-finding, abuse, vilification, denigration; *inf* flak.

vivacious adj lively, full of life, animated, effervescent, bubbling, ebullient, sparkling, scintillating, light-hearted, spirited, high-spirited, gay, merry, jolly, vibrant, vivid, dynamic, vital.

vivacity n liveliness, animation, effervescence, ebullience, sparkle, scintillation, spiritedness, spirit, high-spiritedness, sprightliness, gaiety, merriment, jollity, vibrancy, vividness, dynamism, vitality.

vivid adj **1** *vivid colours* strong, intense, colourful, rich, glowing, bright, brilliant, clear. **2** *a vivid description* graphic, clear, lively, stirring, striking, powerful, impressive, highly coloured, dramatic, memorable, realistic, lifelike, true to life. **3** *a vivid personality* strong, striking, flamboyant, memorable, dynamic, lively, animated, spirited, vibrant, vital.

vocabulary n **1** *have a limited vocabulary* word stock, lexicon, lexis. **2** *there's a vocabulary at the back of the book* word list, dictionary, glossary.

vocal adj **1** *vocal noises* voiced, vocalized, spoken, said, uttered, expressed, articulated, oral. **2** *people vocal in their criticism* vociferous, outspoken, forthright, plain-spoken, free-spoken, blunt, clamorous, strident, loud, noisy.

vocation n profession, calling, occupation, walk of life, career, life's work, *métier*, trade, craft, job, work, employment, business, line, speciality.

vociferous adj **1** *vociferous complaints* loud, noisy, clamorous, vehement, insistent. **2** *vociferous people complaining* vocal, outspoken, forthright, plain-spoken, strident, loud, noisy. *see* VOCAL 2.

vogue n **1** *the vogue for short skirts* fashion, mode, style, trend, taste, fad, craze, rage, latest thing, last word, *dernier cri*; *inf* the

thing. **2** *that hairstyle had a vogue in the '20s* fashionableness, modishness, popularity, currency, prevalence, favour, acceptance.

voice n **1** *lose her voice* power of speech; powers of articulation. **2** *give voice to her feelings* expression, utterance, verbalization, vocalization, airing. **3** *listen to the voice of the people* opinion, view, comment, feeling, wish, desire, vote. **4** *he is the voice of the people* spokesman, spokeswoman, spokesperson, mouthpiece, organ, agency, medium, vehicle.

voice v *voice one's displeasure* put in words, express, give utterance to, utter, articulate, enunciate, mention, talk of, communicate, declare, assert, divulge, air, ventilate; *inf* come out with.

void adj **1** *a void space* empty, emptied, vacant, without contents, bare, clear, free, unfilled, unoccupied, uninhabited, untenanted, tenantless. **2** *void of people* devoid of, lacking, wanting, without, destitute of. **3** *the contract/ticket is now void* null and void, nullified, invalid, cancelled, inoperative, ineffective, not binding, not in force, non-viable, useless, worthless, nugatory.

void n **1** *stare into a void* empty space, emptiness, blank space, blankness, vacuum. **2** *a void left by the death of his wife* space, gap, lacuna, hole, hollow, chasm, abyss.

void v **1** *void the decision* annul, nullify, disallow, invalidate, quash, cancel, repeal, revoke, rescind, reverse, abrogate. **2** *void the bucket/bowels* empty, drain, evacuate. **3** *void faeces* eject, expel, emit, discharge.

volatile adj **1** *a volatile person* mercurial, changeable, variable, capricious, whimsical, fickle, flighty, giddy, inconstant, erratic, unstable. **2** *volatile trading conditions* changeable, variable, inconstant, erratic, unsteady, unstable, irregular, fitful. **3** *a volatile international situation* explosive, eruptive, charged, inflammatory, tense, strained. **4** *volatile substances* evaporative, vaporous, vaporescent.

volition n *of one's own volition* of one's own free will, of one's own choice, by one's own preference, voluntarily.

volley n **1** *the police fired a volley of plastic bullets* barrage, cannonade, battery, broadside, salvo, fusillade, shower. **2** *a volley of questions/insults* barrage, battery, stream, deluge.

volubility n talkativeness, loquaciousness, loquacity, chattiness, articulacy, eloquence, fluency, glibness; *inf* gift of the gab.

voluble adj talkative, loquacious, garrulous, chatty, gossipy, chattering, articulate, eloquent, forthcoming, fluent, glib.

volume n **1** *publish a volume on butterflies* book, publication, tome. **2** *measure the volume* enclosed space, bulk, capacity. **3** *a volume of water escaped* quantity, amount, mass. **4** *turn down the volume | the volume of the music is too loud* loudness, sound, amplification.

voluminous adj *a voluminous cape* capacious, roomy, commodious, ample, full, big, vast, billowing.

voluntarily adv of one's own free will, freely, of one's own volition/accord, willingly, by choice, by preference, spontaneously, without being asked.

voluntary adj **1** *attendance is voluntary* of one's own free will, volitional, of one's own accord, optional, discretional, at one's discretion, elective, non-compulsory, non-mandatory. **2** *undertake voluntary work* unpaid, without payment, honorary, volunteer.

volunteer v **1** *volunteer one's services* offer, tender, proffer, present, put forward, advance. **2** *he volunteered as a helper* offer one's services, present oneself, step forward.

voluptuous adj **1** *voluptuous pleasures* hedonistic, sybaritic, epicurean, pleasure-loving, self-indulgent, sensual, carnal, licentious, lascivious. **2** *a voluptuous woman* curvy, shapely, full-figured, ample, buxom, seductive; *inf* curvaceous.

vomit v **1** *he suddenly vomited* be sick, spew; *inf* throw up, puke; *Amer inf* barf. **2** *vomit blood* bring up, regurgitate, spew up, spit up. **3** *chimneys vomiting smoke* belch, eject, emit, send forth, eruct.

voracious adj **1** *a voracious eater* gluttonous, greedy, ravenous, ravening, starving, hungry. **2** *a voracious appetite* insatiable, insatiate, unquenchable, prodigious, uncontrolled. **3** *a voracious reader* compulsive, enthusiastic, eager.

vortex n whirlpool, maelstrom, eddy, swirl, whirlwind.

vote n **1** *have a vote on who should lead* ballot, poll, election, referendum, plebiscite. **2** *get the vote* right to vote, franchise, suffrage.

vote v **1** *vote for a new president* cast one's vote, go to the polls, mark one's ballot paper. **2** *vote the government in* elect, opt for, return. **3** *I vote that we go home* suggest, propose, recommend, advocate.

vouch v **vouch for 1** *vouch for his honesty* attest to, bear witness to, give assurance of, answer for, be responsible for, guarantee, go/stand bail for. **2** *vouch for the painting's authenticity* certify, warrant, confirm, verify, validate, substantiate.

voucher n chit, slip, ticket, token, document.

vouchsafe v **1** *vouchsafe them a free pardon | vouchsafe a reply* grant, give, accord, confer on, yield to, cede to, favour with. **2** *vouchsafe to reply* deign, condescend.

vow n *take a vow of silence | wedding vows* oath, pledge, promise.

vow v *vow to be true* swear, state under oath, pledge, promise, undertake, give one's word of honour.

voyage n **1** *a sea voyage* crossing, cruise, passage. **2** *voyage by land and sea* journey, trip, expedition; travels.

voyage v **1** *voyage across the Atlantic* sail, cruise. **2** *voyage through space* travel, journey, take a trip.

vulgar adj **1** *vulgar language/jokes* rude, indecent, indecorous, indelicate, unseemly, offensive, distasteful, obnoxious, risqué, suggestive, off-colour, blue, ribald, bawdy, obscene, lewd, salacious, licentious, concupiscent, smutty, dirty, filthy, pornographic, scatalogical; *inf* raunchy. **2** *vulgar table manners* rude, impolite, ill-mannered, unmannerly, ill-bred, common, coarse, boorish, rough, crude. **3** *vulgar decorations* tasteless, gross, crass, unrefined, tawdry, ostentatious, showy, flashy, gaudy; *inf* flash. **4** *the vulgar herd* common, ordinary, low, low-born, ignorant, unsophisticated, unrefined, uneducated, illiterate, uncultured, uncultivated, uncouth, crude.

vulgarity n **1** *the vulgarity of the language/jokes* rudeness, indelicacy, offensiveness, suggestiveness, ribaldry, obscenity, smuttiness; *inf* raunchiness. *see* VULGAR 1. **2** *the vulgarity of his table manners* rudeness, impoliteness, ill manners, coarseness, crudeness. *see* VULGAR 2. **3** *the vulgarity of the decorations* tastelessness, grossness, crassness, tawdriness, ostentation, gaudiness. *see* VULGAR 3. **4** *the vulgarity of the common herd* commonness, lowness, ignorance, unsophisticatedness, lack of refinement, uncouthness, crudeness. *see* VULGAR 4.

vulnerable adj **1** *vulnerable armies/children* open to attack, attackable, assailable, exposed, unprotected, unguarded, defenceless, easily hurt/wounded/damaged, helpless, powerless, weak, sensitive, thin-skinned. **2** *vulnerable to criticism/temptation* open to, wide open to, exposed to, liable to, subject to.

Ww

wad n **1** *a wad of putty* | *wads of cotton wool* lump, mass, chunk, hunk, ball, plug, block. **2** *a wad of bank notes* bundle, roll.

wadding n stuffing, filling, packing, padding, lining.

waddle v sway, wobble, totter, toddle, shuffle.

wade v **1** *wade the stream* | *wade across the snow* ford, cross, traverse. **2** *children wading in the stream* paddle, splash about. **3** *wade through piles of papers* proceed with difficulty, work one's way, plough (through), labour (through), toil/plug/peg away. **wade in** *if we all wade in we'll soon get finished* set to, set to work, pitch in, buckle down, go to it, put one's shoulder to the wheel; *inf* get cracking, get stuck in. **wade into** *wade into the boy who hit/criticized his sister* attack, set about, assault, launch oneself at; *inf* light into, tear into.

waffle n *it was all waffle so we didn't learn anything* meaningless talk/writing, padding, equivocation, prattle, jabbering, verbiage, logorrhoea; *inf* wittering.

waffle v *speakers waffling on to a bored audience* | *waffle without getting to the point* ramble, prattle, jabber, babble; *inf* rabbit, witter.

waft v **1** *leaves wafting down the river* | *smells wafting from the kitchen* float, glide, drift, be carried/borne/conveyed. **2** *the wind wafted the leaves towards us* carry, bear, convey, transport, transmit.

wag[1] n **1** *a wag of the tail* swing, sway, vibration, quiver, shake. **2** *a wag of the finger* wiggle, wobble, wave. **3** *a wag of the head* nod, bob.

wag[1] v **1** *the dog's tail wagged* swing, sway, vibrate, quiver, shake, rock, twitch. **2** *wag one's finger* waggle, wiggle, wobble, wave. **3** *wag one's head* nod, bob.

wag[2] n *he's quite a wag* wit, humorist, jester, joker, jokester, comic, comedian, comedienne, wisecracker, punner.

wage n *on a low wage* pay, remuneration; wages, earnings. *see* WAGES 1.

wage v *wage war* carry on, conduct, execute, engage in, pursue, undertake, devote oneself to, practise.

wager n *lay a wager that he will win* bet, gamble, stake, pledge, hazard; *inf* flutter.

wager v *I wager that he will win* lay a wager, bet, place/make/lay a bet, lay odds, put money on, speculate.

wages npl **1** *low wages* | *collect one's wages* pay, payment, fee, remuneration, salary, emolument, stipend; earnings. **2** *the wages of sin* recompense, requital, retribution; returns, deserts.

waggish adj playful, roguish, impish, mischievous, joking, jesting, jocular, jocose, facetious, witty, amusing, entertaining, droll, whimsical.

waggle v *waggle one's finger/ears/bottom* wiggle, wobble, shake, sway, wag, quiver.

waif n stray, foundling, orphan.

wail n *the wails of the bereaved/abandoned children* cry of grief/pain, lament, lamentation, weeping, sob, moan, groan, whine, complaint, howl, yowl, ululation.

wail v *widows/children wailing* cry, lament, weep, sob, moan, groan, whine, complain, howl, yowl, ululate.

wait v **1** *wait here* stay, remain, rest, linger, tarry, abide. **2** *you'll just have to wait and see* | *wait until you hear from him* be patient, hold back, stand by, bide one's time, hang fire, mark time, cool one's heels; *inf* sit tight, hold one's horses, sweat it out. **3** *wait his arrival* await, wait for, look/watch out for, anticipate, expect, be ready for, be in readiness for. **4** *wait dinner for him* delay, postpone, put off, hold off, hold back, defer. **5** *wait for him* | *wait for his arrival* be ready, anticipate, expect. **wait on** *wait on the dinner guests* act as a waiter/waitress to, serve, attend to. **wait up** *wait up until his daughter returns* stay up, stay awake, keep vigil.

wait n *have a wait of two hours for the bus* period of waiting, interval, stay, delay, hold-up.

waiter, waitress n steward, stewardess, server, attendant.

waive v **1** *waive one's right to appeal* relinquish, renounce, give up, abandon, surrender, yield, cede. **2** *waive the rules* set aside, forgo, disregard, ignore. **3** *waive the decision until tomorrow* postpone, defer, put off, delay, shelve; *inf* put on the back-burner.

wake v **1** *wake at dawn* awake, awaken, waken, wake up, waken up, rouse, stir, come to, get up, arise. **2** *wake the children* wake up, waken, rouse. **3** *wake him out of sloth* rouse, stir up, activate, stimulate, spur, prod, galvanize provoke. **4** *wake to the fact that he is dishonest* become aware/conscious, become alert, become mindful/heedful. **5** *wake old memories* awaken, evoke, call up, conjure up, rouse, stir, revive, resuscitate, revivify, rekindle, reignite.

wake n *hold a wake for his dead mother* vigil, death-watch, watch.

wakeful adj **1** *wakeful children* unsleeping, restless, tossing and turning, insomniac. **2** *wakeful security staff* alert, on the alert, vigilant, on the lookout, on one's guard, on the qui vive, watchful, observant, attentive, heedful, wary.

waken v **1** *waken at dawn* wake, awaken, stir. *see* WAKE v 1. **2** *waken the children* wake, rouse. *see* WAKE v 2. **3** *waken old memories* wake, awaken, evoke, call up, stir, revive, rekindle. *see* WAKE v 5.

walk v **1** *we walked rather than take the car* go by foot, travel on foot, foot it; *inf* go by shank's pony, hoof it. **2** *walk, don't run* stroll, saunter, amble, plod, trudge, hike, tramp, trek, march, stride, step out. **3** *walk her home* accompany, escort, convoy. **walk off/away with 1** *walk off with the firm's takings* make/run off with, carry off, snatch, steal, filch, pilfer, embezzle. **2** *walk off with the match/prize* win easily, win hands down. **walk out 1** *he had a row with the boss and walked out* leave suddenly, make a sudden departure, get up and go, storm out, flounce out; *inf* take off. **2** *the workers walked out at lunch-time* go on strike, call a strike, withdraw one's labour, down tools, stop work, take industrial action. **walk out on** *walk out on his wife and children* desert, abandon, forsake, leave, leave in the lurch, run away from, throw over, jilt; *inf* chuck, dump.

walk n **1** *go for a walk* stroll, saunter, amble, promenade, ramble, hike, tramp, march, constitutional, airing. **2** *he has a distinctive walk* manner of walking, gait, pace, step, stride. **3** *the walk up to the house* road, avenue, drive, promenade, path, pathway, footpath, track, lane, alley. **4** *the postman's usual walk* route, beat, round, run, circuit. **walk of life** social rank/status, sphere, area, line of work, profession, career, vocation, job, employment, trade, craft, *métier*.

walker n pedestrian, hiker, rambler, wayfarer, footslogger.

walk-out n strike, industrial action, stoppage.

walk-over n *winning the prize was a walk-over* easy victory; *inf* piece of cake, child's play, doddle, push-over.

wall n **1** *areas of the house separated by walls* partition, room divider. **2** *the area had a wall around it* enclosure. **3** *the city walls are still standing* fortification, rampart, barricade, parapet, bulwark, stockade, breastwork. **4** *create new tariff walls* barrier, obstacle, impediment, block.

wallet n pocket book, notecase, purse, pouch; *Amer* billfold.

wallow v **1** *the hippopotamus was wallowing in mud* roll, tumble about, lie around, splash around. **2** *wallow in luxury/self-pity* luxuriate in, bask in, take pleasure/satisfaction in, indulge oneself in, delight in, revel in, glory in, enjoy.

wan adj **1** *looking wan after illness* pale, pallid, ashen, white, white as a sheet/ghost, anaemic, colourless, bloodless, waxen, pasty, peaky, tired looking, washed out, sickly. **2** *a wan light* dim, faint, weak, feeble, pale.

wand n baton, stick, staff, twig, sprig, withe, withy.

wander v **1** *wander over the hills* ramble, roam, meander, rove, range, prowl, saunter, stroll, amble, peregrinate, drift; *inf* traipse, mooch. **2** *rivers wandering along* wind, meander, curve, zigzag. **3** *wander from the path/point | wander from the straight and narrow* stray, depart, diverge, veer, swerve, deviate. **4** *the child has wandered off* lose one's way, get lost, go off course, go astray, go off at a tangent. **5** *the old man is wandering* be incoherent, ramble, babble, talk nonsense, rave, be delirious.

wander n *have a wander in the hills | a wander round the shops* ramble, saunter, stroll, amble.

wanderer n rambler, roamer, rover, drifter, traveller, itinerant, wayfarer, nomad, bird of passage, rolling stone, gypsy; vagabond, vagrant, tramp, derelict; beggar, homeless/displaced person; *Amer* hobo; *inf* bum.

wandering adj **1** *wandering bands of people* rambling, roaming, roving, drifting, travelling, itinerant, peripatetic, nomadic, gypsy, vagabond, vagrant, migrant, transient, homeless. **2** *wandering rivers/paths* winding, meandering, curving, bending, zigzagging.

wane v **1** *the moon has waned* pass full moon, decrease, diminish, dwindle. **2** *his power/importance is waning* decrease, decline, diminish, dwindle, shrink, contract, taper off, subside, sink, ebb, dim, fade away, vanish, die out, draw to a close, evanesce, peter out, wind down, be on the way out, abate, fail, become weak, deteriorate, degenerate.

wane n *the wane of his power/importance* decline, decrease, diminution, dwindling, contraction, subsidence, ebb, vanishing, evanescence, abatement, failure, weakening, deteriorating, degenerating. *see* WANE V 2.

want v **1** *children wanting sweets* wish, wish for, desire, demand, call for, long for, hope for, yearn for, pine for, fancy, crave, hanker after, hunger for, thirst for, lust after, covet, need; *inf* have a yen for. **2** *he wants to emigrate* wish, desire, long, yearn. **3** *the garden wants weeding | the car wants petrol* need, be/stand in need of, require. **4** *poor people wanting food* have need of, lack, be lacking, be without, be devoid of, be bereft of, be short of, be deficient in, have insufficient.

want n **1** *for want of time* lack, absence, dearth, deficiency, inadequacy, insufficiency, shortness, paucity, shortage, scarcity, scarceness, scantiness. **2** *children expressing their wants* wish, desire, demand, longing, yearning, fancy, craving, hankering, hunger, thirst, lust, covetousness; *inf* yen. **3** *give aid to people in want* need, neediness, privation, poverty, destitution, penury, indigence.

wanting adj **1** *find the service wanting* lacking, deficient, inadequate, imperfect, not up to standard/par, not good enough, disappointing, not acceptable, not up to expectations, flawed, faulty, defective, unsound, substandard, inferior, secondrate, patchy, sketchy. **2** *something wanting in the machine/organization* lacking, missing, absent, not there, short.

wanting prep *a car wanting an engine* lacking, in need of, without, sans; *inf* minus.

wanton adj **1** *wanton women seducing the soldiers* promiscuous, fast, immoral, loose, immodest, shameless, unchaste, unvirtuous, of easy virtue, impure, abandoned, lustful, lecherous, lascivious, libidinous, licentious, libertine, dissolute, dissipated, debauched, degenerate. **2** *wanton destruction* wilful, malicious, malevolent, spiteful, wicked, evil, cruel, unmotivated, motiveless, arbitrary, groundless, unjustifiable, unjustified, needless, unnecessary, uncalled-for, unprovoked, gratuitous, senseless, pointless, purposefulness. **3** *a wanton wind* capricious, playful, sportive, careless, heedless, impulsive, rash, reckless, devil-may-care. **4** *weeds growing in wan-*

ton profusion wild, unrestrained, uncontrolled, immoderate, lavish, extravagant, abundant, profuse, luxuriant.

wanton n *wantons out to seduce the men in the bar | wantons seducing older women* loose woman, woman of easy virtue, slut, trollop, harlot, strumpet, prostitute, whore; lecher, Casanova, libertine, debauchee, rake.

war n **1** *a state of war between the nations* conflict, strife, hostility, enmity, antagonism, animus, ill will, bad blood. **2** *the war lasted five years | take part in many wars* warfare, conflict, strife, combat, fighting, struggle, armed conflict, battle, fight, confrontation, skirmish; hostilities. **3** *the war against poverty* battle, fight, campaign, crusade.

war v *nations warring with nations* wage/make war, be at war, conduct a war, do combat/ battle, fight, take up arms, cross swords, quarrel, wrangle.

ward n **1** *a hospital ward* room, compartment, cubicle. **2** *counting the votes in the various wards* administrative district, district, division, quarter, zone. **3** *his niece is his ward* charge, protégé, dependant, pupil.

ward v **ward off 1** *ward off a blow* fend off, stave off, parry, avert, deflect, turn aside. **2** *ward off intruders* drive back, repel, repulse, beat back, rout, put to flight, scatter, disperse; *inf* send packing. **3** *ward off the attack* fend off, stave off, keep at bay, keep at arm's length, avert, rebuff, foil, frustrate, thwart, checkmate.

warden n **1** *traffic warden* supervisor, superintendent, steward, overseer. **2** *game wardens* custodian, keeper, guardian, protector, guard, watchman. **3** *a prison warden* prison officer, guard.

warder, wardress n prison officer, guard, warden, jailer, gaoler; *inf* screw.

wardrobe n **1** *put the suits in the wardrobe* clothes cupboard; *Amer* closet. **2** *she has a huge wardrobe | her summer wardrobe* collection/set of clothes, trousseau.

warehouse n store, storehouse, depot, depository, stockroom.

wares npl goods, products, commodities, lines; merchandise, produce, stuff, stock.

warfare n armed conflict, combat, strife, fighting, battle, campaigning, passage at arms; hostilities.

warily adv **1** *tread warily* carefully, with care, cautiously, gingerly, circumspectly, guardedly, on one's guard, on the alert, on the qui vive, watchfully, vigilantly. *see* WARY 1. **2** *treat him warily* cautiously, suspiciously, distrustfully, mistrustfully, charily; *inf* cagily.

wariness n **1** *tread with wariness* care, carefulness, caution, circumspection, alertness, attention, heedfulness, watchfulness, vigilance. **2** *treat the stranger with wariness* caution, circumspection, suspicion, distrust, mistrust.

warlike adj aggressive, belligerent, bellicose, pugnacious, combative, militaristic, militant, martial.

warlock n sorcerer, wizard, male witch, magician.

warm adj **1** *warm water* heated, tepid, lukewarm. **2** *a warm day* sunny, balmy. **3** *a warm person/personality | a warm heart* kindly, kind, friendly, affable, amiable, genial, cordial, sympathetic, affectionate, loving, tender, caring, charitable, sincere, genuine. **4** *receive a warm welcome* hearty, cordial, genial, friendly, hospitable, enthusiastic, eager, sincere, heartfelt, ardent, vehement, passionate, intense, fervent, effusive. **5** *the international situation is getting rather warm* heated, hostile, tense, strained, explosive, dangerous, perilous, hazardous, tricky, difficult, unpleasant, uncomfortable, disagreeable. **6** *players of the guessing game getting warm* close, near.

warm v **1** *warm the food in the oven* warm up, make warm, heat, heat up, reheat. **2** *feel themselves warming to her | warm to the idea* feel well-disposed, feel sympathetic, feel a liking (for), feel attracted. **warm up 1** *warm up the food* heat up. *see* WARM v 1. **2** *warm the party up* liven, enliven, put some life into, cheer up, animate; *inf* get going. **3** *warm up for the race* loosen up, limber up, prepare, exercise, practise, train.

warmed up adj **1** *warmed up food* reheated, heated up. **2** *warmed up ideas/prose* repeated, unoriginal, derivative, stale, hackneyed, trite, stock, banal; *inf* old hat.

warmth n **1** *feel the warmth of the fire/sun* warmness, heat, hotness. **2** *the warmth of her personality* kindness, kindliness, friendliness, affability, amiability, geniality, cordiality, sympathy, sympatheticness, affectionateness, affection, lovingness, love, tenderness, care, charitableness, charity, sincerity, genuineness. **3** *the warmth of the welcome* heartiness, cordiality, geniality, friendliness, hospitableness, hospitality, enthusiasm, eagerness, sincerity, ardour, vehemence, passion, intensity, fervour, effusiveness.

warn v **1** *write to warn them of the approaching confrontation/danger* inform, notify, give notice, give prior notice/tell, let know,

acquaint, give fair warning, forewarn; *inf* tip off, put wise. **2** *warn them to be careful* advise, exhort, urge, counsel, caution, forewarn, prewarn, put on the alert, make aware. **3** *the headmaster warned the unruly pupils* give a warning to, admonish, remonstrate with.

warning n **1** *send them a warning of the approaching confrontation* information, notification, notice, word, forewarning; *inf* tip-off. **2** *deliver a warning that they should be careful* caution; advice, exhortation, counselling. **3** *get a warning from the headmaster* admonition, remonstrance. **4** *he regarded it as a warning of things to come* omen, premonition, foretoken, token, augury, signal, sign, threat, caveat.

warrant n **1** *they are acting under warrant of the king* authorization, consent, sanction, permission, validation, licence, imprimatur, seal of approval. **2** *a warrant for his arrest | a death warrant* authorization, official document, written order; papers. **3** *a sales warrant* voucher, chit, slip, paper.

warrant v **1** *the law warrants the procedure* authorize, consent to, sanction, permit, license, approve of. **2** *her interference was not warranted* justify, vindicate, excuse, be a defence of, explain away, account for, be a reason for, offer grounds for, support. **3** *unable to warrant the truth of the statement* guarantee, swear to, answer for, vouch for, testify to, bear witness to, support, endorse, underwrite, back up, stand by.

warrantable adj **1** *his action was warrantable by the king* authorizable, sanctionable, approvable. *see* WARRANT v 1. **2** *his interference was scarcely warrantable* justifiable, vindicable, excusable, explainable, explicable, reasonable, supportable.

warring adj *warring factions* conflicting, opposing, clashing, hostile, rival; *inf* at each other's throats.

warrior n fighter, fighting man, combatant, soldier, champion.

wary adj **1** *be wary when you walk alone at night* careful, cautious, circumspect, chary, on one's guard, alert, on the alert/look out, on the qui vive, attentive, heedful, watchful, vigilant, observant; *inf* wide awake, on one's toes. **2** *you should be wary of strangers* careful, cautious, chary, suspicious, distrustful, mistrustful; *inf* leery.

wash v **1** *I must wash before breakfast* wash oneself, have a wash, bath, shower, have a bath/shower. **2** *wash one's face | wash the floor* clean, cleanse, sponge, scrub. **3** *wash one's clothes* launder, clean. **4** *wash one's hair* shampoo, clean. **5** *waves washing against the* *rocks* splash against, dash against, break against, beat against. **6** *his story just won't wash* be accepted, be plausible, be convincing, hold up, hold water, stand up, bear scrutiny; *inf* stick. **7** *the current washed the boat away* carry off, bear away, sweep away, convey, transport. **8** *wash away the river bank* erode, abrade, wear, denude. **9** *wash off/out the stain* remove by washing, sponge, scrub.

wash n **1** *have a wash | in need of a wash* clean, cleaning, cleansing, bath, shower. **2** *I must do the wash* washing, laundry. **3** *put the wash in the basket* dirty washing, dirty clothes, soiled linen. **4** *the wash of the waves against the rocks | the ship's wash* surge, swell, roll, flow, splash. **5** *antiseptic wash* liquid, lotion, salve, application, preparation. **6** *put a yellow wash on the walls* paint, stain, varnish, coat, layer, film, overlay, screen.

washed out adj **1** *washed-out jeans* faded, blanched, bleached. **2** *always wear washed-out colours* pale, flat, lacklustre. **3** *a washed-out complexion* pale, wan, pallid, white, anaemic, etiolated, colourless, drawn, haggard. **4** *feeling washed out after a hard day* exhausted, tired out, worn out, weary, fatigued, spent, drained; *inf* all in, done in, dead on one's feet, dead, dog-tired, played out, pooped, knackered.

waspish adj petulant, peevish, querulous, touchy, testy, irritable, irascible, cross, snappish, cantankerous, splenetic, short-tempered, ill-tempered, bad-tempered, crabbed, crotchety, grumpy.

waste v **1** *waste resources/money | jokes wasted on the audience* squander, dissipate, fritter away, misspend, misuse, spend recklessly, throw away, go through, run through; *inf* blow. **2** *his legs are gradually wasting away* grow weak, wither, atrophy, become emaciated. **3** *the disease had wasted his legs* weaken, enfeeble, sap the strength of, wither, debilitate, atrophy, emaciate, shrivel, shrink. **4** *the invading army wasted the land* destroy, devastate, wreak havoc on, pillage, plunder, sack, spoliate, loot, maraud, harry.

waste n **1** *a waste of money/time* squandering, dissipation, frittering away, misspending, misuse, prodigality, unthriftiness. **2** *dispose of the waste* rubbish, refuse, debris, dross; dregs, leavings; *Amer* garbage, trash. **3** *lost in the wastes of Antarctica* desert, wasteland, wilderness, barrenness, emptiness, vastness.

waste adj **1** *waste material* left over, unused, superfluous, supernumerary, unwanted, worthless, useless. **2** *waste land* desert, barren, uncultivated, unproductive, arid, bare, desolate, solitary, lonely, empty, void, uninhabited, unpopulated, wild, bleak, cheerless.

wasted adj **1** *wasted resources* squandered, dissipated, exhausted, used up, misspent, misused. **2** *wasted opportunities* missed, lost, past, bungled. **3** *wasted limbs* weakened, weak, withered, atrophied, emaciated, shrivelled, shrunken.

wasteful adj *wasteful use of the supplies* prodigal, profligate, thriftless, spendthrift, extravagant, lavish.

wastrel n **1** *a wastrel getting through a fortune* waster, spendthrift, prodigal, squanderer, big spender. **2** *she's hard-working but he's a complete wastrel* good-for-nothing, layabout, ne'er-do-well, idler, drone, loafer, shirker, malingerer.

watch v **1** *watch the moon* look at, observe, view, eye, gaze at, stare at, gape at, peer at, contemplate, behold, inspect, scrutinize, survey, scan, examine. **2** *watch his movements | watch the man next door* keep watch on, keep an eye on, keep in sight, follow, spy on; *inf* keep tabs on. **3** *watch and don't get mugged* look out, pay attention, take heed/care, be on the alert/lookout, be watchful. *see* WATCH v watch out. **4** *could you watch the children for me* mind, take care of, look after, supervise, superintend, tend, guard, protect; *inf* keep an eye on. **watch out 1** *watch out and don't get mugged* watch, watch oneself, be watchful, be on the watch, mind out, look out, pay attention, take heed/care, be careful, have a care, be on the alert/lookout, keep a sharp lookout, be vigilant, be wary, be on the qui vive; *inf* keep an eye open, keep one's eyes peeled/skinned. **2** *watch out for the postman* look out for, wait for; *inf* keep an eye open for.

watch over *shepherds watch over the sheep | lawyers watching over our interests* look after, tend, take care of, guard, protect, shield, preserve.

watch n **1** *the time by my watch* wrist-watch, pocket watch, timepiece, chronometer. **2** *on watch at night* guard, vigil.

watchdog n **1** *a watchdog guarding the premises at night* guard dog. **2** *a watchdog of consumers' interests* custodian, guardian, protector, monitor, scrutineer, inspector.

watcher n spectator, onlooker, looker-on, observer, viewer, witness, spy.

watchful adj *keep a watchful eye on the building* observant, alert, vigilant, attentive, heedful, sharp-eyed, eagle-eyed, wary, circumspect.

watchman n security guard/man, guard, custodian, caretaker.

watchword n **1** *quality is meant to be the watchword of the firm* slogan, motto, maxim, catchword, catch-phrase, byword, battle/ rallying cry. **2** *unable to gain entry without the correct watchword* password, magic word, sign, shibboleth.

water n **1** *drink water* Adam's ale; tap water, mineral water, bottled water. **2** *have a picnic by the water* aquatic region; sea, river, lake, loch, pool, reservoir. **hold water** *your theory won't hold water* be tenable, ring true, bear examination, work out.

water v **1** *water the garden* sprinkle, moisten, dampen, wet, water down, douse, hose, spray, drench, saturate, sodden, flood. **2** *his eyes are watering* exude water, moisten, leak. **3** *water the drinks* add water to, water down, dilute, thin, weaken, adulterate, **water down 1** *water down the drinks* water, add water to, dilute. *see* WATER v 3. **2** *water down the extent of the disaster* play down, downplay, tone down, soft-pedal, understate, underemphasize.

waterfall n cascade, cataract; falls.

watertight adj **1** *the boat/jacket is watertight* waterproof, sound. **2** *a watertight excuse* sound, flawless, incontrovertible, indisputable, foolproof, unassailable, impregnable.

watery adj **1** *a watery substance* aqueous, liquid, liquefied, fluid, hydrous. **2** *watery terrain* wet, damp, moist, sodden, soggy, squelchy, saturated, waterlogged, marshy, boggy, swampy, miry. **3** *a watery soup/batter* thin, runny, weak, dilute, diluted, watered down, adulterated, tasteless, flavourless; *inf* wishy-washy. **4** *watery colours* pale, wan, insipid; *inf* wishy-washy. **5** *watery eyes* moist, tearful, teary, weeping, weepy, lachrymose.

wave v **1** *corn waving in the breeze* undulate, ripple, stir, flutter, flap, sway, swing, shake, quiver, oscillate. **2** *wave one's hand/ flag* move up and down, move to and fro, wag, waggle, flutter. **3** *wave a sword in the air* brandish, swing, shake. **4** *wave to them to follow* gesture, gesticulate, signal, sign, beckon, indicate. **5** *her hair waves beautifully* undulate, curl, kink. **wave aside** *wave aside his objections* set aside, dismiss, reject, disregard, ignore.

wave n **1** *children playing in the waves* breaker, billow, roller, comber, ripple, white horse, white cap; swell, surf. **2** *a wave of visitors* stream, flow, rush, surge, flood. **3** *the waves in her hair* undulation, curl, kink. **4** *a wave of enthusiasm* | *a crime wave* surge, upsurge, ground-swell, welling up, rush, outbreak, rash. **5** *waves in the water* | *light waves* ripple, vibration, oscillation, undulation.

waver v **1** *his gaze did not waver* | *his courage began to waver* become unsteady, falter, wobble, hesitate. **2** *we wavered and someone else got in first* | *waver between staying and leaving* be irresolute/indecisive, hesitate, dither, equivocate, hem and haw, vacillate, beat about the bush; *inf* shilly-shally, pussyfoot around, blow hot and cold. **3** *lights wavering* flicker, quiver, tremble. **4** *drunks wavering down the road* weave, reel, totter, teeter, stagger, wobble.

wavy adj undulating, curvy, curling, squiggly, rippled, curving, winding.

wax v **1** *the moon was waxing* approach full moon, get bigger, increase in size, enlarge. **2** *his power waxed in time of war* increase, grow, develop, enlarge, magnify, extend, widen, broaden, spread, mushroom. **3** *wax lyrical about his achievements* become, grow.

way n **1** *walk along the paved way* road, roadway, street, thoroughfare, track, path, pathway, lane, avenue, drive. **2** *is this the way to London?* route, road, course, direction. **3** *the right way to cook the meat* method, course of action, process, procedure, technique, system, plan, scheme, manner, *modus operandi*; means. **4** *admire the way in which she dresses* manner, style, fashion, mode. **5** *dislike his brusque way* conduct, behaviour, practice, wont, manner, style, nature, personality, temperament, disposition, character; habit, custom, characteristic, trait, attribute, mannerism, peculiarity, idiosyncrasy. **6** *a long way from here to London* distance, length, stretch, journey. **7** *make way for the children* room, elbowroom, space. **8** *we've got some way to winning* | *under way* headway, progress, advance. **9** *things are in a bad way* state, condition, situation; *inf* shape. **10** *in some ways it will be useful* | *can I help you in any way?* feature, aspect, detail, point, particular, respect, sense. **by the way** incidentally, by the by, in passing, *en passant*. **give way 1** *the bridge gave way* collapse, give, fall to pieces, crumble, cave in. **2** *he refused to help but finally gave way* yield, back down, make concessions, concede defeat, acquiesce. **on the/one's way** coming, going, proceeding, journeying, travelling.

wayfarer n traveller, walker, hiker, rambler, wanderer, roamer, rover, nomad, gypsy, vagabond, vagrant.

wayfaring adj travelling, journeying, walking, hiking, wandering, roaming, roving, drifting, nomadic, itinerant, peripatetic, on the move/go.

waylay v **1** *the highwaymen waylaid them* lie in wait for, ambush, hold up, attack. **2** *she waylaid the teacher to ask about her child* accost, stop and talk to, intercept, pounce on, swoop down on.

wayward adj **1** *wayward children* wilful, self-willed, headstrong, stubborn, obstinate, obdurate, perverse, contrary, uncooperative, refractory, recalcitrant, contumacious, unruly, ungovernable, unmanageable, incorrigible, intractable, difficult, fractious, disobedient, insubordinate. **2** *wayward fancies/youngster* capricious, whimsical, fickle, inconstant, changeable, changeful, variable, erratic, unpredictable, unstable, mercurial, volatile, flighty.

weak adj **1** *feeling weak after illness | too weak to walk* weakly, frail, fragile, delicate, feeble, infirm, shaky, debilitated, incapacitated, ailing, indisposed, decrepit, puny, faint, enervated, tired, fatigued, exhausted, spent, worn out. **2** *too weak to stand up to his enemies/wife* cowardly, pusillanimous, timorous, timid, spineless, ineffectual, useless, inept, effete, powerless, impotent, namby-pamby, soft; *inf* yellow, weak-kneed. **3** *weak eyes/eyesight* defective, faulty, poor, inadequate, deficient, imperfect, substandard, lacking, wanting. **4** *weak excuses* unsound, feeble, flimsy, lame, hollow, pathetic, unconvincing, untenable, implausible, unsatisfactory. **5** *a weak sound/signal* faint, low, muffled, stifled, muted, scarcely audible. **6** *a weak light* faint, dim, pale, wan. **7** *weak coffee* understrength, dilute, diluted, watery, waterish, thinned down, thin, adulterated, tasteless, flavourless, insipid; *inf* wishy-washy.

weaken v **1** *the illness had weakened her* enfeeble, debilitate, incapacitate, sap one's strength, enervate, tire, exhaust, wear out. **2** *weaken the force of the argument* lessen, reduce, decrease, diminish, moderate, temper, sap. **3** *the force of the storm weakened* abate, lessen, decrease, dwindle, diminish, ease up, let up. **4** *weaken the argument* impair, undermine, invalidate. **5** *they first refused to help but weakened later* relent, give in, acquiesce, yield, give way, accede, come round. **6** *too much milk weakened the coffee* dilute, water down, thin, adulterate.

weakling n coward, mouse, milksop, namby-pamby; *inf* wimp, sissy, drip, wet, doormat, chicken, yellow-belly, fraidy-cat, scaredy-cat.

weakness n **1** *the weakness of the invalid* frailty, fragility, delicateness, delicacy, feebleness, infirmity, debility, incapacity, indisposition, decrepitude, puniness, enervation, fatigue. *see* WEAK 1. **2** *despise his weakness* cowardliness, timidity, spinelessness, ineffectuality, ineptness, powerlessness, impotence. *see* WEAK 2. **3** *the weakness of her eyesight* defectiveness, faultiness, inadequacy, deficiency. *see* WEAK 3. **4** *the weakness of the excuses* unsoundness, feebleness, flimsiness, lameness, untenability, implausibility. *see* WEAK 4. **5** *the weakness of the sound/signal* faintness, low intensity, mutedness. *see* WEAK 5. **6** *the weakness of the light* faintness, dimness. *see* WEAK 6. **7** *the weakness of the coffee* diluteness, wateriness, thinness, tastelessness, flavourlessness; *inf* wishy-washiness. **8** *extravagance is one of her weaknesses* weak point, failing, foible, fault, flaw, defect, shortcoming, imperfection, blemish, Achilles' heel, chink in one's armour. **9** *she has a weakness for chocolate* soft spot, fondness, liking, love, passion, partiality, preference, penchant, predisposition, predilection, leaning, inclination, proneness, proclivity.

wealth n **1** *amass wealth* money, cash, capital, treasure, fortune, finance, property; riches, assets, possessions, resources, goods, funds; *inf* wherewithal, dough, bread. **2** *people of wealth* richness, money, affluence, prosperity, substance; means. **3** *a wealth of beautiful pictures | a wealth of opportunities* mass, abundance, profusion, copiousness, plenitude, amplitude, bounty, cornucopia.

wealthy adj **1** *wealthy people travelling abroad* rich, well off, well-to-do, moneyed, affluent, prosperous, of means, of substance; *inf* well-heeled, rolling in it/money, in the money, made of money, filthy/stinking rich, loaded, flush, on easy street, quids in. **2** *wealthy surroundings* rich, opulent, lavish, luxurious, sumptuous, splendid, magnificent.

wear v **1** *wear beautiful clothes* be dressed in, dress in, be clothed in, cloth oneself in, have on, put on, don, sport. **2** *she wore an anxious expression* have, assume, present, show, display, exhibit. **3** *he wants to leave school but his parents won't wear it* tolerate, stand for, put up with, countenance, accept, allow, permit, brook; *inf* stomach. **4** *wind and rain have worn the rock* erode, corrode, abrade, wash away, rub away, rub down, grind away, wear down. **5** *the carpet is starting to wear* become worn, show signs of wear, wear thin, fray, become threadbare, go into holes. **6** *she is worn by the whole experience* fatigue, tire, weary, exhaust. *see* WEAR v wear out 2. **7** *this carpet has worn well* last, endure, hold up, survive, bear up, stand up to wear, prove durable. **wear away** *the steps have become worn away* wear, erode, corrode, abrade, rub away. *see* WEAR V 4. **wear down 1** *the steps have become worn down* wear, wear away, erode, corrode, abrade, rub down. *see* WEAR V 4. **2** *wear down their resistance/opposition* gradually overcome, slowly reduce/diminish, erode, undermine; *inf* chip away at. **wear off 1** *wear the pattern off the plates* rub away, efface, fade. **2** *the novelty will soon wear off* lose effectiveness/effect, lose intensity/strength, fade, peter out, dwindle, decrease, diminish, disappear, subside, ebb, wane. **wear on** *as time wore on* pass, go by, move on, roll on. **wear out 1** *children wear out their clothes quickly* wear thin, make threadbare, fray. *see* WEAR V 5. **2** *the children/job has quite worn her out* wear, fatigue, tire, weary, exhaust, drain, strain, stress, weaken, enfeeble, prostrate, enervate; *inf* knacker, wear to a frazzle, poop.

wear n **1** *clothes/items for everyday wear* use, service, employment. **2** *pack away her winter wear* clothing, attire, apparel, wardrobe; clothes, garments, outfits; *inf* gear, clobber. **3** *showing signs of wear and tear* use, friction, erosion, detrition, attrition, corrosion, abrasion, deterioration, degeneration, damage.

weariness n *suffering from weariness* fatigue, tiredness, exhaustion, enervation, lassitude, languor, listlessness, lethargy.

wearing adj *have a wearing day | find the children wearing* fatiguing, tiring, wearying, exhausting, draining, stressful, enervating.

wearisome adj *wearisome tasks/journeys* fatiguing, tiring, exhausting, draining, wearing, trying, irksome, boring, tedious, dull, uninteresting, monotonous, humdrum, routine.

weary adj **1** *weary at the end of a hard day's work* fatigued, tired, exhausted, drained, worn, worn out, spent, wearied; *inf* dead tired/beat, dead on one's feet, dog-tired, all in, done in, fagged out, pooped, whacked, bushed, knackered. **2** *the last weary hours/tasks | a weary journey* wearisome, fatiguing, tiring, exhausting, wearing, trying, taxing, irksome, tiresome, laborious, boring, tedious, dull. *see* WEARISOME. **3** *she is weary of the job | the dull job makes her weary* bored, fed up, discontented, jaded, uninterested, listless, lethargic; *inf* browned-off, cheesed-off, sick and tired.

weary v **1** *the hard work wearies them* fatigue, tire, exhaust, drain, wear out; *inf* knacker, wear to a frazzle. **2** *the repetitive job wearies* him bore, irk, make fed up, make discontented/jaded. *see* WEARY adj 3. **3** *she wearied of living abroad* grow weary, tire, get bored, have enough, grow discontented/jaded. *see* WEARY adj 3.

weather n *what's the weather like?* meteorological/atmospheric conditions; temperature, raininess, cloudiness, dryness, humidity, windiness. **under the weather** below par, unwell, not well, off colour, out of sorts, indisposed, ailing, ill, sick; *inf* poorly, seedy, groggy, hung over.

weather v **1** *weather the wood* dry, season, expose, expose to the elements. **2** *wood weathering well | rocks weathered by storms* be exposed, undergo change, erode, wear, bleach, colour, become discoloured. **3** *weather the storm/recession* come/get through, survive, withstand, live/pull through, bear up against, stand, endure, ride out, rise above, surmount, overcome, resist; *inf* stick out.

weave v **1** *weave thread into cloth | weave flowers into garlands* interlace, intertwine, interwork, intertwist, twist together, entwine, braid, plait, interknit. **2** *weave a story to account for his movements* make up, fabricate, put together, construct, invent, create, contrive. **3** *weave in and out of the crowds* zigzag, wind, criss-cross.

web n **1** *a design composed of webs* interlacing, lacework, lattice, latticework, mesh, net, netting. **2** *a web of lies/deceit* network, tissue, tangle, knot, complex.

wed v **1** *they wed tomorrow* get married, marry, become man and wife; *inf* get hitched/spliced, tie the knot. **2** *she weds him tomorrow* marry, take as one's wife/husband. **3** *the local minister wed them* marry, join in matrimony, make one, unite; *inf* hitch. **4** *the two firms have been virtually wedded for years* unite, join, merge, amalgamate, fuse, link, ally. **5** *he is wedded to his work* dedicate, devote.

wedded adj *wedded bliss* married, marital, matrimonial, connubial, conjugal, nuptial.

wedding n *wedding/marriage ceremony,* marriage; nuptials, espousals.

wedge n **1** *insert a wedge* tapered block. **2** *a wedge of cheese/cake* tapered piece, chunk, lump, block; *inf* wodge.

wedge v **1** *wedge packing material round the vase in the box* thrust, stuff, pack, ram, force, cram, squeeze, jam. **2** *the adults wedged the child in* block, jam, squeeze, crowd, pack. **3** *wedge the door open* secure, fasten.

weed v *weed out the less able candidates* separate out, get rid of, remove, dispense with, eliminate, shed, root out, eradicate, extirpate.

weekly adv *the paper is published weekly* once a week, every week, by the week, hebdomadally.

weep v cry, shed tears, sob, blubber, snivel, whimper, whine, moan, lament, grieve, mourn, keen, wail; *inf* boo-hoo, blub.

weepy adj tearful, teary, lachrymose, close to tears, whimpering, crying, sobbing, blubbering.

weigh v 1 *weigh the potatoes* measure/gauge the weight of, put on the scales. 2 *the child weighs 25 kilograms* have a weight of; *inf* tip the scales at. 3 *weigh one plan against the other* balance, compare with, evaluate. 4 *weigh up the situation | weigh up his chances of success* consider, contemplate, think over, mull over, ponder, deliberate upon, meditate on, muse on, brood over, reflect on. 5 *his previous record will weigh with the committee* carry weight with, have influence with, be influential to, count with, tell with, matter to, be important/significant to. 6 *his guilt weighs on his conscience* bear down, burden, oppress, prey on. **weigh down** 1 *he was weighed down by/with heavy luggage* load, overload, burden, overburden. 2 *his responsibilities weighed down on him* weigh, bear down, press down, burden, be a burden to, oppress, prey on, trouble, worry, get one down.

weight n 1 *what is the weight of the flour?* heaviness; poundage, tonnage, avoirdupois. 2 *a weight of potatoes was delivered to everyone* load, quantity. 3 *a weight fell on his head* heavy object. 4 *the weights in the machine* ballast. 5 *lack of money is a real weight on his mind* burden, load, onus, millstone, albatross, oppression, trouble, worry, strain, millstone round one's neck, cross to bear. 6 *how much weight is attached to his statement?* importance, significance, consequence, value, substance, force, influence; *inf* clout. 7 *the weight of the evidence is against him* preponderance, main force, onus.

weighty adj 1 *weighty loads* heavy, massive, burdensome, cumbersome, ponderous; *inf* hefty. 2 *weighty responsibilities* burdensome, onerous, oppressive, troublesome, worrisome, stressful, taxing, vexatious. 3 *weighty matters* important, of great import, significant, momentous, of moment, consequential, of consequence, vital, crucial, serious, grave, solemn. 4 *weighty arguments* cogent, powerful, potent, forceful, effective, effectual, persuasive, authoritative, influential.

weird adj 1 *weird things were happening* strange, queer, uncanny, eerie, mysterious, mystifying, supernatural, preternatural, unnatural, unearthly, ghostly; *Scots* eldritch; *inf* spooky, creepy. 2 *she wears weird clothes* strange, queer, odd, eccentric, bizarre, outlandish, freakish, grotesque; *inf* off-beat, far-out, way-out, out on a limb.

welcome n *receive a welcome from their hostess* greeting, salutation, reception, warm reception.

welcome v 1 *welcome the guests* bid welcome, greet, receive, embrace, receive with open arms, roll out the red carpet for, meet, usher in. 2 *welcome the news of his release* receive with gladness, be pleased by, take pleasure in, feel satisfaction at.

welcome adj 1 *welcome guests* wanted, appreciated, popular, desirable. 2 *welcome news* gladly received, pleasant, pleasing, agreeable, cheering, to one's liking, to one's taste.

welfare n 1 *concern for the welfare of the children/firm* well-being, health, good health, soundness, happiness, comfort, security, prosperity, success, fortune, good fortune. 2 *poor families on welfare* state aid/benefit, public assistance; social security, sickness/unemployment benefit, income support, retirement pension.

well adv 1 *behave well* satisfactorily, in a satisfactory manner/way, correctly, rightly, properly, fittingly, suitably, nicely. 2 *get on well* agreeably, pleasantly, happily; *inf* famously, capitally. 3 *he plays the piano well* ably, competently, proficiently, adeptly, skilfully, with skill, effectively, expertly, with expertise, admirably, excellently. 4 *treat their guests well* kindly, in a kind/kindly way, genially, affably, generously, hospitably, civilly, politely. 5 *polish it well* thoroughly, completely, efficiently, effectively, conscientiously, industriously, carefully. 6 *know the subject well | we don't know her well* thoroughly, fully, deeply, profoundly, intimately, personally. 7 *look at it well | listen to it well* closely, attentively, carefully, conscientiously. 8 *speak well of him* highly, admiringly, with admiration, with praise, glowingly, approvingly, favourably, warmly. 9 *live well* comfortably, in comfort, prosperously. 10 *you may well be right | I can't very well go now* probably, possibly, likely, undoubtedly, certainly, unquestionably, justifiably, reasonably. 11 *he is well over forty* very much, considerably, to a great/marked extent/degree, markedly, substantially. 12 *it bodes well for the future* fortunately, luckily, auspiciously, propitiously.

as well *she left and he went as well too,* also, in addition, besides, into the bargain, to boot. **as well as** *John went as well as Peter* | *take champagne as well as wine* in addition to, besides, along with, over and above.

well adj **1** *the former invalid is quite well now* | *a clinic for well babies/woman* healthy, in good health, fit, strong, robust, hale and hearty, able-bodied, up to par. **2** *all is well now* satisfactory, all right, fine, good, thriving, flourishing; *inf* OK, fine and dandy. **3** *it would be well to leave early* advisable, fitting, proper, wise, prudent, sensible.

well n **1** *a land rich in oil wells* | *get water from the well* sunken/drilled shaft, borehole. **2** *well of knowledge* source, well-spring, fount, reservoir, repository, mine. **3** *hot wells are to be found there* spring, fountain, water-hole, pool.

well v *blood welled from the wound* | *tears welled from her eyes* flow, stream, run, ooze, seep, trickle, pour/rush forth, issue, gush, surge, spurt, spout, jet.

well-advised adj sensible, wise, prudent, judicious, circumspect, far-sighted, sagacious.

well-balanced adj **1** *well-balanced people/personalities* well-adjusted, sensible, reasonable, rational, level-headed, sound, practical, discerning, logical, sane, in one's right mind. **2** *a well-balanced diet* balanced, well-proportioned, well-ordered. **3** *a well-balanced exhibition/room* balanced, symmetrical, well-proportioned, proportional, well-ordered, well-arranged, graceful, elegant.

well-being n welfare, health, good health, happiness, comfort, prosperity, security.

well-bred adj well brought up, mannerly, well-mannered, courteous, polite, civil, ladylike, gentlemanly, gallant, chivalrous, cultivated, refined, polished, cultured, debonair, urbane.

well-built adj strongly built, strong, muscular, brawny, sturdy, robust, strapping, burly, big; *inf* hulking, husky, hefty, beefy.

well-groomed adj neat, neatly dressed, tidy, smart, spruce, well turned out, trim, dapper; *inf* natty, without a hair out of place, out of a bandbox.

well-known adj **1** *well-known facts* | *a well-known figure around the village* known, widely known, familiar, common, usual, everyday. **2** *a well-known artist* famous, famed, renowned, celebrated, noted, notable, illustrious, eminent.

well-nigh adv *well-nigh impossible* virtually, next to, practically, all but, just about, almost, nearly, more or less.

well off adj **1** *his parents are poor but he is very well off* | *well-off people* wealthy, rich, well-to-do, moneyed, affluent, prosperous, of means, of substance; *inf* well-heeled, rolling in it/money, in the money, made of money, filthy/stinking rich, loaded, flush, on easy street, quids in. **2** *he doesn't know when he is well off* fortunate, lucky, comfortable, thriving, successful, flourishing. **3** *we are well off for logs this winter* well-supplied, well-furnished, well-equipped, well-stocked.

well-read adj highly literate, literate, well-educated, educated, well-informed, knowledgeable, erudite.

well-spoken adj articulate, eloquent, fluent, silver-tongued, smooth-talking; *inf* having the gift of the gab.

well-thought-of adj highly thought-of, highly regarded, esteemed, respected, looked up to, acclaimed, revered, venerated.

well-to-do adj *his parents are well-to-do* | *well-to-do parents* wealthy, rich, well off, moneyed, affluent, prosperous, of means, of substance; *inf* well-heeled, in the money, made of money, loaded. *see* WELL OFF.

wet adj **1** *wet clothes/ground* damp, dampened, moist, moistened, wet through, soaked, drenched, saturated, sopping/dripping/wringing wet, sopping, dripping, soggy, waterlogged. **2** *a wet day* rainy, raining, pouring, showery, drizzling, damp, humid, dank, misty. **3** *a wet mixture* aqueous, watery, watered, sloppy. **4** *he's a wet creature* feeble, weak, inept, ineffective, ineffectual, effete, timid, timorous, cowardly, spineless, soft; *inf* namby-pamby, weedy.

wet n **1** *the wet damaged the table/land* wetness, damp, dampness, moisture, moistness, condensation, humidity, water, liquid. **2** *get in out of the wet* | *the wet affects his rheumatism* wet/rainy weather, rain, showery/damp weather, drizzle, damp; rains **3** *he's a real wet* weakling, milksop; *inf* namby-pamby, wimp, weed, drip.

wet v **1** *wet the clothes before ironing them* dampen, damp, moisten, sprinkle, spray, splash. **2** *wet the soil* water, irrigate, sprinkle, spray, douse. **3** *the rain really wet them* wet through, dampen, soak, saturate.

wharf n pier, quay, dock, landing stage, jetty.

wheedle v coax, cajole, beguile, charm, flatter, inveigle, win over, talk into, persuade, induce, entice, influence; *inf* butter up.

wheel n **1** *the wheels of the machine* circular frame, disc. **2** *soldiers making a right-hand wheel* turn, revolution, rotation, circle, pivot, gyration, spin, roll, twirl, whirl. **at the wheel 1** *he was at the wheel when the accident happened* driving, steering, in the driving-seat. **2** *a new man at the wheel in the firm* in charge, in command, in control; *inf* at the helm, in the driving-seat.

wheel v **1** *discs/birds wheeling around* turn, go round, circle, rotate, revolve, spin. **2** *soldiers wheeling round* swivel round, pivot, whirl/twirl round, make a U-turn. **3** *wheel a pram* push, shove, trundle.

wheeze v *asthmatics wheezing* breathe audibly/noisily, gasp, whistle, hiss, rasp.

wheeze n **1** *give a painful wheeze* gasp, whistle, hiss. *see* WHEEZE V. **2** *the school girls thought fooling the teacher was a good wheeze* joke, trick, ruse, ploy, scheme, prank, stunt.

whereabouts n *I don't his whereabouts | the whereabouts of his cottage* location, site, position, situation, place.

wherewithal n *he doesn't have the wherewithal to travel* means, resources, funds, reserves; money, ready money, cash, capital, finance; *inf* dough, bread, loot.

whet v **1** *whet a blade* sharpen, put an edge on, edge, hone, strop, file, grind, rasp. **2** *whet the curiosity/appetite* stimulate, excite, arouse, rouse, kindle, quicken, stir, titillate, tempt.

whiff n **1** *a whiff of air/smoke* puff, breath, gust, draught. **2** *catch a whiff of her perfume* smell, scent, odour, aroma, stink, reek. **3** *a whiff of scandal* hint, suggestion, trace, suspicion, soupçon.

while n *wait for a while* time, spell, period, interval.

while v *while away the hours* laze, idle, loaf, lounge, loiter.

whim n **1** *have a sudden whim to go to the fair* notion, fancy, idea, impulse, urge, caprice, vagary, craze, passion, inclination, bent. **2** *behaviour ruled by whim* whimsy, capriciousness, caprice, volatility, fickleness.

whimper v *dogs/children whimpering* whine, cry, sniffle, snivel, moan, wail, groan; *inf* grizzle.

whimper n *a whimper of fear* whine, cry, moan, wail, groan.

whimsical adj *a whimsical sense of humour | a whimsical children's story* capricious, fanciful, fantastical, playful, mischievous, waggish, quaint, unusual, curious, droll, eccentric, peculiar, queer, bizarre, weird, freakish.

whine v **1** *a dog/child was whining* whimper, cry, wail, groan; *inf* grizzle. *see* WHIMPER V. **2** *he's always whining about the state of the country* complain, grumble, moan, groan, fuss, lament; *inf* grouse, gripe, whinge, bellyache, go on, beef.

whine n **1** *listen to the dog's whines* whimper, cry, wail, groan. **2** *his constant whines about prices* complaint, grumble, moan, groan, fussing, lamenting; *inf* grouse, gripe, whinging, bellyaching, beefing.

whip v **1** *whip the naughty children | whip the reluctant horse* lash, flog, scourge, flagellate, birch, switch, strap, cane, thrash, beat, strike, leather, spank, punish, castigate; *inf* belt, tan, lay into, give a hiding to, beat the living daylights out of. **2** *whip cream* beat, whisk, mix. **3** *whip a handkerchief from his pocket* whisk, flash, snatch, pull, yank, jerk, produce, remove. **4** *he whipped round the corner* whisk, dart, dash, dive, dodge, shoot, tear, rush, fly, bolt, zoom. **5** *he whipped the money* steal, thieve, pilfer, purloin, filch, snatch, seize, pocket; *inf* pinch, swipe, nick, nab. **6** *whip the opposition at football* beat, defeat, overcome, overpower, overwhelm, thrash, trounce, crush, rout. **7** *whip them into a frenzy* rouse, stir up, incite, goad, prod, spur, prompt, agitate. **whip up** *whip up enthusiasm* rouse, stir up, provoke, excite, incite, instigate, work up.

whip n *use a whip on the criminal/horse* lash, scourge, flagellum, horsewhip, bull whip, cat o'nine tails, knout, birch, switch, thong, crop, riding crop, cane.

whipping n **1** *give the child a whipping* lashing, flogging, scourging, flagellation, birching, caning, thrashing, beating, leathering, spanking, castigation; *inf* belting, tanning, hiding. *see* WHIP V 1. **2** *give the opposition a whipping* beating, thrashing, trouncing, routing. *see* WHIP V 6.

whirl v **1** *wheels/dancers whirling* turn round, circle, spin, rotate, revolve, wheel, twirl, swirl, gyrate, reel, pirouette, pivot. **2** *buses whirling past* speed, rush, race, shoot, tear, charge, whip. **3** *my head/brain is whirling* go round, spin, reel, feel dizzy/giddy.

whirl n **1** *give the wheel a whirl | the whirls of the dancers* turn, spin, rotation, revolution, wheel, twirl, swirl, gyration, reel, pirouette, pivot. **2** *the social whirl* activity, bustle, flurry, to-do, hurly-burly. **3** *a whirl of parties* round, merry-go-round, succession, series, sequence, progression, string, chain, cycle. **4** *with heads in a whirl* spin, dither, state of confusion, daze, muddle, jumble. **5** *give the new game a whirl* try, try-out, test; *inf* go, shot, stab.

whirlpool n vortex, maelstrom.

whirlwind n tornado; *inf* dust devil.

whirlwind adj *a whirlwind romance* lightning, swift, rapid, quick, speedy, hasty, headlong, impulsive.

whisk v **1** *the horse whisked its tail* wave, flick, brandish. **2** *whisk the table clean | whisk away the crumbs* brush, sweep, wipe. **3** *whisk a handkerchief out of his pocket* whip, snatch, pull, yank, jerk, produce, remove. **4** *the cat whisked round the corner* dart, dash, dive, dodge, whip, shoot, tear, rush, fly, bolt, zoom. **5** *whisk the guest away* whirl, whip, snatch. **6** *whisk eggs* whip, beat, mix.

whisk n **1** *with a whisk of the tail* wave, flick, brandish. **2** *clean the table with a few whisks* brush, sweep, wipe. **3** *beat eggs with a whisk* beater.

whisky n malt whisky, blended whisky, Scotch whisky, Scotch, Irish whiskey, bourbon, rye whiskey; *Scots* usquebaugh.

whisper v **1** *whisper to her friend* murmur, mutter, speak softly, speak in muted/ hushed tones. **2** *whisper endearments* murmur, mutter, breathe, say/utter softly, say/ utter under the breath. **3** *trees whispering in the wind* murmur, rustle, sigh, sough, swish.

whisper n **1** *speak in a whisper* murmur, mutter, low voice, hushed tone, undertone. **2** *the whisper of trees in the wind* murmur, rustle, sigh, sough, swish. **3** *there's a whisper that he has been promoted* rumour, report, insinuation, suggestion, hint; gossip, word. **4** *a whisper of perfume/hostility about the room* whiff, trace, tinge, hint, suggestion, suspicion.

whit n *not give a whit | not a whit better* particle, bit, jot, iota, mite, little, trifle.

white adj **1** *a white face* white as a ghost/ sheet, chalk-white, pale, wan, pallid, ashen, anaemic, colourless, bloodless, waxen, pasty, peaky, whey-faced, grey. **2** *white hair* grey, silver, hoary, snowy-white, grizzled.

white-collar adj *white-collar workers* non-manual, office, clerical, professional, executive, salaried.

whiten v *clothes whitened by the sun* make white, make pale, bleach, blanch, fade, wash out, etiolate.

whitewash n *regard the report on the accident as a whitewash* cover-up, concealment, camouflage, mask.

whitewash v *try to whitewash his role in the accident* cover up, gloss over, conceal, camouflage, suppress, downplay, make light of, soft-pedal, minimize.

whittle v **1** *whittle wood from the block* cut, hew, pare, shave, trim. **2** *whittle a tent peg from the wood* carve, shape, model. **3** *inflation whittled away their savings* wear away, eat away, erode, consume, use up, undermine, destroy. **4** *the number of employees has been whittled away* reduce, lessen, decrease, diminish, cut back.

whole adj **1** *three whole days | the whole book | a whole cake* entire, complete, full, total, solid, integral, unabridged, unreduced, undivided, uncut. **2** *no glasses left whole | he came home whole* intact, sound, flawless, in one piece, unimpaired, undamaged, unharmed, unhurt, uninjured, unmutilated.

whole adv *eat/cook it whole* in one piece, in one.

whole n **1** *parts making up a whole* entity, unit, ensemble, totality, entirety. **2** *the whole of the year | the whole country rejoiced* all, every part, every person/member/inhabitant. **on the whole 1** *on the whole he is perfect for the job* all in all, all things considered, taking everything into consideration, by and large. **2** *on the whole he works late* as a rule, as a general rule, generally, in general, in the main, for the most part.

wholehearted adj **1** *a wholehearted fan of the group* devoted, dedicated, enthusiastic, eager, keen, zealous, earnest, serious, committed. **2** *give the movement their wholehearted support* unreserved, unqualified, unstinting, complete, committed, hearty, emphatic, real, sincere, genuine.

wholesale adj *the wholesale destruction of animals* indiscriminate, mass, all-inclusive, total, comprehensive, extensive, wide-ranging, sweeping, broad.

wholesale adv *destroy the animals wholesale | throw all the furniture out wholesale* indiscriminately, all at once, in a mass, without exception, on a large scale, comprehensively, extensively.

wholesome adj **1** *wholesome food* nutritious, nourishing, health-giving, healthful, good, good for one, strengthening. **2** *wholesome air/climate* salubrious, invigorating, bracing, stimulating, refreshing. **3** *wholesome literature/advice* moral, ethical, non-erotic, non-violent, uplifting, edifying, helpful, beneficial, prudent. **4** *wholesome country chil-*

dren healthy, fit, in good health, robust, vigorous, lusty, hale and hearty, ruddy-cheeked, innocent, virtuous, righteous, pure.

wholly adv **1** *wholly in favour of the scheme* completely, fully, entirely, totally, utterly, thoroughly, altogether, comprehensively, in every respect, perfectly, enthusiastically, with total commitment, unreservedly, heart and soul; *inf* one hundred per cent. **2** *the burden rests wholly on his shoulders* only, solely, exclusively, purely.

whoop n *whoops of excitement/admiration* cry, call, shout, yell, scream, shriek, hoot, cheer, hurrah; *inf* holler.

whoop v *whoop with excitement/admiration* cry, call, shout, yell, scream, shriek, hoot, cheer; *inf* holler.

whore n **1** *earn her living as a whore* prostitute, call girl, streetwalker, harlot, lady of the night, *fille de joie*, woman of ill repute, fallen woman, strumpet, courtesan, *demimondaine*; *inf* tart, hooker, hustler. **2** *he's very respectable but she is a whore* loose woman, harlot, wanton; *inf* tart.

wicked adj **1** *an evil man* evil, sinful, bad, black-hearted, villainous, base, vile, vicious, dishonourable, unprincipled, unrighteous, criminal, lawless, perverted, immoral, amoral, unethical, corrupt, dissolute, abandoned, dissipated, degenerate, reprobate, debauched, depraved, unholy, impious, irreligious, ungodly, godless, devilish. **2** *his wicked deeds* evil, sinful, iniquitous, wrong, bad, vile, foul, base, mean, gross, odious, obnoxious, nefarious, heinous, flagitious, infamous, dreadful, dire, grim, horrible, hideous, gruesome, monstrous, atrocious, abominable, abhorrent, loathsome, hateful, detestable, reprehensible, dishonourable, disgraceful, shameful, ignoble, ignominious, lawless, unlawful, illicit, illegal, villainous, dastardly, blackguardly, unholy, impious, impure, ungodly, godless, profane, blasphemous, irreverent, irreligious, damnable, devilish, demonic, diabolic. **3** *hurt by her wicked remarks* spiteful, malicious, malignant, nasty, offensive, hurtful, distressing, galling, vexatious. **4** *aim a wicked blow* dangerous, perilous, destructive, harmful, injurious, hurtful, painful, agonizing, ferocious, fierce, terrible, mighty. **5** *give a wicked smile | have a wicked sense of humour* mischievous, impish, roguish, arch, rascally, naughty. **6** *the weather has been wicked* bad, nasty, unpleasant, disagreeable; *inf* dreadful, terrible, awful. **7** *he's a wicked player* excellent, expert, masterly, skilful, proficient, deft,

adept, dexterous, first-rate, outstanding, superior, superlative; *inf* top-notch.

wide adj **1** *a wide river/building* broad, extensive, spacious. **2** *wide hips* broad, large, outspread, spread out, ample. **3** *wide eyes* fully open, dilated. **4** *a wide range of subjects | a wide knowledge* ample, broad, extensive, large, large-scale, vast, far-ranging, wide-ranging, immense, expansive, sweeping, encyclopedic, comprehensive, general, all-embracing, catholic, compendious. **5** *wide trousers* full, loose, baggy, capacious, roomy, generous, commodious. **6** *his shot was wide | his guess was wide of the mark* off target, off course.

wide adv **1** *open your mouth wide* to the fullest/furthest extent, as far as possible, fully, completely. **2** *he shot wide* wide of the mark/target, off target, off course, astray.

wide awake adj **1** *still wide awake at dawn* fully awake, awake, conscious, open-eyed, not asleep. **2** *you have to be wide awake to do business with them* alert, on the alert, on the qui vive, vigilant, wary, chary, watchful, observant, attentive, heedful, aware; *inf* on one's toes, on the ball, keeping a weather eye open.

wide-eyed adj **1** *children wide-eyed at the antics of the clown* surprised, amazed, astonished, astounded. **2** *taking advantage of wide-eyed young girls* naive, impressionable, ingenuous, credulous, trusting, unsuspicious, innocent, simple, unsophisticated, inexperienced, green; *inf* wet behind the ears.

widen v **1** *widen the road* make wider, broaden. **2** *widen her knowledge* broaden, expand, extend, enlarge, increase, augment, add to, supplement. **3** *her eyes widened in surprise* open wide, dilate.

wide open adj **1** *with eyes wide open* open wide, fully open, dilated, gaping. **2** *with legs wide open* open wide, outspread, spread open, outstretched, splayed open, fully extended. **3** *wide open to attack/criticism* exposed, vulnerable, unprotected, unguarded, defenceless, at risk, in danger. **4** *the outcome of the game was wide open* uncertain, unsure, indeterminate, unsettled, unpredictable, in the balance, up in the air; *inf* anyone's guess.

widespread adj *widespread terror/confusion* universal, common, general, far-reaching, far-flung, prevalent, rife, extensive, sweeping, pervasive, epidemic.

width n **1** *the width of the river/cloth* wideness, breadth, broadness, span, diameter. **2** *the width of her hips* wideness, broadness, breadth, largeness, thickness, ampleness.

3 *impressed by the width of his knowledge* wideness, broadness, breadth, scope, range, span, extensiveness, vastness, immensity, immenseness, expansiveness, comprehensiveness, catholicity, compendiousness. *see* WIDE *adj* 4.

wield v **1** *come out wielding a sword* brandish, flourish, wave, swing, shake, use, put to use, employ, handle, ply, manipulate. **2** *wield the power in the country* exercise, exert, be possessed of, have, have at one's disposal, hold, maintain, command, control, manage, be in charge of.

wife n spouse, mate, consort, woman, helpmate, squaw, bride; *inf* better/other half, missus, missis, old woman/lady, the little woman, the lady of the house, 'er/her indoors.

wild adj **1** *wild cats/horses* untamed, undomesticated, unbroken, feral, savage, fierce, ferocious. **2** *wild flowers* uncultivated, natural, native, indigenous. **3** *wild peoples/tribes* uncivilized, primitive, ignorant, savage, barbaric, barbarous, brutish, ferocious, fierce. **4** *wild country/countryside* uncivilized, uncultivated, unpopulated, uninhabited, unsettled, unfrequented, empty, barren, waste, desolate, isolated, forsaken, God-forsaken. **5** *a wild night* stormy, tempestuous, turbulent, blustery, howling, violent, raging, furious, rough. **6** *lead a wild life* | *wild confusion/delight* undisciplined, unrestrained, unconstrained, uncontrolled, out of control, uncurbed, unbridled, unchecked, chaotic, disorderly. **7** *a wild football crowd* rowdy, unruly, disorderly, noisy, turbulent, violent, lawless, riotous, out of control, uncontrolled, unmanageable, ungovernable, unrestrained, excited, passionate, frantic. **8** *when he was killed the crowd went/were wild* beside oneself, berserk, frantic, frenzied, in a frenzy, hysterical, crazed, mad, distracted, distraught, irrational, deranged, demented, raving, maniacal, rabid; *inf* crazy. **9** *the teacher was wild at the children* angry, infuriated, incensed, exasperated, in a temper, seething; *inf* mad. **10** *wild schemes* extravagant, fantastical, impracticable, foolish, ill-advised, illconsidered, imprudent, unwise, madcap, impulsive, reckless, rash, outrageous, preposterous. **11** *wild about rock music* enthusiastic, eager, avid, agog; *inf* crazy, mad, nuts, potty, daft. **12** *a wild guess* arbitrary, random, hit-or-miss, haphazard, uninformed, unknowledgeable. **13** *wild hair* uncombed, unkempt, dishevelled, tousled, wind blown, disarranged, untidy. **run wild** **1** *weeds running wild* grow unchecked, spread like wildfire, ramble, straggle.

2 *children running wild* run free, go undisciplined/unchecked. **3** *demonstrators running wild* run riot, go on the rampage, go berserk, get out of control, cut loose.

wilderness n **1** *the Arctic wilderness* desert, wasteland, waste, jungle, no-man's land; wilds. **2** *a wilderness of abandoned cars* confusion, tangle, jumble, muddle, clutter, miscellany, hotchpotch, bewilderment, maze, labyrinth.

wile n **1** *make use of wile to get her own way* trickery, craftiness, craft, cunning, artfulness, slyness, guile, chicanery, fraud, deception, cheating. **2** *use all her wiles to get her own way* trick, dodge, ruse, subterfuge, ploy, stratagem, lure, artifice, manoeuvre, device, contrivance.

wilful adj **1** *wilful neglect/murder* deliberate, intentional, intended, conscious, purposeful, premeditated, planned, calculated. **2** *coping with wilful children* headstrong, strong-willed, obstinate, stubborn, stubborn as a mule, mulish, pig-headed, bullheaded, obdurate, intransigent, adamant, dogged, determined, persistent, unyielding, uncompromising, intractable, refractory, recalcitrant, disobedient, contrary, perverse, wayward, self-willed.

will¹ v **1** *come when you will* wish, want, desire, please, see/think fit, think best, choose, prefer, apt, elect. **2** *accidents will happen* do, have a tendency to, have a habit of.

will² v **1** *will him to live* impose one's will on, try to make/cause. **2** *God willed it* decree, order, ordain, command, direct, bid, intend, wish, desire. **3** *will him all her books* bequeath, leave, give, hand/pass down, pass on, transfer.

will² n **1** *freedom of the will* volition, choice, option, decision, discretion, prerogative. **2** *he has the will to live* desire, wish, preference, inclination, fancy, mind. **3** *it is the will of God* decree, ordinance, dictate, wish, decision. **4** *he lacks the will to succeed* willpower, determination, resolution, resolve, firmness of purpose, purposefulness, doggedness, single-mindedness, commitment, moral fibre, pluck, mettle, grit, nerve. **5** *draw up his will* last will and testament, testament; last wishes. **6** *bear him ill will* feeling, disposition, attitude. **at will** *come and go at will* as one wishes/pleases, as one thinks fit, to suit oneself, at one's inclination/discretion.

willing adj **1** *willing helpers* ready, eager, keen, enthusiastic, avid. **2** *willing to accept responsibility* prepared, ready, disposed, content, happy, so-minded, consenting, agreeable, amenable, in the mood, compliant; *inf* game. **3** *willing help* cooperative, gladly given, cheerful, accommodating, obliging.

willingly adv **1** *she went with him willingly— she was not forced* voluntarily, of one's own free will, of one's own accord, by choice, by volition, spontaneously, unforced. **2** *I'll willingly help you* cheerfully, happily, with pleasure, readily, without hesitation, ungrudgingly, with all one's heart.

willingness n **1** *their willingness to learn* readiness, eagerness, keenness, enthusiasm, avidity. **2** *their willingness to accept responsibility* readiness, preparedness, consent, agreeableness, amenability. *see* WILLING 2.

will-power n will, strength of will, determination, resolution, resolve, firmness of purpose, purposefulness, doggedness, commitment, single-mindedness, self-discipline, moral fibre, pluck, mettle, grit, nerve.

wilt v **1** *plants wilting* droop, wither, shrivel, lose freshness, sag. **2** *people wilting in the heat* droop, sag, feel weak/faint, languish. **3** *their courage/determination/strength wilted when faced with the enemy* diminish, dwindle, lessen, grow less, flag, fade, melt away, ebb, wane, weaken, fail.

wily adj crafty, cunning, artful, sharp, astute, shrewd, scheming, intriguing, shifty, foxy, sly, guileful, deceitful, deceptive, fraudulent, cheating, underhand; *inf* crooked, fly.

win v **1** *win first prize* achieve, attain, earn, gain, receive, obtain, acquire, procure, get, secure, collect, pick up, come away with, net; *inf* bag. **2** *win the battle/contest* be victorious in, be the victor in, achieve success in, come first in. **3** *may the best side win* be victorious, be the victor, gain the victory, overcome, achieve mastery, carry the day, carry all before one, finish first, come out ahead, come out on top, succeed, triumph, prevail; *inf* win out. **4** *she won them by her beauty* | *win their hearts* charm, attract, lure, disarm. **win over/round** *win over the opposition* | *win them round to our way of thinking* talk/bring round, persuade, induce, influence, sway, prevail upon, convert.

win n *their side needs a win* victory, conquest, success, triumph.

wince v *wince in pain/embarrassment* grimace, start, flinch, blench, shrink, recoil, cringe, squirm.

wince n *give a wince of pain* grimace, start, flinch.

wind[1] n **1** *a day almost entirely without wind* air current, current/stream of air; puff of wind, light air/wind, zephyr, breeze, gust, strong wind, blast, gale, storm, hurricane. **2** *need a lot of wind to play the bagpipes* breath, respiration; *inf* puff. **3** *a pompous fool full of wind* empty talk, talk, babble, blather, blether, boasting, bluster, braggadocio; *inf* hot air, baloney, twaddle, gab, gas. **4** *suffer from wind after a meal* flatulence, flatus, gas. **5** *the deer have got our wind* scent, smell, odour. **6** *there's wind of a pay increase* | *wind of a scandal* rumour, gossip, hint, suggestion, inkling, intimation; news, information, report, intelligence. **in the wind** *sense that redundancies were in the wind* about to happen, in the offing, on the way, coming near, close at hand, approaching, impending, looming; *inf* on the cards.

wind[2] n *the path has many winds* winding, twist, turn, curve, bend, loop, coil, whorl, convolution.

wind[2] v **1** *the road winds up the hill* twist, twist and turn, curve, bend, loop, zigzag, snake, spiral, meander, ramble. **2** *smoke winding up into the sky* curl, spiral, wreathe, snake. **3** *wind the wool into ball* twist, twine, coil, wrap, roll. **wind down 1** *the competitors need to wind down after a race* unwind, relax, become less tense, ease up, calm down, cool off. **2** *we are winding the firm down* bring to a close/end, make less active. **3** *school-work is winding down for the summer* slacken off, ease up, taper off, dwindle, diminish, lessen, decline, come to an end/close. **wind up 1** *the events of the evening really wound her up* | *she gets wound up easily* make tense, strain, make nervous, work up, put on edge, agitate, fluster, discon- cert, discompose. **2** *they aren't serious— they're winding her up* tease, chaff, make fun of; *inf* kid, take one on, pull one's leg, rib, rag, get a rise out of. **3** *it's time to wind up the meeting* bring to an end/conclusion, end, conclude, terminate, finish; *inf* wrap up. **4** *he has wound up his business* close down, dissolve, liquidate, put into liquidation. **5** *we wound up in a small village* end up, finish, find oneself.

winded adj breathless, out of breath, gasping for breath, panting; *inf* puffed out, out of puff.

windfall n piece/stroke of good luck, unexpected gain, godsend, manna from heaven, bonanza, jackpot.

winding adj *a winding road* twisting, twisting and turning, curving, bending, looping, tortuous, zigzagging, snaking, spiralling, meandering, serpentine, sinuous, rambling.

winding n *the road had many windings* wind, twist, turn, bend, loop, coil, curve, convolution, meander.

window n opening, aperture; casement, oriel, bay window, skylight.

windy adj **1** *a windy day* breezy, blowy, blustery, blustering, gusty, gusting, boisterous, squally, stormy, wild, tempestuous, turbulent. **2** *a windy speech* long-winded, loquacious, wordy, verbose, rambling, meandering, prolix, diffuse, turgid, bombastic. **3** *she's a bit windy about living alone* nervous, scared, frightened, alarmed, fearful, timid, timorous, cowardly; *inf* nervy.

wing n **1** *a bird's wings* pennate limb, organ of flight; *Lit* pinion. **2** *the extreme wing of the party* arm, side, branch, section, segment, group, grouping, circle, faction, clique, set, coterie, cabal. **3** *the east wing of the house* side piece, extension, annex, addition; *Amer* ell.

wing v **1** *birds winging through the air* fly, glide, soar. **2** *she winged to the top of her profession | winged to the finishing tape* soar, zoom, speed, race, hurry, hasten. **3** *the bullet winged the bird/soldier* wound, hit, clip.

wink v **1** *wink an eye* blink, flutter, bat, nictate, nictitate. **2** *lights winking across the water* flash, twinkle, sparkle, glitter, gleam. **wink at** *wink at the junior's mistakes* turn a blind eye to, close/shut one's eyes to, blink at, ignore, overlook, disregard, let pass, connive at, condone, tolerate.

wink n **1** *the wink of an eye* blink, flutter, bat, nictation. **2** *the winks of the lights* flash, twinkle, sparkle, glitter, gleam. **3** *I'll be with you in a wink* moment, minute, second, instant; *inf* jiffy, mo, two shakes of a lamb's tail.

winkle v **1** *winkle the splinter out of her hand | winkle the children out of their hiding place* prise out, dig out, extricate, extract, dislodge, remove. **2** *winkle the information from him* draw out, prise out, worm out, extract, extricate.

winner n champion, victor, vanquisher, conqueror, conquering hero; cup winner, prizewinner.

winning adj **1** *the winning team* victorious, successful, triumphant, vanquishing, conquering. **2** *a winning smile/child* captivating, enchanting, bewitching, beguiling, disarming, taking, engaging, endearing, winsome, charming, attractive, fetching, alluring, sweet, lovely, delightful, darling, amiable, pleasing.

winnings npl proceeds, spoils, profits, takings, gains; booty.

winnow v **1** *winnow the grain* blow, fan. **2** *winnow the chaff from the grain* remove, get rid of, divide, separate, part, sort out. **3** *winnow the evidence* sift, go through, examine, comb, sort out.

wintry adj **1** *a wintry day | wintry showers* cold, chilly, icy, frosty, freezing, frozen, snowy, arctic, glacial, biting, piercing, nippy. **2** *a wintry smile/look* unfriendly, cool, chilly, cold, distant, remote, bleak, cheerless.

wipe v **1** *wipe the table* rub, brush, dust, mop, sponge, swab, clean, dry. **2** *wipe the dirt off* rub off, brush off, mop up, sponge off, clean off, remove, get rid of, take off, take away, erase, efface. **wipe out** destroy, demolish, annihilate, exterminate, eradicate, eliminate, extirpate, obliterate, expunge, erase, blot out, extinguish.

wipe n *give the table a wipe* rub, brush, dust, mop, sponge, swab, clean.

wiry adj **1** *wiry children/youths* lean, spare, sinewy, tough, strong. **2** *wiry hair* strong, coarse, tough. **3** *wiry brushes* bristly, prickly, thorny, stiff, rigid.

wisdom n **1** *admire the wisdom of the old man/ sayings* sageness, sagacity, cleverness, intelligence, erudition, learning, education, knowledge, enlightenment, reason, philosophy, discernment, perception, insight. **2** *admire their wisdom in leaving early | the wisdom of her decision* sense, common sense, prudence, judiciousness, judgement, shrewdness, astuteness, smartness, circumspection, strategy, foresight, reasonableness, rationality, logic, soundness, saneness.

wise adj **1** *he's a wise old man | wise sayings* sage, sagacious, clever, intelligent, erudite, learned, educated, well-read, knowledgeable, informed, enlightened, philosophic, deep-thinking, discerning, perceptive, experienced; *lit* sapient. **2** *it was wise to leave early | you were wise to leave | a wise decision* sensible, prudent, well-advised, judicious, politic, shrewd, astute, smart, strategic, reasonable, rational, logical, sound, sane.

wisecrack n quip, witticism, joke, jest, smart remark; *inf* gag, funny.

wish v **1** *wish for a long life* want, desire, long for, hope for, yearn for, pine for, have a fancy for, fancy, crave, hunger for, thirst for, lust after, covet, sigh for, set one's heart on; *inf* hanker after, have a yen for. **2** *wish to die* want, desire, long, yearn, aspire, have an inclination. **3** *they wish you* *to go now* desire, demand, bid, ask, require, instruct, direct, order, command. **4** *I wish you goodbye* bid.

wish n **1** *satisfy her wish to travel* desire, liking, fondness, longing, hope, yearning, want, fancy, aspiration, inclination, urge, whim, craving, hunger, thirst, lust; *inf* hankering, yen. **2** *you must obey their wishes* want, desire, demand, bidding, request, requirement, instruction, direction, order, command.

wishy-washy adj **1** *he's a bit wishy-washy* weak, feeble, puny, ineffectual, effete, spineless, irresolute; *inf* weak-kneed. **2** *wishy-washy colours* pallid, pale, wan, sickly. **3** *wishy-washy soup* tasteless, flavourless, insipid, watery, weak, diluted.

wistful adj yearning, longing, forlorn, disconsolate, melancholy, sad, mournful, dreaming, dreamy, daydreaming, in a reverie, pensive, reflective, musing, contemplative, meditative.

wit n **1** *he didn't have the wit to understand the position* intelligence, intellect, cleverness, wisdom, sageness, sagacity, judgement, common sense, understanding, comprehension, reason, sharpness, astuteness, shrewdness, acumen, discernment, perspicacity, perception, percipience, insight, ingenuity; brains; *inf* nous. **2** *entertained by a person of great wit* wittiness, humour, jocularity, funniness, facetiousness, drollery, waggishness, repartee, badinage, banter, raillery. **3** *one of the great wits of his time* humorist, wag, funny person, comic, jokester, banterer, *farceur*; *inf* card.

witch n sorceress, enchantress, magician, necromancer, hex.

witchcraft n witchery, sorcery, black art/magic, magic, necromancy, wizardry, occultism, the occult, sortilege, thaumaturgy, wonder-working.

withdraw v **1** *withdraw her son from the school | withdraw the poker from the fire* take back, pull back, take away, extract, remove. **2** *asked to withdraw their remarks* take back, retract, recall, unsay. **3** *parliament withdrew the bill* revoke, annul, disannul, nullify, declare void, rescind, repeal, abrogate. **4** *she withdrew into the shadows | withdraw from the group* draw back, go back, absent oneself, detach oneself. **5** *the troops/spectators withdrew* pull back, fall back, retire, retreat, disengage, depart, go, leave; *inf* make oneself scarce.

withdrawal n **1** *his withdrawal from the school | withdrawal of the poker from the fire* extraction, removal. *see* WITHDRAW 1. **2** *the withdrawal of their remarks* retraction, recall,

unsaying. **3** *the withdrawal of the bill* revocation, nullification, rescinding, repeal, abrogation. *see* WITHDRAW 3. **4** *the withdrawal of the troops/spectators* falling back, retiral, retreat, disengagement, departure, leaving, exit, exodus, evacuation. **5** *withdrawal from drugs* cessation (of), abstention, deprivation, absence.

withdrawn adj *a withdrawn person/personality* retiring, reserved, uncommunicative, nonforthcoming, unsociable, taciturn, silent, quiet, introverted, detached, aloof, self-contained, distant, private, shrinking, timid, timorous, shy, bashful, diffident.

wither v **1** *flowers withering in the heat* dry up/out, shrivel, go limp, wilt, die. **2** *heat withering the flowers* dry up/out, desiccate, kill off. **3** *time withered their enthusiasm/hopes* destroy, ruin, kill off, blight, blast. **4** *gradually their enthusiasm/dreams withered* wilt, decline, fade, ebb, wane, disintegrate, die, perish.

withhold v **1** *unable to withhold their laughter* hold back, keep back, restrain, hold/keep in check, check, curb, repress, suppress. **2** *withhold permission* refuse to give/grant/allow, refuse, decline, keep back.

within prep **1** *within the walls of the city* inside, in, within the confines of, enclosed by. **2** *within the speed limit* inside, inside the range/limits of, in the bounds of. **3** *come back within half-an-hour* before, not after, not exceeding, not more than, in the compass of.

without prep **1** *they were three days without food* lacking, short of, wanting, requiring, in want/need of, deprived of, destitute of. **2** *he arrived without her* unaccompanied by, unescorted by, in the absence of. **3** *that is the price without service charge* exclusive of, excluding, not including, not counting.

withstand v *withstand attack/pressure* hold out against, stand up to, stand firm against, resist, fight, combat, oppose, endure, stand, tolerate, bear, put up with, take, cope with, weather, brave, defy.

witness n **1** *taking statements from witnesses | a witness to the accident* eyewitness, observer, spectator, onlooker, looker-on, viewer, watcher, beholder, bystander. **2** *witnesses giving evidence in court* testifier, attestant, deponent. **3** *his ragged clothes were witness of his poverty* evidence, testimony, confirmation, corroboration, proof. **bear witness 1** *several people were asked to bear witness* give evidence, testify, give testimony. **2** *her bruises bore witness to her claim that she had been attacked* testify to, attest to, be evidence of, confirm, corroborate, be proof of, prove, bear out, vouch for, betoken.

witness v **1** *the children witnessed the accident* see, observe, view, watch, look on at, behold, perceive, be present at, attend. **2** *witness his will/signature* endorse, countersign, sign. **3** *his ragged clothes witnessed to his poverty* bear witness to, testify to, attest to, be evidence of, confirm, corroborate, be proof of, prove. **4** *she was asked to witness to the truth of the statement* testify to, give testimony about, attest to, bear witness to, give evidence about.

wits npl *he didn't have the wits to understand the position* wit, intelligence, brains, intellect, cleverness, judgement, common sense, shrewdness, perspicacity; *inf* nous.

witticism n witty remark, clever saying, flash of wit, *bon mot*, quip, sally, pleasantry, riposte, joke, jest, epigram; *inf* wisecrack, crack, one-liner.

witty adj clever, original, ingenious, sparkling, scintillating, humorous, amusing, jocular, funny, facetious, droll, waggish, comic.

wizard n **1** *wizards casting spells* sorcerer, warlock, enchanter, witch, necromancer, magician, magus. **2** *he's a wizard at the piano* expert, master, adept, genius, virtuoso, maestro, star; *inf* dab hand, ace, whiz, wiz.

wizened adj withered, shrivelled, dried-up, shrunken, wasted, wrinkled, lined, gnarled, worn.

wobble v **1** *the table/boat wobbled* rock, sway, see-saw, teeter, shake, vibrate. **2** *she wobbled down the road on high heels* teeter, totter, stagger, waddle, waggle. **3** *her voice wobbled with emotion* shake, tremble, quiver, quaver. **4** *the politicians were wobbling* be undecided, be uncertain, waver, vacillate, hesitate, dither, shilly-shally.

wobble n **1** *try to prevent the wobble of the table/boat* rocking, swaying, teetering, shaking. *see* WOBBLE v 1. **2** *walk with a wobble* teeter, totter, stagger. *see* WOBBLE v 2. **3** *a wobble of emotion in her voice* shaking, trembling, tremor, quiver, quaver.

woe n **1** *a tale of woe* misery, wretchedness, misfortune, disaster, grief, anguish, affliction, suffering, pain, agony, torment, sorrow, sadness, unhappiness, distress, heartache, heartbreak, despondency, desolation, dejection, depression, gloom, melancholy. **2** *she told everyone her woes* trouble, misfortune, adversity, trial, tribulation, ordeal, burden, affliction, suffering, disaster, calamity, catastrophe; trials and tribulations.

woebegone adj *a woebegone face/expression* miserable, sad, unhappy, sorrowful, sorrowing, disconsolate, mournful, downcast, dejected, doleful, desolate, depressed, despairing, tearful.

woeful adj **1** *telling woeful tales of poverty* sad, saddening, unhappy, sorrowful, miserable, dismal, wretched, doleful, gloomy, tragic, pathetic, grievous, pitiful, plaintive, heart-rending, heartbreaking, distressing, anguished, agonizing, dreadful, terrible. **2** *the army will meet a woeful fate* sad, miserable, wretched, harsh, tragic, disastrous, ruinous, calamitous, catastrophic. **3** *a woeful piece of work* poor, bad, inadequate, substandard, lamentable, deplorable, disgraceful, wretched, disappointing, feeble; *inf* rotten, appalling, terrible, lousy, shocking, duff.

wolf n *a wolf trying to seduce the young girl* lady-killer, ladies' man, philanderer, womanizer, seducer, lecher, Casanova, Don Juan, Lothario.

wolf v *wolf his food* devour, gulp down, bolt, gobble, cram down, stuff down, gorge oneself with; *inf* scoff, pack away.

woman n **1** *women and children first* female, lady, girl, she, member of the fair/gentle sex; *derog inf* bird, chick, dame. **2** *he has a new woman* girlfriend, female friend, lady love, sweetheart, partner, lover, wife, spouse. **3** *employ a woman to help in the house* charwoman, domestic help, domestic, maid, maidservant; *inf* char, Mrs Mop.

womanhood n **1** *reach womanhood* maturity, muliebrity. **2** *appreciate her warmth and womanhood* womanliness, feminineness, femininity. **3** *traditionally it is the role of womanhood to raise the children* womankind, women, woman, female sex, womenfolk.

womanish adj *laugh at his womanish ways* effeminate, effete, unmanly; *inf* sissy.

womanizer n lady-killer, ladies' man, philanderer, seducer, lecher, Casanova, Don Juan, Lothario; *inf* wolf.

womankind n women, woman, female sex, womanhood, womenfolk.

womanly adj woman-like, female, feminine, matronly, motherly, warm, tender, gentle, soft.

wonder n **1** *children gazing with wonder at the Christmas tree* wonderment, awe, surprise, astonishment, amazement, bewilderment, stupefaction, fascination, admiration. **2** *one of the wonders of the world* marvel, phenomenon, miracle, prodigy, curiosity, rarity, nonpareil, sight, spectacle.

wonder v **1** *she wondered what to do next | he wondered where she came from* think, speculate, conjecture, ponder, meditate, reflect, deliberate, muse, ask oneself, puzzle, be curious about, be inquisitive about; *inf* cudgel one's brains about. **2** *I wonder you didn't walk out* be surprised, express surprise, find it surprising, be astonished/amazed. **3** *they wondered at the beauty of the church* marvel, stand amazed, stand in awe, be dumbfounded, gape, stare, goggle, look agog; *inf* be flabbergasted, gawk, boggle.

wonderful adj **1** *the church ceiling was wonderful to behold* marvellous, awe-inspiring, awesome, remarkable, extraordinary, phenomenal, prodigious, miraculous, fantastic, amazing, astonishing, astounding, surprising, incredible, unprecedented, unparalleled, unheard-of; *lit* wondrous. **2** *a wonderful mother/piano-player* superb, marvellous, magnificent, brilliant, sensational, stupendous, excellent, first-rate, outstanding, terrific, tremendous, admirable, very good; *inf* great, super, fantastic, smashing, ripping, fabulous, tiptop, ace, A1, wizard, bad, wicked.

wont adj *wont to get up late* accustomed, in the habit (of), used, given.

wont n *it is their wont to rise late* custom, habit, routine, practice, way, rule, convention.

wonted adj *work with his wonted industriousness* customary, accustomed, habitual, usual, normal, routine, regular, common, frequent, familiar, conventional.

woo v **1** *woo the daughter of a millionaire* court, pay court/suit to, seek the hand of, pursue, chase after, set one's cap at, make love to. **2** *woo fame* seek, seek to win/gain, pursue, chase after. **3** *woo the voters* seek the support/favour of. **4** *salesmen wooing householders into buying their goods* importune, press, urge, entreat, beg, implore, supplicate, solicit, coax, wheedle.

wood n **1** *goods made of wood* timber. **2** *wood for the fire* firewood, kindling, fuel. **3** *go for a walk in the wood/woods* forest, woodland, copse, thicket, coppice, grove; trees.

wooded adj woody, forested, tree-covered, tree-clad, timbered, sylvan.

wooden adj **1** *wooden furniture/houses* made of wood, of wood, wood, woody, timber. **2** *give a wooden performance* stiff, stolid, stodgy, expressionless, graceless, inelegant, ungainly, gauche, awkward, clumsy, maladroit. **3** *wearing a wooden expression | give him a wooden look* expressionless, inexpressive, blank, deadpan, empty, vacant, vacuous, glassy, impassive, lifeless, spiritless,

unanimated, emotionless, unemotional, unresponsive. **4** *children seeming completely wooden* stupid, thick, dense, dull, dull-witted, slow, slow-witted, doltish, witless, obtuse, bovine; *inf* dim, dim-witted.

wool n **1** *sheep with dirty wool* fleece, hair, coat. **2** *knit the wool into a sweater* yarn.

wool-gathering n daydreaming, dreaming, reverie, musing, abstraction, preoccupation, absent-mindedness, inattention.

woolly adj **1** *animals with woolly coats* fleecy, fluffy, shaggy, hairy, furry, flocculent. **2** *wearing woolly garments* woollen, made of wool, of wool, wool. **3** *a woolly TV picture* fuzzy, blurred, hazy, cloudy, foggy, indistinct, unclear, ill-defined. **4** *a woolly description | woolly thoughts* vague, hazy, indefinite, muddled, confused, disorganized.

word n **1** *what's another word for fame?* term, expression, name. **2** *he said not a word* remark, comment, statement, utterance, expression, declaration. **3** *she gave him her word that she would be present* word of honour, solemn word, promise, pledge, assurance, guarantee, undertaking, vow, oath. **4** *have a word with the teacher* chat, talk, conversation, discussion, tête-à-tête, consultation, exchange of views; *inf* confab, chit-chat, pow-wow. **5** *they have had word of his death* news, intimation, notice, communication, information, intelligence; tidings, message, report, account, communiqué, dispatch, bulletin; *inf* gen, low-down. **6** *word has it that he is a spy* rumour, talk, hearsay, gossip; *inf* grapevine. **7** *give the word to begin* command, order, signal, go-ahead, thumbs up; *inf* green light. **8** *the king's word is law* command, order, decree, edict, mandate, bidding, will. **9** *our word now must be success* slogan, watchword, password, catchword. **in a word** *in a word he's mad* in short, in a nutshell, briefly, to put it briefly, succinctly, concisely. **word-for-word** verbatim, literal, exact, precise, accurate, close, faithful, strict, undeviating.

word v *word the account differently* express, phrase, couch, put, say, utter, state.

words npl **1** *write the words of the song/opera/play* lyrics, libretto, book, text, script. **2** *she has had words with her sister* angry talk, argument, disagreement, row, altercation.

wordy adj *a wordy description* long-winded, verbose, loquacious, garrulous, voluble, prolix, protracted, discursive, diffuse, rambling, digressive, maundering, tautological, pleonastic.

work n **1** *building a house involves a lot of work* effort, exertion, labour, toil, slog, sweat, drudgery, trouble, industry; *lit* travail; *inf* grind, elbow-grease. **2** *your work is to answer the phone* job, task, chore, undertaking, duty, charge, assignment, commission, mission. **3** *engaged in financial work | out of work | what is his work?* employment, occupation, business; job, profession, career, trade, vocation, calling, craft, line, field, métier, pursuit. **4** *he regards it as his life's work* achievement, accomplishment, deed, feat, handiwork, fulfilment, performance, production. **5** *a work of art* composition, creation, opus, piece, oeuvre, masterpiece. **6** *admire the work that has gone into the stained-glass window* workmanship, art, craft, skill.

work v **1** *he works in industry* be employed, have a job, hold down a job, be engaged, earn one's living, do business, follow/ply one's trade. **2** *you will really have to work to build the house | work hard to pass the exam* exert oneself, put in effort, make efforts, labour, toil, slog, sweat, drudge, slave, peg away; *inf* grind, plug away, knock oneself out. **3** *work the machine* operate, control, drive, manage, direct, use, handle, manipulate, manoeuvre, ply, wield. **4** *this machine won't work* go, operate, function, perform, run. **5** *your idea/plan won't work* succeed, be successful, have success, go well, be effective, be effectual. **6** *work the land* cultivate, till, dig, farm. **7** *they can work miracles* bring about, achieve, accomplish, perform, carry out, execute, create, cause, contrive, effect, implement. **8** *they worked it so that the criminal got off* arrange, handle, manipulate, manoeuvre, contrive, bring off, carry off, pull off; *inf* fix, fiddle, swing. **9** *work the clay* knead, shape, form, mould, fashion, model. **10** *work the peg into the hole* manoeuvre, manipulate, negotiate, guide, engineer, direct, edge. **11** *work one's way through the crowd* manoeuvre, progress, penetrate, move, make, push, elbow. **12** *screws working loose* come, become, move. **13** *his face worked* twitch, convulse, writhe, twist.

work on *work on your mother to let you go* coax, cajole, wheedle, pester, press, nag, importune, persuade, influence, sway.

work out 1 *work out the puzzle/problem* solve, resolve, puzzle out, figure out. **2** *work out the answer* puzzle out, figure out, find out, calculate. **3** *the bill works out at £50* come to, add up to, amount to, totals up to. **4** *work out a plan* develop, evolve, formulate, devise, arrange, organize, elaborate, construct, put together, plan, contrive. **5** *the plan did not work out* work, succeed, be successful, go well, go as planned/arranged/wished, be effective, be effectual. **6** *things worked out well/badly* go, turn out,

come out, develop, evolve, result; *inf* pan out. **7** *work out to keep fit* exercise, do exercises, train, drill, practise, warm up. **work up 1** *work up to a climax* advance, progress, proceed, make headway. **2** *work up an appetite* cause, create, whet, stimulate, arouse, awaken. **3** *unable to work up any enthusiasm* stir up, arouse, rouse, awaken, excite, instigate, prompt, generate, kindle, foment. **4** *the speaker succeeded in working up the crowd* agitate, stir up, arouse, excite, animate, inflame; *inf* get worked up, wind up.

workable adj practicable, practical, viable, doable, feasible, possible.

workaday adj ordinary, everyday, average, commonplace, mundane, run-of-the-mill, routine, humdrum, prosaic.

worker n **1** *workers and employers* employee, hand, workman, workwoman, working man/woman/person, blue-collar worker, white-collar worker, labourer, artisan, craftsman, craftswoman, wage-earner, proletarian. **2** *workers of miracles* doer, performer, perpetrator, executor, operator. **3** *he's a real worker* hard worker, toiler, workhorse, busy bee; *inf* workaholic.

working adj **1** *working mothers* in work, employed, in a job, waged. **2** *working models/machines* functioning, operating, going, running, in working order. **3** *a working majority/plan* effective, viable.

working n **1** *understand the working of the machine* functioning, operation, running process, method of working, modus operandi. **2** *the working of miracles* doing, performing, performance, perpetration, execution, operation. **3** *the children fell down the disused workings* mine, pit, quarry, shaft; diggings, excavations. **4** *mend the workings of the clock* mechanism, machinery; works. *see* WORKS 4.

workman, workwoman n *workmen mending the roof* worker, employee, hand, labourer, artisan, tradesman, tradeswoman, operative.

workmanship n *admire the workmanship of the tapestry/carpentry* craftsmanship, craft, artistry, art, handicraft, handwork, expertise, skill, technique, work.

workout n training/practice session; physical exercise, drill, training; exercises, gymnastics, aerobics; *inf* daily dozen.

works npl **1** *busy at the works* factory, plant, mill, workshop. **2** *the author's complete works* writings, productions; oeuvre, output. **3** *doing good works* deeds, acts, actions. **4** *the works of the clock/engine* workings, working parts, parts; mechanism, machinery, action, movement; *inf* innards, insides, guts. **the works 1** *get the works at the beauty saloon* full treatment, everything available/ required; *inf* the lot. **2** *the enemy gave the prisoners the works* harsh treatment, physical beating, torture.

workshop n **1** *the car's still in the workshop* factory, plant, mill, garage. **2** *craftsmen at work in their workshop* workroom, studio, atelier, shop. **3** *hold a workshop in self-assertiveness* seminar, study/discussion group, class.

world n **1** *the mountains of the world | travel round the world* earth, globe, sphere, planet. **2** *the world was shocked by the nuclear attack* whole world, world at large, mankind, man, humankind, humanity, people everywhere, people, everyone, everybody, public, general public. **3** *God created the world* universe, creation, cosmos, all existence. **4** *the earth and other worlds* planet, satellite, moon, star, heavenly body, orb. **5** *the academic world disliked the novel* society, sector, section, group, division. **6** *he works in the world of finance* area, field, department, sphere, province, domain, realm. **7** *the world of the dinosaurs/Tudors* age, epoch, era, period; times. **8** *it made a world of difference* vast/huge amount; *inf* great deal, immensity. **9** *renounce the world | not interested in the world* secular interests, earthly concerns, human existence.

worldly adj **1** *worldly considerations/pleasures* earthly, terrestrial, secular, temporal, material, materialistic, human, carnal, fleshly, corporeal, physical. **2** *she is worldly but her sister is innocent* worldly-wise, experienced, knowing, sophisticated, cosmopolitan, urbane.

worldwide adj universal, global, international, pandemic, general, ubiquitous, extensive, widespread, far-reaching, wide-ranging.

worn adj **1** *worn carpets/clothes* worn-out, threadbare, tattered, in tatters, ragged, frayed, shabby, shiny. **2** *worn furniture* worn-out, dilapidated, crumbling, broken-down, run-down, tumbledown, decrepit, deteriorated, on its last legs; *inf* clapped-out. **3** *mothers looking worn* haggard, drawn, strained, careworn; *inf* all in, done in, dog-tired, dead on one's feet, fit to drop, played-out, bushed, knackered, pooped. **4** *mothers worn by child-bearing* worn out, exhausted, overtired, tired out, fatigued, weary, wearied, spent. *see* WORN-OUT. **5** *worn ideas/jokes* well-worn, worn-out, obsolete,

antiquated, old, hackneyed, stale; *inf* played-out, clapped-out.

worn-out adj worn, dilapidated, exhausted. *see* WORN 1, 5.

worried adj anxious, disturbed, perturbed, troubled, bothered, distressed, concerned, upset, distraught, uneasy, ill at ease, disquieted, fretful, agitated, nervous, edgy, on edge, tense, overwrought, worked-up, distracted, apprehensive, fearful, afraid, frightened; *inf* uptight, on tenterhooks; *Amer inf* antsy.

worry v **1** *she worries too much* be worried, be anxious, fret, brood. *see* WORRIED. **2** *his absences worry her* cause anxiety, make anxious, disturb, trouble, bother, distress, upset, concern, disquiet, discompose, fret, agitate, unsettle. *see* WORRIED. **3** *stop worrying your mother about new clothes* pester, harass, vex, irritate, annoy, nag, importune, plague, torment, harry, persecute; *inf* hassle. **4** *dogs worrying sheep* tear at, bite, gnaw at, lacerate, savage, go for, attack, shake, pull at.

worry n **1** *the children are a worry to their father* nuisance, pest, plague, trial, trouble, problem, irritation, irritant, vexation, thorn in one's flesh. **2** *their disappearance/behaviour caused him a lot of worry* anxiety, disturbance, perturbation, trouble, bother, distress, concern, care, upset, uneasiness, unease, disquiet, disquietude, fretfulness, agitation, edginess, tenseness, apprehension, fearfulness. *see* WORRIED.

worsen v **1** *his statement simply worsened the situation* make worse, aggravate, exacerbate, damage, intensify, increase, heighten. **2** *the financial situation worsened* get/grow/become worse, take a turn for the worse, deteriorate, degenerate, retrogress, decline, sink, slip, slide; *inf* go downhill.

worship n **1** *worship of God | acts of worship* reverence, veneration, homage, respect, honour, adoration, devotion, praise, prayer, glorification, exaltation, laudation, extolment. **2** *attend morning worship* service; religious rites/acts. **3** *the fan's worship of the rock star* adulation, admiration, adoration, devotion, idolization, hero-worship.

worship v **1** *worship God* revere, venerate, pay homage to, honour, adore, praise, pray to, glorify, exalt, laud, extol. **2** *worship at the local church* attend a service, pray. **3** *he worships his wife | the fans worship the rock star* adore, be devoted to, cherish, treasure, admire, adulate, idolize, hero-worship; *inf* be wild about.

worst v defeat, beat, best, get the better of, gain the advantage over, trounce, rout, thrash, whip, drub, vanquish, conquer, master, overcome, overwhelm, overpower, overthrow, crush, subdue, subjugate.

worth n **1** *the jewels are of little worth* financial value, value, price, cost. **2** *put a low worth on the house* value, valuation, price, assessment, appraisal. **3** *his advice is of little worth to you* value, use, usefulness, advantage, benefit, service, gain, profit, avail, help, assistance, aid. **4** *persons of great worth in the community* worthiness, merit, credit, value, excellence, eminence, importance.

worthless adj **1** *the jewels are worthless* valueless, of little/no financial value, rubbishy, trashy. **2** *his advice was worthless | worthless attempts* valueless, useless, no use, of no benefit, to no avail, futile, ineffective, ineffectual, pointless, nugatory. **3** *their worthless son ended up in prison* good-for-nothing, useless, despicable, contemptible, base, low, vile, corrupt, depraved; *inf* no-good, no-account.

worthwhile adj worth it, worth the effort, valuable, of value, useful, of use, beneficial, advantageous, helpful, profitable, gainful, productive, constructive, justifiable.

worthy adj **1** *worthy people not receiving recognition | lead worthy but boring lives* virtuous, good, moral, upright, righteous, honest, decent, honourable, respectable, reputable, trustworthy, reliable, irreproachable, blameless, unimpeachable, admirable, praiseworthy, laudable, commendable, deserving, meritorious. **2** *worthy of respect* deserving, meriting.

worthy n *local worthies* dignitary, notable, celebrity, personage, luminary, official; *inf* VIP, big shot, bigwig, big cheese, big gun.

wound n **1** *a wound in the leg that is not healing* lesion, cut, graze, scratch, gash, laceration, tear, puncture, slash, injury, sore. **2** *a wound to his pride* blow, injury, insult, slight, offence, affront; hurt, harm, damage. **3** *suffering from mental/emotional wounds* injury, hurt, pain, pang, ache, distress, grief, trauma, anguish, torment, torture.

wound v **1** *the shot wounded his arm* cut, graze, scratch, gash, lacerate, tear, puncture, pierce, stab, slash, injure, hurt, damage, harm. **2** *their words wounded his pride* hurt, harm, damage, injure, insult, slight, offend, affront. **3** *his actions wounded her feelings* hurt, distress, grieve, mortify, pain, shock, traumatize.

wraith n ghost, spectre, shade, phantom, apparition, spirit.

wrangle n *neighbours involved in a wrangle about the upkeep of a dividing wall* dispute,

disagreement, argument, quarrel, row, fight, bickering, squabble, altercation, angry exchange, controversy, tiff, tussle, brouhaha, rumpus, brawl; *inf* falling-out, set-to, dust-up, spat.

wrangle v *wrangle over custody of the children* have a disagreement, argue, quarrel, row, bicker, fight, clash, squabble, have words, brawl; *inf* fall out. *see* WRANGLE n.

wrap v **1** *wrap the child in blankets* envelop, enfold, encase, enclose, cover, swathe, bundle up, swaddle. **2** *wrap the shawl round her* fold, swathe, bundle, draw, arrange. **3** *wrap the present* wrap up, parcel up, package, do up, tie up, gift-wrap.

wrap n shawl, stole, cloak, cape, mantle.

wrap up 1 *wrap up the present* wrap, parcel up, gift-wrap. *see* WRAP v **3**. **2** *try to wrap up the meeting early* finish, end, bring to an end/close, conclude, terminate, wind up. **3** *you must wrap up well in the winter* dress warmly, wear warm clothes. **4** *tell that child to wrap up* be quiet, be silent, hold one's tongue, stop talking; *inf* shut up, shut one's mouth/face/trap, put a sock in it.

wrapper n **1** *sweet wrapper* wrapping, cover, covering, packaging, paper. **2** *book wrappers* cover, jacket, casing. **3** *hot-water tank wrapper* cover, covering, case, casing, sheath, jacket, capsule, pod, shell. **4** *wearing a wrapper and slippers* housecoat, bathrobe, dressing-gown, robe, kimono, negligée, peignoir.

wrath n anger, ire, rage, fury, annoyance, indignation, exasperation, dudgeon, high dudgeon, bad temper, ill humour, irritation, crossness, displeasure, irascibility.

wrathful adj angry, irate, enraged, raging, incensed, infuriated, furious, fuming, ranting, raving, beside oneself, indignant, exasperated, bad-tempered, ill-humoured, irritated, cross, displeased, irascible; *inf* on the warpath.

wreath n **1** *wreaths of flowers* garland, chaplet, circlet, coronet, crown, diadem, festoon, lei. **2** *wreaths of smoke* ring, loop, circle.

wreathe v **1** *the display was wreathed in flowers | her face was wreathed in smiles* cover, envelop, festoon, garland, adorn, decorate. **2** *the snake wreathed itself round the tree trunk* twist, wind, coil, twine, entwine, curl, spiral, wrap. **3** *smoke wreathing from the chimneys* coil, wind, spiral, curl.

wreck n **1** *the divers failed to salvage the wreck* shipwreck, sunken ship/vessel, derelict. **2** *the wreck of the car/house/dreams* wreckage, debris, rubble, detritus; ruins, remains, remnants, fragments, pieces, relics. **3** *upset by the wreck of their car/house/dream* wrecking, wreckage, destruction, devastation, ruination, ruin, demolition, smashing, shattering, disruption, disintegration, undoing.

wreck v **1** *wreck the car* smash, demolish, ruin, damage; *inf* write off. **2** *wreck their plans/hopes* destroy, devastate, ruin, demolish, smash, shatter, disrupt, undo, spoil, mar, play havoc with. **3** *the new crew wrecked the ship* shipwreck, sink, capsize, run aground. **4** *the liner wrecked on its first voyage* founder, run aground, sink.

wreckage n **1** *clear away the wreckage of the car/house/accident* wreck, debris; ruins, remains, remnants, fragments. *see* WRECK n 2. **2** *upset by the wreckage of their car/house/dream* wreck, wrecking, destruction, ruination, ruin, demolition, smashing. *see* WRECK n 3.

wrench n **1** *remove the root at one wrench* twist, pull, tug, yank, wrest, jerk, jolt. **2** *have a wrench in the tool-box* spanner, adjustable spanner; monkey wrench. **3** *the wrist injury is just a wrench* sprain, twist, strain, rick. **4** *leaving home was a wrench* painful parting, distressing separation. **5** *the wrench caused by parting from her children* pain, ache, pang, anguish, distress, trauma.

wrench v **1** *wrench the root from the ground* twist, pull, tug, yank, wrest, jerk, tear, rip, force. **2** *wrench one's ankle/wrist* sprain, twist, strain, rick.

wrest v *wrest the gun from him* twist, wrench, pull, snatch, take away, remove.

wrestle v **1** *men wrestling in the ring* grapple, contend. **2** *wrestle with one's conscience* struggle, grapple, fight, contend, battle, combat. **3** *wrestle with the problem* struggle, contend, come to grips with, face up to, pit oneself against; *inf* plug away at.

wretch n **1** *pity wretches sleeping rough* poor creature/soul/thing, miserable creature, unfortunate, poor devil. **2** *that's the wretch that mugged the old lady* scoundrel, villain, ruffian, rogue, rascal, blackguard, reprobate, criminal, delinquent, miscreant; *inf* rotter, creep, jerk, louse, rat, swine, skunk.

wretched adj **1** *feeling wretched at leaving home* miserable, unhappy, sad, broken-hearted, sorrowful, sorry, distressed, disconsolate, downcast, down, downhearted, dejected, crestfallen, cheerless, depressed, melancholy, gloomy, mournful, doleful, forlorn, woebegone, abject. **2** *feeling wretched during the sea voyage* ill, unwell, sick, sickly, ailing, below par; *inf* under the weather, out of sorts. **3** *lead a wretched existence* miserable, unhappy, poor, hard, harsh, grim, difficult, unfortunate, sorry, pitiful, tragic. **4** *wretched creatures sleeping rough* miserable, poor, unhappy, unfortunate, unlucky, hapless, pitiable. **5** *the wretched burglar is back in prison* contemptible, despicable, base, low, vile. **6** *the food was wretched* poor, bad, substandard, low-quality, inferior, pathetic, worthless.

wriggle v **1** *children wriggling in their seats* twist, squirm, writhe, jiggle, jerk. **2** *wriggle along the ground* twist and turn, zigzag, wiggle, snake, crawl, slink. **3** *wriggle out of the task* avoid, evade, dodge, duck, extricate oneself.

wriggle n *the wriggles of the children* squirming, writhing, jiggling, jerk.

wriggly adj *a wriggly line* wiggly, wiggling, twisting, zigzag, zigzagging.

wring v **1** *wring the clothes* twist, squeeze. **2** *wring the information from him* extract, force, coerce, exact, extort, wrest, wrench, screw. **3** *her poverty wrung their hearts* pierce, stab, wound, harrow, tear at, lacerate, rack, distress, pain, hurt.

wrinkle n *wrinkles in her face | wrinkles in the material* crease, fold, pucker, gather, furrow, ridge, line, corrugation, crinkle, crumple, rumple.

wrinkle v *time had wrinkled her face | sitting wrinkled the dress* crease, pucker, gather, furrow, line, corrugate, crinkle, crumple, rumple.

writ n court order, summons, decree.

write v **1** *write their names* write down, put in writing, put in black and white, commit to paper, jot down, note, set down, take down, record, register, list, inscribe, scribble, scrawl. **2** *write an essay/letter* compose, draft, create, pen, dash off. **3** *don't forget to write* write a letter, correspond, communicate; *inf* drop a line/note. **write down** put in writing, jot down, note, set down, take down, record, register, list. **write off 1** *write off the debt* forget about, disregard, give up for lost, cancel, annul, nullify, wipe out, cross out, score out. **2** *write off the car* damage beyond repair, wreck, smash, crash, destroy, demolish; *Amer inf* total. **3** *don't write off your opponent* disregard, regard as finished, dismiss.

writer n author, wordsmith, penman, hack; novelist, essayist, biographer, journalist, columnist, scriptwriter; *inf* scribbler, penpusher.

writhe v twist about, twist and turn, roll about, squirm, wriggle, jerk, thrash, flail, toss, struggle.

writing n **1** *the writing is illegible* handwriting, hand, penmanship, script, print, calligraphy, chirography scribble, scrawl. **2** *have his writings published* work, *opus*, book, volume, publication, composition.

wrong adj **1** *the wrong answer* | *he is wrong in his calculation* incorrect, inaccurate, in error, erroneous, mistaken, inexact, imprecise, unsound, faulty, false, wide of the mark, off target; *inf* off beam, barking up the wrong tree. **2** *chose the wrong moment to speak* unsuitable, inappropriate, inapt, inapposite, undesirable, infelicitous. **3** *the wrong way to behave on such an occasion* unsuitable, inappropriate, undesirable, unacceptable, unfitting, improper, unseemly, indecorous, unconventional. **4** *it is wrong to steal* unlawful, illegal, illicit, lawless, criminal, delinquent, felonious, dishonest, dishonourable, corrupt, unethical, immoral, bad, wicked, evil, sinful, iniquitous, blameworthy, culpable; *inf* crooked. **5** *he's a wrong 'un* criminal, dishonest, dishonourable, corrupt, bad, wicked, evil, sinful, nasty, vile, base, despicable, contemptible, reprehensible. **6** *something wrong with the phone/heart* amiss, awry, out of order, not right, faulty, defective. **7** *iron the dress on the wrong side* inside, reverse, opposite, inverse.

wrong adv **1** *guess wrong* wrongly, incorrectly, inaccurately, erroneously, mistakenly, inexactly, imprecisely, falsely. **2** *things went wrong* badly, amiss, awry, astray. **get wrong** *get the message wrong* misunderstand, misinterpret, misapprehend, misconstrue. **go wrong 1** *you can't go wrong if you follow the instructions* make a mistake, go astray, err; *inf* slip up, boob, make a booboo. **2** *things went wrong from the start* go

badly, go amiss, go awry. **3** *their plans/marriage went wrong* fail, fall through, come to nothing, misfire, miscarry; *inf* come to grief, flop. **4** *the machine's gone wrong* break down, malfunction, fail, stop working/functioning; *inf* be on the blink, conk out, go phut, go kaput. **5** *young people who go wrong* go astray, err, commit a crime/sin, stray from the straight and narrow, fall from grace; *inf* go to the dogs.

wrong n **1** *not know right from wrong* badness, immorality, sin, sinfulness, wickedness, evil, iniquity, unlawfulness, crime, dishonesty, dishonour, injustice, transgression, abuse; *inf* crookedness. **2** *commit a wrong* | *do us a wrong* bad deed/act/action, misdeed, offence, injury, crime, infringement, infraction, injustice, grievance, outrage, atrocity. **in the wrong** *you were in the wrong to accuse him* in error, mistaken, at fault, to blame, blameworthy, culpable, guilty, off course, off target, wide of the mark; *inf* off beam.

wrong v **1** *he wronged his wife* abuse, mistreat, maltreat, ill-treat, ill-use, harm, hurt, do injury to. **2** *you wrong him by calling him a thief* misrepresent, malign, dishonour, impugn, vilify, defame, slander, libel, denigrate, insult; *Amer inf* bad-mouth.

wrongdoer n lawbreaker, criminal, delinquent, culprit, offender, felon, villain, miscreant, evildoer, sinner, transgressor, malefactor; *inf* wrong 'un.

wrongful adj *wrongful dismissal/arrest* unfair, unjust, improper, unjustified, unwarranted, unlawful, illegal, illegitimate, illicit.

wry adj **1** *make/pull a wry face* twisted, distorted, contorted, crooked, lopsided, askew. **2** *a wry wit/remark* ironic, sardonic, mocking, sarcastic, dry, droll, witty, humorous.

Xx Yy Zz

xerox v *xerox the document* photocopy, copy, duplicate, reproduce, photostat.

Xerox n *get a Xerox of the document* photocopy, copy, duplicate, photostat.

X-ray n X-ray image, radiogram, radiograph.

yank v *yank the weeds out* pull, tug, jerk, wrench.

yank n *remove the tooth with one yank* pull, jerk, wrench.

yap v **1** *dogs yapping* yelp, bark. **2** *people yapping when we're trying to read* chatter, gossip, jabber, prattle, gibber, babble, gabble, clack.

yardstick n measure, standard, gauge, scale, guide, guideline, touchstone, criterion, benchmark, model, pattern.

yarn n **1** *use a fine yarn* thread, fibre, strand. **2** *tell a good yarn* story, tale, anecdote, fable, traveller's tale; *inf* tall tale/story, cock and bull story.

yawning adj *a yawning gap* wide, wide open, gaping, cavernous, chasmal.

year n *have a good year | the academic year* twelve-month period/session; calendar year, fiscal year. **year in, year out** regularly, without a break, unfailingly.

yearly adj *a yearly event* annual, once a year, every year.

yearly adv *published yearly* annually, once a year, per annum.

yearn v *yearn for a child | yearn to go abroad* long, pine, have a longing, crave, desire, want, wish for, hanker after, covet, fancy, hunger for, thirst for; *inf* have a yen for.

yearning n longing, craving, desire, want, wish, hankering, fancy, hunger, thirst, lust, ache, burning; *inf* yen.

yell v *children yelling a warning to their friends* shout, cry out, howl, scream, shriek, screech, squeal, roar, bawl, whoop; *inf* holler.

yell n *give a yell of pain* shout, cry, howl, scream, shriek, screech, squeal, roar, bawl, whoop; *inf* holler.

yen n hankering, desire, want, wish, fancy, longing, craving, hunger, thirst, lust.

yes adv *yes, I'll come* all right, of course, by all means, sure, certainly, in the affirmative; *dial* aye; *inf* yeah, yah, yep, uh-huh, righto.

yet adv **1** *he hasn't appeared yet* as yet, so/thus far, up till/to now, until now. **2** *he is poor, yet he gives to charity* nevertheless, nontheless, however, still, notwithstanding, despite that, for all that, just the same. **3** *there is yet more to come* still, in addition, additionally, besides, also, too, as well, further, into the bargain, to boot. **4** *I wasn't expecting him yet* now, just/right now, by now, already, so soon.

yield v **1** *fields yielding a good crop* produce, bear, give, give forth, supply, provide. **2** *investments yielding a good return* give, return, bring in, fetch, earn, net, produce, supply, provide, generate, furnish. **3** *yield one's place in the team to another | yield the crown to the conqueror* give up, surrender, relinquish, part with, deliver up, turn over, give over, remit, cede, renounce, resign, abdicate, forgo. **4** *the army yielded after a long battle* admit/concede defeat, surrender, capitulate, submit, lay down one's arms, give in, give up the struggle, succumb, raise/show the white flag; *inf* throw in the towel/sponge, cave in. **5** *yield to their demands* submit to, bow down to, comply with, accede to, agree to, consent to, go along with, grant, permit, allow, sanction, warrant. **6** *the material yields on pressure* give, bend, stretch, be flexible/pliant.

yoke n **1** *the yoke of the oxen* harness, collar, coupling. **2** *under the yoke of the tyrant* oppression, tyranny, enslavement, slavery, servitude, bondage, thrall. **3** *the yoke of marriage* tie, link, bond.

yoke v **1** *yoke the oxen* harness, hitch up, couple, join up. **2** *yoked in marriage* join, unite, link, bond, tie.

yokel n rustic, countryman, country-woman, peasant, country bumpkin, provincial; *inf* country cousin; *Amer inf* hayseed, hill-billy.

young adj **1** *young people* youthful, juvenile, junior, adolescent, in the springtime of life, in one's salad days. **2** *young industries* new, recent, undeveloped, fledgling, in the making.

young n *bear young* offspring, progeny, family, issue; little ones, babies, *inf* sprogs.

youngster n young adult/person, youth, juvenile, teenager, adolescent, young hopeful; lad, boy, young man/woman, lass, girl; *inf* kid, shaver, young 'un.

youth n **1** *in their youth they were beautiful* young days, early years, teens; early life, adolescence; boyhood, girlhood. **2** *a youth has been killed* boy, young man, lad, youngster, juvenile, teenager, adolescent; *inf* kid. **3** *the youth of today* young people, the young, younger/rising generation; *inf* kids.

youthful adj **1** *both youthful and elderly dancers* young, juvenile. *see* YOUNG adj 1. **2** *grannies looking very youthful* fresh-faced, young-looking. **3** *he's a youthful sixty-five* young, active, vigorous, spry, sprightly.

zany adj *a zany sense of humour | a zany personality* eccentric, peculiar, odd, ridiculous, absurd, comic, clownish, madcap, funny, amusing; *inf* weird, wacky, daft, screwy; *Amer inf* kooky.

zap v **1** *ordered to zap the enemy* kill, slay, murder, put to death, liquidate, destroy; *inf* do in, knock off. **2** *zap the ball/fly* hit, strike, slap; *inf* whack. **3** *they were zapped by the invading army | zap the opposing team* defeat, beat, conquer, vanquish, trounce, rout, overcome, overpower, overthrow, crush. **4** *zap from place to place* rush, dash, pelt, race, sprint, tear, shoot, fly, scurry, speed, hurry, hasten; *inf* whiz, hare, zoom, zip.

zeal n **1** *his zeal for life/sport* ardour, fervour, fervency, passion, fire, devotion, vehemence, intensity, enthusiasm, eagerness, keenness, earnestness, vigour, energy, verve, gusto, zest, fanaticism; *inf* zing. **2** *upset by their religious/political zeal* zealotry, fanaticism, extremism. *see* ZEALOTRY.

zealot n *a religious/political zealot* enthusiast, fanatic, extremist, radical, militant, bigot; *inf* fiend.

zealotry n *religious/political zealotry* zeal, fanaticism, extremism, single-mindedness, radicalism, militancy, dogmatism, bigotry.

zealous adj *zealous athletes/stamp-collectors* ardent, fervent, fervid, passionate, impassioned, devoted, intense, enthusiastic, eager, keen, earnest, vigorous, energetic, zestful, fanatical.

zenith n *zenith of his achievement/powers* highest/high point, crowning point, height, top, acme, peak, pinnacle, climax, prime, meridian, apex, apogee, vertex; *inf* high noon.

zero n **1** *a series of zeroes* nought, nothing, cipher. **2** *win absolutely zero* nothing, naught, nil; *inf* zilch, not a sausage. **3** *economic growth is at zero* lowest point, nadir, rock bottom.

zero v *zero the stopwatch* adjust to zero point. **zero in on** *his talk zeroed in on the economy* focus on, centre on, concentrate on, home in on, pinpoint.

zero hour n appointed hour/time, crucial/vital/crisis moment, moment of truth.

zest n **1** *approach the project with zest* relish, gusto, enthusiasm, eagerness, zeal, vigour, liveliness, energy, enjoyment, joy, delectation, appetite; *inf* zing, oomph. **2** *add zest to the dish/occasion* piquancy, spice, pungency, flavour, relish, tang, savour, interest; *inf* kick.

zing n zest, enthusiasm, eagerness, gusto, zeal, life, liveliness, spirit, animation, vitality, vivacity, sparkle, vigour, pep, energy, vim, *élan*, dash, brio; *inf* go, oomph, zip, pizzazz.

zip n *a bit of zip to your playing* zest, enthusiasm, eagerness, gusto, life, liveliness, spirit, animation, sparkle, pep, *élan*, brio; *inf* oomph, zing. *see* ZING.

zip v *he zipped off before I could speak* rush, dash, pelt, race, tear, shoot, fly, scurry, speed, hurry, hasten; *inf* whiz, hare, zoom, zap.

zone n area, sector, section, belt, district, region, provinc

zoom v **1** *planes/flies zooming around* fly, buzz. **2** *they zoomed off before he could question them* rush, dash, pelt, race, tear, shoot, fly, scurry, speed, hurry, hasten; *inf* whiz, hare, zip, zap.